SAVILLS

CW01619608

FOR STUD F… …PERTIES

1979-1989. S… …ıase of 34 st… …value in ex…

1985........... Newmarket's biggest stud sale — The Lordship and Egerton Studs were sold jointly by Savills.

1986........... Newmarket's biggest stud sale — The Hadrian and Derisley Wood Studs were sold by Savills.

1987........... Newmarket's largest stud sale — Banstead Manor was handled by Savills.

SAVILLS

Geoffrey van Cutsem, F.R.I.C.S.,
132-135 Sloane Street, London SW1X 9AX
01-730 0822

GALLOPS

Fibresand

Dri-Ex design and construct All-Weather Gallops
to the highest standards and to suit all requirements
Selected contractors to:
The Jockey Club, Newmarket. Leading U.K. Trainers & Training Centres

DRI—EX

For all details and information contact:
David Humbert, Dri-Ex Gallops,
Banks Plant Ltd, Frogham Hill, Fordingbridge
Hampshire SP6 2HW
Telephone: (0425) 54675 Fax: (0425) 55727

UNITED STATES
• CURE THE BLUES
• GENERAL ASSEMBLY
GOLD STAGE
NOBLE DANCER (GB)
• RED ATTACK
• SHIMATOREE
SON ANGE
STAR DE NASKRA
SUN MASTER
VICTORIOUS
• STANDING AT
SPENDTHRIFT FARM
FRANCE
DOM PASQUINI
DOUBLE BED
MILLES BALLES
SCRIPT OHIO
SAINT ANDREWS
AUSTRALIA
NOALCOHOLIC
NO PAROLE
PARTY LEADER
RANCHO RULER
RAVENEAUX
PillarStud
United States: 2651 Russell Cave Road
Lexington, Kentucky 40511. 606 • 293 • 0554
France: Haras de Victot Victot-Pontfol
14430 Dozule, France 31 • 79 • 12 • 39
Australia: Blue Gum Farm, RMB 4115 Euroa,
Victoria 3666, Australia 61 • 57 • 953 • 331

The BRITISH BLOODSTOCK AGENCY plc

Queensberry House, High Street, Newmarket, Suffolk CB8 9BD
Tel: (0638) 665021 Telex: 817157 Fax: (0638) 660283
and at: 1 Chapel View, High Street, Lambourn, Berks RG16 7XL
Tel: (0488) 73111 Fax: (0488) 71219
also: BBA (Ireland) Ltd., 51 Lansdowne Road, Dublin 4, Ireland
Tel: Dublin 686222 Telex: 93850 Fax: Dublin 685634

Jones Lang Wootton
Chartered Surveyors
Country

190 High Street, Newmarket, Suffolk. (0638) 661122

Over 50 Offices in 20 Countries

J. & J. Ransley
IMPORTERS & SUPPLIERS OF TOP QUALITY HAY
AMERICAN MIXTURE HAY:
Timothy, Alfalfa, Red Clover etc.
All from a dependable and well established supplier.
SOUTH AFRICAN ALFALFA:
Grown along the banks of a major river under controlled conditions. Thus ensuring both quality and continuity.
SOLE U.K. IMPORTER.
CANADIAN HAY:
Various mixtures always available.
ENGLISH HAY:
Top quality hay selected countrywide. First year mixtures, i.e. Ryegrass, Red Clover, Lucerne, Timothy etc.
Elms Court, Silver Hill, Willesborough, Ashford, Kent TN24 0NZ.
Tel: Ashford (0233) 624168 – 622055

2 Years In A Row...Number 1.

Saratoga yearling graduate *OPEN MIND*, Eclipse Champion at 2 and again at 3 in 1989.

1988 Graded Stakes Winners	
Fasig-Tipton	**51**
Keeneland	48

1989 Graded Stakes Winners	
Fasig-Tipton	**57**
Keeneland	52

Fasig-Tipton is America's Number 1 sales company for Graded stakes winners.

Statistics verified by *The Blood-Horse* Research Department.

Fasig-Tipton Company

2400 Newtown Pike, Lexington, Kentucky 40583-3610 • (606) 255-1555 • Fax (606) 254-0794

Makes the going better...

The fast and effective all-purpose poultice dressing ideal for the treatment of; cuts, wounds, bruising, swellings, strains, sprains and skin disorders.

Easy to use as a dressing or poultice, Animalintex is impregnated with antiseptics for faster healing and can be cut to size making it suitable for all types of animal.

The unique healing power of easy to use Animalintex helps you care quickly and effectively with your animal's injuries. Every tack box needs Animalintex.

Available from saddlers, tack shops, Agricultural Merchants and Veterinary Surgeries.

ANIMALINTEX
for life's cuts and bruises

ROBINSON

ROBINSON HEALTHCARE, CHESTERFIELD S40 IYF. U.K
TELEPHONE 0246 220022 FAX 0246 208164

97th
YEAR OF PUBLICATION

Raceform HORSES IN TRAINING 1990

ISBN 0 900611 66 9

For anyone or anything (almost) in UK/EIRE/EUROPE.

Unit 27A, Bankside, Kidlington, Oxon OX5 1JE

Tel: 0865 841999 Telex: 83147 'Attn PILOT'

ATOA

CERTIFICATED AIR OPERATOR CAA

Skyborne Air Taxi Service

INDEX TO GENERAL CONTENTS

Editor; Len Bell; Orbit House, Albert Street, Eccles, Manchester, M30 0LJ. Tel: 061 789 3237 Telex 667860, Fax 061 788 9152

Production Editor; Antony Marray; Eclipse Pedigrees, Weatherbys, Sanders Road, Wellingborough, NN8 4BX.

Subscription Orders; Raceform Ltd., Compton, Newbury, Berkshire, RG16 0NL. Tel: 0635 578080

Advertisements; James de Wesselow, Sara Bates; Compton, Newbury, Berkshire, RG16 0NL. Tel: 0635 578128, Fax: 0635 578101

Printed by Woolnough Bookbinding Ltd., Irthlingborough, Northamptonshire, NN9 5SE.

Distributed to the Newstrade by MMC, Waltrix House, Oak Road, Leatherhead, Surrey, KT22 7PN. Tel: 0372 386561

© Raceform Ltd 1990

INDEX TO ADVERTISERS

SPORTSFIELD INDUSTRIES LTD.

Fitter Horses

Cheaper Labour

USE

The PEGASUS Range of Horse Exercisers

Treadmills

Overhead Exercisers (up to 30 Horses)

Swimming Pools

Our machines are widely used by successful Flat and National Hunt Trainers, Show Jumpers, Studs, Eventers etc.

Sportsfield Industries Ltd.,
Athena House,
London Road,
Morden,
Surrey.

Tel: 01-543 0066
Telex: 925985 SBG–G
Fax: 01-543 3618

THE SOCIETY OF MASTER SADDLERS
MEMBER

F. J. CHANDLER

(SADDLER) LTD

HILLIER'S YARD, HIGH STREET,
MARLBOROUGH, WILTS.
Tel. 0672-512633

Specialists in:
RACE AND EXERCISE
SADDLERY,
JOCKEY EQUIPMENT
AND RACE COLOURS

1990

RACING FIXTURES AND SALE DATES

Flat fixtures are in **Black Type**; Jump in Light Type; Irish in *Italic*; asterisk (☆) indicates an evening meeting; † indicates an All Weather meeting. Sale dates are at foot of fixtures.

Fixtures and sales dates are subject to alteration.

Owners names are shown against their horses where this information is available. In the case of Partnerships and Syndicates, the nominated owner is given alongside the horse with other owners listed below the team.

Foaling dates are shown for two-year-olds where these are provided.

Teams which have arrived too late for inclusion in Horses In Training 1990 will be published in the Raceform Handicap Book week ending March 31st.

JANUARY

Sun	Mon	Tues	Wed	Thur	Fri	Sat
	1 Catterick Cheltenham Devon & Exeter Leicester **Southwell†** Windsor *Fairyhouse* *Waterford*	**2** Ayr Cheltenham **Southwell†**	**3** Ayr Lingfield† Sedgefield	**4** **Lingfield†** Nottingham *Thurles*	**5** Edinburgh Folkestone Haydock Southwell† Fasig-Tipton Sales	**6** Haydock Market Rasen Sandown **Southwell†** *Naas* Fasig-Tipton Sales
7 Fasig-Tipton Sales	**8** Chepstow Lingfield† Wolverhampton Keeneland Sales	**9** Leicester **Lingfield†** Newton Abbot Keeneland Sales	**10** Kelso Plumpton Southwell† *Punchestown* Keeneland Sales	**11** **Southwell†** Wincanton *Punchestown* Keeneland Sales	**12** Ascot Edinburgh Lingfield† Wetherby	**13** Ascot **Lingfield†** Market Rasen Newcastle Warwick *Leopardstown*
14	**15** Carlisle Fontwell Southwell†	**16** Folkestone Sedgefield **Southwell†** Worcester	**17** Lingfield† Ludlow Windsor	**18** **Lingfield†** Newton Abbot *Gowran Park*	**19** Catterick Kempton Southwell† Towcester	**20** Catterick Haydock Kempton **Southwell†** Warwick *Navan*
21	**22** Edinburgh Leicester Lingfield†	**23** Chepstow **Lingfield†** Nottingham	**24** Sedgefield Southwell† Wolverhampton *Fairyhouse*	**25** Huntingdon **Southwell†** Taunton *Waterford*	**26** Ayr Doncaster Lingfield† Wincanton	**27** Ayr Cheltenham Doncaster **Lingfield†** *Naas*
28	**29** Plumpton Southwell†	**30** Leicester Sedgefield **Southwell†**	**31** Hereford Lingfield† Windsor *Naas* Doncaster Sales			

THE FIRST NAME IN FLYING HORSES

The Instone AIRSTABLE, the ultimate in safety and comfort for horses travelling by air. Standard equipment on major long-haul airlines.

Wherever in the world you want your horses to go, you can rely on Instone Air Services to get them there safely, efficiently and economically, and with all the creature comforts the care of valuable bloodstock demands.

Instone Air Services' experience, global organisation and attention to detail ensure your horses travel First Class on either scheduled or charter aircraft.

Telephone or fax any of the Instone Air Services offices below for our full colour brochure.

LOS ANGELES	LEXINGTON	SYDNEY	ADELAIDE	HAMILTON
Tel:	Tel:	Tel:	Tel:	Tel:
(213) 318 6504	(606) 276 1977	(02) 669 1566	(08) 374 0071	(071) 295 750
Fax:	Fax:	Fax:	Fax:	Fax:
(213) 374 8705	(606) 276 1978	(02) 669 1452	(08) 374 0072	(071) 295 547

INSTONE AIR SERVICES

LONDON (GATWICK): Unit 13, Church Road, Lowfield Heath, Crawley, Sussex RH11 0PQ.
Tel: (0293) 511271. Fax: (0293) 33650

FEBRUARY

Sun	Mon	Tues	Wed	Thur	Fri	Sat
				1 **Lingfield†** Towcester *Gowran Park*	**2** Bangor Kelso Southwell†	**3** Chepstow Sandown **Southwell†** Stratford Wetherby *Fairyhouse*
4 *Leopardstown*	**5** Fontwell Lingfield† Wolverhampton	**6** Carlisle **Lingfield†** Warwick	**7** Ascot Ludlow Southwell† *Down Royal*	**8** Huntingdon **Southwell†** Wincanton *Clonmel*	**9** Ayr Lingfield† Newbury Sedgefield	**10** Ayr Catterick **Lingfield†** Newbury Uttoxeter *Navan*
11	**12** Nottingham Plumpton Southwell† Goffs Sales	**13** Newton Abbot **Southwell†** Towcester	**14** Folkestone Lingfield† Worcester *Thurles*	**15** Leicester **Lingfield†** Sandown Taunton *Thurles*	**16** Edinburgh Fakenham Sandown Southwell†	**17** Chepstow Newcastle Nottingham **Southwell†** Windsor *Leopardstown*
18	**19** Fontwell Lingfield† Wolverhampton Tattersalls (Ire) Sales	**20** Huntingdon **Lingfield†** Sedgefield Tattersalls (Ire) Ascot Sales	**21** Catterick Southwell† Warwick *Downpatrick*	**22** Folkestone **Southwell†** Wincanton *Tipperary*	**23** Kelso Kempton Lingfield†	**24** Doncaster Edinburgh Kempton **Lingfield†** Stratford *Punchestown*
25	**26** Doncaster Leicester Southwell† Fasig-Tipton Sales	**27** Nottingham Plumpton **Southwell†** Fasig-Tipton Sales	**28** Lingfield† Wetherby Worcester *Leopardstown* Fasig-Tipton Sales			

Trainer Starting Stalls

* DELIVERED TO YOUR U.K. YARD OR DOCKS
* ALL WELDED RECTANGULAR STEEL
* ARTICULATED STEERING PNEUMATIC TYRES
* TOUGH VINYL OVER FOAM PADDING

Established 1955

NEWBOULT & THORP LTD

BRIDGEGATE, RETFORD, NOTTS, U.K. DN22 7X TEL. 0777/703508

MARCH

Sun	Mon	Tues	Wed	Thur	Fri	Sat
				1 **Lingfield†** Ludlow *Wexford* Fasig-Tipton Sales	**2** Haydock Newbury Southwell†	**3** Haydock Hereford Market Rasen Newbury **Southwell†** *Naas*
4	**5** Leicester Lingfield† Windsor	**6** **Lingfield†** Sedgefield Warwick	**7** Bangor Catterick Southwell† *Fairyhouse*	**8** **Southwell†** Stratford Wincanton *Clonmel*	**9** Carlisle Lingfield† Market Rasen Sandown	**10** Ayr Chepstow Doncaster **Lingfield†** Sandown *Navan*
11	**12** Ayr Plumpton	**13** Cheltenham Sedgefield	**14** Cheltenham Newton Abbot	**15** Cheltenham Hexham	**16** Fakenham Lingfield Wolverhampton	**17** Chepstow Lingfield Newcastle Uttoxeter *Down Royal* *Leopardstown* *Limerick*
18	**19** Newcastle Wolverhampton *Leopardstown* *Limerick*	**20** Fontwell Nottingham	**21** Kelso Worcester	**22** Devon & Exeter **Doncaster** Towcester *Gowran Park* Doncaster Sales	**23** **Doncaster** Ludlow Newbury Doncaster Sales	**24** Bangor **Doncaster** Hexham Newbury *Naas*
25	**26** **Folkestone** Hexham **Leicester** *Ballinrobe* Doncaster Sales	**27** **Leicester** Sandown	**28** **Catterick** Worcester *Downpatrick*	**29** **Newcastle** Taunton *Thurles*	**30** **Beverley** Plumpton Wincanton	**31** Ascot **Beverley** Southwell **Warwick** *Curragh* Deauville Sales

SAFETY FIRST
– ALL YEAR ROUND

Minimizing the risk in training begins with choosing the right kind of surface on which to train. Today more and more stables are finding that Melcourt's specially processed wood products are the right kind of surface.

Whatever your requirements, they provide a clean, easily maintained surface of firm yet yielding character which is safe for both horse and rider. Thanks to their excellent drainage properties, they do not become slippery or unpredictable, even in the wettest conditions. They withstand temperature extremes and need only minimal maintenance to keep them in prime condition. Choose from:

EQUICHIP – Flat, profile cut hardwood or conifer woodchips of graduated size range from which virtually all bark and fine particles are removed, greatly reducing the rate of wear. A long lasting surface, Equichip slowly matures from its fresh sandy colour to a soft grey brown which blends in beautifully with natural surroundings.

EQUIFIBRE – A unique blend of carefully selected wood fibres (again with minimal bark content) producing a surface with natural matting characteristics, high resilience and even weight distribution. For large scale applications, a composite surface of Melcourt Walk Chips capped with Equifibre can prove highly cost effective – as well as providing an ideal training surface.

MELCOURT – Putting safety first – Naturally.

MELCOURT
INDUSTRIES LTD

Melcourt Industries Ltd, Tetbury, Glos. GL8 8JG.
Tel: (0666) 502711/503919.
Telex: 43144. Fax: (0666) 504398

APRIL

Sun	Mon	Tues	Wed	Thur	Fri	Sat
1 *Naas* Deauville Sales	**2** **Folkestone** Ludlow **Nottingham** *Roscommon* Ascot Sales	**3** **Hamilton** Sedgefield	**4** **Hamilton** Huntingdon *Navan*	**5** **Brighton** Liverpool *Clonmel*	**6** Devon & Exeter **Kempton** Liverpool	**7** Hereford **Lingfield†** Liverpool *Down Royal* *Phoenix Park* Goffs France Sales
8	**9** Kelso **Wolverhampton** *Limerick*	**10** Fontwell **Pontefract** **Wolverhampton**	**11** **Ascot** **Ripon** Worcester *Gowran Park*	**12** **Ripon** Southwell Taunton Doncaster Sales (at Lingfield)	**13**	**14** Carlisle **Haydock** **Kempton** **Newcastle** Newton Abbot Plumpton Southwell Towcester *Curragh* *Mallow*
15 Carlisle Chepstow Fakenham Hereford Huntingdon **Kempton** Market Rasen **Newcastle**	**16** Newton Abbot **Nottingham** Plumpton Towcester Uttoxeter **Warwick** Wetherby Wincanton *Fairyhouse* *Mallow*	**17** Chepstow **Newmarket** Uttoxeter **Warwick** Wetherby *Fairyhouse* Tattersalls Sales	**18** **Ayr** Cheltenham **Newmarket** **Pontefract** *Fairyhouse* Tattersalls Sales	**19** **Ayr** Cheltenham **Newmarket** *Tipperary* Tattersalls Sales	**20** Ayr **Newbury** **Thirsk**	**21** Ayr Bangor **Newbury** Stratford **Thirsk** *Phoenix Park*
22	**23** **Brighton** **Edinburgh** *Sligo*	**24** **Epsom** Perth Sedgefield *Punchestown*	**25** **Catterick** **Epsom** Perth *Punchestown*	**26** **Beverley** Ludlow Perth Wincanton☆ *Punchestown*	**27** **Carlisle** **Sandown** Southwell Taunton☆	**28** Hexham **Leicester** Market Rasen **Ripon** **Sandown** Uttoxeter Worcester☆ *Curragh*
29	**30** Hexham☆ **Pontefract** **Windsor☆** **Wolverhampton** *Navan☆*					

Sweat Means Lost Performance

Why? **Because when a horse sweats it loses vital fluid and salts.**

As fluid is lost in sweat it is removed from the blood, which itself becomes more viscous, or "thicker". This increases the workload of the heart in pumping blood and causes the horse to tire.

The importance of rehydration, with both fluid and salts, is in helping to bring a horse quickly back to his best after heavy sweating.

Equivite Resorb is a special formulation of salts with glucose for rapid rehydration. It comes as a concentrated liquid in a bottle marked with measured doses. And it can be given in a boiled feed or bran mash, or simply by adding water in a stable bucket.

Equivite Resorb should be given whenever a horse has sweated heavily — be it after racing or work.

Equivite Resorb

restores performance FAST!

Further information from **Dalgety Agriculture Ltd.,** Severn Mill, King Road Avenue, Old Dock, Avonmouth, Bristol BS11 9HE. Telephone: 0272 823882

MAY

Sun	Mon	Tues	Wed	Thur	Fri	Sat
		1 Ascot☆ **Bath** **Nottingham** **Redcar** *Navan☆*	**2** **Ascot** Cheltenham☆ Kelso *Phoenix Park☆*	**3** **Newmarket** Newton Abbot☆ **Salisbury** Sedgefield☆ *Tipperary☆*	**4** **Hamilton** **Newmarket** Newton Abbot	**5** **Haydock** Hereford Hexham☆ **Newmarket** **Thirsk** *Naas*
6 *Gowran Park*	**7** Fontwell **Haydock** **Kempton** Ludlow Newcastle Southwell Towcester **Warwick** *Down Royal* *Killarney☆* Devon & Exeter **Doncaster**	**8** Chepstow **Chester** **Folkestone☆** **Salisbury** *Killarney☆*	**9** **Chester** **Salisbury** **Sandown☆** Wetherby☆ Worcester☆ *Killarney☆* Ascot Sales	**10** **Carlisle** **Chester** Huntingdon☆ Uttoxeter☆ *Waterford☆* Ascot Sales	**11** **Beverley** **Carlisle** **Lingfield** Stratford☆ Taunton☆ *Downpatrick☆* *Phoenix Park☆*	**12** **Bangor** **Bath** **Beverley** **Lingfield** Market Rasen☆ Newcastle☆ Warwick☆ *Downpatrick* *Leopardstown*
13	**14** **Hamilton** **Windsor☆** **Wolverhampton** *Leopardstown☆* Doncaster Sales	**15** **Brighton☆** Newton Abbot **Nottingham☆** Towcester☆ **York** *Limerick☆* Doncaster Sales	**16** **Kempton☆** Newton Abbot☆ Perth☆ Worcester **York** *Gowran Park☆* Doncaster Sales	**17** Huntingdon☆ Perth **York** *Clonmel☆* Doncaster Sales	**18** **Newbury** **Newmarket** Stratford☆ **Thirsk** *Dundalk☆* Doncaster Sales	**19** **Hamilton☆** **Lingfield☆** **Newbury** **Newmarket** **Southwell☆** **Thirsk** Warwick☆ *Curragh*
20	**21** **Bath** **Edinburgh** Folkestone☆ **Wolverhampton** *Mallow☆* *Roscommon☆*	**22** **Beverley** **Salisbury** *Mallow☆*	**23** **Goodwood** Hereford	**24** **Catterick** **Goodwood** *Ballinrobe* *Tipperary☆*	**25** **Haydock** **Pontefract☆** Sedgefield Towcester *Dundalk☆*	**26** Cartmel **Doncaster** **Haydock** Hexham **Kempton** **Lingfield☆** **Southwell☆** **Warwick☆** *Curragh*
27	**28** Hereford Hexham☆ Huntingdon **Leicester** **Redcar** **Sandown** Uttoxeter Wetherby *Down Royal* *Kilbeggan☆* Cartmel **Chepstow** Devon & Exeter **Doncaster** Fakenham Fontwell	**29** **Leicester** **Redcar** **Sandown☆** Uttoxeter☆ *Wexford☆*	**30** **Brighton** Cartmel **Ripon☆** *Phoenix Park☆*	**31** **Brighton** **Carlisle** *Naas☆*		

STRAIGHT FROM THE HORSE'S MOUTH

"THEY CAN ship your Horses by LAND/SEA/AIR to all parts of the world (Horses already shipped to over 53 countries) with experienced personal attention at all times. Excellent stabling available for all horses in transit."

COMPREHENSIVE INSURANCE for all types of Bloodstock — Stud Farms — Racing Stables — Property — Liabilities — Transit — SPECIAL DISCOUNT for Studs — Racing Stables — Groups.

FOR ALL YOUR ENQUIRIES CONTACT:

EDDIE BRENNAN LTD.

129 Strand Road, Sandymount, Dublin 4
Telephone: Dublin: 694512, 694077, 694919
Telex: 30231 BREN E1
Fax no. Dublin: (01) 838720

Office Telephone Numbers during Sales:
R.D.S. (Dublin) 683889 Doncaster (0302) 365088
Tattersalls Ire Ltd (01) 256770/256773
Newmarket (0638) 668251, 665931 (Ex 245), 660701
Ascot (0990) 25350 Goffs (045) 77801, 77211 (Ext 259)

JUNE

Sun	Mon	Tues	Wed	Thur	Fri	Sat
					1 **Goodwood**☆ **Hamilton** **Nottingham** Stratford☆	**2** **Edinburgh** **Lingfield** Market Rasen☆ Stratford *Fairyhouse*
3	**4** **Edinburgh**☆ **Leicester** **Redcar** *Leopardstown* *Tralee* Ascot Sales	**5** **Folkestone** **Yarmouth** *Waterford*☆ Ascot Sales	**6** **Beverley**☆ **Epsom** **Yarmouth** *Curragh*☆	**7** **Beverley** **Epsom** *Clonmel*☆	**8** **Catterick** **Epsom** **Goodwood**☆ **Haydock**☆ **Southwell**	**9** **Carlisle**☆ **Catterick** **Epsom** **Haydock** **Leicester**☆ *Naas*
10 *Roscommon*	**11** **Brighton**☆ **Nottingham** **Pontefract** *Roscommon*☆	**12** **Goodwood** **Pontefract** *Mallow*☆	**13** **Beverley** **Hamilton**☆ **Kempton**☆ **Newbury** *Leopardstown*☆	**14** **Chepstow**☆ **Hamilton** **Newbury** *Tipperary*☆	**15** **Doncaster**☆ **Goodwood**☆ **Sandown** **Southwell** **York**	**16** **Bath** **Lingfield**☆ **Nottingham**☆ **Sandown** **York** *Phoenix Park*
17	**18** **Brighton** **Edinburgh** **Windsor**☆ **Wolverhampton**☆ *Clonmel*☆	**19** **Royal Ascot** **Thirsk** *Sligo*☆	**20** **Royal Ascot** **Ripon** *Sligo*	**21** **Royal Ascot** **Ripon** *Thurles*☆	**22** **Royal Ascot** **Ayr** **Redcar** **Southwell**	**23** **Ascot** **Ayr** **Lingfield**☆ **Redcar** **Warwick**☆ *Leopardstown*
24	**25** **Edinburgh** **Nottingham** **Windsor**☆ *Kilbeggan*☆	**26** **Brighton** **Newbury**☆ **Yarmouth** *Wexford*☆	**27** **Carlisle** **Chester**☆ **Kempton**☆ **Salisbury** *Wexford*☆ Tattersalls (Ire) Doncaster Sales	**28** **Carlisle** **Salisbury** *Gowran Park*☆ Tattersalls (Ire) Sales	**29** **Bath**☆ **Doncaster** **Goodwood**☆ **Lingfield** **Newcastle**☆ **Newmarket** Tattersalls (Ire) Sales	**30** **Chepstow** **Doncaster**☆ **Lingfield**☆ **Newcastle** **Newmarket** **Warwick**☆ *Curragh*

ABIS
Bloodstock Insurance

For all classes
of Racehorse,
Stallion,
Broodmare,
Foal and Yearling

(for Pleasure Horses
please ask for details of
our HORSEPLAN policy)

Telephone us for a Prospectus/Proposal
Form or ask your Insurance Broker/Agent
for details

Agricultural and Bloodstock Insurance Services Ltd.

Specialists in Bloodstock and all Pleasure Horse Insurances

48 East Street, Andover, Hampshire SP10 1ES
Telephone: (0264) 61431 Fax: (0264) 333772

JULY

Sun	Mon	Tues	Wed	Thur	Fri	Sat
1	**2**	**3**	**4**	**5**	**6**	**7**
Curragh	**Edinburgh** **Pontefract** **Windsor☆** **Wolverhampton☆** *Limerick☆* Ascot sales	**Chepstow** **Folkestone** *Bellewstown☆*	**Catterick☆** **Warwick** **Yarmouth** *Bellewstown☆*	**Brighton☆** **Catterick** **Haydock☆** **Yarmouth** *Bellewstown☆*	**Beverley☆** **Haydock** **Sandown** **Southwell**	**Bath** **Beverley** **Haydock** **Nottingham☆** **Sandown** *Phoenix Park*
8	**9**	**10**	**11**	**12**	**13**	**14**
	Edinburgh **Leicester** **Ripon☆** **Windsor☆** *Roscommon☆* *Waterford☆*	**Newmarket** **Pontefract**	**Bath** **Kempton☆** **Newmarket** **Redcar☆** *Dundalk☆* Tattersalls Sales	**Chepstow☆** **Hamilton☆** **Kempton** **Newmarket** *Dundalk* *Tipperary☆* Tattersalls Sales	**Chester☆** **Hamilton☆** **Lingfield** **Warwick** **York** *Down Royal* *Tipperary☆* Fasig-Tipton Sales	**Ayr** **Chester** **Lingfield** **Salisbury** **Southwell☆** **York** *Curragh* *Down Royal* Fasig-Tipton Sales
15	**16**	**17**	**18**	**19**	**20**	**21**
Curragh	**Ayr** **Beverley☆** **Windsor☆** **Wolverhampton** *Killarney☆*	**Ayr** **Beverley** **Folkestone☆** **Leicester☆** *Killarney☆*	**Catterick** **Hamilton** **Sandown☆** **Yarmouth** *Killarney*	**Catterick** **Chepstow☆** **Hamilton** **Sandown** *Killarney*	**Ayr** **Newbury** **Newmarket☆** **Thirsk** *Gowran Park☆*	**Ayr** **Lingfield☆** **Newbury** **Newmarket** **Ripon** **Southwell☆** *Leopardstown*
22	**23**	**24**	**25**	**26**	**27**	**28**
Keeneland Sales	**Ayr** **Bath** **Nottingham☆** **Windsor☆** *Ballinrobe☆* Keeneland Sales	**Folkestone** **Redcar☆** **Yarmouth** *Ballinrobe* Keeneland Sales	**Doncaster☆** **Redcar** **Sandown☆** **Yarmouth** *Phoenix Park☆* Keeneland Sales	**Brighton** **Doncaster** *Tipperary☆*	**Ascot** **Carlisle** **Pontefract☆**	**Ascot** **Hamilton** **Newcastle** **Southwell☆** **Warwick☆** *Leopardstown*
29	**30**	**31**				
	Lingfield **Newcastle** **Windsor☆** **Wolverhampton☆** *Galway☆* Ascot Sales	**Beverley** **Goodwood** **Leicester☆** *Galway☆*				

BOB JONES INTERNATIONAL HORSE TRANSPORT LTD.

Stabling Available For 40 Horses

2 Stall Boxes To 9 Stall Boxes

MANAGER: DEREK MAYS

CRICKET FIELD ROAD.

NEWMARKET CB8 8BT.

(0638) 663492

AUGUST

Sun	Mon	Tues	Wed	Thur	Fri	Sat
			1 **Catterick** **Goodwood** **Southwell☆** *Galway*	**2** **Goodwood** **Yarmouth** *Galway*	**3** Bangor **Edinburgh☆** **Goodwood** **Newmarket☆** **Thirsk** *Galway☆*	**4** **Goodwood** Market Rasen☆ **Newmarket** Newton Abbot **Thirsk** **Windsor☆** *Galway*
5	**6** Newton Abbot **Nottingham☆** **Ripon** *Gowran Park* *Leopardstown*	**7** **Brighton** **Nottingham☆** **Redcar** *Roscommon☆* Fasig-Tipton Sales	**8** **Brighton** Devon & Exeter **Kempton☆** **Pontefract** *Phoenix Park☆* *Sligo☆* Fasig-Tipton Sales	**9** **Brighton** Devon & Exeter **Pontefract** Uttoxeter☆ *Sligo* *Tipperary☆* Fasig-Tipton Sales	**10** **Haydock☆** Market Rasen **Newmarket☆** Plumpton **Redcar** *Kilbeggan☆*	**11** **Haydock** **Lingfield☆** **Newmarket** **Redcar** **Southwell☆** Worcester☆ *Phoenix Park*
12 *Phoenix Park*	**13** **Leicester☆** **Thirsk☆** **Windsor** Worcester *Gowran Park☆* Doncaster Fasig-Tipton Sales	**14** **Bath** **Catterick☆** Devon & Exeter Fontwell☆ **Yarmouth** *Waterford☆* Doncaster Fasig-Tipton Sales	**15** **Beverley** **Folkestone☆** **Salisbury** **Southwell** *Dundalk* *Waterford* Doncaster Sales	**16** **Beverley** Newton Abbot **Salisbury** **Southwell** *Waterford☆*	**17** **Haydock☆** **Newbury☆** Perth **Southwell** ***Laytown*** *Waterford*	**18** **Bangor** **Lingfield☆** **Market Rasen☆** **Newbury** **Perth** **Ripon** **Wolverhampton** *Curragh* Deauville Goffs Sales
19 Deauville Goffs Sales	**20** **Hamilton** **Windsor** *Roscommon☆* *Wexford☆* Deauville Sales	**21** **Folkestone** **York** *Wexford☆* Deauville Sales	**22** Fontwell **Yarmouth** **York** *Mallow☆* Deauville Sales	**23** **Salisbury☆** **Yarmouth** **York** Tattersalls (Ire) Deauville Sales	**24** Devon & Exeter **Goodwood** **Newmarket** *Phoenix Park☆* Tattersalls (Ire) Sales	**25** Cartmel **Goodwood** Hereford Market Rasen **Newcastle** **Newmarket** **Windsor☆** *Curragh* Deauville Sales
26 *Leopardstown* *Tralee* Cartmel **Chepstow** Huntingdon	**27** **Newcastle** Newton Abbot Plumpton **Ripon** **Sandown** Southwell **Warwick** **Wolverhampton** *Downpatrick* *Tralee☆*	**28** Newton Abbot **Ripon** *Tralee*	**29** **Brighton** Newton Abbot **Redcar** *Tralee*	**30** **Lingfield** Worcester *Tralee*	**31** **Chester** **Sandown** **Thirsk** *Tralee*	

★★★ Super Solvitax HORSEGUARD

THE NAME IN HORSE CARE

Seven Seas Veterinary Division, Marfleet, HULL HU9 5NJ. Telephone: 0482-75234. Fax: 0482-74345.

SEPTEMBER

Sun	Mon	Tues	Wed	Thur	Fri	Sat
30 *Curragh*						**1** **Chester** Hereford **Ripon** **Sandown** *Phoenix Park* Deauville Sales
2 *Phoenix Park*	**3** Hexham **Nottingham** *Galway* Ascot Woodbine Sales	**4** **Brighton** **Pontefract** Sedgefield *Galway* Woodbine Sales	**5** Fontwell **York** *Galway*	**6** Newton Abbot **Salisbury** **York** *Tipperary*	**7** **Haydock** **Kempton** Newton Abbot Fasig-Tipton Sales	**8** **Haydock** **Kempton** **Southwell** Stratford **Thirsk** *Curragh* Fasig-Tipton Sales
9 *Curragh* Keeneland Sales	**10** **Hamilton** **Wolverhampton** *Roscommon* Tattersalls Doncaster Keeneland Sales	**11** **Carlisle** **Leicester** **Lingfield** *Limerick* Doncaster Keeneland Sales	**12** Devon & Exeter **Doncaster** Perth *Fairyhouse* Doncaster Keeneland Sales	**13** **Doncaster** **Folkestone** *Thurles* Doncaster Keeneland Sales	**14** **Doncaster** **Goodwood** Huntingdon Doncaster Keeneland Sales	**15** Bangor **Chepstow** **Doncaster** **Goodwood** Worcester *Leopardstown* Doncaster Keeneland Sales
16 Keeneland Sales	**17** **Bath** **Edinburgh** **Leicester** Plumpton Fasig-Tipton Sales	**18** **Sandown** Sedgefield **Yarmouth** Fasig-Tipton Sales	**19** **Ayr** **Beverley** Devon & Exeter **Sandown** **Yarmouth**	**20** **Ayr** **Beverley** **Lingfield** Uttoxeter **Yarmouth**	**21** **Ayr** **Newbury** **Southwell** Worcester A.N.A.C. Sales	**22** **Ayr** **Catterick** Market Rasen **Newbury** Worcester *Curragh* *Down Royal* A.N.A.C. Sales
23	**24** **Folkestone** **Hamilton** **Nottingham** *Ballinrobe* *Listowel* Doncaster Sales	**25** **Kempton** **Nottingham** **Pontefract** *Listowel* Tattersalls (Ire) Sales	**26** **Brighton** Ludlow Perth Southwell *Dundalk* *Listowel* Tattersalls (Ire) Sales	**27** **Ascot** Perth Taunton *Clonmel* *Listowel* Tattersalls (Ire) Sales	**28** **Ascot** **Haydock** **Redcar** *Listowel* Tattersalls (Ire) Sales	**29** **Ascot** Carlisle **Haydock** Hereford **Redcar** Stratford *Downpatrick* *Phoenix Park*

TRI PLARACON

PLARACON FIBRE - WARM UP TRACK - NEWMARKET

ALL WEATHER

SAND AND RUBBER

EQUESTRIAN SURFACES

FOR

GALLOPS–ARENAS–JUMP AREAS

FOR FURTHER DETAILS
REBECCA & PETER DIAMOND
VILLAGE FARM STUD
POTSGROVE, WOBURN, BEDS MK17 9HQ
0525 290203 PAT NO 2142960

OCTOBER

Sun	Mon	Tues	Wed	Thur	Fri	Sat
	1 **Bath** Carlisle Fontwell Southwell **Wolverhampton** *Roscommon* Ascot Sales	**2** **Brighton** Devon & Exeter **Newcastle** **Wolverhampton** Woodbine Tattersalls Sales	**3** Cheltenham **Newmarket** Perth **Salisbury** *Mallow* Woodbine Tattersalls Sales	**4** Cheltenham **Lingfield** **Newmarket** *Navan* Woodbine Tattersalls Sales	**5** **Goodwood** Hexham **Newmarket** Tattersalls Sales	**6** Chepstow **Goodwood** Kelso **Newmarket** Uttoxeter Worcester *Naas* Goffs (France)
7	**8** **Pontefract** **Warwick** *Gowran Park*	**9** **Folkestone** Newton Abbot **Redcar** **Warwick** Goffs Sales	**10** **Haydock** Plumpton Towcester **York** *Punchestown* Goffs Sales	**11** **Haydock** Wincanton **York** *Punchestown* Goffs Sales	**12** **Ascot** Carlisle Market Rasen Goffs Sales	**13** **Ascot** Ayr Bangor Southwell Warwick **York** *Down Royal*
14 *Phoenix Park*	**15** ***Ayr*** *Fontwell* ***Leicester*** *Dundalk* Tattersalls Ascot Sales	**16** **Ayr** **Chepstow** **Leicester** Sedgefield Tattersalls Sales	**17** Cheltenham **Redcar** Wetherby **Wolverhampton** *Fairyhouse* Tattersalls Sales	**18** Hexham **Newmarket** Taunton Uttoxeter *Wexford* Tattersalls Sales	**19** **Catterick** Ludlow **Newmarket** Tattersalls Sales	**20** **Catterick** Kelso Kempton **Newmarket** Southwell Stratford *Curragh* Tattersalls Sales
21	**22** Fakenham **Folkestone** **Nottingham** *Limerick* Deauville Sales	**23** **Chepstow** **Chester** **Nottingham** Plumpton Deauville Sales	**24** Ascot **Chester** **Edinburgh** Newcastle *Navan* Deauville Doncaster Sales	**25** **Newbury** **Pontefract** Southwell Wincanton *Tipperary* Doncaster Sales	**26** Devon & Exeter **Doncaster** Hereford Newbury Doncaster Sales	**27** Catterick **Doncaster** Huntingdon **Newbury** *Leopardstown* Doncaster Sales
28	**29** **Bath** **Leicester** **Lingfield** *Galway* *Leopardstown* Tattersalls Sales	**30** Fontwell **Leicester** **Redcar** **Salisbury** Tattersalls Sales	**31** **Edinburgh** Newbury Sedgefield **Yarmouth** Tattersalls Sales			

Woodbine Sales '90

"Canada's Premier Thoroughbred Marketplace"

SALES DATES

SEPTEMBER YEARLING SALE
September 3, 4

AUTUMN MIXED SALE
October 2, 3, 4

WOODBINE SALES
(Division of the Ontario Jockey Club)
P.O. Box 156 • Rexdale (Toronto) Ontario M9W5L2 • (416) 674-1460 • Fax (416) 675 3985

NOVEMBER

Sun	Mon	Tues	Wed	Thur	Fri	Sat
				1 Kempton **Newmarket** Stratford *Clonmel* Tattersalls Sales	**2** Bangor **Lingfield†** **Newmarket** Wetherby Tattersalls Sales	**3** Chepstow **Newmarket** Sandown Southwell† Wetherby Worcester *Down Royal* *Naas* Tattersalls Sales
4 Keeneland Sales	**5** **Newcastle** Plumpton Wolverhampton Ascot Keeneland Sales	**6** Devon & Exeter **Hamilton** Hereford Nottingham Keeneland Sales	**7** Kelso Newbury **Southwell†** *Curragh* Keeneland Fasig-Tipton Goffs Sales	**8** **Lingfield†** Uttoxeter Wincanton *Gowran Park* Keeneland Fasig-Tipton Goffs Sales	**9** Cheltenham **Doncaster** Hexham Market Rasen Keeneland Fasig-Tipton Goffs Sales	**10** Cheltenham **Doncaster** Newcastle Windsor *Navan* Keeneland Fasig-Tipton Sales
11 *Punchestown* Keeneland Tattersalls (Ire) Sales	**12** Carlisle **Folkestone** Wolverhampton Tattersalls (Ire) Sales	**13** Sedgefield Southwell† Tattersalls (Ire) Sales	**14** Kempton Worcester *Downpatrick* *Punchestown* Tattersalls (Ire) Sales	**15** Ayr Lingfield† Taunton Towcester *Clonmel* Tattersalls (Ire) Sales	**16** Ascot Ayr Huntingdon Tattersalls (Ire) Sales	**17** Ascot Ayr Catterick Warwick *Naas* Tattersalls (Ire) Sales
18 *Leopardstown*	**19** Bangor Leicester Windsor Doncaster Sales	**20** **Southwell†** Wetherby Wolverhampton Doncaster Sales	**21** Haydock Kelso Plumpton *Fairyhouse* Doncaster Sales	**22** Haydock **Lingfield†** Ludlow Wincanton *Tipperary* Doncaster Sales	**23** Leicester Newbury Sedgefield Doncaster Tattersalls (Ire) Sales	**24** Market Rasen Newbury Newcastle Towcester *Navan* Tattersalls (Ire) Sales
25 Tattersalls (Ire) Sales	**26** Catterick Folkestone Nottingham Ascot Sales	**27** Huntingdon Newton Abbot Stratford Ascot Sales	**28** Hereford Hexham *Naas* Tattersalls Sales	**29** Carlisle Lingfield† Taunton Warwick *Thurles* Tattersalls Sales	**30** Bangor Sandown **Southwell†** Tattersalls Sales	

TIPS

DON'T ADD INSULT TO INJURY

LET TIPS PAY YOUR TRAINING FEES WHEN YOUR HORSE IS OUT OF ACTION

If a horse is out of training due to any illness or injury, TIPS will pay the trainer his training fee on the owner's behalf until the horse has recovered sufficiently to go back into training.

TIPS will pay wherever the horse is located for its convalescence, even if that happens to be the owner's stud.

TIPS
P.O. Box 219,
6 Braham Street,
London E1 8ED

	Phone	Fax
John Garrould	01 488 9535	01 480 7450
Emma Crowe	01 488 9535	01 480 7450

DECEMBER

Sun	Mon	Tues	Wed	Thur	Fri	Sat
30	**31** Catterick Leicester Plumpton *Punchestown*					**1** Chepstow Nottingham Sandown Wetherby *Fairyhouse* Tattersalls Sales
2	**3** Kelso Worcester Tattersalls Sales	**4** Fontwell Leicester Newcastle Tattersalls Sales	**5** Catterick Huntingdon Ludlow Southwell† Tattersalls Sales	**6** **Lingfield†** Taunton Uttoxeter Windsor *Thurles* Tattersalls Sales	**7** Cheltenham Devon & Exeter Doncaster Deauville Tattersalls Sales	**8** Cheltenham Doncaster Lingfield Towcester *Clonmel* *Punchestown* Deauville Tattersalls Sales
9 Deauville Sales	**10** Edinburgh Warwick Deauville Goffs Sales	**11** Plumpton Sedgefield Goffs Sales	**12** Haydock Worcester Goffs Sales	**13** Haydock **Southwell†** *Clonmel* Goffs Sales	**14** Catterick Fakenham Hereford Goffs Sales	**15** Ascot Edinburgh **Lingfield†** Nottingham *Navan*
16	**17** Ascot Sales	**18** Folkestone Southwell†	**19** Bangor Lingfield†	**20** Kelso Towcester	**21** Hexham Ludlow Uttoxeter	**22** Chepstow Edinburgh Hereford Lingfield *Navan*
23	**24**	**25**	**26** Huntingdon Kempton Market Rasen Newton Abbot Sedgefield Wetherby Wincanton Wolverhampton *Down Royal* *Leopardstown* *Limerick*	**27** Kempton **Lingfield†** Taunton Wetherby Wolverhampton *Leopardstown* *Limerick*	**28** Carlisle Fontwell Newbury Stratford *Leopardstown* *Limerick*	**29** Folkestone Newbury Newcastle **Southwell†** Warwick *Leopardstown* *Limerick*

COMPTON TRANSPORT

Compton House Newbury Berks. RG16 0NJ

RELIABILITY FLEXIBILITY ECONOMY	**VERY COMPETITIVE RATES**

BY PRIVATE CONTRACT
or PER STALL/MILE
(Concessions for Contract Work)

3 BOXES AVAILABLE 1 4/5's and 2 supersixes	**CONTINENTAL RACING and STUD WORK A SPECIALITY**

HORSES STABLED and
GROOMS AVAILABLE IN
TRANSIT

For further particulars and conditions contact:

Bryan Marshall (operator)

Tel: Compton (0635) 578440 or 578311 (Messages)
Secretary: Mrs Pollock Compton (0635) 578437
Newmarket Sales Office (0638) 661212

"Racings Official Weekly Newspaper"

THE RACING CALENDAR

Each week The Racing Calendar includes:-

- Jockey Club Notices on matters of importance to the sport.
- Accounts of all Stewards' Enquiries, Fines Imposed, etc.
- Changes to the Rules of Racing or Jockey Club Instructions.
- Final conditions and prize money added of races 2½ to 3½ weeks ahead.
- Lists of entries and weights for principal (Early Closing) races.

Subscribers also receive many supplements, featuring:

- All racing colours currently registered with their owners.
- Full Handicap Ratings Lists for qualification in handicaps.
- Information on racecourses.
- Provisional and final Fixture lists.
- Registered names of Two-Year-Olds.

Please tick the appropriate box. (Cheques made payable to The Jockey Club)

☐ **The Racing Calendar 1990**	**£105**
☐ **The Racing Calendar (Hunter Chase Season)**	**£69**
☐ **The Racing Calendar (Flat Turf Season)**	**£73**

NAME: ______________________________

ADDRESS: ______________________________

____

Return to: Jockey Club Publications, Weatherbys, Sanders Road, Wellingborough, Northants, NN8 4BX. Tel. (0933) 440077.

TBA

Can you afford not to join?

For your membership you'll receive:

- The Thoroughbred Breeder monthly magazine
- Over £60 of discounts off various bloodstock publications
- Advice on taxation, stud husbandry, etc.
- Breeders meetings, visits to studs/research centres/Weatherbys
- Breeders prizes/awards – available to TBA members
- Courses of instruction on stud management, for members and their employees. etc.

For your benefit

Through the efforts of the Thoroughbred Breeders' Association many benefits have been achieved

- European Breeders' Fund – over £2.1 million available in Europe in 1989
- Fillies premiums – £511,000 available in 1990
- Equine Fertility Unit research – new facility near Newmarket
- Animal Health Trust veterinary research, incorporating research for a new EHV-1 vaccine
- Capital Transfer Tax – amendment to 1984 Finance Act
- VAT – continued liaison with H.M.C.&E.
- Ratings – the Rating Issue
- National Hunt 5lb mares/fillies allowance

Subscription £50.00

TBA

Join the Thoroughbred Breeders' Association Now

For more information please contact

Nick Musgrave. Stanstead House, Newmarket, Suffolk CB8 9AA

Telephone (0638) 661321 Fax (0638) 665621

AIR SERVICE SHIPPING BLOODSTOCK TO ALL PARTS OF THE WORLD

BROODMARES TO IRELAND,
RUNNERS TO IRELAND,
CONTACT:

DICK MORGAN LIMITED

23 Upper Mount St., Dublin 2
&
Oakdene, Newtown, Waterford, Ireland.

Personal supervision,
at Ports and Airports.

All classes of Bloodstock
Insurance effected.

During Sales
Kill: 045-77510
Newmarket: 0638-665597
Doncaster: 0302-64509
Fairyhouse: 01-256769

Telex: 93893
Fax: 01-619502
Dublin: 01-760434/5
after hours: 01-851833/854295
Waterford: 051-74664

Front cover— A group from Trevor Kersey's Bleak House Stables during morning exercise.

Photograph by Alan Johnson.

INDEX TO TRAINERS

† denotes Permit to train under N.H. Rules only

Name	Team No.
†BELL, MR C. H. P.	049
BELL, MR C. J.	050
BELL, MR M. L. W.	051
BENNETT, MR J. A.	052
BENNETT, MR R. A.	053
†BENSON, MISS M. J.	054
BENSTEAD, MR C. J.	055
BENTLEY, MR W.	056
BERRY, MR J.	057
BETHELL, MR J. D.	058
BEVAN, MR P. J.	059
BILL, MR T. T.	060
†BIRKETT, MR J. J.	061
†BISSILL, MR W. H.	062
BLANSHARD, MR M. T. W.	063
BLOCKLEY, MR P. A.	064
†BLOOM, MRS J.	065
†BLOOR, MR D. R.	066
BLUM, MR G.	067
BLUNDELL, MR J. W.	068
BOLGER, MR J. S.	069
BOLTON, MR M. J.	070
BOOTH, MR C.	071
BOSLEY, MR J. R.	072
BOSS, MR R.	073
BOTTOMLEY, MR J. F.	074
†BOUSFIELD, MR B.	075
BOUTIN, MR F.	076
†BOWEN, MR S. A.	077
BOWER, MISS L. J.	078
BOWKER, MR M. T.	079
†BOWLBY, LADY ANN	080
BOWRING, MR S. R.	081
BRADBURNE, MRS S. C.	082
BRADLEY, MR J. M.	083
BRADLEY, MR N.	084
BRADSTOCK, MR M. F.	085
BRAMALL, MRS S. A.	086
BRASSEY, MR K. M.	087

Name	Team No.
BRAVERY, MR C. V.	088
BRAZINGTON, MR R. G.	089
BRENNAN, MR O.	090
†BREWIS, MR R.	091
BRIDGER, MR J. J.	092
BRIDGWATER, MR K. S.	093
BRISBOURNE, MR A. H.	094
BRITTAIN, MR C. E.	095
BRITTAIN, MR M. A.	096
BROAD, MR C. D.	097
†BROCKBANK, MR J. E.	098
BROMHEAD, MR H. DE	099
BROOKS, MR C. P. E.	100
BROOKS, MR W. G. A.	101
BROTHERTON, MR R.	102
†BROWN, MR M. L.	103
BROWNE, MR DERMOT	104
BROWNE, MR L.	105
†BRUNT, MRS B.	106
BUKOVETS, MR J. M.	107
BURCHELL, MR D.	108
BURGOYNE, MR P. V. J.	109
BYCROFT, MR N.	110
†BYFORD, MR B.	111

C

Name	Team No.
†CAINE, MR E. M.	112
CALDWELL, MR T. H.	113
CALLAGHAN, MR N. A.	114
CALLOW, MR R.	115
CALVER, MR P.	116
CAMACHO, MR M. J. C.	117
CAMBIDGE, MR B. R.	118
CAMPBELL, MR I.	119
CANDY, MR H. D.	120
CARTER, MR W. Y.	121
CASEY, MR W. T.	122
CASTELL, MR M.	123

By appointment
to Her Majesty the Queen
Suppliers of Equine Products

Horse Requisites Newmarket Ltd

BLACK BEAR LANE • NEWMARKET • SUFFOLK CB8 0JT

Telephone 0638-664619 (6 lines) • Fax 0638-661562

SPECIALISTS IN ALL RACING EQUIPMENT

STARTING STALLS
HORSE WALKERS
SOLARIUMS
WEIGH SCALES
LINSEED BOILERS
STEAM CLEANERS
RUBBER FLOORING
PADDOCK PENS
STABLE DOORS
STABLE WINDOWS
IRONMONGARY
CLIPPERS
FARRIERS EQUIPMENT
VET EQUIPMENT
RACING COLOURS
PADDOCK CLOTHING
RACE WEAR & BOOTS
JOCKEY SKULL CAPS
JODHPURS & BOOTS
BALED SHAVINGS

Please Phone or fax today for our comprehensive catalogue

Name	Team No.
CECIL, MR H. R. A.	124
CECIL, MR H. R. A.	125
CHAMBERLAIN, MR A. J.	126
CHAMBERLAIN, MR N.	127
CHAMPION M.B.E., MR R.	128
CHANCE, MR N.	129
CHANNON, MR MIKE	130
CHAPMAN, MR D. W.	131
CHAPMAN, MR M. C.	132
CHARLES, MR M. J.	133
CHARLTON, MR J. I. A.	134
CHARLTON, MR R. J.	135
CHEVALIER DU FAU, MR E.	136
CHRISTIAN, MR S. P. L.	137
CLAY, MR W.	138
†CLYDE M.R.C.V.S., MR D. H.	139
CODD, MR L. J.	140
COLE, MR P. F. I.	141
COLE, MR S. N.	142
COLLET, MR R.	143
COLLINGRIDGE, MR H. J.	144
†COLLINS, MR M. J.	145
CONNOLLY, MR K.	146
CONNORS, MR P. D.	147
CORBETT, MR L. C.	148
CORDELL LAVARACK, MR D.	149
COTTRELL, MR L. G.	150
CRAIG, MR T.	151
CRAWFORD, MR B. T.	152
†CRAWFORD, LT.CD W. H.	153
†CRIDDLE, MR J.	154
CROFT, MRS J. E.	155
†CULHAM, MRS G. P.	156
CUMANI, MR L. M.	157
CUNDELL, MR P. D.	158
CUNNINGHAM, MR M.	159
CUNNINGHAM, MR T. W.	160
CUNNINGHAM-BROWN, MR K.	161
CURLEY, MR B. J.	162
CURTIS, MR R.	163
CUTHBERT, MR T. A. K.	164
CYZER, MR CHARLES	165
CZERPAK, MR J. D.	166

D

Name	Team No.
†DALTON, MR J. N.	167
DAVIES, MR J. D. J.	168
†DAVIES, MR M. W.	169
†DAVIES, MR P. S.	170
†DAVIS, MR N. H.	171
DAVIS, MR P. W.	172
DENSON, MR A. W.	173
DICKIN, MR R.	174
DICKINSON, MR M.	175
†DIXON, MR J. E.	176
DODS, MR R. W.	177
DOIDGE, MR G. C.	178
†DOLLAR, MISS G.	179
DONNELLY, MR T. W.	180
DOOLER, MR JAMES	181
DOW, MR S. L.	182
DREAPER, MR J.	183
†DUFOSEE, MR P.	184
DUNLOP, MR J. L.	185
†DUNSTAN, MR P. R.	186
DURR, MR F.	187

E

Name	Team No.
EARNSHAW, MR R.	188
EASTERBY, MR M. H.	189
EASTERBY, MR M. W.	190
†EASTON, MRS M.	191
EATON, MISS J. M.	192
ECKLEY, MR M.	193
ECKLEY, MR R. J.	194
EDEN, MR GRANT	195

BY APPOINTMENT
TO HER MAJESTY THE QUEEN
SUPPLIERS OF RACING
COLOURS

BY APPOINTMENT
TO H.M. QUEEN ELIZABETH, THE QUEEN MOTHER.
SUPPLIERS OF RACING
COLOURS

RACING COLOURS AND PADDOCK
CLOTHING A SPECIALITY

GIBSON SADDLERS LTD.

SALES PADDOCK LANE,
(OFF THE AVENUE)
NEWMARKET, SUFFOLK
TEL (0638) 662330/663673
FAX (0638) 730049

Comprehensive range of racing and excercise saddlery, made by craftsmen in our extensive workshops using quality materials.

Tack Room and Stable Fittings available.

Catalogues available on request.

Name	Team No.
EDWARDS, MR J. A. C.	196
ELDIN, MR E.	197
ELLERBY, MR M. W.	198
ELLIOTT, MR J. P. D.	199
ELLISON, MR B.	200
ELSEY, MR C. C.	201
ELSEY, MR C. W. C.	202
ELSWORTH, MR D. R. C.	203
ENRIGHT, MR G. P.	204
ETHERINGTON, MR J.	205
ETHERINGTON, MR T. J.	206
†EUBANK, MR A.	207
EUSTACE, MR J. M. P.	208
EVANS, MRS J.	209
EVANS, MR P. D.	210

F

Name	Team No.
FAIRHURST, MR T.	211
FANSHAWE, MR J. R.	212
FEILDEN, MR P. J.	213
FELGATE, MR P. S.	214
FELLOWS, MR J.	215
FETHERSTON-GODLEY, MR M.	216
FFITCH-HEYES, MR J. R. G.	217
FISHER, MR R. F.	218
FITZGERALD, LORD J.	219
FITZGERALD, MR J. G.	220
FLOOD, MR F.	221
FORSEY, MR B.	222
FORSTER, CAPT T. A.	223
†FORT, MR J. R.	224
†FORTE, MR J. E.	225
FOWLER, MR A.	226
FOWLER, MR J. R. H	227
FOX, MR J. C.	228
FRANCIS, MR M.	229
FRANCIS, MR R. B.	230
†FRENCH, MRS S.	231
FROST, MR R. G.	232
†FULLERTON, MRS H. J.	233

G

Name	Team No.
GANDOLFO, MR D. R.	234
GASELEE, MR N. A.	235
†GEE, MR B.	236
GIFFORD, MR J. T.	237
GLOVER, MR J. A.	238
GOLDIE, MR R. H.	239
†GOLDIE, MR T.	240
†GOODFELLOW, MRS A. C. D.	241
†GOSPEL, MRS S. J.	242
GRACEY, MR G. G.	243
GRAHAM, MR N. A.	244
GRASSICK, MR M. J.	245
†GRAY, MR F.	246
†GREATHEAD, MR T. R.	247
GREEN, MISS Z. A.	248
†GREGSON, MR G. G. A.	249
†GREIG, MR D. R.	250
†GRIFFITHS, MR S. G.	251
GRISSELL, MR D. M.	252
GUBBY, MR B.	253
GUEST, MR R.	254

H

Name	Team No.
HAGGAS, MR W. J.	255
HAIGH, MR W. W.	256
HAINE, MRS D.	257
HALDANE, MR J. S.	258
†HALL, MR G. V.	259
HALL, MISS P. J.	260
HALL, MISS S. E.	261
HALLETT, MR T. B.	262
HAM, MR G. A.	263

Your aim is to win races
ours is to win cases.

TAYLOR
VINTERS

SOLICITORS

Contact: Jeremy Richardson or Anna Hall
119, High Street, Newmarket. Telephone (0638) 663571

Name	Team No.
HANBURY, MR B.	264
HANNON, MR R.	265
HANSON, MR J.	266
HARRIS, MR J. L.	267
HARRIS, MR P. W.	268
HARRIS, MR S. T.	269
HARTOP, MR R. W.	270
HARTY, MR E. P.	271
HARWOOD, MR G.	272
HASTINGS-BASS, MR W.	273
HAYDEN, MR JOHN C	274
HAYDN JONES, MR D	275
†HAYNES, MR H. E.	276
HAYNES, MR M. J.	277
HAYWARD, MR P. A.	278
†HEAD, LORD	279
HEAD, MRS C.	280
HEATH, MRS E. H.	281
HEDGER, MR P. R.	282
†HELLENS, MR J. A.	283
†HEMBROW, MRS S. J. R.	284
HENDERSON, MR N. J.	285
†HENRIQUES, MR M.	286
HERN C.V.O., MAJOR W. R.	287
HERRIES, LADY	288
HETHERTON, MR J.	289
HEWITT, MRS A. R.	290
HIDE, MR A.	291
HILLS, MR B. W.	292
HILLS, MR J. W.	293
†HITCHINGS, MR C. J.	294
HOAD, MR R. P. C.	295
HOBBS, MR P. J.	296
†HODGE, MR H. B.	297
HODGES, MR R. J.	298
HOLDEN, MR W.	299
HOLDER, MR R. J.	300
HOLLINSHEAD, MR R.	301
†HOLLY, MR D.	302

Name	Team No.
HOLMES, MR C. J.	303
HOLT, MR L. J.	304
HONEYBALL, MR J.	305
HORGAN, MR C.	306
†HOULBROOKE, MR T. J.	307
HOWLING, MR PAUL	308
†HUBBARD, MR G. A.	309
HUDSON, MR J. P.	310
HUFFER, MR G. A.	311
HUGHES, MR D. T.	312
HUGHES, MR P.	313

I

Name	Team No.
INCISA, DON ENRICO	314
IVORY, MR K. T.	315

J

Name	Team No.
JACKSON, MR C. F. C.	316
†JACKSON, MR F. S.	317
†JACKSON, MRS V. S.	318
JAMES, MR C. J.	319
JAMES, MR M. B. C.	320
†JAMES, MRS M. C.	321
JARVIS, MR M. A.	322
JARVIS, MR W.	323
JEFFERSON, MR J. M.	324
†JEFFREY, MR T. E.	325
JENKINS, MR J. R. W.	326
JERMY, MR D. C.	327
†JERRAM, MR M. J.	328
†JESTIN, MR F.	329
JOHNSON, MR J. HOWARD	330
†JOHNSON, MR M. A.	331
†JOHNSON, MR R. W.	332
JOHNSON HOUGHTON, MR R.	333
JOHNSTON, MR M. S.	334
JONES, MR A. W.	335

THE

Bonner bandage™

"THE FROZEN BANDAGE"

*Tested successfully at leading veterinary institutions worldwide. This remarkable bandage remains **flexible when frozen**, providing both penetrating cold and **all-round compression**.*

Non-toxic, machine washable and virtually indistructable.

From leading tack shops, saddlers and equestrian outlets. All enquiries welcome. Please contact:

EQUETECH LTD.
Plaza 535 Kings Road, London SW10 0SZ
Tel: 01-351 2906 Fax: 01-352 4307

Name	Team No.
†JONES, MR G. E.	336
JONES, MRS G. E.	337
JONES, MR G. H.	338
JONES, MR P. J.	339
JONES, MR T. M.	340
JORDAN, MR F. T. J.	341

K

Name	Team No.
KAUNTZE, MR M.	342
KELLEWAY, MR P. A.	343
KELLY, MR G. P.	344
KEMP, MR W. T.	345
†KENDALL, MRS M. A.	346
KERNICK, MR N.	347
KERSEY, MR T	348
KETTLEWELL, MR S. E.	349
†KEY, MR B. L.	350
KING, MISS A. L. M.	351
KING, MR J. S.	352
KNIGHT, MRS A.	353
KNIGHT, MISS H. C.	354

L

Name	Team No.
LAMB, MR R. R.	355
†LAYLAND, MR J. R. M.	356
†LE BLOND, MR A. J.	357
†LE GRICE, MR T. C.	358
LEACH, MR M. R.	359
LEACH, MR P. S.	360
LEADBETTER, MR S. J.	361
†LEDGER, MR R. R.	362
LEE, MR A. N.	363
†LEE, MR C. F.	364
LEE, MR D	365
LEE, MR FRANCIS H.	366
LEE, MR R	367
LEIGH, MR J. P.	368
LEWIS, MR G.	369
LIDDLE, MR P.	370
†LLEWELLYN, MR B. J.	371
†LOVE, MR J.	372

M

Name	Team No.
MACKIE, MR W. J. W.	373
†MACTAGGART, MR A. H.	374
MADGWICK, MR M. J.	375
MAKIN, MR P. J.	376
MANN, MR W. G.	377
MANNING, MR R. J.	378
MARKS, MR D.	379
MARVIN, MR RICHARD	380
MCCAIN, MR D.	381
†MCCASKILL, MR D	382
MCCORMACK, MR M.	383
MCCOURT, MR M.	384
MCDONALD, MR R.	385
MCGRATH, MR NEIL S.	386
†MCINNES SKINNER, MRS C.	387
†MCKENZIE-COLES, MR W. G.	388
MCKIE, MRS V	389
MCLEAN, MR B.	390
MCMAHON, MR B. A.	391
MCMATH, MR B. J.	392
MEADE, MR N.	393
MELLOR, MR S.	394
†MILLER, MR N.	395
†MILLIGAN, MISS M. K.	396
MILLMAN, MR B. R.	397
†MINNS, MRS S.	398
†MITCHELL, MR C. W.	399
MITCHELL, MR N. R.	400
MITCHELL, MR P.	401
MITCHELL, MR PAT	402
MOFFATT, MR D.	403
MONTEITH, MR PETER	404

TBA

190 Church Road,
Hove, BN3 2DJ

Telephone: 0273-722422

★S.P. or TOTE
★NO LIMITS
★TOP COMMISSION RATES PAID
★WINNING ACCOUNTS NEVER CLOSED, HOWEVER SUCCESSFUL
★NO MAXIMUM STAKE; LARGE WAGERS ARE BROKEN DOWN AMONG MANY OUTLETS TO PRESERVE A TRUE S.P.
★ALL SYSTEMS and STAKING PLANS OPERATED
★"BEST OF THE BIG THREES" ANTE POST or EARLY PRICES MATCHED
★DETAILED COMPUTERISED STATEMENTS

ESTABLISHED OVER 46 YEARS

TO OPEN A DEPOSIT ACCOUNT POST COUPON OR PHONE 0273-722422

Full Name ....

Address ....

....

I enclose cheque value ....

Signature ....**Date**.......................

Name	Team No.
MOORE, MR A.	405
MOORE, MR A. L.	406
MOORE, MR G. M.	407
MORGAN, MR B. C.	408
MORGAN, MR K. A.	409
MORLEY, MR M. F. D	410
MORRIS, MR M.	411
MORRIS, MR W. G.	412
MOUBARAK, MR M.	413
MULDOON, MR S. J.	414
MURPHY, MR M. P. F.	415
MUSSON, MR W. J.	416

N

Name	Team No.
†NASH, MR C. T.	417
NAUGHTON, MR M. P.	418
†NEAVES, MR A. S.	419
†NEEDHAM, MR J. L.	420
NELSON, MR C. R.	421
†NELSON, MR W. M.	422
NICHOLSON, MR D.	423
†NORTH, MRS H. E.	424
NORTON, MR J.	425
NORTON, MR S. G.	426
†NUGENT, MR D. H.	427

O

Name	Team No.
O'BRIEN, MISS G.	428
O'BRIEN, MR M. V.	429
O'CONNOR, MISS P.	430
O'DONOGHUE, MR J.	431
O'GORMAN, MR W. A.	432
O'GRADY, MR E. J.	433
O'LEARY, MR R. M.	434
O'MAHONY, MR F. J.	435
O'NEILL, MR J. J.	436
O'NEILL, MR M. J.	437
O'NEILL, MR O.	438
O'SHEA, MR J. G. M.	439
O'SULLIVAN, MR R. J.	440
O'TOOLE, MR M. A.	441
OLD, MR J. A. B.	442
OLIVER, MR J. K. M.	443
OLIVER, MR M.	444
OLIVER, MRS S.	445
OWEN, MR E. H.	446
OXX, MR J. M.	447

P

Name	Team No.
†PAISLEY, MR R.	448
PALLING, MR BRYN	449
†PARFITT, MR J.	450
PARKER, MR C.	451
PARKES, MR J. E.	452
PARROTT, MRS H.	453
†PAUL, MR W. J. L.	454
†PAYNE, MR J. R.	455
PAYNE, MR J. W.	456
PAYNE, MR S. G.	457
†PEACHEY, MR H. E.	458
PEACOCK, MR R. E.	459
PEARCE, MR J.	460
PEASE, MR J. E.	461
†PERKINS, MR R. A. H.	462
PERRETT, MR A. C. J.	463
PERRIN, MR W. M.	464
PICKERING, MR J. A.	465
PIGGOTT, MRS L.	466
†PIKE, MR S. L.	467
†PILE, MRS P. M.	468
†PILKINGTON, MR J.	469
†PINCOMBE, MR R. W.	470
PIPE, MR M. C.	471
PITMAN, MRS J.	472
†POCOCK, MR R. E.	473

Lester Bowden

HIGH STREET, EPSOM, SURREY KT19 8DT

Tel. Epsom (0372) 42411

Specialist Racing Outfitters since 1902

RACING COLOUR SERVICES

To order in pure silk, best jockey nylon, slipper satin or knitted National Hunt. (Price List Available)

PADDOCK CLOTHING SERVICES

To order in melton, super cloth, medium or heavyweight woollen cloths. (Price List Available)

JOCKEY'S CLOTHING INCLUDES

Exercise jodhpurs, race breeches, race boots, race whips, jockey skulls, race goggles, Epsom range of jodhpur boots, waterproof suits, Puffa jackets and vests, Barbour wax jackets, chaps, race mitts, safety back plates and vests.

RACE SADDLERY INCLUDES

Bates race saddles, full and half tree exercise saddles, irons, race leathers, race bridles, blinkers, visors, girth protectors, girths, surcingles, weight cloths etc.

Please write or call for your 1989 New Edition Race Catalogue with full measure forms sent by return of post. f.o.c.

Name	Team No.
POPHAM, MR C. L.	474
POTTS, MR A. W.	475
†POWELL, MR G. J.	476
PREECE, MR W. G.	477
PRENDERGAST, MR K.	478
PRENDERGAST, MR P.	479
PRESCOTT BT, SIR M.	480
PREST, MR G. R.	481
PRICE, MR G. H.	482
†PRICE, MR J. P.	483
†PRICE, MR T. J.	484
PRICE, MR WILLIAM	485
PRITCHARD, MR P. A.	486
†PRITCHARD, DR P. L. J.	487
PRITCHARD-GORDON, MR G.	488
†PUGH, MR R. C.	489

R

Name	Team No.
RAMSDEN, MRS J. R.	490
RANSOM, MR P.	491
†RATCLIFF, MRS A. E.	492
†RATCLIFFE, MR C. I.	493
REDMOND, MR J. V.	494
REED, MR W. G.	495
REES, MISS G. M.	496
†REID, MR A. S.	497
†REID, MR T.	498
RETTER, MRS J. G.	499
REVELEY, MRS G. R.	500
RICHARDS, MR G. W.	501
†RICHARDSON, MRS S.	502
RICHMOND, MR B.	503
†RIDOUT, MR A. S.	504
RINGER, MR D. J.	505
RIPLEY, MR G.	506
ROACH, MR C. G.	507
ROBERTS, MR J.	508
†ROBERTSON, MR D.	509
ROBINSON, MR M. H. B.	510
ROBINSON, MR W. R.	511
†ROBSON, MR E. H.	512
†ROBSON, MR T. L. A.	513
RODFORD, MR P. R.	514
ROE, MR C. G.	515
†ROE, MR G. L.	516
†ROPER, MR J. H.	517
ROPER, MR W. M.	518
ROUALLE, MR J. DE	519
ROUGET, MR J. C.	520
ROYER-DUPRE, MR A. DE	521
†RUMSEY, MR A. J.	522
†RYALL, MR B. J. M.	523
RYAN, MR M. J.	524

S

Name	Team No.
†SAMPLE, MAJOR W. N.	525
SANDERS, MISS B.	526
†SAUNDERS, MR C. R.	527
SCARGILL, DR J. D.	528
SCOTT, MR A. A.	529
†SCOTT, MR D. D.	530
†SCOTT, MRS E. B.	531
SCOTT, MR M. R.	532
SCUDAMORE, MR M. J.	533
SEMPLE, MR I.	534
SHARPE, MRS N. S.	535
SHAW, MR J. R.	536
†SHEEDY, MR W.	537
SHERWOOD, MR O. M. C.	538
SIDDALL, MISS L. C.	539
SIMPSON, MR R.	540
†SKELTON, MR J.	541
SKINNER, MR M. M.	542
SLY, MRS P. M.	543
SMART, MR B.	544
SMITH, MR A.	545

Flying winners around the world is a one-horse race

If you'd like to know why more owners and trainers trust their mounts to IRT than to any other company, call us.

Your horse couldn't be in better hands.

Robertsbridge Telephone 0580-881122 Fax 0580-880803
Newmarket Telephone 0638-778305 Fax 0638-778118

IRT
INTERNATIONAL RACEHORSE TRANSPORT

Bond Miles Coulter 019 B

Name	Team No.
SMITH, MR C.	546
SMITH, MR D.	547
SMITH, MR J. P.	548
†SMITH, MRS M. M.	549
SMITH, MR N. A.	550
†SMITH, MR R. J.	551
†SMITH, MR S. G.	552
†SMITH, MR W. J.	553
SMYTH, MR R. V.	554
SPARES, MR C. W.	555
SPEARING, MR J. L.	556
†SPICER, MR R. C.	557
STACK, MR T.	558
STEPHENSON, MR W. A.	559
STEVENS, MR B.	560
STEWART, MR A. C.	561
†STICKLAND, MR G.	562
†STOREY, MR F. S.	563
STOREY, MR W.	564
STOUTE, MR M.	565
STRINGER, MR A. P.	566
STUBBS, MR R. W.	567
SUTCLIFFE, MR J.	568
SWAN, CAPT. D.	569
†SWINDLEHURST, MR D. G.	570

T

Name	Team No.
TATE, MR M.	571
TATE, MR T. P.	572
†TAYLOR, MR A. J.	573
†TAYLOR, MR F.	574
†TEAL, MRS V. J.	575
†TEMPLE, MR B. M.	576
†TETLEY, MRS P. A.	577
THOM, MR D. T.	578
THOMAS, MR J. D.	579
THOMPSON, MR R.	580
THOMPSON, MR RONALD	581
†THOMSON, MR A. M.	582
†THOMSON, MRS D.	583
THOMSON JONES, MR H.	584
THORNE, MISS J.	585
THORNER, MR G. E.	586
THORNTON, MR C. W.	587
TINKLER, MR C.	588
TINKLER, MR N.	589
†TINNING, MR W. H.	590
TOLLER, MR J. A. R.	591
TOMPKINS, MR M. H.	592
TOPLEY, MR D. H.	593
†TORR, MR S.	594
†TOWNSEND, MR R. D.	595
TOWNSLEY, MRS P.	596
TRIETLINE, MR C. C.	597
TUCKER, MR D.	598
TUCKER, MR D. R.	599
†TULLIE, MRS A. F.	600
TURNELL, MR A.	601
†TURNER, MR J. S. E.	602
†TURNER, MISS S. J.	603
TURNER, MR W. G.	604
TURNER, MR W. G. M.	605
†TURTON, MR S. F.	606
TWISTON-DAVIES, MR N. A.	607

U

Name	Team No.
†UPSON, MR JOHN R.	608
USHER, MR M. D. I.	609

V

Name	Team No.
†VERNON, MR M. S.	610
VERNON MILLER, MR C. J.	611
VOORSPUY, MR R.	612

Raceform

PRIVATE HANDICAP

The Racing Service which has stood the test for 57 years

BIG PRICED WINNERS OF THE 1989 FLAT

54 at 10/1 or better

Summarised below are the 54 winners at 10/1 or better which were top-rated by Raceform Private Handicap on the Flat during the season just ended. They demonstrate how our private handicappers are not frightened to leave a runner top-rated even though it may not recently have revealed its best form.

1 WON AT 50/1
2 WON at 33/1
2 WON at 25/1
6 WON at 20/1
9 WON at 16/1
10 WON at 14/1
12 WON at 12/1
12 WON at 11/1 and 12/1

Daily Ratings for all meetings
Two-year-olds from mid-May, Jumpers mid-October to Easter
Two full weeks: £23; Three weeks: £30; Five Weeks: £45
Saturdays Only: Four Saturdays: £10.50; Ten Saturdays: £23

RACEFORM LTD,
COMPTON, NEWBURY, BERKS. RG16 0NL

Name	Team No.
W	
†WAGGOTT, MR N.	613
WAINWRIGHT, MR J. S.	614
†WALES, MR W. A.	615
†WALEY-COHEN, MR R. B.	616
WALL, MR C. F.	617
†WALMSLEY, MR J. W.	618
WALWYN, MR F.	619
WALWYN, MR P. T.	620
†WARD, MRS S. A.	621
†WARD, MRS V. C.	622
WARING, MRS B.	623
†WARING, MR L.	624
†WATERMAN, MISS S.	625
WATTS, MR J. W.	626
WEAVER, MR R. J.	627
WEBBER, MR J.	628
WEEDON, MR C. V.	629
WELD, MR D. K.	630
†WELLICOME, MR D. R.	631
†WELLS, MR B. K.	632
WEYMES, MR E.	633
WHARTON, MR J. R. H.	634
WHARTON, MRS V. R. T.	635
WHEELER, MR E. A.	636
†WHEELER, MR N. J.	637
WHITAKER, MR R. M.	638
†WHITE, MR C. J.	639
†WHITE, MRS F. E.	640
WHITE, MR J.	641
WHITE, MR K.	642
WHITFIELD, MISS A. J.	643
WIGHAM, MR P.	644
WIGHTMAN, MR W. G. R.	645
WILDMAN, MR C. P.	646
WILKINSON, MR B. E.	647
†WILKINSON, MRS J. V.	648

Name	Team No.
WILKINSON, MR M. J.	649
WILLIAMS, MR C. N.	650
†WILLIAMS, MR D.	651
WILLIAMS, MR D. L.	652
WILLIAMS, MR R. J. R.	653
WILLIAMS, MR W. R.	654
WILLIS, MR H.	655
WILSON, MR A. J.	656
WILSON, MR D. A.	657
WILSON, CAPT. J. H.	658
WILSON, MR J. S.	659
WILSON, MR W. T. J.	660
WILTON, MISS S. J.	661
WINGROVE, MR K. G.	662
WONNACOTT, MRS J.	663
WOODHOUSE, MR R. D. E.	664
WOODMAN, MR S.	665
WRAGG, MR G.	666
Y	
YARDLEY, MR F. J.	667
YARDLEY, MR G. H.	668
†YOUNG, MR V. P.	669
BELL, MR D. J.	670
BRANDON, MR R.	671
BUTLER, MR P.	672
CHUGG, MR J.	673
FISHER, MR W. E.	674
LONG, MR J. E.	675
MULLINS, MR P.	676
THOMSON JONES, MR T.	677
WATSON, MR F.	678
WELSH, MR D. D. G.	679

NOTED TO WIN

The race-readers, who add such invaluable comments on running to this Annual and Raceform Weekly, are able to amplify their reports in Raceform Note-Book, which is published every Friday throughout the Flat Racing Season. The Note-Book gives basic form details of the first six in each race, plus notes on every worthwhile runner. The race-readers express their opinion about future prospects, the likely two-year-olds, the handicappers returning to form, the potential classic candidates and the promising maidens. They make a point of earmarking future winners. Often their observations will enable the shrewd backer to collect at very remunerative odds.

Subscribers start with the Raceform Note-Book Filing Book, containing the season's returns complete so far including All-Weather Track racing and the famous INDEX TO WINNERS. Loose-leaf issues, including an updated index **with Raceform Private Handicap ratings,** are posted every Wednesday.

Full Turf Season: £86.00
Seven Weeks: £23.00

RACEFORM NOTE-BOOK
1989 COMPLETE
(Specially Bound) £15.00

RACEFORM LTD., COMPTON,
NEWBURY, BERKS. RG16 0NL
Telephone: 0635 578080 Fax: 0635 578101

LONDON THOROUGHBRED SERVICES LTD

International Bloodstock
Transactions

Bloodstock as an investment
Valuations, transport, insurance

**LONDON
THOROUGHBRED
SERVICES
LTD**

7 Phene Street,
London SW3 5NZ

Telephone 01 351 2181/2
Telex 916950 LONTSL G
Fax 01 352 8958

1

PROPERTY OF HER MAJESTY

The Queen

Colours: Purple, gold braid, scarlet sleeves, black cap with gold fringe

Trained by **Mr W. Hastings-Bass,** Hodcott Stables, Newbury

1 **STARLET**, 4, b f Teenoso (USA)—Pas de Deux

THREE-YEAR-OLDS

2 **ALLURE**, b f Bustino—Albany
3 **CHURCH MISSIONARY (USA)**, b f Miswaki (USA)—Christchurch (FR)
4 **ENHARMONIC (USA)**, ch c Diesis—Contralto
5 **HOPSCOTCH**, b f Dominion—Tartan Pimpernel
6 **PIQUANT**, b g Sharpo—Asnoura (MOR)

TWO-YEAR-OLDS

7 **CHESNUT TREE (USA)**, b f 16/1 Shadeed (USA)—Expansive (Exbury)
8 **COLOUR SERGEANT**, b c 9/3 Green Desert (USA)—Tartan Pimpernel (Blakeney)
9 **HIAWATHA'S SONG**, b c 14/2 Dancing Brave (USA)—Soprano (Kris)
10 **LAST MATCH**, b g 7/3 Final Straw—Light Duty (Queen's Hussar)
11 **MIGHTY WIND**, ch c 18/2 Kris—Storm Warning (Tumble Wind (USA))
12 **MOTLEY**, b f 20/3 Rainbow Quest (USA)—Sans Blague (USA) (The Minstrel (CAN))
13 **REVEL**, ch c 8/3 Sharpo—Waltz (Jimmy Reppin)
14 **SHARE HOLDER**, b f 28/1 Shareef Dancer (USA)—Silver Dollar (Shirley Heights)
15 **TALENT (USA)**, b c 27/4 Clever Trick (USA)—Contralto (Busted)
16 **WHITECHAPEL (USA)**, b c 13/5 Arctic Tern (USA)—Christchurch (FR) (So Blessed)
17 **WILY TRICK (USA)**, b f 10/5 Clever Trick (USA)—Highclere (Queen's Hussar)

Trained by **Mr I. A. Balding,** Park House, Kingsclere

18 **VITALITY**, 4, b f Young Generation—Blaze of Glory

THREE-YEAR-OLDS

19 **BAND OF HOPE (USA)**, ch f Dixieland Band (USA)—Reflection
20 **ONCE UPON A TIME**, b f Teenoso (USA)—Pas de Deux
21 **SON ET LUMIERE**, ch f Rainbow Quest (USA)—Soprano

TWO-YEAR-OLDS

22 **BASS ROCK**, b c 12/5 Bellypha—Dunfermline (Royal Palace)
23 **BUDGET**, ch g 5/2 Bustino—Australia Fair (AUS) (Without Fear (FR))
24 **DOMAIN**, b c 20/2 Dominion—Prelude (Troy)
25 **FAR APART**, br/gr f 26/1 Bellypha—Joking Apart (Jimmy Reppin)
26 **FORGE**, ch c 12/2 Formidable (USA)—Red Shoes (Dance In Time (CAN))
27 **MOAT GARDEN (USA)**, b c 14/4 Sportin' Life (USA)—Round Tower (High Top)
28 **PLAYING TRUANT**, b c 17/5 Teenoso (USA)—Elusive (Little Current (USA))
29 **SELF EXPRESSION**, b c 14/3 Homing—Subtlety (Grundy)

Trained by **Major W. Hern, C.V.O.** , West Ilsley Stables, Newbury

30 **TRYING FOR GOLD (USA)**, 4 b f Northern Baby (CAN)—Expansive

THREE-YEAR-OLDS

31 **FULL ORCHESTRA**, b f Shirley Heights—Harpstrings (FR)
32 **MARIENSKI (USA)**, b c Nureyev (USA)—Highclere
33 **RHODES**, ch g Pharly (FR)—Beacon Hill
34 **ROYAL ARCHIVE (USA)**, b f Shadeed (USA)—Round Tower

2

THE PROPERTY OF
H.M. QUEEN ELIZABETH THE QUEEN MOTHER

Colours: Blue, buff stripes, blue sleeves, black cap with gold tassel

Trained by **Fulke Walwyn**, Saxon House Stables, Lambourn.

1 **ADMIRAL'S LEAP,** 6, ch g Quayside—Sailor's Will
2 **DUDLEY,** 7, ch g Owen Dudley—Altruist
3 **FRIARY COURT,** 5, ch g Monkfield—Honours Bless
4 **FURRY KNOWE,** 5, b g Furry Glen—I Know
5 **LUNEDALE,** 12, b g Apollo Eight—Singing Hinny
6 **ROYAL PAVILION,** 7, ch g Royalty—Manushi
7 **SUNSHINE FLIGHT,** 6, b g Sunyboy—Barbella
8 **THE ARGONAUT (NZ),** 12, br g Captain Jason—Syalbi (NZ)

3 MRS V. A. ACONLEY, Weston

Postal: **Stud Farm, Westow, York, YO6 7LX.**
Phone: **(0653) 695042 OR (065381) 594**

1 **CARTHAGENA COTTAGE,** 5, b g Sonnen Gold—Gentle Daisy **Mr P. Aconley**
2 **COSMIC RAY,** 5, b g Comedy Star (USA)—Hey Skip (USA) **Mr P. Aconley**
3 **FIRST LORD,** 4, b g Lord Gayle (USA)—Touquaise (FR) **Mr P. Aconley**
4 4, Ch f Le Bavard (FR)—Kates Wish **Mr P. Aconley**
5 **LANGROVE,** 6, b g Cleon—Dear Lady **Mr P. Aconley**
6 **LANGTON MIST,** 5, b g Grey Ghost—La Raine **Mr P. Aconley**
7 **THE PIKE,** 7, b g Proverb—Daybrook Lass **Mr P. Aconley**

THREE-YEAR-OLDS

8 **SEE THE LIGHT,** b f Relkino—Sun Worshipper **Mr P. Aconley**

TWO-YEAR-OLDS

9 B f 15/3 Marching On—Gambling Wren (Knave To Play) **Mr P. Aconley**

Jockey (NH): John J Quinn (10-0).

4 MR R. P. J. AKEHURST, Epsom

Postal: **South Hatch Stables, 44 Burgh Heath Road, Epsom, Surrey, KT17 4NN.**
Phone: **(0372) 727596 FAX (0372) 721918**

1 **AFRICAN DASH,** 4, b f African Sky—Nibellunga **Mr Peter G. P. Hodgson**
2 **AIR BROKER (NZ),** 9, b g Oakville—Sweet Canyon (NZ) **Food Brokers Ltd**
3 **ATTIKI,** 8, b g Final Straw—Honeypot Lane **Mr Les Randall**
4 **AUCTION TIME,** 7, br g Auction Ring (USA)—Autumn Flush **Mr John Wickins**
5 **BARRISH,** 4, b c Wassl—Rowa **Mr A. D. Spence**
6 **BELDALE STAR,** 7, b g Beldale Flutter (USA)—Little White Star **Mr R. F. Kilby**
7 **BOLD IMP,** 5, br h Dubassoff (USA)—Woodlands Girl **Mr J. T. Heritage**
8 **BROWN PEPPER,** 4, br g Sharpo—Petrary **Mr W. J. Brown**
9 **CHEMIST BROKER (NZ),** 10, b g Oakville—Sweet Canyon (NZ) **Food Brokers Ltd**
10 **COCK A LEEKIE (NZ),** 7, b g Mayo Mellay (NZ)—Summermayo (NZ) **Food Brokers Ltd**

MR R. P. J. AKEHURST—continued

11 **COCKSTOWN LAD,** 4, b g Main Reef—Pasadena Girl **Mr D. W. Baldwin**
12 **COE,** 4, b br g Coquelin (USA)—Gully **Mr Michael Blackburn**
13 **COMBINED EXERCISE,** 6, br g Daring March—Dualvi **Mr M. G. Reilly**
14 **DUDIE,** 12, b g Karabas—En Clair **Halewood Vintners Ltd**
15 **FACT FINDER,** 6, br h Known Fact (USA)—Idealist **Mr A. D. Spence**
16 **FACTOTUM,** 7, b g Known Fact (USA)—Blue Shark **Mr D. M. Stone**
17 **FIRE TOP,** 5, br h Hotfoot—Sirnelta (FR) **Mrs A. Valentine**
18 **FOLLOW THE SEA,** 4, ch g Tumble Wind (USA)—Seapoint **Mr Harry Hutton**
19 **FOODBROKER FLYER (NZ),** 6, b g In The Purple (FR)—Disguise (NZ) **Food Brokers Ltd**
20 **GAASID,** 5, ch h Kings Lake (USA)—Le Melody **Mr Eric Parker**
21 **GHILAN (USA),** 4, b c Linkage (USA)—Chuckle (USA) **Mr Micky Burt**
22 **GLENSTAL ABBEY (USA),** 4, ch g Gregorian (USA)—Full Delivery (USA) **Mr Terry Milson**
23 **GOOD SPARK,** 4, b br g Good Times (ITY)—Bright Spark **Mrs S. R. Crowe**
24 **GRAND PRIX,** 5, b h Formidable (USA)—Mumruffin **Mrs Tracy Stone-Brown**
25 **GULF PALACE (USA),** 5, ch h Green Dancer (USA)—Sanctum Sanctorum (USA) **Mr Colin Mason**
26 **HATS HIGH,** 5, b g High Top—Peculiar One (USA) **Mr E. O'Neill**
27 **HERE HE COMES,** 4, b g Alzao (USA)—Nanette **Mr Peter G. P. Hodgson**
28 **IZIOFF,** 4, ch c Sayyaf—Marova (FR) **Mr D. G. Phillips**
29 **JUVEN LIGHT (FR),** 9, b g Lightning (FR)—Juvenescence **Mr H. P. L. Frost**
30 **KTOLO,** 4, b f Tolomeo—Miss Kate (FR) **Mr Peter G. P. Hodgson**
31 5, B m Layal—Last Trick **Mr T. Batten**
32 **LAZY RHYTHM (USA),** 4, gr c Drone—Ritual Dance **Miss S. A. Hamilton**
33 **LOANINGDALE,** 5, ch g Lomond (USA)—Aliceva **Mrs S. M. Crane**
34 **MADAM JAC,** 4, b f Anfield—Lucky Petina **Mr C. C. Clarke**
35 **MADFA,** 5, b g Prince Tenderfoot (USA)—Vectis **Mr A. D. Spence**
36 **MAKE CONTACT (USA),** 4, b c Fappiano (USA)—Touch (USA) **Mr Harry Hutton**
37 **MAN ON THE LINE,** 7, ch g Whistling Deer—Black Tulip **Mr Les Randall**
38 **MASTER OF LYRIC,** 8, br g Grange Melody—Miss Goodyear **Halewood Vintners Ltd**
39 **METRO LINER,** 4, b g Zino—Bellinzona **Mr Charles Rogers**
40 **MONETARY FUND,** 6, br g Red Sunset—Msida **Mr J. S. Court**
41 **MONTE BRE,** 4, ch c Henbit (USA)—Madame du Barry (FR) **Mr G. S. Beccle**
42 **NATIVE KNIGHT,** 5, b g Be My Native (USA)—Lady Pit **Mr G. S. Beccle**
43 **NEARROE,** 4, ch g Noalto—Incarnadine **Mr A. T. Boanas**
44 **NIKATINO,** 4, b f Bustino—Latakia **Mr H. Austwick**
45 **NONE SO WISE (USA),** 4, ch g Believe It (USA)—Nonesuch Bay **Mr E. Reitel**
46 **OLD VIRGINIA,** 4, ch c Burslem—Molly's Party **Garnmoss Ltd (Parham Bros Builders)**
47 **OPEN ALL HOURS,** 8, b g Martinmas—Land **C. G. O'Brien**
48 **PRINCE SATIRE (USA),** 7, b h Sensitive Prince (USA)—No Comedy (USA) **Britannic Travel Ltd**
49 **PROUD PATRIOT,** 5, ch g Kalaglow—Sandforinia **Mrs S. M. Akehurst**
50 **RAAHIN (USA),** 5, ch h Super Concorde (USA)—Bonnie Hope (USA) **Mr H. P. L. Frost**
51 **RAISE A STAR,** 5, b g Red Sunset—Hill's Realm (USA) **R. J. & S. Styles Ltd**
52 **RICHARD'S LAD,** 5, b g Magnolia Lad—Parton Queen **Mr M. Orloff**
53 **RINGYBOY,** 5, b g Runnett—Graunuaile **Mr Harry Hutton**
54 **ROYAL ASTRONAUT (USA),** 6, ch g Grey Dawn II—Short Stanza (USA) **Mrs Rodney Lambert**
55 **SAILOR BOY,** 4, b c Main Reef—Main Sail **Mrs A. Valentine**
56 **SOLIDASAROCK,** 8, ch g Hardboy—Limefield Rita **Mr Les Randall**
57 **SPANISH SERVANT,** 5, ch g Don—Please Oblige **Mr D. G. Phillips**
58 **TANG,** 5, ch g Mansingh (USA)—Great Blue White **Miss S. A. Hamilton**
59 **THE OIL BARON,** 4, gr g Absalom—Ruby's Chance **Mr R. Carstairs**
60 **THORNFIELD BOY,** 4, b g Homeboy—Pink Blues **Thornfield Securities Ltd**
61 **TILT TECH FLYER,** 5, b g Windjammer (USA)—Queen Kate **Mr Paul De Weck**
62 **VINTAGE PORT (USA),** 8, b g Blood Royal (USA)—Port Au Pass (USA) **Mrs Mary Wickins**
63 **WAGON LOAD,** 5, ch g Bustino—Noble Girl **Dr G. Madan Mohan**

THREE-YEAR-OLDS

64 **BERKELEY HILL BOY,** ch g Castle Keep—Brown Velvet **BHH Group Plc**
65 **BIFOCAL,** b g Vision (USA)—Night Vision **Mr C. F. Sparrowhawk**
66 **LOUKARA GOLD,** b g Taufan (USA)—Blue Parrot (FR) **Mr I. Goldsmith**
67 **LYNE DANCER,** b br f Be My Native (USA)—Martialette **Mr Cecil Holland**
68 **MONKWELL LAD,** br g Town And Country—Brush's Choice **Miss J. Semple**
69 **PLAX,** ch g The Noble Player (USA)—Seapoint **Food Brokers Ltd**

MR R. P. J. AKEHURST—continued

70 **QUINTA ROYALE,** b g Sayyaf—Royal Holly **Mr Peter M. Crane**
71 **RUN HOME,** b g Homeboy—Chiparia **Mrs Valerie N. Greenwood**
72 **SARAH GEORGINA,** b f Persian Bold—Dance By Night **Mr A. R. Perry**
73 **VALIANT WORDS,** br g Valiyar—Wild Words **Mr D. T. Byrne**
74 **WILVICK,** ch g Gabitat—Pas de Chat **Baker Sportswear Ltd**

TWO-YEAR-OLDS

75 **DEVIL'S SOUL,** b c 28/1 Faustus (USA)—Ragged Moon (Raga Navarro (ITY)) **Mr P. F. Roberts**
76 **SUNROOM (USA),** gr f Gato Del Sol (USA)—Redecorate (USA) (Hatchet Man (USA)) **Mr Eric Parker**

Other Owners: Mr William Alexander, Mr R. Bowden, Crown Racing Partnership, Mr Geoffrey C. Greenwood, Mr Alan Guthrie, Mrs Noreen Hodgson, Mr J. P. Jarrett, Mr Nick Norton, Mr Peter Pepper, Mr S. Powell, Mr A. S. Reid, Mr James R. Ritchie, Mr H. Saunders, Mr B. T. E. Shrubsall, Mr John Ullman, Mr John Winchester.

Apprentice: L Carter (7-7).

Conditional: G Heaver, J Leech.

5 MR C. J. T. ALEXANDER, Dollar

Postal: **Woodside, Solsgirth, Dollar, Clackmannanshire, Scotland.**
Phone: **DOLLAR (025 94) 2482**

1 **BALANAKEIL,** 7, b g Bay Express—Deer Forest **Mr C. J. T. Alexander**
2 **DOUBTLESS,** 8, b g Nonoalco (USA)—Consistent **Mr C. J. T. Alexander**
3 5, B g Royal Fountain—Dysie Mary **Mr C. J. T. Alexander**
4 **GOLDEN FANCY,** 13, ch g Gold Form—Our Edith **Mr Nicholas Alexander**
5 **KINNESTON,** 6, b g Night Porter—Dysie Mary **Mr Michael Alexander**
6 **PANEGYRIST,** 15, b g Sweet Story—Pandorana **Mr C. J. T. Alexander**
7 **SNOW BLESSED,** 13, br g So Blessed—Snow Tribe **Mr C. J. T. Alexander**

Amateur: Mr David Mactaggart.

6 MR H. ALEXANDER, Lanchester

Postal: **Partridge Close Stud, Lanchester, Co. Durham.**
Phone: **HOME (0207) 520896 OFFICE (0207) 520066 YARD (0207) 520786**

1 **FREEMASON,** 9, b g Free State—Red Velvet **Mr Hamish Alexander**
2 **WAIT YOU THERE (USA),** 5, b g Nureyev (USA)—Ma Mere L'Oie (FR) **Mr Hamish Alexander**

Jockey (NH): Chris Grant (w.a.).

Amateur: Mr J Walton.

7 MR A. R. ALLAN, Cornhill-on-Tweed

Postal: **Pallinsburn Stables, Cornhill-on-Tweed, Northumberland.**
Phone: **CROOKHAM (089082) 581**

1 **ARPAL BREEZE,** 5, ch g Deep Run—Arpal Magic **R. P. Adam Ltd**
2 **ARPAL FOREVER,** 6, b g Deep Run—Arpal Magic **R. P. Adam Ltd**
3 **BLUE MISCHIEF,** 4, ch f Precocious—Deep Blue Sea **Mr Robert Gibbons**
4 **CLAY COUNTY,** 5, b g Sheer Grit—Make-Up **Mr M. C. Boyd**
5 **COOL JAMIE,** 9, b g Pals Passage—Shangara **Mr T. W. Beaty**
6 **FLOWING RIVER (USA),** 4, b c Irish River (FR)—Honey's Flag (USA) **Mr M. C. Boyd**
7 **GLORIOLE,** 6, b g Indian King (USA)—Escorial **Mr D. J. Fairbairn**
8 **HI WALLIE,** 8, b g Fidel—Donnarabella **Mrs V. Scott Watson**
9 **ITMA,** 7, b g Nicholas Bill—Civic Duty **Mr Robert Gibbons**
10 **JELLY JILL,** 7, ro m Jellaby—Petoria **Miss M. A. Compton**
11 **KHARIF,** 6, b g Formidable (USA)—Pass The Rulla (USA) **Mr R. Allan**
12 **LIGHTFALL (USA),** 6, b g Forli (ARG)—Flood Light (USA) **Alan Munro (Electrical Contractors) Ltd**
13 **MRS JENNIFER,** 5, bl m River Knight (FR)—Wreck-Em-All **B. J. Rousell Ltd**
14 **PAT'S JESTER,** 7, ch g Orchestra—Owey **R. P. Adam Ltd**
15 **SONNY ONE SHINE,** 9, b g Mandalus—Wreck-Em-All **Alan Munro (Electrical Contractors) Ltd**
16 **SPECIAL SETTLEMENT (USA),** 9, b h Riva Ridge (USA)—Laura Bell (USA) **Mr T. W. Beaty**
17 **TOUGH COOKIE,** 5, gr g Lochnager—Jovenita **Mr R. Bowden**
18 **WEE NONIE,** 4, ch f Mljet—Petite Doutelle **James Hickie**

Other Owners: Mr Geoff Adam, Mr R. Q. Dunn, Mr L. Grant, Mr S. Reekie, Mr D. A. Speirs, Mr George B. Turnbull.

Jockeys (Flat): C Dwyer (8-5, w.a.), S Webster (8-3, w.a.).

Jockey (NH): N Doughty (10-2, w.a.).

Conditional: Donal Dunne (9-7).

8 MR C. N. ALLEN, Newmarket

Postal: **Shadowfax Stables, Hamilton Road, Newmarket, Suffolk, CB8 0NQ.**
Phone: **(0638) 667870 FAX (0638) 668005 TELEX 817154 SHADOW G**

1 **ALWAYS TAKE PROFIT,** 4, ch g Noalto—Pour Moi **Eclipse Management Newmarket Ltd**
2 **ANSTEY BOY,** 5, gr g Decoy Boy—Miss Twiggy **Eclipse Management Newmarket Ltd**
3 **BREEZED WELL,** 4, b c Wolverlife—Precious Baby **Mrs Susan Homewood**
4 **ELECTRIC ROSE,** 5, ch m Electric—Rose And The Ring **Mr C. N. Allen**
5 **GAELIC AIR,** 4, b f Ballad Rock—Gaelic Jewel **Mr Andrew Spalding**
6 **GOLDEN ANCONA,** 7, ch h London Bells—Golden Darling **Royal Blue Racing Plc**
7 **GO RABALL GO,** 4, br g All Systems Go—Rabeeb **Mr A. O. Irish**
8 **NIKLAS ANGEL,** 4, b c Petorius—The Woodbird **Winning Post Racing Ltd**
9 **NORTHERN RAIN,** 4, ch g Ballacashtal (CAN)—Summer Rain **Mr A. Anastasiou**
10 **PALACE SONG,** 6, b g Song—Palace of Medina **Mr A. Anastasiou**
11 **PRINCE ZORIN,** 5, b g Bybicello—Evening Surprize **Mr John Hitchin**
12 **REPACKER,** 4, ch f Aragon—Golden October **Brian Yeardley Continental Ltd**
13 **SAO PAULO (USA),** 4, ch c El Gran Senor (USA)—Millingdale Lillie **Winning Post Racing Ltd**
14 **SUIVEZ MOI,** 6, ch g Pas de Seul—Reparata **Mr Paddy Whitby**
15 **SULTANS GIFT,** 4, ch f Homing—Suzannah's Song **Mr B. Homewood**
16 **SURE WILL,** 5, b g Burslem—Wurli **Mr John Hitchin**
17 **VICKENDA,** 5, ch m Giacometti—Phlox **Mr Z. Papastylianou**

MR C. N. ALLEN—continued

THREE-YEAR-OLDS

18 **AUTOBIRD (FR),** b c Procida (USA)—Star of The Stage **Bird Auto-Precision Ltd**
19 **ELA-YEMOU,** ch g Dara Monarch—Micro Mover **Winning Post Racing Ltd**
20 **GORDONS DREAM,** b g Kafu—Dane Valley **Mr G. B. Homewood**
21 **GREY TUDOR,** gr g Import—Grey Morley **Mr G. B. Homewood**
22 **HOUSE OF FRUIT,** b g Mansingh (USA)—Rheinbloom **Mr Norman Harris**
23 **MAISON DES FRUITS,** b f Balidar—Thorganby Tina **Mr Norman Harris**
24 **MR MILANO,** b g Never So Bold—Maid of Milan **Kaydelea Plc**
25 **MY-UGLY-DUCKLING,** ch c Longleat (USA)—Snow Goose **Winning Post Racing Ltd**
26 **NO-NO NADIA,** b f Noalto—Blue Breeze (USA) **Winning Post Racing Ltd**
27 **PLEASANT COMPANY,** b f Alzao (USA)—Keeping Company **Brian Yeardley Continental Ltd**
28 **PSYCHO SONNY,** b g Aragon—Sunny Reproach **Eclipse Management Newmarket Ltd**
29 **SIMPLE TRUTH,** b f Known Fact (USA)—Northern Ballerina **Brian Yeardley Continental Ltd**
30 **UP THE WAGON,** ch c Formidable (USA)—Skiboule (BEL) **Eclipse Management Newmarket Ltd**
31 **YOUNG CHRISTOS,** b c Sayf El Arab (USA)—Pahaska **Mr K. Moustouka**
32 **YOUNG SHADOWFAX,** gr c Absalom—Miss Twiggy **Mr John C. Nelson**

TWO-YEAR-OLDS

33 Gr f 18/3 Valiyar—Bishah **Winning Post Racing Ltd**
34 B c 10/5 Tina's Pet—Buy G's **Mr Guy Shropshire**
35 B f 3/5 Auction Ring (USA)—Classic Choice **Winning Post Racing Ltd**
36 Ch c 5/5 Known Fact (USA)—Cresta (FR) **Shadowfax Racing**
37 B f 21/3 Vision (USA)—Great Alexandra **Winning Post Racing Ltd**
38 Ch f 13/4 Mazaad—Green Idol **Winning Post Racing Ltd**
39 B f 25/1 Dara Monarch—Lady Salinia **Shadowfax Racing**
40 B f 12/4 Balidar—Miss Twiggy **Shadowfax Racing**
41 B c 22/5 Flash of Steel—Prestigious **Shadowfax Racing**
42 **RIVE JUMELLE,** b f 23/2 M Double M (USA)—Riverwave (USA) **Winning Post Racing Ltd**
43 B c 11/4 Nordico (USA)—Romantic Air **Shadowfax Racing**
44 B c 11/5 Taufan (USA)—Star Pursuit **Shadowfax Racing**
45 B f 21/4 Grey Desire—Sweet Delilah **Mr A. Anastasiou**
46 Ch c 6/5 Heraldiste (USA)—Vernair (USA) **Shadowfax Racing**

Other Owners: Mr Chris Andreas, Mr J. L. Eddis, Miss S. J. Hill, Mr S. Homewood, Mr Patrick J. Jarvis, Mr R. Knappett, Mr Barry J. Ross, Mr J. Sim.

Jockeys (Flat): G Bardwell (7-7), G Duffield (8-0, w.a.), R Morse (7-12).

Jockey (NH): J McLaughlin (10-0).

Apprentice: M Denaro (8-10).

Conditional: M Denaro (9-7).

Lady Rider: Miss R Lowes (9-0).

9 MR J. S. ALLEN, Claverdon

Postal: **Little Manor Farm, Manor Lane, Claverdon, Warwick, CV35 8NH.**
Phone: **CLAVERDON (092684) 2026**

1 **CLAVERDON BOY,** 8, ch g Kinglet—Elmir **Mr J. Allen**
2 **CLAVERDON GIRL,** 6, b m Humdoleila—Space Beam **Mr J. Allen**
3 **INCHINA,** 4, ch f Grey Ghost—Chinese Falcon **Mr J. Allen**
4 **PORT OF TIME,** 6, ch g Dance In Time (CAN)—Linguistic **Mr J. Allen**
5 **SINGING HILLS,** 9, b m Crash Course—Purcella **Mr J. Allen**

Lady Rider: Ann Stockell (9-7).

10 MR P. B. ALLINGHAM, Luton

Postal: **Dog Kennel Farm, Lilley, Luton, Bedfordshire.**
Phone: **OFFLEY (046 276) 337**

1 **DICK KNIGHT**, 9, ch g Owen Dudley—Illumination **Miss T. J. Bond**
2 **GALE BOY,** 10, b g Bay Express—Morning Cloud **Mr R. V. Hall**
3 **JEMMA BELLE,** 4, b f Legal Tender—Kandy Belle **Mr P. B. Allingham**
4 **KEENLINE,** 6, b m Bunny Boy—Blue Ginger **Miss J. Stephenson**
5 **VAGABOND VICTOR,** 14, b g Levmoss—Tanndara (FR) **Mr R. V. Hall**
6 **ZIMMERMAN,** 5, b g Windjammer (USA)—Rather Easy **Mr M. T. Branson**

THREE-YEAR-OLDS

7 B g Legal Tender—Kandy Belle **Mr P. B. Allingham**

TWO-YEAR-OLDS

8 B f Royal Vulcan—Kandy Belle (Hot Brandy) **Mr P. B. Allingham**
9 Ch g Tickled Pink—Lamdant (Redundant) **Mr D. Miller**

Amateur: Mr S Andrews (11-0).

11 MR E. J. ALSTON, Preston

Postal: **Edges Farm Stables, Chapel Lane, Longton, Preston.**
Phone: **(0772) 612120**

1 **COQUETA,** 5, ch m Coquelin (USA)—Clara Petacci (USA) **Mr P. J. Lawton**
2 **HERON'S SAM,** 5, b g Proud Knight (USA)—Heron's Mirage **Mr Graham Crompton**
3 **JOHNSTON'S BABY,** 11, ch g Be Friendly—Glimmer of Light **Mr Frank McKevitt**
4 **MARCELLINA,** 8, ch m Welsh Pageant—Connarca **Mrs Maria Charlton**
5 **NO PAY RISE,** 7, b g Faraway Times (USA)—Melfio Miss **Mr Mick Graham**
6 **SUNSET REINS FREE,** 5, b g Red Sunset—Free Rein **Mr M. P. Russell**

THREE-YEAR-OLDS

7 **EL ARAB,** ch g Sayf El Arab (USA)—Sally Conkers **Mr Terence Jones**
8 **GOLDEN FLIGHT,** ch f Remainder Man—Wigeon **Mr G. G. Sanderson**
9 **HAZY HEATH,** b f Wolver Heights—Bumfuzzle (USA) **Mr G. G. Sanderson**

TWO-YEAR-OLDS

10 B g 2/5 Chief Singer—Aristata (Habitat) **Mr Mick Graham**
11 Ch c 30/4 Vencedor—Hunu (Hul A Hul) **Kim Wallwork**
12 **LIFETIMES AMBITION,** b c 15/4 Hotfoot—Consistent Queen (Queen's Hussar) **Mr P. J. Lawton**
13 **MOUNTAIN VISION (IRE),** b f 16/2 Vision (USA)—
Mountain Heather (Daring Display (USA)) **Mr Mick Graham**
14 **NORTHERN NATION,** b c 2/3 Nomination—Ballagarrow Girl (North Stoke) **Mr M. Walsh**
15 Ch f 17/3 Sayf El Arab (USA)—Shining Bright (USA) (Bold Bidder) **Mr Mick Graham**

Other Owners: Mrs S. Y. Alston, Mr A. B. Garside, Mr Derek Hilton, Mr Barry Jones, Mr M. Twentyman.

Jockey (Flat): G Duffield (7-13, w.a.).

Jockeys (NH): K Doolan (9-10), D Dutton (10-0, w.a.).

Conditional: M Alston (9-7).

Lady Rider: Mrs S Y Alston (8-7).

12 MR I. F. ANDERSON, Welshpool

Postal: **Ty Canol, Guilsfield, Welshpool, Powys, Wales.**
Phone: **(0938) 75509 OR (0938) 3340**

1 **BARSTOX BOY,** 5, b g Touch Boy—Siciliana **Mr Ian Anderson**
2 **HYDE,** 13, b g Royalty—Impatience **Mr Ian Anderson**
3 **LISETA,** 6, br m Sonnen Gold—Podzola **Mr Ian Anderson**
4 **MINIZEN MAGIC,** 5, ch h Don—Mayfield Girl **Mr Ian Anderson**
5 **ROUND THE WREKIN,** 7, ch m Peter Wrekin—Iona Flyer **Mr Ian Anderson**
6 **THE MIGHTY DUCK,** 11, b g Push On—Brown Duck **Mr Ian Anderson**

13 MR P. J. ANDERSON, Much Wenlock

Postal: **Top Cottage, Church Preen, Church Stretton, Shropshire.**
Phone: **HOME Longville (069 43) 387 OR YARD Longville (069 43) 377**

1 **BALLYWILLWILL,** 4, b g Wolver Hollow—Nuageuse **Mr A. Lester**
2 **DREAMING STAR,** 5, br g Star Appeal—Yea Misty (USA) **Mr Geoffrey Blythin**
3 **EDGED GOLD,** 13, b g Sharp Edge—Gold of The Day **Mr E. Remmington and Mr S. Thomas**
4 **HABANNE,** 10, gr g Habat—Sister Anne **Mrs Jane Edenborough**
5 **JOHNNY DANGEROUSLY,** 5, ch g Don—Absuleno **Mr J. Milner**
6 **JOSSESTOWN,** 7, gr g Roselier (FR)—Golden Seal **Mr J. Milner**
7 **JUST PERKINS,** 5, ch g Bold Owl—Buckenham Belle **Mr J. J. Guthrie**
8 **LEADING SUPPLIER,** 4, b f Leading Man—Dunoon Court **Wenlock Building Centre Limited**
9 **REWBELL,** 4, ch f Andy Rew—Miss Bell **Mr R. A. Jones**
10 **SMACK ON TARGET,** 5, gr m Smackover—Albine **Mr A. Wall and Mr K. Ford**

Other Owners: Mrs Pat Mullen, Mrs V. A. Stacey.

Jockey (NH): T Wall (9-10).

Conditional: P Verling (9-8).

14 MRS A. B. APPLEYARD, Bristol

Postal: **Clutton Hill Farm, Clutton, Bristol, Avon.**
Phone: **(0761) 52458**

1 **DUSKY'S SPIRIT,** 11, b m Master Spiritus—Dusky Princess II **Mrs A. B. Appleyard**

15 MR D. W. P. ARBUTHNOT, Compton

Postal: **Uplands Stables, Lower Farm, Compton, Newbury, RG16 0RG.**
Phone: **COMPTON (0635) 578427**

1 **BIT OF A LASS,** 4, br f Wassl—Idiot's Delight (USA) **Mr D. N. Larke**
2 **BOURNVILLE,** 4, b f Lochnager—Channing Girl **Mrs B. J. Lee**
3 **DARK SIRONA,** 7, b m Pitskelly—Step You Gaily **Miss C. A. B. Allsopp**
4 **HOLY ZEAL,** 4, b g Alzao (USA)—Crystal Halo **Mr Michael Pescod**
5 **LOVE LEGEND,** 5, ch g Glint of Gold—Sweet Emma **Mr Michael Gliksten**
6 **MOUNT NELSON,** 4, ch g Morston (FR)—Doogali **Mr M. J. Peters**
7 **TIME SHARE,** 5, b g Known Fact (USA)—Midsummertime **Mr R. Crutchley**
8 **YOU MISSED ME,** 4, b c Known Fact (USA)—Milk And Honey **Mr Francis Ward**

MR D. W. P. ARBUTHNOT—continued

THREE-YEAR-OLDS

9 **APPLIANCEOFSCIENCE,** b g Bairn (USA)—Moonlight Serenade **Thompson Cook Distributors Ltd**
10 **MRS HENNY PENNY,** ch f Absalom—Flopsy **Mrs Caroline Holland-Martin**
11 **PERFECT COPY,** ch f Blushing Scribe (USA)—Double Mint **Mrs J. M. Cheeseman**
12 **PLIE,** ch f Superlative—La Pirouette (USA) **Mr John V. Phillips**
13 **PORT SHARER,** b f Runnett—Amorak **Mr David Mushens**
14 **PRINCESS SONATA,** b f Music Boy—Jovenita **S. T. A. Management Ltd**
15 **RINJA (USA),** b c Robellino (USA)—Dijla **Mr O. Zawawi**
16 **STRAT'S LEGACY,** b g Chukaroo—State Romance **Mr Jack Blumenow**
17 **THATCHER'S DILEMMA,** b g Final Straw—Crane Beach **S. T. A. Management Ltd**
18 **TORGHIA,** b f Taufan—Brave Louise **Mr D. R. L. Jones and Mrs D. R. L. Jones**
19 **VISAGE,** b f Vision (USA)—Be Tuneful **Mr Christopher Wright**

TWO-YEAR-OLDS

20 **BESS POOL,** b f 26/2 Sayf El Arab—Bold Apple (Bold Lad (IRE)) **Mr and Mrs E. Leigh-Pemberton**
21 **BLAZING SENSATION,** b c 22/1 Blazing Saddles (AUS)—
La Reine de France (Queen's Hussar) **Miss K. Wheeler**
22 B c 4/5 Vision (USA)—Calvino (Relkino)
23 Ch f Sayf El Arab—Into Harbour (Right Tack) **Mr D. R. L. Jones**
24 **LAMBADA GIRL (IRE),** b f 28/4 Petorius—Spear Dance (Gay Fandango (USA)) **Mrs M. Gutkin**
25 B c 10/3 Precocious—Nonabella (Nonoalco (USA))
26 B c 3/5 Superlative—Patriotic (Hotfoot) **Mrs J. A. Leek**
27 **SIMPLY AFLAME,** ch f 20/5 Simply Great (FR)—Grange Fire (Allangrange) **Mr D. N. Larke**
28 **ZAXIS,** ch f 21/3 Noalto—La Pirouette (USA) (Kennedy Road) **Mr John V. Phillips**

Other Owners: Mrs V. Bampton, Mr K. Gregory, Mr J. A. Leek, Mr W. Lusty, Mrs W. Lusty, Mr George S. Thompson, Mr S. Westwell, Mr N. Woodcock, Mrs P. M. Yeomans.

Apprentice: A Procter (8-0).

Lady Rider: Mrs D Arbuthnot (8-6).

16 MR R. W. ARMSTRONG, Newmarket

Postal: **St Gatien, Newmarket, Suffolk, CB8 8HJ.**
Phone: **(0638) 663333 TELEX 81206 ARMSTRG FAX (0638) 662412**

1 **ALBADR (USA),** 5, ch h Arctic Tern (USA)—Spring Tour (USA) **Mr Hamdan Al-Maktoum**
2 **BEAN KING,** 4, gr g Ardross—Meanz Beanz **Mr James H. Stone**
3 **BEX (USA),** 4, ch f Explodent (USA)—Bay Street **Oceanic Limited**
4 **GREEN EMPEROR,** 4, b br c Head For Heights—La Padma **Mrs F. R. Watts**
5 **NATIVE FLAIR,** 5, b m Be My Native (USA)—Tuyenu **Mr R. J. Arculli**
6 **NATIVE MAGIC,** 4, ch f Be My Native (USA)—Tuyenu **Mr R. J. Arculli**
7 **SOUND MUSIC,** 4, b f Music Boy—Kanvita **Dr Cornel Li**
8 **TAWEEL,** 6, b h Runnett—Silecia **Mr Hamdan Al-Maktoum**
9 **VAL RECIT (FR),** 4, b c Recitation (USA)—Valdecka (FR) **Mr Hamdan Al-Maktoum**

THREE-YEAR-OLDS

10 **BARQAISH,** br c Jalmood (USA)—Adeebah (USA) **Mr Hamdan Al-Maktoum**
11 **BERRY'S DREAM,** b f Darshaan—Berrys Cay (USA) **Oceanic Limited**
12 **BOOK THE BAND,** ch c Be My Guest (USA)—Love Land (FR) **Kennet Valley Thoroughbreds Ltd**
13 **CAMPAI,** b c Try My Best (USA)—Musing **Mrs H. De Burgh**
14 **DISTINCT NATIVE,** ch c Be My Native (USA)—Miami Life **Dr Cornel Li**
15 **ELARRIH (USA),** ch f Sharpen Up—Van Cleef (URU) **Mr Hamdan Al-Maktoum**
16 **FESTIVAL OF MAGIC (USA),** b f Clever Trick (USA)—Santa Linda (USA) **Kennet Valley Thoroughbreds Ltd**

MR R. W. ARMSTRONG—continued

17 **MUIZENBERG,** b c Mashhor Dancer (USA)—Allotria **Mrs G. Webb Bronfman**
18 **NEVER SO HIGH,** b c Never So Bold—High Gait **Mr K. Hsu**
19 **RASAN,** ch c Dominion—Raffle **Mr Hamdan Al-Maktoum**
20 **SAFFAAH (USA),** ch c Secreto (USA)—Somebody Noble (USA) **Mr Hamdan Al-Maktoum**
21 **SHEJRAH (USA),** b f Northjet—Bar J Gal (USA) **Mr Hamdan Al-Maktoum**
22 **TANFITH (CAN),** b c Chief's Crown (USA)—Foxy Olympia (USA) **Mr Hamdan Al-Maktoum**
23 **TASMIM,** b f Be My Guest (USA)—Militia Girl **Mr Hamdan Al-Maktoum**
24 **TOBACCO ROAD,** ch c Burslem—Ishtar **Mrs A. Reid**

TWO-YEAR-OLDS

25 **ARAK (USA),** b c 7/4 Clever Trick (USA)—Twilight Flight (USA) (Quack (USA)) **Mr Hamdan Al-Maktoum**
26 B c 10/2 Simply Great (FR)—Baleen (Lochnager) **Ahmed Al Shaffar**
27 **BANGO SUIVEZ,** b c 11/3 Cragador—Mrs Feathers (Pyjama Hunt)
28 **FACE THE ODDS,** ch c 27/3 Faustus (USA)—Character Builder (African Sky)
29 B c 2/3 Northern Prospect—Faithful Diplomacy (USA) (Diplomat Way) **Kennet Valley Thoroughbreds Ltd**
30 **GIVE ME HOPE (IRE),** b f Be My Native (USA)—Diamond Gig (Pitskelly) **Keith Hsu**
31 **HALOOB (USA),** ch f 30/5 Sharpen Up—Clear Ridge (USA) (Cox's Ridge (USA)) **Mr Hamdan Al-Maktoum**
32 **MAJAZ (USA),** b c 13/5 Elocutionist (USA)—Googalmiss (USA) (Iron Ruler (USA)) **Mr Hamdan Al-Maktoum**
33 **MATAHIF (IRE),** b c 30/3 Wassl—Reves Celestes (USA) (Lyphard (USA)) **Mr Hamdan Al-Maktoum**
34 **MUJADIL (USA),** b c 16/3 Storm Bird (CAN)—Vallee Secrete (USA) (Secretariat (USA)) **Mr Hamdan Al-Maktoum**
35 **MUJTAHID (USA),** ch c 13/3 Woodman (USA)—Mesmerize (Mill Reef (USA)) **Mr Hamdan Al-Maktoum**
36 **MUWAZI,** b c 25/4 Lear Fan (USA)—Sentimental Roses (High Top) **Mr Hamdan Al-Maktoum**
37 **NAJAAH,** b f 14/2 Green Desert (USA)—Sarajill (High Line) **Mr Hamdan Al-Maktoum**
38 B c 23/4 Alzao (USA)—Nesreen (The Parson)
39 B c 11/3 Pitskelly—Nighty Night (Sassafras (FR))
40 **RAHIF,** b c 2/4 Shirley Heights—Vaguely (Bold Lad (IRE)) **Mr Hamdan Al-Maktoum**
41 **SABAAH (USA),** ch f 18/2 Nureyev (USA)—Dish Dash (Bustino) **Mr Hamdan Al-Maktoum**
42 **TAWAAYF (IRE),** ch f 8/2 Be My Guest (USA)—Ardassine (Ahonoora) **Mr Hamdan Al-Maktoum**

Other Owners: Mr R. W. Armstrong, A. R. G. Cherry-Downes, Mr J. J. Hindley, Mr Patrick Hogan, S. Hsu, Mr R. J. C. Upton, Mr P. J. Vela, Mr P. M. Vela.

Jockey (Flat): G Baxter.

Apprentices: R W Price (7-4), A F Shoults (7-12).

Amateur: K Santana (9-0).

17 MR R. C. ARMYTAGE, Middleham

Postal: **Brough Farm, Middleham, Leyburn, North Yorkshire.**
Phone: **(0969) 23970**

1 **BALIDARIUS,** 5, b g Balidar—Siconda **Mrs V. Haslam**
2 **BELINDA VARD,** 8, ch m Le Bavard (FR)—Enslavement **Mr G. Lansbury**
3 **CARATELLI,** 5, ch g True Song—Tagliatelle **Mr R. C. Armytage**
4 **MELEAGRIS,** 6, b g True Song—Fritillaria **Mrs D. Jackson**
5 **MELLOW LIGHT,** 7, b g Wolver Hollow—Mellifont **Mr H. A. Lawrie**
6 **MERRY MASTER,** 6, br g Le Coq d'Or—Merry Missus **Mr G. Lansbury**
7 **STATE LAD,** 6, b g Free State—Lady Bess **Mr D. J. Jackson**
8 **TOO LATE,** 7, b g Mister Tudor—Premier Bond **Miss N. Carroll**

Jockeys (NH): Gee Armytage (9-7), A Orkney.

Amateur: Mr M Armytage (10-4).

18 MRS S. ARMYTAGE, Malmesbury

Postal: **Oliver House Stud, Chedglow, Malmesbury, Wiltshire.**
Phone: **(06667) 238**

1 **ALPHA LADY,** 4, b f Daring March—Fair Persuasion **Mr A. J. Walshe**
2 **BOLD KING'S HUSSAR,** 7, ch g Sunyboy—Oca **Mrs David Plunkett**
3 **DALRYMPLE,** 7, br g Tanfirion—Dark Gold **Mrs R. M. Hepburn**
4 **DAMASKEEN (USA),** 4, b g Caveat (USA)—Double Damask (USA) **Mrs S. Armytage**
5 **FRAGRANT FELLOW,** 6, ch h Hello Handsome—Fragrant Story **Mr D. J. Hillyard**
6 **LIANE BEAUTY,** 4, b f Castle Keep—Princess Fair **Mrs Lesley Piggott**
7 **LORD ADMIRAL (USA),** 8, b g Topsider (USA)—Tumbling Dancer (USA) **Miss N. Carroll**
8 **NO REBASSE,** 8, b g Over The River (FR)—Good Surprise **Mr D. J. Hillyard**
9 **RICKY DICKY DO,** 4, b g Oats—County Clare **D. A. Davies**
10 **ROMANY MONARCH,** 5, b g Nickel King—Gypsy Girl **Mrs R. Legouix**
11 **ROVING GLEN,** 9, b g Proverb—Glenosheen **Mrs L. M. Dresher**
12 **SUNBEAM TALBOT,** 9, b g Sunyboy—Alfetta **Mrs R. Legouix**
13 **TUFTER'S GARTH,** 5, b g Maculata—Magic Minstrel **Mrs S. Armytage**

THREE-YEAR-OLDS

14 **MISTRESS ROSIE,** b f Dubassoff (USA)—Somerford Glory **Mr Valere N. F. Tjolle**

TWO-YEAR-OLDS

15 B f 3/6 Rabdan—Proserpine (Proverb)

Other Owners: Mr C. B. Gasson, Mr N. J. T. Hoggett, Mrs Ann Lacey, Mr Alastair Macgregor, Miss Anne Suter, Mr G. D. W. Swire, Mr D. A. Tupman.

Jockey (NH): Gee Armytage (9-7).

Amateur: Mr M Armytage (10-4).

19 MR P. J. ARTHUR, Aston Tirrold

Postal: **Frimley Stables, Aston Tirrold, Didcot, Oxon, OX11 9EG.**
Phone: **(0235) 850669**

1 **DOUBLE HANDFULL,** 4, gr f Pas de Seul—Love Tangle **Mr Terence Fisher**
2 **FRIMLEY PARKSON,** 6, br g Frimley Park—Frimley Grove **Mr Terence Fisher**
3 **GABRIELLA MIA,** 5, b m Ranksborough—Gin And Lime **Mr Terence P. Lyons II**
4 **HOLLIE DANCING,** 6, br m Frimley Park—Frimleys Junic **Mr Terence P. Lyons II**
5 **LONELY STREET,** 9, b m Frimley Park—Abalone **Mr Terence P. Lyons II**
6 **MIAMI BANKER,** 4, ch c Miami Springs—Banking Coyne **Mr J. J. Amass**
7 **PATRICK JOHN LYONS,** 9, b h Cavo Doro—Latin Spice **Mr Terence P. Lyons II**
8 **SUDDEN IMPACT,** 8, b h Be Friendly—False Evidence **Mr J. R. Rowland**
9 **TACHYON PARK,** 8, b h Frimley Park—Frimley's Alana **Mr J. R. Rowland**

THREE-YEAR-OLDS

10 **ELVOL,** ch f Whistling Deer—Haleys Mark **Mr D. Locke**
11 **MARIOLINO,** b c Buzzards Bay—Banking Coyne **Mr J. D. Wheeler**
12 **PALABORA (USA),** gr c Wolf Power (SAF)—Peeping (USA) **Mrs V. O'Brien**

TWO-YEAR-OLDS

13 B c 2/4 Today And Tomorrow—Banking Coyne (Deep Diver) **Mr H. Saunders and Partners**
14 **DERIS BAY (IRE),** b c 22/4 Gorytus (USA)—Current Bay (Tyrant (USA)) **Mr D. Locke**
15 **HARD TO SNUB,** b c 7/4 Shardari—Snub (Steel Heart) **Mr D. Locke**
16 B f 12/4 Today And Tomorrow—Mia Jubes (Frimley Park) **Mr J. R. Rowland**

Other Owners: Mr B. Azemoudeh.

Jockey (Flat): Nick Adams (7-7).

20 MR C. A. AUSTIN, Wokingham

Postal: **Bill Hill Park, Wokingham, Berkshire.**
Phone: **(0734) 786425**

1 **ATTIC WIT (FR)**, 4, b g Shirley Heights—Laughing Matter **Mr A. J. Richards**
2 **BOLD STRANGER**, 5, br h Persian Bold—Lorna Doon **Mr A. J. Richards**
3 **BOLD TOM (FR)**, 4, b g Bold Lad (IRE)—Tomrousse (FR) **Mr A. J. Richards**
4 **HARDY HAWK (FR)**, 5, br g Zino—My Hawk **Mr A. J. Richards**
5 **HIGH ON HIGH (FR)**, 4, ch f Ginger Brink—Highdinoa **Mr A. J. Richards**
6 **MILTON BURN**, 9, b h Sexton Blake—Neasden Belle **Mr A. J. Richards**
7 **MY MOTHER'S EYES (FR)**, 5, b m Saint Cyrien (FR)—Pollenka (FR) **Mr A. J. Richards**
8 **NATIVE RULER (FR)**, 9, b g King of Macedon—Noble Native **Mr A. J. Richards**
9 **RELIABLE (FR)**, 4, b c Moulin—Glitter **Mr A. J. Richards**

THREE-YEAR-OLDS

10 **LA POMME DE PIN**, b f Ile de Bourbon—Sweep Up **Mr A. J. Richards**
11 **MISS GILLESPIE**, b f Beldale Flutter—Miss Brodie **Mr A. J. Richards**
12 **ROUTINE**, b f Teenoso (USA)—Rue du Pin (FR) **Mr A. J. Richards**
13 **STAN'S STAR (NZ)**, ch c Standaan (FR)—Ewar Star **Mr A. J. Richards**

TWO-YEAR-OLDS

14 **AIR DANCER**, b f 25/4 Teenoso—Lasani (FR) (Appiani II) **Mr A. J. Richards**
15 **BUS STOP (FR)**, b c 25/3 Caerleon (USA)—Tom Rousse (FR) (La Roussiere (FR)) **Mr A. J. Richards**
16 **FROZEN FOREST**, ch c 5/4 Touching Wood—Ever So Cool (FR) (Never Say Die) **Mr A. J. Richards**
17 **SIERRA SUE**, ch f 29/2 Rousillon—St Louis Sue (FR) (Nonoalco (USA)) **Mr A. J. Richards**

21 MR M. AVISON, Nawton

Postal: **Little Manor Farm, High Lane, Nawton, York, YO6 5TU.**
Phone: **HELMSLEY (0439) 71672**

1 **BOTANY BLADE**, 8, ch g Fine Blade (USA)—Vagrant Lass **Mrs P. M. A. Avison**
2 **DOM EDINO**, 7, b g Dominion—Edna **Mr C. Holder**
3 **FARINA STREAM**, 6, ch g Paddy's Stream—Farina **Mr K. Hanson**
4 **GREEN TOPS**, 8, ch g Green Shoon—Gone **Mr K. Hanson**
5 **MUSICAL MYSTERY**, 8, ch g Orchestra—Last Trip **Mr Alan Cairns**
6 **NARROWWATER CASTLE**, 7, br g Tanfirion—Rachel Ruysch **Mr Richard Cadoret and Partners**
7 **POWER BOAT**, 4, ch g Jalmood (USA)—Bedeni **Mr K. Hanson**
8 **QUALITY PRINCE**, 9, b br g Prince Tenderfoot (USA)—Brig O'Doon **Mrs W. M. Crump and Mr S. Reavey**
9 **SUSAN HENCHARD**, 6, b m Auction Ring (USA)—Let Slip **Mr M. Avison**
10 **THE NAWTON STAR**, 10, b m Sunyboy—Star Beauty **Mrs P. M. A. Avison**

THREE-YEAR-OLDS

11 **FURRY BABY**, b f Furry Glen—Another Bless **Mr K. Hanson**
12 **PALATIAL STYLE**, b g Kampala—Stylish Princess **Mrs P. M. A. Avison**
13 **SAFFRON VENTURE**, b f Mufrij—New Saffron **Mr Terence West**

TWO-YEAR-OLDS

14 **SOUNDS GOLDEN**, br g 28/3 Sonnen Gold—Tuneful Queen (Queen's Hussar) **George Coates**

Other Owners: T. Keast, F. Kelly, R. Kelly.

Amateur: Mr R H Brown (10-10).

22 MR N. G. AYLIFFE, Minehead

Postal: **Glebe Stables, Little Ham, Winsford, Minehead, Somerset.**
Phone: **WINSFORD (064385) 265**

1 **BOLD LILLY,** 4, b f Montekin—Topless Dancer **Mrs S. L. Hooper**
2 **DARK ROSAAN,** 6, br m Dalsaan—Miss Robust **Mrs S. L. Hooper**
3 **DRESS UP,** 6, b g Cajun—Prink (USA) **Mr C. M. Shadbolt**
4 **EASY MATCH,** 4, b f Royal Match—Flying Easy **Mr C. John Hill**
5 **HA'PENNY BRIDGE,** 7, br g Tanfirion—Lost Path **Mr Malcolm Bull**
6 **JARPEE,** 4, ch g Bay Express—Romancing **Mr N. G. Ayliffe**
7 **LUCKY THROW,** 4, b g Lucky Wednesday—Sodance **Miss N. L. Peskitt**
8 **SARA LANE,** 6, ch m Sagaro—Maypole Lane **Mr S. Pearce**
9 **SEXTON,** 5, b h Beldale Flutter (USA)—Be Tuneful **Mr N. G. Ayliffe**
10 **STOKE PERO,** 4, ch g Northern Tempest (USA)—Our Mandy **Mr C. John Hill**

Other Owners: Mr M. Austin, Mr Derek Jones, Mr D. B. Roseff, Mr Gerald Withers.

Jockey (NH): M G Ayliffe (10-4).

23 MR A. BAILEY, Newmarket

Postal: **Induna Stables, Fordham Road, Newmarket, Suffolk.**
Phone: **(0638) 661537**

1 **ADORING MAN,** 5, b g Taufan (USA)—Adorit **Castle Farm Stud**
2 **BEECHWOOD COTTAGE,** 7, ch g Malinowski (USA)—Drora **A. Bailey**
3 **CHAMPION GIRL,** 4, br f Blazing Saddles (AUS)—Mercy Cure **Champion Developments (W.A.) Ltd**
4 **CORMAC'S,** 4, gr g Superlative—Tahoume (FR) **Gilt-Edged Thoroughbred Racing Plc**
5 **DOLLAR SEEKER (USA),** 6, b g Buckfinder (USA)—Syrian Song (USA) **Mrs C. M. Nethercott-Hunt**
6 **MAINLY SUNSET,** 4, b f Red Sunset—Mainly Dry **David J. Brown**
7 **RIO PIEDRAS,** 6, b m Kala Shikari—Glory Isle **Mr Nigel S. Scandrett**
8 **ROSE GLEN,** 4, b f Lochnager—Phoenix Rose **Mr D. G. Furlong**
9 **TURN'EM BACK JACK (CAN),** 7, ch g Lord Durham (CAN)—Irish Molly (CAN) **Mr Thomas T. S. Liang**
10 **WING PARK,** 6, ch h Golden Dipper—Puente Primera **Miss C. J. Morris**

THREE-YEAR-OLDS

11 **AIN'TLIFELIKETHAT,** gr c Godswalk (USA)—Blue Alicia **Mr J. T. Hunt**
12 **BOLSHOI PRINCE,** b c Gorytus (USA)—Achafalaya (USA) **Mr M. Tabor**
13 **DIAMOND HILL (USA),** ch c Temperence Hill (USA)—Avant Coureur (USA) **Mr Thomas T. S. Liang**
14 B g Rusticaro (FR)—Directrice (GER) **A. Bailey**
15 B f Prince Tenderfoot—Godwynn **A. Bailey**
16 **JUBI'S SHOES (USA),** b c Tap Shoes (USA)—Jubilant (USA) **Mr Thomas T. S. Liang**
17 **LANZAROTE,** b f Longleat (USA)—Bel Esprit **Mr D. L. Smith**
18 **LONDON ROBERTO (USA),** br c Royal Roberto (USA)—Persistent (USA) **Mr Thomas T. S. Liang**
19 **MISS BEA,** b f Petorius—Stop The Cavalry **Mr J. T. Hunt**
20 **TRANSCRIBER (USA),** b c Transworld (USA)—Scrabbler (USA) **Mr Thomas T. S. Liang**
21 **WALKERWAY BOY,** b c Muscatite—Hadala **Mr K. R. Parker**

TWO-YEAR-OLDS

22 Ch c Gorytus (USA)—Achafalaya (USA) (Apalachee (USA)) **Churchill Bloodstock Ltd**
23 B f Manor Farm Boy—Haverhill Lass (Music Boy) **Manor Farm Dairies (Haverhill) Ltd**
24 Br c Kafu—Joanns Goddess (Godswalk (USA)) **A. Bailey**
25 Ch c Burslem—Lady's Guest (Be My Guest (USA)) **A. Bailey**
26 Br f Green Ruby (USA)—Myna Tyna (Blast) **Mr J. C. Edwards**
27 Ch c Never So Bold—Ring The Changes (Auction Ring (USA)) **Mr J. T. Hunt**
28 B c Bold Owl—Sodina (Saulingo) **A. Bailey**
29 Br c Lidhame—Susie's Baby (Balidar) **A. Bailey**

MR A. BAILEY—continued

Other Owners: Mr Robert C. Edwards, Mr A. E. Freeman, Grange Farm (Barnby Moor) Limited, Mr Peter Jolliffe, Mr Nigel S. Scandrett, Mr R. C. Taylor.

Jockey (NH): A W Carroll (10-0).

Apprentices: S L McKenna (8-0), Melody Town (8-7).

Amateur: Miss S Murgatroyd (8-12).

24 MR K. C. BAILEY, Upper Lambourn

Postal: **The Old Manor, Lambourn, Newbury, Berkshire, RG16 7RG.**
Phone: **LAMBOURN (0488) 71483 FAX LAMBOURN (0488) 72978**

1 **A LAD INSANE,** 9, br g Al Sirat (USA)—Endora **Miss Sarah Wills**
2 **ALLIED LAD,** 5, ch g Monksfield—Miss Evelin **Allied Services**
3 **ANGEL'S DREAM,** 6, b m King's Ride—Angel's Halo **Mr Michael Burley**
4 **BIG OSCAR,** 6, b g Gala Performance (USA)—Lupious **Pell-mell Partners**
5 **BILOXI BLUES,** 8, gr g Blue Refrain—Haunting **Pell-mell Partners**
6 **CAPTAIN FRISK,** 7, bl br h Politico (USA)—Jenny Frisk **C. L. Services Ltd (C. L. S. Group)**
7 **CHURCH LEAP,** 6, b m Pollerton—Phaestus Sister **Blueford Ltd**
8 **DAIRA FORT,** 4, b c Nureyev (USA)—Lady B Gay (USA) **Olympic N.H. Racing**
9 **DEIRDRES DREAM,** 6, b br m The Parson—Deirdre's Joy **Pell-mell Partners**
10 **DOCKLANDS EXPRESS,** 8, b g Roscoe Blake—Southern Moss **Mr R. H. Baines**
11 **FELLOW'S NIGHT,** 7, ch g Deep Run—Chihuahua **Pell-mell Partners**
12 **GOLD HAND,** 6, ch g Nearly A Hand—Way of Life **Mr Robbie Lee**
13 **GOLD HAVEN,** 6, ch g Pollerton—Coolbawn Lady **Pell-mell Partners**
14 **GROGAN,** 8, b g Sapsford—Clear Speech **Miss Sarah Wills**
15 **GUNNER JIM,** 6, b g Gunner B—Well Lined **Eeceethree Ltd**
16 **JUST FOR THE CRACK,** 12, ch g The Parson—Rosesong **Mr G. M. H. Wills**
17 **LOUANDY,** 5, b g Furry Glen—Boreen Queen
18 **MAN O'MAGIC,** 9, br g Manado—Garrucha **Mr James D. Greig**
19 **MERLIN'S CAVE,** 4, b g Reesh—Andalucia **Mrs James Greig**
20 **MISTER BRAMBLE,** 9, b g Brave Invader (USA)—Bramble Mill **Mr J. F. Bance**
21 **MR FRISK,** 11, ch g Bivouac—Jenny Frisk **Mrs Harry J. Duffey**
22 **NATHAN BLAKE,** 5, gr g Sexton Blake—Nana **Mrs J. M. Corbett**
23 **ON REFLECTION,** 8, b g Golden Love—Ballygannon **Eeceethree Ltd**
24 **OXYMERON (USA),** 6, ch g Temperence Hill (USA)—Luv Luvin' (USA) **Mrs Tony Hull**
25 **PERRY WELL,** 6, b g Maculata—Magic Minstrel **Mr A. M. Grazebrook**
26 **POSITIVE,** 8, ch g Posse (USA)—Hello Honey **S. T. A. Management Ltd**
27 **QUEEN'S BISHOP,** 7, b g The Parson—Lady of Desmond **Mr J. G. Ruck Keene**
28 **QUIDDITY,** 7, b g Pollerton—Windbush **Pell-mell Partners**
29 **RAGLAN STREET,** 4, b g Sassafras (FR)—Welsh Maiden **Blaydon Racing Partnership**
30 **STONEY CREEK,** 10, bl g Menelek—Black Lark **Mr Richard Chambers**
31 **TENACIOUS,** 5, b g Tender King—Mantina
32 **THE KULAK,** 9, b g Pollerton—Dowdstown Slipper **Mr Christopher Andrews**
33 **VIGANO,** 4, ch c Lyphard (USA)—Pasadoble (USA) **S.T.A Management Ltd**
34 **VINTAGE VELVET,** 8, ch g Rarity—Funicular
35 **WAAFI,** 8, b g Wolver Hollow—Geraldville **Mrs Anna L. Sanders**
36 **WAPPING REIGN,** 8, b g London Gazette—Queen of Rheims **A. F. Budge (Equine) Limited**
37 **WILL I FLY,** 4, b c What A Guest—Monalda (FR) **Mrs Denise Stamp**
38 **YOUWAITONME,** 8, gr g The Parson—Fort Etna **Mrs Harry J. Duffey**
39 **ZINGARO BOY,** 6, b g Casino Boy—Sukhasana **Mrs V. Allen**

MR K. C. BAILEY—continued

Other Owners: Mr J. Chromiak, Mrs David Clark, Mrs Anne Dunn, Mr J. L. Elwell, Mrs V. Gilder, Mr D. W. R. Harland, Mr C. Hellyer, Mr David Macfarlane, Mrs Christopher Mackarness, Mrs Amanda Milne, Mr Alex Ogilvie, Mr Craig Pearman, P. Rebl, Mr J. W. Russell, Mr I. R. Scott, Mrs J. A. St Clair-Ford, Mr T. R. Thomas, Mr David Todd.

Jockey (NH): R Beggan.

Conditional: I Lawrence (9-7).

Lady Rider: Mrs T Bailey (8-7).

25 MR P. G. BAILEY, Salisbury

Postal: **Springbottom Farm, Wilsford-cum-Lake, Salisbury, Wiltshire , SP4 7BP.**
Phone: **HOUSE (0980) 622964 OFFICE (0980) 622682 TELEX 477346 FAX 0980 624253**

1 **BEE GARDEN,** 9, b g Giolla Mear—Regency View **Mr J. A. H. West**
2 **BILLILLA,** 7, ch g Nicholas Bill—Thorganby Bella **Miss H. Stratton**
3 **BRUNONI,** 6, br m Ovac (ITY)—Bramble Leaf **Mr R. A. Batten**
4 **CHIEF CELT,** 4, ch c Celtic Cone—Chieftain's Lady **Mrs J. J. Peppiatt**
5 **CRAIGMORE,** 6, br g Prince Regent (FR)—Carraig More **Mr Ian S. Steers**
6 **DE PROFUNDIS,** 6, ch g Deep Run—Men's Fun **Mr Ian S. Steers**
7 **DIANA DEE,** 4, b f Blakeney—Deep River (FR) **C. I. Henty**
8 **FELL CLIMB,** 10, ch g Levanter—Rambling **Mr P. G. Bailey**
9 **GREENWINE (USA),** 4, br c Green Dancer (USA)—Princesse Margo **Mr A. L. R. Morton**
10 **HELLO MARK,** 5, ch g Hello Gorgeous (USA)—Fayette **Mr B. H. F. Wright**
11 **IMPERIAL FLIGHT,** 5, b g Pampabird—Queen of Time **Miss S. Douglas-Pennant**
12 **LAUNCH PAD,** 4, br c Score Twenty Four (USA)—Rocket Alert **Mr P. G. Bailey**
13 **LION'S PRIDE,** 4, ch g Longleat (USA)—Stylogram **Mr J. N. Thompson**
14 **MANGROVE,** 6, b g Mandalus—Pine Princess **Mr B. K. Peppiatt**
15 **OGENDEBA,** 10, b g Abednego—Shady Tree **Mr D. G. Sprackland**
16 **RIGHT CARD,** 12, br g Gift Card (FR)—Toranquine (FR) **Mr T. Clyde**
17 **ROXALL CLUMP,** 6, b g Neltino—Wyn-Bank **Mr M. Motley**
18 **SARTORIUS,** 4, b c Henbit (USA)—Salvationist **Mr M. Popham**
19 **SPARKLER GEBE,** 4, b g Be My Native (USA)—Siliferous **Sparkler Filters (Great Britain) Ltd**
20 **THE MASTER GUNNER,** 6, ch g Gunner B—Major Isle **Major-Gen. R. L. T. Burges**
21 **TIGER TED,** 10, b g Night Thought—Linden Light **Mr C. M. Jones**
22 **UNDER OFFER,** 9, br g Rhodomantade—Blue Flash **Miss S. Douglas-Pennant**

Other Owners: Miss D. M. M. Crichton, Mrs J. Dent, Major Basil Heaton, Mrs Ann Lacey, Mrs R. F. Stratton, Mr D. R. Peppiatt, Mrs K. Peyton, Brigadier John Woodroffe.

Jockey (NH): B Powell (9-7, w.a.).

Amateur: Mr E D Bailey (9-7).

26 MR T. N. BAILEY, Hereford

Postal: **Lower Brinsop Court, Brinsop, Hereford, HR4 7AZ.**
Phone: **(0432) 760817 (0432) 761770**

1 **AMETHEA,** 8, ch m True Song—Spartan's Legacy **Lady Bailey**
2 **BASIL THYME,** 10, gr g Scallywag—Savette **Mr W. E. Donohue**
3 **BORDER CHERRY,** 6, b m Deep Run—Brown Cherry **Mr T. N. Bailey**
4 **COVA CAILE,** 6, br m Ovac (ITY)—La Campesina **Mrs K. Lloyd**
5 **FAR OUT,** 4, b g Raga Navarro (ITY)—Spaced Out **Mr T. N. Bailey**
6 **GREAT AUNT SALLY,** 9, ch m Scallywag—Auntie Grace **Mr L. J. A. Phipps**
7 **RAUSAL,** 11, b g Lauso—Aur **Mrs K. Lloyd**

Other Owners: Mrs P. R. Collins.

27 MR J. H. BAKER, Tiverton

Postal: **Steart Racing Stables, Stoodleigh, Tiverton, Devon.**
Phone: **(0398) 5317 HOME (0398) 31646**

1 **ALMOOJID,** 4, b c Sadler's Wells (USA)—Irish Bird (USA) **Kingsley Holidays Ltd**
2 **CINDERELLA DEREK,** 6, ch m Hittite Glory—Leaplet **Mr R. J. Baker**
3 **CLYFFE HAZE,** 8, ch g Bonne Noel—Hazelwel **Mr J. K. Davis**
4 **COOLE DODGER,** 5, gr ro g Scallywag—Coole Streak **Partnership**
5 **DOMINION TREASURE,** 5, b br h Dominion—Chrysicabana **Mr R. B. Payne**
6 **DUCKHAVEN,** 7, b g Duky—Fair Haven **Kingsley Holidays Ltd**
7 **FAST MARKET,** 4, gr f Petong—Sweet Candice **Mr Edward Tanner**
8 **FLYING GOD,** 10, b g Osiris—Purston Express **Mr John Warren**
9 **FRENCH DADDY (USA),** 5, b g Al Nasr (FR)—Surgical Suite (USA) **Mr S. M. McCausland**
10 **FROSTY RECEPTION,** 5, ch g What A Guest—Stormy Queen **Mr P. A. Power**
11 **GAMBLINGWAY,** 9, b m Gambling Debt—Lastway **Mr M. A. F. Searle**
12 **GLENCOMMON,** 9, ch g Forties Field (FR)—Deep Pearl **Mr M. H. Holland**
13 **HOLBROOKE TOWER,** 8, b g Tower Walk—Swing Back **Mr J. B. Radford**
14 **HOME OR AWAY,** 7, b g Homing—Tagik **Mr R. B. Payne**
15 **JACK THE HIKER,** 7, b g Rare One—Royal Dress **Mrs T. Madden**
16 **JASON'S QUEST,** 6, gr g Golden Fleece (USA)—Carose **Mr R. B. Payne**
17 **JUST THE TICKET,** 7, gr m Faraway Times (USA)—Rum Year **Mr Bob Butler**
18 **KALA FAIR,** 5, gr h Kalaglow—Fair Head **Kingsley Holidays Ltd**
19 **LONELLA,** 4, b c Lomond (USA)—Actinella **Mr J. K. Davis**
20 **LOVER'S SECRET,** 5, b g Skyliner—Nistona **Mr H. J. W. Davies**
21 **MASTER CAMERON,** 10, ch g Crash Course—Allocate **Mr Jim Davidson**
22 **MIDNIGHT STRIKE (USA),** 6, b g Topsider (USA)—Revels End **Mr R. B. Payne**
23 **OASIS,** 4, ch f Valiyar—Emaline (FR) **Mr J. W. Buxton**
24 **O B JOYFUL,** 4, b f Jester—Our Bernie **Mr J. H. Baker**
25 **OWTFORNOWT,** 5, ch m Hard Fought—Fast Line **Mr P. Slade**
26 **PASONATE,** 4, b g Pas de Seul—Detonate **Mr R. J. Baker**
27 **PEN BAL PRINCESS,** 5, ch m Whistling Deer—Fairy Tree **Mr M. H. Holland**
28 **PHILOSOPHOS,** 4, b g High Top—Pacificus (USA) **Mr P. Slade**
29 **RUGADAY,** 4, br g Milford—Relma **Mr Graham Streak**
30 **SHOCK ABSORBER,** 6, b g Old Jocus—Please Go **Mrs J. R. Hellier**
31 **STAR PLAYER,** 4, ch c Simply Great (FR)—Star Girl **Kingsley Holidays Ltd**
32 **STAYHAR GOLD,** 8, br g Dubassoff (USA)—Arctic Fern **Mr Mike Rowe**
33 **STERLING SILVER,** 5, b h Star Appeal—Silver Tips **Mr J. K. Davis**
34 **STREETFIGHTER (USA),** 6, b h Roberto (USA)—Excitable Miss (USA) **Mr R. B. Payne**
35 **THE NATIONS WAY,** 8, b g National Trust—Lastway **Mr R. T. C. Searle**
36 **THE QUOHEE,** 8, b g Candy Cane—Canky **Mr B. P. Jones**
37 **TWIGGERS,** 4, gr g Petong—Petulengra **Kingsley Holidays Ltd**
38 **VANISHING BOY,** 8, b g Manor Farm Boy—Vanish **Mr John Warren**
39 **WALCISIN,** 7, b g Balboa—Screen Goddess **Mr R. B. Payne**
40 **WILL BE BOLD,** 5, ch m Bold Lad (IRE)—K-Sera **Mr J. B. Radford**
41 **WINTER HAVEN,** 7, ch g Arctic Tern (USA)—Tia Bella (FR) **Mr J. K. Davis**

MR J. H. BAKER—continued

Other Owners: Mr A. P. Buckingham, Mr D. G. Burns, Mr M. Channon, Mr S. Cornew, Mr A. Drury, Mrs A. M. Foster, Mr K. V. Granger, Mr Andrew Hale, Mr Brian Haydock, Mr M. J. Hubbard, Mr M. R. Lavis, Mr W. E. Northwood, Mr F. R. Radford, Mr M. A. Swift.

Conditional: W McFarland (9-10), Lara Pope (9-0).

28 MR G. B. BALDING, Weyhill

Postal: **Fyfield House, Weyhill, Andover, Hampshire, SP11 8EW.**
Phone: **WEYHILL (026477) 2278 TELEX 477094 BALDIN G FAX (026477) 2935**

1 **AHLAVAI,** 5, ch g Quayside—Play The Part **Mr Irving Young**
2 **ANNA VALLEY,** 4, b f Gleason (USA)—Paperchain **Miss B. Swire**
3 5, Ch g Nearly A Hand—April Belle **Mr A. Solway**
4 **AS GOOD AS GOLD,** 4, ch g Oats—Goldyke **Mr Sydney Mason**
5 **ASK MOSS,** 5, ch g Le Moss—Triple Fire **Duke of Atholl**
6 **ATIG (FR),** 7, gr g Kenmare (FR)—Paradala **Mr M. V. L. Pearce**
7 **BARMOSS,** 5, b g Le Moss—Bartlemy Hostess **Mr B. McGrath**
8 **BASKET WEAVE (FR),** 9, b g Weavers' Hall—Manyra (FR) **Mr J. Sayers**
9 **BEECH ROAD,** 8, ch g Nearly A Hand—North Bovey **Mr Tony Geake**
10 **BISHOPS YARN,** 11, br g Tycoon II—Lilac Veil **British Thoroughbred R. & B. Plc**
11 **BORACEVA,** 7, b g Salluceva—Boreen Queen **Duke of Atholl**
12 **BRENT RIVERSIDE,** 7, b g Track Spare—Queen's Bronze **Mr Sydney Mason**
13 **BURANNPOUR,** 10, br g Wolver Hollow—Bubunia **Mrs Ernest Weinstein**
14 **CAPTAIN AHAB,** 6, b g Balinger—Sea Rambler **Mr R. J. Matthews**
15 **CARMELUS THE GREAT,** 7, gr g General Ironside—Our Charm **Theo Waddington (UK) Ltd**
16 **CASTLE DANCE,** 4, b f Castle Keep—Coming Out **Mrs G. B. Balding**
17 **CHANCERY BUCK,** 7, ch g Pauper—What Vision **Mr Q. J. Jones**
18 **CHATTY FELLOW,** 7, br g Decent Fellow—Fancy Ride **Theo Waddington (UK) Ltd**
19 **CLASSIC HERO,** 9, ch g Over The River (FR)—Hero's Slave **Mrs Kathleen Banville**
20 **CLIVE HOUSE,** 6, b g Nearly A Hand—Royal Dialogue **Mr R. J. Lavelle**
21 5, B g Torus—Craeve **Bishop/Field Partnership**
22 **DEEMSTER WILLOW,** 4, b f Ballacashtal (CAN)—Sprightly Willow **Mr R. G. Bray**
23 **DIRECTLY,** 7, b g Bay Express—Veracious **Miss B. Swire**
24 **DOONLOUGHAN,** 5, b g Callernish—Cora Swan **Mr D. Strauss**
25 **EAST RIVER,** 6, b g Midland Gayle—French Note **Mrs David Russell**
26 **END RESULT,** 5, b g Salluceva—Patricia Brant **Mr Chris Bullmore**
27 **EXPRESS AIR,** 7, ch g Pony Express—Idle Air **Mr M. V. L. Pearce**
28 **FARMLEA BOY,** 10, ch g Kemal (FR)—Nessie B **Mr R. J. Lavelle**
29 **FARM WEEK,** 8, gr g General Ironside—News Letter **Lord Chetwode**
30 **FOLK DANCE,** 8, b g Alias Smith (USA)—Enchanting Dancer (FR) **British Thoroughbred R. & B. Plc**
31 **FORCED MARCH (FR),** 6, b g Direct Flight—Rambling **Mr J. M. Kinnear**
32 **FOREST SUN,** 5, ch g Whistling Deer—Sun Spray **Salehurst Paper Co Ltd**
33 **GANARO,** 8, ch g Sagaro—Nicky's Vulgan **Major Patrick Ness**
34 **GLADYS PUGH,** 4, b f Comedy Star (USA)—Nylon Pirate **Mr Alan Wainwright**
35 **GLENSIDE JERRY,** 10, b g Chas Sawyer—Ruckinge Girl **Mr Q. J. Jones**
36 **GOING GETS TOUGH,** 7, ch g Maystreak—Cham-Ol Bazaar **Mr A. G. F. Leather**
37 **GOLDEN ANN,** 4, b f Absalom—Polly Oligant **Mr Edwin N. Cohen**
38 **GOLD PROSPECT,** 8, b g Wolverlife—Golden Darling **Mr Harvey Spack**
39 **GRANDHAVEN,** 6, ch g Le Bavard (FR)—Sandcast **Mrs John Gee**
40 **HALMAJOR,** 9, b br g Mandrake Major—Counter Coup **Mr Irving Young**
41 **HERBERT UNITED,** 11, b g Sir Herbert—Anglo United **Lady Harris**
42 **HICKORY RUN,** 4, b g Seymour Hicks (FR)—Ardent Runner **Mrs Winston Frost**
43 **HOORAY LADY,** 6, ch m Ahonoora—Song Beam **British Thoroughbred R. & B. Plc**
44 **INDUBITABLE,** 5, ch m Sharpo—Veracious **Miss B. Swire**
45 **IRISH DESTINY,** 7, ch g Henbit (USA)—Trilbys Pearl **Theo Waddington (UK) Ltd**
46 **KAMADOOR,** 7, b g Kambalda—Dirimage **Mr D. E. W. Harvie**
47 **KAMRISE,** 8, br g Kambalda—Riseaway **Mrs L. Field**
48 **KEEP YOUR WORD,** 4, ch f Castle Keep—So True **Miss B. Swire**
49 **KILDIMO,** 10, b g Le Bavard (FR)—Leuze **Lady Harris**

MR G. B. BALDING—continued

50 **LITTLE POLVEIR**, 13, b g Cantab—Blue Speedwell **Mr Edward Harvey**
51 **LITTLE TORO**, 8, b g Torus—Little Echo **Mr J. Bishop**
52 **MAJOR EFFORT**, 5, ro g General Ironside—Julie's Gi-Gi **Mrs F. Harvey**
53 **MALICHO**, 7, b g Malicious—Brava **Eastern Quartet Limited**
54 **MIRACLE WORKER**, 4, b g Saher—Divine Dilly **Mr David Andrews**
55 **MITNER**, 7, b br g Vilgora—Bourges (FR) **Mr A. J. Del-Giudice**
56 **MIZUWARI**, 4, ch f Blazing Saddles (AUS)—River Aire **Mrs James Morrison**
57 **MONDAY CLUB**, 6, ch g Remezzo—Jena **Mr J. Tuck**
58 **MORLEY STREET**, 6, ch g Deep Run—High Board **Salehurst Paper Co Ltd**
59 **MUNJARID**, 5, ch h Habitat—Connaught Bridge **Mrs T. A. Palmer**
60 **MY PILOT**, 6, b g Al Sirat (USA)—Dandyville **Mrs G. Jackson**
61 **NONE TOO DEAR (USA)**, 8, gr g Caro—Service Compris (USA) **The Perseverance Group**
62 **OKAZ (USA)**, 5, b g Temperance Hill (USA)—She Is Gorgeous (USA) **Mr M. Power**
63 **PAR FOR THE COURSE**, 5, ch g The Parson—Awbeg Princess **Michael Jackson Bloodstock Ltd**
64 5, B g Rymer—Pearlyric **Lady Harris**
65 **PEPENON**, 8, b g Fair Season—Pepin **Mr N. G. Castleton**
66 **PETTICOAT POWER**, 4, b f Petorius—Red Realm **Murray, Brogan, Kearney Partnership**
67 **POLO BOY**, 10, ch g Red Alert—Bermuda **Mr G. B. Balding**
68 **RARE FISH**, 4, b g Salmon Leap (USA)—Excellent Fun (USA) **Mr B. D. Maloney**
69 **REACH ME DOWN**, 6, b m Cheval—Tangmalangaloo **The Rumble Racing Club**
70 **RESPECTABLE JONES**, 4, ch g Tina's Pet—Jonesee **Mrs Ernest Weinstein**
71 **RHODBRIDGE**, 8, b g Rhodomantade—Fossebridge **Duke of Atholl**
72 **ROMANY KING**, 6, br g Crash Course—Winsome Lady **Mr L. J. Garrett**
73 **ROYAL SHEPHERD**, 7, br g Red Regent—Shepherds Bush **Mrs K. L. Perrin**
74 **RUNNER DUCK**, 4, ch g On Your Mark—Khaki Cambell (USA) **Mrs B. T. Attenborough**
75 **SALEHURST**, 10, b g Scallywag—Snare **Salehurst Paper Co Ltd**
76 **SEA BUCK**, 4, b g Simply Great (FR)—Heatherside **Mr Colin J. Buckle**
77 **SOBRIETY**, 5, b g Noalcoholic (FR)—Sacred Mountain **British Thoroughbred R. & B. Plc**
78 **SOUTH PARADE**, 6, b g Martinmas—Trust Ann **Miss C. Roberts**
79 **SPRING RAG**, 4, b g Raga Navarro (ITY)—Spring Music **Mr M. A. R. Llewellyn**
80 **SUPER MORNING**, 4, b c Martinmas—Super Lady **Mr Jack Maxwell**
81 **SWIFT MELODY**, 9, b m Grange Melody—Spring Twilight **Mr H. M. F. McCall**
82 **SWING MY WAY**, 5, ch g Swing Easy (USA)—Concern **Mrs G. B. Balding**
83 **TALKING MONEY**, 6, ch g Quayside—Shuil Alainn **Racing Telephone Services Ltd**
84 **THATS THE BUSINESS**, 6, br g Milan—Laragh **Mr G. B. Balding**
85 **THEO'S FELLA**, 6, br g Decent Fellow—Scottish Vulgan **Theo Waddington (UK) Ltd**

THREE-YEAR-OLDS

86 **EUROLINK THE LAD**, b g Burslem—Shoshoni Princess **Eurolink Computer Services Ltd**
87 **GLENSTAL PRIORY**, b f Glenstal (USA)—Jumbolia **British Thoroughbred R. & B. Plc**
88 **HOSTING**, b f Thatching—Hostess **British Thoroughbred R. & B. Plc**
89 **LE PELLEY'S ISLE**, b g Pitskelly—Belitis **Mr D. A. Beaumont**
90 **MALMESBURY**, ch g Burslem—Malmsey **British Thoroughbred R. & B. Plc**
91 **MILLION HEIRESS**, b f Auction Ring (USA)—Irish Isle **British Thoroughbred R. & B. Plc**
92 **MISS EUROLINK**, br f Touching Wood (USA)—Sule Skerry **Eurolink Computer Services Ltd**
93 **PALACE STREET (USA)**, ch f Secreto (USA)—Majestic Street (USA) **Miss B. Swire**
94 **PILGRIM'S PATH**, gr c Godswalk (USA)—Lassalia **British Thoroughbred R. & B. Plc**
95 **POTTER'S DREAM**, ch g Horage—Sally St Clair **Mr W. R. Potter**
96 **PUKKA SAHIB**, b g Jalmood (USA)—So True **Miss B. Swire**
97 **RIVERS RHAPSODY**, b f Dominion—Trwyn Cilan **Mr Rex L. Mead**

TWO-YEAR-OLDS

98 Ch c 31/3 Flash of Steel—Amanzi (African Sky) **Mrs E. Weinstein**
99 **DESIGNER STUBBLE**, b c 11/5 Final Straw—Miami Melody (Miami Springs) **Mrs Gill Waters**
100 B f 29/1 Vaigly Great—Final Act (Decoy Boy) **British Thoroughbred R & B Plc**
101 B c 28/2 Green Ruby (USA)—Jonesee (Dublin Taxi) **Mrs E. Weinstein**
102 B c 10/3 Green Ruby (USA)—Lochmar (Lochnager) **Mrs G. B. Balding**
103 **MAID OF MOONSHINE (IRE)**, b f 3/5 Green Ruby (USA)—
Mount of Light (Sparkler) **British Thoroughbred R & B Plc**
104 B c 28/2 Hard Fought—Reparata (Jukebox) **British Thoroughbred R & B Plc**
105 Br f 2/3 Daring March—River Aire (Klairon) **Mr M. Kerr-Dineen and Mr J. I. Morrison**

Introducing

THE FLECTA-RUG

Unique in every sense

Wyvern Veterinary Co. Ltd. introduce the **FLECTA-RUG** – the stable rug which is equivalent to a jute and two blankets. The material was first developed by I.C.I. and Cardiff University as lightweight thermal suiting for astronauts and is now available for the horse.

The **FLECTA-RUG** is light, reflects radiant heat, is non allergic, non absorbent, equally effective in both wet or dry conditions – and STAYS IN PLACE.

Approved by Toby Balding and David Broome, the **FLECTA-RUG** has been developed and is recommended by veterinary surgeons.

For more information and an order form contact Wyvern's distributor:

J. Roe, Roe Racing Ltd., Hyde Park Farm, Lower Hyde, Chalford, Glos. GL6 8NZ.

Tel: 0453 885487

MR G. B. BALDING—continued

106 SCARED STIFF, br f 13/4 Electric—Petrify (Air Trooper) **Mr M. Kerr-Dineen and Mr J. I. Morrison**
107 Br c 27/1 Gorytus (USA)—Straw Boater (Thatch (USA)) **British Thoroughbred R & B Plc**
108 Gr f 4/2 Be My Guest (USA)—Sweety Grey (Young Emperor) **Eurolink Computer Services Ltd**
109 WICKET MAIDEN, ch f 31/3 Norwick (USA)—Dorriba (Ribero) **Mr Richard Matthews**

Other Owners: Miss Valerie Burton, Mr H. Dalzell Payne, Miss M. A. De Quincey, Mr G. De Speville, Mr Michael Habgood, Mr Leon G. Haley, Mrs F. Harvey, Mr Frank Harvey, Mr T. F. Hornett, Mrs G. Jackson, Mr S. Kent, Mr M. A. F. Leather, Mr A. G. Potter, Mrs R. A. Proctor.

Jockey (Flat): J Williams (8-4, w.a.).

Jockeys (NH): J Frost (10-5), R C Guest (10-0).

Apprentices: M Hunt (7-10), T Purseglove (7-10), D Tierney (7-10).

Conditional: A Charlton (9-12), R Farmer (9-7), S Foster (9-10), S Hodgson (9-10), W McFarland (9-10).

Amateurs: Mr J A Geake (10-7), Mr S Mullins (10-7), Mr H Rowsell (10-7).

Lady Rider: Miss Jane Southcombe.

29 MR I. A. BALDING, Kingsclere

Postal: **Park House, Kingsclere, Newbury, Berkshire, RG15 8PZ.**
Phone: **KINGSCLERE (0635) OFFICE 298210 HOME 298274 TELEX 847142 FAX 298305**

1 CALICON, 4, ch g Connaught—Calgary **Mr Simon Berry**
2 CROWN CREST, 4, ch f Mill Reef (USA)—Crown Treasure (USA) **Mr Paul Mellon**
3 HILLS OF HOY, 4, b g Teenoso (USA)—Fairy Tern **Mr Paul Mellon**
4 INSULAR, 10, b g Moulton—Pas de Deux **Mr I. A. Balding**
5 KNOCK KNOCK, 5, ch g Tap On Wood—Ruby River **Mr G. M. Smart**
6 LADY ROSANNA, 5, b m Kind of Hush—Rosaceae **Mr A. R. G. Cane**
7 MAILMAN, 11, ch g Malacate (USA)—Sallail **Mrs John A. McDougald Farms Inc**
8 MONIGA, 4, b f Blazing Saddles (AUS)—Misuumi **Mrs Duncan Allen**
9 NORTHERN HABIT, 4, ch c Salmon Leap (USA)—Manx Millenium **Mr J. C. Smith**
10 PERFECT APPROACH (USA), 8, b g Alleged (USA)—Fast Approach (USA) **Mr I. A. Balding**
11 PERION, 8, ch g Northfields (USA)—Relanca **E & B Productions (Theatre) Ltd**
12 SIESTA KEY, 5, b g Glint of Gold—Petite Hester **Greenland Park Ltd**
13 SKAZKA (USA), 4, b f Sir Ivor—Winter Words (USA) **Mr Paul Mellon**
14 SONG OF SIXPENCE (USA), 6, b g The Minstrel (CAN)—Gliding By (USA) **Mr Paul Mellon**
15 TIGER CLAW (USA), 4, b g Diamond Shoal—Tiger Scout (USA) **Unity Farm Holiday Centre Ltd**
16 VESTAL HILLS, 4, b g Shirley Heights—Vestal Virgin (USA) **Mr Paul Mellon**
17 WATERLOW PARK, 8, ch g Wollow—Caraquenga (USA) **Mr I. A. Balding**

THREE-YEAR-OLDS

18 BURFORD (USA), ch c Time For A Change (USA)—Windrush Lady (USA) **Sheikh Mohammed**
19 CASUAL FLASH (USA), ch c Sharpen Up—Annie Edge **Mr George Strawbridge**
20 CAXTON (USA), b c Halo (USA)—Printing Press (USA) **Sheikh Mohammed**
21 CLARE COURT, ch f Glint of Gold—Clare Bridge (USA) **Mr Paul Mellon**
22 CRYSTAL SPIRIT, b g Kris—Crown Treasure (USA) **Mr Paul Mellon**
23 DASHING BLADE, b c Elegant Air—Sharp Castan **Mr J. C. Smith**
24 EMERALD SEA (USA), ch g Coastal (USA)—Emerald Reef **Mr Paul Mellon**
25 FAIRY FORTUNE, ch f Rainbow Quest (USA)—Fairy Tern **Mr Paul Mellon**
26 FLIGHTY ANGEL, b f Precocious—Angel Beam (SWE) **Mr J. W. Jennings**

Racing is
a Contact Sport -
make contact now.
MPP
MARTIN PEARCE PROMOTIONS
162 High Street, Newmarket, Suffolk CB8 9AQ
Telephone Newmarket (0638) 666446
Telex 94016660 MPPL G
Fax (0638) 666447
INTERNATIONAL
BLOODSTOCK
AND RACING
INFORMATION
AND PROMOTIONAL
SERVICES

MR I. A. BALDING—continued

27 **FREE THINKER (USA),** b f Shadeed (USA)—Top Hope **Mrs Ronald K. Kirk**
28 **GOLDEN DELLA,** b f Glint of Gold—Shindella **Mrs Galen Weston**
29 **KAIPHAS,** b c Pharly (FR)—Kaiserstadt (GER) **Sheikh Mohammed**
30 **KING'S SHILLING (USA),** b c Fit To Fight (USA)—Pride's Crossing (USA) **Mr Paul Mellon**
31 **LOMOND LADY,** b f Lomond (USA)—Miellita **Mr J. C. Smith**
32 **MAID OF HONOR (USA),** ch f Blushing Groom (FR)—Summer Legend (USA) **Mrs Ronald K. Kirk**
33 **NOBLE MATCH,** ch f The Noble Player (USA)—Marylove **Mrs R. M. Chaplin**
34 **NORTHERN GODDESS,** b f Night Shift (USA)—Hearten **Mr Nigel Harris**
35 **PARTING MOMENT (USA),** ch c The Minstrel (CAN)—Farewell Letter (USA) **Mr Paul Mellon**
36 **RELIANT,** b c Shirley Heights—Swift And Sure (USA) **Sheikh Mohammed**
37 **ROUTILANTE,** b f Rousillon (USA)—Danseuse Classique (CAN) **Mr George Strawbridge**
38 **SAMSOVA,** b f Shareef Dancer (USA)—Deadly Serious (USA) **Sheikh Mohammed**
39 **SANDFORD SPRINGS (USA),** b f Robellino (USA)—Tiger Scout (USA) **Mr N. G. Castleton**
40 **SILVER SINGING (USA),** gr f Topsider (USA)—Early Rising (USA) **Mr Paul Mellon**
41 **SOPHIA GARDENS,** gr f Kalaglow—Mint Julep **Mr R. P. B. Michaelson**
42 **SPINNING,** b br c Glint of Gold—Strathspey **Mr Paul Mellon**
43 **SPRING TO GLORY,** b g Teenoso (USA)—English Spring (USA) **Mr Paul Mellon**
44 **SPURNED (USA),** b f Robellino (USA)—Refill **Mr Marshall W. Jenney**
45 **STEALTHY,** ch f Kind of Hush—Misty Cat (USA) **Mrs Michael Wates**
46 **SUNSET ROSE,** b f Shirley Heights—Rose Bowl (USA) **Mr Paul Mellon**
47 **VESTAL BELL,** b f Shirley Heights—Vestal Virgin (USA) **Mr Paul Mellon**
48 **WEST WITH THE WIND,** b br c Glint of Gold—Mighty Fly **Mr Paul Mellon**

TWO-YEAR-OLDS

49 **AIR OF ELEGANCE,** b f 4/4 Elegant Air—Mighty Fly (Comedy Star (USA)) **Mr Paul Mellon**
50 Ch c 19/2 Sharpen Up—Annie Edge (Nebbiolo) **Mr George Strawbridge**
51 **ARRASTRA,** b f 16/4 Bustino—Island Mill (Mill Reef (USA)) **Mr D. H. Back**
52 **BAY MEADOWS STAR,** b f 23/4 Sharpo—Upper Caen (High Top) **Mr E. F. Maynard**
53 **BEATTLE SONG,** b f 7/5 Song—Betyle (FR) (Hardicanute) **Mr J. C. Smith**
54 **BRANDON PRINCE (IRE),** b c 23/5 Shernazar—
Chanson de Paris (USA) (The Minstrel (CAN)) **Mr R. P. B. Michaelson**
55 **BREAKERS AHEAD (USA),** ch c 28/3 Believe It (USA)—
Emerald Reef (USA) (Mill Reef (USA)) **Mr Paul Mellon**
56 **COUNT ROBERT (USA),** ch c 1/4 Roberto (USA)—Domludge (USA) (Lyphard (USA)) **Sheikh Mohammed**
57 **CRYSTAL RING (RIE),** b f 28/2 Kris—Crown Treasure (Graustark)
58 B c 12/4 Mashhor Dancer (USA)—Crystal's Solo (USA) (Crystal Water (USA)) **Mr J. C. Smith**
59 **DUNSTABLE (IRE),** b c 12/4 Formidable (USA)—Dunoof (Shirley Heights) **Sheikh Mohammed**
60 B f 21/3 Sovereign Dancer—Empress Express (USA) (Private Account (USA)) **Mr George Strawbridge**
61 B c 12/3 Private Account (USA)—Empress of Canada (CAN) (Accomplish) **Mr George Strawbridge**
62 **FAIRY FLAX (IRE),** b f 18/4 Dancing Brave (USA)—Fairy Tern (Mill Reef (USA)) **Mr Paul Mellon**
63 **FATAL FRIENDSHIP (USA),** ch f 21/1 Blushing Groom (FR)—
Leap Lively (USA) (Nijinsky (CAN)) **Mr Paul Mellon**
64 **FIGHT TO WIN (USA),** br c 29/4 Fit To Fight (USA)—
Spark of Life (USA) (Key To The Mint (USA)) **Mr Paul Mellon**
65 **FLASHFOOT,** ch c 20/4 Rousillon (USA)—Miellita (King Emperor (USA)) **Mr J. C. Smith**
66 **FLIGHTY GUEST,** gr ro f 21/2 Be My Guest (USA)—Julia Flyte (Drone (USA)) **Mr R. Meredith**
67 **FRAGRANT HILL,** b f 18/4 Shirley Heights—English Spring (USA) (Grey Dawn II) **Mr Paul Mellon**
68 B c 13/2 Slip Anchor—Glancing (Grundy) **Mr George Strawbridge**
69 **GOLD SLIPPER,** b f 6/6 Glint of Gold—Silk Slipper (Prince Tenderfoot (USA)) **Lord Weinstock**
70 **GRANNY'S GIRL,** b f 7/5 Mummy's Game—Michaelmas (Silly Season) **Mrs Julian Berry**
71 **GREEN LANE (USA),** ch c 28/2 Greinton (USA)—Memory Lane (USA) (Never Bend) **Mr Paul Mellon**
72 B f 13/4 Glint of Gold—Habutai (Habitat) **Mrs Michael Wates**
73 **HEART OF DARKNESS,** br c 11/2 Glint of Gold—Land of Ivory (USA) (The Minstrel (CAN)) **Mr Paul Mellon**
74 **HIGH HABIT,** b f 8/5 Slip Anchor—Manx Millenium (Habitat) **Mr J. C. Smith**
75 **KNIGHT OF HONOUR,** ch c 24/5 Touching Wood (USA)—
Nobly Born (USA) (The Minstrel (CAN)) **Sheikh Mohammed**
76 **KRONPRINZ (IRE),** b c 23/4 Local Suitor (USA)—Kaiserchronik (GER) (Cortez (GER)) **Sheikh Mohammed**
77 **LARK RISE (USA),** ch c 17/2 The Minstrel (CAN)—
Glowing Prospect (USA) (Mr Prospector (USA)) **Mr Paul Mellon**

MR I. A. BALDING—continued

78 **MISS MARTINA,** b f 8/5 Martinmas—Rosaceae (Sagaro) **Mrs W. Protheroe Beynon**
79 **MOONFLUTE (USA),** ch f 17/4 The Minstrel (CAN)—Top Hope (High Top) **Mrs Ronald K. Kirk**
80 **OLD STEINE,** b c 14/4 Elegant Air—Brightelmstone (Prince Regent (FR)) **Sheikh Mohammed**
81 **PAY HOMAGE,** ch c 11/5 Primo Dominie—Embraceable Slew (USA) (Seattle Slew (USA)) **Miss A. V. Hill**
82 **PITT CLUB,** ch c 17/3 King of Clubs—Clare Bridge (USA) (Little Current (USA)) **Mr Paul Mellon**
83 B c 18/2 The Minstrel (CAN)—Royal Dilemma (USA) (Buckpasser) **Mr George Strawbridge**
84 B f 8/3 Mashhor Dancer (USA)—Saniette (Crystal Palace (FR)) **Mr J. C. Smith**
85 **SECRET SILENCE,** br c 19/2 Secretariat (USA)—Dame Margot (USA) (Northern Dancer) **Mr Paul Mellon**
86 Br f 28/4 Chief Singer—Sharp Castan (Sharpen Up) **Mr J. C. Smith**
87 **SMART BLADE,** gr c 23/3 Elegant Air—Alsiba (Northfields (USA)) **Mr J. C. Smith**
88 **SWORD'S POINT,** ch c 25/3 Sure Blade (USA)—Impudent Miss (Persian Bold) **Mr Paul Mellon**
89 **TEST OF GOLD,** b f 12/3 Glint of Gold—Fair Test (Fair Season) **Lady Dunphie**
90 **TRAP DANCER,** gr c 16/5 Mashhor Dancer (USA)—Patraana (Nishapour (FR)) **Mr J. C. Smith**

Other Owners: The Queen, Mr W. Aeberhard, Avon Industries Ltd, Maverick Productions Ltd, Mr B. K. Michaelson, Mr N. Pilkington, Mr Jon Sayers, The Hon. Simon Weinstock.

Jockey (Flat): J Matthias (8-8).

Jockey (NH): J Frost (10-5, w.a.).

Apprentices: F Arrowsmith (8-7), M Bradley (7-8), S O'Gorman (7-8).

Amateur: Miss Clare Balding (10-0).

30 MR J. BALDING, Doncaster

Postal: **12 Narrow Lane, Bawtry, Doncaster, South Yorkshire, DN10 6QJ.**
Phone: **HOME (0302) 710096 STABLES (0777) 818407**

1 **ALWAYS TREASURE,** 4, b f Lochnager—Rosinka **Mrs J. Addleshaw**
2 **B GRADE,** 5, b m Lucky Wednesday—Hitravelscene **Mr J. H. Tunstall**
3 **BLYTON LAD,** 4, b g Skyliner—Ballinacurra **Mrs J. Addleshaw**
4 **DREAMTIME DANCER,** 4, b f Town And Country—Aleda Rose **Mr Earle W. Wright**
5 **JACK BOY,** 5, b g Sparkling Boy—Miss Deed **Mr N. T. Davies**
6 **RUN FOR JOYCE,** 4, br f My Dad Tom (USA)—Assel Zawie **Miss J. Balding**
7 **SINGING STAR,** 4, b g Crooner—Wild Jewel **Mr N. T. Davies**
8 **TALIANNA,** 4, b f Kind of Hush—Friths Folly **Jackson Construction Co Ltd**
9 **THE SINGING MAN,** 4, b c Mansingh (USA)—Opalescent **Mr Bob Leach**

THREE-YEAR-OLDS

10 **CAMMY COME HOME,** b f Camden Town—Thank You Fans **Mrs J. Addleshaw**
11 **HOT TOOTSIE,** b f Hotfoot—Lady of The Isle **Mrs Gwyneth Cooke**
12 **MARTYN'S IDEA,** b f On Your Mark—Key Note **Mrs J. Addleshaw**
13 **OLGA'S PET,** br g Tina's Pet—Aunt Winnie **Mrs O. Tunstall**

TWO-YEAR-OLDS

14 **CLOVER FIELD,** ch f 10/5 Wattlefield—Claral Star (Top Star) **Mr J. Balding**
15 **COMEDIE FLEUR,** b f 7/4 Martinmas—Welsh Flower (Welsh Saint) **Mrs M. Matthews**
16 **LE RUBIS VERT,** br f 15/4 Green Ruby—Dourne (Dom Racine (FR)) **Serlby Racing Ltd**
17 **LINCSTONE BOY (IRE),** b g 23/3 Kafu—Babylon (Hello Gorgeous (USA)) **Mrs J. Addleshaw**
18 **MAY LODGE,** b f 21/4 Country Classic—Irish Blizzard (Fordham (USA)) **Mr L. Dukes**
19 **MISS GREEN GABLES,** br f 7/3 Green Ruby—Redcross Miss (Tower Walk) **Mrs J. Everitt and Mr P. Balding**

MR J. BALDING—continued

20 **RED SPARKY,** b f 25/2 Green Ruby—Electrified (Gunner B) **Mrs J. Addleshaw**
21 **SILVER STONE BOY,** gr c 12/4 Another Realm—Elkie Brooks (Relkino) **Mrs J. Addleshaw**
22 **SKIP CHANGE,** b f 17/5 Hotfoot—Lady of The Isle (Pitskelly) **Serlby Racing Ltd**
23 **STONELEIGH STAR (IRE),** b f 10/5 Muscatite—Canebrake Lady (Formidable (USA)) **Mrs J. Addleshaw**
24 Gr f 17/5 Green Ruby—Susie Hall (Gold Rod) **Mrs J. Everitt and Mr P. Balding**

Other Owners: Mr G. Backhouse, Miss E. Balding, Mr D. C. Bichan, Mr Ivor J. Dowell, Mrs M. C. Hill, Mr H. Leather, Mr M. K. McGuire, Mr N. G. Rollitt.

Jockeys (Flat): M Fry (7-7, w.a.), S Webster (w.a.).

Apprentice: Claire Balding (7-0).

31 MRS P. A. BARKER, Richmond

Postal: **Greenbury Grange, Scorton, Richmond, North Yorks, DL10 6EP.**
Phone: **(0325) 378266**

1 **CAPRICORN BLUE,** 7, b g Blue Cashmere—Aqua Nimba **Mr W. L. Barker**
2 **DUTCH AUCTION,** 6, b g Taufan (USA)—Mock Auction **Mr Christopher Younger**
3 **IN GLORY,** 6, b m Dalsaan—Indigine (USA) **Mr A. Harrison**
4 **MELODY GILL,** 4, br f Tudor Rhythm—Gill Breeze **Mrs G. D. Morrissey**
5 **NEARCTIC BAY (USA),** 4, b c Explodent (USA)—Golferette (USA) **Mrs Elaine Cockrill**
6 **PADDY'S GLEN,** 13, br g Furry Glen—Tricia **Mr W. L. Barker**
7 **RIESENER,** 4, ch c Touching Wood (USA)—Sharp Run **Mrs P. A. Barker**
8 **RYE SPIRIT,** 4, b g Meldrum—Bath Miss **Mr W. L. Barker**
9 **SARNIA SOUND,** 5, ch g Music Boy—St Pauli Girl **Mrs P. A. Barker**
10 **SKOLERN,** 6, b g Lochnager—Piethorne **Mr I. Greaves and Mr A. Fairbairn**
11 **STRAIGHT DOWN,** 13, b g Straight Lad—Down Memory Lane **Mrs P. A. Barker**
12 **SUREST DANCER (USA),** 4, b c Green Dancer (USA)—Oopsie Daisy (USA) **Mr W. L. Barker**

Jockey (NH): C Hawkins (10-0, w.a.).

32 MR G. B. BARLOW, Macclesfield

Postal: **Bradwall Manor, Sandbach, Cheshire, CW11 9RF.**
Phone: **(0270) 762036**

1 **BRADWALL,** 6, br g Strong Gale—Sweet Season **Mr G. B. Barlow**
2 **SHEPPIE'S DOUBLE,** 7, b m Scallywag—Quadrille II **Mr G. B. Barlow**
3 **VALE OF WELTON,** 14, ch g Aglojo—River Minstrel **Mr G. B. Barlow**
4 **WOODEN BEAR,** 7, ch g Orchestra—Release Record **Mr G. B. Barlow**

Amateur: Mr J G R Barlow (12-0).

33 MR M. A. BARNES, Penrith

Postal: **Bank House, Little Salkeld, Penrith, Cumbria.**
Phone: **076881 257**

1 **CHRISADAN,** 4, b g Sweet Monday—Mummy's Rascal **Mr J. G. Graham**
2 **DINSDALE LAD,** 4, ch g Sweet Monday—Forgets Image **Armstrong/Greenwell**
3 **LORDSHIP,** 5, b g Lord Gayle (USA)—All Gold Rose **Mr J. H. Millican**
4 **SPS CREATIVE,** 4, gr f Petong—Rosalina **Mr M. Barnes**

MR M. A. BARNES—continued

THREE-YEAR-OLDS

5 **SCALAMON,** br g Sweet Monday—Mummy's Rascal **Mr Brown**
6 **SECRET DYNASTY,** b f Dynastic—Thelmas Secret **Mr Brown**

Other Owners: Mr T. A. Barnes, Mr R. H. Hayton, Mr V. Shields.

34 MR D. H. BARONS, Kingsbridge

Postal: **Hendham Farm, Woodleigh, Kingsbridge, S. Devon, TQ7 4DP.**
Phone: **KINGSBRIDGE (0548) 550326 (0548) 550411 FAX (0548) 550 160**

1 **AMENHOTEP (NZ),** 5, br h Star Wolf—Pendeen **Partnership**
2 **AUCTION LAW (NZ),** 6, ch g Pevero—High Plateau (NZ) **Mrs Brenda Gittins**
3 **BOLD MONK (NZ),** 8, ch g Pag-Asa (AUS)—Chatalia (NZ) **Partnership**
4 **BRIEF ENCOUNTER (NZ),** 6, b g Foreign Affair—Euphemia (NZ) **Mr Colin Lewis**
5 **BUMBLES FOLLY (NZ),** 9, ch g Sea Anchor—Casurina (NZ) **Mr Colin Lewis**
6 **CELERY RISE (NZ),** 6, b g Palm Beach (FR)—Golden Wedding (NZ) **Mr David Sherman**
7 **DEVON SPIRIT (NZ),** 8, b g Star Wolf—Dac (NZ) **Mrs Donald Campbell**
8 **DUKE OF ABSON (NZ),** 6, ch g Lakenheath (USA)—Moon Goddess (NZ) **Mr Sid Williams**
9 **FORT LINO,** 7, ch g Bustino—Forliana **Mr Colin Lewis**
10 **HANDY LANE,** 9, b m Nearly A Hand—Border Lane **Mr A. D. Stoddart**
11 **HELLOVASTATE,** 5, ch g Enchantment—Brandenbourg **Mrs Gail Gaisford**
12 **HIGH HAM BLUES,** 8, b g White Prince (USA)—Gwentello **Mr D. Crates**
13 **IMADYNA (NZ),** 8, b g Frassino—Volidrill (NZ) **Mr Eric Parker**
14 **JUST AS HOPEFUL (NZ),** 6, b g In The Purple (FR)—Bighearted (NZ) **Mr Michael Padfield**
15 **LADY COGNAC (NZ),** 7, ch m Smuggler—Elamite (NZ) **Mr P. S. Williams**
16 **MAYBE BABY,** 5, b g Don—Treasure Ship **Mr S. J. Lindsey**
17 **MAYORAN (NZ),** 6, b g Mayo Mellay (NZ)—Bundoran (NZ) **Lord Clinton**
18 **MISTER CHRISTIAN (NZ),** 9, b g Captain Jason (NZ)—Grisette (NZ) **Mr R. N. Stevens**
19 **MO'S CHORISTER,** 4, b c Lir—Revelstoke **Mr Clive Fowlie**
20 **MYSTIC PALACE (NZ),** 7, ch g Double Nearco (USA)—Mystic Light (NZ) **Partnership**
21 **OLD DEER PARK,** 4, b g Blakeney—Hurry On Honey **Mr D. H. Barons**
22 **OLVESTON (NZ),** 6, b g Sea Anchor—Statira (NZ) **Mr Colin Lewis**
23 **PLAYSCHOOL (NZ),** 12, b g Valuta—Min Tide (NZ) **Mrs P. M. Cottle**
24 **PORTLEMOUTH (NZ),** 6, br m Rapier II—Fullrate (NZ) **Mr D. H. Barons**
25 **PURPLE POINT (NZ),** 5, br g In The Purple (FR)—Grospoint (NZ) **Mr Eric Parker**
26 **ROCKTOR (NZ),** 5, b g Shy Rambler (USA)—Sobina (NZ) **Mrs G. Watkinson-Yull**
27 **ROYAL BATTERY (NZ),** 7, br g Norfolk Air—All At Sea (NZ) **Mrs P. M. Cottle**
28 **SALCOMBE HARBOUR (NZ),** 6, ch g English Harbour—Faux Leigh (NZ) **Mr R. B. McHardy**
29 **SEA FLOWER (NZ),** 8, ch m Sea Anchor—Golden Flower (NZ) **Mr M. Denton**
30 **SEAGRAM (NZ),** 10, ch g Balak—Llanah (NZ) **Mr Eric Parker**
31 **SEARCHER,** 5, br g Furry Glen—Pollys Flake **Mr S. Hussey**
32 **SIDE BRACE (NZ),** 6, gr g Mayo Mellay (NZ)—Grey Mist (NZ) **Mr Tom Stronge**
33 **SKETCHER (NZ),** 7, b g Candyboy (NZ)—Jezebel (NZ) **Mr S. Hussey**
34 **SOUTHOVER LAD (NZ),** 7, b g Frassino—Tarea (NZ) **Mr Sid Williams**
35 **SOUTH POOL (NZ),** 6, ch g Harbor Prince (USA)—Romany Robe **Mr P. C. Holden**
36 **SUPER EXPRESS,** 9, ch g Hotfoot—Gwynfa **Mr Sid Williams**
37 **THATCHER ROCK (NZ),** 5, b g Le Grand Seigneur (CAN)—Lady Joelyn (NZ) **Mr M. J. Disney**
38 **TOPSHAM BAY,** 7, b g Proverb—Biowen **Mr M. L. Marsh**
39 **TREWITHIEN,** 6, ch m Air Trooper—Balitree **W. H. Williams Turf Accountants Ltd**
40 **YIRAGAN,** 8, ch g Cantab—Foreverusa **Mr M. L. Marsh**
41 **ZUMMERSET (NZ),** 8, b g Star Wolf—Homunga Miss (NZ) **Mr D. W. E. Coombs**

MR D. H. BARONS—continued

Other Owners: Mr J. M. T. Gaisford, Mr Anthony J. Hewitt, Mr Antony Hopkins, Mr P. Maltby, Mr G. N. Noye, Mr Alan Taylor, Mrs D. L. Tucker, Mr Peter J. White.

Jockeys (NH): S Earle (10-0), P Nicholls (10-4).

Conditional: N Hawke (9-7), G Piper (10-0).

Amateurs: Mr R D R Barons (10-7), Mr R Darke (10-0).

35 MR R. E. BARR, Middlesbrough

Postal: **Carr House Farm, Seamer, Stokesley, Middlesbrough, TS9 5LL.**
Phone: **STOKESLEY (0642) 710687**

1 **CAPTAIN CUTE,** 5, br ro g Absalom—Cute **Mrs R. E. Barr**
2 **HAPPY CAVALIER,** 5, b g King of Spain—Happy Donna **Mr I. Dowse**
3 **LIGHT TRAVELLER,** 10, gr ro g Roan Rocket—Balidium **Miss E. A. Curtis**
4 **LISGAYLE,** 7, br m Midland Gayle—Lis Ghorran **Mr G. Taylor**
5 **MRS MUDDLE,** 7, b m Gleason (USA)—Cathy Mont **Mr K. P. Toland**
6 **RAMPANT,** 11, br g Reliance II—Glimmer of Hope **Mr P. Cartmell**
7 **ROWDY,** 4, bl g Lucky Wednesday—Angel Row **Mr C. D. Thomson**
8 **STARLIGHT WONDER,** 4, ch f Star Appeal—My Lady Muriel (USA) **Mr I. G. Thomson**

Other Owners: Mr R. E. Barr, Mr D. R. Walker.

Jockey (NH): A Orkney (10-0).

Conditional: T P White (9-7).

Amateurs: Mr M Brown (10-6), Mr S Swiers (10-6).

36 MR M. F. BARRACLOUGH, Claverdon

Postal: **Claverdon Hall Farm, Manor Lane, Claverdon, Warwickshire, CV35 8NH.**
Phone: **(0926) 843332**

1 **CHRIS'S DELIGHT,** 7, ch m Mycropolis—Florence Eliza **Mr Adrian Salt**
2 **DUNSEL BOY,** 7, b g Dubassoff (USA)—Bobby's Hansel **Mrs E. A. Stokell**
3 **MISSELFORE,** 7, b m Reform—Chalke Valley **Mrs E. A. Stokell**
4 **OXSTALL'S LADY,** 6, b m The Brianstan—Charlotte Mary **Mr J. M. R. Luckett**
5 **PHALIES FOLLY,** 8, ch g Pauper—Lucy Ladybird **Mr M. F. Barraclough**
6 **RELATED SOUND,** 4, b g Uncle Pokey—Darling June **Mr A. G. Hughes**
7 **SIROCKO BAY,** 6, b g Royal Blend—Trapalanda **Mr Mark A. Wall**
8 **SUSSEX QUEEN,** 11, ch m Music Boy—Counsel's Opinion **Mr M. F. Barraclough**
9 **VANDA'S CREATION,** 5, b m Creative Plan (USA)—Vanda **Mr M. F. Barraclough**

Other Owners: Mr G. N. Beckett, Mr K. Morgan, Mr Joseph H. Wall, Mr Nigel Wall, Mr D. Wiseman.

Conditional: Ann Stokell (9-7).

37 MR L. J. BARRATT, Oswestry

Postal: **Bromwich Park, Oswestry, Salop.**
Phone: **(0691) 88209**

1 **BLAZING AWAY**, 4, gr g Blazing Saddles (AUS)—Norton Princess **Mr W. R. Owen**
2 **BROMWICH BILL**, 5, b g Headin' Up—Bilbao **Mr L. J. Barratt**
3 **ELOFAHABIT**, 4, b g Headin' Up—Eleonora **Mr Doug Brereton**
4 **LIVEN UP**, 5, b g Headin' Up—Lonely Dawn (USA) **Mr L. J. Barratt**
5 **LONELY LASS**, 4, b f Headin' Up—Lonely Dawn (USA) **Mr L. J. Barratt**
6 **MAC'S MUSIC**, 4, ch g Music Boy—Annathena **Mr L. J. Barratt**
7 **MISTERITZ**, 5, ch g Headin' Up—Ritzy Dreamer **Mr L. J. Barratt**
8 **MOHSSEN (FR)**, 9, ch g Sharpen Up—Showery Summer (FR) **Mr L. J. Barratt**
9 **NAGEM**, 7, b m Headin' Up—Eleonora **Mr Doug Brereton**
10 **PARK MILL**, 8, ch g Tower Walk—Hodsock Venture **Mr L. J. Barratt**

THREE-YEAR-OLDS

11 **BOAMBER**, ch g Anfield—Rykneld **Mr L. J. Barratt**
12 **DERRY LOVE**, gr f Derrylin—Rough Love **Mr Doug Brereton**
13 **TOLMOSS**, ch g Night Shift (USA)—Viennese Waltz **Mr L. J. Barratt**

TWO-YEAR-OLDS

14 **LONSOM LASS**, ch f 2/3 Headin' Up—Lonely Dawn (USA) (Plenty Old (USA)) **Mr L. J. Barratt**
15 Ro g 15/4 Headin' Up—Lucky Broxted (Broxted) **Mr L. J. Barratt**

Other Owners: Mr Ian Anderson.

Jockey (Flat): Alan Proud.

Lady Rider: Miss Diana Jones.

38 MR T. D. BARRON, Thirsk

Postal: **Maunby House, Maunby, Thirsk, North Yorkshire.**
Phone: **(0845) 587435**

1 **AMENABLE**, 5, b g Kampala—Kirin **Mr W. G. Spink**
2 **ANOTHER MARCH**, 4, b g Marching On—River Sirene **Mr T. M. Wilson**
3 **BEAU DEREK**, 10, b g Derek H—Fashionable Lady **Mr W. G. Spink**
4 **BELLA SEVILLE**, 6, gr m King of Spain—Tempered Wind **Mr H. T. Duddin**
5 **BOLD REPUBLIC**, 4, gr g Nishapour (FR)—Gallant Believer (USA) **Mr Geoffrey Martin**
6 **BRONZE CROSS**, 5, b g Rontino—Make Your Mark **Enderleigh Sport Agencies Ltd**
7 **BURKES PROGRESS**, 4, b br f Tyrnavos—Pushkar **M. P. Burke Plc**
8 **COME TO TERMS**, 4, gr g Welsh Term—Sparkling Time (USA) **Miss S. A. Spink**
9 **ENSHARP (USA)**, 4, b g Sharpen Up—Lulworth Cove **Mrs M. Watt**
10 **EUROCON**, 6, b g Ile de Bourbon (USA)—Consistent **Mr W. G. Spink**
11 **GALA PRINCE**, 13, b g Gala Performance (USA)—Zarabanda **Mrs M. Aston**
12 **GLASTONDALE**, 4, b g Beldale Flutter (USA)—Glastonbury **Mr J. Baggott**
13 **GODS SOLUTION**, 9, gr h Godswalk (USA)—Campitello **Mr Peter Jones**
14 **IRISH PASSAGE**, 7, gr g Welsh Captain—Honey's Queen **Mr T. M. Wilson**
15 **JOE BUMPAS**, 4, b g Noalto—Montana Moss **Mr W. G. Spink**
16 **LIFE'S A LARK**, 5, ch g Wolverlife—Red Lark **Mr Kevin Shaw**
17 **NEW BLUE**, 6, ro g Silly Prices—Blue Haze **Mr T. Hazell**
18 **PATCON**, 5, b g Kafu—Duchess of Howfen **Mr W. G. Spink**
19 **RENTAGHOST**, 12, ro g Grey Ghost—Rosamond **Mrs S. Sturman**
20 **TAWNY**, 4, ch f Grey Ghost—Trim Taxi **Mr E. Buck**
21 **THRINTOFT**, 4, ch g Sandhurst Prince—Finlarrig **Mr T. D. Barron**
22 **TOUCH ABOVE**, 4, b g Touching Wood (USA)—B A Poundstretcher **Mrs J. Hazell**
23 **VALLEY MILLS**, 10, ch g Red Alert—Haunting **Mr T. D. Barron**
24 **YOUNG WILKIE**, 6, br m Callernish—Kincsem **Mr C. H. Greensit**

MR T. D. BARRON—continued

THREE-YEAR-OLDS

25 **ALEZAN,** ch f Dublin Taxi—Mark My Word
26 **ANDREW'S FIRST,** br g Tender King—Dame Kelly **Mr W. G. Spink**
27 **ANOTHER BUMPAS,** br g Pas de Seul—Minstrels Shoe **Mr W. G. Spink**
28 **BRECKENBROUGH LAD,** b g Uncle Pokey—Fabulous Beauty **Mr C. H. Greensit**
29 **CAPTAIN BROWN,** b g Welsh Captain—Belinda Brown **Mr Glyndwr Jones**
30 **CHARM TIME,** ch g Good Times (ITY)—Glamorous Girl **Mr Geoffrey Martin**
31 **EUROBLAKE,** b g Roscoe Blake—Pie Eye **Mr W. G. Swiers**
32 **KILDONAN,** b g Welsh Captain—Madam Import **Express & Star Raceowners Club 1989**
33 **KIRSTENBOSCH,** b c Caerleon (USA)—Flower Petals **Mr W. G. Spink**
34 **MACCONACHIE,** b g Good Times (ITY)—High Point Lady (CAN) **Mr W. G. Spink**
35 **ORCHARD COURT (USA),** ch c Believe It (USA)—Quilting Bee (USA) **Mr Stephen Woodall**
36 **SUPER ONE,** b g Superlative—Josephine Gibney **Mr W. G. Spink**
37 **YOUNG INDIA,** br f Indian King (USA)—Marfisa **Mr Gordon Wilkinson**

TWO-YEAR-OLDS

38 **ADWICK PARK,** b c 1/5 Blazing Saddles (AUS)—Ana Gabriella (USA) (Master Derby (USA))
39 **ALLINSON'S MATE (IRE),** b c 23/2 Fayruz—Piney Pass (Persian Bold)
40 B g 5/6 Swing Easy (USA)—Kastritsa (Royal Palace)
41 Br c 25/4 Reasonable (FR)—Lady Monica (Irish Love)
42 **MATE'S MIRAGE,** ch c 3/5 Music Boy—Gay Shadow (Northfields (USA))
43 **OLIVERS MOUNT (USA),** b c 24/3 Lyphard's Wish (FR)—Olivera (GER) (Kaiseradler)
44 **ON THE EDGE,** b c 16/4 Vaigly Great—Final Request (Sharp Edge)
45 **ORIENT AIR,** br f 9/3 Prince Sabo—Chinese Falcon (Skymaster)
46 Br c 17/3 Petorius—Pitaka (Pitskelly)
47 **SHIMMERING SCARLET (IRE),** br f 6/2 Glint of Gold—Scarlet Slipper (Gay Mecene (USA))
48 **SLY DREAMER,** gr c 30/4 Dreams To Reality—River Vixen (Sagaro)
49 **SPINECHILLER,** gr c 1/4 Grey Ghost—Swinging Gold (Swing Easy (USA))

Other Owners: Mrs Christine Barron, Mr T. E. Barron, Mrs I. M. Boyle, Mr Timothy Cox, Mr B. Elsworth, Mr W. A. Greensit, Mr Donald Moore, Mr T. Nugent, Mr P. D. Savill, Mr W. R. Wilson.

Apprentices: S Gray (7-0), Alex Greaves (8-3), R Lamplugh (7-7).

39 MR A. K. BARROW, Bridgwater

Postal: **Marsh Mills Farm, Over Stowey, Bridgwater, Somerset.**
Phone: **(0278) 732522**

1 **CASH CRISIS,** 10, ch g Hell's Gate—Pound Foolish **Mr C. A. Strawbridge**
2 **CORAL HARBOUR,** 8, ch g Bay Express—Coralivia **Mrs M. Rickards**
3 **DASHING DOMINOE,** 5, ch g Sweet Monday—Autumn Dream **Mr D. W. E. Coombs**
4 **GOODWYNS LAD,** 6, b g Homing—Someone Talked (USA) **Mrs Marilyn Cornish**
5 **HOLY WAR,** 6, b g Northfields (USA)—Bella Carlotta (FR) **Mr M. Watts**
6 **LE CAROTTE,** 8, ch g Balinger—Camargue **Mr M. Hagget and Mr B. Pole**
7 **MISTRESS PARDY,** 8, b m Pardigras—Pettyclose **Mrs Marilyn Cornish**
8 **PANTECHNICON,** 10, b g Pitpan—Avatea **Mr D. W. E. Coombs**
9 **SOVEREIGN STREAM,** 6, b g Paddy's Stream—Noble Lynn **Mrs Marilyn Cornish**
10 **SWIFT ASCENT (USA),** 8, b g Crow (FR)—Barely Flying (USA) **Mr I. J. Williams**
11 **TAGMOUN CHAUFOUR (FR),** 5, ch g Pavo Real (FR)—Bienvenue (FR) **Avalon Surfacing Ltd. and Mrs V. Palmer**
12 **TINKERS BROOK,** 5, b g Last Fandango—Roman Spa **Mr M. S. Taylor**
13 **VALVERDE,** 6, ch m Crofter (USA)—Kindle **Mrs M. Rickards**
14 **WILLESDON (USA),** 6, ch h Master Willie—Dona Maya (USA) **Mrs Vicky Palmer**

Other Owners: Mr T. W. Cornish, Mr F. J. Dolan, Mr R. J. Edwards, Mrs P. A. D. Lloyd, Mr P. C. Lloyd, Mr David Parrish, Mrs E. J. Wilson, Mr F. E. Wilson.

Jockey (NH): B Powell (10-0).

Conditional: J Hurst (9-7), W Irvine (9-7).

40 MR F. M. BARTON, Prestbury

Postal: **Florence Farm, Newton, Macclesfield, Cheshire, SK10 4LH.**
Phone: **(0625) 829633**

1 **KNOWETOP,** 4, ch f Sayyaf—Heirline **Mr F. M. Barton**
2 **SOUTHERNS,** 8, ch g Lord of Arabia—Londoretta **Mr F. M. Barton**

Jockey (NH): Trevor Wall (10-0, w.a.).

41 MR R. B. BARTON, Corsham

Postal: **Manor Farm, Wadswick, Box, Corsham, Wiltshire.**
Phone: **(0225) 810700**

1 **WADSWICK LADY,** 5, b m New Member—Pollys Owen **Mrs M. I. Barton**

Jockey (NH): Richard Dunwoody (w.a.).

42 MR P. BARY, Chantilly

Postal: **5 Chemin des Aigles, 60500 Chantilly, France.**
Phone: **44 57 14 03 TELEX: 145 700 FAX: 44 58 56 12**

1 **LE TEMERAIRE,** 4, b c Top Ville—La Mirande (FR) **P. G. Goulandris**
2 **PRETTY SECRETARY (USA),** 4, ro f Secretariat (USA)—Princess Hattab **I. M. Fares**
3 **SILVER RIVERMAN (USA),** 4, b c Riverman (USA)—Loot (USA) **I. M. Fares**
4 **SOVEREIGN WATER (FR),** 4, b c Gay Mecene (USA)—Paddle (FR) **Mme A. Manning**

THREE-YEAR-OLDS

5 **BAROUF (FR),** gr c Kenmare—Emmanuelle **Mme D. Jacob**
6 **DOUBLE EFFS (USA),** b c Sovereign Dancer (USA)—Meditation (USA) **I. M. Fares**
7 **FAENA (FR),** b f Deep Roots—Sharp Dresser **L. C. Bary**
8 **FIGHT FOR ARFACT,** ch f Salmon Leap—Lady Jeff **H. Minoui**
9 **GO HIGH (FR),** ch f Salmon Leap—High Hollow **L. C. Bary**
10 **GOLDEN ERA (USA),** ch f Hero's Honor (USA)—Golden Secretariat (USA) **Skymarc Farm**
11 **HIGHEST PLEASURE (USA),** b f Foolish Pleasure (USA)—Teisen Lap (USA) **I. M. Fares**
12 **HONOR RAJANA (USA),** b c Hero's Honor (USA)—Rajana (USA) **I. M. Fares**
13 **IVOR JEWEL (USA),** b f Sir Ivor—Adlibber (USA) **I. M. Fares**
14 **LALIFFE (USA),** b f Lypheor—La Francaise (USA) **Skymarc Farm**
15 **LANE END CHAMPION (USA),** b c Alleged (USA)—Wanda's Tear (USA) **I. M. Fares**
16 **LA TRITONA,** ch f Touching Wood (USA)—La Mirande (FR) **Melle C. Goulandris**
17 **L'EXTRA HONOR (USA),** ch f Hero's Honor (USA)—L'Extravagante (CAN) **I. M. Fares**
18 **MISS ALLEGED (USA),** b f Alleged (USA)—Miss Tusculum (USA) **I. M. Fares**
19 **OAKBROOK TERN (USA),** b f Arctic Tern (USA)—Oakbrook Lady (USA) **I. M. Fares**
20 **PRINCESS PLAYER (USA),** b f Play On—Princeline **I. M. Fares**
21 **QUEEN OF COMEDY (USA),** ro f Stage Door Johnny—Winning Laughter **R. S. Gilbert**
22 **RESCUE ME (FR),** gr f Kenmare (FR)—Rebellita (FR) **Melle C. Goulandris**
23 **RHYTHMANIA (USA),** ch f Stop The Music—Lovely Guinevere **R. S. Gilbert**
24 **RICH AND FAMOUS (FR),** b f Deep Roots—Paraxelle (FR) **R. S. Gilbert**
25 **RULING HONOR (USA),** b f Hero's Honor (USA)—Ruling Lark (USA) **I. M. Fares**
26 **SECRET HERO (USA),** b c Secreto—Sans Dot **I. M. Fares**
27 **SECRET JOY,** b br f Fabulous Dancer (USA)—Secretive (FR) **Melle C. Goulandris**
28 **SERAFICA,** b f No Pass No Sale—Servia **Melle C. Goulandris**
29 **SIR HOLLOW (USA),** b f Sir Ivor—My Hollow **I. M. Fares**
30 **SPECIAL SECRETO (USA),** b f Secreto (USA)—Special Team (USA) **I. M. Fares**
31 **SPIRIT OF DARSHAAN,** b c Darshaan—Flut d'Oa (FR) **J. M. Valerio**
32 **UNION EXPRESS (USA),** b c Raise A Native—Our Reunion (USA) **I. M. Fares**
33 **VALIANCE (FR),** b br f Akarad (FR)—Valentina Way (FR) **P. G. Goulandris**
34 **VERTEVOIE (FR),** ch f Tip Moss—La Bate **H. Delloye**

MR P. BARY—continued

TWO-YEAR-OLDS

35 **ABORDABLE,** b f 26/2 Formidable—Absolute (FR) (Luthier) **Melle C. Goulandris**
36 **ALLEDONIA (FR),** ch f Script Ohio—Aloof (Arctic Tern) **I. M. Fares**
37 **BEUSSENT (FR),** b c Dunphy—La Bate (Frontin) **Hugues Delloye**
38 B c Fabulous Dancer—Blushing Saya (Blushing Groom) **O. Yasuda**
39 **CELTIC CROWN (IRE),** ch f 26/5 Shernazar—Guayana (Kronenkranich) **J. Forsythe**
40 Ch f Arctic Tern—Channelette (Seaneen) **Mr Ishida**
41 **CLAIR DE LUNE (FR),** b br f Noblequest—Noce Magique (Concertino) **Mme A. Manning**
42 **DIXIE GENT (GER),** b c Nebos—Divonne (Vieux Chateau) **J. Forsythe**
43 **DOUBLE FORECAST (IRE),** ch c 24/3 Lomond—Typecast (Prince John) **I. M. Fares**
44 **GRAND VOYAGEUR (FR),** b br c Sagace—Athy Angel (Three Dons) **R. S. Gilbert**
45 **HELICE (USA),** b f Slewpy—Hirondelle (Val de L'Orne) **Skymarc Farm**
46 **HIGHMARE (FR),** gr c Kenmare—Highest (High Top) **J. L. Bouchard**
47 **LA BRILLANTE,** b f 29/3 Glint of Gold—La Mirande (Le Fabuleux) **Melle C. Goulandris**
48 **LA CARENE (FR),** gr f Kenmare—La Passionaria (Reform) **I. M. Fares**
49 **LAND SHARK (FR),** b f Pitskelly—Luvia (Cure The Blues) **Melle C. Goulandris**
50 B br f Lashkari—Liberale (Fabulous Dancer) **O. Yasuda**
51 **LUCKY PRINCE (FR),** b c Akarad—Friluck (Judger) **I. M. Fares**
52 **LUNAIRE,** b f 10/2 Try My Best—Lucaya (Mill Reef) **Melle C. Goulandris**
53 **MUSICAL SOUND (FR),** b c Sicyos—Musical Soul (Youth) **I. M. Fares**
54 **MY POPOF (FR),** ch c Gairloch—Vital Spark (Sharpman) **J. Ternynck**
55 **NUMIDIE (FR),** b f Baillamont—Yamuna (Green Dancer) **I. M. Fares**
56 **ON CREDIT (FR),** ch f No Pass No Sale—Noble Tiara (Vaguely Noble) **P. G. Goulandris**
57 **PEGGY FINCH (IRE),** b f 13/2 Law Society—Snow Finch (Storm Bird) **Skymarc Farm**
58 **REBELLIO (FR),** gr c 18/4 Kenmare—Rebellita (Bellypha) **I. M. Fares**
59 **REFORMABLE (IRE),** b c Formidable—Rain Must Fall (Luthier) **O. Yasuda**
60 **REZAIYEH (FR),** gr f Kenmare—Odyssee (Frere Basile) **I. M. Fares**
61 **SLEEPING CAR (FR),** b br c Dunphy—Lorelta (Rose Laurel) **T. Iizuka**
62 **TIGRIS (USA),** b f Halo—Tovalop (Northern Dancer) **Skymarc Farm**
63 **UN CHIC TYPE (FR),** b c Cariellor—Lucky River (River River) **J. G. Murray**
64 **WHISTLE JACKET (FR),** b f Chief Singer—Waterford (Crystal Palace) **O. Yasuda**

Jockeys (Flat): N Jeanpierre, E Legrix.

Apprentice: V Clavreul.

43 MR R. BASTIMAN, Wetherby

Postal: **Cherry Court, Linton, Wetherby, West Yorkshire, LS22 4NT.**
Phone: **(0937) 63050**

1 **DEPUTY TIM,** 7, ch g Crofter (USA)—Kindle **Mr M. Shaw**
2 **LADY'S MANTLE (USA),** 6, ch m Sunny Clime (USA)—Alchemilla (USA) **Mrs P. Bastiman**
3 **RUBY SHOES,** 4, b f Day Is Done—Very Seldom **Mr R. W. Lee**
4 **SILKWORM,** 4, b f Czaravich (USA)—Jemeela **Mr D. Riley**
5 **WASMI,** 7, b h Great Nephew—Hatta **Mr M. Shaw**
6 **WIMBORNE,** 5, b ro g What A Guest—Khadija **Mr David McKenzie**

THREE-YEAR-OLDS

7 **AIRE VALLEY LAD,** b g The Brianstan—Rojael **Mr J. T. Halliwell**
8 **ATEAMBER,** b g Hays—Princess Lamia **Mr R. Churm**
9 **CB SPECIAL,** ch f Absalom—Terre Promise **Mr A. E. Grayshon**
10 **JOHANNA THYME,** b f Reesh—Sea Thyme **Mrs Johanna L. Steinberg**
11 **MISS KNIGHT,** ch f Longleat (USA)—Ethel Knight **Mrs C. B. Bastiman**

MR R. BASTIMAN—continued

TWO-YEAR-OLDS

12 B f 29/2 Tate Gallery (USA)—Arctic Winter (CAN) (Briartic (CAN))
13 Ch c 8/3 Chief Singer—I'll Try (Try My Best (USA))
14 B c 16/5 Reach—Sea Thyme (Persian Bold)

Other Owners: Mr A. D. Bastiman, Mr Robin Bastiman, Mr R. C. Copcutt, Mr J. Moorhouse.

Jockeys (Flat): K Fallon (w.a.), D McKeown (w.a.).

Jockey (NH): M Dwyer (w.a.).

44 MR A. G. BATES, Maisons-Laffitte

Postal: **1 Avenue Champaubert, 78600 Maisons-Laffitte, France.**
Phone: **1-39 62 77 77/1-39 62 03 14**

1 **BALLENCHIVADZE (USA),** 5, b h Pharly (FR)—Bruxelles **Ecurie A. B. U.**
2 **BARON SAMEDI (FR),** 6, gr h Margouillat (FR)—Neasham Star **Alain Bates**
3 **BIRIVER,** 4, b br c Bikala—River Reef **R. Laulhe**
4 **CAPTAIN CAD,** 7, b br g Mad Captain—Cadricka **M. Trecco**
5 **CARNOZI (FR),** 5, b h Zino—Da Swisha (FR) **Alain Bates**
6 **DE LA FONTAINE,** 9, b br g Prince Regent—Ditto **R. Laulhe**
7 **FOYER (USA),** 6, b h Forli—Coral Dance **Mme Arthur Bates**
8 **GRETRY (FR),** 6, b g Gosport—Shedule (FR) **Mr R. Ozenne**
9 **HONDAN,** 6, b h Hand In Hand—Amily **M. Teboul**
10 **HUL HAND,** 7, b h Hand In Hand—Amily **M. Teboul**
11 **ICE ATTACK,** 6, b g Prince Tenderfoot—Villa Primerose **Mme Arthur Bates**
12 **LA CABOUSSE (FR),** 4, ch f Tip Moss (FR)—No Tomorrow **Francis Dunn**
13 **LE MONTMARTROIS,** 7, b br h Matahawk—Place Blanche **Mme Arthur Bates**
14 **MAMAN ZIMBIE (FR),** 4, b f Huntercombe—Neasham Star **Ecurie de Gresse**
15 **OKASHIDO,** 4, ch g Iron Duke—Puntillera **Mme Arthur Bates**
16 **SAIN ET NET (FR),** 4, b c Tanlas (FR)—Cricrac (FR) **J. P. Merigout**
17 **SALSOLA (USA),** 4, ch f Storm Bird—Sea Flavour **Guy Harari**
18 **STAYER (FR),** 6, b h Le Nain Jaune (FR)—Wip **Dr Henri Paul Mignot**
19 **STRANGE TALES,** 5, ch h Niniski—Nostalgic Memory **H. Siber**
20 **THE BOSS,** 6, b br h Fabulous Dancer—Gone With The Wind **Mme Arthur Bates**
21 **VIVA GOUILLAT (FR),** 4, b f Margouillat (FR)—Viva Rosa (FR) **Robert Fournier Sarloveze**
22 **WORDS AND MUSIC (FR),** 7, b g Martinmas—No Tomorrow **Alain Bates**

THREE-YEAR-OLDS

23 **BOMBARDIER WELLS,** gr c Kaldoun—Affection **J-C Cheuvreux**
24 **ELLE EST BIEN,** gr f Julius Caesar—Cricrac **R. Laulhe**
25 **GALLERANDE,** ch f African Song—Fille du Roi **J-C Cheuvreux**
26 **KILDUL,** b c Kilian—Shedule (FR) **Mr R. Ozenne**
27 **OMBRE SOLIDE,** b f Gay Mecene—Adivina **J. L. Perrin**
28 **PENTASYLEE,** b f Sicyos—Lysba **Ecurie Trocadero**
29 **RAPHAEL D'OUILLY,** b c Miliar—Gerda **Alain Bates**

TWO-YEAR-OLDS

30 **CRIFOUTI,** ch f Blue Courtier—Cricrac (FR) **J. P. Merigout**
31 **KANTERING,** b f Kilian—Shedule (FR) **Mr R. Ozenne**

Jockey (Flat): P Parzysz (7-10).

Jockey (NH): J P Godet.

Apprentice: D Barbey (7-4).

Lady Riders: Mrs Chantal Bates, Miss Marie Courreges.

45 MR A. C. BATEY, Stocksfield

Postal: **East Ridley Farm, Stocksfield, Northumberland, NE43 7SB**
Phone: **(0661) 842284 PRESTEL: 661842284**

1 **BLUEHAVEN FLYER,** 5, b h Cure The Blues (USA)—Home Bird **Mr A. C. Batey**
2 **BULLI'S LAD,** 5, b g Bold Owl—Subtle Queen **Mr A. C. Batey**
3 **MASHUM,** 4, br g Humdoleila—Masami **Mr A. C. Batey**
4 **SOYBEAN,** 6, gr g Ardross—Meanz Beanz **Mr A. C. Batey**
5 **WARGAME,** 10, ch g Warpath—Sunshine Holyday **Mr A. C. Batey**

46 MR P. BEAUMONT, Brandsby

Postal: **Foul Rice Farm, Brandsby, Yorkshire, YO6 4SB.**
Phone: **BRANDSBY (03475) 208**

1 **ARCTIC CAMP,** 10, b g Bivouac—Arctic Flight **Mr R. Barclay**
2 **BAY FOX,** 5, b g Bay Express—Gay Vixen **Wing Comdr. P. K. Stead**
3 **CHOCTAW,** 6, gr g Great Nephew—Cheyenne **Mr J. N. Yeadon**
4 **DECENT MAN,** 7, b g Derring Rose—Addies Lass **Mr J. G. Read**
5 **FLEMING,** 10, ch g Royalty—Zulaika **Mrs M. R. Beaumont**
6 **GRACE BECK,** 5, b m Tepukei—Kalrosa **Mrs P. K. Stead**
7 **I'M FINE,** 5, b br m Fitzwilliam (USA)—Quick Thinking **Mrs M. R. Beaumont**
8 **J-J-HENRY,** 11, b br g Ascertain (USA)—Gofton Burn **Mrs J. R. Knowles**
9 **JODAMI,** 5, br g Crash Course—Masterstown Lucy **Mr J. N. Yeadon**
10 **JOES BABY,** 7, b m Deep Run—Kilmorna II **Miss J. Hey**
11 **LADY TRISSIE,** 7, gr m Politico (USA)—Jane Again **Mr J. N. Yeadon**
12 **LA PLUME,** 9, b g Whistling Deer—Air Queen **Mr E. H. Ruddock**
13 **MALTON PRIDE,** 7, b h Blind Harbour—Questionare IV **Mr J. H. Beal**
14 **POTIPHAR,** 4, br g Warpath—Zulaika Hopwood **Mrs M. R. Beaumont**
15 **RELKISSIMO,** 6, br m Relkino—Snow Tribe **Mr J. N. Yeadon**
16 **RENSHAW WOOD,** 10, b m Ascertain (USA)—Annamanda **Mrs J. M. Plummer**
17 **REVILLER'S GLORY,** 6, b g Hittite Glory—Zulaika Hopwood **Mrs M. R. Beaumont**
18 **SARIE MARAIS,** 5, ch m Mansingh (USA)—Zulaika Hopwood **Mrs M. R. Beaumont**
19 **SILENT DREAMS,** 5, b m Day Is Done—Ciao **Mr H. Jackson**
20 **SMART PAL,** 5, b g Balinger—Smart Bird **Mrs J. M. Plummer**
21 **SUPER SUE,** 7, b m Lochnager—Annamanda **Miss J. Hey**

Jockey (NH): P A Farrell (10-0).

Conditional: A G Hickson (9-7).

Amateur: Mrs A L Farrell.

47 MR G. R. BEBBINGTON, Craven Arms

Postal: **The Firs, Norton, Craven Arms, Salop.**
Phone: **(0588) 672511**

1 **MELISSA GOLD,** 9, ch m Deep Run—Imelda **Mr G. R. Bebbington**
2 **RING ME BACK,** 5, b m Ring Bidder—Snippet **Mr G. R. Bebbington**

Jockey (NH): B Dowling (w.a.).

Conditional: R Greene (w.a.).

48 MR C. R. BEEVER, Doncaster

Postal: **Woodfield Farm, Skelbrooke, Doncaster, South Yorkshire, DN6 8NA.**
Phone: **(0302) 725939**

1 **BASIC FUN,** 4, b br f Teenoso (USA)—Sirenivo (USA) **Unique Racing Plc**
2 **COLONNA (USA),** 4, b g Run The Gantlet (USA)—Evolutionary (USA) **Unique Racing Plc**
3 **CRAGSIDE,** 8, b h Hot Spark—Amerella **Mr Jeffrey Ross**
4 **HA'PENNY NAP,** 12, br g Simbir—Strip Poker **Mrs B. Ramsden**
5 **HARVEST BLUES,** 6, ch g Free State—Harvest Reap **Mr John Poynton**
6 **KNOCKAN BOY,** 8, b g Bargello—Lindenise **Mr J. R. Hutton**
7 **LA CASTANA,** 4, ch f Dunbeath (USA)—Din Brown (USA) **Unique Racing Plc**
8 **LIGHTWATER AGAIN,** 8, ch g Celtic Cone—Charmer's Girl **Mrs F. Raper**
9 **MARTINELLI,** 11, b g Martinmas—Panetta (USA) **Mr C. R. Beever**
10 **MESHRARF,** 4, gr c Rusticaro (FR)—Lady Wise **Unique Racing Plc**
11 **NEM CON,** 6, b g Buckskin (FR)—Summerfield Gold **Mr John Poynton**
12 **OLD DUTCH HOLBORN,** 5, ch g Derrylin—Gay City **Unique Racing Plc**
13 **OPENING OVERTURE (USA),** 4, b f At The Threshold (USA)—Rhine Queen (FR) **Unique Racing Plc**
14 **PERSIAN BLADE,** 7, b m Bladon—Persian Bronze **Mr J. P. Thompson**
15 **RUTH'S STAR,** 7, br m Uncle Pokey—Cool Vixen **Mr T. W. Irving**
16 **SHOON WIND,** 7, b g Green Shoon—Gone **Mrs M. B. Scholey**
17 **SLIPPERY MAX,** 6, b g Nicholas Bill—Noammo **Unique Racing Plc**
18 **SOLAR TIME,** 9, br g Another River—Solar Glory **Unique Racing Plc**
19 **TALK NO TRASH,** 6, ch g Deep Run—Woodlore **Mr J. S. Taylor**

THREE-YEAR-OLDS

20 **BOLD ROCKET,** gr g Bold Owl—Marwick **Mrs C. R. Beever**
21 **GOOD SESSION,** ch g Milk of The Barley—Rapid Rhythm **Partnership**
22 **NORTHENER,** ch g Reasonable (FR)—Northampton **Mr J. P. Thompson**

Other Owners: Mr I. M. Johnson, Mr R. H. Scholey, Mr E. G. Vaux, Mr R. Worsley.

Conditional: B McGiff (9-7).

Amateur: J Burley (10-0).

49 MR C. H. P. BELL, Morpeth

Postal: **West Chevington, Morpeth, Northumberland.**
Phone: **(0670) 760560**

1 **DOXFORD HUT,** 6, b g Class Distinction—Tillside Brig **Mr C. H. P. Bell**
2 **NICORIDGE,** 8, b g Riva Ridge (USA)—Nicoletta **Mr C. H. P. Bell**
3 **ORIEL BOY,** 7, b g Humdoleila—Bala Lake **Mr C. H. P. Bell**
4 **RAMBLING PRINCE,** 11, br g Arapaho—Miss Madam **Mr C. H. P. Bell**
5 **REMEMBER HENRY,** 8, b g New Member—The Doyle **Mr C. H. P. Bell**

Amateur: Mr S B Bell (10-2).

50 MR C. J. BELL, Worleston

Postal: **Rookery Park Stud, Main Road, Worleston, Nr. Nantwich, Cheshire, CWS 6DN.**
Phone: **(0270) 623604 OR (0836) 273153**

1 **BEN MACK,** 5, b g Pas de Seul—Fallig Lied **Mr K. Place**
2 **CARIBEAN CONEXION,** 5, b g Indian King (USA)—Borehard **Mr Robert Hughes**

MR C. J. BELL—continued

3 **COLOCRACY**, 8, br g Aristocracy—Coloressa **Mr J. Eddell**
4 **FIRTH OF FORTH**, 7, ch g Deep Run—Belle Mackay **Mr C. J. Bell**
5 **FOCUS ON FOSTER**, 8, ch g Warpath—April **Foster Refrigerator (UK) Ltd**
6 **JUST PRETEND**, 6, b m Sayyaf—Lovely Pretense (USA) **Mr T. Whitfield**
7 **MONRITA**, 8, b g Monksfield—Narita **Mr E. Smith**
8 **OPTIMISM FLAMED**, 7, b g Malinowski (USA)—Sea Swallow (FR) **Mr C. J. Bell**
9 **PRESS FOR ACTION**, 5, b g Croghan Hill—Ballynavin Money **Partnership**
10 **PRINCE METTERNICH**, 9, ch g Tall Noble (USA)—Coloressa **Mr J. Eddell**
11 **RANDOMLY**, 11, ch g Random Shot—Betton's Folly **Mr Michael Thompson**
12 **THE EGG BARON**, 6, b g Revlow—Bois de Rose **Mr Chris Heron**
13 **WAY CLEAR**, 7, b m Bulldozer—Welsh Wise **Mr E. Malkin**
14 **WHITWOOD**, 5, b g Hasty Word—Minetta **Mr J. Hyde**
15 **WOODHOOPOE**, 4, ch f Touching Wood (USA)—Good Try **Mrs Bridget Robinson**

Other Owners: Mrs S. Brown, Mr J. D. Cable, Mr P. J. Dyson, Mr J. H. Eden, Mr B. Hough, Mr N. Peach, Mrs C. A. Ward.

Conditional: Steve Davies (9-12).

Lady Rider: Rachel Halden (9-7).

51 MR M. L. W. BELL, Newmarket

Postal: **Fitzroy House, Newmarket, Suffolk.**
Phone: **(0638) 666567 FAX (0638) 668000 CAR (0836) 769142**

1 **PERION**, 8, ch g Northfields (USA)—Relanca **E & B Productions (Theatre) Ltd**
2 **PLAYING WITH FIRE**, 4, ch f Mr Fluorocarbon—Cinderwench **J. Watts**
3 **POSITIVE ATTITUDE**, 5, b m Red Sunset—Wilderness **K. J. Mercer**
4 **PRESTANCIA (FR)**, 5, br m Ile de Bourbon (USA)—Princesse Kay **Y. Birol**

THREE-YEAR-OLDS

5 **ALAPA**, b g Alzao (USA)—Gay Folly **Mrs B. W. Bell**
6 **BOLD PATRICK**, b c Never So Bold—Baby's Smile **Mr Martin Browne**
7 **BROADWAY STAR**, b c Alzao (USA)—Broadway Royal **Mr A. Stanley Dumbrell**
8 **CHAILEY**, b f Little Wolf—Polygon **Partnership**
9 **DO LOOK**, ch c Doulab (USA)—Gentle Look **P. J. Ransley**
10 **ELMDON PRINCE**, b c Ela-Mana-Mou—Be My Queen **Mr B. J. Warren**
11 **FAIR TITANIA**, b f Fairy King (USA)—Miss Robust **Mr Charles Fairbairn**
12 **FIRST SAPPHIRE**, b f Simply Great (FR)—Yelney **Mr Brian Cooper**
13 **FITZROY BELL**, ch g Red Sunset—Gaychimes **Mr J. R. Boughey**
14 **FLAMING GLORY**, b c Alzao (USA)—Engage **Mr Fahd Salman**
15 **MARJONS BOY**, ch c Enchantment—Nevilles Cross (USA) **Mr J. Harrison**
16 **NEVERDOWN**, ch f Never So Bold—Bourton Downs **Mr M. A. Kirby**
17 **SIMPLY BLUE**, ch f Simply Great (FR)—Bluethroat **C. J. Wates**
18 **STROKE OF LUCK**, br f Be My Native (USA)—Coup de Veine (FR) **Mr A. Stanley Dumbrell**

TWO-YEAR-OLDS

19 **AUNT HESTER (IRE)**, b f 11/4 Caerleon (USA)—Lady Hester (Native Prince) **A. Lillingston**
20 **BLOOD PIGEON (IRE)**, b f 17/2 Thatching—Mariakova (USA) (The Minstrel (CAN)) **Mr Fahd Salman**
21 **CAROMANDOO (IRE)**, b c 2/5 Simply Great (FR)—Tanimara (Sassafras (FR)) **G. Lederman**
22 Ch f 20/5 Star Appeal—Cinderwench (Crooner) **J. Watts**
23 **CORCINA**, gr f 17/4 Kalaglow—Feather Flower (Relkino) **Y. Birol**
24 **CWM DERI (IRE)**, b f 18/5 Alzao (USA)—Cotoneaster (Never Say Die) **Cwmry Racing Club**
25 **DEMOCRATIC (USA)**, ch c 23/4 Miswaki (USA)—Allegra (USA) (Alleged (USA)) **Mr Fahd Salman**
26 **DULCIMAL (IRE)**, b f 16/4 Heraldiste (USA)—Ultimate (Galivanter) **G. Johnson**
27 **GRECIAN REBEL**, b c 5/5 Absalom—Navarino Bay (Averof) **The Hon. E. Biddulph**
28 **HERALDINA (IRE)**, b f 8/2 Heraldiste (USA)—Fotostar (Polyfoto) **Brig. M. Gordon-Watson**

MR M. L. W. BELL—continued

29 **JEWEL OF THE EAST (IRE),** b f 1/3 Pennine Walk—Smash (Busted) **Mr Fahd Salman**
30 **LAND O'THE LEAL (IRE),** b f 4/4 Tate Gallery (USA)—Land Ho (Primera) **Capt. B. W. Bell**
31 **LEGAL WIN (USA),** ch c 10/5 Arctic Tern (USA)—
Banker's Favorite (USA) (Lyphard (USA)) **Sir Gordon White**
32 **LOVEALOCH (IRE),** b f 4/5 Lomond (USA)—Civility (Shirley Heights) **A. Lillingston**
33 **MALE NOIR (USA),** b c 28/1 Solford (USA)—Viewed (USA) (Alydar (USA)) **J. Purcell**
34 Br f 4/4 Prince Sabo—Miskin (Star Appeal) **W. H. Joyce**
35 **MORGANNWG (IRE),** b f 24/1 Simply Great (FR)—Kitty's Sister (Bustino) **K. J. Mercer**
36 B c 28/3 Dominion—Noble Wac (USA) (Vaguely Noble) **Mrs P. Karpidas**
37 B c 8/3 Heraldiste (USA)—Pyjama Game (Cavo Doro)
38 **QUIETLY IMPRESSIVE (IRE),** b f 27/5 Taufan (USA)—Way Ahead (Sovereign Path) **C. J. Wates**
39 **ROMAN FAN (IRE),** b f 15/3 Taufan (USA)—Crepe Myrtle (Crepello) **S. Crown**
40 **ROUTING,** b c 1/5 Rousillon (USA)—Tura (Northfields (USA)) **Mr A. Stanley Dumbrell**
41 **SAINT CALIGULA (IRE),** br c 22/1 Petorius—Saint Cynthia (Welsh Saint) **Mrs P. Howard**
42 **SET UP,** b c 19/2 Sarab—Gitee (FR) (Carwhite) **Mr Fahd Salman**
43 **SIR BASIL (IRE),** b c 8/2 Double Schwartz—Ashbourne Lass (Ashmore (FR)) **M. Talbot-Ponsonby**
44 Ch c 8/2 Sharpo—Snow Tree (Welsh Pageant) **Mrs J. Hambro**
45 **STAR CHALLANGE,** b f 15/3 Baldski (USA)—Challanging (Mill Reef (USA)) **Mr B. J. Warren**
46 B f 25/3 Glow (USA)—Summer Madness (Silly Season) **L. Baxter**
47 **TIMELESS APPEAL (IRE),** b f 26/4 Alzao (USA)—Kazannka (FR) (Wild Risk) **Cheveley Park Stud**

Other Owners: Mr Michael Bell, Mr R. S. W. Bell, A. Bridgewater, Mrs M. A. Dumbrell, Mr Harry French, C. Gordon-Watson, Mr P. W. Kavanagh, D. Kelly, Mr E. D. Kessly, Lady Vivienne Lillingston, Mrs P. H. Lyster, Mr C. Mackenzie, Mrs S. Lee-Robinson, Mr P. A. Philipps, R. Pilkington, S. Sampson.

Jockey (Flat): T R Quinn (w.a.).

Apprentices: W Cahill (7-7), L Healy (7-9), R Price (7-6).

Lady Rider: Mrs G Bell (9-3).

52 MR J. A. BENNETT, Wantage

Postal: **Rectory House Stables, Sparsholt, Wantage, Oxon.**
Phone: **(023 559) 635**

1 **AROUND TOWN,** 9, br g Town And Country—Scottish Circuit **Mr P. D. Purdy**
2 **BOSCEAN CHIEFTAIN,** 6, b g Shaab—Indian Stick **Miss Christine Olds**
3 **BWANA KALI,** 8, b g Kala Shikari—Modom **Mr P. W. Bennett**
4 **EVESHAM BUTCHERS,** 8, b g Moulton—Welsh Carol **Evesham Butchers**
5 **HELLO SAM,** 7, ch g Hello Gorgeous (USA)—Samra **Mr P. W. Bennett**
6 **JABARABA (USA),** 9, b g Raja Baba (USA)—Time To Step (USA) **Mr M. Stephens**
7 **KING OF THE WOOD,** 5, br g Chukaroo—Amore (ITY) **Mr B. E. King**
8 **MR KEWMILL,** 7, b g Homing—Muninga **Mr P. D. Purdy**
9 **PARISIAN,** 5, b g Shirley Heights—Miss Paris **Ridgway Racing Ltd**
10 **SCANNER LAD,** 4, br g Mansingh (USA)—Immodest Miss **Mr David Neal**

THREE-YEAR-OLDS

11 **DYNAMIC QUEST,** ch g Posse (USA)—Do Your Best **Mr John A. Taylor**
12 **NOSMADA,** b g Longleat (USA)—Madame Bleu **Ridgeway Racing Ltd**
13 **TTAYWEN,** br f Noalto—Scotch Thistle **Mr John E. Mutch**
14 **VERRO (USA),** ch c Irish River (FR)—Royal Rafale (USA) **Mr P. D. Purdy**

TWO-YEAR-OLDS

15 B f 29/2 Enchantment—Pts Fairway **Mr P. W. Bennett**

Lady Rider: Miss Alison Purdy.

53 MR R. A. BENNETT, Maidenhead

Postal: **Cedars Farm Racing Stables, Paley Street, Maidenhead, Berkshire, SL6 3JS.**
Phone: **(0628) 30290**

1 **BIDSTON MILL,** 5, ch g Main Reef—Allotria **Mr R. Donohoe**
2 **GARDINIA LAD,** 7, b g Wolverlife—Huntress **Mr Freddie Starr**
3 **ONE TO MARK,** 7, b br g He Loves Me—Markon **Mr R. Donohoe**
4 **ROOF GHOST,** 6, b g Thatching—Vital Spirit **Mr R. A. Bennett**
5 **SHARPENHOE,** 4, ch g Sharpo—Garganey (USA) **Mr A. MacTaggart**
6 **VINTON VA,** 5, b m Crofter (USA)—Bold Flirt (USA) **Mr R. A. Bennett**
7 **WELLOW WINE (USA),** 5, b g Sensitive Prince (USA)—Tempting Lady (USA) **Mr R. A. Bennett**

THREE-YEAR-OLDS

8 **CHRISTIAN SOLDIER,** b c Tickled Pink—Super Princess **Mr R. A. Bennett**
9 **EQUINOR,** b c Norwick (USA)—Cithern **Mr Perry H. Zellick**
10 **FREDDIE'S STAR,** b c Tina's Pet—Wellington Bear **Mr R. A. Bennett**
11 **GLEBELANDS GIRL,** b f Burslem—Genzyme Gene **Mr R. A. Bennett**
12 **PALEY EXPRESS,** ch c Balboa—Our Foxbar **Mr R. A. Bennett**
13 **SWEET VOILA,** b f Sayyaf—Sweet Princess **Mr A. MacTaggart**

TWO-YEAR-OLDS

14 B c 20/5 Le Johnstan—Attendre Moi (Saulingo) **Mr R. A. Bennett**
15 Gr f 23/5 Soughaan (USA)—Divine Apsara (Godswalk (USA)) **Mr R. A. Bennett**
16 B c 23/2 Beldale Flutter (USA)—Eurynome (Be My Guest (USA)) **A. L. Alexander and R. A. Bennett**
17 Ch c 30/5 Stanford—Impailand (Imperial Fling (USA)) **Mr R. A. Bennett**
18 B c 17/3 King Persian—Kellys Risc (Pitskelly) **Mr R. A. Bennett**
19 Br f 30/4 Tender King—Nordic Maid (Vent du Nord (FR)) **Mr R. A. Bennett**
20 B c 28/4 Nomination—Tug Along (Posse (USA)) **Mr R. A. Bennett**
21 B c 2/4 Tina's Pet—Village Lass (No Mercy) **Mr R. A. Bennett**

Other Owners: Mr A. J. Bradley, Mrs A. Davies, Mrs G. Leonard.

Jockeys (NH): D Gallagher (9-7), M Perrett (10-0).

Conditional: Lee O'Hare (9-0).

54 MISS M. J. BENSON, Hexham

Postal: **Chesters, Humshaugh, Hexham, Northumberland.**
Phone: **(043 481) 203**

1 **AIX LA CHAPELLE,** 5, b m Bustino—Charming Thought (USA) **Mrs J. E. Benson**
2 **CALIRA,** 11, ch m Coliseum—Salira **Mrs J. E. Benson**
3 **PALANQUIN,** 8, ch g Royal Palace—Duresme **Mrs J. E. Benson**
4 **SOME FINGERS,** 5, ch g Some Hand—Salira **Mrs J. E. Benson**

55 MR C. J. BENSTEAD, Epsom

Postal: **The Limes, Shepherds Walk, Epsom, Surrey, KT18 6DF.**
Phone: **ASHTEAD (03722) 73152**

1 **BASHAQ,** 4, b c Jalmood (USA)—Welwyn **Mr D. Turner**
2 **DANCING NORTH,** 5, b br g Shareef Dancer (USA)—Icena **Mr Robert Gibbons**
3 **HAWWAM,** 4, b c Glenstal (USA)—Hone **Mr Hamdan Al-Maktoum**
4 **KALAPARTY,** 4, gr f Kalaglow—Firework Party (USA) **Mrs R. Lamb**
5 **MAHRAJAN,** 6, b h Dominion—Dame Julian **Mrs F. A. Harris**

MR C. J. BENSTEAD—continued

6 **MUKHABBR,** 6, b h Taufan (USA)—Ribotingo **Mr D. Turner**
7 **NAWWAR,** 6, ch h Thatching—Priceless Pin **Mr C. J. Benstead**
8 **PULSINGH,** 8, br h Mansingh (USA)—Pulcini **Mr B. W. Hager**
9 **SING THE BLUES,** 6, b g Blue Cashmere—Pulcini **Mr B. W. Hager**
10 **WYKEHAMIST,** 7, ch g Blue Refrain—Flying Portion **Mr M. T. Collins**
11 **ZINBAQ,** 4, ch c Ahonoora—Zaiyundeen (FR) **Mrs R. W. S. Baker**

THREE-YEAR-OLDS

12 **DARAKAH,** ch f Doulab (USA)—Ladytown **Mr Hamdan Al-Maktoum**
13 **ELWADI,** b c Vaigly Great—Final Act **Mr Hamdan Al-Maktoum**
14 **IHSAAS,** b c Niniski (USA)—Justicia **Mr Hamdan Al-Maktoum**
15 **INBIHAR,** br f Doulab (USA)—Silojoka **Mrs R. Lamb**
16 **MONA'S PRINCE,** b br g Class Distinction—Princess Mona **Mr J. P. Saunders**
17 **MOTHERS SON,** b c Mummy's Pet—Miss Suntan **Mr Hamdan Al-Maktoum**
18 **MUARIJ,** ch f Star Appeal—Ivoronica **Mr Hamdan Al-Maktoum**
19 **PHARMOPI,** b f Pharly (FR)—Motion Picture **Mr R. Lamb**
20 **SANAWI,** b c Glenstal (USA)—Russeting **Mr C. F. Sparrowhawk**
21 **TENDER TRAIL,** ch f Tender King—Trail **Mr Zia Ahmad**
22 **WALAYAH,** b f Wassl—Maybe So **Mr Hamdan Al-Maktoum**

TWO-YEAR-OLDS

23 **ALMUHIT,** b f 2/5 Doulab (USA)—Silojoka (Home Guard (USA)) **Mr Hamdan Al-Maktoum**
24 **BARUD (IRE),** b c 9/3 Persian Bold—Pale Moon (Jukebox) **Mr Hamdan Al-Maktoum**
25 **ITHMID,** b c 12/5 Elegant Air—Via Tritus (Sovereign Path) **Mr Hamdan Al-Maktoum**
26 **MAHSUL (IRE),** b c 22/4 Ela-Mana-Mou—Afrah (Our Native (USA)) **Mr Hamdan Al-Maktoum**
27 **MARAASID (IRE),** b f 20/1 High Top—Welwyn (Welsh Saint) **Mr Hamdan Al-Maktoum**
28 **MAZIN,** b c 11/5 Faustus (USA)—Polly Oligant (Prince Tenderfoot (USA)) **Mr Hamdan Al-Maktoum**
29 **RAMZ (IRE),** ch f 29/4 The Minstrel (CAN)—Bear's Affair (Gay Fandango (USA)) **Mr Hamdan Al-Maktoum**
30 **SAKIL (IRE),** b c 20/2 Vision (USA)—Sciambola (Great Nephew) **Mr Hamdan Al-Maktoum**
31 **ZAAGIL (FR),** b c 28/2 Crystal Glitters—La Breloque (Nonoalco (USA)) **Mr Hamdan Al-Maktoum**

Other Owners: Mr F. W. Davey, Mr P. R. Isgar, Mr Richard H. Manson.

56 MR W. BENTLEY, Middleham

Postal: **Highwall Stable, East Witton Road, Middleham, Leyburn, DL8 4PT.**
Phone: **WENSLEYDALE (0969) 22289**

1 **DRU RI'S BRU RI,** 4, b g Kafu—Bru Ri (FR) **Mr D. M. Drury**
2 **LADY SPEED STICK,** 4, b f Tender King—Tetrazzini **Mrs S. Remmington**
3 **NATIVE RIVER,** 5, ch g Deep River—Native Love **Mrs F. Bentley**
4 **PREMIER PRINCESS,** 4, b f Hard Fought—Manntika **Mr D. M. Drury**
5 **PRIMULA AGAIN,** 5, ch g Free State—Silent Prayer **Mr W. Bentley**
6 **REMWOOD GIRL,** 4, b f Remainder Man—Aliwood Girl **Mr A. F. Laws**
7 **THARSIS,** 5, ch g What A Guest—Grande Promesse (FR) **Mr D. M. Drury**

THREE-YEAR-OLDS

8 **CHANTERESSE,** b f Chantro—Miss Friendly **Mr D. M. Drury**
9 **DUNMOUNIN,** ro f Alias Smith (USA)—Poly Negative **Mr A. Kevin Farrell and Mr L. Watts**

TWO-YEAR-OLDS

10 B f 20/2 Faustus—Dame du Moulin (Shiny Tenth) **Mr P. Quinn**
11 B f 5/3 Pitskelly—Daughter of Song (Song)
12 B g 22/2 Say Primula—Miss Primula (Dominion) **Kavli Ltd**
13 B f 19/2 Lochnager—Tricky (Song) **Mr W. Bentley**

Other Owners: Food Brokers Ltd, Mrs June.

57 MR J. BERRY, Cockerham

Postal: **Moss Side Racing Stable, Crimbles Lane, Cockerham, Lancs, LA2 0ES.**
Phone: **FORTON (0524) 791179 CAR (0836) 713192**

1 **ALMOST BLUE,** 4, ch c Ballacashtal (CAN)—Blue Garter **Mr A. Shelton**
2 **DONOVAN ROSE,** 5, b h Song—Piccadilly Rose **Mr P. D. Savill**
3 **GREAT CHADDINGTON,** 5, b h Crofter (USA)—Mainly Dry **Mr C. A. Fry**
4 **MEESON KAMP,** 4, b g Kampala—Turin Rose **Mr J. B. Wilcox**
5 **MIAMI BEAR,** 4, b g Miami Springs—Belinda Bear **Mr J. A. Campbell**
6 **MY TOPIC,** 4, br f Mansingh (USA)—Well Connected **Mr J. Berry**
7 **NO MORE THE FOOL,** 4, ch g Jester—Prima Bella **Mr R. Leah**
8 **OUR FAN,** 4, b g Taufan (USA)—Cruft Wood **Mr J. W. Barrett**
9 **ROSE OF HIGH LEGH,** 4, b f Martinmas—Halka **Brian Durkin Associates Ltd**
10 **SCOTTISH FLING,** 6, ch g Imperial Fling (USA)—Relicia **Mr Peter Hilton**
11 **SO CAREFUL,** 7, br h Dalsaan—Miss Carefree **Mr J. Berry**
12 **SOLARES,** 10, br g Free State—Indian Wells **Mr Sam Berry**
13 **VALDEMOSA,** 4, ch f Music Boy—Astral Suite **Heathaven Stables**

THREE-YEAR-OLDS

14 **AMRON,** b g Bold Owl—Sweet Minuet **Mr Roy Peebles**
15 **ANTIQUE MAN,** b g Sayyaf—Firey Ann **Mr D. Melvin Haughey**
16 **BOOZY,** b f Absalom—The High Dancer **Heathaven Stables**
17 **CANNON'S SPIRIT,** ch g King Persian—Tinsel **Mr Tommy Cannon**
18 **CANTDONOWTRITE,** gr c Belfort (FR)—Miss Tantan **Mr Sam Berry**
19 **CASHTAL DAZZLER,** b g Ballacashtal (CAN)—Miss Meg **Mr G. H. Atkinson**
20 **CEE-JAY-AY,** gr g Free State—Raffinrula **Mr Richard Jinks**
21 **COME HOME KINGSLEY,** ch g Formidable (USA)—Pearl Wedding **Kingsley Homes Ltd**
22 **CROFT IMPERIAL,** ch c Crofthall—Farinara **Mrs B. A. Matthews**
23 **DANCING MUSIC,** ch c Music Boy—Miss Rossi **Mr Norman Harper**
24 **ECHO PRINCESS,** b f Crofter (USA)—What A Breeze **Liverpool Daily Post Echo Ltd**
25 **FAIR WICKET,** ch g Norwick (USA)—Fairford Lass **Mr Sydney Mason**
26 **FOR REAL,** ch f Tina's Pet—Golden Decoy **Moss Side Racing Group**
27 **GREETLAND GRIT,** ch f Ballacashtal (CAN)—Tempered Wind **Mr J. Wilkins**
28 **J R JONES,** b c Blakeney—Bonnie Baiser **Mr T. R. Pearson**
29 **LYNDSEYLEE,** b f Swing Easy (USA)—Miss Merlin **Mr George Syvret**
30 **MISS PINOCCHIO,** b f Noalto—Floral **Mr I. Braganini**
31 **NUCLEAR EXPRESS,** b g Martinmas—Halka **Mr P. Clark**
32 **OYSTON'S WORLD,** br g Reesh—Abrasive **Mrs J. M. Berry**
33 **PROHIBITION,** b g Music Boy—Green Chartreuse **Mr J. K. Brown**
34 **SCOTTISH REFORM,** b g Night Shift (USA)—Molvitesse **Mr P. G. Johnston**
35 **SECOND TO NONE,** b c Superlative—Matinata **Mrs Ann Galvanoni**
36 **SHARP ANN,** gr f Belfort (FR)—Princess Sharpenup **Moss Side Racing Group**
37 **SWATTLING THOMAS,** ch g Ballacashtal (CAN)—Princess Xenia (USA) **Mr P. J. Watson**
38 **TAMARA'S TWINKLE,** ch f Sharpen Up—Lady Tamara **Mr N. A. Souter**
39 **THE JONES BOY (FR),** b g Top Ville—Rhythmeque (CAN) **Mr T. R. Pearson**
40 **TOD,** gr c Petorius—Mainly Dry **Mr C. A. Fry**

TWO-YEAR-OLDS

41 Ch f 24/4 Nicholas Bill—Abrasive (Absalom)
42 B f 15/3 Mansingh (USA)—Anita's Choice (Shantung) **Moss Side Racing Group**
43 Ch f 11/3 Absalom—Astral Suite (On Your Mark) **Heathaven Stables**
44 **BANTEL BAMBINA,** gr f 11/3 Bold Owl—Bantel Baby (Warpath) **Mr Barry L. Brandon**
45 **BEYOND OUR REACH,** br c 20/2 Reach—Over Beyond (Bold Lad (IRE)) **Moss Side Racing Group**
46 **BOLD SPARK,** br c 5/5 Electric—Boldie (Bold Lad (IRE)) **Mr Sydney Mason**
47 Br c 21/5 Belfort (FR)—California Split (Sweet Revenge)
48 **CANNON'S VISION,** ch c 3/5 Fingora—Ribble Reed (Bullrush) **Mr Tommy Cannon**
49 **CARRINKY,** gr f 13/4 Absalom—Nocturnal Bliss (Pyjama Hunt) **Carrprint Ltd**
50 **CHRISTIAN BOY,** b c 9/2 Belfort (FR)—Harem Queen (Prince Regent (FR)) **Mrs C. Robinson**
51 **COOL CALCULATOR,** br g 11/5 Seymour Hicks (FR)—Finlandaise (FR) (Arctic Tern (USA)) **Moss Side Racing Group**
52 Ch f 22/3 King Persian—Crashing Juno (Crash Course) **Moss Side Racing Group**

MR J. BERRY—continued

53 **DAILY SPORT BOY,** b c 20/5 Jalmood (USA)—Knavesmire (Runnymede) **Roldvale Ltd**
54 **DOMINO TRICK,** b f 9/4 Primo Dominie—Tricky Tracey (Formidable (USA)) **Mr John Gibbons**
55 **DOUBLOVA (IRE),** ch f 26/4 M Double M (USA)—Danova (FR) (Dan Cupid) **Moss Side Racing Group**
56 **DOWN THE MIDDLE,** b g 30/3 Swing Easy (USA)—Into The Fire (Dominion) **Mr J. K. M. Oliver**
57 Ch g 24/2 Foolish Ways—Early Doors (Ballad Rock) **Miss Andrea Campion**
58 **ELLEBANNA,** b f 19/2 Tina's Pet—Mainly Dry (The Brianstan) **Mr C. A. Fry**
59 **FIVESEVENFIVEO,** ch f 10/2 Enchantment—Miss Times (Major Portion) **Mr J. Clayton**
60 **FOOD OF LOVE,** ch f 25/4 Music Boy—Shortbread (Crisp And Even) **Mr J. David Abell**
61 **FOURSINGH,** br c 20/2 Mansingh (USA)—Maycrest (Imperial Fling (USA)) **Four Racing**
62 **GO TALLY-HO,** b f 15/3 Gorytus (USA)—Brush Away (Ahonoora) **Mrs Caroline Berry**
63 Ch c 21/4 Gorytus (USA)—Grapette (Nebbiolo) **Moss Side Racing Group**
64 **GREETLAND ROCK,** ch c 2/4 Ballacashtal (CAN)—Zamindara (Crofter (USA)) **Mr J. Wilkins**
65 **HARRY PEA (IRE),** b c 28/1 Runnett—Chiarella (Relkino) **Mr Roy Peebles**
66 **HEAVEN-LIEGH-GREY,** gr f 18/3 Grey Desire—North Pine (Import) **Mr P. Dodd**
67 **HOOTING DON,** bl c 10/3 Bold Owl—Donna Pavlova (Don (ITY)) **H. R. Leetham Ltd**
68 B c 26/3 Prince Sabo—I Don't Mind (Swing Easy (USA)) **Denwis Ltd**
69 **JEAN'S VALENTINE,** gr f 14/2 Green Ruby (USA)—Roanette (Roan Rocket) **Mrs J. Bradford-Nutter**
70 **KESTREL FORBOXES (IRE),** b c 9/5 Seymour Hicks (FR)—Dance Mistress (Javelot) **Laurel Leisure Ltd**
71 **KESTREL KAYSIS (IRE),** b f 27/4 Soughaan (USA)—Faradiya (Rusticaro (FR)) **Laurel Leisure Ltd**
72 **KINLET VISION (IRE),** b f 31/3 Vision (USA)—Verandah (Jaazeiro (USA)) **Wyre Foresters Partners**
73 **KUMMEL KING,** b c 19/3 Absalom—Louise (Royal Palace) **Mr John Gibbons**
74 **L'ACQUESIANA,** ch f 4/5 Crofthall—Well Connected (Bold And Free) **Mr Robert Aird**
75 Ch c 26/3 Thatching—La Troublerie (Will Somers) **H.H. Prince Yazid Saud**
76 **LAUREL QUEEN (IRE),** ch f 18/4 Viking (USA)—Prima Bella (High Hat) **Laurel Leisure Ltd**
77 **LUCKY MANLEY,** b c 8/4 Ballacashtal (USA)—Herminda (King of Spain) **Mr D. Shek**
78 B c 17/3 Belfort (FR)—Miss Merlin (Manacle) **Mr S. Barrett**
79 **MOMENTSOFMUSIC,** ch c 22/4 Music Boy—Sweet Relief (Sweet Revenge) **Mr Geoffrey Adams**
80 **MUSHY BOFF,** ch f 28/5 Tina's Pet—Rely On Guy (Reliance II) **Mr J. K. Brown**
81 **MUSICAL LYRICS,** b f 27/4 Song—Spanish Ribbon (Pieces of Eight) **Mr Robert Aird**
82 B f 20/5 Never So Bold—Nativity (USA) (Native Royalty (USA)) **Heathaven Stables**
83 **NO QUESTIONS,** gr f 20/3 Another Realm—Our Mother (Bold Lad (IRE)) **Dr Nicholas Braslausky**
84 **NORTHERN CONQUEROR (IRE),** ch c 17/4 Mazaad—Gaylom (Lord Gayle (USA)) **Mr T. C. Chiang**
85 Ch f 25/4 Music Boy—Omnia (Hill Clown (USA)) **Hon G. Noel**
86 B c 5/4 General Wade—Palmaria (Be Friendly) **Moss Side Racing Group**
87 Ch f 22/4 M Double M (USA)—Pasadena Lady (Captain James)
88 **PETROPOWER (IRE),** b c 26/4 Petorius—Gay Honey (Busted) **Mr P. D. Savill**
89 **PLAY THE ACE,** b c 26/3 Mansingh (USA)—Boa (Mandrake Major) **Mr E. Thomas**
90 **POACHERS THEME,** b f 12/2 Song—Tickled Trout (Red Alert) **Mrs D. Mason**
91 **PRIMO SUNDAY SPORT,** b c 28/2 Primo Dominie—Miss Import (Import) **Roldvale Ltd**
92 B f 27/2 Mazaad—Princess of Nashua (Crowned Prince (USA)) **Academy Leasing Ltd**
93 **RED TIGER,** ch c 7/5 Blushing Scribe (USA)—Nonpareil (FR) (Pharly (FR)) **Mr R. C. Thompson**
94 **REGAL CREST (USA),** b c 27/2 Gold Crest (USA)—Ambrellita (FR) (Misti IV) **Mr A. Crawford**
95 **RUBY AZELLY,** b f 4/4 Green Ruby (USA)—Azelly (Pitskelly) **Cheshire Racing**
96 **SEASIDE MINSTREL,** ch c 5/5 Song—Blackpool Belle (The Brianstan) **Blackpool Evening Gazette & Herald**
97 **SEQUEL TWO,** gr c 24/4 Nishapour (FR)—Roda Haxan (Huntercombe) **Mr E. Thomas**
98 **SHOT WOOD,** ch c 16/4 Crofthall—Squires Girl (Spanish Gold) **Mr John Galvanoni**
99 **SICKNOTE (IRE),** gr g 11/5 Reesh—Lala (Welsh Saint) **Mrs J. M. Berry**
100 **SINGING MISS,** b f 3/5 Mansingh (USA)—Branston Express (Bay Express) **Mr J. Berry**
101 **SNOWGIRL (IRE),** gr f 18/3 Mazaad—Rust Free (Free State) **Mr A. Slack**
102 **SONSIE LAD,** br g 20/3 Tickled Pink—Charlotte Amalie (No Mercy) **Mr H. Hobson**
103 **STAR CONNECTION,** b f 28/3 Faustus (USA)—Emerald Rocket (Green God) **Mr A. F. S. Bridgwood**
104 B c 28/4 Music Boy—Stepping Gaily (Gay Fandango (USA)) **Heathaven Stables**
105 **SUNDAY SPORT GEM,** ch f 12/2 Lomond (USA)—Gemma Kaye (Cure The Blues (USA)) **Roldvale Ltd**
106 **SUPER SPACEMATE,** gr c 18/2 Absalom—Stedham (Jaazeiro (USA)) **Bloxwich Storage Systems**
107 B f 10/4 Bold Owl—Sweet Minuet (Setay)
108 B f 10/3 Jupiter Island—The High Dancer (High Line)
109 **TIME FOR THE BLUES (IRE),** b c 10/2 Wassl—Azurai (Dance In Time (CAN)) **Mr P. D. Savill**
110 **TOUCH OF BLUE,** ch c 22/3 Ballacashtal (CAN)—Return To Tara (Homing) **Mr A. Shelton**
111 **TRICYCLING (IRE),** b c 5/5 Flash of Steel—Stradavari (Stradavinsky) **Mr J. Nixon**
112 B f 10/5 The Noble Player(USA)—What A Breeze (Whistling Wind) **Moss Side Racing Group**
113 **ZEPPEKI (IRE),** b c 15/2 Taufan (USA)—Avital (Pitskelly) **Mr C. Benford**

MR J. BERRY—continued

Other Owners: M. Aston, Mr Derek Barton, Mr R. S. Bateman, Mr S. Bell, Mr G. Bernacchi, Mr T. Bibby, Mr J. Bigley, Mr C. Bradford-Nutter, Mr D. J. Brown, Mr S. Byfield, Mr A. K. Collins, Mr N. Connop, Mr D. Cook, Mr D. Craven, Mr T. Delaney, Mr D. Disbrey, Mr C. Duke, Mr J. Dunn, Mr R. Farley, The Hon J. Fermor-Hesketh, Mr David Fish, Mr B Hark, Mr S. Hart, Mrs R. Heathcote, Mr J. E. Hector, Mr R. Henriques, Mr R. J. B. Hoare, Mr W. J. Hoey, Mr J. Jackson, Mr J. James, Mr Colin Jarvis, Mr R. Lewis, Mr J. McDowall, Mr J. K. McInerny, Mr R. Moffat, Mr I. Moorhouse, Mrs M. Murphy, Mr J. Murray, Miss T. O'Hanlon, Mr M. Otter, Mr K. Palmers, Mr B. Penine, Mr E. Picton, Mr R. Potts, Mr A. Puc, Mrs A. E. Robertson, Mr B. Scowcroft, Mr M. Seabrook, Mr K. Sharp, Mr B. Shelton, Mrs Josie Shelton, Mr T. D. C. Taylor, Mr D. B. Thompson, Mr J. Thompson, Mr G. Tiribocchi, Mr B. Todd, Mrs I. E. Wallage, Mr D. Wherret, Mr C. J. Williams, Mr R. G. Willis, Mr S. Wright.

Jockeys (Flat): J Carroll (7-13), Kevin Darley (7-3), Eddie Guest (8-6).

Apprentices: Ruth Coulter (7-0), Dermot Fallon (7-7), Simon Giles (7-12), Stephen Hawkes (7-0), Steven Haworth (7-7), William Hollick (7-8).

Amateur: Mr David Parker (8-12).

Lady Rider: Miss L Eaton (9-0).

58 MR J. D. BETHELL, Didcot

Postal: **Downs House, Chilton, Didcot, Oxon, OX11 0RR.**
Phone: **ABINGDON (0235) 834333 TELEX 94017958 JOWB G**

1 **CARPET SLIPPERS,** 4, br f Daring March—Mollified **Mrs G. Fane**
2 **CHAIN SHOT,** 5, b g Pas de Seul—Burnished **Mr H. F. McEwen**
3 **FOLLOW THE DRUM,** 5, b g Daring March—Pretty Miss **Mrs G. Fane**
4 **HACKFORTH,** 4, ch c Hard Fought—Sweet And Sour **Mr L. B. Holliday**
5 **LOFT BOY,** 7, b g Cawston's Clown—Burglar Tip **Mrs Bernie Allwright**
6 **PRECENTOR,** 4, ro c Music Boy—La Magna **Lord Westbury**
7 **ROYAL DIGGER,** 4, ch c Sharpo—Canasta Girl **Al-Deera Bloodstock Holdings Ltd**
8 **ST VILLE,** 4, b c Top Ville—Dame Julian **Mrs David Shirley**
9 **TIN HAT,** 4, b g Tina's Pet—Pretty Miss **Mrs G. Fane**

THREE-YEAR-OLDS

10 **BEST TIMES,** br g Good Times (ITY)—Pretty Miss **Mrs G. Fane**
11 **DONNA BOLD,** b f Never So Bold—Domynga **Mrs David Shirley**
12 **HEAD GROOM,** ch g Shy Groom (USA)—Solarina **Mr R. S. Sawyer**
13 **INDIA'S TWIST,** ch c Exhibitioner—West Bank **Mrs G. Bryant**
14 **LODGING,** ch c Longleat (USA)—Mollified **Mrs G. Fane**
15 **TRUE GEORGE,** ch g King of Clubs—Piculet **Mr T. R. Lock**

TWO-YEAR-OLDS

16 B f Dominion—Black Veil (Blakeney) **Mr L. B. Holliday**
17 B f Heraldiste (USA)—Camden Dancer (Camden Town)
18 B f Mashhor Dancer (USA)—Daring Charm (Daring March) **Mrs David Shirley**
19 B c Daring March—Madam Muffin (Sparkler) **Mr T. R. Lock**
20 B c Glow (USA)—Piculet (Morston (FR))
21 B f Castle Keep—Polly's Teahouse (Shack (USA)) **Mr T. R. Lock**
22 B c Beldale Flutter (USA)—Pretty Miss (So Blessed) **Mrs G. Fane**
23 B f Drumalis—Run Swift (Run The Gantlet (USA)) **Mrs S. M. Burley**
24 Ch f Hard Fought—Sweet And Sour (Sharpen Up) **Mr L. B. Holliday**
25 Ch c Phone Trick (USA)—Wrap It Up (Mount Hagen (FR)) **J. Galvanoni**

Other Owners: Mr J. D. Bethell, Mr Geoffrey C. Greenwood, Dr T. F. Keen, Mr I. D. McEwen, Mr K. McEwen.

59 MR P. J. BEVAN, Uttoxeter

Postal: **The Stables, Black Pitts Farm, Kingstone, Uttoxeter, ST14 8QW.**
Phone: **(0889) 500670 HOME (0889) 500647 STABLES**

1 **BARTINAS STAR,** 10, b g Le Bavard (FR)—Bartina **Mr F. A. Jackson**
2 **BRIMTO PANEDRY,** 5, b g Maculata—Miss Buck **Mr L. E. Goddard**
3 **FAMILY PRIDE,** 5, b g Shareef Dancer (USA)—Our Home **Mr P. Mousikou**
4 **GODLORD,** 10, gr g Godswalk (USA)—Gay Pariso **Mr Patrick Clinton**
5 **HOOCH,** 5, b m Warpath—Brandy **Queensway China Ltd**
6 **JOYFULNESS (FR),** 5, b m Cure The Blues (USA)—Jermaric **Mr E. Bennion**
7 **JURISPRUDENCE (USA),** 7, b h Alleged (USA)—Leliza (USA) **Mr I. W. T. Baugh**
8 **LEAVE IT TO BALLY,** 10, ch g Ballymore—Time To Leave **Mr A. Eaton**
9 **MUCHGRANGE,** 9, ch m Sweet Revenge—Millgrange **Jackson's Marquees**
10 **MY SERENADE (USA),** 6, b m Sensitive Prince (USA)—Mau Mae (USA) **Mr D. B. Holmes**
11 **NOVA LAD,** 6, b g Andy Rew—Safe 'n' Sound **E. Carter**
12 **PLOVER,** 5, b m Kala Shikari—Portella **South Cheshire Racehorses Limited**
13 **POP ABROAD,** 5, b br m Broadsword (USA)—Lady Poppy **Mr A. Eaton**
14 **REGAL SALUTE,** 4, b f Dara Monarch—Forelock **W Cully**
15 **SHIRYON,** 5, b g Tickled Pink—Assel Zawie **Mr Guido Basile**
16 **WEIGHT PROBLEM,** 13, ch g Proverb—Queen of Killonan **Chase Window Company Limited**

Other Owners: Mrs P. J. Bevan, Mrs Suzanne Clinton, Mr D. Elia, J. Forsyth, Mr J. E. Jackson, Mr J. V. Mills.

Jockey (NH): T Wall (10-0).

Conditional: A Skelton.

Amateur: P Clinton (10-7).

60 MR T. T. BILL, Ashby-de-la-Zouch

Postal: **Manor Farm, Smisby, Ashby-de-la-Zouch, Leicestershire.**
Phone: **(0530) 415881 (0530) 416538**

1 **BALA BOY,** 7, b g Black Minstrel—Slave-Lady **Mr F. E. Downes**
2 **BEETEE YOU,** 7, b g Royalty—Jinkin **Alan Merritt A.F.M. (Holdings) Ltd**
3 **BORROWDALE,** 8, b g Golden Love—Fragrant Blossom **Mr A. Godrich**
4 **CELTIC BARD,** 8, b g Celtic Cone—Arctic Lily **Mr G. B. Edmonson**
5 **CELTIC DREAM,** 7, ch m Celtic Cone—Kay's Dream **West Walk House Limited**
6 **CRACK A JOKE,** 11, b g Funny Man—Spin A Yarn **Mr Dennis Randle**
7 **CROSS MASTER,** 13, ch g Master Owen—Swift Mayo **Harlow Bros Ltd**
8 **FICTION WRITER,** 6, ch g Quayside—Chapter Four **Mr A. Godrich**
9 **MASTER REDWOOD,** 6, ch g General Ironside—Chammyville **Harlow Bros Ltd**
10 **PAN ARCTIC,** 11, b g Pitpan—Arctic Sue **Mrs R. Bill**
11 **PERENNELLA,** 4, ch f Kind of Hush—Oranella **Mrs Helen Plumbly**
12 **PRINCESS RYMER,** 7, b m Rymer—Iseult **Mrs R. Bill**
13 **REPINGTON,** 12, br g Grey Mirage—Heron's Dolly **Mr J. R. Gilman**
14 **ROYAL CRACKER,** 9, b g He Loves Me—French Cracker **Harlow Bros Ltd**
15 **WILD ARGOSY,** 11, b g Lucifer (USA)—Mountain Sedge **J. Medler**

Other Owners: Mr T. T. Bill, Mr R. Nichols, Mr P. J. Southgate, Mr J. Watts.

Jockey (Flat): A Proud (7-7, w.a.).

Jockey (NH): J Railton (10-0).

Lady Rider: Miss S Baxter

61 MR J. J. BIRKETT, Workington

Postal: **Garfield House, High Seaton, Workington, Cumbria.**
Phone: **(0900) 604189**

1 **BELLA BANUS,** 8, br m Rapid River—Certain Smile **Mrs K. P. Birkett**
2 **BERMUDA BELLE,** 6, b m Young Man (FR)—Wheel Grace **Mrs K. P. Birkett**
3 **DOWNHILL RUN,** 9, b g Deep Run—Money Spinner **Mrs K. P. Birkett**
4 **KING OF TYRE,** 13, b g Drumbeg—St Georg's Cottage **Mrs K. P. Birkett**
5 **RAMBLING MONK,** 7, ch g Monksfield—Merry Rambler **Mrs K. P. Birkett**

Amateur: Mr Gary Messenger (10-0).

62 MR W. H. BISSILL, Newark

Postal: **Long Acre, Wyke Lane, Farndon, Newark.**
Phone: **(0636) 704221**

1 **TIGERS PET,** 6, b g Tina's Pet—Too Do **Mr W. H. Bissill**

Lady Rider: Mrs M Bissill (11-0).

63 MR M. T. W. BLANSHARD, Lambourn

Postal: **Lethornes Stables, Upper Lambourn, Newbury, Berkshire, RG16 7QT.**
Phone: **LAMBOURN (0488) 71091**

1 **CASTLE CARY,** 4, gr f Castle Keep—Tibouchina **Mr Alan Aikin**
2 **JOIE DE ROSE,** 5, b m Tickled Pink—Joie d'Or (FR) **Mr Alan Aikin**
3 **LUAGA,** 4, b f Tyrnavos—Lady Rushen **Mr A. C. Hall**
4 **LUNA BID,** 7, b g Auction Ring (USA)—Moonscape **Mr A. C. Hall**
5 **PRINCE SOBUR,** 4, b g Jalmood (USA)—Ultra Vires **Mr C. R. Buttery**
6 **SOUTHROP,** 4, b g Auction Ring (USA)—Giovinezza (FR) **Mr Stanley Hinton**
7 **TWILIGHT FANTASY,** 4, b f Red Sunset—Imagination **Mr Charles Philipson**
8 **WELSHMAN,** 4, ch g Final Straw—Joie de Galles **Mr Brian Oxton**

THREE-YEAR-OLDS

9 **MUSICAL NOTE,** ch f Sharpo—Fair And Wise **Mr W. Blanshard**
10 **PHAROAH'S GUEST,** ch g Pharly (FR)—Exuberine (FR) **Lady Page**
11 **RASHEED,** b c Chief Singer—Enchanting Dancer (FR) **Sheikh Mohammed Bin Faleh**
12 **RUST PROOF,** gr c Rusticaro (FR)—Grecian Charter **Mr A. C. Hall**
13 **SABINE'S GULL (USA),** br f Arctic Tern (USA)—Altesse de Loir (USA) **Mr Peter Bedford**

TWO-YEAR-OLDS

14 **DOMIANA,** b f 13/4 Primo Dominie—Tatiana (Habitat) **Mr C. R. Buttery**
15 B f 4/3 Faustus—Fuchsia (Hot Spark) **Mr J. G. Charlton**
16 Br f 14/3 Rusticaro (FR)—Joie d'Or (FR) (Kashmir II) **Mr A. C. Hall**
17 B f 2/2 Bellypha—Rengaine (FR) (Music Boy) **Mr C. R. Philipson**
18 Br c 21/5 Shareef Dancer (USA)—Ultra Vires (High Line)

Other Owners: Mr M. Blanshard, Mr Timothy K. Bullimore, Mrs E. M. Charlton, Mr T. P. Charlton, Mrs Susan Davis, Mr D. W. J. Garrett, Mr H. Nicholas Lund, Mr B. Maynard, Mr Charles McKenna, Mr R. Payne, Mr Peter Pearson, Mr Nigel Rich.

Jockeys (Flat): N Adams (w.a.), R Cochrane (w.a.).

Jockey (NH): M Bastard (10-0).

Apprentice: Philip Skelton (7-12).

64 MR P. A. BLOCKLEY, Catwick

Postal: **Riston Whins, Whins Lane, Catwick, Hull, HU11 5PN.**
Phone: **(0964) 542583 OR (0964) 562440 CAR PHONE (0860) 616294**

1 **ANOTHER STRIPLIGHT,** 7, ch g Pauper—Hill Invader **Niland Construction Co Ltd**
2 **BASTINADO,** 7, ch m Bustino—Strathspey **Sun Rise Racing**
3 **CANESTRELLI (USA),** 5, b g Native Royalty (USA)—Princess Amelia **Mr W. Fletcher**
4 **CHANGE THE NAME,** 7, ch g Celtic Cone—Yogurt **Mr R. A. Bethell**
5 **CLONDROHID,** 9, ch g Lord Ha Ha—White Deer **Mr W. Fletcher**
6 **D'ORS GEM,** 7, b g Brigadier Gerard—Siraf **Mr B. Wilne**
7 **EAT YOUR HAT,** 6, br g Fine Blade (USA)—Honey's Queen **Brenda Bill**
8 **ENERGIA,** 4, b f Alias Smith (USA)—Ermione **Mrs Cheryl L. Owen**
9 **GENNARO,** 10, gr g Dance In Time (CAN)—Landed Lady **Mr P. D. Warne**
10 **HEEMEE,** 4, br f On Your Mark—Beyond The Rainbow **Mr B. S. Adamson**
11 **NON PERMANENT,** 4, b g Niniski (USA)—Perma Fina **Sun Rise Racing**
12 **PIGEON ISLAND,** 8, b g General Ironside—Brown Cherry **Mr R. A. Bethell**
13 **REGAL BRASS,** 6, gr h Royal Palace—Two Friendly **Mr W. Cox**
14 **SILKS VENTURE,** 5, br h Lochnager—Honey Thief **Mr B. S. Adamson**
15 **SPARK OF PEACE,** 8, ch g Royal Match—Geneva **Mr Bill Cahill**
16 **SPORTING CHALLENGE,** 5, b g Artaius (USA)—Karissima **Mr M. J. Gosse**
17 **STEPAULI,** 8, b g Le Bavard (FR)—Charming Ways **Mr Bill Cahill**
18 **SURPRISE STAR,** 7, ch g Sagaro—Star of Light **Mr R. A. Bethell**
19 **TOM KITTY,** 5, b g Broadsword (USA)—Golden Murry **Mrs Susan McDonald**
20 **UNPAID MEMBER,** 6, b g Moorestyle—Sunningdale Queen **Mr W. Fletcher**

THREE-YEAR-OLDS

21 **DARING MINSTREL,** br g Daring March—Miss Twomey **Mr D. A. Brindley**
22 **HANNAH'S CHOICE,** b br f Kampala—Cape of Storms **Mr R. Cromie**
23 **STONEYTHORPEWONDER,** b c Smackover—Holloway Wonder **Mr R. Thornhill**
24 Ch f Flying Tyke—Sunshine State **Mr R. Cromie**
25 **SWIFT WIND,** ro f Dalsaan—Flaretown **Mrs Teresa Blockley**

Other Owners: Mrs M. J. Adamson, Mr Brian Bailey, Mr H. A. Bethell, Lady Jane Bethell, Mr W. A. Bethell, Mr P. A. Blockley, Mr Alan Halsall, Mr Bert Houghton, Mr Peter Mee, Mr W. Millar, Mr Frank Qronez, Mr R. Robey, Mrs G. M. Z. Spink, Exors Of The Late Mr J. B. Woof, Mr P. J. Young.

Jockey (Flat): K Fallon (w.a.).

Jockeys (NH): C Kellet (10-0), Peter Niven (10-0, w.a.).

Conditional: P Midgley (9-7).

Amateur: Mr W A Bethell (11-0).

Lady Rider: Mrs Liddy Bethell (8-2).

65 MRS J. BLOOM, Wymondham

Postal: **Downham Lodge Farm, Wymondham, Norfolk.**
Phone: **WYMONDHAM (0953) 603176**

1 **NERAK SENGA,** 8, ch g Crimson Beau—Ballinkillen **Mr M. Bloom**
2 **PRINCE CARLTON,** 15, b g Autre Prince—Non Such Valley **Mrs J. Bloom**
3 4, Gr g Scallywag—St Lucian Breeze **Mr M. Bloom**

MRS J. BLOOM—continued

THREE-YEAR-OLDS

4 B g Oats—Non Such Valley **Mrs J. Bloom**
5 B br f Celtic Cone—St Lucian Breeze **Mr M. Bloom**

TWO-YEAR-OLDS

6 B f 30/5 Broadsword—Non Such Valley (Colonist II) **Mrs J. Bloom**
7 B g 16/3 Sunyboy—St Lucian Breeze (Vivify) **Mr M. Bloom**

Amateur: Mr N Bloom (11-0).

Lady Rider: Miss C Bloom (10-7).

66 MR D. R. BLOOR, Nuneaton

Postal: **Field Farm, Osbaston, Nuneaton, Warwickshire, CV13 0DR.**
Phone: **(0455) 291739**

1 **CLIFF'S KNIGHT,** 7, gr ro g Supergrey—Jig **Mr D. R. Bloor**
2 **IM PRIVILAGED,** 6, b g Red Sunset—Loch Leven **Mr D. R. Bloor**
3 **PARISH RIGGED,** 12, b g Master Buck—Very Very **Mr D. R. Bloor**
4 **SPORTING MARINER,** 8, b g Julio Mariner—Ma Griffe **Mr D. R. Bloor**
5 **TEAM APPROACH,** 9, ch g Le Bavard (FR)—Overdressed **Mr D. R. Bloor**
6 **TEMPLETOWN,** 11, ch g Laurence O—Bean An Ti **Mr D. R. Bloor**

67 MR G. BLUM, Newmarket

Postal: **Primrose Cottage Stables, The Green, Tuddenham, Bury St. Edmunds, iP28 6SD.**
Phone: **(0638) 713916 OR (0638) 714222**

1 **BEAUTIFUL NINA,** 4, ch f Rabdan—Donna Sirena **Mrs Bridget Blum**
2 **FORGE BEAU,** 5, b g Swing Easy (USA)—Korresia **Mr R. H. Coombes**
3 **SARHAN,** 4, ch c Ahonoora—Rosserk **Mr P. Bradley**

THREE-YEAR-OLDS

4 **KIRBY'S BEST,** ch f Sayf El Arab (USA)—Betty's Bid **Derek Baldwin and G. Blum**
5 **SCORPIO LADY,** ch f Vaigly Great—Buy G's **Mrs Jacqueline Peirce**
6 **SEE MORE INDIANS,** ch g Seymour Hicks (FR)—Border Squaw **G. Blum and P. Kenner**
7 **SHEBA'S PAL,** b f Claude Monet (USA)—Bread 'n Honey **Mr R. J. Peirce**

TWO-YEAR-OLDS

8 **HEAVENLY QUEEN,** b f 5/3 Scottish Reel—Celeste (Sing Sing) **G. Blum**
9 **KIRBY OPPORTUNITY,** ch f 14/4 Mummy's Game—Empress Catherine (Welsh Pageant) **Peter Bradley**
10 **PETITESSE,** gr f 14/3 Petong—Foudroyer (Artaius (USA)) **G. Blum**
11 **ZEPHYR FIRE,** ch c 13/3 Hotfoot—Delta Wind (Tumble Wind (USA)) **G. W. Thorpe**

Other Owners: Miss Lilo Blum.

Jockey (Flat): G Duffield (w.a.).

68 MR J. W. BLUNDELL, Grimsby

Postal: **Wyham House, Ludborough, Grimsby, South Humberside, DN36 5RS.**
Phone: **(0472) 840494 (0472) 840256**

1 **DEADLINE,** 7, br g Strong Gale—Countess Charmere **Mr C. J. Newton**
2 **DEPLETE,** 7, b g Deep Run—Elite Lady **Mrs E. W. Wilson**
3 **FOXY BOY,** 7, b g Chantro—La Sirene **Mrs A. H. Cassell**
4 **HAPPY BREED,** 7, b h Bustino—Lucky Realm **Mr A. Ryan**
5 **JASMIN PATH,** 5, ro m Warpath—Jasmin **Mr R. L. Houlton**
6 **JUST CHARLES,** 5, b g Tepukei—Easter Tinkle **Mrs R. Kirkby**
7 **KING CAP,** 5, ch g Kinglet—Mandycap **Mr T. W. R. Readett-Bayley**
8 **MATRIC,** 9, b br g Mandalus—Bel Arbre **Mrs E. W. Wilson**
9 **MILTON PARK,** 10, b g Derek H—Scotch Flora **Mr J. W. Blundell**
10 **PRINCE OF BABYLON,** 5, ch g Abednego—Princess Grainne **Mrs B. Blundell**
11 **QUOTA ONE,** 6, br g Buckskin (FR)—Sarah Gee **Mr R. A. Wain**
12 **REGARDLESS,** 8, b g Quayside—Bel Arbre **Miss V. R. Wilson**
13 **SAM DA VINCI,** 11, ch g Saucy Kit—Fortilage **Mrs E. W. Wilson**
14 **SMILEY,** 5, b h Blakeney—Laughing Girl **Hugh Bourn Developments (Wragby) Ltd**
15 **STEGSMAN,** 8, b g Fordham (USA)—Charity Concert **Steadfast Scaffold (H'Side) Ltd**
16 **THREE COUNTIES,** 13, b g Little Buskins—Fair Reply **Miss K. Rimell**

THREE-YEAR-OLDS

17 **THE CAN CAN MAN,** b g Daring March—Dawn Ditty **Mr A. W. Robinson and Mr Ian Robinson**

Other Owners: Mr R. N. Beeson, Mr A. H. Cassell.

Jockey (NH): Martin Brennan (10-0).

Conditional: A Leese (9-7).

Lady Rider: Miss K Rimell (9-7).

69 MR J. S. BOLGER, Carlow

Postal: **Glebe House, Coolcullen, Carlow, Ireland.**
Phone: **(056) 43150 OR 43158 FAX (056) 43256**

1 **CAERLESS WRITING,** 4, ch f Caerleon (USA)—Northern Script **Mrs Ogden White**
2 **CIELAMOUR (USA),** 5, b m Conquistador Cielo—Nicole Mon Amour **H. De Kwiatkowski**
3 **ELEMENTARY,** 7, b g Busted—Santa Vittoria **P. C. Green**
4 **FATHER PHIL,** 4, b c Kampala—Kilboy Concorde **C. Ryan**
5 **JAMEEL RIDGE (USA),** 4, b c Cox's Ridge—Jameelapi **Dubai Bloodstock Ltd**
6 **KESHIA,** 4, ch f Buckskin (FR)—Floater **Mark O'Connor**
7 **KYRA,** 4, b f Sadler's Wells—Aunty **Ovidstown Investments Ltd**
8 **MULACH IDE,** 4, b g Salmon Leap (USA)—Place Royale **Mrs D. Mahony**
9 **ORBIS (USA),** 4, b c Conquistador Cielo—Nicole Mon Amour **Mrs C. Shubotham**
10 **ROYAL CLIMBER,** 4, b f Kings Lake (USA)—Ivy **Mrs Ogden White**
11 **STRANGE LADY (USA),** 4, b f Vaguely Noble—Selerina (USA) **Mrs C. Shubotham**
12 **UPWARD TREND,** 4, ch f Salmon Leap (USA)—Ivory Home (FR) **P. C. Green**
13 **VESTRIS ABU,** 4, b c Lyphard's Special—Ishtar Abu **C. De Laubespin**

THREE-YEAR-OLDS

14 **ALL STAR BAND,** br c Ahonoora—Sweet Tones **R. O'Brien**
15 **AMINATA,** b f Glenstal (USA)—Belle Epoque **Mrs C. Shubotham**
16 **ARMANASCO,** br c Ahonoora—For Going **Mrs C. Shubotham**
17 **EASY TO PLEASE,** ch f What A Guest—Clonsella Lady **D. H. W. Dobson**
18 **FREEZING LINE (USA),** b br f It's Freezing (USA)—Maria Line (USA) **Mrs V. Kraft-Payson**

MR J. S. BOLGER—continued

19 **HIGH PRESSURE,** ch f Kings Lake (USA)—Celestial Storm **P. C. Green**
20 **LA COTE FLEURIE (USA),** br f L'Emigrant (USA)—Rosey Ramble (USA) **Miss Kathryn Nikkel**
21 **NIKKICOLA (USA),** br f Damascus (USA)—Belle O'Belgium **T. Gentry**
22 **NORDIC GAYLE,** b c Nordico (USA)—Beparoejojo **Mrs J. S. Bolger**
23 **NORDIC GLADNESS,** b f Nordico (USA)—Gladsome (FR) **H. De Kwiatkowski**
24 **NORDIC MINT,** b f Nordico (USA)—Queen of The Mint **Al-Deera Bloodstock**
25 **NORDIC RACE,** b g Nordico (USA)—Lady Dulcinea **Mrs C. Shubotham**
26 **NORDIC REGION,** b c Nordico (USA)—Favourite Niece **Mrs J. S. Bolger**
27 **NORDIC ROOTS,** b f Nordico (USA)—Red Leaf **D. H. W. Dobson**
28 **NORDIC SPARKLE,** b c Nordico (USA)—Persian Sparkler **Mrs C. Shubotham**
29 **NORDIC SPECIAL,** b f Nordico (USA)—Special Display **D. H. W. Dobson**
30 **NORDIC SURPRISE,** b c Nordico (USA)—Adorable Princess **H. De Kwiatkowski**
31 **NORDIC TOUCH,** b c Nordico (USA)—Scented Cushion **Mrs J. S. Bolger**
32 **PLATINUM BULLET,** b f Auction Ring (USA)—Reload (FR) **Platinum Racing Ltd**
33 **SAVIOUR (USA),** b f Majestic Light (USA)—Victorian Queen **T. Gentry**
34 **WINNING HEART,** ch f Horage—Silver Heart **M. Keogh**

TWO-YEAR-OLDS

35 **ASHCO (IRE),** br f 2/5 Nordico (USA)—Ashaireez (Abernant) **Mrs J. S. Bolger**
36 **ASSURING (IRE),** b c 23/5 Sure Blade (USA)—Exciting (Mill Reef (USA)) **Mrs C. Shubotham**
37 **BACK TO THE FUTURE (IRE),** b f 18/4 Star de Naskra (USA)—
Fair Astrologer (USA) (Quack (USA)) **P. C. Green**
38 **BELOVED VISITOR (USA),** b f 10/2 Miswaki (USA)—Abeesh (USA) (Nijinsky (CAN)) **Maktoum Al Maktoum**
39 B f 21/4 Sure Blade (USA)—Black Crow (Sea Hawk II) **Lady Sarah Barry**
40 **CARPELLI (IRE),** b f 19/4 Law Society (USA)—
Bubbling (USA) (Stage Door Johnny (USA)) **D. H. W. Dobson**
41 B c 13/3 Ballad Rock—Cecily (Prince Regent (FR)) **M. W. J. Smurfit**
42 **DESERT EMERALD (IRE),** b c 23/1 Taufan (USA)—Pavello (Crepello) **Abdullah Ali**
43 **DIANDRA,** b f 6/2 Shardari—Eastern Command (USA) (Far Out East (USA)) **D. H. W. Dobson**
44 **ENERGANCE (IRE),** ch f 22/7 Salmon Leap (USA)—Rosemore (Ashmore (FR)) **D. H. W. Dobson**
45 B c 16/4 Green Desert (USA)—Etoile de Paris (Crowned Prince (USA)) **Maktoum Al Maktoum**
46 **FARINELLA (IRE),** ch f 27/3 Salmon Leap (USA)—Boldella (Bold Lad (IRE)) **Mrs M. O'Dwyer**
47 **FASHION AWARD (IRE),** b f 5/4 Salmon Leap (USA)—
Highly Delighted (USA) (Verbatim (USA)) **Mrs Mary Brennan**
48 **GDANSK VICTORY (USA),** b f 20/3 Danzig Connection—
Lulu Mon Amour (USA) (Tom Rolfe) **H. De Kwiatkowski**
49 B f 4/4 Shareef Dancer—Glasson Lady (GER) (Priamos (GER)) **Mrs J. Corcoran**
50 **HIGH GLIDER,** b f 27/2 High Top—Quietfoot (Grundy) **D. Sharkey**
51 **HOLLYBANK LADY (USA),** b f 9/3 Sir Ivor—Lady Norcliffe (USA) (Norcliffe (CAN)) **P. C. Green**
52 **JET SKI LADY (USA),** ch f 20/2 Vaguely Noble—Bemissed (USA) (Nijinsky (CAN)) **Maktoum Al Maktoum**
53 B f 8/5 Nordico (USA)—Junijo (Junius (USA)) **Mrs J. S. Bolger**
54 B f 19/5 Arctic Tern (USA)—Kazadancoa (FR) (Green Dancer (USA)) **C. W. Clay**
55 **KILCASH (IRE),** b c 25/2 Salmon Leap (USA)—Roblanna (Roberto (USA)) **Mrs Ogden White**
56 B f 31/3 Nijinsky (CAN)—La Dame du Lac (USA) (Round Table) **Maktoum Al Maktoum**
57 **LADY ASHFORD (IRE),** b f 20/2 Top Ville—Tranchard (Sharpen Up) **Mrs J. R. Mullion**
58 **LANSDOWNE,** b c 10/5 High Top—Fettle (Relkino) **D. Sharkey**
59 **LEPALIA (IRE),** b f 12/4 Salmon Leap (USA)—Malia (Malacate (USA)) **Mrs J. S. Bolger**
60 B f 9/5 Sir Ivor—Majestic Peck (USA) (Majestic Light (USA)) **D. H. W. Dobson**
61 **MALVERNICO (IRE),** b c 9/3 Nordico (USA)—Malvern Beauty (Shirley Heights) **Mrs J. S. Bolger**
62 **MUSICAL GEM (USA),** b f 21/2 The Minstrel (CAN)—
Inherit The Flag (USA) (Hoist The Flag (USA)) **P. C. Green**
63 **NEXT TYCOON (IRE),** gr c 5/4 Last Tycoon—Best Gal (FR) (Bonne Noel) **D. H. W. Dobson**
64 B f 26/3 Sadler's Wells—Noble Treasure (Vaguely Noble) **Maktoum Al Maktoum**
65 **NORDIC ADMIRER (IRE),** ch c 22/2 Nordico (USA)—Adoramus (USA) (Believe It (USA)) **H. De Kwiatkowski**
66 **NORDIC BLUE (IRE),** ch f 15/3 Nordico (USA)—Gorm (Majority Blue) **Mrs J. S. Bolger**
67 **NORDIC COMFORT (IRE),** gr f 10/5 Nordico (USA)—Scented Cushion (Rusticaro (FR)) **Mrs J. S. Bolger**
68 **NORDIC DISPLAY (IRE),** b f 14/2 Nordico (USA)—Special Display (Welsh Pageant) **D. H. W. Dobson**
69 **NORDIC ENIGMA (IRE),** b c 3/4 Nordico (USA)—Pollination (Pentotal) **H. De Kwiatkowski**
70 **NORDIC LAKE (IRE),** b f 19/2 Nordico (USA)—High Lake (Quisling) **Mrs J. S. Bolger**
71 **NORDIC OAK (IRE),** ch c 20/5 Nordico (USA)—Red Leaf (Carry Off) **Mrs J. S. Bolger**

MR J. S. BOLGER—continued

72 **NORDIC RELATION (IRE)**, b f 2/4 Nordico (USA)—Favourite Niece (Busted) **D. H. W. Dobson**
73 **NORDIC SOPRANO (IRE)**, b f 8/5 Nordico (USA)—Angor (Lorenzaccio) **Mrs C. Shubotham**
74 **NORDIC SPRING (IRE)**, ch f 16/4 Nordico (USA)—Dream of Spring (Hello Gorgeous (USA)) **Una Bolger**
75 **NORDIC SUN (IRE)**, gr c 29/4 Nordico (USA)—
Cielsoleil (USA) (Conquistador Cielo (USA)) **H. De Kwiatkowski**
76 **NORDIC TIARA (IRE)**, ch f 27/5 Nordico (USA)—Company Royale (King's Company) **Mrs J. S. Bolger**
77 **NORDIC TONES (IRE)**, b c 1/5 Nordico (USA)—Sweet Tones (Lord Gayle (USA)) **Mrs J. S. Bolger**
78 **NORDIC WIND (IRE)**, b c 16/4 Nordico (USA)—Beparoejojo (Lord Gayle (USA)) **Mrs J. S. Bolger**
79 **PARK GUEST (IRE)**, b f 6/5 Last Tycoon—Mimicry (Thatch (USA)) **Patrick H. Burns**
80 **PERANDELLO (IRE)**, ch f 15/3 Coquelin (USA)—Nephrite (Godswalk (USA)) **Mrs C. Shubotham**
81 **ROGER RAMJET (IRE)**, b c 15/4 Law Society (USA)—Saraday (Northfields (USA)) **P. C. Green**
82 **STAR OF GDANSK (USA)**, ch c 4/5 Danzig Connection—
Star Empress (Young Emperor) **H. De Kwiatkowski**
83 **TASHALIN (IRE)**, b f 7/4 Coquelin (USA)—Tasha (Welsh Saint) **D. H. W. Dobson**
84 **TASSA (IRE)**, b c 20/1 Nearly A Nose—Fiesta Femme (Condorcet (FR)) **Mrs J. S. Bolger**
85 **TENNELLE (IRE)**, b f 27/4 Gorytus (USA)—Lady Beck (FR) (Sir Gaylord) **Mrs C. Shubotham**
86 **TIPPERARY AZUL (IRE)**, b c 4/3 Godswalk (USA)—Kilboy Concorde (African Sky) **C. Ryan**
87 **VASSILEVA (IRE)**, ch c 14/5 Gorytus (USA)—Belle Epoque (Habitat) **Mrs C. Shubotham**

Jockey (Flat): C Roche (8-4).

Jockeys (NH): T Carmody (9-10, w.a.), M Flynn (10-0, w.a.).

Apprentices: J A Heffernan (8-0), W J Supple (8-0).

Conditional: Shane Donahoe (9-7), M J Holbrook (9-3).

Amateurs: Mr A P O'Brien (10-0), Mr P O'Donovan (9-10).

Lady Riders: Miss Ann Marie Dunphy (8-7), Miss Joan Kirwin-Lanigan (8-7), Miss Imelda Leahy (8-7).

70 MR M. J. BOLTON, Shrewton

Postal: **The Cleeve, Elston Lane, Shrewton, Wiltshire, SP3 4HL.**
Phone: **(0980) 621059**

1 **DANCING BALLERINA**, 7, b m Record Run—Glanfield **Mrs R. A. Murrell**
2 **DAWES OF NELSON**, 5, b br h Krayyan—Killyhevlin **Mrs Jennie Miller**
3 **ERICA CINEREA**, 7, b m Yukon Eric (CAN)—Steverline **Mrs S. P. Elphick**
4 **MICHELLE CLARE**, 4, b f Good Times (ITY)—Paradise Island **Mr M. M. O'Connor**
5 **O K SON**, 11, b g Oaksam—Dear Liz II **Mr C. I. A. Paterson**
6 **SITEX**, 12, b h Record Run—Glorious Light **Mrs S. P. Elphick**
7 **TA WARDLE**, 6, ch g Import—Zephyr Lady **Mr A. E. Brown**
8 **WELCOME TIDINGS**, 6, b m Record Run—Glanfield **Mr M. J. Bolton**

THREE-YEAR-OLDS

9 **CITY SHOES**, ch c Creetown—Tiny Feet **Mr Parvis Brown**
10 **FALSE PASSPORT**, ch g Alias Smith (USA)—Hussy **Mrs S. P. Elphick**
11 **LIGHT ON HER TOES**, b f Cragador—Oscilight **Mrs S. P. Elphick**
12 **MILDRED SOPHIA**, b f Crooner—Glanfield **Mrs S. P. Elphick**
13 **STAR BLAZE**, b f Alzao (USA)—Space Mark **Commonsidr Racing**

TWO-YEAR-OLDS

14 **SMUGGLERS GOLD**, b f 3/5 Gold Claim—Lareda (Burglar) **Mrs S. P. Elphick**

Other Owners: Mr H. Choules.

Jockey (NH): R Goldstein (10 0).

71 MR C. BOOTH, Flaxton

Postal: **Gravel Pit Farm, Foston, Flaxton, York.**
Phone: **(0653 81) 586**

1 **BILLAN TARA,** 4, b f Nicholas Bill—Celtic Tara **Mr Kenneth Metcalfe**
2 **BOLD CELT,** 7, b br h Brave Shot—Pearl Locket **Mr Richard Ward**
3 **BOULEVARD GIRL,** 5, b m Nicholas Bill—Gay Stampede **Innovative Marketing Int'l**
4 **BURSANA,** 4, b f Burslem—Lady of Surana **Mr A. Lyons**
5 **FIGHTING GORYTUS,** 5, b h Gorytus (USA)—Stella Urbis (GER) **D. Harding**
6 **LOADPLAN LASS,** 4, b f Nicholas Bill—Strathclair **Loadplan Ltd**
7 **PERCY'S PET,** 4, b f Blakeney—Oula-Ka Fu-Fu **Mr A. Lyons**
8 **SYCALUS,** 4, b c Sicyos (USA)—Alcassa (FR) **Mr A. Lyons**

THREE-YEAR-OLDS

9 **MADEMOISELLE CHLOE,** b f Night Shift (USA)—Emerald Rocket **Mr K. H. Jaffa**
10 **MAYFAIR MAIDEN,** b f Fairy King (USA)—De Narde **Mr Thomas G. Cahill**

TWO-YEAR-OLDS

11 **CARDEA CASTLE (IRE),** b f 23/3 Fayruz—Yamba (FR) (Amarko (FR)) **Charles Castle**
12 **CHLOES DIAMOND (IRE),** ch f 28/2 Heraldiste (USA)—
Salique (Sallust) **Mr K. H. Jaffa and Mr A. L. Michaels**
13 Br f Formidable (USA)—Egnoussa (Swing Easy (USA)) **V. Wade**
14 **FAIR DARE,** b f 11/3 Daring March—Fair Madame (Monseigneur (USA)) **Mr A. Lyons**
15 **MUMMY'S EMERALD,** ch f 5/4 Mummy's Game—Emerald Eagle (Sandy Creek) **Mr A. Lyons**
16 Ch f 25/3 Night Shift (USA)—Opalescent (Gulf Pearl)
17 **SHARP GLOW,** ch c 16/2 Reach—Jumra (Thatch (USA)) **Mrs E. Wade**
18 **SYMPOSIUM IDOL (IRE),** b f 23/4 Gorytus (USA)—Estivalia (Persian Bold) **Charles Castle**

Other Owners: Mr C. B. B. Booth, Mr David Hughes, R. Kyle, Mr C. Nickerson, Mr T. A. Welna, Mr R. D. Williams.

Jockey (Flat): K Hodgson (8-6).

Apprentice: P Johnson (7-11).

72 MR J. R. BOSLEY, Bampton

Postal: **Lower Haddon Farm, Bampton, Oxford, OX8 2AT.**
Phone: **BAMPTON CASTLE (0993) 850212**

1 **BALLAFORT,** 5, b m Ballacashtal (CAN)—Fortune's Fancy **Mr C. A. Bentick**
2 **CELTIC CATCH,** 4, br g Celtic Cone—Eyecatcher **Mr J. R. Bosley**
3 **CHEEKY FOX,** 4, b g King of Spain—Diamond Talk **Mrs J. Harmsworth**
4 **CHRISTMAS HOLS,** 4, b g Young Generation—Foston Bridge **Mr Jan Chudzynski**
5 **CURIOUS FEELING,** 4, gr f Nishapour (FR)—Noirima **Mr M. Smith**
6 **KOSEY RUN,** 7, b m Deep Run—Kosey Kitchen **Miss K. S. A. Cuddy**
7 **LADY CATCHER,** 8, b m Free Boy—Eyecatcher **Mr J. Pratt**
8 **MARINER'S STAR,** 8, b g Julio Mariner—Falling Gold (USA) **Mr J. F. Long**
9 **MISS HADDON,** 7, ro m Free Boy—River Dance **Mr J. R. Bosley**
10 **POINT MADE,** 7, b g Tycoon II—Cala Conta **Mr A. L. Deal**
11 **PULL THE PIN,** 4, ch g In Fijar (USA)—Mazzola (FR) **Mr J. L. Hanley**
12 **RUFFINSWICK,** 4, gr g Baron Blakeney—Indiscreet **Mr J. M. A. West**
13 **SOLDIER EVE,** 4, ch f Soldier Rose—Jubilee Eve **Mr J. L. Hanley**
14 **SULETTE,** 6, br m Sunyboy—Aluette **Mrs H. M. Innes**
15 **SWOOPING,** 5, b g Kings Lake (USA)—High Hawk **Mr Tom Casagranda**
16 **TALUS,** 6, gr g Kalaglow—Helcia **J. & D. Contract Cleaners Ltd**

MR J. R. BOSLEY—continued

THREE-YEAR-OLDS

17 **CASTILLO,** b c Dreams To Reality (USA)—Belle Lutine **Mr P. A. Deal**
18 **DIAMOND BAY,** b f Buzzards Bay—Czar's Diamond **Mrs B. A. Long**
19 **DI MODA,** ch c Buzzards Bay—Diamond Talk **Mr Michael Smith**
20 **MUSICAL IVY,** b f Aragon—Dark Parade **Mr J. Westley**

TWO-YEAR-OLDS

21 Ch c 10/4 Jupiter Island—Diamond Talk (Counsel)

Other Owners: Mr Bryan M. Arch, Mr J. I. Porter, Mr M. A. Wilkins.

Jockey (NH): M Bosley (10-2).

73 MR R. BOSS, Newmarket

Postal: **Phoenix Lodge Stables, Rowley Drive, Newmarket, Suffolk, CB8 0NH.**
Phone: **OFFICE (0638) 661335 HOME (0638) 70320**

1 **ACCESS TRAVEL,** 4, b c Auction Ring (USA)—Lady Tippins (USA) **Miss Denise A. Williams**
2 **COME HALLEY (FR),** 4, b g Crystal Glitters (USA)—Edition Nouvelle (FR) **Ligvale Ltd**
3 **CREDIT LINE (FR),** 4, b f Young Generation—Truly Blest **Mrs A. Mackintosh**
4 **DIAMOND PATH,** 4, ch c Morston (FR)—Glide Path **Mrs R. B. Skepper**
5 **EVENING AFFAIR,** 4, b f Red Sunset—Miss Flirt **Mr K. Bethel**
6 **JADEITE (FR),** 4, b g Crystal Glitters—Jawhara **Mr A. M. Foustok**
7 **LAURIES CRUSADOR,** 5, b h Welsh Pageant—Square Note **Mr L. C. James**
8 **SNO SERENADE,** 4, ch g Song—When The Saints **Mrs Judi Gold**
9 **YOUNG TEARAWAY,** 5, br m Young Generation—Chiparia **Mr A. A. Papotto**

THREE-YEAR-OLDS

10 **ACCESS CRUISE (USA),** ch c Wajima (USA)—Lady of Meadowlane (USA) **Miss Denise A. Williams**
11 **ACCESS SKI,** b c Bustino—Crimson Lake (FR) **Miss Elaine D. Williams**
12 **ACCESS SUN,** b c Pharly (FR)—Princesse du Seine (FR) **Miss Elaine D. Williams**
13 **ALL NIGHT DELI,** b g Night Shift (USA)—Tzarina (USA) **Mrs Judi Gold**
14 **BLACKWATERFOOT,** b c Kalaglow—Twelve O'Clock **Mrs Pam Fitsall**
15 **COLIN SELLER,** ch c Noalto—Mallow **Mr David M. Gransby**
16 **FUJAIYRAH,** b f In Fijar (USA)—Ananiyya (FR) **Mr A. M. Foustok**
17 **IKSAB,** b c Lyphard's Special—Some Dame **Mr A. M. Foustok**
18 **I RUN I WIN,** b c Bairn (USA)—Historical Fact **Mr S. Fustok**
19 **LADY SNOOBLES,** b f King of Clubs—Ides of March
20 **LITTLE BIG,** b c Indian King (USA)—Route Royale **Mr L. C. James**
21 **LORD GLEN,** gr c Rabdan—Rage Glen **Mr G. R. Platt**
22 **MIEKA,** ch c Longleat (USA)—Secret Pearl **Mr K. Bethel**
23 **MONYA,** b f Explodent (USA)—Fandangerina (USA) **Mr M. M. Festok**
24 **RATHVINDEN HOUSE (USA),** b c Hostage (USA)—Great Verdict (USA) **Mrs Pam Fitsall**
25 **REASONABLE KID,** ch c Reasonable (FR)—Trust Sally **Mr Maurice Sarkis**
26 **SAN PIER NICETO,** b c Norwick (USA)—Langton Herring **Mrs Elaine-Ann Papotto**
27 **STRADBROKE,** b c Fairy King (USA)—Mattira (FR) **Mrs Pam Fitsall**

TWO-YEAR-OLDS

28 **ACCESS FLYER (IRE),** b c 15/3 Reasonable (FR)—Fenland Queen (King's Troop)
29 **ACCESS HOLIDAYS,** ch c 24/4 Faustus (USA)—Lardana (Burglar) **Partnership**
30 **ACCESS SUPREME,** b c 27/4 Law Society (USA)—Honeypot Lane (Silly Season) **Partnership**
31 Gr c 10/4 Wassl—Ardmay (Roan Rocket) **Mr Saleh Al Homeizi**
32 **BOLT,** ch c 5/4 Precocious—Elope (Jimmy Reppin) **Partnership**
33 **DANNEMAN,** b c 3/5 Daring March—Lillemor (Connaught) **Mr Magnus Berger**
34 **INTERROGATE,** b f 5/3 In Fijar (USA)—Artipiar (Tyrant (USA)) **Mr A. M. Foustok**
35 **KARIM'S KID (IRE),** b c 16/3 Petorius—Light of Eire (USA) (Majestic Light (USA)) **Mr Maurice Sarkis**

MR R. BOSS—continued

36 **MADAGANS GREY,** gr c 19/3 Carwhite—Cheri Berry (Air Trooper) **Madagans**
37 **MARIA CAPPUCCINI,** ch f 19/3 Siberian Express—Mary Martin (Be My Guest (USA)) **Mr A. A. Papotto**
38 **MARIA DONIA,** ch f 13/5 Siberian Express—Nafla (FR) (Arctic Tern (USA)) **Mr A. A. Papotto**
39 **MARIA GRAZIA,** ch f 23/4 Night Shift (USA)—Grace Note (Parthia) **Mr A. A. Papotto**
40 B f 21/2 Flash of Steel—Proper Madam (Mummy's Pet) **Mr Peter Asquith**
41 **RAAWI,** b c 5/3 Be My Guest (USA)—Fast Motion (Midsummer Night II) **Mr A. M. Foustok**
42 **SIXOFUS (IRE),** b c 3/3 Glenstal (USA)—Grace Darling (USA) (Vaguely Noble) **Mr S. Poole**
43 **SNO MARQUE,** ch c 10/5 Carwhite—Hyacine (High Line) **Mrs Judi Gold**
44 **STRAIGHT NO CHASER,** b c 2/5 Norwick (USA)—Pepeke (Mummy's Pet)

Other Owners: Mrs G. F. R. Boss, Mr J. Budgen, Mr John Fuller, Mr Simon Hakim, Lord Howland, Mr R. S. G. Jones, Mr Alex Kelly, Mr J. P. Kenny, Mr Terry A. Leigh, Mr P. E. Mills, Mr N. E. Poole, Mr David Roberts, Marchioness Of Tavistock.

74 MR J. F. BOTTOMLEY, Malton

Postal: **Blinkbonny Stables, Langton Road, Norton, Malton, N. Yorkshire.**
Phone: **HOME (0653) 693511 YARD (0653) 694597**

1 **HOT STAR,** 4, b g Hotfoot—La Camargue **Mr John F. Bottomley**
2 **LUCKY STRAW,** 5, b m Tumble Wind (USA)—Hi Little Gal **Mr P. Bottomley**
3 **QUALITAIR AVIATOR,** 4, b g Valiyar—Comtec Princess **Qualitair Holdings Limited**
4 **QUALITAIR DUTCHESS,** 5, br m Enchantment—Conte Bleu **Mr P. Bottomley**
5 **QUALITAIR FLYER,** 8, b g Kampala—Ziobia **Qualitair Holdings Ltd**
6 **SASKIA'S PRIDE,** 4, ch f Giacometti—Anjamadi **Mr P. Bottomley**
7 **SASKIA'S REPRIEVE,** 6, ch g Giacometti—Anjamadi **Qualitair Holdings Limited**
8 **STANSTED FLYER,** 4, b g Rabdan—Maputo Princess **Qualitair Holdings Limited**

THREE-YEAR-OLDS

9 **CHERRY CROWN,** gr f Uncle Pokey—Cherry Season **Mrs O. K. Steele**
10 **DUXFORD LODGE,** b f Dara Monarch—Simmry **Mr P. Bottomley**
11 B f Mr Fluorocarbon—Grass Emerald **Mr P. Bottomley**
12 **QUALITAIR BLAZER,** ch f Blazing Saddles (AUS)—Midfirna **Mr P. Bottomley**
13 **QUALITAIR DREAM,** b f Dreams To Reality (USA)—Maputo Princess **Mr P. Bottomley**
14 **QUALITAIR FIGHTER,** ch g Hard Fought—Venus of Stretham **Qualitair Holdings Limited**
15 **QUALITAIR SUPREME,** ch f Exhibitioner—Glendalough (USA) **Mr P. Bottomley**
16 **QUALITAIR SWEETIE,** ch g Sweet Monday—Right Abella **Qualitair Holdings Limited**
17 **SASKIA'S HERO,** ch g Bairn (USA)—Comtec Princess **Qualitair Holdings Limited**

TWO-YEAR-OLDS

18 B c 6/4 Mazaad—A Nice Alert (Red Alert) **Qualitair Holdings Ltd**
19 **COMTEC FLYER,** ch f 2/5 Valiyar—Comtec Princess (Gulf Pearl) **Mr P. Bottomley**
20 **FRANCIS ANN,** br f 25/1 Balidar—Supper Party (He Loves Me) **Mr J. F. Bottomley**
21 **QUALITAIR CHOICE (IRE),** b br f 23/4 Stalker—Ardrums (Native Prince) **Mr P. Bottomley**
22 **QUALITAIR DOM,** ch c 28/3 Domynsky—Qualitair Princess (Bay Express) **Qualitair Holdings Ltd**
23 **QUALITAIR MAID,** b f 15/3 Reesh—Wollow Maid (Wollow) **Mr P. Bottomley**
24 **QUALITAIR MELODY,** b c 21/3 Bairn (USA)—Melody Park (Music Boy) **Qualitair Holdings Ltd**
25 **QUALITAIR PROMISE,** ch f 29/3 Reach—Maputo Princess (Raga Navarro (ITY)) **Mr P. Bottomley**
26 **QUALITAIR REALITY,** b f 7/4 Dreams To Reality—Blushing Nurse (Saritamer (USA)) **Mr P. Bottomley**
27 **QUALITAIR RHYTHM (IRE),** b f 11/5 Drumalis—Abbe's Realm (Realm) **Mr P. Bottomley**
28 **QUALITAIR SON,** b c 21/5 Lochnager—Qualitairess (Kampala) **Qualitair Holdings Ltd**
29 **QUALITAIR SONG,** b f 16/2 Song—Hellene (Dominion) **Mr P. Bottomley**

Jockeys (Flat): M Birch (w.a.), S Webster.

Jockeys (NH): D Byrne (10-0, w.a.), J J Quinn (10-0, w.a.).

Conditional: A J Bottomley (10-0).

75 MR B. BOUSFIELD, Brough

Postal: **Glaslyn House, Brough, Kirkby Stephen, Cumbria.**

1 **HAGLER,** 7, br g Silly Prices—Reigate Head **Mrs D. A. Bousfield**
2 **HEAD FOR HOME,** 5, gr m Grey Ghost—Reigate Head **Mrs D. A. Bousfield**
3 **MOVE AHEAD,** 6, ch m Move Off—Reigate Head **Mrs D. A. Bousfield**
4 **WHATS WHAT,** 11, gr g Pongee—Reigate Head **Mrs D. A. Bousfield**

76 MR F. BOUTIN, Lamorlaye

Postal: **Le Mont de Po, 60260 Lamorlaye, France.**
Phone: **(4) 457-16-72 TELEX 140137 F LAGUMA FAX 44 57 44 73**

1 **ALL FORGOTTEN (USA),** 5, b h Alydar—Ole Liz **N. Radwan**
2 **ARK ANGE (USA),** 4, ch f L'Emigrant—Zitherplay **S. Niarchos**
3 **BHAYLIKA,** 4, b f Bikala—Bhaydana **J. L. Lagardere**
4 **ERACER,** 4, b c Niniski—Chalca **S. Niarchos**
5 **ETERNITY'S BREATH (USA),** 4, b c Nureyev—Sham's Princess **J. L. Lagardere**
6 **GUILT (USA),** 4, b c Alleged—Garden of Eden **E. Seltzer**
7 **IDEFIX (USA),** 4, b c Nureyev—Rose du Boele **S. Niarchos**
8 **KARMICHAH,** 4, b f Nice Havrais—Karmisyn **J. L. Lagardere**
9 **LOUIS CYPHRE,** 4, b c Niniski—Princesse Timide **S. Niarchos**
10 **LUXURIOUS,** 4, b f Lyphard—Tropicaro **J. L. Lagardere**
11 **MARZANO,** 4, b c L'Emigrant—Margello **Mme Vukobrat**
12 **MISTER SICY,** 4, b c Sicyos—Mrs Annie **J. L. Lagardere**
13 **MUROTO,** 4, b c Busted—Maresca **G. A. Oldham**
14 **NOSFERATU (USA),** 4, ch c Vice Regent—Ballade **B. Macnall**
15 **RAINIBIK,** 4, b c Bikala—Rains Came **J. L. Lagardere**
16 **SWEET SEATTLE (USA),** 4, b f Seattle Song—Riverdina **F. N. Groves**
17 **TUXEDO,** 4, b c Legend of France—Tavolara **P. Rossier**

THREE-YEAR-OLDS

18 **ACOIBONNISTE,** b c Zino—Radiante **P. Rossier**
19 **ALCHI (USA),** b f Alleged—Campechito **A. Paulson**
20 **ALI GAZIBA (USA),** b c Alydar—Aunt Carol **A. Paulson**
21 **ALLIAGE (USA),** b f Alleged—Professional Dance **Ecurie Skymarc**
22 **ALL MY HEART,** b f Sharpen Up—Red Comes Up **T. Wada**
23 **ASTANAX,** b c Persepolis—Artist's Proof **S. Niarchos**
24 **AVALENGO (USA),** b c L'Emigrant—Cedilla **G. A. Oldham**
25 **BAMBOLELLO,** b c Legend of France—Dunlora **P. Rossier**
26 **BELLA KALA,** b f Bikala—Bhaydana **J. L. Lagardere**
27 **BLUE HOTEL,** b c Procida—Belle d'Arabie **P. Rossier**
28 **BOLDNIKA,** ch f Nikos—Bold Note **J. L. Lagardere**
29 **BOLSENA (USA),** ch f Assert—Irena **Mme Oldham**
30 **CAMILIK,** b c Bikala—Camiriva **J. L. Lagardere**
31 **CAPRAROLA,** b f Bellypha—Olbia **Mme Oldham**
32 **CHATOUILLEUSE,** b f Kings Lake—Chalca **S. Niarchos**
33 **CIEL VIF (USA),** b c Fluorescent Light—New Hope **P. Rossier**
34 **CORSITA,** b f Top Ville—Antrona **Mme Oldham**
35 **CYDALIA (USA),** b f Cresta Rider—Slam Bid **Ecurie Skymarc**
36 **DJENANE (USA),** b f Jacklin Klugman—Bajdara **R. Wright**
37 **ELENITA,** b f Bellypha—Banderole **Mme Oldham**
38 **EVOCATRICE,** b f Persepolis—Northern Trick **S. Niarchos**
39 **GARIMPETRO (USA),** b f Mr Prospector—Far Flying **A. Paulson**
40 **GOLD QUEST,** b f Rainbow Quest—Gipsy Road **Ecurie Skymarc**
41 **GREAT BOY,** b c Bikala—Gairlove **J. L. Lagardere**
42 **GRINKOV (USA),** b c Procida—Melle Chanteuse **Mme Boutin**
43 **HAMI (USA),** b c Jeu de Paille—Spectacular Lady **A. Paulson**
44 **INTIMISTE (USA),** ch c Arctic Tern—Bubble Company **N. Incisa**
45 **KINETIC,** b c Bikala—Karmisyn **J. L. Lagardere**

MR F. BOUTIN—continued

46 **KING WHITE**, b c Ti King—White Alna **S. Franchini**
47 **LACKA**, b f Shareef Dancer—Moudiha **Mme Boutin**
48 **LADY PERSEE**, b f Persepolis—Lady Cornelia **J. L. Lagardere**
49 **LE STREGUE**, ch c Lyphard—Rose du Boele **S. Niarchos**
50 **LIGHT THE SKY**, b f Persepolis—Lighted Glory **Melle Goulandris**
51 **LINAMIX**, gr c Mendez—Lunadix **J. L. Lagardere**
52 **MACHIAVELLIAN (USA)**, b c Mr Prospector—Coup de Folie **S. Niarchos**
53 **MACKLA**, ch f Caerleon—Mariella **Mme Oldham**
54 **MAGICAL MYSTERY**, b f Procida—Mirea **Melle Goulandris**
55 **MAIS OUI (USA)**, b f Lyphard—Affirmatively **Mme Boutin**
56 **MEHTAR (USA)**, ch f Green Dancer—Goldenley **A. Paulson**
57 **MISS D'OUILLY**, b f Bikala—Miss Satin **J. L. Lagardere**
58 **MISS LEGEND**, ch f Legend of France—Miss Diver **J. L. Lagardere**
59 **MURAKALA**, b f Bikala—Muravera **J. L. Lagardere**
60 **MY CLAUDER**, b f Vaguley Noble—Buckles N'Bells **T. Wada**
61 **MY SPECIAL SONG (USA)**, b f Danzig—Tananarive **F. N. Groves**
62 **NOBLISSA (USA)**, b f Vaguely Noble—Sissy's Time **Ecurie Skymarc**
63 **OMBRAGEUX (USA)**, b c Super Concorde—Elk's Ellie **Mme Boutin**
64 **OZAL (USA)**, ch c Lyphard—L'Attrayante **A. Paulson**
65 **PALAVERA**, b f Bikala—Paulistana **J. L. Lagardere**
66 **PAMPHLETAIRE**, b c Pampabird—Elesbed **Mme Boutin**
67 **PANAJAR**, gr c Nadjar—Pachka **J. L. Lagardere**
68 **PINAFLORE**, b f Formidable—Pink Satin **J. L. Lagardere**
69 **PLEASANT RIVER (USA)**, b f Foolish Pleasure—Helga di Russia **Mme Brody**
70 **POLYPHASE**, b f Bikala—Polly's Harde **J. L. Lagardere**
71 **PRIOLO (USA)**, b c Sovereign Dancer—Primevere **Ecurie Skymarc**
72 **REINSTATE**, gr c Kaldoun—Reine Margie **J. L. Lagardere**
73 **RIVER RHYTHM (USA)**, b c Riverman—Moonlight Serenade **Mme Brody**
74 **ROBIN DES BOIS**, b c Nureyev—Rare Mint **S. Niarchos**
75 **ROYAL SMILE**, b f Akarad—Royal Charmer **P. Rossier**
76 **SALVEXPRESS**, gr f Siberian Express—Salve **J. L. Lagardere**
77 **SILVER BULLIT**, b c Procida—Firyal **S. Niarchos**
78 **SILVER SNOW**, b f Kenmare—Skouna **Ecurie Skymarc**
79 **SLEW BOYERA (USA)**, b f Seattle Slew—Boyera **A. Paulson**
80 **SLEW THE SLEWOR (USA)**, b c Slew O'Gold—Featherill **A. Paulson**
81 **SO DESIRABLE (USA)**, b f Seattle Song—Gallina **F. N. Groves**
82 **SOLEIL D'ARGENT (USA)**, b c L'Emigrant—Wield **Ecurie Skymarc**
83 **SOURCE DU CIEL**, ch f Ti King—Salvora **S. Niarchos**
84 **STORMED (USA)**, b f Storm Bird—Absentia **Mme Boutin**
85 **SULMONA (USA)**, b f Miswaki—Spadina **Mme Oldham**
86 **TARVISIO (USA)**, b c Northern Baby—Bold And Bright **G. A. Oldham**
87 **TICKETY**, b f Bikala—Tidy **J. L. Lagardere**
88 **TINY LITTLE (USA)**, b f Diesis—Little Fuzzy **A. Paulson**
89 **TOOTHING STONE**, b c Law Society—Rule Formi **S. Niarchos**
90 **TULSA TIME**, b c Ti King—Godille **S. Niarchos**
91 **TURGUT (USA)**, b c Niniski—Brorita **A. Paulson**
92 **VAGRANCY**, b c Bikala—Vadsa **J. L. Lagardere**
93 **VANYA**, b f Busted—Maresca **Mme Oldham**
94 **VIOLETERA (USA)**, b f Time For A Change—Ardenay **J. Hettinger**
95 **VITOLA**, ch f Sallust—Delmora **Mme Oldham**
96 **VUKOVAR**, b c Esprit du Nord—Margello **Mme Vukobrat**

TWO-YEAR-OLDS

97 B f Tate Gallery—Admit **T. Wada**
98 **AKILESH**, ch c 16/3 Esprit du Nord—All Grey **J. L. Lagardere**
99 **ALTADENA (USA)**, b f Lyphard—Lacovia **G. A. Oldham**
100 B f Timeless Moment—Anjelicco **P. Rossier**
101 **APRES MOI (USA)**, b c Filiberto—Moonlight Serenade **Mme Brody**
102 B c Gold Crest—Ask Me How **Ecurie Skymarc**
103 **AVELLANA**, b f Kaldoun—Avallaneda **R. Malezieux-Dehon**

MR F. BOUTIN—continued

104 **BADLISHAH**, ch c 8/4 Bikala—Belle Promesse **J. L. Lagardere**
105 **BARGYLIA**, ch f 10/4 Ti King—Bold Note **J. L. Lagardere**
106 B f Law Society—Bella Senora **S. Niarchos**
107 **BEOGRAD**, b c 24/3 Dunphy—Gizzeria **Mme Vukobrat**
108 **BHAYANTHUS**, b c 29/2 Antheus—Bhaydana **J. L. Lagardere**
109 **BORMIO**, b c Lichine—Olbia **P. Rossier**
110 **BOSNA**, ch f Cariellor—River Note **Mme Vukobrat**
111 **BUSHIDO**, b c Zino—Neptambre **E. Wiget**
112 **CAMAYAN**, b c 3/4 Nikos—Camiriva **J. L. Lagardere**
113 B f Seattle Song—Carnet Solaire **S. Niarchos**
114 B f Secreto—Carol Jane **Mme Boutin**
115 **CATAGOLD**, b c 13/2 Glint of Gold—Catacomb **J. L. Lagardere**
116 B f Miswaki—Central Figure **Ecurie Skymarc**
117 **CRI VERS ROME**, b c Pampabird—Sokemira **E. Wiget**
118 B f Baillamont—Dame Solitaire **S. Niarchos**
119 B c Foolish Pleasure—Duel At Dawn **W. Pennington**
120 B f Baillamont—Edellic **S. Niarchos**
121 B f Storm Bird—Encorelle **Mme Boutin**
122 **ENNEADER**, b c Sicyos—Dicterna **P. Rossier**
123 **EXIT TO NOWHERE (USA)**, b c Irish River—Coup de Folie **S. Niarchos**
124 B f Baillamont—Firyal **S. Niarchos**
125 **FRECCIA (IRE)**, b f Caerleon—Bold And Bright **G. A. Oldham**
126 **GEBAKLEIA**, b f Kenmare—Gebal **J. L. Legardere**
127 **GEMMOLOGIE**, b f 24/3 Crystal Glitters—Gipsy Road **Ecurie Skymarc**
128 **GIRANNA**, b f 15/4 Antheus—Gironde **Melle Goulandris**
129 **GOKOHOVA**, b f Hellios—Gemia **J. L. Lagardere**
130 B f Shadeed—Her Silver **Ecurie Skymarc**
131 **HONOR BRIGHT**, b c Baillamont—Nicolina **Mme Boutin**
132 **KALYKADIA**, b f River River—Karmiska **J. L. Lagardere**
133 B c Woodman—Korveya **S. Niarchos**
134 **KROUPA**, b f Cariellor—Spilinga **Mme Vukobrat**
135 **LEOCHASA**, b c Ti King—Radiante **P. Rossier**
136 **LETTYFANA (USA)**, b f 12/3 Fappiano—Letty's Pennat **J. L. Lagardere**
137 B f Time For A Change—Lightship **Mme Boutin**
138 **LIGHT THE MOON**, b f Baillamont—Lighted Glory **Melle Goulandris**
139 **LINGERIE**, b f Shirley Heights—Northern Trick **S. Niarchos**
140 **LIRICA (USA)**, b f 27/2 Blushing Groom—Liastra **Melle Goulandris**
141 B f River River—Lisguile **P. Rossier**
142 **LODYPHOS**, b c 28/1 Dunphy—Lady Cornelia **J. L. Lagardere**
143 **LOVE SHACK**, b f Persepolis—Enfant d'Amour **S. Niarchos**
144 B f Arctic Tern—Margie Belle **T. Wada**
145 **MEADOWSWEET (USA)**, b f Meadowlake—Silence Rules **Ecurie Skymarc**
146 **MENTOUHOTEP**, b c Sicyos—Marie de Vermand **P. Rossier**
147 **MYRAKALU**, gr c 6/4 Kaldoun—Muravera **J. L. Lagardere**
148 B f Sovereign Dancer—Mythographer **Mme Boutin**
149 B c Woodman—Nakterjal **S. Niarchos**
150 **NAVALEYA (USA)**, gr f 27/3 Grey Dawn II—Naval Light **J. L. Lagardere**
151 B c Alleged—Nettie Cometti **Mme Manning**
152 **NIKSIC**, ch c 8/5 Hellios—Nostimi **Mme Vukobrat**
153 B f Lord Avie—Normia **S. Niarchos**
154 B c Majestic Light—Northern Eternity **Mme Boutin**
155 **ORAISON DU SOIR**, b f River River—Belle d'Arabie **P. Rossier**
156 **ORNAGORA**, b f Espirt du Nord—Dame Modeste **Mme Vukobrat**
157 B f 11/2 Rainbow Quest—Pluvial **T. Wada**
158 **POLLY'S KAROS**, b c 7/4 Kenmare—Polly's Harde **J. L. Lagardere**
159 **POLYSWARTZ**, b c 16/4 Double Schwartz—Polifontaine **J. L. Lagardere**
160 **PRIERE DE ROSE**, b f Coquelin—Marie de France **P. Rossier**
161 **RASANDIQUEEN**, b f Bikala—Reine des Sables **J. L. Lagardere**
162 **REKHABA**, b f R B Chesne—Rain's Came **J. L. Lagardere**
163 **RIMAVAYR**, b c Vayrann—Reine Margie **J. L. Lagardere**

MR F. BOUTIN—continued

164 **RIOSO,** b c Procida—Revelry **P. Rossier**
165 B f Arctic Tern—Riverdance **Mme Boutin**
166 **ROBIN DES PINS (USA),** b c Nureyev—Rare Mint **S. Niarchos**
167 **ROMANCERO GITAN,** b c Baillamont—Dunlora **P. Rossier**
168 **ROSE HELEN (USA),** b f Lyphard—Why Me Lord **Mme Brody**
169 B c Private Account—Ruby Tuesday **Mme Boutin**
170 **SIDERANT,** ch c Kris—Secretive **T. Wada**
171 **SIKANDER,** b c 27/3 Legend of France—Satanca **J. L. Lagardere**
172 **SISSONIKYA (USA),** b f Vaguely Noble—Sissy's Time **J. L. Lagardere**
173 **SKITHIA,** b f Lichine—Skouna **Ecurie Skymarc**
174 B f Cresta Rider—Slam Bid **Ecurie Skymarc**
175 **STELLINA (IRE),** b f Caerleon—Mariella **G. A. Oldham**
176 B f Green Dancer—Susurrant **Mme Boutin**
177 B c Procida—Sweetly **S. Niarchos**
178 **TAKALAIA,** b f 11/4 Bikala—Tidy **J. L. Lagardere**
179 **TERMOSSOS,** b c 15/2 Hellios—Tracordia **J. L. Lagardere**
180 B c Gate Dancer—Toutski **W. Pennington**
181 **URACANO (IRE),** b c Top Ville—Antrona **G. A. Oldham**
182 **VERICA (USA),** b f Diesis—Verria **Melle Goulandris**
183 **VILLENA,** b f Zino—Barinia **G. A. Oldham**
184 **VIRANSEMIR,** b c Bikala—Vadsa **J. L. Lagardere**
185 **VIVE L'EMPEREUR,** b c Northern Fashion—Vive La Difference
186 **WALK ON TURF,** b f Bikala—Walk On Air **J. L. Lagardere**
187 **ZITO (USA),** b c Arctic Tern—Spadina **G. A. Oldham**
188 **ZULEKHA,** ch f 27/3 Siberian Express—Zulah **J. L. Lagardere**

77 MR S. A. BOWEN, Canterbury

Postal: **Plum Tree Cottage, 112 The Street, Adisham, Canterbury.**
Phone: **OFFICE (0304) 616446 HOME (0304) 841876**

1 **CASTLESIDE,** 4, b f Sonnen Gold—Floor Show **Dr K. W. J. Bowen**

Conditional: Ian Shoemark (9-10).

78 MISS L. J. BOWER, Alresford

Postal: **"Greendowns", Preshaw Road, Beauworth, Alresford, Hampshire, SO24 0PB.**
Phone: **(096279) 552**

1 **AUTUMN CRYSTAL,** 6, gr ro g Stetchworth (USA)—Autumn Lulu **Mr P. Boddy**
2 **AUTUMN ZULU,** 11, gr g Wishing Star—Autumn Lulu **Mr B. R. Edgeley**
3 **BALLERINA GIRL,** 5, b m Hays—Dance Away **Mrs J. B. Knott**
4 **BECTIVE BOY,** 8, ch g Wolverlife—Al Radegonde **Mr Tom Duke**
5 **CAMDEN BELLE,** 8, gr m Camden Town—Haut Lafite **Mr B. R. Edgeley**
6 **CORBALLY BESS,** 10, br m Saulingo—Pretty Janey **Mr P. Boddy**
7 **DONATIST,** 4, b c Dominion—Kaftan **Mr S. Jocham**
8 **DONOSTI,** 6, b g Rusticaro (FR)—Blue Flame (USA) **Lady R. Stuart-Wortley-Hunt**
9 **GEX (USA),** 7, b g Exceller (USA)—Gentle Thoughts (USA) **Mr D. Bass**
10 **MAN IN THE MOON,** 7, b g Mansingh (USA)—Lady Antonia **Mr D. Butt**
11 **MASTER COMEDY,** 6, b g Comedy Star (USA)—Romardia **Miss J. Wilkinson**
12 **PRINCE ROB,** 4, b c Robellino (USA)—Derrain **Mr W. J. Pfann**
13 **RAMAKIED,** 13, b g Deep Run—Tudor Gello **Miss Lindsay Bower**
14 **SMART SLAVE,** 7, b g Smartset—Slave Trade **Mr Anthony Merry**
15 **THE CHAUFFEUR,** 8, b g Crozier—I'm A Taxi **Mr S. Jocham**
16 **TINTO HILL,** 7, br g Mandrake Major—Chantabelle **Mr John Smith**
17 **TOEBOARD,** 4, b g Rushmere—Ile Voleur **Mr R. Page**
18 **WINGETTS,** 14, b br g Mugatpura—Shining Blade **Mr Tom Duke**
19 **WINNING DANCER,** 7, b g Dance In Time (CAN)—Ravenshead **Lady R. Stuart-Wortley-Hunt**
20 **XYLOPHONE,** 8, b m Tap On Wood—Cecily **Mr D. Butt**

MISS L. J. BOWER—continued

THREE-YEAR-OLDS

21 **DUKES HOPE,** b f Idiot's Delight—Furrette **Mr Tom Duke**
22 **MYSTICAL LADY,** ch f Sagaro—L'Angelo di Carlo **Mr Anthony Merry**

Other Owners: Mrs Pamela Merry, Mr D. S. Page, Mr R. Penn, Mr Tom Smith, Mr J. R. Stuart-Wortley-Hunt, Mr C. W. Ward.

Jockeys (NH): Ray Goldstein (w.a.), Tom Grantham (w.a.).

Conditional: S Hodgson (w.a.), D O'Sullivan (w.a.).

Amateurs: Mr C Burnet-Wells (9-7), Mr M Walsh (11-0).

79 MR M. T. BOWKER, Levens

Postal: **Rockfield Racing Stables, Main Street, Levens, Kendal, Cumbria.**
Phone: **(05395) 60533 OR 61074**

1 **ALL ACTION,** 4, b g Rapid River—Palace Tor **Mrs C. P. Townley and Mr M. Keegan**
2 **BICK BENEDICT,** 6, b h Try My Best (USA)—Western Star **Mr P. G. Bowker**
3 **BONFIRE,** 9, ch g Thatch (USA)—Dancing Fire **Mr A. Bowker**
4 **DESIGN WISE,** 6, b g Prince Bee—Wollow Princess **Mrs S. A. Clarke**
5 **RUPERT'S DAUGHTER,** 7, gr m Rupert Bear—Silent Swindler **Mrs R. Townley and Partners**
6 **STORMY AFFAIR,** 17, b br g Prevailing—Romancing
7 **TAXODIUM,** 10, b g Sharpen Up—Lucent **Mr M. T. Bowker**
8 **TIP-TAP,** 8, gr m Tachypous—Dashing Diana **Mr C. Thompson and Mr W. Clarke**

Jockeys (NH): M Bowker, C Grant (10-0).

Conditional: J J Gartland (9-7).

80 LADY ANN BOWLBY, Thirsk

Postal: **Sutton Stables, Felixkirk Road, Sutton, Thirsk, N. Yorkshire, YO7 2PU.**
Phone: **THIRSK (0845) 597331**

1 **CALMATA,** 9, br m Dubassoff (USA)—Raging Calm **Lady Ann Bowlby**
2 **NICKY'S BELLE,** 5, ch m Nicholas Bill—Raging Calm **Lady Ann Bowlby**
3 **RAGROYAL,** 7, ch m Royal Palace—Raging Calm **Lady Ann Bowlby**

Conditional: N Smith (9-7, w.a.).

Amateur: Mr David Kinsella.

81 MR S. R. BOWRING, Edwinstowe

Postal: **Fir Tree Farm, Edwinstowe, Mansfield, Nottinghamshire.**
Phone: **MANSFIELD (0623) 822451**

1 **ASCENMOOR,** 11, b g Ascendant—Honeymoor **Mr S. R. Bowring**
2 **ATTILA THE HONEY,** 5, b m Connaught—Kimbo **Mr S. J. McLaughlin**

MR S. R. BOWRING—continued

3 **CELTIC GERTRUDE,** 10, ch m Celtic Cone—Royal Gertrude **Mr M. Fenton**
4 **MAGNA TRAVAILLE,** 5, br h Mr Fluorocarbon—Bella Travaille **Mrs R. James**
5 **MIA SCINTILLA,** 4, ch f Blazing Saddles (AUS)—Melindra **Mr D. Grant**
6 **RUMBA ROYALE,** 6, b g Ela-Mana-Mou—Regal Way **Mr Mel Jackson**
7 **SERLBY CONNECTION,** 5, ch g Crofthall—Well Connected **Mrs Doreen Jackson**
8 **STAR COVER,** 4, b f Starch Reduced—Rosey Covert **Mr Ken Crow**
9 **TANG DYNASTY,** 5, b g Artaius (USA)—Favant **Mr Ken Crow**
10 **TARISTEAC,** 10, ch g Be My Guest (USA)—Sans Culotte (FR) **Mr S. R. Bowring**
11 **TENNENTS SUPER LAD,** 5, b g Red Sunset—Persian Wind **Mrs Zoe Grant**
12 **VENDREDI TREIZE,** 7, b br g Lucky Wednesday—Angel Row **Mr G. M. Sheppard**

THREE-YEAR-OLDS

13 **COCKED HAT GIRL,** ch f Ballacashtal (CAN)—Screen Goddess **Mr S. R. Bowring**
14 **GO GO BOY,** b c All Systems Go—Sandra's Sovereign **Mrs Irene Pryce**
15 **SANDMOOR DENIM,** b g Red Sunset—Holernzaye **Mr S. R. Bowring**
16 **TITAN,** ch c Domitor (USA)—Per Ardua **Mrs Irene Pryce**

Other Owners: Miss Claire Beardsley, Mr F. P. Dillon, Mr A. L. Hunt, Mrs Jenny Metcalfe, Mr A. H. Ripley, Mr M. Robins, Mrs C. West.

Jockeys (NH): S Mitchell (10-0), M F Murphy (10-0).

82 MRS S. C. BRADBURNE, Cupar

Postal: **Cunnoquhie Cottage, Ladybank, Cupar, Fife, KY7 7RV.**

1 **GENERAL CHANDOS,** 9, ch g Glen Quaich—Kitta **Lady Harris**
2 **INTERIM LIB,** 7, b g Lighter—Ballinew **Mr R. E. Henderson**
3 **OFF THE BRU,** 5, b g General Ironside—Amelieranne **Mr Timothy Hardie**
4 **ON THE HOOCH,** 5, ch m Over The River (FR)—Bit of Fashion **Mr J. G. Bradburne**
5 **PANTO LADY,** 4, br f Lepanto (GER)—Dusky Damsel **David Nimmo**
6 **SCATTERSHOT,** 5, ro g General Ironside—At Random **Mr J. G. Bradburne**
7 **SONSIE MO,** 5, b g Lighter—Charlotte Amalie **Mr Timothy Hardie**
8 **STEPDAUGHTER,** 4, b f Relkino—Great Dancer **Mrs Daphne Pease**
9 **WORK MATE (USA),** 11, ch g Secretariat (USA)—Wedding (USA) **Mrs J. A. M. Smith**

Amateurs: J G Bradburne (10-7),

83 MR J. M. BRADLEY, Chepstow

Postal: **Meads Farm, Sedbury Park, Chepstow, Gwent, Wales, NP6 7HN.**
Phone: **(0291) 622486**

1 **ACHNAHUAIGH,** 6, ch m Known Fact (USA)—Djimbaran Bay **Mr A. P. Stamp**
2 **AT LONG LAST,** 4, b f John French—Atlantica **Mr Stewart G. Martin**
3 **BAKER CONTRACT,** 5, ch g Roman Warrior—Toe Tapper **Mr J. H. Lee**
4 **BOXER REBELLION,** 4, ch f Royal Boxer—Rosefox **Miss E. Edwards**
5 **CAMDORE BOY,** 10, b g Anax—Paddy's Daughter **Mr F. Pritchard**
6 **CELTIC CROW,** 4, ch c Import—Classy Colleen **Mr M. Donovan**
7 **GRAND PARTY,** 5, ch m Revlow—Grand Melody **Mr J. M. Bradley**
8 **GUILTY SPARKLE,** 5, br m Roc Imp—Mayo Melody **Mr E. A. Hayward**
9 **HAYLEY'S LASS,** 4, b f Royal Boxer—Misty Glen **Mrs R. Bradley**
10 **HOME COMMAND,** 10, ch g Home Guard (USA)—Fleurie **Mr Stewart G. Martin**
11 **HO MI CHINH,** 8, ch g Homing—Fiordiligi **Mrs R. Bradley**
12 **INDIAN STREAM,** 6, b m Royal Boxer—Wesley Boat **Mr G. Lucas**
13 **JAGAN SOMBONG,** 7, b g Thatch (USA)—Welsh Pride **Mr Gwilym Fry**
14 **KATHIES CHOICE,** 7, b m Bribe—Montana Queen **Mr J. A. Dunkerton**

MR J. M. BRADLEY—continued

15 **KUMZAR,** 6, br m Hotfoot—Welsh Jane **Mr J. M. Bradley**
16 **LATERAL,** 6, b g Tina's Pet—Wounded Knee **Mr R. Miles**
17 **LIHBAB,** 7, ch g Ballad Rock—Sovereign Bloom **Mrs P. A. Woodfield**
18 **LITTLE HAWTHORNS,** 5, b g Dawn Johnny (USA)—Jingle **Mr J. M. Bradley**
19 **LORD WINDERMERE,** 5, b g Taufan (USA)—Repercussion **Mr R. J. Williams**
20 **MARGAM PARK,** 9, b g Gold Mark—Sovereign Venture **Mrs B. R. Murphy**
21 **MISS MOODY,** 4, ch f Jalmood (USA)—Ice Galaxie (USA) **Mrs C. Day**
22 **MISS RANOVA,** 5, ch m Giacometti—Miss Casanova **Mr John Fitzgerald**
23 **MISTY LEA,** 5, b g Royal Boxer—Misty Glen **Mr L. J. Oxenham**
24 **MY BROTHER JAKE,** 4, b c My Dad Tom (USA)—Silken Sheba **MRH Thoroughbred Racing Ltd**
25 **NATIVE ROSE,** 6, ch m Gone Native—One To Rose **Mr K. Davies**
26 **NUNS JEWEL,** 4, ch f Julio Mariner—Nunswalk **Mr R. H. Williams**
27 **NUNS LITTLE ONE,** 5, ch m Celtic Cone—Nunswalk **Mrs C. Williams**
28 **OLDE CYDER,** 5, b g Royal Boxer—Cider Drinker **Mr J. M. Bradley**
29 **OPAL SURPRISE,** 4, b f Royal Boxer—Opal Lady **Mr S. A. Mailes**
30 **PALACE GARDENS,** 6, b g Royal Boxer—Privy Court **Mr J. Smith**
31 **PERSIAN DYNASTY,** 6, br h Persian Bold—Parez **Mr E. A. Hayward**
32 **RIVER WARRIOR,** 12, b g Forlorn River—Wounded Knee **Mr J. M. Bradley**
33 **ROYAL BEAR,** 8, gr g Rupert Bear—Queens Leap **Mr E. A. Monaghan**
34 **ROYAL MARENGO,** 7, b h Royal Boxer—Lady Zeta **Mr P. M. Wall**
35 **SABRE LONG,** 4, ch c Young Man (FR)—Honey Palm **Mr David Gillespie**
36 **SEASONED EMBER,** 9, ch m Royal Smoke—Spring Vision **Mr R. J. Nelmes**
37 **SILVER AGE (USA),** 4, b c Silver Hawk (USA)—Our Paige (USA) **Mrs S. J. Bird**
38 **SMART MART,** 11, ch g Jimmy Reppin—Fochetta **Mrs L. Spuffard**
39 **SOLAR BREEZE,** 4, b f Tom Noddy—Space Miss **Mr J. Smith**
40 **STAR CITY,** 6, b m Royal Boxer—Staryllis Girl **Mr E. A. Hayward**
41 **STARDUST ROC,** 7, br h Roc Imp—Mayo Melody **Mr E. A. Hayward**
42 **STELLA ALPINA,** 8, ch m Gone Native—Cwm Rhondda **Mr E. M. Vitalini**
43 **SUSAN'S REEF,** 5, b g Main Reef—Susan's Way **Mr Stewart G. Martin**
44 **YANGTSE-KIANG,** 10, gr ro g Rapid River—Au Pair **Mr Gwilym Fry**
45 **YUAN PRINCESS,** 5, ch m Tender King—Skyey **Mr D. Roderick**

THREE-YEAR-OLDS

46 **AGE OF ROMANCE,** b f Chukaroo—Eastern Romance **Mrs C. Day**
47 **BALLA LAD,** b c Ballacashtal (CAN)—Limerick Lace **Mr G. W. Gething**
48 **BEACHLEY,** ch f Brotherly (USA)—Nick Nick **Mrs C. Day**
49 **HANDANLEE,** ro f Battle Hymn—Wedding Guest **Mr J. H. Lee**
50 **OH SO BOLD,** ch g Royal Boxer—Staryllis Girl **Mr E. A. Hayward**
51 **OPAL'S TENSPOT,** b g Royal Boxer—Opal Lady **Mr S. A. Mailes**
52 **SAKURA DANCER,** ch f Viking (USA)—Serenesse **Mr Clifton Hunt**

Other Owners: Mr T. D. Curr, Mr K. E. Deen, Mrs Y. Gillespie, Miss Diane Hill, Mr D. Stone, Mr R. Worsfold.

Jockey (Flat): J Williams.

Jockey (NH): G Davies (10-0).

Conditional: D Williams (9-7).

84 MR N. BRADLEY, Wetherby

Postal: **38 Second Avenue, Wetherby, West Yorkshire.**
Phone: **OFFICE (0937) 62151 HOME (0937) 63142**

1 **BARLEY MOW,** 4, b g Wolverlife—Ellette **Print and Design Limited (Pad Ltd)**
2 **BMH CLASSIC STYLE,** 6, br g Boreen (FR)—Jamestown Girl **BMH Textiles International**

MR N. BRADLEY—continued

3 **CHARLES DEVON LAD,** 5, br h Fitzwilliam (USA)—Devon Maid **Mr Roy Bowes**
4 **COVER WITH HARTS,** 5, b g Indian King (USA)—Roscrea **Hart & Co Insurance Brokers Ltd**
5 **HEART OF YORKSHIRE,** 7, ch g Laurence O—Royal Liatris **Hart & Co Insurance Brokers Ltd**
6 **LEISURETIME SMILE,** 9, b g Arapaho—Darling Smile **Mr W. Newell**
7 **MANHATTAN RIVER,** 4, ch g Gorytus (USA)—East River (FR) **Mr Martin Hirst**
8 4, B g Belfalas—Ring Twice
9 **ROGGAN HALL,** 4, br f Balidar—Star of The Arctic
10 **ROONEY,** 4, b g Geln Quaich—Dashing Bird **Mr M. Kelly**
11 **SOMBRERO GOLD,** 6, ch g Miami Springs—Alleyn **Mr Stanley Warr**
12 **STARJESTIC,** 12, b g Majestic Streak—Star Sheba **Mr M. H. Mitchell**
13 **TINKOSUMTIN,** 4, b f Taufan (USA)—Stapelea (FR)

Other Owners: Mr Tony Mulrooney.

Jockey (NH): G Bradley (10-7, w.a.).

Conditional: Mark Drughan (9-7).

85 MR M. F. BRADSTOCK, Newbury

Postal: **Mabberleys, East Garston, Newbury, Berkshire.**
Phone: **(048839) 8801**

1 **BRAIDA BOY,** 4, b g Kampala—Braida (FR) **Mark Bradstock**
2 **DEEP IMPRESSION,** 11, b g Deep Run—Harmonet **Mr N. G. Mills**
3 **EASTER MOY,** 6, ch g Buckskin (FR)—Cambrian Explorer **Mrs D. Bradstock**
4 **EQUALLY BETTER,** 8, ch g Le Moss—Merette **Racegoers Club Owners Group**
5 **MEDIANE (USA),** 5, b g Dust Commander (USA)—Mlle Quille (USA) **Mr Clive Taylor**
6 **MONTAGNARD,** 6, b g Strong Gale—Louisa Stuart (FR) **Mr N. A. Gill**
7 **PIPER'S SON,** 4, b g Sagaro—Lovely Laura **Mr N. G. Mills**
8 **RUN AGAIN,** 5, br g Runnett—Bee Hawk **Mrs B. Barney**
9 **SCATTERBUCK,** 9, br g Kambalda—Dusky Glory **Mr Clive Taylor**
10 **STILL WATERS,** 6, b g Deep Run—Auburn **E. C. T. Mobile Radio Ltd**
11 **STONE DRUM (USA),** 4, ch c The Minstrel (CAN)—Mists of Time (USA) **Mr Andrew Cohen**
12 **STROKESTOWN LAD,** 6, b g Tanfirion—Misippus **Mr Steve Lee**
13 **TEN IN HAND,** 10, b br g Raise You Ten—Sandrina **Mr J. M. S. Ciechanowski**
14 **WAVE,** 7, br h Mississippi—Wink **Mrs Susan Lee**
15 **WILLIAMSFIELD,** 5, gr g Kafu—Royal Bundle **Mr E. P. K. Weatherall**
16 **ZEPPELIN (GER),** 7, b br g Limbo (GER)—Zandvoort **Mr S. G. Lee**

Other Owners: Mr C. F. Forty, Mrs M. Payne.

Jockey (Flat): B Rouse (8-0, w.a.).

Jockeys (NH): K Mooney (10-0), J White (10-0).

Conditional: M Fitzgerald (9-7).

86 MRS S. A. BRAMALL, Thirsk

Postal: **Burtree House, Hutton Sessay, Thirsk, North Yorkshire.**
Phone: **THIRSK (0845) 401333**

1 **ACROSS THE LAKE,** 6, b g Over The River (FR)—Golden Highway **Mrs S. A. Bramall**
2 4, B f Kemal (FR)—Another Space **Mrs S. A. Bramall**
3 **BREAK EVEN,** 6, b g Decent Fellow—Zepps **Mrs S. A. Bramall**
4 **CASTLEVENNON,** 9, b m Kemal (FR)—Weaver's Fool **Mrs S. A. Bramall**
5 **DARK RECORD,** 7, br g Black Minstrel—Bonny Prepack **Mrs S. A. Bramall**
6 **GENERAL ADVANCE,** 10, b g Push On—En Gal **Mrs S. A. Bramall**
7 **JAAEZ,** 6, b g Ela-Mana-Mou—Almagest **Mrs S. A. Bramall**
8 **KING OF STEEL,** 4, b g Kemal (FR)—Black Spangle **Johnson Structures**
9 4, Ch g Milford—Miss Fanackapan **Mrs S. A. Bramall**
10 **MONKEY HUNTER,** 7, b g Monksfield—Miss Hunter **Mrs S. A. Bramall**
11 **NOW AND THEN,** 5, ch g Over The River (FR)—Lady Rois **Mr I. R. A. Swift**
12 **PEARL MERCHANT,** 9, gr g Precipice Wood—Pearlyric **Mrs S. A. Bramall**
13 4, B g Rymer—Pearlyric **Mrs S. A. Bramall**
14 **RALLYE STRIPE,** 6, gr g Buckskin (FR)—Petit Bleu **Mrs S. A. Bramall**
15 4, Br g Glen Quaich—Ramla Bay **Mrs S. A. Bramall**
16 **ROSSVILLE,** 5, ch g Kemal (FR)—Golden Ingot **Mrs S. A. Bramall**
17 **SHILGROVE PLACE,** 8, ch g Le Bavard (FR)—Petmon **Mrs S. A. Bramall**
18 **THE RIGHT GUY,** 5, ch g Regular Guy—Vulgan's Law **Mr S. C. Rawson**
19 5, B m Le Moss—The Wren's Nest **Mrs S. A. Bramall**
20 **WHAT ABOUT ME,** 7, ch g Condorcet (FR)—Aurora Lady **Mrs Sue Waite**

THREE-YEAR-OLDS

21 B g Kemal (FR)—Agreement **Mrs S. A. Bramall**
22 B g Le Moss—Bavardmore **Mrs S. A. Bramall**
23 Br g Roselier (FR)—Kilbride Madam **Mrs S. A. Bramall**
24 B g Strong Gale—Richest **Mrs S. A. Bramall**
25 **VELEDA II (FR),** ch g Olmeto—Herbe Fine (FR) **Mrs S. A. Bramall**
26 **VIRBAZAR (FR),** b g Grandchant (FR)—Ortie II (FR) **Mrs S. A. Bramall**

Other Owners: Miss Anna Bramall, Mr Brian Sunderland.

Conditional: Joe O'Gorman (9-11).

Amateur: Noel Wilson (10-2).

87 MR K. M. BRASSEY, Upper Lambourn

Postal: **The Old Malt House, Upper Lambourn, Newbury, Berkshire, RG16 7RG.**
Phone: **LAMBOURN (0488) 71508 FAX (0488) 73122**

1 **AMIGO MENOR,** 4, ch c Whistling Deer—Chive **Mr Frank Glennon**
2 **BEAUCADEAU,** 4, b g Alzao (USA)—Pretty Gift **Mr Peter Stroud**
3 **BUESTA,** 4, b f Bustino—Quest **Witham Land & Leisure Services Ltd**
4 **CREEFLEUR,** 4, b f Creetown—Florence Mary **A. D. A. Sutherland and M. Graham**
5 **FAYNAZ,** 4, ch c Tumble Wind (USA)—Ceduna (FR) **N. Y. Aboobaker and A. Sangster Jnr**
6 **FEARSOME,** 4, gr g Formidable (USA)—Seriema **Unicorn Bloodstock and Racing Ltd**
7 **GUNBOAT,** 4, ch g Relaunch (USA)—Ferjima's Gem (USA) **Mr B. R. H. Burrough**
8 **PLAUSIBLE,** 5, b h Neltino—False Evidence **Unicorn Bloodstock and Racing Ltd**
9 **SAXON COURT,** 4, b g Mummy's Game—Blickling **J. P. Sampson**
10 **ZEBOIM,** 4, ch g Stanford—Solarina **D. J. Muir**

MR K. M. BRASSEY—continued

THREE-YEAR-OLDS

11 **ALSHEEN,** br f Alzao (USA)—Miss Olympus **A. Morton**
12 **CHANNOR,** b f Norwick (USA)—Channing Girl **Unicorn Bloodstock & Racing Ltd**
13 **CRIBELLA (USA),** b f Robellino (USA)—Crinoline **Witham Land & Leisure Services Ltd**
14 **C SHARP,** ch g Song—Simply Jane **Mrs N. Myers and Mrs M. Garrard**
15 **FARFELU,** b c Lyphard's Special (USA)—Spring Azure **J. O'Mulloy and Partners**
16 **GO BOY GO,** b g All Systems Go—Chubby Ears **D. J. Muir**
17 **HARLEQUIN LAD (USA),** ch c Erins Isle—Doha (FR) **Unicorn Bloodstock and Racing Ltd**
18 **MUESTA,** b f Bustino—Misguided **Witham Land & Leisure Services Ltd**
19 **PLAYFUL POET,** ch g The Noble Player (USA)—Phamond **P. Bourke and Partners**
20 **PROUD JAK,** gr c Goldhills Pride—Armalou **T. Rowley**
21 **SWEENY TODD,** b c Mansingh (USA)—La Brigitte **I. D. Muir**
22 **THE SWAMP FOX,** b c Mummy's Pet—River Maiden (FR) **Mrs N. Myers and Mrs M. Garrard**

TWO-YEAR-OLDS

23 **ABSENT FOREVER,** gr g 24/4 Absalom—Strawberry Fields (Song) **A. D. A. Sutherland**
24 **ALLEGRO CON BRIO,** b c 26/4 Alleging (USA)—Diami (Swing Easy (USA)) **Mrs Nicole Myers**
25 **CHIARINA,** b f 1/2 Chief Singer—Karine (Habitat) **Witham Land & Leisure Services Ltd**
26 **DANDY KIM (IRE),** b c 21/4 Mazaad—Papoosette (Raise You Ten) **Mrs Nicole Myers**
27 **DEDA,** b f 8/4 Electric—Deed (Derring-Do) **Witham Land & Leisure Services Ltd**
28 **DOMINO DANCING,** bl c 16/3 Lidhame—Atlantic Air (Air Trooper) **Mrs S. Myers and Mr M. Myers**
29 **FIRAGA (IRE),** gr f 8/3 Horage—Fire-Screen (Roan Rocket) **Witham Land & Leisure Services Ltd**
30 **FREEZING (IRE),** gr f 29/2 Siberian Express—Field Day (Northfields (USA)) **A. Mutawa**
31 **HELLO MY DARLING (IRE),** b c 18/4 Law Society (USA)—
Helaplane (USA) (Super Concorde (USA)) **Fayzad Thoroughbreds and Partners**
32 **INKALA,** b f 7/2 Kalaglow—Intoxication (Great Nephew) **Witham Land & Leisure Services Ltd**
33 **LIB'S PET,** b f 22/4 Tina's Pet—Miss Maud (Tennyson (FR)) **Mrs Libby Quayle**
34 **MARYNETTA (IRE),** b f 24/3 Runnett—Mary Mullen (Lorenzaccio) **Witham Land & Leisure Services Ltd**
35 **NAUGHTY REBEL,** b c 5/5 Swinging Rebel—Halma (Hallez (FR)) **Mr Dure**
36 **NETTINA (IRE),** b f 6/3 Runnett—Inner Pearl (Gulf Pearl) **Mrs Libby Quayle**
37 **NOMICA,** b f 9/4 Nomination—Majica (Morston (FR)) **Witham Land & Leisure Services Ltd**
38 **PET SHOP BOY,** gr c 21/4 Petong—Moben (Counsel) **Mrs Nicole Myers**
39 B g 22/4 Fayruz—Pink Fondant (Northfields (USA))
40 B c 23/3 Sportin' Life (USA)—Pleased Miss (USA) (What A Pleasure (USA)) **Mrs B. S. Facchino**
41 B c 25/2 Kafu—Rabuba (Connaught) **D. J. Muir**
42 Ch c 8/5 Whistling Deer—Royal Performance (Klairon)
43 B c 3/3 Prince Tenderfoot—Sandford Lass (Sandford Lad) **Malthouse Racing Club**
44 **SIPOURA,** ch f 17/3 Nishapour (FR)—Silver Form (Formidable (USA)) **Witham Land & Leisure Services Ltd**
45 B c 27/4 Kafu—Taotl (Yellow God) **Malthouse Racing Club**
46 **TRIBELLA,** gr f 3/5 Bellypha—Triple Bar (Jimmy Reppin) **Witham Land & Leisure Services Ltd**

Other Owners: Mrs A. S. Brassey, K. M. Brassey, Change Wear Furniture Ltd, J. Collenette, Mr M. T. O'Brien, Mr T. O'Brien, L. Pickett, Mrs J. Verity.

Apprentice: Kim McDonnell (7-0).

88 MR C. V. BRAVERY, Polegate

Postal: **Jevington Place, Jevington, East Sussex, BN26 5QB.**
Phone: **(03212) 3662**

1 **IRISH DEVIL,** 5, b g Garryowen—Moygara **Mr C. V. Bravery**
2 **LARKAWAY,** 5, b m Furry Glen—The White Lark **Mr C. V. Bravery**
3 **MISTER HAMMY,** 10, b g Dynastic—Forthcoming **Mr C. V. Bravery**
4 **MONJIL,** 9, b g Wolverlife—Priory Miss **Mr C. V. Bravery**
5 **NOBLE FLYER,** 10, ch g Pry—Osbertstown Mill **Mr C. V. Bravery**
6 **RING OUZEL,** 4, ch f Deep Run—Judy Cullen **Mr C. V. Bravery**
7 **ROSTREAMER,** 7, b g Paddy's Stream—Tarqogan's Rose **Miss D. Forsyth**

MR C. V. BRAVERY—continued

8 **ROYAL FLAMINGO,** 4, gr f Deep Run—Crown Bird **Mr C. V. Bravery**
9 **ROYAL PIRANA,** 4, ch f Royal Match—Pirana **Mr C. V. Bravery**
10 **THATS IRISH,** 5, br m Furry Glen—Kilbricken Money **Mr C. V. Bravery**
11 **WOOD BY WOOD,** 12, b g Precipice Wood—Elsea Wood **Mr C. V. Bravery**

THREE-YEAR-OLDS

12 B f Liberated—Dawn Cloud **Miss D. Forsyth**
13 B g Dynastic—Forthcoming **Mr C. V. Bravery**
14 **HIGHLAND BRAVE,** b g Crofter (USA)—Calling Bird **Mr C. V. Bravery**
15 **IRISH EMERALD,** b c Taufan (USA)—Gaelic Jewel **Mr C. V. Bravery**
16 **PUTTINGONTHESTYLE,** ch g Enchantment—Straightaway Style **Mr C. V. Bravery**
17 B g The Parson—Streamon **Mr C. V. Bravery**
18 B f Sunyboy—Wings Ground **Mr C. V. Bravery**

Jockeys (NH): H Davies (w.a.), T Grantham (w.a.).

Lady Rider: Miss A Newton-Smith (9-0).

89 MR R. G. BRAZINGTON, Redmarley

Postal: **Chapel Farm, Redmarley, Gloucestershire, GL19 3JF.**
Phone: **(045284) 384**

1 **AIOLI,** 4, b f Tyrnavos—Coco de Mer **Mr M. Davies**
2 **ASSUMTION,** 7, b m Jimsun—Fullstop **Mrs Christine Davies**
3 **EJREE,** 5, b h Runnett—Carntino **Mr P. J. Duffy**
4 **JIMBALOU,** 7, b g Jimsun—Midnight Pansy **Mr M. Davies**
5 **JIMSINTIME,** 9, b g Jimsun—Midnight Pansy **Mr M. Davies**
6 **MARINERS PET,** 4, b f Julio Mariner—Fullstop **Mr R. G. Brazington**
7 **MARINERS SECRET,** 4, b f Julio Mariner—Midnight Pansy **Mr R. G. Brazington**
8 **SPANISH STREAK,** 13, b g Blue Streak—Native Senorita **Mr Michael Ewbank**
9 **SPARRING,** 5, b m Sagaro—Parabems **Mr B. Owen**
10 **SQUIRE JIM,** 6, b g Jimsun—Squiffy **The Plough Racing Team**
11 **SWINGING MOLLY,** 6, br m Swing Easy (USA)—Molly Cockell **Mr B. Owen**
12 **TAXI LAD,** 6, ch g Dublin Taxi—Midnight Pansy **Mrs Christine Davies**

TWO-YEAR-OLDS

13 Ch f Julio Mariner—Fullstop (Salvo) **Mr R. G. Brazington**
14 Br c Julio Mariner—Ionian Isle (FR) (Jim French (USA)) **Mr R. G. Brazington**
15 B f Julio Mariner—Midnight Lily (Deadly Nightshade) **Mr R. G. Brazington**
16 B c Julio Mariner—Midnight Pansy (Deadly Nightshade) **Mr R. G. Brazington**

Jockey (NH): R Beggan (10-0, w.a.).

90 MR O. BRENNAN, Newark

Postal: **Park Leys, Kelham, Newark, Nottinghamshire, NG23 5RX.**
Phone: **CAUNTON (063 686) 332**

1 **ARTAIUS STAR,** 6, b g Artaius (USA)—Godwyn **Bechers Brook Racing Club**
2 **BALLY SHINE,** 9, ch g Shiny Tenth—Sunny Maid **Mrs M. E. Hounsfield**
3 **BETTY'S GIRL,** 10, b m Menelek—Betty's Money **Mr O. Brennan**
4 **CAMBRIDGE GRADUATE,** 6, ch g Sunotra—Sparkation
5 **CORMEEN CROSS,** 6, ch g Boreen Beag—Shenton Park **Mrs John E. Todd**
6 **GREYSBY,** 8, gr g General Ironside—Kiskadee **Mr R. Marriott**
7 **GUTE NACHT,** 7, ch g Laurence O—Cherry Branch **Mr T. F. Winterton**
8 **IDOL KNIGHT,** 9, b g Tin God—Just Musk **Mrs M. E. Hounsfield**
9 **INDIAN,** 10, ch g Great Nephew—Ardneasken **Mr T. W. R. Bayley**

MR O. BRENNAN—continued

10 **KILCLOONEY FORREST,** 8, b g King's Equity—Carrig-An-Neady **Mr F. Starr**
11 **KINGBIRD,** 6, gr g Neltino—Panda's Gambol **Mr O. Brennan**
12 **KOURON,** 6, b m Pauper—Little Chance **Mr P. Mina**
13 **LOCHERRE,** 6, gr g Lochnager—Chemin de Guerre **Mr G. Chatterton**
14 **PADDYS OYSTER,** 7, b g Tanfirion—Queen's Hussar **Mr O. Brennan**
15 **SAGART AROON,** 10, b g The Parson—Mountain Bell **Mr J. R. Troy**
16 **SAUNTERSON,** 5, b g Saunter—Rosepic **Mr R. Chandler**
17 **SHERWOOD GUNNER,** 8, ch g Gunner B—Wheel Grace **Mr G. Holden**
18 **SKEGBY,** 16, br g Klairon—Leading Breeze **Mr O. Brennan**
19 **STELBY,** 6, ch h Stetchworth (USA)—Little Trilby **Mr Victor Sassie**
20 **THREEOUTOFFOUR,** 5, b g Milford—Smiling **Miss Cindy Brennan**
21 **TUXFORD,** 10, b g Crozier—Dairyguard **Miss Claire Beardsley**
22 **VULRORY'S CLOWN,** 12, b g Idiot's Delight—Vulrory **Mr T. W. R. Bayley**
23 **WHAT IF,** 6, ch m Nicholas Bill—Starproof **Mr O. Brennan**

Other Owners: Mr M. A. Cutts, Havenwood Con'S Ltd, Mr N. R. Starkey, Mr S. Webster, Mr A. J. Winterton.

Jockey (Flat): M J Brennan (8-10).

Jockey (NH): M J Brennan (9-7).

Lady Rider: Miss H Brennan (9-7).

91 MR R. BREWIS, Belford

Postal: **Chester Hill, Belford, Northumberland, NE70 7EF.**
Phone: **(06683) 239**

1 **BLUFF KNOLL,** 7, b g New Brig—Tacitina **Mr R. Brewis**
2 **CANDY CONE,** 10, b g New Brig—Boundary Tale **Mrs R. Brewis**
3 **COCKLEY BRIG,** 13, b g New Brig—Tacitina **Mr R. Brewis**
4 **CORBY CROWN,** 5, br m Royal Fountain—Carney **Mr R. Brewis**
5 **KIMBERLEY ROSE,** 7, b m Monksfield—Fort Rose **Miss R. G. Brewis**
6 **LETRIC,** 9, ch g King Sitric—Scarlet Letch **Mr R. Brewis**
7 **STAG HUNTER,** 6, b g Royal Fountain—Scarlet Letch **Mr R. Brewis**

Jockey (NH): G Harker.

Amateur: Mr A W Robson.

92 MR J. J. BRIDGER, Liphook

Postal: **Upper Hatch Farm, Liphook, Hampshire, GU30 7EL.**
Phone: **(0428) 722528**

1 **AMRULLAH,** 10, br g High Top—Ravenshead **Mr Terry Thorn**
2 **CHURCH STAR,** 6, b m Cajun—Lady of Rathleek **Mr J. J. Bridger**
3 **GENUINE GIFT (CAN),** 5, ch h Blushing Groom (FR)—Barbs Gold (USA) **Mr J. J. Bridger**
4 **GREY TARQUIN,** 18, gr g Tarqogan—Tinker Belle III **Mr J. J. Bridger**
5 **HOT LASS,** 4, ch f Class Distinction—Hot Tramp **Mr J. J. Bridger**
6 **KATIE SCARLETT,** 4, b f Lochnager—Final Request **Mrs M. Bryce-Smith**
7 **MALYA MAL,** 11, gr g Precipice Wood—Replete **Mr J. J. Bridger**
8 **PHILS FRIEND,** 4, ch g Sunley Builds—Our Denise **Mrs M. E. Philpot**
9 **RATION OF PASSION,** 5, b m Camden Town—Bellagold **Mr N. Bryce-Smith**
10 **RED FESCUE,** 8, gr g Warpath—Jasmin **Mr J. W. Plaistowe**
11 **STAMPY,** 9, ch g Sallust—Caer-Gai **Mrs J. M. Stamp**
12 **THORNPUSS,** 4, b f Tachypous—Kiki Mouse **Mr J. J. Bridger**

MR J. J. BRIDGER—continued

THREE-YEAR-OLDS

13 **HOT HOPE,** b f Blazing Saddles (AUS)—Return Home **Mr J. J. Bridger**
14 **THORNZEE,** gr f Belfort (FR)—Trackally **Mr Terry Thorn**
15 **ZHIVAGO'S PASSION,** gr f Another Realm—Crystal Gael **Mr N. Bryce-Smith**

TWO-YEAR-OLDS

16 Gr f 13/2 Petong—Speed The Plough **Mr N. Bryce-Smith**

Other Owners: Mr C. G. Friend, Mrs Barbara McGrath.

Apprentice: Rachel Bridger (7-12).

Conditional: Rachel Bridger (7-12).

93 MR K. S. BRIDGWATER, Lapworth

Postal: **Bear House Farm, Old Warwick Road, Lapworth, Warwickshire.**
Phone: **LAPWORTH 2895**

1 **BRACKAGH RUN,** 6, ch m Deep Run—Sky Green **Mrs C. Kelly**
2 **CHESTER TERRACE,** 6, ch g Crofter (USA)—Persian Mourne **Mrs Thelma Brookhouse**
3 **DEADLY GOING,** 12, b g King Log—Lady Alexandra **Mrs Mary Bridgwater**
4 **DISCOVER GOLD,** 9, br g Junius (USA)—More The Perrier **Ashley Harrison & Co Ltd (Fin Consits)**
5 **EMSLEYS CHOICE,** 4, ch g Windjammer (USA)—Derrygold **Mrs P. Joynes**
6 **FIRST ERROR,** 6, ch g Creetown—Greeana **Mr K. W. Bradley**
7 **GALLEY SONG,** 8, ch m True Song—Galley Light **Mr K. P. Dunne**
8 **GALLOPADE,** 7, ch g True Song—Galley Light **Mr T. Frost**
9 **KARNATAK,** 9, b g Artaius (USA)—Karera **Mrs P. Joynes**
10 **KEEL (GER),** 6, b h Horst-Herbert—Kadmeia (GER) **Mrs M. Christodoulou**
11 **KING OF THE CLOUDS,** 5, b g Sonnen Gold—Misfired **Mrs P. Joynes**
12 **PEAK DISTRICT,** 4, b c Beldale Flutter (USA)—Grand Teton **J. G. J. Racing**
13 **REMWOOD GIRL,** 4, b f Remainder Man—Aliwood Girl **Mr A. F. Laws**
14 **ROMANTIC MELODY,** 4, ch f Battle Hymn—Love Patrol **Mrs Janet Hicken**
15 **ROUGH SAILING,** 6, ch g True Song—Galley Light **Mr I. S. Phipps**
16 **RUSTY IRON,** 8, gr m General Ironside—Wow **Mrs C. Kelly**
17 **STRADEY CASTLE,** 4, gr f Absalom—Comedy Miss **Mr V. A. Harrison**
18 **TIPTONIAN,** 11, gr g Royalty—Pretty Fast **Mr K. Bedworth**
19 **WHISTLING EDGE,** 7, ch m Whistling Deer—Seaville **Mrs P. Joynes**
20 **WINNIE THE WITCH,** 6, b m Leading Man—Star Ruler **Paddocks Thoroughbred Racing Ltd**

THREE-YEAR-OLDS

21 **CAPTAIN CHROME,** b c Welsh Captain—Chrome Mag **Mr A. F. Laws**
22 **RECORD EDGE,** ch g Roman Warrior—Record Red **Mrs P. Joynes**
23 **TRICIA CIP,** ch f Little Wolf—Spring Secret (USA) **Mr A. F. Laws**
24 **VICTORIA'S DELIGHT,** br f Idiot's Delight—Hasty Dawn **Mrs P. Joynes**

TWO-YEAR-OLDS

25 B f 22/3 Kind of Hush—Primrose Way (Young Generation) **Mrs Mary Bridgwater**

Other Owners: Mrs P. A. Allsopp, Miss E. E. Hill, Mr Jerry Wright.

Jockey (Flat): P Darcy (7-12, w.a.).

Jockeys (NH): P Dever, C Llewellyn, A Webb (w.a.).

Apprentices: D Bithell (7-5), M Smith (7-10).

94 MR A. H. BRISBOURNE, Shrewsbury

Postal: **Broomhill Farm, Nesscliffe, Shrewsbury, Shropshire, SY4 1AX.**
Phone: **NESSCLIFFE (074 381) HOME 360 STABLES 536**

1 **PAM'S PRIDE,** 5, b m Bali Dancer—Ensign's Last **Mr A. H. Brisbourne**
2 **ROUSER ROYALE,** 7, b g Rouser—Ensign's Last **Mr A. H. Brisbourne**
3 **ROYAL NORMAN,** 14, b g Normandy—Ensign's Last **Mrs Mary Brisbourne**
4 **ROYAL ROSCOE,** 7, b g Roscoe Blake—Normandy Sign **Mr D. Slingsby**
5 **ROYAL TYCOON,** 12, b m Tycoon II—Ensign's Last **Mr A. H. Brisbourne**
6 **SCALLYMERE,** 7, b m Scallywag—Penny Queen **Mr T. Bebb**

TWO-YEAR-OLDS

7 B f Sonnen Gold—Delbounty **Mr R. M. Evans and Mr Andrew Evans**

Jockey (NH): M Brisbourne (10-2).

95 MR C. E. BRITTAIN, Newmarket

Postal: **'Carlburg', 49 Bury Road, Newmarket, Suffolk, CB8 7BY.**
Phone: **OFFICE (0638) 664347 HOME (0638) 663739 FAX (0638) 661744**

1 **ALFA VITA,** 4, ch f Absalom—Aruba **Mrs C. E. Brittain**
2 **APPETIZER,** 4, ch g Star Appeal—Zedative (FR) **Mr A. J. Richards**
3 **ARMY OF STARS,** 5, b h Posse (USA)—Starawak **Mr C. E. Brittain**
4 **BEAU IDEAL,** 5, b h Brigadier Gerard—Princess Lieven **Mrs J. L. Hislop**
5 **BOLD STRANGER,** 5, b h Persian Bold—Lorna Doone (USA) **Mr A. J. Richards**
6 **CHARMER,** 5, b h Be My Guest (USA)—Take Your Mark (USA) **The Dowager Lady Beaverbrook**
7 **COSSACK GUARD (USA),** 4, br c Nureyev (USA)—Kilijaro **Sheikh Mohammed**
8 **DAWN SUCCESS,** 4, br c Caerleon (USA)—Dawn Echo **Mrs C. Pateras**
9 **JET,** 4, br c Gorytus (USA)—Red Berry **The Dowager Lady Beaverbrook**
10 **KING OF TALES,** 4, b c Sadler's Wells (USA)—Tales To Tell (USA) **Mrs V. Gaucci del Bono**
11 **LA BALLERINE,** 4, b f Lafontaine (USA)—Kirsova **Mrs C. E. Brittain**
12 **LAPIERRE,** 5, b h Lafontaine (USA)—Lucky Omen **Mrs J. M. Khan**
13 **LIKE AMBER,** 4, ch f Aragon—More Fun **Miss M. Carrington-Smith**
14 **LOVELY LAGOON,** 4, b f Mill Reef (USA)—Tweedling (USA) **Wing Cmdr Tim Vigors**
15 **MAID OF ESSEX,** 4, b f Bustino—Magelka **The Dowager Lady Beaverbrook**
16 **MOUNTAIN KINGDOM (USA),** 6, b h Exceller (USA)—Star In The North (USA) **Mr David Thompson**
17 **OPERATION WOLF,** 4, ch c Adonijah—Sesta **N.T.C. (Racing) Limited**
18 **PEDESTAL,** 4, ch f High Line—Mrs Moss **Lord Tavistock**
19 **PRINGIPOULA,** 4, b f Dominion—Another Princess **Mr R. N. Khan**
20 **QUIET ACHIEVER (CAN),** 5, ch g Overskate (CAN)—From Nine To Five (USA) **Mrs C. E. Brittain**
21 **RUNCIBLE CAT (USA),** 4, b c J O Tobin (USA)—Beau Cougar (USA) **Mr R. G. Levin**
22 **SIKESTON (USA),** 4, b c Lear Fan (USA)—Timer (USA) **Mrs V. Gaucci del Bono**
23 **SKISURF,** 4, b c Niniski (USA)—Seasurf **The Dowager Lady Beaverbrook**
24 **SLOE BERRY,** 4, b f Sharpo—Native Berry (FR) **Mr A. J. Richards**
25 **TERIMON,** 4, gr c Bustino—Nicholas Grey **The Dowager Lady Beaverbrook**
26 **TOP CLASS,** 5, b h High Top—Cassina **Aster Racing Limited**
27 **VAGUE SHOT,** 7, ch h Vaigly Great—Cease Fire **The Vague Shot Partnership**
28 **VILANIKA (FR),** 4, b f Top Ville—Kamanika (FR) **Mr W. J. Gredley**
29 **WINGTIP (FR),** 5, ch h Moulin—Highdinoa (FR) **Mr A. J. Richards**

THREE-YEAR-OLDS

30 **AIR MUSIC (FR),** b c Fabulous Dancer (USA)—Santa Musica **Mr A. J. Richards**
31 **ANVARI,** b c Persian Bold—Anne Stuart (FR) **Sheikh Mohammed**
32 **BELUGA GREY,** gr c Bellypha—Lucky For Me **Mr B. H. Voak**
33 **BRIGHTANDBEAUTIFUL,** ch f Sallust—Shopping (FR) **Mr James Miller**
34 **CALL TO ARMS,** b c North Briton—Branitska **Mr W. J. Gredley**
35 **CARNWATH,** b c Auction Ring (USA)—Carroldance (FR) **Mr Noordeen Sarif**
36 **CROUPIER,** b c Night Shift (USA)—Countess Walewski **Mrs J. L. Hislop**

LODDON LOOSE BOXES

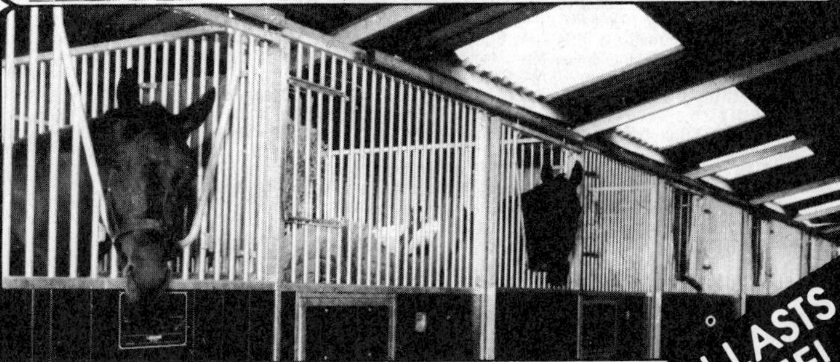

TO FIT NEW OR EXISTING BUILDINGS
Can be tailor made to individual requirements for a FREE quotation and assistance with design call us now on **0508 20744** or fill in the coupon below.

LODDON LASTS A LIFETIME! (0508) 20744

LODDON
LIVESTOCK EQUIPMENT LIMITED
Loddon, Norwich Norfolk NR14 6 JJ

Name: ....

Tel No: ....

Address: ....

....

....

No of horses: .... Student ☐

MR C. E. BRITTAIN—continued

37 **CUVEE ROSE,** b f Lafontaine (USA)—Champers Club **Mrs C. E. Brittain**
38 **DANCING EARL,** gr c Lomond (USA)—Baccalaureate **Mr W. J. Gredley**
39 **DARA DEE,** b f Dara Monarch—Not Mistaken (USA) **Mr R. N. Khan**
40 **DEBACH DAISY,** b f Ahonoora—Princess Seal **Mr James Miller**
41 **DREAMING SPIRES,** b f Sadler's Wells (USA)—Impossibility **Mr N. H. Phillips**
42 **EMVEN,** b f Dara Monarch—La Vosgienne **Mr K. C. Nunn**
43 **ENJOYMENT (NZ),** b c Standaan (FR)—Ascot Belle (USA) **Mr A. J. Richards**
44 **GAME PLAN,** b f Darshaan—Formulate **Mr N. H. Phillips**
45 **GLORIETTA (USA),** b f Shadeed (USA)—Bitty Girl **Mr Saeed Manana**
46 **GLOWING PRAISE,** b c Wassl—Rossitor **Mr N. H. Phillips**
47 **GOODREDA,** b f Good Times (ITY)—Gundreda **Miss M. Carrington-Smith**
48 **GUARANTEE,** b c Persian Bold—Kendie Blue (FR) **Mr A. J. Richards**
49 **HIGH RODING,** b c High Top—Ryoanji **Mr C. T. Olley**
50 **HIGH TIME (FR),** ch f Adonijah—Mortice **Mr N. H. Phillips**
51 **KAYCEN,** b g Kind of Hush—Tomard **Mr K. C. Nunn**
52 **KINGS CLUB,** b c Local Suitor (USA)—Clymene **Mr H. W. King**
53 **KINO,** b c Niniski (USA)—Relkina **The Dowager Lady Beaverbrook**
54 **KRISSOS,** b c Good Times (ITY)—Chrysicabana **Mrs C. Pateras**
55 **LOCAL LASS,** b f Local Suitor (USA)—Sorebelle **Mr A. Notman**
56 **MANTRAKI,** ch c Good Times (ITY)—Tora Tora **Capt. M. Lemos**
57 **MIA FILLIA,** b f Formidable (USA)—As Blessed **Mrs C. Pateras**
58 **MISS FEE FEE,** b f Red Johnnie—Miss Macfee **Mr R. N. Khan**
59 **MY COQUETTE,** ch f Coquelin (USA)—River Lane **Mr H. W. King**
60 **NASAYIM (USA),** ch f Arctic Tern (USA)—So Cozy (USA) **Mr Saeed Manana**
61 **NUNKI (ITY),** b c Clever Trick (USA)—Lacey (USA) **Mrs V. Gaucci del Bono**
62 **NUSAKAN (ITY),** ch c Spring Heights—Present Arms **Mrs V. Gaucci del Bono**
63 **OUR VISION,** b c Vision (USA)—Faiblesse **Mr David Mort**
64 **PHARIAN (USA),** ch f Diesis—Pharlette (FR) **Mr Saeed Manana**
65 **PIER DAMIANI,** b c Shareef Dancer (USA)—All A Lark **Mrs V. Gaucci del Bono**
66 **PORTO HELI,** b c Precocious—Coral Heights **Capt. M. Lemos**
67 **PURSUIT,** ch f Posse (USA)—St Louis Sue (FR) **Mr A. J. Richards**
68 **QUICK TEMPO,** b c Shareef Dancer (USA)—Mineown **The Dowager Lady Beaverbrook**
69 **RAINBOW RING,** b f Rainbow Quest (USA)—Circus Ring **Mr W. J. Gredley**
70 **REGAL THATCH,** ch c Thatching—Kolomelskoy Palace **Mr C. T. Olley**
71 **REGENT'S INLET (USA),** b c It's Freezing (USA)—Lawyer's Wave (USA) **Mr Geoffrey C. Hughes**
72 **RIDGEPOINT,** ch c Gorytus (USA)—Cooliney Princess **Mr R. N. Khan**
73 **RING APPEAL,** ch g Star Appeal—Sally Gal **Mr David Mort**
74 **RUSHMORE (USA),** b c Mt Livermore (USA)—Super Act (USA) **Sheikh Mohammed**
75 **SCOTS LAW,** b c Law Society (USA)—Tweedling (USA) **Wing Cmdr Tim Vigors**
76 **SHAMBO,** b c Lafontaine (USA)—Lucky Appeal **Mrs C. E. Brittain**
77 **STELLA BIANCA (USA),** b f Vaguely Noble—Cahard (USA) **Mr Koichiro Tanikawa**
78 **ST ROBERT,** b c Taufan (USA)—Sainthill **Mr Robin Olley**
79 **SURPASSING,** ch f Superlative—Catherine Howard **Mr D. Sieff**
80 **SWEETWEEQUEEN,** ch f Niniski (USA)—Star of Andros (FR) **The Dowager Lady Beaverbrook**
81 **TOP OF THE WORLD,** b c Top Ville—Une Florentine (FR) **Capt. M. Lemos**
82 **TRICATA,** b br f Electric—Brigata **Mrs C. E. Brittain**
83 **VIGLA,** gr f Siberian Express (USA)—Egnoussa **Capt. M. Lemos**
84 **WATER WELL,** b f Sadler's Wells (USA)—Soba **Mr W. J. Gredley**
85 **ZIZANIA,** ch f Ahonoora—Bolkonskina **Mr Ali Saeed**

TWO-YEAR-OLDS

86 **ALBERTINA,** ch f 20/3 Absalom—More Fun (Malicious) **Miss M. Carrington-Smith**
87 **ANDEMO PIER (IRE),** ch c 22/2 Shardari—Safe Home (Home Guard (USA)) **Mrs V. Gaucci del Bono**
88 **ANDRATH (IRE),** b c 26/2 Commanche Run—Rathvindon (Realm) **The Dowager Lady Beaverbrook**
89 Br c 17/4 Persian Bold—Baheejah (Northfields (USA)) **Maktoum Al Maktoum**
90 **BELLATRIX,** b f 2/5 Persian Bold—Sorebelle (Prince Tenderfoot (USA)) **Mrs C. E. Brittain**
91 **BOLD QUEST (IRE),** ch c 7/4 Persian Bold—Tequesta (Arctic Tern (USA)) **Mr A. J. Richards**
92 **BOY NEXT DOOR,** b c 8/3 Local Suitor (USA)—Krishnagar (Kris) **Mr B. H. Voak**
93 **BRAVEBOY,** b c 12/4 Never So Bold—Relkina (FR) (Relkino) **The Dowager Lady Beaverbrook**
94 **BRIGHT SEA (USA),** b c 15/5 Secreto (USA)—Muriels Dream (USA) (Blue Prince) **Sheikh Mohammed**

MR C. E. BRITTAIN—continued

95 **CAROUSELLA,** b f 27/1 Rousillon (USA)—Salchow (Niniski (USA)) **The Dowager Lady Beaverbrook**
96 **CASTCAREAWAY (FR),** b c 28/4 Caerleon (USA)—Castaway (FR) (Filiberto (USA)) **Mr A. J. Richards**
97 **CHATHAM ISLAND,** ch g 12/2 Jupiter Island—Floreal (Formidable (USA)) **Mr Geoffrey C. Hughes**
98 **CLOCHE D'OR,** b f 25/4 Good Times (ITY)—Chrysicabana (Home Guard (USA)) **Mrs C. Pateras**
99 **COLOSSUS,** ch c 20/1 Good Times (ITY)—Adrana (Bold Lad (IRE)) **Capt. M. Lemos**
100 **COLOUR QUEST,** ch f 20/3 Rainbow Quest (USA)—Formulate (Reform) **Mrs H. Phillips**
101 **DESERT SPLENDOUR,** b c 30/1 Green Desert (USA)—Lost Splendour (USA) (Vaguely Noble) **Mr N. H. Phillips**
102 **EL BABY (IRE),** ch c 15/5 Burslem—Granville Lady (High Hat) **Mrs V. Gaucci del Bono**
103 **GLINTING CURRENCY (USA),** b f 21/3 Glint of Gold—Current Pattie (USA) (Little Current (USA)) **Mr W. J. Gredley**
104 **GO EXECUTIVE,** b c 18/4 Sharpo—Staritsa (USA) (Alleged (USA)) **Mike Dawes**
105 **GREENDALE (FR),** b c 7/4 Green Desert (USA)—Lastcomer (USA) (Kris) **Sheikh Mohammed**
106 **GUSSY MARLOWE,** b f 15/3 Final Straw—Lady Lorelei (Derring-Do) **Mrs Van Geest**
107 **HAILSHAM (CAN),** br c 14/2 Riverman (USA)—Halo's Princess (CAN) (Halo (USA)) **Sheikh Mohammed**
108 B f 23/3 Local Suitor (USA)—Hatta (Realm) **Mr Saeed Manana**
109 **HELLESPONT,** b c 12/3 Beldale Flutter (USA)—Thalassa (Appiani II) **Mr A. J. Richards**
110 **HIGH DEGREE,** b c 19/5 Superlative—St Colette (So Blessed) **Sheikh Mohammed**
111 **HURRICANE BLAKE,** b c 13/2 Blakeney—Nibelunga (Miami Springs) **Mr W. J. Gredley**
112 **HUSO,** ch c 18/5 Sharpo—Husnah (USA) (Caro) **Sheikh Mohammed**
113 **JUPITER SOUND,** b f 7/5 Jupiter Island—Carribean Sound (Good Times (ITY)) **Mr H. W. King**
114 **KALAN (IRE),** ch c 28/4 Sharpo—Zumurrudah (USA) (Spectacular Bid (USA)) **Mrs V. Gaucci del Bono**
115 B f 1/4 Caerleon (USA)—Karissima (Kalamoun) **Mrs V. Gaucci del Bono**
116 **KOHINOOR (IRE),** b c 17/2 Shareef Dancer (USA)—Freddy My Love (Thatch (USA)) **Mrs V. Gaucci del Bono**
117 Ch c Blushing Groom (FR)—La Griffe (Prince John) **Mrs V. Gaucci del Bono**
118 **LATOUR,** b c 4/3 Lafontaine (USA)—Lucky Omen (Queen's Hussar) **Mrs J. M. Khan and Mrs C. E. Brittain**
119 **LIEBSIDE LASS (IRE),** b f 23/3 Be My Guest (USA)—Val's Girl (USA) (Sir Ivor) **Liebside Ltd**
120 **LOUDEST WHISPER,** b c 9/5 Reach—Dancela (Ela-Mana-Mou) **Mr Ray Richards**
121 **MISS HOCROFT,** ch f 10/5 Dominion—As Blessed (So Blessed) **Mrs C. Pateras**
122 **MUNTGIAK (IRE),** b c 2/3 Ela-Mana-Mou—Les Saintes (Kris) **Mrs V. Gaucci del Bono**
123 **MYSTIKO (USA),** ro c 22/2 Secreto (USA)—Caracciola (FR) (Zeddaan) **The Dowager Lady Beaverbrook**
124 **NOUSHY,** ch f 2/3 Ahonoora—Bolkonskina (Balidar) **Mrs W. H. Gerhauser**
125 **PERESKIA,** b f 19/4 Petoski—Mytinia (Bustino) **The Dowager Lady Beaverbrook**
126 **PERFECT RAINBOW,** b f 20/3 Rainbow Quest (USA)—Helpless Haze (USA) (Vaguely Noble) **A. D. Shead**
127 **PERFIDY (FR),** b f 23/3 Persian Bold—Maiyaasah (Kris) **Sheikh Mohammed**
128 **PIGALLE WONDER,** br c 22/1 Chief Singer—Hi-Tech Girl (Homeboy) **Mr W. J. Gredley**
129 **PROPAGANDA,** b c 16/4 Nishapour (FR)—Mrs Moss (Reform) **Lord Tavistock**
130 **SATANIC DANCE (FR),** b f 30/4 Shareef Dancer (USA)—Satanella (GER) (Pentathlon) **Sheikh Mohammed**
131 **SAVANGA (USA),** b c 6/4 Secreto (USA)—Sun Sprite (USA) (Graustark) **Mr David Mort**
132 **SECRET FREEDOM (USA),** b f 22/5 Secreto (USA)—Mary Biz (USA) (T V Lark) **Mrs Celia Miller**
133 Ch c 28/2 Doulab (USA)—Sharrara (CAN) (Blushing Groom (FR)) **Mr Saeed Manana**
134 B f 29/3 Sure Blade (USA)—Silent Movie (Shirley Heights) **Maktoum Al Maktoum**
135 B f 1/5 Taufan (USA)—Silver Glimpse (Petingo) **G. V. Wright**
136 **ST PATRICK'S DAY,** ch c 17/3 Night Shift (USA)—Princess Lieven (Royal Palace) **Mrs J. L. Hislop and Mr J. L. Hislop**
137 **SUNSET STREET (IRE),** b c 2/3 Bellypha—Sunset Reef (Mill Reef (USA)) **Mr A. J. Richards**
138 **SYLVA HONDA,** ch c 25/3 Adonijah—Wolverhants (Wolver Hollow) **E. A. Grimstead & Son Honda Ltd**
139 **TENDER MOMENT,** b f Caerleon (USA)—Cannon Boy (USA) (Canonero (USA)) **Mr Ray Richards**
140 **TRANSCRIPT,** b f 29/3 Transworld (USA)—Lawyer's Wave (USA) (Advocator) **Mr Geoffrey C. Hughes**
141 **TREBLY,** b c 31/1 Top Ville—Jeema (Thatch (USA)) **Mrs V. Gaucci del Bono**
142 B c 29/1 Precocious—Troy Moon (Troy) **Mr H. W. King**
143 **TSUNAMI,** b c 20/4 Niniski (USA)—Seasurf (Seaepic (USA)) **The Dowager Lady Beaverbrook**
144 **TUNED AUDITION,** b c 27/5 Fit To Fight (USA)—Song Test (USA) (The Minstrel (CAN)) **Mr W. J. Gredley**
145 **WAR BEAT,** b c 6/5 Wolver Heights—Branitska (Mummy's Pet) **Mr W. J. Gredley**

Other Owners: Mrs Y. Dawes, Executive & Corporate Financial Services, Hitchcock & Company Ltd, Mr J. G. King, Mr H. Laddie, Mr M. L. Levin, Mr G. Levine, Mrs D. C. Mort.

Apprentice: Brett Doyle (5-6).

96 MR M. A. BRITTAIN, Warthill

Postal: **Northgate Lodge, Warthill, York, YO3 9XR.**
Phone: **(0759) 71472 FAX (0759) 72915 TELEX 57739**

1 **AQUAINTED,** 5, b m Known Fact (USA)—Gay Trinket **Mr Mel Brittain**
2 **BRITANNIA BELL,** 5, br g Pitskelly—Saintly Angel **Mr K. Ward**
3 **DUNESIAN,** 4, ch f Dunbeath (USA)—Polynesian Charm (USA) **Mr Mel Brittain**
4 **JAVERT,** 5, ch g Kings Lake (USA)—Red Berry **Mr J. C. Bredin**
5 **KRISFIELD,** 5, b br h Anfield—Kristallina **Mr Richard Berenson**
6 **NORDIC BRAVE,** 4, b c Indian King (USA)—Belle Viking (FR) **Mr Mel Brittain**
7 **PAYVASHOOZ,** 5, b m Ballacashtal (CAN)—Abercourt **M. D. M. Racing (Thoroughbreds) Limited**
8 **PREVAILING WIND,** 4, b g Night Shift (USA)—Windy Sea **Mr Mel Brittain**
9 **QUEENS TOUR,** 5, b h Sweet Monday—On Tour **Mr Ian Bell**
10 **SINCLAIR LADY,** 6, gr m Absalom—Katysue **Mr Mel Brittain**
11 **SMALL FEE,** 5, ch m Blue Cashmere—Gay Picture **Mr Sidney Eaton**
12 **SUPREME BLUES,** 4, b c Cure The Blues (USA)—Court Barns (USA) **Mr Mel Brittain**
13 **TAKE EFFECT,** 6, b g Tap On Wood—Welsh Partner **Mr Mel Brittain**
14 **TANODA,** 4, b f Tyrnavos—Anoda (FR) **Mr Mel Brittain**
15 **THOMAS LENG,** 5, ch h Homing—Fast Asleep **Mr Mel Brittain**
16 **TOWN MEETING,** 6, ch g General Assembly (USA)—La Marne (USA) **Mr Mel Brittain**
17 **TYRNIPPY,** 4, b c Tyrnavos—Floral **M. D. M. Racing (Thoroughbreds) Limited**

THREE-YEAR-OLDS

18 **APPAREL,** ch f Absalom—Anoda (FR) **Mr Mel Brittain**
19 **BIG ECK,** b g Precocious—Dora's Rocket **Mr Mel Brittain**
20 **COST EFFECTIVE,** ch c Burslem—Perle's Fashion **Miss D. J. Woods**
21 **DIVIDIA,** b f Pas de Seul—Divina (GER) **Miss A. M. Jones**
22 **DUNSTAR,** b c Dunphy—Starlit Way **Royal-Blue Racing Plc**
23 **EIRE LEATH-SCEAL,** b c Legend of France (USA)—Killarney Belle (USA) **Mr Mel Brittain**
24 **GENERAL MEETING,** ch g General Assembly (USA)—La Marne (USA) **Mr Mel Brittain**
25 **GUEST RIGHT,** b c Be My Guest (USA)—Miss Allowed (USA) **Mr Mel Brittain**
26 **INDIAN STAR,** b f Indian King (USA)—Salique **Mr Mel Brittain**
27 **KING DANCER,** b c Kafu—Gay Parthia **Mr R. N. Wellock**
28 **KINGS MEETING,** b g Kings Lake (USA)—Meeting Adjourned **Mr Mel Brittain**
29 **LADY LONGLEAT,** ch f Longleat (USA)—Kip's Sister **Mr Mel Brittain**
30 **MR CHEEKYCHOPS,** ch g Blue Cashmere—Tzu-Hsi **M. D. M. Racing (Thoroughbreds) Limited**
31 **NORTHERN LACE,** gr c Northern Tempest (USA)—Dragon Lace **Mr Mel Brittain**
32 **NORTHGATE KING,** b c Fairy King (USA)—Dollyful **Mr Mel Brittain**
33 **PRESIDENT GEORGE,** b g Be My Native (USA)—Mother White **Mr G. G. Ashton**
34 **SHARQUIN,** b c Indian King (USA)—Lady of The Land **Mr M. A. Murphy**
35 **SINGING DETECTIVE,** gr g Absalom—Smoke Creek **John Mills Office Equipment Limited**
36 **SPANISH REALM,** b f King of Spain—Miss Realm **Mr Mel Brittain**
37 **SWINGING BLUES,** b c Cure The Blues (USA)—Lavender Dance **Mr R. Hebb**
38 **TELEGRAPH CALLGIRL,** b f Northern Tempest (USA)—Northgate Lady **Eclipse Management (Newmarket) Ltd**
39 **TEXAS BLUE,** ch f Jalmood (USA)—Laurel Express **Mr B. S. Creber**

TWO-YEAR-OLDS

40 Br c 23/2 Valiyar—Arianna Aldini (Habitat)
41 Ch c 11/4 Parliament—Barefoot Contessa (Homeric)
42 **BLANKET DECISION (IRE),** ch c 5/2 Touching Wood (USA)—Glomach (USA) (Majestic Light (USA)) **Mr G. G. Ashton**
43 **CARABALI DANCER,** ch c 4/4 Ballacashtal (CAN)—Lillicara (FR) (Caracolero (USA)) **W. Price**
44 B c 23/4 Cragador—Chanita (Averof)
45 Br c 12/4 Lidhame—Cocoban (Targowice (USA))
46 **DESIRED LACE,** gr f 10/3 Grey Desire—Dragon Lace (Dragonara Palace (USA)) **Mr Mel Brittain**
47 **DESIRE'S DOUBLE,** gr c 10/5 Grey Desire—Strip Fast (Virginia Boy) **Mr Mel Brittain**
48 Ch c 19/3 Sayf El Arab (USA)—Djellaba (Decoy Boy)
49 B c 23/5 Wassl—Eloquent Charm (USA) (Private Account (USA))
50 **EMERALD GULF (IRE),** br f 30/3 Wassl—Gaelic Jewel (Scottish Rifle) **P. Rhodes**
51 Ch c 28/3 Tender King—Exotic Dancer (Posse (USA))

MR M. A. BRITTAIN—continued

52 B c 5/3 Good Times (ITY)—Galetzky (Radetzky)
53 Br c 11/5 Grey Desire—Girdle Ness (Pitskelly)
54 **GODSCHARM (IRE),** b f 8/3 Godswalk (USA)—
Polynesian Charm (USA) (What A Pleasure (USA)) **Mr Mel Brittain**
55 **GREY CHIMES,** ch f 22/4 Grey Desire—Cowbells (Mountain Call) **Mr Mel Brittain**
56 **GREY COMMANDER,** gr c 28/2 Grey Desire—Melowen (Owen Dudley) **Mr Mel Brittain**
57 **GREYHILL LADY,** b f 6/5 Grey Desire—Warthill Lady (Hittite Glory) **Mr Mel Brittain**
58 **GREY NORTH,** b f 3/5 Grey Desire—Northgate Lady (Fordham (USA)) **Mr Mel Brittain**
59 **GREY REALM,** ch f 30/1 Grey Desire—Miss Realm (Realm) **Mr Mel Brittain**
60 **GREY RECORD,** gr c 28/2 Grey Desire—Record Lady (Record Token) **Mr Mel Brittain**
61 **GREY STAR (IRE),** gr f 3/4 Grey Desire—Dutch Queen (Ahonoora)
62 **IN CONCERT,** ch f 17/2 Absalom—Hum (Crooner) **Woodberry Ltd**
63 Ch c 12/3 Absalom—Lady Warninglid (Ela-Mana-Mou)
64 B c 8/5 Drumalis—La Marne (USA) (Nashua)
65 **MISS DESIRE,** b f 6/5 Grey Desire—Kamaress (Kampala) **Mr Mel Brittain**
66 B c 21/3 Sayf El Arab (USA)—New Edition (Great Nephew)
67 **NORTHGATE GIRL (IRE),** ch f 5/2 Gorytus (USA)—Red Line Fever (Bay Express) **Mr Mel Brittain**
68 **PAVERS GOOD SHOES,** b f 18/3 Good Times (ITY)—Windy Sea (Sea Hawk II) **M. Paver**
69 B c 13/5 High Top—Raffle (Balidar)
70 Gr c 12/5 Faustus (USA)—Rich Lass (Broxted)
71 Ch c 2/4 Bairn (USA)—Rose And The Ring (Welsh Pageant)
72 **RUNNING GREY,** gr c 14/3 Grey Desire—Running Rainbow (Runnett) **Mr Mel Brittain**
73 **RYEDALE LASS,** ch f 23/5 Ballacashtal (CAN)—Mossy Girl (Ballymoss) **D. A. Pike**
74 **SHARP DECISION,** b f 6/4 Sharpo—Wryneck (Niniski (USA)) **Mrs H. Mills**
75 **STAMFORD BRIDGE,** br c 23/4 Dominion—Meadowbank (Northfields (USA)) **Mr Mel Brittain**
76 **SUPREME DESIRE,** gr f 21/3 Grey Desire—Fire Mountain (Dragonara Palace (USA)) **T. Peel**
77 **SUPRISE ENVOY,** b c 14/4 Grey Desire—Conrara (Balidar) **D. Brotherton**
78 Ch c 5/5 Swing Easy (USA)—Thorganby Bella (Porto Bello)

Other Owners: Mr T. Adams, Mr D. H. Armitage, Mr N. Askey, Mr A. P. Banks, Mr Peter Clowes, Crescent (U.K.) Ltd, Mr Chris Durnan, Mr Gough, Mr Graham Hughes, Mr T. G. Pope, Racing Telegraph, Mr A. Rhodes, Mr R. W. Sansom, Mr Graham Savage, Mr E. V. Stanford, Mr C. Strahl, Mr Peter Wain, Mr P. Wilson.

Jockey (Flat): P Sedgwick (8-0).

Apprentices: S Maloney (7-4), J Marshall, D Wright.

97 MR C. D. BROAD, Westbury-on-Severn

Postal: **Tudor Stables, Elton, Westbury-on-Severn, Gloucestershire, GL14 9XX.**
Phone: **OFFICE (0452) 76835 OR 830015 CAR PHONE (0836) 622858**

1 **AUGHAVOGUE,** 8, b br g Golden Love—Deirdre's Joy **K. W. Bell & Son Ltd**
2 **BELVEL (ITY),** 7, b g Furry Glen—Velatura **K. W. Bell & Son Ltd**
3 **CNOC AN OIR,** 6, br m Goldhill—Castlegannon **Mr Mervyn Jones**
4 4, B c Marechal (FR)—Fiery Kiss **Mrs S. V. Threlfall**
5 **FOR HEAVEN'S SAKE (FR),** 5, br g Be My Guest (USA)—Woolf (FR) **Mr K. W. Bell**
6 **GILT FUTURE,** 8, b g Persian Bold—Connaughts' Trump **K. W. Bell & Son Ltd**
7 **IMSHI WAHEED,** 5, b g Escapism (USA)—Shadytoo **Mr M. J. McGuirk**
8 **KARLOVAC,** 4, ch g Stanford—Croatia **Mr Mark Brookes**
9 **KISSANE,** 9, br g Kemal (FR)—Chamowen **Mr K. W. Bell**
10 **MARINA MEDE,** 6, b m Runnymede—Bodicea **Mr Steve MacDonald**
11 **MILLMERRAN,** 5, b m Jimsun—Sarah's Joy **George Inn (Aylburton) Racing Club**
12 **MUDAHIM,** 4, b g Shareef Dancer (USA)—Mariska (FR) **Mr K. W. Bell**
13 **RAGALOO,** 4, ch g Ragapan—Tangmalang **Mr K. W. Bell**
14 **SPRING TIME PEARL,** 7, b m Black Minstrel—Autumn Pearl **Mr Peter A. Randall**

MR C. D. BROAD—continued

Other Owners: Mrs A. J. Broad.

Jockeys (NH): A Carroll (10-0, w.a.), D Tegg (9-10, w.a.).

Conditional: P S McDermott (9-10).

Amateur: Mr P Fenton (w.a.).

98 MR J. E. BROCKBANK, Carlisle

Postal: **Westward Park, Wigton, Carlisle, Cumbria, CA7 8AP.**
Phone: **WIGTON (0965) 42391**

1 **HIGHRYMER,** 6, gr m Rymer—On High **Mrs J. E. Brockbank**
2 **MIGHTY MATCH,** 6, b g Rymer—Mystic Match **Mr T. Brockbank**
3 **MYSTIC,** 4, b f Leading Man—Mystic Match **Mr J. E. Brockbank**
4 **PAMPERING,** 9, b g Pamroy—Crosswise **Mrs J. E. Brockbank**
5 **THIRTY ALL,** 5, b h Rymer—Mystic Match **Mr J. E. Brockbank**
6 **THRIP THE DYE,** 4, b g Leading Man—Crosswise **Mrs J. E. Brockbank**
7 **TOOTING TIMES,** 4, ch g Leading Man—Saucy **Mrs J. E. Brockbank**
8 **WISE FELLOW,** 5, ch h Leading Man—Crosswise **Mrs J. E. Brockbank**

Jockeys (NH): P Niven, S J O'Neill.

Amateur: Mr T Brockbank (11-3).

99 MR H. DE BROMHEAD, Knockeen

Postal: **Knockeen, Waterford, Ireland.**
Phone: **(051) 75726**

1 **DAPPING,** 6, b m Beldale Flutter (USA)—Sass-Go
2 **FIFI'S MAN,** 4, b br g Mandalus—Fifi L'Amour
3 **FREE FORM,** 5, b m Glenstal (USA)—Free Wheeler
4 **GRAND HABIT,** 6, br g Monksfield—Miss Poohie
5 **GRASSED,** 4, ch f Busted—Greenfly (USA)
6 **IRRAH,** 5, b m Bustino—Spring Is Grey
7 **ISLAND BRIDGE,** 8, br m Mandalus—Malone
8 **WOLF WINTER,** 5, ch g Wolverlife—Windara

Owners: S. A. Aldridge, Mr J. Carroll, Mr Karl Casey, Mr Clive Hartley, Mrs Robert Lanigan, I. H. Stewart Brown, Mr M. J. E. Thornhill.

Jockeys (NH): T Carmody, M Flynn (10-4), T J Ryan (9-7).

Amateurs: Mr P Fenton, Mr T Hyde.

100 MR C. P. E. BROOKS, Lambourn

Postal: **Uplands Stables, Lambourn, Newbury, Berkshire, RG16 7QH.**
Phone: **(0488) 72077 FAX (0488) 71206**

1 **ABBOTTS VIEW,** 6, b g Monksfield—In View Lass **Dr P. P. Brown**
2 **ALL JEFF (FR),** 6, b g Jefferson—Fromentel (FR) **Lady Joseph**
3 **ANOTHER BUCK,** 5, b g Celtic Cone—Clay Duck **Mr D. E. H. Horton**
4 **ANOTHER SCHEDULE,** 9, ch g Beau Tudor—Mo Sgeal Fein **Mrs V. Black**
5 **ARDEN,** 6, b g Ardross—Kereolle **Lord Howard de Walden**
6 **BAIES,** 8, br g Raise You Ten—Peppardstown **Mrs Basil Samuel**
7 **BAJAN SUNSHINE,** 11, b g Reliance II—Nyanga **Mr Paul Green**
8 **BALI DOWN LAD,** 6, b g Balinger—Duckdown **Mr D. E. H. Horton**
9 **BATTALION (USA),** 6, b h Vaguely Noble—Blazon (USA) **Mr R. L. Dormer**
10 **BELL GLASS (FR),** 4, gr g Bellypha—Greener Pastures **C. F. Cronin Ltd**
11 **BITTER BUCK,** 7, ch m Celtic Cone—Clay Duck **Mr D. E. H. Horton**
12 **BLACK HUMOUR,** 6, b g Buckskin (FR)—Artiste Gaye **R. E. A. Bott (Wigmore St) Ltd**
13 **BRIGHT INTERVALS,** 8, br g Condorcet (FR)—Sun Spray **Mrs Miles Valentine**
14 **BRUTON STREET,** 8, b g Pollerton—Raise A Queen **R. E. A. Bott (Wigmore St) Ltd**
15 **CANFORD PALM,** 9, b g Nearly A Hand—Little Tot **Mrs M. J. Cobham**
16 **CELTIC SHOT,** 8, b g Celtic Cone—Duckdown **Mr D. E. H. Horton**
17 **COOKS LAWN,** 5, ch m The Parson—Croom Cross **Mrs M. J. Cobham**
18 **DANCING BEE,** 5, gr g Prince Bee—Dance Mistress **Mrs G. Abecassis**
19 **DEEP AND EVEN,** 10, ch g Deep Run—Drop Even **Mr C. P. E. Brooks**
20 **ESPY,** 7, b g Pitpan—Minorette **R. E. A. Bott (Wigmore St) Ltd**
21 **GLAMIS,** 7, b g Pollerton—Raise A Queen **R. E. A. Bott (Wigmore St) Ltd**
22 **GOLD BEARER,** 10, b g Golden Love—Gina Rose **Lady Joseph**
23 **GOODSHOT RICH,** 6, b g Roscoe Blake—Hunter's Treasure **Mr R. L. Dormer**
24 **HALF FREE,** 14, br g Deep Run—Broken Union **Mr R. Farrell**
25 **HAZY SUNSET,** 13, br g Menelek—Sunset Queen **C. F. Cronin Ltd**
26 **HELLO GRANDAD,** 6, b g Hello Gorgeous (USA)—Emerin **Mr John Galvanoni**
27 **HELLO STEVE,** 5, b g Final Straw—Head First **Mr Jack Joseph**
28 **HYPERBOLE,** 5, ch g Bali Dancer—Third Lady **Mrs William Rees-Davies**
29 **KAMI KING,** 4, gr c Kings Lake (USA)—Karafa **Mrs Miles Valentine**
30 **LARRY-O,** 10, ch g Laurence O—Penthouse Pet **Mr Denis Andrews**
31 **LIASON DANGEREUSE,** 5, ch m Ballacashtal (CAN)—Nelski **Mrs Nicole Myers**
32 **MAROUAT,** 5, ch g Torus—El Reine **Lady Joseph**
33 **MASSINGHAM,** 6, ch g Deep Run—Ballygirl **J. D. Burns**
34 **MIRIYOUN,** 5, b gr h Dalsaan—Minourika (FR) **Mrs Paul Fout**
35 **MY YOUNG MAN,** 5, b g Young Man (FR)—Hampsruth **Mrs W. Tulloch**
36 **OKEETEE,** 7, b g Raise You Ten—Peppardstown **Mrs V. Black**
37 **PENALTY DOUBLE,** 6, b g Deep Run—Silver Doll **Mr N. H. Gardner**
38 **PICA SWORD,** 4, br c Broadsword (USA)—Picotee **Mr Alan Woodley**
39 **REGENT COURT,** 4, br g Prince Regent—Arctic Free **C. F. Cronin Ltd**
40 **ROSCOE HARVEY,** 8, br g Roscoe Blake—Hunter's Treasure **Mr Peter Spicer**
41 **RUN ON STIRLING,** 6, b m Celtic Cone—Night Action **Mr J. L. Rowsell**
42 **SAN OVAC,** 7, b g Ovac (ITY)—Sanvitalia **Miss M. Talbot**
43 **SAYMORE,** 4, ch c Seymour Hicks (FR)—Huahinee (FR) **Mr John Livock**
44 **SMOOTH STYLE,** 6, b br g Smooth Stepper—Hainault **Mr Paul Green**
45 **SOLOMON'S CHOICE,** 5, ch g Proverb—Sweet An
46 **SPEEDY BEAR (USA),** 5, ch g Sir Ivor—Close Control **Miss J. D. Winter**
47 **STAG DINNER,** 7, ch g Le Bavard (FR)—Ethel's Delight **Mr John Galvanoni**
48 **ST ELMO'S FIRE,** 5, br g Electric—Sea Lady **Olympic N. H. Racing**
49 **SUNSET COURT,** 8, ch g Quayside—Shamrock Penny **C. F. Cronin Ltd**
50 **THE GAELCHARN,** 6, ch g Prince Bee—Lady Habitat **Mrs W. Tulloch**
51 **TIBER RIVER,** 6, br g Troy—River Call **G. F. Beddington**
52 **TURNER'S REACH,** 6, b m Enchantment—Nelski **Mr Martin Myers**
53 **UP THE CHERRIES,** 6, b g Official—Crown Bird **Mr Harry Redknapp**
54 **VILLA PARK,** 8, b g Varano—Fethard Flirt **Lady Cooper**
55 **WOLFHANGAR,** 8, ch g Decent Fellow—Vaguely Vulgan **Mrs Basil Samuel**

MR C. P. E. BROOKS—continued

Other Owners: Mr Andrew Baars, Miss S. M. Brien, Mrs Robert Brooks, Mr P. J. Constable, Lady Cooper, Mr D. A. Exton, Miss P. H. Gardner, Heathavon Stables Limited, Mrs B. Mead, Mrs I. Philips, J. Spearman, Stampers Limited, Mrs M. C. Taylor, Mrs Hazel Tiler, Mrs S. Towler, Mr A. Wade, Mrs R. Willis.

Jockeys (NH): B De Haan (10-0), P Scudamore (10-0).

Conditional: C Dempsey (9-10), R Teague (9-10).

Amateurs: Mr J P Durkan (10-0), Mr C Farrell (10-0).

Lady Rider: Miss J Winter.

101 MR W. G. A. BROOKS, Lambourn

Postal: **Delamere Cottage Stables, Folly Road, Lambourn, Newbury.**
Phone: **LAMBOURN (0488) 72140**

1 **BROMO (USA),** 5, b g Sir Ivor—Ciao (USA) **Mrs G. Grant**
2 **BULLY BOY,** 7, ch g Margouillat (FR)—Chere Madame **Mr R. Taylor**
3 **DON'T TELL BOB,** 6, b g Billion (USA)—Pensong **Mrs C. Taylor**
4 **HORWOOD LAD,** 5, b g My Dad Tom—Tavuto **Mr K. Harmsworth**
5 **O-LA-LE,** 6, ch h Virginia Boy—Winning Wave (USA) **Mr E. Tessensohn**
6 **SKY CLOUD,** 4, ch c Formidable (USA)—Cloud Nine **Mr B. R. David**
7 **TALATON FLYER,** 4, b g Kala Shikari—Pertune **Mr D. Coles**

THREE-YEAR-OLDS

8 **BLUE ROOM,** b f Gorytus (USA)—Jokers High (USA) **Mr G. Hicks**
9 **FLIRTY LADY,** b f Never So Bold—Turtle Hill **Mrs J. Harmsworth**
10 **LAKELAND BEAUTY,** b f Mummy's Pet—Skiddaw (USA) **Mrs J. Harmsworth**

TWO-YEAR-OLDS

11 Ch f 27/3 Fayruz—Harp (Ennis) **Mr Stuart Harper**
12 **LARA'S BABY,** ch f 4/2 Valiyar—Tapiola (Tap On Wood) **Larabuild Ltd**
13 **OSCILANTE,** b c 10/3 Swing Easy (USA)—Lillylee Lady (USA) (Shecky Greene (USA)) **Mr G. Hicks**
14 B f 16/4 Dominion—Ulla Laing (Mummy's Pet) **Mr A. W. Boon**

Other Owners: Castell Ceilings Ltd, Mr Costa Kyriakides, Mr Mario Mauro.

Jockey (NH): P Leach (w.a.).

Apprentice: G Thompson (7-12).

102 MR R. BROTHERTON, Evesham

Postal: **2 Church Road, Hampton, Evesham, Worcestershire.**
Phone: **EVESHAM (0386) 443023**

1 **ALL AGREED,** 9, b g Jaazeiro (USA)—Tynwald Hill **Mrs V. Gibson**
2 **ATHLETES' WEEK,** 7, b g Cure The Blues (USA)—Milveagh **Mr Brian A. Robinson**
3 **CHERRYTOWN,** 10, b m Paddy's Stream—Whitestone **Mr J. R. Hall**
4 **CLEAR WATER DRIVE,** 8, ch g Deep Run—Rosecon **Mr S. E. Grove**
5 **DOLLY WARDANCE,** 7, gr m Warpath—April **Mr J. W. Woodward**

MR R. BROTHERTON—continued

6 **HOME ON SUNDAY**, 6, b g Camden Town—Faddle **Mr T. J. Lavin**
7 **IDIOT'S RUN**, 5, b m Idiot's Delight—Credo's Run **Mr D. J. Shorey**
8 **KING OF ARAGON**, 5, b g Aragon—Selina Fair **Mrs Sandra Hall**
9 **MILITARY SALUTE**, 5, b h Sandhurst Prince—Wavetree **Mr Paul Grainger**
10 **NORE HILL**, 5, ch g Town And Country—Hat Hill **Mr J. R. Hall**
11 **SAILORS BANK**, 7, b g Owen Anthony—Sylv **Mr Philip Sloan**
12 **TOWER WATCH**, 7, b br g Tower Walk—Joan Doreen **Mr M. D. Hanmer**

Other Owners: Mr M. R. Aspey, Mr A. J. Britten, Mr Roy Brotherton, Mr J. F. Campbell, Mr B. J. Morse.

Jockeys (NH): S Keightley, K Mooney.

Conditional: Martin Jones, W McFarland.

Amateur: Mr G Hanmer (10-0).

103 MR M. L. BROWN, Llanwrda

Postal: **Llwyntywyll, Llansadwrn, Llanwrda, Dyfed, SA19 8LH, Wales.**
Phone: **LLANGADOG (0550) 777403**

1 **ANOTHER CRUISE**, 5, gr g Cruise Missile—Another Dove **Mr Tom Price**
2 **COUNT TREVISIO**, 6, b h Lochnager—Spring Clump **Mr M. Brown**
3 **DONNA'S TOKEN**, 5, b m Record Token—Lyricist **Mr R. L. Brown**
4 **DRIVER**, 4, b f Motivate—Owen's Hobby **Mr D. A. Hall**
5 **MARSOOM**, 8, b g Full of Hope—Annathena **Mr M. Brown**
6 **MOTOR CLOAK**, 4, b c Motivate—Cavalry Cloak **Mr G. Powell**
7 **RUSTY MUSIC**, 4, b g Rustingo—Lyricist **Mr R. L. Brown**
8 **RUSTY'S SPECIAL**, 8, ch m Rustingo—Newstown **Mrs R. Jones**

Conditional: John Brown (10-4).

104 MR DERMOT BROWNE, Lambourn

Postal: **Upshire Farm Stables, Hungerford Hill, Lambourn, Newbury, Berkshire.**
Phone: **(0488) 72078**

1 **BLAZING SUCCESS**, 4, ch f Blazing Saddles—Relicia **Mrs D. Gleeson**
2 **GET STEPPING**, 4, ch g Posse (USA)—Thanks Edith **Mr J. Gleeson**
3 **I'M ELECTRIC**, 4, b g Electric—Mouletta **Mr A. F. Gleeson**
4 **ROTHERFIELD GREYS**, 8, br g Mummy's Pet—Relicia **Mrs D. Gleeson**
5 **SNIGGY**, 4, b f Belfort—Firey Kim **Mrs D. Gleeson**

THREE-YEAR-OLDS

6 **CELLATICA (USA)**, ch f Sir Ivor (USA)—Sweetsider (USA) **Mr A. F. Gleeson**
7 **HELLO PET**, b f Tina's Pet—Kuwait Night **Mr W. J. Joyce**
8 **LEGEND OF SPAIN**, b f Alleged (USA)—Nikki Winfield **Mr A. F. Gleeson**
9 **MEZZOFORTE**, b c Ballad Rock—Silk Blend **Mr A. F. Gleeson**
10 **OPEN CHAMPION**, br c To-Agori-Mou—Lightening Record **Mr A. F. Gleeson**

TWO-YEAR-OLDS

11 **DASHING PRINCE**, ch c Prince Sabo—Daisy Star (Star Appeal) **Mrs H. Maloney**
12 **HIGHLAND JOHNNY**, b c Stage Door Johnny—Fleur d'Or (USA) (Exclusive Native (USA)) **Mr A. F. Gleeson**
13 Ch f 14/5 Exhibitioner—Kuwait Night (Morston (FR)) **Mrs D. Gleeson**
14 B f Taufan (USA)—Miss Habitat (Habitat)
15 Ch f L'Emigrant—Zitherplay (USA) (Graustark)

MR DERMOT BROWNE—continued

Jockeys (Flat): W Carson (w.a), S Cauthen (w.a.), R Cochrane (w.a.), Pat Eddery (8-4, w.a.), S Whitworth (w.a.).

Jockeys (NH): D W Browne (10-4), B Powell (w.a.).

Apprentices: Shane Aspell (8-0), Beverly Mullins (7-10).

Conditional: D Gallaher (9-7, w.a.), P Hartey (9-7, w.a.).

Amateur: Mr Ray White (10-0, w.a.).

Lady Riders: Miss Carol Browne (8-4), Miss Lorna Vincent (12-0).

105 MR L. BROWNE, The Curragh

Postal: **Maddenstown Lodge, The Curragh, Co. Kildare, Ireland.**
Phone: **THE CURRAGH (045) 41255 OR 41614**

1 **ALL THAT CRACK,** 5, ch m Stanford—Engagement Ring **D. C. Codling**
2 **GREENORE ROSE,** 4, b f Main Reef—Sarah Purser **T. F. Roe**
3 **HEATHER SEEKER,** 4, b f Taufan (USA)—Heather Lark **Mrs T. Gillson**
4 **LADY BYE BYE,** 4, b f Montekin—Glenardina **Mrs T. Gillson**
5 **NAEVOG,** 7, b m Ela-Mana-Mou—Gale Bridge **Mrs J. J. Byrne**
6 **YANKEE GLORY,** 4, b c Welsh Saint—Magloire (FR) **Mrs S. A. Rosenborg**
7 **YOUR BID (FR),** 4, b g Dom Racine—Bid Fair **Mrs M. M. Keogh**

THREE-YEAR-OLDS

8 **ANNIE LAURIE,** b f Aragon—Drama School **T. F. Roe**
9 **AROWVALE,** b c Aragon—Lady Annie Laurie **Bert Cunningham**
10 **BEAUFAN,** b br g Taufan (USA)—Beaume (FR) **Mrs P. J. Conlan**
11 **CLIPPIE LAD,** ch c Bold Lad—Crowdie **J. A. Stewart**
12 **DARASH,** ch c Dara Monarch—Ashken
13 **ELAGUSKA,** ch f Ela-Mana-Mou—Tunguska **Miss Siobhan Browne**
14 **EMPEROR CHANG (USA),** b c Wavering Monarch—Movin Mitzi (USA) **Mrs B. S. Facchino**
15 **FASTBIT,** ch c Henbit (USA)—Fastidious **O. McGillicuddy**
16 **KENNA COURT,** b c Exhibitioner—Rathcoffey Duchy **Mrs B. S. Facchino**
17 **LOVE OF PARIS,** b f Trojan Fen—Danger Signal **Keogh-Browne Syndicate**
18 **MISS GANTLET,** b f Lomond (USA)—Princess John **John Michael**
19 **MOUNTAIN WIND,** b c Tumble Wind (USA)—Bustina (FR) **Mrs Brigitte Wolff**
20 **OBERON'S SON,** b g Fairy King—Glenardina **Mrs T. Gillson**
21 **QUILLAN,** b g Local Suitor (USA)—Goosie **Keogh-Browne Syndicate**
22 **SCIACCA,** ch f Dalsaan—Hill of Howth **Mrs M. M. Keogh**
23 **SOVEREIGN WOLVE,** b c Wolverlife—Moygara **Mr Michael Murray**
24 **TENDERETTA,** ch f Tender King—Fandetta **City of London Racing Club**
25 **THE LIQUIDISER,** ch c Connaught—Frivolity **Mrs B. S. Facchino**
26 **YANKEE SPARKLE,** b f Dara Monarch—Brilleaux **Mrs S. A. Rosenborg**
27 **ZVORNIK,** ch c Thatching—Cairi Bai **Keogh-Browne Syndicate**

TWO-YEAR-OLDS

28 B c 15/4 Touching Wood (FR)—Drama School (Young Generation) **Nabol Racing Syndicate**
29 **DRUMAALER,** b c 8/2 Drumalis—Laois Princess (Crash Course) **Mrs T. Gillson**
30 B c 20/4 Blakeney—Fast Asleep (Hotfoot) **Nabol Racing Syndicate**
31 B gr c 11/4 Kalaglow—Glory Isle (Hittite Glory) **Nabol Racing Syndicate**
32 B f 13/2 Taufan (USA)—Golden Pheasant (Henbit (USA)) **Nabol Racing Syndicate**
33 Ch g 13/4 Ela-Mana-Mou—Habitually Dancing (Habitat) **Park Beech Racing Syndicate**

MR L. BROWNE—continued

34 **IRISH PEACE (IRE),** ch c 15/5 Hold Your Peace (USA)—
Tajniak (USA) (Irish River (FR)) **Nabol Racing Syndicate**
35 B f 25/3 Known Fact (USA)—Lobbino (Bustino)
36 Br f 27/2 Persian Bold—Madame du Barry (FR) (Wollow) **Mrs M. M. Keogh**
37 **MISS GEORGE CINQ (IRE),** ch f 10/4 Be My Guest (USA)—Miss Paris (Sovereign Path) **J. L. C. Pearce**
38 **MUFFY (IRE),** b f 27/4 Soughaan (USA)—Aries Star (King's Leap) **Mrs T. Gillson**
39 B f 9/2 Be My Native (USA)—Parveen (FR) (Kouban (FR))
40 Ch f 21/4 Scottish Reel—Peregrine Falcon (Saulingo)
41 **PERZIN,** ch c 6/3 King Persian—Azina (USA) (Canonero (USA)) **Kay Racing Syndicate**
42 **RAVENSDALE ROSE (IRE),** b f 7/5 Henbit (USA)—Organdy (Blakeney) **T. F. Roe**
43 **REGAL YANKEE (IRE),** b c 22/4 Sandhurst Prince—Concave (Connaught) **Mrs S. A. Rosenborg**
44 Br f 30/4 Shy Groom (USA)—Relda (Relko) **City of London Racing Club**
45 B c 1/4 Scottish Reel—Stufida (Bustino) **Nabol Racing Syndicate**
46 **TENDERLEA (IRE),** b f 18/3 Tender King—Fun Frolic (Sexton Blake) **Hampstead Syndicate**
47 Ch c 10/3 Be My Guest (USA)—Ukraine Girl (Targowice (USA)) **Glenroe Racing Syndicate**
48 **VOLAGE (IRE),** ch f 27/2 Tender King—Tagik (Targowice (USA)) **Michel Rostan**
49 **YANKEE SHOW (IRE),** br c 2/4 Exhibitioner—Skhiza (Targowice (USA)) **Mrs S. A. Rosenborg**

Other Owners: Ray Diffley, Mrs Anne Doyle, Clare Gallagher, Alan Lillingston, Riverside Racing Club, A. S. D. Scott.

Apprentices: Michael Fenton (7-7), Darren O'Sullivan (7-0), Alan Roche (7-12).

Lady Rider: Mrs C B Murphy (9-4).

106 MRS B. BRUNT, Newark

Postal: **The Paddocks, Bogg Lane, Walesby, Newark, Nottinghamshire.**
Phone: **MANSFIELD (0623) 860109**

1 **CARIBBEAN SUN,** 12, ch g Midsummer Night II—Sleepy **Mr Roger Brunt**
2 **VILLA TARANTO,** 5, b m Ashmore (FR)—Gunnard **Mr Roger Brunt**

Amateur: Mr Roger Brunt (10-7).

107 MR J. M. BUKOVETS, Henley-in-Arden

Postal: **Botley Mill Stables, Tanworth Lane, Henley-in-Arden, Solihull, B95 5QZ.**
Phone: **(05642) 4631**

1 **BOREEN JEAN,** 6, ch m Boreen (FR)—Kitty Quin **Mr J. Gilbert**
2 **CAROGROVE,** 7, b g Rusticaro (FR)—Heather Grove **Tewtrell Ltd**
3 **GLINT OF STEEL,** 5, b g Broadsword (USA)—Celtic Well **Steel Plate & Sections Ltd**
4 **GROWING PHASE,** 5, b g Hays—Lovely Linan **Bulls Head Racing**
5 **LAKEFIELD,** 11, b g Pitpan—Chamspex **Tewtrell Ltd**
6 **RIG STEEL,** 10, ch g Welsh Pageant—Fir Tree **Mr Ralph Robbins**
7 **SHEER STEEL,** 10, ch g Precipice Wood—Flora Finching **Steel Plate & Sections Ltd**
8 **TEWTRELL LAD,** 7, ch g Paddy's Stream—May Foliage **Tewtrell Ltd**
9 **THE LAST TUNE,** 6, b m Gunner B—Tempest Girl **Mr J. Casey**
10 **TIKI'S AFFAIR,** 4, b f Bustiki—Rocky Affair **Mr F. J. Lancina**
11 **TROJAN ROSE,** 4, br f Decoy Boy—Firdale Rosie **Mr R. P. Dineen**
12 **WINSOR BOND,** 12, ch g Jimmy Reppin—Romany Girl **Steel Plate & Sections Ltd**

Other Owners: Mr Tom Joyce, Kelmac Developments Ltd, Mrs G. Lancina, Mr P. McElroy, Mr J. A. Rigby, S. V. Wadsworth Ltd, Exors Of The Late Mr M. Treacy.

Jockey (NH): John Shortt.

Conditional: Warren K Bird (9-7).

108 MR D. BURCHELL, Ebbw Vale

Postal: **Drysiog Farm, Briery Hill, Ebbw Vale, Gwent, Wales.**
Phone: **EBBW VALE (0495) 302551**

1 **BACHELOR'S PET,** 4, b c Petorius—Smile For Me Diane **Mr N. Pay**
2 **BEWITCHING WIND,** 5, ch g Windjammer (USA)—Tantra **Mr N. Pay**
3 **BRIGHT SAPPHIRE,** 4, b g Mummy's Pet—Bright Era **Mr T. G. Brooks**
4 **BROWN RIFLE,** 10, bl g Scottish Rifle—Mother Brown **Mr R. D. Forsyth**
5 **COSMIC FLIGHT,** 7, b m Cosmo—Sweet Flight **Mr H. G. Davies**
6 **EVENTIDE,** 4, ch f Red Sunset—Tagik **The Equus Club**
7 **FORCELLO (USA),** 7, b g Forli (ARG)—Heavenly Bow (USA) **Mr S. Cooper**
8 **GAY RUFFIAN,** 4, b g Welsh Term—Alcinea (FR) **Mr Frank Jones**
9 **HIDDEN BEAUTY,** 4, ch f Vaigly Great—Phoebe Ann **Mrs Ross Pitchford**
10 **HOT COMPANY,** 5, ch g Hotfoot—Campagna **Mr T. G. Brooks**
11 **MILLBECK LAD,** 4, b g Millfontaine—Miss Damus **Bedlinog Racing Club**
12 **PECHE D'OR,** 6, ch g Glint of Gold—Fishermans Bridge **Mr S. Cooper**
13 **SEA EXPRESS,** 10, b br g Seaepic (USA)—Expresso **Mr Ralph Morgans**
14 **SILKEN SONG,** 7, b g Taufan (USA)—Courreges **Mr N. Pay**
15 **TENDER WHISPER,** 5, b m Tender King—Queens Message **Mr N. Pay**
16 **TIMES ARE HARD,** 6, b g Bay Express—Raffinrula **Mr E. J. Williams**
17 **WHISTLING TIGER,** 5, b g Whistling Deer—San Estrella **Mr H. G. Davies**

Jockeys (NH): D J Burchell (10-0), Steven Davies (w.a.), Wayne Knox (w.a.).

109 MR P. V. J. BURGOYNE, Childrey

Postal: **Veor Farm, West Street, Childrey, Wantage, Oxon.**
Phone: **CHILDREY (023559) 688**

1 **BARRYSVILLE,** 14, b br g Woodville II—Barryscourt **Andrew Baird Tennis Courts Ltd**
2 **BOHEA DESTROYER,** 5, b g Crofter (USA)—Bold Kate **Mr Tony Smith**
3 **CYNTHIA MAY,** 8, b m Totowah—Rouge El Noire **Mr Steve P. Smith**
4 **DERRY RHYTHM,** 5, b br g Derrylin—French Music **Mr A. W. Byrne**
5 **GLENVALE,** 4, b g Hays—Deira **Mr Dan O'Sullivan**
6 **GREENORE PRIDE,** 13, b br g Menelek—Nenagh Belle **Andrew Baird Tennis Courts Ltd**
7 **MAUREEN'S CAVALIER,** 6, ch g Saher—Aethelflaed **Mr C. H. Cousins**
8 4, B g Seven Hearts—Our Melody **Mr A. Mulrooney**
9 **PLAYFIELDS,** 16, b g Northfields (USA)—Windo **Andrew Baird Tennis Courts Ltd**
10 **SOLDATINO,** 4, b g Chukaroo—Swinging Christmas **Mr I. M. Ledbury**

THREE-YEAR-OLDS

11 **GUILTY CONSCIENCE,** b g Pitskelly—Sweet Shop
12 **HERCULES,** gr g Bay Express—Firdale Rosie **Mr Tony Smith**
13 **PALACE COURT,** br g Anita's Prince—Court Hussar **Mr Steve P. Smith**
14 **TREASURE COURT,** br g Mummy's Treasure—Julia Too **Andrew Baird Tennis Courts Ltd**

TWO-YEAR-OLDS

15 B f 19/2 Today And Tomorrow—All Glorious (Crowned Prince (USA))
16 B c 21/2 Bay Express—Ardverikie (Red Alert) **P. Randall**
17 B c 29/4 Today And Tomorrow—Be Cool (Relkino)
18 B f 9/5 Drumalis—Flower Dell (Wolver Hollow) **P. Randall**
19 B c 5/5 Mummy's Treasure—Make-Up (Bleep-Bleep)
20 B c 9/2 Today And Tomorrow—Rhythm Maker (Song)
21 B c 20/4 Drumalis—Tabriya (Nishapour (FR)) **Mr A. Jolly**
22 B c 6/4 Mummy's Treasure—Thai Sabai (Double Form) **C. O'Donnell**

Other Owners: A. O'Ryan, K. O'Ryan, Mr P. E. Stapleton.

Jockeys (Flat): T Quinn (w.a.), M Wigham (w a).

Jockey (NH): G McCourt (w.a.).

110 MR N. BYCROFT, Brandsby

Postal: **Cotman Rise, Brandsby, York, YO6 4RN.**
Phone: **(03475) 641**

1 **BOREHAM DOWN,** 11, b g High Top—Woodwind (FR) **Mrs Madge Ashton**
2 **CAMDEN KNIGHT,** 5, b h Camden Town—Motionless **Mr D. Pickles**
3 **CREE LEADER,** 5, b g Creetown—Figurehead **Mr B. Lonsdale**
4 **FOLLOW THAT TAXI,** 4, b f Dublin Taxi—Arkengarthdale **Mrs Madge Ashton**
5 **GUNNER MAC,** 7, ch g Gunner B—Take My Hand **Mr F. McHale**
6 **HILLDYKE MAC,** 4, b g Lochnager—Gold Pension **Mr J. A. Swinburne**
7 **JIVE MUSIC,** 4, b f Music Boy—Swift To Conquer **Mr N. Bycroft**
8 **MIDNIGHT IMPERIAL,** 4, b f Night Shift (USA)—Tsar's Bride **Mr A. J. Lavell**
9 **OLD MOTHER GOOSE,** 4, b f Jalmood (USA)—Snow Goose **Mr A. J. Lavell**
10 **SILLY'S BROTHER,** 4, ch g Longleat (USA)—Scilly Isles **Mr G. J. Allison**
11 **STAR MOON,** 4, b c Tyrnavos—Lady of The Manor **Mr S. Mallett**
12 **TEMPTING OFFER,** 4, b f Raga Navarro (ITY)—Strawberry Ice **Mr E. H. Ruddock**
13 **THE DEVIL'S MUSIC,** 6, ch h Music Boy—Obergurgl **Mr David Faulkner**
14 **WESTOW LAD,** 4, b g Rabdan—Wigeon **Mr N. Bycroft**

THREE-YEAR-OLDS

15 **EMMA MAY,** b f Nicholas Bill—Nonsensical **Mrs L. J. Beard**
16 **MAC KELTY,** b c Wattlefield—Thevetia **Mr W. J. Mackenzie**
17 **MAC RAMBLER,** b c Hotfoot—Arkengarthdale **Mrs Madge Ashton**
18 **SAILOR MILAN,** ch c Pas de Seul—Sweet Home **Mr G. C. Morley**

TWO-YEAR-OLDS

19 **AZUL BLUE,** br f 24/2 Tina's Pet—Sailing Brig (Brigadier Gerard) **Mr E. H. Daley**
20 B c 21/4 Fayruz—Bally (Balidar) **Horseshoe Racing Plc**
21 **CALAHONDA SCRIBE,** ch c 16/3 Blushing Scribe (USA)—Smitten (Run The Gantlet (USA)) **Mr D. Faulkner**
22 Ch f 13/3 Stanford—Cast Party (Hello Gorgeous (USA)) **Horseshoe Racing Plc**
23 **CHELSEA MORNING,** b c 16/3 Sayf El Arab (USA)—Chezzy Girl (Manor Farm Boy) **Mrs Dyanne Benjamin**
24 **CLEAN UP,** b g 1/3 Another Realm—Tudor Carnival (Last Fandango) **Milner Cleaning Co Ltd**
25 B c 25/2 King of Spain—Greensward Blaze (Sagaro) **Greensword Racing Co Ltd**
26 B f 10/5 Double Schwartz—Lauribot (Lauso) **Horseshoe Racing Plc**
27 **MACHININGOUN,** b f 5/4 Dunbeath (USA)—Ryoanji (Lyphard (USA)) **Mr J. McDonald**
28 B f 17/2 Blazing Saddles (AUS)—Martin-Lavell Star (Godswalk (USA)) **Mr N. Bycroft**
29 Gr c 20/5 Godswalk (USA)—Miss Kirby (Town Crier) **Mr N. Bycroft**
30 B c 14/5 Anita's Prince—Mooned (Fair Season) **Horseshoe Racing Plc**
31 **NISHARA,** br f 10/5 Nishapour (FR)—Sardara (Alcide) **Mr G. J. Allison**
32 Gr f 31/3 Absalom—Obergurgl (Warpath) **Mr N. Bycroft**
33 Ch c 21/3 Electric—Pushkar (Northfields (USA)) **Mr N. Bycroft**
34 **SHAKEN NOT STIRRED,** b f 4/3 Tremblant—Martini Time (Ardoon) **Milner Cleaning Co Ltd**
35 Ch c 28/4 Dunbeath (USA)—Thimothea (FR) (Timmy My Boy) **Mr N. Bycroft**

Other Owners: Mr M. Bateson, Mr A. Carruthers, Mr C. Hunt, Mr G. H. Leatham, Mr R. Midgley, Mr Duncan Thomson, Mr H. Whitton.

Jockeys (Flat): L Charnock (7-8, w.a.), D Nicholls (w.a.).

Jockey (NH): P Niven (10-0).

Apprentice: C Priest (8-0).

Conditional: C Priest (9-7).

Lady Rider: Miss A S Bycroft (7-12).

111 MR B. BYFORD, Colchester

Postal: **Wash Farm, Halstead Road, Fordham, Colchester.**
Phone: **COLCHESTER (0206) 240235**

1 **CLINT NA GOOLAN,** 6, gr g Scallywag—Major Money **Mr Barry Byford**
2 **FISHING SMACK,** 7, b m Bustiki—Shell Fish **Mr Barry Byford**
3 **LOTHARIO,** 5, ch g Hello Gorgeous (USA)—Fairy Footsteps **Mr Barry Byford**
4 **MCGUIGAN,** 6, b m True Song—Kitengi **Mr Barry Byford**
5 **MISCHIEVOUS ALFIE,** 8, b g Balboa—Up To Mischief **Mr Barry Byford**
6 **MISCHIEVOUS JACK,** 9, b g Scallywag—Up To Mischief **Mr Barry Byford**
7 **TAKE NO TRASH,** 9, b g Deep Run—Karolette **Mr Barry Byford**
8 **TRUE RHYTHM,** 7, ch m True Song—Escartina **Mr Barry Byford**
9 **TUMBLE JACK,** 8, b g Tumble Wind (USA)—Alli-Bee **Mr Barry Byford**

Jockey (NH): G Martin (10-0).

Conditional: T Woolley (9-7).

Amateur: Mr T Moore (10-0).

112 MR E. M. CAINE, Chopgate

Postal. **High Crossett Farm, Fangdale Beck, Chopgate, Cleveland, TS9 7LH.**
Phone: **BILSDALE (043 96) 227**

1 **CAROUSEL CROSSETT,** 9, b m Blind Harbour—Grange Classic **Mr E. M. Caine and Mrs J. Caine**
2 **CAVALIER CROSSETT,** 9, b g Blind Harbour—Majestic Crossett **Mr E. M. Caine and Mrs J. Caine**
3 **COUNTESS CROSSETT,** 8, b m Blind Harbour—Majestic Crossett **Mr E. M. Caine and Mrs J. Caine**
4 **CRESTINA CROSSETT,** 8, b m Gracious Melody—Cresta Crossett **Mr E. M. Caine and Mrs J. Caine**
5 **CROSSETT CRUISADER,** 10, b g Gracious Melody—Portavia **Mr E. M. Caine and Mrs J. Caine**
6 **CROWN CROSSETT,** 8, ch g Blind Harbour—Guide's Ambition **Mr E. M. Caine and Mrs J. Caine**
7 **QUIXALL CROSSETT,** 5, b g Beverley Boy—Grange Classic **Mr E. M. Caine and Mrs J. Caine**

Amateur: Mr J Beardsall (10-0).

113 MR T. H. CALDWELL, Warrington

Postal: **Burley Heyes Cottage, Arley Road, Appleton, Warrington, Lancashire.**
Phone: **ARLEY (056 585) 275**

1 **BADGERS GIFT,** 4, b g Warpath—Bravade **Mrs Fiona Lewis**
2 **BURLEY HILL BOY,** 5, b g Longleat (USA)—Home Sweet Home **Mr T. H. Caldwell**
3 **BURNT PROPHET,** 8, ch g Abednego—Autumn Magic **Mr John Murray**
4 **DOWN FLIGHT,** 10, ch g Run The Gantlet (USA)—Feather Bed **Mr T. H. Caldwell**
5 **FISHY BUSINESS,** 6, gr g Morston (FR)—No Cards **Mr Richard B. Thompson**
6 **NEVER IN,** 4, b g Aragon—Recent Events **Mr T. H. Caldwell**
7 **PARESSE,** 5, ch g Sallust—Parez **Mr D. Ryder and Mr F. Swift**
8 **RODCHENKO (USA),** 5, b h Run The Gantlet (USA)—Golden Jolie (USA) **Miss S. J. Main**
9 **TILSTONE LODGE,** 5, br g Try My Best (USA)—Sabirone (FR) **Mr C. W. Jenkins**
10 **TRUE FAN,** 5, b g Taufan (USA)—Crepe Myrtle **Mr S. M. Street**

Other Owners: Mr Adrian Duckworth, Mr Eric Jones, Mr R. W. Main, Mr M. J. Naughton, Mr Mike Nolan.

Jockey (NH): P H Caldwell (10-0).

Conditional: P A Caldwell (9-11).

114 MR N. A. CALLAGHAN, Newmarket

Postal: **22 Hamilton Road, Newmarket, Suffolk.**
Phone: **HOME (0638) 664040 STABLES (0638) 663441 FAX (0638) 668446**

1 **A LITTLE PRECIOUS,** 4, b c Precocious—The Silver Darling **Mr Don Page**
2 **BANKER MASON (USA),** 4, b c Sadler's Wells (USA)—Alwah (USA) **Mr N. A. Callaghan**
3 **CHART CROSS,** 4, b c Millfontaine—Whichcombe **Mr G. Cawley**
4 **GARGOOR,** 4, ch c Kris—Icena **K. Al-Said**
5 **GENERAL SILKY,** 5, ch g General Assembly (USA)—Silky (USA) **Mr N. A. Callaghan**
6 **HIDDEN CREEK,** 5, ch h Mummy's Game—Brandon Creek **Mr G. Belcher**
7 **JAZETAS,** 7, ch h Jaazeiro (USA)—Mil Pesetas **Mr G. S. B. Cooke**
8 **KISSAVOS,** 4, ch c Cure The Blues (USA)—Hairbrush (USA) **Mr H. Stavrakis**
9 **LA DELIRANTE,** 4, ch f Cure The Blues (USA)—Ventimiglia **Mr M. F. Benacerraf**
10 **MYSTICAL GUEST,** 4, b c Be My Guest (USA)—Saygood (USA) **Mr J. Livock**
11 **NORFOLK THATCH,** 4, b g Thatching—Pellarosa **Mr M. Tabor**
12 **PHANTOM SINGER,** 4, ch f Relkino—Grace Note **A. Kantounas**
13 **RAH WAN (USA),** 4, ch c Riverman (USA)—Thorough **Mr F. M. Kalla**
14 **ROYAL DERBI,** 5, b g Derrylin—Royal Birthday **Mr M. Tabor**

THREE-YEAR-OLDS

15 Ch f Milk of The Barley—Bluejama
16 **CORNWALL PRINCE,** b c Taufan (USA)—Peach Stone **Mr Wafic Said**
17 **CORRIN HILL,** b c Petorius—Pete's Money (USA) **Mr R. K. Carvill**
18 **ETON LAD,** b c Never So Bold—Carolside **Mr Wafic Said**
19 **FOUR AWAY,** br c Valiyar—Edwins' Princess **Mr John Livock**
20 **GENERALS DAUGHTER (USA),** ch f General Holme (USA)—Evelle (USA) **Mr F. M. Kalla**
21 **HERMITAGE LANE,** ch c Habitat—Raminana (USA) **P. Gallagher**
22 **LONG ISLAND,** b f Law Society (USA)—Palm Dove (USA) **M. Hill**
23 **LORICA D'OR,** ch c Hotfoot—Dayana **Mrs O. McFarland**
24 **ORVIETTO,** ch c Try My Best (USA)—Ventimiglia **Mr M. F. Benacerraf**
25 **PRINCE LIVERMORE (USA),** ch c Mt Livermore (USA)—Abbey Leix (USA) **Mr F. M. Kalla**
26 **SHOUT FORE,** gr c Petong—Mavahra **Mr Pip Elson**
27 **SILENT GIRL,** ch f Krayyan—Silent Pearl (USA) **K. Al-Said**
28 **SIR NICK,** gr c Sandhurst Prince—Silecia **Mr G. S. B. Cooke**
29 **TAHADDI (USA),** ch f Northern Baby (CAN)—Nofertiti (FR) **Mr F. M. Kalla**
30 **TOP OF THE BILL,** b c Star Appeal—Cash Limit **Mr John Livock**
31 **TRIPLE BARREL (USA),** b c Sharpen Up—Galexcel (USA) **Mr F. M. Kalla**

TWO-YEAR-OLDS

32 **BOWDEN BOY (IRE),** b c 6/5 Never So Bold—Glebehill (Northfields (USA)) **Mr & Mrs Foreman**
33 Ch c 26/4 Song—Brazilian Beauty (Busted) **M. Hill & N. A. Callaghan**
34 Ch c 14/2 Noalto—Concern (Brigadier Gerard) **S. Griffiths**
35 **CORRUPT (USA),** br c 10/4 Lear Fan (USA)—Nirvanita (FR) (Right Royal V) **Mr F. M. Kalla**
36 Ch c Glow (USA)—Coven (Sassafras (FR)) **Mr Wafic Said**
37 **FREDDIE LLOYD,** b c 23/5 Tate Gallery (USA)—Jemarjo Pet (USA) (Peter Peter) **M. Hill**
38 B br f 7/2 Island Whirl (USA)—Hurry Marie (USA) (Hurry To Market) **M. Hill**
39 Gr f 3/1 Milk of The Barley—Pink Stripes (Pyjama Hunt)
40 Ch c 18/3 Sandhurst Prince—Regal Rhapsody (Owen Dudley) **N. A. Callaghan**
41 Ch c 29/3 Milk of The Barley—Serena Maria (Dublin Taxi)
42 Ch c 28/3 The Noble Player—Sindos (Busted) **Mr John Livock**
43 B f 3/4 Bairn (USA)—Sipapu (Targowice (USA)) **Mr John Livock**
44 Ch f 6/4 Royal Vulcan—Solatia (Kalydon) **G. Hartigan**
45 Ch c 5/2 Nordance (USA)—Tatisha (Habitat) **Mr Wafic Said**
46 Gr f 8/3 Godswalk (USA)—Ventimiglia (Bruni) **Mr M. F. Benacerraf**
47 B c 14/3 Tumble Wind (USA)—Western Wendy (Young Emperor) **Kais Al Said**

Other Owners: Mr R. F. Bailey, Mr J. A. Sheehan.

Apprentice: I Monteith (7-8).

115 MR R. CALLOW, Somerton

Postal: **Badgers Cottage, Compton Dundon, Somerton, Somerset, TA11 6PE.**
Phone: **SOMERTON (0458) 72194**

1 **ALA AMRIK,** 5, gr ro g Prince Tenderfoot (USA)—Negligence **Mrs G. Malone**
2 **BICKERSTAFFE,** 9, br g Workboy—Siciliana **Mr C. T. Brinson**
3 **DUNCAN IDAHO,** 7, b g Busted—Riboreen **Mr A. R. Brown**
4 **GLOW OF KHOBAR,** 5, gr g Kalaglow—Mary of Modena **Mrs Ann Vining**
5 **KNIGHT INSIDE,** 4, ch g Tachypous—Miss Saddler **Mr J. S. Hoare**
6 **MY BOY STAN,** 6, b g Dalsaan—My My Marie **Mr C. T. Brinson**
7 **RANDOM PLACE,** 8, ch g Random Shot—Sicilian Princess **Mr I. J. Pocock**
8 **SUNSET SAM,** 6, b g Dolman—Braeval **Mr E. J. Jones**
9 **THE TORRIDGE,** 5, b g Busted—Red Habit **Mr J. S. Hoare**

Jockey (NH): Simon Earle (10-0).

Amateur: I J Pocock (11-0).

116 MR P. CALVER, Ripon

Postal: **Whitcliffe Grange Farm, Ripon, North Yorkshire, HG4 3AS.**
Phone: **RIPON (0765) 700313**

1 **CETONG,** 4, gr g Petong—My Cecilia **Witham Land and Leisure Services Ltd**
2 **CIRCUIT RING,** 4, b g Electric—Brookfield Miss **Laharna Ltd**
3 **ERADICATE,** 5, b h Tender King—Pushkar **Mr Kenneth MacPherson**
4 **FINEST,** 5, bl m Final Straw—Finest View **Lord Zetland**
5 **GOSPEL ROCK (NZ),** 6, br g Church Parade—Leopard Rock (NZ) **Lord Zetland**
6 **MASKED BALL,** 10, b h Thatch (USA)—Miss Mahal **Mr P. Calver**

THREE-YEAR-OLDS

7 **BETWEEN TIME,** gr f Elegant Air—Beveridge (USA) **Hesmonds Stud**
8 **HICKLAM MILLIE,** ch f Absalom—Embarrassed **Mr L. T. Foster**
9 **ICE MAGIC,** ch g Red Sunset—Free Rein **Mrs Janis MacPherson**
10 **LEAVE IT TO LIB,** b f Tender King—Nuit de Vin **Witham Land and Leisure Services Ltd**
11 **OBOLOV,** ch g Vaigly Great—Dortia **Mrs Janis MacPherson**
12 **PACIFIC GEM,** br g Valiyar—Mary Martin **Laharna Ltd**
13 **PRESET,** ch c Homing—Constanza **Mr Kenneth MacPherson**
14 **VANIE,** b f Niniski (USA)—Vadrouille (USA) **Petra Bloodstock**

TWO-YEAR-OLDS

15 B f 20/4 Shardari—Carmelina (Habitat) **Lord Zetland**
16 B f 27/2 Blakeney—Daring Lass (Bold Lad (IRE)) **J. L. Woolford**
17 Gr f 10/5 Bellypha—Dovetail (Brigadier Gerard) **Lord Zetland**
18 Ch g 19/1 All Systems Go—Jersey Maid (On Your Mark) **Mrs C. Calver**
19 B c 16/4 Song—Sheer Bliss (St Paddy) **Mr Kenneth MacPherson**

Other Owners: Mr J. S. Bloor, Mr P. W. Ratcliffe.

Amateur: Mr S Love (10-7).

117 MR M. J. C. CAMACHO, Malton

Postal: **Star Cottage, Welham Road, Norton, Malton, North Yorkshire.**
Phone: **MALTON (0653) 694901**

1 **BUCKBY FOLLY,** 8, b m Netherkelly—Pavement Artist **Mrs E. C. York**

MR M. J. C. CAMACHO—continued

2 **DRAGONS LAIR,** 4, b br g Homing—Dragonist **G. B. Turnbull Ltd**
3 **FREE MINX,** 4, b g Free State—Musical Minx **Mr D. C. A. Bramall**
4 **GOLDEN SWALLOW,** 4, ch f Creetown—Polysee **Mrs G. E. Davidson**
5 **KILGETTY,** 4, b g Welsh Saint—Duchess **Lord Matthews**
6 **LEDSHAM,** 5, b g Gorytus (USA)—Concert **Mr Brian Nordan**
7 **PRECIOUS LAD,** 4, b g Bay Express—Foothold **Lord Matthews**
8 **SACRED GEM,** 4, b g Mr Fluorocarbon—Skerne Springs **Mr E. Smith**
9 **SEA DEVIL,** 4, gr g Absalom—Miss Poinciana **Mr E. G. Noble**
10 **TIE BACK,** 4, b br f Tender King—Grattan Princess **Mr H. Roberts**
11 **TOMMY OWT,** 4, ch g Mr Fluorocarbon—Helping Hand **Mr E. Smith**
12 **TWILIGHT FALLS,** 5, ch g Day Is Done—Grattan Princess **Mr Clifford Smith**
13 **WARD ONE,** 4, b f Mr Fluorocarbon—Canvas Shoe **G. B. Turnbull Ltd**
14 **WEST BECK,** 4, ch f Mr Fluorocarbon—Hod On **Mr E. Smith**

THREE-YEAR-OLDS

15 **CALACHUCHI,** b f Martinmas—Seleter **Mrs S. Camacho**
16 **CAREFREE TIMES,** b c Good Times (ITY)—Danaka **Lord Matthews**
17 **COLD BLOW,** b f Posse—Warm Wind **Lord Matthews**
18 **CONTRAFLOW,** b f Rainbow Quest (USA)—One Way Street **Lord Matthews**
19 **CRESELLY,** b f Superlative—Gwiffina **Hon I. V. Matthews**
20 **FLAME HAWK,** b f No Lute (FR)—Corsage **Hon. I. V. Matthews**
21 **KNAVE OF CLUBS,** ch g King of Clubs—La Calera (GER) **P. D. Savill**
22 **MENHENIOT,** br g Lochnager—Tremellick **Mr B. P. Skirton**
23 **MISTRESS MONET,** b f Claude Monet (USA)—Skysted **Mrs S. Camacho**
24 **SECRET SOCIETY,** b c Law Society (USA)—Shaara **Lord Matthews**
25 **ZAMBOANGA,** br f Blazing Saddles (AUS)—Maid of The Manor **Mrs S. Camacho**

TWO-YEAR-OLDS

26 **AVRO ANSON,** b c 6/5 Ardross—Tremellick (Mummy's Pet) **Mr B. P. Skirton**
27 **BAHIA FELIZ,** b f 23/3 Domynsky—Bally Tudor (Henry The Seventh) **Mrs S. Camacho**
28 **CHEEKY POT,** b c 21/3 Petoski—Pato (High Top) **Lord Matthews**
29 **EMMA VICTORIA,** b f 19/2 Dominion—Gwiffina (Welsh Saint) **Lady Matthews**
30 **FAMILY LINE,** b c 9/3 High Line—Princess Dina (Huntercombe) **Lord Matthews**
31 **JUNGLE MATE (IRE),** b f 13/4 Thatching—Donna Sabina (Nonoalco (USA)) **Lord Matthews**
32 **LATOSKY,** br c 1/5 Teenoso (USA)—Patosky (Skymaster) **Lord Matthews**
33 **LOCH GARANNE,** br f 1/3 Lochnager—Raperon (Rapid River) **G. S. Wilkinson**
34 B c 29/4 Lochnager—Maybehandy (Some Hand) **Mrs S. Camacho**
35 **MERPET,** b f 19/4 Petong—Spanish Mermaid (Julio Mariner) **G. B. Turnbull Ltd**
36 **MUMMY'S BAIRN,** b f 1/2 Bairn (USA)—Mummy's Glory (Mummy's Pet) **G. B. Turnbull Ltd**
37 B c 31/3 Mummy's Game—Nadron (Thatching) **Mr Brian Nordan**
38 **NICE DICE,** b c 29/4 Double Schwartz—Danaka (FR) (Val de Loir) **Lord Matthews**
39 **ORCHANDA,** b f 24/2 Pennine Walk—My Fair Orchid (Roan Rocket) **Hon. I. V. Matthews**
40 **POOH WEE,** b f 28/4 Music Boy—Nicoletta (Busted) **Lady Matthews**
41 Ch c 26/4 Adonijah—Seleter (Hotfoot) **Mrs S. Camacho**
42 **TUSKY,** b c 9/5 Prince Sabo—Butosky (Busted) **Lord Matthews**

Other Owners: Mr A. L. Goacher, Miss K. A. Wilson, Mr K. P. Wilson, Mrs M. A. Wilson.

Jockeys (Flat): N Connorton (7-13), J Lowe (7-8, w.a.).

Jockeys (NH): M Dwyer (w.a.), P Niven (w.a.).

Conditional: D Garside (10-0).

Lady Rider: Miss J Camacho (9-7).

118 MR B. R. CAMBIDGE, Bishops Wood

Postal: **Park Oak Farm, Tong Road, Bishops Wood, Brewood, Staffordshire, ST19 9AP.**
Phone: **WESTON-UNDER-LIZARD (095 276) 249**

1 **BALLYWEST,** 12, ch g Lord Ha Ha—Bally Decent **Mrs H. Noonan**
2 **BERKANA RUN,** 5, ch g Deep Run—Geraldine's Pet **Mr D. Jones**
3 **BILLSHA,** 4, b f Ahonoora—Sanjana (GER) **A. S. Blackham**
4 **GARRISON PARK,** 7, b g Sagaro—Olympic Visualise **Mr E. Stuart Knape**
5 **ONE OF THE LADS,** 8, ch g Decent Fellow—Medford Lady **Mrs H. Noonan**
6 **RIM OF PEARL,** 7, b m Rymer—Pearl Smoke **Mr E. Stuart Knape**
7 **SEAMERE,** 7, b g Crofter (USA)—Whistling Waltz **Mr B. R. Cambidge**
8 **SHAHNIZAM (USA),** 6, b g Youth (USA)—Shahneez **Mr D. Jones**
9 **TRIKKALA STAR,** 8, b m Tachypous—Emma Chizzet **Mr B. R. Cambidge**

Other Owners: Mr R. G. Starbuck.

Amateur: Mr J R Cambidge (10-0).

119 MR I. CAMPBELL, Newmarket

Postal: **Charlwood Stables, Hamilton Road, Newmarket, Suffolk.**
Phone: **NEWMARKET (0638) 660829**

1 **BAY WINDOW,** 6, b g Bay Express—Broken Record **Mr E. L. Wilkins**
2 **BIG DIAMOND (FR),** 6, br g Bikala—Diathese (FR) **Mrs C. Phipps**
3 **BINKLEY (FR),** 4, ch g Bikala—Jinkitis **Mr I. Campbell**
4 **COMMANDER CARVER,** 4, b g Owen Anthony—Carvers Corah **Mrs Sue Blacker**
5 **FOUR FOR UNCLE,** 8, br g Uncle Pokey—Lake Superior **Mrs J. Young**
6 **KHOREVO,** 5, b g Tyrnavos—Amina **Mr E. Campbell**
7 **REGGAE BEAT,** 5, b g Be My Native (USA)—Invery Lady **Mr E. Campbell**
8 **SIR HUMPHREY,** 10, ch g High Line—Greek Money **Mr I. Campbell**
9 **WILL RAINE,** 6, ch g Nicholas Bill—Chinese Falcon **Mrs J. Young**

THREE-YEAR-OLDS

10 **BARKSTON SINGER,** b f Runnett—Miss Flirt **Mr T. H. Morris**
11 **COSMIC DANCER,** ch c Horage—Royal Cloak **Mr D. Woods**
12 **HIGHLAND BIDDER,** b f Ring Bidder—Highland Rossie **Mr J. McManamon**
13 **LADY ROSEMARY,** b f Burslem—Sweet Foot **Mr S. Anrude**
14 **PEACE TALK,** br f Warpath—War Talk (USA) **Mrs S. E. V. Hinde**
15 **ZEPHYR NIGHTS (USA),** b g Grey Dawn II—Vaslava **Mr D. Woods**

TWO-YEAR-OLDS

16 Ch f 1/4 Giacometti—Bella Chantina (Porto Bello) **Mr I. Campbell**
17 Ch f 1/3 Critique (USA)—Born Anew (USA) (Avatar (USA)) **Mr D. Woods**
18 Ch c 21/2 Noalto—Turtle Dove (Gyr (USA)) **Mr D. Woods**

Other Owners: Mr M. Butcher, Mr B. Gill, Mr A. Gunns, Mr K. P. O'Neill, Mr S. C. Palmer, Mr M. G. Reeder, Mr S. J. Scammel.

Jockey (NH): R Campbell (10-3).

Conditional: V Smith (9-7).

120 MR H. D. CANDY, Wantage

Postal: **Kingstone Warren, Wantage, Oxfordshire, OX12 9QF.**
Phone: **UFFINGTON (036 782) 276/514 TELEX 444601**

1 **BEN ADHEM**, 8, b g Hotfoot—Heaven Chosen **Mr Gerald Kidd**
2 **BILLET**, 7, ch g Nicholas Bill—Cosset **Mrs Henry Candy**
3 **CLIFTON CHAPEL**, 5, b g High Line—Britannia's Rule **Mr J. K. Dale**
4 **FACT OR FICTION**, 4, br g Known Fact (USA)—Noble Wac (USA) **Mr Henry Candy**
5 **FIRST BILL**, 7, ch g Nicholas Bill—Angelica (SWE) **Mr Denis Lennon**
6 **HANDY MO**, 4, b g Rolfe (USA)—Stephouette **G. J. Handy & Co Ltd Garden Machinery**
7 **INCOLA**, 4, b g Liboi (USA)—Sdenka (FR) **Mrs David Blackburn**
8 **MANSIO**, 6, b g Liboi (USA)—Sdenka (FR) **Mrs David Blackburn**
9 **MASTER LINE**, 9, ch h High Line—Fair Winter **Mrs Henry Candy**
10 **MY IMPRESSION**, 4, b g Lomond (USA)—Wish You Were Here (USA) **Mr Gordon Comben**
11 **TOM RUM**, 7, b g Liboi (USA)—Snow Rum **Mrs David Blackburn**
12 **WILLIAM FOUR**, 5, b g Nicholas Bill—Henceforth **Mrs Henry Candy**

THREE-YEAR-OLDS

13 **ANNA KARIETTA**, ch f Precocious—Karietta **Lord Chelsea**
14 **CHOIR PRACTICE**, ch c Chief Singer—Good Try **Mr Fahd Salman**
15 **COOLULAH**, b g Dominion—Phoebe Ann **Mrs Henry Candy**
16 **GULMARG**, b c Gorytus (USA)—Kashmiri Snow **Lord Vestey**
17 **HEBRIDEAN**, b c Norwick (USA)—Pushkar **Mr P. A. Deal**
18 **HIGH BEACON**, ch c High Line—Flaming Peace **Mrs J. E. L. Wright**
19 **INTREPID LASS**, b f Wassl—Risk All **Mr P. A. Deal**
20 **STANDING ROOM ONLY**, b g Stalwart (USA)—Mary Mary Mouse (USA) **Mrs Henry Candy**
21 **ST ARILDA**, b f Pas de Seul—St Isabel **Mr T. A. F. Frost**
22 **TRUE BILL**, b c Nicholas Bill—Cosset **Commander G. G. Marten**
23 **WILLBUTWHEN**, ch c Nicholas Bill—Henceforth **Mr Ruthven Urquhart**

TWO-YEAR-OLDS

24 **ALWAYS FRIENDLY**, ch f 30/4 High Line—Wise Speculation (USA) (Mr Prospector (USA)) **Mr Fahd Salman**
25 **BOLD BOSTONIAN**, b c 16/2 Never So Bold—Miss Boston (FR) (River River (FR)) **Comben Thoroughbreds**
26 **CELIA BRADY**, b f 14/2 Last Tycoon—Lucayan Princess (High Line) **Mrs David Blackburn**
27 **CLOVERMILL**, b f 23/5 Sayf El Arab (USA)—Opinion (Great Nephew) **Mr J. R. White**
28 **COLLIDE**, ch f 8/5 High Line—Collapse (Busted) **Major M. G. Wyatt**
29 **DIBLOOM**, b c 5/5 Nomination—Tosara (Main Reef) **Mr Fahd Salman**
30 Ch c 8/4 Ahonoora—Fair Head (High Line) **R. Barnett**
31 **FLOWER MELODY**, b f 3/3 Liboi (USA)—Milford Moss (Record Token) **Mrs David Blackburn**
32 **HIGHLAND MEETING**, ch c 23/3 Scottish Reel—Neenah (Bold Lad (IRE)) **Mrs M. M. C. Clark**
33 **HOLD FAST (IRE)**, b c 20/5 Dara Monarch—No Flight (Nonoalco (USA)) **Commander G. G. Marten**
34 **HUMSTER**, ch c 22/4 Song—Primrolla (Relko) **Lord Vestey**
35 **IRISH NATIVE (IRE)**, b c 16/2 Be My Native (USA)—Irish Bride (Track Spare) **Mr Fahd Salman**
36 Br c 27/3 Valiyar—Jouvencelle (Rusticaro (FR)) **Mr H. R. Hould**
37 Ch f Master Willie—La Zonga (USA) (Run The Gantlet (USA)) **Mr P. A. Deal**
38 Ch f 25/4 Nicholas Bill—Maryland Cookie (USA) (Bold Hour) **R. Barnett**
39 **PICKLES**, b c 3/3 Petoski—Kashmiri Snow (Shirley Heights) **Lord Vestey**
40 **PIOUS BIRD (IRE)**, b f 4/3 Tender King—Robin Red Breast (Red Alert) **Mr Denis Lennon**
41 **PRESQUE NOIR**, bl c 23/3 Latest Model—Orlaith (Final Straw) **Captain M. M. C. Clark**
42 Ch f 29/3 Master Willie—Regent Miss (CAN) (Vice Regent (CAN)) **R. Barnett**
43 **SOLE CONTROL**, b f 28/4 Jupiter Island—Maureen Mhor (Taj Dewan) **Miss E. Lake and Partners**
44 **USHAK**, b br c 12/3 Baby Turk—Persian Carpet (FR) (Kalamoun) **Mrs David Blackburn**
45 **VENUS OBSERVED**, ch f 22/5 Sharpo—Fair And Wise (High Line) **Mrs C. E. Gross**

Other Owners: Mrs Judith Comben, Mrs T. G. R. Cook, Mr A. L. Deal, Mr J. Heyworth, Mr L. B. Holliday, Miss C. J. Lake, Lady Olivia Waldron.

Jockey (Flat): C Rutter (7-9).

Apprentices: A Armes (7-0), P Brislen (7-12), A Le Jeune (7-12), D J Williams (7-12).

121 MR W. Y. CARTER, Epsom

Postal: **Loretta Lodge Racing Stables, Tilley Lane, Headley, Epsom, KT18 6EP.**
Phone: **(0372) 377209 OR 376028 FAX (0372) 386578**

1 **AL SHANY,** 4, ch f Burslem—Paradise Regained **T. G. Mills Limited**
2 **ASTRASEAL,** 5, ch g Blue Refrain—Lady Farrier **Mr T. E. O'Neill**
3 **BETWEEN THE SHEETS,** 5, b g Crooner—Miss Chianti **T. G. Mills Limited**
4 **DEN'S SONG,** 4, ch g Sallust—Princess Ru **Mr Dennis Cooper**
5 **DIRECTORS' CHOICE,** 5, b g Skyliner—Hazel Gig **Mr P. C. Scarborough**
6 **EURODOLLAR,** 6, gr ro h Sparkler—Silver Berry **K. F. Khan**
7 **IT'S A LONG WAY,** 7, b g Le Moss—Bellejolais **Mr Robert Allen**
8 **LOVE PRINCE,** 4, b g Indian King (USA)—Chanrossa **Mrs Pauline Merrick**
9 **OUR FREDDIE,** 6, br g Cajun—So Valiant **T. G. Mills Limited**
10 **PENDOR DANCER,** 7, b g Piaffer (USA)—Bounding **Mr R. A. Bettney**
11 **PENTAGON ROSE,** 4, b f Kafu—All Gold Rose **T. G. Mills Limited**
12 **PETITE ROSANNA,** 4, b f Ile de Bourbon (USA)—Let Slip **Mr T. G. Mills**
13 **SNOWBALL DAVID,** 5, b g Wolver Hollow—Grace Note **Mr Patrick Hanifan**
14 **TOLO,** 5, b g Bold Lad (IRE)—Thessaloniki **Mr Ian Wicks**
15 **TRECAULDAH,** 6, b m Treboro (USA)—Hannie Caulder **Mr R. Cooper**
16 **WESTERN WOLF,** 5, ch h Wolverlife—Sweet Kate **Mr Robert Allen**

THREE-YEAR-OLDS

17 **BELINDA'S BOY,** b g Swing Easy (USA)—Queen of The Hills **Sherwoods Transport Ltd**
18 **CHEATING HEART,** ch f King of Clubs—Bit of A Fiddle **T. G. Mills Limited**
19 **GOTCHER,** b f Jalmood (USA)—Sipapu **Mr P. E. Stapleton**
20 **IRON MIKE,** b c Glenstal (USA)—Salabella **T. G. Mills Limited**
21 **JAGJET,** ch c Vayrann—Ritsurin **Mr Alan E. Ward**
22 **LA GALERIE,** b c Glenstal (USA)—Tizzy **Mr J. A. Bird**
23 **LONGLYN,** b f Longleat (USA)—Quenlyn **T. G. Mills Limited**
24 **NIGHTMARE KNAVE,** ch c King of Clubs—Mary's Dream **T. G. Mills Limited**
25 **OR NOR,** b f Cure The Blues (USA)—Barely Hot **T. G. Mills Limited**
26 **PETITE BUTTERFLY,** b f Absalom—Girl of Shiraz **Mrs T. G. Mills**
27 **THE FLYING FOUR,** b f Sayf El Arab (USA)—Bar Gold **T. G. Mills Limited**
28 **VALIANT TRIO,** b c Doulab (USA)—So Valiant **T. G. Mills Limited**
29 **WHITE SQUIRREL,** b f Noalto—Lovely Lassie **Mr Rob Frost**

TWO-YEAR-OLDS

30 **AKKAZAO (IRE),** b br f 24/1 Alzao (USA)—Akka **Ernie Penfold**
31 Br f 30/1 Sulaafah (USA)—Babe In The Wood **H. Hanifan**
32 **BARRON'S BOY,** b c 14/5 Track Barron (USA)—Baltic Leap (USA) **Tony Moore**
33 **CAROLE'S KING (IRE),** b c 21/2 Kings Lake (USA)—Senane **Mrs Carole Viney**
34 **CHESHIRE NELL,** b f 16/3 Absalom—Quenlyn **Keith S. Charlesworth**
35 B c 14/4 Balliol—Deer Forest **Inform Partnership**
36 **FLYING BECKEE,** gr f 16/2 Godswalk (USA)—Late Swallow **Joe Dayani**
37 **FRIDAY NIGHT GIRL,** b f 10/2 Good Times (ITY)—Final Call **Robert Lang**
38 **GREENWICH BAMBI,** b f 23/5 Music Boy—Coca **John Humphreys Turf Accountants Ltd**
39 **LEGUARD EXPRESS (IRE),** b c 11/3 Double Schwartz—All Moss **J. P. Devaney**
40 Gr f 4/2 Absalom—Let Slip **Mr P. J. Scarborough**
41 **MAJESTIC MELODY,** ch f 6/6 Crooner—Royal Birthday **Glen Antill**
42 B c 26/4 Bay Express—Miss Milton **Charles V. Cruden**
43 B c 22/4 Horage—Miss Moat **D. R. Hunnisett**
44 **NEPTUNE'S PET,** b c 9/4 Tina's Pet—Abalone **K. B. Symonds**
45 **PROUD BRIGADIER (IRE),** b c 29/4 Auction Ring (USA)—Naughty One Gerard **M. T. Lawrance**
46 **TELSTEAM (IRE),** ch c 8/4 King of Clubs—Ridge The Times (USA) **T. G. Mills Limited**

Other Owners: Mr M. Caine, Mr K. C. Cartwright, Mr John Chequer, Mr P. J. Harding, Mr D. A. Khan, Mr G. W. Mayers, Mr T. J. Oswin, Mr Mark Pointing, Mr Colin Slade, Mr Stephen Williams.

Jockey (Flat): John Reid (w.a.).

Jockey (NH): Dale McKeown.

Apprentice: K F Latchford.

122 MR W. T. CASEY, Banbury

Postal: **Thorpe Mandeville Manor, Thorpe Mandeville, Banbury, Oxon, OX17 2HR.**
Phone: **(0295) 711686**

1 **AFRICAN LASS,** 6, b m Skyliner—Mallabee **Mr J. Connor**
2 **ANDY BOY,** 6, b g Mr Fordette—Killonan Lass **Belmarda Ltd Civil Engineers**
3 **AUGHFAD,** 4, b c Millfontaine—Saulonika **Mr M. Mac Carthy**
4 **BIRKBECK LAD,** 5, b g Rarity—Supreme Pet **Mr T. Casey**
5 **BOLD IN COMBAT,** 7, b g Junius (USA)—Malmsey **J. Browne Construction Co Ltd**
6 **DONNA DEL LAGO,** 4, b f Kings Lake (USA)—Cannon Boy (USA) **Mr M. Mac Carthy**
7 **DUNGANNON,** 4, ch f Hays—Fairham **Mr Graham Burton**
8 **GAULSTOWN LAD,** 11, br g Pitpan—Russian Fun **Mr P. J. Hartigan**
9 **GROVETON (USA),** 8, b g Big Spruce (USA)—Vatican (USA) **Mr Pat Whelan**
10 **HIGH ALOFT,** 6, b h Cut Above—Think Ahead **Mailcom Plc**
11 **IAMA PRINCESS,** 7, gr m Miami Springs—Aughalion **Mrs E. E. Whelan**
12 **JOKERS WILD,** 5, ch g Jester—Brother John **Mr C. V. Unwin**
13 **LAD LANE,** 6, br g Proverb—Quarry Lane **Mr W. Henry**
14 **LEAGAUNE,** 8, br g Over The River (FR)—Cora Princess **Mr Carl Wright**
15 **MONTOOBI,** 5, b g Tickled Pink—Marlotte **Mrs C. A. Trendell**
16 **PENNY DREADFUL,** 7, ch m Nickel King—Catherine Street **Mr Graham Burton**
17 **ROZEL GAMBLE,** 9, b g Sunyboy—Gallic Counsel **Mr L. Connell**
18 **TELL YOU WHAT,** 5, ch g Crested Lark—Andromeda II **Mr R. Vesey**
19 **THE BRAVE GUY,** 7, ch g Le Bavard (FR)—Decisive **Mailcom Plc**

THREE-YEAR-OLDS

20 **LADY GHISLAINE (FR),** b f Lydian (FR)—Planeze (FR) **Mr P. G. Tingey**
21 **LADY MIAMI,** ch f Mansingh (USA)—Miami Star **Oxford and County Roofing Ltd**

Other Owners: Mr D. Curran, Mrs T. McIntyre.

Jockeys (NH): R Dunwoody (w.a.), M Lynch (10-0, w.a.).

Conditional: G Donaldson (9-12), J A McCarthy (9-7).

123 MR M. CASTELL, Clifton-On-Teme

Postal: **Sunnyside Cottage, Clifton-on-Teme, Worcester.**
Phone: **KNIGHTWICK (0886) 21538 CAR (0860) 545144**

1 **CHIEF GERONIMO,** 6, b g Thatch (USA)—Gigiolina **R. C. Grove**
2 **DAISY MILLER,** 5, b m Daring March—Holiday Season **Mr N. Thackeray**
3 **ENCHANTED GODDESS,** 4, ch f Enchantment—Song God **Mr N. Thackeray**
4 **HEADBEE,** 4, b f Head For Heights—Plaits **Julian Graves Ltd**
5 **INDIAN RETREAT,** 11, ch m Country Retreat—Daintylet **Mr M. Castell**
6 **LORETTO COLLECTION (USA),** 4, ch c Raise A Cup (USA)—Indian Queen (USA) **Mr M. Castell**
7 **MONSIEUR TOURBIERE,** 4, ch g Le Moss—Miss Nelly **Mr M. J. Lilley**
8 **SUPERLASSIE,** 4, b f Superlative—Brig of Ayr **Mrs Rosanne Walters**

THREE-YEAR-OLDS

9 B f Paddy's Stream—True Missile **Malvern View Stud**

Jockey (NH): V Slattery (w.a.).

124 MR H. R. A. CECIL, Newmarket

Postal: **Warren Place, Newmarket, Suffolk, CB8 8QQ.**
Phone: **(0638) HOUSE 662387 OFFICE 662192 TELEX 817759 CECIL G FAX 669005**

1 **BLAZE O'GOLD (USA)**, 4, b c Slew O' Gold (USA)—Lady Be Mine (USA) **Mr Peter Burrell**
2 **BRUSH ASIDE (USA)**, 4, b c Alleged (USA)—Top Twig **Sheikh Mohammed**
3 **CITIDANCER**, 4, b c Lomond (USA)—Mrs McArdy **Mr Ivan Allan**
4 **DISSONANT (USA)**, 4, ch c Diesis—Nashualee (USA) **Lord Howard de Walden**
5 **MONSAGEM (USA)**, 4, b c Nureyev (USA)—Meringue Pie (USA) **Sheikh Mohammed**
6 **OLD VIC**, 4, b c Sadler's Wells (USA)—Cockade **Sheikh Mohammed**
7 **REINE D'BEAUTE**, 4, gr f Caerleon—As You Desire Me **Mrs V. Hue-Williams**
8 **SHYOUSHKA**, 4, ch f Shy Groom (USA)—Capsville (USA) **Mrs Henry Cecil**
9 **SPRITSAIL**, 4, b c Kalaglow—Set Sail **Lady Howard de Walden**
10 **ZALAZL (USA)**, 4, b c Roberto (USA)—Salpinx (USA) **Mr M. Al Maktoum**

THREE-YEAR-OLDS

11 **ADAMIK (USA)**, b c L'Emigrant (USA)—Tountinna (USA) **Sheikh Mohammed**
12 **ADVIE BRIDGE**, ch f High Line—Marypark **Sir David Wills**
13 **AILORT**, b f Ardross—Forres **Sir David Wills**
14 **ALIDIVA**, b f Chief Singer—Alligatrix (USA) **Mr Charles H. Wacker III**
15 **APPLECROSS**, b f Glint of Gold—Rynechra **Sir David Wills**
16 **AVRA (FR)**, bl f Mendez (FR)—Vague Bubble (USA) **Mrs H. G. Cambanis**
17 **BELMEZ (USA)**, b c El Gran Senor (USA)—Grace Note (FR) **Sheikh Mohammed**
18 **BE MY CHIEF (USA)**, b c Chief's Crown (USA)—Lady Be Mine (USA) **Mr Peter Burrell**
19 **BIRTHDAY PARADE (USA)**, b f Chief's Crown (USA)—Jubilous (USA) **Sheikh Mohammed**
20 **BONDSTONE**, b c Miller's Mate—Doumayna **Lord Howard de Walden**
21 **CAYMAN BRAC (USA)**, ch c Miswaki (USA)—Biting Wit (USA) **Mr S. Khaled**
22 **CHIMES OF FREEDOM (USA)**, ch f Private Account (USA)—Aviance **Mr S. S. Niarchos**
23 **CUM LAUDE**, b f Shareef Dancer (USA)—With Distinction (USA) **Sheikh Mohammed**
24 **DRESS PARADE**, b c Sadler's Wells (USA)—Steel Habit **Sheikh Mohammed**
25 **DR NO**, b c Be My Guest (USA)—Proskona (USA) **Mr S. S. Niarchos**
26 **ESCRIME (USA)**, b f Sharpen Up—Doubly Sure **Lord Howard de Walden**
27 **FACE UP**, br c Top Ville—Pomade **Lord Howard de Walden**
28 **FRENCH SENOR (USA)**, b c El Gran Senor (USA)—French Poem (USA) **Mr S. Khaled**
29 **GLEN KATE**, b f Glenstal—Miss Kate **Lord Matthews**
30 **GOLAN HEIGHTS**, b c Shirley Heights—Grimpola (GER) **Lord Howard de Walden**
31 **GOLDEN TREASURY (USA)**, b f Lyphard (USA)—Belle Pensee (USA) **Sheikh Mohammed**
32 **GREAT HEIGHTS**, b c Shirley Heights—As You Desire Me **Mrs V. Hue-Williams**
33 **HALSTON PRINCE**, b c Petorius—Repicado Rose (USA) **Mr W. H. Ponsonby**
34 **HERCULE POIROT (FR)**, b c Law Society (USA)—Welsh Berry (USA) **Mr Philip S. Niarchos**
35 **HIGH FOUNTAIN**, ch f High Line—Crystal Fountain **Mr Michael Poland**
36 **JAWZAN**, b g Shareef Dancer (USA)—Abha **Prince A. A. Faisal**
37 **KISU KALI**, ch c Kris—Evita **Lord Howard de Walden**
38 **LASSIA**, b f Teenoso (USA)—Tolmi **Mrs H. G. Cambanis**
39 **LES SYLPHIDES**, b c Top Ville—Nadia Nerina (CAN) **Sheikh Mohammed**
40 **MADAME DUBOIS**, ch f Legend of France (USA)—Shadywood **Cliveden Stud**
41 **MAGNA OF ILLUSIONS (USA)**, ch f Roberto (USA)—Normia **Mr S. S. Niarchos**
42 **MEVLEVI**, b f Shareef Dancer (USA)—Meliora **Lady Howard de Walden**
43 **MIDNIGHT OWL (FR)**, b f Ardross—Midnight Lady (FR) **Mr S. S. Niarchos**
44 **MILLIONAIRE'S ROW**, b c Niniski (USA)—One In A Million **Sheikh Mohammed**
45 **MITAKI (USA)**, ch c Miswaki (USA)—Koketka (USA) **Sheikh Mohammed**
46 **MOON CACTUS**, b f Kris—Lady Moon **Sheikh Mohammed**
47 **MUTAH (USA)**, ch c Topsider (USA)—Bank On Love (USA) **Sheikh Mohammed**
48 **MUZO (USA)**, b c Irish River (FR)—Dance Flower (CAN) **Sheikh Mohammed**
49 **MY SISTER ELLEN**, ch f Lyphard (USA)—Cat Girl (USA) **Mr Charles H. Wacker III**
50 **NADAAWI (USA)**, b c Nijinsky (CAN)—All Rainbows (USA) **Sheikh Mohammed**
51 **NADMA (USA)**, b f Northern Dancer—Beaconaire (USA) **Sheikh Mohammed**
52 **NATIVE TWINE**, b f Be My Native (USA)—Twine **Mr James H. Stone**
53 **NOIRMANT**, ch f Dominion—Krakow **Lord Matthews**
54 **NORTH COUNTRY**, b c Nordico (USA)—Loren **Mr James H. Stone**
55 **ONAWAY**, ch f Commanche Run—Lulubo (USA) **Mr V. E. Barclay**

HORSE U.K.

in association with LEP (Bloodstock) Ltd

Winning Service Not Lip Service

Carroll House, winner of the
1989 Prix de L'Arc de Triomphe

186 High Street,
Newmarket.
Suffolk CB8 9AP

Tel: (0638) 665145
Telex: 818837 HORSUK.G.
Fax: (0638) 660848

MR H. R. A. CECIL—continued

56 **OPENING RUN (USA),** ch c Nureyev (USA)—April Run **Sheikh Mohammed**
57 **PINK BELLS (USA),** ro f Pass The Tab (USA)—Zenica (FR) **Mrs Benjamin Leigh**
58 **PRIVATE TENDER,** b c Shirley Heights—Select Sale **Cliveden Stud**
59 **QUIXOTIC (FR),** b f Caerleon—Idyllic **Mr S. S. Niarchos**
60 **RAFHA,** b f Kris—Eljazzi **Prince A. A. Faisal**
61 **RAHAAM (USA),** gr f Secreto (USA)—Fager's Glory (USA) **Sheikh Mohammed**
62 **RAIN DATE,** ch f Rainbow Quest (USA)—Roussalka **Mr George Strawbridge**
63 **RAZEEN (USA),** b c Northern Dancer—Secret Asset (USA) **Sheikh Mohammed**
64 **RENTINA,** b f Adonijah—Gay Charlotte **Mrs H. G. Cambanis**
65 **RIVER GOD (USA),** b c Val de L'Orne (FR)—Princess Morvi (USA) **Sheikh Mohammed**
66 **ROARING FORTIES (USA),** b c Alleged (USA)—Heavenly Breeze (USA) **Sheikh Mohammed**
67 **ROSE CUT (USA),** ch c Diesis—Sweet Ramblin Rose (USA) **Sheikh Mohammed**
68 **SACRED NUMBER (USA),** ch c Irish River (FR)—Disco Girl (FR) **Mr S. S. Niarchos**
69 **SANCTORUM,** b c Habitat—Sancta **Lord Howard de Walden**
70 **SARDEGNA,** b f Pharly (FR)—Sandy Island **Lord Howard de Walden**
71 **SASPARILLO (USA),** b c Blushing Groom (FR)—Powder Burn (USA) **Mr S. S. Niarchos**
72 **SATIN WOOD,** b c Darshaan—Satanella (GER) **Sheikh Mohammed**
73 **SHAVIAN,** b c Kris—Mixed Applause (USA) **Lord Howard de Walden**
74 **SINGLE STOREY,** b br f Rousillon (USA)—Shorthouse **Cliveden Stud**
75 **SPECKLED BRAID (USA),** b f Miswaki—Pete's Lucky Lady **Kennet Valley Thoroughbreds**
76 **SUNDANCE KID (USA),** b c Fappiano (USA)—Gallanta (FR) **Mrs Maria I. Niarchos**
77 **THUNDERBALL,** gr c Kris—Southern Maid **Mr S. S. Niarchos**
78 **TIGER FLOWER,** b f Sadler's Wells (USA)—Tigresse d'Amour (USA) **Sheikh Mohammed**
79 **TIME GUARDIAN (USA),** ch c Devil's Bag (USA)—Times Are Tough (USA) **Sheikh Mohammed**
80 **TOLEDO (USA),** b c Fappiano (USA)—Visual Emotion (USA) **Sir Gordon White**
81 **TOUR EIFFEL,** b g High Line—Gay France (FR) **Sheikh Mohammed**
82 **TRIFOLIO,** b c Touching Wood (USA)—Triple Reef **Mr Jose M. Soriano**
83 **TYBURN TREE,** b c High Top—Catalpa **Lady Howard de Walden**
84 **VIRELAI,** ch f Kris—Lyric Dance **Mr Saeed Manana**
85 **WAJNA (USA),** b f Nureyev (USA)—Wind Spirit (USA) **Sheikh Mohammed**

TWO-YEAR-OLDS

86 B c 21/4 Auction Ring—Age of Elegance (Troy) **Kennet Valley Thoroughbreds**
87 B c 28/3 Verbatim—Agujita (Vieux Manoir) **Sir Gordon White**
88 Ch f 29/2 Diesis—Alia (Sun Prince) **Prince Khalid Al Saud**
89 **ANAFI,** b f 25/2 Slip Anchor—Linda's Fantasy (Raga Navarro) **Mrs H. G. Cambanis**
90 **ANCHOR LIGHT,** b c 22/1 Slip Anchor—Doumayna (Kouban) **Lord Howard de Walden**
91 **ARATOS,** ch c 9/2 Night Shift—Sariza (Posse) **Mrs H. G. Cambanis**
92 **ARKLET (IRE),** ch f 23/2 Lomond—Timid Bride (Blushing Groom) **Sheikh Mohammed**
93 **ATOURS (USA),** b c 23/4 Chief's Crown—Ataire (What A Pleasure) **Sheikh Mohammed**
94 **AXE,** ch c 21/3 Kris—Russian Ribbon (Nijinsky) **Sir Gordon White**
95 **BALL OF WOOL (FR),** ch f 12/1 Baillamont—Bonny's Niece (Great Nephew) **Mr S. S. Niarchos**
96 **BLISSFUL MOMENT,** gr c 5/6 Rainbow Quest—Magic Vision (Shergar) **Mrs V. Hue-Williams**
97 **BORIS (USA),** b c 21/2 Chief's Crown—Ivory Lady (Sir Ivor) **Mr S. S. Niarchos**
98 B c 15/3 Robellino—Brilliant Dancer (Dancers Image) **Kennet Valley Thoroughbreds**
99 **CAP DIAMANT (USA),** b c 4/3 Secreto—Baby Diamonds (Habitat) **Sheikh Mohammed**
100 B c 7/3 Kris—Cat Girl (Grey Dawn II) **Mr Charles H. Wacker III**
101 **CHANDLERY (USA),** b c 2/3 Woodman—Sail Loft (Shirley Heights) **Sheikh Mohammed**
102 **CHIEF ORNAMENT (USA),** b f 10/2 Chief's Crown—Embellished (Seattle Slew) **Sheikh Mohammed**
103 **CLIPPING,** b f 28/3 Kris—Valkyrie (Bold Lad) **Lord Howard de Walden**
104 **EAT CAKE,** b f 13/4 Legend of France—Guillotina (Busted) **Cliveden Stud**
105 **ELIKI,** b f 24/4 Nishapour—Lovers Light (Grundy) **Mrs H. B. Cambanis**
106 **EYES OF BELIEF,** b f 11/2 Sadler's Wells—Or Vision (Irish River) **Mr S. S. Niarchos**
107 B f 24/5 Elegant Air—Fandangerina (Grey Dawn II) **Mr Charles H. Wacker III**
108 **FLAMING ARROW,** b c 11/2 Dancing Brave—Ma Petite Cherie (Caro) **Saeed Maktoum Al Maktoum**
109 **FLY TO THE MOON (USA),** ch f 24/4 Blushing Groom—
Disconiz (Northern Dancer) **Saeed Maktoum Al Maktoum**
110 **FRIEDLAND (USA),** b c 25/3 Nijinsky—Fenella (Thatch) **Sheikh Mohammed**
111 **FUNKY COLD MEDINA (IRE),** gr f 28/3 Seattle Song—Bernica (Caro) **Mr S. S. Niarchos**
112 **FURRY DANCE (USA),** ch f 6/4 Nureyev—Kenanga (Kris) **Lord Howard de Walden**

ECLIPSE PEDIGREES

Have you seen the light?

Eclipse Pedigrees .....

research the **pedigrees** found in Tattersalls' and Goffs' Sales Catalogues ....

produce **Private Stud Books** for some of the country's leading Studs ......

compile the data contained in the **Weatherbys' Stallion Book** and numerous other publications......

provide a **direct access computer system** utilized throughout the world by the Bloodstock Industry ......

With all this information at our fingertips don't miss out......

For a full range of products contact

ECLIPSE PEDIGREES

SANDERS ROAD, WELLINGBOROUGH,
NORTHANTS NN8 4BX

Telephone (0933) 440077 Fax 440814 Telex 311582

and ask for details.

MR H. R. A. CECIL—continued

113 **GONDOLIER,** b c 5/2 Slip Anchor—Grimpola (Windwurf) **Lord Howard de Walden**
114 **GRAMMOS (USA),** b c 31/1 Bailjumper—Rheine Falls (Rheingold) **Mrs H. G. Cambanis**
115 **GRAVETTE,** ch f 26/4 Kris—Highland Light (Home Guard) **Lord Howard de Walden**
116 B c 12/5 Lyphard—Greedy of Gain (Habitat) **Prince Khalid Al Saud**
117 B c 23/3 Alzao—Hedwige (African Sky) **Prince Khalid Al Saud**
118 **HIGHLY PRAISED,** b c 9/2 Shirley Heights—Ever Genial (Brigadier Gerard) **Cliveden Stud**
119 **HIP TO TIME (USA),** b c 17/3 Roberto—Luv Luvin' (Raise A Native) **Mr S. S. Niarchos**
120 B f 24/3 Mr Prospector—Honey's Flag (Hoist The Flag) **Sheikh Mohammed**
121 **IKEBANA (IRE),** b f 29/3 Sadler's Wells—Miss Toshiba (Sir Ivor) **Mr R. E. Sangster**
122 Ch c 7/2 Diesis—Informatique (Quack) **Sir Gordon White**
123 **JENDALI (USA),** b c 12/2 Nijinsky—Jellatina (Fortino II) **Sheikh Mohammed**
124 **JURA,** ch c 11/4 Rousillon—Reuval (Sharpen Up) **Sir David Wills**
125 **KIT MARLOWE,** b c 7/2 Faustus—Imperial Jade (Lochnager) **Mr H. J. Joel**
126 **KONOTOP,** b c 29/2 Shirley Heights—Konigsalpen (Priamos) **Lady Howard de Walden**
127 **LA SKY (IRE),** b f 7/3 Law Society—Maryinsky (Northern Dancer) **Morven Stud Ltd**
128 **LOVE AND LEGEND (USA),** ch f 8/3 Lyphard's Wish—Lore 'n Legend (Bold Reason) **Mr M. C. Samlalsingh**
129 **LOWAWATHA,** b c 2/5 Dancing Brave—Shorthouse (Habitat) **Cliveden Stud**
130 **MALIK SHAH (USA),** b c 17/3 Shahrastani—Malibran (Spectacular Bid) **Sheikh Mohammed**
131 **MARIE DE FRANCE (USA),** ch f 28/3 Diesis—Fabled Land (Graustark) **Sheikh Mohammed**
132 **MELFORD,** b f 22/3 Petoski—Coral Fury (Mill Reef) **Sheikh Mohammed**
133 B c 22/4 Sadler's Wells—Millerette (Mill Reef) **Mr S. S. Niarchos**
134 **MISS SCHWEPPES,** b f 9/4 Slip Anchor—Alteza Real (Mansingh) **Mr G. A. Fallowes**
135 Ch c 30/1 Nureyev—Nalee's Fantasy (Graustark) **Sheikh Mohammed**
136 B c 15/5 Blushing Groom—Night Light (Northern Dancer) **Sheikh Mohammed**
137 **NORTHERN REALM (IRE),** b c 6/2 Nordico—Petite Realm (Realm) **Mr H. J. Joel**
138 **OH MERCY (FR),** ch f 8/2 Be My Guest—Grammene (Grey Dawn II) **Mr S. S. Niarchos**
139 **OWLER,** b f 11/2 Slip Anchor—Strigida (Habitat) **Lord Howard de Walden**
140 **PEPLUM (USA),** b f 19/2 Nijinsky—Chain Store (Nodouble) **Prince Khalid Al Saud**
141 **PERFAY (USA),** ch c 27/3 Nodouble—Perfect Example (Far North) **Sheikh Mohammed**
142 **PERPENDICULAR,** b c 14/4 Shirley Heights—Pris (Priamos) **Lord Howard de Walden**
143 **POPULARITY (USA),** ch f 21/2 Blushing Groom—Populi (Star Envoy) **Prince Khalid Al Saud**
144 **PRIVY PURSE (USA),** gr f 5/2 Chief's Crown—Add Mint (Vigors) **Sheikh Mohammed**
145 **QUEEN RANAVALONA,** ch f 19/2 Sure Blade—Jungle Queen (Twilight Alley) **Mr P. D. Player**
146 **RAYADO (USA),** b c 18/3 Shadeed—Delray Dancer (Chateaugay) **Sheikh Mohammed**
147 **REDDEN BURN (IRE),** b c 7/2 Green Desert—Red Letter Day (Crepello) **Sheikh Mohammed**
148 **RUDIMENTARY (USA),** b c 17/2 Nureyev—Doubly Sure (Reliance) **Lord Howard de Walden**
149 **SAHARA FOREST,** b f 13/4 Green Desert—Home On The Range (Habitat) **Cliveden Stud**
150 **SAINT OTTO,** b c 11/4 Dancing Brave—Sancta (So Blessed) **Lord Howard de Walden**
151 **SARAWAT,** b c 14/5 Slip Anchor—Eljazzi (Artaius) **Prince A. A. Faisal**
152 **SEDAIR,** b c 25/4 Green Desert—Double Celt (Owen Dudley) **Prince A. A. Faisal**
153 **SERAC,** b c 14/2 Shirley Heights—Slenderella (Alpenkonig) **Sheikh Mohammed**
154 **SHAHI (USA),** ch c 10/3 Shahrastani—First Kiss (Kris) **Sheikh Mohammed**
155 **SHAKEEL (USA),** b c 1/3 Mr Prospector—Mom's Command (Top Command) **Saeed Maktoum Al Maktoum**
156 **SHELEGAI,** b c 19/4 Shernazar—Khandjar (Kris) **Lord Howard de Walden**
157 **SIBERIAN WINTER (USA),** ch f 20/3 Bering—Copperama (Comeram) **Mr R. E. Sangster**
158 B f 24/5 Alleged—Smooth Bore (His Majesty) **Sheikh Mohammed**
159 B c 21/3 Green Desert—Solar (Hotfoot) **Prince Khalid Al Saud**
160 **SOMEONE BRAVE,** b c 17/2 Commanche Run—Someone Special (Habitat) **Mr Peter Tarrant**
161 Gr f 27/1 Al Nasr—Sound of Summer (Drone) **Prince Khalid Al Saud**
162 **SOUTH AUSTRALIA (USA),** b c 28/2 Shadeed—Millicent (Cornish Prince) **Sheikh Mohammed**
163 **SPRING (IRE),** b f 20/3 Sadler's Wells—Gull Nook (Mill Reef) **Sheikh Mohammed**
164 **STRALDI (IRE),** b c 31/3 Ela-Mana-Mou—Cavurina (Cavo Doro) **Sheikh Mohammed**
165 Ch f 10/2 Diesis—Sweet Rambling Rose (Turn-To) **Sheikh Mohammed**
166 **THAMES TIDINGS (USA),** b c 2/3 Riverman—Call The Queen (Hail To Reason) **Sheikh Mohammed**
167 **TOHAMAH,** b f 16/2 Legend of France—Abha (Thatching) **Prince A. A. Faisal**
168 **TORPEDO LOS (FR),** b c 29/4 Baillamont—Artists Proof (Ribot) **Mr S. S. Niarchos**
169 **TWO SIX THREE WEST (FR),** gr f 6/6 Kris—Southern Maid (Northern Dancer) **Mr S. S. Niarchos**
170 **VOLKSRAAD,** b c 5/2 Green Desert—Celtic Assembly (Secretariat) **Sheikh Mohammed**
171 **WAKASHAN,** b c 30/1 Dancing Brave—Lady Moon (Mill Reef) **Sheikh Mohammed**
172 **WAYZGOOSE (USA),** ch f 11/2 Diesis—Indoor (Caracolero) **Lady Howard de Walden**
173 **WESTERN HEIGHTS,** b f 24/4 Shirley Heights—Western Star (Alcide) **Mrs J. McAllister**

Agent Double
Al Bahathri
Alydaress
El Cuite
Hours After
Lacovia
Law Society
Lonely Bird
Melodist
Michelozzo
Midway Lady
Miss Gris
Miss Secreto
Musical Bliss
Northern Trick
Prince of Birds
Prorutori
Rough Pearl
Secreto
Shaadi
Shadeed
Siberian Express
Soviet Star
Triptych
Zaizoom

Keeneland.

The measure of success

Since 1984, horses purchased at Keeneland have won 28 European Classic races – unrivalled success from the world's leading bloodstock auctioneers.

1990 Sales Dates

July 22-24 Selected Yearlings
July 25 Yearlings
September 9-16 Yearlings
November 11-18 Breeding Stock

KEENELAND℠

Source of The Classic Horse

Keeneland Association, Inc.
P.O. Box 1690
Lexington, Kentucky 40592-1690
Telephone 606 254-3412
Fax 606 288-4348
Telex 21-8462

Keeneland's European representative:
Tim Preston, Westfield House
The Links, Newmarket, Suffolk CB8 0TG
Telephone 0638 668026
Fax 0638 668036
Home 0638 730046

MR H. R. A. CECIL—continued

174 ZISKA (USA), gr f 18/4 Danzig—Heavenly Cause (Grey Dawn II) **Sheikh Mohammed**

Other Owners: Mr John Bray, Mrs Mark Burrell, Mr Anthony Cherry-Downes, Mr Leo Collins, Mr J. S. Gutkin, Mr A. L. R. Horton, Mr Maurice Manasseh, Mr R. D. Overall, Mrs P. D. Player.

Jockeys (Flat): S Cauthen (8-7), W Ryan (8-2).

Apprentices: S Davies (7-2), C Hawksley (7-2).

Lady Rider: Mrs J Cecil (9-7).

125 MR H. R. A. CECIL, Newmarket

Postal: **Sefton Lodge Stables, Bury Road, Newmarket, Suffolk, CB8 7BT**
Phone: **(0638) 662233 FAX (0638) 665596**

1 **CAVALCANTI (USA),** 4, b c Sir Ivor—Forelie **Mr C. A. B. St George**
2 **EXCEPTIONAL BID (USA),** 5, b g Spectacular Bill—Gulls Cry **Mr C. A. B. St George**
3 **MICHELOZZO (USA),** 4, b c Northern Baby—Tres Agreable **Mr C. A. B. St George**
4 **PORTER RHODES (USA),** 4, b c Hawaii—Stella Matutina **Mr C. A. B. St George**

THREE-YEAR-OLDS

5 **ADMIRAL BYNG (FR),** ch c Caerleon—Pig Tail **Mr C. A. B. St George**
6 **BEIJA FLOR,** gr c Busted—Rusticello **Mr C. A. B. St George**
7 **BELLEZZA,** b f Ardross—Bobo Emma **Mr C. A. B. St George**
8 **BUONARROTI,** b c Ela-Man-Mou—Amiel **Mr C. A. B. St George**
9 **CAPTAIN HOSTE,** b c Never So Bold—Another Princess **Mr C. A. B. St George**
10 **CARIBBEAN KATIE,** b f Valiyar—Heaven High **Mr Edward St George**
11 **CELIBACY,** b f Thatching—Une Folie **Mr C. A. B. St George**
12 **EMPRESS WU,** b f High Line—Elm Park **Mr C. A. B. St George**
13 **GREAT MARQUESS,** b c Touching Wood—Fruition **Mr C. A. B. St George**
14 **OCTOBER PARKER,** ch c Bustino—Karsavina **Mr C. A. B. St George**
15 **PRESSURE,** b f Pharly—Hay Reef **Mr C. A. B. St George**
16 **PTOLEMY (FR),** gr c Persepolis—Rivoltade **Mr C. A. B. St George**
17 **QUEEN OF SALSA,** b f Dominion—Alma Ata **Mr C. A. B. St George**
18 **SAUMAREZ,** br c Rainbow Quest—Fiesta Fun **Mr C. A. B. St George**

TWO-YEAR-OLDS

19 B c 22/5 Fighting Fit—Angling (Angle Light) **Mr C. A. B. St George**
20 Ch f 25/4 Diesis—Chateau Dancer (Giacometti) **Mr C. A. B. St George**
21 **COLERIDGE,** gr c 31/5 Bellypha—Quay Line (High Line) **Mr C. A. B. St George**
22 **COMANECI,** b f 1/2 Ahonoora—Church Mountain (Furry Glen) **Mr C. A. B. St George**
23 Gr c 6/5 Kalaglow—Creake (Derring-Do) **Mr C. A. B. St George**
24 **ELVIRA (USA),** b f 13/3 Linkeage—Foxhunter's Reel (Majestic Light) **Mr C. A. B. St George**
25 Ch c 3/3 Bering—French Flick (Silent Screen) **Mr C. A. B. St George**
26 **GORT,** b c 3/5 Teenoso—Stemegna (Dance In Time) **Mr C. A. B. St George**
27 **GUECA SOLO,** ch f 24/3 Pharly—Atitlan (Relko) **Mr C. A. B. St George**
28 **JOHN SHAW (USA),** b c 4/2 L'Emigrant—Ivory Wings (Sir Ivor) **Mr C. A. B. St George**
29 Ch c 21/2 Lyphard—Jubilous (Sir Ivor) **Mr C. A. B. St George**
30 Ch f 28/4 Dixieland Band—Keep Me Posted (Stage Door Johnny) **Mr C. A. B. St George**
31 **MARCUS THORPE (USA),** ch c 24/3 Palace Music—Guilty Miss (Mr Redoy) **Mr C. A. B. St George**
32 **PATRICIA (USA),** ch f 3/2 Assert—Passionist (Buckpasser) **Mr C. A. B. St George**
33 **SINGING NELLY,** b f 17/3 Pharly—Nelly Do Da (Derring-Do) **Mr C. A. B. St George**
34 **SUN SURFER (FR),** ch c 20/1 R B Chesne—Sweet Cashmere (Kashmir) **Mr C. A. B. St George**

MR H. R. A. CECIL—continued

35 B f 10/4 Dominion—Sylvania (Luthier) **Mr C. A. B. St George**
36 B c 7/5 Critique—Tres Agreable (Luthier) **Mr C. A. B. St George**
37 **TRUBETZKOY (USA),** ch c 17/3 Master Willie—Travertine (Habitat) **Mr C. A. B. St George**

Other Owners: Dr R. B. Chesne, Mrs Georgia Frontiere, David Howard, Tessona Ltd.

Jockeys (Flat): S Cauthen, Paul Eddery.

126 MR A. J. CHAMBERLAIN, Swindon

Postal: **North End Farm, Ashton Keynes, Swindon, Wiltshire, SN6 6QR.**
Phone: **(0285) 861347**

1 **ANNSOFAIR,** 6, ch m Dubassoff (USA)—Fair Georgina **Mrs A. T. Lodge**
2 **BONUS BOY,** 5, ch g Vital Season—Martini Girl **Mr J. C. P. G. Scutt**
3 **BURLINGTON LAD,** 11, ch g Sweet Revenge—Allegretto **Mr A. J. Chamberlain**
4 **FOURCEES,** 5, b g Balidar—Star Duchess **Mr F. J. Carter**
5 **GEORGIAN QUICKSTEP,** 5, b m Dubassoff (USA)—Fair Georgina **Mrs A. E. Morton**
6 **KINGSBRIDGE FLYER,** 8, ch g Pony Express—River Chant **Mr T. P. Woodbridge**
7 **LORD KILGAYLE,** 6, b g Lord Gayle (USA)—Kilfenora **Mr David Woodward**
8 **LOST PRIDE,** 7, b br g Flatbush—Half Moon Bay **Mr T. W. Edwards**
9 **MASTER THATCHER,** 4, b g Thatching—Mistress Vyne **Mr M. W. Robinson**
10 **NORTHERN HALO,** 9, ch g Northfields (USA)—Halomata **Mr N. B. Moore**
11 **OCEAN LAD,** 7, b g Windjammer (USA)—Elixir **Mr E. H. Lodge**
12 **ROCQUELLE,** 5, ch m Coquelin (USA)—Weapon **Mr M. W. Robinson**
13 **SHAY,** 5, b g Hays—Barefoot Contessa **Mr E. H. Lodge**
14 **SOLENT STEEL,** 5, gr m Undulate (USA)—Tavaro **Mrs A. E. Morton**

Other Owners: Mr G. J. Chamberlain, Mr C. Cowley.

Jockeys (NH): B Powell (10-0, w.a.), Lorna Vincent (10-0).

Conditional: J Duffy (9-7), W McFarland (9-10).

Amateur: Mr C Farrel.

Lady Rider: Lorna Vincent.

127 MR N. CHAMBERLAIN, West Auckland

Postal: **Acrum Lodge, Staindrop Road, West Auckland, Bishop Auckland, DL14 9PB.**
Phone: **(0388) 832465**

1 **GIPSY RAMBLER,** 5, gr g Move Off—Gipsy Silver **Mrs Margaret Underwood**
2 **GIPSY'S TOKEN,** 5, b g Silly Prices—Gipsy Silk **Mr N. Chamberlain**
3 **GO GIPSY,** 8, br m Move Off—Gipsy Silver **Mr N. Chamberlain**
4 **LIOSEAN,** 4, gr g Silly Prices—Manche **Mr N. Chamberlain**
5 **MAGNOX,** 9, ch g Keren—So Blue **Mr K. L. Adey**
6 **MOVING TIME,** 5, ch g Move Off—Ribera **Mr K. L. Adey**
7 **POLARIS,** 4, ro g Move Off—Toadpool **Mrs Margaret Underwood**
8 **ROYAL TRIBUTE,** 5, ch g Ribdale—Dizzy Day **Mr B. R. Rutter**
9 **SIMILE,** 4, br f Silly Prices—Millisles **Mr M. Morley**
10 **SPECIAL PRICE,** 5, ro g Silly Prices—Manche **Mr K. L. Adey**

MR N. CHAMBERLAIN—continued

THREE-YEAR-OLDS

11 **BEYOND MOMBASA,** br f Silly Prices—Elitist **Mr R. W. Chamberlain**
12 **STAR OF THE SEA,** gr f Absalom—River Chimes **Mr N. Chamberlain**

TWO-YEAR-OLDS

13 Br f Silly Prices—Elitist (Keren) **Mr R. W. Chamberlain**
14 Ch g Say Primula—Kerosa (Keren) **Mr N. Chamberlain**
15 Gr g Move Off—Millisles (Pongee) **Mr N. Chamberlain**
16 Ch g Move Off—Ribera (Ribston) **Mr N. Chamberlain**
17 Ch f Say Primula—Rilin (Ribston) **Mr N. Chamberlain**
18 B g Silly Prices—Rimove (Move Off) **Mr K. L. Adey**

Other Owners: Mr W. A. Stephenson.

Conditional: W Urwin (9-7).

128 MR R. CHAMPION M.B.E., Newmarket

Postal: **Bechers, Hamilton Road, Newmarket, Suffolk.**
Phone: **(0638) 666546**

1 **BARUT (USA),** 5, b g Lines of Power (USA)—Brookbourn (USA) **Kenson Contractors (Bennington) Ltd**
2 **COIS NA HABHNA,** 5, ch g Over The River (FR)—Arctic Lou **Mr R. M. Tondut**
3 **FEILE NA HINSE,** 7, b g Cidrax (FR)—Hildamay **Mr R. M. Tondut**
4 **MR FELIX,** 4, b g Camden Town—Mohila
5 **PROVERBIAL ROSE,** 8, b m Proverb—Agapantha **Mr R. M. Tondut**
6 **SEMINOFF (FR),** 4, b g In Fijar (USA)—Borjana (USA) **Mr Ian Watkinson**
7 **TIFFANYS NEDINE,** 4, b g Rymer—Gokatiego **Mr R. M. Tondut**

THREE-YEAR-OLDS

8 **STUBBS ROAD,** b c Blushing Scribe (USA)—Rheinza **Mrs D. F. Champion**

Other Owners: Mr Frank H. Pullen.

Jockey (NH): R Rowe (10-2).

Conditional: Simon Bloss (9-7).

129 MR N. CHANCE, The Curragh

Postal: **Bernard Lodge, Curragh Camp, The Curragh, Co. Kildare, Ireland.**
Phone: **(045) 41397**

1 4, Br c Corvaro—Anglesea Market **Mrs M. Behan**
2 **HAPPY REUNION,** 5, b g Torenaga—Chilita **Mrs L. Skelly**
3 **KNOX'S CORNER,** 5, ch g Green Shoon—Sister Fiona **Mrs M. Behan**
4 **MISTY'S WISH,** 5, b m Furry Glen—Brave Wish **Mrs L. Skelly**
5 4, Ch f Orchestra—Nessie B **Mrs B. Howard**
6 **OUT ON HER OWN,** 4, b f Superlative—On Her Own **John A. Mitchell**
7 **TERRIFFIC STAR,** 4, b f Wolverlife—Spy Girl **Mrs M. Chance**

THREE-YEAR-OLDS

8 B f Tanfirion—Cap d'Antibes **Sean Madigan**
9 B f Seymour Hicks—Dance Mistress **Mr S. Dunne**
10 **HOMOSASSA,** ch f Burslem—Salt **Hugh Curley**
11 **ORLA'S DELL,** b f Muscatite—Flower Dell **Ben Hogan**
12 **YOUNG TYSON,** ch c Coquelin—Gwendolyn **Mr J. Moore**

MR N. CHANCE—continued

TWO-YEAR-OLDS

13 B c 28/5 Rusticaro—Anglesea Market (Sea Hawk II) **Mr L. Rowan**
14 **BELLE OF DREAMS (IRE),** b f 30/3 Sarab—Bells of Ireland (Northfields) **Mr J. Carroll**
15 B f 14/5 Rousillon—Clear Picture (Polyfoto) **Mr M. Hudson**
16 **DUNSALAN,** b f 25/2 Dunbeath—Al Zumurrud (Be My Guest) **Green Island Stud Ltd**
17 **MARIEN PLATZ (IRE),** b f 30/4 Hatim—Blue Bell's Star (Thatching) **Mrs M. Chance**
18 Br f 22/3 Seclude—Play The Fool (Will Somers) **Mr M. McCartan**
19 **SALMON SALBY (IRE),** b f 5/4 Salmon Leap—Telham (No Robbery) **Green Island Stud Ltd**
20 **ZILLER VALLEY (IRE),** ch f 14/5 Mazaad—Riot Girl (Right Boy) **Mrs M. Behan**

Other Owners: F. Burke, N. Chance.

Jockey (Flat): P Shanahan (8-2, w.a.).

Jockey (NH): A Powell (w.a.).

Amateur: Mr J P Dempsey.

130 MR MIKE CHANNON, Lambourn

Postal: **Saxon Gate Stables, Lambourn, Newbury, Berkshire.**
Phone: **(0264) 810225 FAX (0703) 702570**

1 **GOLDEN SCISSORS,** 4, ch f Kalaglow—Hide Out **Colby Bloodstock Agency Ltd**
2 **JEROZA,** 4, b f Shareef Dancer—Tarpoon **Mrs C. Howard**
3 **ROWLANDSONS TROPHY,** 5, b h Vaigly Great—Queen's Parade **Mr S. J. Le Gassick**
4 **SABARAB,** 4, b c Sayf El Arab—Miss Speak Easy **Wessex Bloodstock Agency Plc**
5 **SUPERZOOM,** 4, ch c Ballad Rock—Red Ruby **Mr B. Taylor**
6 **WESSEX WARRIOR,** 4, br c Anfield—Achiever **Wessex Bloodstock Agency Plc**

THREE-YEAR-OLDS

7 **BEAUJOLAIS NOUVEAU,** ch c Aragon—No Halo **Mrs D. Hanson**
8 **CHEVEUX MITCHELL,** ch c Dunbeath—Hide Out **Mrs C. Wood**
9 **EL VOLADOR,** br c Beldale Flutter—Pharjoy **Mr M. Garrido**
10 **PIPERS HILL,** ch c Creative Plan—Kindle **Mr P. Trant**
11 **RUBY SLIPPERS,** ch f Stanford—Tanzanite **Mr G. Herridge**
12 **SLOW EXPOSURE,** b c Pharly—Armure Bleue **Miss K. Stark**
13 **YOU KNOW THE RULES,** b f Castle Keep—Falls of Lora **John Henwood Organisation**

TWO-YEAR-OLDS

14 **CITYPLUMBJO,** b c 30/4 Hotfoot—Vaula (Henbit (USA)) **City Plumbing Supplies plc**
15 B f 17/5 Prince Sabo—Contadina (Memling) **Mr N. F. Swindley**
16 B f 2/5 Fairy King—Dar-A-Meter (Dara Monarch) **Mike Channon Bloodstock**
17 Ch c 3/4 Rabdan—Golderama (Golden Dipper) **Mike Channon Bloodstock**
18 B c 13/2 Red Sunset—Great Land (Friend's Choice) **Mr J. Mitchell**
19 **MISS MOONSHINE,** b f 29/2 Jupiter Island—Third Movement (Music Boy) **Mrs D. Hanson**
20 B c 7/6 Nicholas Bill—Sabala (Tribal Chief) **Mr P. Trant**

Other Owners: Mr P. Beasant, Mr S. Brooks, Mr W. Harrison-Allan, Mr P. Jolliffe, Mr T. Mitchell, Mr M. Quinn, Mrs W. Taylor.

131 MR D. W. CHAPMAN, York

Postal: **Mowbray House Farm, Stillington, York, YO6 1LT.**
Phone: **(0347) 21683 CAR PHONE (0836) 760590 FAX (0347) 23018**

1 **ABSOLUTION,** 6, gr h Absalom—Great Grey Niece **Mr M. F. Hyman**
2 **AUTONOMOUS,** 5, b g Milford—Mandrian **Mr Colin G. R. Booth**
3 **BLACK MARKETEER (NZ),** 5, ch g Sir Tristram—Satina (NZ) **All Aboard Racing**
4 **BREAK LOOSE,** 4, ch f Krayyan—Free Course **Mr Colin G. R. Booth**
5 **BRIGHT HOUR,** 5, ro g Kabour—Amber Vale **Mr William Chapman**
6 **CAMPO,** 5, b g Hill's Forecast—Shagra **Miss Andrea Campion**
7 **CATIMINI,** 5, ch h Coquelin (USA)—Espadrille **Mr Colin G. R. Booth**
8 **CHAPLINS CLUB (USA),** 10, ch g Parade of Stars (USA)—Nautical Rose (USA) **Mr P. D. Savill**
9 **CHERRY CHAP,** 5, b g Kabour—Mild Wind **Mrs M. Hills**
10 **CITY TO CITY,** 4, b f Windjammer (USA)—Beamless **Mr James P. O'Neill**
11 **GLENCROFT,** 6, b g Crofter (USA)—Native Fleet (FR) **Mr David W. Chapman**
12 **KABCAST,** 5, b g Kabour—Final Cast **Mrs M. M. Marshall**
13 **KABELLA,** 4, ch f Kabour—Right Abella **Mr A. Rhodes**
14 **KIBBLE,** 4, ch f Kabour—Hilly's Daughter **Mr David W. Chapman**
15 **LADY KEYSER,** 4, b f Le Johnstan—Fanny Keyser **Mr James P. O'Neill**
16 **LE CHIC,** 4, b g Kabour—Boom Shanty **Mr John Wilman**
17 **MAD HOUSE,** 5, b m Kabour—Open House **Mr David W. Chapman**
18 **MASKOONA,** 5, b m Electric—Hound Song **Mr David W. Chapman**
19 **MASTER OF THE HOUSE,** 4, b g King of Hush—Miss Racine **Mr P. D. Savill**
20 **MILO,** 4, b g Lochnager—Mild Wind **Mrs M. Hills**
21 **MINSK,** 4, ch f Kabour—Wedded Bliss **Mr Michael Hill**
22 **MISS KIVE,** 4, b f Kabour—Final Cast **Mr Michael Hill**
23 **MISTER MARCH,** 7, b g Marching On—Jetwitch **Mr M. F. Hyman**
24 **PRECIOUS MEMORIES,** 5, br g Kabour—Kings Fillet **Mr William Chapman**
25 **RARE VISION,** 4, ch f Salmon Leap (USA)—Silver Glimpse
26 **SCOTCH IMP,** 6, ch m Imperial Fling (USA)—Bunduq **Mr Walter Nelson**
27 **SKY SINGER,** 4, b f Kafu—Singalong Lass **Mr A. C. Whillans**
28 **SOBERING THOUGHTS,** 4, ch g Be My Guest (USA)—Soba **The Hon. I. V. Matthews**
29 **SULLY'S CHOICE (USA),** 9, b g King Pellinore (USA)—Salute The Coates (USA) **Mr William Chapman**

THREE-YEAR-OLDS

30 **BANCROFT,** b f Kabour—Mrs Buzby **Mr Michael Hill**
31 **DARA PRINCE,** ch g Dara Monarch—Dowcester **Mr David W. Chapman**
32 **FINAL HARVEST,** ch f Final Straw—Gas Only **Mr Colin G. R. Booth**
33 B f Kabour—Hilly's Daughter
34 **HYDROPIC,** b g Kabour—Hydrangea **Mr David W. Chapman**
35 **MIDWEST,** ch g Kabour—Boom Shanty **Mr Michael Hill**
36 **REDNET,** b f Tender King—Red For Go **Miss N. F. Thesiger**
37 **SWING NORTH,** b c Night Shift (USA)—Run For Her Life **Miss Andrea Campion**
38 **TIMES GOLD (USA),** b g Gold Stage (USA)—Snow Cone (USA) **Mr Colin G. R. Booth**
39 **TOSS OF THE COIN,** ch g Rabdan—Cedees **Mr Colin G. R. Booth**
40 **TRES AMIGOS,** b g Norwick (USA)—Safeguard **Mr N. Peacock**
41 B f Kabour—Wedded Bliss
42 **WELLSY LAD (USA),** ch c El Baba (USA)—Iwishiknew (USA) **Mr Michael Hill**

TWO-YEAR-OLDS

43 B f 27/3 Kabour—Belhill (Beldale Flutter (USA))
44 Ch f 22/2 Kabour—Boom Shanty (Dragonara Palace (USA)) **Mr Michael Hill**
45 **C'EST MOI,** br f 31/1 Kabour—Woodrush (Mummy's Pet) **Mr C. J. Dennis**
46 B f 4/2 Kabour—Final Cast (Saulingo)
47 **HOMESTEAD LAD,** b g 28/4 Homing—Greenstead Lady (Great Nephew) **Mr J. Eddell**
48 **KABERA,** b g 12/2 Kabour—Boldera (Persian Bold) **Miss N. F. Thesiger**
49 B c 11/5 Scorpio (FR)—L'Angelo di Carlo (Record Token)
50 **LETS GO SABO,** ch g 17/5 Prince Sabo—Run For Her Life (Runnymede) **Mr Bill Waddington**
51 Ch g 12/3 Kabour—Mrs Buzby (Abwah)
52 Ch f 23/5 Kabour—Tang Dancer (Junius (USA))
53 Ch f 14/4 Kabour—Tolly's Best (Hittite Glory) **Mr Michael Hill**
54 Ch f 4/4 Kabour—Wedded Bliss (Relko)

MR D. W. CHAPMAN—continued

Other Owners: Mr P. D. Donoghue, Mr P. H. B. Eddell, Mr Matthew Sharkey, Mrs D. Smith, Mr Reginald Spivey.

Jockey (Flat): K Darley.

Jockey (NH): M Dwyer (w.a.).

Apprentices: A Todd (7-5), S Wood (7-0).

132 MR M. C. CHAPMAN, Market Rasen

Postal: **Woodland Racing Stables, Woodland Lane, Willingham Road, Market Rasen.**
Phone: **(0673) 843663**

1 **BUSORM,** 10, ch g Bustino—Wrekinianne **Mr C. F. Rawlinson**
2 **CHICO VALDEZ (USA),** 6, ch g Valdez (USA)—Lypatia (FR) **Mr L. Naylor**
3 **DAUNTING PROSPECT,** 6, b g Formidable (USA)—Acquire **Mr J. A. Thole**
4 **DRY GIN,** 7, ch g Grundy—Karajinska (USA) **Mr L. Naylor**
5 **GAME TRY,** 5, gr g Mummy's Game—Pariscene **Mr David J. Riggs**
6 **GOLDEN SAMPHIRE,** 5, b m Hays—Sea Shrub **Mr Ian Honeywood**
7 **LYNKIMGEM,** 4, ch g Royal Match—Sweet Millie **Mr R. White**
8 **MACE-BEARER,** 6, b g Martinmas—Annatown **Mr Ron Scott**
9 **PREBEN FUR,** 13, b g Mon Capitaine—Flashing Beauty **Mr J. A. Thole**
10 **SPANISH SONG,** 5, br g King of Spain—Rock Concert **Mr B. Sleath**
11 **VASSAL,** 5, ro g Kalaglow—Vresia **Mr L. Naylor**
12 **VIKING GLORY,** 4, b c Gorytus (USA)—Daness **Mr David J. Riggs**
13 **VULNERABLE,** 9, ch g Le Bavard (FR)—Vulady **Mrs Sheila Freeman**
14 **WISCONSIN,** 6, b m Mummy's Game—Montana **Mr N. Fletcher**
15 **WORLDSPORTFLYER,** 4, b g Hays—Arabian Pearl **Mr R. A. Bromby**
16 **YOUNG GERARD,** 5, ch g Brigadier Gerard—Eastern Queen **Miss Rosemarie Cleary**

Other Owners: Mr M. C. Chapman, Mr S. Dalton, Mr Stan Freeman, Mr C. Hague.

133 MR M. J. CHARLES, Warwick

Postal: **Guys Cliffe Racing Stables, Coventry Road, Warwick, CV34 5YD.**
Phone: **(0926) 493878**

1 **AARON'S ROD,** 4, br c Mansingh (USA)—Belinda Mede **Mr R. H. Harris**
2 **FLEXIBLE FRIEND,** 10, br g Lord Gayle (USA)—My Bonnie **Mr Anthony Smith**
3 **FRAMPTON HOUSE,** 8, b g Fine Blue—Frampton Close **Mr A. J. Wright**
4 **GLENSCAR,** 4, gr c Glenstal (USA)—Caranina (USA) **Group 1 Racing (1989) Ltd**
5 **KURDISH PRINCE,** 6, b g Dunphy—Lea Landing **Mrs Jill Gray**
6 **LOST ART,** 7, ch g Artaius (USA)—Flosshilde **Group 1 Racing (1989) Ltd**
7 **SEAMUS MOR,** 6, b g Capricorn Line—Bon Voyage **Mr R. H. Harris**
8 **SOLAR CLOUD,** 8, ch g Northfields (USA)—Passing Fancy (USA) **Mr R. H. Harris**

THREE-YEAR-OLDS

9 **BROTHER MINSTREL,** ch g Brotherly (USA)—Lady Peggy **Group 1 Racing (1989) Ltd**
10 **LA RAPTOTTE,** b f Alzao (USA)—Maypole Hie **Mr B. R. Baker**
11 **PRETTY DUET,** b f Song—Liberation **Mr G. Morgan**

MR M. J. CHARLES—continued

TWO-YEAR-OLDS

12 B c 23/2 Welsh Captain—Hopeful Waters (Forlorn River) **Dr S. M. Foster**

Other Owners: Mr Graham J. Bradbury, Mr D. A. Davies, Mrs N. Peek, Mr Mike Reynolds, Mr Brian Wildman.

Jockeys (Flat): G Hind (7-7, w.a.), J Quinn (7-7, w.a.).

Jockeys (NH): G Armytage (10-0, w.a.), J Railton (10-0, w.a.).

Conditional: M Sharratt (9-12).

Lady Rider: Miss J Davies (8-7).

134 MR J. I. A. CHARLTON, Stocksfield

Postal: **Mickley Grange, Stocksfield, Northumberland, NE43 7TB.**
Phone: **(0661) 843247**

1 BIXIO, 6, gr g Absalom—Brescianina **Mrs P. Boynton**
2 BLACK SPUR, 8, br g Spur On—Ravenside **Mr James Gibson**
3 BOLD AD, 6, b m Bold Owl—Norma's Way **Mr P. Lockeron**
4 BORDER OAK, 8, b g Majestic Streak—Purple Gem **Mr I. H. Pearson**
5 FERNANDO REYES, 5, gr g Morston (FR)—Setmark **Mr P. Spottiswood**
6 IDA'S DELIGHT, 11, br g Idiot's Delight—Ida Spider **Mr J. I. A. Charlton**
7 JUST FOR JOHN, 7, b m Domitor (USA)—Farm Consultation **Mrs John Brown**
8 MAJOR ROUGE, 8, ch g Mandrake Major—Red Form **Mr J. Herdman**
9 MASTER MAYO, 7, b h Argentinos—Mayo Lassie **Mrs R. C. Carr**
10 MILLTOWN LADY, 6, ch m Deep Run—Elite Lady **Mrs H. Clarke**
11 MUCK OR MONEY, 6, b g Slim Jim—Karena III **Mr J. Herdman**
12 PROUD CON, 11, b g Another River—Farm Consultation **Mr H. Proud**
13 QUE BELLA, 4, b f Hello Handsome—Waterbeck **Mrs C. Thompson**
14 ROMAN DUSK, 10, b g Beatic—Half Moon Bay **Mr W. T. Lockey**
15 ROYAL BOWLER, 11, b g Beau Chapeau—Royal Inquisitor **Miss J. Palmer**
16 SHANKHOUSE GIRL, 6, gr m General Ironside—Truly Fair **Mr Syd Ramsey**
17 STAGSHAW BELLE, 6, b m Royal Fountain—Besciamella **Mrs J. J. Straker**
18 WHO'S SILLY NOW, 4, b f Silly Prices—Who's Free **Mr I. H. Pearson**
19 ZAM'S SLAVE, 5, gr m Zambrano—Cool Date **Mr W. Wylie**

THREE-YEAR-OLDS

20 B f Silly Prices—Hazel's Pet **Mrs J. I. A. Charlton**
21 B g Silly Prices—Who's Free **Mr I. H. Pearson**

TWO-YEAR-OLDS

22 B f 8/5 Silly Prices—Hazel's Pet (Raise You Ten) **Mr J. I. A. Charlton**
23 B f 21/4 Silly Prices—Who's Free (Sit In The Corner (USA)) **Mr I. H. Pearson**

Other Owners: Mr Eric S. Bliss, Mr Ian C. Carr, Mr Charles Hutchinson, Mr T. E. Robinson, Mr J. T. Stobbs.

Jockeys (NH): P Dennis (10-0), B Storey (10-0, w.a.).

Apprentice: P Burke (7-4, w.a.).

Conditional: C Dennis (9-7, w.a.).

135 MR R. J. CHARLTON, Marlborough

Postal: **Beckhampton House, Marlborough, Wiltshire, SN8 1QR.**
Phone: **(067 23) 204/244 TELEX C/O 449703 "TELSER"**

1 **AJANAC,** 6, br g Known Fact (USA)—Majan **Mr Jeremy Tree**
2 **AT PEACE,** 4, b c Habitat—Peace **Mr K. Abdulla**
3 **BECQUEREL (USA),** 4, ch c Sharpen Up—Marie Curie **Mr K. Abdulla**
4 **CAMBO (USA),** 4, b c Roberto (USA)—Cameo Shore **Mr K. Abdulla**
5 **FLAMINGO POND,** 4, b f Sadler's Wells (USA)—Anegada **Mr R. H. R. Dee**
6 **HIGHLY DANGEROUS,** 4, b c Shirley Heights—Slightly Dangerous (USA) **Mr K. Abdulla**
7 **PRIDE OF ARABY (USA),** 4, b c Sovereign Dancer (USA)—Miss Manon (FR) **Mr K. Abdulla**

THREE-YEAR-OLDS

8 **ANGEL FALLS (USA),** b c Nijinsky (CAN)—Angel Island (USA) **Mr K. Abdulla**
9 **ANODYNE (USA),** b g Riverman (USA)—Tongue Tied Muse (USA) **Mr K. Abdulla**
10 **BALLETA (USA),** b f Lyphard (USA)—Navajo Princess (USA) **Mr K. Abdulla**
11 **CROWNING AMBITION (USA),** b f Chief's Crown (USA)—Fabulous Notion (USA) **Mr K. Abdulla**
12 **DEPLOY,** b c Shirley Heights—Slightly Dangerous (USA) **Mr K. Abdulla**
13 **DOMINANCE,** b f Dominion—Juliette Marny **Hon J. I. Morrison**
14 **ELHUDHUD,** ch c Habitat—Green Lucia **Mr Hamdan Al-Maktoum**
15 **EMERALD (USA),** ch f El Gran Senor (USA)—Razyana (USA) **Mr K. Abdulla**
16 **FAVOURED VICTOR (USA),** ch c Diesis—Northern Walk (CAN) **Mr K. Abdulla**
17 **FINDON,** ch f Kris—Fine Honey (USA) **Mr K. Abdulla**
18 **GADABOUT (USA),** ch c Mr Prospector (USA)—Playmate (USA) **Mr K. Abdulla**
19 **GYPSY RIVER (USA),** ch c Alydar (USA)—Seven Springs (USA) **Mr K. Abdulla**
20 **ILLUSORY,** b f Kings Lake (USA)—Bold Fantasy **Mr K. Abdulla**
21 **INTERFACE,** ch c Caerleon (USA)—Intermission **Mr K. Abdulla**
22 **KAWTUBAN,** b c Law Society (USA)—Thunderflash (FR) **Mr Hamdan Al-Maktoum**
23 **MATADOR (USA),** ch c Nureyev (USA)—Allicance (USA) **Mr S. S. Niarchos**
24 **NAWASSI (USA),** b f Shadeed (USA)—Scintillate **Mr Hamdan Al-Maktoum**
25 **QUEST FOR FAME,** b c Rainbow Quest (USA)—Aryenne (FR) **Mr K. Abdulla**
26 **SANGLAMORE (USA),** ch c Sharpen Up—Ballinderry **Mr K. Abdulla**
27 **SPICA (USA),** b f Diesis—Giboulee Era (USA) **Mr K. Abdulla**
28 **STAR QUEST,** b c Rainbow Quest (USA)—Sarah Siddons (FR) **Mr K. Abdulla**
29 **STOP ON RED,** b g Rainbow Quest (USA)—Danger Ahead **Mr Jeremy Tree**
30 **SUNDERLAND (USA),** b g Roberto (USA)—Sunny Bay (USA) **Mr K. Abdulla**
31 **THUNDERCLOUD,** b f Electric—Set Free **Mr A. J. Morrison**
32 **VITAL WITNESS (CAN),** b g Val de L'Orne (FR)—Friendly Witness (USA) **Mr K. Abdulla**
33 **VOODOO CHILD (USA),** b f Seattle Song (USA)—Almata (USA) **Mr S. S. Niarchos**
34 **WRYBILL,** b c Sharpo—Wryneck **Miss M. Sheriffe**
35 **YEMANJA (USA),** b f Alleged (USA)—Korveya (USA) **Mr S. S. Niarchos**
36 **ZONE TIME (USA),** b c Mr Prospector (USA)—Zonely (USA) **Mr K. Abdulla**
37 **ZUBROVKA (FR),** b c Law Society (USA)—Czar's Bride (USA) **Mr Spyros Niarchos**

TWO-YEAR-OLDS

38 B f 13/4 Slip Anchor—Antilla (Averof) **Mrs E. Longton**
39 B f 4/2 Damister—Apply (Kings Lake) **Mr K. Abdulla**
40 B f 1/2 Riverman—Aviance (Northfields) **Mr S. S. Niarchos**
41 BLUE BIRDS FLY, ch f 2/4 Rainbow Quest—Pale Gold (New Chapter) **Mr T. D. Rootes**
42 CHATAIN (USA), ch c 6/4 Sharpen Up—Blushing Redhead (Blushing Groom) **Mr K. Abdulla**
43 B f 23/1 Rainbow Quest—Danger Ahead (Mill Reef) **Mr R. J. McCreery & Partner**
44 Ch f 21/3 Rousillon—Divine Destiny (Sir Ivor) **Mr K. Abdulla**
45 DIVING (USA), b br c 2/3 Silver Hawk—Challenging Stage (Gold Stage) **Mr K. Abdulla**
46 DIXTON (USA), b c 15/4 Dixieland Band—Cosmic Tiger (Tim The Tiger) **Mr K. Abdulla**
47 B f 19/3 Baillamont—Exgravity (Explodent) **Mr S. S. Niarchos**
48 B f 7/5 Pennine Walk—Fair Abode (Habitat) **Mr Christopher Heath & Partner**
49 Ch c 4/5 Diesis—Ivory Smooth (Sir Ivor) **Mr K. Abdulla**
50 B f 12/3 Pharly—Jolly Bay (Mill Reef) **Hon. J. I. Morrison**
51 JUNK BOND, b c 13/4 Last Tycoon—What A Pity (Blakeney) **Lord de la Warr & Partners**
52 B c 28/2 Law Society—Kereolle (Riverman) **Mr K. Abdulla**
53 LADY IN RED (FR), b f 1/5 Shareef Dancer—Dressed In Red (Red Alert) **Mr D. Carleton Paget & Partners**

MR R. J. CHARLTON—continued

54 Br c 1/5 High Top—Lady Zi (Manado) **Mr R. J. McCreery**
55 **LITTLETON (USA),** br f 23/4 El Gran Senor—Daeltown (Dictus) **Mr K. Abdulla**
56 **MADONETTA,** ch f 23/3 Sharpo—Woodwind (Whistling Wind) **Lord & Lady Derby**
57 B f 13/3 Pennine Walk—Majan (Brigadier Gerard) **Mr K. Abdulla**
58 Br c 11/5 Known Fact—Metair (Laser Light) **Mr K. Abdulla**
59 B c 5/4 Pennine Walk—Never Never Land (Habitat) **Mr K. Abdulla**
60 B c 19/2 Blushing Grom—Northernette (Northern Dancer) **Mr S. S. Niarchos**
61 Br f 27/1 Known Fact—Oscura (Caro) **Mr K. Abdulla**
62 B f 8/3 Dancing Brave—Peace (Klairon) **Mr K. Abdulla**
63 **PIPSQUEAK,** gr f 12/3 Alleging—Silver Berry (Lorenzaccio) **Duke of Roxburghe & Partner**
64 Br f 14/4 Glint of Gold—Premiere Danseuse (Saritamer) **Mr A. Stirling**
65 B c 29/3 Law Society—River Goddess (Northern Dancer) **Mr S. S. Niarchos**
66 B f 23/4 Kris—Sephira (Luthier) **Mr K. Abdulla**
67 **SHARPTHORNE (USA),** ch f 17/5 Sharpen Up—Abeer (Dewan) **Mr K. Abdulla**
68 **SHIBUI,** b f 20/2 Shirley Heights—Newquay (Great Nephew) **Mr K. Abdulla**
69 **SOCIAL WISH (USA),** b f 6/3 Lyphard's Wish—Social Column (Vaguely Noble) **Mr K. Abdulla**
70 **STERVIAN,** b c 3/5 Damister—Vian (Far Out East) **Mr K. Abdulla**
71 **THE GLASHA (IRE),** ch c 9/5 Jalmood—Blessed Persian (Persian Bold) **Mr A. Scrimgeour**
72 B c 23/4 Ahoonora—Tikanova (Northern Dancer) **Mr K. Abdulla**
73 **VERTEX,** b c 13/2 Shirley Heights—Rockfest (Stage Door Johnny) **Mr K. Abdulla**

Other Owners: Mr George Baker, Mrs J. Baker, Mr A. N. C. Bengough, Mr Nicolas Crossthwaite, Mr R. S. Dawes, Mr R. Hambro, Lady Sophia Morrison, Mr Philip S. Niarchos, Miss J. Olivier, Mr John Carleton Paget, Mr O. M. Pollard, Mr Hugh Priestly, Mr R. Spring, Mrs M. Storey, Mrs Dare Wigan, Mr S. De Zoete.

Jockeys (Flat): Pat Eddery (8-4), S Raymont (8-5).

136 MR E. CHEVALIER DU FAU, Chantilly

Postal: **29 Avenue de Joinville, 60500 Chantilly, France.**
Phone: **(1) 44573193 OR (1) 44580694**

1 **ARROW HEAD (FR),** 4, b f Fabulous Dancer (USA)—Gadfly (FR) **T. de Ganay**
2 **BAYWOOD (FR),** 7, b g Suvero (FR)—Bayleaf (FR) **Cte E. Decazes**
3 **BRAMBELLE (FR),** 5, ch m Rex Magna (FR)—Blueberry (FR)
4 **DANY CUP (FR),** 4, b g Huntercombe—Dany Cupid (FR) **A. Weisweiller**
5 **FIREBAY (FR),** 7, ch g Phaeton—Blueberry (FR) **Cte E. Decazes**
6 **GARVAL (FR),** 4, b g Garde Royale—Val Lady (FR) **A. Weisweiller**
7 **GAY CARNIVAL (USA),** 4, b c Gay Mecene (USA)—Lyphard's Holme (USA) **Mme H. Stihl**
8 **GOLD CAP (FR),** 5, ch g Noir Et Or—Alkmaar (USA) **E. Chevalier du Fau**
9 **LA MEXICANNA (FR),** 4, b f Crystal Glitters (USA)—High Society (FR) **D. Blum**
10 **MONGINEVRO,** 8, b g Scorpio (FR)—Mobola **E. Chevalier du Fau**
11 **MUIRFIELD (FR),** 4, b f Crystal Glitters (USA)—Deb Marion (USA) **P. Azam**
12 **NIMBLE SKATER (USA),** 4, gr f Icecapade (USA)—Bright Jetty (USA) **H. Stihl**
13 **PEEKABOO (FR),** 4, b g Deep Roots—Prudholme Bay **D. Blum**
14 **PRINCESS BURY (FR),** 5, b m Top Ville—Dandy Bury (FR) **P. Moroney**
15 **RAYDOUN,** 4, b c Darshaan—Sparkling Rose (FR) **Edouard Delanglade**
16 **REACH THE BEACH,** 5, b h Cure The Blues (USA)—Sandina **P. Moroney**
17 **REGALIEN (FR),** 7, b g Valdingran (FR)—Pridonia (FR) **A. Weisweiller**
18 **RESQUILLEUR (FR),** 6, b g Zino—Albonsky (FR) **M. C. de Saint Seine**
19 **RIVER D'AUGE (FR),** 4, b g River River (FR)—Tudor Trophy **T. de Ganay**
20 **ROYAL DUTCH (FR),** 7, b g Rex Magna (FR)—Wilhelmina (FR) **Cte E. Decazes**
21 **SAMBRE D'OR (FR),** 7, b m Noir Et Or—Sainte Sambre (FR) **Prince de Faucigay**
22 **SOLIDO (FR),** 6, b h Solicitor (FR)—Evonsville (FR) **T. de Ganay**
23 **SOUPIKA (FR),** 4, b f Akarad (FR)—Dancilla (FR) **Jean Dolbeau**
24 **VALIBUS (FR),** 5, b g Labus (FR)—Valgrinette (FR) **A. Weisweiller**
25 **VALIGRAND (FR),** 6, br h Valdingran (FR)—Dany Cupid (FR) **A. Weisweiller**
26 **VAL MY WAY (FR),** 5, b g On My Way (USA)—Val Griette (FR) **A. Weisweiller**
27 **WALEWSKA (FR),** 4, ch f Sicyos (USA)—Waterford (FR) **P. Prudhomme**

MR E. CHEVALIER DU FAU—continued

THREE-YEAR-OLDS

28 **ALL THAT GLITTERS (FR),** gr f Crystal Glitters (USA)—All In White (FR) **Mme Love Ammerman**
29 **BIRDBERRY (FR),** br g Pampabird—Loganberry (FR) **Cte E. Decazes**
30 **DANDY SKATER (USA),** gr c Icecapade (USA)—Johnyette (USA) **H. Stihl**
31 **DON BERRY (FR),** b g Don Roberto (USA)—Blueberry (FR) **Cte E. Decazes**
32 **GRANITA (FR),** b f Mille Balles (FR)—Grande Vallee (FR) **M. C. de Saint Seine**
33 **INNOVATRICE (USA),** br f Wild Again (USA)—K A Party (USA) **Eisei Fujita**
34 **LE BOULANGER,** b g Miller's Mate—Bublichka (USA) **Mme Love Ammerman**
35 **PRUDENZIO (FR),** br c Miller's Mate—Piastrella (ITY) **G. Cesetti**
36 **SYMBOLE (FR),** b g R B Chesne—Srilanka (FR) **E. Chevalier du Fau**
37 **VIANN (FR),** gr c Kenmare (FR)—Viou (FR) **Jean Dolbeau**
38 **VILOU (FR),** b f Darshaan—Rosa Mystica (FR) **Jean Dolbeau**

TWO-YEAR-OLDS

39 **HARBINGER (IRE),** b f Sadler's Wells (USA)—Mourwara (Wolver Hollow) **Eisei Fujita**
40 **KARINKA (FR),** br f Mille Balles (FR)—Katarinka (FR) (Emerson) **T. de Ganay**
41 **MAJOR NAG (FR),** b c Major Petingo (FR)—Cantespy (FR) (Grandchant (FR)) **Mme P. Ribes**
42 **MASOCA (FR),** b f Nikos—Sharpriver (FR) (Sharpman) **Mme J. Levesque**
43 **PAMPOUS BIRD (FR),** b f Pampabird—Aeolia (FR) (Versailles) **Cte E. Decazes**

137 MR S. P. L. CHRISTIAN, Severn Stoke

Postal: **The Racing Stables, Kinnersley, Severn Stoke, Worcestershire, WR8 9JR.**
Phone: **SEVERN STOKE (090 567) 233 FAX SEVERN STOKE (090 567) 340**

1 **AHERLOW,** 10, b g Brave Invader (USA)—Cant Pet **Mr P. J. Fahey**
2 **CELTIC WATERS,** 5, ch m Celtic Cone—Moonbreaker **Mr P. T. Petrie**
3 **CORRAVORRIN,** 5, ch g Garda's Revenge (USA)—Pearl Creek **Mrs R. Baxter**
4 **DAUNOU (FR),** 4, b c Fabulous Dancer (USA)—Dourdan **Mr William J. Smith**
5 **ETON ROUGE,** 11, b g The Parson—Rouge Shack **Mrs Bryan P. Jenks**
6 **FLAG OF TRUCE,** 10, b g Arapaho—Darling Smile **Mr P. L. Lee**
7 **GOOD WATERS,** 10, b br g Paddy's Stream—Good Surprise **Mr Lynn Wilson**
8 **HENRY MANN,** 7, br g Mandalus—Little Dipper **Mr Lynn Wilson**
9 5, B g The Parson—Hill Invader **Mr Simon Christian**
10 **HOW MAJESTIC,** 6, b m Majestic Streak—Wits End **Mr P. L. Lee**
11 **LARCHWOOD,** 9, b m Precipice Wood—Last Alliance **Mrs Z. S. Clark**
12 **LOS BUCCANEROS,** 7, br g Neltino—Pirella **Mr Lynn Wilson**
13 **MAYFAIR MINX,** 6, b m St Columbus—Belgrave Queen **Mrs M. D. W. Wilson**
14 **MEMBERS' REVENGE,** 9, b g New Member—Aileens Revenge **Mrs Judith Young**
15 **MIDDLEWICK,** 5, b g Ballacashtal (CAN)—Thunder Bay **Colonel A. H. Parker Bowles**
16 **MIGHTY FINE,** 9, b g Crash Course—Aggvus **Mr T. Anthony Lewis**
17 **MOUNT TORUS,** 6, br g Torus—Mountview Lady **Mrs Padraic Fallon**
18 **OREGON TRAIL,** 10, b g Auction Ring (USA)—Oriental Star **Mr Stephen Crown**
19 **PACTOLUS (USA),** 7, b g Lydian (FR)—Honey Sand (USA) **Mrs David Clark**
20 **PEARLY KING (USA),** 7, b g Tromos—Perfect Mix (USA) **Mr William J. Smith**
21 **PLENTIFUL,** 4, b f Young Generation—Pundy **Mrs F. Walwyn**
22 **ROYAL RELIANCE,** 7, b m Rymer—Last Alliance **Mrs Z. S. Clark**
23 **RYTON GUARD,** 5, br g Strong Gale—Gardez Le Reste **A. F. Budge (Equine) Limited**
24 **SILENT TOM,** 8, b g Tom Noddy—Silent Sleeves **Mr Stephen Crown**
25 **SOUND AND FURY,** 6, ch g Deep Run—Fury Spirit **Mr C. Hellyer**
26 **SWILLY EXPRESS,** 4, b f Ballacashtal (CAN)—Thunder Bay **P. J. Doherty**
27 **THE FOALICULE,** 5, b m Imperial Fling (USA)—Reita **Miss Laura Aitken**
28 **THEPRINCEOFKINGS,** 6, br g Prince Regent (FR)—Betty Sue **Mr William J. Smith**
29 **TOMMYS DREAM,** 7, b m Le Bavard (FR)—Tricia **Mr Gordon Turner**
30 **TYRIAN KING,** 5, ch g Royal Match—Apple Blossom **Mr Stephen Crown**
31 **VITAL BOY,** 9, ch g Vitiges (FR)—Bright Decision **Mr Terry R. Roydon**
32 **VULGAN WARRIOR,** 8, b g Vulgan Slave—Belgrave Queen **Mrs M. D. W. Wilson**
33 **WESTERN GUN (USA),** 5, b h Lypheor—Fandangerina (USA) **Mr Charles H. Wacker III**

MR S. P. L. CHRISTIAN—continued

THREE-YEAR-OLDS

34 **GEORGE JET,** gr c Relaunch (USA)—Eleven Pelicans (USA) **Mr Charles H. Wacker III**
35 **MOUNT KINABALU,** b g Head For Heights—Kaisersage (FR) **Mr Charles H. Wacker III**

Other Owners: Mr F. D. Allison, Mr G. D. Blagbrough, Mr Geoff Buck, Mr J. F. Curran, Mrs Duncan Davidson, Mr N. F. Duckworth, Dr D. R. Edmondson, Mr Colin Edwards, Mr S. A. Evans, Mr H. S. Fuller, Mr Irving Goldstein, Mr J. S. Gutkin, Mr M. H. Hudson, Mrs John Hughes, Mr G. Kindersley, Mrs C. P. Kirwin, Mrs E. C. Knight, Mrs Joan Lewis, Mr Peter McDonald, Mr M. J. M. Petit, Mr W. H. Ponsonby, Mr Tony Pooley, Mr Tony Porter, Mr Nigel Rich, Sir Patrick Sergeant, Mr T. F. Tremlett, Mr E. J. G. Young.

Jockey (NH): J Osborne (10-0, w.a.).

Conditional: A Mulholland (9-7).

Amateur: Mr G Upton (10-2).

138 MR W. CLAY, Stoke-on-Trent

Postal: **Saverley House Farm, Saverley Green, Cresswell, Stoke-on-Trent.**
Phone: **(0782) 392131**

1 **ABOVE THE WIND,** 5, b h High Top—Golden Windlass **Mr G. D. Pointon**
2 **ACEFACE,** 5, ch g Anfield—Silvera **Mr G. D. Pointon**
3 **ALWAYS GREAT,** 4, b g Vaigly Great—Jinja **Mr H. A. Insley**
4 **ANNIE RA,** 8, br m Ra (USA)—Annie **Mrs E. A. Bevan**
5 **BROKEN LINE,** 4, br g Dara Monarch—Bustina (FR) **Mr J. A. Roberts**
6 **COVENT GARDEN (USA),** 12, ch g Stage Door Johnny—Rock Garden **Mr R. Parton**
7 **GINGA JAM,** 7, ch g Leander—Ginseng **Mr Peter G. Freeman**
8 **HAWAIIAN HEIR (USA),** 11, b h Hawaii—Madam Fox (USA) **Mr P. Riley**
9 **HELLBRUNN,** 4, ch c Hotfoot—Midnight Music **Mrs E. A. Bevan**
10 **HILL BEAGLE,** 10, b g Goldhill—Beagle Bay **Mr N. Brown**
11 **HIXON GIRL,** 7, ch m St Columbus—Hillvale **Mr Vic Lockley**
12 **JOHNSTED,** 4, ch g Red Johnnie—Busted Love **Mr P. Riley**
13 **KIMACERO,** 12, b g Tycoon II—La Macera **Mr P. Hamer**
14 **LEON,** 8, gr h Niniski (USA)—Lorelene (FR) **Mr H. A. Insley**
15 **LUCY LASTIC,** 6, b m Tycoon II—Nikancy **Mr Bill Waddington**
16 **MIDNIGHT SECRET,** 6, b m Scallywag—Politely **Mr Ron Ibbs**
17 **PRINCE CELTIC,** 6, b g Celtic Cone—Kam Tsin Princess **Mr H. A. Insley**
18 **ROY PRINCE,** 7, b g Royal Blend—Kam Tsin Princess **Mr H. A. Insley**
19 **SAYANT,** 5, b g Sayyaf—Bodnant **Mr W. Clay**
20 **STAN-PRINCE,** 5, b h Stansted—Kam Tsin Princess **Mr H. A. Insley**
21 **STORMGUARD,** 7, b g Thatching—Silk And Satin **Mr M. D. Page**
22 **SUNDAYSPORT SCOOP,** 5, b h Great Nephew—Heaven Knows **Mr R. D. Cook**
23 **THE BERWICK,** 8, br g Space King—Barneo **Mrs E. A. Bevan**
24 **WYVERN,** 7, ch g Dragonara Palace (USA)—Rosalina **Mr R. Rowlands**

Other Owners: Mr M. J. Bates, Mr M. P. Brooke, Mr Rob Hill, Mr Tommy Ho, Mr G. Huckerby, Mr R. Lawton, Mr M. D. Page, Miss S. Parton.

Conditional: R Bevan (9-7).

Lady Rider: Miss Diane Clay (9-12).

139 MR D. H. CLYDE M.R.C.V.S., Antrim

Postal: **Craigs Stud, Ballyclare, Co. Antrim, Ireland.**
Phone: **(08 493) 22327**

1 5, Br g Tudor Rhythm—Cave Lass **D. H. Clyde**
2 **DICKEYS MOSS,** 5, ch g Sweet Monday—Birdcage **D. H. Clyde**
3 4, Ch g Crofthall—Donnabimba **D. H. Clyde**
4 4, Ch g Bustomi—Mattress **D. H. Clyde**
5 **PEARLING GIRL,** 4, b f Bustomi—Worling Pearl **D. H. Clyde**
6 5, B g Buzzards Bay—Pladda **D. H. Clyde**
7 **RUPERT STANLEY,** 6, ch g Celtic Cone—Lesley Ann **R. D. Wilson**
8 **THE RED MARE,** 5, ch m Sagaro—Lesley Ann **D. H. Clyde**

Other Owners: R. D. Wilson.

Jockeys (NH): P Gill, P Kavanagh, M Sleator.

140 MR L. J. CODD, Evesham

Postal: **Stockwood Stables, Stockwood, Nr Redditch, Worcestershire, B96 6SX.**
Phone: **(0386) 793263**

1 **BELOW ZERO,** 7, ch g Northfields (USA)—Indigine (USA) **Mr T. S. F. Smith**
2 **BERRYS CRUISE,** 5, ch m Cruise Missile—Quick Walk **T. P. Roberts Hindle**
3 **CAPTAIN MANNERING (USA),** 5, b g Tina's Pet—Independentia **Mr P. J. Deer**
4 **GOOD MORROW JACK,** 5, br g Ballymore—Rifflealp **Mr L. J. Codd**
5 **HAMPTON GRANGE,** 6, br m Boreen (FR)—Wild Deer **Mrs Kate Dolan**
6 **HANNAH MILLIE NICK,** 5, b m Balinger—Saucy Eater **Mr M. D. Nickless**
7 **HIGHGATE MILD,** 5, br g Homeboy—Lady Jewel **Bass Mitchells & Butlers**
8 **HONOURS GRADUATE,** 4, b br g Petorius—Princess Virginia **B. W. Hampson**
9 **KILMALOODA,** 4, b f Croghan Hill—Magic Minstrel **Frank O'Rourke**
10 **LIGHT DANCER,** 4, ch g Niniski (USA)—Foudre **Mr L. J. Codd**
11 **LUIGI'S GLORY,** 10, b g Hittite Glory—Glengarry **Mr Les Bevan**
12 **MONTBERGIS (FR),** 7, b g Northern Treat (USA)—Amorina **Mr M. D. Nickless**
13 **PRIOR'S PADDOCK,** 8, b g Monksfield—Keening **Mr P. S. Daly**
14 **SAGAMAN (GER),** 4, b g Solo Dancer (GER)—Scholastika (GER) **Mr Nandor Bayer**
15 5, Ch g Green Shoon—Solaranda **Hugo Merry**
16 **TORNICK,** 5, b g Torus—Madam Nick **Mr R. Owen**
17 **VALTAKI,** 5, b g Valiyar—Taqa **Mr J. R. Salter**

THREE-YEAR-OLDS

18 **ANISESNO,** ch f Mansingh—Missive (FR) **D. L. Claydon**
19 **GAELIC DANCER,** ch c Town And Country—Verily Jane **M. J. Healey**

TWO-YEAR-OLDS

20 Ch f 29/1 Tate Gallery (USA)—Independentia (Home Guard (USA)) **Mr D. J. Deer**
21 **PETRACO,** b c 13/4 Petorius—Merrie Moira (Bold Lad (IRE)) **B. W. Hampson**

Other Owners: Mr Vince Dolan, Mrs Pam Hampson, Mr Robert Harris, Mr Peter McNamara, Miss S. J. K. Scott, Mr Bob Tracey, Mr R. C. Wade.

Jockey (Flat): Nicky Carlisle.

Jockeys (NH): P Leech, T Morgan (w.a.).

141 MR P. F. I. COLE, Whatcombe

Postal: **Whatcombe Estate, Whatcombe, Wantage, Oxon, OX12 9NW.**
Phone: **CHADDLEWORTH (04882) 433 TELEX 849387 FAX 04882 609**

1 **DEBBIE HARRY (USA),** 4, b f Alleged—Tie A Bow **Mr Christopher Wright**
2 **EASY TIME (GER),** 5, b g High Line—Easily **Mr C. J. Wates**
3 **EMPERORS WARRIOR,** 4, ch g High Line—Cocoban **Lowe and Oliver Ltd**
4 **EMPIRE BLUE,** 7, b g Dominion—Bold Blue **Richard Green (Fine Paintings)**
5 **GODLY LIGHT (FR),** 4, b f Vayrann—Western Goddess **Mr E. P. Jameson**
6 **GOLD FLAIR,** 4, ch f Tap On Wood—Suemette **Mr Fahd Salman**
7 **IBN BEY,** 6, ch h Mill Reef (USA)—Rosia Bay **Mr Fahd Salman**
8 **MARINE DIVER,** 4, b c Pas de Seul—Marine Life **Mr C. Shiacolas**
9 **MELICUS (USA),** 5, b h Providential—Melodina **Amerigroup Bloodlines Corporation**
10 **OSTURA,** 5, b h Sir Ivor—Casual (USA) **Mr Fahd Salman**
11 **PRIME DISPLAY (USA),** 4, ch g Golden Act (USA)—Great Display (FR) **Mr F. Jenkins**
12 **ROBERT DEAR (USA),** 4, gr c Caro—Marketess (USA) **Mr G. J. Beck**
13 **RUN DON'T FLY (USA),** 4, b c Lear Fan (USA)—Gantlette **Mr J. S. Gutkin**
14 **SAFE,** 4, b c Kris—Carnival Dance **Mr Fahd Salman**
15 **SALMONID,** 4, ch g Salmon Leap (USA)—Persian Polly **Mr Ray Taylor**
16 **SECRETARY OF STATE,** 4, b c Alzao (USA)—Colonial Line (USA) **Mr W. H. Ponsonby**
17 **SINGULAR RUN,** 4, b g Trojan Fen—Needy **Mr Fahd Salman**
18 **SULTAN'S SON,** 4, b c Kings Lake (USA)—Get Ahead **Mr Fahd Salman**
19 **THE KINGS DAUGHTER,** 4, b f Indian King—Burnished **Mrs M. Simmonds**
20 **TYRIAN BELLE,** 5, b m Enchantment—Chasten **Mr W. H. Ponsonby**

THREE-YEAR-OLDS

21 **AFRICAN CHIMES,** b c Kampala—Rynville **Mr J. S. Gutkin**
22 **AL KHOBAR (USA),** b c Our Native (USA)—Blazing Grace (USA) **Mr Fahd Salman**
23 **ANNELI ROSE,** gr f Superlative—Red Rose Bowl **Mr N. W. L. Abbott**
24 **BARDOLPH (USA),** b c Golden Act (USA)—Love To Barbara (USA) **Sir George Meyrick**
25 **BENZINE (USA),** b c Secreto (USA)—Baby Diamonds **Mr Fahd Salman**
26 **BUBUBU,** ch f Bairn (USA)—Calibina **Mr J. R. Ali**
27 **COURTESY TITLE (USA),** ch c Golden Act (USA)—Social Registry (USA) **Kennet Valley Thoroughbreds Ltd**
28 **CROWN CLASS (USA),** b f Chief's Crown (USA)—Club Class (USA) **Mrs Jane Lewis**
29 **DEAREST,** b f Alzao (USA)—Lover's Rose **Sheikh Mohammed**
30 **DOOLAR (USA),** b c Spend A Buck (USA)—Surera (ARG) **Mr Fahd Salman**
31 **EASTERN PARTNER (USA),** b c Damascus (USA)—Tennis Partner (USA) **Mr Fahd Salman**
32 **EMERITUS,** b c Niniski (USA)—Her Grace **Sheikh Mohammed**
33 **FLANAGAN,** br c Comedy Star (USA)—Bold Blue **Sir George Meyrick**
34 **FLYING FLO JO (USA),** b f Aloma's Ruler (USA)—Madam Cherry (USA) **Mr J. R. Ali**
35 **GREEN'S COROT,** b g Prince Tenderfoot (USA)—Song Beam **Richard Green (Fine Paintings)**
36 **GREEN'S STUBBS,** b c Ballad Rock—Aventina **Richard Green (Fine Paintings)**
37 **HIGH PLATEAU (USA),** ch c Raise A Native—Soft Horizon (USA) **Mr Fahd Salman**
38 **IBN SINA (USA),** b c Dr Blum (USA)—Two On One (CAN) **Mr Fahd Salman**
39 **JAZAF (USA),** b g Hero's Honor (USA)—Fleeing Partner (USA) **Mr Fahd Salman**
40 **KNIGHT'S BARONESS,** b f Rainbow Quest (USA)—Knights Beauty (USA) **Mr Fahd Salman**
41 **KNIGHT'S SPUR (USA),** b c Diesis—Avoid (USA) **Mr Fahd Salman**
42 **LADY VIXEN (USA),** b f Sir Ivor—T V Vixen (USA) **Guiting Stud Limited**
43 **LONDON PRIDE (USA),** b f Lear Fan (USA)—Dance Empress (USA) **Mr Fahd Salman**
44 **LOVE STREET,** b f Mummy's Pet—Crime of Passion **Mr Christopher Wright**
45 **LUCKY AGAIN,** br c Ile de Bourbon (USA)—Soft Pedal **Mr D. A. R. Rowland**
46 **MONARDA,** ch g Pharly (FR)—Emaline (FR) **Mr Fahd Salman**
47 **MY BALLERINA (USA),** b f Sir Ivor—Emmaline (USA) **Mr Fahd Salman**
48 **MYSTERIOUS MAID (USA),** ch f L'Emigrant (USA)—Body Heat (USA) **Mr R. H. Strudwick**
49 **NOT OUT,** ch g Ballacashtal (CAN)—Cricket Bat **Mrs O. M. Lusty**
50 **PIPPA'S DREAM,** b f Doulab (USA)—Chaldea **Mr C. J. Wates**
51 **PRINCE BOLLINGER,** b c Head For Heights—Almuadiyeh **Mr Stephen Crown**
52 **PRINCE JAKATOM,** ch c Ballad Rock—Ballysnip **Mr Stephen Crown**
53 **PRINCESS LUCY,** b f Local Suitor (USA)—Jalapa (FR) **Mrs Sheila Crown**
54 **RIVER NOMAD,** b f Gorytus (USA)—Blue Rider (USA) **Mr Fahd Salman**
55 **RUBDAN (USA),** gr c Lear Fan (USA)—Cindy Jennings (USA) **Mr Fahd Salman**

MR P. F. I. COLE—continued

56 **RUBY TIGER**, gr f Ahonoora—Hayati **Mrs P. Blacker**
57 **SMARTIE LEE**, ch f Dominion—Nosy Parker (FR) **Norman Hill Plant Hire Ltd**
58 **SNURGE**, ch c Ela-Mana-Mou—Finlandia (FR) **Mr M. Arbib**
59 **SWEET GEORGE**, b c Ardross—Madam Slaney **Crown Racing Ltd**
60 **TYRIAN PRINCE**, b g Norwick (USA)—Chasten **Mr Stephen Crown**
61 **ZERO TIME**, br f Alzao (USA)—Queen of Time (USA) **Mr Fahd Salman**
62 **ZOMAN (USA)**, ch c Affirmed (USA)—A Little Affection (USA) **Mr Fahd Salman**

TWO-YEAR-OLDS

63 **AFFAIR OF HONOUR (IRE)**, ch c 26/5 Ahonoora—Good Relations (Be My Guest (USA)) **Mr Fahd Salman**
64 **ALAMIRA (USA)**, ch f 28/2 Affirmed (USA)—Manchester Miss (USA) (Groton) **Mr Fahd Salman**
65 **ALL THE KING'S MEN (IRE)**, b c 31/1 Alzao (USA)—
Hill's Realm (USA) (Key To The Kingdom (USA)) **Mr C. J. Wates**
66 **AMBASSADOR ROYALE (IRE)**, gr c 24/4 Pennine Walk—Hayati (Hotfoot) **Mr Fahd Salman**
67 B f 16/2 Night Shift (USA)—Aphrosina (Known Fact (USA)) **Mr D. A. R. Rowland**
68 **AUSHERRA (USA)**, b f 30/1 Diesis—Princess of Man (Green God) **Mr Fahd Salman**
69 B c 21/4 Lear Fan (USA)—Awenita (Rarity) **Mr J. S. Gutkin**
70 **BALLYRAIN (USA)**, ch f Halo (USA)—Raise Rain (USA) (Raise A Native) **Mr R. H. Strudwick**
71 B f 21/2 Spend A Buck (USA)—Bare Essence (USA) (Youth (USA)) **Guiting Stud Limited**
72 **BATRA (USA)**, b f 17/4 Green Dancer (USA)—Avatar's Court (Avatar (USA)) **Mr Fahd Salman**
73 **BLUSHING BELLE**, b f 12/4 Local Suitor (USA)—Shuteye (Shirley Heights) **Mr Stephen Crown**
74 **BURAIDA**, ch f 5/3 Balidar—Really Sharp (Sharpen Up) **Mr Fahd Salman**
75 B f 8/4 Niniski (USA)—Carnival Dance (Welsh Pageant) **Mr E. Loder**
76 Ch c 27/4 Siberian Express—Chrisanthy (So Blessed) **Lord Sondes**
77 **DASHING FELLOW (IRE)**, b c 19/4 Sure Blade (USA)—Belle Viking (FR) (Riverman (USA)) **Mr Fahd Salman**
78 **FAST RUN (IRE)**, ch c 16/5 Commanche Run—
Starlite Night (USA) (Star de Naskra (USA)) **Mr Fahd Salman**
79 **GARDENER'S BOY**, ch c 10/2 Ballacashtal (CAN)—Rockery (Track Spare) **Mrs O. M. Lusty**
80 **GENEROUS (IRE)**, ch c 8/2 Caerleon (USA)—Doff The Derby (USA) (Master Derby (USA)) **Mr Fahd Salman**
81 **GOLD LAW (IRE)**, b c 27/4 Law Society (USA)—Golden Oriole (USA) (Northern Dancer) **Mr Fahd Salman**
82 **GONE SAVAGE**, b c 9/3 Nomination—Trwyn Cilan (Import) **Mrs Christopher Heath**
83 **HALF A TICK (USA)**, b c 1/4 Timeless Moment (USA)—
Moon Star Miss (USA) (Star Envoy (USA)) **Mr C. J. Wates**
84 **HAYYAN**, b c 6/3 Al Nasr (FR)—Avoid (USA) (Buckpasser) **Mr Fahd Salman**
85 **HIGH GRADE**, b c 20/2 High Top—Bright Sun (Mill Reef (USA)) **Mr Fahd Salman**
86 **IL BAMBINO**, ch g 22/5 Bairn (USA)—Trapani (Ragusa) **Lord Portman**
87 Ch c 7/4 Ahonoora—Infanta (USA) (Intrepid Hero (USA)) **Kennet Valley Thoroughbreds Ltd**
88 **JENDEE (IRE)**, b c 11/3 Dara Monarch—Bunch of Blue (Martinmas) **Mr Fahd Salman**
89 B f 17/2 Roberto (USA)—Kadesh (USA) (Lucky Mel) **Mr Christopher Wright**
90 B c Shareef Dancer (USA)—Marie de Solesmes (FR) (Sassafras (FR)) **Sheikh Mohammed**
91 B c 27/4 Ziggy's Boy (USA)—Matriarchal (USA) (Pronto (ARG)) **Richard Green (Fine Paintings)**
92 B f 3/4 Conquistador Cielo—Minstinguette (USA) (Boldnesian) **Mr Christopher Wright**
93 B f 14/4 Tate Gallery (USA)—Mirkan Honey (Ballymore) **Mr E. P. Jameson**
94 **MOONA (USA)**, b f 8/5 Lear Fan (USA)—Dance Empress (USA) (Empery (USA)) **Mr Fahd Salman**
95 Ch f 31/3 Hagley (USA)—Mrs Hat (Sharpen Up) **Guiting Stud Limited**
96 **MULOOF**, ch c 21/5 Rousillon (USA)—Troyenne (Troy) **Mr Fahd Salman**
97 **NORTHERN RAINBOW**, b c 25/2 Rainbow Quest (USA)—Safe House (Lyphard (USA)) **Mr George Johnson**
98 **PETRUCHIO (IRE)**, ch c 18/4 Ballad Rock—Frances Jordan (Prince Regent (FR)) **Sir George Meyrick**
99 **PHARLY STORY**, b c 28/2 Pharly (FR)—Certain Story (Known Fact (USA)) **Mr E. R. Goodwin**
100 **PLANNING AHEAD (IRE)**, b c 10/5 Lyphard's Special—
Gay Parthia (Gay Fandango (USA)) **Planning Consultancy Ltd**
101 **PRINCE FARELONE (USA)**, b c 26/1 Irish River (FR)—Quilly (USA) (Bagdad) **Mr Fahd Salman**
102 **PRINCE OF THE SEA (IRE)**, gr c 12/2 Double Schwartz—Baracuda (FR) (Zeddaan) **Mr Stephen Crown**
103 B c 31/1 Spend A Buck (USA)—Promising Risk (USA) (Exclusive Native (USA)) **Mr Fahd Salman**
104 **RAINBOW CHASER (IRE)**, b f 9/2 Rainbow Quest (USA)—Scotia Rose (Tap On Wood) **Mr Fahd Salman**
105 **RAINSTONE**, ch f 7/3 Rainbow Quest (USA)—Emaline (FR) (Empery (USA)) **Mr Fahd Salman**
106 Gr f 9/4 Never So Bold—Rectitude (Runnymede) **Richard Green (Fine Paintings)**
107 **ROYAL DECREE**, b c 9/4 Dancing Brave (USA)—
Knights Beauty (USA) (True Knight (USA)) **Mr Fahd Salman**
108 Ch f 6/3 Apalachee (USA)—Royally Rewarded (USA) (Bold Forbes (USA)) **Richard Green (Fine Paintings)**

MR P. F. I. COLE—continued

109 ROYAL OBERON (IRE), b c 17/2 Fairy King (USA)—Broadway Royal (Royal Match) **Mr Fahd Salman**
110 SERENOSKI, b c 20/4 Petoski—Serenesse (Habat) **Mr E. R. Goodwin**
111 SHADIDEEN (USA), ch c 14/2 Shadeed (USA)—Allegretta (Lombard (GER)) **Mr Fahd Salman**
112 SOCIETY PRINCE, b c 27/2 Law Society (USA)—Princess Pati (Top Ville) **Mr Fahd Salman**
113 STRIKE FIRE (IRE), b c 6/3 Touching Wood (USA)—Ascot Strike (USA) (Mr Prospector (USA)) **Sheikh Mohammed**
114 THE LAST EMPRESS (IRE), b f 6/2 Last Tycoon—Beijing (USA) (Northjet) **Binfield Manor Farms Ltd**
115 WIDYAN (USA), b c 29/1 Fappiano (USA)—Hotel Street (USA) (Alleged (USA)) **Mr Fahd Salman**
116 WISE FRIEND (USA), b c Sagace (FR)—Swalthee (FR) (Sword Dancer (USA)) **Sheikh Mohammed**
117 ZONDA, br f 24/4 Fabulous Dancer (USA)—Oh So Hot (Habitat) **Sheikh Mohammed**

Other Owners: Mrs Linda Almeida, Mr Richard Barber, Mr Peter Bickmore, Mr Geoff Buck, Mr P. F. I. Cole, Mr J. L. Green, Mr J. Hayes, Mr A. N. Miller, Mr T. S. Redman, Mrs F. C. Saint Jean, Mr Craig B. Singer, Mr John Smith (Roehampton), Lady Penelope Van Der Woude.

Jockey (Flat): T R Quinn (8-2).

Apprentice: A Simpson (7-10).

Amateur: Miss Jane Allison (9-7).

142 MR S. N. COLE, Tiverton

Postal: **West Batsworthy Farm, Rackenford, Tiverton, Devon.**
Phone: **(088) 488 205 FAX (088) 488 205**

1 ALWAYS FOOLING, 8, b m Crash Course—Many Larks **Mr Tony Fletcher**
2 DISTRESS CALL, 9, b m Saucy Kit—Jolly Pigeon **Mr Reg Jones**
3 EARTHLY PLEASURE, 4, bl f Music Boy—May Fox **M. Willey**
4 EPRYANA, 10, b m English Prince—Ayana (SWE) **Mr Tony Fletcher**
5 FOGGY RIVER, 5, b g Foggy Bell—Little Ulla **Mrs Anita Cole**
6 GOLDEN ACRE, 8, b g Los Cerrillos (ARG)—Pharaoh's Bride **Mr R. Hewitt**
7 GROOM PORTER (USA), 4, ch c Blushing Groom (FR)—Maurita (NZ) **Toffolo & Hughes**
8 KHAREEDAH, 5, b br m Tender King—Miss Teto **Mr M. G. Willey**
9 MAMAMERE, 6, b m Tres Gate—Baidedones **Mr Tony Fletcher**
10 SADDIQUE, 5, b g Skyliner—Danova (FR) **Mr M. G. Willey**
11 SHOREHAM LADY, 5, br m Strong Gale—Tarpon Springs **Mr W. O'Dwyer**
12 SNOW RHAPSODY, 5, ch m Be My Guest (USA)—La Paille **Mr Vernon Frost**
13 STRAIGHT GOLD, 5, ch m Vaigly Great—Merokette **Mrs R. Hughes**

Other Owners: Mrs B. Tompsom, Mr Denis Williams.

Jockey (NH): G McCourt.

Conditional: R Bellamy.

Amateur: Mr S Andrews.

143 MR R. COLLET, Chantilly

Postal: **45/47 Avenue du General Leclerc, 60500 Chantilly, France.**
Phone: **(33) 4457 5927 or 0672 TELEX 150132 FAX 4457 3225**

1 **ALL OF ME,** 4, b c Be My Guest—Arctique Royal **R. C. Strauss**
2 **CRISTAL DE BOHEME (FR),** 4, b f Crystal Glitters—La Toccata **Ecurie Promethee**
3 **DEMAGOGUE (FR),** 4, b c Deep Roots—Rainy Drone **Mr P. Elmoznino**
4 **ELEGANCE,** 4, b f Tap On Wood—Niltava **Mme O'Neill**
5 **FLYING HOPE,** 4, b c Sadler's Wells—Trinity Term **Ecurie Promethee**
6 **JANE'S NEPHEW,** 4, b c Kings Lake—Jem Jem **Prince Sultan Al Kabeer**
7 **JET FOR GOOD (USA),** 4, b g Northjet—Good Fortune **Mr P. Elmoznino**
8 **KERGUELEN,** 4, b c Caerleon—Gay Apparel **R. C. Strauss**
9 **LUFBERRY (USA),** 5, b h Sassafras—La Margalaise **Marius Treco**
10 **MARVEL (FR),** 4, b c Margouillat—Marie de Vercel **Mr P. Elmoznino**
11 **MEHRNAZ,** 4, b f Mendez—Queen of The Mint **Mr P. Elmoznino**
12 **MISTER GILL (FR),** 6, b g April Axe—Remige **Mr Raymonde Wingtans**
13 **MORNING KISS,** 4, b f Kings Lake—Racquette **R. C. Strauss**
14 **NO PASARAN,** 4, b c Be My Guest—No Disgrace **Mme Downing**
15 **OF YANOF (FR),** 4, b c Ile de Bourbon—Stephany's Dream **Ecurie Promethee**
16 **OR ACIER (USA),** 4, b c Lypheor—Secorissa **R. C. Strauss and H. Chalhoub**
17 **PETILLANTE,** 5, b m Rusticaro—Niltava **Mme O'Neill**
18 **PETITE FOLIE,** 4, b f Salmon Leap—Une Folie **Mme O'Neill**
19 **QUELLE CLASSE (FR),** 4, ch f Bikala—Areej **Prince Sultan Al Kabeer**
20 **UNDER A SPELL (USA),** 4, b c Cresta Rider—Gitana **J. P. Binet and R. C. Strauss**
21 **UNKNOWN LORD,** 4, b c Kings Lake—Unknown Lady **R. Collet**
22 **UTAHBEACH (FR),** 4, b g Tadj—Bibiche **R. Collet**
23 **VERY STRONG (FR),** 4, b g Recitation—Werry **Ecurie Promethee**

THREE-YEAR-OLDS

24 **AFFIRMATIF (USA),** ch c Affirmed—Chic Nell **R. C. Strauss**
25 **BUCK DANY (USA),** b c Spend A Buck—Nancy Jr **R. C. Strauss**
26 **DEEP CARE (FR),** b c Deep Roots—Cartune **Mr P. Elmoznino**
27 **DICTATOR'S SONG (USA),** b c Seattle Song—Buck's Dame **H. Chalhoub**
28 **DONA CHARMER (FR),** b f Dom Racine—Our Charmer **Mme Mullion**
29 **DON CAESAR (FR),** b g Julius Caesar—Remige **Mr Raymonde Wingtans**
30 **ERNANI,** b c Sadler's Wells—Godzilla **R. C. Strauss**
31 **EVENING KISS,** b f Kris—Racquette **R. C. Strauss**
32 **FANNING THE FAME,** b f Commanche Run—Flamme d'Amour **R. C. Strauss**
33 **FLYING PASS (FR),** b c No Pass No Sale—Griffade **P. Arnett**
34 **GAIETE DE COEUR,** b f Lomond—Gay Apparel (CAN) **R. C. Strauss**
35 **GOHELLE (FR),** b f R B Chesne—Go Mila **Dr Fialon**
36 **HORSE CHARMING (IRE),** b c Be My Guest—Star Cream **R. Collet**
37 **LADY WISHING WELL,** b f Hero's Honor—Ispahan **H.R.H. Prince Torki M'Saud**
38 **MALOUINE,** b f Commanche Run—North Forland **R. C. Strauss**
39 **MARIE-DE-PHARIS (FR),** ch f Pas de Seul—Marie de Varenne (FR) **R. Collet**
40 **MINILASS (FR),** b c No Pass No Sale—Miniluth **Prince Bendar Al Kabir**
41 **MITROVICA (FR),** b f Cariellor—Nostimi **Mr Elias Zaccour**
42 **NOBLERUSE (FR),** b c Noblequest—Aruse **Prince Bendar Al Kabir**
43 **NOMBRE D'OR,** b c Caerleon—No Disgrace **R. C. Strauss**
44 **NO PASS ME (FR),** b f No Pass No Sale—Areej **Prince Sultan Al Kabeer**
45 **PARTY TIME (FR),** b f Dom Racine—Zone Bleue (FR) **P. Arnett**
46 **PONT AVEN,** b f Try My Best—Basilea (FR) **R. C. Strauss**
47 **PREDILECTION,** b c Be My Guest—Praise (FR) **R. C. Strauss**
48 **RAYONNE,** b f Sadler's Wells—Red Coral (AUS) **Mme W. Wolf**
49 **ROBERT LE DIABLE (USA),** b c Roberto—Sharp Belle (USA) **J. P. Binet and R. C. Strauss**
50 **SILICON BAVARIA (FR),** b f Procida—Siliciana **Mme W. Wolf**
51 **TAVERLEON,** b f Caerleon—Taverne de France **H.R.H. Prince Torki M'Saud**
52 **VIF ESPRIT (FR),** b c Esprit du Nord—Vite Et Belle (FR) **N. Lemaire**
53 **WHO IS COMING,** b c Be My Guest—Niltava **H. Chalhoub**
54 **YES YES EVER (USA),** ch f Miswaki—All In White **H. Chalhoub**
55 **ZAIAGORRI (FR),** b c Prince Mab—Sprinkler **R. Collet**
56 **ZAITZ (FR),** b c Zino—Trenora **Mme Marie Bruneau de la Salle**

MR R. COLLET—continued

TWO-YEAR-OLDS

57 **ANTEA (FR)**, b f Esprit du Nord—Axiane (Mill Reef) **Mr Patrice Brunet**
58 **AQUAVITE (FR)**, b f Script Ohio—Alconaca (Nonoalco) **Mme W. Wolf**
59 **ARMORIQUE (IRE)**, b f Top Ville—Arctic Royal (Royal Regal) **R. C. Strauss**
60 **BENTCHING (FR)**, b f Thatching—Benthose (Dapper Dan) **Cte Paul Leseuleuc de Kerouara**
61 **BERBER PRINCE (IRE)**, b c Try My Best—Kahena (King of The Castle) **Mr A. Boccara**
62 **BOOMING (FR)**, b c Leading Counsel—Donche (Roi Dagobert) **Mr Elias Zaccour**
63 **CAVALIER SEUL (USA)**, b c Alleged—Family Fame (Droll Role) **Mr J. P. Binet and R. C. Strauss**
64 **CHARME SLAVE (FR)**, b c Sicyos—Irish Arm (Irish River) **H. Chalhoub**
65 B c Lomond—Charming Life (Habitat) **Ecurie Promethee**
66 **CINCINNATIAN (IRE)**, b f Script Ohio—Luth Celtique (Thatch) **Prince Sultan Al Kabeer**
67 **CUPID SEA (USA)**, b c Arctic Tern—Phydylla (Lyphard) **H. Chalhoub**
68 **FIRST BABY (FR)**, b f Baby Turk—Djerba (My Swallow) **Mr Elias Zaccour**
69 **FORTUNE'S WHEEL (IRE)**, b c Law Society—North Forland (Northfields) **R. C. Strauss**
70 **FUNAMBULE (IRE)**, b c Be My Guest—Flushing Meadow (Raise A Native) **R. C. Strauss**
71 **GALE WARNING (IRE)**, b f Last Tycoon—Gay Apparel (Up Spirits) **R. C. Strauss**
72 **KENTUCKY COFFEE (FR)**, b c Kenmare—Marie de Fontenoy (Lightning) **H. Chalhoub**
73 **KIPLER (FR)**, b c Crystal Glitters—Nursery Rhyme (Lightning) **P. Arnett**
74 **L'AMOUR FOU (IRE)**, b f Last Tycoon—Flame d'Amour (Gift Card) **R. C. Strauss**
75 **LAS CAJAS (FR)**, b c Lashkari—Mi Casa Su Casa (Dynastic) **Mr Elias Zaccour**
76 **LIGHT FEVER (USA)**, b f Raft—La Magnifique (Emerson) **Mme W. Wolf**
77 **MARMONTEL (USA)**, b c Encino—Mistress Lea (Reverse) **P. Arnett**
78 **MAS DU HOUX (FR)**, b c Dunphy—Fabuline (Djakao) **H. Chalhoub**
79 **MONIMACQ (FR)**, b c Esprit du Nord—Pink Curtain (Mill Reef) **Mr Noel Lemaire**
80 B c Roberto—My Maravilla (Blushing Groom) **Mr Aubert and R. C. Strauss**
81 **OISEAU DE GUERRE (USA)**, b f Storm Bird—Warfever (Luthier) **H. Chalhoub**
82 **ONCE IN MY LIFE (IRE)**, b f Lomond—No Disgrace (Djakao) **R. C. Strauss**
83 **ORFEO NEGRO (FR)**, b c Sadler's Wells—Blue Rider (Wajima) **R. C. Strauss**
84 **POLSKI BOY (USA)**, b c Danzig Connection—Royal Folly (Tom Fool) **Mr Aubert**
85 **ROAN SEAGULL (FR)**, b f Saint Estephe—Areej (Rusticaro) **Prince Sultan Al Kabeer**
86 **SIMINETTE (FR)**, b f General Holme—Royal Cotillon (King Emperor) **Mr Springer**
87 **TEMPLON (FR)**, b c Fabulous Dancer—Ruma (Rheffic) **H. Chalhoub**
88 **THE PERFECT LIFE (IRE)**, b f Try My Best—Mill Princess (Mill Reef) **R. C. Strauss**
89 **TYCOON'S DRAMA (IRE)**, b f Last Tycoon—Drama (Sir Ivor) **R. C. Strauss**
90 **WATCHING (FR)**, b c Thatching—Welsh Game (Pall Mall) **Mme W. Wolf**
91 **WHAT A SHAME**, b f What A Guest— (Shameless (FR)) **R. Collet**

Jockeys (Flat): A Lequeux (8-5), D Regnard (8-1).

Apprentices: D Bourillon (8-3), R Libert (7-6).

144 MR H. J. COLLINGRIDGE, Newmarket

Postal: **Beverley House Stables, Exeter Road, Newmarket, Suffolk, CB8 8LR.**
Phone: **(0638) 665454**

1 **BUZZARDS CREST**, 5, ch g Buzzards Bay—Diamond Talk **Nationcrest Plc**
2 **BUZZARDS SON**, 4, b c Buzzards Bay—Night Cap (SWE) **Corncharm Ltd**
3 **DAME ELUSIVE**, 4, b f Blakeney—Girl On A Swing **Mrs P. A. L. Butler**
4 **DIENAU'S TROVE**, 9, b g Hot Grove—Dienau **Mr and Mrs B. Collinson**
5 **GREENHILLS PRIDE**, 6, b g Sparkling Boy—Soheir **Mr L. Audus**
6 **LATE CUT**, 5, b g Tap On Wood—Sometime Lucky **Mr C. Bain**
7 **LE SAINT GERAN (FR)**, 4, b c Margouillat (FR)—Rain Later (USA) **Fondhart Ltd**
8 **LONG BAY**, 8, b h Song—Sundream **Mr H. J. Collingridge**
9 **MADAM TAYLOR**, 5, b m Free State—Hourglass **Taylors of Soham Ltd**
10 **MISS WILLOW**, 4, b f Horage—Nebanna **Mr P. J. Byrnes**
11 **MOUNT WOOD**, 7, gr m Rupert Bear—Injaka **Mr Michael Kelly**

MR H. J. COLLINGRIDGE—continued

12 **MR TAYLOR,** 5, b g Martinmas—Miss Reliant **Taylors of Soham Ltd**
13 **PINTAIL BAY,** 4, b c Buzzards Bay—Pin Hole **Mr N. H. Gardner**
14 **TAYLOR'S REALM,** 4, gr f Another Realm—Sweet Rosina **Taylors of Soham Ltd**

THREE-YEAR-OLDS

15 **BAYBEEJAY,** b f Buzzards Bay—Peak Condition **Mr D. W. Price**
16 **BOLD ZARD,** b f Buzzards Bay—Bold Kelly **Partnership**
17 **COPPER TOP,** b f Longleat (USA)—Quorn Rocket **Mr J. A. Thomas**
18 **FIGHTING SUN,** ch c Hard Fought—Sunny Waters **The Lime Street Racing Syndicate**
19 **HADLEIGHS CHOICE,** b c Fairy King (USA)—Jillette **Corncharm Ltd**
20 **HARPLEY,** gr c Beldale Flutter (USA)—Jelly Gold **Mr R. W. Hipkin**
21 **NORABLASSIE,** b f Norwick (USA)—Aberdeen Lassie **Nationcrest Plc**
22 **PREMIERE MOON,** ch f Bold Owl—Silvery Moon **Mr B. P. Venner**
23 **TAYLORS PRINCE,** ch c Sandhurst Prince—Maiden's Dance **Taylors of Soham Ltd**
24 **TINAZ,** b f Homing—Claironcita **D. F. Attard**
25 **TYBURN LAD,** gr g Belfort (FR)—Swing Is Back **Mr C. J. T. Graven**
26 **VA TOUJOURS,** b f Alzao (USA)—French Princess **Mr L. Westbury**

TWO-YEAR-OLDS

27 B f Buzzards Bay—Bold Kelly (Pitskelly) **C. Gardiner**
28 B c Lidhame—Burning Ambition (Troy) **B. Kelly**
29 B c Buzzards Bay—Cawston Star (Comedy Star (USA))
30 B f Buzzards Bay—Czar's Diamond (Queen's Hussar) **Mrs R. B. Stokes**
31 B c Lyphard's Special (USA)—High Explosive (Mount Hagen (FR)) **Mr J. A. Thomas**
32 **MILLY SHARP,** ch f Nishapour (FR)—Becky Sharp (Sharpen Up) **Mr R. W. Hipkin**
33 **NOWHISKI,** b c Petoski—Be Faithful (Val de Loir) **Mrs P. Butler**
34 B c Camden Town—Shahrazad (Young Emperor) **M. P. Dennis**
35 **SIR PASS,** b c Chukaroo—State Romance (Free State) **Mr D. W. Price**
36 B c Dunbeath (USA)—Varushka (Sharpen Up)

Other Owners: Mr P. F. Cullinan, Mr M. W. Ginn, Mr P. Houlihan, Mrs J. Justice, Mr Henry Kenner, Miss D. E. Lawes, Mr R. N. Lockhart-Smith, Mrs U. M. Minch, Mr A. W. Orpin, Mr P. Petts, Mr G. W. Short, Mrs S. K. Turton, Mr K. Wakeham.

Jockey (Flat): J Quinn (7-7).

Apprentice: R Grainger (7-7).

Amateur: P Close (9-7).

145 MR M. J. COLLINS, Horley

Postal: **Meadow Cottage, Church Road, Burstow, Horley, West Sussex, RH6 9RG.**
Phone: **Smallfield 2507**

1 **DAMERS GLORY,** 9, b g General Ironside—Lattins Lady **Mr M. J. Collins**
2 **MAJORIAN,** 12, b g Majority Blue—Tinker Lass **Mr M. J. Collins**

Jockey (NH): G M McCourt (10-5).

Lady Rider: Mrs Penny Ffitch-Heyes (9-10).

146 MR K. CONNOLLY, Kildare

Postal: **Westenra, Kildare, Co. Kildare, Ireland.**
Phone: **(045) 21067 FAX NO (045) 22155**

1 **AYN HALI,** 7, ch m Monksfield—Miss Beenie **Mrs. M. Connolly**
2 **CHANUSKA,** 7, b g Lord Gayle (USA)—Vectis **Mr. F. Glennon**
3 **CHEZROCK,** 5, ch m Ballad Rock—Natchez **Mr. F. Glennon**
4 **DOWDINGS TOWN,** 5, b g Jasmine Star—Bermuda Princess **Mr K. Connolly**
5 **FADO'S DELIGHT,** 4, ch f Orchestra—Fado **Mr J. Foley**
6 **IDLE GLEN,** 4, ch g Glen Quaich—Idle Talk **Mr J. Connolly**
7 **LIGHTFOOT PRINCE,** 6, b g Tyrnavos—Wrekinianne **Kevin Connolly**
8 **MARK LAND,** 4, b c Montekin—Nolnocan **Mr S. Mulryan**
9 **MARK SPRITE,** 5, b h On Your Mark—Bermuda Sprite **Mr M. Bergl**
10 4, Ch f Jasmine Star—Miss Beenie **Mr K. Connolly**
11 **ORION DREAM,** 4, b f Skyliner—Kiltartan **Mr M. T. O'Donnell**
12 **PEACE MISSION,** 4, b f Dunbeath—Pichincha **Mr John Malone**
13 **RECKLESS BROOKLINE,** 4, b f On Your Mark—Bermuda Sprite **Mr M. Bergl**
14 **ROSA VAN FLEET,** 4, b f Sallust—Sarah Van Fleet **Miss P. Edwards**
15 **WHISPER WISHES,** 4, ch f Burslem—Carcajou **Mr A. Walsh**

THREE-YEAR-OLDS

16 **AYIA NAPA,** b c Known Fact—Folgoet **Mr B. P. McMahon**
17 **CENTRAL,** b g Taufan—Rinkamire **Mr Kevin Connolly**
18 **CLAN JULIA,** b f Dalsaan—Green Idol **Miss G. Byrne**
19 B f Indian King—Dolphin Bay **Mr K. Connolly**
20 **EMERALD WATERS,** b f Kings Lake—In The Clover **Mr P. Green**
21 **MAID OF MOURNE,** b f Fairy King—Plunket's Choice **Mr P. J. O'Hagan**
22 **MELODIC HABIT,** b f Muscatite—Magyar Melody **Mrs K. Fitzgibbon**
23 Ch f Jasmine Star—Miss Beenie
24 **MOTILITY,** b f Yashgan—Fiodior **Mrs F. D. McAuley**
25 **MR BROOKS,** b c Blazing Saddles—Double Finesse **Mr K. Connolly**
26 **NORTHERN VISION,** b c Vision—Smelter **Mrs Isobel Foley**
27 **REILTON,** b c Cure The Blues—Chanson de Paris **Mr W. J. Hamilton**
28 **RING OF LIGHT,** b f Auction Ring—Giounezza **Mr J. P. Costelloe**
29 **THE CHOODLER,** b f Strong Gale—Cousin Clare **The Choodler Syndicate**
30 **VAN WINKLE,** b c Jalmood—Daydreamer **Mr K. Connolly**

TWO-YEAR-OLDS

31 B c 13/2 Law Society—Arguing (Pharly)
32 B f 2/3 Muscatite—Caroline's Mark (On Your Mark)
33 B f 25/3 Mazaad—Clear Glade (Vitiges)
34 B f 12/5 Burslem—Dolphin Bay (Rarity) **Miss Gabrielle Byrne**
35 B f 25/3 Fast Topaze—Magic In The Air (Home Guard)
36 B f 18/4 King of Clubs—Maria Renata (Jaazeiro) **Mr Paul Green**
37 B c 20/5 Runnett—Plunket's Choice (Home Guard)
38 Ch f 30/4 Hatim—Rags To Riches (High Hat)
39 B f 24/2 Mazaad—Renzola (Dragonara Palace)
40 B f 9/5 Stalker—Smoke Signal (Bleep-Bleep)
41 Ch f Sir Ivor—Sweetsider (Topsider) **Mr J. P. Costelloe**
42 B c 11/5 Nordico—Takachiho's Girl (Takachiho)

Other Owners: Mr P. Dolphin, Mr G. Geraghty, Mr K. McHugh, Mr J. Michael, Mr Liam Mulryan, Mr M. L. Staunton.

Jockey (Flat): Pat Shanahan (8-2).

Amateurs: Mr John Connolly (10-7), Mr T P Spelman (10-0).

147 MR P. D. CONNORS, Hednesford

Postal: **9 Hazel Drive, Hazelslade, Hednesford, Staffordshire.**
Phone: **HEDNESFORD 77823**

1 **BRECKLAND GEM,** 5, b m Good Times (ITY)—Clatter **Mr G. Fierro**
2 **CUCKOO IN THE NEST,** 7, br g Imperial Fling (USA)—Nest Builder **Mr G. Fierro**
3 **FINWOOD,** 12, b m Ashmore (FR)—Souza Rose **Mr G. Fierro**
4 **LOVE WALKED IN,** 9, ch g Hotfoot—Love Resolved **Mr G. Fierro**
5 **MY BROTHER CLIFF,** 4, ch g Brotherly (USA)—Tudor Primrose **Mr G. Fierro**
6 **POACHING POCKET,** 7, gr g Some Hand—Grey Bird **Mr G. Fierro**
7 **SLANEY PRINCE,** 10, b g Sassafras (FR)—Pastina **Mr G. Fierro**
8 **UNTIED,** 5, b g Blakeney—Set Free **Mr G. Fierro**

THREE-YEAR-OLDS

9 **FINWAG,** ro g Scallywag—Finwood **Mr G. Fierro**

TWO-YEAR-OLDS

10 B f Joshua—Finwood (Ashmore (FR)) **Mr G. Fierro**

Jockeys (NH): G Martin, B Powell.

148 MR L. C. CORBETT, Manton

Postal: **Granary Cottage, Manton Grange, Manton, Marlborough, Wiltshire, SN8 4HH.**
Phone: **(0672) 52698**

1 4, B g The Brianstan—Bouboulina
2 4, Br f The Brianstan—Charlotte Mary
3 **FENCHURCH COLONY,** 9, b g Tachypous—Katebird **Mrs T. Coy-Dibley**
4 **KARAKTER REFERENCE,** 8, br g Reformed Character—Windtown Beauty **Winterbourne Construction Ltd**
5 **KIMSWA,** 9, b g Politico (USA)—Messalina **Mrs T. Coy-Dibley**
6 **LET ME THINK,** 6, b g Pollerton—Miss Cathy **Marlborough Homes Ltd**
7 **MERLINSBURG,** 5, br g Dubassoff (USA)—La Merlette **Marlborough Homes Ltd**
8 4, Ch g Deep Run—Scalped
9 **THE BRICHIN,** 9, br g Kambalda—Dream Kuda **Winterbourne Construction Ltd**
10 **TRANSPLANT BLUE,** 7, b g Buckskin (FR)—Slave Light **Transplant Ltd**
11 **WINTER WONDER,** 5, b m Sunyboy—Chancebeg **Winterbourne Construction Ltd**

Jockey (NH): Simon McNeill (10-0).

149 MR D. CORDELL LAVARACK, Bagenalstown

Postal: **Corries House, Bagenalstown, Co. Carlow, Ireland.**
Phone: **(0503) 21667 FAX (0503) 21640**

1 **ALF,** 4, b g Mummy's Treasure—Kazama **Nicholas Cowan**
2 **AN IRISH,** 4, ch c Camden Town—Timely Thatch **Mrs D. Cordell Lavarack**
3 **AZULERO,** 5, b g Cure The Blues (USA)—Misty Hill **Miss Harriet Viner**
4 **BUCKS EXPRESS,** 6, ch g Buckskin (FR)—Express Lady **Mrs C. Kennedy**
5 **CELLOPHANE,** 4, ch f Coquelin (USA)—Lady Pavlova **D. Cordell Lavarack Esq.**
6 **FIFTH GEAR,** 4, b f Red Sunset—Aiguiere (FR) **Mrs D. Cordell Lavarack**
7 **ISOLA (GER),** 4, b f Konigstuhl (GER)—Isabellita (GER) **H. Hintermuller**
8 **LUCAS COURT,** 4, b g Henbit (USA)—Boudoir **Mrs A. M. Folan**
9 **NAUJWAN TOO,** 4, b f Kafu—Mayturn **Tom Waters Esq.**
10 **OVER THE DOWNS,** 5, b g Cure The Blues (USA)—Lady Pavlova **Michael Feld Esq.**
11 **PICK NINE,** 4, b f Tumble Wind (USA)—Oh Carol **Anthony Speelman Esq.**
12 **REVELETTE,** 5, b m Runnett—Al Nadda **W. Patrick Clarke**

MR D. CORDELL LAVARACK—continued

13 **TAWKIN,** 5, b g Taufan (USA)—Kimstar **Mr Dan Tierney**
14 **TOMMY DALY,** 5, b g Dunphy—Bit of A Fiddle **J. Daly**
15 **TRIPLE PRESIE,** 4, b f Decent Fellow—Uzonkopru **Mrs D. Cordell Lavarack**
16 **TUKURUA,** 4, gr f Noalto—Kathinka **Mrs Mary Cordell**

THREE-YEAR-OLDS

17 **BE CHARMED,** b f Fairy King (USA)—Occupation **Mrs E. McClory (Partnership)**
18 **LAST EMPEROR (USA),** b c Forli (ARG)—Image Intensifier (USA) **J. Daly**
19 **NATTY RED,** ch g Coquelin (USA)—Timely Thatch **Stablemate Racing Plc**
20 **OAK QUEEN,** b f King of Clubs—Canton Lightning **K. Fuuii**
21 **OH JACKO,** b g Alzao (USA)—Oh Carol **D. Cordell Lavarack Esq.**
22 **SAKYKO (FR),** b f Sicyos (FR)—Bustelda (FR) **Ronald David Wood**
23 **TELL THE TRUTH (FR),** b f Kenmare (FR)—Kaolette (FR) **Mrs Julia Cowan**
24 **TWENTY TWENTY,** b f Vision (USA)—Grapette **Lady Anne Lambton**
25 **WOODYS COLOURS (USA),** b f Caro—Play Our Song **Ronald David Wood**

TWO-YEAR-OLDS

26 B f 10/4 Bellypha—Ampersand (USA) (Stop The Music (USA)) **Syndicate**
27 B f 24/3 Taufan (USA)—Beaume (FR) (Faraway Son (USA)) **D. Cordell Lavarack Esq.**
28 B f 19/3 Lomond (USA)—Climb The Heights (Majestic Light (USA))
29 **GLENCLOUD (IRE),** b c 17/4 Glenstal (USA)—Clouded Issue (Manado) **Mr Dan Tierney**
30 B f 8/4 Thatching—La Melodie (Silly Season) **D. Cordell Lavarack Esq.**
31 B c 16/4 Shardari—Rebecca's Song (Artaius (USA)) **D. Cordell Lavarack Esq.**
32 Ch f 5/3 Mazaad—Rosebran Ruby (Orchestra) **D. Cordell Lavarack Esq.**
33 B f 16/2 Persian Bold—Snatchingly (Thatch (USA)) **D. Cordell Lavarack Esq.**
34 Ch f 9/5 Commanche Run—Timely Thatch (Thatch (USA)) **D. Cordell Lavarack Esq.**
35 **TINTOMARA (IRE),** b f 4/5 Niniski (USA)—Timbale d'Argent (Petingo) **Miss K. Rausing**

Jockey (Flat): D Gillespie (8-1).

Jockey (NH): Martin Treacy (9-10).

Apprentice: Nial McCullough (7-2).

Amateur: Mr J Treacy (10-3).

Lady Rider: Miss Sarah Gordon (9-6).

150 MR L. G. COTTRELL, Cullompton

Postal: **The Paddocks, Dulford, Cullompton, Devon, EX15 2DX.**
Phone: **KENTISBEARE (08846) 320**

1 **BOULES,** 4, gr g Petong—Placid Pet **Mr Martin Cummings**
2 **CAPE PIGEON (USA),** 5, ch g Storm Bird (CAN)—Someway Somehow (USA) **Mr E. J. S. Gadsden**
3 **CUT UP ROUGH,** 6, b g Mummy's Pet—Albany **Mr M. L. Hookway**
4 **FOURTH PROTOCOL,** 6, ch g Gay Fandango (USA)—Miss Golightly **Mr M. L. Hookway**
5 **KACHINA MAID,** 5, b m Anfield—Grey Twig **Mr A. J. Cottrell**
6 **MERTOLA'S PET,** 4, b f Tickled Pink—Mertola **Mr Roger Hall**
7 **MICRO LOVE,** 6, ch h Vaigly Great—Minne Love **Mr J. B. Stafford**
8 **PREMIER PRINCE,** 4, b g King of Spain—Domicile **Mr John Boswell**
9 **RUIZ MIGUEL,** 4, br c Precocious—Lakshmi **Mr E. J. S. Gadsden**
10 **SIR CROON,** 4, ch g Crooner—Sirette **Mr Martin Cummings**
11 **STORM FREE (USA),** 4, b g Storm Bird (CAN)—No Designs (USA) **Mr E. J. S. Gadsden**
12 **SUPER LUNAR,** 6, gr g Kalaglow—Roxy Hart **Mrs Jenny Hopkins**

MR L. G. COTTRELL—continued

13 **THE REFRIGERATOR,** 6, b g Shirley Heights—Nip In The Air (USA) **S. Morris (Yeovil) Ltd**
14 **VERY ADJACENT,** 5, b h Chukaroo—State Romance **Mr J. Lawrence**
15 **YOUNG INCA,** 12, gr g Young Emperor—Sunny Eyes **Mr John Boswell**

THREE-YEAR-OLDS

16 **CASTLE MAID,** b f Castle Keep—Village Lass **Mrs V. M. Hurst**
17 **HOLY GAIT,** ro f Godswalk (USA)—Deverell's Lady **Mr John Boswell**
18 **LADY BUNTING,** b f Well Decorated (USA)—Lady's Flag (USA)
19 **MONKEY LOVE,** gr c Carwhite—Minne Love **Mr J. B. Stafford**
20 **OLD COMRADES,** ch g Music Boy—Miss Candine **Mr John Boswell**

Other Owners: Mr Phil Bowditch, Mr D. J. Cole, Mrs Nerys Dutfield, Mrs M. Fairbairn, Capt. J. A. George, Mrs H. Macfarlane, Mr J. R. Mitchell, Mr G. H. Perry, Mr Michael Pillans, Mr M. Rogers, Mrs F. L. Selley, Mr R. T. Sercombe, Mrs N. G. Stafford, Mr Ron Stephens, Mrs K. A. Stuart, Mr G. D. W. Swire.

Jockeys (Flat): N Adams, N Carlisle (7-2), M Roberts (w.a.), C Rutter, J Williams (8-2).

Apprentice: T Mayne.

151 MR T. CRAIG, Dunbar

Postal: **Tilton House Stables, West Barns, Dunbar, E. Lothian.**
Phone: **(0368) 62583**

1 **ADEN APOLLO,** 9, ch g Apollo Eight—Fuchsia Cottage **Mr James Sim**
2 **ADEN ROYALE,** 7, gr g Royal Fountain—Spare Maid **Mr James Sim**
3 **ALDAHE,** 5, ch g Dalsaan—Alanood **Mr William Burns**
4 **KWACHA,** 4, b c Reesh—Madame Quickly **Mr T. Craig**
5 **LA CHIQUITA,** 6, b m African Sky—La Cita **Mr I. Bell**
6 **MANS NO ANGEL,** 5, b g Aragon—No Halo **Mr R. R. J. Scott**
7 **PALACE LADY,** 4, b f Ballacashtal (CAN)—Belle (DEN) **Mr T. Craig**
8 **SELF IMPORTANT (USA),** 5, ch g Vigors (USA)—Dear Meme (USA) **Mrs J. McFadyen-Murray**
9 **SEMINOFF (FR),** 4, b g In Fijar (USA)—Borjana (USA) **Mr Dennis L. Dunbar**
10 **SHARBLASK,** 6, b g Sharpo—Blaskette **Mr I. Bell**
11 **SHINNEL WATER,** 4, b c Rolfe (USA)—Linda Dudley **L. P. S. (Cons) Ltd**
12 **SYLOW,** 4, b g Beldale Flutter (USA)—Fleet Noble (USA) **Les Armstrong**
13 **TANFEN,** 9, b g Tanfirion—Lady Mary **Mr William Burns**
14 **TIT WILLOW,** 8, b g He Loves Me—Willow Bird **Mr I. Bell**

THREE-YEAR-OLDS

15 **KEEN BREEZE,** b f Chabrias (FR)—Ginger Tart **Mr Dennis L. Dunbar**
16 **MISS HOSTESS,** gr f Petong—Rosalina **Perthshire Glazing Co Ltd**
17 **RAPID MOVER,** ch g Final Straw—Larive **Mrs J. McFadyen-Murray**

Other Owners: Mr James Anderson, Mr W. R. Birnie, Mr M. C. Boyd, Mr G. S. Brown, Mr R. Francis, Mr A. C. McLeod.

Jockeys (Flat): N Carlisle (7-7, w.a.), A Mackay (7-7, w.a.).

Jockey (NH): J Mooney.

Apprentice: F Scott (8-0).

Conditional: B Hay (9-7).

Amateur: Mr J Grossick.

152 MR B. T. CRAWFORD, Aslockton

Postal: **Abbev Farm Stables, Abbey Lane, Aslockton, Nottinghamshire.**
Phone: **WHATTON (0949) 50238**

1 **CHEAP METAL,** 5, br g Sonnen Gold—Economy Pep **Mr H. G. Norman**
2 **HAWAIIAN PRINCE,** 6, b g Hawaiian Return (USA)—Wrong Decision **Mr P. B. Short**
3 **MASTER FRENCH,** 10, b g Ancient Monro—Miss French **Mr D. S. R. Watson**
4 **MURCAF,** 10, b g Tekoah—Delia Ross **Mr J. Barlow**
5 **POINTER MAN,** 9, ch g Major Point—Spanish Empress **Mrs Susan Bellamy**

Amateur: Mr S Andrews.

153 LT.CD W. H. CRAWFORD, Haddington

Postal: **Huntington, Haddington, E. Lothian, EH41 3SP.**
Phone: **(062082) 2229**

1 **ACHILTIBUIE,** 6, b g Roscoe Blake—Gorgeous Gertie **Mrs W. H. Crawford**
2 **DEVON DISCOVERY,** 8, b g Brave Invader (USA)—Yellow Smoke **Mrs W. H. Crawford**
3 **GLEN MORVERN,** 4, ch f Carlingford Castle—Why Ask **Lt.-Commander W. H. Crawford**
4 **LOTHIAN CAPTAIN,** 5, b g Roscoe Blake—Lothian Lady **Lt.-Commander W. H. Crawford**
5 **LOTHIAN ROSE,** 4, b f Roscoe Blake—Lothian Lady **Lt.-Commander W. H. Crawford**
6 **SCOTTISH SIMBIR,** 10, ch g Simbir—Mary Money **Mrs W. H. Crawford**

Jockey (NH): N Doughty (w.a.).

154 MR J. CRIDDLE, Newport

Postal: **Merrills Bungalow, Carrow Hill, Llanvaches, Magor, Newport, Wales.**
Phone: **(0633) 400491**

1 **HEAD OF DEFENCE,** 5, ch g Tachypous—Headliner **Mr J. V. Criddle**
2 **JOYCE'S PET,** 6, b m Tina's Pet—Resurgence **Mr J. V. Criddle**

Amateur: Mr S Shinton (10-8).

155 MRS J. E. CROFT, Banbury

Postal: **Swerbrook Farm, Wigginton, Banbury, Oxon, OX15 4LH.**
Phone: **(0295) 721261**

1 **BALMUR,** 5, b g Balinger—Merebimur **Mr Roger Croft**
2 **BARTRYN,** 5, b m Barley Hill—Tarylin **Mr Roger Croft**
3 **BENTLEY,** 7, ch g Legal Tender—Dream Isle **Mrs D. Fallows**
4 **CHELSEA PRINCESS,** 5, b m Ranksborough—Eaton Clown **Mr M. E. J. Kilgariff**
5 **DRACAN HILL,** 5, b g Barley Hill—Dracandale VII **Mr Roger Croft**
6 **ERINS DANCER,** 9, b g Brave Invader (USA)—Geisha Dancer **Mr T. Bowman**
7 **FIRST RANK,** 7, b g Ranksborough—Streetcar **Mr R. Nicholls**
8 **HOME TO TARA,** 6, b g Prince Tenderfoot (USA)—Gayshuka **Mrs J. E. Croft**
9 **LUCY KING,** 9, b m Kinglet—Elucidation **Mr Roger Croft**
10 4, Ch f Roman Warrior—Merebimur **Mr Roger Croft**
11 4, B f Hey Romeo—Tarylin **Mr Roger Croft**
12 **TOCHENKA,** 6, ch m Fine Blue—Authors Daughter **K & R Minton-Price**

MRS J. E. CROFT—continued

THREE-YEAR-OLDS

13 B f Maori King—Dracandale VII **Mrs J. E Croft**

Other Owners: Mrs Barbara Bacon.

Jockey (NH): M Bosley (10-1).

Conditional: P Harley (9-7), W G Humphreys (9-7).

Amateur: Mr M Fields (9-7).

156 MRS G. P. CULHAM, Dumfries

Postal: **Boreland of Southwick, Nr Dumfries, Scotland, DG2 8AN.**
Phone: **(038 778) 225**

1 **FRENCH AGGRESSION,** 9, ch g Flandre II—Aggress **Mrs D. F. Culham**
2 **GO CRAZY,** 8, ro g Pongee—Petoria **Mr T. Culham**
3 **TOURAQUE (FR),** 5, b g Caerleon (USA)—Ange Gris (USA) **Mrs D. F. Culham**

Conditional: P Harte (w.a.).

157 MR L. M. CUMANI, Newmarket

Postal: **Bedford House Stables, Bury Road, Newmarket, Suffolk, CB8 7BX.**
Phone: **NEWMARKET (0638) 665432 TELEX 817512 FAX (0638) 667160**

1 **BE FRESH,** 4, ch c Be My Guest (USA)—Fresh **Dr M. Boffa**
2 **BLACK MONDAY,** 4, b c Busted—Lightning Legacy (USA) **Mr Mark Horne**
3 **EMTYAAZ (USA),** 4, b c Danzig (USA)—The Wheel Turns (USA) **Sheikh Mohammed**
4 **KHAYDARA,** 4, b f Indian King (USA)—Khatima **H.H. Aga Khan**
5 **LEGAL CASE,** 4, b c Alleged (USA)—Maryinsky (USA) **Sir Gordon White**
6 **MARKOFDISTINCTION,** 4, b br c Known Fact (USA)—Ghislaine (USA) **Mr Gerald Leigh**
7 **MILITARY FASHION,** 4, ch c Mill Reef (USA)—Smarten Up **Sheikh Mohammed**
8 **PIRATE ARMY (USA),** 4, b c Roberto (USA)—Wac (USA) **Sheikh Mohammed**
9 **PRINCESS ACCORD (USA),** 4, b f d'Accord (USA)—Cohutta Princess (USA) **Cheveley Park Stud**
10 **ROSEATE TERN,** 4, b f Blakeney—Rosia Bay **Mr Peter M. Brant**
11 **SHELLAC,** 4, b c What A Guest—Lacquer **Sheikh Mohammed**
12 **STATOBLEST,** 4, b c Ahonoora—Statira **Mr Richard L. Duchossois**
13 **TRUE DIVIDEND (USA),** 4, ch c Blushing Groom (FR)—Singing Rain (USA) **North Ridge Farm**

THREE-YEAR-OLDS

14 **AL DAMOUR (USA),** b c Lypheor—Visual Effects (USA) **Mrs Karin B. Richards**
15 **ALWATHBA (USA),** b f Lyphard (USA)—d'Arqueangel (USA) **Sheikh Ahmed Al Maktoum**
16 **AMERINDIAN,** b f Commanche Run—Supremely Royal **Sheikh Mohammed**
17 **ARZANNI,** gr c Darshaan—Astara **H.H. Aga Khan**
18 **AYOUN,** gr c Mouktar—Aytana (FR) **H.H. Aga Khan**
19 **BALLET RUSSE (USA),** b f Nijinsky (CAN)—Mariella (USA) **Sheikh Mohammed**
20 **BARRYMORE,** b c Robellino (USA)—Screenable (USA) **Mr O. Miles Pollard Jun**
21 **BAYLIS,** b c Sadler's Wells (USA)—Noblanna (USA) **Sheikh Mohammed**
22 **BERRY BERRY GOOD (USA),** b f Shadeed (USA)—Quilloquick (USA) **Mrs Virginia Knott Bender**
23 **BLUSHING BLOOM (USA),** ch f Blushing Groom (FR)—Catherine's Bet (USA) **Mr John C. Mabee**
24 **BRIDAL TOAST,** b c Rousillon (USA)—Romantic Feeling **Sheikh Mohammed**
25 **CALL BOX,** b f Caerleon (USA)—Cistus **Sir Michael Sobell**

MR L. M. CUMANI—continued

26 **CHIRONE (USA),** b c Lypheor—Distaff Magic (USA) **Studcrown Limited**
27 **CLEMENZA (USA),** ch f Vaguely Noble—Laday (USA) **Fittocks Stud Limited**
28 **CLEONTE,** b c Dominion—Be Faithful **Studcrown Limited**
29 **CULLINAN (USA),** b c Diamond Prospect (USA)—Meshuggenah **Sheikh Mohammed**
30 **DANCING BERRY,** b f Sadler's Wells (USA)—Red Berry **Mr D. F. Bradstock**
31 **DR ROBERT,** ch c Commanche Run—Fresh **Dr M. Boffa**
32 **DURKHAN (USA),** ch c Irish River (FR)—Dukayna **H.H. Aga Khan**
33 **EDWARD SEYMOUR (USA),** b c Northern Baby (CAN)—Regal Leader (USA) **Sheikh Mohammed**
34 **EL PASO,** b c Alzao (USA)—Invery Lady **Mr J. P. Kenny**
35 **EPHEMERAL,** b f Shernazar—Swanilda (FR) **Fittocks Stud Limited**
36 **FIRE THE GROOM (USA),** b f Blushing Groom (FR)—Prospector's Fire (USA) **Mr Richard L. Duchossois**
37 **GOLDEN DARLING (USA),** ch f Slew O' Gold (USA)—Close Control (USA) **Mr John C. Mabee**
38 **GREY SHIMMER (USA),** gr c Caro—Beauty's Image (USA) **Mr R. R. Dodderidge**
39 **HAJADE,** b c Ile de Bourbon (USA)—Timbale d'Argent **Sir Gordon White**
40 **HAROON,** ch c Ahonoora—Gold Paper (FR) **Fittocks Stud Limited**
41 **HERBERTO (USA),** b c Roberto (USA)—Her Silver (USA) **Mr Richard L. Duchossois**
42 **INVITATION WALTZ,** b br f Be My Guest (USA)—Sabre Dancer (AUS) **Mr L. P. Alidenes**
43 **KALAMIYA,** gr f Kalaglow—Kaliala (FR) **H.H. Aga Khan**
44 **KASHTALA,** b f Lord Gayle (USA)—Khatima **H.H. Aga Khan**
45 **KINASREEN,** b f Vayrann—Kadissya (USA) **H.H. Aga Khan**
46 **KING CRACKER,** ch c King of Clubs—Brenda **Mr R. I. Khan**
47 **KIVETON KOMET,** ch f Precocious—Beaufort Star **Kiveton Park (Holdings) Ltd**
48 **LATVIAN,** gr c Rousillon (USA)—Lorelene (FR) **Fittocks Stud Limited**
49 **LINE OF THUNDER (USA),** b f Storm Bird (CAN)—Shoot A Line **Mr Peter M. Brant**
50 **LIVE ACTION,** b c Alzao (USA)—Brig O'Doon **Mrs Angela Sherif**
51 **LORD FLOREY (USA),** b c Blushing Groom (FR)—Remedia (USA) **Sheikh Mohammed**
52 **LORD MAGESTER (FR),** ch c Magesterial (USA)—Lady Zia (FR) **Mr Nicola Mesiano**
53 **MADIRIYA,** ch f Diesis—Majanada **H.H. Aga Khan**
54 **MADIYLA,** gr f Darshaan—Manntika **H.H. Aga Khan**
55 **MANOR HOUSE (USA),** b c El Gran Senor (USA)—Rose Cream (USA) **Mr John C. Mabee**
56 **MILL RUN,** b f Commanche Run—Gay Milly (FR) **Lord Weinstock**
57 **MINIMIZE,** b c Alzao (USA)—Timinala **Mr R. Shannon**
58 **MINSTREL DANCER (USA),** b c The Minstrel (CAN)—Belle Gallante (USA) **Mr Edward P. Evans**
59 **MONTENDRE,** b c Longleat (USA)—La Lutine **Skeltools Ltd**
60 **NARWALA,** b f Darshaan—Noufiyla **H.H. Aga Khan**
61 **NIGHT AT SEA,** gr f Night Shift (USA)—Into Harbour **Lady Juliet De Chair**
62 **NIGHT CEREMONY (USA),** b c Danzig (USA)—Flying Buttress (USA) **Mr Peter M. Brant**
63 **POINT TAKEN (USA),** b c Sharpen Up—Furry Friend (USA) **Sir Michael Sobell**
64 **RATIFY,** br c Shirley Heights—Rattle (FR) **Mr Abbas Yussef**
65 **REGORDES,** b f Commanche Run—Smageta **Mr L. Salice**
66 **RIVERULLAH (USA),** br c Riverman (USA)—Mama Kali (USA) **Mr Richard L. Duchossois**
67 **RUDY'S FANTASY (USA),** b c Nureyev (USA)—Rainbow's Edge (USA) **Sir Gordon White**
68 **SARAFIA,** ch f Dalsaan—Safaya (FR) **H.H. Aga Khan**
69 **SHAADIN (USA),** ch f Sharpen Up—La Dolce **Sheikh Mohammed**
70 **SHILINSKI,** b c Niniski (USA)—Sushila **Mr Richard L. Duchossois**
71 **SOCIETY BRIDE (USA),** b f Blushing Groom (FR)—Chic Belle (USA) **Sheikh Mohammed**
72 **STAPLEFORD MANOR (USA),** br c Riverman (USA)—Round The Rosie (USA) **Mr Richard L. Duchossois**
73 **SUNDAR,** b c Darshaan—Sunny Valley **Lord Weinstock**
74 **SYLVANUS (USA),** b c Chief's Crown (USA)—Sylvan's Girl (USA) **Sheikh Mohammed**
75 **TAMARPOUR (USA),** b c Sir Ivor—Tarsila **H.H. Aga Khan**
76 **TAMBORA,** b f Darshaan—Tameen (FR) **H.H. Aga Khan**
77 **TIDEMARK (USA),** b c Riverman (USA)—Remarkably (USA) **Mrs Maurice Jenkins**
78 **TOP BERRY,** b f High Top—Falcon Berry (FR) **Mr D. F. Bradstock**
79 **UPPER CIRCLE,** b f Shirley Heights—Odeon **Helena Springfield Ltd**
80 **UPSAIL,** b f Top Ville—Sherman Oaks **Mrs A. L. Chapman**
81 **WESTGATE ROCK,** b c Jalmood (USA)—Westgate Sovereign **Mr Robert A. Gladdis**
82 **WINTERHALTER,** b c Busted—Winter Queen **Mrs A. L. Chapman**
83 **WODAABE (USA),** b c Chief's Crown (USA)—Althea (USA) **Mrs Helen K. Groves**
84 **YALANOURA,** b f Lashkari—Yashina (FR) **H.H. Aga Khan**

Whenever you insure a horse

BLOODSTOCK & GENERAL INSURANCE SERVICES LTD 162 HIGH ST NEWMARKET TEL 661411

THINK
BGI

BLOODSTOCK & GENERAL INSURANCE SERVICES LTD.

SIMON TAIT
WILL BE IN ATTENDANCE AT
ALL THE PRINCIPAL ENGLISH AND IRISH BLOODSTOCK SALES

Douglas Hay our Northern Representative will also be at most sales.

Bloodstock & General Insurance Services Ltd.,
162 High Street, Newmarket, Tel: 661411
Facsimile: (0638) 665013

or Northern Representative:
Langbaurgh Cottage, Great Ayton, N. Yorks
Tel: (0642) 722089

MR L. M. CUMANI—continued

TWO-YEAR-OLDS

85 B c 13/4 Ahonoora—African Doll (African Sky) **Mr Richard L. Duchossois**
86 B f 1/2 Lyphard (USA)—Allicance (USA) (Alleged (USA)) **Sheikh Mohammed**
87 Ch f 12/3 Lomond (USA)—Amber Fizz (USA) (Effervescing (USA)) **Mr Saeed Manana**
88 **ANDRASSY,** ch c 25/3 Ahonoora—Anna Matrushka (Mill Reef (USA)) **Sheikh Mohammed**
89 **BAREILLY (USA),** b f Lyphard (USA)—Barger (USA) (Riverman (USA)) **Sheikh Mohammed**
90 **BASSAM FERAIHA (USA),** b c 14/3 Roberto (USA)—
Tea And Roses (USA) (Fleet Nasrullah) **Sheikh Ahmed Al Maktoum**
91 B f 21/4 Slip Anchor—Bercheba (Bellypha) **E. De Rothschild**
92 **BERLIN WALL (IRE),** b c 25/2 Thatching—Friedrichsruh (FR) (Dschingis Khan) **Mr R. E. Sangster**
93 **BOLD AS LOVE,** b f 4/4 Lomond (USA)—Domynga (Dominion) **Aziz Merza**
94 **BORDER MATE (IRE),** b f 16/2 Be My Guest (USA)—Scots Lass (Shirley Heights) **Lord Weinstock**
95 B c 28/4 Ahonoora—Brickfield Queen (High Top) **Bedford House Racing Partnership**
96 B c 12/3 Pennine Walk—Busca (USA) (Mr Prospector (USA)) **Mr J. P. Kenny**
97 **CINNAMON FERN,** b f 3/3 Sadler's Wells (USA)—Osmunda (Mill Reef (USA)) **Sheikh Mohammed**
98 B c 3/6 Last Tycoon—Clarina (Klairon) **Bedford House Racing Partnership**
99 **CLOUD PEAK (USA),** b f 12/3 Storm Bird (CAN)—Good Lassie (Moulton) **Sheikh Mohammed**
100 B f 29/4 Mr Prospector (USA)—Coiffure (USA) (Sir Gaylord) **Mr James Mayor**
101 B f 18/4 Caerleon (USA)—Cornish Heroine (USA) (Cornish Prince) **Sheikh Amin Dahlawi**
102 **CORONADO (IRE),** br c 12/2 Rainbow Quest (USA)—Moon Parade (Welsh Pageant) **Sir Gordon White**
103 Ch f 8/3 Greinton—Countess Belvane (USA) (Ribot) **Mr R. Mould**
104 Ch f 5/2 Be My Guest (USA)—Crown Godiva (Godswalk (USA)) **Kennet Valley Thoroughbreds**
105 Ch f Riverman (USA)—Damana (FR) (Crystal Palace (FR)) **H.H. Aga Khan**
106 Ch c Alydar (USA)—Dancers Countess (USA) (Northern Dancer) **Mr Alan Clore**
107 **DESIGNATE (USA),** b f Nureyev (USA)—Elect (USA) (Vaguely Noble) **Sheikh Mohammed**
108 B f Forli (ARG)—Dukayna (Northfields (USA)) **H.H. Aga Khan**
109 Ch c 17/3 Aragon—Dusty Bluebell (Sky Gipsy) **Studcrown Ltd**
110 **ENCORE AU BON,** gr c 18/4 Petong—White's Pet (Mummy's Pet) **Mr P. Ratti**
111 **EVERSET (FR),** b c 12/3 Green Desert (USA)—
Eversince (USA) (Foolish Pleasure (USA)) **Mr L. Gatto Roissard**
112 B c 2/2 Shahrastani (USA)—Excellent Spirit (USA) (Damascus (USA)) **Mr John C. Mabee**
113 **FIRST CRUSADE (FR),** b c Rainbow Quest (USA)—Saint Osyth (Blakeney) **Lady Juliet de Chair**
114 B c Mogambo (USA)—Forever Command (USA) (Top Command (USA)) **Mr Peter M. Brant**
115 B f 24/2 The Minstrel (CAN)—French Cutie (USA) (Vaguely Noble) **M. S. Anderson**
116 **GRACE BRIDGE (USA),** ch f 30/1 Miswaki (USA)—Ball Star (ARG) (Snow Ball) **Mr R. J. Shannon**
117 Ch c Shadeed (USA)—Heavenly Blue (USA) (Raise A Native) **Mr Alan Clore**
118 **HOT RUN (DEN),** b c 23/2 Commanche Run—Barely Hot (Bold Lad (IRE)) **Mr W. Bechmann**
119 **HUMANITY,** b f 8/2 Ahonoora—Helietta (Tyrnavos) **Fittocks Stud Ltd**
120 Ch f 5/2 Sharpen Up—Irish Royal (USA) (Irish River (FR)) **Mr John C. Mabee**
121 **ISLAND UNIVERSE (USA),** b c Lyphard (USA)—Carefully Hidden (USA) (Caro) **Shiekh Mohammed**
122 Ch c 21/4 Topsider (USA)—Ivor's Honey (Sir Ivor) **Sheikh Mohammed**
123 B f Alydar (USA)—Just A Game (Tarboosh (USA)) **Mr R. Levy**
124 Ch c 9/4 Ballad Rock—Kaliala (FR) (Pharly (FR)) **H.H. Aga Khan**
125 **KEMPINSKI (IRE),** b c 4/3 Valiyar—Kalista (Bellypha) **Lord Weinstock**
126 **KIJAFA (USA),** b f Chief's Crown (USA)—Herb Wine (USA) (Full Pocket (USA)) **Miss Helen Alexander**
127 **KILLIGREW,** b c 18/5 Sadler's Wells (USA)—Sensibility (USA) (Hail To Reason) **Sheikh Mohammed**
128 B c 6/3 Sadler's Wells (USA)—Krakow (Malinowski (USA)) **Sir Gordon White**
129 **LABURNUM,** b c 2/3 Glint of Gold—Lorelene (FR) (Lorenzaccio) **Fittocks Stud Ltd**
130 B c 28/3 Sagace (FR)—Lequilla (Mill Reef (USA)) **Mr Alan Clore**
131 Br c 2/4 Nureyev (USA)—Little Bonny (Bonne Noel) **Sheikh Mohammed**
132 B c 1/2 Dixieland Band (USA)—Lodging (USA) (King Pellinore (USA)) **D. B. Thompson**
133 B c 18/5 Darshaan—Majanada (Tap On Wood) **H.H. Aga Khan**
134 **MATA CARA,** b f 9/3 Storm Bird (CAN)—Fatah Flare (USA) (Alydar (USA)) **Sheikh Mohammed**
135 B c 28/4 Alzao (USA)—Merriment (USA) (Go Marching (USA)) **Mr Richard L. Duchossois**
136 Ch f 22/2 Chief's Crown (USA)—Modiste (USA) (Sir Ivor) **Sheikh Mohammed**
137 **MOUNTAIN BLOOM (IRE),** b f 5/2 Shirley Heights—Sally Rose (Sallust) **Lord Weinstock**
138 **MUROOJ (USA),** ch f 20/5 Diesis—Sancta Rose (Karabas) **Aziz Merza**
139 Gr c 12/2 Mouktar—Naiymat (Troy) **H.H. Aga Khan**
140 B f Caro—Najidiya (USA) (Riverman (USA)) **H.H. Aga Khan**
141 B c Storm Bird (CAN)—Nervous Pillow (USA) (Nervous Energy (USA)) **Mr John C. Mabee**

The Winning Formula . . .

WF High Tech is a unique blend of wood fibre designed to provide a regular training programme no matter what the weather conditions. Formulated to ensure that your horse will stay fit and well, and ready to run all year round.

In creating WF High Tech, special consideration has been given to horses with suspensory or tendon troubles as it provides a natural giving surface for gallops, menages and lunge rings.

The complete installation is handled efficiently and professionally from design to construction.

For a competitive quote and the best advice contact
Willy Fogarty,
WF Equestrian Surfaces, Old Quarry Works,
Chedworth, Nr. Cheltenham, Glos. GL54 4NW
Tel: (0285) 720769, 720770 or 657764

. . .for the Winning Favourite

MR L. M. CUMANI—continued

142 NEW TYCOON (IRE), b f 28/1 Last Tycoon—Go Feather Go (USA) (Go Marching (USA)) **Edward P. Evans**
143 NIBBS POINT (IRE), b f 3/4 Sure Blade (USA)—Fanny's Cove (Mill Reef (USA)) **Earl of Halifax**
144 B c 26/3 Roberto (USA)—Nile Empress (USA) (Upper Nile (USA)) **Mr Richard L. Duchossois**
145 B c 23/3 Caerleon (USA)—Noah's Acky Astra (USA) (Ack Ack (USA)) **Mr Alan Clore**
146 B f Shareef Dancer (USA)—Oh So Sharp (Kris) **Sheikh Mohammed**
147 B c 27/2 Darshaan—Parakara (Great Nephew) **H.H. Aga Khan**
148 PERKY DANCER (USA), b f Green Dancer (USA)—Pert (USA) (Damascus (USA)) **Mr Richard L. Duchossois**
149 PETER GRIMES, b c 12/2 Sadler's Wells (USA)—La Grange (Habitat) **Sheikh Mohammed**
150 B c 1/5 Sharpen Up—Petillante (USA) (Riverman (USA)) **Bedford House Racing Partnership**
151 PRIME MOVER, b c 12/4 Mummy's Game—Feast-Rite (Reform) **R. J. Thompson**
152 PURPLE PROSE, b f 13/2 Rainbow Quest (USA)—Coryana (Sassafras (FR)) **Chevely Park Stud**
153 RADICAL CHIC, b c 26/1 Sadler's Wells (USA)—Santa Roseanna (Caracol (FR)) **Mr G. Leigh**
154 Ch f Blushing Groom (FR)—Ranpoura (Kashmir II) **H.H. Aga Khan**
155 RATAFIA, b f 21/1 Rousillon (USA)—Smageta (High Top) **Mr L. Salice**
156 REHAAN (USA), b c 9/5 Storm Bird (CAN)—Playmate (USA) (Buckpasser) **Sheikh Ahmed Al Maktoum**
157 REPIQUE (USA), ch f 1/4 Sharpen Up—Repetitious (Northfields (USA)) **Sheikh Mohammed**
158 RETURN FLIGHT (USA), b br c 10/4 Riverman (USA)—Dictina (FR) (Dictus (FR)) **Sir Gordon White**
159 B c 17/5 Be My Guest (USA)—Ribera (FR) (Wittgenstein (USA)) **Mr Alan Clore**
160 RIVERWISE (USA), b c 5/3 Riverman (USA)—Village Sass (USA) (Sassafras (FR)) **Sheikh Mohammed**
161 ROAD TO AU BON (USA), b c 24/4 Strawberry Road (AUS)—Village Lady (Seven The Quadrant) **Mr P. Ratti**
162 B f 26/4 Alzao (USA)—Romanee Conti (Will Somers) **Mr Peter M. Brant**
163 ROSEWATER (USA), br f 3/3 Riverman (USA)—Round The Rosie (USA) (Cornish Prince) **Sheikh Mohammed**
164 ROUGE DRAGON (IRE), b c 13/5 Heraldiste (USA)—Peach Melba (So Blessed) **Mrs Amanda Skiffington**
165 B c 26/5 Secreto (USA)—Royal Suite (Habitat) **Mr Peter M. Brant**
166 RUN RINGS, b c 13/3 Commanche Run—Fai La Bella (USA) (Fifth Marine (USA)) **Fittocks Stud Ltd**
167 Gr c 23/4 Darshaan—Safaya (FR) (Zeddaan) **H.H. Aga Khan**
168 B c 28/1 Alzao (USA)—Sarong (Taj Dewan) **Mrs Christopher Heath**
169 B f Secreto (USA)—Satilla (FR) (Targowice (USA)) **Mr Alan Clore**
170 B c 11/1 Alzao (USA)—Say Something (Reform) **Bedford House Racing Partnership**
171 B f Track Barron (USA)—Scoot (Double Jump) **Mr Peter M. Brant**
172 Br c 8/5 Rousillon (USA)—Sea Chant (Julio Mariner) **Kiveton Park (Holdings) Ltd**
173 SHAMSHIR, ch f 21/2 Kris—Free Guest (Be My Guest (USA)) **Sheikh Mohammed**
174 SHARDELISADA (USA), br f Sharpen Up—Flordelisada (USA) (Drone (USA)) **Mr Richard L. Duchossois**
175 SHERE (IRE), b c 6/5 Shernazar—Top Mouse (High Top) **Sheikh Mohammed**
176 B c 10/3 Rainbow Quest (USA)—Short Rations (Lorenzaccio) **Bedford House Racing Partnership**
177 SOAR ABOVE (IRE), ch f 21/2 Commanche Run—Road To The Top (Shirley Heights) **Lord Weinstock**
178 SOUK (IRE), b f 27/4 Ahonoora—Soumana (FR) (Pharly (FR)) **Fittocks Stud Ltd**
179 B c 17/4 High Top—State Ball (Dance In Time (CAN)) **Studcrown Limited**
180 SUOMI (IRE), b c 20/3 Tate Gallery (USA)—Finlandia (FR) (Faraway Son (USA)) **Sheikh Mohammed**
181 B c 16/3 Woodman (USA)—Tentamount (USA) (Tentam (USA)) **Bedford House Racing Partnership**
182 B f 2/4 Last Tycoon—Tulalanee (Habitat) **Cheveley Park Stud**
183 TURBULENT RIVER (USA), b c Riverman (USA)—Star Pastures (Northfields (USA)) **Cheveley Park Stud**
184 B f Riverman (USA)—Vidor (USA) (Vaguely Noble) **Mr Alan Clore**
185 B f 21/3 Alydar (USA)—Wac (USA) (Lt Stevens) **Mr John C. Mabee**
186 WHERE'S MY SHADES (USA), ch c Shahrastani (USA)—Margaritaville (USA) (Tom Rolfe) **Mr Richard L. Duchossois**
187 ZAMANAYN (IRE), gr c 24/3 Mouktar—Zariya (USA) (Blushing Groom (FR)) **H.H. Aga Khan**

Other Owners: Mr D. Aykroyd, L. Del Balzo, Mr O. Baring, Mr A. N. C. Bengough, Colonel Sir Piers Bengough, Mr A. Cronk, Hugh Van Cutsem, Mr P. A. Deal, Lady De La Warr, Lord De La Warr, Mr P. J. Dore, Mr Anthony Freeland, Mr L. Gagosian, Gracebridge Ltd, T. Hyde, Mr J. G. Jagelman, Mr G. Keller, Mr R. D. A. Kelly, Mr D. A. Lucie-Smith, Lord Portsmouth, Mr Peter R. Pritchard, Mrs Amschel Rothschild, Mr David Russell, Mrs Angie Silver, Miss Helena Weinfeld, Mr M. Weinfeld, Mr Simon Weinstock, Mr John Wetherell, The Marquess Of Zetland.

Jockeys (Flat): L Dettori (8-0), R McGhin (8-3), C Rate (8-5), C Wigham (7-12).

Apprentices: D Dunnachie (7-10), I M Monteith (7-7), J Weaver (7-10).

Lady Riders: Mrs S Cumani (9-0), Miss E Hare (8-5).

158 MR P. D. CUNDELL, Newbury

Postal: **Roden House, Compton, Newbury, Berkshire, RG16 0QR.**
Phone: **(0635) 578267**

1 **AFRICAN SAFARI,** 6, b g Daring March—African Berry **Lord Carrick**
2 **BOLD GUARD,** 5, ch g Bold Lad—Mrs Foodbroker
3 **BROAD RYDE,** 4, ch f Broadsword (USA)—Rydewell **Mrs K. I. Hayward**
4 **CELTIC CRACKLE,** 10, ch g Celtic Cone—Birds Well **Mr P. D. Cundell**
5 **EASTER BABY,** 4, ch f Derrylin—Saintly Miss **Mr P. D. Cundell**
6 **GAELIC FROLIC,** 7, ch g Connaught—Frivolity **Mr Peter S. Winfield**
7 **GOLDEN GIANT,** 5, ch g True Song—Catherine Rose **Mr P. D. Cundell**
8 **PECHE D'OR,** 6, ch g Glint of Gold—Fishermans Bridge **Mr P. D. Cundell**
9 **RYDE AGAIN,** 7, ch g Celtic Cone—Rydewell **Mrs K. I. Hayward**
10 **RYDEWELLS DAUGHTER,** 5, ch m Celtic Cone—Rydewell **Mrs K. I. Hayward**
11 **SAINTLY LAD,** 8, b g Derrylin—Saintly Miss **Mr P. D. Cundell**
12 **SAINTLY LASS,** 6, b m Derrylin—Saintly Miss **J. S. Anderson**
13 **TARCONEY,** 10, ch g Celtic Cone—Tarqoretta **Mr R. A. B. Whittle**

Other Owners: Mr K. S. Cundell, Mr J. B. Fenwick, Mrs Eve Slatcher.

159 MR M. CUNNINGHAM, Navan

Postal: **Gormanstown Stables, Kildalkey, Navan, Co.Meath, Ireland.**
Phone: **(046) 31672**

1 **AMBER GIOTTO,** 6, b m Wolverlife—Amber Gift **Mrs E. T. Naughton**
2 **AMERICAN LADY,** 6, b m Ile de Bourbon (USA)—Perchance **John Michael**
3 **AWESOME POWER,** 4, b g Vision (USA)—Majestic Nurse **Garrett J. Freyne**
4 **BALLAD SONG,** 7, b g Ballad Rock—Apt **Mrs Michael Cunningham**
5 **FERGAL'S DELIGHT,** 7, b g Welsh Chanter—Telemonia **Noel McGrady**
6 **GOLDEN DECISION,** 9, b g Royal Trip—Wrong Decision **J. M. O'Malley**
7 **GRAHAM COURSE,** 7, b m Crash Course—Graham Dieu **Noel McGrady**
8 **IT'S TOUGH,** 11, ch g Mandao—Fourth Chance **P. J. Kennedy**
9 **JAN VAN RIEBEECK,** 4, b c Mummy's Treasure—Caramica **Ms Mary Hynes**
10 **LITTLE HIGHNESS,** 4, b f Head For Heights—Little Red Hut **Alexander Pereira**
11 **LYPHARD'S LADY,** 4, b f Lyphard's Special (USA)—Molly Pitcher **Philip Fleming**
12 **MAC'S GLEN,** 6, b g Furry Glen—Graham Dieu **Noel McGrady**
13 **MARSHALLSTOWN,** 8, b br m Callernish—Venette **O. Clarke**
14 **MICHAEL'S DON,** 6, ch g Don—Cordenton Girl **Leo McGrady**
15 **MIRAGE DAY,** 7, br g Our Mirage—Superday **Leo McGrady**
16 **NA CLOCHA LIATHA,** 5, b h Red Sunset—Oileann Carrig **Omicron Industries Ltd.**
17 **PANALPINA,** 4, b f Petorius—Tinktura **Mrs Michael Cunningham**
18 5, Ch g Don—Royal Performance **Mrs Michael Cunningham**
19 **SIR SIMPLE,** 4, ch c Simply Great (FR)—Miralife **Michael J. Heaslip**
20 **SPRINKLING STAR,** 5, br m Strong Gale—Fillo **Mrs Michael Byrne**
21 **WEE SHIRLEY,** 5, gr m Nishapour (FR)—Haco **Mrs Michael Cunningham**

THREE-YEAR-OLDS

22 **FREUDENAU,** b f Wassl—Ferjima's Gem (USA) **Alexander Pereira**
23 **GEISHA TREASURE,** b f Mummy's Treasure—Geisha Dancer **Mrs B. Lynch**
24 **MAYDEATAYMER,** b f Mummy's Treasure—Sacola **Mrs Grace McGonagle**

160 MR T. W. CUNNINGHAM, Northallerton

Postal: **Hollins Stables, East Rounton, Northallerton, North Yorkshire, DL6 2LG.**
Phone: **(060982) 695**

1 **BATTLE OF WITS,** 9, b g Tug of War—Glenvale Princess **Developmore Ltd (Beta Construction)**
2 **BE KAFUL,** 4, b f Kafu—Lobela **Mr T. W. Cunningham**
3 **COLNEY HEATH LAD,** 6, ch g Import—Pass-A-Deaney **Mr A. Doyle**
4 **COMPENSATOR,** 5, b g Sweet Monday—Grayshott Hall **Developmore Ltd (Beta Construction)**
5 **DEBACH DARKNESS,** 4, b f Dara Monarch—Lenticular **Mr T. W. Cunningham**
6 **HEATHER MOTH,** 8, b g Candy Cane—Rumdora **Developmore Ltd (Beta Construction)**
7 **IMPERTAIN,** 10, br g Ascertain (USA)—Swift Imp **Developmore Ltd (Beta Construction)**
8 **IN THE BREEZE (FR),** 9, ch g Mount Hagen (FR)—Starval (FR) **Mr M. Sams**
9 **MURPHY'S CHOICE,** 7, ch g Crash Course—Purlane (FR) **Developmore Ltd (Beta Construction)**
10 **PRAGAS BETA,** 5, gr g Pragmatic—Alcide Inn **Developmore Ltd (Beta Construction)**
11 **SAMONIA,** 10, b m Rolfe (USA)—Nevilles Cross (USA) **Mr J. W. Barker**
12 **SLATYFORD LANE,** 9, ch m Le Bavard (FR)—Kathleen Beag **Mr J. Hugill**
13 **SLOSHED,** 6, b g Tug of War—Lager **Developmore Ltd (Beta Construction)**
14 **THE FINK SISTERS,** 7, ch m Tap On Wood—Mount Hala **Mr R. Martin**
15 **TUMBLE JIM,** 11, b g Tumble Wind (USA)—Little Rastro **Mr R. Martin**

Other Owners: Mr Ron Finch, Mr R. Lee, Mr L. Norman.

Jockey (NH): C Grant (w.a.).

Conditional: S Cunningham (9-7).

161 MR K. CUNNINGHAM-BROWN, Stockbridge

Postal: **Danebury Place, Stockbridge, Hampshire.**
Phone: **(0264) 781061 OR 781611 TELEX 477212 FAX (0264) 781709**

1 **CRUMBLE,** 8, b g Skyliner—Chantry Pearl **K. O. Cunningham-Brown**
2 **DISTANT RELATION,** 5, b m Great Nephew—Perchance **Mr D. Bass**
3 **OWL CASTLE,** 7, b h Bold Owl—My Duty **Mr John W. Mitchell**
4 **REALISM,** 5, b g Known Fact (USA)—Miss Reasoning (USA) **Mr D. Bass**
5 **SABARAB,** 4, b c Sayf El Arab (USA)—Miss Speak Easy (USA) **Wessex Bloodstock**
6 **THABEH,** 4, b f Shareef Dancer (USA)—Loveshine (USA) **Mr D. Bass**
7 **THE TANSEY MAN,** 4, ch g Millfontaine—Kindle **Mr P. Trant**
8 **TWO REALMS,** 4, b f Another Realm—Two Shots **Mrs E. Jackman**
9 **UPTOWN BEAT,** 5, ch g Town And Country—Samba **Mrs Lucy Lawson**

THREE-YEAR-OLDS

10 **CETAGLOW,** b f Kalaglow—Avocet **Mr D. Bass**
11 **CHEVEUX MITCHELL,** ch c Dunbeath (USA)—Hide Out **Mrs Carolyn Wood**
12 **SLOW EXPOSURE,** b c Pharly (FR)—Armure Bleue (FR) **Miss K. Stark**
13 **SPIDER WOMAN,** b f Touching Wood (USA)—Red Spider **Mr D. Bass**
14 **WITH GUSTO,** b c Taufan (USA)—Finesse **Mr Michael D. Brunton**
15 **YOU KNOW THE RULES,** b f Castle Keep—Falls of Lora **John Henwood Organisation**

TWO-YEAR-OLDS

16 Ch c Adonijah—Fedra **Mrs Fiona Brunton**
17 B c Vin St Benet—Sandy Keerie **Danebury Racing Stables**

Other Owners: Mr S. Brooks, Mr M. Channon, Grand Foods Ltd, Mrs D. Hanson, Mr W. A. Harrison-Allan, Mr G. A. Jackman, Mrs Jean Keegan, Mr Trevor Mitchell, Mr B. J. Taylor.

162 MR B. J. CURLEY, Newmarket

Postal: **Harraton Court Stables, Exning, Newmarket, Suffolk.**
Phone: **(0638) 768251**

1 **APPLE LANE (USA)**, 10, ch g Star Envoy (USA)—Queen of Diamonds (USA) **Mrs B. J. Curley**
2 **ARDBRIN**, 7, ch g Bulldozer—Hazels Fancy **Mrs B. J. Curley**
3 **ASSULTAN**, 6, ch g Troy—Plum Run (USA) **Mr Don Cantillon**
4 **DOING THE DOUBLE**, 5, b g Prince Bee—Prancer **Mrs B. J. Curley**
5 **GOLDEN DISPLAY**, 6, b h Golden Fleece (USA)—Minnie Hauk (USA) **Mrs B. J. Curley**
6 **GOLDEN ISLE**, 6, b h Golden Fleece (USA)—Dunette (FR) **Mrs B. J. Curley**
7 **HENRYK**, 6, ch g Gay Fandango (USA)—Clouds **Mrs B. J. Curley**
8 **HEY BOSS**, 6, b g Furry Glen—Clarrie **Mrs B. J. Curley**
9 **KEEP HOPE ALIVE**, 6, b g Corvaro (USA)—Widschi (GER) **Mrs J. Donnelly**
10 **SARYAN**, 7, b g Try My Best (USA)—High Fidelyty (FR) **Mrs B. J. Curley**
11 **SPARE US ALL**, 6, b g Moorestyle—Second Generation **Mrs B. J. Curley**
12 **THE HACIENDEROS**, 11, b g Deep Run—Farina **Mrs B. J. Curley**
13 **THE PAPPARAZI**, 10, ch g Boreen (FR)—Marble Owen **Mrs B. J. Curley**

Jockey (NH): Declan Murphy (10-0).

163 MR R. CURTIS, Epsom

Postal: **Ermyn Lodge Stables, Shepherds Walk, Epsom, Surrey, KT18 6DF.**
Phone: **(0372) 277645**

1 **ADBURY**, 7, gr g Bustino—Fair Melys (FR) **Mr M. J. Rogers**
2 **ANDROBOTE (FR)**, 4, ch g The Wonder (FR)—Andromeda (FR) **Albury Racing Limited**
3 **BARN POOL**, 8, br g High Season—Mint Express **Mrs L. Buckerfield**
4 **BAY MOUNTAIN**, 4, b g Tyrnavos—Just You Wait **Mr David Kirk**
5 **BOSCHENDAL**, 8, b g Orange Bay—Bronze Princess **Mrs Loretta Harris**
6 **BURNING BRIGHT**, 7, b g Star Appeal—Lead Me On **Mrs E. M. English**
7 **BYWELL LAD**, 5, ch g Mandrake Major—Juliette **Mrs Iris E. Evans**
8 **CHAIS DU FONDATEUR**, 10, ch g Hot Brandy—Venture More **Mr Michael Groombridge**
9 **DEBBIES CHOICE**, 4, br f Record Run—Anna's Pet **T. W. Nicholls**
10 **DISK MAKER**, 5, b g Crooner—Sirette **Mrs Sylvia E. M. McGarvie**
11 **DOUBLE ENTENDRE**, 4, br f Dominion—Triumphant **Miss Tina Pile**
12 **DUNRAVEN ROYAL**, 7, b g Le Bavard (FR)—Vulstar **Mr S. B. Glazer**
13 **FLYING ZIAD (CAN)**, 7, ch g Ziad (USA)—Flying Souvenir (USA) **Mr Henry Flouty**
14 **GROVELANDS**, 8, ch g Balinger—Oca **Mr Peter A. Smith**
15 **HAWAIIAN ROMANCE**, 4, ch f Hawaii—Chateau Princess (USA) **Mr David Kirk**
16 **INHERIT**, 8, ch g Homing—Royal Descent (FR) **Mr Gerald Saunders**
17 **JUSTTHEWAYYOUARE (CAN)**, 7, ch g Ziad (USA)—Helen Dickerman **Mr M. J. Rogers**
18 **KEMALS SECRET**, 10, b g Kemal (FR)—Secret Warfare **Exol Office Systems Ltd**
19 **KRAYMARK**, 4, ch g Krayyan—Caroline's Mark **Mr Duncan Gray**
20 **KRUSAVITCH**, 4, ch f Sunley Builds—Dipsicato **Mr S. P. Hayklan**
21 **LIGHT OF LIFE**, 5, b g Wolverlife—Australite **Mr Eric G. Trout**
22 **LONG TALL SALLY**, 4, b f Adonijah—Double Shuffle **Mr S. B. Glazer**
23 **MISTER ED**, 7, ch g Monsieure Edouarde—Are You Poaching **Gilt-Edged Thoroughbred Racing Plc**
24 **MR GEE**, 5, b g Crooner—Miss Desla **Mr M. G. Ferrett**
25 **PALMION**, 8, b g Dominion—Blessed Palm **Mrs Iris E. Evans**
26 **PEARLS A RUNNER**, 5, b m Record Run—Wild Jewel **Miss Tina Pile**
27 **PEN BAL QUEEN**, 4, b f Record Run—Dazzling Hue **Miss Tina Pile**
28 **PRAIRIE OYSTER**, 7, ch g Northfields (USA)—Huahinee (FR) **Mr P. A. Sells**
29 **RAJANPOUR**, 5, ch h Riverman—Rajpoura **Mrs R. Smith**
30 **SALLYS WON**, 6, b g Free State—Arbatina **Communidata Ltd**
31 **SERIOZHA**, 7, b g Cut Above—Anna Karenina **Mrs L. Buckerfield**
32 **SHAMROCK STAR**, 4, ch g Horage—Alfarouse **Albury Racing Limited**
33 **SINGING SEAL**, 9, ch g Privy Seal—Blue Song **Ian Adair**
34 **STARGAZE**, 10, b g Busted—Star of Bagdad **Mr Peter A. Smith**

MR R. CURTIS—continued

35 **ST ATHANS LAD,** 5, b g Crooner—Greasby Girl **Geyer Estates Limited (St.Athans Hotel)**
36 **TAGLIO DE CHAMPFEU (FR),** 5, ch g Pamponi (FR)—Gazelle Blonde (FR) **Mr Darren King**
37 **THE YOMPER (FR),** 8, ch g Arctic Tern (USA)—Grundylee (FR) **Ian Adair**
38 **TRING PARK,** 4, b c Niniski—Habanna **Exol Office Systems Ltd**
39 **WARM WINTER,** 4, gr f Kalaglow—Fair Head **Gilt-Edged Thoroughbred Racing Plc**
40 **WILDWOOD,** 10, gr g Yankee Gold—Hop Step **Mr Peter A. Smith**

THREE-YEAR-OLDS

41 **CHEREN LADY,** br f Comedy Star (USA)—Lillylee Lady (USA) **Mrs L. Buckerfield**
42 **JUDGED LUCKY (FR),** br g Vayrann—Friluck (USA) **Albury Racing Limited**
43 **SPROUTING VENTURE,** ch f Crooner—Two Diamonds **Miss D. A. Mynett**

Other Owners: Steven Astaire, Mr D. Chatten, Mr J. Daniels, Mr S. R. Davies, R. M. Harris, Mr G. Lansbury, Mr John McIntyre, Mohammed Safadi, Mr Joe Sheehan, Robert N Silverstone, Mr Bill Simmons, Mr Ted Yorke.

Jockey (Flat): W Newnes (w.a.).

Jockeys (NH): Ray Goldstein (10-0), Derrick Morris (10-0).

Apprentice: Alex Lappin (7-3).

Conditional: Scott Mason (9-7).

Amateur: Andy Gudgeon (9-10).

Lady Rider: Miss Tina Pile (8-0).

164 MR T. A. K. CUTHBERT, Carlisle

Postal: **26 Eden Grange, Little Corby, Carlisle, Cumbria, CA4 8QW.**
Phone: **(0228) 60822**

1 **ARUM LILY,** 6, b m Bustino—Lys River (FR) **Mr Roderick A. MacLeod**
2 **CASUAL PASS,** 7, ch g Formidable (USA)—Pitapat **Mr J. A. Walker**
3 **COOL FOUNTAIN,** 6, b m Royal Fountain—Cool Date **Mr I. C. Copeland**
4 **GLENLAW,** 7, b m Pitpan—Glenreeba **Mr A. T. Peffers**
5 **LORD'S WAY,** 9, b m Lord Nelson (FR)—Craigie Way **Mr I. C. Copeland**
6 **MADAM CHEVALIER,** 9, b m Kinglet—Chanter Mark **Miss J. Campbell**
7 **MERCIA GOLD,** 7, ch g Roman Warrior—Maygold **Mr T. A. K. Cuthbert**
8 **MIGHTY SUPREMO (USA),** 9, b g Raja Baba (USA)—Glut's Kin (USA) **Mr John Mitchell**
9 **RECEPTIVE,** 9, b m Decoy Boy—Reigning Grace **Mr T. A. K. Cuthbert**
10 **SHE'S ALL THERE,** 5, ch m Hello Handsome—Waterbeck **Mr T. A. K. Cuthbert**
11 **SWANK GILBERT,** 4, b g Balliol—Song To Singo **Mrs Joyce Cuthbert**
12 **TEN A PENNY,** 10, ch m Whistlefield—Ten Knots **Mr Charles Kevans**
13 **VICTORY BOY,** 12, b g Lord Nelson (FR)—Three Oaks **Mr S. W. Millar**
14 **WARDSOFF,** 13, b g Dubassoff (USA)—Greensward II **Mr Roy Thorburn**

Jockey (NH): B Storey (9-10).

Conditional: Carol Cuthbert (9-7).

165 MR CHARLES CYZER, Horsham

Postal: **Elliotts, Maplehurst, Horsham, West Sussex, RH13 6QX.**
Phone: **(0403) 730255 FAX (0403) 730787**

1 **CARDS AND KISSES (USA),** 4, b f Wind And Wuthering (USA)—Heat Haze (USA)
2 **FOND KISS,** 5, b m Young Generation—Firente
3 **GLITZ,** 6, b g Posse (USA)—Rotisserie
4 **PAR AVION,** 5, b g Beldale Flutter (USA)—Pitroyal
5 **SPRINGS WELCOME,** 4, b f Blakeney—Tomfoolery

THREE-YEAR-OLDS

6 **AGE OF MIRACLES,** b c Simply Great (FR)—Single Gal
7 **AMERICAN DREAM,** ch f Dreams To Reality (USA)—Lardana
8 **ARMED FORCE,** b g Shernazar—Skittish (USA)
9 **ART FORM (USA),** b g Little Current (USA)—Christi Dawn (USA)
10 **BANKROLL,** b g Chief Singer—Very Nice (FR)
11 **BLOW A KISS,** b f Auction Ring (USA)—Follow Me Follow
12 **BOX OFFICE,** ch g Taufan (USA)—Vera Van Fleet
13 **COMMANDING OFFICER,** b c Be My Guest (USA)—Honeypot Lane
14 **GOOD GRACE,** b f Longleat (USA)—Shaky Puddin
15 **HYPNOTIST,** b g High Top—Tamilian
16 **LAND OF WONDER (USA),** b g Wind And Wuthering (USA)—Heat Haze (USA)
17 **MATTER OF LAW,** ch g Blakeney—Opera Star (FR)
18 **MODERN BRITISH,** b g Elegant Air—Song of Gold
19 **MOLLY SPLASH,** b f Dunbeath (USA)—Nelly Do Da
20 **PASSION AND MIRTH,** b f Known Fact (USA)—Bustling Nelly
21 **TOUCH OF DANGER,** b c Gorytus (USA)—All Beige
22 **TRIOMPHE MODEST,** b f Petorius—Tinktura
23 **UNDER OATH,** b g Blakeney—Shere Beauty

TWO-YEAR-OLDS

24 **BEY D'AO (FR),** b c 22/3 Baillamont (USA)—Ondoa (FR) (President (FR))
25 **BOLD RESOLUTION (IRE),** b c 14/4 Shardari—Valmarine (FR) (Val de Loir)
26 **CAVIAR QUEEN (IRE),** ch f 10/2 Kings Lake (USA)—Syrian Sea (USA) (Bold Ruler)
27 **CHILLS AND HILLS,** b c 13/5 Sharpo—Lady Oriana (Tudor Melody)
28 **DAZZLE THE CROWD (IRE),** b c 15/4 Simply Great (FR)—Katie Roche (Sallust)
29 B f 3/4 Wind And Wuthering—Diamond Oyster (Formidable (USA))
30 **HIGHLY INFLAMMABLE (USA),** b f 7/4 Wind And Wuthering—Heat Haze (USA) (Jungle Savage (USA))
31 **ISLAND WINGS,** b f 5/6 Siberian Express—City Sound (On Your Mark)
32 **LEGAL LEGACY,** b f 22/2 Norwick (USA)—Jambalaya (Amboise)
33 **MAJOR BOLD (IRE),** b c 24/3 Glenstal (USA)—Misty Hill (Hill Clown (USA))
34 **NASTY BOSS,** b c 3/5 Nicholas Bill—Dark Finale (Javelot)
35 **ONE MAGIC MOMENT (IRE),** b f 14/4 Thatching—Debutante (Silly Season)
36 **PANIC RISING (USA),** b c 6/2 Master Willie—Sticky Habit (Habitat)
37 **PRICELESS LOOT,** b f 21/4 Ardross—Pulcinella (Shantung)
38 **RISING TEMPO (IRE),** b c 13/3 Lomond (USA)—May Hill (Hill Clown (USA))
39 **SMILING CHIEF (IRE),** ch c 11/2 Montelimar (USA)—Victa (Northfields (USA))
40 **SPICE IS NICE,** ch f 8/6 Pharly (FR)—Single Gal (Mansingh (USA))
41 **SWEET BUBBLES (IRE),** ch f 5/3 Dominion—Regal Decoy (Troy)
42 **SWEET DECREE,** ch f 19/5 Known Fact (USA)—Skiddaw (USA) (Grey Dawn II)
43 **TACTICAL MISSION (IRE),** b c 17/2 Rainbow Quest (USA)—Our Village (Ballymore)
44 **TEA AND HONEY,** ch f 5/5 Night Shift (USA)—Tactless (Romulus)

Owners: Amity Finance Ltd, Mr C. A. Cyzer, Mrs E. A. Cyzer, Mrs Elayne Cyzer, Mr R. M. Cyzer, Mr Cyril Fenton, Intaplas Ltd, Mr L. Jarvis, Mrs M. Jarvis, Mr M. Morrison, Napier Industries Limited, Mrs Muriel Rosner.

Jockeys (Flat): M Fry (7-8), M Wigham.

Jockey (NH): M Bosley.

Apprentice: A Morris (7-13).

166 MR J. D. CZERPAK, Farnham

Postal: **Dockenfield Farm, Dockenfield, Farnham, Surrey.**
Phone: **(025) 125 3505 FAX (025) 125 3505**

1 **COUNTESS BLAKENEY,** 4, ch f Baron Blakeney—Waterside **Owner Not Registered**
2 **DICKENS AND BROWNE,** 5, b br g Vayrann—Ravela II **Orlaford Ltd**
3 **FLYING REFRAIN,** 5, b m Blue Refrain—Abercorn Flyer **Mrs L. May**
4 **MING HO GOLD,** 5, b m Homing—Pandoras Gold **Mrs M. T. Taylor**
5 **SOLEIL EXPRESS,** 4, b g Bay Express—Peters Pleasure **Mrs M. T. Taylor**

THREE-YEAR-OLDS

6 **KHAIRULLAH,** b c Adonijah—Naamullah **Mr B. N. Hamoud**
7 **NAAR CHAMALI,** ch f Salmon Leap (USA)—Reliant Nell **Mr David Hammett**
8 **ROCKY'S MATE,** b f Young Man (FR)—Gold Spangle **Mr B. Lee**
9 **SALMIYA,** b f Superlative—The Firebird **Mr B. N. Hamoud**
10 **SCRIBBLING,** b f Blushing Scribe (USA)—Captain Bonnie **Mr Brian Taylor**

TWO-YEAR-OLDS

11 Ch f 12/3 Creetown—Cody (USA) (Giacometti)
12 Gr br c 1/2 Electric—Elfinaria (Song) **Rajmad (Horse Racing) Ltd**
13 B f 30/3 Enchantment—Hunny Bunny (Streetfighter)
14 B c 1/5 Enchantment—Liana Louise (Silly Season) **Mr M. R. Javaid**
15 B c 23/3 Melyno—Maid of Erin (USA) (Irish River (FR)) **Mr B. N. Hamoud**
16 B c 12/5 Magic Mirror—Malise (Royal Palace) **Mr T. Robertson**
17 B f 12/3 Be My Guest (USA)—Mannevillette (USA) (Foolish Pleasure (USA)) **Mr B. N. Hamoud**
18 B c 26/4 Nordance (USA)—Ninotchka (Niniski (USA))
19 B f 24/4 Miramar Reef—Pandoras Gold (Wishing Star) **Mr John Douglas**
20 B f 25/5 Vaigly Great—Peters Pleasure (Jimsun)
21 B c 10/5 Creetown—Rugby Princess (El Gallo) **Mr K. Payne**
22 B f 11/5 Mazaad—Settled (Blue Cashmere)
23 Gr f 9/4 Sunley Builds—Sioux Princess (Habat)
24 Gr c 28/4 Tina's Pet—Spanish Chestnut (Philip of Spain) **Mrs L. May**
25 B c 11/5 Runnett—Tarte Tatin (FR) (Busted)
26 **TIGER BAY,** br c 15/4 Newski (USA)—Caswell Bay (Coronash) **Mr Dave Holly**
27 B c 17/3 Ilium—Valiant Dancer (Northfields (USA))
28 B c 15/3 Scottish Reel—Visitation (Tarqogan)
29 B f 23/4 Kafu—Walnut Tree (Run The Gantlet (USA))
30 B f 25/5 Monsanto (FR)—Welsh Fashion (Welsh Saint)
31 B f 4/5 Tumble Wind (USA)—Winter Harvest (Grundy) **Mrs L. May**

Other Owners: Mrs A. Al Homezi, Mr David Driver, La Grange Ltd, Mr R. Sturley, Mr James Underwood.

Jockey (Flat): N Howe (8-0).

Conditional: D Cooney (9-7).

167 MR J. N. DALTON, Shifnal

Postal: **Sutton House Farm, Shifnal, Shropshire, TF11 9NF.**
Phone: **NORTON 656 (095 271)**

1 **CRESTELLA,** 5, b m Cruise Missile—Stellata Donna **Mr J. N. Dalton**
2 **PERNOIC,** 10, b m Peter Wrekin—Pernel **Mr J. N. Dalton**
3 4, Ch f Cruise Missile—Stellata Donna **Mr J. N. Dalton**

MR J. N. DALTON—continued

THREE-YEAR-OLDS

4 Ch f Riberetto—Pteridium **Mr J. N. Dalton**

Jockey (NH): B De Haan (w.a.).

Amateur: Mr A N Dalton (11-0).

168 MR J. D. J. DAVIES, Ashford

Postal: **Bellinzona Stables, Eastbridge Road, Dymchurch, Romney Marsh, Kent, DN29 OPG.**
Phone: **(0303) 874089**

1 **BLUE MISSILE,** 4, br g Cruise Missile—Blue Basket **Mr P. Claringbold**
2 **BROKEN FLIGHT,** 13, b g Busted—Shortwood **Mr Lawrence Wells**
3 **FLORI WONDER,** 10, b m Floriana—Greek Wonder **Mrs Mary H. Davies**
4 **JAY-DEE-JAY,** 7, b m Mljet—Tagliatelle **Mrs V. E. Maunders**
5 **LANDMARK,** 7, b h Mill Reef—Christchurch **Mr M. I. Forbes**
6 **LORD ROLFE,** 4, ch g Rolfe (USA)—Stepout **Mr Lawrence Wells**
7 **MANTINIK,** 5, b g Sayyaf—Bonny Rand (USA) **Mr J. M. Quinn**
8 **MARLIN DANCER,** 5, b g Niniski (USA)—Mullet **Mr J. M. Quinn**
9 **WHOEVER,** 8, b g Flashback—Sealac **Mr Charles Faris**

Other Owners: Mr A. F. Ablett, Mr B. Agar, Mr D. Baxter, Mr Charles Blunt, Miss J. H. Jenner, Mr Andreas N. Katsaris, Mr Malcolm J. Williams.

Jockey (NH): S Woods (9-11).

Conditional: M Brown (10-0).

169 MR M. W. DAVIES, Abergavenny

Postal: **Home Farm, Llwyndu, Abergavenny, Gwent, Wales.**
Phone: **(0873) 2292**

1 **CHICAS DELIGHT,** 4, ch f Rustingo—La Chica **Mr M. W. Davies**
2 **DERISTONE,** 5, b h Rustingo—Deriside **Mr G. Davies**
3 **POLECROFT,** 7, b g Crofter (USA)—Grange Kova **Mrs D. M. Davies**
4 **RUSTY ROC,** 9, b g Rustingo—La Chica **Mr M. W. Davies**

Jockey (NH): W Knox.

170 MR P. S. DAVIES, Bromyard

Postal: **19 Hatton Park, Bromyard, Herefordshire, HR7 4EY.**
Phone: **(0885) 482567 OR (0885) 482516**

1 **FREDDIE SWALLOW,** 5, ch g Swing Easy (USA)—Rose Bridges **Mr D. L. Davies**
2 **HAZELEELS DELIGHT,** 10, b g Raga Navarro (ITY)—Aibrean **Mr D. L. Davies**
3 **LORD KAMBEE,** 8, b g Kambalda—Lady Bee **Mr P. S. Davies**
4 **SKYLANDER,** 11, b g African Sky—Lagosta (USA) **Mr P. S. Davies**

171 MR N. H. DAVIS, Bridgwater

Postal: **Lawson Farm, Burton, Stogursey, Bridgwater, Somerset.**
Phone: **(0278) 732722**

1 **GOLDSPIC,** 7, ch g Spanish Gold—Spic And Span **Mrs E. M. Davis**
2 **LAWSON PRINCESS,** 6, b br m Latest Model—Calamity **Mrs E. M. Davis**
3 **NEAT AND TIDY,** 5, b g Dubassoff (USA)—Spic And Span **Mrs E. M. Davis**
4 **PARDI'S POPPET,** 6, br m Pardigras—Used Notes **Miss L. A. Davis**
5 **PRIM AND PROPER,** 4, ch f Dubassoff (USA)—Spic And Span **Mrs E. M. Davis**
6 **UPSTANDING,** 8, b g Latest Model—Calamity **Miss L. A. Davis**

THREE-YEAR-OLDS

7 **NEAT AND TRIM,** ch f Whistlefield—Spic And Span **Mrs E. M. Davis**

172 MR P. W. DAVIS, Feckenham

Postal: **The Paddocks, Astwood Lane, Feckenham, Redditch, Worcestershire, B96 6HS.**
Phone: **ASTWOOD BANK (052789) 3174**

1 **BEDROCK,** 7, b g Town And Country—Restful **Mr Tim Underwood and Mr A. Bray**
2 **BORDER LOCH,** 6, b h Lochnager—Sea Chant **Mr Peter Davis**
3 **COME ON FLAN,** 7, b m Royalty—Enchanted Evening
4 **FRENCH HABITAT (NZ),** 8, br g Le Fripon (NZ)—Abode (NZ) **Mrs Judy Arthur**
5 **JOLIE GAZELLE,** 8, b g Panco—Spring Gazelle **Mr Alan Clarke**
6 **MONASTIC CALM,** 6, b g Majestic Maharaj—Cantabrae **Mr Peter Davis**
7 **NUMERATE,** 11, b g Paddy's Stream—Flying Music **Mr Malcolm F. Giles**
8 **OLYMPUS REEF,** 5, b g Main Reef—Elizabethan **Mr Peter Davis**
9 **PADDY'S OWEN,** 8, b m Paddy's Stream—Ellerslie Owen **Mr Peter Davis**
10 **PRINCESS HECATE,** 15, b m Autre Prince—April Witch
11 **QUIET STAR (NZ),** 9, br g Big Hush (NZ)—Astronomy **Mr John Brook**
12 **RAPIER SWAN (NZ),** 6, b g Rapier II—My Swan (NZ) **Mr Peter Davis**
13 **STIRABOUT,** 10, b g Oats—Magic Light **Mr J. G. Boyce**
14 **TREMAR LAD,** 8, ch g Monsanto (FR)—Greyburn **Mr Peter Davis**
15 **WELSH MANSION,** 4, b g Longleat (USA)—La Gallia **Mr Peter Davis**

TWO-YEAR-OLDS

16 B c Country Retreat—Come On Flan (Royalty)

Other Owners: A. Ball, Mr J. G. Boyce, Mrs Wendy Davis, Richard Griffiths, K. Hansen, John Marsden, Roy Northall.

Jockeys (NH): Tarnya Davis (9-0), R Dunwoody (w.a.).

Conditional: Rikki Davis (10-0).

173 MR A. W. DENSON, Epsom

Postal: **Chalet Racing Stables, 89 Burgh Heath Road, Epsom, Surrey.**
Phone: **EPSOM (0372) 729398**

1 **ALLIED FORCE,** 8, b g High Line—Summer Madness **Mr A. W. Denson**
2 **AMWAJ,** 6, gr h Tumble Wind (USA)—Centennial Rose **Mr K. A. Platten**
3 **BAHRAIN BRIDGE,** 5, b g Formidable (USA)—Hide Out **Mr V. J. Walsh**
4 **CELTIC CHIMES,** 6, ch m Celtic Cone—Dyna Bell **Mr H. M. J. Davis**
5 **GROWING POWER,** 6, b g Red Sunset—Margaree **Mr R. L. Moore**

MR A. W. DENSON—continued

6 **INCREDIBLE LADY**, 5, gr m Rusticaro (FR)—Lady d'Arbanville (FR) **Mr A. W. Denson**
7 **JOLLY SURPRISE**, 5, b g Jolly Me—Madame Decoy **Mr A. W. Denson**
8 **SAN FRANCISCO JOE (USA)**, 6, b br g Plum Bold (USA)—Destacion (USA) **Mr J. R. Irving**
9 **SOURCE OF MAGIC**, 8, br g Golden Love—Ballinlonig Lass **Mr P. J. Bryan**
10 **SPRING PLAY**, 6, ch g Hard Fought—Spring Snow **Mr P. J. Bryan**

THREE-YEAR-OLDS

11 **VILLAGE DANCER**, b g Creetown—Autumn Ballet **Mr K. J. Rosser**
12 **YELLOW METAL**, b g Reesh—Madame Decoy **Mr A. W. Denson**

Jockey (Flat): W Newnes (w.a.).

Jockeys (NH): R Goldstein (w.a.), L Harvey (w.a.), M Perret (w.a.).

Conditional: S F Hazell (9-7).

Lady Rider: Miss K Marks.

174 MR R. DICKIN, Newent

Postal: **Fairfield Stables, Welsh House Lane, Newent, Gloucestershire, GL18 1LR.**
Phone: **053 185 644**

1 **BUCKSKIN'S BEST**, 8, b g Buckskin (FR)—Bond's Best **Mr Derek C. Holder**
2 **COTSWOLD CASTLE**, 4, ch g Carlingford Castle—Last Trip **Mr Graham Brown**
3 **DR ROCKET**, 5, b g Ragapan—Lady Hansel **Mr G. C. Downey**
4 **FAIRFIELD'S BREEZE**, 5, b m Buckskin (FR)—Mistic Breeze **Mr A. S. Hawes**
5 **FAIRFIELDS CONE**, 7, ch m Celtic Cone—Bond's Best **Mrs Cheryl Holder**
6 **FAIR MINSTREL**, 6, ch m Longleat (USA)—Western Vale **Mr Graham Brown**
7 **GARDA'S GOLD**, 7, b g Garda's Revenge (USA)—Mielee **Mr T. Little**
8 **IMPETULENCE**, 4, ch f Kind of Hush—Longgoe **Mr T. H. Couchman**
9 **JANE CRAIG**, 7, b m Rapid Pass—Pride of Towy **Mrs Jo Duckett**
10 **K C'S DANCER**, 5, ch g Buckskin (FR)—Lorna Lass **Mr Pete Holder**
11 **LADY BE BRAVE**, 7, b m Laurence O—Miss Argument **Mr J. F. Roberts**
12 **MARIE SWIFT**, 5, b m Main Reef—Sarus **Mr Daniel**
13 **MASTER MERLIN**, 5, b g Straight Knight—Salmon Spirit **Miss A. Stone and Mr M. Stone**
14 **MIDNIGHT RUN**, 11, ch g Deep Run—Night Spot **Alan P. Brewer (Plmbg & Htg) Ltd**
15 **MISS CHEQUERS ISLE**, 4, ch f Cruise Missile—Chequers Girl **Mr P. Potts**
16 **MISS FERN**, 5, b m Cruise Missile—Fernshaw **Phipps, Bailey, Duane & Company**
17 **MISTER BOBBINS**, 7, b h Thatching—Bobbins (FR) **Mr David C. Hudd**
18 **MISTER TICKLE**, 5, b g Deep Run—Desert Maid **Mr C. R. McDonagh**
19 **MONASIRA**, 5, ch m Lord Ha Ha—Westburn VII **Mr Norman Angell**
20 **MOTTRAM'S GOLD**, 5, ch g Good Times (ITY)—Speed The Plough **Mr Graham Brown**
21 **MOUNTAIN MAN**, 14, b g Wolver Hollow—Beck **Mr C. R. McDonagh**
22 **MOUNT OLIVER**, 12, b g No Argument—Bayview Rambler **Mr D. A. Smith**
23 **SEVERN INVADER**, 5, b g Al Sirat—Wunder Madchen **Severn Office Supplies**
24 **SHY HIKER**, 7, ch m Netherkelly—High Seeker **Mr M. J. Lilley**
25 **TEACHER'S DRAM**, 4, b f Strong Gale—Top Marks **Wm Teacher & Sons Ltd**
26 **THE HUCKLEBUCK**, 5, ch g Buckskin (FR)—Iron Star **Mrs C. M. Dickin**
27 **TUNS HILL**, 8, ch g True Song—Aggreccles **Mr Brian Eacott**
28 **WAYWARD LUKE**, 6, b g Bustiki—Lukes Lass **Mr J. D. Sanders**
29 **WINABUCK**, 7, ch g Buckskin (FR)—Mistic Breeze **Mr W. R. Bullivant**

THREE-YEAR-OLDS

30 **CORINTHIAN GIRL**, b f Welsh Captain—Combe Grove Lady **Mrs P. P. Dunn**
31 **COTSWOLD COMEDY**, b f Flying Tyke—Comedy Spring **Mr N. G. Tucker Brown**
32 **WOOD HOLLOW**, b f Chukaroo—Belle Year **Mrs P. P. Dunn**

MR R. DICKIN—continued

Other Owners: Mr D. L. Abbott, Mr R. J. Adams, Mr Ray Baverstock, Mr D. R. Bridge, Mr Ray Cawthorn, Mr R. H. Cook, Mr T. A. Couchman, Mr Roger F. Downes, Mr Malcolm Eustace, Mr K. G. Hughes, Mr Ian D. Newman, Mrs F. M. Terry, Mr J. Turner, Mr P. D. Whitehouse.

Jockeys (Flat): S Keightley, John Williams (8-0, w.a.).

Jockeys (NH): Richard Dunwoody (10-2, w.a.), S Earle (w.a.).

Apprentice: D Meredith (8-0).

Conditional: Martin P Jones (9-0), D Meredith (8-0).

Amateur: Dr P L J Pritchard (10-0, w.a.).

175 MR M. DICKINSON, Melton Mowbray

Postal: **Cornsafe Ltd, Jericho Lodge Farm, Stapleford Road, Leesthorpe, Melton Mowbray, Leics, LE14 2XG.**

Phone: **WHISSENDINE (066 479) 752**

1 **EDOZIEN,** 11, ch g Sun Prince—Lady Mouse **Mrs M. Lethbridge**
2 **HANDSOME FIND,** 6, ch g Scallywag—College Brief **Mr C. F. Moore**
3 **JAMES MY BOY,** 10, ch g Jimmy Reppin—College Brief **Mrs R. A. Dickinson**
4 **MOONLIGHT SHIFT,** 4, ch g Night Shift (USA)—Rana **Mrs F. L. Dickinson**
5 **SPRINGFIELD RIFLE,** 7, b g Sunyboy—Gracemount **Mrs M. Lethbridge**
6 **STANITAS,** 9, b g Stanford—The Wig **Mrs R. A. Dickinson**
7 **TITUS FILLE,** 4, b f Lucky Wednesday—Maiden d'Or **Wendlebury Racing Club**
8 **TITUS GOLD,** 5, b g Sonnen Gold—Chemin de Guerre **Mr A. Dickinson**
9 **TITUS ROCK,** 4, b g Bay Express—La Balconne **Mr A. Dickinson**

TWO-YEAR-OLDS

10 B c 4/5 Green Ruby (USA)—Step Softly **Mr A. Dickinson**

Other Owners: Mr M. Dickinson.

Jockeys (NH): P Dever, G McCourt (w.a.).

Conditional: Adele Jackson (9-7).

176 MR J. E. DIXON, Carlisle

Postal: **Moor End, Thursby, Carlisle, Cumbria, CA5 6QP.**

Phone: **DALSTON (0228) 710318**

1 **ANOTHER FOUNTAIN,** 4, b g Royal Fountain—Another Joyful **Mrs E. M. Dixon**
2 **BALLYLANE,** 6, ch g Touch Paper—Angelic Princess **Mrs S. F. Dixon**
3 **TWISTED HOLLY,** 5, b m Coded Scrap—Holly Lodge **Mrs E. M. Dixon**
4 **WILLY MAC,** 9, b g Ancient Monro—Minny Mouse **Mrs E. M. Dixon**

177 MR R. W. DODS, Darlington

Postal: **Denton Hall, Piercebridge, Darlington, Co. Durham.**
Phone: **(0325) 374270**

1 **BLUE GRIT,** 4, b g Thatching—Northern Wisdom **Mr C. M. Wilson**
2 **BRIERY FILLE,** 5, b m Sayyaf—Zeddera (FR) **C. D. Cole**
3 **FLASHY DANCER,** 5, ch g Young Man (FR)—Gem-May **Mr T. M. Andrews**
4 **GOLDEN IMAGE,** 4, ch f Bustino—Kingston Rose **Mr R. W. Dods**
5 **GOMEZ,** 6, b br g Formidable (USA)—Alpine Niece **Mr J. A. Moore**
6 **HUTNER,** 5, b g Henbit (USA)—Fountain **Mr R. W. Dods and Mr R. Howe**
7 **LIHAR,** 4, ch g Lomond (USA)—Mpani **Mr M. C. J. Sunley**
8 **LYNDEN LASS,** 4, ch f Say Primula—Fishermans Lass **Mr R. W. Dods**
9 **OXALIS,** 6, b m Connaught—Phlox **Mr C. D. Cole**
10 **ROSE'S PRIDE,** 4, b f Ballacashtal (CAN)—Tropingay **Mr R. W. Dods**
11 **ROYAL INVADER,** 6, b g Silly Prices—Fishermans Lass **Mr R. W. Dods**
12 **YOUNG PAGEANT,** 6, ch g Welsh Pageant—Young Mementa **Mr R. W. Dods**

THREE-YEAR-OLDS

13 B f Idiot's Delight—Fishermans Lass **Mr R. W. Dods**

Other Owners: Mr I. Brown, Mr Alan Craggs, Mr Peter Earl, Mr Ned Jones, Mr P. Walsh, Mr T. Wood.

Conditional: S Woods (9-10).

178 MR G. C. DOIDGE, Ivybridge

Postal: **Little Orcheton Farm, Modbury, Ivybridge, Devon, PL21 0TF.**
Phone: **(0548) 830515**

1 **BUSREV,** 6, b g Revlow—Holiday Flair **Mr Nic Szeremeta**
2 **EN GOUNASI THEON,** 9, ch g New Member—Vidi's First **Mrs M. J. Snow**
3 **GOLDEN RAPIER,** 9, ch g Rapier II—Dashing Nymph **Westward Developments Ltd**
4 **GREAT WISHFORD,** 10, br m Laggards Lane—Last Bequest **Mr G. C. Doidge**
5 **HANDBAWN,** 6, ch g Nearly A Hand—Royal Dialogue **Mr G. C. Doidge**
6 **IOWA,** 11, br g So Blessed—Montana **Mr G. C. Doidge**
7 **SNOOZA DOWN,** 7, bl m Fine Blue—The Shrub **Mr G. C. Doidge**

TWO-YEAR-OLDS

8 **MAKER,** ch g 5/6 Northern Game—Bassinet (Sagaro) **Mrs M. E. Doidge**

Jockeys (NH): H Davies, P Holley (9-7).

179 MISS G. DOLLAR, East Hendred

Postal: **Framptons, Newbury Road, East Hendred, Wantage, OX12 8LG.**
Phone: **(0235) 834537**

1 **CASHMOOR,** 12, b g Ashmore (FR)—Go Friendly **Miss G. Dollar**
2 **COMPASITA,** 4, b f Old Jocus—Lucky Tango **Miss G. Dollar**
3 **FLUTTER MONEY,** 6, b g Beldale Flutter (USA)—Berthe Manet **Miss G. Dollar**
4 **MARQUEE CAFE,** 6, ch g Sallust—Royal Sensation **Miss G. Dollar**
5 **POWER CRAZY,** 5, b g Electric—Divetta **Miss G. Dollar**
6 **RICHARDS PET,** 4, ch g Noalto—Whipalash **Miss G. Dollar**
7 **STRIKE A CHORD,** 5, b m Song—Marguerite Gerard **Miss G. Dollar**

Other Owners: Mr L. S. Dollar, Mrs S. J. Dollar.

180 MR T. W. DONNELLY, Burton-on-Trent

Postal: **Calke Abbey Racing Stables, Heath Lane, Hartshorne, Burton-on-Trent, DE11 7AY.**
Phone: **(0283) 226046 FAX (0283) 550193**

1 **BELL BRIDGE GIRL,** 5, b m Coded Scrap—Three Oaks **Mrs J. Goodfellow**
2 **BETHEL ORCHARD,** 5, b m Tyrnavos—Skysted **Mrs Barbara Mersh**
3 **BREAK THE RULER,** 7, b g Busted—Chellita **Mr H. Harpur-Crewe**
4 **BROKERS CHOICE,** 8, ch g Malinowski (USA)—Mehudenna **Mr Pat McCourt**
5 **DORWOOD LADY,** 8, b m Orchestra—Lost Angel **Mr H. Harpur-Crewe**
6 **FULL OF PORT,** 4, ch f Krayyan—Galva **Mr H. Harpur-Crewe**
7 **INVERINATE,** 5, b g Lomond (USA)—Major Concession **Mr C. J. Ewart**
8 **JIMMY BRIG,** 8, b g New Brig—Woodburn Kizzie **Mr C. J. Ewart**
9 **KATY QUICK,** 9, b m Saucy Kit—Tesco Maid **Mr H. Harpur-Crewe**
10 **MOYMET,** 4, b c Jester—Majesta **Mr F. K. Baxter**
11 **MY SKIWAY,** 7, b g Newski (USA)—Good Way **Mr H. Harpur-Crewe**
12 **NONSTOP,** 11, ch g Nonoalco (USA)—Fast Motion **Mr H. Harpur-Crewe**
13 **ROMERHOF,** 9, b g Orchestra—Ghana's Daughter **Calke Abbey Racing Plc**
14 **ROWAN VILLE,** 5, b m Sexton Blake—Hello Stranger **Ibra Racing Co.**
15 **STRANGELY QUIET,** 8, b g Paddy's Stream—Cora Rose **Mr H. Harpur-Crewe**
16 **TINA'S BRIG,** 9, b m Majestic Streak—Cliburn New Cut **Mr K. Milligan**
17 **WILLOW HOLDING,** 5, b g Some Hand—Catherines April

Other Owners: Mrs K. Batey, Mr John Gilligan, Mrs L. Monkhouse.

Conditional: John Burke (10-0).

Amateur: Mark Ashton (10-7).

181 MR JAMES DOOLER, Goole

Postal: **Lowgate Stud Farm, Balne, Goole, N. Humberside.**
Phone: **(0405) 861903**

1 **CROGHAN STAR,** 9, br m Furry Glen—Star Treasure **Mrs E. M. Adair**
2 **DREAM ACADEMY,** 7, b m Town And Country—Figurehead **Mr Edward Jones**
3 **EDWARD'S CORNER,** 12, b br m Sit In The Corner (USA)—Guid Tassie **Mrs Sandra C. Dooler**
4 **FAST APPROACH,** 4, b f Daring March—Honest Opinion **Mr D. Leech**
5 **GINGEMBRE,** 4, ch f Mr Fluorocarbon—Doyles Folly **Mr D. Leech**
6 **I'M STILL STANDING,** 5, b g Blue Refrain—Kikalong **Mrs Noelene Hebblethwaite**
7 **JANIE-O,** 7, ch m Hittite Glory—Tweezer **Mr D. Leech**
8 4, Gr f Warpath—Jasmin **Mr D. Leech**
9 **MELODY'S HONOUR,** 6, b br m Unknown Melody—Honour Girl **Miss C. Oates**
10 **MILL DE LEASE,** 5, b g Milford—Melting Snows **Mr Stuart Leadbetter**
11 **MOTHERS DAY MAGIC,** 4, ch f Kabour—Gay Walk **Mr James Dooler**
12 **REEF PATRICK,** 5, b g Main Reef—Dooneena **Mr Adrian Salt**
13 **SANDRA'S SECRET,** 13, b m Most Secret—Grovenka (FR) **Mrs Sandra C. Dooler**
14 **SEVERN SOLITAIRE,** 11, b g Spitsbergen—Cleo Baby **Mr Adrian Salt**
15 **SKY WATCHER,** 4, b g Skyliner—Holernzaye **Mr James Dooler**

THREE-YEAR-OLDS

16 **FINALLY,** ch f Final Straw—Boswellia **Mr G. A. Russell**

MR JAMES DOOLER—continued

TWO-YEAR-OLDS

17 **CAMERON PRIDE,** b c 17/4 Kabour—Sandra's Sovereign (Workboy) **Mrs Sandra C. Dooler**
18 **HAYSAR,** ch c 15/2 Kabour—Sandra's Secret (Most Secret) **Mrs N. Hebblethwaite and Mr J. Dooler**
19 **LUKE'S BRAVE BOY,** ch c 18/5 Prince Ragusa—Golden Baby (Sharpen Up) **Mr D. Leech**
20 Ch f 2/3 Prince Ragusa—No Bello (Porto Bello) **Mr D. Leech**

Jockey (Flat): N Connorton (8-0).

Jockey (NH): W Worthington (10-0).

Amateur: Mr P McMahon (10-0).

182 MR S. L. DOW, Epsom

Postal: **Wendover Stables, Burgh Heath Road, Epsom, Surrey, KT17 4LX.**
Phone: **EPSOM (0372) 721490**

1 **ALBERTS WAY OUT,** 4, ch g Camden Town—Grunhilde **Mr Anthony A. Etheridge**
2 **BLUE ENSIGN,** 5, b g Beldale Flutter (USA)—Blue Rag **Mrs C. Nutting**
3 **CHILDREN'S JOIE,** 4, b g Auction Ring (USA)—Port La Joie **Mr Philip Langton**
4 **CIVILISED,** 5, b h Habitat—Dingle Bay **Mr S. A. Walker**
5 **COMEDY SAIL,** 6, b h Comedy Star (USA)—Set Sail **Under Orders Racing Plc**
6 **COUNT FREDERICK,** 10, b g Rheingold—Miss Pinkie **Mr Ralph Cross**
7 **CREVE COEUR,** 5, b g Aragon—Friths Folly **Mr Malcolm J. Moss**
8 **DARK HONEY,** 5, b g Marechal (FR)—Caillou **Mr Roger Sayer**
9 **DORVER (USA),** 6, b br g Irish River (FR)—Tudor Gleam (USA) **Under Orders Racing Plc**
10 **FORGET THE BLUES,** 5, b g Blue Refrain—Regency Wood **Mr Anthony A. Etheridge**
11 **FREE TWIST,** 7, b m Free Boy—No More Twist **Mr William Fisher**
12 **GOLDEN SONATA,** 5, ch g Star Appeal—Song of Gold **Mrs J. Harmsworth**
13 **GOLDEN VINTAGE,** 4, ch c Glint of Gold—Boissiere **Mr Geoffrey C. Greenwood**
14 **GUIDOBALDO,** 4, b c Sir Ivor—Hankow Willow **Mrs M. Charalambous**
15 **HIGHLAND BOUNTY,** 6, b g High Line—Segos **Mr Anthony A. Etheridge**
16 **KORYPHEOS,** 11, b g He Loves Me—Silly Song **Mr C. Papaioannou**
17 **LEGAL TINA,** 5, ch m Ballacashtal (CAN)—Pitapat **Mr S. A. Walker**
18 **LOCH BLUE,** 8, b g Lochnager—Miss Sinope **Mr R. A. S. Castle**
19 **MACINTYRE,** 5, b g Morston (FR)—Walk By **Under Orders Racing Plc**
20 **MUIRFIELD VILLAGE,** 4, b c Lomond (USA)—Ukelele (USA) **Mr Roger Sayer**
21 **MURMURING,** 4, b f Kind of Hush—Beryl's Jewel **Mr J. A. Redmond**
22 **NAHAR,** 5, b br h Known Fact (USA)—Muznah **Mr Ralph Cross**
23 **NEARLY RED,** 4, b f Pitskelly—Amber Breeze **Mr J. A. Redmond**
24 **NIGHTBOURNE,** 4, ch g Night Shift (USA)—Catulle **Under Orders Racing Plc**
25 **PELLS CLOSE,** 7, gr g He Loves Me—Seriema **Mrs H. Goalen**
26 **PRECOCIOUSLY,** 4, ch f Precocious—Grankie (USA) **Mrs G. Goodman**
27 **ROUGH JEWEL,** 7, b g Candy Cane—Stolen Diamond **Mr Ray Hawthorn**
28 **SAILORS LUCK,** 5, b g Idiot's Delight—Sarasail **Mr Geoffrey C. Greenwood**
29 **SAULIRE,** 5, b g High Top—Strathoykel **Mr Roger Sayer**
30 **SHORE LIGHT,** 6, b g Sparkler—Sabotage **Mr K. Overington**
31 **STARRLYN,** 4, gr ro f Star Appeal—Petingalyn **Visual Identity Ltd-Design Studio**
32 **TWO TOTAL,** 4, b g Noalcoholic (FR)—Double Shuffle **Mr S. Dow**
33 **WATER SPRITE,** 6, ch m Pry—Sun Spray **Mr Ray Hawthorn**

THREE-YEAR-OLDS

34 **ACROSS THE BAY,** ch c Krayyan—Siofra Beag **Mr J. A. Redmond**
35 **BIRDIE CHANCE,** b f Dominion—Lucky Life **Mr Roger Sayer**
36 **BROOK DANCE,** b g Mashhor Dancer (USA)—Bracey Brook **Mr S. A. Walker**
37 **CLOSED SHOP,** b f Auction Ring (USA)—Silent Sun **Mrs P. K. White**

MR S. L. DOW—continued

38 **CRICKET FAN,** br g Gorytus (USA)—Nollet **Mr J. R. Redmond and Mrs J. R. Redmond**
39 **DIMPLE STAR,** b g The Brianstan—Hanovia Gold **Mr A. Wix**
40 **FIGHTING BREEZE,** b f Hard Fought—Be Gustful **Mr S. Dow**
41 **HOUSEWARMING,** ch c Habitat—Be Sweet **A. Speyer**
42 **MISS TENAVILLE,** b f Kala Shikari—La Bambola **P. Chakko**
43 **NORTHERN VILLAGE,** ch g Norwick (USA)—Merokette **Mr R. Dove**
44 **PETIVARA,** b f Petong—Avahra **Mrs J. Harmsworth**
45 **PINE RIDGE LADY,** gr f Castle Keep—Red Lady **Mr J. S. Culiffe**
46 **SHARAGIL,** b g Muscatite—Cameo Dancer **Mr Ray Hawthorn**
47 **TORGHIA,** b f Taufan (USA)—Brave Louise **Mr D. R. L. Jones and Mrs D. R. L. Jones**

TWO-YEAR-OLDS

48 **BIJOU RESIDENCE,** ch f 24/1 Bustino—Little Madam **Beaufort Bloodstock Ltd**
49 **BLAZONET (IRE),** b c 10/5 Heraldiste (USA)—Jillette **Mrs S. R. Crowe**
50 **BYE BYE BABY (FR),** b f 25/2 Baby Turk—Busteldo (FR) **Sagittarius Bloodstock Agency**
51 **EBONY ENTERTAINER (IRE),** br c 9/4 Kafu—Naval Artiste **Mrs A. Merritt**
52 B f 12/5 Alleging (USA)—Flight Feathers (USA) **Mr C. Sparrowhawk**
53 **ITSAGAME,** br c 22/3 Mummy's Game—Immodest Miss **P. Ang**
54 **MING COURT,** br f 12/2 Daring March—Slick Chick **P. Chakko**
55 **WINDY HEIGHTS,** b f 19/5 Wolver Heights—Cadenza **Mrs B. White**

Other Owners: Mr A. J. Baker, H. Beaufort, C. Clarke, Mr P. Coletti, Mr Paul Deakin, G. Dunn, Mr E. G. King, Mrs A. Naylor, Mr R. Nicol, D. Redman, Mr H. R. Siegle, Mr S. J. Webster.

Jockey (NH): R Guest (10-0).

Apprentice: C Campbell (7-4).

Conditional: A Dicken (9-7), A J Knight (9-10).

183 MR J. DREAPER, Kilsallaghan

Postal: **Greenogue, Kilsallaghan, Dublin, Ireland.**
Phone: **DUBLIN (0001) 350187**

1 **BALDA BOY,** 6, b g Kambalda—Lady Coleman **J. Dreaper**
2 **BOLD FLYER,** 7, b g Peacock—Bold And True **S. N. N. Collen**
3 **BOSPHORUS,** 9, b g Deep Run—Bargara **Brig. A. D. R. Wingfield**
4 **CARVILL'S HILL,** 8, b g Roselier—Suir Valley **Mrs J. McMorrow**
5 **CLONOGUE,** 10, b g Pauper—Clonrochenell **Mrs M. W. Griffin**
6 **EBONY STAR,** 7, br g Irish Star—Rainy Season **Mr P. J. Conway**
7 **FOULKSRATH CASTLE,** 6, b g Niels—Castle Demon **Eromnova Ltd.**
8 **KING OF ASH,** 5, b g Kings Ride—Baronston **Mrs S. Hussey**
9 **LONGUEVILLE,** 5, br g Be My Native—Atanya **Mr S. W. Collen**
10 **MOSES ROD,** 7, br g Le Moss—Magic Quiz **Sir John Thomson**
11 **OAKLAND BUCK,** 6, ch g Buckskin—Slavesville **J. J. Brennan**
12 **RIVER TARQUIN,** 6, br g Over The River (FR)—Tarqogan's Rose **Robinstown Racing Syndicate**
13 **SOUND JUDGEMENT,** 11, b g Deep Run—Legal Argument **Sir John Thomson**
14 **STAR CAST,** 10, br g Lucifer—Glamorous Night **Sir John Thomson**
15 **STUNNING STUFF,** 5, br g Boreen—Mayfield Grove **Mr J. McNeill**
16 **TOP OF THE PACK,** 6, b g Furry Glen—Strip Poker **Mrs Ann Smurfit**

Other Owners: Mrs E. Hussey, Countess Of Mount Charles, Lady Thomson.

Jockey (NH): K Morgan (10-7).

Amateurs: Mr M McNulty (9-5), Mr P Stafford (9-10).

184 MR P. DUFOSEE, Warminster

Postal: **Manor Farm, Monkton Deverill, Warminster, Wiltshire, BA12 7EU.**
Phone: **(09853) 250**

1 **MEMBERSON,** 12, ch g New Member—Miss Stalbridge **Mr P. Dufosee**
2 **NEARBRIDGE,** 10, b g Nearly A Hand—Miss Stalbridge **Mr P. Dufosee**
3 **SAMBRIDGE,** 8, ch g New Member—Miss Stalbridge **Mr P. Dufosee**

185 MR J. L. DUNLOP, Arundel

Postal: **Castle Stables, Arundel, W. Sussex, BN18 9AB.**
Phone: **ARUNDEL (0903) 882194 TELEX-87475 RACDEL FAX (0903) 884173**

1 **AFWAJ (USA),** 4, ch c Caro—Just A Kick (USA) **Mr Hamdan Al-Maktoum**
2 **ALQUOZ (USA),** 5, br h Caerleon (USA)—I Understand (USA) **Mr Hamdan Al-Maktoum**
3 **AMADORA,** 4, b f Beldale Flutter (USA)—Zerbinetta **Lady Cohen**
4 **CASTLE SECRET,** 4, b c Castle Keep—Baffle **Lavinia Duchess of Norfolk**
5 **DUMFRIES,** 10, b g Scottish Rifle—Dashing Diana **Mr J. L. Dunlop**
6 **DUST DEVIL,** 5, b h Horage—Witch of Endor **Mr Aubrey Ison**
7 **ECCOLINA,** 4, ch f Formidable (USA)—Chili Girl **Mrs H. J. Heinz**
8 **ECRAN,** 4, b f Kings Lake (USA)—High Finale **Sir Robin McAlpine**
9 **ELZAEEM (USA),** 4, b c Secreto—Billy Sue's Rib **Mr Hamdan Al-Maktoum**
10 **EXCELSIS,** 4, b c Shirley Heights—Sacred Ibis **Mr Peter S. Winfield**
11 **HIGHLAND CHIEFTAIN,** 7, b h Kampala—La Primavera **Mr D. R. Hunnisett**
12 **HIT THE HIGH SPOTS,** 4, b f High Top—Criminelle **Lavinia Duchess of Norfolk**
13 **MANHUNT,** 4, b f Posse (USA)—Macarte (FR) **Mr J. L. Dunlop**
14 **MURANGO,** 4, b c Shirley Heights—Eldoret **Lavinia Duchess of Norfolk**
15 **PRINCE IBRAHIM,** 4, b c Be My Guest (USA)—Fanny's Cove **Mr D. R. Hunnisett**
16 **SAPPHO COMET,** 4, b c Habitat—Sunbittern **Sir Thomas Pilkington**
17 **SILK PETAL,** 4, b f Petorius—Salabella **Mr Nicholas Jones**
18 **TAJIKA,** 4, gr f Rusticaro (FR)—Taj Princess **Mr M. J. Silver**
19 **TARTIQUE TWIST (USA),** 4, b f Arctic Tern (USA)—
Professional Dance (USA) **Witham Land and Leisure Services Ltd**
20 **THIRTY FIRST,** 5, gr g Castle Keep—January (FR) **Mr J. L. Dunlop**
21 **TOP-BOOT,** 4, b c High Top—Sauceboat **Mr S. P. Hornung**
22 **TRIPLICATE,** 4, b c Mill Reef (USA)—Triple First **Mr J. L. Dunlop**
23 **TRUST TROY,** 4, br c Gorytus (USA)—Gay Fantasy **Windflower Overseas Holdings Inc**
24 **VALVILLE (FR),** 4, gr c Top Ville—Valse Exquise (FR) **Mr Hamdan Al-Maktoum**

THREE-YEAR-OLDS

25 **AL BATAL (USA),** ch c Blushing Groom (FR)—Salpinx (USA) **Mr Hamdan Al-Maktoum**
26 **ALHAJRAS (USA),** b c Northern Dancer—Call Me Goddess **Mr Hamdan Al-Maktoum**
27 **ANNA PETROVNA (FR),** b f Wassl—Anna Paola (GER) **Sheikh Mohammed**
28 **AZZAAM (USA),** ro c Chief's Crown (USA)—Princess Oola (USA) **Mr Hamdan Al-Maktoum**
29 **BALIGH,** b c Sadler's Wells (USA)—Santa's Sister (USA) **Mr Hamdan Al-Maktoum**
30 **BEAUCHAMP EVE,** ch f Jalmood (USA)—Buss **Mr E. Penser**
31 **BEAUCHAMP EXPRESS,** b c Castle Keep—Jubilee **Mr E. Penser**
32 **BIG NEPHEW,** ch c Adonijah—Little Niece **Mr J. A. Haverhals**
33 **BULLACE,** ch c Bustino—Brush **Mr Ian Pilkington**
34 **CASTEL VISCADO,** b g Castle Keep—Myrtle Grove **Mr J. L. Dunlop**
35 **CHEERING,** b f Chief Singer—Midaan **Miss J. Bradford**
36 **CHILIBOY,** gr c Precocious—Chili Girl **Mrs H. J. Heinz**
37 **CHIRRUP (FR),** b f Chief Singer—Bempton **Lord Halifax**
38 **DONNA VENEZIANA,** b f Ela-Mana-Mou—Camogie **Mr Peter S. Winfield**
39 **HARDIHEROINE,** b f Sandhurst Prince—Hardirondo **Mrs A. V. Ferguson**
40 **HIGHLY SECURE,** b c Shirley Heights—Caring **Lord Swaythling**
41 **HIGH SPIRITED,** b f Shirley Heights—Sunbittern **Mrs E. M. Burke**
42 **KID LEWIS,** b c Thatching—Mirkan Honey **Mrs A. V. Ferguson**
43 **KING HIGH,** b c Shirley Heights—Regal Twin (USA) **Lord Swaythling**

MR J. L. DUNLOP—continued

44 **LIFFEY LACE (USA),** b f Sagace (FR)—Liffey (FR) **Sheikh Mohammed**
45 **LUCKY GUEST,** b c Be My Guest (USA)—Gay Fantasy **Windflower Overseas Holdings Inc**
46 **LUCKY MOON,** b c Touching Wood (USA)—Castle Moon **Lavinia Duchess of Norfolk**
47 **MARASOL,** gr f Siberian Express (USA)—Carte (FR) **Mr J. L. Dunlop**
48 **MASTER SANDY (USA),** b c Master Willie—Whose Broad (USA) **Mr John Darby**
49 **MAY HINTON,** ch f Main Reef—Jeanne Avril **Sir Thomas Pilkington**
50 **NAJMAH (USA),** ch f Nijinsky (CAN)—Double's Nell (USA) **Mr Hamdan Al-Maktoum**
51 **NIKOLAYEVICH,** b c Niniski (USA)—Rexana **Mrs Douglas Riley-Smith**
52 **NOBLE PATRIARCH,** b c Alzao (USA)—Pampala **Mr Peter S. Winfield**
53 **PORT OF SPAIN (USA),** b c El Gran Senor (USA)—Four Runs (USA) **Sheikh Mohammed**
54 **PRINCE HANNIBAL,** b c High Top—Fluctuate **Mr D. R. Hunnisett**
55 **ROYAL HUNTER (USA),** b c Dr Carter (USA)—Royal Suite **Mr S. Khaled**
56 **RUBICUND,** b c Niniski (USA)—Rosananti **Sheikh Mohammed**
57 **RUDDY CHEEK (USA),** b c Blushing Groom (FR)—Hail Maggie (USA) **Lavinia Duchess of Norfolk**
58 **SAJJAYA (USA),** ch f Blushing Groom (FR)—Lady Cutlass **Mr Hamdan Al-Maktoum**
59 **SALSABIL,** b f Sadler's Wells (USA)—Flame of Tara **Mr Hamdan Al-Maktoum**
60 **SHAMYL,** ch c Ahonoora—Salidar **Lavinia Duchess of Norfolk**
61 **SHARP RUNNER (FR),** gr c Star Appeal—Assembly Day **Mr Aubrey Ison**
62 **SHAWWAL (USA),** b br c Shirley Heights—Lady of Camelot (FR) **Mr Hamdan Al-Maktoum**
63 **STORM JIB,** b c Elegant Air—Calvet **Mr M. C. C. Armitage**
64 **SYRTOS,** b c Shareef Dancer (USA)—Wayward Lass (USA) **Sheikh Mohammed**
65 **TRADE SECRET,** b c Ela-Mana-Mou—For Your Eyes **Sheikh Mohammed**
66 **USAYLAH,** ch f Siberian Express (USA)—Nawara **H.R.H. Prince A. A. Faisal**
67 **VITAL CLUE (USA),** b c Alleged (USA)—Where You Lead (USA) **Lavinia Duchess of Norfolk**
68 **WASNAH (USA),** b f Nijinsky (CAN)—Highest Trump (USA) **Mr Hamdan Al-Maktoum**
69 **YAJIB (USA),** b c El Gran Senor (USA)—Chocolate Puff (USA) **Mr Hamdan Al-Maktoum**
70 **ZAWAHIR (USA),** ch f Nureyev (USA)—Solariat (USA) **Mr Hamdan Al-Maktoum**

TWO-YEAR-OLDS

71 **AIMAAM (USA),** b c 6/2 Danzig (USA)—Lucky Lucky Lucky (USA) (Chieftain II) **Mr Hamdan Al-Maktoum**
72 **ALKUWAH,** b f 1/3 Sure Blade (USA)—Buthayna (Habitat) **Mr Hamdan Al-Maktoum**
73 **ALNAAB (USA),** b br c 17/4 Mr Prospector (USA)—Hail Maggie (USA) (Hail To Reason) **Mr Hamdan Al-Maktoum**
74 **ALQWANI (USA),** b f 5/3 Mr Prospector (USA)—Dire (USA) (Roberto (USA)) **Mr Hamdan Al-Maktoum**
75 **ALSAAYBAH (USA),** b f 10/5 Diesis—Secretarial Queen (USA) (Secretariat (USA)) **Mr Hamdan Al-Maktoum**
76 B f 3/2 Never So Bold—Altara (GER) (Tarim) **Sir Thomas Pilkington**
77 **ANDREYEVICH,** b c 17/4 Petoski—Park Parade (Monsanto (FR)) **Mrs Douglas Riley-Smith**
78 B f 15/2 Music Boy—Ariadne (Bustino) **Lady Cohen**
79 **BEAUCHAMP FIZZ,** ch c 26/4 Jalmood (USA)—Buss (Busted) **Mr E. Penser**
80 **BEGGARS POINT (IRE),** b c 14/1 Shirley Heights—Lady's Bridge (USA) (Sir Ivor) **Mrs P. Jamison**
81 **BREAKFAST RIDE,** ch f 14/4 Formidable (USA)—Beautiful Dawn (USA) (Grey Dawn II) **Mrs P. G. Goulandris**
82 **CELERY SALT (USA),** ch c 6/5 Miswaki (USA)—Sea Flavour (Sea Bird II) **Lady Chelsea**
83 **CIRCUS LIGHT,** ro c 20/1 Kalaglow—Circus Plume (High Top) **Sir Robin McAlpine**
84 **COOL CHILI,** ch gr c 12/3 Formidable (USA)—Chili Girl (Skymaster) **Mrs H. J. Heinz**
85 **CUT THE MUSTARD (IRE),** b c 15/4 Niniski (USA)—Cutler's Corner (Sharpen Up) **Mr John Darby**
86 **DAWNING STREET (IRE),** ch c 3/3 Thatching—Dawn Star (High Line) **Windflower Overseas Holdings Inc**
87 **DIAMOND ICE (IRE),** b c 15/2 Nordico (USA)—Kristal's Pride (Kris) **Windflower Overseas Holdings Inc**
88 **ELMARJU (IRE),** b c 12/3 Last Tycoon—Flame of Tara (Artaius (USA)) **Mr Hamdan Al-Maktoum**
89 Ch f 13/4 Bustino—Explosiva (USA) (Explodent (USA)) **Duke of Marlborough**
90 **FARAT (USA),** ch c 19/5 Woodman (USA)—Solac (FR) (Gay Lussac) **Lady Swaythling**
91 **FLYING BRAVE,** b c 14/3 Persian Bold—Flying Sauce (Sauce Boat (USA)) **Lord Swaythling**
92 **GLENORTHERN,** ch c 6/2 Glenstal (USA)—Lady Tyrrel (Pall Mall) **Mr Peter S. Winfield**
93 **HENBURY HALL (IRE),** gr c 13/3 Bellypha—Rustic Stile (Rusticaro (FR)) **Lady Chelsea**
94 **HIGHLAND CEILIDH (IRE),** b f 5/3 Scottish Reel—Savage Love (Wolver Hollow) **Mr C. Humphris**
95 **JIDAL (IRE),** b c 24/2 Taufan (USA)—Al Khazaama (USA) (Alydar (USA)) **Mr Hamdan Al-Maktoum**
96 **JIMMY BARNIE,** ch c 9/2 Local Suitor (USA)—Sharper Still (Sharpen Up) **Summerhill Stud Ltd**
97 **KALININ,** ch c 24/2 Niniski (USA)—Kalaya (Tanerko) **Miss K. Rausing**
98 **LAHIB (USA),** b c 23/4 Riverman (USA)—Lady Cutlass (USA) (Cutlass (USA)) **Mr Hamdan Al-Maktoum**
99 **LALLAPALOOSA,** b f 29/4 Superlative—Tsar's Bride (Song) **Mr J. Barber**

RACEFORM BOOKS
Spring 1990

RACEFORM 1989 FLAT ANNUAL. All last season's form on the Flat with comments on running.
The Jockey Club's Official Record £19.00

SYSTEMATIC BETTING. C. Van Der Wheil steers the backer towards a more sensible and methodical approach to betting £2.95

TIMECHECK '89. All Speed Figures of 30 and above achieved last Flat, showing where, when, at what distance and on what going £8.95

100 WINNERS FOR 1990. Pen portraits by Raceform experts on horses likely to do particularly well during the coming Flat season £2.95

HOW TO WIN AT HANDICAP RACING by Patrick Killgallon £4.95

GREYHOUND RACING FOR PROFIT by Sean Connolly £2.95

HOW TO FIND VALUE WHEN BETTING by Malcolm Howard £4.95

CHASEFORM ANNUAL 1988-89. All last season's N.H. form with comments on how they ran and jumped £17.00

All prices include postage and packing
Remit with order to

RACEFORM LTD.
COMPTON, NEWBURY, BERKSHIRE, RG16 0NL

Access and Visa cardholders can order by telephone at any time on 0635 578080

MR J. L. DUNLOP—continued

100 **LANYARD,** b c 6/3 Sure Blade (USA)—Prudence (Grundy) **Sheikh Mohammed**
101 B g 30/4 Jalmood (USA)—Macarte (FR) (Gift Card (FR)) **Mr J. L. Dunlop**
102 **MARAAKIZ (USA),** ch c 13/2 Roberto (USA)—
River of Stars (USA) (Riverman (USA)) **Mr Hamdan Al-Makotum**
103 **MIGHTY DRAGON (IRE),** b c 19/3 Taufan (USA)—Honagh Lee (Main Reef) **Mrs Michael Liddiard**
104 **MISALLAH (IRE),** b f 22/4 Shirley Heights—Turkish Treasure (USA) (Sir Ivor) **Mr Hamdan Al-Maktoum**
105 **MISSED AGAIN,** b f 15/3 High Top—Out of Shot (Shirley Heights) **Capt J. MacDonald-Buchanan**
106 **MISS FOXTROT,** b f 19/4 Bustino—Java Jive (Hotfoot) **Mr Nicholas Jones**
107 **MOY RIVER (IRE),** b c 22/4 Dominion—Alhargah (Be My Guest (USA)) **Mrs N. Elwes**
108 **MUKHAYYALAH,** b f 5/2 Dancing Brave (USA)—Elzaahirah (Irish Ball (FR)) **Mr Hamdan Al-Maktoum**
109 B g 18/5 Castle Keep—Myrtlegrove (Scottish Rifle) **Mr J. L. Dunlop**
110 **OWER (IRE),** b f 18/2 Lomond (USA)—Argon Laser (Kris) **Dr J. A. E. Hobby**
111 B c 25/4 Commanche Run—Peacefully (Nonoalco (USA))
112 B c 13/4 Rousillon (USA)—Pellinora (USA) (King Pellinore (USA)) **Mr D. R. Hunnisett**
113 B c 18/4 Kings Lake (USA)—Risk All (Run The Gantlet (USA))
114 **SHADAYID (USA),** gr f 10/4 Shadeed (USA)—Desirable (Lord Gayle) **Mr Hamdan Al-Maktoum**
115 **SHEDAD (USA),** ch c 11/4 Diesis—Love's Reward (Nonoalco (USA)) **Mr Hamdan Al-Maktoum**
116 **SHENTIT (FR),** b f 8/3 Shirley Heights—Porte des Lilas (FR) (Sharpman) **Mr F. Stronach**
117 **SIBAIRN LAD,** ch c 4/4 Bairn (USA)—Patois (I Say) **Mr J. L. Dunlop**
118 **SINGLE FILE (USA),** ch c 30/3 Blushing Groom (FR)—
Singletta (USA) (Nodouble (USA)) **Sheikh Mohammed**
119 **SUBSONIC (IRE),** b c 31/1 Be My Guest (USA)—Broken Wide (Busted) **Mrs H. J. Heinz**
120 **THE BLUE BOY (IRE),** ch c 9/2 Tate Gallery (USA)—Blue Lookout (Cure The Blues (USA)) **Lady Cohen**
121 **THE FELTMAKER,** b c 3/3 Shernazar—Miss Siddons (Cure The Blues (USA)) **Mr Peter S. Winfield**
122 **THIRD WATCH,** b f 4/3 Slip Anchor—Triple First (High Top) **Mr P. G. Goulandris**
123 **TIME GENTLEMEN,** ch c 5/3 Night Shift (USA)—Final Orders (USA) (Prince John) **Mrs A. Ison**
124 **TOUCH IN FLIGHT (IRE),** b c 14/2 Formidable (USA)—Tilia (ITY) (Dschingis Khan) **Mr P. Tomei**
125 B br f 7/5 Desert Wine (USA)—Turn The Key (Home Guard (USA)) **H.R.H. Prince A. A. Faisal**
126 **ZARISSA (USA),** b f 4/3 Lyphard (USA)—I Want To Be (USA) (Roberto (USA)) **Sheikh Mohammed**

Other Owners: Mrs Dan Abbott, Mr Michael J. Arnold, Mrs T. Brennan, Sir Gordon Brunton, Mr Ian Cameron, Mr N. Clark, Mrs Harry J. Duffey, Mrs G. Fenston, J. Gomez-Hall, Mrs A. Hulkx, Mrs P. Kegerries, Mrs M. Morris, Mr J. Nash, Mrs N. R. Nutting, F. Parlade, Sir Philip Payne-Gallwey, Mr R. A. Pilkington, Mrs D. Sieff, Mr A. Struthers, Mr E. Tudor-Evans, Mr T. C. Wilson, Mr Philip Wroughton.

186 MR P. R. DUNSTAN, Chard

Postal: **Holditch Court, Holditch, Chard, Somerset.**
Phone: **(02977) 353**

1 **COUNT KARLINSKY,** 4, b c Karlinsky (USA)—Five To Four **Mrs Sue Dunstan**
2 **GRAND CELEBRATION (USA),** 8, ch g Monteverdi—Blackfly (USA) **Mrs Sue Dunstan**
3 **MIDNIGHT SOUZY,** 9, br m Sousa—Five To Four **Mrs Sue Dunstan**
4 **QUEEN OF THE HOURS,** 6, ch m Sousa—Five To Four **Mrs Sue Dunstan**

Jockey (NH): R Dennis (10-0, w.a.).

187 MR F. DURR, Newmarket

Postal: **Vicarage Racing Stables, Kirtling, Newmarket, Suffolk, CB9 9HL.**
Phone: **NEWMARKET (0638) 730030 OR 730004**

1 **ALA HOUNAK,** 6, gr h Sexton Blake—Negligence **Capt F. Samdan**
2 **ERRIS EXPRESS,** 5, b g Bay Express—Royal Home **Mr J. S. Ruddy**
3 **FAR MORE,** 4, ch c Gorytus (USA)—Demare **Mrs O. M. Spann**
4 **PHANAN,** 4, ch c Pharly (FR)—L'Ecossaise **Mr A. Saleh**

MR F. DURR—continued

THREE-YEAR-OLDS

5 **CHINA MOON,** ch f Blushing Scribe (USA)—Derring Venture **Mr H. Lee**
6 **COSMIC DANCER,** ch c Horage—Royal Cloak **Mr D. Woods**
7 **KALALEE,** ch c Doulab (USA)—Silk Empress **Mr A. Saleh**
8 **KHIOS (USA),** b c Lord Gaylord (USA)—Monelia (USA) **Mr K. Abdulla**
9 **ONE FOR THE BOYS,** ch c Superlative—Contenance (GER) **Mr J. S. Ruddy**
10 **ZANOBA,** ch f Precocious—Zanubia **Mr A. Saleh**

TWO-YEAR-OLDS

11 **SEVERALS CLARE (IRE),** ch f 4/4 Tender King—Nutgrove (Thatching) **Newmarket Hotels Ltd**
12 Gr f 7/5 Hatim (USA)—Silk Empress (Young Emperor) **Mr A. Saleh**
13 **SWEET REVIVAL,** b f 26/4 Claude Monet—Semperflorens (Don) **Mr C. S. Tateson**

Other Owners: Mr E. Devereaux, Mrs F. Durr, Mr Nigel Fenner-Fownes, Mr J. Gibson, Mr B. Noel, Mr G. Spann, Mr D. Sullivan.

Apprentice: G Mitchell (7-7).

Conditional: S Woods (9-7).

Lady Rider: Miss C O'Shea (9-4).

188 MR R. EARNSHAW, Harrogate

Postal: **High Warren Farm, Otley Road, Killinghall, Harrogate, HG3 5LZ.**
Phone: **(0423) 567790**

1 **ALAICBRUN,** 5, b g Golden Love—Carrigal **Mrs M. W. Kenyon**
2 **CAPTAIN CAVEMAN,** 5, gr g Scallywag—Canadian Pacific **North West Racing Club Owners Group 1988**
3 **CEVA PARK,** 5, b g Salluceva—South Park **Mrs P. A. Morrison**
4 **FAST FREEZE,** 4, b g Vision (USA)—Gohar (USA) **Mr A. Duckworth**
5 **FUSION,** 6, b g Mill Reef (USA)—Gift Wrapped **Mr Frank Sharp**
6 **KAMBALDA RAMBLER,** 6, br g Kambalda—Stroan Lass **Mr J. Dudgeon**
7 **MAN OF MAUM,** 5, ch g Stanford—Kitty Ellis **Mr Frank Sharp**
8 **PAPER SHOES,** 4, b f Workboy—Two Friendly **Mrs D. A. Earnshaw**
9 **PERFECTLY POSSIBLE,** 5, b g Pitpan—Wine List **Quest Design Print Ltd**
10 **SILAS,** 7, b g Pollerton—Money Spinner **Mr Guy Faber**
11 **THE PROHIBITIONIST,** 4, gr g Warpath—Brandy **Mrs P. A. Morrison**

THREE-YEAR-OLDS

12 **MANSE KEY GOLD,** ch f Vaigly Great—Carafran **Mr Steve Radcliffe**

TWO-YEAR-OLDS

13 **DOVEHOUSE,** b f Petoski—Karietta (Wollow) **Canners Racing Club (Bilton)**
14 B f Blakeney—Horton Line (High Line) **Mr T. K. Kindon**
15 B f Sweet Monday—Moonlight Bay (Palm Track)
16 Br f Kafu—Santa Maria (GER) (Literat (GER)) **Mrs A. Witt**

MR R. EARNSHAW—continued

Other Owners: Mrs M. Ashby, Mrs R. H. Beardsworth, Mr P. S. Cresswell, Mrs M. Crossley, Mrs P. Day, Mr M. Mulholland, Mr M. Parkyn, Mr James Ray, Mrs Michele Varmen.

Jockey (Flat): John Carroll (7-12, w.a.).

Jockey (NH): Ger Lyons (10-0, w.a.).

Apprentice: Jimmy Fortune (w.a.).

Conditional: A D Whitham (9-7).

189 MR M. H. EASTERBY, Malton

Postal: **Habton Grange, Great Habton, Malton, North Yorkshire.**
Phone: **(0653) 86600 FAX (0653) 86621**

1 **ANTINOUS,** 6, ch g Hello Gorgeous (USA)—Marthe Meynet **Lt-Col. R. Warden**
2 **AUTO ALICK,** 6, b g Amboise—Auto Sam **Mr S. Childs**
3 **BARNABY BENZ,** 6, b g Lochnager—Miss Barnaby **Mr T. H. Bennett**
4 **BEAN BOY,** 12, ch g Some Hand—Battling **Mrs Sarah Easterby**
5 **BEAR'S PICNIC,** 4, b g Furry Glen—Three Dieu **Gymcrak Thoroughbred Racing Plc**
6 **BEAU BENZ,** 6, b g Camden Town—War Lass **Gymcrak Thoroughbred Racing Plc**
7 **BELGOOLY,** 5, b g Bulldozer—Canoe **Lt-Col. R. Warden**
8 **BEN OLIVER,** 5, ch g Celtic Cone—Lor Darnie **Mr Paul Green**
9 **BENZ BEST,** 4, gr g Busted—Howzat **Mr T. H. Bennett**
10 **BERLIN OR BUST,** 6, b g Sonnen Gold—Milly Monroe **Mrs Anne Henson**
11 **BOLLIN PATRICK,** 5, b h Sagaro—Bollin Charlotte **Sir Neil Westbrook**
12 **BURGOYNE,** 4, b c Ardross—Love Match (USA) **Mr P. D. Savill**
13 **CARBONATE,** 5, b g Mr Fluorocarbon—Girl On A Swing **Mr P. D. Savill**
14 **CELTIC RAINBOW,** 9, ch m Celtic Cone—Candy Stripe **Mr S. Wright**
15 **CRAKAFU,** 4, b g Kafu—Gayles Bambina **Gymcrak Thoroughbred Racing Plc**
16 **CUMBRIAN EXPRESS,** 5, b g Bay Express—Astral Suite **Cumbrian Industrials Ltd**
17 **CUMBRIAN WALTZER,** 5, ch g Stanford—Mephisto Waltz **Cumbrian Industrials Ltd**
18 **DENHAM GREEN,** 4, b g Dominion—Ariadne **Gymcrak Thoroughbred Racing II Plc**
19 **DUCKINGTON,** 6, b h Bustino—Cribyn **Lady Murless**
20 **ELDER PRINCE,** 4, ch g Final Straw—Particular Miss **Mr W. Pratt**
21 **FISH QUAY,** 7, ch g Quayside—Winkle **Gymcrak Thoroughbred Racing II Plc**
22 **FURRY QUEEN,** 4, b f Furry Glen—Release Record **Gymcrak Thoroughbred Racing Plc**
23 **GEORGE OWEN,** 5, b g Furry Glen—Daisy Owen **Lt-Col. R. Warden**
24 **GO WIN GOLD,** 5, b m Sonnen Gold—Gowyn **Mrs S. J. Mason**
25 **GRIMSTON AGAIN,** 4, b f Lochnager—Lush Gold **Gymcrak Thoroughbred Racing Plc**
26 **GYMCRAK DAWN,** 5, b g Rymer—Edwina's Dawn **Gymcrak Thoroughbred Racing Plc**
27 **HAVERTHWAITE,** 8, ch g Palm Track—Goldwis **Gymcrak Thoroughbred Racing Plc**
28 **ICARUS (USA),** 4, b g Wind And Wuthering (USA)—Cedar Waxwing (USA) **Mr N. A. Ryall**
29 **ISLAND JETSETTER,** 4, ch g Tolomeo—Baridi **Mr Paul Green**
30 **JALMUSIQUE,** 4, ch g Jalmood (USA)—Rose Music **Mrs Jennifer E. Pallister**
31 **JAMARJ,** 5, br m Tyrnavos—Veneziana **Mr Ian Armitage**
32 **KARENOMORE,** 12, b g Karabas—Leomor **Lt-Col. R. Warden**
33 **KIRKLAND GREEN,** 5, b m Lochnager—Spring Gala **Mr J. J. Lawson**
34 **MACROBIAN,** 6, b g Bay Express—White Domino **Miss E. G. Macgregor**
35 **MISTER POINT,** 8, ch g Ahonoora—Rozmeen (FR) **Mr M. Battle**
36 **NAVAL FAN,** 4, b g Taufan (USA)—Naval Artiste **Mr P. D. Savill**
37 **NINEOFUS,** 4, b g Lochnager—Mountain Child **Mr Fred Wilson**
38 **NOHALMDUN,** 9, b g Dragonara Palace (USA)—Damsel **Ulceby Farms Ltd**
39 **NORTON WARRIOR,** 7, gr g King of Spain—Sylvanecte (FR) **Maj J. S. Linley**

MR M. H. EASTERBY—continued

40 **NOS NA GAOITHE,** 7, br g Strong Gale—Abroad **Mr Paul Green**
41 **ON TAP,** 6, ch g Tap On Wood—Joshua's Daughter **Lt-Col. R. Warden**
42 **ROYAL FAN,** 7, br g Taufan (USA)—Miss Royal **Mr Ian Armitage**
43 **RUBYDORA,** 6, b m Buckskin (FR)—Superdora **Mr S. Wright**
44 **SAMFEN,** 8, ro g Sonnen Gold—Ensign Steel **Mr F. C. Ballard**
45 **SCARLET BRAVE,** 5, b g Buckskin (FR)—Cherrywood **Gymcrak Thoroughbred Racing Plc**
46 **SHADING,** 6, gr g Homing—Silver Shadow **Mr A. Fawcett**
47 **SKY CAT,** 6, b g Skyliner—Spring Kitten **Gymcrak Thoroughbred Racing Plc**
48 **SMITHS VENTURE,** 5, b g Bustineto—April Shade **Smith Mansfield Meat Co Ltd**
49 **SPRITEBRAND,** 10, br g Workboy—Benedetta da Castello **Mr P. A. Sullivan**
50 **STATED CASE,** 5, b g Beldale Flutter (USA)—High Point Lady (CAN) **Gymcrak Thoroughbred Racing Plc**
51 **ST NINIAN,** 4, ch c Ardross—Caergwrle **Lady Murless**
52 **SUNNABROWN,** 6, br g Lochnager—Tinella **Mrs M. Christian**
53 **SUPER BENZ,** 4, ch g Hello Gorgeous (USA)—Investiture **Mr T. H. Bennett**
54 **SWORD BEACH,** 6, ch g Scallywag—Bargello's Lady **Mrs S. J. Mason**
55 **WITHY BANK,** 8, b g Blakeney—Chiltern Lass **Mr H. J. B. Cooper**
56 **YEARSLEY,** 4, b g Anfield—Mantina **Mr Ian Armitage**
57 **YOUNG BENZ,** 6, ch g Young Generation—Cavalier's Blush **Mr T. H. Bennett**

THREE-YEAR-OLDS

58 **BARONESS GYMCRAK,** b f Pharly (FR)—My Therape **Gymcrak Thoroughbred Racing II Plc**
59 **BOLLIN HARRIET,** b f Lochnager—Bollin Charlotte **Sir Neil Westbrook**
60 **CUMBRIAN CEILIDH,** ch g Simply Great (FR)—Elm **Cumbrian Industrials Ltd**
61 **CUMBRIAN SINGER,** b c Chief Singer—Bloomsday **Cumbrian Industrials Ltd**
62 **DANCE OF GOLD,** b c Jalmood (USA)—Prima Ballerina (FR) **Gymcrak Thoroughbred Racing II Plc**
63 **DAWSON CITY,** ch g Glint of Gold—Lola Sharp **Lt-Col. R. Warden**
64 **DREAM OF JENNY,** b f Caerleon (USA)—Summer Dreams (CAN) **Mr Paul Green**
65 **DUN SHINING,** b c Lochnager—Miss Barnaby **Mr R. G. Spencer**
66 **FINAL SHOT,** br f Dalsaan—Isadora Duncan **Mr Peter Hurst**
67 **GO ELECTRIC,** ch g Electric—Anadyomene **Mr T. H. Bennett**
68 **GUTHRIE COURT,** b f Daring March—Gangawayhame **Mr P. D. Savill**
69 **GYMCRAK LOVEBIRD,** b f Taufan (USA)—Waadi Hatta (USA) **Gymcrak Thoroughbred Racing II Plc**
70 **HARVEST MINSTREL,** ch g Final Straw—Smagiada **Gymcrak Thoroughbred Racing II Plc**
71 **HIGHLAND HERO,** b g Doc Marten—Lush Secret **Gymcrak Thoroughbred Racing II Plc**
72 **HUGGATE,** b c Mummy's Pet—Polly Peachum **Mrs Anne Henson**
73 **INDIAN PLUME,** b g Commanche Run—Fettle **Gymcrak Thoroughbred Racing II Plc**
74 **JUDGEMENT CALL,** b c Alzao (USA)—Syllabub **Mr P. D. Savill**
75 **JUST GO,** ch f All Systems Go—Argostone **Mrs Sarah Easterby**
76 **KINGS CRESCENT,** b g Fairy King (USA)—Pennycress **British Thoroughbred R. & B. Plc**
77 **LAIRD OF BALMORAL,** b c Lochnager—Baggin Time **Gymcrak Thoroughbred Racing II Plc**
78 **LUCKY BLUE,** b g Blue Cashmere—Cooling **Mr Alfred Watson**
79 **NORTON CHALLENGER,** gr c Absalom—Klaire **Maj J. S. Linley**
80 **PETROL BLUE,** b c Tumble Wind (USA)—Petrina **Mr T. H. Bennett**
81 **PLEASE BELIEVE ME,** b f Try My Best (USA)—Believer **Mr Paul Green**
82 **RAGE,** ch g Final Straw—Nasty Niece (CAN) **Lady Murless**
83 **RASCHESTER,** ch g Good Times (ITY)—Killifreth **Retail Advertising Services Ltd**
84 **SANDMOOR JACQUARD,** ch c Noalto—Grand Opera **Sandmoor Textiles Co Ltd**
85 **SHARINSKI,** ch g Niniski (USA)—Upanishad **Gymcrak Thoroughbred Racing II Plc**
86 **SHERIFF'S BAND,** ch g Posse (USA)—Willis (FR) **Mr Ian Armitage**
87 **SONG OF GYMCRAK,** b f Chief Singer—Dusty Letter (USA) **Gymcrak Thoroughbred Racing II Plc**
88 **SOVEREIGN HILL,** ch f Dominion—Tuft Hill **Mr T. H. Bennett**
89 **SUGGIA,** b f Alzao (USA)—Marthe Meynet **Lt-Col. R. Warden**
90 **WINE CELLAR,** br f Muscatite—Passage Falcon **Mr J. F. Farrington**

TWO-YEAR-OLDS

91 **BELLE CHOSE,** b f 9/4 Bairn (USA)—Dingle Belle (Dominion) **Mr P. D. Savill**
92 **BOLLIN MAGDALENE,** b f 8/4 Teenoso (USA)—Klairlone (Klairon) **Sir Neil Westbrook**
93 **BOLLIN SHARON,** b f 6/3 Nishapour (FR)—Royal Yacht (USA) (Riverman (USA)) **Lady Westbrook**
94 **DOMINION GOLD,** b c 20/3 Domynsky—Lush Gold (Goldhill) **Mr H. Boswell**
95 **DOMINION PLEASURE,** b f 8/3 Domynsky—Pleasing Prospect (Imperial Fling (USA)) **Mr H. Boswell**

MR M. H. EASTERBY—continued

96 **DOTTEREL (IRE)**, b c 23/4 Rhoman Rule (USA)—Miysam (Supreme Sovereign) **Lt.-Col R. Warden**
97 **DR BILL**, b c 18/2 Domynsky—Miss Barnaby (Sun Prince) **Mr M. H. Easterby**
98 **GYMCRAK FORTUNE (IRE)**, b g 2/3 Kafu—Forlorn Chance (Fighting Don) **Gymcrak Thoroughbred Racing III Plc**
99 **GYMCRAK GAMBLE**, b c 4/4 Beldale Flutter (USA)—Baridi (Ribero) **Gymcrak Thoroughbred Racing III Plc**
100 **GYMCRAK PREMIERE**, b c 26/2 Primo Dominie—Oraston (Morston (FR)) **Gymcrak Thoroughbred Racing III Plc**
101 **GYMCRAK SOVEREIGN**, b c 20/1 Ballacashtal (CAN)—Get Involved (Shiny Tenth) **Gymcrak Thoroughbred Racing III Plc**
102 **GYMYNSKY**, b c 19/2 Domynsky—Swinging Baby (Swing Easy (USA)) **Gymcrak Thoroughbred Racing III Plc**
103 **IMAGINARY PLANE**, b c 4/2 Petoski—Dalmally (Sharpen Up) **Mr G. H. Leatham**
104 **INFINITY ZOOM (IRE)**, b c 22/2 Alzao (USA)—Carthagian (Thatch (USA)) **Mr P. D. Savill**
105 **JOB LOT**, b c 22/5 Precocious—Do Your Best (Try My Best (USA)) **Milbank Foods Ltd**
106 **MARVAL**, b f 14/1 Dara Monarch—Lola Sharp (Sharpen Up) **Lt.-Col R. Warden**
107 **NAME THE BRAVE (IRE)**, b c 23/3 Nomination—Bold Loren (Bold Lad (IRE)) **Mr J. David Abell**
108 **NIGHT FANCY**, b c 11/3 Night Shift (USA)—Smooth Siren (USA) (Sea Bird II) **Miss E. Pratley**
109 **ON THE LINE**, b c 7/5 Belfort (FR)—Queen's Parade (Sovereign Path) **Mr P. D. Savill**
110 **PHALAROPE (IRE)**, b c 17/5 Petorius—Magee (Weavers Hall) **Lt.-Col R. Warden**
111 **SALLY FAY (IRE)**, b f 30/4 Fayruz—Trust Sally (Sallust) **Mr T. A. Morris and Partners**
112 **SING 'N SWING**, b c 30/4 Chief Singer—Foston Bridge (Relkino) **Mr G. Graham**
113 **ST GREGORY**, b c 8/3 Ardross—Crymlyn (Welsh Pageant) **Lady Murless**
114 **TEN O'CLOCKS**, b f 5/4 Domynsky—Mashin Time (Palm Track) **Mr P. Baillie and Mr M. H. Easterby**
115 **VICTORIA ROAD (IRE)**, b c 29/2 Runnett—That's Swiss (Thatching) **Mr T. H. Bennett**
116 **VINTAGE ONLY**, b c 5/3 Sayf El Arab (USA)—Bias (Royal Perogative) **Mrs B. Ward**
117 **WASPY (IRE)**, b f 6/3 Horage—Persian Caprice (Persian Bold) **Mr T. A. Morris and Partners**
118 **WESTHOLME (USA)**, b c 25/4 Lyphard's Wish (FR)—Shroud (USA) (Vaguely Noble) **Mr T. H. Bennett**
119 **WHO'S TEF (IRE)**, b c 16/5 Muscatite—Eternal Optimist (Relko) **TEF Freight (Scarborough) Ltd**

Other Owners: Mr C. R. Bainbridge, Mr Ken Croft, Mr B. Elsworth, Mr James Glass, Mrs Jenny Green, Miss I. G. Macgregor, Mr A. Robinson, Mr Arthur Smith, Mr G. W. Turner.

Jockey (Flat): M Birch (8-2).

Jockeys (NH): R Marley (9-7), L Wyer (10-0).

Conditional: R Garritty (9-7).

190 MR M. W. EASTERBY, Sheriff Hutton

Postal: **New House Farm, Sheriff Hutton, York, YO6 7TN.**
Phone: **(03477) 368 FAX (03477) 204**

1 **ALMONDBURY**, 9, b g Moulton—Phoenix Rose **Mr S. H. J. Brewer**
2 **ANDROS PRINCE**, 5, b g Blakeney—Ribamba **Mr M. W. Easterby**
3 **BLAKES SON**, 5, b g Blakeney—Susanna (USA) **Mr A. Fawcett**
4 **CHERRY BRAVE**, 9, b g Le Bavard (FR)—Cherry Stack **Mr S. H. J. Brewer**
5 **CRACKLE MOOR**, 5, b m Don—Carol Day **Mr D. P. Travers-Clark**
6 **DIEGO RIVERA**, 6, b g Shirley Heights—Brazen Faced **Mr A. Fawcett**
7 **EMIFIVE**, 5, b m Kind of Hush—Close Secret **Mrs P. G. Wragg**
8 **FINAL PLAYER**, 4, gr g Absalom—Oakwoodhill **Mr J. David Abell**
9 **FOSTON**, 7, br g Sonnen Gold—Gay Ribbon **Mr J. Griffin**
10 **GUSHY**, 4, ch g Hard Fought—Be Gustful **Mr P. D. Savill**
11 **HARRY HULL**, 7, ch g Sagaro—Polly Peachum **Mrs Carol J. Welch**
12 **HOUGHTON**, 4, b g Horage—Deirdre Oge **Lady Manton**
13 **KEEP BIDDING**, 4, br g Hays—Keep Chanting **Mr C. R. Bainbridge**
14 **LAKE VALENTINA**, 9, br g Blakeney—La Levantina **Mr J. R. Chester**

MR M. W. EASTERBY—continued

15 **MACARTHUR,** 5, b g Ardross—Polly Peachum **Mrs Anne Henson**
16 **MERANO (FR),** 7, ch h Tip Moss (FR)—Association (FR) **Mr C. A. B. St. George**
17 **MILITARY HONOUR,** 5, b g Shirley Heights—Princess Tiara **Mr D. Hilton Cox**
18 **MOWTHORPE,** 5, ch g Ballad Rock—Simeonova **Mr M. W. Easterby**
19 **PLANET ASH,** 7, b g Star Appeal—Cinderwench **Mr C. R. Bainbridge**
20 **POLDER,** 4, b c Lochnager—Dutch Girl **Mr Gerald Geraghty**
21 **ROOSTERS TIPPLE,** 4, b g Henbit (USA)—Amiel **Mr A. Fawcett**
22 **ROYAL ESTIMATE,** 4, br g Tender King—Nistona **Mr J. David Abell**
23 **SAWDUST JACK,** 6, b g Rarity—Ribero's Overture **Mr S. H. J. Brewer**
24 **TEN OF CLUBS,** 9, b g Raise You Ten—Sno-Cat **Mr S. H. J. Brewer**
25 **TOO EAGER,** 4, b g Nishapour (FR)—Double Habit **Mr P. D. Savill**
26 **TRESIDDER,** 8, b g Connaught—Twenty Two (FR) **Mr S. H. J. Brewer**
27 **WATERDALE (USA),** 7, b g Caucasus (USA)—Green Girl **Mr M. J. Silver**
28 **WYTHERSTONE,** 4, b g Hotfoot—Jurassic **Mr D. J. Bushnell**
29 **YAHEEB (USA),** 6, b h Alleged (USA)—Rissa (USA) **Mr A. Fawcett**
30 **YOUTHFUL PIP,** 5, b g Young Generation—Pipina (USA) **Mr A. Fawcett**

THREE-YEAR-OLDS

31 **ADONITA,** ch f Adonijah—Latakia **Mr B. H. Farr**
32 **GOLD DIVER,** ch g Main Reef—Ice Baby **Mrs L. Brotherton**
33 **NOTHING'S FREE,** b f Free State—Wayward Polly **Roldvale Limited**
34 **PUFFY,** ch g Wolverlife—Eskaroon **Mr P. D. Savill**

TWO-YEAR-OLDS

35 **ARRACK PRINCESS,** b f 15/3 Precocious—Petrary (Petingo) **Mr B. Swain**
36 **BANKSY BOY (IRE),** ch c 27/2 Gorytus (USA)—Kampai (General Assembly (USA)) **Mr G. E. Shouler**
37 B f 18/3 Precocious—Clean Canasta (Silly Season) **Mr J. David Abell**
38 **COMMANCHE RHYTHM,** b f 7/3 Commanche Run—Hear My Song (Song) **Mr G. E. Shouler**
39 B c 12/4 Damister (USA)—Copt Hall Royale (Right Tack) **Mr G. E. Shouler**
40 Ch f 3/5 Sweet Monday—Dutch Girl (Workboy) **C. F. Buckton**
41 Ro f 26/4 Grey Desire—Dutch May (Maystreak) **C. F. Buckton**
42 **FEEL THE HEAT (IRE),** b g 28/2 Shy Groom (USA)—Granny Bunn (Wolver Hollow) **Mr P. D. Savill**
43 B c 22/3 Sayf El Arab (USA)—Gleneagle (Swing Easy (USA)) **Ancabrand Ltd**
44 Br c 20/3 Belfort (FR)—Gold Duchess (Sonnen Gold) **C. F. Buckton**
45 **HYSSOP,** ch c 8/3 Absalom—Willow Herb (Habat) **Mr J. David Abell**
46 Br f 20/5 Lochnager—Jane Roy (Royalty) **Mrs J. H. Holt**
47 B g 19/3 Reasonable (FR)—Kilteelagh Lady (King's Leap) **Mr Richard Edwards**
48 B f 29/2 King of Spain—Linguistic (Porto Bello) **Mr J. David Abell**
49 **LITTLE FLASHER (IRE),** ch g 15/1 Exhibitioner—Eskaroon (Artaius (USA)) **Mr P. D. Savill**
50 **MICK'S CHOICE,** b c 30/3 Petoski—Holy Day (Sallust) **Lord Belper**
51 **MISS CALCULATE,** ch f 4/4 Mummy's Game—Antique Bloom (Sterling Bay (SWE)) **Mr G. Clark**
52 **MISS MEASURE,** b f 14/5 Electric—Gentle Gypsy (Junius (USA)) **Mr G. Clark**
53 **N R FOUNTAIN,** gr c 5/3 Bellypha—Rainfall (Relko) **Mr G. E. Shouler**
54 Ch f 3/3 Raise A Native (USA)—Pitty Pal (USA) (Caracolero (USA)) **Mr Gerald Geraghty**
55 Br f 20/2 Touching Wood (USA)—Plaits (Thatching) **Mr G. Clark**
56 B c 8/3 Sweet Monday—Podzola (Royal Prerogative) **Corse of Kinnoir**
57 **ROBINS RETURN,** b f 24/4 Music Boy—Baidedones (Welsh Pageant) **Mr B. Swain**
58 **SABRICIOUS (IRE),** ch g 31/3 Precocious—Pale Silk (FR) (Shantung) **Mr P. D. Savill**
59 **STUFFY (IRE),** ch c 15/4 Doulab (USA)—Natural Sunshine (Manado) **Mr P. D. Savill**
60 B g 7/3 Prince Sabo—Wayward Polly (Lochnager) **Ancabrand Ltd**
61 **WHERE'S CAROL,** gr f 5/2 Anfield—Ludovica (Bustino) **Mr D. F. Spence**

Other Owners: Mr R. S. Anand, Mrs S. R. Brook, Sir Gordon Brunton, Mrs P. B. E. P. Farr, Mrs C. M. Geraghty, Mr M. S. H. Hartley, Mr D. Marley, Mr T. Morris, Mrs Vyvien Randall, Mr J. M. Roy, Mrs V. M. C. Watson.

Conditional: G Lyons, C Ryan (9-13).

Lady Rider: Mrs S E Mason (11-0).

191 MRS M. EASTON, Fordingbridge

Postal: **Harris Farm, Martin, Fordingbridge, Hampshire, SP6 3LD.**
Phone: **MARTIN CROSS (072589) 375**

1 **ALICE BRIGHT,** 7, ch m Jolly Lolly—Golden Breeze **Mrs M. Easton**
2 **LAST HOUSE,** 7, ch m Vital Season—Parkhouse **Mrs M. Easton**
3 **LOCH DEVA,** 6, b g Lochnager—Deva Rose **Mrs M. Easton**

Jockeys (NH): Arun Jones (10-0), Trevor Wall (10-0).

Amateur: Mr M J Batters (11-10).

192 MISS J. M. EATON, Wennington

Postal: **Wenning Cottage, Wennington, Lancaster, Lancashire, LA2 8NN.**
Phone: **(0468) 21374**

1 **ARCTIC ADVENTURE,** 7, b g Slim Jim—Lady Marcia **Mr M. A. Proudfoot**
2 **ARCTIC RYMES,** 7, b m Rymer—Lakeland Lady **Miss Judy Eaton**
3 **CASHEL PALACE,** 5, b m Sweet Monday—Sunny Maid **Mr M. A. Proudfoot**
4 **COP FOR THAT,** 8, gr g Meldrum—Splendid Lines **Mr J. H. Smith**
5 **CROSS COUNT,** 12, b g Crozier—The Reckoning **Miss Judy Eaton**
6 **DARING TO GO,** 5, b m Daring March—Summer Lightning **Miss Judy Eaton**
7 **HARLEY,** 10, ch g Cranley—Harmony Rose **Miss Judy Eaton**
8 **HEADLEYS BRIDGE,** 8, b g Artaius (USA)—Gale Bridge (USA) **Mr John J. Byrne**
9 **KINGSWOOD,** 8, ch g Meldrum—Kingsbay **Mr G. R. Eaton**
10 **YALISKARI,** 9, br g Meldrum—Kingsbay **Miss Judy Eaton**

Jockey (NH): Ger Lyons (10-0).

Amateur: Miss Lisa Eaton (9-0).

193 MR M. ECKLEY, Ludlow

Postal: **Alma House, Brimfield, Ludlow, Salop, SY8 4NG.**
Phone: **BRIMFIELD (058 472) 372**

1 **AAARGH,** 4, b f The Brianstan—Miss Binki **Mr Malcolm W. Eckley**
2 **BOLD ILLUSION,** 12, ch g Grey Mirage—Savette **Mr H. M. Thursfield**
3 **C U TECHNIMECH,** 4, b f Chukaroo—Karyobinga **Mr Malcolm W. Eckley**
4 **EXPLETIVE,** 10, ch m Shiny Tenth—Pemba (FR) **Mr Malcolm W. Eckley**
5 4, Ch f Humdoleila—Psidette **Mr B. A. Cullen**
6 **RAG TIME BELLE,** 4, ch f Raga Navarro (ITY)—Betbellof **Mr R. A. Hughes**
7 **SPANISH MOU,** 5, b m King of Spain—Baggage **Mr Malcolm W. Eckley**
8 **THE SCARLET DRAGON,** 4, b f Oats—Dragon Fire **Mr R. A. Hughes**
9 **TUDOR ROMANCE,** 5, b g Aragon—Dovey **Mr T. J. Arnold**

THREE-YEAR-OLDS

10 B g Leading Man—Her Excellency **Mr Malcolm W. Eckley**
11 Ch g Rymer—Love Another **Mr H. M. Thursfield**

TWO-YEAR-OLDS

12 B f 10/5 Rymer—Karyobinga (So Blessed) **Mr Malcolm W. Eckley**

MR M. ECKLEY—continued

Other Owners: Mr Philip A. Fitzpatrick, Mr John H. Foulds, Mrs Patricia S. Foulds, Mr Stephen J. Piggott, Mr Steven Rowlinson.

Jockeys (Flat): S Cauthen (8-6, w.a.), J Reid (8-4, w.a.), T Williams (7-7, w.a.).

Jockey (NH): R Dunwoody (w.a.).

Conditional: S P Arnold (9-7).

Amateur: Miss S Murgatroyd.

194 MR R. J. ECKLEY, Kington

Postal: **The Holme, Lyonshall, Kington, Herefordshire, HR5 3JP.**
Phone: **(05448) 216**

1 **BLUEGRASS LADY,** 4, b f Last Fandango—Gifted Lady **Mr Roger Buck**
2 **BOLD FRED,** 8, br g Bold Owl—Kit-O-Kate **Mrs C. W. Middleton**
3 4, B f Sunyboy—Chaffcombe **Mr R. C. F. Faiers**
4 **DWALE (USA),** 5, b g Bates Motel (USA)—Chip O'Chocolate (USA) **Mrs K. M. Lifely**
5 **EXACT ANALYSIS (USA),** 4, br g Verbatim (USA)—Mity Nice Girl (USA) **Mr E. J. Townley-Berry**
6 **GOLDEN FARE,** 5, ch g Scallywag—Katie Fare **Mr Jeffrey J. Hancorn**
7 **HANDY MARK,** 16, ch g Pinicola—Dhobi Mark **Mr P. R. Eckley**
8 **KARAKA,** 4, ch f Good Times (ITY)—Buff Beauty **Mrs S. C. Barker**
9 **MUMMY'S TOY BOY,** 4, br g Mansingh (USA)—Easterly Gael **Mrs David Williams**
10 **PHYLLIDA FOX,** 7, ro m Healaugh Fox—Fastidium **Mrs C. W. Middleton**
11 **PORRIDGE OATS,** 5, gr m Oats—Bellarina **Mr R. C. F. Faiers**
12 4, Ch f Oats—Royaldyne **Mr R. J. Eckley**
13 4, Ch g Ardross—Sahara Goddess **Mr R. J. Eckley**
14 **SAPPHIRE FLIGHT,** 5, gr m Scallywag—Last Flight **Mr R. J. Eckley**
15 **SERGEANT SILVER,** 5, gr g General Ironside—Coolentallagh **Mr R. C. F. Faiers**
16 4, Br g Broadsword (USA)—Spartaca **Mr R. J. Eckley**
17 **SUPER REGAL,** 8, b g Fordham (USA)—Little Angle **Mr R. C. F. Faiers**
18 **TEACLOTH,** 4, br f Raga Navarro (ITY)—Dishcloth **Exors of the Late Mr Melville Higgins**
19 **THE PARSON'S NUN,** 6, ch m The Parson—Hill Invader **Mr T. C. Court**
20 **VENTURE LADY,** 6, b m Joshua—Aurelia **Mr N. G. Addis**
21 **WHAT'S THAT,** 4, br g Lepanto (GER)—Crendle Hill **Mr R. J. Eckley**

THREE-YEAR-OLDS

22 **DEEP DELIGHT,** b f Idiot's Delight—Browne's Return **Mr R. C. F. Faiers**
23 Ch g Rustingo—Emerald Flight **Mr R. J. Eckley**
24 **PEARLY FLIGHT,** b g Rustingo—Last Flight **Mr R. J. Eckley**

TWO-YEAR-OLDS

25 Ch f 17/5 Celtic Cone—Emerald Flight (Cantab) **Mrs M. A. Eckley**
26 Br c 7/4 Julio Mariner—Last Flight (Saucy Kit) **Mrs R. J. Eckley**
27 Gr f 15/5 Glasgow Central—Pickled Tink (Tickled Pink) **Mrs C. W. Middleton**

Other Owners: Mr S. C. Barker, Mr Peter S. Hill, Mr David C. Lowe, Mr M. B. Roberts, Miss Judith Weeden.

Conditional: M Jackson (9-10).

Amateur: Mr T M Richards (10-10).

195 MR GRANT EDEN, Newmarket

Postal: **Charlcombe Lodge, Hamilton Road, Newmarket, Suffolk, CB8 0TE.**
Phone: **(0638) 667938**

1 **HANDSOME LEADER (USA),** 4, b g Green Forest (USA)—Mazyoun **Charlcombe Holdings**
2 **HELEN RED,** 4, b f Trojan Fen—Spindle Berry **Mrs J. R. Peers**
3 **PRINCESS CAERLEON,** 4, ch f Caerleon (USA)—Tigeen **Mr R. V. Young**
4 **SO RHYTHMICAL,** 6, b g Dance In Time (CAN)—So Lyrical **Miss C. A. Barrow**

THREE-YEAR-OLDS

5 **APRIL CRACKER,** b f Cragador—Chanita **Mrs J. R. Peers**
6 **PRINCESS TANIMARA,** b f Vision (USA)—Tanimara **The Hall Stud Ltd**

TWO-YEAR-OLDS

7 **BARBARY REEF (IRE),** b c 13/4 Sarab—Brown's Cay (Formidable (USA))
8 **DANSE D'ESPRIT,** br f 2/3 Lidhame—Bel Esprit (Sagaro) **Mr J. Robson**
9 **FLOWER REEF,** b f 13/4 Cragador—Kellys Reef (Pitskelly) **Mr R. A. Mohammed**
10 **GALAXY EXPRESS,** ch g 23/3 Bay Express—Heaven And Earth (Midsummer Night II) **Mr M. Eden**
11 **IN THE FRAME,** br g 14/3 Claude Monet (USA)—Venetian Joy (Windjammer (USA))
12 **PRINCESS EMMYLOU (IRE),** ch f 26/2 Gorytus (USA)—Emmylou (Arctic Tern (USA)) **Mr R. V. Young**
13 **PRINCESS ROSANANTI (IRE),** b f 23/3 Shareef Dancer (USA)—Rosananti (Blushing Groom (FR)) **Mr R. V. Young**
14 **TOP TERN,** b f 29/3 Doulab (USA)—Golden Tern (FR) (Arctic Tern (USA))

Other Owners: Mr R. Coombes, Mr C. Eden, Mrs E. Robson.

196 MR J. A. C. EDWARDS, Ross-on-Wye

Postal: **Caradoc Court, Sellack, Ross-on-Wye, Herefordshire.**
Phone: **(098987) 259/315 TELEX 35679 JACED G FAX (098987) 329**

1 **AFARISTOUN (FR),** 6, b g Top Ville—Afrique (FR) **Mr H. Kaye**
2 **ALPHIN PIKE,** 5, b g Lochnager—Bombay Duck **Mrs J. P. Bissill**
3 **ASK FOR MORE,** 5, b g Proverb—Primrose Walk **D. Stern**
4 **AUTUMN SPORT,** 9, b g Mossberry—Bounteous Sport **Mr C. W. Jenkins**
5 **BALLYEDEN,** 6, br m Beau Charmeur (FR)—Mac's Wish **Express & Star Raceowners Club 1989**
6 **BEN THE BOMBER,** 5, b g Beau Charmeur (FR)—Barnwellsgrove **Mr D. A. Davies**
7 **BIRLING JACK,** 9, b g Bronze Hill—Fortilage **Mrs J. K. Peutherer**
8 **BOB TISDALL,** 11, ch g Deep Run—Amphibian **K. Al-Said**
9 **BONNIE DUNDEE,** 6, b g Leading Man—Dragon Lass **Mrs C. P. Fairbairn**
10 **BOOK OF RUNES,** 5, b g Deep Run—Wychelm **Mr D. Jones**
11 **CASTLE BANKS,** 6, ch g Proverb—In The Forest **Mr Roy Padgham**
12 **CASTLERICHARDKING,** 5, b br g Matching Pair—Dont Rock **Mrs Maureen J. Russell**
13 **CASTLE WARDEN,** 13, br g Trombone—Tu-Ukumah **Mr M. L. Shone**
14 **CHARTER HARDWARE,** 8, b g Hardboy—Unsinkable Sarah **Charter Racing Ltd**
15 **CITY COMMENT,** 6, b g Furry Glen—Marty Mann **Mrs A. Bell**
16 **CLEAR CALL (FR),** 5, br g Bikala—Catacomb (USA) **Mr D. Jones**
17 **CLIFFALDA,** 7, ch g Young Man (FR)—Hampsruth **Mr R. J. McAlpine**
18 **CWM GWAUN,** 6, ch g Le Bavard (FR)—Glenbawn Lady **Mr Simon Davies**
19 **DAYKINS BOY,** 5, ch g Deep Run—Mawbeg Holly **Mr Alan Parker**
20 **DEEP FLASH,** 7, b g Deep Run—Sirrahdis **Mr Eric Parker**
21 **DIRECT,** 7, b g The Parson—Let The Hare Sit **Mr H. Kaye**
22 **ES-PORT,** 5, b g Mummy's Game—Bella Lisa **Mr R. Lawton**
23 **FALLOPOLIS (FR),** 5, b g Persepolis (FR)—Fancy's Child (USA) **P. F. M. Civil Eng Co Ltd**
24 **FALSE ECONOMY,** 5, ch g Torus—Vulvic **Mr M. L. Shone**
25 **FIRM PRICE,** 9, b g Our Mirage—Strip Poker **Mr Howard Parker**
26 **FOREST RANGER,** 8, b g The Parson—Nora Grany **K. Al-Said**
27 **FORMULA ONE,** 8, b g Ardoon—Little Dipper **Mr D. A. Davies**
28 **GENTLEMAN'S JIG (CAN),** 5, gr g Jig Time (USA)—Sunny Season (USA) **Mr R. J. McAlpine**

MR J. A. C. EDWARDS—continued

29 **GERAMI,** 10, gr g Grey Mirage—Psidette **Mr R. J. McAlpine**
30 **HAWKSMOOR,** 7, b g Certingo—Lefkara **Mr B. A. O'Brien**
31 **HERE COMES CHARTER,** 5, b g Le Moss—Windtown Fancy **Charter Racing Ltd**
32 **HIGHLAND CHAIN,** 5, b m Furry Glen—Keep The Link **D. Gyle-Thompson**
33 **HIGHLAND TREAT,** 6, b g Northern Treat (USA)—Cereal Queen **Mr Robert L. Thompson**
34 **HILARION (FR),** 6, br g Gay Mecene (USA)—Helvetie II **Mr D. J. Nichols**
35 **HILL'S HALO,** 4, b g Kampala—Clanjingle **Mr Peter S. Hill**
36 **HITCHCOCK,** 7, b g Beau Charmeur (FR)—Laurabeg **Mr Roy Padgham**
37 **HOLLY KING (USA),** 6, b g Key To The Kingdom (USA)—Chargealero (USA) **Mr Roy Padgham**
38 **INDIAN SET,** 6, b m Windjammer (USA)—Bourges (FR) **J. Halsey**
39 **JUNIOR PARKER,** 6, br g Al Sirat (USA)—Black Zeta **Mr M. L. Shone**
40 **KAMBA LAD,** 7, b g Kambalda—Kylenora **Mr A. J. Whitehead**
41 **KEMBERTON CORACLE,** 6, br g Lighter—Evelith **Mrs J. Poole**
42 **KEMY'S COMMANDER,** 5, ch g Monksfield—Rockwood Lady **Mr Glynne Clay**
43 5, B g General Ironside—Kova's Daughter **A. Insley**
44 **LAMPASS,** 6, b br g Never Got A Chance—Annagh Delight **Mrs I. Phillips**
45 **MASTER WILLIAM,** 6, b g Pollerton—Ballyea Jacki **Mrs Eva Ellis**
46 **MISTER GEBO,** 5, b g Strong Gale—Miss Goldiane **Mr D. Jones**
47 **MISTER HARTIGAN,** 10, b g Menelek—Fortrition **Mrs Eva Ellis**
48 **MOUNTAIN CRASH,** 10, b g Crash Course—Cross Pearl **Mr Alan Parker**
49 **MOUNTEBOR,** 6, b g Prince Regent (FR)—Land **Mrs Jean Turpin**
50 **MULTUM IN PARVO,** 7, b g Proverb—Kova's Daughter **Mr Alan Parker**
51 **OBSERVER CORPS,** 9, b g Celtic Cone—Listen Here **Mr Glynne Clay**
52 **PARSONS LAW,** 7, ch m The Parson—Wrekalong **Mr P. R. Brooks**
53 **PEARLYMAN,** 11, b g Mandamus—Pearlyric **Mrs P. Shaw**
54 5, B g Amoristic (USA)—Pitpans Star **Mr J. A. C. Edwards**
55 **POL SLAK,** 7, ch g Pollerton—Kilbrack **Mr Richard J. Edwards**
56 **PRINCE VALMY (FR),** 5, br g Mill Reef (USA)—Princesse Vali (FR) **Mrs Jean Turpin**
57 **PROPLUS,** 8, ch g Proverb—Castle Treasure **Mrs P. Shaw**
58 **PROVERITY,** 9, ch g Proverb—Calamity Jane **Mrs P. Shaw**
59 **QUARRY TOWN,** 7, b g Mandalus—Weary Lil **Mrs Eva Ellis**
60 **RAIDO,** 5, ch g Black Minstrel—Fair Songstress **Mr D. Jones**
61 **RIVER BED (FR),** 6, ch g Sharpman—River Craft **Mr Roy Padgham**
62 **ROBCOURT HILL,** 5, b g Callernish—Cooney Island **Mr M. B. Roberts**
63 **ROYLE SPEEDMASTER,** 6, ch g Green Shoon—Cahermone Ivy **Royle Machinery Limited**
64 **RU VALENTINO,** 6, ch g Deep Run—Tape Mary **Mrs S. A. Jones**
65 5, B g Tudor Rhythm—Saxon Slave **Mr J. A. C. Edwards**
66 **SOONER STILL,** 6, b g Tachypous—Sooner Or Later **Mr J. J. Smith**
67 **ST LOUIS BLUES,** 5, b g Cure The Blues (USA)—Flaretown **Mr H. D. White**
68 **STORM ISLAND,** 5, b g Strong Gale—Sleemana **K. Al-Said**
69 **TARGET PRACTICE,** 5, b m Rymer—Spring Rocket **B. Messer Bennetts**
70 **THE CITY MINSTREL,** 5, br g Black Minstrel—Miss Diga **Mrs Jean Turpin**
71 **TINAS LAD,** 7, b g Jellaby—Arbatina **Mr Geoffrey Johnson**
72 **TOP O' TH' GREEN,** 7, b g Take A Reef—Fanny Green **Mrs J. P. Bissill**
73 **TRUSTY FRIEND,** 8, b g True Song—Princess Camilla **Mrs C. P. Fairbairn**
74 **VALASSY,** 7, b g Northern Value (USA)—Plum Sassy **Mr Hector H. Brown**
75 **WESTERN LEGEND,** 6, ch g Proverb—Calamity Jane **Miss Jennifer Laing**
76 **YAHOO,** 9, b g Trombone—Coolroe Aga **Mr Alan Parker**
77 **YREKA BAY,** 8, b g Le Bavard (FR)—Maureens Dote **Mrs Ian Wasserman**

Other Owners: Mr R. A. N. Bonnycastle, Mr T. C. Court, Mr R. A. Dalton, Mrs B. C. Dice, Mr John Dyson, Mr Richard J. Edwards, Mr W. E. Ellis, Mr R. B. Fielding, Mr B. J. Gibbens, Mr Roger Graham, Mr Richard J. Grainger, Mr Richard Hall, Mr W. Jenks, Mr Reg Key, Mr David C. Lowe, Mr H. K. Porter, Mr A. H. Rachlin, Mrs A. E. Robertson, Mr Alan Saville, Mrs W. D. Sykes, Mr D. N. P. Woodcock, Mrs Ann Yearsley.

Jockeys (NH): T Morgan (10-6), D Tegg (10-0).

Conditional: M Doyle (9-7), N Williamson (9-11).

197 MR E. ELDIN, Newmarket

Postal: **Loder Stables, Hamilton Road, Newmarket, Suffolk, CB8 0NQ.**
Phone: **OFF. (0638) 662036 HOME 663217 FAX (0638) 660998**

1 ANGEL BRIGHT, 4, ch f Krayyan—Godhood **Mr A. K. Gawthrop and Partners**
2 BUT OF COURSE, 5, b h Tap On Wood—Aldern Stream
3 MY OPINION, 4, br f Beldale Flutter—Opinion **Mr Kevin Moorcroft**
4 RANGERS LAD, 5, b g Sallust—Flaxen Hair **St. Andrews Ltd**
5 THE SHANAHAN BAY, 5, b h Hays—Tanala Bay **Mr E. Eldin**

THREE-YEAR-OLDS

6 CEE TEE ELL, ch f Coquelin (USA)—Stamina **Mr A. N. Fiber and Partners**
7 DALLAS FAB, b c Pas de Seul—Sun Lassie (FR) **Dallas Fabrications**
8 HARD TO NAME, b c Connaught—Printafoil **Mr C. A. Blackwell**
9 LAMBTON LAD, b g Saher—Illaqua (USA) **Mr Kevin Moorcroft**
10 LUCKY GIFT, b c Krayyan—Hung Pao **Mr E. Eldin**
11 MONTYKOSKY, b g Montekin—Reliable Rosie **Mr E. Eldin**
12 Ch g Tower Walk—Needless
13 SHINING JEWEL, b c Exhibitioner—Vaguely Jade **Mr E. Eldin and Mr D. W. Rolt**
14 B f Sayf El Arab (USA)—Sterlonia **Mr E. Eldin and Mr M. H. Yong**
15 TAYLORS CASTLE, b f Castle Keep—How Audacious **Taylors of Soham Ltd**

TWO-YEAR-OLDS

16 COLNE STAR, br f 10/4 Primo Dominie—Broomstick Cottage (Habitat) **Mr C. A. Blackwell**
17 ELECTRIC KNIGHT, b c 16/3 Electric—Moonlight Fling (Imperial Fling (USA)) **Mr Kevin Moorcroft**
18 B f 12/2 Noalto—Fallen Angel (Quiet Fling)
19 HUBBERS FAVOURITE, ch f 29/3 Anfield—Printafoil (Habat) **Mr C. A. Blackwell**
20 HUSH KATIE, b f 18/3 Kind of Hush—Perlesse (Bold Lad (USA)) **Mr Kevin Moorcroft**
21 KEVINSLINE (IRE), b c 7/5 Montelimar (USA)—
Priceless Pin (Saint Crespin III) **Mr Kevin Moorcroft and Mr E. Eldin**
22 B f 4/5 Dunbeath (USA)—Little Fire (Bold Lad (IRE))
23 B f 25/3 Belfort (FR)—Manna Green (Bustino)
24 B c 24/3 Montelimar (USA)—Rathcoffey Daisy (Pampapaul) **Churchill Bloodstock Ltd**
25 SCOTS GREY LASSIE, gr f 28/4 Absalom—
Jose Collins (Singing Bede) **Mr Kevin Moorcroft and Mr T. Anderson**

Other Owners: Mr D. Moore.

Jockey (Flat): A Mackay (7-7).

Apprentices: C Pollard (7-9), P White (7-13).

198 MR M. W. ELLERBY, Pickering

Postal: **Westgate Carr Farm, Westgate Carr Road, Pickering, North Yorkshire.**
Phone: **(0751) 74092**

1 CONNAUGHT CARD, 8, b g Connaught—No Cards **Mr N. Hartas**
2 COTTAGE LEAS, 11, b m Ra (USA)—Border Cottage **Mr N. Hartas**
3 INDIAN SPIRIT, 4, ch g Mansingh (USA)—Funny-Do **Mr R. Grayson**
4 5, Ch g Kabour—Lady Meade
5 MISS SHERBROOKE, 6, b m Workboy—Miss Kadir **Mrs A. P. Hartas**
6 MULLED WINE, 9, b m Bivouac—Lady Mede **Mrs H. J. Ellerby**
7 TRAVEL HOME, 10, ch g Genuine—Marys Twiggy **Mrs H. J. Ellerby**

MR M. W. ELLERBY—continued

THREE-YEAR-OLDS

8 B g Mufrij—Cape Farewell **Mrs H. J. Ellerby**
9 **FRIARS HILL,** b g Doc Marten—Dancing Amber **Mrs A. P. Hartas**
10 B f Marching On—Lady Meade **Mrs H. J. Ellerby**
11 Br g Goldhills Pride—Tubes Care **Mr T. M. Harper**

TWO-YEAR-OLDS

12 **ALBERTS TREASURE,** b g 24/4 Sweet Monday—Dancing Amber (Broxted) **Mrs A. P. Hartas**
13 **ILIKEHIMDONTYOU,** b g 6/6 Sonnen Gold—Hopeful Gift (Bounteous) **Mr N. Hartas**
14 **OLIROAN,** gr g 11/4 Vin St Benet—Olibanum (Frankincense)
15 **WOODY EXPRESS,** b g 6/5 Today And Tomorrow—Dewberry (Bay Express)

Jockey (Flat): S Morris (8-0).

Jockey (NH): G Harker (10-0, w.a.).

Conditional: N Smith (9-7).

199 MR J. P. D. ELLIOTT, Alton

Postal: **Croft Farm, Paice Lane, Medstead, Alton, Hampshire, GU34 SPT.**
Phone: **ALTON (0420) 63733**

1 **APETA'S SUN,** 14, ch g Petersham—Sundowns **Mrs C. F. Elliott**
2 **BLANDELL BEAUTY,** 6, b m Mummy's Pet—Maria Luiza **Mrs K. J. Collard**
3 **CASTLE JESTER,** 5, gr g Castle Keep—Peters Pleasure **Mrs C. F. Elliott**
4 **DENROSS,** 9, b g Pauper—Teryak **Mr A. C. Ayres**
5 **GRAND EDOUARD,** 7, ch g Rare One—Lady Mobile **Mr Rowan Cole**
6 **HETTA LOUISE,** 5, gr m Comedy Star (USA)—Ruetina **Mr M. Mitchell**
7 **LEIA MECENE (FR),** 4, b g Gay Mecene (USA)—Dekeleia **Miss N. S. Henton**
8 **MILLADY,** 7, b m Chas Sawyer—Laydoney **Mr J. A. Brett**
9 **NEVER A PENNY,** 7, b g Nearly A Hand—Pilicina **Mr J. T. Mooney**
10 **NIGHT ATTACK,** 14, ch g Midsummer Night II—Surfacing **Mrs F. Burgess**
11 **PROA,** 5, gr g Kalaglow—Bedeni **Mr G. J. Symonds**
12 **SMART BROAD,** 5, b m Broadsword (USA)—Mary Mod **Mrs C. F. Elliott**

Other Owners: Mr Laurence B. Butters, Mr R. Dipre, Mr D. J. McDonald, Mr R. H. Neville.

Lady Rider: Mrs C F Elliott (9-7).

200 MR B. ELLISON, Malton

Postal: **12 Ryedale Close, Norton, Malton, North Yorkshire, YO17 9DQ.**
Phone: **(0653) 600158**

1 **AINSTY FOX,** 6, b g Majestic Current (USA)—Roba's Folly **Mr C. B. Burton**
2 **ARGELITH,** 4, b g Runnett—Miss Redmarshall **Miss Diane Hill**
3 **BANK JOB,** 5, ch g Don—Royal Performance **Mr Charles Castle**
4 **COMME CI COMME CA,** 4, ch g Buzzards Bay—Morstons Maid **Mrs S. J. Strangeway**
5 **CORBITT'S DIAMOND,** 6, b g Le Bavard (FR)—Diamonds Gift **Mr Charles Castle**
6 **CORBITTS MILITARIA,** 8, ch g Pauper—Gurtreeva **Mrs S. J. Strangeway**
7 **DARLING ELLEN,** 5, b m Leading Man—Queen Maeve **Mrs Linda Eddy**
8 **LOG CABIN,** 9, b g Connaught—Haida **Mr R. Harnett**
9 **LORD TAURO,** 7, b g Tachypous—Living Free **Mr Charles Castle**

MR B. ELLISON—continued

10 **MIRANDINHA,** 6, ch g Nicholas Bill—Matsui **Mr Michael Philip Jonas**
11 **QUEL ECLAT,** 5, b g Creetown—Coriace **Mr G. Dunne**
12 **ROCHES ROOST,** 7, b m Pauper—Okie **Mrs S. J. Strangeway**
13 **RYECROFT,** 12, b g Condorcet (FR)—Moonlight Story **Mrs S. J. Strangeway**

Other Owners: Mr D. Eddy, Mr J. Goodman, Mr R. Harnett, Mr K. Jonas.

Jockeys (NH): M Dywer, P Niven.

Conditional: D Byrne.

201 MR C. C. ELSEY, Lambourn

Postal: **Felstead Court Stables, Folly Road, Lambourn, Newbury, RG16 7QE.**
Phone: **LAMBOURN (0488) OFFICE 71242 HOME 72859 FAX 71859**

1 **ALL ELECTRIC,** 5, b g Electric—Miss Tweedie **Mr C. C. Elsey**
2 **BLOODLESS COUP,** 8, b g Free State—Freely Given **Mr T. C. Marshall**
3 **COURT CHARMER,** 4, b c Enchantment—Abercourt **Mr T. C. Marshall**
4 **DIAMONDING (USA),** 4, b c Diamond Shoal—Gwynn (USA) **Mr S. Hollis**
5 **DURZI,** 5, b g High Line—Sookera (USA) **White Horse Racing Ltd**
6 **EASTERN EMBER,** 4, br f Indian King (USA)—Pithead **Mr J. E. Marsden**
7 **ERICA MAY,** 8, b m Streak—Ulrica **Mrs B. Skinner**
8 **IBN ZAMAN (USA),** 4, b c Graustark—Wake Robin **Mr Christopher McHugh**
9 **OCCAMIST (USA),** 5, ch g Diesis—Solo Naskra (USA) **White Horse Racing Ltd**
10 **PANTOSCOPE,** 4, b f Lepanto (GER)—Surfacing **Mrs W. J. Elsey**
11 **POLAR VISION,** 4, b g Lyphard's Special (USA)—Arctic Drama **Mr R. Berenson**
12 **RAPPORTEUR (USA),** 4, b g His Majesty (USA)—Sweet Rapport (USA) **Mr Richard Alcock**
13 **ROSY DIAMOND,** 4, ch f Jalmood (USA)—Sun Approach **Mr C. C. Elsey**
14 **SALAR'S SPIRIT,** 4, ch g Salmon Leap (USA)—Indigine (USA) **Mrs Anastasia Keane**
15 **TOPPER TWO,** 4, b g High Top—Polly Packer **Mr S. Hollis**

THREE-YEAR-OLDS

16 **NICQUITA,** ch f Nicholas Bill—Jacquinta **White Horse Racing Ltd**
17 **REEF WIND,** b g Tumble Wind (USA)—Hollow Reef **Mr J. E. Marsden**
18 **SHAHRIZA,** br f Persian Bold—Amalee **Mr T. C. Marshall**

TWO-YEAR-OLDS

19 Ch c 20/3 Prince Sabo—Gentle Gael (Celtic Ash) **Mr T. C. Marshall**
20 Br c 21/3 Indian King (USA)—Pithead (High Top) **Christoff Stud**
21 B f 17/2 King of Spain—Razor Blade (Sharp Edge) **Mr T. O'Brien**

Other Owners: Mr W. Apperley, Mrs Pamela Cann, Mr J. R. Hall, Mr Michael P. Holmes, Mr A. R. V-A. Merrett, Mr R. J. Parish.

202 MR C. W. C. ELSEY, Malton

Postal: **Highfield House, Beverley Road, Malton, North Yorkshire, YO17 9PJ.**
Phone: **(0653) 693149 FAX (0653) 600260**

1 **BIRSTWITH (USA),** 5, gr h Valdez (USA)—La Chaumiere **Mr D. Aykroyd**
2 **CHORAL SUNDOWN,** 4, b f Night Shift (USA)—Choir **Mr D. Ford**
3 **HONDEGHEM,** 4, gr g Kalaglow—Kajetana (FR) **Mrs M. C. Butler**
4 **JOLEJESTER,** 5, b m Relkino—Mirthful **Mr Eric Barber**
5 **JUST MY BILL,** 4, ch g Nicholas Bill—Misnomer **Mr N. Hetherton**
6 **K-BRIGADE,** 5, b h Brigadier Gerard—Kajetana (FR) **Mrs M. C. Butler**

MR C. W. C. ELSEY—continued

7 **LINPAC WEST,** 4, b c Posse (USA)—North Page (FR) **Linpac Group Limited**
8 **MARIE ZEPHYR,** 6, b m Treboro (USA)—Thimothea (FR) **Mr C. W. C. Elsey**
9 **MR DORMOUSE,** 4, b g Comedy Star (USA)—Tea-Pot **Mrs M. A. Rae Smith**
10 **ONLY ROSES,** 4, b f Dominion—Ramsar **Mrs Noel Harwerth-Melhado**
11 **PHILJOY,** 4, b f Bustino—Formana **Mr C. D. Barber-Lomax**
12 **SAGE BRUSH,** 4, ch f Sagaro—Tentwort **Mr A. J. Massingberd-Mundy**
13 **SCANDAL (USA),** 4, b g Blood Royal (USA)—Affair **Mr D. Aykroyd**

THREE-YEAR-OLDS

14 **GET GOING,** b f Petorius—Regal Promise **Mr Russell Bradley**
15 **GOLDEN,** ch f Don—Roll Up **Mr Russell Bradley**
16 **HALA,** b f Persian Bold—True Respect (USA) **Mrs V. Leary**
17 **HEAD OF AFFAIRS (USA),** ch f Full Pocket (USA)—Affair **Mr D. Aykroyd**
18 **LINPAC LIGHT,** gr f Kalaglow—North Page (FR) **Linpac Group Limited**
19 **MASCULINE,** ch g High Line—Never A Lady **Mr Cyril Humphris**
20 **PALMY (USA),** b f Buckfinder (USA)—Pampas **Mr D. Aykroyd**
21 **PASSAGE HOME,** b f Blakeney—Maze **Mr D. Ford**
22 **RAGTIME,** b c Pas de Seul—Boldella **Mr H. Murray Wells**
23 **SURCOAT,** b c Bustino—Mullet **Mr A. D. G. Oldrey**

TWO-YEAR-OLDS

24 **BONNY'S GAME,** b f 2/4 Mummy's Game—Ribonny (FR) (Fast Hilarious (USA)) **Mrs M. C. Butler**
25 **KATEENA,** b f 27/2 Teenoso (USA)—Kajetana (FR) (Caro) **Mrs M. C. Butler**
26 **KHOJOHN,** ch c 29/2 Chief Singer—Pirate Lass (USA) (Cutlass (USA)) **Mr C. D. Barber-Lomax**
27 **LYNCARA,** b f 4/5 Lyphard's Special—Nicara (Rusticaro (FR)) **Mrs M. C. Butler**
28 **PENNINE STAR (IRE),** b f 29/2 Pennine Walk—Sterna Regina (Royal And Regal (USA)) **Lady Grinstead**
29 **PETONY (IRE),** b f 16/5 Petorius—Norme (FR) (Dark Tiger) **Mr C. W. C. Elsey**
30 **ZAFRA,** b f 11/3 Dunbeath (USA)—White's Ferry (Northfields (USA)) **D. Adams**
31 **ZEN HUTTE (IRE),** b f 11/1 Zino—Villasanta (Corvaro (USA)) **Mr C. W. C. Elsey**

Other Owners: Mr A. Ashton, Mr W. D. J. Ropner, Mr Eugene Ryan.

Apprentice: R Turner (7-7).

203 MR D. R. C. ELSWORTH, Whitsbury

Postal: **Whitsbury Manor Stables, Whitsbury, Fordingbridge, Hampshire.**
Phone: **ROCKBOURNE (072 53) HOME 220 OFFICE 528 TELEX 477965 FAX (072 53) 589**

1 **AFTERKELLY,** 5, b g Le Moss—Vamble **Mr D. R. C. Elsworth**
2 **AMELIANNE (FR),** 4, b f Bustino—My Candy **Mr H. J. Senn**
3 **BARNBROOK AGAIN,** 9, b g Nebbiolo—Single Line (USA) **Mr Mel Davies**
4 **CAVVIES CLOWN,** 10, b g Idiot's Delight—Cavallina **Mrs J. Ollivant**
5 **CHARDEN,** 4, b g Touching Wood (USA)—Fighting Lady **Mr Charles Drake**
6 **COMPELLING,** 8, b m Mandamus—Lunar Bug **Mrs P. A. McConnel**
7 **DESERT ORCHID,** 11, gr g Grey Mirage—Flower Child **Mr R. Burridge**
8 **DEVASTATION,** 6, br g Strong Gale—Lady Beg **Miss Juliet E. Reed**
9 **ELITE LEO,** 5, b g Longleat (USA)—Abielle **Miss Nicola Cooper**
10 **FANNY DILLON,** 6, b m Orchestra—Sunshot **Mrs B. M. McCourt**
11 **FERRYMAN,** 14, b g Forlorn River—La Miranda **Mr John Angus**
12 **FIELD CONQUEROR,** 9, b g Busted—Divine Thought **Miss A. O'Connell**
13 **FIT FOR FIRING (FR),** 6, b m In Fijar (USA)—Elizabeth Wales **Mr F. A. P. Chapman**
14 **FLIGHT HILL,** 6, br g Relkino—Firella **Mrs Richard Stanley**
15 **FLOYD,** 10, ch g Relko—Honey Palm **Mr M. V. Walsh**
16 **FOXBOROUGH LAD,** 11, ch g Some Hand—Liza Paul **Mr P. Lamb**
17 **GHOFAR,** 7, ch g Nicholas Bill—Royale Final **Sir Hugh Dundas**
18 **GIVUS A BUCK,** 7, br g Buckskin (FR)—My Pet **Mr K. Costello**
19 **HYMN OF HARLECH,** 7, b g Welsh Chanter—Church Bay **Mr Timothy K. Bullimore**

MR D. R. C. ELSWORTH—continued

20 **HYPNOSIS (USA)**, 11, ch g Unconscious (USA)—Puzzesca **Major G. D. Snell**
21 **IMPERIAL BRUSH**, 6, b g Sallust—Queen of The Brush **Mr Peter Pullon**
22 **JOHNS JOY**, 5, b g Martin John—Saybya **Mr R. Bastian**
23 **JUST MEASURE**, 5, b m Broadsword (USA)—Fair Measure **Sir Gordon Brunton**
24 **KARIWAK**, 9, b g Rhodomantade—Lucky Tango **Mr Alan Moralee**
25 **KHETA KING**, 7, b g Hittite Glory—Matala (FR) **Sir Gordon Brunton**
26 4, B g Alzao (USA)—Konigin Kate (GER) **Mr C. Smith**
27 4, B g Nearly A Hand—Lavilla **Mr C. Smith**
28 **LOCAL WHISPER**, 6, b g Deep Run—Dream Toi **Mrs Chris Harrington**
29 **LUGANA BEACH**, 4, br c Tumble Wind (USA)—Safe Haven **Mr Ray Richards**
30 **LYPHARD'S CANDY**, 4, ch c Lyphard's Wish (FR)—What A Candy (USA) **Mrs B. M. McCourt**
31 **MAGNUS PYM**, 5, b h Al Nasr (FR)—Full of Reason (USA) **Mr R. P. Standbridge**
32 **MAJOR INQUIRY (USA)**, 4, b c The Minstrel (CAN)—Hire A Brain (USA) **Mrs Tracy Stone-Brown**
33 **MALIBASTA**, 4, b f Auction Ring (USA)—Basta **Mrs Shirley Thornton**
34 **MALLYPHA (FR)**, 6, b g Bellypha—Marzala (USA) **Mr R. Firth**
35 **MELARKA**, 5, b m Dara Monarch—Melka **Trident Inns Ltd**
36 **MIGHTY FALCON**, 5, br g Comedy Star (USA)—Lettuce **Mr R. J. Tory**
37 **MINIM**, 7, b m Rymer—Court Circles **Mrs J. R. Crockett**
38 **MUSCLETON**, 5, gr g Le Moss—Countless **Mr M. M. Kingsley**
39 **MY KEY SILCA**, 5, ch g Deep Run—La Flamenca **Aldridge Racing Limited**
40 **ONEUPMANSHIP**, 5, ch g Derrylin—Lucky Janie **Mr J. R. Stott**
41 **OUT OF RANGE**, 7, b m Faraway Times (USA)—Namur **Mr R. Bastian**
42 **PONTENUOVO**, 5, b g Kafu—Black Gnat **Mr Walter Mariti**
43 **POWER TAKE OFF**, 4, b f Aragon—Law And Impulse **Mrs B. Skinner**
44 **POYLE GEORGE**, 5, br h Sharpo—Hithermoor Lass **Mr Cecil Wiggins**
45 **POYLE PRINCESS**, 4, br f Valiyar—Questa Notte **Mr Cecil Wiggins**
46 **REAL CLASS**, 7, b g Deep Run—Our Cherry **Mr J. N. G. Moreton**
47 **RIVERHEAD (USA)**, 6, b h Riverman (USA)—Tertiary (USA) **White Horse Racing Ltd**
48 **ROLL A DOLLAR**, 4, b g Spin of A Coin—Handy Dancer **Mr K. Higson**
49 **RUN BY**, 6, br g Runnett—Losenger **Mr H. P. L. Frost**
50 **RUSTIC COMEDY**, 5, br g Comedy Star (USA)—Cecilia Gallerani **White Horse Racing Ltd**
51 **SANTELLA PAL (USA)**, 9, b g Effervescing (USA)—Hempens Pal (USA) **Mrs H. Macfarlane**
52 **SEVEN OF DIAMONDS**, 5, b g Comedy Star (USA)—Priceless Gem **Mr T. J. Keeping**
53 **SILCA SUPREME**, 4, b g Chief Singer—Miss Silca Key **Aldridge Racing Limited**
54 5, B g The Parson—Somer's Castle **Mr P. Watson**
55 **SUMMER FASHION**, 5, b m Moorestyle—My Candy **Dr D. B. Davis**
56 **SUNNINGHILL CELTIC**, 6, ch g Celtic Cone—Aunt Livia **Mr J. C. Berry**
57 **TABELLINA**, 6, ch m Tina's Pet—Abielle **Mr S. A. Cooper**
58 **TAKE HEART**, 4, b f Electric—Hollow Heart **Mr C. J. Harper**
59 **TANGLED STRING**, 6, b g Idiot's Delight—Heartstring **Mrs J. Ollivant**
60 **TEMPERED POINT (USA)**, 4, br c Temperence Hill (USA)—Parissaul **Mrs LeRoy Hurlbert**
61 **THE ANTIPODEAN (NZ)**, 6, ch g Royal Plume—Della Dossi (NZ) **Mr Peter S. Winfield**
62 **URIZEN**, 5, ch g High Line—Off The Reel (USA) **K. Al-Said**
63 **WINGED MELODY**, 4, gr f Song—Fancy Flight (FR) **A. H. Warren (Coombe Farm) Limited**
64 **WINK GULLIVER**, 6, gr g Strong Gale—Pale Maid **Mrs T. M. Moriarty**
65 **WONDER BEE**, 7, ch g Grandiose—Honey Wonder **White Horse Racing Ltd**
66 **YOUNG FACT**, 5, b g Known Fact (USA)—Yelming **Mr J. Hoyer**

THREE-YEAR-OLDS

67 **ARDNAMURCHAN**, b f Ardross—Starlite Night (USA) **Mrs Anne Coughlan**
68 **BEAU ROU**, br c Rousillon (USA)—Beautiful Dawn (USA) **Mr P. G. Goulandris**
69 **BOLD MERIT**, b c Persian Bold—Basta **Wm Martin Group (Holdings) Ltd**
70 **BOOKCASE**, b c Siberian Express (USA)—Colourful (FR) **Miss R. Wakeford**
71 **CHIEFTESS**, br f Chief Singer—Gravad Lax **Mr J. C. Smith**
72 **COME ON ROSI**, b f Valiyar—Victory Kingdom (CAN) **Mr Wafic Said**
73 **DAUNTESS**, ch f Formidable (USA)—Cantico **Mr J. C. Smith**
74 **DEAD CERTAIN**, b f Absalom—Sirnelta (FR) **Commander G. G. Marten**
75 **DEADLOCK**, ch c The Minstrel (CAN)—Roses To Rachel **Mr Ray Richards**
76 **DESERT WARBLER (USA)**, ch c The Minstrel (CAN)—Thats The Reason (USA) **Anglo Thoroughbred Racing**
77 **EVERDENE**, b f Bustino—Deed **Mr S. P. Tindall**

ALL WEATHER SURFACE ?

IN ANY WEATHER, top trainers nationwide continue to rely on Dormit's tried and tested surfaces for all year round use.

Dormit's natural, graded woodfibre has, and will continue to have, all the cost effective answers

Take Dormit's advice
Contact us on:

Tel 0285 860781
Fax 0285 861033

or write to:

Dormit Riding Surfaces
Lakeside Sawmills
Broadway Lane
South Cerney
Cirencester, Glos. GL7 5UH

Dormit

MR D. R. C. ELSWORTH—continued

78 **FENOUILLE**, b g Ile de Bourbon (USA)—Foreseen **Mrs P. G. Goulandris**
79 **HEJAZ**, b g Electric—Daisy Warwick (USA) **Mr R. J. McCreery**
80 **IN THE GROOVE**, b f Night Shift (USA)—Pine Ridge **Mr Brian Cooper**
81 **KIBREET**, ch c Try My Best (USA)—Princess Pageant **K. Al-Said**
82 **MARYLAND WILLIE**, b c Master Willie—Maryland Cookie (USA) **K. Al-Said**
83 **MOVING FORCE**, b g Muscatite—Saint Simbir **Mr H. P. L. Frost**
84 **OH SO RISKY**, b c Kris—Expediency (USA) **The Oh So Risky Syndicate**
85 **POLLY MULDOWNEY**, ch f Precocious—Follow The Stars **Mrs T. M. Moriarty**
86 **POWERSURGE**, b c Electric—Ladysave **Mrs H. Ryan Price**
87 **PREOBLAKENSKY**, b c Blakeney—Preobrajenska **Mr W. J. Gredley**
88 **SHAFFIC (FR)**, b c Auction Ring (USA)—Tavella (FR) **Mr Ray Richards**
89 **SHEERWIND**, b c Shernazar—Windy Cheyenne (USA) **Anglo Thoroughbred Racing**
90 **SILCA AN' KEY**, b c Commanche Run—Miss Silca Key **Aldridge Racing Limited**
91 **SLICK CHERRY**, b f Noalto—Slick Chick **Mr Harry Redknapp**
92 **SPIRIT OF INDIA**, b f Indian King (USA)—Sacred Mountain **Miss E. Drax**
93 **SUNSET AND VINE**, gr g Norwick (USA)—Starky's Pet **Sunset & Vine Plc**
94 **TAULELA**, b f Taufan (USA)—Balela **Mrs A. M. Upsdell**
95 **VICTORIA PRINCESS**, b f King of Spain—Renira **Mr N. T. Chappell**

TWO-YEAR-OLDS

96 **AXIAPREPIS**, ch c 4/5 Formidable (USA)—Nicholas Grey (Track Spare) **Mr P. G. Goulandris**
97 B f 29/2 Ahonoora—Ballys Princess (Salvo) **Mr W. Gerhauser**
98 **BOSA**, ch f 3/3 Kris—Tralthee (USA) (Tromos) **Sheikh Ahmed Al Maktoum**
99 Ch f 27/2 The Noble Player—Carolynchristensen (Sweet Revenge) **Doublet Ltd**
100 B f 9/4 Alzao (USA)—Chrism (Baptism) **Mr Wafic Said**
101 Ch c 26/2 Ahonoora—Crimson Royale (High Line) **Mr Wafic Said**
102 **ENGLISH RAJ (USA)**, ch c Raja Baba (USA)—Salem Ho (USA) (Salem (USA)) **Major H. S. Cayzer**
103 **FAMOUS DANCER**, b c 29/3 Top Ville—Dancing Place (FR) (Green Dancer (USA)) **Mr A. R. Thompson**
104 Ch f 4/5 Lyphard's Special—Ferry Lane (Dom Racine (FR)) **Wm Martin Group (Holdings) Ltd**
105 Ch c 26/4 Red Sunset—Fleur-de-Luce (Tumble Wind (USA)) **Mr J. Stafford**
106 Ch f 12/5 Fast Topaze (USA)—Forever Mary (Red Alert) **Mr M. S. Saunders**
107 B f 24/5 Mashhor Dancer (USA)—Gravad Lax (Home Guard (USA)) **Mr J. C. Smith**
108 B f 25/5 Chief Singer—In The Shade (Bustino) **Mr C. J. Harper**
109 B f 2/6 Bustino—Its A Romp (Hotfoot) **Mr C. J. Harper**
110 Ch c 17/3 Ahonoora—Joshua's Daughter (Joshua) **Mr S. Coughlan**
111 **LOVE TALK**, br f 29/3 Hotfoot—Sirnelta (FR) (Sir Tor) **Mr Ray Richards**
112 **MARINE SOCIETY**, b c 2/2 Petoski—Miranda Julia (Julio Mariner) **J. Karageorgis**
113 B f 21/2 Simply Great (FR)—Mexican Two Step (Gay Fandango (USA)) **Mrs C. Argeband**
114 **MIGHTY NOBLE**, b c 4/4 Shirley Heights—Expediency (USA) (Vaguely Noble) **Mr P. Watson**
115 Ch c 14/3 Caerleon (USA)—Miss Silca Key (Welsh Saint) **Aldridge Racing Limited**
116 B f Ziggy's Boy (USA)—Our Feast (Banquet Table (USA)) **Mr D. R. C. Elsworth**
117 B f 19/2 Sharpo—Pennies To Pounds (Ile de Bourbon (USA)) **Mr J. C. Smith**
118 **PENNY DOUBLE (IRE)**, ch f 15/3 Double Schwartz—Needlewoman (Moorestyle) **Mr H. J. Senn**
119 **PICODEAN BOY (IRE)**, b c 1/4 Krayyan—Asta (Captain's Gig (USA)) **B. Peters, Tulsa (Holdings) Ltd**
120 **PUESTO DEL SOL (IRE)**, b c 21/3 Red Sunset—Mount Isa (Miami Springs) **Mrs J. R. Mullion**
121 Br c Phone Trick (USA)—Quick Nurse (USA) (Dr Fager) **J. Karageorgis**
122 B c Cormorant (USA)—Raise The Bridge (USA) (Raise A Cup (USA)) **Mr D. R. C. Elsworth**
123 Ch f 14/3 Mummy's Game—Renira (Relkino) **Mr D. R. C. Elsworth**
124 **RIDGEWAY WALK (IRE)**, ch c 7/4 Godswalk (USA)—Late Date (Goldhill) **B. Peters, Tulsa (Holdings) Ltd**
125 Br c 29/4 Precocious—Rosalka (ITY) (Relko) **Mrs H. P. Ralton**
126 **SIANEMA**, b f 29/4 Persian Bold—Seriema (Petingo) **Mr P. G. Goulandris**
127 **SILVER BRAID (USA)**, ch f Miswaki (USA)—Chalice of Silver (USA) (Graustark) **Mr L. H. J. Ward**
128 Br c 25/1 Simply Great (FR)—Silver Mantle (Bustino) **Mr D. R. C. Elsworth**
129 **SILVER MOOD**, gr f 28/3 Jalmood (USA)—Silver Tips (High Top) **Mr Ray Richards**
130 **SKI DANCER**, b c 1/5 Dancing Brave (USA)—
Ski Sailing (USA) (Royal Ski (USA)) **Sheikh Ahmed Al Maktoum**
131 B c 3/5 Mashhor Dancer (USA)—Solo Vacation (Pas de Seul) **Mr J. C. Smith**
132 **STANE STREET (IRE)**, b f 29/3 Gorytus (USA)—Tumble Ria (Tumble Wind (USA)) **Mr M. Sugden**
133 B c 10/3 King of Clubs—Statira (Skymaster) **Mr M. Slade**
134 B c 20/2 Local Suitor (USA)—Strike It Rich (FR) (Rheingold) **Mr Wafic Said**

MR D. R. C. ELSWORTH—continued

135 SUPER SECRET, b c Super Concorde (USA)—Embroglio (USA) **Mr Ray Richards**
136 Br c Golden Act (USA)—Taipan's Lady (USA) (Bold Hour) **J. Karageorgis**
137 TUDOREALM (USA), b f Palace Music (USA)—Lock's Dream (USA) (Youth (USA)) **Mr L. H. J. Ward**
138 Ch c 9/3 Hatim (USA)—Tuna (Silver Shark) **Mr P. Craven**
139 WICKED THINGS (FR), b c Vayrann—Daffodil Walk (Furry Glen) **Mr Ray Richards**
140 WILD AND LOOSE, b c 9/3 Precocious—Regain (Relko) **Mr Ray Richards**
141 B c 3/3 Petorius—Wollow Princess (Wollow) **Mr I. Sandell**

Other Owners: Adept (80) Ltd, Mr N. B. Attenborough, Mr T. Britland, Mr Bill Brown, Mr S. Bullimore, Mr James Burridge, Mrs M. S. Charrington, Mrs P. V. Close, Mr Peter Coe, Mr P. G. J. Cooper, Mr D. F. Cowley, Mr T. M. Dawson, Mr S . Doherty, Mr R. C. Dollar, Mr G. F. Dursley, Mr Geoffrey C. Greenwood, Miss C. A. Haw, Mr Sid Hooper, Mr W. Hoyer, Mr Anthony Hunt, Mr Jack Joseph, Mr T. J. Keeping, Mr J. A. Lewis, Mr T. F. McGee, Mr Denis O'Dell, Mr C. O'Grady, Mrs S. O'R iordan, Mr R. G. Patton, Mr Ray Penney, Mr R. P. Plewka, Mr David F. Powell, Mr J. Powell, Mrs E. W. Richards, Miss Kate Richards, Mr M. A. Richards, Mr T. J. Richards, Mr John Rumble, Lt-Col Sir James Scott, Lady Scott, Lord Shaftesbury, Mr s P. R. Sheppard, Mr Derek Simester, Mr Peter M. Stevens, Mr C. A. Sutton, Mr Don Taffner, Mr D. Thompson, Mrs Hazel Tiler, Mrs V. A. Tory, Mr P. Trant, Mrs Kathleen Twomey, Mr P. A. Tylor, Mr David R. Watson, Mr F. W. Watson, Mrs C. L. Wilk , Mr A. Wilkinson, Mrs R. Willis, Mr R. V. Wright.

Jockeys (Flat): D Brown (7-7), S Cauthen (8-6, w.a.), Pat Eddery (8-4, w.a.).

Jockeys (NH): R Arnott (10-0), G Bradley, B Powell.

Apprentice: J Hunter (7-0).

Conditional: P Holley (9-7), A McCabe (9-7).

Amateur: Mr D Townsend (10-3).

204 MR G. P. ENRIGHT, Lewes

Postal: **The Oaks, Old Lewes Racecourse, Lewes, East Sussex, BN7 1UR.**
Phone: **LEWES (0273) 479183**

1 **ALL GOLD BOY,** 5, ch g Golden Dipper—Golden Columbine **Mr J. M. Boodle**
2 **BACKPACKER,** 10, b g New Brig—Preston Deal **Mr Chris Wall**
3 **BAD HABITS,** 10, b g Habat—Ribofleur **Mrs M. Enright**
4 **BEST SMILE (USA),** 7, ch g Blushing Groom (FR)—Hartebeest (USA) **Mrs C. I. A. Matheson**
5 **DUTCH RHYMES,** 5, b m Rymer—Dutch Princess **Mr Leonard Fuller**
6 **ENBORNE LAD,** 6, gr g Celtic Cone—Blue Delphinium **Mr D. L. Seward**
7 **FEARLESS FIGHTER,** 5, b g Formidable (USA)—Wild Asset **Mr T. Corcoran**
8 **GOLDEN FOX,** 8, b g Tyrnavos—Red Spider **Mr Leonard Fuller**
9 **INDIAN BABA,** 5, b g Indian King (USA)—Norfolk Bonnet **Mr E. Benfield**
10 **MARTIAL COMMANDER (USA),** 10, br g Bold Commander (USA)—Mijanou **Mr G. P. Enright**
11 **PARSONIFY,** 5, b g The Parson—Kosey Kitchen **Mr Mel Halstead**
12 **REEDLING (USA),** 5, b g Riverman (USA)—Mary Biz (USA) **Mr D. J. Butler**
13 **RISLAN (USA),** 4, b c Diesis—Sanctum Sanctorum (USA) **Mrs Penny Hamilton**
14 **ROYAL BRUSH,** 5, b m King of Spain—Broomstick Corner (USA) **Mr Chris Wall**
15 **SHOT AND SHELL (USA),** 5, b g Damascus (USA)—Leap Lively (USA) **Mr Gerry Ryan**
16 **SPEEDY BOY,** 8, ch g Tachypous—Grandpa's Legacy **Mr Leonard Fuller**
17 **STEEL CYGNET,** 7, gr g Taufan (USA)—Swan Girl **Mr P. Hall**

MR G. P. ENRIGHT—continued

Other Owners: Mrs Catherine Boodle, Mrs C. Butler, Mr Peter Hopkins, Mrs T. H. Johnson, Mr R. F. H. Vanderpump.

Jockey (NH): M Perrett (10-0).

Conditional: R W Moore (9-7).

Lady Rider: Mrs M Enright (8-0).

205 MR J. ETHERINGTON, Malton

Postal: **Wold House, Langton Road, Norton, Malton, North Yorkshire, YO17 9QG.**
Phone: **MALTON (0653) 692842**

1 **COME ON CHASE ME,** 6, ch g Sharpo—Dragonist **Duncan Norvelle**
2 **DRAMATIC EVENT,** 5, br g Kind of Hush—Welsh Jane **G. Butchers**
3 **ECONOMY RUN,** 4, b g Sweet Monday—Mylotta **G. Winstanley**
4 **PATTIE'S GREY,** 4, gr f Valiyar—Katysue **Lady Matthews**
5 **SUPERBRAVE,** 4, b c Superlative—Tribal Feast **Mrs P. L. Yong**
6 **THATS THE ONE,** 4, br c Known Fact (USA)—Kesarini (USA) **Hon I. V. Matthews**
7 **WHIPPER IN,** 6, b h Bay Express—Whip Finish **Mr G. Cafearo**

THREE-YEAR-OLDS

8 **AMOOD POINT,** ch c Jalmood (USA)—Nice Point **Mrs E. W. Ambrose**
9 **BECOCIOUS,** b c Precocious—Baheejah **Mr T. A. Stephenson**
10 **BIDING TIMES,** gr f Bellypha—Biding **Lord Matthews**
11 **BRAVE MUSCATEER,** ch c Muscatite—Amazing Gretts **Mr R. L. Bedding**
12 **BURR TEAK,** br g Sonnen Gold—Posy of Simethio VII **Miss A. Sykes**
13 **DIAMOND SPRITE (USA),** b c Diamond Prospect (USA)—Implicit **Mr T. A. Stephenson**
14 **EASTFIELD BOY,** br g Sayf El Arab (USA)—Dog's Bay **Mr E. E. Collingwood**
15 **FINAL ACE,** ch c Sharpo—Palmella (USA) **Mr S. Fustok**
16 **MAGIC BULLET,** b f Northern Baby (CAN)—Probation (USA) **Mr S. Fustok**
17 **MANALAPAN,** b f Superlative—Hsian **Mr S. Fustok**
18 **MYSTIC BID,** br c Auction Ring (USA)—Relic Spirit **Mr M. O'Horan**
19 **NICE DAY,** br f Shirley Heights—Keyboard **Mr S. Fustok**
20 **REGAL NORTH,** b c Regalberto (USA)—Nell of The North (USA) **Mr N. S. Yong**
21 Gr f Kalaglow—Six Ashes **G. Haywood**
22 **STAINLESS STEVEN,** ch g Balliol—Chebs Honor **P. Simmonite**
23 **SUPERCHIP,** ch g Superlative—Crockfords Green **Mrs P. L. Yong**
24 **TRISTIORUM,** ch g Crofthall—Annie-Jo **Mr J. R. Rowbottom**

TWO-YEAR-OLDS

25 Br f 12/3 Green Ruby (USA)—Avon Royale (Remainder) **Miss M. Gledhill**
26 Br c Proud Appeal (USA)—Bold Mermaid (USA) (Sea Bird II) **Triangle Thoroughbreds Ltd**
27 **CRAZY HORSE DANCER (USA),** b c Barachois (USA)—Why Pass (USA) (Pass (USA)) **D. Wosskow**
28 **DANCING TUDOR,** b c 8/3 Absalom—String of Beads (Ile de Bourbon (USA)) **W. N. Lumley**
29 **FLIP 'N GLOW (USA),** gr f Silver Buck (USA)—Flip For Luck (USA) (Flip Sal (USA)) **Triangle Thoroughbreds Ltd**
30 **FOR PETE'S SAKE,** br f 17/5 Kirchner—Bunnycraft (The Go-Between) **P. Heap**
31 Ch f Lyphard's Wish (USA)—Green Lass (Green God) **Triangle Thoroughbreds Ltd**
32 **IMITATE (IRE),** b f 27/2 Tate Gallery (USA)—Exemplary (Sovereign Lord) **Lord Matthews**
33 **IVY COTTAGE,** br f 24/5 Damister (USA)—Debutina Park (Averof) **Mrs A. Liversidge**
34 **LOSMANAR,** b c 1/4 Los Santos (FR)—Mana (GER) (Windwurf (GER)) **Hon I. V. Matthews**
35 Gr f 6/4 Kalaglow—Moberry (Mossberry) **G. Haywood**
36 **PRINCESS NELL,** b f 21/4 Damister (USA)—Nell of The North (USA) (Canadian Gil (CAN)) **Mr N. S. Yong**
37 B c 24/3 Night Shift (USA)—Rapidus (Sharpen Up) **D. Wosskow**

MR J. ETHERINGTON—continued

38 Gr c 26/2 Kalaglow—Regal Flutter (USA) (Beldale Flutter (USA)) **D. Wosskow**
39 B c Barachois (USA)—Same Tyme (Delaware Chief) **Triangle Thoroughbreds Ltd**
40 **SAM SPADE,** b c 26/3 Balliol—Song Book (Saintly Song) **S. Demanuelle**
41 **SATALITE BOY,** ch c 2/5 Blazing Saddles (AUS)—Persiandale (Persian Bold) **W. Turner**
42 B f Explodent (USA)—Sometimes Perfect (USA) (Bold Bidder) **D. Wosskow**
43 **SUNNYSIDE ROCK (IRE),** ch c 9/5 Ballad Rock—Havana Moon (Ela-Mana-Mou) **S. J. Durkin**
44 **TARNSIDE BANDIT (IRE),** b c 3/5 Alzao (USA)—Really (Sovereign Gleam) **Miss A. Gill**
45 **WOLD GUEST (IRE),** b c 10/3 Kafu—Opera Guest (Be My Guest (USA)) **R. Watkins**

Other Owners: Mr W. L. Armitage, J. Etherington, Mr B. Freer, Mr M. McDonnell, D. J. Parsons, Mrs C. M. Rowbottom.

Apprentices: G Forster (8-0), G Rollinson (8-0).

Amateur: Mr T Etherington (10-0).

206 MR T. J. ETHERINGTON, Dorking

Postal: **Henfold House Cottage, Henfold Lane, Beare Green, Dorking, RH5 4RW.**
Phone: **NEWDIGATE (0306) 77529**

1 **BAYRAM (FR),** 8, br g Blakeney—Zarin (GER) **Mr A. T. A. Wates**
2 **BELLASIS,** 9, b g Over The River (FR)—Sweet Coronation **Mr Paul C. R. Wates**
3 **BOLD SINGER,** 4, b g Ballad Rock—Grande Maison **Mr K. Higson**
4 **CRANCHETER,** 6, br h Red Sunset—French Cracker **Mr A. T. A. Wates**
5 **DRAMATIC EVENT,** 5, br g Kind of Hush—Welsh Jane **Mr Guy Butchers**
6 **ETHIOPIAN KING,** 7, ch g Avocat—Meneleck Queen **Mr A. T. A. Wates**
7 **GOOD TONIC,** 7, b g Goldhill—Quinine's Girl **Lady Wates**
8 **PLENTY OF CHAT,** 8, b g Le Bavard (FR)—Bartina **Mr A. T. A. Wates**
9 **PRAIRIE STORM,** 6, br g Strong Gale—Meadow Wings **Mr A. T. A. Wates and Mrs H. D. McKinnon**
10 **RADWHAW,** 9, gr g Abwah—Darwin Tulip **Mr R. L. Bedding**
11 **REFFOLDS,** 7, ch g Green Shoon—Penthouse Pet **Mr David Wates**
12 **REPEAT THE DOSE,** 5, b g Abednego—Bahia de Palma **Mr A. T. A. Wates**
13 4, B g Deep Run—Vamble **Mr A. T. A. Wates**

Other Owners: B. Freer, T. A. Stephenson.

Jockeys (NH): E Murphy (10-0, w.a.), R Rowe (10-2, w.a.).

Conditional: R Martin (10-0).

207 MR A. EUBANK, Cockermouth

Postal: **Millstone Moor, Cockermouth, Cumbria, CA13 0QA.**
Phone: **(0900) 823027**

1 **ANOTHER GHOST,** 6, ro g Grey Ghost—Bronze Chariot **Mrs A. Eubank**
2 **HIGHMOOR LADY,** 6, ch m Slim Jim—Highmoor Lass **Mr A. Eubank**
3 **TRUELY ROYAL,** 6, b g Royal Fountain—True Friend **Mr A. Eubank**

208 MR J. M. P. EUSTACE, Newmarket

Postal: **Park Lodge Stables, Park Lane, Newmarket, Suffolk, CB8 8AX.**
Phone: **TEL (0638) 664277 FAX (0638) 664156**

1 **CHECKPOINT CHARLIE,** 5, b g Artaius (USA)—Clouded Issue **Mr J. M. P. Eustace**
2 **MOON REEF,** 4, ch f Main Reef—Malmsey **Park Lodge Racing Partners**

THREE-YEAR-OLDS

3 **NUJOOM (USA),** b f Halo (USA)—Bird of Dawning (USA) **Mr J. R. Ali**
4 **SHARP INVITE,** ch f Sharpo—Invitation **Mr Matthew Sharkey**
5 **WAKE UP,** ch c Night Shift (USA)—Astonishing **Park Lane Racing**

TWO-YEAR-OLDS

6 **BECKONING,** b c 27/4 Bellypha—Courtesy Call (Northfields (USA)) **Milton Park Partnership**
7 **BLUE CARNATION,** gr f 16/5 Carwhite—Eyry (Falcon) **Mrs J. M. Birchenough**
8 **BRIGGSMAID,** b f 28/2 Elegant Air—Merry Yarn (Aggressor) **Mr F. W. Briggs**
9 B f 27/4 Chief Singer—Cantico (Green Dancer (USA)) **Mr J. C. Smith**
10 **COLONIAL SPIRIT,** b c 5/3 Primo Dominie—Persian Case (Upper Case (USA)) **Mr Francis Lui**
11 **FALCON'S DOMAIN (IRE),** b c 21/3 Hegemony—Cova Kestrel (Ovac (ITY)) **Mr R. Carstairs**
12 **GREAT AFFAIR,** ch c 22/4 Mummy's Game—Pretty Great (Great Nephew) **G. B. Turnbull Ltd**
13 **HARBOUR KNIGHT (IRE),** b c 11/1 Caerleon (USA)—So Directed (Homing) **Mr Francis Lui**
14 Ch c 27/1 Hawaii—Hawaiian Luau (USA) (State Dinner (USA)) **Mr Russell B. Jones Jr**
15 B f 16/4 Nemerino (USA)—Manor Farm Toots (Royalty) **Mr C. Franks**
16 **PENNY MINT,** ch f 27/1 Mummy's Game—School Road (Great Nephew) **Mr A. G. Norman-Thorpe**
17 **TAPATCH (IRE),** b c 7/2 Thatching—Knees Up (USA) (Dancing Champ (USA)) **The Fando Partnership**
18 B c 9/3 Gregorian (USA)—Vainly Noble (USA) (Vaguely Noble) **Mr Russell B. Jones Jr**
19 **VELVET ASITY,** ch f 25/4 Superlative—The Firebird (Busted) **The Hon Mrs T. R. H. Eustace**

Other Owners: Mr D. Batten, Miss D. Birtwhistle, Mr N. Elliott, Major T. R. H. Eustace, Mr N. Fyler, Mr J. George, Sir Stephen Hastings, Mr J. Honeywood, Mr R. Jack, Mrs J. Jarvis, Captain Ryan Jarvis, Mrs R. Leach, Mrs Pamela Matthews, Mr J. McKeever, Mr A. M. Mitchell, Mrs A. P. Murray, Mr R. Purkis, Mr J. Ratcliffe, Miss J. Rees, Lady Sells, Mr R. St. Aubyn, Mrs A. Sutcliffe, Mr J. Tomalin, Mr A. Watson, Mr D. Wiseman.

Apprentice: J Vale (8-0).

209 MRS J. EVANS, Llanymynech

Postal: **The Paddocks, Sarnau, Llanmynech, Powys, Wales, SW22 6QL.**
Phone: **GUILSFIELD (093 875) 316**

1 **BILL NORMAL,** 5, ch g Ballyglitter—Petite Piece **Mr G. Hutton**
2 **BRIGAND GIRL,** 8, b m New Brig—Tillside **Mr C. B. McNeil**
3 **BROTHER IN ARMS,** 9, b g Balgaddy—Sun Spray **Mr T. Hopkins**
4 **CARTREF,** 4, b f Homing—Kentucky **Mr T. Hopkins**
5 **CRAIG-Y-BWGAN,** 4, b g Hubble Bubble—Boncath **Mr T. Hopkins**
6 **IDREASE,** 6, b g Dunphy—Moonscape **Mr T. Hopkins**
7 **JESSIE ELLIS,** 7, ch m Condorcet (FR)—Gay Friend **Mr R. Pitchford**
8 **KATHYS GIRL,** 10, b m Hasty Word—Stretton Queen **Mrs Jill Evans**
9 **LADY PAY,** 4, b f Hubble Bubble—Princess Pay **Mr D. T. Edwards**
10 **MORVERN,** 11, b g Thatch (USA)—Sleat **Mr T. B. Evans**
11 **MY PRAYER,** 6, ch m Buckskin (FR)—Yellow Idol **Mrs Jill Evans**
12 **RAGENS BOY,** 9, b g Rajen—Princess Pay **Mr D. T. Edwards**

Other Owners: Mr L. J. Barratt, Mr D. Chesworth, Mr J. Rothwell.

210 MR P. D. EVANS, Welshpool

Postal: **Long Mountain Farm, Leighton, Welshpool, Powys, Wales, SY21 8JB.**
Phone: **(093874) 288**

1 **ABBERLEY,** 5, br m Idiot's Delight—Polarita **Mrs Claire Massey**
2 **DONFIL,** 5, ch g Don—Philanderess **Mr K. Halliwell**
3 **FINGEST,** 7, b g Imperial Fling (USA)—Derry Daughter **Mr Roy Ashford**
4 **LOVE ON THE ROCKS,** 5, b m Martinmas—Love Is Blind (USA) **Mr Roy Ashford**
5 **MISS DELILAH,** 4, b f Humdoleila—Pem Pem **Mrs E. A. Davies**
6 **PEACONPALA,** 5, br m Kampala—Kilpeacon **Mr Roy Ashford**
7 **RARE WORDS,** 5, b g Sandhurst Prince—Julie Be Quick (USA) **Mr M. J. Clarke**
8 **RED COCKADE,** 4, ch g Royal Blend—Miss Plumes **Mr G. Guest**
9 **ROUGE ROI,** 5, b g Hays—Restless Morn **Mr Roy Ashford**
10 **SEQUESTRATOR,** 7, b g African Sky—Miss Redmarshall **Mr A. Cooke**
11 **WHAT A BEWT,** 7, b g Anax—Mantavella **Mrs D. Kellner**

THREE-YEAR-OLDS

12 **MISS KERRY,** ch f Royal Blend—Miss Plumes **Mr G. Guest**

TWO-YEAR-OLDS

13 **CLARRY'S BOY,** b g 5/7 Starch Reduced—Miss Plumes (Prince de Galles) **Mr G. Guest**

Other Owners: Mr G. C. Chipman, Mrs Jenny Havenhand, Mr Guy Massey, Mr R. Morris.

Jockey (NH): T Wall (10-0, w.a.).

211 MR T. FAIRHURST, Middleham

Postal: **Glasgow House, Middleham, Leyburn, North Yorkshire.**
Phone: **WENSLEYDALE (0969) 23362**

1 **BARRYS GAMBLE,** 4, gr c Nishapour (FR)—Scoby Lass **North Cheshire Trading & Storage Ltd**
2 **DALESIDE LADYBIRD,** 4, b f Tolomeo—Dawn Redwood **Daleside Nurseries Ltd**
3 **GODOUNOV,** 7, b g Godswalk (USA)—Grilse Run **Miss Diane Sanderson**
4 **HENRY WILL,** 6, b g Nicholas Bill—Silver Cygnet **Mr George H. Leggott**
5 **HOLDENBY,** 5, b h Henbit (USA)—Isadora Duncan **Mr D. Bowker**
6 **MARCHING STAR,** 4, ch f Marching On—Elegant Star **Mr T. Fairhurst**
7 **PANSONG,** 4, b c Absalom—Sea Chant **Mr C. D. Barber-Lomax**
8 **PHOTINIA,** 5, b g Tender King—Permutation **Mr W. F. Perratt**
9 **QUEENS MAN,** 8, ch g Remainder Man—Dior Queen **Mrs Annette Stenner**
10 **WOOD SPOILER,** 9, br g Blue And Grey—Souriciere **Mr T. Fairhurst**

THREE-YEAR-OLDS

11 **BRISAS,** ch c Vaigly Great—Legal Sound **Mr Brian Cann**
12 **GREAT SONG,** ch f Vaigly Great—Suzannah's Song **Mr R. K. Franklin**
13 **HARTLEY,** gr g Final Straw—She Who Dares **Mr J. A. Turney**
14 **HIGH WATER,** ch g High Line—Sextant **Mr C. D. Barber-Lomax**
15 **HOT PERFORMER,** ch f Hotfoot—Show Business
16 **JUST IMAGINE,** b f Head For Heights—Lochboisdale **Mr T. Fairhurst**
17 **LIBERTO,** b c Seymour Hicks (FR)—Countess Decima (USA) **Mr M. J. Rozenbroek**
18 **MARGS GIRL,** b f Claude Monet (USA)—Aquarian Star **Mr G. Stephenson**
19 **PHILSTAY,** b f Bustino—Magelka **Mr C. D. Barber-Lomax**
20 **SUGAR THE PILL,** b c Blue Cashmere—Maple Syrup **Mrs D. E. Kain**
21 **TUNEFUL CHARTER,** gr g Song—Martin-Lavell Star **Mr J. P. Treasure**

TWO-YEAR-OLDS

22 **CHEVELEY CHIEF,** ch c 25/2 Chief Singer—Hawks Nest (Moulton) **C. H. Newton Jnr Ltd**
23 **CROFT PARK,** b c 26/3 Elegant Air—Session (Reform) **J. A. Turney**
24 **DALESIDE,** gr c 22/4 Full Out (USA)—All Regal (Run The Gantlet (USA)) **Daleside Nurseries Ltd**
25 **FLASS VALE,** br c 21/3 Final Straw—Emblazon (Wolver Hollow) **C. H. Newton Jnr Ltd**

MR T. FAIRHURST—continued

26 **FRIENDLY SONG,** ch f 23/5 Song—Friendly Jester (Be Friendly) **T. Fairhurst**
27 **MAGDALENE (IRE),** br f 26/4 Runnett—Grattan Princess (Tumble Wind (USA)) **C. H. Newton Jnr Ltd**
28 **MAGGIES LAD,** b c 24/4 Red Johnnie—Busted Love (Busted) **B. Brownsword**
29 **PATSY'S PET,** b f 1/4 Tina's Pet—Emperor Star (King Emperor (USA)) **M. J. Rozenbroek**
30 **PELAW,** b c 20/3 Persian Bold—No Restraint (Habitat) **C. H. Newton Jnr Ltd**
31 **PRETTY MUCH,** gr f 23/4 Absalom—Pakpao (Mansingh (USA)) **Mrs M. I. Morley and C. D. Barber Lomax**

Other Owners: Mr J. G. Brearley, Mr J. Jackson, Mr J. A. Leach, Mrs Margaret G. Robson, Mr R. Sanderson, Mr D. W. Young.

Jockey (NH): J Fanning (9-0).

Apprentices: K Brownsword (7-10), S G Smith (7-7).

Lady Rider: Miss Judy Fairhurst (9-10).

212 MR J. R. FANSHAWE, Newmarket

Postal: **Pegasus Stables, Snailwell Road, Newmarket, Suffolk, CB8 7DJ.**
Phone: **(0638) 664525 FAX (0638) 664523 TELEX 817821 JRFANS G**

1 **ORIGINAL BID (USA),** 4, ch f Topsider (USA)—No Duplicate (USA) **Mr H. R. Mould**
2 **PETRULLO,** 5, b h Electric—My Therape **Mr C. A. Webster**

THREE-YEAR-OLDS

3 **ALL WELCOME,** b c Be My Guest (USA)—Pepi Image (USA) **Sheikh Mohammed**
4 **BLACK SAPPHIRE,** ch g Lomond (USA)—Star of India **Sheikh Mohammed**
5 **BLIND SHOT,** b c Kris—Shuteye **Sheikh Mohammed**
6 **BURAN (USA),** ch f Blushing Groom (FR)—Born A Lady (USA) **Sir Gordon White**
7 **ELEMIS (USA),** ch f Sir Ivor—Tis A Kitten (USA) **Cheveley Park Stud Ltd**
8 **FIRST EXHIBITION,** b f Claude Monet (USA)—All Hail **Mr J. M. Greetham**
9 **GOLDSTREAM (USA),** b c Slew O' Gold (USA)—Someway Somehow (USA) **Sheikh Mohammed**
10 **NO SHARPS OR FLATS (USA),** ch f Sharpen Up—Orientate **Cheveley Park Stud Ltd**
11 **PACIFIC FIGHTER (USA),** b c Seattle Slew (USA)—Pushy **Sheikh Mohammed**
12 **REPECHAGE,** b f Tina's Pet—Lady's Walk **Mr J. Ward-Hill**
13 **SPEARMAN,** b c Diesis—Oh So Bold (USA) **Sheikh Mohammed**
14 **WHITE BULLET (USA),** ch c Shadeed (USA)—Eye Drop (USA) **Maktoum Al Maktoum**

TWO-YEAR-OLDS

15 B c 20/2 Vaigly Great—Atoka (March Past) **C. I. T. Research**
16 **BIRTHDAY'S CHILD,** b f 30/4 Caerleon (USA)—Shaara (FR) (Sanctus II) **Birthday's Card Shops**
17 B f 6/6 Chief Singer—Blue Queen (Majority Blue) **Miss Lavinia Thompson**
18 **CLARE HEIGHTS,** b f Shirley Heights—Clare Island (Connaught) **The Snailwell Stud Company Limited**
19 **COPPER BURN,** ch f Electric—Divetta (Ribero) **Mr I. Wills**
20 **DON'T BE SHY (IRE),** b f Kafu—Cat O'Mountaine (Ragusa) **Mr S. Yamada**
21 **ENVIRONMENT FRIEND,** gr c Cozzene (USA)—Water Woo (USA) (Tom Rolfe) **Mr W. J. Gredley**
22 **FREEDOM WEEKEND (USA),** ch f Shahrastani (USA)—Glorious Quest (USA) (Hawaii) **Mr R. N. Clay**
23 **HIGH STEPPE,** b f Petoski—High Gait (High Top) **Mr P. D. Player**
24 B c 17/3 Dunbeath (USA)—Integrity (Reform) **Lord Vestey**
25 **LEVADE,** b c Elegant Air—Silent Pool (Relkino) **Mr A. MacDonald-Buchanan**
26 **MEALLWASHA (IRE),** b f 24/4 Wassl—Nathacha (Thatch (USA)) **Mr I. Wills**
27 **PASADENA PET (IRE),** b c Petorius—Magic Quiz (Quisling) **Mr D. Russell**
28 **ROSE ALTO,** ch f Adonijah—Rose Music (Luthier (FR)) **Mr T. Vestey**
29 **SAPIEHA (IRE),** b c Petorius—Sugarbird (Star Appeal) **Baron G. De Geer**

MR J. R. FANSHAWE—continued

30 STYLISH SENOR (USA), ch c El Gran Senor (USA)—Gladiolus (USA) (Watch Your Step) **Mr Michael J. Ryan**
31 B c 22/2 Soughaan (USA)—Terracotta (GER) (Nebos (GER)) **Mrs J. J. Hindley**
32 WALAADIH, b f Dancing Brave (USA)—Basoof (USA) (Believe It (USA)) **Maktoum Al Maktoum**

Other Owners: Mr J. Beatson-Hird, Mr James R. Fanshawe, Mr A. Ison, Mrs H. G. Lascelles, Captain J. Macdonald-Buchanan, Mr Bryan Robson, Mr K. Smith-Bingham, Mrs K. Smith-Bingham, Mrs Doreen M. Swinburn, Mr J. Vestey, Mr R. Vestey, Mr P. Webber, Mr Ron Wood.

213 MR P. J. FEILDEN, Newmarket

Postal: **Harraton Stables, Exning, Newmarket, Suffolk.**
Phone: **(0638) 77637**

1 BILL MOON, 4, ch g Nicholas Bill—Lunar Queen **J-Tec Shoes Ltd and Partners**
2 CHAPEL CHIMES, 4, b f Song—Lady Spey **Mr Roy Bennett**
3 CORKSCREW, 5, b g Bold Lad (IRE)—Devil's Alternative **Mrs Richard Casey**
4 CROWN COUNSEL, 11, ch g Simbir—Edie's Court **Mr P. J. Feilden**
5 EASY LINE, 7, ch g Swing Easy (USA)—Impromptu **Mr Roy Bennett**
6 FAST AND FREE, 4, b g Kafu—Santa Maria (GER) **Mrs V. L. Walker**
7 FINAL SOUND, 5, b g Final Straw—Sound Type **J-Tec Shoes Ltd (Raunds)**
8 FUTURE GAMBLE, 5, b g Auction Ring (USA)—Silja (FR) **Mr D. Lakin**
9 GLENMERE PRINCE, 4, b g Prince Tenderfoot (USA)—Ashbourne Lass **Mr R. N. J. Robinson**
10 GOOD MEDICINE, 5, b g Star Appeal—Jacoletta **Mr David G. Sutherland**
11 HENRY'S WOLFE, 5, b g Coquelin (USA)—Grangemore **Mr P. J. Feilden**
12 HOGMANAY (CAN), 8, b g Halo (USA)—Annie Laurie (CAN) **Mrs Richard Casey**
13 JIM BRIDGER, 5, ch g Little Wolf—Candid Queen **Mr A. Piller**
14 PRINCE HENDRICK, 5, b g Town And Country— **R. V. King**

THREE-YEAR-OLDS

15 DORSEY, ch g Music Boy—Miss Trilli **P. J. Feilden**
16 UNMATCHED, b f Local Suitor (USA)—Mousil **Mr H. B. E. Van Cutsem**

TWO-YEAR-OLDS

17 Ch f 30/3 Formidable (USA)—Palmella (USA) (Grundy) **P. J. Stedman**
18 B c 13/3 Aragon—Sweet Louise (Sweet Revenge) **A. Piller**

Other Owners: Mrs Anne Overstall, R. J. Coles, Miss Audrey L. Forbes, Mr C. A. Potter, Mrs A. E. Roberts, Mr James Wigan.

Amateur: Miss. J Feilden (8-4).

214 MR P. S. FELGATE, Melton Mowbray

Postal: **Grimston Stud, Grimston, Melton Mowbray, Leicestershire.**
Phone: **(0664) 812019**

1 BERNSTEIN BETTE, 4, b f Petong—Glenfield Portion **Manny Bernstein (Racing) Ltd**
2 EVENING HOUR, 5, ch m Glenstal (USA)—Field Lady **Miss Johanna Milward**
3 FABULOUS SHAUN, 4, b g Petong—High State **Mr P. S. Felgate**
4 FIFTH ATTEMPT, 8, b g Vulgan Slave—Dingle Poke **Mr E. Rollinson**
5 FREE SKIP, 6, b m Free State—Economy Pep **Mr H. G. Norman**
6 JOKIST, 7, ro g Orchestra—What A Picture **Mr John Virgo**
7 MIMINING, 4, ch f Tower Walk—Louisianalightning **Mr A. C. Birkle**
8 NO QUARTER GIVEN, 5, b g Don—Maggie Mine **Mr J. David Abell**
9 PENNY LOVER, 6, gr ro h Sonnen Gold—Continental Divide **Mr P. S. Felgate**

MR P. S. FELGATE—continued

10 **PRAIRIE AGENT,** 5, b m Main Reef—Regal Guard **Mrs B. Stevenson**
11 **SANDITTON PALACE,** 7, gr g Dragonara Palace (USA)—Petona **Mr J. David Abell**
12 **SHUTTLECOCK CORNER (USA),** 4, b c Cresta Rider (USA)—Sweet Ellen (USA) **Mr J. David Abell**
13 **SILVER HELLO,** 4, gr g Nishapour (FR)—Si **Mr J. David Abell**
14 **STRAWBERRY SPLIT,** 7, ro m Anax—Continental Divide **Mrs P. S. Felgate**

THREE-YEAR-OLDS

15 **AZUBAH,** b f Castle Keep—Louisianalightning **Mr A. C. Birkle**
16 **DANNY BLANCHFLOWER,** ch c Rabdan—Caffre Lily **Mr G. J. Tully**
17 **ESTEFAN,** b f Taufan (USA)—Benita **Mr J. David Abell**
18 **FRENCH HOUSE,** ch g Coquelin (USA)—Ottina (GER) **Mr J. Walsh**
19 **LARS PORSENA,** b br c Trojan Fen—Apocalypse **Mr J. David Abell**
20 **MACS MAHARANEE,** b f Indian King (USA)—High State **Mr G. Holgate**
21 **RAINBOW BRIDGE,** br c Godswalk (USA)—Regal Entrance **Mr J. David Abell**
22 **TRICOTRIC,** br f Electric—Orpheline **Mr G. E. Stevenson**
23 **WITHIN REASON,** ch f Reasonable (FR)—Nom de Plume **Mr P. S. Felgate**

TWO-YEAR-OLDS

24 B f Prince Sabo—Adduce (USA) (Alleged (USA)) **Havenwood Cons Ltd**
25 **COLONEL NORTH (CAN),** b c Far North (CAN)—Slow March (Queen's Hussar) **Mr J. David Abell**
26 Gr g Belfort (FR)—Continental Divide (Sharp Edge) **Mr P. S. Felgate**
27 Ch f Gabitat—Glenfield Portion (Mummy's Pet) **Mr P. S. Felgate**
28 B f Primo Dominie—Highest Tender (Prince Tenderfoot (USA)) **Havenwood Cons Ltd**
29 **JUST VIRGINIA,** b f Petong—First Experience (Le Johnstan) **Mr J. David Abell**
30 **SIZZLING SAGA (IRE),** b c Horage—Alsazia (FR) (Bolkonski) **Mr J. David Abell**
31 Br c Believe It (USA)—Willow Court (USA) (Little Current (USA)) **Mr J. David Abell**

Other Owners: Mr B. Gilford, Mr C. McGilway, Mr J. B. A. Randall, Mr D. J. Sandell, Mr P. Ward.

Jockey (Flat): W Ryan.

Jockey (NH): S Johnson (10-0, w.a.).

Lady Riders: Mrs Margaret Crawford, Mrs J Saunders.

215 MR J. FELLOWS, Chantilly

Postal: **4 Avenue du General Leclerc, 60500 Chantilly, France.**
Phone: **44582061 OFFICE 44585178 HOME 150154 TELEX 44581078 FAX**

1 **AIR DE NOBLESSE,** 4, b f Vaguely Noble—Ancient Regime (USA) **R. Scully**
2 **ANAGRAMME (FR),** 5, b h In Fijar (USA)—Manoline (FR) **J. Fellows**
3 **CALLISTINE (FR),** 6, b m Arctic Tern (USA)—Loterie (FR) **Mrs J. Fellows**
4 **CAPTAIN FLAMME (FR),** 6, b h Zino—Starry Field **Mrs P. Sutton**
5 **FLORES LANE (FR),** 6, ch m Malestrom Lake—Petticoat Lane (FR) **Mr B. Arbib**
6 **GONE FISHIN,** 4, b f Gay Mecene (USA)—Paresseuse (FR) **J. Fellows**
7 **KICKS (USA),** 6, b h Run The Gantlet (USA)—Fun Palace (USA) **Miss P. Augustus**
8 **L'AMOUR TOUJOUR (USA),** 4, b f Blushing Grooom (FR)—Paint The Town (USA) **P. Augustus**
9 **NAF A NAF (FR),** 6, b h Home Guard (USA)—Moitie Moitie (FR) **Mrs P. Sutton**
10 **OPERA (FR),** 5, b m Lou Piguet (FR)—Ole Miss (FR) **Ecurie Lingfield**
11 **PERPETUAL GUEST,** 4, b f Arctic Tern (USA)—Separate Checks **P. Augustus**
12 **RESERVE BANK,** 4, b c Dom Alaric (FR)—Quat'sous (CAN) **D. Volkert**
13 **SWING IT (FR),** 5, b h Gay Mecene (USA)—Sand Dancer (FR) **J. Fellows**
14 **TIAVANITA,** 4, b f J O Tobin (USA)—Nirvanita (FR) **Mrs P. Sutton**

MR J. FELLOWS—continued

THREE-YEAR-OLDS

15 **AFTER SHOW,** ch f Stage Door Johnny—Duck Flighting (USA) **R. Scully**
16 **ALBERTITO,** b c Esprit du Nord—Aranita **R. Scully**
17 **AND HOW,** b c Enchantment—Bondoe **L. Keele**
18 **CLOSELY LINKED,** ch c Vaguely Noble—Assez Cuite (USA) **R. Scully**
19 **CRY FOR JOY,** b f Northern Fashion—Weeping Well (FR) **P. Augustus**
20 **DOM SALLUST,** ch c Sallust—Riverwave (USA) **D. Volkert**
21 **FIASCO ARGENTO,** b f Silver Hawk—Misty Light **R. Scully**
22 **HAUT D'ESPRIT,** ch c Graustark—Battle Dress (FR) **R. Scully**
23 **HAUTE PUISSANCE,** ch f Irish River—Royal Procession (USA) **R. Scully**
24 **JUDICAL REVIEW,** b c Law Society—Epsiba **R. Lanigan**
25 **LURING,** gr f Mendez—Hybla (FR) **D. Volkert**
26 **MRS RYAN,** b f L'Emigrant—Zitherplay **Dr M. Marenchic**
27 **NAD,** ch c Maelstrom Lake—Nimini (FR) **J. Livock**
28 **NOUKHA,** b f Dom Racine—Nuit Fabuleuse **J. Fellows**
29 B f Assert—Overdove **D. Miller**
30 **POM DU NORD,** b f Esprit du Nord—Pommes Sautees (USA) **J. Fellows**
31 **SENEB,** b c Romildo—Orfila **J. Livock**
32 **SENOR GRANDE,** b c El Gran Senor—Summer Review (USA) **R. Scully**
33 **SHIP OF STATE,** b f Silver Hawk—Star Ship II **R. Scully**
34 **SPENDOMANIA,** b f Roberto—La Trinite (FR) **R. Scully**
35 **SUMMER PARADE,** b f Sir Ivor—River Zara (FR) **Mrs D. Miller**
36 **SYMPHONIE CELEBRE,** gr f Foolish Pleasure—Keep In Step **R. Scully**
37 **WATERLESS,** b f Esprit du Nord—Waterford (FR) **D. Miller**

TWO-YEAR-OLDS

38 B f Exceller—Adept (Grey Dawn II) **R. Scully**
39 Gr c El Gran Senor—Ancient Regime (Olden Times) **R. Scully**
40 Ch f Raise A Native—Assez Cuite (Graustark) **R. Scully**
41 **BAGDAD CAFE,** ch c Script Ohio—Intimate (Be My Guest) **Mme D. Ferran-Boulenger**
42 **CALM DAWN,** b f In Reality—Colophon (Nijinsky) **R. Scully**
43 **COWLEY MANOR,** ch f Irish River—Summer Review (Graustark) **R. Scully**
44 Ch f Lemhi Gold—Dedicated To Sue (Su Ka Wa) **K. Eustace**
45 Ch c Sharpen Up—Duck Flighting (Far North) **R. Scully**
46 B c Slew O'Gold—Emociones (Con Brio) **Mrs P. Vandervoort-Kumble**
47 **EXOTIC ISLE,** ch f Shahrastani—Cameo Native (Raise A Native) **R. Scully**
48 **HEAT OF THE NIGHT,** b f Deep Roots—Kanga (Arctic Tern) **J. Fellows**
49 Ch f Play Fellow—Jolie Sirene (Timmy My Boy) **J. Fellows**
50 **LOUIS,** b c Sovereign Dancer—La Pompadour (Vaguely Noble) **P. Augustus**
51 B c Irish River—Perliere (Rheingold) **B. Arbib**
52 **PIERRE AU ROUGE,** b f Comrade In Arms—Silver Fly (Royal And Regal) **Ecurie Lingfield**
53 **RILLY,** b c Esprit du Nord—Royal Charmer (Wolver Hollow) **R. Scully**
54 **RUSSIAN MAGIC,** gr f Magic Mirror—Anne of Russia (Bold Reason) **J. Fellows**
55 **TRES CHIC,** b f Northern Fashion—Plucky Miss (Plugged Nickle) **P. Augustus**
56 **TROJAN DU NORD,** b c Esprit du Nord—Trojan Queen (Troy) **Mrs J. Fellows**
57 **VAL ROMAND,** gr g Romildo—Petite Vallee (Val de L'Orne) **J. Fellows**
58 **WEDDING PRESENT,** b f Private Account—Beaming Bride (King Emperor) **P. Augustus**
59 **WINDSOR FOREST,** ch c Spectacular Bid—Royal Procession (Lyphard) **R. Scully**
60 B c Esprit du Nord—Zone Bleue (Rose Laurel) **R. Scully**

Other Owners: Mr C. Darty, Mr Jim Fleming, Mr Jim Keele, Mr Fred Kelly, Dr F. Krief, Mr R. La Pointe, Mr Stanley Meadows, Mr J. Messara.

Apprentice: S Legall.

216 MR M. J. FETHERSTON-GODLEY, East Ilsley

Postal: **Kennett House, East Ilsley, Newbury, Berkshire.**
Phone: **(063 528) 250**

1 **MIDNIGHT FLAME,** 4, gr g Kalaglow—Midnight Flit **Mr M. J. Fetherston-Godley**
2 **SUPER GUNNER,** 5, ch g Busted—Lunaria (USA) **Mr Robert Moffatt**
3 **SUPER TRIP,** 9, b g Windjammer (USA)—Esker Rose **Mrs M. J. Fetherston-Godley**
4 **TAKENHALL,** 5, b g Pitskelly—Great Dora **Mr Craig Pearman**
5 **TL QUARTER PINT,** 4, b c Prince Tenderfoot (USA)—Tumble Royal **The TL Group Ltd**
6 **WHERE'S THE MONEY,** 4, b f Lochnager—Balearica **Mrs I. M. Jamieson**

THREE-YEAR-OLDS

7 **ARETHUSA LEISURE,** gr f Homing—Birch Creek **Aretusa Club Ltd**
8 **BEAT THE INTRO,** br f Swing Easy (USA)—Welsh Carol **Mrs M. J. Fetherston-Godley**
9 **BOLD ENDEAVOUR,** b g Try My Best (USA)—Explorelka **Mr J. G. Ross**
10 **CAMDEN'S RANSOM (USA),** b c Hostage (USA)—Camden Court (USA) **Mr Peter H. Belott**
11 **FACTUELLE,** ch f Known Fact (USA)—Cayla **Mr R. Hamer**
12 **LOCHDOR,** br f Lochnager—Cindys Gold **Miss Linda Agran**
13 **LONGDRUM,** ch c Sayf El Arab (USA)—Geppina Umbra **Mr P. Fetherston-Godley**
14 **MARTINSTAR,** b f Norwick (USA)—Martin Place **Mr J. A. L. Burton**
15 **OMORSI,** b f Prince Tenderfoot (USA)—Her Name Was Lola **Miss Jill Chambers**
16 **SPARKS WILL FLY,** ch c Longleat (USA)—Ladyswood **Mrs Ann Botten**

TWO-YEAR-OLDS

17 B c 21/5 Norwick (USA)—Auto Elegance (Brave Shot) **K. Beaumont**
18 B f 29/4 Pitskelly—Bradden (King Emperor (USA))
19 **CAESARS NIECE (IRE),** b f 17/5 Rhoman Rule (USA)—Great Dora (Great Nephew)
20 **HIGHLAND MAGIC (IRE),** b c 29/4 Stalker—Magic Picture (Deep Diver) **Mr P. Fetherston-Godley**
21 B f 24/4 Trojan Fen—Instant Beauty (USA) (Pronto (ARG)) **I. Jerrard**
22 **MACFARLANE,** b c 29/4 Kala Shikari—Tarvie (Swing Easy (USA)) **Mr P. Fetherston-Godley**
23 Ch f 22/2 The Noble Player—Making Tracks (Sagaro) **C. Bexx**
24 B f 19/3 Pitskelly—Miss Galwegian (Sandford Lad)

Other Owners: Mr D. E. G. Berry, Mr R. Bolam, Mr Colin Clay, Dr B. L. Coulton, Mr N. J. Dent, Dr Christopher Elia, M. Hammer, P. W. A. Lake, Mrs Lyndy Lifford, Mr J. McGregor, Mrs J. McGregor, Mr Phil Needham, Mr C. J. G. Norman, Mrs E. W. Pitman.

217 MR J. R. G. FFITCH-HEYES, Lewes

Postal: **The Racing Stables, Old Lewes Racecourse, Lewes, E. Sussex, BN7 1UR.**
Phone: **(0273) 480804 FAX (0273) 478709**

1 **AFFAIRE DE COEUR,** 6, b m Imperial Fling (USA)—Creake **Mrs D. R. Hunnisett**
2 **AZAIYMA,** 4, br f Corvaro (USA)—Aytana (FR) **Mr Graham Pasquill**
3 **BLANDELL BEAUTY,** 6, b m Mummy's Pet—Maria Luiza **Miss Wendy Hart**
4 **CAROL SINGING,** 4, b c Lyphard's Special (USA)—Welsh Pride **Mrs C. J. Howard**
5 **CARPET CAPERS (USA),** 6, b g Dance Bid (USA)—Cofimvaba (FR) **Mrs B. Rankin**
6 **COGNIZANT,** 5, b m Known Fact (USA)—Alia **Mr Robert Digby-Ware**
7 **FLEETWOOD LASS,** 6, b m Lochnager—Lively Lassie **Mr Robert Digby-Ware**
8 **FOUR SPORT,** 8, ch m Swing Easy (USA)—Kingsfold Flash **Miss Bobby Quibell**
9 **GABISH,** 5, b g Try My Best (USA)—Crannog **Mr Chris Steward**
10 **GOLDEN MOSS,** 5, ch g Le Moss—Call Bird **Mrs D. R. Hunnisett**
11 **GREY FELLOW,** 4, gr c Absalom—Follow The Brave **Mr Chris Steward**
12 **GUICI'S RAG,** 7, b g Ragapan—Barradan Lass **Mr Chris Steward**
13 **HETTINGER,** 10, b g Maximilian—Fawnamore **Miss Lynda Quick**
14 **KILBREEDY,** 7, b m The Parson—Fawnamore **Mr John Ffitch-Heyes**
15 **MAJUBA ROAD,** 10, ch m Scottish Rifle—Cleo Baby **Mr A. Benn**
16 **MANHATTAN BOY,** 8, b g Oats—Into Harbour **Mrs D. R. Hunnisett**

MR J. R. G. FFITCH-HEYES—continued

17 MILTON BRYAN, 5, ch g Red Sunset—Priddy Moun **Mr A. L. A. Markham**
18 MR FFITCH, 4, b g Hays—Lady Topknot **Mrs C. J. Howard**
19 NOBBY, 4, b c Dalsaan—Parkeen Princess **Woodstow Antique Developments Ltd**
20 PRIME WARDEN, 4, b c Blakeney—Misguided **Dr Madan Mohan Gaytri**
21 SECOND MORTGAGE, 9, gr g Tack On—Gables Grey **Miss Wendy Hart**
22 TAKE THE MICKY, 7, b g Reform—Hedonist **Mrs C. J. Howard**

TWO-YEAR-OLDS

23 B c Blakeney—Classy Nancy (USA) (Cutlass (USA)) **Mr Robert Digby Ware, Mr J. Ffitch-Heyes**

Other Owners: Mr B. Green, Mr John K. Mowat, Mr Geoffrey Ware, Mr D. Wright.

Jockeys (NH): P Ffitch-Heyes, Ray Goldstein (10-0).

Conditional: Jason Atkinson.

218 MR R. F. FISHER, Ulverston

Postal: **Great Head House, Priory Road, Ulverston, Cumbria, LA12 9RX.**
Phone: **ULVERSTON (0229) 55664 OFFICE 55819 TELEX 65261 FAX (0229) 55079**

1 ANDERO, 8, b g Tug of War—Scotch News **Mr A. J. MacDonald**
2 BALLYDURROW, 13, ch g Doon—Even Tint **Mr S. P. Marsh**
3 BENCANNA, 6, b m Niels—Lackamore **Mr S. P. Marsh**
4 BIZARRE CASE, 6, b g Gleason (USA)—Little Cygnet **Mrs Catherine Brennan**
5 BRILLIANT WISH, 7, b g Green Shoon—Shinaro **Mr N. Jaffer**
6 CARSWELL'S CHOICE, 7, ch g Belfalas—Santal Air **Mr A. J. MacDonald**
7 CASINO RUN, 7, ch m Deep Run—Kassina **Mr R. F. Fisher**
8 CRASH MARKET, 8, b g Crash Course—Anail **Mr A. J. MacDonald**
9 DEEP SECRECY, 5, br g Deep Run—Rusheen's Girl **Mrs D. Miller**
10 IMPERIAL RAIN, 7, ch m Imperial Fling (USA)—El Chaperall **Mrs Carol Reed**
11 KATES FLING (USA), 7, b m Quiet Fling (USA)—Dancers Fairlight (USA) **Mrs Kate Bateson**
12 KRISTENSON, 13, b g Menelek—Chantry Bay **Mr S. P. Marsh**
13 MISS KAMSY, 6, b br m Kambalda—Daisy Owen **Mr D. Rogers**
14 RIEN NE VA PLUS, 7, ch g Green Shoon—Poker Face (SWE) **Mr S. Hussey**
15 SMART JACK, 9, b g Pollerton—Smart Money **Mr S. P. Marsh**
16 SPRINGVALE CRUSADE, 7, b g Callernish—Harlem Lady **New Springvale Co-Operative Ltd**
17 STRONG BREEZE, 6, br g Strong Gale—Salty Breeze **Mrs D. Miller**
18 TELEMETER GEM, 9, b m Decent Fellow—High Energy **Telemeter Engineering Ltd**
19 THREEPLAND, 7, b g Rugged Man—Prosper Lion **Mr A. J. MacDonald**
20 VALE OF SECRECY, 9, b g The Parson—Arctic Rhapsody **Mrs D. Miller**

THREE-YEAR-OLDS

21 AILEEN'S JOY, b br c Runnett—Originality **Mrs Eleanor Fisher**

Other Owners: Mr P. Morrell, Mr S. Morris, Mr Ray Penney, Mr David N. Smith, Mr Peter Stephenson.

Jockeys (Flat): J Lowe (7-7), D Nicholls (8-4).

Jockeys (NH): C Grant, P Niven.

219 LORD J. FITZGERALD, Newmarket

Postal: **Graham Lodge, Birdcage Walk, Newmarket, Suffolk, CB8 ONE.**
Phone: **(0638) 660605**

1 **ANTHONY LORETTO**, 5, b g Mummy's Game—Miss Silly **Stuncroft Ltd**
2 **BID LATER**, 4, b f Auction Ring (USA)—Twenty Two **Mrs B. Long**
3 **SIMPLY SWELL**, 4, br g Simply Great (FR)—Nelly Gail **Mrs Mary Watt**

THREE-YEAR-OLDS

4 **AVOCA HOLMES**, ch f Be My Guest (USA)—Bid For Freedom **Mr C. T. Spencer-Phillips**
5 **BUNDLE OF LUCK**, ch f Touching Wood (USA)—Best Offer **Baron F. C. Oppenheim**
6 **CALLIPOLI (USA)**, br f Green Dancer (USA)—Minstrelete (USA) **Mrs B. Long**
7 **CERTAIN CREATOR (USA)**, b c Alleged (USA)—Producer (USA) **Mr W. J. Gredley**
8 **DUMDUMSKI**, b c Niniski (USA)—Live Ammo **Mr J. E. Nash**
9 **LA COMBATTANTE**, br f Darshaan—La Commere (USA) **Miss K. Rausing**
10 **LADY TOPPING (USA)**, b f Lyphard (USA)—Miss Derby (USA) **Miss K. Rausing**
11 **LOLITA**, b f Wassl—Lady Bennington **Miss K. Rausing**
12 **MAGIC CRYSTAL**, b f Ahonoora—Carntino **Mr W. J. Gredley**
13 **MISTRESS LIL (USA)**, b f Master Willie—Gala Occasion (USA) **Brian Yeardley Continental Ltd**
14 **ROMAN WALK**, b f Petorius—Plum Bold **Mr D. Di Paolo**
15 **TELL NO LIES**, b f High Line—No Cards **Mrs A. Johnstone**

TWO-YEAR-OLDS

16 **BELLEROFONTE (IRE)**, b c 22/2 Tate Gallery (USA)—Faapette (Runnett) **Mr D. Di Paolo**
17 B c 11/4 Caerleon (USA)—Interviewme (Olden Times) **Mr W. J. Gredley**
18 **KIMTECH**, ch c 4/4 Pharly (FR)—Kissin' Cousin (Be Friendly) **W. T. Yip**
19 **LITTLE BANG**, ch f 11/2 Bustino—Live Ammo (Home Guard (USA)) **J. E. Nash**
20 **MUPHRID**, br c 30/4 Sharpo—Favorable Exchange (USA) (Exceller (USA)) **Mr D. Di Paolo**
21 B f 30/4 Alzao (USA)—Native Flower (Tumble Wind (USA)) **Mrs B. Long**
22 B f 26/4 Song—Peckitts Well (Lochnager) **J. C. Smith**
23 Br f 26/3 Chief Singer—Pine Away (Shirley Heights) **Mrs Mary Watt**
24 B f 2/3 Ardross—Ruda (FR) (Free Round (USA)) **Eduardo Hinojosa**
25 B f 28/5 Alzao (USA)—Saranita (Thatch (USA)) **Mr D. Di Paolo**
26 B f 13/3 Rousillon (USA)—Snowtop (Thatching) **Mrs B. Long**
27 B c 24/4 Dom Alaric (FR)—Trojan Bounty (CAN) (Shecky Greene (USA)) **Mr D. Di Paolo**

Other Owners: Mr Khaled Al-Ahmed, Wing Cmdr Tim Vigors, Major M. G. Wyatt.

Jockey (Flat): R J Hills (7-12).

220 MR J. G. FITZGERALD, Malton

Postal: **Norton Grange, Norton, Malton, North Yorkshire, YO17 9EA.**
Phone: **MALTON (0653) 692718 FAX MALTON (0653) 600214**

1 **ANDORRA**, 8, gr g Godswalk (USA)—Lady Sioux (USA) **Mr J. G. Fitzgerald**
2 **ARNHALL**, 8, b g Hello Gorgeous (USA)—First Round **Mrs D. D. Osborne**
3 **AVOPORT**, 10, ch g Avocat—Portballintrae **Mrs J. Mulkeen**
4 **BALKAN LEADER**, 6, b g Balidar—Perfect Lady **A. F. Budge (Equine) Limited**
5 **BLACKSBURG**, 5, b g Black Minstrel—Meneplete **A. F. Budge (Equine) Limited**
6 **BOUTZDAROFF**, 8, ch g Dubassoff (USA)—Love Seat **Robinson Publications Limited**
7 **BUCKO**, 13, b g Royal Buck—Tame Cindy **Mr J. P. McManus**
8 **BUSH HILL**, 5, b g Beldale Flutter (USA)—Butosky **Mr W. H. O'Gorman**
9 **COLLISON LANE**, 4, b f Reesh—Everingham Park **Mr A. D. Bottomley**
10 **DEMOKOS (FR)**, 5, ch g Dom Racine (FR)—Eagletown (FR) **Mr D. Walsh**
11 **DUAL VENTURE**, 8, ch g Brigadier Gerard—Selham **Mr A. Soulsby**
12 **EDWARD LEAR (USA)**, 4, b c Lear Fan (USA)—Coed (USA) **Mr J. G. Fitzgerald**
13 **EVICHSTAR**, 6, ch g Jasmine Star—Chive **Mr Gwyn Meredith**

MR J. G. FITZGERALD—continued

14 **FORGET THE REST**, 5, gr g Palm Track—Precipienne **Mrs B. D. McGowan**
15 **FRAGRANT DAWN**, 6, br g Strong Gale—Aridje **Mr W. H. O'Gorman**
16 **GOLD OPTIONS**, 8, ch g Billion (USA)—Foggy Park **Mr J. McCaghy**
17 **GREEK FLUTTER**, 5, b g Beldale Flutter (USA)—Greek Blessing **Mr J. G. Fitzgerald**
18 **GUERNSEY GIRL**, 5, ch m Deep Run—Falcade **Mr A. Phillips**
19 **HALF OILED**, 6, b g Forties Field (FR)—One Pint **Mr J. G. Fitzgerald**
20 **HALLBOROUGH**, 5, ch g Warpath—Bargain Line **Mr Joseph Ogden**
21 **HALLO LIGHTNING**, 4, gr g Zambrano—Artlight **Mrs J. C. B. Cookson**
22 **HAPPYOATS**, 5, b g Oats—Gay Nipper **Catfoss Farming & Developments Ltd**
23 **HILL STREET (FR)**, 8, b g Grandchant (FR)—Tetlin (FR) **A. F. Budge (Equine) Limited**
24 **HIT THE BOX**, 5, ch g Quayside—Three Dieu **Mr R. Haggas**
25 **IBN MAJED**, 8, gr g Godswalk (USA)—La Meme **Mr P. O'Donnell**
26 **ICE VALLEY**, 8, b g Bronze Hill—Ice Blossom **Mrs D. D. Osborne**
27 **IN THE FASHION**, 8, br g Never Slip—Smashing Style **Mrs H. Ogden**
28 **ISTIKRAR**, 4, b f In Fijar (USA)—Sajeda **Mr A. Foustok**
29 **JANE'S DELIGHT**, 6, b g Royal Palace—Violate **Mrs K. M. Berry**
30 **JASAGLORE**, 4, ch g Simply Great (FR)—Caithness **Mrs J. Hyland**
31 **JIM'S TOP**, 7, ch g Lucifer (USA)—Betty Sue **Mr R. Haggas**
32 **JUST ANOTHER SIP**, 6, b m Lochnager—Sipped **Mr J. F. Slade**
33 **KEELBY**, 5, b g Kemal (FR)—Peter's Pet **A. F. Budge (Equine) Limited**
34 **KEVINSFORT**, 12, b g Will Somers—Hinemoa **Mrs R. Haggie**
35 **LUMBERJACK (USA)**, 6, b g Big Spruce (USA)—Snip **A. F. Budge (Equine) Limited**
36 **MAHANA**, 6, b g Tepukei—Easby Saint **Mr R. Haggas**
37 **MAJOR ROW**, 10, b br g Kambalda—Vina's Last **Mr J. G. FitzGerald**
38 **MAN OF THE WEST**, 7, br g Mandalus—Belle of The West **A. F. Budge (Equine) Limited**
39 **MEADOWVALE**, 5, b g Furry Glen—In View Lass **Mr R. Haggas**
40 **MEIKLEOUR**, 11, b g Reliance II—Videmanette **Mrs A. C. Leggat**
41 **MILL POND (FR)**, 4, gr c Mill Reef (USA)—Royal Way (FR) **Marquesa de Moratalla**
42 **MIND YOUR BACK**, 7, b g Random Shot—Cant Pet **Mr R. Haggas**
43 **MISS CLUB ROYAL**, 7, b m Avocat—Miss Leap Year **Halewood Vintners Ltd**
44 **NATIVE FRIEND**, 4, b g Be My Native (USA)—Wet Powder **Mr J. Dick**
45 **NEWHOLME FARM**, 7, ch g Mart Lane—Aplomb **Mr Ronald Howe**
46 **NICHOLCONE**, 7, b m Celtic Cone—Candy Stripe **Mrs P. Nicholson**
47 **NOBLE RAIDER**, 6, b g Sir Mordred—Clonroche Hawk **A. F. Budge (Equine) Limited**
48 **ONE FOR THE NORTH**, 5, b g Old Jocus—Coach Tour **Mr R. Haggas**
49 **OTTERBURN HOUSE**, 6, b g Proverb—High Energy **Mr R. Haggas**
50 **PHOENIX GOLD**, 10, ch g Precipice Wood—Valeria **Phoenix Waterproofing Limited**
51 **PRINCIPAL**, 8, ch g Deep Run—Lulu Dee **Mr W. A. A. Farrell**
52 **PROUD PILGRIM**, 11, ch g Jimmy Reppin—Plain Pilgrim **Lady Blacker**
53 **QUEEN'S DARLING**, 8, ch m Le Moss—King's Darling **Kilroe Group Limited**
54 **QUINTANA**, 8, ch g Quayside—Clerihan **A. F. Budge (Equine) Limited**
55 **RAPIER THRUST**, 8, ch g Fine Blade (USA)—Zoom Zoom **Mr R. L. White**
56 **RAZEEN**, 5, ch g Be My Guest (USA)—Fast Motion **Mr A. Foustok**
57 **ROCKET LAUNCHER**, 4, b g Strong Gale—Adell **Mr W. H. O'Gorman**
58 **RODOMONT**, 6, b g Shirley Heights—Louise Moulton **Marquesa de Moratalla**
59 **ROSTHERNE**, 8, ch g Crimson Beau—Correct Approach **Mr J. G. Fitzgerald**
60 **RYTON RENOWN**, 5, b g Strong Gale—Rose's Best **A. F. Budge (Equine) Limited**
61 **SALADAN KNIGHT**, 5, b g Dalsaan—Exciting Times **Mrs A. F. Budge**
62 **SANDY'S BEACON**, 5, b g Foggy Bell—Ditchling Beacon **Mrs Margaret Brock**
63 **SAPIENCE**, 4, ch c Niniski (USA)—Claretta (USA) **Mr W. H. O'Gorman**
64 **SEE YOU THERE**, 8, ch g Prominer—Mariner's Leap **Mr J. S. Murdoch**
65 **SIOBHAN MARIE**, 4, b f Lochnager—Kilroe's Calin **Kilroe Group Limited**
66 **SIP OF ORANGE**, 8, ch m Celtic Cone—Sipped **Mrs R. Haggie**
67 **SOLO CORNET**, 5, br g Furry Glen—Royal Willow **Mr W. A. A. Farrell**
68 **SOME MACHINE**, 11, b br g Prominer—Peking **Mr T. J. Fitzgerald**
69 **SYBILLIN**, 4, b g Henbit (USA)—Tea House **Marquesa de Moratalla**
70 **TEKLA (FR)**, 5, b g Toujours Pret (USA)—Hekla des Sacart (FR) **A. F. Budge (Equine) Limited**
71 **TEMPLE TUOHY**, 11, gr g Precipice Wood—Fairy Temple **Racegoers Club Owners Group**
72 **TERMINATOR**, 7, b g Tachypous—Petit Secret **Mr W. H. O'Gorman**
73 **THE SHUFFLER**, 9, br g Decent Fellow—Royal Pothole **Mrs J. G. O'Neill**

MR J. G. FITZGERALD—continued

74 **THIRD IN LINE**, 7, ch g Proverb—Snipkin **Mr R. Haggas**
75 **TYGER KING**, 4, br g Indian King (USA)—Quality Blake **Mr Chr Marner**
76 **UNCLE ERNIE**, 5, b g Uncle Pokey—Ladyfold **A. F. Budge (Equine) Limited**
77 **UNDERWAY (FR)**, 4, b g Djarvis (FR)—Jamaica (FR) **A. F. Budge (Equine) Limited**
78 **VALIANT PILGRIM**, 10, b g Jimmy Reppin—Plain Pilgrim **General Sir Cecil Blacker**
79 4, B f Kambalda—Verenda **A. F. Budge (Equine) Limited**
80 **WHITE SAPPHIRE**, 5, br h Sparkler—On A Bit **Mr A. D. Bottomley**
81 **YANK BROWN**, 10, b g Giolla Mear—Lorinda **Mr C. C. Longstaff**

THREE-YEAR-OLDS

82 **ALLEZ-OOPS**, ch f Moulin—Ever So Cool (FR) **A. F. Budge (Equine) Limited**
83 **ARABIAN STAR**, ch g Sayf El Arab (USA)—Tahoume (FR) **A. F. Budge (Equine) Limited**
84 **ARMORY SHOW (FR)**, b g Mille Balles (FR)—Bamburi **Mr P. Asquith**
85 **AS D'EBOLI (FR)**, b g What A Guest—Ana d'Eboli (FR) **Mr Norman Jackson**
86 **CASA BELLA**, b f Belfort (FR)—Cassiar **Mr J. G. Fitzgerald**
87 **COMSTOCK**, ch g Coquelin (USA)—Maura Paul **A. F. Budge (Equine) Limited**
88 **FALCON BLUE**, ch g Blue Cashmere—Tralee Falcon **A. F. Budge (Equine) Limited**
89 **FAR TOO LOUD**, b g Taufan (USA)—Octet **Mrs Mark Smyly**
90 **KARAZAN**, gr c Nishapour (FR)—Celestial Path **Mr J. Dick**
91 **MATASIETE (USA)**, b g Diamond Shoal—Babalowa (USA) **Marquesa de Moratalla**
92 **NATIVE MISSION**, ch g Be My Native (USA)—Sister Ida **A. F. Budge (Equine) Limited**
93 **PHOENIX JULE**, b g Coquelin (USA)—Ariel Sands (USA) **Phoenix Roofclad Limited**
94 **SHOOT TO KILL**, ch f Posse (USA)—Sorata (FR) **Robinson Publications Limited**
95 **SUPERENFER**, b c Superlative—Moment In Time **Marquesa de Moratalla**
96 **SURSAS**, b g Chief Singer—Dignified Air (FR) **Marquesa de Moratalla**
97 **TRAINGLOT**, ch c Dominion—Mary Green **Marquesa de Moratalla**
98 **WALLINGFEN LANE**, b g Lochnager—On A Bit **Mr A. D. Bottomley**

TWO-YEAR-OLDS

99 B c 28/3 Nishapour (FR)—Aquarula (Dominion)
100 B c 29/1 Mazaad—Ashbocking (Dragonara Palace (USA)) **A. F. Budge (Equine) Limited**
101 **ASLAN (IRE)**, gr g 18/4 Ela-Mana-Mou—Celestial Path (Godswalk (USA)) **Mr J. Dick**
102 Gr c 26/3 Bellypha—Celestial Air (Rheingold)
103 B g 22/1 Indian King (USA)—Chaldea (Tamerlane)
104 **DARI SOUND (IRE)**, b c 26/3 Shardari—Bugle Sound (Bustino) **Mrs K. Leckenby**
105 **KANDARA (FR)**, b f 24/4 Dalsaan—Kantado (Saulingo)
106 B c 4/3 Elegant Air—Laugharne (Known Fact (USA)) **Marquesa de Moratalla**
107 B c 8/4 Absalom—My Pink Parrot (Pirate King)
108 Gr c 18/3 Hatim (USA)—Originality (Godswalk (USA))
109 B f 6/5 Elegant Air—Quaver (Song)
110 Ch c 13/2 Pharly (FR)—Quelle Chance (General Assembly (USA)) **Marquesa de Moratalla**
111 B g 11/5 Reasonable (FR)—Skyway (Skymaster)
112 **SUNKALA SHINE**, ch c 18/3 Kalaglow—Allander Girl (Miralgo) **A. F. Budge (Equine) Limited**
113 Ch f 21/5 Touching Wood (USA)—Turtle Hill (Home Guard (USA))

Other Owners: Mr L. G. Allgood, Mr G. T. Andrewartha, Mr D. H. Armitage, Mr J. F. Brignall, Mr D. A. Coltman, Lady Darling, Mrs B. V. Eve, Mrs Christoper Heath, Mr Martin Horner, Mrs C. C. Longstaff, The Hon. Gerald Maitland-Carew, Mrs Fred Patten, Mrs L. E. Rudd, Mrs C. M. Smalley, Mr Sandy Wyllie.

Jockey (Flat): K Fallon (8-3).

Jockey (NH): M Dwyer (10-2).

Apprentice: V Deering (8-4).

Conditional: J Burton (9-10), D Byrne (9-10), W Dwan (9-7).

221 MR F. FLOOD, Grangecon

Postal: **Ballynure, Grangecon, Co. Wicklow, Ireland.**
Phone: **(045) 53136**

1 **ABBENOIR,** 8, br g Radical—White Abbess
2 **ABOVE THEM ALL,** 6, b g Cut Above—Great Dora
3 **AGILE LADY,** 5, b m Kemal—Galliano
4 **AHEEMA COTTAGE,** 4, br g Kemal—Clyde Avenue
5 **ANOTHER LIABILITY,** 5, ch g Caribo—Valary
6 **BOBSLINE,** 14, ch g High Line—Golden Delicious
7 **BONNE SANTE,** 8, ch g Bonne Noel—Grange Belle
8 **CONSTRUCTION,** 5, b g Torus—Contrivance
9 **COPPER NOB,** 8, ch g Pollerton—Penny Wise
10 **DAVIDS DUKY,** 8, ch g Duky—Cross Pearl
11 **DUFFINS TRALEE,** 5, ch m Buckskin (FR)—Friendly Cherry
12 **DUHALLOW RUN,** 6, ch g Deep Run—Bawnaro
13 **EL SID SENOR,** 7, b g Bonne Noel—Canute Villa
14 **FARMERS CROSS,** 6, b g Derring Rose—Kylogue Daisy
15 **GAIETY LASS,** 6, ch m Le Moss—Gaels of Laughter
16 **GREAT TRUTH,** 5, ch h Great Nephew—Brilliant Reay
17 **I'M A RAMBLER,** 6, b g Buckskin (FR)—Must Ramble
18 **JUST DON'T KNOW,** 5, br m Buckskin (FR)—My Friend Fashion
19 **LA CERISE,** 7, ch g Le Bavard (FR)—French Cherry
20 **LIAMS PRIDE,** 7, ch g Mart Lane—Miss Manhattan
21 **LUCISIS,** 11, ch g Lucifer—Thesis
22 5, B m The Parson—Move Along Gypsey
23 **NANCY MYLES,** 5, ch m The Parson—Break The Bank
24 **NEVER BE GREAT,** 8, b g Merrymount—Contrivance
25 **REELIN SURPRISE,** 7, b m Royal Match—Reelin Bridge
26 **RISKA'S RIVER,** 8, b g Over The River (FR)—Meel Garrow
27 **ROBIN OF SHERWOOD,** 8, ch g Pollerton—Oriental Run
28 **SUPPLICATE,** 4, br f Furry Glen—Gift Seeker
29 **SWIFTS BUTTERFLY,** 5, b m Furry Glen—Baloney
30 **TRIO ROYAAL,** 6, br m Kings Ride—Castle Creeper
31 **TRUMPET PLAYER,** 7, b g Trombone—Linda Lovelace
32 **VICAR HILL,** 5, b g The Parson—Swift Lady
33 **VILLAGE FABLE,** 5, b m Ballymore—Welsh Tale
34 **WHIP ALONG,** 8, b m Deep Run—Peg Whip
35 **WHISKY MAC,** 7, gr g Roselier (FR)—San Remi

Owners: Ballymore Eustace Racing Club, Mr M. J. Bergen, Mr Noel Brannigan, Clones Racing Club, Mr R. G. Coughlan, Mr A. Crowther, Mr N. Doyle, Mr Patrick Doyle, Mr T. S. Doyle, Mrs G. Duffin, Emerald Racing Club, Mr R. Ferguson, Mr J. D. Flood, Foster & Allan, Mr M. Holly, Mr P. Hore, Mr Jim Horgan, Mr John Horgan, Mrs Kate Horgan, Mr J. J. Howlett, Mr C. McCarthy, Mr Rowan McGhie, Mr T. McPharland, Mr T. Miley, Mrs A. Mitchell, Mr D. Mullins, Rathsallagh Racing Club, Mr T. F. Roe, Mr John Rowley, Mrs K. L. Urquhart, Mrs M. Wheelan.

Jockey (NH): C O'Dwyer (9-9).

Conditional: Roy O'Neill (9-10).

Amateurs: Mr H Cleary, Mr F J Flood (9-0), Mr Thomas Flood (9-7).

222 MR B. FORSEY, Taunton

Postal: **Triscombe Racing Stables, Bishops Lydeard, Taunton, Somerset.**
Phone: **CROWCOMBE (09848) 270**

1 **ARBITRAGE,** 9, b g Monsanto (FR)—Sideshow **Mr D. A. Bay**
2 **CLOUD CHASER,** 7, ch g Hardgreen (USA)—Tudor Zara **Mrs C. R. Hayton**
3 **COMTEC PRINCE,** 8, b g Remainder Man—Moon Mirth **Mr B. Forsey**
4 **LONGGHURST,** 7, b g Camden Town—Olanrose **Mr M. L. Constance**
5 **MICKLEHAM,** 5, ch g Ahonoora—Cliona (FR) **Mrs S. A. Maddock**
6 **THE FLY BOYS,** 8, ch g Sousa—Ravenna **Mr B. Forsey**
7 **TUDOR SUN,** 8, b g Sunyboy—Cottage Melody **Mr P. D. Purdy**

Other Owners: Mr E. G. M. Beard, Mr Graham Dennis, Mr R. P. Finch, Mr David Sullivan.

Jockeys (NH): N Coleman (10-0), C Llewellyn (10-0).

Lady Rider: Mrs S Forsey (8-7).

223 CAPT T. A. FORSTER, Wantage

Postal: **The Old Manor House, Letcombe Bassett, Wantage, Oxon, OX12 9LP.**
Phone: **WANTAGE (023 57) 3092**

1 **ABSOLUTE BEGINNER,** 8, ch g Crash Course—Move Along Gypsy **Mrs M. Kelsey Fry**
2 **AIM TO PLEASE,** 6, gr ro m Gunner B—Declamation **Exors of the late Mrs J. de Rothschild**
3 **ALL AFLOAT,** 6, b g Oats—Flotilla **Mr C. V. MacSwiney**
4 **AMARI KING,** 6, b g Sit In The Corner (USA)—Maywell **Mr M. Ward-Thomas**
5 **BASILEA,** 7, b g Strong Gale—Katie Kumar **Mr Simon Sainsbury**
6 **BEN HEAD,** 8, b g Crash Course—Arctic Deer **Anne Duchess of Westminster**
7 **BLUE BUCCANEER,** 7, b g Fine Blue—Port Dancer **Mrs D. K. Price**
8 **BLUE DART,** 10, ch g Cantab—Maisie Owen **Mr H. K. Padfield**
9 **BRIMSTONE HILL,** 7, br g Dynastic—Trysting Day **Lord Chelsea**
10 **BROADWELL,** 6, ch g Floriferous—Dromos **C. J. Leigh Travel Ltd**
11 **BUDDINGTON,** 5, b g Celtic Cone—Goolagong **Mr Simon Sainsbury**
12 **CAPUCHON,** 7, ch g New Member—Hattie **Mrs M. J. Trickey**
13 **CAROWAG,** 6, b m Scallywag—Morgan's Mark **Mr B. G. Hellyer**
14 **CELTIC SERF,** 6, ch m Celtic Cone—Branded Slave **Mr T. F. F. Nixon**
15 **CELTIC WALK,** 6, b g Celtic Cone—Bushwalks Daughter **Mrs A. L. Wood**
16 **CHATSBY,** 9, b g Sunyboy—Scotch Oats **Mr T. F. F. Nixon**
17 **CHERRYKINO,** 5, b g Relkino—Cherry Stack **Anne Duchess of Westminster**
18 **CLARA MOUNTAIN,** 11, b g Furry Glen—Oona More **Mr Simon Sainsbury**
19 **CLOVEN ROCKS,** 10, gr g Scallywag—Jenny Owen **Mr R. J. W. Fisher**
20 **CONA GLEN (NZ),** 9, ch g Lomond—Talento (NZ) **Mrs M. Wiggin**
21 **COPPER STREAK,** 8, ch g Streak—Copper Cloud **Lord Cadogan**
22 **CRYSTAL BEAR (NZ),** 5, b g Veloso (NZ)—Euphemia (NZ) **Lady Knutsford**
23 **EASTSHAW,** 8, b g Crash Course—What A Duchess **Mr Simon Sainsbury**
24 **EVENLODE,** 6, b g Netherkelly—Miss Curiso **J. Carleton-Paget**
25 **FENCE JUDGE,** 8, b g Green Shoon—Bramble Belle **Mr S. Preston**
26 **FIDDLERS THREE,** 7, ch g Orchestra—Kirin **Mr Simon Sainsbury**
27 **FILS DU PARC,** 7, b g Politico (USA)—Merry Leap **Mr James R. Adam**
28 **FIRE AT WILL,** 7, br g Random Shot—Kindly **Mrs Jeremy Cotton**
29 **FRIENDLY BANKER (AUS),** 6, b g Old Crony (USA)—Doubly Bold (AUS) **Gamston Equine**
30 **HARBOUR WALK,** 7, ch g Quayside—Shuil Alainn **Mrs A. Reid Scott**
31 **HOLLIST,** 7, b g Pollerton—Inagh's Image **Mr Simon Sainsbury**
32 **MAJOR MATCH (NZ),** 8, b g Frassino—Burks Rainbow (NZ) **Lady Zetland**
33 **MARRADONG BROOK,** 5, ch g Giacometti—Freuchie **Lord Cadogan**
34 **MOUNT PATRICK,** 6, b g Paddy's Stream—Hills of Fashion **Anne Duchess of Westminster**

CAPT T. A. FORSTER—continued

35 **NO POLITICS,** 10, b m Politico (USA)—Frockham Brae **Mr M. Ward-Thomas**
36 **PAYLINS,** 6, ch g Crash Course—Game Sunset **Mr Simon Sainsbury**
37 **PEGWELL BAY,** 9, b g Tobique—Multigrey **Major A. K. Barlow**
38 **PLAT REAY,** 6, b g Uncle Pokey—Hejera **Anne Duchess of Westminster**
39 **QUICK RAPOR,** 5, b g Rapid Pass—Dark Sensation **Major A. K. Barlow**
40 **RIO HIANA,** 5, ch g St Columbus—Kruganko **Lady Pilkington**
41 **ROYAL REFRAIN,** 5, ch g True Song—Polaris Royal **Mrs A. L. Wood**
42 **SALTY FARE,** 6, b g Furry Glen—Royal Account **G. S. Beccle**
43 **SOCIAL CLIMBER,** 6, b br g Crash Course—What A Duchess **Mr L. G. Kimber**
44 **SOUND OF ISLAY,** 5, b g Deep Run—Sharpaway **Lord Chelsea**
45 **SOUND OF JURA,** 5, b g Deep Run—Arctic Chatter **Lord Chelsea**
46 **TEAM LEADER,** 7, ch g Le Bavard—July's Pet **Lord Chelsea**
47 **THE DOORMAKER,** 8, ch g Balinger—Romany Queen **A. Harvey Ltd Maidenhead**
48 **THE KENDALIST,** 6, ch g Scallywag—Kenda **Mr T. F. F. Nixon**
49 **THE MOSSES,** 5, br g Kinglet—Yutoi Lady **Lord Leverhulme**
50 **THURLESTONE (NZ),** 7, ch g Balkan Knight (USA)—Tabessia (NZ) **Mr Ron Miller**
51 **THURSBY,** 7, br g Abyssinia—Dane Hole **Anne Duchess of Westminster**
52 **TIDAL STREAM,** 7, b g Paddy's Stream—Sea Empress **Mr S. Preston**
53 **TIME STAR (NZ),** 6, br g Drums of Time (USA)—Crescent Star (NZ) **Mrs C. H. Antrobus**
54 **TREMAYNE,** 7, b g Trimmingham—Beagle Bay **Miss V. Z. R. Cotton**
55 **UNCLE MERLIN (USA),** 9, b g Easy Gallop (USA)—Aunt Sheila (USA) **Mrs R. V. Chapman**
56 **WANTAGE,** 8, b g Relkino—Alma **Lord Chelsea**
57 **WHARRY BURN,** 9, b g Gunner B—Sarum Lady **Mrs G. C. McFerran**
58 **WHAT A TO DO,** 6, b g Le Bavard (FR)—Alfie's Wish **Mr J. B. Sumner**
59 **WOODGATE,** 9, ch g Quayside—Owen Money **Mr Simon Sainsbury**

Other Owners: Mr S. E. Allday, Mrs I. Cameron, Mrs J. E. Cannon, Mrs C. Clatworthy, Mr G. W. Cleaver, Miss H. Clegg, Mrs C. D'Arvo, G. Down, Countess Of Eglinton & Winton, Capt T. A. Forster, Mr Roger G. Gibbs, Mr R. L. Hinton, Mr J. Hornsey, Mr B. E. Luby, Mrs T. H. Luckock, Mrs G. D. Macswiney, Mrs M. M. Marnan, Lady McGowan, Mrs D. Padfield, Dr George Scott, Mr T. F. D. Simmons, Mr D. F. Sumpter, Mr R. Van Gelder, Mr D. H. Weller.

Jockeys (NH): H Davies (10-4), C Llewellyn (10-0).

Conditional: J Railton (10-0).

Amateur: Mr E Bailey (10-0).

224 MR J. R. FORT, Brandon

Postal: **27 High Shaws, Brandon, Co Durham, DH7 8QT.**
Phone: **DURHAM (091) 3782319**

1 **ALL OVER THE WORLD,** 6, b g Kind of Hush—Bosworth Moll **Mr J. R. Fort**
2 **BOY PAINTER,** 7, ch g Gunner B—Sister Anne **Mr J. R. Fort**
3 **HENISKI,** 7, b g Henbit (USA)—Noble Girl **Mr J. R. Fort**
4 **ROYAL ROUSER,** 7, b g He Loves Me—Royal Sensation **Mr J. R. Fort**
5 **SECRET FINALE,** 11, ro g Warpath—Fox Covert **Mr J. R. Fort**

225 MR J. E. FORTE, Teignmouth

Postal: **Barton Close Stables, Bishop Stainton, Teignmouth, Devon.**
Phone: **TEIGNMOUTH (062 67) 779211 OR 775377**

1 **DASSELLS,** 9, b g Thatching—Fallen Rose **Mr J. E. Forte**
2 **EMPEROR NAPOLEON,** 13, gr g Young Emperor—Polly Charlot **Mrs V. Forte**
3 **MISHY'S STAR,** 8, b m Balliol—Conte Bleu **Mrs V. Forte**
4 **MORNING TIDE,** 5, ch m Dubassoff (USA)—Tinatwo **Mrs V. Forte**
5 **MOYA MOWA,** 13, b m My Swallow—La Mariposa (USA) **Mrs V. Forte**
6 **MY MOYALE,** 7, b m Grandiose—Moya Mowa **Mrs V. Forte**
7 **OPTIMOSA,** 8, ch g Full of Hope—Wimosa **Mr J. E. Forte**
8 **SPRINGLAKE'S LADY,** 4, b f Music Boy—North Pine **Mr J. E. Forte**

Jockey (NH): A Forte (9-12).

Conditional: R Bellamy.

Amateur: A Wonnacott.

226 MR A. FOWLER, Scarborough

Postal: **1 Willerby Wold Cottage, Willerby Wold Farm, Staxton, Scarborough, YO12 4TF.**
Phone: **(0944) 70088**

1 **BALDWIN MILL,** 5, b g Milford—Irish Holiday **Mrs Rita Petcher**
2 **MARTIN O'SHAUNESSY,** 7, b g Martinmas—O'Shaunessy **Mr Ian Guise**
3 **QUIDEST,** 7, ch g Ovac (ITY)—Gothic Arch **Mrs G. C. Fairlie**
4 **ST SUNDAY'S BECK,** 4, ch g Nicholas Bill—Lingdale Lady **Mr Simon Marsh**
5 **WOODCHESTER GLEN,** 6, b g Furry Glen—Brave Wish **Mr C. McKinney**

Other Owners: Mr Peter Allwood, Mr Anthony Fowler, Mrs L. A. Fowler.

Jockey (NH): D Byrne (9-7).

Amateur: Mr A Fowler (11-3).

Lady Rider: Miss Alyson Deniel.

227 MR J. R. H FOWLER, Summerhill

Postal: **Rahinston, Summerhill, Co. Meath, Ireland.**
Phone: **(0405) 57014**

1 **ALTNABROCKY,** 6, br g Ovac (ITY)—Lady Talisman **Brian Smith**
2 **A TOUT A L'HEURE,** 6, b g Random Shot—Andromache (GER) **Baroness B. Von Stengl**
3 **BANKERS BENEFIT,** 10, b g Le Bavard—Credit Card **Mrs B. J. Fowler**
4 **BID'S DELIGHT,** 6, b m Furry Glen—Atlantic Hope **Brian Connon**
5 **BITOFADIFFERENCE,** 8, b g Laurence O—Gardinela **Mrs F. Barry**
6 **CHATTERING,** 5, ch m Le Bavard—Laurello **Lady J. Fowler**
7 **DORRHA DAISY,** 5, b m Buckskin (FR)—Quit The Hassle **Mrs F. Carroll**
8 **FACE TO FACE,** 6, b m The Parson—Helen's Tower **Mrs K. M. Johnson**
9 **FIRST OFFENDER (USA),** 5, ch g Hostage (USA)—McCooey (USA) **Michael Stroud**
10 **JEWEL STAR,** 6, b m Furry Glen—Quit The Hassle **Ms N. McGrath**

MR J. R. H FOWLER—continued

11 **MAID OF MONEY**, 8, b m Crash Course—Hansel Money **Mrs H. A. McCormick**
12 **MAIN AVENUE**, 8, b g Lucifer (USA)—Quick Miss **Mrs W. Cribbin**
13 **METELMI**, 4, b g Strong Gale—Steady Flow **S. P. Tindall**
14 **MISTER CHATTERBOX**, 9, b g Le Bavard—Farthest South **Mrs S. Reeves Smyth**
15 **MITSUBISHI COLOUR**, 4, ch f Cut Above—Bruntlaw **Mrs E. M. Burke**
16 **MUCH OBLIGED**, 7, b m Crash Course—Ahadoon **Mrs H. M. Robinson**
17 **NAMAJIRA**, 5, b g Furry Glen—Lady Grosvenor **Lady J. Fowler**
18 **NORTHERN LION**, 7, b g Northfields—Pride of Kilcarn **Miss P. F. O'Kelly**
19 **SUWANNEE**, 5, b g Black Minstrel—Fleeting Sunshine **C. S. Bird**
20 **TIME FOR GOLD**, 8, gr g Yankee Gold—Huluva Time **J. G. Graham**

Jockeys (NH): D P Fagan (9-7), A Powell (10-0, w.a.).

Conditional: M Fitzsimons (9-0).

Amateur: Mr A Coonan (10-0).

228 MR J. C. FOX, Amesbury

Postal: **Scotland Lodge Farm, Winterbourne Stoke, Salisbury, Wiltshire, SP3 4TF.**
Phone: **SHREWTON (0980) 620861 FAX (0980) 620270**

1 **ACROW LINE**, 5, b g Capricorn Line—Miss Acrow **Orthopaedic Bedding Advisory Service**
2 **BAGS**, 6, br m Heres—Dream Buck **Mr D. A. Ward-Smith**
3 **BALLAROCK**, 4, b f Ballacashtal (CAN)—Rockery **Mr J. C. Fox**
4 **BOUSHIE BOY**, 6, b g Red Man—Crendle Hill **Mr J. C. Fox**
5 **CUT'N DRY**, 10, b g Dubassoff (USA)—Dissipation (USA) **Orthopaedic Bedding Advisory Service**
6 **FRIENDLY HENRY**, 10, ch g Be Friendly—Henrys Lady **Mr R. V. Wright**
7 **GODIVA BEARINGS**, 8, b g Martinmas—Belle Fillette **Godiva Bearings Southern Ltd**
8 **JOMANA**, 4, ch f Roman Warrior—Tina's Magic **Mr M. M. Nashar**
9 **OBAS GIRL**, 5, b m Mansingh (USA)—Chinese Princess **Orthopaedic Bedding Advisory Service**
10 **PINK PUMPKIN**, 6, b m Tickled Pink—Wild Pumpkin **Mr P. J. Cleary**
11 **SUPREME NEPHEW**, 6, b g Sallust—Country Niece **Mrs P. Fox**
12 **TINKLING STAR**, 6, b g Lepanto (GER)—Tinkling Sound **Unregistered Partnership**

THREE-YEAR-OLDS

13 **TINA'S ANGEL**, b f Martinmas—Tina's Magic **Mr F. Deely**

TWO-YEAR-OLDS

14 **GLEN FINNAN**, ch f Ballacashtal (CAN)—Glen Kella Manx (Tickled Pink) **Bar Equipment and Refridgeration**

Conditional: S Fox (9-7), M Kane (9-7).

Amateur: J Saunders (9-7).

229 MR M. FRANCIS, Lambourn

Postal: **Folly House, Upper Lambourn Road, Lambourn, Newbury, RG16 7QG.**
Phone: **LAMBOURN (0488) 71700 FAX (0488) 72787**

1 **ALKINOR REX**, 5, ch g Welsh Pageant—Glebehill **Mr M. C. Peraticos**
2 **BOURBON SPIRIT**, 5, b g Ile de Bourbon (USA)—Indoor Games **Mr K. H. Fischer**
3 **DARK DESIRE**, 4, b g Alzao (USA)—Treble Cloud **Mr Jeremy Jones**
4 5, Ch m Last Fandango—Lyaaric **Mrs B. Bishop**

MR M. FRANCIS—continued

5 **METANNEE,** 6, b br m The Brianstan—Lyaaric **Mrs B. Bishop**
6 **POLYKRATIS,** 8, b h He Loves Me—Blue Persian **Mr M. C. Peraticos**
7 **PRINCE MERANDI,** 7, b g Blakeney—Copt Hall Princess **Merandi Bloodstock Ltd**
8 **SIEGERIN,** 6, b m Wolver Hollow—Sigtrudis **Mr K. H. Fischer**
9 **SILK DYNASTY,** 4, b g Prince Tenderfoot (USA)—Mountain Chase **Mrs V. Neill**
10 **THARROS,** 4, b c Nishapour (FR)—Bold Maiden (USA) **Mr M. C. Peraticos**
11 **WELSH PAGEANTRY,** 7, b m Welsh Pageant—Sacred Mountain **Mr K. H. Fischer**

THREE-YEAR-OLDS

12 **ATHLON,** b c Kings Lake (USA)—Antilla **Mr M. C. Peraticos**
13 **DARBY SKY (USA),** b c Darby Creek Road (USA)—Wimborne Sky (USA) **Mrs Virginia Kraft Payson**
14 **GREAT MILL,** b c Simply Great (FR)—Milly Lass (FR) **Mr Jeremy Jones**
15 B c Fairy King (USA)—Hillberry Corner
16 **MAPLE WALK,** b f Tumble Wind (USA)—Littoral **Mr K. H. Fischer**
17 **MERANDI SPECIAL,** b g Coquelin (USA)—Mountain Chase **Merandi Bloodstock Ltd**
18 **PERSPICACITY,** b f Petorius—Grattan Princess **Mr Merrick Francis**
19 **YASLOU,** ch g Yashgan—Lough Graney **Mr Mohammed Al-Sabah**

TWO-YEAR-OLDS

20 B f 7/3 Mazaad—Lydja (Hethersett)
21 B c 4/4 Green Ruby (USA)—Miami Blues (Palm Track) **Mr Merrick Francis**
22 B c 17/3 King of Clubs—Perfect Guest (What A Guest)
23 Ch c 6/3 Vaigly Great—Silent Prayer (Queen's Hussar)
24 B c 10/3 Nomination—Top Stream (Highland Melody) **Mr Mohammed Al-Sabah**
25 Ch c 3/4 Hatim (USA)—Vivungi (USA) (Exbury)

Other Owners: Mr J. R. Chitty, Mr Ron Parsons, Mr M. B. Small, Mrs Dagmar Vogelsang.

Jockeys (Flat): Paul Eddery (8-0, w.a.), John Reid (8-4, w.a.), Chris Rutter (7-7).

Jockey (NH): Mark Richards (10-0, w.a.).

Lady Rider: Miss J Russell (9-0).

230 MR R. B. FRANCIS, Malpas

Postal: **Cliffe Bank, Carden, Malpas, Cheshire.**
Phone: **(082 98) 515**

1 **AFTER FOUR,** 6, gr g Roselier (FR)—Caherelly Cross **Anne Duchess of Westminster**
2 **ALICE'S BOY,** 9, b g Tycoon II—Small Dragon **Mrs S. E. Roberts**
3 **CHIPPED METAL,** 11, b g Crash Course—Car Shine **Sir John Barlow B.T.**
4 **DOUBLE DANGER,** 6, b g Scorpio—Hemlock Cup **W. D. Francis**
5 **EYE SIGHT,** 7, b m Roscoe Blake—Pie Eye **Lord Leverhulme**
6 **GAELIC CHERRY,** 7, b g Gleason (USA)—Cherry Stack **Anne Duchess of Westminster**
7 **GOLDEN REDEEMER,** 12, ch g Gold Rod—Second Redeemer **Mrs E. J. Misa**
8 **HOWGILL,** 4, b g Tower Walk—In Form **Mrs Charles Lochart**
9 **MAJESTIC MISS,** 6, ch m Majestic Current (USA)—Moette **Mr M. W. E. Ritchie-Noakes**
10 **RATH WONDER,** 9, b g Golden Love—Ardglass Belle **Anne Duchess of Westminster**
11 **ROYAL CELT,** 6, ch m Celtic Cone—Doubly Royal **Anne Duchess of Westminster**
12 **STAR BURST,** 13, b g Busted—Pearl Star **W. D. Francis**
13 **TARA BOY,** 5, b g Rusticaro (FR)—Flosshilde **Mr D. O. Pickering**
14 **TEMPORARY AFFAIR,** 6, br m Mandalus—Jackie B **Sir John Barlow B.T.**

MR R. B. FRANCIS—continued

THREE-YEAR-OLDS

15 **HIGHFLYER TROOPER,** ch g State Trooper—Highflyer Park **Miss M. Arkle**
16 Ch g Red Sunset—Stunog Wood **R. J. McAlpine**

Other Owners: Mrs J. M. I. Ockleston.

Jockey (NH): S J O'Neill (10-0).

Amateurs: Mr D Barlow (10-6), Mr W Barlow (11-7).

231 MRS S. FRENCH, Meopham

Postal: **Ashmere Farm, Camer Park Road, Meopham, Gravesend, DA13 0AL.**
Phone: **(0474) 814397**

1 **BLOODHOUND,** 11, b g Armagnac Monarch—Miss Angle **Mrs J. R. French**
2 **ELOOT BRIGADE,** 12, b g Light Brigade—Diana Harwell **Mrs J. R. French**
3 **JUST A GHOST,** 14, gr g Rugantino—Just Snuff **Miss S. French**
4 **MORETON BAY (NZ),** 8, br m Bally Royal—Aramusha (NZ) **Miss S. French**
5 **PENNY HEDGE,** 6, gr m Neltino—Supreme Penny **Miss S. French**

Amateur: Miss S French (10-0).

232 MR R. G. FROST, Buckfastleigh

Postal: **Hawson Stables, Buckfastleigh, Devon, TQ11 0HP.**
Phone: **(0364) 42267**

1 **ALMOST CAUGHT,** 9, ch m Nearly A Hand—Kitty Fisher **Mr R. G. Frost**
2 **APACHE RYTHEM,** 7, b g Elvaston—Semi Quaver **Mrs P. Chase**
3 **BACKSTREET GIRL,** 6, b m Joshua—Lady C
4 **BRIGHT CORNER,** 5, br m Sit In The Corner (USA)—Bright Performance **Mr P. A. Tylor**
5 **BRYN TANGLE,** 11, b m Peter Wrekin—Phigaro's Tangle **Mr R. G. Frost**
6 **COMBERMERE,** 6, b g Absalom—Queen's Parade **Mr Jack Joseph**
7 **CORN MERCHANT,** 9, ch g Winden—Erra **Mrs Lynn Osborne**
8 **CRYSTAL COMET,** 6, gr m Cosmo—Neezerbel **Mr Victor G. Palmer**
9 **HOLD ON TIGHT,** 5, ch m Battlement—Holdmetight **Mr R. G. Frost**
10 **KINGSWOOD KITCHENS,** 10, b g General Ironside—Tyrone Typhoon **Mrs E. M. R. Ludlow**
11 **LASTING MEMORY,** 4, b f Ardross—Irreprochable **Mr B. P. Burnard**
12 **LITTLE MAN,** 6, br g Mandalus—Time Ago **Mrs Florence M. Lake**
13 **LOCKWOOD PRINCE,** 7, b g Tanfirion—Mink Fur (CAN) **Mrs J. McCormack**
14 **MASTER BARN,** 10, ch g Celtic Cone—Rummara **Mr Philip Rogers**
15 **MIRAMAC,** 9, b g Relkino—Magical **Mr R. G. Frost**
16 **MOUNTAIN RUN,** 6, b g Deep Run—Palaska **Mr M. J. Mulgrew**
17 **NORTHERN IMAGE,** 4, ch f Northern Tempest (USA)—Charlotte's Image **Mrs Cynthia Rogers**
18 **ON HER TOES,** 6, b m Hotfoot—Remeta **Mr R. G. Frost**
19 **PLAGUE O' RATS,** 6, b g Pitskelly—Hillbrow **Mrs Cynthia Rogers**
20 **PLAYPEN,** 6, b g Sit In The Corner (USA)—Blue Nursery **Mr P. A. Tylor**
21 **REGAL FLAME,** 7, b m Royalty—Firella **Mr P. A. Tylor**
22 **ROYAL GURKHA,** 10, b g Royalty—Nepal **Miss D. M. Eden**
23 **SEATON GIRL,** 6, b m Ovac (ITY)—Forest Music **Mrs J. McCormack**
24 **SHIPWRIGHT,** 9, br g Hotfoot—Ripeck **Mr Chris Unwin**
25 **SISTER CHERYL,** 5, ch m Vaigly Great—Miss Merlin **Mr B. P. Burnard**
26 **TERRERA,** 5, ch m Hard Fought—Bonne Femme **Mr R. G. Frost**

MR R. G. FROST—continued

27 **THE BAKEWELL BOY,** 8, br g Kemal (FR)—Warham Fantasy **Mr N. W. Lake**
28 **TIGHT TURN,** 11, ch g Avocat—Rufter **Mr R. G. Frost**
29 **TORRE TRADER,** 7, b g Ascertain (USA)—Warham Fantasy **Mr N. W. Lake**

Other Owners: Mrs M. J. Britton, Mrs B. P. Burnard, Mr Peter C. Clarke, Mr M. Cox, Mr C. S. Hawnt, Mr C. Roberts, Mrs Richard Stanley, Mr Nick Wright.

Jockey (NH): J Frost (10-0).

Conditional: P M Johnson (9-7).

Amateur: Mr P Hosegood (10-10).

233 MRS H. J. FULLERTON, Dorchester

Postal: **Park Farm Stud, Wanchard Lane, Charminster, Dorchester, DT2 9RP.**
Phone: **(0305) 65323**

1 **BACHELOR OF LAW,** 9, br g Cantab—Tangle Down **Mrs H. Fullerton**
2 **EGDON HEATH,** 7, ch g Some Hand—Alice Sweethorn **Mrs H. Fullerton**
3 **MAYFAIR MOSS,** 5, b g Telsmoss—Fair Frederica **Mrs H. Fullerton**
4 **MR MAJINTY,** 6, gr g Formidable (USA)—Boule de Suif **Mrs H. Fullerton**

234 MR D. R. GANDOLFO, Wantage

Postal: **Downs Stables, Manor Road, Wantage, Oxon, OX12 8NF.**
Phone: **(02357) 3242**

1 **AFALTOUN,** 5, b g High Line—Afeefa **Mr Harry W. Hopgood**
2 **ARDCRONEY CHIEF,** 4, ch g Connaught—Duresme **W. H. Dore**
3 **AUGHWILLIAM,** 10, ch g Le Bavard (FR)—Snipe Walk **Mr Roy Dale**
4 **BIETSCHHORN HUT,** 8, gr g Bruni—Hopeful Step **Mr A. W. F. Clapperton**
5 **BLUE DANUBE (USA),** 6, ch g Riverman (USA)—Wintergrace (USA) **Mr W. H. Dore**
6 **BOCA CHIMES,** 5, b g Welsh Saint—Howzat **Mr T. J. Whitley**
7 **CASTLE OAKS,** 7, br g Strong Gale—Gillogue **J. W. Prew & Sons (Garage Group)**
8 **CHEEKY CHAPLIN,** 4, b g Anfield—Saroan Meed **Miss E. A. Gandolfo**
9 **CLASSY BIRD,** 6, b m Sparkler—Slick Chick **Mr W. H. Dore**
10 **CLEANING UP,** 8, b g Carlburg—The Charwoman **Miletrian Limited**
11 **CURRAGH CADET,** 5, ch g Sandhurst Prince—Dunstells **Mr D. R. Gandolfo**
12 **DOOLIN,** 4, ch g Krayyan—Blunted **Mr D. R. Gandolfo**
13 **GARRY PIERRO,** 5, b g Pauper—Mrs Cafferty **Mr T. J. Whitley**
14 **GIOLLA WAY,** 11, b g Giolla Mear—Tina's Toi **J. W. Prew & Sons (Garage Group)**
15 **GO MILETRIAN,** 6, b g Sonnen Gold—Chestnut Hill **Miletrian Limited**
16 **GRANGE EXPRESS,** 6, b m Buckskin (FR)—Grange Hansel **Mr D. R. Gandolfo**
17 **HI' UPHAM,** 8, ch m Deep Run—Highly Acceptable **Mr R. E. Brinkworth**
18 **IMMORTAL IRISH,** 5, b g Lord Gayle (USA)—Royal Meath **J. W. Prew & Sons (Garage Group)**
19 **KING KAS,** 8, b g Pollerton—Lady Dikler **Miletrian Limited**
20 **LANDA'S TIPPLE,** 6, b m Jimsun—Beychevelle **Mrs Barry Marlin**
21 **LOTSCHEN LADY,** 6, b m Prince Regent (FR)—Irish Aunt **Mr A. W. F. Clapperton**
22 **MARSHLANDER,** 11, b g Sheshoon—Dinamarsh **Mr Osbert Pierce**
23 **MISS WRENSBOROUGH,** 7, b m Buckskin (FR)—Brieflet **Platinum Racing Ltd**
24 **NOBLE EYRE,** 9, br g Aristocracy—Jane Eyre **Mr A. E. Smith**
25 **PAGE OF GOLD,** 10, b m Goldhill—Chapter Four **Mrs A. E. Smith**

MR D. R. GANDOLFO—continued

26 **PREWSTYLE,** 5, b m Rymer—Darling Eve **Mr D. R. Gandolfo**
27 **REALLY NEAT,** 4, gr f Alias Smith (USA)—Tiddley **Mr R. A. Ellis**
28 **REMULA,** 7, gr m Remezzo—Consula **Mr D. R. Gandolfo**
29 **SARAH'S INFLUENCE,** 4, b c Orchestra—Markon **Mr D. R. Gandolfo**
30 **SHAHEAT,** 9, b g Parole—Golden Grove **Mr T. W. Newton**
31 **SHOPWELL,** 6, b g The Parson—Zitas Toi **Mr T. J. Whitley**
32 **STORMWATCH,** 7, b g Kambalda—Glenbrien Dusky **Mr T. J. Whitley**
33 **TRIBAL MASCOT (USA),** 5, b g Our Native (USA)—Little Lady Luck (USA) **Mr W. H. Dore**
34 **UPHAM RAINBOW,** 7, b g Pitpan—Kintrout **Mr R. E. Brinkworth**
35 **UPHAM VIEW,** 5, b m Oats—Real View **Mr R. E. Brinkworth**
36 **WATERMEAD,** 5, b g Oats—Mangro **Mr J. E. Brown**
37 **WELSH OAK,** 10, gr g Jimsun—Besselsleigh Lass **Mr G. E. Amey**

Other Owners: Mr C. P. Billot, Mr P. F. Boggis, Mr H. Candler, Mrs L. A. Deeley, Mr C. Dockar-Drysdale, Mr Stephen Freud, Mr A. E. P. Hayward, Mr A. J. Hayward, Mr J. Kelly, Mr G. Macdonald, Mr C. Mackenzie, Mr J. J. Mansworth, Mrs P. G. Melotti, Mr P. L. Mitchell, Mr T. J. Prew.

235 MR N. A. GASELEE, Upper Lambourn

Postal: **Saxon Cottage, Upper Lambourn, Newbury, Berkshire, RG16 7QN.**
Phone: **LAMBOURN (0488) 71503 FAX (0488) 71585**

1 **ALLEN'S ROCK,** 6, b g Abednego—Larne **Miss Anthea Gibson Fleming**
2 **ALTO CUMULUS,** 8, gr g Random Shot—Aughalion **Mr R. E. Morris-Adams**
3 **BARON TWO SHOES,** 4, gr g Baron Blakeney—Win Shoon Please **Mrs Terence A. M. Cockram**
4 **BRICKET WOOD,** 5, b g Black Minstrel—Royal Bonnet **The Hon. Diana Holland-Hibbert**
5 **CARVING KNIFE (AUS),** 8, ch g Sharp Edge—Royal Feast **Mr Simon Harrap**
6 **CINNAMON RUN,** 6, ch m Deep Run—Clarahill **Mr R. J. Jenks**
7 **DEVILS ELBOW,** 6, ch g Remezzo—Spartan's Legacy **H.R.H. The Prince of Wales**
8 **DUKE OF HAZARD,** 7, b g Royal Palace—Hot Lips Moll **Mrs Mary Crowdy**
9 **DUKE OF MILAN,** 13, br g Milan—Smart Answer **Mr N. A. Gaselee**
10 **FARMER BRYAN,** 4, ch g Deep Run—Erra **Mr B. A. Hawker**
11 **FOREST RAIN,** 7, b g Paico—Super Money Fan **Mr R. E. Morris-Adams**
12 **GARVENISH,** 5, b m Balinger—Wayward Pam **Miss F. M. Fletcher**
13 **GOWAN HOUSE,** 11, gr g Pongee—Carbia **Robert Ogden CBE**
14 **HOPE COVE (NZ),** 8, b m Mayo Mellay (NZ)—Bundoran (NZ) **Mr Simon Harrap**
15 **HOPE DIAMOND,** 7, b br g Sparkler—Canaan **C.G.A. (Horseracing 1988) Ltd**
16 **INSIGHT STAR,** 6, b g Record Run—Talahache Bridge **Insight Cartons Ltd**
17 **KENTISH PIPER,** 5, br g Black Minstrel—Toombeola **Mr M. G. S. Gibson**
18 **KILLERTON,** 6, b m Raise You Ten—Soave **Lady Carden**
19 **LIGHTNING WIND,** 7, b g Windjammer (USA)—Grace Note **Mr A. W. Schiff**
20 **LIVELY MEASURE,** 5, b g Nearly A Hand—Way of Life **Mrs R. W. S. Baker**
21 **MAJESTIC BRUNO,** 6, b g Majestic Maharaj—Palestine Fairey **Mrs Derek Fletcher**
22 **MARKET FORCES,** 7, b g Soldier Rose—Cover Your Money **Mrs R. W. S. Baker**
23 **MATERIAL GIRL,** 4, b f Busted—First Huntress **Mr T. E. S. Egerton**
24 **MORCINDA,** 4, ch g Ballacashtal (CAN)—Montelimar **Mr Neil A. McConnell**
25 **MOUNTAIN MUSE,** 6, b m Sunyboy—Royal Pam **Mr J. G. Charlton**
26 **MR ENTERTAINER,** 7, br g Neltino—Office Party **M. A. Boddington**
27 **MR PINKERTON,** 11, ch g Pauper—Chalk Slipper **M. A. Boddington**
28 **NECOCHEA,** 6, b m Julio Mariner—Mar Del Plata **Mrs L. G. M. Hannen**
29 **NEVADA MIX,** 6, gr h Alias Smith (USA)—Northern Empress **Mr Neil A. McConnell**
30 **PARTY POLITICS,** 6, br g Politico (USA)—Spin Again **Mr D. R. Stoddart**
31 **PRIVATE VIEWS,** 9, b g Radical—Informal Vue **Mrs G. Webb Bronfman**
32 **PRIZE COMMAND,** 13, br g Mandamus—Prize Catch **Lt Col J. C. Currie**
33 **PUCKS PLACE,** 9, ch g Midsummer Night II—Pirate's Cottage **Mr Julian Belfrage**
34 **PYLEIGH COURT,** 8, br g National Trust—Langton Water **Mrs M. Bradley**
35 **RADICAL VIEWS,** 5, b g Radical—Regency View **Mr D. R. Stoddart**
36 **SEA VALE,** 6, ch g Vital Season—Valeria **Mr J. G. Charlton**

MR N. A. GASELEE—continued

37 **SPACIAL (USA),** 6, b g Star Appeal—Abeer (USA) **Colonel John Ward**
38 **SPICE MERCHANT,** 4, b g Lucifer (USA)—Betty Sue **Mrs Richard Jenks**
39 **SQUIRE LAMB,** 5, gr g Absalom—Caroline Lamb **Robert Ogden CBE**
40 **TARN,** 12, b g Deep Run—Rambling **Mr Simon Harrap**
41 **UNSHAKEABLE,** 4, b g Oats—Another Breeze **Lady Carden**
42 **WESTERN DANDY,** 7, b g The Parson—Whisht Lassie **Mrs Derek Fletcher**

TWO-YEAR-OLDS

43 **PRINCE TINO,** b c Bustino—Northern Empress (Northfields (USA)) **Mr Sidney Mason**
44 Ch f Dominion—Zanubia (Nonoalco (USA)) **Sheikh Ali Abu Khamsin**

Other Owners: Mr Peter Bickmore, Colonel A. H. Parker Bowles, Mr Edgar M. Bronfman, Mr T. P. Charlton, Mr J. C. Crowdy, Mr M. E. T. Davies, Mr Simon Day, Mrs B. P. Hall, Mr P. Hannen, Mrs Tom Holt, Mrs D. Mayhew, Mrs M. A. Paravicini, Mrs Ann Parkinson, Mrs M. C. Peel, Mrs Gordon Pepper, Mrs Tim Perkins, Mr Robin Petherick, Mrs R. Pitman, Mrs D. J. Tellwright.

Jockeys (NH): K Mooney (w.a.), B Powell (w.a.).

Conditional: A Adams (9-7), E O'Donovon (9-7).

236 MR B. GEE, Worksop

Postal: **Highfield Bungalow, Greenway, Carlton-in-Lindrick, Worksop, S81 9EX.**
Phone: **OFFICE (0909) 567571 HOME 730306 FAX 569627 TELEX 547229 CONSOR G**

1 **LE JACOBIN,** 7, br g Rare One—Cooleen **Mr Brian Gee**
2 **MAJESTIC MASK,** 9, br g Majestic Streak—Newmaskin **Mr Brian Gee**
3 **MILFORD DOXY,** 6, br m Record Token—Malmaison **Mr Brian Gee**
4 **YORK IMPERIAL,** 9, br g Belfalas—Regency Princess **Mr Brian Gee**

Amateur: Patrick Gee (9-7).

237 MR J. T. GIFFORD, Findon

Postal: **The Downs, Findon, Worthing, W. Sussex, BN14 0RR.**
Phone: **FINDON (0903) 872226**

1 **ABBREVIATION,** 7, b g Torus—Worldling **Mr Peter Hopkins**
2 **ABLE LEADER,** 4, b g Beldale Flutter (USA)—Buckham Barn **Mr Fergus Conroy**
3 **BALLYHANE,** 9, ch g Crash Course—Golden Approach **Mr H. J. Joel**
4 **BEAU PARI,** 6, b g Beau Charmeur (FR)—Raised-In-Paris **Mr G. T. Radmore**
5 **BEDFORD BOY,** 5, b g Mandrake Major—Dalesview **Mrs T. F. Bliss**
6 **BIGNOR HILL,** 5, b g Hardboy—Marvellous Risk **Mr Maurice E. Pinto**
7 **BISHOPS ROCK,** 5, b g The Parson—Noctiluca (FR) **Mrs S. N. J. Embiricos**
8 **BOLLINGER,** 4, ch g Balinger—Jolly Regal **Mr R. Eliot**
9 **BOOK OF GOLD,** 5, b g The Parson—Bright Record **Mr H. J. Joel**
10 **BRADBURY STAR,** 5, b g Torus—Ware Princess **Mr James Campbell**
11 **BRONZE FINAL,** 7, br g Track Spare—Bronze Foliage **Mr S. D. Musson**
12 **BROOKMOUNT,** 8, ch g Bonne Noel—Neater **Mr H. T. Pelham**
13 **CARDINAL RALPH,** 6, b g Ovac (ITY)—Alice Minkthorn **Mrs S. N. J. Embiricos**
14 **CHARLTON YEOMAN,** 5, b g Sheer Grit—Bell Walks Breeze **Mrs Heather Alwen**
15 **CHIEF IRONSIDE,** 10, br g General Ironside—Killiney Lady **Mr H. J. Joel**
16 **CITY KID,** 5, br g Black Minstrel—Glenarold Lass **Pell-mell Partners**
17 **COMANDANTE,** 8, b g Candy Cane—Meakstown **Mr Maurice E. Pinto**
18 **COPSE AND ROBBERS,** 8, b g Hot Grove—Pearl Star **Mr J. N. Hutchinson**
19 **CORBITT'S DIAMOND,** 6, br g Le Bavard (FR)—Diamonds Gift **Mr H. J. Joel**

Triple Crown Products Ltd

Performance Horses Need Performance Feeds
The Triple Crown Concept of Equine Nutrition
Offers your horses feeds which are:-

1. Safe To Use – All Feeds are guaranteed free from all substances prohibited under Jockey Club Rules.

2. Simple and Flexible – Equipower can either be used in conjunction with other triple crown products or with conventional feeds such as clipped oats and bran.

3. Nutritionally Correct – Specific diets can be calculated for individual horses – A free service unique to Triple Crown.

For Free Presentation Brochure and Further details contact:-
Triple Crown, Portfield, Chichester, West Sussex. PO19 2NT
or Telephone 0243 774400.

MR J. T. GIFFORD—continued

20 **CORUSCATE,** 8, ch g Lucifer (USA)—Ten Again **Mr H. J. Joel**
21 **COUNTERPUNCH,** 6, b g Torus—Candy Belle **Pell-mell Partners**
22 **CYTHERE,** 6, gr g Le Soleil—Vinotino **Mr Ken Carr**
23 **DADDY'S DARLING,** 5, b m Mummy's Pet—Annie Get Your Gun **Southern Caravan Group**
24 **DARE SAY,** 7, b g Kris—Pampered Dancer **Mr Peter Hopkins**
25 **DAVY'S WEIR,** 10, ch g Paddy's Stream—Tevie **Mrs R. C. Lacy**
26 **DEEP COLONIST,** 8, ch g Deep Run—New Colonist **Mr Gordon G. H. Adcock**
27 **DEEP SENSATION,** 5, ch g Deep Run—Bannow Bay **Mr R. F. Eliot**
28 **DOOR LATCH,** 12, ch g Cantab—Kelly's Door **Mr H. J. Joel**
29 **EARL SOHAM,** 7, ch g Alias Smith (USA)—Lavenham Rose **Mr G. A. Hubbard**
30 **EDDIE KYBO,** 5, ch g Cidrax (FR)—Claragh Run **Mr I. Kerman**
31 **ENVOPAK TOKEN,** 9, ch g Proverb—Luck Token **Mr Frank Arthur**
32 **FIGHTING WORDS,** 4, ch g Prince Bee—How Hostile **Pell-Mell Partners**
33 **FINCHGLOW,** 7, ch g Some Hand—Lartway **Mr Jack Tully**
34 **FOYLE FISHERMAN,** 11, b g No Argument—Cute Peach **Mr J. N. Hutchinson**
35 **GENERAL CHRYSON,** 10, gr g General Ironside—Tropical Gold **Mr M. C. Peraticos**
36 **GENERAL GLORY,** 6, ch g General Ironside—Kilkileen's Glory **Mrs H. Ryan Price**
37 **GENERAL JAMES,** 7, ch g General Ironside—Royal Bonnet **Mrs Tracy Stone-Brown**
38 **GOLDEN MINSTREL,** 11, ch g Tudor Music—Ethel's Delight **Mr W. E. Gale**
39 **GOLD SHAFT,** 7, b g Kambalda—Golden Goose **Mrs A. N. Sturt**
40 **GRANYTE PALACE,** 6, b g Royal Palace—Aequanimitas **Mrs J. V. Yates**
41 **GREEN WILLOW,** 8, ch g Callernish—Kilwillow **Mr Peter Hopkins**
42 **HAIRY HAT,** 7, ch g Deep Run—Arctic Rhapsody **Mr H. T. Pelham**
43 **HARBINGER,** 5, b g Mandalus—Harvull **Pell-mell Partners**
44 **HEART OF KINGS,** 6, ch g Proverb—Biowen **Mr R. G. Fairbarns**
45 **LAKE TEEREEN,** 5, ch g Callernish—Gusserane Lark **Mrs A. T. Grantham**
46 **LOTHIAN SULTAN,** 6, b g Roscoe Blake—Lothian Lady **Mrs William Gunnery**
47 **LOUGH BROWN,** 7, ch g Ardoon—Nayleen **Mr Jim McCarthy**
48 **LUMLEY LAKE,** 7, ch g Le Bavard (FR)—Penthouse Girl **Mr H. Haskins**
49 **LYPHENTO (USA),** 6, b h Lyphard's Wish (FR)—Hasty Viento (USA) **Pell-mell Partners**
50 **MARK KYBO,** 6, b g Niels—Raglan Lane **Mrs I. Kerman**
51 **MIDNIGHT COUNT,** 10, b g Lauso—Rising Prices **Mr H. J. Joel**
52 **MISSING MAN,** 10, ch g Proverb—Castle Treasure **Mrs Leonard Simpson**
53 **MISTRAL STORY,** 5, b g Pitpan—Flashy Flake **Mr J. N. Hutchinson**
54 **MONTALINO,** 7, br g Neltino—Montage **Mrs Meriel Humphrey**
55 **MOZE TIDY,** 5, b g Rushmere—Church Belle **Mr Mervyn Greenway**
56 **MURPHY'S MAN,** 6, b g Belfalas—Speckled Leinster **Mr M. Rimell**
57 **NOBLE YEOMAN,** 6, b g King's Ride—Baronston **Mrs Heather Alwen**
58 **NODFORM,** 6, b g Good Thyne (USA)—Matriarch **Mr H. J. Joel**
59 **PADDYBORO,** 12, ch g Paddy's Progress—Kellsboro **Capt F. Tyrwhitt-Drake**
60 **PARADISE PARK,** 6, b h Nicholas Bill—Pandoras Gold **Parafix Tapes & Conversions Ltd**
61 **PELHAM SUITE,** 5, ch g Ovac (ITY)—Treasured Gift **The Pelham Hotel Racing Club**
62 **PENSIONER PATCH,** 8, ch g Grey Ghost—Final Edition **Mr Barry Fearn**
63 **PERSIAN STYLE,** 6, br g Persian Bold—Marcela **Mr Peter Hopkins**
64 **PRAGADA,** 7, b g Pragmatic—Adare Lady **Mrs M. G. L. McGlone**
65 **PROPERO,** 5, b g Electric—Nadwa **Mrs S. A. Willis**
66 **PROVING,** 6, ch g Proverb—Golden Strings **Mr R. F. Eliot**
67 **REGGAE YEOMAN,** 6, b g Black Minstrel—Toombeola **Mrs Heather Alwen**
68 **RETAIL RUNNER,** 5, b g Trimmingham—Deep Rose **Mrs A. N. Sturt**
69 **RUNNING SANDS,** 6, b g Record Run—Sirette **Mrs S. A. Willis**
70 **RYDAL PRIDE,** 5, b g Pry—Will Preach **Mr W. E. Gale**
71 **SCAMPERED,** 6, b m Scallywag—Quick Worker **Mrs G. C. Maxwell**
72 **SHORT LIST,** 7, b g Octavo (USA)—Allitess **Mr John Ingram**
73 **SIR'S AT THE GIN,** 9, ch g Al Sirat (USA)—Gin An Tonic **Lady Gibbings**
74 **SO PROUD,** 5, b g Idiot's Delight—Deep Pride **Mr S. P. Tindall**
75 **SOUTHERN SUPREME,** 7, b g Dunphy—Miss Etta **Southern Caravan Group**
76 **STUPID CUPID,** 6, b m Idiot's Delight—Trianqo **Mr D. T. Ellingham**
77 **SUN PEARL,** 5, ch m Le Soleil—Seed Pearl **Mr W. Tyrwhitt-Drake**
78 **SUPER SENSE,** 5, b g Pragmatic—Killonan Lass **Miss N. Hughes**
79 **SUPREME DEALER,** 5, ch g The Parson—Vul's Money **Mr John Galvanoni**

MR J. T. GIFFORD—continued

80 **TARAHUMARA,** 8, b m Soldier Rose—Cover Your Money **Southern Caravan Group**
81 **TENIENTE,** 6, ch g Smooth Stepper—Ballynavin Run **Mr Shaun Lawson**
82 **TEXAN COWBOY,** 6, b br g Prince Tenderfoot (USA)—Hy Carol **Miss J. Semple**
83 **THE ARTFUL RASCAL,** 6, b g Scallywag—Quick Exit **Mrs Richard Banks**
84 **THE WIDGET MAN,** 4, br g Callernish—Le Tricolore Token **Mr A. Ilsley**
85 **TOM TROUBADOUR,** 7, b br g Black Minstrel—Graceland **Mr S. D. Musson**
86 **VINCANTO,** 8, ch g Orchestra—Subiacco **Mrs C. Clatworthy**
87 **VODKA FIZZ,** 5, ch g Don—Doon Royal **Dick Richardson Horse Racing Limited**
88 **VODKATINI,** 11, b g Dubassoff (USA)—Olympic Visualise **Dick Richardson Horse Racing Limited**
89 **YABOYAA,** 6, b g Pragmatic—Trim **Mr H. J. Joel**
90 **YEOMAN FARMER,** 6, br g Trombone—Ballykeel Owen **Mrs Heather Alwen**
91 **YEOMAN METRO,** 6, ch g Pollerton—Plassey Queen **Mrs Heather Alwen**
92 **ZAMIL (USA),** 5, b g Lyphard (USA)—Wayward Lass (USA) **Mr Jim McCarthy**

Other Owners: Mr Roger Alwen, Mrs M. J. Arnold, Mr Clifford Benford, Mrs B. M. Biddlecombe, Mr P. F. Chalcraft, Mr R. Clarke, Mr J. W. Clement, Mrs P. V. Close, Mr Peter Fagan, Mr A. P. Furlong, Mr G. N. Garbutt, Mrs D. Hill-Wood, Mr T. Keogh, Mr Joe Kirtikar, Mr P. Langmead, Mr M. J. Marchant, Mrs E. A. Mason, Mr E. V. McGlone, Mr Geoff Meadows, Mrs J. I. S. Musson, Mr Paul Naret-Barnes, Mr W. R. Pelham, Mrs E. C. Pinto, Mrs L. Pinto, Mr Georges N. Robin, Mr C. Robinson, Mr G. R. Sones, Mr S. M. Speller, Mr B. T. Stewart-Brown, Miss M. J. Symonds, Mr T. F. Villiers-Smith, Mrs Derek Wigan, Lord Wolverton, Miss Carrie Zetter.

Jockeys (NH): T Grantham (10-2), Peter Hobbs (10-1), E McKinley (9-7), E Murphy (10-0), R Rowe (10-0).

Conditional: S Neighbour (9-7), T Pinfield (9-10), G Rowe (10-1).

Amateurs: Mr C Burnett-Wells (9-7), Mr P Lewis (10-0).

238 MR J. A. GLOVER, Worksop

Postal: **Pinewood Stables, Carburton, Worksop, Nottinghamshire.**

Phone: **WORKSOP (0909) 475425 (OFFICE) 475962 (HOUSE)**

1 **CALYMAR,** 4, gr c Bay Express—Tula Singh **Mr E. Bennett**
2 **COGENT,** 6, b g Le Bavard (FR)—Cottstown Breeze **Pell-mell Partners**
3 **CORAKI,** 4, b g Crofter (USA)—Eyry **Mr D. B. Ziff**
4 **COWLEY,** 5, gr h Kalaglow—Loralane **Lady Anne Bentinck**
5 **FIGHTER COMMAND,** 4, ch g Milford—Olga Wagner (ITY) **Mr D. Jenkins**
6 **FOOLISH AFFAIR,** 6, b g Decent Fellow—Silly Carina **Lady Anne Bentinck**
7 **FOR NOTHING,** 5, gr h Bay Express—Flitterdale **Mr Andrew I. Derry**
8 **GIDGEGANNUP,** 4, b c Magnolia Lad—Vulrory's Lass **Mrs A. Phipps**
9 **HIRAM B BIRDBATH,** 4, b g Ragapan—At The King's Side (USA) **Gilt Edge Thoroughbred Racing Plc.**
10 **HYDEONIUS,** 5, b g Crystal Palace (FR)—Razannda (FR) **Miss Charlotte Peters**
11 **INVASION,** 6, b g Kings Lake (USA)—St Padina **Lady Anne Bentinck**
12 4, B g Furry Glen—Last Princess **Lady Anne Bentinck**
13 **POWYS PRINCE,** 7, b g Roscoe Blake—Darling Eve **Atherton and Greens**
14 **RIVER FORTRESS,** 5, b g Swan's Rock—Wishing Trout **Lady Anne Bentinck**
15 **SANTO BOY,** 7, b br g Monsanto (FR)—Mandrian **Mr J. Rose**
16 4, B f Bustiki—Slings And Arrows **Mr R. W. Metcalfe**
17 **THATCHENNE,** 5, b m Thatching—Enterprisor **Mr J. McCann**
18 **THIS NETTLE DANGER,** 6, b g Kambalda—Golden Goose **Lady Anne Bentinck**
19 **YORKSHIREMAN (USA),** 5, ch g Our Native (USA)—Queen Vega (USA) **Hyde Sporting Promotions Limited**

MR J. A. GLOVER—continued

THREE-YEAR-OLDS

20 **HYDE AND PEAK,** b f King of Spain—Vivchar **Hyde Sporting Promotions Limited**
21 **MR MOCCASIN,** b g Doc Marten—Some Cherry **Mrs S. R. Brook**
22 **UNDERTONES,** b f Song—Tattle **Atherton and Greens**

TWO-YEAR-OLDS

23 **BEAUCROFT,** ch c Crofthall—Patent Pending (Goldhill) **Mr Nowicki (Crofthall Racing Ltd)**
24 B f Lyphard's Special (USA)—Bright Era (Artaius (USA)) **Mrs S. Glover**
25 **HELLO VANOS,** b g King of Spain—Flaming Peace (Queen's Hussar) **Mr M. P. C. Watson**
26 Ch f Scorpio (FR)—Kefhalik (Precipice Wood) **Mrs S. Glover**
27 B f King of Spain—Mondoodle (Monsanto (FR)) **Mr D. Bloy**
28 B g Valiyar—Naturally Fresh (Thatching) **Mr A. Morgan**
29 **SAMSOLOM,** b c Absalom—Norfolk Serenade (Blakeney) **Mr B. Dixon**
30 **SIBERIAN BREEZE,** gr c Siberian Express (USA)—Zepha (Great Nephew) **Mr Russ Rogers**

Other Owners: Mr S. Astaire, Mr A. W. Black, Mr Ken Boot, Mr R. F. Boot, Mr Colin G. R. Booth, Mr Bruno E. Ceser, Mr W. I. Derry, Mr M. Dews, Mr A. D. Downing, Mr Granville J. Harper, Mr Leslie Jones, Mr Jeffrey Newton, Miss Nicola Phipps, Mr N. K. Siegel.

Jockeys (Flat): G Carter (w.a.), D McKeown.

Jockey (NH): J J Quinn.

Apprentices: Thomas Ashley, Stephen Williams (8-0).

Conditional: Stephen Williams.

239 MR R. H. GOLDIE, Kilmarnock

Postal: **Harpercroft, Old Loans Road, Dundonald, Kilmarnock, Scotland, KA2 9DD.**
Phone: **TROON (0292) 314323/317222**

1 **BAITIN TIME,** 4, b g Sweet Monday—Mashin Time **Mr W. McIntosh**
2 **BROWNHILL LASS,** 9, ch m Sunyboy—Miss Craigie **Mr Andrew L. Paton**
3 **BUCK TO,** 5, b m Buckskin—Laurbon **Mr Robert H. Goldie**
4 **CELTIC SOMERS,** 7, ch g Celtic Cone—October Fair **Mr Robert H. Goldie**
5 **LADY MING,** 7, b m Flatbush—Mingside **Mr David K. Watt**
6 **SHIONA ANNE,** 6, b m Royal Fountain—Miss Craigie **Mr Andrew L. Paton**
7 **SUNY ZETA,** 6, b m Sunyboy—Blue Zeta **Mrs R. H. Goldie**
8 **THOMAS THE TANK,** 6, ch g Palm Track—Galah Bird **Mr Robert H. Goldie**
9 **WHISPERING KNIGHT,** 12, b g Rugged Man—Reynoldstown Maid II **Mrs R. H. Goldie**
10 **WILLS DAGG,** 7, b g Indiaro—Persian Stitch **Mrs R. H. Goldie**

THREE-YEAR-OLDS

11 **EASTER OATS,** b f Oats—Ice Lass **Mrs R. H. Goldie**

TWO-YEAR-OLDS

12 B g 28/6 Sunyboy—Ice Lass (Heroic Air) **Mrs R. H. Goldie**

Other Owners: Mr P. Baillie, Mrs A. Macdonald.

Conditional: G J Scope (9-7).

240 MR T. GOLDIE, Kilwinning

Postal: **'Oorain', Patterton Farm, Kilwinning, Ayrshire, Scotland.**
Phone: **TORNYARD (029485) 385**

1 **COLONEL ROSE,** 13, b g Fez—Rose Maroc **Mr T. Goldie**
2 **KALEIDOSCOPE,** 5, gr g Kalaglow—Pot Pourri **Mr T. Goldie**
3 **OORAIN LASS,** 7, b m Lord Nelson (FR)—Little Shewalton **Mr T. Goldie**

241 MRS A. C. D. GOODFELLOW, Earlston

Postal: **Leadervale House, Earlston, Berwickshire, TD4 6AJ.**
Phone: **EARLSTON (089 684) 541**

1 **DELIGHTFULPROSPECT,** 5, b m Idiot's Delight—Miss Prospect **Mr J. D. Goodfellow**
2 **JESTERS PROSPECT,** 6, b g Idiot's Delight—Miss Prospect **Mr J. D. Goodfellow**
3 **KING KANDA,** 12, br g Arctic Kanda—Red Satin **Mr J. D. Goodfellow**
4 **LARRY HILL,** 15, b g Laurence O—Must Run **Mrs J. D. Goodfellow**
5 **POLITICAL PROSPECT,** 8, b m Politico (USA)—Miss Prospect **Mr J. D. Goodfellow**
6 **SHERMAGO,** 8, b m Humdoleila—Tartarbee **Mrs J. D. Goodfellow**

Jockey (NH): B Storey.

Amateur: Mr P Doyle.

242 MRS S. J. GOSPEL, Kirbymoorside

Postal: **Low Wold Farm, Farndale, Kirbymoorside, York, YO6 6LB.**
Phone: **KIRBYMOORSIDE (0751) 33219**

1 **CANNIE'S CASTLE,** 7, b m Gypsy Castle—Cannes Beach **Mrs S. J. Gospel**
2 **MOONS QUADRILLE,** 14, b g Quadriga—Tailor Don **Mrs S. J. Gospel**
3 **THISTLE REEF,** 9, b m Take A Reef—Thistle **Mrs S. J. Gospel**

THREE-YEAR-OLDS

4 **PRI NEUKIN,** br g Mufrij—Cessy **Mrs S. J. Gospel**

TWO-YEAR-OLDS

5 **GOODWILL HILL,** b g State Diplomacy—Cessy (Burglar)

243 MR G. G. GRACEY, Ascot

Postal: **Lakeside Farm, Fifield Lane, Winkfield, Windsor, Berks, SL4 4QA.**
Phone: **WINKFIELD ROW (0344) 890461**

1 **ANNETTE'S DELIGHT,** 11, b g Idiot's Delight—On Safari **Coteville Group**
2 **BELHAVEN BILL,** 4, ch g Windjammer (USA)—Correct Approach **Mr Joe Gilio**
3 **FABLED ORATOR,** 5, b g Lafontaine (USA)—Brompton Rose **Dr P. Ash**
4 **GLENRUE,** 13, ch g Carnival Night—Naomi **Mr C. S. Harvey**
5 **HOLYBOURNE,** 6, br g Kind of Hush—Lady Antonia **Mrs Denise Stamp**
6 **JALEES,** 4, b g Precocious—Walladah (USA) **Mr W. R. Mann**
7 **LAKESIDE LASS,** 4, b f Import—Celtic Love **Mr Joe Gilio**
8 **L'ENCHERE,** 5, b m Lafontaine (USA)—Lady Bidder **Racing Thoroughbreds Plc**
9 **MR CARACTACUS,** 9, b g Hittite Glory—Carol Service **Mr John Mandeville**
10 **ROBERT FROST,** 8, gr g Fine Blade (USA)—Zagapu **Mr C. S. Harvey**
11 **SPLENDID FELLOW,** 9, br g Decent Fellow—Forest Fun **Mrs Denise Stamp**
12 **YANKEE SILVER,** 9, gr m Yankee Gold—Cup Bearer **Mr Thomas King**

MR G. G. GRACEY—continued

THREE-YEAR-OLDS

13 DJANILA, ch f Fabulous Dancer (USA)—Happy River **Racing Thoroughbreds Plc**
14 RING OF THE SOUTH, b g Jalmood (USA)—Saturne **Mr Joe Gilio**

Other Owners: Mr D. A. Ash, Miss Z. C. Davison, Mrs B. A. Hammond, Mr J. A. Judd, Mr Paul Stamp, Mrs Anthony Thorne.

Apprentice: Colin Munday (7-7).

Lady Rider: Miss Z Davison (8-7).

244 MR N. A. GRAHAM, Newmarket

Postal: **Coronation Stables, Newmarket, Suffolk, CB8 9BB.**
Phone: **TEL (0638) 665202 FAX (0638) 667849**

1 HIGH QUINTA, 4, ch f High Line—Jacquinta **Sue Warner**
2 MASTER PAT, 10, b g Paddy's Stream—Background **Lesley Graham**
3 NIGHT OF STARS, 4, b f Sadler's Wells—Glinting **Ovidstown Bloodstock**
4 VILLA BIANCA, 4, b f Mummy's Game—Belinda **M. J. Silver**

THREE-YEAR-OLDS

5 FIGHTIING BRAVE, b g Gorytus—Lady Habitat **Sir G. Brunton**
6 GAY GLINT, b g Glint of Gold—Gay Hellene **P. Jacobs**
7 SILKEN LINES (USA), b f Lines of Power (USA)—Bluebell **Lord Carnarvon**
8 SILKEN WAGER, b f Beldale Flutter (USA)—Satin Box **Lesley Graham**
9 VOLPEDO (USA), ch c Secreto (USA)—Votre Altesse (FR) **Saeed Manana**

TWO-YEAR-OLDS

10 ALWAYS ALLIED (IRE), b c 15/3 Dalsaan—Novesia (Sir Gaylord) **Allied Services**
11 BE A HONEY, ch f 7/2 Be My Guest (USA)—Reltop (High Top) **A. S. Leftwich**
12 FIRST EMERALD, b f 9/4 Sulaafah (USA)—Mavela (USA) (Empery (USA)) **Lesley Graham**
13 HELEN'S BOWER (IRE), b br f 15/4 Bellypha—Queen Helen (Troy) **Lord Weinstock**
14 MAPATO (IRE), ch c 13/4 Dara Monarch—Edansa (Majority Blue) **P. Jacobs**
15 B f Riverman (USA)—Noble Lady (USA) (Vaguely Noble) **Mrs T. Schumann**
16 B f 25/3 Nishapour (FR)—Photo Flash (Match III) **R. Greenwood**
17 ROUND TRIP (IRE), b f 23/2 Auction Ring (USA)—La Fortune (Le Haar) **Lord Weinstock**
18 Gr f 29/1 Another Realm—Shebeen (Saint Crespin) **A. S. Leftwich**
19 T V PITCH (FR), b f 7/2 Fast Topaze (USA)—Allatum (USA) (Alleged) **W. Rosenthal**

Other Owners: Leslie Harrison, Hon Simon Weinstock.

245 MR M. J. GRASSICK, Naas

Postal: **16 The Sycamores, Naas, Co. Kildare, Ireland.**
Phone: **HOME (045) 79858 FAX (045) 79858**

1 BLAZING DANCER, 4, b f Blazing Saddles—Take More (FR) **Mr David Laurencson**
2 CORVALLINA, 4, b f Corvaro—Carmelina **M. G. Hynes**
3 DOCHAS, 9, ch g Cawstons Clown—Greenwood Girl **Mr S. J. Mullin**
4 DOWNTOWN BOY, 7, br g Camden Town—Maxi Girl **Mr Robert H. Griffin**
5 FUCHSIA BELLE, 4, b f Vision—Judy's Pinch **Mrs M. J. Grassick**
6 HALIMAH, 4, ch f Be My Guest (USA)—Crannog **Mrs E. M. Cafolla**
7 JEMIMA YORKE, 4, b f Be My Guest (USA)—Noble Dust (USA) **Mr Robert H. Griffin**

MR M. J. GRASSICK—continued

8 **JUST FOR KICKS**, 4, br g Saher—Kix **Mr J. Gallagher**
9 **MAN OF STRAW**, 4, ch c Ela-Mana-Mou—House of Straw **M. G. Hynes**
10 **MO PHEATA**, 4, b f Petorius—Our Village **Oliver Murphy**
11 **NORTHERN MARINER**, 4, ch g Salmon Leap—Pitmarie **Miss P. F. O. Kelly**
12 **PERSIAN VALLEY**, 5, b g Persian Bold—Empress Valley **Mr P. Pender**
13 **QUELLE VITASSE**, 4, b f Henbit—Bureaucracy **Mr M. Mullally**
14 **STRONG EMOTION**, 5, b g Taufan (USA)—Stormy Princess **M. G. Hynes**
15 **TAMANGO LADY**, 5, b m Shack—Good Opportunity **John F. Ryan**
16 **WELSH LOVE**, 4, b f Ela-Mana-Mou—Welsh Flame **Miss P. F. O. Kelly**
17 **ZIZULA**, 4, b f Try My Best (USA)—Home Glo (USA) **Mrs R. M. Smyth**

THREE-YEAR-OLDS

18 **ALTEREZZA (USA)**, b c Alleged (USA)—Hester Bateman **M. G. Hynes**
19 **ANNER PRINCESS**, b f Prince Tenderfoot—Gay Krystyna **Lt Col J. Silcock**
20 **APPROVED AGENT (USA)**, ch c Caro—Attirance **Oliver Murphy**
21 **CONTRAPASATURA**, br f Kings Lake (USA)—Chapelet **Lugi Spa**
22 **CORLY SPECIAL**, b g Lyphard's Special—Courreges **Mr Leo Dowling**
23 **CREGGAN VALE LASS**, b f Simply Great (FR)—Silk Trade **Armagh Racing Club**
24 **DOPPIO FILO**, b f Vision (USA)—Dankalia **Lugi Spa**
25 **EMERALD RULER**, b c Tender King—Blue Gulf **Mrs M. J. Grassick**
26 **GLENFORM**, b c Glenstal (USA)—In Form **Mike Samlalsingh**
27 **GRECIAN QUEEN**, b f Fairy King (USA)—Grecian Sky **Mrs M. Power**
28 **HEAVENLY FEAT**, ch c Godswalk (USA)—Simingia **Mrs M. J. Grassick**
29 **IN WITH A CHANCE**, b f Assert—Dead End **Mr Robert H. Griffin**
30 **ORINOCO FLOW**, ch f Henbit (USA)—Sabrewing **Mrs M. Power**
31 **RATTLE AND HUM**, br c Vision (USA)—Geraldville **M. G. Hynes**
32 **RITUAL GIRL**, b f Ballad Rock—Liturgy **Oliver Murphy**
33 **ROMANZZINO**, b c Alzao (USA)—Pass Friend **Mr Paul Ronan**
34 **SAGASTINI (USA)**, br c Sagace (FR)—Martessana **M. G. Hynes**
35 **SUSSED OUT**, ch f Dara Monarch—Sussita **Oliver Murphy**
36 **THUNDER GIRL**, b f Horage—Sandcliff Girl **Waterside Stud**
37 **TWO MAGPIES**, ch f Doulab (USA)—Captive Audience **Mrs M. J. Grassick**
38 **WHO'S THE BLONDE**, ch f Cure The Blues (USA)—Tigeen **M. G. Hynes**

TWO-YEAR-OLDS

39 B c 18/2 Formidable (USA)—Exotic (Jaazeiro (USA)) **M. G. Hynes**
40 B f 25/3 Thatching—In Form (Formidable) **Mr Dermot O'Brien**
41 B f 27/5 Pennine Walk—Pendulina (Prince Tenderfoot) **Mrs S. Grassick**
42 B c 15/3 Horage—Pitlessie (Hook Money) **Mrs E. McLoughlin**
43 **PRINCE OF TARA (IRE)**, b c 28/2 Caerleon (USA)—Welsh Flame (Welsh Pageant) **Miss P. F. O. Kelly**
44 Ch f 15/5 Krayyan—Rashana (Sharpen Up) **Mrs M. J. Grassick**
45 B f 29/4 Drumalis—Victorian Pageant (Welsh Pageant) **Mrs M. J. Grassick**

Other Owners: Ted Naughton, Dr Tony O'Reilly.

Apprentices: T Daly (7-2), R Hughes (7-0).

Amateurs: Mr M J Grassick (11-7), Mr R Neylon (9-10).

246 MR F. GRAY, Haywards Heath

Postal: **Bulls Wood, Warninglid, Haywards Heath, West Sussex, RH17 5TE.**
Phone: **(044 485) 235 FAX (044 485) 485**

1 **KWI**, 4, b g Krayyan—Angevin **Mr Frederick Gray**
2 **LIZZIES LASS**, 5, br m Sandalay—Kiltegan **Mrs Liz Creber**

MR F. GRAY—continued

3 **MERRY MATIC,** 7, gr g Pragmatic—Victor's Valley **Mr Frederick Gray**
4 **SLIP UP,** 10, b g Quiet Fling (USA)—Artemis **Mr Frederick Gray**
5 **VIRGINIA PAGEANT,** 8, b g Welsh Pageant—Virginia Wade **Mrs Liz Creber**
6 **ZAMZAM,** 5, b m High Top—Nebiha **Mr Frederick Gray**

Other Owners: Mrs Jeanne Gray.

Jockey (NH): M Crosse (9-7).

247 MR T. R. GREATHEAD, Chipping Norton

Postal: **Chalford Oaks, Oxford Road, Chipping Norton, Oxon, OX7 5QP.**
Phone: **CHIPPING NORTON (0608) 642954**

1 **FIB,** 8, br g Sagaro—Ruskaja **Mrs S. Greathead**
2 **LITTLEGOOD GAMBLER,** 7, ch g Doctor Wall—Littlegood Lass **Mrs S. Greathead**
3 **METELA,** 14, b g Cheval—Litani River **Mrs S. Greathead**
4 **SANAMAR,** 6, ch g Hello Gorgeous (USA)—Miss Markey **Mrs S. Greathead**

Jockey (NH): William Humphreys (9-13).

Amateur: J Trice-Rolph (11-0).

248 MISS Z. A. GREEN, Carlisle

Postal: **Snittlegarth, Ireby, Carlisle, Cumbria.**
Phone: **(09657) 219**

1 **DIZZY DORA,** 10, b m Rubor—Little Dora **Miss Z. A. Green**
2 **DOLITINO,** 6, gr m Neltino—Sandoli **Miss Z. A. Green**
3 **DUNDEE VIOLET,** 4, ch f Ballacashtal (CAN)—Treatise **Mr Graeme K. Oram**
4 **HOMERIGG LAD,** 6, b g Spur On—Most Kind **Mr Graeme K. Oram and J. Ritchie**
5 **HYDARNES,** 7, b g Persian Bold—Callixena **Mr J. F. Brock**
6 4, Ro g Heroic Air—Just Millie **Miss Z. A. Green**
7 **NITE OF SPRING,** 12, ch g Hessonite—Hazel Spring **Mr D. R. Green**
8 **STARLIGHT ROCKY,** 14, b g This Above All—Anna Star **Miss Z. A. Green**
9 **VAN DER PUP,** 7, ch g Gypsy Castle—Cheap Gem **Miss Z. A. Green**
10 4, Ch g Tepukei—Vultop **Mr D. R. Green**
11 **WITERO,** 7, b g Heroic Air—Wits End **Mr D. R. Green**

TWO-YEAR-OLDS

12 B f 22/7 Majestic Streak—Grey Shade VII **Mrs S. Mohacs**
13 Ro f 25/4 Majestic Streak—Just Millie **Miss Z. A. Green**
14 B c 10/5 Gypsy Castle—Vultop (Vulgan Slave) **Mr D. R. Green**

Other Owners: Mr A. Hastie, Mrs K. E. Phillips.

Jockey (Flat): S Keightley (8-8, w.a.).

Jockey (NH): M Meagher (w.a.).

Conditional: J O'Gorman (9-7, w.a.).

249 MR G. G. A. GREGSON, Shepton Mallet

Postal: **Beech Tree Stud, Upton Noble, Shepton Mallet, Somerset, BA4 6AX.**
Phone: **(0749) 85245**

1 **LEAVE IT OUT,** 8, b g Over The River (FR)—Tevie **Mr G. G. A. Gregson**
2 **ROCK SAINT,** 13, ch g St Columbus—Moon Venture **Mr G. G. A. Gregson**
3 **SIDEBUCK,** 6, b g General Ironside—Angels Mount **Mr G. G. A. Gregson**

250 MR D. R. GREIG, Cranleigh

Postal: **Pittance Farm, Smithwood Common, Cranleigh, Surrey, GU6 8QY.**
Phone: **CRANLEIGH (0483) 272737**

1 **BOLD CARL,** 7, b g Carlburg—Aerial Orchid **Mr D. R. Greig**
2 **GEE UP,** 7, b g Buckskin (FR)—Sarah Gee **Mr D. R. Greig**
3 **HUMANITY DICK,** 9, ch g Laurence O—Carraig Cottel **Mr D. R. Greig**
4 **JUVENILE PRINCE,** 12, b g Pitpan—Juveno **Mr D. R. Greig**
5 **MOUNT EATON FOX,** 7, b g Buckskin (FR)—Town Fox **Mr D. R. Greig**
6 **PUNDIT,** 6, gr g Bellypha—Pundy **Mr D. R. Greig**
7 **TARTAN TRIUMPH,** 11, ch g Deep Run—Farranfore **Mr D. R. Greig**

251 MR S. G. GRIFFITHS, Carmarthen

Postal: **Rwyth Farm, Nantgaredig, Carmarthen, Dyfed, Wales.**
Phone: **(02672) 90321**

1 **FAIR AGNES,** 6, b m Official—Miss Pat **Mr S. G. Griffiths**
2 **NORTON'S COIN,** 9, ch g Mount Cassino—Grove Chance **Mr S. G. Griffiths**
3 **OFFICIAL LADY,** 6, b m Official—Kick About **Mr S. G. Griffiths**

252 MR D. M. GRISSELL, Heathfield

Postal: **Brightling Park, Robertsbridge, East Sussex, TN32 5HH.**
Phone: **BRIGHTLING (042 482) 241**

1 **BARNSDALE,** 5, ch g Ahonoora—Marfisa **Mr M. F. Sanderson**
2 **BREAKFAST BELLE,** 5, b m Oats—Beau Wonder **Mr F. T. Parsons**
3 **BREAKFAST CAR,** 8, b g Oats—Drawing Room Car **Mr John Grist**
4 **CLEVER DICK,** 5, b g Cosmo—Princess Albertina (FR) **Mrs P. S. Donkin**
5 **FAARIS,** 9, b g Troy—Real Snug **Mrs Eric Boucher**
6 **JUST A BOOZER,** 6, b g Just A Monarch—Vineyard **Mrs A. E. Piper**
7 **KETTI,** 5, br m Hotfoot—Nigrel **Mr John Lister (Reigate)**
8 **LE CHAT NOIR,** 7, br g Paico—June **Lady Harmsworth-Blunt**
9 **MAYBOURNE,** 6, ch g Deep Run—Easy Can **Mr M. F. Sanderson**
10 **MEN OF YORKSHIRE,** 7, b g Uncle Pokey—Hejera **Mrs Jean R. Bishop**
11 **NO WAY JOSE,** 6, b m Sunyboy—Metaxa **Mr J. O'Reilly-Cicconi**
12 **RODELINDA,** 4, br f Ranksborough—Frimley Grove **Mrs M. de Jong**
13 **SERIOUS MAN,** 7, b g Sexton Blake—Lorna Doone (USA) **Mr John W. Musson**
14 **STATELY LOVER,** 7, b g Free State—Maid In Love **Mrs Jean R. Bishop**
15 **SUMMERHILL SHADOW,** 5, gr g Alias Smith (USA)—New Top **Summerhill Stud Ltd**
16 **URBAN SURFER,** 6, b g Le Bavard (FR)—Reynella **Mrs John Grist**
17 **YELLOW SPRING,** 5, b g Buckskin (FR)—Carrigello **Lady Harmsworth-Blunt**

MR D. M. GRISSELL—continued

Other Owners: Mr M. Bridger, Mrs D. M. Grissell, Mr S. R. W. Houghton, Mr J. Keighley, Mr H. G. Musson, Mr Robert D. Simpson.

Jockey (NH): H Davies (w.a.).

Conditional: P Collins (9-7).

Amateur: Mrs Diana Grissell (8-7).

253 MR B. GUBBY, Bagshot

Postal: **Dukes Wood, Bracknell Road, Bagshot, Surrey.**
Phone: **DAY (0276) 63282 EVENING (0276) 71030 TELEX: 858956 FAX: 0276 26964**

1 **BEAU'S DELIGHT (USA),** 4, b f Lypheor—Beauvoir **The Forum Ltd**
2 **CONE LANE,** 4, ch g On Your Mark—Cee Beauty **Brian Gubby Ltd**
3 **JUST SEYMOUR,** 4, ch g Seymour Hicks (FR)—Pennycress **Brian Gubby Ltd**
4 **RED DOLLAR,** 5, ch g Tachypous—Burglars Girl **Brian Gubby Ltd**

THREE-YEAR-OLDS

5 **BELFORT RULER,** b c Belfort (FR)—Call Me Kate **Brian Gubby Ltd**
6 **GABARDOON,** b g Gabitat—Its For Sure **Brian Gubby Ltd**
7 **USA DOLLAR,** b c Gabitat—Burglars Girl **Brian Gubby Ltd**

TWO-YEAR-OLDS

8 **EAST SUNRISE,** ch c Gabitat—Rueful Lady (Streetfighter)
9 **FORLORN DIVER,** ch c Ballacashtal (CAN)—Four Lawns (Forlorn River)
10 **GABIBTI (IRE),** ch f Dara Monarch—Torriglia (USA) (Nijinsky (CAN))
11 **LUCAYA,** br c Gabitat—Queen's Bidder (Auction Ring (USA))
12 **MY HOSTESS,** b f Gabitat—Its For Sure (Ardoon)
13 **NISHAPOUR KID,** b c Nishapour (FR)—Crane Beach (High Top)
14 **ONE DOLLAR MORE,** b c Gabitat—Burglars Girl (Burglar)
15 **PLAYSAYYAF (IRE),** br c Sayyaf—Playtime (Primera)

254 MR R. GUEST, Newmarket

Postal: **Chestnut Tree Stables, Exeter Road, Newmarket, Suffolk, CB8 8LR.**
Phone: **(0638) 661508 FAX (0638) 661508**

1 **ALDBOURNE,** 4, b f Alzao (USA)—Steady The Buffs **Mr Vijay Mallya**
2 **BID LATER,** 4, b f Auction Ring (USA)—Twenty-Two (FR) **Mrs B. Long**
3 **GRAMINIE (USA),** 4, gr g Graustark—Etoile d'Orient **Mrs B. Long**
4 **HEROES SASH (USA),** 5, b h Lypheor—Salish **Mr Norman Jones**
5 **RUN FREE,** 5, b g Julio Mariner—Lucky Appeal **Mrs R. Smith**

THREE-YEAR-OLDS

6 **ALICANTE,** b c Alzao (USA)—Safe And Happy **Mrs R. Smith**
7 **BOURBONVILLE (DEN),** b f Mashhor Dancer (USA)—Indoor Games **Mr J. Mathiesen**
8 **CAFFARELLI,** b c Mummy's Pet—Klewraye **Mrs B. Long**
9 **CELESTIAL GUEST (USA),** b c Northjet—Tobira Celeste (USA) **Dr J. E. Hennau**
10 **CONYGAR PARK,** b c Mummy's Treasure—Whistling Girl **Mr Christopher P. J. Brown**
11 **CORRIANNE,** ch f Balidar—Serdarli **Mr Mehmet Hassan**
12 **CURTAIN UP (FR),** ch c Sicyos (USA)—Angelina d'Or **Lord Delfont**
13 **EMERALD KING,** b c Fairy King (USA)—So Serene **Mrs Seamus Purcell**
14 **GLAZERITE,** b c Dunphy—Rust Free **P. G. Glazerite Ltd**

MR R. GUEST—continued

15 **LADY LITA,** b f Jalmood (USA)—Lady of The Manor **Mr Ettore Landi**
16 **NORTH BASE,** b c Hard Fought—Bases Loaded (USA) **Mr Ettore Landi**
17 **RAINBOW STRIPES,** ch c Rainbow Quest (USA)—Pampas Miss (USA) **Mr Jorgen Strecker**
18 **SYRING (FR),** ch c Sicyos (USA)—Lady Ring **Mr A. Branchini**
19 **TAWJIH (USA),** b c Lyphard's Wish (FR)—Chop Towhee (USA) **Mrs Seamus Purcell**
20 **VAIRAGYA (FR),** gr c Mendez (FR)—Exigence (USA) **Mr D. Woods**

TWO-YEAR-OLDS

21 **ALKABAR,** ch c 2/3 Nordance (USA)—The Ice Maiden (Native Bazaar) **Mr R. J. Wilkinson**
22 **FORT SORENO (DEN),** gr c 14/1 Belfort (FR)—Gavea (African Sky) **Mr W. Bechmann**
23 **GALLERY ARTIST (IRE),** ch c 7/5 Tate Gallery (USA)—Avec L'Amour (Realm) **Mrs Seamus Purcell**
24 **NIGEL'S LUCKY GIRL,** gr f 19/2 Belfort (FR)—Haiti Mill (Free State) **Mr N. Greening**
25 **STRECKINSKI,** ch c 2/5 Niniski (USA)—Princesse Timide (USA) (Blushing Groom (FR)) **Mr Jorgen Strecker**

Other Owners: Mr R. Axford, Mr R. Brichart, Mr J. Chapman, Mr D. Davenport, Mr K. Greening, Mr P. Greening, Mr R. Greening, Mr Rae Guest, Mr P. S. Hubbard, Mr C. J. Mills, Mrs Lesley Mills, Capt W. J. Pratt, Mr B. J. Randall, Rhodabourne Ltd, Mr T. P. Singleton, Mr John E. Smith, Mr D. J. Willis.

Jockeys (Flat): P Brette (7-12), Paul Eddery (w.a.).

Jockey (NH): Richard Guest (w.a.).

Apprentices: S Eiffert (7-4), B W Foote.

Lady Rider: Mrs Britt Guest.

255 MR W. J. HAGGAS, Newmarket

Postal: **Somerville Lodge, Fordham Road, Newmarket, Suffolk, CB8 7AA.**
Phone: **NEWMARKET (0638) 667013 FAX (0638) 660534**

1 **BURN BRIDGE (USA),** 4, b c Linkage (USA)—Your Nuts (USA) **Mr B. Haggas**
2 **COLD MARBLE (USA),** 5, b g Told (USA)—Coney Dell **Mr A. J. Green**
3 **FAG IN HAND,** 5, ch g Music Boy—Brig of Ayr **Mrs M. M. Haggas**
4 **MERRY NUTKIN,** 4, ch g Jalmood (USA)—Merry Cindy **Mr R. F. S. Newall**
5 **THRESHFIELD (USA),** 4, b c Northern Prospect (USA)—French Cutie (USA) **Mr B. Haggas**
6 **TYLER'S WOOD,** 5, br g Homing—Beryl's Jewel **Mrs J. A. Redmond**

THREE-YEAR-OLDS

7 **AIREDALE (USA),** b c Dixieland Band (USA)—Good Hart (USA) **Mr B. Haggas**
8 **ALTAIA (FR),** gr f Sicyos (USA)—Haloom **Mr P. A. Deal**
9 **DAYMER BAY,** b f Lomond (USA)—Clarista (USA) **Mr C. T. Spencer-Phillips**
10 **DODGY,** b g Homing—Beryl's Jewel **Mr J. A. Redmond**
11 **DRUDWEN,** ch f Sayf El Arab (USA)—Roller Bird (FR) **Mr J. E. Lloyd**
12 **FACILITY LETTER,** gr g Superlative—Facetious **Mr A. M. Shead**
13 **FUGLER'S FOLLY,** b g King of Spain—Djellaba **Mr R. C. Thompson**
14 **HIGHLY DESIRABLE,** b f High Top—Snub **Cheveley Park Stud**
15 **MIDNIGHT FLUTTER,** b f Beldate Flutter (USA)—Brickfield Queen **Mr T. M. Saud**
16 **NUMBER ONE LADY,** ch f Shernazar—Yankee Lady **Mr G. J. H. Carroll**
17 **PIMSBOY,** b g Tender King—Hitopah **Pims International Plc**
18 **PLEASURE FLIGHT,** b f Jalmood (USA)—Third Movement **Cheveley Park Stud**
19 **RAW TALENT,** b g Gorytus (USA)—Welcome Break **Hon M. S. K. Greenway**
20 **REGAL HAND,** br g King of Spain—Llanddona **Mrs M. M. Haggas**
21 **SHAMPOO,** ch c Sharpo—Wasslaweyeh (USA) **Mr Ali K. Al Jafleh**
22 **SMART MAGICIAN (USA),** b c Clever Trick (USA)—Straight Edition (USA) **Mr B. Haggas**
23 **WISH QUICK (CAN),** br f Lyphard's Wish (FR)—Quicksand (USA) **Mrs Mary A. Sullivan**

MR W. J. HAGGAS—continued

TWO-YEAR-OLDS

24 **ARABIAN BOLD (IRE)**, b c 7/4 Persian Bold—Bodham (Bustino) **Sheikh Amin Dahlawi**
25 **AUTUMNAL (IRE)**, b f 22/2 Fast Topaze (USA)—Awatef (Ela-Mana-Mou) **Mr P. A. Deal**
26 **BOG TROTTER (USA)**, ch c 9/4 Irish River (FR)—Chaleur (CAN) (Rouge Sang (USA)) **Mr B. Haggas**
27 **BORBOLETA (USA)**, b f 29/3 General Holme (USA)—Naskrahoney (USA) (Naskra (USA)) **Countess Trevisio**
28 **BRASS MONKEY (USA)**, ch c 11/3 It's Freezing (USA)—Josalee (USA) (Jolie Jo (USA)) **Mr B. Haggas**
29 **BUBBLE AWAY (USA)**, b f 12/4 Tonzarun (USA)—
Sister Sophie (USA) (Effervescing (USA)) **Cheveley Park Stud**
30 **CEDRELA (USA)**, ch c 7/2 Assert—Hot Princess (Hot Spark) **Mr B. Haggas**
31 Ch c 26/2 Sagace (FR)—Formartin (USA) (Forli (ARG)) **Mr B. Haggas**
32 **GREEN'S FERNELEY (IRE)**, gr c 12/4 Taufan (USA)—
Rossaldene (Mummy's Pet) **Richard Green (Fine Paintings)**
33 **GWENNOL (IRE)**, b f 20/5 Sayf El Arab (USA)—Roller Bird (FR) (Ribocco) **Mr J. E. Lloyd**
34 **HIGH LOW (USA)**, b c 26/4 Clever Trick (USA)—En Tiempo (USA) (Bold Hour) **Mr B. Haggas**
35 **LATIN QUARTET**, b c 16/2 Chief Singer—Pampas Miss (USA) (Pronto (ARG)) **Mr A. M. Shead**
36 **LOADER**, b c 19/4 Jester—Savahra (Free State) **Miss J. H. Ashbourne**
37 **MISS MIRROR**, gr f 23/4 Magic Mirror—Rhein Symphony (Rheingold) **O. M. J. Bassett**
38 B f 3/5 Hagley (USA)—My Mademoiselle (USA) (Buckaroo (USA)) **Richard Green (Fine Paintings)**
39 **NISHA**, gr f 8/2 Nishapour (FR)—Eary Glas (Reform) **Mrs M. M. C. Clark**
40 **PARFUM D'AUTOMNE (FR)**, b f 29/4 Sharpen Up—Leaf Fall (FR) (Lyphard (USA)) **Mrs M. M. C. Clark**
41 **PERSIAN HAT (IRE)**, ch c 16/3 Hatim (USA)—Persian Myth (Persian Bold) **Mr D. B. Thompson**
42 **PIMS GUNNER (IRE)**, b g 11/2 Montelimar (USA)—My Sweetie (Bleep-Bleep) **Pims International Plc**
43 **PUNCH THE AIR**, ch f 13/3 Northjet—Joyfully (FR) (Dilettante II) **Mr R. L. Burton**
44 **ROMOLA NIJINSKY**, b f 10/5 Bustino—Verchinina (Star Appeal) **Mr W. J. Gredley**
45 **RYEWATER DREAM**, b f 14/4 Touching Wood (USA)—Facetious (Malicious) **Mrs R. Farrell**
46 **SHUTTLE (IRE)**, b g 3/4 Alzao (USA)—Albeni (Great Nephew) **Mr Ali K. Al Jafleh**
47 **SO PERSISTENT**, b f 11/2 High Top—Alcassa (FR) (Satingo) **Mr C. T. Spencer-Phillips**
48 **ST ENODOC**, gr c 10/3 Bellypha—Girton (Balidar) **Mr C. T. Spencer-Phillips**
49 Br f 23/3 Tsunami Slew (USA)—Summertime Lady (USA) (No Robbery) **Richard Green (Fine Paintings)**
50 Ch c 28/3 The Minstrel (CAN)—Thats The Reason (USA) (Bold Reason) **Kennet Valley Thoroughbreds Ltd**
51 **TOP COPY**, b f 13/3 High Top—Minsden's Image (Dancer's Image) **Mr I. A. Southcott**
52 B f 3/3 Doulab (USA)—Tunguska (Busted) **Richard Green (Fine Paintings)**
53 B f 31/1 El Gran Senor (USA)—Une Amazone (USA) (Youth) **Mr G. J. H. Carroll**
54 **WINE TASTER (IRE)**, br c 10/2 Rousillon (USA)—Choire Mhor (Dominion) **Mr B. Haggas**

Other Owners: Mr J. Bogie, Mr T. Cheshire, Mr B. Fugler, Mr G. C. R. Griffiths, Mr W. P. Jenks, Mr A. E. Lloyd, Mr E. J. Lloyd, Mr I. W. T. Loftus, Mrs F. Phillips-Browne, Mrs M. Rosenthal, Miss D. A. Shead.

Apprentice: Ron Hillis (7-12).

Lady Rider: Mrs M Haggas (9-0).

256 MR W. W. HAIGH, Malton

Postal: **Spring Cottage Stables, Langton Road, Norton, Malton, North Yorkshire.**
Phone: **MALTON (0653) 694428**

1 **ARCTIC OATS**, 5, ch m Oats—Arctic Festival **Mr R. P. Dineen**
2 **EAST LIMERICK**, 7, b g Sexton Blake—Shonna (USA) **Mr W. W. Haigh**
3 **HANSOM LAD**, 7, b g Dublin Taxi—Trackalady **Mrs V. Haigh**
4 **HINARI HI FI**, 5, b m Song—Sarah Siddons **J. E. Abbey**
5 **LEACROFT**, 6, b g Domitor (USA)—Whitmarsh **Mr W. W. Haigh**
6 **RED INDIAN**, 4, ch c Be My Native (USA)—Martialette **Mr Dave Marshall**
7 **SAINT TRISTAN**, 6, b g Tyrnavos—Greyburn **Mr A. L. Robinson**
8 **STEPPEY LANE**, 5, b m Tachypous—Alpine Alice **Dr C. I. Emmerson**
9 **SUPER TRUCKER**, 7, br g Lochnager—The Haulier **J. R. Adams**
10 **TENDER TILLY**, 4, b f Tender King—Nightly Dip **Mr A. Marucci**

MR W. W. HAIGH—continued

THREE-YEAR-OLDS

11 **AMIRA T' SAHRRA,** b f Little Wolf—Mummy's Whistler **Gary International Ltd**
12 **BELDALE LADY,** b f Beldale Flutter (USA)—Knavesmire **Mr C. B. Rennison**
13 **BRIGHT START,** ch c Precocious—Perma Fina **Dr C. I. Emmerson**
14 **CARLTON MOOR,** gr f Mandrake Major—Greyburn **Mr A. L. Robinson**
15 **CLAUDIA MISS,** b f Claude Monet (USA)—Palace Travel **Mr W. W. Haigh**
16 **COLVIN LAD,** gr g Rusticaro (FR)—Twice Regal **Mrs M. Molloy**
17 **GOODFELLOWS LOT,** br g Blazing Saddles (AUS)—Just Kidding
18 **PRINCESS OF BASRA,** ch f Bairn (USA)—Miss Nelski **Tim Hawkins**

TWO-YEAR-OLDS

19 **DERRING PET,** br c 30/3 Daring March—Mummy's Whistler **Gary International Ltd**
20 **FALCON BERRY (FR),** b c 25/3 Precocious—
21 Br c 27/2 Balidar—Flashy Looker **B. A. Shovelton (North Wales) Ltd**
22 **ON THE REBOUND,** b f 20/4 Lidhame—Janlarmar **Mrs P. Valentine**
23 Ch f 23/4 Ballacashtal (CAN)—Parabems
24 **SILKEN DREAM (IRE),** b f 6/4 Cataldi—Bonny Bertha
25 Ch c 25/5 All Systems Go—Tzu-Hsi

Other Owners: Mrs E. A. Barber, Mr N. Barber, Mr Gordon Harris, Mr T. G. Kelso, Mr J. L. Medd, Mr Kevin Smith, Mr G. Whorton.

Jockey (NH): R Fahey.

Conditional: S P Richardson.

257 MRS D. HAINE, Newmarket

Postal: **Midsummer Cottage, Snailwell, Newmarket, Suffolk.**
Phone: **HOME (0638) 77719 STABLE (0638) 662346**

1 **CATCH THE CROSS,** 4, gr g Alias Smith (USA)—Juliette Mariner **Mr P. L. Shilton**
2 **DEMI-MONDAINE,** 5, b m Rymer—Alan's Girl **Mrs Solna Thomson Jones**
3 **DUKE DE VENDOME,** 7, b g Amboise—Sweet Duchess **Mrs Solna Thomson Jones**
4 **DUO DROM,** 5, ch m Deep Run—Lady Dromara **Mr F. J. Haggas**
5 **GOOD SAILING,** 6, b m Scorpio (FR)—Mother of The Wind **Mr M. P. Coxhead**
6 **ICKWORTH,** 8, ch g Northfields (USA)—Syrsanta (FR) **Lord Bristol**
7 5, B m Mandalus—Like Now **Mrs D. Haine**
8 **OFFICER GROWLER,** 6, br g Mandalus—Deep Cristina **Mr M. P. Coxhead**
9 **PIRACY,** 6, gr g Rusticaro (FR)—All At Sea **Mrs Solna Thomson Jones**
10 **QANNAAS,** 6, br h Kris—Red Berry **Mrs Ann Leat**
11 **RYTON RUN,** 5, b g Deep Run—Money Spinner **A. F. Budge (Equine) Limited**
12 **SMOOTH ESCORT,** 6, b g Beau Charmeur (FR)—Wishing Trout **A. F. Budge (Equine) Limited**
13 5, Ch g Le Bavard (FR)—Westford **Mr R. Upton**
14 **WHITEWASH (USA),** 5, ch h Majestic Light (USA)—Clear Ceiling (USA) **Mr Harry R. D. McCalmont**

Other Owners: Mr H. De Burgh, Mr Andrew Pavlo, Capt R. M. Smyly.

Jockey (NH): S Smith Eccles.

258 MR J. S. HALDANE, Kelso

Postal: **Hendersyde Stables, Kelso, Roxburghshire, Scotland.**
Phone: **KELSO (0573) 24956**

1 **BORDER FOLLY,** 5, b g Dalsaan—My Folly **Mrs L. A. Fraser**
2 **BROWNSIDE BRIG,** 5, b g Goldhill—Tumlin Brig **Miss C. H. Bartholomew**
3 **DUBALEA,** 7, b g Dubassoff (USA)—Thirkleby Kate VII **Mrs Hugh Fraser**
4 **EQUATOR,** 7, ch g Nijinsky (CAN)—Sound of Success (USA) **Mr J. T. Blacklock**
5 **ICE BREAKER (FR),** 7, b h Arctic Tern (USA)—Figure de Proue (FR) **Mr F. S. Williams**
6 **KING'S IMAGE,** 5, b g Indian King (USA)—Cooliney Dancer **Mr J. S. Haldane**
7 **MATRACE,** 5, ch m Mummy's Game—Sospirae **Mr J. S. Haldane**
8 **MEIGLE STREET,** 5, b m Balgaddy—Golden Owen **Mr J. S. Haldane**
9 **NEW BEGINNING,** 7, b br h Persian Bold—Bumble-Bee **Mr Peter Henderson**
10 **SHELBOURNE,** 8, br g Shirley Heights—Super Dancer **Mr A. Dawson**
11 **TEPULEA,** 6, ch m Tepukei—Thirkleby Kate VII **Mrs Hugh Fraser**

THREE-YEAR-OLDS

12 **BOWMONT IMP,** b f Import—Streets Ahead **Mr W. P. S. Johnson**

259 MR G. V. HALL, Hartlepool

Postal: **Woodside, Three Gates, Dalton Piercy, Hartlepool, Cleveland.**
Phone: **(0429) 279511**

1 **CROWFOOT'S COUTURE,** 9, ch g Sweet Revenge—Soft Moss **Mr Vic Hall**
2 **DALTON DANDY,** 8, b g Dubassoff (USA)—Donna Sight **Mr Vic Hall**
3 **LUBUS,** 8, b m Fordham (USA)—Candescent (USA) **Mr Vic Hall**
4 **TIME CARRIAGE,** 4, br g Carriage Way—Harmony Thyme **Mr Vic Hall**

Jockey (NH): A Orkney (9-11).

Amateur: Mr P J Jenkins (10-7).

260 MISS P. J. HALL, Melton Mowbray

Postal: **Hawthorn Farm, Saltby, Melton Mowbray, Leicestershire, LE14 4QW.**
Phone: **(0476) 860891**

1 **ANOTHER-KAYE,** 7, ch m Jimmy The Singer—Kerema **Mrs Margaret Marston**
2 **BANANA BOAT,** 5, b br g Furry Glen—Bells Hollow **Albury Racing Limited**
3 **FLUTTERBY BELLE,** 4, b f Beldale Flutter—Briar **Mr A. Vrona**
4 **GROSSEN,** 6, gr g Bustomi—Novina **Mr B. Wade**
5 **HOSTILE ACT,** 5, b g Glenstal (USA)—Fandetta **Mr J. E. Titley**
6 **POLLY-LOO,** 6, b m Owen Anthony—Meg Potter **Miss L. Pick**
7 **QUINTO,** 4, b g Tumble Wind (USA)—Con Carni **Mr J. E. Titley**
8 **RED BILLY,** 7, ch g Red Johnnie—Golden Lania **Mr T. A. Waldrom**
9 **RUN BY JOVE (USA),** 7, gr g Northern Jove (CAN)—Running Eagle (USA) **Mr A. W. Darke**
10 **STAR ROUTE,** 9, b m Owen Dudley—Fleet Fen **Miss Pauline Hall**

Other Owners: Mr S. J. Cooley, Mr D. Gillespy, Mr J. E. Harley, Mr A. M. Wright.

Jockey (NH): R Dunwoody (10-2, w.a.).

Lady Rider: Miss Celia Radband (8-7).

261 MISS S. E. HALL, Middleham

Postal: **Brecongill, Coverham, Leyburn, North Yorkshire, DL8 4TJ.**
Phone: **(0969) 40223**

1 **FUTURE GLORY,** 4, b g Ile de Bourbon (USA)—Bombshell **Mr R. Ogden**
2 **GOING ON,** 4, ch g Move Off—Young Lamb **Mrs Joan Hodgson**
3 **IT'S ME,** 4, gr f Good Times (ITY)—Rynkeld **Jack Hanson**
4 **JOYCE'S CARE (USA),** 4, gr f Green Dancer (USA)—Imminent (USA) **Jack Hanson**
5 **JUSSOLI,** 6, b m Don—Torino **Mr C. Platts and Miss S. E. Hall**
6 **SHEVAJI,** 4, b g Indian King (USA)—Brave Ivy **Mrs M. C. Grant**
7 **TWOTIME BID,** 4, b g Taufan (USA)—Avebury Ring **Mrs C. M. Geraghty and Miss S. E. Hall**

THREE-YEAR-OLDS

8 **BATTLE ON,** b f Blakeney—Perfect Picture (FR) **Lord Matthews and The Hon I. V. Matthews**
9 **CRAVEN,** b f Thatching—Rustle of Silk **Mr R. Ogden**
10 **CURRENT EXPRESS,** b g Siberian Express (USA)—Current Raiser **Lord Matthews**
11 **DIVILMINT,** b g Absalom—Miss Diaward **Mrs M. C. Grant**
12 **FARA,** gr f Castle Keep—Faridetta **Miss H. K. Monteith**
13 **FORMIDABLE TASK,** ch f Formidable—Light O'Battle **Jack Hanson**
14 **IMPORTANT GUEST,** b f Be My Guest—Riboule **The Hon I. V. Matthews**
15 **KNOWING,** br f Lochnager—Caroline Lamb **Mrs T. Hall**
16 **MOUNTAIN GLOW,** gr c Siberian Express (USA)—Bombshell **Mr R. Ogden**
17 **PANICO,** b c Superlative—Ex Dancer **Jack Hanson**
18 **PINK GIN,** ch g Tickled Pink—Carrapateira **Mr C. Platts**
19 **ROYAL GIRL,** b f Kafu—Royal Aunt **Miss S. E. Hall**
20 **SLADES HILL,** b c Lochnager—Mephisto Waltz **Jack Hanson**
21 **SPANISH VERDICT,** b c King of Spain—Counsel's Verdict **Cox & Allen (Kendal) Ltd**

TWO-YEAR-OLDS

22 **BYZANTINE,** b c 21/1 Damister (USA)—Rustle of Silk (General Assembly (USA)) **Mr R. Ogden**
23 **GASCOIGNE WOOD,** b c 7/5 Petoski—Be My Queen (Be My Guest (USA)) **Jack Hanson**
24 **GOLD EMBLEM,** b f 26/5 Tina's Pet—Bar Gold (Lucky Brief) **The Hon I. V. Matthews and Mr C. Platts**
25 **JIGGING,** ch c 15/3 Scottish Reel—Kesarini (USA) (Singh (USA)) **Lord Matthews**
26 Gr c 10/3 Formidable (USA)—Longest Day (FR) (Lyphard (USA)) **Lord Matthews**
27 **PERSIAN MISTRESS (IRE),** ro f 22/4 Persian Bold—Beloved Mistress (Rarity) **Corbally Stud**
28 **RADIO CAROLINE,** b g 21/3 All Systems Go—Caroline Lamb (Hotfoot) **Mrs T. Hall**
29 **SECRET HAZE,** ch f 6/4 Absalom—Secret Gill (Most Secret) **Mrs Joan Hodgson**
30 **STORMHEAD,** ch g 22/4 Move Off—Young Lamb (Sea Hawk II) **Mrs T. Hall**
31 **SWISS BEAUTY,** b f 4/5 Ballacashtal (CAN)—Cocked Hat Supreme (Uncle Pokey)

Jockeys (Flat): M Birch (8-3, w.a.), A Culhane (7-12), R Hills (8-0, w.a.).

Amateur: Mr C Platts (10-6).

262 MR T. B. HALLETT, Saltash

Postal: **Woodside Stables, Carkeel, Saltash, Cornwall.**
Phone: **(0752) 846829/842064 MOBILE (0831) 108913**

1 **ALEXA'S BOY,** 6, b g African Sky—Regal Step **Mr J. T. Weekes**
2 **BABY BOY,** 9, b h Mummy's Pet—Lucent **Mrs J. Hicks**
3 **BENJAMIN LANCASTER,** 6, b g Dubassoff (USA)—Lancaster Rose **Mr M. Griffin**
4 **BRENDAN OLIVIA,** 10, b g Belfalas—Three Rings **Mr Chris Rendle**
5 **BUTLERS PET,** 11, b g Mummy's Pet—Reluctant Maid **Mrs J. Hicks**
6 **COTEHELE,** 7, ch m Paddy's Stream—Primrose Cotton **Mr A. Foster**
7 **EARTH WOOD,** 5, ch m Glenstal (USA)—Faiblesse **Mr Chris Coleman**
8 **EXPEDITIOUS,** 10, b g Tachypous—My Own II **Mr G. H. Taylor-Webber**
9 **HENSHAW,** 6, ch g Crofter (USA)—Jabula **Mrs M. I. Hallett**

MR T. B. HALLETT—continued

10 **HI-TECH BOY,** 8, ch g Tickled Pink—Jetwitch **Mr A. Burchell**
11 **LORENTEGGIO (USA),** 5, b g Al Nasr (FR)—Clairvoyance (USA) **Mr B. R. Langdon**
12 **PERFECT STRANGER,** 6, b g Wolver Hollow—Mrs Walmsley **Mr Joseph Bryant**
13 **ROSOGLIO (FR),** 6, ch g Roi de Carreau (FR)—Salopette (FR) **Mrs G. Le Marquand**
14 **TURNBERRY DAWN,** 8, ch g Fair Turn—Shuil Alainn **Palladium Ltd (Builders Merchants)**

Other Owners: Mr A. B. Barraclough, Mrs J. Cash, Mr T. C. Le Grice, Mr P. D. Warren.

Jockey (Flat): N Adams (7-7).

Jockeys (NH): P Richards, A Webb (10-0).

Conditional: Sharon Pengelly (9-7).

263 MR G. A. HAM, Axbridge

Postal: **Rose Farm, Rooksbridge, Axbridge, Somerset.**
Phone: **HOME (0934) 750331 CAR (0860) 823338**

1 **AWKWARD HARRY,** 4, b g Glenstal—Roscrea **Devon Fish**
2 **BILLBOARD,** 5, b m Martin John—Bella Berenice **Mr E. W. Jones**
3 **BILLBROOK,** 8, b g Pardigras—Gay Heath **Mr E. W. Jones**
4 **BUSHDO,** 7, br g Great Nephew—Lucky For Me **J. Whitburn**
5 **CLARE LAD,** 7, ch g Garda's Revenge (USA)—Sea Dike **Travail Employment Group Ltd**
6 **CLASSEY BOY,** 7, ch g Celtic Cone—Tresspassing **A. J. Kaplan**
7 **COMRA,** 11, b g Moulton—Armelle **Mr Paul Dales**
8 **GLEN GEORGE,** 10, b g Furry Glen—Paiukiri **Mrs Janet Ostler**
9 **GODFATHER'S GIFT,** 8, br g Don—Mexican Charity **Mr R. D. Starke**
10 **GROTIUS,** 6, ch g Ardross—Tudor Whisper **Travail Employment Group Ltd**
11 **HAPPY WONDER,** 10, ch m Levanter—Gretna Wonder **Mr Paul A. Jones**
12 **HUBLI,** 10, br g Kinglet—Perrytate **Mr John Williams**
13 **KNOCKBRACK,** 10, b g Pitpan—Highway Mistress **Mr Gerard Holmes**
14 **MEAT THE FOULKES (NZ),** 9, b g Sea Anchor—Divinity (NZ) **Mr M. Foulkes**
15 **MOON RUN,** 7, ch h Deep Run—Etoile de Lune **Miss Claire Burge**
16 **MYLIEGE,** 6, b h Lord Gayle (USA)—My Natalie **Miss Claire Burge**
17 **NIGHT FALL,** 4, b g Night Shift (USA)—Empress Victoria **Hubbards Animal Feed Supplements Ltd**
18 **PADDY'S POND,** 12, ch g Paddy's Stream—Clerihan **Mr Christopher Dodson**
19 **PUNCHBAG,** 4, b g Glint of Gold—Casseys Pet **Hubbards Animal Feed Supplements Ltd**
20 **RHODETTE,** 9, br m Rhodomantade—The Shrub **Hubbards Animal Feed Supplements Ltd**
21 **ROSE MASTER,** 7, b g Derring Rose—Toy Flag **Guiseppe Zaccariello**
22 **ROSSMICHAEL,** 5, ch g On Your Mark—Sea Dike **Mrs Philippa L. C. Wyer**
23 **SCARLET DYMOND,** 8, b m Rymer—Eight of Diamonds **Mrs M. A. Smith**
24 **SCORCH MAN,** 5, b g Ya Zaman (USA)—Cailin Oir **Miss Claire Burge**
25 **SHY MISTRESS,** 7, b m Cawstons Clown—Shy Talk **Mr N. J. Coulson-Stevens**
26 **SILVERHILLS,** 7, ch g Touch Paper—Rosie Probert **Miss Claire Burge**
27 **SPINNING HAND,** 8, b m Nearly A Hand—Cindermouse **D. Barlow**
28 **STEARSBY,** 11, br g Politico (USA)—Lucky Sprite **Miss Claire Burge**
29 **TERRYS TOWN,** 4, b g Creetown—Precious Love **Devon Fish**
30 **TIARUM,** 8, b g Tiran (HUN)—Contessa (HUN) **Mrs S. Hutchings**
31 **TORKABAR (USA),** 5, ch h Vaguely Noble—Tarsila **Mr N. Coulson-Stevens**
32 **TRAVAIL GIRL,** 9, b m Forties Field—Ma Principaute (FR) **Mrs Phillipa L. C. Wyer**
33 **TROPICAL MIST (FR),** 10, b br g Faraway Son (USA)—Tropical Cream (USA) **Mrs S. Hutchings**
34 **WARLEGGAN,** 9, br g Star Appeal—Dauphiness **Mr D. A. Malam**
35 **WESTWAY,** 7, br g Paddy's Stream—Halcyon Years **Miss Claire Burge**
36 **WHISKEY GRAIN,** 8, b g Laurence O—Pry's Delight **Mr N. Coulson-Stevens**
37 **YOZZER HUGHES,** 5, br g Tumble Wind (USA)—Miss Britain **Miss Claire Burge**

MR G. A. HAM—continued

Other Owners: Mr W. G. Adolpho, Mr Gerald Clarke, Mr J. J. Doyle, Mr P. J. Dugdale, Mr David Edwards, Mr Dennis Fisher, Mr C. Rogers, Mr N. Shore, Mr P. R. Waite, Mr John Wallington, Mrs Amanda Webber, Mr J. S. Wright.

Jockey (NH): B Powell (10-0).

Conditional: S Mackey (10-0).

Amateur: Mr S Burrough (10-0).

Lady Rider: Lorna Vincent.

264 MR B. HANBURY, Newmarket

Postal: **Diomed Stables, Hamilton Road, Newmarket, Suffolk, CB8 0PD.**
Phone: **(0638) 663193 OR (0638) 664799 HOME (0440) 820396 FAX (0638) 667209**

1 **BATSHOOF,** 4, b c Sadler's Wells (USA)—Steel Habit **Mr Muttar Salem**
2 **BEAU SHER,** 7, b h Ile de Bourbon (USA)—Mai Pussy **Mr O. Zawawi**
3 **FIGURE OUT (USA),** 4, b c Alleged (USA)—Preceptress (USA) **Mr R. E. Hibbert**
4 **FIRELIGHT FIESTA,** 5, ch g Sallust—Caithness **Mrs John Lamb**
5 **GULSHA,** 4, b f Glint of Gold—Mai Pussy **Mr O. Zawawi**
6 **LIGHT OF MORN (USA),** 4, b c Alleged (USA)—Flaming Leaves (USA) **Mr R. E. Hibbert**
7 **PERFECT CHANCE,** 4, b f Petorius—Perfect Line **Mr M. Kura**
8 **PER QUOD (USA),** 5, b g Lyllos (FR)—Allegedly (USA) **Mr H. Turney McKnight**

THREE-YEAR-OLDS

9 **AAL EL AAL,** b c High Top—Last Card (USA) **Mr O. Zawawi**
10 **ALIM (CAN),** gr c The Minstrel (CAN)—Jiving Queen (CAN) **Mr M. Kura**
11 **BALLET CLASSIQUE (USA),** b f Sadler's Wells (USA)—Estaciones (USA) **Mr G. J. H. Carroll**
12 **CHOIR LEADER,** b br f Chief Singer—View **Mr R. J. McAulay**
13 **CUP OF TRICKS (USA),** br f Clever Trick (USA)—Cup of Honey (USA) **Mr Luis De Hechavarria**
14 **DOWN THE FLAG (USA),** ch c Stalwart (USA)—Hunt's Lark (CAN) **Mr M. Kura**
15 **EASTERN WHISPER (USA),** gr c Arctic Tern (USA)—Mazyoun (USA) **Mr Hamad Ali**
16 **FALSE ALLEGATION (USA),** b c Alleged (USA)—Reckoning (USA) **Mr R. E. Hibbert**
17 **JOLLIFICATION,** b c Habitat—Jovial Josie **Mr M. Kura**
18 **KALISHA,** gr f Rainbow Quest—Kalazero **Miss K. Rausing**
19 **KING MARCOS (USA),** b c His Majesty (USA)—Spanish Fake (USA) **Mr Robert B. Trussell Jr**
20 **LIP SING (USA),** b f Clever Trick (USA)—Spanish Tune (USA) **Mr Robert B. Trussell Jr**
21 **MASERU,** b f Lomond (USA)—Sepideh **Mr M. Kura**
22 **MY SHAFY,** ch f Rousillon (USA)—Lys River (FR) **Mr Hilal Salem**
23 **NATIVE TRIBE,** b g Be My Native (USA)—More Fuss **Mrs J. M. Beeby**
24 **NOBLE FELLOW,** b c The Noble Player (USA)—Fravelot **Mrs B. Newton**
25 **NODOLYA,** b f Niniski (USA)—Press Corps **Mr R. J. McAulay**
26 **PLAY THE BLUES,** gr f Cure The Blues (USA)—Casual Pleasure (USA) **Mr Richard G. Guess**
27 **PROSEQUENDO (USA),** b c Robellino (USA)—Allegedly (USA) **Mr H. Turney McKnight**
28 **RAWDA (USA),** b f Green Forest (USA)—Reham **Mr Saeed Suhail**
29 **REGAN (USA),** b f Lear Fan (USA)—Twice A Fool (USA) **Mr G. J. H. Carroll**
30 **RUBY REALM,** ch f Valiyar—Mai Pussy **Mr O. Zawawi**
31 **SAIF CROWN (USA),** ch c Chief's Crown (USA)—Dimant Rose (USA) **Mr Mohamed Suhail**
32 **SASHTAL,** ch c Ballacashtal (CAN)—Salala **Mr O. Zawawi**
33 **SILVER SALVER,** b br c Known Fact (USA)—Sauceboat **Maktoum Al Maktoum**
34 **SOY ROBERTO (USA),** ch c Roberto (USA)—Ocean's Answer (USA) **Mrs M. E. Miglietti**
35 **SPODE'S BLUE,** b f Sadler's Wells (USA)—Wedgewood Blue (USA) **Mrs Lillie F. Webb**
36 **SUPERBLY SHARP (USA),** b c Diesis—Super Belle (USA) **Maktoum Al Maktoum**

MR B. HANBURY—continued

37 **SUPER DEB,** ch f Superlative—Debutina Park **Mr H. R. Mould**
38 **TAMONO DANCER (CAN),** b c Northern Dancer—Running Around (USA) **Mr K. Nakamura**
39 **TANBURE,** b f Law Society (USA)—Transit **Mr M. Kura**
40 **TICKLE TOUCH (USA),** b f Stop The Music (USA)—Abeesh (USA) **Maktoum Al Maktoum**
41 **TISLAM,** b c Formidable (USA)—Habutai **Mr Muttar Salem**
42 **WILLFY (USA),** ch c Diesis—Little Mandy (USA) **Mr Abdullah Ali**
43 **YAHALABEAK,** b br c Glint of Gold—Spring Rose **Mr Muttar Salem**

TWO-YEAR-OLDS

44 **AGBAL WA FAAZ,** b c 25/3 Touching Wood—Dimant Blanche (Gummo) **Maktoum Al Maktoum**
45 B c 20/2 Doulab—Baddaweeya (Formidable) **Mr Saeed Suhail**
46 Ch f 10/4 Thatching—Badiya (Sir Ivor) **Maktoum Al Maktoum**
47 **BEYNOUNAH (IRE),** b f 12/2 Shareef Dancer—Rare Roberta (Roberto) **Mr Muttar Salem**
48 Br c 2/1 Alleged—Don't Joke (Shecky Greene) **Mr M. Kura**
49 **EN ATTENDANT (FR),** ch c 18/5 Bairn—Vizenia (Vitiges) **B. C. Newton**
50 Ch f 30/3 Secreto—Followeveryrainbow (Mehmet) **Mr Muttar Salem**
51 **GLOWLAMP (IRE),** br f 8/3 Glow—Astania (Arratos) **Mrs S. M. Rogers**
52 B c 2/5 Trojan Fen—Gohar (Barachois) **Mr H. R. Mould**
53 **HAYAT (IRE),** b f 5/3 Sadler's Wells—Stylish Genie (Bagdad) **Sheikh Ahmed Al Maktoum**
54 **IKTESHAF,** b c 1/3 Green Desert—Colourful (Gay Mecene) **Mr Muttar Salem**
55 B f 11/3 Roberto—Journey (What A Pleasure) **Mr H. R. Mould**
56 B c 22/4 Shareef Dancer—Juliette Marny (Blakeney) **A. S. Cronk**
57 **KASHTEH (IRE),** b f 12/5 Green Desert—Klarifi (Habitat) **Mr Hilal Salem**
58 **KAYFAAT (USA),** br c 26/4 Spend A Buck—Duped (On The Sly) **Mr Muttar Salem**
59 Gr c 20/2 Touching Wood—Lune de Minuit (Song) **Maktoum Al Maktoum**
60 **MANHAL,** b c 29/3 Sure Blade—Nordica (Northfields) **Sheikh Ahmed Al Maktoum**
61 **MARDEF,** ch c 28/3 Ahonoora—Zeyneb (Habitat) **Mr Hamdan Al-Maktoum**
62 **MASAKEN,** ch f 8/3 Doulab—Amalee (Troy) **Mr Muttar Salem**
63 **MIDIFINA,** b f 14/3 Green Desert—Vielle (Ribero) **Mr Muttar Salem**
64 B c 6/3 Bering—Mondialite (Habitat) **Mr M. Kura**
65 B f 12/5 State Trooper—Musical Piece (Realm) **R. R. Prettie**
66 Ch f 27/2 Dominion—Nawadder (Kris) **Mr Saeed Suhail**
67 Br f 12/2 Touching Wood—Nihad (Alleged) **Mr Saeed Suhail**
68 **OTTOM,** b f 27/5 Shirley Heights—Hayloft (Tudor Melody) **Sheikh Ahmed Al Maktoum**
69 Ch f 14/2 Sir Ivor—Patia (Don) **Mr M. Kura**
70 **RABSHA (IRE),** b f 29/3 Taufan—Serraj (Seattle Slew) **Mr Mohamed Obaida**
71 **SALLY SAAD,** gr f 22/5 Green Desert—Biding (Habat) **Sheikh Ahmed Al Maktoum**
72 **SAMBOLI (USA),** ch f 12/2 Northjet—Shoag (Affirmed) **Mr Mohamed Suhail**
73 **SHAHIMA (USA),** b f 7/3 Diesis—Reham (Mill Reef) **Mr Saeed Suhail**
74 **SNOW MAIDEN (USA),** b f 23/4 Arctic Tern—Professional Dance (Nijinsky) **Mr Muttar Salem**
75 **SPRINGDALE HALL (USA),** ch f 24/2 Bates Motel—Locksley Hall (Raja Baba) **Mrs M. Hartley**
76 **SWEET SHARPO,** ch f 10/2 Sharpo—Tumble Judy (Tumble Wind) **J. Grady**
77 **TERRITORIAL KING,** ch c 17/2 Sharpo—Pretty Pol (Final Straw) **Mr Abdullah Ali**
78 **TISWA (USA),** b f 28/3 Lyphard—Happy Bride (Royal Match) **Mr Abdullah Ali**
79 **TO-SEVERALS (IRE),** b c 21/5 Horage—Sacred Ibis (Red God) **Newmarket Hotel Dev.-Severals Hotel**
80 **TUMBLE TWIST (IRE),** b c 31/3 Tumble Wind—Reshuffle (Sassafras) **J. Grady**
81 **UMNIYATEE,** b f 6/3 Green Desert—Midway Lady (Alleged) **Mr Hamdan Al-Maktoum**
82 B c 10/5 Fairy King—Vaguely Jade (Corvaro) **A. S. Cronk**
83 Gr f 26/2 Kenmare—Venise Pleasure (Honest Pleasure) **M. Parrish**
84 **WALEEF,** b c 17/1 Persian Bold—Henaadi (Affirmed) **Maktoum Al Maktoum**
85 **WASSIFA,** b f 27/1 Sure Blade—Rye Tops (Ile de Bourbon) **Mr Muttar Salem**
86 **XALISCO (USA),** b c 23/3 Shahrastani—Irlanda (Tom Rolfe) **R. N. Clay**

Other Owners: Mr Tim Franey, Mr B. Hanbury.

Jockey (Flat): B Raymond (8-5).

Apprentice: Robert Smith (7-11).

WORCESTERSHIRE COLLEGE OF AGRICULTURE

HINDLIP, WORCESTER

THE COLLEGE THAT SPECIALIZES IN EQUINE HUSBANDRY COURSES FOR STAFF DEVELOPMENT, TRAINING AND EDUCATION

The Successful and highly acclaimed two-week residential course for trainers, assistant trainers and senior yard staff.

The instruction on equine husbandry facets of horses in training is directed at those working in training establishments who, though skilled in breaking, riding and training routines, require more background and technical instruction on the biology and nature of the animals in their charge. An intensive two weeks covering conformation, skeleton (muscles, legs, joints), feeding and digestion, the physiology of training (blood, respiration, etc.), parasites and diseases.

Course fee: currently £35 plus Board Residence £45–£50 per 5 day week for those living in.

The Course The Professionals Use (Usually held in January each year) has enjoyed the support of leading trainers and staff at home, Ireland, Europe, Africa and the Far East.

Explanatory leaflet of all our Equine Stud and Stable Husbandry courses available from the Principal,

R. B. BRIGHTON

or

Telephone: Worcester (0905) 51310

265 MR R. HANNON, Marlborough

Postal: **East Everleigh Stables, Marlborough, Wiltshire.**
Phone: **(0264) 850 254 FAX (0264) 850 820 TELEX 477068**

1 **BRASSY NELL**, 4, b f Dunbeath (USA)—Raashideah **Mrs Derek Strauss**
2 **D'ALTAGNAN**, 4, ch g Dalsaan—Fresh As A Daisy **Mr David Allen**
3 **DOWN THE VALLEY**, 4, b f Kampala—Abertywi **Mr R. J. Shannon**
4 **ESCAPE HATCH**, 4, b g Thatching—La Troublerie **Mr G. Howard-Spink**
5 **FIRST VICTORY**, 4, gr c Concorde Hero (USA)—Cestrefeld **Mr David Seale**
6 **GRAN ALBA (USA)**, 4, gr c El Gran Senor (USA)—Morning Games (USA) **Mr C. R. Kilroy**
7 **GRAND FRERE**, 4, br g Gorytus (USA)—Balista **Mr Robert Whitworth**
8 **IRON KING**, 4, gr c Tender King—Zanskar **Mrs L. M. Davies**
9 **KNIGHT OF MERCY**, 4, b g Aragon—Little Mercy **Mr C. A. Blackwell**
10 **MAJOR JACKO**, 7, b h Mandrake Major—Toreadora **Mr John Horgan**
11 **NAIL DON**, 5, b g Don—Vivungi (USA) **Mr G. Howard-Spink**
12 **PITSEA**, 4, b c Tina's Pet—Here's Sue **Mr D. F. Cock**
13 **READY WIT**, 9, br g Bay Express—Brevity **Mrs R. Tennant**
14 **SAVAHRA SOUND**, 5, b h Song—Savahra **A. F. Budge (Equine) Limited**
15 **SHARP N' EARLY**, 4, b c Runnett—Irish Kick **A. F. Budge (Equine) Limited**
16 **YOU ARE A STAR**, 4, b g Persian Bold—Flinging Star (USA) **Mr Jim Horgan**

THREE-YEAR-OLDS

17 **ABSONAL**, gr c Absalom—Aldbury Girl **Capt R. W. Hornall**
18 **ADANAR (USA)**, gr g Irish River (FR)—Adjanada **Mr George C. Scudder**
19 **ALBEDO**, b g Daring March—Alicia Markova **Mrs J. Reglar**
20 **ALMAGHRIB**, b c Red Sunset—Another Match **Anglo Thoroughbred Racing**
21 **ARABIAN SILENCE**, ch c Sayf El Arab (USA)—Silent Prayer **Mr P. F. Boggis**
22 **AUCTION NEWS**, b g Auction Ring (USA)—Cestrefeld **Mr David Seale**
23 **CHANDANNE**, ch f Ballad Rock—Affirmation (FR) **Talon Construction Ltd**
24 **CLAYSUUMAR**, b f Montekin—Good Court **Mr S. Rayner**
25 **CONJURER**, gr c Magic Mirror—Morning Miss **Mr David Allen**
26 **DANCING DELIGHT**, ch c Music Boy—Open Country **Mrs P. M. Tarrant**
27 **DAZZLINGLY RADIANT**, gr f Try My Best (USA)—Elvina (FR) **Mrs M. L. Davis**
28 **DONNA KATRINA**, gr f Kings Lake (USA)—Rocketina **Mrs E. J. Wood**
29 **DONNA LORENZA**, br f Ahonoora—Lockwood Girl **Mr Peter S. Winfield**
30 **DOUNHURST**, b f Saher—Wernlas **Mr Angus Whiteside**
31 **DUCK AND DIVE**, ch c Lomond (USA)—Avec L'Amour **Mr Jim Horgan**
32 **ELFING**, b f Fairy King (USA)—Near The End **Mr James Murphy**
33 **FOX CHAPEL**, b g Formidable (USA)—Hollow Heart **A. F. Budge (Equine) Limited**
34 **GALACTIC SCHEME (USA)**, b c Exclusive Era (USA)—Cosmic Time (USA) **A. F. Budge (Equine) Limited**
35 **GENTLY GENTLY**, b c Prince Tenderfoot (USA)—Domani **Mr Jim Horgan**
36 **GREY AREA**, gr c Petong—Little Mercy **Mr C. A. Blackwell**
37 **HARD SELL**, ch g Hard Fought—Misoptimist **Mr G. Howard-Spink**
38 **HASTY THRILL (USA)**, b c Lines of Power (USA)—Ashbud **Mr R. I. Khan**
39 **HAVERTON**, b g Carwhite—Rosie Pug **Mr Jim McCarthy**
40 **INDIAN CHIEF**, b c Indian King (USA)—Gay Broad **Mr John Horgan**
41 **JEBALI**, ch c Good Times (ITY)—Penitent **Anglo Thoroughbred Racing**
42 **KEEN MELODY (USA)**, b f Sharpen Up—Sweet Abandon (USA) **A. F. Budge (Equine) Limited**
43 **KNIGHT OF KIRKTON**, b g State Trooper—Musical Piece **Mrs D. Hammerson**
44 **LIFT AND LOAD (USA)**, b c Lyphard's Wish (FR)—Dorit (USA) **Mr G. Howard-Spink**
45 **LITTLE KRAKER**, b f Godswalk (USA)—Wyn Mipet **Mr D. B. Gallop**
46 **MUSICAL FLASH**, ch c Music Boy—Martin-Lavell News **M. W. Grant**
47 **NOBLE BRAVE**, b g Indian King (USA)—Windy Lady **Mr David Allen**
48 **NOTLEY**, b c Formidable (USA)—Riviere Bleue **Mr D. F. Cock**
49 **ONLY THE LONELY**, b g Mummy's Game—Izobia **Mr L. Brady**
50 **OSARIO**, b c Kind of Hush—Welsh Jane **Mr J. G. Davis**
51 **PETIPA (USA)**, gr c Encino (USA)—Connie O (USA) **Mr J. A. Lazzari**
52 **PUSEY STREET BOY**, ch c Vaigly Great—Pusey Street **Mr M. A. Wilkins**
53 **ROCK CITY**, br c Ballad Rock—Rimosa's Pet **A. F. Budge (Equine) Limited**
54 **RUSHANES**, ch c Millfontaine—Saulonika **Mr M. Mac Carthy**
55 **SHARP N' EASY**, b f Swing Easy (USA)—Dulcidene **Mr C. W. Rogers**

MR R. HANNON—continued

56 SHARP N' SMOOTH, ch c Sharpo—Winning Look **Mr Derek Joseph**
57 SHORT STRAW, b c Thatching—Makeacurtsey (USA) **Anglo Thoroughbred Racing**
58 STANWAY, b c Sandhurst Prince—Spring Bride **Mr D. F. Cock**
59 STRATHELLA, b f Ela-Mana-Mou—Strathdearn **J. W. Mann**
60 THE PRODIGAL, b g Aragon—Patois **Mrs P. W. Talbot-Ponsonby**
61 THEY ALL FORGOT ME, b g Tender King—African Doll **Mr T. Hyde**
62 TIROL, br c Thatching—Alpine Niece **Mr John Horgan**
63 WALKING SAINT, b f Godswalk (USA)—Saintly Tune **Mr John Horgan**
64 WALK UP THE MALL, gr f Godswalk (USA)—Pall Nan **Mrs C. A. Orme**
65 WHAT A SAVE, b f Law Society (USA)—Merriment **Mr P. L. Shilton**
66 WOODSIDE HEATH, ch c King Persian—Saga's Humour **Mr M. Power**

TWO-YEAR-OLDS

67 ABSO, b c 8/3 Absalom—Classical Vintage (Stradavinsky) **P. Oliver**
68 Ch c Golden Act (USA)—Avie's Gold (USA) (Lord Avie (USA)) **Kennet Valley Thoroughbreds**
69 B f 17/1 Sagace (FR)—Bammell (USA) (Tell (USA)) **A. F. Budge (Equine) Limited**
70 BID FOR ELEGANCE, b f 19/3 Nordance (USA)—Single Bid (Auction Ring (USA)) **W. F. Hawkings**
71 BILLY LOMOND (IRE), b c 4/4 Lomond (USA)—Relko's Belle (FR) (Relko) **Mr George C. Scudder**
72 BOLD NEPHEW, b c 6/2 Never So Bold—Cornelian (Great Nephew) **R. C. Thompson**
73 Ch f 28/3 Tate Gallery (USA)—Caelidh (Silly Season) **Mr C. A. Blackwell**
74 Ch c 22/4 Red Sunset—Cafe Au Lait (Espresso) **A. F. Budge (Equine) Limited**
75 B c 8/3 Forzando—Champ d'Avril (Northfields (USA)) **A. F. Budge (Equine) Limited**
76 CITY SOLACE, b c 30/3 Last Tycoon—Sheeog (Reform) **D. A. Caruth**
77 Br f 24/5 Jester—Clear Belle (Klairon) **J. Sasserath Racing**
78 B c 9/4 Tumble Wind—Cruise Port (Homeric) **A. F. Budge (Equine) Limited**
79 DANZARIN (IRE), b c 20/4 Kings Lake (USA)—Sodium's Niece (Northfields (USA)) **Mrs J. Reglar**
80 DREAM CARRIER (IRE), b c 21/4 Doulab (USA)—Dream Trader (Auction Ring (USA)) **Mrs J. Reglar**
81 Ch c 18/3 Thatching—Enigma (Ahonoora) **Mr D. F. Cock**
82 Ch c 23/3 Crofthall—Farinara (Dragonara Palace (USA)) **Kyros Kleanthous**
83 FLYING DOWN TO RIO (IRE), b c 21/5 Try My Best (USA)—Gay France (FR) (Sir Gaylord) **D. Lucie-Smith**
84 Ch c 27/3 Sallust—Gang Plank (Tower Walk) **F. J. Broom**
85 B c 4/5 Red Sunset—God's Kiss (Godswalk (USA)) **Mrs S. Popovich**
86 HALLAND PARK LAD, ch c 19/4 Sayf El Arab (USA)—Sallytude (Tudor Music) **Mrs B. E. Burchett**
87 Gr f 1/3 Bellypha—Ideal Home (Home Guard (USA)) **Mr P. L. Shilton**
88 Ch c 4/3 Noalto—Incarnadine (Hot Spark) **Giles Gleadell**
89 LES ANIMAUX NUAGES (FR), b c 4/5 Primo Dominie—Elmira (FR) (Sir Gaylord) **Richard Green (Fine Paintings)**
90 Gr c 2/4 Stanford—Lucky Song (Lucky Wednesday) **S. Squires**
91 B c 3/4 Lyphard's Special—Maiden Concert (Condorcet (FR)) **Richard Green (Fine Paintings)**
92 MARZOCCO, ch c 3/3 Formidable (USA)—Top Heights (High Top) **Mr J. G. Davis**
93 MISTRAL GIRL (IRE), b f 23/4 Tumble Wind (USA)—Arthashat (Petingo) **Mr J. A. Lazzari**
94 Ch c 25/3 Ballad Rock—Northern Scene (Habitat) **A. F. Budge (Equine) Limited**
95 Ch c 17/4 Fighting Fit (USA)—Ornamental (USA) (Triple Crown (USA)) **Richard Green (Fine Paintings)**
96 B c 8/3 Music Boy—Pasha's Dream (Tarboosh (USA)) **N.T.C. Racing Ltd**
97 PORT SUNLIGHT (IRE), ch c 2/2 Tate Gallery (USA)—Nana's Girl (Tin Whistle) **Mrs C. J. Powell**
98 PUNCH AND RUN, b c 15/4 Forzando—Wrangbrook (Shirley Heights) **R. Bernard**
99 RAPID CORACLE (IRE), b c 29/3 Welsh Term—Canoeing (Tap On Wood) **Mrs L. M. Davies**
100 REED-BED (IRE), b c 13/3 Thatching—Kye-Hye (Habitat) **C. Hamer**
101 B c 15/2 Sharpen Up—Royal Heroine (Lypheor) **A. F. Budge (Equine) Limited**
102 B f 12/4 Dancing Brave (USA)—Santa's Sister (USA) (Middle Brother) **A. F. Budge (Equine) Limited**
103 B f 23/2 Flash of Steel—Silk Lady (Tribal Chief) **A. F. Budge (Equine) Limited**
104 Ch f The Minstrel (CAN)—State Treasure (USA) (Secretariat (USA)) **A. F. Budge (Equine) Limited**
105 SULASTAR, gr c 15/2 Sulaafah (USA)—Bidula (Manacle) **M. W. Grant**
106 SUPER MALT (IRE), ch f 6/3 Milk of The Barley—Sugar Amber (Yellow God) **T. E. Bucknall**
107 B f 3/2 Sharpo—Taiga (Northfields (USA)) **Mr Peter S. Winfield**

Other Owners: Mrs C. A. Cardona, Mr D. G. Churston, Mrs Ingela Cleblad-Raw, Mr T. Clyne, P. Cooper, Mr P. Davies, Mr R. Gander, Mr R. Hannon, Mrs M. Horgan, Mr Archie Hornall, Mrs John Magnier, Mrs Jane Martland, Mr M. V. O'Brien, Mr G. Rowlandson, Mr David Thompson, Mr D. J. Walker, Woodward & Stalder Ltd.

MR R. HANNON—continued

Jockeys (Flat): A McGlone (7-12), B Rouse (8-1).

Apprentices: M Denaro, R Perham (7-12).

Lady Rider: Denise Pomeroy (8-8).

266 MR J. HANSON, Wetherby

Postal: **Crackhill Farm, Sicklinghall, Wetherby, W. Yorkshire, LS22 4BD.**
Phone: **(0937) 62841 FAX: (0937) 67685**

1 **CLEASBY HILL,** 5, ch g Avocat—Strandhill **Mr J. Hanson**
2 **COMEDY ROAD,** 6, br g Old Jocus—Blue Flash **Mr J. Hanson**
3 **HANDY TRICK,** 9, ch g Duky—Deep Sea **Mr J. Hanson**
4 **IT'S ME,** 4, gr f Good Times (ITY)—Rykneld **Mr J. Hanson**
5 **RED RUDDEL,** 7, b g Proverb—Mountain Bell **Mr J. Hanson**
6 **THE RED ONE,** 6, b g Derring Rose—Fairy Island **Mr J. Hanson**

Jockey (Flat): E Johnson (7-9).

Jockeys (NH): G Bradley, M Dwyer.

267 MR J. L. HARRIS, Melton Mowbray

Postal: **Eastwell Hall Stables, Eastwell, Melton Mowbray, Leicestershire.**
Phone: **HARBY (0949) 60671**

1 **BREAKOUT,** 6, ch g High Line—Wolverhants **Mr David Cahal**
2 **CAJUN DANCER,** 6, ch g Cajun—Gay Folly **Mr David Mitchell**
3 **CARBON LADY,** 5, ch m Mr Fluorocarbon—Lady Marmalade **Mr J. South**
4 **CARNBREA FRED,** 4, b g Montekin—Vote Barolo **Mr Dick Emery**
5 **DARE DAGO,** 6, b g Homeboy—Tallishire Beverley **Mr J. L. Harris and Partners**
6 **EBOR NOVA,** 4, b g Krayyan—Turbo Lady **Mr J. L. Harris**
7 **ESSBEEDEE,** 6, ch g Mr Fluorocarbon—Silent Pearl (USA) **Mr J. Sheppard**
8 **EXPOUND (USA),** 5, b h Far North (CAN)—Speaking of Sweets (USA) **Mr Dick Emery**
9 **FILM LIGHTING GIRL,** 4, ch f Persian Bold—Mey **Mr Dick Emery**
10 **FLYAWAY (FR),** 5, ch h Touching Wood (USA)—Flying Sauce **Mr Dick Emery**
11 **GEMTINO,** 7, b g Neltino—Dolben Gem **Miss J. Wood**
12 **GRAVITY FORCE,** 6, ch g Henbit (USA)—Gradiva **Mr J. L. Harris**
13 **HOSKINS (USA),** 4, b g Hostage (USA)—Shalimar Gardens (USA) **Mr J. L. Harris**
14 **JUST SUSANNA (USA),** 4, b f Master Willie—Whose Broad (USA) **Mrs A. E. Harris**
15 **MANDY'S SWORD,** 4, b f Broadsword (USA)—Mandy's Melody **Miss J. Wood**
16 **MANDY'S TINO,** 5, b g Neltino—Mandy's Melody **Miss J. Wood**
17 **MY WILLIE MAN,** 7, b g Young Man (FR)—Preference **Mr J. South**
18 **NORTH VERDICT (USA),** 7, b g Far North (CAN)—Best Dressed List (USA) **Mr Dick Emery**
19 **POLAR ICE,** 14, b g Crozier—Ice C Ice **Mrs M. Bostock**
20 **RAIN-N-SUN,** 4, gr g Warpath—Sun Noddy **Mrs M. Bostock**
21 **SILENT PRINCESS,** 4, b f King of Spain—Silent Dancer **Mr P. Short**
22 **SIR DUBEL,** 9, b g Al Sirat (USA)—Killanny Bridge **Mr A. E. Walton**
23 **SWELL ROMANCE,** 5, b g Formidable (USA)—Geopelia **Mrs R. T. Watson**

THREE-YEAR-OLDS

24 **BRINK,** ch f Ginger Brink (FR)—Gaybells **Mrs A. E. Harris**
25 B g Royal Vulcan—Dark Echo **Mrs A. E. Harris**

MR J. L. HARRIS—continued

Other Owners: Mr Daryl Cashmore, Mr H. A. Cushing, Mr H. Doubtfire, Mr A. J. Morton, Mr P. P. O'Brien, Mr R. Rose, Mr T. R. Williamson.

Jockey (NH): J A Harris (10-0).

Amateur: Mr A E Walton (9-7).

Lady Rider: Vicki M Harris (9-7).

268 MR P. W. HARRIS, Berkhamsted

Postal: **Sallow Copse, Ringshall, Berkhamsted, Herts, HP4 1LZ.**
Phone: **(044284) 2480 FAX (044284) 2521**

1 **BUCKFAST ABBEY,** 10, ch g Deep Run—High School **Mrs P. W. Harris**
2 **CELTIC FLAME,** 9, ch g Celtic Cone—Dandy's Last **Mrs G. A. Godfrey**
3 **CHRISTINE DAAE,** 4, b f Sadler's Wells (USA)—Chiltern Red **Mrs P. W. Harris**
4 **FORT SUMTER,** 7, b g Belfalas—Coniscliff Bell **Mrs P. W. Harris**
5 **LANDING BOARD,** 12, ch g Deep Run—High School **Mrs P. W. Harris**
6 **NEW CHANDELIER,** 4, b g Alzao (USA)—New Light **Mrs P. W. Harris**
7 **OPERA GHOST,** 4, b c Caerleon (USA)—Premier Rose **Mrs P. W. Harris**

THREE-YEAR-OLDS

8 **BRIGHT RED,** ch c Kris—Chiltern Red **Mrs P. W. Harris**
9 **CLASS ADORNS,** b f Sadler's Wells (USA)—Connaught Bridge **Mrs P. W. Harris**
10 **INVISIBLE HALO (USA),** b f Halo (USA)—Placer Queen **Mrs P. W. Harris**
11 **LAST BLESSING,** b f Final Straw—Bless The Match **Mrs P. W. Harris**
12 **LUCY MANETTE,** ch f Final Straw—Lady Tippins (USA) **Mrs P. W. Harris**
13 **MARIAN EVANS,** b f Dominion—Kindjal **Mrs P. W. Harris**
14 **ON WITH THE DANCE,** ch f Formidable (USA)—Plie (USA) **Mrs P. W. Harris**
15 **PRAYER FLAG (USA),** ch f Forli (ARG)—Forever Waving (USA) **Mrs P. W. Harris**
16 **PROVENCE,** ch c Rousillon (USA)—Premier Rose **Mrs P. W. Harris**
17 **SWORD EXCALIBUR,** b c Kings Lake (USA)—Etching **Mrs P. W. Harris**
18 **TO MUSIC,** ch f Rousillon (USA)—Sing Softly **Mrs P. W. Harris**

TWO-YEAR-OLDS

19 Ch c 29/2 Bairn (USA)—Angels Are Blue (Stanford)
20 B br c 8/3 Persian Bold—Awakening Rose (Le Levanstell)
21 B c 15/2 Last Tycoon—Chapelet (Habitat)
22 **COPPER PLATING,** b c 4/4 Rousillon (USA)—Etching (Auction Ring (USA)) **Mrs P. W. Harris**
23 **IN PLACE (USA),** b c Roberto (USA)—Placer Queen (Habitat) **Mrs P. W. Harris**
24 **JESTERS TEAR (USA),** ch f The Minstrel (USA)—
Forever Waving (USA) (Hoist The Flag (USA)) **Mrs P. W. Harris**
25 **LIZZIE HEXHAM,** b f 25/3 Primo Dominie—Lady Tippins (USA) (Star de Naskra (USA)) **Mrs P. W. Harris**
26 **LYDIA MARIA,** b f 19/2 Dancing Brave (USA)—Connaught Bridge (Connaught) **Mrs P. W. Harris**
27 **SHARP THOUGHT,** ch c 1/4 Kris—Good Thinking (USA) (Raja Baba (USA)) **Mrs P. W. Harris**
28 **SUPERTOP,** b c 4/5 High Top—Myth (Troy) **Mrs G. A. Godfrey**
29 **VALLANCE,** b c 18/3 Top Ville—Kindjal (Kris) **Mrs P. W. Harris**

Other Owners: Mr P. Donnelly, Mrs H. G. Hufford.

Conditional: D Skyrme (9-7).

269 MR S. T. HARRIS, High Wycombe

Postal: **Penn Wood Stables Ltd, Gravelly Way, Penn Bottom, High Wycombe, Buckinghamshire, HP10 8PH.**

Phone: **(0494) 715446**

1 **ARMALA,** 5, ch g Deep Run—Bardicate **Mrs C. Houston**
2 **CHALIAND,** 5, ch g Hard Fought—Behroz **Mr Alan Chandler**
3 **DOREEN'S DELIGHT,** 4, ch c Bay Express—Elizabeth Howard **Mrs D. A. Carter**
4 **GIDDY BRIG,** 9, b g New Brig—Giddy Goat **S. T. Harris**
5 **LOST MOMENT,** 6, b m Hotfoot—Elizabeth Howard **Mrs D. A. Carter**
6 **PUPPET SHOW,** 6, b g Mummy's Pet—Contralto **Mr J. J. Clarke**
7 **TAXIADS,** 8, b g Radetzky—Florabette **Mrs Kathy Lansbury**

THREE-YEAR-OLDS

8 **FORTAN PRINCE,** b c Burslem—Hark Hark **Mrs Anthea Bond**
9 **SHIKARI'S SON,** br c Kala Shikari—Have Form **Alan Spargo Ltd**

TWO-YEAR-OLDS

10 **ARMATEUR (FR),** b c 15/4 Miller's Mate—Artistically (USA) (Ribot) **Alan Spargo Ltd**
11 **BEAU DADA (IRE),** b f 25/2 Pine Circle (USA)—Beauvoir (Artaius (USA)) **Mr J. J. Clarke**
12 B c 21/3 Vision (USA)—Captive Audience (Bold Lad (IRE)) **Alan Spargo Ltd**
13 Gr c 12/3 Absalom—Elizabeth Howard (Sharpen Up) **Mrs D. A. Carter**
14 B c 18/4 Mazaad—Trendy Princess (Prince Tenderfoot (USA)) **Alan Spargo Ltd**

Other Owners: Mrs Paula Marzouk.

270 MR R. W. HARTOP, Farnsfield

Postal: **Lower Hexgreave Stables, Farnsfield, Newark, Nottinghamshire.**

Phone: **MANSFIELD (0623) 883081**

1 **FOOL'S ERRAND,** 5, b m Milford—Daisy Chain **Mr R. W. Hartop**
2 **GAMESMANSHIP,** 9, b g Lepanto (GER)—Silly Games **Mr Peter Evans**
3 **GOOD POINT,** 6, b g Try My Best (USA)—Point Gammon (USA) **Mr Peter Evans**
4 **GRIDGER,** 8, b g Lepanto (GER)—Native Wings **Mr G. Appleby**
5 **KATIE'S JOKER,** 4, b g Idiot's Delight—Roller Skate **Mr J. Russell**
6 **KOO,** 4, b f Crofter (USA)—Sue's Dolly **Mr Peter Evans**
7 **PROUD POMPEY,** 9, ch g Ragapan—Fyjia **Mr J. Russell**
8 **WE'RE IN THE MONEY,** 6, ch m Billion (USA)—Fandance **Falcon Metal Products Ltd**

Other Owners: Mrs C. Barclay.

271 MR E. P. HARTY, The Curragh

Postal: **Strawhall House, Strawhall, The Curragh, Co. Kildare, Ireland.**

Phone: **(045) 41284/41515 TELEX 60699 KEC FAX (045) 21438**

1 **BONNY HECTOR,** 6, b g Bonne Noel—Miss Bustle
2 **CROSS CHAPEL,** 5, ch g Good Thyne—Doll Acre
3 **FLY FOR US,** 4, b f Cut Above—Flying Spice
4 **GRAND INQUISITOR,** 8, b g Pry—Sassenach Girl
5 **GROUNDSMAN,** 6, ch g Ardoon—Terrestrail
6 **KEPPOLS DIAMOND,** 4, b br f Kampala—Keppols
7 7, B g Tanfirion—Lunar Star
8 **PROUD PEGASUS,** 5, b g Jimsun—Nikali
9 **PYLON SPARKS,** 5, b h Electric—Sparkler
10 **SACAJAWEA,** 4, b f Tanfirion—Sun Spray
11 **THEO'S CHOICE,** 5, b g Jimsun—Brush's Choice
12 **VIENNA OPERA,** 5, b g Pitskelly—Light Opera
13 **WRITERS QUAY,** 7, b g Quayside—Chapter Four

MR E. P. HARTY—continued

THREE-YEAR-OLDS

14 **BALLYSAX,** b g Crystal Glitters (USA)—Dear Lorraine
15 **CAUTIOUS REBEL,** ch g Shy Groom (USA)—Riot Girl
16 **JONJAS CHUDLEIGH,** ch g Aragon—Lizabeth Chudleigh
17 **KEPPOLS PRINCE,** b br c Kampala—Keppols
18 **LA SCALA DA SETA,** ch f Dalsaan—Turin Rose
19 **PELICAN BAY,** b f Strong Gale—Doll Acre
20 B br f Hard Fought—Reparata
21 **SILKEN STRAND,** ch g Stanford—Beecom Silk
22 Ch c Deep Run—Sun Spray
23 **TAUFAN'S PATH,** b c Taufan (USA)—Bonny Hollow
24 **TOMMY'S MONEY,** ch c Ahonoora—Persian Royale

TWO-YEAR-OLDS

25 Br g 30/5 Godswalk (USA)—Beecom Silk (English Prince)
26 Ch g 23/6 Le Bavard (FR)—Sun Spray (Nice Guy)

Owners: Sir Tristan Antico, J. S. Bellingham, Mrs D. A. Breen, H. Breen, Mr Edward Doyle, Mrs Edward Doyle, F. G. French, Ms Teresa Hanney, Mrs E. P. Harty, John Houghton, Thomas Ludlow, Mrs H. T. Murphy, Carl O'Neill, Theo Waddington.

Jockey (NH): Nial Madden.

Amateur: Mr E P Harty Jnr (11-0).

272 MR G. HARWOOD, Pulborough

Postal: **Coombelands Stables Ltd, Pulborough, W. Sussex, RH20 1BP.**
Phone: **PULBOROUGH (07982) 3011/2 TELEX 87669 FAX 07982 5163**

1 **ALPHASONIC (USA),** 6, b g Super Concorde (USA)—My Kinda Lady (USA) **Mrs Paul Locke**
2 **ARIZELOS,** 5, b h Shirley Heights—Swanilda (FR) **Mr Athos Christodoulou**
3 **ASHFOLD COPSE,** 4, ch g Broadsword (USA)—Celtic Well **Mrs Paul Locke**
4 **ASSATIS (USA),** 5, b h Topsider (USA)—Secret Asset (USA) **Mr S. Harada**
5 **BIENNIAL (USA),** 4, b c Lear Fan (USA)—Six Months Long (USA) **Mr K. Abdulla**
6 **BOLD FOX,** 4, b c Ballad Rock—Spadilla **Blue Chip Racing Plc**
7 **BOUNDEN DUTY,** 4, b c His Majesty—Inward Bound
8 **CACOETHES (USA),** 4, b c Alydar (USA)—Careless Notion (USA) **Lady Harrison**
9 **CARLINGFORD (USA),** 4, ch c Irish Castle (USA)—Delta Sal (USA) **Mr K. Abdulla**
10 **CARMAGNOLE (USA),** 4, b c Lypheor—La Bonzo (USA) **Mrs Monica Watson-Smyth**
11 **CHAFOLD COPSE,** 5, ch g Deep Run—Yellow Idol **Mrs Paul Locke**
12 **DANCE SPECTRUM (USA),** 4, b c Lyphard (USA)—Rainbow Connection (CAN) **Sheikh Mohammed**
13 **EXBOURNE (USA),** 4, br c Explodent (USA)—Social Lesson (USA) **Mr K. Abdulla**
14 **GOLDBUSTER,** 5, b h Busted—Coryana **Mr B. R. J. Hearse**
15 **GOLD MINORIES,** 6, b h Baptism—Viva La Weavers
16 **GREEN ADVENTURE (USA),** 5, b h Green Dancer (USA)—Simply Furious (USA) **Mr J. Garcia-Roady**
17 **HORN DANCE (USA),** 4, b c Green Dancer (USA)—Fair Salinia **Sheikh Mohammed**
18 **HURRY UP HENRY,** 11, b br g Bargello—Lucille **Mr G. Harwood**
19 **ILE DE CHYPRE,** 5, b h Ile de Bourbon (USA)—Salamina **Mr Athos Christodoulou**
20 **KILN COPSE,** 6, b g Celtic Cone—Blast's Queen
21 **LIMEBURN,** 4, b c Young Generation—Brickfield Queen **Lady Harrison**
22 **LOMAX,** 4, b g Lomond (USA)—Cornish Heroine (USA) **Mr K. Abdulla**
23 **LOREN'S COURAGE (USA),** 5, ch g Solford (USA)—Roman Luster (USA) **Mr Roy Taiano**
24 **MAMALUNA (USA),** 4, ch f Roberto (USA)—Kadesh (USA) **Mr Athos Christodoulou**
25 **NOBLE SAVAGE,** 4, ch c Caerleon (USA)—Indian Maid **Sheikh Mohammed**
26 **PARADOR,** 4, ch c Be My Guest (USA)—Keep Shining (USA) **Mr Anthony Speelman**
27 **PEACE KING,** 4, ch g Adonijah—Flaming Peace

MR G. HARWOOD—continued

28 **PENULTIMATION,** 5, b h Young Generation—Maiden Pool **Mrs Lynda Ward**
29 **PIPERS COPSE,** 8, ch g Celtic Cone—Tarqoretta **Mrs Paul Locke**
30 **POLPERRO (USA),** 4, b g Cox's Ridge—Populi
31 **ROYAL SQUARE (CAN),** 4, ch c Gregorian (USA)—Dance Crazy (USA) **Mrs B. R. J. Hearse**
32 **SADEEM (USA),** 7, ch h Forli (ARG)—Miss Mazepah (USA) **Sheikh Mohammed**
33 **SANTELLA BOBKES (USA),** 5, b h Solford (USA)—Ambiente (USA) **Mr Roy Taiano**
34 **SOVEREIGN ROCKET (USA),** 5, b h Sovereign Dancer (USA)—Jeffs Miss Rocket (USA) **Mr K. Abdulla**
35 **STAR OF SCREEN (USA),** 10, b g Vaguely Noble—Slip Screen (USA) **Mr G. Harwood**
36 **VAGADOR (CAN),** 7, ch g Vaguely Noble—Louisador **Miss Amanda Harwood**
37 **VAYRUA (FR),** 5, ch g Vayrann—Nabua (FR) **Mrs Lynda Ward**
38 **YOUNG JAZZ,** 4, b c Young Generation—River Music

THREE-YEAR-OLDS

39 **ABEL PROSPECT (USA),** b c Mr Prospector (USA)—Able Money (USA) **Mr Nicholas De Savary**
40 **ADDING (USA),** ch c Summing (USA)—Miss Zadig **Mrs S. Buchanan**
41 **AHEAD,** b f Shirley Heights—Ghislaine (USA) **Mr Gerald Leigh**
42 **AKAMANTIS,** b f Kris—Graecia Magna (USA) **Mr Athos Christodoulou**
43 **ALLEZ MILADY (USA),** b f Tom Rolfe—Why Me Lord (USA) **Mr Jerome Brody**
44 **ANTOINETTE JANE,** b f Ile de Bourbon (USA)—Hability **Mr Paul H. Locke**
45 **ARCANE (USA),** ch c Blushing Groom (FR)—I Will Follow (USA) **Mr K. Abdulla**
46 **ARDLUI,** b c Lomond (USA)—Rocket Alert **Mr K. Abdulla**
47 **ARGAKIOS,** b c Busted—Salamina **Mr Athos Christodoulou**
48 **ARISTOCRATIC PETER (USA),** b c Sir Ivor—Glimmer Glass (USA) **Mr Paul H. Locke**
49 **AROMATIC,** b c Known Fact (USA)—Mint **Mr K. Abdulla**
50 **AVISHAYES (USA),** b c Al Nasr (FR)—Rose Goddess **Mr Nicholas De Savary**
51 **AZADEH (USA),** ch f Compliance (USA)—Mervat (USA) **Mr Jerome Brody**
52 **BERILLON,** b c Rousillon (USA)—Obertura (USA) **Mr K. Abdulla**
53 **CHILDREY (USA),** ch c Chief's Crown (USA)—Batna (USA) **Mr Nicholas De Savary**
54 **CLAIM HIGH (USA),** b c Alleged (USA)—Shine High (USA) **Mr A. N. Solomons**
55 **CLOUD FREE (USA),** ch f Conquistador Cielo (USA)—Pleasant Flight (USA) **Mr K. Abdulla**
56 **DEFENSIVE PLAY (USA),** b c Fappiano (USA)—Safe Play (USA) **Mr K. Abdulla**
57 **DIAMOND SHOES (USA),** b f Diamond Shoal—Raise A Baby (USA) **Mr & Mrs Moretti degli Adimari**
58 **DIGRESSION (USA),** b c Seattle Slew (USA)—Double Axle (USA) **Mr K. Abdulla**
59 **DOVEKIE,** b c Ela-Mana-Mou—Sacred Ibis **Sheikh Mohammed**
60 **DUKE OF PADUCAH (USA),** gr c Green Dancer (USA)—Flordelisada (USA) **Mr J. Garcia-Roady**
61 **DULVERTON,** ch c Ela-Mana-Mou—Parsimony **Mr G. M. Rivkin**
62 **EMPSHOTT (USA),** b c Graustark—Call The Queen (USA) **Mr Nigel Grandfield**
63 **FLORET (USA),** b c Roberto (USA)—Florera (USA) **Mr K. Abdulla**
64 **FLOWN,** b c Hotfoot—My Own II **Mr Edward P. Winfield**
65 **FREE AT LAST,** b f Shirley Heights—Brocade **Mr Gerald Leigh**
66 **GALAGAMES (USA),** ch c Lyphard (USA)—Morning Games (USA) **Mr Jerome Brody**
67 **GOLDEN MILL (USA),** b f Mr Prospector (USA)—Mill Queen **Mr K. Abdulla**
68 **GREENHAM (USA),** b c Green Dancer (USA)—Cameo Shore **Mr K. Abdulla**
69 **HAIL CAESAR (USA),** ch c Roberto (USA)—Princess Roycraft (USA) **Sir Gordon White**
70 **ISAMBARD,** b c Star Appeal—Mertola **Mrs Archie Kidd**
71 **KALMADENE,** gr c Kalaglow—Almadena **Mrs Archie Kidd**
72 **LOVER'S MOON,** b c Ela-Mana-Mou—Ce Soir **Sheikh Mohammed**
73 **MARLINGFORD,** ch g Be My Guest (USA)—Inchmarlo (USA) **Mr K. Abdulla**
74 **MARQUETRY (USA),** ch c Conquistador Cielo (USA)—Regent's Walk (CAN) **Mr K. Abdulla**
75 **MIND THE STEP,** b c Shareef Dancer (USA)—Mytinia **Sheikh Mohammed**
76 **MINGUS (USA),** b c The Minstrel (CAN)—Sylph (USA) **Mr K. Abdulla**
77 **MODIFY (USA),** ch c Nijinsky (CAN)—Mofida **Mr K. Abdulla**
78 **NATARAYA (USA),** b f Nijinsky—Beautiful Morning
79 **NOW LISTEN (USA),** b c Miswaki (USA)—Nowanna (USA) **Mr K. Abdulla**
80 **PERPIGNAN,** br f Rousillon (USA)—Heart 'n' Soul **Mr J. H. Richmond-Watson**
81 **PETERHOUSE,** b c Habitat—Kanz (USA) **Sheikh Mohammed**
82 **RAJ WAKI (USA),** b c Miswaki (USA)—Script Approval (USA) **Mr Roy Taiano**
83 **REGAL STING (USA),** b c Drone—Momma Taj (USA) **Sir Ernest Harrison**
84 **RESEARCHING (USA),** b c Mr Prospector (USA)—Solartic (CAN) **Mr K. Abdulla**
85 **ROBELLATION (USA),** b c Robellino (USA)—Vexation (USA) **Francis Lever (Partners)**

Tattersalls Sales Dates for 1990
TATTERSALLS ENGLAND
BREEZE-UP SALE April 17 - 19
JULY SALE July 11 - 12
SEPTEMBER SALE September 10
HIGHFLYER YEARLING SALE October 2 - 5
OCTOBER YEARLING SALE October 15 - 20
AUTUMN SALE October 29 - November 3
DECEMBER SALE November 28 - December 8
TATTERSALLS (Ireland) Ltd
FEBRUARY SALE February 19 - 20
DERBY SALE June 27 - 29
AUGUST NATIONAL HUNT SALE August 23 - 24
FAIRYHOUSE YEARLING SALE September 25 - 27
NOVEMBER NATIONAL HUNT SALE November 8 - 9
November 11 - 17
NOVEMBER FLAT BRED SALE November 23 - 27
W
E
The Classic place to sell
Classic Horses in Europe
Tattersalls
Tattersalls
Terrace House, Newmarket, Suffolk CB8 9BT
Telephone: (0638) 665931
Fax: (0638) 660850. Telex: 817582 HAMMER G
Tattersalls
Tattersalls (Ireland) Ltd
Fairyhouse, Ratoath, Co. Meath, Ireland
Telephone: Dublin (01) 256777
Fax: Dublin (01) 256789 Telex: 91737 TATTS EI

MR G. HARWOOD—continued

86 **RUSCINO,** br c Rousillon (USA)—Eastern Shore **Sheikh Mohammed**
87 **SCATTER,** b c Sharpo—Visitation **Mr Murray Gordon**
88 **SCOTTISH JESTER (USA),** b c Northern Baby (CAN)—Foolish Lady (USA) **Sir Gordon White**
89 **SEATTLE BRAVE,** b c Seattle Song (USA)—Oraston **Mr Nigel Grandfield**
90 **SHOUT AND SING (USA),** ch c The Minstrel (CAN)—Godetia (USA) **Mr J. Garcia-Roady**
91 **STEREO (USA),** b c The Minstrel (CAN)—Silver In Flight (USA) **Mr K. Abdulla**
92 **STUMPS,** ch c King of Clubs—Musicienne (FR) **Mr J. Livock**
93 **TAKEOVER TALK (USA),** b c Conquistador Cielo (USA)—Love Words (USA) **Mr A. E. Bodie**
94 **TORCELLO,** b c Procida (USA)—Millieme **Mr J. B. Austin**
95 **VILLEROI,** ch c Kris—Vilikaia (USA) **Sheikh Mohammed**

TWO-YEAR-OLDS

96 **ADVERSARY (CAN),** b c 27/4 Alleged—Imperturbable Lady
97 **AELLOPOUS,** b f 12/2 Kris—Graecia Magna
98 **ALGUA BALVA (USA),** b f 8/4 Solford—Watership
99 B c 18/3 Caro—All Dance
100 B c 26/2 Rainbow Quest—Aryenne
101 B f 21/2 Ela-Mana-Mou—Be Discreet
102 **BE THE BEST,** b c 5/3 Rousillon—Shady Wood
103 B c 29/4 Indian King—Blyth's Folly
104 **BONDI (USA),** b c 21/4 Diesis—Sunshine Law
105 **BOSAMBO (USA),** b c 27/4 Our Native—Grey Dawn Girl
106 Ch c 10/2 Cox's Ridge—Cairn Rouge
107 B c 10/5 Green Desert—Casual
108 Ch c 15/2 Sir Ivor—Colinear
109 Ch c 23/1 Arctic Tern—Date
110 **DI STEFARNO,** b c 29/1 Chief Singer—Doree Moisson
111 Ch c 5/2 Blushing Groom—Double Axle
112 **DUC DE BERRY (USA),** ch c 9/4 Chief's Crown—L'Extravagante
113 **DUKE OF MONMOUTH (USA),** b c 2/4 Secreto—Queen For The Day
114 **EL DOUBLE (IRE),** b c 11/3 Doulab—Eulalie
115 **EL PERSA (USA),** gr c 18/3 Persepolis—A Realgirl
116 **FATHER NORTH (USA),** b c 14/2 Far North—Princess Morvi
117 **FICHU (USA),** b c 29/5 Sharpen Up—Mousseline de Soie
118 Ch c 17/1 Northern Baby—Foolish Lady
119 **FROSCH (USA),** b c 6/4 Irish River—Valderna
120 B c 3/5 Greinton—Gay Current
121 B c 4/4 Sadler's Wells—Gertrude Lawrence
122 **GOLDEN REVERIE (USA),** b c 28/2 Golden Act—Our Reverie
123 **GUIDING STAR (USA),** b c 28/2 Majestic Light—Bethamane
124 **HAREDEN (USA),** b c 26/2 Cougar II—Chippewa
125 **HUNTING GROUND,** b c 5/5 Dancing Brave—Ack's Secret
126 B c 21/2 Known Fact—Ides of March
127 B c 3/5 Shirley Heights—If
128 **INHERITANCE (IRE),** b c 25/3 Last Tycoon—Unknown Lady
129 B c 21/5 Dancing Brave—Intermission
130 **KELTIE (USA),** ch c 29/2 Storm Bird—Classy Twist
131 **KILMARNOCK,** br c 29/1 Sagace—Killapata
132 B c 16/4 Lear Fan—Lady Blackfoot
133 **LEASE BACK (USA),** ch c 26/4 Secretariat—Go Leasing
134 Ch c 2/2 Nepal—Line of Duty
135 **LODESTAR (IRE),** b c 26/1 Rainbow Quest—Air Distingue
136 **LUCKY NOIRE,** b f 30/4 Aragon—Noire Small
137 **LYPHAR DANCER,** b c 27/4 Bellypha—Western Gem
138 **MAN FROM ELDORADO (USA),** b c 21/2 Mr Prospector—Promising Girl
139 **MANGALORE (USA),** ch c 7/2 Blushing Groom—Miss Manon
140 **MEMORIVE (USA),** b f Riverman—Le Vague A L'Ame
141 **MILLERS TALE (USA),** b c 7/3 Nureyev—Mill Queen
142 **MOOT POINT (USA),** b c 24/3 Sharpen Up—Gaelic Logic
143 Ch c 2/4 Mr Prospector—Over Your Shoulder

Horse Dentistry

Robin Abel Smith

Member of International Association of Equine Dental Technicians

Barleythorpe, Oakham,
Rutland, LE15 7EQ
Telephone : (0572) 756762

Car Telephone: (0836) 637704

MR G. HARWOOD—continued

144 POLISH PATRIOT (USA), b c 24/3 Danzig—Maria Waleska
145 B c 27/4 Baillamont—Praise
146 REBEL CHIEF (IRE), b c 23/2 Dancing Brave—Primatie
147 RINGLAND (USA), b c 7/4 Gate Dancer—Tinnitus
148 RIVER CONSORT (USA), b c 21/4 Riverman—Queens Only
149 ROGERDOR (USA), b c Tom Rolfe—Grand Bonheur
150 RONEO (USA), ch c 18/4 Secretariat—Zaizafon
151 RUSSIAN SKY (USA), b c 14/5 Conquistador Cielo—Nijinsky Star
152 Ch c 1/3 The Minstrel—Sahsie
153 B c 15/4 Rainbow Quest—Salidar
154 B f 4/2 Law Society—Santa Luciana
155 SEA BREAKER (IRE), b c 17/2 Glow—Surfing
156 Ch c 21/2 Mr Prospector—Seven Springs
157 B c 23/4 Lear Fan—Sugar Hollow
158 TIERCE (USA), ch c 2/4 Diesis—Ethics
159 TORODIN (USA), ch c 16/3 Northern Baby—Bonnie And Gay
160 TRADE PRESS (USA), ch c 8/2 Affirmed—Sans Pareil
161 Ch c 20/4 Never So Bold—Trinida
162 B c 24/2 Red Sunset—Vahila
163 VIGANO (USA), ch c 27/3 Nijinsky—Playful Queen
164 ZABAR, b c 1/2 Dancing Brave—Brocade

Other Owners: Mr Victor Behrens, Mr T. C. Collyer, Mr J. Egan, Mrs P. Elsbury, Mrs Michael Ennever, Mr J. Fisher, Mr T. Furey, Mr Harrison, Mrs Harrison, Mr Cecil J. Hedigan, Mr R. A. Kirstein, Mrs S. E. Lakin, Mr J. Livock, Mrs Paul Locke, Mr Samuel L. Lyon, Mr Keith Nicklin, Mr C. J. Petyt, Mr C. Radin, Mr R. M. F. Ross, Mr P. Savill, Mr R. H. Smith, Mrs C. B. Thompson, Mr B. Townsley, Mr J. T. Vanner, Mr F. Zarb.

Jockeys (Flat): A Clark (7-12), R Cochrane, S Griffith (7-9).

Jockey (NH): M Perrett (10-0).

Apprentices: G O'Neill (7-7), D Stather (7-12).

Conditional: Gary Crone (9-7).

Lady Riders: Miss Amanda Harwood (9-7), Miss Gaye Harwood (8-0).

273 MR W. HASTINGS-BASS, Newbury

Postal: **Hodcott Stables, West Ilsley, Newbury, Berkshire, RG16 OAE**
Phone: **OFFICE (0635) 28747 HOME (0635) 28725 FAX (0635) 28720**

1 BASHFUL BOY, 5, b g Jalmood (USA)—Sesta **Mrs David Butter**
2 DISCORD, 4, b g Niniski (USA)—Apple Peel **Mrs Evan Williams**

NOW AVAILABLE IN THE UK!

HORSE HEALTH PRODUCTS LTD

THE TOP AMERICAN RANGE!

"The choice of leading trainers!"

RED CELL

OUR WIDELY USED LIQUID BLOOD TONIC, FOR USE AS AN EVERY-DAY FEED ADDITIVE.

EQUALIZER

PROTEIN BASED VITAMIN AND MINERAL SUPPLEMENT FOR YEARLINGS.

MAXUM

THE COMPLETE ADDITIVE FOR STUDS.

ELECTRO-DEX

AMERICA'S LEADING ELECTROLYTE SALTS.

VITA-POULTICE

READY-MIXED CLAY POULTICE FOR SORE SHINS etc.

ABSORBA-PAD

PRESSURE DISPLACEMENT BACK PAD

Also included in our range:

VITAMIN E POWDER

VITAMIN E AND SELENIUM POWDER (and crumbles).

VITA BIOTIN CRUMBLES - to aid hoof growth.

DICALCIUM PHOSPHATE

FOR FURTHER INFORMATION PLEASE CALL US AT:

Broomers Park, Broomers Hill Lane, Pulborough,
West Sussex RH20 2HY. Tel: (07982) 5337 Fax: (07982) 2202

MR W. HASTINGS-BASS—continued

3 **EL REY**, 6, b h King of Spain—Powderhall **Lady Newman**
4 **INDIAN QUEEN**, 5, ch m Electric—Taj Princess **Sir Gordon Brunton**
5 **KIYA (USA)**, 4, b f Dominion—Melodrama **Lord McAlpine**
6 **LADY TAP**, 4, ch f Red Sunset—Park Lady **Mr Irwin H. Kramer**
7 **LUNCH BOX**, 5, ch m Great Nephew—Supper Time **Mrs Amanda Skiffington**
8 **MR PINTIPS**, 6, gr h Kris—Bempton **Lord Halifax**
9 **PERANG PERCY**, 4, b c Bay Express—Carcosa **Lord Crawshaw**

THREE-YEAR-OLDS

10 **BLUE GUM**, ch g Cure The Blues (USA)—Honey **Mr Robert Holmes a Court**
11 **CHIPPER ROTH (USA)**, gr f Blushing Groom (FR)—Zabolina **Mr Michael Doyle Riordan**
12 **EYES ON THE PRIZE**, ch f Lomond (USA)—Girl Friday (USA) **Mr Robert Holmes a Court**
13 **GREY POWER**, gr f Wolf Power (SAF)—Periquito (USA) **Mr J. C. Smith**
14 **LURKING**, b f Formidable (USA)—Hiding **Mr James Wigan**
15 **MONTPELIER LAD**, br g Elegant Air—Leg Glance **Sir Michael Sandberg**
16 **NIGHT JAR**, b f Night Shift (USA)—Fodens Eve **Mr J. T. Thomas**
17 **NOW BOARDING**, b f Blazing Saddles (AUS)—Strictly Swing **Mr Robert Holmes a Court**
18 **OFF THE WALL**, b g Auction Ring (USA)—Fraudulent **Sir G. Loder**
19 **OK CORRAL (USA)**, gr g Malinowski (USA)—Tiger Trap (USA) **Mr M. L. Oberstein**
20 **OK RECORDS**, b c Cure The Blues (USA)—Last Clear Chance (USA) **Mr M. L. Oberstein**
21 **PLATINUM DISC**, b c Song—Pennies To Pounds **Platinum Racing**
22 **PRIORITY PAID**, ch f Try My Best (USA)—Anna Carla (GER) **Mr Robert Holmes a Court**
23 **RELIEF MAP**, ch f Relkino—Montania **Lord Derby**
24 **STYLISH GENT**, br g Vitiges (FR)—Squire's Daughter **Mr N. H. Phillips**
25 **SUNFLOWER SEED**, b f Mummy's Pet—Bright Sun **Mr Christopher Wright**
26 **TAJ VICTORY**, ch f Final Straw—Taj Princess **Sir Gordon Brunton**
27 **THE MINDER (FR)**, b br g Miller's Mate—Clarandal **Mrs Peter Hastings**

TWO-YEAR-OLDS

28 **AMPHIGORY**, b c 5/3 Gorytus—Peculiar One (USA) (Quack (USA)) **L. M. Schott**
29 B c 25/3 Bering—Baltic Sea (CAN) (Danzig (USA)) **Kennet Valley**
30 B c 17/5 Bellypha—Celebrity (Troy) **Lord Carnarvon**
31 **COLTRANE**, b c 10/4 Dominion—Rainbows End (Swallow) **Lord Carnarvon**
32 **CORLEY LAD**, b c 27/4 Elegant Air—Corley Moor (Shirley Heights) **Laharna Ltd**
33 **FEN PRINCESS (IRE)**, b f 21/3 Trojan Fen—Cenerentola (Caro) **Hon S. Weinstock**
34 **GREEN DANUBE (USA)**, ch f 29/1 Irish River—Chere Amie (FR) (Gay Mecene) **Hon S. Weinstock**
35 **ISLAND DESERT (IRE)**, b f 18/3 Green Desert—Salote (Forli (ARG)) **Hon S. Weinstock**
36 **JACK'S CROFT**, b c 14/4 Damister—Smagiada (Young Generation) **Lady Lonsdale**
37 B c 20/4 Elegant Air—Jove's Voodoo (USA) (Northern Jove (CAN)) **Mr Elliot**
38 B f Persian Bold—Lady Habitat (Habitat) **Sir G. Brunton**
39 B f Lear Fan—Melodrama (Busted) **Lord Carnarvon**
40 B f Taufan—Miss Reasoning (USA) (Bold Reasoning (USA)) **Irwin H. Kramer**
41 **MRS BUNN**, b f Millers Mate—Clarandal (Young Generation) **Mrs Peter Hastings**
42 Br c 22/2 Chief Singer—Periquito (Olden Times) **J. C. Smith**
43 B c 22/4 Tender King—Persian Apple (USA) (No Robbery) **Kennet Valley**
44 **RAZOR'S EDGE**, ch c 28/4 Rousillon—Sharp Girl (FR) (Sharpman) **Hon S. Weinstock**
45 **RINGAROSES**, br f 16/3 Auction Ring—Coupe d'Hebe (Ile de Bourbon) **E. Loder**
46 **RUSSIAN MINK (USA)**, ch f 5/5 L'Emigrant—Furry Friend (USA) (Bold Bidder) **Hon S. Weinstock**
47 B f Bustino—Wide of The Mark (Gulf Pearl) **Lord Carnarvon**

Other Owners: The Queen, Mr S. Hastings-Bass, Mrs Jacqueline Getty Phillips, Mr George Strawbridge, Mrs K. M. Thomas, Lord Weinstock.

Apprentices: Dale Gibson (7-6), David Harrison (7-0), Mark Simpson (7-12).

EVERY SUCCESS TO WILLIAM HASTINGS-BASS IN 1990 ON UNIT PLATES

BRITISH PLATES ARE BEST

Designed and developed over 40 years to be the winners in British Conditions.

Unit Plates give:–

MAXIMUM GRIP WITHOUT DANGER (even in the wettest conditions)

- ✻ Strip steel insert to retard wear without ever protruding or being thick and burred.

EASY FITTING

- ✻ Extruded aluminium is inherently harder and tougher yet more malleable to shape adjust than cast plates.
- ✻ Extra nailability with nail holes all round including the toe (16–19 per plate).
- ✻ Better balance with standard, short or upright heel finishes.
- ✻ Four section widths including extra broad.
- ✻ Arab or thoroughbred shapes.

For a free sample contact
UNIT RACING PLATES
Unit 6, West Station Yard
Maldon, Essex CM9 6TR
Maldon (0621) 858252

274 MR JOHN C HAYDEN, Kildare

Postal: **Castlemartin Abbey House Stables, Kilcullen, Co. Kildare, Ireland.**

1 **CRAFTY DESERT,** 4, b g Crafty Prospector (USA)—Desert Pet **Dr A. J. F. O'Reilly**
2 **FLYING JENNIE,** 4, b f Burslem—Lady Abbess **Mr Robert M. Burns**
3 **HERNE,** 4, ch f Miami Springs—Tarvie **Mr Niall Moriarty**
4 **SHARP SLIPPER,** 4, b f Sharpo—Evening Slipper **Dr A. J. F. O'Reilly**

THREE-YEAR-OLDS

5 **COMMENCEMENT,** b f Trojan Fen—Better Begin **Mr Francis O'Toole**
6 **GUEST PLAYER,** ch f Horage—Guestaway **Dr A. J. F. O'Reilly**
7 **LADY OF VISION,** b f Vision (USA)—Lady of The House **Mr Francis O'Toole**
8 **NEEDY THATCH,** b f Thatching—Needy **Dr A. J. F. O'Reilly**
9 **NO DOWRY,** ch f Shy Groom (USA)—Collateral **Mr J. V. Moore**
10 **REASONABLY FRENCH,** b f Reasonable (FR)—French Pearl **Mr Stanley Ridgeway**
11 **RELAXING LADY,** b f Norwick (USA)—Belle (DEN) **Mr Hugo Merry**
12 **SIMPLY GREEDY,** b f Simply Great (FR)—Greedy **Dr A. J. F. O'Reilly**
13 **SUSAN'S PET,** b g Gorytus (USA)—Susan's Way **Dr A. J. F. O'Reilly**

TWO-YEAR-OLDS

14 B f 16/4 Green Ruby (USA)—Bauhinia (Sagaro) **Mrs B. Hayden**
15 B c 4/4 Krayyan—Bold Anna (Bold Lad (IRE)) **Miss Niamh Keating**
16 Ch f 15/2 Sallust—Claremont Girl (Will Hays) **Mrs B. Hayden**
17 Ch c 25/5 Tender King—Flo Kelly (Florescence) **Castlemartin Racing Club**
18 Ch c 21/5 Thatching—Flower Petals (Busted) **Miss Niamh Keating**
19 B c 28/3 Tender King—French Pearl (Gulf Pearl) **Dr A. J. F. O'Reilly**
20 B f 11/4 Runnett—Island Goddess (Godswalk (USA)) **Mrs B. Hayden**
21 B br f 3/2 Last Tycoon—Karella (Jukebox) **Dr A. J. F. O'Reilly**
22 B c 19/3 Bay Express—Marie Galante (Shirley Heights) **Castlemartin Racing Club**
23 B c 9/2 Vision (USA)—Payola (Auction Ring (USA)) **Mr W. Cribben**

Other Owners: Mr T. Bruton, Mr E. D. Gilmartin, Mrs A. Hayden, Mr Peter McCutcheon.

Jockey (Flat): K J Manning (8-6).

Jockey (NH): Brian Nolan (9-3).

Apprentice: Ronan P Hurley (6-10).

Lady Riders: Miss Sarah Collen (9-0), Miss Ann O'Rourke (7-4).

275 MR D. HAYDN JONES, Pontypridd

Postal: **Garth Paddocks, Efail Isaf, Pontypridd, Mid Glamorgan, Wales.**
Phone: **(0443) 202515**

1 **BALLYVAUGHAN LADY,** 4, ch f Burslem—Liangold **Mr John C. Howard**
2 **BORN WITH A VEIL,** 4, b g Thatching—Star Harbour **Mr Kevan R. Kynaston**
3 **CAREER BAY,** 8, b g Orange Bay—Career **Mr Norman J. Phillips**
4 **COOL EMM,** 5, b h Miami Springs—Wise Countess (USA) **North Cheshire Trading & Storage Ltd**
5 **DOLLY BEVAN,** 4, ro f Another Realm—Elkie Brooks **Mr C. Thomas**
6 **GARTH LADY,** 4, ch f Jalmood (USA)—Lady Capilano **Mr H. G. Collis**
7 **GEE DOUBLE YOU,** 4, ch g Tap On Wood—Repicado Rose (USA) **Mr J. A. Cartwright**

MR D. HAYDN JONES—continued

8 **JUST JENNINGS**, 5, ch g Horage—Sally St Clair **Mrs E. M. Haydn Jones**
9 **LANGHAM LADY**, 4, b f Dunbeath (USA)—Rosinante (FR) **North Cheshire Trading & Storage Ltd**
10 **LEVITT LADY**, 4, gr f Another Realm—My Cervantes **Mr C. G. Johns**
11 **PENHILL FLAME**, 4, ch f Main Reef—Debian **Mr C. Gapper**
12 **REGALCROFT**, 6, b h Crofter (USA)—Regal Ray **Mr Ian Purchase**
13 **STONEBROKER**, 8, ch m Morston (FR)—Overspent **Edwards and Cartwright (Cont) Ltd**
14 **WHITE RIVER**, 4, ch c Pharly (FR)—Regain **Mr C. Thomas**

THREE-YEAR-OLDS

15 **CARDIFF ARMS**, b f Another Realm—Gemgem **Mr W. V. Williams**
16 **CORIO BAY**, br c Blue Cashmere—Rushley Bay **Mr C. G. Johns**
17 **DOMINIANA**, b f Dominion—Lady Capilano **Mrs Olga Collis**
18 **EASY PURCHASE**, br c Swing Easy (USA)—Dauphiness **Mr Ian Purchase**
19 **FRENCH BAY**, ch c Pharly (FR)—Finbay (ITY) **Mr H. G. Collis**
20 **GARISSA (FR)**, b f Gorytus (USA)—Reasonable Mona (USA) **Mr Peter Powell**
21 **GLENCOE LADY**, b f Thatching—Borgia (GER) **North Cheshire Trading & Storage Ltd**
22 **KRISTIS GIRL**, ch f Ballacashtal (CAN)—Fleur d'Amour **Mrs A. Taylor**
23 **PREMIER DANCE**, ch g Bairn (USA)—Gigiolina **Premier Offices Limited**
24 **RUDRY PRINCESS**, ro f Blazing Saddles (AUS)—Rudry Park **Miss Karen Harris**
25 **SIAN'S LADY**, b f Dunbeath (USA)—Hawaiian Joss (USA) **Mr John Dalgleish**
26 **TRIBUTE TO DAD**, b g Aragon—Bourienne **Mrs E. M. Haydn Jones**

TWO-YEAR-OLDS

27 B f 30/1 Kafu—Cancaniere (Hotfoot) **Garth Park Racing Ltd**
28 B f 23/3 Kafu—First Contact (Simbir) **North Cheshire Trading & Storage Ltd**
29 Ro f 11/5 Blushing Scribe (USA)—Milnsbridge (Dragonara Palace (USA)) **Garth Park Racing Ltd**
30 Ch c 12/5 Absalom—Nyeri (Saint Crespin III) **Garth Park Racing Ltd**
31 B c 6/4 Reesh—Palace Travel (High Top) **Mr Gordon Vine**
32 B f 16/3 Bold Owl—Piccadilly Rose (Reform) **Mrs E. M. Jones**
33 Ch c 25/4 Dalsaan—Rixensart (Credo) **Mr J. Gibbs**
34 Ch f 28/3 Final Straw—Skiboule (BEL) (Boulou) **Garth Park Racing Ltd**
35 **THRILL**, ch f 22/1 Good Times (ITY)—Naughty Party (Parthia) **Mrs Louise Parry**
36 B c 9/5 Kafu—Waadi Hatta (USA) (Upper Nile (USA)) **Garth Park Racing Ltd**

Other Owners: Mr W. Haydn Jones.

Jockeys (Flat): S Cauthen (8-5, w.a.), John Reid (8-4, w.a.).

276 MR H. E. HAYNES, Swindon

Postal: **Reddown Farm, Highworth, Swindon, Wiltshire, SN6 7SH.**
Phone: **(0793) 762437**

1 **HOW'S BETTY**, 5, b m New Member—Brown Gull **Mrs H. E. Haynes**
2 **JIM BROWN**, 9, b g Jimsun—Brown Gull **Mrs H. E. Haynes**
3 **TEDS TACTICS**, 7, ch g New Member—Alice Clarke **Mrs H. E. Haynes**

Amateur: Mr A Tory (10-0).

Lady Rider: Miss Fiona Haynes (9-7).

277 MR M. J. HAYNES, Epsom

Postal: **21 Chantry Hurst, Epsom, Surrey.**
Phone: **HOME EPSOM (03727) 22664 STABLES BURGH HEATH (0737) 351140**

1 **BIN DAAHIR (USA),** 4, ch g Blushing Groom (FR)—Bolt From The Blue (USA) **S. Bell**
2 **CABALLINE,** 6, ch g Last Fandango—Rosalia **Mr Peter Lancaster**
3 **CAROLES CLOWN,** 4, gr f Another Realm—Show Business **Mrs C. Grimshaw**
4 **CROSBY PLACE,** 4, gr f Crooner—Royal Bat **Miss P. I. Westbrook**
5 **DUTYFUL,** 4, b f Bold Owl—My Duty **Green Curtis Blomfield Assoc. (UK) Ltd**
6 **HOLTERMANN (USA),** 6, b g Mr Prospector (USA)—Royal Graustark (USA) **Mr R. J. Bell**
7 **OLLIE-P,** 5, ch g Red Sunset—Rosemary's Rhythm **Mrs Dawn Pettis**
8 **SONIC SIGNAL,** 4, b f Trojan Fen—Danger Signal **Mr M. J. Haynes**
9 **WIZZARD MAGIC,** 7, ch h Ahonoora—Siofra Beag **Mr David Myers**

THREE-YEAR-OLDS

10 Ch c Good Times (ITY)—Aiglon (HOL) **Mrs R. Bell**
11 **BOLD LEZ,** b c Never So Bold—Classy Nancy (USA) **Mrs M. L. Ansell**
12 **MAID WELCOME,** br f Mummy's Pet—Carolynchristensen **Doublet Ltd**
13 **ON THE SAUCE,** b g Kala Shikari—Kingsfold Flash **J. Rosbotham & Partners**
14 **PLEASURE AHEAD,** b c Taufan (USA)—Nan's Mill **M. Boxon & Partners**
15 **POPSI'S LEGACY,** ch f Little Wolf—Popsi's Poppet **Mr M. J. Haynes**
16 **POSSEBELLE,** ch f Posse (USA)—Belle Origine (USA) **Mr T. A. Daniels**
17 Gr c Town And Country—Royal Bat
18 **SUPER VIRTUOSA,** b f Wassl—Resolve **Mr David J. Chapman**
19 **THE ISLAND,** ch f Bairn (USA)—Redhead **Mr J. Durkin**

TWO-YEAR-OLDS

20 **CLASSICS PEARL (IRE),** gr f Reasonable—Zanskar (Godswalk (USA)) **Miss L. Comer & Partners**
21 B f Mazaad—Faddle (St Paddy)
22 Gr c Kafu—Nuageuse (Prince Regent (FR)) **J. Loong & Partners**
23 **PRINCESS JESTINA (IRE),** b f Jester—Royal Aunt (Martinmas) **Mrs M. Day**
24 Ch f Adonijah—Ptarmigan (Hill Clown (USA))
25 **SCENT OF BATTLE,** ch c Rousillon—Light O'Battle (Queen's Hussar) **W. Carpenter**

Other Owners: Mr B. C. Ansell, Mr C. G. Ansell, Mr D. E. Chambers, Miss Y. Haynes, Mr D. H. Jones, Mr Joseph Nally, Mrs B. H. Nye, Mr Bob Pettis, Mr Keith Turner.

Apprentices: M Smith (8-3), D Toole (7-0).

Lady Rider: Miss Y Haynes.

278 MR P. A. HAYWARD, Netheravon

Postal: **Copperfield, Haxton, Netheravon, Wiltshire.**
Phone: **(0980) 70585**

1 **ATLANTIC CEDAR,** 4, b g Touching Wood (USA)—Enchanted **Mr P. Hayward**
2 **CANONESS,** 9, b m St Paddy—Sea Fable **Mr A. J. Byrne**
3 **CASTLE ORCHARD,** 6, br g Lepanto (GER)—Cora **Beaconsfield Developments**
4 **CLINKER,** 10, gr g Saritamer (USA)—Burning Deck **Mr A. P. King**
5 **COMBE HAY,** 8, br g Rhodomantade—Safeguard **Mr K. P. Neill**
6 **FELSPAR,** 4, gr c Coquelin (USA)—Candide **Mr P. Hayward**
7 **HACKLESTON,** 11, ch g Indigenous—Dracula's Daughter **Mr P. Hayward**
8 **JAYELLS DREAM,** 8, b m Space King—Sam's Song **Beaconsfield Developments**
9 **SOROPTIMISTER,** 5, br g Swing Easy (USA)—Cora **Mrs R. H. Till**
10 **STAGS LANE,** 5, b g Magnolia Lad—Larullah **Mr P. Hayward**
11 **STEADY LOVE,** 5, br m Swing Easy (USA)—Lucky Love **Mr R. H. Till**
12 **WILTSHIRE YEOMAN,** 10, ch g Derrylin—Ribo Pride **Mr J. Sawyer**

MR P. A. HAYWARD—continued

TWO-YEAR-OLDS

13 Ch f Noalto—Cora (Current Coin) **Mr R. H. Till**
14 Ch f 12/5 Capricorn Line—Silver Empress (Octavo (USA)) **Mr P. Hayward**

Other Owners: Mrs A. M. Gilbert, Mr R. J. McGrath, Brig A. A. Sisson, Mrs C. T. Woodley.

Jockeys (NH): G Armytage (10-0, w.a.), B Wright (10-7, w.a.).

279 LORD HEAD, Salisbury

Postal: **Throope Manor, Bishopstone, Salisbury, Wiltshire, SP5 4BA.**
Phone: **(072 277) 318**

1 **ABBOTSBURY ABBOT,** 8, ch g Monksfield—Lucky Money **Lord Head**
2 **MOUNT EREBUS,** 8, ch g Quayside—Well Mannered **Lord Head**

280 MRS C. HEAD, Chantilly

Postal: **32 Avenue du General Leclerc, 60500 Chantilly, France.**
Phone: **44 57 01 01**

1 **ALYPHEOR (USA),** 4, br g Lypheor—Alik (FR) **Mr J. Wertheimer**
2 **CONQUISTACKY (USA),** 4, b c Conquistador Cielo (USA)—Really Lucky (USA) **Ecurie Aland**
3 **DRUGSTORE (USA),** 4, ch c Nijinsky (CAN)—Egalite (FR) **Mrs P. Morange**
4 **HAUT DE FORME,** 4, b c Gay Mecene (USA)—Heres To You (FR) **Ecurie Aland**
5 **MY RIVER (USA),** 4, ch f Irish River (FR)—Messenie (FR) **Mrs P. Morange**
6 **PHARMINE (USA),** 4, ch c Lyphard (USA)—Minstrel Girl (FR) **Mr J. Wertheimer**
7 **ROI DES VILLES (FR),** 4, ch c Ti King (FR)—Yerville (FR) **Mr J. Wertheimer**
8 **SOLDIER OF FORTUNE (FR),** 4, b c Saint Cyrien (FR)—Lucky For Me **Mr C. Humphris**
9 **TIMIDE ESPION (FR),** 4, b g Saint Cyrien (FR)—Wind Spring (FR) **Maktoum Al Maktoum**
10 **VAL DES BOIS (FR),** 4, gr f Bellypha—Vallee des Fleurs **Mr J. Wertheimer**
11 **VENECUELA (USA),** 4, b c Riverman (USA)—Vintage (USA) **Mrs Plesch**

THREE-YEAR-OLDS

12 **ALLEGED JAPI (USA),** b c Alleged (USA)—Jameelapi (USA) **Maktoum Al Maktoum**
13 **ANITRALINE (FR),** b f Crystal Glitters (USA)—Anitra's Dance (FR) **Mr J. Wertheimer**
14 **BALYCIA (FR),** b f Sicyos (USA)—Balsamique (FR) **Mrs A. Head**
15 **BAZILIA (USA),** b f Mr Prospector (USA)—Brillante (FR) **Ecurie Aland**
16 **BEL EXOCTIC (FR),** b c Saint Cyrien (FR)—Biblia (FR) **Mrs A. Head**
17 **BLANC SEING (FR),** b c Shirley Heights—Blanche Reine (FR) **Ecurie Aland**
18 **BLUSHING AWAY (USA),** ch f Blushing Groom (FR)—Sweet Revenge (USA) **Mr J. Wertheimer**
19 **BLUSHING PINK (USA),** b f Blushing Groom (FR)—Ma Biche (USA) **Maktoum Al Maktoum**
20 **COMPANY (USA),** ch f Nureyev (USA)—Sigy (FR) **Mr J. Jones**
21 **CRYSTAL LAND,** ch f Kris—Greenland Park **Maktoum Al Maktoum**
22 **DERNIERE DANSE,** b f Gay Mecene (USA)—Dance Quest (FR) **Ecurie Aland**
23 **DIAVOLINA (USA),** b f Lear Fan (USA)—Diamond Spring (USA) **Ecurie Aland**
24 **DIRECT SEA (USA),** ch f Arctic Tern (USA)—La Dorga (USA) **Mr J. Wertheimer**
25 **DOUBLE SOCIETY (USA),** b f Nodouble (USA)—Noble Society (USA) **Mrs P. Morange**
26 **DOUCEUR (USA),** b f Shadeed (USA)—Jamila **Mr J. Jones**
27 **DR SOMERVILLE (USA),** b c Chief's Crown (USA)—Icing **Maktoum Al Maktoum**
28 **FABULOUS TEASER (FR),** b c Fabulous Dancer (USA)—Moquerie (FR) **Mr J. Wertheimer**
29 **FILAGO (USA),** ch c Foolish Pleasure (USA)—Derly (FR) **Mrs Plesch**
30 **FIRSTWAKI (USA),** ch c Miswaki (USA)—Premiere Danseuse (FR) **Mr J. Wertheimer**

MRS C. HEAD—continued

31 **FLEET FAIRY (USA)**, b f Teeneso (USA)—Fairy Footsteps **Mr R. Smith**
32 **FLYING TALENT (USA)**, b c Blushing Groom (FR)—Egalite (FR) **Sir Gordon White**
33 **FUNAMBULE (USA)**, b c Lyphard (USA)—Sonoma (FR) **Mrs Plesch**
34 **FURTHER LOVE (USA)**, ch f Kris—Breath Taking (FR) **Mr J. Jones**
35 **GALAVA (USA)**, ro f Graustark—Overpowering (USA) **Maktoum Al Maktoum**
36 **GOLD TINA (FR)**, b br f Glint of Gold—Santina (FR) **Mr J. Wertheimer**
37 **GOOFALIK (USA)**, b c Lyphard (USA)—Alik (FR) **Mr J. Wertheimer**
38 **GRACIOUS LINE (FR)**, b br f Fabulous Dancer (USA)—Gracious **Mr J. Wertheimer**
39 **GREENEGED (USA)**, b c Alleged (USA)—Greenway (FR) **Mr J. Wertheimer**
40 **GREENJINSKY (USA)**, b c Nijinsky (CAN)—Green Valley (FR) **Mr J. Wertheimer**
41 **HAVINIA**, ch f Habitat—Lavinia (FR) **Mr J. Wertheimer**
42 **HECQUET (USA)**, ch c Arctic Tern (USA)—Haidee (FR) **Sir Gordon White**
43 **HERSANDE (FR)**, ch f Pink (FR)—Young Hostess (FR) **Mr J. Wertheimer**
44 **HILDITCH (USA)**, b c Al Nasr (FR)—Dumfries (USA) **Mr J. Wertheimer**
45 **HISTORIQUE (FR)**, ch c Rainbow Quest (USA)—Histoire (FR) **Ecurie Aland**
46 **HOPEBLOOMSETERNAL (USA)**, b f Lyphard (USA)—Revidere (USA) **Mr R. K. Eamer**
47 **IMPATIENTE (USA)**, b f Vaguely Noble—Sangue **Mrs P. Morange**
48 **IRISH SUN**, b c Shernazar—L'Irlandaise (USA) **Mr J. Wertheimer**
49 **JUST FABULOUS (FR)**, b f Fabulous Dancer (USA)—Pink Valley (USA) **Mr J. Wertheimer**
50 **LINORA (FR)**, b br f Esprit du Nord (USA)—Princesse Vali (FR) **Mr J. Wertheimer**
51 **MABROVA**, gr f Prince Mab (FR)—Makarova (USA) **Mr J. Wertheimer**
52 **MABVILLE (FR)**, ch f Prince Mab (FR)—Yerville (FR) **Mr J. Wertheimer**
53 **MAD TAX (USA)**, b c Green Dancer (USA)—Alexandrie (USA) **Mr J. Wertheimer**
54 **MONCLAR (USA)**, b c Alydar (USA)—Mother of Pearl (FR) **Ecurie Aland**
55 **MONTAGNARD (USA)**, gr c Nureyev (USA)—Mistretta (FR) **Mrs A. Head**
56 **NEVER BLACK (USA)**, b c Riverman (USA)—Reine de Saba (FR) **Mr J. Wertheimer**
57 **NOBLELY (USA)**, b c Lyphard (USA)—Nonoalca (FR) **Ecurie Aland**
58 **NORTH WALES (USA)**, b f Sir Ivor—Violet (USA) **Mrs R. Guest**
59 **ORANGE BAG (USA)**, ch c Devil's Bag (USA)—L'Orangerie (USA) **Sir Gordon White**
60 **OVER SWING (FR)**, b br f Saint Cyrien (FR)—Charlata (FR) **Mr H. De Kwaitkowski**
61 **PALLAVA (USA)**, b f Lyphard (USA)—Perlita (FR) **Mr H. De Kwaitkowski**
62 **PATAQUES (USA)**, b c Shadeed (USA)—Rivermaid (FR) **Ecurie Aland**
63 **PERLE FINE (USA)**, ch f Devil's Bag (USA)—River Rose (FR) **Mr J. Jones**
64 **PHEORELDA (USA)**, b br c Lypheor—Smeralda **Maktoum Al Maktoum**
65 **PLAY OFF (FR)**, ch c Zino—Popaway **Mr H. De Kwaitkowski**
66 **POSKA (FR)**, b c Posse (USA)—Malenka (FR) **Mr J. Wertheimer**
67 **PRESSIGNY (USA)**, b c Alleged (USA)—Peruvienne **Sir Gordon White**
68 **PROSTAR (FR)**, b f Procida (USA)—Divine Etoile (USA) **Mr J. Wertheimer**
69 **RAYON BLEU (FR)**, b c Bellypha—Blue River (FR) **Mr J. Wertheimer**
70 **REINE DES ILES (USA)**, b f Nureyev (USA)—Reine Mathilde (USA) **Ecurie Aland**
71 **REINE DE THEBES (FR)**, b br f Darshaan—Reine d'Egypte (USA) **Mr J. Wertheimer**
72 **REVE DE VALSE (USA)**, ch c Conquistador Cielo (USA)—Dancing Vaguely (USA) **Sir Gordon White**
73 **REVE (FR)**, b c Fabulous Dancer (USA)—Satu **Haras D'Etreham**
74 **RIVE DU SUD (USA)**, b f Nureyev (USA)—Riviere Doree (USA) **Ecurie Aland**
75 **ROI DE ROME (USA)**, b c Time For A Change (USA)—Reve de Reine (USA) **Ecurie Aland**
76 **SEIGNEUR ET MAITRE (FR)**, ch c Saint Cyrien (FR)—Serenita (FR)
77 **SEPTIEME CIEL (USA)**, b c Seattle Slew (USA)—Maximova (FR) **Mr J. Jones**
78 **SIGNORELLI (USA)**, b c Cox's Ridge (USA)—Silvermine (FR) **Mrs A. Head**
79 **SINGIRI (FR)**, ch c Sicyos (USA)—Wild River (FR) **Mrs Plesch**
80 **SOUS ENTENDU (USA)**, ch f Shadeed (USA)—It's In The Air (USA) **Maktoum Al Maktoum**
81 **SUMMER SONGA (USA)**, b c Nureyev (USA)—Miss Summer **Sir Gordon White**
82 **SWEET GLOW (FR)**, b c Crystal Glitters (USA)—Very Sweet **Mr J. Wertheimer**
83 **THYSSIENNE (USA)**, ch f Lydian (FR)—Princesse Kathy (FR) **Mr J. Wertheimer**
84 **TREVILLARI (USA)**, b f Riverman (USA)—Trevilla (USA) **Mrs A. Head**
85 **TRICK TERN (USA)**, ch c Arctic Tern (USA)—Trick Chick (USA) **Mr J. Wertheimer**
86 **VAILLANT CHEVALIER**, b c Saint Cyrien (FR)—Vallee Dansante (USA) **Mr J. Wertheimer**
87 **VAL FLEURI (FR)**, b br c Sicyos (USA)—Vallee des Fleurs **Mr J. Wertheimer**
88 **VALPIERRE (USA)**, b c Northern Baby (CAN)—Salva (USA) **Mr J. Wertheimer**

GAINSBOROUGH STUD Stallions for 1990

Standing at Whitsbury Manor Stud, Hampshire

CADEAUX GENEREUX

chesnut 1985 by Young Generation - Smarten Up
Champion European Sprinter 1988 and 1989
Won Carroll Foundation July Cup **G.1**, William Hill Sprint Championship **G.1**
RETIRES to STUD in 1990

Standing at Shadwell Stud, Norfolk

GREEN DESERT

bay 1983 by Danzig - Foreign Courier
Won Norcros July Cup **G.1**, Vernons Sprint Cup **G.2**, Flying Childers S. **G.2**, Anglia Television July S. **G.3**
Ladbroke Free H'cap with record top weight, 2nd General Accident 2000 Guineas **G.1**.
FIRST CROP 2-y-olds in 1990

Standing at Haras du Quesnay, France

LEAD ON TIME

bay 1983 by Nureyev - Alathea
Won Prix Maurice de Gheest **G.2**, Criterium de Maisons-Laffitte **G.2**, **Never out of the first two**
FIRST CROP of YEARLINGS in 1990

Standing at Rathbarry Stud, Ireland

JAREER

bay 1983 by Northern Dancer - Fabuleux Jane
Won Shadwell S. by 6 lengths, finished lame in Dewhurst Stakes **G.1**, cost $7,100,000 as a yearling
FIRST CROP of FOALS in 1990

Standing at Ardoon Stud, Ireland

NASHAMAA

brown 1983 by Ahonoora - Balidaress
Won Hennessy Ballymacoy S. **G.3**, Breeders' Cup Classic Trial **LR**, Doyle Hotels Mooresbridge S. **LR**
FIRST CROP YEARLINGS in 1990

Standing at Gainsborough Farm, Kentucky

SHADEED

bay 1982 by Nijinsky - Continual
Won General Accident 2000 Guineas **G.1**, Queen Elizabeth II S. **G.2** in record time, Craven S. **G.3**
A LEADING FIRST SEASON SIRE in 1989

Standing at Dalham Hall Stud, Newmarket

SHAREEF DANCER

bay 1980 by Northern Dancer - Sweet Alliance
Won Irish Sweeps Derby **G.1**, King Edward VII S. **G.2**
Sire in 1989 of the winners of £500,000 and GWs **SHARNFOLD, COLORADO DANCER**
and 2-y-o **SWs ROCK HOPPER, NOBLE BALLERINA**

Standing at Gainsborough Farm, Kentucky

ZILZAL

chesnut 1986 by Nureyev - French Charmer
Champion European Miler 1989
Won Swettenham Stud Sussex S. **G.1**, Queen Elizabeth II S. **G.1**, Jersey S. **G.3**, Van Geest Criterion S. **G.3**
RETIRES to STUD in 1990

Enquiries to:
M.H. Goodbody, **Gainsborough Stud**, Newbury, Berkshire. Telephone: (0635) 253273. Fax: (0635) 254690. Telex: 849436.

MRS C. HEAD—continued

TWO-YEAR-OLDS

89 **AL DUJA (USA)**, ch c 15/4 Arctic Tern (USA)—Bonnie Hope (USA) (Nijinsky (CAN)) **Sheikh Maktoum Al Maktoum**
90 **ALIKA'S DANCE (USA)**, b f Green Dancer (USA)—Alik (FR) (Targowice (USA)) **Mr J. Wertheimer**
91 **ALY SANGUE (USA)**, b f Alydar (USA)—Sangue (Lyphard (USA)) **Mr R. Smith**
92 **ANATHERA (FR)**, b f Antheus (USA)—Reine des Fleurs (FR) (Sharpman) **Mr J. Wertheimer**
93 **ANTHEQUO (FR)**, b c Antheus (USA)—Quemora (FR) (Riverman (USA)) **Mr J. Wertheimer**
94 B f Lyphard (USA)—Arewehavingfunyet (USA) (Sham (USA)) **Prince Khalid Abdulla**
95 **BEAU SULTAN (USA)**, b c Bering—Devalois (FR) (Nureyev (USA)) **Mrs Alec Head**
96 **BELLETERRE (USA)**, b f Arctic Tern (USA)—Beaune (FR) (Lyphard (USA)) **Mrs Alec Head**
97 **BROOKLYN'S DANCE (FR)**, b f Shirley Heights—Vallee Dansante (USA) (Lyphard (USA)) **Mr J. Wertheimer**
98 **BURN A BUCK (USA)**, b c Spend A Buck (USA)—Apachee (FR) (Sir Gaylord) **Mr J. Wertheimer**
99 **CIKALI (USA)**, ch c Miswaki (USA)—La Dorga (USA) (Northern Dancer) **Mr J. Wertheimer**
100 **CYRAMINE (FR)**, b f Saint Cyrien (FR)—Mineralogie (USA) (Nureyev (USA)) **Mr J. Wertheimer**
101 **DAME DE TREFLE (FR)**, b f Antheus (USA)—Dagora (FR) (Roi Dagobert) **Mr J. Wertheimer**
102 B f Bering—Dance Machine (Green Dancer (USA)) **Mr C. Humphris**
103 **DAVIDEUS (FR)**, b c Antheus (USA)—Lakara (FR) (Le Fabuleux) **Mr J. Wertheimer**
104 **DESERT BRIDE (USA)**, b f Key To The Kingdom (USA)—Madge (FR) (Roi Dagobert) **Sheikh Maktoum Al Maktoum**
105 **DIVINE DANSE (FR)**, b f Kris—Dance Quest (FR) (Green Dancer (USA)) **Ecurie Aland**
106 **EGYPTALE**, b f 17/4 Crystal Glitters—Reine d'Egypte (USA) (Val de L'Orne (FR)) **Mr J. Wertheimer**
107 **FABULOUS HOSTESS (FR)**, ch f Fabulous Dancer (USA)—Young Hostess (FR) (Arctic Tern (USA)) **Mr J. Wertheimer**
108 **FALASTANI (USA)**, ch c 14/1 Shahrastani (USA)—Fallacieuse (Habitat) **Ecurie Aland**
109 **FIRST DROP (FR)**, ch f Antheus (USA)—Comtesse Anne (USA) (Secretariat (USA)) **Mr J. Wertheimer**
110 **GENIE CIVIL (FR)**, b br c Top Ville—White Lightning (FR) (Baldric) **Mr J. Wertheimer**
111 Ch f Deputy Minister (CAN)—Godetia (USA) (Sir Ivor) **Prince Khalid Abdulla**
112 **GOODGLOW (FR)**, ch c Kalaglow—Charmante Dame (FR) (Bellypha) **Mr J. Wertheimer**
113 **GREYQUEST (FR)**, gr c Rainbow Quest (USA)—Makarova (USA) (Nijinsky (CAN)) **Mr J. Wertheimer**
114 **HECKLEY (USA)**, b c Shirley Heights—Harifa (FR) (Habitat) **Madame Plesch**
115 **HERING (USA)**, ch c Bering—Haidee (FR) (Irish River (FR)) **Mr J. Wertheimer**
116 **HYPERTEUS (FR)**, b c Antheus (USA)—Pink Valley (Never Bend) **Mr J. Wertheimer**
117 **ICY MISTRESS (FR)**, b f Esprit du Nord (USA)—Mistrella (FR) (Arctic Tern (USA)) **Mr J. Wertheimer**
118 B c Sharpen Up—Idle Gossip (USA) (Lyphard (USA)) **Mrs Morange**
119 **INTOUCHABLE (USA)**, b c Irish River (FR)—Benicia (Lyphard (USA)) **Mrs Morange**
120 **IWICH (FR)**, b f Kris—Baiser Vole (USA) (Foolish Pleasure (USA)) **Mr J. Jones**
121 **IXTAPA**, b f Chief's Crown (USA)—Tertiary (USA) (Vaguely Noble) **Prince Khalid Abdulla**
122 **JESSIRA (FR)**, ch f Antheus (USA)—Blue River (FR) (Riverman (USA)) **Mr J. Wertheimer**
123 **JEWISH PRINCESS (FR)**, b f Sharpo—Habigael (FR) (Habitat) **Haras d'Etreham**
124 **KALGREY (FR)**, gr c Kaldoun (FR)—Very Sweet (Bellypha) **Mr J. Wertheimer**
125 **KATHYFAN (USA)**, b f Lear Fan (USA)—Princesse Kathy (FR) (Luthier (FR)) **Mr J. Wertheimer**
126 **KOPELMAN (FR)**, b c Kenmare (FR)—Moquerie (FR) (Beaugency (FR)) **Mr J. Wertheimer**
127 **KOTASHAAN (FR)**, b c Darshaan—Haute Autorite (USA) (Elocutionist (USA)) **Mr J. Wertheimer**
128 **LA DEESSE (USA)**, b f Nureyev (USA)—Louisville (FR) (Val de L'Orne (FR)) **Ecurie Aland**
129 **LANSKOY (USA)**, b c Nureyev (USA)—Sonoma (FR) (Habitat) **Madame Plesch**
130 Ch c 28/1 Bering—Lavender Mist (FR) (Troy) **Sheikh Maktoum Al Maktoum**
131 **LIDALA (USA)**, b f Alleged (USA)—Princesse Lida (USA) (Nijinsky (CAN)) **Mr J. Wertheimer**
132 **LOUMVILLE (FR)**, ch f Antheus (USA)—Yerville (FR) (Luthier (FR)) **Mr J. Wertheimer**
133 **MAGE (FR)**, b c Rainbow Quest (USA)—Made of Pearl (USA) (Nureyev (USA)) **Mr J. Wertheimer**
134 **MAKALDA (IRE)**, gr f 4/3 Kaldoun (FR)—Malenka (FR) (Fabulous Dancer (USA)) **Mr J. Wertheimer**
135 B c Blushing Groom (FR)—Maniches (USA) (Val de L'Orne (FR)) **Prince Khalid Abdulla**
136 **MA QUEEN (USA)**, b f Nureyev (USA)—Riverqueen (FR) (Luthier (FR)) **Mrs Morange**
137 **MASHOURA**, b f 24/3 Shareef Dancer (USA)—Massorah (FR) (Habitat) **Sheikh Maktoum Al Maktoum**
138 **MAURANICA (FR)**, b f Esprit du Nord (USA)—Mondovision (FR) (Luthier (FR)) **Mrs Alec Head**
139 B c Blushing Groom (FR)—Maximova (FR) (Green Dancer (USA)) **Mr J. Jones**
140 **MEDIATIC FOOL (USA)**, ch c Foolish Pleasure (USA)—Mediation (FR) (Fabulous Dancer (USA)) **Mr J. Wertheimer**
141 **MILESIME (USA)**, ch f Riverman (USA)—Vintage (USA) (Foolish Pleasure (USA)) **Mrs Morange**
142 **MINT TI (FR)**, b br f Gay Minstrel (FR)—Multitude (USA) (Lyphard (USA)) **Mr J. Wertheimer**
143 **MIPHY (FR)**, b c Dunphy—Grande Amie (FR) (Bellypha) **Mr J. Wertheimer**

MRS C. HEAD—continued

144 B c Bering—Molly Moon (FR) (Kalamoun) **Prince Khalid Abdulla**
145 **MULTAHIB (USA)**, ch c 17/5 Shadeed (USA)—
It's In The Air (USA) (Mr Prospector (USA)) **Sheikh Maktoum Al Maktoum**
146 **NO DEVIL (USA)**, b c Devil's Bag (USA)—Nonoalca (FR) (Nonoalco (USA)) **Mr J. Wertheimer**
147 **NUSBAUM**, ch c 20/4 Touching Wood (USA)—Lavinia (FR) (Run The Gantlet (USA)) **Mr J. Wertheimer**
148 **ONLY SEULE (USA)**, ch f Lyphard (USA)—Elle Seule (USA) (Exclusive Native (USA)) **Mr J. Wertheimer**
149 **PLANIA**, ch f 3/3 Kris—Pallanza (USA) (Lyphard (USA)) **Ecurie Aland**
150 **PLESSAYA (USA)**, b f Nureyev (USA)—Perlita (FR) (Baldric) **Ecurie Aland**
151 **PRICIMA (FR)**, ch f Sicyos (USA)—Princess Mab (Turn-To) **Mr J. Wertheimer**
152 **PRIVATE RIVER (USA)**, b f Private Account (USA)—Rivermaid (FR) (Riverman (USA)) **Mrs Morange**
153 B f Bering—Pure Music (FR) (Pure Flight (USA)) **Mr Stephenson**
154 **REVE DE FORTUNE (USA)**, b c 20/3 Cox's Ridge (USA)—
Reve de Reine (USA) (Lyphard (USA)) **Ecurie Aland**
155 **RING BEAUNE (USA)**, b f Bering—Alexandrie (USA) (Val de L'Orne (FR)) **Mr J. Wertheimer**
156 **ROSA NAY (USA)**, b f Lyphard (USA)—Riviere Doree (USA) (Secretariat (USA)) **Ecurie Aland**
157 Ch c 8/5 Arctic Tern (USA)—Rumman (USA) (Lyphard (USA)) **Sheikh Maktoum Al Maktoum**
158 **SAQUIACE (USA)**, b f Sagace (FR)—Laquiola (FR) (Lyphard (USA)) **Mr J. Wertheimer**
159 **SHALIR (FR)**, b c Darshaan—Figure Libre (USA) (Northern Dancer) **Mr J. Wertheimer**
160 **SHERMICK (FR)**, ch c Shernazar—Miquette (FR) (Fabulous Dancer (USA)) **Mr J. Wertheimer**
161 **SIEYEV (USA)**, b c Nureyev (USA)—Sigy (FR) (Habitat) **Mr J. Jones**
162 **SILLERY (USA)**, b c Blushing Groom (FR)—Silvermine (FR) (Bellypha) **Mrs Alec Head**
163 **SLIP SEA**, b c 22/3 Slip Anchor—Isabella Moretti (ITY) (Sir Gaylord) **Mr J. Wertheimer**
164 **SPAULDING (USA)**, b f Devil's Bag (USA)—Sainte Croix (USA) (Nijinsky (CAN)) **Mrs Morange**
165 **ST HONORE (USA)**, b f Bering—Fourteen (FR) (Bellypha) **Mr H. De Kwiatkowski**
166 **STYLE SHARP**, b c Sharpo—Such Style (Sassafras (FR)) **Mr H. De Kwiatkowski**
167 **SUDDEN COLD (FR)**, b br c Esprit du Nord (USA)—Sudden Glory (FR) (Luthier (FR)) **Mr J. Wertheimer**
168 **SWIMDANCE (USA)**, ch f Riverman (USA)—
Premiere Danseuse (FR) (Green Dancer (USA)) **Mr J. Wertheimer**
169 **TOUCH AND LOVE (IRE)**, b f 5/4 Green Dancer (USA)—
Clunk Click (Star Appeal) **Sheikh Maktoum Al Maktoum**
170 **TOUTE PUISSANCE (USA)**, b f Shadeed (USA)—Tower of London (USA) (Quadrangle (USA)) **Ecurie Aland**
171 **TRACIDA (USA)**, b f Procida (USA)—Anitra's Dance (FR) (Green Dancer (USA)) **Mr J. Wertheimer**
172 B f Riverman (USA)—Trevilla (USA) (Lyphard (USA)) **Mr Stephenson**
173 **TUMBLING (USA)**, b c Irish River (FR)—Trephine (FR) (Viceregal (CAN)) **Sheikh Maktoum Al Maktoum**
174 **VALIANTHE (FR)**, b c Antheus (USA)—Princesse Vali (FR) (Val de L'Orne (FR)) **Mr J. Wertheimer**
175 **VILLE D'AMORE (USA)**, ch f 26/2 Irish River (FR)—
Hanoof (USA) (Northern Dancer) **Sheikh Maktoum Al Maktoum**
176 **WALEWSKA (IRE)**, br f 1/5 Slip Anchor—Frenetique (FR) (Tyrant (USA)) **Mr H. De Kwiatkowski**
177 **WASSILA (FR)**, b f Wassl—L'Irlandaise (USA) (Irish River (FR)) **Mr J. Wertheimer**
178 **WILD BILL (FR)**, b c 24/1 Lear Fan (USA)—Wild Lover (USA) (Lyphard (USA)) **Ecurie Aland**

Jockeys (Flat): Guy Guignard (8-3), Freddy Head (8-7).

Apprentice: O Doleuze (7-2).

Amateur: P Hamel.

281 MRS E. H. HEATH, Royston

Postal: **Upper Coombe Farm, Kelshall, Royston, Hertfordshire, SG8 9SA.**
Phone: **(0763 87) 345**

1 **BANKERS CREDIT**, 7, b g Pollerton—Blue Bleep VII **R. E. A. Bott (Wigmore St) Ltd**
2 **BRULEE**, 6, b m Balinger—Rough Crossing **Brazier Investments Ltd**
3 **CORKED**, 11, b g Tumble Wind (USA)—Bristol Milk **Mrs A. Villar**
4 **DOCKSIDER**, 7, ch g Hotfoot—Tanara **Mrs E. H. Heath**

MRS E. H. HEATH—continued

5 **DOUBLE TURN,** 9, b g Comedy Star (USA)—Pearl River (NZ) **Mrs A. Villar**
6 **FINE TUDOR,** 4, b g Jimsun—Mill Haven **Mrs A. P. Wilson**
7 **HAWKES DALE,** 6, ch g Hard Fought—Bird Reserve **Mr Barry Clayden**
8 **IT'S A PRY,** 9, b g Pry—Clogga Girl **Mrs A. Villar**
9 **LAKMON,** 4, br g Final Straw—Tanagrea **Andutra Ltd**
10 **LIMAVADY,** 11, b br g Quayside—Tender Eyes **Mrs E. H. Heath**
11 **POWYS,** 10, b g Busted—Caer-Gai **R. E. A. Bott (Wigmore St) Ltd**
12 **QUICK REACTION,** 7, b g Main Reef—Swift Response **Mrs A. Villar**
13 **TAM'S ARIA,** 8, b g True Song—Tamoretta **Mrs E. H. Heath**

Other Owners: Mr S. R. Clayden, Mr Miles Rivett-Carnac.

Jockey (NH): F Leavy (10-0).

Amateur: Mr P Harding-Jones (10-5).

282 MR P. R. HEDGER, Chichester

Postal: **Eastmere Stables, Eastergate Lane, Eastergate, Chichester.**
Phone: **(0243) 543863**

1 **AL ASOOF (USA),** 5, gr g Shareef Dancer (USA)—Jet Quick (USA) **Mr Peter Redding**
2 **BALVENIE,** 6, ch g Le Bavard (FR)—Arctic Free **Mr J. J. Whelan**
3 **BLACK MONKEY,** 8, b g Monksfield—Black Grouse **Mr J. J. Whelan**
4 **CHEZ POLLY,** 4, ch f Homing—My Pink Parrot **Mrs Lynne J. Collins**
5 **GANOON (USA),** 7, ch g Northern Baby (CAN)—Tropical Island (USA) **Mrs R. H. Morris**
6 **GLORY HILL,** 5, br m Cleon—Mezel Hill **Mr J. J. Whelan**
7 **JANUS,** 12, ro g Ragstone—January (FR) **Mr K. A. Little**
8 **KILKILMARTIN,** 8, b g Rarity—Kilkilwell **Mr Keith Moore and Partners**
9 **L B LAUGHS,** 7, b g Final Straw—Gay Charlotte **City & Essex Travel Ltd**
10 **LISSAHANE LASS,** 4, b br f Daring March—The Suestan **Mr J. J. Whelan**
11 **LYPH (USA),** 4, b g Lypheor—Scottish Lass **Mr Graham Angell and Mr John Lemon**
12 **MARCH FOLLY,** 4, gr f Daring March—Creme de La Creme **Mr J. J. Whelan**
13 **MINIMUM RISK,** 5, gr g Kris—Bare Minimum **Mrs Jacqueline Elizabeth Murray**
14 **MSHAHARA,** 12, ch g Beau Chapeau—Immortal Queen **Mr M. Mitchell**
15 **NICKY'S JOY,** 14, b g Beau Lavender—Slippery Della **Mr M. Smith**
16 **NOIRE SMALL (USA),** 8, b m Elocutionist (USA)—Small Indulgence (USA) **Mrs Carol Harrison**
17 **PROUD SIHK,** 8, br g Mansingh (USA)—Lavington **Mr P. R. Hedger**
18 **SCOTTISH EXPRESS,** 5, b g Celtic Cone—Travellers Cheque **Mr J. J. Whelan**
19 **SILENT RING (USA),** 4, b br g Silent Cal (USA)—Rafters Ring (USA) **Mr Keith Moore**
20 **THE NIGELSTAN,** 9, b g Fine Blade (USA)—Owenette **Mr S. Powell**
21 **TYRED N'SNOOKERD,** 6, b g Le Johnstan—Dobella **Mr J. J. Whelan**

Other Owners: Mr Rodger Carter, Mr J. H. Harrison, Mr Jon Jones, Mr M. Lysaght, Mr David R. Wickins.

Jockey (NH): M Richards (10-0, w.a.).

Conditional: R Goddings (9-12).

283 MR J. A. HELLENS, Chester-le-Street

Postal: **Felledge Farm, Walldridge Lane, Chester Moor, Chester-le-Street, DH2 3RX.**
Phone: **(0913) 885403**

1 **ANY MORE,** 7, b m Space King—Indy-Ann **Mr J. A. Hellens**
2 **FLYING DISPLAY (USA),** 6, ch g Le Fabuleux—Wild Wings **Mr J. A. Hellens**
3 **GRANGE OF GLORY,** 9, ch g Hittite Glory—Neptune's Daughter **Mr J. A. Hellens**
4 **MISTER MOODY (FR),** 5, ch h Master Thatch—Moonly (FR) **Mr J. A. Hellens**
5 **RUN ETOILE,** 6, ch m Deep Run—Etoile de Lune **Mr J. A. Hellens**
6 **WIRE LASS,** 6, b m New Brig—Anotherwire **Mr J. A. Hellens**

284 MRS S. J. R. HEMBROW, Taunton

Postal: **Chico, Lipe Lane, Henlade, Taunton, Somerset.**
Phone: **(0823) 442546**

1 **MR PIPKIN,** 4, b g Casino Boy—True Minstrel **Mrs S. J. R. Hembrow**
2 **MR SEAGULL,** 12, ch g Deep Run—Marsa **Mrs S. J. R. Hembrow**

285 MR N. J. HENDERSON, Lambourn

Postal: **Windsor House, Lambourn, Newbury, Berkshire.**
Phone: **LAMBOURN (0488) 72259 OR 72300 FAX (0488) 72596**

1 **ACCLAIM,** 10, b g Record Token—Acolyte **Mr J. R. Henderson**
2 **ACRE HILL,** 6, gr g Alias Smith (USA)—Acolyte **Mr J. R. Henderson**
3 **AFTERTHOUGHT (NZ),** 5, b g Prince Simbir (NZ)—Two Lettres (NZ) **Mr David Montagu**
4 **ALMERIMAR,** 6, b g Home Guard (USA)—Melaleuca **Mr R. J. McAlpine**
5 **ALONE SUCCESS,** 7, br g Strong Gale—Tabankulu **Sheikh Amin Dahlawi**
6 **BADRAKHANI (FR),** 4, b g Akarad (FR)—Burnished Gold **Mr W. A. Fagan**
7 **BALLYNICK,** 6, ch g Balinger—Ellen Mavourneen
8 **BERRYFELL,** 5, b g Le Bavard (FR)—Reynella **Mrs E. H. Vestey**
9 **BLANTON RESERVE (USA),** 6, b g Recitation (USA)—Ruth's Nite Out (USA) **Mr J. E. H. Collins**
10 **BOLD LAMENT,** 9, b g Rhett Butler—Ameliorate **Mr David Montagu**
11 **BRAVE DEFENDER,** 6, ch g Niniski (USA)—Hirsova **Lady Cohen**
12 **BROWN WINDSOR,** 8, b g Kinglet—Cauldron **Mr W. Shand Kydd**
13 **BUDDY HOLLY (NZ),** 5, b g Leader of The Band (USA)—Annie Day (NZ) **Mr R. A. N. Bonnycastle**
14 **BUSTEELE,** 6, b g Bustino—Narration (USA) **Mr D. J. Wilkinson**
15 **CALABRESE,** 5, ch g Monsanto (FR)—Salsafy **Mrs Ann Fagan**
16 **CLASS ACT,** 4, b g Shirley Heights—Thespian **Mr G. Howard-Spink**
17 **CLEAN THROUGH (NZ),** 5, b g Rapier II—Spotless (NZ) **Mr Peter V. McCalmont**
18 **FIRST BOUT,** 9, b g Nishapour (FR)—Right Swinger (USA) **Mr Wharton Shober**
19 **FOX'S FROLIC (NZ),** 5, b g Solaboy (USA)—Fox Mondo (NZ) **Mr N. C. Clark**
20 **FREELINE FINISHING,** 6, b g Furry Glen—Superday **Mr Irving Struel**
21 **FREESTONE,** 5, b g Great Nephew—Free Dance (FR) **Mr Raymond Tooth**
22 **FURRY VENTURE,** 5, b m Furry Glen—Multeen **Mrs P. Sherwood**
23 **GINGERLAND,** 7, ch g Bustino—Zerbinetta **Miss M. A. Stuart-Hunt**
24 **HAPPY HIGGINS,** 6, b g Strong Gale—Quayville **Catfoss Farming & Developments Ltd**
25 **HAPPY PERCY,** 5, ch g Deep Run—Purcella **Catfoss Farming & Developments Ltd**
26 **INCAMELIA,** 9, br m St Columbus—Indamelia **Mrs M. W. Thorne**
27 **INDE PULSE,** 8, b g Troy—Divine Thought **Mr R. J. McAlpine**
28 **INDIAN CRUISE,** 5, b m Cruise Missile—Indian Diva **Lord Grimston of Westbury**
29 **JOHN'S BIRTHDAY,** 8, ch g True Song—Polaris Missile **Mrs M. W. Thorne**
30 **LE PICCOLAGE,** 6, b g The Parson—Daithis Coleen **Mrs M. L. Clark**
31 **LOFTINESS,** 4, ch g High Line—Waltz **Mr A. C. D. Ingleby-Mackenzie**
32 **MANDAVI,** 9, b g Mandalus—Kimin **Mrs Keith Anderson**
33 **MASTER BOB,** 10, b g Pitpan—Good Calx **Mr Ian Wills**

MR N. J. HENDERSON—continued

34 **MOLOJEC (POL),** 9, b g Frombork—Malwa (POL) **Mrs R. Vaughan**
35 **MR GOSSIP,** 8, b g Le Bavard (FR)—Regency View **Mr G. A. Rogers**
36 **NO ONE TO BLAME,** 8, gr g Roselier (FR)—San Remi **Furlong Bros (Construction) Ltd**
37 **OBLATION (USA),** 5, b g Master Willie—Bold Caress **Lady Rose Musker**
38 **PARSONS GREEN,** 6, b g The Parson—Move Along Gypsy **Mr Raymond Tooth**
39 **PENDENNIS,** 7, ch g Pollerton—Lady Reporter **Comtesse De Brye**
40 **PETER PIPER,** 6, ch g True Song—Indian Diva **Mrs A. J. Sloan**
41 **PUNCHING GLORY,** 6, b g Idiot's Delight—Hitting Supreme **Mr Gerard Nock**
42 **REGAL CASTLE,** 7, b g Tachypous—Right Mall **Edward & Susan Dexter Ltd**
43 **REMITTANCE MAN,** 6, b g Prince Regent (FR)—Mittens **Mr J. E. H. Collins**
44 **RIVER CEIRIOG,** 9, ch g Broxted—Quarry Wood **Mr R. J. McAlpine**
45 **RUE DE CHAILLOT,** 4, b g Al Nasr (FR)—Heidi Badgett (USA) **Mr David Montagu**
46 **RUSTLE,** 8, b g Homeboy—Plunder **Mr Robert Waley-Cohen**
47 **SEE YOU THEN,** 10, br g Royal Palace—Melodina **The Stype Wood Stud Ltd**
48 **SIR JAMESTOWN (USA),** 6, b g Pleasant Colony (USA)—Magnificent Lady **H. & T. Walker Ltd**
49 **SOME DO NOT,** 6, b g Maculata—Ballynavin Money **Catfoss Farming & Developments Ltd**
50 **SUNNY SLAVE,** 9, b g Sunyboy—Slavetown **Mr R. J. Parish**
51 **TAPSTER LAD,** 6, b g Strong Gale—Tip Your Toes **Mrs Jane Lane**
52 **TENNFORES,** 9, b g Raise You Ten—Coolfores IV **Mrs E. H. Vestey**
53 **THE HUMBLE TILLER,** 7, b g Rarity—Bardicate **Mrs F. M. De Moraville**
54 **THE RAPIDS,** 8, ch g Deep Run—Lulu's Daughter **Lord Pembroke**
55 **TINRYLAND,** 6, b g Prince Regent (FR)—Tonduff Star **Mr Michael Buckley**
56 **TSARELLA,** 8, b m Mummy's Pet—Madame Russe **Mrs Hugh Maitland-Jones**
57 **UP AND COMING,** 7, b g Avocat—Cummin Hill **Mrs Caroline Holland-Martin**
58 **VANDENBERG (NZ),** 9, b g Le Fripon (NZ)—Elana (NZ) **Mrs LeRoy Hurlbert**
59 **VERSATILE,** 6, ch g Final Straw—Expansive **Mrs P. Sherwood**
60 **VICOMPT DE VALMONT,** 5, b g Beau Charmeur (FR)—Wish Again **Mr Raymond Tooth**
61 **VODAFONE DAWES,** 6, b g The Parson—Three Ladies **Racal-Vodafone Limited**
62 **WHATEVER YOU LIKE,** 6, b g Deep Run—Garravogue **Mr T. Hyde**
63 **WHISTLING EDDY,** 6, ch g Whistling Deer—Silver Tongue **Mr C. J. Edwards**
64 **WHY SO HASTY,** 9, b g Proverb—Well Caught **Mr Michael Buckley**
65 **WONT BE GONE LONG,** 8, b g The Parson—Most Seen **Mr Robert Waley-Cohen**
66 4, B g Uncle Remus—Yorkshire Mist **Lady Cohen**

Other Owners: Mr Steven Astaire, Mrs John A. Barbara Jnr, Mr V. E. Barclay, Lady Bevan, Mr Patrick A. M. Carr, Mr A. K. Collins, Mrs Sally Cronk, Mr Jeff Dartnall, Mr Michael Diffenderffer, Miss A. M. Edwards, Mr R. J. B. Edwards, Mrs S. P. Edwards, Mr Jim Furlong, Mr Ken Furlong, Mrs D. B. Gallop, Mrs D. A. Henderson, Mr J. J. Hindley, Mrs J. J. Hindley, Martin Dawes Communications, Mrs C. A. Morrison, Mr Douglas Romain, Duke Of Roxburghe, Mr Nicholas Soames, Mr J. L. Spearing, Mr B. Townsley, Mrs F. R. Watts, Mr S. G. Weber-Brown, Mr Michael White.

Jockeys (NH): R Dunwoody (10-0), J White (10-1).

Conditional: P Harley (9-7), C Huggan (9-10), R Milner (9-7).

Amateur: Mr G Johnson-Houghton (10-0).

286 MR M. HENRIQUES, Cirencester

Postal: **Winson Manor, Winson, Cirencester, Gloucestershire, GL7 5ES.**
Phone: **FOSSEBRIDGE (028572) 304 OFFICE 400 FAX: (0285) 72614**

1 **BRONZE EFFIGY,** 8, ch g Vaigly Great—Sea Fern **Mr M. Henriques**
2 **FOURTH LAD,** 6, gr ro g Rarity—Ginkgo **Mrs M. R. Q. Henriques**
3 **KNOWAFENCE,** 4, b f Idiot's Delight—Master Suite **Mr M. Henriques**

Jockey (NH): G McCourt (10-2, w.a.).

NOTED TO WIN

The race-readers, who add such invaluable comments on running to this Annual and Raceform Weekly, are able to amplify their reports in Raceform Note-Book, which is published every Friday throughout the Flat Racing Season. The Note-Book gives basic form details of the first six in each race, plus notes on every worthwhile runner. The race-readers express their opinion about future prospects, the likely two-year-olds, the handicappers returning to form, the potential classic candidates and the promising maidens. They make a point of earmarking future winners. Often their observations will enable the shrewd backer to collect at very remunerative odds.

Subscribers start with the Raceform Note-Book Filing Book, containing the season's returns complete so far including All-Weather Track racing and the famous INDEX TO WINNERS. Loose-leaf issues, including an updated index **with Raceform Private Handicap ratings,** are posted every Wednesday.

Full Turf Season: £86.00
Seven Weeks: £23.00

RACEFORM NOTE-BOOK
1989 COMPLETE
(Specially Bound) £15.00

RACEFORM LTD., COMPTON,
NEWBURY, BERKS. RG16 0NL
Telephone: 0635 578080 Fax: 0635 578101

287 MAJOR W. R. HERN C.V.O., West Ilsley

Postal: **West Ilsley Stables, West Ilsley, Newbury, Berkshire.**
Phone: **EAST ILSLEY (063528) 219 OFFICE 251 HOME 675 FAX 848362 TELEX**

1 **GOLD SEAM (USA),** 4, b c Mr Prospector (USA)—Ballare (USA) **Mr Peter M. Brant**
2 **MYTASKI,** 4, b c Niniski (USA)—Mytinia **The Dowager Lady Beaverbrook**
3 **NAD ELSHIBA (USA),** 4, b c Nijinsky's Secret (USA)—Terska (USA) **Mr Hamdan Al-Maktoum**
4 **PILOT,** 4, ch f Kris—Sextant **Mr R. D. Hollingsworth**
5 **SHABANAZ,** 5, b h Imperial Fling (USA)—Claironcita **Mr Hamdan Al-Maktoum**
6 **VINTAGE,** 5, b g Noalcoholic (FR)—Good To Follow **Major W. R. Hern**

THREE-YEAR-OLDS

7 **AROUSAL,** br f Rousillon (USA)—Model Girl (FR) **Lord Weinstock**
8 **CHOIR MASTER (CAN),** b g Assert—Choral Group (CAN) **Sheikh Mohammed**
9 **CURIA REGIS (USA),** b c Deputy Minister (CAN)—Katie Cochran (USA) **Sheikh Mohammed**
10 **DANCING HIGH,** b c Shirley Heights—The Dancer (FR) **Sir John Astor**
11 **DANCING WAY,** b c Sadler's Wells (USA)—Waterway (FR) **Lord Weinstock**
12 **DAYJUR (USA),** br c Danzig (USA)—Gold Beauty (USA) **Mr Hamdan Al-Maktoum**
13 **EIDOLON,** b f Rousillon (USA)—Eider **Lord Rotherwick**
14 **ELMAAMUL (USA),** ch c Diesis—Modena (USA) **Mr Hamdan Al-Maktoum**
15 **ENDOLI (USA),** b c Assert—Grabelst (USA) **The Dowager Lady Beaverbrook**
16 **EREVNON,** b c Rainbow Quest (USA)—Embryo **The Dowager Lady Beaverbrook**
17 **FREESIA,** b f Shirley Heights—Free Dance (FR) **Lord Rotherwick**
18 **GHASHTAH (USA),** b f Nijinsky (CAN)—My Charmer (USA) **Mr Hamdan Al-Maktoum**
19 **GHZAALH (USA),** ch f Northern Dancer—Give Thanks **Mr Hamdan Al-Maktoum**
20 **HAREFOOT,** b f Rainbow Quest (USA)—Swiftfoot **Lord Rotherwick**
21 **IJTIHAAD (USA),** b c Arctic Tern (USA)—Corita **Mr Hamdan Al-Maktoum**
22 **LANGUEDOC,** b c Rousillon (USA)—Can Can Girl **Sheikh Mohammed**
23 **MUKDDAAM (USA),** b c Danzig (USA)—Height of Fashion (FR) **Mr Hamdan Al-Maktoum**
24 **MUSE,** ch g High Line—Thoughtful **Lord Rotherwick**
25 **MYHAMET,** b c Gorytus (USA)—Honey Bridge **The Dowager Lady Beaverbrook**
26 **NAVAL PAGEANT,** gr c Kalaglow—Sea Pageant **Mr R. D. Hollingsworth**
27 **POTAMOS (USA),** b br c Riverman (USA)—Cautious Bidder (USA) **The Dowager Lady Beaverbrook**
28 **RUBY SETTING,** b f Gorytus (USA)—Sun Princess **Lord Weinstock**
29 **SERENADER (FR),** b c Ela-Mana-Mou—Seattle Serenade (USA) **Sheikh Mohammed**
30 **SHEMALEYAH,** b f Lomond (USA)—Burghclere **Sheikh Ahmed Al Maktoum**
31 **SNOWSPIN,** b f Carwhite—Spin **Mrs Hugh Dalgety**
32 **TRIREME,** ch c Rainbow Quest (USA)—Bireme **Mr R. D. Hollingsworth**

TWO-YEAR-OLDS

33 **ALFAARES (USA),** b c 16/2 Danzig (USA)—Palm Reader (USA) (Sir Ivor) **Mr Hamdan Al-Maktoum**
34 **ALRAYED (USA),** b c 25/2 Alydar (USA)—Life's Magic (USA) (Cox's Ridge (USA)) **Mr Hamdan Al-Maktoum**
35 **BALLET QUEEN (IRE),** b f 16/4 Sadler's Wells (USA)—Sun Princess (English Prince) **Lord Weinstock**
36 **BRAVEFOOT,** b c 19/2 Dancing Brave (USA)—Swiftfoot (Run The Gantlet (USA)) **Lord Rotherwick**
37 **CHEDZOY,** ch g 20/2 Niniski (USA)—Pine (Supreme Sovereign) **Mrs W. R. Hern**
38 **CLARET (IRE),** b c 8/2 Rousillon (USA)—Consolation (Troy) **Lord Rotherwick**
39 **CUTABYE,** b f 21/2 Chief Singer—Cut Loose (High Top) **Sir John Astor**
40 **GRACIOUS BEAUTY (USA),** b f 8/3 Nijinsky (CAN)—
Gold Beauty (USA) (Mr Prospector (USA)) **Mr Hamdan Al-Maktoum**
41 **HONOR YER PARTNER,** b c 21/4 Ahonoora—Lady Gaylass (USA) (Sir Gaylord) **Sir William McAlpine**
42 **HOT DESERT,** b c 9/5 Green Desert (USA)—Hayya (FR) (Shergar) **Sheikh Ahmed Al Maktoum**
43 **JAHAFIL,** b c 22/2 Rainbow Quest (USA)—River Spey (Mill Reef (USA)) **Mr Hamdan Al-Maktoum**
44 **LAAHIJ (USA),** b br c 14/3 Roberto (USA)—
My Royal Guest (Be My Guest (USA)) **Sheikh Ahmed Al Maktoum**
45 **LUCHIROVERTE (IRE),** b c 26/4 Slip Anchor—
Green Lucia (Green Dancer (USA)) **The Dowager Lady Beaverbrook**
46 **MANWAH (USA),** ch f 1/5 Lyphard (USA)—Height of Fashion (FR) (Bustino) **Mr Hamdan Al-Maktoum**
47 **NASHAAT (USA),** b c 14/3 El Gran Senor (USA)—
Absentia (USA) (Raise A Cup (USA)) **Mr Hamdan Al-Maktoum**
48 **PINKFOOT (IRE),** b f 30/3 Gorytus (USA)—Grayfoot (Grundy) **Lord Rotherwick**
49 **RED SISTER (IRE),** b f 7/2 Gorytus (USA)—Happy Kin (USA) (Bold Hitter (USA)) **Lord Weinstock**

BY APPOINTMENT
TO HER MAJESTY QUEEN ELIZABETH II
HORSE FEED MANUFACTURERS
DODSON & HORRELL LIMITED KETTERING

DODSON & HORRELL
LIMITED

Horse Feed Specialists

OFFER THE LARGEST THOROUGHBRED FEEDS
IN THE COUNTRY

INCLUDING UNIQUE HIGH
PERFORMANCE MIXES AND OAT
BALANCERS FOR RACEHORSES
AND THE BEST REARING DIETS
FOR YOUNG STOCK.

Specialists in the Manufacture & Supply
of Quality Feeds to the Equine World
Particular Feeds for Particular Horses

For free nutritional advice
and feed analysis/costings etc
contact John Sharp, Christopher Gordon and Deborah Lucas MSC.

We feed more winners!

RINGSTEAD NORTHAMPTONSHIRE NN14 4BX
TELEPHONE WELLINGBOROUGH (0933) 624221
FAX (0933) 625461

MAJOR W. R. HERN C.V.O.—continued

50 **SARIAH,** ch f 26/2 Kris—Nouvelle Star (AUS) (Luskin Star (AUS)) **Mr Hamdan Al-Maktoum**
51 **SEA CADET,** ch c 4/3 Precocious—Sea Power (Welsh Pageant) **Mr R. D. Hollingsworth**
52 **SEA CRAFT,** gr f 11/3 Nishapour (FR)—Sea Pageant (Welsh Pageant) **Mr R. D. Hollingsworth**
53 **SEA WAR (IRE),** ch c 2/5 Gorytus (USA)—Corinth Canal (Troy) **Lord Weinstock**
54 **SHIMMERING SEA,** b f 21/4 Slip Anchor—Sushila (Petingo) **Miss Kirsten Rausing**
55 **SIJJAAL (USA),** b br c 14/2 Mr Prospector (USA)—South Sea Dancer (USA) (Northern Dancer) **Mr Hamdan Al-Maktoum**
56 B f 20/4 Fappiano (USA)—Tax Holiday (USA) (What A Pleasure) **Mr Peter M. Brant**
57 **TRUST DEED (USA),** ch c 2/4 Shadeed (USA)—Karelia (USA) (Sir Ivor) **Lord Weinstock**
58 **WINOSKI,** b c 17/3 Petoski—Persevering (Blakeney) **The Dowager Lady Beaverbrook**

Other Owners: The Queen, Hon Simon Weinstock.

Jockey (Flat): B Proctor (8-3).

288 LADY HERRIES, Littlehampton

Postal: **Angmering Park, Littlehampton, W. Sussex, BN16 4EX.**
Phone: **HOME (090674) 421 YARD (090674) 460 FAX (090674) 530**

1 **AITCH N'BEE,** 7, ch g Northfields (USA)—Hot Case **Lavinia Duchess of Norfolk**
2 **CANOSCAN,** 5, ch g Grey Ghost—Canny's Tudor **Lady Sarah Clutton**
3 **CASTLE CLOWN,** 5, ch g Castle Keep—Peteona **Lady Mary Mumford**
4 **CASTLE MOAT,** 5, b g Jalmood (USA)—Fotheringay **Lavinia Duchess of Norfolk**
5 **CASTLE ROCK,** 7, b g Shirley Heights—Fotheringay **Lady Herries**
6 **DERCANDER,** 8, br g Derek H—Canny's Tudor **Mr Nigel Clutton**
7 **DRUMOAK,** 9, gr g Dubassoff (USA)—Sister Chatters **Lady Herries**
8 **JINGA,** 5, b g Castle Keep—Eldoret **Lavinia Duchess of Norfolk**
9 **KING OF MILEEN,** 4, b g Castle Keep—Port Meadow **Mrs Eileen Sheehan**
10 **MEGAN'S FLIGHT,** 5, ch m Welsh Pageant—Escape Me Never **Mr M. C. Cowdrey**
11 **PENIELHEUGH,** 8, ch g Politico (USA)—Rubors Law **Lady Herries**
12 **PETAVIOUS,** 5, b g Mummy's Pet—Pencuik Jewel **Lavinia Duchess of Norfolk**
13 **RIGHTEOUS REAVER,** 5, b g Feelings (FR)—Wedderburn **Mr James R. Drummond**
14 **SHERIFF'S STAR,** 5, gr h Posse (USA)—Castle Moon **Mr M. Nishiyama**

THREE-YEAR-OLDS

15 **CASTLE COURAGEOUS,** b g Castle Keep—Peteona **Lady Mary Mumford**
16 **GEMINI STAR,** ch f Castle Keep—Teftu **Mr George Johnson**
17 **MOLO,** b g Castle Keep—Eldoret **Lavinia Duchess of Norfolk**
18 **NORFOLK GEM,** b f Blakeney—Pencuik Jewel **Lavinia Duchess of Norfolk**
19 **RUBY CLUSTER,** b f Posse (USA)—Red Ruby **Lavinia Duchess of Norfolk**
20 **UNDER THE WING,** b f Aragon—Royal Custody **Mrs Sue Horwood**
21 **WONDERMENT,** b f Mummy's Pet—Baffle **Lavinia Duchess of Norfolk**

TWO-YEAR-OLDS

22 B f 16/5 Formidable (USA)—Baffle (Petingo) **Lavinia Duchess of Norfolk**
23 **CASTLE CAVALIER,** br g 19/4 Castle Keep—Peteona (Welsh Saint) **Lady Mary Mumford**
24 **CLIFTON HAMPDEN,** b c 15/2 Blakeney—Red Ruby (Tudor Melody) **Mr Roger G. Gibbs**
25 **CONQUISTA,** ch f 24/1 Aragon—Divine Fling (Imperial Fling (USA)) **Mrs P. Lewis**
26 Ch f 3/3 Aragon—Entrancing (Posse (USA)) **Lavinia Duchess of Norfolk**
27 **LADY WINKINS,** ch f 26/1 Forzando—Pilley Green (Porto Bello) **Mr David Blacker**
28 **MOON FESTIVAL,** gr f 8/5 Be My Guest (USA)—Castle Moon (Kalamoun) **Lavinia Duchess of Norfolk**
29 **RABBIT'S FOOT,** b f 9/5 Touching Wood (USA)—Royal Custody (Reform) **Mr Clive J. Horwood**
30 **SANTI SANA,** b f 1/5 Formidable (USA)—Eldoret (High Top) **Lavinia Duchess of Norfolk**

Other Owners: Mr John M. D. Knight, Mr Tom Stacey.

289 MR J. HETHERTON, Malton

Postal: **Highfield Stables, Beverley Road, Malton, North Yorkshire, YO17 9PJ.**
Phone: **(0653) 696778**

1 **EDGE OF THE WIND,** 8, b g Arapaho—Chammyville **Col S. Lycett Green**
2 **FRESH LINE,** 4, b f High Line—Snow Tribe **Mr N. Hetherton**
3 **NANCY ARDROSS,** 4, b f Ardross—Classy Nancy (USA) **Mr David Hetherton**
4 **PAST GLORIES,** 7, b h Hittite Glory—Snow Tribe **Mr N. Hetherton**
5 **PRECIOUS BALLERINA,** 5, ch m Ballacashtal (CAN)—Jenny's Rocket **Mr Michael Jackson**

THREE-YEAR-OLDS

6 **FLASH BULB,** b g Electric—Saffron Ring **Mr Timothy Hetherton**
7 **JODASCO,** b f Reesh—Creta **Mr David Hetherton**
8 **PANALO,** gr g Magic Mirror—Radinka **Mrs Caroline Ashworth**
9 **QUITE A FIGHTER,** b f Hard Fought—Snow Tribe **Mr N. Hetherton**

TWO-YEAR-OLDS

10 Ch c 31/3 Primo Dominie—Baby's Smile (Shirley Heights)
11 B f 9/3 Auction Ring (USA)—Bernique (Hello Gorgeous (USA))
12 **BILL OF RIGHTS,** b c 10/4 Nicholas Bill—Cold Line (Exdirectory)
13 B f 9/5 Kind of Hush—Courting Day (Right Boy)
14 **HALF A BILLION,** b c 23/5 Nicholas Bill—Half Asleep (Quiet Fling (USA))
15 B f 2/3 Ballacashtal (CAN)—La Perricholi (FR) (Targowice (USA))
16 B f 2/5 Song—Moonlight Serenade (Crooner)
17 B f 20/4 Salmon Leap (USA)—San Salu (Sallust)
18 B f 10/3 Superlative—Strapless (Bustino)

Other Owners: Mr C. D. Barber-Lomax, Mr Walter Bulmer, Mr Craig Glover, Mr Ron Hart, Mr J. Hetherton, Mr John S. Hirst, Mr Jack Prest.

290 MRS A. R. HEWITT, Malpas

Postal: **The White House, Duckington, Malpas, Cheshire, SY14 8LH.**
Phone: **BROXTON (082 925) 314**

1 **BROXTON,** 8, b m Funny Man—Raise Away **Mrs A. R. Hewitt**
2 **COMEDY SPY,** 6, br g Scallywag—Ida Spider **Mrs A. R. Hewitt**
3 **CROESONEN,** 6, ch m Balinger—Rock Rose **Mrs A. D. Paterson**
4 **DANCING SPY,** 5, b g Bali Dancer—Ida Spider **Mrs A. R. Hewitt**
5 **MR ROBINSON,** 6, b g Cawston's Clown—Viduli **Edwin Robinson (Sheffield) Ltd**
6 **NEVILLE,** 4, br g Full of Hope—Vidlli **Mrs A. R. Hewitt**
7 4, Br g Julio Mariner—Sandby **Mrs A. R. Hewitt**
8 **SIKERA SPY,** 8, b m Harvest Spirit—Ida Spider **Plancon Builders Tarporley Ltd**
9 **SILLIAN,** 8, ch g Billion (USA)—Celtic View **Mr G. S. Williams**
10 **SPY'S DELIGHT,** 4, b g Idiot's Delight—Ida Spider **Mrs A. R. Hewitt**
11 **WIGGBURN,** 11, ch g Dalesa—Rayvox **Mr John Butler**

THREE-YEAR-OLDS

12 B g Town And Country—Doubtful Request **Mrs A. R. Hewitt**

Other Owners: Mr Simon Carden, Mr R. A. Clarke, Mr M. Hanson, Mr Stephen J. Stringer.

291 MR A. HIDE, Newmarket

Postal: **Machell Place, Old Station Road, Newmarket, Suffolk, CB8 8DW.**
Phone: **NEWMARKET (0638) 662063**

1 **COMINO GIRL,** 4, b f Indian King (USA)—Arab Art **Mr J. L. Napier**
2 **EVENING STAR,** 4, b f Red Sunset—Avereen **Mrs C. T. Bletsoe**
3 **GLASS CASTLE (FR),** 6, b g Crystal Palace (FR)—Halliana (USA) **Mr Anthony Hide**
4 **NAZMIAH,** 4, b f Free State—Irish Ballad **Mr A. S. Helaissi**
5 **ROYAL ACCLAIM,** 5, ch g Tender King—Glimmer **Mrs B. Wilkinson**

THREE-YEAR-OLDS

6 **DARTINGTON HALL,** ch g Free State—Westonbirt **Mr M. F. Cartwright**
7 **NIGHT TRANSACTION,** ch f Tina's Pet—Beech Tree **Mr Brian Pollins**
8 **SILVER LODGE,** ch f Homing—Silverhall **Mrs C. T. Bletsoe**

TWO-YEAR-OLDS

9 **DAISY GREY,** gr f 7/5 Nordance (USA)—Great Grey Niece (Great Nephew) **T. Charlton**
10 B f 8/5 Good Times (ITY)—Hampton Court (Town And Country) **Mr Anthony Hide**
11 Ch c 19/2 Nicholas Bill—Pullaiyar (Try My Best (USA)) **Mr Anthony Hide**
12 **SCENIC DANCER,** b c 2/5 Shareef Dancer (USA)—Bridestones (Jan Ekels) **A. Al Helaissi**
13 **SMART ENDEAVOUR,** br c 14/5 Elegant Air—Good Try (Good Bond) **F. Judson**
14 **WAYPOST,** br g 27/2 Belfort (FR)—Golden Slade (Octavo (USA)) **Mrs C. T. Bletsoe**

Other Owners: P. Barnett, Mr J. P. Carrington, J. Chapman, R. Chapman, Mrs Roy Chapman, D. Curran, R. Flack, Mrs M. Hayes, J. Judson, Mr Chris Ring, Mr K. Wilkinson.

Jockey (Flat): G Carter.

Amateurs: Miss L J Hide (8-4), Mr P E Hide (8-7).

292 MR B. W. HILLS, Marlborough

Postal: **Manton House Estate, Marlborough, Wiltshire, SN8 1PN.**
Phone: **OFFICE MARLBOROUGH (0672) 514901 HOUSE 514871 FAX 514907 TELEX 44322**

1 **DISTANT RELATIVE,** 4, b c Habitat—Royal Sister II **Mr Wafic Said**
2 **ECOSSAIS DANSEUR (USA),** 4, ch c Arctic Tern (USA)—Northern Blossom (CAN) **Mrs June Doyle**
3 **FURTHER FLIGHT,** 4, gr g Pharly (FR)—Flying Nelly **Mr S. Wingfield Digby**
4 **JUSTAGLOW,** 4, b f Kalaglow—Justicia **Mrs Susan Al Said**
5 **LORD DAVID S (USA),** 4, b c Nijinsky (CAN)—Mirthful Flirt (USA) **Mr Howard Kaskel**
6 **MONTEROS BOY,** 5, ch g Crofter (USA)—Prima Bella **Mr B. W. Hills**
7 **NOMADIC WAY (USA),** 5, b h Assert—Kittyhawk **Mr R. E. Sangster**
8 **OBSERVATION POST,** 4, b c Shirley Heights—Godzilla **Mr R. E. Sangster**
9 **SCENIC,** 4, b c Sadler's Wells (USA)—Idyllic (USA) **Sheikh Mohammed**
10 **SINCLAIR BOY,** 4, b g Aragon—Amber Flyer **Mr B. W. Hills**
11 **STRIKE FORCE,** 5, br g Gorytus (USA)—Helaplane (USA) **Mr R. E. Sangster**
12 **SUDDEN VICTORY,** 6, ch g Kings Lake (USA)—Shebeen **Mr R. E. Sangster**
13 **TAILSPIN,** 5, b g Young Generation—Mumtaz Flyer (USA) **Mrs Arne Larsson**
14 **WASSL PORT,** 4, b c Wassl—Sea Port **Mr Howard Kaskel**

THREE-YEAR-OLDS

15 **ATOLL,** b f Caerleon (USA)—Shirley Reef **Mr R. E. Sangster**
16 **AUGUST CLIMB,** b g Kings Lake (USA)—May Hill **Mr R. E. Sangster**
17 **BESTOW,** br f Shirley Heights—Clandestina (USA) **Mr R. E. Sangster**
18 **BLUE STAG,** b c Sadler's Wells (USA)—Snow Day (FR) **Mr R. E. Sangster**
19 **BLUE VERYAN,** b f Kalaglow—Head First **Mr A. D. Shead**
20 **BOLD AMBITION,** br c Ela-Mana-Mou—Queen of The Dance **Mrs David Thompson**

MR B. W. HILLS—continued

21 **BOLD RUSSIAN**, b c Persian Bold—Russian Ribbon (USA) **Sir Gordon White**
22 **CAMEO PERFORMANCE (USA)**, b br f Be My Guest (USA)—Nancy Chere (USA) **Mr R. E. Sangster**
23 **CHATEAUNEUF**, b c Niniski (USA)—Valois **Mr R. E. Sangster**
24 **CORMORANT CREEK**, b f Gorytus (USA)—Quarry Wood **Mr R. J. McAlpine**
25 **CRUISING HEIGHT**, b f Shirley Heights—Nomadic Pleasure **Mr K. Abdulla**
26 **DANCING PARTY (USA)**, b f Danzig (USA)—Irish Party (USA) **Mr Howard Kaskel**
27 **DEFICIT (USA)**, ch c Deputy Minister (CAN)—Go Leasing **Mr K. Abdulla**
28 **DEMONSTRABLE (USA)**, b c Alleged (USA)—Lovin' Lass (USA) **Mr K. Abdulla**
29 **DEVIOSITY (USA)**, b c Spectacular Bid (USA)—Reinvestment (USA) **Mrs June Doyle**
30 **DRESS PERFORMANCE (USA)**, b f Nureyev (USA)—Hortensia (FR) **Mr R. E. Sangster**
31 **ELAPSE (USA)**, gr c Sharpen Up—Bygones (USA) **Mr R. E. Sangster**
32 **FALLOW DEER**, ch f Jalmood (USA)—Regent's Fawn (CAN) **Mr B. W. Hills**
33 **FLYING DIVA**, b f Chief Singer—Flying Fantasy **Mr Howard Kaskel**
34 **HOME TRUTH**, ch f Known Fact (USA)—Dance Card **Mr D. J. Deer**
35 **HORN PLAYER (USA)**, ch c The Minstrel (CAN)—Qualique (USA) **Mr R. E. Sangster**
36 **IDLE CHAT (USA)**, ch f Assert—Gossiping (USA) **Mr R. E. Sangster**
37 **I SEE ICE**, b f High Top—Climb The Heights (USA) **Mr A. D. Shead**
38 **ISLAND SPIRIT**, b c Ile de Bourbon (USA)—Zeyneb **K. Al-Said**
39 **JUBILEE TRAIL**, b f Shareef Dancer (USA)—Miss Petard **Mr K. Abdulla**
40 **KATSINA (USA)**, b f Cox's Ridge (USA)—Katsura (USA) **Mr K. Abdulla**
41 **KING ARBRO**, b c Tumble Wind (USA)—Double Habit **Mr Brian Kingham**
42 **KITTY RUSSE**, b f Nureyev (USA)—Kittyhawk **Mr R. E. Sangster**
43 **LAXEY BAY**, b c Caerleon (USA)—Franconia (AUS) **Sir Gordon White**
44 **LLANDOVERY**, br c Caerleon (USA)—Copy Conforme (FR) **Mr R. E. Sangster**
45 **LOCH FRUIN**, b c Lomond (USA)—Miralove **Sheikh Mohammed**
46 **LORD OF TUSMORE**, b c Al Nasr (FR)—Princess Toy **Mr Wafic Said**
47 **LOST EMPIRE**, b c Lomond (USA)—Fantasy Land **Mrs June Doyle**
48 **LOTHIAN**, b g Top Ville—Cojean (USA) **Mrs June Doyle**
49 **MIDDLE KINGDOM (USA)**, b c Northern Dancer—Puget Sound **Mr R. E. Sangster**
50 **MISSIONARY RIDGE**, ch c Caerleon (USA)—Shellshock **Sir Gordon White**
51 **MODEL VILLAGE**, ch f Habitat—It's Terrific **Sheikh Mohammed**
52 **MR C FOX (USA)**, ch c Devil's Bag (USA)—Sugar Plum Time (USA) **Mr Howard Kaskel**
53 **NATIVE GUILE**, b f Lomond (USA)—Merlins Charm (USA) **Mr R. E. Sangster**
54 **NEGLIGENT**, gr f Ahonoora—Negligence **Mrs J. M. Corbett**
55 **NORWICH**, b c Top Ville—Dame Julian **Sheikh Mohammed**
56 **OBLIST (CAN)**, gr f Exceller (USA)—Grey Sister (USA) **Mr R. M. Anderson**
57 **ORBIT (USA)**, ch f Sunny's Halo (CAN)—Female Star (USA) **Mr R. E. Sangster**
58 **ORIENTAL MYSTIQUE**, ch f Kris—Miss Toshiba (USA) **Mr R. E. Sangster**
59 **OSHAWA**, br f Alzao (USA)—O'Shaunessy **Sheikh Mohammed**
60 **OZONE FRIENDLY (USA)**, ch f Green Forest (USA)—Kristana **Mr W. J. Gredley**
61 **PASHTO**, b c Persian Bold—Epure **Sir Gordon White**
62 **PATH OF CONDIE**, b c Vaigly Great—Goosie-Gantlet **Sir Raymond Brown**
63 **PAY THE BANK**, b f High Top—Zebra Grass **Mr Wafic Said**
64 **PERFORMING ARTS**, ch f The Minstrel (CAN)—Noble Mark **Mr R. E. Sangster**
65 **POLAR BIRD**, b f Thatching—Arctic Winter (CAN) **Mr R. E. Sangster**
66 **POLAR LICHEN**, b f Lichine (USA)—Polaregina (FR) **Mr A. Sangster**
67 **PORT SODERICK (USA)**, b c Affirmed (USA)—Queen of Cornwall (USA) **Mr R. E. Sangster**
68 **PURE CLASS**, ch c Habitat—On The Fringe (USA) **Mrs David Thompson**
69 **RECTILLON**, b c Rousillon (USA)—Rectitude **Anglo Thoroughbred Racing**
70 **REGIMENTAL ARMS (USA)**, b c Sir Ivor—Durtal **Sir Gordon White**
71 **REINE DE DANSE (USA)**, gr f Nureyev (USA)—Bernica (FR) **Mr R. E. Sangster**
72 **REVOKE (USA)**, ch f Riverman (USA)—Queens Only (USA) **Mr K. Abdulla**
73 **RISEN MOON (USA)**, b c Hawaiian Sound (USA)—Uvula (USA) **Mr R. E. Sangster**
74 **RIVA (USA)**, b f Riverman (USA)—Valderna (FR) **Mr K. Abdulla**
75 **RUSSIAN FRONTIER**, gr c Nureyev (USA)—Lovelight **Mr R. E. Sangster**
76 **SAFETY (USA)**, b c Topsider (USA)—Flare Pass (USA) **Mr K. Abdulla**
77 **SHARP MOVER**, b f Sharpo—Matoa (USA) **Mr K. Abdulla**
78 **SHARP SALUTE (USA)**, ch c Sharpen Up—Topolly (USA) **Sir Gordon White**
79 **SHOEHORN**, br c Prince Tenderfoot (USA)—Relkalim **Mr R. E. Sangster**
80 **SILK SLIPPERS (USA)**, b f Nureyev (USA)—Nalee's Fantasy (USA) **Mr R. E. Sangster**

MR B. W. HILLS—continued

81 **SINGING (USA)**, b f The Minstrel (CAN)—Social Column (USA) **Mr K. Abdulla**
82 **SOUTH SHORE**, b f Caerleon (USA)—Shore Line **Mr R. E. Sangster**
83 **SPANISH EMPIRE (USA)**, b c El Gran Senor (USA)—Tea And Roses (USA) **Mr R. E. Sangster**
84 **STAR OF THE FUTURE (USA)**, b f El Gran Senor (USA)—Promising Girl (USA) **Mr K. Abdulla**
85 **SURE SHARP (USA)**, b c Sharpen Up—Double Lock **Sheikh Mohammed**
86 **SWORDSMITH (USA)**, b c Diesis—Lettre d'Amour (USA) **Sheikh Mohammed**
87 **TOPASANNAH**, b f Commanche Run—Princess Tracy **Mr R. E. Sangster**
88 **TRIUMPHAL SONG**, ch c Caerleon (USA)—Zither **Mr R. E. Sangster**
89 **UNCERTAIN DATE**, b f Habitat—Sooner Or Later **Mr A. Sangster**
90 **VALIRA (USA)**, ch f Nijinsky (CAN)—Condessa **Mr R. E. Sangster**
91 **VERDEUSE (FR)**, ch f Arctic Tern (USA)—Toujours Vert **Sir Tristan Antico**
92 **VICTORY PIPER (USA)**, ch c Nijinsky (CAN)—Arisen (USA) **Mr R. E. Sangster**
93 **WARM FEELING**, b c Kalaglow—Height of Passion **Mr R. J. C. Upton**

TWO-YEAR-OLDS

94 **ADJACENT (IRE)**, ch f 1/3 Doulab (USA)—Near The Door (USA) (Stage Door Johnny (USA)) **Mrs J. M. Corbett**
95 **AROKAT (USA)**, gr c 25/4 Caro—Katsura (USA) (Northern Dancer) **Mr K. Abdulla**
96 **BALLETOMANE (IRE)**, b f 8/2 Sadler's Wells (USA)—Franconia (AUS) (Rheingold) **Mr R. E. Sangster**
97 Gr f 31/3 Golden Act (USA)—Bergluft (GER) (Literat (GER)) **Mrs J. M. Corbett**
98 **BERLIN BREAKOUT**, b c 19/2 Never So Bold—Rostova (Blakeney) **Mr W. J. Gredley**
99 B c 29/4 Clever Trick (USA)—Bluebell (Town Crier) **Manton Bloodstock**
100 **CAERDYDD (IRE)**, ch c 2/3 Caerleon (USA)—Resooka (Godswalk (USA)) **Mr R. E. Sangster**
101 **CHIMAYO (IRE)**, b c 14/2 Sure Blade (USA)—Seattle Siren (USA) (Seattle Slew (USA)) **Sheikh Mohammed**
102 **CLOSE FRIEND (IRE)**, gr c 3/2 Law Society (USA)—Bellifontaine (FR) (Bellypha) **Mr Wafic Said**
103 **COCHINEAL (USA)**, br f 20/3 Vaguely Noble—Crimson Queen (USA) (Crimson Satan) **Mr R. E. Sangster**
104 B f 21/3 Rousillon (USA)—Destina (USA) (Youth (USA)) **Mr K. Abdulla**
105 **EASTERN AURA (IRE)**, ch f 21/2 Ahonoora—Sybaris (Crowned Prince (USA)) **Morven Stud Ltd**
106 **EMILIA ROMAGNA (USA)**, b f 19/4 Forli (ARG)—Pailleron (USA) (Majestic Light (USA)) **Sheikh Mohammed**
107 Br c 27/5 Topsider (USA)—Evening Silk (USA) (Damascus (USA))
108 B f 10/3 Green Desert (USA)—Fear Naught (Connaught) **Y. Ito**
109 **FIFE (IRE)**, b f 26/4 Lomond (USA)—Fiddle-Faddle (Silly Season) **Sheikh Mohammed**
110 B c 27/1 Pennine Walk—First Blush (Ela-Mana-Mou) **Mr Wafic Said**
111 B f 18/2 Niniski (USA)—Fleet Girl (Habitat) **Mr K. Abdulla**
112 **FLY TOWER (IRE)**, b c 30/3 Sadler's Wells (USA)—Dazzling Light (Silly Season) **Sheikh Mohammed**
113 **FORMAL OCCASION (IRE)**, b f 27/4 Shirley Heights—Princess Tiara (Crowned Prince (USA)) **Mr R. E. Sangster**
114 B c 6/4 Lomond (USA)—Gift Wrapped (Wolver Hollow) **Y. Ito**
115 **GUADALCANAL (IRE)**, b c 10/4 Sadler's Wells (USA)—Red Coral (AUS) (Red God) **Mr R. E. Sangster**
116 **ITQAN (IRE)**, b f 11/3 Sadler's Wells (USA)—Photo (Blakeney) **Mr Hamdan Al-Maktoum**
117 **JENNY'S CALL**, gr f 9/3 Petong—Jenny Splendid (John Splendid) **Lady Harrison**
118 B c 13/2 Thatching—Joanne's Joy (Ballymore) **Mr K. Abdulla**
119 B c 9/5 Taufan (USA)—Jovial Josie (USA) (Sea Bird II) **Mr Wafic Said**
120 **KISKA (USA)**, ch f 7/2 Bering—Hortensia (FR) (Luthier (FR)) **Mr R. E. Sangster**
121 **LANNER (USA)**, ch c 30/3 Diesis—Syndaar (FR) (Lyphard (USA)) **Mr K. Abdulla**
122 **LLANGOLLEN (IRE)**, b f 16/3 Caerleon (USA)—Keep The Thought (USA) (Valdez (USA)) **Mr R. E. Sangster**
123 **LOFTY LADY (IRE)**, b f 6/5 Head For Heights—Octavia Girl (Octavo (USA)) **Mr John Leat**
124 **MATTER OF FACT**, br f 13/2 Known Fact (USA)—Matoa (USA) (Tom Rolfe) **Mr K. Abdulla**
125 **MINSKIP (USA)**, ch f 6/5 The Minstrel (CAN)—Fabulous Native (USA) (Le Fabuleux) **Mr K. Abdulla**
126 B c 11/2 Al Nasr (FR)—Modena (USA) (Roberto (USA)) **Mr K. Abdulla**
127 B f 23/4 Sovereign Dancer—Mofida (Right Tack) **Mr K. Abdulla**
128 B c 23/2 Kris—Mountain Lodge (Blakeney) **Mr K. Abdulla**
129 **MY SHOUSHOU**, b f 23/3 Shirley Heights—Crystal Fountain (Great Nephew) **Mr Wafic Said**
130 B c 1/3 Tate Gallery (USA)—Natuschka (Authi) **Mr Howard Kaskel**
131 **NOBLE FLUTTER (IRE)**, ch f 29/2 The Noble Player—Night of Wind (Tumble Wind (USA)) **Mr Alan Townsend**
132 Ch f 26/3 Ahonoora—Nomadic Pleasure (Habitat) **Mr K. Abdulla**
133 **NORTH WIND (IRE)**, b f 10/2 Lomond (USA)—Spirit of The Wind (USA) (Little Current (USA)) **H.R.H. Princess Michael of Kent**
134 B c 4/2 Lomond (USA)—One Way Street (Habitat) **Mr R. E. Sangster**

MR B. W. HILLS—continued

135 **PLECTRUM,** b f 15/3 Adonijah—Cymbal (Ribero) **Mr R. D. Hollingsworth**
136 **PRECIOUS AIR (IRE),** ch f 25/1 Precocious—Astra Adastra (Mount Hagen (FR)) **Mrs Barbara Mallett**
137 Ch f 11/3 Secretariat (USA)—Prodigious (FR) (Pharly (FR)) **Mr K. Abdulla**
138 **PROFESSIONAL (IRE),** b c 28/4 Sadler's Wells (USA)—
Miss Allowed (USA) (Alleged (USA)) **Mr R. E. Sangster**
139 **RACHEL'S DANCER (IRE),** b f 30/3 Lomond (USA)—Passing Fancy (USA) (Buckpasser) **Mr M. Olden**
140 Gr c 12/5 Blakeney—Red Rose Bowl (Dragonara Palace (USA)) **Mr K. Abdulla**
141 **RELENTLESS PURSUIT (IRE),** b c 6/2 Thatching—Daring Way (USA) (Alydar (USA)) **Mr R. E. Sangster**
142 **RIVER PATROL,** b f 6/2 Rousillon (USA)—Boathouse (Habitat) **Mr R. D. Hollingsworth**
143 **RIVER SUIR (USA),** ch f 18/2 Irish River (FR)—Viendra (USA) (Raise A Native) **Mr R. E. Sangster**
144 **SANDICLIFFE WAY (IRE),** ch c 15/2 Doulab (USA)—Plainsong (FR) (Amen (FR)) **Sandicliffe Motor Group**
145 B f 26/4 El Gran Senor (USA)—Satin Ribera (USA) (Mickey McGuire (USA)) **Mr K. Abdulla**
146 **SEA LEVEL (FR),** b c 19/2 Kind of Hush—Packet (Royal Palace) **Mr R. D. Hollingsworth**
147 **SHARP CIRCLE (IRE),** b f 18/2 Sure Blade (USA)—Centre Piece (Tompion (USA)) **Morven Stud Ltd**
148 **SHILTON (USA),** gr c 26/2 Topsider (USA)—Save (USA) (Sadair) **Sheikh Mohammed**
149 **SHOKA (FR),** gr f 2/4 Kaldoun (FR)—Sassika (FR) (Arratos (FR)) **Sheikh Mohammed**
150 **STONE MILL,** b c 10/2 Caerleon (USA)—Millers Creek (USA) (Star de Naskra (USA)) **Sheikh Mohammed**
151 **SUPREME CHOICE (USA),** b c 6/2 Sovereign Dancer—Editors Choice (USA) (Sir Ivor) **Morven Stud Ltd**
152 **SURE SIGN,** b f 22/3 Sure Blade (USA)—Hyroglyph (USA) (Northern Dancer) **Morven Stud Ltd**
153 **SWORDSTICK,** b c 16/2 Sure Blade (USA)—Lypharita (FR) (Lightning (FR)) **Sheikh Mohammed**
154 **TINTAGEL CASTLE (IRE),** br c 11/2 Caerleon (USA)—
Merlins Charm (USA) (Bold Bidder) **Mr R. E. Sangster**
155 **TITIAN RED (CAN),** ch f 30/4 Diesis—Carrot Top (High Hat) **Sheikh Mohammed**
156 **TRACY'S PRINCE (IRE),** ch c 18/3 Be My Guest (USA)—Princess Tracy (Ahonoora) **K. J. Flynn**
157 **TROUPE,** b c 2/5 Sadler's Wells (USA)—Lovelight (Bleep-Bleep) **Mr R. E. Sangster**
158 **VOODOO RHYTHM,** ch c 28/3 Be My Guest (USA)—Melody (USA) (Lord Gayle (USA)) **Mr R. E. Sangster**
159 **WORLD'S CREATION (USA),** b c 29/1 Cormorant (USA)—
Worlds Fair (USA) (Our Hero (USA)) **Morven Stud Ltd**

Other Owners: Mr M. Arbib, Mr Arnold H. Bachner, Mrs G. Webb Bronfman, Mr N. N. Browne, Deln Ltd, Mr Albert Finney, Mr J. J. Hindley, Mrs J. J. Hindley, Mr John T. L. Jones Jr, Mr K. G. Knox, Mr Bob Lanigan, Mr Arne Larsson, Mr John Magnier, Mrs R. McCreery, Mr W. McDonald, Lady Rose Musker, Mr William Du Pont 111, Duke Of Roxburghe, Mr B. V. Sangster, Trans Media Park Stud, Mr B. R. Wilsdon.

Jockeys (Flat): Pat Eddery (8-4), M Hills (8-0).

Apprentice: D Holland (7-0).

293 MR J. W. HILLS, Lambourn

Postal: **South Bank, Lambourn, Newbury, Berkshire, RG16 7LL.**
Phone: **(0488) 71548 TELEX (0488) 848479 FAX (0488) 72823**

1 **CAROL'S TREASURE,** 6, b h Balidar—Really Sharp **Mrs Carol Lane**
2 **GILDERDALE,** 8, ch g Gunner B—Mertola **Abbott Racing Partners**
3 **GOVERNORSHIP,** 6, ch g Dominion—Angel Beam (SWE) **Mr Christopher Wright**
4 **PANDY,** 4, b c Thatching—Hot Stone **Mr R. J. McAlpine**
5 **SCALES OF JUSTICE,** 4, br f Final Straw—Foiled Again **Mr Christopher Wright**
6 **SILLY HABIT (USA),** 4, b f Assert—Habitassa **Amity Finance Ltd**

MR J. W. HILLS—continued

THREE-YEAR-OLDS

7 **AFFIRMATION,** b f Tina's Pet—Affirmative **Mr L. H. J. Ward**
8 **CHAMBROS,** ch c Krayyan—Chilcombe **Mr D. I. Chambers**
9 **DANCING SENSATION (USA),** b f Faliraki—Sweet Satina (USA) **Mr R. E. Sangster**
10 **FRAGRANT PARK,** ch f Gorytus (USA)—Park Lady **Amity Finance Ltd**
11 **MASELLA,** ch f Aragon—Winter Resort **Mr Tim Newsome**
12 **PHILHARMONIA,** ch f Caerleon (USA)—Melody (USA) **Mr R. E. Sangster**
13 **POSTAGE STAMP,** ch c The Noble Player (USA)—Takealetter **Mr R. E. Sangster**
14 **SLIPPEROSE,** gr f Persepolis (FR)—Scholastika (GER) **Mr D. J. Deer**
15 **SUPERETTA,** ch f Superlative—Brown's Cay **Mr N. N. Browne**
16 **SUPRETTE,** b f Superlative—Blaskette **Mrs S. Owen-George**
17 **UNTITLED (USA),** br c Far Out East (USA)—Majestic Gina (USA) **Deln Ltd**

TWO-YEAR-OLDS

18 **ADEVA,** gr f 10/4 Bustino—Faakirah (Dragonara Palace (USA)) **Mr Christopher Wright**
19 Gr c 12/4 Petong—Balearica (Bustino) **Passelande Syndicate**
20 **BLACK THREE (IRE),** b c 4/5 Double Schwartz—Two's Company (Sheshoon) **Mr P. McNamara**
21 **COLONIAL LEGEND,** ch f 3/3 Dominion—Dynamic Mistress (No Mercy) **Mr L. H. J. Ward**
22 **ETERNAL FLAME,** b f 19/3 Primo Dominie—Cameroun (African Sky) **Mr Christopher Wright**
23 B c 3/5 Faustus (USA)—Hithermoor Lass (Red Alert) **Mr R. J. Arculli**
24 B c 4/5 Secreto (USA)—I'll Be Around (USA) (Isgala) **Mr N. N. Browne**
25 **JENUFA (IRE),** b f 24/1 Last Tycoon—Love Lost (Home Guard (USA)) **Mrs R. Hastings**
26 **LIAR'S POKER (IRE),** b c 11/4 Alzao (USA)—Goldwyn Princess (Native Prince) **Mr A. G. Waldie**
27 **LOMINDA (IRE),** b f 6/2 Lomond (USA)—Olinda (Sassafras (FR)) **Mr L. H. J. Ward**
28 **LUNAR LUNACY (IRE),** b f 1/5 Ahonoora—Flinging Star (USA) (Northern Fling (USA)) **Mr R. E. Sangster**
29 **MISS U LIKE CRAZY (USA),** ch f 19/4 Miswaki (USA)—
Summersault (USA) (Vaguely Noble) **Mr Christopher Wright**
30 **MY POLISHED CORNER (IRE),** ch f 12/2 Tate Gallery (USA)—Mettle (USA) (Pretendre) **Mr R. W. Bulfield**
31 **REPLICATE,** ch f 24/4 Vaigly Great—Remould (Reform) **Mrs R. Wigley**
32 B c 14/4 Lear Fan (USA)—Runaway Lady (USA) (Caucasus (USA)) **Kennet Valley Thoroughbreds Ltd**
33 **SALINGER,** b c 5/4 Rousillon (USA)—Scholastika (GER) (Alpenkonig (GER)) **Mr D. J. Deer**
34 B c 26/2 The Minstrel (CAN)—Street Savy (USA) (Foolish Pleasure)
35 **TEGERE (IRE),** ch f 8/2 Thatching—La Duse (Junius (USA)) **Amity Finance Ltd**
36 **TIP OF MY TONGUE,** b f 7/3 Beldale Flutter (USA)—Foiled Again (Bold Lad (IRE)) **Mr Christopher Wright**
37 **TURBOFAN (IRE),** b c 30/4 Taufan (USA)—Timinala (Mansingh (USA)) **Mr A. G. Waldie**

Other Owners: Mr M. Arbib, Mr K. E. Chambers, Mr D. Goodenough, Mr G. Howard-Spink, Mr C. W. Jenkins, Mr Howard Kaskel, Mr Brian Kingham, Mr John Nash, Mrs L. H. J. Ward.

Jockeys (Flat): M Hills (8-0), R Hills (8-0).

Apprentice: N Perry (7-12).

Amateur: Mr James Unett (9-7).

Lady Riders: Miss Suzie Francome (8-2), Miss Celia Radband (8-7).

294 MR C. J. HITCHINGS, Worcester

Postal: **Tyre Hill House, Hanley Swan, Worcester, WR8 0EQ.**
Phone: **EX-DIRECTORY**

1 **ANOTHER RUMOUR,** 6, b br m The Parson—Another Lady VI **Mr C. J. Hitchings**
2 **ASIA MINOR,** 10, b g Hittite Glory—Paresseuse **Mr C. J. Hitchings**

MR C. J. HITCHINGS—continued

3 **FOOLISH HERO,** 14, b g Run The Gantlet (USA)—Flibbertigibbet **Mr C. J. Hitchings**
4 **GREY WHISKERS,** 7, gr g Scallywag—Happy Returns **Mr C. J. Hitchings**
5 **HILLS HOPE,** 7, b g Random Shot—Jeanette Marie **Mr C. J. Hitchings**
6 **HOMER'S NOD,** 7, b g Quayside—Gilded Empress **Mr C. J. Hitchings**

295 MR R. P. C. HOAD, Lewes

Postal: **Windmill Lodge Stables, Spital Road, Lewes, East Sussex.**
Phone: **(0273) 477124**

1 **CARFAX,** 5, ch g Tachypous—Montana Moss **Mrs K. W. Sneath**
2 **CAYMAN QUEEN,** 5, b m Tina's Pet—Harpers Girl **Mr A. Walton**
3 **COUNT ME OUT,** 5, ch g Vaigly Great—Balatina **Mrs K. W. Sneath**
4 **HEARD IT BEFORE (FR),** 5, b h Pharly (FR)—Lilac Charm **Mr A. Walton**
5 **JACK LAPPER,** 6, br g Swing Easy (USA)—Seaknot **Mr A. Walton**
6 **LARCH IMAGE LADY,** 5, ch m Music Maestro—Unexpected **Mr A. Walton**
7 **LE BON CHANCE,** 5, b g Crooner—Saratoga Maid **Mrs J. Hoad**
8 **LOVE TO DANCE,** 5, b g Dominion—Atoka **Mr J. A. Christmas**
9 **LUCKY OAK,** 4, ch g Tap On Wood—Zalinndia (FR) **Miss Janet Moorey**
10 **MASTER TYKE,** 5, gr g Flying Tyke—Habatashie **Mr Jeffrey Ross**
11 **TERRY JO,** 6, b g Royal Blend—Barby's Girl **Miss Janet Moorey**
12 **TOURMALIEN,** 5, ch g Caerleon (USA)—Jacinth **Mrs D. E. Small**

Other Owners: Mr C. M. Bradfield, Miss Valerie Myson.

Conditional: M Hoad (9-10).

Amateur: Mr Phil Collins (9-0).

296 MR P. J. HOBBS, Minehead

Postal: **Bournstream, Bilbrook, Minehead, Somerset, TA24 6HB.**
Phone: **(0984) 40366 CAR PHONE (0860) 729795**

1 **BORDER ARCHER,** 6, br g Lighter—Inishdooey **Mr R. M. E. Wright**
2 **BRACELET,** 5, ch m Balidar—Asnoura (MOR) **Mr Paul R. Warren**
3 **BRIGHT BARLEY,** 6, ch g Native Bazaar—Laughing Corn **Miss J. Birt**
4 **BROAD BEAM,** 10, b g Averof—Angel Beam (SWE) **Mr George James Webb**
5 **CLOSE ESCAPE,** 7, b g Sunyboy—Tarquann **Mrs J. A. Debenham**
6 **COIRE VANNICH,** 6, b m Celtic Cone—Deepness **Mrs J. A. George**
7 **CREAM BY POST,** 6, b m Torus—Lady Manta **Mr T. C. Frost**
8 **EDGE O' BEYOND,** 5, ch m Monksfield—Bright Society **Mr E. C. Eveleigh**
9 **ELEGANT BAR,** 7, b m Latest Model—Evening Bar **Mrs A. Frank**
10 **FREEMANTLE,** 5, ch g Welsh Pageant—Reno (USA) **Mr Frank Habberfield**
11 **FRESH-MINT,** 6, b g Giacometti—What A Mint **Mr John Cockerill**
12 **GALLIC PRINCE,** 11, b g Kinglet—Camargue **Mr C. C. B. Mathew**
13 **GAY CRISELLE,** 7, b m Decoy Boy—Giselle **Mr Derek R. Price**
14 **GAY EDITION,** 8, b m New Member—Gay Park **Mr A. L. Hobbs**
15 **GAY TICKET,** 6, ch m New Member—Gay Park **Mr A. L. Hobbs**
16 **GOODASNEW,** 7, b g Godswalk—Fast Motion **Mr M. Brookes**
17 **GORSE HUNTER,** 7, ch g Bivouac—Joyous Day **Mr P. J. Hobbs**
18 **GUIBURN'S NEPHEW,** 8, ch g National Trust—Arran Sunset **Mrs R. O. Steed**
19 **IAMA ZULU,** 5, ch g Son of Shaka—Quick Sort **Mrs Anona Taylor**
20 **JOINT SOVEREIGNTY,** 10, b g Status Seeker—Sovereign's Choice **Mr G. J. Giddy**
21 **LANACRE BRIDGE,** 13, b g Langton Heath—So Gay **Mr R. M. E. Wright**

MR P. J. HOBBS—continued

22 **LUCKY ROMANY,** 8, b g High Season—Romany Lone **Mrs D. Parr**
23 **MARSH KING,** 9, b g Kinglet—Camargue **Mrs Mary Hill**
24 **MARSH MINK,** 8, b m Our Jimmy (USA)—Swinging Mink **Mr Frank Habberfield**
25 **MIDFIELDER,** 4, ch g Formidable (USA)—Pampas Flower **Bournstream '7'**
26 **MOODY MAN,** 5, b g Ela-Mana-Mou—Princess Redowa **Mr James Burley**
27 **PARTY BOY,** 7, b g Pardigras—Guyana **Mrs J. A. Debenham**
28 **PICADOR,** 6, b g Piaffer (USA)—Go Gently **Mr M. T. Lockyer**
29 **PRINCE OF DIAMONDS,** 7, b g Remezzo—Queen's Crystal **Mr P. J. Gwyn**
30 **PRIZE ASSET,** 10, b g Levanter—Not Often **Mrs C. James**
31 **ROSCOFF,** 8, b m Roscoe Blake—Kaminaki **Mr N. J. Knott**
32 **RULER'S GOLD,** 6, b g Majestic Maharaj—Treasury **Mrs Mary Hill**
33 **SILVER SKYLARK,** 6, ch g True Song—Silver Spartan **Mr C. G. M. Lloyd-Baker**
34 **SOFTLY,** 4, b c Beldale Flutter (USA)—Soft Pedal **Mr T. C. Frost**
35 **SPORTSNEWS,** 8, b g New Member—Dicopin **Mrs J. A. Debenham**
36 **STAR LANE,** 7, br g Comedy Star (USA)—Border Lane **Mr A. D. Stoddart**
37 **SUPREME WARRIOR,** 4, b c Simply Great (FR)—Sindo **Mr Derek R. Price**
38 **TERRA DI SIENA,** 8, ch g Manor Farm Boy—Paddys Tern **Cliffstar Labels Ltd**
39 **TERRYWARNER SPORTS,** 5, b g Furry Glen—Granny Knot **Terry Warner Sports**
40 **TINKERS GOLD,** 8, ch g Levanter—Rose Cottage **Mrs C. James**
41 **TULLOMAGRANGE,** 11, b g No Argument—Turn Back **Mr J. E. Moloney**
42 **WARNER FOR LEISURE,** 12, b g Jimsun—Besselsleigh Lass **Terry Warner Sports**
43 **WATERSMEET DOWN,** 7, ch g Carlburg—Brians Vulgan **Mr R. M. E. Wright**
44 **WEBBS WONDER,** 5, b g Latest Model—Gay Park **Mrs Megan Webb**

Other Owners: Mr J. P. Brooks, Mr Ray Bulled, Mrs R. H. Dunn, Miss I. D. Du Pre, Mr W. McKibbin, Mr J. C. Milton, Mr D. Parkes, Mr C. J. Sexton, Mr I. L. Shaw, Unity Farm Holiday Centre Ltd., Mr C. J. M. Walker.

Jockey (NH): Peter Hobbs (10-2).

Conditional: D G W Hood (9-12).

Amateur: Mr B Clifford (9-7).

Lady Rider: Mrs S L Hobbs (9-7).

297 MR H. B. HODGE, Ware

Postal: **Rickneys Cottage, Rickneys Farm, Chapmore Lane, Ware, Hertfordshire, SG12 0HD.**
Phone: **(0992) 587413**

1 **ANNIE'LL DO,** 5, ch m Horage—Anaglogs Daughter **Mr H. B. Hodge**
2 **CELTIC BARLE,** 6, ch g Celtic Cone—Pelant Barle **Mrs Irene Hodge**

298 MR R. J. HODGES, Somerton

Postal: **Cedar Lodge, Charlton Adam, Somerton, Somerset.**
Phone: **CHARLTON MACKRELL (045822) 3922**

1 **AMETHYSTINE (USA),** 4, ch f Barachois (CAN)—Amathus **Mr J. W. Mursell**
2 **ANOTHER MEMBER,** 6, b g New Member—Silver Peace **Mr J. L. Frampton**
3 **BALIGAY,** 5, b m Balidar—Gaygo Lady **Mr E. W. Carnell**
4 **CAERNARVON ROYAL,** 5, ch g Main Reef—Berserk **Mr C. John Hill**

MR R. J. HODGES—continued

5 **CALAMITY JOE,** 7, ch g Gay Palm—Calamint **Mr D. R. Whigham**
6 **DARK GISELLE,** 5, b m King of Spain—Giselle **Mr C. John Hill**
7 **DESERT PALM,** 5, b m Palm Track—Diascia **Mr C. T. Wells**
8 **DIAMOND DIGGER,** 8, ch g Lepanto (GER)—Priceless Gem **Mrs V. A. Tory**
9 **EVENING RAIN,** 4, b c Hays—Fine Form (USA) **B. J. Rousell Ltd**
10 **HIGHTOWN FONTANA,** 9, b m Gunner B—Fountain **Hightown Finance & Bloodstock Agency**
11 **JUVENARA,** 4, b g Young Generation—Sharrara (CAN) **Mr R. J. Hodges**
12 **LAPIAFFE,** 6, b g Piaffer (USA)—Laval **Mr R. A. Atkin**
13 **LEADING GUEST,** 5, b g What A Guest—Light House **Mr R. J. Hodges**
14 **MASTER SOUTH LAD,** 6, b g Shrivenham—Miss Rosewyn **Mr N. J. Case**
15 **MELODY LANE,** 5, b br m Horage—Melody Ryde **R. Arnold Engineers**
16 **MEMBERS METTLE,** 5, ch m New Member—Armagnac Spirit **Mr M. L. Chorlton**
17 **MUNDY MOON,** 5, b m Nearly A Hand—Lake Victoria **Mr W. F. Fry**
18 **NAVARESQUE,** 5, b m Raga Navarro (ITY)—Esquinade **Mrs D. Pickford**
19 **NEARLY MEDINA,** 8, ch m Nearly A Hand—Miss Medina **Mrs Stanley Perry**
20 **PARKLANDS BELLE,** 6, b m Stanford—Kelly's Curl **Mr C. John Hill**
21 **PENDINE SANDS,** 5, ch m Rolfe (USA)—Llanmilo **Mr R. J. Hodges**
22 **PERMANENTLY PINK,** 4, b c Auction Ring (USA)—Hawaiian Joss (USA) **Mr R. J. Hodges**
23 **RAMROD,** 5, ch g Giacometti—Come On Girl **B. J. Rousell Ltd**
24 **RARE BID (NZ),** 7, br g Balak—So Rare (NZ) **Mrs S. J. Maltby**
25 **RECIDIVIST,** 4, b f Royben—On Remand **Mr C. John Hill**
26 **RECORD FLIGHT,** 6, ch m Record Token—Lady Relka **Mr Frank E. Crumpler**
27 **RED RIVER BOY,** 7, b g Latest Model—Count On Me **Mr J. W. Mursell**
28 **RUNAWAY TRAIN,** 7, ch g Deep Run—Apair **Mr Patrick Parnell**
29 **RUSHLUAN,** 6, gr g Kalaglow—Labista **Mrs K. M. Burge**
30 **SECRET MEMBER,** 6, ch g Peacefull Member—Ennis Rose **Mr J. L. Frampton**
31 **SETTER COUNTRY,** 6, b m Town And Country—Top Soprano **Mr D. Barber**
32 **ST WILLIAM,** 13, b g St Paddy—Lower Slade **Mrs E. A. Tucker**
33 **SUNDAY FOR MONDAY,** 7, ch g Pal's Bambino—Gin An Tonic **Mr Richard J. Evans**
34 **TACHADOR,** 9, ch g Tachypous—Adored **Mr P. E. Axon**
35 **TINSEL ROSE,** 7, ch m Porto Bello—Love Is Blind (USA) **Mr J. Jamouneau**
36 **TRUST THE GYPSY,** 8, br g National Trust—Zingarella **Mrs B. Whettam**

Other Owners: Mr R. Alley, Mr David Chilton, Mr B. Dennett, Lt.-Col. P. G. C. Dunn, Mrs M. Frampton, Mrs Barbara Lock, Mr Jack Miller, Mr C. H. Rillstone, Mr A. M. Stevens, Mrs P. P. Surtees, Mr R. J. Tory, Mr Philip Webster, Mr C. M. Wilson, Mr John Young.

Conditional: M Fitzgerald, W S Irvine.

Amateur: Mr C Maude.

299 MR W. HOLDEN, Newmarket

Postal: **Exeter Stables, Exning, Newmarket, Suffolk.**
Phone: **EXNING (063 877) 384**

1 **CHANTRY BOY,** 6, b g Balliol—Glebe **Prof A. R. Sanderson**
2 **COUNT BERTRAND,** 9, b h Brigadier Gerard—Gingerale **Serological Reagents Ltd**
3 **DELLWOOD RENOWN,** 8, b g Connaught—Erstung **Mr W. Holden**
4 **EDGEWISE,** 7, b br g Tanfirion—Regency Girl **Mr John Peters**
5 **FIRE LADY,** 4, ch f Hotfoot—Hindu Flame **Mr R. Biller**
6 **GYPSY'S BARN RAT,** 6, br m Balliol—Chebs Lass **Miss Kathryn Holden**
7 **IRISCAR,** 4, b f Valiyar—Dellwood Iris **Mr W. Holden**
8 **JAUNTER,** 10, ch g St Columbus—Jaunting **Whitting Commodities Ltd**
9 **KAWWAS,** 5, b h Persian Bold—Tifrums **Whitting Commodities Ltd**
10 **LES YEUX D'AMOUR,** 4, br f Vision (USA)—Adorit **Castle Farm Stud**
11 **SICILIAN SWING,** 5, b g Swing Easy (USA)—Mab **Mr N. A. Springham**

MR W. HOLDEN—continued

THREE-YEAR-OLDS

12 **BURSAR,** b f Balliol—Trading **Mr W. Holden**
13 **DELLA PETINA,** ch f Tina's Pet—Dellwood Iris **Mr W. Holden**
14 **RED BLISTER,** ch g Hotfoot—Hindu Flame **Serological Reagents Ltd**

TWO-YEAR-OLDS

15 **HORSEFLY,** b f 26/5 Balliol—Erstung (Shantung) **Mr W. Holden**

Other Owners: Mr William Terence Brown, Mrs M. Clutten, Mr Paul Anthony Green, Mr J. W. Orbell, Mr Craig M. Springham, Mr D. A. Wallace, Mr S. L. Wallace.

Apprentice: B Russell (7-7).

Lady Rider: Miss K Holden (8-7).

300 MR R. J. HOLDER, Bristol

Postal: **Racecourse Farm, Portbury, Bristol, Avon, BS20 9SN.**
Phone: **OFFICE (027 581) 2192 FAX (027 581) 4185**

1 **ABLE VALE,** 4, b f Formidable (USA)—Valeur **Mr Andy Bailey**
2 **ANOTHER CANFORD,** 5, ch g Humdoleila—Little Tot **Mrs S. King**
3 **AVONMOUTHSECRETARY,** 4, b f Town And Country—Star Display **Mr John M. Tutton**
4 **BERESFORDS GIRL,** 5, b m Furry Glen—Hansel's Queen **Mr Beresford Mills**
5 **BERTIE WOOSTER,** 7, ch g Homeboy—Peace of Mind **Miss Amanda J. Rawding**
6 **BEST EFFORT,** 4, ch g Try My Best (USA)—Lunaria (USA) **Mr Raymond Miquel**
7 **BETRIM,** 6, b g Dubassoff (USA)—Horoscope **Mr H. Gooding**
8 **BLUE BOURBON,** 6, b g Ile de Bourbon (USA)—Habanna **Mr P. A. Williams**
9 **CAPE MANTON,** 9, b m Mandamus—Cape Thriller **Partnership**
10 **CELTIC MEMBER,** 6, ch g New Member—Qebir Celtice **Mr P. S. Rawlings**
11 **COMEDY BASIN,** 7, b g Comedy Star (USA)—Porcupine Basin **Mrs John Spielman**
12 **CONNEMARA DAWN,** 6, ch g Viking (USA)—Amendola (FR) **Avondurn Limited**
13 **DOREEN'S PRIDE,** 4, ch f Celtic Cone—Quae Supra **Mrs Marion C. Morgan**
14 **EDDIES FELLA,** 5, b g New Member—Daniel's Fancy **Mr Ken Edwards**
15 **FAYGATE,** 4, ch f Vaigly Great—Fayette **Mr M. Dallimore**
16 **FROME BOY,** 5, ch g New Member—Groundsel **Mr C. C. Lowe**
17 **GUN HAPPY,** 6, b g Formidable (USA)—Naughty One Gerard **P.S.B. (Racing) Ltd**
18 **GUNNERS BEST,** 6, b g Gunner B—Swakara **M. & N. Plant Ltd**
19 **GUNNER STREAM,** 6, ch g Gunner B—Golfers Dream **Mr Val Kelly**
20 **HAND BASIN,** 5, ch g Nearly A Hand—Porcupine Basin **Mrs John Spielman**
21 **IKDAM,** 5, b h Glint of Gold—Run To The Sun **LBI Law (873) Ltd**
22 **JOHNS PRESENT,** 12, b g Gift Card (FR)—Kirmeen (FR) **Mr Paul Dening**
23 **KERRYS CASTLE,** 5, ch m Deep Run—Legaun **Castle Farm Stud**
24 **LADY WESTOWN,** 6, b m Town And Country—Hay-Hay **Mrs Jackie Jarrett**
25 **LEAVENWORTH,** 6, ch g Bustino—Hide The Key (USA) **Mr A. Gardiner-Hill**
26 **LONGRIVER LADY,** 7, b m Town And Country—Peggy Wig **Mr David A. Brown**
27 **LORD CAPILANO,** 7, ch g Busted—Finbay (ITY) **Mr Barclay Watson**
28 **LORD MURPHY,** 8, ch g Oats—Lady Pavlova **Mr Bram Davies**
29 **MAGIC MELISSA,** 8, ch m New Member—Cape Mandalin **Febry's Haulage and Warehousing Ltd**
30 **MAN FROM MARS,** 4, b g Wolver Hollow—Articmars **Mr M. Burley**
31 **MATCHING WOOD,** 5, b g Touching Wood—Matloch **Mr Geoffrey C. Greenwood**
32 **MISS POKEY,** 4, b f Uncle Pokey—Silken Swift **Mr David A. Brown**
33 **MR ACACIA,** 4, b g Enchantment—Lightening Blue **Mr V. Centamore**
34 **NORSE IMP,** 4, b f Impecunious—Norsemen's Lady **Mrs A. G. Sims**
35 **PHYL'S LEGACY,** 5, ch m Cruise Missile—Sober Sue **Miss Alison Broyd**
36 **SILVER THORN,** 6, b m Record Run—Victory Corner **Mrs P. W. Talbot-Ponsonby**
37 **SIR CRUSTY,** 8, b g Gunner B—Brazen **Mr M. Ash**

MR R. J. HOLDER—continued

38 **SLEEPLINE FANTASY**, 5, ch h Buzzards Bay—Sleepline Princess **Sleepline Holdings**
39 **SLEEPLINE ROMANY**, 5, b g Buzzards Bay—Sleepline Comfort **Sleepline Holdings**
40 **SLEEPLINE ROYALE**, 4, ch g Buzzards Bay—Sleepline Princess **Sleepline Holdings**
41 **SONNY HILL LAD**, 7, ch g Celtic Cone—Honey Dipper **Mr Paul Dening**
42 **STAR SEASON**, 6, b g Newski (USA)—Silly Moo **Mr Marc Wheeler**
43 **TRUST THE IRISH**, 9, b g Ile de Bourbon (USA)—Trusted Maiden **Mr A. Gardiner-Hill**
44 **TUDOR D'OR**, 7, br m Mister Tudor—Petit d'Or **Mr Tony Raggett**
45 **VA LUTE (FR)**, 6, b g No Lute (FR)—Viverba (FR) **Castle Farm Stud**
46 **VICEROY JESTER**, 5, br g Jester—Midnight Patrol **Mr Frank J. Broom**
47 **WAHIBA**, 6, b g Tumble Wind (USA)—Lady Kasbah **Mr J. M. Brown**
48 **YOUTHFUL CAPITANA**, 6, ch m Hardboy—La Capitana **Mr E. Anderson**

THREE-YEAR-OLDS

49 **BALISHY**, ch f Shy Groom (USA)—Bally **Mr B. N. Schafer**
50 **COMPOS MENTIS**, b g Homeboy—Rhythm **Mr Geoffrey C. Greenwood**
51 **DANCE OF A GUNNER**, ch f Gunner B—Kilttaley **M. & N. Plant Ltd**
52 **DELIGHTFUL DIANE**, b f Kalaglow—Whip Finish **Mr Raymond Miquel**
53 **FAILAND**, b f Kala Shikari—What A Mint **Mr James Neville**
54 **GORDANO**, ch g Muscatite—Coral Star **Mr B. K. Symonds**
55 **HIGH CASTE**, ch c Carwhite—Brazen **Mr R. M. West**
56 **I'LL SOON KNOW**, ch f Known Fact (USA)—Soolyn **Mr C. C. Jones**
57 **JAGGED EDGE**, ch c Sharpo—Tura **Mr N. Robinson**
58 **LOGICAL LADY**, b f Tina's Pet—Lady Andrea **Mr D. Tylden-Wright**
59 **MIDNIGHT MOVES**, ch f Coquelin (USA)—Puss Moth **Mr Henry D'Abo**
60 **MONSIEUR MORUE**, b g Pas de Seul—Footway **Partnership**
61 **PATSBERIC**, b g Blushing Scribe (USA)—Manageress **Mr E. A. Bicknell**
62 **SIGWELL'S GOLD**, b f Sonnen Gold—Manna Green **Mr Andy Bailey**
63 **SLEEPLINE PALACE**, b f Homing—Sleepline Princess **Sleepline Holdings**

TWO-YEAR-OLDS

64 **CAPITAL BOND (IRE)**, b c Hegemony—Have A Flutter **Mr D. Mort**
65 **CASIENNE (IRE)**, ch f Doulab—Borshch **Restoration (South West) Ltd**
66 **CONKWELL**, b g Sula Bula—Pita **Conkwell Grange Stud Ltd**
67 **EASTER TERM**, b f Welsh Term—Silly Woman **Mr D. L. C. Hodges**
68 B f Town And Country—Ganadora **Mr S. Glenn**
69 B f Millfontaine—Get Ready **Mr R. J. Holder**
70 Gr f Absalom—Kilttaley **M. & N. Plant Ltd**
71 B f Lidhame—Lady Antonia **Mr J. M. Brown**
72 Ch c Homing—Rocas **Sleepline Holdings**
73 Ch c Absalom—Safeguard **Mr K. Neill**
74 Ch f Good Times (ITY)—Sandy Looks **Sleepline Holdings**
75 Ch c Buzzards Bay—Sleepline Princess **Sleepline Holdings**

Other Owners: Mr John Brookman, Mr David Dowell, Mr H. G. Gwyn, Mr E. Kendrick, Mr J. Law, Mr David Lawson, Mr M. J. Lee, Mr Harry Lewis, Mr I. D. Macdonald, Mrs A. S. Moore, Mr T. M. Newman, Mr H. O'Neill, Mr B. Pemberton, Mr Chris Scott, Mr E. Simmons, Mrs S. M. Somers, Mr R. J. Tanner, Mr R. H. Taylor, Mr M. Telford Turner, Mr A. Townend, Mr B. White, Mr J. C. White.

Jockey (Flat): A Dicks (8-0).

Jockey (NH): N Coleman (10-0).

Conditional: N Mann.

Amateurs: Mr A Farrant (9-7), Mr R Farrant (8-7), Mrs L Murphy (9-7).

301 MR R. HOLLINSHEAD, Upper Longdon

Postal: **Lodge Farm, Upper Longdon, Rugeley, Staffordshire.**
Phone: **ARMITAGE (0543) 490298**

1 **AICNAL,** 4, br f Ile de Bourbon—Skelbrooke **Mr T. Connop**
2 **BALAO,** 4, ch f Mr Fluorocarbon—Bombay Duck **Mrs J. P. Bissill**
3 **BIRMINGHAM'S PRIDE,** 4, br f Indian King (USA)—Cooliney Dancer **Daily News Ltd (Birmingham)**
4 **BLUFF COVE,** 8, ch g Town Crier—Dolly Dickins **Dickins Ltd**
5 **BUTLERS WHARF,** 5, b g Burslem—Regal Promise **Mrs Thelma White**
6 **CENTENARY STAR,** 5, b g Broadsword (USA)—Tina's Gold **Daily News Ltd (Birmingham)**
7 **DANCING MONARCH,** 5, ch h Dara Monarch—Maiden's Dance **Mr S. C. Reakes**
8 **GRACE CARD,** 4, b g Ela-Mana-Mou—Val de Grace (FR) **Mr G. A. Farndon**
9 **HILDA,** 4, b f Ile de Bourbon (USA)—Palovna (FR) **Mr R. Hollinshead**
10 **INDIVISIBLE,** 4, ch f Remainder Man—Red Ragusa **Mrs A. Mutch**
11 **KATHY COOK,** 5, b m Glenstal (USA)—Belmont Blue **Mrs R. Hollinshead**
12 **KENILWORTH CASTLE,** 4, b c Dunbeath (USA)—Ravenshead **Mr G. A. Farndon**
13 **KIND OF SHY,** 4, ch f Kind of Hush—Peta **Mr T. G. Holdcroft**
14 **LILAC TIME,** 4, b f Town And Country—Harp Strings (FR) **Mrs M. A. Power**
15 **MAGIC QUEST,** 4, ch f Posse (USA)—Satina **Mr Patrick Rugg**
16 **MISS SARAJANE,** 6, b m Skyliner—Taffeta **Mr Gordon Smyth**
17 **MOHARABUIEE,** 4, b f Pas de Seul—Clonavee (USA) **Mr Noel Sweeney**
18 **NIPOTINA,** 4, b f Simply Great (FR)—Mothers Girl **Mr G. A. Farndon**
19 **OUT OF FUNDS,** 4, b g Ela-Mana-Mou—Overspent **Mr Trevor Painting**
20 **PERSIAN EMPEROR,** 5, ro h Persepolis (FR)—Rosananti **Mrs Christine Painting**
21 **PETITE ANGEL,** 5, ro m Burslem—Lavinia **Mr R. Hollinshead**
22 **PYTCHLEY PRINCE,** 7, b g Tyrnavos—Athenia Princess **Mr S. C. Reakes**
23 **RED PENCIL,** 5, ch g Krayyan—Blue Gulf **Mrs P. T. Tellwright**
24 **SQUIRSKY,** 4, b c Tina's Pet—Targos Delight **Mr Stanley Squires**
25 **SULCIS,** 5, ch g Castle Keep—Skiboule (BEL) **Mr N. Connop**
26 **SULUK (USA),** 5, b h Lypheor—Cheerful Heart **Mr Anthony White**
27 **TELL'S TOWER,** 4, b f Dunbeath (USA)—Gallatin Valley (USA) **Mr L. Briggs**
28 **THEKKIAN,** 6, ch h Thatching—Debian **Mr C. D. Owens**
29 **TOPHAMS,** 4, b br c Good Times (ITY)—Sun Lamp **Mr Roland Topham**
30 **URRAY ON HARRY,** 6, b g Anfield—Noorina **Mr D. Coppenhall**

THREE-YEAR-OLDS

31 **ANKARA'S PRINCESS (USA),** ch f Ankara (USA)—Tales of Long Ago (USA) **J. D. Graham**
32 **BARACHOIS PRINCESS (USA),** b f Barachois (USA)—Egregious (USA) **J. D. Graham**
33 **BEAU QUEST,** b c Rainbow Quest—Elegant Tern **Mr G. A. Farndon**
34 **BESITO,** b f Wassl—Field Day **Mr Trevor Painting**
35 **CALABALI,** b f Persian Bold—Bedfellow **Mrs Thelma White**
36 **CAVALLA,** b f The Brianstan—Bombay Duck **Mrs J. P. Bissill**
37 **CRIMINAL LAW,** b c Law Society (USA)—Indian Maid **Mrs B. Facchino**
38 **DEMESNE FLYER,** ch g Tower Walk—Covenant **Mr J. F. Bower**
39 **DODGER DICKINS,** gr g Godswalk (USA)—Sronica **Dickins Ltd**
40 **EAGER DEVA,** b c Lochnager—Deva Rose **Dubanscam Racing Ltd**
41 **EMERALD MOON,** b c Auction Ring (USA)—Skyway **Mrs Christine Painting**
42 **FAMOUS BEAUTY,** br f Vision (USA)—Relfo **Mr J. E. Bigg**
43 **ISLE OF ARRAN,** b c Ile de Bourbon (USA)—Marzooga **Mr P. D. Savill**
44 **LAWNSWOOD JUNIOR,** gr c Bairn (USA)—Easymede **Mr A. S. Hill**
45 **LOVING OMEN,** ch c Touching Wood (USA)—Etoile d'Amore (USA)
46 **METAL BOYS,** b c Krayyan—Idle Gossip **North Staffs Racing Club**
47 **MISTRAL'S DANCER,** br f Shareef Dancer—Mythical Assembly
48 **MY TAI-PAN,** b c King of Clubs—Orchestration **Mrs G. E. Maloney**
49 **NICE AND SHARP,** b c Sharpo—Lune de Miel **Mr J. E. Bigg**
50 **PYTCHLEY NIGHT,** b c Red Sunset—Lili Bengam **Mr D. Demetri**
51 **RES IPSA LOQUITUR,** b c Law Society (USA)—Bubbling (USA) **Mr Trevor Painting**
52 **ROYAL STEEL,** ch g Kings Lake (USA)—All Souls **Mr Ralph Robbins**
53 **SILVERDALE FOX,** ch c Sweet Monday—Its My Turn **Mr Anthony White**
54 **SINCLAIR PRINCE,** ch c Local Suitor (USA)—Mothers Girl **Sinclair Developments Limited**
55 **SOUTER'S HILL (USA),** b c Temperence Hill (USA)—Kissapotamus (USA) **Mrs B. Facchino**

MR R. HOLLINSHEAD—continued

56 **STARCHY COVE,** br f Starch Reduced—Rosey Covert **Mr Cecil W. Wardle**
57 **STAR EXHIBIT,** ch c Exhibitioner—Star Bound **Mrs M. Guthrie**
58 **STAR LEADER,** b f Kafu—Sweet Relief **Express & Star Raceowners Club 1989**
59 **STATE OF AFFAIRS,** b c Free State—Trigamy **Mr P. D. Savill**
60 **SUNNYSIDE,** ch f Doulab (USA)—Sunny Look **Mr Noel Sweeney**
61 **VESTIGE,** ch c Remainder Man—Starchy **Mrs Carol Cooper**
62 **YARRAMAN,** b g Ya Zaman (USA)—Isa **Mr P. D. Savill**

TWO-YEAR-OLDS

63 B f 17/4 Magnolia Lad—Amber Windsor (Windjammer (USA)) **Mr J. B. Wilcox**
64 **BIT OF A LARK,** b c 15/2 Nomination—Straffan Girl (Sallust) **Mr R. E. Mason**
65 B f 11/3 Head For Heights—Blaze of Light (Blakeney)
66 Ch c 5/4 Doulab—Dankalia (Le Levanstell)
67 **DAVID'S FLIGHT,** ch c 26/4 Absalom—Djimbaran Bay (Le Levanstell) **Mr J. E. Bigg**
68 **DEVA'S GEM,** b f 15/4 Green Ruby—Deva Rose (Chestergate) **Dickins Ltd**
69 B c 20/4 Music Maestro—Eastern Romance (Sahib)
70 B c 28/3 Cragador—Gold Spangle (Klondyke Bill)
71 B c 20/1 Aragon—Little Egret (Carwhite) **Rykneld Thoroughbred Racing Ltd**
72 Ch c 4/3 Bairn (USA)—Octavia (Sallust) **Mr P. J. White**
73 **OLIFANTSFONTEIN,** b c 11/4 Thatching—Taplow (Tap On Wood) **Mr Trevor Painting**
74 Ch f 7/4 Shernazar—Penny Habit (Habitat) **Mr R. Hollinshead**
75 B c 22/2 Legend of France—Polly's Pear (USA) (Sassafras (FR)) **Mr R. Hollinshead**
76 **READER'S REWARD,** b f 7/3 Oats—Red Ragusa (Homeric) **Mrs A. Mutch**
77 **ROUSITTO,** ch c 16/4 Rousillon (USA)—Helenetta (Troy) **Mrs G. E. Maloney**
78 B c 9/4 Wassl—Sabrine (Mount Hagen (FR)) **Rykneld Thoroughbred Racing Ltd**
79 B f 29/4 Red Sunset—Sabura (Busted)
80 **SENTIMENTALITY (IRE),** b br c 2/4 Reasonable (FR)—Good Reliance (Good Bond) **Mrs G. E. Maloney**
81 **SINCLAIR LAD (IRE),** ch c 28/2 Muscatite—
Kitty Frisk (Prince Tenderfoot (USA)) **Sinclair Developments Limited**
82 B f 16/4 Bairn—Sindo (Derring-Do)
83 B c 7/4 Legend of France—Snow Goose (Santa Claus) **Dickins Ltd**
84 **STONELEIGH ABBEY (IRE),** b c 5/3 Sallust—Yellow Creek (Sandy Creek) **Mr G. A. Farndon**
85 B f 16/1 Precocious—Zalatia (Music Boy)

Other Owners: Miss B. Connop, Mr M. J. Cooper, Mr R. Davidson, Mr G. Hamilton, Mr K. W. Hogg, Mrs T. G. Holdcroft, Miss Sarah Hollinshead, Mr J. D. Jones, Mr E. H. Maloney, Mr Tom Mowbray, Pegasus Racing Thoroughbreds Limited, Mrs P. A. Sherwin, Mr J. Smyth.

Jockey (Flat): S Perks (8-5).

Apprentices: Jason Fordham, A Garth (6-7), G Hind (7-5), C Hodgson (7-12), M B Humphries (7-0), E Husband, G Husband (7-6).

Conditional: G Lyons (10-0).

Amateur: Mr A N Hollinshead (10-9).

Lady Riders: Ms Maxine Juster, Mrs Geraldine Rees.

302 MR D. HOLLY, Pontyclun

Postal: **Llwyngibbon Farm, Peterstone-super-Ely Road, Grosefaen, Pontyclun, Mid Glamorgan, Wales.** Phone: **(0446) 760001**

1 **GUARENA (USA),** 5, b g Run The Gantlet (USA)—Trenton North (USA) **Mrs A. H. Holly**

Amateurs: Mr P Hamer (10-10), Mrs R Vickery (9-0).

303 MR C. J. HOLMES, Gerrards Cross

Postal: **Windmill Farm, Bowstridge Lane, Chalfont St. Giles, Buckinghamshire.**
Phone: **(02407) 5964 FAX (02407) 4276**

1 **ANQUETIL**, 4, b br g Valiyar—Racemosa **Cross Lorraine Limited**
2 **BATCHWORTH HILL**, 8, b g Balinger—Royal Rally **Mrs Diana Price**
3 **DENITZ (FR)**, 8, ch g Sharpman—Djerba **Mrs Phoenix Raisbeck**
4 **DOUBLEUAGAIN**, 16, b g Double-U-Jay—Halfsixagain **Mr Clive Holmes**
5 **DUCATUS**, 9, b br g Duky—Fortrition **Mr Clive Holmes**
6 **LARA'S LUCK**, 5, b m Julio Mariner—Lara's Song (USA) **Mrs S. Jacobs**
7 **LIGHT DEMON**, 13, br g Lucifer (USA)—Menloe **Mr Clive Holmes**
8 **MASTER NIBBLE**, 15, b g Master Owen—Chambolle **Mr Clive Holmes**
9 **MISS BATCHWORTH**, 4, ch f Ballacashtal (CAN)—Soft Secret **Mrs Diana Price**
10 **SLANEY RAMBLER**, 9, ch g Tepukei—Difoolish **Mr Clive Holmes**

THREE-YEAR-OLDS

11 **HARDALE**, b f Beldale Lark—Jachar **Mrs S. Jacobs**

Other Owners: Mr B. Crawley, Mrs P. A. Garner.

Jockeys (NH): D Bennyworth, L Harvey.

304 MR L. J. HOLT, Basingstoke

Postal: **Tunworth Downs Stables, Tunworth, Basingstoke, Hampshire.**
Phone: **BASINGSTOKE (0256) 463376**

1 **ALWAYS READY**, 4, b g Tyrnavos—Merchantmens Girl **Mr G. Steinberg**
2 **AMBER NECTAR**, 4, ch g Sallust—Curtana **Mr M. V. Kirby**
3 **BEAUMONT'S KEEP**, 4, b g Castle Keep—Powderhall **Mrs Margaret Bates**
4 **COPPERMILL LAD**, 7, ch g Ardoon—Felin Geri **Mrs J. K. Sargood**
5 **MALLAU**, 4, b g Runnett—Brierley Lodge **Mr J. Sargood Snr**
6 **PADDY CHALK**, 4, gr c Tina's Pet—Guiletta **Mrs R. G. Wellman**

THREE-YEAR-OLDS

7 **ARGENTUM**, br c Aragon—Silver Berry **Mr K. F. Khan**
8 **KHULM**, b c Kafu—Little Wild Duck **Mr J. S. Khan**
9 **MASTER PIERRE**, b br g Gabitat—Emerglen **Mr J. A. G. L'Heureux**
10 **NAGORNOKARABACH**, ch c Glenstal (USA)—Abelina **Mr J. S. Khan**
11 **NAZAKAT**, ch f Known Fact (USA)—Royal Home **Mr T. H. Barma**
12 **NOT QUITE FREE**, b f Gabitat—Free Range **Mr P. Callard**
13 **SWIFT RUNNER**, b g Runnett—Celeritas **Mr G. W. Knight**

TWO-YEAR-OLDS

14 **DESERT FOREST**, ch c 21/2 Hotfoot—Sequoia (Sassafras (FR)) **Mr D. Scott and Mr J. Smith**
15 **GREY ILLUSIONS**, gr c 14/4 Nishapour (FR)—Morica (Moorestyle) **Mr J. R. Redfern**
16 **MAMALAMA**, ch f 24/2 Nishapour (FR)—Gauloise (Welsh Pageant) **Mr P. Cook**
17 B f 1/5 Nomination—Olderfleet (Steel Heart) **Mr R. J. F. Brothers**
18 **POWERFUL PIERRE**, br c 5/3 Mummy's Game—Harmonious Sound (Auction Ring (USA)) **Mr J. A. G. L'Heureux**
19 **TIME LORD**, ch c 6/5 Good Times (ITY)—Miss Trilli (Ardoon) **Mr K. F. Khan**
20 **TRAVEL TOKEN**, b c 20/4 Tina's Pet—Guiletta (Runnymede) **Mrs R. G. Wellman and Mrs M. Payne**

Other Owners: Mr A. T. Barma, Mr John Henwood, Mr L. J. Holt, Mr D. Khan, Mr Michael Knight, Mrs Pamela Lewendon, Mrs Josie Ridgers, Mr G. Le Rossignol, Mrs George Steinberg.

Jockeys (Flat): N Adams, J Reid (w.a.).

Apprentice: C Avery (7-7).

305 MR J. HONEYBALL, Bridgwater

Postal: **Manor Farm, Waterpitts, Broomfield, Bridgwater, Somerset.**
Phone: **KINGSTON ST. MARY (082 345) 451266**

1 **BUCKMINSTER BOY,** 9, ch g Sweet Revenge—Tintale **Mrs Marion Bowden, Mrs Jenifer Fletcher**
2 **DAYBROOK VERB,** 8, ch g Proverb—Daybrook Lass **Mr Roy Brown**
3 **FIDUCIARY DUTY,** 10, b g Top Star—Kirsch II **Mr David Cridland**
4 **GRINGO (HUN),** 11, br g Seebirk (EG)—Guanabara (HUN) **Mr Roy Brown**
5 **MR T BEAR,** 6, b g Neltino—Racer Jess **Mrs Joyce Morris**
6 **MULLION COVE,** 7, ch g Deep Run—News Letter **Mrs Joyce Morris**
7 **NOTRE CHEVAL,** 11, b g Weavers' Hall—Polar Point **Mrs Joyce Morris**
8 **PADDY BUCK,** 10, ch g Caribo—Buck's Rose **Mrs Joyce Morris**
9 **SIZZLING SUN,** 5, b m Sunyboy—Royal Blast **Mr Roy Brown**
10 **TACHYLINE,** 9, b m Tachypous—Top Line **Mr A. R. Page**

Other Owners: Mr P. Gunn, Mr C. J. Herring, Mr L. Jaume, Mr J. W. Prew.

Jockey (NH): Peter Hobbs (10-0).

306 MR C. HORGAN, Billingbear

Postal: **Billingbear Racing Stables, Billingbear Park, Wokingham, Berkshire, RG11 5RZ.**
Phone: **(0344) 425382**

1 **CABRA,** 4, ch f Red Sunset—Shangara **Mr K. C. Rohan**
2 **DECRETO,** 9, ch h Touch Paper—Tacora **Mrs Jackie Kendall-Davis**
3 **ELECTRIC DANCER,** 4, br g Electric—Chicory **Mr H. Lodge**
4 **EMPIRE JOY,** 5, ch g Sallust—Vivchar **Mr R. Del Rosario**
5 **HALLOW FAIR,** 5, b g Wolver Hollow—Fingers **Mr N. J. Spencer**
6 **KARBAJ,** 6, ch g Arctic Tern (USA)—Jadhringa **Mr A. Kinghorn**
7 **LORD VANITY,** 5, b g Sallust—Chaldea **Mr R. Del Rosario**
8 **MANGO MANILA,** 5, b h Martinmas—Trigamy **Mr R. Del Rosario**
9 **NABIL,** 9, ch g Malinowski (USA)—Clara Petacci (USA) **Mr M. P. Ayres**
10 **PARKBHRIDE,** 4, b g Wolver Hollow—Gulistan **Mr A. Kinghorn**
11 **SCHOOL DINNERS,** 4, ch f Sharpo—Patois **Roldvale Limited**
12 **SHALBANEY,** 6, br g The Brianstan—Aldbury Girl **Mrs L. M. McNalley**
13 **SPORTING WEDNESDAY,** 5, b g Martinmas—Philogyny **Mr M. D. Brunton**
14 **STAR OF THE GLEN,** 4, b c Glenstal (USA)—Bamstar **Mr Ken Orrell**
15 **THORLI,** 7, b g Thatch (USA)—Grey Autumn **Mrs D. J. McKinley**
16 **VAIGLY BLAZED,** 6, ch g Vaigly Great—Monkey Tricks **Mr L. J. Spencer**
17 **WESTERN DANCER,** 9, b g Free State—Polyandrist **Mr L. J. Spencer**

THREE-YEAR-OLDS

18 **ANATROCCOLO,** b f Ile de Bourbon (USA)—Art Deco **Mr G. Killoran**
19 **INDIANA SCARLETT,** ch f Blazing Saddles (AUS)—Littleton Song **Mrs D. J. McKinley**
20 **PHIL-BLAKE,** br c Blakeney—Philogyny **Mr K. W. C. Readings**

TWO-YEAR-OLDS

21 **CROESO,** b c Sayf El Arab (USA)—Coral Princess (Imperial Fling (USA))
22 B g Aragon—Ginnies Pet (Compensation)
23 **GRUNDONIAN,** b c Tina's Pet—Sound Type (Upper Case (USA)) **S. Grundon (Waste) Ltd**
24 B f Nordico (USA)—Raj Kumari (Vitiges (FR))
25 B c Final Straw—Trigamy (Tribal Chief)

Other Owners: Mr G. J. Ayrton-Grime, Mr P. Ayrton-Grime, Mr Colin Drinkwater, Mr John Duggan, Mr C. A. Horgan, Mr Mike Hurley, Mr A. Kaplan, Mr Michael Leon, Mr Ian Thompson.

Lady Rider: Miss D Albion (8-0).

307 MR T. J. HOULBROOKE, Ledbury

Postal: **Bickerton Court, Much Marcle, Ledbury, Herefordshire, HR8 2NR.**
Phone: **MUCH MARCLE (053184) 368 OR (053184) 225**

1 **DAWN BUSTER,** 5, b g Dawn Johnny (USA)—Amber Palace **Mr T. J. Houlbrooke**
2 **ONLY TROUBLE,** 9, b br m Trasi's Son—Kadella **Mr T. J. Houlbrooke**
3 **ROYAL BOUNCER,** 4, b g Royal Palace—Amber Palace **Mr T. J. Houlbrooke**

THREE-YEAR-OLDS

4 **CELTIC ROMPER,** ch g Celtic Cone—Amber Palace **Mr T. J. Houlbrooke**

Jockey (NH): H Davies (w.a.).

Amateur: Mr T Houlbrooke (11-5).

308 MR PAUL HOWLING, Surrey

Postal: **Charlcombe Stables, Off Park Lane, Brook, Nr. Godalming, Surrey, GU8 5LA.**
Phone: **OFFICE (042 879) 4065 HOME (048 68) 24210**

1 **ALL SHOOK UP,** 4, b c All Systems Go—Mary of Scots **Mr C. N. Wright**
2 **AL-TORFANAN,** 6, b g Taufan (USA)—Powder Box **Mr Tor Sandgren**
3 **AQUARIAN PRINCE,** 5, ch g Mansingh (USA)—Princess Story **Miss S. French**
4 **CAYMANIA,** 4, b f Wolver Hollow—Takachiho's Girl **Mr John A. Furze**
5 **CAYMAN QUEEN,** 5, b m Tina's Pet—Harpers Girl **Mr John A. Furze**
6 **CHIEF RUNNER,** 8, b g Arapaho—Waterhen **Mr Andrew Baker**
7 **DEMI JOHN,** 8, br g Alias Smith (USA)—Indian Wells **Mr P. D. Woodward**
8 **GIBBOT,** 5, b g Taufan (USA)—Gaychimes **Mr Barrie Lewis-Ranwell**
9 **INDIAN SET,** 6, b m Windjammer (USA)—Bourges (FR) **Mr John Halsey**
10 **JENDRA,** 4, b f Horage—Mother White **Mr J. W. Harwood**
11 **MRS PEOPLEATER,** 7, b m Ancient Monro—Flea Pit **Mr G. C. H. Lawson**
12 **NIKKI DOW,** 4, b g Tanfirion—Amboselli **Mr T. Melki**
13 **PUNTERS LAD,** 10, br g Home Guard (USA)—Arioza (FR) **Miss S. French**
14 **RUNNING FLUSH,** 8, ch g Lord Gayle (USA)—Hidden Hand (USA) **Mr P. Cook**
15 **SERGEANT MERYLL,** 6, b g Marching On—Mistress Meryll **Mrs Jenine Moodie**
16 **SKI CAPTAIN,** 6, b g Welsh Captain—Miss Nelski **Mr B. P. Dickson**
17 **SNOW WONDER,** 4, gr f Music Boy—Grey Charter **Mr Ronny S. Lamb**

THREE-YEAR-OLDS

18 **ABSOLATUM,** ro c Absalom—Omnia **Mr T. Melki**
19 **BLUEFONTAINE,** b f Rolfe (USA)—Annarise
20 **BRIGARA,** ch f Aragon—Brig of Ayr **Mr K. M. Campbell**
21 **DANCING MAY,** b f Tina's Pet—Breckland Lady **Mr Basheer Kielany**
22 **EVER SO ARTISTIC,** ch c Claude Monet (USA)—Ever So **Mr J. Dwight**
23 **KABAKA,** b f Krayyan—Miss Merryweather **Mr T. Melki**

TWO-YEAR-OLDS

24 Ch c 30/4 Horage—Alldyke (Klondyke Bill)
25 B c 31/3 Tina's Pet—Breckland Lady (Royalty) **Mr F. P. Howling**
26 **BULLET PROOF (IRE),** ch c 28/4 Mazaad—Natija (Vitiges (FR)) **Mr R. Dollar**
27 B c 18/4 Reach—Burglar Tip (Burglar) **Mr H. Reed**
28 **FIVESEVENFIVEO,** br f 25/2 Petong—Miss Timed (Monseigneur (USA)) **Mr Barrie Lewis-Ranwell**
29 B c 20/3 Touching Wood (USA)—Katharina (Frankincense)
30 Ch f 25/3 Mummy's Game—Toccata (USA) (Mr Leader (USA)) **Mr J. Dwight**

MR PAUL HOWLING—continued

Other Owners: Mr B. R. Allen, Mrs Eric Boucher, Mr N. Capon, Mr M. J. Codd, Mr A. J. Cousins, Mr Mark Hollingsworth.

Jockey (Flat): N Adams (7-7).

Apprentice: L Chambers.

Conditional: G A Heaver (10-0).

Amateur: Miss S French.

309 MR G. A. HUBBARD, Woodbridge

Postal: **Worlingworth Hall, Worlingworth, Woodbridge, IP13 7NS.**
Phone: **(072 876)243 OR 554 TELEX 98291 FAX (072 876) 250**

1 **BLUE MARBLE,** 8, ch g Flair Path—Blue Nimbus **Mr G. A. Hubbard**
2 **BRANDESTON,** 5, b g Northern Treat (USA)—Fussy Budget **Mr G. A. Hubbard**
3 **CAMPSEA-ASH,** 6, gr g Rusticaro (FR)—Lady d'Arbanville (FR) **Mr G. A. Hubbard**
4 **CLAY HILL,** 11, ch g Menelek—Vul's Money **Mr G. A. Hubbard**
5 **CLOPTON,** 6, ch g General Assembly (USA)—Senthia **Mr G. A. Hubbard**
6 **CUDDY DALE,** 7, b g Deep Run—Verbana **Mr G. A. Hubbard**
7 **EMSEE-H,** 5, b g Paddy's Stream—Kincsem **Mr G. A. Hubbard**
8 **EYE EYE,** 5, b g Scallywag—My Annassar **Mr G. A. Hubbard**
9 **FIDDLE A LITTLE,** 5, b g Deep Run—Brideweir **Mr G. A. Hubbard**
10 **FRANNIGAN,** 7, b g Candy Cane—Continuity Lass **Mr G. A. Hubbard**
11 **FREDS HEAD,** 8, ch g Callernish—Dreamwell **Mr G. A. Hubbard**
12 **GEE-A,** 11, br g Arapaho—Arctic Daisy **Mr G. A. Hubbard**
13 **GENERAL BEE,** 8, ch g Decent Fellow—Arctic Daisy **Mr G. A. Hubbard**
14 **HALLO MATEY,** 9, b g Al Sirat (USA)—Vulgan's River **Mr G. A. Hubbard**
15 **JAN-RE,** 6, ch g Deep Run—Khalketta **Mr G. A. Hubbard**
16 **JOHN O'DEE,** 7, b g Kambalda—Lady Parkhill **Mr G. A. Hubbard**
17 **KNOCKERRA,** 10, br g Giolla Mear—Mariner's Dash **Mr G. A. Hubbard**
18 **MR PARKER,** 8, br g Al Sirat (USA)—Black Zeta **Mr G. A. Hubbard**
19 **MR-PAW,** 7, b g Deep Run—Khalketta **Mr G. A. Hubbard**
20 **NOTARY-NOWELL,** 4, b g Deep Run—Hamers Flame **Mr G. A. Hubbard**
21 **ON THE TWIST,** 8, b g Callernish—Irish Beauty **Mr G. A. Hubbard**
22 **PARHAM,** 7, b g Pauper—Clonrochenell **Mr G. A. Hubbard**
23 **PRY'S-JOY,** 6, b g Pry—Charmaines Joy **Mr G. A. Hubbard**
24 **REYDON,** 6, ch g Deep Run—Rent A Card **Mr G. A. Hubbard**
25 **SANDY-BRANDY,** 5, gr g Scallywag—Rose of Daveen **Mr G. A. Hubbard**
26 **SCOLE,** 5, b g Deep Run—Verbana **Mr G. A. Hubbard**
27 **SIBTON ABBEY,** 5, b g Strong Gale—Bally Decent **Mr G. A. Hubbard**
28 **SIMMIE,** 5, b g Buckskin (FR)—Miss Dunbrody **Mr G. A. Hubbard**
29 **TANNINGTON,** 7, b g Deep Run—Kertina **Mr G. A. Hubbard**
30 **TURBO KING,** 7, b g Abednego—Ice Folly **Mr G. A. Hubbard**
31 **VAGUELY ARTISTIC,** 8, gr g Vaigly Great—Roanette **Mr G. A. Hubbard**
32 **YALE,** 8, ch g Orchestra—Treasure Boat **Mr G. A. Hubbard**

Apprentices: T Cloke (9-6), B Murphy (9-7).

Lady Rider: Miss G Armytage (8-0).

310 MR J. P. HUDSON, Lambourn

Postal: **Al-Deera Stables, Mile End, Lambourn, Newbury.**
Phone: **TEL (0488) 71485/73161 FAX (0488) 71262**

1 **BALLAD BAY,** 4, ch c Ballad Rock—Swan Upping **Al-Deera Bloodstock Holdings Ltd**
2 **BLAKENEYS GIFT,** 4, gr c Blakeney—Teleflora **Al-Deera Bloodstock Holdings Ltd**
3 **CAREFUL LAD,** 4, b c Precocious—Arenetta **Al-Deera Bloodstock Holdings Ltd**
4 **CREAKE'S PET,** 5, b br h Mummy's Pet—Creake **Al-Deera Bloodstock Holdings Ltd**
5 **GENERAL THOUANY,** 4, b c General Assembly (USA)—Bahrain Star **Al-Deera Bloodstock Holdings Ltd**
6 **GORYTUS STAR,** 4, ch c Gorytus (USA)—Bean Siamsa **Al-Deera Bloodstock Holdings Ltd**
7 **KASHMIRI WIND,** 4, b f Tumble Wind (USA)—Lady Cromer **Al-Deera Bloodstock Holdings Ltd**
8 **LAMBOURN CITIZEN (USA),** 4, ch c L'Emigrant (USA)—Journey (USA) **Al-Deera Bloodstock Holdings Ltd**
9 **LAMBOURN RAJA,** 4, b c Indian King (USA)—Take A Chance (FR) **Al-Deera Bloodstock Holdings Ltd**
10 **LOMOND EXPRESS,** 4, b c Lomond (USA)—Checker Express **Al-Deera Bloodstock Holdings Ltd**
11 **LOVELY EARS,** 4, b f Auction Ring (USA)—Baldritta (FR) **Al-Deera Bloodstock Holdings Ltd**
12 **MAJESTIC GROOM (USA),** 7, ch br h Blushing Groom (FR)—Sweetbidder (USA) **Al-Deera Bloodstock Holdings Ltd**
13 **MARCH GENERATION,** 4, b c Young Generation—Walk By **Al-Deera Bloodstock Holdings Ltd**
14 **NO COSMETIC,** 4, ch f Gorytus (USA)—Face Lift (USA) **Al-Deera Bloodstock Holdings Ltd**
15 **ROCK BALLAD,** 5, b h Ballad Rock—Our Village **Al-Deera Bloodstock Holdings Ltd**
16 **ROYAL DIGGER,** 4, ch c Sharpo—Canasta Girl **Al-Deera Bloodstock Holdings Ltd**
17 **SAGLAWY,** 4, ch c Krayyan—Willow Bird **Al-Deera Bloodstock Holdings Ltd**
18 **SHARP ROMANCE (USA),** 8, ch h Sharpen Up—Sir Ivor's Favour (USA) **Al-Deera Bloodstock Holdings Ltd**
19 **SHEIKH'S PET,** 4, b c Mummy's Pet—Parlais **Al-Deera Bloodstock Holdings Ltd**
20 **SOUND OF VICTORY,** 5, b h Thatching—Bugle Sound **Al-Deera Bloodstock Holdings Ltd**
21 **STORM RUNNER,** 5, b m Runnett—Glimmer of Hope (USA) **Al-Deera Bloodstock Holdings Ltd**
22 **SWEET 'N' SHARP,** 4, ch f Sharpo—Smagiada **Al-Deera Bloodstock Holdings Ltd**
23 **TREAD LIKA PRINCE,** 4, b c Prince Tenderfoot (USA)—Flat Refusal (USA) **Al-Deera Bloodstock Holdings Ltd**
24 **WEST CHINA,** 6, b h Habitat—Sorbus **Al-Deera Bloodstock Holdings Ltd**

THREE-YEAR-OLDS

25 **ABSOLUTELY PERFECT,** ch c Absalom—Petalina **Al-Deera Bloodstock Holdings Ltd**
26 **AKHT MARIAM,** b f Ahonoora—Bahrain Star **Al-Deera Bloodstock Holdings Ltd**
27 **A LITTLE HOT,** gr f Petong—Hot Money **Al-Deera Bloodstock Holdings Ltd**
28 **ALMOOSS,** ch f Sharpo—Bellma (FR) **Al-Deera Bloodstock Holdings Ltd**
29 **ARABIAN SULTAN,** b c Muscatite—Church Bay **Al-Deera Bloodstock Holdings Ltd**
30 **BAY BURSLEM,** b c Burslem—Wild Romance **Al-Deera Bloodstock Holdings Ltd**
31 **BAY TO STAY,** b c Shareef Dancer (USA)—Costly Wave (FR) **Al-Deera Bloodstock Holdings Ltd**
32 **BINT AL ARAB,** ch f Ahonoora—Corcomroe **Al-Deera Bloodstock Holdings Ltd**
33 **BOLD HABIBTI,** b f Never So Bold—Cardinal Palace **Al-Deera Bloodstock Holdings Ltd**
34 **DANCING BRIDE,** ch f Caerleon (USA)—Bahrain Vee (CAN) **Al-Deera Bloodstock Holdings Ltd**
35 **DELMON LASS,** ch f Pas de Seul—Dolmen Ballad **Al-Deera Bloodstock Holdings Ltd**
36 **FAST OPERATIVE,** ch c Absalom—Thorganby Victory **Al-Deera Bloodstock Holdings Ltd**
37 **HAWAIIAN REEF,** b c Henbit (USA)—Raffmarie **Al-Deera Bloodstock Holdings Ltd**
38 **HELLO LADY,** b f Wolverlife—Lady Cromer **Al-Deera Bloodstock Holdings Ltd**
39 **HURRICANE POWER,** br c Wolverlife—Libby Jayne **Al-Deera Bloodstock Holdings Ltd**
40 **JUDICIAL HERO,** b c Law Society (USA)—Prattle On **Al-Deera Bloodstock Holdings Ltd**
41 **MIDSUMMER BREEZE,** b f Tumble Wind (USA)—Pam Story **Al-Deera Bloodstock Holdings Ltd**
42 **NORTHERN PORT,** b c Glenstal (USA)—Cramond **Al-Deera Bloodstock Holdings Ltd**
43 **NORTHERN STREET,** ch c Glenstal (USA)—Moaning Low **Al-Deera Bloodstock Holdings Ltd**
44 **PHARAOH'S DANCER,** b c Fairy King (USA)—Marie Louise **Al-Deera Bloodstock Holdings Ltd**
45 **PHARAOH'S DELIGHT,** b f Fairy King (USA)—Ridge The Times (USA) **Al-Deera Bloodstock Holdings Ltd**
46 **PLEASANT EXHIBIT,** ch c Exhibitioner—Miss Fandango **Al-Deera Bloodstock Holdings Ltd**
47 **RAJPUT RAJAH,** b c Indian King (USA)—Take A Chance (FR) **Al-Deera Bloodstock Holdings Ltd**
48 **ROUSILLON TO BE,** b c Rousillon (USA)—Triple Bar **Al-Deera Bloodstock Holdings Ltd**
49 **SAUB (CAN),** ch c Shadeed (USA)—Overpraised (USA) **Al-Deera Bloodstock Holdings Ltd**
50 **SEXY MOVER,** ch c Coquelin (USA)—Princess Sinna **Al-Deera Bloodstock Holdings Ltd**

311 MR G. A. HUFFER, Newmarket

Postal: **La Grange Racing Stables, Snailwell Road, Newmarket, Suffolk.**
Phone: **(0638) 667997 TELEX-81606 HUFFER G FAX (0638) 661701**

1 **AUTO CONNECTION,** 4, b f Blushing Scribe (USA)—Smitten **Mr N. Iordanou**
2 **CHEROKEE SQUAW,** 4, gr f Rusticaro—Natchez **R. Cutler Esq MRCVS**
3 **ILE DE NISKY,** 4, b c Ile de Bourbon (USA)—Good Lass (FR) **H.R.H. Prince Yazid Saud**
4 **JUST PULHAM,** 5, b g Electric—Lady Acquiesce **C. M. C. Carpets (Norwich) Ltd**
5 **MEL'S ROSE,** 5, ch g Anfield—Ragtime Rose **Mr R. Sabey**
6 **MYSTERY BAND (USA),** 4, b c Dixieland Band (USA)—Lindaria (USA) **H.R.H. Prince Yazid Saud**
7 **R AND B UPDATE,** 4, b g Longleat (USA)—Neringulla **La Grange Ltd**
8 **TOUCH OF WHITE,** 4, ch f Song—Cayla **L. Ellinas**

THREE-YEAR-OLDS

9 **AL ANBA (USA),** b f Lear Fan (USA)—Dacquoise (USA) **La Grange Ltd**
10 **BARFORD LAD,** b c Nicholas Bill—Grace Pool **Barford Bloodstock**
11 **BARHOOM,** ch c Nicholas Bill—Strathclair **La Grange Ltd**
12 **BIDWEAYA (USA),** b f Lear Fan—Sweet Snow **La Grange Ltd**
13 **BONNY ROSA,** b f Dunbeath (USA)—Emmuska (USA) **Mr M. Khalid**
14 **BOTTLES (USA),** b c North Pole (CAN)—Fooling Around **Bottles Restaurant Sheringham**
15 **BULAITH,** gr c Blazing Saddles (AUS)—Travois **La Grange Ltd**
16 **CITRUS KING,** ch c Tender King—Lucy Limelight **L. Ellinas**
17 **CLEAR LIGHT,** ch c Exhibitioner—Beach Light **J. Adams**
18 **CUTTING NOTE (USA),** ch c Diesis—Hasty Key (USA) **H.R.H. Prince Yazid Saud**
19 **DANAS TURN,** ch f His Turn—Bay Foulard **La Grange Ltd**
20 **DANDOON,** b c Rainbow Quest (USA)—Good Lass (FR) **H.R.H. Prince Yazid Saud**
21 **GERAGHTYFIRSTPAST,** b c Kafu—Swan River **M. F. Geraghty Racing Ltd**
22 **GULF REESH,** b c Reesh—Ro **La Grange Ltd**
23 **HABIBTI DALLAL,** b f High Line—Tudor Whisper **La Grange Ltd**
24 **HABIBTI DANA,** ch f Bairn—Southern Swanee **La Grange Ltd**
25 **HALIA MARIE,** b f Formidable—Milk And Honey **H.R.H. Prince Yazid Saud**
26 **HIGH PURSE,** ch c High Line—Petty Purse **H.R.H. Prince Yazid Saud**
27 **JACK TULLY,** b c Mouktar—Fabulous Luba **Mrs Elaine-Ann Papotto**
28 **JARBA,** b f Dalsaan—Idealist **La Grange Ltd**
29 **LA GRANGE MUSIC,** ch c Music Boy—Great Care **La Grange Ltd**
30 **MISHAB,** ch c Local Suitor (USA)—Jeema **La Grange Ltd**
31 **NADI AL QADISIYA,** b c Reesh—Swinging Baby **La Grange Ltd**
32 **POLONEZ PRIMA,** ch g Thatching—Taiga **Mr M. Afdhal**
33 **RAMBO EXPRESS,** b br c New Express—Saul Flower **Mr R. S. Cutler**
34 **REMTHAT NASER,** b f Sharpo—Warning Sound **Sheikh Mohammed Nasser Al Sabeh**
35 **RIPYANA,** ch f Bairn (USA)—Correct Number **La Grange Ltd**
36 **SMART TURN,** b f His Turn—Smashing Pet **La Grange Ltd**
37 **SUNSET DREAMS,** b c Habitat—Pennyweight **La Grange Ltd**
38 **ZARYA,** b f Shelter Half—Ice Blue **B. Butterworth**

TWO-YEAR-OLDS

39 **AHO-REMTHA NOORA (IRE),** b c 13/4 Vision (USA)—Warning Sound (Red Alert) **Imad Al Sagar**
40 B f 2/4 Primo Dominie—Atilla The Hen (Hot Spark)
41 **BALLERINA BAY,** ch f 11/5 Myjinski (USA)—Lady Seville (Orange Bay) **Mrs C. Whitwood**
42 B c 7/6 King of Clubs—Crazyfoot (Luthier (FR)) **Imad Al Sagar**
43 Ch c 17/3 Burslem—Crimson Crest (Pampapaul) **Sheikh Mohammed Nasser Al Sabeh**
44 **DR-MAN,** b c 27/4 Dreams To Reality—Village Idol (Blakeney)
45 B c 29/2 Dreams To Reality—Elbandary (Shirley Heights) **La Grange Ltd**
46 B f 7/4 Ballad Rock—El Pina (Be My Guest (USA)) **Ms Z. A. Hussein**
47 **FARA NOU RIYA (IRE),** b f 14/4 Lomond (USA)—Millieme (Mill Reef (USA)) **Imad Al Sagar**
48 Ch c 23/4 Tate Gallery (USA)—Firdosa (Relic) **Imad Al Sagar**
49 B c 21/4 Dreams To Reality—Hairbrush (USA) (Sir Gaylord) **La Grange Ltd**
50 B f 7/4 Kafu—Hydro Princess (Pitskelly) **Imad Al Sagar**
51 Ch f 10/4 The Noble Player—Phamond (Pharly (FR))
52 B f 10/3 Formidable (USA)—Relatively Sharp (Sharpen Up) **Mr A. Bianchi**
53 **REZA,** gr c 20/2 Superlative—Moon Charter (Runnymede) **Mr Z. A. Hussein**

MR G. A. HUFFER—continued

54 Ch f 30/3 Tender King—Rhumb Line (Right Tack) **Mr A. Bianchi**
55 B f 12/5 Commanche Run—Ribamba (Ribocco)
56 Ch f 1/4 Dreams To Reality—Runaway Girl (FR) (Homeric) **La Grange Ltd**
57 B f 18/4 Dara Monarch—Shenachie (Sheshoon) **Imad Al Sagar**
58 B f 28/4 Kafu—Swan River (Roan Rocket) **Imad Al Sagar**
59 B f 4/5 Prince Sabo—Val Brilliant (USA) (Val de L'Orne (FR))
60 B f 11/3 Sadler's Wells (USA)—Very Bissy (BRZ) (Harken (URU)) **T. Nerses**
61 Ch f 21/3 Salmon Leap (USA)—Villars (Home Guard (USA)) **Imad Al Sagar**
62 Ch f 10/4 Absalom—Vivchar (Huntercombe) **Saleh Al Homeizi**

Other Owners: Mrs A. Al Homezi, Mr Khalid M. Al Khalid, Mr M. Culley, Mr John M. Magnier, Mr Y. A. Matrouk, Mrs H. McConville, Mr Z. Papastylianou, Mr M. Tipper.

Apprentice: Lee Newton (7-0).

312 MR D. T. HUGHES, Kildare

Postal: **Osborne Lodge, Kildare, Co. Kildare, Ireland.**
Phone: **(045) 21490**

1 **AMARI PRINCE,** 5, ch g Rarity—Polyxena (FR) **Michael Ward Thomas**
2 **BALLYCHORUS DREAM,** 9, ch m Over The River—Efficiency **Patrick J. Kinsella**
3 **BOLD GUARD,** 5, ch h Bold Lad (IRE)—Mrs Foodbroker **Mrs Margaret O'Leary**
4 **CORVASSIO,** 6, b m Corvaro (USA)—Naas **Mrs Thomas Matthews**
5 **CROWNING GLORY,** 4, b g Be My Guest (USA)—Princess Tiara **G. J. Keary**
6 **DAVID GARRICK,** 4, b g Seymour Hicks (FR)—Gentle Rain **Patrick Corr**
7 **DOTRECUIG,** 5, b g Welsh Saint—Sallywell **F. Kenny**
8 **FINBAR FUREY,** 5, br g Rymer—Pal Alley **Mark O'Connor**
9 **FOILACLUG FURRY,** 5, b g Furry Glen—Con's Dual Fair **Frank Ward**
10 **GARBALLY PARK,** 7, b g Cut Above—Godwyn **Mrs Maureen Graham**
11 4, B g Good Thyne (USA)—Highland Party **Charles Greyston**
12 **KAM ROYALE,** 6, br g Kambalda—Hopeful Bar **Niall Clarkin**
13 5, B m Glint of Gold—Lady Phoebe (CAN) **John P. Iburg**
14 **LASTING LEGACY,** 6, b m Buckskin (FR)—Arctic Moonshine **Mrs D. T. Hughes**
15 **LEAP FIELD,** 6, b g Monksfield—Maggies Daughter **Mrs D. T. Hughes**
16 **LEOPOLD BLOOM,** 4, b g Le Moss—Barhopper **John P. Iburg**
17 4, B f Furry Glen—Lough Sholin **Mrs T. Doherty**
18 4, B g Flower Robe—Lucifer's Dream **O. B. P. Carroll**
19 **MARKET MOVER,** 4, b c Lord Gayle (USA)—Kavali **Racing Management Services**
20 **MONK'S DELIGHT,** 6, b g Monksfield—Hardyglass Lass **Mrs Pauline Donnelly**
21 **MOON TIGER,** 4, b g High Top—Rivers Maid **Colm O'Connell**
22 **OLDE CRESCENT,** 4, b g Kambalda—Bush Mistress **Beaumont Racing Club**
23 **OPEN THE GATE,** 5, b g The Parson—Etrenne **Mrs T. Doherty**
24 **RATHMICHAEL,** 4, b g Petorius—Always Smiling **Michael Garrigan**
25 **ROYAL RECORD,** 9, br g Bluerullah—Lucifer's Dream **Mrs D. M. Donohue**
26 **SHUIL NA MARA,** 7, ch g Pollerton—Shuil Na Greine **Mr R. A. B. Whittle**
27 **SLANEY SAM,** 7, ch g Crash Course—Foolish Lady **A. Redmond**
28 **TROWBRIDGE (USA),** 4, b g Sauce Boat (USA)—Not A Clue (USA) **P. J. Fitzpatrick**
29 **WINE BROKER,** 5, b g Corvaro (USA)—Peak Time **Mrs J. Nicholson**

THREE-YEAR-OLDS

30 **BAJAN PRINCESS,** b f Head For Heights—Red Rag **Mrs J. R. Mullion**
31 **DECOR LIGHTS,** b f Head For Heights—Corny Story **Mrs W. Fennessy**
32 **FAIRWAY LASS,** b f Montekin—Wurli **Bay Syndicate**
33 B g Strong Gale—Kylogue Lady **A. Delaney**
34 **MERVILLE,** b f Fairy King—Margo's Mink **Stuart Mullion**
35 B g Red Sunset—Royal Daughter **T. Corbett**

MR D. T. HUGHES—continued

36 SELECT TENDER, b c Prince Tenderfoot—Nonnita **Mrs T. J. Cross**
37 TOUCHDOWN, ch f Hard Fought—Forest Fortune **Mrs D. T. Hughes**
38 WATERSTOWN GIRL, ch f Ahonoora—French Falcon **Kathleen Colgan**

TWO-YEAR-OLDS

39 B c 11/5 Exhibitioner—Aria (Saintly Song) **Mrs M. Holleran**
40 B c 7/4 Flash of Steel—Cereal Queen (Oats) **Mrs D. T. Hughes**
41 B f 19/2 Krayyan—Cheri Bond (Relkino) **Conor P. O'Brien**
42 B f 3/5 M Double M (USA)—Crecora (Royal Captive) **Mrs D. T. Hughes**
43 Br f 25/4 Dalsaan—Maypole Hie (Bold Lad (IRE)) **Mrs D. T. Hughes**
44 B c 29/4 Vision (USA)—Tithe Barn (Zarathustra) **Mrs D. T. Hughes**
45 B c 25/5 Mummy's Treasure—Whistling Girl (Whistling Wind) **Martin J. Connolly**

Other Owners: John Byrne, W. Forde.

Jockeys (NH): James D Collins (9-0), C F Swan (8-12).

Apprentices: Richard D Hughes (6-7), Jerome McKeon (6-7).

Conditional: James D Collins (9-0).

Amateurs: Mr J R Banahan (10-5), Mr P J Dreeling (10-6).

313 MR P. HUGHES, Bagenalstown

Postal: **Fenniscourt, Bagenalstown, Co. Carlow, Ireland.**
Phone: **(0503) 21250/21882**

1 ABBEY GLEN, 8, b g Furry Glen—Light Jumper **Mrs G. T. McKey**
2 ASHFORD CONNECTION, 5, b g Ashford (USA)—Italian Connection **T. Donohoe**
3 BALLYMACCON, 7, b g Paddy's Stream—Madam Helen **P. N. Moran**
4 CASTING VOTE (USA), 4, ch f Monteverdi—Myra's Best **P. Hughes**
5 DOLLAR DECADE, 6, b m Black Minstrel—Penny Maes **P. Hughes**
6 4, B g Strong Gale—Fillo **O. R. Cantwell**
7 FURRY BANK, 6, b g Furry Glen—Watch The Birdie **Seamus Hughes**
8 HAPPY ELIZA, 7, b m Laurence O—Whipper Snapper **Mrs T. A. Connolly**
9 INDEX LADY, 6, b m Decent Fellow—Holy Hills **Mrs N. P. Connelly**
10 LOWER STREAM, 7, b g Pitpan—Lady Rex **J. M. Foley**
11 PARKAVOUREEN, 5, b m Deep Run—Poll's Turn **Mrs Brenda Byrne**
12 REMEMBER DON, 5, b m Don—Nimble Rose **M. J. Clancy**
13 RUSTY COIN, 5, ch g Baragoi—Penny Levy **P. Hughes**
14 SKOMAL, 8, br g Beau Charmeur (FR)—Dust Cloud **M. F. O'Sullivan**
15 THE SHAUGHRAUN, 4, b g Alzao (USA)—Light Jumper **Mrs G. T. McKey**

THREE-YEAR-OLDS

16 IRISH TAN, b g Tanfirion—Anglesea Market **Miss Esther Feeney**

TWO-YEAR-OLDS

17 Br c 29/5 Last Tycoon—Tweedling (USA) (Sir Ivor)

Other Owners: N. Carter, Patrick F. Kehoe, John Larkin, G. Meaney.

Jockey (NH): M Duffy (9-7).

Amateurs: Mr J M Fleming (10-0), Mr Seamus O'Donnell (9-7).

314 DON ENRICO INCISA, Coverham

Postal: **Thorngill, Coverham, Middleham, Leyburn, DL8 4TJ.**
Phone: **WENSLEYDALE (0969) 40653 FAX (0969) 40694**

1 **BREGUET**, 7, b m Rouser—Span **Don Enrico Incisa**
2 **BRUSQUE (USA)**, 6, b g Assert—Cecelia (USA) **Don Enrico Incisa**
3 **CALAFURIA**, 4, b f Chief Singer—Cattarina Ginnasi (ITY) **Don Enrico Incisa**
4 **FIESOLE**, 4, ch f Sharpo—Flaming Peace **Don Enrico Incisa**
5 **FILICAIA**, 4, ro f Sallust—Fine Flame **Don Enrico Incisa**
6 **LOCALITY**, 5, b m Lochnager—Declamation **Don Enrico Incisa and Partner**
7 **NUGOLA**, 8, ch m Derrylin—Nell Trent **Don Enrico Incisa**
8 **OAKES DAY**, 5, ch m Derrylin—Persian Breakfast **Don Enrico Incisa**

THREE-YEAR-OLDS

9 **ISOLA FARNESE**, b f Hotfoot—Immaculate Girl **Don Enrico Incisa**
10 **LADY VIOLET**, gr f Superlative—Declamation **Don Enrico Incisa and Partner**
11 **MINSKIP MISS**, ch f Lucky Wednesday—Sofica **Don Enrico Incisa**

Other Owners: Count Federico Radicati.

Jockey (Flat): Kim Tinkler (7-7).

315 MR K. T. IVORY, Radlett

Postal: **Harper Lodge Farm, Harper Lane, Radlett, Hertfordshire, WD7 7HU.**
Phone: **(0923) 855337 or (0836) 606397**

1 **BUNNYLOCH**, 6, b m Lochnager—Bunnycraft **Mr P. J. C. Simmonite**
2 **CARVER LAD**, 5, b g Balinger—Chevulgan **Mr V. E. Randell**
3 **DAWN'S DELIGHT**, 12, b g Dawn Review—Bird of Passage **Mr K. T. Ivory**
4 **FIRST FLUSH**, 4, b c Precocious—Rosananti **Mr Roy Skeggs**
5 **GO BANANA'S**, 9, b g Young Generation—Miss Lucian **Mr K. T. Ivory**
6 **JOSHYKIN**, 4, b g Montekin—Miss Annie **Mr K. T. Ivory**
7 **JUST CRUISE**, 4, ch c Milford—Glenside Lady **Mr Michael Howard**
8 **MAJORITY HOLDING**, 5, b g Mandrake Major—Kirkby **Wallace Farms (Stud) Ltd**
9 **SWING LUCKY**, 5, b g Swing Easy (USA)—Bounding **Mrs L. S. Ward**
10 **YEOMAN FORCE**, 4, b c Crofter (USA)—High Voltage **Mrs Sarah Lee-Robinson**

THREE-YEAR-OLDS

11 **IVORY'S OF RADLETT**, b g Alzao (USA)—La Croisette **K. T. Ivory Limited**
12 **MYFONTAINE**, b c Persepolis (FR)—Mortefontaine (FR) **Mr K. T. Ivory**
13 **SPRING HIGH**, b f Miami Springs—High Voltage **Mrs P. A. Brown**
14 **YEOMAN BID**, b g Longleat (USA)—Bounding **Yeoman Bloodstock Ltd**

Other Owners: Mrs Thomas Buffett, Mr Peter Goy, Mr L. H. J. Ward.

Jockey (Flat): R Cochrane (w.a.).

Jockey (NH): Mark Richards (10-0).

Apprentice: C Scally.

Amateur: Mr D Marshall.

316 MR C. F. C. JACKSON, Malvern

Postal: **Whitehouse Farm, Tanhouse Lane, Cradley, Malvern. Worcestershire.**
Phone: **(0886) 880463**

1 **BOLD CADET,** 5, b g Sandhurst Prince—Bold Lady **Classical Enterprises Ltd**
2 **CAROLS BELLE,** 7, ch m Ballymore—Love For Money **Mr C. F. C. Jackson**
3 **DARK MERCHANT,** 6, ch m Irish Rifle—Princess Adventure VII **Mr Joe Lyons**
4 **GAELGOIR,** 6, gr g Godswalk (USA)—Sagosha **Mr D. Craddock**
5 **MODERN MUSIC,** 11, br g You Sir—Ceili Mor **Mr C. F. C. Jackson**
6 **RONALD IVOR,** 4, b c Bold Lad (IRE)—Lady Probus **Mr C. F. C. Jackson**
7 **TANCRED WALK,** 11, b g Farm Walk—Darling Do **Mr D. J. Pardy**
8 **THE BUCKWHEAT,** 9, b g Golden Love—Autumn Pearl **Mr S. Nixon**
9 **VISCOUNT TULLY,** 5, b g Blakeney—Cymbal **Fumel Securities S.A.**
10 **ZALINA,** 4, b f Tyrnavos—Cymbal **Mr C. F. C. Jackson**

Other Owners: Mr R. H. Atkins, Mr K. J. Maile, Mr A. Perry.

Jockeys (Flat): A McGlone (w.a.), W Newnes (w.a.).

Jockey (NH): J Bryan (10-0).

317 MR F. S. JACKSON, Gonalston

Postal: **Holme Farm, Gonalston, Nottinghamshire.**
Phone: **(0602) 663832 OR 663970**

1 4, B g Boco (USA)—Hannah Princess **Mr F. S. Jackson**
2 **LADYWOOD LAD,** 8, b g Country Retreat—Mannion's Queen **Mr F. S. Jackson**
3 **MAX CLOWN,** 7, b g Cawston's Clown—Maxine's Here **Mr F. S. Jackson**
4 **SCOTGAVOTTE (FR),** 4, b f Dunbeath (USA)—French Minuet (FR) **Mr F. S. Jackson**
5 **SUSSEX OVERSEAS,** 8, b g Anax—Go Perrys **Mr F. S. Jackson**

THREE-YEAR-OLDS

6 Ch f Dawn Johnny (USA)—Hannah Princess **Mr F. S. Jackson**
7 Gr f Dawn Johnny (USA)—Porto Louise **Mr F. S. Jackson**

TWO-YEAR-OLDS

8 Gr c Dawn Johnny (USA)—Porto Louise (Porto Bello) **Mr F. S. Jackson**

318 MRS V. S. JACKSON, Ponteland

Postal: **Ogle Flatts, Ogle, Ponteland, Newcastle Upon Tyne, NE20 OAU.**
Phone: **(0670) 75388**

1 **BUSH GUIDE,** 14, b g Flatbush—Guide Post **Mrs V. S. Jackson**
2 **PARK SLAVE,** 8, b g Park Row—Cool Date **Mrs V. S. Jackson**

Lady Rider: Mrs Valerie Jackson (10-0).

319 MR C. J. JAMES, Newbury

Postal: **Mask Cottage, East Garston, Newbury, Berkshire.**
Phone: **GREAT SHEFFORD (0488 39) 280**

1 **ALCANDO,** 4, b f Alzao (USA)—Kaniz **Mr Nicholas Cowan**
2 **BORRETO,** 6, b br g Treboro (USA)—Fiji Express **Mr C. James**
3 **CAPULET,** 7, b h Henbit (USA)—Lady Juliet (USA) **Mr Ian Fry**
4 **DEXTROUS LADY,** 4, b f Vital Season—Skilla **Mr R. A. Shaw**
5 **EVE FROM EDEN,** 7, ch m Riboboy (USA)—Fair Saint **Major R. P. Thorman**
6 **FREMONT BOY,** 8, b h Ahonoora—Shoshoni Girl (USA) **Miss S. Previte**
7 **GISSMO,** 5, ch g Native Bazaar—Torlonia **Mr Brian Trotman**
8 **GREAT AIM,** 4, b f Great Nephew—Perfect Aim **Mr Gordon Comben**
9 **HIGH TILT,** 4, b f My Dad Tom (USA)—Torlonia **Mr D. Smith (Benson)**
10 **NOBLE PATROL,** 16, ch g Golden Dipper—Ermine Socks **Mr C. James**
11 **RUSINGA ISLAND,** 4, ch f Oats—Gretta's Girl **Mrs J. N. Humphreys**
12 **SHARP 'N SHINE,** 4, b g Sharpen Up—Repetitious **Comben Thoroughbreds**

THREE-YEAR-OLDS

13 **ALCANDANCE,** b f Alzao (USA)—Dancing Sun **Mr Nicholas Cowan**
14 **ALCHIEA,** b f Alzao (USA)—Dancing Lass **Mr Ronnie Wood**
15 **MRS SKINNER,** ch f Electric—Equal Chance **Mr A. Emrys Davies**

TWO-YEAR-OLDS

16 Ch f 30/4 Coquelin (USA)—Djory (USA) **Mr C. James**
17 B f 30/4 Martinmas—Khatti Hawk **Mr Nick Townsend**
18 Ch c 19/4 Glenstal (USA)—Quite Sweet **Mrs J. M. Browne**
19 Ch f 29/5 Thatching—Red Roman **Mr Nicholas Cowan**
20 Ch f 11/4 Hotfoot—Trackalley **Mr C. James**

Other Owners: Mrs Judith Comben, Mr A. Shaw.

320 MR M. B. C. JAMES, Whitchurch

Postal: **Warren Stables, Prees Heath, Whitchurch, Salop.**
Phone: **(0948) 4067**

1 **ANBAK (USA),** 5, ch g Riverman (USA)—Virgin (FR) **Mr J. Mansfield**
2 **COMPOSER,** 12, ch h Music Boy—Contadina **Mr P. A. Thomas**
3 **DANE ROSE,** 4, b f Full of Hope—Roella **Mr C. H. Lorne**
4 4, Ch c Ring Bidder—Elfen Queen **Mr R. Darlington**
5 **FALCONWOOD,** 4, b c Sharpo—Treeline **Mr P. A. Thomas**
6 **GLOSS,** 5, b g Town And Country—Star Display **Miss Sheila Lavery**
7 **INDEBAR TWO,** 9, b m Java Sea—Indebar **Mr A. Goold**
8 **MIAMI PRIDE,** 4, b f Miami Springs—Gwynpride **Mr J. Mansfield**
9 **MISSILE MAGGIE,** 5, b m Cruise Missile—Big Maggie **Mr F. Holbrook**
10 **POLEMISTIS,** 11, b g Hittite Glory—Swing The Cat **Mr B. Sinners**
11 **PURE-LITE,** 5, b m Imperial Fling (USA)—The Huyton Girls **Mr John C. Harrison**

TWO-YEAR-OLDS

12 B f Dubassoff (USA)—Jubilee Joy (Burglar) **Mr R. Darlington**
13 Ch f Brotherly (USA)—The Huyton Girls (Master Sing) **Mr J. C. Harrison**

Other Owners: Mr T. Roberts.

Jockey (Flat): Sharron James (8-6).

Jockey (NH): Sharron James (9-7).

Lady Rider: Miss Elaine James (9-0).

321 MRS M. C. JAMES, Cheltenham

Postal: **Cotswold Stud, Lower Slaughter, Cheltenham, Gloucestershire, GL54 2HP.**
Phone: **(0451) 20288 TELEX 838779 FINEWD G FAX (0451) 20993**

1 **BASSE TERRE**, 6, b g Mill Reef (USA)—Land Ho **Mrs Mary James**
2 **CARTOONESS (USA)**, 5, b m Achieved—Silly Symphony **Mrs Mary James**
3 **TEARFUL REUNION**, 6, b m Pas de Seul—Sweet Eliane **Mrs Mary James**

322 MR M. A. JARVIS, Newmarket

Postal: **Kremlin House Stables, Fordham Road, Newmarket, Suffolk, CB8 7AQ.**
Phone: **(0638) OFFICE 661702 HOME 662519 TELEX 817786 (JARVIS G) FAX 667018**

1 **ARDROSS BEST**, 4, ch c Ardross—Do Your Best **Elisha Holding**
2 **BEAUMOOD**, 4, br c Jalmood (USA)—Falcon Berry **Mr V. Raibin**
3 **CARROLL HOUSE**, 5, ch h Lord Gayle (USA)—Tuna **Mr Zenya Yoshida**
4 **CHELSEA GIRL**, 4, b f Pas de Seul—Buffy **Mr Michael Hill**
5 **DIACO**, 5, b g Indian King (USA)—Coral Cave **Mr J. R. Good**
6 **FEDORIA**, 4, b c Formidable (USA)—Zepha **Mr Mark Christofi**
7 **L'AQUINO**, 5, ch m Kings Lake (USA)—Willowy **Mr J. R. Good**
8 **PRORUTORI (USA)**, 4, b c Providential—Miss Flower Belle (USA) **Mr Antonio Balzarini**
9 **RELEKTO**, 8, b g Relko—Heaven Knows **Mrs Gay Jarvis**
10 **TOP DREAM**, 5, br h High Top—Pleasant Dream **Mr Raymond Anderson Green**

THREE-YEAR-OLDS

11 **ACQUISITION**, b g Petorius—Steady The Buffs **T. G. Holdcroft (Motors) Ltd**
12 **ALOSAILI**, ch c Kris—Vaison La Romaine **Sheikh Ahmed Al Maktoum**
13 **BASENITE**, br f Mansingh (USA)—Iridium **Mr T. G. Warner**
14 **CHATEAU DE BERNE (USA)**, b c Fit To Fight (USA)—Liberally Laced (USA) **Mr W. F. Muddyman**
15 **COSMIC PRINCESS**, b f Fairy King (USA)—Come True (FR) **Mr Bob Young**
16 **DEVA SPRINGS**, b f Elegant Air—Precious Jade **Mr F. C. T. Wilson**
17 **FRONT LINE ROMANCE**, ch f Caerleon (USA)—Bottom Line **Mr Jerry Sung**
18 **GILT DIMENSION**, b c Dara Monarch—Nastassia (FR) **G. E. Racing**
19 **GILT PREFERENCE**, b c Pitskelly—Mandolin **G. E. Racing**
20 **GILT PREMIUM**, b c Precocious—Nonabella **G. E. Racing**
21 **HARBOUR BAR (USA)**, b c Cure The Blues (USA)—Little Deep Water **Mr Antonio Balzarini**
22 **INDIAN FASHION (USA)**, ch f General Holme (USA)—Your Place Or Mine (USA) **Mr Gregory A. Peters**
23 **KINKAJOO**, b f Precocious—Skyey **Mrs G. M. Peel**
24 **LADY OF PERSIA (USA)**, ch f Persian Bold—Tants **Mr Gregory A. Peters**
25 **MORNINGHASBROKEN**, ch f Ballad Rock—Dawn Star **Mr G. J. H. Carroll**
26 **NEGATORY (USA)**, ch c Secreto (USA)—Negation (USA) **Sheikh Ahmed Al Maktoum**
27 **ODILEX**, b g Mummy's Pet—Odile **Mr T. G. Warner**
28 **PHOTO CALL**, b f Chief Singer—Photo **Mr J. R. Good**
29 **PRIMO GENITO**, ch g Vaigly Great—Arbor Lane **Mr A. A. Papotto**
30 **PRINCE VALIYAR**, b g Valiyar—Lusitanica **Mr J. M. Poland**
31 **RAZZBERRY (FR)**, br f Be My Guest (USA)—Wool Princess (FR) **Mr G. J. H. Carroll**
32 **ROYAL PASSION**, ch f Ahonoora—Courtesy Call **Mr J. R. Good**
33 B c Mummy's Pet—Shadow Play **Mr T. G. Warner**
34 **SKIPPER TO BILGE**, b c Night Shift (USA)—Upper Deck **Crescent (UK) Ltd**
35 **STORMY BELLE**, ch f Tumble Wind (USA)—Never So Lovely **Mr K. H. Fischer**
36 **TARTAR'S BOW**, b c Gorytus (USA)—Sweet Eliane **Mr R. L. Capon**
37 **TEODORICO**, b c Simply Great (FR)—Tin Goddess **Mr G. Mazza**
38 **TERNIMUS (USA)**, ch c Arctic Tern (USA)—Lustrious (USA) **Mr J. Goodman**
39 **THE DARA QUEEN**, b f Dara Monarch—Ladyfish **Mr G. J. H. Carroll**
40 **TREBLE EIGHT**, ch c Kings Lake (USA)—Persian Polly **Mrs P. L. Yong**
41 **TRISTAN'S COMET**, br c Sayf El Arab (USA)—Gleneagle **Mr K. G. Powter**
42 **VAIN SEARCH (USA)**, gr f Vigors (USA)—Hunt The Thimble (USA) **Mr J. R. Carroll**
43 **VIRGIN GORDA**, b f Law Society (USA)—Betsy Bay (FR) **Mr L. Monaldi**
44 **WINDMILL PRINCESS**, b f Gorytus (USA)—Cley **Mr Bob Young**
45 **ZANONI**, b c Mummy's Pet—Princely Maid **Mr T. G. Warner**

MR M. A. JARVIS—continued

TWO-YEAR-OLDS

46 **ANOTHER BOB (USA),** b br c 22/3 Roberto (USA)—
Spicy Stuff (USA) (Reviewer (USA)) **Mr Antonio Balzarini**
47 **BDOORE (IRE),** b f 4/3 Petoski—Princess Biddy (Sun Prince) **Sheikh Ahmed Al Shaffar**
48 Ch c 10/4 Jester—Beach Light (Bustino) **Lord Harrington**
49 **CLAREMONT BOY,** b c 1/2 Another Realm—Lady Eton (Le Dieu d'Or) **Mr M. A. Jarvis**
50 **DALE HILL IDEA,** b c 28/5 Alleging (USA)—Late Idea (Tumble Wind) **Manjina Ltd**
51 B f 15/2 Naskra (USA)—Dream Play (USA) (Blushing Groom (FR)) **Mr G. J. H. Carroll**
52 Ch c 4/4 Flash of Steel—Ever So (Mummy's Pet) **Mr M. Bailey**
53 **GOLDLINE SEEKER,** b c 12/2 Damister (USA)—Bottom Line (Double Jump) **Mr Jerry Sung**
54 B f 29/4 Bustino—Gold Rupee (Native Prince) **Mr Michael Hill**
55 **HELENSVILLE (IRE),** ch f 27/4 Horage—Calaloo Sioux (USA) (Our Native (USA)) **Lord Harrington**
56 **HIGH SAVANNAH,** ch f 5/5 Rousillon (USA)—Stinging Nettle (Sharpen Up) **Mrs Mary Taylor**
57 **IMCO AFFIRMATION (IRE),** b c 18/3 Glow (USA)—Affirmation (FR) (Affirmed (USA)) **Mr Antonio Balzarini**
58 **IMCO DOUBLE (IRE),** ch c 14/2 Double Schwartz—Cupids Hill (Sallust) **Mr Antonio Balzarini**
59 **IRON RED,** b f 19/3 Never So Bold—Rosie Pug (Mummy's Pet) **Mr R. P. Marchant**
60 B f 17/2 Glenstal (USA)—Lady Regrets (FR) (Sir Gaylord) **Mr J. R. Good**
61 B c 13/2 Trojan Fen—Little Loch Broom (Reform)
62 **MANDIKA,** b c 10/3 Flash of Steel—Bushti Music (Bustino) **Mr R. L. Capon**
63 **MAZARINE BLUE,** b f 4/2 Bellypha—Maiden Pool (Sharpen Up) **Mrs Mary Taylor**
64 **MEZAAJ (USA),** br c 24/3 Shadeed (USA)—Honor To Her (USA) (Sir Ivor) **Sheikh Ahmed Al Maktoum**
65 **MIRANDA JAY,** b br f 3/2 Night Shift (USA)—Assisi (Habitat) **Crescent (UK) Ltd**
66 Ch c 26/3 Lomond (USA)—Moonscape (Ribero) **Mr Raymond Anderson Green**
67 **MUTHHIL (IRE),** b c 6/5 Green Desert (USA)—Cockade (Derring-Do) **Sheikh Ahmed Al Maktoum**
68 **OFF STUMP,** b g 8/2 Forzando—Lady's Walk (Pall Mall) **Mr C. Buckle**
69 **OLFA,** b f 27/1 Rousillon (USA)—Wassl's Sister (Troy) **Sheikh Ahmed Al Maktoum**
70 **PARISIAN EXPRESS (FR),** br f 18/2 Siberian Express—Parisana (FR) (Gift Card (FR)) **Mr A. A. Papotto**
71 Ch f 18/4 Spectacular Bid (USA)—Pleasant Flight (USA) (Bold Ruler) **Mr G. J. H. Carroll**
72 **PRIME PROSPECT,** b c 7/3 Damister (USA)—Sunningdale Queen (Gay Fandango (USA)) **Mrs P. L. Yong**
73 **RIVAL BID (USA),** b c 1/3 Cannonade (USA)—Love Triangle (USA) (Nodouble (USA)) **Mr David Altham**
74 **SAVOYARD,** b c 14/3 Sayf El Arab (USA)—Ballad Island (Ballad Rock) **Lady Butt**
75 **SHEROOG (USA),** b f 28/2 Shareef Dancer (USA)—Fall Aspen (USA) (Pretense) **Sheikh Ahmed Al Maktoum**
76 Gr f 29/2 Godswalk (USA)—Silent Sail (Aglojo) **Mr J. R. Good**
77 Ch c 5/5 Kings Lake (USA)—Sly Wink (Song) **Mr L. Monaldi**
78 Ch c 7/3 Fighting Fit (USA)—Sonseri (Prince Tenderfoot (USA)) **Mr L. Monaldi**
79 B c 13/3 Taufan (USA)—Stop The Cavalry (Relko) **Mr Michael Hill**
80 **THORNBURY (IRE),** b f 15/2 Tender King—Glastonbury (Grundy) **Lord Harrington**
81 **TOP SHEREEK,** b c 24/3 High Top—Shereeka (Shergar) **Sheikh Ahmed Al Maktoum**
82 **WILD WALTZ (USA),** b br c 23/2 Wild Again (USA)—
Waltz Me Sue (USA) (Olden Times) **Mr Antonio Balzarini**

Other Owners: Mr C. J. Barker, Mr J. D. W. Birts, Sir Kenneth Butt, Mrs J. R. Collins, Mr A. R. G. Else, Mrs P. Good, Mr David Humphreys, Mr A. J. Kelly, Mr P. A. Lee, Sqdn Ldr R. A. Milsom, Mr P. Newton, Mr W. R. H. Reid, Mr M. Roper, Mrs M. Sharkey Kelly, Mr H. Turner.

Jockeys (Flat): B Marcus (8-1), B Raymond (8-5, w.a.).

Lady Rider: Mrs Gay Jarvis (9-0).

323 MR W. JARVIS, Newmarket

Postal: **Phantom House Stables, Fordham Road, Newmarket, Suffolk, CB8 7AA.**
Phone: **NEWMARKET HOME-(0638) 662677 OFFICE-(0638) 669873 FAX (0638) 667328**

1 **BRIGGSCARE,** 4, b g Chief Singer—Magonis **Mr F. W. Briggs**
2 **GREEN'S CANALETTO (USA),** 4, b c Hagley (USA)—Gaucherie (USA) **Richard Green (Fine Paintings)**

MR W. JARVIS—continued

3 **LOCH DUICH,** 4, ch c Kris—Sleat **Sir David Wills**
4 **LOVELY FLOWER,** 4, ch f Hello Gorgeous (USA)—Apricot Rose **Tasso Syndicate**
5 **PELORUS,** 5, b h High Top—St Isabel **Mr James H. Slade**
6 **PODRIDA,** 4, gr f Persepolis (FR)—Pot Pourri **Lord Howard de Walden**
7 **SCARLET VEIL,** 4, b f Tyrnavos—Red Velvet **Mr Hugh McCalmont and Mr P. McCalmont**
8 **SUGAR PLUM FAIRY,** 4, b f Sadler's Wells (USA)—Epithet **Mrs S. Page**
9 **TAFILA,** 4, ch f Adonijah—Brigata **Mrs David Butter and Mr N. H. Phillips**
10 **TEMPERING,** 4, b g Kris—Mixed Applause (USA) **Lord Howard de Walden**
11 **WELD,** 4, ch c Kalaglow—Meliora **Lord Howard de Walden**

THREE-YEAR-OLDS

12 **ACROW LORD,** b c Milford—Miss Acrow **Mr W. A. De Vigier**
13 **AKAROA,** ch c Kalaglow—St Isadora **Mr James H. Slade**
14 **AMIENS,** b g Noalto—Two Stroke **Mr and Mrs R. Payne**
15 **BENAZIR,** b f High Top—Crusader's Dream **Mr J. M. Greetham**
16 **COMHAIL (USA),** ch f Nodouble (USA)—Bronislava **Mr D. Macrae**
17 **CONTRACT LAW (USA),** b c Lypheor—Permissible Tender (USA) **Kennet Valley Thoroughbreds Ltd**
18 **DIAMOND HILL (USA),** b g Temperence Hill (USA)—Avant Coureur (USA) **Mr Thomas T. S. Liang**
19 **DRUM SERGEANT,** b c Elegant Air—Cala-Vadella **Kennet Valley Thoroughbreds Ltd**
20 **EAVESDROP,** ch f Final Straw—Queens Message **Mr and Mrs P. D. Player**
21 **FAR TOO SMART,** br f Trojan Fen—Bonnie Bess **Mr P. Graeme Wedgwood**
22 **FETLAR,** ch f Pharly (FR)—Reuval **Sir David Wills**
23 **GREEN'S GUARDI (USA),** b g Hagley (USA)—Carobreuse (FR) **Richard Green (Fine Paintings)**
24 **LAND AFAR,** b c Dominion—Jouvencelle **Mrs F. G. Allen**
25 **LA STUPENDA,** ch f Chief Singer—Lap of Honour **Mr T. C. Blackwell**
26 **LOVE RETURNED,** b f Taufan (USA)—Miss Loving **Mr J. M. Ratcliffe**
27 **MARISTON MAIDEN,** b f Night Shift (USA)—Rapidus **The Hon. H. M. Lopes**
28 **PAPPAGALLO,** ch c Lomond (USA)—Glasshouse (AUS) **Mr G. E. Sangster**
29 **RED FORMATION,** b f Formidable (USA)—Red Velvet **Mr Hugh McCalmont and Mr P. McCalmont**
30 **REGINA ROYALE (USA),** br f Eternal Prince (USA)—Lizzie's Light (USA) **Mr D. Baigler**
31 **SARANTE,** ch f Bold Lad (IRE)—Billante (USA) **Mrs James McAllister**
32 **SKERRYVORE,** ch f Kalaglow—Highland Light **Lord Howard de Walden**
33 **SPOOF,** b f Precocious—Thimblerigger **Mr T. C. Blackwell**
34 **SUPREME DANCER (FR),** b g Alzao (USA)—Supreme Solar **Richard Green (Fine Paintings)**
35 **TESORA,** ch f Busted—Savahra **Mrs Shona St. George**
36 **TINKERBIRD,** b f Music Boy—Quaranta **Mr Michael Worth**
37 **TRANSCRIBER (USA),** b c Transworld (USA)—Scrabbler (USA) **Mr Thomas T. S. Liang**
38 **VALCENA,** ch f Glint of Gold—Baltimore Belle **Mr and Mrs A. R. Boyd-Rochfort**
39 **ZENELLA,** b f Precocious—Zepha **Mrs S. A. Randall**

TWO-YEAR-OLDS

40 **ATTADALE,** b c 30/4 Ardross—Marypark (Charlottown) **Sir David Wills**
41 **BLUE CASHMERE (USA),** b f 29/2 Secreto (USA)—
Bruces Blue Lou (USA) (Storm Bird (CAN)) **Mr Fahd Salman**
42 B f 18/4 Night Shift (USA)—Brittle Grove (Bustino) **Richard Green (Fine Paintings)**
43 **CATUNDRA (IRE),** ch f 18/3 Far North (CAN)—Tis A Kitten (USA) (Tisab (USA)) **Mr Michael Worth**
44 B c 7/3 Elegant Air—Chase Paperchase (Malinowski (USA)) **Mr J. Bray**
45 B c 10/4 Diesis—Chickery Chick (USA) (Hatchet Man (USA)) **Kennet Valley Thoroughbreds**
46 **DEDICATED,** b c 18/4 Valiyar—Mischiefmaker (Calpurnius) **Mr D. B. Thompson**
47 **DESERT DITTY,** b f 26/1 Green Desert (USA)—Royal Loft (Homing) **The Hon. H. M. Lopes**
48 **DOSSERI,** b c 15/5 Bellypha—Hants (Exbury) **Mr Fahd Salman**
49 B f 17/2 Absalom—Double Stitch (Wolver Hollow) **Sir Rupert Mann**
50 **ELEVATED LANDING,** b f 4/4 Shirley Heights—Bright Landing (Sun Prince) **Mr J. W. Rowles**
51 **ENCHANTED FOREST,** b f 14/4 Reach—Migiyas (Kings Lake (USA)) **Mr Fahd Salman**
52 **FANCY ME,** b f 28/4 Dunbeath (USA)—
Friendly Thoughts (USA) (Al Hattab (USA)) **Mr H. J. W. Steckmest and Mrs Sue Davis**
53 **FARSI,** gr c 23/1 Nishapour (FR)—Pot Pourri (Busted) **Lord Howard de Walden**
54 **GALAXY RANGER,** b c 21/2 Caerleon (USA)—Fallen Rose (Busted) **Mr Jerry Sung**
55 **GENPAT,** b f 25/4 Mashhor Dancer (USA)—
Russeting (Mummy's Pet) **Richard Green and Mr D. B. Thompson**

MR W. JARVIS—continued

56 **GREEN'S TRILOGY (USA),** b c 22/3 Lyphard's Wish (FR)—
Capitol Caper (USA) (Senate Whip (USA)) **Richard Green (Fine Paintings)**
57 **IN OTHER WORDS (USA),** b c Vaguely Noble—
Halo Again (USA) (Halo (USA)) **Richard Green (Fine Paintings)**
58 **KAIKOURA,** br f 1/2 Full On Aces (AUS)—Jandell (NZ) (Shifnal) **Mr James H. Slade**
59 **KRIUS,** b c Shirley Heights—Meliora (Crowned Prince (USA)) **Lord Howard de Walden**
60 **LA STRAVAGANZA,** b f Slip Anchor—St Isadora (Lyphard (USA)) **Lord Howard de Walden**
61 **LEGION OF HONOUR,** b c 22/2 Ahonoora—Shehana (USA) (The Minstrel (CAN)) **Mr Fahd Salman**
62 **LITERARY SPARK,** ch c 20/4 Kalaglow—My Lady Muriel (USA) (Visible (USA)) **Lensfield Racing**
63 **LIVING IMAGE,** b c 19/2 Taufan (USA)—Visible Form (Formidable (USA)) **Mr H. J. Joel**
64 **MANAGEMENT,** b c 12/3 Faustus (USA)—
Rosana Park (Music Boy) **Mr R. C. Thompson and Mr D. B. Thompson**
65 **MILITARY TATTOO (IRE),** b c 11/2 Lomond (USA)—Tenea (Reform) **Mr B. V. Sangster**
66 **MILLY BLACK (IRE),** b f 8/4 Double Schwartz—Milly Lass (FR) (Bold Lad (USA)) **Mr and Mrs M. Page**
67 **NIMIGEN,** b c 6/2 Niniski (USA)—Petty Purse (Petingo) **A. F. Budge (Equine) Ltd**
68 **PHERON,** b c Pharly (FR)—Magic Flute (Tudor Melody) **Lord Howard de Walden**
69 **PORT,** b f Blakeney—Historical Fact (Reform) **Mr J. M. Greetham**
70 **RED CRESCENT,** b c 4/2 Red Sunset—Temple Heights (Shirley Heights) **Mr J. Garfield and Mr A. Hitchins**
71 **REGAL LOOK (IRE),** b f 25/4 Vision (USA)—Latin Guest (Be My Guest (USA)) **Cheveley Park Stud**
72 **REGAL VALUE,** b c 18/4 Nomination—Be Royal (Royal Pale) **A. F. Budge (Equine) Ltd**
73 **REGENT'S FOLLY (IRE),** ch f 5/3 Touching Wood (USA)—
Regent's Fawn (CAN) (Vice Regent (CAN)) **The Hon. H. M. Lopes**
74 **SEA GODDESS,** b f Slip Anchor—Elysian (Northfields (USA)) **Lord Howard de Walden**
75 **SHADOW THEM,** gr c 31/5 Absalom—River Chimes (Forlorn River) **Mr Bernard Hathaway**
76 **SLOVENIA (IRE),** b c 4/4 Slip Anchor—Cider Princess (Alcide) **A. F. Budge (Equine) Ltd**
77 **STRIMMER,** ch c Sharpo—Toppeshamme (USA) (Topsider (USA)) **Lord Howard de Walden**
78 **STYRIAN (USA),** b c Storm Bird (CAN)—Vachti (FR) (Crystal Palace (FR)) **Lord Howard de Walden**
79 **TERESA,** ch f 3/3 Superlative—Astonishing (Jolly Good) **Mrs E. G. Lambton**
80 **TIBBY HEAD (IRE),** b c 3/4 Lyphard's Special—Deer Park (FR) (Faraway Son (USA)) **Mrs Nigel Farmer**
81 B c 9/3 Sadler's Wells (USA)—Tifrums (Thatch (USA)) **Mr A. Smurfitt**
82 **TREMENDOUS (USA),** b c 10/2 Spectacular Bid (USA)—
Returned Conqueror (USA) (Danzig (USA)) **Mr Fahd Salman**
83 **TRISETTE,** ch f 20/3 Adonijah—Canasta Girl (Charlottesville) **Mrs David Butter and Mr N. H. Phillips**
84 **VELOCITY,** b f Glint of Gold—Volida (Posse (USA)) **Mr R. E. Waugh**
85 B f 24/5 Marfa (USA)—Volatile Gal (USA) (Explodent (USA)) **Mr M. S. H. Hartley**
86 B c 3/3 Thatching—Waveguide (Double Form) **Kennet Valley Thoroughbreds**
87 **WEEKDAY CROSS (IRE),** b c 26/3 Taufan (USA)—Isoldes Tower (Balliol) **Mrs F. G. Allen**
88 **WET WILBUR (USA),** b c 22/4 Air Forbes Won (USA)—
Princess Aurora (USA) (Grey Dawn II) **Mrs Gwen Boyle**

Other Owners: Mr D. A. Beaumont, Mr R. A. C. Furber, Mr Peter Hart, Mr F. E. Harvey, Miss V. H. Owen, Mr M. A. Shenfield, Mr J. F. Slade, Miss K. A. Slade, Captain R. M. Smyly.

Jockeys (Flat): Bruce Raymond (8-5), M Tebbutt (8-4).

Apprentices: S J Hobbs (7-10), B Tervit (7-10).

324 MR J. M. JEFFERSON, Malton

Postal: **Newstead Cottage Stables, Norton, Malton, North Yorkshire.**
Phone: **(0653) 697225**

1 **ANOTHER NICK,** 4, ch g Nicholas Bill—Another Move **Mr A. Fawcett**
2 **ASTURIAS,** 7, b g Artaius (USA)—Tanaka **Mrs A. Dawson**
3 **CHOPYATT,** 5, b g Kabour—Argostone **David Scott**
4 **CLIPPERS DREAM,** 7, b g Heroic Air—Robbies Girl **Mrs M. E. Dixon**
5 **MORE DISTINCT,** 6, b m Class Distinction—Coliemore **Yorkshire Racing Club Owners Group**

MR J. M. JEFFERSON—continued

6 **OUTSTANDING BILL**, 4, ch g Nicholas Bill—Hardwick Amber **Mr J. C. Hibbitt**
7 **POSSETIVE PLANT**, 5, ch g Posse (USA)—Sakeena **Mrs Jock Armstrong**
8 **SCHIEHALLION**, 5, ch m Scallywag—Hardwick Sun **The Caledonian Racing Club**
9 **STORMSEAL BOY**, 4, b g Tyrnavos—Firente **Tony Knowles**
10 **SWIFT CARRIAGE**, 4, br f Carriage Way—River Petterill **R. J. Elliott**
11 **TANCRED SAND**, 7, ch g Nicholas Bill—Another Move **Mr A. Fawcett**
12 **THIRD SON**, 4, b br c Oats—Angodeen **Mrs M. Barker**
13 **TOWNY BOY**, 4, b g Camden Town—Serenesse **Mr Stephen Dorsey**
14 **WEST ENDER**, 7, gr g Pongee—Three Oaks **Fenstone (Quarries) Limited**

THREE-YEAR-OLDS

15 **BEN ROYALE**, b g King of Spain—Fille de General **B. Coulthard**
16 **PERSIAN HOUSE**, ch g Persian Bold—Sarissa **B. Coulthard**

Other Owners: Mrs R. N. Crossley, Mr D. H. Lock.

Jockey (Flat): W Ryan (w.a.).

Jockeys (NH): N Doughty (w.a.), R Marley.

Conditional: B Dalton (9-7).

325 MR T. E. JEFFREY, Alnwick

Postal: **Cold Harbour Farm, Christon Bank, Alnwick, Northumberland.**

1 **MONTAZ DANCER**, 7, b g Bajan Dancer—Montaz **Mr T. E. Jeffrey**
2 **NATIONAL VELVET**, 7, b g Torus—Teachers Pet VI **Mr T. E. Jeffrey**
3 **STARCHY BLAKE**, 5, b g Starch Reduced—Pem Pem **Mr T. E. Jeffrey**

Amateur: Mr T Jeffrey (10-0).

326 MR J. R. W. JENKINS, Royston

Postal: **Kings Ride, Baldock Road, Royston, Hertfordshire, SG8 9NN.**
Phone: **(0763) 241141 FAX (0763) 248 223 TELEX 818441**

1 **ACONITUM**, 9, b g Fair Season—The Yellow Girl **Mr Philip Burley**
2 **ACTINIUM (FR)**, 7, br h Labus (FR)—Activity (FR) **Mr Tony Millar**
3 **ALI' CARRENA**, 5, br g Town And Country—Classic Hand **Mr Humphrey Solomons**
4 **ANOTHER BARNEY**, 6, ch g Stetchworth (USA)—Another Reef **Mr P. Byrne**
5 **ANOTHER RHYTHM**, 6, b g Music Boy—Just You Wait **Mr P. Byrne**
6 **ATLAAL**, 5, b g Shareef Dancer (USA)—Anna Paola (GER) **Mr Oliver Donnelly**
7 **BALASANI (FR)**, 4, b c Labus (FR)—Baykara **Mr M. D. Smith**
8 **BALLATICO**, 7, b br h Ballad Rock—Sweetham **Mr A. Manning**
9 **BLUE DISC**, 5, br g Disc Jockey—Kaotesse **Mr M. J. Moore**
10 **BLUE FINCH**, 6, b g Bustino—Blue Linnet **Mr C. W. Cooper**
11 **BRIGGS BUILDERS**, 6, b g Absalom—Quenlyn **Mr J. G. Chapman**
12 **BROAD BRIDGE**, 4, b f Broadsword (USA)—Tye Bridge **Mr H. Gibbon**
13 **BROOKENFIELD**, 5, ch g Town And Country—Classic Lady **Brooke (Enfield Wash) Ltd**

MR J. R. W. JENKINS—continued

14 **CRYSTAL SONG (FR),** 7, gr g Crystal Palace (FR)—Our Song (FR) **Miss Wendy Redman**
15 **DAILY SPORT SOON,** 5, b h Star Appeal—Pritillor **Mr John Livock**
16 **DR ZEVA,** 4, b c Busted—Dance In Rome **Mr G. R. Butterfield**
17 **ESCRIBANA,** 5, b m Main Reef—Amorak **Mrs J. A. Larkin**
18 **ESKIMO MITE (USA),** 6, b g Northern Baby (CAN)—Astania (GER) **Mr P. Byrne**
19 **GO SOUTH,** 6, b g Thatching—Run To The Sun **Mr Rex Joachim**
20 **GREY SALUTE (CAN),** 7, gr g Vice Regent (CAN)—Night Out (USA) **Mr Tony Hayward**
21 **HARKEN PREMIER,** 5, gr g Hard Fought—Maraquiba (FR) **Mr C. J. Donovan**
22 **JIM'S MUSHROOM,** 6, b m Skyliner—Red Rose **Mr P. Byrne**
23 **KAFARMO,** 7, b h High Line—Fashion Club **Mr J. D. H. Mackenzie**
24 **KEYNES,** 10, ch g Relkino—Rheola **Mr D. H. W. Dobson**
25 **LANDSKI,** 7, b g Niniski (USA)—Misacre **Mr Broderick Munro-Wilson**
26 **LOBRIC,** 5, b g Electric—Light O'Battle **Mr T. H. Ounsley**
27 **MR JERSEY,** 8, b m Crash Course—Belle Mackay **Mr D. R. Plaskett**
28 **NEW ARRANGEMENT,** 4, b g Trojan Fen—Cariole **Mr Robin Billingsley**
29 **OPERATIC SCORE,** 6, ch g Kind of Hush—Grand Opera **Mrs B. V. Tuckwell**
30 **PLAZA GIZON (USA),** 5, ch g Little Current (USA)—Regal Endeavour (USA) **Mr Louis Frederick**
31 **POCKETED (USA),** 4, b c Full Pocket (USA)—Duchess of Malfi (USA) **Mr John Andrew Loxton**
32 **PRIORY BAY,** 4, b f Petong—Salt of The Earth **Mr J. Pepper**
33 **RAKES LANE,** 5, b g Pitskelly—Mrs Cullumbine **Mr John Livock**
34 **RICMAR (USA),** 7, ch g Lydian (FR)—Regency Tale (CAN) **Mr Paul Walker**
35 **SANTELLA BOY,** 8, b h Sparkler—Hors Serie (USA) **Gallagher Enterprises Ltd**
36 **SENOJOJ,** 5, b g Tachypous—Merency **Mr Norman Jones**
37 **SHORT SHOT,** 4, b c Young Generation—Blessed Damsel **Mr Norman Jones**
38 **SHOULD NEVER BE,** 9, bl gr g Native Admiral (USA)—Whizzing **Mr Patrick Woodford**
39 **SOUTHERNAIR,** 10, b g Derrylin—Port La Joie **Mr S. Powell**
40 **SPHINX,** 6, b g Auction Ring (USA)—The Yellow Girl **Mr J. R. Bostock**
41 **SPLASHMAN (USA),** 4, ch c Riverman (USA)—L'Extravagante (USA) **Mr John Livock**
42 **STAR NEPHEW,** 5, b g Great Nephew—Sa-Vegas **Mr Tony Millar**
43 **SWINGING MOON,** 11, ch g Swing Easy (USA)—Moon Gem (USA) **Mr T. W. King**
44 **TAJROBA (USA),** 5, b g Solford (USA)—You're So Vain (USA) **Mr D. Badham**
45 **THE MALDIVE LADY,** 4, b f Oats—Kaotesse **Mrs Toni De Laroque**
46 **THIN RED LINE,** 6, b br g Brigadier Gerard—Golden Keep **Mr John Shipley**
47 **VANROY,** 6, b g Formidable (USA)—Princess Tavi **Mr Derek Garrad**
48 **YANBU,** 5, b g Artaius (USA)—Belle Bretonne **Mr J. Pepper**

THREE-YEAR-OLDS

49 **FORBIDDEN CITY (NZ),** b c Babaroom (USA)—The Empress (NZ) **C. S. Europe Limited (CSE)**
50 **SWORD BRIDGE,** b f Broadsword (USA)—Tye Bridge **Mr H. Gibbon**
51 **VICEROY EXPRESS,** ch f Jalmood (USA)—Viceroy Princess **Mr Michael A. Rust**
52 **WOODCOCK WONDER,** ch c Royal Vulcan—Deandar **Mr B. J. Barrett**

TWO-YEAR-OLDS

53 B c Two Punch (USA)—Lady Roberta (USA) (Roberto (USA)) **J. Pepper**
54 Ch c Carwhite—Nosey (Nebbiolo) **Sheikh Mohammed Bin Khalifa**

Other Owners: Mr B. T. Buckley, Mr Richard Bulgin, Mrs Ann Bull, Miss O. M. Davidson, Mr C. J. Donovan, Mr P. A. French, Mr Tony Hayward, Mr R. W. Hipkin, Mr Neil Holmes, Mr Bernard H. Hutchinson, Mr Rex Joachim, Norman Jones Jnr., Mr Leonard Kitter, Mr J. W. Lemon, Mr Denis Milne, Mr B. P. Monkhouse, Mr K. Nielsen, Mr R. Philip, Mr H. B. Shouler, Mr P. D. Silvester, Miss N. F. Thesiger, Mrs B. E. Tutt, Mr Paul Ward, Mr Robin C. Williams, Mr Adrian Wyatt.

Jockey (NH): R Dunwoody (10-12).

Conditional: M Ahern (9-12).

Amateur: R Massey (9-7).

327 MR D. C. JERMY, Warminster

Postal: **Ludlow Farm, Bradley Road, Warminster, Wiltshire.**
Phone: **WARMINSTER (0985) 213155**

1 **BET OLIVER,** 7, b m Kala Shikari—Lor Darnie **Mr M. Harrod**
2 **CHALKHILL BLUE,** 5, b m Dunphy—Lady Probus **Mr Mike Marsh**
3 **CORNCHARM,** 9, b g Thatch (USA)—Just Larking (USA) **United Racing Services Ltd**
4 **MISS KILPATRICK,** 4, ch f Noalto—Ann Wilson **Mr John James**
5 **OWER QUAY,** 14, b g Coronash—Brown Hen (USA) **Mr Alastair Elliott**
6 **QUELLE CHEMISE,** 4, b f Night Shift (USA)—Quaranta **Mr Alastair Elliott**
7 **SCOTS LAD,** 9, b g Lochnager—Marbella II **Mr W. C. D. Sleeman**
8 **WILD GEESE,** 12, b g Kashmir II—Ring Rose **Mr Alastair Elliott**

THREE-YEAR-OLDS

9 **DASHWOOD (USA),** ch g The Minstrel (CAN)—Jane Austen (USA) **Mr W. C. D. Sleeman**
10 **DIAMOND LIGHT,** ch c Roman Warrior—Another Jo **Mr A. R. Sleeman**
11 **JAMESIE,** ch c Noalto—Ann Wilson **Mr John James**

TWO-YEAR-OLDS

12 B f 4/2 Swing Easy—Ann Wilson (Tumble Wind (USA)) **Mr John James**

Other Owners: Mr R. B. A. Gale.

328 MR M. J. JERRAM, Dunmow

Postal: **Collins Farm, Aythorpe Roding, Dunmow, Essex.**
Phone: **(024531) 215 OR 794**

1 **COMPANY POLICY,** 12, ch g Peter Wrekin—Polite **Mr M. J. Jerram**
2 **ELSEA'S IMAGE,** 9, ch g Vulgan Slave—Elsea Wood **Mr M. J. Jerram**
3 **FOUR EIGHTS,** 5, b g Le Soleil—Madam Constance **Mr M. J. Jerram**
4 **MACANJAC,** 11, b br g Random Shot—Moonraker VI **Mr M. J. Jerram**
5 **MASTER STRIDES,** 7, b g Peter Wrekin—Polite **Mr M. J. Jerram**
6 **ONE LAW,** 8, gr g Charlaw—Limewood **Mr M. J. Jerram**
7 **YORK ROYAL,** 8, ch g Baptism—Annagh Girl **Mr M. J. Jerram**

Amateur: Mr Tim Moore.

329 MR F. JESTIN, Wigton

Postal: **Hilltop, Brocklebank, Wigton, Cumbria.**
Phone: **(06998) 439**

1 **ANTIGUAN MOON,** 12, ch g Articulate—Mavala **Mr F. Jestin**
2 **FINAL TRIP,** 5, ch m Final Straw—Tripolitaine (FR) **Mr F. Jestin**
3 **HOME TO ROOST,** 10, b br g Peacock (FR)—La Belle Dame **Mr F. Jestin**
4 **JASON COLE (NZ),** 6, b g Captain Jason (NZ)—Caravine Girl (NZ) **Mr F. Jestin**
5 **KINROYAL,** 5, br g Royal Fountain—Most Kind **Mrs E. Jestin**
6 **LITTLE BAVARD,** 10, ch g Le Bavard (FR)—Kathleen Beag **Mr F. Jestin**

Amateur: F Jestin (11-7).

330 MR J. HOWARD JOHNSON, Crook

Postal: **White Lea Farm, Crook, Co. Durham, DL15 9QN.**
Phone: **BISHOP AUCKLAND HOME (0388) 762113 CAR PHONE (0860) 319064**

1 **ABNEGATION,** 5, b g Abednego—Autumn Magic **Mr Joe Henderson and Mr J. S. Robinson**
2 **BIG CAHOONA,** 5, b g Jasmine Star—Vale of Peace **Mr J. Duffy**
3 **BOYNTON,** 7, b g Riboboy—Lingdale Lady **Mrs K. Hawkey and Mr J. Howard Johnson**
4 **CHESWOLD,** 6, b g Dominion—Soft Voice **Mr M. B. Frazer**
5 **CNO CAPILL,** 6, ch g Lucifer—Innocent Laura **Mr George Tobitt**
6 **COOL CATCH,** 7, b g Patch—Coole Park **Mr Ian Simpson**
7 **COPELAND LAD,** 8, b g Radical—No Dice **Mr R. Seagrave**
8 **COUNTRY CARNIVAL,** 6, b m Town And Country—Fairabunda **Agnewtree Ltd (Thwaites Country)**
9 **EDBERG,** 6, br g Strong Gale—White Shoes **Mr R. Darby**
10 **FALCONERS PRIDE,** 4, ch f Grey Ghost—Final Edition
11 **GARRY ODDER,** 6, ch g Garryowen—Deceptive Day **Mr W. M. G. Black**
12 **GINGER PINK,** 4, b g Strong Gale—Zitas Toi **Mr Allen Walton**
13 **HIGHLY DECORATED,** 5, b g Sharpo—New Ribbons **Mr J. Hodgson**
14 **LACIDAR,** 10, b br g Radical—No Dice **Mrs E. Seagrave**
15 **MAUDLINS CROSS,** 5, ch g Vaigly Great—Pepin **Mr G. W. Fletcher and Mr David Bell**
16 **NIAD,** 6, b g Lighter—Taxi Freight **Mr T. G. J. Gadd**
17 **OISINS CASTLE,** 11, b g Bluerullah—Japonica **Mr George Tobitt**
18 **OLD APPLEJACK,** 10, ch g Hot Brandy—Windfall VI **Mr George Tobitt**
19 **OPTIMISTIC LADY,** 5, ch m Full of Hope—Red Lady **Mr P. Needham**
20 **OUR DESSA,** 7, br m Derek H—Jeanne du Barry **Norbri Stud Ltd**
21 **PIKE'S PEAK,** 9, br g High Top—Sometime Lucky **Mr R. Tallentire**
22 **ROCKMARTIN,** 8, b g Fair Season—Aunt Eva **Mr Duncan Gill**
23 **SHACKMAN,** 4, ch g Shack (USA)—Peperonia **Mr A. G. Watson**
24 **SHAMIRANI,** 4, gr g Darshaan—Sharmada (FR) **Mr A. G. Watson**
25 **TARLOGIE,** 4, b g Touching Wood—Soft Chinook **Mr P. G. Cavey and Mr J. McEwan**
26 4, B g Royal Fountain—Taxi Freight **Mr T. G. J. Gadd**
27 **WHITEGATES LADY,** 9, b m Le Coq d'Or—Katie Little **Mr R. W. L. Bowden**
28 **YAMANOUCHI,** 6, b g Hard Fought—Noreena **Mr J. Duffy**

THREE-YEAR-OLDS

29 **AVONSIDE,** b f Ile de Bourbon (USA)—Lady Abernant **Mr P. G. Cavey and Mr J. McEwan**
30 **CHLOE SUSAN,** b f Adonijah—Be Still **Mr P. G. Cavey and Mr J. McEwan**
31 Gr f Grey Ghost—Final Edition **Mr T. F. Shepherd**
32 **GARSCUBE,** gr g Petong—Brigado **Mr P. G. Cavey and Mr J. McEwan**
33 **HANOVER STREET,** b g Doc Marten—Carnation **Mr P. G. Cavey and Mr J. McEwan**
34 **LUNA PROBE,** b f Pas de Seul—Dancing Song **Mr P. G. Cavey and Mr J. McEwan**
35 **PA-JO,** b g Uncle Pokey—Darling June **Mr J. Howard Johnson**
36 **PANDESSA,** b f Blue Cashmere—Jeanne du Barry **Norbri Stud Ltd**
37 **SIDI BARANI,** br g Coded Scrap—Merrywren **Agnewtree Ltd (Thwaites Country)**
38 **SUPREME COURT,** b g Yashgan—My Natalie **Mr P. G. Cavey and Mr J. McEwan**
39 **WELL BANK,** b g Tudor Diver—Technical Merit **Mrs S. Johnson**

TWO-YEAR-OLDS

40 Ch g Say Primula—Technical Merit **Mr J. Howard Johnson**

Other Owners: Mrs S. Baudouin, Mrs Sandra Blair, Mr John Hamilton, Mr Tom Harty, Mrs H. Johnson, Mr John Mullins, Mr David S. Nimmo, Mr J. R. Raine, Mr P. Seagrave, Tyneside Frozen Foods Ltd.

Jockeys (NH): T Reed (10-0), B Storey (10-0).

Conditional: A G Smith (9-7).

Amateur: Mr Shaun Bowden (10-7).

331 MR M. A. JOHNSON, Buntingford

Postal: **Glebe House, Little Hormead, Buntingford, Hertfordshire, SG9 OLT.**
Phone: **GREAT HORMEAD (076389) 372 (0860) 322778**

1 **DOUBLE LIGHT,** 8, b g Lighter—Salira **Mrs A. Johnson**
2 **LITTLE HORMEAD,** 5, b m Cruise Missile—Ballygoman **Mrs A. Johnson**
3 **NEWNHAM,** 13, ch g Cantab—Ribon Perfume **Mr Michael A. Johnson**
4 **PEACEFUL LANE,** 12, b g Crozier—Denmead **Mr Michael A. Johnson**

332 MR R. W. JOHNSON, Newcastle-on-Tyne

Postal: **Grange Farm, Newburn, Newcastle-on-Tyne, NE15 8QA.**

1 **BRAVE THE STORM,** 8, b g Brave Invader (USA)—Little Tina **Mr Robert Johnson**
2 **JUPITER PRINCE,** 11, ch g Jupiter Pluvius—Lady Rois **Mr Robert Johnson**
3 **ORMOND HALL,** 6, b g Balboa—Ahoy Dolly **Mr Robert Johnson**
4 **STRONG SILVER (USA),** 5, b g Silver Hawk (USA)—Brave Mimi (FR) **Mrs Ann Johnson**
5 **UPWELL,** 6, b g Tanfirion—Debnic **Mr Robert Johnson**

TWO-YEAR-OLDS

6 **LIBERTY RANGE,** b f Liberated—Inrange (Connaught) **Mr Robert Johnson**

Amateurs: Mr K Johnson (9-7), Mr P Johnson (10-9).

333 MR R. F. JOHNSON HOUGHTON, Didcot

Postal: **Woodway, Blewbury, Didcot, Oxon, OX11 9EZ.**
Phone: **(0235) 850480 FAX (0235) 851045**

1 **AKDAM (USA),** 5, b h Arctic Tern (USA)—Dancers Countess (USA) **Mrs G. T. Johnson Houghton**
2 **ALEXANDRA KATRINE,** 4, b f Precocious—Sipapu **Mrs S. Arnold**
3 **CASTORET,** 4, b c Jalmood (USA)—Blaskette **Lady D'Avigdor-Goldsmid**
4 **CHARLOTTE GRAY,** 5, ro m Rolfe (USA)—Madame Russe **Mr G. P. P. Stewart**
5 **COINAGE,** 7, br gr g Owen Dudley—Grisbi **Mr R. F. Johnson Houghton**
6 **HABITANCY,** 4, b f Habitat—Bright Landing **Mr J. W. Rowles**
7 **JASCHA,** 4, b f Music Boy—Ardmay **Lady D'Avigdor-Goldsmid**
8 **KHAYAMOUR,** 4, gr c Habitat—Khayra (FR) **Mr Anthony Pye-Jeary**

THREE-YEAR-OLDS

9 **AMBROSE,** b c Ile de Bourbon (USA)—Famous Band (USA) **Mrs G. T. Johnson Houghton**
10 **BAWBEE,** gr f Dunbeath (USA)—Fee **Exors of the late Mrs J. de Rothschild**
11 **CLOCK GOLF,** b f Mummy's Game—Stuff And Nonsense **Exors of the late Mrs J. de Rothschild**
12 **DARMENT,** b f Darshaan—Nijinsky Sentiment (USA) **H.H. Prince Yazid Saud**
13 **EMPRESS OF CANADA,** b f Dominion—Canadian Charisma **Mrs Hilly Beaufort**
14 **FAR FROM HOME,** b f Habitat—Miss By Miles **T. D. Holland-Martin**
15 **LONGSHOREMAN,** gr g Longleat (USA)—Cabotage **Exors of the late Mrs J. de Rothschild**
16 **MAHAT,** b f Rainbow Quest (USA)—Rivers Maid **H.H. Prince Yazid Saud**
17 **PULPIT ROCK,** ch f Lomond (USA)—Piney Ridge **Mrs David Crossley Cooke**
18 **QUICK PROFIT,** b f Formidable (USA)—Penny Blessing **T. D. Holland-Martin**
19 **RED VICTOR,** b g Bellman (FR)—Red Sharp (FR) **Mr William Wallace**
20 **REPLY,** b f Derrylin—Repoussee **Lady D'Avigdor-Goldsmid**
21 **SECRET WATERS,** b f Pharly (FR)—Idle Waters **Mr R. Crutchley**
22 **STRANGER TO FEAR,** ch f Never So Bold—Acadie (FR) **Mr J. W. Rowles**
23 **TIMUR'S KING,** b g King of Spain—Timur's Daughter **Lord Leverhulme**
24 **TODA,** ch f Absalom—Lambay **Exors of the late Mrs J. de Rothschild**
25 **WALTZING HOME,** b c Habitat—State Ball **Mr R. B. Holt**
26 **WATER GOD,** b c Dominion—Silent Pool **Mr S. J. D. Posford**

MR R. F. JOHNSON HOUGHTON—continued

TWO-YEAR-OLDS

27 **ACKERS WOOD**, b c 31/3 Castle Keep—Gloria Maremmana (King Emperor (USA)) **Lord Leverhulme**
28 **ARTURIAN**, b c 4/3 Vaigly Great—Aspark (Sparkler) **Mr R. F. Johnson Houghton**
29 **BAYONNE**, ch f 29/4 Bay Express—Lambay (Lorenzaccio) **Exors of the late Mrs J. de Rothschild**
30 B c 27/4 Last Tycoon—Berengaria (ITY) (Teodoro Trevulzio) **Mr R. F. Johnson Houghton**
31 **CLEAR LEADER**, ch c 2/2 Caerleon (USA)—Moulin Rapide (USA) (Roberto (USA)) **Mr S. J. D. Posford**
32 **GLEAMING WATER**, gr f 13/3 Kalaglow—Idle Waters (Mill Reef (USA)) **Mr R. Crutchley**
33 B c 13/4 Doulab (USA)—Helcia (Habitat) **Mr R. F. Johnson Houghton**
34 **LONGLEAVE**, b c 3/2 Night Shift (USA)—
Stuff And Nonsense (Crooner) **Exors of the late Mrs J. de Rothschild**
35 B c 22/4 Ballad Rock—Prasia (Prince Regent) **Mr R. F. Johnson Houghton**
36 **SEARCY**, b c 25/2 Good Times (ITY)—Fee (Mandamus) **Exors of the late Mrs J. de Rothschild**
37 **TAKE TWO**, b c 20/2 Jupiter Island—Dancing Daughter (Dance In Time (CAN)) **Lord Leverhulme**
38 **TOO CLEVER BY HALF**, b g 2/4 Pragmatic—
Acushla Macree (Mansingh (USA)) **Mrs R. F. Johnson Houghton**
39 **TRAINBLEU**, b c 18/5 Siberian Express—Skyey (Skymaster) **Mr R. F. Johnson Houghton**

Other Owners: Mr P. Arnold, Mrs Bruce Bossom, Mr D. G. Churston, Mr J. Coggan, Mrs R. E. Crutchley, Mr A. P. Hamilton, Hawkridge Farmhouse Cheese Limited, Mr Saleh Al Homeizi, Mr John Merrwether, Mr M. C. Talbot-Ponsonby.

Amateur: Mr G F Johnson Houghton (9-13).

334 MR M. S. JOHNSTON, Middleham

Postal: **Kingsley House Racing Stables, Middleham, Leyburn, North Yorkshire, DL8 4PH.**
Phone: **(0969) 22237 FAX (0969) 22484**

1 **CRAFT EXPRESS**, 4, b c Bay Express—Lydia Rose **Mrs V. G. Rowland**
2 **CRAIL HARBOUR**, 4, b g Don—Broccoli **Mr S. A. B. Dinsmore**
3 **HELEN HOTEL**, 5, ch g High Line—Orange Sensation **Mr G. Agodino**
4 **HINARI SUNRISE**, 4, ch c Tap On Wood—Miss Markey **Mr J. Cowan**
5 **HINARI TELEVIDEO**, 4, b f Caerleon (USA)—Red Jade **Mark Johnston Racing Ltd**
6 **HINARI VIDEO**, 5, b g Sallust—Little Cynthia **Mr Richard Wheeler**
7 **SIMPLY PERFECT**, 4, b c Wassl—Haneena **Mrs M. A. Jones**
8 **SOLOMON'S SONG**, 4, b g Night Shift (USA)—Judeah **Miss Caroline Spurrier**
9 **STISTED PARK**, 5, b g Be My Native—Up To You **Mr J. Clark**

THREE-YEAR-OLDS

10 **ADDISON'S BLADE**, b c Pas de Seul—Addison's Jubilee **Mr Edward N. Addison**
11 **ALJANAN**, b c Pitskelly—Charley's Aunt **M.H.T.B. Racing**
12 **CAREFORALLSEASONS**, ch f Try My Best (USA)—Crimson Crown **Mr Billy Morgan**
13 **DERAILED**, ch g Siberian Express (USA)—Lasani (FR) **Mr A. J. Richards**
14 **FIRST DREAM**, b f Dreams To Reality (USA)—Khloud **Mr S. A. B. Dinsmore**
15 **GO BUY BAILEY'S**, b c Rousillon (USA)—Geoffrey's Sister **G. R. Bailey Ltd (Baileys Horse Feeds)**
16 **HIGH ELEGANCE**, b f Elegant Air—Tula Singh **Tony Cuthbert Cartoons Ltd**
17 **HINARI VISION**, b f Kings Lake—Get Ahead **Mr P. Venner**
18 **JAYDEEGLEN**, b f Bay Express—Friendly Glen **Miss T. Longstaff**
19 **KINGSLEY**, b f Kings Lake (USA)—Bushti Music **Mrs S. Hanby**
20 **LIFEWATCH CHECK**, b c Tumble Wind (USA)—Habilite **Dr Anne J. F. Gillespie**
21 **LIFEWATCH VISION**, b c Vision (USA)—Maellen **Dr Anne J. F. Gillespie**
22 **MISTER'S SISTER**, ch f Tumble Wind (USA)—Joanelle **Mr Frank Thornton**
23 **PAPER CRAFT**, b c Formidable—Civility **Michael Craft Ltd**
24 **SAUCY SAINT**, b c Show-A-Leg—Stolen Halo **Mr Peter Mee**
25 **SILENT LOCH**, b f Lochnager—Keep Silent **Mr M. I. Marsh**
26 **STARSTREAK**, b c Comedy Star (USA)—Kochia **Skeltools Ltd**

MR M. S. JOHNSTON—continued

TWO-YEAR-OLDS

27 B c 21/3 Vision—Belitis **Mark Johnston Racing Ltd**
28 B c 14/5 Glenstal—Fandetta **Mark Johnston Racing Ltd**
29 Ch f 17/5 Bairn—Marie Galante **Mr R. Searle**
30 B f 6/2 Taufan—Premiere Cuvee **Mr & Mrs D. Hicks**
31 B c 14/4 Vision—Princess John **Mark Johnston Racing Ltd**
32 Ch c 4/5 Hostage—Run Amber Run **Mark Johnston Racing Ltd**
33 **SMALL DOUBLE (IRE),** b f 18/5 Double Schwartz—Little Cynthia **Mr A. Phair and Mr D. Clark**
34 B f 8/2 Sadler's Wells—Soba **Dr Anne J. F. Gillespie**
35 **VENICE IN PERIL (IRE),** ch c 11/4 Lomond—Rising Tide **Mr S. A. B. Dinsmore**

Other Owners: Mrs K. Audibert, Mr D. Bosomworth, Mrs M. R. Boxall, Mrs R. A. Godsell, Mr D. J. Kerr, Mr W. Millar, Dr C. J. Nicholls, Mrs R. M. Wells.

Jockeys (Flat): A Bacon (7-13), R P Elliot (7-13, w.a.).

Jockey (NH): D Condell (10-0).

Apprentice: S Rabjohn (8-4).

335 MR A. W. JONES, Oswestry

Postal: **Pentre David, Oswestry, Salop, SY10 7EA.**
Phone: **(0691) 659720**

1 **ABC SUPERSTAR,** 10, b g Undulate (USA)—Paddy's Rose **Mr J. E. Abbey**
2 **BILLION MELODY,** 8, b g Billion (USA)—Thistle **Mr F. E. Phillips**
3 **BRAVE SONG,** 11, b g Busted—Net Call **Mr I. J. Glenister**
4 **CAPEABILITY POUND,** 7, gr g Balboa—Olibanum **Martin Pound Racing Ltd**
5 **FOURTH TUDOR (USA),** 8, ch g Horatius (USA)—Fourth Dimension (USA) **Mr Doug Brereton**
6 **GUN-CARRIAGE,** 10, b g Gunner B—Miss Little **Mr A. W. Jones**
7 **HAPPY DEAL,** 4, b g Mon Cheval—Straight Look **Mr F. E. Phillips**
8 **OPALKINO,** 5, ch m Relkino—Opalescent **Mrs M. H. Leslie**
9 **RUSSIAN WINTER,** 15, b g King Emperor (USA)—Am Stretchin' (USA) **Miss Victoria Jones**
10 **THE STAMP DEALER,** 7, b br g Runnett—Royal Meath **Miss G. Woods**
11 **THUNDERING,** 5, b g Persian Bold—Am Stretchin' (USA) **Calmac (Tool & Engineering) Ltd**
12 **TOP ROW,** 7, b g Beldale Flutter (USA)—Connaught Nymph **Mr John Zochonis**

THREE-YEAR-OLDS

13 **ABSTONE LAD,** b g Blazing Saddles (AUS)—Abbey Rose **Mr J. E. Abbey**
14 **FAIRE FAILLITE,** b f Bustino—Coverham Lass **Mrs Irene C. Anderton**
15 **SHEWHOMUSTBEOBEYED,** ch f Miami Springs—Sleepline Promise **Mr J. T. Fairhurst**

TWO-YEAR-OLDS

16 **LAST STRAW,** b c Blushing Scribe (USA)—Straw Reef (Final Straw) **Lady Leighton**

Amateur: Miss Diana Jones (9-0).

MR A. W. JONES—continued

336 MR G. E. JONES, Lampeter

Postal: **Lluestnewydd, Bettws, Lampeter, Dyfed, Wales, SA48 8PB.**
Phone: **(057045) 261**

1 **CHARLIE BURTON,** 8, b g My Chopin—Judy Burton **Mr G. Elwyn Jones**
2 **FOSSARD,** 6, b g Mummy's Game—Pinaka **Mr G. Elwyn Jones**
3 **MILFORD PET,** 6, ch g Milford—Mi Favorita **Mr G. Elwyn Jones**

Jockey (NH): H Davies (10-4).

Amateur: Mr D Jones (10-7).

337 MRS G. E. JONES, Upton-on-Severn

Postal: **Whitefield Court, Upton-on-Severn, Worcester.**
Phone: **UPTON-ON-SEVERN (06846) 2691**

1 **ACE OF SPIES,** 9, b g He Loves Me—Belle Bergere **Mr Michael Groom**
2 **CONVINCING,** 6, ch g Formidable (USA)—Star of Bagdad (USA) **Mrs Mary Rose Hickman**
3 **COOL MOVE,** 5, ch g Prince Tenderfoot (USA)—Tranquil Love **Mr E. Ryan**
4 **DEEP PROSPECT,** 11, b g Deep Run—Tudor Gello **Mr N. J. Jones**
5 **FINAL SPRING,** 6, b g Hubble Bubble—Final Answer **Miss J. C. Gibson**
6 **FOWLING PIECE,** 5, ch g Kinghaven—Bonny Hollow **Mrs Gill E. Jones**
7 **FULL BLOOM,** 6, ch m Le Johnstan—Floral Light **Mr A. H. Grant**
8 **GOLDEN CAJUN,** 6, ch h Cajun—Miscellaneous **Mrs P. I. Fuller**
9 **JACK AND JILL,** 10, gr g Scallywag—Royal Cottage **Mr N. J. Jones**
10 **KATE KELLY,** 9, b m Netherkelly—Spring Offer **Paula Garrett**
11 **LOUGH ROAD,** 8, ch g Laurence O—Vixen's Red **Mr M. J. McNamee**
12 **MINERAL DUST,** 7, ch g Callernish—Magnesium **Mr Michael Groom**
13 **NEWBAWN DALE,** 7, ch g Ovac (ITY)—Hunea **Mr P. J. Beswick**
14 **SHELLY'S FOLLY,** 5, b h Music Boy—Gay Maria **Mr P. J. Beswick**
15 **SKELBY,** 6, b g Torus—Chantry Blue **Mrs Gill E. Jones**
16 **SPARTAN CHIEF,** 9, ch g True Song—Silver Spartan **Mr Henry Taylor**
17 **SPARTAN SOLDIER,** 9, b g Soldier Rose—Sparella **Miss J. C. Gibson**
18 **TILL IT HURTS,** 4, b g Owen Anthony—High Authority **Mr E. Ryan**
19 **WALKSFAR,** 9, ch g Class Distinction—High Walk **Mr Michael Groom**
20 **WINTER MEASURE,** 10, b g Pamroy—Funny Baby **Mr N. J. Jones**

TWO-YEAR-OLDS

21 B f 17/5 Brewery Boy—Buffy (French Beige) **Mr E. Ryan**
22 B f 2/4 Pia Fort—Sleepline Group (Jukebox) **Mr E. Dalton**

Other Owners: Mr D. J. Holland, Mr A. W. C. Morris.

Jockey (Flat): W Carson (w.a.).

Jockey (NH): B Powell.

Amateur: Mr N Jones (10-7).

338 MR G. H. JONES, Tenbury Wells

Postal: **The Juggis, Leysters, Leominster, Herefordshire.**
Phone: **(056887) 305**

1 **FERNS BUNYIP,** 8, b m Rustingo—Royal Fern **Mrs A. R. Piggott**
2 **FRANK DALE,** 7, b g Space King—Mileciptic **Mrs R. Jones**
3 **LUCKACTIVE,** 4, ch g Lucky Wednesday—Swakara **Mr D. Pugh and Mr M. Mifflin**
4 **MCA LUCKY STAR,** 4, gr f Lucky Wednesday—Starkist **Mrs R. Jones**
5 **MOST INTERESTING,** 5, b m Music Boy—Quick Glance **Mr John Priday**
6 **RAINBOW BRITE (FR),** 5, b g Maelstrom Lake—Orfila (FR) **Mr John Priday**
7 **SLEEPERS,** 6, b m Swing Easy (USA)—Jenny's Rocket **Mrs R. Jones**
8 **STORMY MONARCH,** 9, b g Fordham (USA)—Stormy Queen **Mr T. G. Mulkeen and Partners**

THREE-YEAR-OLDS

9 B c Lucky Wednesday—Swakara **Mrs R. Jones**

Other Owners: Mr D. Borthwell, Mr T. Ingles.

339 MR P. J. JONES, Marlborough

Postal: **Fox Twitchen, East Kennett, Marlborough, Wiltshire.**
Phone: **LOCKERIDGE (067286) 427**

1 **DARA DOONE,** 4, b g Dara Monarch—Lorna Doone (USA) **Mr T. K. Pearce**
2 **FAREWELL TO ALMS,** 8, b g Pauper—Cracked Bell **Mrs George Tricks**
3 **JAYLAND,** 4, ch c Kings Lake (USA)—Santarelle **Mr T. K. Pearce**
4 **LEGAL SUGAR,** 12, b g Legal Eagle—Sugar Sugar **Mrs Gillian Jones**
5 **MISTER BUTLER,** 11, b g Menelek—Golden Number **Mr John Amor**
6 **NEW GAME,** 8, b m New Member—Rare Game **Mr M. P. Fear**
7 **NOBLE STORM,** 8, b g Morston (FR)—Brave Ballard **Mrs S. Hart**
8 **NONSUCH HERO,** 6, ch m Leander—Karella (FR) **Mrs I. A. McNeile**
9 **OH SO RIPE,** 5, ch m Deep Run—Perished **Mrs A. E. Goodwin**
10 **RARE LUCK,** 7, b m Rare One—Silly Millie **Mrs D. Hammerson**
11 **RONDEAU,** 7, ch m Orchestra—Sunshot **Mr P. J. Jones**
12 **VICTORY LANE,** 4, b g Valiyar—Open Country **Mr David Cliff**

Other Owners: Mr G. D. Blagbrough, Mr F. J. Burrows, Mr Bonar Mackie, Mrs B. Read.

Jockey (NH): M Kinane (10-0).

Lady Rider: Heather Mumford (9-7).

340 MR T. M. JONES, Guildford

Postal: **Brook Farm, Albury, Guildford, Surrey, GU5 9DJ.**
Phone: **SHERE (048 641) 2604**

1 **BARA PEG,** 9, b m Random Shot—Borderina **Mr D. H. Smith**
2 **MOOR FROLICKING,** 4, ch f Morston (FR)—Woodland Frolic **Mr Mervyn J. Evans**
3 **MR FOG PATCHES,** 8, ch g Patch—Cashelgarran **Mr Ian Macauley**
4 **NICOLAKI,** 5, gr g Busted—Nicholas Grey **Mr B. T, E. Shrubsall**
5 **RING OF SECRETS,** 8, b g Belfalas—Jeanette Marie **Mr Mervyn J. Evans**
6 **THANK YOURSELF,** 6, ch m Le Bavard (FR)—So Called **Mr Ray Hawthorn**
7 **TRYUMPHANT LAD,** 6, gr g Roselier (FR)—Blackbog Lass **Try Group PLC**

MR T. M. JONES—continued

THREE-YEAR-OLDS

8 **AUTUMN MORNING,** b c Elegant Air—Short And Sharp **Mr J. P. Crouch**
9 **BEHIND THE CLOCK,** b c Sula Bula—Hale Lane **Mr T. M. Jones**

TWO-YEAR-OLDS

10 B c Sula Bula—Hale Lane **Mrs C. G. Miliam**
11 Ch g Funny Man—Palimony **Mrs P. Scott-Dunn**
12 Ch c Nicholas Bill—Rest Hill Dolly **Mrs J. Brookes**

Other Owners: Mr Darrell P. Hinds, Miss J. C. Holden-Baker, Mr R. F. Kilby, Mr Rodney Palmer, Mr H. Saunders, Mr A. J. G. Taylor.

Jockey (NH): H Davies (w.a.).

341 MR F. T. J. JORDAN, Leominster

Postal: **Butt Oak Farm, Risbury, Leominster, Herefordshire.**
Phone: **(056882) 281**

1 **ARDRA DUKE,** 6, ch g Deep Run—Astrella Celeste **Royal Oak Racing**
2 **BLOXHAM,** 5, b g The Brianstan—Sur Les Roches **Mr Carl Wright**
3 **CELTIC SUNLIGHT,** 5, b g Celtic Cone—Hilliana **Mrs M. I. Kimpton**
4 **CHARLY MUTUAL (NZ),** 4, ch g Husha (AUS)—Golden Talaria (NZ) **Mrs Joy Green**
5 **CHIUSO,** 5, ch g Main Reef—Losenger **Free Foresters Haulage Limited**
6 **DOCTOR RHYTHM,** 5, ch g Cure The Blues (USA)—Mombones **Mr A. Townend**
7 **EMBARKATION,** 4, ch g Main Reef—Pointe de Grace (FR) **Mr F. Jordan**
8 **FEELING BETTER,** 4, b g Cure The Blues (USA)—La Mortola **Three Counties Bloodstock Agency Limited**
9 **FIRST CRACK,** 5, b m Scallywag—Furstin **Mr D. Pugh**
10 **FLIGHTING MOON,** 5, gr g Moorestyle—Perlesse **Mr R. Gunthorpe**
11 **FOX PATH,** 6, b g Godswalk (USA)—Precious Egg **Mrs Jean Lewis**
12 **FRENDLY FELLOW,** 6, b g Grundy—Relfo **Mr C. D. Norton**
13 **GENERAL PERSHING,** 4, br c Persian Bold—St Colette **Three Counties Bloodstock Agency Limited**
14 **GIRL IN GREEN,** 6, b m Connaught—Hindu Flame **Mr R. Gunthorpe**
15 **GO GO GORGEOUS,** 4, b g Hello Gorgeous (USA)—Go Mays **Three Counties Bloodstock Agency Limited**
16 **GREAT SALING,** 5, b g Vaigly Great—Goosie-Gantlet **Mr Bill Woodward**
17 **HELMAR (NZ),** 4, b g Gay Apollo—War Field (NZ) **Mrs Joy Green**
18 **INNOVATOR,** 4, ro g Relkino—Gunnard **Mr R. H. Lewis**
19 **JARRAS,** 5, b g Touching Wood (USA)—Hilary's Hut **Mr Carl Wright**
20 **JEFFREY GRAHAM,** 9, b g Mandrake Major—Lanchard **Mr F. T. J. Jordan**
21 **KAMEO STYLE,** 7, b g Kambalda—Smashing Style **Three Counties Bloodstock Agency Limited**
22 **KUWAIT LEEL,** 8, b g Ile de Bourbon (USA)—Love And Care (USA) **Mr J. B. Wilcox**
23 **LULA BLAKE,** 5, b m Roscoe Blake—Ablula **Mr T. W. Kinsey**
24 **MEESON SCRAP,** 4, b g Coded Scrap—Meeson Secret **Mr J. B. Wilcox**
25 **MIGHTY CHANCE,** 5, b g Furry Glen—Cant Pet **Mr Bill Woodward**
26 **MRS DODD,** 4, b g Petorius—Standing Ovation **Mr R. Laughlid**
27 **PANT LLIN,** 4, b g Mummy's Pet—Goosie-Gantlet **Mrs M. Cooper**
28 **PATRICK JAMES,** 5, b g Kampala—Up The Gates **Mr D. J. West**
29 **PRIDE HILL (NZ),** 8, b g Diamante D—Purple Dream (NZ) **Mrs Brenda Gittins**
30 **QUICK FLING,** 9, b g Bay Express—Arrangement **Mr I. Jones**
31 **REEF LARK,** 5, b g Mill Reef (USA)—Calandra (USA) **Mr A. F. Guy**
32 **RETURN TO ROMANCE,** 4, b f Trojan Fen—Honest Penny (USA) **Mr Carl Wright**
33 **ROCHE'S,** 6, b g Monsanto (FR)—Sur Les Roches **Mr Carl Wright**
34 **SPACE CHASER,** 7, b g Space King—Bow Baby **Mrs Gwen Meacham**
35 **SPIN (NZ),** 4, ch g Lakenheath (USA)—Casurina (NZ) **Mrs Helen Holdsworth**
36 **STAGE QUEEN,** 4, br f Dawn Johnny (USA)—Queen of The Kop **Miss E. J. Davis**
37 **THE BANK (USA),** 4, br c Clever Trick (USA)—Quick Reason (USA) **Three Counties Bloodstock Agency Limited**

MR F. T. J. JORDAN—continued

38 **TOUCHING STAR,** 5, b g Touching Wood (USA)—Beaufort Star **Mr Derek R. Price**
39 **TUDOR JUSTICE,** 8, b g Mister Tudor—True Verdict **Mr Glyn Jones**
40 **ULLSWATER,** 4, b g Wassl—Dignified Air (FR) **Mr R. Thomas**
41 **UNCLE PARKS (NZ),** 4, b g Diagramatic (USA)—Talento (NZ) **Mr Martin Green**
42 **VALLEY OF DANUATA,** 5, b g Taufan (USA)—Dane Valley **Mrs Margaret Cooper**
43 **WOODKNOT,** 5, b g Tap On Wood—Sister Connie **Miss Monica Campbell**
44 **YAMASHITA (USA),** 5, b g Vaguely Noble—Princesse Aglae (FR) **Mr F. Jordan**

THREE-YEAR-OLDS

45 **ANDY-TOM,** b c My Dad Tom (USA)—Queen of The Kop **Free Foresters Haulage Limited**
46 **AUCTION DAY,** b c Runnett—Valediction **Mrs Brenda Gittins**
47 **DUKE OF IMPNEY,** b c Roscoe Blake—Top Secret **Impney Hotels (Chateau)**

Other Owners: Mr Anthony Palmer, Mr Jeffrey A. Smith.

Apprentice: C Simpson (8-7).

Conditional: Jonathan Lodder (9-7), Paul Williams (9-7).

Amateur: Damien Duggan (10-7).

342 MR M. KAUNTZE, Ashbourne

Postal: **Bullstown, Ashbourne, Co. Meath, Ireland.**
Phone: **DUBLIN (01) 350440 FAX DUBLIN (01) 351606**

1 **BLUE SCEPTRE,** 4, b f Tender King—Blue Button **C. S. Gaisford St Lawrence**
2 **CHESAPEAKE BAY,** 5, br g Rusticaro—Gulf Girl **Mrs Michael Kauntze**
3 **DOBEY THATCHER,** 7, b h Thatching—Lancette **Mrs L. C. Ronan**
4 **EEDUFF,** 4, b br f Auction Ring—Limbara **Mrs R. W. Hanson**
5 **OREMBO,** 6, ch g Tap On Wood—Arab Art **Mrs R. W. Hanson**

THREE-YEAR-OLDS

6 **CASLA,** b f Lomond—Princess Arabella **Major V. McCalmont**
7 **CASPIAN TALK,** ch f Persian Bold—No Jargon **Lady Clague**
8 **CATCH TWENTY TWO,** b c Taufan—Dancing Decoy **Sheikh Mohammed**
9 **CRY IN THE DARK,** b f Godswalk—Embustera **M. C. Throsby**
10 **FINAL VEIL (USA),** b f Sadler's Wells—A Streaker **Mrs G. W. Bronfman**
11 **FOURP'NY ROCK,** ch f Ahonoora—Sixpenny **Major V. McCalmont**
12 **FREAKY DEAKY,** br g Prince Tenderfoot—Marylands **N. J. F. Robinson**
13 **GOOD AND GENTLE,** ch g Good Thyne—Gentle Down **J. L. Allbritton**
14 **KILARNEY RING,** b f Scorpio—Corbalton **Major V. McCalmont**
15 **LOTTE LENTA,** ch f Gorytus (USA)—Jeanie Duff (USA) **C. S. Bird III**
16 **LYRAKEEN,** br f Melyno—Tiptoe **T. J. Rooney**
17 **MAID OF ASTORAL,** b f Caerleon—Bold Meadows **Mrs A. S. O'Brien**
18 **MINNIE HABIT,** b f Habitat—Minnie Tudor **Mrs E. M. Burke**
19 **PERFECT SWINGER,** gr f Shernazer—Aldern Stream **Knockanally Golf Club**
20 **PERSIAN FLIRT,** b f Persian Bold—Flatteuse **Mrs Michael Kauntze**
21 **REASONABLY SUNNY,** br g Reasonable—Sunny Eyes **Michael Doyle**
22 **ROSE WREATH,** b f Thatching—Rosolini **Major V. McCalmont**
23 **UP UP AND AWAY,** b g Tumble Wind—Pennyhabit **K. Rohan**
24 **VAUDEVILLE LADY,** b f Top Ville—Air Distingue (USA) **Sheikh Mohammed**

MR M. KAUNTZE—continued

TWO-YEAR-OLDS

25 **COME TO TEA (IRE),** ch f 3/4 Be My Guest (USA)—Tea House (Sassafras (FR)) **Major V. McCalmont**
26 B f 16/3 Try My Best (USA)—Delightful Time (Manado) **T. J. Rooney**
27 **FERNLEA (USA),** ch f Sir Ivor—Pampas (Pampapaul) **T. K. Cooper**
28 **FOIE GRAS (IRE),** ch f 6/3 Ballad Rock—Goosalley (Run The Gantlet (USA)) **C. S. Gaisford St Lawrence**
29 Ch c 24/4 Pennine Walk—Golden Grundy (Grundy) **Mrs Michael Kauntze**
30 B c 5/2 Sovereign Dancer—Grace Joie (FR) (Top Ville) **Sheikh Mohammed**
31 Br f 19/2 Simply Great (FR)—Happy Nun (Habitat) **H. R. D. McCalmont**
32 B f 26/3 Sadler's Wells (USA)—Jalapa (FR) (Luthier (FR)) **Sheikh Mohammed**
33 **KOOYONGA (IRE),** ch f 12/5 Persian Bold—Anjuli (Northfields (USA)) **M. C. Throsby**
34 B f Glow (USA)—Lancette (Double Jump) **Mrs L. C. Ronan**
35 Br f 21/6 Sure Blade (USA)—Limbara (Espresso) **Mrs R. W. Hanson**
36 B f 21/1 Pitskelly—Margery (FR) (Cadmus II) **Antonio Boesso**
37 **MAZOVIA (FR),** b f 26/1 Taufan (USA)—Warsaw (Salvo) **C. S. Gaisford St Lawrence**
38 **MISTY VALLEY (USA),** ch c 24/4 Majestic Light (USA)—
Orchid Vale (USA) (Gallant Man) **Sheikh Mohammed**
39 B f 25/4 Flash of Steel—Nelly Gail (Mount Hagen (FR)) **Aerhorseracing Ltd**
40 **OLYMPIA FIELDS (IRE),** ch f 18/4 Tate Gallery (USA)—Mille Fleurs (USA) (Jacinto) **M. C. Throsby**
41 **OPINIONATED (IRE),** b g 22/4 Shernazar—Melodramatic (Tudor Melody) **Mrs C. S. Gaisford St Lawrence**
42 **PERSIAN HALO (USA),** br c 4/5 Sunny's Halo (CAN)—
Persian Susan (USA) (Herbager) **Tematron Racing Club**
43 **PLAY THE QUEEN (IRE),** br f 30/5 King of Clubs—Orchestration (Welsh Pageant) **Major V. McCalmont**
44 B c 12/2 Sadler's Wells (USA)—Sweet Posey (Envoy) **Ovidstown Bloodstock**
45 **TEN TALES,** b c 10/4 Prince Tenderfoot—Pam Story (Sallust) **Tematron Racing Club**
46 **TREBLE HOOK (IRE),** ch f 9/5 Ballad Rock—Three Piece (Jaazeiro) **Major V. McCalmont**
47 **TWO WAY MIRROR (IRE),** ch c 16/5 Double Schwartz—Alice Kyteler (Crepello) **Major V. McCalmont**
48 **WHITESVILLE,** b f 22/3 Top Ville—White Star Line (USA) (Northern Dancer) **Sheikh Mohammed**

Other Owners: David Aykroyd, R. A. Bonnycastle, J. R. Brown, J. D. Clague, J. Duggan, Mrs John Horgan, W. Mackinnon, John Magnier, A. V. Nicoll.

Jockey (Flat): P Shanahan (8-3, w.a.).

343 MR P. A. KELLEWAY, Newmarket

Postal: **Paul Kelleway Bloodstock, Shalfleet, 17 Bury Road, Newmarket, CB8 7BX.**
Phone: **(0638) 661461 FAX 0638 666238**

1 **ARTIC ENVOY (USA),** 4, ch c Arctic Tern (USA)—Eternity (FR) **Mr G. Mazza**
2 **CECILIANO (USA),** 4, ch g Irish River (FR)—Derly (FR) **Mr R. B. Belderson**
3 **ELMAYER (USA),** 4, ch c Sharpen Up—Dancing Lesson (USA) **Mr R. G. Whalley**
4 **STONE FLAKE (USA),** 4, ch c Diesis—Wyandra **Mr N. Mandell**

THREE-YEAR-OLDS

5 **AGALEION (FR),** ch c Esprit du Nord (USA)—Algaselle (FR) **Mr R. G. Whalley**
6 **BLACK ADDER (USA),** br c Riverman (USA)—Star Guide (FR) **Fares Stables and Partners**
7 **CRYSTAL BEAM,** b c Crystal Glitters (USA)—Jem Jen **Fares Stables and Partners**
8 **GOLD NOSTALGIA,** ch f Glint of Gold—Crepellora **Fares Stables and Partners**
9 **GRONDOLA,** b f Indian King (USA)—Trysting Place **Mr A. A. Papotto**
10 **LUCKY FROSTY (USA),** br c What Luck (USA)—Frosty Stare **Fares Stables and Partners**
11 **MISS WASSL,** b f Wassl—Arena **Fares Stables and Partners**
12 **POINTE OF LAW (FR),** b f Law Society (USA)—Ninoushka (USA) **Fares Stables and Partners**
13 **ROYAL VERSE (FR),** b c Recitation (USA)—Sauce Royale **Mr B. Lynch**
14 **SCARLET EXPRESS,** b g Precocious—Scarlet Slipper **Miss S. A. Hamilton**
15 **SHANNON EXPRESS,** gr c Magic Mirror—Tatisha **Mr R. B. Hill**
16 **SOBER MIND (USA),** b c Caro—Lolly Dolly **Fares Stables and Partners**
17 **SWAGMAN (USA),** ch c Graustark—Mawgrit (USA) **Mr C. W. Reynolds**
18 **TOP COMPANY (FR),** b c Lomond (USA)—Highest (FR) **Mr R. G. Whalley**
19 **WAKI GOLD (USA),** ch c Miswaki (USA)—Sainte Croix (USA) **Fares Stables and Partners**

MR P. A. KELLEWAY—continued

TWO-YEAR-OLDS

20 B f 27/3 Star Appeal—Alpine Alice (Abwah) **Roldvale Ltd**
21 Gr c Caro—Binky (FR) (Faraway Son (USA)) **Mr N. Mandell**
22 B c 3/3 Wassl—Blue Shark (Silver Shark)
23 B f 20/4 Jalmood (USA)—Celtic Twilight (Varano) **Roldvale Ltd**
24 ELIZA WOODING, b f 2/3 Faustus (USA)—Red Gloves (Red God) **Mrs E. Papotto**
25 B c Vacarme (USA)—Force Nine (FR) (Lutheir (FR)) **Mr R. Whalley**
26 GIPSY KING, br c 22/2 Magic Mirror—Sarah Gillian (USA) (Zen (USA)) **Mrs G. E. Kelleway**
27 HUNDRA (USA), ch c Arctic Tern (USA)—Nur Jahan (USA) (Raja Baba (USA)) **Mr Y. Nasib**
28 B f 3/4 Green Desert (USA)—Jem Jen (Great Nephew) **Roldvale Ltd**
29 Ch f 29/1 Star Appeal—Justine (GER) (Luciano) **Roldvale Ltd**
30 B f 4/5 Chief Singer—Lumiere (USA) (Northjet) **Mr Y. Nasib**
31 B f Gold Crest (USA)—Miss Derby (USA) (Master Derby (USA))
32 MONESTA, ch f 1/4 Claude Monet (USA)—Esta Bonita (USA) (To-Agori-Mou) **Mr P. Evans**
33 B c 8/5 Milles Balles (FR)—Prosodie (FR) (Relko)
34 B f 1/4 Star Appeal—Rapid Glory (Hittite Glory) **Roldvale Ltd**
35 B f 8/2 Nordance (USA)—Screenable (USA) (Silent Screen (USA))
36 B f 31/3 Star Appeal—Targos Delight (Targowice (USA)) **Roldvale Ltd**

Other Owners: Mr J. G. Devonport, Mr G. M. Hantson, Mr J. James, Mrs A. L. Jones, Mr P. A. Kelleway, Mr D. Margolis, Mr Lewis H. Norris, Mr N. J. Phillippo, Mr Derek C. Primett, Mr H. Rosenblatt, Mr P. H. Wagstaffe.

Amateur: Miss S Kelleway (7-10).

344 MR G. P. KELLY, Sheriff Hutton

Postal: **Golden Flatts Farm, Torrington Road, Sherriff Hutton, York, YO6 1RS.**
Phone: **(03477) 518**

1 ALWAYS NATIVE (USA), 9, b br g Our Native (USA)—Mountain Memory (USA) **Mr Gerald P. Kelly**
2 BARATIJO, 5, b g Krayyan—Another Match **Mr Brian J. James**
3 JANES STAR, 6, br g Reformed Character—Janes Jet **Mr Gerald P. Kelly**
4 JUST A SPARK, 11, b m Sparkler—Pontresina **Mr Gerald P. Kelly**
5 KING BOO, 4, b c Van Der Linden (FR)—Star Bella **Mr G. P. Henderson**
6 LADY KHADIJA, 4, b f Nicholas Bill—Chenkynowa **Mr A. Barrett**
7 LURBECK WARRIOR, 8, b g Court Circus—Valpolicella **Mr Gerald P. Kelly**
8 NO RESPONSE, 5, ch m Connaught—Ritratto **Mr Brian J. James**
9 REBECCA'S PET, 8, br m Court Circus—French Secret **Mr R. H. Oxendale**
10 ROYAL COURSE, 5, ch g On Your Mark—Debnic **Mr Stuart Kelly Grant**
11 SHERPAMAN, 8, b h Northfields (USA)—McCoy (USA) **Mr Gerald P. Kelly**

THREE-YEAR-OLDS

12 FIRST BORN, br f Be My Native (USA)—Feat of Arms **Mr G. Murray**
13 SHAMAL, b f Exhibitioner—Kilpeacon **Mr G. Murray**

TWO-YEAR-OLDS

14 B f Cragador—Rodi **Mr N. Crawshaw**

Other Owners: Mr T. Hainsworth, Miss K. Watson.

Jockeys (NH): G Armytage (9-0), P A Farrell (9-7), P Midgley (9-7), A Orkney (10-0).

Amateur: Mr Ian McInnes (9-7).

Lady Riders: Miss Jane Armytage (8-7), Miss Lizzie Hare (8-7).

345 MR W. T. KEMP, Ashford

Postal: **Park Wood Cottage, Smeath, Ashford, Kent, TN25 6SY.**
Phone: **(0233) 72525 or (0860) 398157**

1 **BELLA NOAL,** 4, b f Noalto—Nimble Fingers **Mrs J. C. Ware**
2 **BORENCO,** 9, br m Boreen (FR)—Enco's Lek **Mrs S. Martin**
3 **CEROMERE,** 4, br f Rushmere—Cerolane **A. M. Newport and R. M. Wright**
4 **FOREVER TOGETHER,** 4, ch f Hawaiian Return (USA)—Lightfoot Lady **Mrs Elaine Mitchell**
5 **ISLAND PEARL,** 10, ch g Gulf Pearl—Island Woman **Southchase Limited (Buman Insulations)**
6 **LOCHCROSS,** 4, b f Lochnager—Cross Your Heart **Mr Eric Gleadall**
7 **MISTY JOY,** 5, gr m General Ironside—Darjoy **Mr G. A. Fordham**
8 **MY DOMINION,** 8, b g Dominion—Madge **Mrs S. Martin**
9 **NARCONE,** 9, b m Kambalda—Lady Coleman **Mr Eric Gleadall**
10 **OWEN SOMER,** 5, br g Tudorville—Floral Somer **H. Lowe**
11 **POWER PUNCH,** 6, b g Black Minstrel—Kellsboro Star **Mr A. Mawson**
12 **TEENAGE SCRIBBLER,** 5, br g Over The River (FR)—Balldado **Miss Alison Langmead**
13 **TUMBLED BRIDE,** 4, b f Tumble Wind (USA)—Bridewell Belle **Mr A. Mawson**

THREE-YEAR-OLDS

14 **PERSIAN SULTAN,** br c Persian Bold—Florita **Mr Mike Culling**

Other Owners: Mr J. B. Mitchell, Mr A. Ross, Mrs Caroline Spooner.

Conditional: S McKeever (9-7).

Amateur: Mr H Finegan (10-5).

346 MRS M. A. KENDALL, Penrith

Postal: **Wood Side, Great Strickland, Penrith, Cumbria, CA10 3DX.**
Phone: **HACKTHORPE (09312) 318**

1 **COOL CRYSTAL,** 4, b f Dynastic—Cool Baby **Mrs M. A. Kendall**
2 **GILLANBONE,** 8, ch g Baptism—Joplin **Mrs M. A. Kendall**
3 **MY MERLIN,** 4, b g My Chopin—Miss Rubor VII **Mrs M. A. Kendall**

Lady Rider: Mrs M A Kendall (9-7).

347 MR N. KERNICK, Buckfastleigh

Postal: **Top-of-the-mark-Stables, Higher Wallaford Farm, Buckfastleigh, Devon, TQ11 0HG.**
Phone: **(0364) 42755**

1 **FLAME FLOWER,** 8, gr m Runnymede—Headliner **Mr R. U. Hall**
2 **LINDANJAN,** 6, b m Radetzky—Cherio Honey **Mr A. L. Hawkings**
3 **OCKY'S FLIER,** 6, bl g Aban—Ceile **Mrs S. M. Walters**
4 **REVEREND MOTHER,** 4, b f Class Distinction—Black Veil **Mr A. L. Hawkings**
5 **TAR'S HILL,** 9, gr g Hill Farmer—Tar's Tart **Mrs Beryl Somerton**
6 **XEROMEDE,** 6, b g Runnymede—Nervous Cough **Mr R. U. Hall**

THREE-YEAR-OLDS

7 **ARTISTIC PEACE,** b f Prince of Peace—Rising Artist **Mrs Pamela Yeo**

MR N. KERNICK—continued

TWO-YEAR-OLDS

8 **FLAME BURST,** ro c 15/4 Prince of Peace—Flame Flower (Runnymede) **Mrs Pamela Yeo**
9 **JOLLY FLIER,** br g 26/4 Prince of Peace—Ceile (Galivanter) **Mrs S. M. Walters**
10 **NEIL'S WAY,** b g 2/4 Prince of Peace—My Always (Kalimnos) **Mrs Pamela Yeo**
11 **WHY FOR,** b g 16/5 Prince of Peace—Rising Artist (Mandamus) **Mr Colin Sorrell**

Other Owners: Mr W. J. Francis, Mrs B. E. Kernick, Kingswood Thoroughbred Racing Ltd, Mr C. R. Manvell.

Jockey (Flat): R Street (7-7, w.a.).

Jockey (NH): S Foster (9-12, w.a.).

348 MR T. KERSEY, Rotherham

Postal: **Bleak House Stable, 16 Packman Road, West Melton, Rotherham.**
Phone: **(0709) 873166**

1 **AVARICE,** 4, ch c Persian Bold—Parsimony **Mr T. Kersey**
2 **BARCHAM PRINCE,** 8, b g Balliol—Barcham Bride **Mr T. Kersey**
3 **BELLE DE MONT,** 4, b f Montekin—Magic Lady **Mr J. W. Baker**
4 **BURTONWOOD'S BEST,** 4, b g Longleat (USA)—Abbey Rose **Mr T. E. Mellor**
5 **CHARLOTTES GIFT,** 6, b m Welsh Captain—Mandys Gift
6 **DUFFERS DANCER,** 8, ch g Miami Springs—Evening Chorus
7 **EJAY HAITCH,** 5, br g Be My Native (USA)—Miss Spencer
8 **FAILIQ (FR),** 6, b h Bustino—Salvationist **Mr T. E. Mellor**
9 **FANDANGO KISS,** 7, ch m Gay Fandango (USA)—Bridewell Belle **Mr T. Kersey**
10 **IN DREAMS,** 7, b g High Line—Blissful Evening **Mr H. R. Rushworth**
11 **IRISH DILEMMA,** 7, b g Jaazeiro (USA)—Southern Swanee **Mr T. Kersey**
12 **JEAN DUKE'S LAD,** 4, ch g Bay Express—Pounakha (USA) **Mrs Jean Duke**
13 **JOHN'S REEF,** 5, ch g Main Reef—Embustera **Mr M. E. Taylor**
14 **KEELLEB,** 5, ch h Gorytus (USA)—Miss Upward **Mr T. Kersey**
15 **MAJOR FREDIE,** 4, ch g Major Petingo (FR)—Piber **Mr T. E. Mellor**
16 **MANDALAY PRINCE,** 6, b g Nishapour (FR)—Ops **Mr H. R. Rushworth**
17 **MEADOW TERRACE,** 6, br g Young Man (FR)—Rebecca Sarah **Mr T. Kersey**
18 **MEDIA STAR,** 5, ch m Star Appeal—Linduna **Mr T. Kersey**
19 **MISS VAL,** 4, gr f Nishapour (FR)—Light Opera (FR)
20 **NEWMARKET SAUSAGE,** 9, ch g Owen Dudley—Manoeuvre **Mr T. Kersey**
21 **OHILL SKY,** 6, b g Skyliner—Royal Inheritance **Mr T. Kersey**
22 **ROMAN CHIMES,** 4, ch g Sallust—Mingoon Bell
23 **ROYAL-BLUE BELLE,** 4, b f Castle Keep—Pat Pong **Mr T. Kersey**
24 **SIR EDWARD,** 5, b g Formidable (USA)—Pearl Wedding **Mr H. R. Rushworth**
25 **SOARING EAGLES,** 6, b m Piaffer (USA)—Circumstance **T. Kersey**
26 **SWEETEN GALE,** 4, ch f On Your Mark—Betty Bun **Mr H. R. Rushworth**
27 **UPTOWN RANDB'S,** 7, b m Uncle Pokey—Mountain Child **T. Kersey**
28 **YOUNG BENJAMIN,** 5, b g Tyrnavos—Pearling **Mrs Jean Duke**
29 **ZAGADKA (FR),** 5, gr m Carwhite—Fille du Roi (FR) **Mrs Ruth Roper-Tye**

THREE-YEAR-OLDS

30 **BRACKEN BAY,** gr f All Systems Go—War Bird
31 **DENHAM HOUSE,** ch g Jalmood (USA)—Ariadne

MR T. KERSEY—continued

TWO-YEAR-OLDS

32 Ch c Vaigly Great—Assya (Double Form) **Mr T. E. Mellor**
33 Ch g Scottish Reel—Aunt Winnie (Wolver Hollow) **Mr T. E. Mellor**
34 B f Lyphard's Special—Hasty Goddess **Mr T. E. Mellor**
35 B c Nordance (USA)—Headfirst (Welsh Pageant) **Mr T. E. Mellor**
36 **LADYCROFT,** ch f Crofthall—War Bird **Mr T. Kersey**
37 Gr c Hotfoot—Loving Doll (Godswalk) **Mr T. E. Mellor**
38 B c Prince Sabo—Miss Rossi

Other Owners: Mrs K. M. Ballard, Mr P. T. Ballard, Mr Peter Coles, Mr A. G. Duke, Mrs S. D. Lynam, Mr J. Winterbottom.

Jockey (NH): Susan Kersey (9-10).

Apprentice: Sharon Kersey (8-0).

Conditional: Susan Kersey (10-0).

Amateurs: Mr T Kersey (11-0), Miss Julie Middleton (9-0).

349 MR S. E. KETTLEWELL, Middleham

Postal: **Tupgill Park Stables, Middleham, Leyburn, North Yorkshire.**
Phone: **WENSLEYDALE (0969) 40295**

1 **CALLAGHAN,** 5, b g Cut Above—Super Restless (USA) **Mr K. J. Lawson**
2 **CASSANOVA LAD,** 4, b c Swing Easy (USA)—Sallusteno **Mrs G. A. Cawthorn**
3 **DEINOPUS,** 6, b g Hittite Glory—Flying Fire **Mrs B. R. Powell**
4 **HALF SHAFT (USA),** 9, b g Broadway Forli (USA)—One Quest **Mr K. J. Lawson**
5 **LIFESONG,** 4, b f Song—Blakesware Saint **Mr D. J. Vernon**
6 4, B g Full of Hope—Linden Dolly **Mr G. R. Orchard**
7 **MARKET HIGH,** 7, b g Native Bazaar—First Flight **Mr K. J. Lawson**
8 **PRINTER,** 8, ch g Velvet Prince—Potterlane **Mr G. R. Orchard**
9 **ROSCOE THE BRAVE,** 6, br g Roscoe Blake—My Plucky Lady **Mr G. R. Orchard**
10 **VALIANT BOY,** 4, b g Connaught—Irish Amber **Mr Roy Chadwick**
11 **VALIANT DASH,** 4, b g Valiyar—Dame Ashfield **Mr G. R. Orchard**

THREE-YEAR-OLDS

12 B g Oats—Lost Valley **Mr G. R. Orchard**
13 **MAY QUEEN,** b f Dara Monarch—Markon **Mrs G. A. Cawthorn**
14 Ch c Nearly A Hand—Moate Queen VII **Mr G. R. Orchard**
15 **PRINCESS ARABRAB,** ch f Jalmood (USA)—Princess Zeddera **Mrs B. R. Powell**

TWO-YEAR-OLDS

16 B g 24/4 Idiot's Delight—Be Spartan (Spartan General) **Mr G. R. Orchard**
17 B c 3/4 Tudor Rhythm—Colly Cone (Celtic Cone) **Mr G. R. Orchard**

Other Owners: Mr J. R. Kettlewell, Mr T. E. Kettlewell.

Jockey (Flat): S Webster (w.a.).

Jockey (NH): B Storey (w.a.).

Conditional: R Garritty (w.a.).

350 MR B. L. KEY, Malvern

Postal: **Moat Court Farm, Sherrards Green, Malvern, Worcestershire, WR13 5AS.**
Phone: **(0684) 573830**

1 **BELPENEL,** 4, ch g Pharly (FR)—Seldovia **Mrs Brenda Key**
2 **STOCKSIGN (USA),** 9, b g King's Bishop (USA)—Ruff Up (USA) **Mrs Brenda Key**

Other Owners: Mr B. L. Key, Mrs D. A. Smith.

Jockey (NH): Craig Smith (10-0).

Lady Rider: Mrs D Smith.

351 MISS A. L. M. KING, Stratford-on-Avon

Postal: **Warren Chase, Wilmcote, Stratford-on-Avon, Warwickshire.**
Phone: **OFFICE (0789) 205087 YARD (0789) 297121 HOME (0789) 298346**

1 **BIG MINSTREL,** 5, b g Black Minstrel—Magic Money **Queensway Securities Limited**
2 **COMPLETE OPTIMIST,** 6, b g Midland Gayle—No Hunting **Mr Brian J. D. Lewis**
3 **CREETOWN SALLY,** 7, b m Creetown—Brocton Queen **Mr Douglas King**
4 **DIAMOND BOY,** 4, b g Sparkling Boy—Haddon Anna **Mr John Brooke**
5 **GLENCAIRN LASS,** 6, b m Buckskin (FR)—Tony's Sister **Mr Brian J. D. Lewis**
6 **HADDON LAD,** 7, b g Dragonara Palace (USA)—Gresham Girl **I. T. S. Ltd**
7 **HARD TO RESIST,** 5, b g Oats—Anchor Lady **Mrs J. Madden**
8 **LADY ROSABELLE,** 4, ch f Broadsword (USA)—T V Star **Mr H. P. Naden**
9 **MULLAUN,** 6, b br m Deep Run—Quadro **Mr M. F. D. Bartley**
10 **QUEENSWAY BOY,** 11, ch g Kemal (FR)—Oscillation **Queensway Securities Limited**
11 **SHELLEYS ROCKY GEM,** 4, b f Kemal (FR)—Kintullagh **Queensway Securities Limited**
12 **STANS JOY,** 6, b g Buckskin (FR)—Just Our Luck **Queensway Securities Limited**
13 **STORMY SAGA,** 5, ch g Sagaro—Tempest Girl **Mr B. McReynolds**
14 4, Ch g Julio Mariner—Tempest Girl **Miss A. L. M. King**
15 **VIRIDIAN,** 5, b g Green Shoon—Cahermone Ivy **Mr Brian J. D. Lewis**
16 **WHY NOT FLOPSY,** 5, b m Quayside—Realinda **Mr Brian J. D. Lewis**

THREE-YEAR-OLDS

17 B f Oats—Tempest Girl **Miss A. L. M. King**

TWO-YEAR-OLDS

18 B f 20/4 Rymer—Creetown Sally (Creetown) **Mr Douglas King**

Other Owners: Mr Andrew L. Cohen, Mr N. J. Darbourne.

Jockey (NH): Allan Webb (10-0).

Conditional: Pat O'Dwyer (9-10).

Amateur: Mr N Bradley (9-7).

352 MR J. S. KING, Swindon

Postal: **Elm Cross House, Swindon Road, Broad Hinton, Swindon, SN4 9PF.**
Phone: **(0793) 731481 MOBILE (0836) 245393**

1 **ADELAURE (FR),** 5, b g Rose Laurel—Sonade (FR) **Mr Mark O'Connor**
2 **BEACH TIGER,** 6, gr g Java Tiger—Lido Light **Mrs A. J. Garrett**
3 **BLENDERS CHOICE,** 8, b g Cavo Doro—Harriny **Mr Mark O'Connor**
4 **BUCK AND SKIP,** 6, ch g Buckskin (FR)—Cool Amanda **Mrs A. T. Pollard**
5 **CHANGE WEAR,** 4, b g Alzao (USA)—Piccadilly Lil **Change Wear Furniture Ltd**
6 **CHUCKLESTONE,** 7, b g Chukaroo—Czar's Diamond **Mr Mark O'Connor**
7 **CLEVER FOX,** 10, b g Kambalda—Leaney Escort **Sportswords Ltd**
8 **COMPTON PARK,** 9, ch g Eastwood Prince—Mighty Grand **Lord Vestey**
9 **DEMOCRATIC BOY,** 8, b g Free State—Klaire **Mr Alan Lee**
10 **DUSKEY COMIC,** 8, br m Comedy Star (USA)—Dusky Damsel **Mr J. S. King**
11 **FLYING JUNCTION,** 4, ch g Burslem—Windy City **Mrs P. M. King**
12 **FURZEN HILL,** 11, b g Jimsun—Lady Maggie **Mrs P. M. King**
13 **GALLIC BELLE,** 4, b f Roman Warrior—Belle Lutine **J. K. Dale**
14 **HUNTERS FEN,** 8, b g Bonne Noel—Positioned **Mr F. J. Carter**
15 **LAST SHOWER,** 5, ch m Town And Country—Rainbow's End **Mrs S. A. McLeod**
16 **LAUDERDALE LAD,** 8, b g Politico (USA)—Cannes Beach **Hills Of Swindon Limited**
17 5, B g Nearly A Hand—Lost In Silence **Mr Mark O'Connor**
18 **MARCHMAN,** 5, b g Daring March—Saltation **Mr Matt McBride**
19 **MISTER FEATHERS,** 9, b g Town And Country—Nikali **Mrs M. Forde**
20 **MISTER ODDY,** 4, b g Dubassoff (USA)—Somerford Glory **Mr Valere N. F. Tjolle**
21 **PLEATED (USA),** 8, b g Grey Dawn II—Kick Pleat **Mr Peter Hopkins**
22 **SHARPRIDGE,** 6, ch g Nearly A Hand—Maria's Piece **Mr John Skull**
23 **SILENT TWIRL,** 7, b m Piaffer (USA)—Lost In Silence **Mr Matt McBride**
24 **TEE QU,** 5, b g Jimsun—Stephouette **T. Quality Ltd**
25 **TOM CAXTON,** 9, b g Nearly A Hand—Lost In Silence **Mr Mark O'Connor**
26 **TURPIN'S GREEN,** 7, b g Nearly A Hand—Maria's Piece **Lord Vestey**
27 **VISION OF WONDER,** 6, b g Tyrnavos—Valeur **Mr F. J. Carter**

THREE-YEAR-OLDS

28 **APHELINA,** b f Belfort (FR)—Aphaia **Mrs P. M. King**

Other Owners: Mr P. A. Deal, Mr James A. Hamilton, Miss Elizabeth Knight, Mr G. Otway, Mr Eric Penny, Mrs A. M. Whatley.

Conditional: T Barry (10-0).

Lady Rider: Michelle Sawyer (9-7).

353 MRS A. KNIGHT, Cullompton

Postal: **The Racing Stables, Garland Hayes, Clayhidon, Cullompton, Devon, EX15 3TT.**
Phone: **(0823) 680959**

1 **ALKIONIS,** 4, b c Dominion—Norfolk Gal **Mrs R. M. Davies**
2 **BACCAROLE,** 5, b g Ballad Rock—Eastern Saint **Mr Andy Strickland**
3 **CHANTILLY LACE (FR),** 6, ch m Carwhite—Frenchouan (FR) **Mr Alan Samuel**
4 **DOMARC,** 7, b g Moorestyle—Head First **Mr Gary Cooper**
5 **FASHION PRINCESS,** 4, gr f Van Der Linden (FR)—Pendle's Secret **Mr J. A. F. Cairns**
6 **FIVE QUARTERS,** 7, gr m Native Bazaar—Pippaluk (FR) **Mr R. Jefferies**
7 **GOOD APPEAL,** 5, ch m Star Appeal—Good Larker **Mr Derek V. Bolt**
8 **GRANDANGUS,** 7, b g Creetown—Woolcana **Mr Ian Abrahams**
9 **HELLO SWEETIE,** 4, ch f Hello Gorgeous (USA)—My Sweetie **Mr Stephen Shears**
10 **IN ORBIT,** 5, b h Habitat—Aryenne (FR) **Mr Gary Cooper**

MRS A. KNIGHT—continued

11 **KOWZA,** 4, ch f Young Generation—Follow The Stars **Mr Vivian Guy**
12 4, Ch f Telsmoss—Laveche **Mrs R. M. Davies**
13 **MAPLE HAYES,** 4, b f Pas de Seul—Sweet Eliane **Mr Vivian Guy**
14 **MARLBOROUGH LADY,** 4, gr f Rusticaro (FR)—Noir Afrique **Poppe Inne Racing**
15 4, Ch f Julio Mariner—Miss Colleen **Mr J. A. F. Cairns**
16 **MOST OF ALL,** 4, gr f Absalom—Beech Tree **Mr Gary Cooper**
17 **MY DARK ROSALEEN,** 4, br f King of Spain—Irish Holiday **Mr Gary Cooper**
18 **ONLY JOKING,** 6, b m Balinger—Comical **Mr Gordon Salter**
19 **POPPE INNE BELLE,** 4, b f Magnolia Lad—Parton Belle **Mr N. Foote**
20 **PURSTON STAR,** 10, b g Osiris—Purston Nigella **Mrs J. H. Turner**
21 **RED BREWSTER,** 4, b g Burslem—Red Magic **Mr D. A. Cooper**
22 **RISATINA,** 4, ch f Sallust—Saga's Humour **Mr G. Demery**
23 **SATURN MOON,** 5, ch m Monsanto (FR)—Ritruda (USA) **Mrs R. M. Davies**
24 **SKRAGGS PLUS TWO,** 6, ch h Owen Anthony—Carvers Corah **Mr A. F. Guy**
25 **TASKALADY,** 4, ch f Touching Wood (USA)—Damaska **Mr Geo Taylor**
26 **TIME ON MY HANDS,** 4, ch f Warpath—Midsummer Madness **Mr L. G. Howkings**

Other Owners: Mr Graham Amery, Mr Jim Camwell, Mr Derek Conibeer, Mr K. J. Corcoran, Mr John Flynn, Miss Heather Gregory, Mrs Vicki Guy, Mr N. J. Harris, Mr Langlois.

Jockey (NH): George Knight (9-7).

Apprentice: B Lane.

Conditional: David Matthews (9-7).

354 MISS H. C. KNIGHT, Wantage

Postal: **West Lockinge Farm, Wantage, Oxon, OX12 8QF.**
Phone: **(0235) 833535**

1 **AMBER BLOSSOM,** 8, ch g Amoristic (USA)—Hidden Blossom **Mrs J. K. Peutherer**
2 **ASSAGLAWI,** 8, b g Troy—Queen's Counsellor **Richard Green (Fine Paintings)**
3 **BALLINCAR BOY,** 7, b g Deep Run—Rugged More **Lord Hartington**
4 **CRAFTY STYLE,** 7, b g Crafty Codger—Hi Style **Mrs J. K. Peutherer**
5 **DECIDED (CAN),** 7, b g Affirmed (USA)—Expediency (USA) **Richard Green (Fine Paintings)**
6 **DIAMOND RUN,** 6, ch g Deep Run—Yellowstone Park **Mrs F. E. Wigley**
7 **DIVINE PROBLEM,** 8, gr g Roselier (FR)—Group Problem **Mrs I. A. K. Dipple**
8 **EMPLOYMENT LAW,** 6, ch g Import—Pepin **Mr Frank Walton**
9 **ESPECIALLY BOLD,** 4, b f Lyphard's Special (USA)—Bold Design **Castle Farm Stud**
10 **FAIR PROSPECT,** 4, b c Shirley Heights—Sans Blague (USA) **Richard Green (Fine Paintings)**
11 **FLEMISH FUDGE,** 8, b g Candy Cane—Leuze **Mrs David Gardiner**
12 **GARRELGUM,** 7, b g Deep Run—Toombeola **Lord Hartington**
13 **GAY GUNNER,** 9, b g Gunner B—Gay Ribbon **Mrs Denise Stamp**
14 **GOLDEN CELTIC,** 6, b g Rare One—Cooleen **Mrs H. Brown**
15 **HARP OF GOLD,** 4, b g Chief Singer—Blue Queen **Lord Chelsea**
16 **INCIDENTAL,** 5, br g Swing Easy (USA)—Luckley Brake **Mr R. E. Morris-Adams**
17 **ITS ALL VERY FINE,** 9, ch g Deep Run—Flat Refusal **Mr J. R. Collins**
18 **JOHNNY WILL,** 5, b g Salluceva—Hellfire Hostess **Lord Chelsea**
19 **KINDLED'S CLOWN,** 4, b g Idiot's Delight—Kindled Spirit **Castle Farm Stud**
20 **MANDER'S WAY,** 5, b g Furry Glen—Art Mistress **Lord Vestey**
21 **MIDNIGHT STORY,** 5, gr g Pragmatic—Midnight Oil **Mr Paul Stamp**
22 **MORE ACTION,** 8, b g Deep Run—Una's Pride **Mr Peter Hemelik**
23 **OUR SURVIVOR,** 6, b g Trimmingham—Lougharue **Mr P. E. Simpson**
24 **PEARL PROSPECT,** 7, br g Kambalda—Georgette **Mrs Valerie Lewis**

MISS H. C. KNIGHT—continued

25 **ROYAL BOROUGH,** 5, b g Bustino—Lady R B (USA) **Lord Chelsea**
26 **SMILE AGAIN,** 7, b g Sagaro—Heckley Surprise **Mr Paul Stamp**
27 **STRAIGHT MILE LAD,** 9, b g Free Boy—Palimony **Mrs P. Scott-Dunn**
28 **THE GREY GUNNER,** 10, gr g Pry—Willsie's Blunder **Mr J. C. Newton-Taylor**
29 **THE TAN MAN,** 7, b g Tanfirion—Lady Begorra **Mr John Foreman**
30 **TOPPING-THE-BILL,** 5, b g Nicholas Bill—Top-N-Tale **Mrs I. A. K. Dipple**
31 **TOUREEN PRINCE,** 7, b g Cheval—Lauregeen **Mr Paul Stamp**
32 **WHATS THE CRACK,** 7, b g The Parson—Mighty Crack **Mr J. Wright**
33 **WHATS YOUR PROBLEM,** 7, b g Buckskin (FR)—Laurenca **Lord Vestey**
34 **WHISTLE BLOWER,** 5, ch g Le Bavard (FR)—Grangeclare Lady **Mrs G. N. Morris-Adams**
35 **YOUNG LINE,** 4, b g Young Generation—Quay Line **Mr R. Brazier**
36 **YOUNG WARRIOR,** 6, ch g Roman Warrior—Teenager **Sir Charles Morrison**

Other Owners: Mr Paul Barnes, Miss Desi Dillingham, Mrs P. Donner, Mr J. L. Dunlop, Mr P. J. Ensor, Mrs I. Kelsey-Fry, Mr Jim Lewis, Mrs David Naylor-Leyland, Mr J. Rigby, Sir John Saville, Mrs David Sieff, Mr S. Sohmer, Lady Tavistock, Mrs Lorna Walton, Mr Edward Wood, Mr J. W. Woolley, Mr John Zochonis.

Jockey (NH): R J Beggan (10-2).

Amateur: Mr G Cosgrove.

355 MR R. R. LAMB, Seahouses

Postal: **East Fleetham, Seahouses, Northumberland, NE68 7UX.**
Phone: **(0665) 720260**

1 **ANOTHER FOLLY,** 6, b m Lighter—Goodfellow's Folly **Mr S. J. Watson**
2 **BRIG HOUSE,** 10, b m New Brig—Forlorn Lady **Mrs Margaret W. Lamb**
3 **CASPER,** 5, ch g Grey Ghost—Marcus Lady **Mrs Margaret W. Lamb**
4 **CHARLIEWAM,** 7, ch g White Speck—Canute Lady **Mr R. R. Lamb**
5 4, B g Grey Ghost—Forlorn Lady
6 5, Gr g Montreal Boy—Forlorn Lady
7 **LA BOEUF,** 14, br g Bing II—True Grit **Mr R. R. Lamb**
8 **MARCOMTE,** 7, ch g Vicomte—Marcus Lady **Mrs Margaret W. Lamb**
9 **MEADOW MOOR,** 7, b h Comedy Star (USA)—Miss Golightly **Mr L. Munro**
10 **MISTOSH,** 6, b m White Speck—Keyvaca **Mrs M. Crooks**
11 **SPOT ON,** 7, b g White Speck—Singing Span **Mr K. L. Larnach**
12 **TOSHEN BOY,** 10, ch g White Speck—Keyvaca **Mrs Margaret W. Lamb**
13 **WAR HOUSE,** 7, ch m Tug of War—Brilliant Girl **Mr R. R. Lamb**
14 **WILLIEWAM,** 8, b g White Speck—Canute Lady **Mr R. R. Lamb**
15 **YOUNG ADVENTURER,** 11, gr g Pongee—Fleetham Irene **Mrs Margaret W. Lamb**

Other Owners: Miss S. M. Anderson, Mr D. A. Lamb.

Jockey (NH): K Jones (10-4).

356 MR J. R. M. LAYLAND, Clitheroe

Postal: **Demesne House, Newsholme, Gisburn, Clitheroe, Lancashire, BB7 4JF.**
Phone: **(0200) 445 490 or (0270) 258822 FAX (0200) 445 795 or (0270) 500029**

1 **ANCIENT CROSS,** 6, ch m Celtic Cone—Crossacres **Mr R. Layland**
2 **BALINGLANCE,** 8, b g Balinger—Greek Glance **Mr R. Layland**
3 **KEMCROSS,** 10, ch m Kemal (FR)—Crossacres **Mr R. Layland**

MR J. R. M. LAYLAND—continued

4 **MYSTERY'S NIECE,** 7, b m Belfalas—Place Pigalle **Mr R. Layland**
5 **PARKLYN,** 12, b g Bivouac—Moette **Mr R. Layland**
6 **RAGING RIVER,** 8, b g Tachypous—Rivers Maid **Mr R. Layland**

Amateur: Ross McGhie (10-0).

357 MR A. J. LE BLOND, Hetton-le-Hole

Postal: **South Lodge Farm, North Road, Hetton-le-Hole, Houghton-le-Spring, DH5 9TY.**
Phone: **(091) 5263442**

1 **CHLOROPHYLL,** 7, b m Ballymore—Mandy Girl **Mr A. J. Le Blond**
2 **FLAXON WORRIOR,** 6, ch g Roman Warrior—Domino Smith **Miss B. Baker**
3 **SHADY STAR,** 4, b f Lochnager—Shady Desire **Mr A. J. Le Blond**

THREE-YEAR-OLDS

4 **SHADY MOON,** b f Lochnager—Shady Desire **Miss B. Baker**

358 MR T. C. LE GRICE, Penzance

Postal: **Trereife Farm, Penzance, Cornwall.**
Phone: **PENZANCE (0736) 62750**

1 **CORNISH SUMMER,** 7, ch m Vital Season—Cornish Saffron **Mr T. C. Le Grice**
2 **ROMAN STARGAZER,** 5, b h Shaab—Roman Candy **Mr T. C. Le Grice**
3 **ROMANY WALK,** 8, b g Saunter—Roman Candy **Mr T. C. Le Grice**
4 **TREVAYLOR (NZ),** 6, ch g Rapier II—Regal Bride (NZ) **Mr T. C. Le Grice**

359 MR M. R. LEACH, Newark

Postal: **Rose Cottage, Long Lane, Barnby In The Willows, Newark, Nottinghamshire, NG24 2SG.**
Phone: **(0636) 626518**

1 **ASONESS,** 4, b f Laxton—Asicion **Mr A. Snipe**
2 **BLAKENESS,** 5, b m Blakeney—Nesreen **Mr A. Snipe**
3 **POMPUSE LORD,** 4, ch g Posse (USA)—Laxay **Mr A. Snipe**

THREE-YEAR-OLDS

4 **DAWN DECISION,** br c Dawn Johnny (USA)—Asicion **Mr A. Snipe**
5 **DAWN SECRET,** b c Dawn Johnny (USA)—Sasol **Mr A. Snipe**

TWO-YEAR-OLDS

6 Ch c Laxton—Berrio **Mr A. Snipe**
7 Gr f Dawn Johnny (USA)—Lallax **Mr A. Snipe**
8 Gr c Dawn Johnny (USA)—Laxay **Mr A. Snipe**
9 B f Dawn Johnny (USA)—Mayab **Mr A. Snipe**

Jockeys (Flat): A Barclay (8-4, w.a.), D Nicholls (8-4, w.a.).

Apprentice: Neil Leach (8-7).

360 MR P. S. LEACH, Taunton

Postal: **1 Dobins Cottage, West Bagborough, Taunton, Somerset, TA4 3EP.**
Phone: **(0823) 433249 MOBILE (0860) 482908**

1 **ARIBIE,** 4, b br f Konigsstuhl (GER)—Arita (FR) **Mr G. Whittaker**
2 **AUCTIONEERS MOLL,** 7, b m Pardigras—Jostling **Mr R. G. Williams**
3 **BOURBON ROSE,** 4, b f Ile de Bourbon (USA)—Tantot **Mrs B. M. L. Davis**
4 **CANTUS FIRMUS,** 4, b c Lyphard's Special (USA)—Capricious (FR) **Mr A. H. Kosky**
5 **CAORAN MONA,** 5, b g Dominion—Maddelena **Mrs Lynne Webb**
6 **FERENTINO,** 5, b g Sparkler—Sa Fille **Mrs B. M. L. Davis**
7 **FRANCESCA-BELLE,** 5, ch m Shaab—Orvotus **Mr F. B. Colwill**
8 **FRAUD SQUAD,** 11, ch g Gambling Debt—Jostling **Mr R. G. Williams**
9 **HEART OF STONE (USA),** 8, ch h Dust Commander (USA)—Grankie (USA) **Mr Paul Leach**
10 **HIGH IMP,** 10, ch g Import—High Walk **Mrs Marie-Christine Jacobs**
11 **MISS CHEERFUL,** 5, ch m Last Fandango—Meadow Nymph **Mr D. H. Currie**
12 **MR MURDOCK,** 5, b g Last Fandango—Moss Pink (USA) **Mr F. A. Clegg**
13 **PURPLE PRINCE (USA),** 7, b g Sensitive Prince (USA)—Roses For The Lady (USA) **Mrs Lynne Webb**
14 **ROYAL HERO,** 9, b g Heres—Royal Rondo **Mr D. Bryant**
15 **SEDGEWELL LAD,** 8, ch g Proud Challenge—Meadow Nymph **Mr D. H. Currie**
16 **SEDGEWELL ORCHID,** 5, gr m John de Coombe—Lyn Affair **Mrs Lynne Webb**
17 **SUMMERHILL SALLY,** 4, b f Dunbeath (USA)—Sharper Still **Mr J. R. Wilmington**

Other Owners: Mr J. Hodges, Mr H. Newman, Mr T. Wallace.

Jockey (NH): H Davies (10-3).

Conditional: S Burden (10-0).

361 MR S. J. LEADBETTER, Berwick-upon-Tweed

Postal: **Ladykirk Stables, Berwick-upon-Tweed, TD15 ISU.**
Phone: **(0289) 82519**

1 **ANDREW,** 7, b g Le Coq d'Or—Turkish Suspicion **Mr G. McGuinness**
2 **ARISHAN,** 6, ch g Relkino—Second House **Mrs W. A. Griffiths**
3 **DAVARA,** 4, gr g Dawn Johnny (USA)—News Belle **Mr D. W. Nicholson**
4 **DAWN COYOTE (USA),** 7, ch g Grey Dawn II—Beanery (USA) **Mr James Baxter**
5 **DUNDYVAN,** 8, ch g Crimson Beau—Flora Day **Mr S. J. Leadbetter**
6 **IMPAGE,** 12, br g Enbrage—Swift Imp **Mr D. W. Nicholson**
7 **MONTEVIOT,** 6, b m Scallywag—Mikadora **Mr J. B. Lees**
8 **MOULTON BULL,** 4, ch g Chabrias (FR)—Welsh Cloud **Mrs B. Ward**
9 **PADDY HAYTON,** 9, br g St Paddy—Natenka **Mrs M. P. Wares**
10 **ROY'S DREAM,** 7, b g Down The Hatch—Promising Dream **Mr C. Bird**

THREE-YEAR-OLDS

11 Br g Politico (USA)—Bravade
12 **DAISY BRAE,** gr f Brotherly (USA)—Tudor Primrose **Mr C. Bird**
13 **MAGIC LAW,** b f Majestic Current (USA)—Lawsuitlaw
14 B g Oats—Rapenna

Other Owners: Mr W. Hogarth, Mrs M. Lees.

Amateur: Mr R Shiels (10-10).

362 MR R. R. LEDGER, Sittingbourne

Postal: **Sorrento, School Lane, Borden, Sittingbourne, ME9 8JS.**
Phone: **(0795) 423360**

1 **JOHNNY TARQUIN,** 17, br g Tarqogan—Fanny O'Dea **Mr R. R. Ledger**
2 **NORHAM CASTLE,** 7, b g Scott Joplyn—Gay Amanda **Mr R. R. Ledger**
3 **SEA CHALLENGER,** 9, ch m Seaepic (USA)—Escallop **Mr R. R. Ledger**
4 **SILVER SLEEK,** 5, gr m Royal Palace—War Bird **Mr R. R. Ledger**
5 **THE FRUIT,** 11, ch g Kambalda—Beautiful Night **Mr R. R. Ledger**

Amateur: Mrs Nicky Ledger (9-0).

363 MR A. N. LEE, Newmarket

Postal: **Hackness Villa Stables, Exeter Road, Newmarket, Suffolk, CB8 8LP.**
Phone: **(0638) OFFICE 669783 HOME 662734**

1 **CASPIAN GATES,** 6, b g Persian Bold—Galka **Mr B. N. Fulton**
2 **JANET'S FOSS,** 4, b f Idiot's Delight—Pennulli **Miss Betty Duxbury**

THREE-YEAR-OLDS

3 **ABIGAIL'S DREAM,** gr f Kalaglow—Moss Pink (USA) **Mr Tom King**
4 **BETWS-Y-COED,** b f Petong—Glyn Rhosyn **Mr John Livock**
5 **BUSTALA,** ch f Bustino—B A Poundstretcher **Mr R. A. Clowes**
6 **DAISY TOPPER,** b f Top Ville—Fairlawne **Miss Z. Whitmore**
7 **GILDED PAST,** ch c Glint of Gold—Historia **Lt Col A. K. Sharp**
8 **THE WEIR,** ch g Salmon Leap (USA)—Galka **Mr B. N. Fulton**

TWO-YEAR-OLDS

9 Ch f 24/2 Claude Monet (USA)—Arbor Lane (Wolverlife) **Mr A. A. Papotto**
10 Gr c 31/3 Never So Bold—Celestial City (Godswalk (USA)) **Mr John Livock**
11 **CIXI,** b f 19/2 Far Out East (USA)—Hasty Key (USA) (Key To The Mint (USA)) **Miss Z. Whitmore**
12 **CLOSE THE DEAL,** ch f 30/3 Nicholas Bill—Cateryne (Ballymoss) **Miss Lisa Kelly**
13 B f 27/3 Persian Bold—Hanna Alta (FR) (Busted) **Mr A. A. Papotto**
14 B f 11/4 Tate Gallery (USA)—Linda Dudley (Owen Dudley) **Mr John Livock**
15 **MAY REEF (IRE),** b f 2/3 Simply Great (FR)—Mey (Canisbay) **Invoshire Ltd**
16 **PLEASE PLEASE ME (IRE),** b f 21/4 Tender King—Tacama (Daring Display (USA)) **Mr John Livock**
17 **PRIOR'S RAKES,** ch c 23/3 Bairn (USA)—Lucky Petina (Mummy's Pet) **Miss Betty Duxbury**
18 **RAVATHATCH (USA),** b c 16/2 Thatching—Realisatrice (USA) (Raja Baba (USA)) **Mr D. M. Dick**

Other Owners: Mr C. R. Buckle, Mr Jeremy Bull, Mr D. Douglas, Mr Gifford Eccles, Mr Jeremy Edge, Mr Finlay Gordon, Mr John Howard, Miss A. Pierson, Mr D. Sears, Mr R. A. Spicer, Mr B. W. Wetenhall.

Apprentice: J Quinn (7-7, w.a.).

364 MR C. F. LEE, Nottingham

Postal: **Coneygre Farm, Haveringham, Nottingham, NG14 7JX.**
Phone: **NEWARK (0636) 830318**

1 **PILOT WILL,** 7, ch g Gay Pilot—Seven Threes **Mr C. F. Lee**
2 **TIPPER LAD,** 8, b g Ascendant—Seven Threes **Mrs J. M. Lee**

365 MR D. LEE, Kirkbymoorside

Postal: **Manor Farm, Fadmoor, Kirkbymoorside, York, YO6 8HY.**
Phone: **(0751) 32425 OR 32894**

1 **ALICIAN BRIDGE,** 9, br g Over The River (FR)—Pontnos **Mr D. Lee**
2 **ATTAVANTE,** 8, ch m Derrylin—Angor **Mrs D. R. Lee**
3 **JACK DASH,** 8, ch g Celtic Cone—Melodist **Mr D. Lee**
4 **RAPID SLANE,** 6, ch g Rapid River—Slane Lady **Mr J. H. Richardson**
5 **RAVEN VENTURE,** 10, b g Le Coq d'Or—Bride's Burn **Mrs Rosalind Pearcy**
6 **SKIPLAM WOOD,** 4, b f Cree Song—Mab **Mrs D. R. Lee**
7 **SUNSET CRUISE,** 5, b g Cruise Missile—Suntino **Mr H. P. Hogarth**
8 **TEWIT CASTLE,** 8, b g Enbrage—Slane Lady **Mr J. H. Richardson**
9 **TOMMY FARMER,** 8, b g Roselier (FR)—Fannie Farmer **Mr D. Lee**
10 **WHO IS HE,** 6, b g Smooth Stepper—Ross Lady **Mrs G. D. H. Armitage**

Other Owners: Mrs G. F. Armitage, Mr C. Booth, Mr C. J. Cundall, Mr R. Cundall, Mrs E. Dixon, Mr J. Hogarth, Mr P. H. Hogarth, Mr R. D. Moody.

366 MR FRANCIS H. LEE, Wilmslow

Postal: **Little Stanneylands Racing Stables, Stanneylands Road, Wilmslow, Cheshire, SK9 4ER.**
Phone: **(0625) 533250/529672 TELEX 635435 FAX (0625) 539489**

1 **AAHSAYLAD,** 4, b c Ardross—Madam Slaney **Mr M. Stapleton**
2 **ASTRONOMER,** 4, b c Head For Heights—Diamonds In The Sky **Exors of the late Mr J. Collinson**
3 **ELEGANT MONARCH,** 4, ch c Ardross—Supremely Royal **Mr Peter Barr**
4 **KOLINSKY,** 4, ch g Dunbeath (USA)—Kolomelskoy Palace **Mr J. Goodman**
5 **MOFADOR (GER),** 6, br h Esclavo (FR)—Mantilla (GER) **Mr F. H. Lee**
6 **NATIVE SCOT,** 4, ch f Be My Native (USA)—Bunduq **Mr Tony Hooper**
7 **ON MY MERIT,** 4, ch c Bold Lad (IRE)—Borehard **Wm Martin Group (Holdings) Ltd**
8 **PETER MARTIN,** 9, ch g Monsanto (FR)—Bouboulina **Mr F. H. Lee**
9 **QUESSARD,** 6, ch g Ardross—Marquessa d'Howfen **Mr F. H. Lee**
10 **STRING PLAYER,** 8, ch g Orchestra—Ghana's Daughter **Mr F. H. Lee**
11 **TALL MEASURE,** 4, b g High Top—Millimeter (USA) **Mrs Joan Jones**
12 **TENDER BID,** 4, ch c Tender King—Princess Biddy **Mr Peter Barr**
13 **YOUNG JASON,** 7, ch g Star Appeal—Smarten Up **Mrs Gillian Lee**

THREE-YEAR-OLDS

14 **ANOTHER MARQUESSA,** b f Beldale Flutter (USA)—Marquessa d'Howfen **Mr F. H. Lee**
15 **DIADAD,** ch c Doulab (USA)—Numidia **Mr Peter Barr**
16 **GREAT PRECOCITY,** b c Precocious—Rip Roaring **Mrs Joan Jones**
17 **I PERCEIVE,** b c Vision (USA)—Wavetree **Mrs Joan Jones**
18 **KUMADA,** b g Vision (USA)—Fan The Flame **Mrs Joan Jones**
19 **OH SO CUTE,** b f Kings Lake (USA)—Shirley's Joy **Mrs P. Good**
20 **RESOLUTIONIST (USA),** b g Stalwart (USA)—Trackmist **Mr F. H. Lee**
21 **SHEER PRECOCITY,** b c Precocious—Age of Elegance **Mr Peter Barr**
22 **SIR ARTHUR HOBBS,** b c Lyphard's Special (USA)—Song Grove **Mr John Hardman**

TWO-YEAR-OLDS

23 Ch f 18/4 Doulab (USA)—Borehard (Bonne Noel) **K. J. Merret**
24 **CRYSTAL JACK (FR),** b c Crystal Glitters (USA)—Cackle (USA) (Crow (FR))
25 **FINAL DEED,** ch gr c 27/4 Final Straw—Birch Creek (Carwhite) **Mr J. Burke and Partners**
26 Ch c 16/4 Ahonoora—Flying Anna (Roan Rocket) **Mr Peter Barr**
27 B c 20/3 Beldale Flutter (USA)—Foil 'em (USA) (Blade (USA)) **North West Racing Club**
28 B c 4/3 Tender King—Fruit of Passion (High Top)
29 B c 1/4 Damister (USA)—Full of Reason (USA) (Bold Reason) **Mr D. Gransby**
30 Ch f 29/4 Kalaglow—Hide Out (Habitat) **Mrs J. Keegan**
31 B c Temperence Hill (USA)—Honorine (USA) (Blushing Groom (FR))
32 B c Palace Music (USA)—Intensive (USA) (Sir Wiggle (USA)) **Mr Peter Barr**

MR FRANCIS H. LEE—continued

33 B f 28/4 Ardross—Marquessa d'Howfen (Pitcairn) **Mr Gary F. Lee**
34 Ch f 15/2 Persian Bold—Militia Girl (Rarity) **Mr F. H. Lee**
35 B c Danzig Connection (USA)—Miss Hatco (USA) (Damascus (USA)) **Mr D. Jones**
36 Ch f 9/4 Exhibitioner—Morelia (Murrayfield) **Mr J. Lee and Partners**
37 B c 14/5 Secreto (USA)—Mythilene (FR) (Targowice (USA))
38 B c Explodent (USA)—Old Westbury (USA) (Francis S) **Mr D. Gransby**
39 B f 22/4 Beldale Flutter (USA)—Report 'em (USA) (Staff Writer (USA)) **Mrs Gillian Lee**
40 **SAIL PAST (FR),** b c No Pass No Sale (FR)—All In White (FR) (Carwhite) **Wm Martin Group (Holdings) Ltd**
41 B c 10/5 Doulab (USA)—Song Grove (Song)
42 B c 13/3 Commanche Run—Supremely Royal (Crowned Prince (USA))
43 Ch f 26/4 Pharly (FR)—Sweet Emma (Welsh Saint) **Mr J. Lee and Partners**
44 B c 6/4 Persian Bold—Tattle (St Paddy)

Other Owners: Mr P. Asquith, Mrs B. Barr, Mrs B. Collinson, Mr M. Dinneen, Mr Simon A. D. Gleave, Mr D. Holt, Mr William McGhee, Mrs E. Merret, Mr J. S. Sheen.

Jockey (Flat): S Perks (w.a.).

Jockey (NH): C Hawkins (w.a.).

Apprentices: D Barrett (7-0), R Lappin (7-12).

Conditional: K Wilkinson (9-7).

367 MR R. LEE, Presteigne

Postal: **Bell House, Byton, Presteigne, Powys, Wales.**
Phone: **(0544) 267672 OR (0836) 537145 (MOBILE)**

1 **ANNICOMBE RUN,** 6, b m Deep Run—Purcella **Mr T. M. J. Curry**
2 **ARDMORE CLASSIC,** 7, b g He Loves Me—Classical Music **Mrs Nicola Shields**
3 **BAVARD ASH,** 7, ch g Le Bavard (FR)—Merrybash **Mrs Lynda Lewis**
4 **BIT OF A CHANCE,** 6, br m Lord Ha Ha—Romany Miss **Mr R. Yates**
5 **CELTIC ORIGINAL,** 6, b g Celtic Cone—Ice Bird **Mrs Lynda Lewis**
6 **CHARLIE DAGG,** 9, br g Indiaro—Persian Stitch **Mr Richard Lee**
7 **COME ON CLOVER,** 4, br f Oats—National Clover **Mr J. Bowen**
8 **COURTBROOK,** 9, b g Hard Fact—Donington Queen **Mr R. W. Guilding**
9 **DAMERS CAVALRY,** 7, b g Stanford—Margery (FR) **Mrs Nicola Shields**
10 **DELIUS,** 12, ch g The Parson—More Melody **Mr John Renton**
11 **DIXONS HOMEFINDER,** 6, b g Strong Gale—Julia Too **Mr Brian J. D. Lewis**
12 **DOCK BRIEF,** 9, br g Pauper—Flying Lady **Mr P. L. Parkinson**
13 **EVEN SMARTER,** 7, b g Proverb—Smart Money **Mr G. D. Thorp**
14 **FAMOUS LAD,** 7, b g Bold Lad (IRE)—Famous Band (USA) **Mr W. J. George**
15 **GADBROOK,** 8, b g Rymer—Quelles Amours **Osborne House Limited**
16 **HARD TO HOLD,** 7, b g He Loves Me—Run Swift **Mrs Virginia Hambly**
17 **I LIKE IT A LOT,** 7, ch g Proverb—Jupiters Jill **Mrs Lynda Lewis**
18 **KING OF THE LOT,** 7, br g Space King—Nicola Lisa **Major R. Yule**
19 **LITTLE MYND,** 11, b m Space King—Lady Mynd **Mr T. R. Pearson**
20 **LONDON LEADER,** 8, ch g London Bells (CAN)—Stop Thinking **Champion (Safety Headwear) Ltd**
21 **MARKET LEADER,** 10, b br g Kala Shikari—Natflat **Mr Ernie Flello**
22 **MISS NERO,** 9, br m Crozier—Romany Miss **Mr R. Yates**
23 **MONK'S MISTAKE,** 8, ch g Monksfield—Hardyglass Lass **Mr G. A. Goldstein**
24 **MY NEW BEST FRIEND,** 6, b g Prince Bee—Tender Song **Mr J. J. Smith**
25 **ORCHIPEDZO,** 5, ch g Le Moss—Jupiters Jill **Mrs Lynda Lewis**
26 **PEMBROKESHIRE LAD,** 9, ch g Nearly A Hand—Lady Columbus **Mr T. S. Warner**

MR R. LEE—continued

27 **PIKEMAN,** 8, b g Turnpike—Cavallina **Mr Richard Edwards**
28 **RYNODE,** 7, b m Rymer—Pernel **Mr J. N. Dalton**
29 **SANDICLIFFE BOY,** 9, b g Jaazeiro (USA)—Almost **Mr G. H. S. Bailey**
30 **SPACE FAIR,** 7, b g Space King—Katie Fare **Osborne House Limited**
31 **SPRING BASH,** 5, b g Crash Course—Spring Hat **Mr T. R. Pearson**
32 **SWARDEAN,** 8, b g Le Coq d'Or—Katie Little **Mrs Ann Starkie**
33 **TANDERAGEE,** 9, ch m Trasi's Son—Whitney **Mr J. Bowen**
34 **TARKOVSKY,** 5, b g Moorestyle—Fallen Rose **Mr J. Watkins**
35 **THE WELDER,** 12, b g Bargello—Chantarella **Mr R. Yates**
36 **TOPHARD,** 4, b g Lyphard's Special (USA)—Tomard **Mr Bob Brazier**
37 **TRAVEL OVER,** 9, b g Over The River (FR)—Kincsem **Mrs C. E. Feather**
38 **TREE POPPY,** 7, b m Rolfe (USA)—Caribs Love **Miss G. Stuart Evans**
39 **TROSTREY,** 6, b br g Tom Noddy—Trefair **Mr Nigel Lilley**
40 **TURN UP THE WICK,** 7, b m Over The River (FR)—Lovely Daisy **Mr J. O. Beavan**
41 **WHAT A MOUNT,** 7, b g Merrymount—Ribots Fancy **Military Quartet**
42 **WHYBROWS,** 4, b g Star Appeal—Haida **Miss Sallie Blair**

THREE-YEAR-OLDS

43 **FOUR LEAF CLOVER,** ch f Sunyboy—National Clover **Mr J. Bowen**

Other Owners: Mrs Janie Blake, Mrs G. M. Brisbane, Mrs C. J. Cole, Mr John Collinge, Mr D. E. Edwards, Mr Robert C. Edwards, Mr Peter Greenall, Mr L. J. Gwynne, Mr R. L. C. Hartley, Mr P. J. M. Hoskin, Mr Dave Kings, Mr D. I. Price, Mr Paddy Renton, Mr Will Roseff.

Jockey (NH): B Dowling (10-0).

Conditional: Andrew David (9-7), Leanne Eldredge (9-7), Roddy Greene (9-7).

Amateur: Mr Al Hambly (10-0).

368 MR J. P. LEIGH, Gainsborough

Postal: **Mount House Stables, 12 Long Lane, Willoughton, Gainsborough, Lincolnshire, DN21 5SQ.** Phone: **(042 773) 210**

1 **ALONE CYGNET,** 7, ch g Swan's Rock—Anona-Anona **Mr S. Robinson**
2 **BARN BRAE,** 8, b g Derek H—La Raine **Mr J. Barton**
3 **BECKINGHAM BEN,** 6, gr g Workboy—Pickwood Sue **Mr H. T. Pickering**
4 **CATCH AT STRAWS,** 4, ch g Hayrick—Nanking **Mr J. W. Rowles**
5 **CONSCRIPTION,** 10, ch g Gunner B—Needless **Mr C. G. Rowles Nicholson**
6 **EAMONS OWEN,** 13, br g Master Owen—Clerihan **Mr W. G. N. Morgan**
7 **GEOSTAR,** 6, b g Runnett—Oriental Star **Mr W. G. N. Morgan and Mrs B. Morgan**
8 **JUST INCREDIBLE,** 4, b g Auction Ring (USA)—Elated **Mr Colin G. R. Booth**
9 **KNOCK AGAIN,** 6, ch g Floriferous—Santimwen **Mr J. V. Hales**
10 **PRESAGE,** 4, b c Petong—Discreet **Mr J. G. Leyland**
11 **RECORD PRICE,** 4, b g Simply Great (FR)—Silk Trade **Mr J. W. Rowles**
12 **SEA ARROW,** 5, gr m Sagaro—Seajan **Mr J. Barton**
13 **SECOND AWARD,** 5, ch m Cruise Missile—Cash Award **Mrs E. M. Hall**
14 **SILVER SUSAN,** 4, gr f Ampney Prince—Pickwood Sue **Mr H. T. Pickering**
15 **TOUCH GO GO,** 5, b g Touch Boy—Lucky Donation **Mrs D. E. Pickering**
16 **WOLVER DAN,** 8, b g Wolver Hollow—Danilla (USA) **Mr William P. Iceton**

THREE-YEAR-OLDS

17 **LADY PENNINGTON,** b f Blue Cashmere—Lady Carol **Mr C. Tomkins**
18 **MORPICK,** gr g Morston (FR)—Pickwood Sue **Mr H. T. Pickering**
19 **NORTHERN ROCKET,** b c Northern Tempest (USA)—Scotch Rocket **Mr K. G. Bridges**

Other Owners: Mr G. A. Bridges.

369 MR G. LEWIS, Epsom

Postal: **Thirty Acre Barn, Shepherds Walk, Headley, Epsom, KT18 6BX.**
Phone: **ASHTEAD (0372) 277662 OR 277366 TELEX 9413320 GNMPGL FAX (0372) 277366**

1 **ABOU MINJAL (MOR),** 4, ch g Asandre (FR)—Honeyou (MOR) **Mr Gerald Godfrey**
2 **CASPIAN MIST,** 5, b m Remainder Man—Bay Foulard **Mr B. Nelson**
3 **CRONK'S COURAGE,** 4, ch g Krayyan—Iresine (GER) **Cronk Garages Ltd**
4 **CRONK'S QUALITY,** 7, b g Main Reef—Ozone **Cronk Garages Ltd**
5 **EFFERVESCENT,** 5, ch h Sharpo—Never So Lovely **Mrs S. Khan**
6 **POUR ENCOURAGER,** 5, ch g Kind of Hush—Divine Penny **Mr T. J. Gregory**
7 **REGENT LIGHT (USA),** 4, b c Vice Regent (CAN)—I Like To Watch (USA) **Elisha Holding**
8 **RESTORE,** 7, ch g Habitat—Never So Lovely **Mrs S. Khan**
9 **TIGANI,** 4, b c Good Times (ITY)—She Who Dares **Capt. M. Lemos**

THREE-YEAR-OLDS

10 **ARCTIC HEIGHTS (USA),** ch c Arctic Tern (USA)—Dols Jaminque (USA) **Mrs S. Khan**
11 **ARDEARNED,** b f Ardross—Divine Penny **Mr T. J. Gregory**
12 **BALUOD,** ch f Doulab (USA)—June Darling **Mr A. Jones**
13 **BRADMORE'S CLASSIC,** ch c Jalmood (USA)—Water Pageant **Mr T. Brady**
14 **BROWN CARPET,** b br c Never So Bold—Geopelia **Mr R. Del Rosario**
15 **CHILIPOUR,** gr g Nishapour (FR)—Con Carni **Mr M. J. E. Thornhill**
16 **CLEAN AND POLISH,** ch g Superlative—Greek Blessing **Mr P. J. Oliver**
17 **COLOUR SCHEME,** ch g Rainbow Quest (USA)—Much Pleasure **Mrs N. Lewis**
18 **DANCER'S FIRST (USA),** b f Green Dancer (USA)—Beauvoir **Mr Robert Cox**
19 **DECEIT,** b g On Your Mark—Second Movement **Mr N. Bedack**
20 **DUKE'S DUET (USA),** b c Seattle Song (USA)—Haute Sanga **Mr P. J. Canty**
21 **FAULTLESS SPEECH,** ch c Good Times (ITY)—Fine Asset **Mr Gerald Godfrey**
22 **HERMITAGE ROCK,** ch c Ballad Rock—Verde Dimora **Gallagher Contractors Ltd**
23 **INTUITIVE JOE,** b g Petorius—Super Girl **Mr J. Ward Hill**
24 **IT'S THE PITS,** b c Tender King—Pithead **Mr P. D. Savill**
25 **KATIES FIRST (USA),** b f Kris—Katies **Mr Robert Cox**
26 **KOLONAKI,** b c Busted—Nuppence **Capt. M. Lemos**
27 **MADAM BOLD,** b f Never So Bold—Sophisticated Lady **Mr Robert Cox**
28 **MILNE'S WAY,** ch f The Noble Player (USA)—Daring Way (USA) **Mr M. Jameson**
29 **MY KIA,** ch f Good Times (ITY)—Troy Moon **Capt M. Lemos**
30 **RENTAL AGREEMENT,** b f Sayf El Arab (USA)—Tsar's Bride **Archer Van & Truck Hire Ltd**
31 **SALINAMAR,** b g Muscatite—Bells of Ireland **Mr J. C. Walters**

TWO-YEAR-OLDS

32 **AS ALWAYS (IRE),** ch f 20/1 Hatim (USA)—Red Magic (Red God) **Mr David Barker**
33 Ch c 17/4 Reach—Errol Emerald (Dom Racine (FR))
34 **FOREIGN ALLIANCE,** br c 21/3 Lidhame—Pour Moi (Bay Express) **Mr N. Topche**
35 B c 11/4 Electric—Garnette Rose (Floribunda)
36 **HEARD A WHISPER,** b c 3/2 Bellypha—Breadcrumb (Final Straw) **Mr David Barker**
37 B c 9/5 Krayyan—Lady Anna Livia (Ahonoora) **Plan Flow (Leasing) Ltd**
38 Ch c 10/5 Reasonable (FR)—Lady Pitt (Pitskelly) **Mr G. Archer**
39 Gr f 14/2 Prince Sabo—La Magna (Runnymede)
40 B c 23/3 Law Society (USA)—Lighted Lamp (USA) (Sir Gaylord) **Elisha Holding**
41 **LOKI (IRE),** ch c 16/4 Thatching—Sigym (Lord Gayle (USA)) **Mr T. K. Laidlaw**
42 **PENTRIDGE,** ch f 20/5 Pennine Walk—Pennycuick (Celtic Ash) **Lady McIndoe**
43 **SHADES OF VERA,** b f 23/5 Precocious—More Reliable (Morston (FR)) **Mr A. R. Perry**
44 Ch c 20/3 Bay Express—Sophie Avenue (Guillaume Tell (USA))
45 B c 10/2 Law Society (USA)—Sweet Soprano (High Line) **Gallagher Contractors Ltd**
46 B c 3/5 Superlative—Venetian Sky (Touch Paper)
47 **WINGS OF FREEDOM (IRE),** b c 11/5 Fairy King (USA)—Wingau (FR) (Hard To Beat) **Mr P. D. Savill**

Other Owners: Mr S. Archer, Mr C. Gaventa, Mr D. Khan, Mr J. S. Khan, Mr K. F. Khan, Mr T. P. Milne, Mr H. R. Mould, Mr Noordeen Sarif.

Jockey (Flat): Pat Eddery (8-4).

Apprentices: R Berry (7-7), J Williams (7-10).

370 MR P. LIDDLE, Chester-le-Street

Postal: **Ouston Villa Farm, Ouston, Chester-le-Street, Co. Durham, DN2 1LN.**
Phone: **TYNESIDE (091) 4102072 MOBILE (0860) 271532**

1 **ALBERT THE GREAT,** 7, ch g Meldrum—Bath Miss **Mr I. Rodden**
2 **ALWAYS FLAT BROKE,** 6, b br g Flatbush—Poor Girl **Mr P. Liddle**
3 **BUSH MAID,** 7, ch m Flatbush—Sewing Maid **Mr P. Liddle**
4 **FARM BOY,** 5, b h Some Hand—Poor Girl **Mr P. Liddle**
5 **FOSSWAY MERCHANT,** 5, b g Arapahos (FR)—Super Valu **Mr D. Neale**
6 **HORSESHOE BAY,** 10, ch m Duc d'Orleans—Wall Street **Mrs F. Hodgson**
7 **LOCHNDOM,** 5, b m Lochnager—Domino Smith **Mr A. J. Le Blond**
8 **LOOKATTHOSELEGS,** 6, ch m Velvet Prince—Red Title **Mr P. Liddle**
9 **MISS SIMONE,** 4, b f Ile de Bourbon (USA)—Nanga Parbat **Mr P. Liddle**
10 **OUR HERO,** 7, ch g Posse (USA)—Blonda **Mr David Cook**
11 **RED PROCESSION,** 6, ch g Red Sunset—Procession **Mr Iain R. Sykes**
12 **STAND AT EASE,** 5, b g The Brianstan—Plush **Mr D. Neale**
13 **TERRACOTTA ARMY,** 4, ch g Red Sunset—Xian **Mr P. Liddle**
14 **TERRACOTTA WARRIOR,** 4, ch c Roman Warrior—Derek's Folly **Mr P. Liddle**
15 **WALTER STREET,** 5, b g Lochnager—Shady Desire **Mr A. J. Le Blond**
16 **WAYSIDE,** 8, br g Smokey Rockett—Rosamond **Mr James Donnelly**

Other Owners: Mrs Julie Kirtley, Mr K. J. Mastaglio, Mr F. W. Oates, Mr John G. Watson.

Jockey (NH): Mark Dwyer (w.a.).

Conditional: Graham Cook (9-7).

Amateur: Mr A Kirtley (11-0).

371 MR B. J. LLEWELLYN, Bargoed

Postal: **Ffynonau Duon Farm, Pentwyn Fochriw, Bargoed, Mid Glam, Wales, CF8 9NR.**
Phone: **(0685) 841259**

1 **ARRAN VIEW,** 4, br g Aragon—Shadow Play **Mr B. Llewellyn**
2 **EL CAPISTRANO,** 9, b g Song—Abide **Mr B. Llewellyn**
3 **MAJESTICIAN (GER),** 7, b g Honduras (GER)—Marlova (FR) **Mr B. Llewellyn**
4 **RECTORY BOY,** 7, b g Rustingo—Ron's Girl **Mr B. Llewellyn**

Amateurs: Miss Beth Llewellyn (9-7), Mr John Lewis Llewellyn (10-0).

372 MR J. LOVE, Kilbarchan

Postal: **Moniabrook Farm, Kilbarchan, Johnstone, Renfrewshire, Scotland, PA10 2QA.**
Phone: **BRIDGE OF WEIR (0505) 612135**

1 **AYR BAY,** 5, br g Vaigly Great—Hopeful Subject **Mrs J. Love**
2 **TARLETON'S OAK,** 7, br g Town Crier—Stately Gala **Mrs J. Love**

Amateur: Mr S Love (10-7).

373 MR W. J. W. MACKIE, Church Broughton

Postal: **The Bungalow, Barton Blount, Church Broughton, Derbyshire, DE6 5AN.**
Phone: **SUDBURY (028378) 604 MOBILE (0836) 768773**

1 **BEAUDENE,** 4, b g Song—Princess Tavi **S. Taberner**
2 **BEST EMPEROR,** 4, gr g Secreto (USA)—Port Aransas (USA) **B. Brewer**
3 **BLACK COMEDY,** 7, b h Blakeney—Laughing Goddess **S. V. Wadsworth Limited**
4 **COUTURE COLOR,** 7, br g Wolver Hollow—Home Sweet Home **Couture Marketing Ltd**
5 **COUTURE QUALITY,** 4, gr g Absalom—Miss Couture **Couture Marketing Ltd**
6 **COUTURE STOCKINGS,** 6, b g Free State—Miss Couture **Couture Marketing Ltd**
7 **COUTURE TIGHTS,** 5, b g Mummy's Game—Miss Couture **Couture Marketing Ltd**
8 **FALCON FLIGHT,** 4, ch g Tampero (FR)—Kemoening **M. D. M. Racing (Thoroughbreds) Limited**
9 **GOLDEN VEST,** 6, b g Sonnen Gold—Key Harvest **Mr A. W. Smith**
10 **GO WITH THE FLO,** 4, br f Indian King (USA)—Doon Belle **D. Hodgkinson**
11 **INDIAN UPRISING,** 4, b g Indian King (USA)—Infanta (USA) **D. Hodgkinson**
12 **JAHZEEN,** 4, b g Shareef Dancer (USA)—Dancing Meg (USA) **D. Hodgkinson**
13 **LEAN ORT,** 12, ch g Proverb—Carry On Jackie **Mr T. H. S. Wragg**
14 **OCEANUS,** 9, b g Julio Mariner—Princess Zena **Mr R. M. Mitchell**
15 **OLYMPIC CHALLENGER,** 6, b g Anfield—Calibina **Mrs Isobel Ryles**
16 **PRIDEAUX,** 6, b g Mill Reef (USA)—Gallic Pride (USA) **S. V. Wadsworth Limited**
17 **PRINCE OF RHEIMS,** 5, ch g Sandhurst Prince—Fairmile **Mr Douglas H. Francis**
18 **RANDY BAY,** 5, b g Bay Express—Kiara **S. Taberner**
19 **RED JAM JAR,** 5, ch g Windjammer (USA)—Macaw **Mr F. Reacher**
20 **SACRE D'OR (USA),** 5, b g Lemhi Gold (USA)—Dedicated To Sue (USA) **Mr J. W. H. Fryer**
21 **SALINE,** 5, ch m Sallust—Silk Rein **S. V. Wadsworth Limited**
22 **SANTARAY,** 4, ch c Formidable—Stockingful **S. Taberner**
23 **SHINING DEEP,** 6, ch g Deep Run—Ever Shining **Mr T. H. S. Wragg**
24 **SNEVES,** 5, b g Bali Dancer—Tuneful Queen **Mr G. L. Jones**
25 **SOLDIERS DUTY (USA),** 6, b g Golden Act (USA)—Fuzier (USA) **Four Oaks Syndicate**
26 **STUMBLE,** 6, ch g Sayyaf—Tumble Royal **J. Cowan**
27 **TORT,** 6, b g Le Moss—Stead Flow **Mr T. H. S. Wragg**
28 **TRAVELLERS TRIP,** 9, ch g Royal Trip—Bohemian Girl **A. J. Winterton**
29 **TRIVET,** 7, ch g Thatching—Borana **Steve Lilley Racing Ltd**
30 **WIGTOWN BAY,** 7, br g Young Nelson—Bonnie Bladnoch **Provan Hatch Holdings Ltd**

THREE-YEAR-OLDS

31 **BALCO,** ch g Noalto—Stracy **S. Taberner**
32 **FASCINATION WALTZ,** b f Shy Groom (USA)—Cuckoo Weir **F. Havercroft**

Other Owners: Mr C. R. Gilman, Mr J. F. Hickling, Mr Joesph F. Lomas, Mrs J. Mackie, Mrs C. A. Riley, Mr L. F. J. Piacenti, Mr J. M. Smith, Mr D. Tivey, Mrs P. M. Wilson, Mr R. J. Wright.

Jockeys (NH): S J O'Neill (w.a.), D Shaw.

Conditional: J Manson.

Amateurs: T Eley (10-0),

374 MR A. H. MACTAGGART, Hawick

Postal: **Hallrule, Bonchester Bridge, Hawick, Roxburghshire, Scotland, TD9 8JF.**
Phone: **(0450) 86314**

1 **BUCKLE IT UP,** 5, br g Buckskin (FR)—The Hofsa **Mr A. H. Mactaggart**
2 **DEEP CREEK,** 6, ch m Deep Run—Bramble Lane **Mr A. H. Mactaggart**
3 **LAST OF THE FLIES,** 9, ch g Kemal (FR)—Gledswing **Mrs A. H. Mactaggart**
4 **ROUGHSIDE,** 5, br g Black Minstrel—Glazing Lady **Mr A. H. Mactaggart**

Amateurs: Mr D Mactaggart (10-0), Mr J Mactaggart (11-0).

375 MR M. J. MADGWICK, Denmead

Postal: **Forest Farm, Forest Road, Denmead, Hampshire, PO7 6UA.**
Phone: **(0705) 258313**

1 **B Q MACAW,** 6, ch g Morston (FR)—Macaw **Mr M. Madgwick**
2 **BU-SOFYAN,** 6, b g Runnett—London Spin **Mr Ian Macavoy**
3 **CANON'S COURT,** 5, b g Main Reef—My Fawn **Mr M. Madgwick**
4 **CHATTERIS,** 4, b g Shareef Dancer (USA)—Fenella **Mr D. J. Willis**
5 **COLTOWN BOY,** 5, b h Town And Country—Miscontent **Mr Frank W. Golding**
6 **CREECH WOOD,** 5, b h Record Run—Flyweight **Mr M. Madgwick**
7 **GILD THE LILY,** 5, b m Ile de Bourbon (USA)—Meliora **Mr D. M. Drury**
8 **GOING UP,** 5, b g Henbit (USA)—Mill Hill (USA) **Mr M. N. Kemp-Gee**
9 **HARREEK,** 5, ch g Tap On Wood—Footway **Mr D. J. Willis**
10 **OUR NOBBY,** 8, br g McIndoe—Fair Arctic **Mr R. Bastian**
11 **PALM REEF,** 6, b g Main Reef—Fingers **Mr D. J. Willis**
12 **R LAD,** 6, b g Rushmere—Brismaid **Mr W. V. Roker**
13 **ROYAL HUNT,** 5, b g Mill Reef (USA)—Glass Slipper **Mr P. Beach**
14 **SNITTERFIELD,** 12, b g Royal Match—Mile Cross **Mr K. Lockstone**
15 **SPOT ON ANNIE,** 4, gr f Miami Springs—Hallo Rosie **Mr T. G. N. Burrage**
16 **STRIDE HOME,** 5, ch m Absalom—Another Treat **Mr Peter Taplin**
17 **THE GRIFTER,** 6, gr g Treboro (USA)—Mary Crooner **Mr T. G. N. Burrage**
18 **TRAFALGAR BUOY,** 6, b g Radetzky—Changan **Mr D. Knight**

THREE-YEAR-OLDS

19 **GROWN AT ROWAN,** b f Gabitat—Hallo Rosie **Mrs Linda Burrage**

Other Owners: Mrs Jean Bastian, Mr A. T. Lonsdale.

Jockey (Flat): J Matthias (8-5).

Jockeys (NH): H Davies, R Dunwoody.

Conditional: D Madgwick (10-0).

Amateur: Mr A Madgwick (9-7).

376 MR P. J. MAKIN, Marlborough

Postal: **Bonita Racing Stables, Ogbourne Maisey, Marlborough, Wiltshire, SN8 1RY.**
Phone: **MARLBOROUGH (0672) 512973 FAX (0672) 514166**

1 **CHIC ANTIQUE,** 6, ch m Rarity—What A Picture **Mr J. M. Wakefield**
2 **CURTAIN CALL,** 4, ch c Final Straw—Hathaway **Mr A. R. C. Hobbs**
3 **EARTH BEAM,** 4, b g Kampala—Amore Mare **Mr J. M. Wakefield**
4 **EVER SHARP,** 6, b g Sharpo—Blue Jane **E. Franklin Robbins**
5 **FAIRWAY ROYALE,** 5, b g Runnett—Lady Salinia **Mrs P. J. Makin**
6 **FESTIVE FALCON,** 4, ch c Sandhurst Prince—Caelidh **Mr T. W. Wellard**
7 **GOLD JUSTICE,** 6, b g Taufan (USA)—Nordic Maid **Mr E. Benfield**
8 **GOLD TOUCH,** 7, b g Strong Gale—Nordic Maid **Mr E. Benfield**
9 **HERONS ROSIE,** 5, b m Import—Leger Bar **Mr J. M. Wakefield**
10 **JEALOUS LOVER,** 6, gr m Alias Smith (USA)—Drawing Room Car **Miss R. Hill**
11 **LUCKY FLINDERS,** 4, ch f Free State—Lucky Kim **Mrs P. J. Makin**

MR P. J. MAKIN—continued

12 **MIRROR BLACK,** 4, b c Alzao (USA)—Flaxen Hair **Mrs C. A. Webster**
13 **OLD EAGLE,** 4, b g Bold Lad (IRE)—Home Bird **Peter R. Pearce**
14 **PORTOFINO,** 4, ch g Coquelin (USA)—Decoy Duck **Mr R. P. Marchant**
15 **RED PADDY,** 5, ch g Red Sunset—Irish Bride **Mr J. M. Wakefield**
16 **SPANISH HEART,** 5, b m King of Spain—Hearten **Avon Industries (Bath) Ltd**
17 **TOUR DE FORCE,** 10, ch g Reliance II—Set To Work **Mrs Derek Strauss**
18 **TUGBOAT,** 11, ch g Grundy—Pirate Queen **Mr E. Benfield**
19 **UGANDAN AFFAIRS,** 5, b g Kampala—Karens Pet **Mr P. H. C. Dyson**

THREE-YEAR-OLDS

20 **AMATHUS GLORY,** b f Mummy's Pet—Copt Hall Realm **Mascalls Stud Farm Limited**
21 **BALZAON KNIGHT,** b g Alzao (USA)—April Sal **Miss S. G. Barton**
22 **CALGARY REDEYE,** gr c Kalaglow—River Call (FR) **Mr A. Hollingworth**
23 **CELEBRATION TIME,** gr c On Your Mark—Raise The Roof **Mr T. W. Wellard**
24 **COUTURE INNOVATORS,** b c Music Boy—Miss Couture **Couture Marketing Ltd**
25 **ELBIO,** b c Precocious—Maganyos (HUN) **Mr Brian Brackpool**
26 **ENTERPRISE LADY (FR),** ch f Gorytus (USA)—Calder Hall **Bakewell Bloodstock Ltd**
27 **FINAL ENIGMA,** ch c Final Straw—Mystery Ship **Mr B. H. Simpson**
28 **GOLD TRUST,** b c Bellypha—Abbey (FR) **Mr E. Benfield**
29 **HARIFA,** b f Local Suitor (USA)—Fariha **Lt. Col. W. Whetherly**
30 **JALINGO,** ch g Jalmood—Linguistic **E. Franklin Robbins**
31 **JOKERS PATCH,** ch g Hotfoot—Rhythmical **Mr David J. Lacey**
32 **KATZAKEENA,** b f Gorytus (USA)—Current Bay **Miss R. Hill**
33 **KING FERDINAND,** b c King of Spain—Gundi **Mr S. H. J. Brewer**
34 **RUNWAY ROMANCE (FR),** gr c Julius Caesar (FR)—Airstrip **Mrs Joy Dilley**
35 **SCARLETT HOLLY,** b f Red Sunset—Wilderness **Mrs Jacqueline McColl**
36 **SHARPER BLUE,** b c Sharpo—Riverlily (FR) **Mr Stewart McColl**
37 **SINGH HOLME,** b g Mansingh—Ivy Holme **E. Franklin Robbins**
38 **SPANISH WHISPER,** b g Aragon—Whisper Gently **Mascalls Stud Farm Limited**
39 **TELYX,** b f Mansingh (USA)—Spritely **Mr T. G. Warner**
40 **TRANSITIONAL,** b c Dalsaan—Parkeen Princess **Mr R. P. Marchant**

TWO-YEAR-OLDS

41 B f 31/3 Alzao (USA)—Abertywi (Bounteous) **Mrs P. J. Makin**
42 Gr f 31/1 Petong—Adana (FR) (Green Dancer (USA)) **Mr T. G. Warner**
43 B c 23/4 Gorytus (USA)—Almuadiyeh (Thatching) **D. M. Ahier**
44 B c 12/2 Petoski—Cristalga (High Top) **J. P. Carrington**
45 B f 20/3 Red Sunset—Free Rein (Sagaro) **D. M. Ahier**
46 **GARTH,** b c 22/2 Petong—Doppio (Dublin Taxi) **B. Whitehouse**
47 Gr f 26/1 Petong—Glyn Rhosyn (Welsh Saint) **Mr Gazie Kadi**
48 **GOLD GLEN (IRE),** b f 22/4 Red Sunset—Park Lady (Tap On Wood) **E. Benfield Esq**
49 Ch f 26/4 Norwick (USA)—Hat Hill (Roan Rocket) **D. F. Powell**
50 **LOGARITHM,** b f 24/4 King of Spain—Hearten (Hittite Glory) **Avon Industries (Bath) Ltd**
51 B f 24/4 Norwick (USA)—Mumtaz Mayfly (Tap On Wood) **Mrs P. J. Makin**
52 **NORTH LODGE,** b c 28/5 Norwick (USA)—Horns Lodge (High Line) **J. W. Malins**
53 **ROSIETOES,** b f 28/2 Master Willie—Desrose (Godswalk (USA)) **F. J. Reeder**
54 B f 28/2 Salmon Leap (USA)—Sainthill (St Alphage) **R. A. Henley Esq**
55 **SPANIARDS CLOSE,** b c 12/2 King of Spain—Avon Belle (Balidar) **Avon Industries (Bath) Ltd**
56 B c 24/4 Gorytus (USA)—State of Mind (Mill Reef (USA)) **Mr Gazie Kadi**
57 **TEA DUST (IRE),** b f 1/5 Pennine Walk—Ridalia (Ridan) **R. P. Marchant**
58 **WELL WICKED (IRE),** b f 24/2 Sallust—Carose (Caro) **Mascalls Stud Farm Limited**
59 B f 24/4 Bay Express—Whisper Gently (Pitskelly) **Mascalls Stud Farm Limited**

Other Owners: Jeremy Baker, Mr K. Brackpool, Mr A. K. Collins, Miss Gloria Dollar, Mr R. C. Dollar, L. S. Dollar, Mrs Linda Donald, Mr Phil Field, Keith Fisher, Mrs Nicolas Kairis, Mr Keith Mac Master, R. D. A. Kelly, Mr R. G. Percival, Mr D. A. Poole, Mr A. N. R. Rudd, Mr Jeremy J. Thompson, Mr G. L. Watson, Mrs P. J. Whitehouse, Mr David R. Wickins, M. G. Yates.

Apprentice: T Sprake (7-10).

377 MR W. G. MANN, Leamington Spa

Postal: **The Cottage Stables, Bishops Itchington, Leamington Spa, Warwickshire.**
Phone: **(0926) 612659**

1 **CLEO LADY,** 7, ch m Cleon—Dear Lady **Mr P. C. Nichols**
2 **HIGH HAGBERG,** 4, br g Cree Song—Persian Breakfast **Mrs T. A. Goodall**
3 **IVORDALE,** 5, b g Beldale Flutter (USA)—Ivoronica **Mr Anthony Weaver**
4 **JOLLY JAUNT,** 5, ch g St Columbus—Jaunting **Mrs Jessie F. Hayward**
5 **MARIE'S VALENTINE,** 7, br m Piaffer (USA)—Tavuto **Mr W. J. Kelly**
6 **SOVEREIGN QUAY,** 8, gr g Quayside—Happy Princess **Mrs T. A. Goodall**
7 **SPINNEY LIGHT,** 7, b g Seaepic (USA)—Sara's Light **Mr P. R. Mann**

Other Owners: Mr R. Austin, Mrs J. C. Fox, Mr F. Mann, Mr D. R. Wilson.

Jockey (NH): J D Doyle (9-12).

Amateur: Mr D Verco (10-2).

378 MR R. J. MANNING, Winterbourne

Postal: **Kendleshire Farm, Down Farm, Winterbourne, Bristol, BS17 1AU.**
Phone: **WINTERBOURNE (0454) 773274**

1 **FEARLESS NATIVE,** 4, br c Final Straw—Nativity (USA) **Mrs Julie Ann Holmes**
2 **FLYING,** 4, b f Head For Heights—Pine **R. J. Manning Racing Partnerships**
3 **MUMMY'S CHANCE,** 6, b g Mummy's Game—Kalopia **Mr S. C. Godden**
4 **ROCKY REEF,** 5, b m Diamond Shoal—Gohar (USA) **Mr Arthur Holmes**
5 **SOLDIER BRAVE,** 4, b g Persian Bold—Gilwanigan **Mrs Ena Rolfe**
6 **THE YOKEL,** 4, b g Hays—Some Dame **Mrs R. J. Manning**
7 **TREMMIN,** 5, b m Horage—Ballinavail **R. J. Manning and Andrew Mildon**

THREE-YEAR-OLDS

8 **NEW PROBLEM,** b f New Member—Light of Zion **Mr R. J. Manning**

Other Owners: Mrs Gina G. Angeletta, Mr Jay Angeletta, Mrs J. Fowler, Mr Pat Kelly, Mr John W. Wall, Mr Edward Wood.

Jockeys (NH): M Bowlby (w.a.), C Llewelyn (w.a.).

Conditional: Andrew McKellan (9-7).

Amateur: Mr G Upton.

379 MR D. MARKS, Lambourn

Postal: **Lethornes, Lambourn, Newbury, Berkshire, RG16 7QS.**
Phone: **(0488) 71767**

1 **CORICK BRIDGE,** 4, b c Homing—Sussex Queen **Mr Gary Potter**
2 **EAGLES LAIR,** 4, b c Head For Heights—Just A Shadow **Mr George Cannon**
3 **FIREPROOF,** 7, ch g Vitiges (FR)—Marie Mancini **Mrs E. R. Stevens**
4 **LUCKY NATIVE,** 4, br c Be My Native (USA)—Change of Luck **Mr George Cannon**
5 **MISCELLANY,** 6, b g Taufan (USA)—Karens Pet **Mr D. Marks**
6 **MSHATTA PALACE,** 7, br g Big Spruce (USA)—Carmelize (USA) **Mr Robert M. Pegg**
7 **TOSCANA,** 9, ch m Town And Country—Constanza **Mr D. Marks**

MR D. MARKS—continued

THREE-YEAR-OLDS

8 **CHILTERNS,** b f Beldale Flutter (USA)—Ballad Island **Mr M. G. Turner**

TWO-YEAR-OLDS

9 **FOO FOO,** ch f The Noble Player—Unmistakeable **Mr C. R. Buttery**
10 **KEEP IN TOUCH,** ch f Pharly (FR)—Silverhall **Mr George Cannon**
11 **TANAYESTELIGN,** gr f Bellypha—Opale **Mr G. J. King**

Other Owners: Mr C. R. Davis, Mr Denis Marchant, Mr G. Oliver.

Jockey (Flat): W Carson.

Jockey (NH): H Davies.

Lady Rider: Miss Kelly Marks (8-12).

380 MR RICHARD MARVIN, Budby

Postal: **North Farm Stables, Budby, Nr. Newark, Nottinghamshire, NG22 9EX.**
Phone: **(0623) 822714**

1 **ASTRABEE,** 5, b g Show-A-Leg—Manatay **Mr M. Antoniou**
2 **BRADBURY HALL,** 7, b g Comedy Star—Grayshott Hall **Mr M. Watterson**
3 **DANDY GIRL,** 5, ch m Record Token—Miss Rockefeller **Mr W. Baylis**
4 **DRUSO,** 6, b g Raise A Cup—Pretty Pride **Mr A. Whitehouse**
5 **GOULDS DELIGHT,** 4, b f Deep Roots—Brun's Toy **Windmill Club**
6 **HELLRAISER,** 11, ch g Hell's Gate—Solfield **J. G. Thorpe**
7 **INFALLIBLE,** 5, ch g Tumble Wind (USA)—Nous **Mrs C. Lord**
8 **LAUDIBLE,** 5, ch g Formidable—Clouds **Mr E. Turner**
9 **NICKYLEE,** 5, b g Son of Shaka—Fragrant Coffee **Mrs V. Hobson**
10 **SHELBERRY,** 4, b f Jester—Dainty Eden **Mr G. Peat**
11 **THEHELLHEIS,** 5, b g Posse (USA)—Hail To Vail **Mr E. Turner**

THREE-YEAR-OLDS

12 **SAXONDALE,** ch g Ballad Rock—Joanne's Joy **Mrs M. A. Marvin**
13 **VALIANT FRIEND,** b g Hell's Gate—Fleur-de-Chriose **Mr W. Baylis**

TWO-YEAR-OLDS

14 B c 11/4 Show-A-Leg—Elsaca (Ela-Mana-Mou) **Mr E. Turner**
15 Ch c 17/5 Hell's Gate—Fleur-de-Chriose (Dragonara Palace) **Mr W. Baylis**
16 Ch c 17/4 Hell's Gate—Velocidad (Balidar) **Mr W. Baylis**

Jockeys (NH): J Harris (10-0), S Johnson (10-7).

Conditional: S Harris (9-7).

381 MR D. MCCAIN, Southport

Postal: **Upper Aughton Stables, Birkdale, Southport, Merseyside, PR8 5NA.**
Phone: **(0704) 69677 OR 66007**

1 **BELLA DELITE,** 4, b f Uncle Pokey—Lady Letitia **W. W. Bellamy (Bakers) Ltd**
2 **CILERNA'S LAD,** 5, b g Pablond—Cilerna Rock **Mr G. Clark**

MR D. MCCAIN—continued

3 **COLLEGE SILK,** 8, b g Balliol—Cheb's Honour
4 5, B g Over The River (FR)—Cullagh's Girl
5 4, Br g Ring Bidder—Eastern Flight
6 **FERVENT HOPE,** 8, b g Full of Hope—Parbold **Mr D. A. Lunt**
7 **FOREST LORD,** 6, br g Lord Gayle (USA)—Heart 'n' Soul **Mr Robin Billingsley**
8 **GENOBRA,** 6, b g Young Generation—Dobra Star (FR) **Mr G. Clark**
9 **GOLDEN CROFT,** 7, ch g Crofter (USA)—Rossian
10 **GRAND VALUE,** 7, ch g Kambalda—Candy Slam **Mr Martin Jump**
11 **GRANNY'S BAY,** 7, b g Tycoon II—Lorien Wood **Mrs S. K. Dimond**
12 **HEY COTTAGE,** 5, ch g Pablond—Cottage Myth **Mrs S. K. Dimond**
13 **HOTPLATE,** 7, ch g Buckskin (FR)—Pencil Lady **W. W. Bellamy (Bakers) Ltd**
14 **JUST A HALF,** 8, ch g Most Secret—Alentejo **Mr F. S. Markland**
15 **KATICA,** 4, b f Jester—Gwen Somers **Mrs D. McCain**
16 **LEANDER LAD,** 5, b g Paico—Miss Leander **Mr Robin Billingsley**
17 **MASTER ATTORNEY,** 8, b g General Ironside—Miss Leap Year **Halewood Vintners Ltd**
18 **MEINE VONNE LADY,** 5, br m Jalmood (USA)—Gold Rupee **Mr B. Scowcroft**
19 **METEORS WAY,** 5, ch g Scallywag—Maid of Lorien **Meteor Freight Ltd**
20 **NADIAD,** 4, b g Darshaan—Naveen **Mr John J. Gray**
21 **NORTH HOLLOW,** 5, b g Tyrnavos—Philigree
22 **ORTY,** 5, b g Wolverlife—Diana's Choice
23 **PALS GALORE,** 8, b br g Paddys Stream—Ballygoman Maid **Mr John Singleton**
24 **PINK PANTHER,** 10, ch g Moulton—Pink Moss
25 **SANTAC,** 5, b g Tachypous—Sandy Keerie **Mr G. Clark**
26 5, B g Buckskin (FR)—Sayanarra
27 **SEBEL HOUSE,** 7, b g Buckskin (FR)—Lulu Dee **Mr G. Clark**
28 **SHEDARBO,** 5, ch g Sagaro—Song of Grace **Mr David P. Rimmer**
29 **SHINING ART,** 5, ch g Artaius (USA)—Moonlight Sonata **Champ Chicken Co Ltd**
30 **SNAPPIT,** 8, b g Billion (USA)—Snippet **Mr D. McCain**
31 **SPRING PAUPER,** 9, b g Pauper—Spring Campaign **Mr Robin Billingsley**
32 **SURE METAL,** 7, b g Billion (USA)—Sujini **Nolan Hardman & Partners Ltd**
33 **SWIFT WARRIOR,** 9, ch g Tug of War—Swift Jay **Mr W. Hargreaves**
34 **TRIBAL RULER,** 5, b g Prince Tenderfoot (USA)—Candolcis **Mr John Singleton**
35 **TWENTY ONE RED,** 5, br g Dunphy—Monalda (FR) **Mr B. Scowcroft**
36 **WATER ORCHID,** 5, b g Lafontaine (USA)—Johnnie's Lass **Mr Robin Billingsley**

THREE-YEAR-OLDS

37 Br f Swinging Rebel—Eastern Flight
38 B c Joshua—Snippet

TWO-YEAR-OLDS

39 B c 15/5 Dubassoff (USA)—Snippet (Ragstone)

Other Owners: Mr J. P. Sidebottom, Mr C. Wilby.

Jockey (NH): G McCourt (w.a.).

Amateurs: Mr Donald McCain (Jr) (9-12), Mr Greg Robertson (9-7).

382 MR D. MCCASKILL, Chester-le-Street

Postal: **Lingeyfine Stables, Pennyfine Road, Sunniside, Tyne and Wear.**
Phone: **STABLES (091) 4887062 HOME (091) 4102938**

1 **APPLE MAGIC,** 4, ch g Current Magic—Lucky Apple **Mr David McCaskill**
2 **KEEP DREAMING,** 13, br g Seaepic (USA)—Moitie **Mr David McCaskill**

MR D. MCCASKILL—continued

3 **LEARNING FAST,** 5, b g Bold Lad (IRE)—Sarajill **Mr David McCaskill**
4 **LOCHAR BRIG,** 11, b g Bilsborrow—Lochar Lass **Mr David McCaskill**
5 **LORD LENEY,** 12, b br g Deep Run—Dame Leney **Mr David McCaskill**
6 **PARPANTO,** 9, ch g Lepanto (GER)—Pardalina
7 **POLAR DELTA,** 8, b g Polar Jinks—Delemar **Mr David McCaskill**
8 **RED DESIREE,** 8, gr ro m Piaffer (USA)—Rikis **Mr David McCaskill**
9 **USARIO,** 6, ch g Abednego—Frozen Ground **Mr David McCaskill**

Other Owners: Mrs Sandra McCaskill.

Jockeys (NH): T Reed (w.a.), B Storey (w.a.).

Conditional: Julie Dodds (9-7).

Amateur: Mr L Crosswaite (10-7).

Lady Rider: Miss Jane Morton (10-0).

383 MR M. MCCORMACK, Wantage

Postal: **East Manton Stables, Sparsholt, Wantage, Oxon, OX12 9PJ.**
Phone: **CHILDREY (023 559) 433**

1 **JUST A STEP,** 4, br c Lochnager—My Louise **Mr G. S. B. Cooke**
2 **JUST THREE,** 4, b c Tina's Pet—Mio Mementa **Mr B. McGee**
3 **NO BEATING HARTS,** 7, b g London Bells (CAN)—Movement **Mr C. B. D. Taylor**
4 **RATHBAWN DAN,** 7, b g Homeboy—Last Trick **Mr M. McCormack**
5 **SPANISH LOVE,** 4, b f Precocious—San Marguerite **Orchid Racing & Bloodstock Ltd**
6 **TAFFY JONES,** 11, br g Welsh Pageant—Shallow Stream **Mr M. McCormack**

THREE-YEAR-OLDS

7 **ALFEREZ,** gr g Petong—Sarah's Venture **Mr Maurice E. Pinto**
8 **HALF A PINK JO,** ch c Absalom—Habitual Beauty **Feeny Holdings Ltd**
9 **KILLIMOR LAD,** b c Tina's Pet—Jeldi **Mr James Clasby**
10 **KNIGHT'S GLANCE,** b g Castle Keep—Coming Out **Mr Brian North**
11 **MAC'S BEST,** ch g Borzoi (USA)—Happy Satan (USA) **Mr M. McDonnell**
12 **MOTCOMBS,** gr f Glenstal (USA)—Roof **Mrs Margie Fearn**
13 **RACECALL GOLD CARD,** ch g Camden Town—Polly Royal **Racegoers Club Owners Group**
14 **SILENT STEPS,** ch c Kind of Hush—On The Turn **Mr R. K. Curtis**
15 **SOLEIL GRAND,** b g Red Sunset—Becassine **Mr David Mort**

TWO-YEAR-OLDS

16 B c 28/3 Hatim (USA)—African Bloom **Mr M. Holleran**
17 B c 10/3 Stalker—Angelica (SWE)
18 Ch f 26/1 Sayf El Arab (USA)—Collegian **Mr Maurice E. Pinto**
19 B c 4/5 High Top—Crimbourne **Mr Maurice E. Pinto**
20 B c 28/3 Mazaad—Golden Arum
21 Ch gr c 22/3 Carwhite—Marymount **J. J. Durkan**
22 **MORE LARKS (IRE),** b br c 20/2 Godswalk (USA)—Charmeuse **Mr Dennis G. Clarke**
23 Gr br f 4/3 Lidhame—Norton Princess **Mr Maurice E. Pinto**
24 **RINCE DEAS (IRE),** b f 29/4 Alzao (USA)—Flaxen Hair **Mr G. Mills**
25 Ch c 21/3 The Noble Player—Sea Palace
26 **SOLEIL DANCER (IRE),** b c 2/3 Fairy King (USA)—Cooliney Dancer **Mr David Mort**
27 **SOUTARI,** b br c 11/5 Scorpio (FR)—Sousocks **Mrs Satu Marks**

MR M. MCCORMACK—continued

28 WILL I OR WONT I (IRE), b c 26/1 The Noble Player—Dusty Highway **Mr Z. Papastylianou**
29 Ch c 10/4 M Double M (USA)—Wolver Rose **Mr Maurice E. Pinto**

Other Owners: Mr John Davey, Mr D. L. Ellis, Mr David Lee, Mr Peter Newell, Mr Kevin Roberts, Mr Peter Savery, Mr P. B. Sheehy, Mrs Lynn Waight, Mr J. W. Wells.

Jockeys (Flat): S Cauthen (w.a.), P Eddery (w.a.), J Reid (w.a.).

Amateur: Mr C Maude (9-7, w.a.).

384 MR M. MCCOURT, Wantage

Postal: **Antwick Stud, Letcombe Regis, Wantage, Oxon, OX12 9LH.**
Phone: **WANTAGE (02357) 4456**

1 BUSY MITTENS, 9, ch m Nearly A Hand—Busy Buskins **Mrs Heather Bare**
2 CEE-EN-CEE, 6, b g Junius (USA)—Lady Red Rose **Orbit Precision Machining Ltd**
3 COUNTRY DIARY, 7, b m Town And Country—Royal Dialogue **Mrs Heather Bare**
4 EARLY BREEZE, 4, b c Tumble Wind (USA)—Dawn Hail **Mr N. A. Gill**
5 IN ORDER, 7, ch g Relkino—Expansive **Mr T. Dunbar**
6 INTREPID LAD, 8, ch g Hot Grove—Mountain Rescue **Mr B. E. Walsh**
7 JUST TOO BRAVE, 7, b g Beldale Flutter (USA)—Georgina Park **Mr M. Stoneman**
8 MERCURY MOON, 5, gr g Belfort (FR)—Tringa (GER) **Mr J. F. Watson**
9 TAMI, 5, ch m Miami Springs—Tenoria **Mrs B. Taylor**
10 VICK THE BUSKER, 13, b g Little Buskins—Vickie's Bell **Mrs Heather Bare**

THREE-YEAR-OLDS

11 MISS MATTERS, b f Strong Gale—Miss Filbert **Mr D. E. McDowell**

TWO-YEAR-OLDS

12 B c Mashhor Dancer (USA)—Dark Amber **Mr N. A. Gill**
13 B c Mazaad—Putt Wood **Mr M. McCourt**

Jockey (NH): G McCourt (10-5).

385 MR R. MCDONALD, Duns

Postal: **Kelloe Mains, Duns, Berwickshire, Scotland, TD11 3PT.**
Phone: **CHIRNSIDE (089 081) 218**

1 ABOVE BOARD, 5, ch g Cut Above—Lady Ector (USA) **Mr G. W. Reid**
2 ARCTIC STRIKE, 6, ch g Golden Love—Gorryelm **Mr R. McDonald**
3 BANQUE D'OR, 6, b m Le Coq d'Or—Gilzie Bank **Mr R. McDonald**
4 BIRSBY, 16, br g New Brig—Buzz About **Mr R. McDonald**
5 GILZIE'S TOUCH, 4, b f Feelings (FR)—Gilzie Bank **Mr R. McDonald**
6 HAZEL LEAF, 4, b f Le Moss—Camden **Mr R. McDonald**
7 ROWAN LEAF, 7, ch g Dynastic—Young Ash Leaf **Mr R. McDonald**
8 ROYAL JESTER, 6, b g Royal Fountain—Tormina **Mrs A. D. Wauchope**
9 SOMERLED, 11, b g Dynastic—Young Ash Leaf **Mr R. McDonald**
10 YOUNG MOSS, 4, b g Le Moss—Young Ash Linn **Mr R. McDonald**

MR R. MCDONALD—continued

THREE-YEAR-OLDS

11 Ch f Feelings (FR)—Camden **Mr R. McDonald**
12 B g Feelings (FR)—Gilzie Bank **Mr R. McDonald**
13 Ch g Le Moss—Young Ash Leaf **Mr R. McDonald**

TWO-YEAR-OLDS

14 B f 10/6 Uncle Pokey—Camden (David Jack) **Mr R. McDonald**

Other Owners: Mr I. Anderson.

Jockey (NH): C Hawkins (10-3).

386 MR NEIL S. MCGRATH, Kildare

Postal: **Brownstown House, Curragh, Kildare, Ireland.**
Phone: **(045) 41303 (045) 41817 FAX 41215**

1 CARRICK MINES, 5, ch g Deep Run—Gallant Breeze **F. Shaw**
2 COME ON THE BEACH (USA), 4, ch c Spectacular Bid—One For Cuz **Due Process Stables**
3 CORRECTED (USA), 5, b g Cojak (USA)—Dihela (USA) **Brian Boudreau**
4 MASTER OF PARIS (USA), 6, b g Master Willie—Woman of Paris **P. W. McGrath**

THREE-YEAR-OLDS

5 BRIDGE OF SPIES (USA), b g Belted Earl—Cabinbinini **P. W. McGrath**
6 ELA KORU MOU (USA), gr f Slew's Royalty—Travelin' Joan **Mrs Andry Muinos**
7 HEAVENLY WAY, ch f Godswalk—Chaumine **Mrs P. W. McGrath**
8 HERO'S WELCOME, br c Simply Great—Airport **M. J. Dargan**
9 LEGAL VERDICT, b c Law Society—True Rocket **Legal Verdict Syndicate**
10 LINEKER, ch g Exhibitioner—Golden Dividend **F. Shaw**
11 MANAMOU, b f Ela-Mana-Mou—Idle Threat **Mrs P. W. McGrath**
12 SALLY BAGGER, ch f Be My Guest—Astra Adastra **S. McGrath**

TWO-YEAR-OLDS

13 B f 15/5 Gorytus (USA)—Airport (Warpath) **M. J. Dargan**
14 B c 12/4 Formidable (USA)—Amalancher (USA) (Alleged (USA)) **Currarevagh Racing Club**
15 B c 9/3 Alzao (USA)—Elvire (Dominion) **Currarevagh Racing Club**
16 B c 28/2 Krayyan—Frisky Matron (On Your Mark) **Currarevagh Racing Club**
17 Gr c 6/5 Sarab—Legs And Things (Three Legs) **Currarevagh Racing Club**
18 Ch c 5/5 Tumble Wind (USA)—My Louise (Manado) **Currarevagh Racing Club**
19 Ch f Nijinsky (CAN)—Strictly Raised (Raise A Native) **Richard Brooks**
20 Ch c 5/3 Superlative—Swordlestown Miss (Apalachee (USA)) **Currarevagh Racing Club**

387 MRS C. MCINNES SKINNER, Melton Mowbray

Postal: **John O'Gaunt House, Melton Mowbray, Leicestershire, LE14 2RE.**
Phone: **(066) 477 327**

1 ANOTHER BOXER, 10, br g Hardboy—Oriental China **Mrs T. J. McInnes Skinner**
2 CRUDEN BAY, 10, bl g Lucky Wednesday—Floragold **Mrs T. J. McInnes Skinner**
3 DIE IN THE SKY, 9, ch g Welsh Pageant—Heaven And Earth **Mrs T. J. McInnes Skinner**
4 TARCOLA, 11, b g Tarqogan—Game Hen **Mrs T. J. McInnes Skinner**

Jockey (NH): S J O'Neill (10-0, w.a.).

388 MR W. G. MCKENZIE-COLES, Taunton

Postal: **Bells Cottage, Lydeard St Lawrence, Taunton, Somerset, TA4 3RN.**
Phone: **LYDEARD ST LAWRENCE (09847) 334**

1 **BOAT TRAIN,** 4, b f Lighter—Biggsie's Bird **Mr W. G. McKenzie-Coles**
2 **MISS BUNCE,** 6, b m Mummy's Game—Autumn Breeze **Mr W. G. McKenzie-Coles**
3 **MONTGOMERY,** 9, b g Push On—Mirror Back **Mr W. G. McKenzie-Coles**
4 **PROVERBIAL SESSION,** 9, ch g Proverb—Courting Session **Mr W. G. McKenzie-Coles**
5 **TRAIN ROBBER,** 5, b g Sharp Deal—Biggsie's Bird **Mr W. G. McKenzie-Coles**

Jockey (NH): B Powell.

389 MRS V. MCKIE, Twyford

Postal: **'Twyford Mill', Twyford, Buckinghamshire.**
Phone: **STEEPLE CLAYDON (029) 6730707**

1 **ANOTHER BOLUS,** 8, gr g Yankee Gold—Pretty Candy **Mr J. B. Sumner**
2 **BATTLE STANDARD,** 4, ch g Battle Hymn—Rose Bridges **Alfordshire Ltd**
3 **BIT OF A CLOWN,** 7, b g Callernish—Gusserane Lark **Mr J. B. Sumner**
4 **DUBLIN SAGA,** 5, ch m Sagaro—Dublin Express **Mr J. B. Sumner**
5 **FLORA LOUISA,** 5, b m Rymer—Star Ruler **Mrs D. Barnett**
6 **FRAMFIELD,** 8, br g Monksfield—Framboise **Mrs Ian McKie**
7 **LARRY'S BOTTLE,** 13, ch g Golden Love—Breaking Point **Mrs Ian McKie**
8 **M I BABE,** 5, ch m Celtic Cone—Cover Your Money **Mr Tony Kay**
9 **MINT-MASTER,** 5, ch g Deep Run—Bold Penny **Captain Miles Gosling**
10 **MOSS CONNELL,** 8, ch g Carnival Night—Doon Mist **Unregistered Partnership**
11 **MRS PEPPERPOT,** 7, b m Kinglet—Nostra **Mrs Ian McKie**
12 **ONE MORE KNIGHT,** 7, b g Roselier (FR)—Ballyadam Lass **Mr Richard West**
13 **RISK A BET,** 11, ch g Kinglet—Imperial Stake **Mrs Ian McKie**
14 **ROLLING DICE,** 7, b m Balinger—Imperial Stake **Mrs A. M. Murray**
15 **ROYAL GOSSIP,** 8, ch g Le Bavard (FR)—Royal Intrigue **Mr J. B. Sumner**
16 **ROYAL SUNSHINE,** 5, ch g Sunyboy—Royal Intrigue **Mrs Ian McKie**
17 **SPRUCER,** 5, b g Prince Regent (FR)—Knollwood Court **Alfordshire Ltd**
18 **TERRY'S PROBLEM,** 5, b g Lepanto (GER)—Annie Louise **Mrs Ian McKie**
19 **THE GREY BOREEN,** 5, gr g Boreen (FR)—Grey Daisy **Mrs Ian McKie**

Other Owners: Mr K. Borrett, Mr P. Burton, Mr T. Hall, Mr C. Hodgson.

Jockey (NH): L Harvey (10-0).

Amateur: Mr I McKie (10-12).

Lady Riders: Miss K Ellis (8-7), Miss K Holmes (9-7).

390 MR B. MCLEAN, Morpeth

Postal: **Burgham Farming Co, Burgham Farm, Felton, Morpeth, Northumberland, NE65 8TJ.**
Phone: **FELTON (0670) 787314**

1 **FLYING DANCER,** 8, b g Niniski (USA)—Topbird **Mr D. C. A. Bramall**
2 **GEEANTEE,** 5, ch g Abednego—Covette **The G. & T. Syndicate**
3 **INTO THE MYSTIC,** 8, br g Kemal (FR)—Rochetta **Mrs Dianne McLean**

MR B. MCLEAN—continued

4 **JACK OF CLUBS,** 10, b g Kinglet—Laughing Stock **Mr Brian McLean**
5 **KING FLIPPER,** 4, b g King's Ride—Natasha Ann **Mr H. B. Shouler and Mr T. Ounsley**
6 **LINDEN BRIG,** 8, br m New Brig—Velvet Cap II **Mr Brian McLean**
7 **RIBO MELODY,** 7, b m Riboboy (USA)—Sovereign Melody **Mr T. Hurst**
8 **SNOW ROSE,** 5, ch m Deep Run—Kilmanahan **Mr R. S. Brown**
9 **SUKAAB,** 5, gr g Nishapour (FR)—Nye (FR) **Mr T. Hurst**
10 **THE PROGRAMMER,** 5, b g Paddy's Stream—Articogan **Systemcare Ltd**
11 **WORTHY KNIGHT,** 9, ch g Dubassoff (USA)—Quidsworth **Mr H. B. Shouler and Mr T. Ounsley**

Other Owners: Mrs C. Bell, Mr Ian Davison, Mr Ron Davison, Mr K. McLean, Mrs E. M. Patrick, Mr R. Alan Robson.

Jockey (NH): B Storey (w.a.).

391 MR B. A. MCMAHON, Tamworth

Postal: **Woodside Farm, Hopwas Hill, Tamworth, Staffordshire.**
Phone: **(0827) 62901**

1 **ANOTHER NORFOLK,** 9, ch g Pamroy—Norfolk House **Mr N. Smith**
2 **BIG WHITE CHIEF,** 9, gr g Warpath—Compulsion **Mr E. A. Lee**
3 **BRIGADIERS GLORY,** 4, ch f Castle Keep—Join The Club **Mr D. E. Gregory**
4 **CANDESCO,** 4, b f Blushing Scribe (USA)—Madame Mim **Mrs Brenda Jeffery**
5 **CASHEW KING,** 7, b g Faraway Times (USA)—Sinzinbra **Mr P. Moss**
6 **CAUSLEY,** 5, br g Swing Easy (USA)—Four Lawns **Mr Henry Pearce**
7 **DALBY DASH,** 5, ch g Bustiki—Wensum Girl **Mr J. H. H. Benbow**
8 **FARRIERS LAD,** 5, b h Smackover—Kirkmaiden **West Midlands Telecom**
9 **GOLDEN MADJAMBO,** 4, ch c Northern Tempest (USA)—Shercol **Mr Tony S. K. Wong**
10 **GREENACRES LAD,** 7, ch g Billion (USA)—Moon Lady **Mr M. J. Talbot**
11 **HUNG OVER,** 4, b f Smackover—Passionate **Mr Chris Melville**
12 **MAY OVER,** 5, ch g Smackover—May Bond **Mr K. O. Warner**
13 **MEESON KING,** 9, br g Space King—Meeson Girl **Mr J. B. Wilcox**
14 **PEANUTS PET,** 5, b h Tina's Pet—Sinzinbra **Mr L. Perry**
15 **R A EXPRESS,** 5, b g Bay Express—Pinaka **R. A. Holdings Ltd**
16 **ROAD UP,** 4, ch c Smackover—Road To Somewhere **Swinnerton Transport Ltd**
17 **SCHWEPPES TONIC,** 4, br c Persian Bold—Gay Shadow **Mr J. B. Wilcox**
18 **SINGALETTO,** 6, b m Neltino—Sweet Singer **Peter Haughton**
19 **TACOMA HEIGHTS,** 4, b c Taufan (USA)—Good Relations **Mr Tony F. H. Man**
20 **TEE WALL,** 4, b c Tampero (FR)—Wallpark Princess **Mrs J. McMahon**
21 **THE MISSISSIPPIAN,** 9, b g Tumble Wind (USA)—Dolly-Longlegs **Mr J. E. Abbey**
22 **WEETMANS WAGON,** 6, ch g Welsh Chanter—Judy Green **Ed Weetman (Haulage & Storage) Ltd**

THREE-YEAR-OLDS

23 **BAND ON THE RUN,** ch c Song—Sylvanecte (FR) **Mr D. J. Allen**
24 **DARING JOY,** b f Daring March—African Berry **Miss A. O'Malley**
25 **GALATEA PEARL,** b f Rabdan—Bridal Wave **Mr A. J. Whitehead**
26 **KATY'S LAD,** b c Camden Town—Cathryn's Song **Mr J. W. Butler**
27 **KINLACEY,** b f Aragon—Mimika **Mr R. L. Shaw**
28 **LEGAL STREAK,** b c Mr Fluorocarbon—Streakella **Mr J. W. Hall**
29 **PETRADARE,** ch f Wolver Heights—Petlady **Mr Michael G. T. Stokes**

TWO-YEAR-OLDS

30 Ch f Creetown—Aldington Cherry **Mr Henry Pearce**
31 **GONE OVER,** ch c Smackover—Condec **Alfred Hui-Sik-Yin**
32 **JURISPRUDENCE (IRE),** b f 15/5 Law Society (USA)—Virginia Sham (USA) **Mr and Mrs D. J. Allen**
33 **JUST JOHN,** ch c 15/3 Smackover—Saint Motunde **Antony Ting-Yuk Wu**
34 **NICKY RA RA,** ch f Nicholas Bill—Ra Ra Girl **R. A. Holdings Ltd**

MR B. A. MCMAHON—continued

Other Owners: Mrs Ann Coombes, Mr K. P. Holland, Mr M. Mumford, Mr D. A. Thompson.

Jockey (NH): Trevor Wall (9-8).

Apprentices: Paul Farmer (6-12), Ian Hughes (7-7), Sebastian Sanders (7-0).

Conditional: Adam Roper (9-7).

Amateur: Mr Edward McMahon (10-8).

Lady Rider: Miss Stephanie Baxter (8-9).

392 MR B. J. MCMATH, Bury St Edmunds

Postal: **Dalmer Lodge, Timworth Green, Timworth, Bury St Edmunds, Suffolk, IP33 1HS.**
Phone: **CULFORD (0284) 84439**

1 **BIG COUNTRY,** 7, b g Town And Country—Top Soprano **Mr B. Belchem**
2 **DEEP WATER BAY,** 6, b g Lochnager—Cateryne **L. E. Neep & Co Limited**
3 **FIRM FOUNDATIONS,** 13, br g Pieces of Eight—Streetcar **Mr M. F. Quiller**
4 **IDIOT'S BEAUTY,** 9, b m Idiot's Delight—Oyston Beauty **Mr B. Belchem**
5 **JORGE MIGUEL,** 11, b g Welsh Pageant—Sheralda **K. Martin (Sudbury) Ltd**
6 **KING OF COMEDY,** 8, b g Comedy Star (USA)—Sunbird **Mr J. H. Corre**
7 **KING OF KNOWLEDGE,** 6, ch g Known Fact (USA)—Parsimony **Ms A. Coates**
8 **LOVE ANEW (USA),** 5, b g Sensitive Prince (USA)—Armure Bleue (FR) **Mr David L. Bowkett**
9 **NAUTICAL FESTIVAL,** 5, ch g Windjammer (USA)—The Festival Chat **Mrs D. Crage**
10 **PRINCE YAMADORI,** 6, b g Riboboy (USA)—Orange Tip **L. E. Neep & Co Limited**
11 **RUTHS MELODY,** 7, b m Healaugh Fox—Ruths Image **Mr H. Spencer**
12 **SLIP STITCH,** 6, b m Vivify—Talentira **C. E. Willcox**
13 **TAYLORS QUEEN,** 4, b f Tender King—Fenland Queen **Miss Sue Chubb**
14 **YUVRAJ,** 6, b g Final Straw—Never Never Land **Mr A. B. Reason**

Other Owners: Mr R. A. Fincham, Mr Alan Kaufman, Mr Lennard Lazarus, Mr B. J. McMath, Mr Ray Powell, Mr M. A. Stein.

Jockeys (NH): R Beggan (10-0), A Carroll (10-0).

393 MR N. MEADE, Navan

Postal: **Tu Va Stables, Castletown, Navan, Co. Meath, Ireland.**
Phone: **(046) 54197 or 54278 FAX (046) 54459**

1 **ACTION DANCER,** 4, b g Viking (USA)—Action Girl **Mr R. McCarthy**
2 **BLAKICA,** 5, gr m Sexton Blake—Makica (USA) **Mr N. Coburn**
3 **DARING STEPS,** 4, b c Daring March—Gold Rule **Mrs M. Cahill**
4 **DUBLINS COQ HARDI,** 5, ch g Stanford—Caramica **Mrs Catherine Howard**

MR N. MEADE—continued

5 **FANE BANKS,** 8, b g Random Shot—Vulgans Princess **Mrs M. Cahill**
6 **ICE PRINCESS,** 5, ch m Known Fact (USA)—Blue Shark **Joseph Michael Clarke**
7 **IL TROVATORE (USA),** 4, b c Chief Singer—Last Flair **Mr J. Hunt**
8 **IMPI,** 6, b g Kampala—Masai Princess **Mrs A. Kaufman-Lehn**
9 **JACKIE HEAD,** 4, b f Head For Heights—Lucky Life **Noel Meade**
10 **JOIN THE QUE,** 5, b g Kafu—Royal Express **Mrs P. J. Carr**
11 **LITTLE BIGHORN,** 5, b h Blakeney—Nip In The Air **J. Hunt**
12 **LOUGH KEY,** 4, b g Creetown—Figurehead **P. M. Hunt**
13 **MERRY DANCE,** 5, ch g Merrymount—Kohrain **David A. Jackson**
14 **MILLENNIUM FALCON,** 4, b c Dunbeath (USA)—Peregrine Falcon **Ms Michelle Hadley**
15 **NATURAL ABILITY,** 5, ch g Billion (USA)—Confident Girl **Miss Anne Halpin**
16 **NEWBAWN GROVE,** 7, br g He Loves Me—Gavina **Donal Kinsella**
17 **OCEAN PEARL,** 7, ch g Wrens Hill—Ballintra Lady **David A. Jackson**
18 **RANDOM PRINCE,** 6, br g Random Shot—Tonys Lass **Mr N. Coburn**
19 **RENOIR,** 4, ch c Ahonoora—Lagolette **Mr F. Towey**
20 **ROCKET DANCER,** 4, b c Niniski (USA)—Dora's Rocket **Mr P. Garvey**
21 **SEE NOW,** 5, ch g Tumble Wind (USA)—Rosie O'Grady **Mrs Rita Polly**
22 **THE HYACE DRIVER,** 7, ch g Proverb—Annalys Last **Donal Kinsella**
23 **WINSTON MURPHY,** 4, ch g Don—Annais Nin **Stewart Jamieson**

THREE-YEAR-OLDS

24 **BEAU BEAUCHAMP,** b g Thatching—El Pina **Donal Kinsella**
25 **CLARE'S FIZZY,** b f Kafu—Fizzy **Arthur Joseph O'Neill**
26 Br g Anita's Prince—Curragh Gold **Mrs Anita Quinn**
27 **DANCE OR BURST,** ch f Try My Best (USA)—Court Ballet **Dr F. J. Healy**
28 **DEAN SWIFT,** br g Anita's Prince—Speedwriter **Mrs Anita Quinn**
29 **DOMINION DANCER,** b f Dominion—Cara Rose **Stewart Jamieson**
30 **EVER SO BOLD,** ch c Never So Bold—Spinelle **Patrick White**
31 **HAWAIIAN GODDESS (USA),** b f Hawaii—Destiny's Reward (USA) **Stewart Jamieson**
32 **JIMMY THE JACKDAW,** b c Henbit (USA)—Organdy **Michael Murray**
33 **MASTER GLAZE,** b f Camden Town—Flying Beauty **Mrs J. T. Murphy**
34 **MOOSE MALLOY,** ch c Try My Best (USA)—Brilliant Rosa **Mr J. Hunt**
35 **REUBEN JAMES,** ch g Tumble Wind (USA)—Winter Harvest **Anne Halpin**
36 **TRUE OPTIMIST,** b g Try My Best (USA)—Lenticular **Sportsmans Club**
37 **VICEROY OF INDIA (CAN),** b c Vice Regent (CAN)—Damascene Lady (USA) **Mr J. Hunt**
38 **VISIONS PRIDE,** gr ro g Vision (USA)—Danielle Delight **Mrs M. Brennan**
39 **WIND OF CHANGE (FR),** ch f Sicyos (USA)—Nip In The Air (USA) **Mrs Maureen Hunt**

TWO-YEAR-OLDS

40 B c 9/3 High Line—Al Washi (USA) (The Minstrel (CAN))
41 Br c 19/4 Persian Bold—Am Stretchin (USA) (Ambiorix II) **Mr Stewart Jamieson**
42 Ch c 3/2 Camden Town—Favant (Faberge II)
43 Br c 27/3 Irish River (FR)—Gala Evening (Try My Best (USA)) **Mr J. Hunt**
44 Ch f 19/4 Pennine Walk—Gruntled (Grundy) **Joseph Michael Clarke**
45 B f 1/3 Flash of Steel—Kew Gift (Faraway Son (USA)) **Mr Denis Howard**
46 B f 25/4 Anita's Prince—Lady of Man (So Blessed) **Stablemate Plc.**
47 B f 24/5 Anita's Prince—Mashid (Fordham (USA))
48 Ch c 1/4 Dominion—Misfire (Gunner B) **Mr John Moore**
49 B c 17/4 Sicyos (USA)—Nip In The Air (USA) (Northern Dancer) **Mr J. Hunt**
50 B c 11/4 Dominion—Oriental Star (Falcon)
51 B c 22/5 Elegant Air—Pearlesque (Gulf Pearl)
52 Gr f Rusticaro (FR)—Shoshoni Girl (USA) (Winning Hit (USA)) **Mr T. Hunt**
53 B f 22/3 Mashhor Dancer (USA)—Speedy Rose (On Your Mark) **P. F. Towey**
54 B c 10/4 Robellino (USA)—Street Ballet (USA) (Nijinsky (CAN))
55 Ch f 23/5 Yashgan—Tower Bank (Tower Walk) **Mr J. McKeown**

Apprentice: Warren O'Connor (8-6).

Conditional: Peter McLoughlin (9-0), Mark White (9-0).

394 MR S. MELLOR, Swindon

Postal: **Pollardstown Racing Stables, Foxhill, Wanborough, Swindon, SN4 0DR.**
Phone: **(0793) 790230**

1 **ASTRE RADIEUX (FR),** 5, b g Gay Mecene (USA)—Divine Etoile (USA) **Mr Trevor Hemmings**
2 **BILLY STRAYHORN,** 6, b g Northfields (USA)—Tanaka **Mr S. P. Tindall**
3 **BOREEN KING,** 9, b br g Boreen (FR)—Proverb's Bride **Mr P. Winkworth**
4 **CRACKERJACKIE GEE,** 5, ch g Rymer—Song Without Words **Mrs Jackie Gill**
5 **CRASHING BORE,** 6, ch g Boreen (FR)—Ware Princess **Mr C. J. Ells**
6 **GREEN RIDGE,** 11, br g Green Shoon—Amazakove **Mr David Mullen**
7 **HACKENBUCH,** 5, ch g Proverb—Giolla Beag **Miss Maria Mai**
8 **INFINITY RULES,** 9, b g Mandamus—Catherine Rose **Metal-Woods Ltd**
9 **INTRUM BOY,** 5, b g Boreen (FR)—Ullard Lady **Miss Maria Mai**
10 **JESSOP,** 5, b g Gleason (USA)—Perusia **Mr S. P. Tindall**
11 **JUMP,** 5, gr g General Ironside—Maroon Well **Mr E. T. Wright**
12 **KING'S CURATE,** 6, b g King's Ride—Parnessa **Mr C. J. Ells**
13 **LAUNDRYMAN,** 7, b g Celtic Cone—Lovely Laura **The Burford District Laundry Co Ltd**
14 **LEAN AR AGHAIDH,** 13, ch g Proverb—Carry On Jackie **Mrs W. Tulloch**
15 **MACROOM,** 8, b g Furry Glen—Crashing Juno **Mrs M. M. Tindall**
16 **NEWLAR,** 11, br g Dominion Day—Star Strip **Mr S. P. Tindall**
17 **NUMBER CRUNCHER,** 5, ch g Orchestra—I'm No Saint **Mr P. Winkworth**
18 **ORLEANS SOUND,** 6, b g Duc d'Orleans—What A Performance **Dickins Ltd**
19 **ROSIE MAY DICKINS,** 4, b f King of Spain—Gipsy Scott **Dickins Ltd**
20 **ROSITARY (FR),** 7, b m Trenel—Houri V (FR) **Mr P. Winkworth**
21 **RUBIKA (FR),** 7, b g Saumon (FR)—Eureka III (FR) **Mr Trevor Hemmings**
22 **SENEGALAIS (FR),** 6, b g Quart de Vin (FR)—Divonne (FR) **Mr S. P. Tindall**
23 **THAMESDOWN TOOTSIE,** 5, b m Comedy Star (USA)—Lizzie Lightfoot **Mrs S. C. Haine**
24 **TRUBLION (FR),** 5, b g Cherubin (FR)—Mirella II (FR) **Mr Trevor Hemmings**
25 **TUROLDUS (FR),** 5, b g Toujours Pret (USA)—Katy Collonge (FR) **Mr Stan Mellor**
26 **UNEXIS,** 5, ch g Salluceva—Caddy Girl **Mr David Mullen**
27 **UNICOL,** 8, ch g Manado—Ragatina **Mr David Mullen**
28 **WATERHAY,** 7, b g Callernish—Crookhaven **Mr Peter Forsdike**
29 **WAY OF LIFE (FR),** 5, ch g No Lute (FR)—My Beloved (FR) **Mr Trevor Hemmings**
30 **ZUKO (CHI),** 9, b g Kimono (CHI)—La Saudade (CHI) **Mr S. Powell**

Other Owners: Mr J. G. Bailey, Mr F. O. A. Bennett, Mr K. H. Jaffa, Mr G. R. Seymour, Mr M. E. Thompsett, Lord Wolverton.

Jockey (Flat): Dana Mellor (7-2).

Jockeys (NH): S Cowley (10-0), G Charles Jones (10-0).

Conditional: P Barnard (9-0), I Shoemark (9-7).

Amateur: Mr R Griffiths (10-0).

Lady Rider: Miss L Mellor (7-0).

395 MR N. MILLER, Ferryhill

Postal: **Chilton Grange Farm, Gypsy Lane, Ferryhill, Co Durham, DL17 0LF.**
Phone: **(0388) 721565**

1 **CELESTIAL INVADER,** 8, b g Brave Invader (USA)—Astrella Celeste **Mr Norman Miller**
2 **CHILTON LADY,** 5, ch m Liberated—Jedhart Lass **Mr Norman Miller**

MR N. MILLER—continued

3 **EMMET STREET,** 10, ch g Avocat—Carnival Beauty **Mr Norman Miller**
4 **GAV'S DELIGHT,** 12, b g Furry Glen—Lauch Berg **Mr Norman Miller**
5 **JAY DOUBLE YOU,** 9, b g Free State—Touch of Dutch **Mr Norman Miller**
6 **PRINCE BISHOP,** 4, br g Sparkling Boy—Indian Tea **Mr Norman Miller**
7 **RUN 'N SEEK,** 6, ch g Deep Run—Gift Seeker **Mr Norman Miller**

396 MISS M. K. MILLIGAN, Middleham

Postal: **Hazeldene, Kirkgate, Middleham, Leyburn, North Yorkshire.**
Phone: **(0969) 22990**

1 **SCANDALOUS RUMOUR,** 7, b g Le Bavard (FR)—Reynella **Mrs J. M. L. Milligan**
2 **SPARTAN RANGER,** 5, b g Lochnager—Spartan Flutter **Mrs J. M. L. Milligan**
3 **WILL COWAN,** 5, b br g Tudor Diver—Pemrock **Mrs J. M. L. Milligan**

397 MR B. R. MILLMAN, Cullompton

Postal: **The Paddocks, Kentisbeare, Cullompton, Devon, EX15 2DY.**
Phone: **(0884) 6620**

1 **BAYSHAM (USA),** 4, b c Raise A Native—Sunny Bay (USA) **Mr W. Butt**
2 **BRIGHT MORNING,** 12, b g Duc d'Orleans—Top of The Morning **Mrs N. Dutfield**
3 **CHARCOAL BURNER,** 5, b g Royal Match—Resist **Mrs A. Schwolm**
4 **DEE AND EM,** 5, ch g Crofter (USA)—Cousin Clare **Mr P. Tracey**
5 **DEEP REEF,** 4, ch g Main Reef—Kareela **Mrs M. Rowe**
6 **GOLDEN GENERATION,** 4, b g Young Generation—Song of Gold **Mr Danny Furneaux**
7 **HANSOM MARSHAL,** 4, br g Daring March—Fille de Phaeton **Mr J. Boswell**
8 **HONEST GLORY,** 4, b f Al Nasr (FR)—Mistress Lea **Mr R. Withers**
9 **MAGIC MILLY,** 4, b f Simply Great (FR)—Supreme Fjord **Mr R. Withers**
10 **MONTECATINI,** 4, b g Tyrnavos—Gunnera **Mrs N. Dutfield**
11 **ROYAL DARTMOUTH (USA),** 5, ch g Czaravich (USA)—Blushing Emy (USA) **Axminster Carpets**
12 **SPORTING SIMON,** 5, ch g Vaigly Great—City Link Lass **Mrs N. Dutfield**

THREE-YEAR-OLDS

13 **BIGHAYIR,** gr g Petong—Nook **Mrs N. Dutfield**
14 **BOSTON BILL,** gr g Magic Mirror—Barrow Girl **Mr B. R. Millman**
15 **DAISY MY LOVE,** b f Sharpo—Carmen Maria **Mrs N. Dutfield**
16 **EDEN'S DAWN,** ch g Godswalk (USA)—Fresh As A Daisy **Mrs N. Dutfield**
17 **PENNIES WOOD,** b g Star Appeal—Deep River **Mrs M. Rowe**

TWO-YEAR-OLDS

18 Ch g Coquelin (USA)—Doushkina (Dubassoff (USA)) **Mrs N. Dutfield**
19 **RED HOT ROSIE,** gr f Absalom—Cloister Rose (Track Spare) **Mrs N. Dutfield**

Other Owners: Mr G. Anstey, Mr D. M. Brain, Mr W. H. Dutfield, R. J. A. Earle, Mr R. C. Ewin, K. D. Kidd, A. Lynn, Mrs Woodgate.

Jockeys (NH): Simon Earle (10-0), Andy Forte (10-0).

398 MRS S. MINNS, Droitwich

Postal: **Woodfield House Cottage, Woodford Lane, Woodford, Ombersley, Worcestershire.**
Phone: **(0905) 621201 DAYTIME (0905) 620347 EVENINGS**

1 **JUNAC,** 6, b m Cajun—Be In Touch **Mrs Sylvia Minns**
2 **PETIT PAIN,** 9, b g Ile de Bourbon (USA)—Shortbread **Mrs Sylvia Minns**
3 **POWER HAPPY,** 5, ch m Instant Fame—Dawn Dreamer **Mrs Sylvia Minns**
4 **PRINCELY HEIR,** 9, b g Royalty—Petitpoint **Mrs Sylvia Minns**
5 **ROYAL FAME,** 6, ch g Instant Fame—Royal Chanter **Mrs Sylvia Minns**

Jockey (NH): Nigel Coleman (10-0).

Conditional: Derek Byrne (9-7).

399 MR C. W. MITCHELL, Dorchester

Postal: **White House, Buckland Newton, Dorchester, Dorset, DT2 7DE.**
Phone: **(03005) 276**

1 **FLOATING LOVER,** 11, ch g Crawter—Floating Dreams **Mr C. W. Mitchell**
2 **MAJESTIC DREAM,** 6, b m Majestic Maharaj—Floating Dreams **Mr C. W. Mitchell**
3 **ROMFUL PRINCE,** 7, b g White Prince (USA)—Romfultears **Mr C. W. Mitchell**
4 **TEARFUL PRINCE,** 6, b g White Prince (USA)—Romfultears **Mr C. W. Mitchell**

400 MR N. R. MITCHELL, Dorchester

Postal: **Whitcombe Racing Stables, Dorchester, Dorset, DT2 8NY.**
Phone: **DORCHESTER (0305) 251429 FAX (0305) 251217**

1 **ALARM CALL (USA),** 7, b h Alleged (USA)—Sunelianne (USA) **Whitcombe Manor Racing Stables Limited**
2 **AUCTION FOLLY,** 10, b g Diamonds Are Trump (USA)—Khios **Whitcombe Manor Racing Stables Limited**
3 **BLAKEINGTON,** 4, b c Baron Blakeney—Camina **Miss I. L. Ritchie**
4 **BLONDE BELLA,** 5, b m Pablond—Donna Bellina **Miss I. L. Ritchie**
5 **CAME DOWN,** 7, gr g Nearly A Hand—Bellentina **Major N. D. Martin**
6 **CARNEADES,** 10, b g Homing—Connarca **Whitcombe Manor Racing Stables Limited**
7 **CLEAR CHOICE (NZ),** 8, b g Tierra Fuego—Flower Bird (NZ) **Mrs John W. Finding**
8 **COOL GROUND,** 8, ch g Over The River (FR)—Merry Spring **Whitcombe Manor Racing Stables Limited**
9 **CUT ABOVE THE REST,** 8, b m Indiaro—Towpath **Mr N. R. Mitchell**
10 **EURODIX,** 7, ch g Touch Paper—Sun Empress **Whitcombe Manor Racing Stables Limited**
11 **FLEET ASSERT (USA),** 4, b g Assert—Fleet Bidder (USA) **Whitcombe Manor Racing Stables Limited**
12 **GODS FOX,** 8, b g Paico—Lilgarde **Whitcombe Manor Racing Stables Limited**
13 **GRANNY PRAY ON,** 8, ch m Proverb—My Copper **Whitcombe Manor Racing Stables Limited**
14 **GREEN MARBLE,** 8, bl g Green Shoon—Ten-Cents **Whitcombe Manor Racing Stables Limited**
15 **G W SUPERSTAR,** 7, ch m Rymer—Miss Lara **Great Western Developments Ltd**
16 **HAMPER,** 7, ch g Final Straw—Great Care **Whitcombe Manor Racing Stables Limited**
17 **HANKIR,** 10, ch g Avocat—Miss Ballyhill **Mrs E. Mitchell**
18 **HEAVENLY BROTHER,** 7, b g Baptism—High Above **Whitcombe Manor Racing Stables Limited**
19 **HELOONIUM,** 5, br g Green Shoon—Helenium **Whitcombe Manor Racing Stables Limited**
20 **INTO THE TREES,** 6, b g Over The River (FR)—Diana's Flyer **Whitcombe Manor Racing Stables Limited**
21 **IRISH GUEST,** 9, b g Northern Guest (USA)—Laikipia **Whitcombe Racing Limited**
22 **LAURENBEL,** 9, b g Dublin Taxi—Betbellof **Mr G. H. Hussey**
23 **LIBILLARY (USA),** 7, b g Liloy (FR)—Nobiliary (USA) **Whitcombe Racing Limited**
24 **MACKY'S AXXON,** 10, br g Super Slip—Up First **Mrs E. Mitchell**
25 **MAITREDEE,** 11, b g Le Patron—No Cert **Whitcombe Manor Racing Stables Limited**
26 **MOONTALK,** 4, br f Dubassoff (USA)—Gay Picture **Whitcombe Manor Racing Stables Limited**

MR N. R. MITCHELL—continued

27 **MORE ONE WAY,** 9, b br g Arapaho—Safe Return **Mr G. H. Hussey**
28 **MOUNTAICO,** 8, b g Paico—Mount Rainier **Whitcombe Manor Racing Stables Limited**
29 **MR LION,** 8, ch g Windjammer (USA)—Polly Darling **Whitcombe Manor Racing Stables Limited**
30 **NAATELL (USA),** 7, b br g Cox's Ridge (USA)—Lisanninga **Mr P. Turner**
31 **NONSUCH PALACE,** 6, b g Glint of Gold—Starlight Roof (USA) **Mr J. A. King**
32 **OBEE FAST,** 6, ch m Dubassoff (USA)—In Confidence **Mr M. Wackett**
33 **ON HIS OWN,** 7, br g Paico—Luvvy Duvvy **Whitcombe Manor Racing Stables Limited**
34 **OWEN'S PRIDE,** 8, b g Owen Dudley—Beech Tree **Mr C. Gapper**
35 **PABREY,** 4, gr g Pablond—Grey Receipt **Mr S. L. Mitchell**
36 **POWIS LASS,** 5, ch m Buckskin (FR)—Random View **Mr J. A. King**
37 **PRETTY PANTOES,** 6, br m Lepanto (GER)—Lustful Lady **Mrs E. Mitchell**
38 **PRINCESS SIHAM,** 5, ch m Chabrias (FR)—Fickle Fortune **Mr R. L. Scorgie**
39 **PULSATE,** 9, gr g Orcis—Impulsive Lady **Whitcombe Manor Racing Stables Limited**
40 **RANDOM WIND,** 9, ch m Random Shot—Hulava Time **Whitcombe Racing Limited**
41 **RIVERS NEPHEW (FR),** 7, b g Great Nephew—River Deep (FR) **Whitcombe Manor Racing Stables Limited**
42 **SIRRAH JAY,** 10, b br g Tug of War—Dellasville **Whitcombe Manor Racing Stables Limited**
43 **SOULFUL STRUT,** 9, ch g Derrylin—Russellia **Whitcombe Manor Racing Stables Limited**
44 **SWINGING NOE JOE,** 4, b g Swing Easy (USA)—Palace Pet **Mr John Stevens**
45 **THE BEAT OF IT,** 7, ch g Golden Love—Sister Belinda **Mrs C. A. Holmes**
46 **THE QUIETSTAN,** 7, ch g Gay Fandango (USA)—Viduli **Whitcombe Manor Racing Stables Limited**
47 **WHITCOMBE WARRIOR,** 4, br g Tina's Pet—Minuetto **Whitcombe Manor Racing Stables Limited**

THREE-YEAR-OLDS

48 **BORN TO BE ME,** b c Sandhurst Prince—Sabura **Whitcombe Manor Racing Stables Limited**
49 **KIND A LUCKY,** br c Kind of Hush—Joker's Luck **Mr A. K. Royle**
50 **OH SO FINE,** b c Welsh Term—Miss Ultra Sound (USA) **Whitcombe Manor Racing Stables Limited**
51 **PANALLEY,** b f Lepanto (GER)—Camina **Miss I. L. Ritchie**
52 **PETMER,** b c Tina's Pet—Merency **Whitcombe Manor Racing Stables Limited**
53 **PRINCE SANMAR,** b g Sandhurst Prince—Miss Markey **Whitcombe Manor Racing Stables Limited**
54 **SLIP-A-SNIP,** b f Wolverlife—Stramenta **Whitcombe Manor Racing Stables Limited**
55 **TUMBLECOMBE,** b c Tumble Wind (USA)—Ching A Ling **Whitcombe Manor Racing Stables Limited**
56 **WHITCOMBE PRINCE,** b c Anita's Prince—Hello Stranger **Whitcombe Racing Limited**

Other Owners: Mr P. B. Haycock, Mr Michael Holmes, Mr F. Pitman.

Conditional: A S Tory (10-0).

Amateurs: Mr Nick Mitchell (10-10), Mr T Mitchell (11-0).

Lady Rider: Miss S Mitchell (9-7).

401 MR P. MITCHELL, Epsom

Postal: **Downs House, Epsom Downs, Surrey.**
Phone: **(0372) 273729**

1 **ALTOBELLI,** 6, b g Northern Treat (USA)—Imagination (FR) **Mrs M. Beuttell**
2 **APOLLO KING,** 4, b g Indian King (USA)—Mehudenna **Mrs Barbara Edwards**
3 **BRAVO STAR (USA),** 5, b g The Minstrel (CAN)—Stellarette (CAN) **Mrs R. S. Triefus**
4 **CELTIC BHOY,** 4, b g Red Sunset—Nighty Night **St. Andrews Ltd**
5 **COWORTH PARK,** 5, gr g Wolver Hollow—Sparkling Time (USA) **Mr Mark Gibbon**
6 **DRIVERS BUREAU,** 6, ch m Proverb—Pal Alley **Drivers Bureau Ltd**
7 **FINAL ALMA,** 7, b g Final Straw—Alma Ata **Mrs P. L. Isaacs**
8 **IT'S VARADAN,** 6, ch h Rabdan—Miss Casanova **Mrs M. A. Bayliss**
9 **KEEN EDGE,** 6, b h Good Times (ITY)—Razor Blade **Mr T. Tobin**

MR P. MITCHELL—continued

10 **LONDON STANDARD,** 5, b g Shack (USA)—Red Realm **Mr John Leese**
11 **MAZANO (USA),** 5, ch g Vaguely Noble—Itsamaza (USA) **St. Andrews Ltd**
12 **MISS BUTTERFIELD,** 4, b f Cure The Blues (USA)—Be My Queen **Mr B. J. Warren**
13 **MY PAL POPEYE,** 5, br g Runnett—Staderas **Mr G. Grant**
14 **PROPERS,** 4, ch f Noalto—Budget Queen **K. F. Butler and Co**
15 **RIVERTINO,** 6, ch g Ivotino (USA)—River Damsel **Mr R. Cheetham**
16 **ROSGILL,** 4, ch c Mill Reef (USA)—Speedy Rose **Brigadier Racing**
17 **RUN HIGH,** 7, b g Thatch (USA)—Fleet Noble (USA) **Mrs Patricia Mitchell**
18 **SYLVAN TEMPEST,** 4, b br g Strong Gale—Hedwige **Mrs R. A. Johnson**
19 **WHAT A GUY,** 6, b br g What A Guest—Khadija **Mr B. J. Warren**

THREE-YEAR-OLDS

20 **CHESS PIECE,** b f Castle Keep—Princess Log **Mr Graham J. Hough**
21 **CHINA CRISIS,** b f Tina's Pet—Yellatown **Mr C. R. Basson**
22 **GENTLE SATIN,** b c Anita's Prince—Drora **Mr Peter R. Fraser**
23 **HUNZA'S CHOICE,** b c Exhibitioner—Romantic Air **St. Andrews Ltd**
24 **LYPHAROS,** b c Lyphard's Special (USA)—Cocarde **Mr F. J. Crouch**
25 **RAIL D'OR (FR),** ch c Brustolon—Rain Or Shine (FR) **Mrs R. A. Johnson**
26 **SIBERIAN STEPPES,** b br f Siberian Express (USA)—La Palma **Mr A. G. Speake**
27 **SYLVAN SIROCCO,** b c Known Fact (USA)—Juddmonte **Mrs R. A. Johnson**
28 **THE SWINGE,** b c Thatching—Hi Gorgeous **Mrs Jill Eyles**
29 **VALOUROUS,** b f Bold Lad (IRE)—Midsummer Madness **Mr B. D. Miller**
30 **WILD SAGE,** ch f Noalto—Jenny's Rocket **Mrs Barbara Edwards**

TWO-YEAR-OLDS

31 B c Grey Desire—Canty Day (Canadel II) **Mrs Patricia Mitchell**
32 B f Kafu—Miss Merryweather (Sexton Blake) **Mrs Barbara Edwards**
33 **POLICIANE (FR),** ch f Policeman (FR)—Pharlane (FR) (Pharly (FR)) **Mr S. Lever**

Other Owners: Mr Nigel Benstead, Mr J. D. Hurd, Mr D. W. Johnson, Mrs F. Kuler, Baron Kuler-Von Der Luhe, Mr D. A. Lucie-Smith, Mr D. C. G. Ollis, Peter Urwin (Holdings) Ltd, Mr B. M. Redden, Mr N. H. Silbery, Mr G. P. Triefus, Mr H. Wallace-Smith.

Apprentice: R Lawson (7-12).

Conditional: I Todd (9-0).

Amateur: Mr R Teal (10-0).

402 MR PAT MITCHELL, Newmarket

Postal: **Hamilton Stables, Hamilton Road, Newmarket, Suffolk.**
Phone: **NEWMARKET (0638) 660013**

1 **BOLD PROTEST,** 6, b m Indian King (USA)—Lady Tycoon **Mr F. Pyne**
2 **FORTUNE AND GLORY,** 4, b f Rusticaro (FR)—Souza Rose **Mr J. Stringer**
3 **HENRY WILLIAM,** 5, b g Known Fact (USA)—Kesarini (USA) **Mr Stanley J. Sharp**
4 **JOY'S TOY,** 4, ch f Wolverlife—Tanzanite **Mrs D. Willett**
5 **MALACHI LAD,** 6, b g Manor Farm Boy—Cala Galera **Mrs B. A. Mitchell**
6 **MOSSY ROSE,** 4, b f King of Spain—Mosso **Mr Stanley J. Sharp**
7 **SAALIB,** 7, b g Tyrnavos—Velvet Habit **Mr Stanley J. Sharp**
8 **SONAR,** 4, b br c Pitskelly—Diana's Choice **Mrs D. Willett**
9 **SPITZABIT,** 6, br g Pitskelly—Marsabit **Mrs Catherine Reed**
10 **TAUBER,** 6, b g Taufan (USA)—Our Bernie **Mrs Catherine Reed**

MR PAT MITCHELL—continued

THREE-YEAR-OLDS

11 **DANCING BREEZE,** ch f Horage—Lady's Guest **Mr A. Robins**
12 **FIRST HOME,** b c Homing—Mill Wind **Mrs B. A. Mitchell**
13 **PALABORA (USA),** gr c Wolf Power (SAF)—Peeping (USA) **Mrs V. O'Brien**
14 **PRIOR CHARGE,** ch f Tender King—Priors Mistress **Mrs Susan Quinn**
15 **SNOW SHY,** gr f Shy Groom (USA)—Snow Maid **Mr J. Stringer**
16 **TUDOR ACE,** b c Stanford—Lusaka **Mrs B. A. Mitchell**

TWO-YEAR-OLDS

17 Ch f 29/2 Reasonable (FR)—Fair Colleen (King Emperor (USA))
18 Ch c 3/4 Double Schwartz—Hay Knot (Main Reef)
19 B c 24/2 Tender King—Storm Lass (Typhoon)
20 **TODAY'S FANCY,** b c 29/2 Today And Tomorrow—Fancy Pages (Touch Paper) **Mrs V. O'Brien**
21 B f 23/5 Petorius—Travel (Saritamer)

Other Owners: Mr Ron Ashdown, Mr P. R. Dixon, Mrs Rita Godfrey, Mr D. W. Johnson, Mrs R. A. Johnson, Mr Alan Westmarland.

403 MR D. MOFFATT, Cartmel

Postal: **Pit Farm Racing Stables, Cartmel, Grange-over-Sands, Cumbria.**
Phone: **CARTMEL (05395) 36689 FAX (05395) 36236**

1 4, B f Gleason (USA)—Adventure Run
2 **BORLEAFRAS,** 10, b g Sassafras (FR)—Levers Leap **Mr M. A. Warner**
3 **BROMPTON ROAD,** 7, b g Derring Rose—London Gem **Mr J. Piercy**
4 **DEB'S BALL,** 4, b f Glenstal (USA)—De'b Old Fruit **Miss M. Faragher**
5 **ORIENTAL CHARM,** 5, ch h Krayyan—Little Angle **Mr David F. Jefferson**
6 **POKEREE,** 7, gr g Uncle Pokey—Border Squaw **Mr Mike Flynn**
7 **PRETTY IN PINK,** 4, b f Formidable—Londonderry Air **P. S. B. Racing Ltd**
8 **PROCURATOR,** 4, b c Alleged (USA)—North Eastern (USA) **Mrs Dorothy Mason and Mr David Jefferson**
9 **REGAL ESTATE,** 6, ch g Royal Palace—Salira **Mr Ian Ives**
10 **RISK FACTOR,** 4, b g Auction Ring (USA)—Flying Anna **Mr Marten Julian**
11 **SILVER'S GIRL,** 5, b m Sweet Monday—Persian Silver **Haydock Exhibitions Ltd**
12 **SIMBAD,** 14, b g Simbir—Amsterdam Lassie **Mr J. Piercy**
13 **SNOW BABU,** 8, b h Foggy Bell—Fleur-Babu **Mr A. Mansley**

THREE-YEAR-OLDS

14 B f Mr Fluorocarbon—Rekindle

Other Owners: Mr J. Calvert, Mr Richard Day, Mr T. Glendinning, Mrs P. Jefferson, Mr J. E. Mottram, Mr Graham Mullen, Mrs Mavis Munro.

Conditional: D J Moffatt (9-7).

Lady Rider: Mrs J A Moffatt (8-0).

404 MR PETER MONTEITH, Rosewell

Postal: **Whitebog Farm, Rosewell, Midlothian, Scotland, EH24 9AY.**
Phone: **(031 440) 2309**

1 **AULD YUD,** 9, ch g Scallywag—Lucy Lady **Mrs Maud Monteith**
2 **BELDINE,** 5, b g Belfort (FR)—Royal Celandine **Lt.-Col. W. L. Monteith**
3 **BENNAN HILL,** 5, ch g Stanford—Floraventure **C. Sheenan**

MR PETER MONTEITH—continued

4 **BOLD ARMOUR,** 5, b m Belfort (FR)—Swing Is Back **Mrs Sybil Howe**
5 **CHERRY FIELD,** 11, gr m Precipice Wood—Cherish **Mr J. Kendal**
6 **FLOATER (USA),** 7, b g Vaguely Noble—Need A Dime (USA) **William McKinlay Limited**
7 **HABIOLA,** 5, b g Hays—Warbiola **W. McKinlay**
8 **HALCANOR,** 6, ch g Irish River (FR)—Princess Gayle **Matchsemi Limited**
9 **HAZEL BANK,** 11, gr m Pongee—Petoria **Mr William McKinlay**
10 **LAMANCHA LAD,** 9, b g Indiaro—Sal's Guide **Mr J. Bogue and Mrs J. Bogue**
11 **MAJESTIC RING (CAN),** 8, b g Majestic Prince—Savage Call (USA) **Lt-Col W. L. Monteith**
12 **MALIPIERO,** 6, ch g Persian Bold—Fear Naught **Mr A. L. Hay**
13 **MOMENT OF TRUTH,** 6, b g Known Fact (USA)—Chieftain Girl (USA) **P. Purcell**
14 **NEW KINGSGROVE,** 11, b g Kinglet—Maidensgrove **Drummhor Investments Ltd.**
15 **NIGHT GUEST,** 8, br g Northern Guest (USA)—Night Rose **Mr J. A. G. Fiddes**
16 **SCARNING DALE,** 7, b g Cawston's Clown—Within Bounds **Lt-Col W. L. Monteith**
17 **THE FIXER,** 9, ch g Our Mirage—Carambola **Mr I. Ross**
18 **TREYARNON (USA),** 8, b g Superbity (USA)—Lagrange Belle (USA) **Lt-Col W. L. Monteith**
19 **WALL STREET SLUMP,** 4, gr g Belfort (FR)—Running Dancer (FR) **Lt-Col W. L. Monteith**

Other Owners: Mr P. Monteith.

Jockey (NH): D Nolan (10-4).

Lady Rider: Val Jackson.

405 MR A. MOORE, Brighton

Postal: **10 Holt View Road, Woodingdean, Brighton, E. Sussex, BN2 6DH.**
Phone: **BRIGHTON (0273) 681679**

1 **BENDICKS,** 8, b g Young Generation—Mint **Mr David Humphreys**
2 **BE SURPRISED,** 4, ch g Dubasoff (USA)—Buckenham Belle **Mr F. L. Hill**
3 **CARELESS KISS,** 6, ch m Persian Bold—More Kisses **Mr A. Moore**
4 **COLNE VALLEY KID,** 5, ch g Homing—Pink Garter **Mr Glynne Owen**
5 **COLONEL CHINSTRAP,** 5, ch g Milford—Deep Blue Sea **Mr F. L. Hill**
6 **CORDILLERO,** 4, br g Head For Heights—Petipa (FR) **Mr K. Higson**
7 **DALBURY,** 12, br g Royal Palace—Tikki Tavi **Mr Roger Smale**
8 **DISCO DUKE,** 5, b g Record Token—Grandgirl **Mr A. Moore**
9 **EL-PAYASO,** 4, b c Cure The Blues (USA)—Baroness (FR) **Mr F. Willson**
10 **FAMOUS FLASK,** 8, ch g New Member—Regal Bristol **Mr J. G. Blackwell**
11 **FANDANGO LIGHT,** 9, ch g Gay Fandango (USA)—Crystal Light **Mr A. Moore**
12 **FIGHTING DAYS (USA),** 4, ch g Fit To Fight (USA)—August Days (USA) **Mr Peter L. Higson**
13 **FLASHING SILKS,** 5, b m Kind of Hush—Hit The Line **Mr A. G. Russell**
14 **FORT WAPPING,** 6, b g Ile de Bourbon (USA)—Hot Press **Mr John Denver**
15 **GINGER WINGS,** 6, ch m Ginger Boy—Sticky Wings **Mr D. Forehead**
16 **GOLD COLLAR,** 5, ch m Sayyaf—Colonial Line (USA) **John Humphreys (Turf Accountants) Ltd**
17 **HASTY GAMBLE,** 10, ch g Hasty Word—Stormation **Mr K. Higson**
18 **JENOOD (USA),** 4, b g Diamond Shoal—Rajput Princess **Mr A. Moore**
19 **JIM'S NEPHEW,** 4, b g Connaught—Grandgirl **Mr A. Moore**
20 **KINGSWOOD RESOPAL,** 6, br g Comedy Star (USA)—Solhoon **Mr Gary Brown**
21 **LA SHAKA,** 7, b m Son of Shaka—Lady Sylvania **Mr A. Moore**
22 **LIRCHUR,** 4, b f Lir—Amberush **Mr K. Higson**
23 **MANNYS CHOICE,** 5, br g Netherkelly—Sporting Image **Mr Roger Smale**
24 **NORTHERN ALLIANCE,** 6, ch g Northfields (USA)—Plight **Mr Danny Thomas**
25 **OUTCAST,** 6, b g Final Straw—Persian Market **Mr B. Lennard**
26 **PALMERSTON BOY,** 7, b g Tickled Pink—Silver Swallow **Palmerston Business Centre Ltd**
27 **RHODE ISLAND RED,** 7, ch g Henbit (USA)—Embarrassed **Mr J. C. Bruton**
28 **SHOWDOWN,** 4, ch c Final Straw—Sideshow **Mr J. G. Blackwell**

MR A. MOORE—continued

29 **UGLY,** 4, b g Cleon—Lammas **Mr A. Moore**
30 **USELESS MEMBER,** 8, ch g Whistling Top—Bow-Bar **Mr A. Moore**
31 **VICTORY GATE (USA),** 5, b g Lydian (FR)—Pago Miss (USA) **Mrs P. S. Donkin**
32 **WAR CHILD,** 6, br m Welsh Chanter—Winter Sunshine **Mr J. Bird**

THREE-YEAR-OLDS

33 **MACREE,** b f Another Realm—Mrs Willie **Mr John Denver**
34 **SAYSANA,** b f Sayf El Arab (USA)—Rosana Park **Mr F. L. Hill**

Other Owners: Mr E. T. Bateman, Mr C. A. Blackwell, Mr M. J. Jones, Mrs C. E. Mason-Smale, Mr M. O. Owens, Mr J. A. Smyth, Mr F. G. Taylor, Mr M. Vyner.

Jockey (Flat): B Rouse (8-4, w.a.).

Jockey (NH): G Moore (10-2).

Conditional: J Clarke (9-7).

Lady Rider: Miss Candy Moore (8-10).

406 MR A. L. MOORE, Naas

Postal: **Dereens, Naas, Co. Kildare, Ireland.**
Phone: **NAAS (045) 76292**

1 **AU COURANT,** 5, b g Runnett—La Garde **Peter Horgan**
2 **BARKHILL (USA),** 5, b g Sassafras (FR)—Dear Irish (USA) **T. Ryan**
3 **BONALMA,** 10, ch g Bonne Noel—Realma **C. Hanbury**
4 **CHAMOIS BOY,** 6, ch g Buckskin (FR)—Levandia **W. Tyrell**
5 **CHIASSO FORTE (ITY),** 7, b g Furry Glen—Cassai (ITY) **Mrs Rita Hale**
6 **CHRISTY RING,** 6, b g Hardboy—Christy's Bow **Mrs A. L. T. Moore**
7 **COCTAIL BID,** 7, b m Mandalus—Early Start **Mrs A. L. T. Moore**
8 **COURSING GUY,** 8, ch g Crash Course—Lady Aylmer **Mrs Mary T. Burke**
9 **DUBLIN CITY,** 5, b g Bulldozer—Purranna **Stephen Lanigan O'Keeffe**
10 **FERODA,** 9, b g Ashmore—Dedham Vale **N. McCarthy**
11 **FIT AS A FIDDLE,** 6, ch g Slim Jim—Lady Marcia **F. P. Taaffe**
12 **FLASHY BUCK,** 6, b g Buckskin (FR)—Flashy Money **C. Jones**
13 **GARRYDUFF MOVER,** 6, b g Rarity—Hansel's Trouble **D. J. O'Keeffe**
14 **GOOD FOR A LAUGH,** 6, b g Idiot's Delight—Mekhala **Frank Conroy**
15 **HAVE A BARNEY,** 9, ch g Laurence O—Barney's Girl **Pierre Doyle**
16 **HOLY AWL,** 5, b g Buckskin (FR)—Saint Audrey **Mrs A. L. T. Moore**
17 **IMPRESSARIO,** 5, b g Rarity—Turbina **G. Gorey**
18 **INCA CHIEF,** 6, b g Rubor—Mayo Lassie **Mrs Y. F. de Alvarez**
19 **JOYFUL NOISE,** 7, b g Lighter—Roadway Mistress **Spencer Wood**
20 **JUST SUBLIME,** 5, b g Corvaro (USA)—Tiepoless **Mrs A. Dunlop**
21 **LOUGHLINSTOWN BOY,** 5, b g Ela-Mana-Mou—Tante Yvonne **Mrs P. Duffy**
22 **NEW MILL HOUSE,** 7, ch g Tobique—Ascess **J. Lyons**
23 **ON YOUR WAY,** 8, b g Ragapan—Fourteen Carat **Mrs A. L. T. Moore**
24 **RARE ORDER,** 6, b g Rarity—Caramore Again **F. Conroy**
25 **SET YOUR SIGHTS,** 7, b g Celtic Cone—Even Fair **Mrs A. L. T. Moore**
26 **SHEEPHAVEN,** 6, b g Relkino—Suffolk Broads **Mrs A. L. T. Moore**
27 **SOFT DAY,** 5, b g Strong Gale—Arctic Track **Frank Conroy**
28 **SPREAD THE NEWS,** 5, b g Impecunious—Royal Snip **Mrs A. L. T. Moore**
29 **STRONG SUSPICION,** 6, b g Strong Gale—Shady Doorknocker **Stephen Lanigan O'Keeffe**

MR A. L. MOORE—continued

30 **THATS THE LIFE,** 5, b g Wolverlife—Culleenamore **A. L. Moore**
31 **THE VIBES,** 7, ch g Le Bavard—So Called **T. J. Murray**
32 **THINKING CAP,** 9, ch g Bargello—Grangeclose Lady **Mrs. S. Barrett**
33 **TORRENT BAY,** 8, b g Roselier (FR)—Peaceful Girl **R. Horton**
34 **WAZAFELLA,** 7, b g Decent Fellow—Miss Corrientes **C. Hanbury**

Other Owners: Mrs T. K. Cooper, J. Duffy.

Jockeys (NH): P Malone (9-7), T J Taaffe (10-3).

Amateurs: Mr G Allen (9-9), Mr R Davis (10-0), Mr D Geoghegan (10-0), Mr C O'Shea (10-0), Mrs M Shepherd (10-2).

407 MR G. M. MOORE, Middleham

Postal: **Warwick Lodge Stables, Middleham, Leyburn, North Yorkshire, DL8 4PB.**
Phone: **WENSLEYDALE (0969) 23823**

1 **A GENTLEMAN TWO,** 4, b c All Systems Go—Solar Honey **Mr W. M. Boothroyd**
2 **ALDRA BOND,** 5, ch g Gold Song—Petite Case **Mr M. R. Johnson**
3 **ALWAYS DANGEROUS,** 8, b g Celtic Cone—Sally Ann III **Mr R. I. Graham**
4 **AMBUSCADE (USA),** 4, ch c Roberto (USA)—Gurkhas Band (USA) **Mrs Lynne Firth**
5 **ASTON EXPRESS,** 7, b g Decent Fellow—Kilbride Lady VI **Mr J. R. Featherstone**
6 **ATALL ATALL,** 7, b h Kampala—Bint Africa **Mr S. Monaghan**
7 **AVENIO (FR),** 6, ch g Connaught—Poppea Sabina (FR) **Mrs Eva Richardson**
8 **AWKAS,** 5, b g Busted—Moreno **Mr Charles MacMillan**
9 **BALI SUNSET,** 4, b f Balidar—Orange Silk **Mr J. R. Featherstone**
10 **BALLYMORE PARK,** 5, b g Ballymore—Tiltress **Mr A. J. Davenport**
11 **BLAKESWARE GOLD,** 4, ch g Vaigly Great—Presentable **Mr John Hamilton**
12 **CHAPERALL LADY,** 4, br f Mansingh (USA)—El Chaperall **Mr M. Wilson**
13 **COOL STRIKE,** 9, ch g Royal Match—Coolrobin **Mr Tony Knowles**
14 **DUNLORING,** 7, b br g Dunphy—Blessingtonia **Mr J. Tennant**
15 **EASY OVER (USA),** 4, ch c Transworld (USA)—Love Bunny (USA) **Miss V. Foster**
16 **FARNWORTH,** 7, b g Quayside—Brave Trudy **Mrs M. Bird**
17 **FOREVER ASTON,** 5, b g Le Moss—Go Mays **Mr J. R. Featherstone**
18 **GENAIR (FR),** 5, ch h General Assembly (USA)—Metair **Mr Norman Firth**
19 **GILSAN GREY,** 7, gr m Grey Ghost—Noble Hart **Mr G. W. Fenwick**
20 **GLASS MOUNTAIN,** 8, gr g Scallywag—Miss Maskin **Mr B. Whitehorn**
21 **GREY CLOUD,** 5, gr h Warpath—Alexandra **Mr I. Bray**
22 **KILMOND WOOD,** 5, ch g Monsanto (FR)—River Belle **Mr I. Bray**
23 **KING'S HARVEST,** 7, ch g Oats—Sovereign Court **Mr I. Bray**
24 **LAID BACK,** 9, ch g Bonne Noel—Babu Saar **Mr John Evans**
25 **LEIGH BOY (USA),** 4, b c Bates Motel (USA)—Afasheen **Mr John Robson**
26 **LIVING FIRE,** 11, b g Le Bavard (FR)—Lovely Pine **Michael Watterson Ltd**
27 **LORD POTTER,** 5, b g Nemorino (USA)—Double Cri **Mrs J. R. Morris**
28 **MAGIC AT DAWN (USA),** 5, ch g Diamond Prospect (USA)—Implicit **Mrs Julie Gray**
29 **MARK-EDEN,** 7, b g On Your Mark—Dainty Eden **Mr D. Melvin Haughey**
30 **MERITMOORE,** 7, b g Moorestyle—More Treasure **Mr G. Borek**
31 **MIZAJ,** 6, ch g Thatching—Stickpin **Mr W. B. Marshall**
32 **PARIS MATCH,** 8, b br g Bold Lad (IRE)—Miss Paris **Mrs J. Jordan**
33 **PINISI,** 5, ch g Final Straw—Bireme **Mr R. Pitman**
34 **RAISABILLION,** 8, b g Billion (USA)—Small Problem **Mrs S. Blane**
35 **ROBSIM,** 8, br g Garda's Revenge (USA)—Aunty Peg **Wetherby Racing Bureau Plc**
36 **ROYAL GREEK,** 8, ch g Royal Captive—Greek Empress **Mr John Renton**
37 **ROYAL ILLUSION,** 6, b g Creative Plan (USA)—Semper Fi **Mr John Lishman**
38 **RUNNING FORTUNE,** 5, b m Goldhills Pride—Kingdom Come **Wetherby Racing Bureau Plc**

MR G. M. MOORE—continued

39 **RUSCAROFF,** 4, gr c Rusticaro (FR)—Fair Or Foul **Mrs J. R. Morris**
40 **SHESHELLS,** 5, b m Zino—Sandy Doll **Mrs Desmond Magrath**
41 **SOUTH CROSS (USA),** 5, ch g Valdez (USA)—Blue Cross Nurse (USA) **Mr W. H. Green**
42 **SOUTHEND SCALLYWAG,** 4, b f Tina's Pet—By The Lake **Mrs V. Mason**
43 **SPITTIN MICK,** 6, b g The Brianstan—La Fille **Sandmoor Textiles Co Ltd**
44 **STAGS FELL,** 5, gr g Step Together (USA)—Honey's Queen **Mr Richard Johnson**
45 **THE POD'S REVENGE,** 5, b g Pollerton—Fair People **Mr W. H. Williams**
46 **THIMONI,** 5, ch m Ahonoora—Thimothea (FR) **Mr K. Johnson**
47 **TOP D'OR (FR),** 5, b g Pot d'Or (FR)—Jupe de Laine (FR) **Mr D. J. Bushell**
48 **UNEX-PLAINED,** 7, b g Last Fandango—Miss Pinkerton **Mr B. V. Eddishaw**
49 **WATERTIGHT (USA),** 5, b g Affirmed (USA)—Brookward (USA) **Mr J. Good**

THREE-YEAR-OLDS

50 **AZUBAH,** b f Castle Keep—Louisianalightning **Mr A. C. Birkle**
51 **BELFORT PRINCE,** b g Belfort (FR)—Turtle Dove **Mr J. Lishman**

Other Owners: Mr C. J. Allister, Mr C. Anderson, Mr P. Barrett, Mr John C. Berry, Mr C. Bircham, Mr J. Chapman, Mr B. Collier, Mr S. R. Counsell, Mr G. Daubney, Miss C. Foster, Mr I. Grudgings, Mrs C. Hamilton, Mr P. A. Hine, Mr M. G. R. Hoskins, Mr D. M. Howarth, Mr P. Sellars, Mr Alasdair Simpson, Mr P. Sowerby, Mr D. W. Thomas, Mr V. J. Walsh, Mr A. P. Ward, Mr J. Wardle, Mr Roy E. Watson, Mr R. Whitehorn, Mr J. R. Yates.

Apprentice: Neil Kennedy (7-0).

Conditional: J Callaghan (9-7), J Winterbottam (9-7).

408 MR B. C. MORGAN, Burton-on-Trent

Postal: **Stoneyford Farm, Barton-under-Needwood, Burton-on-Trent, Staffordshire, DE13 8BW.**
Phone: **HOAR CROSS (0283 75) 304**

1 **APPLIED SIGNS,** 5, b m Tycoon II—Arctic Lion **Applied Signs Ltd**
2 **BROMLEY BOY,** 5, b g Maris Piper—Willmore Joyce **Royal Oak Racing**
3 **CLARE'S DELIGHT,** 5, b m Viking (USA)—Miss Inglewood **Mr Jeremy C. Barnes**
4 **DUNSTALL,** 13, b br g Bivouac—Phillopene **Mr J. Drewry**
5 **EL-EM-BEE,** 5, b m Workboy—Simbirica **Mr Les Baker**
6 **GRUNDY LANE,** 8, b g Grundy—Tamilian **Mr A. R. Fletcher**
7 **HIGH RIVER,** 8, br m Joshua—High Value **Mr Tim Leadbeater**
8 **NEEDWOOD FOREST,** 7, b m Tycoon II—Arctic Lion **Needwood Turf Accountants Ltd**
9 **NEEDWOOD IMP,** 4, ch g Joshua—The Doe **Needwood Turf Accountants Ltd**
10 **NEEDWOOD SPRITE,** 4, ch f Joshua—Sea Dart **Needwood Turf Accountants Ltd**
11 **ROLFESON,** 6, b h Rolfe (USA)—Do Something **Mrs Nicky Griffiths**
12 **STATFOLD PAM,** 7, gr m Pamroy—Statfold Pride **Mr L. Gilman**
13 5, B m Tycoon II—Tina Fort **Needwood Turf Accountants Ltd**
14 **VICKSTOWN,** 8, b h Town And Country—Empress Victoria **Hon A. J. Baillie**

THREE-YEAR-OLDS

15 **COMIC RELIEF,** br f Comedy Star (USA)—Moberry **Needwood Turf Accountants Ltd**
16 **NEEDWOOD NIGHTLIFE,** b f Decoy Boy—Johnny's Pride **Needwood Turf Accountants Ltd**
17 Br f Anfield—Sandra Bella **Mr P. L. de Weck**
18 B g Rolfe (USA)—Sea Dart **Needwood Turf Accountants Ltd**
19 **STIG,** b c The Brianstan—The Crying Game **Mr Paddy Barrett**

MR B. C. MORGAN—continued

TWO-YEAR-OLDS

20 **AS TEARS GO BY,** b f 14/3 King of Spain—The Crying Game (Manor Farm Boy) **Mr Paddy Barrett**
21 **BRENDA FROM HUBY,** ch f 18/5 Tina's Pet—Dominion Blue (Dominion) **Mr Geoff Whitaker**
22 B f 17/5 Rolfe (USA)—Needwood Nap (Some Hand) **Needwood Turf Accountants Ltd**
23 **NEWARK ANTIQUEFAIR,** b c 25/5 Rolfe (USA)—
Sea Dart (Air Trooper) **The Int. Antique & Collectors Fair Ltd**
24 B c 8/5 Rolfe (USA)—The Doe (Alcide) **Needwood Turf Accountants Ltd**

Other Owners: Mrs Lucy Barnes, Mr C. J. Dytham, Mrs N. G. G. Herrtage.

Conditional: C Prince (9-7).

409 MR K. A. MORGAN, Melton Mowbray

Postal: **Hall Farm Stables, Waltham On The Wolds, Melton Mowbray, Leicestershire.**
Phone: **WALTHAM ON THE WOLDS (066 478) 711 OR 488**

1 **ANBAK (USA),** 5, ch g Riverman (USA)—Virgin (FR) **Mr J. C. Fretwell**
2 **ARTFUL CHARLEY,** 10, br g Articulate—Green Monkey **Mr T. J. Riley**
3 **BEAUCHAMP CREST,** 5, b m Jalmood (USA)—Jubilee **Mr Jim Short**
4 **BIG BEAR,** 4, ch c Tolomeo—Alma Ata
5 **BILL AND COUP,** 5, br m Nicholas Bill—Counter Coup **Mrs C. E. Brown**
6 **CARPACCIO (USA),** 4, b g Blazing Saddles (AUS)—Reine du Nil **Mr Peter Watson**
7 **COMPANY MAGIC,** 8, b br g Dragonara Palace (USA)—Magic Maiden **Mr Mike Murphy**
8 **CURVET (USA),** 5, b m Ack Ack (USA)—Jingle Jan (USA) **Mrs C. A. Morgan**
9 **DUSTY EMERALD (USA),** 4, ch g Green Forest (USA)—Grey Reliance (USA) **Mr D. H. Lee**
10 **FANTASIE IMPROMPTU,** 5, gr m Ballad Rock—Gay Nocturne **Mr D. S. Cooper**
11 **GAN ON LAD,** 9, ch g On Your Mark—Fado **Mr D. S. Cooper**
12 **GREY ADMIRAL,** 5, gr g Alias Smith (USA)—Beech Tree **Mr G. Horsford**
13 **HIDDEN QUIVER (USA),** 4, b c Secreto (USA)—Feather Bow (USA) **Mr Rex Norton**
14 **ISLAND SET (USA),** 8, b h Hawaii—Desk Set (USA) **Mr Jim Short**
15 **JUBAIL,** 5, b g Sandhurst Prince—Fluella **Mr V. C. Bootle**
16 **KIND'A SMART,** 5, ch g Kind of Hush—Treasure Seeker **Mr David G. Smith**
17 **KIRTLINGTON,** 5, b g Gay Mecene (USA)—Cley **Mrs E. M. Wakefield**
18 **KRYSTLE SAINT,** 9, ch m St Columbus—Clear Thinking **Mr D. J. Wheatley**
19 **MONDRIAN (USA),** 4, ch g Sir Ivor—Turban (USA) **Royston Racing Club Ltd**
20 **MUTARID (USA),** 5, ch h Kris—Voie Lactee (FR) **Brooklands Civil Engineering Limited**
21 **NESSFIELD,** 4, b f Tumble Wind (USA)—Ceiling **Royston Racing Club Ltd**
22 **SHAHRAYAR (MOR),** 4, b f Happy Lord (FR)—Bellinga (FR) **Mr James Hughes**
23 **SHARP KING (FR),** 7, ch g Sharpman—Princesse Kay (FR) **Mr Rex Norton**
24 **SMOKEY TRACK,** 5, b m Uncle Pokey—Malmar **Mr Graham Large**
25 **SUPER SOL,** 6, ch m Rolfe (USA)—Solo Waltz **Miss Isobel McMillan**
26 **WASSELNI,** 4, br g Wassl—Monongelia **Mr Jim Short**
27 **WELSH KING,** 4, ch c Kings Lake (USA)—Daffodil Day
28 **WOODCRAFT,** 5, ch g Tap On Wood—Irish Isle **Mr D. H. Lee**

Other Owners: Mr W. H. Berry, Mr Eric Brown, Mr Richard Brown, Mr P. A. Bullen-Smith, Mr P. Dobson, Fairlord Wholesale Confectioners Ltd, Mr Patrick Fanning, Mr Robert Hendry, Mr R. W. Jaines, Mr Brian Jenkins, Mr R. A. Juggins, Mr T. J. Kenny, Mr J. Marks, Mr J. McCarthy, Mr Peter McDonald, Mr D. P. McLaughlin, Mr P. Milne, Mr A. W. Murphy, Mr B. Parker, Mr S. W. Parsons, Mr T. R. Pryke, Mr Jack Rubins, Mr S. H. Wilkinson.

Jockeys (NH): H Davies (10-4), J Osborne (10-0), S Turner (10-0), A Webb (10-0).

Conditional: Janine Henfrey (9-7).

410 MR M. F. D. MORLEY, Newmarket

Postal: **High Havens Stables, Hamilton Road, Newmarket, Suffolk, CB8 0NQ.**
Phone: **NEWMARKET (0638) 667175 FAX (0638) 667913**

1 **ELADHAM,** 4, b br c Lyphard's Special (USA)—Derrede **Mr D. R. Hunnisett**
2 **NEW MEXICO,** 6, br g Free State—Trigamy **Mrs M. F. D. Morley**
3 **SAN ROQUE,** 5, b g Aragon—Arch Sculptress **Mr Graham T. Mann**
4 **SESAME,** 5, b m Derrylin—Hot Spice **Mr Christopher Spence**
5 **TOUSHTARI (USA),** 4, b g Youth (USA)—Taduska (FR) **Mr C. H. Williams**
6 **TURMERIC,** 7, ch g Alias Smith (USA)—Hot Spice **Mrs M. F. D. Morley**
7 **ZUCCHINI,** 4, ch g Absalom—Hot Spice **Mr Christopher Spence**

THREE-YEAR-OLDS

8 **APACHE PRINCE,** gr g Red Sunset—Maxi Girl **Mr D. R. Hunnisett**
9 **ARBOR VITAE,** b c Dominion—Plain Tree **K. Al-Said**
10 **BELAFONTE,** b c Derrylin—Ulla Laing **Mr C. J. Allan**
11 **BIMBO,** b f Bustino—Brazen Face **Lord Halifax**
12 **BROOKAL,** b g Relkino—Rapid Glory **Mr A. N. Scarfe**
13 **CABOCHON,** b g Jalmood (USA)—Lightning Legacy (USA) **Colonel Sir Piers Bengough**
14 **CAPABILITY BROWN,** b c Dominion—Tomfoolery **Mr A. R. Perry**
15 **CHAPMAN'S PEAK,** b g Top Ville—Cape Race (USA) **Mr R. E. Sangster**
16 **CHOBE RIVER,** b f Dara Monarch—Fair Or Foul **Mr John Carleton Paget**
17 **DUBAI VIEW,** b c Doulab (USA)—Anglo Irish **Mr Hamdan Al-Maktoum**
18 **GOMARLOW,** gr c Belfort (FR)—Tringa (GER) **Mr K. J. Underwood**
19 **LIGHTNING THUNDER,** b g Dara Monarch—Royal Sister II **Mr Wafic Said**
20 **MAKBUL,** b c Fairy King (USA)—Royaltess **Mr Hamdan Al-Maktoum**
21 **MERTON MILL,** b f Dominion—Brookfield Miss **Lord Clinton**
22 **PALMAS PRIDE,** b g Dalsaan—Sabirone (FR) **Finneys Homes**
23 **PRECIOUS DAMSEL,** b f Precocious—Blessed Damsel **Normanby Stud Ltd**
24 **PRINCE CARNEGIE,** b g Taufan (USA)—Phar Lapa **Mr D. R. Hunnisett**
25 **RASHITA,** b f Alzao (USA)—Apapa Port **Mr Wafic Said**
26 **SASHIMI,** ch g Kind of Hush—Falaka **Mr Christopher Spence**
27 **SNAFEE,** b c Mummy's Pet—Miss Kuta Beach **Mr Ali K. Al Jafleh**
28 **SWING DANCER,** br f Swing Easy (USA)—Four Lawns **Mrs F. G. Gorst**
29 **TOM CLAPTON,** b g Daring March—Embroideress **Mrs William McAlpine**
30 **TOPCLIFFE,** b f Top Ville—Sandford Lady **Lord Hartington**
31 **ZIZI JEAN MAIRE,** ch f Chief Singer—Ring Lady **Miss J. Proudfoot**

TWO-YEAR-OLDS

32 **CAMOMILE,** b f 23/4 Bay Express—Hot Spice (Hotfoot) **Mr Christopher Spence**
33 **CASCADE,** b f 21/4 Shirley Heights—Spin Turn (Homing) **Lord Hartington**
34 **CYPRUS (FR),** b c 8/2 Crystal Glitters—Sihame (Crystal Palace (FR)) **Mr Hamdan Al-Maktoum**
35 Ch c 30/4 Tumble Wind (USA)—Devil's Drink (Red God)
36 **DOIRE,** gr c 9/4 Belfort (FR)—Derrygold (Derrylin) **Mr W. Smith**
37 **ERNIE,** b c 17/5 Miller's Mate—Bempton (Blakeney) **Lord Halifax**
38 **HALUCINATION,** b c 16/4 Miller's Mate—Calder Hall (Grundy) **Mr O. Miles-Pollard Jnr**
39 **HAMOUDI,** b c 29/3 Miller's Mate—Wanton (Kris) **Mr A. Razzak**
40 B f 27/5 Shareef Dancer (USA)—House Tie (Be Friendly) **Mr Wafic Said**
41 **IWAN,** b c 20/2 Elegant Air—Clouded Vision (So Blessed) **Mr Hamdan Al-Maktoum**
42 **JEWEL OF THE NILE,** b f 30/3 Glenstal (USA)—Miller's Daughter (Mill Reef (USA)) **Mr A. R. Perry**
43 **JURHUM (IRE),** b c 23/5 Fairy King (USA)—Grecian Blue (Majority Blue) **Mr Hamdan Al-Maktoum**
44 **LAHIN,** b f 9/3 Rainbow Quest (USA)—Rivers Maid (Rarity) **Mr Hamdan Al-Maktoum**
45 **MAAMUR (USA),** gr c 9/4 Robellino (USA)—Tiger Trap (USA) (Al Hattab (USA)) **Mr Hamdam Al-Maktoum**
46 **MABTHUL (USA),** b c 11/4 Northern Baby (CAN)—
Persuadable (USA) (What A Pleasure (USA)) **Mr Hamdan Al-Maktoum**
47 **MARJORIE RAMSAY,** b f 12/2 Daring March—Game For A Laugh (Martinmas) **Mrs William McAlpine**
48 **MASHHOR JOHN,** br c 6/5 Mashhor Dancer (USA)—Dastina (Derring-Do) **Mr Wafic Said**
49 **MAY SQUARE (IRE),** ch c 6/2 Nicholas Bill—Casa Rosada (Known Fact (USA)) **Mrs M. E. Lockwood**
50 **MIDSUMMER COMMON,** b f 24/2 Hotfoot—Summer Fayre (Reform) **Lord Fairhaven**
51 **NASAB,** ch c 14/4 Nordance (USA)—Piccadilly Etta (Floribunda) **Mr Hamdan Al-Maktoum**
52 **NO SID NO STARS (USA),** ch c Diamond Shoal—Side Saddle (USA) (Codex (USA)) **Marshall W. Jenney**

MR M. F. D. MORLEY—continued

53 B f 3/3 Tina's Pet—Our Katy (Dragonara Palace (USA)) **Mr D. R. Hunnisett**
54 Ch c 20/5 Tate Gallery (USA)—Reveal (Pitskelly) **Mr O. Miles-Pollard Jnr**
55 SACQUE, b f 13/4 Elegant Air—Embroideress (Stanford) **The Hon. Mr W. McAlpine**
56 SHABAAB (USA), ch c 25/2 L'Emigrant (USA)—
Bid For Manners (USA) (Raise A Bid (USA)) **Mr Ali K. Al Jafleh**
57 SUSHI, gr f 15/2 Nishapour (FR)—Falaka (Sparkler) **Mr Christopher Spence**
58 SWAALIF (USA), ch f 27/2 Secretariat (USA)—
Queen Louie (USA) (Crimson Satan) **Mr Hamdan Al-Maktoum**
59 SWITCH HITTER, b c 22/4 Tate Gallery (USA)—Gay Surrender (Sir Gaylord) **Mr J. J. Hindley**
60 TARBUSH (IRE), br c 12/2 Bustino—Akaaleel (Tyrnavos) **Mr Hamdan Al-Maktoum**
61 TATHIR (CAN), ch c 29/2 Blushing Groom (FR)—Great Verdict (Le Fabuleux) **Mr Hamdan Al-Maktoum**
62 WATCH IT MATEY, b g 20/2 Tina's Pet—Mouletta (Moulton) **Lord Hartington**

Other Owners: Mr A. N. C. Bengough, Mrs Cheryl Cripp, Mrs J. V. Green, Mr C. J. Heath, Mr Mark Horne, Mr J. G. Jagelman, Mr J. S. Lockwood, Lady Manton, Mr Nick Scotland, Sir Reginald Sheffield, Mrs A. Skiffington, Mr Charles Sutton, Lord Vestey, Mrs G. Webb Bronfman.

Jockeys (Flat): M Birch (w.a.), G Duffield (w.a.).

Apprentice: Eliot Bentley (7-7).

Amateur: Mrs A Wilson (9-0).

Lady Rider: Mrs M F D Morley (9-7).

411 MR M. MORRIS, Fethard

Postal: **Everardsgrange, Fethard, Co. Tipperary, Ireland.**
Phone: **(052) 31474 FAX (052) 31654**

1 AIGUILLE ROUGE, 7, b g Buckskin—Master Nidee **Mrs T. Hyde**
2 ALBERTA CLIPPER, 4, b g Strong Gale—Tu-Ukumah **R. Carrier**
3 ATTITUDE ADJUSTER, 10, ch g Deep Run—Careless Biddy **Mrs Shanny Morris**
4 BRIDEVALLEY, 5, b m Deep Run—Arctic Cut **Michael O'Flynn**
5 BROWNSKIN, 5, b m Buckskin (FR)—Summerfield Gold **Mrs A. W. Buller**
6 CAHERVILLAHOW, 6, b g Deep Run—Bargara **Mrs Miles Valentine**
7 CHORTLE, 5, b g Deep Run—Chuckle Hansel **Mrs P. F. N. Fanning**
8 COURSE OF ACTION, 5, b g Crash Course—Narita **A. J. O'Reilly**
9 CRANLOME, 12, b g Menelek—Austrian Maid **Mrs P. F. N. Fanning**
10 5, B g Buckskin (FR)—De Lafield **A. J. O'Reilly**
11 DOORSLAMMER, 5, b m Avocat—Candora **Mrs B. M. Browne**
12 EMERALD GEM, 4, b g Henbit—Mary Arden **Mrs Shanny Morris**
13 5, B g Celtic Cone—Flora Finching **A. J. O'Reilly**
14 GRANVILLE HOTEL, 6, br g Random Shot—Behistina **R. H. Strudwick**
15 HI HARRY, 12, ch g Fidel—Deity **Mrs Shanny Morris**
16 I DON'T KNOW, 6, b g Buckskin—The Wren's Nest **Mrs John Magnier**
17 4, Ch f Boreen—Jamestown Girl **M. Fahy**
18 LASTOFTHEBROWNIES, 10, b g Giolla Mear—Another Rose **Mrs A. M. Daly**
19 LEATHERS, 6, b g Buckskin—Keeping Company **Major Victor McCalmont**
20 4, B g Furry Glen—Lovely Pine **R. H. Strudwick**
21 MIXED BLENDS, 8, b m The Parson—Biowen **John Spearman**
22 NED OF THE HILL, 4, b g The Parson—Little Credit **Mrs P. F. N. Fanning**
23 PROSPECTOR'S WAY (CAN), 5, b g Crafty Prospector (USA)—Justine's Way (USA) **A. J. O'Reilly**
24 RAWHIDE, 6, ch g Buckskin—Shuil Eile **Mrs Harry McCalmont**

MR M. MORRIS—continued

25 4, Ch g Carlingford Castle—Reapers Run **Mrs David Austin**
26 **ROCKLANDER,** 6, b g Smokey Rockett—Clevelander **Mrs P. F. N. Fanning**
27 4, B g Wolver Hollow—Saffron Ring
28 **SANGIO,** 6, b g Kings Ride—Happy View **James Horgan**
29 **SHAKIMA,** 9, br g Crash Course—Linmoss **Mrs Sharon C. Nelson**
30 4, B g Carlingford Castle—Shanagarry Gazette **L. Kiely**
31 4, B g Be My Native—Sniff
32 **THE BULL MCCABE,** 5, b g Deep Run—Miss Cheeky **Mrs John Magnier**
33 **THE SLICED PAN,** 6, b g Pitpan—Believe It Or Not **Major Victor McCalmont**
34 **THOMASTOWN CASTLE,** 4, ch g Carlingford Castle—Determined Sara **Mrs P. F. N. Fanning**
35 **TLAQUEPAQUE,** 6, ch g Deep Run—Saucy Society **K. McCreery**
36 **TRAPPER JOHN,** 6, b g The Parson—Blueola **Mrs P. F. N. Fanning**
37 **TWO BOB,** 6, ch g Billion—Hazar **James Horgan**
38 **WESTERN HEARTBEAT,** 6, b m Buckskin—Highland Party **Arnold E. Lowe**
39 **WINDS OF WAR,** 5, br g Strong Gale—Kind Rose **Mrs Miles Valentine**
40 **WINSCOMBE COURT,** 6, ch g Deep Run—Desmorona **Mrs Miles Valentine**
41 **WITCHFINDER,** 6, b g The Parson—Vul's Money **Clonmel Racecourse Supporters Club**
42 **YOUKNOWHATIMEAN,** 5, b g Monseigneur—Miss Galwegian **Patrick G. Ford**
43 **YOU'RE IN CHARGE,** 8, b g Pitpan—Esparta **Mr D. Ashby**

Other Owners: Mr S. Barrett, Alfred Buller, J. D. Clague, Mr Frank Conroy, Mrs John Horgan, Mrs M. V. Horgan, Harry McCalmont, Mr P. McCormack, Mrs Noreen McManus, Mrs D. Nagle, Mrs Catherine O'Byrne, Mr M. G. Ryan.

Jockeys (NH): T Carmody (w.a.), C F Swan.

Conditional: M Davey.

Amateur: Mr J Queally.

412 MR W. G. MORRIS, Kidderminster

Postal: **Unwicks Farm Stables, Station Road, Hartlebury, Kidderminster, DY11 7YL.**
Phone: **(0299) 250953**

1 **ALANERRY,** 10, br g Alanrod—Kerry B **Mr D. W. Dacosta**
2 **BRIARQUEEN,** 6, b br m The Brianstan—Queen of The Kop **Mr Andrew Plumb**
3 **GEORGE GREY,** 4, gr c Runnymede—Miss Moritz **Mr Graham Parker**
4 **GOLD DUST,** 5, b h Golden Fleece (USA)—Soba **Robert Reynolds (Commercials) Ltd**
5 **KAMUR,** 4, b f Kafu—Namur **Mr B. K. Wells**
6 **ORIENTAL DREAM,** 6, ch g Northfields (USA)—Jenny **Mr B. S. Port**
7 **PATCHOULI'S PET,** 7, b m Mummy's Pet—Primage **Mr Graham Parker**
8 **RUN OF GOLD,** 5, ch m Deep Run—The Ceiriog **Mr E. F. Birchall**
9 **RUN OF WELD,** 7, ch g Deep Run—The Ceiriog **Mr Graham Parker**
10 **TINY STEAL,** 6, b g Pollerton—Spray **Mr Graham Parker**
11 **UNIHOC,** 11, ch g Maris Piper—Cute Smokey **Mr D. J. Weaver**

THREE-YEAR-OLDS

12 B f Idiot's Delight—The Ceiriog **Mr E. F. Birchall**

MR W. G. MORRIS—continued

TWO-YEAR-OLDS

13 B f Rymer—The Ceiriog **Mr E. F. Birchall**

Other Owners: Mr M. V. Darby, Mrs Valerie Wells.

Jockey (Flat): John Williams.

Jockey (NH): W A Morris (9-7).

Conditional: A B Mulholland.

Amateur: Mr M V Darby.

Lady Rider: Mrs Candy Morris.

413 MR M. MOUBARAK, Newmarket

Postal: **Green Ridge Stables, Hamilton Road, Newmarket, Suffolk, CB8 0NQ.**
Phone: **NEWMARKET (0638) 666553**

1 CHARBATTE (FR), 4, b f In Fijar (USA)—Evonsville (FR) **Mr Sleiman Moubarak**
2 FOREST MONARCH (USA), 4, b g Green Forest (USA)—Uncommited (USA) **Ecurie Fustok**
3 GRAND BLUSH (USA), 4, gr f Blushing Groom (FR)—Versatile (FR) **Ecurie Fustok**
4 GREEN LINE EXPRESS (USA), 4, ch c Green Forest (USA)—Laylitna (USA) **Ecurie Fustok**
5 NORFOLKIEV (FR), 4, b c In Fijar (USA)—Touraille (FR) **Ecurie Fustok**

THREE-YEAR-OLDS

6 BLACK FIGHTER (USA), br f Secretariat (USA)—Faten (USA) **Ecurie Fustok**
7 CENTERLAND (USA), ch c Green Forest (USA)—Pompoes (DEN) **Ecurie Fustok**
8 INSTANT DESIRE (USA), ch f Northern Dancer—Pink Topaze (FR) **Ecurie Fustok**
9 MAGIC EXPRESS (USA), ch c Green Forest (USA)—Secretariat Flag (USA) **Ecurie Fustok**
10 PURE GREEN (USA), ch f Green Forest (USA)—Malakya **Ecurie Fustok**
11 SHANNON FLOOD, b c In Fijar (USA)—Gracious Girl (USA) **Ecurie Fustok**
12 SONIC MUSIC (USA), ch c Green Forest (USA)—Laylitna (USA) **Ecurie Fustok**
13 STARLIGHT FLYER, b c In Fijar (USA)—Nareen (USA) **Ecurie Fustok**
14 STATE DANCER (USA), b c El Gran Senor (USA)—Bimbo Sue (USA) **Ecurie Fustok**
15 TURKISH STAR (USA), b c Blushing Groom (FR)—Perlee (FR) **Ecurie Fustok**

TWO-YEAR-OLDS

16 EXPLOSIVE SPEED (USA), b c 23/2 Exceller (USA)—Strait Lane (USA) (Chieftain (USA)) **Ecurie Fustok**
17 FIVE STAR EXPRESS, gr f 28/3 Siberian Express—Rose of The Sea (USA) (The Minstrel (CAN)) **Ecurie Fustok**
18 Ch f 7/4 Crystal Glitters—Flower Parade (USA) (Mill Reef (USA)) **Ecurie Fustok**
19 FLYING SPEED (USA), b c 5/5 Far North (CAN)—Diatoma (FR) (Sicambre (FR)) **Ecurie Fustok**
20 GRACIOUSLY (FR), b f 12/3 Fast Topaze (USA)—Gracious Girl (USA) (Forli (ARG)) **Ecurie Fustok**
21 GREEN MEADOWS (USA), ch f 16/1 Green Forest (USA)—Perlee (FR) (Margouillat (FR)) **Ecurie Fustok**
22 KARNAK (FR), b c 19/4 Fast Topaze (USA)—Sasetto (FR) (St Paddy) **Ecurie Fustok**
23 MAGNIFICENT STAR (USA), b f 5/3 Silver Hawk (USA)—Gulanar (Val de Loir (FR)) **Ecurie Fustok**
24 MOUNTAIN HARVEST (FR), b f 2/5 Shirley Heights—Bitter Rice (Sassafras (FR)) **Ecurie Fustok**
25 RING OF FORTUNE (FR), b c 25/4 Fast Topaze (USA)—Forgata (FR) (Bolkonski) **Ecurie Fustok**
26 SHARP GLITTERS, ch c 12/3 Crystal Glitters—Sharp Valley (USA) (Sharpen Up) **Ecurie Fustok**
27 STAR OF FORTUNE (FR), b f 1/3 Fast Topaze (USA)—Star Kris (FR) (Kris) **Ecurie Fustok**
28 SUPERIOR HAWK (USA), b c 5/3 Silver Hawk (USA)—Ruby Green (USA) (J O Tobin (USA)) **Ecurie Fustok**

414 MR S. J. MULDOON, Malton

Postal: **Auburn Hill Stables, Langton Road, Norton, Malton, North Yorkshire, YO17 9PZ.**
Phone: **OFF. (0653) 696409 HOME 693795 MOBILE (0836) 652729 FAX (0653) 696409**

1 **HIGHFLYING,** 4, br g Shirley Heights—Nomadic Pleasure **Mr B. Batey and Mr R. Murray**
2 **ISOBAR,** 4, b g Another Realm—Lady Eton **Mr S. Dalton**
3 **POSITIVE WAY,** 6, b g Ardross—Abbe's Realm **Mr S. J. Muldoon**

THREE-YEAR-OLDS

4 **CON'S DREAM,** b f Final Straw—Bright Era **Mr S. J. Muldoon**
5 **FRANGELICO,** b f Kampala—Solo Stream **L. Muldoon**
6 **ON CUE,** b g Magic Mirror—Tug Along **Mr S. J. Muldoon**
7 **SI SAWAT,** ch g Superlative—Soft Chinook (USA) **Mr J. J. May**
8 **SMUTS,** b f Local Suitor (USA)—Firework Party (USA) **Mr D. B. Lamplough**

TWO-YEAR-OLDS

9 B g Aragon—Aunt Charlotte (Charlottown)
10 Ch g Dominion—Brilliant Rosa (Luthier (FR))
11 Ch c Rousillon (USA)—Cellist (USA) (Bagdad)
12 B c Coquelin (USA)—Donna Cressida (Don (ITY))
13 B f Hotfoot—Farandella (English Prince)
14 Ch c Primo Dominie—Formidable Dancer (Formidable (USA))
15 Ch c Scottish Reel—Green Pool (Whistlefield)
16 B f Tumble Wind (USA)—Lady Mary (Sallust)
17 Ch f Final Straw—Rosie Black (Roan Rocket)
18 B f M Double M (USA)—Suba (GER) (Limbo (GER))

Other Owners: Auburn Hill Racing Club, Mr J. Carr (Durham), Mr Eddleston, A. Fawcett, Mr R. E. Graham, D. Johnson, Mr P. L. Muldoon, W. Polland, Sea Pigeon Thoroughbred Racing, G. West.

Jockey (Flat): J H Brown (8-1).

Jockey (NH): M Hill (9-7).

415 MR M. P. F. MURPHY, Bury St Edmunds

Postal: **Green Farm Stables, Timworth, Bury St. Edmunds, Suffolk, IP33 1HS.**
Phone: **NEWMARKET (0638) 665328 HOME CULFORD (028 484) 8980 STABLE**

THREE-YEAR-OLDS

1 **INTRIGUE,** b c Mummy's Pet—Subtlety **East Coast Racing Club**
2 **MEESON CODE,** b c Coded Scrap—Meeson Secret **Mr B. J. Wilcox**

TWO-YEAR-OLDS

3 **BENHALL GREEN,** b f Blushing Scribe (USA)—Rheinza (Rheingold) **Homefield Racing & Bloodstock Ltd**
4 **BLAKENEY MARSH,** b f Blakeney—High Caraval (High Top) **Homefield Racing & Bloodstock Ltd**
5 **GREAT YELDAM,** ch f Blushing Scribe (USA)—
Super Fortune (USA) (Super Concorde (USA)) **Homefield Racing & Bloodstock Ltd**
6 B f Hotfoot—H R Micro (High Award) **Mrs S. Sands**
7 B c Sonnen Gold—Meeson Secret (Most Secret) **Mr B. J. Wilcox**
8 **SANDHURST TYPE (IRE),** ch f Sandhurst Prince—Double Type (Behistoun) **Mr M. Forbes**
9 **SANDON CROWN,** b f Sandhurst Prince—Grand Teton (Bustino) **Homefield Racing & Bloodstock Ltd**
10 **TOOTSIE WOOTSIE,** b f Hotfoot—Hippona (Red God) **Mr D. Crocket**

416 MR W. J. MUSSON, Newmarket

Postal: **Saville House, St Mary's Square, Newmarket, Suffolk, CB8 OHZ.**
Phone: **(0638) 663371 TELEX 817083 MUSSON G FAX (0638) 667979**

1 **ANURAG,** 4, br g Indian King (USA)—Merta (USA) **Mr Brian Donald**
2 **ASBAAB,** 5, b g Young Generation—The Yellow Girl **Mr J. Remblance**
3 **AUTHORSHIP (USA),** 4, b g Balzac (USA)—Piap (USA) **Mr Jim E. Nelson**
4 **DUAL CAPACITY (USA),** 6, b g Coastal (USA)—Fenney Mill **Mr A. P. Field**
5 **FOOLISH TOUCH,** 8, b g Hot Spark—Nushka **Broughton Thermal Insulation**
6 **FULL HEARTED (USA),** 6, b g Full Out (USA)—Heladi **Mr Victor Chandler**
7 **KING'S LADY (FR),** 4, ch f Ti King (FR)—Harold's Girl (FR) **B. T. Chambers**
8 **MEGABUCKS,** 5, b m Buckskin (FR)—Floater **J. R. Hawksley**
9 **MY BID,** 6, b m Cleon—Pleasure Bid **R. D. Musson**
10 **SHARP THISTLE,** 4, b f Sharpo—Marphousha (FR) **Angley Stud Limited**
11 **SHARP TIMES,** 7, b g Faraway Times (USA)—Sharp Venita **Mr F. W. Briggs**
12 **SOME SPEAK,** 7, b br g Paddy's Stream—Clerihan **Mrs J. J. F. Francis**
13 **TADBIR,** 5, b g Try My Best (USA)—La Grange **Mr A. P. Field**
14 **TRAVELLING TRYST (USA),** 4, ch g Pilgrim (USA)—King's Courtesan (USA) **Broughton Thermal Insulation**

THREE-YEAR-OLDS

15 **BRENDANS SUPERIOR,** b f Kind of Hush—Waltham Terrace **F. G. Construction**
16 **BROUGHTINO,** b g Sandhurst Prince—Modest Maiden (FR) **Broughton Thermal Insulation**
17 **BROUGHTON BAY,** b c Trojan Fen—Rose Noir **Broughton Thermal Insulation**
18 **CAPTAIN FAWLEY,** br g Petorius—Lady Fawley **Mr Keith Brown**
19 **CONFUCIUS,** b g Stanford—Carrhae **Mr R. Conway**
20 **ECONOMY PRINT,** b g Muscatite—Scarlet O'Harlot **Economy Print**
21 **FLITCHAM,** br f Elegant Air—Seldom **R. W. Hipkin**
22 Ch g Superlative—Gandoorah **Mrs Rita Brown**
23 **HI-LI,** b f High Top—Leipzig **Angley Stud Limited**
24 **INDIAN FLUTE,** br f Indian King (USA)—Corista **C. S. Goldsmith**
25 **KINGS ALDERMAN,** b g Kings Lake (USA)—Keep The Thought (USA) **Equity Provincial Ltd**
26 **LINGFIELD LASS (USA),** b f Advocator—Royal Caprice (USA) **Angley Stud Limited**
27 **LISA ROSA,** b f Ardross—Macaw **A. C. L. Sturge**
28 **SAVILLE WAY,** ch g Gorytus (USA)—Claretta (USA) **Saville House Racing Limited**
29 **SWIFT SILVER,** gr c Bairn (USA)—Asmalwi **Mr O. Zawawi**
30 **WAIKANINI,** br f Mummy's Pet—Harmonise **Angley Stud Limited**

TWO-YEAR-OLDS

31 **ASWAMEDH,** gr c Ore—Asmalwi (Averof) **Mr O. Zawawi**
32 **ECONOMY EXPRESS,** b f Bay Express—Massawa (FR) (Tennyson (FR)) **Economy Print**
33 Br f Ilium—Raffinrula (Raffingora) **S. Holmes**
34 **SAAFEND,** br f Sayf El Arab (USA)—Gilt Star (Star Appeal) **Mr J. Remblance**
35 B f Trojan Fen—Smash Hit (Roan Rocket) **Broughton Thermal Insulation**
36 B f Never So Bold—Yelney (Blakeney) **Broughton Thermal Insulation**

Other Owners: Mr David Brewer, Mr M. E. Broughton, Mr Roy Conway, Mr T. Crawford-Gray, Mr John F. Difford, Mr Ken Furlong, Mr David Gallyer, Mr Tony Hayward, Mr R. Levy, Mr T. D. Lofts, Mr M. J. Miserotti, Mr Gavin Patmore, Mr Clive Pettigrew, Mr R. A. Powell, Mr Paul Tacon, Victor Chandler (Knightshill) Ltd, Mr I. L. Weaver.

Jockey (Flat): M Wigham (8-3).

Jockeys (NH): D J Murphy (10-0), C Smith (10-0).

Conditional: P McEntee (9-9).

Amateur: D J S Cosgrove (10-10).

Lady Rider: Mrs Judy Musson (8-7).

417 MR C. T. NASH, Wantage

Postal: **Raceyard Cottage, Kingston Lisle, Wantage, Oxon, OX12 9QH.**
Phone: **(036782) 510**

1 **BALLIMINSTER,** 5, b g Balinger—Merry Minuet **Mr C. T. Nash**
2 **CELTIC REMORSE,** 8, b m Celtic Cone—Armagnac Bay **Mrs P. L. Nash**
3 **CHANCE BUY,** 7, b g Rolfe (USA)—Astonishment **Mr C. W. Nash**
4 **DEEP N' DANGEROUS,** 4, b f Balinger—Deepness **Mr C. W. Nash**
5 **HOT HANDED,** 9, ch m Nearly A Hand—Fiery Sol **Mrs P. L. Nash**
6 **JIMSTER,** 8, b g Jimsun—Merry Minuet **Mr C. W. Nash**
7 **ROADSTER,** 14, b g Streetfighter—Malin **Mr C. W. Nash**
8 **SIR LESTER,** 14, br g Bend A Bow (USA)—Treaty Girl **Mrs P. L. Nash**

Jockey (NH): M Bosley (10-2).

Amateur: Mr T Jones (11-0).

Lady Rider: Mrs P L Nash (8-7).

418 MR M. P. NAUGHTON, Richmond

Postal: **High Gingerfield Lodge, Hurgill Road, Richmond, N. Yorkshire.**
Phone: **(0748) 2803**

1 **ABIGAILS PORTRAIT,** 4, ch f Absalom—Corr Lady **Miss Sarah J. Naughton**
2 **ALLTEN GLAZED,** 13, b g Ragapan—Elands Kop **Mrs W. Widdall**
3 **DAMART (USA),** 6, b g Verbatim (USA)—Ice Wave (USA) **Mr Philip Davies**
4 **DOMINICUS,** 4, b g Dominion—Pulcinella **Mr W. J. Kelly**
5 **FRESCOBALDO (USA),** 4, b g Run The Gantlet (USA)—Voice of The River (USA) **Miss Sarah J. Naughton**
6 **GEMINI FIRE,** 6, br g Mansingh (USA)—Sealady **Mr P. McMahon**
7 **GENTLE HERO (USA),** 4, ch g Hero's Honor (USA)—Tender Camilla **Mr Michael O'Grady**
8 **GOLDEN BEAU,** 8, b g Crimson Beau—Kantado **Mr J. E. Mottram**
9 **MR CHRIS CAKEMAKER,** 6, ch m Hotfoot—Polonaise **Mr Peter J. Davies**
10 **NED'S AURA,** 5, br g Dalsaan—My Natalie **Mr D. J. Soley**
11 **NOBLE SON,** 4, b g Thatching—Eden Quay **Miss Sarah J. Naughton**
12 **PENDLEY GOLD,** 9, ch g Le Bavard (FR)—Angel's Song **Mrs Helen Greenshields**
13 **PHAISTOS (FR),** 5, gr g Bellypha—Sainte Gemme (FR) **Mr D. J. Soley**
14 **POSITIVELY GREAT (USA),** 4, ch g Achieved—Sable Linda (USA) **N.T.C. (Racing) Limited**
15 **QUIP,** 5, ch g High Line—Sans Blague (USA) **Mr R. H. Summers**
16 **SAY YOU WILL,** 6, b g Riboboy (USA)—Polita **Mr G. Noble**
17 **STEM GINGER,** 5, ch g Mr Fluorocarbon—Hope Baggot **Miss J. M. Thompson**
18 **SWEET BAY,** 4, b f Sweet Monday—Moonlight Bay **Mr W. J. Kelly**
19 **TOOZAN TAK,** 4, b g Sadler's Wells (USA)—Calandra (USA) **D. Scullion and M. P. Naughton**
20 **WARWICK SUITE,** 8, b g Orchestra—Place To Place (USA) **Mr Philip Davies**
21 **YOUNG COMMANDER,** 6, br g Bustino—Bombshell **Mr Philip Davies**

THREE-YEAR-OLDS

22 **MISSISSIPPI BEAT (USA),** b g Dixieland Band (USA)—Jungle Dance (USA) **Mrs R. Olivier**
23 **REAL STUNNER,** ch f Chief Singer—Real Party **Philip Davies and M. P. Naughton**
24 **SACOSHE,** b f Swing Easy (USA)—Just Irene **Mr G. Noble**
25 **SMOOTH FINISH,** b g Welsh Term—Chantry Pearl **Mr P. Jillings**

TWO-YEAR-OLDS

26 **ROCK OPERA (IRE),** ch c Ballad Rock—Time For Romance (Cure The Blues (USA)) **Philip Davies**
27 **SEVERALS PRINCESS,** gr f Formidable (USA)—Justicia (Nonoalco (USA)) **M. Southin**
28 B f Indian King—Sweet Melody (Alcide) **Killoran Engineering and P. McMahon**
29 Gr f Marching On—Tootsie Jay (Alias Smith (USA)) **Mrs J. Leadbitter**

MR M. P. NAUGHTON—continued

Other Owners: Mr Ian P. Davies, Mr D. J. Graham, Mr Ned Jones, Mr G. Lowe, Mr Fred Moreton, Mr Gordon Stead, Tow-Star Limited, Mr C. R. Utting, Mr J. F. Widdall, Mr S. H. Widdall, Frank Wilson, Mrs C. T. Woodley.

Jockeys (Flat): K Fallon, M Roberts (w.a.).

Apprentice: Jason Eales (7-0).

Lady Rider: Miss J Davies (9-0).

419 MR A. S. NEAVES, Faversham

Postal: **Arnolds Oak Farm, Eastling, Faversham, Kent.**
Phone: **EASTLING (079589) 274**

1 **ASHMAE,** 8, b g Anax—Solentown **Mr A. S. Neaves**
2 **GOLA'S IMP,** 8, b br m Impecunious—Anagola **Mr A. S. Neaves**
3 **MANDERLEY BOY,** 4, b g Absalom—Phlox **Mr A. S. Neaves**
4 **NOAH'S ARK,** 10, b g Habat—Rainbow's End **Mr A. S. Neaves**

THREE-YEAR-OLDS

5 **ALPARLER,** b g Kampala—Westafrica **Mr A. S. Neaves**
6 **CERTAIN LOOK,** b g Yawa—Best Lady **Mr A. S. Neaves**
7 **CERTAIN STAR,** b g Good Times (ITY)—Summer Fayre **Mr A. S. Neaves**
8 **COOLAGOWN,** b g Castle Keep—Little Oncer **Mr A. S. Neaves**
9 **DO OR BUST,** b f Posse (USA)—Fardella (ITY) **Mr A. S. Neaves**
10 **MULSHING,** b g Song—Petit Secret **Mr A. S. Neaves**

420 MR J. L. NEEDHAM, Ludlow

Postal: **Gorsty Farm, Mary Knoll, Ludlow, Salop.**
Phone: **(0584) 874826/872112 FAX: (0584) 873256**

1 **BAYMOUNT,** 9, br g Al Sirat (USA)—Light Moment **Mr J. L. Needham**
2 **CARLINGFORD BELLE,** 4, ch f Carlingford Castle—Swiftly Belle **Mr J. L. Needham**
3 **CHICK WAY,** 12, ch g Menelek—Nursery **Mr J. L. Needham**
4 **IMAGINE THAT,** 8, b g Our Mirage—Saul Flower **Mr J. L. Needham**
5 **KIRI'S SONG,** 7, b m True Song—Mekhala **Mr J. L. Needham**
6 **LASTOFTHEVIKINGS,** 5, ch g Cisto (FR)—Vivyiki **Mr J. L. Needham**
7 **LEINTHALL FOX,** 4, b br f Deep Run—Winter Fox **Mr J. L. Needham**
8 **LEINTHALL PRINCESS,** 4, b f Prince Regent (FR)—Due Consideration **Mr J. L. Needham**
9 **PADDY IN PARIS,** 7, ch g Paddy's Stream—Wrekin Rose **Mr J. L. Needham**
10 **PRINCE OF BARODA,** 6, b g Torenaga—Princess Baroda **Mr J. L. Needham**
11 **QUAYSIDE BUOY,** 7, br g Quayside—Ivernia **Mr J. L. Needham**

Jockey (NH): A Gorman.

Conditional: S Graham (9-7), V Smith.

421 MR C. R. NELSON, Lambourn

Postal: **Kingsdown, Lambourn, Newbury, Berkshire, RG16 7QX.**
Phone: **(0488) 71391 OR 71878 TELEX 846357 KINGSD FAX (0488) 73235**

1 **BEC ROUGE,** 4, ch c Ballad Rock—Mrs Tittlemouse **Mrs J. Yarnold**
2 **DISTANT RULER,** 6, b h Indian King (USA)—Faraway Places **Mr C. R. Nelson**
3 **DOUBLE ENCORE (USA),** 4, ch c Nodouble (USA)—Flo Russell (USA) **Mrs J. Yarnold**
4 **GIN AND ORANGE,** 4, b c Mummy's Pet—Amberetta **R. E. A. Bott (Wigmore St) Ltd**
5 **LIFFEY REEF,** 4, ch f Main Reef—Sloane Ranger **Mr Kevin J. Molloy**
6 **LUNAR MOVER (USA),** 4, b c Sharpen Up—Intentional Move (USA) **Mr Edward P. Evans**
7 **NO SUBMISSION (USA),** 4, b c Melyno—Creeping Kate (USA) **Mr P. F. Warren**
8 **SIR RUFUS,** 4, ch c Thatching—La Melodie **Mr J. C. Driscoll**
9 **SPITFIRE,** 4, b c Shirley Heights—Home Fire **R. E. A. Bott (Wigmore St) Ltd**
10 **WISH YOU WELL,** 4, b f Sadler's Wells (USA)—Happy Thought (FR) **R. E. A. Bott (Wigmore St) Ltd**

THREE-YEAR-OLDS

11 **AKIMBO,** ch c Bold Lad (IRE)—Western Gem **Mrs D. Weatherby**
12 **BRIC LANE (USA),** br c Arctic Tern (USA)—Spring Is Sprung (USA) **Mr M. Bennett**
13 **DE WINTER,** b c Formidable (USA)—Mrs Danvers **R. E. A. Bott (Wigmore St) Ltd**
14 **GO DUTCH (USA),** ch c Lyphard's Wish—Parema (USA) **Mr R. J. Lorenz**
15 **LA DOMAINE,** b f Dominion—La Galette **Mr John W. Mitchell**
16 **LAWFUL,** b f Law Society (USA)—Dunette (FR) **R. E. A. Bott (Wigmore St) Ltd**
17 **LEGAL FANTASY,** br c Law Society (USA)—Never Never Land **Mrs J. Yarnold**
18 **MELBURY (USA),** ch f Forli (ARG)—Her World (USA) **Mrs D. Weatherby**
19 **MISS BOBBY BENNETT,** b f Kings Lake (USA)—Karen Lee M (USA) **Mr B. A. Kilpatrick**
20 **MOUNT IDA (USA),** b f Conquistador Cielo (USA)—Suspicious (USA) **R. E. A. Bott (Wigmore St) Ltd**
21 **NEENAWN,** gr f Bairn (USA)—Rustling **Mr George Ward**
22 **PHANTOM BELLE,** br f Taufan (USA)—Spinning Jenny **Lt-Col John Silcock**
23 **POKE THE FIRE,** ch c Never So Bold—Home Fire **R. E. A. Bott (Wigmore St) Ltd**
24 **SAUCIER VOLANT (USA),** ch c Sauce Boat (USA)—Intentional Move (USA) **Mrs J. Yarnold**
25 **SHOUT OUT,** b c Auction Ring (USA)—Manora (USA) **Dr Carlos E. Stelling**
26 **SMOKEY NATIVE (USA),** b c Our Native (USA)—Smokey Spender (USA) **Mr J. W. Robb**
27 **SOUTHERN BEAU (USA),** b c Dixieland Band (USA)—Love For Love (USA) **Mrs W. Tulloch**
28 **TEREBRID,** ch c Coquelin (USA)—Hone **Miss D. A. Colvile**
29 **TUPPY (USA),** ch f Sharpen Up—Petradia **R. E. A. Bott (Wigmore St) Ltd**
30 **YARRA GLEN,** ch f Known Fact (USA)—Sloane Ranger **Mr Kevin J. Molloy**

TWO-YEAR-OLDS

31 **AUNT DICEY,** b f 26/4 Never So Bold—Mrs Danvers (Balidar) **R. E. A. Bott (Wigmore St) Ltd**
32 **BOLD DOUBLE,** ch c 29/2 Never So Bold—Bold Flawless (USA) (Bold Bidder) **Mrs D. Weatherby**
33 **DOMINORA,** b f 19/3 Dominion—True Nora (Ahonoora) **R. E. A. Bott (Wigmore St) Ltd**
34 B c 30/3 Crafty Prospector—Illustrious Joanne (USA) (Illustrious (USA))
35 **KIMBERS,** b c 24/4 Lomond (USA)—Take Your Mark (USA) (Round Table) **Mrs W. Tulloch**
36 **LEAR LEADER (USA),** b c Lear Fan (USA)—Tolstoya (Northfields (USA)) **Dr Carlos E. Stelling**
37 B c 4/4 Far North (USA)—Make An Attempt (USA) (Nashua) **R. H. Horriss**
38 **PANCHOS PEARL (USA),** b f Pancho Villa (USA)—Jackie Pearl (USA) (Ruffled Feathers) **Mrs J. Yarnold**
39 **REGAL MATE (USA),** ch c Woodman (USA)—Regal Response (USA) (Viceregal (CAN)) **Dr Carlos E. Stelling**
40 **SING OUT (FR),** b c Auction Ring (USA)—Manora (USA) (Stop The Music (USA)) **Dr Carlos E. Stelling**
41 Ch c 11/3 Try My Best (USA)—Sloane Ranger (Sharpen Up)
42 B c 10/5 Tanks Prospect (USA)—Snow Pearl (USA) (Boldnesian)

Other Owners: Mr D. Bagler, Mr T. L. Boyd, Mr Lionel Godfrey, Guiting Stud Limited, Mr William J. Patterson, Mr M. D. K. Read, Mr Nick Wilson.

Jockey (Flat): J Reid (8-4, w.a.).

Apprentice: Lee Davis.

Lady Rider: Miss J Winter (8-7).

422 MR W. M. NELSON, Torthorwald

Postal: **Longrigg, Torthorwald, Dumfries, Scotland, DG1 3PS.**
Phone: **(038775) 237**

1 **ROTATE,** 10, ch g Roman Warrior—Waterbeck **Mr W. M. Nelson**
2 **THISTLEHOLM,** 4, ro g Hello Handsome—Private Path **Mr W. M. Nelson**

Amateur: Mr Frank Nelson (10-0).

423 MR D. NICHOLSON, Stow On The Wold

Postal: **Cotswold House, Condicote, Stow-on-the-Wold, Cheltenham, Gloucestershire, GL54 1ES.**
Phone: **(0451) 30417 OR 30296 FAX (0451) 32271**

1 **AGAINST THE GRAIN,** 9, b g Oats—Bench Game **Mr Ben Brooks**
2 **AGATHIST (USA),** 7, ch g Bon Mot III—We Try Harder **Mrs J. Mould**
3 **ALASKA RUN,** 8, ch g Deep Run—Snow Slave VI **Mrs M. J. Rogers**
4 **AL HASHIMI,** 6, b g Ile de Bourbon (USA)—Parmesh **Mr J. Hobbs**
5 **ANOTHER CORAL,** 7, br g Green Shoon—Myralette **Mr M. R. Deeley**
6 **ASCOT LAD,** 5, ch g Broadsword (USA)—Aunt Livia **Mr J. C. Berry**
7 **BANBRIDGE,** 7, ch g Paddy's Stream—Glenroid **Mr M. W. Vestey**
8 **BANKER'S GOSSIP,** 6, b g Le Bavard (FR)—Gracious View **Mrs R. J. Skan**
9 **BEECH PARK,** 6, b g Salluceva—Whitford **Mr J. B. R. Morris**
10 **BELSTONE FOX,** 5, br g Buckskin (FR)—Winter Fox **Mrs R. J. Skan**
11 **BIGSUN,** 9, b g Sunyboy—Stella Roma **Mr John F. Horn**
12 **BOBBY KELLY,** 8, ch h Le Bavard (FR)—Very Very **Save & Prosper Group Ltd**
13 **BROTHER GEOFFREY,** 11, b g Sheshoon—Eilan Aigas **Straight Deal Racing Plc**
14 **CANON CLASS,** 9, b g The Parson—Pallatess **H.R.H. The Princess Royal**
15 **CAOIMHE,** 8, br m Pollerton—Cottage View **Mrs Claire Smith**
16 **CELTIC HAMBRO,** 7, b g Celtic Cone—Ice Bird **Mrs M. J. Rogers**
17 **CHARTER PARTY,** 12, b g Document—Ahoy There **Mrs Claire Smith**
18 **CORRY'S CAPER,** 5, b g Mandalus—Glad Rain **Mrs Claire Smith**
19 **COTTAGE RUN,** 10, b g Deep Run—Cottage View **Mrs M. J. Rogers**
20 **DARTON RI,** 7, b g Abednego—Boogie Woogie **Brig C. B. Harvey**
21 **DEADLY CHARM (USA),** 4, b br f Bates Motel (USA)—Certain Something **Mrs A. J. Davies**
22 **DUKE'S WHISTLE,** 7, gr g Whistling Deer—Ruemaro **Mrs Claire Smith**
23 **DUNTREE,** 5, ch g Day Is Done—Bay Tree (FR) **Mrs J. Mould**
24 **EMRYS,** 7, ch g Welsh Pageant—Sun Approach **Mr Brian Gregory**
25 **FAST STUDY,** 5, b g Crash Course—Mary May **Brig C. B. Harvey**
26 **FOR THE GRAIN,** 6, b g Nishapour (FR)—Some Dame **Mr H. J. Joel**
27 **GENERALLY RIGHT,** 8, b g Fine Blade (USA)—Nire's Pride **Mr H. J. Joel**
28 **HARD STUFF,** 6, ch g Hardboy—Spritestown **Miss M. Lane**
29 **HOPING FOR GLORY (USA),** 4, b c L'Emigrant (USA)—Hope For All (USA) **Sheikh Mohammed**
30 **IRON GRAY,** 8, gr g General Ironside—Yvonne's Delight **Mrs J. Mould**
31 **LAKE MISSION,** 5, b g Blakeney—Missed Blessing **Mr W. T. Montgomery**
32 **LISALEEN LADY,** 5, b m Miner's Lamp—Chestnut Fire **Mr D. P. Hornby**
33 **LITTLE-NIPPER,** 5, ch g Derrylin—Emily Kent **Mrs J. Mould**
34 **LODDON LAD,** 8, ch g Anax—Emily Kent **Mrs J. Mould**
35 **LONG ENGAGEMENT,** 9, b g Mandalus—Selk Fly **Mr A. M. Armitage**
36 **MULLOCH BRAE,** 6, b m Sunyboy—Stella Roma **Mr P. G. Lowe**
37 **NINJA,** 4, ch g Niniski (USA)—Buckhurst **Mr H. R. Mould**
38 **OLNISTAR (FR),** 4, b f Balsamo (FR)—Star Light (FR) **Mrs Claire Smith**
39 **PERSIAN SWORD,** 4, b g Broadsword (USA)—Sorraia **Mr Peter Hepworth**
40 **PITCHCOTT HILL,** 5, b br g Pollerton—Khalice **Mr J. E. Brown**
41 **POTTERTON LADY,** 5, ch m Deep Run—Fly Swift **Potterton International Ltd**
42 **PRISCILLIAN,** 6, b g Runnett—Douala (GER) **Mr H. R. Mould**
43 **QUEEN'S CHAPLAIN,** 6, b g The Parson—Reginasway **Mrs J. Mould**
44 **RANDOLPH CRESCENT,** 7, b g Le Bavard (FR)—Cailin Meireach **Lord Vestey**
45 **RANDOM ROMANCE,** 7, b m Eric—Embuscade **Mrs M. P. Sutton**

MR D. NICHOLSON—continued

46 **RED TIMBER,** 6, ch g Nishapour (FR)—Welsh Miniature **Cavaliers Sporting Society**
47 **RELATIVELY EASY,** 7, b m Relkino—Linguistic **Mr A. R. Macdonald-Buchanan**
48 **RUN ROUND THE PARK,** 5, ch g Deep Run—Miel Crepe **Mrs M. J. Rogers**
49 **SALAMANDER JOE,** 5, br g Salluceva—Fast And Clever **Mr G. C. Mordaunt**
50 **SHAMANA,** 4, b f Broadsword (USA)—Celestial Bride
51 **SICILIAN PASSAGE,** 8, gr g Pals Passage—Hiriwa **Mrs Stewart Catherwood**
52 **SPLITTHEDIFFERENCE,** 6, br g Pollerton—Glen Rambler **Mr V. E. Barclay**
53 **SPRING HAY,** 4, gr c Wassl—Spring Silver **Mr Ali Saeed**
54 **SPRINGHOLM,** 8, br g Mandalus—Lady Hiltop **Brig C. B. Harvey**
55 **STRAIGHT BRANDY,** 7, b g Sit In The Corner (USA)—Fair Spirit **Mrs D. Anderson**
56 **STRONG BEAU,** 5, br g Strong Gale—Red Pine **Mrs G. Maxwell-Jones**
57 **TRIBUTE TO YOUTH (USA),** 6, b g Youth (USA)—Merkel (USA) **Mr R. Maryan Green**
58 **TROOP THE COLOUR,** 10, ch g Soldier Rose—Clear Beat **Mr M. R. Deeley**
59 **TRUE CLOWN,** 8, b m True Song—Copperclown **Mrs Susan Orton**
60 **TUG OF GOLD,** 5, gr g Tug of War—Grey Squirrell **Mrs J. Mould**
61 **UNCLE MOGY,** 4, ch g Monsanto (FR)—Primrolla **Lord Vestey**
62 **UNCLE RAGGY,** 7, b g Monksfield—Lorna Doone **Prowting Homes**
63 **VERY PROMISING,** 12, br g The Parson—No Hitch **Mr David Nicholson**
64 **WATERLOO BOY,** 7, ch g Deep Run—Sapphire Red **Mr M. R. Deeley**
65 **WHEEL TAPPER,** 6, ch g True Song—Spartan Clown **Mr H. Hutsby**
66 **WOODSIDE ROAD,** 10, ch g Paddy's Stream—White Trout **Prowting Homes**

Other Owners: Mrs J. M. Battersby, Mr B. Bennett, Mr J. S. Dale, Mr S. R. J. Garretty, Miss S. L. M. Gold, Capt. J. Macdonald-Buchanan, Mrs C. A. Maryan Green, Mr J. F. Mawle, Mr C. G. Nicholl, Mrs E. Roberts, Mr R. J. Rymer, Mr H. B. Shouler, Mrs J. M. Snell, Mrs H. Taylor, Mr T. W. Upfield, Mr J. A. H. West, Mrs Eileen Wiseman.

Jockey (NH): Richard Dunwoody (10-0).

Conditional: Robert Bellamy (9-10), David Bridgwater (9-7), Warren Marston (9-7).

Lady Rider: H. R. H. The Princess Royal (9-3).

424 MRS H. E. NORTH, Withiel Florey

Postal: **Swansea Farm, Withiel Florey, Brendon Hill, Watchet, Somerset, TA23 OLH.**
Phone: **BROMPTON REGIS (03987) 202**

1 **DRUM DOBBIN,** 8, b g Dubassoff (USA)—Vulrusika **Mr H. Handel**
2 **JUST JOSHUA,** 11, ch g Joshua—Delk Lass **Mr H. Handel**
3 **MARCH AMADEUS,** 8, ch g Sousa—Dotted Swiss **Mrs C. Handel**
4 **RANDOM MISS,** 8, b m Random Shot—Astral Fairy **Mr H. Handel**

Amateur: Miss A Handel (11-0).

425 MR J. NORTON, Barnsley

Postal: **Globe Farm, High Hoyland, Barnsley, S. Yorkshire, S75 4BE.**
Phone: **(0226) 387633**

1 **BELFORT GIPSY,** 4, b g Belfort (FR)—Tringa (GER) **Mr John Richard Norton**
2 **BHARKAT,** 4, b g Beldale Flutter (USA)—Cienaga **Mr W. D. T. Scott**
3 **CAWSTON BAY,** 5, b m Cawston's Clown—Princess Davinia **Mr J. Norton**
4 **CLASSY BOY,** 5, b g Country Classic—Cherry Volante **Mr J. Norton**

MR J. NORTON—continued

5 **FLYING HYDE,** 4, b f Petong—Campagna **Mr Tony Yates**
6 **HOWARDS WAY,** 5, ch g Touch Boy—Canty Day **Tow-Star Limited**
7 **MEANIE MINNA,** 4, b f Derrylin—Pirate Maid **Mr J. Norton**
8 **ROYAL FOREST,** 4, b f Royal Fountain—Princess Davinia **Mr V. F. Walsh**
9 **SO GIFTED,** 4, b f Niniski (USA)—Maybe So **Mr Tony Yates**
10 **TOW-STAR'S LADY,** 4, b f On Your Mark—Miss Tehran **Tow-Star Limited**
11 **WIL-TOT,** 13, br g Peacock (FR)—Ulster Belle **Mr John Richard Norton**

THREE-YEAR-OLDS

12 **AL BADETO,** b f Hays—Atedaun **Mr A. L. Watson**
13 **HILLMOOR BELLA,** ch f Creetown—Confleur **Mr R. E. Evans**
14 **ZAMBRINIA,** b f Zambrano—Princess Davinia **Mr J. Norton**

TWO-YEAR-OLDS

15 Ch f 22/4 Millfontaine—Atedaun (Ahonoora) **Mr P. N. Howard**
16 B f 7/5 Blakeney—Ribaria (Ribero) **Mr J. Norton**

Other Owners: Mr B. S. Brereton, Mrs E. C. Carberry, Mr A. F. Guy, Mr R. Milner, Mr B. D. Petty, Mr C. Widdowson.

Conditional: S Woods (9-10).

426 MR S. G. NORTON, Barnsley

Postal: **Longsides, Jebb Lane, High Hoyland, Barnsley, S. Yorkshire, S75 4BS.**
Phone: **(0924) 830450/830406 TELEX 557946**

1 **EASTERN EMBER,** 4, br f Indian King (USA)—Pithead **Mr J. E. Marsden**
2 **GAZZYMAZ,** 4, ch g Longleat (USA)—Vaguely Hopeful **Ian Redford Ltd**
3 **GIANTS CASTLE,** 6, b g Great Nephew—Our Home **Mr J. M. Plowright**
4 **RAMBO CASTLE,** 4, b g Castle Keep—Rampage **Mrs J. H. Tyrrell**
5 **SALMAN (USA),** 4, b c Nain Bleu (FR)—H M S Pellinore (USA) **Mr S. G. Norton**
6 **THIMBALINA,** 4, ch f Salmon Leap (USA)—Maestrette **Mrs James Hartley**

THREE-YEAR-OLDS

7 **ALSAAMER (USA),** ch c Megaturn (USA)—Regal Nip (USA) **Sheikh Rashid Al Khalifa**
8 **BACK RAISE (USA),** ch c Raise A Man (USA)—Double Polite (USA) **P & M**
9 **BARHOOM,** ch c Nicholas Bill—Strathclair **La Grange Ltd**
10 **CAUGHT UNAWARES,** ch g Longleat (USA)—Mrs Cullumbine **Mr A. K. Smeaton**
11 **DAKIN BROOK,** b f Prince Ragusa—Minster Melody **Mr J. M. Plowright**
12 **DENCAST,** b c Battle Hymn—Ishiyama **Mr Charles A. Green**
13 **FIRST VINTAGE (USA),** b c Ruthie's Native (USA)—Champagneandlace (USA) **Mr G. Charlesworth**
14 **GOD BLESS YOU,** b c Vision (USA)—Maestrette **Mr Salman Alkhalifa**
15 **GOZONE,** ro g Carwhite—Perlesse **Mrs A. M. Upsdell**
16 **HOT RUMOUR,** ch g Hotfoot—Clear As Crystal **Mr Graham Gill**
17 **JUST JEAN,** b f Kala Shikari—Curzon House **Mr David G. Robinson**
18 **KAWARAU QUEEN,** b f Taufan (USA)—Hasty Goddess **Mr W. Jardine**
19 **PETLOVA,** b f Petorius—Vlassova (FR) **Mr P. A. Deal**
20 **PIC NEGRE,** b c Lochnager—Sallusteno **Mrs C. P. Chapman**
21 **REEF WIND,** b g Tumble Wind (USA)—Hollow Reef **Mr S. G. Norton**
22 **SATIN LAKE (USA),** b f Well Decorated (USA)—Bunny Lake **Mrs N. J. Sutton**
23 **SHIKARI KID,** b g Kala Shikari—Muffet **Mr G. Corbett**
24 **SPIRIT AWAY,** b f Dominion—Jove's Voodoo **Lord Haddington**
25 **TORTUGA BAY,** gr f Try My Best (USA)—Miss Caribbean **British Thoroughbred R & B Plc**
26 **TRIXIE'S GUEST,** gr f What A Guest—Winter Lady **Mr C. J. Corlett**

MR S. G. NORTON—continued

TWO-YEAR-OLDS

27 Ch f 18/4 Dreams To Reality—Beechwood (USA) (Blushing Groom (FR)) **Mr S. G. Norton**
28 MINDY (IRE), b c 27/5 Salmon Leap (USA)—Malija (FR) (Malicious) **Mr G. S. B. Cooke**
29 B f 15/3 Blakeney—Mrs Cullumbine (Silly Season) **Mr A. K. Smeaton**
30 B c 13/5 Affirmed (USA)—Sheika (USA) (Minnesota Mac) **Mr D. Scott**
31 B c 21/5 Taufan (USA)—Spring Bride (Auction Ring (USA)) **P & M**
32 TRACK MONARCH (USA), b c 16/3 Track Barron (USA)—Coasting Home (USA) (Coastal (USA)) **Mr Philip England**
33 B f Miswaki (USA)—Untitled (USA) (Far Out East (USA)) **Mrs J. H. Tyrrell**
34 ZENISKA (USA), b c 5/2 Cozzene (USA)—Istiska (FR) (Irish River (FR)) **Mr J. E. Marsden**

Other Owners: Mr S. A. Al-Khalifa, Mr K. Bennett, Mr R. Bu-Rashid, Mr A. L. Deal, Mr J. D. Graham, Mrs Angela Norton, Mr Brian Padgett, Vickers Shopfitters Ltd.

427 MR D. H. NUGENT, Upper Lambourn

Postal: **Chaddleworth House, Newbury, Berkshire, RG16 0EB.**
Phone: **CHADDLEWORTH (04882) 209 ALSO LAMBOURN OFFICE (0488) 71452**

1 AESTHETIC, 5, ch g Hello Gorgeous (USA)—Tootens **Lady Eliza Nugent**
2 BATTLE DRUM, 9, b br g Bustino—Ring Rose **Lady Eliza Nugent**
3 BRAMBLE TWIG, 5, b g Monksfield—Bramble Mill **Lady Eliza Nugent**
4 MULLAGHMEEN, 4, b f Kinglet—Joedes Janet **Mr David H. L. Nugent**
5 WAY UNDER, 10, b g Menelek—In The Limelight **Lady Eliza Nugent**

THREE-YEAR-OLDS

6 FARREN CONNELL, b g Kinglet—Joedes Janet **Mr David H. L. Nugent**

TWO-YEAR-OLDS

7 B g Kinglet—Joedes Janet (Bahrain) **Mr David H. L. Nugent**

Jockey (NH): M Perrett (10-0).

428 MISS G. O'BRIEN, Castletown

Postal: **Painstown, Castletown, Navan, Co. Meath, Ireland.**
Phone: **(046) 64197 FAX (046) 54459**

1 HAEPENNY WELL, 9, ch g General Ironside—Moyle Majic **Mrs J. Hurley**
2 IRISH MOSS, 5, ch g Le Moss—Moyle Majic **Mrs J. Hurley**
3 JADE SHOON, 5, b g Green Shoon—Milparinka **O. K. Chung**
4 MARY BRADY, 5, ch m Day Is Done—Ce La Vie **Mrs J. Kinsella**
5 MIDDLESEX YEOMAN, 7, ch g First Council—Ballindoon **Capt. K. J. L. Beaumont**
6 5, B g Proverb—Moppit-Up **Mrs A. S. O'Brien**
7 4, B f Carlingford Castle—Reaper's Pride **Mrs J. Magnier**
8 SOCKEYE, 6, ch g Deep Run—Polar Vixen **Mrs M. Valintine**
9 SPRING JINKS, 9, b g Laurence O—Arctic Moonshine **Mrs J. M. Law**
10 TORRISH, 5, b g Over The River—Good Surprise **T. E. Hyde**

Other Owners: Mitchell McLeish.

429 MR M. V. O'BRIEN, Cashel

Postal: **Ballydoyle House, Cashel, Co. Tipperary, Ireland.**
Phone: **(062) 61222 TELEX 70714 FAX (062) 61677**

1 **ESPRIT D'ETOILE (USA),** 5, b h Spectacular Bid—Star Pastures **R. E. Sangster**
2 **GREAT LAKES,** 4, b c Lomond—Costly Wave **Classic Thoroughbreds**
3 **PUISSANCE,** 4, b c Thatching—Girton **Classic Thoroughbreds**
4 **SOCIETY BAY (USA),** 4, b c Alleged—Meadow Blue **Classic Thoroughbreds**

THREE-YEAR-OLDS

5 **ANCIENT AIR,** br c Thatching—Zenga **Classic Thoroughbreds**
6 **ARTISTIC IDEA (USA),** ch f Kris—Dandy Bury **Classic Thoroughbreds**
7 **BOOKER PRIZE,** b c Caerleon—Prudent Miss **R. E. Sangster**
8 **CAMBRINA,** b f El Gran Senor—Crown Godiva **Mrs M. V. O'Brien**
9 **CLASSIC LEGEND (USA),** b c Nijinsky—Pump **Classic Thoroughbreds**
10 **CLASSIC MEMORY,** b c Sadler's Wells—Vaguely **Classic Thoroughbreds**
11 **CLASSIC MUSIC (USA),** b c Northern Dancer—Fairy Bridge **R. E. Sangster**
12 **CLASSIC OPERA,** ch f Lomond—Drama **R. E. Sangster**
13 **DAYLIGHT HOUR (USA),** gr c Caerleon—Hat Tab Girl **Mrs M. V. O'Brien**
14 **DRURY LANE (USA),** b c Nijinsky—Exotic Bride **R. E. Sangster**
15 **FACE THE FACTS,** b f Lomond—Intrepid Lady **R. E. Sangster**
16 **FOLK SONG (USA),** ch f The Minstrel—Native Banner **Charles P. B. Taylor**
17 **GRAND RAPIDS (USA),** b c Riverman—Moralisme **Classic Thoroughbreds**
18 **HEAD HOME,** b c Taufan—Salagangai **Classic Thoroughbreds**
19 **HOTEL DU LAC,** b f Lomond—Hotel de Ville **Classic Thoroughbreds**
20 **IVORY LANE (USA),** gr f Sir Ivor—Turban **R. E. Sangster**
21 **KARRI VALLEY (USA),** b f Storm Bird—Lisadell **Mrs M. V. O'Brien**
22 **LAW CHAMBERS,** b c Law Society—Amata **Mrs John Magnier**
23 **LEGAL ADVISER,** b c Law Society—Kiama **Mrs M. V. O'Brien**
24 **LYREBIRD (USA),** ch f Storm Bird—Vallee Secrete **Classic Thoroughbreds**
25 **MEDIA AWARD,** b c Thatching—Bellinzona **Classic Thoroughbreds**
26 **MIDDAY SHOW (USA),** br c Roberto—Worlds Fair **Mrs M. V. O'Brien**
27 **NETWORK,** b c Caerleon—Alshandegha **Mrs M. V. O'Brien**
28 **PASSER-BY,** b g Lomond—Inisfree **Mrs M. V. O'Brien**
29 **ROYAL ACADEMY (USA),** b c Nijinsky—Crimson Saint **Classic Thoroughbreds**
30 **SPLASH OF COLOUR,** ch c Rainbow Quest—Cockade **Classic Thoroughbreds**
31 **STADLER,** b c Sadler's Wells—Santa Roseanna **Classic Thoroughbreds**
32 **SUMMING UP,** b g Law Society—Etoile de Paris **Mrs M. V. O'Brien**
33 **SUNNY MORNING,** b f Law Society—Golden Oriole **R. E. Sangster**
34 **THRESHOLD,** b f Alleged—All Ashore **Mrs M. V. O'Brien**
35 **TIME SLOT (USA),** ch c Secreto—Ebbing Tide **Mrs M. V. O'Brien**
36 **TRIBUTARY (USA),** b br f Seattle Slew—Woodstream **R. E. Sangster**
37 **WEDDING BOUQUET,** b f Kings Lake—Doff The Derby **Mrs M. V. O'Brien**
38 **WYNDALIA (USA),** b f Seattle Slew—Northernette **R. E. Sangster**

TWO-YEAR-OLDS

39 **ADJUDICATE (IRE),** b c 3/4 Law Society (USA)—Fairy Dancer (USA) (Nijinsky (CAN)) **R. E. Sangster**
40 **ARCHWAY (IRE),** ch c 23/2 Thatching—Rose of Jericho (USA) (Alleged (USA)) **A. Heffernan**
41 **BALLET REVIEW (IRE),** b f 28/4 Sadler's Wells (USA)—Fantasy Land (Nonoalco (USA))
42 B c Alleged (USA)—Bold Bikini (USA) (Boldnesian) **W. S. Farish**
43 B c 19/4 Alzao (USA)—Bonny Hollow (Wolver Hollow) **Classic Thoroughbreds**
44 B f 2/3 Alzao (USA)—Clanjingle (Tumble Wind (USA)) **R. E. Sangster**
45 **CLASSICAL MELODY (IRE),** b f 9/5 Fairy King (USA)—Nigel's Star (Ashmore (FR)) **Classic Thoroughbreds**
46 **CLASSICAL RHYTHM (IRE),** br c 3/3 Ballad Rock—Non Casual (Nonoalco (USA)) **Classic Thoroughbreds**
47 **CLASSIC CHARM,** ch c 17/2 Be My Guest (USA)—Triagonal (Formidable (USA)) **Classic Thoroughbreds**
48 **CLASSIC CHEER (IRE),** b c 21/2 Lomond (USA)—Plume Au Vent (Posse (USA)) **Classic Thoroughbreds**
49 **CLASSIC MATCH (IRE),** ch c 5/2 Ballad Rock—Ballymaloe Girl (Nonoalco (USA)) **Classic Thoroughbreds**
50 **CLASSIC MINSTREL (USA),** b c 6/3 The Minstrel (CAN)—Bold Caress (Bold Lad (IRE)) **Classic Thoroughbreds**
51 **CLASSIC TRUST (IRE),** b c 9/3 Tate Gallery (USA)—Trusted Maiden (Busted) **Classic Thoroughbreds**
52 **CLASSIC VENTURE (IRE),** b c 3/4 Fairy King (USA)—Allorette (Ballymore) **Classic Thoroughbreds**

Q What are the 3 most important words in the stallion business?

LEADING SIRE OF EUROPEAN 2-Y-O GROUP WINNERS

YEAR	HORSE	LOCATION
1986	THATCHING	COOLMORE
1987	LOMOND	COOLMORE
1988	CAERLEON	COOLMORE
1989	AHONOORA	COOLMORE

A *1. Location 2. Location 3. Location*

COOLMORE

Contact: **Bob Lanigan**: 353-52-2198 or **Christy Grassick**: 353-52-31313.
Coolmore Stud, Fethard, Co. Tipperary, Ireland. Tel: 353-52-31298. Telex: 80695. Fax: 353-52-31382.

STALLIONS FOR 1990
AL HAREB
ALZAO
BARBAROLLI
BE MY GUEST
BLUEBIRD
CAERLEON
COMMANCHE RUN
DANEHILL
DON'T FORGET ME
ENTITLED
GALLIC LEAGUE
GLENSTAL
HIGH ESTATE
LAST TYCOON
LAW SOCIETY
LOMOND
PERSIAN HEIGHTS
SADLER'S WELLS
SALMON LEAP
TATE GALLERY
THATCHING
TRY MY BEST
VACARME
WAAJIB

U.S.A. STALLIONS
ASSERT
EL GRAN SENOR
SEATTLE DANCER
STORM BIRD
WOODMAN

N.H. STALLIONS:
BUCKSKIN
CARLINGFORD CASTLE
ELECTRIC
EXECUTIVE PERK
HENBIT
LANCASTRIAN
LE MOSS
SUPREME LEADER

All Coolmore Stallions nominated to the European Breeders Fund.

MR M. V. O'BRIEN—continued

53 **DEPENDABLE (IRE),** ch c 28/2 Caerleon (USA)—Caring (Crowned Prince (USA)) **Classic Thoroughbreds**
54 B f 11/4 Nijinsky (CAN)—Exotic Bride (USA) (Blushing Groom (FR)) **Classic Thoroughbreds**
55 B c 26/3 Tate Gallery (USA)—Fair Flutter (Beldale Flutter (USA)) **Mrs M. V. O'Brien**
56 B c 9/5 Storm Bird (CAN)—Fairy Bridge (USA) (Bold Reason (USA)) **R. E. Sangster**
57 **FAIRY FOLK (IRE),** b f 23/5 Fairy King (USA)—Tripoli (Great Heron (USA)) **Denis McCarthy**
58 **FAVOURED NATIONS (IRE),** br c 31/1 Law Society (USA)—
Lady Lavery (USA) (Northern Dancer) **R. E. Sangster**
59 B f 26/3 El Gran Senor (USA)—Fleur Royale (Mill Reef (USA)) **R. E. Sangster**
60 B c 15/4 Alleged (USA)—Gallanta (FR) (Nureyev (USA)) **Classic Thoroughbreds**
61 B f 16/2 Sadler's Wells (USA)—Giada (USA) (Vaguely Noble) **Mrs M. V. O'Brien**
62 Ch g 16/3 The Noble Player—Grande Madame (Monseigneur (USA)) **Classic Thoroughbreds**
63 **HEAD OF CHAMBERS (IRE),** b c 31/3 Alleged (USA)—
Woodstream (USA) (Northern Dancer) **R. E. Sangster**
64 **HIGH KING (IRE),** b c 3/3 High Top—Marwell (Habitat) **Classic Thoroughbreds**
65 **KALAHARI PRINCE (IRE),** b c 1/3 Green Desert (USA)—Lauretta (Relko) **Classic Thoroughbreds**
66 B c 28/4 El Gran Senor (USA)—Keep Off (Bold Lad (IRE)) **Mrs M. V. O'Brien**
67 B f 8/2 Thatching—Kiama (Be My Guest (USA)) **Mrs M. V. O'Brien**
68 Ch c 21/3 Nijinsky (CAN)—Kuja Happa (USA) (Tell (USA)) **Classic Thoroughbreds**
69 **LAKE ISLE (IRE),** b g 6/3 Lomond (USA)—Inisfree (USA) (Hoist The Flag (USA)) **Mrs M. V. O'Brien**
70 **LEGAL PROFESSION (IRE),** b c 1/2 Law Society (USA)—
Palais Rose (USA) (Northern Dancer) **Mrs M. V. O'Brien**
71 B c 14/4 Tate Gallery (USA)—Melody Hour (Sing Sing) **Mrs M. V. O'Brien**
72 **MONTE CARLO (IRE),** b c 12/3 Last Tycoon—Thistlewood (Kalamoun) **John Colleran**
73 **OPERA QUEEN (IRE),** b f 30/4 Sadler's Wells (USA)—Intrepid Lady (USA) (Bold Ruler) **Mrs M. V. O'Brien**
74 Ch c 19/4 Secreto (USA)—Plains And Simple (USA) (Twist The Axe (USA)) **Classic Thoroughbreds**
75 **POET'S DREAM (IRE),** br c 13/5 Storm Bird (CAN)—Lisadell (USA) (Forli (ARG)) **Mrs M. V. O'Brien**
76 **PORTRAIT PAINTER (IRE),** gr c 26/2 Sadler's Wells (USA)—
Daring Grey (Bold Lad (IRE)) **Classic Thoroughbreds**
77 **QUARTER DECK (IRE),** b f 19/2 Storm Bird (CAN)—
Rosa Mundi (USA) (Secretariat (USA)) **Mrs M. V. O'Brien**
78 Br f 23/3 Ahonoora—Riverlily (FR) (Green Dancer (USA)) **Mrs John Magnier**
79 **RUSSIAN BALLET (USA),** ch f 5/4 Nijinsky (CAN)—Sex Appeal (USA) (Buckpasser) **Mrs M. V. O'Brien**
80 **SAN LORENZO (USA),** b c 17/3 El Gran Senor (USA)—
Wising Up (USA) (Smarten (USA)) **Classic Thoroughbreds**
81 Ch f 22/1 Lomond (USA)—Sheristadar (Shergar) **R. E. Sangster**
82 **SUB JUDICE (IRE),** br c 16/4 Law Society (USA)—
Thunderflash (FR) (Northfields (USA)) **Classic Thoroughbreds**
83 B f 28/3 El Gran Senor (USA)—Thorough (Thatch (USA)) **Mrs M. V. O'Brien**
84 **TYCHE (FR),** b f 18/4 Last Tycoon—Believer (Blakeney) **Classic Thoroughbreds**

Jockey (Flat): J Reid (8-4).

430 MISS P. O'CONNOR, Andover

Postal: **Midlecote House Racing Stables, Cholderton Road, Quarley, Andover, Hampshire.**
Phone: **HOME GRATELEY (026 488) 691 OFFICE CHOLDERTON (098 064) 498**

1 **BALLYSEEDY HERO,** 12, gr g Supreme Sovereign—Knocknagrena **Mr John W. Ford**
2 **DYLAN'S PRIDE (NZ),** 11, ch g First Consul (USA)—Val's Dream (NZ) **Miss Elaine Edwards**
3 **ENBYAR DAN,** 10, ch g Porto Bello—Alleyn **Mr Colin L. Clarke**
4 **JERSEY PEARL,** 5, b m Last Fandango—Snow Chief **Mr R. W. Stebbing**
5 **KILROY,** 5, b g Shirley Heights—Hyroglyph (USA) **Mr P. Trant**
6 **LEIA MECENE (FR),** 4, b g Gay Mecene (USA)—Dekeleia **Miss Elaine Edwards**
7 **LIKEABLE LADY,** 6, gr m Piaffer (USA)—Lady Andrea **Mr P. Trant**
8 **LUREX STAR,** 4, b g Thatching—Stellarevagh **Mr D. Gladwyn**
9 **PADDY'S DREAM,** 10, b g Paddy's Stream—Fairyslave **Mr A. Grodno**
10 **RUNCINA,** 4, b f Runnett—Seldom **Mr P. Trant**

MISS P. O'CONNOR—continued

11 **SAFE DISTANCE,** 5, ch g Lord Gayle (USA)—Our Sarah **Miss Elaine Edwards**
12 **TROUT ANGLER,** 9, br g Rarity—Gun Tana (FR) **Mr P. Trant**

Other Owners: Mr K. Bloom.

Jockeys (NH): G McCourt, B Powell (w.a.).

Amateur: Mr G Upton.

431 MR J. O'DONOGHUE, Reigate

Postal: **Priory Racing Stables, Reigate, Surrey, RH2 8JU.**
Phone: **(0737) 245241**

1 **HONEY PLUM,** 6, b m Kind of Hush—Rosaceae **Mr J. O'Donoghue**
2 **NEOLOGIST,** 4, b c Bold Owl—Neophyte II **Mrs E. Williams**
3 **PRINCE GREMIN,** 4, gr g Scallywag—Tuneful Queen **Mrs C. S. Ockwell**
4 **ROMAN CRACKSHOT,** 6, b g Roman Glory—Ogeno **Mrs C. S. Ockwell**

THREE-YEAR-OLDS

5 **MOREIRWEN,** b br f Bold Owl—Neophyte II **Mrs E. Williams**
6 **SIMPLY DES,** b f Simply Great—Kashida **Mr Brian Mitten and Mr Ted Powell**

TWO-YEAR-OLDS

7 **LADY SHALOTT (IRE),** b f 18/3 Caveat (USA)—
Carillon Miss (USA) (The Minstrel (CAN)) **James Harrow and Partners**

Other Owners: D. K. Budia, D. V. Patel.

Jockey (Flat): R Fox (7-8, w.a.).

Jockey (NH): M Furlong (10-0).

Amateurs: Mr D Evatt, Mr W W Sim (10-8).

432 MR W. A. O'GORMAN, Newmarket

Postal: **Seven Springs, Newmarket, Suffolk.**
Phone: **(0638) 663330 FAX (0638) 663160**

1 **MAC'S FIGHTER,** 5, ch h Hard Fought—Geoffrey's Sister **Mr M. McDonnell**
2 **NUCLEON (USA),** 4, ch c Mr Prospector (USA)—Nonoalca (FR) **Peter Milner**
3 **SALLY'S SON,** 4, b c Beldale Flutter (USA)—Sally Chase **Mr Jed M. Cohen**
4 **TAKDEER,** 4, ch c Sharpo—Red Gloves **Mrs Elaine O'Gorman**
5 **WORK ON AIR,** 4, ch g Doc Marten—Set To Work **Peter Milner**

MR W. A. O'GORMAN—continued

THREE-YEAR-OLDS

6 **DR MACCARTER (USA),** gr c Dr Carter (USA)—Now Voyager (USA) **Tamdown Ltd**
7 **GUNS AND ROSES,** ch c Ballad Rock—Sweet Reprieve **Mrs P. L. Yong**
8 **IN EXCESS,** b c Siberian Express (USA)—Kantado **Mr A. Foustok**
9 **PROST (USA),** b c Raise A Cup (USA)—Wrap It Up **Mrs P. L. Yong**
10 **RED HENRY (USA),** ch c Red Ryder (USA)—Bay Line Girl (USA) **Tamdown Ltd**
11 **SEARCHING,** b br c Ballad Rock—Cristalga **H.H. Prince Yazid Saud**
12 **SILVER ORE (FR),** ch f Silver Hawk (USA)—Forever Mary **Mr A. Foustok**
13 **SUPERFORCE,** b c Superlative—Loup de Mer **Mrs P. L. Yong**
14 **SUPER SALLY,** ch f Superlative—Sally Chase **Mr Jed M. Cohen**
15 **TARA'S GIRL,** b f Touching Wood (USA)—Esquire Lady **Tamdown Ltd**
16 **TROPIC POWER,** b c Petorius—Investiture **Mrs P. L. Yong**

TWO-YEAR-OLDS

17 **ABLE JET (USA),** br c Northjet—Princess Nicketti (USA) (Tom Rolfe) **Peter Milner**
18 **ABLE MAC (USA),** ch c Red Ryder (USA)—Amber Amethyst (USA) (Staff Writer (USA)) **Peter Milner**
19 **BURNT SUGAR (USA),** b c Raised Socially (USA)—Carmelize (USA) (Cornish Prince) **R. A. Meadows**
20 **CHINA BEACH,** ch f Superlative—Alanood (Northfields (USA)) **S. Fustok**
21 **CRYSTAL HEIGHTS (FR),** ch c Crystal Glitters (USA)—Fahrenheit (Mount Hagen (FR)) **Mr A. Foustok**
22 **DERBY CUP (USA),** ch c Raise A Cup (USA)—Pretty Derby (USA) (Master Derby (USA)) **Tamdown Ltd**
23 **ELECTRAVATION (USA),** b g Elocutionist (USA)—
Brava (GER) (Arratos (FR)) **Carley O'Gorman and W. A. O'Gorman**
24 **GOLD FUTURES (IRE),** b c Fayruz—Fair Chance (Young Emperor) **Mrs P. L. Yong**
25 **GOLDVEIN (SWE),** b c Superlative—Follow Me Follow (Wollow) **Mrs P. L. Yong and Times of Wigan**
26 **HAKY (FR),** b c Miswaki (USA)—Honey Stage (USA) (Stage Door Johnny (USA)) **Mrs P. L. Yong**
27 **KAYRUZ,** b g Fayruz—Rheinbloom (Rheingold) **Mr A. Foustok**
28 **KNIGHTARTIC (USA),** br c Arctic Tern (USA)—Zabolina (Busted) **Knight Group**
29 **MAC'S IMP (USA),** b c Imp Society (USA)—Flaming Reason (USA) (Limit To Reason (USA)) **Tamdown Ltd**
30 **MAC'S PRINCESS (USA),** b f Sovereign Dancer (USA)—
Jungle Princess (USA) (Jungle Road) **Tamdown Ltd**
31 **MAKEMEASTAR (IRE),** ch f Horage—Sally St Clair (Sallust) **S. Fustok**
32 **MYSTIC CRYSTAL (IRE),** b f Caerleon (USA)—Bolivia (GER) (Windwurf (GER)) **S. Fustok**
33 **PACIFIC RIM,** ch g Absalom—Spare Wheel (Track Spare) **P. Bonner**
34 **SALLY'S PRINCE (IRE),** ch c Prince Sabo—Sally Chase (Sallust) **Mr Jed M. Cohen**
35 **SCOTTISH CASTLE,** ch c Scottish Reel—Show Home (Music Boy) **Mrs P. L. Yong**
36 **SCREAMER,** br f Chief Singer—Palumba (Derring-Do) **S. Fustok**
37 **SEA WATCH,** b f Chief Singer—Brave Advance (USA) (Bold Laddie (USA)) **S. Fustok**
38 **SHERGARS SECRET (USA),** b c Desert Wine (USA)—Public Sympathy (Shergar) **Peter Milner**
39 **SILKEN SAILED (USA),** b c Gold Crest (USA)—Lady of Camelot (FR) (Bolkonski) **W. A. O'Gorman**
40 **SMILING SUN (IRE),** ch c Thatching—Charites (Red God) **S. Fustok**
41 **SOUTH CROFTY (USA),** ch g Imp Society (USA)—Pia's Estonia (USA) (Nikoli) **P. Bonner**
42 **TIMELESS TIMES (USA),** ch c Timeless Moment (USA)—Lovely Hobo (USA) (Noholme II) **Times of Wigan**

Other Owners: Mr Saleh Al Homeizi, Mrs M. E. O'Gorman, Mr P. M. Wells, Mr N. S. Yong.

Jockey (Flat): A Munro (7-10).

Apprentices: David Eddery (8-1), Emma O'Gorman (7-7).

433 MR E. J. O'GRADY, Thurles

Postal: **Killeens, Ballynonty, Thurles, Co. Tipperary, Ireland.**
Phone: **(052) 56156 FAX:(052) 56466**

1 **ANY GOSSIP,** 7, b g Proverb—Bartina **John P. McManus**
2 **BLITZKREIG,** 7, gr g General Ironside—Tyrone Typhoon **Peter Hopkins**

MR E. J. O'GRADY—continued

3 **CHEEKY DEVIL,** 6, b g Lucifer (USA)—Queen Aston **G. J. D. Wragg**
4 **CUTTY SARK,** 5, b m Strong Gale—Speedy Lady **Charles Hansard**
5 **DON LEONE,** 5, b g Don—Saintly Tune **John Horgan**
6 **FERROMYN,** 5, b g Green Shoon—Ferrajo **M. McGread**
7 **FLAMESKIN,** 5, b g Buckskin (FR)—Santa Ponsa **Paschal Phelan**
8 **GOD'S BANKER,** 4, br g Red Sunset—Aria **P. Senezio**
9 **GOLDEN SHARE,** 4, br f Reesh—Swinging Baby **Miss M. Delaney**
10 **HOT PURSUIT,** 4, b g Krayyan—Starlina **G. K. O'Reilly**
11 **MANTA,** 11, b g Oats—Fishfinger **John P. McManus**
12 **MARKS REFRAIN,** 6, b g Blue Refrain—Markup **H. Hardiman**
13 **MIRIAM'S FANCY VI,** 6, b g The Parson—Deep Sea **Mrs A. Thompson**
14 **MOI,** 5, br m Rymer—Boherdeel **G. J. D. Wragg**
15 **MORE OF IT,** 5, b g Furry Glen—Homewrecker **J. J. Power**
16 **MOTHER AIKENHEAD (USA),** 6, b m Mac Diarmida (USA)—The Neurologist **Dr R. Torsney-Durkin**
17 **ON DEPOSIT,** 4, b g Gorytus (USA)—Papsie's Pet **James Horgan**
18 **PUKI PUKI,** 6, b m Roselier (FR)—Dorset Belle **Mrs A. Thompson**
19 **VIRGINIA IRONSIDE,** 5, gr m General Ironside—Mrs Popple **Mrs W. T. O'Grady**
20 **WHATS HE BY,** 6, ch g Deep Run—Highly Acceptable **Mrs A. Thompson**

THREE-YEAR-OLDS

21 **AL FROLIC,** b c Alzao (USA)—Fun Frolic **James Glass**
22 **BELUGA PRINCE,** b c Siberian Express (USA)—Maiden's Walk **Mrs A. Thompson**
23 **BONTDOU,** ch c Godswalk (USA)—Eirene Oge **P. Gallagher**
24 **BREAK THE HABIT (FR),** gr c Habitat—Hippodrone (USA) **J. S. Gutkin**
25 **C'EST BON,** gr g Vaigly Great—Cracked Up **Mr Robert Salter Townshend**
26 **DINGLE TRIP,** b f Tumble Wind (USA)—Jane Bond **Aziende Agricole Associate S.R.L.**
27 **EOLAS,** b c Lomond (USA)—Glomach (USA) **J. P. Lynch**
28 **GAYLE EILE,** ch g Lord Gayle (USA)—Junella **Mrs E. J. O'Grady**
29 **INFANCY (USA),** b f Northern Baby (CAN)—Better 'n' Bold (USA) **Arthur B. Hancock III**
30 **INSPIRED GUESS (USA),** b c Robellino (USA)—Inspire (USA) **James Glass**
31 **LOOSE ENDS,** ch c Persian Bold—Crimson Royale **R. J. Rooney**
32 **PARTY GUEST,** ch f What A Guest—Tremiti **Thomas J. Murphy**
33 **PLAYING SAFE,** b c Reasonable (FR)—Crystal Halo **Mrs Norah Kennedy**
34 **SUNSHINE MIRROR,** b f Magic Mirror—Brazilian Beauty **Mrs C. Young**
35 **TENDER,** ch f Tender King—Frederika (USA) **Mrs M. Valentine**

TWO-YEAR-OLDS

36 B f 23/2 Burslem—Annais Nin (Dominion)
37 B c 30/4 Pennine Walk—Danger Signal (Red God) **A. Senezio**
38 Br c 20/3 Mazaad—Idle Gossip (Runnett)
39 B c 26/4 Last Tycoon—Ladytown (English Prince)
40 Gr c 8/4 Absalom—Matinata (Dike (USA))
41 B f 22/4 Procida (USA)—Moretta (Artaius (USA)) **P. Gallagher**
42 Ch f 2/1 Ballad Rock—Penny Halfpenny (Sir Ivor) **R. McCrann**
43 B f 4/4 Krayyan—Randolina (Wolver Hollow) **Mark A. Synnott**
44 B c 1/3 Nordance (USA)—Rose And Honey (Amber Rama (USA))
45 Br f 17/2 Godswalk (USA)—Scoby Lass (Prominer) **R. E. Sangster**
46 **SOLCHOID (USA),** b br f 12/3 Solford (USA)—Small Heist (USA) (No Robbery) **Dr E. O'Brien**
47 B c 8/5 Try My Best (USA)—Sooner Or Later (Sheshoon) **Mrs Norah Kennedy**
48 B f 24/2 Tumble Wind (USA)—Swan Upping (Lord Gayle (USA))
49 B f 14/5 In Fijar (USA)—Vallee Sarthoise (FR) (Val de Loir)

Other Owners: J. Clague, John Magnier, F. McNulty, P. Meenan, Ian Murphy, M. O'Malley, The Hon. Mrs E. Wood.

Jockeys (NH): T J Ryan (9-7), A J Slattery (9-7).

Apprentice: Timothy J O'Sullivan (6-0).

Amateur: Mr P Fenton (10-0).

434 MR R. M. O'LEARY, Malton

Postal: **Clarence House, Great Habton, Malton, North Yorkshire, YO17 0TU.**
Phone: **(0653) 86684**

1 **BETSY BOOP,** 5, b m Pauper—Day Fiddle **Mr John Watson**
2 **BOOKIE BASHER,** 7, b br g Derring Rose—Wine Spy **Mrs E. Murphy**
3 **DONTPUSHME,** 9, ch g Pauper—Miss Victor **Mrs Julia Ward**
4 **EMERALD ROYALE,** 6, b m Skyliner—Miss Royal **Mrs Vicky O'Leary**
5 **HIGHFIELD PRINCE,** 4, b g Prince Tenderfoot (USA)—Parler Mink **Mr John Watson**
6 **ORWELL OPINION,** 8, br g Roselier (FR)—Brief Summary **Seagrave Haulage & Civil Eng Ltd**
7 **YOUGOTIT,** 4, b f Orange Reef—Costerini **Mrs E. Murphy**

THREE-YEAR-OLDS

8 **BOUGAINVILLEA,** ch f Longleat (USA)—Diamante **Mr E. H. Maloney**
9 **EXCHANGE FAYRE,** ch c Burslem—Sanibel **Mrs Ann Smurfit**
10 **INTEGRITY BOY,** b c Touching Wood (USA)—Powderhall **Mr John M. Jackson**
11 **LADY IN THE LAKE,** b f Kings Lake (USA)—Trouble Me Not (USA) **Mrs Ann McCarthy**
12 **OXFORD PADDY,** b c Taufan (USA)—Spyglass **Mrs Ann Smurfit**
13 **SLEEKBURN LADY,** b f Rapid River—Sophia Western **Mr Bennett Charlton**

Other Owners: Mr T. Conway, Mr John Knotts.

Jockeys (NH): M Dwyer (w.a.), L Wyer (w.a.).

435 MR F. J. O'MAHONY, Lingfield

Postal: **Ford Manor Racing Stables, Ford Manor Road, Dormansland, Lingfield, RH7 6NZ.**
Phone: **OFFICE (0342) 833238**

1 **BRAVE SETANTA,** 5, b g Hillandale—Kasarose **Miss Janet Menzies**
2 **CALL A TRUCE,** 5, b g Hard Fought—Celestial Star **Ernist Smith**
3 **CONDOVER SILK,** 7, b br m Record Run—Silk Fashion
4 **DENRY,** 5, ch g Burslem—Escalado **Mr W. A. Rooney**
5 **INVOLVED AGAIN,** 5, b g Ballacashtal (CAN)—Get Involved **Hugh Morris and D. Greener**
6 **QUAI D'ORSAY,** 5, b g Be My Guest (USA)—Noblanna (USA) **Mrs Vivienne O'Mahony**
7 **RONNIE BOLINSKI,** 4, b g Balidar—Watch Lady **Mrs Virginia Toft**
8 **SALVAGER,** 6, b g Balinger—Mahnaz **Miss V. Willes**
9 **SAY YOU,** 6, b g Sayyaf—Braida (FR) **Mr Terry Prebble**

Other Owners: Mr B. Baldwin, Mr R. A. Butler, Mrs L. J. Gatward, Mr M. J. Hoare, Mr J. H. Lewis, Mr M. Lowry.

Jockeys (NH): M Kinnane (9-7), E Murphy (9-7).

436 MR J. J. O'NEILL, Penrith

Postal: **Ivy House, Skelton Wood End, Penrith, Cumbria.**
Phone: **(08534) 555 FAX (08534) 559**

1 **ALMA GOLD,** 5, b g Sonnen Gold—Au Pair **Mr David Alan Harrison**
2 **ALMARREEKH (FR),** 5, b g Glint of Gold—Formulate **Miss L. McShane**
3 **BARNEY O'NEILL,** 4, gr c Ballad Rock—Lapis Lazuli **Mr G. B. Davidson**

MR J. J. O'NEILL—continued

4 **BUILDERS GOLD,** 4, b g On Your Mark—Linanbless **Mr Eric Scarth**
5 **CABBIE'S BOY,** 4, ch g Dublin Taxi—Petriva **Mr A. Burns**
6 **CANEY RIVER,** 7, ch g Over The River (FR)—High Town Jackie **Mrs June Doyle**
7 **CHANCE REMARK (USA),** 7, b g Elocutionist (USA)—Lucky Sway (USA) **Mr A. K. Collins**
8 5, Ch g Le Moss—Cold Arctic **Mr G. B. Davidson**
9 **DANNY CONNORS,** 6, b g Furry Glen—Steady Lady **Mr J. P. McManus**
10 **DAWN BLADE,** 7, b m Fine Blade (USA)—Watch The Birdie **Mr Mark O'Connor**
11 **DEEP CLIFF,** 8, ch g Deep Run—Woodcliffe **Mr J. D. Graham**
12 **DUTCH CALL,** 7, br g Callernish—Castle-Lady **Mr John Davey**
13 **EXCITING PROSPECT,** 6, ch g North Summit—Hopefull Polly **Mr Paul Green**
14 **FURLANA WONDER,** 8, b g Miami Springs—Furlana **Mr Liam Mulryan**
15 **GENERALS BOY,** 8, b g General Ironside—Even More **Mr P. F. Craggs**
16 **GRANNY'S PRAYER,** 9, br g Boreen (FR)—Ace Blue **Mr Peter Hopkins**
17 **GURTEEN BOY,** 8, ch g Tickled Pink—Joie d'Or (FR) **Mr J. E. Lane**
18 **HIT THE CEILING,** 7, br g Buckskin (FR)—Star of Hope **Mr J. E. Lane**
19 **HUNTING COUNTRY,** 6, b g Wolver Hollow—Drag Line **Mr David Alan Harrison**
20 **I KID YOU NOT,** 7, ch g Laurence O—Miss Kilbride **Jonjo Thoroughbred Racing Plc**
21 **IMPANY,** 11, br g Parasang—Swift Imp **Mr Jim McGrath**
22 4, Br g Callernish—Ingenious **Mrs June Doyle**
23 **INSTANT TAN,** 6, b g Tanfirion—Instanter **Mr John Poynton**
24 **J J FRANK,** 5, b g Le Moss—Kanturk Lady **T. G. Beighton Ltd**
25 **JOGALOT,** 4, b g Lochnager—Key Harvest **Mr T. Birkbeck**
26 **KANGAROO COURT,** 4, br g Tumble Wind (USA)—Wild Justice **Mr A. N. R. Rudd**
27 **KINGS QUEST,** 5, ch g Touch Paper—Leapallez **Mr A. McLuckie**
28 **KONVEKTA,** 6, gr g Rymer—Moselle Mist **Konvekta Ltd**
29 5, B g Selko—Lady Affair **F. K. Roofing Ltd**
30 **MACHO MAN,** 5, br g Mummy's Game—Shoshoni **Mr G. V. Wilson**
31 **MAELKAR (FR),** 6, b g Maelstrom Lake—Karabice **Mr P. Byrne**
32 4, B br g Taufan (USA)—Maltese Pet **J. J. O'Neill**
33 **MASTER LAMB,** 7, gr g Absalom—Caroline Lamb **Mr R. E. Graham**
34 **MILS MIJ,** 5, br g Slim Jim—Katie Grey **Mr Joe Hurst**
35 **MISS LAMB,** 6, ch m Relkino—Young Lamb **Jonjo Thoroughbred Racing Plc**
36 **NATIONAL VELVET,** 7, b g Torus—Teachers Pet VI **Mr T. E. Jeffrey**
37 **NOBLE PROSPECT,** 6, b m Tall Noble (USA)—Prosper Lion **Mr S. Tonge**
38 **OH DEAR,** 8, b m Paico—Coniscliff Bell **Dr Roy Palmer**
39 **OUT ON A FLYER,** 6, b m Comedy Star (USA)—Listen To Me **Mr David Alan Harrison**
40 **PACO'S BOY,** 5, b g Good Thyne (USA)—Jeremique **F. K. Roofing Ltd**
41 **POLO PRINCE,** 7, gr g Nishapour (FR)—Tiepoless **Mr Tom Doran**
42 **PRUSSIAN GUARD,** 4, b g Lomond (USA)—Friedrichsruh (FR) **Mr A. K. Collins**
43 **RAISE AN ARGUMENT,** 11, b g No Argument—Ten Again **Mr John Poynton**
44 **REMEMBER THE ALAMO,** 4, b g Scorpio (FR)—Chelsea Charmer **Mr M. Corbett**
45 **ROLIAD,** 6, br g Rolfe (USA)—Clear Whistle **Mr A. K. Collins**
46 **STAY AWAKE,** 4, ch g Anfield—Djimbaran Bay **Mr Austin Donnellon**
47 **SUPER BAR,** 8, b g Le Bavard (FR)—Super Queen **Mr J. B. Gilruth**
48 **TINA'S HIDEAWAY,** 5, b br m Kabour—Tina Glitters **Hyde Production Engineering Co Ltd**
49 **VICARIO DI BRAY (ITY),** 7, b g Furry Glen—Via Del Tabacco **Mr Peter Hopkins**
50 **WAR HOUSE,** 7, ch m Tug of War—Brilliant Girl **Mr J. J. Power**

THREE-YEAR-OLDS

51 **GO FOR GLORY,** b br c My Dad Tom (USA)—Ardtully Lass **Jonjo Thoroughbred Racing Plc**
52 **MR OPTIMISTIC,** ch c King Persian—Saybya **Jonjo Thoroughbred Racing Plc**
53 Ch g Red Johnnie—Sequoia **Mr A. K. Collins**
54 Ch f Import—Sponsorship **Miss V. Hetherington**

TWO-YEAR-OLDS

55 B c Bairn (USA)—Miss Cindy (Mansingh (USA)) **J. J. O'Neill**
56 B f Red Sunset—Miss Spencer (Imperial Fling (USA)) **J. J. O'Neill**

MR J. J. O'NEILL—continued

Other Owners: Mr W. Breckons, Mr J. P. Carrington, Mr M. F. Cartwright, Mr Peter Davey, Mr F. P. Graham, Mr Reg Griffin, Mr G. P. Henderson, Mrs L. Joughin, Mr John Lowthian, Mr A. A. McCluskey, Mrs Angela Norton, Mr L. Payne, Mr Walter G. Pritchard, Mr G. H. Smith.

Jockeys (NH): Mark Dwyer (w.a.), Lorcan Wyer (w.a.).

Apprentice: A Dobbin (7-12).

Conditional: F Murtagh (9-0), R J Supple (9-0).

Amateurs: Mr P Moloney (10-7), Mr S O'Sullivan (10-0).

437 MR M. J. O'NEILL, Lydiate

Postal: **Oaklea Racing Stables, 'Oaklea', Southport Road, Lydiate, Merseyside, L31 4EB.**
Phone: **(051) 5319616**

1 **ADMIRALTY WAY,** 4, b g Petorius—Captive Flower **Mr C. J. Murphy**
2 **BOBBY ON THE BANK,** 4, ch g Monsanto (FR)—Dewberry **Mr Rob Molyneux**
3 **DANRAB,** 4, b g Rabdan—Friendly Pet **Mr Lee Heaven**
4 **DARK JESTER,** 5, b g Jester—Chilcombe **Mrs S. Blane**
5 **GENERAL TROY,** 4, ro c General Ironside—Silly Twit **Mr Lee Heaven**
6 **HITCHENSTOWN,** 7, b g Town And Country—Veinarde **Oaklea Bloodstock Limited**
7 **HONEY BOY SIMBA,** 4, ch g Mansingh (USA)—Continental Divide **Roscoe Scaffolding Ltd**
8 **JOVEWORTH,** 7, gr g Monsanto (FR)—Flitterdale **Mr D. C. G. Cooper**
9 **LINKSIDE,** 5, b h Good Thyne (USA)—Laurel Wood **Linkside Fabrications**
10 **NORTHERN PRINTER,** 5, ch g Baptism—Stradey Lynn **Oaklea Bloodstock Limited**
11 **PAPAJOTO,** 5, b g Ahonoora—Papukeena **Mr D. A. Price**
12 **ROBCHRIS,** 4, b br c Dunphy—Whispering Star **Mr A. E. Hamill**
13 **RUNNING SHOT,** 9, b g Random Shot—Figdale **Mr Barry Norman**
14 **SELEUCIA,** 5, ch m Persian Bold—Cienaga **Mr A. E. Hamill**
15 **TAP DANCING,** 4, ch g Sallust—Amorak **Mr C. P. Cleary**
16 **TIEITOFF,** 5, b g Monksfield—Hypolite **T. C. Staffolding**
17 **TONGADIN,** 4, b g Petong—River Vixen **Mr G. D. J. Linder**

THREE-YEAR-OLDS

18 **FALCONS DAWN,** b g Exhibitioner—African Bloom **Mr A. Stannard**
19 **FORD KING,** b f Sandhurst Prince—Douala (GER) **Ford Asphalt**
20 **IRISH FLASHER,** b g Exhibitioner—Miss Portal **Oaklea Bloodstock Limited**
21 **ITDOESNTMATTER,** b f Saher—Debnic **Mr Barry Norman**
22 **LOMBARD FLYER,** b g Exhibitioner—Quirina (GER) **Mr Barry Norman**
23 **LOMBARD SHIPS,** ch f Orchestra—Tina's Star **L. S. F. Warehousing Limited**
24 **LOMBARD THATCH,** ch f Thatching—Molly Malone **L. S. F. Warehousing Limited**

TWO-YEAR-OLDS

25 **EL SHADDAI,** br c 7/2 Green Ruby (USA)—Miss Serlby (Runnett) **Mrs S. Blane**
26 **PRIVATE THOUGHTS,** b c 12/4 Jupiter Island—Placid Pet (Mummy's Pet) **Miss C. S. Brown**

Other Owners: Mr David Currie, Mr Ron Currie, Mr J. A. Hassall, Mr J. Heymans, A. D. Middleton, Mr A. N. Morgan, Mrs Jean Norman, Mr R. Squires, System Drive Ltd.

Jockey (NH): Michael Meagher (10-0).

Apprentices: Jimmy Fortune (7-8), Martin O'Reilly (7-13).

Conditional: Andrew Laird (9-7), Anthony Stanford (9-7).

438 MR O. O'NEILL, Cheltenham

Postal: **Cleeve Lodge, Cleeve Hill, Cheltenham, Gloucestershire, GL52 3PW.**
Phone: **(0242 67) 3275**

1 **BONNE ARME,** 9, ch g Bonne Noel—Laud **Miss J. C. Gibson**
2 **BY FAR (USA),** 4, b f Far North (CAN)—Countess Babu (USA) **Mr Hugh Ellis**
3 **CELTIC BOB,** 10, ch g Celtic Cone—Quaife Sport **Mrs Carol Cooper**
4 **CELTIC RULER,** 5, ro g Celtic Cone—Binney **Mr R. F. Denmead**
5 **CHRISTIAN SCHAD,** 8, br g Tumble Wind (USA)—Lorna Doone (USA) **Miss M. Pratten**
6 **CLOUD BASE,** 4, b g Another Realm—A-Bye
7 **ELEGANT ROSE,** 4, ch f Noalto—Shapina **Mr E. A. Badger**
8 **FARRANRORY,** 6, br m Mandalus—Caisepuca **Miss J. C. Gibson**
9 **HIGHFIRE,** 8, b g High Top—Home Fire **Mr G. Monahan**
10 **HONEY MILL,** 4, b f Milford—Sharp Venita **Mr E. A. Badger**
11 **IMPECCABLE TIMING,** 7, ch g Paddy's Stream—Wynchy Comby **Mr W. T. Robinson**
12 **JOSIE SMITH,** 6, gr m Alias Smith (USA)—Josilu **Mr Chris Scott**
13 **MODEL PUPIL,** 10, b g Tudor Music—Ballygoman Maid **Mr T. Treacy**
14 **PASHM,** 4, ch c Morston (FR)—Poshteen **Mr Hugh Ellis**
15 **PITY'S PET,** 5, b m Stanford—Irish Kick **Mr D. A. Hunt**
16 **PRECIPICE RUN,** 5, ch g Deep Run—Lothian Lassie **Kinch Bulk Haulage (Leicester) Limited**
17 **SAINT SUPREME,** 7, b g Condorcet (FR)—Princess Concorde **Mr Roger Champness**
18 **SANTOPADRE,** 8, gr g Welsh Saint—Shanty **Mrs Jill Holland**
19 **SCORPIO SAM,** 5, b g Scorpio (FR)—Copocabana **Mrs Carol Cooper**
20 **SHADY ROAD,** 8, b g Laurence O—Aprils End **Kinch Bulk Haulage (Leicester) Limited**
21 **SPECIAL VENTURE,** 9, b m Giolla Mear—Winsome Lady **Mr J. I. Roche**
22 **STEPHENS PET,** 7, ch g Piaffer (USA)—Mrs Stephens **Mrs M. A. T. Potter**
23 **STEVEYVUL,** 6, ro h Whistlefield—Persian Water **Miss H. Smith**
24 **THE BARON GREY,** 4, gr g Baron Blakeney—I-Ching **Mr E. H. Lodge**
25 **THE FARMERSKITCHEN,** 8, ch g General Ironside—Cambrian Explorer **Mr V. Hever and Partners**
26 **WOODENBRIDGE,** 7, ch g Thatch (USA)—December Blossom **Mrs Celia Murray**

THREE-YEAR-OLDS

27 **ABRIGO,** b c Aragon—Poshteen **Mr Hugh Ellis**

Other Owners: Mrs A. G. Blackman, Mr R. Brittain, Mr M. J. Brown, Mr Billy Burke, Mr P. L. Clayton, Mr R. P. Denton, Mr M. C. Fry, Mrs M. Haslum, Mr J. Jordan, Mr R. T. Macauley, Mr D. McCarthy, Mr S. McCarthy, Mr John McKenna, Mr C. B. O'Neill, Mrs L. J. O'Neill, Mr G. J. Roberts, Mr C. B. Sanderson, Mr G. Smith, Mr R. T. Wilkins, Mrs A. Rosato Yates.

Conditional: D Murray (9-7), V Slattery (9-7).

439 MR J. G. M. O'SHEA, Kidderminster

Postal: **Berkley Farm, Summerway Lane, Torton, Hartlebury, Worcestershire, DY11 7SE.**
Phone: **OFFICE (0299) 250905 HOME (0562) 823160**

1 **BIRCHGREY LADY,** 5, b m Strong Gale—Willow Hand **Gary Blunden**
2 **EYE STUNNER,** 5, b m Sayyaf—Weavers Love **D. E. Watts**
3 **GLENCOE BOY,** 7, b g Pry—Rainella **Mr D. J. Ward**
4 **GOLD 'N SOFT,** 6, br m Whistling Deer—Wine Lake **Mr Ger Foley**
5 **LOCH BRAN LASS,** 6, ch m General Ironside—Coolentallagh **T. G. K. Construction Ltd**
6 **PULLOVER,** 5, ch m Windjammer (USA)—Woolcana **Mrs Eileen Sadik**
7 **RHYTHM DANCER,** 7, b m Rarity—Party Dancer **Mr J. A. Morrison**
8 **SINGING FLAME,** 8, b g Royal Match—Pilots Row **D. E. Watts**

MR J. G. M. O'SHEA—continued

THREE-YEAR-OLDS

9 **AVRILS CHOICE,** b f Montelimar—Tack **Mr Ger Foley**
10 **BOOTON,** b f Welsh Captain—Diese Girl **Mrs Anne M. Booton**
11 **CONDOVER FLYER,** b f Krayyan—Messie **Mr J. A. Morrison**
12 **MISS EMMAJANE,** b f Dublin Taxi—Linanbless **Mrs D. E. Watts**
13 **PRINCE OF DREAMS,** ch c Gabitat—Icacos Bay **Mrs D. E. Watts**

TWO-YEAR-OLDS

14 B c 28/4 Gabitat—Icacos Bay (Martinmas) **Mrs Anne M. Booton**

Other Owners: Mr W. E. Catstrey, Mr J. A. Edge, Mr G. M. Evans, Mr Alex Nisbet, Mr S. O'Shea, Mrs P. M. B. Tandy.

Jockey (NH): D Byrne.

Conditional: S Hodgson (7-0).

440 MR R. J. O'SULLIVAN, Bognor Regis

Postal: **Sefter Lodge, Sefter Road, Rose Green, Bognor Regis, W. Sussex, P02 13EE.**
Phone: **PAGHAM (0243) 267563/263767**

1 **ARROW DANCER,** 4, b g Gorytus (USA)—Rose And Honey **Mr C. Lane**
2 **BARAOORA,** 8, gr g Bruni—Tory Island **Mr R. J. O'Sullivan**
3 **BELMOREDEAN,** 5, ch g Be My Guest (USA)—Hanna Alta (FR) **Mr J. Hartnett**
4 **BUSTED'S FANCY,** 4, b f Busted—Fancy Work **Mr M. Hickey**
5 **CUT A CAPER,** 8, b g Gay Fandango (USA)—Brilliant Gem **Mr Richard G. Brown**
6 **DREAM MERCHANT,** 8, ch g Welsh Pageant—Waladah **Mr G. A. Jones**
7 **HERON'S JAKE,** 5, gr g Humdoleila—Heron's Mirage **Mr G. A. Jones**
8 **HOMME D'AFFAIRE,** 7, br g Lord Gayle (USA)—French Cracker **Mrs Laurette R. Baerlein**
9 **INTERPLAY,** 5, ch g Be My Guest (USA)—Intermission **Mr R. J. O'Sullivan**
10 **LOOTING (USA),** 4, b br g Pirate's Bounty (USA)—Bank Examiner (USA) **Mr M. Hickey**
11 **MASNUN (USA),** 5, gr g Nureyev (USA)—Careless Kitten (USA) **Mr I. W. Page**
12 **OTTERBURN (USA),** 4, b c Raise A Man (USA)—Summertime Lady (USA) **Mr D. O. Elton**
13 **PEALLA,** 5, b g Dara Monarch—Nofertiti (FR) **Mrs Gillian Willard**
14 **RIGHT STEP (FR),** 5, ch g Noalcoholic (FR)—Right Dancer **Mr P. Chipchase**
15 **ROSE FESTIVAL,** 4, br f Ile de Bourbon (USA)—Vendemmia **Mrs J. Hickey**
16 **SCOTONI,** 4, ch g Final Straw—Damiya (FR) **Mrs Laurette R. Baerlein**
17 **SINGLE SHOOTER (USA),** 5, b g Nodouble (USA)—Irish Sister (USA) **Mr I. W. Page**
18 **SUZY LORENZO,** 5, b br m Swing Easy (USA)—Love Beach **Mr J. W. De Mestre**
19 **WINDSOR PARK (USA),** 4, br g Bold Forbes (USA)—Round Tower **Mr A. P. Caton**

TWO-YEAR-OLDS

20 **FULL OF TRICKS,** ch c Mossberry—Duchess of Hayling VII **Mr White**

Other Owners: Mr W. F. Dearan, Mr R. Ellis, Mr Bryan Fry, Mrs Cecilia Jones, Mr B. D. Morris, Mr F. O. Spanton.

Conditional: D O'Sullivan (9-12).

441 MR M. A. O'TOOLE, Kildare

Postal: **Maddenstown, Kildare, Ireland.**
Phone: **OFFICE (045) 41317 HOME (045) 41486**

1 **BENBURB,** 4, ch g Salmon Leap (USA)—Molokai **P. J. Donohoe**
2 **BISHOP'S STAFF,** 5, b g Monksfield—Knockaville **Mrs M. A. O'Toole**
3 **BRONZE HALL,** 4, b g Rusticaro (FR)—Spring Spray **J. O'Sullivan**
4 **DAIL EIREANN,** 4, ch c Ballymore—Grangemore **Mrs Joseph Keeling**
5 **DESTRIERO,** 4, b g Ile de Bourbon (USA)—Tipperary Tartan **Miss M. O'Toole**
6 **FOSBURY,** 5, b g Kambalda—Joyful Luck **Mrs M. A. O'Toole**
7 **FOURTH OF JULY,** 6, b g Rymer—Wayward Pam **Mrs Joseph Keeling**
8 **IMPOUNDED,** 6, b g Furry Glen—Mervins **Mrs M. A. O'Toole**
9 **LES PARVENUS,** 6, b g Smartset—Entry Hill **Mrs M. A. O'Toole**
10 **LIVE SHOW (USA),** 4, b g Marshua's Dancer—Star Formation (USA) **Mrs M. A. O'Toole**
11 **LOUGH GALE,** 6, br g Strong Gale—Lough Street **R. G. Hogan**
12 4, B g Monksfield—Maggie's Daughter **Mrs M. A. O'Toole**
13 **MAGIC MILLION,** 4, b g Gorytus (USA)—Beach Light **P. J. Donohoe**
14 **MANSION HOUSE,** 4, b c Thatching—El Pina **P. J. Donohoe**
15 5, Ch g Pas de Seul—Marine Life **Mrs M. A. O'Toole**
16 **MECHLIN,** 4, b f Dunphy—Margaree **Mrs M. A. O'Toole**
17 4, B g Furry Glen—Milkmaid **Mrs M. A. O'Toole**
18 **NET CALL (USA),** 4, gr f Quack (USA)—Sarcenet (USA) **Mrs M. A. O'Toole**
19 **OFFICIAL RECEPTION (USA),** 4, b g State Dinner (USA)—Petals 'n Lace **Mrs Joseph Keeling**
20 **PORTSTEWART,** 5, ch g Le Bavard (FR)—Gay Countess **Mrs M. Eastwood**
21 4, Gr g Warpath—Precipienne **Mrs M. A. O'Toole**
22 **SIMENON,** 4, b g Oats—Mirthful **P. J. Donohoe**
23 **SMOGGY SPRAY,** 6, ch g Smoggy—Spring Spray **J. O'Sullivan**
24 **SUPER TUESDAY,** 4, b g Lyphard's Special—Margery (FR) **Mrs M. A. O'Toole**
25 5, B br g Black Minstrel—Suspicious Vulvic **Mrs M. A. O'Toole**
26 **TOUCH OF WINTER,** 4, b g Strong Gale—Ballyhoura Lady **Mrs M. A. O'Toole**
27 **WHITE LINEN,** 4, ch f Nishapour (FR)—In The Clover **Mrs M. A. O'Toole**

THREE-YEAR-OLDS

28 **BOARDING SCHOOL,** b c Glenstal (USA)—Amenity (FR) **Mrs M. A. O'Toole**
29 **BOLD STARLET,** b f Precocious—Cadasi **Mrs M. A. O'Toole**
30 **CORNERED,** b g Whistling Deer—Boxted **Mrs M. A. O'Toole**
31 **EMANATION,** b c Vision (USA)—Durun **Mrs M. A. O'Toole**
32 **FIERY SPARK,** b g Red Sunset—Rathcoffey Dodd **Mrs M. A. O'Toole**
33 **HAVE A PARTY,** b c Cure The Blues (USA)—Carnival Dance **Mrs M. A. O'Toole**
34 **HEGEMONIC,** gr br g Godswalk (USA)—Tomona **Mrs M. A. O'Toole**
35 **KAFFIR ALMANAC,** b g Kafu—Flo Kelly **Mrs M. A. O'Toole**
36 **KAURI,** b c Ela-Mana-Mou—Crannog **Mrs M. A. O'Toole**
37 **MAIN ATTRACTION,** ch g What A Guest—Spring Spray **Mrs M. A. O'Toole**
38 **NO INHIBITIONS,** ch g Exhibitioner—Australite **Mrs M. A. O'Toole**
39 **ONE LAST LOOK,** br g Final Straw—One Last Glimpse **Mrs M. A. O'Toole**
40 **OUTGOING,** ch c Exhibitioner—Bombalurinaby **Mrs M. A. O'Toole**
41 **TIE THE KNOT,** ch c Shy Groom (USA)—Polifontaine (FR) **Mrs M. A. O'Toole**
42 **TROJAN STEEL,** gr c Bellypha—Troja **Mrs M. A. O'Toole**

TWO-YEAR-OLDS

43 B c 1/3 Glenstal (USA)—Aces Full (USA) (Round Table) **Mrs M. A. O'Toole**
44 B c 13/4 Alzao (USA)—Balela (African Sky) **Wafic Said**
45 Ch c 1/3 Glow (USA)—Charlotteen (Charlottown) **Mrs Elizabeth Furlong**
46 Ch c 11/5 Ballad Rock—Con Carni (Blakeney) **Mrs M. A. O'Toole**
47 **DANCING BELVOIR,** b c 22/5 Lidhame—Rosalina (Porto Bello) **Mrs M. A. O'Toole**
48 Ch f 25/4 Glow (USA)—Dismantle (Aureole) **John L. Wood**
49 Ch c 9/4 Thatching—Gitane Blue (Cure The Blues (USA)) **Mrs M. A. O'Toole**
50 B f 13/4 Kings Lake (USA)—In The Clover (Meadow Mint (USA)) **Mrs Elizabeth Furlong**
51 B c 31/5 Kings Lake (USA)—Norfolk Gal (Blakeney) **Mrs M. A. O'Toole**
52 B c 10/4 Mansingh (USA)—Parmassia (Pampered King) **Mrs M. A. O'Toole**
53 Ch f 19/4 Dominion—Sea Trial (Blakeney) **Mrs M. A. O'Toole**

MR M. A. O'TOOLE—continued

54 B c 15/4 Baillamont (USA)—Star of The Stage (Nureyev (USA)) **Mrs M. A. O'Toole**
55 Ch c 2/4 Exhibitioner—That's Easy (Swing Easy (USA)) **Mrs M. A. O'Toole**
56 B f 16/2 Trojan Fen—Tipperary Tartan (Rarity) **Mrs M. A. O'Toole**
57 Ch f 21/5 Superlative—Velvet Pigeon (Homing) **Mrs M. A. O'Toole**

Other Owners: Mrs D. M. Donohoe, Mrs G. Houlihan, W. McDonald, Mrs M. O'Sullivan, J. Turley.

Jockey (Flat): D Gillespie (8-0).

Jockeys (NH): J W Cullen (9-9), F O'Connor, P Ryan (9-7).

Apprentices: M Kelly (7-0), M Ryan (7-0).

Amateurs: Mr J R Banahan, Mr T M Walsh.

442 MR J. A. B. OLD, Shepton Mallet

Postal: **Heighes House, Ditcheat, Shepton Mallet, Somerset.**
Phone: **(0749) 86656 CAR (0836) 721459**

1 **AND THERES MORE,** 8, b g Le Bavard (FR)—Judiths Treasure **Hunt & Co (Bournemouth) Ltd**
2 **ARISTOS,** 6, b g Derring Rose—Forest Fun **A. J. & R. G. Barber Ltd**
3 **BARGE BOY,** 6, b g Jimsun—Barge Mistress **Mr C. P. House**
4 **CASTLEBAY LAD,** 7, br g Crozier—Carbery Star **Spaceage Plastics Limited**
5 **CATHOS (FR),** 5, b g Bellman (FR)—Charming Doll **Mr W. E. Sturt**
6 **CHATTY CORNER,** 6, ch m Le Bavard (FR)—Whisht Lassie **Mr Nigel Dempster**
7 **CHESHIRE COVE,** 7, ch g Belfalas—Fairy **Mr Peter J. White**
8 **CIMA,** 12, br g High Top—Lemon Blossom **Mr J. A. B. Old**
9 **COUNTRY DAMSEL,** 6, b m Town And Country—Dusky Damsel **Mr Richard Barber**
10 **CRISP NOTE,** 6, ch g Kris—Airgead Beo **Mr Mike Cornish**
11 **DROMINA STAR,** 9, b br g Pauper—Kitty The Hare **Mr Paul K. Barber**
12 **HASTY DIVER,** 9, ch g Crash Course—Tara Babu **Mr K. R. Britten**
13 **MOLE BOARD,** 8, br g Deep Run—Sharpaway **Mr W. E. Sturt**
14 **MON REGRET,** 5, ch g Record Token—Charlotte's Image **Mr N. H. S. New**
15 **MOSSAL BAY,** 9, ch g Goldhill—Kortisso **Mr J. A. B. Old**
16 **MY PURPLE PROSE,** 9, b m Rymer—Lady Marcia **Mr Nigel Dempster**
17 **PLASTIC SPACEAGE,** 7, b g The Parson—Chestnut Fire **Spaceage Plastics Limited**
18 **POSTLEBURY,** 7, ch g New Member—Barge Mistress **Mr C. P. House**
19 **REHAB VENTURE,** 6, ch g Deep Run—Hansel's Princess **Mr P. R. E. Venn**
20 **ROBUSTI,** 8, ch g Bustino—Juliette Marny **Mr P. J. Carter**
21 **SAND-DOLLAR,** 7, ch h Persian Bold—Late Spring **Mr R. P. Fry**
22 **SANDWALK,** 5, ch g Sandalay—Beach Walk
23 **SHANNAGARY,** 9, ch g Deep Run—Farranfore **Hunt & Co (Bournemouth) Ltd**
24 **SIMPSON,** 5, ch g Royal Match—Black Penny **Mr K. R. Britten**
25 **SNOWY AUTUMN,** 6, ch m Deep Run—Autumn Queen **Mr D. C. Sharpe**
26 **SUPER JULES (FR),** 5, ch g Trio (FR)—Silver Plate (FR) **Mr Derek Petrie**
27 **TUFF STICK,** 5, b g Welsh Saint—Corr Lady **Mr J. M. Sage**
28 **WHISTLE FOR FRY,** 7, b g Whistlefield—Injudicious **Mr R. P. Fry**
29 **WICK POUND,** 4, b c Niniski (USA)—Hors Serie (USA) **Mr K. R. Britten**

MR J. A. B. OLD—continued

Other Owners: Mr Nazar Abdulla, Mr R. Blumberg, Cheshire Paper Sales Ltd, Mr J. M. Connolly, Mr Stephen Freud, Mr M. S. Jarvis, Mr B. J. Jones, Mr C. Mackenzie, Mr D. S. Mahany, Mr George Murray, Mr C. M. Phillimore, Mr D. W. Redpath, Mr J. S. B. White.

Jockeys (NH): C Llewellyn (10-0, w.a.), S McNeill (10-0, w.a.).

Apprentice: D Kent (7-10).

Conditional: P W Davies (9-7).

Amateur: G Densley (10-7).

443 MR J. K. M. OLIVER, Hawick

Postal: **Hassendean Bank, Hawick, Roxburghshire, Scotland, TD9 8RX.**
Phone: **(0450) 87216**

1 **ABDICATOR,** 10, ch g Levanter—Saffron Princess **Colonel D. C. Greig**
2 **ABERCROMBY CHIEF,** 5, br g Buckskin (FR)—Free For Ever **Abercromby Corporation**
3 **ABERCROMBY COMET,** 5, br g Strong Gale—Star-Pit
4 **BACK BEFORE DARK,** 6, b g Silly Prices—Willow Path **Partnership**
5 **BANTEL BUCCANEER,** 8, b g Jellaby—Highview Jill **Mr Barry L. Brandon**
6 **BELON BRIG,** 9, b m New Brig—Oyster Eye **Mrs D. A. Coltman**
7 **BOLD SPARTAN,** 7, b g Bold Owl—Spartan's Girl **Mr R. M. Kirkland**
8 **BOTHAM,** 10, ch g Deep Run—Ballyowen **Mr J. A. Price**
9 **BOYSTEROUS BOY,** 6, br g Balinger—Oyster Eye **Mrs M. Graham**
10 **CHARLOTTE'S OLIVER,** 5, b g Tumble Gold—Candy Belle **Mr W. R. Woods**
11 **CORSTON BLAZE,** 6, ch g Vitiges (FR)—Corston Lass **Mr A. S. Lyburn**
12 **HIGH EDGE GREY,** 9, gr ro g Precipice Wood—China Bank **Mr J. B. Stone**
13 **INTARSIA,** 6, b g Smartset—London Fancy **Mr J. N. Hinchliffe**
14 **IRON PRINCE,** 4, gr g General Ironside—Pry Princess **Mrs J. B. Stone**
15 **MAJESTIC RIDE,** 6, b g Palm Track—Lakeland Lady **Mr T. J. Summerfield**
16 **MARLEFIELD,** 8, ch g Le Bavard (FR)—Ballyowen **Mr W. Stuart Wilson**
17 **MOIETY,** 5, gr g General Ironside—Pry's Delight **Mrs S. M. Robinson**
18 **POLLIBRIG,** 6, br m Politico (USA)—Taras Brig **Mr A. Goram**
19 **QUARNDON,** 5, ch g Deep Run—Dame Lucy **Mr R. M. Kirkland**
20 **RED DUSK,** 6, ch m Deep Run—Bannow Bay **Mrs A. Maiden**
21 **SAINTLY PATH,** 7, ch g Deep Run—Shuil Le Dia **Guiderise Ltd**
22 **SILLY JUDGE,** 7, b g Silly Prices—Rookery Judge **Mr R. M. Kirkland**
23 **TRAPRAIN LAW,** 7, b g Politico (USA)—Pops Girl **Mr J. Stephenson**

Other Owners: Mr J. T. Duxbury, Miss L. M. Gold, Mrs Sybil Howe, Mr S. M. Jepson, Miss M. Lane, Mr J. K. M. Oliver, Mr R. Campbell Pearson, Mr C. J. Price, Mrs P. H. Wilkins, Mr W. Wishart.

Jockey (NH): T Reed (10-5).

Conditional: G Thomson (9-7).

444 MR M. OLIVER, Droitwich

Postal: **New House Farm, Elmley Lovett, Droitwich, Worcestershire.**
Phone: **HARTLEBURY (0299) 250500 OR (0299) 250159**

1 **BORDER LAD,** 9, b g Rymer—Solgift **Mr R. C. F. Faiers**
2 **CADDLESTOWN,** 6, b br g Derring Rose—Quick Romance **Mr Michael Oliver**
3 **CALLOPE (USA),** 6, b m Recitation (USA)—Caramba (FR) **Robert Reynolds (Commercials) Ltd**
4 **CHUFFBUTTONS,** 6, ch g Buckskin (FR)—Georgette **Mr R. C. F. Faiers**
5 **ELITE BOY,** 8, ch g Deep Run—Elite Lady **Mrs C. J. Black**
6 **GATTERSTOWN,** 7, ch g Over The River (FR)—Larkins Mills **Mr Peter Luff**
7 **HAROLD MICHEL,** 6, br g Slippered—I'm A Buck **Mr Peter Luff**
8 4, Ch g Le Moss—Hogan's Cherry **Mr M. E. Oliver**
9 4, Ch g Torus—Honey Roast **Mr F. H. Parkes**
10 **MOORSTOWN RAMBLER,** 7, ch g Push On—Miss Moorstown **Mr Phillip Hughes**
11 **MR DIBBS,** 9, ch g Random Shot—Hopestown **Mr Patrick Bancroft**
12 **ONEFACE,** 6, b m General Ironside—Green Face **Mr Jack Harbutt**
13 **PEA SAL,** 7, b g Peacock (FR)—Fighting Sal **Mr D. J. Ward**
14 4, B g Quayside—Ragadoon **Mr F. H. Parkes**
15 **REDMARLEY,** 8, ch g Malinowski (USA)—Meadow Rhapsody **Mrs Ernest Weinstein**
16 **SAPELLO,** 4, gr f General Ironside—Topeka **P. Luff**
17 **SILVER PALE,** 9, ch g Carnival Night—Doon Mist **Mr P. Scammell**
18 **STOP TWO,** 6, b g Buckskin (FR)—Natanya **Mr D. Mills**
19 **TANTALITE,** 5, b br m Tanfirion—Capricorn Lady **Mr Martin Oliver**
20 **TELE CALL LADY,** 6, b m The Parson—Noctiluca (FR) **Mrs S. Sharpstone**
21 **THE BEAR LOVER,** 8, br g Random Shot—Miss Mouri **Mr R. C. F. Faiers**
22 **WAYCROSS,** 5, ch g Deep Run—Topeka **Mr Peter Luff**
23 **WEST TIP,** 13, b g Gala Performance (USA)—Astryl **Mr Peter Luff**
24 **WHAT A WALLY,** 8, gr g General Ironside—Saint Malva **Mr R. C. F. Faiers**

Other Owners: Mr R. Baylis, Mr A. J. Brazier, Mr John Duggan, Mrs Michael Oliver, Mr C. H. Rillstone.

Jockey (NH): J Railton.

Amateur: Mr M Harris.

445 MRS S. OLIVER, Wombourne

Postal: **The Demesne, Himley Park Stables, Stourbridge Road, Wombourne, Staffordshire, CV5 0SN.**
Phone: **WOMBOURNE (0902) 892017 OR 892648**

1 **ALAOUI,** 8, ch g Al Sirat (USA)—Sunny Sunset **Mr E. Lloyd Lewis**
2 **ARCTIC WOLF,** 5, gr h Belfort (FR)—Shahnavaz **Mrs L. E. Pyne**
3 **BOLSHOI BOY,** 6, ch g Proverb—Cherrywood **P. R. D. Fasteners Ltd**
4 **BUCKMILLER,** 4, b c Gorytus (USA)—Bandit Queen (FR) **W. G. Ash Ltd**
5 **FEARLESS KING,** 4, b g Kings Lake (USA)—Intrepid Lady (USA) **Mr Peter Gormley**
6 **FOREST NYMPH (NZ),** 5, b m Oak Ridge (FR)—Lively Lass (NZ) **Henry Oliver**
7 **FORWARD MARCH (NZ),** 8, b g March Legend (NZ)—Naughty Marie (NZ) **Mrs J. M. Stennett**
8 **GENEROUS SCOT,** 6, b g Rarity—Galloping Santa **Mr T. N. Siviter**
9 **HEIGHT O'BATTLE,** 4, b c Shirley Heights—Light O'Battle **Mrs Johanna Shone**
10 **NOEL LUCK,** 10, ch g Deep Run—Monavalla **Mr Peter Gormley**
11 **RONANS BIRTHDAY,** 8, b g Furry Glen—Mountain Sedge **Breener Fabrications & Reinforcement Ltd**
12 **RYMOLBREESE,** 5, gr m Rymer—Moll **Breener Fabrications & Reinforcement Ltd**
13 **SHU FLY (NZ),** 6, ch g Tom's Shu (USA)—Alycone (NZ) **Severn Second Partnership**

MRS S. OLIVER—continued

THREE-YEAR-OLDS

14 B g Strong Gale—Milan United **Henry Oliver**
15 B g Le Moss—Santimwen **Mr T. N. Siviter**

Other Owners: Mr Tony Ash, Mrs H. Blunt, Mrs S. M. Braziek, Mr Adrian Harbord, Mr Steven Jones, Mr Martin Legge, Mr N. D. Mardell, Mr Elwyn Morse, Mr Martin Owen, Mr M. K. Penny, Mr A. Stennet, Mr C. J. A. Stennett, Mr Stephen Symonds, Mrs J. A. Taylor, Mrs Anita Trowbridge.

Jockey (Flat): J Williams (8-2).

Jockey (NH): R Hyett (10-2).

Conditional: W Hayes (8-0).

Lady Rider: Mrs J Hayes (9-7).

446 MR E. H. OWEN, Denbigh

Postal: **Y Wern, Llandyrnog, Denbigh, Clwyd, Wales.**
Phone: **LLANDYRNOG (08244) 264**

1 ACCESSOFHORNCHURCH, 4, ch g Coquelin (USA)—The Saltings (FR) **Mr A. Bailey**
2 BLACK ROCK, 5, br m Rymer—Gadabout **Mr John A. Owen**
3 CHIEF'S CHOICE, 5, b g Coquelin (USA)—Douschkina **Mr J. L. Beckwith**
4 DICKIE'S LADY, 4, b f Le Bavard (FR)—Gigondas **Mrs H. F. Richards**
5 GRAYROSE DOUBLE, 7, b m Celtic Cone—Mangro **Dr G. M. Thelwall Jones**
6 IORWERTH, 4, b c Rymer—Wicker Basket **Mrs W. B. Higgin**
7 PALMER'S GOLD, 9, b g Palm Track—Golden Pinelopi **Mr P. J. Rothery**
8 PURPLE SILK, 6, b m Belfalas—Lucky Money **Mrs Elizabeth Owen**

THREE-YEAR-OLDS

9 ARBITRAGEUR, b c Ile de Bourbon (USA)—Jenny Diver (USA) **Mr R. S. G. Jones**
10 GINGER'S GONE, b f Ginger Brink (FR)—Away And Gone **Mr R. S. G. Jones**

TWO-YEAR-OLDS

11 BLIMPERS, gr c 31/5 Alias Smith (USA)—Melton Grange (Song) **Echoline Ltd**
12 FALLEN ANGEL, b f 17/4 Scottish Reel—Autumn Gift (Martinmas) **Mr R. S. G. Jones**
13 MANIBEN, b f 22/3 Grey Desire—Comedy Miss (Comedy Star (USA)) **Echoline Ltd**
14 B f 24/3 Domynsky—May Kells (Artaius (USA)) **Mr R. S. G. Jones**
15 B c 10/5 Scorpio (FR)—Rosie Tudor (Tudor Treasure) **D. G. Scott**
16 B c 7/5 Ballad Rock—The Way She Moves (North Stoke) **Mr R. S. G. Jones**

Other Owners: N. S. H. Virani.

Jockey (NH): D J Burchell (9-10).

Conditional: D Skyrme (9-7).

447 MR J. M. OXX, Currabeg

Postal: **Creeve, Currabeg, Kildare, Ireland.**
Phone: **KILDARE (045) 21310 TELEX 60905 (OXX E1) FAX (045) 22236**

1 **CALEVA,** 4, b f Ahonoora—Madelon **Miss E. B. C. Laidlaw**
2 **ENTHUSIASTIC,** 4, b c Ela-Mana-Mou—Gruntled **Mrs P. A. Love**
3 **EUROBUS,** 4, b c Sadler's Wells—Sorbus **G. W. Jennings**
4 **TOKYO ROSE,** 4, br f Krayyan—Crecora **Dundalk Racing Club**

THREE-YEAR-OLDS

5 **ADARAK,** b c Top Ville—Adariysa **H. H. Aga Khan**
6 **AGAINST YOU,** b g Auction Ring—Saranita **Hon R. Hesketh**
7 **ANNE DE BEAUJEU,** gr f Ahonoora—Honey Buzzard **M. E. Parrish**
8 **AUCALE (USA),** gr f Nijinsky—Lady's Slipper **Sheikh Mohammed**
9 **BAKHTARAN,** b c Mouktar—Badalushka **H. H. Aga Khan**
10 **BALADIYA,** b f Darshaan—Bayazida **H. H. Aga Khan**
11 **BEN ALISKY,** ch c Dunbeath—Oh So Sharp **Sheikh Mohammed**
12 **BLACKDOWN,** b c Rainbow Quest—Cider Princess **Sheikh Mohammed**
13 **CANDY'S LION,** b c Shernazar—What A Candy **J. F. Malle**
14 **CARIBBEAN DAWN (USA),** b c Majestic Light—Islands **Sheikh Mohammed**
15 **CASTOR (USA),** b c Hostage—Likely Double **Sheikh Mohammed**
16 **CHIRKPAR,** b c Shernazar—Callianire **H. H. Aga Khan**
17 **CLASSICAL BALLET,** b c Shareef Dancer—Musique Classique **Sheikh Mohammed**
18 **CROWN ROSE,** b f Dara Monarch—Darling Bud **Mrs M. Beaumont**
19 **DEAR AND NEAR,** ch f Ahonoora—Dellear (FR) **J. L. Mamakos**
20 **FABLIAU (USA),** b f Slew O'Gold—Ancient Fables **Sheikh Mohammed**
21 **FANTASTIC FLYER,** b c Ela-Mana-Mou—Protasis (USA) **Frank Lynch**
22 **GALA DANSANT (USA),** b f Shadeed—Mild Deception **M. J. W. Ryan**
23 **GERTRUDES DAUGHTER,** b f Niniski—Gertrude Lawrence **Mrs J. R. Mullion**
24 **GLASS BLOWER,** b g Shareef Dancer—Glasson Lady **Sheikh Mohammed**
25 **HAROUNIYA,** gr br f Siberian Express—Hazy Idea **H. H. Aga Khan**
26 B f Fairy King—Hyperborei **P. F. McManus**
27 **IONE (USA),** ch f Diesis—Mythilene **Sheikh Mohammed**
28 **ISABEAU,** b f Law Society—Elodie **M. E. Parrish**
29 **JACKIE'S WISH,** b f Fairy King—Clifden Bottoms **Mrs M. Togher**
30 **JANE DOE,** ch f The Noble Player (USA)—Kimangao **Mrs B. M. McCourt**
31 **KAUSAR (USA),** b c Vaguely Noble—Kozana **H. H. Aga Khan**
32 **KEMIRIAN,** b c Habitat—Kermiya **H. H. Aga Khan**
33 **KHALAFIYA,** b f Darshaan—Khalisiyn **H. H. Aga Khan**
34 **LAW TERM,** b c Law Society—Tranchard **Sheikh Mohammed**
35 **LOCAL TRIBE,** b c Local Suitor—Iceni Star **Sheikh Mohammed**
36 **MARIE DE SOLOGNE,** b f Lashkari—Marie de Solesmes **M. E. Parrish**
37 **MARWAZI,** gr c Darshaan—Modiyna **H. H. Aga Khan**
38 **MITSUBISHI FAX,** b f King of Clubs—Diamond Land **Dundalk Racing Club**
39 **MY POTTERS (USA),** br f Irish River—My Bupers **Lady Clague**
40 **NIGHT SAILING (USA),** ch c Riverman—Lunar Destiny **Sheikh Mohammed**
41 **OLD DOWNIE,** ch f Be My Guest—Rising Tide **Simon Fraser**
42 **PARTING HOUR,** b c Top Ville—Cri de Coeur **Sheikh Mohammed**
43 **PETRASHAR,** b c Petorius—Loushara (FR) **Mrs K. Bredin**
44 **POOLMAN-IA,** br f Koenigsstuhl (GER)—Olivana **Montrose Racing Club**
45 **RAYSIYA,** ch f Cure The Blues—Rilasa **H. H. Aga Khan**
46 **REQUESTED,** b c Rainbow Quest—Melody Hour **Sheikh Mohammed**
47 **ROCK SUPREME,** b c Ballad Rock—Salus **B. Kearney**
48 **ROSATI (USA),** gr f Caro—Satilla **Sheikh Mohammed**
49 **SANAMIA,** b f Top Ville—Santalina **H. H. Aga Khan**
50 **SARATOGA WORLD,** b f Saratoga Six—Go March **Miss Makiko Kuroiwa**
51 **SAYMARI,** b c Mouktar—Sellasia **H. H. Aga Khan**
52 **SEA FOWL,** b f Salmon Leap (USA)—Sea Swallow (USA) **J. Cojuangco Jr**
53 **SELERET (USA),** b f Lear Fan—Shahneez **H. H. Aga Khan**
54 **SHILSILA,** b f Darshaan—Shahdiza **H. H. Aga Khan**
55 **SHIYRA,** b br f Darshaan—Sharya **H. H. Aga Khan**

MR J. M. OXX—continued

56 **SPY SCHOOL (USA),** gr c Green Dancer—Head Spy **Sheikh Mohammed**
57 **SUNNY DAYS,** b f Seattle Slew—So Fine **Sheikh Mohammed**
58 **TANGARA LADY (USA),** b f Sovereign Dancer—Dance Hall Girl **Sheikh Mohammed**
59 **TEL E THON,** b c Ela-Mana-Mou—Costa Rossa (ITY) **T. Keena**
60 **THETFORD FOREST,** b c Blakeney—Leylandia **Sheikh Mohammed**
61 **VATERSAY (USA),** ch f Far North—Salish **Sheikh Mohammed**
62 **VENTUARI,** ch c Simply Great—Parima **Sheikh Mohammed**
63 **YASA,** gr f Indian King—Contrail **Miss E. B. C. Laidlaw**
64 **ZELDEYNN,** br c Lightning—Zelda **M. Clifford**

TWO-YEAR-OLDS

65 Br f 7/4 Akarad—Adariysa (Shirley Heights) **H. H. Aga Khan**
66 Gr c 3/6 Nishapour (FR)—Afkaza (Labus (FR)) **H. H. Aga Khan**
67 **ARABIAN BIRD (IRE),** b f 13/3 Sure Blade (USA)—Arab Heritage (Great Nephew) **Sheikh Mohammed**
68 **ARBELA (IRE),** b f 10/3 Persian Bold—Callixena (Kalamoun) **Miss E. B. C. Laidlaw**
69 **ATHCLARE (IRE),** ch c 2/3 Glow (USA)—Athry (Be Friendly) **Sheikh Mohammed**
70 B c 9/3 Kings Lake (USA)—Badalushka (Rex Magna (FR)) **H. H. Aga Khan**
71 B f 14/3 Caerleon (USA)—Bayazida (Bustino) **H. H. Aga Khan**
72 B f 20/4 Danzig (USA)—Belle Pensee (USA) (Ribot) **G. W. Jennings**
73 **BLAZE OF MAJESTY (USA),** b c 4/3 Majestic Light (USA)—
Uncommitted (USA) (Buckpasser) **Sheikh Mohammed**
74 **BLUE DAISY (USA),** gr f 15/3 Shahrastani (USA)—
Bleu Angel's Image (USA) (Ruritania (USA)) **Sheikh Mohammed**
75 **BLUSH RAMBLER (IRE),** ch f 28/2 Blushing Groom (FR)—Nikitina (Nijinsky (CAN)) **R. More O'Ferrall**
76 B br c 28/4 Mouktar—Callianire (Sir Gaylord) **H. H. Aga Khan**
77 B c 21/4 Dalsaan—Chishtiya (Try My Best (USA)) **H. H. Aga Khan**
78 Ch f 13/5 Nijinsky (CAN)—Continuation (USA) (Forli (ARG)) **G. W. Jennings**
79 **COOPERS SPOT ON,** b c 28/2 Glenstal—Shikari Rose (Kala Shikari) **M. Fitzgibbon**
80 **DANTE'S VIEW,** ch c 10/2 Cox's Ridge (USA)—Only Star (USA) (Nureyev (USA)) **Sheikh Mohammed**
81 **DISGUISED (USA),** ch f 10/3 Vaguely Noble—Sister Sal (USA) (Delta Judge) **M. Clifford**
82 **DUHARRA (IRE),** ch c 19/4 Flash of Steel—Mrs Walmsley (Lorenzaccio) **Mrs M. Togher**
83 **EAGLE ROCK (USA),** b c 28/4 Green Dancer (USA)—
Village Jazz (USA) (Stage Door Johnny (USA)) **Sheikh Mohammed**
84 **EILEEN JENNY (IRE),** ch f 9/3 Kris—Sorbus (Busted) **G. W. Jennings**
85 **FLASH CARD,** ch f 21/4 Flash of Steel—Malossol (Gulf Pearl) **Sheikh Mohammed**
86 B f 26/4 Pennine Walk—For Your Eyes (Gay Fandango) **Miss Marie Gibbs**
87 Gr c 12/4 Flash of Steel—Gay Nocturne (Lord Gayle (USA)) **Lady Clague**
88 **GEORGE AUGUSTUS (USA),** b c 28/5 El Gran Senor (USA)—
Surely Georgie's (USA) (Alleged (USA)) **Sheikh Mohammed**
89 Ch f 29/1 Lomond (USA)—Gold And Purple (Golden Fleece (USA)) **M. E. Parrish**
90 **HASHAR (IRE),** b c 8/5 Darshaan—Hazy Idea (Hethersett) **H. H. Aga Khan**
91 B f 17/6 Darshaan—Hurry Down (High Line) **H. H. Aga Khan**
92 **ISLE OF GLASS (USA),** b f 2/2 Affirmed (USA)—Liffey Lass (USA) (Irish River (FR)) **Sheikh Mohammed**
93 **KABASHAN (IRE),** b br c 25/4 Dalsaan—Kabbaala (Brigadier Gerard) **H. H. Aga Khan**
94 B c 28/3 Dalsaan—Karayasha (Posse (USA)) **H. H. Aga Khan**
95 **KHAZARI (USA),** ch c 6/3 Shahrastani (USA)—Kozana (Kris) **H. H. Aga Khan**
96 **KOTI,** b f 24/3 Shardari—Kottna (USA) (Lyphard (USA)) **Sheikh Mohammed**
97 **LYNCH LAW (IRE),** b c 5/2 Law Society (USA)—Hogan's Sister (USA) (Speak John) **Sheikh Mohammed**
98 **LYNDONVILLE (IRE),** b f 16/5 Top Ville—Diamond Land (Sparkler) **Sheikh Mohammed**
99 **MARAMOURESH (IRE),** b c 15/4 Lashkari—Modiyna (Nishapour (FR)) **H. H. Aga Khan**
100 **MELTING ICE,** b f 2/2 Sure Blade (USA)—Sledge (Young Generation) **Sheikh Mohammed**
101 B f 22/3 Saint Estephe—Miknasa (Hot Grove) **H. H. Aga Khan**
102 **MISTFLOWER (USA),** b f 19/2 Alleged (USA)—Swoonmist (USA) (Never Bend) **Sheikh Mohammed**
103 **MONCHITCH (IRE),** b f 18/4 Montelimar (USA)—Safe Haven (Blakeney) **Miss Makiko Kuroiwa**
104 **REDCLYFFE (USA),** b c 3/4 Secreto (USA)—Regal Heiress (English Prince) **Sheikh Mohammed**
105 **REED BUCK (IRE),** b c 23/3 Thatching—Fleur de Lyphard (USA) (Lyphard) **Sheikh Mohammed**
106 B c 8/5 Darshaan—Rosy Moon (FR) (Sheshoon) **H. H. Aga Khan**
107 **SEME DE LYS (USA),** b f 4/2 Slew O'Gold (USA)—Blazon (USA) (Ack Ack (USA)) **Sheikh Mohammed**
108 B f 2/6 Vayrann—Shahdiza (Blushing Groom) **H. H. Aga Khan**
109 B gr f 12/5 Shareef Dancer (USA)—Shaiyneen (Kalamoun) **H. H. Aga Khan**

MR J. M. OXX—continued

110 B f 17/3 Dom Racine (FR)—Sharya (FR) (Lord Gayle (USA)) **H. H. Aga Khan**
111 SHOOSKA (USA), ch f 18/3 Storm Bird (CAN)—Raise A Ten (USA) (Raise A Native) **Sheikh Mohammed**
112 SIMPLY CANDY (IRE), b f 26/3 Simply Great (FR)—What A Candy (Round Table) **J. F. Malle**
113 B c 30/4 Secreto (USA)—Staunch Lady (USA) (Staunchness) **Sheikh Mohammed**
114 SUNSET VILLAGE (USA), gr f 25/3 Spectacular Bid (USA)—
Quickening Dawn (USA) (To The Quick (USA)) **Sheikh Mohammed**
115 TAUNTING (IRE), b c 23/2 Taufan (USA)—Dancing Decoy (Troy) **Sheikh Mohammed**
116 B c 14/3 Devil's Bag (USA)—Tennis Partner (USA) (Northern Dancer) **Sheikh Mohammed**
117 THORNBERRY (USA), b c 9/4 Diesis—Oxslip (Owen Dudley) **Sheikh Mohammed**
118 B br f 16/1 Shahrastani (USA)—Tikarna (FR) (Targowice) **H. H. Aga Khan**
119 VITSA (USA), b f 9/4 Diesis—Gypsy Talk (USA) (Alleged) **Sheikh Mohammed**
120 B f 3/2 Glow (USA)—Welsh Dancer (Welsh Saint) **Lady Clague**
121 B f 26/4 Ela-Mana-Mou—Yankee Lady (Lord Gayle) **P. Caiani**

Jockeys (Flat): D Hogan (8-1), Ron Quinton (8-2).

Apprentices: K Maher (7-12), J Murtagh (7-9), D O'Shea (7-0).

448 MR R. PAISLEY, Langholm

Postal: **Hallcrofts, Langholm, Dumfriesshire, Scotland.**
Phone: **(03873) HOUSE 80698 OFFICE 80308**

1 **BRUFF ACADEMY,** 9, b br g Crash Course—My Dayan **Mr R. Paisley**
2 **COOL BREW,** 12, b g Menelek—Maximum Bonus **Mr R. Paisley**
3 **TAVERN TIME,** 9, br g Pitpan—My Copper **Mr R. Paisley**

449 MR BRYN PALLING, Cowbridge

Postal: **Ty-With Farm, Ystradowen, Cowbridge, South Glamorgan, Wales.**
Phone: **COWBRIDGE (044 63) 2089**

1 **BIRCHGROVE CENTRAL,** 6, b g Free State—Grand Central **Mr T. H. Stuart**
2 **BRYMA,** 10, b br g Rymer—Saucy Walk **Mrs M. M. Palling**
3 **CONCERT PITCH,** 11, ch g Royal Match—Ballychord (DEN) **Bryn Palling Limited**
4 **HANNAH'S SECRET,** 4, ch f Starch Reduced—Lana's Secret **Mr K. L. Merriman**
5 **KINGFISHER BAY,** 5, b g Try My Best (USA)—Damiya (FR) **Mr D. Chilcott**
6 **LITTLE BRYMA,** 8, b g Rymer—Saucy Walk **Mrs M. M. Palling**
7 **MISS PATDONNA,** 4, b f Starch Reduced—Karousa Girl **Mr S. D. Williams**
8 **MY LIZZIE,** 4, br f Starch Reduced—Darlinski **Mr J. Hamilton-Jones**
9 **PRINCE'S DRIVE,** 12, b g Sovereign Path—Fille de Fizz **Mr Brian Manning**
10 **RICKESTON LAD,** 7, b g Piaffer (USA)—Jolly Smooth **Mr James F. Knowles**
11 **SILVER STRINGS,** 10, b g Blakeney—Melody Hour **Bryn Palling Limited**
12 **WILLIE MCGARR (USA),** 5, ch g Master Willie—Pay T V (USA) **Mr P. Jones (Bridgend)**

THREE-YEAR-OLDS

13 **ATLANTIC CLEAR,** b c Starch Reduced—Kathy King **Mr D. Egan**
14 **STARCHY BELLE,** b f Starch Reduced—Ty-With-Belle **Mrs M. M. Palling**
15 **TASHANITZA,** b f Starch Reduced—Mrs Dumbfounded **Mr D. Egan**

MR BRYN PALLING—continued

TWO-YEAR-OLDS

16 B c 28/4 Anita's Prince—Clodianus (Bay Express) **Mr Harry Barnbrook**
17 B c 25/2 Green Ruby (USA)—Habitab (Sovereign Path) **Mr K. L. Merriman**
18 B c 8/3 Starch Reduced—Karousa Girl (Rouser) **Mr R. Edwards and Mr S. D. Williams**
19 B c 8/4 Starch Reduced—Kathy King (Space King)
20 B f 18/5 Nishapour (FR)—La Pythie (FR) (Filiberto) **D. T. Williams**
21 B f 17/5 Another Realm—Meadow Wood (Meadow Court) **Mr James F. Knowles**
22 B f 7/4 Nicholas Bill—Ozra (Red Alert) **Mr James F. Knowles**
23 **PLYNLIMON,** b c 11/4 Starch Reduced—Joie de Galles (Welsh Pageant) **Mrs J. A. P. Hamilton Jones**
24 B f 14/5 Sacrilege—Tender Manx (Owen Dudley) **Bryn Palling Limited**
25 **WATWICK BAY,** b c 12/5 Green Ruby (USA)—Jolly Smooth (Jolly Jet) **Mr James F. Knowles**

Other Owners: Mr G. Henderson, Mr D. M. Price.

Jockey (NH): C Evans (10-0).

Conditional: D C Rees (9-7).

Amateur: Mrs Katherine M Christopher.

450 MR J. PARFITT, Rhymney

Postal: **Swn-yr-Afon, Rhymney Bridge, Rhymney, Gwent, Wales.**
Phone: **STABLE OFFICE (0685) 841715 HOME 840137 BUSINESS OFFICE 840329**

1 **BOB-CAM,** 6, ch g Scallywag—Stolen Girl **Mr J. Parfitt**
2 **BOLD IMPRESSION,** 9, b g Random Shot—Jeanette Marie **Mr J. Parfitt**
3 **EGGINGTON,** 12, ch g Baragoi—Primeapple **Mr J. Parfitt**
4 **GAVENNY GIRL,** 5, b m Rustingo—Stiperstones **Mr J. Parfitt**
5 **PHOEBE MERYLL,** 4, br f Marching On—Mistress Meryll **Mr J. Parfitt**
6 **TARVILLE,** 12, b g Woodville II—Stella's Art **Mr J. Parfitt**

451 MR C. PARKER, Lockerbie

Postal: **Douglas Hall Farm, Lockerbie, Dumfries, Scotland.**
Phone: **KETTLEHOLM (05765) 232**

1 **BRABINER KING,** 5, ch g Posse (USA)—High Finale **Mr S. Hartley**
2 **BRANDY HAMBRO,** 9, b g Hot Brandy—Ice Bird **Mr Raymond Anderson Green**
3 **BROKEN BRAE,** 6, b g Silly Prices—Penny Pink **Mr Raymond Anderson Green**
4 **FAIR ECHO,** 10, b m Quality Fair—Early Echo **Mr Chilton Fawcett**
5 **GREEN SPUR,** 8, b g Status Seeker—Arctic Goose **Mr Raymond Anderson Green**
6 **JOLI EXCITING,** 5, b m Tepukei—Merry Leap **Mr James R. Adam**
7 **KING SPRING,** 5, br g Royal Fountain—K-King **Mrs D. B. Johnstone**
8 **KUSHBALOO,** 5, b h Kambalda—Cushla **Mr Raymond Anderson Green**
9 **LUPY MINSTREL,** 5, br h Black Minstrel—Lupreno **Mr Raymond Anderson Green**
10 **MADJDEC,** 8, b g Roscoe Blake—Chukka **Mr A. F. Stewart**
11 **MAGWOOD,** 10, b g Precipice Wood—Big Maggie **Mr Raymond Anderson Green**
12 **PLENARY,** 7, b g Proverb—Sinarga **Mr S. Hartley**
13 **TODDLIN HAME,** 8, br g Bronze Hill—Pandorana **Mr D. P. Gourlay**
14 **TOWER STEPS,** 5, b g Tower Walk—Rosia Steps **Mr A. R. Bell**
15 **VIKING ROCKET,** 6, ch m Viking (USA)—Calcine **Mr Raymond Anderson Green**

Other Owners: Mr C. Parker.

Apprentice: D Dobson.

Conditional: A Parker (10-0).

452 MR J. E. PARKES, Malton

Postal: **12 Whitewall Cottages, Norton, Malton, North Yorkshire.**
Phone: **(0653) 697570**

1 **APRIL FLOWER,** 5, ch m Parva Stella—Paddys Flyer **Mr J. H. Myers**
2 **BEAU GUEST (FR),** 8, ch g Be My Guest (USA)—Belle Zed (FR) **Mr W. A. Sellers**
3 **BONNE NUIT,** 7, b br g Windjammer (USA)—Reine d'Etat **Mr J. Parkes**
4 **BULLET TRAIN,** 7, ch g Paddy's Stream—Irish Beauty **Mr J. Parkes**
5 **CALL COLLECT,** 9, ch g Ballymore—Regal Bell **Mr James Clements**
6 **CHICA MIA,** 6, b m Camden Town—Backwoodsgirl **Mr J. C. Parsons**
7 **CORRIENDO LIBRE,** 6, b g Tumble Wind (USA)—Bouganville **Mr J. Myers**
8 **JACQUELINE'S GLEN,** 4, b f Furry Glen—June's Slipper **Mr Tony Nunnari**
9 **JENNY'S JOY,** 5, ch m Le Bavard (FR)—Blackrath Girl **Mrs J. N. Askew**
10 **KITTY'S DAUGHTER,** 5, ch m Le Moss—Kitty Killowen VII **Mr P. S. Mehaffey**
11 **LECALE LADY,** 6, ch m Torus—Lucy's Pal **Mr G. Whorton**
12 **MILITARY BLAZE,** 4, ch g Sandhurst Prince—Echo Repeating **Mr C. Flear**
13 **MISS TRISTRAM (NZ),** 5, b m Sir Tristram—Coole Park **Mr Tony Nunnari**
14 **MOURNE ENDEAVOUR,** 5, ch g Parva Stella—Fair Eva **Mr Paul Hardy**
15 **NOBLE SCAMP,** 5, gr m Scallywag—Gouly Duff **Mrs C. Ford**
16 **OUR PHIL,** 12, ch g Sandford Lad—Four Queens **Mr James Clements**
17 **PRINCE ENGELBERT,** 5, br g Persian Bold—Polyester Girl **Miss Lynn Whiffen**
18 **RANDOM WARRIOR,** 6, b g Random Shot—Regency Cherry **Mrs G. Lister**
19 **RINGMORE,** 8, ch g Porto Bello—Dirrie Star **Mr W. A. Sellers**
20 **R NANCY,** 9, ch m Immortal Knight—Lovesome Hill **Mrs L. Holloway**
21 **STORMY DOMAIN,** 5, b g Dunphy—Lea Landing **Mr J. Parkes**
22 **SUDBROOKE PARK,** 12, ch g Duc d'Orleans—Miss Hill **Mr Cecil Hague**
23 **THE ETRUSCIAN,** 4, b g Young Man (FR)—Seven Year Itch **Mr Colin Flear**
24 **THE RIGHT TIME,** 5, b g King of Spain—Noddy Time **Mr J. H. Myers**
25 **TIBO HINE,** 4, b f Scorpio (FR)—Evening Flight **Mr W. A. Sellers**
26 **TRISTRAM'S LAKE (NZ),** 4, b f Sir Tristram—Coole Park **Mr Christopher Plowman**
27 **WINGED FOOT,** 4, b f Tap On Wood—Goirtin **Mr John Leslie**
28 **YELLOW BEAR,** 8, ch g Gold Form—Dumb Kathy **Mr J. Bousfield**

THREE-YEAR-OLDS

29 **BELLAGHY BRIDGE,** b f Dublin Taxi—Red Solitaire **Mr J. C. Parsons**

Other Owners: Colfax Window Systems Ltd, Mr K. Hall, Mrs G. M. Z. Spink, Mr J. A. Sutton, Mr B. Valentine.

Jockey (NH): R A Fahey (9-7, w.a.).

Conditional: N Smith (9-7).

Amateur: S Charleton (10-0).

453 MRS H. PARROTT, Coombe Hill

Postal: **Highfield Farm, Tewkesbury Road, Deerhurst, Nr Tewkesbury, Gloucester.**
Phone: **TEWKESBURY (0684) 292214**

1 **BIG ORDER,** 6, b g Buckskin (FR)—Newcastle Lady **Mr D. J. Shorey**
2 **BROCHE (FR),** 9, b g Nonoalco (USA)—Tyrant's Vale (FR) **Mr T. G. Bish**
3 **CAPELI CONE,** 8, b g Celtic Cone—Capelena **Mr T. J. Parrott**
4 **CELTIC RIFLE,** 6, b g Celtic Cone—Busted Rifle **Mrs I. L. Brewster**
5 **CHATANOOGACHOOCHOO,** 7, b g London Gazette—Pet Jackdaw **Mr B. Snape**
6 **COLWALL PARK,** 5, br g Furry Glen—Regent's Gina **Mrs Yvonne Allsop**
7 **COURT BEAUTY,** 7, b m Scallywag—Marchiness Drake **Miss E. E. Hill**

MRS H. PARROTT—continued

8 **COURT RAPIER,** 8, ch g Pardigras—Weepers Laura **Mr H. V. Perry**
9 **DEERHURST,** 5, b g Swing Easy (USA)—Bonzolena **Mr Roger Allsop**
10 **DIAMOND FORT,** 5, b g Mirror Boy—Fortina Lass **Mr D. J. Shorey**
11 **FARMCOTE AIR,** 8, ch m True Song—Mandy Lou **Miss S. Pratt**
12 **GENERAL OFFICER,** 7, gr g General Ironside—Storybook Child **Mr M. O'Keogh**
13 **HOPE END,** 12, b g Politico—Kate Bird **Mrs Yvonne Allsop**
14 **INKY BAY,** 9, b g Proverb—Straight Heiress **Mr D. J. Shorey**
15 **KING SEAR,** 8, br g Dubassoff (USA)—Noble Device **Mrs Yvonne Allsop**
16 **MENINGI,** 9, ch g Bustino—Miss Filbert **Mr H. V. Perry**
17 **MONUMENTAL LAD,** 7, ro g Jellaby—Monumental Moment **Mr T. J. Parrott**
18 **MOVE ABOUT,** 6, ch g Move Off—Toadpool **Mrs Yvonne Foster**
19 **PALLETINE,** 9, b g African Sky—Pro Patria **Mr T. J. Parrott**
20 **PURBECK DOVE,** 5, gr g Celtic Cone—Grey Dove **Mr H. V. Perry**

Other Owners: Mr G. E. Parr, Mrs H. Parrott.

Jockeys (NH): Robert Bellamy (9-7), Simon Earle (10-0).

Amateur: J Pritchard (10-7).

454 MR W. J. L. PAUL, Tring

Postal: **Drayton, Holloway, Tring, Hertfordshire, HP23 4LB.**
Phone: **OFFICE (044282) 6669 HOME (0296) 681762**

1 **CELTIC SHOWMAN,** 5, b g Celtic Cone—Spin Again **Mrs Sally Paul**
2 **GREY GATE,** 13, gr g Grey Mirage—Contentment **Mrs Sally Paul**

Conditional: D Skyrme (9-7).

455 MR J. R. PAYNE, Dulverton

Postal: **Lower Holworthy Farm, Brompton Regis, Dulverton, Somerset.**
Phone: **(03987) 244**

1 **HOLWORTHY,** 7, gr g Latest Model—Anchor Wood **Mr J. R. Payne**
2 **INDIAN SUNRISE,** 9, ch m Gambling Debt—Indian Whistle **Mr J. R. Payne**
3 **KINGS BROMPTON,** 4, b c Latest Model—Idson Lass **Mr J. R. Payne**
4 **WIMBLEBALL,** 10, b br h Sunrising—Polly Wall **Mr J. R. Payne**
5 **WIMBLEBALL LASS,** 5, b m Wimbleball—Idson Lass **Mr J. R. Payne**

Amateur: Mr R J Payne (10-7).

456 MR J. W. PAYNE, Newmarket

Postal: **Frankland Lodge, Hamilton Road, Newmarket, Suffolk, CB8 7JQ.**
Phone: **NEWMARKET (0638) 668675**

1 **CHIC CAROLE,** 4, ch f Dalsaan—Valley of Diamonds **Mr Maurice Downey**
2 **CROSBY,** 4, b c Music Boy—Yelney **Mr J. H. Etherton**
3 **DAM INQUISITIVE,** 6, br g Don—Inquisitive Girl **Mr Maurice Downey**
4 **JUDGMENT DAY,** 8, b g Mandamus—Vimaday **Mr Raymond Tooth**
5 **KALI KOPELLA,** 4, ch f Ahonoora—Restless Lady **Mrs J. W. Payne**
6 **LAKE DANCER,** 4, b c Kings Lake (USA)—Windy Cheyenne (USA) **Mr Raymond Tooth**
7 **RIVER DRAGON,** 5, b g Rarity—Wet Powder **Mr Raymond Tooth**

MR J. W. PAYNE—continued

THREE-YEAR-OLDS

8 **BELLWICK,** b f Norwick (USA)—Dusty Bluebell **Mr A. Wilkinson**
9 **CORAL FLUTTER,** b f Beldale Flutter (USA)—Countess Olivia **Mr D. Waller**
10 **KIMBOLTON KRACKER,** ch f Gabitat—One Sharper **Mr N. F. Tebbutt**
11 **MATUSADONA,** br f Tumble Wind (USA)—Ceiling **Mr Raymond Tooth**
12 **NAZELA,** gr f Another Realm—Alezan Dore **Mr J. P. A. Wolff**
13 **NICHOLAS PAYNE,** ch c Salmon Leap (USA)—Erin Lassie (USA) **Mr Raymond Tooth**
14 **ROUSKI,** b c Rousillon (USA)—Missy Baldski (USA) **Mr D. Waller**
15 **SHOCKING AFFAIR,** ch f Electric—Bedspring **Mr A. Wilkinson**
16 **STRATH ISLA,** br f Tina's Pet—Quick Kick **Mr J. H. Etherton**

TWO-YEAR-OLDS

17 B f 5/4 Tumble Wind (USA)—Avise La Fin (Scottish Rifle) **The Frankland Partnership**
18 **MEDAILLE D'OR,** ch c 4/4 Primo Dominie—Alezan Dore (Mountain Call) **Mr J. G. K. Borrett**
19 B g 22/3 Formidable (USA)—Miss Shirley (FR) (Shirley Heights) **Nagy El Azar**
20 Ch c 3/4 Music Boy—Morgiana (Godswalk (USA))
21 **PARIOS (FR),** ch c Sicyos (USA)—Parga (FR) (Gay Mecene (USA)) **Nagy El Azar**
22 **PERJURY (IRE),** b c 5/3 Try My Best (USA)—Riverine (FR) (Riverman (USA)) **Mr Raymond Tooth**
23 B f 12/3 Last Tycoon—Sometime Lucky (Levmoss) **Andrew Irish**
24 Ch f 24/3 Primo Dominie—Song of Gold (Song) **The Frankland Partnership**
25 Ch f 4/6 Music Boy—Soosjoy (Sexton Blake) **The Frankland Partnership**
26 **TANAGROS,** b c 1/3 Dunbeath (USA)—Tanagrea (Blakeney) **Mr Raymond Tooth**
27 B f 20/2 Primo Dominie—Zinzi (Song) **Mr Raymond Tooth**

Other Owners: Richard Brett, Mr Gerald Cooper, Mrs J. A. Crawshay, Mr D. E. Harman, Mr G. Jabre, Mr Alan Jervis, Mr S. Lycett Green, Mr N. Ttofalli.

Apprentice: Peter Hutton (8-0).

Lady Rider: Miss Sally Waugh (7-12).

457 MR S. G. PAYNE, Carlisle

Postal: **Rydal Mount Farm, Gilcrux, Carlisle, Cumbria, CA5 2QD.**
Phone: **ASPATRIA (0965) 20010**

1 **AISKEW FLUTTER,** 7, b br g Move Off—Flicka **Mr Michael M. Gunn**
2 **BILLY TOBIN,** 10, br g Bivouac—Romayne **Mr John Golding**
3 **FRIENDLY VENTURE,** 6, b br m Young Man (FR)—Melash **Mrs C. Payne**
4 **GALA LOCH,** 6, br m Lochnager—Spring Gala **Mr Bill Farrell**
5 **LOS GIGANTES,** 6, b m Formidable (USA)—Safety Measure **Mr S. G. Payne**
6 **LUDA LADY,** 7, b m Red Regent—Crepine **Mr John Wills**
7 **RAMPSBECK LAD,** 5, b g Davout—Story Writer **Mr S. G. Payne**
8 **SEASON'S AHEAD,** 7, ch m Politico (USA)—Early Echo **Mr David W. Hill**
9 **STAN'S FOLLY,** 9, b g Lighter—Cumbria Lass **Mr John Golding**
10 **VICO EQUENSE,** 5, gr m Absalom—Miss Diaward **Mr John Wills**

TWO-YEAR-OLDS

11 **IMGONNAWIN,** b f 9/4 Meadowbrook—Spring Gala (Ancient Monro) **Mr G. Payne**

Other Owners: Mr John Carter, Mr P. M. Gunn.

Jockeys (NH): J K Kinane (9-7), B Storey (10-0).

Lady Rider: Mrs J Thurlow (9-0).

458 MR H. E. PEACHEY, Stratford-on-Avon

Postal: **The Woodlands, 2 The Ridgeway, Stratford-on-Avon, Warwickshire, CV37 9JL.**
Phone: **STRATFORD-ON-AVON (0789) 294520**

1 **ELEGANT HEART,** 5, ch m Sunyboy—Arctic Elegance **Mr H. E. Peachey**
2 **GIFT VOUCHER,** 13, ch g Gift Card (FR)—Karmala (FR) **Mr H. E. Peachey**

THREE-YEAR-OLDS

3 B g Cruise Missile—Arctic Elegance **Mr H. E. Peachey**

Lady Rider: Miss Ann Stokell (9-7).

459 MR R. E. PEACOCK, Tarporley

Postal: **Tilstone Paddocks, Tilstone Fearnall, Tarporley, Cheshire, CW6 9HU.**
Phone: **(0829) 732716**

1 **AL-AMARADY,** 8, ch g Tumble Wind (USA)—Allanooka **Mr N. J. Barrowclough**
2 **CAPTAIN MAY,** 6, b g Welsh Captain—Maygo **Miss N. C. Taylor**
3 **COBBLERS CROSS,** 5, ch m Hasty Word—Stormation **F. Lloyd (Penley) Ltd**
4 **EASY KIN,** 8, ch g Great Nephew—Ardneasken **Mr S. Mercer**
5 **EDWARDS LAST,** 6, b g Edwards Hill—Jolly Pigeon **Mr A. L. Holland**
6 **HEAD LAD,** 7, ch g Headin' Up—Authors Daughter **F. Lloyd (Penley) Ltd**
7 **JUPITER EXPRESS,** 12, ch g Jupiter Pluvius—La Perla **Mr R. E. Peacock and N. J. Barrowclough**
8 **KEMBLE,** 4, b c Habitat—Sarah Siddons (FR) **F. Lloyd (Penley) Ltd**
9 4, B f Sweet Monday—Maygo **Mr R. E. Peacock**
10 **MUQADAR (USA),** 9, b h Stop The Music (USA)—Final Compliment (USA) **The Kilroe Group Limited**
11 **NAFPLION,** 5, b m Young Generation—Time For Thought **Miss P. Kissock-Smith**
12 **OAKLAND JASON,** 12, b g No Argument—Affectionately **Mr D. A. Davies**
13 **PATRICK'S FAIR,** 14, br g Tudenham—Little Squaw **Mr W. R. Slater**
14 5, Br g Celtic Cone—Roadway Mistress **Mr T. O. Peacock**
15 **ROYAL TREATY,** 6, ch g Tower Walk—Covenant **Mr T. H. Davies**
16 **RUSHMOOR,** 12, br g Queen's Hussar—Heathfield **Mrs R. E. Peacock**
17 **SPACE GEM,** 9, b g Space King—Nicola Lisa **Mr T. H. Davies**
18 **SPRING FORWARD,** 6, b h Double Form—Forward Princess (USA) **Mr G. Whittaker**
19 **SPRING PALM,** 7, br g Palm Track—Springdamus **Mr D. Hutchinson**
20 **SUPREME OPTIMIST,** 6, b g Absalom—Cachucha **Mr Allan White**

THREE-YEAR-OLDS

21 **DAL MISS,** b f Dalsaan—Loyal And Regal **Mr James Keogh**

Other Owners: Mr Niall Boden, Mr Jim Ennis, Mr J. P. McGinn, Mr J. D. McLuckie, Mr C. M. Spann.

Jockey (NH): S J O'Neill (10-0, w.a.).

Lady Rider: Mrs Carmen Peacock (8-12).

460 MR J. PEARCE, Newmarket

Postal: **Sackville House, Sackville Street, Newmarket, Suffolk, CB8 8DX.**
Phone: **NEWMARKET (0638) 664669**

1 **BARRY OWEN,** 4, b g Owen Anthony—Tacita **Mr Arthur Meadows**
2 **BARTON PARK,** 4, br c Lucky Wednesday—Bronzamer **Mr Keith Parker**
3 **BOLD INTENTION,** 6, ch g Baptism—Fines Herbes **Mrs M. E. Taylor**

MR J. PEARCE—continued

4 **CASBATINA,** 4, b f Castle Keep—Balatina **Mrs M. E. Taylor**
5 **DANISH CHIEF,** 9, b g Brave Invader (USA)—Just Darina **Mrs Valerie Anne Wood**
6 **FREELANCE,** 11, b g Free Boy—Princess Fortina **Miss C. J. Morris**
7 **HAND PAINTED,** 6, br g Rabdan—Morkulla (SWE) **Mr Jeff Pearce**
8 **HELLENIC PRINCE,** 4, b g Ela-Mana-Mou—Pipina (USA) **Mr Kevin Moorcroft**
9 **HERESHEIS,** 4, b f Free State—Gambela (USA) **Mrs Mary Hepworth**
10 **KING MENELAOS,** 5, b g Ile de Bourbon (USA)—Be Sweet **Mr Kevin Moorcroft**
11 **LOTS OF LUCK,** 7, gr m Neltino—Safe Passage **Mr Roger Patrick**
12 **MARKSTYLE,** 5, b g Moorestyle—Alicia Markova **Mr T. Wood**
13 **PODSNAP (USA),** 7, b g Lord Gaylord (USA)—Cougar Cat (USA) **Mr Kevin Moorcroft**
14 **QUITE SO,** 6, br m Mansingh (USA)—Chiquitita **Adrott Ltd**
15 **SHAKERS HALL,** 8, ch g Shiny Tenth—Ripatip **Mrs Ruby Lanham**
16 **SPECKYFOUREYES,** 7, b m Blue Cashmere—Sprightly Sprite **Mr K. Sayles**
17 4, Gr br g Monsanto (FR)—Stance **Mr Jeff Pearce**
18 **STAR MAESTRO,** 8, br g Music Maestro—Maryland Star **Mr T. Wood**
19 **TEPYLON,** 11, b g Maystreak—Just-A-Honey **Mr Kevin Moorcroft**
20 **ZODIAC BOY,** 5, b g Monseigneur (USA)—Hannie Caulder **Mr T. Wood**

THREE-YEAR-OLDS

21 **BERT DAVEY,** b c Homing—Tea-Pot **Mr Arthur Old**
22 B g Balliol—Burdigala **Mrs Lydia Pearce**
23 **FLORIDA SECRET,** b c Miami Springs—Close Secret **Mr Roger Patrick**
24 **FREEDOM,** b f Free State—Pied A Terre **Miss Audrey Lanham**
25 **LATIN LEEP,** b c Castle Keep—Balatina **Mrs K. W. Sneath**
26 **NOCTURNAL REVERIE (USA),** b f Assert—Grey Dream **Mr Kevin Moorcroft**
27 **PINNACLE POINT,** b c Lochnager—Wollow Maid **Mr A. S. Goodjohn**
28 **S'AGAPO,** ch f Prince Ragusa—No Bello **Mr A. Watford**
29 **TESEKKUREDERIM,** b br g Blazing Saddles (AUS)—Rhein Symphony **Mr V. C. Smith**

TWO-YEAR-OLDS

30 B c 20/3 Enchantment—Lost Valley **Mrs Mandy Elliott**
31 **SHAR EMBLEM,** b f 12/3 Shardari—Lady's Flag (USA) **Mrs Eileen Blyth**
32 Gr br c 6/3 Another Realm—Tory Blues **Mr James Stephenson**

Other Owners: Mr Robert Barton, Mrs Marcia Fairbairn, Mr W. J. Goddard, Mr D. Leech, Mr S. J. Mear, Mr R. G. Thurston, Mr R. Whiting.

Jockey (Flat): W Newnes (w.a.).

Jockeys (NH): John McLaughlin (9-7), John Ryan (9-7).

Conditional: M Coglan (9-7).

Lady Rider: Mrs Lydia Pearce (8-7).

461 MR J. E. PEASE, Chantilly

Postal: **'Villa Primerose', Chemin des Aigles, 60500 Chantilly, France.**
Phone: **OFFICE 44 58 19 96 HOME 44 57 23 09 TELEX 155101 SWINKCO FAX 44575990**

1 **BELIEVE IN GOLD (USA),** 7, b h Bellypha—Lady Gold **J. E. Pease**
2 **BOBBY'S DREAMER,** 4, b f Roberto—Tash **R. K. Eamer**
3 **DAZZLING HEIGHTS,** 4, b f Shirley Heights—Cape Chesnut **P. R. Pritchard**
4 **FOOL'S GOLD,** 4, b c Glint of Gold—Amazer
5 **FORETASTE,** 5, ch m Forli—Suni **T. D. Rootes**

MR J. E. PEASE—continued

6 **FRANC ARGUMENT,** 4, b f Argument—Franca **G. Strawbridge**
7 **GALA SONG,** 4, ch c The Minstrel—Revedire **R. K. Eamer**
8 **RIOSAMBA,** 4, b f Caerleon—Immensity **P. R. Pritchard**
9 **ROMAN PROSE,** 5, ch g Sallust—Mothers Girl **H. Seymour and Partners**
10 **SHREAKE,** 4, b g Shirley Heights—Creake **C. Budgett**
11 **SILICON LADY,** 4, b f Mille Balles—Siliciana **J. Goelet**
12 **SUITE FOLIE,** 4, b f Top Ville—Cymbaline **R. K. Eamer**
13 **TURGEON,** 4, gr c Caro—Reiko **G. Strawbridge**
14 **VERY VIGORS,** 4, gr c Vigors—Dynamite **Mrs H. Cole**

THREE-YEAR-OLDS

15 **ADAGIETTO,** b c Green Dancer—Hence (USA) **C. N. Ray**
16 **ANNA'S HONOR,** b f Alleged—Honor To Her (USA) **Joanna Beresford**
17 **ASSRAR,** b f Foolish Pleasure—Smokey Legend **S. Abdul Karim**
18 **BABY ARABIAN,** ch c Northern Baby—Southern Baby **R. K. Eamer**
19 **BABY SAS,** ch c Northern Baby—Aransas (USA) **B. McNall**
20 **DARA ROSE,** b f Dara Monarch—Rose Chanelle **Sir G. Brunton**
21 **EXCEPTED,** b c Procida—L'Exception (FR) **R. K. Eamer**
22 **FEMME GRISE,** gr f Auction Ring—Pizziri **J. L. Moore**
23 **FORECENE,** b f Formidable—Suni **T. D. Rootes**
24 **FOR THE CUP,** b f L'Emigrant—Barre **B. McNall**
25 **FRANQUEVAL,** b c Fabulous Dancer—Tuneria **R. K. Eamer**
26 **GAGE D'AMOUR,** ch f Diamond Shoal—Dana Dana (FR) **J. Goelet**
27 **GORDION,** b c Gay Mecene—Gortynia (FR) **R. K. Eamer**
28 **ISLINGTON SPA,** b c Sadler's Wells—St Padina **G. Strawbridge**
29 **KING AMOS,** b c His Majesty—Amaryllia (USA) **C. N. Ray**
30 **LOCAL ARTIST,** b c Green Dancer—Lucky Spell (USA) **R. K. Eamer**
31 **NORTH COL,** b c Head For Heights—Night Encounter **S. Emmet**
32 **OCTOGENARIAN,** ch c Czaravich—Arantelle (FR) **B. McNall**
33 **OLVARRIA,** b f Bikala—Marie de Vez **H. Liebrecht**
34 **PERFECT SISTER,** ch f Perrault—Franca **B. McNall**
35 **PHARGETTE,** b f Lyphard—Logette (USA) **B. McNall**
36 **QUEEN OF WOMEN,** b f Sharpen Up—Tash (USA) **R. K. Eamer**
37 **RAIN MELODY,** b f Nijinsky—Ida Delia (USA) **Aaron Jones**
38 **REMIND ME,** b f Riverman—Fourteen (FR) **G. Strawbridge**
39 **SAINTE ADRESSE,** b f Esprit du Nord—Sainte Gemme (FR) **R. K. Eamer**
40 **SANTIAGO ROB,** b c Robellino—Santiago Sweetie (USA) **C. N. Ray**
41 **SHARP SASS,** b f Sharpen Up—Village Sass (USA) **C. N. Ray**
42 **SHIMMERING NATIVE,** b f Our Native—Shimmering Spruce **C. N. Ray**
43 **SPANKY'S GANG,** gr c Bellypha—Martha Spanks **R. K. Eamer**
44 **SUN BRANDY,** b f Storm Bird—Mazama (USA) **Aaron Jones**
45 **THE MINOTAUR,** gr c Mendez—Lorelei Lea (USA) **J. Goelet**
46 **WARFIELD,** b c Glint of Gold—Alys **T. D. Rootes**

TWO-YEAR-OLDS

47 B f Shadeed—Attirance (Crowned Prince) **J. Wigan**
48 **BORAGE,** b c Carwhite—Balsamine (Gosport) **Hon Mrs Pease**
49 **CRODELLE (IRE),** gr f Formidable—Pizziri (Artaius) **Mrs J. L. Moore**
50 B f Red Sunset—Dance Partner (Graustark) **J. Goelet**
51 **DYNAMIQUE,** ch c Kenmare—Madiyma (Top Ville) **B. McNall**
52 B f Slip Anchor—Flashy (Sir Ivor) **G. Strawbridge**
53 B f Liloy—Fohre (Menes) **H. Liebrecht**
54 **FOX CUB,** b f Mille Balles—Fox Oa (French Friend) **Hon Mrs Pease**
55 Ch c Argument—Franca (Viceregal) **B. McNall**
56 **GOOBER PEA,** b f Akarad—Lyphaora (Lyphard) **R. K. Eamer**
57 **MANTECA,** b c Cariellor—With You All (Free Round) **R. K. Eamer**
58 **MRS MERRY MAN,** b f Bellypha—Bessie Wallis (Prince de Galles) **T. D. Rootes**
59 B f Big Spruce—Nice Noble (Vaguely Noble) **H. Liebrecht**
60 B f Taufan—Nuit de Vin (Nebbiolo) **S. Emmet**
61 B f Nijinsky—Palmistry (Forli) **Mr Kashiwagi**

MR J. E. PEASE—continued

62 B f Herat—Pink Princess (Tickled Pink) **G. Strawbridge**
63 RAIN MEDLEY, ch f Storm Bird—Lituya Bay (Empery) **G. V. Jones**
64 REDCOAT, ch c Nureyev—Grabelst (Graustark) **G. V. Jones**
65 Ch f Northjet—Reiko (Targowice) **G. Strawbridge**
66 SHATISH, b c Nijinsky—Belle Marie (Candy Spots) **G. V. Jones**
67 Ch c Palace Music—Shore Route (Vice Regent) **Mrs D. Beresford**
68 B c Rainbow Quest—Singapore Girl (Lyphard) **G. Strawbridge**
69 B f Law Society—Snow Day (Reliance II) **G. Strawbridge**
70 B f Sharpen Up—Summer Fling (Nijinsky) **G. Strawbridge**
71 WAYLAND, b c Lashkari—Valentina Way (Fabulous Dancer) **R. K. Eamer**
72 WINDSOR HERALD, b c Formidable—Alys (Blakeney) **T. D. Rootes**

Jockeys (Flat): A S Cruz (second claim), M De Smyteer.

Amateur: Mr J Portman.

462 MR R. A. H. PERKINS, Burton-on-Trent

Postal: **Bretby Park, Burton-on-Trent, Staffordshire, DE15 0RB.**
Phone: **(0283) 215195 OR 221323 FAX (0283) 224679**

1 GREENBANK PARK, 13, ch g Twilight Alley—Rustella **Mr R. A. H. Perkins**
2 MYNAH KEY, 9, ch g Kemal (FR)—Galah Bird **Mr R. A. H. Perkins**
3 PHILOSOPHERS WOOD, 10, ch g Golden Love—Knight's Princess **Mr R. A. H. Perkins**
4 ROCHESTOWN LASS, 4, b f Deep Run—Knockatippaun H. Perkins
4 ROCHESTOWN LASS, 4, b f Deep Run—Knockatippaun **Mr R. A. H. Perkins**
5 VAZON EXPRESS, 4, b c Le Bavard (FR)—Grangecon Express **Mr R. A. H. Perkins**
6 VINO FESTA, 11, ch m Nebbiolo—Madrilon (FR) **Mrs R. S. Perkins**

463 MR A. C. J. PERRETT, Cheltenham

Postal: **Yew Trees, Shipton Oliffe, Cheltenham, Gloucestershire.**
Phone: **CHELTENHAM (0242) 820244 OR 820841**

1 LADY BLUES SINGER, 4, ch f Chief Singer—Moaning Low **Mr P. Perrett**
2 MASCALLS GIRL, 5, ch m Moorestyle—Copt Hall Realm **Mr K. J. Perrett**
3 WESTERN DIVIDE (USA), 5, b g Sharpen Up—River Nile (USA) **Mr K. J. Perrett**

Jockeys (Flat): E Johnson (7-7), R Street (7-7).

Jockeys (NH): B Dowling (10-0, w.a.), L Harvey (10-0, w.a.).

464 MR W. M. PERRIN, Buntingford

Postal: **Silkmead Farm, Hare Street, Buntingford, Hertfordshire.**
Phone: **(076 384) 8113**

1 **CASCADING,** 7, br m Casino Boy—Carolina Star **Mr L. A. White**
2 **DERRING VALLEY,** 5, b g Derrylin—Chalke Valley **Mr Harry Hobson**
3 **FLEMINGTON,** 11, b g Bargello—Leuze **Mrs Jacqueline Perrin**
4 **HERON VALLEY,** 6, b m Remezzo—Garbally Girl **Mr N. Blair**
5 **LEXDEN,** 4, b c Blakeney—Annabella **Mr A. A. Goodman**
6 **MARSDALE,** 5, b m Royal Palace—Jamuna **Mr L. A. White**
7 **MEDITATOR,** 6, ch g High Line—Thoughtful **Mrs Jacqueline Perrin**
8 **REINDEER WALK,** 8, gr g Godswalk (USA)—Carcajou **Mr L. A. White**
9 **ROWHEDGE,** 4, ch c Tolomeo—Strident Note **Mrs Jacqueline Perrin**
10 **SPROWSTON BOY,** 7, ch g Dominion—Cavalier's Blush **Mr G. Whiting and Mr K. Blanch**

Jockey (NH): M Bowlby.

465 MR J. A. PICKERING, Hinckley

Postal: **Cottage Farm, Wigston Parva, Sharnford, Hinckley, Leicestershire, LE10 3AP.**
Phone: **(0455) 220535**

1 **ABADARE (USA),** 6, b g Robellino (USA)—Latonia Thrush **Mr D. Lowe**
2 **ABBEY BRAVE,** 7, ch g Avocat—Garnerstown Queen **Mr L. G. Jones**
3 **AFTER THE GLOOM,** 5, ch g Bay Express—Heaven And Earth **Mr D. Lowe**
4 **BUTTONWOOD SOUND,** 6, ch g True Song—Ballena **Mrs J. K. Oldring**
5 **MONTY'S GIFT,** 6, b g Park Lane—Solgift **Mr C. N. Nimmo**
6 **SIDEWINDER,** 12, ch g Country Retreat—Woodland Wedding **Mr J. A. Pickering**
7 **TRUE TIP,** 7, b m True Song—Copperclown **Mr I. D. James**
8 **WOODLAND RETREAT,** 10, ch m Country Retreat—Woodland Wedding **Mrs J. A. Pickering**

Conditional: D J Dennis (9-7).

466 MRS L. PIGGOTT, Newmarket

Postal: **Eve Lodge, Hamilton Road, Newmarket, Suffolk, CB8 0NY.**
Phone: **(0638) 662584 OFFICE 660229 FAX (0638) 665283**

1 **BUSTED ROCK,** 5, b h Busted—Mexican Two Step **Mr H. Furuoka**
2 **EBRO,** 4, ch g Aragon—Caribbean Blue **Mrs F. A. Veasey**
3 **HOW,** 4, b c Horage—Rathcoffey Dodo **Mrs Susan Rudolf**
4 **MONASTERY,** 4, b g General Assembly (USA)—Sweet Habit **J. D. Ashenheim**
5 **NORTHANTS,** 4, b g Northern Baby (CAN)—Astania (GER) **J. Atrib**
6 **SAXON LAD (USA),** 4, b c Lear Fan (USA)—Presto Youth (USA) **Mr W. E. Norton**
7 **SCARLET LEGEND,** 4, b g Legend of France (USA)—Orillia **Mr A. Miller**
8 **VERSAILLES ROAD (USA),** 7, b h Blushing Groom (FR)—Lucinda Lea (USA) **Mrs Joyce Wood**

THREE-YEAR-OLDS

9 **BATZUSHKA (USA),** b c Danzig (USA)—Nicole Mon Amour (USA) **Mr Henryk De Kwiatkowski**
10 **BIG IDEA,** ch c Sharpo—Wild Idea **Mr Richard Strong**
11 **COMMANCHE NATION,** b c Commanche Run—Rally **Mr K. Abdulla**

MRS L. PIGGOTT—continued

12 **DEAUVILLE DUCHESS,** gr f Ballad Rock—Miss Deauville **Mr K. H. Fischer**
13 **DZET (USA),** b c Caerleon (USA)—Tendresse (USA) **Mr Henryk De Kwiatkowski**
14 **ERIK ODIN,** b c Nordico (USA)—Assurance (FR) **Mr Geoffrey C. Greenwood**
15 **FRONT PAGE,** ch g Adonijah—Recent Events **Mr Geoffrey C. Greenwood**
16 **GOLDEN DAFFODIL,** gr f Jalmood (USA)—Katysue **Mr Tony S. K. Wong**
17 **HOZAY (USA),** b c Cresta Rider (USA)—Chellita **Mr Charles H. Wacker III**
18 **INVOCATION,** ch c Kris—Royal Saint (USA) **Mr K. Abdulla**
19 **MASROUG,** b c Dunbeath (USA)—Fleur Rouge **Mrs Lester Piggott**
20 **MEXICAN VISION,** b c Vision (USA)—Mexican Two Step **Mr D. Moore**
21 **OKAKU,** b c Be My Guest (USA)—Be My Darling **Mr H. Furuoka**
22 **PRINCESS DANCER,** b f Alzao (USA)—Singing In The Sun **Mrs Peggy O'Connor**
23 **REEL FOYLE (USA),** ch f Irish River (FR)—Abergwaun **W. J. Gredley**
24 **ROBERT'S REJECT (USA),** ch f Assert—Bold Sands (USA) **Mrs Darryl Myers**
25 **ROYAL FI FI (USA),** b f Conquistador Cielo (USA)—Apple Betty (USA) **Mr Henryk De Kwiatkowski**
26 **SHERJAMAL (USA),** ch c Raise A Native—Sedra **Mrs S. Khan**
27 **SHINING SILVER,** gr c Kalaglow—Lustrous **Sheikh Mohammed**
28 **SLAVE TO LOVE,** ch f Song—Presentable **R. A. Popely**
29 **STONE OR SCISSORS,** ch c Ballad Rock—Take The Option (USA) **Lady Clague**
30 **SUSANNA'S SECRET,** b c Superlative—Queens Welcome **Miss Maha Kalaji**
31 **TENDER CHARM,** ch g Tumble Wind (USA)—Best Bidder **Mr K. H. Fischer**

TWO-YEAR-OLDS

32 **AFFORDABLE,** b c 21/4 Formidable (USA)—Ophrys (Nonoalco (USA)) **Abdulla Mazen Kalaji**
33 B c 5/3 Alleging (USA)—Be My Darling (Windjammer) **J. Atrib**
34 Ch f 7/2 Master Willie—Bold Sands (USA) (Wajima (USA)) **Mr B. T. Stewart-Brown**
35 **BRERA (IRE),** b f 3/4 Tate Gallery (USA)—Anoint (Connaught) **Tony Hirschfeld**
36 **BROWN AS A BERRY (IRE),** b c 31/1 Glow (USA)—Sun Bed (Habitat) **Mrs Sonia Rogers**
37 **CARELESS LOVE,** b f 5/4 Top Ville—La Carlotta (USA) (J O Tobin (USA)) **M. J. Simmonds**
38 **CHANTILLY LOVE,** b f 13/3 Alleging (USA)—Ruff's Luck (USA) (Ruffinal (USA)) **Mr W. E. Norton**
39 B c 2/5 Fairy King (USA)—Clifden Bottoms (Wolver Hollow) **Naim Mazen Kalaji**
40 **COUNTESS OF POLAND (USA),** b f 5/3 Danzig Connection—Priceless Countess (Vaguely Noble) **Mr Henryk de Kwiatkowski**
41 **F-TROOP (IRE),** b f 8/5 Nordico (USA)—Adorable Princess (Royal Palace) **Roger Speechley**
42 **IVORY TIME,** ch c 4/3 Time For A Change—Ivory Waltz (USA) (Sir Ivor) **W. J. Gredley**
43 **JANE'S AFFAIR,** b f 10/2 Alleging (USA)—Blue Jane (Blue Cashmere) **R. A. Popely**
44 B f 6/4 Never So Bold—Lady Regent (Wolver Hollow) **Brook Stud**
45 **LIFFEY RIVER (USA),** ch c 11/3 Irish River (FR)—Close Comfort (USA) (Far North (CAN)) **Mrs Heather Hirschfeld**
46 **LOUFAGH (USA),** ch f 24/5 Bering—Nibabu (FR) (Nishapour (FR)) **Abdullah Ali**
47 **MAOUJOUD,** b c 9/4 Green Desert (USA)—Anne Stuart (FR) (Bolkonski) **Abdullah Ali**
48 **NORTHERN GALLERY (IRE),** ch c 12/2 Tate Gallery (USA)—Cliona (FR) (Ballymore) **Mrs R. Minshall**
49 **PLAYUP,** ch f 11/4 High Line—Putupon (Mummy's Pet) **Lord Tavistock**
50 Gr f 28/2 Niniski (USA)—Plum Blossom (USA) (Gallant Romeo (USA)) **Mr Charles H. Wacker III**
51 **REGAL EMBERS (IRE),** b c 14/3 Glow (USA)—Royal Sister II (Claude (ITY)) **J. D. Ashenheim**
52 **RIDGE END (USA),** b f 9/3 Cox's Ridge (USA)—Lipika (USA) (Nijinsky (CAN)) **Mr Henryk de Kwiatkowski**
53 **ROVIRIS,** b c 18/4 Sir Ivor—Royal Caprice (USA) (Swaps) **Mrs H. McConville**
54 **SHAFOURI (IRE),** b c 19/2 Alzao (USA)—Sauntry (Ballad Rock) **Ali K. Al Jafleh**
55 B c 23/2 Tate Gallery (USA)—Vaguely Deesse (USA) (Vaguely Noble) **Wafic Said**

Other Owners: Mrs C. A. Dickson, Mr R. Miller, Mr J. Palmer-Brown, Mr Michael Quinn, Lady Tavistock, Mr J. S. Threadwell, S. M. Threadwell.

Jockeys (Flat): R Cochrane (w.a.), B Crossley (7-10).

Conditional: J P Darby (9-0).

Lady Rider: Mrs Jennie Crossley (8-7).

RED MILLS

IRISH RACEHORSE FEEDS

Already a
PROVEN WINNER

amongst top English Trainers.

(and fed by 9 of Ireland's current Top 10 National Hunt Trainers of 1989/90)

16% HI-PRO RACEHORSE CUBES
14% RACEHORSE CUBES
14% RACING COARSE MIXTURE
25% OAT BALANCER PELLETS
TOP QUALITY RACEHORSE OATS

Available throughout the U.K. from:

J. Toomer & Sons Ltd. Blunsdon, **Swindon**. 0793-721408
W. F. Banks Ltd. Askrigg, **Leyburn** , N. Yorks. 0969-50229
B.A.T.A. Ltd. **Malton**, N. Yorks. 0653-693234
Gowlett Grain Ltd. Gt. Abingdon, **Newmarket**. 0223-893737
Hill House Stud, Hambledon, **Hants**. 070132-446
Shearing & Loader Ltd. Grateley, **Andover**, Hants. 026488-333
Badcock & Evered Ltd. **Washford**, Somerset. 0984-40412
John Hogarth Ltd. **Kelso**. 0573-24224
Birniehill Trading, **Maybole** Ayrshire. 0655-82103
Agriservice, Long Bennington, **Newark**, Notts. 0400-81421
Equimix Feeds, **Stourport** (Worcs)/**Penkridge** (Staffs). 078571-2223
C. & W. Farmers Ltd, **Penrith/Wigton/Longtown/Kendal**. 0768-63764
Hay & Brecon Farmers Ltd. **Hay-On-Wye**. 0497-820516
Park & White, Crook, **Bishop Auckland.** 0388-762103
Marshall & Forsyth, **Wooler.** 0668-81567
Paddock Star, **Ascot.** 0276 856009
W. M. Lillico, **Epsom.** 0737 247666
Preston Farmers, **Preston.** 0772 794621

RED MILLS - *Always a winner!*

Colour brochure and full information on the Red Mills range of specialist racing and stud diets are available from our UK Representatives:

Mrs Nicola Baird B. A., Tel:0762-881637 or
Miss Vicky Jones, Pentre David, Oswestry, Shropshire SY10 7EA. Tel:0691-659720

467 MR S. L. PIKE, Sidmouth

Postal: **Synderborough Farm, Sidbury, Sidmouth, Devon, EX10 0QJ.**
Phone: **(03957) 485**

1 **LADY GENEVA,** 8, b br m Royalty—Jinkin **Mr Stewart Pike**
2 **SIDBURY HILL,** 14, br g Cheval—Watermark II **Mr Stewart Pike**
3 **SWEATSHIRT,** 5, ch g Leander—Roman Lilly **Mr Stewart Pike**
4 **TOFFEE APPLE,** 7, b g Comedy Star (USA)—Apple of My Eye **Mr Stewart Pike**
5 **VANASHING TANNER,** 10, ch g Rugantino—Bridle Lane **Mr Stewart Pike**

Amateur: Mr A Walter.

468 MRS P. M. PILE, Leamington Spa

Postal: **Splash Leys, Avon Dassett, Leamington Spa, Warwickshire, CV33 0AZ.**
Phone: **(0295) 89661**

1 **LITTLE DASSETT,** 5, ch m St Columbus—Dassett Wood **Mrs P. M. Pile**
2 **TRUE HOLLOW,** 8, ch g True Song—Wilspoon Hollow **Mrs D. Mitchell**

469 MR J. PILKINGTON, Malvern

Postal: **The Leys, Birt Street, Birtsmorton, Malvern, Worcestershire, WR13 6AW.**
Phone: **BIRTSMORTON (068 481) 580**

1 **BUCKSHEE BOY,** 8, ch g Buckskin (FR)—Old Hand **Mr J. Pilkington**
2 **GOLDFINGER,** 7, ch g Billion (USA)—Old Hand **Mr J. Pilkington**
3 5, B m Oats—Old Hand **Mr J. Pilkington**
4 **SECOND HAND,** 6, ch m Sagaro—Old Hand **Mr J. Pilkington**

Jockey (NH): Peter Dever (10-0, w.a.).

470 MR R. W. PINCOMBE, South Molton

Postal: **Town Living Farm, Mariansleigh, South Molton, Devon.**
Phone: **BISHOPS NYMPTON (07697) 331**

1 **DARKTOWN STRUTTER,** 4, ch g Pas de Seul—Princess Henham **Mr R. W. Pincombe**
2 **GAMBLERS REFRAIN,** 5, b g Blue Refrain—Blue Fire Lady **Mr R. W. Pincombe**
3 **IRISH NOBLE,** 15, ch g Crepello—Miss Ireland **Mr R. W. Pincombe**
4 **KEN LAKE,** 17, ch g Appiani II—Lake Constance **Mr R. W. Pincombe**
5 **THE RECTOR,** 16, ch g Royal Cavalier—Gypsy Touch **Mr R. W. Pincombe**
6 **VIGI'S GREY,** 11, gr g Come On Grey—Vigi **Mr R. W. Pincombe**

Jockeys (NH): Mark Williams, David Wonnacott (10-3).

471 MR M. C. PIPE, Wellington

Postal: **Pond House, Nicholashayne, Wellington, Somerset.**
Phone: **OFFICE (0884) 40715 FAX (0884) 41343**

1 **AFFORD,** 5, b m Silly Prices—Fabrica **Mr M. C. Pipe**
2 **AMAREDO,** 4, gr g Akarad (FR)—Amila **Pipe Scudamore Racing Plc**

MR M. C. PIPE—continued

3 **AMBASSADOR,** 7, ch g General Assembly (USA)—Klairlone **Fairlord Wholesale Confectioners Ltd**
4 **ANGEL'S KISS (SWE),** 5, b g Atlantic Boy—Cielo Azzurro **Mr L. G. R. Jonsson**
5 **ARDOUR,** 4, b g Ardross—Evita **Pipe Scudamore Racing Plc**
6 **BAR FLY (FR),** 4, ch g Salmon Leap (USA)—Breathalyser **Roldvale Limited**
7 **BLAKE'S PROGRESS,** 4, b g Blakeney—Patosky **Mr B. A. J. Lake**
8 **BLUE RAINBOW,** 7, ch m Balinger—Metaxa **Mr A. J. Lomas**
9 **BOARDMANS STYLE,** 12, b g Giolla Mear—Caroline's Money **Mr A. F. Walls**
10 **BODFARI,** 5, b m Lighter—Connaughts' Trump **Lord Mostyn**
11 **BONANZA BOY,** 9, b g Sir Lark—Vulmid **Mr S. Dunster**
12 **BONANZA REBEL,** 8, ch g Belfalas—Speckled Leinster **Mr S. Dunster**
13 **BRAMBER,** 4, b f Castle Keep—Hartnell Dream **Mr R. H. Lewis**
14 **CACHE FLEUR (FR),** 4, ch g Kashneb (FR)—Blanche Fleur (FR) **Mr B. A. Kilpatrick**
15 **CASH FLOW BAY,** 5, gr g Cawston's Clown—Saragail **Mr T. Flaherty**
16 **CELCIUS,** 6, b g Ile de Bourbon (USA)—Cistus **Mr M. C. Pipe**
17 **CHATAM (USA),** 6, b g Big Spruce (USA)—Cristalina (FR) **Dr B. Nolan**
18 **CYPHRATE (USA),** 4, b br g Saint Cyrien (FR)—Euphrate (FR) **Mr M. C. Pipe**
19 **DANCING EYES,** 5, b m Jester—Le Chat **Mr M. C. Pipe**
20 **DAWN PRINCE,** 7, b g King of Spain—The Dupesdawn **Unity Farm Holiday Centre Ltd**
21 **DELTIC (USA),** 4, br c Far North (CAN)—Moon Delta (USA) **Pond House Racing**
22 **DUSTY DIPLOMACY (USA),** 7, b g Run Dusty Run (USA)—Faithful Diplomacy (USA) **Mr R. Brichart**
23 **ETERNAL CREDIT,** 8, ch g Quayside—Fair Vic **Mr G. P. Rees**
24 **FATU HIVA (GER),** 6, b m Marduk (GER)—Faehna (GER) **Mr L. W. Cooper**
25 **FIT FOR COUNSEL,** 4, b f Hotfoot—Rose of Shenfield **Pond House Racing**
26 **FLAXEN KING,** 8, ch g Carnival Night—Doravaun **Mr Freddie Starr**
27 **FU'S LADY,** 8, b m Netherkelly—Cindyr **Mr S. Dunster**
28 **GALWEX LADY,** 4, gr f Mendez (FR)—Shadiliya **Avondurn Limited**
29 **GOLD SERVICE,** 5, b g Glint of Gold—House Maid **Mr W. E. Norton**
30 **GO WEST,** 6, b g Akarad (FR)—Western Goddess **Mrs June Dodd**
31 **GREEN'S FINE ART,** 4, ch g Kind of Hush—L'Hawaienne (USA) **Richard Green (Fine Paintings)**
32 **HARLEY STREET MAN,** 9, b g Maris Piper—Poppy-Jill **Mr J. P. Powis**
33 **HARRY LIME,** 5, b g Beldale Flutter (USA)—Zither **Mr Bernard Newton**
34 **HERECOMES FLANAGAN,** 6, b g Crozier—Daffydown Lady **Mrs M. Mara**
35 **HUNTWORTH,** 10, ch g Funny Man—Tamorina **Mr W. H. Walter**
36 **IN-KEEPING,** 4, b f Castle Keep—Primmy **Mrs H. M. Read**
37 **JABRUT,** 5, b g Young Generation—Migoletty **Mr A. J. Lomas**
38 **KALSHAN,** 6, b g Lightning (FR)—Carota (FR) **Mr R. Brichart**
39 **KINGS RANK,** 5, br g Tender King—Jhansi Ki Rani (USA) **Mr D. J. Few**
40 **K O ISLAND,** 7, b g Garda's Revenge (USA)—Tudor Story **Mr Ciaran A. McClintock**
41 **L'ANE ROUGE,** 9, b g Deep Run—Imperial Leather **Mr Paul Green**
42 **LEVANTINE ROSE,** 10, br m Levanter—Gambling Rose **Mrs D. Jenks**
43 **LIADETT (USA),** 5, b g Lydian (FR)—Provincia (CHI) **Mr Frank A. Farrant**
44 **LONELY REEF,** 5, b h Pas de Seul—Merriment (USA) **Mr R. Brichart**
45 **LUCKY VERDICT,** 4, b g Touching Wood (USA)—Noor **Richard Green (Fine Paintings)**
46 **MALAMUTE SALOON (USA),** 4, ch c Arctic Tern (USA)—Square Generation **Mr N. R. J. Wellington**
47 **MIGHT MOVE,** 7, ro g Town And Country—Strathdearn **Hortray Builders Ltd**
48 **MIGHTY PRINCE,** 5, ch g Pharly (FR)—Anne Stuart (FR) **Mr R. Garbett**
49 **MIINNEHOMA,** 7, b br g Kambalda—Mrs Cairns **Mr Freddie Starr**
50 **MILFORD QUAY,** 7, ch h Milford—Miss Quay **Mr W. A. Jones**
51 **MILINETTA,** 5, b m Milford—Golden Linnet **Mr R. Meredith**
52 **MISS CHALK,** 4, ch f Dominion—Stoney **Mr A. J. Lomas**
53 **MONARU,** 4, b g Montekin—Raubritter **Mr R. Meredith**
54 **MYFOR,** 4, ch c Be My Guest (USA)—Forliana **Mr A. J. Lomas**
55 **NORTH LANE,** 13, b g Dusky Boy—Carlow Smile **Mr G. C. Bisgrove**
56 **NOTTAGE (USA),** 4, b c Northern Baby (CAN)—Salinidad (CHI) **Pipe Scudamore Racing Plc**
57 **OLD KILPATRICK,** 5, b br g Touching Wood (USA)—Mother Brown **Mr B. E. Tomlinson**
58 **PARLEZVOUSFRANCAIS,** 6, b g Blakeney—Oula-Ka Fu-Fu **Fairlord Wholesale Confectioners Ltd**
59 **PENNY ROSE,** 9, b m Whistlefield—Gambling Rose **Mrs D. Jenks**
60 **PERISTYLE,** 4, br f Tolomeo—Persevering **Mrs E. King**
61 **PERTEMPS NETWORK,** 6, br g Touching Wood (USA)—No Relation **Pertemps Limited**
62 **PHAROAH'S LAEN,** 9, b g Laen—Pharaoh's Lady **Mr T. A. Johnsey**

MR M. C. PIPE—continued

63 **POLLOCK (FR),** 7, b g Arctic Tern (USA)—Golden Gleam (FR) **Mrs M. A. Bisgrove**
64 **REDALLY,** 7, b g Ballymore—Red Aster **Miss Helen L. Pengelly**
65 **REGAL AMBITION,** 6, b g Royal Palace—Quick Aim **Skeltools Ltd**
66 **REIN DE TOUT,** 7, b g Al Sirat (USA)—Not At All **Pipe Scudamore Racing Plc**
67 **RE-RELEASE,** 5, ch m Baptism—Release Record **Mr Jim Ennis**
68 **ROCHALLOR,** 4, ch g Dara Monarch—Ballymaloe Girl **Pipe Scudamore Racing Plc**
69 **ROCKARIA,** 5, b h Ballad Rock—Grazia **Pertemps Limited**
70 **ROCK OF AGES,** 6, ro m Blakeney—Rockery (FR) **Mr Brian Ward**
71 **ROYAL RUFFIN (USA),** 6, ch h Snow Knight—Rubye Brooks (USA) **Pond House Racing**
72 **ROYAL WONDER,** 4, b f Welsh Saint—Collectors' Item **Pond House Racing**
73 **RUN FOR FREE,** 6, b g Deep Run—Credit Card **Mr Ralph Freethy**
74 **RUSCH DE FARGES (FR),** 7, ch g Italic (FR)—Bielly (FR) **Mr Frank A. Farrant**
75 **SABIN DU LOIR (FR),** 11, b g Go Marching (USA)—Star Light (FR) **Mr B. A. Kilpatrick**
76 **SEXTON ASH,** 8, b g Sexton Blake—Golden Ash **Mr D. A. Beswick**
77 **SHADEUX,** 4, ch g Valiyar—A Deux (FR) **Mr John Billington**
78 **SHIP OF STATE,** 7, b g Troy—Sea Venture (FR) **Mr Leon B. Fisk**
79 **SILVER ACE,** 11, b g Son of Silver—Bunny Club **Mr M. C. Pipe**
80 **SILVER KING (FR),** 4, ch f Son of Silver—Lakala (FR) **Pipe Scudamore Racing Plc**
81 **SIRE NANTAIS (FR),** 6, br g Meisir (FR)—Farala (FR) **Mr N. C. Biggs**
82 **SISTER CHABRIAS,** 5, b m Chabrias (FR)—Ginger Tart **Mr P. McMahon**
83 **SKIPPING TIM,** 11, b g Deep Run—Skiporetta **Miss H. A. Bisgrove**
84 **STAR OF KUWAIT,** 6, b m Crooner—Miss Kuwait **Mr R. N. Short**
85 **STAR'S DELIGHT,** 8, gr g John de Coombe—Vanity Surprise **Mr F. Barr**
86 **STRANDS OF GOLD,** 11, b g Le Coq d'Or—Sweet Fanny **Independent Twine Manufacturing**
87 **STRAW BLADE,** 4, ch f Final Straw—Little Niece **Pond House Racing**
88 **TARQOGAN'S BEST,** 10, b g Tarqogan—Balldado **Mr Jim Ennis**
89 **TEL-ECHO,** 6, ch h Nishapour (FR)—Rhodante **Pertemps Limited**
90 **THE LEGGETT,** 7, b g Faraway Times—Mrs McNicholas **Mr A. E. Ford**
91 **TORSIDE,** 11, ch g Funny Man—Annaghmore **Mr G. C. Bisgrove**
92 **TRAVEL MYSTERY,** 7, b m Godswalk (USA)—Sugar Cookie **Mrs J. H. Johnson**
93 **TREFELYN CONE,** 6, ch m Celtic Cone—Trefelyn Heather **Mrs J. K. L. Watts**
94 **TREFELYN ROSE,** 7, b m Tom Noddy—Trefelyn Heather **Mrs J. K. L. Watts**
95 **TRES SPORTIF,** 4, br f Daring March—Impeccable Lady **Mr T. A. Johnsey**
96 **TRIDENT TESTED,** 5, b g Cruise Missile—Coombe Valley
97 **TRI FOLENE (FR),** 4, b f Nebos (GER)—Jefty (FR) **Pipe Scudamore Racing Plc**
98 **VOYAGE SANS RETOUR (FR),** 5, ch g Le Nain Jaune (FR)—Mativa (FR) **Mrs J. A. Leeper**
99 **WACKERS MAGIC,** 6, b g Celtic Cone—Jackyda **Mr G. A. Mallaber**
100 **WALK OF LIFE (USA),** 5, b h Northern Baby (CAN)—Ballena Ridge (USA) **Mr N. R. J. Wellington**
101 **WALNUT WAY,** 11, ch m Gambling Debt—Pickled Walnut **Mrs J. Robshaw**
102 **WILL JAMES,** 4, ch g Raga Navarro (ITY)—Sleekit **Mr R. J. K. Roberts**
103 **WINGSPAN (USA),** 6, b g Storm Bird (CAN)—Miss Renege (USA) **Mr P. L. Shilton**
104 **WONDERINE (FR),** 5, br m The Wonder (FR)—Tarpeienne (FR) **Pipe Scudamore Racing Plc**
105 **WOODLIGHT FANTASY,** 8, ch m Happy Match—Fair Dream **Mr J. F. Morse**
106 **ZULU (FR),** 5, b h Zino—Marilu (FR) **Pipe Scudamore Racing Plc**

THREE-YEAR-OLDS

107 **MAGIC ANA,** b f Magic Mirror—Ana Gabriella (USA) **Miss Ana Archer**

Other Owners: Mr T. G. Bish, Mr R. Blumberg, Mr Mark Bovingdon, Mr T. M. Chandler, Colonnade Racing Limited, Mrs B. M. L. Davis, Mrs Alison C. Farrant, Mr F. W. Fern, Mr T. M. Few, Mr E. Fraenkel, Mr E. R. D. Goldsmith, Mr Gordon Gray, Mr Michael J. Hill, Mr Grant Howells, John Doyle Construction Limited, Mrs Sally Leggett, Mr T. P. Macdonald, Mr M. H. D. Madden, Mr Bob McMillan, Mr Gwyn Meredith, Mr Adrian F. Nolan, Mrs V. O'Leary, Mr Trevor Painting, Miss N. Parker, Miss Helen L. Pengelly, Mr J. Rodgers, Mr Mark Ruffell, Mrs G. D. Spencer, Mr M. A. Swift, Mr I. A. Taylor, Mr Ray Washbourne, Mr Bob Wheatley, White Bros (Taunton) Ltd.

Jockeys (NH): J Lower (10-0), P Scudamore (10-0).

Conditional: M R Foster (9-7), R Macneice (9-7), D Richmond (9-7).

Amateurs: Mr L Jefford (9-7), Mr A Walter (11-0).

472 MRS J. PITMAN, Upper Lambourn

Postal: **Weathercock House, High Street, Lambourn, Newbury, Berkshire.**
Phone: **LAMBOURN (0488) 71714 FAX (0488) 72196**

1 **ABBA LAD,** 8, ch g Le Bavard (FR)—Rosina Royal **Abba Double Glazing Co Ltd**
2 **AKRASH VALLEY,** 5, gr ro g Ardross—Haloom **Mr Jeremy Hollowell**
3 **ALMANZORA,** 6, ch g Proverb—Serrulata **Mrs Elizabeth Hitchins**
4 **APPLETON,** 4, ch c Quayside—Beagle Bay **Mr E. Hirst**
5 **ARCTIC CAVALIER,** 8, br g Paddy's Stream—Charming Hostess **Segray Properties Limited**
6 **AUDLEY LADY,** 4, ch f Deep Run—Lulu's Daughter **Mr Asil Nadir**
7 **BAGGRAVE LAD,** 5, ch g Over The River (FR)—Bawnaro **Mr Asil Nadir**
8 **BIZAGE MOTORS,** 6, b g Oats—Cherry Lodge **Mr B. Nadir**
9 **BLACKGUARD (USA),** 4, ch g Irish River (FR)—Principle (USA) **Mr M. L. Oberstein**
10 **BLACK MOCCASIN,** 7, b g Buckskin (FR)—Lovely Bio **Platinum Racing**
11 **CANTAMEGA,** 6, b g Deep Run—Una's Pride **Larkhall Natural Health Ltd**
12 **CASH IS KING,** 6, b g Tug of War—Norhamina **Mr Martin Myers**
13 **CLASSIC STATEMENT,** 4, ch c Mill Reef (USA)—Lady Graustark (USA) **Mrs Elizabeth Hitchins**
14 **COBO BAY,** 5, ch g General Assembly (USA)—Top Hope **Mrs Elizabeth Hitchins**
15 **COKENNY BOY,** 5, b g Abednego—Northern Push **Mr S. D. Hemstock**
16 **COOL SUN,** 10, b g Deep Run—Stroll On **Mr L. Hamilton**
17 **CROIX DE GUERRE,** 9, b g Proverb—Josephine **Mr J. Shaw**
18 **DANDY MINSTREL,** 6, br g Black Minstrel—Julanda **Mr W. V. Robins**
19 **DANNY HARROLD,** 6, b g Deep Run—Chillaway **Mrs Shirley Robins**
20 **DAN RAISE,** 9, b g Raise You Ten—Arctic Cut **Mrs Jane Saunders**
21 **DAT TRAIN,** 6, b g Mandalus—Early Start **Mr M. L. Oberstein**
22 **DEVIL'S VALLEY,** 7, ch g Lucifer (USA)—Barrowvale **Mrs Ann Galvanoni**
23 **DISNEYLAND (POL),** 6, ch g Dixieland (POL)—Dzungaria (POL) **Mr W. V. Robins**
24 **DIS TRAIN,** 6, ch g Deep Run—Bunkilla **Mr M. L. Oberstein**
25 **DO BE BRIEF,** 5, ch g Le Moss—Right Performance **Mr Errol Brown**
26 **DON VALENTINO,** 5, ch g Don—Hells Mistress **Mr Asil Nadir**
27 **EGYPT MILL,** 5, b g Deep Run—Little Dipper **Mr S. R. Webb**
28 **ESHA NESS,** 7, b g Crash Course—Beeston **Dubanscam Racing Ltd**
29 **FEDERAL TROOPER,** 9, ch g Ascertain (USA)—Rough Crossing **Mr Peter Bonner**
30 **FIFTH AMENDMENT,** 5, b g The Parson—Biowen **Mr W. V. Robins**
31 **FILE CONCORD,** 6, br g Strong Gale—Lady Reporter **The Jet Stationery Company Limited**
32 **FIRE REFINED,** 7, b g Cut Above—Life Began **Mrs Ruth Bonner**
33 **GAINSAY,** 11, br g Tepukei—Swift Response **Mr Errol Brown**
34 **GARRISON SAVANNAH,** 7, b g Random Shot—Merry Coin **Autofour Engineering**
35 **GEORGIC,** 7, b m Tumble Gold—Miss Pet Tina **Mr Peter Harvey**
36 **GOLDEN FREEZE,** 8, b g Golden Love—Freezeaway **Mr Asil Nadir**
37 **GOLDEN LANTERN,** 7, b g Smartset—Swanee Mistress **Mrs Shirley Robins**
38 **HALF BROTHER,** 8, br g Faraway Times (USA)—Sinzinbra **Mr Peter Bonner**
39 **HEYFLEET,** 7, b g Tachypous—Heyford **Mrs Richard Allen**
40 **HOW NOW,** 9, b g Pollerton—Tape Mary **Dubanscam Racing Ltd**
41 **IDLEIGH'S TUDOR,** 5, b g Tudorville—Green Monkey **Mr W. V. Robins**
42 **IVEAGH HOUSE,** 4, b c Be My Guest (USA)—Waffles **Mrs Shirley Robins**
43 **IVORS GUEST,** 4, b c Be My Guest (USA)—Ivor's Date (USA) **Mrs Elizabeth Hitchins**
44 **KANTARA BOY,** 4, b g Belfalas—Smashing Run **Mr Asil Nadir**
45 **LAFOSSE,** 9, b g Status Seeker—Meelgarrow **Mr Robert Hitchins**
46 **L'UOMO PIU,** 6, b g Paddy's Stream—Easter Vigil **L'Uomo Menswear Ltd**
47 **MICK'S STAR,** 10, br g Orange Bay—Starboard Belle **Mr P. Scammell**
48 **MIDNIGHT TRAIN,** 9, b g Oats—Gail Borden **Mr M. L. Oberstein**
49 **MISTER LAWSON,** 4, ch g Blushing Scribe (USA)—Nonpareil (FR) **Mr Peter Bonner**
50 **MONKSCOMBE,** 7, b g Monksfield—Doone Valley **Mr David Rose**
51 **MOSSGARA,** 5, b g Le Moss—Bargara **Mr Robert Hitchins**
52 **NARE POINT,** 5, ch g Floriferous—Rather Grand **Mr A. L. Deal**
53 **NORTHERN HEATHER,** 6, b g Gleason (USA)—Darren's Heather **Mr Ted Steed**
54 **PAT CASH,** 6, b g Deep Run—Stormy Breeze **Mrs Nicole Myers**
55 **PATROL LEADER,** 5, br g Trimmingham—Arctic Actress **Mr Peter Bonner**
56 **PEMBROKE BAY,** 7, b g Paddy's Stream—Tudor Gello **Mrs Elizabeth Hitchins**
57 **QUINTIN DERWOOD,** 4, gr g Mr Fluorocarbon—Donallan **Mr Peter Bonner**

MRS J. PITMAN—continued

58 **RANDOM TRAVELLER,** 9, b g Random Shot—Con's Dual Fair **Alan Phelp**
59 **REGAL LAKE,** 4, b br c Kings Lake (USA)—Thistlewood **Platinum Racing**
60 **RI-NA-RITHANN,** 5, b g Deep Run—Casacello **Dubanscam Racing Ltd**
61 **RIVA ROSE,** 9, b g Caribo—Rose of The West **Mr W. A. Gaff**
62 **ROCHESTER,** 4, gr g Entre Nous—Satans Daughter **Mrs Elizabeth Hitchins**
63 **ROCQUAINE,** 4, ch g Ballad Rock—Lola Sharp **Mr Robert Hitchins**
64 **ROYAL ATHLETE,** 7, ch g Roselier (FR)—Darjoy **Mr Gary Johnson**
65 **RUN TO FORM,** 5, br g Deep Run—Let The Hare Sit **Mrs Richard Allen**
66 **SADDLERS NIGHT,** 8, ch g Crash Course—Barge Royal **The Jet Stationery Company Limited**
67 **SOCKS DOWNE,** 11, b br g Paddy's Stream—Kincsem **Mr C. Cowley**
68 **SPIRIT OF KIBRIS,** 5, ch g Quayside—Golden Shuil **Mr Asil Nadir**
69 **STRONG GOLD,** 7, b g Strong Gale—Miss Goldiane **Mrs Shirley Robins**
70 **SUPERIOR FINISH,** 4, b g Oats—Emancipated **Drawact Ltd**
71 **SWIFT WATERS,** 4, b c Sadler's Wells (USA)—Rapids (USA) **Mrs Elizabeth Hitchins**
72 **TARTAN TRIX,** 7, b g Pitpan—Blue Trix **Mrs Enid M. Boucher**
73 **TAURUS,** 4, br g Lucifer (USA)—Jane Eyre **Mrs Elizabeth Hitchins**
74 **TEAM CHALLENGE,** 8, ch g Laurence O—Maid O'The Wood **Mrs Elizabeth Hitchins**
75 **THE A TRAIN,** 8, b g Tumble Gold—Wrong Decision **Mr M. L. Oberstein**
76 **THE ILLYWHACKER,** 5, b g Dawn Review—Trucken Queen **Mr J. Hitchins**
77 **THE PINK'UN,** 5, gr g Deep Run—Silver Doll **Mrs Elizabeth Hitchins**
78 **THE PUTNEY LARK,** 6, b g Merrymount—Blue Lagoon **Larkhall Natural Health Ltd**
79 **THE SHY CONTROLLER,** 5, b g Kind of Hush—Heyford **Mr Mike Bateman**
80 **TIMELY STAR,** 9, b g Faraway Times (USA)—Star Pearl **Mr Ben Smith**
81 **TOBY TOBIAS,** 8, b g Furry Glen—Aurora Lady **Mrs Elizabeth Hitchins**
82 **VAZON BAY,** 6, b g Deep Run—Fair Argument **Mr Robert Hitchins**
83 **VILLA RECOS,** 5, b g Deep Run—Lovely Colour **Mr Robert Hitchins**
84 **WILLSFORD,** 7, b g Beau Charmeur (FR)—Wish Again **Mr A. M. Kaplan**
85 **WONDER MAN (FR),** 5, ch g The Wonder (FR)—Juvenilia (FR) **Mrs Shirley Robins**

THREE-YEAR-OLDS

86 **ANDRELOT,** b c Caerleon (USA)—Seminar **Mr Robert Hitchins**
87 **CRAZY RIVER,** b g Vision (USA)—Etty **Mr Peter Bonner**
88 **L'UOMO CLASSICS,** b g Indian King—Sperrin Mist **Mr Colin Pratt**
89 **MR SMILEY,** b c Pharly (FR)—Yelming **Mrs Shirley Robins**

Other Owners: Mr B. R. H. Burrough, Mr C. W. Foreman, Mrs Maureen Garrard, Mr I. R. Hadfield, Mr N. S. Hadfield, Mr J. C. Hitchins, Mrs Leroy Hurlbert, Mr B. R. Jervis, Mr David Johnson, Mr L. Johnson, Mr Rex Johnson, Mr Robert Johnson (Harborne), Mr E. N. Kronfeld, Mr A. V. Marchfield, Mr K. T. McCourt, Mr M. C. Noble, Mr Tom Scott, Mr N. Shulman, Mrs I. M. Silver, Mr M. J. Silver, Mr D. W. Stait, Mr Ian Stewart, Mr F. G. Thorne, Mr Robert Tyrrell, Mr David P. Walker, Mr David Webster.

Jockeys (NH): M Bowlby (10-0), B De Haan (10-0), M Pitman (10-7).

Conditional: F Perratt (9-7), J Tuite (10-0).

Amateurs: Mr S Kerr (9-10), Mr G Morrow (9-7).

Lady Rider: Mrs A Bowlby.

473 MR R. E. POCOCK, Bridgwater

Postal: **Stringston Farm, Holford, Bridgwater, Somerset.**
Phone: **(027874) 236**

1 **INDIAN KNIGHT,** 5, b g Kinglet—Indian Whistle **Mr T. E. Pocock**
2 **INDIAN MINOR,** 6, b g Jimsun—Indian Whistle **Mr T. E. Pocock**

MR R. E. POCOCK—continued

3 **INDIAN ROSE,** 8, ch m Kinglet—Indian Whistle **Mr T. E. Pocock**
4 **KILTON PARK,** 8, b g Jimsun—Park End **Mr T. E. Pocock**
5 **RED MATCH,** 5, ch g Royal Match—Hi Mary **Mr T. E. Pocock**

Jockey (NH): P L Richards.

474 MR C. L. POPHAM, Taunton

Postal: **Bashford Racing Stables, West Bagborough, Taunton, Somerset.**
Phone: **(0823) 432769**

1 **AMATORY,** 7, ch g Junius (USA)—Amatrice **Quantocks Racing Ltd**
2 **ANOTHER SEEKER,** 8, ch g Status Seeker—Foolish Lady **Mr R. I. Brafield**
3 **BARACUS,** 7, br g Lepanto (GER)—Pendon Fare **Quantocks Racing Ltd**
4 **CANTORIAL,** 9, ch g Cantab—Signal Melody **Mrs C. R. Hayton**
5 **CLASSICAL QUARTET,** 5, b g Relkino—Daughter of Song **A. P. Hill**
6 **COMMANCHE BRAVE,** 7, ch g Royal Blend—Billie Jean **Mr Vernon Colhoun**
7 **COURT APPEAL,** 8, b g Star Appeal—Londonderry Air **Arthur Souch**
8 **DANRIBO,** 7, b g Riboboy (USA)—Sheridans Daughter **Mr K. L. Dare**
9 **DOUBLE U DEE,** 7, b g Rapid Pass—Abbyrama **Mr M. L. Stoddart**
10 **GOLDEN OZY,** 9, br g Golden Love—Ozyett **Mr Robert Allen**
11 **GREY TORNADO,** 9, b ro g Rugantino—Tornadora **Mr D. R. Short**
12 **HIGH NODDY,** 5, b m Tom Noddy—High Lee **Mr Rhys Thomas Williams**
13 **KING RETAIN,** 7, b g Cut Above—De'b Old Fruit **Mr David Paul Corfield**
14 **KNOWSTONE,** 7, ch g Reassurance—Miss Moritz **Mrs J. R. Bulled**
15 **KOO-MING,** 5, b m Mansingh (USA)—Jenny Splendid **Mrs L. M. Warren**
16 **NORTHERN CREST,** 4, ch g Anfield—Contadina **Mr D. R. Short**
17 **OH SO NIPPY,** 4, b g Martinmas—Listen To Me **Mr Anthony Hunt**
18 **PANTO PRINCE,** 9, br g Lepanto (GER)—Native Wings **Mrs L. M. Warren**
19 **PRIORS COPPICE,** 8, b g Monksfield—Just Darina **Miss Anna Bucknall**
20 **ROLL-A-JOINT,** 12, ch g Take A Reef—Sark **Mr Rhys Thomas Williams**
21 **SHAH'S CHOICE,** 7, b g Persian Bold—Royal Display **Mr A. Skidmore**
22 **SKYLARK WONDER,** 8, gr g Idiot's Delight—Rainbow Wonder **Mr Anthony Hunt**
23 **SPORTING IDOL,** 5, b g Mummy's Game—Village Idol **R. G. Turvey**
24 **TELEMACHUS,** 6, b g Runnett—Bee Hawk **Mr J. Warren**
25 **THATS NICE,** 7, ch g Grundy—Copt Hall Realm **Mr D. R. Short**

THREE-YEAR-OLDS

26 **GREY SONATA,** gr f Horage—The Grey (GER) **S. Dare**

Other Owners: Mr W. M. Burton, Mr J. P. Carrington, Mr R. D. A. Kelly, Mr C. L. Popham, Mr Christopher Rogers, Mr A. Staple, Mrs C. A. Webster.

Jockey (NH): Brendan Powell (10-0).

475 MR A. W. POTTS, Barton-on-Humber

Postal: **Manor Stables, Horkstow, Barton-on-Humber, S. Humberside.**
Phone: **SAXBY-ALL-SAINTS (065261) 750**

1 **MILL TERN,** 8, ch g Milford—Mitsuki **Mr A. W. Potts**
2 **MOON SUNSHINE,** 5, b h Welsh Saint—Relko's Pride **Mr D. Kerr**
3 **PALAIS DE DANSE,** 6, ch h Dance In Time (CAN)—Dunfermline **Mr G. Simpson**
4 **RIGTON SALLY,** 10, b m Joshua—Rigton Caprice **Mrs I. Willford**
5 **TAMERTOWN LAD,** 9, b g Creetown—Gay Tamarind **Mr D. Kerr**

MR A. W. POTTS—continued

THREE-YEAR-OLDS

6 **ALIBI WARNING,** b c Belfort (FR)—Carymara (FR) **Mr Brian Robb**

TWO-YEAR-OLDS

7 B f 25/1 Lightning Dealer—Balmenoch (Queen's Hussar) **Mr R. Lindsay**
8 B c 2/2 Full On Aces (AUS)—Hard To Forget (AUS) (Mount Hagen (FR)) **Mr Jim Cowan**
9 B f 9/3 Today And Tomorrow—La Verte Gleam (Bustomi) **Mr E. Judge**
10 B f 31/3 Gianchi—Marzia Fabricotti (Ribero) **Mr E. Judge**

Other Owners: Mr L. C. Maultby, Mr P. J. Williams, Mr David Wraith.

Jockey (Flat): S Webster.

Conditional: T M Potts (9-7).

Lady Rider: Miss R Judge (9-0).

476 MR G. J. POWELL, Abbeydore

Postal: **Tan House Farm, Abbeydore, Herefordshire.**
Phone: **GOLDEN VALLEY (0981) 240204**

1 **ABBEYDORE,** 8, b g Rouser—Cagaleena **Mr G. J. Powell**
2 **DORE RIVER,** 5, br g Cruise Missile—Cagaleena **Mr G. J. Powell**

Jockey (NH): David Tegg (10-0).

Conditional: R Bellamy (9-7).

477 MR W. G. PREECE, Telford

Postal: **Uppington Smithy, Uppington, Telford, Salop, TF6 5HN.**
Phone: **(095 286) 249 MOBILE (0860) 336943 FAX (095 286) 447**

1 **AT LONG LAST,** 4, b f John French—Atlantica **Bill Preece**
2 **BALUCHI,** 9, b g Gunner B—Atlantica **Mr D. E. Squire**
3 **BILLHEAD,** 4, b g Nicholas Bill—Time-Table **K. &. M. Construction Ltd**
4 **CARJUJEN,** 6, b g Tumble Wind (USA)—Baldritta (FR) **Shropshire Race Horses Ltd**
5 **CROWECOPPER,** 11, b g Netherkelly—Cammy **Mrs Mary Price**
6 **DEE JAY PEE,** 4, ch g Electric—Lady Gaston **Mr D. Jones**
7 **ELITE ETOILE,** 5, b m Gorytus (USA)—Antipol **Mr K. H. Fischer**
8 **HUMDECOLA,** 5, ch g Humdoleila—Nicola Lisa **Mr J. S. Ritter**
9 **MITHRAS,** 12, b g Centaurus—Timidora **Mrs H. F. Richards**
10 **MY SON JOHN,** 7, ch g Plenty Spirit—Lady Keeper **Mrs S. M. Graves**
11 **RAMBLING WILD,** 9, ch g Deep Run—Rockaway Rose **Mrs H. F. Richards**
12 **RICARDO BOOTS,** 4, gr g Remainder Man—Mountainette **Mr Nial G. Boden**
13 **SELF RAISING,** 5, ch g Boreen (FR)—Just Image **Mr D. A. Davies**
14 **STORM WARRIOR,** 5, b g Main Reef—Spadilla **Mr W. J. Sinker**
15 **THE LIGHTER SIDE,** 4, br g Comedy Star (USA)—Moberry **Mr D. A. Davies**
16 **ZACTOO,** 4, br g Tycoon II—Maidensgrove **Mr D. Jones**
17 **ZAFIRO,** 4, br g Starch Reduced—Miss Admington **Mrs E. M. Yates**

MR W. G. PREECE—continued

THREE-YEAR-OLDS

18 **ZAFOD,** b c Silly Prices—Coatham **Mr R. H. Gill**

Other Owners: Mrs M. A. Baldwin, Mr A. J. French, J. A. D. Engineering Ltd, Mr R. Knight, Mr G. Thomas.

Jockeys (NH): G Landau (10-0, w.a.), P Scudamore (10-0, w.a.).

478 MR K. PRENDERGAST, Kildare

Postal: **Rossmore Lodge Stables, Kildare, Co. Kildare, Ireland.**
Phone: **(010) 353 45 21387 FAX (010) 353 45 22264 TELEX 60695 KEUNEI**

1 **CHILLY RAJAH,** 4, b c Indian King (USA)—Chilblains **Mr Hugo Merry**
2 **DANZIG HARBOUR (USA),** 4, b f Private Account (USA)—Ship 'n Shore **G. McNulty**
3 **ISLET TIME,** 5, b m Burslem—Island Time **Mrs C. van C. Anthony**
4 **NANARCH (USA),** 6, ch g Dara Monarch—Natuschka **H. de Burgh**
5 **NEWTON JOHN,** 4, b g Head For Heights—Natuschka **H. de Burgh**
6 **NORTHERN DESCENT,** 4, ch g Salmon Leap (USA)—Donna Sabina **Noel Carter**
7 **RESERVE JUDGEMENT (USA),** 4, b g Alleged (USA)—Green Reef **G. McNulty**
8 **SADIE JORDAN (USA),** 6, b m Hail The Pirates (USA)—Lexacon (USA) **A. D. Brennan**
9 **SEMIWILD (USA),** 4, b br f Rumbo (USA)—African Desert **Mrs Kevin Prendergast**

THREE-YEAR-OLDS

10 **AHD,** b c Linkage (USA)—Old Gypsy (USA) **Hamdan Al Maktoum**
11 Ch f Mt Livermore (USA)—As Hot As (USA) **H. de Burgh**
12 **ASSERTION,** b f Assert—Yes Please **Peter Leon**
13 **BEDGELLERT (USA),** ch g Wolf Power (SAF)—Sonseri **John L. Wood**
14 **CUPID MISS,** b f Anita's Prince—Lady of Man **Mrs Anita Quinn**
15 **DEVIL WORSHIP,** b f Yashgan—Hell's Mistress **Mrs C. Magnier**
16 **EINSEKTSOLLBRENNEN (USA),** b c Country Pine (USA)—Plage (FR) **G. Berger**
17 **FRENCH LEGIONNAIRE,** b g Legend of France—Angail **J. C. Harley**
18 **GHAADAH (USA),** b f Linkage (USA)—Strings Attached (USA) **Mr Hamdan Al-Maktoum**
19 **HELEN'S DYNASTY,** b f Habitat—Dismantle **John L. Wood**
20 **ISLAND BREEZE,** b g Tumble Wind (USA)—Slaney Maid **Mrs M. O'Connell**
21 **ITEN SON,** b c Millfontaine—Couture d'Argent (FR) **Ernst Iten**
22 **JAYIZ (USA),** ch c The Minstrel (CAN)—Celebrity Guest (USA) **Mr Hamdan Al-Maktoum**
23 **KING OF ZURICH,** b c Alzao (USA)—Perfect Choice **Louis Mayer**
24 **LITTLE MOLL,** b f Coquelin (USA)—Bunch of Blue **Mrs Patrick J. Conlan**
25 **MASAI WARRIOR,** b c Petorius—Spear Dance **J. C. Harley**
26 **MISTRAL'S LOVE,** b f Adonijah—Still More **Mrs D. H. Solomon**
27 **MONTEZUMA,** b c Commanche Run—Quisissanno **Mr C. A. B. St George**
28 **MOONLIGHT SAIL,** ch f Main Reef—Moonlight Sonata **M. Ferguson**
29 **MOUNAMARA,** b f Niniski (USA)—Mounara (FR) **A. D. Brennan**
30 **MUDARRIS (USA),** ch c Lyphard's Wish (FR)—Speciously Bold (USA) **Mr Hamdan Al-Maktoum**
31 **MUTAFANI,** b c Top Ville—Nepula **Mr Hamdan Al-Maktoum**
32 **NORTHERN PET,** b f Petorius—Northern Chance **Mrs Patrick J. Conlan**
33 **POLISH DANCER (USA),** b f Malinowski (USA)—Ygraine **A. D. Brennan**
34 **RATHBAWN REALM,** b f Doulab (USA)—Lucky Realm **Mrs J. W. Reynolds**
35 **ROUSINETTE,** ch f Rousillon (USA)—Clarina **R. More O'Ferrall**
36 **SOUTHERN RULE,** b c Law Society (USA)—Isobelline (USA) **Noel Carter**
37 **TAKWIM,** br f Taufan (USA)—Brush Away **Mr Hamdan Al-Maktoum**
38 **TANWI,** br f Vision (USA)—Shine The Light **Mr Hamdan Al-Maktoum**
39 **TWINKLE BRIGHT (USA),** b br f Star de Naskra (USA)—Lady May (FR) **N. D. Biddle**
40 **WELSH BLEND,** b c Welsh Term—Port-O-Call **Noel Carter**
41 **WICKED FOLLY,** ch f Exhibitioner—Glencoe Lights **Mrs C. Magnier**

MR K. PRENDERGAST—continued

TWO-YEAR-OLDS

42 **AL SUMMAN (USA),** ch f 14/2 Secretariat (USA)—Hasty One (USA) (Delta Judge) **Mr Hamdan Al-Maktoum**
43 **ANSAB (IRE),** b c 14/1 Doulab (USA)—Magic Slipper (Habitat) **Mr Hamdan Al-Maktoum**
44 Br c 12/4 Sharpen Up—Bank Examiner (USA) (Buckfinder (USA)) **Mr Hugo Merry**
45 B f 27/4 Pennine Walk—Dominica (GER) (Zank) **Dr Michael Smurfit**
46 **DOWN EASTER ALEXA (USA),** ch f 4/3 Red Ryder (USA)—Phils Fancy (Irish Love) **G. McNulty**
47 **DUAL ASSET (IRE),** b f 27/2 Double Schwartz—Lady Moorfield (Sallust) **David Prentice**
48 **ERINDALE STAR (IRE),** br c 8/4 Fairy King (USA)—My Fawn (Hugh Lupus) **Mrs D. M. Donohoe**
49 **FLAME FLICKER (IRE),** b f 2/4 Doulab (USA)—Fluella (Welsh Pageant) **Patrick J. Conlan**
50 **GORTLEMON STAR (IRE),** br c 31/3 Try My Best (USA)—Swift Reply (He Loves Me) **Mrs D. M. Donohoe**
51 **ISLAND HEATHER (IRE),** ch f 23/4 Salmon Leap (USA)—Princess Sinna (Sun Prince) **Mrs M. O'Connell**
52 **JADA (IRE),** ch c 15/4 Shy Groom (USA)—La Loie Fuller (FR) (Rheffic (FR)) **Mr Hamdan Al-Maktoum**
53 **LAKE OF ZURICH (IRE),** ch c 13/3 Salmon Leap (USA)—Naomi Joy (Sun Prince) **Louis Mayer**
54 **LAWAHED (USA),** ch f 18/4 Riverman (USA)—Sweet Simone (FR) (Green Dancer (USA)) **Mr Hamdan Al-Maktoum**
55 **LUCAS CARTON (IRE),** b c 17/3 Nordico (USA)—Bentinck Hotel (Red God) **Mrs Cathrine McNulty**
56 **MUBADIR (USA),** ch c 18/3 Nodouble (USA)—Hapai (Nijinsky (CAN)) **Mr Hamdan Al-Maktoum**
57 **MUTABAKHTIR (USA),** ch c 27/3 The Minstrel (CAN)—Street's Glory (USA) (Dr Fager) **Mr Hamdan Al-Maktoum**
58 **MUTARJJAM (USA),** b c 26/3 Stop The Music (USA)—So Smooth (USA) (Third Martini) **Mr Hamdan Al-Maktoum**
59 **PERFORMANCE,** ch c 15/4 Shadeed (USA)—Pushy (Sharpen Up) **Mr Hamdan Al-Maktoum**
60 **QUEEN OF ZURICH (IRE),** b f 26/3 Fairy King (USA)—Perfect Choice (Bold Lad (IRE)) **Louis Mayer**
61 **RAGHIB (IRE),** b c 21/5 Vision (USA)—Naqiyah (USA) (In Reality (USA)) **Mr Hamdan Al-Maktoum**
62 **RASMI (IRE),** b c 11/2 Last Tycoon—Alhaan (Tap On Wood) **Mr Hamdan Al-Maktoum**
63 **ROYAL RECREATION (USA),** b f 9/4 His Majesty (USA)—Break In (USA) (Wajima (USA)) **Dr Michael Smurfit**
64 **SAMAR (IRE),** b f 5/4 Wassl—Haneena (Habitat) **Hadi Al Tajir**
65 B f 20/3 Try My Best (USA)—St Clair Star (Sallust) **G. McCullagh**
66 **THIN ICE (IRE),** b f 6/2 Try My Best (USA)—Pudibunda (Bold Lad (IRE)) **Patrick J. Conlan**
67 **THUHOOL,** b c 3/3 Formidable (USA)—Wurud (USA) (Green Dancer (USA)) **Mr Hamdan Al-Maktoum**
68 **TONY'S DELIGHT (IRE),** b c 29/3 Krayyan—Tina's Image (He Loves Me) **Mrs Chris Harrington**
69 **TOOMUCH TOOSOON (IRE),** b c 24/1 Glenstal (USA)—Star of India (General Assembly (USA)) **J. C. Harley**
70 **TURFTEARER (IRE),** b g 30/4 Exhibitioner—Movement (Daring Display (USA)) **J. C. Harley**
71 **WILTON PLACE (IRE),** br c 8/5 Flash of Steel—Up The Gates (Captain James) **Mrs Cathrine McNulty**
72 **YAQATHA (IRE),** b f 15/2 Sadler's Wells (USA)—Two Rings (USA) (Round Table) **Mr Hamdan Al-Maktoum**

Jockey (Flat): D Parnell (8-2).

Jockey (NH): J R Sullivan (10-0).

Apprentices: R Burke (7-10), J F Clarke (7-12), U Halliday (7-7), B P Harding (7-1), A Murray (7-12), G Tormey (7-7).

479 MR P. PRENDERGAST, Kildare

Postal: **Melitta Lodge, Kildare, Co. Kildare, Ireland.**
Phone: **(045) 21288 OR 21401 FAX 353 45 21875**

1 **AMBER KING,** 6, b br g Indian King—Bean Siamsa **Mr Sean T. McElligott**
2 **BILLY BATHGATE,** 4, ch g Gala Performance—Royal River **Michael Buckley**
3 **CALLY'S KINGDOM,** 7, b h Rarity—Oblige **Herb M. Stanley**
4 **DR BOBBY,** 5, gr g Torus—Flower Dust **Mrs Patrick Prendergast**
5 **ENIGMATIC,** 4, b br g Welsh Term—Sammlerina **Michael Buckley**
6 **FESTIVAL DREAMS,** 5, b br g Strong Gale—Gala Noon **Mrs N. Dutfield**
7 4, B g Billion (USA)—Forest Music **Mrs Patrick Prendergast**
8 **GALLEY BAY,** 4, b f Welsh Saint—Locust Grove **Mrs Patrick Prendergast**

MR P. PRENDERGAST—continued

9 4, B g Prince Bee—Hidden Hand **Mrs Patrick Prendergast**
10 **JUST A MEMORY,** 4, b br c Kafu—Souveniers **Mr Patrick Prendergast**
11 **PROUD POINT,** 5, b m Over The River—High Town Jackie **Mrs Patrick Prendergast**
12 **RAGLAN ROAD,** 6, b g Furry Glen—Princess Concorde **Mrs Patrick Prendergast**
13 **SANDFORD SAINT,** 4, b c Welsh Saint—Sandford Star **Mrs Patrick Prendergast**
14 4, Br g Deep Run—Shuill Donn **Mrs Patrick Prendergast**
15 **SUDAF,** 4, b f Welsh Saint—Perfect Choice **C. Twomey**
16 **TURKISH TRUTH,** 4, b c Wolverlife—Turkish Suspicion **Mrs Patrick Prendergast**

THREE-YEAR-OLDS

17 **BALBRIGGAN,** b br f Dublin Taxi—Racy Lady **Mr P. J. Gallagher**
18 **BELLIVEAU,** b g Blakeney—Gilt Star **John Holleran**
19 **BLUES QUARTET,** b f Cure The Blues—Ringawoody **Mrs Patrick Prendergast**
20 **DIVINE BLOOM,** b f Yashgan—Second Bloom **Thomas R. Capehart**
21 **GAELIC HOPE,** ch g Horage—Amiga Mia **Mrs N. Dutfield**
22 **GONE FISHIN,** ch c Kris—Le Melody **Mr Patrick Prendergast**
23 Ch g Nicholas Bill—Hi-Conkers **Mrs Philomena Purcell**
24 **SLIPPERY PEER,** ch c Lord Gayle—Evening Slipper **Mr P. J. Gallagher**
25 **SOME FUN,** b f Wolverlife—Northern Wisdom **Lady Clague**
26 **TRUE LIBERTY,** br g Indian King—Takawin **Mr Patrick Prendergast**

TWO-YEAR-OLDS

27 Gr f 20/4 Glow (USA)—Hazy Lady (Habitat) **Mrs A. Moran**
28 Ch f 18/4 Fayruz—Instanter (Morston (FR))
29 Ch c 7/3 Commanche Run—Lassalia (Sallust) **Motohide Aoki**
30 Ch c 19/4 Flash of Steel—Manx Retreat (Habitat) **Lady Clague**
31 Ch f 16/3 Ela-Mana-Mou—No Distractions (Tap On Wood) **Mr Y. Akazawa**
32 B f 11/3 King of Clubs—Northern Chance (Northfields (USA))
33 **OTHER RANKS (IRE),** b c 27/4 Trojan Fen—Wernlas (Prince Tenderfoot (USA)) **Mr P. J. Gallagher**
34 B f 3/4 Ahonoora—Princess Seal (Prince Tenderfoot (USA))
35 **SIMPLY AMBER (IRE),** b f 10/5 Simply Great (FR)—Inishannagh (St Alphage) **Mr Sean T. McElligott**

480 SIR M. PRESCOTT BT, Newmarket

Postal: **Heath House, Newmarket, Suffolk, CB8 8DU.**
Phone: **(0638) 662117 FAX (0638) 666572**

1 **HELAWE,** 7, ch g Last Fandango—Pigmy **Mr A. R. C. Finn**
2 **MILLIGAN,** 5, ch h Tap On Wood—Rose Music **Mr B. Haggas**
3 **PLAIN FACT,** 5, b g Known Fact (USA)—Plain Tree **Mrs Peter Atkinson**
4 **PUSSY FOOT,** 4, b f Red Sunset—Cats **Mrs C. R. Philipson**
5 **SERIOUS TROUBLE,** 4, ch c Good Times (ITY)—Silly Woman **Mr G. Moore**

THREE-YEAR-OLDS

6 **AMOUR DU SOIR (USA),** b c L'Emigrant (USA)—Evening Kiss (USA) **Mr T. J. Rooney**
7 **ARPERO,** b f Persian Bold—Arvel **Mr P. G. Goulandris**
8 **BABICOS,** b f Free State—Chellaston Park **Mr David M. Adams**
9 **CASE LAW,** ch c Ahonoora—Travesty **Mr John Livock**
10 **DANCE BUSTER,** b g Bustino—Dance In Rome **Mr Neil Greig**
11 **DANCING COVE,** b c Shareef Dancer (USA)—Fanny's Cove **Mr B. Haggas**
12 **DUNMAGLASS,** b g Sayf El Arab (USA)—Stubble **Lady Hayward**
13 **FIGMENT,** b f Posse (USA)—Honey Thief **Lady Henrietta St. George**
14 **LOCO TYCOON,** ch c Nicholas Bill—Sabala **Mr William West**
15 **MARTIN-LAVELL POST,** b f Tina's Pet—Stradey Park **Mr A. Lavell**
16 **MATHEMA,** ch f Rousillon (USA)—Blue Doc **Mr Fahd Salman**
17 **MISTY EYES,** b f High Top—Ringed Aureole **Capt. J. Macdonald-Buchanan**
18 **MONA,** b f Auction Ring (USA)—Sovereign Rose **Lady Henrietta St. George**
19 **NIDOMI,** ch c Dominion—Nicholas Grey **Mr P. G. Goulandris**
20 **NIGHT-SHIRT,** b g Night Shift (USA)—Vestina **Mr Garth Insoll**

SIR M. PRESCOTT BT—continued

21 **NUMBER ELEVEN,** b f Local Suitor (USA)—Babycham Sparkle **Mrs John Hayter**
22 **ROCK FACE,** b f Ballad Rock—Misty Halo **Mrs C. R. Philipson**
23 **SAPPHIRINE,** b f Trojan Fen—By Surprise **Mrs F. R. Watts**
24 **SERIOUS HONOUR (SWE),** ch g Ballacashtal (CAN)—Blue Garter **Mr G. Moore**
25 B f Ardross—Sombreuil **Lady Henrietta St. George**
26 **TWILIGHT RAIN,** b g Hays—Fine Form (USA) **Mr G. Rock**
27 **TWO LEFT FEET,** b c Petorius—Whitstar **Mr P. W. W. Molins**
28 **TYRIAN,** b f Elegant Air—Character Builder **Lady Yarrow**
29 **VICTORIOUS PRINCE,** b c Bold Lad (IRE)—Stracomer Queen **Mr Neil Greig**
30 **VOGOS ANGEL,** b f Song—Lovage **Mrs John Hayter**
31 **YANKEE TRADER,** b f Stanford—Amboselli **Mr G. D. Waters**

TWO-YEAR-OLDS

32 **ASPIRANT,** b c 21/3 High Top—Yen (AUS) (Biscay (AUS)) **Lord Derby**
33 **CARMEN'S JOY,** br f 12/3 Chief Singer—Bag Lady (Be My Guest (USA)) **Mr P. G. Goulandris**
34 **CORYPHEE,** b f 25/2 Touching Wood (USA)—Dance In Rome (Dance In Time (CAN)) **Major General Sir George Burns**
35 **GIJON,** b c 29/2 Coquelin (USA)—Elan's Valley (Welsh Pageant) **Mr David M. Adams**
36 **GILDED OMEN,** b f 24/2 Faustus (USA)—Fine Asset (Hot Spark) **Miss E. Aldous**
37 **GLENASLENA (IRE),** b f 11/4 Gorytus (USA)—Scalded (Hotfoot) **Mr John Davis**
38 **HAZAR (IRE),** b f 20/4 Thatching—Etoile des Galles (Busted) **Mr Fahd Salman**
39 **HENPOT (IRE),** b f 2/3 Alzao (USA)—Whispered Wishes (High Top) **Lady Henrietta St. George**
40 **HIGHLAND GIRL,** b f 17/3 Scottish Reel—Girl On A Swing (High Top) **Mr P. D. Savill**
41 **INDIGO LADY (IRE),** b f 18/3 Salmon Leap (USA)—Late Spring (Silly Season) **Mrs F. R. Watts**
42 **JAHZEELAN,** b c 23/3 Never So Bold—Misty Halo (High Top) **Mr Fahd Salman**
43 **JAMESTOWN BOY,** b c 8/3 King of Clubs—Jhansi Ki Rani (Far North) **Lady Henrietta St. George**
44 **JUST GILL,** ch f 26/3 Tina's Pet—City Link Lass (Double Jump) **Mr David M. Adams**
45 **JUST READY (IRE),** b c 2/4 Petorius—Lacey Brief (Roi Dagobert) **Mr W. E. Sturt**
46 **KINA (USA),** ch f 17/5 Bering—Sanctum Sanctorum (USA) (Secretariat (USA)) **Mr Fahd Salman**
47 **MANGROVE MIST,** b f 10/4 Nishapour (FR)—Antiguan Cove (Mill Reef (USA)) **Mr W. E. Sturt**
48 **MERRY ROUS,** b f 10/5 Rousillon (USA)—Merry Weather (Will Somers) **Major J. L. L. Green**
49 **MIDNIGHT SAGA,** b c 10/5 Mashhor Dancer (USA)—Honey Pot (Hotfoot) **Lady Henrietta St. George**
50 **MOVING OUT,** b c 20/2 Slip Anchor—New Generation (Young Generation) **Mr Fahd Salman**
51 **MR CONFUSION,** b c 26/4 Kafu—Mrs Foodbroker (Home Guard) **Mr John Livock**
52 **MR SNAIL,** b c 1/4 Petorius—Spring Lane (Forlorn River) **Lady Henrietta St. George**
53 **ORUJO (IRE),** b c 14/3 Try My Best (USA)—Oyace (Hogarth) **Mr T. J. Rooney**
54 **PERSIAN PUSSYCAT (IRE),** b f 22/4 Persian Bold—Gracious Consent (Prince Regent) **Mr E. J. Loder**
55 **PUCK'S BOSS (IRE),** b c 9/2 Fairy King (USA)—Mullaghroe (Tarboosh) **Mrs David Russell**
56 **QUINZII MARTIN,** b c 10/4 Song—Quaranta (Hotfoot) **Lady Fairhaven**
57 **RIVER CHASE (IRE),** ch f 18/1 Salmon Leap (USA)—Amboselli (Raga Navarro (ITY)) **Mr G. D. Waters**
58 **SERIOUS HURRY,** ch c 20/3 Forzando—Lady Bequick (Sharpen Up) **Mr G. Moore**
59 **SERIOUS TIME,** ch c 10/3 Good Times (ITY)—Milva (Jellaby) **Mr G. Moore**
60 **SKI BABY,** b f 23/2 Petoski—Babycham Sparkle (So Blessed) **Mr John Livock**
61 **SUNNY DAVIS (USA),** ch f 20/3 Alydar (USA)—Goldie Hawn (USA) (Northern Dancer (USA)) **Hesmonds Stud**
62 **TOBY HENRY,** b c 14/2 Jalmood (USA)—Wave Dancer (Dance In Time (CAN)) **Mr David M. Adams**
63 **TRUTH ENDURES,** b f 25/3 Absalom—Truth Will Out (Blakeney) **Miss Pearl Lawson Johnston**
64 B c 1/5 Final Straw—Warm Wind (Tumble Wind (USA)) **Sir Mark Prescott**
65 **WILL PLASI,** b c 10/3 Elegant Air—Miss Plasi (Free State) **Mr Garth Insoll**
66 **YAKITORI,** b c 6/5 Petoski—Epithet (Mill Reef (USA)) **Mr David M. Adams**

Other Owners: Mrs O. Fox-Pitt, Mr M. A. Hudson, Mr Fenton James Kirwan, Mr J. W. Malins, Mr P. McSwiney, Mrs Sam Whitbread, Mr A. Whitfield.

Jockeys (Flat): G Duffield (7-13), C Nutter (8-0).

Apprentice: B Lang (7-7).

Amateur: Miss Jane Armitage (8-0).

481 MR G. R. PREST, Newbury

Postal: **Cullimore Stables, Peasemore, Newbury, Berkshire, RG16 0JN.**
Phone: **(OFFICE) & (HOME) 0635 248036**

1 6, B g Dubassoff—Idyll-Liquor
2 OCEAN LINK, 6, gr g Cunard—La Chatelaine **Mr J. M. G. Andrews**
3 4, B g Goldhill—Orra Beg
4 4, B g Nearly A Hand—Papa's Paradise
5 SPARTAN RAFT, 9, ch g Lighter—Tanaway

Other Owners: Mr A. Lawes, Mrs G. Joyce Prest, Mr G. R. Prest.

Jockey (NH): A Gorman (10-0).

482 MR G. H. PRICE, Leominster

Postal: **Hamnish Farm, Leominster, Herefordshire.**
Phone: **STEENSBRIDGE (056882) 235**

1 BRIEF GLANCE, 5, b m Official—Second Glance **Mrs S. Fawcett-Gandy**
2 COPPERITE, 7, b g Rapid Pass—Present Fantasy **Mrs M. O. James**
3 I WONDER WHEN, 9, ch g Levanter—Gretna Wonder **Mr M. F. Oseman**
4 NIMBLE DOVE, 14, b m Starch Reduced—Red Dove **Mrs V. E. Price**
5 PEARL RUN, 9, ch g Gulf Pearl—Deep Down **Mr R. Squires**
6 SALFORD RAPHAELLA, 6, ch m Deep Run—Hazeldean **Mrs K. Oseman**
7 SALLY'S DOVE, 5, ch m Celtic Cone—Nimble Dove **Mrs V. E. Price**
8 TRUE SPARTAN, 10, b g True Song—Madge Spartan **Mr T. J. Eckley**
9 VICTORY WIND, 5, ch g Asdic—Cool Wind **Mr D. W. Gladwyn**

THREE-YEAR-OLDS

10 PEARL DOVE, b f Oats—Nimble Dove **Mr Cecil J. Price**

Other Owners: Mr J. E. Heymans.

483 MR J. P. PRICE, Leominster

Postal: **The Day House, Kingsland, Leominster, Herefordshire, HR6 9SW.**
Phone: **(0568) 81264**

1 GENERAL HINTON, 6, b g General Assembly (USA)—Cherry Hinton (USA) **Mr J. P. Price**
2 MARDOOD, 5, b h Ela-Mana-Mou—Tigeen **Mr J. P. Price**

484 MR T. J. PRICE, Chepstow

Postal: **Bradbury Farm, Crick, Portskewett, Newport, Wales.**
Phone: **(0291) 421596**

1 NEVER EVER, 5, gr g Bradbury Master—Gillian Rosemary **Mr T. J. Price**

Jockey (NH): Granville Davies (10-0).

Lady Rider: Mrs Rosemary Price (9-10).

485 MR WILLIAM PRICE, Ebbw Vale

Postal: **3 Garth Dan-y-Bryn, Beaufort, Ebbw Vale, Gwent, Wales, NP3 5RU.**
Phone: **(0495) 303655**

1 **ARCTIC KEN,** 7, ch g Stanford—Peggy Dell **Mr Michael Deren**
2 **CONNAUGHT CLEANERS,** 10, br g Raise You Ten—Bramble Rose **Mr A. D. Phillips**
3 **CRYMLYN SWING,** 6, ch m Swing Easy (USA)—Royal Tactic **Mr A. D. Phillips**
4 **HIGH BID,** 5, b m Auction Ring (USA)—High Move **Mrs Sharon Jenner**
5 **HIGH LAWS,** 6, b g Royal Fountain—Dunlean **Mrs Thora Lewis**
6 **KARFIA,** 4, b f Royal Match—Kasarose **Mr T. G. Price**
7 **KINGS FOLLY,** 8, b g Hillandale—Sovereign's Folly **Mrs A. Gregg**
8 **ORIGAMI,** 5, ch g Horage—Demeter **Mr F. O. Trickett**
9 **SMITHY BEAR,** 8, b g Rupert Bear—Avonteous **Mrs J. V. John**
10 **TA CHANCE,** 4, ch f On Your Mark—Telstop (FR) **Mr W. Wright**

Other Owners: Mr Cliff Brown, Mr Stan Huish, Mr D. L. Jones, Mr A. J. Price.

Conditional: A Price (10-0).

486 MR P. A. PRITCHARD, Shipston-on-Stour

Postal: **The Gate House, Whatcote, Shipston-on-Stour, Warwickshire.**
Phone: **TYSOE (029 588) 689**

1 **ANNIES ROSE,** 5, br g Soldiers Rose—Easy Action **Mrs N. R. Matthews**
2 **BALLAD RULER,** 4, ch g Ballad Rock—Jessamy Hall **Miss M. J. Preece**
3 **DORNVALLEY LAD,** 9, ch g Anax—Lovely Diana **Mr Bryan Gordon**
4 **GREEN DOORS,** 6, b g Swing Easy (USA)—Rouge Song **Mr M. B. Maunsell**
5 **LUCKY VINTAGE,** 13, br g French Vine—Al Mansoura **Miss M. J. Preece**
6 **ROUTE MARCH,** 11, ch g Queen's Hussar—Wide of The Mark **Miss M. J. Preece**
7 **TOUR VIEILLE,** 7, b g Bold Lad (IRE)—Noreena **B. B. Cocken**
8 **WOODLAND GENERATOR,** 11, ch g True Song—Dainty **Miss M. J. Preece**
9 **WOODLANDS GENHIRE,** 5, ch g Celtic Cone—Spartella **Miss M. J. Preece**
10 **WOODLANDS GENPOWER,** 8, b g Celtic Cone—April Sovereign **Miss M. J. Preece**
11 **WOODLANDS GREY,** 4, gr g Nishapour (FR)—Topling **Miss M. J. Preece**
12 **WOODLANDS LAD,** 15, ch g Jimmy Reppin—Ptelea **Mr P. A. Pritchard**
13 **WOOLY RAGS,** 4, ch f Raga Navarro (ITY)—Woolcana **Mr P. A. Pritchard**

Amateur: Mr J Pritchard (10-7).

487 DR P. L. J. PRITCHARD, Purton

Postal: **Scrumpy Cottage, Purton, Berkeley, Gloucestershire, GL13 9HY.**
Phone: **(0453) 811881**

1 **CERTAIN SPARK,** 10, ch g Ascertain (USA)—Sparkling Sugar **Mr Ray Pritchard**
2 **FOOTSTICK,** 14, b g Tarqogan—Troon **Mrs T. Pritchard**
3 **FOUR FROM THE EDGE,** 7, b g Pollerton—Honey Toi **Dr P. L. J. Pritchard**
4 **JILLY WOOD,** 6, gr m Pragmatic—Bartlemy Fair **Mr Ray Pritchard**
5 **MR GUMBOOTS,** 16, b g Eucalyptus—White Slave **Dr P. L. J. Pritchard**
6 **NEEDWOOD LEADER,** 9, b g Averof—The Doe **Dr P. L. J. Pritchard**
7 **SANDMOOR PRINCE,** 7, b g Grundy—Princesse du Seine (FR) **Mrs T. Pritchard**

Amateur: Dr P L J Pritchard (9-9).

Follow The Leader

*During the 365 days of 1989, the progeny of Gainesway Farm stallions won or placed more than **650** times in stakes races worth over **$60,000,000**, including **195** times in Graded or Group stakes and **65** times in Grade I or Group I events.*

*Sheikh Mohammed's **Local Talent**, perhaps the last Group I winner by **NORTHERN DANCER**, won the 1989 Prix Jean Prat, Fr-I, from champion and classic winner **KENDOR***

GAINESWAY FARM

William Graham's ***BLONDEINAMOTEL****, winner of the classic Canadian Oaks, Can-I, was one of five 1989 stakes winners to represent* ***Bates Motel***

February

20th ***Advocator's*** MARTIN A. won the Copa Jorge Washington, PR-I
26th ***Stop the Music's*** MUSIC MERCI won the San Rafael S., gr. II

March

4th ***Lyphard's Wish's*** GIORDANO won the Handicap Hidalgo, Mex-II
7th ***Explodent's*** MI SELECTO won the Pan American H., gr. I
25th ***Blushing Groom's*** BLUSHING JOHN won the Razorback H., gr. II

April

18th ***Lyphard's*** ENSCONSE won the Nell Gwyn S., Eng-III
21st ***Green Dancer's*** FANTASTIC LOOK won the Fantasy S., gr. I
22nd ***Lyphard's*** MAZILIER won the San Simeon H., gr. III
23rd ***Local Talent*** won the Prix de Guiche Fr-III
29th ***Lyphard's Wish's*** LYPHARD'S RIDGE won the Ark-La-Tex H., gr. III
30th ***Lear Fan's*** SIKESTON won the Italian Two Thousand Guineas, Ity-I

May

4th ***Explodent's*** HOLST won the Prix de Saint-Georges, Fr-III
6th ***Blushing Groom's*** NASHWAN won the Two Thousand Guineas, Eng-I

Sheikh Hamdan al Maktoum's ***NASHWAN****, by* ***Blushing Groom****, with four Group I victories—the 2000 Guineas, Derby, Eclipse, and the King George VI and Queen Elizabeth Diamond Stakes—became the first horse in history to score such a single-season grand slam*

11th ***Exceller's*** MOUNTAIN KINGDOM won the Ormonde E.B.F. Stakes, Eng-III

14th ***Lyphard's*** PEARL BRACELET won the French One Thousand Guineas, Fr-I

16th ***Blushing Groom's*** SNOW BRIDE won the Musidora S., Eng-III

17th ***Green Dancer's*** TORJOUN won the Dante S., Eng-III

18th ***Exceller's*** MOUNTAIN KINGDOM won the Yorkshire Cup, Eng-III

27th ***Lyphard's*** ENSCONSE won the Irish One Thousand Guineas, Ire-I

27th ***Stop the Music's*** MUSIC MERCI won the Illinois Derby, gr. II

28th ***Local Talent*** won the Prix Jean Prat, Fr-I

28th ***Temperence Hill's*** IMBIBE won the Peter Pan S., gr. II

28th ***Explodent's*** HOT OPTION won the Honeymoon H., gr. III

28th ***Wolf Power's*** ALEMANIA won the Clasico Rafina, Mex-III

June	July

June

3rd ***Stop the Music's*** SQUILL won the Premio Emilio Turati, Ity-II

7th ***Blushing Groom's*** NASHWAN won the Derby S., Eng-I

18th ***Bates Motel's*** BLONDEINAMOTEL won the Canadian Oaks, Can-I

20th ***Blushing Groom's*** TWO TIMING won the Prince of Wales's S., Eng-II

25th ***Blushing Groom's*** BLUSHING JOHN won the Hollywood Gold Cup H., gr. I

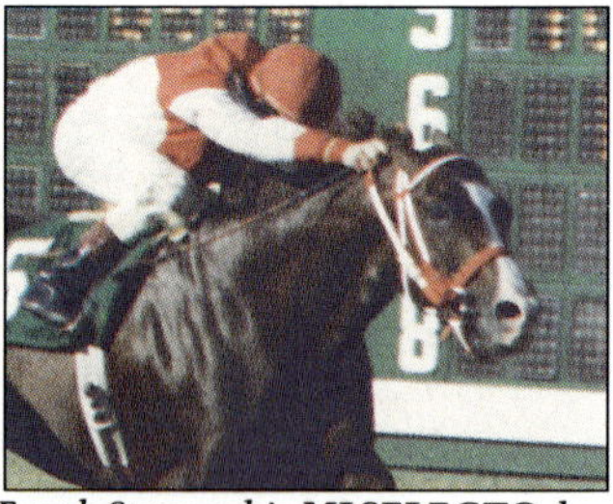

Frank Stronach's ***MI SELECTO****, by* ***Explodent****, won both the $300,000 Pan American Handicap, gr. I, and the $500,000 Meadowlands Cup Handicap, gr. I, in 1989*

July

1st ***Explodent's*** MI SELECTO won the Dominion Day H., gr. III

8th ***Blushing Groom's*** NASHWAN won the Eclipse S., Eng-I

12th ***Big Spruce's*** SPRUCE FIR won the Matchmaker S., gr. II

14th ***Riverman's*** RIVER WARDEN won the Prix Eugene Adam, Fr-II

16th ***Blushing Groom's*** RAHY won the Bel Air H., gr. II

22nd ***Blushing Groom's*** NASHWAN won the King George VI and Queen Elizabeth Diamond S., Eng-I

30th ***Blushing Groom's*** BLUSHING KATY won the Dutchess S., Can-III

August

5th ***Arts and Letters'*** SUNSHINE ALWAYS won the Queen's H., gr. III

5th *Riverman's* QIRMAZI won the Prix de Cabourg, Fr-III

19th *Czaravich's* BLACK CZARAVICH won the Clasico Anahuac, Mex-I

20th *Riverman's* UNDERWORLD won the Norsk Derby, Nor-I

September

1st *Green Dancer's* CONFIRMED DANCER won the Arlington Oaks, gr. III

4th *Irish River's* DRAPEAU TRICOLORE won the Norristown H., gr. III

9th *Blushing Groom's* BLUSHING JOHN won the Washington Park H., gr. II

16th *Riverman's* RIVER MEMORIES won the Flower Bowl H., gr. I

16th *Czaravich's* BLACK CZARAVICH won the Clasico Independencia, Mex-II

17th *Green Dancer's* SENOR PETE won the Futurity S., gr. I

23rd *Green Dancer's* GREEN BARB won the Laurance Armour H., gr. II

23rd *Blushing Groom's* BLUSHING KATY won the Etobicoke H., Can-III

Mr. and Mrs. Jerome Moss' ***Garthorn*** *won the 1986 Metropolitan Handicap, gr. I, in the second fastest time in the history of the event—1:33 3/5 for the mile*

October

1st *Lyphard's* Funambule won the Prix des Chenes, Fr-III

4th *Czaravich's* BLACK CZARAVICH won the Clasico Jacarandas, Mex-II

7th *Irish River's* DRAPEAU TRICOLORE won the Fayette H., gr. II

8th *Czaravich's* TURFAH won the Niagara H., gr. III

13th *Explodent's* MI SELECTO won the Meadowlands Cup H., gr. I

*Allen Paulson's **BLUSHING JOHN**, by **Blushing Groom**, maintained his edge as the leading candidate for Eclipse Award honors as champion older male with his courageous run in the Breeders' Cup Classic, gr. I*

*Lawrence C. Pendleton and Royal T Stable's **MUSIC MERCI**, by **Stop the Music**, won or placed in seven 1989 stakes, six of which were Graded*

14th *Riverman's* NAYRIZI won the Herbert Power H., Aus-II

14th *Blushing Groom's* SNOW BRIDE won the Princess Royal S., Eng-III

15th *Wolf Power's* ALEMANIA won the Clasico Northern Dancer, Mex-I

29th *Irish River's* SEVEN RIVERS won the Volante H., gr. II

30th *Explodent's* BEX won the Prix de Flore, Fr-III

Mike Rutherford's homebred ***SENOR PETE*** *won the Futurity Stakes, gr. I, and was one of three Graded stakes winners for* ***Green Dancer*** *in a span of 14 days in September*

Mahmoud Fustok's ***PEARL BRACELET*** *won the 1989 classic Poule d'Essai des Pouliches, Fr-I, and became one of 21 champions, classic performers and/or millionaires sired by* ***Lyphard***

November

12th ***Blushing Groom's*** HEART OF GROOM won the Premio Roma Vecchia, Ity-III

20th ***Wolf Power's*** ALEMANIA won the Clasico Veinte de Noviembre, Mex-II

December

26th ***Stop the Music's*** MUSIC MERCI won the Malibu S., gr. II

The Stallions

ADVOCATOR
AFLEET
APALACHEE
ARTS AND LETTERS
BATES MOTEL
BIG SPRUCE
BLUSHING GROOM
BROAD BRUSH
CANNONADE
COZZENE
CZARAVICH
DR. CARTER
EXCELLER
EXPLODENT
GARTHORN
GREEN DANCER
HATCHET MAN
IRISH RIVER
LEAR FAN
LEMHI GOLD
L'EMIGRANT
LOCAL TALENT
LYPHARD
LYPHARD'S WISH
MT. LIVERMORE
PANCHO VILLA
RIVERMAN
SILENT SCREEN
SMILE
STAGE DOOR JOHNNY
STOP THE MUSIC
SUPERBITY
TANK'S PROSPECT
TEMPERENCE HILL
TREMPOLINO
WOLF POWER
KEY TO THE MINT

All Gainesway stallions are nominated to the Breeders' Cup

GAINESWAY FARM

Graham J. Beck, President 3750 Paris Pike, Lexington, KY 40511 606/293-2676

488 MR G. A. PRITCHARD-GORDON, Newmarket

Postal: **Trillium Place, Birdcage Walk, Newmarket, Suffolk, CB8 ONE.**
Phone: **(0638) 665281 OR 662824 or 664685 FAX 665234**

1 **CRAFTSMAN,** 4, b c Balinger—Crafty Look **Mr George Paul**
2 **GOOD FOR THE ROSES,** 4, b c Kampala—Alleyn **Mr M. J. Stewart**
3 **GULFLAND,** 9, ch g Gulf Pearl—Sunland Park **Mr Gavin A. Pritchard-Gordon**
4 **HENRIETTA PLACE,** 6, b m Sayyaf—Gilana **Mr Gavin A. Pritchard-Gordon**
5 **LETTEREWE,** 4, b f Alias Smith (USA)—Princess Nefertiti **Mr E. H. Vestey**
6 **LILY'S LOVER (USA),** 4, b g Sensitive Prince (USA)—Rushing Stream (USA) **Mr A. Leonard**
7 **MATOU,** 10, b h Mummy's Pet—Great Optimist **Mrs T. C. Pick**
8 **PEER PRINCE (USA),** 5, br h Vaguely Noble—Sweet Maid (USA) **Mr C. Pick**
9 **PROMEGG,** 4, ch c Music Boy—Rosy Lee (FR) **Miss H. F. Gevers**
10 **STEFFI,** 4, ch f Precocious—Western Gem **Mrs S. W. O'Brien**
11 **VERDON CANYON,** 6, b g African Sky—Windy City **Mr Gavin A. Pritchard-Gordon**

THREE-YEAR-OLDS

12 **BARCHAM,** b g Blakeney—La Pythie (FR) **Mrs A. P. B. Allen**
13 **BODGE,** b f Horage—The Flying Sputnik **Miss H. F. Gevers**
14 **BREEZY MONARCH,** b f Tender King—Airy Queen (USA) **Mr Gavin A. Pritchard-Gordon**
15 **DARTING MOTH,** br f Mansingh (USA)—Crescent Dart **Lady Durham**
16 **EASY PREP,** b g Reasonable (FR)—Professor's Choice **Mr A. K. Collins**
17 **GLITTERBIRD,** br f Glint of Gold—Dovetail **Lord Ronaldshay**
18 **GOOD SKILLS,** b f Bustino—Gunner's Belle **Mr Gavin A. Pritchard-Gordon**
19 **HINTLESHAM HARRY,** b g Pas de Seul—Silver Glimpse **Hintlesham Hall Ltd**
20 **KALOGY,** gr f Kalaglow—Coyote **Lord Derby**
21 **LAKE MISTASSIU,** b f Tina's Pet—Kakisa **Mr John Lambton**
22 **LOCH SPEY,** ch f Formidable (USA)—River Spey **Mr I. H. Stewart-Brown**
23 **MILITARY SHOT (USA),** b g Lyphard's Wish (FR)—Pavahra **Mrs Shona St. George**
24 **MISTRESS CARROLL,** ch f Simply Great (FR)—Cariole **Mr M. A. Carroll**
25 **NAKORA BISTRAYA (USA),** b f Robellino (USA)—Calypsa (USA) **Mrs D. MacRae**
26 **PARKING BAY,** b g Bay Express—Sophie Avenue **Lord Cadogan**
27 **PRAYER WHEEL,** b f High Line—Heaven Knows **Mr Giles W. Pritchard-Gordon**
28 **SHADOW BIRD,** b f Martinmas—In The Shade **Mrs R. C. Buxton**
29 **SPOFFORTH,** b g Jalmood (USA)—Visible Form **Mr S. P. Tindall**
30 **TARDA,** ch f Absalom—Ixia **Lady Durham**
31 **TIGNANELLO,** ch g Burslem—Ms Yvonne **Mr Walter Mariti**
32 **WAVE MASTER,** b g Chief Singer—Sea Fret **Mr A. W. Anderson**
33 **WEAREAGRANDMOTHER,** b f Prince Tenderfoot (USA)—Lady Bettina **Sir Clement Freud**

TWO-YEAR-OLDS

34 Gr c 22/3 Bold Owl—Bri-Ette (Brittany)
35 **CARD TRICK,** ch f 2/2 Good Times (ITY)—Double Shuffle (Tachypous) **The Hon. David Sieff**
36 B c 19/2 King of Clubs—Carntino (Bustino)
37 **FENTON LAKE,** b c 5/5 Tina's Pet—Kakisa (Forlorn River) **Lady Durham**
38 Br c 15/3 King of Spain—Firdale Rosie (Town Crier)
39 **FOXTROT PIE,** ch f 24/3 Shernazar—Round Dance (Auction Ring (USA)) **Mr E. H. Vestey**
40 B f 13/4 Balliol—Glebe (Tacitus) **Newmarket Club Plc**
41 B c 29/3 Kafu—Golden Empress (Cavo Doro)
42 B br c 27/3 Sayf El Arab (USA)—Home In Pasadena (Home Guard (USA)) **Mr John J. McLaren**
43 B f 11/5 Tina's Pet—Ixia (I Say) **Lady Durham**
44 Br c 30/4 On Your Mark—June Lady (Junius) **Mrs M. Carr**
45 **MARSH WARBLER,** b c 1/6 Wattlefield—Be Lyrical (Song) **Mr J. M. Greetham**
46 **MINARET,** ch f 4/4 Jalmood (USA)—Montania (Mourne) **Lord Derby**
47 **MIRACLES HAPPEN,** ch f 24/2 Superlative—Pilfer (Vaigly Great) **Mr Giles W. Pritchard-Gordon**
48 **MIRROR'S IMAGE,** ch f 19/2 Never So Bold—Mirabiliary (USA) (Crow (FR)) **Mrs D. Scott-Harden**
49 Ch c 28/1 Dara Monarch—Miss Victoria (Auction Ring (USA)) **Sheikh Amin Dahlawi**
50 **RED POPPY (IRE),** b f 25/2 Coquelin (USA)—Special Thanks (Kampala) **Mr S. A. Meacock**
51 **RESTAPOUR,** gr f 25/4 Nishapour (FR)—Restive (Relic) **Mr R. N. Richmond-Watson**
52 **RUNAWAY LAD,** b c 11/5 Runnett—Kingston Rose (Tudor Music) **Mr G. J. Butts**
53 Ch c 30/3 Be My Native (USA)—Sunland Park (Baragoi) **Sir John Mowbray**

MR G. A. PRITCHARD-GORDON—continued

54 **SURVEY,** b f 26/4 Glint of Gold—Old Domesday Book (High Top) **Lord Derby**
55 **SWEEP ALONG (IRE),** b f 12/4 Persian Bold—Bristle (Thatch (USA)) **Mr I. H. Stewart-Brown**
56 B c 19/4 Red Sunset—Tippity Top (High Top) **Mr M. Ennever**
57 **TUPPAT,** ch f 6/5 Noalto—Stratch (FR) (Thatch (USA)) **Mr Giles W. Pritchard-Gordon**
58 **VOSTOK,** ch f 3/5 The Noble Player—The Flying Sputnik (Touch Paper) **Mrs D. MacRae**
59 B f 14/4 Nomination—Wild Asset (Welsh Pageant)

Other Owners: Miss D. Birkbeck, Mr P. Burnett, Mr A. L. Don, Lord Dundas, Mr J. Jones, Lord Lambton, Mrs R. Leonard, The Countess Of Lonsdale, Mr M. J. Meacock, Mr Paul Morrison, P. Myerscough, Mr J. H. Richmond-Watson, Mr Ian Robertson, Mr John R. Sims, Mrs E. Stokes, Lord Zetland.

Jockey (Flat): W Hood (8-4).

Jockey (NH): S Smith-Eccles (10-2).

Apprentice: Paul Smith-Eccles (7-9).

Conditional: Terence John Kent (10-0).

489 MR R. C. PUGH, Worcester

Postal: **Ashfields Farm, Peachley Lane, Hallow, Worcestershire.**
Phone: **(0905) 640547**

1 **MISS CANNIBAL,** 9, gr m Buckskin (FR)—No Nonsence (FR) **Mr R. C. Pugh**
2 **SALA BLUE,** 4, b f Fine Blue—Ashfields Kanda **Mr R. C. Pugh**
3 **SENNA BLUE,** 5, ch g Fine Blue—Ashfields Kanda **Mr R. C. Pugh**

490 MRS J. R. RAMSDEN, Thirsk

Postal: **Breckenbrough House, Sandhutton, Thirsk, North Yorkshire, YO7 4EL.**
Phone: **(0845) 587226 FAX (0845) 587427**

1 **AHSANTA SANA,** 4, b g Nicholas Bill—Dancing Valerina **Mr R. E. Sangster**
2 **ARBORY STREET,** 5, b g Anfield—Melvin **Mr James P. Stewart**
3 **COOL ENOUGH,** 9, ch g Welsh Captain—Sundrive **Mrs J. R. Ramsden**
4 **DARING TIMES,** 5, gr g Good Times (ITY)—She Who Dares **Mr Colin Webster**
5 **GREEN ARCHER,** 7, b g Hardgreen (USA)—Mittens **Mr R. C. Moody**
6 **KIND OF USEFUL,** 4, b g Kind of Hush—Klaire **R. H. Lewis**
7 **LYPHEORIC (USA),** 5, b g Lypheor—Fabulous Salt (USA) **Mr Nicholas De Savary**
8 **ONE FOR THE POT,** 5, ch g Nicholas Bill—Tea-Pot **Mr K. E. Wheldon**
9 **REVARO,** 4, b g Corvaro (USA)—Quick Dream **Mr George Ridley**
10 **STANDING COUNT,** 4, ch g Stanford—Barefoot Contessa **Mr Nicholas De Savary**
11 **TRAVELLING LIGHT,** 4, b g Electric—La Levantina **Mrs A. E. Sigsworth**
12 **VERBARIUM (USA),** 10, br g Verbatim (USA)—Havre **Mrs J. R. Ramsden**

THREE-YEAR-OLDS

13 **DERRY REEF,** b f Derrylin—Ballyreef **Mrs J. R. Ramsden**
14 **ESCAPE TALK,** gr f Gabitat—Getaway Girl **Mr Jonathan Ramsden**
15 **FOOT SOLDIER,** b g Hotfoot—Gunnard **Mr J. Grondona**
16 **GOLDEN TORQUE,** br g Taufan (USA)—Brightelmstone **Mr Colin Webster**
17 **HIGHLAND RALLY (USA),** b g Highland Blade (USA)—Fast Trek (FR) **Mr Colin Webster**

MRS J. R. RAMSDEN—continued

18 **HIGH LIVING,** b g Good Times (ITY)—Visible Asset **Mrs D. Ridley**
19 **LINE OF VISION (USA),** gr c Liloy (FR)—Invision (USA) **Mrs Nicholas De Savary**
20 **MANX PRINCESS,** b f Roscoe Blake—Princess Scarlett **Mrs M. E. White**
21 **MATCHING LINES,** ch f Thatching—Irish Limerick **Mrs Henry Meakin**
22 **OWT ON,** ch g Sweet Monday—Young April **Mr J. Brisco**
23 **PLATONIQUE,** b f Dunbeath (USA)—Plato's Retreat **Mr Peter Thompson-Hill**
24 **PULIGNY,** b g Glenstal (USA)—No Distractions **Mr N. R. Munton**
25 **SUREFOOT SILLARS,** ch g Hotfoot—Make A Signal **Sillars Civil Engineering**

TWO-YEAR-OLDS

26 **ACTIVE MOVEMENT,** ch f 17/2 Music Boy—Royal Agnes (Royal Palace) **Cheveley Park Stud**
27 **ADMIRALS SEAT,** ch c 3/5 Ardross—Sombreuil (Bold Lad (IRE)) **Mr Nicholas De Savary**
28 **CHALLENGE,** ch c 30/1 Never So Bold—Ravaro (Raga Navarro (ITY)) **R. C. Thompson**
29 **DEGREE OF FORCE,** b c 21/3 Stanford—Scotch Rocket (Roan Rocket) **R. D. Binns**
30 **FIZZ TIME,** b c 24/2 Good Times (ITY)—More Fizz (Morston (FR)) **Mr Nicholas De Savary**
31 **HIGH PREMIUM,** b c 9/3 Forzando—High Halo (High Top) **D. B. Thompson**
32 **KING OF CHANCE (IRE),** b c 22/3 Indian King (USA)—
Midnight Chance (Run The Gantlet (USA)) **Mr Nicholas De Savary**
33 **LINCOLN GREEN (IRE),** b f 5/3 Ela-Mana-Mou—Verde Dimora (Sir Ivor) **Mr R. E. Sangster**
34 **MIDDLETHORPE MAID,** ch f 20/2 Nicholas Bill—Floricelle (Derring-Do) **C. Stevenson**
35 **NEVER SO SURE,** br c 27/5 Never So Bold—Amerella (Welsh Pageant) **R. C. Thompson**
36 **SENOR POQUITO,** b c 7/5 Primo Dominie—Poquito (Major Portion) **Mrs D. Gillam**
37 **SHADY PIMPERNEL,** b c 21/5 Blakeney—Upanishad (Amber Rama) **Mr Nicholas de Savary**
38 **SILLARS STALKER (IRE),** b c 11/5 Stalker—Mittens (Run The Gantlet (USA)) **Sillars Civil Engineering**
39 **SOVEREIGN NICHE,** gr c 15/5 Nishapour (FR)—Sovereign Flash (FR) (Busted) **Mrs H. P. J. Meakin**
40 Ch c 3/3 The Noble Player—Tallantire (USA) (Icecapade (USA)) **Mr R. E. Sangster**
41 **THE YELLOW VEST,** b c 24/4 Superlative—Foolish Things (Song) **M. Old**
42 **TRAVELLING BLUES (IRE),** gr c 18/4 Ballad Rock—Danielle Delight (Song) **Mrs A. E. Sigsworth**
43 **TWILIGHT FIESTA (IRE),** b c 22/4 Burslem—Caithness (Connaught) **P. D. Savill**
44 **VALDO VIA,** b f 18/4 Ardross—Brigado (Brigadier Gerard) **Mrs J. R. Ramsden**
45 **WELSH SECRET,** b f 17/5 Welsh Captain—Bridge of Gold (Balidar) **R. H. Lewis**

Other Owners: Mr J. D. Clague, Mr D. Morrison, Mr A. Swindle.

Jockey (Flat): A Munro (7-10).

Apprentice: M A Giles (7-7).

491 MR P. RANSOM, Leominster

Postal: **Chapel Farm, Wigmore, Leominster, Herefordshire, HR6 9UQ.**
Phone: **WIGMORE (056 886) 253**

1 **ARNOLD'S CHOICE,** 6, ch g Vitiges (FR)—Never A Lady **Mr Duncan Ferguson**
2 **BRONZE AGE,** 5, ch m Celtic Cone—Sharelle **Mr A. Reed**
3 **HEAVENLY PEACE,** 7, b g Welsh Saint—Sweet Accord **Argent Thoroughbred Racing Plc**
4 **KILFORD,** 10, b g Northfields (USA)—Ashaireez **Mr F. E. Ransom**
5 **KYLE PRINCE,** 11, ch g Prince Hansel—Ceol An Ghra **Mr Ivor Chaddock**
6 **QAJAR,** 6, gr g Nishapour (FR)—Gravina **Mrs D. Claessen-Brierton**
7 **SERGEANT SPRITE,** 10, gr g General Ironside—Miss Sprite **Mr David Worth**
8 **TOKYO JOE,** 7, b g Double Form—Moortown Lady **Argent Thoroughbred Racing Plc**
9 **TOYTOWN,** 9, b g Pitpan—Sinarga **Mrs P. Ransom**
10 **TRUE BRIT (FR),** 6, ch g Grundy—Charlotteen **Mr Duncan Ferguson**

MR P. RANSOM—continued

Other Owners: Mrs Carole Broadley, Mr N. K. Chapman, Mr T. R. Chapman, Mr M. A. Charlton, Mr P. Ransom.

Jockeys (NH): B Powell (w.a.), S Smith-Eccles (w.a.).

Conditional: T Protheroe (9-7).

492 MRS A. E. RATCLIFF, Norton Lindsey

Postal: **Claverdon Lodge, Norton Lindsey, Warwick, CV35 8JT.**
Phone: **CLAVERDON (092 684) 2209**

1 **EASTER LASS,** 4, b f Workboy—Cuenca **Mr G. R. Ratcliff**
2 **FISHING SEASON,** 5, ch g Vital Season—Golden Mullet **Mr G. R. Ratcliff**
3 **SWEET SIRENIA,** 8, br m Al Sirat (USA)—Sweet Imelda **Mr G. R. Ratcliff**

Conditional: J Lodder.

Amateur: Mr M Wellings.

493 MR C. I. RATCLIFFE, Scouthead

Postal: **Hillcliffe Stables, 1 Doctor Lane Head Cottages, Highmoor, Scouthead, OL4 3RZ.**
Phone: **SADDLEWORTH (0457) 872097**

1 **FALLING FOSS,** 6, br g Workboy—Lorna Dell **Mrs Karen Ratcliffe**
2 **HIGHMOOR SCALLYANN,** 4, ch f Scallywag—Ancat Girl **Mrs Karen Ratcliffe**
3 **PRICKLY NATIVE,** 8, br g Mandalus—Thistle Dell **Mrs Karen Ratcliffe**

Jockey (NH): P A Farrell (10-0, w.a.).

Amateurs: Mr R Ford (10-7), Mr C I Ratcliffe (10-7).

494 MR J. V. REDMOND, Guildford

Postal: **Centaur Place, Foxborrow Hill, Bramley, Guildford, Surrey, GU5 0BL.**
Phone: **GUILDFORD (0483) 892233**

1 **BALLYGLUNIN,** 10, b g Simbir—Patsy Fagan **Mr M. Sullivan**
2 **BRAMLEY BOY,** 4, ch c Burslem—Louisa Jane **Mr D. B. Underwood**
3 **DANCING BLISS,** 6, b m Bladon—Ballymalisimo **Mr Terence Enticknap**
4 **ELEPHANT BOY,** 8, br g Tanfirion—Theban Queen **Mr Stanley J. Sharp**
5 **MARMION,** 5, b br g Sweet Monday—Parrot Fashion **Mr Gordon E. Curzon**
6 **PADDYCOUP,** 8, ch g Julio Mariner—Sociable **Mr Stanley J. Sharp**
7 **REX TREMENDA,** 5, b g Bustino—Elfinaria **Mr Stanley J. Sharp**
8 **RISING DEXY,** 5, b g Bay Express—Maladie d'Amour **Mrs Carole Bokenham**
9 **RIVER KINGDOM,** 7, b g Riverman (USA)—Victory Kingdom (CAN) **Mr Gary A. Smith**
10 **ROCKY PIT,** 8, b g Pitpan—Prellgo **Mrs Pat Sullivan**
11 **ROYAL HALO (USA),** 9, b g Halo (USA)—Lady Gordon (USA) **Mrs Doris Campbell**
12 **TALAB,** 5, b g Beldale Flutter (USA)—Glen Dancer **Mrs N. Funke**
13 **TRUE POETRY,** 9, ch m True Song—Mid-Day Milli **Mrs J. K. Underwood**

Other Owners: Mr P. Bradley, Mr Keith Griffin.

Jockeys (NH): R Goldstein (10-0), K Mooney (10-0).

495 MR W. G. REED, Hexham

Postal: **Moss Kennels, Haydon Bridge, Hexham, Northumberland, NE47 6NL.**
Phone: **HALTWHISTLE (0434) 344201**

1 **ALISTAIRS GIRL,** 7, b m Connaught—Miss Hubbard **Miss E. Reed**
2 **CASTLE PAN,** 9, b g Pitpan—Clashdermot Lady **Mrs P. Ruff**
3 **FLYING OATS (USA),** 10, b g Delta Flag (USA)—Kelly Keim (USA) **Mr W. W. McGhie**
4 **REGAL BEE,** 7, br m Royal Fountain—Brown Bee III **Mr W. G. Reed**
5 **ROYAL BEE,** 6, br g Royal Fountain—Brown Bee III **Mr W. G. Reed**
6 **THETCHU,** 12, b g Averof—Cavalier's Blush **Mrs G. Reed**
7 **ZAM BEE,** 4, br g Zambrano—Brown Bee III **Mr W. G. Reed**

THREE-YEAR-OLDS

8 **HERE COMES TIBBY,** b f Royal Fountain—Miss Hubbard **Mrs G. Reed**
9 **MOSS BEE,** br g Zambrano—Brown Bee III **Mr W. G. Reed**

Other Owners: Mr R. C. Reed.

Jockey (NH): W T Reed (10-2).

496 MISS G. M. REES, Scunthorpe

Postal: **'Grangehill', Burringham Road, Ashby Decoy, Scunthorpe, DN17 2AA.**
Phone: **(0724) 863347**

1 **BATH STREET BOY,** 5, b g Baptism—Lancashire Lass **Mrs J. Addleshaw**
2 **BATTLEAXE,** 6, b g Kampala—Fine Flame **Mr R. A. Ball**
3 **BOLD ANSWER,** 7, b g Bold Owl—Subtle Answer **Mr B. Evison**
4 **BREAK THE DUCK,** 4, b f Absalom—Bally Tudor **Mrs J. Addleshaw**
5 **BRIDGETTS SECURITY,** 4, b f Camden Town—Knight Security **Mrs J. Addleshaw**
6 **COLONEL POPSKI,** 8, ch g Niniski (USA)—Miss Jessica **Mr Bruce Finch**
7 **EASTERN PLAYER,** 7, ch g Royal Match—Cigarette **Mr Bruce Finch**
8 **EMERKALA,** 6, b m Kala Shikari—Emerglen **Mrs J. Worthington**
9 **MAID MARINER,** 8, br m Julio Mariner—Molly Polly **Mrs J. Worthington**
10 **PHILOTAS,** 6, b g Pitskelly—Damaring (USA) **Mrs J. Addleshaw**
11 **RASPBERRY COPSE,** 5, b m Riboboy (USA)—Stepout **Mr Brian Critten**
12 **RHYTHM GIRL,** 4, b f Tudor Rhythm—Vintage Girl **Mr G. Batty**

TWO-YEAR-OLDS

13 B f 12/6 Royal Vulcan—Grangehill (Goldhill) **Miss G. M. Rees**

Other Owners: Mr Glen Bannister, Mr Gordon Batty, Mrs Ruth Cawood, Mr Steven Goldthorpe, Mr F. E. Hodgkinson, Mr N. G. Rollitt, Mr Adrian Salt, Mr Robert Thompson.

Jockey (NH): Bill Worthington (10-0).

Conditional: Tim Potts (9-7).

497 MR A. S. REID, Thurleigh

Postal: **Park End Farm, Robin's Folly, Thurleigh, Bedfordshire.**
Phone: **TEL 01 723 1824/0234 771350 FAX 01 723 4741 TELEX 296170**

1 **AQUA VERDE,** 11, b g Auction Ring (USA)—Regal Guard **Mr A. S. Reid**
2 **CHINA'S WAY (USA),** 4, b br f Native Uproar (USA)—China Tea (USA) **Mr A. S. Reid**

MR A. S. REID—continued

3 **ELA-AYABI-MOU,** 4, ch f Absalom—Fairfields **Mr A. S. Reid**
4 **FOXE'S CASTLE,** 10, b br g Little Buskins—Heather Lady **Mr A. S. Reid**
5 **KONIG,** 4, ch g Jalmood—Spring Lane **Mr A. S. Reid**
6 **RECHARGEABLE,** 4, b g Music Boy—Ciliata **Mr A. S. Reid**
7 **REDMINT,** 6, ch m Lucifer (USA)—Quefort **Mr A. S. Reid**
8 **SAMMY LUX,** 12, br g Come On Grey—Last Spirit **Mr A. S. Reid**

THREE-YEAR-OLDS

9 **TASKFORCE FIXED IT,** b g Aragon—Broken Accent **Mr A. S. Reid**

Amateur: Tim Rogers.

498 MR T. REID, Haywards Heath

Postal: **Broxmead Farm, Broxmead Lane, Cuckfield, Haywards Heath, RH17 5JH.**
Phone: **(0444) 413914**

1 **AFTER YOU,** 7, b g Choral Society—Scoupland **Mr T. Reid**
2 **STEP TO STARDOM,** 5, ch g Julio Mariner—Starbright **Mr T. Reid**
3 **SWORD EDGE,** 13, ch g Sharpen Up—Coulter Belle **Mrs P. J. Reid**
4 **TARTAN ARMY,** 13, b g Milan—Tartan Rain **Mr T. Reid**
5 **THUNDERWOOD,** 8, ch g Lombard (GER)—Calibre **Mr T. Reid**

Jockey (NH): M E Perrett.

Amateur: Mrs P J Reid (9-7).

499 MRS J. G. RETTER, Exeter

Postal: **Glebe Farm, Whitestone, Exeter, Devon, EX4 2HP.**
Phone: **(0392 81) 410**

1 **ALLYFAIR,** 5, gr m Scallywag—Spartan Blonde **Mrs K. A. Stuart**
2 **BISCUIT TRADER,** 6, b g Enchantment—Lovely Kate **Mrs J. G. Retter**
3 **CELTIC DIAMOND,** 5, b m Celtic Cone—Eight of Diamonds **Mrs K. A. Stuart**
4 **CELTIC LORD,** 8, ch g Celtic Cone—Mrs Stephens **Mr J. P. Carrington**
5 **CROWN AND HORNS,** 6, b g Song—Dash On **Miss Sarah Stott**
6 **CRYSTAL HEIGHTS,** 4, ch g Wolver Heights—Crystal's Solo (USA) **Mrs K. A. Stuart**
7 **FANDANGO BOY,** 7, b g Last Fandango—African Doll **Mrs M. Channing**
8 **FAUX PAVILLON,** 6, ch g Alias Smith (USA)—Beech Tree **Mrs J. C. Coyne**
9 **GREYFRIARS BOBBY,** 4, ch g Hard Fought—Victorian Pageant **Mrs B. Taylor**
10 **KASHILL,** 12, b g Gulf Pearl—Wolver Hill **Mrs J. G. Retter**
11 **MILITARY BAND (FR),** 12, b g Sassafras (FR)—Melody Hour **Mr T. J. R. Jones**
12 **MZIMA SPRING,** 11, gr m Scallywag—Lady Colonist **Mrs K. A. Stuart**
13 **NURSES NIECE,** 6, b m Sallust—Tranquil Love **Mr P. D. Warren**
14 **SABAKI RIVER,** 6, br g Idiot's Delight—Keen Lass **Mrs K. A. Stuart**
15 **TRUISM,** 5, b g Known Fact (USA)—Great Care **Mrs K. A. Stuart**

Other Owners: Mr E. T. Crawshaw, Mr Anthony Gross, Mr Martin Hill, Mr A. Hollingworth, Mr J. Knowles, Mrs Jacqueline May, Mrs R. P. Rising, Mr Mark Sweet, Mr David I. Taylor.

Jockey (NH): Brendan Powell (w.a.).

500 MRS G. R. REVELEY, Malton

Postal: **16 Whitewall Cottages, Norton, Malton, North Yorkshire.**
Phone: **(0287) 50456 OR (0653) 600295**

1 **ABSONANT,** 8, ch m Absalom—Chance Belle **A. Flannigan**
2 **ATKINSONS,** 9, gr g Oats—For Sure **Mrs T. A. Metcalfe**
3 **BRIGADIER BILL,** 5, ch g Nicholas Bill—Sailing Brig **M. Bailey**
4 **BRIGHT DANCER,** 5, ch m Move Off—Toadpool **Mr J. H. Newson**
5 **BROCTUNE GREY,** 6, gr m Warpath—Hitesca **Mr D. Playforth**
6 **BURNDITCH GIRL,** 4, ch f Raga Navarro (ITY)—Queen of The Nile **R. A. Hughes**
7 **CAB ON TARGET,** 4, br g Strong Gale—Smart Fashion **Target Taxis Ltd**
8 **CHRISTMAS HOLLY,** 9, b g Blind Harbour—Holly Doon **Mr R. S. Wood**
9 **COWGATE FOUNTAIN,** 4, b f Royal Fountain—Cowgate Lady
10 **DALKEY SOUND,** 7, gr m Crash Course—Silver Doll **Mr G. S. Brown**
11 **ELEVEN LIGHTS (USA),** 6, ch g Lyphard (USA)—Eleven Pelicans (USA) **Mr A. Roe**
12 **FAIRWAYS ON TARGET,** 4, b g Billion (USA)—Aileen's Belle **Target Taxis Ltd**
13 **FLEET FOOTED,** 7, b h Tachypous—More Or Less **Laurel Leisure Ltd**
14 **FRISKNEY DALE LAD,** 5, b g Side Track—Midi Run **Mr R. P. Tilley**
15 **GODS LAW,** 9, gr g Godswalk (USA)—Fluently **Mrs V. Robson**
16 **GOLDEN ASSETT,** 8, b g Golden Love—Mehitabel **Wm Hoey**
17 **HEY RAWLEY,** 5, b g Sagaro—Silly Games **Mr C. C. Buckley**
18 **JANE'S JAUNT,** 7, ch m Move Off—Jaunty Jane **Mr W. G. Barker**
19 **JANE'S JOY,** 5, ch g Move Off—Jaunty Jane **Mr W. G. Barker**
20 **JOFF,** 4, br g Move Off—Janes Tan **Mrs Spensley**
21 **KATY KEYS,** 6, b m Tepukei—Arctic Flight **Miss J. K. Gladstone**
22 **KING CHARLEMAGNE,** 11, gr g Habat—Calibina **Mrs G. R. Reveley**
23 **LAURIE-O,** 6, b g Deep Run—Eight of Diamonds **Mr B. L. Parry**
24 **LEHMANS LOT,** 4, ch f Oats—Lottie Lehmann **Mrs G. R. Reveley**
25 **LEVY FREE,** 5, ch g Kinglet—Metaxa **Mr B. L. Parry**
26 **LONG JOHN SILVIA,** 9, ch m Celtic Cone—Hidden Treasure **Mr P. A. Tylor**
27 **MAJOR IVOR,** 5, ch g Mandrake Major—Double Birthday **P. Colquhoun**
28 4, B f Oats—Mangro **Mr C. C. Buckley**
29 **MASTER VULGAN,** 11, br g Master Buck—Kathleen Beag **Mrs S. Raines**
30 **MELLOTTIE,** 5, b br g Meldrum—Lottie Lehmann **Mrs J. G. Fulton**
31 **MISS RELSUN,** 6, ch m Le Soleil—Relax **Mrs V. Robson**
32 **MR WOODCOCK,** 5, b g Sit In The Corner (USA)—Grey Bird **Mr P. A. Tylor**
33 **PADAVENTURE,** 5, b g Belfalas—Cardamine **D. Sundin**
34 **PEACEWORK,** 6, br m Workboy—Flower Child **S. Burridge**
35 4, B g Candy Cane—Pixelated **K. Reveley**
36 **RAMILIE,** 8, b m Rambah—Millipede **Miss A. H. Sykes**
37 **ROSCAM LADY,** 5, ch m Cruise Missile—Willmon **Mr Michael Duffy**
38 **SECRET CONTRACT,** 5, b g Caruso—Sealed Contract **Mr D. Playforth**
39 **SMITHONIAN,** 6, ch g Stetchworth (USA)—Inkflash **Mr G. Smyth**
40 **TAXI ON TARGET,** 5, gr g Roselier (FR)—Violet Glade **Target Taxis Ltd**
41 **THE BARFITTER,** 4, b g Le Bavard (FR)—Harlave **William Cowan & Son Ltd**
42 **THE BUILDER,** 11, ch g Deep Run—Bramble Leaf **William Cowan & Son Ltd**
43 **TULUM,** 5, b g Blakeney—Inca Girl **A. Flannigan**
44 **TYPHOON LUCY,** 6, br m Laurence O—Tyrone Typhoon **Mr G. G. Stevenson**
45 **WHAT A LINE,** 8, ch g High Line—Something To Hide **Mr D. Playforth**
46 **WORKING SUCCESS,** 5, b m Workboy—Key To Success **William Cowan & Son Ltd**
47 **YORKSHIRE HOLLY,** 7, br g Bivouac—Holly Doon **Mr R. S. Wood**

THREE-YEAR-OLDS

48 **ANYTIME ANYWHERE,** br f Daring March—Martini Time **Mr C. C. Buckley**
49 **EASTDENE MAGIC,** ch f Nicholas Bill—Step Softly **Mr C. C. Buckley**
50 **IVORS MELODY,** b f Music Maestro—Double Birthday **P. Colquhoun**
51 **LEVEN BABY,** b f Blazing Saddles (AUS)—Fara Baby **Mrs Lamb**

MRS G. R. REVELEY—continued

TWO-YEAR-OLDS

52 **FIT THE BILL,** b c Nicholas Bill—Golden Windlass **P. D. Savill**
53 **SWIFT SWORD,** gr c Sayf El Arab (USA)—Lydiate **G. Peacock**

Other Owners: Mr Cecil Atkinson, Mr Ralph Bailey, Miss M. Barber, P. Collings, Mr C. Graham, Mr G. E. C. Graham, Mr David A. Green, Mr N. O. Hugill, Mr E. J. Kirby, Mr David T. J. Metcalfe, Mr James Murray (Ballymena), Mrs Cheryl L. Owen, Mr K. W. Paley, Mr G. W. Peirson, Mr G. A. Robinson, Mr R. Lindsay Smith, Mr P. Willis.

Jockey (Flat): John Lowe (w.a.).

Jockey (NH): P Niven (10-0).

Conditional: R Hodge.

Amateur: Mr M Buckley (9-7).

501 MR G. W. RICHARDS, Penrith

Postal: **The Stables, Greystoke, Penrith, Cumbria.**
Phone: **(08533) 392**

1 **ABAN WAY,** 8, br g Aban—Good Way **Mrs A. C. Wakeham**
2 **ABBOT OF FURNESS,** 6, b g The Parson—Chestnut Fire **Mr Hugh Cavendish**
3 **ANOTHER DYER,** 6, ch g Deep Run—Saint Society **The Edinburgh Woollen Mill Ltd**
4 **ARCTIC SKYLIGHT,** 6, ch g Lighter—Arctic Dawn **Mrs D. A. Whitaker**
5 **BALLYDALY EXPRESS,** 7, b g Distinctly (USA)—Indien Wine **J. Martin Engineers (Wishaw) Ltd**
6 **BENGAIRN,** 7, br g Pitpan—Star Deb **Mr Peter J. Cox**
7 **BESSACARR BOY,** 9, b g Ahonoora—Falcade **Mr P. Hinchliff**
8 **BETTER TIMES AHEAD,** 4, ro g Scallywag—City's Sister **Mr E. Briggs**
9 **BLAKEHOLME,** 5, ch g Over The River (FR)—Fun Princess **Mr H. Youdell**
10 **BORDER RAMBLER,** 10, ch g Scallywag—Matanza **Mr R. Tyrer**
11 **BORDER SPARK,** 7, br g Lighter—Border Gloria **Mrs V. J. Gilmour**
12 **BOWLANDS WAY,** 6, b g Al Sirat (USA)—Kilbride Lady VI **Mrs Lynn Campion**
13 **CANDLEBRIGHT,** 6, ch m Lighter—Arctic Ander **Mrs D. A. Whitaker**
14 **CARRICK HILL LAD,** 7, b g Royal Fountain—Indian Lace **Mr A. M. Picken**
15 **CENTRE ATTRACTION,** 11, b g Little Buskins—Money For Fun **N. B. Mason (Farms) Ltd**
16 **CLEVER FOLLY,** 10, b g Idiot's Delight—Lilac Veil **N. B. Mason (Farms) Ltd**
17 **CLEVER SHEPHERD,** 5, b g Broadsword (USA)—Reluctant Maid **The Edinburgh Woollen Mill Ltd**
18 **COLONEL ARTHUR,** 6, ch g Politico (USA)—Selborne Lass **Miss Melissa Jardine Paterson**
19 **CONCLUSIVE,** 11, ch g Crash Course—French Cherry **Mr Richard Shaw**
20 **DAMANOUR (USA),** 4, gr c Lypheor—Damana (FR) **Mr W. J. Peacock**
21 **DORONICUM,** 11, ch g Deep Run—May Foliage **Dr Kenneth S. Fraser**
22 **FOUR TRIX,** 9, gr ro g Peacock (FR)—Merry Chariot **Mrs Stewart Catherwood**
23 **FULL STRENGTH,** 7, b g Strong Gale—Richest **Mr J. N. G. Moreton**
24 **HIGHFRITH,** 7, ch m Deep Run—Lulu's Daughter **Mr Hugh Cavendish**
25 **IMPALE,** 6, b br g Crash Course—Show Rose **Miss Juliet E. Reed**
26 **JIM THORPE,** 9, ch g Gunner B—Burriana **M.C. Inns Limited**
27 **JINXY JACK,** 6, b g Random Shot—True Or False **Mrs B. M. McKinney**
28 **LARLOCH,** 6, br g Young Generation—Black Fire **Mr A. C. Leggat**
29 **LOTHIAN ADMIRAL,** 8, b g Roscoe Blake—Lothian Lady **Mr W. C. Morrison**
30 **MAGIC SOLDIER,** 5, br g Mandrake Major—Dior Queen **Mrs B. M. McKinney**

MR G. W. RICHARDS—continued

31 **MANHATTAN CHASE,** 7, b g Deep Run—Price Rise **Mr P. Hinchliff**
32 **MISTER TUFTIE,** 5, b g Black Minstrel—Articinna **Major I. C. Straker**
33 **MR GLEN,** 5, ch g The Parson—Park Blue **N. B. Mason (Farms) Ltd**
34 **NICKEL SILVER (FR),** 6, ch g Son of Silver—Dana's Return (USA) **Mr E. Q. Melville**
35 **OVER THE STYX,** 5, br g Over The River (FR)—My Dear Good Woman **Mrs Caroline Shaw**
36 **OYDE HILLS,** 11, br g Night Sky—My Affair **Mrs B. N. Bletsoe**
37 **PALM HOUSE,** 5, ch g Coquelin (USA)—Kew Gift **Mr R. Tyrer**
38 **PALM LAD,** 7, b g Palm Track—Captain Frances **Mr F. Tyldesley**
39 **PINEMARTIN,** 7, b g Pry—Sassenach Girl **Mrs A. G. Martin**
40 **PURA MONEY,** 8, b g Mugatpura—Bell Money **Mr John D. Hamilton**
41 **PYJAMAS,** 9, ch g Lighter—Arctic Dawn **Mrs D. A. Whitaker**
42 **QUASSIMI,** 6, gr g Ahonoora—Silk Empress **Dr Kenneth S. Fraser**
43 **RANDOLPH PLACE,** 9, br g Pitpan—French Cherry **The Edinburgh Woollen Mill Ltd**
44 **RINUS,** 9, br g Netherkelly—Pirella **Mr A. M. Proos**
45 **SASSY BONNE,** 4, ch f Good Thyne (USA)—Saucy Slave **Mr E. R. Madden**
46 **SICILIAN ANSWER,** 13, b g No Argument—Sicilian Girl **Mr G. Lennox Cotton**
47 **SLOTAMATICS,** 7, b g Royal Fountain—Sardan **Slotamatics (Bolton) Ltd**
48 **STAR OATS,** 4, ch g Oats—Starproof **Mr Alistair Duff**
49 **STAR OF ESK,** 8, b g Bybicello—Simprim Lady **Mr J. E. Clarkson**
50 **SUPER TRIX,** 7, gr g Bonne Noel—Merry Chariot **Mrs Stewart Catherwood**
51 **SWEET CITY,** 5, ch g Sweet Monday—City's Sister **Mr David T. Little**
52 **TARTAN TABARD,** 8, b g Le Bavard (FR)—Serrulata **The Edinburgh Woollen Mill Ltd**
53 **TARTAN TAILOR,** 9, b g Patch—Court Time **The Edinburgh Woollen Mill Ltd**
54 **TARTAN TAKEOVER,** 8, b g Tycoon II—Tina Fort **The Edinburgh Woollen Mill Ltd**
55 **TARTAN TEMPEST,** 7, br g Crozier—Frello **The Edinburgh Woollen Mill Ltd**
56 **TARTAN TRADEMARK,** 8, ch g Deep Run—Golden Shuil **The Edinburgh Woollen Mill Ltd**
57 **TEACAKE,** 6, b g Deep Run—Another Adventure **Mrs Alix Stevenson**
58 **THE ANTARTEX,** 7, ro g Vital Season—Rue Talma **The Edinburgh Woollen Mill Ltd**
59 **THE DEMON BARBER,** 8, b g Fine Blade (USA)—Mingy **Mr Ronald Cuppa**
60 **THE LANGHOLM DYER,** 11, b br g Crash Course—Belle Artiste **The Edinburgh Woollen Mill Ltd**
61 **THUNDER FLOWER,** 5, ch m Deep Run—Lulu's Daughter **Mr G. Richards**
62 **WAYSIDE BOY,** 5, b g Deep Run—Ciotog **Mr E. R. Madden**
63 **WESTWARD DRIFT,** 5, ch g Paddy's Stream—Quay Blues **Mr Peter J. Cox**

THREE-YEAR-OLDS

64 **LORD RINUS,** b g Strong Gale—Jamie's Girl **Mr A. M. Proos**

Other Owners: Mr G. Bartholomew, Mr Patrick Burling, Lt.-Commander W. H. Crawford, Mr J. A. Dudgeon, Mrs D. E. Knox, Mr Stanley Little, Mr Alex Penman, Mrs Gordon Richards, Mrs T. R. Riley.

Conditional: N Leach (9-7), M Moloney (9-7), L O'Hara (9-7).

Amateur: Mr P Doyle (10-0).

502 MRS S. RICHARDSON, Cheltenham

Postal: **Owdeswell Manor, Andoversford, Cheltenham, Gloucestershire, GL54 4LD.**
Phone: **(0242 820) 297**

1 **FLORENCE MAY,** 11, ch m Grange Melody—Florrie Green **Mr R. G. Fairbarns**
2 **GOLDEN SHOON,** 6, ch g Green Shoon—Marigold **Mrs P. J. Fairbarns**
3 **L FOREVER,** 7, ch g Laurence O—Immortal Queen **Mr R. G. Fairbarns**
4 **THAMES AIR,** 10, b m Crash Course—Santal Air **Mrs S. L. Richardson**

Amateur: Mr P Verling.

503 MR B. RICHMOND, Wellingore

Postal: **Hall Stables, Wellingore, Lincoln, LN5 0HX.**
Phone: **(0522) 810578**

1 **BRIGHT HONEY,** 10, ch m Duc d'Orleans—Honey Bright **Mr B. Richmond**
2 **DONOSA,** 5, ch m Posse (USA)—Love Supreme **Mr B. Richmond**
3 **DRAW THE LINE,** 11, b g High Line—Minibus **Mrs Margot Stewart**
4 **ELEANOR CROSS,** 5, br m Kala Shikari—Riboflеur **Mr P. Shilton**
5 **FAMOUS RUN,** 10, ch g Deep Run—Milwaukee Famous **Mrs J. M. Curson**
6 **GAELIC LOVER,** 6, b g He Loves Me—Argalie (USA) **Mr D. Eaton**
7 **IBN NAAS (USA),** 4, ch g Diesis—La Vie (USA) **Mrs J. M. Curson**
8 **LOOK AT ME NOW,** 4, b f Blushing Scribe (USA)—Shortigal **Mr Les Baker**
9 **NO CREDIBILITY,** 8, ch g Ahonoora—Karlaine **Mr M. J. Stewart**
10 **OPAL GLEN,** 8, br g Kampala—Greek Opal **Mrs J. M. Curson**
11 **ROYAL TAFI,** 4, b g Tanfirion—Queen's Pet **Mr Les Baker**
12 **WISE CRACKER,** 9, b g Hittite Glory—Exquisite **Mr M. Webster**

THREE-YEAR-OLDS

13 **SIGGLESTHORNE,** ch f Claude Monet (USA)—Le Levandoll **Mr M. Webster**

Other Owners: Mr R. Baker, Mrs Marjorie Greenacre, Mrs Joy Thomas.

Jockeys (NH): D Byrne (w.a.), S Keightley.

504 MR A. S. RIDOUT, Fordingbridge

Postal: **Mintys Hill, Rockbourne, Fordingbridge, SP6 3NB.**
Phone: **TEL (07253) 646 FAX (07253) 376**

1 **HILL-STREET-BLUES,** 12, b g White Prince (USA)—Crendle Hill **Mr A. S. Ridout**
2 **HILL-WAY BLUES,** 5, b g Uncle Pokey—Carnation **Mr A. S. Ridout**
3 **MILE END,** 5, b g Camden Town—Lady of Primrose **Mr A. S. Ridout**
4 **POONA EXPRESS,** 9, b g Amen (FR)—Bold Strike (FR) **Mr A. S. Ridout**
5 **PROVIDENCE BEAU,** 4, b g Anfield—Sandra Bella **Mr A. S. Ridout**

Conditional: M Bellisario (9-7).

Amateur: Mr M Batters (11-0).

505 MR D. J. RINGER, Newmarket

Postal: **Saffron House, Hamilton Road, Newmarket, Suffolk, CB8 0NY.**
Phone: **STABLES (0638) 662653 HOME 666021**

1 **ALCATRAZ (FR),** 6, b g Nadjar (FR)—Ancholia **Mr P. Garner**
2 **ARROW EXPRESS (USA),** 7, b g Clev Er Tell (USA)—Cornish Express **Mr D. S. Ringer**
3 **BOTTLE BASHER,** 5, b m Le Soleil—Mrs Walker **Mr P. Rackham**
4 **BRODERIE ANGLAISE,** 4, b f Night Shift (USA)—Emblazon **Mr D. S. Ringer**
5 **FLOWER OF TINTERN,** 8, b br m Free State—Welsh Flower **Mrs A. M. Chatten**
6 **HIGHLAND LAIRD,** 6, b g Kampala—Bonny Hollow **Mr D. S. Ringer**
7 **LUCIFER LIGHT,** 7, b g Salluceva—Boyne Light **Mr P. Garner**
8 **MOORE STYLISH,** 7, br m Moorestyle—Coralivia **Mr D. A. Beaumont and Partners**
9 **PATRICIA BRIDGET,** 4, ch f Sagaro—Tinted Blonde (USA) **Mr D. S. Ringer**
10 **ROMANTIC PLAYBOY,** 5, b g Balliol—Bils Romance **Mr D. A. Howes**
11 **SOSPIRANDO,** 5, b g Music Boy—Andalucia **Mr Chris Trussell**
12 **TAMATOUR (USA),** 7, b g Caro—Taduska (FR) **Mr Jim Furlong**
13 **TIMBER'S BOY,** 5, b g Nemorino (USA)—Ludorum's Praise **Mr Jim Furlong**

MR D. J. RINGER—continued

THREE-YEAR-OLDS

14 **FLAMBOYANCE,** b f Exhibitioner—Mock Auction **Mr P. Garner**
15 **HAYLEY CLAIRE,** b f Free State—Lucky Love **Mr Chris Trussell**
16 **MAURICE MINOR,** br g Mandrake Major—Kind Thoughts **Mr D. S. Ringer**
17 **MUSCADINE,** b f Muscatite—Bee Hawk **Mr Jim Furlong**
18 **ROSE OF TOUGET,** b f Dreams To Reality (USA)—Loredana **Mr R. W. Ellis**
19 **ROYAL SCOTS GREYS,** ch f Blazing Saddles (AUS)—Relicia **Mrs M. A. Hutton**

Other Owners: Mr K. G. Burke, Mr Ian Church, Mr Anthony Cooper, Mr Royston Evans, Mr Ken Furlong, Mr T. J. Judd, Mr J. Prentice, Mr D. A. Shekells, Mr P. G. Simcock, Mr V. C. Smith, Mr A. N. Taylor, Mr G. P. Yandell.

Jockey (NH): S McNeill (10-0).

506 MR G. RIPLEY, Ashford

Postal: **Glebe Farm, Shadoxhurst, Ashford, Kent.**
Phone: **HAMSTREET (023373) 2438/2462**

1 **ALEDAN,** 9, b g Raise You Ten—Melodic Beat **Mr B. G. Daley**
2 **COVER INN,** 7, gr m Tachypous—Greyburn **Mrs L. Ripley**
3 **DIAMOND WAY,** 4, b c Carriage Way—Ackastar **Mrs L. Ripley**
4 **GRAND LOU,** 4, b f Joshua—Grand Melody **Mrs L. Ripley**
5 **HAWTHORN JACKS,** 10, b g Paddy's Stream—Strawberry Mess **Mr M. V. Johnston**
6 **HIYA JUDGE,** 12, b g Ashmore (FR)—Grey Home **Mrs L. Ripley**
7 **NEVER GAMBOL,** 7, b m Neltino—Panda's Gambol **Mrs L. Ripley**
8 **PINEY POINT,** 5, ch g Buzzards Bay—Rockaway **Mrs L. Ripley**
9 **SEVRINO,** 5, ch g Swing Easy (USA)—Melissa Jane **Mrs L. Ripley**
10 **SPIGOT SHAFT (USA),** 10, b g Upper Nile (USA)—Reckless Date (USA) **Mrs L. Ripley**
11 **WALKING CANE,** 14, b g Candy Cane—Visitare **Mr A. Ripley**
12 **ZAGAZIG (USA),** 7, b g Chieftain II—I'll Take It (USA) **Mr M. V. Johnston**

Other Owners: Mr G. Ripley.

507 MR C. G. ROACH, St Austell

Postal: **Prideaux House, St Blazey, Par, St Austell, Cornwall, PL24 2SS.**
Phone: **(0726) 850701 TELEX 45613**

1 **ADDINGTON LAD,** 5, b g Le Moss—Santimwen **Gott Foods Limited**
2 **DEEP KASH,** 5, ch g Deep Run—Beatrix **Mr K. G. Manley**
3 **GAMBLING ROYAL,** 7, ch g Royal Match—Chance Belle **Roach Foods Limited**
4 **GROCER JACK,** 7, br g Derrylin—Kessella **Roach Foods Limited**
5 **HARD EDGE,** 6, b g Hardboy—Wild Piper **Roach Foods Limited**
6 **LUXULYAN LAD,** 7, b g Idiot's Delight—Sarasail **Roach Foods Limited**
7 **MOORCROFT BOY,** 5, ch g Roselier (FR)—Well Mannered **Mrs H. L. Manley and Mrs J. M. Roach**
8 **MORNING CRY,** 6, ch g Royal Match—Gay Seeker **Adams Homes (U.K.) Limited**
9 **PRIDEAUX BOY,** 12, b g Idiot's Delight—Firella **Roach Foods Limited**
10 **ROYAL DUCHY,** 8, b g Charlottesvilles Flyer—Hill Sixty **Roach Foods Limited**
11 **SLICE OFTHE ACTION,** 7, b g Random Shot—Tangle Tut **Roach Foods Limited**
12 **WHEAL PROSPER,** 5, b g Strong Gale—Kells Bay **Roach Foods Limited**

508 MR J. ROBERTS, Taunton

Postal: **Haynes Down Farm, Skilgate, Taunton, Somerset, TA4 2DG.**
Phone: **BAMPTON (0398) 31626**

1 **BOLD FURY,** 7, ch g Bold Lad (IRE)—Falassa **Hawkridge Farmhouse Cheese Limited**
2 **CELTIC BANJO,** 5, b m Celtic Cone—Allende **Mr D. J. Hunt**
3 **DAWN BELL,** 5, b m Belfort (FR)—Dobrina (FR) **Mr B. W. Crockett**
4 **DUART,** 10, b g Saunter—Traverser **Mrs J. Scrivens**
5 **FLYING ROOFER,** 4, b f Jester—Forest Glen **Edwards & Cartwright Ltd**
6 **GLEN OAK,** 5, b g Glenstal (USA)—Neeran **Mrs Diana Payne**
7 **JAY JAY'S VOYAGE,** 7, b h Saunter—Traverser **Mrs J. Scrivens**
8 **JUST BLAKE,** 9, b g Blakeney—Just A Dutchess (USA) **Mrs Dinah Beer**
9 **JUST SO,** 7, bl br g Sousa—Just Camilla **Mr H. T. Cole**
10 **LITTLE ERNIE,** 4, b g Idiot's Delight—Allende **Mr D. J. Hunt**
11 **MERRY MARIGOLD,** 4, b f Sonnen Gold—Manna Green **Mrs I. E. Penfold**
12 **MUSICAL MOMENTS,** 4, b f Vision (USA)—Miami Melody **Mr J. D. Roberts**
13 **REMEMBER NODDY,** 5, ch g Tom Noddy—Member's Lady **Mr A. L. Roberts**
14 **SELF AID,** 7, b m Fine Blade (USA)—Laurolin **Mr R. V. Safe**
15 **SPAR LADY,** 7, b m Tanfirion—Royal Reserve **Mr A. G. Mogford**
16 **STATIONERS DREAM,** 5, b g Enchantment—Just Janie **Mr L. Cornall**
17 **SUN-SID-ROSE,** 5, b m Tom Noddy—Heulwen **Mr A. L. Roberts**
18 **TELEMAHOS,** 8, b g Tap On Wood—The Woodbird **Mr P. L. Parkinson**
19 **YOUNG NICHOLAS,** 9, b g Young Generation—Nicholas Grey **Mr R. V. Safe**

THREE-YEAR-OLDS

20 **WOLVER GOLD,** b f Wolverlife—Mahele (USA) **Mr A. L. Roberts**

Other Owners: Mr Ron Bawden, Mr P. A. Brewer, Mr Christopher Chanter, Mr C. G. Gadd, Mr R. W. Guppy, Mr Cedric Price, Mr S. D. Sherring.

Conditional: S Turner (9-7).

Amateur: Mr G Upton (10-3).

509 MR D. ROBERTSON, Kilmarnock

Postal: **Gateside Farm, Craigie, Kilmarnock, Ayrshire, Scotland.**
Phone: **(0563) 86201**

1 **CENTRAL PACIFIC,** 6, ch g Stanford—Derrynane **Mr D. Robertson**
2 **MAGALLURE,** 4, b f Magnolia Lad—Allured **Mrs A. L. Robertson**
3 **MERCURIUS,** 8, ch g Roman Warrior—Just Splendid **Mrs A. L. Robertson**
4 **NELION'S LASS,** 5, b m Sonnen Gold—Nelion **Mr D. Robertson**

Amateurs: Mrs A Robertson (9-0), Mr D Robertson (10-5).

510 MR M. H. B. ROBINSON, Wantage

Postal: **Ginge Farm Cottage, Ginge, Wantage, Oxon, OX12 8QS.**
Phone: **HOME (0235) 835050 OFFICE (0235) 833919 FAX (0235) 832630**

1 **ALCHEMIC (NZ),** 6, br g Bold Venture (NZ)—Poldhullie **Mrs J. M. Howell**
2 **ATTRACTIVE (NZ),** 6, ch g Imposing (AUS)—Mi Gold (NZ) **Dr B. Alexander**
3 **CAZAUDEHORE,** 5, ch g Callernish—Clashdermot Lady **Mr George Johnson**

MR M. H. B. ROBINSON—continued

4 **COURAGEOUS BIDDER,** 5, b g Known Fact (USA)—Hysterical **Mrs A. D. Steel**
5 **EPILENY,** 6, br g Random Shot—Charming Hostess **Mr A. W. Gooda**
6 **EPITROT,** 7, b g Pollerton—Irish Invade **Mr A. W. Gooda**
7 **EUROPA POINT,** 5, ch g Deep Run—Regal Dawn **Mr L. G. Randall**
8 **FLOLINE,** 6, b g Floriferous—Marline **Mr P. L. Lee**
9 **GAY MOORE,** 9, b g Raise You Ten—Knockaville **Miss Caroline Beasley**
10 **IMPERIAL BOLT (NZ),** 6, b g Imperial Guard—Alan's Girl (NZ) **Mrs Pat Beasley**
11 **KIWI TAUKA (NZ),** 7, b g Auk (USA)—Talama (NZ) **Mrs Julia Ward**
12 **LOGANBANK,** 7, ch g General Ironside—Polygala **Mr Tommy Newell**
13 **MAIORO (CAN),** 4, b f Bates Motel (USA)—Toys Are Fun (USA) **Mr D. W. Samuel**
14 **MIDNIGHT MISS (NZ),** 6, br m Princes Gate—Princess Jane (NZ) **Mr P. M. H. Robinson**
15 **NEWELLS ROAD (NZ),** 5, b g Princes Gate—d'Or Veille (NZ) **Mr D. W. Samuel**
16 **OUT THE GAP,** 7, ch g Cheval—Clashdermot Lady **Mr Jonathan Harvey**
17 **PEAJADE,** 6, b g Buckskin (FR)—Kaminaki **Mrs Pauline Vernon**
18 **POLYFEMUS,** 8, ch g Pollerton—Bardicate **Mr George Johnson**
19 **PRINCE VINCENNE (NZ),** 5, b g So Bold (NZ)—Hoream's Wonder (AUS) **Mr A. K. Johnson**
20 **REMEDY THE MALADY,** 9, b g Crash Course—Promiscuous **Mr Jeremy Beasley**
21 **ROCKVILLE,** 4, b g Hardboy—Our Chrisy **Mr George Johnson**
22 **ROYAL STING,** 4, b g Prince Bee—Dolly-Longlegs **Mrs Julia Ward**
23 **SLALOM,** 9, ch g Deep Run—Arctic Nook **Mrs M. J. Russell**
24 **STRONTINO,** 5, b g Rontino—Fair Pirouette **Mr George Johnson**
25 **SUNSET AGAIN,** 5, ch g Al Sirat (USA)—Noddy **Mr John Hooper**
26 **TUDOR ORCHID,** 5, b m Tudor Rhythm—Flower Child **Mrs R. M. Maclean**
27 **VALRODIAN (NZ),** 7, b g Allgrit (USA)—Nyleva (NZ) **Mr D. W. Samuel**
28 **WEIRPOOL,** 8, ch g Le Bavard (FR)—Vulplume **Mr Howard Spooner**
29 **YOUNG GENERAL,** 4, br g Young Generation—Amerella **Mr George Johnson**

Other Owners: Mrs A. Aldrete, Mr P. J. Blackmore, Mr S. Bullimore, Miss F. Burridge, Mrs Janine Hall, Mr R. J. Osborne, Andy Ross, Mrs Ruth Smith, Mrs Caroline Spooner, Mrs H. R. A. Spooner, Mrs Mary Wells, Mr Peter Wiegand.

Jockeys (NH): J Duggan (10-0), J White (10-0, w.a.).

511 MR W. R. ROBINSON, Scarborough

Postal: **Charm Park, Wykeham, Scarborough, North Yorkshire, YO13 9QV.**
Phone: **(0723) 862162**

1 **BROAD STEET,** 7, br g Balliol—Ballyarctic **Mr E. Steinton**
2 **BRYN FLIER,** 5, b g Shaab—Chingley Lass **Mr Roy Robinson**
3 **CHANGE GUARD,** 4, b f Day Is Done—Mittens **Mr E. Steinton**
4 **ESCUDERO,** 6, ch g Cut Above—Haralda (FR) **Mr Roy Robinson**
5 **GOLD MIRAGE,** 11, b g Gold Rod—Ishka **Mrs J. A. Booth**
6 **MANOSA MILL,** 5, b g Red Sunset—Egyptian Moon **Mr J. Hall**
7 **MARSIR,** 7, b g Sir Mago—National Day **Mr Roy Robinson**
8 **MON BILL,** 4, ch g Nicholas Bill—Fair Madame **Mr Roy Robinson**
9 **RUDDA CASS,** 6, b g Rapid River—Glaven **Mr J. B. Slatcher**
10 **RUDDA STAR,** 5, b m General David—Glaven **Mr J. B. Slatcher**

TWO-YEAR-OLDS

11 Br f Wonderful Surprise—Swift Embrace (Enbrage) **Mr Roy Robinson**

Other Owners: Mr I. F. Burn, Mr W. H. Jackson, Mr J. P. Peace.

Jockey (NH): D Condell (9-7).

Amateur: Mr H Brown (10-7).

512 MR E. H. ROBSON, Morpeth

Postal: **East Shaftoe, Morpeth, Northumberland, NE61 4EA.**
Phone: **(0830) 30207**

1 4, Ch f Politico (USA)—Melmin **Mrs E. H. Robson**
2 **MELSONBY,** 8, br g Politico (USA)—Melmin **Mrs E. H. Robson**

Jockeys (NH): G Harker, T Reed, B Storey (w.a.).

Amateur: Mr D Mactaggart.

513 MR T. L. A. ROBSON, Alnwick

Postal: **Appletree Cottage, Edlingham, Alnwick, Northumberland, NE66 2BL.**
Phone: **(066574) 307**

1 **CELTIC SANDS,** 7, b m Celtic Cone—Rapenna **Mr T. L. A. Robson**
2 **HASTY IMPORT,** 11, ch g Import—Isis Rapide **Mr T. L. A. Robson**
3 **POLITICAL ISSUE,** 6, b g Politico (USA)—Red Stockings **Mr T. L. A. Robson**
4 **REDHALL ROYALE,** 6, b m Royal Fountain—Isis Rapide **Mr T. L. A. Robson**
5 **SILENTINA,** 4, b f Tina's Pet—Keep Silent **Mr T. L. A. Robson**

Lady Rider: Mrs Rosemary Robson (8-10).

514 MR P. R. RODFORD, Martock

Postal: **Lavenoak House, Ash, Martock, Somerset.**
Phone: **MARTOCK (0935) 823459**

1 **DARING CLASS,** 4, b f Class Distinction—Darymoss **Mrs C. J. Blezard**
2 **FILL THE JUG,** 9, br m Derrylin—Fleur d'Amour **Mr Jamie Reid**
3 **PADDY O'BRIEN,** 10, gr g Scallywag—Penrith **Mr S. N. Burfield**
4 **PLAID,** 7, b g Martinmas—Lanata **Miss H. L. Gantlett**
5 **STAFFORD LAD,** 4, b g Tachypous—Frizzante **Mr J. E. Staddon**
6 **STORMY PRAISE (USA),** 6, ch h Storm Bird (CAN)—Prayers'n Promises (USA) **Mr Keith Stokes**
7 **TUFOLI,** 6, b m Mljet—Tagliatelle **Mr Mike Tebbut**
8 **WINART,** 12, br g Scottish Rifle—Alice **Mr P. R. Rodford**

Other Owners: Mr C. T. Brinson, Mr S. Goss-Turner, Mr G. J. Waters.

Jockey (NH): P Richards (10-1).

Conditional: W Irvine (9-7).

515 MR C. G. ROE, Chalford

Postal: **Hyde Park Farm, Lower Hyde, Chalford, Gloucestershire.**
Phone: **(0453) 885487 TELEX 0453 88 437105 FAX (0453) 88 5204**

1 **ANGLIA VALE,** 5, ch g Chukaroo—Silmira **Feeny Holdings Ltd**
2 **APRIL'S MODEL LADY,** 4, b f Shaab—Dream Lady **Miss Lis McKechnie**
3 **BOBO THE GREEK,** 5, b g Balboa—Grecian Victory **Mrs C. Barclay**

MR C. G. ROE—continued

4 **DRUSILLUS,** 12, b br g Furry Glen—Agrippina **Roe Racing Ltd**
5 **KOKOSCHKA,** 8, gr ro g Alias Smith (USA)—Opinion **John McNair and Roe Racing Ltd**
6 **LE GRAND MAITRE,** 9, ch g Over The River (FR)—Cora Swan **Mrs K. Haddon**
7 **POPPLE,** 7, ch g Country Retreat—Poppy Lansdowne **Miss Lis McKechnie**
8 **PRINCESS FALCON,** 5, ch m Chukaroo—Coxmoore Sweaters **Falcon Metal Products Ltd**
9 **QUEEN RUN,** 5, ch m Irish Rifle—Babs Reflection VII **Mr E. Walker**
10 **RADICAL REQUEST,** 7, br g Derring Rose—Kitty Laurence **Mrs C. Barclay**
11 **ROSIE'S JUMPER,** 7, br g Rhodomantade—Coxmoore Sweaters **Mr T. R. Beston**
12 **UTOPIAN,** 12, b g Radical—Tuti **Partnership**
13 **WELSH BLUEBELL,** 8, b m Manado—Welsh Sapphire **Mrs M. C. Wilson**

Other Owners: Dr Susan Barnes, Mrs M. Holme, Mr M. J. Keane, Mrs Jean Roe.

Jockey (Flat): John Williams (8-4).

Jockey (NH): Richard Guest (10-0).

Conditional: P McDermott.

Lady Rider: Miss Sarah Farrant (8-0).

516 MR G. L. ROE, Yelverton

Postal: **Belliver Farm, Hoo Meavy, Yelverton, Devon, PL20 6PZ.**
Phone: **(0822) 852850**

1 **ATHOS,** 5, br g High Season—Keen Lass **Mr G. Roe**
2 **BELLIVER PRINCE,** 10, ch g Rugantino—Sharon **Mr G. Roe**
3 **FLIRTINO,** 9, gr m Rugantino—Native Flirt **Mr G. Roe**
4 **POP SONG,** 6, b g High Season—Top of The Pops II **Mr G. Roe**
5 **WIGFORD LAD,** 6, ch g Charlie's Pal—Golden Festival **Mr G. Roe**

517 MR J. H. ROPER, Suckley

Postal: **Lower House, Suckley, Worcester, WR6 5DQ.**
Phone: **SUCKLEY (0886) 884 368**

1 **SCALE MODEL,** 8, b m Latest Model—Ruby Sherry **Mr Joe Roper**
2 **WALD KONIGIN,** 4, ch f Kinglet—Nightwood **Mr Joe Roper**

Jockey (NH): R Hyett (10-1).

Amateur: J Roper (11-0).

518 MR W. M. ROPER, Newbridge

Postal: **C/O Baroda Stud, Newbridge, Co. Kildare, Ireland.**
Phone: **(045) 31194**

1 **AHEAD OF THE LAW,** 6, b g Garda's Revenge (USA)—Amy's Choice **Mrs M. Sinanan**
2 **APPLE BETTY,** 5, b m Runnett—Cut The Cake **Mr Evan Newell**
3 **BUZZ ALONG,** 4, ch f Prince Bee—Killyhevlin **Mr D. Cornwall**

MR W. M. ROPER—continued

4 **HURRICANE DANDY,** 7, b m Strong Gale—Dandy Brush **Mr W. P. Roper**
5 **IN THE DOCK,** 10, br g Garda's Revenge (USA)—Amy's Choice **Mr P. Dennis**
6 **KINKY LADY,** 5, b m River Knight (FR)—Slinky Persin **Mrs M. Sinanan**
7 **VIKINGS DAUGHTER,** 5, ch m Viking (USA)—Roman Folly **Mr T. Lombard**

THREE-YEAR-OLDS

8 **APPRAISAL,** b c Critique—Glad Tidings **Mr N. B. Wachman**
9 **SILK CORD,** b f Sallust—Silk Rein **Sir Michael Sobell**

Other Owners: Mr B. Burke, Mr F. Clarke, Mrs Piers Dennis, Mr P. Finlay, Mr A. Hamilton, Mr R. J. Osborne, Mr M. Taylor, Lord A. Weinstock, Hon S. A. Weinstock.

Jockey (NH): B Sheridan (10-0, w.a.).

519 MR J. DE ROUALLE, Chantilly

Postal: **17 Rue Charles Pratt, 60260 Lamorlaye, France.**
Phone: **44 21 37 37 FAX: 44 21 37 28 TELEX: 145 950 F EASTERN**

1 **A LITTLE MUSIC (USA),** 4, b f Stop The Music—Rickadoo **R. E. Hibbert**
2 **AUTANT POUR MILLE,** 4, b c Mille Balles—Samana **Mr E. Di Nella**
3 **BAKANAL,** 5, b h Two River—Randa **Mr Diarte**
4 **DARTMOUTH QUEEN,** 4, b f Mehmet—Winter Princess **A. Appleton**
5 **FARACHITO,** 4, b c Lightning—Faracha **Mrs P. Beck**
6 **GOLLESTAN,** 4, b c Gay Mecene—Sun Breiz **Ecurie Ayaros**
7 **GREEN BUTTERFLY,** 4, ch c Tip Moss—Darling Lass **Mme de Forest**
8 **KEY TO STARDOM,** 4, ch f The Minstrel—Pleasure Key Fager **A. Appleton**
9 **LOCH LANE,** 4, b f Gairloch—Double Lane **Mme de Forest**
10 **RAIN OR ZINO,** 4, ch f Zino—Rain Or Shine **Mrs A. de Villiers**
11 **RHINE GLADE,** 4, b c Deep Roots—Rhine Lane **Mme de Forest**
12 **SILVER LANE,** 5, b h Son of Silver—Stony Lane **Mme de Forest**
13 **SOLEIL D'AUTOMNE,** 4, b c General Holme—Feuille d'Automne **Mrs P. Beck**
14 **TOWFIK'S GOLD,** 4, b c Glint of Gold—Lamalinne **Mrs P. Beck**

THREE-YEAR-OLDS

15 **ALIVEWITHPLEASURE (USA),** b f Alleged—Rashana **A. Appleton**
16 **AL'S KATE (USA),** b f Al Nasr—Sid's Kate **R. K. Eamer**
17 **AU CASSIS (IRE),** gr f Mendez—Brigitte Laveau **R. K. Eamer**
18 **BE GRISE,** ch f Be My Guest—Grizabella **Horse Bred Ltd**
19 **BET A MILLION (USA),** b f Alleged—Pleasure Key Fager **A. Appleton**
20 **BRIGHT LINE,** ch f High Line—Birthday Star **Mme de Forest**
21 **CREBEK,** gr c Kaldoun—Rhine Lane (FR) **Mme de Forest**
22 **DUEDALE,** ch f Iron Duke—Nessedal **Mme de Forest**
23 **FUNNY DOLLY,** b f Lashkari—Fancy's Child (USA) **Mr H. Chalhoub**
24 **GIROFLEE D'ETE,** gr f No Pass No Sale—Gentop (FR) **R. C. Strauss**
25 **GROOM OF LIR (IRE),** ch c Shy Groom—Child of Lir **D. Al Johar**
26 **HERR MAESTRO,** b c Brustolon—Starmania **Mr Grisel**
27 B f Mille Balles—Kakinka **Mr E. Di Nella**
28 **KILLEKENNY,** ch f Pampabird—Blue Design **A. Stewart**
29 **L'AVANIE (USA),** b f L'Emigrant—Avanie **R. K. Eamer**
30 **LICHIMA,** b f Lichine—Marwana **Mr P. Joncoux**
31 **LUTHIER ENCHANTEUR (USA),** b c General Holme—Margis Lute **Mrs P. Beck**
32 Ch c General Holme—Madame Premier (USA) **Ecurie I. Fares**
33 Ch c Green Dancer—Martha Reinhart **Horse Bred Ltd**
34 **MINK GLOVES,** gr f Persepolis—Cut Velvet (USA) **Mme de Villiers**
35 B f Lomond—Miss Protege (USA) **Horse Bred Ltd**
36 **MISTRESS SYLVIE (USA),** b f The Minstrel—Lady Sylvie **A. Appleton**
37 **MY STYLE,** ch c Kings Lake—Miss Mulaz (FR) **R. C. Strauss**
38 **NOBLE TEA,** b f Noblequest—Tisaniere (FR) **Mr H. Chalhoub**

MR J. DE ROUALLE—continued

39 **PAS DE PANIQUE,** b f No Pass No Sale—Bernique **R. C. Strauss**
40 **PRETTY POINT,** b f Crystal Glitters—Pointe Alezane (FR) **Mr H. Chalhoub**
41 **PURISTE,** b c Cariellor—Phalangine **Mme de Villiers**
42 B f No Pass No Sale—Rapids **Brandon Hayes**
43 **SAIL ON (IRE),** b f No Pass No Sale—Canoeing **Brandon Hayes**
44 **SECRET FOLY,** b f Procida—Secret Ground **Mr P. Bamberger**
45 **STRUMICA,** b f King of Macedon—Darling Lass (FR) **Mme de Forest**
46 **SUPER CHINO,** b c Bates Motel—Volume Two **J. F. Gribomont**
47 **VASSY,** b f Lou Piguet—Vaucouleurs **Mme Thieriot**

TWO-YEAR-OLDS

48 B c Glenstal—Albenga **J. F. Gribomont**
49 **BALLEROY (USA),** gr c 14/4 Kaldoun—Blanche Reine **R. K. Eamer**
50 **BONNY BAIRN,** ch c 11/3 Blue Courtier—Scottish Bride **Mme de Forest**
51 **CAERLINA (IRE),** b f Caerleon—Diva Lina **R. C. Strauss**
52 **CHIRAZ,** ch f 22/2 Sicyos—Prophetesse **Mme de Villiers**
53 Gr f 8/3 Procida—Daisy's Stem **R. K. Eamer**
54 **EROIKO,** b c 25/3 Nikos—Edina **Mme de Villiers**
55 **ETOILE DE JOUR,** ch f 5/4 Saint Cyrien—Florenly **J. P. Van Gysel**
56 **FIERTY,** ch c 15/4 Pharly—Iskeba **Mme de Villiers**
57 **GALTO,** ch c 9/5 Gairloch—Alto Mortale **J. F. Gribomont**
58 **GRAUBUNDEN,** b c 26/3 Deep Roots—Rhine Lane **Mme de Forest**
59 **KALDAN,** gr c 11/3 Kaldoun—Stony Lane **Mme de Forest**
60 B f Fast Topaze—Lamalinne **Mrs P. Beck**
61 **LA REINE DES DUNES,** b f 20/5 Dunphy—Bergara **Mr Fournier**
62 **MARID D'OR,** b f 31/3 Procida—Marie de Rethondes **Mme Thieriot**
63 **MARINAIO,** ch c 15/2 Mille Balles—Dancing Guest **Mr E. di Nella**
64 **MEMPHIS TENNESSEE (IRE),** b c 4/3 No Pass No Sale—Mill Mulaz **R. C. Strauss**
65 **ONE MORE,** b f 24/4 Lashkari—Renewed Interest **Mme de Forest**
66 **OVER FLYING,** b f Zino—High Society **Narvick International**
67 **PEARL NOBLE,** b f 23/1 Noblequest—Pearl Harbour **Mme Thieriot**
68 **QUANDAHAR,** b f 23/3 Akarad—Quilaba **Mme Thieriot**
69 **QUETILA,** ch f 22/2 Fabulous Dancer—Queen's Mystery **Mme Thieriot**
70 **RAPADISSIMO,** b c 16/2 Bikala—Dancing Fame **Mrs P. Beck**
71 B f Galant Vert—Sarah Anita **Mrs P. Beck**
72 **SINJAR,** b c Crystal Glitters—Dame de Carreau **D. Al Johar**
73 **SKAY,** ch f 23/1 Sicyos—Princesse Kay **P. Joncoux**
74 **SUSY STAR,** b f 11/3 Brustolon—Bad Start **P. Bamberger**
75 **TRUEDAL,** b f 18/2 Truculent—Nessedal **Mme de Forest**
76 **TYCOON DAZZEL (USA),** b f Last Tycoon—Davao **J. R. Arriola**

Jockeys (Flat): Cash Asmussen (8-5), Eric Legrix (8-5).

Amateur: Mr J F Portos (9-4).

520 MR J. C. ROUGET, Pau

Postal: **Chemin de la Foret, Bastard, 64000 Pau, France.**
Phone: **59 33 27 90 TELEX 570 873**

1 **AKARA D'ESPIENS,** 4, br c Labus—Tativa **Mrs A. Soueges**
2 **ALL FOR THE BEST,** 4, b f Cure The Blues—Broken Up **O. Reglade**
3 **ARRANZALEAK (FR),** 4, b c R B Chesne—Intemperies (FR) **Mrs P. Saget**
4 **BALANCE SHEET (FR),** 5, b m Ile de Bourbon (USA)—Ymirkhan (FR) **J. Biraben**
5 **BEAU ROI (FR),** 8, ch h Rex Magna (FR)—Nikbelle (FR) **P. H. Martin**
6 **BRILAUREL (FR),** 4, br c Rose Laurel—Brink Miss (FR) **J. P. Rios**
7 **BRINK SYMBOL (FR),** 6, gr g Brinkmanship (USA)—Symbolique (FR) **C. Gour**
8 **BRIQUOQUET (FR),** 7, br h Brinkmanship (USA)—Brixia (FR) **C. Gour**

MR J. C. ROUGET—continued

9 **CENTURY PORT (FR),** 5, b h Iron Duke (FR)—Lots of Money **C. Gour**
10 **CHESRESY,** 4, b c R. B. chesne—Heresie **P. Lanouilh**
11 **CLEAR CUT,** 4, gr f Kenmare—Gloria Prince **A. Lapoterie**
12 **EBENE WOOD,** 4, b c Touching Wood (USA)—Lassalia **C. Gour**
13 **FORTUNATELLO (FR),** 4, br c Bikala—Sasetto (FR) **Y. Renaud**
14 **FORTUNE TELLER (FR),** 6, b h Solicitor (FR)—Carolia (FR) **P. Nogues**
15 **GENTLE TOUCH (FR),** 5, gr h Bellypha—Barbotte (FR) **J. C. Rouget**
16 **KENALYA (FR),** 4, b f Kenmare (FR)—Alliaria (FR) **K. Benfell**
17 **KNIGHT DREAM (FR),** 5, ch h Zino—Playing For Keeps **Ecurie I. M. Fares**
18 **LOS VERDES,** 5, b h Persian Bold—Lucy Limelight **C. Gour**
19 **LUCKY SHIP (FR),** 5, b h Brinkmanship (USA)—Red Lupus **C. Gour**
20 **LUTH SINCERE (FR),** 4, b f No Lute (FR)—Heartfelt **Mrs F. Adam De Raquine**
21 **NIGHT STAKER,** 4, ch f Northrop—Startling **J. Muldoon**
22 **ONCLE TOTO (FR),** 7, br h Perouges (FR)—Royalka **J. P. Rios**
23 **ORIENTAL SON (FR),** 7, br g Kashtan (FR)—Belle Affaire (FR) **B. Cazenave**
24 **PITCH AND RUN,** 4, b c Runnett—Merrie Laughter **C. Gour**
25 **RESILIA (FR),** 7, br m Katowice (FR)—Capta (FR) **B. Belinguier**
26 **SEVIGNE LIBERTINE (FR),** 6, b m Ramsin (FR)—La Libertine (FR) **Mrs A. Nobili**
27 **SIR KING (FR),** 5, b h King of Macedon—Surprise d'Hermite (FR) **Mrs P. Saget**
28 **TACHNY D'ESPIENS (FR),** 5, b h Kashnil (FR)—Tativa (FR) **B. Cazenave**
29 **TAXIS DRIVER (FR),** 5, ch h Gorfou (USA)—Tour En Taxis (FR) **B. Cazenave**
30 **WILD HAWAII,** 4, ch c Hawaii—Wild Wings **Ecurie I. M. Fares**

THREE-YEAR-OLDS

31 **ALL A QUIVER,** b f Gorytus—Broken Up **Mrs B. R. Firestone**
32 **AMORGOS,** b c Kaldoun—Amrela **C. Gour**
33 **BALTER,** b c Beldale Flutter—Belle Zed **Ecurie I. M. Fares**
34 **BAMBINA,** b f Brinkmanship—Badiniere **J. P. Rios**
35 **BARDONELLA,** b f Beaudelaire—Binky **C. Gour**
36 **BOIS DE MAI,** b c Kaldoun—Belle de Mai **Mrs P. Saget**
37 **CORRIB QUEEN,** ch f Bon Sang—Mona Mou **R. Bousquet**
38 **CUT MY HEART,** b f General Assembly—Highland Girl **C. Gour**
39 **DAME GALANTE,** b f Gallant Vert—Indian Lady **P. H. Martin**
40 **FIK EL BARRAKI,** b c Crystal Glitters—Crillion **Ecurie I. M. Fares**
41 **FRONTIER GALLANT,** b c Sir Wimborne—Mother Courage **J. M. Soriano**
42 **FUNAMBULIEN,** ch c L'Emigrant—Charming Pan **B. Cazenave**
43 **GATSBY LE FASTUEUX,** b c Cimon—Finarose **P. Nogues**
44 **GIRL OF IRON,** b f Son of Silver—Liona **C. Gour**
45 **HEARTNOBLE,** b c Noblequest—Heartfelt **C. Gour**
46 **HOLLY BOY,** b c Noblequest—Hollybella **H. Chamarty**
47 **HYDE PARK,** gr c Persepolis—Ciao Bella **C. Gour**
48 **INESPERADA,** b f Cariellor—Faracha **Cte. de Quintanilla**
49 **JMERINKA,** b c R B Chesne—Tsarine Sophie **R. Labeyrie**
50 **JOLI BIJOU,** b c Solicitor—Yakapa **J. M. Lorca**
51 **JONES BEACH,** b c Sandhurst Prince—Classic Choice **C. Gour**
52 **KANORSONG,** b c African Song—Une Nordique **C. Gour**
53 **LADY LUCK,** b f Karkour—Lady Bee **Baronne De Lassus**
54 **LA TACUNGA,** b f R B Chesne—La Meslerie **C. Gour**
55 **LEGAL PARK,** ch f Highland Park—Keep It Legal **Ecurie I. M. Fares**
56 **LOT'S MORE,** b c Gorytus—Ladyship **C. Gour**
57 **MAHYOUBI,** b f African Song—Playing For Keeps **Ecurie I. M. Fares**
58 **MIRUS,** b c American Stress—Milda **J. C. Rouget**
59 **MOUCHA,** b f Fabulous Dancer—Ricabie **V. Resk**
60 **NAJJINA,** b f Fabulous Dancer—Barbotte **Ecurie I. M. Fares**
61 **PRESERVATIONIST,** b f Sadler's Wells—Prestigious **Mrs B. R. Firestone**
62 **PROFIT MAKER,** b c Crystal Glitters—Cutie Kiss **C. Gour**
63 **REDSTONE,** b f Pampabird—Saadia **Baronne de Nervo**
64 **REFLECT MIRACLE,** b f Magic Mirror—Lady Caubeta **Mrs J. F. Dupont**
65 **ROCKET RICHARD,** b c Darshaan—Clear Picture **C. Gour**
66 **SAM SAM,** b f Kaldoun—Winbella **P. Vernier-Rayer**

MR J. C. ROUGET—continued

67 **SEKONDI,** b c R B Chesne—Petite No **J. Laborde**
68 **SHOESHINE,** b c Saint Cyrien—Bellatrice **C. Gour**
69 **SIPS,** b c Procida—Guilledine **F. Adam**
70 **SWEET JUSTICE,** b f Law Society—Hilo Girl **Mrs B. R. Firestone**
71 **SWEET SHAMROCK,** ch f Vacarme—Batioushka **Mrs R. Bousquet**
72 **SYRDARIO,** b c L'Emigrant—Aztec **A. Lapoterie**
73 **TOP MOSS,** b c Tip Moss—Top Queen **B. Belinguier**
74 **TROISIEME BRIGADE,** b c R B Chesne—Voie Royale **C. Gour**
75 **WONDERSHIP,** b c The Wonder—Carminsha **Mrs P. Saget**
76 **YELLOW DUKE,** b c Iron Duke—Yellow Sky **C. Gour**

TWO-YEAR-OLDS

77 **AGROS,** b c Fabulous Dancer—Circassienne **Haras D'Etreham**
78 **ANCIEN HERITAGE,** b c Saint Estephe—Grand Flame **Ecurie I. M. Fares**
79 **ARTEAGA,** b c Fabulous Dancer—Santa Musica **La Clauzade Agriculture S. A.**
80 **ATAYO,** b c Crystal Glitters—Izosta **Ecurie I. M. Fares**
81 **BACK TO ONE,** b f Doulab—Lucy Limelight **C. Gour**
82 **BERING GIFTS,** b c Bering—Southern Fable **C. Gour**
83 **BOYDARA,** b f Darly—Boyarina **La Clauzade Agriculture S. A.**
84 **BRAIN TRUST,** b c Critique—Traviata **Ecurie I. M. Fares**
85 **BREVE,** b f Alla Breva—Super Naskra **J. M. Soriano**
86 **CELLULOID HEROES (IRE),** b c Sandhurst Prince—Miss Slip **J. P. Rios**
87 **DAME DE MONROSE,** b f Saint Estephe—Sirinndi **C. Gour**
88 **DANSHUKAI,** b c Fabulous Dancer—Akline **Ecurie I. M. Fares**
89 **DINNER OUT,** b f Al Nasr—Gourmet Dinner **C. Gour**
90 **DO THE TRICK,** b c Phone Trick—Notte d'Amore **B. Cazenave**
91 **FAIRY DREAM,** b f Lashkari—Bid Fair **Mr M. Daguzan Garros**
92 **FANTASY TRICK,** b f Clever Trick—Sweetest Fantasy **Ecurie I. M. Fares**
93 **FAST RIVER,** b f Zino—Tolga **La Clauzade Agriculture S. A.**
94 **HEARTY KING,** b c Ti King—Heartfelt **C. Gour**
95 B c Sham—Iceland **C. Gour**
96 **JOUR DE REINE,** b c Saint Cyrien—Tien Wice **C. Gour**
97 **KOLAMA,** b f Cariellor—White Face **Mme O. Nicol**
98 **KOLOMBAR,** b c Kaldoun—Chester County **C. Gour**
99 **KYPIRINE,** b c Our Native—Gin And Juice **C. Gour**
100 **LOISAIDA,** b f Sicyos—Solidarite **Haras D'Etreham**
101 **MAELSTROM BAY,** b c Maelstrom Lake—Fille de Villedieu **Mr R. W. Denechere**
102 **MARIKANA,** b f R. B. chesne—Matriona **La Clauzade Agriculture S. A.**
103 **MARIMANDONA (IRE),** b f Gorytus—Cutie Kiss **A. Lapoterie**
104 **MILBURN,** b c Maelstrom Lake—Milford Sound **A. Lapoterie**
105 **MISS HERESIE,** b f Bon Sang—Heresie **P. Lanouilh**
106 **NEW HORIZON,** b f Fast Topaze—Flamethrower **Ecurie I. M. Fares**
107 **NOBLESTA,** b f Noblequest—Nono Algea **P. Vernier Rayer**
108 **NOUGAYORK,** b c Palace Music—Gaite **C. Gour**
109 **PARIS DEAUVILLE,** b c Noblequest—Phalangine **H. Chamarty**
110 **PILINSKI,** b c Lichine—Pinski **Mrs P. Saget**
111 **PLAY THE QUEEN,** b f Ti King—Playing For Keeps **Ecurie I. M. Fares**
112 **PROCIDAGE,** b c Procida—Savage Princess **C. Gour**
113 **PRO SUGAR,** b f Miswaki—Hot Fudge **La Clauzade Agriculture S. A.**
114 **QUALIDO,** b c Procida—Quality Stripe **Ecurie I. M. Fares**
115 **QUEENEMARA (IRE),** b f King of Clubs—Vaison La Romaine **C. Gour**
116 **SAD SAMBA,** b c Kaldoun—Tyranesque **Haras D'Etreham**
117 **SATIS,** b c Mille Balles—Missing Guest **Mr and Mrs R. Bousquet**
118 **SEFIROS,** b c Petoski—Servia **Mrs F. Adam De Raquine**
119 **SONG OF PEACE,** b f Brinkmanship—Song of Tonga **Mrs P. Saget**
120 **TRY OA (IRE),** b c Try My Best—Flut d'Oa **Mr J. M. Valerio**
121 **VALOMBREUSE,** b f Nikos—Riverina **A. Lapoterie**
122 **WINDSIDER (USA),** b c Lear Fan—Bottom Drawer **C. Gour**

Jockeys (Flat): J R Dubosc, P Dumortier.

Jockeys (NH): P Boisgontier, T Lepeltier.

521 MR A. DE ROYER-DUPRE, Chantilly

Postal: **3 Chemin des Aigles, 60500 Chantilly, France.**

1 **BEHERA,** 4, b f Mill Reef—Borushka **H. H. Aga Khan**
2 **BELLE BRAVA (USA),** 4, b f El Baba—Brava **Mme Sven Hanson**
3 **BOQUEN (FR),** 6, gr h Kenmare—Belledune **Marquise de Moratalla**
4 **CHIVALROUS (FR),** 4, ch c Crystal Glitters—Some Thing **Mme Robert Bousquet**
5 **CHOCOLATE ECLAIR (FR),** 4, ch c Pampabird—Pinkski **Mr Robert Lalemant**
6 **CRYSTAL GREEN (FR),** 4, ch c Crystal Glitters—Green Pastures **Mr Robert Lalemant**
7 **DELIORMAN,** 4, ch c Pharly—Dedra **H. H. Aga Khan**
8 **GRAPHUS (BRZ),** 6, b h Depressa—Al Sabah **Mr A. Grumser Filho**
9 **HARTANI,** 4, b c Kalaglow—Herila **H. H. Aga Khan**
10 **HELIANTHEMUM (USA),** 4, b f Lyphard—Summer Review **Ecurie Kadjar**
11 **INVERNESS (FR),** 4, b c Son of Silver—Kaoline **Mr Robert Lalemant**
12 **KALZARI (USA),** 5, b br h Riverman—Kamisha **H. H. Aga Khan**
13 **LIGHTS OUT (FR),** 4, b br c Crystal Glitters—Light A Star **Marquise de Moratalla**
14 **LYPHARD'S MELODY (USA),** 4, b f Lyphard—Luth Music **Mr E. J. Sabato**
15 **MADJARISTAN (USA),** 4, ch c Irish River—Masarika **H. H. Aga Khan**
16 **NAVARZATO,** 7, b h Dominion—Sharp Castan **Marquise de Moratalla**
17 **PORT DE LANNE (FR),** 4, b c Bellypha—Porte des Lilas **Mr Walter Nilsen**
18 **SOMORMUJO (FR),** 5, gr h Known Fact—Kaliopa **Marquise de Moratalla**
19 **SPARKING PLENTY (FR),** 4, b f Crystal Glitters—So Gay **Mr E. J. Sabato**
20 **TABOUSHKAN,** 6, b h Posse—Talaja **H. H. Aga Khan**
21 **TALNAR,** 4, b c Auction Ring—Talaja **H. H. Aga Khan**
22 **TORCECUELLOS (FR),** 4, b c Top Ville—Jacobean Stairs **Marquise de Moratalla**
23 **VALDALI,** 4, b c Darshaan—Val Divine **H. H. Aga Khan**

THREE-YEAR-OLDS

24 **ABYAD,** b c Kenmare—Abalvina **H. H. Aga Khan**
25 **AFSHAN (FR),** b c Lashkari—Afrique **H. H. Aga Khan**
26 **AKSAR (USA),** b c Sharpen Up—Akila **H. H. Aga Khan**
27 **ARDASHER (FR),** ch c Lashkari—Anafa **H. H. Aga Khan**
28 **ASHTARKA,** gr f Dalsaan—Asharaz **H. H. Aga Khan**
29 Ch f Ela-Mana-Mou—Azaarika **H. H. Aga Khan**
30 **BAKILANI (FR),** b c Darshaan—Baykara **H. H. Aga Khan**
31 **BAROURA (FR),** b f Lashkari—Burnished Gold **H. H. Aga Khan**
32 **BEAU MATIN (FR),** b g Crystal Glitters—Bille En Tete **Mr Robert Lalemant**
33 B f King's Lake—Borushka **H. H. Aga Khan**
34 **CAN'T GET STARTED (FR),** b c Lashkari—Fiquefleur **Mr Robert Lalemant**
35 **CASH AND HURRY (USA),** b c Star de Naskra—Miss Secretariat **Mr Robert Lalemant**
36 **DANAKALA,** b f Mouktar—Demo **H. H. Aga Khan**
37 **DARIDSTANN,** gr c Mouktar—Darazina **H. H. Aga Khan**
38 **DEDARA,** b f Head For Heights—Denia **H. H. Aga Khan**
39 **DEYLAMAAN (FR),** b c Vayrann—Dedra **H. H. Aga Khan**
40 B c Lashkari—Drazinnda **H. H. Aga Khan**
41 **ERDELISTAN (FR),** b br c Lashkari—Eunomia **H. H. Aga Khan**
42 **ERGANA,** b f The Wonder—Eloura **H. H. Aga Khan**
43 **EVEN DANCER (USA),** b g Fabulous Dancer—Even Song **Mr Jose Gonzalez**
44 **EVRANA (USA),** b f Nureyev—Euliya **H. H. Aga Khan**
45 **FLECHE DE CRYSTAL (FR),** gr f No Pass No Sale—Aurore de Crystal **Mme S. Cino del Duca**
46 **FONZERN,** b c Dalsaan—Faramoush **Mrs Regula Wurz**
47 **FOREST HILLS (FR),** ch f Sicyos—Fille de Ferme **Mme Yolande Seydoux**
48 **HAMALIYA,** b f High Line—Haughty Manner **H. H. Aga Khan**
49 **HAZARA (FR),** b f Vayrann—Hecalene **H. H. Aga Khan**
50 **HIKAYA,** b f Darshaan—Herila **H. H. Aga Khan**
51 **HOUMAYOUN (FR),** b c Shernazar—Halwah **H. H. Aga Khan**
52 **IN A MELLOTONE (USA),** b f Shadeed—Matachanna **Mr Robert Lalemant**
53 **ISFANDIYAR,** ro c Mouktar—Iroma **H. H. Aga Khan**
54 **JARDINERITO,** ch c Lashkari—Jacobean Stairs **Marquise de Moratalla**
55 **JIM CROW (FR),** b br c Noblequest—Kaoline **Mr Robert Lalemant**
56 **KALANNDI (FR),** b c Lashkari—Kalisa **H. H. Aga Khan**

MR A. DE ROYER-DUPRE—continued

57 **KALAPA (FR)**, b f Mouktar—Kamada **H. H. Aga Khan**
58 B c Recitation—Kaleema **H. H. Aga Khan**
59 B c Mouktar—Kaloudiya **H. H. Aga Khan**
60 **KANNBANIYA**, gr f Mouktar—Kabbaala **H. H. Aga Khan**
61 **KANNDABIL**, b c Nishapour—Katana **H. H. Aga Khan**
62 **KARLAFSHA**, gr f Top Ville—Karosa **H. H. Aga Khan**
63 **KASTALANIYA**, gr f Darshaan—Kastiliya **H. H. Aga Khan**
64 **KATAD (FR)**, b c Akarad—Khadaeen **H. H. Aga Khan**
65 **KAYTAK (FR)**, b c Mouktar—Kaythama **H. H. Aga Khan**
66 **KOLDIA**, b f Darshaan—Koblenza **H. H. Aga Khan**
67 **LARIANA (FR)**, ch f Vayrann—Larannda **H. H. Aga Khan**
68 **LASHKARINA (FR)**, ch f Lashkari—Una Capitana **Mme S. Cino del Duca**
69 **LA TIRANA (FR)**, b br f Akarad—Arosa **Marquise de Moratalla**
70 **MAHSHARI**, b c Mouktar—Majieda **H. H. Aga Khan**
71 **MASAMIYDA**, ch f Lyphard—Masarika **H. H. Aga Khan**
72 **MOUJANNA**, ch f Posse—Mounayn **H. H. Aga Khan**
73 **NAZEERA (FR)**, b f Lashkari—Niece Divine **H. H. Aga Khan**
74 **NIMRAN**, b c Commanche Run—Nilmeen **H. H. Aga Khan**
75 **NORTH POLLY (USA)**, b c Esprit du Nord—Typhoon Polly **Mr Robert Lalemant**
76 **NORTH WATER (FR)**, b br c No Pass No Sale—Paddle **Mme O. Bryant**
77 **RAWAAN (FR)**, b c Labus—Rose Ness **H. H. Aga Khan**
78 **RIVERLYPH (USA)**, ch f Lyphard—Rivermande **Mr Henri Mastey**
79 **ROZGAR**, b c Darshaan—Roziyna **H. H. Aga Khan**
80 **SARTAK (FR)**, b c Mouktar—Stoyana **H. H. Aga Khan**
81 **SEBA LE ROUGE (FR)**, b br c No Pass No Sale—Quintefolle **Mr Afonso Burlamaqui**
82 **SHAHYAD**, ch c Cure The Blues—Barbra **Ecurie Kadjar**
83 **SHAKOURA (FR)**, b f Labus—Shapaara **H. H. Aga Khan**
84 **SHALAYARI**, b c Auction Ring—Shayina **H. H. Aga Khan**
85 **SHAMDINAN**, b c Dalsaan—Sharmaya **H. H. Aga Khan**
86 **SHAMKOUR (FR)**, b br c Deep Roots—Sharsha **H. H. Aga Khan**
87 **SHAM PRINCESS (USA)**, b f Lyphard—Paradise **Ecurie Kadjar**
88 **SHENAR (FR)**, b c Akarad—Shashna **H. H. Aga Khan**
89 **SUETAGAR**, gr f Zino—Reine Mere **Marquise de Moratalla**
90 **SULTANPOUR**, b c Akarad—Sega Ville **H. H. Aga Khan**
91 **TAKOUDAR**, gr c Mouktar—Takrana **H. H. Aga Khan**
92 **TALAMA (FR)**, gr f Shakapour—Talosca **H. H. Aga Khan**
93 Ch c Lashkari—Tasskeen **H. H. Aga Khan**
94 **THE TENDER TRACK (USA)**, b c Topsider—Articulate Robbery **Mr Robert Lalemant**
95 **TRACKING SHOT (USA)**, b c Lypheor—Chieftain's Native **Mr Robert Lalemant**

TWO-YEAR-OLDS

96 B c Darshaan—Afrique (Exbury) **H. H. Aga Khan**
97 B c Riverman—Akila (Top Ville) **H. H. Aga Khan**
98 B c Lightning—Aladja (Mill Reef) **H. H. Aga Khan**
99 **ALAZANI (IRE)**, ch c Shardari—Aleema (Red God) **H. H. Aga Khan**
100 **ALTA LOMA (FR)**, ch f Fast Topaze—Kasala (Blushing Groom) **Mr Henri Mastey**
101 B c Darshaan—Anafa (Faristan) **H. H. Aga Khan**
102 **AZAKI (FR)**, ch f Niniski—Azahara (Exclusive Native) **Mme S. Cino del Duca**
103 Ch f Shardari—Baykara (Direct Flight) **H. H. Aga Khan**
104 **BLUSHING TAMARA (USA)**, ch f Blushing Groom—Tamara Alain (Judge Kilday) **Mr Henri Mastey**
105 B f Vayrann—Burnished Gold (Breton) **H. H. Aga Khan**
106 **CINCO DE COPAS (FR)**, b br c Chief's Crown—Tamarinda (Relkino) **Marquise de Moratalla**
107 Ch c Vayrann—Darbaka (Relkino) **H. H. Aga Khan**
108 B c Shardari—Demo (Abdos) **H. H. Aga Khan**
109 **DON'TWARY (FR)**, ch f Lomond—Batioushka (Guillaume Tell) **Mr Robert Bousquet**
110 Gr c Mouktar—Eloura (Top Ville) **H. H. Aga Khan**
111 B c Arctic Tern—Euliya (Top Ville) **H. H. Aga Khan**
112 B f Vayrann—Hereke (Blakeney) **H. H. Aga Khan**
113 **HORA DANCER (FR)**, b f Lashkari—Disco Dancer (Green Dancer) **Melle M. C. de Saint Seine**
114 **HUSSAIN (FR)**, ch c Vayrann—Eurissia (Sir Gaylord) **H. H. Aga Khan**

MR A. DE ROYER-DUPRE—continued

115 B f Kenmare—Ilyaara (Huntercombe) **H. H. Aga Khan**
116 I WISH YOU LOVE, b c Shahrastani—Silent Bidder (Bold Bidder) **Mr Robert Lalemant**
117 B c Deep Roots—Kalisa (Exceller) **H. H. Aga Khan**
118 KALITA MELODY, b f Chief Singer—Belle Reef (Mill Reef) **Mr Luay al Swaidi**
119 B f Labus—Kalsena (Ile de Bourbon) **H. H. Aga Khan**
120 B c Lashkari—Kamada (Blushing Groom) **H. H. Aga Khan**
121 Ch f Fast Topaze—Kariya (Irish River) **H. H. Aga Khan**
122 KENA (FR), b br c Caro—Intrepidora (Intrepid Hero) **Mme Robert Bousquet**
123 LITTLE STANY (FR), ch c Shahrastani—Little Deep Water (General Assembly) **Mme S. Cino del Duca**
124 B f No Pass No Sale—Marmana (Blushing Groom) **H. H. Aga Khan**
125 B c Nikos—Nabita (Akarad) **H. H. Aga Khan**
126 B c Akarad—Nashkara (Shirley Heights) **H. H. Aga Khan**
127 B c Shakapour—Naveen (Sir Gaylord) **H. H. Aga Khan**
128 B f Darshaan—Niece Divine (Great Nephew) **H. H. Aga Khan**
129 B br f Critique—Nofertiti (Exbury) **Mr Afonso Burlamaqui**
130 POOR BUTTERFLY, b c Sharpo—Eastern Shore (Sun Prince) **Mr Robert Lalemant**
131 PRINCE DE CRYSTAL (FR), b c Crystal Glitters—Una Capatina (Sanctus) **Mme S. Cino del Duca**
132 B c Mouktar—Rasseema (Youth) **H. H. Aga Khan**
133 SETH (FR), b c Script Ohio—Some Thing (Will Somers) **Mme Robert Bousquet**
134 B c The Wonder—Shalta (Targowice) **H. H. Aga Khan**
135 B c Lashkari—Shapaara (Rheingold) **H. H. Aga Khan**
136 B c Mouktar—Sharsha (Labus) **H. H. Aga Khan**
137 B f Darshaan—Shashna (Blakeney) **H. H. Aga Khan**
138 SHINE HIGH, b br c High Top—Somalia (Formidable) **Mr Beniamino Arbib**
139 SLOBODAN, b c Shirley Heights—Jacobean Stairs (Welsh Pageant) **Marquise de Moratalla**
140 B c Lashkari—Stoyana (Abdos) **H. H. Aga Khan**
141 SVETLANA (FR), b f Darshaan—Belle Doche (Riverman) **Marquise de Moratalla**
142 B f Akarad—Taeesha (Mill Reef) **H. H. Aga Khan**
143 B c Last Tycoon—Talaja (Kalamoun) **H. H. Aga Khan**
144 B c Labus—Tasskeen (Lyphard) **H. H. Aga Khan**
145 B f Lashkari—Yasiyn (Brigadier Gerard) **H. H. Aga Khan**
146 ZAGOR, b c Zino—Carrozzella (Vaguely Noble) **Mr Robert Lalemant**
147 B f Akarad—Zanata (African Sky) **H. H. Aga Khan**

Jockeys (Flat): A S Cruz, William Mongil.

522 MR A. J. RUMSEY, Stourbridge

Postal: **Upper Whittimere Farm, Bobbington, Stourbridge, West Midlands, DY7 5EP.**
Phone: **BOBBINGTON (038 488) 269**

1 MESEMBRYANTHEMUM, 5, br m Warpath—Delphinium **Mr A. J. Rumsey**
2 RENO'S JEM, 4, b f Starch Reduced—Miss Purchase **Mr A. J. Rumsey**
3 RENO'S QUEST, 7, gr g Roscoe Blake—Auto Sam **Mr A. J. Rumsey**

Jockey (NH): W J Hayes (9-7, w.a.).

523 MR B. J. M. RYALL, Yeovil

Postal: **Higher Farm, Rimpton, Yeovil, Somerset, BA22 8AD.**
Phone: **MARSTON MAGNA (0935) 850222**

1 HONEYDEER MEAD, 8, ch g Le Bavard (FR)—Midnight Oil **Mr B. J. M. Ryall**

524 MR M. J. RYAN, Newmarket

Postal: **Cadland, 35 Old Station Road, Newmarket, Suffolk, CB8 8DT.**
Phone: **(0638) 664172 TELEX 817777**

1 **ABEROY,** 11, ch g Abercorn—Maroyal **A. Gregory**
2 **AJALITA,** 4, ch f Move Off—Citrine **S. Potter**
3 4, Br g Vaigly Great—Couteau **Mrs W. L. Sole**
4 **GREENHILLS STAR,** 5, ch m Mansingh (USA)—Soheir **Mr L. Audus**
5 **GREENHILLS WARRIOR,** 4, ch g Tina's Pet—Soheir **Mr G. Davies and Mr L. Audus**
6 **KAMAKAZE GIRL,** 4, b f Kampala—Glencara **M. J. Baxter**
7 **KATIE JO,** 4, b f Taufan (USA)—Wyn Mipet **R. Scott**
8 **LANGTRY LADY,** 4, b f Pas de Seul—Arianna Aldini **Teresa Baron**
9 **LINK MARKET (USA),** 4, b f Linkage (USA)—Motor Mouse **P. J. Flavin**
10 **MACKENZIES,** 5, ch m Homing—Miss Henry **Mr M. J. Ryan**
11 **MERCHANT'S DREAM,** 5, ch g Hard Fought—Victorian Pageant **M. J. Baxter**
12 **MOMSER,** 4, ch g Mr Fluorocarbon—Jolimo **Mrs M. J. Ryan**
13 **OSRIC,** 7, b g Radetzky—Jolimo **Mr Richard Scott**
14 **PRADEL,** 6, br g Monsanto (FR)—Couteau **Mrs W. L. Sole**
15 **REBEL RAISER (USA),** 6, ch g Raise A Native—Lady Oakley **Mr Richard E. Scott**
16 **SANDCASTLE,** 9, ch g Tap On Wood—Pacific Sands **Mr D. C. Rees**
17 **SHARP JUSTICE,** 4, ch c Sharpo—Lady Justice **Malpass Bros Ltd**
18 **SILKS DOMINO,** 5, ch g Dominion—Bourgeonette **Mr R. W. Malpass**
19 **SILKS PRINCESS,** 4, b f Prince Tenderfoot (USA)—Pitlessie **Mrs J. McFadden**
20 **TROJAN DEBUT,** 4, b g Trojan Fen—Debutina Park **Mr M. J. Ryan**
21 **WESTERN DYNASTY,** 4, ch g Hotfoot—Northern Dynasty **M. F. Kentish**
22 **YET,** 5, gr m Last Fandango—Rana of Coombe **Mr D. C. Rees**

THREE-YEAR-OLDS

23 **EVERY ONE A GEM,** ch g Nicholas Bill—Lady Bequick **Miss C. Coyne**
24 **FENAMICA,** b f Trojan Fen—My Tootsie **F. Ellis**
25 **GONDO,** br g Mansingh (USA)—Secret Valentine **T. Childs**
26 **LADY MADINA,** br f Legend of France (USA)—Double Touch **J. Enright**
27 **LANGTRY LASS,** br f Tina's Pet—Nimble Star **A. Baron**
28 **LES AMIS,** b f Alzao (USA)—Les Sylphides (FR) **Mrs W. L. Sole**
29 Gr g Petong—Lucky Orphan **Mrs M. J. Ryan**
30 **MONA CHIC,** ch g Noalto—Lady Justice **Mr C. I. Garrad**
31 **RUPPLES,** b g Muscatite—Miss Annie **Mrs M. J. Ryan**
32 **SATIS DANCER,** br f Mashhor Dancer (USA)—Chrisanthy **N. Morris**
33 **TARA'S DELIGHT,** b f Dunbeath (USA)—Tickton Bridge **Stevenage Printing**

TWO-YEAR-OLDS

34 **ASCOT SILKS,** b f Commanche Run—Les Sylphides (FR) **R. Scott**
35 **BIG BLOW,** b c Last Tycoon—Tuxford Hideaway **Miss C. Coyne**
36 **DOMICKSKY,** br c Dominion—Mumruffin **Enterprise Markets**
37 **EVERLOVING (IRE),** b f Alzao (USA)—Moorland Chant **C. Cronin Ltd**
38 Ch f Vaigly Great—Jolimo
39 Br f Prince Sabo—Joli's Girl
40 **POLYPLATE,** b f Song—Countless Countess **M.H.M. Ltd**
41 **SALUTING WALTER (USA),** b c Verbatim (USA)—Stage Hour **P. J. Flavin**
42 **SHARP TOP,** b f Sharpo—Two High **Malpass Bros Ltd**
43 **SILKS JANJO,** b f Petoski—Elegida **Mrs J. McFadden**
44 Br c Another Realm—Stardyn **F. Cosgrove**
45 Gr f Kalaglow—Tickton Bridge **Asad Meerza**

Other Owners: G. Battochi, C. Blackmore, P. Dickson, W. Dixon, Ellis And Roukin Limited, K. Mansfield, K. Marriott, P. Marron, D. McKey, G. W. Mills, W. B. Payn, Mr B. Schmidt-Bodner, M. Soames, M. Stoneman.

Jockey (Flat): P Robinson (7-11, w.a.).

MR M. J. RYAN—continued

Jockeys (NH): G McCourt (10-3, w.a), J McLaughlin (9-8).

Apprentices: G Bardwell (7-0), N Gwilliams (7-3), J Ryan.

Lady Rider: Mrs Maureen Howes (9-4).

525 MAJOR W. N. SAMPLE, Morpeth

Postal: **The Low House, South Middleton, Scotsgap, Morpeth, Northumberland.**
Phone: **SCOTSGAP (067 074) 627**

1 **GROUND MASTER,** 13, b g Master Owen—Background **Major W. N. Sample**

Amateur: Mr C J Sample (10-7).

526 MISS B. SANDERS, Epsom

Postal: **Chalk Pit Stables, Headley Road, Epsom, Surrey.**
Phone: **ASHTEAD (037 22) 78453 FAX (037 22) 276137**

1 **BIG FINISH,** 5, b h Persian Bold—Azurn **Mr A. G. Bayliss**
2 **CALAPAEZ,** 6, gr g Nishapour (FR)—Charter Belle **Mr T. J. Blake**
3 **CHAROSSA,** 5, b m Ardross—Charter Belle **Mr T. J. Blake**
4 **COLORTAG,** 4, b g Runnett—Two's Company **Mr N. M. Goymer**
5 **DON KEYDROP,** 6, b g Don—Tomrousse (FR) **Mrs V. Dalton**
6 **DOUBLE DUTCH,** 6, b m Nicholas Bill—Dutch Princess **Mr Leonard Fuller**
7 **DUTCH MAJESTY,** 4, b f Homing—Dutch Princess **Mr Leonard Fuller**
8 **EXHAUST MAN,** 6, b g Crooner—Silk Fashion
9 **FARAYAR (USA),** 5, b g Alleged (USA)—Felix Culpa **Mr Alan Kinghorn**
10 **HAVE FAITH,** 9, b g Sunyboy—Credo's Daughter **Mr N. M. Goymer**
11 **KATY LOU,** 4, gr f Nishapour (FR)—Emmylou **Miss Brooke Sanders**
12 **LIZAWAY,** 6, ch m Casino Boy—Mahogany Lady **Miss S. J. Weyman**
13 **MIAMI IN SPRING,** 7, ch g Miami Springs—Fado **Mr N. M. Goymer**
14 **OLD EROS,** 6, ch g Bold Owl—Piccadilly Rose **Mr T. Childs**
15 **OUBLIER L'ENNUI (FR),** 5, b m Bellman (FR)—Cassowary **Mr R. J. Reip**
16 **POLYROLL,** 4, b c Kampala—Hail To Feathers (USA) **Mr F. T. Adams**
17 **QUEEN ANGEL,** 4, b f Anfield—More Or Less **Mrs M. Fairbarns**
18 **SALMON PRINCE,** 4, ch g Salmon Leap (USA)—Princesse Anglaise **Mr L. M. Bush**
19 **SODA FOUNTAIN,** 4, b f Lafontaine (USA)—Sugar Lump
20 **SOLITARY REAPER,** 5, b g Valiyar—Fardella (ITY) **Harefield Cricket Club**
21 **SOUPCON,** 4, b f King of Spain—Duck Soup **Mrs Jayne Clark**
22 **SPAROS,** 6, ch g Prince Mab (FR)—Spare Change **Mr N. M. Goymer**
23 **SULLI BOY (NOR),** 5, b g Sparkling Boy—Lady Sullivan
24 **VIRGINIA'S BAY,** 4, b g Uncle Pokey—Carnation **Mrs Virginia Toft**
25 **WILLOW GORGE,** 7, ch g Hello Gorgeous (USA)—Willowy **Mr J. R. Barr**
26 **WYARDS WONDER,** 4, b g Hotfoot—Tenth Hussar **Mr P. Cook**
27 **YAMRAH,** 6, b m Milford—Silojoka **Miss Brooke Sanders**

THREE-YEAR-OLDS

28 **CRABBY BILL,** br g Blakeney—Dancing Kathleen **Mr W. Gerhauser**
29 **DUTCH MONARCH,** br g Homing—Dutch Princess **Mr Leonard Fuller**
30 **FLIRTY FILLY,** b f Bay Express—Romancing **P. J. Meyer**
31 **MISTER MISTRAL,** ch g Formidable (USA)—Landlady **Mrs Myra Fuller**
32 **PAISINGH,** br f Mansingh (USA)—Patience Unlimited **Sheet & Roll Convertors Ltd**
33 **SAM THE MAN,** b g Aragon—First Temptation (USA) **Mr E. Fenarol**

MISS B. SANDERS—continued

TWO-YEAR-OLDS

34 **DUTCH CZARINA,** b f 21/2 Prince Sabo—Dutch Princess (Royalty) **Mr Leonard Fuller**
35 B f 25/2 Dunbeath (USA)—First Temptation (USA) (Mr Leader (USA)) **Mr N. M. Goymer**
36 **SHEZNICE (IRE),** ch f 6/5 Try My Best (USA)—Miss Kate (FR) (Nonoalco (USA)) **Mr P. Cook**

Other Owners: Mrs A. Billison, Mr R. M. Ellis, Mrs L. J. Gatward, Mr J. F. Hansberry, Mr David Hudd, Mr P. C. M. Jones, Mrs Pauline Moran, Mr John J. Morrissey, Mr Larry Murphy.

Jockey (Flat): W Newnes (w.a.).

Apprentice: Dana Mellor (7-2).

Conditional: Jason Halls (9-10).

Lady Riders: Miss T Bird (7-7), Miss B Sanders (8-7).

527 MR C. R. SAUNDERS, Northampton

Postal: **Holdenby North Lodge, Spratton, Northampton, NN6 8LG.**
Phone: **(0604) 770234**

1 **BALLINAVEEN,** 10, b g Peacock (FR)—Fugacity **Miss C. Saunders**
2 **SONGELLA,** 5, ch m True Song—Tenella **Mr C. R. Saunders**
3 **TENECOUNT,** 6, ch g Country Retreat—Tenella **Mr C. R. Saunders**
4 **TENESAINT,** 9, ch g St Columbus—Tenella **Mr C. R. Saunders**

Amateur: Mr A Sansome (10-10).

Lady Rider: Mrs J Saunders (9-0).

528 DR J. D. SCARGILL, Newmarket

Postal: **Red House Stables, Hamilton Road, Newmarket, Suffolk, CB8 0PE.**
Phone: **(0638) 663254**

1 **CHINA'S WAY (USA),** 4, b f Native Uproar (USA)—China Tea (USA) **Mr A. S. Reid**
2 **FILLE DE FRAISE,** 4, b f Mr Fluorocarbon—Strawberry Fields **Mr Basil White**
3 **FROZEN MINSTREL,** 6, b g Black Minstrel—Arctic Sue **Mr Jonathan Crisp**
4 **GO MOTORPLAN,** 8, ch g Beau Tudor—Another Lady VI **Mr Jonathan Crisp**
5 **MERSEYSIDE MAN,** 4, b g My Dad Tom (USA)—Chanita **Mrs Susan Scargill**
6 **MILLFORD HAVEN,** 5, b g Welsh Saint—Flute (FR) **Mr Roger Myers**
7 **MISTER BYBLOS,** 4, b g Lomond (USA)—Current Jargon (USA) **Mr Jonathan Crisp**
8 **ORSETT (USA),** 4, b g Our Native (USA)—Ornamental (USA) **Mr R. A. Dalton**
9 **SIGN PEOPLE,** 4, ch c Sayyaf—Maura Paul **A. C. Edwards Ltd**
10 **SPIRITUALIST,** 4, ch c Simply Great (FR)—Parima **Mr Mark Gibbon**
11 **TROJAN LANCER,** 4, b c Trojan Fen—Dunsters Cream **Mr Ashley Graham**

THREE-YEAR-OLDS

12 **AURORA GLITZA,** ch f Sayf El Arab (USA)—Linda's Design **Mrs Janet Stevenson**
13 **DEGANNWY,** br f Caerleon (USA)—Delagoa (FR) **Mrs Celia Miller**
14 **HALEIM,** ch c Formidable (USA)—Miss Reasoning (USA) **Stableline Limited**
15 **HOSTESS QUICKLY,** b f Hotfoot—Linda Dudley **Mr Bruce Willey**
16 **KING AL,** b c Indian King (USA)—Impudent Miss **Mr A. P. Smith**
17 **MISS GOLDIE LOCKS,** ch f Dara Monarch—Really Sharp **Mrs S. Weiss**
18 **MRS PEEBODY,** ch f Trampler—Midsummer Sparkle **Mr J. Hammond**

DR J. D. SCARGILL—continued

19 **NAJAT,** b f Tender King—Brave Ivy **Stableline Limited**
20 **PAN E SALAM,** gr g Ile de Bourbon (USA)—Norton Princess **Aziende Associate Agricole SRL**
21 **PIPISTRELLE,** b f Shareef Dancer (USA)—Latin Melody **Mrs Celia Miller**
22 **PRINCESS TAUFAN,** b f Taufan (USA)—Guindilla **Mr Bob Young**
23 **PROOF OF PURCHASE,** b c Wassl—Anjuli **Mr R. A. Dalton**
24 **SIGN PERFORMER,** ch g Longleat—Grandgirl **A. C. Edwards Ltd**
25 **SOLO COURT,** ch f King of Clubs—Mrs Tittlemouse **Mrs Gill Willey**
26 **SOLOMONS NEPHEW,** b c Absalom—Strawberry Fields **Mr Basil White**
27 **TASKFORCE FIXED IT,** b g Aragon—Broken Accent **Mr A. S. Reid**
28 **TEES WHEELIE BIN,** b f Balliol—Mead Lane **Little Cornard Racing**
29 **TO BE FAIR,** ch c Adonijah—Aquarula **Mr M. Reditt**

TWO-YEAR-OLDS

30 B f 17/3 Tumble Wind (USA)—Ange de Feu **Mrs S. Weiss**
31 **CARNBREA CUDDY (IRE),** ch c 21/4 King of Clubs—Mrs Tittlemouse **Mrs S. M. Crompton**
32 B f 5/4 Soughaan (USA)—Dame Ross **Rightbetter Ltd**
33 B c 9/5 Hatim (USA)—Divine Fleece **Aziende Associate Agricole SRL**
34 B c 4/4 Red Sunset—Dominia **A. C. Edwards Ltd**
35 **ELUSIVE SPIRIT,** ch f 29/2 Absalom—Sister Jinks **Mrs J. Martin**
36 B c 7/4 Last Tycoon—Fabled Lady **Mrs R. Jones**
37 **FRIEND OF A FRIEND,** b f 18/5 Nishapour (FR)—Marista **Three Shires Bloodstock**
38 **KATIE VALENTINE,** gr f 14/2 Belfort (FR)—Call Me Kate **Mr R. Oxley**
39 B f 19/2 Trojan Fen—Key of The Kingdom **Mrs Susan Scargill**
40 **NIP,** b f 13/3 Bay Express—Broken Accent **Mr A. S. Reid**
41 B f 4/5 Swing Easy—Only Miranda **Mrs Shirley Scargill**
42 B f 20/3 Indian King (USA)—Persian Royale **Rightbetter Ltd**
43 **ROCKIN' ROSIE,** b f 23/3 Song—Almarose **Mrs P. Reditt**
44 B c 23/5 Mashhor Dancer (USA)—Sunset Ray **Mr J. McCourt**
45 **SWEET JUSTICE,** b f 17/4 Law Society (USA)—Sweet And Lovely **Mrs M. Field**
46 **WAY OFF BEAT,** b c 5/2 Ballad Rock—Astral Way **Mr M. Reditt**

Other Owners: Mrs Teresa Dexter, Mrs V. Drake, B. Field, D. Fitzgerald, Mrs S. Girvan, Mrs Beryl Graham, Mr D. Guest, Mr B. Norris, Mr G. A. Raggett, Mr R. Roberts, Mr G. Robinson, Peter Sowerby, Mr B. Westgate, Mr Martin Wickens.

Jockeys (Flat): R Cochrane (w.a.), J Lowe (w.a.), W Newnes (w.a.).

Jockeys (NH): C Llewellyn (w.a.), P Tuck (w.a.).

Apprentice: K Rutter (7-12).

Conditional: J Driscoll (9-7).

529 MR A. A. SCOTT, Newmarket

Postal: **Oak Stables, Hamilton Road, Newmarket, Suffolk, CB8 OTE.**
Phone: **(0638) 661998 TELEX: 81518 TELEFAX: (0638) 667394**

1 **GO ON SMILE (USA),** 4, ch c Diesis—Key To The Minstrel (USA) **Maktoum Al Maktoum**
2 **GREAT COMMOTION (USA),** 4, b c Nureyev (USA)—Alathea **Maktoum Al Maktoum**
3 **MAGIC GLEAM (USA),** 4, b f Danzig (USA)—All Agleam (USA) **Maktoum Al Maktoum**
4 **NABEEL DANCER (USA),** 5, b h Northern Dancer—Prayers'n Promises (USA) **Maktoum Al Maktoum**
5 **SKY CONQUEROR (USA),** 5, ch h Conquistador Cielo (USA)—Blushing Cathy (USA) **Maktoum Al Maktoum**

MR A. A. SCOTT—continued

THREE-YEAR-OLDS

6 **A KISS IN DEED (USA),** b f Shadeed (USA)—Passakiss (USA) **Maktoum Al Maktoum**
7 **ALRIYAAH,** b f Shareef Dancer (USA)—Sharpina **Mr Hadi Al-Tajir**
8 **AZIM,** b c Mummy's Pet—Dimant Blanche (USA) **Maktoum Al Maktoum**
9 **BEDOUIN PRINCE (USA),** b c Danzig (USA)—Regal Heiress **Maktoum Al Maktoum**
10 **BINT SHAHEEN (USA),** b f Shadeed (USA)—Avum (USA) **Maktoum Al Maktoum**
11 **CARTEL,** b c Kris—Meis El-Reem **Maktoum Al Maktoum**
12 **CROWN BALADEE (USA),** b br c Chief's Crown (USA)—Naseem Baladee **Maktoum Al Maktoum**
13 **DANCE MOVE,** b f Shareef Dancer (USA)—Rapide Pied (USA) **Maktoum Al Maktoum**
14 **DEMI LUNE,** b f Dominion—Lune de Minuit (USA) **Maktoum Al Maktoum**
15 **DIVINE HEROINE,** b f Valiyar—Pellinora (USA) **Cheveley Park Stud**
16 **INSIDER DEALER (USA),** ch g Secreto (USA)—Acquisitor (USA) **Maktoum Al Maktoum**
17 **MAGICAL DEED (USA),** b c Shadeed (USA)—Cornish Genie (USA) **Maktoum Al Maktoum**
18 **MISCHAK (USA),** b c Miswaki (USA)—Chuckles (USA) **Maktoum Al Maktoum**
19 **MODEST HOPE (USA),** b c Blushing Groom (FR)—Key Dancer (USA) **Maktoum Al Maktoum**
20 **MY MAVOURNIN (USA),** b f L'Emigrant (USA)—Maid of Erin (USA) **Abigail Limited**
21 **NUWIRAH (USA),** b f Pleasant Colony (USA)—Secretarial Queen (USA) **Mr Hamdan Al-Maktoum**
22 **POLISHING,** ch c Touching Wood (USA)—Loveshine (USA) **Maktoum Al Maktoum**
23 **POSSESSIVE LADY,** ch f Dara Monarch—Possessive **Mrs Doreen M. Swinburn**
24 **SHALFA (USA),** b f Riverman (USA)—Bon Gout (USA) **Sheikh Ahmed Al Maktoum**
25 **SWISS AFFAIR (USA),** ch c Private Account (USA)—Ten Cents A Kiss (USA) **Maktoum Al Maktoum**
26 **TABDEA (USA),** b f Topsider (USA)—Madame Secretary (USA) **Mr Hamdan Al-Maktoum**
27 **TAJFAH (USA),** b f Shadeed (USA)—Alathea **Maktoum Al Maktoum**
28 **THEATRICAL CHARMER,** b c Sadler's Wells (USA)—Very Charming (USA) **Maktoum Al Maktoum**
29 **TRINCOMALEE,** ch f Electric—Copt Hall Princess **Lt-Col Sir James Scott**
30 **WAATHIG,** ch c Sharpen Up—Clunk Click **Sheikh Ahmed Al Maktoum**
31 **WELL FURNISHED,** ch c Salmon Leap (USA)—Mimicry **Mr Philip Afia**

TWO-YEAR-OLDS

32 **ALSAARIYAH (USA),** b f Diesis—Welden (USA) (Danzig (USA)) **Mr Hamdan Al-Maktoum**
33 **AL ZOUD (USA),** ch f Sharpen Up—Queen's Visit (Top Command (USA)) **Maktoum Al Maktoum**
34 **ANJIZ (USA),** b c Nureyev (USA)—
Prayers'n Promises (USA) (Foolish Pleasure (USA)) **Maktoum Al Maktoum**
35 B f 13/4 Alleged (USA)—April Fancy (No Argument) **Mr A. A. Scott**
36 **BALWA (USA),** b f 22/3 Danzig (USA)—Princess Oola (USA) (Al Hattab (USA)) **Sheikh Ahmed Al Maktoum**
37 **BASHOOSH (USA),** b f Danzig (USA)—Condessa (Condorcet (FR)) **Maktoum Al Maktoum**
38 **BE DEVIOUS,** b f Bering—Ulterior Motive (Pyjama Hunt) **Morven Stud Ltd**
39 **BESHAARH (USA),** b f Blushing Groom (FR)—Scintillate (Sparkler) **Mr Hamdan Al-Maktoum**
40 **BOLD HEART,** ch c 24/3 Pennine Walk—June Maid (Junius) **Mr R. C. Thompson**
41 B f 7/4 Prince Tenderfoot—Breezy Answer (On Your Mark) **Hambleton Million Thoroughbred Plc.**
42 Ch f 18/3 Nureyev (USA)—Bright Omen (USA) (Grey Dawn II) **Maktoum Al Maktoum**
43 **BUCKLE KNIGHT (USA),** br c 7/3 Spend A Buck (USA)—Knightly Belle (USA) (Knightly Manner)
44 **BUSH BIRD (USA),** b c Chief's Crown (USA)—Naseem Baladee (Kris) **Maktoum Al Maktoum**
45 Ch c 22/3 Saratoga Six (USA)—Caline (USA) (Ack Ack (USA))
46 **CHIEF'S EXAMPLE (USA),** ch c Chief's Crown (USA)—
Bold Example (USA) (Bold Lad (USA)) **Maktoum Al Maktoum**
47 **CONVIVIAL,** b f 16/4 Nordance (USA)—Rensaler (USA) (Stop The Music (USA)) **Cheveley Park Stud**
48 B c 19/3 Horage—Corozal (Corvaro (USA)) **Hambleton Million Thoroughbred Plc.**
49 B f 12/4 Forzando—Cow Pastures (Homing) **Mr D. G. Churston**
50 **CREAM SILK LADY (FR),** b f 8/4 Dancing Brave (USA)—
Loveshine (USA) (Gallant Romeo (USA)) **Maktoum Al Maktoum**
51 B c 6/4 Al Nasr (FR)—Dabbiana (CAN) (Fappiano (USA)) **A. F. Budge (Equine) Ltd**
52 **DESERT BRIDE,** b f 9/4 Green Desert (USA)—Sharpina (Sharpen Up) **Mr Hadi Al-Tajir**
53 B f 7/3 Dixieland Band (USA)—Did She Agree (USA) (Restless Native) **Mr A. A. Scott**
54 **DUL DUL (USA),** b f Shadeed (USA)—Cassy's Pet (Sing Sing) **Maktoum Al Maktoum**
55 **FISHIN' TACKLE (USA),** b c Sportin' Life (USA)—
Perilune (USA) (Soy Numero Uno (USA)) **Sir Anthony Page-Wood**
56 **FURAJET (USA),** ch f 25/3 The Minstrel (CAN)—Zummerudd (Habitat) **Maktoum Al Maktoum**
57 Ro f 25/4 Spectacular Bid (USA)—Geiger Countess (USA) (Mr Prospector (USA))
58 **GOLDEN SHOULDERS (USA),** b f Alleged (USA)—Eye Drop (USA) (Irish River (FR)) **Maktoum Al Maktoum**

MR A. A. SCOTT—continued

59 **GUYUM,** b f 27/2 Rousillon (USA)—Lady of Chalon (USA) (Young Emperor) **Mr Hamdan Al-Maktoum**
60 **HIDEAWAY (USA),** ch f 25/3 Secreto (USA)—Out Distance (USA) (Forli (ARG))
61 **HUD HUD (USA),** b f Alydar (USA)—Tax Dodge (USA) (Seattle Slew (USA)) **Maktoum Al Maktoum**
62 **INSEYAB,** b f Persian Bold—Strike Home (Be My Guest (USA)) **Maktoum Al Maktoum**
63 **LA MASAAS (USA),** br c 7/1 Miswaki (USA)—Skeeb (USA) (Topsider (USA)) **Maktoum Al Maktoum**
64 **LYNABERACK,** b f 24/3 Ardross—Happy Hannah (Absalom) **Mrs Alexander Scott**
65 **MARWAD (IRE),** b c 14/4 Runnett—Splendid Chance (Random Shot) **Mr Hamdan Al-Maktoum**
66 **MAYAASA (FR),** b f 24/3 Green Desert (USA)—Fitnah (Kris) **Miss H. Al-Maktoum**
67 Br c 29/4 Gate Dancer (USA)—Meditation (USA) (Private Thoughts (USA))
68 **MISS FYOR (USA),** b f Danzig (USA)—Ma Biche (USA) (Key To The Kingdom (USA)) **Maktoum Al Maktoum**
69 **MUKAAFAH (USA),** b c 17/1 Chief's Crown (USA)—
Taylor Park (USA) (Sir Gaylord) **Mr Hamdan Al-Maktoum**
70 **RAINBOW TRUST,** b c 22/3 Rainbow Quest (USA)—Bandit Queen (FR) (Jim French (USA))
71 **RAJAYA (USA),** b c Nureyev (USA)—Don't Sulk (USA) (Graustark) **Maktoum Al Maktoum**
72 B c Secreto (USA)—Rephrase (USA) (Affirmed (USA)) **Mr D. B. Thompson**
73 B c 19/2 Copelan—Rock Fever (Hawaii) **A. F. Budge (Equine) Ltd**
74 **RUSSIAN LIAISON,** b f 19/3 Law Society—Veruschka (Lorenzaccio) **Cheveley Park Stud**
75 **SAFA,** b f 22/4 Shirley Heights—Beveridge (Spectacular Bid) **Sheikh Ahmed Al Maktoum**
76 **SAINT CIEL (USA),** b c Skywalker—Holy Tobin (J O Tobin) **Mr R. C. Thompson**
77 **SHAFFAAF (USA),** b c 5/3 Shadeed—Refill (Mill Reef) **Mr Hamdan Al-Maktoum**
78 **SHEIKH ALBADOU,** b c Green Desert (USA)—Sanctuary (Welsh Pageant) **Mr Hilal Salem**
79 **SHIHAMA (USA),** b f 31/1 Shadeed (USA)—Dubian (High Line) **Mr Mohammed Obaida**
80 Ch c 2/2 Be My Guest—Smarten Up (Sharpen Up) **Maktoum Al Maktoum**
81 **TAUTINA,** b f 8/5 Taufan—Wintina (Tumble Wind) **Morven Stud Ltd**
82 **TOP BEAUTY,** b f High Top—American Beauty (Mill Reef (USA)) **Morven Stud Ltd**
83 **TRAHIN,** ch c Kris—Mangayah (USA) (Spectacular Bid (USA)) **Maktoum Al Maktoum**
84 **UN SOUVERAIN,** b c 19/3 Kenmare—Serenita (Lyphard) **Maktoum Al Maktoum**

Other Owners: Mrs J. R. Crockett, Mr C. J. Harper, Mr Dale Hobson, Mr Peter Newell, Mr Maurice E. Pinto, Lady Scott.

530 MR D. D. SCOTT, Minehead

Postal: **East Lynch, Minehead, Somerset, TA24 8SS.**
Phone: **(0643) 702430**

1 **MASTER PEPPER,** 9, b g Latest Model—Miss Pepper **Mr D. D. Scott**
2 **TIME MODULE,** 6, b g Latest Model—Gemini Miss **Mrs D. D. Scott**

Amateur: Mr J A Scott (10-0).

531 MRS E. B. SCOTT, Wysall

Postal: **Church Site Farm, Thorpe-in-the-Glebe, Wysall, Nottinghamshire, NG12 5QX.**
Phone: **WYMESWOLD (0509) 880489**

1 **RAPID BOY,** 6, b br g Rapid River—Silver Thread **Mrs Elizabeth B. Scott**
2 **SILVER SNOW,** 12, gr m Abwah—Silver Yarn **Mrs Elizabeth B. Scott**

Amateur: Miss J M Scott (8-7).

532 MR M. R. SCOTT, Moate

Postal: **Farnagh Stud, Moate, Co. Westmeath, Ireland.**
Phone: **(0902) 81484**

1 **AREWEDANCINGYET,** 6, ch m Boreen—Grey Daisy **Mrs K. Keegan**
2 **NIGHT NUN,** 6, b m Monksfield—Capo Willow **Mrs. B. B. Scott**

THREE-YEAR-OLDS

3 B f Sexton Blake—Night Course **Mrs B. B. Scott**
4 B f Boreen—Speckled Leinster **Mrs M. Scott**

Amateurs: Mr M Scott (10-7), Mr P Scott (11-0).

533 MR M. J. SCUDAMORE, Hoarwithy

Postal: **Prothither, Hoarwithy, Herefordshire, HR2 6QJ.**
Phone: **CARY (043 270) 253**

1 **BALLINAGORE GAA,** 9, br g Random Shot—Duessa **Mr R. C. F. Faiers**
2 **BIRD OF SPIRIT,** 10, b g Hot Brandy—Bird of Honour **Mr E. J. Praill**
3 **DAWN QUEST,** 6, gr m Nadjar (FR)—Invery Lady **Mr R. C. F. Faiers**
4 **MOUNTAIN SHADOW,** 5, b g Tyrnavos—Follow Me Follow **The Praill Group**
5 **RECORD WING,** 12, b g Record Run—O'Flynn **Mr Keith Howard**
6 **ROMAN DART,** 6, b g Roman Warrior—Angodeen **Mrs M. Barker**
7 **SARAH'S WROATH,** 5, b g Morston (FR)—All Our Yesterdays **Mrs V. Stockdale**
8 **WALLY WOMBAT,** 12, b g Abwah—Enlighten **Mr E. J. Praill**

THREE-YEAR-OLDS

9 **MARINERS MIRROR,** b f Julio Mariner—Sujono **Partnership**

Other Owners: Mr T. C. Court, Mr Peter S. Hill, Mr A. M. Porter, Mrs M. G. Scudamore, Mr P. W. Talbot-Ponsonby.

Jockey (NH): P Scudamore (10-0, w.a.).

534 MR I. SEMPLE, Carluke

Postal: **Waygateshaw Lodge, Braidwood, Carluke, Lanarkshire, Scotland, ML8 5PX.**
Phone: **OFFICE (0555) 71994 HOME (0555) 50660**

1 **BELLA SOFIE,** 6, ch m Sallust—Kath **Mr J. G. Hickie**
2 **CAPITAL BUILDER,** 4, b g Pas de Seul—Double Touch (FR) **Silverbell Racing Ltd**
3 **DUTCH SCHULTZ,** 4, b g Uncle Pokey—Double Duchess **Mr J. G. Hickie**
4 **ERIVAN,** 4, ch c Shakapour—Eurissia (FR) **Beta Racing**
5 **GOOD MOOD,** 5, b g Jalmood (USA)—Key of The Kingdom **Alpha Racing**
6 **I'M ALERT,** 5, b g Kampala—Last Trip **Mr James A. Cringan**
7 **IZADYAR,** 6, b g Akarad (FR)—Ilyaara **Mr R. F. Baker**
8 **J-TEC BOY,** 4, gr g Orange Reef—Fotostar **Mr James A. Cringan**
9 **KAIM PARK,** 7, b g Ovac (ITY)—Liffey's Choice **Mr T. J. Filshie**
10 **OFF AND ON,** 4, b f Touching Wood (USA)—Off The Reel (USA) **Mr J. G. Hickie**
11 **RICHARDS BAY,** 9, b g Record Run—Gowyn **Mr James Ratter**
12 **RIX WOODCOCK,** 9, br g Lord Gayle (USA)—Silk Lady **Mr John Anderson**
13 **SKIMMING,** 5, b h Mill Reef (USA)—Mighty Fly **Mr James Carrigan**
14 **TAYLORS PET,** 5, b m Tina's Pet—Quick Kick **Taylors Of Soham**
15 **THE RANNOCH,** 7, b g Relkino—Jamelah **Mr Dennis McGuinness**
16 **VELVET PEARL,** 7, ch m Record Token—Pearlinda **Mr James A. Cringan**

MR I. SEMPLE—continued

THREE-YEAR-OLDS

17 **HONEY'S FORTUNE,** gr c Magic Mirror—Close To You **Mr Dennis McGuinness**

TWO-YEAR-OLDS

18 Ch c 28/4 Stanford—Covenant (Good Bond) **Silverbell Racing Ltd**
19 B f 16/5 Valiyar—Fardella (ITY) (Molvedo) **Silverbell Racing Ltd**
20 Ch c 28/4 Reach—Miss Kimmy (Tower Walk) **Silverbell Racing Ltd**

Other Owners: Mr R. Cox, Mrs E. Hewitson.

535 MRS N. S. SHARPE, Leominster

Postal: **Upper Wall End, Monkland, Leominster, Herefordshire.**
Phone: **DAYTIME (0568) 2673 EVENINGS (0432) 356104**

1 **COLONEL JAMES,** 8, br g Captain James—Faraday Girl **Miss Diane F. Smith**
2 **DAVID'S TREASURE,** 10, b g Pitskelly—Cecilia's Will **Mr Tony Raggett**
3 **MASTER OF SHANE,** 11, b g Cantab—Miss Goodyear **Andrews Freight Services Ltd**
4 **MUSIC MY SON,** 9, b g Tumble Wind (USA)—Negante **Mr S. J. Yeomans**
5 **RED BOLT,** 8, ch g Stanford—Amy Jane **Stella Harvard**
6 **SLAVE KING,** 11, b g Kinglet—Slavetown **Andrews Freight Services Ltd**
7 **SMOKEY GEM,** 8, gr g Oats—Miss Kalamaloo **Mr M. J. Perry**
8 **VYNZ SUPREME,** 10, b g Supreme Sovereign—High Drama **Mr P. A. George**

Other Owners: Miss J. Davenport, Mrs V. Grundy, Mr L. Samuel.

Jockey (Flat): J Williams.

Conditional: I Lawrence.

536 MR J. R. SHAW, Newmarket

Postal: **Albert House Stables, Bury Road, Newmarket, Suffolk, CB8 8DU.**
Phone: **NEWMARKET (0638) 661680 OR 667954 OFFICE (0638) 731139 FAX 731138**

1 **BALLY KNIGHT,** 4, b g Balidar—Silk's Suggestion **Mr J. R. Shaw**
2 **BANANA CUFFLINKS (USA),** 4, b c Peterhof (USA)—Heather Bee (USA) **Mr R. C. Clifford-Turner and J. R. Shaw**
3 **FLOCKTON'S OWN,** 4, b c Electric—Tree Mallow **Ian Flockton Developments Limited**
4 **GREAT LEGEND,** 4, ch g Vaigly Great—Chinese Legend **Skeltools Ltd**
5 **MALUNAR,** 5, gr g Mummy's Pet—Tranquility Base **Mrs V. J. Brudenell and Partners**

THREE-YEAR-OLDS

6 **BALI LADY,** b f Balidar—Silk's Suggestion **Skeltools Ltd**
7 Ch f Busted—Summer Silks **Skeltools Ltd**

TWO-YEAR-OLDS

8 B f 5/4 Star Appeal—Kochia (Firestreak) **Skeltools Ltd**
9 **PEPPERBOY,** b f 18/3 King of Spain—Bunduq (Scottish Rifle) **Hon. Mrs M. V. Chaworth-Musters**

Other Owners: Mr T. M. Brudenell, Major R. P. Chaworth-Musters.

537 MR W. SHEEDY, Newport

Postal: **North Hey, Llandevaud, Newport, Gwent, Wales.**
Phone: **(0633) 400646**

1 **ROYS DILEMMA,** 8, b m Bold Owl—Spartan's Girl **Mr William Roy Sheedy**
2 **SHOTINGO,** 10, b g Rustingo—Pennyshot **Mr William Roy Sheedy**
3 **STAR OF IRELAND,** 10, b g Star Appeal—Belligerent **Mr William Roy Sheedy**

538 MR O. M. C. SHERWOOD, Upper Lambourn

Postal: **Rhonehurst, Upper Lambourn, Newbury, Berkshire, RG16 7RG.**
Phone: **(0488) OFFICE 71411 HOSTEL 72263 TELEX 946240 CWEASY G FAX 72786**

1 **ACHILLEAN,** 7, b g Wolver Hollow—Prime Thought **Mr Roger K. Simmons**
2 **AFTER THE NUMBER,** 5, b g Le Moss—Fly Fuss **Mr N. Gratton**
3 **AIR COMMANDER,** 5, br g Strong Gale—Southern Slave **Mr David Knox**
4 **ALDINO,** 7, ch g Artaius (USA)—Allotria **Mr A. Boyd-Rochfort**
5 **ALWAYS TALKING,** 9, b g Bishop of Orange—Brogeen Lass **Mr T. F. Parrett**
6 **ARCTIC CALL,** 7, b g Callernish—Polar Lady **Mr B. T. Stewart-Brown**
7 **ARCTIC TEAL,** 6, b g Town And Country—Arctic Warbler **Mrs P. Robeson**
8 **ATRABATES,** 10, b m Precipice Wood—Stanegate **The Atrabates Cricket Club**
9 **BLUSTERY FELLOW,** 5, b g Strong Gale—Paulas Fancy **Mrs R. A. Humphries**
10 **BORDEAUX BEAU,** 6, b g French Vine—Fiddlers Bee **Mr D. Naylor-Leyland**
11 **BREMHILL ROSIE,** 7, b m Celtic Cone—Bay Rambler **Mrs J. M. F. Dibben**
12 **CERTAIN STYLE,** 7, b g Connaught—Nushka **Mr Paul Stamp**
13 **CHIEF MOLE (USA),** 5, gr g Caro—Head Spy (USA) **Mrs Christopher Heath**
14 **CHILD OF THE MIST,** 4, b c Lomond (USA)—Lighted Lamp (USA) **Mrs Christopher Heath**
15 **CREDIT CUT,** 8, b g Fine Blade (USA)—Vul's Money **R. E. A. Bott (Wigmore St) Ltd**
16 **CROCK-NA-NEE,** 9, b g Random Shot—Saucy Slave **Mr D. E. Harrison**
17 **CRUISING ALTITUDE,** 7, ch g Celtic Cone—Carmarthen Honey **Mrs Christopher Heath**
18 **DRAW POKER,** 5, b g Uncle Pokey—Hejera **Mr H. M. Heyman**
19 **DROWSY,** 8, b g Mississippi—Siesta **Stablemates Partnership**
20 **DWADME,** 5, b g High Top—Durun **Olympic N. H. Racing**
21 **EL GALILEO,** 8, b g Comedy Star (USA)—Spanish Sail **Mr J. C. South**
22 **FIRST HAND,** 5, b g Manor Farm Boy—Fairies First **Mrs K. H. Lewis**
23 **FIVE LAMPS,** 10, b g Paddy's Stream—Ballinarose **Mr R. C. G. Smith**
24 **FLIGHT OF STEEL,** 5, ch g Le Moss—Mary Deen **Lake & Elliot Industries Ltd**
25 **GALLIC AIR,** 6, ch g Le Moss—Country Tune **Mrs Christopher Heath**
26 **GENERAL MOSS,** 5, b g Le Moss—Merendas Sister **Mrs Christopher Heath**
27 **GOLDEN SOUND,** 6, b g Goldhill—Regal Sound **Mr N. S. Hadfield**
28 **GURTEEN WOOD,** 10, b g The Parson—Castlejane **Mrs Christopher Heath**
29 **HALLCROSS,** 6, br g Junius (USA)—Time To Leave **Mr Christopher J. Wilkinson**
30 **HEIGHT OF FUN,** 6, b g Kambalda—Moongello **Mrs Basil Samuel**
31 **JUST PATRIMONY,** 6, br g Petrassi (GER)—Quilpee Mai **Mrs F. L. Langton**
32 **KNIGHT OIL,** 7, b g Miner's Lamp—Fair Argument **R. E. A. Bott (Wigmore St) Ltd**
33 **KNIGHTON LAD,** 9, gr g Peacock (FR)—Buscarina **Mr J. C. South**
34 **KODIAK ISLAND,** 8, br g Green Shoon—Poker Face (SWE) **Mrs Christopher Heath**
35 **LATENT TALENT,** 6, b g Celtic Cone—Fra Mau **Mrs Christopher Heath**
36 **MAJESTIC PRINCESS,** 4, b f Majestic Maharaj—Miss Merida **R. K. Bids Ltd**
37 **MANDRAKI SHUFFLE,** 8, b g Mandalus—Indictment **Mrs J. M. F. Dibben**
38 **MIDNIGHT STORM,** 6, br g Strong Gale—Gala Noon **Mr John Bolsover**
39 **MISTER BOOT,** 11, b g Arapaho—Nevada-Credo **Mr R. G. Morcom Snr.**
40 **MURPHY,** 6, ch g Touch Paper—Iamstopped **Mr J. P. J. Coles**
41 **NICE DYNASTY (FR),** 6, ch g Nice Havrais (USA)—Danesta (USA) **Mrs Christopher Heath**
42 **NIGHT SESSION,** 7, ch g Roselier (FR)—Love The Irish **Mr J. Dougall**
43 **NODFORMS DILEMMA (USA),** 7, ch g State Dinner (USA)—Princess Jo Jo **Mr Paul Stamp**
44 **PARK STREET,** 5, b g Runnett—Chieftain Girl (USA) **Mr P. A. Idris**
45 **PATRICO,** 7, b g Boreen (FR)—Patrician Maid **Mr P. A. Idris**
46 **PICASSO MOODS,** 6, b g Idiot's Delight—Alpogemy **Mr Irvin S. Naylor**

MR O. M. C. SHERWOOD—continued

47 **PREDOMINATE,** 9, ch g Thatch (USA)—Miss Noname **501 Club Racing Group**
48 **PROUD CREST (USA),** 6, ro h Cox's Ridge (USA)—Nancy Be Good (USA) **Sheikh Mohammed**
49 **RAMBLING ECHO,** 9, b g Rymer—Tarquann **Mr R. C. G. Smith**
50 **REBEL SONG,** 8, b g Tug of War—Country Tune **Mrs Christopher Heath**
51 **SACRED PATH,** 10, br g Godswalk (USA)—Crepe Rose (FR) **Mrs Christopher Heath**
52 **SENOR TOMAS,** 7, b g Sparkler—Pearlemor **Mr M. Berger**
53 **SNUGFIT'S IMAGE,** 4, b g Music Boy—Sinzinbra **Mr A. Greenwood**
54 **SOUTHERLY BUSTER,** 7, b g Strong Gale—Southern Slave **Mr M. D. S. Dorey**
55 **STEEPLE VIEW,** 9, b g The Parson—Deep View **Mrs Christopher Heath**
56 **STIRRUP CUP,** 6, b g Majestic Maharaj—Gold Gift **Mrs Christopher Heath**
57 5, B m Royal Match—Straightlace **Mr N. G. Brummitt**
58 **STRATFORD PONDS,** 5, b h High Top—Opinion **Mr R. Waters**
59 **STREAM BRIDGE,** 9, b g Carlburg—Hay Casta **Mrs Denise Stamp**
60 **SUM INSURED,** 7, br g Mandalus—Knocklow VI **Mr Michael Jenner**
61 **SUNSTANE,** 6, ch m Sunyboy—Stanegate **Mr N. E. C. Sherwood**
62 **THE JOGGER,** 5, br g Deep Run—Pollychant **Mrs E. M. Stockwell**
63 **THE MILROY,** 7, b g Buckskin (FR)—Sno-Cat **R. E. A. Bott (Wigmore St) Ltd**
64 **THE WEST AWAKE,** 9, b g Green Shoon—Ballygoman Maid **Mrs Christopher Heath**
65 **TILDARG,** 6, ch g Black Minstrel—Real Treasure **Mr M. L. Oberstein**
66 **TOAD ALONG,** 5, b g Daring March—Fille de Phaeton **Mr Nigel Stafford**
67 **TONIGHTS THE NIGHT,** 9, ch g Simbir—Sarejay Day **Mr John Poynton**
68 **VAULT (USA),** 4, b c Golden Act (USA)—Open Gate (USA) **Mrs Christopher Heath**
69 **VICARS LANDING,** 7, b g Rusticaro (FR)—Rhinestone **Mr M. L. Oberstein**
70 **WENTBRIDGE,** 5, b g Royal Fountain—Tacitina **Mr Paul Stamp**
71 **WORK TO WIN,** 5, ch g That's Swanee—Lady Cherry **Mr A. L. R. Morton**
72 **YOUNG POKEY,** 5, b g Uncle Pokey—Young Romance **Mr M. L. Oberstein**
73 **YOUNG SNUGFIT,** 6, ch g Music Boy—Sinzinbra **Mr John Poynton**

Other Owners: Mrs A. R. Boyd-Rochfort, Mr Richard Cunis, Mr M. Duff, Mr R. F. Eliot, Mr R. W. Fothergill, Mr I. R. Hadfield, Mr A. P. Hamilton, Mrs John Ind, Mr E. N. Kronfeld, Mr J. M. Layton, Mr E. A. Matthews, Mr K. T. McCourt, Mr D. R. Monroe, Mrs R. G. Morcom, Mr R. G. Morcom Jnr, Mr J. Palmer-Brown, Mr Leonard F. Ratcliff, Mr F. D. Shallow, Miss D. M. Stafford, Mr M. J. Wainwright, Mr H. D. Wilkinson.

Jockeys (NH): C Cox (10-0), J Osborne (10-0), M Richards (10-0).

Conditional: D Benneyworth (9-7), A Smith (9-7).

Amateur: Mr D McCain (9-7).

539 MISS L. C. SIDDALL, Tadcaster

Postal: **Stonebridge Farm, Colton, Tadcaster, N. Yorkshire, LS24 8EP.**
Phone: **(090484) 291**

1 **BIG CHIEF,** 5, b g Gorytus—Maybe So **Miss L. C. Siddall**
2 **BRUTUS,** 6, ch g Junius (USA)—Orangery **Mr R. J. Wilkinson**
3 **CASHMERE 'N' CAVIAR,** 6, gr m Bustino—Nelly Do Da **Mrs P. Hinton**
4 **MEGA BLUE,** 5, gr m Scallywag—Town Blues **B. G. Riley & Son Ltd**
5 **MISS TIMBER TOPPER,** 6, b m Liberated—Tacitina **B. G. Riley & Son Ltd**
6 **NOT SO SHY,** 5, b m Star Appeal—Nanushka **Mr Kenneth Dancer**
7 **PACIFIC SOUND,** 7, b g Palm Track—Pacific Dream **Mr D. A. Stephenson**
8 **REGENT LAD,** 6, b g Prince Regent (FR)—Red Laser **Mr F. Tyldesley**
9 **SHEAN LAD,** 10, b g Deep Run—Shean Lass **Miss L. C. Siddall**
10 **THE MAGUE,** 6, br g Bold Owl—Silvery Moon **Mr R. Jenkinson**
11 **TOUCHLIN PRIDE,** 4, b g Touch Boy—Lindrake's Pride **Mr J. G. Rookes**
12 **TRIPLE TOP,** 5, b g High Top—Dalmally **Mr B. Roberts**
13 **WOODLAND STEPS,** 4, ch f Bold Owl—Sweet Minuet **Mr R. Oliver-Smith**

MISS L. C. SIDDALL—continued

THREE-YEAR-OLDS

14 **ASCOT LASS,** b f Touching Wood—Second Generation **Mrs D. S. Bailey**
15 **BOLD-BRI,** gr f Bold Owl—Bri-Ette **Mrs Jack Fulton**
16 Ch g What A Guest—Corofin (USA) **Mr T. A. Charlesworth**
17 **EDUCATED RITA,** b f The Brianstan—Sobriquet **Mrs James Bloor**
18 **GREY MERLIN,** gr g Derrylin—Sea Kestrel **Mrs P. Hinton**
19 **KATSUE,** ch g Noalto—Gamma (GER) **Mrs S. C. Waring**
20 **LILLY CAMILLY,** ch f Electric—Be Sharp **Mrs D. J. Morris**
21 **LOVEYA LYNSEY,** b f Relkino—Guiletta **Mr R. Jenkinson**
22 B f Relkino—Tactless **Mrs D. J. Morris**

TWO-YEAR-OLDS

23 **BELDRAKE'S PRIDE,** gr g 25/1 Belfort (FR)—Lindrake's Pride (Mandrake Major) **Mr J. G. Rookes**
24 B c 7/4 Commanche Run—Miss Upward (Alcide) **Mr F. Tyldesley**
25 Ch f 8/5 Music Boy—Sobriquet (Roan Rocket)

Other Owners: Mrs R. M. Arundale, Mr M. J. Ashworth, Mrs K. M. Cornforth, Mr S. R. Counsell, Mr K. M. Dacker, Mrs D. Ibbotson, Mr R. A. Speight.

Apprentices: T G McLaughlin (7-5), Carmen Roberts (7-12).

Conditional: A J Quinn (9-9).

540 MR R. SIMPSON, Upper Lambourn

Postal: **Neardown Racing Stables, Lambourn, Newbury, Berkshire, RG16 7QP.**
Phone: **LAMBOURN (0488) 72688**

1 **ARD T'MATCH,** 5, b g Ardross—Love Match (USA) **Mr John Rumble**
2 **CAVENDISH DIAMOND,** 4, b f Decoy Boy—Tactile **Mr Shaun Millard**
3 **COUNTRY LIFE (USA),** 4, br g Key To Content (USA)—Roseliere (FR) **Mr Rod Simpson**
4 **DEERCAL DANCER,** 4, ch g Ballacashtal (CAN)—Lookslike Reindeer **Mr M. J. Lewin**
5 **IXOR (FR),** 6, ch g Yours—Brouette (FR) **Mr D. Gerrard**
6 **KALAKATE,** 5, gr g Kalaglow—Old Kate **Darfam Racing**
7 **MISS A TURN,** 4, b f Tyrnavos—Misacre **Planflow Leasing Ltd**
8 **NA LA GIRI,** 4, b g Nishapour (FR)—Les Sylphides (FR) **Mrs Carol Darby**
9 **PINCTADA,** 8, b g Mummy's Pet—Pinaka **Mrs Carol Darby**
10 **PROBLEM CHILD,** 7, b g Daring March—Lena's Girl **Amity Finance Ltd**
11 **ROUYAN,** 4, b g Akarad (FR)—Rosy Moon (FR) **Darfam Racing**
12 **SHOKRAN,** 5, b g Top Ville—Celtic Twilight **Mrs R. Bonner**
13 **SOLO ARTIST,** 5, ch g Young Generation—Jubilee Song **Mrs Lyn Washington**
14 **TORIUS,** 4, b g Petorius—Princess Martina **Mr G. C. Darby**
15 **XHAI,** 8, b g Brave Shot—Wild Thyme **Mrs Carol Darby**

THREE-YEAR-OLDS

16 **ALKILONG,** b g Longleat (USA)—Alkion **Mr M. J. Lewin**
17 **BALLARAT BAY,** b g Longleat (USA)—Terex **Mr P. Bonner**
18 Ch f Saher—Colonial Line (USA) **Mr R. Shaw**
19 **DOWNTOWN BELLE,** b f Belfort (FR)—Chance Match **Bob Menzies Ltd**
20 **LADY MAGENTA,** ch f Rolfe (USA)—Heliotrope **Partnership**
21 **MILLFIELDS LADY,** b f Sayf El Arab (USA)—Ma Pierrette **Mr Robert Cox**
22 **TUDOR BRAVE,** b g Indian King (USA)—Stickpin **Mrs Lyn Washington**

MR R. SIMPSON—continued

TWO-YEAR-OLDS

23 **DANCE WITH A DEVIL,** br c Superlative—Crystallize (Reliance II) **Mr T. Painting**
24 **HELIOS,** b c Blazing Saddles (AUS)—Mary Sunley (Known Fact (USA)) **Mr T. Painting**
25 B f Green Ruby (USA)—Lookslike Reindeer (Bonne Noel) **Mr C. Perry**
26 **NAOCHA,** b f Sallust—Her Name Was Lola (Pitskelly) **Mr R. Smith**

Other Owners: Dr Chris Bruton, Mr R. D. Cowell, Fairbourne Ltd, Mrs Jennifer Fletcher, Gordian Troeller Bloodstock, Mrs Francis Hives, Mr A. G. Marley, Mr M. J. Morrison, Mr J. Poole, Miss Claire Saward.

Jockeys (Flat): Stephen Whitelam (8-2), Simon Whitworth (8-2).

Apprentice: Byron Thomas (7-0).

Conditional: Dean Gallagher (10-0).

541 MR J. SKELTON, Skipton

Postal: **Kennels Cottage, Gledstone, Skipton, North Yorkshire, BD23 3JR.**
Phone: **(0282) 842503**

1 **NIPPER SMITH,** 7, b g Chantro—Alice Springs **Mr John Skelton**

542 MR M. M. SKINNER, Snetterton

Postal: **Holly Lodge, North End, Snetterton, Norfolk, NR16 2LD.**
Phone: **GREAT HOCKHAM (095 382) 8132**

1 **BEACHAMWELL,** 8, b g Record Run—Mishabo **Mrs M. McInnes Skinner**
2 **BIRDTOWN,** 7, gr g Peacock (FR)—Miss Bro **Mr Jeremy Hancock**
3 **FLYING TREAT,** 5, b m Dutch Treat—Flying Question
4 **GENIE'S BOTTLE,** 5, b m Le Soleil—Spring Kingdom **Mr Paul Rackham**
5 **MET OFFICER,** 10, b g Sunyboy—Metaxa **Mr Jeremy Hancock**
6 **MUBAARIS,** 7, ch g Hello Gorgeous (USA)—Aloft **T. W. Suiter & Son Ltd**
7 **OXNEAD,** 6, ch m Balinger—Blades **Capt. W. H. Bulwer-Long**
8 **POLARIS SONG,** 6, ch m True Song—Polaris Royal **Mrs M. McInnes Skinner**
9 **SADDLER'S CHOICE,** 5, b g Buckskin (FR)—Lady Perry **Mrs F. D. McInnes Skinner**
10 **SPRING TIDE,** 6, b m Take A Reef—Spring Kingdom **Mr Paul Rackham**
11 **TAR KNIGHT,** 13, b g Tarqogan—Hero's Slave **Mr M. Skinner**
12 **WHISKEY BLUES,** 5, b g Cure The Blues (USA)—Ozone **Mr Jeremy Hancock**

Jockey (NH): R Dunwoody (10-2, w.a.).

Conditional: S Woods (9-7).

543 MRS P. M. SLY, Peterborough

Postal: **Singlecote, Thorney, Peterborough, PE6 0PB.**
Phone: **(0733) 270212**

1 **BROOKTINO,** 5, b g Neltino—Binney Brook **Mr R. G. Pike**
2 **BURNHAM,** 5, br g Blakeney—Derry Daughter **Mr R. P. O'Connor**
3 **EASTER FESTIVAL,** 9, b g Tycoon II—Arctic Festival **Mr M. S. Smith**
4 **EMINENCE VERTE,** 5, ch m High Line—Greenfly (USA) **Mr Rex Carter**

MRS P. M. SLY—continued

5 **LEAMLARA LAD,** 10, b gr g Antwerp City—Beths' Bermudas **Mrs P. Sly**
6 **MEHTAB,** 4, b f Touching Wood (USA)—Zaheen **Mrs P. Sly**
7 **RELKOORA,** 6, b g Ahonoora—Giddy Lyn (USA) **Mrs P. Sly**
8 **ROSIE CONE,** 8, ch m Celtic Cone—Arctic Festival **Mr M. S. Smith**
9 **SAADOUN (FR),** 7, br g Grandchant (FR)—Rose Valery (FR) **Mr T. Crowson Jr**
10 **SINGLESOLE,** 5, ch g Celtic Cone—Milly Kelly **Mrs P. Sly**

Other Owners: Mr C. R. Bird.

544 MR B. SMART, Lambourn

Postal: **Hill House Stables, Folly Road, Lambourn, Newbury, Berkshire, RG16 7QE.**
Phone: **LAMBOURN (0488) 71632 CAR (0860) 532596**

1 **ANOTHER EARL (USA),** 6, ch h Belted Earl (USA)—Aloran (USA) **Mr M. F. Ando and Mr A. D. Bright**
2 **BOLD GRENADIER,** 9, b g Soldier Rose—Classical Air **Mr M. Pattimore**
3 **BREEZY GLORY,** 4, b f Strong Gale—My Halo **Mrs J. M. F. Dibben**
4 **CORRIE'S GIRL,** 5, ch m Whistling Deer—Soave **J. I. Corrie Hill and J. A. Corrie Hill**
5 **FESTIVE QUIZ,** 8, b g Quisling—Bright Festive **Mr M. K. Radbourne**
6 **FIRST CITIZEN,** 6, b br g Nishapour (FR)—Graunuaile **Mrs D. J. Smart**
7 **GLENGOOLE,** 7, b g Glen Quaich—Blush **Mr M. Pattimore**
8 **HARBOURS WELL,** 5, b m Pitpan—Palmers Well **Mr Philip Brown and Mr P. Huins**
9 **HARD HOLLOW,** 5, b g Hard Fought—Boudoir **Mr J. Cooper and Mr P. Cooper**
10 **JOFEN,** 5, b m Sonnen Gold—Ensign Steel **Mr Dwight Makins and Mrs C. Colman**
11 **JOSEY WALES,** 8, b g Carnival Night—Graceful Grange **The Spinal Injuries Association**
12 **KEEP TALKING,** 5, b g Le Bavard (FR)—Keep Faith **Mrs Margaret Radbourne**
13 **KILBARRY LAD,** 5, b g Mr Fluorocarbon—Gosforth Lady **Burt & Travica Contractors Ltd**
14 **LARS NILSEN,** 8, ch g Paddy's Stream—Michelle Telegrams (USA) **Mrs D. J. Smart**
15 **MASTER TIM,** 6, ch g Timolin (FR)—Straight Beauty **Mrs D. J. Smart and Partners**
16 **NEARLY TIME,** 7, gr m Nearly A Hand—Half A Minute **Mrs J. M. F. Dibben**
17 **OWEN,** 6, b g Pollerton—Princess Charmere **Burt & Travica Contractors Ltd**
18 **PAMBER PRIORY,** 7, b g Balinger—Miset **Mr Dwight Makins**
19 **PREACHERS POPSY,** 4, ch f The Parson—Ballycold **Mrs J. M. F. Dibben**
20 **RAMPALLION,** 7, b g Riboboy (USA)—Rampage **Mrs D. J. Smart and Mr Dwight Makins**
21 **RAMSDELL,** 8, ch g Paddy's Stream—Strawberry Mess **Mr Dwight Makins**
22 **RHOECUS (FR),** 11, b g Rheingold—Polly Cotton (USA) **Mrs Margaret Radbourne**
23 **RUBIN'S BOY,** 4, ch g Riberetto—Gaie Pretense (FR) **Mr J. Cooper and Mr P. Cooper**
24 6, Ch m Funny Man—Sister Broncho **Mr M. Pattimore**
25 7, Ch g Funny Man—Space Project **Miss M. E. Sherrington**
26 **SUPERGRASS,** 11, b g Thatch (USA)—Pepi Image (USA) **Mrs D. J. Smart**
27 **TENESONG,** 11, ch g True Song—Teuella **Miss B. Tyler**
28 **THE HILL,** 8, b g Tula Rocket—Choral Speech **Mr A. D. Bright and Partners**
29 **TOTAL LINKING,** 6, gr m Prince Regent (FR)—Happy Princess **Mr William N. Benson**

THREE-YEAR-OLDS

30 **GABRIELLE'S ANGEL,** br f Another Realm—Leaplet **Burt & Travica Contractors Ltd**
31 **PRINCESS JESSICA,** ch f Anfield—Maid of Warwick **Burt & Travica Contractors Ltd**

TWO-YEAR-OLDS

32 **BRANCO LAURIAN,** br c 12/5 Another Realm—Leaplet **Burt & Travica Contractors Ltd**

Other Owners: Mr J. Downes, Mr James G. Smith, Mrs G. Tudor.

Jockey (Flat): W Newnes (8-2).

Jockeys (NH): R Dunwoody (10-0), K Mooney (10-0), B Powell (10-0).

Conditional: S McDougall (9-7), T Pinfield (9-10).

545 MR A. SMITH, Beverley

Postal: **Heath Racing Stables, Newbold Road, Beverley, N. Humberside.**
Phone: **(0482) 882520**

1 **HUNMANBY GAP,** 5, ch g Flying Tyke—Another Mufsie **Mr John Wiles**
2 **ICHI BAN SON,** 6, b h Hotfoot—My Bushbaby **Mr B. A. Kilpatrick**
3 **INTROVERT,** 6, b h Niniski (USA)—Consister **Miss Georgina Purkiss**
4 **MISCHIEVOUS TYKE,** 4, ch f Flying Tyke—Habatashie **Mr David Tate (Louth)**
5 **PHILS PRIDE,** 6, b h Sunotra—La Furze **Mr A. Bayman**
6 **SPRINGMAN,** 6, b g Young Man (FR)—Spring Secret (USA) **Mr S. G. Stacey**
7 **TOM TOWLEY,** 4, b g Reformed Character—Darwin Tulip **Mrs G. Wood**

THREE-YEAR-OLDS

8 **CROFTY BOY,** ch g Crofthall—Floral Light **Mr A. H. Grant**
9 **HOTFOOT HENRY,** ch g Hotfoot—Courting Day **Mr M. J. Buck**
10 **MILBURN LEISURE,** br g Kala Shikari—Paperwork **Mr John Allan Milburn**

TWO-YEAR-OLDS

11 Gr c Flying Tyke—Habatashie **Mr David Tate**
12 **THE WADKIN,** b c Creetown—Thinkluckybelucky **Mr T. Mulrooney**
13 Ch f Giacometti—Thorganby Tina **Mr A. Smith**

Other Owners: Mr J. Fotherby, Mr P. G. Leadley, Mr L. Mason.

Jockey (Flat): S Webster (w.a.).

546 MR C. SMITH, Wellingore

Postal: **Thompsons Bottom Farm, Temple Bruer, Wellingore, Lincoln, LN5 ODE.**
Phone: **(0526) 833245**

1 **ABLE SAILOR,** 10, gr g Abwah—Shipwrecked **Mr J. F. Dean**
2 **AMANDA JANE (USA),** 6, b m State Dinner (USA)—Roman Edge (USA) **Mr B. A. Hill**
3 **CARRY THE CAN,** 6, ch m Deep Run—Ingenious **Mr J. R. Cornwall**
4 **DAN THE MAN,** 4, b c Rabdan—Liberty Light **Mr B. A. Hill**
5 **HEILEN LULLABYE,** 4, ch f True Song—Princess Mey **Lady Anne Scott**
6 **HOISTED,** 6, ch g Posse (USA)—Miss Petard **Mr David J. Thompson**
7 **MASTER BUSTER,** 5, b g Master Sing—Dona Ferentes **Mr Charles Smith**
8 **PAT'S LITTLEACRE,** 5, b m Scallywag—Saucy Pat **Mr W. Sergent**
9 **REFRAIN NO MORE,** 5, ch m Blue Refrain—More Rheola **Mr David J. Thompson**
10 **TRENTSIDE VALOUR,** 5, br g Tudorville—Trent Valley **Mr J. Payne**
11 **YOUNG FOOL,** 6, br g Young Man (FR)—Fool 'em **Mr Charles Smith**

Other Owners: Mrs V. Hope, Mrs Y. Robinson.

Amateur: Mr M Ranger (10-0).

547 MR D. SMITH, Bishop Auckland

Postal: **Holdforth Farm, Bishop Auckland, Co. Durham, DL14 6DJ.**
Phone: **(0388) 603317 OR 606180**

1 **ALL OVER THE WORLD,** 6, b g Kind of Hush—Bosworth Moll **Mrs Rowena Coleman**
2 **AUGUST (USA),** 9, b g Sensitive Prince (USA)—Polynesian Charm (USA) **Mr R. Coleman**
3 **BALLINROSTIG,** 7, ch g General Ironside—Mavar's Choice **Mr H. J. Thompson**

MR D. SMITH—continued

4 **BIG BELL BOY,** 5, ch h Scallywag—Miss Quay **Mr C. J. Spencer**
5 **BRADSHAW,** 5, b br g Bay Express—Time-Table **Duke of Sutherland**
6 **CORNET,** 4, b g Coquelin (USA)—Corny Story **Duke of Sutherland**
7 **DENSBEN,** 6, b g Silly Prices—Eliza de Rich **Mrs Janet M. Pike**
8 **DIRECT INTEREST,** 7, ch g Al Sirat (USA)—Honey Come Home **Mr Denys Smith**
9 **FESTIVE FLING,** 5, b g Last Fandango—Pandomyne **Mrs Janet Madeley**
10 **FULL MONTY,** 4, ch g Raga Navarro (ITY)—Miss Quay **Mrs C. Croft**
11 **GALLOWAY BREEZE,** 5, b g Day Is Done—Whispering Breeze **Mr Denys Smith**
12 **GALLOWAY RAIDER,** 6, br g Skyliner—Whispering Breeze **Mr J. A. Bianchi**
13 **GREY MINSTREL,** 6, gr g Black Minstrel—Sam's Can **Mr John Madeley**
14 **GYDAROS,** 5, b h Ardross—Handy Dancer **Mr K. Higson**
15 **IVOROSKI,** 8, b g Malinowski (USA)—Fado **P. & I. Darling**
16 **KING WILLIAM,** 5, b g Dara Monarch—Norman Delight (USA) **Mr C. J. Pennick**
17 **LAS RAMPAS,** 8, b g Le Bavard (FR)—Highway Mistress **Mr John Madeley**
18 **MAJESTIC PLAYER,** 6, ch m Torus—Blackrath Girl **Mr J. A. Bianchi**
19 **MASNOON (USA),** 7, ch g Sharpen Up—A Twinkling (USA) **Mr J. L. Eyre**
20 **MIDLAND EXPRESS,** 7, ch g Midland Gayle—Queens County **Mr John Madeley**
21 **OAKEN,** 9, b g Connaught—Syringa **Duke of Sutherland**
22 **POTATO KING,** 5, b g Hard Fought—Fenland Queen **Mrs John N. Park**
23 **RED PLANET,** 5, b g Sir Ivor—Miss Mars **Carlton Appointments (Aberdeen) Ltd**
24 **RIVERS SECRET,** 6, b m Young Man (FR)—Pendle's Secret **Mr James Simpson**
25 **SONALTO,** 4, br g Noalto—Sanandrea **Mr J. A. Bianchi**
26 **TAYLORMADE BOY,** 7, b g Dominion—Ash Gayle **Mr Bryan Robson**
27 **TRY SCORER,** 8, b g Gulf Pearl—Just Frolicking **Mr H. J. Thompson**
28 **WILLILOV,** 4, ch g Rabdan—Miss Love **Mr W. Love**

THREE-YEAR-OLDS

29 B g Sweet Monday—Canty Day **Mr Denys Smith**
30 **CHAMPAGNE GOLD,** ch c Bairn (USA)—Halkissimo **Mrs Claire Massey**
31 **DARUSSALAM,** ch f Tina's Pet—Chinese Falcon **Mr Jim Richardson**
32 **FRANCIS FURNESS,** b f Burslem—Sodium's Niece **Mrs Audrey Healy**
33 **HICKORY WIND,** ch c Dalsaan—Derrain **Lord Durham**
34 **HOLDFORTH,** b c Sayyaf—Chief Dilke **Mr R. Coleman**
35 **IRISH SUNSET,** b f Red Sunset—Meisha **Mrs Audrey Healy**
36 **KARINGA BAY,** ch c Ardross—Handy Dancer **Mr K. Higson**
37 **KIRKLEES ROCK,** br f Kala Shikari—Lady Farrier **Kirklees Rock Asphalt Ltd**
38 **MADELEY'S PET,** ch f Tina's Pet—Thorganby **Mr John Madeley**
39 **MISS ALCAZAR,** b f Aragon—Permutation **Mr J. Askew**
40 **ROMANTIC SAGA,** b f Prince Tenderfoot (USA)—Sirena **Mrs C. G. R. Booth**
41 **SAY A PRAYER,** ch f Sayf El Arab (USA)—Careless Flyer **Mr Denys Smith**

TWO-YEAR-OLDS

42 **BUSTERS PAL,** gr c 3/4 Scottish Reel—Tula Singh (Mansingh) **Mr K. Higson**
43 B f 12/5 Carriage Way—Central Carpets (Garda's Revenge (USA)) **Mr Denys Smith**
44 B c 31/3 Lidhame—Darlinga (Derring-Do) **Mr B. Hathaway**
45 B c 14/3 Ardross—Fiordiligi (Tudor Melody) **Mr C. J. Pennick**
46 **GRANADA ROCK (IRE),** b c 2/5 Kreisler—Rock Blues (Ballad Rock) **Mr Sydney Rae Jnr**
47 **IANOVITCH,** b c 26/3 Lightning Dealer—Misty Arch (Starch Reduced) **P. & I. Darling**
48 **MANAOLANA,** b f 17/2 Castle Keep—Ladysave (Stanford) **Mr K. Higson**
49 **MASILIC,** gr f 22/2 Grey Desire—Pendle's Secret (Le Johnstan)
50 Br f 1/4 Sandhurst Prince—North North West (Northfields) **Mr Denys Smith**
51 B f 2/4 Carriage Way—Parade Girl (Swing Easy (USA)) **Mr Denys Smith**
52 **PAULINUS,** b c 4/4 Nomination—New Ribbons (Ribero) **P. & I. Darling**
53 B c 10/1 Sulaafah (USA)—Roncastella (Royal Palace) **Mr R. Coleman**
54 **SLENDER,** b f 10/3 Aragon—Handy Dancer (Green God) **Mr K. Higson**
55 **SOVEREIGN HEIGHTS,** b c 16/4 Elegant Air—Blubella (Balidar) **Mr C. J. Pennick**
56 B f 23/2 Good Times (ITY)—Stage Revue (Comedy Star) **Mr C. J. Pennick**
57 **VALATCH,** ch c Valiyar—Love Match (Affiliate) **Mr D. Eccleston**
58 B f 19/5 Myjinski (USA)—Ventrex (Henry The Seventh) **Mr C. J. Pennick**
59 **VISIBILITY,** b c 17/4 Vision (USA)—Yvonne's Choice (Octavo) **Mr K. Higson**
60 **WYCLIFFE,** ch c 4/4 Dunbeath (USA)—Blakewood (Blakeney) **Mr Denys Smith**

MR D. SMITH—continued

Other Owners: B. L. Banbridge, Mr Fred Birch, Mr Philip Black, Mr D. Lambert, Mrs D. Lambert, Lord Lambton, Mr T. P. Macdonald, Mr John Mason, Mr D. Mossop, Mrs D. Mossop, Mr W. Robinson, Mr Gerard Taylor, Mr Brian Thexton, Mr W. G. Walton.

Jockey (NH): Chris Grant (10-0).

Apprentice: Pat Dalton (7-0).

Conditional: P Carr, D Crossman (9-7), J L Neilson (9-7).

Amateur: Mr Peter Waggott (9-7).

548 MR J. P. SMITH, Rugeley

Postal: **Coldwell Cottage, Coldwell, Gentleshaw, Rugeley, Staffordshire.**
Phone: **BURNTWOOD (054 36) 6587**

1 **BIRDLESS GROVE,** 6, ch m Final Straw—Pilley Green **Mr M. G. Ferrett**
2 **BISPHAM BAY,** 6, ch g Caruso—Miss Sunacelli **Mr P. R. Wheeler**
3 **EVER SO SHARP,** 7, br h Caruso—Sealed Contract **Mr P. R. Wheeler**
4 **INSPECTOR BEN,** 11, br g Bold As Brass—Christmas Gorse **Mrs H. J. Bannister**
5 **IRENE'S DAUGHTER,** 8, ch m Al Sirat (USA)—Aunt Irene **Mr J. T. Stimpson**
6 **LIVING PROOF,** 6, ch g Known Fact (USA)—Lady Esmeralda **Mrs M. Hillback**
7 **MALACANANG,** 6, b m Riboboy (USA)—Gold Spangle **Mr J. T. Stimpson**
8 **MY SWAN SONG,** 5, b g Soul Singer—Palmaria **Mr M. G. Ferrett**
9 **NIGHT CLUB (GER),** 6, ch g Esclavo (FR)—Nightlife (GER) **Mr J. P. Smith**
10 **TIME-BEE,** 9, ch g Manado—Alli-Bee **Mr J. T. Stimpson**
11 **WELSH SPY,** 9, ch g Welsh Pageant—Spey **Mr M. G. Ferrett**
12 **ZIO PEPPINO,** 9, ch g Thatch (USA)—Victorian Habit **Mr Brian Marsh**

THREE-YEAR-OLDS

13 **IRISH GROOM,** b c Shy Groom (USA)—Romany Pageant **Mr J. T. Stimpson**
14 **MOTHERUBBADSCUBBAD,** ch f Blushing Scribe (USA)—Lady of Primrose **Mrs M. Hillback**

Other Owners: Mr Ronald Sennett.

Jockey (NH): S J O'Neill (w.a.).

Amateur: Mr Peter Hammersley (10-3).

549 MRS M. M. SMITH, Launceston

Postal: **Treburland Farm, Lewannick, Launceston, Cornwall.**
Phone: **TIVETSHALL (037 977) 278**

1 **BARMER CONE,** 8, ch m Celtic Cone—Barmer **Mrs M. M. Smith**
2 **BLACK BEETLE,** 10, br g Tarqogan—Hansels Mood **Mrs M. M. Smith**
3 **COME ON VALLEY,** 6, b m Sousa—Valley Mist **Mrs M. M. Smith**
4 **RISING MIST,** 8, gr m Sousa—Valley Mist **Mrs M. M. Smith**

550 MR N. A. SMITH, Pershore

Postal: **Victoria Cottage Stables, Hill Furze, Bishampton, Nr. Pershore, Worcestershire, WR10 2NB.**
Phone: **EVESHAM (0386) 860131**

1 **APPLE TARTAN,** 7, b br g Pollerton—Swan of The Bride **Gain Racing**
2 **CITY INDEX (USA),** 4, b g J O Tobin (USA)—Fannie Annie (USA) **The Horizon Partnership**
3 **FRENCH CASTLE,** 4, b c Millfontaine—La Chamelle **Mr N. A. Smith**
4 **HOLT PLACE,** 7, b g Be My Guest (USA)—Ya Ya **Mr Edwin Smith**
5 **LISAHANE LAD,** 4, b g Daring March—Puff Pastry **Mrs P. L. Aldersey**
6 **LITTLE TUGBOAT,** 6, br m Duky—Loobagh Bridge **Mr N. A. Smith**
7 **ROYAL SUMMIT,** 5, b g Thatching—Hill of Tara **The Pershore Partnership**
8 **SOCIAL CIRCLE,** 5, b m Henbit (USA)—Princesse Anglaise **Mr N. A. Smith**
9 **TOUGH OUT,** 6, b g Tumble Wind (USA)—Ragatina **The Toffy Nuts**
10 4, B f Castle Keep—Viennese Waltz **Mrs P. L. Aldersey**
11 **VILLAGE PRINCESS,** 7, br m Rolfe (USA)—Saffron Princess **Mrs G. C. List**

Other Owners: M. A. Wellman.

Jockey (NH): R Dunwoody (w.a.).

Conditional: W Irvine (9-7, w.a.), T Pinfield (10-2, w.a.).

551 MR R. J. SMITH, Loughborough

Postal: **Fox Covert Farm, Narrow Lane, Wymeswold, Loughborough, Leicestershire, LE12 6SD.**
Phone: **(0509) 881250**

1 **SMITH'S LAD,** 8, b g Normandy—Scrahan **Mr Roy J. Smith**

552 MR S. G. SMITH, Grimsby

Postal: **Glebe Farm, Ludborough, Grimsby, S. Humberside, DN36 5SQ.**
Phone: **GRIMSBY (0472) 840276**

1 **CHUCKBUCK,** 13, ch g Roebuck—Chuckling **Mr S. G. Smith**
2 **CHUCKLING BOY,** 9, b g Rambah—Chuckling **Mr S. G. Smith**
3 **NIKABUCK,** 5, b g Roebuck—Nikea **Mr S. G. Smith**
4 **SEND IT DOWN,** 6, b g Lochnager—Mashin Time **Mr S. G. Smith**
5 **SKIDDY LAD,** 8, ch g Music Maestro—Skiddy River **Mr S. G. Smith**
6 **SKIDDY MISS,** 5, ch m Roebuck—Skiddy River **Mr S. G. Smith**
7 **TWILIGHT LAD,** 9, b g Master Sing—Twilight Princess **Mr S. G. Smith**

553 MR W. J. SMITH, Oxford

Postal: **Logg Farm, Oddington, Islip, Oxford, OX5 2QU.**
Phone: **(086 733) 224**

1 **ANOTHER COLUMBUS,** 7, b m St Columbus—Milk River **Mr W. John Smith**
2 **ANOTHER VULGAN,** 9, b g Vulgan Slave—Milk River **Mr W. John Smith**
3 **DETAILS GALORE,** 9, ch h Octavo (USA)—Barefoot Contessa **Mr W. John Smith**

Jockey (NH): Luke Harvey.

Amateur: Jonathan V Smith.

554 MR R. V. SMYTH, Epsom

Postal: **Clear Height, Downs Road, Epsom, Surrey, KT18 5LR.**
Phone: **EPSOM (037 27) 20053**

1 **DISMISS,** 5, b m Daring March—Sweet Jane **Lord McAlpine and Mrs G. R. Smith**
2 **LADDERMAN,** 4, ch g Salmon Leap (USA)—Joanne's Joy **Michael Everett**
3 **MARCH ON,** 4, b g Daring March—Dualvi **Miss Dian Smyth**
4 **OUR JOCK,** 8, br h Daring March—Sweet Jane **Lord McAlpine**
5 **PHAETONS GLORY,** 6, b g Hittite Glory—Fille de Phaeton **Mrs K. R. Ensten**
6 **ROBBIE BURNS,** 4, br c Daring March—Gangawayhame **Mr D. R. Hunnisett and Lord McAlpine**
7 **SILVER OWL,** 4, gr c Daring March—Bird's Custard **Mr D. R. Hunnisett and Lord McAlpine**
8 **SMITH'S PEAK,** 6, ro g Alias Smith (USA)—Sacred Mountain **Mr T. J. Wood**

THREE-YEAR-OLDS

9 **BINGO BONGO,** gr f Petong—Daring Display **Lord McAlpine and Mrs G. R. Smith**
10 **COPPERBOTTOM,** b c Night Shift (USA)—Crimson Damask **Crescent (UK) Ltd**
11 **LIGHT GREEN (USA),** b c Green Dancer (USA)—Linklighter **K. Abdulla**
12 **MAKESHIFT,** b f Night Shift (USA)—Fall To Pieces (USA) **K. Abdulla**
13 **ORLEANS GIRL,** b f Dixieland Band (USA)—Philassa (USA) **Nationcrest Plc**
14 **OUR RON,** b g Daring March—Sweet Jane **Lord McAlpine**
15 **SHIFT SURPRISE (USA),** ch f Night Shift (USA)—Al-Burak **Crescent (UK) Ltd**
16 **THOMPSON FLYER,** b c Swing Easy (USA)—Off The Mark **Mr Geoffrey S. Bishop**
17 **TIDDLY WINKS,** b g Daring March—Party Game **Miss Dian Smyth**

TWO-YEAR-OLDS

18 **BELL BOY,** b c Daring March—Belle Tower (Tower Walk) **Lord McAlpine and Mrs G. R. Smith**
19 **CARN MAIRE,** b f Northern Prospect (USA)—
Samsara (PER) (Golden Spur (USA)) **Giles W. Pritchard-Gordon**
20 **COIR 'A' GHAILL,** b f Jalmood (USA)—Karsavina (Silly Season) **Giles W. Pritchard-Gordon**
21 B c Nicholas Bill—Devils Alternative (Hotfoot) **Miss Dian Smyth**
22 **IT'S NATIONCREST,** ch g Tremblant—Dawn Ditty (Song) **Lord McAlpine and Nationcrest Plc**
23 Ch c Adonijah—Jolie Pelouse (USA) (Riverman (USA)) **K. Abdulla**
24 **KILLICK,** b f Slip Anchor—Enthralment (USA) (Sir Ivor) **K. Abdulla**
25 B c Riverman (USA)—Linklighter (Busted) **K. Abdulla**
26 **PIPING HOT,** b g Daring March—Rosette (Red Alert) **Lord McAlpine**
27 **TREMBALINO,** b g Tremblant—Balinese (Balidar) **Lord McAlpine and Mrs G. R. Smith**
28 **TRIANGULATION,** b g Tremblant—Gangawayhame (Lochnager) **Lord McAlpine**
29 **VERY DICEY,** b g Tremblant—Party Game (Red Alert) **Lord McAlpine and Mrs G. R. Smith**

Jockeys (Flat): Pat Eddery (8-4, w.a.), S Whitworth (7-12).

Apprentice: T Martinez (7-10).

Conditional: L Dace (8-10).

555 MR C. W. SPARES, Aslockton

Postal: **The Stables, Dawns Lane, Aslockton, Nottinghamshire, NG13 9AD.**
Phone: **WHATTON (0949) 50099**

1 **ARC LAMP,** 4, b g Caerleon (USA)—Dazzling Light **Mr A. G. Wakley**
2 **CATHEDRAL PEAK,** 6, b g Tyrnavos—Honeypot Lane **Mr C. W. Spares**
3 **CHAGHATAI (USA),** 4, ch c Sir Ivor—Clutch Hitter (USA) **Mrs M. Robertson**
4 **CRY FOR THE CLOWN,** 6, b h Cawston's Clown—Bayberry **Mr James E. Blott**
5 **KAMAROCK,** 8, b h Kampala—Hey Dolly **Mr C. W. Spares**
6 **SAYYAF'S LAD,** 5, ch h Sayyaf—Opinebo **Minizen Ltd**
7 **SHALBOOD,** 4, b c Runnett—Deer Park (FR) **Mr V. M. Donnelly**
8 **TROJAN WAR,** 6, b h Troy—Sea Venture (FR) **Mr Roger Langley**
9 **VUCHTERBACHER,** 4, b c Longleat (USA)—Queensbury Star **Mrs D. Carvalho**

MR C. W. SPARES—continued

THREE-YEAR-OLDS

10 **BILLIEWHO,** b f Blue Cashmere—Petite Maman **Minizen Ltd**
11 **CUT OUT,** ch c Claude Monet (USA)—Luscinia **Minizen Ltd**
12 **MINIZEN LEADER,** ch f Salmon Leap (USA)—Red Line Fever **Minizen Ltd**
13 **ROY HOBBS,** b c Glint of Gold—Glory of Hera **Minizen Ltd**

TWO-YEAR-OLDS

14 Ch c 10/4 Forzando—Grand Opera (Great Nephew) **Minizen Ltd**
15 B c 6/4 Anita's Prince—Northern Amber (Shack (USA)) **Minizen Ltd**
16 B c 22/3 Fulmar (USA)—Reperage (USA) (Key To Content (USA)) **Minizen Ltd**
17 Ch c 8/2 Thatching—Rose Linnet (USA) (Mr Prospector (USA)) **Minizen Ltd**
18 B c 26/4 Fayruz—Sassess (Sassafras (FR)) **Minizen Ltd**

Other Owners: Mr G. F. Hurved.

Jockey (Flat): A Proud (7-7).

Jockey (NH): J McLaughlin (9-7).

Apprentice: S Drowne (7-4).

Conditional: R Carson (9-7), C Dennis (9-7).

556 MR J. L. SPEARING, Alcester

Postal: **Moor Hall Stables, Wixford, Nr. Alcester, Warwickshire.**
Phone: **(0789) 772639**

1 **ANOTHER NONSENSE,** 6, ch g Mr Fluorocarbon—Gosforth Lady **Mr E. E. Bowers**
2 **APPEAL FOR HELP,** 5, br h Star Appeal—Sovereign Help **Heathavon Stables Limited**
3 **BANGKOK BOSS,** 4, b f Balinger—Fare **Mr M. Sheridan**
4 **BASIC FUN,** 4, br f Teenoso (USA)—Sirenivo (USA) **Group 1 Racing (1989) Ltd**
5 **BICKERMAN,** 7, b h Mummy's Pet—Merry Weather **Mr B. Dowling**
6 **CASINO MAGIC,** 6, b g Casino Boy—Gypsy Girl **Mrs Maureen Wilson**
7 **CHELWORTH RAIDER,** 4, ch g Oats—Driven Snow **Mr R. A. Giles**
8 **CREE BAY,** 11, b g Bay Express—Porsanger (USA) **Mr D. J. Oseman**
9 **CROPDATE,** 7, b g Lucifer (USA)—Chamowen **Premier Crops Limited**
10 **DOMINUET,** 5, b m Dominion—Stepping Gaily **Mrs Robert Heathcote**
11 **FLUTTER BLUE,** 4, ch f Blue Refrain—Kivulini **Mrs B. Badger**
12 **HIGH CHATEAU,** 6, b g Amboise—High Seeker **Mr M. J. Lilley**
13 **HIGH POKEY,** 4, b f Uncle Pokey—High Seeker **Mr C. J. Brent**
14 **INDAMU,** 5, b g Indian King (USA)—Kilfenora **Vax Appliances Ltd**
15 **IN SEPTEMBER,** 4, b f Head For Heights—Maylands **Mrs J. Shine**
16 **LESCLACHA,** 5, b m Homing—Skelbrooke **Mr Brian A. Robinson**
17 **LUCEDEO,** 6, gr g Godswalk (USA)—Lucy Limelight **Mr Tom Coleman**
18 **MOORES METAL,** 10, b h Wolverlife—Torino **Group 1 Racing (1989) Ltd**
19 **MY LADY MINSTREL,** 4, ch f Brotherly—Lady Peggy **Mr S. Foster**
20 **PAGEANT LINE,** 8, ch m Balinger—Clothes Line **Mr Graham Treglown**
21 **PRETTY PRECOCIOUS,** 4, b f Precocious—Siouxsie **Mr Graham Treglown**
22 **RABA RIBA,** 5, gr g Oats—Erica Alba **Mr R. A. Beswick**
23 **RAPID LAD,** 12, b g Rapid River—Seacona **Mr Stephen Borsberry**
24 **ROYALTY BAY,** 7, b g Royalty—Warham Trout **Mr Brian A. Robinson**
25 **RUN AND SKIP,** 12, b g Deep Run—Skiporetta **Mr Jeff McCarthy**
26 **SHARI LOUISE,** 7, br m Radetzky—Jenny Splendid **Dr S. M. Foster**
27 **SUKEY TAWDREY,** 4, gr f Wassl—Jenny Diver (USA) **Mr Alan Corfield**
28 **SWANBOURNE LAD,** 7, b g Pollerton—Tu-Ukumah **Mr K. L. Cooper**

MR J. L. SPEARING—continued

THREE-YEAR-OLDS

29 **COMEDY RIVER,** br c Comedy Star (USA)—Hopeful Waters **Group 1 Racing (1989) Ltd**
30 **FIELDS OF FORTUNE,** ch f Anfield—Suffolk Broads **Mrs Lynne Crowden**
31 **INFEB,** gr f Another Realm—Sweet Rosina **Mr J. Shine**
32 **VAX LADY,** ch f Millfontaine—Opinebo **Vax Appliances Ltd**

TWO-YEAR-OLDS

33 **BLUES BALIDAR,** ch c 14/5 Balidar—Kimble Blue (Blue Refrain) **Mike Hawkett**
34 Br f 12/4 Jester—Cape of Storms (Fordham) **Vax Appliances Ltd**
35 B f 14/5 Coquelin—Demeter (Silly Season)

Other Owners: Mr John F. Billington, Mr A. Bosley, Mr N. A. Burton, Mr J. L. Chamberlain, Mr J. G. Freeland, Mr Bill Gerhauser, Mr P. D. Jones, Mr G. Lansbury, Mrs L. A. Marsh, Mr W. Marzouk, Mr S. L. McFarlane, Mr Simon P. Mills, Mr A. R. Nicholas, Mr David C. Spencer, Mr Alexander J. Taylor, Mr Bob Tunnicliffe, Mrs Carol J. Welch, Mr Arthur Wilson.

Jockeys (NH): Gee Armytage, G McCourt, P Scudamore (w.a.), A Webb.

Conditional: Dawson Lees (9-7).

Lady Riders: Miss Caroline Spearing (9-0), Miss Teresa Spearing (8-0).

557 MR R. C. SPICER, Spalding

Postal: **Glenhurst, Slipe Drove, West Pinchbeck, Spalding, Lincolnshire, PE11 3QF.**
Phone: **(077587) 444 FAX (077587) 637**

1 **BARSBRIDGE LAD,** 10, b g Little Buskins—Hills of Fashion **Mr R. C. Spicer**
2 **BARSHARE,** 5, ch g Longleat (USA)—Grill Room **Mr R. C. Spicer**
3 4, Ch f Broadsword (USA)—Bit of A Wit **Mrs P. M. Spicer**
4 **COOL FELLOW,** 6, b g Decent Fellow—Coolcanute **Mr R. C. Spicer**
5 **FOXTREE,** 7, b g Dubassoff (USA)—High Value **Mrs P. M. Spicer**
6 **JOSHING,** 9, b g Joshua—Topolass **Mr R. C. Spicer**
7 **NOM DE FORT,** 5, gr g Belfort (FR)—French Strata (USA) **Mrs P. M. Spicer**
8 **OPTIONAL CHOICE (USA),** 6, b g Northern View—Muchisma (USA) **Mr R. C. Spicer**
9 **TWICKNAM GARDEN,** 7, b g Mandrake Major—Dame Aux Bijoux **Mr R. C. Spicer**

Jockeys (NH): S Johnson (10-10), S McNeil (10-0), S O'Neil (10-0).

558 MR T. STACK, Golden

Postal: **Thomastown Castle, Golden, Co. Tipperary, Ireland.**
Phone: **(062) 54129 TELEX 70686 TC3G FAX (062) 54399**

1 **ICE KINGDOM (USA),** 4, b c Nijinsky—Laide Festa
2 **IT'S SO (USA),** 4, b c Vaguely Noble—Halo Dotty
3 **KOSTROMA,** 4, b f Caerleon—Katie May
4 **MOLDAVIA,** 4, ch f Glenstal (USA)—Sooner Or Later
5 **PIROUETTE,** 4, b f Sadlers Wells—True Rocket
6 **TALES TO TELL,** 4, b g Kings Lake (USA)—Hard To Tell

THREE-YEAR-OLDS

7 **ALLENDALE,** b c Alzao—Mountain High
8 **AMEX KID (USA),** b c Sagace—Darlin Momma
9 **BASTILLE DAY,** ch c Persian Bold—Marie Antoinette
10 **BATTLE STANDARD (CAN),** b c Storm Bird—Hoist Emy's Flag

MR T. STACK—continued

11 **BRIDGE PLAYER,** ch f The Noble Player—Auction Bridge
12 **CHILDHOOD MEMORIES (USA),** ch f The Minstrel—All My Memories
13 **CLEAN CUT,** ch c Formidable—Cutlers Corner
14 **CLIFTON BEACH,** b f Auction Ring—Lady Aladdin
15 **COALITION,** gr c Law Society—Spindle Berry
16 **CUT IN STONE (USA),** b f Assert—Ballyknockan
17 **DIVINE HERO (USA),** b c Baldski—Full Reign
18 **FAIRY BALLERINA,** b f Fairy King—Primed
19 **FLUORESCENT FLO,** ch f Ballad Rock—Ridans Girl
20 **GAELIC MYTH (USA),** b c Nijinsky—Irish Valley
21 **GAIETY,** b f Sadler's Wells—Wish You Were Here
22 **GLASS GOBLET (USA),** b f Storm Bird—Table of Contents
23 **GOLDEN BOUGH (USA),** b f Graustark—Seeker's Gold
24 **HOLY DEVOTION,** ch f Commanche Run—Sister Sassafras
25 **JIVE,** b f Ahonoora—Rince Si
26 **KINGCLIP,** b f Kings Lake—Reo Racine
27 **LAUREON,** b f Caerleon—Lauretta
28 **LOCHEARNHEAD (USA),** b c Lomond—Carmelize
29 **LUNAR WALK,** gr c Godswalk—Kurrie Kurrie
30 **MISSING YOU,** br f Ahonoora—Saving Mercy
31 **MOEL-Y-GUEST,** ch c Be My Guest—Freemanche
32 **NICE TO HAVE YOU (USA),** br c Alleged—Halo Dotty
33 **PAPAL LEGATE (USA),** ch c Deputy Minister—Youcanbelieveit
34 **POCKATELLO,** b f Commanche Run—Jakomima
35 **QUELLE CHANSON (USA),** b f Nijinsky—Luth Music
36 **QUIET VICTORY,** b f Never So Bold—Les Saintes
37 **RANDOM CHANCE,** b f Glenstal—Aces Full
38 **REZA KHAN,** b c Persian Bold—Lady Pavlova
39 **SABLE COATED,** b f Caerleon—Sutton Place
40 **SASKATCHEWAN,** gr c Commanche Run—Perla
41 **SECRET DIARY (USA),** b f Forli—Quat' Sous
42 **SINGLE COMBAT (USA),** b c Nijinsky—La Dame du Lac
43 **SOCIETY NEWS,** b f Law Society—Bandit Queen
44 **SONG GIRL,** ch f Caerleon—Popular Win
45 **VICTORIOUS DEED (USA),** ch c Roberto—Golden Highlights
46 **WAFFLING,** b f Lomond—Waffles
47 **WORLDWISE,** ch c Persian Bold—Priddy Blue

TWO-YEAR-OLDS

48 **APPELLATE COURT,** b c 26/2 Law Society—Vicomtesse (Relko)
49 B c The Noble Player—Bellinote (Noir Et Or)
50 **BONE CHINA (IRE),** b f 3/3 Sadler's Wells—Wedgewood Blue (Sir Ivor)
51 Gr br c 18/2 Godswalk—Castleisland (Deep Diver)
52 **CHOREOGRAPHER (IRE),** b c 27/3 Sadler's Wells—Dunette (Hard To Beat)
53 **CIRCUIT COURT (IRE),** gr c 30/1 Law Society—Spindle Berry (Dance In Time)
54 **DANGEROUS LIASON,** b c 14/3 Never So Bold—Fortune Teller (Troy)
55 Ch f 23/3 Golden Act—Dewan's Niece (Dewan)
56 B c Caerleon—Divina (Alpenkonig)
57 B c 21/3 Vision—Gay Shore (Gay Fandango)
58 **IL CORSARO (USA),** b c Northern Dancer—Gleaming Smile (Gleaming)
59 **JOE JEFF,** b c 14/2 Adonijah—Squire's Daughter (Bay Express)
60 **JUSTIFIED (FR),** b c Law Society—Megara (Thatching)
61 b br f Spend A Buck—Broas (Wig Out)
62 B c 5/4 Star Appeal—Lady Constance (Connaught)
63 **LE JONGLEUR (USA),** gr c The Minstrel—La Koumia (Kaldoun)
64 **LUTTRELLSTOWN,** b c 11/3 Precocious—La Mortola (Bold Lad (IRE))
65 **MAGIC ARTS (IRE),** b f 24/4 Fairy King—Maura Paul (Bonne Noel)
66 B c 19/2 Sure Blade—Melting Moments (His Majesty)
67 **NAIADOORA (IRE),** b f 4/6 Ahonoora—Naiad Queen (Pampered King)
68 B f 6/2 Sadler's Wells—North Broadway (Bold Ruler)

MR T. STACK—continued

69 B c 18/5 Sadler's Wells—Poquito Queen (Explodent)
70 Ch c Shahrastani—Quilloquick (Graustark)
71 **RISING WATERS (IRE),** b c 30/3 Sure Blade—Over The Waves (Main Reef)
72 **SAINTS DAY,** b br c Artichoke—Santa Quilla (Sanctus II)
73 **SEARCH FOR SPRING (IRE),** ch f 30/3 Rainbow Quest—Katie May (Busted)
74 **SIDE WINGER (USA),** b c Topsider—Fancy Wings (Wing Out)
75 **SIMPLY OUTSTANDING (IRE),** b c 14/2 Simpy Great—Sweet Repose (High Top)
76 **SPANISH GRANDEE (USA),** b c El Gran Senor—Stealthy Lady (J O Tobin)
77 B c 21/3 Tate Gallery—Steaua Romana (Pitskelly)
78 **TITLE ROLE (IRE),** ch f 2/2 Tate Gallery—Tough Lady (Bay Express)
79 Ch f 10/4 Pennine Walk—Tootens (Northfields)
80 **TURN UP TRUMPS (IRE),** ch c 8/2 Glenstal—Four Leaf Clover (Irish River)
81 Ch c 9/4 Persian Bold—Zedative (Zeddaan)

Other Owners: Mrs D. Atwood, Mr M. A. Begley, Mrs Heather Bielenberg, Mr Glenn S. Bromagen, Mr C. De Burgh, Major J. De Burgh, P. V. Burns, Mr Kevin Doyle, Mrs Kevin Doyle, Glenbeigh Racing Syndicate, Mrs John Horgan, Mr R. D. Hubbard, Mr V. L. Kilkenny, Mrs John Magnier, Mrs Betty G. Marcus, Mr M. McLeish, Morven Stud, Mrs David Nagle, A. V. Nicoll, Mr John G. O'Neill, Ovidstown Inv Ltd, Mr John J. M. Power, Maurice M Power, Mr Michael J. Ryan, Mr B. V. Sangster, Mrs R. E. Sangster, Mr R. E. Sangster, Mrs T. Stack, Mr Albert M. Stall, Mrs W. J. Taylor, Mr John L. Wood.

Jockey (Flat): S Craine (8-3).

Apprentices: J O'Dwyer (7-10), S Stack (7-5).

Amateurs: M F Barrett (10-7),

559 MR W. A. STEPHENSON, Bishop Auckland

Postal: **Crawleas, Leasingthorne, Bishop Auckland, Co. Durham, DL14 8EQ.**
Phone: **(0388) 720213**

1 **ALPHA ONE,** 5, ch g Belfalas—Clonaslee Foam **Mr W. A. Stephenson**
2 **AMBERGATE,** 9, b g Forlorn River—Jackie's Joy **Mr W. A. Stephenson**
3 **BISHOPDALE,** 9, ch g Proverb—Garryduff Lady **Mr Ray Causer**
4 **BLAZING WALKER,** 6, ch g Imperial Fling (USA)—Princess Kofiyah **Mr P. Piller**
5 **BONNIE ARTIST,** 6, ch g Caruso—Bonnie Ribema **Mr P. Piller**
6 **BORDER GAMBLER,** 6, br m Strong Gale—Golden Hansel **Mr W. A. Stephenson**
7 **BREAK THE CHAIN,** 5, br g Callernish—Lovely Daisy **Mrs A. L. Brown**
8 **CANBRACK COTTAGE,** 4, ch f Gorytus (USA)—Cottage Style **Mr T. McDonagh**
9 **CAUTIOUS PETE,** 7, ch g Kambalda—Tarsilogue **Mr W. A. Stephenson**
10 **COOL RECEPTION,** 9, ch g Decent Fellow—Arctic Daisy **Mr P. Piller**
11 **COULD BE GOLD,** 5, ch g Ovac (ITY)—My Gold **Mr W. A. Stephenson**
12 **CROSSGLEN,** 6, gr g Bybicello—Sister Chatters **Mr W. A. Stephenson**
13 **DAILY QUEST,** 5, br g Sandalay—Sunquest **Mr W. A. Stephenson**
14 **DANCING RIVER,** 4, b g Niniski (USA)—River Chimes **Mr Bernard Hathaway**
15 **DIVINE PROBLEM,** 8, gr g Roselier (FR)—Group Problem **Mr W. A. Stephenson**
16 **DURHAM EDITION,** 12, ch g Politico (USA)—Level Stakes **Mr Robert Oxley**
17 **EASTERN MINSTREL,** 6, ch g Black Minstrel—Shackle Walk **Mr P. Piller**

MR W. A. STEPHENSON—continued

18 **EXPRESS REALE,** 5, b g Al Sirat (USA)—Real Path VII **Mr W. A. Stephenson**
19 **EXTRA SPECIAL,** 5, ch g Avocat—Cummin Hill **Mr R. Ogden**
20 **FETTUCCINE,** 6, ch g Bybicello—Reel Keen **Mr J. Wilson Walker**
21 **FIGHTING FINISH,** 6, ch g Lucky Mickmooch—Fighting Sal **Mr W. A. Stephenson**
22 **FOREVER BLUE,** 7, b g Buckskin (FR)—Blue Zeta **Mr P. Piller**
23 **GHOSTDANCER,** 5, ch g Rontino—Bartlemy Fair **Mr W. A. Stephenson**
24 **GRAAL LEGEND,** 5, br h Cosmo—Lysippe **Mr W. A. Stephenson**
25 **GREAT LAW,** 5, b g Glint of Gold—Bedfellow **Mr J. Walby**
26 **GREEK LOVER,** 5, b g Mandalus—Smashing Lady **C. H. Taylor & Co Ltd (Taylorsteel)**
27 **GREENHEART,** 7, br g Green Shoon—Giollaretta **The Morley Stud**
28 **HARBOUR RETREAT,** 6, ch g Quayside—Winkle **Mr W. A. Stephenson**
29 **HE WHO DARES WINS,** 7, b g Le Bavard (FR)—Brave Air **Mr I. D. Cheesbrough**
30 **INK SPLASH,** 6, b g Relkino—Galosh **The Morley Stud**
31 **INTO THE GLEN,** 7, b g Over The River (FR)—Margerval **Mr P. Piller**
32 **IRISH RED,** 8, ch g Trombone—Smiling Diplomat **Hathaway Roofing Ltd**
33 **JAUNTY GIG,** 4, b g Dunphy—Hazel Gig **Mr W. A. Stephenson**
34 **JUPITER'S GLORY,** 6, b g Derring Rose—The Blazing Star **Mr W. A. Stephenson**
35 **KAMSEL,** 7, b g Kambalda—My Hansel **Mrs A. R. Page**
36 **KILLONE ABBEY,** 7, b g The Parson—Michelle's Fancy **Mr P. Piller**
37 **LUCKY JORDON,** 7, ch g Bybicello—Sister Chatters **Mr W. A. Stephenson**
38 **MILLEONE,** 4, b g Milford—Mama Leone **Mr P. Piller**
39 **MR WINKLE,** 5, gr g Royal Blend—Kefhalik **The Morley Stud**
40 **NARANA,** 6, b g Don—Broccoli **Mr P. Piller**
41 **NAUTICAL JOKE,** 11, b g Sea Catch—Carnival Jest **Mr P. Piller**
42 **PARK PRINCE,** 9, b g Shackleton—Proud Rain **Mr P. Piller**
43 **PARSON'S CROSS,** 6, b g The Parson—Croom Cross **Mr P. Piller**
44 **PEOPLE'S CHOICE,** 5, br g Strong Gale—Carrig-An-Neady **Hathaway Roofing Ltd**
45 **POACHER'S PAL,** 5, br h Golden Love—Easter Noddy **Mr W. A. Stephenson**
46 **POLAR NOMAD,** 9, br g Mandalus—Polar Lady **James Stoddart Ltd**
47 **PRIMROSE STAR,** 5, ch m Le Coq d'Or—Star Attention **Mr W. A. Stephenson**
48 **RIVER HOUSE,** 8, ch g Over The River (FR)—Kinsella's Choice **P. Cheesbrough**
49 **RIVERNOT,** 8, br g Over The River (FR)—Tabithatouchmenot **Mr P. Piller**
50 **ROBINSON'S CLASSIC,** 6, ch m Ashbro Laddo—Hasty Arrow **Simon J. Robinson (MGA) Ltd**
51 **ROSSHELM,** 5, ch g Ardross—Ice Cream Soda **Mr W. A. Stephenson**
52 **ROYAL MILE,** 5, b g Tyrnavos—Royal Rib **C. Leader**
53 **SAILOR'S DELIGHT,** 6, b g Idiot's Delight—Sarasail **T. P. M. McDonagh Ltd**
54 **SECRET LIFE,** 5, b g Corvaro (USA)—Intriguing **Mr W. A. Stephenson**
55 **SHOON HILL,** 6, br g Green Shoon—Carrig-An-Neady **Mr W. A. Stephenson**
56 **SID PRICE,** 9, b g Random Shot—Royal Rally **Mr W. A. Stephenson**
57 **SIR JEST,** 12, b g Sea Catch—Carnival Jest **Mr P. Piller**
58 **SOME HERO,** 6, b g Boreen Beag—Tipperary Star **Mrs A. R. Page**
59 **SOUTHERN MINSTREL,** 7, ch g Black Minstrel—Jadida (FR) **Hathaway Roofing Ltd**
60 **SPEECH,** 7, ch g Salluceva—Malone **Mr P. Piller**
61 **STAY ON TRACKS,** 8, gr g Roselier (FR)—Bee In Bonnet **Mr P. Piller**
62 **STEPFASTER,** 5, gr m Step Together (USA)—Pollyfaster **Mr W. A. Stephenson**
63 **STRONG CALLING,** 5, br g Strong Gale—Knowing Card **Hathaway Roofing Ltd**
64 **SWINDLE BECK,** 6, ch g Deep Run—Castle River **Mr P. Piller**
65 **SWIRL HOWE,** 10, ch g Tug of War—Couriette **Mr W. A. Stephenson**
66 **TASAR,** 9, gr g Pongee—Foreign Bird **Charlotte Lady Reay**
67 **THE BURLEYMAN,** 8, br g Belfalas—Taitu **Mrs J. Porter**
68 **THE PLAIN WAIN,** 7, br m Majestic Streak—Medwyn Heiress **Mrs Mary Aitchison-Meek**
69 **THE THINKER,** 12, ch g Cantab—Maine Pet **T. P. M. McDonagh Ltd**
70 **THE WILK,** 11, b g Pongee—Oh Look **Mr F. T. Scotto**
71 **TRIGPOINT CHARLIE,** 10, b g Bronze Hill—Salambo II **James Stoddart Ltd**
72 **VILLIERSTOWN,** 11, b g Giolla Mear—Chammyville **Mr P. Piller**
73 **WALTINGO,** 7, b g Certingo—Honeyglen **Mr P. Piller**
74 **WATERSIGN,** 9, b g Camden Town—Larkview **Mr Tony Lapping**
75 **WREKIN HILL,** 8, b g Duky—Cummin Hill **Mr P. Piller**
76 **ZARIBEE,** 5, b g Prince Bee—Zariba **Mr J. Walby**

MR W. A. STEPHENSON—continued

THREE-YEAR-OLDS

77 **CANBRACK STYLE,** b f Glenstal (USA)—Cottage Style **Mr T. McDonagh**
78 **STAR OF THE SEA,** gr f Absalom—River Chimes **Mr Bernard Hathaway**
79 **STAR TRACKER,** br f Lochnager—Star Attention **Mr P. Piller**

Other Owners: Mr M. McDonagh, Mr P. McDonagh.

Jockeys (NH): C Grant (10-0), A Merrigan (10-0).

Conditional: J Dillon (9-7), A Heywood (9-7), A Larnach (9-7), A Parker (9-7), J Supple (9-7), T P White (9-7).

Amateur: Mr K Johnson (9-7).

560 MR B. STEVENS, Winchester

Postal: **Red House Racing Stables, Main Road, Littleton, Winchester, Hampshire.**
Phone: **(0962) 883030**

1 **AMBIANCE,** 11, gr g Three Legs—Ambient **Mr N. Pay**
2 **ANNETTE'S VENTURE,** 8, ch g Kemal (FR)—Boon Adventure **Mr L. W. Worner**
3 **BOLD SPIRIT,** 7, b g Derrylin—Bold Pioneer **Mr Barry Stevens**
4 **COOL OPERATOR,** 7, ch g Song—Gentildonna **Mr T. Beresford**
5 **DENBOY,** 8, ch g On Your Mark—Petal **Royal Blue Racing**
6 **FAY'S PET,** 5, b g Tina's Pet—Gipsy Scott **D. L. Maund**
7 **FOLIGNO,** 5, ch m Crofter (USA)—Alpine Morn **Mrs F. Fisk**
8 **FRANCIS ROSE,** 4, ch f Salmon Leap (USA)—Brief Agenda **Mrs F. Fisk**
9 **GEORGIAN BAY,** 10, b g Laurence O—Georgette **Mr L. W. Worner**
10 **GERAGHTY AGAIN,** 7, b g Hard Fought—Ottoline **G. A. Associates**
11 **HANDSOME JINKO,** 5, ch h Some Hand—Nelodor **Mr Barry Stevens**
12 **INDIAN PONY,** 11, br g Arapaho—Temba **Pauseroy Limited (Picture Palace)**
13 **LAVROSKY (USA),** 6, b g Nijinsky (CAN)—Just A Game **Mr Max Jenkins**
14 **MOTUS,** 6, b m Anfield—Lady Cox **C. Kardisky**
15 **NEW MARKET,** 6, b g Niels—Bella Berenice **Mr Clive Thorpe**
16 **ODYN PRINCE,** 4, br g Andy Rew—Silver Water **Mr N. Pay**
17 **SEISMIC LINE,** 5, br g Ardoon—Too Soon **Mr Barry Stevens**
18 **SIR COSMO,** 4, b c Simply Great (FR)—Singing Away **Mr Barry Stevens**
19 **SOLENT LAD,** 7, b h Undulate (USA)—River Palace **Mr D. Solan**
20 **SOLENT SUN,** 5, b g Undulate (USA)—River Palace **Mr A. M. Gibson**
21 **SWEET THURSDAY,** 4, ch f Sunley Builds—Adrift **Mrs Carol Cruddace**
22 **VAIGLY PERCEPTIVE,** 4, b c Vaigly Great—Ash Gayle **Mr Andrew Shenston**
23 **VILTASH,** 7, ch g Tachypous—Swynford's Pride **W. J. Marshal**
24 **WEFFIE,** 4, ch f On Your Mark—Catch Crop **Mr G. Brown**

THREE-YEAR-OLDS

25 **ALPINE TROOPER,** ch c Burslem—Alpina **Mrs M. J. Stevens**
26 **ARAGANT MAN,** b g Aragon—Cuillin Gael **Mr Barry Stevens**
27 **LUSTREMAN,** ch c Sallust—Miss Speak Easy (USA) **Smiths Cleaning Service**
28 **PERSIAN SPRING,** ch f King Persian—Northern Amber **Miss J. L. Shennan**

Other Owners: Mr D. M. Anderson, Mr D. Richardson, Mr T. I. Smith.

Jockey (Flat): Dennis Mackay.

Jockey (NH): Kevin Mooney.

Conditional: Mark Stevens (9-12).

561 MR A. C. STEWART, Newmarket

Postal: **Clarehaven, Bury Road, Newmarket, Suffolk, CB8 7BY.**
Phone: **(0638) 667323 TELEX 817929 FAX (0638) 666389**

1 **ALPHABEL,** 4, b c Bellypha—Absolute (FR) **Mr Hamdan Al-Maktoum**
2 **BRAASHEE,** 4, b c Sadler's Wells (USA)—Krakow **Maktoum Al Maktoum**
3 **NASHID,** 5, b g Be My Guest (USA)—Whispering Sands **Mr Hamdan Al-Maktoum**
4 **STAR LORD,** 4, b c Lord Gayle (USA)—Crack of Light **Mrs Christopher Heath**
5 **WHITE GLOW,** 4, b c Kalaglow—Bianca Lancia (FR) **Mr D. Harris**

THREE-YEAR-OLDS

6 **ABSAAR (USA),** b f Alleged (USA)—My Nord (USA) **Mr Hamdan Al-Maktoum**
7 **ALMARAI (USA),** b f Vaguely Noble—Waterbuck (USA) **Mr Hamdan Al-Maktoum**
8 **ALYSARDI (USA),** ch f Alydar (USA)—Passamaquoddy (USA) **Dr Michael Smurfit**
9 **AMAZAKE,** ch c Rousillon (USA)—Kesarini (USA) **Mr A. R. Macdonald-Buchanan**
10 **BARAKAT,** b f Bustino—Rosia Bay **Mr Hamdan Al-Maktoum**
11 **CHAPALA,** ch f Pharly (FR)—Amatrice **Mr K. McCreery**
12 **COLOURIST,** b c Petorius—Flaxen Hair **Mr R. Collins**
13 **DASHING SENOR,** b c El Gran Senor (USA)—Zillionaire (USA) **Sheikh Ahmed Al Maktoum**
14 **DJEBEL PRINCE,** b c Ile de Bourbon (USA)—Noirmont Girl **Mr M. R. Soames**
15 **DUTEST,** b c Aragon—Indian Call **Mr Khalifa Dasmal**
16 **FARMIN,** b br c Rousillon (USA)—Jendeal **Mr Hamdan Al-Maktoum**
17 **FIELD RUNNER,** ch c Precocious—Orange Squash **Mr J. A. Haverhals**
18 **GHARAM (USA),** ch f Green Dancer (USA)—Water Lily (FR) **Mr Hamdan Al-Maktoum**
19 **GOLDEN DIVOT,** b c Chief Singer—Action Belle **Mr M. A. Heffernan**
20 **GOOD FOR A LOAN,** b c Daring March—Game For A Laugh **Mrs William McAlpine**
21 **HAWWAR (USA),** b br c Lypheor—Berkeley Court **Mr Hamdan Al-Maktoum**
22 **HEADREST,** b f Habitat—Guillotina **Cliveden Stud**
23 **HUNTED,** ch c Busted—Madam Cody **Sir Thomas Pilkington**
24 **INNERGLOW,** gr f Kalaglow—Intoxication **Brook Bloodstock plc**
25 **ISLAND RULER,** b br f Ile de Bourbon (USA)—Dominant **Mr C. M. Budgett**
26 **KAHEEL (USA),** ch c Caro—Escaline (FR) **Mr F. M. Kalla**
27 **KAHER (USA),** b c Our Native (USA)—June Bride (USA) **Mr F. M. Kalla**
28 **LEOTARD,** b c Lyphard's Special (USA)—Tondbad **Mrs Christopher Heath**
29 **MAHRAH (USA),** b f Vaguely Noble—Montage (USA) **Mr Hamdan Al-Maktoum**
30 **NAJEEBA (USA),** ch f Blushing Groom (FR)—La Noblesse (USA) **Sheikh Ahmed Al Maktoum**
31 **NOBLE ENDEAVOUR,** b c Try My Best (USA)—Lady Probus **Mr R. C. Stewart**
32 **PALE WINE,** b c Rousillon (USA)—Opale **Sheikh Ahmed Al Maktoum**
33 **PLATINUM ROYALE,** b c Dominion—Zerbinetta **Platinum Racing**
34 **PLAYTHING,** b f High Top—Round Dance **Mr A. J. Simpson**
35 **REALM (USA),** b f Mr Prospector (USA)—State (USA) **Mrs A. B. Hancock Jr**
36 **RECITAL (USA),** b f Danzig (USA)—Dancealot (USA) **Mrs A. B. Hancock Jr**
37 **RED TOTO,** ch c Habitat—Soumana (FR) **Mr M. Hawkes**
38 **SILVER SHIFTER,** b f Night Shift (USA)—The Silver Darling **Mr Trevor Hemmings**
39 **SPRING TO THE TOP,** b c Thatching—Queen of The Brush **Mr G. Jabre**
40 **STARA,** b f Star Appeal—Saucy Flirt **Mr B. H. Farr**
41 **STRIKING DISTANCE,** ch c Never So Bold—Gallatin Valley (USA) **Brook Bloodstock plc**
42 **TIMBERLAND,** b c Hotfoot—Tanara **Mr A. Villar**
43 **WOODHEAD,** br f Touching Wood (USA)—Ravenshead **Mr B. H. Farr**
44 **YAAZI,** b c Mummy's Pet—Ica **Sheikh Ahmed Al Maktoum**

TWO-YEAR-OLDS

45 **AL MUTAHM (USA),** b c 18/3 Green Dancer (USA)—Musical Medicine (FR) (Margouillat (FR)) **Mr Hamdan Al-Maktoum**
46 **AL SHAQRAH (USA),** ch f 28/4 Sir Ivor—Emmaline (USA) (Affirmed (USA)) **Mr Hamdan Al-Maktoum**
47 **AL THERAAB (USA),** ch f 18/5 Roberto (USA)—Golden Lamb (USA) (Graustark) **Mr Hamdan Al-Maktoum**
48 **AMAAKI,** ch c 10/2 Kris—Rowa (Great Nephew) **Sheikh Ahmed Al Maktoum**
49 **ARYLH (USA),** b f 13/3 Lyphard (USA)—Riviere Enchantee (FR) (Riverman (USA)) **Mr Hamdan Al-Maktoum**
50 **BE MAGIC,** ch f 1/4 Persian Bold—Be Sweet (Reform) **Cliveden Stud**
51 B f 17/3 Northern Prospect—Blushing Emy (USA) (Blushing Groom (FR)) **Dr Michael Smurfit**

MR A. C. STEWART—continued

52 **CAVEAT VENDOR,** b c 25/5 Auction Ring (USA)—Star Court (Aureole) **Cliveden Stud**
53 B c 28/5 Shirley Heights—Cley (Exbury) **Mr C. M. Budgett**
54 B c 2/5 Fairy King (USA)—Concensus (Majority Blue) **Mr F. M. Kalla**
55 **ELATHIR (USA),** ch c 24/1 Alydar (USA)—Mohair (FR) (Blue Tom) **Mr Hamdan Al-Maktoum**
56 B f 21/4 Devil's Bag (USA)—Foolish Passion (USA) (Secretariat (USA)) **Dr Michael Smurfit**
57 B c 29/3 High Line—Heather Croft (Kala Shikari) **Mr A. C. Stewart**
58 **IDOL MIO (USA),** b f 22/5 Shadeed (USA)—Ionian Idol (USA) (Prince John (USA)) **Gainsborough Stud**
59 **JADIDH,** b f 17/4 Touching Wood (USA)—Petrol (Troy) **Mr Hamdan Al-Maktoum**
60 **JASOOR,** b c 2/3 Dancing Brave (USA)—Amethysta (Gulf Pearl) **Sheikh Ahmed Al Maktoum**
61 B f 20/2 Persian Bold—Labista (Crowned Prince (USA)) **Duke of Roxburghe**
62 B f 22/4 High Top—Latakia (Morston (FR)) **Mr B. H. Farr**
63 Ch c 14/2 Burslem—Lavinia (Habitat) **Newmarket Club**
64 **LIME ST NIGHTMAIR,** b c 25/5 Elegant Air—Bernice Clare (Skymaster) **Mr A. R. Bavin**
65 **LITTLE ROUSILLON,** b c 29/2 Rousillon (USA)—Carolside (Music Maestro) **Fayzad Thoroughbreds**
66 **LYNAM PRINCE (IRE),** br c 7/5 Fairy King (USA)—Come True (FR) (Nasram II) **Mr M. Hawkes**
67 B c 3/5 Thatching—Madam Loving (Vaigly Great) **Mohamed Obaida**
68 **MAHAASIN,** b f 26/5 Bellypha—Dame Ashfield (Grundy) **Sheikh Ahmed Al Maktoum**
69 B f 4/5 Shareef Dancer (USA)—Mahabba (USA) (Elocutionist (USA)) **Mr T. Dartford**
70 **MAHFIL,** b c 19/4 Head For Heights—Polavera (FR) (Versailles II) **Mr Hamdan Al-Maktoum**
71 **MAKHAALIB,** b f 12/5 Caerleon (USA)—Index To Forli (USA) (Forli (ARG)) **Mr Hamdan Al-Maktoum**
72 **MARCHING PAST,** br c 9/3 Daring March—Storm Crest (Lord Gayle (USA)) **Mrs William McAlpine**
73 Ch c 24/4 Lyphard (USA)—Miss Summer (Luthier (FR)) **Sheikh Ahmed Al Maktoum**
74 **MUTHHIL (USA),** b c 27/3 Shahrastani (USA)—Icing (Prince Tenderfoot (USA)) **Sheikh Ahmed Al Maktoum**
75 **NASEEM ELBARR (USA),** ch c 10/2 The Minstrel (CAN)—
Doubling Time (USA) (Timeless Moment (USA)) **Sheikh Ahmed Al Maktoum**
76 **NEGEEN (USA),** b f 31/3 Danzig (USA)—Sunny Smile (Boldnesian) **Sheikh Ahmed Al Maktoum**
77 **NUNIVAK (USA),** ch f 2/4 Bering—Snow The Judge (USA) (Court Recess) **Mrs M. Moran**
78 B f 3/2 Commanche Run—Papsies Pet (Busted) **Mr Shack**
79 Ch c 1/2 Miswaki (USA)—Petit Rond Pont (USA) (Round Table) **Mr F. M. Kalla**
80 B c 6/2 Palace Music (USA)—Principle (USA) (Viceregal (CAN)) **Dr Michael Smurfit**
81 **REVIF (FR),** gr c 18/3 Kenmare (FR)—Reverente (FR) (Riverman (USA)) **S. Corman Ltd**
82 **SAN (USA),** b f Danzig (USA)—Alluvial (USA) (Buckpasser) **Mrs A. B. Hancock Jnr**
83 B c 11/4 Dominion—Short And Sharp (Sharpen Up) **Mohamed Obaida**
84 B f 24/2 Slip Anchor—Sibley (Northfields (USA)) **Mr B. H. Farr**
85 **SOHA (USA),** b f 17/2 Dancing Brave (USA)—Paris Royal (Mill Reef (USA)) **Sheikh Ahmed Al Maktoum**
86 **SWEET REQUEST,** b c 16/4 Rainbow Quest (USA)—Attica Meli (Primera) **Cliveden Stud**
87 Ch f 13/5 Busted—Taniokey (Grundy) **Mr Shack**
88 **THARIF,** b c 10/3 Green Desert (USA)—Mrs Bacon (Balliol) **Mr Hamdan Al-Maktoum**
89 **TOP MILL,** b c 30/3 High Top—Mill On The Floss (Mill Reef) **Cliveden Stud**
90 Ch f 26/1 Devil's Bag (USA)—Treizieme (USA) (The Minstrel (CAN)) **Sheikh Ahmed Al Maktoum**
91 **TURJUMAN (USA),** b c 26/4 Topsider (USA)—Harbor Wine (USA) (Herbager) **Mr Hamdan Al-Maktoum**
92 B c 20/5 Lomond (USA)—Waffles (Wollow) **F. D. Nastasi**
93 B c 18/5 Busted—Winter Queen (Welsh Pageant) **Mrs Christopher Heath**
94 **YASMEEN VALLEY (USA),** b f 17/2 Danzig Connection—
Friendly Circle (USA) (Round Table) **Sheikh Ahmed Al Maktoum**

Jockey (Flat): M Roberts (7-11).

Apprentice: M Cassidy.

Lady Rider: Mary-Ann Clark (8-7).

562 MR G. STICKLAND, Stalbridge

Postal: **Triangle Farm, Stalbridge, Sturminster Newton, Dorset.**
Phone: **(0963) 62492**

1 **BABY SIGH,** 8, bl br g African Sky—Frances Jordan **Mr G. Stickland**
2 **JUST A TRIFLE,** 8, gr m Jellaby—Just Jolly **Mr G. Stickland**
3 **SPECIAL RESERVE,** 5, b g Auction Ring (USA)—Grande Madame **Mr G. Stickland**

563 MR F. S. STOREY, Carlisle

Postal: **Low Dubwath, Kirklinton, Carlisle, Cumbria, CA6 6EF.**
Phone: **KIRKLINTON (022 875) 331**

1 **BREGA,** 6, ch g Free State—Dauphiness **Mr F. S. Storey**
2 **MR DUDLEY,** 5, b g Riboboy (USA)—Arctic Jewel **Mr F. S. Storey**

Jockey (NH): B Storey (9-10).

564 MR W. STOREY, Consett

Postal: **Grange Farm & Stud, Muggleswick, Consett, Co. Durham.**
Phone: **(0207) 55259**

1 **BAY CHASER,** 7, b g Hasty Word—Darlinski **Mr C. B. Rennison**
2 **BELLEPHERON,** 7, b h Bellypha—Une Pavane (FR) **Mr C. B. Rennison**
3 **DARK EMPEROR,** 9, b g Park Spirit—Pin Up Girl **G Banks**
4 **EYE BEE AITCH,** 5, b m Move Off—River Petterill **I. B. H. Ltd**
5 **FIEFDOM,** 10, ch g Home Guard (USA)—Eastwood Bounty **Mr C. A. Clark**
6 **HEAVENLY HOOFER,** 7, b g Dance In Time (CAN)—Heavenly Chord **Mr G. Bramley**
7 **HOME STRAIGHT,** 4, b c Homing—Fast Asleep **W Storey**
8 **INDISPENSABLE,** 5, ch g Glenstal (USA)—Santa Vittoria **Mr Ron Price**
9 **MADONIJAH,** 4, ch f Adonijah—Linda's Design **Linda Watson**
10 **MEGAN'S MOVE,** 7, ch m Move Off—River Petterill **Mr H. S. Hutchinson**
11 **MOD SQUAD,** 4, ch f Montekin—Fauchee **F Watson**
12 **NO FRILLS,** 5, ch m Glenstal (USA)—No Fuss **F Watson**

THREE-YEAR-OLDS

13 **MOLLY'S MOVE,** ch f Kabour—Sallyanda **Mr H. S. Hutchinson**

Other Owners: N. Bowden, R. Harrop, Mr R. W. Hurst, Mr Peter Imrie, D. Neale, Mr A. Whiting.

Jockey (NH): K Doolan (10-0).

Amateur: Mr M Hindmarsh (9-7).

Lady Riders: Miss F J Storey (10-0), Miss S Storey (8-7).

565 MR M. STOUTE, Newmarket

Postal: **Freemason Lodge, Bury Road, Newmarket, Suffolk, CB8 7BT.**
Phone: **NEWMARKET (0638) 663801 TELEX 817811 FAX (0638) 667276**

1 **BY CHARTER,** 4, b f Shirley Heights—Time Charter **Mr R. Barnett**
2 **DOLPOUR,** 4, b c Sadler's Wells (USA)—Dumka (FR) **H.H. Aga Khan**
3 **KRIBENSIS,** 6, gr g Henbit (USA)—Aquaria **Sheikh Mohammed**
4 **NANGARAR (USA),** 4, b c Topsider—Nawazish **H.H. Aga Khan**
5 **PATIENCE CAMP,** 4, b f Bustino—Short Rations **Mr J. M. Greetham**
6 **PHOUNTZI (USA),** 4, ch c Raise A Cup (USA)—Pushy **H.H. Aga Khan**
7 **SABOTAGE (FR),** 4, ch c Kris—Subject To Change (USA) **Sheikh Mohammed**
8 **SAFAWAN,** 4, ch c Young Generation—Safita **Mrs David Thompson**
9 **TEAMSTER,** 4, br c Known Fact—Rosetta Stone **Philip Newton**
10 **THE PRUSSIAN (USA),** 4, b c Danzig (USA)—Miss Secretariat (USA) **Sir Gordon White**

THREE-YEAR-OLDS

11 **ADJARISTAN,** b c Akarad (FR)—Adjarida **H.H. Aga Khan**
12 **AFAFF (USA),** b f Nijinsky (CAN)—Continual (USA) **Maktoum Al Maktoum**
13 **AFKAR,** gr c Mouktar—Afeefa **H.H. Aga Khan**
14 **AJAAYEB (USA),** b c Shadeed (USA)—Connie Knows (USA) **Maktoum Al Maktoum**
15 **ALDERHEY (USA),** b c Blushing Groom (FR)—Native Nurse (USA) **Sheikh Ahmed Al Maktoum**
16 **ALIMANA,** b f Akarad (FR)—Alannya (FR) **H.H. Aga Khan**
17 **BARAKISH,** b c Mummy's Pet—Blissful Evening **H.H. Aga Khan**
18 **BOY EMPEROR,** ch c Precocious—Much Too Risky **Mr J. M. Greetham**
19 **BRILLIANT TIMING (USA),** ro f The Minstrel (CAN)—Timely Roman **Cheveley Park Stud**
20 **CHARLOTTE AUGUSTA (USA),** b f Chief's Crown (USA)—Noble Damsel (USA) **Sheikh Mohammed**
21 **COLORSNAP,** b f Shirley Heights—Reprocolor **Helena Springfield Ltd**
22 **CONSTANT DELIGHT,** b f Never So Bold—Lady Constance **Cheveley Park Stud**
23 **COOL DANCER,** ch f Fabulous Dancer (USA)—Sarajill **Mr R. Barnett**
24 **DANCING HOME,** b f Shareef Dancer (USA)—Our Home **Sheikh Mohammed**
25 **DANESH,** gr c Kalaglow—Demia **H.H. Aga Khan**
26 **DEAR MIMI (USA),** b f Roberto (USA)—Carnival Princess (USA) **Mr John C. Mabee**
27 **DESERT OF STARS (USA),** b c Desert Wine (USA)—Vesuvius (USA) **Mr John C. Mabee**
28 **DOSTOYEVSKY (USA),** b c Nureyev (USA)—Mairzy Doates (USA) **Sheikh Mohammed**
29 **DUMAYLA,** b f Shernazar—Dumka (FR) **H.H. Aga Khan**
30 **EXCELLENT PROSPECT (USA),** b f Mr Prospector (USA)—Par Excellance (CAN) **Maktoum Al Maktoum**
31 **FABULOUS DEED (USA),** ch f Shadeed (USA)—Fabulous Salt (USA) **Hanson Leigh Racing**
32 **FANELLAN,** b f Try My Best (USA)—Scotia Rose **Mr Simon Fraser**
33 **FEARLESS REVIVAL,** ch f Cozzene (USA)—Stufida **Cheveley Park Stud**
34 **FIELD GLASS (USA),** b c Mr Prospector (USA)—Stellarette (CAN) **Sheikh Mohammed**
35 **FIRE AND SHADE (USA),** ch f Shadeed—Fatah Flare **Sheikh Mohammed**
36 **HEART OF JOY (USA),** b f Lypheor—Mythographer (USA) **Mr John C. Mabee**
37 **HEBBA (USA),** b f Nureyev (USA)—Likely Exchange (USA) **Sheikh Mohammed**
38 **HELLENIC,** b f Darshaan—Grecian Sea (FR) **Sir Michael Sobell**
39 **HUNTING HORN (USA),** b c Northern Dancer—Buzz My Bell (USA) **Sheikh Mohammed**
40 **ISLAND WEDDING (USA),** b f Blushing Groom (FR)—South Sea Dancer (USA) **Maktoum Al Maktoum**
41 **IVREA,** b f Sadler's Wells (USA)—Ivy (USA) **Sheikh Mohammed**
42 **JOVIAL,** b c Northern Jove (CAN)—Rensaler (USA) **Kennet Valley Thoroughbreds Ltd**
43 **KARTAJANA,** b f Shernazar—Karamita **H.H. Aga Khan**
44 **KENTFIELD,** b f Busted—Girton **C. T. Spencer-Phillips**
45 **LOCAL COLOUR,** b c Rainbow Quest (USA)—Dancing Shadow **Sir Michael Sobell**
46 **LOST INNOCENCE (USA),** ch c Blushing Groom (FR)—Olamic (USA) **Sheikh Mohammed**
47 **MAGICAL SPIRIT,** b f Top Ville—Anegada **Mr Michael J. Ryan**
48 **MAZAG (USA),** b c Mr Prospector (USA)—Rose O'Riley (USA) **Maktoum Al Maktoum**
49 **MEQDAAM (USA),** b c Storm Bird (CAN)—Nobiliare (USA) **Maktoum Al Maktoum**
50 **MOSCOW DYNAMO,** br c Siberian Express (USA)—County Line **Mr J. D. Burns**
51 **NAFZAWA (USA),** ch f Green Dancer (USA)—Nawazish **H.H. Aga Khan**
52 **NEELAM (USA),** ch f Arctic Tern (USA)—Nasseem (FR) **H.H. Aga Khan**
53 **OOGIE POOGIE (USA),** b f Storm Bird (CAN)—Cascapedia (USA) **Mr D. B. Garvin**
54 **PERDIKKAS (USA),** b br c Chief's Crown (USA)—Oeuf Ivoire (USA) **Maktoum Al Maktoum**
55 **QUI DANZIG (USA),** b c Danzig (USA)—Qui Royalty (USA) **Sir Gordon White**

DARLEY STUD

MANAGEMENT

Stallions

FOR 1990

- **DANCING BRAVE 1983** *by Lyphard - Navajo Princess by Drone*
  Champion European 3-year-old of 1986. First crop 2-year-olds in 1990.
- **POLISH PRECEDENT 1986** *by Danzig - Past Example by Buckpasser*
  Won Prix du Moulin de Longchamp **G.1,** Prix du Haras de Fresnay-le-Buffard Jacques le Marois **G.1.** Retires to Stud in 1990.
- **REFERENCE POINT 1984** *by Mill Reef - Home on the Range by Habitat*
  Champion European 2 and 3 year old. First crop yearlings in 1990.
- **SHAREEF DANCER 1980** *by Northern Dancer - Sweet Alliance by Sir Ivor*
  Sire of **COLORADO DANCER, DABAWEYAA, NEDIYM, NOBLE BALLERINA, RASLAAN, ROCK HOPPER, SHAMSHOON, SHARKA, STAR SHAREEF, TRIPLE KISS** etc.
- **SOVIET STAR 1984** *by Nureyev - Veruschka by Venture*
  Champion European Sprinter 1988. Won 5 Group 1 races. First crop foals in 1990.
- **MTOTO 1983** *by Busted - Amazer by Mincio*
  Champion European 4 and 5-year-old. First crop foals in 1990.
- **SHAADI 1986** *by Danzig - Unfurled by Hoist The Flag*
  Unbeaten 2-y-old, won Airlie/Coolmore Irish 2000 Guineas **G.1,** St James's Palace S. **G.1.** Retires to Stud in 1990.
- **SURE BLADE 1983** *by Kris - Double Lock by Home Guard*
  Won St James's Palace S. **G.2,** Queen Elizabeth II S. **G.2,** Laurent Perrier Champagne S. **G.2,** Coventry S. **G.3.** First Crop 2-year-olds in 1990.
- **DUNBEATH 1980** *by Grey Dawn - Priceless Fame by Irish Castle*
  Won William Hill Futurity **G.1.** Sire in 1989 of 18 individual winners from his first crop, and 9 from his second crop.
- **JALMOOD 1979** *by Blushing Groom - Fast Ride by Sicambre*
  Group 1 winner. Sire of winners of 95 races and over £500,000 from 3 crops.
- **MASHHOR DANCER 1983** *by Northern Dancer - Zonely by Round Table*
  Won his only race at 2 years. First season sire 1989 of 2 winners from 6 runners.
- **TEENOSO 1980** *by Youth - Furioso by Ballymoss*
  Champion Older Horse in Europe at 4. Won Derby **G.1,** King George VI & Queen Elizabeth S. **G.1.** Sire of winners in England and Italy from his first 2 crops.
- **MILLER'S MATE 1982** *by Mill Reef - Primatie by Vaguely Noble*
  Won Wood Ditton Stakes. First season sire 1989 with 7 individual winners.
- **LOCAL SUITOR 1982** *by Blushing Groom - Home Love by Vaguely Noble*
  Won Rokeby Farms Mill Reef Stakes **G.2,** beaten a head and same in Dewhurst Stakes **G.1.** First Crop 3-year-olds 1990.
- **TOP VILLE 1976** *by High Top - Sega Ville by Charlottesville*
  Sire of Group 1 winners **DARARA, PRINCESS PATI, SAINT ESTEPHE, SHARDARI** and **TOP SUNRISE.**

Darley Stud Management Company Ltd.,
Dalham Hall Stud, Duchess Drive, Newmarket, Suffolk
Telephone: Newmarket (0638) 730070. Telex: 818823 (DALHAM G).
Fax: (0638) 730167.

MR M. STOUTE—continued

56 **RAINHAM**, b c Sadler's Wells—Edge of Town **Sheikh Mohammed**
57 **RANDAMA**, b f Akarad (FR)—Ramanouche (FR) **H.H. Aga Khan**
58 **RECIPE**, ch f Bustino—Rosetta Stone **Philip Newton**
59 **REFERENCE LIGHT (USA)**, b c Diesis—Lulworth Cove **Sir Gordon White**
60 **RIDWAN**, b c Rousillon (USA)—Ring Rose **H.H. Aga Khan**
61 **ROCK HOPPER**, b c Shareef Dancer (USA)—Cormorant Wood **Maktoum Al Maktoum**
62 **ROYAL DESIGN**, b c Habitat—Gift Wrapped **Mr David Thompson**
63 **RULING PASSION**, b c Bairn—Unbidden Melody **P. D. Savill**
64 **SAGAR ISLAND (USA)**, b br f Sagace (FR)—Star River (FR) **Sheikh Mohammed**
65 **SAHARA BALADEE (USA)**, b f Shadeed (USA)—Splendid Girl (USA) **Maktoum Al Maktoum**
66 **SAMAIN (USA)**, ch f Caerleon—Samarta Dancer **Sheikh Mohammed**
67 **SASAKI**, b c Sadler's Wells (USA)—Sairshea **Sheikh Mohammed**
68 **SAYYARA**, gr f Kris—Safita **H.H. Aga Khan**
69 **SELAAH**, b c Rainbow Quest (USA)—Marwell **Sheikh Ahmed Al Maktoum**
70 **SHAHANNDEH**, b c Assert—Shademah **H.H. Aga Khan**
71 **SHAJAN**, b f Kris—High Hawk **Sheikh Mohammed**
72 **SHAMARZANA**, b f Darshaan—Sharmeen (FR) **H.H. Aga Khan**
73 **SHAMSHAD**, b c Darshaan—Shannfara (FR) **H.H. Aga Khan**
74 **SNAADEE (USA)**, br c Danzig (USA)—Somfas (USA) **Maktoum Al Maktoum**
75 **SONG OF KINGS (CAN)**, ch c The Minstrel (CAN)—Nabora (USA) **Sheikh Mohammed**
76 **STAGECRAFT**, b c Sadler's Wells (USA)—Bella Colora **Sheikh Mohammed**
77 **TALABAYRA**, b f Darshaan—Takariyna **H.H. Aga Khan**
78 **TAMISE**, b f Dominion—Miss Thames **Mrs Denis Haynes**
79 **TARIKHANA**, gr f Mouktar—Tremogia (FR) **H.H. Aga Khan**
80 **THEHOOL (USA)**, gr c Nureyev (USA)—Benouville (FR) **Maktoum Al Maktoum**
81 **TIMIYA**, b f High Top—Triumphant **H.H. Aga Khan**
82 **TRAFUL (USA)**, b c Riverman (USA)—Wintergrace (USA) **Maktoum Al Maktoum**
83 **VAIG APPEAL**, b c Star Appeal—Dervaig **Mr T. E. Sellier**
84 **VOLTA (USA)**, b c Nureyev (USA)—Ivory Lady (USA) **Sheikh Mohammed**
85 **WACE (USA)**, b c Nijinsky (CAN)—La Mesa (USA) **Sheikh Mohammed**
86 **WADOOD (USA)**, b c Danzig—Foreign Missile **Sheikh Mohammed**
87 **WESTERN OCEAN**, ch c Pharly—Pretty Pol **R. H. Cowell**
88 **WITHOUT EQUAL (USA)**, ch c Sharpen Up—Key Tothe Minstrel (USA) **Mrs David Thompson**
89 **YSATIROUS**, gr c Ahonoora—Amalancher (USA) **Mrs V. Hue-Williams**
90 **ZABARRJAD (USA)**, b f Northern Dancer—Smooth Bore (USA) **Sheikh Mohammed**
91 **ZARNA**, ro f Shernazar—Zahra **H.H. Aga Khan**

TWO-YEAR-OLDS

92 **AJAAD (USA)**, ch c 23/3 Nureyev—Execution (The Axe II) **Maktoum Al Maktoum**
93 B c 16/5 Lashkari—Alannya (FR) (Relko) **H.H. Aga Khan**
94 B f Green Desert (USA)—Allegedly Blue (Alleged) **Maktoum Al Maktoum**
95 **AMEERAT JUMAIRA (USA)**, ch f 25/5 Alydar—French Charmer (Le Fabuleux) **Sheikh Ahmed Al Maktoum**
96 **ANAGRAM (USA)**, ch f 13/4 Shahrastani—Troyanna (Troy) **Lord Weinstock**
97 B c 26/3 Sadler's Wells (USA)—Aunty (FR) (Riverman (USA)) **Maktoum Al Maktoum**
98 **AVE VALEQUE (USA)**, ch c 28/3 Diesis—Hail Proudly (Francis S) **Sheikh Mohammed**
99 Ch c 27/2 Blushing Groom (FR)—Awaasif (CAN) (Snow Knight) **Sheikh Mohammed**
100 **AYAH (USA)**, b f 23/5 Secreto—Native Nurse (Graustark) **Sheikh Mohammed**
101 B c 8/5 Sir Ivor—Banasiya (Mill Reef (USA)) **H.H. Aga Khan**
102 **BAO LACK (USA)**, br c 29/4 Blushing Groom—Break Through (Hail To Reason) **Maktoum Al Maktoum**
103 **BARKERVILLE (USA)**, b c 14/5 Mr Prospector (USA)—Euryanthe (USA) (Nijinsky (CAN)) **Sheikh Mohammed**
104 **BELSALAAMA (USA)**, b c 28/1 Alydar—Softly (Solo Landing) **Sheikh Ahmed Al Maktoum**
105 Ch c 10/5 Northern Baby (CAN)—Carnival Princess (USA) (Prince John) **John C. Mabee**
106 **CHIEF CELEBRITY (USA)**, b f 29/4 Chief's Crown (USA)—My Nord (USA) (Vent du Nord (USA)) **Cheveley Park Stud**
107 B f 6/4 Nijinsky (CAN)—Classy Cathy (USA) (Private Account (USA)) **Sheikh Mohammed**
108 **CLIPPERINA (USA)**, b f 2/3 L'Emigrant—Wield (Judger) **Aubrey Ison**
109 B c 24/2 Sadler's Wells (USA)—Colorspin (FR) (High Top) **Sheikh Mohammed**
110 **CROWN DERBY**, b c 19/2 Chief's Crown—Mrs Warren (Hail To Reason) **Sheikh Mohammed**
111 **DAFRAH (USA)**, b f 2/2 Danzig—Capo di Monte (Final Straw) **Maktoum Al Maktoum**

AIRLIE STUD, Dublin

Postal: **Airlie Stud, Lucan, Co. Dublin.**

Phone: **DUBLIN (01) 280267/281548/280597 TELEX 31049 TROG EI FAX (01) 283109**

1 **BALLAD ROCK,** 16, ch h Bold Lad (IRE)—True Rocket
2 **ELA-MANA-MOU,** 14, b h Pitcairn—Rose Bertin
3 **GLOW,** 7, b h Northern Dancer—Glisk
4 **KING OF CLUBS,** 9, ch h Mill Reef (USA)—Queen Pot
5 **SALT DOME (USA),** 7, ch h Blushing Groom (FR)—Buda Lady (USA)
6 **STANDAAN,** 14, gr h Zeddaan—Castania (GER)

YEARLINGS

7 Ch f 1/3 Ela-Mana-Mou—Adjala (Northfields (USA))
8 B c 24/1 Niniski (USA)—Adrana (Bold Lad (IRE))
9 B f 30/1 Ballad Rock—Alaria (GER) (Kaiseradler)
10 B f 30/4 Darshaan—Alruccaba (Crystal Palace (FR))
11 B f 22/3 Glow (USA)—Astania (GER) (Arratos (FR))
12 Ch c 29/3 Ela-Mana-Mou—Babilla (USA) (Raja Baba (USA))
13 Ch c 26/3 Ballad Rock—Bay Laurel (Habitat)
14 B c 29/4 Dixieland Band (USA)—Bold Example (USA) (Bold Lad (IRE))
15 B c 18/2 Alzao (USA)—Brilleaux (Manado)
16 B c 5/3 Glow (USA)—Cipriani (Habitat)
17 Br f 23/4 Glow (USA)—Clouded Issue (Manado)
18 B c 1/3 Niniski (USA)—Dingle Bay (Petingo)
19 B f 17/2 Alleged (USA)—Dream Play (USA) (Blushing Groom (FR))
20 B f 20/2 Glow (USA)—Fair of The Furze (Ela-Mana-Mou)
21 B c 27/1 Northern Baby (CAN)—Glim (USA) (Damascus (USA))
22 B f 12/5 King of Clubs—Habanna (Habitat)
23 B c 24/2 Ela-Mana-Mou—Highland Ball (Bold Lad (IRE))
24 B f 9/2 Kris—Irish Bird (USA) (Sea Bird II)
25 B f 10/4 Glow (USA)—Jadhringa (Petingo)
26 B c 30/3 Shirley Heights—Kristar (Kris)
27 B c 19/4 Reference Point—La Mer (NZ) (Copenhagen)
28 Ch c 8/4 Lord Ballina (AUS)—Margaret's Ruby (Tesco Boy)
29 B f 27/2 Slip Anchor—Noble Girl (Be Friendly)
30 Br c 10/2 Pennine Walk—Olivana (GER) (Sparkler)
31 Br c 8/4 Glow (USA)—Peacehaven (Home Guard (USA))
32 B f 1/3 King of Clubs—Petite Bourguoise (Crowned Prince (USA))
33 Ch f 5/5 King of Clubs—Ramiana (USA) (Blushing Groom (FR))
34 B f 7/3 Glow (USA)—Salvationist (Mill Reef (USA))
35 B c 7/4 Sure Blade (USA)—Secala (USA) (Secretariat (USA))
36 B f 9/4 Standaan (FR)—Sleeping Car (Scorpio (FR))
37 Ch f 24/4 Diesis—Sweet Simone (FR) (Green Dancer (USA))
38 B f 16/5 Ballad Rock—Virna (USA) (Coursing)
39 B c 14/5 Saint Estephe (FR)—White Alna (FR) (Carwhite)

Owners: Airlie Stud and Partners, Airlie Stud.

Airlie

MR M. STOUTE—continued

112 DANCE AHEAD, b f 17/1 Shareef Dancer—Shoot Clear (Bay Express) **Mrs J. D. Burns**
113 DARTREY (IRE), b f 27/2 Darshaan—Secala (Secretariat) **Sheikh Mohammed**
114 DEPOSKI, ch c 23/1 Niniski (USA)—Deposit (Thatch (USA)) **W. H. Scott**
115 DESERT DIRHAM (USA), ch c 11/3 Blushing Groom—Capricorn Belle (Nonoalco) **Maktoum Al Maktoum**
116 DESERT SPORT (FR), b c 8/2 Green Desert—Majestic Kahala (Majestic Prince) **Maktoum Al Maktoum**
117 B c 14/2 Lyphard (USA)—Dolka (Shergar) **H.H. Aga Khan**
118 DOME LAWEL (USA), b f 30/3 Blushing Groom—Par Excellance (L'Enjoleur) **Maktoum Al Maktoum**
119 DRAGON'S WAY (IRE), b c 26/3 Caerleon—Waterway (Riverman) **Lord Weinstock**
120 ENQELAAB (USA), b c 13/2 Chief's Crown—Affirmatively (Affirmed) **Sheikh Ahmed Al Maktoum**
121 EVASIVE PRINCE (USA), b c 4/4 Secreto—Overstate (Speak John) **Sir Gordon White**
122 EXCITING GIRL (USA), b f 10/3 Lyphard—Sophisticated Girl (Stop The Music) **Mr John C. Mabee**
123 EXCLUSIVE VIRTUE (USA), b f 20/3 Shadeed—Exclusive Order (Exclusive Native) **Cheveley Park Stud**
124 FARISI (USA), ch c 12/1 Shahrastani (USA)—Fashada (USA) (Riverman (USA)) **H.H. Aga Khan**
125 FENNEL, b f 18/2 Slew O'Gold—Fenney Mill (Levmoss) **Sheikh Mohammed**
126 FREEZING (IRE), b f 23/1 Alleged (USA)—Field Dancer (Northfields (USA)) **R. E. Sangster**
127 GLOWING ARDOUR (IRE), b f 18/2 Dancing Brave—Cocotte (Troy) **Lord Weinstock**
128 GOLDEN AWARD (IRE), b f 12/3 Last Tycoon—Golden Glint (Vitiges) **Cheveley Park Stud**
129 GUAPA, b f 4/5 Shareef Dancer—Sauceboat (Connaught) **Maktoum Al Maktoum**
130 GULF SAILOR (IRE), b c 12/4 Darshaan—Grecian Sea (Homeric) **Lord Weinstock**
131 B c 6/4 Never So Bold—Gunner's Belle (Gunner B) **R. I. Khan**
132 Gr c 1/4 Danzig (USA)—Heatherten (USA) (Forceten (USA)) **Sheikh Mohammed**
133 Ch c 29/3 Nureyev (USA)—Hitting Irish (USA) (Irish Ruler (USA)) **Maktoum Al Maktoum**
134 B f 15/2 Sagace (FR)—Hydahs (USA) (Cheiftain II) **H. R. Mould**
135 IVANOV (USA), b c 20/1 Nijinsky—Fine Spirit (Secretariat) **Sheikh Mohammed**
136 JOUD, b f 26/4 Dancing Brave—Rapide Pied (Raise A Native) **Maktoum Al Maktoum**
137 JUBILATA (USA), ch f 16/2 The Minstrel—All Gladness (Alydar) **Sheikh Mohammed**
138 JUNGLE DANCER (IRE), b c 23/5 Sadler's Wells—Forlene (Forli) **Sir Gordon White**
139 Ch c 10/2 Assert—Kabiyla (Busted) **H.H. Aga Khan**
140 B c 22/6 Shernazar—Karamita (Shantung) **H.H. Aga Khan**
141 Ch f 25/2 Shahrastani—Kareena (Riverman) **H.H. Aga Khan**
142 LAXMI (USA), b c 26/2 Lyphard's Wish—Camarina (Vaguely Noble) **Mrs I. Phillips**
143 LILIAN BAYLISS (IRE), b f 4/4 Sadler's Wells—Godzilla (Gyr) **R. E. Sangster**
144 B c 21/4 Shernazar—Lisana (Alleged) **H.H. Aga Khan**
145 Ch f 3/4 Shahrastani—Mabira (Habitat) **H.H. Aga Khan**
146 MAGICAL VEIL, ch f 26/3 Majestic Light—Jameelapi (Blushing Groom) **Maktoum Al Maktoum**
147 MAJLOOD (USA), b c 13/3 Danzig—Qui Royalty (Native Royalty) **Sir Gordon White**
148 MASTER'S CROWN (USA), ch c 12/2 Chief's Crown—Mastoora (Raise A Native) **Maktoum Al Maktoum**
149 MISTING RAIN (USA), gr c 7/2 Cozzene—North Mist (Far North) **Mr John C. Mabee**
150 MORN OF SONG (USA), b f 20/3 Blushing Groom (FR)—
Glorious Song (CAN) (Halo (USA)) **Sheikh Mohammed**
151 MUDAAHIM (USA), b c 4/4 Danzig—Continual (Damascus) **Maktoum Al Maktoum**
152 MUJAAZIF (USA), b c 9/3 Alydar—Miss Snowflake (Snow Sporting) **Maktoum Al Maktoum**
153 B f 11/3 Shadeed (USA)—Optimistic Lass (USA) (Mr Prospector (USA)) **Sheikh Mohammed**
154 PARR (IRE), b c 10/3 Salmon Leap—Mums (Mummy's Pet) **Mrs Denis Haynes**
155 PEKING OPERA (IRE), b c 14/3 Sadler's Wells—Braneakins (Sallust) **Sheikh Mohammed**
156 PFALZ, b f 4/2 Pharly—Leipzig (Relkino) **Snailwell Stud Co Ltd**
157 POLISH KING (USA), gr c 16/3 Danzig—Sintra (Drone) **Sir Gordon White**
158 PORT ISAAC (USA), br f 22/1 Seattle Song—Key Link (Bold Ruler) **C. T. Spencer-Phillips**
159 PRICELESS BOND (USA), ch f 28/1 Blushing Groom—Pied Princess (Tom Fool) **Cheveley Park Stud**
160 B c 11/3 Diesis—Privy (USA) (Tisab (USA)) **Dr Michael Smurfit**
161 QUELUZ (USA), b f 13/2 Saratoga Six—Mariella (Roberto) **Sheikh Mohammed**
162 RAHDARI (IRE), br c 18/4 Darshaan—Ramanouche (Riverman) **H.H. Aga Khan**
163 RECHERCHEE, b f 22/2 Rainbow Quest—Princess Arabella (Crowned Prince) **Miss K. Rausing**
164 REEM ALBARAARI, b f 5/3 Sadler's Wells—Habibti (Habitat) **Maktoum Al Maktoum**
165 B c 26/3 Damister—Roman River II (Bonconte di Montefeltro) **Kennet Valley Thoroughbreds Ltd**
166 RUN AND DELIVER (USA), gr c 9/4 Danzig—Belga (Le Fabuleux) **Cheveley Park Stud**
167 SADDLERS' HALL (IRE), b c 26/5 Sadler's Wells—Sunny Valley (Val de Loir) **Lord Weinstock**
168 SAFE ARRIVAL (USA), gr f 8/3 Shadeed—Flyingtrip (Vaguely Noble) **Mrs V. Hue-Williams**
169 SANDUSKY (USA), b c 17/2 Al Nasr—Sandy Blue (Windy Sands) **Sheikh Mohammed**
170 SEDUCTRESS, ch f 31/3 Known Fact—Much Too Risky (Bustino) **Mr J. M. Greetham**

NOW AVAILABLE from Weatherbys

The Statistical Record Annual 1989 £59

The Stallion Book Hardbound £49

Softback £35

SPECIAL INTRODUCTORY OFFER

The Stallion Book for 1990 (hardbound),
The Statistical Record Annual 1989
and the Return of Mares 1989 £100

Weatherbys, Sanders Road, Wellingborough,
Northants. NN8 4BX

Access

Telephone: 0933 440077
Telex: 311582
Fax: 0933 440814

AMERICAN EXPRESS

MR M. STOUTE—continued

171 **SHADY LEAF (IRE),** b f 8/5 Glint of Gold—Dancing Shadow (Dancer's Image) **Lord Weinstock**
172 **SHAMAALY BABY (USA),** ch c 26/1 Northern Baby—Shining Skin (Fappiano) **Maktoum Al Maktoum**
173 Br c 29/3 Top Ville—Sharmada (FR) (Zeddaan) **H.H. Aga Khan**
174 **SHESLIKETHEWIND,** b f 1/4 Shareef Dancer—Green Leaf (Alydar) **Maktoum Al Maktoum**
175 **SNOW PLOUGH (IRE),** b f 12/2 Niniski—River Dancer (Irish River) **Lord Weinstock**
176 **SNOWY OWL (USA),** b c 11/4 Storm Bird—Nafees (Raja Baba) **Sheikh Mohammed**
177 Ch c 1/5 El Gran Senor (USA)—Somebody Noble (USA) (Vaguely Noble) **John C. Mabee**
178 **SOUGHT OUT (IRE),** b f 17/3 Rainbow Quest—Edinburgh (Charlottown) **Lord Weinstock**
179 **STOP PRESS (USA),** b f 22/4 Sharpen Up—Glad Tidings (Gaily) **Lord Weinstock**
180 B c 25/4 Northern Prospect—Swan Song (USA) (Ribot) **R. C. Thompson**
181 Ch f 11/4 Shahrastani—Taduska (Daring Display) **H.H. Aga Khan**
182 **TANGALOA (USA),** b c 29/4 Lyphard—Angel Island (Cougar II) **Sheikh Mohammed**
183 **TUFRAJ (USA),** ch c 26/3 Kris—Greenland Park (Red God) **Maktoum Al Maktoum**
184 **UNFOLD,** ch f 9/3 Kris—Untold (Final Straw) **Sheikh Mohammed**
185 **VANNOZZA,** ch f 24/1 Kris—Vilikaia (Nureyev) **Sheikh Mohammed**
186 **VERY BOLD,** b f 27/2 Never So Bold—La Nureyeva (Nureyev) **Mrs V. Hue-Williams**
187 **WALIM (USA),** ch c 31/3 Nijinsky—Splendid Girl (Golden Eagle) **Maktoum Al Maktoum**
188 **WILAYIF (USA),** b f 26/3 Danzig—Kamar (Key To The Mint) **Maktoum Al Maktoum**
189 **WOLF HALL (IRE),** b c 18/5 Green Desert—Lady Seymour (Tudor Melody) **Sheikh Mohammed**
190 **WRETHAM HOUSE,** b c 26/3 Bellypha—Hayley Warren (Habitat) **Mrs Denis Haynes**
191 **ZABELINA (USA),** ch f 14/5 Diesis—Intentional Move (Tentam) **Sheikh Mohammed**

Other Owners: Mr G. Hahn, Mr S. Hanson, Mr Gerald Leigh, Mr P. A. Leonard, Lord Tavistock, Mr Simon Weinstock, Mr W. T. Young.

Jockey (Flat): W R Swinburn (8-6).

Apprentices: Vincent Bray (7-4), Elaine Stannard (8-0).

Lady Rider: Maxine Juster (8-7).

566 MR A. P. STRINGER, Thirsk

Postal: **Common Hall, Kilburn Parks, Carlton Husthwaite, Thirsk, North Yorkshire, YO7 2BX.**
Phone: **(0845) 401329**

1 **AH JIM LAD,** 6, b g Jimsun—Gigante Rossa **Mr R. J. Cooper**
2 **ALMARREEKH (FR),** 5, b g Glint of Gold—Formulate
3 **AUCTION FEVER,** 7, b g Hello Gorgeous (USA)—Auction Bridge **Mr E. Reitel**
4 **BEAU NASH,** 6, b g Prince Tenderfoot (USA)—Dominica (GER) **Mrs Rowena Coleman**
5 **FAR GLOW,** 4, gr c Kalaglow—Faridetta **Mrs A. Taylor (Co Durham)**
6 **FURNACE MILL,** 5, b br g Tumble Wind (USA)—Jane Bond **Mr B. Morton**
7 **GLOWING DARKNESS,** 5, gr m Kalaglow—Guama **Mr D. Walsh**
8 **HEIR OF EXCITEMENT,** 5, b g Krayyan—Merry Choice **Mr D. M. Hetherington**
9 **KAMAL SIDDIQI,** 10, b g Proverb—Artic Sue **Mr R. J. Cooper**
10 **KOOKY'S PET,** 7, br g Baptism—Great Aunt II **Mr A. P. Stringer**
11 **MON MISTRAL,** 4, b f Kemal—Deep Sea Diver **Mr C. Wardman**
12 **REJOINUS,** 5, ch g Blue Refrain—Teesdale **Mr C. R. Galloway**
13 **SCOTS GAP,** 5, b g Relkino—Suffolk Broads **Mr Marten Julian**
14 **SILVER PATROL,** 5, gr g Rusticaro (FR)—Goccia d'Oro (ITY) **Mr J. E. Vowles**
15 **SPRING MORN,** 5, b g Alleged (USA)—Valinciennes (USA) **Mrs A. Taylor (Co Durham)**
16 **TIMMINION,** 8, ch g Dominion—My Baby Love **Mr R. Dawson**

THREE-YEAR-OLDS

17 **DUMBRECK,** b f Another Realm—Eagles Quest **Mr H. O'Donnell**
18 **PRIORY CLOUD,** b f Castle Keep—Misfired **Mrs A. E. Julian**
19 **THE GOOFER,** b g Be My Native (USA)—Siliferous **Mrs Rowena Coleman**

MR A. P. STRINGER—continued

TWO-YEAR-OLDS

20 **COLWAY CROWN,** b c 4/2 Wassl—Dignified Air (FR) (Wolver Hollow) **Mr R. Coleman**
21 B c 29/4 Prince Tenderfoot—El Cerrito (Tribal Chief)
22 Ch c 15/4 Commanche Run—Lake Tawa (Cure The Blues (USA))
23 B c 23/2 Nordance (USA)—Sense of Pride (Welsh Pageant)
24 B f 4/2 Nomination—Sharp Run (Sharpen Up)

Other Owners: Mr S. Andrew, Mr M. Court, Mr L. E. Cureton, Mr M. Glennon, Mr G. Griffin, Mr A. Hannah, Mr P. Hardy, Mrs B. J. Hetherington, Mr D. Howell, Mr C. McDonald, Dr S. Nam, Mr J. P. Peers, Mr J. G. Rookes, D. Thomas.

Jockeys (Flat): P Burke (7-7), M Hindley (8-6).

Jockeys (NH): C Grant (10-0, w.a.), J J Quinn (10-0).

Conditional: N O'Connor (10-0).

Amateur: Mr S Brisby (10-4).

567 MR R. W. STUBBS, Newmarket

Postal: **Carriageway Stables, Hamilton Road, Newmarket, Suffolk, CB8 7JQ.**
Phone: **(0638) 560014**

1 **AZEB,** 4, br c Young Generation—Visible Form **Mr R. A. Brazier**
2 **CARRY ON CARY,** 4, b g Carriage Way—Greenhill Lass **Mr Ian W. Glenton**
3 **PRINCESS WU,** 4, b f Sandhurst Prince—Hsian **Mr J. C. Buckland**
4 **SMOOTH FLIGHT,** 4, ch f Sandhurst Prince—Female Mudwrestler **Mr T. Clement**
5 **YERIF NOGARD,** 4, b br f Don—Firey Dragon **Mrs Diana Lake**

THREE-YEAR-OLDS

6 **ANGLOINTERNATIONAL,** b f Millfontaine—Brigadiers Nurse **Anglo International Bloodstock Plc**
7 **GLOBAL DRAGON,** b c Reasonable (FR)—Real Sure **Mrs Diana Lake**
8 **KRISTIN'S LIGHT,** b f Noalto—Parez **Anglo International Bloodstock Plc**
9 **NIKKRIS,** ch f Song—Java Jive **Miss Nicky Taylor**
10 **PHILIPPA'S HEIR,** b f Elegant Air—Ebb And Flo **Anglo International Bloodstock Plc**
11 **SARAH CARTER,** b f Reesh—Second Swallow **Mr C. I. Garrad**
12 **WINSLOW LAD,** br g Horage—Rathcoffey Daisy **Winslow Racing**

TWO-YEAR-OLDS

13 **BIRLING ASHES,** gr c Magic Mirror—Morning Miss (Golden Dipper) **Mrs Stella Garrad**
14 Br f 20/3 Bay Express—Calidore (Scottish Rifle) **E. Dolan**
15 **CAPTAIN KAGAR,** b c 15/3 Tina's Pet—Captain Bonnie (Captain James) **Mr M. S. Griffiths**
16 **CAPTAIN OF THE GUARDS,** ch c 29/5 Prince Sabo—Keeps (Roan Rocket) **Mr P. G. Shorrock**
17 Br c 3/6 Prince Tenderfoot—Louisa Stuart (FR) (Ruysdael II) **Mr C. I. Garrad**
18 B c 23/3 Ballacashtal (CAN)—Northern Hope (FR) (Fabulous Dancer (USA)) **Carriageway Racing Co Ltd**
19 Ch c 7/5 Salmon Leap (USA)—Persian Polly (Persian Bold) **Mr C. I. Garrad**
20 Ch f 4/5 Norwick (USA)—Powderhall (Murrayfield) **Carriageway Racing Co Ltd**
21 B c 12/2 Petorius—Special Guest (Be My Guest (USA)) **Miss Zelda Blakey**
22 B c 2/3 Norwick (USA)—Two Shots (Dom Racine (FR)) **Carriageway Racing Co Ltd**
23 B c 16/3 Two Davids (USA)—Vaguely Sensitive (USA) (Sensitive Prince (USA)) **Carriageway Racing Co Ltd**
24 Ch c 27/3 Sayf El Arab (USA)—Winsong Melody (Music Maestro) **Carriageway Racing Co Ltd**

Other Owners: Mr Leslie F. Allett, Mr J. H. Caplin, Mr A. R. Goulding, Mr Harry Groenen, Mr T. Howarth, Mr Peter Lake, Mr T. Pulford, Mr R. Reynolds, Mr R. W. Stubbs.

Jockey (Flat): D Nicholls (w.a.).

568 MR J. SUTCLIFFE, Epsom

Postal: **Woodruffe House, Headley Road, Epsom, Surrey, KT18 6BH.**
Phone: **(0372) 272825 FAX (0372) 277852**

1 **A PRAYER FOR WINGS,** 6, gr g Godswalk (USA)—Late Swallow **Mr S. Powell**
2 **ASHTINA,** 5, b g Tina's Pet—Mrewa **Mr R. P. Maughan**
3 **BE MY RUNNER,** 4, b g Runnett—Ivorysguest **Mr Stanley Myers**
4 **CHASE THE DOOR,** 5, br g Red Sunset—Clonsella Lady **C. Dodson**
5 **GO FORUM,** 5, ch g Tumble Wind (USA)—Devine Lady **The Forum Ltd**
6 **HALOX (USA),** 4, b g Little Current (USA)—Noble Legion (CAN) **Lawrence Industries Plc**
7 **MARCH BIRD,** 5, ch g Dalsaan—Late Swallow **A. Nolan**
8 **PENNY FORUM,** 6, b g Pas de Seul—Kind Thoughts **Mr R. J. Surridge**
9 **SUNWIND,** 4, b g Windjammer (USA)—Mrewa **Mr R. P. Maughan**
10 **SUPEROO,** 4, b g Superlative—Shirleen **Mr Albert Finney**
11 **TAKE ISSUE,** 5, b g Absalom—Abstract **Mr R. M. Flower**
12 **VITE VITE,** 4, ch g Kind of Hush—Swiftacre **Mrs S. Powell**

THREE-YEAR-OLDS

13 **AMERICAN CONNEXION,** ch g Tender King—Chieftain Girl (USA) **Mr D. A. Johnson**
14 **BROTHER RAY,** b g Chief Singer—Havara **Mr Albert Finney**
15 **CHIPANDABIT,** b c Mummy's Pet—Parlais **Mrs B. Facchino**
16 **GO PATHFINDER,** b g Swing Easy (USA)—Pollinella **Mr S. Powell**
17 **IN THE PAPERS,** b f Aragon—Mistress Gay **Mr S. Powell**
18 **LORD BERTIE (USA),** b c Roberto (USA)—Honorine (USA) **Mrs B. Facchino**
19 **MULL HOUSE,** b g Local Suitor (USA)—Foudre **Mrs B. Facchino**
20 **MY CROFT,** b f Crofter (USA)—Randolina **Mrs B. Facchino**
21 **PARK FORUM,** ch g Dunbeath (USA)—Heavenly Gaze (FR) **The Forum Ltd**
22 **RICKSHAW QUEEN,** b f Alzao (USA)—Sorrow **Mrs B. Facchino**
23 **SISTER SAL,** ch f Bairn (USA)—Mercy Cure **C. Dodson**

TWO-YEAR-OLDS

24 B f 14/5 Last Tycoon—Chilblains (Hotfoot)
25 **COUNTESS BRUSSELS,** ch f 25/4 Scottish Reel—Net Call (Song)
26 Ch f 16/4 Soughaan (USA)—Cousin Clare (Pontifex (USA))
27 B c 9/5 Homing—Duboff (So Blessed)
28 B f 19/4 Storm Bird (CAN)—Euphrosyne (USA) (Judger (USA))
29 B f 21/5 Nordico (USA)—Havara (African Sky)
30 **IN THE SPOTLIGHT (IRE),** b c 26/2 The Noble Player—On Her Own (Busted)
31 **KINCHERINCHEE,** b f 5/3 Dunbeath (USA)—Kaisersage (FR) (Exbury)
32 B c 8/5 Sarab—Lanata (Charlottown)
33 **LYPHARD'S SONG (IRE),** b f 20/4 Lyphard's Special—Supreme Song (Supreme Sovereign)
34 Ch c 15/4 Tate Gallery—Parlais (Pardao)
35 **PAY TO DREAM (IRE),** b c 16/3 Runnett—Pursue (Auction Ring (USA))
36 B c 14/5 Last Tycoon—Sherkraine (Shergar)
37 B c 4/5 Tate Gallery—Sister Eucharia (Oats)
38 **THATCH AND GOLD (IRE),** b c 7/4 Thatching—Tuck (Artaius (USA))
39 B c 1/4 Ardross—Twine (Thatching)

Other Owners: Mr J. E. Cama, Mr D. F. Cowham, Mrs P. A. Garner, Mr Michael R. Jaye, Miss Victoria Markowiak, M. J. N. Peacock, Roldvale Ltd, J. St George, Mr John Sutcliffe, Mrs B. Wolff.

Apprentices: S Cairns (7-10), D Cripps (7-10).

569 CAPT. D. SWAN, Cloughjordon

Postal: **Modreeny, Cloughjordon, Co. Tipperary, Ireland.**
Phone: **(0505) 42221 FAX (0505) 42128**

1 **ATTESES,** 6, br m Smooth Stepper—Sesetta **Capt D. G. Swan**

CAPT. D. SWAN—continued

2 **BAR THE GOSSIP,** 5, ch m Le Bavard—Bar You Try **Gal-Ros Syndicate**
3 **CHAPEL FIELD,** 4, br f Kampala—Eiger Sanctions **Capt D. G. Swan**
4 **DIRTY DIANA,** 5, br m Boreen—Sesetta **Mr T. Austin**
5 **EALA,** 5, br m Smooth Stepper—Cool As Ice **Miss T. A. Chaloner**
6 **ELLIS TOWN,** 5, br m Camden Town—Maroua **Mr T. Melia**
7 **LORD DE MONTFORD,** 6, b g Godswalk (USA)—Fog **Mrs A. Keane**
8 **LOUGH EGISH,** 8, b g Tug of War—Johnnie's Lass **Mr J. F. Keane**
9 **LUCKY BALOO,** 8, ch m The Parson—Lane Baloo **Kevin Clarke**
10 4, B f The Parson—Miss Buck **Capt D. G. Swan**
11 **MOSS THE BOSS,** 6, ch g Le Moss—Palukiri **Miss T. A. Chaloner**
12 **PILOT PROJECT,** 4, b g Maculata—Ceoil Eireann **Mr J. McIntyre**
13 **POLLYS PUB,** 5, br m Delamain—Caladors Polly **Mr E. Moran**
14 **POLLY TINKERTON,** 6, ch m Pollerton—Fair Tinker **Gal-Ros Syndicate**
15 **POSSIBLE AMBITION,** 5, ch g Perrault (USA)—Its Possible (USA) **Mrs A. Keane**
16 **QUIET ONE,** 5, b m Bustineto—Another Reef **Mr J. Dalton**
17 **RAHINANE,** 7, ch g Super Slip—Goose Loose **Miss T. A. Chaloner**
18 **SPRINGALEAK,** 5, br m Lafontaine (USA)—Union Rules **Mr J. H. Ramsden**
19 **SUZY STEPPER,** 6, br m Smooth Stepper—Alligate **Capt D. G. Swan**

THREE-YEAR-OLDS

20 **CINNAMON SEDGE,** b f Farhaan—Ceoil Eireann **Mr M. J. Collison**
21 **FANTAN LATOUR,** b f Lafontaine (USA)—Brompton Rose **Mr J. A. Dene**

Jockeys (NH): P Gill (9-0, w.a.), C F Swan (9-0, w.a.).

Apprentice: Caroline Treacy (7-7).

Conditional: Joseph Donnelly (9-0).

Amateur: Mr K McCarthy (9-0).

Lady Riders: Miss M L Olivefalk (9-0), Miss N Swan (9-7).

570 MR D. G. SWINDLEHURST, Carlisle

Postal: **Lynefoot, Westlinton, Carlisle, Cumbria, CA6 6AJ.**
Phone: **(0228) 74289**

1 **IMPORTED SCRAP,** 5, gr m Coded Scrap—Award For Export **Mrs M. A. Swindlehurst**
2 **INCENSE,** 10, b g Martinmas—Cabochard **Mrs M. A. Swindlehurst**

THREE-YEAR-OLDS

3 **TAUVALERA,** b f Taufan (USA)—Halva **Mr D. J. Swindlehurst**

Amateur: Mr D J Swindlehurst (10-4).

571 MR M. TATE, Kidderminster

Postal: **Winterfold Farm, Chaddesley Corbett, Kidderminster, Worcestershire, DY10 4PL.**
Phone: **(056 283) 243**

1 **DOCTOR'S REMEDY,** 4, br g Doc Marten—Champagne Party **Mr R. J. Gadsby**
2 **DYFED,** 5, b g Daring March—Regency Brighton **Mr D. A. Morris**

MR M. TATE—continued

3 **LYSANDER,** 8, br g Ile de Bourbon (USA)—Helcia **Mr D. H. Cowgill**
4 **MAUJENDOR,** 10, b g Rose Laurel—Mark My Word **Mr M. Tate**
5 **NICKLE JOE,** 4, ro g Plugged Nickle (USA)—Travois (USA) **Mrs E. Tate**
6 **PRINCESS JENNY,** 8, b m Home Guard (USA)—Princess of Verona **Mrs Jenny Adlington**
7 **RAVEN'S AFFAIR,** 4, b g Tower Walk—Femme Fatale **Mr M. Tate**
8 **ROGERS PRINCESS,** 8, b m Owen Anthony—Ask For Roger **Mr R. C. Smith**
9 **SAINTHILLS SON,** 5, b g Dunphy—Sainthill **Mr M. Tate**
10 **TAGIO,** 10, b g Martinmas—Harford Belle **Mr M. Tate**
11 **THE LIDGATE STAR,** 7, b g Pitskelly—Gold Pollen **Mrs Julie McHugh**
12 **USEFUL ADDITION,** 8, b m Royalty—Facade **Mr D. H. Cowgill**

Jockeys (NH): R Hyett (10-1, w.a.), P Scudamore (10-0, w.a.), C Smith (10-0).

572 MR T. P. TATE, Otley

Postal: **Castle Farm, Hazlewood Castle, Tadcaster, North Yorkshire, LS24 9NH.**
Phone: **(0937) 836036**

1 **ANNE'S GLEN,** 4, b f Furry Glen—Lovely London **Mrs A. P. Wallace**
2 **BEAU ROSE,** 7, b g Beau Charmeur (FR)—Rosantus **Mr A. E. Dickinson**
3 **BRINCADOR,** 5, ch g Funny Man—Sister Broncho **Mrs L. Stewart-Brown**
4 **CHERRY BEE,** 6, ch g Pollerton—Tanner Hill **Mr M. Hellyer**
5 **COLLEGE MASTER,** 6, b g Balliol—Poosie Nansie **Mrs T. P. Tate**
6 **CRAWN HAWK,** 5, br g Croghan Hill—Gin An Tonic **Mr R. A. Clegg**
7 **DICKIE'S GIN,** 6, b g Mr Fordette—Gin An Tonic **Mr A. E. Dickinson**
8 **EDWARDS VISION,** 9, ch g Pollerton—Comeragh Vision **Mr M. Hellyer**
9 **GLANMOORE,** 6, br g Amboise—Michaelmas Daisy **Mr B. Leatherday**
10 **HONEST PLAYER,** 5, b g Decent Fellow—Sun Chimes **Mr T. P. Tate**
11 **OLIVERS HILL,** 7, b g Decent Fellow—Walnut Hill **Mr R. A. Clegg**
12 **QUAY ANCHOR,** 7, ch g Quayside—Charming Girl **Mr T. P. Tate**
13 **RIFLE RANGE,** 7, b g Torus—Miss Bavard **Mr C. J. Murphy**
14 **RUSSIAN CATHERINE,** 5, ch m Starch Reduced—Dawn Catherine **Mr R. Darlington**
15 **SHUTTLE HILL,** 5, b g Green Shoon—Shinaro **Mr R. Morrow**
16 **SKELETOR,** 7, b g Scallywag—Wayside Dancer **Mr T. P. Tate**
17 **ST GABRIEL,** 9, b g Furry Glen—French Honey **Mr T. P. Tate**
18 **WARRIORS MOTTO,** 7, ch g Tug of War—Mikimoto **Mrs T. P. Tate**
19 **WITHOUT A DOUBT,** 8, br g Prominer—Shinaro **Mr T. P. Tate**

Other Owners: Mrs M. Dickinson.

Conditional: W Fry (9-7).

Amateur: Mr R Ford (10-7).

573 MR A. J. TAYLOR, Hassocks

Postal: **Captains Farm, Streat, Hassocks, West Sussex.**
Phone: **PLUMPTON (0273) 890318**

1 **CLEAR GIN,** 6, b g Ginger Boy—Cool Straight **Mr A. J. Taylor**
2 **STRAIGHT GIN,** 9, b m Ginger Boy—Cool Straight **Mr A. J. Taylor**

Amateur: A J Taylor (10-4).

574 MR F. TAYLOR, Richmond

Postal: **Micklow Hill, Aldbrough St John, Richmond, N. Yorkshire, DL11 7TS.**
Phone: **DARLINGTON (0325) 374394**

1 **NO INTERFERENCE,** 5, b m Silly Prices—Ereka Oak **Mr F. Taylor**
2 **PRICE OF OAK,** 7, br m Silly Prices—Ereka Oak **Mr F. Taylor**
3 **SCOTTO'S REGRET,** 6, ch m Celtic Cone—Backcheiss **Miss D. A. Taylor and Mrs A. B. Collins**

Conditional: P Barnard (9-7), P Harte (w.a.).

Amateur: Mr J Beardsall (10-0).

575 MRS V. J. TEAL, St Clears

Postal: **Little Burrows, Laugharne, St Clears, Dyfed, Wales, SR3 4RS.**
Phone: **(0994) 427396**

1 **CALDERA,** 4, ch g Jasmine Star—Marks Aba **Mrs Vicky Teal**
2 **MAWDLYN GATE,** 7, br g Artaius (USA)—Fiordiligi **Mrs Vicky Teal**
3 **MELODY RUN,** 8, b g Grange Melody—Carnbane Princess **Mrs P. W. John**

Jockey (NH): D Morris.

Amateur: Mr R Teal (10-0).

576 MR B. M. TEMPLE, Driffield

Postal: **Wold Farm, Driffield, N. Humberside, YO25 0BB.**
Phone: **(0377) 42321**

1 **CONEY BAY,** 9, ch g Bunny Boy—Rozel Bay **Mr B. M. Temple**
2 **TIERIKI,** 7, b g Riki Lash—Tiepola **Mr B. M. Temple**

THREE-YEAR-OLDS

3 **EASY RHYTHM,** b g Tudor Rhythm—Tiebell **Mr B. M. Temple**
4 **MANWELL,** b g Tudor Rhythm—Tiemandee **Mr B. M. Temple**

TWO-YEAR-OLDS

5 **CERTAIN PRIDE,** b f 3/4 Crofthall—Tiemandee **Mr B. M. Temple**
6 **JUST WOODY,** b g 28/5 Tudor Rhythm—Tiebell **Mr B. M. Temple**
7 **POSITIVE JOY,** b f 8/4 Crofthall—Mandrake Honey **Mr B. M. Temple**

577 MRS P. A. TETLEY, Cranleigh

Postal: **Norley Farm, Horsham Road, Cranleigh, Surrey, GU6 8EH.**
Phone: **(0483) 274013 FAX (0306) 79747**

1 **ARTIC CHIEF,** 9, b g Owen Anthony—Freezing Point **Mrs P. A. Tetley**
2 **COURAGEOUS CHARGER (USA),** 8, ch g Bold Bidder—Charger's Star (USA) **Mrs P. A. Tetley**
3 **LORD SOLENT,** 11, b g Smokey Rockett—Mill Court **Mrs P. A. Tetley**
4 **NICKNAVAR,** 5, ch g Raga Navarro (ITY)—Bay Girl **Mr Brian Tetley**

Amateur: Mr A Hickman (10-3).

578 MR D. T. THOM, Newmarket

Postal: **Harraton Court, Exning, Newmarket, Suffolk, CB8 7HQ.**
Phone: **OFFICE (0638) 77288 HOME (0638) 77675**

1 **ALL IS REVEALED,** 8, b g Welsh Pageant—Senorita Rugby (USA) **Mrs Irene Norman**
2 **BINGDON BUILDERS,** 6, br m Derrylin—Forini **Mr D. J. Rowland**
3 **BLICO,** 6, b g Miner's Lamp—Ethiopia **Mr N. Cabburn**
4 **EVER RECKLESS,** 4, ch f Crever—Gold Spangle **Mr B. P. Monkhouse**
5 **FRIENDLY COAST,** 4, b g Blakeney—Noreena **Mr Bob Honess**
6 **GRAND OCCASION,** 8, b m Great Nephew—All Hail **Mrs Alison Thom**
7 **HOPEA,** 4, ro f Drone (USA)—Hope So (USA) **Stanley C. Bass**
8 **JOPANINI,** 5, b g Homing—Honeybuzzard (FR) **Hodwell Group Plc**
9 **JUST GREAT,** 4, br g Simply Great (FR)—Bourton Downs **Mr Jack Ashurst**
10 **NORTHWOLD STAR (USA),** 4, br f Monteverdi—Its A Romp **Mr T. M. Jennings**

THREE-YEAR-OLDS

11 **CLWYD LODGE,** b g Blakeney—High Caraval **P. & D. Leisure (Clwyd) Ltd**
12 **DEAR OLD GIRL,** gr f Carwhite—Curfew **Mr J. Perry (Syndicate)**
13 **MEDITATE,** b f Red Sunset—Time For Thought **Mr D. T. Thom**
14 **PREMIER LADY,** b f Red Sunset—Be A Dancer **Mr T. M. Jennings**
15 **SHORT ENCOUNTER,** b g Blakeney—Double Stitch **Mr P. L. E. Baxter**
16 B f Superlative—Spin Dry **Mr John Livock**
17 **THREE JAYS,** b c Blakeney—Photo Flash **Mr John Griffiths**
18 **WALKERN WITCH,** b f Dunbeath (USA)—Emblazon **Mr J. M. Dyson**
19 **WYNS VISION,** br f Vision (USA)—First Round **Hodwell Group Plc.**

TWO-YEAR-OLDS

20 Gr f 29/4 Norwick (USA)—Belle (DEN) (Comedy Star (USA)) **Mr T. M. Jennings**
21 **DASHING APRIL,** b f 8/4 Daring March—Ritruda (Roi Dagobert) **Mrs J. E. Copp and Partners**
22 **FINAL BOUT,** br f 13/4 Final Straw—Bourton Downs (Philip of Spain) **Mr T. M. Jennings**
23 B f 10/4 Montekin—Gay Barbarella (Gay Fandango (USA)) **Mr T. M. Jennings**
24 **INDEPENDENT AIR,** gr c 25/6 Elegant Air—Tranquility Base (Roan Rocket) **Mrs J. E. Copp and Partners**
25 **JETPET,** b c 31/3 Tina's Pet—Spinnaker Lady (Windjammer (USA)) **Mr B. P. Monkhouse**
26 **WATERMILL GIRL,** b f 13/5 Blakeney—Absurd (Absalom) **Mr T. M. Jennings**
27 **YES,** b f 27/1 Blakeney—Arrapata (Thatching) **Mr D. T. Thom**

Other Owners: Mr B. Gower, Mrs L. Gower, Mrs P. Hamilton, Mr Alastair Hodge, Mr D. Shah, Mr John Wills.

Jockey (NH): D Murphy.

579 MR J. D. THOMAS, Cowbridge

Postal: **Plwcca Dafydd Farm, Pendoylan, Cowbridge, S. Glamorgan, Wales.**
Phone: **OFFICE (0446) 760861 HOME (0446) 760815**

1 **CRYSTAL BALL,** 6, b g Formidable (USA)—Clouded Vision **Terry Price and Partners**
2 **DESERT LOMOND,** 5, b g Lomond (USA)—Lighted Lamp (USA) **Mrs Madeline Burgin**
3 **EVERMETT,** 4, ch g Milford—Myna Tyna **Mrs Madeline Burgin**
4 **FANNY'S YOUR AUNT,** 5, b m Great Nephew—Sweet And Lovely **Mrs C. Norris**
5 **FIRST WHIP,** 4, ch g Dublin Taxi—Whip Finish **Mrs Madeline Burgin**
6 **GWENNI,** 4, gr f Gwynfi Ni—Tanwen **Mr Wyn R. Griffiths**
7 **INDIAN SOVEREIGN,** 6, br g Indian King (USA)—Sovereign Dona **Ken Richards**
8 **JAPLING,** 12, gr g Brittany—Dalcius **Mrs J. A. Thomas**
9 **KING OF THE RING,** 5, b g Rusticaro (FR)—Coumfea **Mrs Madeline Burgin**
10 **MARTIN THOMAS,** 7, br g Auction Ring (USA)—Canelle
11 **MY RATBAG,** 5, ch m Main Reef—Trina's Girl **Mrs Madeline Burgin**
12 **SIMON'S SONG,** 4, b c Reesh—Queen Swallow **Mr J. D. Thomas**

MR J. D. THOMAS—continued

13 **SOLAR MASTER,** 6, b g Old Lucky—Space Miss **Mr P. M. Rich**
14 **TEMPERABLE,** 6, ch g Touching Wood (USA)—On Demand **Mr P. M. Rich**
15 **TENOFUS,** 5, ch g Crofter (USA)—Valley of Diamonds **Mr D. Powell**
16 **ZEPAGAS,** 4, b c Gorytus (USA)—Wampum **Mr J. D. Thomas**

Other Owners: W. Adams, G. Roberts, Mr P. D. Stephenson, P. Thomas.

Amateur: Mr T Jones (10-7).

580 MR R. THOMPSON, Grantham

Postal: **The Racing Stables, Potters Hill, Castle Bytham, Grantham, Lincolnshire.**
Phone: **STABLES/OFFICE (0780) 410812**

1 **BEATT'YS LAD,** 6, gr g Cawston's Clown—Donallan **Mr W. G. Wright**
2 **BORUFUS,** 4, b g Sunley Builds—Song of Pride **Mr N. P. Coley**
3 **BREEZY SAILOR,** 4, ch g Tumble Wind (USA)—Bouganville **Mr Sydney Mason**
4 **BRIGLEN,** 5, b m Swing Easy (USA)—Blou Hemel **Mr B. Yule**
5 **CAPTAIN'S BIDD,** 10, ch g Captain James—Muffet **Mr R. Ryan**
6 **FRED FOR FUN,** 4, b g Crofthall—Jolly Sweet **Mr Shane Snelling**
7 **KING OF SAILORS,** 6, br g King of Spain—Found At Sea (USA) **Mr Richard Halling**
8 **NORTHERN RULER,** 8, br g Rolfe (USA)—Sanandrea **Mr R. R. H. Whiting**
9 **POLYNIXOS,** 4, b g Raga Navarro (ITY)—Whistler's Princess **Mr Colin Jones**
10 **SAILOR'S TALES,** 7, b g Double Form—Petalca (USA) **Mrs Marion Thompson**
11 **TARTAR TUDOR,** 9, b g Mister Tudor—Tartarbee **Mr Richard Halling**
12 **WELSH FLUTE,** 4, b f Welsh Captain—Spanish Flute **Mr R. Ryan**

THREE-YEAR-OLDS

13 Ch g Kirchner—Jolly Sweet **Mr Sydney Mason**
14 **MISS KELLYBELL,** ch f Kirchner—California Split **Mr John J. Smith (Nottingham)**
15 **NICNATLOU,** ch f Van Der Linden (FR)—Double Pebble **Mr T. A. Waldrom**
16 **O'BERON'S DAUGHTER,** b f Fairy King (USA)—Precocious Angel **Mr R. Thompson**
17 **ORATEL FLYER,** gr c Kirchner—Hyperion Princess **Mrs Marion Thompson**

TWO-YEAR-OLDS

18 B f 14/1 Fairy King (USA)—Grace de Bois (Tap On Wood) **Mr W. G. Wright and Partners**
19 **GREENSIDE,** b f 3/5 Hotfoot—Akola (Hard Tack) **Mr R. Thompson**
20 Br f 23/4 Goldhills Pride—Lucy Brotherton (Pieces of Eight) **Mr R. Thompson**
21 B c 11/3 Myjinski (USA)—Song of Pride (Goldhills Pride) **Mr R. Thompson**

Other Owners: J. Delahunt, A. Macaley, Mr Michael F. Maguire, Mr Peter Monaghan, Oratel Racing Circle.

Jockey (Flat): W Carson (w.a.).

Jockey (NH): Martin Brennan (w.a.).

Apprentice: Thomas Ashley.

581 MR RONALD THOMPSON, Doncaster

Postal: **No 2 Bungalow, Haggswood Racing Stable, Stainforth, Doncaster, S. Yorkshire.**
Phone: **(0302) 845904**

1 **ABHA GUYA,** 7, b g Over The River (FR)—Peg's Guya Guya **Haggs Wood Racing Club Ltd**
2 **BOLD GAMBLE,** 4, ch g Bold Owl—Subtle Queen **Mr J. Billings**
3 **ENTERPRISE PRINCE,** 4, b g Lucky Wednesday—Avona **Mr E. H. Lunness**
4 **FAITHFULL,** 4, b f Skyliner—Windsagale **Haggs Wood Racing Club Ltd**
5 **FLORAFORD,** 4, b g Stanford—Floraventure **Haggs Wood Racing Club Ltd**
6 **HELEN BOY,** 7, b g Swing Easy (USA)—Tassel **South Yorkshire Pneumatics Ltd**
7 **HOT TAN,** 4, ch f Hotfoot—Tanara **Mr A. G. Watson**
8 **ORIENTAL EXPRESS,** 7, b g Whitstead—Miss Argyle **Mr A. G. Watson**
9 **OUR GINGER,** 6, ch m Le Johnstan—Summersoon **Haggs Wood Racing Club Ltd**
10 **OXFORD PLACE,** 6, br g Derrylin—Garden Party **Haggs Wood Racing Club Ltd**
11 **ROCK PULSE,** 4, ch g Ballad Rock—Muscadina **Haggs Wood Racing Club Ltd**
12 **SOUTH STACK,** 4, b g Daring March—Lady Henham **Mr A. G. Watson**
13 **SPENT FORCE,** 5, gr g Mummy's Pet—Tamer Grange **Mr Ronald Thompson**
14 **TIGER TIGER,** 5, ch g Enchantment—Fleur d'Amour **Haggs Wood Racing Club Ltd**
15 **TRAFALGAR BLUE,** 10, ch g Tug of War—Arcticanute **Mr Jack Faulkner**
16 **WELSH GUARD,** 8, br g Welsh Pageant—Mariinsky **Haggs Wood Racing Club Ltd**
17 **WENTBRIDGE GIRL,** 4, gr f Petong—Naughty Party **Mr K. Morrell**

THREE-YEAR-OLDS

18 **AYODESSA,** b f Lochnager—Melody Song **Mrs B. D. Georgiou**
19 **GREAT SERVICE,** ch c Vaigly Great—Janlarmar **Mr J. T. Hunt**
20 **MYLORDMAYOR,** ch g Move Off—Sharenka **Mr P. Roberts**
21 **SHEEN CLEEN LAD,** ch c On Your Mark—Mishcasu **Sheen Cleen Ltd**
22 **WHAT HAPPENS NEXT,** ch c Lucky Wednesday—Delayed Action **Mrs P. A. Barrett**
23 **YUKOSAN,** ch f Absalom—K-Sera **Mr Ronald Thompson**

TWO-YEAR-OLDS

24 B c Bold Owl—Kareela (FR) (Deep Diver)
25 Ch c Domynsky—Melody Song (Saintly Song)
26 B c Faustus (USA)—Solo Singer (Song)
27 Ch c Aragon—Sun Lamp (Pall Mall)
28 **WATTO (IRE),** b c Mazaad—Jolie Brise (Tumble Wind (USA)) **Wentdale Con**

Other Owners: Mrs P. Baker, Mr K. Roberts.

Jockey (Flat): R P Elliott (7-12, w.a.).

Conditional: Marin Lees.

582 MR A. M. THOMSON, Greenlaw

Postal: **Lambden Burn, Greenlaw, Duns, Berwickshire, TD10 6UN.**
Phone: **GREENLAW (03616) 514**

1 **BENGHAZI,** 6, b br g Politico (USA)—Numerous **Mr A. M. Thomson**
2 **CALEDONIAN LAD,** 5, b g Cragador—Carriemear **Mrs B. K. Thomson**
3 **MACMURPHY,** 5, ch g Deep Run—Millymeeta **Mr D. M. Thomson**
4 **WILLOW WOOD,** 9, gr m Precipice Wood—Silk Willoughby **Mrs B. K. Thomson**

Amateur: Mrs B Thomson (10-0).

583 MRS D. THOMSON, Milnathort

Postal: **Tillyrie House, Milnathort, Kinross-shire, KY13 7RW.**
Phone: **(0577) 63418**

1 **TYCOON MOON,** 9, b m Tycoon II—Moonbreaker **Mrs Dorothy Thomson**

THREE-YEAR-OLDS

2 Ch f Nearly A Hand—Moonbreaker

Jockey (NH): Brian Storey (10-0).

Amateur: Mr David Mactaggart (10-0).

584 MR H. THOMSON JONES, Newmarket

Postal: **Green Lodge, The Severals, Newmarket, Suffolk, CB8 7BS.**
Phone: **NEWMARKET (0638) 664884 OR 663640 FAX (0638) 660885**

1 **ALJARIH (USA),** 4, b c Nijinsky (CAN)—Love Words (USA) **Mr Hamdan Al-Maktoum**
2 **ANNAF (USA),** 4, b c Topsider (USA)—Kawkeb (USA) **Mr Hamdan Al-Maktoum**
3 **ASHAL,** 4, b c Touching Wood (USA)—Johara (USA) **Mr Hamdan Al-Maktoum**
4 **INAAD,** 6, b h Mill Reef (USA)—Rambling Rose **Mr Hamdan Al-Maktoum**
5 **JURRAN,** 5, ro g Formidable (USA)—Queen's Counsellor **Mr Hamdan Al-Maktoum**
6 **LUZUM,** 6, ch h Touching Wood (USA)—Velvet Habit **Mr Hamdan Al-Maktoum**
7 **POLEMOS,** 6, ch h Formidable (USA)—Polemia (USA) **Mr Hamdan Al-Maktoum**
8 **PONTIN BOY,** 11, b g Prince Tenderfoot (USA)—Buenaventura II **Mr H. Thomson Jones**

THREE-YEAR-OLDS

9 **ABS (USA),** b c Nureyev (USA)—Reyah **Mr Hamdan Al-Maktoum**
10 **ALHAWRAH (USA),** b f Danzig (USA)—Khwlah (USA) **Mr Hamdan Al-Maktoum**
11 **ALMUINJJID (USA),** ch c Blushing Groom (FR)—Herb Wine (USA) **Mr Hamdan Al-Maktoum**
12 **AQIQ,** b c Shareef Dancer (USA)—Miss Gris (USA) **Mr Hamdan Al-Maktoum**
13 **DAARIK,** b c Diesis—Bay Street **Mr Hamdan Al-Maktoum**
14 **DOULAB'S IMAGE,** ch c Doulab (USA)—Haneena **Mr Hadi Al-Tajir**
15 **ELMAFTUN,** b c Rainbow Quest (USA)—Shoot Clear **Mr Hamdan Al-Maktoum**
16 **ELMAJARRAH (CAN),** ch f Caro—Play Around Honey (USA) **Mr Hamdan Al-Maktoum**
17 **FAYAFI,** b f Top Ville—Muznah **Mr Hamdan Al-Maktoum**
18 **FLOWER GIRL,** ch f Pharly (FR)—Dancing Meg (USA) **Mr W. J. Gredley**
19 **HAFHAFAH,** b f Shirley Heights—Shurooq (USA) **Mr Hamdan Al-Maktoum**
20 **HAITHAM,** b c Wassl—Balqis (USA) **Mr Hamdan Al-Maktoum**
21 **HASBAH,** ch f Kris—Al Bahathri (USA) **Mr Hamdan Al-Maktoum**
22 **HIDDEN (USA),** ch f Secreto (USA)—Shark Song **Mrs H. T. Jones**
23 **HIMMAH (USA),** b f Habitat—Charmie Carmie (USA) **Mr Hamdan Al-Maktoum**
24 **ITTISAAL,** b br f Caerleon (USA)—House Tie **Mr Hamdan Al-Maktoum**
25 **JATHIBIYAH (USA),** b f Nureyev (USA)—Carefully Hidden (USA) **Mr Hamdan Al-Maktoum**
26 **KADIM (USA),** ch c Diesis—Alghuzaylah **Mr Hamdan Al-Maktoum**
27 **KAHIN,** br c Diesis—Kawkeb (USA) **Mr Hamdan Al-Maktoum**
28 **KASAYID,** b c Niniski (USA)—Raabihah **Mr Hamdan Al-Maktoum**
29 **NAFHAAT (USA),** ch f Roberto (USA)—Distant Horizon (USA) **Mr Hamdan Al-Maktoum**
30 **QATHIF (USA),** b c Riverman (USA)—Al Bayan (USA) **Mr Hamdan Al-Maktoum**
31 **RA'A (USA),** ch f Diesis—Shicklah (USA) **Mr Hamdan Al-Maktoum**
32 **SAWAKI,** br f Song—Roxy Hart **Mr Hamdan Al-Maktoum**
33 **TATWIJ (USA),** b f Topsider (USA)—Infantes (USA) **Mr Hamdan Al-Maktoum**
34 **THUBUT (USA),** b f Tank's Prospect (USA)—Social Lesson (USA) **Mr Hamdan Al-Maktoum**

MR H. THOMSON JONES—continued

TWO-YEAR-OLDS

35 **ALAMIR (USA),** b c 8/2 Shadeed (USA)—Glamour Girl (FR) (Riverman (USA)) **Mr Hadi Al-Tajir**
36 **ALMAASEH (IRE),** b f 10/2 Dancing Brave (USA)—
Al Bahathri (USA) (Blushing Groom (FR)) **Mr Hamdan Al-Maktoum**
37 **ASSARAAYIR,** ch f 5/2 Kris—Al Sylah (Nureyev (USA)) **Mr Hamdan Al-Maktoum**
38 **BAATISH (USA),** b c 4/2 Slew O'Gold (USA)—
Shukey (USA) (Key To The Mint (USA)) **Mr Hamdan Al-Maktoum**
39 **ELFASLAH (IRE),** b f 1/3 Green Desert (USA)—Fair of The Furze (Ela-Mana-Mou) **Mr Hamdan Al-Maktoum**
40 **FITAHL (USA),** br c 28/1 Chief's Crown (USA)—Love's Dream (FR) (Rheingold) **Mr Hamdan Al-Maktoum**
41 **FRAAR (USA),** b c 21/3 Topsider (USA)—
Alchaasibiyeh (USA) (Seattle Slew (USA)) **Mr Hamdan Al-Maktoum**
42 **FUTUH (USA),** gr f 18/2 Diesis—Hardship (USA) (Drone (USA)) **Mr Hamdan Al-Maktoum**
43 **HTHAAL (USA),** br c 7/1 Caro—Endurable Heights (USA) (Graustark (USA)) **Mr Hamdan Al-Maktoum**
44 **ISHAARAH (IRE),** b f 20/2 Top Ville—Nadirah (Mill Reef (USA)) **Mr Hamdan Al-Maktoum**
45 **JACKSON FLINT,** b c 26/1 Nishapour (FR)—Scamperdale (French Beige) **Mrs H. T. Jones**
46 **JANBIYA (IRE),** ch f 31/3 Kris—Spark of Fire (Run The Gantlet (USA)) **Mr Hamdan Al-Maktoum**
47 **JAZILAH (FR),** b br c 29/2 Persian Bold—Muznah (Royal And Regal (USA)) **Mr Hamdan Al-Maktoum**
48 **JURZ (IRE),** b c 1/6 Pennine Walk—Kawkeb (USA) (Vaguely Noble) **Mr Hamdan Al-Maktoum**
49 **KAHHAL (IRE),** gr f 27/4 Doulab (USA)—Queen's Counsellor (Kalamoun) **Mr Hamdan Al-Maktoum**
50 **LIBK,** b c 16/2 Kalaglow—Balqis (USA) (Advocator (USA)) **Mr Hamdan Al-Maktoum**
51 **MADRAJ (IRE),** b br c 15/3 Double Schwartz—
Poka Poka (FR) (King of Macedon) **Mr Hamdan Al-Maktoum**
52 **MARAATIB (IRE),** b f 15/5 Green Desert (USA)—Shurooq (USA) (Affirmed (USA)) **Mr Hamdan Al-Maktoum**
53 **MASAAWM,** ch c 12/2 Kris—Tarib (Habitat) **Mr Hamdan Al-Maktoum**
54 **MATHKURH (USA),** b br f 24/3 Riverman (USA)—Manal (FR) (Luthier (FR)) **Mr Hamdan Al-Maktoum**
55 **MOUSAIHA (USA),** b f 19/3 Shadeed (USA)—Chain (USA) (Herbager) **Mr Hamdan Al-Maktoum**
56 **MRS THATCHER,** br f 13/2 Law Society (USA)—Hardihostess (Be My Guest (USA)) **Mr W. J. Gredley**
57 **MU-ARRIK,** b br c 13/3 Aragon—Maravilla (Mandrake Major) **Mr Hamdan Al-Maktoum**
58 **MULAWIH (USA),** b c 3/4 Secreto (USA)—
'n Everything Nice (USA) (Damascus (USA)) **Mr Hamdan Al-Maktoum**
59 **MUSAWWM (USA),** ch c 10/3 Blushing Groom (FR)—
Heavenly Breeze (USA) (Lyphard (USA)) **Mr Hamdan Al-Maktoum**
60 **MUTAMARRID,** br c 11/2 Sure Blade (USA)—Raabihah (Shirley Heights) **Mr Hamdan Al-Maktoum**
61 **RAWAABE (USA),** ch f 30/3 Nureyev (USA)—Passerine (USA) (Dr Fager (USA)) **Mr Hamdan Al-Maktoum**
62 **RAZIK (IRE),** b c 10/2 Last Tycoon—Warm December (He Loves Me) **Mr Hamdan Al-Maktoum**
63 **SHAARID (USA),** b c 26/1 El Gran Senor (USA)—
Summer Silence (USA) (Stop The Music (USA)) **Mr Hamdan Al-Maktoum**
64 **SHABBABA (USA),** ch f 18/3 Arctic Tern (USA)—
Shicklah (USA) (The Minstrel (CAN)) **Mr Hamdan Al-Maktoum**
65 **THIBAAIN (USA),** b c 23/3 El Gran Senor (USA)—
Catherine's Bet (USA) (Grey Dawn II) **Mr Hamdan Al-Maktoum**
66 **WISH OF LUCK (USA),** ch f 5/2 Diesis—Kesar Queen (USA) (Nashua (USA)) **Mr Hadi Al-Tajir**
67 **ZAHR (IRE),** b br f 10/2 Touching Wood (USA)—
Haraabah (USA) (Topsider (USA)) **Mr Hamdan Al-Maktoum**
68 **ZUHAL,** b f 16/2 Busted—Divine Thought (Javelot) **Mr Hamdan Al-Maktoum**

Jockeys (Flat): N Carlisle (7-7), R Hills (8-0).

Apprentice: L McWilliam (8-0).

MR T. THOMSON JONES, Lambourn

The Team for the above trainer can be found in the Stop Press.

Weekend winners begin with Raceform Handicap Book every Thursday
56 Page Issue
Every Thursday
Raceform
HANDICAP BOOK
ADVANCE RACECARDS FOR THE WEEKEND
WITH ALL THE AIDS TO HELP YOU WIN
THE LIVELIEST RACING WEEKLY
INSIDE
• FORM BOOK PULL OUT
• REFLECTIONS ON RUNNING
• RACING NEWS FROM THE TOP WRITERS
• POOLS AND GREYHOUNDS
• Start checking out the weekend racecards on Thursday with Raceform Handicap Book.
• Complete information on every runner.
• Expert previews on all meetings.
• Collect the Weekly form-book pull-outs.
There is a full index every week.
• Latest news from Newmarket, Epsom, Ireland and many more.
It's all this and so much more which gives Raceform Handicap Book its winning image. So order your copy from your newsagent now - and make next Saturday your most successful yet.
The best informed weekly racing newspaper
RACEFORM HANDICAP BOOK
EVERY THURSDAY
95p

585 MISS J. THORNE, Bridgwater

Postal: **Lilstock Farm, Kilve, Bridgwater, Somerset, TA5 1SU.**
Phone: **OFFICE HOLFORD (0278 74) 588 HOME HOLFORD (0278 74) 457**

1 **ARCTIC BARON,** 5, b g Baron Blakeney—Learctic **Mr C. Raymond**
2 **ARCTIC ELLE,** 4, gr f Baron Blakeney—Learctic **Mr C. Raymond**
3 **BALLYANTO,** 5, b g Lepanto (GER)—Ballyarctic **Mr J. Chard**
4 **CAPTAIN DIMITRIS,** 5, ch h Dubassoff (USA)—Proud Gipsy **Mr G. Redwood**
5 **DISCREET CHARM,** 5, ch m Moorestyle—La Meme **Mr J. Chard**
6 **FEROCIOUS KNIGHT (USA),** 11, b g Fearless Knight—Fallaha's Love (USA) **Miss Jacqui Thorne**
7 **RECOLLECT,** 8, b g Vaigly Great—Archaic **Mrs S. J. Thorne**
8 **SALAMART,** 7, br g Aban—Hespera **Mr M. C. Lawrence**
9 **SAUCY MINSTREL,** 6, b m Black Minstrel—Billeragh Girl **Mrs S. J. Thorne**

THREE-YEAR-OLDS

10 B f Baron Blakeney—Leartic **Mr C. Raymond**
11 Ch g Royal Match—Madame Rochas **Mr M. C. Lawrence and Miss S. Hiscox**

TWO-YEAR-OLDS

12 B f 13/5 Sulaafah (USA)—Madame Rochas (Midsummer Night II) **Mr M. C. Lawrence and Miss S. Hiscox**

Other Owners: Mrs A. V. Cheshire, D. W. Coombes, Mrs R. M. Crichton, Mac'S Garage (Weston) Ltd, Mrs A. Porteous, Mrs M. Raymond.

Jockey (NH): N J Dawe (10-0).

586 MR G. E. THORNER, Wantage

Postal: **Manor Farm, Letcombe Regis, Wantage, Oxon, OX12 9LD.**
Phone: **WANTAGE (02357) 3003**

1 **ALL INTENT (USA),** 8, b g Alleged (USA)—Dear Intent (USA) **Mr P. P. Byfield**
2 **BARTONDALE,** 5, br m Oats—Miss Boon **Mr S. Bishop**
3 **GENERALISE,** 8, ch g Young Generation—Miss Petard **J. Browne Construction Co Ltd**
4 **HAZY DANCER,** 4, b c Hays—Miami Dancer **Graham Thorner**
5 **HONEYWALL LAD,** 5, ch g Revlow—Honey Beam **Mr W. S. Ivens**
6 **MANHATTAN BEACH,** 6, b g Tepukei—Open House **Mr Keith Ogden**
7 **MISTRESS ROSS,** 7, b m Impecunious—Rostresse **Dr Jane Van Tilborg**
8 **SAM SHORROCK,** 8, b br g Vivadari—To Windward **Mr Keith Ogden**

THREE-YEAR-OLDS

9 **THE PORTSOY LOON,** b c Miami Springs—Glittering Gem **Brian Crossman**

Other Owners: Mr Dennis Chantry, Mr M. M. Kingsley, Mr Paul K. Lacy, Mrs G. W. Lugg.

Conditional: J Duffy.

587 MR C. W. THORNTON, Middleham

Postal: **Spigot Lodge, Middleham, Leyburn, N. Yorkshire.**
Phone: **(0969) 23350 LADS HOSTEL (0969) 22252 TELEX-58140**

1 **BARONY ISLE,** 9, b g Cagirama—Specific Day **Mr Michael D. Abrahams**
2 **BEN,** 4, ch g Seymour Hicks (FR)—Kirin **Mr Guy Reed**
3 **CHANTRY BARTLE,** 4, ch g Say Primula—Sallametti (USA) **Mrs J. J. Kirk Scott**

MR C. W. THORNTON—continued

4 **GREEN GORSE,** 10, br g Green Shoon—Gorteen **Mr S. Lycett Green**
5 **HOPPING AROUND,** 6, b g Prince Tenderfoot (USA)—Wurli **The Racegoers Club H. A. Owners Group**
6 **I'LL TAKE YOU HOME,** 4, b g Ile de Bourbon (USA)—Dancing Kathleen **Mr Guy Reed**
7 **NORTHUMBRIAN KING,** 4, b g Indian King (USA)—Tuna **Mr Norman Robinson**
8 **PANTOMIME PRINCE,** 7, b g Lepanto (GER)—Annie Louise **Mr P. A. D. Gargon**
9 **SECRET FRIEND,** 4, br g Relkino—Aunt Eva **Mrs Janet Pallister**
10 **TRIP TO THE MOON,** 4, b g Red Sunset—Mile By Mile **Mr Guy Reed**
11 **WHITE JASMIN,** 4, ch f Jalmood (USA)—Willowbed **Simon Brown**
12 **YOU'RE THE TOPS,** 4, b g Head For Heights—Relatively Sharp **Mr Guy Reed**

THREE-YEAR-OLDS

13 **ALBERT,** b c Kings Lake (USA)—Darine **Mr Guy Reed**
14 **BARRICADE,** b g Viking (USA)—Avebury Ring **Mr Guy Reed**
15 **BOLD RELATIVE,** ch g Superlative—Relko's Pride **Mr D. B. Dennison**
16 **BONANZA,** ch g Glenstal (USA)—Forliana **Mr Guy Reed**
17 **CALL RACECALL,** b g Reasonable (FR)—Miel **Racegoers Club Owners Group**
18 **RAGTIME COWBOY,** b g Indian King (USA)—F Sharp **Mr Guy Reed**
19 **STRAIGHTASANARROW,** ch g Siberian Express (USA)—Blue Queen **Mr Guy Reed**
20 **TOMAHAWK,** ch c Be My Guest (USA)—Siouan **Mr Guy Reed**
21 **TOUCH THE CLOUDS,** b f Precocious—Siouxsie **Mr Guy Reed**
22 **VALIANT VICAR,** b g Belfort (FR)—Shagra **Mr H. R. Vickers**
23 **WASHITA,** b f Valiyar—Ardneasken **Mr Guy Reed**
24 **WHITE CLOUD,** ro c Vaigly Great—Cheyenne **Mr Guy Reed**
25 **WILL,** gr g Tender King—Fine Flame **Mr Guy Reed**

TWO-YEAR-OLDS

26 **CHERRY DANCE,** ch f 26/2 Nordance (USA)—Cherry Picking (Queen's Hussar) **A. J. Wilson**
27 Gr c 22/4 Nishapour (FR)—Geoffrey's Sister (Sparkler) **Mr Guy Reed**
28 **PETITE AMIE,** gr f 21/3 Petoski—Amourette (Crowned Prince (USA)) **Mr S. Lycett Green**
29 Br f 12/5 Nomination—Rebecca (Quorum) **E. H. Covell**
30 **WILL O'THE WISP,** b c 25/5 Trojan Fen—Heavenly Spark (Habitat) **G. H. Brittan**

Other Owners: Mr Paul Alster, Mr A. Claypole, Mr D. Coates, Mr J. Dent, Mrs Mary Dodds, Miss L. M. Gold, Mr M. Hayler, Dr Roy Heylings, Mr W. P. McKeown, Mr P. Sadler, Mrs Jo Anne Storre, Mr C. J. Taylor, Mr A. Wells, Mr R. Woodhead.

Jockey (Flat): J Bleasdale (8-0).

Jockey (NH): D Wilkinson (10-0).

588 MR C. TINKLER, Malton

Postal: **The Mews House, Musley Bank Stud, Malton, N. Yorkshire, YO17 0TD.**
Phone: **MALTON (0653) 695981 FAX (0653) 600241**

1 **BAWNRUADH,** 5, ch g Wrens Hill—Old Town Princess VI **T. Dyer**
2 **BLUE CHATEAU,** 4, ch g Longleat (USA)—La Sinope (FR) **Mr I. B. Littlewood**
3 **GAELIC ISSUE,** 5, ch h Lord Gayle (USA)—Tissue Paper **Mrs G. Simpson**
4 **GOTHIC FORD,** 6, b g Stanford—Gothic Lady **Mrs C. M. Tinkler**
5 **HOGAN'S RUN,** 5, br h Tender King—Moment To Remember (USA) **Mrs M. Anderson**
6 **J CHEEVER LOOPHOLE,** 5, gr g King of Spain—Sally's Silver **Mr Steven Astaire**
7 **LUCKY CONQUEROR,** 4, ch c On Your Mark—Rekolette **T. Dyer**
8 **MIGHTY GLOW,** 6, gr g Kalaglow—Faridetta **Mrs Anne Rubin**
9 **MORE ICE,** 4, b f Runnett—Spoons **T. Dyer**
10 **NORMHURST,** 4, ch g Lucky Wednesday—Bronze Princess **Mrs G. Simpson**
11 **TIMSOLO,** 7, ch g Remainder Man—Miss Tehran **Mr T. Hainsworth**
12 **TOPEKA EXPRESS (USA),** 7, b g Topsider (USA)—Watch Out **Mrs C. M. Tinkler**
13 **WALTZ ON AIR,** 4, b f Doc Marten—Young Romance **Mrs C. M. Tinkler**

MR C. TINKLER—continued

THREE-YEAR-OLDS

14 **BANTON LOCH,** br g Lochnager—Balgownie **Mr R. Young**
15 **BEACHY GLEN,** b c Glenstal (USA)—Ampersand (USA) **E. R. Edmonds**
16 **BOLD STREET BLUES,** b c Bold Owl—Basin Street **Mr P. D. Savill**
17 **BURSLEM BEAU,** gr g Burslem—Divine Apsara **Miss C. Mitchell**
18 **CORPORATE MEMBER,** ch g Exhibitioner—Sciambola **Mr J. A. Birch**
19 **HYDEONIAN,** ch g Viking (USA)—Precious Lady **Hyde Sporting Promotions Limited**
20 **LUSTY RON,** ch c Sallust—Roya **W. Bulmer**
21 **MISS ABBI,** b f Jalmood (USA)—The Shrew **Mr T. Hainsworth**
22 **NEEDS MUST,** gr c Another Realm—Miss Monte Carlo **Mr G. Shiel**
23 **PAGO,** ch c Sallust—Fire Dance (FR) **Mr J. J. Mulligan**
24 **TROJAN EXCEL,** b f Trojan Fen—War Ballad (FR) **Mrs C. M. Tinkler**
25 **WATTLE SYKE,** ch g King Persian—Sandforgold **Mr G. C. Morley**
26 **WILD DANCER,** br g Gorytus (USA)—Rosserk **G. Dyson**

TWO-YEAR-OLDS

27 **AMARASH,** b c 19/2 Good Times (ITY)—Mistress Bowen (Owen Anthony) **S. Holt**
28 **BLASTER BINS,** b c 29/4 Vision (USA)—Trail (Thatch (USA)) **Mr P. D. Savill**
29 **HAXBY LAD,** gr c 17/1 Faustus (USA)—Vignargenta (Absalom) **W. Granger**
30 B c 2/3 Glenstal (USA)—Hotbee (Hotfoot) **Miss T. Mitchell**
31 **JINGLEBY JIM,** b c 19/2 Glenstal (USA)—Miss Noora (Ahonoora) **A. H. Jackson**
32 **JUST PIP,** b c 8/2 Petorius—Swift Verdict (My Swallow) **J. Barber**
33 Gr c 15/4 Primo Dominie—Katysue (King's Leap) **Miss T. Mitchell**
34 **KAYEMBEE,** b c 16/4 Trojan Fen—By Surprise (Young Generation) **K. M. Barker**
35 Ch c 19/5 Montekin—Maiden's Dance (Hotfoot) **R. J. Montague**
36 **MANTON MEMORIES,** bl c 2/4 Uncle Pokey—Carnation (Runnymede) **Mrs M. Pett**
37 Ch c 23/5 Precocious—Midaan (Sallust) **Mrs C. M. Tinkler**
38 **MINSTER TIMES,** ch c 4/4 Good Times (ITY)—Gunnera (Royal Gunner (USA)) **W. Bulmer**
39 **POD'S DAUGHTER,** b f 5/3 Tender King—Make Your Bid (Auction Ring (USA)) **Mrs H. Rowbottom**
40 **PRELECTOR,** bl c 12/4 Primo Dominie—Pearl Wedding (Gulf Pearl) **A. G. Black**
41 **SATANIC PRINCE,** b c 6/2 Anita's Prince—Lady Ingrid (Taufan (USA)) **C. Monty**
42 B f 12/4 Claude Monet (USA)—Scilla (ITY) (Court Martial) **Prince Sultan**
43 Bl c 24/3 Uncle Pokey—Strath of Orchy (Lochnager) **D. Gorton**
44 B c 20/3 Fairy King (USA)—To Oneiro (Absalom) **M. Yiapatos**
45 **TRAMONTANA,** b c 7/2 Drumalis—Blunted (Sharpen Up) **A. G. Black**
46 **WALJON,** b c 20/5 Exhibitioner—Sanjana (GER) (Priamos (GER)) **W. Bulmer**
47 **WILD FLYER,** ch c 20/4 Double Schwartz—Magyar Melody (Prince Tenderfoot (USA)) **G. Dyson**
48 **WILD PROSPECT,** b c 29/5 Homing—Cappuccilli (Lorenzaccio) **G. Dyson**
49 **ZERMANSKY,** bl c 23/3 Camden Town—Middle Verde (USA) (Sham (USA)) **Mrs S. Brook**

Other Owners: Mr E. A. Brook, Mr David Cheetham, Mr G. Cockcroft, J. Croft, Equiform Nutrition Limited, Mr Ron Hart, Mr Michael Jackson, Mr J. D. Peet, Mr C. Ryan, Mr David Scott, Mr K. Westman, Tony S. K. Wong.

Jockeys (Flat): M Birch (8-3, w.a.), P Burke (7-7).

Jockey (NH): Richard Fahey.

Apprentice: Tracey Brown (8-0).

Lady Riders: Mrs S Brook, Mrs J Goulding.

589 MR N. TINKLER, Malton

Postal: **Woodland Stables, Langton, Malton, N. Yorkshire, YO17 9QR.**
Phone: **(065 385) 245 FAX (0653) 85542**

1 **ATHENS GATE (USA),** 6, ch h Lydian (FR)—Pago Miss (USA) **Mr Dave Douglas**
2 **BANK VIEW,** 5, ch g Crofter (USA)—Stony Ground **Date Bloodstock Ltd**
3 **BEAU ROLANDO,** 4, b g Teenoso (USA)—Fabulous Luba **Mr Neil McAndrews**
4 **BOLD TRY,** 5, ch g Try My Best (USA)—Persian Polly **Full Circle Thoroughbreds F Plc**
5 **CLEAVERS GATE,** 5, ch h Touching Wood (USA)—Thimblerigger **Langton Syndicate**
6 **CORN LILY,** 4, ch f Aragon—Ixia **Full Circle Thoroughbreds F Plc**
7 **CRIME PASSIONNEL (USA),** 5, b g Rich Cream (USA)—Fresh And Fancy **Mr Raymond Gomersall**
8 **DALE PARK,** 4, b c Kampala—Coshlea **Full Circle Thoroughbreds F Plc**
9 **DARKORJON,** 9, b g Whistling Top—Hildamay **Full Circle Thoroughbreds F Plc**
10 **DESERT EMPEROR,** 5, gr h Ahonoora—Silk Empress **Full Circle Thoroughbreds F Plc**
11 **ESTONIA,** 4, b f Kings Lake (USA)—Paddy's Joy **Full Circle Thoroughbreds F Plc**
12 **FAMILIAR SPIRIT,** 4, b c Pitskelly—Witch of Endor **Full Circle Thoroughbreds F Plc**
13 **FENFIRE,** 4, b f Trojan Fen—Unpanishad **Full Circle Thoroughbreds F Plc**
14 **FISHERMAN'S CROFT,** 4, b c Dunbeath (USA)—Russeting **Full Circle Thoroughbreds F Plc**
15 **GHADBBAAN,** 6, b h Kalaglow—Firework Party (USA) **Full Circle Thoroughbreds F Plc**
16 **GROOM STAR (USA),** 4, ch c Blushing Groom (FR)—Guiding Star (SWE) **Robinson Publications Limited**
17 **HERCLE (FR),** 4, b c Fabulous Dancer (USA)—L'Exception (FR) **Full Circle Thoroughbreds F Plc**
18 **JACK DWYER,** 6, br g Mr Fordette—Daraheen Gate **Langton Syndicate**
19 **KOSCIOSKO (USA),** 4, b c Arctic Tern (USA)—Ancient Jewel (USA) **Mr Raymond Gomersall**
20 **LADYKHADIJA,** 4, b f Nicholas Bill—Chenkynowa **A. B. Barrett**
21 **LOCALITY,** 5, b m Lochnager—Declamation **Don Enrico Incisa**
22 **LOGAMIMO,** 4, b c Lord Gayle—Miss Morgan **Peter Savill**
23 **LOTUS ISLAND,** 6, gr h Ile de Bourbon—Be Easy **Mike Hurst**
24 **MODESTINO (USA),** 4, b c Fappiano (USA)—Demitasse (USA) **Full Circle Thoroughbreds F Plc**
25 **MONANORE,** 13, ch g Prefairy—Mouskouri **Full Circle Thoroughbreds F Plc**
26 **NORQUAY (USA),** 5, ch g Arctic Tern (USA)—Godetia (USA) **Full Circle Thoroughbreds F Plc**
27 **NORTHERN BRAVE,** 4, ch c Mill Reef (USA)—Sharpina **Full Circle Thoroughbreds F Plc**
28 **PERSILLANT,** 6, b h Persian Bold—Gauloise **Mr Raymond Gomersall**
29 **PHILIP,** 8, b g Kala Shikari—Canteen Katie **Mr D. Marley**
30 **QUESTION OF DEGREE,** 4, b c Known Fact (USA)—Bernice Clare **Langton Syndicate**
31 **RACEY NASKRA (USA),** 4, b f Star de Naskra (USA)—Langness (USA) **Full Circle Thoroughbreds F Plc**
32 **RED ROSEIN,** 4, b f Red Sunset—Vain Deb **Mr A. C. Findlay**
33 **ROYAL BEQUEST (CAN),** 4, b c Mill Reef (USA)—Regal Heiress **Robinson Publications Limited**
34 **RUNUN,** 4, b c Sharpo—Silent Movie **David Stokes**
35 **SAYYURE (USA),** 4, b c Lydian (FR)—Periquito (USA) **Mr Brian Lovrey**
36 **SELF IMPROVEMENT (USA),** 4, b c Sharpen Up—Imaflash (USA) **Date Bloodstock Ltd**
37 **SHEILAS HILLCREST,** 4, b c Hotfoot—Be Honest **Full Circle Thoroughbreds F Plc**
38 **SMART PERFORMER,** 5, b g Formidable—Brilliant Rosa **Mr Raymond Gomersall**
39 **SUPER RELATIVE,** 4, b g Superlative—Breton's Sister **Mr Joe Jennings**
40 **TRANQUIL WATERS (USA),** 4, ch c Diesis—Ebbing Tide (USA) **Robinson Publications Limited**
41 **TWICE AS VAGUE,** 4, b c Two Davids (USA)—Vaguely Sensitive **Amy Lee Tinkler**
42 **WESSEX,** 8, b h Free State—Bonandra **Full Circle Thoroughbreds F Plc**
43 **YESICAN,** 4, gr c Kalaglow—Geoffrey's Sister **Robinson Publications Limited**

THREE-YEAR-OLDS

44 **ALARCO,** b c Alzao—Raashideah **Peter Savill**
45 **DOMRUN,** b f Runnett—Dominion Blue **Mr Y. Spink**
46 **ELLA STREET,** b f King of Spain—More Fun **Jim Hacking**
47 **HIGHER HAMILL,** b c Taufan—Judys Pinch **Date Bloodstock Ltd**
48 **LINDA'S HILLCREST,** b f Aragon—Cavalier's Blush **Mr Dave Douglas**
49 **LUCK O' THE IRISH,** ch g Sallust—Sweet Hostess **A. Booth**
50 **PRECELLA THE HUN,** b f Precocious—Amerella **Neill Jackson**
51 **ROYAL MAC,** br c Pas de Seul—Royal Wolff **Mr J. McAllister**
52 **SO KNOWLEDGEABLE,** b f Night Shift—Sister Hannah **P. W. Bradbury**
53 **TENDERLOIN,** b g Tender King—Samkhya **Full Circle Thoroughbreds F Plc**
54 **TITE SPOT,** ch f Muscatite—Luan Causca **Mrs Christine Cawley**
55 **VAIN PRINCE,** b g Sandhurst Prince—Vain Deb **Mr A. C. Findlay**

MR N. TINKLER—continued

TWO-YEAR-OLDS

56 B c Nicholas Bill—Barrie Baby (Import) **Don Enrico Incisa**
57 **BURSLEM BELLE,** b f Burslem—Hy Carol (High Hat) **D. B. White**
58 B g King of Spain—La Bambola (Be Friendly) **Full Circle Thoroughbreds F Plc**
59 B f Another Realm—Lady Killane (Reform)
60 **LIBEL ACTION (IRE),** b f Ahonoora—Verette (Posse) **A. Booth**
61 **NO HARD FEELINGS (IRE),** b f Alzao (USA)—Coshlea (Red Alert) **Peter Savill**
62 B c Green Ruby (USA)—Pearl Pet (Mummy's Pet) **Sheila Oakes**
63 Ch c Red Sunset—Pink Rose (Ragusa)
64 Br f Belfort (FR)—Rainbow Vision (Prince Tenderfoot) **Full Circle Thoroughbreds F Plc**
65 B c Glow (USA)—Red Val (Red God) **Date Bloodstock Ltd**
66 Gr f Fayruz—Regency Girl (Right Boy)
67 B f Mandrake Major—Rock Psalm (Saintly Song)
68 B c Red Sunset—Shangara (Credo) **Sheila Oakes**
69 B c Taufan (USA)—Shopping (FR) (Sheshoon)
70 Gr f Belfort (FR)—Tresanna (Treboro (USA))

Jockey (Flat): Kim Tinkler (7-7).

Jockey (NH): Graham McCourt (10-5, w.a.).

Conditional: Dermot Sullivan (9-7).

590 MR W. H. TINNING, Harrogate

Postal: **Lund Head Farm, Kirkby Overblow, Harrogate, N. Yorkshire, HG31 1HY.**
Phone: **(0532) 886260**

1 **MOORLANDER,** 5, b g River Knight (FR)—Lady Perrin **Mrs J. A. Tinning**
2 **WESTERN REVIVAL,** 8, ch g Alias Smith (USA)—Resurgence **Mr W. H. Tinning**

Jockey (NH): K Jones (10-2).

591 MR J. A. R. TOLLER, Newmarket

Postal: **Wellbottom Lodge, Moulton Paddocks, Bury Road, Newmarket, Suffolk.**
Phone: **(0638) 668503**

1 **ANNABRIANNA,** 4, ch f Night Shift (USA)—Aviceda **Mr B. S. McElney**
2 **DRY POINT,** 4, ch c Sharpo—X-Data **Duke of Devonshire**
3 **LOW DALBY,** 4, ch f Longleat (USA)—Bridestones **Mr Alan Gibson**
4 **SKIRBECK,** 4, b c Ahonoora—Grecian Sky **Mrs Charles Vere Nicoll**
5 **SUGEMAR,** 4, ch c Young Generation—Jade Ring **Mr B. S. McElney**

THREE-YEAR-OLDS

6 **AGNES DODD,** b f Homing—Mosso **Miss U. D. Toller**
7 **ALWAYS REMEMBER,** b c Town And Country—Try To Remember **Mr Derek R. Price**
8 **CATBALLOU,** b f Tina's Pet—Blue Brocade **Mr Jonathan Bevan**
9 **EMPEROR FOUNTAIN,** b c Chief Singer—Set Sail **Duke of Devonshire**
10 **FOXTROT OSCAR,** b c Mummy's Game—Glint of Silver **Foxtrot Restaurants Ltd**
11 **GRACE O'MALLEY,** ch f Yashgan—Perestrella
12 **INTO THE FUTURE,** b g Mummy's Game—Valley Farm **Mr B. V. Sangster**
13 **LORD OF THE FIELD,** b c Jalmood (USA)—Star Face **Duke of Devonshire**
14 **MAY BE BOLD,** b f Never So Bold—Plum Run (USA) **Mr Derek R. Price**
15 **STROBE LIGHT,** b c Electric—Sequin Lady **A. Morrison**

MR J. A. R. TOLLER—continued

TWO-YEAR-OLDS

16 **BENNO,** ch c Chief Singer—Swan Ann (My Swanee) **Duke of Devonshire**
17 **FELIM BLWM,** b c Sayf El Arab (USA)—Dawn Loch (USA) (Grey Dawn II) **Lord Mostyn**
18 **SHINE ON BRIGHTLY (USA),** b f Majestic Light (USA)—
Golden Secretariat (USA) (Secretariat (USA)) **C. Wright**

Other Owners: Lady Aitken, Mr J. W. Becher, Mr A. N. C. Bengough, Colonel Sir Piers Bengough, Mr A. K. Collins, Mr Harry R. D. McCalmont, Mrs F. J. Munson, Mr J. E. Fitzroy Newdegate, Mr J. A. R. Toller.

Jockey (Flat): G Duffield (8-0, w.a.).

Apprentice: Jaki Houston (7-0).

592 MR M. H. TOMPKINS, Newmarket

Postal: **Flint Cottage Stables, Rayes Lane, Newmarket, Suffolk, CB8 7AB.**
Phone: **NEWMARKET (0638) 661434 FAX (0638) 668107**

1 **A FRIEND OF MINE,** 4, b g Noalto—Merency **Manchester Evening News**
2 **ASITAPPENS,** 4, ch g Music Maestro—Dalchroy **Flint Cottage Stables Ltd**
3 **BENNY LEONARD,** 4, b g Henbit (USA)—Brenda **Mr B. Schmidt-Bodner**
4 **BLAKESWARE PRINCE,** 4, ch g Morston (FR)—Ming **Mr R. R. Kalman**
5 **BRABAZON (USA),** 5, b g Cresta Rider (USA)—Brilliant Touch (USA) **P. H. Betts (Holdings) Ltd**
6 **CHRONOLOGICAL,** 4, b g Henbit (USA)—
Forward Princess (USA) **Hirst Kidd & Rennie Ltd-Oldham Chronicle**
7 **DORKING LAD,** 8, b g Cawston's Clown—High Voltage **Mr John Freedman**
8 **DOVEDON LADY,** 4, ch f Castle Keep—Copt Hall Princess **Mr Michael C. Whatley**
9 **DOVEDONS GRACE,** 4, b g Netherkelly—Grace of Langley **Mr Michael C. Whatley**
10 **ECHO CHAMBER,** 4, ch f Music Boy—Abalone **Northampton Mercury Co Ltd**
11 **ELEGANT STRANGER,** 5, b g Krayyan—Tumvella **Mr Barrie Betts**
12 **FATHER TIME,** 6, ch g Longleat (USA)—Noddy Time **Mrs Angela Hollest**
13 **HALKOPOUS,** 4, b c Beldale Flutter (USA)—Salamina **Mr Athos Christodoulou**
14 **HARD AS IRON,** 7, b g Ardoon—Prancer **Mr Martin Wickens**
15 **KADAN (GER),** 6, b g Horst-Herbert—King Lady (GER) **Mr Michael C. Whatley**
16 **KREMLIN GUARD,** 5, ch m Home Guard (USA)—Laurel Wreath **Mr N. A. Cawthorne**
17 **LARISTON GALE,** 4, b f Pas de Seul—Gigiolina **Lariston Apartments Ltd**
18 **LIGHT HAND,** 4, b f Star Appeal—No Cards **Mr John A. Furze**
19 **MEDUCK,** 5, b g Connaught—Wheatley **Mr Bill Orr**
20 **MUSIC REVIEW,** 7, ch g Music Boy—Right View **Flint Cottage Stables Ltd**
21 **NDITA,** 4, b f Be My Native—Orangery **Mr Peter Lord**
22 **OBELISKI,** 4, b g Aragon—Pasha's Dream **Mr A. B. Atkins**
23 **ONE DEVONSHIRE,** 4, b g Sandhurst Prince—Raregirl **Mr P. J. Stedman**
24 **POKEY'S PRIDE,** 7, b g Uncle Pokey—Strawberry Ice **Mr Michael C. Whatley**
25 **PRIVATE AUDITION,** 8, b g Crimson Beau—Loren **P. H. Betts (Holdings) Ltd**
26 **ROSEATE LODGE,** 4, b g Habitat—Elegant Tern (USA) **Wharf Racing**
27 **SEATTLE PRIDE (CAN),** 4, b c Seattle Song (USA)—Minstrelsy (USA) **Mrs J. S. Wootton**
28 **TIEMPO,** 4, b f King of Spain—Noddy Time **Mrs Angela Hollest**
29 **TRING PARK,** 4, b c Niniski (USA)—Habanna **P. H. Betts (Holdings) Ltd**
30 **XAFU XAFU,** 4, b g Kafu—On The Road **Mr J. H. Ellis**

THREE-YEAR-OLDS

31 **APPELANIA,** b f Star Appeal—Penna Bianca **Mr J. H. Ellis**
32 **ARANY,** b c Precocious—Bellagio **Mrs Patricia M. Kalman**
33 **BARANYKA,** b f Horage—Sister Jenks **Mr R. R. Kalman**
34 **BETWEEN THE STICKS,** gr f Pharly (FR)—Sandstream **Mr Peter Shilton**
35 **BURTONWOOD HARP,** ch g Mandrake Major—Misty Arch **Mr A. B. Atkins**
36 **DORIMAR,** br g Wolverlife—Ahoy Dolly **Mr A. V. Marchfield**

MR M. H. TOMPKINS—continued

37 **DOVEDON'S PRINCESS,** gr br f Baron Blakeney—Grace of Langley **Mr Michael C. Whatley**
38 **DUBLIN BREEZE,** b g Dublin Taxi—Dusty Foot **Mr W. J. Hall**
39 **EXPRESS EDITION,** b f Comedy Star (USA)—June Fayre **Aberdeen Journals Limited**
40 **GABBIADINI,** b g Taufan (USA)—Galerida **Mr D. Grant**
41 **GIPPESWYCK LADY,** b f Pas de Seul—Estivalia **Ipswich Bloodstock Agency Ltd**
42 **GREEN TIN HUT (USA),** b g Strike Gold (USA)—Cazeez (USA) **The Gentlemen of Leisure Partnership**
43 **KAHSHED,** ch g Wolverlife—Lady Margaret **Mrs M. Barwell**
44 **KERRY BOY,** ch g Sallust—Silk Imp **Mr A. Piller**
45 **KIRALYI (FR),** b f Kings Lake—Vivante **Mr R. R. Kalman**
46 **MISS ADVENTURE,** b f Adonijah—Sunset Ray **Roalco Ltd**
47 **PASSED PAWN,** b g Blakeney—Miss Millicent **Mr H. A. Illingworth**
48 **POPPY CHARM,** b f Star Appeal—Pop Music (FR) **Flint Cottage Stables Ltd**
49 Br f Strong Gale—Prancer **Flint Cottage Stables Ltd**
50 **RAMBADALE,** ch f Vaigly Great—Corinthia **Mr M. Sinclair**
51 **RAMSEY STREET,** b f Mummy's Game—Green Jinks **Mrs R. Heath**
52 **RUN FOR ROSEMARY,** b f Petorius—Class Will Tell
53 **SANDSUMO,** ch g Sandhurst Prince—Mursuma **Mr H. R. Hewitt**
54 **SNUGGLE,** ch f Music Boy—Sinzinbra **Mr G. V. Lockett**
55 **SWEET 'N' LOW,** b c Kampala—Karin Maria **Mr A. Piller**
56 **THIRD EVENT,** b f Thatching—Second Event **Mr B. Schmidt-Bodner**
57 **WOLFGANG,** ch g Music Boy—Hello Honey **Mrs R. M. S. Neave**
58 **WYLAM,** b c What A Guest—Wish You Wow **Mrs J. S. Wootton**

TWO-YEAR-OLDS

59 **ALL PRESENT,** b c 4/2 Reach—Mar Del Plata (Crowned Prince (USA)) **Mr A. Frost**
60 B f 31/3 Final Straw—Appealing (Star Appeal)
61 **BARLOGAN,** b f 3/4 Dunbeath—Corinthia (USA) (Empery (USA)) **Mr J. Sacs**
62 **BASTIN,** ch c 3/4 Alzao (USA)—Benita (Roan Rocket) **Mr D. Fisher**
63 **CASPIAN GREY,** gr c 1/4 Absalom—Sea Aura (Guillaume Tell (USA)) **Mr B. Schmidt-Bodner**
64 **DALEY BRIOCHE,** b c 29/5 Pharly (FR)—Flaretown (Town Crier) **Mr G. Cole**
65 **DON'T PRESUME,** b f 23/3 Pharly (FR)—Roxy Hart (High Top) **Flint Cottage Stables Ltd**
66 **ELEGANT FRIEND,** ch c 15/6 Music Boy—Cardinal Palace (Royal Palace) **Mr Barrie Betts**
67 **FIABA,** b f 13/3 Precocious—Historia (Northfields (USA)) **Mr H. R. Reuben**
68 B f 12/4 Prince Tenderfoot—Flame Up (Bustino) **Lady Nelson of Stafford**
69 B f 6/3 Music Boy—Frozen Asset (FR) (Northern Treat (USA)) **Mrs P. Sealey**
70 **FULLER,** b c 30/4 Wolverlife—Carnation For Me (Kala Shikari) **Mr J. A. Fuller**
71 **GAPTON PREY,** b c 19/5 Auction Ring (USA)—Double Eagle (Goldhill) **Mr P. F. Riseborough**
72 **GLITTERING EYES,** ch c 2/4 Crystal Glitters—Seventeen Roses (USA) (Lyphard (USA)) **Ecurie Fustok**
73 **GOLDEN GUNNER,** ch c 8/2 Mazaad—Sun Gift (Guillaume Tell (USA)) **Mr R. J. Levitt**
74 B c 12/5 Doulab (USA)—Habanna (Habitat) **P. H. Betts (Holdings) Ltd**
75 B c 18/3 Glenstal (USA)—Huppel (Huntercombe) **P. H. Betts (Holdings) Ltd**
76 **INDIAN OCEAN,** b f 29/1 Commanche Run—Inland Sea (Kings Lake (USA)) **Mr Stuart Andrews**
77 **IN THE HOG,** ch f 16/5 Music Boy—Emlyn Princess (Julio Mariner) **Mrs M. A. Smithson**
78 **IVORY BRIDE,** b f 23/4 Domynsky—Ivoronica (Targowice (USA)) **Mr B. Stuttaford**
79 **JACKSON SQUARE,** b c 5/2 Prince Tenderfoot—Double Habit (Double Form) **Lariston Apartments Ltd**
80 Gr c 13/4 Music Boy—Jenny Diver (USA) (Hatchet Man (USA))
81 B c 10/5 Daring March—Laisser Aller (Sagaro)
82 **LOVE OF THE ARTS (IRE),** b f 15/3 Tate Gallery—Royal Daughter (High Top) **Mr John E. Sims**
83 B c 25/5 Auction Ring (USA)—Madame Fair (Monseigneur (USA))
84 B f 17/4 Prince Tenderfoot—Mock Auction (Auction Ring (USA))
85 **MRS CLAYPOOL,** br f 22/3 Petong—Rare Legend (Rarity) **Mr M. Sinclair**
86 **MY BEDTIME,** b f 5/6 Blakeney—Noddy Time (Gratitude) **Mrs Angela Hollest**
87 **ON STRIKE,** b c 2/4 Caerleon (USA)—Kaysanniya (Nishapour (FR)) **Mr P. D. Saville**
88 **PEGGY SUE,** ch f 14/4 Hotfoot—Presentable (Sharpen Up) **Mr R. R. Kalman**
89 B f 13/4 Northern Tempest—Penna Bianca (My Swallow) **Mr G. S. Grant**
90 **PERSPECTIVE,** b f 21/2 Never So Bold—Geopelia (Raffingora) **Cheveley Park Stud Ltd**
91 B c 28/3 Horage—Rare Find (Rarity) **Mr A. Piller**
92 B gr f 1/5 Petong—Second Event (Fine Blade (USA)) **Mr B. Schmidt-Bodner**
93 **SO APT,** b c 28/3 Taufan (USA)—Anita's Princess (Miami Springs) **Mr T. W. Taylor**
94 **STATUS FLO,** b f 8/2 Never So Bold—Ranyas's Pet (Busted) **Mr M. I. George**

MR M. H. TOMPKINS—continued

95 TIME LINE, ch c 8/4 Hatim (USA)—Up To You (Sallust) **Mrs B. Loftus**
96 TUDORGATEWAY, b c 30/3 Martinmas—Shikra (Sea Hawk II) **Mr Stuart Andrews**
97 Ch f 19/4 Chief Singer—Uranus (Manacle) **Northampton Mercury Co Ltd**
98 VILANY, b f 21/4 Never So Bold—Bellagio (Busted) **Mrs Patricia M. Kalman**

Other Owners: Mr W. J. Bridge, Mr William Clarke, Mr Jack Fisher, Mr Pat Fitzgerald, Mr Michael Flannagan, Mr V. Gibbons, Mr J. A. Grainger, Mr Henry Harding, Mr H. Hatton, Mr A. B. Milford, Movedive Ltd (Coronet Racing Newmarket), Mr P. Stuart-Buttle, Mr M. H. Tompkins, Mr W. A. Weaver, Mr Jack Webster, Mr J. W. Wishart.

Jockeys (Flat): Ray Cochrane (8-3, w.a.), P Robinson (7-11, w.a.), Tyrone Williams (7-7, w.a.).

Jockeys (NH): R T J Dennis (10-0), S Smith Eccles (10-3, w.a.).

Amateurs: Mr M Armytage (10-7, w.a.), Mr J Wheymes (10-3).

Lady Rider: Miss Sarah Beard (9-12).

593 MR D. H. TOPLEY, Esh

Postal: **Hill Top Farm Stables, Esh, Durham, Co. Durham, DH7 9RN.**
Phone: **OFFICE (091) 373 5460 HOME (091) 373 0312**

1 AKID (USA), 4, ch c Secreto (USA)—Raise The Bridge (USA) **Mr D. Franks**
2 APPELLANT, 5, b h Star Appeal—St Louis Sue (FR) **Mrs R. Bostock**
3 ATHENE NOCTUA, 5, b m Aragon—Lady Lorelei **Mr W. Wilson**
4 KATHTEEN, 4, b f Teenoso (USA)—Kath **Mr D. R. Franks**
5 PRINCEABLE LADY, 6, b m Saher—Douriya **Mr D. Franks**
6 ROSTOVOL, 5, b g Vaigly Great—Emerin **Mr J. G. Lumsden**
7 WHAT A SNIP (USA), 5, b g Water Bank (USA)—Snip **Antony G. Wharton Ltd**
8 WINDWARD ARIOM, 4, ch g Pas de Seul—Deja Vu (FR) **Mrs A. B. Drury**

THREE-YEAR-OLDS

9 DEERNESS LAD, b g Kala Shikari—Il Regalo **Mr J. G. Lumsden**
10 STEVEN JOHN, b br g Carriage Way—Harmony Thyme **Mr Pat Brennan**
11 ZACCIUS, ch c Burslem—Vesperale **Mr D. Franks**

TWO-YEAR-OLDS

12 Ch c 28/3 All Systems Go—Carreg-Wennol (Dublin Taxi)
13 Br f 26/5 Anita's Prince—Chanrossa (High Top)
14 B f 5/4 Kind of Hush—Fuddled (Malacate (USA))

Other Owners: Mr A. J. Carroll, Mr Gerard Cuan, Kendal White & Co Ltd, Mr D. Maloney, Miss R. F. Mead, Mr Andrew Shaw.

Apprentices: Ron Hillis (w.a.), Alan Munro (w.a.).

Conditional: Jason Callaghan (9-7, w.a.).

Amateur: Mr D Franks (10-0).

594 MR S. TORR, Leek

Postal: **Roche Grange, Meerbrook, Leek, Staffordshire.**
Phone: **BLACKSHAW (053834) 266**

1 **LUCKY LENA,** 10, b m Leander—Quiet Sailing **Mr S. A. Torr**
2 **MISTY MIRAGE,** 10, b g Grey Mirage—Will She Win **Mr S. A. Torr**
3 **ROCHE ROSIE,** 6, b m Mossberry—Quiet Sailing **Mr S. A. Torr**
4 **ROCHE RUBY,** 8, ch m Humdoleila—Quiet Sailing **Mr S. A. Torr**

595 MR R. D. TOWNSEND, Charing

Postal: **Dormestone Farm, Hart Hill, Charing, Ashford, Kent.**
Phone: **CHARING (023 371) 2586**

1 **ANOTHER TROUP,** 8, b g Beau Charmeur (FR)—Ballinabranna **Mr Rodney D. Townsend**
2 **BARRERA LAD (USA),** 10, ch g Barrera (USA)—Misty Joy (USA) **Mr Rodney D. Townsend**
3 **COUNTRY CAP,** 9, ch g Pollerton—Farm Hat **Mr Rodney D. Townsend**
4 **DOVEHILL,** 4, gr g Pragmatic—Arconist **Mr Rodney D. Townsend**
5 **JOKER JACK,** 5, ch g Garryowen—Deceptive Day **Mr Rodney D. Townsend**
6 **MR TEE,** 7, br g Ancient Monro—Jolly Jacqueline **Mr Rodney D. Townsend**
7 **TANGO IN THE NIGHT,** 5, b g River Knight (FR)—Rock'n Roll **Mr Rodney D. Townsend**

Amateur: Mr D J Townsend (10-3).

596 MRS P. TOWNSLEY, Dorking

Postal: **Burnt Oak Manor Farm, Cudworth Lane, Newdigate, Dorking, Surrey.**
Phone: **(030677) 492**

1 4, Ch f Broadsword—Centaur Star **Mrs P. Townsley**
2 **CLOVER SONG,** 8, ch m True Song—Spartan Clover **Mr E. Easton**
3 **GRAHAMES PADDY,** 10, b g Precipice Wood—Paddy's Delight **Mr Grahame A. Dedman**
4 **HALE'S MELODY,** 5, b m Dubassoff (USA)—Hale Lane **Mrs P. Townsley**
5 **JORDENS SCALLYWAG,** 6, ch m Scallywag—Paddy's Delight **Mr Grahame A. Dedman**
6 **LADY RUN,** 8, b m Deep Run—Abbeylands Lass **Mr Erik Gale**
7 5, B m Dubassoff (USA)—Paddy's Delight **Mr Grahame A. Dedman**
8 **SPITE AND MALICE,** 8, b g Hot Grove—La Mirabelle **Mr J. A. Porteous**
9 **VIRGINIA'S PET,** 7, b m Virginia Boy—Gayles Bambina **Mr J. A. Porteous**

Other Owners: Mr D. Dewdney.

Jockey (NH): M Furlong.

Conditional: Lucy Townsley (9-7).

Amateur: Mr P Townsley (10-7).

Lady Rider: Miss L Townsley (9-7).

597 MR C. C. TRIETLINE, Stratford-on-Avon

Postal: **Upper Welford House, Welford-on-Avon, Stratford-on-Avon, Warwickshire, CV37 8HD.**
Phone: **HOME (0789) 750294 OFFICE (0789) 750833 CAR MOBILE (0836) 617417**

1 **ALDINGTON BELL,** 7, b g Legal Eagle—Dear Catalpa **Mr C. J. Wheatley**
2 **ALDINGTON PRINCE,** 4, b g Creetown—Dear Catalpa **Mr C. J. Wheatley**
3 **ALWAYS AWAY,** 6, ch g Quayside—Safe Return **Mr Alan Stadler**
4 **ARROW VALLEY LAD,** 5, b g Gone Native—Runaway Girl (FR) **Arrow Valley Transport Ltd**
5 **B B S BIDFORD,** 5, b m Legal Eagle—Dear Catalpa **Bidford Building Supplies**
6 **BEJAYJAY,** 6, b m Ya Zaman (USA)—Happy Ridan **Mr J. Doran**
7 **BENGAL WAY,** 5, b h Boreen (FR)—Santal Air **Mr J. A. Taylor**
8 **BIBULOUS,** 6, b g Bybicello—Ginger Up **Mr E. M. Russon**
9 **BIG DON,** 7, ch g Don—Artillery Row **Mr C. C. Trietline**
10 **COOL DISTINCTION,** 7, b g Class Distinction—Arctic Flight **Mr J. Huckle**
11 **DACANI'S GUEST,** 5, ch g What A Guest—Dacani **Mr C. C. Trietline**
12 **DYNAMIC STAR,** 6, b g Lord Gayle (USA)—Stellarevagh **West Midlands Racing Club Owners Group**
13 **EASTEND BLAKE,** 6, b g Blakeney—Dalmally **West Midlands Racing Club Owners Group**
14 **EMMADILL,** 10, b m New Member—Em Gee Bee **Mrs G. E. Reeve**
15 **EXCAVATOR,** 6, b g Bulldozer—Lucky Favour **Mr J. Huckle**
16 **GEMBRIDGE JUPITER,** 12, b g Jupiter Pluvius—Some Ana **Mr Anthony Carver**
17 **GIFT LIGHTER,** 6, br g Lighter—Ride Light **Arrow Valley Transport Ltd**
18 **GOLDEN BAVARD,** 9, ch g Le Bavard (FR)—Tamer Island **West Midlands Racing Club Owners Group**
19 **INTO THE RED,** 6, ch g Over The River (FR)—Legal Fortune **Mr J. Huckle**
20 **JUDGES FANCY,** 6, b g Monksfield—Knollwood Court **Mr J. C. de C. Scott**
21 **KILCORVINO,** 5, br g Corvaro (USA)—Kilboy Concorde **Miss E. Saunders**
22 **KILLBANON,** 8, b g Imperius—Flail **Mr W. Ebury**
23 **LADY LAX,** 6, ch m Henbit (USA)—Spoilt Miss (USA) **Mr J. Doran**
24 **ORARION,** 8, b g Blakeney—Love Story **Mr Brian J. D. Lewis**
25 **RETTINO,** 5, ch g Revlow—Nuttino **Mr J. Doran**
26 **RIVER FLY,** 5, ch g Over The River (FR)—Diana's Flyer **Miss E. Saunders**
27 **ROUND THE BLOCK,** 8, ch g Push On—War Queen **Mr N. G. King**
28 **TAPSTER VALLEY,** 7, br m Politico (USA)—Game Reward **Mr A. Rogers**
29 **THE LATE MAN,** 9, ch g Tudor Rocket—Kytton **Mr C. C. Trietline**
30 **THE UNDERGRADUATE,** 11, gr g Scallywag—Mrs Cantab **Mr J. A. Taylor**
31 **VALLEY JUSTICE,** 10, ch g Avocat—Cherry Valley **Mr Anthony Carver**
32 **WISECOURSE (USA),** 6, b g Irish River (FR)—Strigida **West Midlands Racing Club Owners Group**
33 **WORTHY LIGHT,** 9, b m Lighter—Sardan **Mr R. P. J. Taylor**

Other Owners: Mr R. M. Ackrill, Mr T. P. Grainger, Mr Graham Pickering.

Jockeys (NH): P Dever, W Humphreys.

Conditional: C Gibbons, A Plester.

598 MR D. TUCKER, Frome

Postal: **Feltham Farm, Frome, Somerset.**
Phone: **(0373) 62383**

1 **GOLDEN JUNE,** 8, ch m Undulate (USA)—Irene Louise **Mr P. R. Tennant**
2 **ON THE BLUE,** 5, b br h Blue Cashmere—Key Wind **Mr Mike Tebbut**
3 **WOODLANDS CROWN,** 7, ch g Milford—Town Girl **Miss J. M. Heritage**
4 **YOUNG VITAL,** 6, ch g Vital Season—Irene Louise **Mr Donald C. Tucker**

THREE-YEAR-OLDS

5 **KALABUCK,** gr c Kalaglow—Buckhurst **Mr Donald C. Tucker**
6 **PADDY'S LINE,** ch g Crimson Line—Paddys Belle **Mr Donald C. Tucker**

MR D. TUCKER—continued

TWO-YEAR-OLDS

7 **BELLE LOCK,** ro f 23/4 Lock And Load (USA)—Paddys Belle (St Paddy)
8 **IRENE LOCK,** b c 11/5 Lock And Load—Porto Irene (Porto Bello)
9 **VITAL TYCOON,** b f 4/6 Vital Season—Tycoons Belle (Tycoon II)

599 MR D. R. TUCKER, Cullompton

Postal: **Haydon Farm, Blackborough, Culmstock, Cullompton, Devon.**
Phone: **HEMYOCK (0823) 680159**

1 **CALA CONE,** 7, ch m Celtic Cone—Cavo Varka **Mr John Williams**
2 **CORSTON SPRINGS,** 8, gr g Bruni—Corston Lass **Mr D. R. Tucker**
3 **JUNE'S FANCY,** 4, ch f Mr Fluorocarbon—Havaneza **Mr John Williams**
4 **KRYPTON KNIGHT,** 5, ch g Star Appeal—Bold Pioneer **Mr John Williams**
5 **LA FRITE,** 4, b f John French—Saratoga Chip (USA) **Mr D. Martin**
6 **LUREX GIRL,** 6, ch m Camden Town—Klairelle **Mr J. Power**
7 **MEZIARA,** 9, b g Dominion—Abertywi **Mr G. Willey**
8 **RANWELI REEF,** 4, b g Superlative—Grace Poole **Mr D. R. Tucker**
9 **ZANUSSI LINE,** 6, b g High Line—Angelica (SWE) **Mr Bryan Scott**

TWO-YEAR-OLDS

10 B f 16/5 Skyliner—Kitty Come Home (Monsanto (FR)) **Mr D. R. Tucker**
11 B f 26/4 Moor House—Peggy Wig (Counsel) **Miss E. J. Southall and Mr J. Williams**

Other Owners: Mr John Livock.

Jockey (NH): N Coleman (w.a.).

Conditional: W Sterry (9-7).

Lady Rider: Miss J Southall (7-10).

600 MRS A. F. TULLIE, Eyemouth

Postal: **Auchencrow Mains, Reston, Eyemouth, Berwickshire, Scotland, TD14 5LT.**
Phone: **CHIRNSIDE 226 OR 8848 STD CODE 089-081**

1 **ADMIRE-A-MORE,** 6, b m Le Coq d'Or—Wynsomemore **Mrs W. R. Tullie**
2 **BWANA SIMBA,** 5, b g Mljet—Uzuri **Mrs M. P. Nisbet**
3 **RISK ANOTHER,** 7, ch g Hot Spark—Speadon **Mrs W. R. Tullie**

THREE-YEAR-OLDS

4 **MASIKA,** br f Royal Fountain—Fala Kalima **Mrs W. R. Tullie**

TWO-YEAR-OLDS

5 **SHAMBA MAJI,** br f 15/4 Meadowbrook—Fala Kalima (Sousa) **Mrs W. R. Tullie**

Amateur: Mr J G Grossick.

601 MR A. TURNELL, Wantage

Postal: **Orchard Stables, East Hendred, Wantage, Oxon, OX12 8JP.**
Phone: **(0235) 833297**

1 **AROUND AND ABOUT,** 6, br g Roselier (FR)—Like Now **Pell-mell Partners**

MR A. TURNELL—continued

2 **BIG RED,** 6, ch g Final Straw—Cut Loose **Mr L. G. Kimber**
3 **BLUEBERRY KING,** 7, b g Sunyboy—Messalina **Pell-mell Partners**
4 **BOWL OF OATS,** 4, ch g Oats—Bishop's Bow **Mrs Anthony Morley**
5 **CARROL'S CROSS,** 7, br m Decent Fellow—Sallys Wish **Mrs Heather Chittem**
6 **CEDAR SHELL,** 5, b g Sharpo—Cedrella **Mr J. S. Lammiman**
7 5, B g The Brianstan—Charlotte Mary **Mr L. A. H. Ames**
8 **DIE BROKE,** 6, b br g Pollerton—Gillogue **Pell-mell Partners**
9 **ELECTRESS,** 4, ch f Baron Blakeney—Elect **Lt. Col. W. Wetherly**
10 **FERNANDO (CZE),** 6, b g Silvaner (CZE)—Felos (HUN) **Mr David Codling**
11 **FIRST AVENUE,** 6, b g Tina's Pet—Olympus Girl **Mr C. J. Drewe**
12 **FISHERMAN'S TALE,** 7, b g Deep Run—Spin A Yarn **Mr H. J. Joel**
13 **GUN RULE,** 6, ch g Posse (USA)—Brave Lass **Mr David Milburn**
14 **HOOK HEAD,** 6, ch g Pollerton—Deep View **Mr H. J. Joel**
15 **KATABATIC,** 7, br g Strong Gale—Garravogue **Pell-mell Partners**
16 **KING'S ADVOCATE,** 8, ch g Avocat—Wesleyan **Mr J. S. Lammiman**
17 **KITTINGER,** 9, b g Crash Course—Mandaloch **Mr J. S. Lammiman**
18 **MIKE'S DIAMOND (NZ),** 6, b g Trictrac (NZ)—Subdue (NZ) **Mrs Heather Chittem**
19 **MORETON'S MARTHA,** 5, b m Derrylin—Kissimmee (FR) **Mrs M. R. Taylor**
20 **MOUNT PARSON,** 10, ch g The Parson—Salwood **Mr H. J. Joel**
21 **PROTECTION,** 8, ch g Thatch (USA)—Fairy Fans **Mr H. J. Joel**
22 **RING RUSSELL,** 7, ch g Belfalas—Ring Twice **Mr Russell McLoughlin**
23 **RUNCIBLE,** 6, ch g Deep Run—Lady Dromara **Pell-mell Partners**
24 **SECRET TURN (USA),** 4, b g Secreto (USA)—Changing (USA) **Mrs C. C. Williams**
25 **SOCIETY GUEST,** 4, ch c High Line—Welcome Break **Robinson Webster (Holdings) Ltd**
26 **SPRING CORN,** 4, ch f Oats—Springbow **Mrs Anthony Morley**
27 **SQUEEZE PLAY,** 5, b g Gleason (USA)—Cherry Leaf **Pell-mell Partners**
28 **TEBITTO,** 7, b g Derrylin—Over Beyond **Mr L. A. H. Ames**
29 **TOM BIR,** 8, ch g Deep Run—Clontinty Queen **Mr K. C. B. Mackenzie**
30 **TOP VILLAIN,** 4, b g Top Ville—Swan Ann **Mr H. J. Joel**
31 **WISE CUSTOMER,** 6, ch g Deep Run—Clontinty Queen **Mr H. J. Joel**
32 **WODEHOUSE,** 5, b g Sunyboy—Flammula **Mr M. H. L. Stevens**

THREE-YEAR-OLDS

33 **MYVERYGOODFRIEND,** b g Swing Easy (USA)—Darymoss **Mr Robert Long**

TWO-YEAR-OLDS

34 **CITY BOUQUET,** b f 21/2 Top Ville—Roses To Rachel (Artaius) **Mr David Codling**
35 Ch c 23/3 Bustino—Duck Soup (Decoy Boy) **Mr J. S. Lammiman**

Other Owners: Mr M. V. S. Aram, Mr Bill Haine, Mr P. G. Huxtable, Mr M. W. Richings.

Conditional: D Bentley (9-7), R Boucher (9-7), A Durnin (9-7).

Amateur: Mr R H M Westropp (10-7).

Lady Rider: Mrs Louise Turnell (8-7).

602 MR J. S. E. TURNER, Whitchurch

Postal: **Heath Paddocks, Prees Heath, Whitchurch, Salop, SY13 2AF.**
Phone: **(0948) 3527 TELEX: 35756 A/B TURNER G FAX: (0948) 5949**

1 **RAIN MARK,** 9, b g Politico (USA)—Rightful Ruler **Mrs J. S. E. Turner**
2 **SITRIC SOL,** 6, gr g King Sitric—Sailor's Sol **Mrs J. S. E. Turner**
3 **VERY CHEERING,** 7, b g Gleason (USA)—Cherry Joy **Mrs J. S. E. Turner**

603 MISS S. J. TURNER, Ripon

Postal: **The Farm, Skelton-on-Ure, Ripon, North Yorkshire, HG4 5AJ.**
Phone: **(042332) 4096**

1 **CARBIA'S LAST**, 5, ch m Palm Track—Carbia **Miss S. J. Turner**
2 **DEEP THINKING**, 6, b g Deep Run—Muriel's Pet **Miss S. J. Turner**
3 **JOHN NORTH**, 10, b g Pongee—Norgill **Miss S. J. Turner**
4 **PALM READER**, 6, b g Palm Track—Carbia **Miss S. J. Turner**
5 **SAFELY AWAY**, 7, ch g Politico (USA)—Carbia **Miss S. J. Turner**

604 MR W. G. TURNER, Tavistock

Postal: **Ley Farm Racing Stables, Peter Tavy, Tavistock, Devon.**
Phone: **(082281) 237**

1 **BISHOPRIC**, 9, b g Crozier—Frello **Mr W. G. Turner**
2 **BORVACALL**, 6, b m Ovac (ITY)—Call God **Mrs E. Grainey**
3 **DURATIVE**, 5, gr g Moorestyle—Zedative (FR) **Mr P. W. Bayley**
4 **ELECTRIC MONEY**, 4, b c Kafu—Silver Bullion **Mr W. G. Turner**
5 **INDOMITABLE (FR)**, 6, b m Indian King (USA)—Dominant **Mr W. G. Turner**
6 **LEPUS**, 7, b g French Vine—Spectra **Mr W. G. Turner**
7 **MASCALLS LADY**, 5, b m Nicholas Bill—Whisper Gently **Mr G. A. K. Moore**
8 **PAILIN**, 4, b f Blue Refrain—Petploy **Mr W. G. Turner**
9 **PENSIVE BEAUTY**, 5, b m Penmarric (USA)—Guanabara (GER) **Mr W. G. Turner**
10 **PLAZA TORO**, 11, ch g Ashmore (FR)—Duke Street (USA) **Mr David Fisher**
11 **PONTEVECCHIO NOTTE**, 5, b h Blakeney—Oula-Ka Fu-Fu **Mr W. G. Turner**
12 **TABACOS**, 7, ch g Sagaro—Shere Beauty **Mr George Ball**
13 **VICEROY MAJOR**, 7, ch g Bay Express—Lady Marmalade **Mr R. N. Short**
14 **WEISS ROSE (FR)**, 5, b m Pilgrim (USA)—Seul **Mr W. G. Turner**

Other Owners: Mrs Susan Baker, Mr John Bathurst, Mr Stephen Clasper, Mr P. Hayward, Mrs Renate Mahmoud, Mrs Sandra E. Turner.

Jockey (NH): Gareth Charles-Jones (10-0).

Conditional: C Dempsey (9-7).

605 MR W. G. M. TURNER, Sherborne

Postal: **Sigwells Farm, Sigwells, Corton Denham, Sherborne, Dorset.**
Phone: **CORTON DENHAM (096322) 523**

1 **BORE HILL PRINCESS**, 5, b m Imperial Fling (USA)—Domicile **Mr O. J. Stokes**
2 **BUILDMARK**, 4, ch f Longleat (USA)—Crescentia **Mr Graham Emery**
3 **CADFORD GIRL**, 6, ch m Nearly A Hand—Claverton **Mr P. F. Coombes**
4 **CHAMPAGNE RUN**, 5, b g Runnett—Tolaytala **Mr T. R. Connor**
5 **FLORIDA ISLAND**, 4, b f Miami Springs—Honiara **Mr O. J. Stokes**
6 **FOUR STAR LINE**, 5, ch g Capricorn Line—Florida Girl **Mr F. H. Smith**
7 **JADEBELLE**, 4, b f Beldale Flutter (USA)—Precious Jade **Mr Tony J. Smith**
8 **LES'S GIRL**, 4, br f Uncle Pokey—Fair Louise **Mr E. Goody**
9 **LOVE AND LIFE**, 4, b br f Lyphard's Special (USA)—Miss Olympus **Mr R. A. Wilkins**
10 **MARTINSMOON**, 5, ch m Homeboy—Moonvein **Mr Norman Berry**
11 **MILLER'S GILT**, 5, b h Glint of Gold—Hecalene (FR) **Mr Julian Batchelor**
12 **NICK THE DREAMER**, 5, ch g Nicholas Bill—Dream of Fortune **Somerset and Dorset Racing Limited**

MR W. G. M. TURNER—continued

13 **ORCHARD'S PET,** 4, gr g Petong—Toccata (USA) **Mr P. Stranger**
14 **PRECIOUS LINK,** 7, gr g Relkino—The Silver Darling **Mr E. Goody**
15 **QUEEN MATILDA,** 6, b m Castle Keep—Daydreamer **Mr O. J. Stokes**
16 **RALEIGH GAZELLE,** 8, gr m Absalom—Haven Bridge **Mr R. A. Newton**
17 **SECRET LIASON,** 4, b g Ballacashtal (CAN)—Midnight Mistress **Mr Patrick Ward**
18 **SHASTON,** 5, ch g Rolfe (USA)—Nicaline **Kavanagh Roofing Southern Limited**
19 **SIMON DAMIAN,** 7, ch g Roman Warrior—Our Polly **Mr F. H. Smith**
20 **THANKS A MILLION,** 4, ch f Simply Great (FR)—Friendly Thoughts (USA) **Mr R. N. Short**
21 **THE SLATER,** 5, ch g Town And Country—Yashama **Kavanagh Roofing Southern Limited**

THREE-YEAR-OLDS

22 **CADFORD BALARINA,** b f Adonijah—Jarama **Mr P. F. Coombes**

TWO-YEAR-OLDS

23 **ABSALOUI,** gr f 29/2 Absalom—Agreloui **Mr A. Poole**
24 **JUST RUN (IRE),** b f 13/1 Runnett—Wild Justice **Mrs M. Tevesham**
25 **KATHY FLYNN,** b f 1/2 Import—Runasca **Mr E. Goody**
26 **PARITSIS,** b f 4/5 Lochnager—September Fire **Mr E. Goody**
27 **ROSY SAKER,** ch f 4/5 Absalom—Anoda **Mr E. Goody**

Other Owners: Mr B. G. Bunn, Burton And Smith (U.K.) Ltd.

Jockey (NH): H Davies (w.a.).

Conditional: P Holley, J Neaves (9-7).

606 MR S. F. TURTON, Yealmpton

Postal: **Oakhill Farm, Worston, Yealmpton, Plymouth, PL8 2LN.**
Phone: **(0752) 880105**

1 **CELTIC WARRIOR,** 6, b g Celtic Cone—Great Aunt Emily **Mr S. F. Turton**
2 **GET AWAY,** 8, ch g Posse (USA)—Dash On **Mr S. F. Turton**
3 **KERICHO,** 6, b g Joshua—Miss Jeroco **Mr S. F. Turton**
4 **MOLISE,** 4, b f Town And Country—Quaint
5 **RUGGED SPIRIT,** 10, gr g Rugantino—Express Spirit **Mr S. F. Turton**
6 **THIONVILLE,** 10, b g African Sky—Mariska (FR) **Mr S. F. Turton**

607 MR N. A. TWISTON-DAVIES, Cheltenham

Postal: **Grange Hill Farm, Naunton, Cheltenham, Gloucestershire, GL54 3AY.**
Phone: **(04515) 278**

1 **ANOTHER SWORD,** 5, ch m Broadsword (USA)—Alex M **Partnership**
2 **BABIL,** 5, b g Welsh Pageant—Princess Eboli **Mr Mark Christofi**
3 **CAMDEN SOUL,** 6, ch g Camden Town—Pilgrim Soul **Mr N. A. Twiston-Davies**
4 **CELTIC PRINCE,** 4, ch g Celtic Cone—Lothian Countess **Mrs G. Maxwell-Jones**
5 **FLYING FRANKIE,** 5, b g Tower Walk—Tarte Aux Pommes
6 **GUIENNE,** 14, b g Normandy—Pantala **Miss Sarah Gordon Cumming**
7 **MASTER MUCK,** 7, b g Sagaro—Emperor's Gift **Mr N. A. Twiston-Davies**
8 **MRS MUCK,** 9, b m Air Trooper—Emperor's Gift **Mr N. A. Twiston-Davies**
9 **NOUGAT RUSSE,** 9, b g Sweet Story—Natasha VI **Mr David Langdon**
10 **REGULAR VULGAN,** 7, b g Regular Guy—Vulgan's Law **Mr N. A. Twiston-Davies**

MR N. A. TWISTON-DAVIES—continued

11 **RONNIE WILL,** 7, b g Balinger—Donna May **Mr N. A. Twiston-Davies**
12 **SPARKLING CINDERS,** 6, b m Netherkelly—Cindyr **Mr G. M. MacEchern**
13 **TIPPING TIM,** 5, b g King's Ride—Jeanarie **Mrs J. Mould**

Other Owners: Mr C. Edwards, Mr H. R. Mould.

Jockey (NH): P Scudamore (10-0).

Lady Rider: Mrs C Twiston-Davies (9-0).

608 MR JOHN R. UPSON, Towcester

Postal: **Highfields House, Adstone, Towcester, Northants, NN12 8DS.**
Phone: **(0327) 860043 TELEX 826921 EROS G**

1 **BALLINHASSIG,** 6, b g Slippered—Rathcreevagh **Mr John R. Upson**
2 **CAFFIERI (USA),** 7, b g Youth (USA)—Effeffvee (USA) **Mr John R. Upson**
3 **CENTRASPIREBUILD,** 6, ch g Black Minstrel—Vickies Rambler **Mr John R. Upson**
4 **DEEP DARK DAWN,** 5, ch g Deep Run—Swinging Sovereign **Mr John R. Upson**
5 **DIANES DESTINY,** 6, b g Kambalda—Kinsella's Choice **Mrs Diane Upson**
6 **DUHALLOW BOY,** 10, b g Ardoon—Mallow Isle (USA) **Mr John R. Upson**
7 **EROSTIN FLOATS,** 6, ch g Paddy's Stream—Zeta's Daughter **Mrs Diane Upson**
8 **FLYING FREEHOLD,** 5, b g Callernish—Flying Music **Mr John R. Upson**
9 **KNOCKUMSHIN,** 7, ch g Kambalda—Vina's Last **Mr John R. Upson**
10 **MALISTRANO,** 9, b g Malinowski (USA)—Kilistrano **Mr John R. Upson**
11 **MANDRAY,** 7, br g Mandalus—Kimin **Mr John R. Upson**
12 **NEARLY READY,** 7, br g Matching Pair—Orcatina **Mr John R. Upson**
13 **NICK THE BRIEF,** 8, b g Duky—Roman Twilight **Mr John R. Upson**
14 **OVERHEREOVERTHERE,** 7, ch g Green Shoon—Cool Madam **Mr John R. Upson**
15 **OVER THE ROAD,** 9, ch g Over The River (FR)—Legal Fortune **Mr John R. Upson**
16 **SOUTHERN REAPER,** 8, ch g Kambalda—Ingenious **Mr J. A. Upson**
17 **SUASANAN SIOSANA,** 5, b br g Frigid Aire—Efficiency **Mr John R. Upson**
18 **THAR-AN-BHARR,** 8, b g Over The River (FR)—Another Bird **Mr John R. Upson**
19 **THE GREEN STUFF,** 5, ch g Green Shoon—Cottage View **Mr John R. Upson**
20 **THE VATMAN COMETH,** 5, b g Lafontaine (USA)—Sugar Lump **Mr John R. Upson**
21 **TONY MURPHYS MAN,** 5, br g Strong Gale—Bold Aroon **Mr John R. Upson**
22 **TRY ME NOW,** 4, b g Try My Best (USA)—Sapientia (FR) **Mr John R. Upson**
23 **WAYWARD SINGER,** 7, ch g The Parson—Fairy Island **Mr John R. Upson**
24 **ZETA'S LAD,** 7, ch g Over The River (FR)—Zeta's Daughter **Mrs Diane Upson**

THREE-YEAR-OLDS

25 **LETTERFORE,** br f Strong Gale—Ruby Girl **Mr John R. Upson**
26 **WALLISTRANO,** br g Indian King (USA)—Kilistrano **Mr John R. Upson**

Jockey (NH): Robbie Supple (9-7).

Conditional: G Bohane (9-7).

Amateur: David Finn (10-7).

609 MR M. D. I. USHER, East Garston

Postal: **The Stables, Parsonage Farm, East Garston, Newbury, Berkshire, RG16 7ER.**
Phone: **(0488) 398953 OR (0488) 398954 TELEX 265451 WKK158 FAX (0488) 398950**

1 **BRILLIANT BAY,** 5, b g Hello Gorgeous (USA)—Cala-Vadella **Lambourn Racing Ltd**
2 **FEARLESS DANCER,** 4, ch g Ballacashtal (CAN)—Miss Anniversary **Mrs Jane Black**
3 **HOLYPORT VICTORY,** 8, br g Free State—Snow Goose **Mr G. Hughes**
4 **KINGS VICTORY,** 6, ch g What A Guest—Directrice (GER) **Mr G. Hughes**
5 **MY CHIARA,** 4, b f Ardross—My Tootsie **Mr John P. Pitt**
6 **MY DIAMOND RING,** 5, b m Sparkling Boy—Bells of St Martin **Mrs Marion Wickham**
7 **OTHET,** 6, b g Thatch (USA)—Hot Pad **Mr C. Budd**
8 **PALEY PRINCE (USA),** 4, b c Tilt Up (USA)—Apalachee Princess (USA) **Mr John P. Pitt**
9 **PERUZZI,** 4, ch g Simply Great (FR)—Okavamba **Mr Trevor Barker**
10 **PILLAR OF FIRE (USA),** 5, b g Master Willie—As You Would (USA) **Temple Insulation**
11 **STAR NORTH,** 6, b g Star Appeal—Highly Polished **Orchid Racing & Bloodstock Ltd**

THREE-YEAR-OLDS

12 **ALDWICK COLONNADE,** ch f Kind of Hush—Money Supply **Colonnade Racing Limited**
13 **CANDAVIA,** b f Ardross—Sly Wink **Mrs Nicolas Kairis**
14 **CAROMISH (USA),** br f Lyphard's Wish (FR)—Carom (USA) **Mr John P. Pitt**
15 **CHLOE'S PET,** ch f Local Suitor (USA)—Mischiefmaker **Mrs S. J. Stovold**
16 **COLSAN BOY,** b c Remainder Man—Wimbledon's Pet **Mrs S. J. Stovold**
17 **CUILLIN RIDGE,** ch c Dalsaan—Cailin Oir **Mr M. D. I. Usher**
18 **ERIC'S PET,** gr g Petong—When I Dream **Colonnade Racing Limited**
19 **GINGERNUT (USA),** ch c Timeless Moment (USA)—United Appeal (USA) **Mrs John P. Pitt**
20 **JOVIAL KATE (USA),** gr f Northern Jove (CAN)—Flashy Feet (USA) **Mr John P. Pitt**
21 **LADY GRENVILLE,** b f Aragon—Tri'as **Mr D. H. Currie**
22 **LITTLE RIPPER,** br f Belfort (FR)—Harem Queen **Mr M. Rowles**
23 **MOGUL PRINCE,** br g Mansingh (USA)—Valadon **Mrs Nicolas Kairis**
24 **MOHINI,** ch f Sharpo—Girl's Brigade **Mr Trevor Barker**
25 **MY RUBY RING,** b f Blushing Scribe (USA)—Bells of St Martin **Mrs Marion Wickham**
26 **SIRSE,** gr f Enchantment—Sea Farer Lake **Mr Trevor Barker**
27 **STERLING BUCK (USA),** b c Buckfinder (USA)—Aged (USA) **Mrs M. P. Pearson**
28 **TREACLE MINE,** ch c Ballacashtal (CAN)—Miss Anniversary **Mrs Jane Black**

TWO-YEAR-OLDS

29 **CIBOURE,** ch f 18/4 Norwick (USA)—Brandon Creek (Be My Guest (USA)) **Mr Trevor Barker**
30 **FIORENTIA,** br f 4/2 Final Straw—Chellaston Park (Record Token) **Mrs Nicholas Kairis**
31 Ch f 9/4 Enchantment—Formula (Reform) **Backcroft Racing & Bloodstock Ltd**
32 B f 12/2 Fayruz—Granny Stock (Imperial Fling (USA)) **Backcroft Racing & Bloodstock Ltd**
33 **JIM'S WISH (IRE),** b c 26/1 Heraldiste (USA)—Fete Champetre (Welsh Pageant) **Mr J. P. Pitt**
34 B f 21/3 Sulaafah (USA)—My Sweet Melody (Music Boy) **Mr M. Jaggs**
35 **NO BIG DEAL,** b c 2/3 Kris—Sophisticated Lady (FR) (Habitat) **Mrs Nicholas Kairis**
36 B f 6/5 King of Spain—Princess Story (Prince de Galles) **Mr P. Warren**
37 Gr f 19/2 Enchantment—Seafarer Lake (Gairloch) **Mrs Jane Black**
38 B c 27/4 Ballacashtal (CAN)—Take To Heart (Steel Heart) **Mr P. A. Deal**

Other Owners: Mr L. D. Darrell, Mr W. Hinshelwood, Mr Dick Tapper, Mr M. S. C. Thurgood, Mr Tim Vignoles, Mr Carl West-Meads, Mr D. V. Williams.

Jockey (Flat): M Wigham (8-2).

Apprentices: M Marshall (7-12), A Tate (7-7).

Conditional: S Harris (9-7).

Lady Rider: Mrs Ann Usher (7-7).

610 MR M. S. VERNON, Darlington

Postal: **New House Farm, Heighington, Darlington, Co Durham, DL2 2XW.**
Phone: **(0325) 300590**

1 **ALLENELLA,** 10, br g Derek H—Nella The Nipper **Mr M. S. Vernon**
2 **PRICEY,** 6, b br m Silly Prices—Nella The Nipper **Mr M. S. Vernon**
3 **WEDDING BELLE,** 7, ch m Derek H—Nella The Nipper **Mr M. S. Vernon**

611 MR C. J. VERNON MILLER, Shipston-on-Stour

Postal: **Blackwell Grange, Blackwell, Shipston-on-Stour, Warwickshire.**
Phone: **HOME AND YARD ILMINGTON 357**

1 **BABY ALEX,** 6, br g Derrylin—Nello (USA) **Mrs L. Vernon Miller**
2 **BUSKINA,** 10, b g Little Buskins—Fair Corina **Mr T. N. Siviter**
3 **ESPERO (CHI),** 9, ch g El Oriental (ARG)—Elfish (CHI) **Mrs L. Vernon Miller**
4 **FORT FLUTTER,** 4, b f Beldale Flutter (USA)—Shindella **Mr C. J. Vernon Miller**
5 **MISTS OF TIME,** 7, gr ro g Grey Dawn II—Hyroglyph (USA) **Mr J. W. Noden**
6 **PALAIS ROSE (FR),** 9, gr g Crystal Palace (FR)—Texan Belle (FR) **Mrs L. Vernon Miller**
7 **QUILANTARO (CHI),** 9, b g Tantoul (USA)—Baluta (CHI) **Mrs Peggy Siviter**
8 **SIR NODDY,** 7, ch g Tom Noddy—Pinzarose **Mr J. W. Noden**
9 **TRULY HOT,** 5, b m True Song—Duiker **Mr J. P. Thorne**

Other Owners: Mrs P. Butler, Mr Max Pearce, Mr Robert C. Williams.

612 MR R. VOORSPUY, Polegate

Postal: **The Coach House, Folkington, Polegate, E. Sussex, BN26 5SD.**
Phone: **POLEGATE (032 12) YARD 5006 HOUSE 7133 TELEX 877440 (P. BURNS G)**

1 **BALLANTRAE,** 6, b m Creetown—Tecllyn **Mr M. A. De Gara**
2 **DONOSA,** 5, ch m Posse (USA)—Love Supreme **Mrs D. Brazier**
3 **FORULI,** 5, b m Last Fandango—Unbeknown **Mr Jeremy Edwards**
4 **HUNTERS BERG,** 7, ch g One Little Boy—Highland Jingle **Mr R. Voorspuy**
5 **MEADS BROW,** 4, b c Petong—Pams Gleam **Mr I. J. Paterson**
6 **MERDON MONARCH,** 9, ch g Relko—Palmavista **Mrs Yvonne Hicks**
7 **PATROCLUS,** 5, b g Tyrnavos—Athenia Princess **Mr Alan W. Clarke**
8 **RUNLAD,** 6, gr ro g Runnett—Queensworthy **Mrs Yvonne Hicks**
9 **RUSSBOROUGH,** 9, ch g Astrapi—Melpo **Mrs C. M. Leeson**
10 **SAMOAAN CHARGER,** 4, b g Aragon—Sea Charm **Mr R. G. Wasey**
11 **SAY SHANAZ,** 4, b br f Tickled Pink—Wild Pumpkin **Mrs Wendy Smith**
12 **SILVER CANNON (USA),** 8, gr g Lot O'Gold (USA)—So High (USA) **Mr M. P. Wood**
13 **SNAPSHOT BABY,** 6, br m Faraway Times (USA)—Firecat **W. Clarke**
14 **SOLSTICE BELL,** 8, br m Record Token—Nasty Niece (CAN) **Mr J. D. T. Wall**
15 **SONIC LORD,** 5, b g Final Straw—Lucent **B. F. H. P. Racing**
16 **THE WOODEN HUT,** 7, ch g Windjammer (USA)—Bunduq **F. Bull**

THREE-YEAR-OLDS

17 **GUNRUNNER GIRL,** ch f Longleat (USA)—Witchingham Lass **Mr R. A. Waight**
18 **TROPICAL ACE,** b f Final Straw—Rampage **Mr Robin D. Hendry**

TWO-YEAR-OLDS

19 Br f 9/2 Nomination—Sister Hannah (Monseigneur (USA)) **Mr Robin D. Hendry**
20 **TENDER REACH,** b f 30/4 Reach—Betty's Bid (Auction Ring (USA)) **Mrs B. Sands**
21 Br c 12/5 Tickled Pink—Wild Pumpkin (Auction Ring (USA)) **Mr R. Voorspuy**

MR R. VOORSPUY—continued

Other Owners: Mr A. L. Ainslie, Mr B. T. Chamberlain, Mr I. T. Hawkins, Mr T. M. J. Keep, Miss J. Newell, Mr M. A. R. Pummell, Mr C. J. A. Ross, Mr N. Topche, Mr S. D. Tyndall, Mr J. P. C. Wall.

Jockeys (Flat): M Roberts (7-10, w.a.), S Whitworth (8-0).

Jockey (NH): M Furlong (10-0).

613 MR N. WAGGOTT, Spennymoor

Postal: **Ingledene, Vyners Close, Merrington Lane, Spennymoor, Co. Durham, DL16 7HB.**
Phone: **(0388) 819012**

1 **ALASKAN GOODWILL,** 7, b g Snow Warning—Runaway Bay **Mrs J. Waggott**
2 **BERTHELIER,** 6, ch g Mandrake Major—Marton Lady **Mrs J. Waggott**
3 **BISHOPSFORD,** 4, b g Henbit (USA)—Arena **Mrs J. Waggott**
4 **CARD PARTY,** 5, ch g Lucky Wednesday—Hutton Barns **Mrs J. Waggott**
5 **CODED PRINCESS,** 8, b m Coded Scrap—Gala Queen **Mrs J. Waggott**
6 **DROVERS ROAD,** 9, br m Netherkelly—Bally Mitty **Mrs J. Waggott**
7 **EAST PARK,** 10, b g Some Hand—Bally Mitty **Mrs J. Waggott**
8 **HAKEDMA,** 4, ch c Van Der Linden (FR)—Duty Watch **Mrs J. Waggott**
9 **KILRONA,** 6, gr h Rusticaro (FR)—Firdosa **Mrs J. Waggott**
10 **LIGHTCLIFFE LADY,** 7, b m Royal Blend—Oujarater **Mrs J. Waggott**
11 **SABDABEANI,** 5, b g Good Times (ITY)—Canvas Shoe **Mrs J. Waggott**
12 **SCOTCH DOUBLE (USA),** 4, b g Duns Scotus (CAN)—Role Twice (USA) **Mrs J. Waggott**

Amateur: Mr N Waggott Jnr (11-0).

Lady Rider: Miss Tracy Waggott (9-7).

614 MR J. S. WAINWRIGHT, Malton

Postal: **Hanging Hill Farm, Kennythorpe, Malton, North Yorkshire.**
Phone: **(0653) 85537**

1 **BE TENDER,** 4, b f Prince Tenderfoot (USA)—The Habit of Being **Mr J. M. Gahan**
2 **FLOATING NOTE,** 5, ch m Music Boy—Red Crest **Fir Trading Ltd**
3 **FOUR ALLS LADY,** 4, b f Broadsword (USA)—Hazeldean **Mr W. Price**
4 **JESTMENOT,** 4, gr g Jester—Petite Ville **Mr P. Tierney**
5 **SUM MUSIC,** 5, b m Music Boy—Sum Star **Fir Trading Ltd**
6 **WAVERLEY BOY,** 8, br g Scallywag—Mansina **Mr S. Pedersen**
7 **WAVERLEY GIRL,** 4, b f Seymour Hicks (FR)—Iamstopped **Mr N. F. Strange**
8 **WAVERLEY STAR,** 5, br g Pitskelly—Quelle Blague **Mr S. Pedersen**

THREE-YEAR-OLDS

9 **BLUELLA,** b f Blue Cashmere—Set To Work **Mr M. Stanard**
10 **BOLD ANGEL,** b c Lochnager—Lobela **Mr A. M. Wragg**
11 **BYKER LASS,** b f Superlative—Golden Tern (FR) **Mrs Vida McGiven**
12 **DIAMOND SINGH,** b c Mansingh (USA)—Prime Thought **Mr S. Pedersen**
13 **KING PHILIP,** b c King of Spain—Midnight Music **Mr A. Fawcett**
14 **LADY ELLEN,** b f Horage—Hillbrow **Mrs Chris Harrington**
15 **RATHBRIDES JOY,** gr c Kafu—Great Meadow **Mrs Chris Harrington**

MR J. S. WAINWRIGHT—continued

TWO-YEAR-OLDS

16 B c 5/5 Rusticaro (FR)—Directrice (GER) (Zank)
17 B c 18/2 Le Johnstan—Flore (Dance In Time (CAN))
18 **GREAT MUSIC,** ch c 6/4 Music Boy—Amadina (Great Nephew) **Mr J. H. Pickard**
19 B c 9/4 Kafu—La Mascotte (Hotfoot)
20 **MINKES BOY,** ch c 31/3 Krayyan—Willow Bird (Weepers Boy) **Mr J. H. Pickard**
21 Ch c 25/3 Hatim (USA)—On The Road (On Your Mark) **Mr P. Tierney**
22 Ro c 13/5 Godswalk (USA)—Rocket Lass (Touch Paper)
23 Ch c 1/5 Mazaad—Sharpwinds (Tumble Wind (USA))
24 **TOTAL SHAMBLES,** b c 7/3 Taufan—Home Bird (Ragusa) **Mr B. Wake**

Other Owners: Mr J. H. Bellerby, Mrs Gubi Forrest, Mrs B. Hall, Mr Ian Nicholson, Mr P. E. Wragg.

Jockeys (Flat): K Darley (w.a.), S Morris (7-12).

Jockeys (NH): G Harker (10-0, w.a.), J J Quinn (10-0, w.a.).

Conditional: M Carter (9-7).

615 MR W. A. WALES, Fakenham

Postal: **Abbey Farm, Binham, Fakenham, Norfolk, NR21 ODQ.**
Phone: **(0328) 75580**

1 **ICEBANK,** 5, b m Roscoe Blake—Wood Bank **Mr W. A. Wales**
2 **KILRUDDERY,** 11, ch g Laurence O—Ballycold **Mr W. A. Wales**
3 **PENDLE LYRIC,** 8, b m Roscoe Blake—Penny Princess **Mr W. A. Wales**
4 **PENDLE PRINCE,** 10, b g Broxted—Pendella **Mr D. A. Wales**
5 **TAR FLAME,** 11, b g Tarqogan—Some Flame **Mr W. A. Wales**

Amateur: Mr W A Wales (10-12).

616 MR R. B. WALEY-COHEN, Banbury

Postal: **Upton Viva, Banbury, Oxon, OX15 6HT.**
Phone: **(01 244) 6022 OR (029587) 242**

1 **DROMORE CASTLE,** 10, b g Tepukei—Glen Rambler **Mr Robert Waley-Cohen**
2 **FIRST WARNING,** 7, br g Foggy Bell—Premier Nell **Mr Robert Waley-Cohen**
3 **FLEETING PASSION,** 11, br g Golden Love—Rambling Gift **Mr Robert Waley-Cohen**
4 **THE DRAGON MASTER,** 8, br g Pollerton—Glen Rambler **Mr Robert Waley-Cohen**

617 MR C. F. WALL, Newmarket

Postal: **Wroughton House Stables, Old Station Road, Newmarket, Suffolk, CB8 9DT.**
Phone: **OFFICE (0638) 661999 HOME (0638) 668896 FAX (0638) 667279**

1 **COUNT MY BLESSINGS,** 5, b g Touching Wood (USA)—Topaz Too **Mr Michael H. Gadsby**
2 **DONNA ELVIRA,** 4, b f Chief Singer—Countess Olivia **Lady Juliet De Chair**
3 **FISHERMANS FRIEND,** 4, ch c Pal O Mine—Sardine **Mr J. C. Jakes**
4 **HIGH I KEW,** 4, b c High Top—Klewraye **Sir Stanley Grinstead**
5 **NOBLE LUSTRE (USA),** 4, br f Lyphard's Wish (FR)—Crowned **Mrs Yoshiko Allan**
6 **THE CHERRY MAN,** 8, b g Paddy's Stream—Bonny Wild **Mr I. A. Low**

MR C. F. WALL—continued

THREE-YEAR-OLDS

7 **BATTLE OF FLOWERS,** b f Shernazar—Valiant Cry **Mr Peter R. Pritchard**
8 **CANDY GLEN,** b c Glenstal (USA)—Maiden Concert **Mr Antonio Balzarini**
9 **DAME D'AMOUR,** ch f Ballad Rock—Behroz **Mr A. E. Baxter**
10 **HUDSON BAY TRADER (USA),** b c Sir Ivor—Yukon Baby (USA) **Mr Brownell Combs II**
11 **IVOR ROSE,** b c Nemorino (USA)—Last Rose **Mr John MacNae**
12 **KORACLE BAY,** b f Kind of Hush—Sea Aura **Mr J. A. Stimpson**
13 **MAGIA (USA),** b f Vaguely Noble—My Sister **Mr G. Algranti**
14 **MISS TATTING (USA),** ch f Miswaki (USA)—Petit Rond Point (USA) **Mr Peter R. Pritchard**
15 **NYONYA BESAR,** b f Ballad Rock—Nekhbet **Mr Peter R. Pritchard**
16 **PROSPECTORS MOON (USA),** ch f Miswaki (USA)—Moon Min (USA) **Lady Juliet De Chair**
17 **ROYAL MAZI,** b f Kings Lake (USA)—Seven Seas (FR) **Sir Philip Oppenheimer**
18 **SAFFRON LACE,** b f Rabdan—French Music **Mrs O. D. Beets**
19 **SHOWMANSHIP,** b g Shernazar—Melodramatic **Mrs C. A. Wall**

TWO-YEAR-OLDS

20 **CHANCE ALL,** ch f 16/4 Glenstal (USA)—Auction Bridge (Auction Ring (USA)) **Lady Juliet De Chair**
21 **CHIPAYA,** b f 14/3 Northern Prospect—Flaming Rose (USA) (Upper Nile (USA)) **Mr G. Algranti**
22 **DESERT VICTRESS (USA),** ch f Desert Wine (USA)—Elegant Victress (USA) (Sir Ivor) **Mr M. Malmuth**
23 **FANLIGHT,** b c 28/1 Beldale Flutter—Carib Flash (Mill Reef (USA)) **Sir Philip Oppenheimer**
24 B c 24/6 Shardari—Fire And Ice (FR) (Reliance II) **Mr David Allan**
25 **HALLOWED GROUND (IRE),** b f 23/3 Godswalk (USA)—Stony Ground (Relko) **Mr G. Hampton**
26 **JARZON DANCER,** bl c 19/3 Lidhame—Long Valley (Ribero) **Jarzon Plastics Ltd**
27 **LOOK KEW,** b f 18/5 Precocious—Klewraye (Lord Gayle (USA)) **Sir Stanley Grinstead**
28 B f 8/5 Kafu—Miss Redmarshall (Most Secret)
29 **MODEL CHILD,** ch f 1/5 Bairn (USA)—Reform Princess (Reform) **Lady Juliet De Chair**
30 **NAI HARN,** b br c 29/3 Petong—Pacific Polly (Mount Hagen (FR)) **Mr C. J. A. Hughes**
31 **O MY DARLING (USA),** b f 13/4 Mr Prospector (USA)—
Midnight Pumpkin (USA) (Pretense) **Mr Peter R. Pritchard**
32 **PEARL ESSENCE (USA),** br f 26/1 Conquistador Cielo—
Frau Daruma (ARG) (Frari (ARG)) **Mr Peter R. Pritchard**
33 **SKY SIGN (USA),** br c Skywalker (USA)—J O Nurse **Mr M. Malmuth**
34 **SWEET TASSA,** b f 12/2 Forzando—Granny's Bank (Music Boy) **Mrs C. A. Wall**
35 **WESTERN MIST,** ch f 24/3 Damister—Western Line (High Line) **Mrs James McAllister**
36 Ro c 7/4 Northern Jove—Winthataway (Blushing Groom (FR))

Other Owners: Mrs J. R. Collins, Mr S. S. De Chair, Mrs A. J. Dorey, Mr Stuart R. Gibson, Mr S. Leckie, Mrs John J. Melk, A. J. O'Connell (Plasterers) Ltd, Mrs Constance V. Pathy, Mr J. A. Rippon, Mrs G. F. Schwier, Mr A. J. Stannard, Mr J. H. Wall, Mr J. R. Westgarth.

Jockey (Flat): N Day (8-2).

Apprentice: W Litwin (7-8).

618 MR J. W. WALMSLEY, Tadcaster

Postal: **East Garth, Catterton, Tadcaster, North Yorkshire.**
Phone: **(0937) 833380**

1 **FOSTERS FOLLY,** 4, gr g Petong—Dastina **Mrs A. E. Walmsley**
2 **INTREPID WORLD (USA),** 4, b g Transworld (USA)—Intrepid Mary Ann (USA) **Mr J. W. Walmsley**
3 **LUDERMAIN,** 5, ch m Oats—Peacock Vain **Mr J. W. Walmsley**
4 **OLU DENIZ,** 5, b m Oats—Sotuta **Mr J. W. Walmsley**

619 MR F. WALWYN, Lambourn

Postal: **Saxon House Stables, Lambourn, Newbury, Berkshire, RG16 7QL.**
Phone: **LAMBOURN (0488) 71555**

1 **BUTT AND BEN,** 6, b g Crofter (USA)—Aileen's Belle **Lady Aitken**
2 **BY LINE,** 6, b m High Line—Mount Hala **Mrs S. W. Smart**
3 **CAPITAL PUNISHMENT,** 4, ch g Capitano—Loophole **Mrs M. L. Giles**
4 **CAPSIZE,** 4, ch g Capitano—Fused Light **Mrs F. Walwyn**
5 **DON'T TELL RUTH,** 8, b g Miami Springs—Mount of Light **Mr Mike Murphy**
6 **FALWORTH (USA),** 6, b g Sir Ivor—Real Wisdom (USA) **Mr W. H. Whitbread**
7 **HILL'S PAGEANT,** 11, b g Welsh Pageant—Reita **Mrs F. Walwyn**
8 **HYPNOTIC,** 10, b g Royben—Magic Mountain **Mrs J. M. Corbett**
9 **KILBRITTAIN CASTLE,** 14, ch g Dike (USA)—Now Or Never **Mr W. H. Whitbread**
10 **LIFELINE,** 8, b g Fine Blade (USA)—Quiet Life **Mrs F. Walwyn**
11 **LORD TORENAGA,** 7, b br g Ballymore—Tudor Bay (FR) **Mr M. B. J. Kimmins**
12 **MISS MAGIC,** 5, b m Cruise Missile—Magic Mountain **Mrs J. M. Corbett**
13 **PETE'S SAKE,** 5, b g Scorpio (FR)—Pete's Money (USA) **Mr W. H. Whitbread**
14 **PRINCE'S COURT,** 7, b g Kinglet—Court Scene **Crown Racing Ltd**
15 **PROVIDENCE LODGE,** 8, b m The Parson—Pallatess **Mr Charles S. Bird III**
16 **QUAY WALL,** 7, b m Paddy's Stream—Polar Sprite **Duke of Devonshire**
17 **RED SAILS,** 4, b f Town And Country—Helm **Mrs S. W. Smart**
18 **ROSIE MARCHIONESS,** 7, br m Neltino—Maid of Honor II **Mr V. E. Barclay**
19 **SAFFRON PALM,** 6, b g Palm Track—New Saffron **Mrs F. Walwyn**
20 **SLIGHTLY GONE,** 5, b g Balinger—Nearly Straight **Mrs F. Walwyn**
21 **SMAYMAN,** 6, br g Touching Wood (USA)—Monaco Melody **Mr J. H. Thursby**
22 **SUNSHINE BLUES,** 7, b g Sunyboy—Fatal Hour **Mr J. E. Hewett**
23 **TEN OF SPADES,** 10, b g Raise You Ten—Hansel Money **Mr W. H. Whitbread**
24 **THE PURSEWARDEN,** 7, b g Down The Hatch—Miss Sonnet **Mrs F. Walwyn**
25 **TROOP LEADER,** 11, b g Queen's Hussar—Lizzie Lightfoot **Mrs G. S. Forbes**
26 **TRUE LOOP,** 8, ch g True Song—Loophole **Mrs F. Walwyn**
27 **TRUE SPARK,** 8, ch g True Song—Fused Light **Mrs F. Walwyn**

Other Owners: Queen Elizabeth, Mr Nick Blair, Mr Keith Gregory, Mrs Katharine Knott, Mr C. D. Pilkington, Mr P. H. Rawson, Mr Jack Rubins.

Jockeys (NH): R Chapman (10-0), K Mooney (9-7).

Conditional: S Pearson (9-7).

Amateur: Mr G Oxley (10-4).

620 MR P. T. WALWYN, Lambourn

Postal: **Seven Barrows, Lambourn, Newbury, Berkshire, RG16 7UJ.**
Phone: **LAMBOURN 71347 TELEX 94013727 FAX (0488) 72664**

1 **ARRAGUANIE,** 4, gr c Tolomeo—Princess Runnymede **Mr L. A. Smith**
2 **BRAMDEAN,** 4, b f Niniski (USA)—Elizabethan **Mr A. D. G. Oldrey**
3 **COLLAGE,** 4, b f Ela-Mana-Mou—Cojean (USA) **Hesmonds Stud**
4 **COMMAND PERFORMER,** 4, b f Comedy Star (USA)—Freely Given **Mrs W. Wallace**
5 **DRUMHEAD,** 4, ch g High Line—Wig And Gown **Mr A. D. G. Oldrey**
6 **FORT RUPERT,** 8, gr g Busted—Princess Runnymede **Mr L. A. Smith**
7 **FRAMLINGTON COURT,** 7, gr h High Top—Princess Runnymede **Mr L. A. Smith**
8 **GREY GYPSY,** 4, gr f Absalom—Nyeri **Mrs P. T. Walwyn**
9 **HATEEL,** 4, b c Kalaglow—Oatfield **Mr Hamdan Al-Maktoum**
10 **HUSYAN (USA),** 4, b c Alleged (USA)—Close Comfort (USA) **Mr Hamdan Al-Maktoum**

MR P. T. WALWYN—continued

11 **MUKIR,** 4, ch c Kris—Velvet Habit **Mrs P. T. Walwyn**
12 **OTTERGAYLE,** 5, br h Lord Gayle (USA)—Otterhill **Mrs Lionel Wigram**
13 **PARANG,** 9, b g Sharpen Up—Parmelia **Mr P. T. Walwyn**
14 **RELIEF PITCHER,** 4, b c Welsh Term—Bases Loaded (USA) **Mrs John Wallinger**

THREE-YEAR-OLDS

15 **ALYANAABI (USA),** ch f Roberto (USA)—Fair (CHI) **Mr Hamdan Al-Maktoum**
16 **BASIC THOUGHTS,** b f Simply Great (FR)—Final Thought **Bloodstock And Stud Investment Co Ltd**
17 **BLAKE'S FINESSE,** br f Baron Blakeney—True Finesse **Miss C. A. James**
18 **BOLD RAB,** ch c Rabdan—Herbary (USA) **Mr Peter Kuehnel**
19 **CHARMING,** ch f Glenstal (USA)—Threes A Charm **Mrs R. B. Kennard**
20 **COUNTRY COTTAGE (USA),** ro f Full Out (USA)—La Chaumiere **Mr D. Aykroyd**
21 **DENYS HATTON,** br c Kampala—Nordic Maid **Seven Barrows Racing**
22 **DREAMAWHILE,** b f Known Fact (USA)—Forgotten Dreams (FR) **Hesmonds Stud**
23 **ELMURAQASH,** b c Ela-Mana-Mou—Queen's Counsellor **Mr Hamdan Al-Maktoum**
24 **FARM STREET,** b c Henbit (USA)—Mill Hill (USA) **Mr Leonard Sainer**
25 **FINJAN,** b c Thatching—Capriconia **Mr Hamdan Al-Maktoum**
26 **FUNUN (USA),** b f Fappiano (USA)—Toutski (USA) **Mr Hamdan Al-Maktoum**
27 **GHARAH (USA),** b f Shadeed (USA)—Bolt From The Blue (USA) **Mr Hamdan Al-Maktoum**
28 **GHAYAAT (USA),** ch f Lyphard (USA)—Goodbye Shelley (FR) **Mr Hamdan Al-Maktoum**
29 **HEARTHRUG,** br f Persian Bold—Chauffeuse **Mr D. Aykroyd**
30 **HIGH BARON,** br g Baron Blakeney—High Finesse **Miss C. A. James**
31 **LA CABRILLA,** b ro f Carwhite—La Tuerta **Mrs R. B. Kennard**
32 **LAND OF HOPE,** b f Dominion—Vielle **Mrs Caroline Holland-Martin**
33 **LAW STUDENT,** ch f Precocious—Star Court **Cliveden Stud**
34 **MUWFIQ,** b c Formidable (USA)—Triple First **Mr Hamdan Al-Maktoum**
35 **NOBLE SOUL,** ch f Sayf El Arab (USA)—Fleet Noble (USA) **Seven Barrows Racing**
36 **NORTHERN HAL,** b c Sadler's Wells (USA)—Northern Script (USA) **Mrs Roger Waters**
37 **OLYMPIAN,** ch c High Line—Elysian **Mr A. D. G. Oldrey**
38 **OXBOW,** b c Trojan Fen—Shannon Princess **Mr A. D. G. Oldrey**
39 **PERSIAN SOLDIER,** b c Sandhurst Prince—Persian Case **Seven Barrows Racing**
40 **PHARYNX,** b c Pharly (FR)—Pamina **Lord Howard de Walden**
41 **RAMI (USA),** br c Riverman (USA)—Ancient Regime (USA) **Mr Hamdan Al-Maktoum**
42 **SALMON SPARKLE,** ch c Salmon Leap (USA)—Sparkling Air **Seven Barrows Racing**
43 **SAWSAN,** b f Top Ville—Al Washl (USA) **Mr Hamdan Al-Maktoum**
44 **SINDEED (USA),** ch c Northern Baby (CAN)—Kit's Double (USA) **Mr Hamdan Al-Maktoum**
45 **SUPER GLOW,** gr g Kalaglow—Super Lady **Jack Maxwell**
46 **TABYAN (USA),** b f Topsider (USA)—Wink (USA) **Mr Hamdan Al-Maktoum**
47 **TADWIN,** ch f Never So Bold—Songs Jest **Mr Hamdan Al-Maktoum**
48 **TRIGON,** b c Kris—Triagonal **Mr P. G. Goulandris**
49 **TRYING DAYS,** b c Teenoso (USA)—April Days **Mr Michael Kent**
50 **VISION OF INDIA,** b f Vision (USA)—Flying Bid **Mrs Roger Waters**
51 **WHISPERING SEA,** b f Bustino—Sound of The Sea **Beechgrove Stud Farm Ltd**
52 **ZAMMAH,** b f Jalmood (USA)—Petrol **Mr Hamdan Al-Maktoum**

TWO-YEAR-OLDS

53 B c 30/3 Robellino (USA)—Affair (Bold Lad (IRE)) **Mr D. Aykroyd and Mr A. D. G. Oldrey**
54 **AFFAIR TO REMEMBER,** b f 4/3 Persian Bold—Princess Eboli (Brigadier Gerard) **Ian Pilkington and Mrs C. Holland-Martin**
55 **AGHNIYAH (USA),** ch f 7/4 Lyphard (USA)—Goodbye Shelley (FR) (Home Guard (USA)) **Mr Hamdan Al-Maktoum**
56 **ALLAYAALI,** b f 13/3 Dunbeath (USA)—Walladah (USA) (Northern Dancer) **Mr Hamdan Al-Maktoum**
57 **BALAAT (USA),** b c 28/3 Northern Baby (CAN)—Bar J Gal (USA) (Key To The Mint (USA)) **Mr Hamdan Al-Maktoum**
58 B f 31/3 Sulaafah (USA)—Blakesware Gift (Dominion) **Mrs R. H. Dunn and D. J. Bennett-Baggs**
59 **CADENCY,** b c 4/5 Teenoso (USA)—Mullet (Star Appeal) **Mr D. Aykroyd and Mr A. D. G. Oldrey**
60 Br f 14/2 Lidhame—Capel Curig (Welsh Pageant) **Mrs Julian Sheffield**
61 B br c 29/5 Vision (USA)—Chauffeuse (Gay Fandango) **Mr D. Aykroyd and Mr A. D. G. Oldrey**
62 B c 28/3 Bates Motel (USA)—Coquelicot (CAN) (L'Enjoleur (CAN)) **Salisbury Farms Ltd and Mrs P. T. Walwyn**

MR P. T. WALWYN—continued

63 **DOMINIO,** b f 27/3 Dominion—La Tuerta (Hot Spark) **Mrs R. B. Kennard and Partners**
64 **EARLY ALICE,** b f 10/3 Lidhame—Fayette (Dom Racine (FR)) **Mr Michael Kent**
65 B f 22/3 Thatching—Good To Follow (Wollow) **Lady Lillingston and Mrs P. T. Walwyn**
66 **GREAT IMPOSTOR,** ch c 13/4 Vaigly Great—Lady Waverton (Huntercombe) **Mrs Dan Abbott and Partners**
67 **HILLZAH (USA),** ch c 29/2 Blushing Groom (FR)—Glamour Girl (ARG) (Mysolo) **Mr Hamdan Al-Maktoum**
68 **JAHIZ,** b c 22/2 Damister (USA)—Tribal Feast (Tribal Chief) **Mr Hamdan Al-Maktoum**
69 **JALLAD (USA),** b c 30/3 Blushing Groom (FR)—Petrava (NZ) (Imposing (AUS)) **Mr Hamdan Al-Maktoum**
70 **KAFIYAH (USA),** ch f 2/4 Shadeed (USA)—
Bolt From The Blue (USA) (Blue Times (USA)) **Mr Hamdan Al-Maktoum**
71 **LOVELY MONEY,** br c 7/4 Primo Dominie—Linda's Design (Persian Bold) **Lord McAlpine**
72 **MAFATIN,** b f 27/2 Sadler's Wells (USA)—Glass Slipper (Relko) **Mr Hamdan Al-Maktoum**
73 Ch f 17/1 Absalom—Marcela (Reform) **Turf Club**
74 **MOONJID,** br c 23/1 Shirley Heights—Psylla (Beldale Flutter) **Mr Hamdan Al-Maktoum**
75 **MUBIN,** b c 5/5 Wassl—Mashteen (USA) (Majestic Prince (USA)) **Mr Hamdan Al-Maktoum**
76 **MUKADDAMAH (USA),** b c 21/3 Storm Bird (USA)—Tash (USA) (Never Bend) **Mr Hamdan Al-Maktoum**
77 **MUSABIQ,** gr c 7/3 Superlative—Lammastide (Martinmas) **Mr Hamdan Al-Maktoum**
78 **NORTHERN FLYER,** ch c 21/3 Bairn (USA)—
Fly The World (USA) (Empery (USA)) **R. P. Worthington and C. Hume**
79 **PAPER DANCE,** b c 13/5 Mashhor Dancer (USA)—April Days (Silly Season) **Mr Michael Kent**
80 **PAPER DART (USA),** b c 5/2 Lear Fan (USA)—Forelie (Formidable (USA)) **Mrs John Wallinger**
81 B f 25/4 Daring March—Pirate Maid (Auction Ring) **Mr Michael White and Mrs P. T. Walwyn**
82 **SALIC DANCE,** b c 11/4 Shareef Dancer (USA)—Sandy Island (Mill Reef (USA)) **Lord Howard de Walden**
83 **SEARCHING STAR,** b f 6/4 Rainbow Quest (USA)—Little White Star (Mill Reef (USA)) **Mr P. G. Goulandris**
84 **SHALEEL,** b c 14/3 Last Tycoon—Wood Violet (USA) (Riverman (USA)) **Mr Hamdan Al-Maktoum**
85 **SUPER DELIGHT,** b f 29/4 Norwick (USA)—Super Melody (Song) **Jack Maxwell and David Harris**
86 **TAKADDUM (USA),** ch c 29/4 Riverman (USA)—
Lyphard's Holme (USA) (Lyphard (USA)) **Mr Hamdan Al-Maktoum**
87 **THE ORGAN GRINDER,** b c 27/4 Scottish Reel—Sideshow (Welsh Pageant) **Lord McAlpine**
88 B f 24/4 Nordance (USA)—Town Lady (Town Crier) **Turf Club**
89 Ch f 31/3 Stalker—Ultra (Stanford) **Patrick Helmore and Partners**
90 **ZAKARIF,** b f 29/1 Lomond (USA)—Lady Capulet (USA) (Sir Ivor) **Mr Hamdan Al-Maktoum**

Other Owners: Mr James Barber, Mr G. S. Beccle, Mrs Elizabeth Birks, Mrs Nicola Clarke, Lord Clinton, Mr R. J. B. Hoare, Mrs Anna Hulks, Mrs Ann Humphries, Mr Peter Kirrage, Miss Peggy Kwoh, Mrs Jack Maxwell, Mr S. F. Oldrey, Stoneleigh Investment Ltd, Mr R. N. Tikkoo, Mr G. S. Tuck, Mr Arthur D. P. Williams, Mr Malcolm J. Williams.

Jockeys (Flat): P Eddery (w.a.), N J Howe (7-13).

Jockey (NH): Dermot Browne (w.a.).

Lady Rider: Mrs Carolyn Eddery (7-8).

621 MRS S. A. WARD, Northallerton

Postal: **High Park House, Winton, Northallerton, N. Yorkshire, DL6 2TB.**
Phone: **EAST HARLSEY (060 982) 293**

1 **AVEC COEUR (USA),** 8, b g Cinteelo (USA)—Cadeau de Coeur (USA) **Mrs S. A. Ward**
2 **BATTLE STING,** 6, b g Hard Fought—Mrs Bee **Mrs S. A. Ward**
3 **DUKE OF HAMILTON,** 5, b g Hard Fought—Piazza Navona **Mrs S. A. Ward**
4 4, B g Capricorn Line—Greek Glance **Mrs S. A. Ward**
5 **LINDSEY DOYLE,** 4, ch f Stanford—Sans Blague **Mrs S. A. Ward**
6 **WIDE RECEIVER,** 5, ch g Posse (USA)—Red Partridge **Mrs S. A. Ward**

Conditional: D Byrne (w.a.), R Supple (w.a.).

622 MRS V. C. WARD, Grantham

Postal: **Aisby House, Aisby, Grantham, Lincolnshire.**
Phone: **(052) 95 260**

1 **BATTLE'S TOWN BOY,** 8, b g Crash Course—Fair Trouble **Mrs V. C. Ward**
2 **FATHER FLINN,** 5, b g Wolver Hollow—Trouble Pocket (USA) **Mrs V. C. Ward**
3 **TANWORTH,** 5, ch m Stetchworth (USA)—Fotopan **Mrs V. C. Ward and Mrs R. F. Key**

623 MRS B. WARING, Chippenham

Postal: **Luckham Park Stud, Colerne, Chippenham, Wiltshire, SN14 8AZ.**
Phone: **BOX (0225) 742044**

1 **BUCKSWILL,** 6, b g Liboi (USA)—Berganza **Mr J. W. Storkey**
2 **CRACKERMAC,** 5, b m Sparkler—Mac's Melody **Mr J. Robson**
3 **EMMA TOM BAY,** 5, b g Bay Express—Counsel's Verdict **Mrs Barbara Waring**
4 **FROGS FIRST,** 4, b f Beldale Flutter (USA)—Lareyna **Mr J. Friel**
5 **FULL QUIVER,** 5, br g Gorytus (USA)—Much Pleasure **Mr E. A. Davies**
6 **JANISKI,** 7, b g Niniski (USA)—Seasurf **Mr S. Mustoe**
7 **LAUGHING GRAVY,** 10, b g Monsanto (FR)—Poppy Time **Mr Harry Chisman**
8 **MEAN TO ME,** 4, b f Homing—Mac's Melody **Mr T. McCarthy**

THREE-YEAR-OLDS

9 **ALWAYS ALEX,** b f Final Straw—Two High **Mr Harry Chisman**
10 B g Niniski (USA)—Favorite Prospect (USA) **Mr Harry Chisman**
11 **GREEK LAD,** ch c Decoy Boy—Corinth Canal **Mrs Barbara Waring**
12 B g Law Society (USA)—Hardiemma **Mrs Barbara Waring**
13 **ILDERTON ROAD,** br f Noalto—Mac's Melody **Mr T. McCarthy**
14 Ch f Valiyar—Landlady **Mr Harry Chisman**
15 **NAZARE BLUE,** b c Absalom—Top Stream **Mrs C. J. Williams**
16 **VANISKI,** b g Niniski (USA)—Voltigeuse (USA) **Mr Harry Chisman**

TWO-YEAR-OLDS

17 **CURLILOCKS,** ch f 17/4 Glenstal—Merry Sharp (Sharpen Up) **Mr A. R. Perry**
18 **DEEP SELECTION (IRE),** b f 25/1 Deep Run—Random Select (Random Shot) **Mr D. Smith**
19 Gr f 1/2 Belfort (FR)—La Bleu (Blue Cashmere) **Mrs Barbara Waring**
20 B g 14/2 Noalto—Mac's Melody (Wollow) **Mr T. McCarthy**
21 B g 17/3 Macmillion—Mrs Currie (He Loves Me) **Mr Harry Chisman**
22 B f 11/4 Macmillion—My Charade (Cawston's Clown) **Mr T. McCarthy**
23 B g 10/4 Macmillion—River Damsel (Forlorn River) **Mr Harry Chisman**
24 B g 7/3 Macmillion—Valsette (Anfield) **Mr T. McCarthy**
25 Br g 21/3 Macmillion—Willington House (Comedy Star (USA)) **Mr Harry Chisman**

Other Owners: Mr N. Perry, Mr B. L. Wilton.

Jockeys (Flat): N Howe, D McKay, J Williams (8-6).

Jockey (NH): J Robson (10-0).

624 MR L. WARING, Wellington

Postal: **Southey Farm, Higher Wrangway, Wellington, Somerset, TA21 9QG.**
Phone: **(0823) 662660 MOBILE (0831) 132859**

1 **CITY NATIVE,** 4, b g Be My Native (USA)—Blue Kingsmill **Mr L. Waring**
2 **COOMBE,** 5, b g Beldale Flutter (USA)—Nullah **Mr L. Waring**
3 **GERYON,** 9, b g Exdirectory—Floreat Salopia **Mr L. Waring**
4 **PENNILESS IMP,** 5, br m Impecunious—Munlochy **Mr L. Waring**

Amateur: Mrs Jenny Matthews (10-0).

625 MISS S. WATERMAN, Dorchester

Postal: **Melbury Bubb Cottage, Nr Evershot, Dorchester, Dorset, DT2 0NQ.**
Phone: **(093583) 394**

1 **BACK TO FORM,** 5, ch g Homing—Alezan Dore **Miss S. Waterman**
2 **BIRMINGHAM'S GLORY,** 4, b f Hays—Exmoor Lass (FR) **Miss S. Waterman**
3 **JUDYS LINE,** 6, b m Capricorn Line—Gold Braid **Miss S. Waterman**

Lady Rider: Miss S E Waterman (9-5).

626 MR J. W. WATTS, Richmond

Postal: **Hurgill Lodge, Richmond, North Yorkshire, DL10 4TA.**
Phone: **(0748) 850444 OR (0836) 224721 FAX (0748) 850374**

1 **ABBOTSLEY,** 4, b f Chief Singer—Abbeydale **Mrs Anne Sutton**
2 **DANCING DAYS,** 4, ch c Glenstal (USA)—Royal Agnes **Mr R. Coleman**
3 **FANATICAL (USA),** 4, b c Lear Fan (USA)—Gal A Tic (USA) **Sheikh Mohammed**
4 **GOOD HAND (USA),** 4, ch g Northjet—Ribonette (USA) **Mrs M. M. Haggas**
5 **HABETA (USA),** 4, ch c Habitat—Prise **Developmore Ltd (Beta Construction)**
6 **MAYDAY MIRACLE,** 4, b f Superlative—Mayday Melody **Mrs Rowena Nurse**
7 **NAFUAT,** 6, b g Taufan (USA)—Jerusalem **Duke of Sutherland**
8 **OVERPOWER,** 6, b g Try My Best (USA)—Just A Shadow **Mr Gerald Cooper**
9 **ROYALIST (CAN),** 4, b c Commemorate (USA)—Hangin Round (USA) **Sheikh Mohammed**
10 **UPTON PARK,** 5, b g High Top—Polly Packer **Philip Newton**

THREE-YEAR-OLDS

11 **BERBERANA,** b f Never So Bold—Ricura **Hamish Alexander**
12 **BILIMBI,** ch f Nicholas Bill—Scrub Oak **Duke of Sutherland**
13 **BILLOW,** br f Nicholas Bill—Time-Table **Duke of Sutherland**
14 **BOXTOP,** ch f Final Straw—Polly Packer **Philip Newton**
15 B f Vaigly Great—Classy Dame **G. C. Morley**
16 **COME AND STAY,** ch f Be My Guest (USA)—Julip **Mrs J. J. Hindley**
17 **CONFIDENCE,** ch f Noalto—Orange Silk **Mrs Gerald Cooper**
18 **GRACEWING,** br f Gorytus (USA)—Bellinote (FR) **Mr R. E. Sangster**
19 **HACIENDA,** b c Habitat—Bare Minimum **Mr B. Haggas**
20 **HARVEST SPLENDOUR (USA),** b f Solford (USA)—Autumn Splendour (AUS) **Mr R. E. Sangster**
21 **HATTA FORT,** bl g Formidable (USA)—Hatta **Sheikh Mohammed**
22 **HUCKLEBERRY WIN (USA),** ch c Riverman (USA)—Waterloo **Mr Joe L. Allbritton**
23 **JEAN DOUGAL,** ch f Star Appeal—Brandy **Lord Bolton**
24 **LE SAULE D'OR,** br f Sonnen Gold—Richesse (FR) **Mr Carleton Wright**
25 **LOCAL DERBY,** ch c Local Suitor—Honey Match **Sheikh Mohammed**
26 **MESSAGE PAD,** ch c Rousillon (USA)—Ouija **Lord Derby**
27 **MISS PORTIA,** ch f Import—Mistress Meryll **Mr James Westoll**
28 **OFFICER CADET,** b g Shernazar—Selection Board **Lord Derby**
29 **RANCHO MIRAGE,** ch g Superlative—Que Sera **Mr J. A. Redmond**

MR J. W. WATTS—continued

30 **ROYAL WARRANT (USA),** ch g Wavering Monarch (USA)—Gay Lady J (USA) **Mr David Montagu**
31 **SAN GRECO,** b g Mandrake Major—Rich Lass **Mr J. A. Redmond**
32 **SARSAPARILLA (FR),** br f Shirley Heights—Sassika (GER) **Sheikh Mohammed**
33 **SILVER STICK,** gr g Absalom—Queen's Parade **Lord Manton**
34 **SOCIETY BALL,** b f Law Society (USA)—Mariakova (USA) **Mr R. E. Sangster**
35 **SOOTY TERN,** br c Wassl—High Tern **Sheikh Mohammed**
36 **VINTAGE TYPE,** b g Import—Marock Morley **Mr J. N. Anthony**
37 **YODELLING,** b g Head For Heights—Saucy Singer (USA) **Sheikh Mohammed**

TWO-YEAR-OLDS

38 **ADELPHI PRINCESS,** br f 15/5 Anfield—Princess Pageant (Welsh Pageant) **Hon Michael A. J. Oakshott**
39 **ADJUSTING (IRE),** b f 11/4 Busted—Julip (Track Spare) **Mrs S. W. Smart**
40 **AUVILLAR (USA),** b br c 6/2 Temperence Hill (USA)—Exquisita (Cougar (CHI)) **Mr David Montagu**
41 **BRILLIANT,** ch f 5/5 Never So Bold—Diamond Hill (High Top) **Lord Derby**
42 **BROOM ISLE,** b f 14/4 Damister (USA)—Vynz Girl (Tower Walk) **Lord Bolton**
43 B f 31/3 Kalaglow—Can Can Girl (Gay Fandango (USA))
44 **COLONEL FAIRFAX,** ch gr c 2/5 Alias Smith—Mistress Meryll (Tower Walk) **Mr James Westoll**
45 **COLWAY DOMINION,** ch c 22/1 Dominion—My Therape (Jimmy Reppin) **Mr K. Stringer**
46 **FLEUR D'ETE (IRE),** gr f 9/2 Miller's Mate—Lily of The Valley (GER) (Pentathlon) **Sheikh Mohammed**
47 B c 10/3 Sure Blade (USA)—Headin' Home (Habitat)
48 **KANANGA,** br f 18/4 Local Suitor (USA)—Kandia (Luciano) **Sheikh Mohammed**
49 **KAZOO,** gr f 29/3 Shareef Dancer (USA)—Kallista (Zeddaan) **Sheikh Mohammed**
50 **KILLINGHALL (IRE),** b c 11/5 Glow—Joma Kaanem (Double Form) **Mrs M. Irwin**
51 **MOLLERS,** ch f 25/3 Foolish Pleasure—Musical Sally (The Minstrel (CAN)) **Lord Ronaldshay**
52 **PERU,** b c 23/3 Conquistador Cielo—Dance Flower (CAN) (Northern Dancer) **Sheikh Mohammed**
53 **RHEIN VALLEY (IRE),** b f 10/5 Kings Lake (USA)—Rhein Bridge (Rheingold) **Mr R. E. Sangster**
54 **ROYAL CHERUB (USA),** b br f 9/1 Sovereign Dancer—Cherubim (Stevward) **Lord Derby**
55 **SESAME SEED (IRE),** b c 14/3 Wassl—Halva (Troy) **Sheikh Mohammed**
56 **STEAM AHEAD,** b g 22/2 All Systems Go—Mature (Welsh Pageant) **Mrs Susan Rudolf**
57 Br c 29/3 Sharpo—Sunita (Owen Dudley)
58 **TIP AND RUN (IRE),** b c 18/2 Alleged (USA)—Keep In Step (Dance In Time (CAN)) **Sheikh Mohammed**
59 **WOLFSKIN,** ch f 8/3 Sharpo—Wolverene (Relko) **Lord Derby**
60 **WORLDBETA (IRE),** ch c 22/2 Hatim (USA)—
Celestial Star (So Blessed) **Developmore Ltd (Beta Construction)**

Other Owners: Peter Bickmore, Miss E. A. Morley, Lady Rose Musker, A. D. Shead, Mr B. Shephard, Mr T. Umpleby, Mr J. W. Watts, Mrs P. M. Watts.

Jockey (Flat): Dean McKeown (8-1, w.a.).

627 MR R. J. WEAVER, Markfield

Postal: **Ulverscroft Racing Stables, Priory Lane, Ulverscroft, Markfield, Leicestershire.**
Phone: **OFFICE MARKFIELD (0530) 243105 HOME (0533) 414112**

1 **DISTRICT NURSE,** 4, b f Country Retreat—Furious Babs **Mr L. R. Gasson**
2 **ELLTEE-ESS,** 5, ch g Lighter—Verosina **Mr D. A. Johnson**
3 **ENGLISH RIVER (USA),** 6, b g Irish River (FR)—Belle Sorella (USA) **Ulverscroft Racing Stables Ltd**
4 **HARVEST FAIR,** 5, b m Oats—Breamish Belle **Mr H. W. Turcan and Mr W. J. Turcan**
5 **HIGH FINANCE,** 5, ch g Billion (USA)—Miss Plumes **Mr D. A. Johnson**
6 **MANOR PARK CRUMPET,** 6, ch m True Song—Madge Spartan **Mr Eddie Jordan**
7 **MANOR PARK LASS,** 6, b m Torus—Evening Primrose **Mr Eddie Jordan**
8 **O'CONNELL STREET,** 6, ch g Dublin Taxi—The Danstan **Ulverscroft Racing Stables Ltd**
9 **ROYAL EFFIGY,** 7, b g Henbit (USA)—Queen's Penny **Rugby Finance (Midlands) Ltd**
10 **SHIRLEY ANN,** 7, ch m Buckskin (FR)—Doone Gate **Mr D. A. Johnson**
11 **TIKITAMA,** 7, b m Bustiki—Tarama **Mr F. H. Gilman**

Other Owners: Mr Rick Gorne.

Conditional: Vicki Salt (8-7).

628 MR J. WEBBER, Banbury

Postal: **Cropredy Lawn, Mollington, Banbury, Oxon, OX17 1DR.**
Phone: **(0295) 750226 FAX (0295) 758482**

1 **ARTFUL ABBOT,** 6, ch g The Parson—She's Clever **Mr Peter S. Thompson**
2 **AUNTIE DOT,** 9, b m Hallodri (ATA)—Dream Isle **Mrs R. Wilson**
3 **COUSIN FLO,** 5, ch m True Song—Dream Isle **Mrs R. Wilson**
4 **ELFAST,** 7, b g Neltino—Niagara Rhythm **Mr John Webber**
5 **FATHER PADDY,** 8, b g Mandamus—Dream Isle **Mr P. J. Morgan**
6 **FOXCOPSE,** 7, b g Healaugh Fox—Belinka **Mrs M. Thomlinson**
7 **GLENFORRES,** 5, ch g Callernish—Clever Noel **Mr Peter S. Thompson**
8 **MWEENISH,** 8, b g Callernish—No Trix **Mr Peter S. Thompson**
9 **RESIDENCY,** 6, b g Dominion—Restive **Mr R. N. Richmond-Watson**
10 **RIVERVALE,** 7, ch g Over The River (FR)—Sweetville **Mr John Webber**
11 **SABRE STAR,** 5, b br m Broadsword (USA)—Mexican Star **Mrs R. Wilson**
12 **SAMSUN,** 8, b g Sunyboy—Etoile de Lune **Exors of the late Major George Rodwell**
13 **SHALYMYRRH,** 6, b m Rymer—Shahzadeh **Mrs Peter Hall**
14 **SPRING WEDDING,** 5, ch m Tudorville—St Lucian Breeze **Mr John Webber**
15 **TAPLYCH D'AIRY (FR),** 5, b g Lychee (FR)—Capeline (FR) **Mrs Mary Grant**
16 **TILDEBO,** 6, b g Ile de Bourbon (USA)—Thereby **Mrs David Blackburn**
17 **WARNER'S END,** 9, ch g Legal Tender—Yoriet **Lady Lyell**

Other Owners: Mr Ivor Chaddock, Mrs Sheila Cole, Mrs M. E. Dalzell, Major R. P. G. Dill, Captain P. R. Doyne, Mr Richard Hall, Col Ivo Reid, Mr David Wade-Jones, Mrs C. Watson, Mrs E. M. Wharton, Mr William Wilson.

Jockey (NH): M M Lynch (10-0).

Lady Rider: Miss Joanna Henry (9-7).

629 MR C. V. WEEDON, Chiddingfold

Postal: **Robins Farm, Fisher Lane, Chiddingfold, Surrey, GU8 4TB.**
Phone: **042879 3344**

1 **BAY TERN (USA),** 4, b c Arctic Tern (USA)—Unbiased (USA) **Mr T. Dyer**
2 **COQUILLAGE,** 5, b g Coquelin (USA)—Legs And Things **Miss A. K. Bayliss**
3 **CROSSLAND LEISURE,** 5, b g Torus—Kathleen Beag **Mr D. Cross**
4 **FISTFUL OF BUCKS,** 4, b g Lochnager—Crimson Ring **Mr T. Dyer**
5 **LITTLE GENERAL,** 7, ch h General Ironside—Coolentallagh **Mr N. R. Robinson**
6 **RICH NEPHEW,** 5, b br g Great Nephew—Strike It Rich (FR) **Mr D. Jonathan McDougall**
7 **SQUADRON (CAN),** 7, ch g Vice Regent (CAN)—Quadrillion (USA) **Miss Maria West**
8 **TOP ENTERTAINER,** 4, ch g Be My Guest (USA)—Her Review (USA) **Mr I. C. Fenwick-Smith**

Other Owners: Mr T. J. Harrington, Mr C. A. Johnson, Mr P. G. Simcock, Mr Colin Weedon, Mr Peter Wiegand.

Jockeys (NH): P Hobbs, A Webb.

630 MR D. K. WELD M.V.B. M.R.C.V.S., The Curragh

Postal: **Rosewell House, The Curragh, Co. Kildare, Irish Republic.**
Phone: **THE CURRAGH 41273/41476 TELEX 60689 WELD EI FAX 045/41119**

1 **GENERAL IDEA,** 5, ch g General Assembly—Idealist
2 **KIICHI (USA),** 5, b g Perrault—Kahaila
3 **LONE RUNNER,** 4, br c Chief Singer—Helpless Haze (USA)
4 **MILIEU,** 5, b h Habitat—Lady Graustark
5 **PERRIS VALLEY,** 9, b g Le Bavard—Margerval
6 **RARE HOLIDAY,** 4, ch g Caerleon—Temporary Lull
7 **SLENDER STYLE (USA),** 4, b f Alleged—Cold Buns
8 **TWILIGHT AGENDA (USA),** 4, b c Devil's Bag—Grenzen
9 **WIDE SUPPORT,** 5, br g Be My Guest—Riva Ring

THREE-YEAR-OLDS

10 **APPLEDORN,** ch f Doulab—Mythical Lady
11 **ARABIAN KNIGHTS,** br c Ela-Mana-Mou—Return To Paris
12 **BANATEE,** ch f Thatching—Faraway Places
13 **CAMDEN FOX,** ch f Camden Town—Lucky Monday
14 **CAREFREE DANCER (USA),** ch c Nijinsky—Blue Wind
15 **CHEERING NEWS,** b c Shernazar—Florentink
16 **CLEAR ISSUE (USA),** ch f Riverman—Grenzen
17 **COMMITTED DANCER,** b c Nijinsky—Committed
18 **CROCKADORE (USA),** ch f Nijinsky—Flo Russell
19 **DLIADORE,** b c Law Society—Catopetl
20 **EASY'N GOLD (USA),** ch f Slew O'Gold—Easy To Copy
21 **ENCHANTED FLYER,** b g Doulab—Enchanted
22 **GO AND GO,** ch c Be My Guest—Irish Edition
23 **GUARANTEED INCOME,** b c Saratoga Six—Talking Picture
24 **HANALEI (USA),** b c Fit To Fight—Loaded Gun
25 **IN REVIEW,** b f Ela-Mana-Mou—Istiea
26 **INSIDER'S VIEW,** b f Caerleon—Sweet Mint
27 **LORD ABBEYDALE,** b c Habitat—Abbeydale
28 **LOTUS POOL,** b c Spectacular Bid—Golden Petal
29 **MISHNOCK,** ch c Persian Bold—Gerardmer
30 **MUNSIF (FR),** b c Akarad—Primitive Troikas
31 **NASSAU,** b c Cure The Blues—Nanticious
32 **NAVY ADMIRAL,** b c Be My Guest—Nana Mana Mou
33 **NAYDO MAY,** b f Shirley Heights—Smeralda
34 **PADIORD,** ch c Caerleon—Osmunda
35 **PERFECT WELCOME,** b f Taufan—Areola
36 **PRE EMINENT,** b c Local Suitor—Fluella
37 **PRUDENT MANNER,** ch c Cure The Blues—Prudent Girl
38 **QUICKSHINE (USA),** b f The Minstrel—Bubinka
39 **SADLER'S CONGRESS,** b c Sadler's Wells—Congress Lady
40 **SHAGUDINE,** ch f Shadeed—Lady Norcliffe
41 **SHANDRYANN (USA),** b f Shadeed—Esna
42 **SHARP FLASH,** ch f Kris—Spark of Fire
43 **SLEET SKIER,** b c Niniski—Fleet Girl
44 **SPENDING RECORD,** ch c Topsider—Final Figure
45 **TEACH DHA MHILE,** b c Kampala—Mittens
46 **THE CARETAKER,** b f Caerleon—Go Feather Go
47 **WELSH MUFFIN,** b f Caerleon—Muffitys
48 **ZUIDER ZEE (USA),** b c Sagace—Cycylya Zee

TWO-YEAR-OLDS

49 **ALAROOS (IRE),** b f Persian Bold—Pilot Bird (Blakeney)
50 B c Caerleon—Bean Siamsa (Solinus)
51 **BIT OF FAITH (USA),** b f Affirmed—Falafel (Northern Dancer)
52 **CAPTURE THE FLAIR (IRE),** b f Darshaan—Going Digital (Northern Baby)
53 B f Green Desert—Costly Wave (Caro)

MR D. K. WELD M.V.B. M.R.C.V.S.—continued

54 **FLOURISHING STYLE (IRE),** ch f Shardari—Florentink (The Minstrel)
55 B c Tate Gallery—Hard To Tell (Buckpasser)
56 B c Danzig—Helen Street (Troy)
57 **ISHRAAQ (USA),** ch c Alydar—Water Lily (Riverman)
58 **KALABA,** gr c Kalaglow—Izba (Thatching)
59 **LADY KRIS (IRE),** ch f Kris—Lady Graustark (Graustark)
60 B c Storm Bird—La Noblesse (Key To The Mint)
61 **LATEST CREATION (USA),** b f Affirmed—High Competence (The Minstrel)
62 **MAIDEN OF IRON (IRE),** ch f Flash of Steel—Takastroll (Hello Gorgeous)
63 B f Sure Blade—Marble Run (Run The Gantlet)
64 **MARSHAD (USA),** b c El Gran Senor—Hatton Gardens (Auction Ring)
65 **MINSTREL'S FOLLY (USA),** b f The Minstrel—Fiscal Folly (Foolish Pleasure)
66 **MISSING LOVE (IRE),** ch f Thatching—Miss Love (Northfields)
67 B c Wolf Power—Morelle (Vitelio)
68 **MYSTERY MISSION (IRE),** b c King's Lake—Sefka (Masetto)
69 **NOUSCHKA,** ch f Ahonoora—Place of Honour (Be My Guest)
70 **OKHIRO (USA),** b c Stalwart—Hiroko (Alydar)
71 **OTHER INCOME (IRE),** b c Shernazar—Honey Bend (Never Bend)
72 **OVERSEAS HOLDING (USA),** ch c Super Concorde—Overall Image (Nijinsky)
73 **OVERSEAS MARKET (IRE),** b c Super Concorde—Melodic (Song)
74 **PARIS IN SPRING (USA),** ch f The Minstrel—Need For Cash (Raise A Native)
75 B f Nijinsky—Pass A Glance (Buckpasser)
76 B c Commanche Run—Practical (Ballymore)
77 B f Danzig—Queen Sucree (Ribot)
78 **QUICK SHUFFLE (USA),** b f Super Concorde—Raise Your Skirts (Elevation)
79 **RENEWED BID (USA),** ch c Chief's Crown—Bubinka (Nashua)
80 Ch c Nijinsky—Roycon (High Top)
81 B f Kings Lake—Saving Mercy (Lord Gayle)
82 Gr c Topsider—Shindy (Roberto)
83 **SLIP AND SLIDE (IRE),** b c Pennine Walk—Polaregina (Rex Magna)
84 **SLIP ASHORE (IRE),** b f Slip Anchor—Muffitys (Thatch (USA))
85 **SMOOTH PERFORMANCE (USA),** b c Seattle Slew—Seasonal Pickup (The Minstrel)
86 **SOLO SAIL,** b c Slip Anchor—Soluce (Junius (USA))
87 B c The Minstrel—South Ocean (New Providence)
88 **SPARK OF SUCCESS (USA),** b f Topsider—Social Lesson (Forum)
89 **SPRING TO LIGHT (USA),** ch f Blushing Groom—Holiday Dancer (Masked Dancer)
90 Ch f Diesis—Srping Adieu (Buckpasser)
91 B c Be My Guest—Steel Habit (Habitat)
92 **STRATEGIC PUZZLE (IRE),** b c Taufan—Software (Lyphard)
93 **STRONG RESISTANCE (USA),** ch c Affirmed—Sweetened Offer (General Assembly)
94 **SUPER IMAGE (USA),** b c Shahrastani—Starushka (Sham)
95 B c Lomond—Tree of Knowledge (Sassafras)
96 B c Nureyev—Tremulous (Gregorian)
97 **TWO TYCOONS (IRE),** b f Last Tycoon—Reo Racine (Dom Racine)
98 **UNREACHABLE,** b f Reach—On The Top (High Top)
99 B c Seattle Song—Waterloo (Bold Lad)
100 **WEEKEND BREAK (IRE),** ch f Caerleon—Sally's Wish (Sensitivo)

Owners: Y. Akazawa, Bernard Cooke, Dana Stud Ltd, Hamdan Al Maktoum, Sheikh Mohammed, Mount Juliet, Moyglare Stud, Mrs J. R. Mullion, A. Mutawa, A. J. O'Reilly, Allen E. Paulson, N. H. Phillips, Mrs Sonia Rogers, R. E. Sangster, Michael W. J. Smurfit, Stablemate Racing Plc, C. E. P. Taylor, Mrs C. L. Weld.

Jockey (Flat): M J Kinane (8-3).

Apprentice: D V Smith (7-12).

GET ON TARGET
with a BBA Ireland Stallion
at Corbally Stud
PENNINE WALK
PERSIAN BOLD
PRINCE RUPERT
VISION
at Ennistown Stud
SHY GROOM
at Athassel House Stud
REASONABLE
at Knocktoran Stud
ASTRONEF
at The Irish National Stud
BE MY NATIVE
at Ardoon Stud
EXHIBITIONER
NASHAMAA
Enquiries to:
B.B.A. (Ireland) Ltd., 51, Lansdowne Road, Dublin 4, Ireland
Tel: Dublin (01) 686222. Telex: 93850 (BBAEI) Fax: (01) 685634

631 MR D. R. WELLICOME, Northampton

Postal: **Washbrooke Farm, Naseby, Northampton, NN6 7DW.**
Phone: **NORTHAMPTON (0604) 740587**

1 **FAIR SEAS,** 4, b f General Assembly (USA)—Seven Seas (FR) **Mr D. R. Wellicome**
2 **FAST REALM (USA),** 7, b g Tromos—Fast Ride (FR) **Mr D. R. Wellicome**
3 **ROYAL CHARGE (USA),** 9, b g King Pellinore (USA)—Reload (FR) **Mr D. R. Wellicome**
4 **TRAVEL MUSIC,** 5, b m Kafu—Octet **Mr D. R. Wellicome**

Jockey (NH): M Bastard (10-0).

632 MR B. K. WELLS, Kidderminster

Postal: **The Tanwood Stud, Chaddesley Corbett, Kidderminster, Worcestershire.**
Phone: **(056283) 296**

1 **AYRES ROCK,** 9, b h Shirley Heights—Brazen Faced **Mrs Valerie Wells**
2 **BALLYFER,** 13, br m Sovereign Bill—Ballyarctic **Mr B. K. Wells**
3 **BIBSKELLY,** 8, br g Pitskelly—Piedita **Mr B. K. Wells**
4 **BOURGEOIS,** 15, ch g Crowned Prince (USA)—Paris Label (USA) **Mr B. K. Wells**
5 **CAR GEE,** 12, gr m Pongee—Carbia
6 **CROMWELL GIRL,** 11, br m Forlorn River—Ballyarctic **Mrs Valerie Wells**
7 **KAMUR,** 4, br f Kafu—Namur **Mr B. K. Wells**
8 **LA BELLE OF SANTO,** 7, b m Monsanto (FR)—Henrietta Belle **Mr B. K. Wells**
9 **MAHSERYAH,** 5, b m Kafu—Pure Perfection **Mr B. K. Wells**
10 **OUTWOOD LASS,** 12, br m Most Secret—Birgeen **Mr B. K. Wells**
11 **ROYAL DESTINY,** 4, b f King of Spain—Avon Belle **Mr B. K. Wells**
12 **ST ANLO,** 8, b m Sir Nulli—Bridport **Mrs Valerie Wells**
13 **SWIFT CHARLIE,** 5, br g Shua Jo—Bridport **Mr B. K. Wells**
14 **TASHONYA,** 8, b g Grundy—Explorelka **Mrs Valerie Wells**

THREE-YEAR-OLDS

15 **BONNIE DE LYON,** b f Silver Season—Mummy's Pride **Mrs Valerie Wells**

Other Owners: Miss Susan Yardley.

Jockeys (NH): Gareth Charles-Jones (10-0, w.a.), A Forte (9-7), W A Morris (9-10).

Conditional: J Dacosta (9-7).

Amateur: Mr M V Darby (10-8).

Lady Riders: Miss Sally Ann Billot (8-7), Miss Jeannetta Hancox (8-0), Miss Susan Yardley (8-7).

633 MR E. WEYMES, Leyburn

Postal: **Ashgill, Coverham, Leyburn, N. Yorkshire, DL8 4TJ.**
Phone: **(0969) 40229**

1 **CARBISDALE,** 4, ch g Dunbeath (USA)—Kind Thoughts **Mr E. Weymes**
2 **CHORUS BOY,** 5, br g Sonnen Gold—Toccata **Mrs N. Napier**
3 **CROWTHERS,** 4, gr g Mandrake Major—Milnsbridge **Mrs P. M. Weymes**
4 **FORMATION,** 4, br g Tanfirion—Imagination (FR) **Mr R. L. Heaton and Mrs R. L. Heaton**
5 **GRAND ISLAND,** 5, ch g Thatching—Okavamba **Mrs P. M. Weymes**

MR E. WEYMES—continued

6 **LAST 'O' THE BUNCH,** 6, ch h Meldrum—Golden Royalty **Mr G. Middlebrook**
7 **MANHATTAN RIVER,** 4, ch g Gorytus (USA)—East River (FR) **Mr Martin Hirst**
8 **NOT YET,** 6, b g Connaught—Ritratto **Mrs V. Moorey**
9 **OH DANNY BOY,** 6, br g Rabdan—Musical Princess **Mrs N. Napier**
10 **PREPOLLO,** 4, gr g Precocious—Rosie Black **Mr T. A. Scothern**
11 **TRILL ALONG,** 4, ch g Longleat—Cabaletta **Mrs N. Napier**
12 **VAGUE DANCER,** 4, br c Vaigly Great—Step You Gaily **Mr and Mrs Norman Blyth**

THREE-YEAR-OLDS

13 **BELDONAYR,** ch f Rabdan—Pearl Cove **Mr K. Coxon**
14 **CASH POINT,** b g Sweet Monday—Kindling **Miss R. Duckitt**
15 **FINLUX SKY DESIGN,** br g Ballad Rock—Slip The Ferret **Mr T. A. Scothern**
16 **KALVEE DANCER,** b f Kalaglow—Clonavee **Mrs A. Birkett**
17 **OSGATHORPE,** ch c Dunbeath (USA)—Darlingka **Mrs L. Middlebrook**

TWO-YEAR-OLDS

18 Ch f 27/4 Vaigly Great—Cracked Up (Busted)
19 **NOT JUST YET,** b f 11/5 Mandrake Major—Okavamba (Wollow) **Mrs V. Moorey**

Apprentice: G Barnes (8-0).

Amateur: J Weymes (10-0).

634 MR J. R. H. WHARTON, Melton Mowbray

Postal: **Shipmans Barn Stud, Saxby Road, Melton Mowbray, Leicestershire, LE14 4RZ.**
Phone: **HOME (0664) 65225 OFFICE (0664) 78334**

1 **BELTALONG,** 4, gr f Belfort (FR)—Gentian **Mr J. L. Ashby**
2 **BESCABY BOY,** 4, b g Red Sunset—Charo (FR) **Pennells Estates**
3 **BLUES INDIGO,** 5, b m Music Boy—Bluit (FR) **Mrs R. T. Watson**
4 **CREEAGER,** 8, b g Creetown—Teenager **Mr J. M. Berry**
5 **CRYSTAL PARK,** 4, b f Head For Heights—So Precise (FR) **Mr G. W. Mills**
6 **DEEP IN THE WOOD,** 7, ch g Deep Run—Elsea Wood **Mr G. G. H. Adcock**
7 **FRED ASTAIRE,** 9, b g Be Friendly—Floor Show **Mr H. Morton**
8 **GINA'S CHOICE,** 4, b f Ile de Bourbon (USA)—Modern Romance **Dr W. J. Heffernan**
9 **GLEBE SPINNEY,** 8, b g Netherkelly—My Darling **Mr R. M. Micklethwait**
10 **MR QUICK,** 11, b g Saucy Kit—Tesco Maid **Mr Richard Sanderson**
11 **NAE BOTHER,** 5, b g Neltino—Pirella **Mr W. Wharton**
12 **PRIESTGATE,** 5, ch g Stanford—Change of Luck **Mr Roger Speechley**
13 **ROLAMPAGO,** 7, ch g Hardgreen (USA)—Candolcis **Mrs A. V. Ferguson**
14 **SELDOM IN,** 4, ch g Mummy's Game—Pinzamber **Mrs V. Craggs**
15 **SNAKE EYE,** 5, b g Tina's Pet—Dingle Belle **Mr T. Civil**
16 **WHISTLING BLUES,** 4, ch f Stanford—Whistling Girl **Lord Gainsborough**

THREE-YEAR-OLDS

17 **ADVANCE TO GO,** ch f Horage—La Bellilotte **Mrs L. E. Penny**
18 **BIG SURPRISE,** br g Comedy Star (USA)—Maxine's Here **Mr C. R. Bird**
19 **BOLD PERFORMER,** b c Bold Lad (IRE)—Miss St Cyr **Mr W. Wharton**
20 **CHARLES THE GREAT,** b g Vaigly Great—Tin Tessa **Mr M. J. Yarrow**
21 **EASTERN PLEASURE,** gr g Absalom—First Pleasure **Mr J. L. Ashby**
22 **HARD TO GET,** b g Rousillon (USA)—Elusive **Mr Tom Tayler**
23 **ILEWIN,** br g Ile de Bourbon (USA)—City Swinger **Dr W. J. Heffernan**
24 **ILLOGICAL,** br f Ile de Bourbon (USA)—Modern Romance **Dr W. J. Heffernan**
25 **MARSH'S LAW,** br g Kala Shikari—My Music **Mr Adrian J. Moore**
26 **PARKBORO LAD,** b g Kala Shikari—Great Lass **Parkers of Peterborough Plc**
27 **WALTZING WEASEL,** b f Nemorino (USA)—Branston Express **Mr P. Willett**
28 **YONGE TENDER,** b f Tender King—St Clair Star **Dr T. J. Molony**

MR J. R. H. WHARTON—continued

TWO-YEAR-OLDS

29 **ABLAZE,** ch g 8/4 Absalom—Great Lass (Vaigly Great) **Mr P. W. Lambert**
30 **ARRIVEZ DEUX,** ch f 16/5 Reach—Apair (Red Slipper) **Mr Tom Tayler**
31 Ch f 15/4 Burslem—Courreges (Manado)
32 **DRINKS PARTY,** b f 17/1 Camden Town—Holy Water (Monseigneur (USA)) **Mr David H. Lee**
33 Ch c 4/6 Lyphard's Special—Fire Risk (Thatch (USA))
34 **GALLERY LADY,** b f 10/4 Tender King—London Spin (Derring-Do) **Mr M. C. Mugglestone**
35 Ch f 19/4 Soughaan (USA)—Hard Riche (Hard Fought)
36 **MARTINA,** b f 22/5 Tina's Pet—Tin Tessa (Martinmas) **Mr M. J. Yarrow**
37 **MYSTICAL MELI,** ch f 1/3 Faustus (USA)—La Millie (Nonoalco) **Mr Tom Tayler**
38 **PANIKIN,** gr g 9/4 Red Sunset—Haunting (Lord Gayle) **Mr P. W. Lambert**
39 B c 24/2 Runnett—Spoons (Orchestra)
40 **WILD COINCIDENCE,** ch g 19/4 Faustus (USA)—Wild Rosie (Warpath) **Mr Tom Tayler**

Other Owners: Mrs J. A. Adams, Mrs L. J. Berry, Mr W. Botterill, Mr J. Browne, Mr Peter Churchman, Mr T. Crowson Jnr, Mr J. W. H. Davis, Mr M. J. Hanlon, Mr Peter J. Kerry, Mrs P. Knowles, Mrs A. C. Lambert, Mr Peter W. Marsh, Mr Peter McDonald, Mrs V. McGeough, Mr Geoffrey W. Mills, Mr J. H. Mills, Mr Adrian J. Moore, Mr J. Rose, Mrs T. Rothery, The Sunflower Partnership, Mr D. C. Tye, Mr M. A. Wells, Mr A. C. Wilkinson, Mr P. V. Williams, Dr H. Yarrow.

Jockeys (Flat): Peter Walsh (7-9), Wally Wharton (8-4).

Jockey (NH): S J O'Neill (10-0).

635 MRS V. R. T. WHARTON, Middleham

Postal: **Manor House Stables, Middleham, Leyburn, North Yorkshire, DL8 4QL.**
Phone: **(0969) 23173**

1 **ANGLO BRASIL,** 5, ch g Hardboy—Unsinkable Sarah **Mr J. D. Gordon**
2 **AUSTHORPE SUNSET,** 6, b g Majestic Maharaj—Kings Fillet **Mr A. Walker**
3 **BIDDERS CLOWN,** 5, b g Ring Bidder—Lucky Joker **Mr G. A. Farndon**
4 **COPPER MARKET,** 7, ch g Native Bazaar—Copper Cloud
5 **FOGGY SCOTCH,** 6, br g Chantro—Sirene River **Mrs Dorothy Horner**
6 **KAREN'S STARLET,** 4, b f Ampney Prince—Karen's Girl **Mrs P. Lester**
7 **KELDHOLME,** 8, b m Derek H—Bobby's Hansel **Mrs Roxanne Wharton**
8 5, B g Ballynockan—Kelly's Move **Mrs Roxanne Wharton**
9 **SNOWFIRE CHAP,** 7, ch g Salluceva—Fainne Nua **J. Pickles (Harrogate) Limited**
10 **SOLICITOR'S CHOICE,** 7, b g Cagirama—Girostar **Mr Anthony Sugare**
11 **STRONG FANCY,** 7, br g Royal Match—Sugar Lump **Mr P. Macklam**
12 **THE MALTKILN,** 7, br g Sonnen Gold—Kittaspec Gal **Mr H. Young**
13 **THORNFIELD GROVE,** 6, b g Royal Fountain—Joyous Sound **Citygrove Thornfield Limited**
14 **VALIANT STAR,** 4, br g Noalto—Duns Tew **Mr D. S. Arnold**

THREE-YEAR-OLDS

15 **KARENS PRINCE,** b c Ampney Prince—Karen's Girl **Mr Geoffrey Clarkson**
16 **REFLECTIVE,** br g Magic Mirror—Thanks Edith **Mrs D. E. Sharp**
17 **REKLAW,** b g Hard Fought—Rubina Park **Mr A. Walker**
18 **SAXBY STORM,** ch f Northern Tempest (USA)—Rigton Sally **Mrs I. Willford**
19 **THE QUIET GENIUS,** b f Reesh—Gay Ribbon **Mr A. Walker**

Other Owners: Mr J. Arnold, Mr J. Burns, Mr T. Mulrooney, Mr E. I. Speight, Mrs E. Stoker, Mr D. F. Ward.

Apprentice: Paul Harte (9-0).

Conditional: Paul Harte (9-7).

636 MR E. A. WHEELER, Lambourn

Postal: **Rose Hill Stables, Mile End, Lambourn, Newbury, Berkshire.**
Phone: **(0488) 71650**

1 **ALI MOURAD,** 5, ch g Final Straw—Paper Sun **Mr Tim Kelly**
2 **BRONZE RUNNER,** 6, gr g Gunner B—Petingalyn **Austin Stroud & Co Ltd**
3 **CARPE DIEM,** 5, b m Good Times (ITY)—Olympic Visualise **Mr M. V. Kirby**
4 **CHARMED KNAVE,** 5, b g Enchantment—Peerless Princess **Mrs M. E. Olsson**
5 **ELYSIAN WARRIOR,** 5, b g Full of Hope—Paddock Princess **Mr Alan Williams**
6 **FAYADPOUR,** 6, b g Dalsaan—Fille du Tonnerre (FR) **Austin Stroud & Co Ltd**
7 **FLEET SPIRIT,** 4, b g Ranksborough—Gin And Lime **Mr G. D. Groarke**
8 **FOREST FAWN (FR),** 5, b m Top Ville (FR)—Red Deer **Mr E. Wheeler**
9 **GREEN DOLLAR,** 7, b g Tickled Pink—Burglars Girl **Mr B. Azemoudeh**
10 **HATAAM,** 4, b c Shirley Heights—Nophe (USA) **Mrs E. A. Keating**
11 **KILCONNEY PRINCE,** 8, br g Martinmas—Dark Gold **Mr Alan Williams**
12 **LADY HOMILY,** 6, b m Homing—Taryn **Mr J. Canney**
13 **MICRONOVA,** 4, ch g Homing—Tula Music **Mr A. P. Whittaker and Mr J. Canney**
14 **ROTTEN FOR DAPHNE,** 4, b f Beldale Flutter (USA)—Canadian Charisma **Mr P. V. Mendoza**
15 **SEA SHADOW,** 5, ch g Hello Gorgeous (USA)—Marie Antoinette **Mr P. V. Mendoza**
16 5, B g Lighter—Sponsorship **Mr J. Canney**
17 **SWEET AND SURE,** 5, gr m Known Fact (USA)—Fair Melys **Mr B. Attwood**
18 **TREASURE LORD,** 7, b g Don—Treasure Ship **Mrs P. Michael and Mr J. Graham**

THREE-YEAR-OLDS

19 **FONTAINE LADY,** b f Millfontaine—Lady Begorra **Mrs P. Michael and Mr J. Graham**
20 **GAMEFISHER,** br c Claude Monet (USA)—Resurgence **Austin Stroud & Co Ltd**
21 **LEAH JAY,** ch c Sayyaf—Patriots Day **Mr Jas Jackson**
22 **SHAREUBELLE,** b f Saher—Blue Kingsmill **Mrs F. E. Bacon**
23 **SHARPALTO,** br c Noalto—Sharp Venita **Millprew Bloodstock**
24 **SLIGHT INDULGENCE,** b g Runnett—Celeritas **Mr M. V. Kirby**
25 **SUNGROVE BEST,** ch g Buzzard's Bay—Judann **Mr W. Gibson**

TWO-YEAR-OLDS

26 Ch c 9/3 Bairn—Calibina (Caliban) **Millprew Bloodstock**
27 B c 30/4 Dreams To Reality—Pendona (Blue Cashmere) **Millprew Bloodstock**
28 B f 25/5 Dreams To Reality—Sharp Venita (Sharp Edge) **Millprew Bloodstock**
29 B f 27/1 Runnett—Soudchika (GER) (Dschingis Khan) **Millprew Bloodstock**

Jockey (NH): J White (10-0, w.a.).

Apprentice: L Riggio (7-12).

Conditional: P Barnard (9-7, w.a.).

Amateur: Mr R White (10-0, w.a.).

637 MR N. J. WHEELER, Battle

Postal: **Slivericks Farm, Ashburnham, Battle, E. Sussex, TN33 9PE.**
Phone: **(0435) 830571**

1 **ARMATRIST,** 11, ch g Armagnac Monarch—La Tristesse **Mr N. J. Wheeler**
2 **BATU,** 9, ch g Sparkler—Amber Star **Mr N. J. Wheeler**
3 **SCYLLA'S CHIP,** 8, b g Armagnac Monarch—Just Scylla **Mr N. J. Wheeler**
4 **SHERALAM,** 11, b g Carvin—Sursum Corda (FR) **Mr N. J. Wheeler**

Amateur: Mr N J Wheeler (10-7).

638 MR R. M. WHITAKER, Wetherby

Postal: **Grange Stables, Grange Park, Wetherby, West Yorkshire, LS22 5DY.**
Phone: **(0937) 62122 FAX (0937) 66906**

1 **AARDVARK,** 4, ch g On Your Mark—Vaguely Jade **Mrs M. Pollard-Gill**
2 **AFRICAN AFFAIR,** 5, br g Be My Native (USA)—Moment of Weakness **Wetherby Racing Bureau Plc**
3 **AFRICAN SPIRIT,** 6, b g African Sky—Relic Spirit **Mr G. H. Tufts**
4 **ANFIELD SALLY,** 4, b f Anfield—Bargain Line **Mr Joseph Ogden**
5 **ANNACERAMIC,** 5, b m Horage—Miss Redmarshall **Mr D. Gill**
6 **ARROGANZA,** 5, ch m Crofthall—Redgrave Design **Partnership**
7 **BARRYPHILIPS DISCO,** 13, br g Firestreak—Appollo Fourteen **Mr I. B. Ender**
8 **BAYFORD ENERGY,** 4, ch g Milford—Smiling **Mrs Jean Turner**
9 **BURCROFT,** 6, ch g Crofthall—Two's Up **Mrs D. W. Verity**
10 **CLASSIC SUITE,** 4, b c Ya Zaman (USA)—Lady Bidder **Mr G. A. Farndon**
11 **IMPUNITY,** 5, b g Blakeney—Lantern Light **Mr G. H. Tufts**
12 **JOE SUGDEN,** 6, b g Music Boy—Sum Star **Mr T. F. Bell**
13 **KINGS ASH,** 4, gr f Hill Farmer—Mentone-Lillie **Mr R. G. Creber**
14 **KING TREVISIO,** 4, b c King of Spain—Gundi **Mr M. S. H. Hartley**
15 **KIRKBY FLYER,** 6, b m Gay Pilot—Impatience **Mr D. Gill**
16 **LE PIAT D'OR,** 9, ch g Le Coq d'Or—Game Gypsy **Mrs R. M. Whitaker**
17 **MARCROFT,** 5, ch m Crofthall—Squires Girl **Mrs M. A. Clayton**
18 **MARK AIZLEWOOD,** 5, b g Nicholas Bill—Lunar Queen **Mr D. Gill**
19 **MELANCOLIA,** 4, b f Legend of France (USA)—Fardella (ITY) **Mr G. H. Tufts**
20 **MERRYACRES,** 7, b g Homing—Joking **Mrs D. W. Verity**
21 **MRS MEYRICK,** 9, br m Owen Dudley—Social Bee **Mr D. Gill**
22 **NICHOLAS MARK,** 6, ch g Gunner B—Bargain Line **Mr Joseph Ogden**
23 **NIGHT GIFT,** 4, b f Longleat (USA)—Lucky Tonight **Mr G. I. Thomas**
24 **PARLIAMENT PIECE,** 4, ch c Burslem—Sallywell **Mr G. A. Farndon**
25 **PERCHCOURT,** 5, b g Red Sunset—Faddle **Perchcourt Ltd**
26 **PREDICTABLE,** 4, ch g Music Boy—Piccadilly Etta **Mr G. F. Pemberton**
27 **RESOLUTE BAY,** 4, b g Crofthall—Spinner **Mr D. I. Buckley**
28 **SECRET DANCER,** 4, ch g Last Fandango—Secret Isle (USA) **Mrs Greta Sparks**
29 **SNOWY KITE,** 5, ch m Connaught—Malicious Love **Mr David F. Jackson**
30 **STILL SURPRISED,** 5, ch g Nicholas Bill—Noammo **R. M. Whitaker**
31 **SWEET N' TWENTY,** 4, b f High Top—Royal Home **Mr Frazer Hines**
32 **TENDER TYPE,** 7, b g Prince Tenderfoot (USA)—Double Type **Mr G. H. Tufts**
33 **TOBERMORY BOY,** 13, b g Mummy's Pet—Penny Pincher **Mrs R. T. Watson**

THREE-YEAR-OLDS

34 **ANOTHER LANE,** b f Tina's Pet—Spinner **London & Blenheim Estates**
35 **CALAHONDA DAVE,** gr g Song—Great Grey Niece **Mrs E. G. Faulkner**
36 **CROFT VALLEY,** ch c Crofthall—Sannavally **Miss Vivian Pratt**
37 **DINNINGTON BUMBLE,** ch f Miramar Reef—Sandra's Secret **Mr D. I. Broadbent**
38 **DOUBLE STRAND,** ch f Crofthall—Excavator Lady **Mr Frazer Hines**
39 **EURO GALAXY,** ch c Crofthall—Patent Pending **Europrint Promotions Ltd**
40 **FASTAUFAN,** b g Taufan (USA)—Maggie Mine **Mrs Audrey Tudor**
41 **FIRST BID,** ch c Crofthall—Redgrave Design **Thomlinson's**
42 **FOUNTAIN LOCH,** b f Lochnager—Fountain **Mr G. A. Farndon**
43 **FRIVOLOUS,** ch f Bairn (USA)—Wild Asset **R. M. Whitaker**
44 **GANT BLEU (FR),** ch c Crystal Glitters (USA)—Gold Honey **Mr David Cecil**
45 **GRANITTON BAY,** b c Prince Tenderfoot (USA)—Miss Redmarshall **Mr D. Gill**
46 **HORALDO,** ch g Horage—Nebanna **Mr D. B. Walker**
47 **LAMBSON,** b c Petorius—Julie Be Quick (USA) **Mr Ian Hall**
48 **LA PLACE,** ch f Mansingh (USA)—Pegs Promise **Mr G. H. Leatham**
49 **MASTER DANCER,** b c Mashhor Dancer (USA)—Silent Dancer **Mr T. F. Bell**
50 B c Dutch Treat—My Polyanna **Mr A. Forty**
51 **NATASHA NADINE,** b f Bay Express—Sweet Candice **Trueperch International Ltd**
52 **ONE FOR IRENE,** gr f Hotfoot—Vila Real **Mr J. Wilkins**
53 **PRINCETHORPE,** b g Ring Bidder—Sparkling Jenny **Mr G. A. Farndon**
54 **QUATRE FEMME,** b f Petorius—Irish Kick **Mr G. C. Morley**
55 **SHARP TO OBLIGE,** ch g Dublin Taxi—Please Oblige **Equestrian & Racing Developments Ltd**

MR R. M. WHITAKER—continued

56 SYSTEM TWO, ch f All Systems Go—Two's Up **Mr R. A. Lee**
57 THE HEALY, b f Blushing Scribe (USA)—Smitten **Tim Healy (Entertainments) Ltd**

TWO-YEAR-OLDS

58 B c 9/3 Chief Singer—Action Belle (Auction Ring (USA))
59 B f 12/5 Mashhor Dancer—Baltimore Belle (Bold Lad (IRE))
60 BIDDERS LOVE LANE, b f 5/5 Ring Bidder—Bundling Bed (Welsh Pageant) **Mr G. A. Farndon**
61 Ch f 9/2 Primo Dominie—Blueit (FR) (Bold Lad (IRE))
62 B c 18/4 Fairy King—Burren Star (Hardgreen (USA))
63 B c 13/4 Prince Sabo—Choral Park (Music Boy)
64 Ch f 27/4 Scottish Reel—Florence Street (Final Straw)
65 B g 30/1 Jupiter Island—Friendly Pet (Be Friendly)
66 MY ALMA (IRE), b f 23/1 Reasonable—Lady Bidder (Auction Ring (USA)) **Mr G. A. Farndon**
67 Ch f 23/3 Scottish Reel—Salacious (Sallust)
68 SOUSON (IRE), b c 27/2 Soughaan (USA)—Down The Line (Brigadier Gerard) **Mr J. David Abell**
69 STRAW BABY, ch f 17/4 Final Straw—Miss Bretonne (Huntercombe) **Mr B. Samson**
70 B f 22/5 Vision—Tender Niece (Prince Tenderfoot (USA))
71 WHAT A SHOW OFF, ch c 10/3 Exhibitioner—Berserk (Romulus) **Mr L. S. Smith**

Other Owners: Mr A. Barnes, Mr D. I. Buckley, Mrs Jose Button, Mr H. Cooper, Mr M. Granger, Mrs M. Granger, Mr Chris Moreno, Mr T. A. Morton, Mrs E. J. Mulkeen, Mr B. Pratt, Mrs G. L. Rastrick, Mr J. Richardson, Mr E. Richmond, Mrs E. M. Ridding, Mr J. Rowlands, Mr M. Schofield, Mr David Scott, Mr Brian Thompson, Mr H. Tuck.

Jockeys (Flat): J Carr (8-0), A Culhane (7-12).

Jockey (NH): Stuart Turner (9-7).

Amateurs: Mr Frazer Hines (11-0), Mr Simon Richard Whitaker (11-3).

639 MR C. J. WHITE, Steyning

Postal: **Annington Mere Farmhouse, St Botolphs, Steyning, West Sussex.**
Phone: **(0903) 816258**

1 BACKTONICA, 5, b m Rolfe (USA)—Minica **Mr C. J. White**
2 SEE YOU ANON, 6, b g Longleat (USA)—Huntergirl **Mr C. J. White**

TWO-YEAR-OLDS

3 B f Lightning Dealer—The Mopolli (Spartan General)

640 MRS F. E. WHITE, Chelmsford

Postal: **The Lodge, Nipsells Farm, Nipsells Chase, Mayland, Chelmsford, Essex, CM3 6EJ.**
Phone: **MALDON (0621) 742161**

1 HARD UP, 9, br g Impecunious—Anagola **Mr W. White**
2 HENRY MAJOR, 6, ch g Roman Warrior—Pretty Girl **Mr W. White**
3 NINTH TERM, 4, b c Welsh Term—Dusty Bluebell **Mr W. White**
4 POINT CLEAR, 10, b g Le Bavard (FR)—Vulstar **Mr W. White**

Amateur: Miss S White (9-0).

641 MR J. WHITE, Wendover

Postal: **Russell Farm, Cobblers Hill, Wendover, Buckinghamshire, HP22 6QD.**
Phone: **(0296) 623387**

1 **AL SAHIL (USA),** 5, b h Riverman (USA)—Tobira Celeste (USA) **Mr M. Broadley**
2 **AL'S SON,** 9, br g Al Sirat (USA)—Fanny's Daughter **Mr R. F. Warwick**
3 **ALZAMINA,** 4, b f Alzao (USA)—Timinala **Mr K. Panos**
4 **BARLEY LOAF,** 7, b g Barley Hill—Motherly Love **Mr P. A. Oppenheimer**
5 **BONDAID,** 6, b g Main Reef—Regency Gold **Mr A. J. Allright**
6 **BOY JAMIE,** 6, ch g Nicholas Bill—Petard **Mrs Wrighton**
7 **BRINKWATER,** 14, b g Super Slip—Yes Gail **Mr John R. White**
8 **BURNT FINGERS,** 6, ch g Busted—Madame's Share **Mr M. R. Pascall**
9 **BUSTAMENTE,** 7, b g Busted—Blessed Damsel **Mrs A. Gittins**
10 **CAIRNCASTLE,** 5, b g Ardross—Brookfield Miss
11 **CHESS MISTRESS (USA),** 5, b m Run The Gantlet (USA)—Bishop's Fling (USA) **Mr R. Brand**
12 **COOL SEASON,** 6, ch g Vital Season—Iced Lolly **Mrs J. D. M. Kempe**
13 **DUNCTON HILL,** 4, ch f Formidable (USA)—Hazel Bush **Mrs Rita Bates**
14 **FINAL SELECTION,** 7, ch g Final Straw—Contralto **Mrs E. D. Robinson**
15 **GOLD STRATA,** 4, b g Gold Song—French Strata (USA) **Mr Frank Brant**
16 **MASTER VINCE,** 12, b g Menelek—Oh Babe **Mr Stanley Squires**
17 **MERYETT (BEL),** 6, b m Le Grand Meaulnes—Maji **Mr M. Nelmes-Crocker**
18 **PACIFIC RUN,** 5, ch h Deep Run—Little Welly **Mr S. Cartmel and Mrs S. Cartmel**
19 **PRESIDIO,** 4, ro g Beldale Flutter (USA)—Danielle Delight **Mrs C. M. Dartford**
20 **QUIET RIOT,** 8, b g Hotfoot—Tuyenu **Mrs Evelyn Gittins**
21 **ROCK ON KELLY,** 6, b g Netherkelly—Escallop **Mr C. K. Parker**
22 **SALLY'S GEM,** 5, b g Hasty Word—China Bank **Mr M. H. Smith**
23 **SASSANOCO,** 9, b g Nonoalco (USA)—Sassanian **Mr M. R. Pascall**
24 **SHANGOSEER,** 9, b g Record Token—Fly For Home **Direct Salt Supplies Ltd**
25 **SHERINGHAM HOUSE,** 7, b g Crash Course—Deep Grey **Sheringham Hotel Ltd Reading**
26 **SICILIAN VESPERS,** 5, b m Mummy's Game—Orange Silk **Mr Chris Page**
27 **SOHAIL (USA),** 7, ch g Topsider (USA)—Your Nuts (USA) **Mrs Evelyn Gittins**
28 **SOMEBODY,** 6, b h Bustino—Kashmir Lass **Mr C. Cheesman**
29 **STRONG LANGUAGE,** 5, ch m Formidable (USA)—Linguistic **Mr T. G. N. Burrage**
30 **SWEETING,** 5, b g Lighter—Snare **Mr Raymond Singer**
31 **TAKEAWAY,** 4, ch g Ivotino (USA)—Come On Doll **Mr H. K. Man**
32 **TALK OF GLORY,** 9, b g Hittite Glory—Fiddle-Faddle **Mrs Carys Gadsden**
33 **TARANGA,** 7, b g Music Boy—Emblazon **Mr Stanley Squires**
34 **TIVIAN,** 10, b g Busted—Jovian **Mrs E. D. Robinson**
35 **TOPKAPI,** 7, b g Beldale Flutter (USA)—Pithead **Mr C. Cheesman**
36 **TUCK BOX,** 4, ch g Bustino—Sweet Hour **Mr Jim White**

THREE-YEAR-OLDS

37 **BODAMIST,** b c Swing Easy (USA)—Diorina **Mrs Evelyn Gittins**
38 **PHISUS,** b f Henbit (USA)—Daring Lass **Mr P. Higson**
39 **SIREESH,** b g Reesh—Record Lady **Mr P. Higson**
40 **SUPADUPA,** ch f Superlative—Maysina **Print and Design Limited (Pad Ltd)**

TWO-YEAR-OLDS

41 Gr br c 25/3 Nishapour (FR)—Bustling Nelly (Bustino) **Mrs C. Dartford**
42 B c 10/3 Belfort (FR)—Firey Kim (CAN) (Cannonade (USA)) **Mr K. Kleanthous**
43 Gr br c 27/2 Petong—Infelice (Nishapour (FR)) **Mr K. Kleanthous and Mr K. Panos**
44 B c 17/3 Swing Easy (USA)—Mummy's Chick (Mummy's Pet) **Mrs C. Dartford**
45 Ch c 5/5 Red Sunset—Saintly Game (Welsh Saint) **Mr K. Kleanthous**
46 B f 18/2 Sayf El Arab (USA)—Scotch Thistle (Sassafras (FR)) **Mr K. Kleanthous**
47 B f 14/2 Ballacashtal (CAN)—Within A Whisper (Welsh Pageant) **SPS Bloodstock**

Other Owners: Mr K. Craddock, Mr A. Gibbon, Mr J. Graham, Mr Martin C. Ingram, Mr G. Maclean, Mr Leslie Rose, Mr T. Sheeran.

Jockeys (NH): K Burke (10-0), D Skyrme.

Conditional: B Hanley (10-0), N Roche (10-0).

642 MR K. WHITE, Aston Munslow

Postal: **Little London Farm, Aston Munslow, Craven Arms, Salop, SY7 9ES.**
Phone: **(058 476) 200**

1 **ASTLEY JACK,** 4, gr c Belfort (FR)—Brigado **Mrs H. M. Knott**
2 **AUK EYE (NZ),** 6, b g Auk (USA)—Horafama (NZ) **Mrs H. F. Richards**
3 **BUSTED SPRING,** 9, b g Crash Course—Rose of Spring **Mr Alan Millard**
4 **CHAIN SHOT,** 5, b g Pas de Seul—Burnished **Mr H. F. McEwen**
5 **CREAM AND GREEN,** 6, b g Welsh Chanter—Jumana **Andea (The South American Shop) Limited**
6 **DUE DILLIGENCE,** 8, ch h General Assembly (USA)—Mrs McArdy **Mr R. D. Griffiths**
7 **FLEURCONE,** 8, ch g Celtic Cone—Little Fleur **Mrs B. Wynn**
8 **GIGONDAS,** 11, b m Brigadier Gerard—Gingerale **Mrs H. F. Richards**
9 **GOLFER'S SUNRISE,** 5, b g Red Sunset—Miss Stradavinsky **Mr Rod Taylor**
10 **GREAT ASPECT,** 6, b br h Great Nephew—Broad Horizon **Mr Garry Roberts**
11 **HEADIN' ON,** 10, b g Headin' Up—Olisa **Mrs H. M. Knott**
12 **LEGAL COIN,** 6, ch m Official—Anxious Coin **Mr Bob Moseley**
13 **MISS DELILAH,** 4, b f Humdoleila—Pem Pem **Mrs E. A. Davies**
14 **RESTLESS RHAPSODY,** 7, ch g Young Generation—Bohemian Rhapsody **Mr Garry Roberts**
15 **RISE OVER,** 4, ch f Smackover—Stewart's Rise **Mr Garry Roberts**
16 **SHARP CHARTER,** 4, ch g Kris—Centrocon **Mr A. H. Bennett**
17 **TARA TONG,** 4, b f Bold Fort—Lucinski **Mrs L. M. Tong**
18 **WILLOWSON,** 9, b g Vulcott—Goldie's Willow **Mr G. R. S. Allsopp**

THREE-YEAR-OLDS

19 **LARA'S ELEGANT,** b c Elegant Air—Lara's Song (USA) **Mr J. L. Mason**
20 **URFAN,** br c Valiyar—Nafla (FR) **Mr Rod Taylor**
21 **XAI-TANG,** gr g Petong—Northern Dynasty **Andea (The South American Shop) Limited**

TWO-YEAR-OLDS

22 B f Hasty Word—Butchers Barn (Space King) **Mr K. B. White**
23 B f 12/4 Pennine Walk—Treeline (High Top) **Mr Garry Roberts**

Other Owners: Mr M. A. Coombs, Mr K. C. G. Edwards, Mrs H. M. Knott, Derek Pugh.

Jockey (Flat): John Williams (w.a.).

Jockey (NH): A O'Hagan (10-0).

Apprentice: Karen Gurney (8-4).

Amateur: Mr J Hay (10-7).

Lady Rider: Miss L Wallace (8-7).

643 MISS A. J. WHITFIELD, Lambourn

Postal: **Windy Hollow, Sheepdrove, Lambourn, Newbury, Berkshire, RG16 7XA.**
Phone: **(0488) 72342 FAX (0488) 72248**

1 **ALGAIHABANE (USA),** 4, b c Roberto (USA)—Sassábunda **Mr Andreas Sofroniou**
2 **ATHENS BY NIGHT (USA),** 4, ch f London Bells (CAN)—Senorita Poquito **Mr Andreas Sofroniou**
3 **EXECUTIVE STAR,** 4, b f Raga Navarro (ITY)—Belligerent **Mr S. Sofroniou**
4 **GOLDUST (FR),** 5, ch m Dublin Taxi—Aberklair **Mr Andreas Sofroniou**
5 **HIGHLAND CLIPPER,** 11, b g Pitcairn—Mother Brown **Miss A. Whitfield**

MISS A. J. WHITFIELD—continued

6 **HONEY DANCER,** 6, b g Tyrnavos—Hello Honey **Mr Andreas Sofroniou**
7 **NIKITAS,** 5, b g Touching Wood (USA)—Hi There **Mrs Peter Liddiard**
8 **NUMISMATIST,** 11, b g Vitiges (FR)—Mile By Mile **Miss A. Whitfield**
9 **PLEASURE DANCER,** 5, b g Monsanto (FR)—Moment's Pleasure (USA) **Mr A. Sofroniou**
10 **SEA SIESTA,** 4, b f Vaigly Great—Janlarmar **Mr Andreas Sofroniou**
11 **SILENT WISH (USA),** 4, ch g Silent Screen (USA)—Petita **Mrs P. Carson**
12 **STONE FOREST,** 5, b br h Thatching—Senta's Girl **Mr Andreas Sofroniou**

THREE-YEAR-OLDS

13 **BUBULINA,** b f Dunphy—Hi There **Mr Andreas Sofroniou**
14 **DRAGONS NEST,** b c Welsh Term—Laxmi **The French Garden Ltd**

TWO-YEAR-OLDS

15 B c 17/2 Bellypha—Ivor's Date (USA) (Sir Ivor)
16 Ro c 22/3 Show-A-Leg—Land of Ginger (Young Man (FR))
17 B c 12/5 Niniski (USA)—Miss Saint-Cloud (Nonoalco (USA))
18 B f 30/4 Slip Anchor—Nepula (Nebbiolo)
19 B c 3/4 Mashhor Dancer (USA)—Raina Perera (Tyrnavos)
20 B c 24/2 Lidhame—Rainbow Star (Star Appeal)
21 B c 7/3 Plugged Nickle (USA)—Slewvindaloo (USA) (Seattle Slew (USA))
22 **SUPER HEIGHTS,** b c 21/2 Superlative—Shadha (Shirley Heights)

Other Owners: Mr George Ward.

Jockey (Flat): J Carter (7-7).

Jockey (NH): S McNeill (10-0).

644 MR P. WIGHAM, Malton

Postal: **Underbrow Farm, Scagglethorpe, Malton, N. Yorkshire, YO17 8EA.**
Phone: **(09442) 332**

1 **AMY'S STAR,** 4, b f Touch Boy—Keep Believing **Mrs J. L. Wigham**
2 **CAVALIERAVANTGARDE,** 8, b g Rarity—Erica **Cavalier Carpets Limited**
3 **SKI RUN,** 15, b g Workboy—Snow Rum **Mrs J. L. Wigham**
4 **SPRINGFIELD MATCH,** 5, b m Royal Match—Petoria **Mr G. Lowe**

THREE-YEAR-OLDS

5 Br f Warpath—Foil **Mrs J. L. Wigham**
6 **SEABTIC,** br c Sayf El Arab (USA)—Tickled To Bits **Mrs J. L. Wigham**

TWO-YEAR-OLDS

7 Ch c 12/3 Bairn (USA)—County Line (High Line)
8 B c 22/4 Electric—Famous Band (USA) (Banderilla (USA))
9 Ch c 3/4 Hatim (USA)—Serriyya (Tap On Wood)
10 B c 1/5 Sarab—Whilst (Dalsaan)

Other Owners: Mr J. E. Mottram, Mr P. Wigham.

Jockeys (Flat): C Wigham (8-0, w.a.), M Wigham (8-2).

Jockey (NH): J J Quinn.

645 MR W. G. R. WIGHTMAN, Upham

Postal: **Ower Farm, Upham, Southampton, Hampshire, SO3 1HW.**
Phone: **BISHOPS WALTHAM (0489) 89 2565**

1 **ALL WEATHER,** 4, b g Air Trooper—Modom **Mr W. G. R. Wightman**
2 **DI BRAVURA,** 4, b g Noalto—Diorina **Mr A. G. Lansley**
3 **DIVINE PET,** 5, br g Tina's Pet—Davinia **Mrs A. J. Taylor**
4 **INSWINGER,** 4, br g Swing Easy (USA)—Cheri Berry **Mr W. G. R. Wightman**
5 **IN THE ZONE,** 5, b g Martinmas—Modom **Mr W. G. R. Wightman**
6 **KINGSBROOK,** 8, b g Kinglet—Miss Bubbly **Mr J. A. Leavett-Shenley**
7 **KINGSTRACK,** 4, b f King's Ride—Cinder Belle **Mr W. G. R. Wightman**
8 **MARTINOSKY,** 4, b g Martinmas—Bewitched **Mr D. B. Clark**
9 **MILCLERE,** 4, ch f Milford—Great Lass **Mrs M. A. Saunders**
10 **POPESWOOD,** 7, b g Nicholas Bill—Villarrica (FR) **Mr N. J. Hitchins**
11 **ROYAL PROGRESS,** 4, b g King's Ride—Saucy Melody **Mr D. B. Clark**
12 **SINGLE,** 8, br g Jellaby—Miss Solo **Mr A. G. Lansley**
13 **SISTER-IN-LAW,** 7, ch m Legal Tender—Sister Brown **Mrs P. Scott-Dunn**
14 **TOLOMENA,** 4, b f Tolomeo—Meg's Pride **Mr T. R. Mountain**

THREE-YEAR-OLDS

15 **ALLSORTS,** br g Noalto—Cheri Berry **Mrs J. A. Thomson**
16 **BUFFS EXPRESS,** ch f Bay Express—Buff Beauty **Mrs R. Newton**
17 **ELUSIVE LADY,** b f Blakeney—Bewitched **Mr D. B. Clark**
18 **LILY'S SUN,** gr g Kala Shikari—Lily of France **Dorothea Viscountess Kelburn**
19 **MAGNETIZE,** b f Electric—Silver Birch **Mrs R. Newton**
20 B f Idiot's Delight—Modom **Mr W. G. R. Wightman**
21 **RUSSIAN RED,** ch c Kind of Hush—Green Diamond **Mrs E. N. Pyle**
22 **SIMPLY SPIM,** b f Simply Great (FR)—Spimpinina **Mrs R. Newton**
23 **STAR HILL,** b c Star Appeal—Pook's Hill **Mr T. R. Mountain**

TWO-YEAR-OLDS

24 **BACHELOR BOY,** b c 22/4 Ballacashtal (CAN)—Miss Solo (Runnymede) **Mrs Hunt**
25 **GOLDEN BIRCH,** gr c 20/4 Heights of Gold—Silver Birch (Silver Shark) **Mrs R. Newton**
26 **GOLDEN GENERAL,** ch c 28/4 Blushing Scribe (USA)—Broken Paws (Busted) **Mr J. Baring**
27 **MARDIOR,** b f 7/3 Martinmas—Diorina (Manacle) **Mrs J. A. Thomson**
28 **MARWELL BIANCA,** b f 30/3 Carwhite—Lily of France (Monsanto (FR)) **Lady Kelburn**
29 Ch f 8/3 Jupiter Island—Spimpinina (Be My Guest (USA)) **Mrs R. Newton**

Other Owners: P. J. Brain, Lady R. Dacre, Miss D. Downes, Mr R. D. Dunley, Mr J. Hunt, Mr S. J. Lansley, J. Light, Sir Arthur Norman, Mr G. W. Pyle, Mr G. M. Thomson.

646 MR C. P. WILDMAN, Salisbury

Postal: **South View Stables, Larkhill, Salisbury, Wiltshire, SP4 8PY.**
Phone: **(0980) 52226**

1 **AVERON,** 10, b g Averof—Reluctant Maid **Beaconsfield Developments**
2 **BUZANCHAR,** 5, b g Taufan (USA)—La Primavera **Mr C. P. Wildman**
3 **CRISP HEART,** 6, b m Dominion—Persevering **Mr Cyril Elford**
4 **CUMLODEN,** 4, ch g Creetown—Melinda Jane **Mr David Allen**
5 **DOC'S COAT,** 5, b g Tower Walk—Gold Loch **Beaconsfield Developments**
6 **FOREST FAWN (FR),** 5, b br m Top Ville—Red Deer (FR) **Mr J. Bull**
7 **LESBET,** 5, b m Hotfoot—Remeta **Mrs L. W. Carlson**
8 **LITTLE GOOSE GIRL,** 4, ch f Alias Smith (USA)—Mother Goose **Mr C. P. Wildman**
9 **PATIENCE CREEK,** 4, ch f Mummy's Game—Brandon Creek **Rockhouse Stud**
10 **SARUM,** 4, b g Tina's Pet—Contessa (HUN) **Mr W. Wildman**

MR C. P. WILDMAN—continued

THREE-YEAR-OLDS

11 **KNIPHOFIA,** ch c Norwick (USA)—Miss Hippolyta **Mr A. Csaky**
12 **LIZZY CANTLE,** b f Homing—Muninga **Mr Brian D. Cantle**

TWO-YEAR-OLDS

13 **CLASSIC ACCOUNT,** ch c 7/4 Pharly (FR)—Money Supply (Brigadier Gerard) **Mr P. Watts**
14 **RIACE,** ch c 7/3 Town And Country—Cygne (Piaffer (USA)) **Mr A. Csaky**
15 Ch c 9/5 Nishapour (FR)—Tasimah (FR) (Petingo) **Mr C. P. Wildman**

Other Owners: Dame Elizabeth Csaky, Mr D. Lee.

Jockey (Flat): N Adams (7-7).

Jockey (NH): B Wright (10-7).

Conditional: D Dengel (9-7).

647 MR B. E. WILKINSON, Middleham

Postal: **Fell View Stables, 41 East Witton, Middleham, Leyburn, N. Yorkshire, DL8 4SL.**
Phone: **(0969) 23385**

1 **ANTIGUAN SMILE,** 5, ch g Croghan Hill—Evan's Love **Mr Denis Lennon**
2 **ARMAGRET,** 5, b g Mandrake Major—Friendly Glen **Miss T. Longstaff**
3 **CHIPCHASE,** 10, b g New Brig—Tillside **Mr S. R. Orchard**
4 **CRACKHILL,** 11, b g Legal Eagle—Mexican Music **Mr A. Suddes**
5 **EBORACUM,** 12, ch g Sheshoon—Swift Fire **Mrs A. Harker**
6 **FLODDEN FIELD,** 7, b g New Brig—Tillside **Mr A. T. Taylor**
7 **KEYANLOCH,** 8, b m Lochnager—Key Harvest **Mr M. J. Holley**
8 **KNOCK THRICE,** 8, b g Ballynockan—Quibba **Mr W. R. Lofthouse**
9 **MOORFIELD LADY,** 6, ch m Vicomte—Aberklair **Mr D. W. Dresser**
10 **PARTRIDGE FLATT,** 5, ch g Known Fact (USA)—Castleisland **Mr Robert Parker**
11 **ROMAN NAUT,** 4, b g Connaught—Green Menelek **Mr W. T. Lockey**
12 **TRAUMATIC LAURA,** 5, gr m Pragmatic—Trim **Mrs S. J. Newbould**
13 **TWEED VALLEY,** 4, b g Le Coq d'Or—Tillside **Mr A. T. Taylor**
14 **VERONA CHIEF,** 7, ch g Viking Chief—Verona Star **Mrs S. J. Newbould**

Other Owners: Mr Paul Jackson.

Jockeys (NH): G Harker (10-0), A Orkney (10-0).

648 MRS J. V. WILKINSON, Sarratt

Postal: **White Oaks Farm, Dawes Lane, Sarratt, Rickmansworth, Hertfordshire, WD3 6BQ.**
Phone: **KINGS LANGLEY (09277) 65624**

1 **MUSSEL BED,** 13, ch g Deep Run—Artella **Mrs J. V. Wilkinson**
2 **NOVASCOPE,** 11, ch m New Member—Horoscope **Mrs J. V. Wilkinson**

Amateur: Mrs J V Wilkinson (8-7).

649 MR M. J. WILKINSON, Banbury

Postal: **Trafford Bridge, Edgcote, Banbury, Oxon, OX17 1AG.**
Phone: **CHIPPING WARDEN (0295 86) 713 CAR (0836) 727693**

1 **ALIDAN,** 6, b g Golden Love—Priest's Sister **Woodrock Investments Ltd**
2 **ARTESIUM,** 8, b g Artaius (USA)—Idle Waters **Mr R. J. Fox**
3 **CAPTAIN TOM,** 7, b g Blue Refrain—Icy Look **Mr John Clegg**
4 **CATCHAPENNY,** 5, br g True Song—Quickapenny **Mr C. J. Courage**
5 **CUT ABOVE AVERAGE,** 5, br g McIndoe—Adroit **Mr J. A. Cunningham**
6 **DEEP AUBURN,** 11, b g Deep Run—Auburn **Mr K. W. Walker**
7 **DISCIPLINE,** 5, b m Roman Warrior—Steadily **Mrs R. A. Budgett**
8 **EL POLITICASTRO,** 6, b g Politico (USA)—Jedhart Lass **Mr R. J. Campbell**
9 **FARMER'S TOAST,** 8, b g True Song—Zanetta **Mrs L. F. Rathbone**
10 **FIRST REVIEW,** 7, b m Dawn Review—Opening Order **Woodrock Investments Ltd**
11 **FRANKTON,** 9, ch g Extra—Quadrilette **Mrs Pam Slawson**
12 **HURRY ON HARRY,** 6, b g Workboy—Merry Marion **Woodrock Investments Ltd**
13 **KESWOOD JACK,** 7, b g The Parson—Petite Bally **Mr Roger K. Simmons**
14 **LOVER BILL,** 8, b g Golden Love—Billeragh Girl **Dr P. P. Brown**
15 **MET STATION,** 7, b g Royal Fountain—Lido Light **Mr Mark Wilkinson**
16 **MR STRIDER,** 6, b g Charlaw—Queen of Myshal **Woodrock Investments Ltd**
17 **NESAGA,** 6, ch m Sagaro—Netley **Mr Michael J. Hair**
18 **PARSONS PLEASURE,** 7, b g Pry—Will Preach **Mr John Wilkinson**
19 **QUEEN OF SPARTA,** 5, b m Idiot's Delight—Spartan's Girl **Lady Helen Smith**
20 **RATTLIN' JACK,** 11, ch g True Song—Marinella **Mr John Wilkinson**
21 **RED COLUMBIA,** 9, ch g St Columbus—Red Tan **Mrs J. Webster**
22 **ROMAN FORTUNE,** 8, b g Billion (USA)—Denaria **Mrs Karen Sinclair**
23 **SAFARI KEEPER,** 4, b g Longleat (USA)—Garden Party **Mrs T. Lawther**
24 **SMART CHICK,** 7, b m True Song—I'm Smart **Mrs E. R. Courage**
25 **SMART TAR,** 9, b g Seaepic (USA)—I'm Smart **Mrs E. R. Courage**
26 **SNEAKAPENNY,** 8, ch g Levanter—Quickapenny **Mrs E. R. Courage**
27 **SPEAKERS CORNER,** 7, ch g Politico (USA)—Gusty Lucy **Baxter & Walsh Ltd**
28 **SUNCIA,** 6, br m Sunyboy—Ascencia **Mrs W. Morrell**
29 **TOMMY ARR,** 4, b g Neltino—Promenade Concert **Mr W. Ward**
30 **VERITATE,** 6, b m Roman Warrior—Empress of England **Mrs John Wilkinson**
31 **WICKET,** 5, b m Deep Run—Knock Off **Mr John Wilkinson**

Other Owners: Mr Colin Gee, Mr Peter Hair, Mr A. L. Jones.

Jockey (NH): C Llewellyn (9-10).

Conditional: P Kelly.

Amateur: Mr J Rees (9-7).

650 MR C. N. WILLIAMS, Newmarket

Postal: **'Queensbury Lodge', 198 High Street, Newmarket, Suffolk, CB8 9AP.**
Phone: **(0638) 665116 FAX (0638) 660935**

1 **DO-I-KNOW-YOU,** 4, b f Kafu—Galaxy Scorpio **Mr Robin Myddelton and Partners**
2 **GAILAN'S MAGIC,** 4, b g Montekin—Densidal **Mrs Gail Dunlop**
3 **PEERGLOW,** 6, br m Raga Navarro (ITY)—Go Perrys **Mrs Gail Dunlop**
4 **SHARP REMINDER,** 6, b h Sharpo—Fallen Rose **Mr R. T. Jacobson**

MR C. N. WILLIAMS—continued

THREE-YEAR-OLDS

5 **GO HOLIMARINE,** gr f Taufan (USA)—Standing Ovation **Mrs Gail Dunlop and Miss B. J. Falkus**
6 **MICDAN,** gr c Exhibitioner—Galaxy Scorpio **Mrs Gail Dunlop**
7 **POWER OF PRAYER,** ch f The Noble Player (USA)—Sandra's Choice **Mrs B. T. Morrissey**
8 **SANDY STORM,** ch c Lomond (USA)—Holly Deb (USA) **Mrs R. Jacobson**
9 **SOCKEM,** b g Nordico (USA)—Floating Petal **Mrs Gail Dunlop**

TWO-YEAR-OLDS

10 B f 29/4 Daring March—Airlanka (Corvaro (USA))
11 B c 26/4 Top Ville—Bird Point (USA) (Alleged (USA)) **Mrs Gail Dunlop**
12 **CANUTELL,** b f 9/2 Persepolis (FR)—Dry Land (Nonoalco (USA)) **Mrs Gail Dunlop**
13 **DANUBE,** b c 19/2 Kings Lake (USA)—Alpine Niece (Great Nephew) **Mrs Gail Dunlop**
14 **ESTRELLE,** b f 10/4 Claude Monet (USA)—Queensbury Star (Wishing Star) **Mrs D. Carvelho**
15 Gr f 13/5 Nishapour (FR)—Gallant Believer (USA) (Gallant Romeo (USA)) **Mrs Gail Dunlop**

Other Owners: Mr R. Collins, Mr Eamonn Curtin, Mr E. Harrington, Mr J. F. Jennings, Peerglow Developments Ltd, Mr B. Townsley, Mr Christopher Wright.

Apprentice: Ian Ferguson (7-12).

651 MR D. WILLIAMS, Exeter

Postal: **Chiverstone Farm, Kenton, Exeter, Devon, EX6 8NL.**
Phone: **(0626) 890268**

1 **BOLT THE GATE,** 11, ch g Bustino—Madame Quickly **Mr Denis Williams**
2 **BUCKOAK,** 8, br g Buckskin (FR)—Tycoonello **Mr Denis Williams**
3 **ESS-KAY-DEE,** 5, b g Jasmine Star—Theft **Mr Denis Williams**
4 **NIGHT BLOOMER (USA),** 5, b m Told (USA)—Ms Bloomers (USA) **Mr Denis Williams**
5 **SKY SOCIETY,** 6, b g Charlie's Pal—Septieme Ciel **Mr Denis Williams**

652 MR D. L. WILLIAMS, Broadway

Postal: **Buckland Racing Limited, Little Buckland Farm, Broadway, Worcestershire, WR12 7JH.**
Phone: **BROADWAY (0386) 852569 OR (0386) 858489 FAX (0386) 852269**

1 **ARCTIC CIDER (USA),** 5, br h Arctic Tern (USA)—All Dance (USA) **Mr Michael Berrow**
2 **BUCKLAND HAZE,** 4, b f Hays—Frensham (FR) **Mr Michael Berrow**
3 **CHEEKY KING,** 8, b g Space King—Pearlyric **Mr Michael Berrow**
4 4, B g Chiavari—Fair Detail **Mr Michael Berrow**
5 **FIR TRADING,** 6, gr g Tachypous—Melfio Miss **Mrs Angie Evans**
6 **GARCIA,** 6, b g Thatching—Song Grove **Mr Michael Berrow**
7 **GOLD CHILD,** 7, b g Goldhill—Aggvus **Mrs M. J. Gee**
8 **HALLO POLI,** 8, ch g Politico (USA)—Artlight **Mr Gavin Wragg**
9 **HIGH TENSION,** 8, ch g Vitiges (FR)—Montania **Mr Michael Berrow**
10 4, B f Roscoe Blake—La Foire II **Mr Michael Berrow**
11 **LONDON WINDOWS,** 8, b g Balliol—Chebs Lass **Mr T. C. Hartley**
12 **MR CHRIS GATEAUX,** 8, gr g Gay Fandango (USA)—Snap Cobwebs **Mrs M. J. Gee**
13 **MY ARWAY,** 4, br g Ardar—Good Way **Mr Michael Berrow**
14 **POKEY'S BELLE,** 6, b m Uncle Pokey—Belle of Sark **Miss B. W. Palmer**
15 4, B f Impecunious—Royal Snip **Mr Michael Berrow**
16 **SPIRITED HOLME (FR),** 5, b g Gay Mecene (USA)—Lyphard's Holme (USA) **Mr Michael Berrow**
17 **TAUREAN TYCOON,** 6, b g Octogenarian—Eastling **Mrs Angie Evans**
18 **TOUCH OF SPEED,** 6, b g Touch Paper—Maggie Mine **Mr Michael Berrow**
19 **WARRIOR'S PROMISE,** 5, ch g Mansingh (USA)—Pegs Promise **Miss B. W. Palmer**
20 **WILLOWESQ,** 7, ch g Octogenarian—Tenon Saw **Mrs Angie Evans**

MR D. L. WILLIAMS—continued

THREE-YEAR-OLDS

21 B f Auction Ring (USA)—Dame Brisene (FR) **Mr Michael Berrow**
22 **HI DUCHESS,** ch f Carwhite—Good Larker **Mr J. A. Lewis**
23 B g Sparkling Boy—Topolino Sauro **Mr M. Wooldridge**

TWO-YEAR-OLDS

24 **HERMES HARVEST,** b g 27/5 Oats—Swift Messenger (Giolla Mear) **Miss B. W. Palmer**
25 Ch f 19/4 Carlingford Castle—Liebeslied (Dike (USA)) **Mr Michael Berrow**
26 B f 14/5 Lafontaine (USA)—Mil Pesetas (Hotfoot) **Mr Michael Berrow**
27 B f 4/4 Deep Run—Phalaborwa (Oats) **Mr Michael Berrow**

Other Owners: Mr G. Blunden, Mr Gareth Cheshire, Mr Ray Eke, Mr Martin Evans, Mr J. A. Hewitt, Richard Kirkland M.R.C.V.S., Mr Paddy Moore, Mr I. Whittock, Mr David Yearsley.

Conditional: B Doran (10-0).

Amateur: Mr Luke Neale (10-7).

653 MR R. J. R. WILLIAMS, Newmarket

Postal: **Marriott Stables, Hamilton Road, Newmarket, Suffolk, CB8 0NY.**
Phone: **NEWMARKET (0638) 663218 FAX (0638) 660145**

1 **CANTORIS,** 4, b f Song—Singing Witch **Mr David Robinson**
2 **LONDON LOUISE,** 4, b f Ile de Bourbon (USA)—Miss St James's **Mr Peter Bedford**
3 **MR WISHING WELL,** 4, ch g Dunbeath (USA)—Little Change **Mr Colin G. R. Booth**
4 **SIR BLESSED,** 11, b g So Blessed—Morinda **Marriott Stables Limited**
5 **SWIFT TROOPER,** 7, br h Air Trooper—Kemoening **Mr Colin G. R. Booth**
6 **TONGUE TIED JOHNNY (USA),** 4, b c Sir Ivor—Tongue Tied Muse (USA) **Mr Jonathan Crisp**
7 **VAGUE DISCRETION,** 5, b g Vaigly Great—Discreet **Marriott Stables Limited**

THREE-YEAR-OLDS

8 **ACQUA NOIR,** ch c Kings Lake (USA)—Late Sally **Mr D. C. Brady**
9 **ALL FIRED UP,** b f Song—Honey Pot **Mr Christopher Wright**
10 **ARIAL STAR,** b c High Line—Premiere Danseuse **A. F. Budge (Equine) Limited**
11 **ASH AMOUR,** b f Hotfoot—Loving Doll **Mr Terry Minahan**
12 **CAGLIARI,** ch c Dominion—Bedeni **Mr David Robinson**
13 **CHARMING GIFT,** b f Petorius—Aubretia (USA) **Mrs M. Linney**
14 **DUGGAN,** b c Dunbeath (USA)—Silka (ITY) **Notcarl Publishing Ltd**
15 **ENDLESS JOY,** b f Law Society (USA)—La Joyeuse **Cheveley Park Stud**
16 **EXECUTIVE LADY,** ch f Night Shift (USA)—Rosier **Mr Mervyn Ayers**
17 **EXPRESS ACCOUNT,** b f Carr de Naskra (USA)—Miss Audimar (USA) **Marriott Stables Limited**
18 **GREY WOLF,** gr g Bellypha—Matinee **Lord Carnarvon**
19 **JR'S PET,** b f Auction Ring (USA)—What A Pet **Mr John Rathmell**
20 **LE PASSE TEMPS,** ch c King Persian—Darius Royal **Mr Colin G. R. Booth**
21 **ON Y VA (USA),** ch f Victorious (USA)—Golden Moony **Notcarl Publishing Ltd**
22 **RETURN TO SENDER,** b c Auction Ring (USA)—Tarte Tatin (FR) **Mrs C. J. Powell**
23 **SHELTER,** b c Teenoso (USA)—Safe House **Lord Carnarvon**
24 **THORESBY,** ch c Thatching—Nana's Queen **A. F. Budge (Equine) Limited**
25 **WILD ONE,** gr f Nordico (USA)—To-Oneiro **M. Yiapatos**

TWO-YEAR-OLDS

26 **ABEL LEPITRE (IRE),** ch f 16/2 Hatim (USA)—Rose In Time (Hello Gorgeous (USA)) **Mr R. L. Capon**
27 B f 4/3 Dominion—Bahamas Princess (Sharpen Up) **Mr Christopher Wright**
28 B f 13/3 Godswalk (USA)—Cathryn's Song (Prince Tenderfoot) **Marriott Stables Limited**
29 B f 14/2 Northern Baby—Chepstow Vale (Key To The Mint) **Kennet Valley Thoroughbreds Ltd**
30 B f 18/1 Primo Dominie—Cottage Pie (Kalamoun) **Mr D. J. Harrison**
31 Ch c 21/5 Song—Faraway Grey (Absalom) **Mr Jonathan Crisp**

MR R. J. R. WILLIAMS—continued

32 Ch c 22/3 Jester—Hasta (Skymaster) **Mr C. P. Linney**
33 **IRISH IMPULSE (USA),** b f 14/4 Irish River (FR)—Exclusively Raised (USA) (Exclusive Native (USA)) **Cheveley Park Stud**
34 **NO COMEBACKS,** b f 28/2 Last Tycoon—Dead End (Bold Lad (IRE)) **Mr D. J. Wilson**
35 B c 3/2 Gorytus (USA)—Pepi Image (USA) (National) **Mr Colin G. R. Booth**
36 **SANS FRAIS,** b f 21/3 Forzando—Shere Beauty (Mummy's Pet) **Miss Victoria Hull**
37 **SMASHER,** b f 25/2 Simply Great (FR)—Star Face (African Sky) **Robin Dollar**
38 **SO REWARDING,** ch f 15/2 Never So Bold—Haitienne (FR) (Green Dancer (USA)) **Cheveley Park Stud**

Other Owners: Colin W. Ayers, Mrs M. I. Booth, D. F. Cowham, Mr L. S. Dollar, Mr M. A. B. Jenks, D. A. Johnson, Mr J. R. Maybank, Lord Porchester, Mr D. F. Powell, Mr F. J. Reeder, Mr M. J. Ronson, Mr R. M. F. Ross, Kevin M. Selvester, Mr H. C. Velissarides.

Jockey (Flat): R Cochrane (8-3).

Apprentices: D Biggs (7-5), Alison Harper (7-12).

654 MR W. R. WILLIAMS, Exeter

Postal: **Lower Horrells, Idestone, Longdown, Exeter, EX6 7BL.**
Phone: **(0392) 81558**

1 **RAZZLE DAZZLE BOY,** 8, ch g Some Hand—Fair Georgina **Mr W. R. Williams**
2 **STRUELL ROYALE,** 9, ch g Royal Captive—Greek Empress **Mr Nicholas Lenygon**
3 **TOM'S LITTLE BET,** 6, gr m Scallywag—Fleet Street Fifty **Mr T. Staddon**
4 **TOM'S LITTLE WILL,** 7, br g Celtic Cone—Fleet Street Fifty **Mr T. Staddon**
5 **TORULA BRIDGE,** 6, b m Torus—Killanny Bridge **Westward Developments (Totnes) Ltd**

TWO-YEAR-OLDS

6 **TOM'S ARCTIC DREAM,** br f 14/5 Oats—Tom's Nap Hand (Some Hand)
7 **TOM'S CAMPUZANO,** b g 8/5 Julio Mariner—Tom's Hideaway (Country Retreat)
8 **TOM'S GEMINI STAR,** ch g 3/6 Celtic Cone—Je Dit (I Say)
9 **TOM'S HALWELL LAD,** b g 19/5 Oats—Tom's Comedy (Comedy Star (USA))

Other Owners: Mr D. J. Cartwright, C.I.T. Research Ltd, S. Pitts, Stewart Stunt.

Jockey (NH): Mark Williams (10-0).

Amateur: Mr Ian Williams (11-0).

655 MR H. WILLIS, Winchester

Postal: **Hazeley Down Stables, Morestead, Winchester, Hampshire.**
Phone: **(0962) 712159**

1 **FINAL TOP,** 5, ch g Chaparly (FR)—Peg Top **Mr W. Wood**
2 **HAZELY CHASE,** 6, ch m Jolly Me—Owslesbury **Capt Alan Smith**
3 **KEN SAUCE,** 7, gr g Kenmare—Sauce Royale **Mr N. Shammas**
4 **MAJOR TOM,** 13, b g Cantab—Ice Folly **Mrs Jill Pelly**
5 **MERALTO,** 4, ch f Noalto—Miss Merlin **Capt Alan Smith**
6 4, Ch f Netherkelly—Miniwonder **Mr H. Willis**
7 **REEMAN,** 12, b g Star Appeal—Mary Morison **Mrs Jill Pelly**

MR H. WILLIS—continued

THREE-YEAR-OLDS

8 B f Town And Country—Hentmore **Mrs C. Taylor**
9 B c Kala Shikari—Rota **Mr D. W. Hill**

TWO-YEAR-OLDS

10 Ch c 13/4 Undulate—April Rose (Wollow) **Mr E. Saunders**
11 B c 8/4 My Dad Tom (USA)—Helmstone (Dominion) **Mr E. Saunders**
12 Br c 7/4 Undulate—Midsummer Girl (Midsummer Night II) **Mr E. Saunders**
13 SHADES OF JADE, gr f 4/5 General Wade—Gellifawr (Saulingo) **Mr W. Wood**

Other Owners: Mrs D. J. Flaherty.

Jockey (NH): B Powell.

Conditional: J Leech (9-7).

Amateur: Mr M Kilford (10-11).

656 MR A. J. WILSON, Cheltenham

Postal: **Glenfall Stables, Ham, Charlton Kings, Cheltenham, Gloucestershire.**
Phone: **(0242) 244713 OR (0242) 226319**

1 AIR STREAK, 6, br m Air Trooper—Regent Street **Mr J. G. Phillips**
2 BUMPTIOUS BOY, 6, b g Neltino—Bellardita **Mr T. D. Pilkington**
3 CAMROC, 10, b g Vivadari—Milady Luck **Mr M. F. Heaton**
4 CRACKER D'OR, 6, ch g Le Coq d'Or—Little Cracker **Mrs M. J. Wilson**
5 ELVERCONE, 9, b g Celtic Cone—Capalena **Mrs C. M. Scott**
6 FREE JUSTICE, 6, br g Impecunious—Old Brief **Lt Col B. J. Lockhart**
7 FUEGO BOY (NZ), 10, b g Tierra Fuego—Silver Melody (NZ) **Mr A. M. Darlington**
8 GALTERIO (USA), 8, b br g Christopher R (USA)—Oyace (ITY) **Miss Nicola S. Harvey**
9 GLENBROOK D'OR, 6, b g Le Coq d'Or—Wedderburn **Mr Tim Leadbeater**
10 HIGH DEAL, 6, gr g Warpath—Royal Handful **Mrs J. Alford**
11 HOLY JOE, 8, b g The Parson—Doonasleen **Mr T. D. Pilkington**
12 JEASSU, 7, b g Whistlefield—Menhaden **Mrs R. H. Y. Mills**
13 KITCHI KOO, 6, b m Imperial Fling (USA)—Hard To Follow **Mr Phil Price**
14 LADY OF BALDWIN, 9, b m Decent Fellow—Star O'Solway **Mr P. M. C. Rabl**
15 LADY SEEKER, 7, ch m Royal Match—Gay Seeker **Miss Louise Wood**
16 MAYGON, 10, b m Maystreak—Greenfield Girl **Mr P. G. F. Oliver**
17 MORPION, 8, b m Scallywag—Greenfield Girl **Mr P. G. F. Oliver**
18 PORKINSON BANGER, 6, br g Golden Love—Tarabelle **Mr P. M. C. Rabl**
19 RED SCORPION, 6, b g Furry Glen—Glamorous Night **Mr A. J. Sutton**
20 SEVENS OUT, 8, ch g Touch Paper—Rosie Probert **Mr Gerard Nock**
21 SHIRKOUK (FR), 6, b g Rubloff (USA)—Insoumise (FR) **Mrs M. P. Moore**
22 SPIRESLAKE, 7, ch g Paddy's Stream—Hero's Slave **Mr Gerard Nock**
23 SUNSET VINE, 7, b g French Vine—Suntino **Mrs A. Penney**
24 TABERNA LORD, 9, b g Le Coq d'Or—Norwich Girl **Mr Tim Leadbetter**
25 TRIUMPHANT CHIEF (NZ), 5, b g Triumphal March (USA)—Lefette (NZ) **Mr A. M. Darlington**
26 URCCA (FR), 4, b g Mont Basile (FR)—Malacca II (FR) **Mrs Carol Bloom**

Other Owners: Mr Brian Basham, Mr S. N. Bedward, Mr J. B. Charlesworth, Mr T. Corden, Mr J. B. Holt, Mr J. R. Latham, Mr G. P. D. Milne, Mr Alan Moore, Mr Bill Muirhead, Mrs P. M. Phillips, Mr Renny Platt, Mrs P. Rabl, Mrs H. M. Robertson, Mr W. S. Rogers.

Jockey (NH): S Cowley (10-0).

Conditional: B T O'Dowd (9-7).

657 MR D. A. WILSON, Epsom

Postal: **Cedar Point Racing Stables, Headley Road, Epsom, Surrey.**
Phone: **OFFICE (03722) 78327 HOME (03722) 73839 ANSAPHONE**

1 **CITY LINK PET,** 4, b f Tina's Pet—City Link Rose **Mr R. J. Thomas**
2 **GREAT HAND,** 4, b c Tumble Wind (USA)—Great Aunt **Mr T. S. M. S. Riley-Smith**
3 **KOVALEVSKIA,** 5, ch m Ardross—Fiordiligi **Mr T. S. M. S. Riley-Smith**
4 **LA BELLE VIE,** 4, b f Indian King (USA)—Engage **Mr Robin Lawson**
5 **LOVELY WONGA,** 4, b c Tanfirion—Teala **Palmerston Business Centre Ltd**
6 **MAIDEN BIDDER,** 8, b m Shack (USA)—Wolverina **MR J. S. S. Hollins**
7 **MOON WARRIOR,** 5, b g The Brianstan—Brigannie Moon **Mr Peter J. Allen**
8 **ORDER OF MERIT,** 5, b g Cut Above—Lady Habitat **Mr Thomas J. McLoughlin**
9 **PLATONIC AFFAIR,** 9, b g Kemal (FR)—Deep Shine **Mr Ken Brant**
10 **PROFIT A PRENDRE,** 6, b g Tina's Pet—Brave Ballard **Mr Peter Thorne**
11 **VIKING VENTURE,** 5, ch g Viking (USA)—Mattira (FR) **Mr Nigel Spreadbury**

THREE-YEAR-OLDS

12 **BLAZING SUNSET,** ch f Blazing Saddles (AUS)—Krishnagar **Mr Marti J. Jacobs**
13 **FLORIDA GOLD,** b c Hard Fought—Klairelle **Mr K. W. Elcock**
14 **ISIPINGO,** b g Pitskelly—Nemoralis **Mr Nigel Spreadbury**
15 **KALA'S PRINCESS,** b f Kampala—Dasa Girl **Mr T. S. M. S. Riley-Smith**

TWO-YEAR-OLDS

16 Ch f 25/3 Music Boy—City Link Rose (Lochnager) **Mr R. J. Thomas**

Other Owners: Mr Martin Kersh, Mr K. Kitzwegerer, Mr David Mills.

Jockeys (Flat): W Newnes (8-2), B Rouse (8-0), T Williams (7-7).

Jockeys (NH): C Llewellyn (10-0), D Murphy (10-0), P Scudamore (10-1).

Lady Rider: Miss Elaine Bronson (9-0).

658 CAPT. J. H. WILSON, Preston

Postal: **Moor Farm, Sollom, Tarleton, Preston, Lancashire, PR4 6HR.**
Phone: **(0772) 812780 OR 812876**

1 **BRAVE MELODY,** 4, b c Heroic Air—Kaymay **Mrs G. S. Rees**
2 **CHEMMY,** 6, b m Billion (USA)—Gambling Girl **Mrs J. Wilson**
3 **I'VE GOTTA TELL YA,** 4, b g Petong—Super Jennie **Mrs G. S. Rees**
4 **MINE'S A DOUBLE,** 5, b g Crofter (USA)—Modena **Red Rose Racing Plc**
5 **NORTH OF WATFORD,** 5, ch h Jasmine Star—Wallie Girl **Mr R. S. Aylward**
6 **PROFILIC,** 5, b h Ballacashtal (CAN)—Sea Charm **Mr J. Goodman**
7 **RATHER GORGEOUS,** 5, br m Billion (USA)—Fair Sara **Major P. Bailey**
8 **RUNNING MONEY,** 6, b g Billion (USA)—Streets Ahead **Red Rose Racing II**

THREE-YEAR-OLDS

9 Ch c Final Straw—Bargouzine **Mrs G. S. Rees**
10 B c Hays—Honavos **Mrs G. S. Rees**
11 **HUNKY DORIUS,** b f Petorius—Always Smiling **Red Rose Racing Plc**
12 **NORTHERN GLINT,** b c Glint of Gold—Bernice Clare **Mr R. S. Aylward**
13 B c Dunphy—Raskaska **Mrs G. S. Rees**
14 **SKY FIGHTER,** b f Hard Fought—Sky Valley **Red Rose Racing Plc**
15 **SOLEMN MELODY,** b c Jalmood (USA)—Garganey (USA) **Mr J. Goodman**
16 **WELL GROOMED,** ch g Shy Groom (USA)—Great Dora **Red Rose Racing II**

CAPT. J. H. WILSON—continued

TWO-YEAR-OLDS

17 B c 2/5 Ballacashtal (CAN)—Florence Mary **Mrs G. S. Rees**
18 B f 26/3 Germont—Kaymay **Mrs G. S. Rees**
19 Gr f 6/3 Enchantment—Ramona **Mrs G. S. Rees**

Other Owners: Mr D. M. Beresford, Mr Peter W. Clarkson, Mrs S. K. Dimond, Mr Geoffrey Kenyon, Mr H. M. Rees.

Jockey (Flat): K Darley (7-13).

Apprentices: C Roberts (6-7), S Spence (7-4).

Amateurs: Mrs M Ranger (9-0), Mrs G S Rees (8-10).

659 MR J. S. WILSON, Ayr

Postal: **Cree Lodge, 47 Craigie Road, Ayr, Scotland, KA8 OHD.**
Phone: **(0292) 266232 FAX (0292) 611974**

1 ALPHA HELIX, 7, b g Double Form—Daidis **Mr J. W. M. M. Richard**
2 ARTHURS STONE, 4, ch c Kings Lake (USA)—Two Rock **Mr J. J. McLaren**
3 BIT ON EDGE, 4, b f Henbit (USA)—Border's Edge **Mr N. J. Angus**
4 BORDER'S LEGACY, 5, br m Cut Above—Border Honour **Mr G. N. Perratt**
5 CAROUSEL ROCKET, 7, ch h Whistling Deer—Fairy Tree **Mr A. Saccomando**
6 DIET, 4, b g Starch Reduced—Highland Rossie **Mrs M. S. J. Clydesdale**
7 DRUMLEY DAWN, 5, b m Red Sunset—Bamstar **Mr Gabriel Politakis**
8 DURGAM (USA), 4, b c Nureyev (USA)—Famed Princess (USA) **Mr W. M. Johnstone**
9 DUSTY MILLER, 4, b c Current Magic—Royal Barb **Mr I. Peebles**
10 EASTERN WAY, 5, ch g Mansingh (USA)—Kate Kimberley **Mr R. M. Morrison**
11 FURRY PATH, 5, b g Furry Glen—Troubled Heart **Mr Daniel A. Couper**
12 GRANARY GRAIN, 4, b g Deep Run—Poula Scawla **Lightbody's of Hamilton Ltd**
13 IMPECUNIOSITY, 8, gr g Free State—Lydiate **Mr David Landa**
14 JAKE MORGAN, 5, b g Battlement—Bally Morgan **Mr S. Smillie**
15 JUBRAN (USA), 4, b g Vaguely Noble—La Vue (USA) **Mrs E. Scullion**
16 KIRSTY'S BOY, 7, b g Majestic Streak—Cute Peach **Mrs K. McClelland**
17 KIRSTY'S COMET, 4, b g Le Coq d'Or—Cute Peach **Mrs K. McClelland**
18 LAST GRAIN, 8, b g Remainder Man—Wheatley **Lightbody's of Hamilton Ltd**
19 MASTER PLAN (FR), 4, b g Carwhite—Manene (FR) **Mr J. S. Wilson**
20 METROPOLIS DANCER, 5, b g Hard Fought—Reliant Nell **Mr J. Fox**
21 MISS ABOYNE, 5, b m Lochnager—Mia Cosa (USA) **Dr I. F. Davies**
22 NIGHT CHARMER, 4, b f Burslem—Wind Shadow **Mrs H. Beattie**
23 ORDER PAPER, 5, b g Taufan (USA)—Lady of Surana **Mr J. S. Wilson**
24 PIT PIECE, 4, b g Pumps (USA)—On The Wing **Mrs Jane Tait**
25 PIT PONY, 6, b g Hittite Glory—Watch Lady **Mrs H. Beattie**
26 RAITH HOMES, 4, ch g Import—Gay Dawn **Raith Property Co Ltd**
27 RHYMING KATE, 5, b m Rymer—Gokatiego **Mr Roy Peebles**
28 RIVER PEARL, 5, b m Oats—Dark Pearl **Mrs A. G. Martin**
29 RUADH ADHAR, 4, b f Heroic Air—Rosemarkie **Mr D. J. Gordon Wright**
30 SCOTTISH FLAME, 4, b br g Blazing Saddles (AUS)—Firnelta (FR) **Mr J. S. Wilson**
31 SCOTTISH GOLD, 6, b g Sonnen Gold—Calaburn **Mrs F. Honig**
32 SE-AQ, 5, b g Krayyan—Messie **Mr Gabriel Politakis**
33 SHAWINIGA, 4, b f Lyphard's Wish (FR)—Shining Bright (USA) **Mr Duncan Leggat**
34 THISTLE MONARCH, 5, b g Rontino—Lavender Blue **Mr J. A. Gordon**
35 TREBONKERS, 6, b g Treboro (USA)—Sally Conkers **Mrs C. M. Richard**
36 WICINGA, 4, ch g Viking (USA)—Lazy Belle (USA) **Mr J. Leeming**
37 ZODE, 4, b g Simply Great (FR)—Star Face **Mr S. Smillie**

MR J. S. WILSON—continued

THREE-YEAR-OLDS

38 **AYR RAIDER,** ch c Claude Monet (USA)—Thimothea (FR) **Mr Peter Orr**
39 **CAPRONI,** b c Lomond (USA)—Helaplane (USA) **Mr W. G. McHarg**
40 **DRINNY'S DOUBLE,** ch g Connaught—Caramel **Mr J. Hamilton**
41 **FOREVER DIAMONDS,** ch c Good Times (ITY)—Mel Mira **Mrs J. B. Russell**
42 **GOLDEN ALCHEMIST,** ch g Ballacashtal (CAN)—Pts Fairway **Mr Thomas Broster**
43 **GO ON THE GRAIN,** ch g Remainder Man—Femme Fatale **Lightbody's of Hamilton Ltd**
44 **IN SHARP FOCUS,** ch f Final Straw—Little Change **Mr S. A. B. Dinsmore**
45 **PADDY CASH,** b g Pas de Seul—Kachela **Mr P. D. Savill**
46 **PERSUASIVE,** b f Sharpo—Queen's Eyot **Mr W. G. McHarg**
47 **ROMANY HOME,** ch f Gabitat—Warrior's Sister **Mr G. H. Pollock**
48 **SHIKARI SUNSHINE,** b g Kala Shikari—Sunshine Holyday **Mr L. W. Dunbar**
49 **WESTERN MUSIC,** ch f Music Boy—Tripolitaine (FR) **Western Meeting Club Owners Group**
50 **WESTERN SECRET,** br g Kind of Hush—My Ginny **Western Meeting Club Owners Group**

TWO-YEAR-OLDS

51 **AYR GAIETY,** ch f 21/3 Destroyer—Win Shoon Please (Sheshoon) **Mr Peter Orr**
52 **CASHEROOSKI (IRE),** b c 25/4 Ballad Rock—Kachela (Kalamoun) **Mr P. D. Savill**
53 **DARAGENCY,** b f 7/2 Dara Monarch—Rashah (Blakeney) **Smacs Racing Quartet**
54 **GLENAIRLIE (IRE),** b f 6/3 Glow (USA)—Celtic Symphony (Orchestra) **Mr W. M. Johnstone**
55 **ODIN'S FLAME (IRE),** b c 13/2 Viking (USA)—Sunley Saint (Artaius (USA)) **Mr G. Milne**
56 **RED TEMPEST (IRE),** b c 15/2 Red Sunset—Msida (Majority Blue) **Mr L. W. Dunbar**

Other Owners: Mr Gordon Cowan, Mr J. H. Etherton, Mr N. Fleming, Mr T. Hughes, Mr R. B. Johnstone, Mr Charles Martin, Mr J. C. Murdoch, Lt-Col Tom Park.

Jockey (Flat): G Duffield (w.a.).

Jockey (NH): C Grant (10-0, w.a.).

Conditional: Alan Linton (9-0), James O'Ware (9-2).

Lady Rider: Miss Linda A Perratt (9-0).

660 MR W. T. J. WILSON, Newmarket

Postal: **Ten Yard, Hamilton Stables, Hamilton Road, Newmarket, Suffolk.**
Phone: **HOME (0638) 661393 YARD (0638) 667400**

1 **BILLY'S DANCER,** 7, ch h Piaffer (USA)—Hay-Hay **Mr F. J. Phoenix**
2 **COME ON KATE,** 7, b m Tycoon II—Lantao Lady **Mrs E. Wilson**
3 **JUST ONE KISS,** 5, ch m Tower Walk—Mistress Royal **Mr R. G. Giles**
4 **MR PRESLEY,** 4, b g Tender King—Theda **Mr Nicholas Roteman**
5 **PHARAMINEUX,** 4, ch g Pharly (FR)—Miss Longchamp **Mr Nicholas Roteman**
6 **SIMASCALA,** 4, b g Electric—Elegida **Mr K. Russell and Partners**

THREE-YEAR-OLDS

7 B f Kind of Hush—Elaine Anne **Mr D. Parker**
8 **ESH WINNING,** ch f Tender King—Migoletty **Mrs E. Wilson**
9 **GIFT OF LIFE,** b c Formidable (USA)—Mattagirl **Mr T. J. Wall**
10 **KATANGO BEAT,** b f Dunbeath (USA)—Kittycatoo Katango (USA) **Partnership**
11 **PINK BUBBLES,** ch f Blushing Scribe (USA)—Swing The Cat **Mrs B. P. Cannell**
12 **SERENIKI,** b f Dublin Taxi—Highdrive **Mr K. Russell and Partners**

MR W. T. J. WILSON—continued

TWO-YEAR-OLDS

13 Ch c Superlative—Bushy Top (Thatching) **Mr P. Butler**
14 B c Kafu—La Quinta (Thatch (USA)) **Mr P. Butler**
15 B f Precocious—Larive (Blakeney) **Mr R. Milburn**
16 B f Teenoso (USA)—Mosso (Ercolano (USA)) **Mr R. Milburn**
17 B f Sayf El Arab (USA)—Perchance (Connaught) **Mr P. Butler**
18 B c Gorytus (USA)—Sparkling Air (Malinowski (USA)) **Mr P. Butler**
19 Ch f Fayruz—Very Seldom (Rarity) **Mr J. Carrigan**

Other Owners: Mr A. Edwards, Mr Frank Parker, Mr P. Rommerrl, Mr M. Russell, Mr K. R. Snellings, Mrs P. Targett, Mrs C. W. Traylen, Mr C. Williams, Mr Brian Wiseman, Mr B. Wright.

Jockey (Flat): C Dwyer.

Jockeys (NH): Ross Campbell, R Guest.

Amateur: Miss Ginny Belding (9-7).

661 MISS S. J. WILTON, Stoke-on-Trent

Postal: **Round Meadow Racing Stables, Rownal Road, Wetley Rocks, Stoke-on-Trent, ST9 OBP.**
Phone: **HOME (0782) 550861 OFFICE (0782) 550115**

1 A 1 PAPER CHASER, 6, ch g The Parson—Summerville Lass **A1 Paper Plc**
2 ARDORAN, 4, ch g Little Wolf—Smoke Creek **Mr B. Molloy**
3 ARTY SCHWEPPES (USA), 4, ch g Super Concorde (USA)—Mon Solange (USA) **Mr John Pointon**
4 BROWN BEAR BOY (USA), 8, b g San Feliou (FR)—Gabriele (USA) **Mr John Nolan**
5 CHEDDLETON WHIFF, 8, b g Crooner—Sirette **Mr Carl Pointon**
6 CONCERT PAPER, 6, b g Over The River (FR)—Good Surprise **Mr John Pointon**
7 COURT RULER, 7, b g Rolfe (USA)—Sanandrea **Mr Barry Winfield**
8 FOUJITA (USA), 5, b h Tap Shoes (USA)—Ivory Smooth (USA) **Mr Barry Winfield**
9 GOLDEN AZELIA, 7, b m Jimsun—Persian Swallow **Mr M. Cooper**
10 GOOD CAUSE, 6, ch h Kris—Goodwin Sands (USA) **Mr John Pointon**
11 HENRY PADWICK, 7, ch g Balidar—Lucky Janie **Mr John Pointon**
12 JANEYS DELIGHT, 9, b m New Henry—Keep Shining **Mr Walter Moss**
13 JOHNNY SHARP (USA), 6, ch g Sharpen Up—Crimson Flame (USA) **Mr Peter Ashmore**
14 KILSYTH, 11, b m Jolly Good—Harmony Thyme **Mr Martin Pointon**
15 MARSHAL BLAKE, 7, b g Roscoe Blake—Off The Pill **Mr Brian White (Rocester)**
16 MO ICHI DO, 4, b g Lomond (USA)—Engageante (FR) **Miss Sue Wilton**
17 NOBLE BID, 6, b h Kings Lake (USA)—First Round **Mr George Byatt**
18 OVERT (USA), 5, b m Ben Fab (CAN)—Lady More Friendly (USA) **Mr G. C. Chipman**
19 PARKERS JOY, 6, b g Final Straw—Blakewood **Mrs Joy Parker**
20 PIGEON ENGLISH, 6, b br g Homing—Particular Miss **Mr George Byatt**
21 PRINCE BOLD (FR), 7, b g Rex Magna (FR)—Lady Bold **J. & J. Slitting Services**
22 QUEENS PALACE, 12, ch g Altosa Palace—Melche **Mr R. Rowlinson**
23 RIPSTER, 6, b g Ahonoora—Goirtin **Mr Martin Pointon**
24 SCOBIE DOUGH, 4, br g Over The River (FR)—Clerihan Miss **A1 Paper Plc**
25 SHARP ORDER, 5, ch g Sharpo—Cardinal Palace **Mr B. Molloy**
26 SIXTY MINUTES, 6, b g Formidable (USA)—Dialogue **Mr Martin Pointon**
27 SORORITY, 5, ch m Tap On Wood—Restless Lady **A1 Paper Plc**
28 TAKE A LIBERTY, 5, ch m Aragon—Liberty Tree **Mr P. W. Saunders**
29 VISTULE (USA), 8, ch g Dust Commander (USA)—Riverdance (FR) **Mrs S. E. Bibby**
30 WHITEHOUSE GEM, 7, ch m Amboise—Golden Pinelopi **Mr K. M. Bebbington**
31 WOODLANDS LADY, 4, b f Oats—Sand Lady **Mr John Pointon**

MISS S. J. WILTON—continued

THREE-YEAR-OLDS

32 **FARNDALE,** gr c Vaigly Great—Beloved Mistress **Mrs Sheila Pointon**
33 **UNCLE BOBBY,** ch c King Persian—Honi Soit **Mr Bob Jacobs**

Other Owners: Mr George Basnett, Ceilings & Interiors (Midlands) Ltd, Mr T. Connop, Mr Clive Fenton, Mr A. Harriott, Mr J. B. Holt, Mr Paul Lipton, Mr Frank Longman, Mr Kieran McGee, Mr Michael McRitchie.

Jockeys (NH): Graham McCourt (10-4), Steve Smith-Eccles (10-3).

Conditional: John Bates.

662 MR K. G. WINGROVE, Leamington Spa

Postal: **Fox Farm, Bascote Heath, Southam, Leamington Spa, Warwickshire.**
Phone: **SOUTHAM (0926) 813958**

1 **ANTIGUAN STING,** 4, b g Head For Heights—Honey Bridge **Mr R. A. Jeffries**
2 **BEAULIEU BAY,** 6, b g Longleat (USA)—Peta's Bay **Mr R. A. Jeffries**
3 **HYDRO-ELECTRIC,** 5, b m Electric—Lady Spey **Mr P. F. Rawbone**
4 4, Br f Callernish—Madam Beau **Stud Power Limited**
5 **MARY O'REILLY,** 5, br m Callernish—Monavalla **Stud Power Limited**
6 **PALACE YARD,** 8, ch g Town And Country—Escorial **Mr R. A. Jeffries**
7 **PRESENT TIMES,** 4, b g Sayf El Arab (USA)—Coins And Art (USA) **Stud Power Limited**
8 **PRIX DU NORD (USA),** 4, b g Northern Prospect (USA)—Bisouloun (FR) **Mr M. J. Stiles**
9 4, Ch f Floriferous—Speedy Willow **Mr G. J. Wingrove**
10 **SUPER IDEA,** 5, b m Red Sunset—Priors Mistress **Mrs M. V. Creasey**
11 4, Gr f Modern Dancer—Tepon Gail **Mr G. J. Wingrove**
12 **TOUCH ME TOUCH ME,** 5, ch m Last Fandango—Lombardia **Mr R. A. Jeffries**
13 **TROMEROS,** 9, b h Camden Town—Silky Starlet (USA) **Mr R. A. Jeffries**
14 **YUFFROUW ANN,** 5, b m Tyrnavos—Recline **Mr R. A. Jeffries**

THREE-YEAR-OLDS

15 **CASTLERAE FAIR,** b f Sweet Monday—La Bird **Mr M. Usher**
16 B g Teenoso (USA)—North Queen **Mr M. J. Stiles**
17 **POWER'S MONET,** b f Claude Monet (USA)—Mummy's Glory **Stud Power Limited**

TWO-YEAR-OLDS

18 Ch c 12/5 Dragon Palace (USA)—Dear Alicia (Runnymede) **Stud Power Limited**
19 B f 25/4 Rusticaro (FR)—Lady Portobello (Porto Bello) **Mr M. Usher**
20 B c 5/4 Siberian Express—Three Waves (Cure The Blues (USA)) **Stud Power Limited**

Jockey (NH): Joe Lodder (w.a.).

Conditional: Tarnya Stone (9-7).

663 MRS J. WONNACOTT, Tavistock

Postal: **Hurlditch, Lamerton, Tavistock, Devon.**
Phone: **(082287) 215**

1 **ANOTHER BROWNIE,** 11, br g Giolla Mear—Another Rose **Miss Linda Wonnacott**
2 **BEN LEDI,** 6, b g Strong Gale—Balacco **Mr A. C. D. Joynson**

MRS J. WONNACOTT—continued

3 **CARTA TITLE,** 4, ch f Runnymede—Headliner **Mr Colin A. Pester**
4 **DENNING (USA),** 8, b h Advocator—Sunbeam Sal (USA) **Mr Colin A. Pester**
5 **DOUBLE U DEE,** 7, b g Rapid Pass—Abbyrama **Mr Colin A. Pester**
6 **HORATIAN,** 5, b g Horage—Assurance (FR) **Mrs J. Wonnacott**
7 **JOIST,** 8, ch g Malinowski (USA)—Junella **Mr Tony Butler**
8 **LEG UP,** 11, ch g Quality Fair—Early Echo **Mr Colin A. Pester**
9 **LIZZY LONGSTOCKING,** 8, br m Jimsun—Darling Emma **Miss Linda Wonnacott**
10 **MISS HISSY,** 4, b f Tyrnavos—Hissy Missy **Mrs J. Wonnacott**
11 **OIL FEVER,** 10, ch g Deep Run—Ivernia **Mr Colin A. Pester**
12 **SAKR,** 8, ch g Hotfoot—Grande Fille **Mr Colin A. Pester**
13 **SEW HIGH,** 7, b g Nicholas Bill—Sew Nice **Mr Tony Butler**
14 **SHALCHLO BOY,** 6, gr g Rusticaro (FR)—Mala Mala **Mr S. N. Burfield**
15 **STOCKWOOD,** 4, ch f Oats—Sur Les Roches **Mrs J. Wonnacott**
16 **TORENAGA'S TRIUMPH,** 4, b g Mummy's Game—Autumn Breeze **Mr Tony Butler**
17 **VERTIGO,** 5, b g Shirley Heights—Western Partner (USA) **Mr S. N. Burfield**

Jockey (NH): D Wonnacott (10-0).

Amateurs: Mr A Wonnacott (10-7), Mrs Claire Wonnacott (10-0).

664 MR R. D. E. WOODHOUSE, York

Postal: **Teal House, Greets Farm, Welburn, York, YO6 7EJ.**
Phone: **WHITWELL ON THE HILL (065381) 637**

1 **CASTLE SAINT,** 6, b g Welsh Saint—French Swallow **Mr C. F. Colquhoun**
2 **DELPIOMBO,** 4, br g Lochnager—Precious Petra **Mr Paul Coulter**
3 **DOC LODGE,** 4, b f Doc Marten—Cooling **Mr M. K. Oldham**
4 **DUBIOUS JAKE,** 7, b g Dubassoff (USA)—Coliemore **Mr M. K. Oldham**
5 **EARL HANSEL,** 9, b g Hardboy—Cool Amanda **Mr C. F. Colquhoun**
6 **GOLDEN WAVE,** 5, b g Glint of Gold—Grecian Sea (FR) **Mr R. D. E. Woodhouse**
7 **HELLO SPARKLER,** 5, b h Hello Gorgeous (USA)—Rheinsparkle **Mr M. K. Oldham**
8 **HIGH KABOUR,** 4, b f Kabour—High Walk **Mr R. D. E. Woodhouse**
9 **LEVISHAM,** 5, ch g Valiyar—Bridestones **Mr A. Woodhouse**
10 **LUCKY RHUMBA,** 7, b g Rambah—Old Currency **Mr M. A. Humphreys**
11 **MR BOSTON,** 5, b g Halyudh (USA)—Edith Rose **Mr M. K. Oldham**
12 **NIDD BRIDGES,** 4, br f Grey Ghost—Bargello's Lady **Hymas Hire Ltd**
13 **READ ALL ABOUT IT,** 9, ch g London Gazette—Pet Jackdaw **Mr Harry Atkinson**
14 **ROCKLINE,** 5, ch g Inline—Honey Rock **Mr M. K. Oldham**
15 **SIDVIC,** 11, b g Harvest Spirit—Olisa **Mr C. F. Colquhoun**

Other Owners: Mr M. W. Easterby, Mr Philip Parker.

Jockey (NH): L Wyer (10-0).

Conditional: R Garritty (10-0), C Woodall (10-0).

Amateur: Mr R D E Woodhouse (11-0).

665 MR S. WOODMAN, Chichester

Postal: **Parkers Barn Stables, East Lavant, Chichester, West Sussex, PO18 OAU.**
Phone: **OFFICE (0243) 527136 HOME (0243) 528227**

1 **CHANCE AGAIN,** 7, br m Balinger—Chance A Look **Mrs Diane Bryant**
2 **CONNABEE,** 6, b g Connaught—Sera Sera **Mrs Brenda Serjeant**
3 **CREDORA BAY,** 6, b m Orange Bay—Credo's Daughter **Mr P. G. Williams**
4 **JOANN'S CREDO,** 4, b f Tachypous—Credo's Daughter **Mr G. Gornall**
5 **JOLLIENNE,** 6, ch m Absalom—Bourienne **Mr D. J. Flint**
6 **KING CREDO,** 5, b g Kinglet—Credo's Daughter **Mr R. W. Lacey**
7 **SONEETO,** 4, b g Teenoso (USA)—Flying Bid **Mr Brian Plaistowe**
8 **SUN OF CHANCE,** 6, b g Sunyboy—Chance A Look **Mr M. Bryant**
9 **TREBLE CHANCE,** 8, b m Balinger—Chance A Look **Mr M. Bryant**
10 **UNIQUE NEW YORK,** 7, b g Balinger—Credo's Daughter **Mr J. C. Bolam**

THREE-YEAR-OLDS

11 **HENRI LE COMTE,** gr g Sunley Builds—Countess Mariga **Mrs J. E. M. Powell**
12 B f Castle Keep—My Pink Parrot **Mrs Sally Woodman**
13 **YOU JEST,** b g Comedy Star (USA)—Paradise Straits **Miss Jane Lane**

Other Owners: Miss Susan Jameson, Mr Peter Wiegand.

Jockey (NH): R Dunwoody (w.a.).

666 MR G. WRAGG, Newmarket

Postal: **Abington Place, Bury Road, Newmarket, Suffolk, CB8 7BT.**
Phone: **OFFICE (0638) 662328 TELEX 94016161 WRAG G FAX (0638) 663576**

1 **AIGUE,** 4, b f High Top—Cecilia Bianchi (FR) **Sir Robin McAlpine**
2 **BRAISWICK,** 4, b f King of Spain—Laughing Girl **Sheikh Mohammed**
3 **ELMSTEAD,** 4, b c Shirley Heights—Cherry Hinton (USA) **Sheikh Mohammed**
4 **JEHOL,** 4, b c Teenoso (USA)—Buz Kashi **Sir Philip Oppenheimer**
5 **LOVERS' PARLOUR,** 4, b f Beldale Flutter (USA)—Ready And Willing **Mrs H. H. Morriss**
6 **MBULWA,** 4, ch c Be My Guest (USA)—Bundu (FR) **Sir Philip Oppenheimer**
7 **NAYLAND,** 4, ch g Be My Guest (USA)—Troytops **Sheikh Mohammed**
8 **PRINTERS PIE,** 4, b g Known Fact (USA)—Boule de Suif **Mr H. H. Morriss**
9 **TAKE ONE,** 4, b c Teenoso (USA)—Old Kate **Sheikh Mohammed**

THREE-YEAR-OLDS

10 **AMARANTHUS,** b f Shirley Heights—Amaranda **Earl of Halifax**
11 **ANCIENT CITY,** gr c Persepolis (FR)—Fair Melys (FR) **Sir Philip Oppenheimer**
12 **CASAMURRAE,** b f Be My Guest (USA)—Loralane **Sir Philip Oppenheimer**
13 **CHAFF,** b c Final Straw—Silky (USA) **Sheikh Mohammed**
14 **CHEERFUL NOTE,** b f Cure The Blues (USA)—Strident Note **Sheikh Mohammed**
15 **CHEZ JARRASSE,** b c Pharly (FR)—Miss Saint-Cloud **Mr J. L. C. Pearce**
16 **COPFORD,** b c Teenoso (USA)—Chalkey Road **Sheikh Mohammed**
17 **DORSET DUKE,** b c Beldale Flutter (USA)—Youthful (FR) **Sir Robin McAlpine**
18 **GLENFINLASS,** b f Lomond (USA)—Glowing With Pride **Sir Philip Oppenheimer**
19 **GREGORAVICH,** ch c Nijinsky (CAN)—Pagan Queen **Sir Philip Oppenheimer**
20 **HELEN'S GUEST,** ch f Be My Guest (USA)—Helenetta **Sheikh Mohammed**
21 **ILE DE ROMA,** b c Ile de Bourbon (USA)—Romara **Sheikh Mohammed**
22 **JAMIN,** b c Teenoso (USA)—Miss Longchamp **Mr J. L. C. Pearce**
23 **KATAHDIN,** b c Sandhurst Prince—Grand Teton **Mrs H. H. Morriss**
24 **KATES CABIN,** ch f Habitat—Old Kate **Sheikh Mohammed**
25 **LET FLY,** ch c Kris—Cut Loose **Sir John Astor**
26 **MA PETITE CHOU,** gr f Known Fact (USA)—Boule de Suif **Mr H. H. Morriss**
27 **MATOMANI,** b f Beldale Flutter (USA)—Bundu (FR) **Sir Philip Oppenheimer**
28 **MISS JAVA,** ch f Persian Bold—Miss Bali **Mr J. L. C. Pearce**

MR G. WRAGG—continued

29 **MISS ORIENTAL,** ch f Habitat—Miss Bangkok **Mr J. L. C. Pearce**
30 **NEVER SO FAIR,** b f Never So Bold—Favoletta **Sheikh Mohammed**
31 **PIPITINA,** b f Bustino—Pipina (USA) **Sheikh Mohammed**
32 **POST CODE,** b c Teenoso (USA)—Home Address **Sheikh Mohammed**
33 **RAND LORD,** b c Rainbow Quest (USA)—Dancing Rocks **Sir Philip Oppenheimer**
34 **RIVIERA MAGIC,** ch c Niniski (USA)—Miss Beaulieu **Mr J. L. C. Pearce**
35 **ROCKRIDGE,** b c Chief Singer—Croda Rossa (ITY) **Sir Philip Oppenheimer**
36 **ROMANY MARSH (USA),** b c Lomond (USA)—Zinzara (USA) **Sir Philip Oppenheimer**
37 **SALLY ROUS,** br f Rousillon (USA)—Sassalya **Sir Philip Oppenheimer**
38 **STRANGER STILL,** b f Cragador—No Relation **Sir Philip Oppenheimer**
39 **TENESA,** gr f Teenoso (USA)—Be Easy **Sir Philip Oppenheimer**
40 **TOTHAM,** b f Shernazar—Susanna (USA) **Sheikh Mohammed**
41 **TULWAR,** b c Kris—On The House (FR) **Sir Philip Oppenheimer**
42 **VOTE IN FAVOUR,** b f General Assembly (USA)—Favoridge (USA) **Sheikh Mohammed**
43 **WELNEY,** b br c Habitat—On Show **Sir Philip Oppenheimer**

TWO-YEAR-OLDS

44 **ABLE SUSAN,** b f Formidable (USA)—Susanna (USA) (Nijinsky (CAN)) **Exors of the late Mr E. B. Moller**
45 **ARCADIAN HEIGHTS,** b c Shirley Heights—Miss Longchamp (Northfields (USA)) **Mr J. L. C. Pearce**
46 **ARCOT,** b c Formidable (USA)—Pagan Queen (Vaguely Noble) **Sir Philip Oppenheimer**
47 **BALI SURFER,** ch c Pharly (FR)—Miss Kuta Beach (Bold Lad (IRE)) **Mr J. L. C. Pearce**
48 **BILDESTON,** b c Teenoso (USA)—Sue Grundy (Grundy) **Sheikh Mohammed**
49 **BUSHY TAILED,** br c Teenoso (USA)—Bundu (FR) (Habitat) **Sir Philip Oppenheimer**
50 **CHELSWORTH,** b f Never So Bold—Ash Ridge (USA) (Bold Reason) **Exors of the late Mr E. B. Moller**
51 **CIRCE'S ISLE,** b f Be My Guest (USA)—Sassalya (Sassafras (FR)) **Sir Philip Oppenheimer**
52 **CROSSILLION,** b c Rousillon (USA)—Croda Rossa (ITY) (Grey Sovereign) **Sir Philip Oppenheimer**
53 B f Trojan Fen—Crown Witness (Crowned Prince (USA)) **Edmund Loder**
54 **DAUNT NOT,** gr f Kalaglow—Dare Me (Derring-Do) **Sir John Astor**
55 **DEBENHAM,** b f Formidable (USA)—Top Shot (Grundy) **Sheikh Mohammed**
56 **DREAMS END,** ch c Rainbow Quest (USA)—Be Easy (Be Friendly) **Sir Philip Oppenheimer**
57 **EVERGLADES (IRE),** b c Green Desert (USA)—
Glowing With Pride (Ile de Bourbon (USA)) **Mr A. E. Oppenheimer**
58 **FLORALIA,** b f Auction Ring (USA)—Norpella (Northfields (USA)) **Sheikh Mohammed**
59 **GABY,** b c Sure Blade (USA)—Mpani (Habitat) **Sir Philip Oppenheimer**
60 **GAI BULGA,** b f Kris—Dancing Rocks (Green Dancer (USA)) **Sir Philip Oppenheimer**
61 **GRAND GUIGNOL,** ch c Superlative—Boule de Suif (Major Portion) **Mr H. H. Morriss**
62 **HERIZ,** ch c Persian Bold—Home Address (Habitat) **Sheikh Mohammed**
63 **KALAMIS,** gr f Kalaglow—Buz Kashi (Bold Lad (IRE)) **Sir Philip Oppenheimer**
64 **KERSEY,** b c Glint of Gold—Favoridge (USA) (Riva Ridge (USA)) **Sheikh Mohammed**
65 **MOHAWK CHIEF,** b c Ahonoora—Ringtail (Auction Ring (USA)) **Lt Col N. E. Frieze**
66 **OLD GLORY,** ch c Valiyar—Old Kate (Busted) **Sheikh Mohammed**
67 **PEBMARSH,** b c Law Society (USA)—Pipina (USA) (Sir Gaylord) **Exors of the late Mr E. B. Moller**
68 **PERCY'S GIRL (IRE),** b f Blakeney—Laughing Girl (Sassafras (FR)) **Sheikh Mohammed**
69 **PHAMILLA (IRE),** b f Bellypha—Mill Dance (Mill Reef (USA)) **Sir Philip Oppenheimer**
70 **RECALDE,** b c King of Spain—Kissimmee (FR) (Petingo) **Palmbridge Services Limited**
71 **RENDALLS,** b c Top Ville—On The House (FR) (Be My Guest (USA)) **Sir Philip Oppenheimer**
72 **RIVIERA RAINBOW,** b c Rainbow Quest (USA)—Miss Beaulieu (Northfields (USA)) **Mr J. L. C. Pearce**
73 **ROMANY RYE,** ch c Nijinsky (CAN)—Zinzara (USA) (Stage Door Johnny) **Sir Philip Oppenheimer**
74 **SAVEUR,** b f Ardross—Youthful (FR) (Green Dancer (USA)) **Sir Robin McAlpine**
75 **SHE'S THE TOPS,** b f Shernazar—Troytops (Troy) **Sheikh Mohammed**
76 **SOHRAB (IRE),** ch c Shernazar—On Show (Welsh Pageant) **Sir Philip Oppenheimer**
77 **SO ROMANTIC (IRE),** b f Teenoso (USA)—Romara (Bold Lad (IRE)) **Sheikh Mohammed**
78 **STREET KID,** b c Teenoso (USA)—Chalkey Road (Relko) **Sheikh Mohammed**
79 **SUGGESTION,** b c Teenoso (USA)—Suggestive (Bold Lad (IRE)) **Sir Robin McAlpine**
80 **SUMONDA,** b f Lomond—Soemba (General Assembly (USA)) **Sir Philip Oppenheimer**
81 **TORCHON,** b c High Top—Cecilia Bianchi (FR) (Petingo) **Sir Robin McAlpine**
82 **WELCOMING,** b f Sharpo—Warm Welcome (General Assembly (USA)) **Sheikh Mohammed**
83 **WILD PAVANE,** b f Dancing Brave (USA)—Loralane (Habitat) **Mrs A. E. Oppenheimer**
84 **YOUNG BUSTER (IRE),** b c Teenoso (USA)—Bustara (Busted) **Exors of the late Mr E. B. Moller**

Jockey (Flat): Gary Carter (7-11).

667 MR F. J. YARDLEY, Droitwich

Postal: **Daneswood Farm, Boreley, Nr Ombersley, Droitwich, Worcestershire.**
Phone: **WORCS (0905) 620477**

1 **ABSENT LOVER,** 9, ch m Nearly A Hand—Straight Avenue **Mr F. J. Yardley**
2 **COT LANE,** 5, ch g Remainder Man—Smokey Princess **Mr R. H. Griffiths**
3 **ILE DE ROI,** 7, b h Ile de Bourbon (USA)—Regal Lady (FR) **Maltsword Ltd**
4 **INSPIRED LOVE,** 5, gr m Dalsaan—Inspiring **Mr R. H. Griffiths**
5 **JORURI,** 5, ch g High Line—Dancing Sally **Maltsword Ltd**
6 **KOFFI (GER),** 8, b g Horst-Herbert—Kalliope (GER) **Mr F. J. Yardley**
7 **MISS STOCKIN,** 6, b m Balinger—Reine d'Armagnac **Mrs Valerie Turley**
8 **PECKING ORDER,** 6, b m Henbit (USA)—Daring Lass **Mr F. J. Yardley**
9 **TAWNY HAWK,** 6, ch m Crofthall—Honeybuzzard (FR) **Mr F. J. Yardley**
10 **TOKANDA,** 6, ch g Record Token—Andalucia **Mr F. J. Yardley**
11 **WARFLIGHT,** 11, b h Warpath—Brief Flight **Mr F. J. Yardley**

THREE-YEAR-OLDS

12 **CAPALLUS,** b g Big Connaught—Chatley's Seedling **Mr F. J. Yardley**
13 **MECADO,** b g Ballacashtal (CAN)—Parma Nova **Maltsword Ltd**
14 **MY LADYS TEARS,** gr f Godswalk (USA)—Vital Spirit **Maltsword Ltd**
15 **PARTY BLUES,** gr f Ballacashtal (CAN)—Party Cloak **Maltsword Ltd**

TWO-YEAR-OLDS

16 B f 5/3 Claude Monet (USA)—Miss Twights (Hopeful Venture) **Mr F. J. Yardley**

Jockey (Flat): I Johnson (8-4).

Lady Rider: Miss Carol Yardley (8-4).

668 MR G. H. YARDLEY, Malvern

Postal: **Upper Woodsfield Farm, Newland, Malvern, Worcestershire.**
Phone: **WORCESTER (0905) 830245**

1 **ANHAAR,** 5, b m Ela-Mana-Mou—Chilblains **Mr John H. Marston**
2 **BEL CREATION,** 6, br m Creative Plan (USA)—Linbel **Mr John H. Marston**
3 **HAVON AIRCO,** 4, b g Lafontaine (USA)—Sunland Park **Mr John H. Marston**
4 **PITHY,** 8, ch g Orange Bay—Pranky **Mr P. C. Harris**
5 **PRINZ EUGEN,** 12, gr g Pitcairn—Nice Hostess **Mr G. H. Yardley**
6 4, B g Sunyboy—Royal Russe **Mr G. H. Yardley**
7 **SPARRING,** 5, b m Sagaro—Parabems **Mr B. Owen**
8 **SPRING MIST,** 4, b f Cruise Missile—Springs To Mind **Miss A. Pound**

TWO-YEAR-OLDS

9 **KINGSTHORPE,** ch g Brotherly (USA)—Miss Kewmill (Billion (USA)) **Mr Mervyn Jones**
10 B f Brotherly (USA)—Royal Russe (Bally Russe) **Mr G. H. Yardley**

Other Owners: Mr Philip Jones.

Jockey (NH): M Bosley.

Conditional: W McFarland.

Lady Rider: Miss A Yardley (8-7).

669 MR V. P. YOUNG, Hastings

Postal: **37A Saxon Road, Hastings, TN35 5HJ.**
Phone: **(0424) 438425**

1 **ADANUS,** 4, ch g General Assembly (USA)—Mirkan Honey **Mr V. Young**
2 **AL SKEET (USA),** 4, b g L'Emigrant (USA)—Processional (USA) **Mr V. Young**
3 **ESPRIT DE FEMME (FR),** 4, b f Esprit du Nord (USA)—Bustelda (FR) **Mr V. Young**
4 **ITTIHAAD,** 7, gr g Rusticaro (FR)—Perfect Bid (USA) **Mr V. Young**
5 **SHARPGUN (FR),** 4, ch c Sharpo—Whitegun (FR) **Mr V. Young**
6 **YOUNG ALFIE,** 5, b g Neltino—Anglophil **Mr V. Young**

Amateur: Mr Alan Deeprose (9-7).

STOP PRESS

The following trainers entries were received too late for inclusion in the appropriate section of Horses in Training.

670 MR D. J. BELL, Banbury

Postal: **2 Nill Farm Cottages, Hook Norton, Banbury, Oxon.**
Phone: **(0608) HOOK NORTON 730070**

ARDILES, 6, b g Windjammer (USA)—Primmy **Mr Dennis Mill**
COLLISTO, 9, ch g Lombard (GER)—Colinetta **Mrs Simon Aldridge**
DEPUTY GOVERNOR, 7, b h Tower Walk—Come On Girl **Mr M. Harker**
FANILLE, 4, b c Top Ville—Flying Fantasy **Mr Dennis Mill**
KEEP GUESSING, 4, b c Bay Express—Guess Again (GER) **Mr M. Harker**
PIN CUSHION, 4, ch f Blue Cashmere—Tribal Princess **Combined Racing Limited**
SHARP SHAPE (USA), 5, ch h Sharpen Up—Love That Girl (USA) **Mr M. Harker**
THE GANNOCHY (USA), 4, ch g Coastal (USA)—Bright View **Mr B. Lynch**
TOTALY PICKLED, 9, ch g Tickled Pink—Noble Nugget **Denise E. Smith**
YOUNG DRIVER, 13, b g Linacre—Pepe **Mr M. Harker**

Other Owners: Mr George Darling, Mrs Angus Irvine, Mr Steve Woods.

Jockeys (NH): Jimmy Duggan (10-0), Lorna Vincent (9-5).

Conditional: Paul Harley (9-0).

671 MR R. BRANDON, Doncaster

Postal: **Chez Nous, Green Lane, Scawthorpe, Doncaster, DN5 7UT.**
Phone: **(0302) 721015**

FUTURE REFERENCE, 6, b g Ardoon—Melanie Jane **Mr R. Brandon**
MISS EUTOPIA, 5, b m Dunphy—Fair Colleen **Mrs C. Turner**
POSSESSED, 6, b g Posse (USA)—Mariinsky **Mrs C. Turner**

672 MR P. BUTLER, Lewes

Postal: **Homewoodgate Farm, Novington Lane, East Chiltington, Lewes, BN7 3AU.**
Phone: **(0273) 890124 OR (0273) 477254**

BRANSTOWN SUNSET, 6, b g Red Sunset—Lydja **Mr M. Murray**
CRASH CALL, 9, br m Crash Course—Lady Piersfield **Mrs K. Baldry**
DUNSANY PLAYBOY, 6, ch g Salluceva—Lagore Lady **Mr M. Murray**
GREAT STANDS BY, 6, br g Welsh Captain—Same Date **Mr O. J. Henley**
HJANI, 9, b g Tanfirion—Ikatina **Mr O. J. Henley**
MANOUSHKA, 5, b m Ile de Bourbon (USA)—Gilwanigan **Crisptrend Ltd**
MATTA MIA FLYER, 5, b br m Boreen (FR)—Wild Deer **Mr C. Hume and Mrs N. Porter**
NATHIR (USA), 4, b c Diesis—As You Would (USA) **Mr A. J. Taaffe**

MR P. BUTLER—continued

NOMELAP, 5, b g Palemon—Coronation Heath **Mr O. J. Henley**
PANEL GAME, 6, ch m Lepanto (GER)—Silly Games **Mrs J. N. O'Connor**
POWER REIGNS, 5, ch h Star Appeal—All Risks **Mrs K. Baldry**
PRESIDENTIAL STAR (USA), 4, b f President (FR)—Out of This World **Mr E. H. Whatmough**

THREE-YEAR-OLDS

PERSIAN PEACH, b br f Persian Bold—Derry Daughter **Mr H. James**

Other Owners: Mr P. Butler, Mr Fraser Graham, Miss N. Lucey, Mrs Ann Sainty, Dr O. Studd.

Amateur: Mr A R Burnham (9-7).

Lady Rider: Mrs E L Butler (8-7).

673 MR J. CHUGG, Milton-under-Wychwoo

Postal: **Heath Farm, Milton-under-Wychwood, Oxford, OX7 6LR.**
Phone: **(0993) 830219**

BEAU VITE, 15, ch g Celtic Cone—Hasty Belle **Milton Heath Farm Ltd**
GENERAL HIGHWAY, 7, b g General Ironside—Highway Mistress **Mrs P. Glenn**
HARVEST BEAU, 4, ch g Oats—Bowtina **Mrs P. Glenn**
MASTER RAJH, 6, b g Majestic Maharaj—Miss Medina **Mrs P. Glenn**
MIGHTY'S IMAGE, 5, b m Oats—Mighty Nice **Unregistered Partnership**
MR RUMPOLE, 6, b g Whistlefield—Mighty Nice **Mr P.S. Mistry and Milton Heath Farm Ltd**
PIPER TAMSON, 4, b g Chantro—Veno Star **Mrs P. Glenn**
RYMER KING, 8, b g Rymer—Belinda Pocket **Mr G. Hutsby**
SCHOOL RUN, 6, ch m Deep Run—High School **Mrs P. Glenn and Partners**
THE NUNS STORY, 5, b m The Parson—Nora Grany **Mrs P. Glenn**

THREE-YEAR-OLDS

MIGHTY FROLIC, b f Oats—Mighty Nice **Milton Heath Farm Ltd and Mr P.S. Mistry**

Other Owners: Mrs Jennifer Chugg, Mrs Katie Hutsby.

Jockeys (NH): M M Lynch (10-0), J Shortt (10-0).

674 MR W. E. FISHER, Bath

Postal: **Bathway Farm, Chewton Mendip, Bath, Avon.**
Phone: **(076 121) 283**

COURTLANDS GIRL, 8, ch m Crimson Beau—Queen's Treasure **Mr M. S. Saunders**
DUBATINI, 5, b m Dubassoff (USA)—Queen's Wild **Mr B. B. Akerman**
ELLA ROSA, 9, ch m Le Bavard (FR)—High School **Mr P. Tosh**
GEORGE BUCKINGHAM, 5, b g Royal Palace—Flying Idol **Mr P. F. Hatherell**
HONEST MEMBER, 9, ch g New Member—Truly Sincere **J. P. Thorner**
KELLYANN, 7, b m Jellaby—Queen's Treasure **Mr R. K. Kelly**
KING UNIVERSE, 9, b g Kinglet—Miss Universe **Mrs I. R. Millar**
LEVANT WAY, 10, br g Levanter—Lartway **Mr D. S. Mutton**
WILD DEAL, 9, b g Levanter—Queen's Wild **Mr B. B. Akerman**

MR W. E. FISHER—continued

THREE-YEAR-OLDS

MISS PURBECK, br f Ranksborough—Party Miss **B. Curtis**

Other Owners: Mr Mike Cornish, Mr K. G. Nicholls, Mr B. S. Thatcher.

Amateur: Miss H Chard (9-0).

675 MR J. E. LONG, Plumpton

Postal: **Southern Stables, The Ridge, Plumpton Green, Lewes, East Sussex.**
Phone: **PLUMPTON (0273) 890244**

AIRDRIE FLYER, 5, ch g Beldale Lark—Rock Angel **Mrs Fiona Irvine**
BAYTINO, 7, ro m Neltino—Fleet Fen **Mr Michael Thomas**
CELTIC HAMLET, 11, ch g Celtic Cone—Royal Gertrude **Churchills Racehorse One Hundred Ltd**
CHAN FU, 5, b g Kafu—Chanrossa **J. S. Gowling**
DECIDING BID, 4, ch c Valiyar—Final Call **Mr B. Baldwin**
DIADEM DANCER, 4, b g Solford (USA)—Pure Music (FR) **Mr J. A. Porteous**
EASTERN EVENING, 5, gr g Runnett—Sacola **Mr K. D. Poulton**
ELPLOTINO, 8, br g Bustino—Explosiva (USA) **Mr Michael Thomas**
GEBLITZT, 6, b h Tumble Wind (USA)—Tatty Kay **Mr Phil Cook**
KIRAM (USA), 5, b h Gold Stage (USA)—Alight (FR) **J. S. Gowling**
LAABAS, 7, br g Ile de Bourbon (USA)—Lyric Dance **Mr John Nicholson**
LOOSE RUCK, 6, b g Runnett—Where Is It **Churchills Racehorse One Hundred Ltd**
MISS SARAHSUE, 4, br f Van Der Linden (FR)—Blakesware Dancer **Gary Marney**
MISS STYLE, 6, b m Tack On—Amber Amsel **Mrs Ann Nash**
ORIENTESSA, 5, b m Don Roberto (USA)—Green Bay (FR) **Westcliff Bloodstock Ltd**
PARENTUS, 7, b g Derrylin—Flaxen Hair **Churchills Racehorse One Hundred Ltd**
SERGEANT AT ARMS, 5, b g Shirley Heights—Sunningdale Queen **Churchills Racehorse One Hundred Ltd**
TESTAROSSA, 7, b m Tower Walk—Floor Show **T. Kenward**
VAGUELYNNIGHT, 5, b h Victor Hugo—Night Work **Mr J. King**
VICTORIAN FAIR, 4, br f Victor Hugo—Straight Face **Mr P. McQuillan**

THREE-YEAR-OLDS

TACK ON TWO, b g Tack On—Amber Amsel **Mrs Ann Nash**

Other Owners: Mr J. D. Barling, Mr Dave Foster, Mr Brian Arthur Pearce, Mr C. A. Pike, Mr Steve Pitman.

Jockeys (NH): R Goldstein, R Rowell (10-0).

Apprentice: J Stenning (7-12).

Conditional: Leesa Long (9-7).

Amateur: Mr J Poulton (10-0).

676 MR P. MULLINS, Goresbridge

Postal: **Doninga, Goresbridge, Co. Kilkenny, Ireland.**
Phone: **(0503) 75121**

ANTRIM COUNTY, 5, ch g Deep Run—Gothic Arch

MR P. MULLINS—continued

ARCH DUCHESS, 4, b f Tender King—Mag
BAPTISMAL FIRE, 6, ch g Baptism—Levi's Star
BARKMILLS, 7, b g Maculata—Fairy Snow
BART OWEN, 5, b g Belfalas—Ten Again
BEGORSHUR, 7, b g Deep Run—Peg Whip
BORO SMACKEROO, 5, b g Deep Run—Boro Nickel
CLOUGHTANEY, 9, b g Quayside—Coady's Fancy
DELIFFIN, 4, b g Wolverlife—Teletype
DERRINORE, 5, b g Castle Keep—Cheribond
DERRYMORE BOY, 8, br g Bonne Noel—Sweet Melody
DEVIL'S LOCK, 6, ch g Lucifer—Barrowvale
DONE INSTANTLY, 5, b g Day Is Done—Instanter
DOZING BULL, 6, b g Bulldozer—Gorgeous Gael
FAIR BOREEN, 7, ch g Boreen—Fair Rullath
FORGESTOWN, 9, br m Al Sirat—Collatian Tale
GRABEL, 7, b m Bold Owl—Gay Dawn
IRISH WIND, 7, b g In Fijar—Zagray
KERFONTAINE, 5, b m Lafontaine—Kero Code
LIKE A MELODY, 6, gr g Grange Melody—Don't Like
LOUIS ROYALE, 5, ch g Sallust—Turkish Song
MINORETTES GIRL, 5, b m Strong Gale—Minorette
MONASTERADEN, 7, ch g Le Moss—Loygara
MOONEE O'VALLEY, 5, b g Kings Ride—Longford Lady
NORMAN VALLEY, 7, b br g Normandy—Suir Valley
PARESA, 4, b f Saher—Parijatak
PARGAN, 11, b g Tarqogan—Parijatak
PIT RUNNER, 5, b m Deep Run—Pitalina
POTENTIAL PIN, 7, ch g Pollerton—Bank Rate
PRINCE KILLINOIS, 6, b h Tina's Pet—Solea
QUEEN OF FINNS, 4, ch f Viking (USA)—Mullaghroe
REDUNDANT PAL, 7, ch g Redundant—Palesa
RFL STEEL, 4, br g Borcon—Siba Vione
ROSE APPEAL, 4, ch g Star Appeal—Rose And The Ring
SAYPAREE, 5, b g Saher—Paritajak
SCALLY OWEN, 6, br g Scallywag—Owen Belle
TCHIFFLEY'S RIDE, 5, b g Argentinos—Quarry Hill Legend
THE GOOSER, 7, b g Torus—Gracious View
US AND JOE, 7, b g Candy Cane—How Ready

THREE-YEAR-OLDS

FOREST MIST, ch f Dalsaan—Magic Miss
GALWAY STAR, b c Kampala—Lady Kiara
GRENANE BAYLEAF, ch f What A Guest—Barratt Oak
HABIRA, b f Fairy King—Mink Fur
LUX AETERNA, b f Sandhurst Prince—Northern Twilight
PATTIS PALA, b f Kampala—Tamen John
SIMPLY SWIFT, b f Simply Great—Run Swift

TWO-YEAR-OLDS

LIGHT AND DARKNESS, ch f Dalsaan—Winds Light
SAUCE MAKER, ch c Sauceboat—Hooplah
THROUGH THE MILL, b f Millfontaine—What Ya Want

Owners: Miss V. A. Charlton, Clounacour Racing Syndicate, J. Cullen, J. M. Cusack, Miss Marion Delaney, Thomas J. Farrell, S. Forrest, N. Grant, Mrs Audrey Healy, Peter C. Heron, J. P. Hill, W. J. Kavanagh, P. J. Keary, Patrick F. Kehoe, Rory F. Larkin, Charles O. M. S. Mansergh, C. Maye, Hugh McCann, Mrs Sandra McCarthy, Mrs C. A. Moore, George Mullins, Gerard Mullins, Capt Luke Mullins, Mrs P. Mullins, Thomas Mullins, W. P. Mullins, John M. Murphy, Mrs Michael O'Dwyer, Mrs M. O'Leary, Mrs P. J. O'Mears, P. S. O'Neill, Mrs Antonia Peters, Heinz Pollmeier, Michael Reidy, Mrs R. A. Shaw, F. P. Taaffe, P. S. Taggart.

MR P. MULLINS—continued

Jockeys (NH): P Kavanagh, A Mullins.

Apprentice: N English.

Amateurs: Mr P McCarthy (11-4), Mr George Mullins (11-0), Mr Tom Mullins (10-11), Mr W P Mullins (10-11).

Lady Rider: Mrs Sandra McCarthy (9-0).

677 MR T. THOMSON JONES, Lambourn

Postal: **The Croft, Lambourn, Newbury, Berkshire, RG16 7QH.**
Phone: **LAMBOURN (0488) 71596**

ALREEF, 4, b g Wassl—Joey (FR) **Mr Harry Sibley**
BLUE RHYTHM, 5, b m Blue Cashmere—Abalone **Mr Richard F. Green**
5, Br g Royal Fountain—Constant Rose **Miss C. O'Sullivan**
CROSSROAD LAD, 4, b g Beldale Flutter (USA)—Croda Rosa (ITY) **Miss K. George**
DEERNESS SPOOK, 7, gr g Grey Ghost—Part Rum **Mrs L. G. Turner**
ELFIE'S SON, 6, b h Sonnen Gold—Elf Trout **Miss K. George**
FIDWAY, 5, b g Fidel—Galway Maid **Mr A. R. Coley**
FORTUNES WOOD, 4, b g Town And Country—Top Soprano **Melbury Park Stud**
FURMORE, 5, b m Furry Glen—Vulmore **Mr K. Young**
FUSILIER, 8, b g Habitat—Formentera (FR) **Mrs Caroline Humphrey**
GILDED YOUTH, 5, ch g Young Generation—Woodwind (FR) **Miss K. George**
GO NOBLEY, 4, b g Gorytus (USA)—Noblanna (USA) **Mrs E. M. H. Ogden White**
MARIANO, 5, b g Aragon—Macarte (FR) **Mrs D. Buckett**
PALM SWIFT, 4, b f Rabdan—Swiftsand **Mr Paul Lay and Mr M. Gomez**
PUKKA MAJOR (USA), 9, gr g Le Fabuleux—Pakeha (FR) **Mrs Solna Thomson Jones**
REHEARSING (USA), 7, gr g Nijinsky (CAN)—Zerelda (USA) **Miss K. George**
SAGA GIRL, 5, ch m Sagaro—Town Belle **Mrs S. N. J. Embiricos**
SKINNHILL, 6, b g Final Straw—Twenty Two (FR) **Mrs T. Binnington**
SOVEREIGN TRUST, 5, gr g Rymer—Moselle Mist **Mrs T. Binnington**

THREE-YEAR-OLDS

BLAKE'S TREASURE, b c Mummy's Treasure—Andamooka **Mr P. J. Blake and Mr T. Reape**
DERWENT WATERS, b c Lomond (USA)—Jemarjo Pet (USA) **Mr K. Beaumont**
DORSET DELIGHT, gr f Red Sunset—Tippity Top **Mr Timothy N. Chick**
HEAR A NIGHTINGALE, br g Pitskelly—Calarette **Miss Charlotte Bingham**
LADY TOPAZ, b f Jalmood—Town Lady **Sir E. de Rothschild**
LA FUMATA, br f Valiyar—Manela Lady **Mr Peter V. McCalmont & Mrs N. O'Neill**
B f Oats—Palace Pet **Mr R. J. Veryard**
PUMPKIN, b f Top Ville—Bumpkin **Mrs E. M. H. Ogden White**
ROMANOVNA, b f Mummy's Pet—Empress of Russia **Mrs Solna Thomson Jones**
SAND DAISY, b f Precocious—San Marguerite **Mrs P. Robeson**
SHIFTING BREEZE, ch f Night Shift (USA)—Easterly Wind **Mr C. Donald and Mrs T. Binnington**
VALIANT HOPE, ch f Valiyar—Lucky Fingers **Miss Jackie Rich**

TWO-YEAR-OLDS

Ch f Doulab (USA)—Aldern Stream **Partnership**
CINDEROSA, b f Kings Lake (USA)—Rosalita **Mr C. Donald and Mr W. Swindon**
B c Godswalk—Circus Lady **Mr T. Thomson Jones**
B c Relkino—Great Aunt Emily **Mr D. Makin**
Br c Daring March—Jacoletta **Mr F. Pike**

MR T. THOMSON JONES—continued

B c Burslem—La Calera **Mr E. Faber**
Br f Alleging (USA)—Lucky Engagement (USA) **Mr Harry Sibley**
PERSONALITY CLASH, b f High Top—Five Farthings **Mr R. E. Sangster**
Ch f Burslem—Senama **Partnership**
STEVE RACE, br c Mansingh—My Music **Mrs Solna Thomson Jones**
B c Legend of France (USA)—Young May Moon **Mr E. Steadman and Mrs B. Allen**

Other Owners: Mrs B. M. L. Davis, D. Jones, Mrs C. A. Morrison, E. Nicolson, Mrs J. G. O'Neill, Mrs S. W. Smart, Mr R. Veryard.

Apprentice: L Mahoney (7-10).

Conditional: B J Farley (9-7).

Lady Rider: S A Billot (8-10).

678 MR F. WATSON, Sedgefield

Postal: **Beacon Hill Farm, Sedgefield, Stockton-on-tees, Cleveland, TS21 3HN.**
Phone: **(0740) 20582**

AMOYNO GENIUS, 10, ch g Tepukei—Carry On Jackie **Ramside Estates Ltd**
BONN JOVY GREY, 5, gr g Grey Ghost—Gemma Jean **Mr J. D. Blythe**
BUY NORDAN, 6, ch m Camden Town—Mivanwy **Mr F. Watson**
DALMORE, 4, b g Runnett—Fade To Grey **Mr F. Watson**
HIGHLAND PARK, 4, ch g Simply Great (FR)—Perchance **Mr Ray Craggs**
MR ABINGTON, 10, ch g Avocat—Donnarabella **Mr J. D. Blythe**
SINGALONG SAM, 13, b g Master Sing—Sam's Song **Mr F. Watson**
SUBURBIA, 4, b f Another Realm—Leaplet **Mr F. Watson**
THARALEOS (USA), 10, ch g Junction (USA)—Right About (USA) **Mr F. Watson**
4, Gr g Highlands—Umtali **Mr F. Watson**
4, Ch f Highlands—Unique Lady **Mr F. Watson**
WREKIN MELODY, 9, b g Peter Wrekin—Sam's Song **Mr G. Childs**

THREE-YEAR-OLDS

Gr g Highlands—Umtali **Mr F. Watson**
B f Highlands—Unique Lady **Mr F. Watson**

TWO-YEAR-OLDS

Ch g 29/1 Highlands—Friendly Wonder **Mr F. Watson and Mrs R. Birtwistle**

679 MR D. D. G. WELSH, Meopham

Postal: **Dairy House Farm, Hodsoll Street, Meopham, Wrotham.**
Phone: **MEOPHAM (0474) 813132**

BYNACONDRA, 9, b g Pitpan—Nothing Fancy **Mr D. Welsh**
CARNIVAL ISLE, 9, br g Spur On—Scotch Isle **Mr D. Welsh**
INKPEN LADY, 6, ch m Sharpman—Bourton Downs **Mrs B. D. Welsh**
MR BLAYZARR, 4, b c Pry—Troopers Friend **Mr D. Welsh**
PERSIAN LUCK, 4, br g Persian Bold—Ansedonia **Mrs B. D. Welsh**
TANGARAX, 6, br m Tanfirion—Shangara **Mr D. Welsh**
TEN BEARS, 14, ch g Salvo—Lunar Bug **Mr D. Welsh**

Amateur: Mr Adam Welsh (9-7).

STOP PRESS

TWO-YEAR-OLDS

Trained by Mr J. Berry, Cockerham

	Named
b c 17/3 Belfort (FR)—Miss Merlin	AVONDALE LAD
b c 28/4 Music Boy—Stepping Gaily	RHYTHMIC DANCER
b f 27/2 Mazaad—Princess of Nashua	IT'S ALL ACADEMIC
b c 26/3 Prince Sabo—I Don't Mind	DOKKA OYSTOM

Trained by Mr P. F. I. Cole, Whatcombe

b f 3/4 Conquistador Cielo—Minstinguette	SWEET SOUL DREAM
b c 21/4 Lear Fan—Awenita	FLY AWAY SOON
Gr f 9/4 Never So Bold—Rectitude	GREEN'S BONHEUR
PETRUCHIO (IRE) Ch c 18/4 Ballad Rock—Frances Jordan	CARMEL HEAD (IRE)

Trained by Mr B. Hanbury, Newmarket

Gr c 20/2 Touching Wood—Lune de Minuit	GALLATEEN

Trained by Mr W. Jarvis , Newmarket

NIMIGEN b c 6/2 Niniski (USA)—Petty Purse	NIJMEGEN
SLOVENIA (IRE) b c 4/4 Slip Anchor—Cider Princess	CRUISE PARTY (IRE)

ADDITIONS TO TEAMS

Trained by Mr J. Berry, Cockerham

DREAM TALK, 3 ch c Dreams to Reality (USA)—Lala
BANTEL BARONET, 2 b g Tickled Pink—Bantel Bouquet (Red Regent) **Barry L. Brandon**

Trained by Mr R. W. Armstrong, Newmarket

ARITA, 3 br f Never So Bold—Exotic **Duke of Roxburghe**
BLUEFIELD BAY, 3 br c Never So Bold—Bahamas Princess **Oceanic Ltd.**
MIAD, 3 b f Wassl—Al Khazaama **Hamdan Al-Maktoum**

INDEX TO HORSES

The Figure before the name of the horse refers to the number of the team in which it appears and **The Figure after** the horse supplies a ready reference to each animal. Horses are indexed strictly alphabetically, e.g. THE CENTAUR appears in the T's , MR LINNET in the MR's, ST ALEZAN in the ST's etc.

Owners names are shown against their horses where this information is available. In the case of Partnerships and Syndicates, the nominated owner is given alongside the horse with other owners listed below the team.

LOCATION OF TRAINING QUARTERS

References show squares as on map
IN SEVERAL CASES THE NEAREST MAIN CENTRE IS SHOWN TO LOCATE SITUATION OF STABLES

Trainer	Square
Aconley, Mrs V. A., Westow	C5
Akehurst, R. P. J., Epsom	F5
Alexander, C., Dollar	A2
Alexander, H. H., Lanchester	C4
Allan, A. R., Cornhill-on-Tweed	B3
Allen, C. N., Newmarket	E6
Allen, J. S., Warwick	E4
Allingham, P. B., Luton	F5
Alston, E. J., Preston	D3
Anderson, I. F., Welshpool	E2
Anderson, P. J., Church Stretton	E3
Appleyard, Mrs A. B., Bristol	F3
Arbuthnot, D., Newbury	F4
Armstrong, R. W., Newmarket	E6
Armytage, R. C., Middleham	C4
Armytage, Mrs S., Malmesbury	F3
Arthur, P. J., Aston Tirrold	F4
Austin, C. A., Wokingham	F5
Avison, M., Nawton	C4
Ayliffe, N. G., Minehead	F2
Bailey, A., Newmarket	E6
Bailey, K. C., Lambourn	F4
Bailey, P. G., Salisbury	F4
Bailey, T. N., Hereford	E3
Baker, J. H., Tiverton	G2
Balding, G. B., Weyhill	F4
Balding, I. A., Kingsclere	F4
Balding, J., Doncaster	D4
Barker, Mrs P. A., Richmond	C4
Barlow, G. B., Sandbach	D3
Barnes, M. A., Penrith	C3
Barons, D. H., Kingsbridge	G2
Barr, R. E., Middlesbrough	C4
Barraclough, M. F., Claverdon	E4
Barratt, L. J., Oswestry	E2
Barron, T. D., Thirsk	C4
Barrow, A. K., Bridgwater	F3
Barton, F. M., Macclesfield	D3
Barton, R. B., Corsham	F3
Bastiman, R., Wetherby	D4
Batey, A. C., Stocksfield	C4
Beaumont, P., Brandsby	C4
Bebbington, G. R., Craven Arms	E2
Beever, C. R., Doncaster	D4
Bell, C. H. P., Morpeth	B4
Bell, C. J., Nantwich	D4
Bell, M., Newmarket	E6
Bennett, R. A., Maidenhead	F5
Benson, Miss M. J., Hexham	C3
Benstead, C. J., Epsom	F5
Bentley, W., Middleham	C4
Berry, J., Cockerham	C3
Bethell, J. D. W., Didcot	F4
Bevan, P. J., Uttoxeter	E4
Bill, T. T., Ashby-de-la-Zouch	E4
Birkett, J. J., Workington	C2
Bissill, W. H., Newark	D5
Blanshard, M. T. W., Lambourn	F4
Blockley, P. A., Hull	D5
Bloom, Mrs J., Wymondham	E7
Bloor, D. R., Nuneaton	E4
Blum, G., Bury St. Edmunds	E6
Blundell, J. W., Grimsby	D6
Bolton, M. J., Shrewton	F6
Booth, C. B. B., Flaxton	C5
Bosley, J. R., Bampton	F4
Boss, R., Newmarket	E6
Bottomley, J. F., Malton	C5
Bousfield, B., Brough	C3
Bowen, S. A., Canterbury	F7
Bower, Miss L. J., Alresford	G4
Bowker, M. T., Levens	C3
Bowlby, Lady Ann, Thirsk	C4
Bowring, S. R., Mansfield	E4
Bradburne, Mrs S. C., Fife	A3
Bradley, J. M., Chepstow	F3
Bradley, N., Wetherby	D4
Bradstock, M. F., East Garston	F4
Bramall, Mrs S. A., Thirsk	C4
Brassey, K. M., Lambourn	F4
Bravery, C. V., Jevington	G6
Brazington, R. G., Redmarley	F3
Brennan, O., Newark	D5
Brewis, R., Belford	B4
Bridger, J. J., Liphook	G4
Bridgwater, K. S., Lapworth	E4
Brisbourne, A. H., Shrewsbury	E3
Brittain, C. E., Newmarket	E6
Brittain, M. A., Warthill	D4
Broad, C. D., Westbury-on-Severn	F3
Brockbank, J. E., Carlisle	C3

Location of Training Quarters – Continued

Brooks, C. P. E., Lambourn F4
Brooks, W. G. A., Lambourn F4
Brotherton, R., Evesham F3
Brown, M. L., Llanwrda E2
Browne, D., Lambourn F4
Brunt, Mrs B., Newark D5
Bukovets, J. M., Henley-in-Arden E4
Burgoyne, P. V. J., Childrey F4
Bycroft, N., Brandsby C4
Byford, B., Fordham F6

Caine, E. M., Chopgate C5
Caldwell, T. H., Warrington D3
Callaghan, N. A. J., Newmarket E6
Callow, R., Somerton F3
Calver, P., Ripon C4
Camacho, M. J. C., Malton C5
Cambidge, B. R., Bishop's Wood E3
Campbell, I., Newmarket E6
Candy, H. N. D., Wantage F4
Carter, W. Y., Epsom F5
Casey, W. T., Banbury E4
Castell, M., Clifton-on-Teme E3
Cecil, H. R. A., Newmarket E6
Chamberlain, A. J., Swindon F4
Chamberlain, N., West Auckland C4
Champion, R., Bury St. Edmunds E6
Channon, M., Lambourn F4
Chapman, D. W., York C4
Chapman, M. C., Market Rasen E5
Charles, M. J., Warwick E4
Charlton, J. I. A., Stocksfield B3
Charlton, R. J., Marlborough F4
Christian, S., Kinnersley E3
Clay, W., Stoke-on-Trent E3
Codd, L. J., Redditch E4
Cole, P. F. I., Wantage F4
Cole, S. N., Tiverton G2
Collingridge, H. J., Newmarket E6
Collins, M. J. Horley G5
Connors, P. D., Hednesford E3
Corbett, L. C., Manton F4
Cottrell, L. G., Cullompton G2
Craig, T., Dunbar A3
Crawford, B. T., Aslockton E5
Crawford, W. H., Haddington A3
Criddle, J., Magor F3
Croft, Mrs J. E., Banbury E4
Culham, Mrs G. P., Dumfries B2
Cumani, L. M., Newmarket E6
Cundell, P. D., Newbury F4
Cunningham, T. W., Northallerton C4
Cunningham-Brown, K., Stockbridge F4
Curley, B. J., Newmarket E6
Curtis, R., Epsom F5
Cuthbert, A. J., Tetsworth F4
Cuthbert, T. A. K., Carlisle C3
Cyzer, C., Horsham F5
Czerpak, J. D., Farnham F5

Dalton, J. N., Shifnal E2
Davies, J. D. J., Dymchurch F7
Davies, M. W., Abergavenny F2
Davies, P. S., Bromyard E3
Davis, N. H., Bridgwater F3
Davis, P. W., Feckenham E3
Denson, A. W., Epsom F5
Dickin, R., Newent F3
Dickinson, M., Melton Mowbray E5
Dixon, J. E., Carlisle C3
Dods, R. W., Darlington C4
Doidge, G. C., Ivybridge G3
Dollar, Miss G., East Hendred F4
Donnelly, T. W., Burton-on-Trent C3
Dooler, J., Goole D5
Dow, S. L., Epsom F5
Dufosee, P., Warminster F3
Dunlop, J. L., Arundel G5
Dunstan, P. R., Chard G3
Durr, F., Newmarket E6

Earnshaw, R., Harrogate D4
Easterby, M. H., Malton C5
Easterby, M. W., Sheriff Hutton C4
Easton, Mrs M., Fordinbridge G4
Eaton, Miss J. M., Wennington C3
Eckley, M. W., Ludlow E3
Eden, G., Newmarket E6
Edwards, J. A. C., Ross-on-Wye E3
Eldin, E., Newmarket E6
Ellerby, M. W., Pickering C5
Elliot, J. P. D., Alton F4
Ellison, B., Malton C5
Elsey, C. C., Lambourn F4
Elsey, C. W. C., Malton C5
Elsworth, D. R. C., Whitsbury G4
Elwyn Jones, G., Lampeter E2
Enright, G. P., Lewes G6
Etherington, J., Malton C5
Etherington, T. J., Dorking F5
Eubank, A., Cockermouth C2
Eustace, J. M. P., Newmarket E6
Evans, Mrs J. J., Llanymynech E2
Evans, P. D., Welshpool E2

Fairhurst, T., Middleham C4
Fanshawe, J. R., Newmarket E6
Feilden, P. J., Newmarket E6
Felgate, P. S., Melton-Mowbray E5
Fetherson-Godley, M. J., East Ilsley F4
Ffitch Heyes, J., Lewes G6
Fisher, R. F., Ulverston C2
FitzGerald, Lord John., Newmarket E6
FitzGerald, J. G., Malton C5
Forsey, B., Taunton F3
Forster, Capt. T. A., Wantage F4
Fort, J. R., Brandon C4
Forte, J. E., Teignmouth G2
Fowler, A., Scarborough C5
Fox, J. C., Salisbury F4

Location of Training Quarters – Continued

Francis, M. E. D., Lambourn F4
Francis, R. B., Malpas D3
French, Mrs S., Gravesend F6
Frost, R. G., Buckfastleigh G2
Fullerton, Mrs H. J., Dorchester G3

Gandolfo, D. R., Wantage F4
Gaselee, N. A., Lambourn F4
Gee, B., Worksop D4
Gifford, J. T., Findon G5
Glover, J., Worksop D4
Goldie, R. H., Kilmarnock B1
Goldie, T., Kilwinning B1
Goodfellow, Mrs A. C. D., Earlston B3
Gospel, Mrs S. J., Kirbymoorside C5
Gracey, G. G., Winkfield F5
Graham, N. A., Newmarket E6
Gray, F., Haywards Heath G5
Greathead, T. R., Chipping Norton F4
Green, Miss Z. A., Carlisle C3
Gregson, G. G. A., Cranleigh F5
Greig, D. R., Cranleigh F5
Griffiths, S. G., Carmarthen F1
Grissell, D. M., Robertsbridge F6
Gubby, B., Bagshot F5
Guest, R., Newmarket E6

Haggas, W. J., Newmarket E6
Haigh, W. W., Malton C5
Haine, Mrs D., Newmarket E6
Haldane, J. S., Kelso B3
Hall, G. V., Hartlepool C4
Hall, Miss P. J., Melton Mowbray E5
Hall, Miss S. E., Middleham C4
Hallett, T. B., Saltash G3
Ham, G. A., Axbridge F3
Hanbury, B., Newmarket E6
Hannon, R. M., Marlborough F4
Hanson, J., Wetherby D4
Harris, J. L., Melton Mowbray E5
Harris, P. W., Berkhamsted F5
Harris, S. T., High Wycombe F5
Hartop, R. W., Farnsfield E4
Harwood, G., Pulborough G5
Hastings-Bass., West Ilsley F4
Hadyn Jones, D., Pontypridd F2
Haynes, H. E., Swindon F4
Haynes, M. J., Epsom F5
Hayward, P. A., Netheravon F4
Head, Lord, Salisbury F4
Heath, Mrs E. H., Royston E5
Hedger, P., Chichester G5
Hellens, J. A., Chester-le-Street C4
Hembrow, Mrs S. J. R., Taunton F2
Henderson, N. J., Lambourn F4
Henriques, M., Cirencester F3
Hern, Major W. R., West Ilsley F4
Herries, Lady, Littlehampton G5
Hetherton, J., Malton C5
Hewitt, Mrs A. R., Malpas D3
Hide, A. G., Newmarket E6
Hills, B. W., Marlborough F4
Hills, J. W., Lambourn F4
Hitchings, C. J., Worcester E3
Hoad, R. P. C., Lewes G6
Hobbs, P. J., Minehead F2
Hodge, H. B., Ware E6
Hodges, R. J., Somerton F3
Holden, W., Newmarket E6
Holder, R. J., Bristol F3
Hollinshead, R., Upper Longdon E4
Holly, D., Pontyclun F2
Holmes, C. J., Chalfont St. Giles F5
Holt, L. J., Basingstoke F4
Honeyball, J., Bridgwater F3
Horgan, C. A., Wokingham F5
Hoswood, Miss J. E., Swerford E4
Houlbrooke, T. J., Ledbury E3
Howling, P., Godalming F5
Hubbard, G. A., Woodbridge E7
Hudson, J. P., Lambourn F4
Huffer, G. A., Newmarket E6

Incisa, Don Enrico, Coverham C4
Ivory, K. T., Radlett F5

Jackson, C. F. C., Malvern E3
Jackson, F. S., Gonalston E4
Jackson, V. S., Ponteland B4
James, C. J., Newbury F4
James, M. B. C., Whitchurch E3
James, Mrs M. C., Cheltenham F3
Jarvis, M. A., Newmarket E6
Jarvis, W., Newmarket E6
Jefferson, J. M., Malton C5
Jeffrey, T. E., Alnwick B4
Jenkins, J. R., Royston E6
Jermy, D. C., Warminster F3
Jerram, M. J., Dunmow F6
Jestin, F., Wigton C2
Johnson, J. H., Crook C4
Johnson, M. A., Buntingford F6
Johnson, R. W., Newcastle-on-Tyne C4
Johnson Houghton, R. F., Didcot F4
Johnston, M. S., Middleham C4
Jones, A. W., Oswestry E2
Jones, Mrs G. E., Upton-on-Severn E3
Jones, G. H., Leominster E3
Jones, Mrs M. A., Lambourn F4
Jones, P. J., Marlborough F4
Jones, T. M., Guildford F5
Jordan, F. T. J., Leominster E3

Kelleway, P. A., Newmarket E6
Kelly, G. P., Sheriff Hutton C4
Kemp. W. T., Ashford F7
Kendall, Mrs M. A., Penrith C3
Kernick, N., Buckfastleigh G2
Kersey, T., West Melton D4
Kettlewell, S, E., Middleham C4

Location of Training Quarters – Continued

Key, B. L., Malvern E3
King, Miss A. L. M., Stratford-upon-Avon E4
King, J. S., Swindon F4
Knight, Mrs A., Cullompton G2
Knight, Miss H. C., Wantage F4

Lamb, R. R., Seahouses B4
Layland, J. R. M., Clitheroe D3
Le Blond, A. J., Hetton-Le-Hole C4
Le Grice, T. C., Penzance G1
Leach, M. R., Newark D5
Leach, P. S., Taunton F2
Leadbetter, S. J., Berwick-upon-Tweed B4
Ledger, R. R., Sittingbourne F6
Lee, A. N., Newmarket E6
Lee, C. F., Nottingham E4
Lee, D., Kirkbymoorside C4
Lee, F. H., Wilmslow D3
Lee, R., Presteigne F2
Leigh, J. P., Gainsborough D5
Lewis, G., Epsom F5
Liddle, P., Chester-le-Street C4
Llewellyn, B. J., Bargoed F2
Love, J., Kilbarchan B1

Mackie W. J. W., Church Broughton E4
Mactaggart, A. H., Hawick B2
Madgwick, M. J., Denmead G4
Makin, P. J., Marlborough F4
Mann, W. G., Leamington Spa E4
Manning, R. J. Winterbourne F3
Marvin, R., Newark D5
McCain, D., Southport D2
McCaskill, D., Chester-le-Street C4
McCormack, M., Wantage F4
McCourt, M., Wantage F4
McDonald, R., Duns B3
McInnes Skinner, Mrs C. A. P., Melton Mowbray E4
McKenzie-Coles, W. G., Taunton F2
McKie, Mrs V., Twyford F5
McLean, B., Morpeth B4
McMahon, B. A., Tamworth E3
McMath, B. J., Bury St. Edmunds E6
Mellor, S., Wanborough F4
Miller, N., Ferryhill C4
Milligan, Miss M. K., Middleham C4
Millman, B. R., Cullompton G2
Minns, Mrs S., Woodford E3
Mitchell, C. W., Dorchester G3
Mitchell, N. R., Dorchester G3
Mitchell, P., Epsom F5
Mitchell, P. K., Newmarket E6
Moffat, D., Cartmel C2
Monteith, P., Rosewell B2
Moore, A., Brighton G5
Moore, G. M., Middleham C4
Morgan, B. C., Burton-on-Trent E4
Morgan, K. A., Melton Mowbray E5
Morley, M. F. D., Newmarket E6
Morris, W. G., Kidderminster E3
Moubarak, M., Newmarket E6
Muldoon, S. J., Malton C5
Murphy, M. P. F., Newmarket E6
Musson, W. J., Newmarket E6

Nash, C. T., Wantage F4
Naughton, M. P., Richmond C4
Neaves, A. S., Faversham F6
Needham, J. L., Ludlow E3
Nelson, C. R., Lambourn F4
Nelson, W. M., Torhoswald C2
Nicholson, D., Stow-on-the-Wold F4
North, Mrs H. E., Withiel Florey F2
Norton, J., Barnsley D4
Norton, S. G., Barnsley D4
Nugent, D. H., Lambourn F4

O'Connor, Miss P., Andover F4
O'Donoghue, J., Reigate F5
O'Gorman, W. A., Newmarket E6
O'Leary, R. M., Malton C5
Old, J. A. B., Shepton Mallet F3
Oldroyd, G. R., Malton C5
Oliver, J. K. M., Hawick B3
Oliver, M. E., Droitwich E3
Oliver, Mrs S., Wombourne E3
O'Mahony, F. J., Lingfield F5
O'Neill, J. J., Penrith C3
O'Neill, M. J., Lydiate D2
O'Neill, O., Cheltenham F3
O'Shea, J. G. M., Hartlebury E3
O'Sullivan, R. J., Bognor Regis G5
Owen, E. H., Denbigh D2

Paisley, R., Langholm B2
Palling, B., Cowbridge F2
Parfitt, J., Rhymney F2
Parker, C., Lockerbie B2
Parkes, J. E., Malton C5
Parrott, Mrs H., Deerhurst F3
Paul, W. J. L., Tring E5
Payne, J. R., Dulverton G2
Payne, J. W., Newmarket E6
Payne, S. G., Carlisle C3
Peachey, H. E., Stratford-on-Avon E4
Peacock, R. E., Tarporley D3
Pearce, J., Newmarket E6
Perkins, R. A. H., Burton-upon-Trent E4
Perrett, A. C. J., Cheltenham F3
Perrin, W. M., Buntingford F5
Pickering, J. A., Hinckley E4
Piggott, Mrs L., Newmarket E6
Pike, S. L., Sidmouth G3
Pile, Mrs P. L., Leamington Spa E4
Pilkington, J., Malvern E3
Pincombe, R. W., South Molton F2
Pipe, M. C., Wellington F2
Pitman, Mrs J. S., Upper Lambourn F4

Location of Training Quarters – Continued

Trainer	Location
Pocock, R. E., Bridgwater	F3
Popham, C. L., Taunton	F3
Potts, A. W., Barton-on-Humber	D5
Powell, G. J., Abbey Dore	E3
Preece, W. G., Telford	E3
Prescott, Sir M., Newmarket	E6
Prest, G. R., Newbury	F4
Price, G. H., Leominster	E3
Price, J. P., Leominster	E3
Price, T. J., Newport	F3
Price, W., Ebbw Vale	F2
Pritchard, Dr. P. L. J., Berkeley	F3
Pritchard, P. A., Shipston-on-Stour	E4
Pritchard-Gordon, G. A., Newmarket	E6
Pugh, R. C., Hallow	E2
Ramsden, Mrs J. R., Thirsk	C4
Ransom, P. B., Leominster	E3
Ratcliff, Mrs A. E., Norton Lindsey	E4
Ratcliffe, C. I., Southead	D3
Redmond, J. V., Guildford	F5
Reed, W. G., Hexham	C3
Reed, W. J., Umberleigh	F1
Rees, Miss G. M., Scunthorpe	D5
Reid, A. S., Thurleigh	E5
Reid, T., Haywards Heath	G5
Retter, J. G., Exeter	G2
Reveley, Mrs G. R., Malton	C5
Richards, G. W., Penrith	C3
Richardson, Mrs S., Cheltenham	F3
Richmond, B. A., Wellingore	D5
Ridout, A. S., Fordingbridge	G4
Ringer, D. J., Newmarket	E6
Ripley, G., Ashford	F6
Roach, C. G., St. Austell	G1
Roberts, J., Taunton	F3
Robertson, D., Kilmarnock	B1
Robinson, M. H. B., Wantage	F4
Robinson, W. R., Scarborough	C5
Robson, A. M., Leyburn	C4
Robson, E. H., Morpeth	B4
Robson, T. L. A., Alnwick	B4
Rodford, P. R., Martock	F2
Roe, C. G., Chalford	F3
Roe, G. L., Yelverton	G1
Roper, J. H., Suckley	E3
Rumsey, A. J., Stourbridge	E3
Ryall, B., J. M., Yeovil	G3
Ryan, M. J., Newmarket	E6
Sample, Major W. N., Morpeth	B4
Sanders, Miss B., Epsom	F5
Saunders, C. R., Northampton	E5
Scargill, Dr. J., Newmarket	E6
Scott, A. A., Newmarket	E6
Scott, D. D., Minehead	F2
Scott, Mrs E. B., Wysall	E4
Scudamore, M. J., Hoarwithy	F3
Semple, I., Carluke	B2
Sharpe, Mrs N. S., Leominster	E3
Shaw, J. R., Newmarket	E6
Sheedy, W., Newport	F3
Sherwood, O. M. C., Upper Lambourn	F4
Siddall, Miss L. C., Tadcaster	D4
Simpson, R., Upper Lambourn	F4
Skelton, J., Skipton	D4
Sly, Mrs P. M., Peterborough	E5
Smart, B., Lambourn	F4
Smith, A., Beverley	D5
Smith, C., Wellingore	D5
Smith, D., Bishop Auckland	C4
Smith, J. P., Rugeley	E4
Smith, Mrs M. M., Launceston	G1
Smith, N. A., Bishampton	E4
Smith, R. J., Loughborough	E4
Smith, S. G., Grimsby	D6
Smith, W. J., Oxford	F4
Smyth, R. V., Epsom	F5
Spares, C. W., Aslockton	E4
Spearing, J. L., Alcester	E4
Spicer, R. C., Spalding	E6
Stephenson, W. A., Bishop Auckland	C4
Stevens, B., Winchester	F4
Stewart, A. C., Newmarket	E6
Stickland, G., Sturminster Newton	G3
Storey, F. S., Carlisle	C3
Storey, W., Consett	C4
Stoute, M. R., Newmarket	E6
Stringer, A., Carlton Husthwaite	C4
Stubbs, R. W., Newmarket	E6
Sutcliffe, J. R. E., Epsom	F5
Swindlehurst, D. G., Carlisle	C3
Tate, M., Kidderminster	E3
Tate, T. P., Tadcaster	D4
Taylor, A. J., Hassocks	G5
Taylor, F., Richmond	C4
Teal, Mrs V. J., St. Clears	F1
Temple, B. M., Driffield	F3
Tetley, Mrs P. A., Cranleigh	F5
Thom, D. T., Newmarket	E6
Thomas, J. D., Cowbridge	F2
Thompson, R., Grantham	D5
Thompson, Ron, Doncaster	D4
Thomson, A. M., Duns	B4
Thomson, Mrs D., Milnathort	A2
Thomson Jones. H., Newmarket	E6
Thorne, Miss J., Bridgwater	F3
Thorner, G. E., Wantage	F4
Thornton, C. W., Middleham	C4
Tinkler, C., Malton	C5
Tinkler, N., Malton	C5
Tinning, W. H., Harrogate	D4
Tompkins, M. H., Newmarket	E6
Topley, D. H., Durham	C4
Torr, S., Leek	D4
Townsend, R. D., Charing	F6
Townsley, Mrs P., Dorking	F5
Trietline, C. C., Stratford-on-Avon	E4

Location of Training Quarters – Continued

Tucker, D. R., Cullompton G2
Tullie, Mrs A. F., Eyemouth B3
Turnell, A. R., Wantage F4
Turner, J. S. E., Whitchurch E3
Turner, Miss S. J., Ripon C4
Turner, W. G., Tavistock G1
Turner, W. G. M., Sherborne F3
Turton, S. F., Plymouth G1
Twiston-Davies, N. A., Cheltenham F3

Upson, J. R., Adstone E5
Usher, M. D. I., Lambourn F4

Vernon, M. S., Darlington C4
Vernon-Miller, C. J., Shipston-on-Stour E4
Voorspuy, R., Polegate G6

Waggott, N., Spennymoor C4
Wainwright, J. S., Malton C5
Wales, W. A., Fakenham E6
Waley-Cohen, R. B., Banbury E4
Wall, C. F., Newmarket E6
Walmsley, J. W., Tadcaster D4
Walwyn, F., Lambourn F4
Walwyn, P. T., Lambourn F4
Ward, Mrs S. A., Northallerton C4
Ward, Mrs V. C., Grantham E5
Wardle, I., Wells F3
Waring, Mrs B. H., Chippenham F3
Waring, L., Somerset F3
Waterman, Miss S., Dorchester G3
Watts, J. W., Richmond C4
Weaver, R. J., Markfield E4
Webber, J., Banbury F4
Weedon, C. V., Chiddingfold G5
Wellicome, D. R., Northampton E5
Wells, B. K., Kidderminster E3
Weymes, E., Leyburn C4
Wharton, J. R. H., Melton Mowbray E5
Wharton, Mrs R., Leyburn C4
Wheeler, E. A., Lambourn F4
Wheeler, N. J., Battle G5
Whitaker, R. M., Wetherby D4
White, C. J., Steyning G5
White, Mrs F. E., Chelmsford F6
White, J., Wendover F5
Whitfield, Miss A. J., Lambourn F4
Wightman, W. G. R., Upham G4
Wildman, C. P., Salisbury F4
Wilesmith, M., Dymock E3
Wilkinson, B. E., Middleham C4
Wilkinson, J. V., Sarratt F5
Wilkinson, M. J., Banbury E4
Williams, C. N., Newmarket E6
Williams, D., Exeter G2
Williams, D. L., Broadway E4
Williams, R. J. R., Newmarket E6
Williams, W. R., Exeter G2
Willis, H., Winchester G4
Wilson, A. J., Cheltenham F3
Wilson, D. A., Epsom F5
Wilson, Capt. J. H., Preston D3
Wilson, J. S., Ayr B1
Wilson, W. T. J., Newmarket E6
Wilton, Miss S. J., Stoke-on-Trent E3
Wingrove, K. G., Leamington Spa E4
Wonnacott, Mrs J., Tavistock G1
Woodhouse, R. D. E., York D4
Woodman, S., Chichester G5
Wragg, G., Newmarket E6

Yardley, F. J., Droitwich E3
Yardley, G. H., Malvern E3
Young, V. P., Hastings G6

Teams which have arrived too late for inclusion in Horses In Training 1990 will be published in the Raceform Handicap Book week ending March 31st.

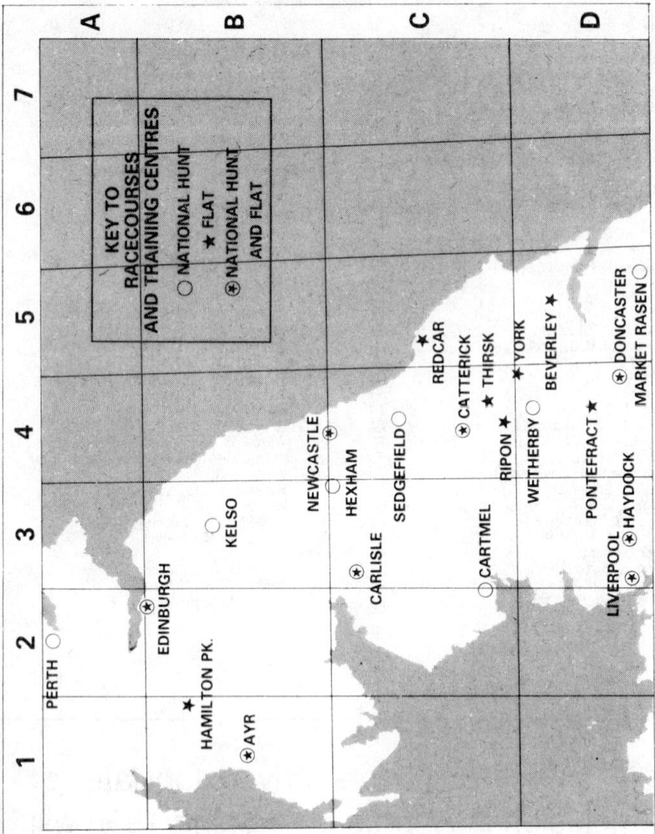
KEY TO
RACECOURSES
AND TRAINING CENTRES
NATIONAL HUNT
FLAT
NATIONAL HUNT
AND FLAT
A
B
C
D
1
2
3
4
5
6
7
PERTH
EDINBURGH
HAMILTON PK.
AYR
KELSO
NEWCASTLE
HEXHAM
CARLISLE
SEDGEFIELD
REDCAR
CATTERICK
THIRSK
RIPON
YORK
CARTMEL
WETHERBY
BEVERLEY
PONTEFRACT
DONCASTER
MARKET RASEN
LIVERPOOL
HAYDOCK

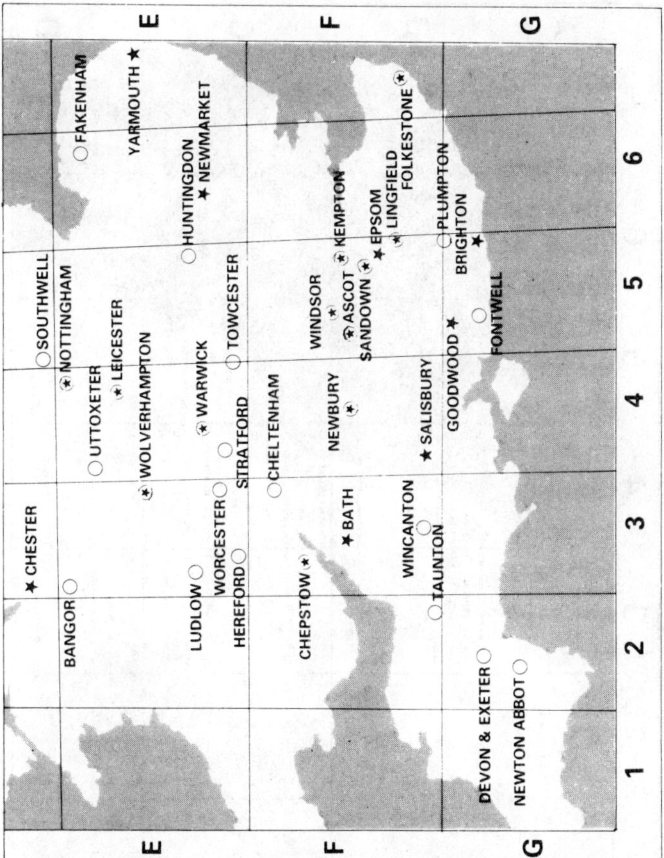
E
F
G
1
2
3
4
5
6
CHESTER
BANGOR
SOUTHWELL
NOTTINGHAM
UTTOXETER
LEICESTER
WOLVERHAMPTON
FAKENHAM
YARMOUTH
HUNTINGDON
NEWMARKET
LUDLOW
WORCESTER
HEREFORD
STRATFORD
WARWICK
TOWCESTER
CHELTENHAM
CHEPSTOW
BATH
NEWBURY
WINDSOR
ASCOT
SANDOWN
KEMPTON
EPSOM
LINGFIELD
FOLKESTONE
WINCANTON
TAUNTON
SALISBURY
GOODWOOD
FONTWELL
BRIGHTON
PLUMPTON
DEVON & EXETER
NEWTON ABBOT

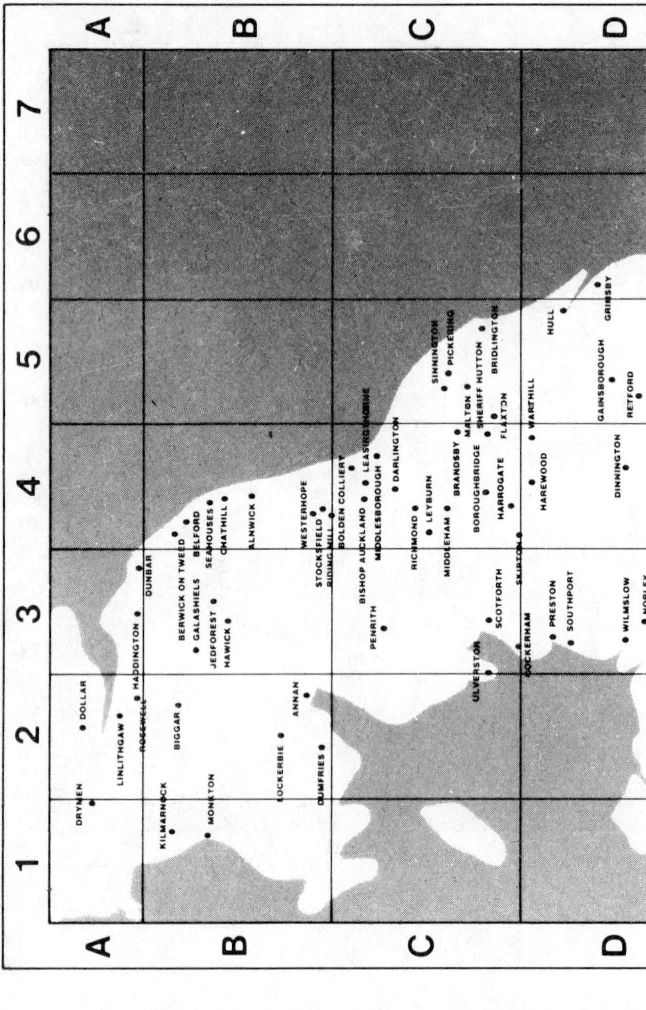
A
B
C
D
1
2
3
4
5
6
7
DRYNEN
DOLLAR
LINLITHGAW
ROSEWELL
HADDINGTON
DUNBAR
KILMARNOCK
MONKTON
BIGGAR
BERWICK ON TWEED
GALASHIELS
BELFORD
SEAHOUSES
JEDFOREST
HAWICK
CHATHILL
ALNWICK
LOCKERBIE
ANNAN
DUMFRIES
WESTERHOPE
STOCKSFIELD
RIDING MILL
BOLDEN COLLIERY
BISHOP AUCKLAND
MIDDLESBOROUGH
DARLINGTON
PENRITH
RICHMOND
LEYBURN
MIDDLEHAM
BRANDSBY
SINNINGTON
PICKERING
MALTON
BOROUGHBRIDGE
SHERIFF HUTTON
FLAXTON
BRIDLINGTON
HARROGATE
SKIPTON
ULVERSTON
SCOTFORTH
COCKERHAM
PRESTON
SOUTHPORT
HAREWOOD
WARTHILL
HULL
GRIMSBY
GAINSBOROUGH
RETFORD
DINNINGTON
WILMSLOW
NORLEY

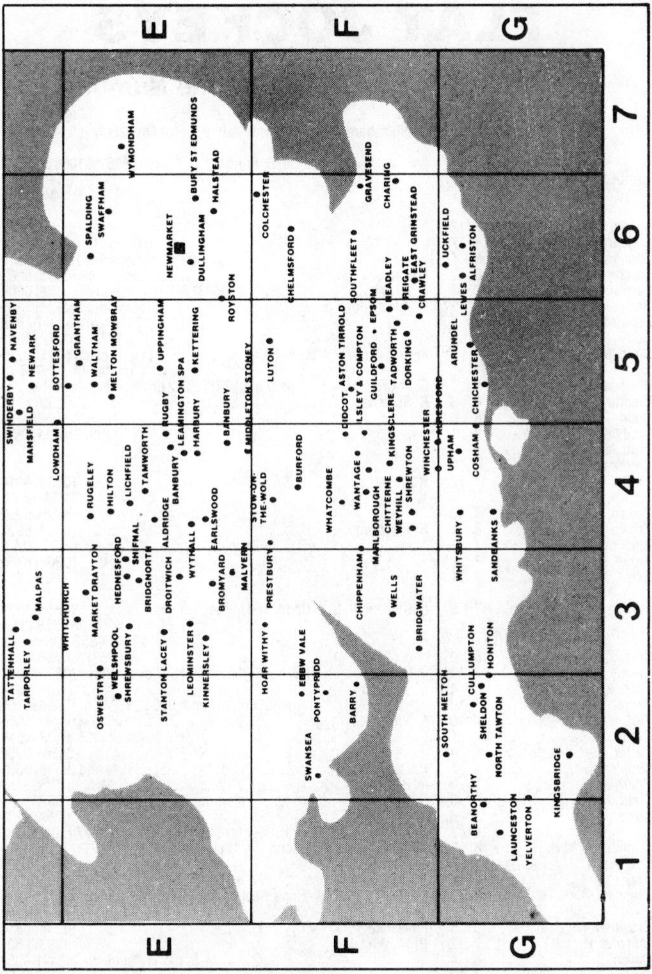
E
F
G
1
2
3
4
5
6
7
TATTENHALL
TARPORLEY
MALPAS
WHITCHURCH
MARKET DRAYTON
OSWESTRY
WELSHPOOL
SHREWSBURY
HEDNESFORD
SHIFNAL
BRIDGNORTH
STANTON LACEY
DROITWICH
LEOMINSTER
KINNERSLEY
WYTHALL
ALDRIDGE
BROMYARD
MALVERN
EARLSWOOD
RUGELEY
HILTON
LICHFIELD
TAMWORTH
BANBURY
RUGBY
LEAMINGTON SPA
HARBURY
LOWDHAM
MANSFIELD
SWINDERBY
NEWARK
NAVENBY
BOTTESFORD
GRANTHAM
WALTHAM
MELTON MOWBRAY
UPPINGHAM
KETTERING
SPALDING
SWAFFHAM
WYMONDHAM
NEWMARKET
DULLINGHAM
BURY ST EDMUNDS
HALSTEAD
ROYSTON
COLCHESTER
CHELMSFORD
LUTON
MIDDLETON STONEY
BANBURY
STOW-ON-THE-WOLD
BURFORD
PRESTBURY
HOAR WITHY
EBBW VALE
PONTYPRIDD
SWANSEA
BARRY
CHIPPENHAM
WHATCOMBE
WANTAGE
MARLBOROUGH
DIDCOT
ASTON TIRROLD
ILSLEY & COMPTON
GUILDFORD
EPSOM
SOUTHFLEET
GRAVESEND
CHARING
HEADLEY
REIGATE
EAST GRINSTEAD
CRAWLEY
TADWORTH
DORKING
KINGSCLERE
CHITTERNE
WEYHILL
SHREWTON
WELLS
BRIDGWATER
WINCHESTER
ALRESFORD
UPHAM
COSHAM
CHICHESTER
ARUNDEL
LEWES
ALFRISTON
UCKFIELD
WHITSBURY
SANDBANKS
SOUTH MELTON
CULLUMPTON
HONITON
SHELDON
NORTH TAWTON
BEANORTHY
LAUNCESTON
YELVERTON
KINGSBRIDGE

FLAT JOCKEYS

Their Employers and Telephone Numbers

Jockey	st	lb	Employers	Telephone
Adams, J. A.	8	0		(0932) 243913
Adams, N. M.	7	7	M. Blanshard, T. B. Hallett, P. Arthur C. P. Wildman, L. J. Holt, R. Smyly	(0488) 72004 or (0903) 873780 (agent) and (0836) 501688 (carphone)
Asmussen, C.	7	12		1-47-20-07-50
Atkinson, D. J.	8	5		(04882) 433
Bacon, A. E.	7	12		(0969) 22237
Balfour, R. T.	8	7		c/o Clipston (085886) 255
Banner, M. A.	8	6		Newmarket (0638) 751517
Barclay, A.	8	2	Freelance	Chevington (0284) 850554
Bardwell, G.	7	7	C. N. Allen	(0638) 668484 (agent) or (0638) 660621
Baxter, G.	8	1	R. Armstrong	Newmarket (0638) 730541
Beecroft, M. C.	8	2		(0609) 70194 or (0734) 581877
Berry, R. J.	8	2		(0372) 386167
Birch, M.	8	3	M. H. Easterby, Miss S. Hall	Hovingham (065 382) 578 or (0860) 245768 (car)
Bleasdale, J.	8	0	C. Thornton	Bedale (0677) 22222 or Wensleydale (0969) 23350
Bloomfield, P.	8	3	B. Stevens	(0638) 731113
Bond, A. M.	8	0		(0638)76681
Bradshaw, K.	8	1		(0937)62112/62522
Bradwell, P.	7	12		
Brennan, M. J.	8	10		
Brette, P.	7	12	R. Guest	c/o (0638) 661508
Brown, D. L.	7	7		(07253) 657/528
Brown, G.	7	13		(0638) 669944
Brown, J. H.	8	1	S. Muldoon	(0653) 697768
Buckton, S.	7	12		(03475) 641
Burke, P. A.	7	8		(0904) 647213
Byrne, N.	8	11		01-285480
Carlisle, N. A.	7	8	L. G. Cottrell, L. J. Codd, H. Thomson Jones	(0638) 663863 or (0638) 666431 and (0827) 880652 (Winter only)
Carr, J. M.	8	0		(0653) 692695/693365
Carroll, J.	7	12	J. Berry	(0524) 791697 or carphone (0836) 326084
Carroll, R.	8	4	D. K. Weld	(045) 21863
Carson, W.	7	10		(0638) 660947 and (063 528) 348 or (0836) 315000
Carter, G. A.	7	10	A. Hide, G. Wragg,	(0638) 668484/665950
Carter, J. P.	7	7		(0488) 72925 or(09442) 419
Carter, R. P.	8	4		(0638) 663688
Cauthen, S.	8	7	H. Cecil	(0235) 833544 and (0638) 768262
Charnock, L.	7	9	N. Bycroft	Malton (0653) 5004
Clark, A. S.	8	0	G. Harwood	Pulborough (079 82) 0788 and 3028 (home)
Coates, C.	8	6		(0969) 23823
Cochrane, R.	8	3	G. Harwood, M. Tompkins	Newmarket (0638) 743045/743047
Connorton, N. B.	8	0	J. Dooler, M. J. Camacho	Richmond (0653) 692132 or (09442) 419
Coogan, B.	8	8		(045) 33038
Craine, S.	8	6	P. Hughes, T. Stack	(045) 22032
Crossley, B. G.	7	10	Mrs L. Piggott, A. Scott	Newmarket (0638) 751367 or (0638) 667624 (agent)
Crowther, N.	8	5	Freelance	(0638) 731002
Culhane, P.	7	12	R. M. Whitaker	c/o (0937) 62122
Cullen, E. M.	8	4		c/o Wokingham (0344) 425382
Curant, J. A.	7	13		(01876) 0250

Flat Jockeys – Continued

Name	st	lb	Retained by	Telephone
Curant, R. D.	7	12	A. P. Ingham	(0225) 810171
Curran, G.	8	8		(045) 24560
D'Arcy, P.	7	12		Newmarket (0638) 750005/76686
Darley, K.	7	13	Capt. J. H. Wilson, D. W. Chapman	Easingwold (0347) 22588 or (0860) 231240 (car)
Dawe, N. J.	8	6		Arundel (0903) 884749
Dawson, S.	7	7		(0488) 72261 or (0903) 873780 (agent)
Day, N. P.	8	2	C. F. Wall	Home (0638) 730012, office (0638) 660811
Dettori, L.	8	0	L. Cumani	(0638) 666431
Dicks, A. C.	9	0	R. Holder	(0272) 519184 or (027581) 2192
Duffield, G. P.	8	1	Sir Mark Prescott (1st claim), J. S. Wilson, W. J. Pearce	Stetchworth (063 876) 544 (agent) or (0638) 668484
Dwyer, C. A.	8	6	W. T. J. Wilson	(0638) 665533
Eddery, Pat	8	6	(Mr K. Abdulla's horses and Maktoum Al Maktoum, 2nd retainer)	Haddenham (0844) 290282 and 201427
Eddery, Paul	8	0		Mildenhall (0638) 714672/712426
Egan, J. F.	7	7		(045) 21829
Elliott, R. P.	8	0	R. Thompson	Wensleydale (0969) 22884
Fallon, K. F.	8	1		(0904) 647213 (agent)
Farrell, P. A.	8	7		(03475) 273/208
Fox, R.	7	9	J. O'Donoghue,	(0638) 778188
Fozzard, M. G.	7	7		(0476) 870178
Fry, M. J.	7	9	J. Balding	(0737) 246416 or (0932) 243913
Gibson, D. J.	7	13		Newmarket (0638) 665512
Giles, M. S.	8	0		c/o Newmarket (0638) 661999
Gill, P.	8	10		(056) 26207
Gillespie, D.	8	0	M. V. O' Brien, D. McMillan, D. Lavarack, H. de Bromhead, M. A. O'Toole	(045) 21048
Gilson, P. V.	8	5		(045) 31337
Griffith, S.	7	9	G. Harwood	(07982) 3011/2
Griffiths, S. P.	7	12		(0937) 835541
Guest, E. J.	8	6		(0524) 792367
Guest, R.	8	5		(0638) 730005 or (0734) 581877
Gunn, G. P.	8	4	Freelance	Newmarket (0638) 668724 (home) or 668484 (office)
Hagen, H. P. M.	7	7		(0276) 71030
Hamblett, P. A.	7	12		Newmarket (0638) 750454
Hayes, W. J.	8	0		(0488) 72649
Helfenbein, A.	7	13	B. Schutz	(0221) 7407029
Higgins, J. J.	8	6		(0638) 720723 (agent)
Hill, P. D.	7	7		(0543) 490490
Hillis, J. D.	8	4		(045) 21183
Hills, M.	8	0	B. W. Hills, J. W. Hills	Newmarket (0638) 750379 or 751421
Hills, R.	8	0	B. W. Hills, H. Thomson Jones, Lord Fitzgerald	(0638) 750379 or (0638) 751421
Hindley, M. G.	8	4	A. Stringer	(0653) 693628
Hodgson, K.	8	6	G. Oldroyd, C. Booth	(0653) 696651
Hogan, D.	8	6	J. M. Oxx	(045) 21858
Hood, W.	8	5	G. Pritchard-Gordon	(0638) 778366
Horsfall, S. F.	8	3		c/o (0302) 710096
Howard, P. T.	7	7		(0638) 660013
Howe, N. J.	7	13	P. Walwyn, J. Czerpak, Mrs B. Waring	Wantage (023 57) 68227 or (02357) 69742

Flat Jockeys – Continued

Name	st	lb	Retained by / Contact
Ives, T. A.	8	4	W. O'Gorman, (0638) 79414 or (09442) 419
James, Miss S. E.	9	7	(0948) 4067
Johnson, E.	7	9	J. Hanson, A. Perrett (0285) 5020
Jones, Lee	8	0	(0264) 333520
Keightley, S. L.	8	7	Newmarket (0638) 666070
Kennedy, J. B.	8	2	(0488) 72734
Kettle, M.	8	4	Freelance (0672) 54966
Kimberley, A.	8	6	Newmarket (0638) 663267
Kinane, J. K.	9	0	(0835) 23814
Kinane, M. J.	8	3	D. K. Weld (045) 21739
King, G. N.	7	7	(0638) 668163/76686
Lacy, T. F.	8	12	(0405) 37032
Lang, T. L.	8	2	(08846) 419
Lawes, S. D.	8	2	Beverley (0482) 869885
Leech, P.	8	12	Navan 22107
Legrix, E.	7	12	44-21-44-10
Lequeux, A.	7	12	P. Bary 44-21-21-41
Lowe, J. J.	7	7	R. Fisher.... York (0904) 708871 and (0347) 810103 or (0860) 244284 (car)
Lowry, P.	8	4	(045) 32207
Mackay, A.	7	10	E. Eldin, (0638) 730306/662036
Mader, Lutz	8	3	B. Schutz (0221) 5904670
Manning, K. J.	8	6	J. Hayden (045) 26846
Manning, P. N.	8	7	(09276) 5337
Marcus, B.	8	1	M. A. Jarvis c/o (0638) 661702
Marshall, R. C.	8	4	c/o (0638) 668675
Matthias, J. J.	8	6	I. A. Balding, M. Madgwick, (0635) 298423
McAndrew, M. A.	7	13	
McGhin, R.	8	2	L. Cumani (0638) 660920
McGlone, A.	7	11	R. Hannon (0423) 871624 or (0836) 242788 (car)
McKay, D.	7	9	B. Stevens, Mrs B. Waring (0672) 40802
McKeown, D. R.	8	1	Wetherby (0937) 63301 and (01 381) 9318 (agent)
McKeown, T. P	7	10	(0638) 661589
McNamee, C. J.	7	10	Marlborough (0672) 55453
Mellor, Dana	7	2	S. Mellor (03727) 20843
Mercer, A.	7	11	Richmond (0748) 811103/5640
Montgomery, D. J.	7	7	
Morris, Mrs C. L.	8	9	W. G. Morris (0635) 254920
Morris, S.	7	12	M. W. Ellerby, J. Wainwright (0653) 692098
Morse, R. R.	7	9	C. N. Allen (09442) 419
Murray, J. G.	8	4	(0403) 730255
Murtagh, J.	7	8	(045) 32228
Nesbitt, H. A.	7	7	(0638) 730703/663801
Newnes, W.	8	2	D. A. Wilson, B. Smart Uffington (036782) 276 and (01674) 3673 (agent)
Nicholls, D.	8	6	N. Bycroft (0347) 23094 and York (0904) 647213 or (0836) 713418 (car)
Nolan, A. J.	7	9	(045) 34193
Nutter, C.	7	13	Sir Mark Prescott Newmarket (0638) 668153
Parnell, D.	8	2	K. Prendergast (045) 32366
Perks, S. J.	8	5	R. Hollinshead Yoxall (0543) 491594
Powdrell, K. M.	7	7	Freelance Lambourn (0488) 72419
Powell, B. G.	8	9	(0793) 782286 or (0860) 314745
Proctor, B.	8	3	W. Hern East Ilsley (063 528) 596

Flat Jockeys – Continued

Name	st	lb	Trainers	Telephone
Proud, A.	7	9	Mrs N. J. Macauley, C. Spares, L. J. Barratt	Bingham (0949) 43350/50099
Quinn, T. R.	8	0	P. Cole	(0488) 72576 or (0860) 287172 (car)
Quinton, R.	8	2	J. Oxx	c/o Kildare (045) 81500
Radcliffe, K.	8	0		(051531) 9616
Rate, C.	8	4		(0638) 665432
Raymond, B.	8	0	M. Jarvis, W. Jarvis, B. Hanbury	Newmarket(0638) 730387/666431 (agent)
Raymont, S.	8	1		Seagry (0249) 817007 or (06723) 573
Reid, J.	8	5	M. V. O'Brien, W. Carter	(036 782) 214
Richardson, M. A.	8	4		(03476) 622
Rimmer, M.	8	4		Newmarket (0638) 666581
Roberts, M.	7	12	A. Stewart	Newmarket (0638) 661026 and East Ilsley (063 528) 331
Robinson, P.	8	0	M. Tompkins	Newmarket (0638) 668484 and 667353 (home)
Roche, C.	8	4		(045) 21464
Rouse, B. A.	8	0	R. Hannon	(0293) 871547
Russell, D. H.	8	3		c/o (0638) 663333
Russell, D. H.	9	7		(0638) 664172
Rutter, C.	7	10	M. Francis, H. Candy	(02357) 65263 or (036782) 276 and (0295) 68619 (agent)
Ryan, J. B.	9	7		(0638) 664172
Ryan, M. J.	8	0		(0638) 66547
Ryan, T. J.	9	7	E. J. O'Grady	(052) 56378
Ryan, W.	8	2	H. Cecil, P. S. Felgate	(0423) 871624 or (0860) 243295 (car)
Salmon, I. P. A.	7	10		(0653) 694285
Salmon, S. E. W.	7	10		(09443) 411
Sedgwick, Paul	8	0	M. Brittain	(0759) 71472
Sexton, G.	8	2		Newmarket (0638) 660252 and Thetford (0842) 66365
Shanahan, P.	8	3	M. Kauntze, K. Connolly	(010 353 45) 24184 or c/o (045) 21067/24545
Shoults, A. F.	7	12		(0638) 730371
Smith, V.	9	7		(0638) 668972
Still, R. W.	7	6		Newmarket (0638) 750755
Street, R.	7	8	J. Perrett	Lambourn (0488) 71412 and 71548
Swan, C. F.	8	12	D. T. Hughes, M. Morris	(045) 21490/22217
Swinburn, W. R.	8	6	M. Stoute	Wickhambrook (0440) 820277 or (0638) 660811 and 660258 (agent)
Tebbutt, M.	8	4	W. Jarvis	(0638) 666625
Thomas, M. L.	7	7		Newmarket (0638) 666431/720723 (agent)
Tinkler, Mrs K.	7	7	N. Tinkler, Don Enrico Incisa	(0653) 85245
Tulk, P.	8	2		Newmarket (0638) 663209
Wallace, P.	8	5		(0344) 425382
Walsh, M. P.	7	10		J. R. Wharton (0664) 65225
Weaver, R. I.	8	5		Newbury (0635) 46778
Webster, S. G.	8	0	J. Bottomley	Elvington (090 485) 458
Wernham, R.	8	3		Abingdon (0235) 833754
Wharton, W.	8	4		Uffington (036782) 710 or (0638) 665533
Whitehall, A.	7	10	I. Balding	(0372) 724018
Whitelam, S. M.	8	2	R. Simpson	(0488) 72688
Whitworth, S.	8	2	R. V. Smyth	(0860) 324314 (car) or agent (01 969 3517)
Wigham, C.	7	12	P. Wigham, L. Cumani	(09442) 332
Wigham, M.	8	2	A. Scott, M. Usher	(0904) 488008, (0836) 229685 (car) and (0638) 669011
Williams, J. A. N.	8	3	Mrs N. Sharpe	Badminton (045 421) 622
Williams, M.	8	2		(0398) 31028
Williams, T.	7	7	D. A. Wilson	Lambourn (0488) 72734
Wood, M.	7	13		(065385) 412 or (0836) 326084

1989 RACEFORM APPRENTICE CHAMPIONSHIP

	1st	2nd	3rd
Lanfranco Dettori (L. Cumani)	71	57	55
Alan Munro (M. Brittain)	37	36	51
Jimmy Fortune (M. O'Neill)	28	36	29
Dale Gibson (W. Hastings-Bass)	28	34	27
Tony Culhane (R. Hollinshead)	24	44	24
Gary Hind (R. Hollinshead)	23	19	17
Jimmy Quinn (A. Bailey)	19	24	23
Paul Burke (C. Tinkler)	14	19	15
Darren Biggs (R. Williams)	11	14	14
Steve Wood (D. Chapman)	11	15	15
Seamus O'Gorman (I. Balding)	10	7	13
Russell Price (M. Bell)	10	2	6
Andrew Bacon (J. Berry)	8	12	7
Tim Sprake (P. Makin)	8	8	13
Stephen Maloney (M. Brittain)	7	9	8
Dana Mellor (Miss B. Sanders)	7	9	7
Ron Hillis (G. Huffer)	7	8	8
Lee Newton (G. Huffer)	6	8	6
Richard Perham (R. Hannon)	6	7	5
Michael Tebbutt (W. Jarvis)	6	2	4
Richard Fahey (S. Muldoon)	6	0	3
John Carr (Mrs G. Reveley)	5	9	7
Neil Gwilliams (M. Ryan)	5	8	6
Carl Hodgson (R. Hollinshead)	5	5	8
Barry Lane (Sir M. Prescott)	5	3	2
Gavin Husband (R. Hollinshead)	5	2	9
Danny Dunnachie (L. Cumani)	5	1	4
Roddy Lappin (R. Hollinshead)	4	7	6
Rikki Morse (C. Allen)	4	7	6
David Eddery (R. Williams)	4	3	8
Mark Giles (Mrs J. Ramsden)	4	3	5
Kim McDonnell (K. Brassey)	4	0	0
Philip Barnard (S. Mellor)	3	8	11
Neil Kennedy (G. Moore)	3	7	10
Victor Deering (J. FitzGerald)	3	3	1
Dewi Williams (H. Candy)	3	2	4
Julie Bowker (N. Tinkler)	3	2	2
Simon Giles (W. Haggas)	3	2	2
Jaki Houston (J. Toller)	3	2	2
Andrew Riding (J. White)	3	2	0
Adam Shoults (R. Armstong)	3	1	5
John Murray (C. Cyzer)	3	1	0
Melody Town (A. Bailey)	3	1	0
Darren Stather (G. Harwood)	3	0	2
Gary Forster (J. Etherington)	3	0	1
Allan Morris (C. Cyzer)	3	0	0
Pat Dalton (Denys Smith)	2	14	16
Michael Marshal (M. Usher)	2	8	8
David D'Arcy (J. Gosden)	2	4	7
Jason Swift (R. Simpson)	2	4	2

Armes, Miss A.	7	0	Mr H. Candy	c/o (036782) 276/514
Arrowsmith, F. P.	8	0	Mr I. Balding	c/o (0635) 298210
Ashley, T.	7	0	Mr R. Thompson	(0780) 410812
Ashley, T. L.	7	0	Mr J. A. Glover	c/o (0909) 475425
Aspell, J. S.	7	10	Mrs J. Pitman	c/o (0488) 71714
Aspell, S.	8	0	Mr D. Brown	c/o (0488) 72078
Avery, C. M.	7	8	Mr L. J. Holt	c/o (0256) 463376
Baird, P. J.	7	2	Mr M. Ryan	c/o (0638) 664172
Balding, Miss C.	7	4	Mr J. Balding	c/o (0302) 710096
Bamford, P. R.	7	9	Mr B. W. Hills	c/o (0672) 54901
Barnard, P. J.	8	10	Mr S. Mellor	c/o (0793) 790230
Barrett, D.	7	4	Mr F. H. Lee	c/o (0625) 533250
Beeching, Miss K.	7	12	Mr R. Chapman	c/o (085 886) 255
Bentley, E.	7	7	Mr D. Morley	c/o (0638) 667175
Berry, D. P.	8	0	Mr P. Burgoyne	c/o (023559) 688
Berry, R.	7	7	Mr G. Lewis	c/o (0372) 277662
Best, Andre.	7	6	Mr B. Schutz	c/o (0221) 743010
Biggs, D.	7	4	Mr R. J. R. Williams	c/o (0638) 663218
Bithell, D. P.	7	5	Mr K. S. Bridgwater	c/o (05643) 2895
Bridger, Miss R. J.	7	9	Mr J. J. Bridger	(0428) 722528
Brown, Miss Tracey	7	10	Mr C. Tinkler	c/o (0653) 695981
Brownsword, K.	7	10	Mr T. Fairhurst	c/o (0969) 23362
Bowe, P. D. P.	7	5	Mr W. Musson	c/o (0638) 663371
Bradley, M. P.	7	8	Mr I. A. Balding	c/o (0635) 298 210

Apprentices – Continued

Name	st	lb	Trainer	Telephone
Bray, V.	7	4	Mr M. R. Stoute	c/o (0638) 663801
Brislen, P.	7	10	Mr Henry Candy	c/o (036782) 276
Brown, G.	7	12	Mr R. M. Whitaker	c/o (0937) 62122
Burke, Miss F.	8	0	Mr N. A. Callaghan	c/o (0638) 664040
Burke, R.	7	7	Mr K. Prendergast	c/o (045) 21387
Burns, A. C.	7	12	Mr J. P. Hudson	c/o (0488) 71729
Bycroft, Miss P. J.	7	7	Mr N. Bycroft	c/o (03475) 641
Byrne, D. C.	8	7	Mr J. G. FitzGerald	c/o (0653) 692718
Cahill, W.	7	4	Mr M. Bell	c/o (0638) 666567
Cairns, S.	7	10	Mr J. Sutcliffe	c/o (0372) 272825
Campbell, Colin	7	4	Mr S. Dow	c/o (03727) 21490 or (01) 9693517
Carr, J. M.	7	11	Mrs M. C. Reveley	(0653) 692695/693365
Carr, P. A.	8	0	Mr Denys Smith	c/o (0388) 603317
Carroll, G. J.	7	7	Mr A. R. Davidson	(0883) 44523
Carroll, John	7	12	Mr J. Berry	c/o (0524) 791179
Carter, J. P.	7	8	M. Usher	(0488) 39384 or (09442) 419 (agent)
Carter L. A.	7	0	Mr R. P. J. Akehurst	c/o (03727) 27596
Carter, R. P.	7	12	Mr A. Bailey	(0638) 661537
Casselbury, Miss E.	7	12	Mr P. Calver	c/o (0765) 700313
Cassidy, M. P.	7	12	Mr A. Stewart	c/o (0638) 667323
Cecil, P.	8	4	Mr G. Lewis	c/o (03722) 77662
Chambers, Miss L.	7	7	Mr P. Howling	c/o (042879) 4065
Childs, M.	8	7	Mr A. C. Stewart	c/o (0638) 667323
Childs, S. L.	8	7	Mr A. C. Stewart	c/o (0638) 667323
Chisnell, S. L.	8	0	Mr G. A. Pritchard Gordon	c/o (0638) 662824
Clark, A. A.	7	12	Mr C. A. Horgan	c/o(0344) 425382
Clark, Miss C.	7	9	Mr A. G. Hide	c/o (0638) 662063
Clark, J. F.	7	12	Mr K. Prendergast	c/o (045) 21387
Clarke, A. J.	8	0	Mr J. R. Jenkins	c/o (0763) 41141
Clayton, W.	7	7	Mr W. Pearce	c/o (0845) 597373
Clements, Miss E. D.	7	0	Miss Sharon Oliver	c/o (08864) 539
Coates, C.	8	3	Mr G. Moore	(0969) 23823
Cochrane, Miss N.	7	12	Mr W. J. Musson	c/o (0638) 663371
Corrigan, J. A. P.	7	9	Mr G. Harwood	c/o (07982) 3011
Cosgrove, D. W.	6	10	Mr C. W. C. Elsey	c/o (0653) 693149
Coulter, Miss R.	6	12	Mr J. Berry	c/o (0524) 791179
Coyle, P. J.	7	8	Mr D. T. Hughes	(045) 21490
Cripps, D.	8	0	Mr John Sutcliffe	c/o (0372) 272825
Crowe, T.	6	13	Mr H. Thomson Jones	c/o (0638) 664884
Cunningham, A.	8	0	Mr J. Balding	c/o (0302) 710096
Dace, L. A.	8	11	Mr R. V. Smyth	c/o (03727) 20053
Dacombe, Miss M.	7	7	Mr R. W. Armstrong	c/o (0638) 663333
Dalton, P. J.	7	0	Mr D. Smith	c/o (0904) 647213 (agent)
Daly, T.	7	2	Mr M. Grassick	(045) 79858
D'Arcy, D. J.	7	7	Mr J. Gosden	c/o (0933) 772671 (agent)
Davies, L.	7	4	Mr C. R. Nelson	c/o (0488) 71391
Deacon, Miss D.	7	7	Mr Paul Howling	c/o (042879) 4065
Deering, M. V.	7	12	Mr J. G. FitzGerald	c/o (0653) 692718
Denaro, M.	9	7	Mr C. N. Allen	(026485) 254 or (0638) 552017
Dobbin, A.	7	10	Mr J. J. O'Neill	c/o (08534) 555
Dobson, D. G.	8	0	Mr J. Watts	c/o (0748) 5811
Doyle, B.	5	6	Mr C. E. Brittain	c/o (0638) 664347
Drowne, S. J.	7	4	Mr C. Spares	c/o (0949) 50099
Druce, M.	7	7	Mr G. Thorner	c/o (02357) 3003
Drugan, M. J. J.	8	0	Mr S. G. Norton	c/o (0924) 830450
Dunn, R. J.	7	12	Mr J. M. Bradley	c/o (02912) 2486
Dunnachie, D.	7	10	Mr L. Cumani	c/o (0638) 665432
Eades, Miss J.	7	0	Mr N. Tinkler	(0653) 85245

Apprentices – Continued

Name	st	lb	Trainer	Telephone
Eddery, J. D.	7	10	Mr R. J. R. Williams	(0638) 663218 or (0748) 5640 (agent)
Eeles, J.	7	0	Mr A. M. Robson	c/o (0969) 40431
Eiffert, S.	7	0	Mr Rae Guest	(0638) 661508
Ennis, P. J.	8	4	Mr H. R. A. Cecil	c/o (0638) 662192
Evely, P. C. H.	8	11	Mr G. Pritchard-Gordon	c/o (0638) 662824
Fahey, R. A.	10	0	Mr S. J. Muldoon	(0904) 647213 (agent)
Fallon, D.	7	7	Mr J. Berry	(0524) 791179
Fanning, J. K.	7	6	Mr H. Candy	c/o (036782) 276
Farmer, P.	6	12	Mr B. McMahon	c/o (0827) 62901
Farmer, R. B.	9	0	Mr I. A. Balding	c/o (0635) 298210
Fenton, M.	7	7	Mr L. Browne	c/o (045) 41255
Ferguson, I.	7	12	Mr C. N. Williams	(0638) 665116
Ferriday, J. D.	7	0	Mr Bill Preece	c/o (095286) 249
Foote, B. W.	7	9	Mr R. Guest	c/o (0638) 661508
Fordham, J. R.	7	0	Mr R. Hollinshead	c/o (0543) 490298
Forster, G.	8	0	Mr J. Etherington	c/o (0653) 692842
Fortune, J. J.	7	4	M. O'Neill	c/o (051) 5265235 or (0836) 326084 (agent)
Gallagher, D.	8	10	Mr R. Simpson	c/o (0488) 72688
Gardner, M.	7	7	Mr R. M. Whitaker	c/o (0937) 62122
Garth, A. R.	6	2	Mr R. Hollinshead	c/o (0543) 490298
Gibson, D. R.	7	5	Mr W. Hastings-Bass	(0635) 28725/28747
Giles, M. A.	7	7	Mrs J. R. Ramsden	(0845) 587226/2559/5
Giles, Simon	7	12	Mr J. Berry	c/o (0524) 791179
Glindoni, I. J.	7	10	Mr N. A. Callaghan	c/o (0638) 664040
Gordon, R.	7	7	Mr J. Wharton	c/o (0664) 65225
Granger, R. Y.	7	7	Mr H. J. Collingridge	(0638) 665454
Gray, S. A.	6	7	Mr T. D. Barron	c/o (0845) 587435
Greaves, Miss A. A.	8	3	Mr T. D. Barron	c/o (0845) 587435
Gregory, S.	8	0	Mr P. W. Harris	c/o (044284) 2480
Gurney, Miss K. A.	8	0	Mr K. B. White	c/o (058476) 200
Gwilliams, N.	7	3	Mr M. Ryan	c/o (0638) 668484
Hagger, D. S.	7	12	Mr J. Berry	c/o (0524) 791179
Haigh, I.	7	2	Mr H. Rohan	c/o (0653) 692337/600277
Halliday, U.	7	7	Mr K. Prendergast	c/o (045) 21387
Hall, Miss Joanne	7	3	Mr R. Voorspuy	c/o (03212) 7133
Hall, Nicholas	7	9	Mr R. M. Whitaker	c/o (0937) 62122
Harding, B. P.	7	1	Mr K. Prendergast	c/o (045) 21387
Harper, Alison	7	12	Mr R. J. Williams	c/o (0638) 663218
Harrison, D. P.	7	0	Mr William Hastings-Bass	c/o (0635) 28725/28747
Hart, B.	8	0	Mr G. M. Moore	c/o (0969) 23823
Harte, P. G.	9	0	Mrs R. Wharton	c/o (0969) 23307
Hawkes, S.	7	2	Mr J. Berry	c/o (0524) 791179
Hawksley, C. L.	7	0	Mr H. R. A. Cecil	c/o (0638) 662192
Hawksley, W. A.	7	2	Mr A. Bailey	c/o (0638) 661537
Haworth, S. M.	7	7	Mr J. Berry	(0524) 791179
Hayman, Miss D. M.	7	12	Mr W. O'Gorman	c/o (0638) 663330
Hayne, Miss T. M.	8	0	Mrs L. G. Cottrell	c/o (08846) 320
Healy, L.	7	10	Mr M. Bell	c/o (0638) 666567
Heffernan, J. A.,	8	0	Mr J. Bolger	(056) 43150/8
Hills, R. P.	8	0	Mr W. Haggas	c/o (0638) 667013/660767
Hills, G.	7	5	Mr P. F. I. Cole	c/o (04882) 433
Hindmarch, G. W.	7	7	Mr R. Thompson	c/o (078081) 526
Hobbs, S. J.	7	7	Mr William Jarvis	c/o (0638) 669873
Hodgson, C.	7	12	Mr R. Hollinshead	c/o (0543) 490298
Holland, D.	7	0	Mr B. W. Hills	c/o (0672) 514901
Hollick, William John	7	7	Mr W. Berry	c/o (0524) 791179
Houston, Miss J.	7	0	Mr J. Toller	c/o (0638) 668503
Hughes, Ian	7	10	Mr B. McMahon	c/o (0827) 62901

Apprentices – Continued

Name	st	lb	Trainer	Telephone
Hughes, R. D.	7	0	Mr M. Grassick	c/o (045214) 90
Humphries, M. B.	7	2	Mr R. Hollinshead	c/o (0543) 490298
Hunt, M. R.	7	12	Mr G. B. Balding	c/o (026477) 2278
Hunter, J. J.	7	0	Mr D. R. C. Elsworth	c/o (07253) 528
Hurley, R. P.	6	10	Mr D. Lavarack	c/o (0503) 21381
Hurley, R. P.,	6	10	Mr J. Hayden	(045) 81598
Husband, E.	7	0	Mr R. Hollinshead	c/o (0543) 490298
Husband, G.	7	6	Mr R. Hollinshead	c/o (0543) 490298
Hutton, P.	8	0	Mr J. W. Payne	(0733) 263816 or (0638) 668675
Huurdeman, A.	9	7	Mr J. D. J. Davies	(0303) 874089
Hyde, J.	8	6	Mr D. K. Weld	(045) 41273
James, M. J.	7	12	Mr P. T. Walwyn	c/o (0488) 71347
Johnson, Lee	7	7	Mr C. W. C. Elsey	c/o (0653) 693149
Johnson, P. A.	7	10	Mr C. B. B. Booth	c/o (0653) 81586
Juckes, A. G.	8	0	Mr R. Juckes	c/o (029921) 471
Judge, Miss S. L.	7	4	Mr M. Johnston	c/o (050785) 8146
Kaid, B. A.	7	12	Mr D. H. Jones	c/o (0443) 202515
Kelly, Miss J.	6	13	Lord John FitzGerald	c/o (0638) 660605
Kennedy, N.	6	10	Mr G. M. Moore	c/o (0638) 660212 (agent)
Kent, D. R.	7	12	Mr J. Old	(0727) 642756/781340
Kenyon, Miss J.	7	0	Mrs S. E. Piggott	c/o (0638) 662584
Kersey, Miss S.	8	0	Mr T. Kersey	c/o (0709) 873166
Lamplugh, R.	7	0	Mr T. Barron	c/o (0845) 587435
Landau, G. L.	8	2	Mr S. Mellor	(0488) 71729
Lane, B. B.	7	7	Sir Mark Prescott	(0638) 662117 or (0933) 772671 (agent)
Langlands, M. D.	8	0	Mr M. R. Stoute	c/o (0638) 663801
Lanigan, S.	6	12	Mr D. J. G. Murray-Smith	c/o (0488) 71041
Lappin, A.	7	7	Mr R. Curtis	c/o (0372) 277645
Lappin, R. T.	7	12	Mr F. Lee	(0625) 533250/525033
Lawson, R.	7	12	Mr P. Mitchell	c/o (0372) 273729
LeJeune, A. J.	7	2	Mr Henry Candy	c/o (036782) 276
Leech, J. P.	9	0	Mr R. Akehurst	c/o (03727) 27596
Litwin, Miss L. A.	7	0	Mr C. A. Austin	c/o (0734) 786425
Litwin, W. B.	7	8	Mr C. F. Wall	(0252) 510823 (home) or c/o (0638) 661999
Lloyd, C. O.	8	2	Mr R. Boss	c/o (0638) 661335
Long, Miss L. G.	8	7	Mr J. Long	c/o (0273) 890244
Lynch, B.	7	12	Mrs N. Macauley	c/o (0476) 860578
Lynch, M. J.	7	11	Mr B. A. McMahon	c/o (0827) 62901
Mabb, Miss F.	7	10	Mr G. Harwood	c/o (07982) 3011
Mabb, Miss S.	8	0	Mr R. Hoad	(0273) 477124
MacKenzie, A.	7	10	Mr G. Harwood	c/o (07982) 3011/2
Maher, K.	7	12	Mr J. Oxx	(045) 21310
Maher, P. J.	7	0	Mr R. Hannon	c/o (0264) 850254
Mahoney, L. D.	7	10	Mr T. Thomson Jones	c/o (0488) 71596
Maloney, S.	7	4	Mr M. Brittain	c/o (0759) 71472
Marshall, J.	7	10	Mr M. Brittain	c/o (0759) 71472
Marshall, M.	7	12	Mr M. Usher	(048839) 8953/8954 (0271) 883813 (agent)
Martinez, A. L.	7	10	Mr R. Smyth	c/o (03727) 20053
Mayne, Miss T. M.	7	8	Mr L. G. Cottrell	c/o (08846) 320
McCabe, D.	7	0	Mr N. Meade	(046) 54197
McConnell, M. R.	7	10	Mr P. Cundell	c/o (063) 522 267
McCullough, N.	7	2	Mr D. Lavarack	c/o (0503) 21381
McDonnell, Miss K. S.	7	0	Mr K. M. Brassey	c/o (0488) 71508
McGinn, J.	7	0	Mr D. Laing	c/o (0488) 71825
McGlone, B. E.	7	10	Mr W. Jarvis	c/o (0638) 669873
McKeever, N.	8	7	Mr P. Hughes	(0503) 21882/21891
McKenna, S. L.	8	0	Mr A. Bailey	c/o (0638) 661537

Apprentices – Continued

Name	st	lb	Trainer	Telephone
McKeown, J.	6	7	Mr D. T. Hughes	c/o 04521490
McLaughlin, T. G.	7	0	Miss L. C. Siddall	c/o (090484) 291
McMahon, H. I.	9	0	Mr J. Ffitch-Heyes	c/o (0273) 477529
McWilliam, Miss L. J.	8	0	Mr H. Thomson Jones	c/o (0638) 664884/663640
Meade, D. N.	7	12	Mr P. Walwyn	c/o (0488) 71347
Mellor, Miss A. D.	7	2	Miss B. Sanders	(0488) 71485 or (0836) 278602 (car phone)
Meredith, D.	8	0	Mr R. Dickin	c/o (053) 185644
Middleton, Miss A.	7	7	Mr C. Austin	(0734) 786425
Mitchell, G. C.	7	7	Mr F. Durr	c/o (0638) 730030
Monteith, I.	7	8	Mr N. Callaghan	c/o (0638) 664040
Moore, Miss C. L.	8	9	Mr A. Moore	c/o (0273) 681679
Morris, A.	7	12	Mr C. Cyzer	c/o (0403) 730255
Morris, P. J.	6	12	Mr J. R. Jenkins	c/o (0363) 241141
Moss, G. P.	8	0	Mr R. Thompson	c/o (078081) 526
Mullins, Miss B. J.	7	10	Mr E. Wheeler	c/o (0488) 71650
Munday, C. J. A.	7	7	Mr G. Gracey	c/o (0344) 890461
Munro, A. K.	7	7	Mr W. A. O'Gorman	(0904) 645887 or (0860) 288254 (agent)
Murphy, M. D.	8	0	Mrs S. Oliver	c/o (0902) 892017/892648
Murray, A.	7	12	Mr K. Prendergast	c/o (045) 21387
Murtagh, J.	7	9	Mr J. Oxx	(045) 21618

Name	st	lb	Trainer	Telephone
Naylor, J.	8	2	Mr R. Armstrong	c/o (0638) 663333
Newey, A. S.	7	13	Mr J. A. C. Edwards	c/o (098987) 259/315
Newton, L.	7	0	Mr G. Huffer	c/o (0638) 76686 or (0993) 772671
Nichol, B. P.	7	7	Mr Pat Mitchell	c/o (0638) 660013
Norman, Miss K. P.	7	0	Mr G. A. Huffer	c/o (0638) 667997
Norton, F.	7	0	Mr A. Bailey	c/o (0638) 661537

Name	st	lb	Trainer	Telephone
O'Connor, W.	8	6	Mr N. Meade	c/o (046) 54197
O'Gorman, S. M.	7	8	Mr I. A. Balding	c/o (0365) 298210
Oliver, Miss J.	8	7	Mrs S. Oliver	(0902) 892017
O'Neill, G. J.	7	7	Mr G. Harwood	c/o (07982) 3011/2
O'Reilly, M. G.	7	7	Mr Mike O'Neill	c/o (051) 5316887
O'Shea, D.	7	0	Mr J. Oxx	c/o (045) 21310
O'Sullivan, D.	7	0	Mr B. Schutz	c/o (0221) 743010
O'Sullivan, J. J.	8	0	Mr G. Balding	(026477) 2278

Name	st	lb	Trainer	Telephone
Parkes, T. A.	8	0	Mr R. Stubbs	c/o (0969) 40680
Parkinson, D.	7	9	Lord John FitzGerald	c/o (0638) 660605
Payne, P. G.	8	7	Mr H. O'Neill	(0306) 711723
Perham, R.	7	13	Mr R. Hannon	(026485) 254
Perratt, W. F.	8	1	Mr T. Fairhurst	c/o (0969) 23362
Perry, N. L.	7	12	Mr J. W. Hills	c/o (0488) 71548
Pollard, C.	7	9	Mr E. Eldin	c/o (0638) 662036
Popely, A.	7	9	Miss L. C. Siddall	(0904) 799783
Porter, J. J.	7	7	Mr J. W. Watts	c/o (0748) 850444
Porter, S. P.	7	3	Mr M. J. Ryan	c/o (0638) 664172
Price, R. W.	7	4	Mr M. Bell	c/o (0638) 666567 and (0638) 76686 or (0993) 772671 (agent)
Priest, C.	8	0	Mr N. Bycroft	c/o (03475) 641
Procter, A. R.	7	12	Mr D. Arbuthnot	c/o (0635) 578427 or (0993) 772671 (agent)
Prys-Jones, Miss B. L.	7	8	Mr K. T. Ivory	c/o (0923) 855337
Puddle, J. B.	8	5	Miss A. King	c/o (0789) 205087
Purseglove, Miss T. N.	8	0	Mr G. B. Balding	c/o (026477) 2278
Pyne, Miss J. A.	8	7	Mr D. Dale	c/o (0638) 661586

Name	st	lb	Trainer	Telephone
Quane, S. H. N.	8	0	Mr C. Allen	c/o (0638) 664568 or (0993) 72671
Quinn, J. A.	7	6	Mr H. Collingridge	(0638) 665454

Name	st	lb	Trainer	Telephone
Rabjohn, S. D.	8	2	Mr Mark Johnston	(0969) 22237
Riding, A.	7	11	Mr J. R. White	(0638) 660212 (agent)

Apprentices – Continued

Name	st	lb	Employer	Telephone
Riggio, L.	7	12	Mr E. Wheeler	(0488) 71650 or (01) 7698263
Rimell, K. M.	8	6	Mr H. O'Neill	c/o (0306) 711723
Roberts, Miss C. A.	7	12	Miss L. Siddall	c/o (090484) 291
Roberts, C. N.	6	7	Capt. James Wilson	c/o (0772) 812780
Roberts, M.	8	0	Mr M. Naughton	(0748) 2803
Roche, A.	7	12	Mr L. Browne	c/o (045) 41255
Roffey, Paul	7	12	Mr D. W. P. Arbuthnot	c/o (0635) 57842
Rollinson, G.	8	0	Mr J. Etherington	c/o (0653) 692842
Roper, A. J.	8	1	Mr N. Callaghan	c/o (0638) 664040
Rourke, R. R.	7	11	Mr J. R. Jenkins	c/o (0763) 241141
Russell, B. J.	7	7	Mr W. Holden	c/o (063877) 384
Rutter, K.	7	10	Dr. J. D. Scargill	c/o (0638) 663254
Ryan, J. B.	9	0	Mr M. J. Ryan	c/o (0638) 664172
Sanders, S.	7	0	Mr B. McMahon	c/o (0827) 62901
Sargent, P. J.	7	10	Mr G. Roe	c/o (0453) 885487
Scally, C.	7	9	Mr K. T. Ivory	c/o (0923) 855337
Schikora, A.	7	6	Mr B. Schutz	c/o (0221) 743010
Scorer, Miss H.	7	7	Mr R. Smyth	c/o (03727) 20053
Scott, E.	7	0	Mr W. T. Wilson	c/o (0638) 667400
Scott, Miss F.	8	0	Mr T. Craig	c/o (0368) 62583
Severn, A.	7	0	Mr P. Calver	c/o (0765) 700313
Shoults, A. F.	7	12	Mr R. W. Armstrong	c/o (0638) 666431
Simms, P.	7	12	Mr M. Brittain	c/o (0759) 71472
Simpson, A. J.	7	9	Mr P. F. I. Cole	(04882) 433
Simpson, Miss C. A.	8	7	Mr F. Jordan	c/o (056882) 281
Simpson, M.	7	12	Mr William Hastings-Bass	c/o (0635) 28725/28747
Skelton, P. R.	7	12	Mr M. Blanshard	c/o (0488) 71091
Slattery, J. V.	9	7	Mr O. O'Neill	c/o (024267) 3275
Smith, D.	7	12	Mr D. K. Weld	(045) 41273/41476
Smith, Miss M.	8	3	Mr M. Haynes	c/o (03727) 22664
Smith, M. J.	8	0	Mr K. Bridgwater	c/o (05643) 2895
Smith, R. O.	7	10	Mr B. Hanbury	c/o (0638) 663193
Smith, S. J.	7	6	Mr T. Fairhurst	c/o (0969) 23362
Smith, V.	9	7	Mr I. Campbell	(0638) 668972
Smith-Eccles, P.	7	9	Mr Gavin A. Pritchard-Gordon)	(0638) 662824
Snowdon, Miss V. F.	7	10	Mr D. R. C. Elsworth	c/o (07253) 528
Soar, R.	6	7	Mr W. Wharton	c/o (0664) 65225/78334
Spence, A. J.	7	10	Mr W. Musson	c/o (0638) 663371
Spence, S. D.	7	4	Capt. James Wilson	c/o (0772) 812780
Sprake, T. J.	7	10	Mr P. J. Makin	c/o (0672) 52973
Stannard, Miss E. C.	8	0	Mr M. R. Stoute	c/o (0638) 663801
Stather, D. M.	7	12	Mr G. Harwood	c/o (07982) 3011
Stenning, J.	7	12	Mr J. Long	(0273) 890244
Strickland, Miss C. L.	6	7	Mr D. Haydn Jones	c/o (0443) 202515
Strange, G.	7	7	Mr Ronald Thompson	c/o (0302) 845904
Supple, W.	8	0	Mr J. Bolger	(056) 43150/8
Surrey, D.	7	12	Mr G. Wragg	c/o (0638) 662328
Tate, A. B.	7	6	Mr M. D. I. Usher	c/o (0488) 71307
Tate, J.	7	2	Mr P. Arthur	c/o (0235) 850338
Taylor, S. D.	7	0	Mr G. M. Moore	c/o (0969) 23823
Tervitt, B. G.	7	12	Mr W. Jarvis	c/o (0638) 669873
Thomas, B.	7	2	Mr Rod Simpson	(0488) 72688
Thomas, Miss N. J.	7	10	Mr M. J. Ryan	c/o (0638) 664172
Thompson, G.	7	12	Mr W. Brook	c/o (0488) 72140
Tierney, D. P.	7	10	Mr G. B. Balding	c/o (026477) 2278 or (0264) 57517
Timms, C. C.	6	0	Mr D. Haydn Jones	c/o (0443) 202515
Todd, A. W.	7	5	Mr David W. Chapman	c/o (0347) 21683
Todd, I.	8	7	Mr A. P. Jarvis	(0763) 47444
Toole, D.	7	0	Mr M. Haynes	c/o (03727) 22664

Apprentices – Continued

Tormey, G.	7	7	Mr K. Prendergast	c/o (045) 21387
Towler, D. L.	7	8	Mr R. W. Stubbs	c/o (0969) 40644
Town, Miss M	8	0	Mr A. Bailey	c/o (0638) 661537
Treacy, Caroline	7	7	Capt. D. Swan	c/o (0505) 42221
Tucker, A. P.	7	8	Mr M. McCormack	c/o (023559) 433 or (0638) 76686
Turner, P. J.	7	7	Mr M. H. Tompkins	c/o (0653) 693149
Turner, R. D.	7	0	Mr C. W. C. Elsey	c/o (0653) 693149
Vale, John	7	12	Mr J. Eustace	c/o (0638) 664277
Want, D.	7	5	Mr R. Thompson	c/o (078081) 812
Ward, J.	7	0	Mr W. Wharton	c/o (0664) 65225/78334
Ward, J. R.	7	11	Mr M. Johnston	c/o (050785) 8146
Watts, G. B.	7	7	Mr P. Cundell	(063522) 267
Weaver, J. C.	7	7	Mr L. M. Cumani	c/o (0638) 665432
Webster, Miss S.	8	0	Mr O. Brennan	c/o (063686) 332
White, P. A.	7	13	Mr E. Eldin	c/o (0638) 662036
Whitham, A. D.	9	7	Mr R. Earnshaw	c/o (0423) 567790
Widger, G.	7	7	Mr P. Burgoyne	c/o (023559) 688
Widger, M.	7	0	Mr P. F. I. Cole	c/o (04882) 433
Widger, P.	7	7	Mr W. Pearce	(0845) 597373
Wilhelms, R.	7	10	Mr B. Schutz	c/o (0221) 743010
Williams, D. J.	7	10	Mr H. Candy	c/o (036782) 276
Williams, J.	7	10	Mr G. Lewis	c/o (03722) 77662
Williams, N. G.	7	0		(0638) 667997
Williams, S. A. G.	7	0	Mr S. Kettlewell	c/o (0969) 40295
Williams, S. D.	9	0	Mr J. Glover	(0909) 475425/475962
Williams, T. G. A.	7	8	Mr N. Callaghan	c/o (0638) 664040
Wilson, C.	8	0	Mr P. Feilden	c/o (0638) 77637
Winterbotom, G.	8	0	Sir M. Prescott	c/o (0638) 662117
Woodall, N. C.	8	4	Mr J. S. Wainwright	c/o (0653) 85537
Woods, S.	7	2	Mr D. W. Chapman	c/o (0347) 21683 or (0347) 6482 (agent)
Wright, D.	6	12	Mr M. Brittain	c/o (0759) 71472
Wright, M. G.	7	0	Mr P. F. I. Cole	c/o (04882) 433

Raceform 1989 Flat Annual

£18 FROM NEWSAGENTS **£19** BY POST

ISB NO: 0 900611 46 4

A complete cloth-bound reprint of last Flat Racing Season's Raceform (The Official Form Book). Every fact of form about every race, embellished by abbreviated comments on the runners by Raceform's own team of expert race-readers. Almost 1,500 pages. Extra features include Speed Figures and Standard and Record Times for each course.

N.H. JOCKEYS

Weights, Phone Numbers, Stables

* Jockeys shown with an asterisk hold a "conditional" licence or a claiming licence. They are entitled to claim 7lb. until they have won 15 races, thereafter 4lb. until they have won 30 races.
† Restricted to Conditional Jockeys Races and National Hunt Flat Races only.

Adams, A. J., 9-7 .... (N. Gaselee) Lambourn (0488) 72238 or (0235)819093 agent
†Adams, D. J., 9-2 .... (T. Forster)
Adshead, K. R., 9-7 c/o Wensleydale (0969) 23269
Ahern, M. J., 9-9 ...... (J. Jenkins) (0763) 241141
Akehurst, J. C., 10-3 .... (G. Beeson) (04352) 4713
Allen, J., 10-0 ....(I. Jordon) Newcastle-upon-Tyne (0632) 868 803
*Alston, M. E., 9-12......... (E. Alston, R. Scholey) (0772) 612120
*Andrews, D., 9-7 (Mr R. Lee) c/o (0544) 267672
Armytage, Gee, 10-0 ....(A. G. Blackmore, Mrs S. Armytage) (063528) 273
*Arnold, S. P., 9-7 ....(Mr Malcolm W. Eckley) (0584) 72372
Arnott, T. R., 10-0........................(D. Elsworth) (072 53) 504
*Ashworth, L. R.9-7 ....(Mr A. R. Davison)
†Atkinson, J. K., 10-0.......(Mr John Ffitch-Heyes) (0273) 480804
*Atwell, M. E., 9-7..................... (P. O'Connor) c/o (0283) 226046
†Ayles, W. J., 9-7 ....(Mr W. T. Kemp) c/o (0233) 72525
Ayliffe, M. G., 10-4 ....(N. Ayliffe) Winsford Somerset (064385) 265

Babbage, N., 10-12...... Cheltenham (0242) 33090
Balfour, R., 9-7 ....(J. Parkes)
Barker, J. C., 8-10.......... (J. Dreaper) 01 350486
Barlow, J., 10-0......... Newmarket (0638) 713018
*Barnard, P. J. 8-10... (Mr F. Taylor) (0638) 76686 or (0793) 790230
†Barry, D. J. P., 9-7 .... (Mr G. Richards) c/o (08533) 392
†Barry, T. P., 9-9 (Mr J. S. King) c/o (079373) 1747
Barton, Paul D., 10-2.............. (J. A. C. Edwards, M. McCormack, G. Thorner) Frilford Heath (0865) 390750
Bastard, M. H., 10-0 .... (M. Blanshard) Lambourn (0488) 72747
†Bates, J. M., 9-7 ....(Miss Sue Wilton) c/o (0782) 550861
Beardwood, W. A. J., 10-0 ....(0704) 75352
Beggan, R. J., 10-0.......................... (K. Bailey, B. McMath, Mrs A. Knight) Great Shefford (car phone) (0836) 507 343 (0672) 40868
*Begley, Miss A. J., 9-7... Newbury (0635) 253164
†Belding, Miss G. V., 9-7 .... (R. Champion) (028484) 278
†Bell, C. D., 9-0.........................(R. Champion)
*Bellamy, R. J., 9-7 .... (D. Nicholson Mrs H. Parrott, A. Forte) c/o (0451) 30417/32472 (043 270) 448 Agent (0836) 747 694 Car
*Bellisario, M., 9-7..........................(A. Ridout) c/o (07253) 646
*Bennyworth, D. C., 9-7.. (Mr O. M. C. Sherwood) (0488) 72760/72928
†Bentley, D. B., 9-7 .... (Mr Andrew Turnell) c/o (0235) 833297
*Berry, M. 9-7 ....c/o Lambourn (0488) 72259
Berry, R. J., 9-4...................................(A.J. Pitt) Epsom (03727) 23408
*Bevan, R. C., 10-0 ....(W. Clay) c/o (0767) 260618
†Bielby, M. P., 9-7 .... (J. Harris) (0949) 60671
*Bird, W. K., 9-7 (Mr J. M. Bukovets) (05642) 4631
†Birrane, P. F., 9-12.................... (J. Spearing)
Blakeney, Judy, 9-12...................(R. Blakeney) c/o (048641) 2604
Bloomfield, L. A., 10-0.................. (S. Holmes) Weston Super Mare (0934) 29547
†Bloss, S., 9-9 (R. Champion) c/o (0638) 666546
*Bohane, G., 9-6 .... (Mr John R. Upson) (0327) 860043
†Bond, K. J., 9-7 .... (P. Hayward) c/o Netheravon (098 07) 585
Bosley, M. R., 10-2.............. (J. Bosley, C. Nash C. Cyzer, Mrs J. E. Croft, G. Yardley) (0993) 850212 or (0367) 22224
†Bottomley A. J., 10-0 ....(J. Bottomley) (0653) 693511
*Boucher, R. A., 9-7 .... (A. Turnell, R. Smyly) (0488) 71027 or (0235) 833297
†Bourne, C., 9-9 .... (D. Tucker)
Bowens, C. N., 9-7 .... (045) 53100
Bowlby, M. S. S., 10-0... (J. Wilson, W. M. Perrin, P. T. S. Bowlby, Mrs J. Pitman) c/o Lambourn (0488) 72259 or 72210 and (0836) 249472 (car)
*Bowman, P., 9-7 .... (Mr I. Wardle) c/o (0749) 870592
†Boxhall, A. P., 9-7...............(Mr C. L. Popham) c/o (0823) 432769
Bradley, G. J., 10-5...................... (N. Bradley, J. Hanson, D. Elsworth) (023559) 533 carphone (0860) 327649

N.H. Jockeys – Continued

Bradshaw K., 8-0 ....(R. Whitaker) (0937) 62122
†Brennan, Miss H., 10-0.............. (O. Brennan) (063686) 332
Brennan, M. J., 8-10 .... (J. Blundell, O. Brennan, D. Thom) (0636) 815161 or (0937) 66556/64441 agent and (0836) 287640 (car)
*Bridger, Miss R. J., 7-9.......... (Mr J. J. Bridger) c/o (0428) 722528
†Bridgwater, D. G., 9-0 ....(Mr D. Nicholson) c/o (0451) 30417
*Bridle, S. R., 9-7 .... (Mr K. S. Bridgewater) c/o (05643) 2895
†Brisbourne, Mrs P. J., 9-7 .... (A. Brisbourne) (074 381) 536
Brisbourne, W. M., 10-2......... c/o (0980) 620861 Nesscliffe (074 381) 360
Brooke E., 9-10 .... Tern Hill (063083) 433
*Brough, J. H., 9-11 .... (R. W. Jeffrey) (0704) 892781
*Brown, J. L., 10-5........................ (M. Brown) (0550) 777403
*Brown, M. P., 10-0 .... (Mr J. D. J. Davies) c/o (0303) 874089
Browne, D. W., 10-3 ...... Lambourn (0488) 39706 72078 or (0860) 398166 (car)
Bryan, J. R., 10-0 (W. Hickman, C. F. C. Jackson) Ridgway Cross (088 684) 748 or (0886) 880273
Buckley, E., 10-2 ....(T. Casey, J. J. Costello) Towcester (0327) 62351
Buckton, S., 8-0 ....(0845) 597373
Burchell, D. J., 10-0.....................(D. Burchell, E. H. Owen jun.) c/o Ebbw Vale (0495) 302551
†Burden, S. J., 10-0........................ (P. Leech) c/o (0823) 433249
*Burke, J. H., 10-0 .... (Mr T. W. Donnelly) c/o (0283) 226046
Burke, K. R., 10-0 .... (J. White) (0636) 84522 or (0860) 744172 carphone
†Burland, Miss D. M., 9-7 .... (Mr K. Bishop) c/o (027867) 437
*Burton, J. N., 9-7 .... (Mr J. G. FitzGerald) c/o (0653) 692718
Butler, Denise, 9-7......................... (K. Bishop) (027867) 511
†Byles, M. J., 9-7.....................(R. E. Blakeney)
*Byrne, D. C., 9-7 .....(Mr K. Stone, Mrs S. Minns, J. FitzGerald, B. Ellison, A. Fowler) (0836) 278374 and (0653) 692288 (home) or (0904) 647213 (agent)
*Byrne, F., 9-7 .... (J. Jenkins, C. C. Trietline)
Byrne, J. P., 9-7 .... (J. R. Cox) 046 28026
Byrne, L. A., 9-4 .... c/o (065 386) 600
Byrne, M. J. 9-10 .... (062) 61775
Byrne, N., 8-11 01-285480
Byrne, R., 9-7 .... (045) 81729

*Caldwell, Pat, 9-11 ......T. Caldwell (056 585) 275
Caldwell, Peter H., 10-0.................(T. Caldwell) Warrington (0925) 602679
*Callaghan, J. G., 9-7 ....(G. Moore) c/o (0969) 23823
Campbell, R., 9-13 .... (I. Campbell, W. T. J. Wilson) Newmarket (0638) 664117
*Caplen, K. J., 9-7......................... (D. Wilson) (0372) 377209 and (03722) 73839
*Carcary, D. R., 9-7 .... (R. Hollinshead) c/o (0543) 490298
Carmody, T., 9-9 .. (J. Mulhearn, H. De Bromhead) (045) 41729
†Carr, P. A., 9-7 .... (Mr Denys Smith) c/o (0388) 603317
Carroll, A. W., 10-0............. (A. Bailey, A. Jarvis, P. M. Taylor, D. Wintle, B. McMath) (0638) 751607 or (03677) 723
†Carson, A., 9-7 ...... (C. W. Spares) (0949) 50099
†Carson, R. W., 9-7 .... (Mr C. Spares) c/o (0949) 50099
*Carter, M., 9-7.................. (Mr J. Wainwright) c/o (0653) 85537
†Carter, R., 8-7 .... (P. Mitchell)
†Carter, S. R., 9-7 .... (B. Palling)
*Cassidy, M., 8-7.... (N. Gracey) c/o (0883) 40922
Castell, M., 10-9 .... Knightwick (0886) 21538
Caswell, M., 10-0......................(024 267) 6216
Chamberlain, A. J., 10-5 Cirencester (0285) 861347
*Chandler, L. E., 9-7 .... (Mrs D. Haine) c/o 0638) 77719
†Chapman, Miss Kerry, 9-0 ....(B. Wise)
†Chapman, M., 9-7... (M. Chapman) (0858) 86255
Chapman, R. H., 10-0...... (0488) 71555 or (0531) 820448
Charles-Jones, G., 10-0 .... (S. Mellor W. G. Turner) Swindon (0793) 790317
*Charles-Jones, Mrs J. K., 9-7........ (R. Simpson) c/o (0488) 72688
Charles, M. J., 10-0 .... Warwick (0926) 499403
*Charlton, A., 10-0.... (G. Balding) (0264) 772583
Chatburn, E. R., 10-0 c/o Codford St Mary (0985) 50477
Chinn, D., 10-0 ......(Miss E. Sneyd) (060884) 739
*Clarke, J., 9-10 .... (A. Moore) (0273) 681679
Clarke, P., 9-0........................... (E. P. Harty) c/o (045) 22161
*Clay, Miss Diane, 9-7 ....(W. Clay) (0767) 260618
*Cloke, T. N., 9-0................ (Mr G. A. Hubbard) c/o (072) 876250
*Cockburn, D. A., 9-7................ (090 084) 306
†Coglan, M. V., 9-7 .... (J. Pearce) (0638) 664669
*Colbert, G. J., 9-7 .... (Mr P. W. Harris) c/o (044284) 2480
Coleman, N. F., 10-0 .... (R. Holder, Mrs S. Minns) Torquay (0803) 615843 or (0860) 529486 (car)
Collen, Sarah., 9-0 .... (Mr J. Hayden) (045) 97736

N.H. Jockeys – Continued

*Collett, M. K., 9-0 .... (Mrs G. Jones)
Condell, D., 9-7 .... (W. R. Robinson) (0969) 24039/22237
Collins, J. D., 9-0 .... (D. T. Hughes) (045) 21490
†Collins, P. M., 9-7 .... (Mr D. M. Grissell) c/o (042482) 241
*Conlon, S. P. 9-7 .... (M. S. Johnston) (0969) 22237
†Cook G., 9-7 .... (P. Liddle) c/o (091) 4102072 or 3886329
†Cooney, D., 9-7 .... (Mr Julian Czerpak) (025125) 3505
*Cooney, P., 9-0 .... (F. Gray) (044485) 235
†Corkell, J. D., 10-0 .... c/o (0751) 31066
Corrigan, P. P., 10-0 .... (P. Haynes) (0444) 881594
*Cotter, K. P., 10-0 ... (P. Charlton) (0653) 693356
†Cottey, Miss S. J., 9-7 .... (W. Fisher) c/o (076121) 283
Cowley, S., 10-0 .... (A. J. Wilson, B. Smart) (0242) 528634/580092
Cox, C. G., 10-0 .... (O. Sherwood, M. Churches, Mrs S. Minns, F. Yardley) (0488) 72418 or(0860) 744799 (car)
Coyle, M., 9-7 .... Netheravon (09807) 358
Crank, R. W., 10-2 .... (T. Hall, C. Dingwall, P. Blockley) Tattenhall (0829) 70672 and (051356) 0025
†Crone, G. S., 9-7 .... (Mr G. Harwood) c/o (07982) 2423/3011
Cross, Miss Angela, 8-7 .... Chatton (06685) 247
Crosse, M., 10-0 .... (F. Gray) (044485) 586
*Crossman, D. R., 9-7 .. (D. Smith) (0388) 603317
Cullen, J. W., 9-10 .... (045)41837
*Cunningham, W. S., 9-7 ..... (T. W. Cunningham) (060982) 695
Cusack, L. P. 10-2 .... (0507) 31544
*Cusack, S. P., 9-7 .... (J McConnochie)
†Cuthbert, Miss C., 9-7 .. (Mr T. A. K. Cuthbert) c/o (0228) 60822

†Dable, D. K., 9-7 .... (J. Blundell) c/o Grimsby (0472) 840387
†Dace, L. A., 8-11 .... (Mr R. V. Smyth) c/o (03727) 20053
†Dacosta, J. W., 9-7 .... (B. K. Wells) (056283) 296
*Dalton, M. P., 9-7 .... (A. Scott)
*Dalton, P., 9-7 .... (Mr J. M. Jefferson) c/o (0653) 697225
†Darby, J. P. F., 9-0 .... (Mrs Lester Piggott) c/o (0638) 660229
†Darling, D. S., 9-7 .... (D. Gandolfo) c/o (02357) 3242
†David, A. N., 9-7 .... (Mr J. P. D. Elliot)
†Davies, C. H., 9-7 .... (B. Stevens)
Davies, G., 10-0 .... (J. Bradley) (0291) 622486
Davies, H. J., 10-4 ...... (T. Forster, R. Champion, C. S. Wates, J. Sayers, E. Jones, P. Leach) (079371) 395 or (0860) 324826 car phone
Davies, J. D., 10-0 .... (0823) 432769
Davies, J. H., 9-12 .... c/o (023559) 276
*Davies, P. W., 9-7 .... (Mr J. A. B. Old) c/o (0749) 86656
*Davis, R. S., 10-4 .... (Mr P. W. Davis) c/o (052789) 3174
*Davis, S. R., 10-4 .... (P. W. Davis) c/o (052789) 3174
*Davies, P. W., 9-7 .... (J. Old) (0272) 642756/787240
*Davies, S., 9-12 .... (Mr C. J. Bell) (0831) 419841
Davies, T. G., 10-0 .... (W. A. Stephenson) Bishop Auckland (0388) 720133
Davis, Miss T. M. J., 9-7 .... (0488) 72677 or (052789) 3174
Dawe, N., 10-0 .... (M. Pipe, Miss J. Thorne) (0903) 884749 or (0295) 68619 agent and (027874) 457
Deegan, J., 8-0 .... (E. O'Grady) (045) 41575
De Haan, B., 10-0 .... (Mrs J. Pitman, C. Brooks, B. Smart) (0488) 72163 or (0831) 104574
†Dempsey, C., 9-7 .... (Mr C. P. E. Brooks, Mr W. G. Turner) c/o (0488) 72077 and (082281) 237
†Denaro, M. J., 9-7 .... (Mr C. N. Allen) c/o (0638) 76767
Dengell, D., 9-7 .... (Mr C. Wildman) c/o (0980) 52226
*Dennis, C. P., 9-7 ... (Mr C. Spares) (0949) 50099
†Dennis, D. J., 9-7 .... (Mr J. A. Pickering) (0455) 220535
Dennis, P. J., 10-0 .... (J. Charlton, R. Scholey, (060 983) 357
Dennis, R. T. J., 10-0 .... (C. Bell, P. Dunstan, M. Tompkins) (0638) 750191
Dever, P., 10-0 .... (J. Cosgrave, C. Trietline, K. S. Bridgwater) (0386) 858988 or (0860) 742424 carphone
†Dicken, A., 9-10 .... (S. L. Dow) Epsom (03727) 21490
Dicks, A. C., 9-0 .... (R. Holder) (0272) 519184 or (027581) 2192
†Dillon, J. E., 9-7 .... (W. A. Stephenson) (0388) 720213
Dineley, D., 9-0 .... (B. McMahon) (0488) 72712
*Diplock, G., 9-0 .... (A. R. Davison)
*Dixon, Miss K. N., 9-7 .... (Mr C. J. Holmes) c/o (02407) 3436
†Dobson, D. G., 9-7 .... (C. Parker) c/o (05765) 232
*Dodds, Miss J., 9-7 .... (Mr D. McCaskill) c/o (091) 4102938
*Donaldson, G. P., 10-0 .... (T. Casey) c/o (0295) 711686
Doolan, K. J., 10-0 .... (D. McCain, E. Alston, W. A. Stephenson, W. Storey) (05765) 275/232 or (020750) 2341
Donahoe, S., 9-7 ...... Mr J. Bolger (056) 43150/8
Donnelly, Joseph 9-0 (Capt. D. Swan) (0505) 42221

N.H. Jockeys – Continued

*Doran. B. N., 9-7 .... (D. L. Williams) c/o (0386) 858605
Double, P. F., 10-5 .... (D. Oughton) (090 671) 2926 or c/o 2113
Doughty, D. N., 10-5 .... Penrith (0768) 63575 or (0860) 711122 carphone
Dowling, B., 10-0 .... (R. Lee) (056888) 460 or (0684) 298227
Doyle, J. C. M., 10-7 .... Wetherby (0937) 63855
Doyle, J. D., 9-10 .... (W. G. Mann, J. M. Bukovets) (0562) 67266 or (0384) 793263
†Doyle, M. A., 9-7 .... (J. Edwards)
Doyle, Mark, 9-0 .... (E. O'Grady) (052) 56156
†Driscoll, J. P., 9-7 .... (Dr J. Scargill) c/o (0638) 663254
*Drugan, M., 9-7 .... (Mrs N. Bradley) (0937) 62151
†Duffy, J. A., 9-7 .... (G. Thorner) c/o (02357) 3003/770359
Duffy, M. 10-0 .... c/o(0503) 21250
Duggan, J., 10-0 .... (D. J. Bell, M. Eckley, M. Robinson) Wantage (02357) 3986, or (0295) 710297
Dun, T. G., 10-8 .... (K. Oliver, J. S. Wilson) Heriot (087 535) 230 or 225
†Dunne, D., 9-7 .... (Mr A. R. Allan) c/o (089082) 581
*Dunster, Miss Samantha, 9-7 .... (R. T. Juckes)
Dunwoody, T. R., 10-0 .... (D. Nicholson, N. Henderson, B. Smart, R. Barton, A. G. Blackmore, J. R. Jenkins) (023559) 287 or (0836) 502290 (car)
†Durnin, A., 9-7 .... (Mr Andrew Turnell) c/o (0235) 833297
Dutton, D., 10-0 .... (G. Harman) Malton (0653) 695637
*Dwan, W. J., 9-7 .... (Mr J. G. FitzGerald) c/o (0653) 692718
Dwyer, M. P., 10-3 .... (J. Hanson, J. J. O'Neill, P. Liddle, D. Ellison) Malton (09442) 8841 or (0759) 71586 (agent) or (0860) 366672 (car)

Earle, S. A., 10-0 .... (K. Bishop, D. H. Barons, R. Callow, Mrs H. Parrott) (0823) 433346 and (0860) 252348 (car)
Earnshaw, R., 10-0 .... (0423) 67790
*Eatwell, M., 9-7 ... (J. E. Long) c/o (0273) 890244
†Edwards, Miss G., 8-10 .... (Mr R. W. Swiers) c/o (0423) 322226
*Edwards, S., 9-7 .... c/o (063 528) 253
†Eldredge, Miss L. C., 9-7 .... (Mr Richard Lee) c/o (0544) 267672
†Ellis, T., 9-7 .... (G. Morgan)
Ellison, B., 10-2 .... (0653) 695935
Ennis, M. A., 10-0 .... (R. M. Whitaker) (0937) 62122
Enright, G. P., 10-0 .... (J. Gifford) Bolney (044 482) 761
Evans, C., 10-0 .... (B. Palling) (0443) 673630
*Evans, G. C., 9-10 .... (0584) 3969
*Evans, K. A., 9-0 .... (02357) 3420
Evely, P. C. H., 8-11 ...... (Mr G. Pritchard-Gordon) c/o (0638) 662824

Fagan, D. P., 9-7 .... (J. Fowler) (0405) 57401
Fahey, R. A., 10-0 .... (C. Tinkler, J. E. Parkes, W. W. Haigh) (0904) 647213 agent and (0653) 86635/695450 and (0836) 567580 (car)
*Fanning, J. K., 9-0 .... (Mr T. Fairhurst) c/o (0969) 23362
†Farley, B. J., 9-7 .... (Mr T. Thomson-Jones)
†Farmer, R. B., 9-7 .... (Mr G. B. Balding) c/o (026477) 2278
Farrell, P. A., 9-10 .... (Freelance) (03475) 273 and 208
†Fear, R. C., 9-7 (D. H. Barons) c/o (0548) 550326
Fearn, N. K., 10-0 .... (P. A. Blockley) (0203) 419322
Ffitch-Heyes, Miss P. A., 9-10 .... (J. Ffitch-Heyes, M. J. Collins) (0372) 276106 or (0273) 480804
*Finch, P. J., 10-0 .... (06846) 2691/2396
†Fisher, Miss Belinda, 9-0 .... (G. Prest)
Fisher, D. L. C., 9-0 .... (A. Fisher) Leicester (0533) 605907
†FitzGerald, M. P., 9-7 .... (Mr Mark Bradstock) c/o (0488) 39258
*FitzGerald, S., 9-7 .... (P. Bailey) (0980) 23542
*FitzGerald, M. 9-10 ...... (R. J. Hodges) c/o (0458) 223922
Fitzsimons, M., 9-0... (J. Fowler) c/o (0405) 57014
†Flood, D. J. D., 9-7 .... (R. W. Morris)
Flynn, M., 10-0 .... (0405) 53313
Forte, A. M., 9-12 .... (B. K. Wells, J. Forte) (0626) 779211 or (0626) 779006
*Foster, M. R., 9-7 .... (Mr M. C. Pipe) c/o (0823) 672969
*Foster, S. J., 9-10 .... (Mr G. B. Balding) c/o (026477) 2278 or (0264) 57517
*Fox, S., 9-7 .... (J. C. Fox) (0980) 620861
Frost, J. D., 10-4 ...... G. B. Balding (036 44) 2267
*Frost, K., 10-0 .... (R. Frost)
†Fry, W. S., 9-7 (Mr T. P. Tate) c/o (0937) 836036
†Fuller, T., 8-12 (Mr D. J. Wintle) c/o (045276) 459
Furlong, C. J., 9-7 .... Epsom (037 27) 21832
Furlong, M. J., 10-0 .... (R. Howe, J. Scallan, J. D. Davies, R. Voorspuy, J. O'Donoghue) Brighton (0273) 476515

Gallagher, D., 9-7 ...... (D. T. Hughes) (045) 21490
Gallagher, D. T., 9-7 ...... (R. Simpson, R. Bennett) (0672) 40809 or (0932) 243913 agent
†Galvin, B. W., 9-7 .... (A. Turnell) (02357) 69351 or (0235) 833297
†Garner, Miss V. C., 8-7 .... (Mr J. W. Payne) c/o (0638) 668675

N.H. Jockeys – Continued

*Garrity, R. J., 10-0 .... (M. H. Easterby, R. Woodhouse) (0653) 600221 or (0836) 326084
†Garside, D. W., 10-0.......... (Mr M. J. Camacho) (0653) 694901
†Gartland, J. J. J., 9-7 .... (Mr M. T. Bowker) c/o (05395) 60533
Gill, P., 8-10.................. (D. Clyde) (056) 26207
†Goddings, R. W., 9-10 .... (P. R. Hedger) (0243) 551808
Goldstein, R., 10-0 .... (R. Curtis, J. Long J. Redmond) (0273) 476755 or (0372) 277645 (office)
†Goodin, A. J., 9-7 .... (A. Ingham)
†Goodwin, R. A., 9-7..................... (04882) 586
Gorman, A. F., 10-0 ...... (P. Cundell, J. Needham) (0635) 248036/248660
*Goswell, P. W., 9-9 .... (C. Horgan)
Goulding, J. L., 9-10 .... (D. W. MacDonald) Cockermouth (0900) 825393
*Gracey, P. J. D., 9-7, ... (G. Gracey) (0883) 40922
†Graham, S. J., 9-7 .... (Mr J. L. Needham) (0584) 874826
Grant, C., 10-0 .... (W. A. Stephenson, R. F. Fisher) Bishop Auckland (0388) 710425
Grantham, T., 10-0 .... J. Gifford (0903) 815360 or (0836) 221988 (car)
Gray, C. J., 9-7.......................... (M. Stephens) Martock (0935) 825306
Gray, G. W., 10-0.............. Malton (0653) 7536
*Greene, R. J., 9-7 .... (Mr Richard Lee) c/o (0544) 267672
Griffiths, A., 10-0 .... (0443) 222265
Griffiths, L., 9-7...................... (M. McCormack) c/o (023 559) 433
†Griffiths, Miss V. J., 9-7 .... (A. James)
†Grimwood, O. T. A., 10-0 ...... (Mr Barry Stevens) c/o (0962) 883030
Guest, R. C., 10-0 .... (M. J. Collins, S. Dow, C. Roe, W. T. J. Wilson) (026477) 2278 and (0836) 781938 (car)
Gwilliam, C. K., 9-4........ Amesbury (0980) 24010

†Hagen, P. H., 7-8........................ (0276) 71030
*Halden, Miss R., 9-7 (Mr C. J. Bell) (0270) 623604
†Halls, J. I., 9-10 .... (Miss B. Sanders) c/o (03722) 78453
†Hanley, B. A., 9-7 .... (Mr John R. White) c/o (0296) 625310
Harker, G. A., 10-0 .... (D. Barrons, R. Thompson, B. E. Wilkinson, E. Robson) Eaglescliff (0325) 378634
*Harley, P. M., 9-7 .... (N. J. Henderson, Mrs J. E. Croft, D. J. Bell) (0432) 70448 agent or (0831) 136088 and (0488) 72259 and (0295) 721261
Harris, J. A., 10-0 .... (J. Harris)
†Harris, S. D., 9-3 .... (Mr M. D. I. Usher) c/o (0488) 398953 Harby (0949) 60671 and 43408 (evenings)
*Harris, S. A., 9-7 .... (M. Usher) c/o (0488) 398953
*Harris, Vicky M., 10-0 ... (J. Harris) (0949) 60671
*Harrison, Miss Mandy R., 9-7 .. (W. R. Robinson) (0723) 863988
*Harte, P. G., 9-7.................. (Mrs R. Wharton) (0759) 71586 (agent) or (0969) 23307
Harvey, L. J., 10-0........... (C. Nash, W. J. Smith, A. Perrett) (0398) 31478
*Hathaway, G., 9-6...................... (R. Whittaker)
*Hawke, N., 9-7 .... (D. Barons, John Brooks) (0548) 550411
Hawkins, C., 10-0 .... (R. McDonald) Bedale (0677) 22342 or (0347) 810103 and (0325) 378266 (office)
*Hay, B. T., 10-7 .... (T. Craig) c/o Dunbar (0368) 62583
Hayes, Mrs J., 9-7..................... (Mrs S. Oliver) (0488) 72649 or (0902) 892017/892648
*Hayes, W. J., 9-7....... (Mrs S. Oliver, J. Colston) (0488) 72649 or 892017/892648
*Haynes, J. M., 9-7 .... (Mr J. G. FitzGerald c/o (0653) 692718
*Hazell, M. G., 10-5...................... (N. Gaselee)
†Hazell, S. F., 9-7................. (Mr A. W. Denson) c/o (0372) 729389
*Head, Miss Susan, 9-0.................. (R. Morris)
*Heaver, G., 9-7 (R. Akehurst) c/o (0372) 727596
Heeney, T. J., 9-12 ..... Newmarket (0638) 663333
*Hegarty, P., 9-2 .... (D. Lee) c/o (0751) 32425
†Henfrey, Miss J., 10-0 .... (K. Morgan) c/o (066478) 711
*Hensman, Miss Georgina., 10-0... (0638) 663371
†Herbert, Miss Georgina, 9-7 .... (F. Coton) c/o Nottingham (0602) 663048
*Heywood, A. N., 9-7 .... (Mr W. A. Stephenson) c/o (0388) 720213
†Hickey, S., 9-0..................... (Mr P. J. Arthur) c/o (0235) 850338
†Hickson, A. G., 9-7.................. (P. Beaumont) c/o (03475) 208
Hill, M. R., 10-2........ (S. Muldoon) (065385) 245
*Hoad, M. R., 10-0 (R. P. C. Hoad) (0273) 477124
Hobbs, P. D., 10-0 .... (J. Gifford, P. J. Hobbs, J. B. Sayers, J. Honeyball) (0903) 743928 or (0860) 729794 (car)
Hobbs, Philip J., 10-0 .... (A. Hobbs) (0984) 40366
*Hodge, R. J., 9-7 Mrs G. Reveley (0653) 600295
*Hodgson, S. P., 9-12 (G. Balding) (026477) 2278
Holbrook, M. J., 9-3.... Mr J. Bolger (056) 43150/8
*Holley, P., 9-11... (W. G. M. Turner, D. Elsworth) c/o (072 53) 528/520
Holmes, P. F., 10-5......... c/o Malton (0653) 3149
*Hood, D. G. W., 9-12 .... (P. J. Hobbs) (0860) 370777 (car) or (0903) 208758 (agent)
Hopwood, C. J., 10-0 (R. Frost) c/o (0364) 42267 or (0823) 680959
†Hoskings, Miss Penelope, 9-7 .... (J. Webber)
*Howe, P. R., 10-0 .... (A. Ingham) (0482) 860513
†Howell, I., 9-5 .... (P. Haslam) (0638) 664525

N.H. Jockeys – Continued

Hower, Miss P., 7-13 (B. Schutz) (0221) 7407029
†Howitt, M. A., 9-0 .... (T. Bulgin)
*Huggan, C. H., 9-10 .... (Mr N. J. Henderson) (0488) 71784
†Hughes, P., 9-7 .... (Mr T. N. Bailey) c/o (0432) 760817
Hughes, R. G., 10-0 ... Burgh Heath (07373) 59995
Humphreys, W., 9-0 ... (T. Greathead, C. Trietline, Mrs J. E. Croft) (0242) 39531 or (0666) 825385 and (043270) 460 agent.
Hurst, J. S., 9-12 .... (D. Barons) (0548) 550411/550006
†Hutchinson, I., 9-12 (0532) 886536 and 886256
Hyde, D. M., 10-0 .... (G. Balding) c/o Weyhill (026 477) 2278
Hyett, R. G., 10-1 (M. Tate, C. F. Jackson, Mrs S. Oliver, J. S. Wright, J. Roper) Bosbury (053 186) 312

*Irvine, W. S., 9-7 .... (R. Hodges, P. Rodford, A. K. Barrow) c/o (045 822) 3922/3292

†Jackson, Andrew, 9-7 .... (D. Gandolfo) c/o (02357) 3242
*Jackson, Miss A. E., 9-7 .... (M. Dickinson)
†Jackson, D. A., 9-10 .... (Mrs M. Reveley) (0287) 50456
*Jackson, M. J., 9-10 .... (Mr R. J. Eckley) c/o (05448) 216
*Jackson, N., 9-7 .... (N. Tinkler) c/o (0653) 85245
James, Miss Sharron, 9-7 .... (M. James) (0948) 4067/2679
†Jarvis, D. A., 9-0 .... (H. Owen) (0495) 302551
†Jenkins, L. E., 9-7 ... (D. Oughton) (090 671) 2113
†Jenner, M., 9-7 .... (T. P. McGovern)
†Johnsey, L. D., 8-6 .... (P. Arthur)
*Johnson, P. M., 9-7 .... (Mr R. G. Frost) c/o (0364) 42267
Johnson, S. N., 10-7 ..... (G. G. Horgan, R. Spicer) (0949) 50752
†Jones, A. D., 9-7 .... (H. Beasley) (027874) 231
Jones, A. E., 10-7 .... (Mrs M. Easton) Great Shefford (048839) 712/742
Jones, C. H., 10-0 .... (0531) 821341
*Jones, D., 9-7 .. (P. Monteith) c/o (031 440) 2309
†Jones, Miss D., 9-7 .... (D. Burchell, L. J. Barratt)
Jones, G. H., 10-7 .... (B. Cambidge) Leysters (056887) 676
Jones, K., 10-2 .... (R. R. Lamb, W. Tinning) (0665) 720260 or (066576) 722
*Jones, M. P., 9-2 .... (R. Dickin) c/o (053) 185644
†Jones, Miss Wendy, 8-4 ..... (Mrs C. Lloyd-Jones) c/o Willington Kelsall (0829) 51143
*Juckes, A. G., 9-7 .... (Mr R. T. Juckes) c/o (0299) 896471

†Kalirai, D. S., 9-7 .... (G. Balding) c/o Weyhill (026 477) 2278
Kane, M. A., 9-7 .... (J. Fox) c/o (0980) 620861
Kavanagh, P. 9-7 ...... (D. Clyde) c/o (0503) 75121
Keightley, S. L., 10-0 ..... (J. Cosgrave, J. Redfern, R. Brotherton) Newmarket (0638) 666070
Kellett, C., 10-0 .... P. Blockley (0964) 562684
†Kelly, P. P., 9-7 .... (Mr Mark Wilkinson) c/o (092586) 713
†Kent, T. J., 9-7 .... (Mr G. A. Pritchard-Gordon) c/o (0638) 662824
†Keogh, M., 9-7 .... (0299) 250953
*Kersey, Miss Susan, 10-0 .... (T. Kersey) (0709) 873166
Kinane, J. K., 9-7 .... (J. K. Oliver, S. G. Payne) (0750) 22110 or (0835) 23814
Kinane, M. J., 9-7 .. (N. Lee-Judson, F. O'Mahony) Worthing (0903) 884935
Kinane, P. P., 9-7 .... c/o (052) 56248
Kinane, T. Jun., 10-0 .... (045) 21739
*Knight, A. J., 9-10 (Mr S. Dow) c/o (03727) 21490
Knight, Stephen Charles, 10-2 .... (D. A. Wilson) (0793) 740710
Knight, Steven George, 9-7 .... (J. F. Cann, Mrs A. Knight) Kentisbeare (0823) 680959
Knox, W., 10-7 .... (M. W. Davies) Abergavenny (0873) 6776
*Kobler, N., 9-10 .... (Mr J. R. Jenkins) c/o (0763) 41141

†Labbe, Miss Wendy, 9-7 .... (M. Stephens) c/o North Curry (0823) 490335/490656
†Laird, A. P., 9-7 .... (Mr Mike O'Neill) c/o (051) 5316887
Landau, G., 10-0 ... (0638) 660212 or (0672) 40809 carphone (0836) 224644
†Larnach, A. A., 9-7 .... (Mr W. A. Stephenson) c/o (0388) 720213
*Lawrence, I. R., 9-7 .... (Mrs N. Sharpe Mr K. C. Bailey) (0860) 823336 (car), (02357) 69671 or c/o (0488) 71483
*Lawson, R., 9-7 .... (P. Taylor, T. Bailey) c/o (0432) 760817
*Leach, N. R., 9-7 .... (Mr G. W. Richards) c/o (08533) 392
Leach, P., 10-5 (M. Pipe, M. Morley) (0488) 71105
*Leahy, D., 9-7 .... c/o (090 567) 233
Leavy, J. F., 10-0 .... (Mrs E. H. Heath) (0763) 87227 and c/o (0763) 41141
*Leech, J. P., 9-7 ...... (R. Akehurst) (0488) 72259 73245 or (0372) 727596
Leech, P., 9-0 .... Navan 54150
*Leech, T. M., 9-7 .... (J. Redmond)
*Leech, T. M., 9-7 ... (J. Redmond) (0483) 892233
*Lees, D., 9-7 .... (Mr J. Spearing) c/o (0789) 772639

N.H. Jockeys – Continued

*Leese, A., 9-10 .... (J. Blundell, Mrs S. Pepper) c/o (0472) 840256
†Leese, M., 9-7 .... (Mr Ronald Thompson) c/o (0302) 845904
*Liddle, P. A., 9-7 .... (M. Chapman) c/o Clipston (085 886) 255
†Linton, A., 9-0 .... (Mr J. S. Wilson) c/o (0292) 266232
Llewellyn, C., 10-0 ... (T. Forster, J. Old, B. Smart, M. Wilkinson, B. Forsey, K. S. Bridgwater) (02357) 3410 (car) (0836) 255286
†Lodder, J., 9-7 .... (F. Jordan, Mrs A. Ratcliff) (0568) 611068 and (0831) 486302 (car)
*Long, Miss Leesa, 9-7 .... (J. Long) Plumpton 0233 890 244
*Loughlin, P., 9-0 ...... (Mr N. Meade) (046) 54197
Lovejoy, J. M., 10-0 .... (P. Haynes, Mrs L. C. Clay) Midhurst (073081) 2403
*Lovejoy, S. P., 9-7 .... (N. Painting) Worcester (0905) 641743
Lower, J. A., 10-0 .... (M. Pipe) Wellington (082347) 3580
Lowry, P., 8-4 .... (045) 32207
Lynch, M. M., 10-0 .... (J. Chugg, J. Webber) (029586) 713 or (0860) 823322 (car) or (0295) 76769
*Lyons, Gary, 10-0 .... (Mr R. Hollinshead) c/o (0543) 490298
*Lyons, Ger., 9-10 .... (Mr M. W. Easterby) c/o (03477) 368 and (0836) 747727 (car)

*Mackey, S. C., 10-0 .... (G. Ham) (093472) 331
*MacNeice, R. J. J., 9-7 .... (M. Pipe) (0823) 289275
Madden, N. P., 10-3 .... (M. Morris, E. P. Harty) (045) 79432/7932
*Madgwick, D. S., 10-3 .... (M. Madgwick) (0705) 258313
†Maguire, M. A., 9-7 c/o Bishop Auckland (0388) 720432
Maher, J. J., 9-7 .... c/o(062) 54129
†Maher, S. J. J., 8-11 .... (Mr R. F. Fisher) c/o (0229) 55819
*Maiden, N. A., 9-7 (Mrs S. Austin) (0751) 31637
Malone, P., 10-3 .... (A. L. Moore) 01 288 2424
*Mann, N. J. W., 9-0 .... (Mr R. J. Holder) c/o (027581) 2192
†Mansell, B. J., 9-7 .... (P. Duggins) c/o (0782) 550115
*Manson, J. P. P., 9-7(Mr J. Mackie) (0283) 78604
Marley, R. J., 10-0 .... (M. H. Easterby) c/o (0653) 696205 or (03476) 482 (agent) and (0836) 326084
†Marston, W. J., 9-7 .... (Mr David Nicholson) c/o (0451) 30417
Martin, A., ... (O. Sherwood)
†Martin, D. M., 9-7 .... (Mr P. Liddle)
Martin, G. J., 9-7 .... (03475) 641 or (0206) 240235
*Martin, R., 10-0 (Mr T. Etherington) (0306) 77529
†Martin, S. D., 9-7 .... (J. Ffitch-Heyes) c/o (0273) 477529 or (0748) 2118
*Mason, S. T., 9-7 .... (Mr R. Curtis) (0372) 277645
†Matthews, D. D., 9-7 .... (Mrs Angela Knight) (0823) 680959
†McCabe, A. J., 9-7 (D. Elsworth) c/o (07253) 528
†McCarthy, J. A., 9-7 .... (Mr T. Casey) c/o (0295) 711686
†McCaskill, G., 9-0 .... c/o (0388) 832465
McCormack, N. P., 9-7 .... (W. Storey) c/o (020755) 259
McCormack, P., 10-5 .... c/o (045) 68148
McCourt, G. M., 10-5 .... (R. Champion, M. McCourt, M. Ryan, S. N. Cole, Miss P. O'Connor, Miss S. Wilton, J. Spearing) Wantage (023559) 501 or (0836) 749191/236625
McCourt, T. G., 9-12 .... (M. Cunningham) (01) 285829
†McCrorie, A., 9-10 .... (K. Bishop)
*McCrystal, S., 9-7 .... (J. D. Davies, W. M. Perrin, H. O'Neill) (076 384) 8113
*McDermott, P. S., 9-11 .... (C. Broad) (0453) 885487 or (045276) 835
McDonald, E., 10-0 .... (M. Connolly) (045) 21465
*McDonald, S. E., 9-12 .... (O. Sherwood) Lambourn (0488) 72263
*McDougall, S. J., 9-7 .... (Mr B. Smart) c/o (0488) 71632
*McEntee, P. S., 9-7 .... (Mr W. Musson) c/o (0638) 663371
*McFarland, W. J., 9-10 .... (Mr G. B. Balding, R. T. Juckes, J. H. Baker, G. Yardley) (0235) 765135 and (0836) 507631 (car)
McGhin, R., 9-0 .... c/o Ashtead (03722) 74059
*McGiff, B. C., 9-7 .... (C. R. Beever) (0347) 6482 (agent) or (0302) 725939
McGivern, T. P., 10-8 .... (0405) 46006
McGlinchey, G., 9-7 .... (0808662) 670272
McIlfatrick, C., 9-7 .... (G. G. Morgan) Market Rasen (0673) 842633
McKeever, N., 9-7 .... (P. Hughes) 0503 21882/21891
*McKeever, S. W., 9-8 .... (Mr W. T. Kemp) c/o (0233) 72525
McKeown, D. W. E., 10-0 .... (W. Carter) (01 381) 9318 (agent) or (0836) 672574 carphone
McKinley, E., 9-7 .... (J. Gifford) (090 387) 2226
McLaughlin, J. F. S., 9-10 ... (M. Ryan, S. McNeill, C. Allen, C. Spares, J. Pearce) (0638) 668115
†McLellan, A. D., 9-7 .... (Mr R. J. Manning) c/o (0454) 773274
*McLelland I. W., 9-7 .... (0653) 692835
McNeill, S. R. O., 10-0 ..... (A. Madwar, D. Ringer, R. Spicer, L. Corbett, R. Robinson) Great Shefford (048839) 8861
*Meade, D. N., 9-7 .... (Mr D. R. Gandolfo) c/o (02357) 3242

N.H. Jockeys – Continued

Meagher, M. G., 10-0 .... (M. O'Neill) (0772) 612120 or (051531) 6887 or (051) 5482521
Melia, P., 9-7 .... c/o (045 276) 459
†Meredith, D., 8-0 .... (Mr Robert Dickin) c/o (053185) 644
Merrigan, A., 10-0 .... (W. A. Stephenson) c/o Rushyford (0388) 720213 or 813877 (night)
*Midgley, P. T., 9-7 .... (Mr P. A. Blockley, G. Kelly) c/o (0964) 542583
†Milburn, S., 9-10 (M. H. Easterby) (065 386) 600
*Millar, P. N. E., 9-7 .... (Mr W. G. Preece) c/o (095286) 249
*Millen, Miss F. E., 8-6 .... (Miss A. Sinclair) (0580) 62076
Millman, B. R., 10-0 .... M. Stephens) (0884) 41247/253070
†Milner, R. G. A., 9-7 .... (Mr N. Henderson) c/o (0488) 72259
Mitchell, Shaun. 10-0 .... (0623) 823800
†Moffatt, D. J., 9-7 (Mr D. Moffatt) (05395) 36689
*Moloney, M. J., 9-7 .... (Mr G. Richards) c/o (08533) 392
Mooney, J. W., 10-7 ...... (T. Craig (031665) 8616
Mooney, K. P., 10-0 .... (F. Walwyn, M. Bradstock, J. Redmond, B. Smart, R. Brotherton) Lambourn (0488) 71555/72176
Moore, Miss C. L., 8-10 (A. Moore) (0273) 681679
Moore, G. L., 10-4 .... (J. J. Bridger, A. Moore) Brighton (0273) 681679
Moore, J. S., 10-0 .... (0264) 50706 or (0985) 6286
*Moore, R. W., 9-7 .... (Mr G. P. Enright) c/o (0273) 479183
Moran, M., 9-7 .... (0504) 31012
*Morgan, A. P., 10-0 .... (0793) 790230
*Morgan, G. P., 9-7 .... (Mr R. J. Manning) c/o (0454) 773274
Morgan, K., 10-7 .... (J. Dreaper) (01) 350023
*Morgan, P. M., 9-7 .... (J. Berry) (02407) 3436
†Morgan, Paul, S., 9-7 .... (D. H. Jones) (0443) 202515
Morgan, Tom, 10-3 .... (0594) 60555
Morgan, T. W., 10-2 .... (0989) 63228
Morris, Mrs C. L., 8-10 .... c/o (0273) 681679
Morris, Derrick, 10-0 ...... (R. Curtis) (0420) 22629 or 0372 277645 (office)
Morris, S., 10-0 .... (G. Balding) (0264) 50706
Morris, W. A., 10-0 ..... (W. G. Morris, B. K. Wells) (0299) 250686 (0836) 363666 (car)
Morshead, S. R., 10-4 .... (J. Roberts) Birtsmorton (068 481) 275
*Mowen, C., 9-7 .... (Mr J. R. White)
*Muggeridge, M. P., 9-7 .... (N. A. Smith)
*Muggeridge, R. J., 9-7 .... (B. Stevens) Guildford (0483) 898902
*Mulholland, A. B., 9-10 .... (S. Christian, W. G. Morris) (090567) 382 and (0836) 784439 (car)
†Mullaney, L. A., 9-12 .... (M. H. Easterby)
*Mulligan, M., 9-7 .... (J. W. Mooney) c/o (031 665) 6876
Mullins, A., 9-10 .... (088) 553867
*Murphy, A. T., 9-10 .... (D. McCain) c/o Southport (0704) 66007/69677
†Mumford, Miss H., 9-7 .... (Mr P. Jones) (067286) 472
†Murphy, B. J., 9-10 .... (Mr G. A. Hubbard) c/o (072876) 250
Murphy, D., 10-0 .... (B. Curley) (0638) 77702
Murphy, D. J., 10-0 .... (D. A. Wilson, W. Musson) c/o (0638) 77645
Murphy, E. R., 10-0 .... (J. Gifford F. O'Mahony, T. Etherington) Worthing (0903) 60687 and (090387) 3957
*Murphy, F. J. C., 9-0 .... (A. Davison)
Murphy, M. F., 10-0 .... (Mr S. R. Bowring) (0623) 883081/823800
*Murphy, S. J. C., 9-0 .... (A. Davison)
†Murray, D., 9-7 .... (Mr Owen O'Neill) c/o (0242) 673275
*Murtagh, F. P., 9-7 .... (Mr J. J. O'Neill) c/o (08534) 555
*Mustow, D. J., 9-7 .... (Mr. A. Turnell) (02357) 68614

†Neaves, J. P., 9-0 .. (Mr Bill Turner) (096322) 523
*Neighbour, S. P., 9-9 .... (J. Gifford) (0903) 872521
†Neilson, J. L., 9-7 .... (Mr D. Smith) c/o (0388) 603317
†Newey, A. S., 9-7 .... (Mr J. A. C. Edwards) c/o (098987) 259
Newman, G., 10-0 .... (A. Jarvis) Tewkesbury (0684) 294153
Nicholls, P. F., 10-4 .... (D. Barons, P. W. Davis) (0548) 550326 or (0454) 612900
Niven, P., 10-0 .... (Mrs G. R. Reveley, B. Ellison, J. E. Brockbank, N. Bycroft, R. F. Fisher) (0904) 647213 (agent) or (0860) 260999 (car) and (0751) 32630
†Nixon, A., 9-7 .... (J. Eyre)
Nolan, B., 9-3 .... (J. Hayden) (0503) 41592
*Nolan, C. D., 9-5 .... (F. Lee)
Nolan, D. A., 10-5 .... (P. Monteith, Mrs A. Bell) Edinburgh (031 440) 2309

O'Brien, A. J., 10-0 .... (052) 38258
O'Brien, K. F., 9-11 .... (061) 88300
†O'Connor, C., 9-7 ..... (Mr D. J. G. Murray-Smith)
O'Connor, D. H., 9-12 .... (053) 58942
*O'Connor, N., 10-0 .... (Mr A. Stringer) c/o (0845) 401329
O'Donnell, P. F., 9-10 c/o Tarporley (08293) 2716
†O'Donovan, E. F., 9-7 .... (N. Gaselee) (0488) 71503

N.H. Jockeys – Continued

†O'Dowd, B., 9-7 .... (Mr A. J. Wilson) (0242) 244713
O'Dwyer, C. 9-10 .... (045) 32544
*O'Dwyer, P. M., 9-11 .... (Miss A. L. M. King) c/o (0789) 205087
*O'Gorman, J. M., 9-11 .... (Mrs S. A. Bramall) (0845) 401287
O'Hagan, A. T., 10-0 .... (K. White) (0584) 810627
*O'Hara, L., 9-7 .... (R. Bennett) (0628) 30290 and (0759) 71586 (agent)
†O'Hare, L. N., 9-0 .... (Mr R. A. Bennett)
Old, G., 9-12 .... (Dorchester (0305) 62313
†Oldershaw, D. B., 9-7 .... (C. Roach) c/o (0726) 850701
Olivefalk, Miss M., 9-0 .... c/o (0505) 42221
†O'Neill, E. M., 9-0 .... (G. Gracey)
O'Neill, G. M. 9-9 .... c/o (063) 90676
O'Neill, S. J., 10-0 .... (P. Brookshaw, J. Wharton, F. Hall, W. R. Whiston, R. Spicer, J. Brockbank, R. Francis) Bunbury (0829) 3260660
O'Neill, T., 9-7 .... (01) 354386
Orkney, R. A., 10-0 .... (R. C. Armytage, R. E. Barr, B. Wilkinson) (03476) 482 (agent) or (0836) 326084
O'Rourke, Ann, 7-4 .... (J. Hayden) (045) 81403
†Orton, N. A. P., 10-0 .... (K. Bridgwater)
Osborne, J. A., 10-0 .... (W. M. Perrin, K. Morgan, O. Sherwood) (0488) 398931 or (0860) 533422 (car)
*O'Sullivan, D. K., 9-12 .... (Mr R. J. O'Sullivan) c/o (0243) 267563
†O'Ware, J., 9-2 .... (Mr J. S. Wilson) c/o (0292) 266232

*Parker, A., 9-7 .... (W. A. Stephenson) c/o (0388) 720213
†Pearson, S. L., 9-10 .... (F. Walwyn) (0488) 71555
†Peill, M. A., 9-7 .... (Mrs G. R. Reveley)
†Pengelly, Miss S., 9-7 .... (Mr T. B. Hallett) c/o (0752) 846829
Pepper, M. N., 10-0 .... (E. Carter, H. Fleming) (0889) 567310
*Perratt, W. F., 9-7 .... (Mrs J. Pitman) c/o (0488) 71714
Perrett, M. E., 9-7 .... (R. Bennett, D. Nugent, G. Harwood) (0903) 892895 or (0836) 221273 (car)
*Pike, D. R., 10-0 .... (Mr W. Clay) c/o (0782) 392131
*Pinfield, T. R., 10-0 .... (J. Gifford, B. Smart) (0903) 873984 or (090671) 3984
†Pipe, D., 9-12 (Miss S. J. Wilton) (0782) 550861
†Piper, G. E., 9-7 (D. Barrons) c/o (0548) 550411
Pitman, M. A., 10-3 .... (M. Pipe, Mrs J. Pitman) (08844) 41222 and (0488) 71714
†Plester, A. G., 9-7 .... (C. Trietline) (0789) 750752
*Plumb, P., 9-7 .... (Mrs J. Pitman) c/o (0488) 71714
†Plumridge, S. C., 9-9 .... (N. B. Thomson)
*Poole, D., 9-7 .... c/o (0555) 851851
†Pope, Miss L., 8-12 .... (J. Baker) (0398) 31646
*Potts, T. M., 9-7 ...... (Mr A. W. Potts) (9261) 750
Powell, A., 10-0 .... (J. Fowler) (045) 81645
Powell, B. G., 10-0 ... (G. Ham, R. S. C. Robinson, B. Smart, D. Elsworth, G. Roe, Mrs G. E. Jones, H. Willis A. K. Barrow, W. McKenzie-Coles, P. Connors) (0793) 782286 or (0860) 314745
†Powell, T. J., 9-8 .... (A. Moore) c/o Brighton (0273) 681679
*Price, A. J., 10-0 ..... (W. J. Price) (0495) 303655
Price, C. M., 10-0 .... (G. M. Price) Llangorse (087 484) 212
Price, M. I., 10-0 .... (G. H. Price) (056882) 235
†Pridham, Miss H. A., 9-7 .... (Mr H. O'Neill) c/o (0306) 711723
†Priest, C., 8-0 .... (Mr N. Bycroft) (03475) 641
*Prince, C. J., 9-7 ... (B. Morgan) c/o (028375) 304
*Protheroe, T., 9-7 .... (Mr P. Ransom) c/o (056886) 253
†Pullin, J. R., 9-7 .... (J. McConnochie)

*Quinn, A. J., 9-9 (Miss L. Siddall) (0532) 842982
Quinn, J. J., 10-0 .... (P. Wigham) (0653) 695450
*Quinn, J. R. J., 10-0 .... (076885) 374

*Railton, J. A., 10-0 .... (T. Forster M. Oliver, T. Bill) (0488) 71890 or (0860) 282467 (car)
*Rayner, N. J., 9-12 .... (Mr D. Gandolfo) c/o (02357) 3242
Reed, W. T., 10-2 .... (E. Robson, J. J. O'Neill, W. G. Reed, J. Johnson) (0434) 344201 and (0836) 326084 (car)
†Rees, D. C., 9-7 ..... (B. Palling) c/o (04463) 2089
*Reynolds, P., 9-7 .... c/o (0372) 377209
†Richardson, S. P., 9-7 .... (W. W. Haigh) c/o (0653) 694428
Richards, M. R., 10-0 .... (Mrs L. Clay, K. Ivory, O. Sherwood) (0243) 551440
Richards, P. L., 10-2 .... (R. Pocock, T. B. Hallett, P. Rodford) Day: Holford (027 874) 405 and Evening: Nether Stowey (0278) 733203
Richmond, C., 9-12 .... (0522) 810578
*Richmond. D. S., 9-7 .... (Mr M. C. Pipe) c/o (0823) 338358
*Ricketts, J. M., 9-7 .... (N. J. Henderson) c/o 0488 72259
Robson, J. M., 10-2 .... (Mrs B. Waring) (0793) 740611
*Roche, N., 10-0 .... (John White) c/o (0372) 724018
Rogers, H. 9-10 .... (041) 53353
*Rolls, A. M., 9-11 ..... (A. Turnell) (023 57) 67885

N.H. Jockeys – Continued

†Roper, A. J., 9-7 .... (Mr B. A. McMahon) c/o (0827) 62901
†Rose, D., 10-0 .... (H. O'Neill) c/o Dorking (0306) 711723
†Rowe, G. T., 9-10 .... (J. T. Gifford) c/o (0903) 872226
Rowe, R., 10-0 .... (R. Chapman, J. Gifford T. Etherington, J. Sayers) Storrington (0903) 742871 or (0860) 398167 (car)
Rowell, R., 10-0 .... (M. J. Bolton, J. Long) Polegate (03212) 4681
Ryan, C., 9-12 .... (J. Cosgrave, J. P. Smith M. W. Easterby) (03477) 368
*Ryan, C. J. M., 9-10 .... (M. W. Easterby) c/o (03477) 368 or (03477) 794 or (0904) 647213 (agent)
*Ryan, J. B. 9-0....... (Mr M. Ryan) (0638) 664172
Ryan, K. A., 9-12 .... (J. P. Smith) c/o (044854) 689
Ryan, T. J., 9-7 .... (E. O'Grady) (052) 56378

†Salt, Miss V. M., 9-0 .... (Mr R. J. Weaver) c/o (0530) 243105
*Saltmarsh, S. A., 9-7 .... (Mr E. Wheeler) c/o (0488) 71650
*Scope, G. J., 9-7 .... (R. Goldie) (0292) 314323/317222
Scudamore, P. M., 10-0 (D. A. Wilson, C. Brooks, M. Pipe, N. Twiston-Davies) (04515) 741 or (0836) 514820 carphone
Seward, C., 9-2 .... Cowbridge (04463) 2089
Sharpe, A. J., 10-0 .... (0531) 81408
*Sharratt, M., 9-12 (M. J. Charles) (0926) 493878
†Sharratt, M. R., 9-7 .... (E. Owen, Jun.) c/o (08244) 264
Shaw, D., 9-10 .... (R. Hobson, W. Mackie F. Gibson) c/o Mansfield (0623) 743661 or 94748811
Sheridan, B., 10-0 .... (045) 77511
Shilston, S. R. W., 10-0 .... (James Bennett) Lambourn (0488) 72387
Shoemark, I. W., 9-10 ..... (S. Mellor, R. Akehurst, S. A. Bowen) (0793) 8288054 or (0836) 638615 (car)
Shortt, J., 10-0 .... (J. Chugg, P. O'Connor, C. C. Trietline, J. Bukovets) c/o (0789) 750833/773296 or (0860) 823366 (car)
†Simpson, W. R., 10-3 .... (R. Hodges) c/o (045 822) 3922
Sims, K. R., 10-4 .... (050 982) 2288
†Skelton, J. A., 9-0 .... (Mr P. J. Bevan) c/o (0889) 500670
*Skyrme, D. V., 9-7 ...... (P. Harris, W. J. L. Paul, R. S. C. Robinson, J. White (044282) 7830
Slattery, A. J., 9-7 .... (E. O'Grady) (052) 56530
*Slattery, J. V., 9-7 .... (O. O'Neill) 0242 673275

Sleator, P. M., 10-12 .... (D. Clyde) (045) 53190
*Smith, A. G., 9-7 .... (J. Howard Johnson) c/o (0388) 762113
*Smith, A. S., 9-7 .... (O. Sherwood) (0488) 72406
Smith, C. A., 10-2 .... (M. Tate, W. Musson, B. Key) (06845) 5900
*Smith, C. N., 9-7 .... (J. Parkes) (03476) 482 and (0836) 326084 (car)
Smith-Eccles S., 10-3 .... (N. Henderson, Mrs D. Haine, Miss S. Wilton, G. Pritchard-Gordon) Newmarket (0638) 77590 and (0836) 241780 (car)
†Smith, J. P., 9-10 .... (N. Henderson) c/o (0488) 72259
*Smith, N., 9-7 .. (Mr J. Parkes, Lady Ann Bowlby) (0287) 39312
*Smith, V., 9-7 .... (I. Campbell, J. White) (0638) 668972
*Smyth, U. P., 10-0 .... (Mr N. J. Henderson) (0964) 562991
*Somers, A. B., 10-5 .... (P. Daly)
*Stanford, A. M., 9-7 .... (M. O'Neill) c/o (051) 5316887
*Stephens, W. E., 9-7 .... (G. Oldroyd) (09442) 8126 (0653) 695911
†Sterry, W. A., 9-7 .... (Mr D. R. Tucker) c/o (0823) 681059
*Stevens, M., 9-12 .... (B. Stevens) (0962) 883030
*Stirk, D., 9-0 .... (J. Leigh)
*Stockell, Ann., 9-7 .... (Mr M. Barraclough) (092684) 3332
†Stone, Mrs T., 9-7 .... (Mr K. G. Wingrove) c/o (092681) 3958
Storey, B., 10-0 ..... (F. Storey, S. Payne, I Jordan, A. Goodfellow, Mrs D. Thomson, J. Johnson) Kirkinton (022 875) 331/376
Storey Miss F. J., 10-5 .... (0207) 55259
Stronge, R. M., 10-0 ... (M. Naughton, B. Stevens) Great Shefford (048 839) 650
†Sullivan, D. A., 9-7 (N. Tinkler) c/o (0653) 85245
Sullivan, J. M., 10-0 (K. Prendergast) (045) 21387
†Supple, J. A., 9-7 .... (Mr W. A. Stephenson) c/o (0388) 720213
Supple, K. R., 9-7 (R. Shaw, J. Upson) (08534) 555
*Supple, R. J., 9-0 .... (Mr J. J O'Neill) (0609) 748241 (agent)
Swan, C. F. 9-0...... (D. T. Hughes, Capt. D. Swan) (045) 21490/22217
Swan, Miss N., 9-7 .... c/o (0505) 42221
*Sweeney, A. P., 9-7 ... (B. Curley) c/o Exning 8386

Taaffe, T. J., 10-0 .... (A. L. Moore) (045) 31455
†Taylor, J. A., 9-7 .... (Mr J. Spearing) c/o (0789) 772639
*Teague, R. J., 9-7 .... (Mr C. P. E. Brooks) c/o (0488) 72077
Tegg, D. R., 10-0 .... (B. Smart, G. J. Powell, R. S. C. Robinson) (0432) 352674

N.H. Jockeys – Continued

*Telfer, D. M., 10-0 .... (Mrs S. Lamyman) (065883) 764/260
†Tenanty, A. P., 9-7 .. (P. Burgoyne) (023 559) 688
*Tierney, E., 9-7 .... (Mr A. P. James) (053186) 319/264
*Thomson, G. J., 9-7 .... (J. Oliver) (045087) 216
Tinker, N. D., 10-7 Burythorpe (065 385) 245/512
†Tinker, S. P., 9-10 .... (Mr J. M. Jefferson) c/o (0653) 697225
*Tinkler, S., 9-7 .... (0653) 695981
†Tinlin, Miss J., 8-3 .... (Miss M. J. Benson) c/o (043481) 203
†Todd, I., 9-0 .. (Mr P. Mitchell) c/o (0372) 273729
*Tory. A. S., 10-0 .... (Mr N. R. Mitchell) c/o (0305) 68069
Townend, K., 10-0.......... (J. Wardle, D. Weeden) (0761) 232705
Townend, T., 10-0........................ (J. Murphy) (058) 56129 and (021) 642311
†Townsley, Lucy., 9-7 .... (Mrs P. Townsley) (030677) 492
*Traylor, K. G., 9-7................. (W. G. M. Turner) Corton Denham (096 322) 523
Treacy, M., 9-10 .... (D. Lavarack) (0503) 73484
Treacy, S., 10-0......................... (0502) 26539
*Trevor-Jones, R., 9-7......................... (T. Bill) c/o (0530) 415881/416538 or c/o (0401) 62991
†Trueman, P., 9-7 (J. R. Jenkins) c/o (0763) 41141
Tuck, P. C., 10-2.......... Calthwaite (076 885) 374 or (0759) 71586 (agent) or (0836) 719795 (car)
*Tuite, J. M., 10-0.................. (Mrs J. Pitman) c/o (0488) 71714
*Turner, S., 9-7.......... (P. O'Connor, J. Roberts, K. A. Morgan, R. M. Whitaker) (0937) 62690 or (0609) 748241 (agent) and (0860) 343470 (car)
*Turner, Miss Tracy., 9-7.............. (082281) 237
Twite, J., 9-12 .... (C. Holmes) c/o 02407 5964
†Tynan, T. A., 9-7 .... (P. Howling)
Tyrrell, E., 9-7........................... (045) 31650

†Urwin, W. D., 9-7 .... (Mr N. Chamberlain) (0388) 832465

*Verling, P. M., 9-10... (Mr D. J. G. Murray-Smith) (0488) 73125 or (0903) 208758 (agent)
Vincent, Miss Lorna, 9-2.................. (D. J. Bell, Miss E. Sneyd, A. Chamberlain) (0793) 782286

Waite, E. G., 10-4..................... (02357) 69732
†Walker, Miss E., 8-0 .... (S. T. Harris) (02403) 4138
Wall, T. R., 9-7.............. (H. Dale, R. T. Juckes, B. McMahon, P. J. Anderson, P. J. Bevan, Mrs M. Easton) (095289) 743 or (0860) 256211 (car)
Walsh, K. B., 9-7 .... (045) 32544
*Ward, R. J., 9-7 .... (Mr I. P. Wardle) c/o (0749) 75293
*Wathen, J. Q., 9-10 .... (D. Wintle) c/o Westbury-on-Severn (045 276) 459
Webb, A., 10-0.............. (P. Haynes, K. Morgan, Miss A. King, N. Painting, Mr C. Weedon, T. Hallett) Stratford (0789) 68812 (0451) 31685
*Welsh, A., 9-7 .... (J. R. Jenkins) 03727
*West, Miss Alyson, 9-0..................... (B. Wise)
†West, R. D., 9-7.......................... (R. Holder) c/o (027 581) 2192/4185
*Wheatley, G., 10-5.................. (Mr W. Bentley) c/o (0969) 22289
White, J. A., 10-0........... (J. Jenkins (1st claim), N. Henderson, M. Bradstock) Lambourn (0488) 72831
White, M., 9-0 ...... (N. Meade) (046) Navan 54197
*White, T. P., 9-7.............. (W. A. Stephenson, T. W. Cunningham, R. E. Barr) (0388) 720432
†Whitham, A. D., 9-7 .... (Mr R. Earnshaw) c/o (0423) 567790
Wilkinson, D., 9-7 (Mrs S. M. Austin, P. C. Curtis, C. Thornton) (0969) 22798 or (0488) 72670
†Wilkinson, K., 9-7 (F. H. Lee) c/o (0625) 533250
*Willey, C. E., 9-10... (D. Wintle) c/o (045 276) 459
†Williams, D. J., 9-7 .... (Mr J. M. Bradley) c/o (0291) 622486
Williams, D. L., 10-10............... (D. L. Williams) (0386) 852569
Williams, G. S., 10-0 .... (T. Bill, B. C. Morgan) (0283) 225358
Williams, John A. N., 10-0............... (G Balding, Mrs B. Waring) Badminton (045421) 622
Williams, Mark., 9-10 .... (W. R. Williams) c/o (0392) 81558
Williams, Michael, 10-0............ (M. Scudamore) (0823) 665156 and (0836) 588690 (carphone)
†Williams, P. D., 9-7 (F. Jordan) c/o (056882) 281
*Williams, S. D., 9-0 .... (Mr J. A. Glover) c/o (0909) 475425
*Williams, T. J., 9-7................. Bishops Cleeve (0242 67) 3275
Williamson, N., 9-0...................... (023) 41217
*Williamson, N., 9-7 .... (Mr J. A. C. Edwards) c/o (098987) 259
*Wilson, A. C., 9-10.................... (G. Richards) c/o (08533) 392
†Wilson, G. M., 10-3..................... (A. Madwar) c/o (063877) 429
†Wilson, R. J., 9-0 .... (0969) 23350
*Wilton, Miss S. J., 9-7...................... (H. Dale)
†Winterbotham, J. R., 9-10 .... (G. Moore) c/o (0969) 23823
Wonnacott, D. J., 10-3.................... (T. Hallett, Miss J. Wonnacott, R. Pincombe) (0822) 66416 or (082287) 215 (day)
†Woodall, C., 9-7......... (Mr R. D. E. Woodhouse) c/o (065381) 637
†Woods, A. T., 9-4 .... (Mr J. A. C. Edwards) c/o (098987) 259/315

N.H. Jockeys – Continued

Woods, F., 9-7 .... (01) 350189
Woods, S. P. C., 9-11 .... (F. Durr, M. Skinner, H. Collingridge, J. Norton, J. A. C. Edwards, R. Dods) (0638) 715755 or (0860) 334898 (car)
*Woolley, T. I. 9-7 .... (B. Byford) (0206) 240235
Worthington, W. M., 10-0 .... (K. S. Bridgwater, Mrs G. M. Rees, J. Dooler) (0724) 863347
Wright, B. J., 10-7 .... (T. Hallett, S. Holmes, C. Wildman) (0488) 72688
*Wright, I. C., 9-12 .... (0984) 40941
Wyer, L. A., 10-0 .... (M. H. Easterby, J. J. O'Neill) Kirby Misperton (0653) 694776 or (0759) 71586 (agent)
Wyner, H., 9-7 ..... (R. Hodges) c/o (045822) 3922

Yeoman, M. H., 10-0 .... (062682) 442

Handicap Book every Thursday

- Start checking out the weekend racecards on Thursday with Raceform Handicap Book.
- Complete information on every runner.
- Expert previews on all meetings.
- Collect the Weekly form-book pull-outs.

There is full index every week.

- Latest news from Newmarket, Epsom, Ireland and many more.

It's all this and so much more which gives Raceform Handicap Book its winning image. So order your copy from your newsagent now and make next Saturday your most successful yet.

AMATEUR RIDERS

Riding weights and telephone numbers.

Akehurst, J., 10-7, ... (037 27) 27596
Albion, Miss D. A., 8-7, ... (0734) 774582
Allison, Miss J. K., 9-5, ... (04882) 433
Allison, Miss K., 9-0, ... (0488) 72140
Alner, R., 11-3, ... (025 86) 271
Alston, Mrs S. Y., 8-10, ... (0772) 612120
Anderson, K., 10-0, ... (0461 15) 482
Andrews, S., 10-12, ... (0582) 21325
Andrews, S. R., 11-2, ... (046 276) 263
Arbuthnot, Mrs D., 8-6, ... (0635) 578427
Armytage, Miss J., 8-0, ... (0638) 660142
Armytage, M. D., 10-3, ... (0638) 664680
Ashton, M., 10-7, ... (0283) 226046
Avery, P. J., 9-7, ... (0226) 790685

Bailey, E., 10-0, ... (02357) 67547
Bailey Mrs T. L., 8-7, ... (0488) 71483
Baillie, Maj. H. A., 11-7, ... (057 32) 4684
Balding, Miss C., 10-0, ... (0635) 298274
Banahan, J. R., 10-5, ... (045) 21490
Barham, K. N., 10-3, ... (0526) 861023
Barker, D., 10-7, ... (9378) 266
Barkes, G. W. N., 10-3, ... (066 16) 230
Barlow, D., 10-6, ... (02357) 3128
Barlow, J. G. R., 12-0, ... (0270) 762036
Barlow, W., 11-7, ... (082 922) 316
Barons, R. D. P., 10-7, ... c/o (0548) 550326
Barrow, Miss J., 10-7, ... (0278) 732413
Batters, M., 11-10, ... (072589) 375 or
c/o (07253) 646
Baxter, Miss S. E., 8-7, ... c/o (0827) 62901
Bealby, C. J., 11-3, ... (0476) 72749
Beasley, Miss C. J., 9-0, ... (0952) 460636
Belamy, R., 9-7, ... (043) 270277
Belcher, Miss S. J., 9-11, ... (0580) 200039
Belding, Miss G. V., 9-7, ... (0638) 662009
Bell, Mrs G. P., 9-3, ... c/o (0638) 666567
Bellamy, R. J., 9-7, ... (0884) 41276
Benneyworth, D. C., 9-10, ... c/o (0488) 72928
Berry, A., 11-7, ... (0524) 791179
Berry, Mrs J., 9-7, ... (0524) 791179
Berry, J., 9-7, ... (0235) 833297
Bethell, Mrs L., 8-2, ... (0964) 562996
Bethell, W. A., 11-0, ... (0964) 562996
Bilborough, Miss S., 7-10, ... (0638) 667997
Billings, D. M., 11-10, ... (0789) 292526
Billot, Miss S. A., 8-11, ... (0488) 84285
Bishop, K., 10-7, ... (027 874) 255
Bissell, G. J., 9-7, ... (0544) 267221
Bissill, W. H., 10-3, ... (0949) 50226
Blackford, Miss L. A., 10-8, ... (0964) 562996
Black, Miss D., 9-7, ... (0930) 51354
Blakeney, Miss J., 9-10, ... (038086) 245
Bloom, Miss C. A., 10-7, ... (0953) 603137
Bloom, N., 11-1, ... (0953) 603137
Bloor, D. R., 11-0, ... (0455) 291739
Boggis, Mrs J. E., 8-12, ... (0993) 71868
Bosley, M., 10-0, ... (0993) 850212
Bowker, M. T., 10-7, ... (0448) 60533
Bowlby, Mrs A., 9-6, ... (0488) 72210
Bowlby, A. A. F. S., 10-9, ... (05295) 242
Bradburn, J. G., 10-7, ... (033781) 325
Bradburn, Mrs S. C., 7-10, ... (033781) 325
Bradley, Mr N., 9-7, ... c/o (0789) 205087
Bradstock, M., 9-7, ... (048 839) 258
Brait, F., 9-7, ... (0626) 65899
Bridge, Miss H., 9-7, ... (0562) 730284
Bridgett, C. J., 10-0, ... (063087) 2501
Broad, Miss B. F., 8-4, ... (094 881) 226
Brockbank, T., 11-3, ... (0965) 21582
Bronson, Miss E., 8-7, ... (0689) 54749
Brookes, N. H., 10-12, ... (024 267) 5037
Brown, R. H., 10-10, ... (0439) 71672 or
(0751) 71650
Brown, Miss S. R., 8-10, ... (0638) 662063
Brown, Mr S. R., 8-9, ... (0638) 662063
Browne, Miss C. B., 9-4, ... c/o Curragh (045) 41255
Brunt, R. J., 10-7, ... (0623) 860109
Buckley, M. A., 9-7, ... (0653) 600295
Buckley, Miss V. J., 10-0, ... (0924) 474440
Budd, Mrs C., 10-0, ... (0278) 662902
Bulgin, Mrs N., 8-12, ... (0747) 811648
Bullard, S. R., 10-7, ... (0638) 669780
Burke, Mrs E. M., 9-3, ... (0763) 45006
Burley, J. M., 9-7, ... (0302) 725939
Burnett-Wells. C., 9-7, ... (0903) 872226
Burnham, A. R., 9-7, ... (9786) 526
Bush, N., 11-4, ... (0225) 891293
Bush, S., 10-7, ... (0249) 782317
Butler, Mrs E. L., 8-7, ... (0273) 477254
Bycroft, Miss A. S., 7-12, ... (03475)641

Camacho, Miss J., 9-7, ... (0653) 694901
Cambidge, J. R., 10-0, ... c/o (095276) 249
Campbell, C. W., 9-7, ... (054781) 627
Cannon, Mrs L., 10-0, ... (09328) 67021
Carden, Miss C. M., 8-12, ... (0625) 829748
Carden, J., 10-12, ... (0625) 829748
Carr, Miss Y. E., 9-12, ... (0388) 710014
Carrier, Mrs J. S., 10-7, ... (028 484) 278
Carter, Miss G., 8-7, ... (0653) 3522
Cazalet, E. S., 12-0, ... (0273) 890207
Cecil, Mrs J., 9-0, ... (0638) 662387
Champness, R. G. S., 11-5, ... (0242) 529280
Chard, Miss H., 9-0, ... (0749) 72648
Charlesworth, M., 9-7, ... (978) 73564
Charlton. S., 9-7, ... (0287) 50456
Chesney, Dr. D., 10-3, ... (0305) 65450

Amateur Riders – Continued

Clark, Miss M., 8-7, ... (0638) 730052
Clay, Miss D., 9-12, ... (0782) 392131
Clay, T., 11-7, ... (0243) 551440
Clifford, B. M., 9-7, ... (0984) 40253
Clinton, P., 10-7, ... (0889) 590614
Close, P. L., 9-7, ... (0638) 730480
Cockram, D. D. L., 11-0, ... (023 57) 2399
Collen, Miss S., 9-0, ... (045) 97736
Collins, P., 9-0, ... (0273) 477124
Constantine, T., 9-7, ... (0993) 3594
Coonan, A., 10-0, ... (01) 605704
Cope, A. R., 10-0, ... (0223) 834592
Cornelius, Miss M., 9-0, ... (0903) 892895
Cosgrove, D. J. S., 10-10, ... (0638) 661961
Cosgrove, G. D., 10-0, ... (0235) 833535
Costello, T. S., 10-0, ... (061) 71242
Cowell, R. M. H., 10-3, ... (0638) 730329
Cowell, S. A., 10-0, ... (0621) 87310
Cowley, S., 9-7, ... (0242) 580092
Cox, Mrs J. R., 9-7, ... (042) 34391
Craggs, P. F., 10-4, ... (067 072) 260
Crawford, Mrs J., 9-0, ... (0530) 60279
Crawford, Miss M. A., 8-12, ... c/o (0664) 812019
Crossland, M. R., 9-7, ... (0482) 882520
Crossley, Mrs J., 8-5, ... (0638) 751367/660229
Crothers, Miss C., 8-8, ... c/o (0502) 29017
Cumani, Mrs S., 9-0, ... (0638) 665432
Cundall, C. J., 10-4, ... (09444) 70676
Curling, Miss P., 10-5, ... (027874) 405
Curran, P. P., 9-7, ... (062) 54322

Dalton, A. N., 11-0, .. (095 271) 656/(0989) 62250
Danahar, J. A., 11-4, ... (0242) 42000
Darby, K., 10-10, ... (0768) 63141/65315
Darby, M. V., 10-7, ... (0299) 60251
Dare, Miss A., 9-7, ... (0454) 778778
Darke, R., 10-7, ... c/o (0548) 550411
Darling, D. W., 10-0, ... (0361) 83569
Davenport, Miss N., 8-0, ... (0568) 2673
Davey, F. W., 10-13, ... (01-699) 8393
Davies, Miss J., 9-7, ... (0748) 4630
Davis, R. J., 9-0, ... (038 682) 600
Davison, Miss Z. C., 7-12, ... (040376) 700 or (0344) 890461
Deeprose, A., 9-7, ... (0424) 712241 and (0831) 109947
Deniel, Miss A. J., 8-10, ... (0653) 692288
Denson, A., 9-10, ... (038 684) 1070
D'Esterré Roberts, Miss S., 8-9, ... (0638) 662824
Dickin, Mrs K., 9-7, ... (095 286) 439
Dickin, S., 10-7, ... (095 286) 439
Dore, C., 10-7, ... (061) 88389
Downing, R. S., 10-4, ... (0787) 61766
Doyle, P. J., 9-10, ... (08533) 392
Dreeling, P. J., 10-6, ... (045) 21490
Drysdale, J. C., 10-10, ... (031 332) 7148
Drysdale, R., 10-9, ... (033 77) 238
Dudgeon, A. S., 10-7, ... (0360) 22391
Duggan, D., 10-7, ... c/o (056) 882281
Dukes, J., 10-0, ... (096 274) 231
Dukes, P. J., 11-0, ... (096 274) 231
Dun, J. M., 10-13, ... (087 535) 300
Dun, P. J., 9-7, ... (087 535) 225
Dun, W. G., 11-0, ... (087 535) 219
Dunn, Miss A. M., 8-4, ... (0388) 603317
Dunn, N. G. H., 10-12, ... (082 342) 530
Dunphy, Anne Marie, 8-7, ... (056) 43150/8
Durkan, J. P. P., 10-0, ... (0488) 72077/73241

Easterby, Miss S. E., 10-10, ... (03477) 368
Easterby, T., 10-0, ... c/o (065386) 600
Eaton, Lisa, 9-0, ... (0468) 21374
Eckley, B. J., 9-7, ... (0874) 2422
Eddery, Mrs C. J., 7-10, ... (0844) 290282
Edmunds, K., 10-7, ... (030 05) 272
Edwards, G. F., 10-12, ... (064 383) 549
Eley, T., 10-0, ... (0283) 78604
Elliott, Mrs C. F., 9-0, ... (0420) 63733
Ellis, Miss K., 8-7, ... (03643) 457
Elvin, M. A., 9-7, ... (0283) 78604
Enright, Mrs M., 8-0, ... (0273) 479183
Etherington, T., 10-3, ... (0653) 692842
Eubank, A., 10-7, ... (0900) 823027
Evans, John, 9-7, ... (0724) 863347
Evatt, D. B., 10-8, ... (0342) 810482

Fairhurst, Miss J., 9-10, ... (0969) 23362
Fanshawe, J., 10-7, ... (0638) 667504
Farrant, A., 9-7, ... (027581) 2192
Farrant, J., 10-0, ... (0580) 880558
Farrant, R. A., 8-7, ... (027581) 2192
Farrell, Mrs A. L., 8-7, ... (03475) 208/273
Farrell, C., 10-0, ... (0488) 72909 or (0672) 40868
Feilden, Miss J., 8-7, ... (063 877) 637
Fellows, Miss J., 9-4, ... (0684) 310275
Fellows, Miss L. K., 9-4, ... (0684) 310275
Felton, M. J., 11-0, ... (07255) 267
Fenlon, Mrs K., 10-0, ... (0570) 480231
Fennessy, J. F., 10-5, ... (0388) 720432
Fenton, P., 10-0, ... (052) 56156
Finegan, H., 10-5, ... c/o (0233) 72525
Finn, D., 10-7, ... (0327) 860043
Fisher, Miss P., 9-10, ... (0548) 2919
FitzGerald, T., 11-0, ... c/o (0653) 692718
Fleming, J. M., 10-0, ... c/o (0503) 21891
Fogarty, L. C., 10-5, ... (0252) 332392
Ford, R., 10-7, ... (0900) 826092 or c/o (0937) 836036
Forsey, Mrs S., 8-7, ... (09848) 270
Forsyth, Miss M., 9-0, ... (0439) 70566
Fowler, A., 11-3, ... (0664) 840203
Francome, Miss S. C., 8-2, ... (0488) 71548
Franks, D. R., 10-3, ... (0388) 819188 or (091373) 0459
Freeman, E., 10-5, ... c/o (0653) 2718
French, Miss S., 9-7, ... (0474) 814397

Gandolfo, Miss E. A., 9-0, ... (02357) 3242
Garton, T., 10-12, ... (0625) 827892
Gately, C., 10-7, ... Guildford 61987

Amateur Riders – Continued

Geake, J., 10-2, ... c/o (026477) 2278 or (026477) 2020
Geary, M., 10-0, ... (0206) 240235
Gee, M. P., 9-7, ... (0909) 566666/732647
Gibberd, Miss L., 9-0, ... (0748) 5816
Gibbon, Mrs L. J., 9-7, ... (0206) 250832
Gibson, I. R., 10-7, ... (089 682) 2716
Gill, H. J., 10-7, ... (0532) 813273
Gladders, R., 10-8, ... (058 06) 3265
Gladders, Miss S., 8-8, ... (058 06) 3265
Gooding, Miss A., 8-4, ... (0373) 827774
Gordon, Miss S., 9-6, ... (0503) 73484
Grassick, J., 10-10, ... (0875) 52115
Grassick, M. J., 11-7, ... (045) 79858
Greaves, Mrs V. A., 8-7, ... (0609) 779199
Greenall, J. E., 11-6, ... (082786) 238
Greene, R. J., 9-6, ... (027867) 437
Greenway, C. E. R., 10-10, ... (0606) 882387
Griffith, A. D. W., 10-0, ... (01402) 2572
Griffith, E. J. W., 11-0, ... (074574) 633
Griffiths, R., 10-0, ... (0793) 790230
Griffiths, S., 10-6, ... (0584) 810430
Grissell, Mrs D., 8-7, ... (042 482) 241
Grossick, J., 10-10, ... (0875) 52115
Guest, Mrs B., 8-11, ... (0638) 661508

Hacking, W. P., 11-4, ... (090 671) 3984
Haggas, Mrs M., 9-0, ... (0638) 667013
Hale, R. A., 9-10, ... (08533) 564
Hall, Miss P. J., 9-7, ... (0635) 297248
Hambly, Mr A., 10-4, ... (0638) 662383 or (0544) 267672
Hamer, M. P., 10-10, ... (0656) 860275
Hammersley, P., 10-3, ... (0827) 896250
Hancox, Miss J., 8-0, ... (0527) 79184
Handel, Miss A., 11-0, ... c/o (03987) 202
Hanmer, G., 10-2, ... (0283) 550035
Harding-Jones, P., 10-3, ... (037882) 2183
Hare, Miss E., 8-5, ... (0638) 730763
Harker, G., 10-0, ... (0642) 780995
Harley, J. C., 10-7, ... (0489) 877207
Harper, R., 10-10, ... (0295) 810997
Harris, M. C. M., 10-0, ... c/o (0299) 250500
Harrison, S., 9-12, (095289) 664 or (069185) 443
Harty, E. P., 11-0, ... (045) 41284
Harvey, Miss A. J., 9-10, ... (0488) 72210
Harvey, R., 9-7, ... (02357) 3092
Harwood, Miss A., 9-7, ... (07982) 2195/3011
Harwood, Miss G., 8-0, ... (07982) 2195/3011
Hawke, N., 9-7, ... (090 671) 2226
Hayes, Miss F., 9-7, ... (0793) 762437
Hayes, J., 9-7, ... (052) 31474
Haynes, Miss Y., 9-0, ... (037 27) 22664
Hembrow, Mrs J., 9-10, ... (0823) 442546
Henderson, Mrs D. A., 8-3, ... (0488) 72259
Hennessy, Miss K., 8-0, ... (0992) 464586
Hetherington, W. R., 10-7, ... (0900) 2959
Hide, Miss L. J., 8-4, ... (0638) 662063
Hide, P. E., 8-7, ... (0638) 662063
Hill, A., 11-7, ... (0844) 51268

Hills, Miss S., 8-4, ... (0937) 842812
Hills, T., 10-10, ... (023 371) 2224
Hindmarsh, M., 9-7, ... (020755) 259
Hines, F. S. F., 10-13, ... (01 581) 2478
Hitches, Miss C., 8-0, ... (067 284) 292
Hobbs, Mrs S. L., 9-7, ... (0984) 40366
Hobson, Miss L., 9-0, ... (0623) 822835
Hobson, S., 10-0, ... (023 57) 3420
Holden, N., 10-7, ... (0488) 72412
Hollinshead, A. N., 10-8, ... (0543) 490490
Holmes, C. J., 11-10, ... (0753) 887832
Holmes, Miss K., 9-7, ... (0296730) 707
Holmes, Miss T., 8-0, ... (0753) 887832
Holt, Miss H., 9-3, ... (021 1445) 4458
Holt, J. R., 10-5, ... (04557) 4608
Hook, N. G., 10-7, ... (0803) 525547
Horner, Miss S. L., 9-7, ... (060982) 695
Hosgood, P. J., 10-12, ... (0364) 42267
Hosie, Miss F., 8-7, ... (082 585) 228
Houghton, Johnson, Mrs G., 9-0, ... (0488) 72259/73125
Houghton, Johnson, G. F., 9-13, ... (0488) 72259/73125
Houlbrooke, Mr T. J., 11-0, ... (053184) 368/225
Howes, Miss K., 9-4, ... (0638) 77456
Howes, Mrs M. L., 9-0, ... (0638) 77456
Hudson, L. T., 10-12, ... (06993) 726
Hutchinson, R. R., 10-3, ... (073 72) 42132

Jackson, Mrs J., 9-10, ... (0683) 20127
Jackson, T. H., 10-0, ... Ridgeway 457
Jackson, Mrs V. S., 10-0, ... (067 075) 388
James, Miss E., 9-0, ... (0948) 4067
James, Mrs V., 9-7, ... (048 839) 280
Jarvis, Mrs G., 9-0, ... (0638) 661702/662519
Jefford, Mr L., 9-7, ... c/o (0884) 40715
Jeffrey, T. E., 10-10, ... (066576) 664
Jenkins, P. S., 10-7, ... (0429) 275048
Jenks, R. J., 11-7, ... (025672) 2859
Johnston, J. P., 10-7, ... (0900) 91831523
Johnson, K., 9-7, ... (091) 2674464 or c/o (0388) 720213
Johnson, P., 10-7, ... (091) 2674464
Jones, C., 10-0, ... c/o (Naas (045)) 76292
Jones, Miss D., 9-3, ... (0691) 659720 or (0836) 369587
Jones, D. S., 10-7, ... (026723) 6661
Jones, G., 9-7, ... (023 559) 291
Jones, Miss I. D. W., 9-3, ... (0691) 659720
Jones, N., 10-7, ... (06846) 2691
Jones, N. E. M., 11-4, ... (0642) 712382
Jones, T. L., 11-0, ... (0222) 882217
Jones, T. T., 10-3, ... (0488) 71596
Juster, Miss M., 8-7, ... (0638) 662915

Keegan, Miss E. J., 9-7, ... c/o (029921) 471
Kelleway, A. S., 10-0, ... (0638) 661461
Kelleway, Miss S., 8-0, ... (0638) 661461
Kendall, Mrs M., 9-7, ... (093 12) 318
Kerr, S., 9-10, ... c/o (0488) 71714

Amateur Riders – Continued

Kersey, T., 11-0, ... (0709) 873166
Kinsella, D. A., ... (060982) 272
Kirkby, L. P., 10-4, (065 261) 362 or (0652) 32248
Kirtley, A., 11-0, ... (410)2072
Knight, A. J., 9-7, ... (0372) 374011
Knight, S., ... (0488) 84428

Lane, C. W. S., 9-8, ... (082 281) 477
Larkin, P., 10-12, ... (0405) 55151
Lawrence, Miss S., 9-7, ... (0488 39) 258
Lay, A. L., 11-0, ... (060 883) 608
Leavy, B., 9-7, ... (0296) 623387
Ledger, Mrs N., 9-0, ... (0795) 423360
Leonard, Miss M., 7-10, ... (0990) 20858
Lewis, P., 10-0, ... (0903) 872226
Llewellyn, Miss B., 9-7, ... (0685) 841259
Llewellyn, J., 10-7, ... (04463) 3633
Llewellyn, J. L., 10-0, ... (0685) 841259
Lloyd-Jones, Mrs C., 10-0, ... (0829) 51143
Love, S., 10-12, ... (041330) 5700 or (041956) 5306
Low, M., 10-0, ... (068 481) 651
Lumsden, Mr C. J., 11-7, ... c/o (0453 88) 437105
Lyttle, J., 9-7, ... c/o (0902) 81484

MacEwan, A. G., 10-5, ... (0638) 669796
MacTaggart, B., 11-7, ... (0450) 72086
MacTaggart, D. C., 10-0, ... (0450) 86314
MacTaggart, J., 10-0, ... (0450) 86314
MacTaggart, S., 10-7, ... (0488) 72922
Madgwick, A., 9-7, ... (0705) 258313
Magnier, C., 10-10, ... c/o (Meath 046) 32218
Manley, S., 10-0, ... (0452) 76459
Mann, N., 9-7, ... (027581) 2192
Mann, R., 11-7, ... (0926) 613717
Marks, Miss A. K., 9-0, ... (0488) 71767
Marshall, D. G., 9-10, ... (01 845) 1467
Martin, A. J., 10-10, ... (Meath 046) 35129
Mason, Mrs S. E., 11-0, ... c/o (03477) 368
Massey, R., 9-7, ... c/o (0763) 241141
Mathet, H., 9-7, ... c/o (4) 421-54-30
Matthews, Mrs J., 10-0, ... (0823) 662660
Maude, C. G., 9-8, ... (0458) 223922
Maundrell, G., 11-3, ... (067 284) 202
Mccain, D. R., 9-12, ... c/o (0488) 72406 or 71411
McCarthy, K., 9-0, ... c/o (0505) 4221
McGhie, R., 10-0, ... c/o (0200) 445305/445490
McInnes, I., 9-7, ... (03477) 518
McKeever, A., 10-2, ... (0488) 71609
McKie, I., 10-12, ... c/o (0296730) 707
McMahon, E., 10-7, ... (0827) 62901
McMath, Mrs J., 9-5, ... (0206) 211376
McNulty, M., 9-5, ... c/o (0001) 433165
McPherson, A. S., 9-7, ... (0506) 842815
Mead, J. H., 10-10, ... (0672) 62365
Meddes, R. L., 11-7, ... (0306) 730115
Mee, S., 10-7, ... c/o 0302 842 857
Mellor, Miss L., 8-0, ... (0524) 751911 or (0488) 71485

Messenger, G., 10-0, ... (0900) 604189
Middleton, Miss L., 9-0, ... (0709) 873166
Mitchell, Miss, 9-7, ... (0305) 251429
Mitchell, Mrs E., 10-10, ... (030 05) 272
Mitchell, N., 10-10, ... (0305) 251429
Mitchell, T., 11-0, ... (0305) 251429/68069
Moffatt, Mrs J. A., 8-0, ... (044 854) 689
Moloney, P. J., 10-5, ... (08534) 555
Moore, Miss C., 8-10, ... (0273) 681679
Moore, D. A., 11-0, ... (021) 668416
Moore, T. W., 10-0, ... (0371) 821013
Moorhead, Mrs R., 8-7, ... (0969) 23823
Morley, Mrs M. F. D., 9-7, ... (0638) 667175
Morley, M. R., 11-0, ... (0751) 74240
Morris, R. W., 10-0, ... (0400) 72072
Morrow, G. T., 9-7, ... (0229) 55664
Muir, W., 10-5, ... (048 82) 463
Mullins, J. W., 10-5, ... (0653) 697861
Mullins, S., 10-5, ... c/o (026477) 2278
Munro-Wilson, B., 11-7, ... (09547) 347
Murgatroyd, Miss S. C., 8-12, ... (0638) 751607
Murphy, D., 10-0, ... c/o (0638) 77288
Murphy, D. G., 10-2, ... (021) 64234
Murphy, Mrs L., 9-7, ... c/o (027581) 2192
Murphy, M., 11-0, ... c/o (0229) 55664
Murphy, M. A., 10-0, ... (021) 64234
Musgrave, Miss J., 9-0, ... (0783) 262 965
Musgrave, Maj N., 10-7, ... (0980) 43225
Musson, Mrs J. A., 8-7, ... (0638) 663371

Nash, Mrs P. L., 8-7, ... (036782) 510
Naylor-Leyland, D., 11-0, ... (0491) 680320
Neale, L., 10-2, ... c/o (0386) 859605
Nelson, F. M., 10-0, ... (038775) 237
Newport, C., 10-10, ... c/o (0233) 32720
Newton-Smith, Miss A., 9-0, ... (032 12) 4681
Neylon, R., 9-10, ... (045) 79858
Nichols, Mrs P., 9-0, ... (0327) 61476
Nimmo, C. N., 10-6, ... (060 125) 798

O'Brien, A. P., 10-0, ... (056) 43273
O'Brien, J. L., 9-7, ... (030384) 215
O'Donnell, S., 9-7, ... c/o (0503) 21891
O'Dononvan, 9-10, ... (056) 43273
O'Donovan, S. H., 9-12, ... (0503) 27133
O'Leary, B., 9-7, ... (01641) 0491
O'Leary, B. P., 10-5, ... (0372) 376468
Oliver, Miss S., 10-2, ... (088 64) 539
O'Reilly, P., 10-7, ... (0984) 40532
O'Rourke, Miss A., 7-4 .... (045) 81403
Osbourne, J., 10-0, ... (0969) 23049
O'Shea, Miss C. D., 9-4, ... (0638) 667028
O'Sullivan, S., 10-0, ... (08534) 555
O'Toole, C., 9-10, ... (0638) 662549
Oxley, J. A. G., 10-5, ... (0488) 71556

Palmer, Mrs P., 11-0, ... (0622) 39112
Parker, D., 8-12, ... c/o (0524) 791179
Payne, R. J., 10-7, ... (0398) 7244
Peacock, Mrs C., 9-0, ... (0829) 732716

Amateur Riders – Continued

Pearce, Lydia., 8-0, ... (0638) 664669
Penn, Miss J. M., 8-12, ... (0672) 52316
Perratt, Miss L. A., 8-11, ... (03553) 3425
Peters, J., 10-0, ... (022029) 885
Pickering, C., 10-3, ... (0325) 321443
Pidgeon, Miss J., 9-7, ... (029 576) 8237
Pile, Miss T., 8-0, ... (01 668) 8814
Pile, Miss T. P., 8-0, ... (0372) 277645
Pilgrim, N., 11-0, ... (023 587) 8119
Pilkington, Miss S., 9-7, ... (036782) 214
Pitcher, D. F., 10-7, ... (06286) 66177
Platts, C., 10-12, ... (0274) 871522
Pocock, I. J., 11-0, ... (0458) 210324
Pomeroy, Miss D. A., 8-7, ... (0264) 790936
Portman, J., 10-2, ... (0235) 59205
Poulton, Mr J. C., 10-2, ... (0273) 890 244
Price, A., 10-0, ... (0495) 304794
Price, M. I., 10-0, ... (04973) 254
Price, Miss R. H. R., 9-10, ... (0291) 421596
H. R. H. The Princess Royal, 9-3, c/o (0451) 30417
Pritchard, J., 10-7, ... (0684) 297119
Pritchard, Dr P. L. J., 9-9, ... (0453) 811881
Pritchard, Mrs J., 10-7, ... (029587) 383
Provan, J. A., 10-12, ... (0889) 590987

Radband, Miss C., 8-8, ... (0488) 71119
Ranger, M., 10-0, ... (0526) 833245
Ranger, Mrs M. A., 8-5, ... (0772) 812780
Ratcliffe, C. I., 10-10, ... (04577) 2097
Rees, Mrs D. 9-0, ... (082346) 424
Rees, Mrs G., 8-10, ... (077473) 4409
Rees, J., 9-7, ... (0280) 701991
Reid, Mrs P. J., 9-7, ... (0444) 413914
Rice, Miss G. M., 9-7, ... (0604) 844836
Richards, M. D. R., 9-13, ... (087386) 219
Richards, M., 9-12, ... (0600) 85552
Richards, T. M., 10-10, ... (05448) 216
Rigby, Mrs P., 10-0, ... (0978) 822198
Riley, D., 9-10, ... c/o (0924) 848468
Rimell, Miss K., 9-8, ... (090 567) 233
Ringer, D. J., 10-1, ... (0638) 662653/666021
Roberts, J., 10-0, ... (043270) 328
Roberts, P., 10-7, ... (0488) 71717
Robertson, Mrs A., 9-7, ... (056386) 201
Robertson, D., 11-0, ... (056 386) 201
Robertson, Greg., 9-7, ... (0704) 69677
Robinson, D. H., 10-12, ... (09328) 60601
Robinson, G., 10-0, ... (04612) 2852/2792
Robinson, R., 10-5, ... (04612) 2852/2792
Robinson, R. S. C., 10-7, ... (0278) 760479
Robson, A. W., 11-0, ... (066 589) 276
Robson, Mrs R. A., 8-10, ... (066 574) 307
Roe, G., 10-7, ... (045 38) 885487
Rogers, T., 10-10, ... (08012) 2241/4923
Rohan, Miss L., 9-7, ... (0653) 692337
Rooney, T. P., 10-7, ... (0633) 895878
Roper, J., 11-0, ... (0886) 884368
Rosoman, Miss J., 10-0, ... (0562) 822026
Rowsell, H., 10-7, ... c/o (026477) 2278
Rudge, J., 10-0, ... (0905) 820333

Russell, Miss J. M., 9-0, ... c/o (0488) 71700

Sample, C. J., 10-5, ... (067 074) 245
Sanders, Miss B., 8-7, ... (037 22) 77459
Sansome, A., 10-10, ... (0604) 770991
Santana, K., 9-0, ... (01 651) 6482
Saunders, Mrs J., 9-0, ... (060124) 739
Saunders, J., 9-0, ... c/o (0980) 620861
Sawyer, Miss M. A., 9-7, ... (0672) 514857
Scallan, S. P., 9-0, ... (0206) 262613
Scholfield, P. M., 10-9, ... (0626) 890764
Schutz, A., 9-11, ... (0221) 742474
Scott, D. W., 11-0, ... (043473) 313
Scott, J. A., 10-0, ... (0643) 702430
Scott, Miss J. M., 8-7, ... (0509) 880489
Scott, M., 10-7, ... c/o (0902) 81484
Sharp, J., 11-2, ... (08012) 4578
Sheedy, Mrs L., 10-0, ... (0633) 400 386
Sheppard, M. I., 10-0, ... c/o (090 567) 233
Sheridan, D. N., 10-0, ... (05643) 2011
Shiels, R., 10-10, ... (0289) 82519
Shinton, S. N., 10-10, ... (0633) 250489
Shone, C., 10-7, ... (024 267) 3275
Sim, W., 10-8, ... (0737) 242190
Simpson, Mrs G. L., 9-7, ... (043473) 413
Slack, Miss H. D. 10-0, ... (0930) 51354
Smallman, Mrs C., 9-7, ... (038 081) 3304
Smith, Mrs D., 9-7, ... (0684) 573830
Smith, K. H., 10-12, ... (023371) 2768
Smith, Nadine., 9-7, ... (0532) 886536/886256
Smith, T. E. G., 10-4, ... (0734) 761116
Southall, Miss E. J., 7-10, ... (0823) 680159
Southcombe, Miss J. A., 9-0, ... c/o (026477) 2278
Sowersby, M. E., 10-5, ... (026 288) 212
Spearing, Miss A., 8-7, ... (0789) 772639
Spearing, Miss C. M., 9-0, ... c/o (0789) 772639
Spearing, Miss T. S., 8-0, ... (0789) 772639
Spence, Mrs R., 9-7, ... c/o (0482) 882520
Sporborg, W. H., 11-0, ... (0279) 74444
Staight, Dr. G. B., 11-4, ... (01 584) 6511
Staneley, A., 9-12, ... c/o (03722) 77645
Staples, P., 10-0, ... (0584) 810430
Stephenson, T. M., 10-0, ... (068481) 312
Stickland, S. G., 10-10, ... (0963) 64292
Stone, Miss D. E., 8-7, ... (0653) 693586
Storey, C., 10-2, ... (069 77) 3810
Storey, Miss F. J., 10-0, ... (0207) 55259
Storey, Miss S., 8-12, ... (0207) 55259
Stubbs, Mrs L., 9-0, ... (0969) 40680
Studd, Dr. C., 10-10, ... (0273) 890303
Swiers, S. J., 10-7, ... (0423) 324155
Swindlehurst, D., 10-4, ... (022874) 376/289

Tate, T., 11-0, ... (0532) 842982
Taylor, A. J., 10-4, ... (0273) 890318
Taylor, S., 11-0, ... c/o (0488) 71767
Teal, R., 10-0, ... (0994) 427396
Thompson, M., 10-7, ... (066 576) 272
Thomson, Mrs B. K., 10-0, ... (03616) 514
Thomson Jones, T., 10-2, ... (0488) 71596

Amateur Riders – Continued

Thorne, Miss J., 9-7, (0278) 74216
Thurlow, Mrs J., 9-0, (0965) 20576
Tinning, Mrs J. A. 9-7, (0532) 886260
Todd, Miss L., 10-0, (0673) 858242
Tomkins, Mrs A., 9-12, (0638) 661434
Toner, K., 9-10, (085 33) 392
Tosdevin, D., 10-0, (0306) 711635
Towers, B. J., 9-7, (0548) 550411
Townsend, D. J., 10-4, (023371) 2586
Townsley, P., 10-9, (030 677) 492
Townson, J. G., 11-0, (025 482) 3412
Treacy, J., 10-3, (0503) 24367
Treloggen, R., 10-0, (0458) 45933
Trice-Rolph, J. C., 11-0, (0451) 32039
Tsakarisianos, Mrs D., 8-7, (0452) 22606
Turnell, Mrs L., 8-7, (0235) 833297
Turner, Miss A. J., 9-7, (075539) 231
Turner, Miss M., 9-6, (075 539) 231
Tutty, N. D., 10-9, (060983) 624 or (0642) 781894
Twiston-Davies, Mrs C., 9-0, (04515) 278

Unett, J. W., 9-7, (0488) 71548
Upton, G., 10-3, ... (06846) 3710 or (036782) 710
Urquhart, Mrs M., 9-0, (069) 65244

Venn, B., 10-12, (082346) 322
Verco, D. I., 10-2, (97317) 150
Vergette, G., 11-5, (0778) 344993
Vergette, G. Jnr., 11-7, (0778) 344993
Vickery, Mrs R., 9-0, (0963) 40421
Vittadini, Miss F. G., 8-10, (0638) 730173/730335

Wade, J., 11-0, (0388) 720480
Waggot, E. S., 11-0, (0385) 780719
Waggot, N. jun., 11-0, (0388) 819012
Waggot, P., 9-7, c/o (0388) 603317
Waggot, Miss T., 9-7, (0388) 819012
Wales, P. R., 11-7, (03664) 213
Wales, W., 10-12, (032875) 580
Walford, T., 9-7, (03477) 382
Wallace, Miss A., 9-0, (0488) 71907
Wallace, Miss L., 8-7, (0743) 860387
Walsh, M. E. J., 11-0, (057 62) 2680
and (096279) 552
Walsh, T. M., 10-8, (045) 77818
Walter, A., 11-0, c/o (0884) 40715
Walter, A. H., 11-0, (045) 421751
Walton. A.. 9-0 (0400) 50531
Walton, J. B., 10-12, (0669) 40253
Wanless, S., 10-10, (056 283) 296
Ward, Miss S. M., 10-4, (0388) 527402
Ware, Miss L., 8-7, (0638) 730763
Waterman, Miss S., 9-1, (093 583) 394
Waugh, Miss S. M., 8-2, (0483) 38297
Webber, P., 11-0, (0638) 664459
Webster, G., 10-7, (0984) 40941
Wellings, M., 10-2, (0384) 52060
Welsh, A., 9-7, (0474) 813132
West, S., 11-0, (0752) 822686
Westrop, P. R., 10-7, (02357)3128
Weymes, J. R., 10-0, (0969) 40229
Whales, T. P., 11-7, (0328) 701788
Wharton, J., 10-12, (0644) 65225
Wheeler, N. J., 10-10, (043583) 0571
Whettam, E., 11-0, (0300) 20311
Whitaker, S. R., 11-3, (0532) 892265
White, R., 10-0, (0488) 72831
White, Miss S., 9-0, (0621) 742161
Wight, A. J., 10-0, (03683) 219
Wikinson, Mrs J. U., 8-7, (09277) 65624
Wilkinson, Miss J. A., 9-7, (060 28) 542
Wilkinson, M. J., 11-3, (063 528) 294
Willett, C. T., 10-12, (089 283) 3746
Williams, Mrs A. D., 9-0, (038 483) 2318
Williams, D., 10-0, (023 57) 3420
Williams, Mrs D., 9-0, (038487) 3965
Williams, I., 11-0, c/o (0488) 71714
Williams, Miss V. M., 9-6, (043270) 217
Williamson, Miss S. L., 9-0, (032 574) 839
Wilson, C. R., 10-7, (032 574) 595
Wilson, Miss M., 9-10, (0780) 782323
Wilson, Miss S. J., 8-0, (0638) 667400
Winter, Miss J., 8-7, (0488) 72928
Wintle, Miss J., 9-7, (0452) 76459
Wonnacott, A. J., 10-7, (082287) 215
Wonnacott, Mrs C., 10-0, (0822) 616416
Woods, S., 9-7, (023 57) 3003
Wragg, G. J. D., 11-0, (01 370) 0980
Wrathall, J., 11-0, (0858) 32075
Wrathall, T. J., 10-12, (0858) 32075
Wyatt, J. J., 10-10, (072 589) 312

Yardley, Miss A., 8-7, (0905) 830245
Yardley, Miss C. J., 8-4, (0905) 620477
Yeomans, Miss D., 8-6, (063 522) 427
Yearsley, D. K., 10-9, c/o (0823) 78604

Foaling dates are shown for two-year-olds where these are provided.

RACECOURSES OF GREAT BRITAIN

AINTREE (L.H.)
(N.H.)

Two L.H. courses. A triangular circuit of nearly 2¼ miles with a flat run in 494 yards for the Grand National (30 unique fences) and the Mildmay Course, approx. 1½m round with conventional fences.

Clerk of the Course and Managing Director: Mr. J. Parrett, Aintree Racecourse Co. Ltd., Aintree, Liverpool, L9 5AS.
Phone: 051-523 2600.

Admission: County Enclosure: Sat £27.00 Thurs/Fri £11.00; three days £38.00 Aintree and Paddock ; Sat £15.00; Thurs/Fri £7.00.

Photography: By prior permission only.

Enquiries: including party bookings, to be addressed to the Racecourse.

Railway Station: Aintree, Lancs.

Car Park: Western £12.00 (Sat); £4.00 (Thurs/Fri)

Nearest airfield: Speke, Liverpool.

ASCOT (R.H.)

A triangular testing course of 1m 6f 34yds, the first 3f downhill and the last half (including the Old Mile which starts in a chute) uphill with a straight run-in of 2½f. The Hunt Cup Course is 1m straight and is undulating with an uphill finish. All races of less than 1m are run on the Hunt Cup Course.

Draw: Advantage doubtful.

Clerk of the Course and Secretary to the Ascot Authority: Captain the Hon. Nicholas Beaumont, C.V.O., D.L., Royal Enclosure Lodge, Ascot, Berks. SL5 75N. Phone: Ascot (0990) 22211: Going: Ascot 23127 (Evening): Fax 0990–28299.

Admission: Members £8-£15 (not including Royal Meeting) according to meeting; Grand Stand £6-£15; Silver Ring £2.50.

Railway Station: Ascot, Berks, (From Waterloo).

Car Park: Adjoining course and on Ascot Heath. For reservations apply to the Secretary, Ascot Racecourse, Ascot, Berkshire SL5 7JN. Phone 0990–20768

ASCOT (N.H.)

Circular course of 1¾ miles in circumference with an uphill finish. The course is laid out on the inside of the flat race track and was opened for N.H. racing in the 1965-66 Season.

AYR (L.H.)

A wide flat oval course of just over 1m 4f with a straight run-in of 4f, 5f and 6f courses are quite straight. Good galloping track.

Draw: 5f, 6f—High; 7f and up—Low.

Joint Clerk of the Course: Mr David W. McHarg and Miss Morag Chalmers, Racecourse Office, 2 Whitletts Road, Ayr. KA8 0JE Phone: Ayr (0292) 264179.

Racecourses of Great Britain – Continued

General Manager: Mr D. W. McHarg, address as above.

Secretary: Mr David W. McHarg, address as above.

Admission: Club £10.00-£15.00 according to meeting; Eglinton Stand and Paddock £5.00-£7.00; Carrick/Craigie Stand £1.00-£2.50 (April-Sept.) children under 16 free. Special party rate. Racecards free.

Railway Station: Ayr (from Glasgow Central) 30 mins. service. Journey time, 45 minutes. Buses and taxis to course. 1 hour by car from Glasgow (Abbotsinch) Airport, 10 minutes from Prestwick (International) Airport.

Car Park: Free for buses and cars.

AYR (N.H.)

1½ miles in circumference; Oval. Run in 210 yds.

BANGOR-ON-DEE (L.H.) (N.H.)

1½ miles in circumference. Perfectly flat and all grass. Run in 325 yards. Full watering system installed.

Clerk of the Course: B. R. Davies, Home: New House Farm, Much Marcle, Ledbury, Hereford. HR8 2PH. Phone: 053184 604, Office: Shepherds Meadow, Eaton Bishop, Hereford, HR2 90A. Phone: 0981 250436. Fax: 0981 250192

Secretary and Manager: P. W. Ockleston, Chorlton Hall, Malpas, Cheshire. SY14 7ET. Phone: 0948860 438.

Admission: Course £3.00; Tattersalls £7.00; Annual Membership £55.00

Stabling: Contact the Secretary as above.

Railway Station: Wrexham, Denbighshire (Paddington)

Car Park: Free.

Location: 11 miles from Whitchurch, Salop, and 22 miles from Shrewsbury.

BATH (L.H.)

An oval course of 1½ miles 25yds. with a straight uphill run-in of 4f. The 5f 167 yds course is a continuation of 5f course. The mile and the mile and a quarter courses have over a quarter of a mile straight at the start.

Draw: 5f-1m—Low

Clerk of the Course and Secretary: Capt. C. B. Toller, "Greenfields", Little Rissington, Nr. Cheltenham, Glos. GL54 2NA Phone: Cotswold 20517.

Admission: Members £9.00; Tattersalls £6.00; Silver Ring £2.00; Course £1.00.

Railway Station: Bath, Somerset (from Paddington).

Car Park: Unlimited free car and coach parking space immediately behind the stands. Special bus services operate from Bath and Bristol to the racecourse.

BEVERLEY (R.H.)

An oval course of 1m 3f with a straight run-in of 2½f rising to the winning post. The 5f course is on the ascent throughout and bends slightly at half-way. Testing track for two-year-olds.

Draw: High numbers.

Clerk of the Course and Manager: Mr J. G. Cleverly F.R.I.C.S., Wells Cundall, 19 North Bar Within, Beverley N. Humberside. HU17 8DB. 'Phone: North Grimston (09446) 203 (night), Hull (0482) 867816 (day). Racecourse foreman: Hull (0482) 882587. Office: Hull (0482) 867488. Racecourse: (Race days only) Hull (0482) 882645.

Racecourses of Great Britain – Continued

Admission: Club £10.00; No.1 Ring £6.00; No.2 Ring £2.50; No.3 Ring £1.00.

Railway Station: Beverley, (from Kings Cross). 1½m from course with bus service.

Car Park: Free.

Location: M62 within 10m.

BRIGHTON (L.H.)

The course forms a figure like three sides of a square with easy turns and is 1½ miles in length. The first three furlongs are slightly uphill. There is then a slight descent and rise to about four furlongs from home when the ground falls more steeply until two furlongs from the finish when there is a slight rise with the last 100 yards level. The straight run-in measures about 3½ furlongs.

Draw: 5f, 6f—Low.

Clerk of the Course: Mr C. E. Griggs, 11 Boltro Road, Haywards Heath, Sussex, RH 16 1BP. Phone: 0444-441111. Brighton (0273) 603580 on race days.

Racecourse Managers: Pratt & Co., 11 Boltro Road, Haywards Heath, Sussex, RH 16 1BP. Phone: 0444-441111. Brighton (0273) 603580 on race days.

Admission: Club £10.00; Tattersalls £7.00; Grand Stand £3.00. Annual Club membership £80.00 (includes car parking).

Railway Station: Brighton, Sussex (from Victoria, London Bridge or Portsmouth). Bus service to the course.

Car Park: Free.

CARLISLE (R.H.)

A pear-shaped, undulating course of 1m 5f with a straight uphill run-in of 3½f. On the ascent until the distance post from which it is almost level, the 6f course, of which the 5f forms part, bears right for the first 1½f with a further right-hand bend to the run-in after another furlong. Test of stamina for two-year-olds.

Draw: 5f, 6f, 7f, 8f—High.

Clerk of the Course: Major T. R. Riley, Burbank House, Blencowe, Penrith, Cumbria, CA11 ODB 'Phone: Greystoke (085 33) 246, (Evening). Hackthorpe (09312) 392 (By Day)

Managing Director: Mr T. E. Robinson, Grandstand Office, Carlisle Racecourse, Durdar, Carlisle CA2 4TS. Phone (0228) 22973

Secretary & Club Secretary: Mrs A. Bliss, Moorthwaite, Wigton, Cumbria CA7 0LZ. Phone Wigton (06973) 42634 - Race Day tel. no. Carlisle (0228) 22973

Admission: Club Day Badges £8; Sats. & Bank Holidays £10; Tattersalls £4; Premium Meetings £5; (Premium Meetings are Easter & 9th June – 29th September 1990 inclusive); O.A.P.s at a reduced rate. Accompanied Children free. Special party rates – minimum 10 people.

Railway Station: Carlisle, Cumbria.

Car Park: Free to buses and cars. Trackside car parking £2.00 – except for Premium Meetings.

Location: Easy access off M6 from Junction 42.

CARLISLE (N.H.)

1 mile 5 furlongs circuit. Undulating. Run in 250 yds New 2m start (1989).

Racecourses of Great Britain – Continued

CARTMEL (L.H.)
(N.H.)

Quite sharp left-handed oval course, about 1 mile. Chase course run in about 4½ furlongs.

Clerk of the Course: Major T. R. Riley. Home address: Burbank House, Blencowe, Penrith, Cumbria CA11 0DB. Phone: Home, Greystoke (085 33) 246 and Estate Office, Lowther, Penrith, Cumbria, CA10 2HG; Phone: (09312) 392. Racedays: (05395) 36340.

Club Secretary: Mrs R. H. C. Bray, Bleacott Farm, Witherslack, Grange Over Sands, Cumbria LA11 6RZ. Witherslack (044852) 228 Racedays (044854) 340.

Admission: Paddock: £7.00, O.A.P's £4.00; Course: £3.00, O.A.P's £1.50; Children (accompanied by an adult) Free; Club membership and party rates on application to Club Secretary.

Car Park: Paddock £5.00; course free.

CATTERICK (L.H.)

A sharp oval course of 1m 1f, uphill along the back stretch, with a straight run-in of 3f. An almost straight 5f joins to round course down a sharp slope after 2f.

Draw: 5f, 6f, 7f—Low.

Clerk of the Course: Mr J. F. Sanderson, F.C.A., Ebor Court, First Floor, Westgate, Leeds LS1 4ND. Home: (0904) 489669.

Secretary: Mrs M. Rose, The Racecourse, Redcar, Cleveland TS10 2BY. Phone: Redcar (0642) 484068.

Admission: Club £8.00; Tattersalls £5.00; Course £1.50.

Railway Station: Darlington (Bus service to course).

Car Park: Free.

Location: Course adjacent to A1.

CATTERICK (N.H.)

Oval Course, 1 mile 127 yds., almost flat. Run in approx, 240 yds.

N.H. Clerk of the Course: Major C. Enderby, The Riding, Hexham, Northumberland. Phone: Hexham (0434) 606881.

CHELTENHAM (L.H.)
(N.H.)

Two oval courses, approx. 1½ miles round. Undulating. Run in about 237 yds., uphill. The National Hunt Course, 4 miles, for the National Hunt Steeplechase, 24 fences, is run over the old course, after starting from the 4 mile chute in the centre of the course.

Clerk of the Course: Major P. W. F. Arkwright, Shirley Farm, Little Wolford, Shipston-on-Stour, Warwickshire. Phone: Long Compton (060884) 460.

Club Secretary: Mrs R. Hammond, address and phone as Gen. Manager.

General Manager: E. W. Gillespie, The Steeplechase Company, Prestbury Park, Cheltenham Glos. GL50 4SH. Phone: Cheltenham (0242) 513014.

Racecourses of Great Britain – Continued

Admission:

	Club Daily	Junior Badge (16-24)	Tattersalls	Course
STANDARD Days	£9	£6	£6	£3
FEATURE Days	£10	£7	£7	£3
PREMIER Days	£15	£8	£8	£3
HUNTER Evening	£8	£5	£8	£3

NATIONAL HUNT FESTIVAL

	Club Daily	Tattersalls	Fosters Enclosure	Festival Grandstand Seat
Tuesday	£25	£12	£5	£12
Wednesday	£25	£12	£5	£12
Thursday	£30	£15	£5	£18
3 Day	£70	–	–	–

Railway Station: Cheltenham, Spa.

Car Park: Free, except during the N.H. Festival (£5.00; three-day voucher £12.00).

CHEPSTOW (L.H.)

An oval course of about 2m in circumference, undulating with a straight run-in of 5f. This run-in rises sharply for about half its length, then gradually levelling out to the winning post. All races up to 1m are run on the straight course which is downhill until joining the round course 5f from the finish.

Draw: 5f, 6f, 7f, 8f—High.

Clerk of the Course and Manager: Mr Rodger Farrant, Chepstow Racecourse, Chepstow, Gwent, NP6 5YH. Phone: Chepstow (0291) 622260.

Secretary: Mr G. C. Francis, 17 Welsh Street, Chepstow, Gwent NP6 5YH.

Admission: Club £9.00; Tattersalls £6.00; Public Enclosure £3.00; (Open April 16 and 17, May 28, and August 27); Centre Course (including picnic car park) £3.00 (Open April 16 and 27, May 28, and August 27), Car Park Free.

Railway Station: Chepstow, Gwent. 1m from course.

CHEPSTOW (N.H.)

Oval course. 2 mile circuit. Undulating but no steep gradients. Run in 240 yds.

CHESTER (L.H.)

A perfectly flat saucer-shaped course 1m 73yds in circumference, with a straight run-in of 230yds. All races from 5f to 2¼m are run on this course.

Draw: All distances:—Low.

Clerk of the Course: Captain C. B. Toller. "Greenfields," Little Rissington, Nr. Cheltenham Glos. GL54 2NA. Phone: Home, Cotswold 20517. Racedays: Chester 23170.

Secretaries: Lowndes McLintock, 2 George Street, Chester. CHI 3EQ Phone: Chester 27171.

Admission: Apply secretaries.

Railway Station: Chester General (from Euston, Paddington, and Northgate).

Car Park: Owners and trainers' car park immediately behind stand. Public in centre of the course.

Racecourses of Great Britain – Continued

DEVON AND EXETER (R.H.) (N.H.)

Circuit of 2m 40yds. Undulating. Run in about 250 yds.

Clerk of the Course: R. H. Merton, Pump Close, Denbury, Newton Abbot. Devon, TQ12 6DN. Phone: Ipplepen (0803) 812289.

Manager: R. H. Merton, Devon & Exeter, Steeplechases Ltd., The Racecourse, Kennford in Exeter, (0392) 832599.

Membership Secretary: B. Kennedy, 20, Queen Street, Exeter. Phone: Exeter (0392) 59395.

Admission: Daily Member £7.50; Tattersalls £7.50; Course £3.00.

Stabling: Apply Mrs J. Browning, Exeter (0392) 832816.

Car Park: Rails £1.00; remainder free.

Location: The course is at Haldon, six miles from the centre of Exeter 2 miles East of Chudleigh on the main Exeter to Plymouth Road (A38). Frequent bus services ('specials' on race days) to and from the Course.

DONCASTER (L.H.)

There is a straight course of about 1m which is approximately 88ft wide and tapers from the start to 60ft wide at the winning post. A round Mile Course joins the Straight Course at a tangent. The Round Course is about 1m 7½f in circumference, and all races over a mile are run upon this course. The run in is 5f 140yds of the Straight Course. The St. Leger Course is part of the Round Course, the distance being about 1m 6f 127yds. Flat galloping track.

Draw: 5f, 6f, 7f, 8f—No advantage, 8f (round)—Low.

General Manager: Mr D. A. H. Cox, Leger Way, Doncaster DN2 6BB. Phone (0302) 320066. Home (0904) 644474.

Admission: Club £12.00-£22.00 according to meeting; Grand Stand £6.00-£11.00; Second Ring £2.00-£5.00; Racecards free subject to availability.

Stables: Mr T. Harrison, Phone: (0302) 349337. Phone (0302) 536404.

Railway Station: Doncaster Central, Yorks. Eastern Region Inter-City. Motorways linked to Racecourse: M18, M62 and A1(M).

Car Park: Large car parks adjacent to the course (Free).

Air Landing Facilities: On Doncaster Airport adjoining Racecourse. Full details from South Yorkshire Airport Limited. Phone: Doncaster 535666.

DONCASTER (N.H.)

About 2 miles in circumference, conical in shape, no steep gradients. Run in 247 yds.

EDINBURGH (R.H.)

The course is situated at Musselburgh, 6 miles east of Edinburgh on the A1. The track is a flat oval of 1¼m with a straight run-in of 4f. There is a nearly straight 5f course.

Draw: 5f, 7f, 8f—High.

Clerk of the Course: Mr Sam Morshead, Racecourse Office, 2 Whitletts Road, Ayr. KA8 0JE. Phone: Ayr (0292) 264179. Race days: 031-665 2859.

Secretary: Morag Chalmers. Address as above.

Racecourses of Great Britain – Continued

Admission: Club £8.00, Tattersalls £4.00 (Discounts for pensioners and unemployed). Special party rates. Racecards Free.

Railway Station: Edinburgh. Frequent bus service from Edinburgh passes the course. A new train service from Edinburgh also operates.

Car Park: Free for buses and cars.

EDINBURGH (N.H.)

1m 3f in circumference; Oval Right handed run in 150 yds.

EPSOM (L.H.)

The present Derby Course (1872) rises about 150ft at varying gradients for the first 6f and then falls until the final 50yds which is uphill. The first 6f is not straight but the width of the course minimises the effect of the bend. The next 2f is in a gradual turn leading to Tattenham Corner. The straight run-in is 4f. The Epsom Mile is the last 1m 110yds of the Derby Course. The new 6f and 7f Courses start on short arms projecting from the Derby Course into which they run shortly after their start. The Egmont course is 5f straight. The City and Suburban Course is the last 1m 2f. of the Derby Course.

Draw: 5f, 6f, 7f, 8f—Low. 10f, 12f—Middle.

Clerk of the Course: Major R. M. O. Webster. Epsom Racecourse, Racecourse Paddock, Epsom, Surrey, KT18 5NJ.

General Manager and Secretary: Mr M. J. Carmichael, F.C.A., Address as above. Phone: Epsom 26311 (4 lines).

Managing Director: Mr Timothy P. Neligan. Address as above.

Admission:	Derby Day	Oaks Day	Other Days
†Club (daily)	£40.00†	£20.00†	£12.00
Club Junior (16–25 yrs)	–	£13.00†	£9.00
Grand Stand	£16.00	£12.00	£8.00
Paddock Supplement	£4.00	FREE	FREE
Paddock only	£9.00	£6.00	£4.00
Lonsdale Stand	£9.00	£6.00	£4.00
Finishing Straight (Derby Week only)	£5.00	£4.00	£3.00
Anglesey Stand-Reserved seat	£35.00	–	–

Accompanied children under 16 free to all enclosures except the Club on Derby Day.
† Admission to Club Enclosure by voucher only.

Railway Stations: Epsom, Epsom Downs and Tattenham Corner, Surrey.

Car Park: Phone Epsom (03727) 26311 for charges.

FAKENHAM (L.H.) (N.H.)

Circuit 1 mile. Run in 200 yards

Clerk of the Course: P. B. Firth, Fakenham Racecourse Ltd., The Racecourse, Fakenham, Norfolk, NR21 7NY. Phone: Fakenham (0328) 862388.

Admission: (16th February, 16th March, 22nd October, 14th December) Course and Paddock Combined £3.50 Members £8.00 (16th April and 28th May) Course £3.00, Grandstand and Paddock £6.00 members £8.00. Fakenham Race Club: Annual Subscription Double £36.00. Single £25.00. Children if accompanied by adult admitted free.

Stabling: 66 boxes, Phone Fakenham (0328) 862388.

Car Park: Free (except members car park £5.00 on 16th April and 28th May; £4.00 on 16th February, 16th March, 22nd October and 14th December)

Racecourses of Great Britain – Continued

FOLKESTONE (R.H.)

Circuit 1m 3f, somewhat undulating, with a straight, run-in of 3f. Races up to 6f, first ½m undulating with a slight rise over the final furlong, are run on the straight course.

Draw: 5f, 6f—Low.

Clerk of the Course: Mr D. E. Cameron, 11 Boltro Road, Haywards Heath, Sussex RH16 1BP. Phone: 0444-441111.

Secretaries: Messrs. Pratt & Co. Address as above.

Admission: Club £9.00; Tattersalls and Paddock £5.50. Accompanied children under 16 free. Course £2.00

Railway Station: Westenhanger, Kent. (from Charing Cross) adjoins course.

Car Park: Adjoining stands. Free except Course Enclosure £3.00.

Location: Those coming by car should leave the M20 at Junction 11

FOLKESTONE (N.H.)

Circuit approx. 1m 2f. Undulating. Run in 220yds. steeplechases, 250yds. hurdles.

FONTWELL PARK (L.H.) (N.H.)

Course for hurdle racing approx. 1 mile round. Undulating, 9 hurdles per 2¼m. Run in about 230 yds. Steeplechase course: Figure of eight. Steeplechase course run-in has slight left hand bend.

Clerk of the Course: C. Griggs, 11 Boltro Road, Haywards Heath, Sussex, RH16 1BP. Phone: Haywards Heath (0444) 441111, Racecourse; (0243) 543335.

Club Secretaries: Messrs. Pratt & Co., 11, Boltro Road, Haywards Heath, Sussex, RH16 1BP. Phone: Haywards Heath (0444) 441111.

Admission: Club day badge £10.00; Tattersalls and Paddock £7.00; Silver Ring £3.00.

Club Subscription: £75.00 + £5.00 Car Label (Personal Badge only).

Stabling: If arriving day before meeting: Phone Eastergate (024368) 3335.

Railway Station: Barnham, Sussex (from Victoria and London Bridge).

Public Car Park: Free; Silver Ring picnic car park; car £3.00 (occupants extra).

GOODWOOD (R.H.)

The Cup course is about 2m 5f, starting by the winning post and running the reverse way of the course, turning left after about 4f, and returning to the straight 5f run-in by the top bend. The Stakes Course is the last 2m 3f, the Bentinck course is the last 1m 6f and the Gratwicke Course is the last 1½m of the Cup Course. The Craven Course is 1m 2f, starting in almost the same spot as the Gratwicke Course but running in the reverse direction returning to the straight 5f run-in by the top bend. The Old Mile and 7f courses start on the Cup Course and join the 5f course on the lower bend. The 5f and 6f (Stewards Cup) courses are dead straight, the first furlong of the latter being uphill followed by a descent for 4f. Distance events test for stamina.
A new race distance was introduced in 1989 over 1m 1f. This 9f start is the same as the 1m 2f start on the Craven Course but entering the straight on the lower bend as per the 7f and 8f races.

Draw: 5f, 6f—High numbers favoured when stalls drawn on stands side but a quick start is essential.

Clerk of the Course and General Manager: Mr R. N. Fabricius, Goodwood Racecourse Limited, Chichester, Sussex PO18 0PX. Phone: Chichester 0243-774107, (Race-days 0243-774838).

Admission: Richmond enclosure £12.00 (n/a July); Grand Stand and Paddock £8.00 (£6.00 May to June); (£15.00 July); Public Enclosure £3.00;.
For further details apply to the Manager.

Racecourses of Great Britain – Continued

Railway Station: Chichester, Sussex. (from Victoria and London Bridge) 4½m from course.

Car Park: Adjacent to course. Apply: Goodwood Racecourse Limited.

Air Travel: Chicester (Goodwood) Aerodrome is situated 2 miles south of the Racecourse.

Helicopter landing pad at racecourse by p.p.o. (all inquiries to Blades Helicopters Ltd. Phone: Chichester (0243) 779222.

HAMILTON (R.H.)

A handle with loop course of 1m 5f from a start in front of the stands with a straight run-in of over 4f. 5f and6f courses are straight with an uphill finish. The course lies at the head of a valley, the hollow of which cuts the straight about 2¼f from the winning post.

Draw: 5f, 6f—Middle upwards.

Clerk of the Course: Miss Morag Chalmers, Racecourse Office, 2 Whitletts Road, Ayr, KA8 0JE. Phone: Ayr (0292) 264179.

Secretary: Miss J. I. C. Grant, Penrose Hill , Moffat, Dumfriesshire, Scotland DG10 9BX. Phone: Moffat (0683) 20131.

Admission: Club £10.00; Grand Stand and Paddock: £5.00 (special family admission prices and reduction for pensioners and registered unemployed). Special party rates. Racecards free.

Railway Station: Hamilton West. Frequent bus service from Glasgow passes course.

Car Park: Free for buses and cars.

Location: Course adjacent to the A74 and M74. 10 miles from Glasgow. Glasgow Airport 40 minutes by car.

HAYDOCK PARK (L.H.)

A flat oval course of 1m 5f with a straight run-in of 4f. 5f and 6f courses are straight.

Draw: 5f, 6f—High on soft ground, 7f, 8f—Low.

Clerk of the Course: Major P. W. F. Arkwright, Shirley Farm, Little Wolford, Shipston-on-Stour, Warwickshire, Phone: Long Compton (060884) 460.

Secretary: Mr F. Smith, Haydock Park Racecourse Company Limited, Newton-le-Willows, Merseyside WA12 0HQ. Phone: Ashton-in-Makerfield (0942) 727345 or 728017.

Admission: (Mid-week) County Stand £9.00; Tattersalls £5.50; Newton Stand £2.00. Saturdays and Bank Holiday Monday: County Stand £12.00; Tattersalls £6.00; Newton Stand £2.50. Pensioners half-price in Tattersalls and Newton Stand. Accompanied children under 16 free. Reductions for parties of 25 or over.

Railway Station: Newton-le-Willows, 2½ miles.

Car Park: On course. (Free)

Air Travel: Landing ground centre of course for planes not exceeding 10,000lb, laden weight.

HAYDOCK PARK (N.H.)

Undulating, 1 mile 5 furlongs circuit. Run in 440 yds.

HEREFORD (R.H.)
(N.H.)

About 1½ miles in circumference. Run in 200yds.

Clerk of the Course: J. Williams, F.R.I.C.S Shepherds Meadow, Eaton Bishop, Hereford HR2 9UA. Phone: (0981) 250436 Golden Valley (0981) 250291 (evenings): Hereford (0432) 273560 (race days).

Racecourses of Great Britain – Continued

Admission: Course £3.00; Tattersalls £6.00.

Stabling: Apply The Stabling Manager, The Racecourse House, Roman Road, Holmer, Hereford. Phone: Hereford (0432) 273560.

Railway Station: Hereford 1 mile.

Car Park: Free.

HEXHAM (L.H.) (N.H.)

Circuit approx. 1½ miles. Short hill just before straight. Run in 250yds. Full view from all enclosures.

Clerk of the Course and Manager: S. C. Enderby, The Riding, Hexham, Northumberland. Phone: Hexham (0434) 606881.

Admission: Club £8.00; Paddock £5.00 - Racecards free.

Club Subscription: Apply Secretary and Club Secretary: S. C. Enderby, The Riding, Hexham, Northumberland, NG46 4PF. Phone: Hexham (0434) 606881.

Railway Station: Hexham, Northumberland (E.R). Free bus service from station

Car Park: Free.

HUNTINGDON (R.H.) (N.H.)

Flat circuit of 1½ miles. Run in 200yds.

Clerk of the Course: H. Bevan, The Old House, Little Everdon, Daventry, Northants NN11 6B6. Phone: Preston Capes (032-736) 266: Racedays (0480) 454610.

Manager and Secretary: R. A. Juggins, Huntingdon Racecourse, Huntingdon, Cambs PE18 8NN. Phone: Huntingdon (0480) 453373 or 453235.

Admission: Club £8.00; Tattersalls £6.00; Course £3.00.

Car Park: Free (£1 on rails).

Club Subscription: Apply Club-Secretary, R. Arnold, Huntingdon Racecourse, Huntingdon, Cambs.

Stabling: 100 Boxes available. Allotted on arrival.

Railway Station: Huntingdon (E.R.).

KELSO (L.H.) (N.H.)

Circuit of hurdle course is 1 mile 330yds. Circuit of Steeplechase course is, 1 mile 600yds. Run in 440yds.

Clerk of the Course: Sam Morshead, Racecourse Office, 2 Whitletts Road, Ayr. KA8 0JE. Phone: Ayr (0292) 264179.

Secretary: R. M. Landale, 18-20 Glendale Road, Wooler, Northumberland. Phone: (0668) 81611.

Admission: Club £8.00 – £10.00; Paddock £5.00 (O.A.P's £2.50); (Free Racecards); Special Party Rates.

Stabling and Accommodation: For lads and girls at the racecourse. Phone: Kelso (0573) 24822.

Car Park: Free for buses and cars.

Racecourses of Great Britain – Continued

KEMPTON (R.H.)

The 1m 5f round or inner course joins the Jubilee course (1m 2f) for a 3½f straight run-in. The Jubilee course upon which are also run 7f and 1m races, has one right-hand turn into the straight. 5f and 6f races are run over a separate straight diagonal course.

Draw: Straight Course—No advantage. Round and Jubilee Course—High,

Clerk of the Course: Major R. M. O. Webster, Kempton Park, Sunbury-on-Thames TW16 5AQ. Phone: Sunbury (0932) 782292.

Club Secretary: Mrs Carol Milburn-Lee. Address as above. Phone: as above.

Admission: Club £10.00; (normal days) £12.00 (premium day); Grandstand £6.00 (normal) £8.00 (premium); Silver Ring £4.00 (Boxing Day £5.00) Boxing Day Club £18.00; Grandstand £12.00. All prices include a free racecard. Accompanied children under 16 free.

Railway Station: Kempton Park, Middlesex.

Car Park: Main car park £2.00; Silver Ring and Centre Free.

KEMPTON (N.H.)

Triangular circuit of 1 mile 5 furlongs practically flat. Run in 200yds. approx.

LEICESTER (R.H.)

An oval, galloping course of approx. 1m 5f with a straight run-in of 5f. Races of 1m and less are run on a dead straight course which joins the round course 5f from the finish, the first half being mainly downhill, followed by an ascent gradually levelling off to the winning post.

Draw: 5f, 6f—Low

Clerk of the Course: Captain N. E. S. Lees, The Racecourse, Leicester LE2 4AL. Phone: Leicester (0533) 716515 or Newmarket 664151.

Secretary: Mr D. C. Henson, The Racecourse, Leicester LE2 4AL. Phone: Leicester (0533) 716515. Enquiries concerning going etc., Leicester 712115.

Admission: Members £10.00; Tattersalls £7.00; Silver Ring £3.00 (includes free racecard and free car parking).

Railway Station: Leicester.

Car Park: Silver Ring Car Park (facing track) £10.00 admits car plus four occupants.

LEICESTER (N.H.)

Rectangular undulating circuit of 1¾ miles. Run in about 250yds.

LINGFIELD (L.H.)

Straight 7f 140yds is on a slightly falling and rising gradient from start to finish, the first 4f shows an average decline of 1 in 76 and last 4f a decline of 1 in 200. Round course intersects the straight at the 4f post with easy gradients to summit of slight hill. Derby Trial (1½m) Course is very similar to the Epsom Derby Course.

Draw: 5f, 6f, 7f 140yds—High numbers.

Clerk of the Course: G. R. Stickels, Lingfield Park Racecourse, Surrey, RH7 6PQ. Phone: Lingfield (0342) 834800.

Chairman: F. Clarke, Lingfield Park Limited, Lingfield, Surrey RH7 6PQ. Phone: Lingfield (0342) 834800.

Admission: Members Badge £10.00; Grandstand £6.00. Accompanied Juniors under 16 free. Pensioners (Grandstand only) £4.00; Saturday 12th May Members Badge £15.00; Grandstand £8.00; Pensioners (Grandstand only) £4.00.

Racecourses of Great Britain – Continued

Annual Membership: To all mettings £180 double; £100 single (22 turf meetings; 10 All-Weather Track).

Railway Station: Lingfield, Surrey. Regular service to and from London (Victoria) & London Bridge.

Car Park: Free. Reserved car park £2.00

LINGFIELD (A.W.T.)

The new configuration of Lingfield Racecourse incorporates a 1¼ mile all weather racecourse, with an extended chute to give a 1 mile 5 furlongs start. The re-aligned turf track which incorporates both Flat racing and National Hunt racing, extends around the outside of the all weather track, disposing of the tight Racecourse Road bend and the Flat course intersection of the old grass track. This now makes a very gradual bend into the back straight and joins the old turf course at the 2½ mile National Hunt start, commonly known as Weir Cottage bend. The angle of this bend has been considerably reduced. The original straight course is untouched by the all weather track, as is the downhill bend into the straight.

Admission: Members Badge £5.00; Grandstand £3.00; Accompanied Juniors under 16 Free. Group discounts do not apply.

LINGFIELD (N.H.)

Conical shaped course; circuit of 1 mile 2 furlongs; down-hill into straight. Run in 200 yds. approx.

LUDLOW (R.H.)
(N.H.)

Oval course. Circuit of 1½ miles. Steeplechase course is perfectly flat. Hurdle course slightly undulating. Run in 450yds.

Club Secretary & Clerk of the Course: B. R. Davies
Home: New House Farm, Much Marcle, Ledbury, Hereford, HR8 2PH. Phone: (053 184) 604.
Office: Shepherds Meadow, Eaton Bishop, Hereford, HR2 9UA. Phone: (0981) 250436. Fax: (0981) 250192

Admission: Course £3.00; Tattersalls £6.00; Members £9.00.

Railway Station: Ludlow

Club Subscription: For application for Membership apply to Secretary. Annual £50.00. Junior under 21 £25.00.

Car Park: Free.

Location: The course is situated at Bromfield, 2m north of Ludlow on the A49.

MARKET RASEN (R.H.)
(N.H.)

Oval in shape. Circuit of approx. 1¼ miles. Run in 220yds.

General Manager and Clerk of the Course: Major Charles L. Moore, The Weighing Room, Legsby Road, Market Rasen, LN8 3EA. Fax: (0673) 844532.

Secretary: Mrs S. Al-Soudani, Weighing Room, The Racecourse, Market Rasen, LN8 3EA. Phone: Market Rasen (0673) 843434.

Admission: Daily Club £8.00; Tattersalls £6.00; Silver Ring £3.50. (Racecards Free)

Club Subscription: Apply to Secretary.

Stabling: 98 boxes on Course, allocated on arrival. Please book overnight accomodation for stable staff.

Railway Station: Market Rasen, Lincs. (E.R.).

Racecourses of Great Britain – Continued

Car Park: Free, except Picnic Park at £2.00 per car.

Aircraft: Land facilities for helicopters only.

Caravan Club: Caravan site, 9-hole Golf Course opens Easter 1990.

NEWBURY (L.H.)

An oval course of about 1m 7f, 80 ft wide, with a straight mile slightly undulating. The 1m and the 7f 60yds on the round course start on a chute from the round course and both join the straight about 5f from the finish.

Draw: No material advantage.

Clerk of the Course: Captain C. B. Toller, The Racecourse, Newbury, Berks RG14 7NZ. Phone: Newbury (0635) 40015.

Manager and Secretary: Mr F. W. Osgood, The Racecourse, Newbury, Berks. RG14 7NZ Phone: Newbury (0635) 40015.

Admission: Club £11.00 weekdays, £15.00, Feb., Aug., Sept., Nov., all others £11.00 Saturdays; Tattersalls Saturdays, Feb., Aug., Sept., Nov., £8.00, all others £7.00, weekdays £6.00; Silver Ring £2.00; Picnic car park £2.00 plus £2.00 per adult

Railway Station: Racecourse Station.

Car Park: Car and coach parks: Free.

Air Travel: Aircraft landing ground, 1,100yds long by 50yds east to west.

NEWBURY (N.H.)

1 mile, 7 furlongs in circumference. Oval and slightly undulating. Run in 255yds.

NEWCASTLE (L.H.)

A flat oval course of 1¾m with a straight run-in of 4f gradually uphill with level 200yds at the finish. A straight seven furlongs, almost flat, joins the round course about 3½f from the post. Testing track.

Draw: No advantage.

Managing Director: Mr D. G. Parmley.

Clerk of the Course: Mr D. G. Parmley, High Gosforth Park, Newcastle-upon-Tyne, NE3 5HP. Phone: Tyneside (091) 236 2020 or (091) 236 5508

Admission: Club £12.00; £15.00 for Plate and Fighting Fifth Meeting; Tattersalls £7.00; Silver Ring £2.50.

Railway Station: Newcastle-on-Tyne (from Kings Cross). Bus service to the course from Four Lane Ends, Metro Station.

Car Park: All car and coach parking free.

NEWCASTLE (N.H.)

An oval course 1¾ miles in circumference with a level, straight finish of 4f, constructed inside the flat racecourse; run in 220yds.

Racecourses of Great Britain – Continued

NEWMARKET

The course is shaped roughly like the letter Y with straight arms and the tail bent to the right. The tail is represented by the Beacon Course which turns right at the Junction into the July Course on the right and the Rowley Mile Course on the left.

Clerk of the Course: Captain N. E. S. Lees, Westfield House, The Links, Newmarket, Suffolk, CB8 OTG. Phone: Newmarket 663482.

Admission: Members £12.00; Feature days 2000 Gns and Champion Stakes £20; 1000 gns, Cambridgeshire and July Meeting £17; Tattersalls 4 feature days £9; other days £7.50. Silver Ring 4 feature days £4; other days Rowley Mile £3. July Course Family Enclosure £2.00.

Railway Station: Newmarket (E.R. from Liverpool Street).

Car Park: At rear of enclosure free of charge. Members car park: £1.00 all days.

Rowley Mile Course (R-H)

This course is used for all except the Summer meetings. All races up to 1m 2f inclusive are perfectly straight with little rise or fall as far as "the Bushes," about two furlongs from the finish. From that point the course runs downhill for a furlong to "the Dip," the final furlong being uphill. Races exceeding 1m 2f start on the Beacon course and have a right-hand turn into the straight.

The lengths of the various courses are shown below:
R.C.=Rous Course (5 furlongs)
Bret=Bretby Stakes Course (6 furlongs)
Dew=Dewhurst Stakes Course (last 7 furlongs of Rowley Mile)
R.M.=Rowley Mile (1 mile)
Cambs.=Cambridgeshire Course (last 1m 1f of A.F.)
A.F.=Across the flat (1m 2f straight)
CES=Cesarewitch Course (1½m, 1¾m, 2m, 2½m, finishing A.F).

JULY COURSE (R.H.)

The meetings in June, July and August are held on this course. All races up to one mile inclusive are straight with a steadily increasing downhill gradient after two furlongs, the final furlong being uphill. Races of 1m 2f and over, start on the Beacon Course, turning right into the straight mile.
The lengths of the course are shown below:
C.C.=Chesterfield Course (5 furlongs)
B.M.=Bunbury Mile (6f, 7f, 1m)
S.S.=Suffolk Course (1¼m. 1½m)
S.C.=Summer Course (1m 6f 171y, 2m 24y)

NEWTON ABBOT (L.H.) (N.H.)

Oval circuit of just over 1 mile. Run in about 300yds.

Clerk of the Course: I. S. G. Lang, Higher Humber, Bishopsteignton, Teignmouth, Devon, TQ14 9TD. Phone: (0626) 77252

Secretary: C. Nekola, The Racecourse, Kingsteignton Road, Newton Abbot TQ12 3AF. Phone: Newton Abbot (0626) 53235 Night: 52853.

Admission: Course £3.00; Tattersalls £7.00.

Stabling: Apply to Secretary.

Railway Station: Newton Abbot, Devon (W.R.).

Car Park: Coaches free; cars free (£1.00 on rails).

Racecourses of Great Britain – Continued

NOTTINGHAM (L.H.)

This course consists of a perfectly flat straight 6f with a left-hand oval loop running into it giving a straight run-in of about 5f.

Draw: 5f, 6f—High. Round Course—Low.

Clerk of the Course and Manager: Mr D. C. Henson, 2 Lower Mounts, Northampton. NN1 3DE. Phone (0604) 30757 Fax (0604) 30758

Company Secretary: Mr R. J. Goodman, Prestbury Park, Cheltenham, Glos GL50 4SH.

Admission: Tattersalls £8.50; Silver Ring £4.00 (including free car parking and racecard with form guide).

Railway Station: Nottingham, Midland

Car Park: Silver Ring car park £12.00 (admits car and four occupants).

NOTTINGHAM (N.H.)

Oval circuit of 1½ miles. Flat run in 240yds.

PERTH (R.H.) (N.H.)

Circuit of about 1¼ miles. Racecourse equipped with own watering system.

Clerk of the Course: Sam Morshead, Racecourse Office, 2 Whitletts Road, Ayr. KA8 0JE. Phone: Ayr (0292) 264179.

Secretary: Miss J. I. C. Grant, Penrose Hill, Moffat, Dumfriesshire. Phone: Moffat (0683) 20131.

Admission: Club £8.00; Paddock £5.00; Course £2.00; Special Party Rates (Free Racecards).

Stabling: 100 boxes and accommodation for lads and girls. Apply to the Head Groundsman. Racecourse Telephone No.: Perth (0738) 51597.

Railway Station: Perth.

Car Park: Free.

PLUMPTON (L.H.) (N.H.)

Undulating, oval circuit of 1 mile, 1 furlong. Run in 200 yds.

Clerk of the Course: C. E. Griggs, 11 Boltro Road, Haywards Heath, Sussex, RH16 1BP. Phone: Haywards Heath (0444) 441111.

Admission: Annual Club membership £75.00 & £5.00 car label if required. Club daily badge £10.00; Tattersalls and Paddock £7.00; Course Enclosure £3.00

Stabling: If arriving day before meeting, Phone: Plumpton 890383.

Railway Station: Plumpton, Sussex (from Victoria and London Bridge) adjoining Course.

Car Park: 50p and £3.00 centre course.

PONTEFRACT (L.H.)

An undulating oval-shaped course of 2m 125yds, with a sharp bend into the 2f straight; 5f and 6f courses are part of the main course, the last 3f of which is on the ascent.

Draw: 5f, 6f—Low.

Clerk of the Course and Secretary: Mr J. Norman Gundill, 33 Ropergate, Pontefract, West Yorks. WF8 1LE. Phone: Pontefract (0977) 703224 (Secretary's Office) 702210 (Course Office Racedays only) 702323 (Stables/Foreman).

Racecourses of Great Britain – Continued

Admission: Club £10.00; Paddock £6.00; Silver Ring £2.50; Third Ring (car with four occupants) £5.00 or £1.50 per person through turnstyle. Accompanied children under 16 free. Reduced rates for parties (all enquiries to secretary).

Railway Station: Pontefract (Baghill).

Car Park: Adjacent to course, free.

REDCAR (L.H.)

A flat, oval galloping course of 1m5f, with a straight run-in of 5f. All races up to 1m are run on a straight course which joins the round course at the run-in.

Draw: 5f, 6f, 7f, 8f—High.

Clerk of the Course: Mr J. G. Cleverly F.R.I.C.S., Wells Cundall, 19 North Bar Within, Beverley, N. Humberside, HU17 8DB. Phone: N. Grimston (09446) 203. Office: Hull (0482) 867816.

Secretary: Mrs M. Rose, The Racecourse, Redcar, Cleveland TS10 4BY. Phone: Middlesbrough (0642) 484068.

Admission: Club £10.00; Grand Stand and Paddock £6.00; Course £1.50.

Railway Station: Redcar, Yorks.

Car Park: Free for buses and cars. Adjoining course.

Air Travel: Teesside Airport: 18 miles west of Redcar, taxi service to course.

RIPON (R.H.)

A sharp, oval course of 1m 5f with a straight run-in of 5f, the 6f course is also straight. The straight course is slightly on the ascent except for a shallow dip at the distance.

Draw: 5f, 6f—Low. 8f—High.

Clerk of the Course: Mr A. C. Newton, The White House, Myton-on-Swale, York, YO6 2QY. Phone: Boroughbridge (0423) 360643.

Secretary: Mr M. C. H. Hutchinson, 77 North Street, Ripon, Yorks HG4 1DS. Phone: Ripon 2156.

Admission: Club £10.00; Tattersalls £6.00; Silver Ring £2.50; Course £1.50.

Car Park: Free for buses and cars. Ample accommodation. For reservation, apply secretary.

SALISBURY (R.H.)

This course consists of a loop with "arm" of about 4f for the finish of all races. Races up to 1m are almost straight but for a slight right-hand elbow halfway. For 1¾m races, horses start opposite to Club Enclosure and, running away from the stands, diverge to the left, go round the loop and re-enter the "straight" (as is the case in all races of more than 1m) at the 7f starting gate. The last 5f are on the ascent.

Draw: 5f, 6f, 7f—High.

Clerk of the Course: I. Renton, Holywell Farmhouse, Holywell, Dorchester, Dorset. DT2 OLQ Tel: 0772 26461 (Office); 0935 83570 (Home).

Secretary: Mrs F. M. Gomersall, The Bibury Club, Salisbury Racecourse, Netherhampton, Salisbury, Wilts SP2 8PN. Phone: Salisbury (0722) 26461.

Admission: Members £9.50; Annual Member £60; Tattersalls £6.00; Course Enclosure £2.50.

Railway Station: Salisbury, Wiltshire (facilities from Waterloo). Bus service to course.

Car Park: Adjoining course, free.

Racecourses of Great Britain – Continued

SANDOWN PARK (R.H.)

This is a testing oval course of just over 1m 5f with a straight run-in of 4½f. The course is practically level until entering the straight, which rises increasingly to the winning post. The 1m course starts on a projecting arm which is straight and level for 2f where it enters the round course. 5f races are run on a separate straight course which runs inside the main circuit and is uphill the whole way.

Draw: 7f, 8f—High.

Clerk of the Course: Nick Cheyne, Sandown Park, Esher KT10 9AJ. Phone: Esher 63072/64348.

Club Secretary: Miss Karen Winterbourne, address and phone as above.

Managing Director: Mr Timothy P. Neligan

Admission: Club £10.00 or £12.00 according to meeting (Whitbread Gold Cup day and Coral Eclipse day £20.00); Tattersalls £6.00 or £8.00 according to meeting (Whitbread Gold Cup day and Coral Eclipse day £12.00); Park Enclosure £3.00 (Whitbread Gold Cup day and Coral Eclipse day £4.00). Club Junior (16-25 yrs) £7.00 or £9.00 according to meeting. (Whitbread Gold Cup Day and Coral Eclipse Day £13.00). All prices include a free racecard. Children under 16 free.

Railway Station: Esher, Surrey (from Waterloo), adjoins course.

Car Park: Members entrance in More Lane (£2); parking off Portsmouth Road free.

SANDOWN PARK (N.H.)

Oval circuit approx. 1m 5f. Uphill finish. 1st fence in 3 mile chase on down gradient. Run in approx. 300 yds.

SEDGEFIELD (L.H.) (N.H.)

Approx. 1¼ miles in circumference. Run in: Chases 500 yds. hurdles 200 yds.

Clerk of the Course: J. G. Cleverly, F.R.I.C.S., Wells Cundall, 19 North Bar Within, Beverley, N. Humberside, HU17 8DB. Phone: (Home) 09446 203: (Office) 0482 867816.

Secretary: D. McW. Riley, 23a The Green, Billingham, Cleveland, TS23 1ES. Phone: (0642) 557081, 559050.

Course Foreman: Sedgefield (0740) 20366.

Admission: Paddock £6.00, Course £2.50

Car Park: Free

SOUTHWELL (L.H.) (A.W.T.)

Oval track. Circuit 1¼ miles, 5 furlongs straight.

Clerk of the Course: R. Muddle, Southwell Racecourse, The Racecourse, Rolleston, Newark, Notts. NG25 0TS

Secretary: Mr J. P. Harris, Southwell Racecourse, The Racecourse, Rolleston, Newark, Notts. NG25 0TS. **Phone:** (0636) 814481; Fax: (0638) 812271

Admission: Day Membership £8.00; Paddock Enclosure £5.00; Pensioners £3.00. Children accompained by adult free.

Group Bookings: 11-20 £4.50; 21-50 £4.00; 51-100 £3.50; over 100 £3.00. Over 20 boxes discount of 50p; over 50 in Restaurant discount of £1.00.

Racecourses of Great Britain – Continued

Stabling: 94 boxes on the course.

Railway Station: Rolleston Junction, (main Nottingham to Lincoln line) adjoins the Course.

Car Park: Public Car Park Free; Coach Park Free; Members Car Park £2.00; Picnic Car Park £5.00

SOUTHWELL (L.H.) (N.H.)

Triangular course. Circuit approx. 1¼ miles. Run in 150 yds.

STRATFORD-ON-AVON (L.H.) (N.H.)

Circuit of 1 mile, 2 furlongs. Run in 200 yds.

Clerk of the Course: Lt.-Comdr. J. W. Ford, The Gables, Everdon, nr. Daventry, Northants. NN11 6BL. Phone: Preston Capes 221. (On racedays phone Stratford (0789) 67949 or 294272).

Company Secretary and Racecourse Manager: Mrs A. L. N. Gale, The Racecourse, Stratford-on-Avon CV37 9SE. (0789) 67949.

Club Secretary: R. M. Dunstan, Rickstaddles, Snitterfield, Stratford-on-Avon. Phone: Snitterfield 322.

Admission: Club £8.50; Tattersalls £6.00; course £3.00

Stabling: 96 boxes available. Allotted on arrival. Racecourse Phone: 0789-67949 (office), 294272 (weighing room).

Railway Station: Stratford-on-Avon (1 mile).

Car Park: Free (forward parking £2.50)

Location: Course is 1 mile from town centre, just off the Evesham road.

TAUNTON (R.H.) (N.H.)

Circuit approx 1¼ miles. Run in 150 yds.

Clerk of the Course and Secretary: Lt. Col. A. G. M. Shewen, The Racecourse, Taunton. Phone: Taunton (0823) 337172

Admission: Daily Member £8.00; Paddock £6.00; Course £3.00.

Club Subscription: £80.00 double badge, £50.00 single. 12 days racing.

Stabling: Approx. 100 boxes. Allotted on arrival.

Railway Station: Taunton, Somerset (from Paddington).

Car Park: Free for Members; either £1.00 or free parking for the public.

Location: Course is 2 miles from town centre on the Honiton road.

THIRSK (L.H.)

A perfectly flat oval course of 1m 2f, with a straight run-in of 4f. The 5f and 6f course is straight, undulating until it joins the round course at the run-in.

Draw: 5f, 6f—High. 7f, 8f—Low.

Racecourses of Great Britain – Continued

Clerk of the Course: Mr John Smith, The Racecourse, York, YO2 1EX. Phone: (0904) 620911.

Managing Director and Company Secretary: Mr Christopher Tetley, The Racecourse, Station Road, Thirsk, North Yorkshire.

Registered Office: Thirsk Racecourse Limited, The Racecourse, Station Road, Thirsk, N. Yorks YO7 1QL. Phone: Thirsk (0845) 22276.

Admission: Club £10.00; Tattersalls £6.00; Silver Ring £2.50; No. 3 Ring £1.50.

Stables: Phone (race days only): Thirsk 22096.

Railway Station: Thirsk, North Yorks. (from King's Cross). 1m from course.

Car Park: Free for buses and cars.

TOWCESTER (R.H.) (N.H.)

Circuit about 1¾ miles. Undulating. Run in about 140 yds.

Clerk of the Course and Manager: H. Bevan, The Old House, Little Everdon, Daventry, Northants NN11 6BG. Phone: Preston Capes (032 736) 266.

Secretary: F. P. Brangwyn, Easton Neston, Towcester, Northants, NN12 7HS. Phone: (0327) 50672.

Railway Station: Northampton (Buses to Towcester).

Admission: Day Member £8.00; Tattersalls £6.00; Course £3.00.

Car Park: £10.00 (admits car and occupants to course); free otherwise.

Location: Exit 16 from M1 North: Exit 13 from M1 south.

UTTOXETER (L.H.) (N.H.)

Approx. 1¼ miles in circumference. Run in 170 yards.

Clerk of the Course: David McAllister, Wychnor Nurseries, Wychnor, Burton Upon Trent. Tel: 0283 790127

Racecourse Tel: 0889 562561 (5 lines)

Manager and Club Secretary: D. McAllister, The Racecourse, Wood Lane, Uttoxeter. Phone: Uttoxeter (0889) 562561.

Stabling Manager: Phone: Uttoxeter (0889) 562561 for reservations. There are 78 boxes, allotted on arrival.

Admission: Club £9.00; Tattersalls £6.50; Silver Ring £4.50; Course (Infield) £2.50

Car Park: Free

Railway Station: Uttoxeter, Staffs. (Adjoining course).

WARWICK (L.H.)

The Mile Course is perfectly straight for the first 4f and the run-in is about 2½f. The 5f course is run with a dog-leg at halfway.

Draw: 5f, 7f, 8f—Low.

General Manager and Clerk of the Course: Mr E. W. Gillespie, Warwick Racecourse Co. Ltd., Prestbury Park, Cheltenham, Glos. GL50 4SH. Phone: Racedays: Warwick (0926) 491553, Office: (0242) 513014.

Club Secretary: P. R. McNeile, address and phone as General Manager.

Admission: Members £9.00; Tattersalls £6.00; Course £3.00.

Railway Station: Warwick and Leamington Spa.

Car Park: Centre of course £1.00.

Racecourses of Great Britain – Continued

WARWICK (N.H.)

1¾ miles circuit. Run in 240 yds.

WETHERBY (L.H.) (N.H.)

Oval 1½ mile circuit. 200 yds. run in; slight rise to finish.

Clerk of the Course: P. B. Firth, 6 Hayes Lane, Fakenham, Norfolk, NR21 9ER. Phone: (0328) 862388. Racedays only: Wetherby (0937) 62270 and 62035.

Secretary: G. M. Hanson, The Racecourse, Wetherby. LS22 5EJ. Phone: Wetherby (0937) 62035.

Admission: Club £10.00; Tattersalls £5.00; Course £1.50 (O.A.P's 50p). Annual Club: single £50.00; associate £80.00.

Car Park: Free. Excellent bus and coach facilities.

Location: Racecourse adjoins A1. Leeds 13m; York 13m.

WINCANTON (R.H.) (N.H.)

Good galloping course. Rectangular circuit approx. 1 mile 3 furlongs. Run in 200 yds. (approx.)

Clerk of the Course and Manager: R. I. Renton, Holywell Farmhouse, Holywell, Dorchester, Dorset. DT2 OLQ. Tel: 0963 32344 (Office); 0935 83570 (Home).

Secretary: Mrs J. Michell, Wincanton Racecourse, Wincanton, Somerset BA9 8BJ. Phone: (0963) 32344.

Admission: Members £9.00; Tattersalls £6.00; Course £3.00; Annual member £60.

Stabling: Apply Racecourse Secretary, Wincanton. Phone: Wincanton (0963) 32344.

Railway Station: Gillingham (from Waterloo); Castle Cary (from Paddington).

Car Park: Free.

WINDSOR (R.H. and L.H.)

Situated 20 minutes out of London on the M4 and additionally served by the M3 and M25, this 1m 4f course is shaped like a figure eight and is almost dead level. 5f and 6f are run from chute starts and are straight except for a slight bend approaching half-way.

Draw: 5f, 6f—High.

Clerk of the Course: Mr H. Bevan, The Old House, Little Everdon, Daventry, Northants. NN11 6BG. Phone: 032 736 266.

Phone: Windsor (0753) 865234 or 864726. Stables: 865350.

Admission: Club £10.00; Tattersalls and Paddock £6.00; Silver Ring £3.00. Accompanied children under 16 free.

Railway Station: Windsor Central (from Paddington). Windsor Riverside (from Waterloo).

Car Parks: £1.00, £1.50, £2.00. Coaches £1.00.

Air Travel: London Airport, 15 minutes by M4 motorway. Also White Waltham Airfield, Near Maidenhead.

Racecourses of Great Britain – Continued

WINDSOR (N.H.)

Figure of eight, almost dead level. The new western bend has cancelled out much of the sharpness. Circuit 1½ miles. Run in 200 yards.

WOLVERHAMPTON (L.H.)

A pear-shaped course, just over 1m 4f in circumference with a straight run-in of 5f. 5f races are straight.

Clerk of the Course: Lt-Cmdr. J. W. Ford. The Gables, Everdon, nr. Daventry, Northants. NN11 6BL Phone: Preston Capes (032 736) 221.

Secretary: Mr M. J. Legge. The Racecourse, Gorsebrook Road, Wolverhampton WV6 0PE. Phone: Wolverhampton (0902) 24481 or 772038.

Admission: Members £9.00; Tattersalls £6.00; Course £3.00; pensioners £2.50.

Stabling: Phone: Wolverhampton 22673.

Railway Station: Wolverhampton (½ mile).

Car Park: Dunstall Lane entrance and Dunstall Enclosure (on rails) £1.00.

Air Travel: Halfpenny Green, 8m from course. Phone: (038 488) 350 and 328.

Location: 2½ miles south of Exit 2 M54 on A449.

WOLVERHAMPTON (N.H.)

Flat circuit of 1½ miles. Run in 220yds., approx.

WORCESTER (L.H.) (N.H.)

Oval circuit 1 mile 5 furlongs. Run in 220yds.

Clerk of the Course: H. Bevan, The Old House, Little Everdon, Daventry, Northants, NN11 6BG. Phone: Preston Capes (032 736) 266.

Manager: J. H. A. Bennett, The Racecourse, Worcester WR1 3EJ. Phone: Worcester (0905) 25364 or Upton-on-Seven (06846) 2033.

Railway Station: Foregate St. Worcester.

Admission: Club £8.50; Tattersalls £6.50; Centre Course Enclosure £3.00; O.A.P.s. £1.20 (Centre Course only). No annual membership. Racecard 50p. Party discount (12 persons or more); Club £6.50; Tattersalls £4.90; Centre Course Enclosure £2.25.

Car Park: Free.

YARMOUTH (L.H.)

A narrow oblong course approximately 1½m in circumference with a slight fall to a straight run-in of almost 5f. A straight mile joins the round course at the home turn and is perfectly level. The 5f, 6f and 7f courses form part of the straight mile.

Draw: No advantage.

Clerk of the Course: Captain N. E. S. Lees, Westfield House, The Links, Newmarket, Suffolk CB8 0TG. Phone: Newmarket (0638) 663482.

Manager: Paul Sheild Esq., The Racecourse, North Dene, Great Yarmouth, NR30 4AU. Phone: Great Yarmouth (0493) 845227

Racecourses of Great Britain – Continued

Admission: Members £9.00; Tattersalls £6.50; Course and family enclosures £3.

Railway Station: Vauxhall Station, Great Yarmouth, Norfolk. Bus service to course.

Car Park: Large park adjoining course, 50p.

Air Travel: Aircraft landing facilities adjacent to course (Air Anglia Limited).

YORK (L.H.)

A flat wide course of 2m with two bends and a straight run-in of 4½f. 5f and 6f courses are quite straight and join the round course after the 5f gate. The 7f course starts on a 2f chute which curves left to join the round course 5f from home.

Draw: Low numbers best on very soft ground.

Manager, Clerk of the Course and Secretary: Mr J. L. Smith, The Racecourse, York YO2 1EX. Phone: York (0904) 620911.

Admission: Club £25.00 (August), £14.00 (May), £12.00 (others). Tattersalls £9.00 (August), £7.50 (others). Silver Ring £3.00. Course £1.50. Three-day passes available at discount.

Railway Station: York (from Kings Cross).

Car Park: Bookings can be made prior to race meetings (except August) for reserved car park for £2.00 (inc. VAT) per day. All other parking free.

IRISH RACECOURSES

CURRAGH (R.H.)

Horseshoe with no sharp bends, over 2m with a straight run-in of 3f, uphill finish. There are starts at 5f, 6f, 6f 63yds and 7f on a straight course, with a 1m start as a chute on this course, as well as a 1m start on the round course.
A new Outer Course, 2m N.H. is likely to be used occasionally.

Draw: No significant effect.

Clerk of the Course: Mr D. P. Martin.

Manager and Secretary: Mr J. Marsh, M.V.B. M.R.C.V.S. Curragh Racecourse, Co. Kildare. Phone: Curragh 41205 Telex: 60666.

Railway Station: Kildare 3m and Curragh main line platform 500 yards from stands on race days.

Car Park: Adjoining course (free).

LEOPARDSTOWN (L.H.)

A level, oval track of 1¾m, five miles south of Dublin. The sweeping bends and long run-in suit a strong galloper. Straight 6f sprint course.

Draw: Low numbers have a slight advantage over 7f and 1m, otherwise there is no effect. High numbers best on sprint course.

Clerk of the Course: Mr J. Collins.

Manager: A. Corcoran., Leopardstown Club, Foxrock., co. Dublin. Phone: Dublin 893607

Railway Station: Dun Laoghaire 3m.

Racecourses of Great Britain – Continued

PHOENIX PARK (L.H. and R.H.)

A level track four miles west of Dublin with left and right-handed courses. The left-handed course has a sharp turn into the straight.

Draw: 7f–High numbers in big fields.

Clerk of the Course: Mr Peter Martin

Directors: Mr Jonathan Irwin and Mr John Sanderson.

Manager: Mr Teddy Tighe, Phoenix Park Racecourse, Dublin. Phone: Dublin 300837

Railway Station: Ashtown.

Car Park: Ample free car parking adjacent to the racecourse.

Raceform
HANDICAP BOOK

ON SALE EVERY THURSDAY
ORDER NOW!

95p from all good Newsagents.

Includes indexed racecards for Friday and Saturday, comprehensive statistics and Official Jockey Club ratings updated weekly.

RACEFORM STANDARD TIMES

REVISED UP TO 1989 INCLUSIVE

The following represent the standard true-run race times for the varied distances and courses brought to 9st.

ASCOT

5f....1/0.5s
6f....1/13.6s
7f....1/26.5s
1m (str)....1/39.3s
Old Mile....1/39.6s
1m 2f....2/4.5s
1½m....2/29.5s
2m....3/23s
2½m....4/16s
2m 6f 34yds (est)....4/48s

AYR

5f....58s
6f....1/10.4s
7f (est)....1/23.3s
1m....1/37.4s
1m 2f....2/5.5s
1m 3f....2/15s
1m 5f....2/46.5s
1m 7f....3/13s
2m 1f 90yds (est)....3/41s
2m 4f 90yds (est)....4/26s

BATH

5f....1/1.2s
5f 167yds....1/9.2s
7f 8yds....1/27.8
1m 8yds....1/39.3s
1m 2f 50yds....2/7.7s
1m 3f 150yds....2/26.7s
1m 5f 12yds....2/49s
2m 1f 27yds....3/44s
2m 1f 194yds (est)....3/58s

BEVERLEY

5f....1/1.5s
7f 110yds....1/31.6s
1m 100yds....1/43.7s
1¼m....2/2.5s
1½m....2/31.6s
2m 40yds....3/30.7s
2m 3f (est)....4/10s
2m 3f 100yds (est)....4/17s

BRIGHTON

5f 66yds....1/0.7
6f....1/9s
7f....1/20.3s
1m....1/32.5s
1¼m....1/58.3s
1½m....2/27s

CARLISLE

5f....1/0.2s
6f....1/13s
7f(est)....1/26s
1m....1/38.7s
1m 1f 80yds....1/57s
1½m....2/29s

CATTERICK

5f....58.2s
6f....1/11.3s
7f....1/23.7s
1m 3f 40yds....2/23.6s
1½m 40yds....2/36s
1m 5f 180yds....2/58s
1m 7f 180yds....3/23.6s

CHEPSTOW

5f....57s
6f....1/9s
7f....1/20.2s
1m....1/32.5s
1¼m....2/4.5s
1½m....2/31.5s
2m....3/28s

FLAT STANDARD TIMES – *continued*

CHESTER

5f	1/0s
6f	1/13s
7f (est)	1/25.4s
7f 122yds (est)	1/32s
1m 2f 85yds	2/9s
1m 3f 70yds (est]	2/22s
1m 4f 65yds	2/36s
1m 5f 88yds	2/50s
About 2m	3/22.3
2m 2f 97yds	3/59s

CURRAGH

5f	58s
6f	1/11s
6f 63yds	1/14.3s
7f	1/24.5s
1m	1/36s
1m (new mile)	1/36s
1m 1f (est)	1/50.5s
1¼m	2/3s
1m 3f (est)	2/17s
1½m	2/31s
1m 5f (est)	2/44s
1m 6f (est)	2/57s
2m (est)	3/24s

DONCASTER

5f	58.7s
5f 140yds	1/7s
6f	1/11.5s
7f	1/24s
1m (str)	1/36.5s
1m (round)	1/36.6s
1m 2f 50yds	2/7s
1m 3f	2/19s
1½m	2/31s
1m 6f 127yds	3/4s
2m (est)	3/28s
2m 110yds (est)	3/34s
2¼m	3/53.3s

EDINBURGH

5f	57.6s
7f	1/26.2s
1m	1/38.7s
1m 3f	2/20s
1½m	2/32.7s
1m 7f	3/10.7s

EPSOM

5f	55s
6f 9yds	1/8.7s
7f 11yds	1/21.3s
1m 110yds	1/42s
1¼m	2/4.3s
1½m	2/35s
2¼m	3/55s

FOLKESTONE

5f	59s
6f	1/11.3s
7f	1/22s
1m 110yds (est)	1/44s
1m 1f 130yds (est)	1/57s
1¼m	1/58.7s
1½m	2/34s
1m 7f (est)	3/14s
1m 7f 100yds	3/20s
2m 100yds	3/33s

GOODWOOD

5f	58s
6f	1/10.5s
7f	1/25.3s
Old Mile	1/37.7s
1m 1f (est)	1/53.5s
1¼m	2/5s
1½m	2/33s
1m 6f	2/58s
2m 3f	4/8.5s
2m 5f	4/31s

HAMILTON

5f	58.3s
6f	1/10.5s
1m 40yds	1/43.6s
1m 1f	1/54.5s
1m 3f (est)	2/19.5s
1½m	2/32s
1m 5f (est)	2/47s

FLAT STANDARD TIMES – *continued*

HAYDOCK

5f....................59s
6f....................1/12s
7f 40yds....................1/27s
1m 40yds.................1/40.5s
1m 2f 130yds...............2/10s
1½m....................2/27.5s
1m 6f (est)....................2/55s
2m (est)....................3/25s
2m 35yds (est)..............3/26s
2m 1f 130 yds (est)......3/45s
2m 3f (est)....................4/3.3s

KEMPTON

5f....................59s
6f....................1/11.7s
7f (Round)...............1/24.7s
7f (Jubilee)..................1/24s
1m (Round).............1/37.6s
1m (Jubilee)................1/37s
1m 1f (Round) (est).....1/50s
1m 2f (Jubilee)...........2/2.3s
1m 3f 30yds.................2/19s
1½m....................2/30.5s
1m 6f (est)....................2/57s
2m....................3/24s

LEICESTER

5f....................59s
6f....................1/10.4s
7f....................1/22.6s
1m....................1/35s
1¼m....................2/3s
1m 4f....................2/29.5s

LEOPARDSTOWN

5f....................59s
6f....................1/11.2s
7f....................1/26s
1m....................1/38.4s
1m 1f....................1/50.5s
1m 2f....................2/4s
1½m....................2/30s
1m 5f....................2/43s
1m 6f (est)................2/56.5s
2m (est)....................3/27s
2¼m (est)....................3/52s
2½m (est)....................4/18s

LINGFIELD

5f....................57.2s
6f....................1/9s
7f....................1/20.3s
7f 140yds....................1/27s
1m 1f....................1/53.7s
1m 2f....................2/5.3s
1½m....................2/31.5s
1¾m....................2/58s
2m....................3/24.7s

NAAS

5f....................1/0s
6f....................1/12s
7f....................1/24s
1m 1f....................1/51s
1½m....................2/32s
2m (est)....................3/27s

NEWBURY

5f....................1/0.5s
6f....................1/12.3s
7f....................1/25s
7f 60yds..................1/27.3s
1m (Str)....................1/37s
1m (Round).................1/36s
1¼m....................2m 3.4
1m 3f (est)...............2/17.4s
1½m....................2/30.3s
1m 5f 60yds.............2/46.3s
2m....................3/26.7s

NEWCASTLE

5f....................59.5s
6f....................1/12s
7f....................1/24.2s
1m (est)....................1/39s
1m 1f 20yds..............1/52.3
1m 2f 40yds....................2/7s
1m 4f 80yds.................2/39s
2m....................3/25s
2m 2f (est)....................3/52s

FLAT STANDARD TIMES – *continued*

NEWMARKET

(ROWLEY MILE COURSE)

Rous Course (5f) 59.4s
Bretby Stakes Course (6f) 1/11.7s
Dewhurst Stakes Course (7f) 1/24s
R.M. (1m)................ 1/37.7s
New Cambridgeshire Course (1m 1f) 1/50.6s
A.F. (1m 2f)................2/3.7s
Last 1½m Cesarewitch Course........................2/31s
Last 1¾m Cesarewitch Course........................2/57s
Last 2m Cesarewitch Course.........................3/25s
Cesarewitch Course (2m 2f) 3/50.6s
2½m Cesarewitch Course (est).............................4/19s

(JULY COURSE)

Chesterfield Course (5f) 59s
Last 6f of B.M........... 1/11.5s
Last 7f of B.M........... 1/24.7s
B.M. (1m).....................1/38s
Last 1m 2f Suffolk Stakes Course........................2/3.5s
Suffolk Stakes Course (1m 4f) 2/29s
Last 1m 6f 175yds of Summer Course (est) 3/7s
Summer Course (2m 24yds) 3/23.4s
2½m Summer Course (est).............................4/21s

NOTTINGHAM

5f.....................................59s
6f............................. 1/11.4s
1m 50yds 1/40.4s
1¼m 2/2.5s
1m 5f............................2/45s
1m 6f (est)............... 2/58.5s
2m........................... 3/25.3s
2m 2f (est)....................3/52s

PHOENIX PARK

5f.....................................57s
6f....................................1/9s
7f..................................1/18s
1m................................1/34s
1m 1f....................... 1/46.6s
1m 2f............................1/59s
1m 3f (est).............. 2/12.5s
1m 4f............................2/29s
1m 6f (est)............... 2/56.3s
2m...............................3/22s
2m 1f (est)............... 3/34.5s

PONTEFRACT

5f................................1/1.3s
6f..................................1/14s
1m........................... 1/41.6s
1¼m 2/8.3s
1m 4f....................... 2/34.5s
2m 1f (est)....................3/39s
2m 2f...........................3/52s
2m 5f 125yds(est) 4/41s

REDCAR

5f.................................57.5s
6f.................................1/9.7s
7f............................. 1/22.2s
1m........................... 1/35.4s
1m 1f (est)............... 1/49.5s
1¼m 2/2.5s
1m 3f(est) 2/16s
1½m 2/30.3s
1m 5f 125y (est)....... 2/50.4s
1m 6f (est)....................2/57s
2m (est) 3/25s
2m 115yds (est)...........3/32s
2m 3f (est)......................4/3s

RIPON

5f.................................58.3s
6f............................. 1/11.6s
1m........................... 1/37.6s
1m 1f...........................1/50s
1¼m 2/4s
1½m 70yds 2/32.5s
1m 6f 132yds..............3/8.2s
2m........................... 3/24.5s
2m 2f (est)....................3/51s

FLAT STANDARD TIMES – *continued*

SALISBURY

5f	1/0s
6f	1/12.8s
7f	1/26.5s
1m	1/40s
1¼m	2/4.7s
1½m	2/32.7s
1¾m	2/58.4s

SANDOWN

5f	1/0s
7f	1/26.7s
1m	1/39.5s
1m 1f (est)	1/51.6s
1¼m	2/4s
1m 3f 100yds (est)	2/21.5s
1¾m	2/54s
2m	3/30s

THIRSK

5f	59.5s
6f	1/10s
7f	1/24.2s
1m	1/38s
1½m	2/31s
2m	2/23s
2m 1f	3/39.4s
2m 2f	3/56.5s

WARWICK

5f	59.3s
6f	1/12s
7f	1/24s
1m	1/36.7s
1m 2f 170yds	2/13.5s
1m 4f 52yds (est)	2/37s
1m 6f 180yds (est)	3/8s
2m	3/26s
2m 2f 180yds (est)	4/5s

WINDSOR

5f	59.3s
6f	1/11.3s
1m 70yds	1/41.7s
1m 2f 22yds	2/3.4s
1m 3f 150yds	2/22s

WOLVERHAMPTON

5f	57.3s
7f	1/24s
1m	1/37.5s
1m 1f	1/49.3s
1m 3f (est)	2/15s
1m 4f 100yds	2/32s
1m 7f 70yds	3/7s
2m 1f 130yds	3/39s

YARMOUTH

5f 25yds	1/0.3s
6f	1/10.6s
7f	1/22.6s
1m	1/35s
1¼m	2/4.4s
1m 3f 110yds (est)	2/23s
1m 6f	2/58.5s
2m 2f 26yds	3/57s

YORK

5f	58s
6f	1/10.2s
7f	1/22.6s
1m	1/36s
1m 1f	1/49.4s
1m 2½f	2/7.5s
1½m	2/27s
1m 6f	2/55s
2m	3/20s

From all good newsagents every Thursday

RACEFORM HANDICAP BOOK

FLAT RACE DISTANCES SURVEY 1989

All Flat race distances in the UK (34 racecourses) were re-measured during the winter '88-'89 and, as a result of discrepancies at eleven tracks, action has been taken as shown below. Although some starts have been moved (col 3), the majority of the conflicting distances have a new description for 1989 (col.4)

Course	1988 Distances	Alteration to Start	1989 Description
Beverley	7f about 100y	None	7f about 110y
	2m	None	2m about 40y
Brighton	About 5f	None	5f about 66y
Chester	1m 7f 186y	None	About 2m
Haydock	6f	Stalls 10y back	No change
	About 1m 2f	None	1m 2f about 130y
	2m 28y	None	2m about 35y
	2m about 3f	None	2m 2f about 130y
Newcastle	7f	Stalls 4y forward	No change
	1m	Stalls 9y forward	No change
	1m 1f	None	1m 1f about 20y
	1m 2f	None	1m 2f about 40y
	1m 4f 60y	None	1m 4f about 60y
Newmarket July	1m 6f 171y	None	1m 6f 175y
Pontefract	2m 1f 24y	None	About 2m 1f
	2m 5f 133y	None	2m 5f about 125y
Redcar	6f	Stalls 23y forward	6f
Ripon	5f	Stalls 6y forward	No change
	6f	Stalls 10y forward	No change
	1m	Stalls 5y forward	No change
	1m 1f	Stalls 7y forward	No change
	1m 2f	Stalls 7y forward	No change
	About 1½m	None	1m 4f about 70y
	2m	Stalls 20y back	No change
	2m 2f	Stalls 6y forward	No change
Thirsk	7f	Stalls 7y back	No change
	1m	Stalls 5y forward	No change
	1m 4f	Stalls 14y forward	No change
Wolverhampton	About 1m 4f	None	1m 4f about 100y
	About 1m 6½f	None	1m 7f about 70y
	About 2m 1f	None	2m 1f about 130y

TOP SPEED FIGURES RECORDED 1989

TWO-YEAR-OLDS

COLTS		FILLIES	
1. Rock City	79	1. Negligent	76
2. Balla Cove	77	2. Chimes of Freedom (USA)	75
3. Be My Chief (USA)	74	3. Pharoah's Delight	75
4. Duck and Dive	74	4. Tanwi	74
5. Daarik	73	5. The Caretaker	70

SPRINTERS

5f–6f

3-Y-O		OLDER HORSES	
1. Danehill (USA)	96	1. Cadeaux Genereux	104
2. Dancing Dissident (USA)	95	2. Chummy's Favourite	97
3. Golden Opinion (USA)	91	3. Carol's Treasure	94
4. Statoblest	88	4. Mac's Fighter	94
5. Silca Supreme	87	5. Ajanac	93

MILERS

7f–9f

3-Y-O		OLDER HORSES	
1. Zilzal (USA)	98	1. Warning	98
2. Green Line Express (USA)	89	2. Most Welcome	94
3. Nashwan (USA)	89	3. Llyn Gwynant	92
4. Distant Relative	86	4. Beau Sher	85
5. Exbourne (USA)	86	5. Hello Vaigly	83

MIDDLE DISTANCE

10f–12f

3-Y-O		OLDER HORSES	
1. Aliysa	94	1. Ile de Chypre	97
2. Nashwan (USA)	93	2. Sheriff's Star	93
3. Old Vic	92	3. Emmson	89
4. Snow Bride (USA)	88	4. Beau Sher	88
5. Roseate Tern	87	5. Most Welcome	88

STAYERS

13f–20f

3-Y-O		OLDER HORSES	
1. Michelozzo (USA)	88	1. Sadeem (USA)	89
2. Weld	84	2. Zero Watt (USA)	82
3. Demawend	79	3. Upper Strata	80
4. Free Sweater (USA)	78	4. Zaffaran (USA)	79
5. Polar Run (USA)	77	5. Nomadic Way (USA)	78

FLAT SPEED FIGURES 1989

The following list, based on Standard Times, shows speed figures of 40 and upwards, returned on British and selected Irish tracks. All the ratings are given at 9st. after allowances for going and distance behind winners. Additional information in parentheses following the speed figure shows the distance of the race in furlongs, course, state of going and the date on which the figure was recorded. Going abbreviations are: H (hard), F (firm), G (good), Y (yielding), S (soft), Hvy (Heavy).

THREE-YEAR-OLDS AND UPWARDS

Aahsaylad 41 (11f, Red, F, Oct 31)
Aardvark 44 (8f, Tsk, H, June 20)
Absolution 76 (5f, Yrk, F, May 17)
Access Travel 80 (5f, Nmkt, F, May 6)
Ack Va Vite (USA) 65 (8f, Nby, F, May 20)
Adamlyi (USA) 40 (10f, Yar, F, July 19)
Adbass (USA) 49 (7f, Leo, G, Aug 27)
Adjriyna 45 (8f, Gwd, F, July 25)
Admiralty Way 54 (7f, War, F, Oct 10)
Aerobics Plus 68 (10f, Nmkt, F, July 29)
African Dash 46 (7f, Gwd, F, May 25)
African Light 47 (10f, Nby, F, May 19)
African Safari 49 (6f, Kem, F, May 27)
African Spirit 57 (7f, Nmkt, G, Oct 7)
Afriyd 62 (10½f, Yrk, F, July 15)
Afwaj (USA) 71 (6f, Yrk, G, Oct 14)
Ahsanta Sana 48 (6f, Ayr, Y, Sep 23)
Ahwak 58 (11f, Red, F, Aug 1)
Aim To Please 69 (12f, Hay, G, Sep 1)
Aitch N'Bee 58 (7½f, Bev, G, Apr 21)
Ajanac 93 (6f, Ayr, Y, Sep 22)
Ajraas (USA) 46 (8f, Bri, F, June 19)
Akdam (USA) 53 (10f, Nwc, G, Oct 28)
Akin To Fame 48 (7f, Yrk, F, May 17)
Ala Hounak 65 (16f, San, F, May 29)
Albadr (USA) 55 (12f, Nby, Y, Oct 28)
Albazm 45 (12f, Flk, F, Oct 10)
Alcando 71 (10f, Phx, F, Sep 2)
Aldahe 51 (5f, Edn, F, Sep 18)
Aldbourne 79 (8f, Cur, F, May 27)
Al Diffa (USA) 43 (12f, Tsk, H, June 20)
Aldino 68 (12f, Eps, G, Apr 26)
Alexandra Katrine 52 (5f, Red, F, Aug 4)
Algaihabane (USA) 49 (11f, Red, F, May 30)
Al Hanash (USA) 54 (10f, Eps, F, Aug 29)
Aliocha (USA) 65 (7f, Asc, F, June 21)
A Little Precious 44 (6f, Not, S, Mar 27)
Aliysa 94 (12f, Eps, F, June 10)
Aljarih (USA) 43 (10½f, Hay, F, Sep 29)
Alkinor Rex 60 (10f, Kem, Y, Mar 27)
Allasdale (USA) 40 (10f, Lei, S, Apr 3)
Alleged Savage (USA) 40 (10f, Phx, Y, May 3)
Allez Au Bon 65 (8f, Nwc, F, June 30)
Allied Force 56 (12f, Lin, F, June 3)
All Saints Day (USA) 44 (10f, Bri, F, June 19)
Al Maheb (USA) 50 (10f, Rip, F, May 31)
Almost Blue 79 (5f, San, F, July 8)
Al Mufti (USA) 60 (12f, Eps, F, June 8)
Al Najah (USA) 46 (8½f, Eps, F, June 9)
Alnasric Pete (USA) 43 (9f, Kem, F, June 14)
Alo Ez 68 (6f, Nmkt, F, May 5)
Alphabel 69 (12f, Gwd, F, July 25)
Alpha Helix 47 (12f, Ham, G, May 5)
Alpine Pass 73 (8f, Cur, G, Oct 21)
Alpine Spring 57 (10f, Phx, Y, May 3)
Alqirm (USA) 57 (10f, Sal, F, June 28)
Alquoz (USA) 74 (7f, War, F, Oct 10)
Al Raja 51 (10f, Nby, F, Sep 22)
Alreef 44 (10½f, Hay, F, Sep 30)
Al Skeet (USA) 41 (12f, Kem, F, July 13)
Al-Torfanan 56 (7f, Wol, G, May 3)
Always Fair (USA) 66 (7f, Hay, F, June 10)
Always On A Sunday 60 (10f, Nmkt, F, Nov 3)
Always Ready 50 (5f, San, G, Sep 19)
Always Valiant 81 (10f, Nmkt, F, Oct 21)
Alydaress (USA) 84 (12f, Cur, F, July 15)
Amber King 65 (6f, Cur, F, May 27)
Amber Loch (USA) 65 (10f, Gwd, G, Aug 26)
Amber Nectar 45 (6f, Yar, F, Aug 3)
Amelianne (FR) 58 (14f, Yrk, F, Aug 22)
Amenable 55 (8f, Tsk, Y, Apr 14)
Amigo Menor 79 (6f, Nby, F, May 19)
Amoodi (USA) 60 (13f, Nby, G, June 27)
Anadax 58 (9f, Red, F, July 26)
Angel Bright 47 (10f, Nby, Y, Oct 26)
Angels Kiss 49 (8f, Rip, F, May 31)
Annabelle Royale 55 (7½f, Lin, F, Oct 5)
Annabrianna 52 (12f, Sal, F, May 23)
Anodyne 75 (6f, Hay, F, July 7)
Another Rhythm 57 (5f, San, F, May 30)

FLAT SPEED FIGURES – continued

Anthony Loretto 70 (6f, Nby, Y, Oct 28)
Antipathy 46 (7f, Phx, Hvy, Apr 15)
Apache 69 (12f, Nmkt, F, July 1)
Apollo King 46 (10f, Lei, F, May 30)
A Prayer For Wings 89 (6f, Hay, G, Sep 2)
Aptitude 54 (10f, Yar, F, June 27)
Aquaglow 67 (7f, Nmkt, F, July 13)
Aquatic 44 (6f, Yar, F, July 6)
Aradu 77 (8f, Asc, G, Oct 14)
Arizelos 68 (16f, Nmkt, G, May 4)
Army of Stars 68 (10½f, Hay, Y, Oct 12)
Arsaan (USA) 62 (10f, Nby, F, June 14)
Artic Envoy (USA) 64 (12f, Asc, F, June 20)
Asbaab 62 (7f, Nmkt, F, May 19)
Ashtina 81 (5f, Asc, F, Sep 29)
Asitappens 42 (8f, Yar, G, Aug 24)
Assatis (USA) 87 (12f, Asc, F, June 23)
Assignment 46 (7f, Nby, Y, Oct 26)
Astraeus (USA) 77 (6f, Phx, F, Aug 12)
Atall Atall 64 (6f, Ayr, G, Aug 7)
Athens Gate (USA) 62 (9f, Yrk, F, June 17)
Aughfad 49 (6f, Not, F, June 2)
August Agent (USA) 67 (7f, Phx, G, May 10)
Auto Connection 40 (10f, Yar, F, Aug 2)
Autumn Festival (USA) 40 (8f, Bth, F, May 6)
Averax 40 (8f, Ham, F, Sep 11)
Awa'wi'ye 44 (5f, Flk, G, Apr 3)
Awayed (USA) 74 (8f, Leo, F, Aug 7)
Awkas 52 (13f, Ham, F, May 15)
Azeb 54 (8f, San, S, Apr 29)

Babiana (CAN) 53 (6f, Nby, F, May 19)
Babil 48 (11½f, San, G, July 8)
Bailey's Comet 41 (10f, Phx, S, Apr 29)
Baldomero 72 (7f, Yrk, G, Oct 14)
Baligay 40 (7f, Chep, F, July 4)
Balizara 61 (8f, Tsk, H, June 20)
Balkan Leader 58 (5f, Edn, F, July 28)
Ballad Dancer 47 (5f, Don, G, Mar 31)
Ballafort 46 (6f, Not, F, Sep 26)
Ballinascreena 59 (16f, Cur, G, Oct 1)
Ballydurrow 43 (12f, Bev, F, Sep 20)
Baraz 42 (10f, Asc, F, Sep 29)
Barrish 43 (12f, Bri, F, Aug 17)
Barrys Gamble 64 (5f, San, F, May 29)
Bashful Boy 58 (8f, Nby, F, June 14)
Bastinado 52 (10f, Flk, F, July 4)
Batshoof 78 (10½f, Yrk, F, June 17)
Bawnanell 66 (5f, Cur, G, Aug 26)
Bay Bay 68 (6f, Yrk, F, Aug 22)
Bay Bird (USA) 61 (12f, Kem, F, July 13)
Bay Tern (USA) 49 (10f, Not, Y, May 2)
Bay Window 57 (11f, Ayr, Y, Sep 21)
Bean King 51 (10f, Wind, F, May 8)
Beau Benz 46 (10f, Bev, G, May 13)
Beaucadeau 59 (5f, Pon, F, July 11)
Beauchamp Cactus 54 (17½f, Wol, F, May 15)
Beauchamp Dream 68 (14f, Nmkt, F, Oct 19)
Beau Guest (FR) 52 (10f, Don, G, Mar 31)
Beau Ideal 63 (11½f, San, G, July 8)
Beaumont's Keep 44 (6f, Flk, F, Aug 22)
Beaumood 52 (13f, Ham, Y, Sep 25)
Beau Sher 88 (10f, Asc, F, June 20)
Beckingham Ben 45 (5f, Pon, F, Sep 5)
Becquerel (USA) 73 (8f, Yrk, F, June 17)
Bedford Ranger (USA) 46 (14f, Leo, G, May 15)
Beechwood Cottage 57 (7f, Bri, F, Sep 14)
Beekman Street 42 (16f, Nmkt, G, Oct 4)
Be Fresh 73 (6f, Nmkt, F, Oct 21)
Bel Byou 65 (7f, Tsk, F, May 20)
Belhomme 57 (7f, War, F, Oct 10)
Bella Rossi 65 (5f, San, F, July 7)
Bella Seville 57 (5f, Pon, F, Oct 9)
Bell Toll 42 (10f, Eps, F, June 9)
Bell Tower 57 (6f, Phx, G, May 10)
Belmartin 48 (8f, Cur, G, Oct 1)
Belmoredean 83 (12f, Nmkt, F, Oct 20)
Belpenel 46 (10f, Nby, F, June 15)
Be My Idle 50 (11f, Phx, G, June 17)
Be My Runner 49 (7f, San, G, July 7)
Ben Adhem 44 (12f, Tsk, G, Nov 11)
Bequest (USA) 53 (6f, Bri, G, Apr 13)
Bernstein Bette 48 (6f, Yar, F, Sep 12)
Bertie Wooster 75 (6f, Yrk, F, Sep 6)
Bescaby Boy 55 (8f, Lei, G, Apr 22)
Better Now 40 (7f, War, F, Aug 28)
Bex (USA) 63 (10f, Phx, G, Oct 7)
Beyond The Lake 59 (12f, Leo, G, June 14)
Bid Later 49 (6f, Flk, F, July 4)
Biennial (USA) 72 (10f, Gwd, F, July 28)
Big Bear 42 (10f, Nmkt, F, Aug 5)
Big Shuffle (USA) 81 (6f, Cur, G, May 20)
Billet 62 (10f, Don, G, May 1)
Bin Hathlain (USA) 53 (12f, Leo, G, June 14)
Birstwith (USA) 43 (8f, Don, F, Apr 1)
Black Jewel 54 (6f, Cur, Hvy, Mar 25)
Black Monday 65 (12f, Gwd, F, July 27)
Blasted Heath 65 (7f, Leo, F, July 22)
Blaze O'Gold (USA) 53 (10f, Lei, G, Apr 22)
Bluebird Lady 51 (5f, Yar, G, Sep 14)
Blue Mischief 49 (5f, Edn, F, Oct 25)
Blue Orca 50 (10f, Eps, F, Aug 29)
Blue Rhythm 48 (7f, Tsk, Y, Apr 14)
Blue Sceptre 57 (7f, Phx, G, Aug 25)
Blues Indigo 66 (5f, Yrk, F, July 14)
Blyton Lad 70 (5f, Nby, G, Sep 22)
Bocas Rose 54 (8f, Nmkt, F, July 12)
Boldden 47 (10f, Pon, F, July 3)
Bold Fox 58 (10f, Nwc, G, Oct 28)
Bold Habit 52 (6f, Car, F, June 28)
Bold Pillager 52 (8f, Lei, F, Oct 17)
Bold Republic 49 (9f, Yrk, F, July 14)
Bold Stranger 48 (16f, Nwc, F, July 1)
Bold Try 51 (8f, Chep, F, July 1)
Bollin Patrick 59 (12f, Tsk, Y, Apr 15)
Bollin Zola 62 (7f, Yrk, F, Sep 7)
Boot Polish 66 (8f, Red, F, May 29)
Bourbon Topsy 43 (16f, San, F, May 29)
Bournville 67 (7f, Nmkt, F, July 13)
Braashee 77 (12f, Asc, F, Sep 30)

FLAT SPEED FIGURES – continued

Braiswick 82 (10f, Nmkt, G, Oct 7)
Bramdean 40 (12f, Sal, G, May 3)
Brassy Nell 41 (7½f, Lin, F, Sep 12)
Breezed Well 59 (7f, Nmkt, F, Nov 4)
Briery Fille 42 (7f, Lin, G, Aug 31)
Brigadier Bill 43 (10½f, Hay, G, Aug 11)
Briggscare 42 (16f, Nmkt, G, Oct 4)
Bright Aisle 48 (10f, Don, G, Mar 30)
Brizlincote 52 (7f, Nmkt, F, May 19)
Broadway Rosie 60 (6f, Cur, F, July 15)
Broctune Grey 50 (16f, Nmkt, F, Aug 4)
Bronze Cross 52 (7f, Tsk, Y, Apr 14)
Brush Aside (USA) 64 (10f, Nmkt, G, May 4)
Brutus 50 (5f, Rip, F, June 21)
Budapest 61 (7f, Kem, G, Sep 1)
Burcroft 48 (12f, Pon, Y, Apr 19)
Burgoyne 57 (11f, Red, F, Oct 31)
Burkan 67 (10f, Eps, F, June 7)
Burning Volcano 45 (10f, San, F, May 30)
Bush Hill 45 (12f, Asc, F, Sep 30)
Bu-Sofyan 55 (8f, Sal, H, Oct 4)
Busted Rock 59 (10f, Nmkt, F, July 29)
Butlers Wharf 45 (12f, Asc, F, June 21)
Buzzards Son 52 (7f, Eps, F, June 10)
Bywell Lad 44 (12f, Lei, S, Apr 3)

Cacoethes (USA) 84 (10½f, Yrk, F, Aug 22)
Cadeaux Genereux 104 (6f, Nmkt, F, July 13)
Caerforme 48 (6f, Cur, F, Sep 9)
Caerless Writing 51 (12f, Cur, F, July 15)
Caleva 57 (9f, Leo, G, Aug 27)
Calltheminstrel (CAN) 62 (7f, Cur, F, Sep 10)
Cambo (USA) 52 (10f, Not, Y, May 2)
Camden Knight 41 (8½f, Bev, G, Apr 22)
Camden's Gift 40 (14f, Leo, G, May 15)
Cantoris 49 (5f, Bri, F, Oct 3)
Cape Pearl 44 (7f, Kem, F, June 14)
Cape Pigeon (USA) 58 (7f, Gwd, G, Aug 26)
Captain's Bidd 46 (5f, Cat, F, July 19)
Captive Heart 44 (7f, Chep, F, July 13)
Cara Deilish 43 (7f, Phx, G, June 17)
Careafolie 74 (8f, Cur, F, July 2)
Carlingford (USA) 67 (12f, Asc, F, June 22)
Carmagnole (USA) 45 (13f, Bth, F, July 8)
Carmencita 42 (10f, Cur, F, May 27)
Carnival Spirit 62 (8f, Asc, G, Oct 14)
Carol's Treasure 94 (5f, Yrk, F, July 14)
Carotic (USA) 52 (12f, Nmkt, F, Oct 20)
Carpe Diem 48 (7f, Wol, G, May 3)
Carroll House 85 (10f, Cur, F, May 20)
Carry On Cary 52 (8f, Yar, F, July 5)
Cartier Bijoux 53 (5f, Gwd, G, Oct 6)
Caspian Gates 47 (12f, Bev, F, Sep 20)
Caspian Mist 59 (10f, Don, G, Mar 30)
Castleacre 43 (10f, Not, F, June 26)
Castle Clown 61 (10f, Kem, Y, Mar 27)
Castle Peak 51 (12f, Tsk, F, May 20)
Castle Secret 55 (16f, Asc, G, Oct 13)
Catalani 46 (6f, Ayr, G, Aug 7)
Cathedral Peak 40 (10f, Kem, F, July 13)
Causa Sua 60 (10f, Cur, F, May 20)
Causley 54 (8f, Hay, Y, Oct 11)
Ceciliano (USA) 51 (12f, Lin, F, May 13)
Cee-En-Cee 48 (5f, San, F, Aug 19)
Celtic Bhoy 42 (12f, Eps, F, Aug 29)
Celtic Monarch 43 (7f, Phx, F, May 31)
Chadenshe 44 (7f, Lei, G, Apr 22)
Chain Shot 59 (5f, Flk, F, June 6)
Chaplins Club (USA) 71 (6f, Ayr, Y, Sep 22)
Charbatte (FR) 50 (7f, Yrk, F, Aug 24)
Charcoal Burner 40 (7f, Bri, F, May 10)
Charden 53 (14f, Sal, F, Aug 10)
Charmer 74 (10f, Nmkt, F, Oct 21)
Checkpoint Charlie 61 (10f, Nmkt, F, July 29)
Cheerful Times 47 (12f, Hay, G, July 8)
Chelsea Girl 56 (18f, Nmkt, F, Oct 21)
Chica Mia 49 (7f, Ayr, F, Aug 7)
Chief's Image 65 (8f, Nwc, F, July 1)
Child of The Mist 50 (12f, Don, F, May 29)
Chilly Rajah 69 (6f, Cur, F, May 27)
China Blue 55 (6f, Phx, F, May 31)
Chinese Justice (USA) 55 (10f, Phx, Y, May 3)
Choral Sundown 49 (10f, Bev, F, June 14)
Chouchounova 44 (12f, Lin, F, May 13)
Christian's Gold 40 (15½f, Flk, F, May 22)
Chucklestone 51 (16f, Asc, F, July 21)
Chummy's Charm 59 (6f, Not, G, July 8)
Chummy's Favourite 97 (6f, Asc, G, Sep 30)
Church Light 62 (10f, Nby, F, May 19)
Cielamour (USA) 64 (7f, Cur, Hvy, Apr 8)
Ciren Jester 44 (8f, Pon, Y, Apr 19)
Citidancer 83 (9f, Leo, G, Sep 16)
City Link Pet 40 (5f, San, G, Sep 19)
Clarentia 66 (5f, Yrk, F, Oct 11)
Class Act 44 (12f, Eps, F, June 9)
Classic Fame (USA) 62 (8f, Cur, F, May 20)

SCALE OF CONVERSION

5 & 6 furs		7-9 furs.		10-14 furs.		15 furs. & over	
1 len...	= 4pts	1 len...	= 3pts	1 len...	= 2pts	1 len...	= 1pt
¾ len...	= 3pts	¾ len...	= 2pts	¾ len...	= 2pts	¾ len...	= 1pt
½ len...	= 2pts	½ len...	= 2pts	½ len...	= 1pt	½ len...	= 1pt
nk, hd or sh-hd	= 1pt	nk, hd or sh-hd	= 1pt	nk, hd or sh-hd	= 1pt		

FLAT SPEED FIGURES – continued

Classic Secret (USA) 55 (10f, Phx, G, June 17)
Classic Sport (USA) 65 (12f, Leo, G, Oct 30)
Clifton Chapel 53 (11f, Nby, Y, Oct 28)
Closette (FR) 61 (7f, Leo, G, Aug 27)
Cluzo 56 (7½f, Bev, F, May 23)
Code Satin (USA) 40 (12f, Leo, F, July 29)
Coeur de Miel (USA) 58 (8f, San, F, May 29)
Coincidental 55 (7f, Nby, F, Sep 22)
Cold Marble (USA) 60 (16f, Asc, F, July 21)
Collage 41 (8f, Kem, F, Sep 2)
Collison Lane 46 (6f, Not, F, Sep 26)
Colway Rally 81 (8f, Cur, F, Aug 19)
Come On Chase Me 71 (5f, San, F, June 16)
Come On The Beach (USA) 40 (11f, Phx, G, July 8)
Come To Terms 48 (12f, Bev, F, June 7)
Comfort And Style 71 (5f, Cur, G, Aug 26)
Comic Talent 70 (8f, San, F, May 29)
Command Performer 46 (8f, Gwd, F, June 13)
Compleat 51 (7f, Eps, S, Apr 26)
Condor Pan 43 (14f, Leo, F, June 5)
Connie's Gift (USA) 65 (10f, Nmkt, F, July 22)
Cooks Gorse 47 (8f, Sal, F, May 23)
Cool Enough 54 (8f, Pon, Y, Apr 19)
Cool Run 60 (10f, Nmkt, F, July 22)
Coppermill Lad 66 (6f, Ayr, Y, Sep 22)
Coral Sword 64 (8f, Nwc, F, July 22)
Corwyn Bay 76 (6f, Cur, G, Oct 1)
Cossack Guard (USA) 61 (12f, Asc, F, June 22)
Cottenham 73 (7f, Asc, F, June 21)
Count My Blessings 49 (18f, Don, F, May 29)
Court Town 46 (8f, Sal, F, Aug 10)
Cowley 65 (10f, Pon, F, May 26)
Craft Express 82 (6f, Nby, Y, Oct 28)
Cree Bay 42 (5f, Edn, F, June 5)
Cricket Ball (USA) 93 (6f, Hay, G, Sep 2)
Crime Passionnel (USA) 44 (17½f, Wol, F, May 15)
Crimson Sails 46 (7f, Phx, G, June 17)
Crofter's Cline 57 (6f, Ham, F, June 2)
Cronk's Quality 52 (5f, San, F, July 8)
Crosby 47 (7f, Lin, F, Sep 12)
Crown Crest 66 (10f, Nmkt, F, July 12)
Crowthers 52 (7f, Eps, F, June 10)
Crystal Spray 47 (10f, Ches, F, Sep 8)
Crystal Sprite 45 (5f, San, F, July 20)
Cumbrian Express 54 (5f, San, F, May 30)
Cumbrian Melody 54 (5f, Bev, G, July 8)
Cumbrian Waltzer 76 (5f, Nwc, F, June 30)
Curtain Call 61 (8f, Yrk, F, Oct 12)
Cut Ahead 65 (10f, Chep, F, Aug 28)
Cut Up Rough 51 (6f, Chep, F, July 13)
Cuvee Charlie 55 (8f, Asc, F, June 21)

Daarkom 77 (16f, San, F, May 29)
Dail Eireann 55 (8f, Leo, S, Apr 1)
Dalby Dancer 41 (15f, War, F, July 22)
Dale Park 45 (10f, Ayr, Y, Sep 22)
d'Altagnan 50 (7f, Kem, G, Sep 1)
Damanour (USA) 44 (8f, Yrk, F, Sep 6)
Damaskeen (USA) 59 (5f, Yrk, F, Sep 7)
Dame Kiri 48 (10f, Phx, F, Aug 12)
Danbury (USA) 41 (8f, Lei, F, Oct 16)
Dance Festival 70 (8f, Cur, F, May 27)
Dance Spectrum (USA) 63 (12f, Yrk, F, Sep 7)
Dancing Dissident (USA) 95 (6f, Nby, F, May 19)
Dancing Monarch 72 (8f, Yrk, F, Aug 24)
Dancing Tribute (USA) 77 (8f, Nby, F, Sep 23)
Danehill (USA) 96 (6f, Hay, G, Sep 2)
Darcy's Thatcher 67 (7f, Phx, G, May 10)
Daring Times 55 (8f, Nwc, F, June 30)
Dash of Red 53 (7f, Phx, G, May 10)
Dateline Avalon 53 (10f, Nmkt, F, Oct 21)
Dawn Love 44 (12f, Pon, F, Aug 2)
Dawn's Delight 74 (6f, Hay, Y, Oct 11)
Dawn Storm 51 (7f, Yrk, G, Oct 14)
Dawn Success 70 (8f, Kem, S, Mar 25)
Deadly Charm (USA) 42 (12f, Sal, F, Aug 24)
Debbie's Next (USA) 43 (7f, Nby, Y, Apr 15)
Dee And Em 45 (6f, Tsk, F, Aug 7)
Deep Idol 55 (10f, Phx, S, Apr 29)
Deep Reef 53 (6f, Gwd, F, May 23)
Defence Policy 76 (10½f, Hay, G, Sep 2)
Demawend 79 (16f, Asc, F, June 21)
Denham Green 60 (5f, Yrk, F, June 16)
Densben 50 (5f, Don, G, Mar 31)
Den's Song 40 (7f, Red, F, Sep 29)
Deputy Tim 45 (7f, Ayr, F, July 15)
Derab (USA) 57 (14f, Yrk, F, Aug 22)
De Rivera (USA) 66 (12f, Nmkt, F, Oct 5)
Desert Bluebell 52 (10f, Chep, F, July 20)
Desert Dawn 80 (5f, San, F, July 8)
Destiny Dance (USA) 60 (12f, Asc, G, Oct 14)
Devils Dirge 48 (5f, Bri, H, Aug 3)
Dhakrah 42 (10f, Chep, F, July 20)
Diaco 48 (7f, Lin, F, Sep 12)
Diamond Appeal 56 (6f, Ches, F, Sep 8)
Diamond Path 57 (12f, Lin, F, May 13)
Didicoy (USA) 65 (6f, Yrk, F, June 17)
Diego Rivera 41 (10f, Bev, G, May 13)
Diet 50 (7f, Edn, F, June 26)
Dimmer 68 (8f, San, G, Aug 18)
Directly 50 (12f, Hay, S, May 1)
Discord 46 (13f, Nby, G, June 27)
Dismiss 65 (10f, Eps, F, Aug 29)
Dissonant (USA) 65 (10f, Nmkt, G, Oct 4)
Distant Relative 86 (8f, Gwd, G, Aug 26)
Distant Ruler 67 (5f, San, F, July 8)
Divine Pet 61 (6f, Gwd, F, July 29)
Dobey Thatcher 56 (7f, Cur, F, Aug 19)
Doctor Fell (USA) 50 (5f, Sal, G, May 4)
Dolpour 83 (10f, Nmkt, F, Oct 21)
Domus 62 (7½f, Ches, F, Sep 9)
Don Martino 61 (7f, Nmkt, F, July 11)
Donna Elvira 72 (7f, Nmkt, F, Nov 4)
Donode 50 (10f, Phx, F, Sep 30)
Donovan Rose 62 (7f, Don, G, Sep 14)
Dorking Lad 65 (6f, Yrk, F, Sep 6)
Dotrecuig 72 (5f, Phx, G, Oct 7)

FLAT SPEED FIGURES – continued

Double Dutch 72 (16f, Nmkt, F, Nov 3)
Double Encore (USA) 54 (8f, Hay, F, May 26)
Doubtfire 41 (10f, Nwc, Y, Mar 25)
Dragons Lair 41 (12f, Pon, F, Aug 2)
Dramatic Event 45 (8f, San, G, Sep 9)
Dr Brook 72 (10f, Phx, G, Aug 13)
Dream of Fame 62 (10f, Nmkt, F, July 12)
Drefflane Star 43 (8f, Cur, G, Oct 21)
Drumhead 59 (14f, Nmkt, F, Oct 19)
Drum Taps (USA) 75 (10f, Nby, G, Oct 28)
Dubai Lady 41 (10f, Nby, Y, Oct 26)
Duchy of Cornwall (USA) 42 (7f, Flk, S, Apr 10)
Duck Flight 40 (5f, San, S, Apr 28)
Duckington 69 (6f, Yrk, F, May 16)
Durasingh 49 (5f, Hay, F, May 27)
Dust Devil 73 (10f, Asc, F, July 22)
Dusty Emerald (USA) 44 (10f, Lin, F, May 13)
Dutyful 48 (12f, Sal, F, Aug 24)
Dwadme 64 (15f, Ayr, F, July 17)
Dwell (USA) 64 (6f, Nmkt, G, May 4)
Dyflin 53 (10f, Phx, F, June 18)

Eagles Lair 52 (10f, Nmkt, G, May 4)
Early Breeze 46 (7f, San, G, July 7)
Eastern Diamond (USA) 50 (12f, Hay, Y, Oct 12)
Eastern Ember 65 (5f, Rip, F, Aug 29)
Easy Line 68 (6f, Gwd, F, July 29)
Easy Time (GER) 45 (12f, Flk, F, July 31)
Ebro 41 (10f, Flk, F, May 22)
Echo Chamber 44 (6f, Nmkt, G, Oct 6)
Ecran 51 (18f, Don, G, Sep 14)
Edward Lear (USA) 50 (11f, Red, F, Oct 31)
Eezepeeze 48 (7f, Red, F, Aug 30)
Effervescent 42 (8f, San, F, July 19)
Elarqam 50 (12f, Ches, F, May 10)
Elder Prince 45 (6f, Hay, F, July 6)
Electric Lady 69 (8f, Kem, S, May 1)
Elegance In Design 73 (8f, Cur, F, May 27)
Elegant Rainbow 73 (7f, Asc, F, Sep 30)
Elegant Stranger 46 (8f, Lei, F, Oct 17)
Elementary 77 (12f, Cur, F, July 2)
Elenos 44 (12f, Lin, F, July 1)
Eliakim 58 (12f, Naas, H, July 20)
Ella Mon Amour 42 (9f, Wol, G, Sep 11)
Eloquent Minister (USA) 74 (5f, Yrk, F, Aug 24)
El Rey 53 (8f, San, G, July 8)
Emarati (USA) 58 (8f, Yrk, F, Sep 6)
Emerald Ring 42 (6f, Nby, G, Aug 11)
Emmson 89 (12f, Asc, F, June 23)
Emperor To Be 42 (9f, Leo, G, Sep 16)
Empire Blue 74 (11f, Nby, Y, Oct 28)
Empire Joy 45 (7f, Nmkt, F, July 28)
Emtyaaz (USA) 55 (6f, Nmkt, F, May 6)
Enaam 44 (9f, Wol, G, Sep 11)
Enigma (CAN) 50 (8½f, Bev, F, June 14)
Ensconse (USA) 85 (8f, Cur, F, May 27)
Ensharp (USA) 52 (7f, San, F, May 29)
Eradicate 75 (8f, Nby, G, Aug 11)
Erivan 48 (10½f, Wind, F, June 19)
Erris Express 61 (6f, Rip, F, Aug 28)
Etoit 46 (7½f, Ches, F, Sep 9)
Evening Affair 51 (9f, Red, F, Oct 10)
Evening Rain 51 (8f, Lei, G, Apr 22)
Evening Star 51 (8f, Yrk, F, Sep 6)
Ever Sharp 69 (5f, San, F, July 8)
Ever Welcome 41 (10f, Sal, F, May 23)
Evichstar 52 (10f, Eps, F, Aug 29)
Exact Analysis (USA) 43 (10f, Lin, F, May 13)
Exbourne (USA) 86 (8f, Nmkt, F, May 6)
Excavate 47 (10f, Phx, Y, May 3)
Excelsis 43 (10f, Bri, H, Aug 3)
Exceptional Bid (USA) 59 (10f, Rip, F, May 31)
Executive Perk 82 (10f, Cur, F, May 20)
Eye In The Sky 43 (8½f, Bev, F, Sep 20)
Ezy Koter 66 (10f, Phx, F, June 18)

Fabled Orator 56 (7f, Chep, F, May 29)
Fact Finder 50 (8f, Don, F, Apr 1)
Fag In Hand 61 (7½f, Ches, F, May 9)
Fair Prospect 57 (11f, Nby, S, Apr 14)
Fairway Royale 44 (10f, Gwd, G, Oct 7)
Fairy Feet 47 (11f, Red, F, May 30)
Falcon Flight 51 (7f, Tsk, F, May 20)
False Start (USA) 51 (10f, Asc, G, Oct 13)
False Tenet (USA) 48 (12f, Sal, G, May 3)
Familiar Spirit 45 (10f, Don, F, May 29)
Familiar (USA) 49 (8f, Yar, F, June 27)
Fanatical (USA) 57 (12f, Nmkt, F, Oct 5)
Far Glow 40 (10½f, Wind, F, June 19)
Farmer Jock 62 (5f, Yar, F, July 25)
Fast Chick 67 (10½f, Hay, F, Sep 30)
Father Phil 57 (8f, Leo, G, June 23)
Father Time 46 (8f, Pon, F, Aug 2)
Faux Pavillon 49 (16f, Nmkt, F, Aug 4)
Faynaz 47 (8f, Wind, F, July 24)
Fecamp (USA) 73 (8f, Nby, G, Aug 11)
Fenjaan 48 (7f, Nby, F, Sep 22)
Fenlass 41 (7f, Lin, F, Oct 5)
Ferox 44 (6f, Nmkt, F, May 6)
Ferryman 45 (5f, Gwd, F, Aug 25)
Fettle Flame 55 (7f, Yar, G, Sep 14)
Figure Out (USA) 54 (12f, Yrk, F, Sep 7)
Fine A Leau (USA) 45 (5f, Gwd, F, June 30)
Finest 47 (11f, Red, F, June 23)
Firelight Fiesta 84 (12f, Tsk, G, Nov 11)
Fire Top 81 (10f, Asc, G, Oct 13)
First Bill 49 (12f, Pon, F, July 12)
First Fastnet 51 (5f, Wind, F, July 29)
First Victory 46 (12f, Lei, G, Nov 6)
Fish Merchant 48 (11f, Phx, G, July 8)
Fit For A Queen (USA) 49 (6f, Rip, F, July 31)
Fitzrovia (USA) 56 (7f, Phx, Y, May 3)
Flamingo Pond 53 (10½f, Yrk, F, May 17)
Fleet Special 52 (10f, Bri, H, May 31)
Flockton's Own 57 (10½f, Yrk, F, May 17)
Flower From Heaven 51 (5f, Phx, F, July 8)
Fluters Ball 70 (6f, Phx, F, May 31)
Flyaway (FR) 44 (12f, Tsk, Y, Apr 15)

FLAT SPEED FIGURES – continued

Fly By Knife 58 (12f, Nby, G, Aug 12)
Flying 41 (12f, Lei, F, Sep 18)
Folk Dance 58 (14f, San, S, Apr 28)
Folly Foot 71 (7f, Nmkt, G, Apr 19)
Foolish Touch 63 (7f, Nmkt, F, May 19)
Footstool 42 (10f, Flk, F, July 4)
For Action (USA) 73 (16f, Asc, F, July 21)
Foreign Asset (USA) 69 (14f, Yrk, F, Aug 22)
Foreshadowing (USA) 43 (12f, Tsk, F, May 20)
Forest Glade (USA) 52 (12f, Leo, G, June 14)
Forest Monarch (USA) 42 (8f, Yrk, F, June 17)
Four-Legged Friend 59 (5f, Kem, F, May 17)
Four Star Thrust 48 (12f, Ches, F, May 11)
Fourwalk 54 (6f, Not, G, July 8)
Frank Harris 47 (10f, Nmkt, F, July 21)
Free Sweater (USA) 79 (12f, Asc, F, Sep 30)
Fremont Boy 40 (6f, Lin, G, Aug 31)
French Gondolier (USA) 41 (12f, Edn, Y, Apr 17)
French Riviera 71 (10f, Nmkt, F, July 12)
French Stress (USA) 73 (8f, San, S, Apr 28)
Frendly Persuasion 66 (8f, Leo, F, Aug 7)
Frequent Flyer 72 (7f, San, G, July 7)
Frescobaldo (USA) 43 (10f, Lei, G, Apr 22)
Frimley Parkson 56 (5f, Nby, Y, Oct 26)
Full Quiver 57 (8f, San, F, July 19)
Full Story 44 (10f, Phx, Y, May 3)
Fundraiser 71 (6f, Phx, G, May 10)
Fusilier 47 (7f, Edn, F, Oct 25)
Fusion 42 (11½f, San, F, June 17)
Future Success 52 (12f, Nmkt, F, Oct 20)
Future Treasure 56 (7f, Nby, Y, Apr 15)

Gaasid 77 (12f, Eps, F, June 9)
Gaijin 49 (7f, Eps, F, Aug 28)
Galatrix 56 (7f, Cur, F, Sep 9)
Gale Yaka 47 (8f, Rip, F, July 31)
Gallant Hope 71 (6f, Eps, F, June 9)
Gallic League 93 (5f, Leo, F, June 5)
Gathering Speed 56 (7f, Nwc, F, July 24)
Gazettalong 49 (10f, Yar, F, June 7)
Gemini Fire 75 (5f, Tsk, Y, Nov 11)
Genair (FR) 54 (8f, Rip, F, June 21)
Genotin 40 (10f, Chep, F, July 1)
Gentle Hero (USA) 75 (6f, Ayr, Y, Sep 23)
Gentleman's Jig (CAN) 48 (10f, Ches, F, May 9)
Gentleshaw 40 (7f, Yrk, F, May 17)
Genuine Gift (CAN) 48 (11½f, Yar, F, July 5)
George Philips 54 (8f, Cur, F, July 2)
Gershwin 47 (6f, Bri, F, June 27)
Ghassanah 48 (7f, Kem, Y, May 1)
Ghathanfar (USA) 45 (8f, Edn, F, Oct 25)
Gibbot 42 (10f, Don, G, Mar 30)
Gilderdale 71 (8f, Asc, G, Oct 14)
Gild The Lily 63 (16f, Nmkt, F, Nov 3)
Gin And Orange 46 (8f, Nmkt, F, May 5)
Glacial Storm (USA) 81 (12f, Eps, F, June 8)
Glenbeigh Summer 64 (8f, Cur, F, May 27)
Glencroft 80 (5f, Nwc, F, June 30)
Glory Gold 43 (7f, Ayr, F, Aug 7)
Glowing Picture 44 (16f, Don, F, June 16)
Glowing Star 64 (12f, Cur, F, July 2)
Gods Law 40 (12f, Pon, F, Aug 2)
Gods Solution 48 (6f, Tsk, F, June 20)
Go Forum 52 (11½f, San, G, July 8)
Gold Dust 60 (12f, Tsk, F, May 6)
Golden Ancona 77 (6f, Hay, F, June 9)
Golden Beau 52 (7f, Ayr, F, Aug 7)
Golden Flats 61 (5f, Hay, F, Sep 29)
Golden Garter 54 (6f, Hay, S, Apr 29)
Golden Opinion (USA) 91 (6f, Nmkt, F, July 13)
Golden Pheasant (USA) 78 (12f, Ches, F, May 9)
Golden Rhythym 45 (10f, Phx, F, June 26)
Golden Share 41 (5f, Phx, Y, Apr 29)
Gold Minories 70 (7½f, Lin, F, Aug 12)
Gold Pavilion (USA) 55 (10f, Lei, G, Apr 22)
Gold Prospect 56 (8f, Hay, F, June 10)
Gold Seam (USA) 78 (7f, Don, G, Sep 14)
Golfe du Lion 47 (8f, Ham, G, Aug 21)
Good Hand (USA) 47 (16f, Nmkt, G, Oct 4)
Goodnight Moon 58 (8f, San, F, May 29)
Good Partners 61 (7½f, Lin, F, May 13)
Go On Smile (USA) 56 (10f, Gwd, F, July 28)
Gorytus Star 49 (6f, Sal, F, June 28)
Goscar 64 (10f, Red, F, May 29)
Go South 47 (16f, Not, F, May 16)
Got Away 67 (6f, Don, F, May 27)
Gothic Ford 40 (7f, Ayr, F, June 23)
Gott's Desire 46 (7f, Nmkt, F, Aug 25)
Governorship 61 (8f, Yrk, F, May 18)
Gran Alba (USA) 70 (12f, Eps, F, June 7)
Grand Frere 59 (8f, Nby, G, Aug 11)
Grand Prix 63 (8f, Bri, F, July 6)
Great Chaddington 64 (5f, Don, G, Mar 31)
Great Commotion (USA) 75 (8f, Gwd, G, Aug 26)
Great Dilemma 58 (7f, Chep, F, May 29)
Great Lakes 52 (8f, Phx, Y, May 3)
Great Ocean 43 (7f, Naas, F, June 24)
Great Relations (USA) 65 (14f, Gwd, G, Aug 26)
Green Adventure (USA) 87 (12f, Eps, F, June 8)
Green Dollar 65 (5f, San, F, July 8)
Green Emperor 64 (10f, Asc, G, Oct 13)
Green Flag (USA) 71 (11f, War, F, July 4)
Greenhills Pride 40 (10f, Don, G, Mar 30)
Green Line Express (USA) 89 (8f, Gwd, F, July 26)
Green's Canaletto (USA) 80 (6f, Nby, F, July 14)
Green's Fine Art 47 (10f, Lei, G, Apr 22)
Greensmith 80 (8f, Asc, F, June 20)
Green's Seascape 68 (7f, Nmkt, F, July 13)
Greenwich Papillon 66 (10f, Gwd, F, May 24)
Grey Rum 40 (7f, Red, F, Sep 30)
Grey Salute (CAN) 57 (18f, Ches, F, May 10)

FLAT SPEED FIGURES – continued

Groom Star (USA) 59 (12f, Lei, F, Oct 16)
Gualdo (USA) 55 (10½f, Hay, G, Sep 2)
Guest Artiste 62 (8f, Nmkt, F, July 12)
Gulf Palace (USA) 63 (12f, Gwd, F, July 29)
Gunboat 56 (6f, Nmkt, F, May 6)
Gun Rule 59 (7f, Don, F, June 16)
Gushy 41 (8f, Ham, F, Sep 11)

Habitancy 68 (5f, Nmkt, F, Oct 21)
Hadif (USA) 85 (5f, Nmkt, G, Oct 4)
Haebeh (USA) 50 (10f, Chep, H, Sep 9)
Hafir 76 (7f, Nmkt, F, Oct 19)
Halkopous 60 (9f, Yrk, F, May 16)
Hall of Mirrors (USA) 69 (10f, Nmkt, F, July 29)
Hallow Fair 40 (10f, Not, F, Aug 8)
Halstead 53 (10f, Sal, F, Sep 7)
Handsome Sailor 79 (5f, Phx, F, Sep 2)
Hard As Iron 71 (9f, Yrk, F, Aug 23)
Hard To Come By 48 (16f, Not, F, May 16)
Hard To Figure 55 (5f, Bth, F, July 12)
Harmonica (USA) 43 (6f, Phx, F, May 31)
Harreek 41 (17f, Bth, F, May 6)
Harry's Coming 41 (6f, Not, F, June 12)
Hasty Vessel (USA) 40 (8f, Kem, F, July 5)
Hateel 57 (12f, Asc, G, Oct 13)
Hauwmal 63 (12f, Eps, F, June 9)
Hawwam 70 (8f, Nby, G, Aug 11)
Hazy Vision 57 (7f, Leo, Y, Nov 19)
Head of The Abbey 50 (7f, Leo, F, July 22)
Head of The House 59 (8f, Cur, F, Sep 9)
Headquarters 43 (8f, Nmkt, F, May 5)
Headstrong 48 (6f, Yar, F, Sep 12)
Hear Me 41 (7f, Cur, Hvy, Apr 8)
Heavenly Note 57 (8f, Yrk, F, May 17)
Helawe 50 (5f, Flk, F, Sep 5)
Helenikos 70 (10f, Phx, F, June 18)
Helens Dreamgirl 59 (10f, Bri, F, May 10)
Helen's Song (USA) 47 (10f, Nmkt, F, July 12)
Hello Vaigly 83 (8f, San, G, July 8)
Henry William 42 (5f, Lin, F, July 22)
Here He Comes 49 (7f, Lin, F, May 12)
Herne 75 (5f, Phx, G, Aug 13)
Heroes Sash (USA) 70 (7f, Asc, G, Sep 30)
Heron's Rock 42 (11½f, Yar, F, July 5)
He's A Flyer 63 (7f, Leo, F, July 29)
Hibernian Gold (USA) 69 (10f, Asc, F, June 20)
Hidden Creek 51 (5f, San, F, Sep 9)
High Estate 61 (10f, Gwd, F, May 24)
Highest Praise (USA) 61 (7f, Yrk, F, Sep 7)
High Holborn 41 (8f, San, F, May 11)
High I Kew 50 (11f, Ayr, Y, Sep 21)
Highland Chieftain 46 (10f, San, F, May 30)
Highland Rowena 53 (5f, Cat, F, July 19)
Hilton Brown 50 (8f, Asc, F, June 20)
Hinari Sunrise 50 (12f, Sal, F, June 28)
Hinari Televideo 52 (5f, Asc, F, June 24)
Hinari Video 46 (5f, Ham, G, May 5)
Hocus 60 (10f, Nby, F, Sep 22)
Hollia 41 (5f, Edn, F, July 3)
Holtermann (USA) 46 (7½f, Lin, F, June 3)
Holy Zeal 47 (16f, Hay, F, Oct 11)
Homely Touch 57 (8f, Yrk, F, May 17)
Home Rule (FR) 44 (6f, Phx, Hvy, Apr 15)
Homo Sapien 66 (8f, Tsk, F, May 6)
Hong Kong Girl 73 (5f, Hay, F, Sep 29)
Honoria (USA) 74 (8f, Cur, F, May 27)
Honour's Degree 44 (5f, War, F, July 4)
Honour The Wind 48 (8f, Yar, G, Aug 24)
Hooray Lady 71 (8f, San, G, Aug 18)
Hopping Around 46 (15f, Ayr, S, Oct 16)
Horatian 57 (10f, Bri, H, May 31)
Horn Dance (USA) 48 (14f, Yrk, F, Aug 23)
Hot Pursuit 51 (7f, Phx, S, Apr 29)
Houghton 44 (8f, Rip, Y, Apr 29)
House of Commons 60 (7½f, Ches, F, May 9)
How's Yer Father 50 (5f, San, G, Aug 18)
Hoy 78 (8f, Kem, F, May 27)
Hufoof 62 (5f, Hay, G, Aug 5)
Hunter Valley 46 (12f, Pon, F, Aug 2)
Husyan (USA) 75 (12f, Asc, F, Sep 28)
Hymn of Harlech 69 (8f, Nby, G, Aug 11)

Ibn Bey 75 (16f, San, F, May 29)
Icarus 41 (10½f, Hay, F, June 9)
Icarus (USA) 41 (10½f, Hay, G, June 9)
Icelander 40 (12f, Don, G, May 1)
Ice Queen 46 (7f, Nby, S, Apr 14)
Icona (USA) 80 (10f, Nmkt, F, Nov 3)
If Memory Serves (USA) 66 (10f, Lei, G, Nov 6)
Ile de Chypre 97 (10½f, Yrk, F, Aug 22)
Ile de Nisky 79 (12f, Cur, F, July 2)
Ile de Roi 62 (18f, Don, F, May 29)
Impala Lass 69 (5f, Eps, F, Aug 28)
Inaad 73 (10f, Red, F, May 29)
Indian Maestro 49 (6f, Yar, F, July 6)
Indian Queen 66 (10f, Gwd, Y, Sep 15)
Indian Ridge 71 (5f, Asc, F, June 23)
Indian Skimmer (USA) 68 (10f, San, G, July 8)
Indian Sovereign 41 (6f, Ayr, F, June 23)
Indian Uprising 40 (6f, Gwd, F, May 24)
Inisfail 42 (7f, Cur, F, Sep 9)
Inishpour 68 (8f, Tsk, Y, Apr 14)
Insan (USA) 49 (10f, Gwd, F, May 24)
Intimidate 66 (6f, Kem, Y, Mar 27)
Invertiel 44 (8f, Pon, F, June 13)
Irene's Charter 55 (8f, Chep, F, July 1)
Irish Passage 47 (8f, Red, F, May 2)
Iron King 65 (5f, Sal, F, Sep 7)
Isabella Ra (USA) 55 (12f, Eps, F, Aug 28)
Is King 67 (5f, Cur, G, Aug 26)
Island Mead 52 (8f, Gwd, F, July 25)
Islet Time 48 (10f, Phx, S, Apr 29)
It's Me 40 (10f, Rip, F, Aug 28)
Ivordale 44 (7½f, Bev, F, June 8)
Ivory Way (USA) 49 (10f, Kem, F, June 14)

Jacamar 66 (8f, Nwc, F, July 22)
Jadeite (FR) 48 (10½f, Hay, F, May 26)

FLAT SPEED FIGURES – continued

Jalmusique 69 (8f, Nwc, F, July 22)
Jalopy 45 (6f, Car, H, May 31)
Jamarj 67 (8f, Rip, F, Aug 28)
Janet Oliphant 49 (9f, Cur, G, Sep 23)
Janiski 59 (16f, Nmkt, F, Aug 4)
J Cheever Loophole 76 (5f, Sal, F, Sep 7)
Jigs And Reels 44 (7f, Kem, G, Sep 1)
Jinga 52 (14f, San, S, Apr 28)
Joe Sugden 73 (5f, Nmkt, G, Aug 26)
John Bowles (USA) 56 (8f, Rip, Y, Apr 29)
Johns Joy 59 (8f, San, G, July 8)
Joie de Rose 52 (7f, Yar, F, June 7)
Join The Que 41 (7f, Phx, Y, May 3)
Jokist 40 (6f, Kem, S, Apr 7)
Jomana 49 (5f, Bth, F, July 12)
Joveworth 83 (6f, Nby, Y, Oct 28)
Joytotheworld 79 (5f, San, F, June 16)
Jumby Bay 56 (8f, Chep, F, Oct 16)
Jungle Pioneer (USA) 69 (10f, Pon, F, June 13)
Jurran 40 (8f, Bri, F, June 19)
Just A Flutter 58 (8f, San, S, Apr 28)
Justaglow 44 (8f, Ayr, F, July 17)
Just Jennings 44 (5f, San, F, May 30)
Just My Bill 67 (10f, Ayr, Y, Sep 22)
Just Precious 43 (8f, Don, G, Mar 31)
Just Susanna (USA) 40 (8f, Yrk, F, Sep 6)
Just Three 79 (7f, Nmkt, F, Oct 19)

Kabcast 68 (5f, Eps, F, Aug 28)
Kachina Maid 57 (7f, Bri, G, Sep 14)
Kadan (GER) 44 (8f, Wol, F, Oct 18)
Kafkin 44 (5f, Yar, G, Sep 14)
Kafu Lady 43 (5f, Ches, F, May 9)
Kaliberto (FR) 40 (12f, Gwd, F, May 24)
Kali Kopella 47 (5f, Cat, F, June 9)
Kamakaze Girl 54 (7f, Red, F, Sep 29)
Kassiyda 73 (10f, Chep, F, Aug 28)
Katherines Emerald 44 (5f, Bev, G, Apr 22)
Kawwas 44 (6f, Eps, F, Aug 29)
K-Brigade 56 (8f, Nwc, G, Mar 27)
Keen Edge 67 (6f, Gwd, F, June 16)
Keep Your Word 42 (9f, San, G, Aug 18)
Kemosabe 53 (12f, Nmkt, F, July 29)
Kerita 70 (7f, Gwd, G, Oct 6)
Kerrera 86 (5f, Hay, F, May 27)
Keswa 58 (12f, Nby, F, May 19)
Key To The Music (USA) 57 (6f, Nwc, F, July 1)
Khaydara 75 (6f, Yrk, G, Oct 14)
Kikala 54 (7½f, Lin, F, May 13)
Kilronan 42 (6f, Flk, F, May 22)
Kilsheelan Lad 56 (16f, Cur, F, June 7)
King Charlemagne 46 (5f, Ham, F, July 14)
King of Mileen 50 (10f, Nmkt, F, Oct 21)
King's Beeches 41 (7f, Flk, F, July 4)
Kingsfold Flame 79 (10f, Eps, F, June 7)
Kings Quest 40 (16f, Sed, F, Sep 26)
Kintail 41 (10f, Nwc, F, Oct 3)
Kirla (CAN) 46 (10f, Phx, F, Aug 12)
Kissavos 40 (6f, Not, G, Oct 24)
Kiwayu (USA) 55 (8½f, Eps, F, Aug 28)
Kiya (USA) 54 (8f, Asc, F, Sep 29)
Klammering 61 (7f, Hay, F, June 10)
Knight of Mercy 70 (6f, Nby, F, June 14)
Knights Secret 45 (8f, Red, F, Sep 30)
Knock Knock 58 (10f, San, F, Aug 19)
Knoosh (USA) 76 (12f, Eps, F, June 10)
Knowlton 59 (12f, Bri, F, May 10)
Known Ranger 77 (8f, Yrk, F, Aug 24)
Konig 45 (11f, Nby, F, June 15)
Konigsberg 74 (16f, Asc, F, June 21)
Ko Samat 53 (6f, Leo, G, May 13)
Kostroma 64 (11f, Phx, G, June 17)
Kovalevskia 45 (12f, Flk, G, Oct 23)
Kremlin Guard 56 (8f, Nby, G, Aug 11)
Krisalya 58 (10½f, Yrk, F, May 17)
Kris Kringle 52 (10f, Cur, F, May 20)
Ktolo 50 (12f, Flk, F, Oct 10)
Kyra 69 (8f, Cur, F, May 27)

La Ballerine 42 (9f, Wol, G, Sep 11)
La Chiquita 62 (5f, Hay, F, July 6)
Lady In Pace 67 (11f, Phx, G, July 8)
Lady In White 54 (10½f, Hay, F, June 10)
Lady Lane 50 (12f, Leo, G, June 23)
Lady of The Sea 55 (10f, Bev, F, Sep 20)
Lady Rosanna 64 (12f, Eps, F, Aug 29)
Lady Shipley 70 (10f, Gwd, F, May 25)
Lady's Mantle (USA) 48 (5f, Cat, F, July 19)
La Grande Affaire 51 (7f, Lin, G, Aug 31)
Lake Dancer 43 (7f, War, S, May 1)
Lake Magic 56 (8f, Phx, Hvy, Apr 15)
Lambourn Citizen (USA) 46 (8f, Nby, F, May 20)
Lanchester (USA) 68 (6f, Nby, F, May 19)
Langtry Lady 40 (6f, Not, S, Mar 17)
Lapierre 77 (10f, Asc, F, June 20)
Lariston Gale 44 (11f, Ayr, Y, Sep 21)
La Rosette 48 (10½f, Yrk, F, May 17)
La Tanque (USA) 55 (5f, Leo, G, June 14)
Laura Dear (USA) 46 (10f, Lin, F, May 13)
La Visir (USA) 44 (12f, Sal, F, Aug 24)
Lazaz (USA) 73 (14f, Cur, G, Sep 23)
Lazy Rhythm (USA) 54 (8f, Hay, F, Oct 11)
Leacroft 40 (8f, Car, F, June 28)
Legal Case 84 (10f, Nmkt, F, Oct 21)
Legal Legend (USA) 55 (10f, Leo, Y, Oct 28)
Legal System (USA) 51 (10f, Phx, S, Apr 29)
Lepoushka 57 (8f, Cur, G, Oct 21)
Letsbeonestaboutit 48 (5½f, Bth, F, May 6)
Life At The Top 68 (10f, Nmkt, G, Oct 7)
Light Hand 41 (10f, Pon, F, Oct 9)
Lightning Bug 57 (16f, Cur, G, Oct 1)
Light of Morn (USA) 82 (9f, Yrk, F, Aug 23)
Light Romance 50 (12f, Nmkt, F, Oct 5)
Like A Dove 54 (10f, Phx, F, Aug 12)
Like Amber 51 (5f, Yrk, F, June 16)
Lily's Lover (USA) 59 (12f, Asc, F, June 22)
Limeburn 64 (12f, Asc, G, Oct 13)
Linpac West 68 (10f, Red, G, Nov 10)
Liquid Asset 53 (10f, Yar, G, Sep 14)

FLAT SPEED FIGURES – continued

Little Bighorn 63 (8f, Cur, F, July 2)
Little Douglas 58 (7f, Nby, F, May 19)
Littlepace 45 (5f, Phx, G, Aug 13)
Lively Cockney (USA) 50 (7f, Flk, S, Apr 17)
Live Show (USA) 53 (10f, Phx, F, Aug 12)
Llyn Gwynant 92 (8f, Cur, F, Aug 19)
Loaningdale 59 (10f, Phx, F, Aug 12)
Loft Boy 58 (5f, Asc, F, Sep 29)
Logamimo 56 (10f, Bth, F, Sep 18)
Lomax 53 (7f, Gwd, F, July 28)
Lonely Street 72 (6f, Kem, S, Apr 7)
Lone Runner 63 (10f, Phx, G, Aug 13)
Lord Balmerino (USA) 59 (12f, Nmkt, F, July 28)
Lord David S (USA) 65 (10f, Nmkt, G, Oct 4)
Loren's Courage (USA) 66 (12f, Hay, G, July 7)
Lots of Luck 49 (10½f, War, S, May 1)
Lough Key 46 (6f, Leo, G, May 13)
Love Legend 60 (6f, Hay, Y, Oct 11)
Lovely Flower 43 (7f, Lin, G, Aug 31)
Love Prince 42 (5f, San, F, May 11)
Lucedeo 57 (5f, Cat, G, Oct 20)
Lucky Flinders 45 (7f, Kem, G, Sep 1)
Lucky Round 50 (10f, Bri, F, Aug 17)
Lucky Song 64 (10f, Gwd, F, May 25)
Lucky Song (USA) 53 (16½f, Don, G, Sep 13)
Lucky Verdict 50 (16f, Asc, G, Oct 13)
Lugana Beach 85 (5f, Yrk, F, Aug 23)
Luna Bid 73 (6f, Kem, F, June 14)
Lunar Mover (USA) 72 (8f, Kem, S, Mar 25)
Lust of Love 43 (6f, Nmkt, F, Oct 6)
Luzum 43 (8f, Bri, F, Apr 24)
Lyphard's Candy 59 (10f, Phx, F, Sep 30)
Lypheor's Honour (CAN) 66 (10½f, Yrk, F, June 17)
Lyreen River 48 (10f, Yar, F, Aug 24)

Macrobian 82 (6f, Nwc, G, Oct 28)
Mac's Fighter 94 (6f, Asc, F, June 23)
Madame Bovary 56 (9f, Yrk, F, July 14)
Madraco 66 (6f, Gwd, G, Aug 26)
Magical Strike (USA) 80 (7f, Nmkt, F, May 19)
Magic Gleam (USA) 82 (8f, Nmkt, F, July 12)
Magistro (USA) 45 (12f, Cur, F, July 2)
Magnus Pym 72 (12f, Hay, S, May 1)
Mahrajan 40 (9f, Kem, Y, Mar 27)
Maiden Bidder 55 (6f, Gwd, F, June 16)
Maiden Fair 59 (10f, Cur, F, May 20)
Main Objective 83 (10f, Eps, F, June 7)
Majestic Ace (USA) 40 (8f, Tsk, F, July 29)
Majority Holding 40 (10½f, Hay, Y, Oct 11)
Major Ivor 58 (9f, Yrk, F, Aug 23)
Makarim (FR) 47 (10f, Chep, F, July 13).
Make Or Mar 68 (6f, Nby, F, May 20)
Malamute Saloon (USA) 41 (12f, Car, G, Oct 27)
Malevich (USA) 61 (8f, Gwd, F, July 27)
Malhamdale (USA) 45 (8f, Tsk, F, Sep 8)
Malibasta 45 (8f, Gwd, F, June 2)
Mallau 42 (6f, Not, F, July 24)
Malunar 57 (6f, Nmkt, G, May 4)
Mamaluna (USA) 82 (12f, Eps, F, June 10)
Mango Manila 60 (7f, Nmkt, F, July 21)
Mansion House 68 (7f, Phx, G, May 10)
Maradit 47 (6f, Yar, F, Aug 3)
Marbella Silks 82 (6f, Nmkt, G, May 4)
Marchinella 40 (8f, Kem, F, Sep 2)
Marchman 49 (10f, Sal, F, Sep 7)
Marcinkus 80 (10f, Nmkt, F, July 12)
Mardood 55 (12f, Hay, S, May 1)
Marine Diver 65 (10f, Ches, F, May 11)
Mark Aizlewood 49 (11f, Ayr, Y, Sep 23)
Mark Birley 40 (7f, Flk, F, July 4)
Market Maker 43 (6f, Gwd, F, May 24)
Markofdistinction 84 (8f, Gwd, F, July 26)
Mark Sprite 58 (5f, Phx, G, Aug 13)
Marlion 59 (16f, Cur, G, Oct 1)
Martinosky 52 (6f, Wind, F, May 15)
Marvellous Marvin 50 (8f, Cur, F, May 20)
Masked Ball 47 (12f, Hay, F, July 7)
Masnun (USA) 70 (6f, Gwd, G, Aug 26)
Master Ofthe House 53 (6f, Ayr, Y, Sep 23)
Master Plan (FR) 48 (9f, Nmkt, G, Oct 4)
Master Pokey 66 (5f, Nwc, F, July 22)
Matou 40 (7f, Yar, F, Aug 23)
Mauve Reef (USA) 46 (8f, Yar, F, June 7)
Mayday Miracle 43 (6f, Nmkt, F, May 5)
Mayor 52 (6f, Kem, S, Apr 7)
Mazzacano 72 (16f, Asc, G, Apr 22)
Meanie Minna 44 (7f, Gwd, F, May 25)
Meeson Kamp 55 (5f, Gwd, G, Oct 6)
Megan's Flight 54 (12f, Hay, G, Sep 1)
Mega Sport (USA) 58 (16f, Lin, F, Aug 31)
Mehtab 42 (7f, Kem, G, Sep 1)
Melancolia 44 (10f, Nmkt, F, Nov 3)
Mel's Rose 55 (7f, Yar, F, June 7)
Mertola's Pet 49 (5f, Bth, F, May 22)
Miami Banker 69 (5f, San, F, July 7)
Michelozzo (USA) 88 (14f, Gwd, G, Aug 26)
Micro Love 69 (5f, Eps, F, Aug 28)
Midfielder 71 (8f, Nby, F, May 20)
Midnight's Reward 41 (6f, Nmkt, F, May 5)
Midsummer Fun 48 (10f, Phx, F, Aug 12)
Mileeha (USA) 62 (10f, Nmkt, F, July 12)
Milieu 83 (7f, Leo, F, July 22)
Military Fashion 53 (10f, Red, F, Oct 31)
Military Salute 41 (12f, Lin, F, June 3)
Milligan 62 (8f, Gwd, F, July 27)
Mill Pond (FR) 74 (12f, Eps, F, June 7)
Mils Mij 41 (13f, Ham, Hvy, Apr 6)
Milton Burn 46 (12f, Eps, S, Apr 26)
Mine's A Double 40 (7f, Cat, F, Sep 23)
Minstrel Guest 60 (8f, Asc, F, Sep 29)
Mirror Black 76 (8f, Gwd, F, July 27)
Miss Aboyne 40 (8½f, Bev, G, July 8)
Miss Blitz 66 (7f, Nmkt, F, July 13)
Miss Camellia 44 (12f, Ham, G, May 5)
Miss Chrissy 45 (5f, Pon, F, July 11)
Miss Demure 52 (8f, Asc, G, Oct 13)
Miss Emily 40 (8f, Ham, G, Aug 21)
Miss Fancy That (USA) 62 (10f, Gwd, F, May 25)

FLAT SPEED FIGURES – continued

Miss Garuda 59 (10f, Lin, H, Aug 5)
Miss Pisces 49 (7f, Eps, S, Apr 26)
Miss Relsun 46 (10f, Bev, F, Aug 17)
Miss Sarajane 50 (8f, Hay, F, July 6)
Miss Secreto (USA) 45 (7f, Nby, S, Apr 14)
Miss Swansong 40 (7f, Gwd, F, May 25)
Miss Toot 41 (15f, Edn, F, July 3)
Mister Bobbins 50 (5f, War, F, July 4)
Mizaj 49 (10f, Bev, F, June 8)
Mizuwari 42 (7f, Nby, F, Sep 22)
Mo Ceri 54 (12f, Flk, S, Apr 17)
Mofador (GER) 47 (8f, Nwc, F, July 1)
Mo Ichi Do 48 (10f, Pon, F, July 12)
Momtaaz 48 (8f, Lei, F, Sep 19)
Monarch O Th Glen 63 (10½f, Hay, F, June 10)
Monasteroris (USA) 47 (7f, Leo, S, Mar 17)
Monastery 71 (10f, Gwd, G, Oct 6)
Money Saved 43 (16f, Cur, F, June 7)
Moniga 56 (6f, Kem, F, July 13)
Monsagem (USA) 74 (8f, Nmkt, F, May 6)
Montefiore 48 (9f, Leo, G, Aug 27)
Monteros Boy 44 (10f, Bri, F, Oct 3)
Mon Tresor 70 (7f, Nmkt, G, Apr 19)
Moorish Idol 43 (6f, Lei, F, May 30)
Most Welcome 94 (8f, Gwd, F, July 28)
Mother Aikenhead (USA) 58 (14f, Leo, G, May 15)
Mountain Bluebird (USA) 48 (8f, San, G, Sep 19)
Mountain Kingdom (USA) 73 (12f, Eps, F, June 8)
Mountain Retreat 47 (10f, Kem, F, June 14)
Mount Nelson 59 (16f, Lin, F, Aug 31)
Moving Off 46 (7f, Naas, F, June 1)
Mr Boldwood 68 (10f, Phx, F, Sep 30)
Mr Chris Cakemaker 41 (11f, Ayr, F, Aug 7)
Mr Minstrel (CAN) 47 (12f, Leo, G, June 14)
Mr Pintips 67 (16f, Asc, G, Apr 22)
Mrs Pistol 50 (12f, Hay, G, Sep 1)
Mr Waddilove 58 (5f, Hay, G, Sep 1)
Mr Wishing Well 53 (10f, Nmkt, F, July 1)
Muhbubh (USA) 66 (7f, Nmkt, G, Apr 18)
Mukhabbr 55 (7f, Sal, G, May 4)
Mummy's Chance 42 (5f, Edn, F, June 19)
Murango 55 (12f, Nmkt, F, Oct 5)
Musaahim 62 (11f, Red, F, Sep 29)
Musical Bliss (USA) 66 (12f, Eps, F, June 10)
Musical Leader 49 (10f, Yar, F, Aug 24)
Musical Look (USA) 62 (7f, Yrk, F, June 16)
My Chiara 61 (12f, Gwd, G, Oct 6)
Myfor 57 (8f, Yrk, F, Sep 6)
My Lamb 72 (10f, Don, G, May 1)
My Mallet (FR) 51 (10f, Lin, F, July 1)
My Pal Popeye 54 (5f, Ham, F, July 14)
Mysteries (USA) 53 (10½f, Yrk, F, May 16)
Mystery Band (USA) 52 (8f, Pon, F, May 26)
Mystery Music 67 (8f, Kem, F, Sep 2)
Mythyaar (USA) 48 (8f, San, F, May 29)
My Wild Flower (USA) 48 (6f, Cur, F, May 27)
Mzeff 72 (5f, San, F, July 27)
Naatell (USA) 56 (10f, Bri, H, May 31)
Nabeel Dancer (USA) 93 (6f, Asc, F, June 22)
Nadiad 56 (10f, Nmkt, F, July 12)
Nafuat 54 (6f, Hay, F, June 9)
Nail Don 51 (8f, Nby, Y, Apr 15)
Nanarch (USA) 74 (16f, Cur, G, Oct 1)
Nangarar (USA) 40 (8f, Nmkt, F, May 13)
Naoko 49 (8f, Cur, Y, Oct 21)
Nashid 68 (16f, Nmkt, F, Nov 3)
Nashwan (USA) 93 (12f, Eps, F, June 7)
Nathan Blake 49 (16f, Cur, F, June 7)
Native Magic 48 (13f, Nby, Y, Oct 26)
Natural Lad 42 (8f, Cur, G, Oct 1)
Naval Fan 56 (5f, Yrk, F, June 16)
Nawwar 51 (6f, Nmkt, F, Aug 4)
Nayland 41 (8f, Pon, F, Oct 9)
N C Owen 67 (12f, Gwd, F, July 25)
Nearctic Bay (USA) 45 (10f, Nmkt, F, July 12)
Nearctic Flame 66 (10½f, Yrk, F, May 17)
Neatfoot 50 (10f, Nby, G, June 27)
Neat Style 55 (11f, Red, F, Aug 1)
Nebulatis (USA) 54 (16f, Asc, F, June 24)
Ned's Aura 60 (7f, Yrk, F, Sep 7)
Neeha 42 (5f, San, F, June 17)
Nelson River (USA) 60 (8f, Pon, F, Aug 2)
Nemesia 72 (10f, Nby, F, July 15)
Nesaah (USA) 46 (10½f, Hay, F, July 6)
Nevada Mix 49 (6f, Eps, F, Aug 29)
New Chandelier 46 (7f, Lin, F, Oct 5)
New Mexico 49 (8f, Red, G, Oct 31)
Nicholas Mark 47 (12f, War, F, Oct 9)
Nickle Plated 73 (12f, Hay, G, July 8)
Night Lady 44 (6f, Ham, G, Sep 11)
Night Secret 56 (10f, Bev, F, Sep 20)
Nikitas 58 (12f, Lin, F, June 3)
Nikki Dow 59 (5f, San, F, Sep 9)
Nobby 49 (8f, Car, F, June 29)
No Beating Harts 60 (5f, San, F, July 8)
Noble Lustre (USA) 42 (7f, Don, F, July 27)
Noble Savage 70 (16f, Asc, F, June 21)
No Dreaming (USA) 60 (7f, Leo, F, July 29)
Nomadic Way (USA) 78 (16f, Nmkt, F, Nov 3)
No More The Fool 40 (11f, Ayr, F, Aug 7)
Noones Honours 43 (8f, Leo, S, Apr 1)
Noora Abu 65 (10f, Leo, G, June 23)
No Quarter Given 51 (5f, Ham, Y, Nov 2)
Norquay (USA) 52 (8½f, Bev, G, July 8)
Northants 73 (12f, Gwd, G, Oct 6)
Northern Alliance 40 (15½f, Flk, S, Apr 10)
Northern Brave 47 (12f, Sal, F, May 23)
Northern Commander 43 (7f, Nwc, G, Mar 27)
Northern Flagship (USA) 54 (8f, Nby, F, July 14)
Northern Habit 42 (7f, Kem, F, July 13)
Northern Printer 51 (7f, Nmkt, F, Oct 19)
Northern Teller (USA) 53 (8f, Car, G, Apr 28)
Northern Tide 49 (7f, Leo, S, Mar 17)
Northern Tryst (USA) 61 (7f, Nmkt, G, Apr 19)
Northumbrian King 46 (12f, Bev, F, June 7)

FLAT SPEED FIGURES – continued

No Submission (USA) 59 (8f, San, F, May 11)
Not Yet 49 (8f, Nwc, G, Aug 26)

Observation Post 84 (12f, Cur, F, July 2)
Oh Danny Boy 46 (10f, Bev, F, Aug 17)
Old Man River 50 (16f, Cur, F, June 19)
Old Vic 92 (12f, Cur, F, July 2)
Olympic Times (USA) 48 (12f, Lei, S, Apr 3)
One Liner 50 (6f, Not, S, Mar 27)
One Man Band 54 (6f, Not, F, June 12)
On My Merit 50 (8f, War, F, July 22)
Opening Overture (USA) 40 (10f, Kem, F, June 14)
Opening Verse (USA) 81 (8f, Gwd, F, July 26)
Opera Ghost 49 (8f, Chep, F, July 4)
Operation Wolf 46 (8f, Lei, F, Oct 16)
Optaria 69 (5f, Yrk, F, Aug 23)
Orange Grove (USA) 55 (7f, Nmkt, F, Oct 19)
Orbis (USA) 54 (11f, Phx, G, July 8)
Orchard's Pet 49 (5f, Flk, F, June 6)
Orembo 61 (10f, Phx, F, June 18)
Organza 47 (10f, Wind, F, July 10)
Oriental Splendour 49 (7f, Bri, F, Aug 17)
Orpheus (USA) 65 (15f, Ayr, F, July 17)
Osric 75 (12f, Nmkt, F, Oct 20)
Ostora (USA) 44 (8f, Yar, G, Sep 13)
Ostura 71 (10½f, Hay, G, Sep 2)
Ottergayle 68 (10f, Nby, F, Sep 23)
Our Fan 45 (5f, Not, F, Aug 8)
Our Freddie 59 (5f, Sal, F, Sep 7)
Our Jock 60 (7f, Bri, F, May 10)
Outeniqua 58 (7f, Phx, G, Aug 25)
Out of Funds 57 (14f, Yrk, F, Aug 22)
Out On Allege (USA) 40 (11½f, Yar, F, Aug 23)
Overpower 59 (8f, Pon, Y, Apr 19)
Owen Falls 49 (14f, Cat, F, Aug 9)
Own Free Will 48 (10f, Kem, Y, Mar 27)

Paddy Chalk 75 (6f, Nby, F, May 19)
Palace Rebel 46 (8f, Lei, G, Apr 22)
Paley Prince (USA) 84 (5f, Yrk, F, Oct 11)
Pamela Peach 50 (6f, Nby, F, June 14)
Panama Princess 40 (5f, Wol, F, July 17)
Pandy 68 (8f, Yrk, F, Sep 6)
Paper Shoes 45 (5f, Edn, F, Sep 18)
Parador 65 (9f, San, G, Aug 18)
Parliament Piece 65 (7f, Yrk, G, Oct 14)
Passelande 43 (12f, Gwd, F, June 16)
Pass The Peace 70 (7f, Nby, S, Apr 14)
Pastoral Jem 62 (6f, Nby, F, May 19)
Patcon 62 (5f, Ham, F, July 19)
Patience Camp 68 (16f, Nmkt, F, Nov 3)
Patsy Western 44 (6f, Kem, S, May 1)
Pay Corps (USA) 41 (10f, Don, G, Sep 13)
Payvashooz 40 (7f, Edn, F, Oct 25)
Peerage 52 (6f, Cur, G, July 2)
Peleus (USA) 71 (16f, Nmkt, G, May 4)
Pelorus 79 (10f, Gwd, F, July 29)
Pendor Dancer 68 (5f, Eps, F, Aug 28)
Penny Candle 74 (5f, Nmkt, G, Oct 4)
Penny Forum 48 (16f, Nmkt, G, May 4)
Perfect Chance 54 (7f, Eps, F, Aug 28)
Perion 90 (5f, San, F, July 8)
Perosini 53 (10f, Don, G, Sep 13)
Per Quod (USA) 74 (10f, Kem, S, Apr 7)
Persian Emperor 51 (7f, Red, F, June 24)
Persian Moon 55 (6f, Nmkt, G, Oct 4)
Persillant 65 (14f, Hay, F, June 10)
Petavious 49 (8f, Wind, F, Aug 21)
Petite Ile 81 (12f, Cur, F, July 15)
Petite Rosanna 54 (10f, Eps, F, June 8)
Petrullo 72 (10f, Asc, F, June 20)
Petticoat Lane 47 (8f, Phx, Hvy, Apr 15)
Petticoat Power 44 (6f, Flk, G, Oct 23)
Phanan 45 (12f, Cat, F, Aug 10)
Phantom Breeze 69 (12f, Cur, F, July 2)
Phazania 56 (10f, Leo, Y, Oct 28)
Philip 46 (5f, Edn, F, July 3)
Phountzi (USA) 44 (8f, Nmkt, G, May 4)
Pick of The Pops 46 (10½f, Yrk, F, May 16)
Pilot 59 (10½f, Yrk, F, May 16)
Pinctada 70 (7f, Yrk, G, Oct 14)
Pirate Army (USA) 74 (12f, Lin, F, May 13)
Pirouette 71 (7f, Cur, G, Sep 23)
Pitsea 59 (6f, Nmkt, F, May 5)
Plain Fact 82 (6f, Gwd, F, July 25)
Point House 74 (8f, Nby, F, Sep 23)
Point of Light 88 (6f, Nmkt, G, Apr 18)
Pokey's Pride 51 (12f, Gwd, F, July 29)
Polar Boy (USA) 61 (8f, Asc, F, June 23)
Polar Run (USA) 77 (16f, Asc, F, June 21)
Polar Vision 45 (10f, Lin, H, Aug 5)
Polemos 58 (12f, Asc, F, Sep 29)
Polish Precedent (USA) 73 (8f, Asc, G, Sep 30)
Polykratis 74 (6f, Asc, F, July 21)
Polyroll 52 (7f, Eps, F, June 10)
Poniard 42 (8f, Red, F, Sep 30)
Pontevecchio Notte 57 (12f, Gwd, F, May 24)
Popular Glen 72 (9f, Cur, G, Sep 23)
Porter Rhodes (USA) 62 (10f, Cur, F, May 27)
Positive Attitude 66 (8f, Nby, G, Aug 11)
Positively Great (USA) 43 (8f, Yrk, F, June 17)
Power Take Off 48 (10f, Sal, F, Aug 10)
Poyle George 90 (5f, Nmkt, G, Oct 4)
Precentor 44 (5f, San, F, June 17)
Precious Boy 64 (9f, Yrk, F, May 16)
Predictable 41 (5f, Ayr, Y, Sep 23)
Premier Prince 54 (6f, Ham, G, Aug 21)
Pretty Thing 56 (11f, Red, F, July 4)
Prevailing Wind 54 (5f, Pon, F, Sep 5)
Pride of Araby (USA) 44 (10½f, Hay, F, June 9)
Priestgate 62 (5f, San, G, Sep 19)
Prince Ibrahim 62 (10f, Nmkt, F, May 5)
Prince of Dance 82 (10f, Nmkt, F, May 5)
Prince of Tides 50 (5f, San, F, July 27)
Princess Accord (USA) 66 (10f, Nmkt, F, Nov 3)
Princess Athena 84 (5f, Gwd, F, July 27)

FLAT SPEED FIGURES – continued

Princess Sobieska 76 (12f, Asc, G, Oct 14)
Pringipoula 50 (6f, Nmkt, F, July 11)
Procurator (USA) 52 (14f, Nmkt, F, Oct 19)
Profilic 60 (6f, Red, F, Oct 18)
Profit A Prendre 58 (7f, Gwd, Y, Sep 16)
Project Manager 58 (10f, Cur, F, May 20)
Promegg 48 (10f, Ayr, Y, Sep 22)
Prorutori (USA) 41 (9f, Nmkt, G, Apr 18)
Puff Puff 42 (7f, Gwd, F, May 25)
Puissance 69 (6f, Phx, G, May 10)
Pure Genius (USA) 70 (8f, Nmkt, F, May 6)
Pussy Foot 63 (5f, Bri, F, Sep 27)

Qannaas 72 (12f, Nmkt, F, Oct 20)
Queen Angel 59 (12f, Eps, F, June 9)
Queen of Finns 41 (10f, Leo, G, Oct 30)
Queen's Share 61 (5f, Phx, G, Oct 7)
Queens Tour 55 (10f, Kem, Y, Mar 27)
Question of Degree 49 (8f, Ham, G, Aug 21)
Quiche 55 (6f, Wind, F, July 17)
Quiet Awakening (USA) 61 (12f, Asc, G, Oct 14)
Quinlan Terry 68 (10f, Kem, Y, Mar 27)

Raahin (USA) 55 (16f, Asc, F, June 24)
Racey Naskra (USA) 51 (7½f, Lin, F, Oct 5)
Rahik 46 (7f, Asc, F, Sep 28)
Rah Wan (USA) 65 (8f, Yrk, F, June 17)
Rain Burst 64 (8f, Gwd, F, June 13)
Rambo's Hall 84 (10f, Nmkt, F, Nov 3)
Rambushka (USA) 55 (10f, Nmkt, G, May 4)
Rana Pratap (USA) 47 (12f, Flk, F, Aug 22)
Rapid Lad 44 (10f, Bev, F, Aug 8)
Rasheek (USA) 74 (7f, Asc, G, Sep 30)
Rashtoun 49 (10f, Gwd, F, July 29)
Really Brilliant (USA) 62 (10f, Gwd, F, May 24)
Rebel Raiser (USA) 45 (7f, Bri, F, May 10)
Red Glow 64 (12f, Nmkt, F, May 5)
Red Paddy 66 (8f, San, G, Sep 9)
Red River Boy 51 (5f, Gwd, F, Aug 25)
Red Rosein 49 (6f, Yrk, F, July 15)
Reef Galles 43 (8f, Chep, F, July 4)
Regal Reform 67 (16f, Nmkt, F, Aug 4)
Regal Salute 42 (8f, Tsk, F, May 19)
Regent Lad 65 (7½f, Bev, F, Aug 16)
Regent Light (USA) 63 (10f, Gwd, F, July 28)
Reggae Beat 49 (10f, Nmkt, F, July 29)
Rejim 60 (8f, Tsk, F, May 19)
Relief Pitcher 59 (10f, Kem, F, June 14)
Reprimand 83 (8f, Gwd, G, Aug 26)
Re-Release 58 (12f, Tsk, G, Nov 11)
Resolute Bay 58 (6f, Nwc, F, July 1)
Respectable Jones 58 (5f, Nby, Y, Oct 26)
Restless Don 63 (5f, Hay, F, May 27)
Restore 77 (6f, Yrk, F, May 16)
Resucada 45 (6f, Bri, F, May 10)
Retouch 53 (14f, Nmkt, F, Oct 19)
Return To Romance 40 (10f, Not, F, Sep 25)
Revaro 49 (10f, Nwc, Y, Mar 25)
Revelette 53 (8f, Cur, F, Aug 19)
Ridgiduct 45 (5f, Cat, F, July 6)
Rienzi 50 (14f, Leo, G, May 15)
Rifada 70 (12f, Nby, G, Aug 12)
Rincon 46 (12f, Edn, G, July 10)
Ring of Ford 50 (6f, Phx, G, May 10)
Rio Piedras 57 (10f, Red, G, Nov 10)
Riosamba (USA) 59 (10f, Nby, F, Sep 22)
Riptide 48 (10f, San, G, Sep 19)
River Glow 49 (14f, Leo, G, May 15)
Riverhead (USA) 55 (10f, Kem, S, Apr 7)
River of Hope (USA) 49 (7f, Wol, F, May 8)
River Reprise (USA) 47 (6f, Cur, Hvy, Mar 25)
River's Rising (FR) 55 (8f, Nby, F, July 14)
Road To Reason 55 (10f, Ches, F, May 11)
Robert Dear (USA) 53 (8f, Gwd, F, June 16)
Roblet (USA) 76 (12f, Nmkt, F, July 28)
Rocket Dancer 50 (8f, Leo, S, Apr 1)
Rockwell 41 (10f, Phx, G, June 17)
Rocquaine 45 (7f, Kem, G, Sep 1)
Roesboro 50 (6f, Cur, F, May 27)
Rolfeson 40 (10½f, Hay, G, Aug 11)
Roll A Dollar 41 (10f, Wind, F, July 10)
Roman Prose 62 (6f, Nmkt, F, Aug 25)
Romantic Past (USA) 40 (8f, Yar, F, Aug 23)
Roseato Lodge 55 (8f, Car, G, Apr 28)
Roseate Tern 87 (12f, Eps, F, June 10)
Rosebery Avenue 40 (10½f, Hay, G, Aug 4)
Rose Campion 52 (10f, Nby, G, June 27)
Rosen (USA) 47 (10f, Asc, G, Oct 13)
Rose Reef 70 (7f, Cur, Hvy, Apr 8)
Rosie Potts 63 (8f, Yrk, F, May 17)
Rotherfield Greys 76 (6f, Gwd, F, July 25)
Rothko 42 (13f, Ham, Hvy, Apr 6)
Roushayd 74 (12f, Asc, F, Sep 30)
Royal Astronaut (USA) 44 (14f, Not, S, Apr 17)
Royal Borough 67 (12f, Nmkt, F, Oct 20)
Royal Climber 61 (12f, Cur, F, July 15)
Royal Dartmouth (USA) 48 (7f, Wol, G, May 3)
Royal Estimate 53 (8f, Tsk, F, Sep 2)
Royal Fan 59 (5f, Yrk, F, May 17)
Royalist (CAN) 50 (10f, Rip, F, Sep 9)
Royal Run 43 (8f, Cur, G, July 1)
Royal Square (CAN) 55 (10f, Wind, F, May 15)
Royal Vote (USA) 74 (16f, Asc, G, Oct 13)
Rubelite 43 (12f, Yrk, F, Sep 7)
Ruddy Lucky 73 (12f, Asc, F, June 22)
Rudjig (USA) 53 (10f, Ches, F, May 9)
Run Don't Fly (USA) 64 (12f, Asc, F, Sep 30)
Run High 53 (12f, Eps, F, Aug 29)
Run To Jenny 77 (8f, Cur, F, May 27)
Runun 71 (7f, Asc, G, Sep 30)
Russian Bond (USA) 73 (6f, Asc, F, June 22)
Russian Royal (USA) 74 (7f, Asc, F, June 21)
Rustle 52 (16f, Asc, G, Apr 22)

Sabarab 57 (10f, Asc, G, Oct 13)
Sabotage (FR) 63 (8f, Nmkt, G, Apr 19)
Sacre d'Or (USA) 51 (11f, Ayr, Y, Sep 21)

FLAT SPEED FIGURES – continued

Sadeem (USA) 89 (16f, San, F, May 29)
Sadie Jordan (USA) 57 (10f, Leo, Y, Oct 28)
Sadler's Lad 65 (12f, Leo, G, June 14)
Safawan 74 (8f, Gwd, F, July 27)
Safe 41 (12f, Cat, F, June 10)
Saffaanh (USA) 61 (10f, Nby, F, May 19)
Sagamore 52 (6f, Cur, F, May 20)
Sagamore (USA) 60 (7f, Phx, Hvy, Apr 15)
Sailor Boy 42 (12f, Lei, F, July 18)
Sail (USA) 43 (8f, Bth, G, Apr 25)
Saint Joachim 67 (6f, Phx, G, Aug 13)
Saint Navarro 57 (5f, Nmkt, G, Aug 26)
Saline 44 (10½f, War, F, Aug 28)
Sallustar 40 (6f, Leo, F, July 22)
Sallys Won 41 (10f, Don, G, Mar 31)
Salman (USA) 58 (8½f, Bev, F, Sep 20)
Salmonid 43 (10f, Ayr, F, July 22)
Saluti Tutti 41 (5f, Bev, Y, May 12)
Samarzana (USA) 77 (12f, Gwd, G, Oct 6)
Samaza (USA) 40 (10f, Nby, F, May 19)
Sam Cocktail 43 (12f, Tsk, F, Sep 2)
Samhaan 49 (10f, Chep, F, July 1)
Samhoi (USA) 47 (10f, Nmkt, G, May 4)
Samoan (USA) 73 (7f, Nmkt, F, May 19)
Sandhurst Goddess 62 (7f, Phx, G, Aug 25)
Sandicliffe Star 56 (8f, Kem, F, July 5)
Sanditton Palace 51 (5f, Wind, F, June 19)
San Roque 64 (10f, Bth, F, Sep 18)
Santa Tecla 67 (8f, Yrk, F, June 17)
Sao Paulo (USA) 55 (10f, Eps, F, June 8)
Sapience 62 (12f, Asc, F, June 22)
Sappho Comet 71 (7f, Nby, F, Sep 22)
Saraa-Ree (USA) 61 (7f, Nmkt, G, May 4)
Saratogan (USA) 67 (7f, Cur, Y, Apr 22)
Sartorius 61 (10½f, Hay, G, Aug 4)
Saturday Live 56 (6f, Leo, F, July 22)
Savahra Sound 87 (6f, Asc, F, June 22)
Saxon Court 42 (12f, Flk, F, June 6)
Saxon Lad (USA) 48 (7½f, Lin, F, Oct 5)
Saygoodbye 40 (7f, Naas, F, June 24)
Saymore 59 (8f, Sal, F, June 29)
Saynete 63 (8f, Tsk, F, Sep 8)
Say You Will 66 (7f, Nby, Y, Oct 26)
Scandal (USA) 41 (12f, Yrk, F, July 15)
Scarlet Crest 44 (10f, Not, F, May 16)
Scarlet Red 43 (8f, Cur, G, Aug 26)
Scarpanto 44 (11f, Red, F, May 30)
Scarron (USA) 67 (8f, San, F, May 11)
Scenic 79 (10f, Nmkt, F, Oct 21)
Schhh You-Know-Who 61 (7f, Nby, Y, Oct 26)
Scotch Double (USA) 41 (16f, Not, F, June 26)
Scotch Imp 48 (6f, Rip, F, July 10)
Scottish Fling 49 (8f, Red, F, June 24)
Seamere 53 (5f, Pon, F, Sep 5)
Se-Aq 52 (7f, Cat, F, May 25)
Sea Venture (USA) 45 (6f, Nmkt, F, May 6)
Second Guess 60 (12f, Leo, G, Oct 30)
Secret Appeal 69 (7f, Cur, Hvy, Apr 8)
Secretary of State 57 (8f, Chep, F, Oct 16)
Secret Liason 42 (7f, Bri, F, Sep 14)
Secret Obsession (USA) 68 (10f, Nmkt, F, July 1)
Secret Turn (USA) 50 (10½f, Wind, F, June 26)
Sedulous 43 (7f, Phx, Hvy, Apr 15)
Seespotrun 44 (7f, Naas, F, June 1)
Self Improvement (USA) 52 (10f, Flk, F, July 18)
Sergeyevich 52 (14f, Cur, F, July 15)
Serious Trouble 71 (8f, Gwd, F, July 27)
Serlby Connection 41 (8f, Lei, F, Oct 17)
Sesame 77 (12f, Nby, Y, Oct 28)
Settling Down (USA) 52 (7f, Phx, G, Aug 25)
Sew High 46 (6f, Lei, F, June 10)
Shaadi (USA) 86 (8f, Asc, F, June 20)
Shabanaz 44 (8½f, Eps, F, June 7)
Shadow Boxer 43 (8f, Wind, F, Aug 21)
Shady Heights 86 (10½f, Yrk, F, Aug 22)
Shalfleet 46 (5f, Hay, G, Oct 12)
Shamirani 75 (10f, Gwd, F, July 28)
Sharardoun 57 (10f, Ches, F, May 9)
Sharazari 66 (8f, Asc, F, July 22)
Sharka 59 (8f, San, F, May 29)
Sharlie's Wimpy 43 (5f, Edn, F, June 19)
Sharon's Royale 50 (8f, Nwc, G, Aug 26)
Sharpgun (FR) 53 (8f, Lei, G, Apr 22)
Sharp Justice 73 (7f, Yrk, G, Oct 14)
Sharp N' Early 71 (6f, Nmkt, F, July 13)
Sharp Reminder 82 (6f, Nmkt, G, Apr 18)
Sharp Romance (USA) 59 (8f, Kem, F, May 27)
Sharp Slipper 61 (8f, Cur, Hvy, Apr 8)
Sharp Steven 55 (5f, Bri, H, Aug 3)
Sharp Thistle 59 (7f, Nmkt, F, July 13)
Sharp Times 61 (6f, Hay, Y, Oct 11)
Shaynoor 43 (10½f, Hay, F, June 9)
Shayraz 63 (10½f, Yrk, F, May 17)
Shellac 57 (10f, San, F, May 30)
Sheriff's Star 93 (12f, Eps, F, June 8)
Shieling 54 (8f, Asc, F, Sep 29)
Shillelagh 49 (6f, Bri, F, May 10)
Shining Steel 64 (7f, Nmkt, F, May 19)
Shmame (USA) 49 (6f, Nmkt, F, May 5)
Shoot Ahead 40 (10f, Bri, G, Apr 13)
Short Shot 49 (10½f, Wind, F, June 19)
Shotiche (USA) 65 (10f, Lin, F, Aug 4)
Showdown 46 (8f, Yar, F, July 5)
Shuttlecock Corner (USA) 76 (5f, Yrk, F, Aug 24)
Shyoushka 66 (10f, Nby, F, June 14)
Siesta Key 68 (16f, Asc, F, July 21)
Sigama (USA) 52 (5f, Ches, F, May 9)
Sign People 52 (7f, Lei, F, June 10)
Silca Supreme 87 (6f, Nby, F, May 19)
Silk Petal 58 (7f, Wol, F, May 8)
Silks Princess 41 (6f, Kem, Y, Mar 25)
Silver Fling (USA) 93 (6f, Nmkt, F, May 6)
Silver Haze 71 (8f, Tsk, Y, Apr 14)
Silver Owl 71 (12f, Eps, F, Aug 28)
Simjour 58 (12f, Asc, F, June 22)

FLAT SPEED FIGURES – continued

Simply Henry 61 (7f, Nwc, F, July 24)
Single 65 (8f, Nby, G, Aug 11)
Sir Rufus 47 (10f, Lei, F, May 30)
Sister Chabrias 56 (7f, Wol, G, May 3)
Sixslip (USA) 57 (13f, Nby, G, June 27)
Skazka (USA) 52 (10f, Nby, F, July 14)
Ski Captain 78 (5f, San, F, July 8)
Skolern 47 (8f, Tsk, F, May 6)
Sky Cat 54 (8f, Don, G, Mar 31)
Sky Cloud 43 (7f, Cat, G, Oct 20)
Sky Conqueror (USA) 72 (8f, San, F, June 17)
Sleepers 45 (5f, Sal, F, Sep 7)
Sleepline Fantasy 60 (7f, Sal, G, May 4)
Sleepline Royale 52 (7f, War, S, May 1)
Sleepy Mountain 81 (7f, Yrk, G, Oct 14)
Slender Bender 59 (8f, Kem, F, Sep 2)
Slender Style (USA) 62 (11f, Phx, G, June 17)
Sloe Berry 63 (5f, Asc, F, Sep 29)
Small Scotch 50 (6f, Phx, G, May 10)
Smaoineamh 56 (12f, Leo, G, June 23)
Smoggy Spray 52 (8f, Cur, F, May 20)
Smokey Lad 47 (5f, Cur, F, June 7)
Smooth Flight 42 (8f, Kem, F, Sep 2)
Snake Song 42 (6f, Not, G, Oct 24)
Sno Serenade 56 (10f, Lin, F, July 15)
Snow Bride (USA) 88 (12f, Eps, F, June 10)
Snow Glint 49 (12f, Cat, F, July 19)
Snow Huntress 53 (10f, Don, G, Mar 31)
Sobriety 47 (7f, Nby, Y, Oct 26)
So Careful 62 (6f, Chep, F, Oct 16)
Society Bay (USA) 60 (10f, Leo, Y, Oct 28)
Society Glide 43 (7f, Naas, F, June 24)
Softly Spoken 57 (5f, Ayr, Y, Sep 20)
Sola Mia 46 (7f, Edn, F, Oct 25)
Solar Myth (USA) 46 (6f, Cur, F, May 27)
Solo Act 66 (14f, Yrk, F, Aug 22)
Solo Artist 55 (10f, Bev, F, Sep 21)
Solomon's Song 50 (6f, Ham, G, Aug 21)
Somebody 43 (13f, Ham, Hvy, Apr 6)
Song of Hope 41 (8f, Nwc, F, July 1)
Song of Sixpence (USA) 68 (10½f, Hay, G, Sep 2)
Songstead 57 (6f, Yrk, F, July 15)
Sonic Lord 46 (10f, Yar, F, Aug 24)
Sonilla 70 (6f, Nmkt, G, Oct 6)
Soporific 46 (10f, Nmkt, F, July 12)
So Rhythmical 68 (6f, Kem, F, May 27)
Southern Sky 66 (7f, Gwd, G, Aug 26)
Southrop 56 (5f, Nby, S, Apr 14)
South Sands 48 (12f, Tsk, F, Sep 2)
Sovereign Rocket (USA) 59 (10f, Nmkt, F, July 29)
Spanish Heart 68 (8f, Sal, H, Oct 4)
Spanish Love 45 (7f, Gwd, F, May 25)
Spanish Reel 42 (10½f, War, F, June 24)
Specialised Boy 59 (7f, Kem, Y, May 1)
Sphinx 52 (8f, Pon, Y, Apr 19)
Spiritualist 41 (12f, Lei, G, Apr 22)
Spitfire 64 (10f, Lin, F, June 3)
Spittin Mick 43 (5f, Edn, F, June 19)
Splashman (USA) 42 (10½f, Hay, Y, Oct 12)
Splendid Career (USA) 73 (10½f, Hay, G, Sep 2)
Splintering 76 (6f, Gwd, F, July 25)
Spoilt Son 49 (6f, Nmkt, F, May 5)
Sporting Simon 41 (7f, Gwd, F, July 28)
Spot On Annie 47 (5f, San, F, July 27)
Spottiswode 51 (8f, Cur, G, Oct 21)
Spring Hay 69 (12f, Asc, F, June 20)
Spring Sparkle 55 (7f, Nby, S, Apr 14)
Springs Welcome 59 (10f, Ches, F, Sep 8)
Spritsail 71 (12f, Asc, F, Sep 28)
Squeaky Wheel (USA) 42 (10f, Pon, Y, Apr 19)
Stage Player 44 (10f, Rip, F, Aug 28)
St Ame 69 (5f, Phx, G, Aug 13)
Standing Count 40 (8f, Sal, G, May 4)
Stanwell (CAN) 60 (10f, Nmkt, F, July 1)
Star Lord 70 (11f, Nby, Y, Oct 28)
Star of A Gunner 43 (10½f, War, S, May 1)
Star of The North 47 (7f, Phx, G, June 17)
Staten Island 71 (12f, Eps, F, June 9)
Statoblest 88 (5f, Don, G, Sep 13)
St Cadoc 58 (12f, Hay, G, Sep 1)
Steel Cygnet 40 (10f, Flk, Y, Apr 3)
Steel Spark 54 (10f, Nmkt, G, May 4)
Steffi 46 (11½f, Yar, F, Aug 23)
Stelby 42 (7f, Ayr, F, June 23)
St Elmo's Fire 58 (8f, Yrk, F, May 18)
Steppey Lane 49 (10f, Don, G, May 1)
Still Surprised 52 (10f, Red, F, May 29)
St Ninian 44 (10f, Don, F, May 29)
Stocious 60 (5f, Yrk, F, June 16)
Stone Drum (USA) 63 (12f, Cur, F, July 2)
Stone Flake (USA) 48 (7f, Nby, Y, Apr 15)
Stop Day (USA) 57 (6f, Gwd, G, Oct 7)
Storm Force (USA) 67 (10f, Lin, F, Aug 4)
Stormline (USA) 57 (10f, San, F, Aug 19)
Storm Runner 43 (7½f, Lin, F, May 12)
Stormy Praise (USA) 48 (6f, Gwd, F, June 16)
Stormy Reef 45 (12f, Sal, F, Aug 24)
Straight Gold 48 (8f, Bth, F, July 12)
Stratford Ponds 69 (12f, Hay, G, July 8)
Strover (USA) 50 (7f, Leo, F, July 29)
Sudaf 44 (7f, Cur, F, Sep 9)
Sudden Love (FR) 71 (10f, Gwd, F, July 29)
Sudden Victory 79 (12f, Nby, Y, Oct 28)
Sugar Plum Fairy 43 (10f, Gwd, G, Oct 6)
Suhail Dancer 51 (8f, Tsk, H, June 20)
Sully's Choice (USA) 63 (6f, Rip, F, Aug 12)
Suluk (USA) 49 (12f, Car, H, July 21)
Summa Cum Laude 56 (7f, Yrk, G, Oct 14)
Summer Fashion 51 (10f, Sal, F, Aug 9)
Summerhill 71 (6f, Phx, F, May 31)
Summer Senate (USA) 45 (8f, Leo, G, June 23)
Sunday Sport Star 66 (10f, Kem, Y, Mar 27)
Sunset Reins Free 43 (12f, Hay, S, May 1)
Sunwind 44 (6f, Flk, G, Oct 23)
Super Benz 42 (6f, Not, F, June 12)

FLAT SPEED FIGURES – continued

Super Lunar 60 (9f, San, F, July 27)
Super Neon 42 (7f, Bri, F, May 10)
Superoo 68 (7f, Don, G, Sep 14)
Superpower 86 (5f, Nmkt, F, May 6)
Sure Gold 59 (6f, Yrk, F, June 17)
Suren 67 (16f, Cur, G, Oct 1)
Surest Dancer (USA) 47 (10f, Bri, F, May 10)
Surreal 44 (5f, War, Y, Mar 27)
Susan's Angel 45 (10f, Cur, F, May 27)
Sutosky 42 (10f, Kem, Y, Mar 27)
Sweeping 60 (8f, Yrk, F, May 17)
Sweet Chesne (FR) 74 (8f, Asc, F, June 20)
Sweet Dragon 40 (6f, Wind, F, Aug 21)
Swing Lucky 54 (5f, Lin, F, July 22)
Swing Shift 64 (8f, Bri, F, June 19)
Sylvan Mistral 58 (6f, Lin, F, May 12)
Sylvan Tempest 61 (7f, Nmkt, F, Nov 4)

Tachyon Park 71 (5f, Lin, F, Oct 5)
Taffeta And Tulle (USA) 56 (8f, Yrk, F, Sep 6)
Tafila 48 (10f, Bev, F, May 23)
Tailspin 58 (16f, Asc, F, Sep 28)
Takdeer 48 (8f, Cur, F, May 20)
Takenhall 70 (7f, Yrk, F, Sep 7)
Talitha 40 (12f, Tsk, F, May 20)
Tancred Sand 64 (12f, Hay, G, Sep 1)
Tappen Zee 40 (8f, Leo, F, Aug 17)
Tarsho 75 (10f, Nmkt, F, July 12)
Tatsfield 54 (7f, Yrk, F, Aug 24)
Tauber 54 (7f, Wol, G, May 3)
Tawny 44 (5f, Yrk, F, June 16)
Taylor's Realm 47 (11½f, Yar, F, Aug 23)
Tay Wharf 55 (7f, Nmkt, F, July 1)
Teamster 43 (12f, Ches, F, May 10)
Teeming Shore (USA) 75 (5f, Phx, F, Sep 2)
Teletrader 41 (10f, Don, G, Mar 30)
Tempering 55 (12f, Nby, F, May 19)
Tendency 56 (6f, Lei, F, Sep 19)
Tender Bid 45 (7f, Edn, F, June 26)
Tender Type 51 (15f, Ayr, F, July 17)
Tenter Close 40 (11f, Red, F, Oct 18)
Terimon 83 (12f, Eps, F, June 7)
Tessla (USA) 71 (12f, Eps, F, June 10)
Test Case 65 (8f, San, F, May 29)
That's The One 69 (5f, Yrk, F, Aug 23)
The Devil's Music 56 (6f, Cat, G, Mar 29)
The Footman 51 (8f, Pon, Y, Apr 19)
The Freshes 40 (12f, Lei, F, June 5)
The Kings Daughter 62 (5f, San, F, July 27)
Thekkian 51 (5f, Pon, F, Oct 9)
The Mague 46 (10½f, War, F, June 24)
The Mazall 43 (7f, Cat, F, June 10)
The Prussian (USA) 74 (10f, Nmkt, F, July 12)
The Queen of Soul 54 (5f, San, F, July 20)
The Right Time 40 (6f, Ayr, G, Aug 7)
The Shanahan Bay 43 (5f, Rip, F, Aug 29)
Thethingaboutitis (USA) 73 (16f, Asc, F, June 24)
Thirty First 64 (18f, Don, F, May 29)
Thomas Leng 46 (8f, Tsk, Y, Apr 14)
Thorn Dance (USA) 80 (5f, Hay, F, May 27)
Thornfield Boy 71 (6f, Gwd, G, Aug 26)
Tigani 87 (5f, Yrk, F, Aug 24)
Tiger Claw (USA) 48 (10f, Lei, F, May 30)
Tikhomirov 72 (10f, Phx, F, June 1)
Tilt Tech Flyer 42 (7f, Nmkt, F, July 11)
Timothy's Toy 79 (10f, Asc, G, Oct 13)
Timourtash (USA) 60 (10f, Wind, F, May 8)
Tinco Paleno 47 (6f, Leo, F, Aug 7)
Titchwell 48 (10f, Not, F, June 26)
Tobermory Boy 43 (6f, Not, G, July 8)
To Die For (USA) 55 (7f, Cur, F, Aug 19)
Tokyo Rose 51 (10f, Leo, Y, Oct 28)
Tolo 63 (6f, Asc, F, July 21)
Tonkawa 61 (13f, Bth, F, Aug 15)
Too Eager 45 (6f, Ayr, F, July 22)
Top-Boot 75 (8f, San, S, Apr 29)
Top Class 84 (12f, Asc, F, June 23)
Top Dream 66 (7f, Nmkt, F, Oct 19)
Topeka Express (USA) 41 (8f, Nwc, G, Mar 27)
Top One 51 (6f, Chep, F, July 13)
Tops All (USA) 62 (8f, San, S, Apr 29)
Torius 62 (5f, San, G, Aug 18)
Torjoun (USA) 74 (10½f, Yrk, F, May 17)
Tornabuoni 68 (6f, Cur, F, May 27)
Torrance 45 (7f, Bri, F, Sep 14)
Touch Above 47 (10f, Bev, F, Aug 17)
Touching Star 58 (10½f, Hay, F, June 9)
Touch of White 44 (5f, Bev, Y, May 12)
Toushtari (USA) 43 (10½f, Hay, F, June 10)
Towny Boy 59 (10f, Ayr, Y, Sep 22)
Toxotis 52 (6f, Wind, F, June 26)
Tralos (USA) 88 (12f, Asc, F, Sep 28)
Travelling Light 43 (12f, Pon, F, June 13)
Travelling Tryst (USA) 46 (8f, Tsk, Y, Apr 15)
Travel Mystery 76 (18f, Ches, F, May 10)
Triode (USA) 62 (8f, Lei, F, Oct 17)
Trojan Lancer 43 (10f, Yar, F, July 6)
Trojan River (USA) 40 (10f, Nby, Y, Oct 26)
True Panache (USA) 68 (8f, Asc, F, June 21)
Trust Troy 62 (9f, Red, F, Oct 10)
Trying For Gold (USA) 49 (12f, Sal, F, Aug 24)
Tudor Pilgrim 42 (7f, Cat, Y, Apr 26)
Tuppenny Red 47 (10f, Nby, F, June 15)
Turbine Blade 51 (10f, Yar, F, July 19)
Turbo Speed 68 (7½f, Ches, F, May 9)
Turgot 69 (12f, Eps, F, June 9)
Turmeric 51 (12f, Cat, F, Sep 23)
Tursanah (USA) 55 (8f, Cur, F, May 27)
Twilight Agenda (USA) 74 (7f, Leo, F, July 29)
Twin Jet (USA) 62 (8f, Tsk, F, July 29)
Two Seats 66 (5f, Leo, G, June 14)
Twotime Bid 42 (8f, Ayr, S, Oct 16)
Two Timing (USA) 76 (10f, Asc, F, June 20)
Tylers Wood 56 (5f, Yar, F, June 6)
Tyrian Belle 55 (5f, San, S, Apr 28)
Tyrnippy 53 (8f, Bth, G, Apr 25)
Tyrone Bridge 69 (14f, Cur, G, Sep 23)

FLAT SPEED FIGURES – continued

Ulanova (USA) 49 (8f, Tsk, F, Sep 2)
Ultra Light 54 (10f, Don, G, June 30)
Uncle Ernie 50 (12f, Hay, S, May 1)
Unexpected Guest 48 (11½f, San, G, July 8)
Unfuwain (USA) 81 (12f, Nmkt, F, May 5)
Unknown Quantity 68 (10f, San, F, July 7)
Unpaid Member 49 (10f, Don, G, Mar 31)
Upper Strata 80 (16f, Nmkt, F, Nov 3)
Upton Park 59 (16f, Hay, F, Oct 11)
Upward Trend 75 (8f, Leo, F, Aug 7)
Urray On Harry 47 (8f, Don, F, July 26)
Usran 65 (10f, Lin, F, July 15)
Uxontorius 45 (6f, Gwd, F, May 24)

Vague Dancer 68 (6f, Yrk, F, Sep 6)
Vague Discretion 44 (6f, Not, G, July 8)
Vague Melody 42 (10½f, War, S, May 1)
Vague Shot 69 (8f, Asc, F, July 22)
Valldemosa 55 (5f, Cat, G, Oct 20)
Valls d'Andorra 42 (15f, Ayr, S, Oct 16)
Val Recit (FR) 63 (12f, Asc, F, June 20)
Valville (FR) 60 (16f, Hay, Y, Oct 11)
Vanished Land (USA) 45 (10f, Nmkt, F, May 5)
Vanishing Spirit 42 (7f, Bri, F, Sep 14)
Vanroy 57 (7f, Nmkt, F, May 19)
Vault (USA) 65 (7f, Nmkt, F, Nov 4)
Veltion 51 (9f, Yrk, F, July 14)
Verbarium (USA) 42 (10½f, War, F, Aug 28)
Verdant Boy 55 (6f, Rip, G, Sep 9)
Versailles Road (USA) 53 (10f, Not, F, May 16)
Very Adjacent 62 (6f, Bri, H, Aug 3)
Vestris Abu 65 (9f, Leo, G, Sep 16)
Viceroy Jester 55 (7f, Sal, G, May 4)
Vieste 63 (8f, Cur, Hvy, Apr 8)
View From Above 40 (7f, Kem, F, July 13)
Vilandrado 47 (10f, Nmkt, G, May 4)
Vilanika (FR) 53 (7f, Don, F, July 27)
Vintage 62 (12f, Sal, F, Sep 7)
Viqueen 59 (10f, Phx, Y, May 3)
Vitality 70 (10f, Nmkt, F, July 12)
Volcanoes Spark 47 (12f, Tsk, F, Sep 2)
Vouchsafe 41 (12f, Lei, F, June 5)

Wabil (USA) 70 (10f, Asc, F, Sep 29)
Waki Rainbow (USA) 53 (5f, San, F, July 7)
Wantage Park 73 (6f, Nmkt, G, May 4)
Ward One 49 (8f, Ham, G, Oct 9)
Warning 98 (8f, Asc, F, June 20)
Warrshan (USA) 77 (12f, Asc, F, Sep 28)
Wassling 46 (10½f, Hay, S, Apr 29)
Wassl Port 45 (8f, Nby, Y, Oct 26)
Waterfield 65 (16f, Asc, G, Apr 22)
Waterlow Park 56 (10f, Don, G, Mar 31)
Waverley Star 55 (5f, Ham, F, May 20)
Weld 84 (16f, Asc, F, June 21)
Weldnaas (USA) 61 (7f, Hay, F, June 10)
Welsh Love 59 (10f, Phx, G, Oct 7)
Welsh Siren 45 (7f, Don, G, June 30)
West Beck 50 (7f, Eps, F, June 10)
West China 60 (16f, San, F, May 29)
Western Dancer 51 (16f, Hay, Y, Oct 11)
Western Wolf 61 (8½f, Bev, F, Sep 20)
What A Rowley 46 (6f, Hay, F, May 26)
Where Is She 55 (8f, San, G, Sep 19)
Where's The Money 55 (5f, Nby, S, Apr 14)
Whipper In 54 (5f, San, F, May 30)
Whippet 78 (5f, Gwd, F, July 27)
Whipp's Cross 73 (10f, Phx, Y, May 3)
Whirlygigger 46 (7f, Nmkt, G, May 4)
Whisper The Wind 43 (6f, Flk, F, Aug 22)
White Sapphire 52 (10f, Rip, F, Aug 12)
White-Wash 66 (12f, Eps, F, June 9)
Wick Pound 42 (12f, War, F, Oct 9)
Wide Support 63 (10f, Leo, G, June 23)
Wild Jester 58 (5f, Phx, G, Oct 7)
William Four 49 (10f, Don, G, Sep 13)
Windatum 46 (7½f, Lin, F, Aug 12)
Windbound Lass 48 (13f, Bth, H, July 24)
Windsor Park (USA) 41 (10f, Gwd, G, Oct 6)
Winking Winner 53 (7f, Nwc, Y, Mar 25)
Winning Gallery 42 (13f, Nby, F, June 14)
Wishiah 59 (10f, Red, F, Oct 18)
Wizzard Artist 47 (16f, Chep, F, July 1)
Wizzard Magic 41 (8f, Chep, F, July 1)
Wolverstar 72 (5f, Cur, G, Aug 26)
Wonder Dancer (USA) 76 (8f, San, G, July 8)
Wood Dancer (USA) 76 (8f, San, G, July 8)
Woodside Mill 72 (7f, Nmkt, F, Oct 19)
Wootton (USA) 43 (12f, Sal, F, Sep 7)
Wrapping 58 (10f, Phx, G, Oct 7)

Xafu Xafu 43 (6f, Yar, F, July 6)

Yamashita (USA) 44 (10f, Red, F, July 25)
Yamrah 43 (11½f, San, G, July 8)
Yankee Glory 49 (10f, Phx, F, Sep 30)
Yankee Star 44 (7f, Naas, F, June 1)
Yearsley 56 (8f, Tsk, F, July 29)
You Are A Star 48 (7f, San, F, June 16)
You Missed Me 50 (8f, Lei, F, Aug 1)
Young Benz 45 (11f, Ayr, Y, Sep 21)
Young Commander 47 (8f, Pon, Y, Apr 19)
Young General 48 (10f, Nby, F, Sep 23)
Young Hal 70 (5f, Gwd, F, July 27)
Young Inca 66 (6f, Gwd, F, June 16)
Young Jason 64 (7½f, Ches, F, Sep 9)
Young Oak 43 (5f, Chep, F, July 1)
Young Tearaway 70 (6f, Nmkt, G, Oct 6)
Young Turpin 58 (8f, San, F, May 11)
Young Woodley (USA) 48 (10f, Lei, G, Nov 6)
Youpon (USA) 53 (14f, Leo, G, May 15)

Zaffaran (USA) 79 (16f, San, F, May 29)
Zakhir (USA) 59 (8f, Nmkt, F, May 5)
Zalazl (USA) 65 (10½f, Yrk, F, May 17)
Zayyani 77 (12f, Asc, F, June 20)
Zeffirella 64 (7f, Gwd, F, May 25)
Zero Watt (USA) 82 (16f, San, F, May 29)
Zia (USA) 63 (12f, Yrk, F, Sep 7)
Zilzal (USA) 98 (8f, Gwd, F, July 26)
Zucchini 45 (7f, Ayr, F, July 17)

FLAT SPEED FIGURES – continued

TWO-YEAR-OLDS

Able Express (USA) 41 (5f, Nmkt, F, May 6)
Absolutely Perfect 51 (5f, Kem, Y, May 1)
Abs (USA) 52 (7f, Lei, F, Sep 19)
Access Sun 47 (8f, Yrk, F, Oct 11)
Across The Bay 52 (5f, Gwd, F, July 28)
Adding (USA) 47 (8f, Hay, Y, Oct 11)
Advie Bridge 43 (8f, Lei, F, Sep 18)
Affirmation 41 (5f, San, G, Sep 19)
Agri Dagi (USA) 57 (6f, Nmkt, F, July 1)
Ahd (USA) 54 (6f, Naas, F, June 1)
Air Music (FR) 46 (8f, Asc, G, Sep 30)
Akamantis 46 (7f, Asc, F, Sep 29)
Alidiva 62 (6f, Nmkt, F, Oct 20)
All Fired Up 49 (5f, Cat, F, Aug 10)
Al Mujil 56 (5f, Red, F, Sep 29)
Alriyaah 53 (5f, Flk, F, Aug 8)
Altered Beast (USA) 51 (6f, Nby, S, Oct 28)
Alwathba (USA) 47 (6f, Asc, F, Sep 28)
Amathus Glory 47 (5f, San, F, July 7)
Amazake 41 (8f, Tsk, Y, Nov 11)
Amber Lightning 42 (5f, Nby, Y, Apr 15)
Ambrose 40 (8f, Yrk, F, Oct 11)
American Connexion 41 (6f, Wind, G, Aug 26)
Aminata 66 (6f, Phx, G, Aug 25)
Amron 41 (5f, Ham, Hvy, Apr 6)
Ankara's Princess (USA) 41 (5f, Ayr, Y, Sep 21)
Anne de Beaujeu 45 (6f, Phx, G, June 17)
Annie Laurie 50 (8f, Cur, G, Oct 21)
Anshan 65 (7f, Nmkt, F, Oct 20)
Antoinette Jane 41 (7f, Nmkt, F, Aug 5)
Appledorn 43 (6f, Phx, G, June 17)
Aquatic (USA) 59 (7f, Yrk, F, Aug 22)
Arany 58 (6f, Cat, G, Oct 21)
Argentum 68 (5f, Asc, G, Oct 14)
Arita 47 (5f, Bri, F, Sep 27)
Armanasco 60 (8f, Cur, G, Oct 21)
Aromatic 51 (8f, Pon, F, Sep 5)
Arousal 45 (8f, Asc, G, Sep 30)
Arpero 40 (7f, Bri, F, Aug 17)
Ashdren 45 (6f, Gwd, G, Oct 7)
Asian Pete 45 (8f, Bri, F, Oct 3)
Astrid Gilberto 44 (6f, War, F, July 14)
Atoll 62 (7f, Nmkt, F, Oct 21)
Aucale (USA) 47 (7f, Phx, G, Aug 25)
Ayodessa 47 (5f, Wol, G, Sep 11)
Azzaam (USA) 53 (7f, Yrk, F, Oct 11)

Baligh 62 (8f, Nwc, G, Oct 28)
Balla Cove 77 (6f, Nmkt, F, Oct 5)
Ballysax 44 (7f, Phx, F, Sep 2)
Barakish 65 (7f, Ayr, Y, Oct 17)
Bartat 42 (8f, Ayr, S, Oct 16)
Barton Dene 49 (5f, Gwd, F, May 24)
Batzushka (USA) 55 (5f, Lin, F, Sep 21)
Beachy Glen 45 (6f, Pon, F, Oct 9)
Beata 57 (6f, Phx, F, July 26)
Beehive Boy 40 (6f, Nwc, F, Aug 28)
Belmez (USA) 69 (8f, Nmkt, F, Nov 3)
Be My Chief (USA) 74 (8f, Nwc, G, Oct 28)
Ben Alisky 47 (7f, Cur, S, Nov 8)
Bermuda Lily 43 (5f, Nby, F, June 14)
Berry's Dream 53 (7f, Nby, S, Oct 28)
Between The Sticks 53 (6f, Kem, G, Sep 2)
Bijlee 43 (6f, Cur, F, Aug 19)
Bimbo 42 (8f, Tsk, F, Sep 2)
Blue Stag 40 (10f, Not, G, Oct 23)
Bold Angel 55 (7f, Yrk, F, Oct 11)
Bold Butterfly 49 (7f, Cur, S, Nov 8)
Bold Russian 47 (6f, Hay, G, July 8)
Bold Starlet 44 (7f, Cur, F, Aug 19)
Book The Band 66 (7f, Cur, F, Sep 9)
Boozy 54 (5f, Eps, F, June 10)
Bop Shop 52 (7f, Cur, G, Oct 1)
Born To Swing (USA) 43 (5f, Yrk, F, Aug 23)
Bridal Toast 48 (8f, Asc, G, Sep 30)
Bright Flower (USA) 49 (6f, Rip, F, June 22)
Brisas 53 (5f, Nby, F, Sep 23)
Broughton Bay 62 (6f, Nmkt, F, Oct 19)

Caffarelli 46 (5f, Pon, F, Aug 3)
Call To Arms 66 (7f, Nmkt, F, Oct 20)
Candy Glen 59 (6f, Asc, F, June 20)
Cantdonowtrite 40 (5f, Cat, G, Apr 26)
Caromish (USA) 64 (6f, Kem, G, Sep 1)
Casamurrae 42 (7f, Lei, F, Aug 1)
Case Law 41 (5f, Nmkt, F, Oct 5)
Cashtal Dazzler 44 (7f, Nwc, F, Aug 28)
Castle Courageous 49 (8f, Lei, F, Nov 7)
Castor (USA) 49 (8f, Leo, G, Sep 16)
Catch Twenty Two 40 (7f, Leo, F, July 29)
Champagne Gold 44 (5f, Pon, F, May 26)
Charming Ballerina 42 (7f, Nby, F, Sep 22)
Childrey (USA) 58 (6f, Flk, G, Oct 23)
Chimes of Freedom (USA) 75 (6f, Cur, F, Sep 10)
China Moon 42 (5f, Flk, F, Oct 10)
City Life 54 (5f, Cur, F, July 15)
Close The Till 55 (8f, Leo, G, Sep 16)
Coalition 46 (7f, Cur, S, Nov 8)
Cold Blow 48 (7f, Lin, F, Sep 12)
Contract Law (USA) 49 (6f, Gwd, F, July 26)
Cordoba (USA) 63 (6f, Nmkt, F, Oct 5)
Cosmic Princess 50 (7f, Nby, S, Oct 28)
Country Cottage (USA) 41 (5f, Bth, F, Oct 2)
Croft Imperial 70 (5f, Nmkt, F, July 11)
Croupier 43 (6f, Nmkt, F, Oct 5)
Cullinan (USA) 68 (6f, Gwd, Y, Sep 15)
Curia Regis (USA) 60 (7f, Ches, F, Sep 9)
Curved Blade (FR) 49 (7f, Yar, G, Aug 24)
Cutting Note (USA) 50 (8f, Nwc, G, Oct 28)

Daarik 73 (6f, Asc, F, Sep 28)
Daawi 63 (6f, Kem, G, Sep 2)
Dame Rousara 50 (7f, Asc, G, Oct 13)
Dancing Music 61 (5f, Ayr, Y, Sep 23)

FLAT SPEED FIGURES – continued

Dancing Party (USA) 55 (6f, Nmkt, F, July 1)
Darakah 44 (5f, Lin, F, Sep 12)
Darby Sky (USA) 46 (6f, Asc, G, Oct 13)
Dashing Blade 69 (7f, Cur, F, Sep 9)
Dashing Senor 40 (7f, Yar, G, Sep 13)
Dawson City 41 (6f, Rip, F, June 22)
Dayjur (USA) 61 (6f, Nby, F, July 15)
Dead Certain 67 (6f, Nmkt, F, July 11)
Deer Emily 54 (6f, Leo, G, May 13)
Defensive Play (USA) 50 (8f, Nmkt, F, Oct 19)
Deploy 47 (8f, Nby, S, Oct 28)
Diamond Shoes (USA) 46 (7f, Nmkt, F, Nov 4)
Dickens Lane 44 (6f, Naas, G, Nov 4)
Digression (USA) 57 (8f, Asc, G, Sep 30)
Doolar (USA) 47 (7f, Yrk, F, Aug 22)
Drayton Special 44 (5f, Asc, F, June 22)
Dreamawhile 48 (5f, Flk, F, Oct 10)
Dream Talk 49 (5f, San, F, Sep 9)
Drum Sergeant 44 (6f, Nby, Y, Oct 26)
Duck And Dive 74 (6f, Phx, G, Aug 13)
Duke of Paducah (USA) 61 (7f, Nmkt, F, Oct 21)
Dumbreck 45 (6f, Ayr, Y, Sep 21)

Easy Prep 52 (5f, Ham, G, Sep 11)
Echo Princess 41 (5f, Ayr, Y, Oct 16)
Eire Leath-Sceal 46 (7f, Yrk, F, Oct 11)
Elapse (USA) 43 (5f, Lei, F, June 5)
Elmaamul (USA) 63 (8f, San, G, Sep 19)
Empshott (USA) 43 (7f, Asc, G, Oct 13)
Enchanted Flyer 44 (7f, Cur, G, Sep 23)
Endless Joy 63 (8f, Leo, G, Sep 16)
Enharmonic (USA) 47 (6f, Pon, F, Oct 9)
Ereng (USA) 40 (7f, Phx, G, Aug 13)
Euchan Glen 43 (7f, Edn, G, Nov 1)
Eurolink The Lad 56 (6f, Nby, S, Oct 28)

Facility Letter 58 (6f, Nby, S, Oct 28)
Factuelle 47 (5f, Kem, S, May 1)
Falcons Dawn 40 (5f, Rip, S, Apr 12)
Fantastic Flyer 71 (7f, Leo, Y, Oct 28)
Farfelu 44 (5f, Lin, F, May 13)
Fearless Revival 61 (7f, Nmkt, F, Oct 20)
Felin Special 57 (6f, Cur, F, Aug 19)
Fern Heights 47 (8f, Leo, Y, Oct 28)
First Dream 40 (6f, Ham, S, Nov 2)
Fragrant Park 40 (8f, Yrk, F, Oct 11)
Free At Last 65 (7f, Nby, G, Sep 22)
Front Line Romance 61 (8f, Leo, G, Sep 16)
Fujaiyrah 43 (8f, Asc, G, Sep 30)
Full Volume 50 (5f, Eps, Y, Apr 25)
Fyfield House 41 (6f, Wind, F, July 24)

Galway Star 49 (6f, Naas, G, Nov 4)
Garscube 49 (7f, Yrk, F, Aug 22)
General Practice 56 (7f, Cur, G, Sep 23)
Generals Daughter (USA) 41 (6f, Nby, G, Aug 11)
Gharam (USA) 61 (7f, Nmkt, F, Aug 5)
Gilt Note 56 (6f, Leo, G, May 13)
Go And Go 58 (7f, Cur, F, Aug 19)
Go Dutch (USA) 45 (6f, Nmkt, G, Oct 7)
Going Supersonic (USA) 42 (7f, Leo, F, July 29)
Golan Heights 45 (7f, Yar, G, Sep 13)
Golden Torque 41 (8f, Ayr, S, Oct 16)
Great Heights 40 (7f, Nmkt, F, Nov 4)
Great Service 41 (5f, Ayr, Hvy, Apr 12)
Green's Belle 44 (6f, Rip, F, Aug 19)
Green's Leader (USA) 54 (7f, Nmkt, G, Oct 6)

Halston Prince 45 (6f, Lin, F, Oct 5)
Hana Marie 53 (5f, Nmkt, F, July 11)
Harbour Bar (USA) 42 (8f, Asc, G, Oct 14)
Hasbah 46 (6f, Asc, F, Sep 28)
Haunting Beauty (USA) 59 (6f, Nmkt, G, Oct 4)
Hear A Nightingale 43 (5f, Bth, F, May 6)
Heart of Joy (USA) 65 (6f, Nby, Y, Oct 26)
Hero's Welcome 46 (8f, Cur, G, Sep 23)
Higher Hamill 57 (7f, Nwc, G, Oct 28)
Himmah (USA) 42 (7f, Tsk, Y, Nov 11)
Hintikka 43 (5f, Lei, F, May 29)
Horrofic 40 (7f, Phx, F, July 26)

Ibn Sina (USA) 45 (8f, Nmkt, F, Nov 3)
Illusory 49 (6f, Nby, Y, Oct 26)
In Excess 48 (6f, Red, G, Oct 31)
Insider's View 57 (8f, Leo, G, Seo 16)
In The Groove 55 (7f, Phx, G, Oct 7)
In The Papers 58 (5f, San, F, Sep 9)
I Perceive 42 (7f, Tsk, Y, Nov 11)
Irish Emerald 42 (5f, Kem, S, Mar 25)
Ishtihaar (USA) 43 (7f, Nby, F, July 14)
Island Ruler 42 (7f, Nby, G, Sep 22)
Ivrea 49 (7f, Lei, F, Oct 16)

Jacomino 47 (6f, Gwd, G, Oct 7)
Jagged Edge 41 (5f, Cat, G, Oct 21)
Jagjet 49 (7f, Lei, F, Aug 14)
Janubi 58 (5f, Cur, F, July 15)
Jayiz (USA) 48 (8f, Leo, G, Sep 16)
Jonjas Chudleigh 47 (6f, Phx, G, Aug 13)
Jovial 56 (7f, Phx, G, Oct 7)
Joviality 50 (6f, Phx, F, July 26)
Judgement Call 59 (5f, San, F, Sep 9)

Kaapstad 40 (7f, Wol, F, Aug 28)
Kadim (USA) 40 (7f, Red, F, Sep 29)
Kaheel (USA) 58 (7f, Asc, F, Sep 29)
Karazan 49 (8f, Red, G, Oct 31)
Karinga Bay 49 (7f, Nby, G, Aug 11)
Katsina (USA) 47 (7f, Nmkt, F, Nov 4)
Katzakeena 46 (5f, Red, F, Oct 31)
Keep On Runnin' 42 (5f, Nwc, G, Mar 27)
Kenna Court 44 (6f, Leo, G, May 13)
King Al 50 (6f, Pon, F, Sep 5)
Kissogram Girl (USA) 49 (5f, San, F, May 29)
Kuma Chan 53 (7f, Phx, F, Sep 2)

La Cabrilla 50 (6f, Asc, F, July 22)

FLAT SPEED FIGURES – continued

La Cote Fleurie (USA) 45 (7f, Phx, F, July 26)
La Domaine 61 (6f, Ayr, Y, Sep 21)
La Galerie 58 (5f, Ayr, Y, Sep 21)
Laird of Balmoral 56 (6f, Ham, G, Aug 21)
Lakeland Beauty 57 (6f, Red, F, Oct 18)
Lake Mistassiu 56 (5f, Bth, F, Sep 18)
Land Afar 48 (6f, Kem, G, Sep 2)
Lars Porsena 43 (5f, Nwc, F, June 30)
Lassia 51 (6f, Nmkt, G, Oct 7)
Laxey Bay 59 (8f, Nwc, F, Oct 3)
Legal Verdict 47 (7f, Cur, F, Sep 9)
Le Saule d'Or 44 (8f, Tsk, F, Sep 2)
Lifewatch Vision 55 (6f, Hay, G, July 8)
Lift And Load (USA) 61 (8f, Tsk, Y, Nov 11)
Line of Thunder (USA) 67 (6f, Gwd, Y, Sep 15)
Linpac Light 44 (8f, Tsk, Y, Nov 11)
Lip Sing (USA) 45 (5f, Red, G, Oct 31)
Lochearnhead (USA) 46 (6f, Phx, G, May 10)
Loch Fruin 52 (8f, Nwc, G, Oct 28)
Lord Florey (USA) 53 (7f, Asc, F, Sep 29)
Lord Glen 68 (5f, Nmkt, F, July 11)
Lord of The Field 47 (7f, Nmkt, F, Nov 4)
Love Returned 50 (5f, Sal, F, May 23)
Lover's Moon 54 (8f, Lei, F, Nov 7)
Loving Omen 45 (8f, Tsk, F, Sep 2)
Lucky Frosty (USA) 46 (5f, Red, F, Sep 29)
L'Uomo Classics 48 (6f, Yrk, F, Oct 12)
Lyndseylee 52 (5f, Ches, F, May 9)

Madeley's Pet 43 (5f, Rip, F, June 22)
Mademoiselle Chloe 70 (5f, Ayr, Y, Sep 21)
Maid of Mourne 50 (6f, Naas, F, Oct 14)
Makbul 64 (6f, Asc, F, June 24)
Marasol 41 (5f, Flk, F, Aug 8)
Marienski (USA) 48 (7f, Nmkt, G, Aug 25)
Marquetry (USA) 46 (7f, Nby, G, Aug 11)
Masai Warrior 43 (7f, Phx, F, Sep 2)
Master Pierre 42 (6f, Wind, F, July 24)
Mazag (USA) 41 (7f, Don, G, Sep 13)
Megyaas (CAN) 53 (6f, Hay, G, July 8)
Melbury (USA) 59 (5f, San, F, July 7)
Message Pad 51 (7f, Don, G, Sep 13)
Metal Boys 50 (5f, Nmkt, F, Nov 3)
Military Medium (USA) 54 (6f, Wind, F, July 24)
Milne's Way 49 (6f, Nmkt, G, Oct 7)
Mine Dancer (USA) 43 (7f, Phx, G, Aug 25)
Missing You 47 (7f, Phx, F, Sep 2)
Missionary Ridge 50 (7f, Nby, Y, Oct 26)
Mistral's Collette 58 (8f, Leo, G, Sep 16)
Montendre 42 (6f, Yrk, G, Oct 14)
Moon Cactus 60 (6f, Nmkt, F, July 12)
Mr Brooks 52 (7f, Leo, Y, Oct 28)
Munsif (FR) 40 (8f, Leo, G, Sep 16)
Musical Major 44 (5f, Ham, G, Sep 11)
Music Prospector (USA) 66 (5f, Cur, G, July 1)
Mutah (USA) 48 (6f, Don, F, July 27)
Muwfiq 47 (6f, Yrk, F, Oct 11)
Myhamet 40 (8f, Bth, F, Oct 2)
My Lord (USA) 45 (8f, Lei, F, Nov 7)

Nailem 40 (5f, Flk, F, July 18)
Native Twine 59 (6f, Lei, F, Oct 16)
Nauty Vicki Oyston 42 (5f, Red, F, Sep 29)
Navy Admiral 59 (7f, Leo, Y, Oct 28)
Nazakat 49 (5f, Flk, F, Oct 10)
Nazare Blue 41 (5f, Lin, Hvy, Apr 8)
Neat Dish (CAN) 67 (7f, Leo, Y, Oct 28)
Needham Hope 47 (8f, Nmkt, F, Nov 3)
Negligent 76 (7f, Nmkt, F, Oct 20)
Network 56 (7f, Cur, S, Nov 8)
Never Wrong 54 (5f, Naas, F, May 6)
New Romantic (USA) 40 (6f, Not, F, July 24)
Night At Sea 62 (6f, Nmkt, F, Oct 19)
Noble Match 51 (5f, Gwd, F, July 25)
Noble Patriarch 52 (8f, Gwd, G, Oct 6)
Nobodys Sweetheart 48 (6f, Not, G, Oct 23)
No Dowry 41 (7f, Cur, G, Oct 1)
Nordican 44 (7f, Cur, F, Aug 19)
Nordic Sparkle 55 (6f, Leo, G, May 13)
Nordic Surprise 61 (7f, Leo, Y, Oct 28)
North Country 42 (6f, Asc, G, Oct 13)
Northern Goddess 46 (5f, Eps, F, June 10)
Northern Pet 51 (7f, Cur, G, Sep 23)
Northern Zenith 43 (5f, Red, F, Aug 30)
Norton Challenger 49 (5f, Tsk, Y, Apr 27)
Norwich 47 (7f, Asc, F, Sep 29)
Notley 62 (6f, Nby, Y, Oct 26)
Nout 53 (5f, Lin, F, Aug 4)
Nuclear Express 47 (5f, Tsk, Y, Apr 27)
Number Eleven 43 (5f, Lin, F, Sep 12)

Oh So Risky 40 (6f, Wind, G, Aug 26)
Old Alliance (USA) 67 (5f, Yrk, F, Aug 23)
Old Comrades 47 (5f, Bth, F, Sep 18)
Old Talka River 54 (5f, Phx, G, Apr 29)
Olympic Hero 54 (5f, Sal, F, May 3)
One At A Time 40 (5f, Nmkt, Y, Apr 20)
Orchard Court (USA) 40 (7f, Edn, G, Nov 1)
Osario 68 (6f, Red, G, Oct 31)
Outgoing 52 (5f, Naas, F, May 6)
Ozone Friendly (USA) 61 (6f, Nmkt, F, July 12)

Palace Street (USA) 51 (6f, Nby, G, Aug 11)
Parting Moment (USA) 48 (8f, Don, G, Sep 14)
Pencarreg 57 (7f, Yrk, F, Oct 11)
Performing Arts 54 (6f, Gwd, G, May 24)
Peterhouse 41 (6f, Red, G, Nov 10)
Petillante 68 (5f, Nby, G, Aug 12)
Petipa (USA) 53 (7f, Yrk, F, Aug 22)
Pharaoh's Delight 75 (6f, Phx, G, Aug 13)
Pictorial (USA) 65 (7f, Cur, F, Sep 9)
Pippa's Dream 46 (6f, Kem, G, Sep 1)
Piquant 57 (6f, Nby, S, Oct 28)
Platinum Dancer 44 (6f, Sal, F, Aug 10)
Platonique 52 (8f, Don, G, Sep 14)
Platoon 51 (6f, Nby, S, Oct 28)
Playful Poet 43 (5f, Flk, G, Apr 3)
Playing Safe 42 (6f, Naas, G, Nov 4)
Please Believe Me 51 (5f, Yrk, F, May 16)

FLAT SPEED FIGURES – continued

Poke The Fire 61 (5f, San, F, July 19)
Polar Bird 65 (6f, Phx, G, Aug 25)
Potter's Dream 55 (6f, Ham, G, Aug 21)
Power Shift 40 (5f, Flk, F, Oct 10)
Premier Developer 46 (5f, Edn, F, May 22)
Premiere Moon 43 (7f, Lei, F, Aug 14)
Premier Touch 40 (5f, Ham, F, July 20)
Pretty Cool 49 (5f, Pon, F, May 8)
Primacy 62 (8f, War, F, Oct 9)
Prince Jakatom 40 (7f, Tsk, Y, Nov 11)
Princess Taufan 63 (5f, San, F, May 30)
Proud Friend (USA) 56 (7f, Cur, G, Oct 1)
Puffy 56 (7f, Nwc, G, Oct 28)
Purity 46 (6f, Bri, F, Oct 3)

Qathif (USA) 61 (8f, Nwc, G, Oct 28)
Qualitair Dream 57 (6f, Nmkt, G, Oct 7)
Quavering 45 (7f, Nmkt, F, Nov 4)
Quebec 56 (5f, Cur, Y, Apr 22)
Quest For Fame 49 (8f, Nby, S, Oct 28)
Qui Danzig (USA) 53 (6f, Wind, F, June 26)

Ra'a (USA) 66 (5f, Car, G, Oct 27)
Rafha 60 (6f, Nmkt, F, July 1)
Rahaam (USA) 50 (6f, Nmkt, F, Nov 3)
Raj Waki (USA) 62 (7f, Gwd, F, July 28)
Rami (USA) 55 (6f, Nmkt, F, Oct 20)
Rasan 43 (6f, Lin, F, Oct 5)
Raschester 43 (5f, Ham, S, Apr 29)
Rattle And Hum 43 (7f, Cur, G, Sep 23)
Razzberry (FR) 42 (7f, Wol, F, Oct 2)
Reasonably French 45 (6f, Naas, F, Oct 14)
Red Henry (USA) 60 (5f, Gwd, F, July 28)
Reel Foyle (USA) 44 (5f, Wol, G, Sep 11)
Reference Light (USA) 47 (6f, Asc, F, Oct 13)
Regal Peace 41 (5f, Phx, F, Sep 2)
Regal Thatch 56 (7f, Yrk, F, Oct 11)
Regal Victress (CAN) 54 (6f, Naas, F, June 1)
Rejoneo (USA) 44 (6f, Nmkt, F, Oct 20)
Remthat Naser 64 (7f, Phx, G, Oct 7)
Repercutionist (USA) 61 (6f, Nmkt, G, Oct 4)
Ridgepoint 48 (8f, Hay, F, Oct 11)
Ring of Light 56 (6f, Naas, F, Oct 14)
Robellation (USA) 65 (7f, Gwd, F, July 27)
Rock City 79 (6f, Asc, F, June 20)
Roman Walk 54 (6f, Nmkt, G, Oct 7)
Rope Trick 45 (5f, Red, G, Nov 10)
Rosati (USA) 41 (7f, Cur, Y, Oct 21)
Rose of Miami 54 (6f, Hay, G, Sep 2)
Routilante 60 (6f, Asc, F, July 22)
Royal Academy (USA) 53 (7f, Nmkt, F, Oct 20)
Royal Fi Fi (USA) 51 (7f, Nmkt, F, Oct 20)
Royal Verse (FR) 40 (8f, Pon, F, Sep 5)
Ruby Tiger 44 (7f, Eps, F, Aug 28)
Rudy's Fantasy (USA) 55 (7f, Nmkt, F, Oct 21)
Rushmore (USA) 63 (6f, Nby, F, July 15)
Russian Frontier 50 (6f, Nby, Y, Oct 26)

Sadlers Congress 49 (8f, Cur, Y, Oct 21)
Salsabil 64 (6f, Nby, G, Sep 22)
Saltessa 50 (6f, Lei, F, Oct 16)
Samsova 44 (7f, Nby, G, Sep 22)
Sanglamore (USA) 45 (8f, Lei, F, Nov 7)
Sarah Georgina 42 (6f, Wind, F, July 3)
Sasaki 40 (7f, Lei, F, Oct 17)
Satin Wood 64 (8f, Nmkt, F, Nov 3)
Saysana 43 (5f, Flk, F, Sep 5)
Scarlett Holly 49 (6f, Nby, S, Oct 28)
Scatter 56 (6f, Wind, G, Aug 14)
Sea Fowl 42 (7f, Phx, G, Oct 7)
Seven Sons 49 (5f, Bth, F, May 6)
Shambo 40 (7f, Nby, G, Aug 11)
Shamshoon 72 (5f, Nmkt, F, July 11)
Shandryann (USA) 45 (5f, Cur, G, July 1)
Sharpalto 40 (5f, Flk, F, Oct 10)
Sharp Anne 50 (5f, Pon, F, May 8)
Sharp N' Easy 44 (5f, Bth, F, Sep 18)
Sharp N' Smooth 45 (5f, Bth, F, May 6)
Shavian 67 (7f, Asc, F, Sep 29)
Sheer Precocity 54 (6f, Red, G, Oct 31)
Shout Fore 55 (6f, Nmkt, F, Oct 19)
Shunt 42 (5f, Nmkt, F, May 5)
Silent Girl 46 (8f, Nmkt, F, Oct 6)
Silk Slippers (USA) 52 (8f, Asc, G, Sep 30)
Simply Terrific 44 (8f, Cur, G, Sep 23)
Single Combat (USA) 57 (6f, Cur, F, Aug 19)
Sink The Fleet (USA) 41 (5f, Red, F, May 2)
Sir Arthur Hobbs 46 (5f, Cur, G, Sep 23)
Smokey Native (USA) 53 (7f, Yrk, F, Aug 22)
Snurge 45 (8f, Nby, G, Sep 22)
Sober Mind (USA) 46 (7f, Nby, F, July 15)
Soleil Grand 40 (7f, Nmkt, F, July 11)
Some Fun 46 (6f, Cur, F, Aug 19)
Somethingdifferent (USA) 71 (7f, Nmkt, F, July 11)
Song of Angels (USA) 48 (6f, Phx, G, June 17)
Southern Beau (USA) 49 (7f, Yrk, F, Aug 22)
Southern Rule 42 (6f, Leo, F, July 29)
Soy Roberto (USA) 63 (6f, Nmkt, F, Oct 20)
Spanish Empire (USA) 46 (8f, Nby, S, Oct 28)
Spinning 55 (8f, Nmkt, G, Aug 26)
Spoof 53 (6f, Nmkt, G, Oct 7)
Spring High 42 (5f, Flk, F, July 18)
Spurned (USA) 46 (7f, Phx, F, Sep 2)
Spy School (USA) 50 (7f, Cur, F, Aug 26)
Stadler 48 (8f, Leo, G, Oct 30)
Starchy Cove 46 (5f, Wol, F, Oct 18)
Star Hill 69 (6f, Kem, G, Sep 2)
Stereo (USA) 43 (8f, Lei, F, Nov 7)
Stoneythorpewonder 56 (5f, Ham, G, Sep 11)
Stormy Belle 57 (5f, Nmkt, F, July 11)
Sundance Kid (USA) 50 (6f, Nwc, F, Oct 3)
Super Deb 47 (5f, Rip, F, June 22)
Super Flame (CAN) 48 (7f, Phx, G, Aug 25)
Super One 44 (5f, Lin, F, June 3)
Sure Sharp (USA) 65 (6f, Nmkt, F, Nov 3)
Surpassing 43 (7f, Lei, F, Aug 1)
Swiss Affair (USA) 53 (6f, Nby, F, Sep 23)

FLAT SPEED FIGURES – continued

Swordsmith (USA) 42 (7f, Nmkt, F, Oct 20)

Tabdea (USA) 55 (6f, Rip, F, Aug 12)
Tadwin 59 (5f, Ayr, Y, Sep 21)
Takeall 50 (5f, Red, F, Sep 30)
Tanfith (CAN) 60 (8f, Nby, G, Sep 22)
Tanwi 74 (7f, Leo, Y, Oct 28)
Tarnside Club 42 (6f, Nwc, G, Aug 26)
Tatwij (USA) 64 (5f, Ayr, Y, Oct 16)
Tavolara 44 (6f, Nmkt, F, Oct 20)
Teach Dha Mhile 57 (6f, Phx, G, Aug 13)
Tenderetta 41 (6f, Cur, F, Sep 10)
The Caretaker 70 (7f, Phx, G, Oct 7)
The Irish Sheik 55 (5f, Lin, F, May 12)
The Island 40 (5f, Lin, Hvy, Apr 8)
Thetford Forest 55 (7f, Cur, G, Sep 23)
Times Gift 49 (6f, Wind, F, July 29)
Time Slot (USA) 52 (7f, Cur, G, Sep 23)
Tirol 59 (7f, Nby, Y, Oct 26)
Tod 51 (6f, Pon, F, Sep 5)
Tory Conquest (FR) 41 (8f, Nwc, F, Oct 3)
Toshiba Comet 42 (5f, Hay, G, Oct 12)
Toss of The Coin 46 (5f, Red, F, Sep 29)
Totally Complete (USA) 47 (7f, Phx, F, July 26)
Treble Eight 40 (8f, Nmkt, G, Oct 4)
Tribal Lady 40 (6f, Nby, F, June 15)
Trireme 55 (7f, Nmkt, F, July 11)
Tulac An Iarainn 52 (7f, Phx, F, Sep 2)
Two Left Feet 59 (8f, Ham, G, Oct 9)
Tyburn Tree 61 (8f, Nby, S, Oct 28)

Under The Wing 42 (7f, Lei, F, Aug 14)

Va Toujours 68 (7f, Nmkt, F, Oct 7)
Vax Lady 40 (6f, Yrk, G, Oct 14)
Verdeuse (FR) 40 (7f, Chep, F, Oct 16)
Viceroy 56 (5f, Hay, G, Aug 11)
Victory Piper (USA) 62 (8f, Cur, Y, Oct 21)
Villeroi 61 (5f, Red, G, Oct 31)
Vintage Type 41 (5f, Nwc, F, June 30)

Wadood (USA) 67 (6f, Asc, F, June 20)
Waki Gold (USA) 54 (8f, Nby, G, Sep 22)
Walking Saint 53 (7f, Nmkt, F, July 12)
Wanda 45 (5f, Ham, G, Sep 11)
Water Well 45 (7f, Nmkt, F, Nov 4)
Wedding Bouquet 69 (7f, Phx, G, Oct 7)
Welney 71 (6f, Nby, F, Sep 23)
Western Music 44 (5f, Ayr, Y, Oct 16)
Western Ocean 46 (8f, Don, G, Sep 14)
Willbutwhen 55 (5f, Nmkt, F, Nov 3)
Wilnic 41 (6f, Leo, F, July 29)

Young India 42 (5f, Red, F, Sep 30)

Zanoni 58 (6f, Nby, Y, Oct 26)
Zizania 50 (6f, Nmkt, G, Oct 7)
Zoman (USA) 48 (7f, Chep, F, Oct 16)
Zubrovka (FR) 54 (7f, Nmkt, F, Oct 21)
Zvornik 51 (7f, Cur, S, Nov 8)

© RACEFORM LIMITED 1990
COPYRIGHT

Copyright in all Raceform Limited's publications is strictly reserved by the publishers, and no material therein may be reproduced, stored in a retrieval system, or transmitted in any form or by any means, electronic, mechanical, photocopying, recording or otherwise without written permission of Raceform Limited.

1989 TWO-YEAR-OLD RATINGS

JON WILDE'S two-year-old handicap for 1989 runs on a scale of 0-100, with any horse worthy of a rating listed. Two-year-old ratings for 1990 will be published each week in Raceform Handicap Book.

TOP TEN

1	Be My Chief	100
2=	Dashing Blade	98
	Dead Certain	98
	Osario	98
5=	Negligent	97
	Rafha	97
	Tatwij	97
8=	Anshan	96
	Shavlan	96
10=	Berry's Dream	95
	Gharam	95
	Line of Thunder	95

Horse	Rating
Abel Prospect	33
Abigail's Dream	49
Able Express	28
Able Player	59
Abrigo	27
Abs	70
Absolutely Perfect	80
Absonal	12
Abstone Lad	42
Access Cruise	20
Access Leisure	75
Access Ski	51
Access Sun	82
Across The Bay	53
Acrow Lord	30
Adding	80
Addison's Blade	45
Admiral Byng	54
Adorable Cherub	26
Advance To Go	3
Advie Bridge	60
Afaff	22
Affirmation	50
Afrienddroppinging	24
Agaleion	37
Age Of Miracles	57
Agri Dagi	42
Airedale	24
Aire Valley Lad	39
Air Music	76
Air Nymph	46
Akamantis	93
Akhawrah	53
Akimbo	20
Albert	55
Al Anba	57
Alchiea	28
Al Demour	53
Alderhey	52
Alfujairah	55
Alibi Warning	38
Alicante	9
Alidiva	79
Alim	66
Alimana	34
Aljanan	36
Al Khobar	20
Allez-Oops	32
All Fired Up	18
All Night Deli	55
All Welcome	24
Almaghrib	56
Almanama	29
Almuinjjid	40
Al Mujjl	59
Alriyaah	12
Alsaamer	38
Altaia	69
Altered Beast	87
Alvares	31
Alwathba	50
Always Alex	43
Alysardi	48
Amana River	26
Amathus Glory	48
Amazake	74
Amber Lightning	34
Ambrose	59
Amood Point	10

TWO-YEAR-OLD RATINGS - *continued*

Horse	Rating
Amour Du Soir	35
Amron	47
Anatroccolo	47
Andrew's First	43
Anna Petrovna	56
Another Lane	57
Anshan	96
Antique Andy	31
Antoinette Jane	61
Anything Goes	19
Anytime Anywhere	73
Apache Prince	10
Apparel	41
Appelania	28
Applianceofscience	59
Apres Huit	42
April Cracker	14
Aquatic	62
Arabian Nymph	31
Arabian Silence	74
Arany	93
Arbitrageur	14
Arctic Heights	7
Ardelle Grey	54
Ardlui	56
Arethusa Leisure	27
Argentum	22
Arita	72
Aromatic	71
Arousal	73
Arpero	65
Arthur Devis	3
Ascending Dream	25
Ashdren	48
Asian Pete	94
Astrid Gilberto	47
Athlon	37
Atlantic Clear	44
Atoll	71
Auction News	43
Autobird	50
Autumn Morning	20
Avonside	36
Ayodessa	62
Ayr Raider	47
Azadeh	72
Azzaam	94
Back Raise	34
Badgers Dash	52
Baligh	88
Bali Lady	48
Balishy	74
Balla Cove	93
Ballet Bliss	18
Ballyhooly	51
Ballyzao	16
Balzaon Knight	25
Band On The Run	30
Bankroll	58
Banton Loch	30
Barachois Princess	31
Barakish	83
Barbezieux	5
Bardolph	47
Barhoom	23
Barkston Singer	68
Baroness Gymcrak	27
Bartat	86
Barton Dene	48
Basenite	20
Bateau Rouge	77
Batzushka	52
Bawbee	58
Baybeejay	15
Bayfoot	11
Bay Reef	65
Beachy Glen	55
Beau Quest	57
Beau Rou	15
Becocious	24
Beehive Boy	21
Beldomayr	7
Belfort Ruler	20
Belinda's Boy	44
Be My Chief	100
Benazir	77
Benzine	33
Bermuda Lily	26
Berillon	41
Berkeley Hill Boy	17
Berry's Dream	95
Bersey	37
Besito	35
Bestow	44
Betwoen The Sticks	75
Between Time	43
Bid Only	39
Big Bass	47
Big Nephew	44
Bilimbi	11
Bimbo	81
Birthday Parade	40
Bitocal	12
Black Fighter	34
Blackthorn Winter	39
Blazing Sunset	23
Blindmans Double	29
Block The Day	6
Blow A Kiss	40
Blue Bell Ribbons	1
Blue Room	33
Blue Stag	68
Blushing Bloom	28
Bodge	57
Bold Ambition	67
Bold Angel	71
Bold Endeavour	42
Bold Lez	53
Bold Passion	90
Bold Performer	68
Bold Rab	31
Bold Russian	87
Bold Street Blues	58
Bolshoi Prince	26
Bondstone	73
Book The Band	70
Bootscraper	44
Boozy	77
Born To Swing	67
Bougainvillas	8
Bounder Rowe	36
Bourbonville	33
Boy Emperor	44
Bracken Bay	47
Bracken Bells	11
Bradmore's Classic	61
Bric Lane	38
Bridal Toast	78
Bright Flower	15
Brilliant Timing	5
Brisas	4
Broadway Star	12
Brockshill	32
Broughtino	25
Brown Carpet	39
Bruntsfield	36
Bubulina	42
Buffs Express	11
Bullace	30
Bundle Of Luck	29
Buran	15
Burford	35
Burslem Beau	28
Cacophany	15
Caffarelli	52
Calabali	28

TWO-YEAR-OLD RATINGS - *continued*

Calacuchi 22
Calahonda Dave 60
Calgary Redeye 35
Calgroup Lad 16
Callipoli 67
Call To Arms 88
Cameo Performance 52
Campai 49
Candy Glen 54
Cannon's Spirit 30
Camden's Ramsom 27
Capability Brown 75
Cartel 37
Casamurrae 47
Case Law 41
Cashtal Dazzler 83
Castle Courageous 89
Castlerea Fair 13
Casual Flash 46
Caswell 1
Catballou 54
Caught Unawares 54
Cavalla 44
CB Special 5
Cee-Jay-Ay 46
Cellatica 35
Certain Star 9
Chambros 49
Champagne Gold 77
Chandanne 63
Change Of Mood 14
Chanteresse 5
Chapman's Peak 35
Charming Ballerina 76
Charm Time 22
Chateaubaby 23
Chateau de Berne 25
Cheren Lady 20
Chess Piece 51
Chez Jarasse 37
Chief Dancer 21
Childrey 86
Chilling Breeze 27
Chilterns 8
Chimes Of Freedom 94
Chipandabit 57
Chirone 68
Chilterns 31
Choir's Image 33
Chou-Chou Royale 66
Clare Court 75
Claudia Miss 29
Clear Light 43
Clock Golf 23
Clockwork Orange 28
Closed Shop 67
Cocked Hat Girl 46
Cold Blow 52
Colfax Lady 18
Colonia 30
Colourist 47
Colson Boy 22
Colvin Lad 22
Come And Stay 30
Come On Nora 20
Come On Rosi 47
Commanche Nation 27
Compos Mentis 35
Comstock 68
Conjourer 37
Constant Delight 63
Contract Law 91
Cool Dancer 34
Copford 27
Copper Top 33
Coral Flutter 23
Cordoba 90
Corio Bay 23
Cormorant Creek 46
Corrin Hill 63
Corsee 49
Cosmic Dancer 9
Cosmic Princess 92
Country Cottage 36
Courtesy Title 75
Cove Cottage 39
Craven 39
Crazy River 28
Creselly 48
Cribella 51
Cricket Fan 48
Criminal Law 63
Crispy Duck 26
Croft Imperial 67
Croupier 62
Crown Baladee 46
Crown Class 41
Crowning Ambition 31
Crown Of Glass 46
Cross Mags 4
C Sharp 47
Cullinan 83
Cumbrian Singer 28
Cum Laude 36
Cup Of Tricks 47
Curia Regis 82
Curved Blade 87
Cutting Note 76
Daarik 85
Daisy Wheel 70
Dakin Brook 21
Dalsanna 24
Dalston 28
Dame Rousara 94
Dancing May 4
Dancing Music 58
Dancing Party 70
Dancing Scholar 21
Dancing Sensation 10
Dancing Tender 54
Dara Dee 40
Dara Prince 14
Darby Sky 41
Daring Joy 9
Daromann 65
Darting Moth 54
Dashing Blade 98
Dashing Senor 64
Dauntess 47
Dawson City 59
Dayjur 76
Dazzlingly Radiant 24
Dead Certain 98
Deax Anes 57
Debach Daisy 37
Deceit 54
Defensive Play 86
Deficit 31
Deploy 80
Derechef 19
Derry Reef 6
De Winter 29
Dhabiha 40
Diamond Shoes 84
Diamond Sprite 55
Digression 87
Distinct Native 40
Dividia 57
Djanila 20
Dodgy 32
Domrun 37
Donna Bold 28
Dontworryaboutit 35
Dollar 60
Doris Girl 29
Dorset Delight 24

TWO-YEAR-OLD RATINGS - *continued*

Horse	Rating
Dorset Duke	94
Dostoyevsky	28
Doulally	44
Dovekie	50
Drayton Special	64
Dreamwhile	44
Dream Of Jenny	63
Dream Talk	57
Drum Sergeant	69
Dublin Breeze	69
Duck And Dive	58
Duke's Duet	55
Duke Of Paducah	70
Dukhan	23
Dumbreck	73
Dumdumski	65
Dunmaglass	27
Dun Shining	26
Dunstar	46
Dushenka	43
Dustbowl	21
Dutest	23
Easy Prep	82
Echo Princess	74
Eire Leath-Sceal	59
Elapse	58
El Arab	49
Ela-Yemou	40
Elemis	16
Elmaamul	86
Elmdon Prince	17
Elmuraqash	69
El Paso	63
El Volador	50
Empress Wu	32
Empshott	41
Emven	31
Emy's Way	25
Enchanting Habit	51
Endless Joy	56
Endoli	53
Enharmonic	61
Enterprise Lady	70
Equinor	31
Erevnon	35
Erik Odin	53
Ermo Express	47
Escrime	75
Estefan	45
Eterea Leap	25
Eton Lad	45
Euchan Glen	54
Euroblake	53
Euro Galazy	38
Everdene	4
Every one a Gem	55
Exchange Fayre	18
Exhibition Road	40
Express Account	68
Facility Letter	62
Failand	40
Fair Titania	58
Fair Wicket	21
Falcon Blue	30
Falcons Dawn	38
Fallow Deer	14
Fame N Fortune	27
Famous Beauty	52
Fanellan	43
Fara	42
Faraway Blues	50
Farfelu	21
Farmin	48
Farndale	30
Farnley Hey	4
Fascination Waltz	70
Fast Operative	45
Faultless Speech	45
Fayafi	58
Fearless Revival	82
Field Glass	59
Figment	42
Final Ace	44
Final Enigma	38
Final Shot	71
Finette	39
Fine Warrior	2
Fire And Shade	24
Fire The Groom	38
Firjan	62
First Blessed	24
First Choice	42
First Dream	68
First Exhibition	20
First Mistake	10
First Vintage	48
Flamberge	25
Flaming Glory	38
Florida Secret	29
Flower Girl	22
Flying Diva	74
Flying Monarch	74
Foot Soldier	54
Forbidden City	16
Ford King	42
Foreign Currency	48
Forever Diamonds	48
Forever More	21
Formidable Task	29
For Real	53
Fortan Prince	22
Forteto	52
Fox Chapel	45
Fragrant Park	65
Free Thinker	47
Free At Last	88
French Bay	21
Friendship Renewed	46
Front Line Romance	75
Front Page	39
Full Orchestra	44
Funun	28
Fyfield House	45
Galactic Scheme	56
Galatea Pearl	13
Gant Bleu	50
Garissa	7
Gasbbiadiani	85
Gerscube	45
Generals Daughter	14
Gentle Gain	21
Get Going	51
Gharah	42
Gharam	95
Gilded Past	40
Gingernut	19
Gippeswyck Lady	27
Give In	30
Glazerite	50
Glebelands Girl	20
Glencoe Lady	12
Glen Kate	87
Glen Maddie	41
Glenstal Princess	62
Glentor	58
Glitterbird	37
Go All Night	22
Go Buy Baileys	76
God Bless You	33
Godsall	28
Go Dutch	78
Golan Heights	43
Golden Flight	29
Golden Loft	63
Golden Torque	69
Golden Treasury	70

TWO-YEAR-OLD RATINGS - *continued*

Horse	Rating
Gold Nostalgia	53
Gold Of Honour	40
Gomarlow	76
Gondo	64
Goodfellows Lot	53
Goodreda	35
Good Skills	28
Go Pathfinder	9
Gotcha	57
Gozone	35
Granitton Bay	54
Great Heights	78
Great Mill	72
Great Service	16
Green Tin Hut	27
Green's Belle	46
Green's Leader	78
Green's Sisley	50
Green's Stubbs	27
Greetland Grit	16
Grey Duster	82
Grey Merlin	52
Grey Owl	52
Grey Power	20
Grey Tudor	25
Grey Wolf	42
Grown At Rowan	57
Guarantee	14
Gulmarg	62
Gusty Lady	29
Guthrie Court	40
Gymcrak Lovebird	37
Hafhafah	29
Haitham	44
Haleim	32
Half A Pink Jo	7
Halston Prince	57
Hana Marie	61
Hanover Street	24
Harbour Bar	80
Hardiheroine	63
Hard To Get	42
Hard To Name	56
Hartley	54
Hasbah	52
Hasland	12
Hawaiian Reef	20
Hayya Ya Shareef	24
Hazy Heath	23
Hear A Nightingale	78
Heart Of Joy	94
Heaven's Gate	45
Heaven's Highway	13
Hebba	65
Heigh-Ho	45
Heisman	72
Helen's Guest	47
Hellenic	44
Hephzivah	20
Hermitage Rock	69
Hickory Wind	51
Hidden	57
High Beacon	61
High Caste	14
High Elegance	19
Higher Hamill	93
Highly Secure	36
High Purse	55
High Water	47
Himmah	58
Hintikka	69
Holy Gait	49
Homosassa	47
Hopscotch	51
Horn Player	27
Hostess Quickly	38
Hotfoot Henry	5
Hot Rumour	70
Hud	39
Hugli	15
Hunkey Dorius	22
Hunting Horn	32
Ibn Sina	64
Icarnafordit	6
Ice Magic	18
Idle Chat	44
Ijtihaad	44
Ikraaj	29
Ile De Roma	59
Illusory	74
Imhotep	44
Inbihar	22
Indian Fashion	43
Indian Plume	43
India's Twist	66
In Excess	78
Inhibition	10
Instant Desire	69
In The Groove	79
Intransit	49
Intrepid Lass	22
Intrepid Lad	19
Intuitive Joe	68
Invisible Halo	37
I Perceive	58
Irish Emerald	51
I See Ice	40
Ishtihaar	46
Island Ruler	50
Island Wedding	44
Isle Of Arran	53
Ittisaal	36
Ivory's Of Radlett	38
Ivrea	91
I Wanna Dance	3
Jacomino	67
Jagged Edge	73
James's Pet	22
Jamin	13
Jathibiyah	69
Jaydeeglen	41
Jazaf	62
Jebali	37
Jokers Patch	62
Jovial	84
Jovial Kate	56
J R Jones	20
Jubilee Trail	53
Judgement Call	72
Just Go	21
Just Jean	48
Kaapstad	31
Kadim	52
Kaheel	87
Kaher	76
Karazan	94
Karens Prince	18
Karinga Bay	25
Katahdin	57
Katsina	85
Katy's Lad	54
Katzakeena	55
Kawarau Queen	45
Kawtuban	27
Kaycen	38
Keen Hunter	61
Keen Melody	11
Keep On Runnin	48
Kerama	86
Key Shift	46
Khios	26
Kid Lewis	33
Kildonan	48
Killimor Lad	1
King Al	15
King Cracker	61

TWO-YEAR-OLD RATINGS - *continued*

King High 21
King Orpheus 47
King's Shilling 53
Kinlacey 39
Kino 43
Kirstenbosch 37
Kissogram Girl 7
Kitty Russe 42
Klairover 11
Knave Of Clubs 56
Knight's Baroness 94
Koracle Bay 72
Krista Kala 22
Kristin's Light 4
Kristis Girl 61
Kukajoo 28
Kumada 31
La Cabrilla 26
La Domaine 37
Lady Bunting 58
Lady Ellen 69
Lady Grenville 67
Lady Lita 51
Lady Longleat 27
Lady Mainda 20
Lady Of Persia 56
Lady Of Vision 65
Lady Rosemary 10
Lady Snooble 14
Lady Topaz 46
Lady Wishing Well 24
Lafkadio 25
La Galerie 83
Laird Of Balmoral 71
Lakeland Beauty 65
Lake Mahwa 15
Lake Mistassiu 67
Lake Taupo 14
Lance's Lassie 34
Land Afar 70
Land Of Hope 40
Langtry Lass 37
Languedoc 68
La Raptotte 29
Laser Contact 14
Lassia 76
Lassie's Holme 20
Last Emperor 35
Latvian 45
Lawnswood Junior 45
Laxey Bay 81
Leah Jay 5
Leave It To Lib 34
Leenan Bay 44
Legal Streak 5
Legin 16.
Les Amis 68
Le Saule D'Or 64
Les Sylphides 26
Leven Baby 44
Liandtrisant 13
Lifewatch Check 34
Lifewatch Vision 31
Liffey Lace 73
Lift and Load 94
Light On Her Toes 17
Lilly Camilly 3
Line Of Thunder 95
Line Of Vision 19
Lingfield Lass 33
Linpac Light 77
Lip Sing 64
Little Big 35
Little Corporal 60
Little Kraker 20
Llennodo 29
Local Council 34
Loch Fruin 78
Loch Spey 10
Logical Lady 45
Lombok 17
Lomond Lady 19
Long Island 54
Longlyn 1
Lord Bertie 73
Lord Florey 84
Lord Glen 46
Lord Magester 45
Lord Of The Field 85
Lorica D'Or 5
Lost Empire 27
Lost Innocence 49
Love Returned 65
Lover's Moon 61
Love Street 48
Loving Omen 39
Luck O The Irish 16
Lucky Barnes 65
Lucky Blue 36
Lucky Frosty 40
Lucky Lyphard 29
Lucky Moon 25
Luna Probe 28
L'Uomo Classics 44
Lurking 49
Lyndseylee 12
Mac Rambler 16
Mac's Idea 9
Macs Maharanee 79
Madamoiselle Chloe 85
Madam Tudor 34
Madeley's Pet 44
Madriya 59
Magic Bullet 9
Magic Fluke 69
Mahrah 25
Maison Des Fruits 36
Majesty's Room 19
Makbul 74
Make And Mend 11
Malmesbury 17
Manse Key Gold 59
Mantraki 39
Manx Princess 25
Marciana 34
Margs Girl 65
Marian Evans 15
Marienski 57
Mariolino 4
Marjons Boy 66
Marlingford 11
Marquetry 59
Marsh's Law 48
Martini's Courier 46
Martin-Lavell Post 4
Martinstar 4
Maryland Willie 56
Masella 27
Master Dancer 38
Master Pierre 47
Matching Lines 37
May Hinton 67
Mazag 77
Megathrust 19
Megan Blaze 19
Megyaas 68
Melbury 45
Merandi Special 24
Merryfall 56
Metal Boys 79
Mexican Vision 63
Mezhirov 34
Mia Fillia 4
Midnight Moves 27
Midsummer Breeze 40
Mieka 51

TWO-YEAR-OLD RATINGS - *continued*

Horse	Rating
Mildame	5
Military Shot	49
Millfields Lady	52
Million Heiress	9
Mill Run	39
Milne's Way	81
Miltiades	69
Mingus	34
Minimize	68
Minstrel Dancer	46
Miss Adventure	64
Miss Fee Fee	46
Miss Java	26
Missionary Ridge	82
Miss Kellybell	40
Miss Knight	29
Miss Pelota	56
Miss Pinocchio	46
Miss Tenaville	11
Miss Wassl	40
Mister's Sister	19
Mistress Monet	38
Misty Eyes	44
Mitaki	66
Modest Hope	34
Mohini	27
Molly's Move	28
Molly Splash	18
Molo	6
Monarda	34
Monkey Love	57
Moon Cactus	83
Moon Walking	43
Montendre	91
Morpick	7
Moscow Dynamo	58
Motcombs	26
Mountview	18
Mr Optimistic	49
Mrs Gray	39
Mrs Skinner	47
Muarij	56
Mukddaam	85
Mull House	56
Musical Flash	44
Musical Major	67
Musical Note	55
Mutah	76
Muwfiq	88
My Croft	50
Myhamet	56
My Little Bird	5
My Lord	76
My Mavournin	46
My Sister Ellen	35
Mysterious Gent	33
My Ugly Duckling	27
Myverygoodfriend	62
Nafhaat	67
Nafzawa	68
Nailem	73
Nakora Bistraya	37
Najat	13
Narwala	64
Native Gem	53
Native Guile	51
Native Tribe	72
Native Twine	89
Nauty Vicki Oyston	35
Naval Pageant	50
Naval Party	39
Nawassi	32
Nazare Blue	35
Needham Hope	66
Negligent	97
Never So High	52
New Romantic	57
Newsham Bridge	1
Niarbyl Bay	50
Nice And Sharp	53
Nice Day	71
Nicnatlou	8
Nicquita	38
Nidomi	19
Night At Sea	94
Night Duchess	29
Night Floows Day	24
Night Princess	46
Night Shirt	70
Night Transaction	24
Nikkris	30
Nikolaise	45
Noble Match	52
Noble Partner	9
Noble Patriach	85
Nobody's Sweetheart	84
No No Nadia	9
North Country	74
Northern Goddess	38
Northern Hal	26
Northern Heights	50
Northern Rocket	38
Northern Zenith	61
Northgate King	41
Norton Challenger	62
Norwich	76
No Sharps Or Flats	4
Notley	87
Nout	62
Nujoom	16
Number Eleven	54
Number One Son	46
Nusakan	18
Nyonya Besar	48
Oblist	45
Obolov	58
Odilex	18
Oh So Risky	64
OK Corral	34
Old Alliance	84
Old Comrades	68
Olympian	22
Olympic Hero	37
Once Upon A Time	54
One For Irene	19
One Missing	20
On The Wire	18
Oogie Poogie	78
Open Champion	26
Orbit	46
Orchard Court	69
Oriental Mystique	55
Orvietto	51
Osario	98
Osgathorpe	32
Our Ron	50
Oxbow	40
Pago	76
Palace Court	4
Palatial Style	43
Pale Wine	41
Palmas Pride	73
Pandessa	3
Panalo	66
Panoply	13
Parking Bay	60
Parting Moment	77
Passed Pawn	45
Path Of Condie	32
Pay The Bank	55
Pencarreg	56
Performing Arts	67
Persian Sultan	46
Peterhouse	68
Petillante	58
Petivara	25

TWO-YEAR-OLD RATINGS - *continued*

Horse	Rating
Petipa	58
Petite Butterfly	40
Petlova	29
Phantom Row	26
Pharoah's Delight	76
Phil Blake	41
Phil's Folly	6
Phisus	28
Phoenix Jule	57
Photo Call	52
Pier Damiani	41
Pilgrims Path	38
Pinecone Peter	18
Pinnacle Point	8
Piper's Hill	65
Pipitina	72
Pipper's Dream	81
Planters Point	20
Platinum Dancer	53
Platinum Disc	45
Platoon	87
Platonique	72
Plax	44
Playful Poet	17
Play The Blues	7
Play The Game	58
Plaything	42
Please Believe Me	68
Pleasure Ahead	3
Plie	50
Podra	30
Point Taken	56
Poke The Fire	14
Pointe Of Law	40
Polistatic	2
Porto Heli	52
Port Soderick	35
Po Shan	17
Possebelle	21
Potter's Dream	64
Prayer Flag	19
Precella The Hun	34
Precious Spirit	11
Premier Dance	32
Premier Developer	47
Premiere	54
Premier Girl	12
Premier Touch	48
Preset	13
Pretty Cool	53
Priceless Fantasy	51
Prince Hannibal	32
Prince Jakatom	85
Princess Mariella	39
Princess Taufan	58
Prince Valiyar	25
Priority Paid	53
Priory Cloud	23
Prohibition	55
Prospectors Moon	32
Proud Jak	23
Puffy	92
Puligny	64
Pulpit Rock	21
Pumpkin	27
Pundles Pet	46
Purity	49
Pusey Street Boy	55
Pym's Boy	29
Pytchley Night	54
Qaswarah	75
Qathif	87
Qualitair Dream	57
Quavering	83
Quest For Fame	82
Qui Danzig	87
Quick Profit	17
Quinta Royale	44
Ra'a	85
Rafha	97
Rahaam	79
Rail D'Or	43
Rainbow Bridge	39
Raj Waki	74
Rambadale	45
Rambo Express	52
Rami	81
Ramification	31
Ramsey Street	36
Rannoch House	19
Rasan	40
Rasheed	15
Rathbrides Joy	55
Rathvinden House	28
Razzberry	70
Really Squidgeley	14
Realm	42
Reasonable Kid	60
Recipe	41
Rectillon	56
Red Beacon	1
Red Net	25
Red Pippin	45
Red Toto	50
Red Victor	38
Reef Wind	40
Reel Foyle	61
Reference Light	64
Regal North	38
Regal Sting	20
Regal Thatch	76
Regal Touch	32
Regina Royale	37
Rejoneo	54
Remthat Naser	14
Rentina	37
Repercutionist	93
Revoke	33
Richmond Park	53
Ridgepoint	75
Rinja	58
Risen Moon	51
Riva	34
River God	58
Rivers Rhapsody	75
Riviera Magic	46
Robellation	90
Rock City	85
Rock Hopper	94
Romantic Saga	49
Rope Trick	82
Rose Of Miami	34
Rouski	44
Routilante	82
Royal Academy	84
Royal Archive	47
Royal Coquelin	20
Royal Fifi	76
Royal Passion	54
Royal Resort	28
Royal Result	22
Royal Supreme	22
Royal Warrant	28
Rubicund	43
Ruby Tiger	94
Ruby Setting	30
Ruddy Cheek	57
Rudy's Fantasy	76
Ruling Passion	49
Run Home	60
Runway Romance	72
Running Home	19
Ruscino	53
Rushanes	50
Rushmore	80
Russian Red	27

TWO-YEAR-OLD RATINGS - *continued*

Horse	Rating
Russian Frontier	75
Ruthless Boy	41
Sabonis	42
Saddle Bow	58
Sagar Island	43
Sahara Baladee	64
Sailor Milan	13
Sajjaya	71
Sally Rous	66
Salmiya	11
Salsabil	78
Saltessa	33
Samsova	61
Sanawi	44
Sandford Springs	47
Sandmoor Denim	23
Sandmoor Jacquard	31
Sandsumo	13
Sanglamore	52
San Pier Niceot	17
Sanssong	55
Sarah Carter	16
Sarah Georgina	52
Sardegna	66
Sarmatara	60
Sasaki	59
Sashtal	43
Satin Wood	83
Satis Dancer	57
Saucy Saint	24
Saumarez	64
Sawsan	8
Saysana	46
Scarlet Express	25
Scarlett Holly	85
Scatter	35
Scorched Earth	27
Scorpio Lady	67
Scots Law	21
Scottish Reform	64
Scribbling	8
Seabtic	28
Second To None	49
Secret Society	25
Secret Waters	37
Seenachance	26
Serenader	41
Sereniki	8
Set Your Mark	30
Seven Sons	25
Sexy Mover	37
Shambo	44
Shamshoon	72
Shamyl	40
Shannon Express	39
Sharquin	8
Sharpalto	46
Sharp Anne	43
Sharp N Easy	64
Sharp Invite	26
Sharp Mover	55
Sharp N Smooth	11
Sharp Runner	30
Sharp Salute	37
Sharper Blue	23
Shattered Dreams	38
Sharinski	26
Shavian	96
Sheenachance	26
Sheen Cleen Lad	9
Sheer Precocity	84
Shelter	3
Sheriff's Band	17
Sherna Lavender	1
Shewhomustbeobeyed	24
Shifting Breeze	58
Shift Over	6
Shikari Kid	32
Shikari's Son	25
Shoo Bee Doo	41
Shoot To Kill	48
Shout And Sing	77
Shout Fore	87
Shout Out	36
Shunt	52
Sian's Lady	41
Siberian Steppes	56
Sigwell's Gold	22
Silca An Key	53
Silent Girl	31
Silent Steps	26
Silk Slippers	81
Sillars Sandpiper	3
Silverdale Fox	79
Silver Ore	68
Silver Singing	63
Silver Stick	18
Simply Spim	27
Singing	52
Singing Detective	42
Sink The Fleet	85
Sir Arthur Hobbs	29
Sireesh	12
Sirse	32
Sister Sal	93
Sky Fighter	36
Slades Hill	48
Slave To Love	12
Sleepline Palace	47
Slipperose	58
Slow Exposure	14
Smarty Lee	61
Snafee	35
Snowspin	20
Snurge	63
Sober Mind	64
Society Ball	44
Sockem	37
So Knowledgeable	30
Soleil Grand	26
Solo Court	76
Somethingdifferent	96
Song For Europe	37
Song Of Gymcrak	36
Sophia Gardens	33
Southern Beau	71
Soy Roberto	80
Spanish Empire	79
Spanish Realm	59
Spanish Whisper	62
Spanish Verdict	51
Sparkling Nectar	13
Specific Impulse	13
Speckled Braid	48
Spica	52
Spofforth	8
Spring High	37
Spring Run	51
Stagecraft	67
Standing Room Only	60
Stanway	65
Star Blaze	34
Star Child	27
Star Hill	67
Star Leader	24
Star Of Fashion	28
Star Of The Future	60
Starstreak	61
Staunch Rival	54
Stealthy	24
Stereo	74
Steel River	11
Stella Bianca	75
Still Battling	29
Stock Pile	33
Stoneythorpewonder	52

TWO-YEAR-OLD RATINGS - *continued*

Stop High 29
Stormy Belle 23
Stranger Still 18
Strike For Home 16
Strongly Favoured 61
Stylish Gent 73
Suman 9
Sum Mede 67
Sundance Kid 55
Sunday Sport's Pet 8
Sunflower Seed 38
Superenter 40
Superetta 45
Super One 33
Suprette 63
Surcoat 42
Sure Sharp 94
Surpassing 45
Suspect Device 28
Supreme Court 10
Swattling Thomas 53
Sweet Alma 51
Sweet Form 8
Swing North 63
Swiss Affair 78
Swordsmith 79
Syrtos 44
Taylors Prince 15
Tabdea 81
Tabyan 27
Tadeus 30
Tadwin 86
Tahaddi 26
Taittinger Rose 18
Take A Bath 34
Takeall 61
Takeover Talk 42
Talabayra 51
Tamahan 37
Tamara's Twinkle 38
Tanfith 80
Tangle Free 16
Tara's Delight 5
Tarazed 18
Tarikhana 41
Tarnside Club 62
Taroom 14
Tasarli 60
Tashanitza 24
Tatwij 97
Taulela 35
Tavolara 50
Tawjih 50
Tears Of Happiness 62
Telegraph Callgirl 4
Tempestosa 18
Tempting Odds 16
Tender Charm 34
Tenderloin 49
Tender Trail 46
Ternimus 30
Tesora 64
Thakib 25
The Can Can Man 24
The Dara Queen 34
The Daring Sport 45
The Flying Four 9
Thehool 58
The Irish Sheik 37
The Island 29
The Minder 22
The Prodigal 48
The Swamp Fox 39
The Weir 20
Tickle Touch 60
Tidemark 62
Tight Rein 51
Tignanello 27
Times Gift 46
Tinkerbird 37
Tina's Momento 13
Tirol 91
Tite Spot 26
Toast The Host 30
Tobacco Road 26
Tod 42
Toledo 77
Tom Clapton 7
Topasannah 41
Top Berry 47
Topcliffe 24
Top Company 23
Top Of The Bill 49
Torghia 39
Tory Conquest 70
Toshiba Comet 55
Toucan 27
Touch The Clouds 45
Trainglot 63
Transitional 35
Transcriber 52
Treacle Mine 20
Treble Eight 50
Tribute To Dad 15
Tricotric 25
Triomphe Modest 39
Trireme 66
Triumphal Song 31
Trixie's Guest 52
Trojan Excel 46
Trojan Pleasure 29
Trying Days 36
Tudor Ace 18
Tuneful Charter 30
Turs 39
Tuwittuwittuwoo 51
Two Left Feet 88
Two Toffs 34
Tyburn Tree 94
Tyrian Prince 27
Uncle Bobby 21
Undertones 34
Ultra Magic 49
Urfan 1
USA Dollar 9
Usaylah 58
Vain Prince 29
Vain Search 37
Valiant Hope 39
Valiant Vicar 40
Valiant Words 30
Valira 21
Varnish 40
Va Toujours 77
Vax Lady 29
Verdeuse 70
Vermont 42
Vestige 28
Viceroy 74
Victoria Princess 22
Victory Piper 55
Villeroi 76
Vintage Type 43
Virgin Gorda 22
Visage 46
Vision Of India 35
Vital Clue 26
Vogos Angel 40
Vote In Favour 54
Vulcanist 43
Wace 43
Wadood 70
Wajna 79
Wake Up 41
Walkern Witch 51
Walkerway Boy 15

TWO-YEAR-OLD RATINGS - *continued*

Horse	Rating
Walk Well	40
Waltzing Home	78
Wanda	68
Warm Feeling	55
Wasnah	42
Water Well	83
Way Too Much	39
Weareagrandmother	33
Weekender	30
Wellsy Lad	30
Welney	91
We're In	9
Western Music	64
Western Ocean	78
Westgate Rock	34
West With The Wind	50
What A Save	41
What Happens Next	8
Whispering Sea	25
Whistling Gale	29
Whistling Wilde	4
White Squirrel	10
Who Gives A Donald	42
Wild Dancer	32
Wild Sage	4
Wild Warrior	19
Willbutwhen	84
Wilvick	39
Wine Cellar	55
Winslow Lad	53
With Gusto	22
Without Equal	52
Wolver Gold	69
Wonderment	5
Woodcock Wonder	9
Woodside Heath	62
Wrybill	64
Wylam	23
Yaazi	75
Yanabee	34
Yankee Trader	12
Yarra Glen	53
Yaslou	11
Yer No Puggy	23
Yonge Tender	34
You Know The Rules	64
Young George	10
Young India	76
Young Monty	31
Ysatirous	50
Zabarrjad	32
Zalali	34
Zammah	45
Zanoba	19
Zanoni	87
Zarna	29
Zawahir	59
Zephyr Knight	6
Zero Time	3
Zizania	55
Zoman	78
Zurrovka	63

Raceform Note-Book 1989 Complete: £15

This specially trimmed and paper-bound edition of last season's Raceform Note-Book runs to 1,280 pages and provides a unique eye witness record of every race run on the Flat last year. It also includes basic form details of the first six in every race and is fully indexed throughout. Raceform Note-Book 1989 is packed with clues to 1990 winners and, in particular, it is a great guide to the lightly raced three-year-olds. £15 post free from the address below.

RACEFORM LTD.,
COMPTON, NEWBURY, BERKSHIRE
RG16 0NL

RACEFORM RECORD TIMES

As recorded by "Raceform" since 1936. Courses with electrical timing apparatus are indicated—(Electric).

NEWMARKET (Electric)

ROWLEY MILE COURSE

Course	Dist.	Time	Age	Weight		Going	Horse	Date	
Rous	5f	57·4	5	8	9	Firm	Knight's Armour	April 6,	1938
Rous	5f	58·99	2	7	5	Firm	Katysue	Oct. 2,	1980
Bretby Stakes	6f	1. 10·66	5	7	12	Firm	Welsh Blossom	Oct. 1,	1980
Bretby Stakes	6f	1. 11·04	2	9	0	Firm	Junius (USA)	Oct. 5,	1978
			2	9	0	Firm	Balla Cove	Oct. 5,	1989
Dewhurst Stakes	7f	1. 24·14	3	8	6	Firm	Chalon	May 1,	1982
Dewhurst Stakes	7f	1. 23·63	2	9	0	Firm	Goblin	Oct. 1,	1977
Rowley Mile	8f	1. 35·8	3	9	0	Hard	My Babu	April 28,	1948
Rowley Mile	8f	1. 37·43	2	8	7	Firm	Demetrius	Sept. 28,	1977
Cambdgshire	9f	1. 47·45	3	8	3	Firm	Sin Timon	Oct. 1,	1977
A.F.	10f	2. 1·04	3	8	10	Good	Palace Music (USA)	Oct. 20,	1984
A.F.	10f	2. 4·65	2	9	4	Good	Highland Chieftain	Nov. 2,	1985
Cesarewitch	12f	2. 29·75	4	9	6	Firm	Firelight Fiesta	Oct. 5,	1989
Cesarewitch	14f	2. 56·19	4	8	11	Firm	Buckhound	Oct. 1,	1953
Cesarewitch	16f	3. 22·48	3	8	2	Firm	Misalliance	Oct. 1,	1977
Cesarewitch	18f	3. 47·5	3	7	12	Hard	Whiteway	Oct. 15,	1947
Cesarewitch	20f	4. 26·84	8	9	4	Fast	Mayotte	Oct. 28,	1983

JULY COURSE

Course	Dist.	Time	Age	Weight		Going	Horse	Date	
Chesterfield	5f	58·68	3	8	6	Firm	Light Grey	July 3,	1962
Chesterfield	5f	58·8	2	9	0	Hard	Dante	June 17,	1944
			2	8	7	Firm	Cosmohome	June 29,	1938
Bunbury Mile	6f	1. 9·82	4	9	6	Good	Cadeaux Genereux	July 13,	1989
Bunbury Mile	6f	1. 11·32	2	8	9	Fast	Diminuendo (USA)	July 7,	1987
Bunbury Mile	7f	1. 23·6	5	7	8	Hard	Ti-Chin	June 17,	1944
Bunbury Mile	7f	1. 24·93	2	8	7	Firm	Sexton Blake	July 30,	1977
Bunbury Mile	8f	1. 36·8	4	9	7	Hard	Pink Flower	June 6,	1944
Bunbury Mile	8f	1. 40·28	2	9	4	Fast	Lear Fan (USA)	Aug. 27,	1983
Suffolk Stks	10f	2. 2·8	3	9	7	Firm	Borealis	May 2,	1944
			4	7	5	Firm	Alarm Bell	June 29,	1938
Suffolk Stks	12f	2. 28·68	4	9	0	Fast	Celestial Storm (USA)	July 7,	1987
Summer	14f 175y	3. 5·42	3	8	6	Fast	Cockatoo Island	July 9,	1987
Summer	16f 24y	3. 18	4	8	0	Good	Luncheon Hour	Nov. 21,	1940

FLAT RECORD TIMES – *continued*

ASCOT (Electric)

Distance	Time	Age	Weight	Going	Horse	Date	
5f	59·1	3	8 8	Firm	Orient	June 21,	1986
5f	1. 0.57	2	8 11	Firm	Sizzling Melody	June 19,	1986
6f	1. 12·95	3	8 0	Firm	Danehill (USA)	June 22,	1989
6f	1. 13·63	2	8 8	Firm	Minstrella (USA)	June 19,	1986
7f	1. 26·2	3	8 10	Firm	Indian Ridge	June 15,	1988
7f	1. 27·3	2	8 11	Firm	Tour D'Or (USA)	Sept. 28,	1984
8f (rnd)	1. 38·8	3	9 0	Firm	Shadeed	Sept. 28,	1985
8f (rnd)	1. 40·92	2	8 7	Fast	Untold	Sept. 26,	1985
8f (st)	1. 38·17	3	8 7	Firm	Dallas (USA)	June 20,	1986
10f	2. 3·31	4	9 1	Firm	Trepan	June 15,	1976
12f	2. 26·95	5	8 9	Firm	Stanerra	June 17,	1983
16f	3. 20·54	3	8 9	Firm	Weld	June 21,	1989
20f	4. 15·67	5	9 0	Firm	Royal Gait (disq)	June 16,	1988
22f 34y	4. 51·32	4	8 8	Firm	Otabari	June 20,	1986

AYR (Electric)

Distance	Time	Age	Weight	Going	Horse	Date	
5f	57·68	7	7 7	Firm	Red Desire	July 21,	1972
5f	57·8	2	8 0	Hard	Monte Christo	May 17,	1946
6f	1. 10·2	{ 3	8 11	Hard	Toronto	May 18,	1946
		3	6 9	Good	The Country Lane	Sept. 18,	1969
6f	1. 9·73	2	7 10	Good	Sir Bert	Sept. 17,	1969
7f	1. 24·39	5	7 7	Firm	Emerald Eagle	Sept. 20,	1986
7f	1. 26·5	2	8 6	Firm	Ludham	July 19,	1966
8f	1. 36	4	7 13	Firm	Sufi	Sept. 16,	1959
8f	1. 39·21	2	9 0	Firm	Kribensis	Sept. 17,	1986
10f	2. 5·38	4	9 5	Firm	Chil The Kite	July 24,	1976
10f 180y	2. 23·86	6	9 5	Firm	Topeka Express	June 23,	1989
11f	2. 14·51	3	8 3	Firm	Santiki	Sept. 17,	1986
13f	2. 46·34	4	9 7	Firm	Plenty Spirit	May 28,	1977
15f	3. 12·76	7	8 11	Firm	Cagirama	July 18,	1966
17f 90y	3. 45	4	6 13	Good	Curry	Sept. 16,	1955
18f	3. 48·4	4	7 3	Hard	Danger	July 18,	1949
20f 90y	4. 33·86	4	8 6	Good	Charles Stuart (FR)	July 8,	1983

BATH

Distance	Time	Age	Weight	Going	Horse	Date	
5f	1. 0·5	3	8 11	Firm	Elegant Rainbow	May 22,	1989
5f	1. 1·2	2	8 11	Firm	Avon Valley	July 3,	1971
5f 167y	1. 8·1	6	9 0	Firm	Madraco	May 22,	1989
5f 167y	1. 10·3	2	8 11	Hard	Cheri Berry	Aug 26,	1981
7f 8y	1. 27·8	{ 4	8 3	Firm	Diplomatic Cloak	Sept. 2,	1961
		3	8 4	Firm	Star Flare	July 28,	1980
7f 8y	1. 28·6	2	9 0	Firm	Hunting Tower	Aug. 3,	1970
8f 8y	1. 39	5	9 4	Firm	Al-Torfanan	May 22,	1989
8f 8y	1. 40.7	2	8 11	Firm	Myhamet	Oct. 2,	1989
10f 50y	2. 7	3	8 13	Fast	Golden Wave	April 26,	1988
11f 150y	2. 26·3	{ 3	9 0	Firm	Mubarak of Kuwait	April 27,	1982
		3	8 11	Firm	Cypria Sacra (USA)	June 1,	1987
13f 12y	2. 48·3	3	9 7	Firm	Orpheus (USA)	May 22,	1989
17f 27y	3. 44	6	8 10	Hard	Morgan's Choice	July 13,	1983
17f 194y	4. 0·5	3	7 11	Good	Baytree	Aug. 30,	1969

FLAT RECORD TIMES – *continued*

BEVERLEY

Distance	Time	Age	Weight	Going	Horse	Date	
5f	1. 1	4	7 4	Firm	Noble Native	Aug. 27,	1970
5f	1. 2	2	8 11	Firm	Persian Breeze	June 13,	1974
		2	8 8	Firm	Fimi	Aug. 27,	1981
7f 110y	1. 31·3	3	9 7	Firm	Cluzo	May 23,	1989
7f 110y	1. 31.7	2	9 0	Firm	Vanished Land (USA)	Aug. 9,	1988
8f 100y	1. 42.3	3	8 4	Firm	Legal Case	June. 14,	1989
8f 100y	1. 43·3	2	9 0	Firm	Arden	Sept. 24,	1986
10f	2. 2·2	4	7 9	Firm	Coffee House	Aug. 30,	1979
12f	2. 30·6	3	8 1	Hard	Coinage	June 18,	1986
16f	3. 30·1	4	7 7	Firm	Between The Sheets	Sept. 21,	1989
19f 100y	4. 21·5	3	8 9	Firm	Mandalay Prince	July 14,	1987

BRIGHTON

Distance	Time	Age	Weight	Going	Horse	Date	
5f 66y	1. 0·1	5	10 3	Firm	St. Alphage	Aug. 28,	1968
5f 66y	1. 1·1	2	8 9	Firm	Ahonita	Sept. 30,	1987
6f	1. 7·95	3	7 12	Firm	Sound Of The Sea	Sept. 16,	1982
6f	1. 8·7	2	9 0	Firm	Purity	Oct. 3,	1989
7f	1. 19·8	3	8 12	Firm	Last Case	June 9,	1966
7f	1. 19.9	2	8 11	Hard	Rain Burst	Sept. 15,	1988
8f	1. 31·1	5	8 3	Hard	Al-Torfanan	June 19,	1989
8f	1. 32·8	2	9 7	Firm	Asian Pete	Oct. 3,	1989
10f	1. 57·2	3	9 0	Firm	Get the Message	April 30,	1984
12f	2. 25·8 (flag)	4	8 2	Firm	New Zealand	July 4,	1985

CARLISLE

Distance	Time	Age	Weight	Going	Horse	Date	
5f	59.8	4	8 3	Firm	Miss Taurus	July 15,	1971
		3	9 3	Firm	Bollin Emily	July 5,	1984
5f	1. 02	2	8 9	Hard	Metal Boys	June 1,	1989
6f	1. 11·8	6	8 13	Firm	Night Patrol	Aug. 27,	1970
6f	1. 13·8	2	8 11	Firm	Off Scent	Sept. 13,	1973
7f	1. 26·4	5	10 0	Hard	Invertiel	June 1,	1989
7f	1. 28·7	2	8 6	Fast	Margs Girl	June 29,	1989
8f	1. 38·4	5	8 8	Firm	Overpower	June 28,	1989
		3	8 0	Firm	Nasr	June 7,	1984
8f	1. 44·6	2	8 8	Firm	Blue Garter	Sept. 9,	1980
10f	2. 8	3	8 1	Hard	War Eagle	July 5,	1962
12f	2. 28·1	3	8 0	Firm	Auchinlea	July 4,	1985

CATTERICK

Distance	Time	Age	Weight	Going	Horse	Date	
5f	57·1	4	8 7	Firm	Kabcast	July 7,	1989
5f	58·3	2	9 7	Firm	Lord Glen	July 5,	1989
		2	8 10	Firm	A Star Is Born	May 31,	1978
6f	1. 10·4	3	8 8	Firm	Triad Treble	May 31,	1984
		6	8 2	Firm	Mendick Adventure	April 29,	1987
6f	1. 11·4	2	9 4	Firm	Captain Nick	July 11,	1978
7f	1. 23	4	7 12	Firm	Royal Ziska	June 9,	1973
		4	9 7	Firm	Maazi	July 25,	1985
7f	1. 24·1	2	8 11	Firm	Lindas Fantasy	Sept. 18,	1982
12f 40y	2. 33·4	3	8 3	Firm	Watet Khet	June 4,	1982
13f 180y	2. 54·8	3	8 5	Firm	Geryon	May 31,	1984
15f 180y	3. 20·8	4	7 11	Firm	Bean Boy	July 8,	1982

FLAT RECORD TIMES – *continued*

CHEPSTOW

Distance	Time	Age	Weight	Going	Horse	Date	
5f	56·8	3	8 4	Firm	Torbay Express	Sept. 15,	1979
5f	57·6	2	8 11	Firm	Micro Love	July 8,	1986
6f	1. 8·8	4	8 6	Firm	African Rex (FR)	May 12,	1987
6f	1. 9·4	2	9 0	Fast	Royal Fi Fi (USA)	Sept. 9,	1989
7f	1. 19·9	3	9 10	Firm	Prince Titian	Aug. 29,	1978
7f	1. 21·4	2	8 11	Hard	Dijla	Aug. 31,	1981
8f	1. 31·8	6	9 6	Firm	Traditional Miss	June 27,	1981
		6	9 6	Hard	Traditional Miss	Aug. 31,	1981
8f	1. 39·7	2	8 11	Hard	Mamaluna (USA)	Aug 29,	1988
10f	2. 4·1	5	8 9	Hard	Leonidas (USA)	July 5,	1983
		5	7 9	Fast	Its Varadan	Sept. 9,	1989
12f	2. 31	5	8 11	Hard	The Friend	Aug. 29,	1983
		7	9 6	Hard	Maintop	Aug. 27,	1984
		3	8 9	Fast	Spritsail	July 13,	1989
16f	3. 27·7	4	9 0	Fast	Wizzard Artist	July 1,	1989

CHESTER (Electric)

Distance	Time	Age	Weight	Going	Horse	Date	
5f	59·2	3	10 0	Firm	Althrey Don	July 10,	1964
5f	1. 0·4	2	8 11	Firm	Cynara	May 3,	1960
6f	1. 12·8	4	7 5	Good	Welsh Warrior	July 27,	1968
6f	1. 13·4	2	9 3	Good	Stung	July 27,	1968
7f	1. 26·12	3	7 7	Firm	Eight Mile Rock	May 7,	1987
7f	1. 26·6	2	8 5	Firm	No Faith	Sept. 1,	1979
7f 122y	1. 32·4	3	8 8	Firm	Joey	Sept. 2,	1972
7f 122y	1. 35	2	9 0	Firm	Double Value	Sept. 1,	1972
10f 10y	2. 6·2	6	9 7	Good	Colonel Blimp	July 27,	1968
10f 85y	2. 8·6	3	8 12	Firm	Sir Harry Lewis (USA)	May 7,	1987
11f 70y	2. 23·71	3	8 11	Fast	Braiswick	May 10,	1989
12f 65y	2. 34·21	3	8 11	Fast	Old Vic	May 9,	1989
13f 88y	2. 45·43	5	8 11	Firm	Rakaposhi King	May 7,	1987
15f 186y	3. 25	3	8 6	Firm	Seacourt	Sept. 1,	1972
18f 97y	3. 57·26	4	9 8	Firm	Just David	May 6,	1987

CURRAGH

Distance	Time	Age	Weight	Going	Horse	Date	
5f	57·6	3	8 4	Firm	Racefield	June 30,	1979
5f	58·1	2	8 11	Firm	Ausone	May 20,	1970
6f	1. 10·5	4	9 0	Good	Sylvan Express	May 16,	1987
		3	8 1	Firm	Dorney Common	Aug. 19,	1961
6f	1. 10·6	2	9 0	Firm	London Bells	July 4,	1979
6f 63y	1. 12·4	4	9 8	Firm	Bold Tack (disq)	June 11,	1975
6f 63y	1. 15·0	2	8 7	Firm	Gay Challenger	Sept. 2,	1961
		2	8 0	Firm	Blue Nose	July 21,	1979
7f	1. 24	3	8 6	Fast	Snowdonia (USA)	July 21,	1984
7f	1. 25·2	2	8 11	Fast	Concert Hall (USA)	Aug. 18,	1984
8f Old	1. 35	3	9 0	Good	Arctic Storm	May 16,	1962
8f Old	1. 45	2	8 12	Yielding	Pontifex	Oct. 6,	1962
8f New	1. 34·3	4	9 4	Good	Llyn Gwynant	July 19	1989
8f New	1. 38·6	2	9 0	Firm	Padroug (USA)	Sept. 18,	1976
9f	1. 55·8	4	9 11	Yielding	Popular Glen	Sept. 23,	1989
10f	2. 2·1	3	8 9	Firm	Princess Pati	June 30,	1984
11f	2. 21·0	3	8 13	Fast	Montefiore	June 25,	1988
12f	2. 28·6	3	9 0	Fast	Princess Pati	July 21,	1984
13f	2. 49·9	3	8 7	Fast	Esprit D'Etoile	May 21,	1988
14f	3. 0.06	3	8 7	Good	Tyrone Bridge	July 15,	1989
16f	3. 30·8	3	8 12	Good	Orient Rose	Oct. 12,	1986

FLAT RECORD TIMES – *continued*

DONCASTER (Electric)

Distance	Time	Age	Weight	Going	Horse	Date
5f	58·2	3	8 8	Firm	Sir Gatric	Sept. 10, 1959
5f	58·4	2	9 5	Firm	Sing Sing	Sept. 11, 1959
		2	9 0	Good	D'Urberville	Sept. 13, 1967
5f 152y	1. 6·2	3	9 2	Good	Welsh Abbot	Sept. 12, 1958
		6	7 3	Firm	New World	Sept. 11, 1959
5f 152y	1. 8	2	8 10	Good	Crown Flatts	Oct. 25, 1947
6f	1. 10·2	4	7 9	Firm	Ryecroft	May 16, 1959
6f	1. 11·2	2	8 11	Firm	Paddy's Sister	Sept. 9, 1959
7f	1. 22·6	3	9 4	Hard	Pinolil	June 3, 1963
7f	1. 24·4	2	9 0	Good	Chebs Lad	Sept. 12, 1967
8f (st)	1. 35·67	3	8 6	Firm	Asteroid Field (USA)	Sept. 13, 1986
8f (st)	1. 39·6	2	7 8	Firm	Corinthian	Oct. 21, 1955
8f (rnd)	1. 35·6	4	8 1	Hard	Old Tom	June 3, 1963
8f (rnd)	1. 38·32	2	9 0	Firm	Sandy Creek	Oct. 28, 1978
10f 56y	2. 6·4	4	8 7	Firm	Silver Cloud	Sept. 12, 1963
10f 56y	2. 13·47	2	8 8	Good	Yard Bird	Nov. 6, 1981
12f	2. 30·2	5	9 2	Firm	Saraceno	Oct. 24, 1970
14f 127y	3. 2·92	3	8 10	Good	Eastern Mystic	Sept. 11, 1985
16f 110y	3. 27·81	7	9 2	Fast	Western Dancer	July 27, 1988
18f	3. 52·7	3	7 6	Firm	Protection Racket	Sept. 10, 1981

EDINBURGH

Distance	Time	Age	Weight	Going	Horse	Date
5f	57·4	4	7 2	Firm	Palm Court Joe	July 4, 1977
5f	58·2	2	9 0	Fast	Premier Developer	May 22, 1989
7f	1. 26	6	9 0	Firm	Show Of Hands	April 19, 1982
7f	1. 27·5	2	9 1	Firm	Mubdi (USA)	Oct. 6, 1986
8f	1. 38·3	4	8 13	Firm	Churchillian	July 11, 1977
8f	1. 40·9	2	8 11	Firm	Trompe D'Oeil	Oct. 6, 1986
11f	2. 19·7	3	8 10	Firm	Old Court	July 4, 1977
12f	2. 32·2	5	7 9	Good	Glengrigor	April 15, 1946
15f	3. 10·4	3	8 0	Good	Cunningham	Sept. 21, 1953

EPSOM (Electric)

Distance	Time	Age	Weight	Going	Horse	Date
5f	53·6	4	9 5	Firm	Indigenous	June 2, 1960
5f	55·2	2	8 9	Firm	Cerise	June 4, 1954
		2	8 2	Hard	Kerrabee	June 3, 1960
6f 9y	1. 7·91	5	7 7	Firm	Moor Lane	June 7, 1973
6f 9y	1. 8·4	2	9 0	Hard	My Babu	Aug. 4, 1947
		2	8 6	Firm	Mozart	June 3, 1959
7f 11y	1. 20·15	4	8 7	Firm	Capistrano	June 7, 1972
7f 11y	1. 22·4	2	8 8	Fast	Goodnight Moon	Aug. 29, 1988
		2	9 0	Hard	Leonardo	Sept 5, 1964
8f 110y	1. 41	3	8 6	Good	Lauries Warrior	June 3, 1987
8f 110y	1. 42.8	2	8 5	Fast	Nightstalker	Aug 30, 1988
10f	2. 3·5 (unofficial)	5	7 13	Good	Crossbow	June 7, 1967
12f	2. 33·31	4	9 0	Firm	Bustino	June 7, 1975
18f	3. 54	4	6 8	Firm	Gay Ballad	April 23, 1957

FLAT RECORD TIMES – *continued*

FOLKESTONE

Distance	Time	Age	Weight	Going	Horse	Date	
5f	58·8	3	6 10	Good	Tammany	Aug. 12,	1963
5f	58·8	2	8 11	Hard	Merry Monk	July 6,	1971
6f	1. 10·5	4	8 5	Firm	Zipperdi-Doo-Dah	Mar. 31,	1976
6f	1. 11	2	7 13	Hard	Fashion Model	Aug. 31,	1970
7f	1. 21·3	3	8 9	Fast	Cielamour (USA)	Aug. 9,	1988
7f	1. 24·8	2	7 8	Firm	Lord Rochford	Oct. 3,	1977
8f 110y	1. 47.6	3	8 12	Good	Cissbury Boy	July 23,	1974
9f 130y	1. 57·8	4	8 11	Firm	Lord Raffles	June 2,	1980
10f	1. 59·7	3	9 8	Firm	Shardari	July 2,	1985
12f	2. 33·8	3	8 4	Firm	Santella King	June 28,	1983
		3	9 5	Firm	Royal Cracker	July 17,	1984
15f	3. 15·1	6	7 6	Firm	Bonds Best	April 14,	1980
15f 100y	3. 18·8	3	7 13	Firm	Coral Heights	July 17,	1984
16f 100y	3. 32·5	6	7 13	Firm	North West	July 21,	1981
		3	8 5	Firm	On Her Own	Aug. 11,	1981

GOODWOOD (Electric)

Distance	Time	Age	Weight	Going	Horse	Date	
5f	56·92	4	9 0	Firm	Tina's Pet	July 29,	1982
5f	58·07	2	8 10	Firm	Kafu	July 27,	1982
6f	1. 9·58	3	8 4	Firm	Soba	July 27,	1982
6f	1. 11·05	2	8 11	Fast	Vacarme (disq.)	July 27,	1983
7f	1. 24·7	3	7 13	Yielding	Alcindoro	Sept. 14,	1970
7f	1. 26·61	2	9 0	Firm	Be My Chief (USA)	July 27,	1989
8f	1. 36·77	3	8 10	Firm	Zilzal (USA)	July 26,	1989
8f	1. 40·66	2	8 13	Firm	Bonnie Isle	Sept. 18,	1978
9f 40y	1. 56·24	3	8 6	Firm	Awayed (USA)	June 13,	1989
10f	2. 4·72	5	9 0	Good	Rakaposhi King	May 20,	1987
11f 200y	2. 35·1	3	8 3	Good	Karabas	July 30,	1968
12f	2. 32·73	4	9 1	Firm	Capstan	July 30,	1982
14f	2. 57·88	3	8 11	Fast	Ala Hounak	Aug. 29,	1987
19f	4. 8·30	4	9 13	Firm	El Conquistador	May 21,	1987
20f 193y	4. 35·08	4	9 0	Firm	Mr Bigmore	July 29,	1976
21f	4. 30·42	3	7 10	Firm	Sergeyevich	July 30,	1987

HAMILTON

Distance	Time	Age	Weight	Going	Horse	Date	
5f	58	5	8 6	Firm	Golden Sleigh	Sept. 6,	1972
5f	58	2	7 8	Firm	Fair Dandy	Sept. 25,	1972
6f	1. 9·3	4	8 7	Firm	Marcus Game	July 11,	1974
6f	1. 10·1	2	7 5	Hard	Yoohoo	Sept. 8,	1976
8f 40y	1. 42·7	6	7 7	Firm	Cranley	Sept. 25,	1972
8f 40y	1. 45·8	2	8 11	Firm	Hopeful Subject	Sept. 24,	1973
9f 10y	1. 54.2	3	8 2	Hard	Fairman	Aug. 20,	1976
11f	2. 20·5	3	9 3	Firm	Wang Feihoong	July 21,	1983
12f	2. 32	4	7 4	Firm	Fine Point	Aug. 24,	1981
		4	10 0	Firm	Hold Tight	Aug. 22,	1983
13f	2. 46·9	5	8 4	Firm	Point North	July 21,	1983

FLAT RECORD TIMES – *continued*

HAYDOCK (Electric)

Distance	Time	Age	Weight	Going	Horse	Date
5f	58·9	3	7 5	Firm	Fish and Chips	June 6, 1970
5f	59·2	2	9 4	Firm	Money For Nothing	Aug. 12, 1964
6f	1. 11·64	6	7 4	Firm	Roysia Boy	Oct. 4, 1986
6f	1. 11·49 (unofficial)	3	9 0	Firm	Kerrera	May 27, 1989
6f	1. 12·3	2	8 7	Hard	I Believe	June 5, 1970
7f 40y	1. 27·21	4	9 4	Firm	Indian King	June 5, 1982
7f 40y	1. 30·57	2	8 11	Hard	Go Grandly	Sept. 30, 1972
8f 40y	1. 40·9	3	9 6	Firm	Spanish Pool	May 29, 1982
8f 40y	1. 41·42	2	9 5	Firm	Suhailie (USA)	Oct. 4, 1986
10f 130y	2. 11·14	3	8 2	Hard	Hill Top	Sept. 29, 1972
12f	2. 26·4	5	8 2	Firm	New Member	July 4, 1970
14f	2. 58·17	3	8 1	Firm	Red Duster	Aug. 5, 1983
16f	3. 29.99	5	8 9	Fast	El Conquistador	May 28, 1988
16f 35y	3. 27·09	4	8 13	Firm	Prince of Peace	May 26, 1984
17f 130y	2. 59·98	3	8 9	Yielding	Teamster	Sept. 2, 1989
19f	4. 21·09	3	8 1	Fast	Nomadic Way (USA)	Sept 3, 1988

KEMPTON (Electric)

Distance	Time	Age	Weight	Going	Horse	Date
5f	58·07	3	8 1	Firm	Silent Majority	June 25, 1986
5f	58·3	2	9 7	Firm	Schweppeshire Lad	June 3, 1978
6f	1. 10·06	4	7 7	Firm	Gusty's Gift	June 3, 1978
6f	1. 10·8	2	8 10	Good	Zabara	Sept. 22, 1951
7f Jubilee	1. 23·79	3	8 11	Firm	Swiss Maid	Aug. 19, 1978
7f Jubilee	1. 24·92	2	8 11	Firm	Silver Hawk	Sept. 5, 1981
7f (rnd)	1. 25·7	4	7 11	Firm	Gaykart	July 14, 1971
		3	7 9	Good	Glen Na Smole	May 7, 1984
7f (rnd)	1. 27·52	2	8 6	Good	Duke of Ragusa	Sept. 1, 1972
8f (rnd)	1. 35·81	4	9 1	Firm	County Broker	May 23, 1984
8f (rnd)	1. 43·4	2	7 0	Good	Fascinating	Nov. 3, 1956
8f Jubilee	1. 35·93	3	8 5	Firm	Soprano	June 1, 1985
		3	9 4	Firm	Diaglyphard (USA)	June 1, 1985
8f Jubilee	1. 42·5	2	7 4	Good	Bantanolius	Oct. 19, 1962
9f	1. 50·56	3	8 12	Fast	Sky Conqueror	June 29, 1988
10f Jubilee	2. 0·14	4	9 5	Firm	Lord Helpus	May 21, 1977
11f 30y	2. 16·20	4	9 2	Firm	Shernazar	Sept. 6, 1985
12f	2. 30·18	6	8 5	Firm	Going Going	Sept. 7, 1985
14f	2. 59·98	3	8 7	Firm	Teamster	July 5, 1989
16f	3. 23·8	4	7 6	Firm	Incredule	July 26, 1956

LEICESTER

Distance	Time	Age	Weight	Going	Horse	Date
5f	58·6	3	9 2	Firm	Rapid River	Sept. 24, 1973
5f	58·4	2	9 0	Firm	Cutting Blade	June 9, 1986
6f	1. 10	3	8 6	Firm	Preparation	Sept. 20, 1982
		3	9 2	Firm	Dream Chaser	May 27, 1986
6f	1. 10.2	2	8 11	Firm	Native Twine	Oct. 16, 1989
7f	1. 20·8	3	8 9	Firm	Flower Bowl	June 9, 1986
7f	1. 23·4	2	7 10	Firm	Astara	Sept. 20, 1982
		2	8 11	Firm	Avrea	Oct. 16, 1989
8f	1. 34·4	3	8 3	Hard	Mariapolis	Sept. 19, 1961
8f	1. 35·8	2	9 0	Firm	Missionary Ridge	Oct. 17, 1989
10f	2. 2·4	3	8 11	Firm	Effigy	Nov. 4, 1985
10f	2. 7·2	2	8 13	Firm	Hardly Fair	Oct. 21, 1985
12f	2. 28·5	4	7 11	Hard	Gyroscope	Sept. 21, 1964
		3	9 3	Firm	Summer Ridge (USA)	Oct. 21, 1985

FLAT RECORD TIMES – *continued*

LINGFIELD (Electric)

Distance	Time	Age	Weight	Going	Horse	Date	
5f	56·8	3	8 9	Firm	Marguerite	Oct. 7,	1964
5f	57·27	2	9 6	Fast	Batzushka	Sept. 21,	1989
5f	57·36	2	8 12	Firm	Rough Love	June 24,	1977
6f	1. 8·2	6	9 10	Firm	Al Amead	July 2,	1986
6f	1. 8·6	2	9 3	Firm	The Ritz	June 11,	1965
7f	1. 20·2	8	7 10	Hard	Polar Jest	Aug. 19,	1955
7f	1. 21·34	2	7 6	Firm	Mandav	Oct. 3,	1980
7f 140y	1. 26·73	3	8 6	Firm	Hiaam (USA)	July 11,	1987
7f 140y	1. 29·93	2	8 12	Firm	Rather Warm	Nov. 7,	1978
9f	1. 53·6	8	9 9	Firm	Traquair	July 8,	1977
10f	2. 4·61	3	9 3	Firm	Ursan	July 15,	1989
12f	2. 30·89	3	9 0	Firm	Cacoethes	May 13,	1989
14f	2. 57·38	5	9 4	Firm	Lemhill	July 11,	1987
16f	3. 23·71	3	9 5	Fast	Lauries Crusader	Aug. 13,	1988

NEWBURY (Electric)

Distance	Time	Age	Weight	Going	Horse	Date	
5f	59·8	3	8 12	Good	Minstrels Gallery	June 18,	1955
5f	1. 0·6	2	8 7	Firm	Zuccherene	June 25,	1959
6f	1. 10·79	3	8 9	Good	Dancing Dissident	May. 19,	1989
6f	1. 11·61	2	8 6	Firm	Bright Crocus	June 10,	1982
7f (st)	1. 24·4	3	9 7	Firm	Firestreak	May 29,	1959
7f (st)	1. 25·93	2	9 0	Good	Zoffany	Aug. 14,	1982
7f 60y (rnd)	1. 26·8	4	7 1	Firm	Bucktail	June 25,	1959
7f 60y (rnd)	1. 29·12	2	9 7	Firm	Kalaglow	Sept. 19,	1980
8f (rnd)	1. 35·19	3	8 11	Fast	Dancing Tribute	Sept. 23,	1989
8f (rnd)	1. 37·29	2	8 11	Firm	Master Willie	Oct. 1,	1979
8f (st)	1. 36·21	4	9 7	Firm	Kris	May 17,	1980
8f (st)	1. 39·71	2	8 11	Good	Shergar	Sept. 19,	1980
10f	2. 2·76	3	8 4	Fast	Monastery	Sept. 23,	1989
10f	2.2 (hand timed)	3	8 9	Firm	Sudden Love (FR)	May 13,	1988
11f	2. 18·41	3	9 0	Firm	General Khaled (USA)	May 16,	1987
12f	2. 29·2	4	8 9	Hard	Vidi Vici	June 21,	1951
13f 60y	2. 45·79	3	9 10	Fast	Green Adventure (USA)	Sept. 17,	1988
16f	3. 26·41	3	7 13	Firm	Sunyboy	Sept. 8,	1973

NEWCASTLE (Electric)

Distance	Time	Age	Weight	Going	Horse	Date	
5f	58·27	3	8 1	Firm	Dublin Lad	June 27,	1986
5f	59·2	2	8 2	Good	Dunce Cap	Aug. 6,	1962
6f	1. 11·34	3	9 3	Firm	Cumbrian Dancer	June 26,	1986
6f	1. 12·67	2	9 0	Firm	Sundance Kid (USA)	Oct. 3,	1989
7f (st)	1. 23·53	3	8 5	Firm	Beaudelaire (USA)	July 23,	1983
7f (st)	1. 26·82	2	8 8	Firm	Nice Balance	Aug. 10,	1976
7f (rnd)	1. 38·4	5	8 1	Soft	Christmas Cottage	April 2,	1983
8f (rnd)	1. 38·96	3	8 12	Firm	Jacamar	July 27,	1989
8f (rnd)	1. 39·97	2	9 0	Firm	Laxy Bay	Oct. 3,	1989
9f 20y	1. 52.3	3	6 3	Good	Ferniehurst	June 23,	1936
10f 40y	2. 6·61	4	7 8	Firm	Doogali	July 24,	1978
12f 60y	2. 38·4	4	8 13	Firm	Kesrullah	June 25,	1953
16f	3. 22	4	7 12	Good	Nectar II	June 23,	1937

FLAT RECORD TIMES – *continued*

NOTTINGHAM

Distance	Time	Age	Weight	Going	Horse	Date	
5f	58·4	6	8 8	Good	Minstrel King	Mar. 29,	1960
		4	7 7	Firm	Vilgora	Apr. 12,	1976
5f	58·6	2	8 11	Firm	Al Sylah	May 1,	1984
6f	1. 10	4	9 2	Firm	Ajanac	Aug. 8,	1988
6f	1. 11·4	2	8 11	Firm	Jameelapi (USA)	Aug. 8,	1983
8f 50y	1. 39·9	5	7 3	Firm	Sterlonia	July 4,	1981
8f 50y	1. 41	2	9 7	Firm	Mashhur	Oct. 1,	1985
10f	2. 2·3	3	8 8	Firm	Ayaabi	July 21,	1984
10f	2. 5·6	2	9 0	Firm	Al Salite	Oct. 28,	1985
11f	2. 20	3	9 0	Hard	Hurry de Savoie	July 5,	1937
14f	2. 57·8	3	8 10	Firm	Buster Jo	Oct. 1,	1985
16f	3. 24	5	7 7	Firm	Fet	Oct. 5,	1936
18f	3. 59·6	3	9 7	Firm	Sneak Preview	Oct. 25,	1983

PONTEFRACT

Distance	Time	Age	Weight	Going	Horse	Date	
5f	1. 1·1	5	7 7	Hard	Regal Bingo	Sept. 29,	1971
5f	1. 1·4	2	8 9	Firm	Breakaway	Aug. 6,	1987
6f	1. 12·6	3	7 13	Firm	Merry One	Aug. 29,	1970
6f	1. 14	2	9 3	Firm	Fawzi	Sept. 6,	1983
8f	1. 41·4	5	8 12	Firm	Nevison's Lad	May 14,	1965
		4	8 6	Firm	Effulgence	Aug. 29,	1979
		3	7 13	Firm	Whealden	Aug. 5,	1970
		4	7 12	Firm	Paddy's Amour	June 29,	1970
8f	1. 42·8	2	9 13	Firm	Star Spray	Sept. 6,	1983
10f	2. 8·2	3	7 13	Hard	Tom Noddy	Aug. 21,	1972
		4	7 8	Hard	Happy Hector	July 9,	1979
10f	2. 15·5	2	8 3	Firm	One-Cal	Oct. 10,	1977
12f	2. 34·3	4	8 9	Hard	Ezra	June 23,	1975
16f 24y	4. 0·6	4	9 7	Soft	Crusader Castle	April 6,	1983
17f 16y	3. 42·1	3	9 2	Firm	Night Eye (USA)	Sept. 6,	1983
18f	3. 51·1	3	8 8	Firm	Kudz (USA)	Sept. 9,	1986
21f 125y	4. 47·8	4	8 4	Firm	Physical (USA)	May 14,	1984

REDCAR

Distance	Time	Age	Weight	Going	Horse	Date	
5f	56·7	4	7 10	Firm	Mels Choice	Sept. 25,	1982
5f	57·2	2	9 2	Firm	Captain Nick	July 27,	1978
		2	7 8	Firm	English Star	Sept. 24,	1982
6f	1. 9	6	8 4	Firm	Flying William	May 2,	1958
6f	1. 10.7	2	8 9	Firm	Lakeland Beauty	Oct. 18,	1989
7f	1. 22·1	3	8 2	Firm	Marston	July 25,	1978
7f	1. 21·9	2	8 11	Firm	Nagwa	Sept. 27,	1975
8f	1. 35	4	9 3	Firm	Easy Day	June 9,	1986
8f	1. 36·7	2	8 8	Firm	Carbonate	Sept. 15,	1987
9f	1. 50·1	6	10 0	Firm	Hard As Iron	July 26,	1989
9f	1. 54·7	2	8 11	Firm	Cri De Coeur (USA)	Oct. 20,	1983
10f	2. 1·5	5	9 3	Firm	Inaad	May 29,	1989
11f	2. 17·5	3	9 0	Firm	Tenter Close	Oct. 18,	1989
12f	2. 30·1	3	9 0	Firm	High Tension	June 22,	1985
13f 125y	2. 54·7	3	9 0	Firm	Embarkation	June 24,	1989
14f	3. 0	3	8 6	Firm	Groom Porter	July 4,	1989
		3	8 5	Firm	Eastern Diamond	Aug. 5,	1989
14f 160y	3. 8·9	3	8 4	Firm	Tailspin	June 6,	1988
16f	3. 25·7	3	8 6	Firm	Royal Square	Aug. 30,	1989
16f 115y	3. 33·3	4	9 8	Firm	Special Vintage	Aug. 10,	1984
19f	4. 18·5	4	9 2	Firm	Autonomous	Aug. 4,	1989

FLAT RECORD TIMES – *continued*

RIPON

Distance	Time	Age	Weight	Going	Horse	Date	
5f	58	4	7 2	Firm	Castle Mona	July 22,	1966
5f	58·3	2	8 11	Firm	Jonacris	June 2,	1982
6f	1. 9·8	5	7 0	Firm	Quoit	July 23,	1966
6f	1. 11·2	2	9 3	Firm	Domynsky	June 2,	1982
8f	1. 37	4	7 10	Firm	Crown Witness	Aug. 25,	1980
8f	1. 41·2	2	7 2	Good	Roanstreak	Sept. 5,	1970
9f	1. 49·9	3	6 12	Firm	Courtly Lad	May 24,	1972
10f	2. 3·5	3	8 11	Firm	Leysh	July 21,	1984
12f	2. 32·2	{ 6	8 7	Firm	Cholo	Sept. 27,	1941
		{ 7	8 3	Firm	Crusader's Horn	Aug. 8,	1950
14f 134y	3. 8	5	9 13	Good	Grey of Falloden	July 25,	1964
16f	3. 24	4	9 10	Firm	Panama Jack	June 23,	1988
18f	3. 51·3	3	7 8	Firm	Beechwood Seeker	Sept. 1,	1981

SALISBURY (Electric)

Distance	Time	Age	Weight	Going	Horse	Date	
5f	59·78	{ 5	7 12	Fast	Loft Boy	Sept. 8,	1988
		{ 3	9 2	Firm	Iron King	Sept. 7,	1989
5f	59·89	2	8 11	Firm	Blue Tango	June 25,	1986
6f	1. 11·54	4	8 7	Firm	Prince Sky	June 25,	1986
6f	1. 13·06	2	8 11	Firm	Jakomima	Sept. 9,	1971
7f	1. 25·63	3	8 9	Firm	Below Zero	June 26,	1986
7f	1. 26·33	2	9 0	Firm	Bartat	Oct. 4,	1989
8f	1. 39·25	3	8 11	Firm	Schh-You-Know-Who	Oct. 4,	1989
8f	1. 43·86	2	9 3	Fast	Carocrest	Sept. 1st,	1983
10f	2. 4·46	4	7 7	Firm	Kala Nashan	June 25,	1986
12f	2. 32·42	3	8 4	Fast	Buzzbomb	Sept. 8,	1988
14f	2. 58·01	4	10 0	Fast	Dancing Affair	Aug. 16,	1984

SANDOWN (Electric)

Distance	Time	Age	Weight	Going	Horse	Date	
5f	59·31	5	9 2	Fast	Alev	April 27,	1984
5f	59·48	2	9 3	Firm	Times Time	July 22,	1982
7f	1. 26·36	3	9 0	Firm	Mawsuff	June 14,	1986
7f	1. 28·15	2	9 1	Firm	Attempt	Aug. 19,	1983
8f	1. 39·08	3	8 8	Firm	Linda's Fantasy	Aug. 19,	1983
8f	1. 41·14	2	8 11	Firm	Reference Point	Sept. 23,	1986
9f	1. 51·22	3	8 9	Firm	Green's Old Master (USA)	Aug. 21,	1987
9f	1. 54·63	2	8 8	Fast	French Pretender	Sept. 20,	1988
10f	2. 2·14	4	8 11	Firm	Kalaglow	May 31,	1982
11f 100y	2. 21·61	4	8 3	Fast	Aylesfield	July 7,	1984
14f	2. 53·82	3	9 3	Firm	Verdance	Sept. 25,	1985
2m	3. 29·93	6	9 2	Fast	Sadeem	May 29,	1989

FLAT RECORD TIMES – *continued*

THIRSK

Distance	Time	Age	Weight	Going	Horse	Date
8f	57	3	8 8	Firm	Bold and Free	June 3, 1972
5f	57·8	2	8 11	Firm	Fearless Lad	Sept. 5, 1981
		2	7 7	Firm	Be My Bride	May 9, 1987
6f	1. 9·6	3	8 10	Firm	Cedar Grange	Sept. 3, 1977
6f	1. 9.9	2	9 5	Firm	Daarik	July 29, 1989
7f	1. 22·6	5	6 11	Firm	Tuanwun	May 29, 1970
7f	1. 24·6	2	8 12	Firm	Man of Harlech	Aug. 2, 1975
8f	1. 36·2	5	9 0	Firm	Teamwork	May 8, 1982
8f	1. 39·5	2	8 7	Firm	High Port	Sept. 5, 1981
12f	2. 30	4	8 2	Firm	Casting Vote	Aug. 1, 1964
16f	3. 22·3	3	8 11	Firm	Tomaschek	July 17, 1981

WARWICK

Distance	Time	Age	Weight	Going	Horse	Date
5f	57·7	3	9 6	Firm	Truth Will Out	June 21, 1980
5f	58·6	2	9 0	Firm	Tircelyn	June 8, 1957
6f	1. 11·8	4	9 5	Firm	Pride of Kilmalloch	July 1, 1960
6f	1. 12·1	2	7 7	Firm	Sum Mede	July 14, 1989
7f	1. 23·8	6	7 12	Hard	Blackshore	May 19, 1956
7f	1. 24·8	2	9 4	Firm	Nocino	July 28, 1979
8f	1. 36	3	9 0	Firm	Academic World	Aug. 25, 1975
8f	1. 37·5	2	9 3	Firm	Perfect Stranger	Oct. 14, 1986
10f 170y	2. 13·2	3	8 8	Firm	Classic Tale	July 7, 1987
12f 52y	2. 37·2	5	8 12	Hard	Noirmont Buoy	June 19, 1967
14f 150y	3. 8·5	3	9 10	Firm	Kudz (USA)	July 2, 1986
16f	3. 25·8	4	9 7	Fast	Sanamar (disq)	Aug. 29, 1988
		5	8 7	Firm	Tilly Tavi	Aug 31, 1987
18f 180y	4. 3·9	5	9 10	Fast	Fitzpatrick	Aug. 27, 1984

WINDSOR

Distance	Time	Age	Weight	Going	Horse	Date
5f	59·2	3	9 7	Fast	La Tuerta	July 15, 1985
		3	9 7	Good	Possedyno	July 7, 1986
		4	8 1	Firm	Magic Red	June 23, 1945
		6	7 7	Firm	Monk Vendor	Aug. 14, 1936
5f	58·9	2	9 0	Firm	Strictly Private	July 22, 1974
		2	7 0	Firm	Miss Merlin (disq)	Sept. 11, 1978
6f	1. 10·1	3	8 12	Firm	Free Style	June 27, 1964
		3	8 4	Firm	Sweet Relief	Sept. 11, 1978
6f	1. 10·1	2	9 3	Firm	Rosier	Aug. 17, 1981
8f 70y	1. 41·5	4	7 2	Firm	Blowing Bubbles	July. 16, 1984
10f 22y	2. 3	3	9 1	Firm	Moomba Masquerade	May 19, 1980
11f 150y	2. 21·5	3	9 2	Firm	Double Florin	May 19, 1980

FLAT RECORD TIMES – *continued*

WOLVERHAMPTON

Distance	Time	Age	Weight	Going	Horse	Date
5f	56·6	3	7 13	Firm	Balvima	Sept. 17, 1979
5f	57·1	2	9 0	Good	Soverena	July 3, 1967
7f	1. 23·8	3	8 11	Firm	Silk Petal	May 8, 1989
7f	1. 25·7	2	9 1	Firm	Acajou	Aug. 3, 1987
8f	1. 37·3	3	8 8	Firm	Tender Sovereign	July 4, 1983
8f	1. 39·1	2	8 8	Fast	Ivory Tower	Sept. 12, 1988
9f	1. 47·4	3	8 8	Firm	Mailman	May 18, 1982
9f	1. 51·8	2	8 12	Firm	Connaught Bridge	Oct. 9, 1978
		2	8 11	Firm	River Jig (USA)	Oct. 7, 1986
11f 25y	2. 17·5	3	7 12	Firm	Wrong Page	Aug. 15, 1981
12f 100y	2. 38·4	3	8 11	Fast	Samarzana	Aug. 28, 1989
14f 110y	3. 5·6	3	9 7	Firm	Sanchi Steeple	July 8, 1985
17f 130y	3. 36·3	4	9 0	Firm	Dark Proposal	May 17, 1982

YARMOUTH

Distance	Time	Age	Weight	Going	Horse	Date
5f 25y	1. 0·2	3	8 11	Fast	Charm Bird	Sept. 15, 1988
5f 25y	1. 0·9	2	8 8	Firm	Aberbevine	June 14, 1967
		2	8 10	Fast	Sam's Wood	July 13, 1983
6f	1. 10·4	4	8 4	Good	Denikin	July 4, 1951
		3	7 7	Firm	Gold Prospector	Sept. 19, 1978
6f	1. 10·4	2	9 0	Fast	Lanchester	Sept. 15 1988
7f	1. 22·2	3	8 7	Fast	Cielamour (USA)	Sept. 15 1988
7f	1. 22·2	2	9 0	Fast	Warrshan (USA)	Sept. 14, 1988
8f	1. 34·4	3	8 11	Fast	Alderney	Sept. 14, 1988
8f	1. 36·3	2	8 2	Fast	Outrun	Sept. 15, 1988
10f	2. 4·2	3	8 1	Firm	On The Foan	Aug. 17, 1983
		3	9 3	Fast	Aunt Mabel	Aug. 3, 1988
11f 100y	2. 23·8	3	9 0	Firm	Lakenheath	June 10, 1981
		3	9 0	Firm	His Turn	June 9, 1982
14f	2. 58·3	4	8 10	Firm	Top Straight	July 1, 1976
18f 26y	3. 56	6	9 2	Firm	Dolben Lad	Sept. 21, 1978

YORK (Electric)

Distance	Time	Age	Weight	Going	Horse	Date
5f	57·24	4	8 11	Good	Committed (USA)	Aug. 23, 1984
5f	57·84	2	8 12	Fast	Shuttlecock Corner (USA)	Aug. 17, 1988
6f	1. 9·9	3	7 8	Firm	Alphadamus	June 16, 1973
6f	1. 9·84	2	9 0	Fast	Sharp N'Early	Aug. 17, 1988
7f	1. 22·31	4	8 6	Fast	Duckington	Oct. 8, 1988
7f	1. 23·48	2	8 8	Firm	Angelic Note (USA)	Oct. 6, 1988
8f	1. 35·85	3	8 2	Firm	Rosie Potts	May 17, 1989
8f	1. 38·51	2	8 11	Firm	Bocatower (disq)	Oct. 8, 1986
9f	1. 48·90	3	8 5	Fast	Jalmusique	May 16, 1989
9f	1. 52·43	2	8 1	Firm	Oral Evidence	Oct. 6, 1988
10f 110y	2. 6·35	3	8 10	Fast	Persian Heights (disq)	Aug. 16, 1988
12f	2. 25·79	3	9 0	Fast	Diminuendo (USA)	Aug. 16, 1988
14f	2. 52·92	5	8 9	Firm	Mountain Kingdom	May 18, 1989
16f	3. 18·49	3	8 0	Fast	Dam Busters (USA)	Aug. 16, 1988

DATES OF PRINCIPAL RACES

(Subject to alteration)

JANUARY

A.S.W. CHASE (Cheltenham)....Mon. 1
NEW YEAR'S DAY HURDLE (Windsor)....Mon. 1
SPA HURDLE (Cheltenham)....Tue. 2
FEDERATION BREWERY HANDICAP CHASE (Haydock)....Fri. 5
NEW YEAR HANDICAP CHASE (Haydock)....Sat. 6
ANTHONY MILDMAY, PETER CAZALET MEMORIAL HANDICAP CHASE (Sandown)....Sat. 6
TOLWORTH HURDLE (Sandown)....Sat. 6
TATTERSALLS MARES ONLY CHASE (Chepstow)....Mon. 8
JOHN BULL CHASE (Wincanton)....Thur. 11
THUNDER AND LIGHTNING NOVICES' CHASE (Ascot)....Fri. 12
P.M.L. HANDICAP HURDLE (Ascot)....Fri. 12
PETER ROSS NOVICES CHASE (Ascot)....Sat. 13
WARWICK PREMIER CHASE (Warwick)....Sat. 13
LADBROKE HURDLE (Leopardstown)....Sat. 13
PINTAIL HANDICAP CHASE (Newcastle)....Sat. 13
VICTOR CHANDLER CHASE (Ascot)....Sat. 13
PETER DUNCANSON TROPHY NOVICES CHASE (Fontwell)....Mon. 15
GOFFS THYESTES CHASE (Gowran Park)....Thur. 18
CHAMPION HURDLE TRIAL (Haydock)....Sat. 20
PREMIER LONG DISTANCE HURDLE (Haydock)....Sat. 20
PETER MARSH CHASE (Haydock)....Sat. 20
BIC RAZOR LANZAROTE HANDICAP HURDLE (Kempton)....Sat. 20
FULWELL HANDICAP CHASE (Kempton)....Sat. 20
WARWICK NATIONAL (Warwick)....Sat. 20
CLIVE GRAHAM HURDLE (Chepstow)....Tue. 23
WEST OF SCOTLAND PATTERN NOVICE CHASE (Ayr)....Fri. 26
WILLIAM HILL GOLDEN SPURS CHASE (Doncaster)....Sat. 27
CHARTERHOUSE MERCANTILE CHASE (Cheltenham)....Sat. 27
ARLINGTON SECURITIES CHASE FINAL (Cheltenham)....Sat. 27
FOODBROKERS CHASE (Cheltenham)....Sat. 27

FEBRUARY

GAINSBOROUGH HANDICAP CHASE (Sandown)....Sat. 3
OTELEY HURDLE (Sandown)....Sat. 3
PERSIAN WAR PREMIER NOVICES HURDLE (Chepstow)....Sat. 3
SAVE AND PROSPER HANDICAP CHASE (Wetherby)....Sat. 3
BET WITH THE TOTE HANDICAP HURDLE (Wetherby)....Sat. 3
WESSEL CABLE ARKLE PERPETUAL CHALLENGE CUP CHASE (Leopardstown)....Sun. 4
WESSEL CABLE CHAMPION HURDLE (Leopardstown)....Sun. 4
REGENCY HURDLE (Warwick)....Tue. 6
CHARTERHOUSE MERCANTILE CHASE (Ascot)....Wed. 7
REYNOLDSTOWN NOVICES' CHASE (Ascot)....Wed. 7
DAILY TELEGRAPH HURDLE (Ascot)....Wed. 7
STROUD GREEN HURDLE (Newbury)....Fri. 9
FAIRVIEW NEW HOMES CHASE (Newbury)....Fri. 9
TOTE GOLD TROPHY HURDLE (Newbury)....Sat. 10
BYRNE BROTHERS CHASE (Newbury)....Sat. 10
COMPTON CHASE (Newbury)....Sat. 10
GAME SPIRIT CHASE (Newbury)....Sat. 10
P.Z. MOWER CHASE (Thurles)....Wed. 14
FAIRLAWNE CHASE (Windsor)....Sat. 17

Dates of Principal Races – Continued

JOHN HUGHES GRAND NATIONAL TRIAL (Chepstow) .... Sat. 17
WEATHERCALL RISING STARS CHASE (Chepstow) .... Sat. 17
AYNSLEY CHINA CUP CHASE (Chepstow) .... Sat. 17
TOTE EIDER CHASE (Newcastle) .... Sat. 17
CITY TRIAL HURDLE (Nottingham) .... Sat. 17
VINCENT O'BRIEN GOLD CUP (Leopardstown) .... Sat. 17
NATIONAL SPIRIT CHALLENGE TROPHY HURDLE (Fontwell) .... Mon. 19
WOLVERHAMPTON CHAMPION HURDLE TRIAL (Wolverhampton) .... Mon. 19
CHATTERIS FENN HURDLE (Huntingdon) .... Tue. 20
COVENTRY CITY TRIAL NOVICES HURDLE (Warwick) .... Wed. 21
KINGWELL PATTERN HURDLE (Wincanton) .... Thur. 22
JIM FORD CHASE (Wincanton) .... Thur. 22
TOTE PLACEPOT HURDLE (Kempton) .... Sat. 24
RENDLESHAM HURDLE (Kempton) .... Sat. 24
RACING POST CHASE (Kempton) .... Sat. 24

MARCH

ARKELL BREWERY CHASE (Newbury) .... Fri. 2
DE VERE HOTELS HURDLE (Haydock) .... Fri. 2
GEOFFREY GILBEY CHASE (Newbury) .... Sat. 3
PHILIP CORNES SADDLE OF GOLD HURDLE (Newbury) .... Sat. 3
GREENALL WHITLEY GOLD CUP CHASE (Haydock) .... Sat. 3
TIMEFORM CHASE (Haydock) .... Sat. 3
TATTERSALLS MARES ONLY FINAL (Haydock) .... Sat. 3
A. F. BUDGE NOVICES' CHASE (Market Rasen) .... Sat. 3
NEWARK STORAGE JUVENILE HURDLE (Market Rasen) .... Sat. 3
VICTOR LUCAS MEMORIAL NOVICES HURDLE (Market Rasen) .... Sat. 3
COLIN BOOTH HANDICAP CHASE (Market Rasen) .... Sat. 3
BEAUMONT HUNTER CHASE (Market Rasen) .... Sat. 3
CRUDWELL CUP (Warwick) .... Tue. 6
HORSE AND HOUND GOLD CUP CHASE (Sandown) .... Fri. 9
WILLIAM HILL IMPERIAL CUP HANDICAP HURDLE (Sandown) .... Sat. 10
CROWN PAINTS HURDLE (Chepstow) .... Sat. 10
WATERFORD CRYSTAL CHAMPION HURDLE (Cheltenham) .... Tue. 13
WATERFORD CRYSTAL SUPREME NOVICES' HURDLE (Cheltenham) .... Tue. 13
WATERFORD CRYSTAL STAYERS' HURDLE (Cheltenham) .... Tue. 13
ARKLE CHALLENGE TROPHY CHASE (Cheltenham) .... Tue. 13
GRAND ANNUAL HANDICAP CHASE (Cheltenham) .... Tue. 13
KIM MUIR MEMORIAL CHASE (Cheltenham) .... Tue. 13
SUN ALLIANCE CHASE (Cheltenham) .... Wed. 14
SUN ALLIANCE NOVICES' HURDLE (Cheltenham) .... Wed. 14
QUEEN MOTHER CHAMPION CHASE (Cheltenham) .... Wed. 14
CORAL GOLDEN HURDLE FINAL (Cheltenham) .... Wed. 14
MILDMAY OF FLETE CHASE (Cheltenham) .... Wed. 14
NATIONAL HUNT CHASE (Cheltenham) .... Wed. 14
TOTE CHELTENHAM GOLD CUP CHASE (Cheltenham) .... Thur. 15
RITZ CLUB NATIONAL HUNT CHASE (Cheltenham) .... Thur. 15
DAILY EXPRESS TRIUMPH HURDLE (Cheltenham) .... Thur. 15
CHRISTIES FOXHUNTERS' CHASE (Cheltenham) .... Thur. 15
CATHCART CHASE (Cheltenham) .... Thur. 15
COUNTY HURDLE (Cheltenham) .... Thur. 15
BURMAH CASTROL DAY (Leopardstown) .... Sat. 17
BIC RAZOR GOLD CUP (Lingfield) .... Sat. 17
TONY PRESTON CHASE (Chepstow) .... Sat. 17
BASSETT FOODS MILE (Doncaster) .... Thur. 22
BROCKLESBY STAKES (Doncaster) .... Thur. 22
RACEFORM HANDICAP BOOK STAKES (Doncaster) .... Thur. 22
KENCOT HANDICAP CHASE (Newbury) .... Fri. 23

Dates of Principal Races – Continued

BETTERTON CHASE (Newbury) .... Fri. 23
DONCASTER SALES BIDDING STAKES (Doncaster) .... Fri. 23
HOECHST PANACUR HURDLE FINAL (Newbury) .... Sat. 24
BROWN CHAMBERLIN CHASE (Newbury) .... Sat. 24
NEWBURY SPRING HURDLE (Newbury) .... Sat. 24
STEEL PLATE AND SECTIONS CHASE (Newbury) .... Sat. 24
WILLIAM HILL LINCOLN HANDICAP (Doncaster) .... Sat. 24
CAMMIDGE TROPHY (Doncaster) .... Sat. 24
JOSHUA TETLEY STAKES (Doncaster) .... Sat. 24
IRISH LINCOLNSHIRE (The Curragh) .... Sat. 31
KEITH PROWSE LONG DISTANCE HURDLE (Ascot) .... Sat. 31
GOLDEN EAGLE NOVICES CHASE (Ascot) .... Sat. 31

APRIL

MARTELL CUP CHASE (Liverpool) .... Thur. 5
MUMM CLUB NOVICES CHASE (Liverpool) .... Thur. 5
JOHN HUGHES MEMORIAL CHASE (Liverpool) .... Thur. 5
SEAGRAM 100 PIPERS TOP NOVICES HURDLE (Liverpool) .... Thur. 5
SANDEMAN HANDICAP CHASE (Liverpool) .... Thur. 5
ODDBINS HANDICAP HURDLE (Liverpool) .... Thur. 5
GLENLIVET HANDICAP HURDLE (Liverpool) .... Fri. 6
SEAGRAM FOXHUNTERS (Liverpool) .... Fri. 6
PERRIER JOUET NOVICES' CHASE (Liverpool) .... Fri. 6
HEIDSIECK DRY MONOPOLE CHASE (Liverpool) .... Fri. 6
MARTEL HANDICAP HURDLE (Liverpool) .... Fri. 6
WHITE SATIN NOVICES CHASE (Liverpool) .... Fri. 6
SEAGRAM GRAND NATIONAL CHASE (Liverpool) .... Sat. 7
CAPTAIN MORGAN AINTREE CHASE (Liverpool) .... Sat. 7
SANDEMAN AINTREE HURDLE (Liverpool) .... Sat. 7
MUMM PRIZE NOVICE HURDLE (Liverpool) .... Sat. 7
CHEVAS REGAL AMATEUR HANDICAP HURDLE (Liverpool) .... Sat. 7
CHEVAS REGAL NOVICES CHASE (Liverpool) .... Sat. 7
JANNEAU ARMAGNAC HANDICAP HURDLE (Liverpool) .... Sat. 7
2000 GUINEAS TRIAL (Phoenix Park) .... Sat. 7
1000 GUINEAS TRIAL (Phoenix Park) .... Sat. 7
HEY (U.K.) GROUP TROPHY STAKES (Pontefract) .... Tue. 10
BOLLINGER CHAMPAGNE NOVICE CHASE (Ascot) .... Wed. 11
E.B.F. GLADNESS STAKES (The Curragh) .... Sat. 14
E.B.F. MADRID HANDICAP (The Curragh) .... Sat. 14
BONUS PRINT EASTER STAKES (Kempton) .... Sat. 14
BONUS PRINT MASAKA STAKES (Kempton) .... Sat. 14
FIELD MARSHALL STAKES (Haydock) .... Sat. 14
ROSEBERY HANDICAP (Kempton) .... Mon. 16
WELSH CHAMPION HURDLE (Chepstow) .... Mon. 16
WETHERBY HANDICAP CHASE (Wetherby) .... Mon. 16
SILVER JUBILEE CHASE (Fakenham) .... Mon. 16
QUEENS CUP HUNTER CHASE (Fakenham) .... Mon. 16
ROBERT HOARE MEMORIAL HUNTER CHASE (Fakenham) .... Mon. 16
JAMESON IRISH GRAND NATIONAL (Fairyhouse) .... Mon. 16
JAMESON GOLD CUP (Fairyhouse) .... Mon. 16
NELL GWYN STAKES (Newmarket) .... Tue. 17
ABERNANT STAKES (Newmarket) .... Tue. 17
WELSH NOVICES CHAMPION CHASE (Chepstow) .... Tue. 17
BARCLAYS UNICORN HANDICAP HURDLE (Chepstow) .... Tue. 17
POWER GOLD CUP (Fairyhouse) .... Tue. 17
LADBROKE EUROPEAN FREE HANDICAP (Newmarket) .... Wed. 18
PIPER CHAMPAGNE GOLDEN MILLER CHASE (Cheltenham) .... Wed. 18
E.B.F. HURDLE FINAL (Cheltenham) .... Wed. 18
STEEL PLATE & SECTIONS YOUNG CHASERS FINAL (Cheltenham) .... Wed. 18

Dates of Principal Races – Continued

SILVER TROPHY CHASE (Cheltenham) ... Wed. 18
GREAT WESTERN SPRINT (Ayr) ... Wed. 18
DAVID SCOTT PATERN MAKERS HANDICAP (Pontefract) ... Wed. 18
EARL OF SEFTON STAKES (Newmarket) ... Wed. 18
CHARLES HEIDSIECK CHAMPAGNE CRAVEN STAKES (Newmarket) ... Thur. 19
GERRY FEILDEN STAKES (Newmarket) ... Thur. 19
RAPID RACELINE SCOTTISH CHAMPION HURDLE (Ayr) ... Fri. 20
GAINSBOROUGH STUD FRED DARLING STAKES (Newbury) ... Fri. 20
BECKHAMPTON MAIDEN STAKES (Newbury) ... Fri. 20
MAIL ON SUNDAY HANDICAP (Newbury) ... Fri. 20
BIRDFORTH HANDICAP (Thirsk) ... Fri. 20
LANES END JOHN PORTER STAKES (Newbury) ... Sat. 21
GREENHAM STAKES (Newbury) ... Sat. 21
SPRING CUP (Newbury) ... Sat. 21
EBF THIRSK HALL STAKES (Thirsk) ... Sat. 21
BACK A WINNER BY TRAIN CLASSIC TRIAL STAKES (Thirsk) ... Sat. 21
EDINBURGH WOOLLEN MILL FUTURE CHAMPIONS NOVICES' CHASE (Ayr) ... Sat. 21
SEAGRAMS 100 PIPERS NOVICE HURDLE FINAL (Ayr) ... Sat. 21
WILLIAM HILL SCOTTISH NATIONAL (Ayr) ... Sat. 21
SCOTTISH FARM DAIRY FOODS NOV. HAND. HURDLE (Ayr) ... Sat. 21
DONCASTER BLOODSTOCK N.H. FLAT RACE (Ayr) ... Sat. 21
TOTE NOVICES HANDICAP CHASE FINAL (Stratford) ... Sat. 21
WARREN STAKES (Epsom) ... Tue. 24
PRINCESS ELIZABETH STAKES (Epsom) ... Tue. 24
CITY AND SURBURBAN HANDICAP (Epsom) ... Tue. 24
RACAL VODAFONE BLUE RIBAND TRIAL STAKES (Epsom) ... Wed. 25
TATTERSALLS GOLD CUP (Punchestown) ... Wed. 25
GLENEAGLES CHASE (Perth) ... Thur. 26
TRUSTHOUSE FORTE MILE (Sandown) ... Fri. 27
DERMOT McCALMONT TETRARCH STAKES (The Curragh) ... Sat. 28
ATHASI STAKES (The Curragh) ... Sat. 28
MOORESBRIDGE STAKES (The Curragh) ... Sat. 28
BALLYSAX STAKES (The Curragh) ... Sat. 28
MIDLANDS GRAND NATIONAL (Uttoxeter) ... Sat. 28
SIR GORDON RICHARDS STAKES (Sandown) ... Sat. 28
WHITBREAD GOLD CUP CHASE (Sandown) ... Sat. 28
GUARDIAN CLASSIC TRIAL (Sandown) ... Sat. 28
ESHER CUP HANDICAP (Sandown) ... Sat. 28

MAY

WHITE ROSE STAKES (Ascot) ... Wed. 2
INSULPAK VICTORIA CUP (Ascot) ... Wed. 2
INSULPAK SAGARO STAKES (Ascot) ... Wed. 2
GENERAL ACCIDENT 1000 GUINEAS (Newmarket) ... Thu. 3
PRETTY POLLY STAKES (Newmarket) ... Thu. 3
JOCKEY CLUB STAKES (Newmarket) ... Fri. 4
NEWMARKET STAKES (Newmarket) ... Fri. 4
GENERAL ACCIDENT 2000 GUINEAS (Newmarket) ... Sat. 5
PALACE HOUSE STAKES (Newmarket) ... Sat. 5
THIRSK HUNT CUP (Thirsk) ... Sat. 5
CORAL LINE STAKES (Thirsk) ... Sat. 5
FAIREY GROUP SPRING TROPHY (Haydock) ... Sat. 5
SWINTON INSURANCE HURDLE (Haydock) ... Mon. 7
JUBILEE HANDICAP (Kempton) ... Mon. 7
FEDERATION BREWERY NOVICE CHASE FINAL (Limited Handicap) (Newcastle) ... Mon. 7
DALHAM CHESTER VASE (Chester) ... Tue. 8
STATUS HURDLE (Chepstow) ... Tue. 8
R. M. C. CHASE (Chepstow) ... Tue. 8
LADBROKE CHESTER CUP (Chester) ... Wed. 9

Dates of Principal Races – Continued

SHADWELL STUD CHESHIRE OAKS (Chester)......Wed. 9
ORMONDE STAKES (Chester)......Thur. 10
DEE STAKES (Chester)......Thur. 10
MARLEY ROOF TILE OAKS TRIAL (Lingfield)......Sat. 12
CALOR DERBY TRIAL (Lingfield)......Sat. 12
DERRINSTOWN STUD DERBY TRIAL (Leopardstown)......Sat. 12
VETERANS CHASE (Warwick)......Sat. 12
TOP OF THE NORTH NOVICE HURDLE (FINAL) (Newcastle)......Sat. 12
IRISH MUTUAL BUILDING SOCIETY EVENING (Leopardstown)......Mon. 14
TATTERSALLS MUSIDORA STAKES (York)......Tue. 15
WILLIAM HILL-DANTE STAKES (York)......Wed. 16
YORKSHIRE CUP (York)......Thur. 17
DUKE OF YORK STAKES (York)......Thur. 17
NORWEST HOLST HANDICAP (York)......Thur. 17
SIR CHARLES CLORE MEMORIAL STAKES (Newbury)......Fri. 18
ULTRAMAR HANDICAP (Newbury)......Fri. 18
HUE WILLIAMS STAKES (Newbury)......Fri. 18
JUDDMONTE LOCKINGE STAKES (Newbury)......Fri. 18
TRENCHERWOOD MAIDEN STAKES (Newbury)......Fri. 18
CORAL BOOKMAKERS HANDICAP (Newmarket)......Sat. 19
ASTON PARK STAKES (Newbury)......Sat. 19
LONDON GOLD CUP (Newbury)......Sat. 19
WINCHESTER STAKES (Newbury)......Sat. 19
AIRLIE COOLMORE IRISH 2000 GUINEAS (The Curragh)......Sat. 19
TATTERSALLS ROGERS GOLD CUP (The Curragh)......Sat. 19
GREENLAND STAKES (The Curragh)......Sat. 19
MARBLE HILL STAKES (The Curragh)......Sat. 19
BET WITH THE TOTE HANDICAP (Thirsk)......Sat. 19
DIP LUPTON BROOMHEAD CUP (Thirsk)......Sat. 19
JOSHUA TETLEY HANDICAP (Thirsk)......Sat. 19
N.M. SCHRODER'S PREDOMINATE STAKES (Goodwood)......Wed. 23
FESTIVAL STAKES (Goodwood)......Wed. 23
SHERATON PARK TOWER LUPE STAKES (Goodwood)......Thur. 24
DARESBURY HANDICAP (Haydock)......Fri. 25
GEORGE FARNDON HANDICAP (Pontefract)......Fri. 25
MAGINN TV STAKES (The Curragh)......Sat. 26
GOFFS IRISH 1000 GUINEAS (The Curragh)......Sat. 26
HERON STAKES (Kempton)......Sat. 26
VENUS STAKES (Kempton)......Sat. 26
TOTE CREDIT HANDICAP (Haydock)......Sat. 26
SANDY LANE STAKES (Haydock)......Sat. 26
SEARS TEMPLE STAKES (Sandown)......Mon. 28
MAPPIN AND WEBB HENRY II STAKES (Sandown)......Mon. 28
ZETLAND GOLD CUP (Redcar)......Mon. 28
SAXONE FILLIES STAKES (Sandown)......Mon. 28
SELFRIDGES WHITSUN HANDICAP (Sandown)......Mon. 28
PRINCE OF WALES CUP CHASE (Fakenham)......Mon. 28
MERCURY STAKES (Chepstow)......Mon. 28
BRIGADIER GERARD STAKES (Sandown)......Tue. 29
CHARLES HEIDSIECK NATIONAL STAKES (Sandown)......Tue. 29

JUNE

HORSE AND HOUND CUP (Stratford)......Sat. 2
DAILY MAIL LEISURE STAKES (Lingfield)......Sat. 2
BALLYOGAN STAKES (Leopardstown)......Mon. 4
EVER READY DERBY STAKES (Epsom)......Wed. 6
DIOMED STAKES (Epsom)......Wed. 6
NIGHTRIDER HANDICAP (Epsom)......Wed. 6
SILVER SEAL HANDICAP (Epsom)......Wed. 6

Dates of Principal Races – Continued

CORONATION CUP (Epsom) ... Thur. 7
NORTHERN DANCER HANDICAP (Epsom) ... Fri. 8
TOKYO TROPHY HANDICAP (Epsom) ... Fri. 8
BURTONWOOD BREWERY HANDICAP (Haydock) ... Fri. 8
GOLD SEAL OAKS STAKES (Epsom) ... Sat. 9
EBBISHAM HANDICAP (Epsom) ... Sat. 9
JOHN OF GAUNT STAKES (Haydock) ... Sat. 9
HERMITAGE STAKES (Newbury) ... Wed. 13
BALLYMACOLL STUD STAKES (Newbury) ... Wed. 13
COOPERS & LYBRAND STAKES (Newbury) ... Thur. 14
KINGSCLERE STAKES (Newbury) ... Thur. 14
CORK GULLY APPRENTICE HANDICAP (Newbury) ... Thur. 14
TARMAC CONSTRUCTION STAKES (Chepstow) ... Thur. 14
INNOVATIVE MARKETING SPRINT (York) ... Fri. 15
WILLIAM HILL TROPHY (York) ... Sat. 16
WILLIAM PRENN ROYAL YORKSHIRE STAKES (York) ... Sat. 16
KILFRUSH CONCORDE STAKES (Phoenix Park) ... Sat. 16
KING EDWARD VII STAKES (Royal Ascot) ... Tue. 19
ST. JAMES'S PALACE STAKES (Royal Ascot) ... Tue. 19
PRINCE OF WALES'S STAKES (Royal Ascot) ... Tue. 19
COVENTRY STAKES (Royal Ascot) ... Tue. 19
QUEEN ANNE STAKES (Royal Ascot) ... Tue. 19
ASCOT HANDICAP (Royal Ascot) ... Tue. 19
CORONATION STAKES (Royal Ascot) ... Wed. 20
JERSEY STAKES (Royal Ascot) ... Wed. 20
QUEENS VASE STAKES (Royal Ascot) ... Wed. 20
QUEEN MARY STAKES (Royal Ascot) ... Wed. 20
ROYAL HUNT CUP HANDICAP (Royal Ascot) ... Wed. 20
BESSBOROUGH HANDICAP (Royal Ascot) ... Wed. 20
GOLD CUP (Royal Ascot) ... Thur. 21
CORK AND ORRERY STAKES (Royal Ascot) ... Thur. 21
NORFOLK STAKES (Royal Ascot) ... Thur. 21
RIBBLESDALE STAKES (Royal Ascot) ... Thur. 21
CHESHAM STAKES (Royal Ascot) ... Thur. 21
KING GEORGE V HANDICAP (Royal Ascot) ... Thur. 21
HARDWICKE STAKES (Royal Ascot) ... Fri. 22
KINGS STAND STAKES (Royal Ascot) ... Fri. 22
WOKINGHAM HANDICAP (Royal Ascot) ... Fri. 22
BRITANNIA HANDICAP (Royal Ascot) ... Fri. 22
WINDSOR CASTLE STAKES (Royal Ascot) ... Fri. 22
QUEEN ALEXANDRA STAKES (Royal Ascot) ... Fri. 22
WILLIAM HILL HANDICAP (Ascot) ... Sat. 23
WARWICK OAKS (Warwick) ... Sat. 23
RACAL-VODAFONE STAKES (Kempton) ... Wed. 27
VEUVE CLICQUOT CHAMPAGNE STAKES (Salisbury) ... Thur. 28
GOSFORTH PARK CUP HANDICAP (Newcastle) ... Fri. 29
NORTHUMBERLAND PLATE (Newcastle) ... Sat. 30
VAN GEEST CRITERION STAKES (Newmarket) ... Sat. 30
WARWICK VASE (Warwick) ... Sat. 30
FRED ARCHER STAKES (Newmarket) ... Sat. 30
SILVER CUP (Lingfield) ... Sat. 30
WOODPECKER STAKES (Chepstow) ... Sat. 30
BUDWEISER PRETTY POLLY STAKES (The Curragh) ... Sat. 30

JULY

BUDWEISER IRISH DERBY (The Curragh) ... Sun. 1
ANHEUSER-BUSCH RAILWAY STAKES (The Curragh) ... Sun. 1
McGRATH STAKES (The Curragh) ... Sun. 1

Dates of Principal Races – Continued

JAPANESE WHISPERS (BARNSLEY) HANDICAP (Pontefract) .... Mon. 2
TRAVIS PERKINS HANDICAP (Chepstow) .... Tue. 3
JOHNNY OSBORNE HANDICAP (Haydock) .... Thur. 5
JULY TROPHY (Haydock) .... Fri. 6
HONG KONG DAY (Sandown) .... Fri. 6
LANCASHIRE OAKS (Haydock) .... Sat. 7
COCK OF THE NORTH STAKES (Haydock) .... Sat. 7
OLD NEWTON CUP (Haydock) .... Sat. 7
INTERNATIONAL STAKES (Phoenix Park) .... Sat. 7
CORAL-ECLIPSE STAKES (Sandown) .... Sat. 7
SANDOWN E.B.F. STAKES (Sandown) .... Sat. 7
TRAFALGAR HOUSE SPRINT STAKES (Sandown) .... Sat. 7
PRINCESS OF WALES'S STAKES (Newmarket) .... Tue. 10
CHERRY HINTON STAKES (Newmarket) .... Tue. 10
LADBROKE BUNBURY CUP (Newmarket) .... Tue. 10
CHESTERFIELD STAKES (Newmarket) .... Tue. 10
CHILD STAKES (Newmarket) .... Wed. 11
ANGLIA TELEVISION JULY STAKES (Newmarket) .... Wed. 11
ADDISON TOOLS HANDICAP (Newmarket) .... Thur. 12
CARROLL FOUNDATION JULY CUP (Newmarket) .... Thur. 12
BERNARD VAN CUTSEM STAKES (Newmarket) .... Thur. 12
WELSH BREWERS PREMIER STAKES (Chepstow) .... Thur. 12
JOHN SMITH'S MAGNET CUP (York) .... Sat. 14
KILDANGAN STUD IRISH OAKS (The Curragh) .... Sat. 14
SHERNAZAR CURRAGH STAKES (The Curragh) .... Sat. 14
BET WITH THE TOTE TROPHY (Lingfield) .... Sat. 14
SCOTTISH CLASSIC (Ayr) .... Sat. 14
CURRAGH CUP (The Curragh) .... Sun. 15
TENNENT TROPHY (Ayr) .... Mon. 16
DUNSTALL DERBY (Wolverhampton) .... Mon. 16
TOTE BOOKMAKERS SPRINT TROPHY (Ayr) .... Tue. 17
GILBEY'S GIN STAKES (Chepstow) .... Thur. 19
MILCARS STAKES (Sandown) .... Thur. 19
RIDGEWAY HANDICAP (Newbury) .... Fri. 20
HACKWOOD STAKES (Newbury) .... Fri. 20
WILLIAM THE LION HANDICAP (Ayr) .... Fri. 20
KERRIDGE COMPUTER STAKES (Newbury) .... Sat. 21
MANTON ROSEBOWL STAKES (Newbury) .... Sat. 21
MAIL ON SUNDAY HANDICAP (Ayr) .... Sat. 21
FOOD BROKERS TROPHY (Newmarket) .... Sat. 21
GOLDEN PAGES HANDICAP (Leopardstown) .... Sat. 21
P.G. TIPS TEA CUP (Ayr) .... Mon. 23
BROWN JACK HANDICAP (Ascot) .... Fri. 27
THE KING GEORGE VI AND THE QUEEN ELIZABETH DIAMOND STAKES (Ascot) .... Sat. 28
PRINCESS MARGARET STAKES (Ascot) .... Sat. 28
BEESWING STAKES (Newcastle) .... Mon. 30
WILLIAM HILL STEWARDS CUP (Goodwood) .... Tue. 31
LANSON CHAMPAGNE VINTAGE STAKES (Goodwood) .... Tue. 31
GORDON STAKES (Goodwood) .... Tue. 31
OAK TREE STAKES (Goodwood) .... Tue. 31

AUGUST

SUSSEX STAKES (Goodwood) .... Wed. 1
RICHMOND STAKES (Goodwood) .... Wed. 1
DIGITAL GALWAY PLATE HANDICAP CHASE (Galway) .... Wed. 1
GUINNESS GALWAY HANDICAP HURDLE (Galway) .... Thur. 2
GOODWOOD CUP (Goodwood) .... Thur. 2
SCHWEPPES GOLDEN MILE (Goodwood) .... Thur. 2
KING GEORGE STAKES (Goodwood) .... Thur. 2

Dates of Principal Races – Continued

MOLECOMB STAKES (Goodwood) .... Fri. 3
SCHRODERS GLORIOUS STAKES (Goodwood) .... Fri. 3
MALONEY & RHODES HANDICAP (Newmarket) .... Fri. 3
JOHN BELL MEMORIAL HANDICAP (Thirsk) .... Fri. 3
VODAPHONE NASSAU STAKES (Goodwood) .... Sat. 4
CHESTERFIELD CUP (Goodwood) .... Sat. 4
COLMANS OF NORWICH NURSERY (Newmarket) .... Sat. 4
YORKSHIRE TELEVISION HANDICAP (Thirsk) .... Sat. 4
JOE McGRATH SPRINT (Leopardstown) .... Mon. 6
NOTTINGHAM STEWARDS CUP (Nottingham) .... Mon. 6
BRIGHTON CHALLENGE HANDICAP (Brighton) .... Wed. 8
BRIGHTON SPRINT HANDICAP (Brighton) .... Thur. 9
LEISURE COMPANY STAKES (Haydock) .... Fri. 10
CORAL BOOKMAKERS HANDICAP (Haydock) .... Sat. 11
BURTONWOOD BREWERY ROSE OF LANCASTER STAKES (Haydock) .... Sat. 11
NEW ZEALAND HANDICAP (Newmarket) .... Sat. 11
SWEET SOLERA STAKES (Newmarket) .... Sat. 11
HEINZ '57' PHOENIX STAKES (Phoenix Park) .... Sun. 12
IRISH NATIONAL STUD STAKES (Phoenix Park) .... Sun. 12
NORTH YORKSHIRE STAKES HANDICAP (Thirsk) .... Mon. 13
WHITCHURCH STAKES (Salisbury) .... Thur. 16
GARDNER MERCHANTS HUNGERFORD STAKES (Newbury) .... Fri. 17
WASHINGTON SINGER STAKES (Newbury) .... Fri. 17
PENKFORD WEIR HANDICAP (Haydock) .... Fri. 17
GEOFFREY FREER STAKES (Newbury) .... Sat. 18
ST. HUGH'S STAKES (Newbury) .... Sat. 18
GREAT ST. WILFRID HANDICAP (Ripon) .... Sat. 18
ROYAL WHIP STAKES (The Curragh) .... Sat. 18
TARA SIRES DESMOND STAKES (The Curragh) .... Sat. 18
REFERENCE POINT TYROS STAKES (The Curragh) .... Sat. 18
JUDDMONTE INTERNATIONAL STAKES (York) .... Tue. 21
GREAT VOLTIGEUR STAKES (York) .... Tue. 21
MELROSE HANDICAP (York) .... Tue. 21
ACOMBE STAKES (York) .... Tue. 21
LONSDALE STAKES (York) .... Tue. 21
EGLINTON NURSERY (York) .... Tue. 21
YORKSHIRE OAKS (York) .... Wed. 22
TOTE EBOR HANDICAP (York) .... Wed. 22
SCOTTISH EQUITABLE GIMCRACK STAKES (York) .... Wed. 22
ANDY CAPP HANDICAP (York) .... Wed. 22
YORK ROSES STAKES (York) .... Wed. 22
LOWTHER STAKES (York) .... Thur. 23
BRADFORD AND BINGLEY HANDICAP (York) .... Thur. 23
WILLIAM HILL SPRINT CHAMPIONSHIP (York) .... Thur. 23
CITY OF YORK STAKES (York) .... Thur. 23
NUNTHORPE STAKES (York) .... Thur. 23
GALTRES STAKES (York) .... Thur. 23
KNAVESMIRE HANDICAP (York) .... Thur. 23
PRESTIGE STAKES (Goodwood) .... Fri. 24
PHOENIX SPRINT (Phoenix Park) .... Fri. 24
DEBUTANTE STAKES (Phoenix Park) .... Fri. 24
HOPEFUL STAKES (Newmarket) .... Fri. 24
DANEPAK BACON STAKES (Newmarket) .... Sat. 25
PHILIP CORNES NURSERY (Newmarket) .... Sat. 25
MELD STAKES (The Curragh) .... Sat. 25
DUNMURRY STUD ANGLESEY STAKES (The Curragh) .... Sat. 25
CELEBRATION MILE (Goodwood) .... Sat. 25
MARCH STAKES (Goodwood) .... Sat. 25
SPORT ON 2 HANDICAP (Goodwood) .... Sat. 25
HIGHFLYER STAKES (Newmarket) .... Sat. 25

Dates of Principal Races – Continued

VIRGINIA STAKES (Newcastle) .... Mon. 27
BONUS PRINT CHAMPION 2-Y-O TROPHY (Ripon) .... Mon. 27
TOTE SPRINT HANDICAP (Sandown) .... Mon. 27
BANK HOLIDAY HANDICAP (Chepstow) .... Mon. 27
MIDLANDS CAMBRIDGESHIRE (Wolverhampton) .... Mon. 27
MOET AND CHANDON SILVER MAGNUM STAKES (Sandown) .... Mon. 27
SOLARIO STAKES (Sandown) .... Fri. 31
ATALANTA STAKES (Sandown) .... Fri. 31

SEPTEMBER

FLYING FIVE (Phoenix Park) .... Sun. 2
SILVER FLASH STAKES (Phoenix Park) .... Sun. 2
BARRONSTOWN STUD GOLD STAKES (Phoenix Park) .... Sun. 2
PHOENIX CHAMPION STAKES (Phoenix Park) .... Sun. 2
FALMOUTH HANDICAP (York) .... Wed. 5
LAWRENCE BATLEY HANDICAP (York) .... Wed. 5
SUN LIFE OF CANADA GARROWBY STAKES (York) .... Thur. 6
STRENSALL STAKES (York) .... Thur. 6
DICK POOLE STAKES (Salisbury) .... Thur. 6
CLAUDE HARRISON TROPHY (Haydock) .... Fri. 7
GLINT OF GOLD STAKES (Kempton) .... Fri. 7
BONUSPRINT SEPTEMBER STAKES (Kempton) .... Sat. 8
HAMBLIN GRAND TROPHY HANDICAP (Haydock) .... Sat. 8
LADBROKE SPRINT CUP (Haydock) .... Sat. 8
GUINNESS PEAT AVIATION NATIONAL STAKES (The Curragh) .... Sat. 8
LADBROKE SPRINT CUP (Haydock) .... Sat. 8
IRISH CAMBRIDGESHIRE (The Curragh) .... Sat. 8
SIRENIA STAKES (Kempton) .... Sat. 8
RUSH AND TOMPKINS CUP HANDICAP (Thirsk) .... Sat. 8
RUSH AND TOMPKINS NURSERY (Thirsk) .... Sat. 8
MOUNT COOTE STUD MATRON STAKES (The Curragh) .... Sun. 9
MOYGLARE STUD STAKES (The Curragh) .... Sun. 9
MIDLANDS CESAREWITCH (Wolverhampton) .... Mon. 10
PARK HILL STAKES (Doncaster) .... Wed. 12
MAY HILL STAKES (Doncaster) .... Wed. 12
PORTLAND HANDICAP (Doncaster) .... Wed. 12
KIVETON PARK STAKES (Doncaster) .... Thur. 13
DONCASTER CUP (Doncaster) .... Thur. 13
MALLARD HANDICAP (Doncaster) .... Thur. 13
TATTERSALLS YORKSHIRE FILLIES STAKES (Doncaster) .... Thur. 13
LAURENT PERRIER CHAMPAGNE STAKES (Doncaster) .... Fri. 14
SELECT STAKES (Goodwood) .... Fri. 14
COUNTRY LADY STARDOM STAKES (Goodwood) .... Fri. 14
TROY STAKES (Doncaster) .... Fri. 14
FLYING CHILDERS STAKES (Doncaster) .... Sat. 15
SCEPTRE STAKES (Doncaster) .... Sat. 15
BATTLE OF BRITAIN STAKES (Doncaster) .... Sat. 15
ST LEGER STAKES (Doncaster) .... Sat. 15
REFERENCE POINT SCEPTRE STAKES (Doncaster) .... Sat. 15
SKOL SPRINT TROPHY (Goodwood) .... Sat. 15
HENNESSY DAY (Leopardstown) .... Sat. 15
HARP LAGER CUP (Chepstow) .... Sat. 15
DOONSIDE CUP (Ayr) .... Wed. 19
SOTHEBY'S HANDICAP (Ayr) .... Wed. 19
GUINNESS KERRY NATIONAL (Listowel) .... Wed. 19
HARRY ROSEBERY CHALLENGE TROPHY (Ayr) .... Thur. 20
HAYNES, HANSON & CLARK STAKES (Newbury) .... Fri. 21
MAIL ON SUNDAY HANDICAP (Newbury) .... Fri. 21
JACK COLLIER MEMORIAL STAKES (Newbury) .... Fri. 21

Dates of Principal Races – Continued

LADBROKES AYR GOLD CUP HANDICAP (Ayr) .... Fri. 21
LADBROKES AYRSHIRE HANDICAP (Ayr) .... Sat. 22
FIRTH OF CLYDE STAKES (Ayr) .... Sat. 22
PHILIP CORNES NICKEL ALLOYS HANDICAP (Ayr) .... Sat. 22
ROKEBY FARMS MILL REEF STAKES (Newbury) .... Sat. 22
CORAL AUTUMN CUP (Newbury) .... Sat. 22
COURAGE STAKES (Newbury) .... Sat. 22
HIGHCLERE NURSERY (Newbury) .... Sat. 22
FUTURITY STAKES (The Curragh) .... Sat. 22
JEFFERSON SMURFIT MEMORIAL ST. LEGER (The Curragh) .... Sat. 22
ROUND TOWER STAKES (The Curragh) .... Sat. 22
HOOVER CUMBERLAND LODGE STAKES (Ascot) .... Thur. 27
BLUE SEAL STAKES (Ascot) .... Thur. 27
STANLEY LEISURE ORGANISATION DREAM MILE (Haydock) .... Fri. 28
WILLIAM HILL GOLDEN SPURS HANDICAP (Ascot) .... Fri. 28
TAYLOR WOODROW HANDICAP (Ascot) .... Fri. 28
ROYAL LODGE STAKES (Ascot) .... Sat. 29
DIADEM STAKES (Ascot) .... Sat. 29
QUEEN ELIZABETH II STAKES (Ascot) .... Sat. 29
HOOVER FILLIES MILE (Ascot) .... Sat. 29
TOTE FESTIVAL HANDICAP (Ascot) .... Sat. 29
BRENT WALKER HANDICAP (Ascot) .... Sat. 29
BUCKLOW HILL HANDICAP (Haydock) .... Sat. 29
BROOKE BOND FOODS FINAL (Haydock) .... Sat. 29
FASIG-TIPTON STAKES (Phoenix Park) .... Sat. 29
CESAREWITCH HANDICAP (The Curragh) .... Sun. 30
WATERFORD TESTIMONIAL STAKES (The Curragh) .... Sun. 30

OCTOBER

TATTERSALLS CHEVELEY PARK STAKES (Newmarket) .... Wed. 3
ROUS STAKES (Newmarket) .... Wed. 3
TATTERSALLS MIDDLE PARK STAKES (Newmarket) .... Thur. 4
GODOLPHIN STAKES (Newmarket) .... Thur. 4
SOMERVILLE TATTERSALLS STAKES (Newmarket) .... Fri. 5
SUPREME STAKES (Goodwood) .... Fri. 5
FOUNDATION STAKES (Goodwood) .... Fri. 5
MAIN REEF STAKES (Newmarket) .... Fri. 5
JOCKEY CLUB CUP (Newmarket) .... Sat. 6
SUN CHARIOT STAKES (Newmarket) .... Sat. 6
WILLIAM HILL CAMBRIDGESHIRE HANDICAP (Newmarket) .... Sat. 6
TIMEFORM HURDLE (Chepstow) .... Sat. 6
MERCEDES BENZ CHASE (Chepstow) .... Sat. 6
BIRDCATCHER NURSERY (Naas) .... Sat. 6
CIGA PRIX DE L'ARC DE TRIOMPHE (Longchamp) .... Sun. 7
BROCKADALE HANDICAP (Pontefract) .... Mon. 8
OAK HANDICAP (Haydock) .... Wed. 10
BARCLAYS UNICORN TROPHY (York) .... Wed. 10
HORNBEAM HANDICAP (Haydock) .... Thur. 11
ALLIED DUNBAR HANDICAP (York) .... Thur. 11
OCTOBER STAKES (Ascot) .... Fri. 12
ROCKINGHAM STAKES (York) .... Sat. 13
PRINCESS ROYAL STAKES (Ascot) .... Sat. 13
CORNWALLIS STAKES (Ascot) .... Sat. 13
BOVIS HANDICAP (Ascot) .... Sat. 13
CORAL BOOKMAKERS SPRINT TROPHY (York) .... Sat. 13
C.L. WELD STAKES (Phoenix Park) .... Sun. 14
CARTIER MILLION (Phoenix Park) .... Sun. 14
ASTON PARK HANDICAP (Chepstow) .... Tue. 16
TOP FLIGHT LEISURE HURDLE (Ayr) .... Tue. 16

Dates of Principal Races – Continued

BOBBY RENTON MEMORIAL NOVICES' CHASE (Wetherby) .... Wed. 17
BMW NOVICES CHASE (Wetherby) .... Wed. 17
A.R. DENNIS NURSERY (Newmarket) .... Thur. 18
BISQUIT COGNAC CHALLENGE STAKES (Newmarket) .... Thur. 18
DEWHURST STAKES (Newmarket) .... Fri. 19
ROCKFEL STAKES (Newmarket) .... Fri. 19
EBF NURSERY (Newmarket) .... Fri. 19
BARING INTERNATIONAL DARLEY STAKES (Newmarket) .... Fri. 19
DUBAI CHAMPION STAKES (Newmarket) .... Sat. 20
TOTE CESAREWITCH HANDICAP (Newmarket) .... Sat. 20
WARD HILL BENTINCK STAKES (Newmarket) .... Sat. 20
CHARISMA GOLD CUP (Kempton) .... Sat. 20
JUDDMONTE BERESFORD STAKES (The Curragh) .... Sat. 20
BLANDFORD STAKES (The Curragh) .... Sat. 20
MUNSTER NATIONAL CHASE (Limerick) .... Mon. 22
MADEMOISELLE LADIES STAKES (Chepstow) .... Tue. 23
VODAFONE HORRIS HILL STAKES (Newbury) .... Thur. 25
LETCOMBE HANDICAP (Newbury) .... Thur. 25
TERRY BIDDLECOMBE CHASE (Wincanton) .... Thur. 25
WHITELINE HANDICAP (Pontefract) .... Thur. 25
DONCASTER STAKES (Doncaster) .... Fri. 26
GLYNWED INTERNATIONAL CHASE (Newbury) .... Fri. 26
FALCON CATERING EQUIPMENT HURDLE (Newbury) .... Fri. 26
FLAVEL LEISURE HURDLE (Newbury) .... Fri. 26
HALDON GOLD CUP CHASE (Devon) .... Fri. 26
ST. SIMON STAKES (Newbury) .... Sat. 27
THAMES VALLEY EGGS STAKES (Newbury) .... Sat. 27
RADLEY STAKES (Newbury) .... Sat. 27
WILLIAM HILL HANDICAP (Newbury) .... Sat. 27
SOLAGLAS HANDICAP (Doncaster) .... Sat. 27
RACING POST TROPHY (Doncaster) .... Sat. 27
DONCASTER EBF HANDICAP (Doncaster) .... Sat. 27
BAILEYS IRISH CREAM DAY (Leopardstown) .... Mon. 29
BURR STAKES (Lingfield) .... Mon. 29
RACECALL GOLD TROPHY (Redcar) .... Tue. 30
LIONEL VICK CHASE (Newbury) .... Wed. 31
TOM MASSON HURDLE (Newbury) .... Wed. 31
BMW SERIES CHASE QUALIFIER (Newbury) .... Wed. 31

NOVEMBER

GEORGE STUBBS STAKES (Newmarket) .... Fri. 2
JAMES SEYMOUR STAKES (Newmarket) .... Fri. 2
MAIL ON SUNDAY HANDICAP FINAL (Newmarket) .... Sat. 3
JENNINGS THE BOOKMAKERS ZETLAND STAKES (Newmarket) .... Sat. 3
CHARLIE HALL MEMORIAL CHASE (Wetherby) .... Sat. 3
WEST YORKSHIRE HURDLE (Wetherby) .... Sat. 3
WENSLEYDALE JUVENILE HURDLE (Wetherby) .... Sat. 3
WIGHILL HANDICAP CHASE (Wetherby) .... Sat. 3
MARSHALL STAKES (Newmarket) .... Sat. 3
TOTE SILVER TROPHY (Chepstow) .... Sat. 3
CURRIDGE CHASE (Newbury) .... Wed. 7
HALLOWEEN CHASE (Newbury) .... Wed. 7
BADGER BEER HANDICAP CHASE (Wincanton) .... Thur. 8
SILVER BUCK CHASE (Wincanton) .... Thur. 8
WILLIAM HILL NOVEMBER HANDICAP (Doncaster) .... Sat. 10
MACKESON GOLD CUP CHASE (Cheltenham) .... Sat. 10
GEORGE FARNDON ENGINEERING STAKES (Doncaster) .... Sat. 10
WHITBREAD WHITE LABEL HANDICAP HURDLE (Cheltenham) .... Sat. 10
BOXING DAY TRIAL CHASE (Kempton) .... Wed. 14

Dates of Principal Races – Continued

RACECALL ASCOT HURDLE (Ascot) .... Fri. 16
LANG WHANG HURDLE (Ayr) .... Fri. 16
ARLINGTON PREMIER CHASE (Ayr) .... Fri. 16
ST MARY'S TRIAL HURDLE (Warwick) .... Sat. 17
H & T WALKER GOLD CUP CHASE (Ascot) .... Sat. 17
TENNENT SPECIAL CHASE (Ayr) .... Sat. 17
RIP HANDICAP CHASE (Ascot) .... Sat. 17
JOAN MACKAY CHASE (Ayr) .... Sat. 17
N.C.B. NOVEMBER HANDICAP (Leopardstown) .... Sun. 18
EDWARD HANMER MEMORIAL CHASE (Haydock) .... Wed. 21
SAVE AND PROSPER HANDICAP CHASE (Haydock) .... Thur. 22
OXFORD CHASE (Newbury) .... Fri. 23
HENNESSY COGNAC GOLD CUP CHASE (Newbury) .... Sat. 24
GERRY FEILDEN HURDLE (Newbury) .... Sat. 24
FIGHTING FIFTH HURDLE (Newcastle) .... Sat. 24
LINCOLNSHIRE GRAND NATIONAL (Market Rasen) .... Sat. 24
NEWARK STORAGE NOVICES CHASE (Market Rasen) .... Sat. 24
PETERBOROUGH CHASE (Huntingdon) .... Tue. 27

DECEMBER

JOSHUA TETLEY HANDICAP CHASE (Wetherby) .... Sat. 1
WILLIAM HILL HANDICAP HURDLE (Sandown) .... Sat. 1
WILLIAM HILL NOVICES HANDICAP HURDLE (Sandown) .... Sat. 1
TINGLE CREEK HANDICAP CHASE (Sandown) .... Sat. 1
REHERSAL HANDICAP CHASE (Chepstow) .... Sat. 1
CONSTANT SECURITY CHASE (Doncaster) .... Sat. 8
CONSTANT SECURITY HANDICAP HURDLE (Doncaster) .... Sat. 8
FREEBOOTER NOVICES CHASE (Doncaster) .... Sat. 8
ENVOPAK CHASE (Lingfield) .... Sat. 8
GOLD CUP HANDICAP CHASE (Cheltenham) .... Sat. 8
A.F. BUDGE GOLD CUP (Cheltenham) .... Sat. 8
BULA HURDLE (Cheltenham) .... Sat. 8
CHARTERHOUSE MERCANTILE LEISURE NOV. CHASE (Cheltenham) .... Sat. 8
LINGFIELD PARK HANDICAP CHASE (Lingfield) .... Sat. 8
TOMMY WHITTLE CHASE (Haydock) .... Wed. 12
RONNIE JOHNSTON HANDICAP CHASE (Haydock) .... Thur. 13
SGB HANDICAP CHASE (Ascot) .... Sat. 15
LONG WALK HURDLE (Ascot) .... Sat. 15
HSS HIRE SHOP HURDLE (Ascot) .... Sat. 15
CORAL WELSH NATIONAL CHASE (Chepstow) .... Sat. 22
CURRAN GROUPS FINAL HURDLE (Chepstow) .... Sat. 22
RACING INTERNATIONAL HURDLE (Chepstow) .... Sat. 22
KING GEORGE VI RANK CHASE (Kempton) .... Wed. 26
BUTLINS FELTHAM NOVICES CHASE (Kempton) .... Wed. 26
ROWLAND MEYRICK HANDICAP CHASE (Wetherby) .... Wed. 26
JOHN HAGGAS MEMORIAL NOVICES' CHASE (Wetherby) .... Wed. 26
MID SEASON CHASE (Wincanton) .... Wed. 26
DENNY'S CHASE (Leopardstown) .... Wed. 26
DENNY MEATS JUVENILE HURDLE (Leopardstown) .... Wed. 26
TOP RANK CHRISTMAS HURDLE (Kempton) .... Thur. 27
CASTLEFORD HANDICAP CHASE (Wetherby) .... Thur. 27
FINDUS EXTENDED HANDICAP CHASE (Leopardstown) .... Thur. 27
FINDUS HURDLE (Leopardstown) .... Thur. 27
BLACK & WHITE GOLD CUP (Leopardstown) .... Fri. 28
CHALLOW HURDLE (Newbury) .... Fri. 28
BOOKMAKERS HURDLE (Leopardstown) .... Sat. 29
L'OREAL HURDLE (Newbury) .... Sat. 29
SAVE AND PROSPER MANDARIN CHASE (Newbury) .... Sat. 29
PHILIP CORNES HURDLE (Newbury) .... Sat. 29

LADBROKE EUROPEAN FREE HANDICAP

NEWMARKET, CRAVEN MEETING 1990 (ON THE ROWLEY MILE COURSE) WEDNESDAY, APRIL 18th

The Ladbroke European Free Handicap (Listed Race) with £30,000 added for two-yr-olds only of 1989 (including all 2-yr-olds in the 1989 International Classification), to run as three-yr-olds: lowest weight 7st 7lb; highest weight 9st 7lb. Winner after December 16, 1989, 5lb (acceptance February 28). Seven furlongs Dewhurst Stakes Course (SS30).

Rating		st	lb	SF
125	Machiavellian (USA)	9	7	
120	Argentum	9	2	66
	Digression (USA)	9	2	55
	Jade Robbery (USA)	9	2	
119	Contract Law (USA)	9	1	48
118	Be My Chief (USA)	9	0	74
	Elmaamul (USA)	9	0	63
	Linamix (FR)	9	0	
	Negligent	9	0	76
	Rock City	9	0	79
117	Bleu de France (FR)	8	13	
116	Dead Certain	8	12	69
	Qirmazi (USA)	8	12	
	Septieme Ciel (USA)	8	12	
115	Balla Cove	8	11	80
	Funambule (USA)	8	11	
	The Caretaker	8	11	73
114	Bridal Toast	8	10	52
	Moon Cactus	8	10	64
	Qui Danzig (USA)	8	10	57
	Salsabil	8	10	68
	Snurge	8	10	49
	Somethingdifferent	8	10	75
	Welney	8	10	75
113	Air Music (FR)	8	9	51
	Dashing Blade	8	9	74
	Free At Last	8	9	70
	Pharaoh's Delight	8	9	80
112	Anshan	8	8	71
	Call To Arms	8	8	72
	Chimes of Freedom	8	8	81
	Curia Regis (USA)	8	8	66
	Dr Somerville (USA)	8	8	
	Epicarmo	8	8	
	Ernani	8	8	
	Gharam (USA)	8	8	67
	Honor Rajana (USA)	8	8	
	Horatio Luro (USA)	8	8	
	Line of Thunder (USA)	8	8	73
	Pole Position	8	8	
	Rich and Famous (FR)	8	8	
	Satin Wood	8	8	70
	Silk Slippers (USA)	8	8	58
111	Champagne Gold	8	7	51
	Cullinan (USA)	8	7	73
	Follidays (FR)	8	7	
	Golden Era (USA)	8	7	
	Rafha	8	7	67
	Repercutionist (USA)	8	7	68
110	Alchi (USA)	8	6	
	Book the Band	8	6	72
	Duck and Dive	8	6	82
	Filago (USA)	8	6	
	Go and Go	8	6	66
	Haunting Beauty (USA)	8	6	67
	Houseproud (USA)	8	6	
	Intimiste (USA)	8	6	
	Miss Afrique (FR)	8	6	
	Osario	8	6	74
	Ozone Friendly (USA)	8	6	69
	Pont-Aven	8	6	
	Robellation (USA)	8	6	73
	Roi De Rome (USA)	8	6	
	Slew the Slewor (USA)	8	6	
	Tirol	8	6	67
109	Defensive Play (USA)	8	5	59
	Dorset Duke	8	5	
	Duke of Paducah (USA)	8	5	70
	Fearless Revival	8	5	70
	Makbul	8	5	73
	Mukddaam (USA)	8	5	
	Raj Waki (USA)	8	5	71
	Treble Eight	8	5	49
	Wadood (USA)	8	5	76
108	Arousal	8	4	55
	Belmez (USA)	8	4	79
	Candy Glen	8	4	69
	Cordoba (USA)	8	4	73
	Knight's Baroness	8	4	
	Montendre	8	4	52
	Routillante	8	4	70
	Spinning	8	4	65
	Trireme	8	4	65
	Va Toujours	8	4	78
107	Akamantis	8	3	57
	Baligh	8	3	73
	Karinga Bay	8	3	60
	Mademoiselle Chloe	8	3	81
	Native Twine	8	3	70
	Tanfith (CAN)	8	3	71
	Wajna (USA)	8	3	
	Zoman (USA)	8	3	59

106	Adding	8	2	59
	Atoll	8	2	74
	Dancing Music	8	2	73
	Fujaiyrah	8	2	55
	Golan Heights	8	2	57
	Jovial	8	2	68
	Lord Glen	8	2	80
	Missionary Ridge	8	2	62
	Noble Patriarch	8	2	64
	Old Alliance (USA)	8	2	79
	Qathif (USA)	8	2	73
	Ridgepoint	8	2	60
	Rock Hopper	8	2	
	Rushmore (USA)	8	2	75
105	Alidiva	8	1	75
	Blue Stag	8	1	53
	Dayjur (USA)	8	1	74
	Drayton Special	8	1	57
	Harbour Bar (USA)	8	1	55
	Marquetry (USA)	8	1	59
	Princess Taufan	8	1	76
	Red Henry (USA)	8	1	73
	Tabdea (USA)	8	1	68
104	Berry's Dream	8	0	67
	Daarik	8	0	87
	Green's Leader (USA)	8	0	68
	Grey Duster	8	0	
	Heart of Joy (USA)	8	0	79
	In The Groove	8	0	69
	Marienski (USA)	8	0	62
	Message Pad	8	0	65
	Naval Party	8	0	
	Notley	8	0	76
	Olympic Hero	8	0	68
	Palace Street (USA)	8	0	65
	Petillante	8	0	82
	Please Believe Me	8	0	65
	Remthat Naser	8	0	78
	Royal Academy (USA)	8	0	67
	Royal Fifi (USA)	8	0	65
	Ruby Tiger	8	0	58
	Sardegna	8	0	
	Shavian	8	0	81
	Sheer Precocity	8	0	68
	Soy Roberto (USA)	8	0	77
	Swiss Affair (USA)	8	0	67
	Tod	8	0	65
	Victory Piper (USA)	8	0	76

THREE-YEAR-OLDS OF 1989

A handicap for three-year-olds which have been placed in the first three in Great Britain during 1989 and have been allotted a rating of not less than 100.

1¾m plus

Michelozzo (USA)	8	11
Weld	8	4
Lucky Song (USA)	8	1
Sapience	8	0
Princess Sobieska	7	13
Demawend	7	12
Noble Savage	7	7
Orpheus (USA)	7	7
Ashal	7	2

1m 3f plus

Old Vic	9	8
Cacoethes (USA)	9	2
Aliysa	8	10
Roseate Tern	8	8
Observation Post	8	7
Terimon	8	7
Alydaress (USA)	8	6
Snow Bride (USA)	8	5
Zalazl (USA)	8	5
Golden Pheasant (USA)	8	4
Petite Ile	8	4
Pirate Army (USA)	8	4
e de Nisky	8	3
Prorutori (USA)	8	2
Warrshan (USA)	8	1
Tayyani	8	1
rtic Envoy (USA)	8	0
pritsail	8	0
raashee	7	13
noosh (USA)	7	13
eartic Flame	7	13
phabel	7	12
Husyan (USA)	7	12
Free Sweater (USA)	7	11
N C Owen	7	11
Polar Run (USA)	7	10
Shayraz	7	10
Gran Alba (USA)	7	9
By Charter	7	7
Konigsberg	7	7
Quiet Awakening (USA)	7	7
Shellac	7	7
Destiny Dance (USA)	7	6
Timourtash (USA)	7	6
Wrapping	7	6
Trying For Gold (USA)	7	5
Elmayer (USA)	7	4
Val Recit (FR)	7	4
Jehol	7	3
Prime Display (USA)	7	3
Roblet (USA)	7	3
Fair Prospect	7	2
Operation Wolf	7	2
Rifada	7	2

9½f plus

Nashwan (USA)	9	5
Legal Case	8	11
Dolpour	8	10
Opening Verse (USA)	8	8
Citidancer	8	7
Prince of Dance	8	7
Scenic	8	7
Torjoun (USA)	8	7
Braiswick	8	6
Two Timing (USA)	8	6
Mamaluna (USA)	8	3
Pilot	8	2
Alcando	8	1
High Estate	8	1
Porter Rhodes (USA)	8	1
Batshoof	8	0
Brush Aside (USA)	7	13
Greenwich Papillon	7	13
Lady Shipley	7	13
Life at the Top	7	13
Monastery	7	13
Relief Pitcher	7	13
Tessla (USA)	7	13
Bex (USA)	7	12
Drum Taps (USA)	7	12
Icona (USA)	7	12
Shyoushka	7	12
Mysteries (USA)	7	11
Rambushka (USA)	7	10
Spitfire	7	10
If Memory Serves (USA)	7	9
Arsaan (USA)	7	8
Always on a Sunday	7	7
Dimmer	7	7
Flamingo Road	7	7
Really Brilliant (USA)	7	7
Always Valiant	7	6
Nangara (USA)	7	6
Top Boot	7	6
Jungle Pioneer (USA)	7	3
Green Flag (USA)	7	2
Marcinkus	7	2

	st	lb
Marine Diver	7	2
Prince Ibrahim	7	2

7f plus

	st	lb
Zilzal (USA)	9	8
Polish Precedent (USA)	9	3
Golden Opinion (USA)	9	0
Distant Relative	8	12
Green Line Express (USA)	8	11
Exbourne (USA)	8	10
Markofdistinction	8	8
Shaadi (USA)	8	8
Magic Gleam (USA)	8	7
Shining Steel	8	6
Ensconse (USA)	8	5
Greensmith	8	4
Pass the Peace	8	4
Gold Seam (USA)	8	3
Great Commotion (USA)	8	3
Monsagem (USA)	8	3
Musical Bliss (USA)	8	3
Kerrera	8	1
Lunar Mover (USA)	8	1
Magical Strike	8	1
Mirror Black	8	1
Aldbourne	8	0
Cottenham	8	0
Princess Accord (USA)	8	0
Russian Bond (USA)	8	0
Samoan (USA)	8	0
Dancing Tribute (USA)	7	13
Weldnaas (USA)	7	13
Light of Morn (USA)	7	12
Rain Burst	7	12
Russian Royal (USA)	7	12
Sabotage (FR)	7	12
Comic Talent	7	11
Bequest (USA)	7	9
Folly Foot	7	9
Kerita	7	9
Mon Tresor	7	9
Muhbubh (USA)	7	9
Safawan	7	8
Just Three	7	7
Polar Boy (USA)	7	7
Triode (USA)	7	7
Known Ranger	7	6
Moviegoer	7	6
Sharks	7	6
Awayed (USA)	7	5
Guest Artiste	7	5
Serious Trouble	7	5
Sure Gold	7	4
Malevich (USA)	7	2
Tatsfield	7	2

5f plus

	st	lb
Danehill (USA)	8	11
Statoblest	8	7
Tigani	8	7
Dancing Dissident (USA)	8	4
Shuttlecock Corner (USA)	8	0
Superpower (USA)	8	0
Green's Caneletto (USA)	7	12
Lugana Beach	7	11
Wonder Dancer (USA)	7	9
Thorn Dance (USA)	7	8
Didicoy (USA)	7	6
Access Travel	7	5
Blyton Lad	7	5
Desert Dawn	7	5
Hadif (USA)	7	4
Almost Blue	7	3
Paley Prince (USA)	7	3
Silca Supreme	7	3
Four Legged Friend	7	2

FOUR-YEAR-OLDS AND UP OF 1989

A handicap for four-year-olds and upwards which have been placed in the first three in Great Britain during 1989 and have been allotted a rating of not less than 100.

1¾m plus

	age	st	lb
Sadeem (USA)	6	8	6
Mountain Kingdom	5	8	0
Mazzacano	4	7	13
Zaffaran (USA)	4	7	13
Lazaz (USA)	4	7	11
Zero Watt (USA)	5	7	10
Ala Hounak	5	7	7
Arden	5	7	6
Arizelos	4	7	6
Sergeyevich	5	7	4
Upper Strata	4	7	4
Lauries Crusador	4	7	3
Nomadic Way (USA)	4	7	2

1m 3f plus

	age	st	lb
Carroll House	4	9	2
Unfuwain (USA)	4	9	1
Ibn Bay	5	8	12
Assatis (USA)	4	8	9
Sheriff's Star	4	8	8
Highland Chieftain	6	8	7
Top Class	4	8	5
Per Quod (USA)	4	8	4
Tralos (USA)	4	8	2
Apache	4	8	1
Green Adventure	4	8	0
Albadr (USA)	4	7	13
Indian Queen	4	7	11
Waterfield	5	7	11
Atlaal	4	7	10
Glacial Storm (USA)	4	7	10
Sudden Victory	5	7	10
Sesame	4	7	8
Nemesia	4	7	7
Firelight Fiesta	4	7	6
My Lamb	4	7	5

9½f plus

	age	st	lb
Ile de Chypre	4	8	11
Kefaah (USA)	4	8	7
Petrullo	4	8	2
Emmson	4	8	1
Pelorus	4	8	0
Shady Heights	5	8	0
Hibernian gold (USA)	4	7	13
Insan (USA)	4	7	11
Sudden Love (FR)	4	7	10
Dust Devil	4	7	7
Lapierre	4	7	7
Main Objective	4	7	5
Unknown Quantity	4	7	2

7f plus

	age	st	lb
Warning	4	9	1
Most Welcome	5	8	11
Indian Skimmer (USA)	5	8	9
French Stress (USA)	4	8	8
Reprimand	4	8	6
Beau Sher	6	8	5
Luzum	5	7	13
Sweet Chesne (FR)	4	7	13
Charmer	4	7	12
Alquoz (USA)	4	7	11
Rambo's Hall	4	7	11
Always Fair (USA)	4	7	10
Hoy	4	7	10
Hello Vaigly	4	7	7
Vague Shot	6	7	7
Point House	4	7	5
Wood Dancer (USA)	4	7	5
Colway Rally	5	7	3
Tay Wharf	4	7	3
Electric Lady	4	7	2

5f plus

	age	st	lb
Cadeaux Genereux	4	8	12
Indian Ridge	4	8	10
Cricket Ball (USA)	6	8	8
Gallic League	4	8	6
Nabeel Dancer (USA)	4	8	4
Silver Fling (USA)	4	8	4
A Prayer For Wings	5	8	2
Mac's Fighter	4	8	2
Point of Light	4	8	2
Chummy's Favourite	4	8	1
Princess Athena	4	8	1
Carol's Treasure	5	8	0
Savahra Sound	4	8	0
Intimidate	4	7	8
Poyle George	4	7	8
Sharp Reminder	5	7	8
Teeming Shore (USA)	4	7	8
Ajanac	5	7	4
Perion	7	7	2

IRISH CLASSIFICATIONS

TWO-YEAR-OLDS OF 1989

For two-year-olds only that ran in 1989 and are assessed by handicappers Michael T. Byrne and Ciaran Kennelly at a rating of 95 or more relative to the European Classifications. Only winners included for horses trained outside Ireland.

	st	lb
The Caretaker	8	11
Dashing Blade	8	9
Pharaoh's Delight	8	9
Chimes of Freedom (USA)	8	8
Go and Go	8	6
Pictorial (USA)	8	5
Wedding Bouquet	8	4
Aminata	8	0
Royal Academy	8	0
Victory Piper (USA)	8	0
Armanasco	7	12
Mr Brooks	7	12
Polar Bird	7	11
Hero's Welcome	7	9
Teach Dha Mhile	7	9
Quebec	7	8
Legal Verdict	7	7
Missing You	7	7
Simply Terrific	7	7
Single Combat (USA)	7	7
Endless Joy	7	6
Tanwi	7	6
Thetford Forest	7	6
Annie Laurie	7	5
Ereng (USA)	7	5
Gilt Note	7	5
Music Prospector (USA)	7	5
Neat Dish (CAN)	7	5
Sadlers Congress	7	5
War Chest (USA)	7	5

THREE-YEAR-OLDS OF 1989

Weights shown in this handicap are published for information only and are intended as an indication of the relative merit of the horses that have been included. For three year olds only assessed at a rating of 100 or more relative to the 1989 European International Classification. Only winners included for horses trained outside Ireland.

1¾m

Tyrone Bridge	8	1

1m 3f plus

Old Vic	9	8
Alydaress (USA)	8	6
Petite Ile	8	4
Beyond The Lake	7	9
Gran Alba (USA)	7	9
Classic Sport (USA)	7	7

9½f plus

Citidancer	8	7
Phantom Breeze	8	1
Porter Rhodes (USA)	8	1
Bex (USA)	7	12
Tursanah (USA)	7	10
Slender Style (USA)	7	8
Lone Runner	7	4

7f plus

Distant Relative	8	12
Shaadi (USA)	8	8
Ensconse (USA)	8	5
Sagamore (USA)	7	12
Classic Fame (USA)	7	10
Run To Jenny	7	10
Upward Trend	7	10
Honoria (USA)	7	8
Saratogan (USA)	7	8
Elegance In Design	7	7
Just Three	7	7
Tantum Ergo	7	6
Awayed (USA)	7	5
Kyra	7	5
Great Lakes	7	4
Pirouette	7	4
Blasted Heath	7	3

5f plus

Puissance	8	0
Corwyn Bay	7	13
Eloquent Minister (USA)	7	11

FOUR-YEAR-OLDS AND UPWARDS

Weights shown in this handicap are published for information only and are intended as an indication of the relative merit of the horses that have been included. For four year olds and upwards assessed at a rating of 100 or more relative to the 1989 European International Classification. Only winners included for horses trained outside Ireland.

1m 3f plus

	st	lb
Carroll House	9	2
Indian Queen	7	11

9½f plus

	st	lb
Ile de Chypre	8	11
Executive Perk	8	3
Elementary	8	2
Noora Abu	8	0
Little Bighorn	7	11

7f plus

	st	lb
Milieu	7	10
Llyn Gwynant	7	10
Cielamour (USA)	7	7
Wood Dancer (USA)	7	5

5f plus

	st	lb
Gallic League	8	6
Big Shuffle (USA)	8	3
A Prayer For Wings	8	2
Point of Light	8	2
Handsome Sailor	7	12
Astraeus (USA)	7	7

FRENCH FREE HANDICAP

(For two-year-olds of 1989) (Handicap Libre)

	st	lb
Machiavellian (USA)	9	7
Jade Robbery (USA)	9	2
Linamix	9	0
Rock City (IRE)	9	0
Bleu de France	8	13
Qirmazi (USA)	8	12
Septième Ciel (USA)	8	12
Funambule (USA)	8	11
Salsabil (IRE)	8	10
Snurge (IRE)	8	10
Dr. Somerville (USA)	8	8
Ernani (IRE)	8	8
Honor Rajana (USA)	8	8
Horatio Luro (USA)	8	8
Pole Position (GB)	8	8
Rich and Famous	8	8
Follidays	8	7
Golden Era (USA)	8	7
Repercutionist (USA)	8	7
Alchi (USA)	8	6
Filago (USA)	8	6
Houseproud (USA)	8	6
Intimiste (USA)	8	6
Miss Afrique	8	6
Ozone Friendly (USA)	8	6
Pont Aven (IRE)	8	6
Roi de Rome (USA)	8	6
Slew the Slewor (USA)	8	6
Anna's Honor (USA)	8	5
Boston Two Step (USA)	8	5
Boxing Day	8	5
Company (USA)	8	5
Evocatrice (GB)	8	5
Goofalik (USA)	8	5
Houmayoun	8	5
King White	8	5
Lituanien	8	5
Mackla (IRE)	8	5
Noblely (USA)	8	5
Pagan Gold (USA)	8	5
Pas Facile	8	5
Princess Player (USA)	8	5
River of Light (USA)	8	5
Robin des Bois (USA)	8	5
Sharp Sass (USA)	8	5
Sifting Gold (USA)	8	5
Theatre Critic (IRE)	8	5
Zinarelle	8	5

INTERNATIONAL CLASSIFICATION

For three-year-olds only which, during 1989, have run in France, Germany, Great Britain, Ireland or Italy and are jointly assessed at a rating of 112 or above by the official handicappers.

1¾m plus

Trained		st	lb
GB	Michelozzo (USA)	8	11
FR	Turgeon (USA)	8	4
GB	Weld (GB)	8	4
FR	Mardonius (IRE)	8	3
FR	Lou Biella (FR)	8	1
GB	Lucky Song (USA)	8	1
IRE	Tyrone Bridge (IRE)	8	1
GB	Sapience (IRE)	8	0
FR	Sharnfold (IRE)	8	0

1m 3f plus

GB	Old Vic (GB)	9	8
GB	Cacoethes (USA)	9	2
GER	Mondrian (GER)	8	12
FR	Behera (IRE)	8	11
GB	Aliysa (IRE)	8	10
FR	Sierra Roberta (FR)	8	10
FR	Young Mother (FR)	8	10
GB	Roseate Tern (GB)	8	8
GB	Observation Post (IRE)	8	7
GB	Terimon (GB)	8	7
GB	Alydaress (USA)	8	6
FR	Colorado Dancer (IRE)	8	6
GB	Snow Bride (USA)	8	5
GB	Zalazl (USA)	8	5
FR	Borromini (GB)	8	4
FR	Golden Pheasant (USA)	8	4
FR	Louis Cyphre (IRE)	8	4
IRE	Petite Ile (IRE)	8	4
GB	Pirate Army (USA)	8	4
FR	Deliorman (IRE)	8	3
GB	Ile de Nisky (GB)	8	3
FR	Passionaria (FR)	8	3
GB	Prorutori (USA)	8	2
FR	Sherarda (FR)	8	2
FR	French Glory (IRE)	8	1
FR	Mill Pond (FR)	8	1
GB	Taishan (GER)	8	1
GB	Warrshan (USA)	8	1
GB	Zayyani (IRE)	8	1
GB	Artic Envoy (USA)	8	0
FR	Ode (USA)	8	0
GB	Spritsail (GB)	8	0

9½f plus

GB	Nashwan (USA)	9	5
FR	Dancehall (USA)	8	13
FR	Creator (GB)	8	12
GB	Legal Case (IRE)	8	11
GB	Dolpour (IRE)	8	10
FR	Lady In Silver (USA)	8	9
FR	Norberto (CAN)	8	8
FR	Louveterie (USA)	8	8
GB	Opening Verse (USA)	8	8
GB	Citidancer (IRE)	8	7
GB	Prince of Dance (IRE)	8	7
GB	Scenic (IRE)	8	7
GB	Torjoun (USA)	8	7
GB	Braiswick (GB)	8	6
GER	Filia Ardross (GB)	8	6
FR	In The Wings (GB)	8	6
GB	Two Timing (USA)	8	6
FR	Galetto (FR)	8	5
ITY	Yellow King (IRE)	8	5
FR	River Warden (USA)	8	3
FR	Val des Bois (FR)	8	3
FR	Along All (GB)	8	2
GB	Mamaluna (USA)	8	2
GB	Pilot (GB)	8	2
FR	Premier Amour (IRE)	8	2
FR	Rose de Crystal (FR)	8	2
FR	Sovereign Water (FR)	8	2
GER	Turfkonig (GER)	8	2

		st	lb
GB	Alcando (IRE)	8	1
FR	Bellaride (FR)	8	1
GB	High Estate (IRE)	8	1
IRE	Phantom Breeze (IRE)	8	1
GB	Porter Rhodes (USA)	8	1
FR	Tartas (FR)	8	1
GB	Batshoof (IRE)	8	0
FR	J'Ai Deux Amours (FR)	8	0

7f plus

		st	lb
GB	Zilzal (USA)	9	8
FR	Polish Precedent (USA)	9	3
FR	Golden Opinion (USA)	9	0
GB	Distant Relative (IRE)	8	12
FR	Kendor (FR)	8	12
GB	Green Line Express (USA)	8	11
GB	Exbourne (USA)	8	10
FR	Local Talent (USA)	8	8
GB	Markofdistinction (GB)	8	8
GB	Shaadi (USA)	8	8
FR	Aliocha (USA)	8	7
FR	Goldneyev (USA)	8	7
GB	Magic Gleam (USA)	8	7
FR	Ocean Falls (IRE)	8	7
FR	Pearl Bracelet (USA)	8	7
GB	Shining Steel (GB)	8	7
GB	Ensconse (USA)	8	5
GB	Greensmith (GB)	8	4
FR	Navratilovna (USA)	8	4
GB	Pass the Peace (IRE)	8	4
FR	Star Touch (FR)	8	4
FR	Go Milord (FR)	8	3
GB	Gold Seam (USA)	8	3
GB	Great Commotion (USA)	8	3
GB	Monsagem (USA)	8	3
GB	Musical Bliss (USA)	8	3
FR	Lady Winner (FR)	8	2
FR	Lowell (USA)	8	2
GB	Sikeston (USA)	8	2
FR	Keniant (FR)	8	1
GB	Kerrera (IRE)	8	1
GB	Lunar Mover (GB)	8	1
GB	Magical Strike (USA)	8	1
GB	Mirror Black (IRE)	8	1
GB	Aldbourne (IRE)	8	0
FR	Be Exclusive (IRE)	8	0
GB	Cottenham (GB)	8	0
FR	Lightning Fire (GB)	8	0
FR	Lioubovnik (USA)	8	0
GB	Princess Accord (USA)	8	0
GB	Russian Bond (USA)	8	0
GB	Samoan (USA)	8	0

5f plus

		st	lb
GB	Danehill (USA)	8	11
GB	Statoblest (IRE)	8	7
GB	Tigani (GB)	8	7
GB	Dancing Dissident (USA)	8	4
FR	Or Acier (USA)	8	0
IRE	Puissance (GB)	8	0
GB	Shuttlecock Corner (USA)	8	0
GB	Superpower (GB)	8	0

INTERNATIONAL CLASSIFICATION

For four-year-olds and upwards which, during 1989, have run in France, Germany, Great Britain, Ireland or Italy and are jointly assessed at a rating of 112 (8st 0lb) or above by the official handicappers.

1¾m plus

		age	st	lb
FR	Top Sunrise (FR)	4	8	7
GB	Sadeem (USA)	6	8	6
FR	Rachmaninov (FR)	4	8	3
FR	Trebrook (FR)	5	8	2
GB	Mountain Kingdom (USA)	5	8	0
FR	Vaguely Pleasant (FR)	7	8	0

1m 3f plus

		age	st	lb
GB	Carroll House (IRE)	4	9	2

GB	Unfuwain (USA)	4	9	1
FR	Boyatino (FR)	5	8	13
FR	Saint Andrews (FR)	5	8	13
GB	Ibn Bey (GB)	5	8	12
FR	Star Lift (GB)	5	8	11
FR	Robore (FR)	4	8	10
GB	Alwuhush (USA)	4	8	9
GB	Assatis (USA)	4	8	9
GB	Sheriff's Star (GB)	4	8	8
GB	Highland Chieftain (IRE)	6	8	7
ITY	Tisserand (ITY)	4	8	5
GB	Top Class (GB)	4	8	5
GB	Per Quod (USA)	4	8	4
GER	Britannia (GER)	4	8	2
GER	Luigi (GER)	4	8	2
GB	Tralos (USA)	4	8	2
GB	Apache (GB)	4	8	1
ITY	Knight Line Dancer (IRE)	4	8	1
FR	Summer Trip (USA)	4	8	1
GB	Green Adventure (USA)	4	8	0

9½f plus

GB	Ile de Chypre (GB)	4	8	11
GB	Kefaah (USA)	4	8	7
FR	Mansonnien (FR)	5	8	7
ITY	Welsh Guide (IRE)	4	8	7
FR	Fijar Tango (FR)	4	8	5
IRE	Executive Perk (IRE)	4	8	3
FR	Hello Calder (GB)	4	8	3
IRE	Elementary (IRE)	6	8	2
GB	Petrullo (GB)	4	8	2
GB	Emmson (IRE)	4	8	1
GER	Medicus (GER)	5	8	1
ITY	Love the Groom (USA)	5	8	0
IRE	Noora Abu (IRE)	7	8	0
GB	Pelorus (GB)	4	8	0
GB	Shady Heights (GB)	5	8	0

7f plus

GB	Warning (GB)	4	9	1
GB	Most Welcome (GB)	5	8	11
FR	Squill (USA)	4	8	10
GB	Indian Skimmer (USA)	4	8	9
FR	French Stress (USA)	4	8	8
FR	Gabina (USA)	4	8	8
FR	Royal Touch (IRE)	4	8	7
FR	Athyka (USA)	4	8	7
GB	Reprimand (GB)	4	8	7
GB	Beau Sher (GB)	6	8	5
GER	Just A Flutter (GB)	5	8	5
FR	In Extremis (USA)	4	8	3
GB	Red Glow (GB)	4	8	2
GER	Zampano (GER)	5	8	2
FR	Miss Kenmare (FR)	5	8	1
GER	Alkalde (GER)	4	8	0
FR	Malaspina (IRE)	5	8	0
FR	Val des Pres (FR)	5	8	0

5f plus

GB	Cadeaux Genereux (GB)	4	8	12
GB	Indian Ridge (IRE)	4	8	10
FR	Cricket Ball (USA)	6	8	8
GB	Gallic League (GB)	4	8	6
GB	Nabeel Dancer (USA)	4	8	4
GB	Silver Fling (USA)	4	8	4
IRE	Big Shuffle (USA)	5	8	3
CAN	Zadracarta (CAN)	4	8	3
GB	A Prayer for Wings (IRE)	5	8	2
GB	Mac's Fighter (GB)	4	8	2
GB	Point of Light (GB)	4	8	2
GB	Chummy's Favourite (GB)	4	8	1
FR	Holst (USA)	5	8	1
GB	Princess Athena (IRE)	4	8	1
FR	Astronef (IRE)	5	8	0
GB	Carol's Treasure (GB)	5	8	0
GB	Savahra Sound (GB)	4	8	0

RACEFORM BOOKS
Spring 1990

RACEFORM 1989 FLAT ANNUAL. All last season's form on the Flat with comments on running.
The Jockey Club's Official Record £19.00

SYSTEMATIC BETTING. C. Van Der Wheil steers the backer towards a more sensible and methodical approach to betting £2.95

TIMECHECK '89. All Speed Figures of 30 and above achieved last Flat, showing where, when, at what distance and on what going £8.95

100 WINNERS FOR 1990. Pen portraits by Raceform experts on horses likely to do particularly well during the coming Flat season £2.95

HOW TO WIN AT HANDICAP RACING by Patrick Killgallon £4.95

GREYHOUND RACING FOR PROFIT by Sean Connolly £2.95

HOW TO FIND VALUE WHEN BETTING by Malcolm Howard £4.95

CHASEFORM ANNUAL 1988-89. All last season's N.H. form with comments on how they ran and jumped £17.00

All prices include postage and packing
Remit with order to

RACEFORM LTD.
COMPTON, NEWBURY, BERKSHIRE, RG16 0NL

Access and Visa cardholders can order by telephone at any time on 0635 578080

HIGH–PRICED YEARLINGS OF 1989 AT TATTERSALL'S SALES

The following yearlings realised 66,000 guineas and over at Tattersall's Sales in 1989:-

Name and Breeding	Vendor	Purchaser	Gns
Ch c Nureyev (USA)—Hitting Irish (USA)	Mellon Stud	Mr L. Lillingston	700,000
B c Sadler's Wells (USA)—Krakow	Camas Park Stud	B.B.A. (Ireland)	680,000
Soha (USA) B f Dancing Brave (USA)—Paris Royal	Sallyview Estates Stud Farm	Darley Stud Management	600,000
B f Nijinsky (CAN)—La Dame du Lac (USA)	Barronstown Stud	Mr J. S. Bolger	580,000
B c Sadler's Wells (USA)—Miss Allowed (USA)	Camas Park Stud	B.B.A. (Ireland)	580,000
Fitahl (USA) B c Chief's Crown (USA)—Love's Dream (FR)	Mellon Stud	Shadwell Estates	560,000
Axe (GB) Ch c Kris—Russian Ribbon (USA)	ZIW Associates	B.B.A. (Ireland) Ltd	520,000
Reem Albaraari (GB) B f Sadler's Wells (USA)—Habibti	Sussex Stud Ltd.	Darley Stud Management	510,000
B c Green Desert (USA)—Cockade	Stowell Hill	Darley Stud Management	500,000
Mafatin (IRE) B f Sadler's Wells (USA)—Glass Slipper	Camas Park Stud	D. Minton Bloodstock	410,000
B c Rainbow Quest (USA)—Moon Parade	Longfield Stud	B.B.A. (Ireland)	400,000
Rahif (GB) B c Shirley Heights—Vaguely	Floors Stud	Shadwell Estates	380,000
Ch c Lyphard (USA)—Miss Summer	Stowell Hill	Darley Stud Management	380,000
B c Dancing Brave (USA)—True Lady (USA)	Cotswold Stud	Juddmonte Farms	370,000
B c High Top—Marwell	Eyrefield Lodge Stud	Dr. M. V. O'Brien	370,000
Venango (GB) B c Shirley Heights—Val d'Erica	Mount Coote Stud	Juddmonte Farms	360,000
B c Sadler's Wells (USA)—Aunty (FR)	Sussex Stud Ltd.	Gainsborough Stud	350,000
B c Sadler's Wells (USA)—Colorspin (FR)	Meon Valley Stud	Darley Stud Management	340,000
Playup (GB) Ch f High Line—Putupon	Bloomsbury Stud	Countess Esterhazy	330,000
Lady Kris (IRE) Ch f Kris—Lady Graustark (USA)	Sussex Stud Ltd.	British Bloodstock Agency	330,000
Safa (GB) B f Shirley Heights—Beveridge (USA)	Hesmonds Stud	Darley Stud Management	330,000
B c Ahonoora—African Doll	Gurteenard and Kiltinan Farms Inc.	Mrs A. Skiffington	320,000
Un Souverain (GB) B c Kenmare (FR)—Serenita (FR)	Mount Coote Stud	Gainsborough Stud	290,000
Bone China (IRE) B f Sadler's Wells (USA)—Wedgewod Blue	Camas Park Stud	B.B.A (Ireland)	290,000
La Sky (IRE) B f Law Society (USA)—Maryinsky (USA)	Corbally Stud	Mr M. Bramwell	260,000
B c Alleged (USA)—Woodstream (USA)	Lyonstown Stud	Mr M. Bramwell	250,000
B f Green Desert (USA)—Allegedly Blue	Heatherwold Stud	Gainsborough Stud	250,000
Luchiroverte (IRE) B c Slip Anchor—Green Lucia	Stonethorn Stud Farms Ltd.	British Bloodstock Agency	250,000
B f Green Desert (USA)—Clunk Click	Yeomanstown Lodge Stud	Gainsborough Stud	240,000
Sheroog (USA) Br f Shareef Dancer (USA)—Fall Aspen (USA)	Sussex Stud	Darley Stud Management	240,000
Sharp Circle (IRE) B f Sure Blade (USA)—Centre Piece	Lodge Park Stud	Mr M. Bramwell	240,000
B f Sure Blade (USA)—Smeralda (GER)	Mounte Coote and Tsarina Studs	Darley Stud Management	230,000
B f Lomond (USA)—Burghclere	Barronstown Stud	Mr S. Cosgrove	220,000
B f Shirley Heights—Crystal Fountain	Islanmore Stud	Addison Racing	220,000
B c Shadeed (USA)—Millicent (USA)	Mounte Coote Stud	Curragh Bloodstock Agency	210,000
Ch f Sharpen Up—Repetitious	Ballygallon Stud	Darley Stud Management	210,000
Wiorno (GB) B c Wassl—Just You Wait	Mayday Investment Co.	Agencé Fairway	210,000
B f Alzao (USA)—Chrism	Mount Coote Stud	Addison Racing	200,000

Ch c Be My Guest (USA)—Smarten Up	Major and Mrs R. B. Kennard	Z. H. L. Associates	200,000
Jahafil (GB) B c Rainbow Quest (USA)—River Spey	Hesmonds Stud	Shadwell Estates	200,000
Guadalcanal (IRE) B c Sadler's Wells—Red Coral (AUS)	Tullamaine Castle Stud	B.B.A. (Ireland)	200,000
Performance (GB) Ch c Shadeed (USA)—Pushy	Bloomsbury Stud	Shadwell Estates	200,000
B c Storm Bird (CAN)—La Noblesse (USA)	Camas Park Stud	Mr D. Weld	200,000
B c Rainbow Quest (USA)—Salidar	Tullamaine Castle Stud	Miss A. Scrope	190,000
B f Danzig (USA)—Queen Sucree	Cotswold Stud	Mr E. A. Stuner	170,000
Br f Rousillon (USA)—Lady of Chalon (USA)	Whitsbury Manor Stud	Shadwell Estates	170,000
Ch f Sir Ivor—Patia	Cotswold Stud	British Bloodstock Agency	165,000
Ch c Sure Blade (USA)—Impudent Miss	Mount Coote Stud	Mr I. Balding	165,000
Jumped Up (IRE) B c Last Tycoon—Sea Harrier	Hilltown Stud	Juddmonte Farms	160,000
Society Prince (IRE) B c Law Society—Princess Pati	Ardenode Stud	Mr A. Penfold	160,000
Valadina (GB) B f Lomond—Arkadina (USA)	Cotswold Stud	Dr M. Brossman	160,000
B f Slew O'Gold (USA)—Fenney Mill	Airlie Stud	Darley Stud Management	155,000
B c Pennine Walk—First Blush	Airlie Stud	Addison Racing	150,000
B f Sadler's Wells (USA)—Intrepid Lady (USA)	Lyonstown Stud	Mr A. Cooper	150,000
B f Sadler's Wells (USA)—Stylish Genie (USA)	Barronstown Stud	Darley Stud Management	150,000
Formal Occasion (IRE) B f Shirley Heights—Princess Tiara	Camas Park Stud	British Bloodstock Agency	150,000
Classic Charm (GB) Ch c Be My Guest (USA)—Triagonal	Hesmonds Stud	Classic Thoroughbreds	145,000
Llangollen (IRE) B f Caerleon (USA)—Keep the Thought (USA)	Cotswold Stud	Mr T. Stack	145,000
Dartrey (IRE) B f Darshaan—Secala (USA)	Airlie Stud	Darley Stud Management	145,000
Elfaslah (IRE) B f Green Desert—Fair of the Furze	Airlie Stud	Shadwell Estates	145,000
B c Ahonoora—Brickfield Queen	Northmore Stud Farm	Mrs A. Skiffington	140,000
Murooj (USA) Ch f Diesis—Sancta Rose	Pegasus Stud/Champlain Corp.	Darley Stud Management	140,000
Bold As Love (GB) B f Lomond (USA)—Domynga	Mr G. Leigh	Darley Stud Management	140,000
Missing Love (IRE) Ch f Thatching—Miss Loving	Yeomanstown Lodge Stud	Mr S. Cosgrove	140,000
B f Alydar (USA)—Wac (USA)	Cotswold Stud	Mr D. Garvin	135,000
B c Green Desert (USA)—Solar	Charlton Down Stud	Mr A. R. G. Cherry-Downes	135,000
Revif (FR) Gr c Kenmare (FR)—Reverente (FR)	Hesmonds Stud	British Bloodstock Agency	135,000
Ch f Rainbow Quest (USA)—Katie May	Tullamaine Castle Stud	Mr M. Bramwell	135,000
B c Seattle Song (USA)—Waterloo	Mount Coote Stud	Mr D. K. Weld	135,000
Ch c Secreto (USA)—Plains and Simple (USA)	Tullamaine Castle Stud	Mr J. Delahooke	135,000
Secret Silence (GB) Br c Secretariat (USA)—Dame Margot (USA)	Stetchworth Park Stud Ltd.	Mr I. Balding	130,000
B or Br c Roberto (USA)—Tea and Roses (USA)	Campbell Stud	Darley Stud Management	125,000
Regal Embers (IRE) B c Glow (USA)—Royal Sister II	Ballymorris Studs	Mrs S. Piggott	120,000
Ch f Nijinsky (CAN)—Sex Appeal (USA)	Lyonstown Stud	Mr A. Sime	120,000
Raafid (GB) B c Shareef Dancer (USA)—Gerardmer (FR)	Someries Stud	Darley Stud Management	120,000
B c Alzao (USA)—Hedwige	Bellewstown Farm Stud	Mr A. R. G. Cherry-Downes	110,000
Lyphar Dancer (GB) B c Bellypha—Western Gem	Mr J. M. Greetham	Miss A Scrope	110,000
B f Sadler's Wells (USA)—Arrangement	Manor House Stud	D. Minton Bloodstock	110,000
Manhal (GB) B c Sure Blade (USA)—Nordica	Shutford Stud	Darley Stud Management	110,000
Ikteshaf (GB) B c Green Desert (USA)—Colourful (FR)	Sussex Stud Ltd.	Mr B. Hanbury	105,000
B c Law Society (USA)—Queen of the Brush	Mount Coote Stud	B.B.A. (Ireland) Ltd.	105,000

Lot	Vendor	Purchaser	Price
Tiswa (USA) Ch f Lyphard (USA)—Happy Bride	Lanwades Stud	Eagle Stone Farm	105,000
Ch f Lyphard (USA)—Jubilous (USA)	Northmore Stud Farm	Mr D. St. George	105,000
Mahaasin (GB) B f Bellypha—Dame Ashfield	Laharna Ltd.	Darley Stud Management	100,000
B f Dancing Brave (USA)—High and Dry	Windfields Farm (CAN)	British Blodstock Agency	100,000
B c El Gran Senor (USA)—Wising Up (USA)	Camas Park Stud	B.B.A. (Ireland) Ltd.	100,000
B c Green Desert (USA)—Dancing Meg (USA)	Hesmonds Stud	Mr M. Ryan	100,000
B f Pennine Walk—Pyjamarous	Camas Park Stud	Mr D. Weld	100,000
B f Secreto (USA)—Targa (USA)	Cotswold Stud	Curragh Bloodstock Agency	100,000
Alywar (USA) Ch c Alydar (USA)—Black Eyed Lucy (USA)	Campbell Stud	Mr M. Bramwell	98,000
Shadideen (USA) Ch c Shadeed (USA)—Allegretta	Haras d'Etreham	Mr A. Penfold	96,000
Ch c Be My Guest (USA)—Crown Godiva	Cotswold Stud	J. Warren Bloodstock	94,000
B f Law Society (USA)—Bella Senora (USA)	Haras de Fresnay-Le Buffard	D. Minton Bloodstock	94,000
B f Nomination—Olderfleet	Tyrwhitt Stud	British Bloodstock Agency	94,000
B c Al Nasr (FR)—Dabbiana (CAN)	Adstock Manor Stud	British Bloodstock Agency	92,000
Sheikh Albadou (GB) B c Green Desert (USA)—Sanctuary	Highclere Stud	Gainsborough Stud	92,000
Br c Sharpen Up—Bank Examiner (USA)	Stowell Hill	Mr H. Merry	92,000
Ramz (IRE) Ch f The Minstrel (CAN)—Bear's Affair	Tsarina Stud	Shadwell Estates	92,000
High Assault (USA) B f Topsider (USA)—Electric Fanny (USA)	Cotswold Stud	Darley Stud Management	92,000
B f Alzao (USA)—Romanee Conti	Kiltinan Farms Inc.	Mr P. M. Brant	90,000
B f Dancing Brave (USA)—Santa's Sister	Mount Coote Stud	Heron Bloodstock	90,000
Midifina (GB) B f Green Desert (USA)—Vielle	Haresfoot Stud	Mr B. Hanbury	90,000
High Grade (GB) B c High Top—Bright Sun	Littleton Stud	Mr A. Penfold	90,000
Blood Pigeon (IRE) B f Thatching—Mariakova (USA)	Raffin Stud	Mr A. Penfold	90,000
B f Sir Ivor—Lady Norcliffe (USA)	Hesmonds Stud	Mr J. T. Doyle	89,000
Be Devious (GB) B f Bering—Ulterior Motive	Arrow Farm and Stud	Mr M. Bramwell	88,000
Inheritance (IRE) B c Last Tycoon—Unknown Lady (USA)	Knocktoran Stud	Juddmonte Farms	86,000
Ch c Shahrastani (USA)—Quilloquick (USA)	Mounte Coote Stud	Mr T. Stack	85,000
B c Lomond (USA)—Gift Wrapped	Sussex Stud Ltd.	B.B.A. (Ireland) Ltd.	84,000
B c Niniski (USA)—Petty Purse	Overbury Stud	British Bloodstock Agency	84,000
Desert Ditty (GB) B f Green Desert (USA)—Royal Loft	Mr and Mrs P. D. Player	W. Edmeades Bloodstock	82,000
Ch c Persian Bold—Zedative (FR)	Islanmore Stud	Equine Investments	82,000
Occhiobello (GB) B c Sadler's Wells (USA)—Catherines Well	Ashtown House Stud	B.B.A. (Italia)	82,000
B c Sharpen Up—Petillante (USA)	Lordship and Egerton Studs Ltd.	Mrs A. Skiffington	82,000
Sea Breaker (IRE) B c Glow (USA)—Surfing	Airlie Stud	Mr M. Ryan	80,000
B f Lomond (USA)—Millieme	Camas Park Stud	Mr P. Shanahan	80,000
Recherchee (GB) B f Rainbow Quest (USA)—Princess Arabella	Lanwades Stud	Lord John Fitzgerald	80,000
Red Rainbow (GB) B c Rainbow Quest (USA)—Red Berry	Mr D. F. Bradstock	D. Metcalfe Bloodstock	80,000
B c Sadler's Wells (USA)—Poquito Queen (CAN)	Lordship and Egerton Studs	Horse France	80,000
B f Sadler's Wells (USA)—Vive La Reine	Lyonstown Stud	Mr T. Stack	80,000
Duke of Monmouth (USA) B c Secreto (USA)—Queen for the Day (USA)	Tullamaine Castle Stud	Mr M. Ryan	80,000
Marwad (IRE) B c Runnett—Splendid Chance	Islanmore Stud	Curragh Bloodstock Agency	76,000
B c Darshaan—Kamanika (Fr)	Airlie Stud	Mr M. Ryan	75,000
Gr f El Gran Senor (USA)—Flo Russell (USA)	Tullamaine Castle Stud	Mr D. Weld	75,000

B or Br c Green Desert (USA)—Musical Medicine (FR)	Mellon Stud	Shadwell Estates	75,000
B c Kris—Mountain Lodge	Earl of Halifax	Juddmonte Farms	75,000
Ch c Spectacular Bid (USA)—Royal Procession (USA)	Clovelly Stud (USA)	Mr J. Fellows	75,000
Najaah (GB) B f Green Desert (USA) — Sarajill	Adstock Manor Stud	Shadwell Estates	74,000
Russian Liaison (IRE) B or Br f Law Society (USA)—Veruschka	Longfield Stud	D. Minton Bloodstock	74,000
Rainbow Trust (GB) B c Rainbow Quest (USA)—Bandit Queen (FR)	Cotswold Stud	Curragh Bloodstock Agency	74,000
B f Sadler's Wells (USA)—Photo	Sussex Stud Ltd.	B.B.A. (Ireland) Ltd.	74,000
Ch c Sharpo—Pretty Pol	Mr R. H. Cowell	Mr B. Hanbury	74,000
Nouschka (GB) Ch f Ahonoora—Place of Honour	Kiltinan Farms Inc.	J. Warren Bloodstock	72,000
Shafouri (IRE) B c Alzao (USA)—Sauntry	Mr E. Crow	J. Warren Bloodstock	72,000
B c Damister (USA)—Smagiada	Home Stud Inc.	Lady Lonsdale	72,000
B f Glenstal (USA)—Simply Gorgeous	Rathbarry Stud	B.B.A. (Ireland) Ltd.	72,000
Little Rousillon (GB) B c Rousillon (USA)—Carolside	Wickfield Stud	British Bloodstock Agency	72,000
B f Slip Anchor—Bercheba	Overbury Stud	Suprina	72,000
Ch f Golden Act (USA)—Dewan's Niece	Islanmore Stud	B.B.A. (Ireland) Ltd.	70,000
B f Green Desert (USA)—Fear Naught	Mount Coote Stud	B.B.A. (Ireland) Ltd.	70,000
B c Last Tycoon—Clarina	Farmleigh Partners	Mrs A. Skiffington	70,000
Ch c Thatching—Enigma	Islanmore Stud	B.B.A. (Ireland) Ltd.	70,000
Ch f The Minstrel (CAN)—Top Hope	Woods Edge Farm	Mr I. Balding	70,000
B or Br c Topsider (USA)—Evening Silk (USA)	Ballysheehan Stud	B.B.A. (Ireland)	70,000
Ch f Secreto (USA)—Followeveryrainbow (USA)	West Stow Stud	Mr B. Hanbury	68,000
Idol Mio (USA) Ch f Shadeed (USA)—Ionian Idol (USA)	Lanwades Stud	Darley Stud Management	68,000
Bird of Peace (USA) Ch f Sharpen Up—Timotara (USA)	Hesmonds Stud	Classic Thoroughbreds	68,000
Kit Marlowe (GB) B c Faustus (USA)—Imperial Jade	Mr and Mrs D. J. Deer	Mr A. Cherry Downes	66,000
B c Forzando—Champ d'Avril	Mr and Mrs D. A. Hicks	Mr A. F. Budge	66,000
B f Rainbow Quest (USA)—Danger Ahead	Stowell Hill	W. Edmeades Bloodstock	66,000

HIGH – PRICED YEARLINGS OF 1989 AT GOFF'S SALES

The following yearlings realised over 31,000 Irish guineas at Goff's Sales in 1989:-

Name and Breeding	Vendor	Purchaser	Ire Gns
Jungle Dancer (IRE) B c Sadler's Wells (USA)—Forlene	Tullamaine Castle Stud	B.B.A. (Ireland) Ltd.	725,000
Elmarju (IRE) B c Last Tycoon—Flame of Tara	Kilcarn Stud	Shadwell Estate Co. Ltd.	440,000
Nashaat (USA)B c El Gran Senor (USA)—Absentia (USA)	Camas Park Stud	Shadwell Estate Co. Ltd.	420,000
Ch c Nijinsky (CAN)—Kufa Happa (USA)	Camas Park Stud	Classic Thoroughbreds	415,000
Janbiya (IRE) Ch f Kris—Spark of Fire	Gilltown Stud	Shadwell Estate Co. Ltd.	370,000
B c Mr Prospector (USA)—Promising Girl (USA)	Abbeville & Meadow Court	James Delahooke, Esq.	360,000
B f Nijinsky (CAN)—Exotic Bride (USA)	Barronstown Stud	Classic Thoroughbreds	350,000
Gold Law (USA) B c Law Society (USA)—Golden Oriole (USA)	Lyonstown Stud (Agent)	Anthony Penfold Bloodstk.	300,000
B c Shirley Heights—Daisy Warwick (USA)	Stowell Hill	B.B.A. plc.	300,000
Mujadil (USA) B c Storm Bird (CAN)—Vallee Secrete (USA)	Camas Park Stud	Shadwell Estate Co. Ltd.	300,000
B c Green Desert (USA)—Lauretta	Camas Park Stud	James Delahooke, Esq.	280,000
B c Sadler's Wells (USA)—Gertrude Lawrence	Ardenode Stud	Juddmonte Farm Ltd.	260,000
B c Nureyev (USA)—Tremulous (USA)	Camas Park Stud	D. K. Weld, Esq.	260,000
B f Sadler's Wells (USA)—Noble Treasure (USA)	Eyrefield House Stud	Gainsborough Stud Mgt. Ltd.	260,000
Supreme Choice (USA) B c Sovereign Dancer (USA)—Editor's Choice (USA)	Camas Park Stud	H. Branwell, Esq.	250,000
B c Sharpen Up—Royal Heroine	Camas Park Stud	A. S. Budge (Equine) Ltd.	250,000
Lawahed (USA) Ch f Riverman (USA)—Sweet Simone (FR)	Airlie Stud	Shadwell Estate Co. Ltd.	240,000
Classic Cheer (IRE) B c Lomond (USA)—Plume Au Vent	Tullamaine Caste Stud (Agent)	Classic Thoroughbreds	235,000
Shaleel (IRE) B c Last Tycoon—Wood Violet (USA)	Ballysheehan Stud (Agent)	Shadwell Estate Co. Ltd.	230,000
B c Al Nasr (FR)—Modena (USA)	Mount Coote Stud	B.B.A. plc.	220,000
Soderant (GB) B c Kris—Secretive (FR)	Hesmonds Stud	B.B.A. (Ireland) Ltd.	220,000
Slip Ashore (IRE) B f Slip Anchor—Muffitys	Gilltown Stud	J. S. Cosgrove, Esq.	210,000
B c Last Tycoon—Thistlewood	Grangemore Stud	Classic Thoroughbreds	210,000
B c Chief Singer—Dance Card	Tullamaine Castle Stud	Darley Stud Management	205,000
Generous (IRE) Ch c Caerleon (USA)—Doff the Derby (USA)	Partridge Close Stud	Anthony Penfold Bloodstk	200,000
B c Auction Ring (USA)—Age of Elegance	Mount Coote Stud	John Warren Bloodstock	200,000
B f Sadler's Wells (USA)—Osmunda	Grangemore Stud	David Minton Bloodstock	180,000
B c Green Desert (USA)—Etoile De Paris	Tullamaine Castle Stud (Agent)	Curragh Bldstock Agency	175,000
Portrait Painter (IRE) Gr c Sadler's Wells (USA)—Daring Grey	Raffin Stud (Agent)	Classic Thoroughbreds	170,000
Ch c Chief's Crown (USA)—Satinette	Camas Park Stud	Shadwell Estate Co. Ltd.	170,000
Tyche (FR) B f Last Tycoon—Believer	Kirtlington Stud	Classic Thoroughbreds	165,000
Ch c Lomond (USA)—Wish You Were Here (USA)	Tullamaine Castle Stud (Agent)	D. K. Weld, Esq.	165,000
B c Alzao (USA)—Merriment (USA)	Dunmurry Stud Ltd.	Amanda Skiffington	160,000
Jahiz (GB) B c Damister (USA)—Tribal Feast	Yeomanstown Stud	Shadwell Estate Co. Ltd.	160,000
B c The Minstrel (CAN)—Bold Caress	Highclere Stud U.S.A.	Classic Thoroughbreds	155,000
B c Sadler's Wells (USA)—Sensibility (USA)	Gilltown Stud	Mike Ryan (Agent)	155,000
B c Green Desert (USA)—Mrs Bacon	Helescane Stud	Shadwell Estate Co. Ltd.	150,000
B c Last Tycoon—Zillionaire (USA)	Tullamaine Castle Stud (Agent)	Juddmonte Farm, Ltd.	150,000

Gr c Topsider (USA)—Shindy (USA)	Mellon Stud	D. K. Weld, Esq.	150,000
B c Sadler's Wells (USA)—Deadly Serious (USA)	Tullamaine Castle Stud (Agent)	T. Bott, Esq.	145,000
Ch c Sharpen Up—Lavishly Bold (USA)	Tullamaine Castle Stud (Agent)	Curragh Bldstck Agency	140,000
Dependable (IRE) Ch c Caerleon (USA)—Caring	Barronstown Stud	Classic Thoroughbreds	140,000
Razik (IRE) B c Last Tycoon—Warm December	Raffin Stud (Agent)	Shadwell Estate Co. Ltd.	140,000
Eastern Aura (IRE) Ch f Ahonoora—Sybaris	Rathasker Stud	Michael Bramwell, Esq.	140,000
B f Rousillon (USA)—Snowtop	Ballyprior Stud	B.B.A. plc	140,000
B c Slip Anchor—Glancing	Cotswold Stud	Ian A. Balding, Esq	135,000
Ch c Northern Baby (CAN)—Foolish Lady (USA)	Derrygrath Stud	B.B.A. (Ireland) Ltd	130,000
B c Law Society (USA)—Christabelle (USA)	Lyonstown Stud (Agent)	Horse France S.A.	130,000
Richly Deserved (IRE) B f Kings Lake (USA)—Spirit In the Sky	Mellon Stud	J. T. Doyle, Esq.	130,000
B f Sovereign Dancer (USA)—Empress Express (USA)	Mr William J. Betz (Agent)	Ian A. Balding, Esq	125,000
B c Sadler's Wells (USA)—Tifrums	Forenaughts Stud	Horse France Ire. Ltd.	125,000
Ch c Nijinsky (CAN)—Roycon	Gilltown Stud	Richard Galpin Bldstck	125,000
New Tycoon (IRE) B f Last Tycoon—Go Feather Go (USA)	Pipers Hill Stud	Amanda Skiffington	120,000
B c Green Desert (USA)—Red Letter Day	Stackallen Stud	Darley Stud Management	120,000
Ch c Be My Guest (USA)—Ask the Wind	Gilltown Stud	Kay Shigeta/Silky Green	110,000
B c Storm Bird (CAN)—Verset Holiday (USA)	Landscape Stud	Equine Invest. Consultants	110,000
Classic Match (IRE) Ch c Ballad Rock—Ballymaloe Girl	Irish National Stud	Classic Thoroughbreds	110,000
B/br c Chief's Crown (USA)—Taylors Park (USA)	Mellon Stud	Shadwell Estate Co. Ltd.	110,000
B c Storm Bird (CAN)—Nervous Pillow (USA)	Abbeville & Meadow Court	John Warren Bloodstock	110,000
Northern Realm (IRE) B c Nordico (USA)—Petite Realm	Garraun Stud	Cherry-Downes Bldsk Ltd	110,000
B c Woodman (USA)—Tentamount (USA)	Dunmurry Stud Ltd.	Amanda Skiffington	105,000
Ch f The Minstrel (CAN)—State Treasure (USA)	Camas Park Stud (Agent)	A. S. Budge (Equine) Ltd	105,000
B f Ahonoora—Soumana (FR)	Irish National Stud	Amanda Skiffington	105,000
Br c High Top—Lady Zi	Stowell Hill	C. Gordon-Watson, Esq.	100,000
Ch c Miswaki (USA)—Petit Rond Point (USA)	Tullamaine Castle Stud (Agent)	Horse France S.A.	97,000
Ch f Shadeed (USA)—Scythe	Tullamaine Castle Stud Agent	David Minton Bloodstock	95,000
Slip And Slide (IRE) B c Pennine Walk—Polaregina (FR)	Camas Park Stud	John Warren Bloodstock	95,000
Gr/br f Thatching—Perla	Abbeville & Meadow Court	Kay Shigeta/Silky Green	95,000
Flash Card (GB) Ch f Flash of Steel—Malossol	Barouche Stud	Darley Stud Management	92,000
B c Tate Gallery (USA)—Finlandia (FR)	Kilcarn Stud	David Minton Bloodstock	90,000
Ch c Glow (USA)—Coven	Ballysheehan Stud	Tim Bulwer-Long, Esq	90,000
Next Tycoon (IRE) Gr c Last Tycoon—Best Gal (FR)	Grangemore Stud	European Bloodstock Agency	90,000
B/br c Caerleon (USA)—Bean Siamsa	Old Troytown Stud	Richard Galpin Bldstock	90,000
B c Dixieland Band (USA)—Highly Noble (USA)	Landscape Stud	B.B.A. (Ireland) Ltd.	88,000
B c Wassl—Countess Candy	Airlie Stud	Anthony Penfold Bloodstk	88,000
B c Alzao (USA)—Balela	Mount Rivers Stud	Tim Bulwer-Long, Esq	86,000
B c Thatching—Joanne's Joy	Camas Park Stud	Curragh Bldstk Agency	85,000
B c Pennine Walk—Never Never Land	Corbally Stud	Juddmonte Farm Ltd.	85,000
B c Persian Bold—Cryptomeria	Arrow Farm and Stud	Juddmonte Farm Ltd.	82,000
Kooyonga (IRE) Ch f Persian Bold—Anjuli	Corbally Stud	B.B.A. (Ireland) Ltd.	82,000
B c Local Suitor (USA)—Strike It Rich (FR)	Newtownbarry House Stud	C.B.A. Newmarket	80,000
B c Northern Prospect (USA)—Faithful Diplomacy (USA)	Cleaboy Stud	John Warren Bloodstock	78,000

B f Try My Best (USA)—Crestia	Raffin Stud (Agent)	B.B.A. (Ireland) Ltd	77,000
Morny (IRE), Ch c Lomond (USA)—Miralove	Tullamaine Castle Stud (Agent)	German International BA	75,000
East Walk (IRE) B c Pennine Walk—Kolomelskoy Palace	Landscape Stud	Peter J. Doyle, Esq	74,000
B c Tate Gallery (USA)—Hard To Tell	Barronstown Stud	D. K. Weld, Esq	72,000
Classic Trust (IRE) B c Tate Gallery (USA)—Trusted Maiden	Camas Park Stud	Classic Thoroughbreds	72,000
Loki (IRE) Ch c Thatching—Sigym	Irish National Stud Partners	Cormac McCormack Esq	72,000
B c Star Appeal—Lady Constance	Beechgrove Stud Farm Ltd	T. Stack Esq	70,000
B c Lomond (USA)—Gallic Pride (USA)	Barouche Stud	Cormac McCormack Esq	70,000
B c Caerleon (USA)—Divina (GER)	Whitechurch Stud	Michael Bramwell, Esq	70,000
Dashing Fellow (IRE) B c Sure Blade (USA)—Belle Viking (FR)	Tsarina Stud	Anthony Penfold Bldstk	70,000
Ch c Hatim (USA)—Tuna	Dunderry Stud	C. Gordon-Watson Esq	70,000
Final Verdict (IRE) Br f Law Society (USA)—Catopetl (USA)	Tullamaine Castle Stud (Agent)	Horse France S.A.	69,000
Hello My Darling (IRE) B c Law Society (USA)—Helaplane (USA)	Abbeville & Meadowcourt	Kim M. Brassey, Esq	68,000
Straldi (IRE) B c Ela-Mana-Mou—Cavurina	Mellon Stud	Darley Stud Management	68,000
B f Tate Gallery (USA)—Admit	Mount Coote Stud	B.B.A. (Ireland) Ltd	68,000
Jendee (IRE) B c Dara Monarch—Bunch of Blue	Oaklawn Stud	Anthony Penfold Bldstk	67,000
Palner (IRE) Br f Law Society (USA)—Palm Dove (USA)	Ballysheehan Stud (Agent)	Sallyview Estates	67,000
Worlds Creation (USA) B c Cormorant (USA)—Worlds Fair (USA)	Landscape Stud	Michael Bramwell, Esq	66,000
B c Tate Gallery (USA)—Steaua Romana	Churchtown House Stud	B.B.A. (Ireland) Ltd	66,000
Wolf Hall (IRE) B c Green Desert (USA)—Lady Seymour	Eyrefield Lodge Stud	Darley Stud Management	65,000
Marshad (USA) B c El Gran Senor (USA)—Hatton Gardens	Tullamaine Castle Stud (Agent)	Shadwell Estate Co. Ltd	65,000
Symphony Sound (IRE) B c Law Society (USA)—Alpine Symphony	Ballysheehan Stud (Agent)	B.B.A. (Ireland) Ltd	65,000
Mardef (GB) Ch c Ahonoora—Zeyner	Charlton Down Stud	Kevin Prendergast, Esq	65,000
B f Caerleon (USA)—Return to Paris (FR)	Gilltown Stud	Kay Shigeta/Silky Green	65,000
B c Faustus (USA)—Hithermoor Lass	Whitsbury Manor Stud	B.B.A. (Ireland) Ltd	63,000
Ch c Ahonoora—Flying Anna	Yeomanstown Stud	B.B.A. plc	62,000
Ch c Ahonoora—Crimson Royale	Kellistown Stud	Tim Bulwer-Long, Esq	62,000
B c Fairy King (USA)—Clifden Bottoms	Ballysheehan Stud	Cormac McCormack, Esq	62,000
Gr c Law Society (USA)—Bellifontaine (FR)	Roehoe Stud	Tim Bulwer-Long, Esq	62,000
Classic Venture (IRE) B c Fairy King (USA)—Allorette	Rathmore Farm	James Delahooke, Esq	62,000
B c Danzig Connection (USA)—Miss Hatco (USA)	Cotswold Stud (Agent)	B.B.A. plc	60,000
B c Tender King—French Pearl	Cloghran Stud	John Hayden, Esq	60,000
Ro f Lomond (USA)—What A Summer (USA)	Gilltown Stud	Ciaran O'Toole, Esq	60,000
Royal Oberon (IRE) B c Fairy King (USA)—Broadway Royal	Ballysheehan Stud (Agent)	Anthony Penfold Bldstk	60,000
B c Lomond (USA)—Tree of Knowledge	Gilltown Stud	Kay Shigeta/Silky Green	60,000
Desert Emerald (IRE) B c Taufan (USA)—Pavello	Mount Coote Stud	Gainsborough Stud Mgt. Ltd	60,000
B c Sure Blade (USA)—Over the Waves	Mount Coote Stud	B.B.A. (Ireland) Ltd	60,000
B/br c Thatching—Anna Carla (GER)	Mount Coote Stud	David Murray-Smith, Esq	58,000
Thatch And Gold (IRE) B c Thatching—Tuck	Barouche Stud	Peter J. Doyle, Esq	58,000
B f Palace Music (USA)—Locks Dream (USA)	Mellon Stud	C. Gordon-Watson, Esq	56,000
Le Jongleur (USA) Gr c The Minstrel (CAN)—La Koumia (FR)	Camas Park Stud	Michael Bramwell, Esq	55,000
B f Pennine Walk—Dominica (GER)	Loughbrown & Martinstown	Forenaughts Stud	55,000
Don't Be Shy (IRE) B f Kafu—Cat O'Mountaine	Irish National Stud	Tim Vigors Bloodstock	55,000
B c Vision (USA)—Warning Sound	Newtownbarry House Stud	Gulf Racing Bloodstock	55,000

Sapieha (IRE) B c Petorius—Sugarbird	Stackallen Stud	B.B.A. (Ireland) Ltd.	55,000
Glowlamp (IRE) Br f Glow (USA)—Astania (GER)	Airlie Stud	David Minton Bloodstock	54,000
3 c Glow (USA)—Piculet	Islanmore Stud	Equine Bldstk Consultant	53,000
3 c Known Fact (USA)—Ides of March	Whitsbury Manor Stud	Juddmonte Farm Ltd.	52,000
3 c Nordance (USA)—Cerise Bouquet	Abbeville & Meadow Court	J. T. Doyle, Esq.	52,000
3 c Pennine Walk—Busca (USA)	Partridge Close Stud	Derek Lucie-Smith, Esq.	52,000
Classical Rhythm (IRE) B/br c Ballad Rock—Non Casual	Triermore Stud	Classic Thoroughbreds	52,000
Ch f Blushing Groom (FR)—Fashionably Late (USA)	Gilltown Stud	Leinster B'stock Agency	50,000
B c Secreto (USA)—Mythilene (FR)	Dunmurry Stud Ltd.	B.B.A. plc.	50,000
B c Nordico (USA)—Lady Dulcinea (ARG)	Mellon Stud	B.B.A. plc.	50,000
B c Never So Bold—Gunner's Belle	Whitsbury Manor Stud	C.B.A. Newmarket	50,000
Fast And Straight (IRE) B f Shirley Heights—Gulf Girl	Stackallen Stud	Michael Kauntze, Esq.	50,000
B c Glow (USA)—Full Choke	Mellon Stud	Horse France Ire. Ltd.	50,000
Back To The Future (IRE) B f Star De Naskra (USA)—Fair Astrologer (USA)	Tullamaine Castle Stud (Agent)	J. S. Bolger, Esq.	50,000
Banksy Boy (IRE) Ch c Gorytus (USA)—Kampai	Gilltown Stud (Agent)	Kay Shigeta/Silky Green	50,000
Cape Heights (GB) B f Shirley Heights—Cape Chestnut	Mellon Stud	Sallyview Estates	50,000
Broad Haven (IRE) Ch f Be My Guest (USA)—Welsh Fantasy	Ardenode Stud	Tim Vigors Bloodstock	50,000
B f Thatching—Walkyria	Loughbrown & Martinstown	Darley Stud Management	50,000
Peggy Finch (GB) B f Law Society (USA)—Snow Finch	Round Hill Stud	C. Goulandris	50,000
Archway (IRE) Ch c Thatching—Rose of Jericho (USA)	Lyonstown Stud (Agent)	James Delahooke, Esq.	50,000
Imco Double (IRE) Ch c Double Schwartz—Cupids Hill	Ardoon Stud	New Turf	48,000
High Degree (GB) B c Superlative—St. Colette	Partride Close Stud	Mike Ryan Esq, (Agent)	48,000
B c Last Tycoon—Sherkraine	Ardenode Stud Ltd.	Peter J. Doyle, Esq.	48,000
Wilton Place (IRE) Br c Flash of Steel—Up the Gates	Ballysheehan Stud	Mr Frank Barry	47,000
Kimbers (IRE) B c Lomond (USA)—Take Your Mark (USA)	Barronstown Stud	B.B.A. plc.	47,000
Ch f Persian Bold—Militia Girl	Islanmore Stud	B.B.A. plc.	46,000
Ch f Be My Guest (USA)—Hobe Sound	Gilltown Stud	Tim Vigors Bloodstock	46,000
Two Way Mirror (IRE) Ch c Double Schwartz—Alice Kyteler	Raffin Stud (Agent)	C. Gordon-Watson, Esq.	46,000
B c Wolf Power (SAF)—Morelle (ARG)	Newlands House Stud	William McDonald, Esq	45,000
Ch c Tate Gallery (USA)—Miss Anna	Tullamaine Castle Stud (Agent)	Equine Invest Consultants	45,000
Ch c Commanche Run—Lassalia	Landscape Stud	Kay Shigeta/Silky Green	45,000
Jada (IRE) Ch c Shy Groom (USA)—La Loie Fuller (FR)	Ennistown Stud	Shadwell Estate Co. Ltd.	45,000
Ch c Pancho Villa (USA)—Drop the Mark (USA)	Mr William J. Betz (Agent)	William McDonald, Esq.	45,000
Prince Farelone (USA) B c Irish River (FR)—Quilly (USA)	Ballysheehan Stud (Agent)	Anthony Penfold Bldstk.	45,000
B c Miswaki (USA)—Nice Manners (USA)	Mellon Stud	P. Buckley, Esq.	45,000
Exotic Sounds (IRE) B/br f Be My Guest (USA)—Diva Encore	Irish National Stud	John McLoughlin, Esq.	44,000
B c Lomond (USA)—Cheerful Heart	Orchardstown Stud Farm	Sallyview Estates	44,000
Kalan (IRE) Ch c Sharpo—Zumurrudah (USA)	Mowread Stud	Derby Bloodstock	44,000
B c Formidable (USA)—Loreef	Tara Stud	Kay Shigeta/Silky Green	42,000
B f Ela-Mana-Mou—Be Discreet	Raffin Stud (Agent)	David Minton Bloodstock	42,000
B c Thatching—Crimson Robes	Gilltown Stud	Kay Shigeta/Silky Green	42,000
Roger Ramjet (IRE) B c Law Society (USA)—Saraday	Oak Lodge Stud	J. S. Bolger, Esq.	42,000
Ch c Nordance (USA)—Tatisha	Tipper House Stud	Tim Bulwer-Long, Esq.	42,000
B c Petorius—Merrie Moira	Mrs M. W. Beaumont	L. J. Codd, Esq.	40,000
B f Sure Blade (USA)—Marble Run	Pipers Hill Stud	Newmarket Bloodstock	40,000

Lot	Vendor	Purchaser	Price
B c Thatching—Ganna (ITY)	Abbeville & Meadow Court	B.B.A. (Ireland) Ltd.	40,000
B c Lyphard's Special (USA)—Maiden Concert	Croom House Stud	B.B.A.plc.	40,000
B c Persian Bold—Alligatrix (USA)	Tullamaine Castle Stud	B.B.A. (Ireland) Ltd.	40,000
Imco Gallery (IRE) Ro f Tate Gallery (USA)—Sunblast	Corduff Stud	New Turf Bldstk. Agency	40,000
B f Sadler's Wells (USA)—North Broadway (USA)	Barronstown Stud	Billy McDonald, Esq.	40,000
Maiden of Iron (IRE) Ch f Flash of Steel—Takastroll	Eyrefield House Stud	John Warren Bloodstock	39,000
Weekday Cross (IRE) B c Taufan (USA)—Isoldes Tower	Tally-Ho Stud	John Warren Bloodstock	38,000
Athclare (IRE) Ch c Glow (USA)—Athry	Arrow Farm and Stud	Curragh Bldstck. Agency	38,000
Ch c Be My Guest (USA)—Ukraine Girl	Ardenode Stud	European Blstk Agency	38,000
Ch f Secreto (USA)—Classical Suite (USA)	Ballysheehan Stud (Agent)	B.B.A. (Italy)	38,000
B c Doulab (USA)—Song Grove	Ballysheehan Stud (Agent)	B.B.A. plc.	38,000
Phalarope (IRE) B c Petorius—Magee	Prop of Mrs H. McCartan	Curragh Bldstk Agency	37,000
Ballyloop (IRE) B br/c Petorius—Ballysnip	Oak Lodge Stud	John Warren Bloodstock	37,000
B c Be My Guest (USA)—Welshwyn	Collinstown Stud Farm Ltd.	B.B.A. (Italy)	37,000
Fairy Folk (IRE) B f Fairy King (USA)—Tripoli	Derrygrath Stud	European Bldstk Agency	37,000
B f Sagace (FR)—Bammell (USA)	Mellon Stud	A. F. Budge Equine Ltd.	36,000
Imco Affirmation (IRE) B c Glow (USA)—Affirmation (FR)	Round Hill Stud	New Turf Bldstk Agency	36,000
Gr c Glenstal (USA)—Love Locket	Garraun Stud	David Murray-Smith, Esq	35,000
Gr c Sarab—Legs and Things	Carrigbeg Stud	Neil McGrath, Esq.	35,000
Ch c Diesis—Ivory Smooth (USA)	Airlie Stud	Juddmonte Farms	35,000
B c Formidable (USA)—Exotic	Floors Stud	B.B.A. (Ireland) Ltd.	35,000
Gr f Glow (USA)—Hazy Lady	Killarkin Stud	B.B.A. plc.	35,000
Ch f Ahonoora—Redeem Herself	Collinstown Stud Farm Ltd.	P. J. Prendergast, Esq.	35,000
Ch c Never So Bold—Ravaro	Cheveley Park Stud	Alexander Scott, Esq.	35,000
Harbour Knight (IRE) B c Caerleon (USA)—So Directed	Barronstown Stud	James Eustace, Esq.	35,000
Griffith (IRE) Ch c Glow (USA)—Ashton Amber	Ballylea Stud	Derby Bloodstock	34,000
B c M Double M (USA)—Bebe Altesse (GER)	Swordlestown Stud	Hambleton Premier Thoroughbreds	33,000
B c Hatim (USA)—An Tig Gaelige	Irish National Stud	Forenaughts Stud	33,000
Ch c Dixieland Band (USA)—Miss Stark (USA)	Mr William J. Betz (Agent)	William J. Betz, Esq.	32,000
B f Shareef Dancer (USA)—Mahabba (USA)	Monread Stud	B.B.A. plc.	32,000
Ch f Ahonoora—Myra's Best	Tullamaine Castle Stud	German International BA	32,000
Ch c The Noble Player (USA)-Grande Madame	Peter Farrington, Esq.	Mr Frank Barry	32,000
Jackson Squire (IRE) B c Prince Tenderfoot (USA)—Double Habit	Cornhill B/S-Brick Kiln	A. W. J. Perry, Esq.	32,000
Prospecting (GB) B c Damister (USA)—Copt Hall Royale	Corduff Stud	Richard J. O'Gorman Esq	32,000
Ch f Precocious—Astra Adastra	Raffin Stud (Agent)	B.B.A. (Ireland) Ltd.	32,000
Ch c Phone Trick (USA)—Wrap It Up	Orchardstown Stud Farm	Equine Invest Consultants	32,000
B c Double Schwartz—Two's Company	Ballyprior Stud	B.B.A. (Ireland) Ltd.	32,000
Sub Justice (IRE) B/br c Law Society (USA)—Thunderflash (FR)	Landscape Stud	Classic Thoroughbreds	32,000
Ch c Miswaki (USA)—Sea Flavour	Tullamaine Castle Std (Agent)	J. Dunlop, Esq.	32,000
Ch c Golden Act (USA)—Sassy Lane	Tullamaine Castle Std (Agent)	B.B.A. (Italy)	32,000
B c Tender King—Persian Apple (USA)	Clobemon Hall Stud	John Warren Bloodstock	32,000
Adjacent (IRE) Ch f Doulab (USA)—Near the Door (USA)	Raffin Stud (Agent)	B.B.A. (Ireland) Ltd.	32,000
Gr c Taufan (USA)—Rossaldene	Prop. Mr N. Browne	B.B.A. plc.	32,000

WINNERS OF GREAT RACES

LINCOLN HANDICAP
Doncaster—1m

1970 New Chapter 4-8-1 ... 23
1971 Double Cream 4-8-9 ... 26
1972 Sovereign Bill 6-8-12 ... 21
1973 Bronze Hill 4-7-9 ... 26
1974 Quizair 5-7-13 ... 26
1975 Southwark Star 4-7-3 ... 24
1976 The Hertford 5-8-6 ... 26
1977 Blustery 5-7-11 ... 26
1978 Captains Wings 5-7-10 ... 25
1979 Fair Season 5-8-10 ... 23
1980 King's Ride 4-8-12 ... 18
1981 Saher 5-8-12 ... 19
1982 Kings Glory 4-8-3 ... 26
1983 Mighty Fly 4-8-4 ... 26
1984 Saving Mercy 4-8-9 ... 26
1985 Cataldi 4-9-10 ... 26
1986 K-Battery 5-8-4 ... 25
1987 Star of a Gunner 7-8-8 ... 25
1988 Cuvee Charlie 4-8-1 ... 25
1989 Fact Finder 5-7-9 ... 25

GREENHAM STAKES (3y)
Newbury—7f

1970 Gold Rod 8-10 ... 6
1971 Mill Reef 9-1 ... 7
1972 Martinmas 8-10 ... 7
1973 Boldboy 8-10 ... 5
1974 Glen Strae 8-10 ... 8
1975 Mark Anthony 9-1 ... 9
1976 Wollow 9-1 ... 10
1977 He Loves Me 8-10 ... 11
1978 Derrylin 8-10 ... 11
1979 Kris 9-0 ... 9
1980 Final Straw 9-0 ... 9
1981 Another Realm 9-0 ... 6
1982 Cajun 9-0 ... 5
1983 Wassl 9-0 ... 5
1984 Creag-an-Sgor 9-0 ... 8
1985 Bairn 9-0 ... 6
1986 Faustus 9-0 ... 9
1987 Risk Me 9-0 ... 8
1988 Zelphi 9-0 ... 7
1989 Zayyani 9-0 ... 12

JOHN PORTER STAKES
Newbury—1m 4f

1970 Torpid 5-9-5 ... 8
1971 Meadowville 4-9-1 ... 12
1972 Rock Roi 5-9-5 ... 5
1973 Rheingold 4-9-1 ... 15
1974 Freefoot 4-8-6 ... 12
1975 Salado 4-8-10 ... 13
1976 Quiet Fling 4-9-0 ... 11
1977 Decent Fellow 4-8-9 ... 11
1978 Orchestra 4-9-0 ... 10
1979 Icelandic 4-8-11 ... 12
1980 Niniski 4-9-0 ... 16
1981 Pelerin 4-8-8 ... 9
1982 Glint of Gold 4-9-0 ... 11
1983 Diamond Shoal 4-8-8 ... 8
1984 Gay Lemur 4-8-8 ... 13
1985 Jupiter Island 6-8-8 ... 14
1986 Lemhill 4-8-8 ... 8
1987 Rakaposhi King 5-8-10 ... 12
1988 Alwasmi 4-8-10 ... 8
1989 Unfuwain 4-8-13 ... 7

EUROPEAN FREE HANDICAP (3y)
Newmarket—7f

1970 Shiny Tenth 8-3 ... 18
1971 No Mercy 8-5 ... 16
1972 Panama Canal 7-11 ... 16
1973 Pitskelly 8-5 ... 16
1974 Charlie Bubbles 8-3 ... 14
1975 Green Belt 8-9 ... 15
1976 Man of Harlech 8-4 ... 19
1977 Mrs McArdy 8-0 ... 19
1978 Remainder Man 7-10 ... 12
1979 Lyric Dance 8-10 ... 14
1980 Moorestyle 8-10 ... 13
1981 Motavato 8-13 ... 13
1982 Match Winner 9-4 ... 13
1983 Boom Town Charlie 8-11 ... 8
1984 Cutting Wind 8-8 ... 17
1985 Over The Ocean 8-11 ... 11
1986 Green Desert 9-7 ... 8
1987 Noble Minstrel 9-7 ... 11
1988 Lapierre 9-1 ... 9
1989 Danehill 9-1 ... 9

CRAVEN STAKES (3y)
Newmarket—1m

1970 Tamil 8-12 ... 9
1971 Levanter 9-2 ... 6
1972 Leicester 8-5 ... 5
1973 My Drifter 8-5 ... 14
1974 Numa 8-10 ... 12
1975 No Alimony 8-10 ... 10
1976 Malinowski 8-10 ... 7
1977 Limone 8-10 ... 9
1978 Admiral's Launch 8-10 ... 10
1979 Lyphard's Wish 8-7 ... 3
1980 Tyrnavos 8-7 ... 9
1981 Kind of Hush 8-7 ... 9
1982 Silver Hawk 8-7 ... 9
1983 Muscatite 8-7 ... 5
1984 Lear Fan 8-12 ... 5
1985 Shadeed 8-7 ... 6
1986 Dancing Brave 8-7 ... 11
1987 Ajdal 9-0 ... 6
1988 Doyoun 8-9 ... 5
1989 Shaadi 8-9 ... 5

CLASSIC TRIAL (3y)
(Royal Stakes before 1971)
Sandown—1m 2f

1970 Cry Baby 8-7 ... 5
1971 L'Apache 8-7 ... 10

Winners of Great Races – Continued

1972	Pentland Firth 8-12	13
1973	Ksar 8-12	6
1974	Bustino 8-9	9
1975	Consol 9-0	9
1976	Riboboy 9-0	7
1977	Artaius 8-9	5
1978	Whitstead 8-11	8
1979	Troy 8-7	5
1980	Henbit 8-7	6
1981	Shergar 8-7	9
1982	Peacetime 8-7	11
1983	Gordian 8-7	7
1984	Alphabatim 9-0	8
1985	Damister 8-7	4
1986	Shahrastani 8-7	4
1987	Gulf King 8-12	8
1988	Galitzin 8-7	5
1989	Old Vic 8-8	3

VICTORIA CUP

Ascot—7f

1970	Welsh Pageant 4-9-6	14
1971	Mon Plaisir 4-9-8	23
1972	Heave To 4-7-13	10
1973	Royal Prerogative 4-8-7	18
1974	Galiano 5-8-8	11
1975	Rhodomantade 4-8-3	20
1976	Record Token 4-9-4	14
1977	Duke Ellington 4-9-1	16
1978	Private Line 5-8-13	16
1979	The Adrianstan 4-8-6	18
1980	Kampala 4-9-3	16
1981	Columnist 4-9-13	14
1982	Indian King 4-9-3	13
1983	Abandoned	
1984	Mummy's Pleasure 5-8-9	13
1985	Tremblant 4-8-5	22
1986	Ready Wit 5-7-13	14
1987	Fusilier 5-7-9	20
1988	Wing Park 4-9-1	16
1989	Top Dream 4-9-1	23

JUBILEE HANDICAP

Kempton—1m

1970	Blue Yonder 4-8-2	12
1971	Welsh Rarebit 4-7-11	15
1972	Grandrew 6-8-8	14
1973	Brigade Major 4-8-5	12
1974	Jumpabout 4-7-12	11
1975	Jumpabout 5-8-5	14
1976	Royal Match 5-9-0	11
1977	Lord Helpus 4-9-5	16
1978	Sunday Guest 4-8-12	14
1979	Smartset 4-7-0	12
1980	Blue Refrain 4-9-5	10
1981	Greenwood Star 4-9-2	10
1982	Tugoflove 6-8-3	12
1983	Elmar 4-8-10	12
1984	Larionov 4-9-11	11
1985	Portogon 7-7-11	11
1986	Pennine Walk 4-9-11	23
1987	Turfah 4-8-12	15
1988	Just A Flutter 4-9-3	11
1989	Electric Lady 4-9-8	14

JOCKEY CLUB STAKES

Newmarket—1m 4f

1970	Queen of Twilight 4-8-11	9
1971	Meadowville 4-9-6	3
1972	Knockroe 4-8-13	4
1973	Our Mirage 4-9-3	9
1974	Relay Race 4-8-9	5
1975	Shebeen 4-8-10	6
1976	Orange Bay 4-9-8	8
1977	Oats 4-9-1	11
1978	Classic Example 4-9-5	7
1979	Obraztsovy 4-8-11	9
1980	More Light 4-8-11	8
1981	Master Willie 4-8-12	6
1982	Ardross 6-8-12	6
1983	Electric 4-8-10	11
1984	Gay Lemur 4-8-7	6
1985	Kirmann 4-8-7	8
1986	Phardante 4-8-7	3
1987	Phardante 5-8-12	7
1988	Almaarad 5-8-10	4
1989	Unfuwain 4-8-10	6

CHESTER VASE (3y)

Chester—1m 4f 65yds

1970	Politico 8-12	6
1971	Linden Tree 8-12	5
1972	Ormindo 8-8	6
1973	Proverb 8-8	7
1974	Jupiter Pluvius 8-8	8
1975	Shantallah 8-12	7
1976	Old Bill 8-8	6
1977	Hot Grove 8-12	6
1978	Icelandic 8-12	4
1979	Cracaval 8-8	6
1980	Henbit 8-12	5
1981	Shergar 8-12	10
1982	Super Sunrise 8-12	8
1983	Abandoned	
1984	Kaytu 8-8	7
1985	Law Society 8-12	5
1986	Nomrood 8-12	7
1987	Dry Dock 8-11	8
1988	Unfuwain 8-11	4
1989	Old Vic 8-11	5

CHESTER CUP

Chester—2m 2f 97yds

1970	Altogether 4-7-5	21
1971	Random Shot 4-8-1	21
1972	Eric 5-7-0	16
1973	Crisalgo 5-7-7	10
1974	Attivo 4-7-5	7
1975	Super Nova 5-7-7	15
1976	John Cherry 5-9-4	15
1977	Sea Pigeon 7-8-8	15
1978	Sea Pigeon 8-9-7	13
1979	Charlotte's Choice 4-8-4	13

Winners of Great Races – Continued

1980 Arapahos 5-9-5 10
1981 Donegal Prince 5-8-4 15
1982 Dawn Johnny 5-8-8 16
1983 Abandoned
1984 Contester 4-8-2 9
1985 Morgans Choice 8-7-11 16
1986 Western Dancer 5-9-0 22
1987 Just David 4-9-8 13
1988 Old Hubert 7-7-8 17
1989 Grey Salute 6-8-7 14

ORMONDE STAKES
Chester—1m 5f 88yds

1970 Blakeney 4-9-2 5
1971 Quayside 4-8-4 4
1972 Selhurst 4-8-4 7
1973 Ormindo 4-8-12 5
1974 Crazy Rhythm 6-8-9 5
1975 Rouser 4-8-4 7
1976 Zimbalon 4-8-6 4
1977 Oats 4-9-0 8
1978 Crow 5-9-0 7
1979 Remainder Man 4-8-10 4
1980 Niniski 4-9-4 10
1981 Pelerin 4-9-4 5
1982 Six Mile Bottom 4-8-10 6
1983 Abandoned
1984 Teenoso 4-9-4 5
1985 Seismic Wave 4-8-10 8
1986 Brunico 4-8-10 8
1987 Rakaposhi King 5-8-11 5
1988 Mr Pintips 4-8-11 6
1989 Mountain Kingdom 5-8-11 3

OAKS TRIAL (3y fillies)
Lingfield—1m 4f

1970 Pulchra 8-5 5
1971 Maina 8-5 5
1972 Ginevra 9-0 6
1973 Syrona 8-9 10
1974 Riboreen 8-9 7
1975 Juliette Marny 8-9 7
1976 Heaven Knows 9-0 10
1977 Lucent 9-0 5
1978 Suni 9-0 9
1979 Reprocolor 9-0 7
1980 Gift Wrapped 9-0 7
1981 Leap Lively 9-0 7
1982 Tants 9-0 9
1983 Give Thanks 9-0 12
1984 Out of Shot 9-0 7
1985 Kiliniski 8-9 11
1986 Mill on the Floss 8-9 8
1987 Port Helene 8-9 8
1988 Bahamian 8-9 7
1989 Aliysa 8-9 5

DERBY TRIAL (3y)
Lingfield—1m 4f

1970 Meadowville 9-0 11
1971 Homeric 9-0 12
1972 Charling 9-0 9
1973 Ksar 9-0 7
1974 Bustino 9-0 7
1975 Patch 9-0 8
1976 Norfolk Air 9-0 8
1977 Caporello 9-0 8
1978 Whitstead 9-0 6
1979 Milford 9-0 8
1980 Ginistrelli 9-0 7
1981 Riberetto 9-0 8
1982 Jalmood 9-0 6
1983 Teenoso 9-0 11
1984 Alphabatim 9-0 5
1985 Slip Anchor 9-0 8
1986 Mashkour 9-0 6
1987 Legal Bid 9-0 8
1988 Kahyasi 9-0 8
1989 Cacoethes 9-0 7

CORAL BOOKMAKERS HANDICAP (3y)
(formerly Holsten Diat Pils Handicap)
Newmarket—6f

1981 Sharp Venita 7-3 12
1982 Admirals Princess 9-2 13
1983 Bold Secret 8-6 10
1984 Lovers Bid 7-3 14
1985 Zanata 8-4 12
1986 Latch Spring 7-10 14
1987 Bel Byou 8-4 15
1988 Cadeaux Genereux 8-0 16
1989 Didicoy 8-12 11

MUSIDORA STAKES (3y fillies)
York—1m 2½f

1970 Whitefoot 9-0 4
1971 Catherine Wheel 9-0 5
1972 Jakomima 9-0 10
1973 Where You Lead 9-0 6
1974 Escorial 9-0 6
1975 Moonlight Night 9-0 10
1976 Everything Nice 9-0 8
1977 Triple First 9-0 9
1978 Princess of Man 9-0 9
1979 Rimosa's Pet 9-0 10
1980 Bireme 9-0 9
1981 Condessa 9-0 5
1982 Last Feather 9-0 5
1983 Give Thanks 9-0 8
1984 Optimistic Lass 9-0 9
1985 Fatah Flare 9-0 9
1986 Rejuvenate 8-11 7
1987 Indian Skimmer 8-8 3
1988 Diminuendo 8-11 6
1989 Snow Bride 8-8 6

DANTE STAKES (3y)
York—1m 2½f

1970 Approval 9-0 8
1971 Fair World 9-0 8
1972 Rheingold 9-0 9
1973 Owen Dudley 9-0 10
1974 Honoured Guest 9-0 6

Winners of Great Races – Continued

1975 Hobnob 9-0 12
1976 Trasi's Son 9-0 11
1977 Lucky Sovereign 9-0 15
1978 Shirley Heights 9-0 9
1979 Lyphard's Wish 9-0 14
1980 Hello Gorgeous 9-0 8
1981 Beldale Flutter 9-0 6
1982 Simply Great 9-0 6
1983 Hot Touch 9-0 9
1984 Claude Monet 9-0 15
1985 Damister 9-0 5
1986 Shahrastani 9-0 7
1987 Reference Point 9-0 8
1988 Red Glow 9-0 7
1989 Torjoun 9-0 7

YORKSHIRE CUP
York—1m 6f

1970 Rangong 5-9-0 3
1971 Alto Volante 4-8-4 6
1972 Knockroe 4-8-8 8
1973 Celtic Cone 6-8-10 6
1974 Buoy 4-8-13 4
1975 Riboson 4-8-5 4
1976 Bruni 4-9-1 5
1977 Bright Finish 4-8-10 7
1978 Smuggler 5-8-10 7
1979 Pragmatic 4-8-7 10
1980 Noble Saint 4-9-1 8
1981 Ardross 5-8-12 6
1982 Ardross 6-9-1 6
1983 Line Slinger 4-8-4 10
1984 Band 4-8-10 9
1985 Ilium 4-8-7 10
1986 Eastern Mystic 4-8-9 7
1987 Verd-Antique 4-8-9 7
1988 Moon Madness 5-9-0 8
1989 Mountain Kingdom 5-8-9 6

DUKE OF YORK STAKES
York—6f

1970 Fluke 3-7-10 3
1971 The Brianstan 4-9-0 8
1972 Stilvi 3-8-6 7
1973 Abwah 4-9-7 7
1974 Noble Mark 3-8-10 9
1975 Steel Heart 3-8-13 7
1976 Three Legs 4-9-7 9
1977 Boldboy 7-9-12 13
1978 Private Line 5-9-4 16
1979 Thatching 4-9-0 9
1980 Flash N'Thunder 3-8-1 7
1981 King of Spain 5-9-0 10
1982 Jester 3-8-2 11
1983 Vorvados 6-9-0 11
1984 Gabitat 6-9-4 10
1985 Chapel Cottage 4-8-11 10
1986 Grey Desire 6-9-0 10
1987 Handsome Sailor 4-9-0 9
1988 Handsome Sailor 5-9-8 13
1989 Indian Ridge 4-9-4 10

LOCKINGE STAKES
Newbury—1m

1970 Welsh Pageant 4-8-12 6
1971 Welsh Pageant 5-9-2 6
1972 Brigadier Gerard 4-9-5 5
1973 Sparkler 5-8-12 12
1974 Boldboy 4-8-12 8
1975 Abandoned
1976 El Rastro 6-9-0 8
1977 Relkino 4-9-0 9
1978 Don 4-9-4 10
1979 Young Generation 3-8-4 10
1980 Kris 4-9-7 7
1981 Belmont Bay 4-9-0 6
1982 Motavato 4-9-0 7
1983 Noalcoholic 6-9-4 10
1984 Cormorant Wood 4-9-5 6
1985 Prismatic 3-7-13 11
1986 Scottish Reel 4-9-1 8
1987 Then Again 4-9-4 9
1988 Broken Hearted 4-9-4 5
1989 Most Welcome 5-9-1 4

TOTE CREDIT HANDICAP (3y)
(Cecil Frail Handicap before 1986)
Haydock—1m 40yds

1970 Tudor Tinker 9-0 9
1971 Smart Sam 8-5 7
1972 Roy Bridge 9-2 6
1973 Apple King 8-4 9
1974 Votecatcher 8-2 15
1975 Rebec 7-12 9
1976 Gunner B 8-8 12
1977 Owen Jones 7-9 11
1978 Fair Top 7-10 11
1979 Bold Owl 8-1 10
1980 Greenwood Star 7-7 13
1981 Silver Season 9-5 12
1982 Spanish Pool 9-6 12
1983 Schuss 8-5 10
1984 Incisive 7-9 10
1985 Trucidator 9-7 11
1986 Al Bashaama 7-10 13
1987 Mohamed Abdu 7-8 8
1988 Jamarj 9-7 15
1989 Safawan 8-11 13

HENRY II STAKES
Sandown—2m

1978 Smuggler 5-9-0 6
1979 Buckskin 6-9-3 6
1980 Billion 6-8-8 8
1981 No race
1982 Ardross 6-9-3 5
1983 Ore 5-8-11 7
1984 Harly 4-8-11 5
1985 Destroyer 4-8-8 8
1986 Longboat 5-8-11 10
1987 Saronicos 4-8-10 7
1988 Primitive Rising 4-8-10 9
1989 Sadeem 6-9-2 8

Winners of Great Races – Continued

PREDOMINATE STAKES (3y)
Goodwood—1m 2f

1970	Charlton 8-11	4
1971	Levanter 9-0	5
1972	Scottish Rifle 8-11	8
1973	Buoy 8-11	9
1974	English Harbour 9-0	11
1975	No Alimony 9-0	6
1976	General Ironside 8-11	6
1977	Royal Blend 8-11	6
1978	English Harbour 8-11	9
1979	Troy 9-0	4
1980	Prince Bee 8-6	8
1981	No race	
1982	Peacetime 9-0	9
1983	Morcon 8-6	6
1984	Ilium 8-6	12
1985	Lanfranco 9-0	8
1986	Allez Milord 8-12	8
1987	Ibn Bey 8-12	9
1988	Minster Son 9-1	7
1989	Warrshan 8-12	8

LUPE STAKES (3y)
Goodwood—1m 2f

1975	Misoptimist 8-8	7
1976	Laughing Girl 8-3	9
1977	Western Star 8-8	5
1978	Cistus 8-8	7
1979	Britannias Rule 8-3	5
1980	Vielle 8-8	8
1981	Golden Bowl 8-8	4
1982	Height of Fashion 8-11	4
1983	Current Raiser 8-3	8
1984	Miss Beaulieu 8-8	15
1985	Bella Colora 8-11	6
1986	Tralthee 8-11	6
1987	Scimitarra 8-11	16
1988	Miss Boniface 8-11	4
1989	Lady Shipley 8-11	7

TEMPLE STAKES
Sandown—5f

1970	Raffingora 5-9-4	5
1971	Mummy's Pet 3-8-13	6
1972	Shoolerville 3-8-7	4
1973	Saulingo 3-8-7	5
1974	Bay Express 3-8-7	10
1975	Blue Cashmere 5-9-8	12
1976	Lochnager 4-9-4	8
1977	Vilgora 5-9-0	6
1978	*Oscilight 3-8-2	
	*Smarten Up 3-8-2	15
1979	Double Form 4-8-11	12
1980	Sharpo 3-8-2	10
1981	Abandoned	
1982	Mummy's Game 3-8-2	13
1983	Fearless Lad 4-9-8	11
1984	Petorius 3-8-6	9
1985	Never So Bold 5-9-5	6
1986	Double Schwartz 5-9-3	10
1987	Treasure Kay 4-9-3	9
1988	Handsome Sailor 5-9-3	10
1989	Dancing Dissident 3-8-8	6

BRIGADIER GERARD STAKES
(Coronation Stakes before 1973)
Sandown—1m 2f

1970	Hotfoot 4-8-10	8
1971	Pembroke Castle 4-8-10	6
1972	Stubbs Gazette 4-8-10	5
1973	Scottish Rifle 4-8-10	7
1974	Ksar 4-8-10	5
1975	Rymer 4-8-13	7
1976	Anne's Pretender 4-8-11	6
1977	Jellaby 4-8-8	9
1978	Gunner B 5-8-11	8
1979	Jellaby 6-8-11	7
1980	Gregorian 4-8-11	3
1981	Abandoned	
1982	Kalaglow 4-8-11	8
1983	Stanerra 5-8-5	10
1984	Adonijah 4-8-8	9
1985	Commanche Run 4-9-3	5
1986	Bedtime 6-8-10	7
1987	Mtoto 4-8-10	8
1988	Highland Chieftain 5-9-1	7
1989	Hibernian Gold 4-8-10	6

LEISURE STAKES
Lingfield—6f

1978	Gypsy Dancer 3-8-7	6
1979	Absalom 4-9-10	7
1980	The Pug 3-8-3	6
1981	Runnett 4-9-10	7
1982	Sylvan Barbarosa 3-8-3	8
1983	Solimile 3-8-6	7
1984	Habibti 4-9-3	8
1985	Alpine Strings 4-9-4	7
1986	Hallgate 3-8-3	9
1987	Mister Majestic 3-8-3	11
1988	Gallic League 3-8-3	8
1989	Restore 6-9-0	12

DIOMED STAKES
Epsom—1m 110yds

1971	Sparkler 3-9-0	5
1972	Sallust 3-9-4	7
1973	Owen Dudley 3-9-0	4
1974	Averof 3-8-5	9
1975	All Friends 3-8-2	11
1976	All Friends 4-9-5	7
1977	Gunner B 4-9-6	6
1978	Ovac 5-9-9	9
1979	Spring In Deepsea 4-9-4	11
1980	Hardgreen 4-9-3	5
1981	Saher 5-9-6	6
1982	Prima Voce 3-8-3	8
1983	Lofty 3-8-3	6
1984	Adonijah 4-9-9	7
1985	Scottish Reel 3-8-7	7
1986	Pennine Walk 4-9-9	10

Winners of Great Races – Continued

1987 Lauries Warrior 3-8-6 10
1988 Waajib 5-9-9 8
1989 Shining Steel 3-8-7 8

CORONATION CUP
Epsom—1m 4f

1970 Caliban 4-9-0 4
1971 Lupe 4-8-11 6
1972 Mill Reef 4-9-0 4
1973 Roberto 4-9-0 5
1974 Buoy 4-9-0 5
1975 Bustino 4-9-0 6
1976 Quiet Fling 4-9-0 6
1977 Exceller 4-9-0 6
1978 Crow 5-9-0 5
1979 Ile de Bourbon 4-9-0 4
1980 Sea Chimes 4-9-0 4
1981 Master Willie 4-9-0 5
1982 Easter Sun 5-9-0 8
1983 Be My Native 4-9-0 6
1984 Time Charter 5-8-11 6
1985 Rainbow Quest 4-9-0 7
1986 Saint Estephe 4-9-0 10
1987 Triptych 5-8-11 5
1988 Triptych 6-8-11 4
1989 Sheriff's Star 4-9-0 9

JOHN OF GAUNT STAKES
Haydock—7f 40yds

1976 Record Token 4-9-5 6
1977 Gwent 4-9-5 4
1978 Persian Bold 3-8-10 10
1979 Borzoi 3-8-0 4
1980 Hard Fought 3-8-0 8
1981 Last Fandango 4-9-4 7
1982 Indian King 4-9-4 7
1983 Abandoned
1984 Mr Meeka 3-8-3 13
1985 Sarab 4-9-4 8
1986 Firm Landing 3-8-0 11
1987 Linda's Magic 3-8-4 5
1988 Wantage Park 4-8-9 9
1989 Weldnaas 3-8-7 13

WILLIAM HILL GOLDEN SPURS (HANDICAP) (3y)
York—6f

1973 Alphadamus 7-8 8
1974 Roman Warrior 8-2 11
1975 Be Tuneful 8-12 8
1976 Ubedizzy 8-10 13
1977 Mofida 8-13 10
1978 Emperor's Shadow 7-11 14
1979 Eagle Boy 7-8 17
1980 Optimate 8-0 13
1981 Marking Time 7-9 9
1982 Cyrils Choice 9-1 8
1983 Autumn Sunset 7-8 17
1984 Ashley Rocket 7-4 16
1985 Si Signor 8-9 12
1986 *Governor General 8-12
*Sew High 7-7 12
1987 Dowsing 7-10 15
1988 Cadeaux Genereux 8-5 10
1989 Sure Gold 8-11 10

QUEEN ANNE STAKES
Ascot—1m

1970 Welsh Pageant 4-9-5 6
1971 Roi Soleil 4-9-2 7
1972 Sparkler 4-9-2 8
1973 Sun Prince 4-9-5 4
1974 Brook 4-9-2 11
1975 Imperial March 3-7-10 11
1976 Ardoon 6-8-11 9
1977 Jellaby 4-9-8 8
1978 Radetzky 5-9-5 10
1979 Baptism 3-8-5 9
1980 Blue Refrain 4-9-8 11
1981 Belmont Bay 4-9-11 10
1982 Mr Fluorocarbon 3-8-6 10
1983 Valiyar 4-9-5 10
1984 Trojan Fen 3-8-5 6
1985 Rousillon 4-9-5 8
1986 Pennine Walk 4-9-2 9
1987 Then Again 4-9-5 6
1988 Waajib 5-9-2 5
1989 Warning 4-9-8 7

PRINCE OF WALES'S STAKES
Ascot—1m 2f

1970 Connaught 5-9-4 4
1971 Arthur 4-9-2 4
1972 Brigadier Gerard 4-9-8 7
1973 Gift Card 4-9-5 5
1974 Admetus 4-9-5 5
1975 Record Run 4-9-2 6
1976 Anne's Pretender 4-9-1 7
1977 Lucky Wednesday 4-9-1 5
1978 Gunner B 5-9-1 6
1979 Crimson Beau 4-9-1 7
1980 Ela-Mana-Mou 4-9-4 10
1981 Hard Fought 4-9-4 9
1982 Kind of Hush 4-9-1 7
1983 Stanerra 5-8-12 11
1984 Morcon 4-9-1 5
1985 Bob Back 4-9-7 4
1986 English Spring 4-8-12 9
1987 Mtoto 4-9-4 10
1988 Mtoto 5-9-8 4
1989 Two Timing 3-8-4 8

ST JAMES'S PALACE STAKES (3y)
Ascot—1m

1970 Saintly Song 9-0 6
1971 Brigadier Gerard 9-0 4
1972 Sun Prince 9-0 5
1973 Thatch 9-0 2
1974 Averof 9-0 7
1975 Bolkonski 9-0 8
1976 Radetzky 9-0 8

Winners of Great Races – Continued

1977	Don 9-0	7
1978	Jaazeiro 9-0	8
1979	Kris 9-0	5
1980	Posse 9-0	8
1981	To-Agori-Mou 9-0	8
1982	Dara Monarch 9-0	9
1983	Horage 9-0	7
1984	Chief Singer 9-0	8
1985	Bairn 9-0	8
1986	Sure Blade 9-0	7
1987	Half a Year 9-0	5
1988	Persian Heights 9-0	7
1989	Shaadi 9-0	5

COVENTRY STAKES (2y)
Ascot—6f

1970	Mill Reef 9-0	5
1971	Sun Prince 8-11	10
1972	Perdu 8-11	7
1973	Doleswood 8-11	12
1974	Whip It Quick 8-11	18
1975	Galway Bay 8-11	10
1976	Cawston's Clown 8-11	12
1977	Solinus 8-11	17
1978	Lake City 8-11	20
1979	Varingo 8-11	18
1980	Recitation 8-11	13
1981	Red Sunset 8-11	16
1982	Horage 8-11	8
1983	Chief Singer 8-11	14
1984	Primo Dominie 8-11	8
1985	Sure Blade 8-11	12
1986	Cutting Blade 8-11	19
1987	Always Fair 8-13	13
1988	High Estate 8-13	9
1989	Rock City 8-13	16

KING EDWARD VII STAKES (3y)
Ascot—1m 4f

1970	Great Wall 8-6	5
1971	Seafriend 8-10	7
1972	Lord Nelson 8-6	6
1973	Klairvimy 8-10	7
1974	English Prince 9-0	6
1975	Sea Anchor 8-10	8
1976	Marquis de Sade 8-10	5
1977	Classic Example 8-10	10
1978	Ile de Bourbon 8-6	10
1979	Ela-Mana-Mou 8-6	9
1980	Light Cavalry 8-6	10
1981	Bustomi 8-6	10
1982	Open Day 8-6	11
1983	Shareef Dancer 8-6	7
1984	Head for Heights 8-6	10
1985	Lanfranco 8-6	10
1986	Bonhomie 8-8	13
1987	Love the Groom 8-8	8
1988	Sheriff's Star 8-8	8
1989	Cacoethes 8-8	6

JERSEY STAKES (3y)
Ascot—7f

1970	Fluke 8-12	9
1971	Ashleigh 8-3	5
1972	Proof Positive 8-10	16
1973	Pitskelly 8-10	9
1974	Red Alert 8-10	17
1975	Gay Fandango 8-6	13
1976	Gwent 9-2	12
1977	Etienne Gerard 8-10	13
1978	Camden Town 8-10	17
1979	Blue Refrain 9-2	17
1980	Hard Fought 9-2	13
1981	Rasa Penang 8-10	20
1982	Merlins Charm 8-7	21
1983	Tecorno 8-6	13
1984	Miss Silca Key 8-7	16
1985	Pennine Walk 8-10	19
1986	Cliveden 8-10	20
1987	Midyan 9-1	13
1988	Indian Ridge 8-10	12
1989	Zilzal 8-10	12

QUEEN MARY STAKES (2y fillies)
Ascot—5f

1970	Cawston's Pride 8-12	11
1971	Waterloo 8-8	11
1972	Truly Thankful 8-8	14
1973	Bitty Girl 8-8	13
1974	Highest Trump 8-8	10
1975	Rory's Rocket 8-8	18
1976	Cramond 8-8	12
1977	Amaranda 8-8	13
1978	Greenland Park 8-8	21
1979	Abeer 8-8	14
1980	Pushy 8-8	17
1981	Fly Baby 8-8	11
1982	Widaad 8-8	16
1983	Night of Wind 8-8	15
1984	Hi-Tech Girl 8-8	17
1985	Gwydion 8-8	14
1986	Forest Flower 8-8	13
1987	Princess Athena 8-8	15
1988	Gloriella 8-8	12
1989	Dead Certain 8-8	13

CORONATION STAKES (3y fillies)
Ascot—1m

1970	Humble Duty 9-0	3
1971	Magic Flute 9-0	4
1972	Calve 9-0	7
1973	Jacinth 9-0	9
1974	Lisadell 9-0	8
1975	Roussalka 9-0	11
1976	Kesar Queen 9-0	8
1977	Orchestration 9-0	10
1978	Sutton Place 8-8	14
1979	One In A Millon 9-4	13
1980	Cairn Rouge 9-4	8
1981	Tolmi 9-0	10
1982	Chalon 9-0	8

Winners of Great Races – Continued

1983 Flame of Tara 9-0 6
1984 Katies 9-4 10
1985 Al Bahathri 9-4 7
1986 Sonic Lady 9-4 7
1987 Milligram 9-0 6
1988 Magic of Life 9-0 8
1989 Golden Opinion 9-0 12

ROYAL HUNT CUP
Ascot—1m

1970 Calpurnius 4-7-13 18
1971 Picture Boy 6-7-13 18
1972 Tempest Boy 4-8-1 20
1973 Camouflage 5-7-9 20
1974 Old Lucky 4-8-8 30
1975 Ardoon 5-8-3 18
1976 Jumping Hill 4-9-7 16
1977 My Hussar 5-8-10 15
1978 Fear Naught 4-8-0 19
1979 Pipedreamer 4-8-5 24
1980 Tender Heart 4-9-0 22
1981 Teamwork 4-8-6 20
1982 Buzzards Bay 4-8-12 20
1983 Mighty Fly 4-9-3 31
1984 Hawkley 4-8-6 18
1985 Come on the Blues 6-8-2 27
1986 Patriach 4-7-12 32
1987 Vague Shot 4-9-5 25
1988 Governorship 4-9-6 26
1989 True Panache 4-9-4 27

QUEENS VASE
Ascot—2m

1970 Yellow River 3-7-12 16
1971 Parnell 3-7-12 20
1972 Falkland 4-9-4 10
1973 Tara Brooch 3-7-13 13
1974 Royal Aura 3-8-3 13
1975 Blood Royal 4-9-4 20
1976 General Ironside 3-8-5 14
1977 Millionaire 3-8-5 14
1978 Le Moss 3-8-0 12
1979 Buttress 3-8-5 13
1980 Toondra 3-8-0 14
1981 Ore 3-8-0 13
1982 Evzon 4-9-3 14
1983 Santella Man 4-9-8 17
1984 Baynoun 3-8-0 11
1985 Wassl Merbayeh 3-8-0 10
1986 Stavordale 3-7-10 13
1987 Arden 3-8-9 9
1988 Green Adventure 8-9 14
1989 Weld 8-9 11

CORK AND ORRERY STAKES
Ascot—6f

1970 Welsh Saint 4-9-1 4
1971 King's Company 3-8-12 11
1972 Parsimony 3-7-9 6
1973 Balliol 4-9-0 9
1974 Saritamer 3-8-5 17
1975 Swingtime 3-7-8 9
1976 Gentilhombre 3-8-0 11
1977 He Loves Me 3-8-4 15
1978 Sweet Mint 4-8-8 12
1979 Thatching 4-9-0 17
1980 Kearney 3-8-0 20
1981 The Quiet Bidder 3-8-2 16
1982 Indian King 4-9-0 18
1983 Sylvan Barbarosa 4-8-10 17
1984 Committed 4-8-7 15
1985 Dafayna 3-7-11 12
1986 Sperry 3-8-0 10
1987 Big Shuffle 3-8-4 11
1988 Posada 3-7-12 14
1989 Danehill 3-8-0 12

NORFOLK STAKES (2y)
Ascot—5f

1973 Habat 8-11 11
1974 Overtown 8-11 12
1975 Faliraki 8-11 10
1976 Godswalk (USA) 8-11 5
1977 Emboss 8-11 5
1978 Schweppeshire Lad 8-11 8
1979 Romeo Romani (USA) 8-11 10
1980 Chummy's Special 8-11 6
1981 Day Is Done 8-11 8
1982 Brondesbury 8-11 5
1983 Precocious 8-11 5
1984 Magic Mirror 8-11 4
1985 Marouble 8-11 10
1986 Sizzling Melody 8-11 6
1987 Colmore Row 8-13 8
1988 Superpower 8-13 10
1989 Petillante 8-8 6

GOLD CUP
Ascot—2m 4f

1970 Precipice Wood 4-9-0 6
1971 Random Shot 4-9-0 10
1972 Erimo Hawk 4-9-0 8
1973 Lassalle 4-9-0 7
1974 Ragstone 4-9-0 6
1975 Sagaro 4-9-0 8
1976 Sagaro 5-9-0 7
1977 Sagaro 6-9-0 6
1978 Shangamuzo 5-9-0 10
1979 Le Moss 4-9-0 6
1980 Le Moss 5-9-0 8
1981 Ardross 5-9-0 4
1982 Ardross 6-9-0 5
1983 Little Wolf 5-9-0 12
1984 Gildoran 4-9-0 9
1985 Gildoran 5-9-0 12
1986 Longboat 5-9-0 11
1987 Paean 4-9-0 8
1988 Sadeem 5-9-0 13
1989 Sadeem 6-9-0 8

RIBBLESDALE STAKES (3y fillies)
Ascot—1m 4f

1970 Parmelia 8-6 12

Winners of Great Races – Continued

1971 Fleet Wahine 8-10 10
1972 Star Ship 8-10 7
1973 Miss Petard 8-10 9
1974 Northern Princess 8-10 8
1975 Gallina 8-10 6
1976 Catalpa 8-10 7
1977 Nanticious 8-10 9
1978 Relfo 8-10 12
1979 Expansive 8-7 7
1980 Shoot A Line 8-11 9
1981 Strigida 8-7 9
1982 Dish Dash 8-7 10
1983 High Hawk 8-7 14
1984 Ballinderry 8-7 9
1985 Sally Brown 8-7 10
1986 Gull Nook 8-8 12
1987 Queen Midas 8-8 6
1988 Miss Boniface 8-8 11
1989 Alydaress 8-9 6

HARDWICKE STAKES
Ascot—1m 4f

1970 Karabas 5-8-12 5
1971 Ortis 4-8-12 8
1972 Selhurst 4-8-10 5
1973 Rheingold 4-9-0 4
1974 Relay Race 4-8-10 5
1975 Charlie Bubbles 4-8-10 11
1976 Orange Bay 4-9-0 5
1977 Meneval 4-9-0 7
1978 Montcontour 4-8-12 8
1979 Obraztsovy 4-8-9 6
1980 Scorpio 4-9-0 7
1981 Pelerin 4-8-12 9
1982 Critique 4-8-9 8
1983 Stanerra 5-8-9 10
1984 Khairpour 5-8-12 7
1985 Jupiter Island 6-8-9 4
1986 Dihistan 4-8-9 10
1987 Orban 4-8-9 4
1988 Almaarad 5-8-12 8
1989 Assatis 4-8-9 4

WOKINGHAM STAKES
Ascot—6f

1970 Virginia Boy 4-7-4 28
1971 Whistling Fool 5-7-7 21
1972 Le Johnstan 4-9-5 17
1973 Plummet 4-8-2 21
1974 Ginnies Pet 4-8-6 22
1975 Boone's Cabin 5-10-0 20
1976 Import 5-9-4 12
1977 Calibina 5-8-5 13
1978 Equal Opportunity 4-7-12 24
1979 Lord Rochford 4-8-8 28
1980 Queen's Pride 4-7-13 29
1981 Great Eastern 4-9-8 29
1982 Battle Hymn 3-7-7 24
1983 Melindra 4-7-5 27
1984 Petong 4-9-6 28
1985 Time Machine 4-7-12 30
1986 Touch of Grey 3-8-8 28
1987 Bel Byou 3-8-3 29
1988 Powder Blue 6-8-5 30
1989 Mac's Fighter 4-9-12 27

KING'S STAND STAKES
Ascot—5f

1970 Amber Rama 3-8-8 11
1971 Swing Easy 3-8-8 9
1972 Sweet Revenge 5-9-4 7
1973 Abergwaun 5-9-1 7
1974 Bay Express 3-8-9 10
1975 Flirting Around 4-9-4 12
1976 Lochnager 4-9-3 13
1977 Godswalk 3-8-9 11
1978 Solinus 3-8-9 8
1979 Double Form 4-9-3 13
1980 African Song 3-8-9 14
1981 Marwell 3-8-6 12
1982 Fearless Lad 3-8-9 14
1983 Sayf El Arab 3-8-9 16
1984 Habibti 4-9-0 11
1985 Never So Bold 5-9-3 15
1986 Last Tycoon 3-8-9 14
1987 Bluebird 3-8-9 12
1988 Chilibang 4-9-3 8
1989 Indian Ridge 4-9-3 15

NORTHUMBERLAND PLATE
Newcastle—2m

1970 Philoctetes 6-7-12 16
1971 Tartar Prince 4-7-8 18
1972 Scoria 6-7-6 13
1973 Tom Cribb 4-8-4 11
1974 Attivo 4-7-8 11
1975 Grey God 4-8-9 12
1976 Philominsky 5-8-0 11
1977 Tug of War 4-8-7 15
1978 Tug of War 5-9-2 10
1979 Totowah 5-8-2 11
1980 Mon's Beau 5-7-7 15
1981 Dawn Johnny 4-8-6 18
1982 Abandoned
1983 Weavers Pin 6-8-8 14
1984 Karadar 6-9-10 19
1985 Trade Line 4-7-10 13
1986 Sneak Preview 6-8-12 15
1987 Treasure Hunter 8-7-7 20
1988 Stavordale 5-9-2 10
1989 Orpheus 3-7-7 12

VAN GEEST CRITERION STAKES
Newmarket—7f

1981 Dalsaan 4-9-7 8
1982 Noalcoholic 5-9-7 14
1983 Thug 3-8-10 12
1984 Grey Desire 4-9-7 11
1985 Capricorn Belle 4-9-9 12
1986 Mister Wonderful 3-8-5 14
1987 Linda's Magic 3-8-2 5
1988 Cadeaux Genereux 3-8-5 5
1989 Zilzal 3-8-10 4

Winners of Great Races – Continued

SILVER CUP
(formerly Sun Page 3 Silver Cup)
Lingfield—1m 6f

1985	Skaramanga 3-8-6	4
1986	Rakaposhi King 4-8-12	6
1987	Lemhill 5-9-4	6
1988	Waterfield 4-8-12	6
1989	Ibn Bey 5-9-5	3

ECLIPSE STAKES
Sandown—1m 2f

1970	Connaught 5-9-5	3
1971	Mill Reef 3-8-7	6
1972	Brigadier Gerard 4-9-5	6
1973	Scottish Rifle 4-9-5	6
1974	Coup de Feu 5-9-5	12
1975	Star Appeal 5-9-7	16
1976	Wollow 3-8-8	10
1977	Artaius 3-8-8	10
1978	Gunner B 5-9-7	9
1979	Dickens Hill 3-8-8	7
1980	Ela-Mana-Mou 4-9-7	6
1981	Master Willie 4-9-7	7
1982	Kalaglow 4-9-7	9
1983	Solford 3-8-8	9
1984	Sadler's Wells 3-8-8	9
1985	Pebbles 4-9-4	4
1986	Dancing Brave 3-8-8	8
1987	Mtoto 4-9-7	8
1988	Mtoto 5-9-7	8
1989	Nashwan 3-8-8	6

OLD NEWTON CUP
Haydock—1m 4f

1970	New Member 5-8-2	9
1971	Wabash 4-8-2	9
1972	Private Walk 5-7-9	12
1973	Private Walk 6-7-10	3
1974	Belper 5-8-5	9
1975	Fool's Mate 4-9-2	9
1976	Peaceful 5-9-0	8
1977	Mint 3-7-7	11
1978	Move Off 5-9-4	12
1979	St Briavels 5-9-3	7
1980	Shady Nook 5-9-5	10
1981	Dogberry 3-7-5	8
1982	Valentinian 4-10-3	10
1983	Regal Steel 5-8-2	9
1984	Bishop's Ring 3-8-6	6
1985	Clanrallier 5-8-3	10
1986	Rakaposhi King 4-9-7	10
1987	Pipsted 3-8-0	9
1988	Roushayd 4-9-10	9
1989	Nickle Plated 4-9-7	16

LANCASHIRE OAKS (3y)
Haydock—1m 4f

1970	Amphora (FR) 8-12	6
1971	Maina 8-12	6
1972	Star Ship 9-0	7
1973	Istiea 8-6	4
1974	Mil's Bomb 8-6	8
1975	One Over Parr 8-11	5
1976	Centrocon 8-11	9
1977	Busaca (FR) 8-11	5
1978	Princess Eboli 9-1	9
1979	Reprocolor 9-1	5
1980	Vielle 8-11	6
1981	Rhein Bridge 8-11	7
1982	Sing Softly 8-11	8
1983	Give Thanks 9-1	13
1984	Sandy Island 8-11	9
1985	Graecia Magna 8-11	8
1986	Park Express 8-11	9
1987	Three Tails 9-1	6
1988	Andaleeb 8-9	8
1989	Roseate Tern 8-9	8

CHERRY HINTON STAKES (2y)
Newmarket—6f

1970	Hecla 8-3	5
1971	Padrona 8-8	5
1972	Mysterious 8-7	3
1973	Celestial Dawn 8-10	10
1974	Roussalka 8-10	8
1975	Everything Nice 8-13	6
1976	Ampulla 8-10	7
1977	Turkish Treasure 8-10	9
1978	Devon Ditty 8-13	13
1979	Mrs Penny 8-7	10
1980	Nasseem 8-10	11
1981	Travel On 8-10	10
1982	Crime of Passion 8-10	8
1983	Chapel Cottage 8-10	9
1984	Top Socialite 8-10	8
1985	Storm Star 8-10	12
1986	Forest Flower 9-0	10
1987	Diminuendo 8-9	9
1988	Kerrera 8-9	9
1989	Chimes of Freedom 8-9	8

BUNBURY CUP
Newmarket—7f

1970	Golden Orange 4-7-2	10
1971	Grotto 4-7-7	10
1972	Red Mask 5-8-12	6
1973	Fabvista 3-8-5	10
1974	Pitskelly 4-9-9	9
1975	Penny Post 3-8-2	14
1976	Lottogift 5-8-10	7
1977	Kintore 5-8-0	8
1978	Greenhill God 4-8-5	11
1979	Pipedreamer 4-9-3	14
1980	Steeple Bell 4-7-9	14
1981	Captain Nick 5-9-13	11
1982	Paterno 4-9-1	14
1983	Mummy's Pleasure 4-9-3	19
1984	Mummy's Pleasure 5-8-12	17
1985	Tremblant 4-8-12	18
1986	Patriach 4-9-1	16
1987	Individualist 4-8-5	15

Winners of Great Races – Continued

1988 Pinctada 6-8-3 16
1989 Baldomero 4-7-7 18

PRINCESS OF WALES'S STAKES

Newmarket—1m 4f

1970 Prince Consort 4-9-2 6
1971 Lupe 4-9-6 4
1972 Falkland 4-9-5 8
1973 Our Mirage 4-9-9 7
1974 Buoy 4-9-9 9
1975 Libra's Rib 3-7-11 10
1976 Smuggler 3-7-11 6
1977 Lord Helpus 4-9-2 8
1978 Pollerton 4-9-2 4
1979 Milford 3-8-2 6
1980 Nicholas Bill 5-9-2 9
1981 Light Cavalry 4-9-9 8
1982 Height of Fashion 3-7-11 4
1983 Quilted 3-8-0 11
1984 Head for Heights 3-8-6 9
1985 Petoski 3-8-0 5
1986 Shardari 4-9-0 6
1987 Celestial Storm 4-9-0 9
1988 Unfuwain 3-8-0 5
1989 Carroll House 4-9-5 5

CHILD STAKES (fillies)

Before 1974: 3-year-olds only
(Falmouth Stakes before 1975)
Newmarket—1m

1970 Caprera 8-3 4
1971 Favoletta 9-3 3
1972 Waterloo 9-7 4
1973 Jacinth 9-7 4
1974 Himawari 3-7-12 9
1975 Sauceboat 3-8-1 6
1976 Duboff 4-9-6 9
1977 River Dane 3-8-5 6
1978 Cistus 3-8-2 10
1979 Rose Above 4-8-10 7
1980 Stumped 3-7-12 9
1981 Star Pastures 3-8-3 10
1982 Chalon 3-8-11 7
1983 Royal Heroine 3-8-5 8
1984 Meis El-Reem 3-8-5 5
1985 Al Bahathri 3-8-11 9
1986 Sonic Lady 8-11 8
1987 Sonic Lady 4-9-10 4
1988 Inchmurrin 3-8-6 7
1989 Magic Gleam 3-8-6 6

JULY STAKES (2y)

Newmarket—6f

1970 Swing Easy 9-0 4
1971 Deep Diver 8-11 8
1972 Perdu 8-11 3
1973 Dragonara Palace 8-11 4
1974 Auction Ring 8-6 9
1975 Super Cavalier 8-6 6
1976 Sky Ship 8-10 6
1977 Royal Harmony 8-10 4
1978 Main Reef 8-13 6
1979 Final Straw 8-10 7
1980 Age Quod Agis 8-10 3
1981 End of the Line 8-10 11
1982 Horage 9-2 7
1983 Superlative 8-10 6
1984 Primo Dominie 9-1 7
1985 Green Desert 8-10 8
1986 Mansooj 8-10 8
1987 Sanquirico 8-10 7
1988 Always Valiant 8-10 4
1989 Rock City 9-1 4

JULY CUP

Newmarket—6f

1970 Huntercombe 3-8-6 4
1971 Realm 4-9-3 8
1972 Parsimony 3-8-7 5
1973 Thatch 3-8-10 6
1974 Saritamer 3-8-10 9
1975 Lianga 4-9-4 13
1976 Lochnager 4-9-6 10
1977 Gentilhombre 4-9-6 8
1978 Solinus 3-8-11 14
1979 Thatching 4-9-6 11
1980 Moorestyle 3-8-11 14
1981 Marwell 3-8-8 14
1982 Sharpo 5-9-6 16
1983 Habibti 3-8-8 15
1984 Chief Singer 3-8-11 9
1985 Never So Bold 5-9-6 9
1986 Green Desert 3-8-11 5
1987 Ajdal 3-8-11 11
1988 Soviet Star 4-9-6 9
1989 Cadeaux Genereux 4-9-6 11

MAGNET CUP

York—1m 2½f

1970 Timon 4-7-4 15
1971 Prominent 4-8-8 12
1972 Prominent 5-9-4 8
1973 Peleid 3-7-9 8
1974 Take a Reef 3-8-12 13
1975 Jolly Good 3-7-8 15
1976 Bold Pirate 4-9-3 9
1977 Air Trooper 4-9-6 8
1978 Town and Country 4-8-13 9
1979 Tesoro Mio 4-8-3 9
1980 Fine Sun 3-7-8 12
1981 Amyndas 3-8-5 11
1982 Buzzards Bay 4-9-8 6
1983 Bedtime 3-7-9 9
1984 Straight Man 3-8-11 9
1985 Chaumiere 4-9-7 12
1986 Chaumiere 5-9-5 11
1987 *Brave Dancer 3-8-8
*Wolsey 3-8-6 9
1988 Bashful Boy 3-8-2 16
1989 Icona 3-9-8 10

Winners of Great Races – Continued

PRINCESS MARGARET STAKES (2y)

Ascot—6f

Year	Winner	Runners
1970	Boulevard 9-2	6
1971	Secret Kiss 9-1	10
1972	Fiery Diplomat 9-1	4
1973	Celestial Dawn 9-4	10
1974	Roussalka 9-4	6
1975	Outer Circle 9-4	4
1976	Al Stanza 9-4	8
1977	Sarissa 9-1	7
1978	Devon Ditty 9-1	4
1979	Luck of the Draw 8-12	4
1980	Tolmi 8-12	7
1981	Circus Ring 8-12	9
1982	Royal Heroine 8-12	6
1983	Desirable 8-12	4
1984	Al Bahathri 8-12	9
1985	Kingscote 8-12	11
1986	Hiaam 8-8	6
1987	Bluebook 8-8	6
1988	Muhbubh 8-8	6
1989	Pharaoh's Delight 8-8	6

BEESWING STAKES

Newcastle—7f

Year	Winner	Runners
1977	In Haste 3-8-5	9
1978	John de Coombe 3-8-5	7
1979	Jeroboam 3-8-5	3
1980	Kampala 4-9-6	7
1981	Milk of the Barley 4-9-0	6
1982	Silly Steven 3-8-5	8
1983	Beaudelaire 3-8-5	7
1984	Major Don 4-9-3	7
1985	Sarab 4-9-6	7
1986	Hadeer 4-9-0	9
1987	Farajullah 4-9-1	8
1988	Salse 3-8-9	6
1989	Great Commotion 3-8-6	4

STEWARDS' CUP

Goodwood—6f

Year	Winner	Runners
1970	Jukebox 4-8-11	24
1971	Apollo Nine 4-9-5	26
1972	Touch Paper 3-8-2	22
1973	Alphadamus 3-7-11	27
1974	Red Alert 3-9-2	25
1975	Import 4-8-0	21
1976	Jimmy the Singer 3-7-8	17
1977	Calibina 5-8-5	24
1978	Ahonoora 3-8-0	23
1979	Standaan 3-7-10	16
1980	Repetitious 3-7-2	28
1981	Crews Hill 5-9-9	30
1982	Soba 3-8-4	30
1983	Autumn Sunset 3-8-2	23
1984	Petong 4-9-10	26
1985	Al Trui 5-8-1	28
1986	Green Ruby 5-8-12	24
1987	Madraco 4-7-2	30
1988	Rotherfield Greys 6-8-8	28
1989	Very Adjacent 4-7-4	22

GORDON STAKES (3y)

Goodwood—1m 4f

Year	Winner	Runners
1970	Rock Roi 8-7	4
1971	Athens Wood 8-7	5
1972	Scottish Rifle 8-10	3
1973	Duke of Ragusa 8-10	4
1974	Grey Thunder 8-10	8
1975	Guillaume Tell 8-10	9
1976	Smuggler 8-13	6
1977	Pollerton 8-10	4
1978	Sexton Blake 8-10	5
1979	More Light 8-10	6
1980	Prince Bee 8-10	6
1981	Bustomi 9-2	5
1982	Electric 8-13	6
1983	John French 8-10	6
1984	Commanche Run 8-10	8
1985	Kazaroun 8-10	5
1986	Allez Milord 8-10	5
1987	Love the Groom 9-2	6
1988	Minster Son 8-10	5
1989	Warrshan 8-10	4

OAK TREE STAKES

Goodwood—7f

Year	Winner	Runners
1980	Trevita 3-8-5	10
1981	Star Pastures 3-8-11	6
1982	Chalon 3-9-0	5
1983	Fenny Rough 3-8-7	6
1984	Brocade 3-8-5	10
1985	Ever Genial 3-8-5	6
1986	Royal Loft 3-8-7	12
1987	Gayane 3-8-10	6
1988	Ohsomellow 3-8-10	7
1989	Kerita 3-8-7	6

SUSSEX STAKES

Goodwood—1m

Year	Winner	Runners
1970	Humble Duty 3-8-4	5
1971	Brigadier Gerard 3-8-7	5
1972	Sallust 3-8-10	3
1973	Thatch 3-8-10	7
1974	Ace of Aces 4-9-7	10
1975	Bolkonski 3-8-10	9
1976	Wollow 3-8-10	9
1977	Artaius 3-8-10	11
1978	Jaazeiro 3-8-10	6
1979	Kris 3-8-10	7
1980	Posse 3-8-10	9
1981	Kings Lake 3-8-10	9
1982	On the House 3-8-7	13
1983	Noalcoholic 6-9-7	11
1984	Chief Singer 3-8-10	5
1985	Rousillon 4-9-7	10
1986	Sonic Lady 3-8-7	5
1987	Soviet Star 3-8-10	7
1988	Warning 3-8-10	9
1989	Zilzal 3-8-10	8

Winners of Great Races – Continued

RICHMOND STAKES (2y)
Goodwood—6f

1970	Swing Easy 9-0	5
1971	Sallust 8-11	10
1972	Master Sing 9-0	7
1973	Dragonara Palace 8-11	7
1974	Legal Eagle 8-11	6
1975	Stand to Reason 8-11	9
1976	J O Tobin 8-11	5
1977	Persian Bold 8-11	5
1978	Young Generation 8-11	5
1979	Castle Green 8-11	5
1980	Another Realm 8-11	10
1981	Tender King 8-11	7
1982	Gallant Special 8-11	4
1983	Godstone 8-11	9
1984	Primo Dominie 8-11	6
1985	Nomination 8-11	10
1986	Rich Charlie 8-11	8
1987	Warning 8-11	7
1988	Heart of Arabia 9-0	6
1989	Contract Law 8-11	5

KING GEORGE STAKES
Goodwood—5f

1970	Raffingora 5-9-9	4
1971	Constans 6-8-13	6
1972	Stilvi 3-8-5	5
1973	Sandford Lad 3-8-4	5
1974	Singing Bede 5-9-0	9
1975	Auction Ring 3-8-4	8
1976	Music Boy 3-8-5	8
1977	Scarcely Blessed 3-8-2	9
1978	Music Maestro 3-9-1	7
1979	Ahonoora 4-9-3	7
1980	Valeriga 4-9-6	9
1981	King of Spain 5-9-8	8
1982	Tina's Pet 4-9-0	12
1983	Soba 4-9-0	14
1984	Anita's Prince 3-8-8	13
1985	Primo Dominie 3-8-13	11
1986	Double Schwartz 5-9-5	14
1987	Singing Steven 3-8-13	9
1988	Silver Fling 3-8-5	13
1989	Statoblest 3-8-8	13

SCHWEPPES HANDICAP
Goodwood—1m

1987	Waajib 4-9-10	20
1988	Strike Force 3-8-6	21
1989	Safawan 3-8-0	14

GOODWOOD CUP
Goodwood—2m 5f

1970	Parthenon 4-9-0	5
1971	Rock Roi 4-9-0	5
1972	Erimo Hawk 4-9-0	4
1973	Proverb 3-7-10	4
1974	Proverb 4-9-0	4
1975	Girandole 4-9-0	8
1976	Mr Bigmore 4-9-0	6
1977	Grey Baron 4-9-3	8
1978	Tug of War 5-9-0	5
1979	Le Moss 4-9-7	5
1980	Le Moss 5-9-7	5
1981	Ardross 5-9-7	6
1982	Heighlin 6-9-0	8
1983	Little Wolf 5-9-7	7
1984	Gildoran 4-9-7	4
1985	Valuable Witness 5-9-0	7
1986	Longboat 5-9-7	5
1987	Sergeyevich 3-7-10	5
1988	Sadeem 5-9-7	6
1989	Mazzacano 4-9-0	5

EXTEL HANDICAP (3y)
(News of the World Handicap before 1970)
Goodwood—1m 2f

1970	Sol 'Argent 7-7	13
1971	Spoiled Lad 9-3	8
1972	Warpath 8-4	15
1973	Cupid 7-7	12
1974	Take a Reef 9-11	19
1975	Duboff 8-0	12
1976	Il Padrone 8-1	13
1977	Ad Lib Ra 9-0	14
1978	Crimson Beau 8-2	7
1979	Lindoro 9-0	8
1980	Karamita 7-7	10
1981	Indian Trail 8-3	9
1982	Busaco 9-1	10
1983	Millfontaine 8-13	12
1984	Free Guest 8-6	15
1985	Fish 'N' Chips 8-3	13
1986	Chinoiserie 8-11	13
1987	Broken Hearted 9-3	13
1988	Kazaviyna 7-10	14
1989	Biennial 9-2	8

SCHRODERS GLORIOUS STAKES
Goodwood—1m 4f

1979	Bohemian Grove 3-8-3	5
1980	Water Mill 3-8-2	7
1981	Capstan 3-7-1	5
1982	Capstan 4-9-1	4
1983	Seymour Hicks 3-8-5	7
1984	Longboat 3-8-2	6
1985	Shernazar 4-9-1	9
1986	Nisnas 3-8-2	8
1987	Knockando 3-8-5	9
1988	Maksud 3-8-2	4
1989	Knoosh 3-8-5	3

MOLECOMB STAKES (2y)
Goodwood—5f

1970	Cawston's Pride 8-11	3
1971	Pert Lassie 8-8	4
1972	Miss Slip 8-11	3
1973	Bitty Girl 9-11	6
1974	Lady Rowley 8-13	4
1975	Hayloft 8-10	8
1976	Be Easy 8-10	7

Winners of Great Races – Continued

1977	Hatta 8-10	7
1978	Greenland Park 9-4	6
1979	Keep Off 8-10	6
1980	Marwell 8-10	7
1981	Prowess Prince 8-10	6
1982	Kafu 8-10	4
1983	Precocious 9-0	7
1984	Absent Chimes 8-10	8
1985	Hotbee 8-7	9
1986	Gemini Fire 8-12	6
1987	Classic Ruler 8-12	7
1988	Almost Blue 8-12	13
1989	Haunting Beauty 8-7	10

NASSAU STAKES (fillies)

Before 1975 3-year-olds only.
Goodwood—1m 2f

1970	Pulchra 8-4	5
1971	Catherine Wheel 8-4	5
1972	Crespinall 8-8	4
1973	Cheveley Princess 8-8	9
1974	Mil's Bomb 8-8	4
1975	Roussalka 3-8-8	6
1976	Roussalka 4-9-6	10
1977	Triple First 3-8-5	8
1978	Cistus 3-8-5	7
1979	Connaught Bridge 3-8-5	10
1980	Vielle 3-8-5	7
1981	Go Leasing 3-8-8	11
1982	Dancing Rocks 3-8-5	11
1983	Acclimatise 3-8-5	6
1984	Optimistic Lass 3-8-8	5
1985	Free Guest 4-9-8	11
1986	Park Express 3-8-8	7
1987	Nom de Plume 3-8-7	5
1988	Ela Romara 3-8-6	7
1989	Mamaluna 3-8-6	5

HUNGERFORD STAKES

Newbury—7f 60yds

1970	Zingari 3-7-9	7
1971	Welsh Pageant 5-9-4	7
1972	Home Guard 3-8-6	6
1973	Brook 3-8-6	7
1974	Pitcairn 3-8-6	6
1975	Court Chad 3-8-3	14
1976	Ardoon 6-9-4	15
1977	He Loves Me 3-8-11	10
1978	Tannenberg 3-8-6	10
1979	Skyliner 4-9-0	13
1980	Kampala 4-9-0	8
1981	Dalsaan 4-9-0	10
1982	Pas de Seul 3-8-9	10
1983	Salieri 3-8-11	10
1984	Prego 4-9-0	8
1985	Ever Genial 3-8-6	12
1986	Hadeer 4-9-3	11
1987	Abuzz 3-8-3	8
1988	Salse 3-8-9	11
1989	Distant Relative 3-8-11	7

GEOFFREY FREER STAKES

Newbury—1m 5f 60yds

1970	High Line 4-9-3	4
1971	High Line 5-9-5	4
1972	Sol' Argent 5-9-0	7
1973	Attica Meli 4-9-5	8
1974	Realistic 5-9-0	7
1975	Consol 3-8-6	10
1976	Swell Fellow 5-9-0	5
1977	Valinsky 3-8-4	5
1978	Ile de Bourbon 3-8-9	7
1979	Niniski 3-8-1	7
1980	Nicholas Bill 5-9-5	5
1981	Ardross 5-9-8	4
1982	Ardross 6-9-8	4
1983	Khairpour 4-9-0	7
1984	Baynoun 3-8-5	5
1985	Shernazar 4-9-0	5
1986	Bakharoff 3-8-3	6
1987	Moon Madness 4-9-8	4
1988	Top Class 3-8-3	6
1989	Ibn Bey 5-9-8	6

SOLARIO STAKES (2y)

Sandown—7f

1975	Over to You 8-11	10
1976	Avgerinos 8-11	10
1977	Bolak 8-11	9
1978	Lyphard's Wish 9-1	6
1979	Rankin 9-4	4
1980	To-Agori-Mou 9-0	4
1981	No race	
1982	The Fort 9-0	6
1983	Falstaff 9-0	4
1984	Oh So Sharp 8-8	9
1985	Bold Arrangement 9-0	5
1986	Shining Water 8-8	11
1987	Sanquirico 9-0	4
1988	High Estate 9-0	6
1989	Be My Chief 9-0	3

INTERNATIONAL STAKES

(Benson & Hedges Gold Cup before 1986)
York—1m 2½f

1972	Roberto 3-8-10	5
1973	Moulton 4-9-7	8
1974	Dahlia 4-9-4	9
1975	Dahlia 5-9-4	6
1976	Wollow 3-8-10	7
1977	Relkino 4-9-6	8
1978	Hawaiian Sound 3-8-10	10
1979	Troy 3-8-10	10
1980	Master Willie 3-8-10	12
1981	Beldale Flutter 3-8-10	9
1982	Assert 3-8-10	7
1983	Caerleon 3-8-10	9
1984	Cormorant Wood 4-9-3	9
1985	Commanche Run 4-9-6	6
1986	Shardari 4-9-6	12
1987	Triptych 5-9-3	10
1988	Shady Heights 4-9-6	6
1989	Ile De Chypre 4-9-6	7

Winners of Great Races – Continued

GREAT VOLTIGEUR STAKES (3y colts)
York—1m 4f

1970 Meadowville 9-0 4
1971 Athens Wood 9-0 5
1972 Our Mirage 9-0 7
1973 Buoy 9-0 5
1974 Bustino 9-0 3
1975 Patch 9-0 4
1976 Hawkberry 8-7 7
1977 Alleged 8-11 7
1978 Whitstead 8-7 8
1979 Noble Saint 8-7 5
1980 Prince Bee 8-7 5
1981 Glint of Gold 9-0 6
1982 Electric 8-7 7
1983 Seymour Hicks 8-7 5
1984 Rainbow Quest 8-7 7
1985 Damister 8-11 4
1986 Nisnas 8-7 7
1987 Reference Point 9-0 3
1988 Sheriff's Star 8-12 4
1989 Zalazl 8-9 3

YORKSHIRE OAKS (3y fillies)
York—1m 4f

1970 Lupe 9-0 3
1971 Fleet Wahine 9-0 6
1972 Attica Meli 9-0 6
1973 Mysterious 9-0 5
1974 Dibidale 9-0 3
1975 May Hill 9-0 5
1976 Sarah Siddons 9-0 13
1977 Busaca 9-0 8
1978 Fair Salinia 9-0 10
1979 Connaught Bridge 9-0 5
1980 Shoot a Line 9-0 7
1981 Condessa 9-0 11
1982 Awaasif 9-0 7
1983 Sun Princess 9-0 6
1984 Circus Plume 9-0 5
1985 Sally Brown 9-0 7
1986 Untold 9-0 11
1987 Bint Pasha 9-0 9
1988 Diminuendo 9-0 6
1989 Roseate Tern 9-0 5

EBOR HANDICAP
York—1m 6f

1970 Tintagel 5-8-5 21
1971 Knotty Pine 5-8-7 21
1972 Crazy Rhythm 4-8-6 21
1973 Bonne Noel 4-9-2 20
1974 Anji 5-7-8 18
1975 Dakota 4-9-4 18
1976 Sir Montagu 3-8-0 15
1977 Move Off 4-8-1 14
1978 Totowah 4-8-1 22
1979 Sea Pigeon 9-10-0 17
1980 Shaftesbury 4-8-5 16
1981 Protection Racket 3-8-1 22
1982 Another Sam 5-9-2 15
1983 Jupiter Island 4-9-0 16
1984 Crazy 3-8-13 14
1985 Western Dancer 4-8-6 19
1986 Primary 3-8-7 22
1987 Daarkom 4-9-3 15
1988 Kneller 3-8-1 21
1989 Sapience 3-8-4 18

GIMCRACK STAKES (2y)
York—6f

1970 Mill Reef 9-0 8
1971 Wishing Star 8-11 12
1972 Rapid River 9-0 9
1973 Giacometti 9-0 11
1974 Steel Heart 9-0 10
1975 Music Boy 9-0 14
1976 Nebbiolo 9-0 7
1977 Tumbledownwind 9-0 5
1978 Stanford 9-0 11
1979 Sonnen Gold 9-0 7
1980 Bel Bolide 9-0 9
1981 Full Extent 9-0 8
1982 Horage 9-0 7
1983 Precocious 9-0 6
1984 Doulab 9-0 8
1985 Stalker 9-0 6
1986 Wiganthorpe 9-0 11
1987 Reprimand 9-0 6
1988 Sharp N' Early 9-0 8
1989 Rock City 9-3 5

WILLIAM HILL SPRINT CHAMPIONSHIP
(Nunthorpe Stakes before 1976)
York—5f

1970 Huntercombe 3-9-2 3
1971 Swing Easy 3-9-2 8
1972 Deep Diver 3-9-2 7
1973 Sandford Lad 3-9-2 8
1974 Blue Cashmere 4-9-7 12
1975 Bay Express 4-9-7 10
1976 Lochnager 4-9-6 11
1977 Haveroid 3-9-2 8
1978 Solinus 3-9-2 9
1979 Ahonoora 4-9-6 9
1980 Sharpo 3-9-2 11
1981 Sharpo 4-9-0 9
1982 Sharpo 5-9-0 11
1983 Habibti 3-8-7 10
1984 Committed 4-8-11 8
1985 Never So Bold 5-9-0 7
1986 Last Tycoon 3-9-2 8
1987 Ajdal 3-9-2 11
1988 Handsome Sailor 5-9-6 12
1989 Cadeaux Genereux 4-9-6 11

BRADFORD AND BINGLEY HANDICAP
(Rose of York Handicap before 1983)
York—1m

1970 Morris Dancer 9-8-9 12
1971 Dancing Mood 5-8-3 8

Winners of Great Races – Continued

1972 Hardy Scot 3-8-2 12
1973 Summer Knave 3-7-8 11
1974 Father Christmas 4-9-5 9
1975 Chil the Kite 3-9-2 13
1976 Silver Steel 3-7-13 13
1977 Chukaroo 5-7-11 10
1978 Petronisi 4-8-1 15
1979 Piaffer 4-8-6 9
1980 Miner's Lamp 3-8-7 12
1981 Silver Season 3-9-0 9
1982 Indian Trail 4-8-8 11
1983 Mauritzfontein 4-7-11 14
1984 King of Clubs 3-8-12 17
1985 Lucky Ring 3-8-3 14
1986 Digger's Rest 3-9-4 14
1987 Prince Rupert 3-8-8 12
1988 Kingsfold Flame 5-8-5 15
1989 Known Ranger 3-9-4 16

LOWTHER STAKES (2y fillies)
York—6f

1970 Cawston's Pride 9-0 2
1971 Rose Dubarry 8-8 3
1972 Regardia 8-11 6
1973 Bitty Girl 9-0 7
1974 Cry of Truth 8-11 6
1975 Pasty 8-11 7
1976 Icena 8-11 13
1977 Enstone Spark 8-11 9
1978 Devon Ditty 9-0 11
1979 Mrs Penny 9-0 8
1980 Kittyhawk 8-8 5
1981 Circus Ring 8-11 8
1982 Habibti 8-11 8
1983 Prickle 8-11 9
1984 Al Bahathri 8-11 10
1985 Kingscote 8-11 7
1986 Polonia 9-0 9
1987 Ela Romara 8-11 5
1988 Miss Demure 8-11 9
1989 Dead Certain 9-0 6

BLACKBOTTLE SCOTCH WHISKY STAKES (2y)
(Formerly Waterford Candelabra Stakes)
Goodwood—7f

1981 Stratospheric 8-6 6
1982 Flamenco 8-9 9
1983 Shoot Clear 8-9 8
1984 Bella Colora 8-6 6
1985 Asteroid Field 8-6 6
1986 Invited Guest 8-7 6
1987 Obeah 8-9 6
1988 Life at the Top 8-12 7
1989 Moon Cactus 8-12 7

BEEFEATER GIN CELEBRATION MILE
(Formerly Waterford Crystal Mile)
Goodwood—1m

1970 Humble Duty 3-8-4 5
1971 Brigadier Gerard 3-8-6 3
1972 Sallust 3-8-13 3
1973 Jacinth 3-8-10 5
1974 Pitcairn 3-8-8 3
1975 Gay Fandango 3-8-8 8
1976 Free State 3-8-3 6
1977 Be My Guest 3-8-7 6
1978 Captain James 4-8-13 5
1979 Kris 3-8-12 8
1980 Known Fact 3-8-12 6
1981 To-Agori-Mou 3-8-12 6
1982 Sandhurst Prince 3-8-5 8
1983 Montekin 4-8-13 6
1984 Rousillon 3-8-6 5
1985 Abandoned
1986 Then Again 3-8-7 8
1987 Milligram 3-8-7 4
1988 Prince Rupert 4-9-3 6
1989 Distant Relative 3-8-12 5

LADBROKE SPRINT CUP
Haydock—6f

1970 Golden Orange 4-9-10 5
1971 Green God 3-9-6 7
1972 Abergwaun 4-9-7 10
1973 The Blues 2-8-0 8
1974 Princely Son 5-9-10 11
1975 Lianga 4-9-7 7
1976 Record Token 4-9-8 8
1977 Boldboy 7-9-8 7
1978 Absalom 3-9-6 14
1979 Double Form 4-9-8 7
1980 Moorestyle 3-8-12 8
1981 Runnett 4-9-3 6
1982 Indian King 4-9-3 9
1983 Habibti 3-8-9 6
1984 Petong 4-9-3 9
1985 Orojoya 3-8-12 8
1986 Green Desert 3-8-12 8
1987 Ajdal 3-9-0 8
1988 Dowsing 4-9-2 10
1989 Danehill 3-9-5 9

SEPTEMBER STAKES
Kempton—1m 3f 30yds

1979 Cracaval 3-8-10 9
1980 More Light 4-9-2 7
1981 Kind of Hush 3-8-4 11
1982 Critique 4-9-2 7
1983 Lyphard's Special 3-8-4 6
1984 Bedtime 4-9-0 8
1985 Shernazar 4-9-2 5
1986 Dihistan 4-9-2 7
1987 Knockando 3-8-4 8
1988 Percy's Lass 4-8-11 8
1989 Assatis 4-9-5 5

MAY HILL STAKES (2y)
Doncaster—1m

1981 Height of Fashion 8-9 4
1982 Bright Crocus 8-7 8
1983 Satinette 8-6 9
1984 Ever Genial 8-6 7
1985 Midway Lady 8-6 6

Winners of Great Races – Continued

1986 Laluche 8-9 10
1987 Intimate Guest 8-8 6
1988 Tessla 8-8 11
1989 Rafha 8-8 5

PORTLAND HANDICAP
Doncaster—5f 140yds

1970 Virginia Boy 4-7-1 16
1971 Royben 3-8-6 17
1972 Privateer 6-8-1 13
1973 Supreme Gift 3-8-6 15
1974 Matinee 3-8-11 20
1975 Walk By 3-8-10 16
1976 Hei'land Jamie 5-7-13 11
1977 Jon George 3-7-12 12
1978 Goldhills Pride 4-8-10 13
1979 Oh Simmie 4-7-0 21
1980 Swelter 4-8-2 20
1981 Touch Boy 5-8-11 21
1982 Vorvados 5-8-13 14
1983 Out of Hand 4-7-3 15
1984 Dawn's Delight 6-7-8 22
1985 Lochtillum 6-8-1 17
1986 Felipe Toro 3-8-2 23
1987 Dawn's Delight 9-8-13 23
1988 Roman Prose 3-9-3 22
1989 Craft Express 3-8-9 22

PARK HILL STAKES (3y fillies)
Doncaster—1m 6f 127yds

1970 Parmelia 9-0 5
1971 Example 9-0 8
1972 Attica Meli 9-0 7
1973 Reload 9-0 9
1974 Mil's Bomb 9-0 10
1975 May Hill 9-0 7
1976 African Dancer 9-0 9
1977 Royal Hive 9-0 3
1978 Idle Waters 9-0 10
1979 Quay Line 9-0 5
1980 Shoot a Line 9-0 6
1981 Alma Ata 9-0 13
1982 Swiftfoot 9-0 6
1983 High Hawk 9-0 7
1984 Borushka 9-0 13
1985 I Want To Be 9-0 7
1986 Rejuvenate 8-9 12
1987 Trampship 8-9 5
1988 Casey 8-9 9
1989 Lucky Song 8-10 4

KIVETON PARK STAKES
Doncaster—7f

1978 Green Girl 3-8-4 12
1979 Tap on Wood 3-9-3 7
1980 Known Fact 3-9-3 4
1981 Kittyhawk 3-8-5 6
1982 The Quiet Bidder 4-9-10 9
1983 Annie Edge 3-8-4 8
1984 Sarab 3-8-13 10
1985 Lucky Ring 3-8-13 8
1986 Hadeer 4-9-4 12
1987 Guest Performer 3-8-4 12
1988 Salse 3-8-11 6
1989 Gold Seam 3-8-7 6

DONCASTER CUP
Doncaster—2m 2f

1970 Magna Carta 4-8-12 4
1971 Rock Roi 4-8-12 5
1972 Biskrah 5-9-0 5
1973 Attica Meli 4-8-11 4
1974 Proverb 4-9-0 3
1975 Crash Course 4-9-0 3
1976 Sea Anchor 4-9-3 4
1977 Shangamuzo 4-8-12 5
1978 Buckskin 5-9-2 6
1979 Le Moss 4-9-2 5
1980 Le Moss 5-9-2 5
1981 Protection Racket 3-7-6 4
1982 Ardross 6-9-2 8
1983 Karadar 5-8-5 8
1984 Wagoner 4-8-5 4
1985 Spicy Story 4-8-9 8
1986 Longboat 5-9-6 4
1987 Buckley 4-8-13 8
1988 Kneller 3-8-4 4
1989 Weld 3-8-0 3

CHAMPAGNE STAKES (2y)
Doncaster—7f

1970 Breeders Dream 9-0 6
1971 Crowned Prince 8-11 8
1972 Otha 9-0 5
1973 Giacometti 9-0 8
1974 Grundy 9-0 10
1975 Wollow 9-0 8
1976 J. O. Tobin 9-0 6
1977 Sexton Blake 9-0 6
1978 R. B. Chesne 9-0 7
1979 Final Straw 9-0 9
1980 Gielgud 9-0 10
1981 Achieved 9-0 8
1982 Gorytus 9-0 5
1983 Lear Fan 9-0 4
1984 Young Runaway 9-0 6
1985 Sure Blade 9-0 5
1986 Don't Forget Me 9-0 9
1987 Warning 9-0 4
1988 Prince of Dance 8-11 7
1989 Abandoned ....

FLYING CHILDERS STAKES (2y)
(Norfolk Stakes before 1973)
Doncaster—5f

1970 Mummy's Pet 9-0 5
1971 Rose Dubarry 8-8 5
1972 Marble Arch 8-11 8
1973 Gentle Thoughts 8-11 7
1974 Hot Spark 9-4 7
1975 Hittite Glory 9-0 5
1976 Mandrake Major 9-0 9
1977 Music Maestro 9-0 8

Winners of Great Races – Continued

1978 Devon Ditty 8-11 7
1979 Abeer 8-11 6
1980 Marwell 8-11 6
1981 Peterhof 9-0 7
1982 Kafu 9-0 5
1983 Superlative 9-0 10
1984 Prince Sabo 9-0 6
1985 Green Desert 9-0 8
1986 Sizzling Melody 9-0 6
1987 Gallic League 8-11 7
1988 Shuttlecock Corner 8-11 8
1989 Abandoned

AYR GOLD CUP
Ayr—6f

1970 John Splendid 3-8-10 19
1971 Royben 3-8-7 28
1972 Swinging Junior 3-8-11 20
1973 Blue Cashmere 3-8-2 19
1974 Somersway 4-7-12 23
1975 Roman Warrior 4-10-0 23
1976 Last Tango 5-7-5 18
1977 Jon George 3-8-4 25
1978 Vaigly Great 3-9-6 24
1979 Primula Boy 4-7-7 22
1980 Sparkling Boy 3-9-2 24
1981 First Movement 3-7-10 21
1982 Famous Star 3-7-7 14
1983 Polly's Brother 5-8-3 28
1984 Able Albert 4-8-6 29
1985 Camps Heath 4-7-9 25
1986 Green Ruby 5-8-11 29
1987 Not So Silly 3-7-10 29
1988 So Careful 5-7-7 29
1989 Joveworth 6-8-0 29

SELECT STAKES
(Formerly Valdoe Stakes)
Goodwood—1m 2f

1975 Escapologist 3-7-8 7
1976 Obstacle 3-7-12 8
1977 Balmerino 5-9-9 9
1978 Gunner B 5-9-9 3
1979 Bolide (at Sandown) 3-7-13 6
1980 Welsh Chanter 4-9-3 6
1981 Prince Bee 4-9-9 4
1982 Peacetime 3-8-10 6
1983 Morcon 3-8-7 6
1984 Bob Back 3-8-5 5
1985 Iroko 3-8-4 8
1986 Dancing Brave 3-8-13 6
1987 Most Welcome 3-8-6 6
1988 Mtoto 5-9-9 5
1989 Legal Case 3-8-6 5

COURAGE HANDICAP
(Peter Hastings Handicap before 1985)
Newbury—1m 2f

1971 Royal Echo 4-8-2 7
1972 Colum 4-9-1 8
1973 Bright Fire 5-8-7 14
1974 One Night Stand 3-7-9 11
1975 Jolly Good 3-8-11 12
1976 Chil the Kite 4-9-10 9
1977 April 3-8-3 11
1978 Pam's Gleam 5-8-0 8
1979 Effulgence 4-9-4 7
1980 Etching 3-8-5 9
1981 Atlantic Boy 4-9-4 8
1982 Oratavo 4-7-13 13
1983 Mauritzfontein 4-8-2 9
1984 Miss Saint-Cloud 3-8-8 7
1985 Leading Star 3-8-13 15
1986 Power Bender 4-8-1 13
1987 Shabib 3-8-4 9
1988 Ile de Chypre 3-9-3 16
1989 Monastery 3-8-4 16

MILL REEF STAKES (2y)
Newbury—6f

1972 Mon Fils 8-11 4
1973 Habat 9-4 6
1974 Red Cross 8-11 8
1975 Royal Boy 8-11 8
1976 Anax 8-11 6
1977 Formidable 8-11 6
1978 King of Spain 8-11 8
1979 Lord Seymour 8-11 7
1980 Sweet Monday 8-11 7
1981 Hays 8-11 8
1982 Salieri 8-11 5
1983 Vacarme 8-11 7
1984 Local Suitor 8-11 12
1985 Luqman 8-11 9
1986 Forest Flower 8-8 9
1987 Magic of Life 8-6 5
1988 Russian Bond 8-11 4
1989 Welney 8-11 7

CORAL AUTUMN CUP (Handicap)
Newbury—1m 5f 60yds

1970 Golden Love 3-7-9 16
1971 Fidel 3-7-7 9
1972 Danton 3-7-8 13
1973 Sunyboy 3-7-13 11
1974 Inventory 6-8-8 12
1975 Coed Cochion 3-8-2 15
1976 John Cherry (USA) 5-9-6 4
1977 Nearly a Hand 3-8-4 12
1978 Piccadilly Line 5-8-12 8
1979 Greatham House 3-9-1 13
1980 Castle Keep 3-9-1 10
1981 Telsmoss 5-8-4 10
1982 Fitzpatrick 3-8-6 14
1983 Jupiter Island 4-9-8 16
1984 First Bout 3-7-7 13
1985 Eastern Mystic 3-9-4 16
1986 Broken Wave 3-8-3 13
1987 Aim To Please 3-8-2 14
1988 Green Adventure 3-9-10 17
1989 Braashee 3-9-5 16

Winners of Great Races – Continued

CUMBERLAND LODGE STAKES
Ascot—1m 4f

1970 Park Top 6-9-4 5
1971 Knockroe 3-8-5 3
1972 Knockroe 4-9-2 5
1973 Scottish Rifle 4-9-7 5
1974 Shebeen 3-7-11 7
1975 Calaba 5-8-8 15
1976 Bruni 4-9-7 9
1977 Orange Bay 5-9-7 6
1978 Fordham 3-8-2 5
1979 Main Reef 3-8-5 6
1980 Fingal's Cave 3-8-3 5
1981 Critique 3-8-5 8
1982 Lafontaine 5-9-0 7
1983 Band 3-8-5 8
1984 Bedtime 4-9-3 7
1985 Shardari 3-8-6 5
1986 Kazaroun 4-9-3 4
1987 Moon Madness 4-9-7 5
1988 Assatis 3-8-5 6
1989 Tralos 4-9-0 4

HOOVER FILLIES' MILE (2y fillies)
Ascot—1m

1975 Icing 9-1 6
1976 Miss Pinkie 9-1 8
1977 Cherry Hinton 9-1 8
1978 Formulate 9-1 9
1979 Quick as Lightning 8-12 9
1980 Leap Lively 8-12 7
1981 Height of Fashion 9-2 8
1982 Acclimatise 8-9 8
1983 Nepula 8-9 8
1984 Oh So Sharp 8-10 8
1985 Untold 8-7 9
1986 Invited Guest 9-0 12
1987 Diminuendo 8-13 7
1988 Tessla 8-13 8
1989 Silk Slippers 8-10 8

DIADEM STAKES
Ascot—6f

1970 Realm 3-9-2 4
1971 Abergwaun 3-8-13 7
1972 Home Guard 3-9-2 8
1973 Boldboy 3-9-2 5
1974 Saritamer 3-9-2 5
1975 *Roman Warrior 4-9-7
*Swingtime 3-8-13 8
1976 Honeyblest 4-9-7 7
1977 Gentilhombre 4-9-7 6
1978 Creetown 6-9-7 14
1979 Absalom 4-9-7 6
1980 Sovereign Rose 3-9-0 9
1981 Moorestyle 4-9-7 10
1982 Indian King 4-9-7 12
1983 Salieri 3-9-3 12
1984 Never So Bold 4-9-7 9
1985 Al Sylah 3-8-9 8
1986 Hallgate 3-8-12 12
1987 Dowsing 3-8-12 17
1988 Cadeaux Genereux 3-8-12 13
1989 Chummy's Favourite 4-9-2 11

QUEEN ELIZABETH II STAKES
Ascot—1m

1970 Welsh Pageant 4-9-1 5
1971 Brigadier Gerard 3-8-8 3
1972 Brigadier Gerard 4-9-7 4
1973 Jan Ekels 4-9-0 5
1974 Abandoned
1975 Rose Bowl 3-8-4 5
1976 Rose Bowl 4-9-4 8
1977 Trusted 4-9-0 7
1978 Homing 3-8-7 11
1979 Kris 3-9-0 7
1980 Known Fact 3-9-0 7
1981 To-Agori-Mou 3-9-0 6
1982 Buzzards Bay 4-9-0 10
1983 Sackford 3-8-7 9
1984 Teleprompter 4-9-0 6
1985 Shadeed 3-9-0 7
1986 Sure Blade 3-8-11 7
1987 Milligram 3-8-8 5
1988 Warning 3-8-11 8
1989 Zilzal 3-8-11 5

ROYAL LODGE STAKES (2y)
Ascot—1m

1970 Seafriend 9-0 12
1971 Yaroslav 8-11 7
1972 Adios 8-11 12
1973 Straight as a Die 8-11 13
1974 Abandoned
1975 Sir Wimborne 8-11 6
1976 Gairloch 8-11 6
1977 Shirley Heights 8-11 8
1978 Ela-Mana-Mou 8-11 8
1979 Hello Gorgeous 8-11 4
1980 Robellino 8-11 8
1981 Norwick 8-11 9
1982 Dunbeath 8-11 9
1983 Gold and Ivory 8-11 5
1984 Reach 8-11 8
1985 Bonhomie 8-11 7
1986 Bengal Fire 8-11 9
1987 Sanquirico 8-13 10
1988 High Estate 8-13 5
1989 Digression 8-10 9

TOTE FESTIVAL HANDICAP
Ascot—1m 4f

1987 Roushayd 3-8-11 16
1988 Casey 3-8-6 19
1989 Braashee 3-9-4 17

CHEVELEY PARK STAKES (2y fillies)
Newmarket—6f

1970 Magic Flute 8-11 11
1971 Waterloo 8-8 17
1972 Jacinth 8-11 13
1973 Gentle Thoughts 8-11 14

Winners of Great Races – Continued

1974 Cry of Truth 8-11 15
1975 Pasty 8-11 14
1976 Durtal 8-11 15
1977 Sookera 8-11 10
1978 Devon Ditty 8-11 7
1979 Mrs Penny 8-11 12
1980 Marwell 8-11 8
1981 Woodstream 8-11 13
1982 Ma Biche 8-11 9
1983 Desirable 8-11 12
1984 Park Appeal 8-11 13
1985 Embla 8-11 14
1986 Forest Flower 8-11 5
1987 Ravinella 8-11 8
1988 Pass the Peace 8-11 7
1989 Dead Certain 8-11 11

MIDDLE PARK STAKES (2y)
Newmarket—6f

1970 Brigadier Gerard 9-0 5
1971 Sharpen Up 8-11 5
1972 Tudenham 9-0 7
1973 Habat 9-0 7
1974 Steel Heart 9-0 8
1975 Hittite Glory 9-0 8
1976 Tachypous 9-0 11
1977 Formidable 9-0 7
1978 Junius 9-0 10
1979 Known Fact 9-0 7
1980 Mattaboy 9-0 9
1981 Cajun 9-0 13
1982 Diesis 9-0 6
1983 Creag-an-Sgor 9-0 9
1984 Bassenthwaite 9-0 8
1985 Stalker 9-0 6
1986 Mister Majestic 9-0 7
1987 Gallic League 9-0 5
1988 Mon Tresor 9-0 6
1989 Balla Cove 9-0 6

SUN CHARIOT STAKES (fillies)
Before 1974: 3-year-olds only.
Newmarket—1m 2f

1970 Popkins 9-0 4
1971 Hill Circus 8-8 4
1972 Sleat 8-10 6
1973 Cheveley Princess 9-3 2
1974 Sweet Farewell 3-8-7 6
1975 Duboff 3-8-7 11
1976 Ranimer 3-8-7 10
1977 Triple First 3-9-0 7
1978 Swiss Maid 3-8-7 9
1979 Topsy 3-8-7 8
1980 Snow 3-8-7 7
1981 Home on the Range 3-8-6 10
1982 Time Charter 3-9-0 10
1983 Cormorant Wood 3-8-5 9
1984 Free Guest 3-8-4 8
1985 Free Guest 4-9-4 5
1986 Dusty Dollar 3-8-7 7
1987 Infamy 3-8-7 6
1988 Indian Skimmer 4-9-6 6
1989 Braiswick 3-8-7 9

CAMBRIDGESHIRE
Newmarket—1m 1f

1970 Prince de Galles 4-9-7 27
1971 King Midas 3-7-9 29
1972 Negus 5-9-0 35
1973 Siliciana 4-8-5 37
1974 Flying Nelly 4-7-7 39
1975 Lottogift 4-8-2 36
1976 Intermission 3-8-6 29
1977 Sin Timon 3-8-3 27
1978 Baronet 6-9-0 18
1979 Smartset 4-8-8 24
1980 Baronet 8-9-3 19
1981 Braughing 4-8-4 28
1982 Century City 3-9-6 29
1983 Sagamore 4-7-8 30
1984 Leysh 3-8-7 34
1985 Tremblant 4-9-8 31
1986 Dallas 3-9-6 31
1987 Balthus 4-8-1 31
1988 Quinlan Terry 3-8-5 29
1989 Rambo's Hall 4-8-6 34

JOCKEY CLUB CUP
Newmarket—2m

1970 High Line 4-9-6 5
1971 High Line 5-9-6 5
1972 Irvine 4-9-3 5
1973 Parnell 5-9-6 5
1974 Petty Officer 7-9-3 6
1975 Blood Royal 4-9-6 6
1976 Bright Finish 3-8-6 6
1977 Grey Baron 4-9-3 5
1978 Buckskin 5-9-7 6
1979 Nicholas Bill 4-8-11 8
1980 Ardross 4-9-5 5
1981 Centroline 3-8-4 9
1982 Little Wolf 4-9-5 8
1983 Karadar 5-9-3 5
1984 Old Country 5-9-7 4
1985 Tale Quale 3-8-4 10
1986 Valuable Witness 6-9-5 4
1987 Buckley 4-9-3 11
1988 Kneller 3-8-7 5
1989 Weld 3-8-7 3

SUPREME STAKES
Goodwood—7f

1987 Asteroid Field 4-8-6 10
1988 Fair Judgement 4-8-12 8
1989 Kerita 3-8-5 8

PRINCESS ROYAL STAKES
Ascot—1m 4f

1970 Heavenly Thought 3-8-7 6
1971 Hill Circus 3-9-2 7
1972 Attica Meli 3-9-6 5
1973 Mandera 3-8-11 9
1974 Shebeen 3-8-11 5
1975 Shebeen 4-9-6 9

Winners of Great Races – Continued

1976 Abandoned
1977 Aloft 3-8-9 11
1978 Trillionaire 3-8-6 6
1979 Alia 3-8-3 11
1980 Karamita 3-8-7 8
1981 Flighting 3-8-3 11
1982 Believer 3-8-3 14
1983 Sylph 3-8-3 11
1984 One Way Street 3-8-7 11
1985 Free Guest 4-9-7 15
1986 Tashtiya 3-8-9 6
1987 Abandoned
1988 Banket 3-8-6 8
1989 Snow Bride 3-8-11 10

CORNWALLIS STAKES (2y)
Ascot—5f

1970 Cawston's Pride 8-11 5
1971 Deep Diver 8-11 2
1972 The Go-Between 9-0 6
1973 Splashing 8-11 5
1974 Paris Review 9-0 6
1975 Western Jewel 8-11 7
1976 Abandoned
1977 Absalom 9-0 8
1978 Greenland Park 8-11 7
1979 Hanu 9-0 8
1980 Pushy 8-11 7
1981 My Lover 9-0 7
1982 Tatibah 9-0 9
1983 Petorius 9-0 14
1984 Doulab 9-0 11
1985 Hallgate 9-0 13
1986 Singing Steven 8-11 9
1987 Abandoned
1988 Hadif 8-13 13
1989 Argentum 8-13 9

DEWHURST STAKES (2y)
Newmarket—7f

1970 Mill Reef 8-12 3
1971 Crowned Prince 8-11 11
1972 Lunchtime 9-0 8
1973 Cellini 9-0 7
1974 Grundy 9-0 8
1975 Wollow 9-0 7
1976 The Minstrel 9-0 11
1977 Try My Best 9-0 7
1978 Tromos 9-0 6
1979 Monteverdi 9-0 6
1980 Storm Bird 9-0 5
1981 Wind and Wuthering 9-0 9
1982 Diesis 9-0 4
1983 El Gran Senor 9-0 10
1984 Kala Dancer 9-0 11
1985 Huntingdale 9-0 8
1986 Ajdal 9-0 5
1987 Abandoned
1988 *Prince of Dance 9-0
*Scenic 9-0 6
1989 Dashing Blade 9-0 7

ROCKFEL STAKES (2y)
Newmarket—7f

1981 Top Hope 8-8 8
1982 Saving Mercy 8-7 7
1983 Mahogany 8-8 13
1984 Kashi Lagoon 8-5 9
1985 Tralthee 8-6 9
1986 At Risk 8-9 13
1987 Abandoned
1988 Musical Bliss 8-8 9
1989 Negligent 8-8 12

CHALLENGE STAKES
Newmarket—7f

1970 Realm 3-9-2 5
1971 Joshua 4-9-7 5
1972 Abergwaun 4-9-4 10
1973 Boldboy 3-9-2 3
1974 New Model 4-9-7 10
1975 Be Tuneful 3-8-13 7
1976 Star Bird 3-9-0 8
1977 Boldboy 7-9-6 8
1978 Spence Bay 3-9-2 12
1979 Kris 3-9-2 7
1980 Moorestyle 3-9-2 6
1981 Moorestyle 4-9-6 7
1982 Noalcoholic 5-9-6 8
1983 Salieri 3-9-2 10
1984 Brocade 3-8-13 7
1985 Efisio 3-9-2 8
1986 Lucky Ring 4-9-0 12
1987 Asteroid Field 4-8-11 7
1988 Salse 3-8-10 8
1989 Distant Relative 8-13 6

CHAMPION STAKES
Newmarket—1m 2f

1970 Lorenzaccio 5-9-0 8
1971 Brigadier Gerard 3-8-7 10
1972 Brigadier Gerard 4-9-3 9
1973 Hurry Harriet 3-8-7 16
1974 Giacometti 3-8-10 14
1975 Rose Bowl 3-8-7 9
1976 Vitiges 3-8-11 19
1977 Flying Water 4-9-0 8
1978 Swiss Maid 3-8-7 10
1979 Northern Baby 3-8-10 14
1980 Cairn Rouge 3-8-7 13
1981 Vayrann 3-8-10 16
1982 Time Charter 3-8-7 14
1983 Cormorant Wood 3-8-7 19
1984 Palace Music 3-8-10 15
1985 Pebbles 4-9-0 10
1986 Triptych 4-9-0 11
1987 Triptych 5-9-0 11
1988 Indian Skimmer 4-9-0 5
1989 Legal Case 3-8-10 11

CESAREWITCH
Newmarket—2m 2f

1970 Scoria 4-7-0 21

Winners of Great Races – Continued

1971 Orosio 4-8-2 ... 18
1972 Cider With Rosie 4-7-11 ... 21
1973 Flash Imp 4-7-8 ... 29
1974 Ocean King 8-7-7 ... 27
1975 Shantallah 3-8-10 ... 17
1976 John Cherry 5-9-13 ... 14
1977 Assured 4-8-4 ... 11
1978 Centurion 3-9-8 ... 17
1979 Sir Michael 3-7-8 ... 11
1980 Popsi's Joy 5-8-6 ... 27
1981 Halsbury 3-8-4 ... 30
1982 Mountain Lodge 3-7-10 ... 28
1983 Bajan Sunshine 4-8-8 ... 28
1984 Tom Sharp 4-7-5 ... 26
1985 Kayudee 5-8-1 ... 21
1986 Orange Hill 4-7-9 ... 25
1987 Private Audition 5-7-9 ... 28
1988 Nomadic Way 3-7-9 ... 24
1989 Double Dutch 5-9-10 ... 22

HORRIS HILL STAKES (2y)
Newbury—7f 60yds

1970 Good Bond 9-0 ... 7
1971 Disguise 8-5 ... 14
1972 Long Row 9-0 ... 10
1973 Welsh Harmony 9-0 ... 15
1974 Corby 8-9 ... 11
1975 State Occasion 9-0 ... 11
1976 Fair Season 9-0 ... 9
1977 *Derrylin 9-0
*Persian Bold 9-0 ... 12
1978 Kris 9-0 ... 9
1979 Super Asset 9-0 ... 4
1980 Kalaglow 9-0 ... 10
1981 Montekin 9-0 ... 8
1982 Abandoned
1983 Elegant Air 9-0 ... 7
1984 Efisio 9-0 ... 5
1985 Celtic Heir 9-0 ... 12
1986 Naheez 9-0 ... 7
1987 Glacial Storm 8-12 ... 9
1988 Gouriev 8-12 ... 8
1989 Tirol 8-12 ... 8

ST SIMON STAKES
Newbury—1m 4f

1970 Politico 3-8-7 ... 4
1971 Frascati 3-8-7 ... 6
1972 Knockroe 4-9-3 ... 9
1973 Ballyhot 5-9-0 ... 9
1974 Never Return 3-8-7 ... 11
1975 Dakota 4-9-0 ... 4
1976 Mart Lane 3-8-7 ... 12
1977 Hot Grove 3-8-10 ... 11
1978 Obraztsovy 3-8-7 ... 6
1979 Main Reef 3-8-10 ... 7
1980 Shining Finish 3-8-7 ... 9
1981 Little Wolf 3-8-7 ... 7
1982 Abandoned
1983 Jupiter Island 4-9-0 ... 11
1984 Gay Lemur 4-9-6 ... 11
1985 Shardari 3-8-10 ... 8
1986 Jupiter Island 7-8-9 ... 9
1987 Lake Erie 4-9-0 ... 11
1988 Upend 3-8-4 ... 9
1989 Sesame 4-8-11 ... 11

RACING POST TROPHY (2y)
(Observer Gold Cup before 1976)
(Formerly The Futurity Stakes)
Doncaster—1m

1970 Linden Tree 8-12 ... 9
1971 High Top 8-11 ... 13
1972 Noble Decree 9-0 ... 10
1973 Apalachee 9-0 ... 10
1974 Green Dancer 9-0 ... 10
1975 Take Your Place 9-0 ... 11
1976 Sporting Yankee 9-0 ... 6
1977 Dactylographer 9-0 ... 12
1978 Sandy Creek 9-0 ... 11
1979 Hello Gorgeous 9-0 ... 7
1980 Beldale Flutter 9-0 ... 7
1981 Count Pahlen 9-0 ... 13
1982 Dunbeath 9-0 ... 8
1983 Alphabatim 9-0 ... 9
1984 Lanfranco 9-0 ... 10
1985 Bakharoff 9-0 ... 9
1986 Reference Point 9-0 ... 10
1987 Emmson 9-0 ... 6
1988 Al Hareb 9-0 ... 8
1989 Be My Chief 9-0 ... 5

MAIL ON SUNDAY HANDICAP FINAL (3y)
Newmarket—1m 1f

1985 Shellman 7-11 ... 12
1986 Geordie's Delight 9-7 ... 11
1987 Miss Sarajane 7-4 ... 20
1988 Indian Queen 8-4 ... 22
1989 Secretary of State 8-5 ... 17

NOVEMBER HANDICAP
Doncaster—1m 4f

1970 Saraceno 5-9-2 ... 21
1971 Misty Light 3-8-4 ... 20
1972 King Top 3-7-11 ... 16
1973 Only for Jo 3-7-4 ... 22
1974 Gritti Palace 5-7-0 ... 21
1975 Mr Bigmore 3-9-1 ... 12
1976 Gale Bridge 3-8-12 ... 14
1977 Sailcloth 3-7-7 ... 20
1978 Eastern Spring 4-7-10 ... 21
1979 Morse Code 4-8-3 ... 14
1980 Path of Peace 4-8-5 ... 22
1981 Lafontaine 4-8-7 ... 20
1982 *Double Shuffle 3-9-0
*Turkoman 3-8-7 ... 17
1983 Asir 3-8-7 ... 25
1984 Abu Kadra 3-8-12 ... 23
1985 Bold Rex 3-8-7 ... 24
1986 Beijing 3-8-4 ... 25
1987 Swingit Gunner 6-8-11 ... 25
1988 Young Benz 4-8-4 ... 22
1989 Firelight Fiesta 4-9-8 ... 19

Winners of Principal Races in Ireland

IRISH 2000 GUINEAS (3y)
The Curragh—1m

1970 Decies 9-0 13
1971 King's Company 9-0 14
1972 Ballymore 9-0 14
1973 Sharp Edge 9-0 16
1974 Furry Glen 9-0 10
1975 Grundy 9-0 12
1976 Northern Treasure 9-0 17
1977 Pampapaul 9-0 21
1978 Jaazeiro 9-0 12
1979 Dickens Hill 9-0 9
1980 Nikoli 9-0 13
1981 Kings Lake 9-0 13
1982 Dara Monarch 9-0 14
1983 Wassl 9-0 10
1984 Sadler's Wells 9-0 9
1985 Triptych 8-11 16
1986 Flash of Steel 9-0 6
1987 Don't Forget Me 9-0 8
1988 Prince of Birds 9-0 14
1989 Shaadi 9-0 12

IRISH 1000 GUINEAS (3y fillies)
The Curragh—1m

1970 Black Satin 9-0 13
1971 Favoletta 9-0 17
1972 Pidget 9-0 16
1973 Cloonagh 9-0 12
1974 Gaily 9-0 17
1975 Miralla 9-0 11
1976 Sarah Siddons 9-0 14
1977 Lady Capulet 9-0 14
1978 More So 9-0 17
1979 Godetia 9-0 12
1980 Cairn Rouge 9-0 18
1981 Arctique Royale 9-0 15
1982 Prince's Polly 9-0 24
1983 L'Attrayante 9-0 18
1984 Katies 9-0 23
1985 Al Bahathri 9-0 15
1986 Sonic Lady 9-0 19
1987 Forest Flower 9-0 11
1988 Trusted Partner 9-0 16
1989 Ensconse 9-0 13

IRISH DERBY (3y)
The Curragh—1m 4f

1970 Nijinsky 9-0 13
1971 Irish Ball 9-0 15
1972 Steel Pulse 9-0 14
1973 Weavers' Hall 9-0 15
1974 English Prince 9-0 13
1975 Grundy 9-0 13
1976 Malacate 9-0 17
1977 The Minstrel 9-0 15
1978 Shirley Heights 9-0 11
1979 Troy 9-0 9
1980 Tyrnavos 9-0 13
1981 Shergar 9-0 12
1982 Assert 9-0 10
1983 Shareef Dancer 9-0 12
1984 El Gran Senor 9-0 8
1985 Law Society 9-0 13
1986 Shahrastani 9-0 11
1987 Sir Harry Lewis 9-0 8
1988 Kahyasi 9-0 11
1989 Old Vic 9-0 8

IRISH OAKS (3y fillies)
The Curragh—1m 4f

1970 Santa Tina 9-0 13
1971 Altesse Royale 9-0 13
1972 Regal Exception 9-0 12
1973 Dahlia 9-0 12
1974 Dibidale 9-0 8
1975 Juliette Marny 9-0 14
1976 Lagunette 9-0 18
1977 Olwyn 9-0 8
1978 Fair Salinia 9-0 12
1979 Godetia 9-0 13
1980 Shoot A Line 9-0 8
1981 Blue Wind 9-0 10
1982 Swiftfoot 9-0 10
1983 Give Thanks 9-0 12
1984 Princess Pati 9-0 11
1985 Helen Street 9-0 9
1986 Colorspin 9-0 8
1987 Unite 9-0 8
1988 *Diminuendo 9-0
*Melodist 9-0 9
1989 Alydaress 9-0 5

PHOENIX STAKES (2y)
Phoenix Park—6f

1970 Areola 8-11 7
1971 Celtic Twilight 8-11 8
1972 Marble Arch 8-11 9
1973 Noble Mark 8-11 9
1974 Lady Seymour 8-11 9
1975 National Wish 9-0 8
1976 Cloonlara 8-11 7
1977 Perla 8-11 6
1978 Kilijaro 8-11 9
1979 Smokey Lady 8-11 10
1980 Swan Princess 8-11 10
1981 Achieved 9-0 7
1982 Sweet Emma 8-11 11
1983 King Persian 9-0 13
1984 Aviance 8-11 8
1985 Roaring Riva 9-0 13
1986 Minstrella 8-11 10
1987 Digamist 9-0 12
1988 Superpower 9-0 12
1989 Pharaoh's Delight 8-11 10

PHOENIX CHAMPION STAKES
Phoenix Park—1m 2f

1984 Sadlers Wells 3-8-11 12
1985 Commanche Run 4-9-6 11
1986 Park Express 3-8-8 13
1987 Triptych 5-9-3 12

Winners of Principal Races in Ireland – Continued

1988 Indian Skimmer 4-9-3 9
1989 Carroll House 4-9-6 9

NATIONAL STAKES (2y)
The Curragh—7f

1970 King's Company 9-0 9
1971 Roberto 9-0 5
1972 Chamozzie 9-0 7
1973 Cellini 9-0 8
1974 Reap The Wind 8-11 4
1975 Sir Wimborne 9-0 7
1976 Pampapaul 9-0 8
1977 Diamonds Are Trump 9-0 9
1978 Tap on Wood 9-0 10
1979 Monteverdi 9-0 15
1980 Storm Bird (CAN) 9-0 10
1981 Day Is Done 9-0 11
1982 Glenstal 9-0 9
1983 El Gran Senor 9-0 8
1984 Law Society 9-0 9
1985 Tate Gallery 9-0 9
1986 Lockton 9-0 9
1987 Caerwent 9-0 6
1988 Classic Fame 9-0 12
1989 Dashing Blade 9-0 10

IRISH CAMBRIDGESHIRE
The Curragh—1m (Hcap)

1970 Mighty Quin 4-7-6 23
1971 Ryker 3-7-4 30
1972 Assetive 3-8-6 26
1973 Jail Break 5-7-8 22
1974 Port Magee 6-7-10 28
1975 Inis-Gloire 3-8-0 31
1976 Floriferous 3-8-10 25
1977 Poacher's Moon 4-10-0 22
1978 Loyal Son 4-7-13 22
1979 Habituate 3-9-3 19
1980 I'm Ready 3-8-3 24
1981 Majestic Nurse 6-8-3 18
1982 Majestic Star 5-9-5 14
1983 Persian Royale 3-7-13 25
1984 Chammsky 5-9-4 21
1985 National Form 4-9-9 24
1986 Any Song 3-9-1 26
1987 Silius 4-7-10 24
1988 Ben's Pearl 3-7-9 30
1989 Smoggy Spray 5-8-10 17

MOYGLARE STUD STAKES (2y fillies)
The Curragh—6f

1973 Milly Whiteway 8-11 11
1974 Tender Camilla 8-11 10
1975 Petipa 8-11 10
1976 Regal Ray 8-11 8
1977 Ridaness 8-12 9
1978 Phil's Fancy 8-11 9
1979 Daness 8-11 6
1980 Arctique Royale 8-11 14
1981 Woodstream 8-11 14
1982 Habibti 8-11 15
1983 Gala Event 8-11 20
1984 Park Appeal 8-11 13
1985 Gayle Gal 8-11 15
1986 Minstrella 8-11 8
1987 Flutter Away 8-11 11
1988 Flamenco Wave 8-11 11
1989 Chimes of Freedom 8-11 7

IRISH ST LEGER
Before 1983: 3-year-olds only
The Curragh—1m 6f

1970 Allangrange 9-0 8
1971 Parnell 9-0 8
1972 Pidget 8-11 7
1973 Conor Pass 9-0 7
1974 Mistigri 9-0 7
1975 Caucasus 9-0 13
1976 Meneval 9-0 11
1977 Transworld 9-0 9
1978 M-Lolshan 9-0 8
1979 Niniski 9-0 10
1980 Gonzales 9-0 8
1981 Protection Racket 9-0 7
1982 Touching Wood 9-0 10
1983 Mountain Lodge 4-9-4 10
1984 Opale 4-9-4 9
1985 Leading Counsel 3-8-12 12
1986 Authaal 3-8-12 6
1987 Eurobird 8-9 8
1988 Dark Lomond 3-8-9 13
1989 Petite Ile 3-8-9 10

IRISH CESAREWITCH
The Curragh—2m (Hcap)

1970 Bigaroon 4-8-0 25
1971 Bigaroon 5-9-8 31
1972 Polar Fox 7-8-5 24
1973 Bigaroon 7-9-10 26
1974 Golden Lancer 7-8-3 34
1975 Prominent King 3-8-2 21
1976 Cill Dara 4-8-9 29
1977 Cill Dara 5-9-6 28
1978 Chateau Royal 3-8-8 23
1979 Jack of Trumps 7-8-13 23
1980 Potato Merchant 5-7-8 20
1981 The Neurologist 3-9-3 30
1982 Five Nations 5-8-2 29
1983 Five Nations 6-7-11 20
1984 Jean-Claude 3-7-11 24
1985 Ravaro 5-9-12 30
1986 Orient Rose 3-8-12 23
1987 Try a Brandy 5-8-4 29
1988 Midsummer Gamble 7-8-12 26
1989 Marlion 8-7-8 18

CARTIER MILLION STAKES
Phoenix Park—7f

1988 Corwyn Bay 9-0 20
1989 The Caretaker 8-11 20

Winners of Principal Races in France

PRIX GANAY
Longchamp—1m 2f 110yds

1978 Trillion 4-8-13 8
1979 Frere Basile 4-9-2 8
1980 Le Marmot 4-9-2 6
1981 Argument 4-9-2 9
1982 Bikala 4-9-2 10
1983 Lancastrian 6-9-2 7
1984 Romildo 4-9-2 8
1985 Sagace 5-9-2 7
1986 Baillamont 4-9-2 10
1987 Triptych 5-8-13 10
1988 Saint Andrews 4-9-2 5
1989 Saint Andrews 5-9-2 7

POULE D'ESSAI DES POULAINS (3y)
Longchamp—1m

1970 Caro 9-2 6
1971 Zug 9-2 14
1972 Riverman 9-2 10
1973 Kalamoun 9-2 10
1974 Moulines 9-2 11
1975 Green Dancer 9-2 12
1976 Red Lord 9-2 11
1977 Blushing Groom 9-2 6
1978 Nishapour 9-2 14
1979 Irish River 9-2 4
1980 In Fijar 9-2 13
1981 Recitation 9-2 10
1982 Melyno 9-2 9
1983 L'Emigrant 9-2 10
1984 Siberian Express 9-2 14
1985 No Pass No Sale 9-2 9
1986 Fast Topaze 9-2 8
1987 Soviet Star 9-2 14
1988 Blushing John 9-2 10
1989 Kendor 9-2 10

POULE D'ESSAI DES POULICHES (3y)
Longchamp—1m

1970 Pampered Miss 9-2 9
1971 Bold Fascinator 9-2 11
1972 Mata Hari 9-2 11
1973 Allez France 9-2 11
1974 Dumka 9-2 9
1975 Ivanjica 9-2 10
1976 Riverqueen 9-2 11
1977 Madelia 9-2 8
1978 Dancing Maid 9-2 10
1979 Three Troikas 9-2 7
1980 Aryenne 9-2 6
1981 Ukraine Girl 9-2 10
1982 River Lady 9-2 9
1983 L'Attrayante 9-2 10
1984 Masarika 9-2 11
1985 Silvermine 9-2 10
1986 Baiser Vole 9-2 8
1987 Miesque 9-2 8
1988 Ravinella 9-2 8
1989 Pearl Bracelet 9-2 16

PRIX LUPIN (3y)
Longchamp—1m 2f 110yds

1978 Acamas 9-2 11
1979 Top Ville 9-2 9
1980 Belgio 9-2 13
1981 No Lute 9-2 9
1982 Persepolis 9-2 10
1983 L'Emigrant 9-2 7
1984 Dahar 9-2 7
1985 Metal Precieux 9-2 8
1986 Fast Topaze 9-2 7
1987 Groom Dancer 9-2 7
1988 Exactly Sharp 9-2 9
1989 Galetto 9-2 6

PRIX SAINT-ALARY (3y Fillies)
Longchamp—1m 2f

1978 Reine de Saba 9-2 10
1979 Three Troikas 9-2 7
1980 Paranete 9-2 8
1981 Tootens 9-2 10
1982 Harbour 9-2 8
1983 Smuggly 9-2 8
1984 Grise Mine 9-2 11
1985 Fitnah 9-2 10
1986 Lacovia 9-2 9
1987 Indian Skimmer 9-2 9
1988 Riviere d'Or 9-2 8
1989 Behera 9-2 7

PRIX DU CADRAN
Longchamp—2m 4f

1970 Le Chouan 4-9-0 11
1971 Ramsin 4-9-0 9
1972 Rock Roi 5-9-6 10
1973 Lassalle 4-9-0 6
1974 Recupere 4-9-0 13
1975 Le Bavard 4-9-0 13
1976 Sagaro 5-9-2 10
1977 Buckskin 4-9-2 5
1978 Buckskin 5-9-2 9
1979 El Badr 4-9-2 5
1980 Shafaraz 7-9-2 6
1981 Gold River 4-8-13 6
1982 El Badr 7-9-2 5
1983 Karkour 5-9-2 6
1984 Neustrien 5-9-2 6
1985 Balitou 6-9-2 7
1986 Air de Cour 4-9-2 6
1987 Royal Gait 4-9-2 9
1988 Yaka 5-9-2 5
1989 Trebrook 5-9-2 3

PRIX D'ISPAHAN
Longchamp—1m 1f 55yds

1978 Carwhite 4-9-6 10
1979 Irish River 3-8-9 8
1980 Nadjar 4-9-6 10
1981 The Wonder 3-8-9 11
1982 Al Nasr 4-9-6 6
1983 Crystal Glitters 3-8-9 12

Winners of Principal Races in France – Continued

1984 Crystal Glitters 4-9-7 8
1985 Sagace 5-9-6 7
1986 Baillamont 4-9-6 8
1987 Highest Honor 4-9-2 6
1988 Miesque 4-8-13 6
1989 Indian Skimmer 5-8-13 6

PRIX JEAN PRAT (3y)
Longchamp—1m 1f 55yds

1978 Midshipman 4-8-11 9
1979 Campero 6-9-0 8
1980 Hard to Sing 4-9-0 9
1981 Gold River 4-9-1 9
1982 Melyno 3-9-2 5
1983 Kelbomec 7-9-0 9
1984 Magwal 5-8-12 12
1985 Baillamont 3-9-2 8
1986 Magical Wonder 3-9-2 9
1987 Risk Me 3-9-2 9
1988 Lapierre 3-9-2 8
1989 Local Talent 9-2 6

PRIX DU JOCKEY-CLUB (3y)
Chantilly—1m 4f

1970 Sassafras 9-2 15
1971 Rheffic 9-2 14
1972 Hard to Beat 9-2 13
1973 Roi Lear 9-2 16
1974 Caracolero 9-2 15
1975 Val de l'Orne 9-2 11
1976 Youth 9-2 18
1977 Crystal Palace 9-2 14
1978 Acamas 9-2 20
1979 Top Ville 9-2 11
1980 Policeman 9-2 14
1981 Bikala 9-2 12
1982 Assert 9-2 14
1983 Caerleon 9-2 12
1984 Darshaan 9-2 17
1985 Mouktar 9-2 11
1986 Bering 9-2 13
1987 Natroun 9-2 17
1988 Hours After 9-2 16
1989 Old Vic 9-2 12

PRIX DE DIANE (3y fillies)
Chantilly—1m 2½f

1970 Sweet Mimosa 9-2 19
1971 Pistol Packer 9-2 16
1972 Rescousse 9-2 21
1973 Allez France 9-2 25
1974 Highclere 9-2 22
1975 Abandoned
1976 Pawneese 9-2 11
1977 Madelia 9-2 13
1978 Reine de Saba 9-2 17
1979 Dunette 9-2 12
1980 Mrs Penny 9-2 14
1981 Madam Gay 9-2 14
1982 Harbour 9-2 14
1983 Escaline 9-2 17
1984 Northern Trick 9-2 15
1985 Lypharita 9-2 10
1986 Lacovia 9-2 14
1987 Indian Skimmer 9-2 11
1988 Resless Kara 9-2 16
1989 Lady in Silver 9-2 14

GRAND PRIX DE PARIS (3y)
Longchamp—1m 2f
(1m 7f up to 1986)

1978 Galiani 8-11 14
1979 Soleil Noir 8-11 7
1980 Valiant Heart 8-11 14
1981 Glint of Gold 8-11 11
1982 Le Nain Jaune 8-11 11
1983 Yawa 8-11 7
1984 At Talaq 8-12 11
1985 Sumayr 8-11 7
1986 Swink 8-11 9
1987 Risk Me 9-2 9
1988 Fijar Tango 9-2 10
1989 Dancehall 9-2 8

GRAND PRIX DE SAINT-CLOUD
Saint-Cloud—1m 4f

1970 Gyr 3-8-7 8
1971 Ramsin 4-9-8 10
1972 Rheingold 3-8-7 7
1973 Rheingold 4-9-8 9
1974 Dahlia 4-9-5 11
1975 Un Kopeck 4-9-8 11
1976 Riverqueen 3-8-6 8
1977 Exceller 4-9-8 10
1978 Guadanini 4-9-8 9
1979 Gay Mecene 4-9-8 13
1980 *Dunette 4-9-5
*Shakapour 3-8-9 9
1981 Akarad 3-8-9 10
1982 Glint of Gold 4-9-8 9
1983 Diamond Shoal 4-9-8 9
1984 Teenoso 4-9-9 11
1985 Strawberry Road 6-9-8 7
1986 Acatenango 4-9-8 9
1987 Moon Madness 4-9-8 6
1988 Village Star 5-9-8 10
1989 Sheriff's Star 4-9-8 6

PRIX JACQUES LE MAROIS
Deauville—1m

1970 Priamos 6-9-7 13
1971 Dictus 4-9-2 12
1972 Lyphard 3-8-7 9
1973 Kalamoun 3-8-7 11
1974 Nonoalco 3-8-7 10
1975 Lianga 3-8-12 11
1976 Gravelines 4-9-2 13
1977 Flying Water 4-8-12 7
1978 Kenmare 3-8-8 10
1979 Irish River 3-8-8 8
1980 Nadjar 4-9-2 9
1981 Northjet 4-9-2 11

Winners of Principal Races in France – Continued

1982 The Wonder 4-9-2 9
1983 Luth Enchantee 3-8-7 10
1984 Lear Fan 3-8-9 10
1985 Vin de France 3-8-9 11
1986 Lirung 4-9-2 12
1987 Miesque 3-8-6 9
1988 Miesque 4-8-13 6
1989 Polish Precedent 3-8-9 10

PRIX MORNY (2y)
Deauville—6f

1970 My Swallow 8-11 7
1971 Daring Display 8-11 8
1972 Filiberto 8-11 17
1973 Nonoalco 8-11 7
1974 Broadway Dancer 8-8 13
1975 Vitiges 8-11 13
1976 Blushing Groom 8-11 11
1977 Super Concorde 8-11 10
1978 Irish River 8-11 11
1979 Princess Lida 8-11 10
1980 Ancient Regime 8-8 7
1981 Green Forest 8-11 5
1982 Deep Roots 8-11 6
1983 Siberian Express 8-11 7
1984 Seven Springs 8-8 7
1985 Regal State 8-8 11
1986 Sakura Reiko 8-8 8
1987 First Waltz 8-8 8
1988 Tersa 8-8 8
1989 Machiavellian 8-11 7

PRIX DU MOULIN DE LONGCHAMP
Longchamp—1m

1970 Gold Rod 3-8-9 11
1971 Faraway Son 4-9-2 12
1972 Sallust 3-8-9 12
1973 Sparkler 5-9-2 12
1974 Mount Hagen 3-8-9 11
1975 Delmora 3-8-6 11
1976 Gravelines 4-9-2 9
1977 Pharly 3-8-11 7
1978 Sanedtki 4-8-13 10
1979 Irish River 3-8-11 8
1980 Kilijaro 4-8-13 11
1981 Northjet 4-9-2 12
1982 Green Forest 3-8-11 9
1983 Luth Enchantee 3-8-8 8
1984 Mendez 3-8-11 7
1985 Rousillon 4-9-2 12
1986 Sonic Lady 3-8-8 14
1987 Miesque 3-8-8 7
1988 Soviet Star 4-9-2 7
1989 Polish Precedent 3-8-11 11

PRIX VERMEILLE (3y fillies)
Longchamp—1m 4f

1970 Highest Hopes 9-2 13
1971 Pistol Packer 9-2 15
1972 *San San 9-2
*Paysanne 9-2 18
1973 Allez France 9-2 13
1974 Paulista 9-2 15
1975 Ivanjica 9-2 13
1976 Lagunette 9-2 10
1977 Kamicia 9-2 18
1978 Dancing Maid 9-2 12
1979 Three Troikas 9-2 13
1980 Mrs Penny 9-2 12
1981 April Run 9-2 10
1982 All Along 9-2 13
1983 Sharaya 9-2 12
1984 Northern Trick 9-2 10
1985 Walensee 9-2 13
1986 Darara 9-2 8
1987 Bint Pasha 9-2 12
1988 Indian Rose 9-2 8
1989 Young Mother 9-2 7

GRAND CRITERIUM (2y)
Longchamp—1m

1970 My Swallow 8-11 6
1971 Hard to Beat 8-11 14
1972 Satingo 8-11 9
1973 Mississipian 8-11 8
1974 Mariacci 8-11 9
1975 Manado 8-11 11
1976 Blushing Groom 8-11 10
1977 Super Concorde 8-11 13
1978 Irish River 8-11 12
1979 Dragon 8-11 8
1980 Recitation 8-11 11
1981 Green Forest 8-11 10
1982 Saint Cyrien 8-11 8
1983 Treizieme 8-8 9
1984 Alydar's Best 8-8 6
1985 Femme Elite 8-8 11
1986 Danishkada 8-8 8
1987 Fijar Tango 8-11 6
1988 Kendor 8-11 9
1989 Jade Robbery 8-11 8

PRIX DE L'ABBAYE DE LONGCHAMP
Longchamp—5f

1970 Balidar 4-9-11 9
1971 Sweet Revenge 4-9-11 5
1972 Deep Diver 3-9-10 8
1973 Sandford Lad 3-9-10 12
1974 Moubariz 3-9-10 9
1975 Lianga 4-9-7 12
1976 *Mendip Man 4-9-10
*Gentilhombre 3-9-10 10
1977 Gentilhombre 4-9-11 11
1978 Sigy 2-8-5 7
1979 Double Form 4-9-11 13
1980 Moorestyle 3-9-11 9
1981 Marwell 3-9-8 10
1982 Sharpo 5-9-11 13
1983 Habibti 3-9-7 8
1984 Committed 4-9-7 12
1985 Committed 5-9-7 12
1986 Double Schwartz 5-9-11 13
1987 Polonia 3-9-7 9
1988 Handsome Sailor 5-9-11 10
1989 Silver Fling 4-9-7 16

Winners of Principal National Hunt Races

MACKESON GOLD CUP
(H'CAP CHASE)
Cheltenham—2½m

1970 Chatham 6y 10st 3lb 17
1971 Gay Trip 9y 11st 3lb 10
1972 Red Candle 8y 10st 11
1973 Skymas 8y 10st 5lb 15
1974 Bruslee 8y 10st 7lb 11
1975 Clear Cut 11y 10st 9lb 13
1976 *Cancello 7y 11st 1lb 13
1977 Bachelor's Hall 7y 10st 6lb 16
1978 Bawnogues 7y 10st 7lb 11
1979 Man Alive 8y 10st 9lb 11
1980 Bright Highway 6y 11st 1lb 15
1981 Henry Kissinger 7y 10st 13lb 11
1982 Fifty Dollars More 7y 11st 11
1983 Pounentes 6y 10st 6lb 9
1984 Half Free 8y 11st 10lb 10
1985 Half Free 9y 11st 10lb 10
1986 Very Promising 8y 11st 13lb ... 11
1987 Beau Ranger 9y 10st 2lb 14
1988 Pegwell Bay 7y 11st 2lb 13
1989 Joint Sovereignty 9y 10st 4lb 15

*Run at Haydock

H & T WALKER GOLD CUP
(H'CAP CHASE)
Ascot—2½m
1981 Run as Tote Silver Trophy Chase

1981 Wayward Lad 6y 11st 10lb 8
1982 Pay Related 8y 11st 2lb 6
1983 The Tsarevich 7y 11st 6lb 6
1984 Cybrandian 6y 10st 9lb 6
1985 Very Promising 7y 11st 7lb 7
1986 Church Warden 7y 10st 7lb 6
1987 Weather the Storm 7y 11st 11
1988 Saffron Lord 6y 11st 3lb 5
1989 Man O'Magic 8y 11st 5lb 11

HENNESSY COGNAC GOLD CUP
(H'CAP CHASE)
Newbury—3¼m 82y

1960 Knucklecracker 7y 11st 1lb..... 20
1961 Mandarin 10y 11st 5lb 22
1962 Springbok 8y 10st 8lb 27
1963 Mill House 6y 12st 10
1964 Arkle 7y 12st 7lb 9
1965 Arkle 8y 12st 7lb 8
1966 Stalbridge Colonist 7y 10st 6
1967 Rondetto 11y 10st 1lb 13
1968 Man of the West 7y 10st 11
1969 Spanish Steps 6y 11st 8lb 15
1970 Border Mask 8y 11st 1lb 12
1971 Bighorn 7y 10st 11lb 13
1972 Charlie Potheen 7y 11st 4lb 13
1973 Red Candle 9y 10st 4lb 11
1974 Royal Marshal II 7y 10st 13
1975 April Seventh 9y 11st 2lb 13
1976 Zeta's Son 7y 10st 9lb 21
1977 Bachelor's Hall 7y 10st 10lb 14
1978 Approaching 7y 10st 6lb 8
1979 Fighting Fit 7y 11st 7lb 15
1980 Bright Highway 6y 11st 6lb 14
1981 Diamond Edge 10y 11st 10lb 14
1982 Bregawn 8y 11st 10lb 11
1983 Brown Chamberlin 8y 11st 8lb 12
1984 Burrough Hill Lad 8y 12st 13
1985 Galway Blaze 9y 10st 15
1986 Broadheath 9y 10st 5lb 15
1987 Playschool 9y 10st 8lb 12
1988 Strands Of Gold 9y 10st 12
1989 Ghofar 6y 10st 2lb 8

A.F. BUDGE GOLD CUP
(H'CAP CHASE)
Cheltenham—2½m
1970-1981 Run as Massey-Ferguson Gold Cup
1982-1984 Run as Kennedy Construction Gold Cup
1985 Run as Still Fork Trucks Gold Cup
1986-1987 Run as Glen International Gold Cup

1970 Simian 8y 11st 8lb 7
1971 Leap Frog 7y 12st 1lb 12
1972 Arctic Bow 7y 10st 12lb 11
1973 Pendil 8y 12st 7lb 8
1974 Garnishee 10y 10st 6lb 9
1975 Easby Abbey 8y 11st 10lb 9
1976 Abandoned because of frost
1977 Even Melody 8y 11st 2lb 11
1978 The Snipe 8y 10st 14
1979 Father Delaney 7y 10st 10lb ... 12
1980 Bueche Giorod 9y 10st 15
1981 Abandoned because of snow
1982 Observe 6y 10st 11lb 15
1983 Fifty Dollars More 8y 11st 10lb 13
1984 Beau Ranger 6y 9st 10lb 10
1985 Combs Ditch 9y 11st 9lb 7
1986 Oregon Trail 6y 10st 7lb 6
1987 Bishop's Yarn 8y 10st 7lb 5
1988 Pegwell Bay 7y 10st 13lb 10
1989 Clever Folly 9y 10st 4lb 6

TOP RANK CHRISTMAS HURDLE
Kempton—2m
1972-1981 Run as William Hill Christmas Hurdle
1982-1985 Run as Ladbroke Christmas Hurdle

1970 Abandoned because of snow
1971 Coral Diver 6y 12st 5lb 4
1972 Canasta Lad 6y 12st 1lb 6
1973 Lanzarote 5y 12st 1lb 4
1974 Tree Tangle 5y 12st 1lb 5
1975 Lanzarote 7y 11st 13lb 5
1976 Dramatist 5y 11 10lb 6
1977 Beacon Light 6y 11st 10lb 3
1978 Kybo 5y 11st 7lb 6
1979 Bird's Nest 9y 11st 10lb 5

Winners of Principal National Hunt Races – Continued

1980 Celtic Ryde 5y 11st 6lb........... 7
1981 Abandoned because of frost
1982 Ekbalco 6y 11st 13lb................ 4
1983 Dawn Run 5y 10st 12lb............ 4
1984 Browne's Gazette 6y 11st 3lb ... 7
1985 Aonoch 6y 11st 3lb 9
1986 Nohalmdun 5y 11st 3lb............ 7
1987 Osric 4y 11st 3lb 8
1988 Kribensis 4y 11st 3lb................ 7
1989 Kribensis 5y 11st 3lb................ 8

KING GEORGE VI RANK CHASE
Kempton—3m

1956 Rose Park 9y 11st 7lb.............. 6
1957 Mandarin 6y 12st 9
1958 Lochroe 10y 11st 7lb 7
1959 Mandarin 8y 11st 5lb 9
1960 Saffron Tartan 9y 11st 7lb....... 10
1961 Abandoned because of frost
1962 Abandoned because of frost
1963 Mill House 6y 12st..................... 3
1964 Frenchman's Cove 9y 11st 7lb 2
1965 Arkle 8y 12st 4
1966 Dormant 9y 11st......................... 7
1967 Cancelled because of foot and mouth epidemic
1968 Abandoned because of waterlogged course
1969 Titus Oates 7y 11st 10lb 5
1970 Abandoned because of snow
1971 The Dikler 8y 11st 7lb 10
1972 Pendil 7y 12st 6
1973 Pendil 8y 12st 4
1974 Captain Christy 7y 12st............. 6
1975 Captain Christy 8y 12st............. 7
1976 Royal Marshall II 9y 11st 7lb ... 10
1977 Bachelor's Hall 7y 11st 7lb........ 9
1978 Gay Spartan 7y 11st 10lb 16
1979 Silver Buck 7y 11st 10lb.......... 11
1980 Silver Buck 8y 11st 10lb........... 8
1981 Abandoned because of frost
1982 Wayward Lad 7y 11st 10lb........ 6
1983 Wayward Lad 8y 11st 10lb........ 5
1984 Burrough Hill Lad 8y 11st 10lb 3
1985 Wayward Lad 10y 11st 10lb...... 5
1986 Desert Orchid 7y 11st 10lb 8
1987 Nupsala (FR) 8y 11st 10lb 9
1988 Desert Orchid 9y 11st 10lb 5
1989 Desert Orchid 10y 11st 10lb 6

CORAL WELSH GRAND NATIONAL (H'CAP CHASE)
Chepstow—3¾m
1979-1988 Run in December

1970 French Excuse 8y 10st 9lb...... 11
1971 Royal Toss 9y 10st 12lb.......... 13
1972 Charlie H 10y 11st 3lb.............. 9
1973 Deblin's Green 10y 9st 12lb.... 16
1974 Pattered 8y 10st 2lb................ 24
1975 Abandoned because of waterlogged course
1976 Rag Trade 10y 11st 2lb.......... 17
1977 Abandoned because of waterlogged course
1978 Abandoned because of frost
1979 Peter Scot 8y 10st 2lb............ 15
1980 Narvik 7y 10st 11lb................ 18
1981 Peaty Sandy 7y 10st 3lb 23
1982 Corbiere 7y 10st 10lb.............. 10
1983 Burrough Hill Lad 7y 10st 9lb 18
1984 Righthand Man 7y 11st 5lb 18
1985 Run And Skip 7y 10st 8lb 18
1986 Stearsby 7y 11st 5lb 17
1987 Playschool 9y 10st 11lb.......... 13
1988 Bonanza Boy 7y 10st 1lb 12
1989 Bonanza Boy 8y 11st 11lb 12

LADBROKE H'CAP HURDLE
Leopardstown—2m
1970-1975 Run as Irish Sweeps Hurdle
1976-1980 Run as Sweeps H'cap Hurdle
1981-1986 Run as Irish Sweeps H'cap Hurdle
1982-1989 Run in January

1970 *Persian War 7y 12st................ 11
1971 Kelanne 7y 11st 6lb 16
1972 Captain Christy 5y 11st 6lb..... 13
1973 Comedy Of Errors 6y 12st......... 9
1974 Comedy Of Errors 7y 12st......... 8
1975 Night Nurse 4y 11st 5lb............ 9
1976 Master Monday 6y 10st 2lb..... 19
1977 Decent Fellow 4y 11st 4lb....... 18
1978 Chinrullah 6y 10st 6lb 12
1979 Irian 5y 10st............................. 20
1980 Carrig Willy 5y 10st 26
1982 For Auction 6y 10st 10lb 20
1983 Fredcoteri 7y 10st 15
1984 Fredcoteri 8y 10st 4lb............. 18
1985 Hansel Rag 5y 10st................. 20
1986 Bonalma 6y 10st 13lb 22
1987 Barnbrook Again 6y 11st 8lb... 22
1988 Roark 6y 11st 11lb 15
1989 Redundant Pal 6y 10st........... 17
1990 Redundant Pal 7y 11st 5lb...... 27

*Run at Fairyhouse

ARLINGTON PREMIER CHASE FINAL
Cheltenham—2½m
1970-1980 & 1984-1986 Run as Embassy Premier Chase Final
1981-1983 Run as Lambert & Butler Premier Chase Final

1970 L'Escargot 7y 11st 17
1971 Leap Frog 7y 11st 6lb 12
1972 Colebridge 8y 11st 7lb............. 7
1973 Balinese 8y 11st 7lb............... 10
1974 Credibility 6y 11st 7lb............ 12
1975 Ben More 7y 11st 7lb 10
1976 Floating Pound 7y 11st 7lb 13

Winners of Principal National Hunt Races – Continued

1977 Border Incident 7y 11st 7lb 9
1978 The Dealer 8y 11st 7lb 6
1979 Silver Buck 7y 11st 7lb............. 7
1980 Daletta 7y 11st 7lb.................... 7
1981 Royal Bond 8y 11st 7lb 7
1982 Wayward Lad 7y 11st 7lb......... 7
1983 Combs Ditch 7y 11st 7lb 9
1984 Ballinacurra Lad 9y 11st 7lb...... 9
1985 Abandoned because of snow and frost
1986 Very Promising 8y 11st 10lb 8
1987 No Race
1988 No Race
1989 Barnbrook Again 8y 11st 7lb..... 4
1990 Sabin du Loir 11 11st 7lb........... 4

1970-1980 Run at Haydock
1981-1986 Run at Ascot

RACECALL GAINSBOROUGH HANDICAP CHASE
Sandown—3m 118y
Run as Gainsborough Handicap Chase
1977-1979 Leisure Caravan Parks Handicap Chase
1980-1982 Freshfields Holidays Handicap Chase
1987 F.U's Jeans Gainsborough Handicap Chase
1988 Lee Cooper Gainsborough Handicap Chase

1970 Spanish Steps 7y 12st 3
1971 Titus Oates 9y 12st 3
1972 Crisp 9y 12st 3
1973 Royal Toss 11y 11st 9lb 3
1974 Kilvulgan 7y 10st 9lb 6
1975 Abandoned because of waterlogged course
1976 Bula 11y 12st 3
1977 Master H 8y 10st 8lb 7
1978 Master H 9 11st 3lb 6
1979 Diamond Edge 8y 11st 3lb 11
1980 Diamond Edge 9y 12st 7
1981 Tragus 9y 10st 7lb 8
1982 *Bregawn 8y 10st 7lb 9
1983 Observe 7y 11st 3lb 5
1984 Burrough Hill Lad 8y 11st 10lb 5
1985 Burrough Hill Lad 9y 12st ......w.o
1986 Burrough Hill Lad 10y 12st 6
1987 Desert Orchid 8y 11st 10lb 6
1988 Charter Party 10y 10st 11lb 11
1989 Desert Orchid 10y 12st 4

*Run at Kempton

TOTE GOLD TROPHY (H'CAP HURDLE)
Newbury—2m 100y
1970-1986 Run as Schweppes Gold Trophy

1970 Abandoned because of snow & frost
1971 Cala Mesquida 7y 10st 9lb...... 23
1972 Good Review 6y 10st 9lb 26
1973 Indianapolis 6y 10st 6lb 26
1974 Abandoned because of waterlogged course
1975 Tammuz 7y 10st 13lb 28
1976 Irish Fashion 5y 10st 4lb 29
1977 True Lad 7y 10st 4lb 27
1978 Abandoned because of frost
1979 Within The Law 5y 11st 4lb 28
1980 Bootlaces 6y 10st 9lb.............. 21
1981 Abandoned because of frost
1982 Donegal Prince 6y 10st 8lb 27
1983 Abandoned because of snow & frost
1984 Ra Nova 5y 10st 6lb................ 26
1985 Abandoned because of snow
1986 Abandoned because of snow
1987 Neblin 8y 10st 21
1988 Jamesmead 7y 10st................. 19
1989 Grey Salute (CAN) 6y 11st 5lb 10

VINCENT O'BRIEN IRISH GOLD CUP CHASE
Leopardstown—3m

1987 Forgive 'N Forget 10y 12st 9
1988 Playschool (NZ) 10y 12st 5
1989 Carvill's Hill 7y 12st 9

RACING POST HANDICAP CHASE
Kempton—3m

1988 Rhyme 'n' Reason 9y 10st 11lb 12
1989 Bonanza Boy 8y 11st 1lb........... 11

WILLIAM HILL IMPERIAL CUP
Sandown 2m

1960 Farmer's Boy 7y 11st 7lb 20
1961 Fidus Achates 6y 10st 4lb....... 23
1962 Irish Imp 5y 10st 12lb............. 26
1963 Antiar 5y 11st 2lb 21
1964 Invader 6y 11st 4lb 15
1965 Kildavin 7y 10st 7lb................. 19
1966 Royal Sanction 7y 10st 1lb 18
1967 Sir Thopas 6y 11st 8lb 20
1968 Persian Empire 5y 11st 5lb..... 18
1969 Abandoned because of waterlogged course
1970 Solomon II 6y 11st 1lb............. 17
1971 Churchwood 7y 11st 3lb 12
1972 Spy Net (FR) 5y 10st 18
1973 Lanzarote 5y 12st 4lb 14
1974 Flash Imp 5y 10st 9lb 17
1975 Abandoned because of waterlogged course
1976 Nougat (FR) 6y 10st 6lb.......... 11
1977 Acquaint 6y 11st 2lb 20
1978 Winter Melody 7y 11st 3lb....... 15
1979 Flying Diplomat 8y 10st 6lb..... 9
1980 Prayukta 5y 11st...................... 16
1981 Ekbalco 5y 11st 3lb................. 14
1982 *Holemoor Star 5y 11st 7lb 7
1983 Desert Hero 9y 9st 8lb 16

Winners of Principal National Hunt Races – Continued

1984 Dalbury 6y 9st 12lb 13
1985 Floyd 5y 10st 3lb 16
1986 Insular 6y 9st 10lb 19
1987 Inlander 6y 10st 3lb 23
1988 Sprowston Boy 5y 10st 11lb ... 15
1989 Travel Mystery 6y 10st 8lb 8
*Run at Kempton

ARKLE CHALLENGE TROPHY (NOVICES CHASE)
Cheltenham—2m

1969 Chatham 5y 11st 10
1970 Soloning 5y 11st 13
1971 Alpheus 6y 11st 8lb 11
1972 Pendil 7y 12st 1lb 10
1973 Denys Adventure 8y 12st 1lb 10
1974 Canasta Lad 8y 11st 11lb 10
1975 Broncho II 6y 11st 11lb 12
1976 Roaring Wind 8y 11st 8lb 16
1977 Tip The Wink 7y 11st 8lb 10
1978 Alverton 8y 11st 8lb 10
1979 Chinrullah 7y 11st 8lb 8
1980 Anaglogs Daughter 7y 11st 8lb 9
1981 Clayside 7y 11st 8lb 13
1982 The Brockshee 7y 11st 8lb 19
1983 Ryeman 6y 11st 8lb 16
1984 Bobsline 8y 11st 8lb 8
1985 Boreen Prince 8y 11st 8lb 16
1986 Oregon Trail 6y 11st 8lb 14
1987 Gala's Image 7y 11st 8lb 19
1988 Danish Flight 9y 11st 8lb 12
1989 Waterloo Boy 6y 11st 8lb 14

WATERFORD CRYSTAL CHAMPION HURDLE
Cheltenham—2m 200y

1955 Clair Soleil 6y 12st 21
1956 Doorknocker 8y 12st 14
1957 Merry Deal 7y 12st 16
1958 Bandalore 7y 12st 18
1959 Fare Time 8y 12st 14
1960 Another Flash 6y 12st 12
1961 Eborneezer 6y 12st 17
1962 Anzio 5y 11st 12lb 14
1963 Winning Fair 8y 12st 21
1964 Magic Court 6y 12st 24
1965 Kirriemuir 5y 11st 12lb 19
1966 Salmon Spray 8y 12st 17
1967 Saucy Kit 6y 12st 23
1968 Persian War 5y 11st 12lb 16
1969 Persian War 6y 12st 17
1970 Persian War 7y 12st 14
1971 Bula 6y 12st 9
1972 Bula 7y 12st 12
1973 Comedy Of Errors 6y 12st 8
1974 Lanzarote 6y 12st 7
1975 Comedy Of Errors 8y 12st 13
1976 Night Nurse 5y 12st 8
1977 Night Nurse 6y 12st 10
1978 Monksfield 6y 12st 13
1979 Monksfield 7y 12st 10

1980 Distance changed to 2m

1980 Sea Pigeon 10y 12st 9
1981 Sea Pigeon 11y 12st 14
1982 For Auction 6y 12st 14
1983 Gaye Brief 6y 12st 17
1984 Dawn Run 6y 11st 9lb 14
1985 See You Then 5y 12st 14
1986 See You Then 6y 12st 23
1987 See You Then 7y 12st 18
1988 Celtic Shot 6y 12st 21
1989 Beech Road 7y 12st 15

QUEEN MOTHER CHAMPION CHASE
Cheltenham—2m

1959-1979 Run as National Hunt Two Mile Champion Chase

1959 Quita Que 10y 12st 9
1960 Fortria 8y 12st 7
1961 Fortria 9y 12st 5
1962 Piperton 8y 12st 7
1963 Sandy Abbot 8y 12st 5
1964 Ben Stack 7y 12st 5
1965 Dunkirk 8y 12st 6
1966 Flyingbolt 7y 12st 6
1967 Drinny's Double 9y 12st 8
1968 Drinny's Double 10y 12st 5
1969 Muir 10y 12st 11
1970 Straight Fort 7y 12st 6
1971 Crisp 8y 12st 8
1972 Royal Relief 8y 12st 5
1973 Inkslinger 6y 12st 6
1974 Royal Relief 10y 12st 6
1975 Lough Inagh 8y 12st 8
1976 Skymas 11y 12st 7
1977 Skymas 12y 12st 8
1978 Hilly Way 8y 12st 10
1979 Hilly Way 9y 12st 9
1980 Another Dolly 10y 12st 7
1981 Drumgora 9y 12st 9
1982 Rathgorman 10y 12st 9
1983 Badsworth Boy 8y 12st 6
1984 Badsworth Boy 9y 12st 10
1985 Badsworth Boy 10y 12st 5
1986 Buck House 8y 12st 11
1987 Pearlyman 8y 12st 8
1988 Pearlyman 9y 12st 8
1989 Barnbrook Again 8y 12st 8

SUN ALLIANCE NOVICES' CHASE
Cheltenham—3m

1970 Proud Tarquin 7y 11st 12lb 17
1971 Tantalum 7y 11st 7lb 16
1972 Clever Scot 7y 11st 7lb 18
1973 Killiney 7y 11st 3lb 9
1974 Ten Up 7y 11st 12
1975 Pengrail 7y 11st 11
1976 Tied Cottage 8y 11st 15
1977 Gay Spartan 6y 11st 4lb 15
1978 Sweet Joe 6y 11st 4lb 17
1979 Master Smudge 7y 11st 4lb 17
1980 Lacson 8y 11st 4lb 17

Winners of Principal National Hunt Races – Continued

1981 Lesley Ann 7y 11st 4lb 17
1982 Brown Chamberlin 7y 11st 4lb 15
1983 Canny Danny 7y 11st 4lb 14
1984 A Kinsman 8y 11st 4lb 18
1985 Antartic Bay 8y 11st 4lb 11
1986 Cross Master 9y 11st 4lb 30
1987 Kildimo 7y 11st 4lb 18
1988 The West Awake 7y 11st 4lb... 14
1989 Envopak Token 8y 11st 4lb..... 15

DAILY EXPRESS TRIUMPH HURDLE (4-y-o)
Cheltenham—2m 200y

1960 Turpial 10st 10lb 13
1961 Cantab 10st 10lb 15
1962 Beaver II 10st 10lb 11
1963 No Race
1964 No Race
1965 Blarney Beacon 11st 4lb 7
1966 Black Ice 11st 4lb 11
1967 Persian War 11st 8lb 13
1968 England's Glory 10st 10lb 16
1969 Coral Diver 11st 4lb 26
1970 Varma 11st 4lb 31
1971 Boxer 11st 3lb 18
1972 Zarib 11st 16
1970 Varma 11st 4lb 31
1971 Boxer 11st 3lb 18
1972 Zarib 11st 16
1973 Moonlight Bay 11st 18
1974 Attivo 11st 21
1975 Royal Epic 11st 28
1976 Peterhof 11st 23
1977 Meladon 11st 30
1978 Connaught Ranger 11st 14
1979 Pollardstown 11st 28

1980 Distance changed to 2m

1980 Heighlin 11st 26
1981 Baron Blakeney 11st 29
1982 Shiny Copper 11st 29
1983 Saxon Farm 11st 30
1984 Northern Game 11st 30
1985 First Bout 11st 27
1986 Solar Cloud 11st 28
1987 Alone Success 11st 29
1988 Kribensis 11st 26
1989 Ikdam 11st 27

TOTE CHELTENHAM GOLD CUP (CHASE)
Cheltenham—3¼m

1955 Gay Donald 9y 12st 9
1956 Limber Hill 9y 12st 11
1957 Linwell 9y 12st 13
1958 Kerstin 8y 12st 9
1959 Roddy Owen 10y 12st 11
1960 Pas Seul 7y 12st 12
1961 Saffron Tartan 10y 12st 11
1962 Mandarin 11y 12st 9
1963 Mill House 6y 12st 12
1964 Arkle 7y 12st 4
1965 Arkle 8y 12st 4
1966 Arkle 9y 12st 5
1967 Woodland Venture 7y 12st......... 8
1968 Fort Leney 10y 12st 5
1969 What A Myth 12y 12st 11
1970 L'Escargot 7y 12st 12
1971 L'Escargot 8y 12st 8
1972 Glencaraig Lady 8y 12st 12
1973 The Dikler 10y 12st 8
1974 Captain Christy 7y 12st 7
1975 Ten Up 8y 12st 8
1976 Royal Frolic 7y 12st 11
1977 Davy Lad 7y 12st 13
1978 Midnight Court 7y 12st 10
1979 Alverton 9y 12st 14
1980 Tied Cottage 12y 12st (subsequently disqualified on technical grounds and race awarded to Master Smudge 8y 12st) 15
1981 Little Owl 7y 12st 13
1982 Silver Buck 10y 12st 22
1983 Bregawn 9y 12st 11
1984 Burrough Hill Lad 8y 12st 12
1985 Forgive'N Forget 8y 12st 15
1986 Dawn Run 8y 11st 9lb 11
1987 The Thinker 9y 12st 12
1988 Charter Party 10y 12st 15
1989 Desert Orchid 10y 12st 13

MARTELL CUP CHASE
Liverpool—3m 1f
1984-1988 Run as Chivas Regal Cup Chase

1984 Royal Bond 11y 11st 5lb 4
1985 Wayward Lad 10y 11st 5lb 6
1986 Beau Ranger 8y 11st 5lb 4
1987 Wayward Lad 12y 11st 5lb 6
1988 Desert Orchid 9y 11st 5lb 4
1989 Yahoo 8y 11st 5lb 8

GLENLIVET ANNIVERSARY HURDLE (4-y-o)
Liverpool—2m
Previously run under different titles

1980 Starfen 11st 20
1981 Broadsword (USA) 11st 3lb 10
1982 Prince Bless 11st 12
1983 Benfen 11st 9
1984 Afzal 11st 17
1985 Humberside Lady 10st 9lb 15
1986 Dark Raven 11st 16
1987 Aldino 11st 13
1988 Royal Illusion 11st 14
1989 Vayrua (FR) 11st 9

Winners of Principal National Hunt Races – Continued

CAPTAIN MORGAN AINTREE CHASE (LIMITED H'CAP)
Liverpool—2m
Previously run under different titles

1976 Menehall 9y 10st 10
1977 Skymas 12y 12st........................ 9
1978 Even Melody 9y 11st 6lb 14
1979 Funny Baby 8y 10st 7lb 8
1980 Drumgora 8y 10st 7lb 10
1981 Western Rose 9y 10st 7lb 11
1982 Little Bay 7y 11st 7lb 12
1983 Artifice 12y 11st 9
1984 Little Bay 9y 11st 7lb 7
1985 Kathies Lad 8y 11st 7lb 8
1986 Kathies Lad 9y 10st 13lb 6
1987 Sea Merchant 10y 10st 7lb 9
1988 Prideaux Boy 10y 10st 7lb 13
1989 Feroda 8y 10st 7lb 9

SANDEMAN AINTREE HURDLE
Liverpool—2½m
Previously run under different titles

1980 Pollardstown 5y 11st 5lb........... 3
1981 Daring Run 6y 11st 9lb............. 7
1982 Daring Run 7y 11st 9lb............. 5
1983 Gaye Brief 6y 11st 9lb.............. 6
1984 Dawn Run 6y 11st 11lb............ 8
1985 Bajan Sunshine 6y 11st 6lb 7
1986 Aonoch 7y 11st 9lb 9
1987 Aonoch 8y 11st 9lb 7
1988 Celtic Chief 5y 11st 6lb 9
1989 Beech Road 7y 11st 9lb.......... 12

WILLIAM HILL SCOTTISH GRAND NATIONAL (H'CAP CHASE)
Ayr—4m 120y

1970 The Spaniard 8y 10st.............. 10
1971 Young Ash Leaf 7y 10st 2lb 21
1972 Quick Reply 7y 9st 9lb 17
1973 Esban 9y 9st 11lb 21
1974 Red Rum 9y 11st 13lb............ 17
1975 Barona 9y 10st........................ 17
1976 Barona 10y 10st 2lb................ 23
1977 Sebastian V 9y 10st 2lb 18
1978 King Con 9y 9st 13lb.............. 21
1979 Fighting Fit 7y 10st 10lb.......... 19
1980 Salkeld 8y 10st........................ 23
1981 Astral Charmer 8y 9st 10lb 21
1982 Cockle Strand 9y 9st 11lb....... 15
1983 Canton 9y 10st 2lb.................. 22
1984 Androma 7y 10st...................... 19
1985 Androma 8y 10st...................... 18
1986 Hardy Lad 9y 10st.................... 24
1987 Little Polveir 9y 10st................ 11
1988 Mighty Mark 9y 10st 4lb.......... 17
1989 Roll-a-Joint 11y 10st................ 11

WHITBREAD GOLD CUP (H'CAP CHASE)
Sandown—3m 5f 18y
*Run at Newcastle

1959 Done Up 9y 10st 13lb............. 23
1960 Plummers Plain 7y 10st 21
1961 Pas Seul 8y 12st 23
1962 Frenchman's Cove 7y 11st 3lb 22
1963 Hoodwinked 8y 10st 9lb 32
1964 Dormant 7y 9st 7lb.................. 11
1965 Arkle 8y 12st 7lb 7
1966 What a Myth 9y 9st 8lb.............. 8
1967 Mill House 10y 11st 11lb......... 13
1968 Larbawn 9y 10st 9lb............... 16
1969 Larbawn 10y 11st 4lb.............. 18
1970 Royal Toss 8y 10st.................. 17
1971 Titus Oates 9y 11st 13lb 18
1972 Grey Sombrero 8y 9st 10lb..... 28
1973 *Charlie Potheen 8y 12st........... 21
1974 †The Dikler 11y 11st 13lb 16
1975 April Seventh 9y 9st 13lb 13
1976 Otter Way 8y 10st 10lb............ 14
1977 Andy Pandy 8y 10st 12lb 15
1978 Strombolus 7y 10st.................. 15
1979 Diamond Edge 8y 11st 11lb.... 14
1980 Royal Mail 10y 11st 5lb........... 12
1981 Diamond Edge 10y 11st 7lb.... 18
1982 Shady Deal 9y 10st..................... 9
1983 Drumlargan 9y 10st 10lb 15
1984 Special Cargo 11y 11st 2lb..... 13
1985 By The Way 7y 11st 20
1986 Plundering 9y 10st 6lb 16
1987 Lean Ar Aghaidh 10y 9st 10lb... 9
1988 Desert Orchid 9y 11st 11lb 12
1989 Brown Windsor 7y 10st............ 18

(†Proud Tarquin, 11y 10st 3lb came in first, disqualified)

SWINTON INSURANCE BROKERS TROPHY (H'CAP HURDLE)
Haydock—2m
1978-1982 Run as Royal Doulton H'cap Hurdle
1984 Run as Tia Maria H'cap Hurdle

1978 Royal Gaye 5y 10st.................. 20
1979 Beacon Light 8y 11st 1lb......... 17
1980 No Bombs 5y 10st 9lb............. 14
1981 Gaye Chance 6y 10st 10lb...... 18
1982 Secret Ballot 8y 10st 3lb 17
1983 Abandoned due to waterlogged course
1984 Bajan Sunshine 5y 10st 13lb .. 15
1985 Corporal Clinger 6y 10st 3lb ... 21
1986 Prideaux Boy 8y 11st 2lb 20
1987 Inlander 6y 10st 8lb 8
1988 Past Glories 5y 11st 9lb 23
1989 State Jester 6y 10st 18

1000 GUINEAS STAKES (3y fillies) Newmarket—1 mile

Year	Owner	Winner and Price	Jockey	Trainer	Second	Third	Ran	Time
1951	H Tufton's	Belle of All (4/1)	G Richards	N Bertie	Subtle Difference	Bob Run	18	1 44.80
1952	Sir M McAlpine's	Zabara (7/1)	K Gethin	V Smyth	La Mirambule	Refreshed	20	1 40.92
1953	H Wills's	Happy Laughter (10/1)	E Mercer	J Jarvis	Tessa Gillian	Bebe Grande	14	1 45.05
1954	J Dewar's	Festoon (9/2)	A Breasley	N Cannon	Big Berry	Welsh Fairy	12	1 38.90
1955	Lady Z Wernher's	Meld (11/4)	W Carr	C B Rochfort	Aberlady	Feria	12	1 42.16
1956	Sir V Sassoon's	Honeylight (100/6)	E Britt	C Elsey	Midget	Ariletta	19	1 39.15
1957	H H Aga Khan's	Rose Royale (6/1)	C Smirke	A Head	Sensualita	Angelet	20	1 39.15
1958	F Dupre's	Bella Paola (8/11)	S Boullenger	F Mathet	Amante	Alpine Bloom	11	1 38.75
1959	Aly Khan's	Petite Etoile (8/1)	D Smith	N Murless	Rosalba	Paraguana	14	1 40.36
1960	Mrs H Jackson's	Never Too Late (8/11)	R Poincelet	E Pollet	Lady in Trouble	Running Blue	14	1 39.89
1961	Mrs S Costello's	Sweet Solera (4/1)	W Rickaby	R Day	Ambergris	Indian Melody	14	1 38.14
1962	R More O' Ferrall's	Abermaid (100/6)	W Williamson	H Wragg	Display	West Side Story	14	1 39.36
1963	Mrs P Widener's	Hula Dancer (1/2)	R Poincelet	E Pollet	Spree	Royal Cypher	12	1 42.34
1964	Beatrice, Lady Granard's	Pourparler (11/2)	G Bougoure	P J Prendergast	Gwen	*Royal Danseuse *Petite Gina	18	1 38.82
1965	L Holliday's	Night Off (9/2)	W Williamson	W Wharton	Yami	Mabel	16	1 45.43
1966	Mrs J Mills's	Glad Rags (100/6)	P Cook	V O'Brien	Berkeley Springs	Miliza	21	1 40.30
1967	R Boucher's	Fleet (11/2)	G Moore	N Murless	St Pauli Girl	Lacquer	16	1 44.76
1968	Mrs N Murless's	Caergwrle (4/1)	A Barclay	N Murless	Photo Flash	Sovereign	14	1 40.38
1969	R Moller's	Full Dress (7/1)	R Hutchinson	H Wragg	Hecuba	Motionless	13	1 44.53
1970	Jean, Lady Ashcombe's	Humble Duty (3/1)	L Piggott	P Walwyn	Gleam	Black Satin	12	1 42.13
1971	F Hue-Williams's	Altesse Royale (25/1)	Y Saint Martin	N Murless	Super Honey	Catherine Wheel	10	1 40.90
1972	Mrs R Stanley's	Waterloo (8/1)	E Hide	J W Watts	Marisela	Rose Dubarry	18	1 39.49
1973	G Pope's	Mysterious (11/1)	G Lewis	N Murless	Jacinth	Shellshock	14	1 42.12
1974	The Queen's	Highclere (12/1)	J Mercer	R Hern	Polygamy	Mrs Twiggyw'kle	15	1 40.32
1975	Mrs D O' Kelly's	Nocturnal Spree (14/1)	J Roe	S Murless	Girl Friend	Joking Apart	16	1 41.65
1976	D Wildenstein's	Flying Water (2/1)	Y Saint Martin	A Penna	Konafa	Kesar Queen	25	1 37.83
1977	Mrs E Kettlewell's	Mrs McArdy (16/1)	E Hide	M W Easterby	Freeze the Secret	Sanedtki	18	1 40.07
1978	R Bonnycastle's	Enstone Spark (35/1)	E Johnson	B Hills	Fair Salinia	Seraphima	16	1 41.56
1979	Helena Springfield Ltd's	One in a Million (evens)	J Mercer	H Cecil	Abbeydale	Yanuka	17	1 43.06
1980	O Phipps's	Quick as Lightning (12/1)	B Rouse	J Dunlop	Our Home	Mrs Penny	23	1 41.89
1981	H Joel's	Fairy Footsteps (6/4)	L Piggott	H Cecil	Tolmi	Go Leasing	14	1 40.43
1982	Sir P Oppenheimer's	On The House (33/1)	J Reid	H Wragg	Time Charter	Dione	15	1 40.45
1983	Maktoum Al Maktoum's	Ma Biche (5/2)	F Head	Mme C Head	Favoridge	Habibti	18	1 41.71
1984	M Lemos's	Pebbles (8/1)	P Robinson	C Brittain	Meis El-Reem	Desirable	15	1 38.18
1985	Sheikh Mohammed's	Oh So Sharp (2/1)	S Cauthen	H Cecil	Al Bahathri	Bella Colora	17	1 36.85
1986	H Ranier's	Midway Lady (10/1)	R Cochrane	B Hanbury	Maysoon	Sonic Lady	15	1 41.54
1987	S Niarchos's	Miesque (15/8)	F Head	F Boutin	Milligram	Interval	14	1 38.48
1988	E Aland's	Ravinella (4/5)	G W Moore	Mrs C Head	Dabaweyaa	Diminuendo	12	1 40.88
1989	Sheikh Mohammed's	Musical Bliss (7/2)	W R Swinburn	M Stoute	Kerrera	Aldbourne	7	1 42.69

2000 GUINEAS STAKES (3y) Newmarket—1 mile

Year	Owner	Winner and Price	Jockey	Trainer	Second	Third	Ran	Time
1951	Ley On's	Ki Ming (100/8)	A Breasley	M Beary	Stokes	Malka's Boy	27	1 42.00
1952	E Constant's	Thunderhead (100/7)	R Poincelet	E Pollet	King's Bench	Argur	26	1 42.48
1953	W Humble's	Nearula (2/1)	E Britt	C Elsey	Bebe Grande	Oleandrin	16	1 38.26
1954	Sir P Loraine's	Darius (8/1)	E Mercer	H Wragg	Ferriol	Poona	19	1 39.45
1955	D Robinson's	Our Babu (13/2)	D Smith	G Brooke	Tamerlane	Klairon	23	1 38.83
1956	A Samuel's	Gilles de Retz (50/1)	F Barlow	Mrs H Houghton	Chantelsey	Buisson Ardent	19	1 38.76
1957	Sir V Sassoon's	Crepello (7/2)	L Piggott	N Murless	Quorum	Pipe of Peace	15	1 38.24
1958	The Queen's	Pall Mall (20/1)	D Smith	C B Rochfort	Major Portion	Nagami	14	1 39.43
1959	Aly Khan's	Taboun (5/2)	G Moore	A Head	Masham	Carnoustie	13	1 42.42
1960	R Webster's	Martial (18/1)	R Hutchinson	P J Prendergast	Venture	Auroy	17	1 38.33
1961	T Yuill's	Rockavon (66/1)	N Stirk	G Boyd	Prince Tudor	Time Greine	22	1 39.46
1962	G Glover's	Privy Councillor (100/6)	W Rickaby	T Waugh	Romulus	Prince Poppa	19	1 38.74
1963	Miss M Sheriffe's	Only for Life (33/1)	J Lindley	J Tree	Ionian	Corpora	21	1 45.00
1964	Mrs H. Jackson's	Baldric (20/1)	W Pyers	E Fellows	Faberge	Balustrade	27	1 38.44
1965	W Harvey's	Niksar (100/8)	D Keith	W Nightingall	Silly Season	Present	22	1 43.31
1966	P Butler's	Kashmir (7/1)	J Lindley	M Bartholomew	Great Nephew	Celtic Song	25	1 40.63
1967	H Joel's	Royal Palace (100/30)	G Moore	N Murless	Taj Dewan	Missile	18	1 39.37
1968	R Guest's	Sir Ivor (11/8)	L Piggott	V O'Brien	Petingo	Jimmy Reppin	10	1 39.26
1969	J Brown's	Right Tack (15/2)	G Lewis	J Sutcliffe	Tower Walk	Welsh Pageant	13	1 41.65
1970	C Engelhard's	Nijinsky (4/7)	L Piggott	V O' Brien	Yellow God	Roi Soleil	14	1 41.54
1971	Mrs J Hislop's	Brigadier Gerard (11/2)	J Mercer	R Hern	Mill Reef	My Swallow	6	1 39.20
1972	Sir J Thorn's	High Top (85/40)	W Carson	B Van Cutsem	Roberto	Sun Prince	12	1 40.82
1973	Mrs B Davis's	Mon Fils (50/1)	F Durr	R Hannon	Noble Decree	Sharp Edge	18	1 42.97
1974	Mme M Berger's	Nonoalco (19/2)	Y Saint Martin	F Boutin	Giacometti	Apalachee	12	1 39.53
1975	C d'Alessio's	Bolkonski (33/1)	G Dettori	H Cecil	Grundy	Dominion	24	1 39.53
1976	C d'Alessio's	Wollow (evens)	G Dettori	H Cecil	Vitiges	Thieving Demon	17	1 38.09
1977	N Schibbye's	Nebbiolo (20/1)	G Curran	K Prendergast	Tachypous	The Minstrel	18	1 38.54
1978	J Hayter's	Roland Gardens (28/1)	F Durr	D Sasse	Remainder Man	Weth Nan	19	1 47.33
1979	A Shead's	Tap On Wood (20/1)	S Cauthen	B Hills	Kris	Young Generation	20	1 43.60
1980	K Abdulla's (Nureyev fin first disqualified)	Known Fact (14/1)	W Carson	J Tree	Posse	Night Alert	14	1 40.46
1981	Mrs A Muinos's	To-Agori-Mou (5/2)	G Starkey	G Harwood	Mattaboy	Bel Bolide	19	1 41.43
1982	G Oldham's	Zino (8/1)	F Head	F Boutin	Wind and Wuthering	Tender King	26	1 37.13
1983	R Sangster's	Lomond (9/1)	Pat Eddery	V O'Brien	Tolomeo	Muscatite	16	1 43.87
1984	R Sangster's	El Gran Senor (15/8)	Pat Eddery	V O'Brien	Chief Singer	Lear Fan	9	1 37.41
1985	Maktoum Al Maktoum's	Shadeed (4/5)	L Piggott	M Stoute	Bairn	Supreme Leader	14	1 37.41
1986	K Abdulla's	Dancing Brave (15/8)	G Starkey	G Harwood	Green Desert	Huntingdale	15	1 40.00
1987	J Horgan's	Don't Forget Me (9/1)	W Carson	R Hannon	Bellotto	Midyan	13	1 36.74
1988	H H Aga Khan's	Doyoun (4/5)	W R Swinburn	M R Stoute	Charmer	Bellefella	9	1 41.73
1989	Hamdan Al-Maktoum's	Nashwan (3/1)	W Carson	R Hern	Exbourne	Danehill	14	1 36.44

DERBY STAKES (3y) Epsom—1 mile 4 furlongs

Year	Owner	Winner and Price	Jockey	Trainer	Second	Third	Ran	Time
1950	M Boussac's	Galcador (100/9)	W Johnstone	C Semblat	Prince Simon	Double Eclipse	25	2 36.80
1951	J McGrath's	Arctic Prince (28/1)	C Spares	W Stephenson	Sybil's Nephew	Signal Box	33	2 39.40
1952	H H Aga Khan's	Tulyar (11/2)	C Smirke	M Marsh	Gay Time	Faubourg	33	2 36.40
1953	Sir V Sassoon's	Pinza (5/1)	G Richards	N Bertie	Aureole	Pink Horse	27	2 35.60
1954	R Clark's	Never Say Die (33/1)	L Piggott	J Lawson	Arabian Night	Darius	22	2 35.80
1955	Mme L Volterra's	Phil Drake (100/8)	F Palmer	F Mathet	Panaslipper	Acropolis	23	2 39.80
1956	P Wertheimer's	Lavandin (7/1)	W Johnstone	A Head	Montaval	Roistar	27	2 36.40
1957	Sir V Sassoon's	Crepello (6/4)	L Piggott	N Murless	Ballymoss	Pipe of Peace	22	2 35.40
1958	Sir V Sassoon's	Hard Ridden (18/1)	C Smirke	M Rogers	Paddy's Point	Nagami	20	2 41.20
1959	Sir H de Trafford's	Parthia (10/1)	W Carr	C B-Rochfort	Fidalgo	Shantung	20	2 36.00
1960	Sir V Sassoon's	St Paddy (7/1)	L Piggott	N Murless	Alcaeus	Kythnos	17	2 35.80
1961	Mrs A. Plesch's	Psidium (66/1)	R Poincelet	H Wragg	Dicta Drake	Pardao	28	2 36.40
1962	R Guest's	Larkspur (22/1)	N Sellwood	V O'Brien	Arcor	Le Cantilien	26	2 37.60
1963	F Dupre's	Relko (5/1)	Y Saint Martin	F Mathet	Merchant Venturer	Ragusa	26	2 39.40
1964	J Ismay's	Santa Claus (15/8)	A Breasley	M Rogers	Indiana	Dillettante	17	2 41.98
1965	J Ternynck's	Sea-Bird (7/4)	P. Glennon	E Pollet	Meadow Court	I Say	22	2 38.41
1966	Lady Z Wernher's	Charlottown (5/1)	A Breasley	G Smyth	Pretendre	Black Prince	25	2 37.63
1967	H Joel's	Royal Palace (7/4)	G Moore	N Murless	Ribocco	Dart Board	22	2 33.36
1968	R Guest's	Sir Ivor (4/5)	L Piggott	V O Brien	Connaught	Mount Athos	13	2 38.73
1969	A Budgett's	Blakeney (15/2)	E Johnson	A Budgett	Shoemaker	Prince Regent	26	2 40.30
1970	C Engelhard's	Nijinsky (11/8)	L Piggott	V O'Brien	Gyr	Stintino	11	2 34.68
1971	P Mellon's	Mill Reef (100/30)	G Lewis	I Balding	Linden Tree	Irish Ball	21	2 37.14
1972	J Galbreath's	Roberto (3/1)	L Piggott	V O'Brien	Rheingold	Pentland Firth	22	2 36.09
1973	A Budgett's	Morston (25/1)	E Hide	A Budgett	Cavo Doro	Freefoot	25	2 35.92
1974	Mrs N. Phillips's	Snow Knight (50/1)	B Taylor	P Nelson	Imperial Prince	Giacometti	18	2 35.04
1975	Dr C Vittadini's	Grundy (5/1)	Pat Eddery	P Walwyn	Nobiliary	Hunza Dancer	18	2 35.35
1976	N B Hunt's	Empery (10/1)	L Piggott	M Zilber	Relkino	Oats	23	2 35.69
1977	R Sangster's	The Minstrel (5/1)	L Piggott	V O'Brien	Hot Grove	Blushing Groom	22	2 36.44
1978	Lord Halifax's	Shirley Heights (8/1)	G Starkey	J Dunlop	Hawaiian Sound	Remainder Man	25	2 35.30
1979	Sir M Sobell's	Troy (6/1)	W Carson	R Hern	Dickens Hill	Northern Baby	23	2 36.59
1980	Mrs A Plesch's	Henbit (7/1)	W Carson	R Hern	Master Willie	Rankin	24	2 34.77
1981	H H Aga Khan's	Shergar (10/11)	W Swinburn	M Stoute	Glint of Gold	Scintillating Air	18	2 44.21
1982	R Sangster's	Golden Fleece (3/1)	Pat Eddery	V O'Brien	Touching Wood	Silver Hawk	18	2 34.27
1983	E Moller's	Teenoso (9/2)	L Piggott	G Wragg	Carlingford Castle	Shearwalk	21	2 49.07
1984	L Miglitti's	Secreto (14/1)	C Roche	D O'Brien	El Gran Senor	Mighty Flutter	17	2 39.12
1985	Lord H. de Walden's	Slip Anchor (9/4)	S Cauthen	H Cecil	Law Society	Damister	14	2 36.23
1986	H H Aga Khan's	Shahrastani (11/2)	W Swinburn	M Stoute	Dancing Brave	Mashkour	17	2 37.13
1987	L Freedman's	Reference Point (6/4)	S Cauthen	H Cecil	Most Welcome	Bellotto	19	2 33.90
1988	H H Aga Khan's	Kahyasi (11/1)	R Cochrane	L Cumani	Glacial Storm	Doyoun	14	2 33.84
1989	Hamdam Al-Maktoum's	Nashwan (5/4)	W Carson	R Hern	Terimon	Cacoethes	12	2 34.90

OAKS STAKES (3y fillies) Epsom—1 mile 4 furlongs

Year	Owner	Winner and Price	Jockey	Trainer	Second	Third	Ran	Time
1955	Lady Z Wernher's	Meld (7/4)	W Carr	C B-Rochfort	Ark Royal	Reel In	13	2 47.80
1956	Mme L Volterra's	Sicarelle (3/1)	F Palmer	F Mathet	Janiari	Yasmin	14	2 42.00
1957	The Queen	Carrozza (100/8)	L Piggott	N Murless	Silken Glider	Rose Royale	11	2 37.40
1958	F Dupre's	Bella Paola (6/4)	M Garcia	F Mathet	Mother Goose	Cutter	17	2 40.80
1959	Aly Khan's	Petite Etoile (11/2)	L Piggott	N Murless	Cantelo	Rose of Medina	11	2 35.80
1960	Mrs H Jackson's	Never Too Late (6/5)	R Poincelet	E Pollet	Paimpont	Imberline	10	2 39.20
1961	Mrs S Castello's	Sweet Solera (11/4)	W Rickaby	R Day	Ambergris	Anne La Douce	12	2 39.40
1962	G Goulandris's	Monade (7/1)	Y Saint Martin	J Lieux	West Side Story	Tender Annie	18	2 38.20
1963	Mrs J Olin's	Noblesse (4/11)	G Bougoure	P J Prendergast	Spree	Pouponne	9	2 39.60
1964	Sir F Robinson's	Homeward Bound (100/7)	G Starkey	J Oxley	Windmill Girl	La Bamba	18	2 49.36
1965	J C Brady's	Long Look (100/7)	J Purtell	V O'Brien	Mabel	Ruby's Princess	18	2 39.56
1966	C Clore's	Valoris (11/10)	L Piggott	V O'Brien	Berkeley Springs	Varinia	13	2 39.35
1967	Countess M Batthyany's	Pia (100/7)	E Hide	W Elsey	St Pauli Girl	Ludham	12	2 38.34
1968	H Berlin's	La Lagune (11/8)	G Thiboeuf	F Boutin	Glad One	Pandora Bay	14	2 41.66
1969	Lord Rosebery's	Sleeping Partner (100/6)	J Gorton	D Smith	Frontier Goddess	Myastrid	15	2 39.94
1970	Mrs S Joel's	Lupe (100/30)	A Barclay	N Murless	State Pension	Arctic Wave	16	2 41.46
1971	F Hue-Williams's	Altesse Royale (6/4)	G Lewis	N Murless	Maina	La Manille	11	2 36.95
1972	C St George's	Ginevra (8/1)	A Murray	R Price	Regal Exception	Arkadina	17	2 39.35
1973	G Pope's	Mysterious (13/8)	G Lewis	N Murless	Where You Lead	Aureoletta	10	2 36.31
1974	L Freedman's	Polygamy (3/1)	Pat Eddery	P Walwyn	Furioso	Matuta	15	2 39.39
1975	J Morrison's	Juliette Marny (12/1)	L Piggott	J Tree	Val's Girl	Moonlight Night	12	2 39.10
1976	D Wildenstein's	Pawneese (6/5)	Y Saint Martin	A Penna	Roses for the Star	African Dancer	14	2 35.25
1977	The Queen's	Dunfermline (6/1)	W Carson	R Hern	Freeze the Secret	Vaguely Deb	13	2 36.53
1978	S Hanson's	Fair Salinia (8/1)	G Starkey	M Stoute	Dancing Maid	Suni	15	2 36.82
1979	J Morrison's	Scintillate (20/1)	Pat Eddery	J Tree	Bonnie Isle	Britannia's Rule	14	2 43.74
1980	R Hollingsworth's	Bireme (9/2)	W Carson	R Hern	Vielle	The Dancer	11	2 34.33
1981	Mrs B Firestone's	Blue Wind (3/1)	L Piggott	D Weld	Madam Gay	Leap Lively	12	2 40.93
1982	R Barnett's	Time Charter (12/1)	W Newnes	H Candy	Slightly Dangerous	Last Feather	13	2 34.21
1983	Sir M Sobell's	Sun Princess (6/1)	W Carson	R Hern	Acclimatise	New Coins	15	2 40.98
1984	Sir R McAlpine's	Circus Plume (4/1)	L Piggott	J Dunlop	Media Luna	Poquito Queen	15	2 38.97
1985	Sheikh Mohammed's	Oh So Sharp (6/4)	S Cauthen	H Cecil	Triptych	Dubian	12	2 41.37
1986	H Ranier's	Midway Lady (15/8)	R Cochrane	B Hanbury	Untold	Maysoon	15	2 35.60
1987	Sheikh Mohammed's	Unite (11/1)	W R Swinburn	M Stoute	Bourbon Girl	Three Tails	11	2 38.17
1988	Sheikh Mohammed's	Diminuendo (7/4)	S Cauthen	H Cecil	Sudden Love	Animatrice	11	2 35.02
1989	H H Aga Khan's	Aliysa (11/10)	W R Swinburn	M Stoute	Snow Bride	Roseate Tern	9	2 34.22

ST LEGER STAKES (3y) Doncaster—1 mile 6 furlongs 127 yards

Year	Owner	Winner and Price	Jockey	Trainer	Second	Third	Ran	Time
1950	M Boussac's	Scratch (9/2)	W Johnstone	C Semblat	Vieux Manoir	Sanlinea	15	3 8.80
1951	M Boussac's	Talma (7/1)	W Johnstone	C Semblat	Fraise du Bois	Medway	18	3 13.80
1952	H H Aga Khan's	Tulyar (10/11)	C Smirke	M Marsh	Kingsfold	Alcinus	12	3 7.80
1953	W Wyatt's	Premonition (10/1)	E Smith	C B-Rochfort	Northern Light	Aureole	11	3 6.80
1954	R S Clark's	Never Say Die (100/30)	C Smirke	J Lawson	Elopement	Estremadur	16	3 10.60
1955	Lady Z Wernher's	Meld (10/11)	W Carr	C B-Rochfort	Nucleus	Beau Prince	8	3 14.60
1956	R Strassburger's	Cambremer (8/1)	F Palmer	G Bridgland	Hornbeam	French Beige	13	3 12.20
1957	J McShain's	Ballymoss (8/1)	T P Burns	V O'Brien	Court Harwell	Brioche	16	3 15.60
1958	Sir H de Trafford's	Alcide (4/9)	W Carr	C B-Rochfort	None Nicer	Nagami	10	3 6.40
1959	W Hill's	Cantelo (100/7)	E Hide	C Elsey	Fidalgo	Pindari	11	3 4.60
1960	Sir V Sassoon's	St Paddy (4/6)	L Piggott	N Murless	Die Hard	Vienna	9	3 13.20
1961	Mrs V Lilley's	Aurelius (9/2)	L Piggott	N Murless	Bounteous	Dicta Drake	13	3 6.60
1962	L Holliday's	Hethersett (100/8)	W Carr	R Hern	Monterrico	Miralgo	15	3 10.80
1963	J Mullion's	Ragusa (2/5)	G Bougoure	P J Prendergast	Star Moss	Fighting Ship	7	3 5.40
1964	C Engelhard's	Indiana (100/7)	J Lindley	J Watts	Patti	Soderini	15	3 5.40
1965	J Astor's	Provoke (28/1)	J Mercer	R Hern	Meadow Court	Solstice	11	3 18.60
1966	R Sigtia's	Sodium (7/1)	F Durr	G Todd	Charlottown	David Jack	9	3 9.80
1967	C Engelhard's	Ribocco (7/2)	L Piggott	R Houghton	Hopeful Venture	Ruysdael	9	3 5.40
1968	C Engelhard's	Ribero (100/30)	L Piggott	R Houghton	Canterbury	Cold Storage	8	3 19.80
1969	G Oldham's	Intermezzo (7/1)	R Hutchinson	H Wragg	Ribofilio	Prince Consort	11	3 11.80
1970	C Engelhard's	Nijinsky (2/7)	L Piggott	V O'Brien	Meadowville	Politico	9	3 6.40
1971	Mrs J Rogerson's	Athens Wood (5/2)	L Piggott	H T Jones	Homeric	Falkland	8	3 14.90
1972	O Phipps's	Boucher (3/1)	L Piggott	V O'Brien	Our Mirage	Ginevra	7	3 28.71
1973	W Behrens's	Peleid (28/1)	F Durr	W Elsey	Buoy	Duke of Ragusa	13	3 8.21
1974	Lady Beaverbrook's	Bustino (11/10)	J Mercer	R Hern	Giacometti	Riboson	10	3 9.02
1975	C St George's	Bruni (9/1)	A Murray	R Price	King Pellinore	Libra's Rib	12	3 9.02
1976	D Wildenstein's	Crow (6/1)	Y Saint-Martin	A Penna	Secret Man	Scallywag	15	3 13.17
1977	The Queen's	Dunfermline (10/1)	W Carson	R Hern	Alleged	Classic Example	13	3 5.17
1978	M Lemos's	Julio Mariner (28/1)	E Hide	C Brittain	Le Moss	M-Lolshan	14	3 4.94
1979	A Rolland's	Son of Love (20/1)	A Lequeux	R Collet	Soleil Noir	Niniski	17	3 9.02
1980	H Joel's	Light Cavalry (3/1)	J Mercer	H Cecil	Water Mill	World Leader	7	3 11.48
1981	Sir J Astor's	Cut Above (28/1)	J Mercer	R Hern	Glint of Gold	Bustomi	7	3 11.60
1982	Maktoum Al Maktoum's	Touching Wood (7/1)	P Cook	H T Jones	Zilos	Diamond Shoal	15	3 3.53
1983	Sir M Sobell's	Sun Princess (11/8)	W Carson	R Hern	Esprit du Nord	Carlingford Castle	10	3 16.65
1984	I Allan's	Commanche Run (7/4)	L Piggott	L Cumani	Baynoun	Alphabatim	11	3 9.93
1985	Sheikh Mohammed's	Oh So Sharp (8/11)	S Cauthen	H Cecil	Phardante	Lanfranco	6	3 7.13
1986	Duchess of Norfolk's	Moon Madness (9/2)	Pat Eddery	J Dunlop	Celestial Storm	Untold	8	3 5.03
1987	L Freedman's	Reference Point (4/11)	S Cauthen	H Cecil	Mountain Kingdom	Dry Dock	7	3 5.91
1988	Lady Beaverbrook's	Minster Son (15/2)	W Carson	N A Graham	Diminuendo	Sheriff's Star	6	3 6.80
1989	C St George's (Run at Ayr)	Michelozzo (6/4)	S Cauthen	H Cecil	Sapience	Roseate Tern	8	3 20.72

KING GEORGE VI AND QUEEN ELIZABETH STAKES
Ascot—1 mile 4 furlongs

Year	Owner	Winner and Price	Jockey	Trainer	Second	Third	Ran	Time
1951	Mrs V Lilley's	Supreme Court 3-8-4 (100/9)	C Elliott	E Williams	Zucchero	Tantieme	19	2 29.40
1952	H H Aga Khan's	Tulyar 3-8-6 (3/1)	C Smirke	M Marsh	Gay Time	Worden	15	2 33.20
1953	Sir V Sassoon's	Pinza 3-8-4 (2/1)	G Richards	N Bertie	Aureole	Worden	13	2 33.60
1954	The Queen's	Aureole 4-9-4 (9/2)	E Smith	C B-Rochfort	Vamos	Darius	17	2 44.00
1955	P Wertheimer's	Vimy 3-8-4 (10/1)	R Poincelet	A Head	Acropolis	Elopement	10	2 33.60
1956	Marchese Incisa's	Ribot 4-9-4 (2/5)	E Camici	U Penco	High Veldt	Todrai	9	2 40.24
1957	R Strassburger's	Montaval 4-9-7 (20/1)	F Palmer	G Bridgland	Al Mabsoot	Tribord	12	2 41.02
1958	J McShain's	Ballymoss 4-9-7 (7/4)	A Breasley	V O'Brien	Almeria	Doutelle	8	2 36.33
1959	Sir H de Trafford's	Alcide 4-9-7 (2/1)	W Carr	C B-Rochfort	Gladness	Balbo	11	2 31.39
1960	Sir H Wernher's	Aggressor 5-9-7 (100/8)	J Lindley	J Gosden	Petite Etoile	Kythnos	8	2 35.21
1961	Mme E Couturie's	Right Royal 3-8-7 (6/4)	R Poincelet	E Pollet	St Paddy	Rockavon	4	2 40.34
1962	F Dupre's	Match 4-9-7 (9/2)	Y Saint Martin	F Mathet	Aurelius	Arctic Storm	11	2 32.02
1963	J Mullion's	Ragusa 3-8-7 (4/1)	G Bougoure	P J Prendergast	Miralgo	Tarqogan	10	2 33.80
1964	Mrs H Jackson's	Nasram 4-9-7 (100/7)	W Pyers	E Fellows	Santa Claus	Royal Avenue	4	2 33.15
1965	G Bell's	Meadow Court 3-8-7 (6/5)	L Piggott	P J Prendergast	Soderini	Oncidium	12	2 33.27
1966	J Hornung's	Aunt Edith 4-9-4 (7/2)	L Piggott	N Murless	Sodium	Prominer	5	2 35.06
1967	S Joel's	Busted 4-9-7 (4/1)	G Moore	N Murless	Salvo	Ribocco	9	2 33.64
1968	H Joel's	Royal Palace 4-9-7 (7/4)	A Barclay	N Murless	Felicio	Topyo	7	2 33.22
1969	Duke of Devonshire's	Park Top 5-9-4 (9/4)	L Piggott	B van Cutsem	Crozier	Hogarth	9	2 32.46
1970	C Engelhard's	Nijinsky 3-8-7 (40/85)	L Piggott	V O'Brien	Blakeney	Crepellana	6	2 36.16
1971	P Mellon's	Mill Reef 3-8-7 (8/13)	G Lewis	I Balding	Ortis	Acclimatization	10	2 32.56
1972	Mrs J Hislop's	Brigadier Gerard 4-9-7 (8/13)	J Mercer	R Hern	Parnell	Riverman	9	2 32.91
1973	N B Hunt's	Dahlia 3-8-4 (10/1)	W Pyers	M Zilber	Rheingold	Our Mirage	12	2 30.43
1974	N B Hunt's	Dahlia 4-9-4 (15/8)	L Piggott	M Zilber	Highclere	Dankaro	10	2 33.03
1975	Dr C Vittadini's	Grundy 3-8-7 (4/5)	P Eddery	P Walwyn	Bustino	Dahlia	11	2 26.98
1976	D Wildenstein's	Pawneese 3-8-5 (9/4)	Y Saint Martin	A Penna	Bruni	Orange Bay	10	2 29.36
1977	R Sangster's	The Minstrel 3-8-8 (7/4)	L Piggott	V O'Brien	Orange Bay	Exceller	11	2 30.48
1978	D McCall's	Ile de Bourbon 3-8-8 (12/1)	J Reid	F Houghton	Hawaiian Sound	Montcontour	14	2 30.53
1979	Sir M Sobell's	Troy 3-8-8 (2/5)	W Carson	R Hern	Gay Mecene	Ela-Mana-Mou	7	2 33.75
1980	S Weinstock's	Ela-Mana-Mou 4-9-7 (11/4)	W Carson	R Hern	Mrs Penny	Gregorian	10	2 35.39
1981	H H Aga Khan's	Shergar 3-8-8 (2/5)	W Swinburn	M Stoute	Madam Gay	Fingals Cave	7	2 35.40
1982	A Ward's	Kalaglow 4-9-7 (13-2)	G Starkey	G Harwood	Assert	Glint of Gold	9	2 31.58
1983	R Barnett's	Time Charter 4-9-4 (5/1)	J Mercer	H Candy	Diamond Shoal	Sun Princess	9	2 30.78
1984	E Moller's	Teenoso 4-9-7 (13/2)	L Piggott	G Wragg	Sadler's Wells	Tolomeo	13	2 27.95
1985	Lady Beaverbrook's	Petoski 3-8-8 (12/1)	W Carson	R Hern	Oh So Sharp	Rainbow Quest	12	2 27.61
1986	K Abdulla's	Dancing Brave 3-8-8 (6/4)	Pat Eddery	G Harwood	Shardari	Triptych	9	2 29.49
1987	L Freedman's	Reference Point 3-8-8 (11/10)	S Cauthen	H Cecil	Celestial Storm	Triptych	9	2 34.63
1988	Sheikh Ahmed Al Maktoum	Mtoto 5-9-7 (4/1)	M Roberts	A C Stewart	Unfuwain	Tony Bin	10	2 37.33
1989	Hamdan Al-Maktoum's	Nashwan 3-8-8 (2/9)	W Carson	R Hern	Cacoethes	Top Class	7	2 32.27

PRIX DE L'ARC DE TRIOMPHE Longchamp—1 mile 4 furlongs

Year	Owner	Winner and Price	Jockey	Trainer	Second	Third	Ran	Time
1949	M Boussac's	Coronation 3-8-7 (37/10)	R Poincelet	C Semblat	Double Rose	Amour Drake	28	2 33.20
1950	F Dupre's	Tantieme 3-8-10 (5/2)	J Doyasbere	F Mathet	Alizier	L'Amiral	12	2 34.20
1951	F Dupre's	Tantieme 4-9-6 (17/10)	J Doyasbere	F Mathet	Nuccio	Le Tyrol	19	2 32.80
1952	H H Aga Khan's	Nuccio 4-9-6 (74/10)	R Poincelet	A Head	La Mirambule	Dynamiter	18	2 39.80
1953	P Duboscq's	La Sorellina 3-8-7 (65/4)	M Larraun	E Pollet	Silnet	Worden	25	2 31.90
1954	Mme J Cochery's	Sica Boy 3-8-10 (41/10)	W Johnstone	P Pelat	Banassa	Philante	21	2 36.40
1955	Marchese Incisa's	Ribot 3-8-10 (88/10)	E Camici	U Penco	Beau Prince	Picounda	23	2 35.60
1956	Marchese Incisa's	Ribot 4-9-6 (3/5)	E Camici	U Penco	Talgo	Tanerko	20	2 34.80
1957	R Meyer's	Oroso 4-9-6 (52/1)	S Boullenger	D Lescalle	Denisy	Balbo	24	2 33.40
1958	J McShain's	Ballymoss 4-9-6 (39/10)	A Breasley	V O Brien	Fric	Cherasco	17	2 37.90
1959	Aly Khan's	Saint Crespin 3-8-10 (17/1)	G Moore	A Head	Midnight Sun	Le Loup Garou	25	2 33.30
1960	H Aubert's	Puissant Chef 3-8-10 (14/1)	M Garcia	C Bartholomew	Hautain	Point d'Amour	17	2 43.90
1961	E Verga's	Molvedo 3-8-10 (18/10)	E Camici	A Maggi	Right Royal	Misti	19	2 38.40
1962	Mme C del Ducca's	Soltikoff 3-8-10 (40/1)	M Depalmas	R Pelat	Monade	Val de Loir	24	2 30.90
1963	Baron G de Rothschild's	Exbury 4-9-6 (36/10)	J Deforge	G Watson	Le Mesnil	Misti	15	2 34.90
1964	R Ellsworth's	Prince Royal 3-8-10 (16/1)	R Poincelet	G Bridgland	Santa Claus	La Bamba	22	2 35.50
1965	J Ternynck's	Sea-Bird 3-8-10 (6/5)	P Glennon	E Pollet	Reliance	Diatome	20	2 35.50
1966	W Burmann's	Bon Mot 3-8-10 (53/10)	F Head	W Head	Sigebert	Lionel	24	2 39.80
1967	Mme S Volterra's	Topyo 3-8-10 (82/1)	W Pyers	M Bartholomew	Salvo	Ribocco	30	2 38.20
1968	Mrs W Franklyn's	Vaguely Noble 3-8-10 (5/2)	W Williamson	E Pollet	Sir Ivor	Carmarthen	17	2 35.20
1969	S McGrath's	Levmoss 4-9-6 (52/1)	W Williamson	S McGrath	Park Top	Grandier	24	2 29.00
1970	A Plesch's	Sassafras 3-8-10 (19/1)	Y Saint Martin	F Mathet	Nijinsky	Miss Dan	15	2 29.70
1971	P Mellon's	Mill Reef 3-8-10 (7/10)	G Lewis	I Balding	Pistol Packer	Cambrizzia	18	2 28.30
1972	Countess M Batthyany's	San San 3-8-7 (37/2)	F Head	A Penna	Rescousse	Homeric	19	2 28.30
1973	H Zeisel's	Rheingold 4-9-6 (77/10)	L Piggott	B Hills	Allez France	Hard to Beat	27	2 35.80
1974	D Wildenstein's	Allez France 4-9-3 (1/2)	Y Saint Martin	A Penna	Comtesse de Loir	Margouillat	20	2 36.90
1975	W Zeitelhack's	Star Appeal 5-9-6 (119/1)	G Starkey	T Grieper	On My Way	Comtesse de Loir	24	2 33.60
1976	J Wertheimer's	Ivanjica 4-9-1 (71/10)	F Head	A Head	Crow	Youth	20	2 39.40
1977	R Sangster's	Alleged 3-8-11 (38/10)	L Piggott	V O'Brien	Balmerino	Crystal Palace	26	2 30.60
1978	R Sangster's	Alleged 4-9-4 (7/5)	L Piggott	V O'Brien	Trillion	Dancing Maid	18	2 36.10
1979	Mme G Head's	Three Troikas 3-8-8 (88/10)	F Head	Mme C Head	Le Marmot	Troy	22	2 28.90
1980	R Sangster's	Detroit 3-8-8 (67/10)	Pat Eddery	O Douieb	Argument	Ela-Mana-Mou	20	2 28.00
1981	J Wertheimer's	Gold River 4-9-1 (53/1)	G W Moore	A Head	Bikala	April Run	24	2 35.20
1982	H H Aga Khan's	Akiyda 3-8-8 (43/4)	Y Saint Martin	F. Mathet	Ardross	Awaasif	17	2 37.00
1983	D Wildenstein's	All Along 4-9-1 (173/10)	W Swinburn	P Biancone	Sun Princess	Luth Enchantee	26	2 28.10
1984	D Wildenstein's	Sagace 4-9-4 (29/10)	Y Saint Martin	P Biancone	Northern Trick	All Along	22	2 39.10
1985	K Abdulla's	Rainbow Quest 4-9-4 (71/10)	Pat Eddery	J Tree	Sagace	Kozana	15	2 29.50
1986	K Abdulla's	Dancing Brave 3-8-11 (11/10)	Pat Eddery	G Harwood	Bering	Triptych	15	2 27.70
1987	P de Moussac's	Trempolino 3-8-11 (20/1)	Pat Eddery	A Fabre	Tony Bin	Triptych	11	2 26.30
1988	Mrs V Gaucci del Bono's	Tony Bin 5-9-4 (14/1)	J Reid	L Camici	Mtoto	Boyatino	24	2 27.30
1989	A Balzarini's	Carroll House 4-9-4 (19/1)	M Kinane	M Jarvis	Behera	Saint Andrews	19	2 30.80

GRAND NATIONAL STEEPLECHASE (Liverpool)—4m 4f

Year	Winner and Price	Age & Weight	Jockey	Second	Third	Ran	Time
1949	Russian Hero (66-1)	9 10 8	L McMorrow	Rolmond	Royal Mount	43	9 23.80
1950	Freebooter (10-1)	9 11 11	J Power	Wot No Sun	Acthon Major	49	9 23.60
1951	Nickel Coin (40-1)	9 10 1	J A Bullock	Royal Tan	Derrinstown	36	9 47.40
1952	Teal (100-7)	10 10 12	A P Thompson	Legal Joy	Wot No Sun	47	9 20.60
1953	Early Mist (20-1)	8 11 2	B Marshall	Mont Tremblant	Irish Lizard	31	9 21.60
1954	Royal Tan (8-1)	10 11 7	B Marshall	Tudor Line	Irish Lizard	29	9 32.80
1955	Quare Times (100-9)	9 11 0	P Taaffe	Tudor Line	Carey's Cottage	30	10 20.60
1956	E.S.B. (100-7)	10 11 3	D V Dick	Gentle Moya	Royal Tan	29	9 21.40
1957	Sundew (20-1)	11 11 7	F T Winter	Wyndburgh	Tiberetta	35	9 42.40
1958	Mr What (18-1)	8 10 6	A Freeman	Tiberetta	Green Drill	31	10 1.20
1959	Oxo (8-1)	8 10 13	M Scudamore	Wyndburgh	Mr What	34	9 37.20
1960	Merryman II (13-2)	9 10 12	G Scott	Badanloch	Clear Profit	26	9 26.20
1961	Nicolaus Silver (28-1)	9 10 1	H Beasley	Merryman II	O'Malley Point	35	9 22.60
1962	Kilmore (28-1)	12 10 4	F T Winter	Wyndburgh	Mr What	32	9 50.00
1963	Ayala (66-1)	9 10 0	P Buckley	Carrickbeg	Hawa's Song	47	9 35.80
1964	Team Spirit (18-1)	12 10 3	G W Robinson	Purple Silk	Peacetown	33	9 47.00
1965	Jay Trump (100-8)	8 11 5	Mr C Smith, jun	Freddie	Mr Jones	47	9 30.60
1966	Anglo (50-1)	8 10 0	T Norman	Freddie	Forest Prince	47	9 52.80
1967	Foinavon (100-1)	9 10 0	J Buckingham	Honey End	Red Alligator	44	9 49.60
1968	Red Alligator (100-7)	9 10 0	B Fletcher	Moidore's Token	Different Class	45	9 28.60
1969	Highland Wedding (100-9)	12 10 4	E Harty	Steel Bridge	Rondetto	30	9 30.80
1970	Gay Trip (15-1)	8 11 5	P Taaffe	Vulture	Miss Hunter	28	9 38.00
1971	Specify (28-1)	9 10 13	J Cook	Black Secret	Astbury	38	9 34.20
1972	Well To Do (14-1)	9 10 1	G Thorner	Gay Trip	Black Secret	42	10 8.40
1973	Red Rum (9-1)	8 10 5	B Fletcher	Crisp	L'Escargot	38	9 1.90
1974	Red Rum (11-1)	9 12 0	B Fletcher	L'Escargot	Charles Dickens	42	9 20.30
1975	L'Escargot (13-2)	12 11 3	T Carberry	Red Rum	Spanish Steps	31	9 31.10
1976	Rag Trade (14-1)	10 10 12	J Burke	Red Rum	Eyecatcher	32	9 20.90
1977	Red Rum (9-1)	12 11 8	T Stack	Churchtown Boy	Eyecatcher	42	9 30.30
1978	Lucius (14-1)	9 10 9	B R Davies	Sebastian V	Drumroan	37	9 33.90
1979	Rubstic (25-1)	10 10 0	M Barnes	Zongalero	Rough & Tumble	34	9 52.90
1980	Ben Nevis (40-1)	12 10 12	Mr C Fenwick	Rough & Tumble	The Pilgarlic	30	10 17.40
1981	Aldaniti (10-1)	11 10 13	R Champion	Spartan Missile	Royal Mail	39	9 47.20
1982	Grittar (7-1)	9 11 5	E Saunders	Hard Outlook	Loving Words	39	9 12.60
1983	Corbiere (13-1)	8 11 4	B de Haan	Greasepaint	Yer Man	41	9 47.04
1984	Hallo Dandy (13-1)	10 10 2	N Doughty	Greasepaint	Corbiere	40	9 21.04
1985	Last Suspect (50-1)	11 10 5	H Davies	Mr Snugfit	Corbiere	40	9 42.70
1986	West Tip (15-2)	9 10 11	R Dunwoody	Young Driver	Classified	40	9 33.00
1987	Maori Venture (28-1)	11 10 13	S C Knight	The Tsarevich	Lean Ar Aghaidh	40	9 19.30
1988	Rhyme n'Reason (10-1)	9 11 0	B Powell	Durham Edition	Monanore	40	9 53.50
1989	Little Polveir (28-1)	12 10 3	J Frost	West Tip	The Thinker	40	10 6.80

TURF STATISTICS

WINNING TRAINERS, 1989

	Races Won	Stakes £	Per Cent	Last Year
STOUTE, M.R.	117	1,469,158	23.5%	6
CECIL, H. R. A.	116	1,175,041	32.1%	1
HERN, Major W. R.	44	1,096,211	19.2%	15
HARWOOD, G.	109	1,070,813	26.5%	3
CUMANI, L. M.	88	822,022	26.6%	2
HILLS, B. W.	73	479,669	16.0%	4
ELSWORTH, D. R. C.	35	418,001	17.7%	–
HANNON, R.	50	352,506	8.8%	18
TREE, J.	29	323,203	20.1%	8
SCOTT, A. A.	24	314,285	18.1%	–
BALDING, I. A.	41	295,426	11.8%	17
JARVIS, W.	32	258,200	14.6%	–
WRAGG, G.	25	251,524	12.8%	11
DUNLOP, J. L.	60	238,460	14.1%	7
BERRY, J.	92	235,828	14.4%	19
BRITTAIN, C. E.	36	230,024	7.3%	13
COLE, P. F. I.	50	228,174	13.0%	14
HANBURY, B.	40	222,547	18.6%	20
AKEHURST, R.	32	200,478	12.8%	–
STEWART, A. C.	30	197,137	15.2%	5
LEWIS, G.	23	183,191	7.6%	–
EASTERBY, M.H.	57	178,521	11.5%	12
WALWYN, P. T.	34	160,436	10.8%	–
BOSS, R.	21	150,622	12.9%	–
JARVIS, M. A.	26	146,766	9.9%	–
HASTINGS-BASS, W.	25	146,473	15.3%	–
TOMPKINS, M. H.	44	139,606	12.1%	–
THOMSON JONES H	37	134,724	19.5%	16
PIGGOTT Mrs L.	33	133,472	16.1%	–
FITZGERALD J. G.	18	132,578	11.8%	–
CALLAGHAN, N. A.	29	130,313	13.3%	–
JOHNSON HOUGHTON, R. F.	25	122,338	12.3%	–
FABRE, A. (in France)	1	111,946	16.6%	–
PRESCOTT, Sir MARK	40	109,060	16.4%	–
WHITAKER, R. M.	29	98,886	6.8%	–
LADY HERRIES	6	98,479	9.0%	–
ARMSTRONG, R. W.	20	94,156	15.5%	9
HOLLINSHEAD, R.	30	93,808	6.1%	–
MORLEY, D.	23	91,656	12.9%	–
WATTS, J. W.	24	90,189	11.4%	–

Do you *really* know the Form?

- There is one firm which has ***invented*** and implemented computer handicapping.
- There is one firm ***capable*** of producing ratings for jockeys.
- There is one firm ***competent*** to produce ratings for the draw.
- There is one firm ***able*** to evaluate a stable's relative form.
- There is ***only*** one firm in the World which can do these things!

RACING RESEARCH possesses a depth of knowledge and insight way beyond the rest.

Is it surprising then, that their ratings have a better profit/loss record than other published ratings?

They also produce the most sophisticated timefigures in the World. Amongst other things.

RACING RESEARCH PUBLICATIONS

COMPUTER RACING FORM Flat Annual
Complete form of every horse with CRF ratings and timefigures for the past season and their best performances from previous seasons. Jockey ratings and analysis. Trainer analysis. Ratings for the draw. Sires/Dam Sires analysis. £42.

FORMDATA Published every Tuesday. The complete form with CRF ratings and timefigures of every horse for the 12 months up to and including the previous Saturday. Also stable form. £17.

PRINTOUTS The most sophisticated race card available to the serious backer. Posted 4 days before racing. £4.50. Combined Saturday racing edition £8.50.

COMPUTER CHASING FORM National Hunt Annual.
Published September. (Current edition £34).

PROSPECTUS Containing details of all publications and subscription rates. Free.

The above publications can be obtained, post-free, from

RACING RESEARCH,
21 Upper Green Lane, Hove Edge, Brighouse, W. Yorks., HD6 2NZ
Telephone 0484-710979.

WINNING OWNERS, 1989

	Races Won	Stakes £	Last Year
SHEIKH MOHAMMED	130	1,296,032	1
HAMDAN AL MAKTOUM	98	1,222,192	2
ABDULLA, K.	61	683,577	3
MAKTOUM AL MAKTOUM	32	484,688	8
H. H. AGA KHAN	48	484,581	4
MANA AL MAKTOUM	5	397,606	–
SIR GORDON WHITE	20	337,712	–
ST. GEORGE, C. A. B.	17	250,069	7
CHRISTODOULOU, ATHOS	8	213,795	–
COMMANDER G. G. MARTEN	4	198,542	–
BURRELL, P.	6	187,898	–
SMITH, J. C.	3	144,908	–
SANGSTER, R. E.	21	142,119	6
LORD HOWARD de WALDEN	18	142,093	–
LORD CARNARVON	9	136,223	–
SAID, Mr WAFIC	8	120,383	–
A. F. BUDGE EQUINE LTD	16	112,647	–
WHITE LODGE STUD	8	111,190	–
SIR PHILIP OPPENHEIMIER	12	108,482	–
DAVIS, Mr J. G.	2	102,295	–
M. AL MAKTOUM	4	100,699	–
LAVINIA DUCHESS OF NORFOLK	7	100,411	11
SAVILL, Mr P. D.	37	99,836	–
LADY HARRISON	4	96,461	–
HILL, Mr MICHAEL	11	95,848	–
MARQUESA DE MORATALLA	5	85,291	–
SALMAN, Mr FAHD	11	82,847	–
COUGHLAN, Mrs ANNE	2	79,687	–
COHEN, Mr HARVEY	1	79,131	–
KENNET VALLEY T'BREDS LTD.	10	76,058	–
CHEVELEY PARK STUD	13	74,100	–
FULLER, Mr LEONARD	4	72,494	–
DIXON, Mr B.	3	70,469	–
THE QUEEN	14	68,269	–
RICHARD GREEN (Fine Paintings)	15	65,430	–
BALZARINI, Mr ANTONIO	3	53,594	–
HUE-WILLIAMS, MRS V.	4	53,322	–
AL-DEERA BLOODSTOCK LTD.	10	53,315	–
LAWRENCE, Mr J.	1	52,393	–
KNOTT BENDER, Mrs VIRGINIA	2	50,761	–
SAEED MAKTOUM AL MAKTOUM	2	50,149	–
SIR MICHAEL SOBELL	9	49,545	–
SPENCE, Mr A. D.	1	49,452	–

TWO "MUSTS"
FOR THE FLAT

Raceform
1989 Flat Annual

£18 FROM NEWSAGENTS **£19** BY POST

ISB NO: 0 900611 46 4

A complete cloth-bound reprint of last Flat Racing Season's Raceform (The Official Form Book). Every fact of form about every race, embellished by abbreviated comments on the runners by Raceform's own team of expert race-readers. Almost 1,500 pages. Extra features include Speed Figures and Standard and Record Times for each course. A MUST for every serious racegoer. £19 by post from the address below.

Raceform Note-Book
1989 Complete: £15

This specially trimmed and paper-bound edition of last season's Raceform Note-Book runs to 1,280 pages and provides a unique eye witness record of every race run on the Flat last year. It also includes basic form details of the first six in every race and is fully indexed throughout. Raceform Note-Book 1989 is packed with clues to 1990 winners and, in particular, it is a great guide to the lightly raced three-year-olds. £15 post free from the address below.

RACEFORM LTD.,
COMPTON, NEWBURY, BERKSHIRE
RG16 0NL

WINNING BREEDERS, 1989

	Races Won	Stakes £	Last Year
HAMDAN AL MAKTOUM (in USA).	8	834,623	–
KENTUCKY SELECT BLOODSTOCK (in USA)	6	400,180	–
H. H. AGA KHAN,	40	392,672	1
JUDDMONTE FARMS (in USA)	31	390,530	–
OVIDSTOWN INVESTMENTS LTD.	4	277,924	–
JOHNSON HOUGHTON, R. F.	8	229,302	–
PETER E. BURRELL TRUST (in USA)	9	223,761	–
ROWE, CHARLES (in USA)	3	184,162	–
KENNARD, Mrs R. B.	9	182,309	12
DARLEY STUD MANAGEMENT (in USA)	5	171,631	–
WHITE LODGE STUD LTD.	11	156,817	5
LORD PORCHESTER	6	151,461	–
LITTLETON STUD	5	149,210	–
LORD HOWARD DE WALDEN	18	148,959	–
CHRISTODOULOU, ATHOS	5	142,949	–
COX Jr., E. A. (in USA)	2	136,053	–
AIRLIE STUD	11	133,378	–
GORRINGE R. J.	3	109,995	–
JUDDMONTE FARMS	10	105,438	–
KING RANCH INC. (in USA)	2	104,832	–
LAVINIA DUCHESS OF NORFOLK	7	100,411	–
STERLINGBROOK FARM (in USA)	1	98,260	–
STARK, FRAN & RAY (in USA)	4	96,713	–
LONDON T'BRED SERVICES & R. LAPOINTE	3	94,299	–
TELLWRIGHT, P.T.	5	89,133	–
H. H. AGA KHAN (in USA)	8	88,019	–
TARRY, A.	17	85,467	–
McCALMONT, Mrs V.	2	85,083	–
WHITEHEAD, W. & Mrs	4	85,027	–
SWETTENHAM STUD	21	81,374	–
HASCOMBE AND VALIANT STUDS	12	75,277	–
CHEVELEY PARK STUD LTD.	23	74,829	–
CLAIBOURNE FARM & W. L. JONES (in USA)	2	74,223	–
FULLER, L.	4	72,494	–
SHEIKH MOHAMMED	15	72,005	–
SQDN-LDR. FRANK BARRETT	3	70,649	–
STRAWBRIDGE, G (& Ptnrs)	1	69,370	–
HESMONDS STUD LTD	22	69,066	–
FIRESTONE, B. R. & Mrs	4	66,934	–
STOWELL HILL LTD.	5	66,878	–
HUMPHREY Jr. GETAL (in USA)	1	66,291	–
PIN OAK FARM (in USA)	5	66,277	–
MABEE, MR & MRS JOHN (in USA)	11	64,952	–

ROLL OF HONOUR—The Classics

Present Day Trainers & Jockeys with TWO (or more) successes

	2000	1000	DERBY	OAKS	ST LEGER
TRAINERS	M V O'Brien (4) H Cecil F Boutin G Harwood R Hannon W Hern M Stoute	H Cecil (3) Mrs C Head	M V O'Brien (6) W Hern (3) H Cecil M Stoute	W Hern (3) M Stoute (3) M V O'Brien J Tree H Cecil	W Hern (6) H Cecil (4) M V O'Brien (3) F J Houghton H T Jones
JOCKEYS	W Carson (4) G Dettori Pat Eddery G Starkey	F Head	W Carson (3) W R Swinburn Pat Eddery S Cauthen	W Carson (3) Pat Eddery G Starkey S Cauthen W R Swinburn	W Carson (3) S Cauthen (3)
RESULTS	**2000**	**1000**	**DERBY**	**OAKS**	**ST LEGER**
1989	**Nashwan (USA)** W Hern W Carson	**Musical Bliss (USA)** M R Stoute W R Swinburn	**Nashwan (USA)** W Hern W Carson	**Aliysa** M R Stoute W R Swinburn	**Michelozzo (USA)** H Cecil S Cauthen
1988	**Doyoun** M Stoute W R Swinburn	**Ravinella (USA)** Mrs C Head G W Moore	**Kahyasi** L Cumani R Cochrane	**Diminuendo (USA)** H Cecil S Cauthen	**Minster Son** N Graham W Carson
1987	**Don't Forget Me** R Hannon W Carson	**Miesque (USA)** F Boutin F Head	**Reference Point** H Cecil S Cauthen	**Unite** M Stoute W R Swinburn	**Reference Point** H Cecil S Cauthen
1986	**Dancing Brave (USA)** G Harwood G Starkey	**Midway Lady (USA)** B Hanbury R Cochrane	**Shahrastani (USA)** M Stoute W R Swinburn	**Midway Lady (USA)** B Hanbury R Cochrane	**Moon Madness** J Dunlop Pat Eddery

WINNING JOCKEYS, 1989

	1st	2nd	3rd	Unplaced	Total	Last Year
EDDERY, PAT	171	126	91	450	838	1
CAUTHEN, S.	163	92	65	341	661	5
CARSON, W.	137	126	122	482	867	2
COCHRANE, R.	121	97	85	379	682	4
ROBERTS, M.	106	105	88	512	811	3
SWINBURN, W. R.	94	92	91	375	652	7
BIRCH, M.	91	61	75	462	689	6
McKEOWN, D.	86	77	63	496	722	13
REID, J.	84	71	69	363	587	8
DUFFIELD, G.	77	65	63	471	676	9
HILLS, M.	74	61	55	292	482	11
DETTORI, L.	71	58	55	274	458	–
DARLEY, K.	68	58	59	368	553	–
RAYMOND, B.	65	73	66	399	603	10
CARROLL, J.	62	50	54	305	471	18
QUINN, T.	58	55	70	253	436	20
HILLS, R.	58	53	50	294	455	15
STARKEY, G.	52	59	34	157	302	19
RYAN, W.	49	70	43	275	437	14
ROUSE, B.	48	48	59	365	520	17
CARTER, G.	45	48	55	336	484	–
EDDERY, PAUL	44	55	49	370	518	16
NEWNES, W.	40	45	52	398	535	–
CLARK, A.	38	19	19	200	276	–
MUNRO, A.	37	36	51	350	474	–
LOWE, J.	36	44	51	455	586	–
WILLIAMS, TYRONE	34	33	41	429	537	–
WILLIAMS, J.	33	41	37	344	455	–
PERKS, S.	31	40	34	215	320	–
WIGHAM, M.	31	18	27	325	401	–
IVES, T.	30	37	39	191	297	12
FORTUNE, J.	28	36	29	230	323	–
NICHOLLS, D.	28	44	33	232	337	–
GIBSON, DALE	28	34	27	296	385	–
COOK, P.	27	35	39	216	317	–
FALLON, K.	27	37	32	261	357	–
CULHANE, A.	24	44	24	261	353	–
WHITWORTH, S.	24	25	37	286	372	–
HIND, G.	23	19	17	211	270	–
MATTHIAS, J.	22	31	23	143	219	–
WEBSTER, S.	22	23	11	226	282	–
CONNORTON, N.	21	17	26	173	237	–

LEADING SIRES OF 1989 IN GREAT BRITAIN AND IRELAND

STALLION	BREEDING	RNRS	WNRS	WINS	WIN MONEY	PLACES	PLACE MONEY	TOTAL
BLUSHING GROOM (1974)....	by Red God	35	14	24	924809	38	82811	1007619
SADLER'S WELLS (1981)	by Northern Dancer	43	25	41	618962	51	228984	847945
NUREYEV (1977)	by Northern Dancer	40	22	35	636813	46	159351	796165
DANZIG (1977)..................	by Northern Dancer	31	18	31	544753	40	246111	790864
CAERLEON (1980)...............	by Nijinsky	63	34	49	581142	94	133957	715099
ILE DE BOURBON (1975)	by Nijinsky	41	16	27	347098	42	240762	587860
ALLEGED (1974)................	by Hoist the Flag	27	15	29	394828	40	96930	491759
ALYDAR (1975)	by Raise A Native	9	6	10	262702	12	207621	470322
KNOWN FACT (1977)...........	by In Reality	46	19	28	249471	60	187715	437186
HABITAT (1966)	by Sir Gaylord	50	22	37	294016	57	138009	432026
AHONOORA (1975).............	by Lorenzaccio	71	21	33	283531	105	123944	407475
THE MINSTREL (1974).........	by Northern Dancer	41	15	21	233879	57	157803	391681
SHIRLEY HEIGHTS (1975).....	by Mill Reef	50	17	24	123530	55	239263	362792
YOUNG GENERATION (1976)..	by Balidar	46	9	15	310165	52	46697	356863
ABSALOM (1975)...............	by Abwah	70	21	35	284708	76	63448	348156
BE MY GUEST (1974)...........	by Northern Dancer	59	20	32	145805	89	192978	338783
ALZAO (1980)	by Lyphard	65	23	39	172527	90	139206	311732
NORTHERN BABY (1976)	by Northern Dancer	15	7	22	276705	20	29066	305771
PERSIAN BOLD (1975).........	by Bold Lad (IRE)	66	25	40	124634	92	165427	290060
KINGS LAKE (1978)	by Nijinsky	52	19	29	146269	69	135383	281652

LEADING BRITISH AND IRISH BASED SIRES OF 1989
(GREAT BRITAIN, IRELAND AND OVERSEAS)

STALLION	BREEDING	DOMESTIC WNRS	DOMESTIC WINS	WIN MONEY	OVERSEAS WNRS	OVERSEAS WINS	WIN MONEY	TOTAL
HABITAT (1966)	by Sir Gaylord	22	37	294016	19	39	892939	1186955
SADLER'S WELLS (1981)	by Northern Dancer	25	41	618962	14	19	450137	1069099
CAERLEON (1980)..............	by Nijinsky	34	49	581142	25	47	359236	940379
BLUSHING GROOM (1974)....	by Red God	14	24	924809	0	0	0	924809
ELA-MANA-MOU (1976).......	by Pitcairn	14	17	43479	16	31	787756	831234
NUREYEV (1977)	by Northern Dancer	22	35	636813	1	2	152413	789226
LORD GAYLE (1965)	by Sir Gaylord	12	19	208972	9	16	522703	731675
WHAT A GUEST (1979).........	by Be My Guest	3	6	26421	26	46	598810	625231
CURE THE BLUES (1978)	by Stop the Music	6	8	22960	38	72	565032	587992
MILL REEF (1968)	by Never Bend	16	21	143636	17	28	425283	568919
DANZIG (1977)..................	by Northern Dancer	18	31	544753	1	1	12701	557454
BE MY GUEST (1974)...........	by Northern Dancer	20	32	145805	44	71	403896	549701
ILE DE BOURBON (1975)	by Nijinsky	16	27	347098	21	48	182854	529952
GENERAL ASSEMBLY (1976)..	by Secretariat	7	14	84453	30	68	409324	493776
YOUNG GENERATION (1976)..	by Balidar	9	15	310165	17	33	140321	450486
ALLEGED (1974)................	by Hoist the Flag	15	29	394828	1	2	19052	413880
KINGS LAKE (1978)	by Nijinsky	19	29	146269	20	31	247687	393956
POSSE (1977)....................	by Forli	5	8	110711	22	43	278673	389384
AHONOORA (1975).............	by Lorenzaccio	21	33	283531	9	20	103503	387034
ABSALOM (1975)...............	by Abwah	21	35	284708	15	29	96141	380849

LEADING TWO-YEAR-OLD SIRES OF 1989 IN GREAT BRITAIN AND IRELAND

STALLION	BREEDING	RNRS	WNRS	WINS	WIN MONEY	PLACES	PLACE MONEY	TOTAL
CAERLEON (1980)	by Nijinsky	26	11	13	458803	28	38262	497065
ABSALOM (1975)	by Abwah	30	9	17	230371	31	31638	262009
ELEGANT AIR (1981)	by Shirley Heights	14	3	6	229499	11	7671	237170
BALLAD ROCK (1974)	by Bold Lad (IRE)	13	5	11	187922	15	43724	231646
CHIEF'S CROWN (1982)	by Danzig	9	4	11	212133	8	4221	216354
FAIRY KING (1982)	by Northern Dancer	17	8	13	169804	14	37779	207584
PRIVATE ACCOUNT (1976)	by Damascus	5	2	5	135835	6	36268	172103
DIAMOND PROSPECT (1978)	by Mr Prospector	3	2	3	6641	8	161342	167983
PERSIAN BOLD (1975)	by Bold Lad (IRE)	28	9	14	40537	30	121327	161864
KRIS (1976)	by Sharpen Up	16	10	12	80043	12	40506	120550
DANZIG (1977)	by Northern Dancer	13	11	17	67979	13	52292	120271
KIND OF HUSH (1978)	by Welsh Pageant	15	3	4	106235	8	10136	116371
NUREYEV (1977)	by Northern Dancer	16	9	11	104342	11	7681	112023
TAUFAN (1977)	by Stop the Music	34	12	22	73374	44	37811	111185
NIGHT SHIFT (1980)	by Northern Dancer	26	12	20	79083	32	30262	109345
ROUSILLON (1981)	by Riverman	20	8	9	39443	19	60891	100334
NORTH BRITON (1979)	by Northfields	1	1	2	5078	4	87762	92840
GLENSTAL (1980)	by Northern Dancer	20	10	16	65806	24	25602	91408
ALZAO (1980)	by Lyphard	33	9	17	63815	37	26982	90796
AHONOORA (1975)	by Lorenzaccio	19	5	5	54554	17	35568	90122

LEADING FIRST CROP SIRES OF 1989 IN GREAT BRITAIN AND IRELAND

STALLION	BREEDING	RNRS	WNRS	WINS	WIN MONEY	PLACES	PLACE MONEY	TOTAL
ELEGANT AIR (1981)	by Shirley Heights	14	3	6	229499	11	7671	237170
CHIEF'S CROWN (1982)	by Danzig	9	4	11	212133	8	4221	216354
FAIRY KING (1982)	by Northern Dancer	17	8	13	169804	14	37779	207584
ROUSILLON (1981)	by Riverman	20	8	9	39443	19	60891	100334
BAIRN (1982)	by Northern Baby	10	5	10	42373	13	14544	56917
DREAMS TO REALITY (1982)	by Lyphard	12	4	7	39500	9	11282	50782
LAW SOCIETY (1982)	by Alleged	21	6	8	27818	26	20302	48119
NORDICO (1981)	by Northern Dancer	16	6	10	31754	31	15468	47222
DOULAB (1982)	by Topsider	26	8	10	24771	28	16162	40933
NEVER SO BOLD (1980)	by Bold Lad (IRE)	19	5	6	14855	17	15895	30750
SHADEED (1982)	by Nijinsky	12	4	5	10026	16	14936	24962
COZZENE (1980)	by Caro	1	1	2	12219	2	10730	22949
EXHIBITIONER (1982)	by Thatching	26	4	4	12877	16	9360	22237
FATIH (1980)	by Icecapade	1	1	4	19943	2	1924	21867
THE NOBLE PLAYER (1980)	by The Minstrel	10	3	5	12496	7	8918	21414
RAINBOW QUEST (1981)	by Blushing Groom	12	3	3	10049	8	11034	21083
MAGIC MIRROR (1982)	by Nureyev	15	4	5	10597	19	10170	20767
REASONABLE (1982)	by Formidable	15	5	6	12954	15	7033	19988
MT LIVERMORE (1981)	by Blushing Groom	3	1	1	8460	3	10204	18664
SIBERIAN EXPRESS (1981)	by Caro	8	2	2	6158	8	12441	18599

TWENTY YEARS OF LEADING SIRES IN GREAT BRITAIN AND IRELAND

YEAR	STALLION	BREEDING	RNRS	WNRS	WINS	WIN MONEY	PLACES	PLACE MONEY	TOTAL
1989	BLUSHING GROOM (1974)	by Red God	35	14	24	924809	38	82811	1007619
1988	CAERLEON (1980)	by Nijinsky	53	28	46	743152	75	152168	895320
1987	MILL REEF (1968)	by Never Bend	39	12	19	962939	44	280860	1243799
1986	NIJINSKY (1967)	by Northern Dancer	30	14	20	624905	27	58257	683163
1985	KRIS (1976)	by Sharpen Up	31	13	25	434319	35	147801	582120
1984	NORTHERN DANCER (1961)	by Nearctic	24	16	27	848199	44	193147	1041346
1983	NORTHERN DANCER (1961)	by Nearctic	23	11	21	392267	24	49940	442206
1982	BE MY GUEST (1974)	by Northern Dancer	48	19	28	391670	38	77751	469421
1981	GREAT NEPHEW (1963)	by Honeyway	39	12	23	485709	47	74290	559999
1980	PITCAIRN (1971)	by Petingo	23	10	16	388202	38	75491	463693
1979	PETINGO (1965)	by Petition	26	12	21	450488	38	21086	471574
1978	MILL REEF (1961)	by Never Bend	26	14	27	264716	47	48205	312922
1977	NORTHERN DANCER (1961)	by Nearctic	9	6	13	349050	14	31932	380982
1976	WOLVER HOLLOW (1964)	by Sovereign Path	40	20	37	194797	54	15968	210765
1975	GREAT NEPHEW (1963)	by Honeyway	45	17	29	291049	55	22235	313284
1974	VAGUELY NOBLE (1965)	by Vienna	12	5	8	140116	13	11769	151885
1973	VAGUELY NOBLE (1965)	by Vienna	10	3	5	106832	12	21077	127908
1972	QUEEN'S HUSSAR (1960)	by March Past	31	10	23	172502	24	12835	185337
1971	NEVER BEND (1960)	by Nasrullah	3	3	10	125712	2	8138	133850
1970	NORTHERN DANCER (1961)	by Nearctic	7	6	14	230542	14	16908	247450

STALLIONS EARNINGS FOR 1989 IN GREAT BRITAIN AND IRELAND

STALLIONS	RNRS	STARTS	WNRS	WINS	PLACES	TOTAL
ABEDNEGO	10	16	0	0	2	358.34
ABSALOM	70	378	21	35	76	348156.14
ACAMAS	1	2	0	0	1	213.33
ACHIEVED	1	8	0	0	4	1295.50
ACK ACK (USA)	1	5	1	1	1	6177.00
ADONIJAH	23	109	6	7	32	41196.12
AFFIRMED (USA)	3	5	1	1	0	2889.00
AFRICAN SKY	10	46	3	6	16	23473.68
AHONOORA	71	314	21	33	105	407474.80
AKARAD (FR)	5	13	3	3	3	8263.50
ALIAS SMITH (USA)	18	99	4	6	20	30183.10
ALLA BREVA (USA)	1	3	0	0	2	1324.00
ALLEGED (USA)	27	104	15	29	40	491758.84
ALL SYSTEMS GO	11	47	1	1	6	4791.00
AL NASR (FR)	7	45	3	5	5	14296.33
ALOMA'S RULER (USA)	1	5	0	0	4	10543.34
AL SIRAT (USA)	9	19	0	0	4	1257.51
ALYDAR (USA)	9	32	6	10	12	470322.34
ALZAO (USA)	65	311	23	39	90	311732.06
AMBOISE	1	1	0	0	1	324.80
ANAX	1	7	1	1	1	9295.00
ANDY REW	3	9	0	0	1	198.00
ANFIELD	24	149	8	16	33	63691.60
ANITA'S PRINCE	10	29	1	1	7	3046.20
ANKARA (USA)	1	4	1	2	0	7453.00
ANOTHER REALM	20	111	8	12	18	39189.20
ARAGON	57	296	12	21	66	171300.68
ARAPAHO	6	13	1	1	4	2403.33
ARCTIC TERN (USA)	30	100	7	9	29	90417.77
ARDOON	3	19	2	8	2	43640.00
ARDROSS	24	120	11	16	27	74400.10
ARGUMENT (FR)	2	5	1	1	0	2550.00
ARISTOCRACY	4	9	0	0	4	745.00
ARTAIUS (USA)	12	48	4	7	8	17342.64
ASANDRE (FR)	1	4	0	0	1	396.00
ASSERT	12	40	3	4	19	60560.83
ATHENAGORAS (GER)	1	4	1	2	2	2621.68
AT THE THRESHOLD (USA)	1	5	0	0	3	2218.20
AUCTION RING (USA)	42	211	9	17	53	115207.43
AVOCAT	5	11	0	0	3	236.67
BAIRN (USA)	11	44	5	10	13	56916.90
BALBOA	9	41	2	2	6	3204.17
BALDSKI (USA)	1	2	0	0	1	400.00
BALI DANCER	2	8	0	0	1	175.00
BALIDAR	15	84	4	7	22	54283.52
BALINGER	4	10	1	1	1	1416.66
BALLACASHTAL (CAN)	38	202	8	11	35	55575.53
BALLAD ROCK	48	195	9	17	36	255703.11
BALLIOL	11	67	2	3	7	10829.60
BALLYDOYLE (CAN)	1	8	0	0	6	748.34
BALLYMORE	11	30	1	1	9	14086.51
BAPTISM	9	64	2	3	17	35359.28
BARACHOIS (CAN)	6	40	4	7	6	39834.60
THE BART (USA)	4	18	2	5	3	13900.85

Stallions Earnings – Continued

STALLIONS	RNRS	STARTS	WNRS	WINS	PLACES	TOTAL
BATES MOTEL (USA)	2	11	1	1	2	2982.00
BATTLE HYMN	6	22	1	1	6	5391.00
BAY EXPRESS	42	201	12	21	35	139000.66
BEAU CHARMEUR (FR)	22	56	3	4	12	8235.00
BEAUDELAIRE (USA)	1	1	0	0	1	10703.00
BEDFORD (USA)	1	9	0	0	5	991.67
BELDALE FLUTTER (USA)	42	175	8	15	40	103133.24
BELFALAS	6	15	1	1	5	1424.17
BELFORT (FR)	28	176	7	13	33	63656.70
BELIEVE IT (USA)	3	19	1	4	5	13802.80
BELLMAN (FR)	4	13	1	1	2	1182.50
BELLYPHA	10	41	5	8	11	52611.35
BELTED EARL (USA)	1	4	0	0	1	490.50
BE MY GUEST (USA)	59	247	20	32	89	338782.75
BE MY NATIVE (USA)	37	195	12	16	58	79071.85
BIG SPRUCE (USA)	1	2	1	1	0	2469.00
BIKALA	1	5	0	0	1	604.80
BILLION (USA)	5	11	1	1	5	3249.34
BIVOUAC	2	11	1	2	2	6324.00
BLACK MINSTREL	15	28	1	1	2	1304.17
BLAKENEY	38	183	13	18	40	227808.40
BLAZING SADDLES (AUS)	19	87	5	8	20	23670.75
BLOOD ROYAL (USA)	2	7	1	1	3	5840.40
BLUE CASHMERE	21	86	3	4	13	20491.20
BLUE REFRAIN	6	31	2	2	4	8762.00
BLUSHING GROOM (FR)	35	115	14	24	38	1007619.40
BLUSHING SCRIBE (USA)	22	98	4	4	13	15850.50
BOLD FORBES (USA)	3	14	1	3	4	10328.20
BOLD FORT	1	10	0	0	1	816.00
BOLD LAD (IRE)	20	89	7	13	12	36903.17
BOLD OWL	17	102	8	9	20	32104.30
BONNE NOEL	9	18	2	2	5	3222.50
BOREEN (FR)	19	49	4	4	16	7310.01
BOYNE VALLEY	2	4	1	1	0	1725.00
BRAVE SHOT	4	30	1	1	4	5412.00
THE BRIANSTAN	12	61	0	0	10	3850.00
BRIGADIER GERARD	6	34	3	3	8	15439.60
BROADSWORD (USA)	3	9	0	0	2	914.00
BROTHERLY (USA)	1	14	0	0	2	1463.00
BRUSTOLON	1	5	1	1	1	3456.00
BUCKSKIN (FR)	48	116	9	14	27	29704.19
BULLDOZER	5	17	1	2	3	3551.67
BURSLEM	47	252	11	12	51	46866.79
BUSTED	23	108	6	10	29	89373.93
BUSTIKI	1	13	1	4	4	12528.50
BUSTINETO	1	5	0	0	1	118.33
BUSTINO	45	188	12	22	51	265904.62
BUZZARDS BAY	14	73	3	4	13	22040.50
CAERLEON (USA)	63	246	34	49	94	715099.49
CAJUN	6	25	1	2	6	9665.50
CALLERNISH	16	30	6	6	9	8105.84
CAMDEN TOWN	33	154	7	8	27	29885.66
CAPRICORN LINE	2	8	1	1	2	3348.90
CAPTAIN JAMES	5	29	3	6	7	15720.90
CARIBO	1	4	1	2	1	2106.67
CARO	16	51	8	11	15	64572.94
CARR DE NASKRA (USA)	1	2	0	0	2	798.40
CARRIAGE WAY	2	7	0	0	5	3512.00
CARWHITE	14	55	2	3	6	17152.17

Stallions Earnings – Continued

STALLIONS	RNRS	STARTS	WNRS	WINS	PLACES	TOTAL
CASTLE KEEP	38	177	8	11	47	75933.58
CAVEAT (USA)	1	9	1	1	3	4030.00
CAWSTON'S CLOWN	8	47	2	2	9	15252.40
CELTIC CONE	5	12	1	1	5	2354.59
CERTINGO	2	3	0	0	1	40.00
CHABRIAS (FR)	2	7	0	0	1	327.00
CHEVAL	4	10	1	1	5	3097.50
CHIEF'S CROWN (USA)	9	27	4	11	8	216353.80
CHIEF SINGER	33	155	14	22	48	113524.15
CHUKAROO	8	30	2	3	3	68012.25
CIDRAX (FR)	2	3	0	0	1	116.67
CLAUDE MONET (USA)	10	41	2	2	11	10867.30
CLEVER TRICK (USA)	9	37	4	4	15	24209.00
COASTAL (USA)	2	13	1	2	2	6032.60
CODED SCRAP	3	15	0	0	1	364.00
COMBINE HARVESTER	1	4	0	0	2	201.67
COMEDY STAR (USA)	33	163	9	13	26	52308.40
COMMANCHE RUN	15	37	1	1	7	3331.59
COMMEMORATE (USA)	1	4	0	0	2	1283.00
COMPLIANCE (USA)	1	1	1	1	0	2574.00
CONCORDE HERO (USA)	1	6	1	3	0	8963.00
CONDORCET (FR)	4	11	1	3	5	8430.84
CONNAUGHT	17	53	3	4	5	11179.45
CONQUISTADOR CIELO (USA)	11	44	6	11	14	55459.11
COPPER GAMBLE	3	5	1	1	1	2915.00
COQUELIN (USA)	38	154	4	6	26	18001.01
CORVARO (USA)	12	47	4	5	10	12023.30
COUNTRY PINE (USA)	1	2	0	0	1	525.00
COX'S RIDGE (USA)	4	18	4	6	3	16592.14
COZZENE (USA)	1	4	1	2	2	22948.95
CRAFTY PROSPECTOR (USA)	3	11	1	1	7	6736.66
CRAGADOR	7	26	1	1	2	2351.60
CRASH COURSE	9	33	2	2	9	4041.68
CREATIVE PLAN (USA)	10	33	2	2	7	4123.73
CREE SONG	3	11	0	0	3	696.00
CREETOWN	13	48	2	2	5	4696.34
CRESTA RIDER (USA)	2	10	1	1	5	17165.99
CREVER	1	17	1	2	0	3958.80
CRIMSON BEAU	1	17	1	2	3	7458.00
CRITIQUE (USA)	4	8	0	0	2	6838.03
CROFTER (USA)	32	250	15	26	62	107814.86
CROFTHALL	17	101	5	11	23	117894.40
CROGHAN HILL	5	24	0	0	6	1370.01
CROONER	6	33	1	1	4	5111.00
CROZIER	3	6	1	2	1	3718.34
CRYSTAL GLITTERS (USA)	8	42	4	6	8	22806.87
CRYSTAL PALACE (FR)	2	9	0	0	3	1322.20
CURE THE BLUES (USA)	31	143	6	8	27	34712.98
CUT ABOVE	12	51	4	4	18	10395.61
CUTLASS (USA)	3	14	1	1	6	5516.20
CZARAVICH (USA)	4	21	1	1	6	3054.17
D'ACCORD (USA)	1	6	1	5	1	34559.50
DALSAAN	33	188	11	16	50	74793.39
DANCE IN TIME (CAN)	6	35	2	5	4	19777.67
DANZIG (USA)	31	101	18	31	40	790864.06
DARA MONARCH	38	155	8	10	39	62837.50
DARBY CREEK ROAD (USA)	1	2	0	0	1	576.00
DARING MARCH	41	190	10	16	32	82756.90

Stallions Earnings – Continued

STALLIONS	RNRS	STARTS	WNRS	WINS	PLACES	TOTAL
DARSHAAN	23	61	12	14	25	267227.99
DAWN JOHNNY (USA)	1	2	0	0	1	302.40
DAWN REVIEW	2	13	1	2	3	9772.50
DAY IS DONE	15	56	4	4	6	11248.67
DECENT FELLOW	15	42	3	4	7	10909.17
DECOY BOY	6	27	0	0	1	380.00
DEEP RIVER	1	7	0	0	1	208.00
DEEP RUN	52	136	13	19	40	51722.57
DEPUTY MINISTER (CAN)	8	27	3	5	12	44760.40
DERRING ROSE	20	63	2	3	13	6534.18
DERRYLIN	25	104	2	3	15	48765.40
DESERT WINE (USA)	3	14	1	1	3	8518.00
DEVIL'S BAG (USA)	4	12	2	4	2	22152.90
DIAMOND PROSPECT (USA)	5	26	2	3	9	168392.84
DIAMOND SHOAL	7	29	1	3	5	16552.20
DIESIS	41	158	22	32	49	221084.13
DISC JOCKEY	1	6	0	0	2	618.00
DIXIELAND BAND (USA)	8	38	3	7	11	54480.40
DOC MARTEN	7	44	1	1	7	4556.50
DOMINION	58	236	17	23	44	122959.12
DOMITOR (USA)	1	9	1	1	4	4391.60
DOM RACINE (FR)	4	21	1	4	3	15258.80
DON	28	71	3	5	11	13463.58
DON ROBERTO (USA)	3	14	0	0	2	1529.20
DOON	1	12	1	1	4	4928.00
DOUBLE FORM	4	39	3	7	14	22376.61
DOULAB (USA)	26	104	8	10	28	40933.00
DRAGONARA PALACE (USA)	1	10	1	1	2	4853.50
DRAMATIC BID (USA)	1	1	0	0	1	45.00
DR BLUM (USA)	2	9	1	1	3	7833.67
DR CARTER (USA)	2	6	1	1	2	2839.20
DREAMS TO REALITY (USA)	12	41	4	7	9	50782.02
DRONE	4	13	1	2	5	8056.50
DUBLIN TAXI	23	89	2	2	7	8000.46
DUKY	5	9	1	1	2	1060.84
DUNBEATH (USA)	32	169	15	18	42	70439.52
DUNPHY	22	92	4	5	17	15807.84
DUNS SCOTUS (CAN)	1	9	1	1	5	6979.40
EFFERVESCING (USA)	2	6	0	0	3	295.00
ELA-MANA-MOU	47	155	14	17	57	98003.94
EL BABA (USA)	1	5	1	1	2	3570.00
ELECTRIC	39	162	9	15	27	126927.98
ELEGANT AIR	14	55	3	6	11	237170.42
EL GRAN SENOR (USA)	14	44	6	9	19	82011.87
ENCHANTMENT	16	60	2	3	14	14455.80
ENCINO (USA)	1	5	1	2	1	11365.00
ESPRIT DU NORD (USA)	3	14	2	2	3	7217.90
EXCELLER (USA)	4	14	3	4	5	68461.53
EXCLUSIVE ERA (USA)	1	3	1	1	1	3859.00
EXHIBITIONER	26	90	4	4	16	22236.88
EXPLODENT (USA)	5	10	2	3	4	61614.12
FABULOUS DANCER (USA)	7	27	1	1	8	22276.65
FAIRBAIRN	1	8	0	0	1	401.67
FAIR SEASON	2	10	1	1	1	2058.00
FAIRY KING (USA)	17	71	8	13	14	207583.56
FALIRAKI	2	10	0	0	5	2494.60
FAPPIANO (USA)	10	23	3	3	9	15689.90
FARAWAY TIMES (USA)	4	19	2	4	3	21432.50
FARHAAN	1	4	0	0	1	400.00

Stallions Earnings – Continued

STALLIONS	RNRS	STARTS	WNRS	WINS	PLACES	TOTAL
FAR NORTH (CAN)	4	10	1	1	1	428.00
FATIH (USA)	1	7	1	4	2	21866.60
FIDEL	3	7	1	1	1	434.17
FINAL STRAW	45	219	20	27	47	107217.78
FINE BLADE (USA)	4	7	1	1	1	925.84
FIT TO FIGHT (USA)	6	20	0	0	6	5261.00
FLAIR PATH	7	20	0	0	8	1589.17
FLORIFEROUS	7	11	1	1	1	1055.84
FLUORESCENT LIGHT (USA)	1	8	1	2	2	25815.80
FLYING TYKE	4	24	1	1	5	4437.00
FOOLISH PLEASURE (USA)	3	16	0	0	3	1188.00
FORLI (ARG)	13	47	5	6	15	131223.16
FORLORN RIVER	1	6	0	0	2	1952.00
FORMIDABLE (USA)	68	294	20	28	56	174686.39
FREE STATE	24	119	7	11	29	55372.50
FRIGID AIRE	4	12	0	0	2	140.84
FRIMLEY PARK	6	52	1	2	16	25696.60
FULL EXTENT (USA)	2	7	0	0	2	414.00
FULL OF HOPE	10	36	1	1	8	6040.67
FULL OUT (USA)	2	7	1	1	1	2831.60
FULL POCKET (USA)	2	14	0	0	4	939.67
FURRY GLEN	52	155	13	15	41	39666.88
FUZZBUSTER (USA)	1	6	0	0	1	387.00
GABITAT	9	40	2	5	8	14435.20
GARDA'S REVENGE (USA)	9	32	0	0	3	738.33
GARRYOWEN	2	9	1	1	1	914.17
GAY FANDANGO (USA)	6	19	2	2	4	5950.00
GAY MECENE (USA)	6	17	0	0	1	230.00
GAY PILOT	1	10	0	0	5	2185.00
GENERAL ASSEMBLY (USA)	23	105	7	14	33	110558.18
GENERAL HOLME (USA)	5	15	0	0	5	4289.20
GENERAL IRONSIDE	15	35	1	1	8	1707.68
GIACOMETTI	4	17	2	2	3	11752.20
GINGER BRINK (FR)	3	7	0	0	1	627.20
GLEASON (USA)	8	19	2	2	5	2260.01
GLENSTAL (USA)	51	241	24	35	74	206338.21
GLINT OF GOLD	34	108	7	7	34	92311.69
GODSWALK (USA)	37	182	10	16	35	140483.20
GOLDEN ACT (USA)	8	31	4	4	13	36740.30
GOLDEN FLEECE (USA)	3	5	1	1	0	1856.00
GOLDEN LOVE	12	17	1	1	4	1960.01
GOLDHILL	7	24	2	2	9	11304.99
GOLD SONG	4	27	1	1	7	5091.60
GOOD THYNE (USA)	12	28	1	1	2	760.00
GOOD TIMES (ITY)	32	157	9	13	33	106833.58
GORYTUS (USA)	55	242	17	23	57	108169.81
GO STEP (USA)	1	7	1	1	1	1793.33
GRANGE MELODY	5	8	1	1	1	1208.33
GRAUSTARK	5	21	1	1	7	8669.00
GREAT NEPHEW	13	50	3	3	7	42664.43
GREEN DANCER (USA)	18	77	8	16	26	228530.81
GREEN FOREST (USA)	14	68	7	9	20	145547.24
GREEN SHOON	13	22	0	0	4	297.50
GREGORIAN (USA)	4	22	1	2	6	6922.37
GREY DAWN II	6	15	1	2	3	8904.80
GREY GHOST	4	18	0	0	3	2211.00
GRUNDY	8	18	2	2	4	4153.33
GUILLAUME TELL (USA)	2	4	1	1	0	1725.00
GULF PEARL	3	28	0	0	9	4029.20

Stallions Earnings – Continued

STALLIONS	RNRS	STARTS	WNRS	WINS	PLACES	TOTAL
GUNNER B	8	61	2	3	17	27362.05
HABAT	1	6	1	1	2	3348.80
HABITAT	50	191	22	37	57	432025.84
HAGLEY (USA)	1	7	1	1	4	21997.80
HAIL THE PIRATES (USA)	1	14	1	2	8	10814.15
HALO (USA)	5	14	2	2	1	5270.60
HARDBOY	1	2	0	0	1	200.00
HARD FOUGHT	26	136	4	6	21	54557.34
HARDGREEN (USA)	3	11	1	1	2	3897.50
HARLOW (USA)	1	16	1	2	3	5159.20
HASTY WORD	1	2	0	0	1	180.00
HAWAII	4	12	3	4	1	37544.60
HAWAIIAN RETURN (USA)	10	28	0	0	4	476.67
HAYS	21	109	4	9	18	29122.13
HEAD FOR HEIGHTS	29	156	8	11	45	43816.95
HEADIN' UP	5	17	0	0	3	1578.50
HELLO GORGEOUS (USA)	14	55	2	2	16	19889.40
HE LOVES ME	8	53	4	5	14	21757.97
HENBIT (USA)	46	158	11	13	27	39615.75
HEROIC AIR	2	12	0	0	3	1596.00
HERO'S HONOR (USA)	4	13	1	4	4	14591.80
HIGHLAND PARK (USA)	1	3	1	1	1	1825.00
HIGH LINE	39	151	9	10	40	40742.74
HIGH TOP	50	223	17	22	71	255222.25
HILDENLEY	1	3	0	0	1	266.67
HILLANDALE	1	1	0	0	1	660.00
HIS MAJESTY (USA)	2	9	1	1	2	2565.70
HITTITE GLORY	7	33	2	2	5	5738.34
HOMEBOY	7	36	3	5	4	58854.30
HOME GUARD (USA)	5	18	0	0	4	2039.33
HOMING	35	170	5	7	26	30406.80
HORAGE	47	246	13	14	66	62401.29
HORST–HERBERT	1	2	1	1	1	3930.40
HOSTAGE (USA)	5	14	1	1	4	2618.34
HOTFOOT	40	180	8	14	31	91527.70
HOT GROVE	1	1	0	0	1	210.00
HOT SPARK	4	31	2	4	7	29094.75
HUGUENOT (USA)	1	9	0	0	1	583.33
ILE DE BOURBON (USA)	41	178	16	27	42	587859.99
IMMORTAL KNIGHT	1	14	1	1	4	6590.20
IMPECUNIOUS	1	4	0	0	1	190.00
IMPERIAL FLING (USA)	9	51	1	1	12	10754.90
IMPORT	10	31	1	1	5	4264.40
INDIAN KING (USA)	54	344	24	44	80	169289.28
IN FIJAR (USA)	8	25	2	2	8	24345.28
IN REALITY	1	8	1	1	4	2701.68
IRISH CASTLE (USA)	1	2	1	2	0	12836.00
IRISH RIVER (FR)	17	59	4	5	14	15412.75
IRISH STAR	2	6	1	1	2	2391.67
IT'S FREEZING (USA)	2	6	2	2	0	4160.10
JAAZEIRO (USA)	4	7	1	1	1	1211.67
JALMOOD (USA)	56	239	13	18	48	84655.25
JASMINE STAR	7	47	1	2	13	11499.07
JELLABY	5	15	0	0	2	1811.00
JESTER	18	83	3	5	10	21277.41
JIG TIME (USA)	1	4	0	0	1	1160.00
JOSHUA	4	18	1	1	4	4506.00
J O TOBIN (USA)	2	19	0	0	4	2136.67
JULIO MARINER	7	23	2	3	2	16114.83

Stallions Earnings – Continued

STALLIONS	RNRS	STARTS	WNRS	WINS	PLACES	TOTAL
JULIUS CAESAR (FR)	1	1	0	0	1	310.80
JUNIUS (USA)	8	50	3	5	12	22978.66
KABOUR	13	83	1	5	8	21100.20
KAFU	46	238	10	16	38	59115.96
KALAGLOW	48	209	17	29	59	244242.44
KALA SHIKARI	23	111	2	3	17	18142.75
KAMBALDA	28	70	4	5	17	7981.69
KAMPALA	48	228	16	23	70	114630.83
KARLINSKY (USA)	3	6	0	0	3	751.67
KEMAL (FR)	6	11	1	1	1	576.67
KEY TO THE KINGDOM (USA)	2	12	2	4	3	13353.00
KHATANGO (USA)	1	7	1	1	1	2731.20
KIND OF HUSH	36	166	8	14	43	184651.11
KING OF CLUBS	15	47	3	3	9	13863.61
KING OF SPAIN	50	238	11	18	32	133755.62
KING PELLINORE (USA)	1	24	1	3	6	26449.40
KING PERSIAN	10	45	2	2	16	14532.10
KING'S BISHOP (USA)	1	2	0	0	1	833.00
KINGS LAKE (USA)	52	218	19	29	69	281651.99
KING'S RIDE	8	15	1	2	2	2389.16
KNOWN FACT (USA)	46	220	19	28	60	437186.38
KONIGSSTUHL (GER)	2	8	0	0	1	384.00
KRAYYAN	39	198	6	9	49	53689.80
KRIS	56	172	23	29	59	261504.98
LABUS (FR)	3	6	0	0	2	1445.00
LAFONTAINE (USA)	10	48	3	4	12	18839.67
LAOMEDONTE (USA)	1	6	1	1	0	2226.00
LAST FANDANGO	13	58	0	0	6	2464.00
LAST RAISE (USA)	1	6	1	1	2	1281.67
LATEST MODEL	1	16	1	2	4	9052.00
LAW SOCIETY (USA)	21	71	6	8	26	48119.13
LAXTON	3	9	0	0	1	430.50
LEAR FAN (USA)	14	57	8	15	21	115346.12
LE BAVARD (FR)	41	104	8	8	38	15449.21
LEGEND OF FRANCE (USA)	8	36	2	4	11	23824.97
LE JOHNSTAN	6	30	1	1	2	2932.60
LEMHI GOLD (USA)	3	9	2	3	1	7837.00
L'EMIGRANT (USA)	9	39	5	7	14	35938.41
LE MOSS	20	48	2	2	7	16364.10
LE SOLEIL	1	6	1	3	2	10007.40
LIBOI (USA)	3	13	1	1	1	4060.00
LIGHTER	1	1	0	0	1	666.67
LILOY (FR)	1	4	0	0	1	520.00
LINKAGE (USA)	7	33	2	2	8	6786.51
LITTLE CURRENT (USA)	3	6	0	0	2	10899.85
LITTLE WOLF	3	21	1	1	5	4504.00
LOBSANG	1	8	1	1	4	2471.68
LOCAL SUITOR (USA)	12	31	1	1	7	5638.07
LOCHNAGER	45	230	11	12	38	68026.10
LOMOND (USA)	51	148	19	22	46	199334.43
LONDON BELLS (CAN)	4	32	1	1	9	11923.50
LONGLEAT (USA)	44	202	9	15	42	69142.90
LORD GAYLE (USA)	36	161	12	19	40	277202.17
LORD HA HA	5	13	1	1	7	4820.84
LOVE TALE	1	3	1	1	0	862.50
LUCIFER (USA)	2	5	0	0	1	166.67
LUCKY WEDNESDAY	19	93	2	2	8	8249.20
LYDIAN (FR)	4	16	1	1	5	14672.20
LYLLOS (FR)	1	7	1	2	5	30993.25

Stallions Earnings – Continued

STALLIONS	RNRS	STARTS	WNRS	WINS	PLACES	TOTAL
LYPHARD'S SPECIAL (USA)	25	125	8	12	28	67548.86
LYPHARD'S WISH (FR)	15	66	7	10	23	48641.86
LYPHARD (USA)	15	47	4	6	13	166058.53
LYPHEOR	22	86	7	16	18	111422.18
MAC DIARMIDA (USA)	1	13	1	1	6	4149.17
MACULATA	4	9	0	0	1	100.00
MAGESTERIAL (USA)	2	14	1	1	3	4346.67
MAGIC MIRROR	15	72	4	5	19	20766.67
MAIN REEF	36	170	9	13	37	82417.88
MAJESTIC LIGHT (USA)	4	26	3	3	8	9954.67
MAJESTIC MAHARAJ	2	5	0	0	2	1125.00
MAJESTY'S PRINCE (USA)	1	11	1	1	4	3378.35
MAJOR PETINGO (FR)	1	7	0	0	2	446.00
MALACATE (USA)	1	10	1	2	2	5480.40
MALINOWSKI (USA)	8	44	3	5	13	63793.00
MANDALUS	17	46	1	1	13	2141.68
MANDRAKE MAJOR	18	94	6	8	23	40256.97
MANSINGH (USA)	41	192	7	7	21	33386.40
MARCHING ON	10	80	2	4	13	15199.00
MARFA (USA)	1	7	0	0	2	467.60
MARSHUA'S DANCER (USA)	1	10	1	2	5	4680.01
MARTIN JOHN	9	34	1	1	5	1635.01
MARTINMAS	24	121	8	11	16	49815.66
MASHHOR DANCER (USA)	6	24	2	3	8	16286.70
MASTER DERBY (USA)	1	3	0	0	1	176.67
MASTER WILLIE	11	32	1	1	10	7436.67
MATCHING PAIR	1	1	0	0	1	200.00
MEGATURN (USA)	1	3	0	0	1	632.80
MELYNO	3	11	1	1	3	2870.00
MENDEZ (FR)	4	15	1	1	1	4508.50
MIAMI SPRINGS	18	96	7	13	26	48075.22
MICKEY MCGUIRE (USA)	1	6	1	1	2	1336.67
MILAN	1	6	0	0	3	220.84
MILFORD	20	100	2	3	18	17820.50
MILLER'S MATE	4	9	2	2	2	8050.40
MILLFONTAINE	23	129	8	10	24	39518.63
MILL REEF (USA)	36	141	16	21	44	193693.83
MINER'S LAMP	4	7	1	1	0	862.50
THE MINSTREL (CAN)	41	140	15	21	57	391681.37
MISSISSIPPI	8	20	0	0	7	851.67
MISWAKI (USA)	13	36	5	5	11	24132.90
MODERN DANCER	2	6	0	0	1	147.50
MONKSFIELD	17	53	3	3	18	5438.34
MONSANTO (FR)	11	72	3	5	15	65346.20
MONSEIGNEUR (USA)	5	16	0	0	1	205.83
MONTEKIN	33	178	6	9	29	31051.53
MONTELIMAR (USA)	1	3	0	0	2	275.00
MONTEVERDI	4	18	1	1	5	5841.80
MOORESTYLE	10	37	2	4	5	15899.40
MORSTON (FR)	10	42	2	4	9	18947.90
MOULIN	1	4	0	0	2	1272.40
MOULTON	2	6	0	0	1	408.00
MOVE OFF	10	41	0	0	8	3279.40
MR FLUOROCARBON	22	91	3	5	13	18647.23
MR FORDETTE	5	8	0	0	1	87.50
MR PROSPECTOR (USA)	9	26	4	7	9	82076.89
MT LIVERMORE (USA)	3	9	1	1	3	18664.00
MUGATPURA	1	1	0	0	1	176.67
MUMMY'S GAME	33	189	12	15	39	67956.20

Stallions Earnings – Continued

STALLIONS	RNRS	STARTS	WNRS	WINS	PLACES	TOTAL
MUMMY'S PET	60	285	18	22	63	191279.64
MUMMY'S TREASURE	12	38	1	1	3	2816.40
MUSCATITE	15	66	3	5	12	16126.40
MUSIC BOY	56	355	15	23	80	124542.03
MUSIC MAESTRO	7	43	2	5	6	14476.50
MY DAD TOM (USA)	10	45	1	1	8	4869.77
MY TOP	4	27	0	0	3	764.17
NADJAR (FR)	4	7	0	0	1	101.67
NAIN BLEU (FR)	1	3	1	1	1	3582.60
NATIVE UPROAR (USA)	1	6	0	0	1	1000.00
NEARLY A HAND	4	7	0	0	2	1108.00
NEBOS (GER)	1	6	1	2	1	2743.33
NELTINO	5	30	2	2	7	10584.20
NEMORINO (USA)	2	10	0	0	1	428.00
NETHERKELLY	1	4	0	0	1	80.00
NEVER SO BOLD	19	51	5	6	17	30749.80
NEW MEMBER	1	2	0	0	1	321.00
NICHOLAS BILL	41	208	12	15	49	131594.80
NIELS	4	18	2	2	0	4168.67
NIGHT SHIFT (USA)	47	262	20	35	67	203441.05
NIJINSKY (CAN)	29	79	14	21	25	153656.77
NIJINSKY'S SECRET (USA)	2	8	1	1	3	3299.50
NINISKI (USA)	46	177	13	18	57	257017.59
NISHAPOUR (ГП)	31	158	9	12	33	58555.63
NOALCOHOLIC (FR)	5	27	3	7	8	26396.50
NOALTO	40	180	6	6	37	28355.34
THE NOBLE PLAYER (USA)	10	37	3	5	7	21414.34
NODOUBLE (USA)	6	17	2	2	4	7827.00
NO LOITERER	1	5	0	0	3	2345.00
NO LUTE (FR)	3	9	0	0	1	739.20
NO PASS NO SALE	1	3	0	0	2	935.20
NORDICO (USA)	16	79	6	10	31	47222.04
NORMANDY	1	5	1	1	1	1266.67
NORTH BRITON	1	6	1	2	4	92839.50
NORTHERN BABY (CAN)	15	70	7	22	20	305771.12
NORTHERN DANCER	19	65	6	9	30	174154.26
NORTHERN GUEST (USA)	5	8	1	1	0	1151.67
NORTHERN JOVE (CAN)	4	22	1	1	7	13170.76
NORTHERN PROSPECT (USA)	2	6	0	0	1	804.00
NORTHERN TEMPEST (USA)	9	37	1	1	4	4530.40
NORTHERN TREAT (USA)	1	10	1	1	0	3106.00
NORTHFIELDS (USA)	6	25	0	0	7	4447.50
NORTHJET	4	13	1	1	5	10522.83
NORTH POLE (CAN)	2	3	1	1	1	7408.33
NORTH SUMMIT	4	13	2	2	4	5851.66
NORWICK (USA)	16	57	2	3	4	8757.37
NUREYEV (USA)	40	139	22	35	46	796164.57
OATS	11	24	0	0	3	1666.67
OLDEN TIMES	2	4	0	0	2	27615.50
ONE FOR ALL (USA)	1	4	0	0	1	176.67
ON YOUR MARK	33	194	6	8	42	34432.64
ORCHESTRA	13	47	4	5	13	12584.54
OUR NATIVE (USA)	12	31	3	3	5	13239.00
OVAC (ITY)	16	44	3	5	11	7189.18
OVERSKATE (CAN)	1	7	1	1	0	2721.00
OVER THE RIVER (FR)	16	25	3	3	2	3918.34
OWEN DUDLEY	2	10	1	3	0	6775.40
PADDY'S STREAM	9	15	0	0	3	433.34
PAICO	5	14	1	1	2	1575.00

Stallions Earnings – Continued

STALLIONS	RNRS	STARTS	WNRS	WINS	PLACES	TOTAL
PALM TRACK	3	6	1	1	1	2826.00
PARADE OF STARS (USA)	1	14	1	1	5	15646.20
THE PARSON	22	51	2	4	12	7604.17
PAS DE SEUL	42	214	11	18	50	149419.60
PATCH	3	4	1	1	1	1199.98
PAUPER	7	23	1	1	4	4103.33
PEACOCK (FR)	1	6	0	0	2	150.00
PENMARRIC (USA)	3	8	0	0	3	203.34
PERRAULT	2	6	0	0	2	277.00
PERSEPOLIS (FR)	7	32	2	3	8	16454.20
PERSIAN BOLD	66	354	25	40	92	290060.36
PETERHOF (USA)	4	23	0	0	1	957.60
PETONG	43	267	16	20	48	109072.10
PETORIUS	49	265	19	32	72	149740.17
PHARLY (FR)	40	180	18	27	51	116918.50
PIAFFER (USA)	3	19	1	4	4	13921.50
PILGRIM (USA)	4	24	1	1	8	6318.67
PIMPERNELS TUNE	1	1	0	0	1	118.33
PIRATE'S BOUNTY (USA)	1	5	1	1	0	2245.60
PITPAN	9	15	0	0	3	390.83
PITSKELLY	27	150	5	6	34	34182.90
PLAY FELLOW (USA)	1	7	1	1	4	6480.50
PLUGGED NICKLE (USA)	3	9	0	0	1	378.00
POLLERTON	15	38	3	3	11	6139.17
PORTO BELLO	1	10	0	0	2	1832.00
POSITIVELY	1	2	0	0	1	118.33
POSSE (USA)	21	73	5	8	20	144266.00
PRAGMATIC	9	22	4	4	6	3893.32
PRECOCIOUS	44	204	13	15	44	78304.56
PRESIDENT (FR)	1	10	0	0	1	188.00
PRINCE BEE	10	33	3	8	6	22729.17
PRINCE REGENT (FR)	9	47	4	9	13	31328.68
PRINCE RHEINGOLD	1	4	0	0	2	111.67
PRINCE TENDERFOOT (USA)	49	219	14	21	41	84806.90
PRIVATE ACCOUNT (USA)	7	33	3	6	16	177567.14
PRIVATE WALK	2	12	1	1	5	1701.67
PROCIDA (USA)	4	11	0	0	3	1007.00
PROMINER	2	5	0	0	1	147.50
PROUD APPEAL (USA)	1	5	0	0	1	225.00
PROVERB	20	35	3	4	4	6133.34
PROVIDENTIAL	1	3	1	1	1	2398.00
PRY	5	14	0	0	1	29.17
PYJAMA HUNT	1	4	0	0	1	720.00
QUAYSIDE	19	49	3	3	13	7416.69
RABDAN	17	97	5	8	18	31856.00
RADETZKY	4	15	1	1	1	6974.00
RAGA NAVARRO (ITY)	22	87	4	6	5	18064.30
RAGAPAN	4	7	0	0	2	371.67
RAINBOW QUEST (USA)	12	19	3	3	8	21083.36
RAISE A CUP (USA)	6	19	2	2	3	10360.00
RAISE A MAN (USA)	2	7	0	0	2	1040.00
RAISE A NATIVE	5	23	1	1	3	17124.20
RANDOM SHOT	8	26	1	1	8	3688.33
RAPID RIVER	5	25	1	2	6	8712.30
RARE ONE	3	8	0	0	1	133.33
RARITY	10	31	4	4	10	11418.86
R B CHESNE	1	3	1	1	2	23671.44
REASONABLE (FR)	15	69	5	6	15	19987.67
RECITATION (USA)	2	10	2	2	4	8527.50

Stallions Earnings – Continued

STALLIONS	RNRS	STARTS	WNRS	WINS	PLACES	TOTAL
RECORD RUN	3	14	1	1	3	4952.60
RECORD TOKEN	5	14	0	0	3	960.50
RED JOHNNIE	3	19	1	1	6	4527.50
RED REGENT	5	22	2	2	6	3013.32
RED RYDER (USA)	2	9	1	2	3	13083.90
RED SUNSET	63	345	20	31	83	144137.30
REESH	12	62	3	3	8	8613.87
REGALBERTO (USA)	1	5	0	0	1	864.00
RELAUNCH (USA)	1	5	0	0	3	1626.00
RELKINO	21	79	6	7	13	29306.60
REMAINDER MAN	10	65	3	4	12	15771.70
RIBOBOY (USA)	8	34	1	5	5	20420.90
RICH CREAM (USA)	1	7	0	0	3	4013.00
RING BIDDER	4	15	0	0	3	1232.00
RIVER BEAUTY	2	4	1	1	2	791.67
RIVER KNIGHT (FR)	4	11	0	0	5	4686.67
RIVERMAN (USA)	31	95	12	14	30	111312.07
RIVER RIVER (FR)	1	5	1	1	2	4055.60
ROBELLINO (USA)	13	59	5	9	20	65482.10
ROBERTO (USA)	21	78	9	13	33	277238.22
ROLFE (USA)	7	30	1	1	5	4808.80
ROMAN WARRIOR	5	26	0	0	3	710.83
RONTINO	2	25	2	3	8	8703.67
ROSCOE BLAKE	6	25	1	1	4	4409.33
ROSELIER (FR)	10	44	2	2	6	3698.34
ROUSER	1	9	0	0	2	945.60
ROUSILLON (USA)	20	49	8	9	19	100333.72
ROYAL MATCH	13	58	1	1	10	9948.60
ROYAL PALACE	3	9	0	0	2	936.00
ROYBEN	3	24	1	3	4	9940.50
RUNNETT	37	229	17	23	54	116266.58
RUN THE GANTLET (USA)	5	11	1	1	4	4744.67
RUPERT BEAR	1	10	0	0	1	267.50
RUSTICARO (FR)	36	143	6	9	32	31950.67
RUTHIE'S NATIVE (USA)	1	2	0	0	1	319.20
RYMER	4	10	1	1	2	1533.31
SADLER'S WELLS (USA)	43	146	25	41	51	847945.42
SAGACE (FR)	3	6	1	2	2	6696.05
SAGARO	7	32	1	2	3	8119.00
SAHER	14	56	1	1	11	4465.92
SAINT DENYS	1	3	0	0	2	354.17
SALLUCEVA	7	17	0	0	2	386.66
SALLUST	42	185	13	21	42	118871.01
SALMON LEAP (USA)	34	154	8	13	39	98783.37
SANDHURST PRINCE	40	223	7	10	56	42851.46
SARATOGA SIX (USA)	1	1	1	1	0	1725.00
SAYF EL ARAB (USA)	33	173	7	11	41	51645.70
SAY PRIMULA	1	7	1	1	1	3500.00
SAYYAF	35	158	6	8	30	38407.51
SCALLYWAG	2	3	1	1	0	1150.00
SCORPIO (FR)	14	59	1	1	12	3012.50
SEATTLE SLEW (USA)	5	11	2	3	6	74723.29
SEATTLE SONG (USA)	8	32	3	5	8	73426.67
SECRETARIAT (USA)	3	9	1	1	2	6580.00
SECRETO (USA)	18	42	3	4	13	26843.55
SELKO	1	1	0	0	1	116.67
SENSITIVE PRINCE (USA)	6	29	0	0	3	1542.85
SEXTON BLAKE	13	49	5	9	18	72595.09
SEYMOUR HICKS (FR)	14	54	1	2	8	12459.57

Stallions Earnings – Continued

STALLIONS	RNRS	STARTS	WNRS	WINS	PLACES	TOTAL
SHACK (USA)	12	46	1	2	3	9600.75
SHADEED (USA)	12	33	4	5	16	24961.77
SHAKAPOUR	1	3	1	1	1	1849.00
SHAM (USA)	1	2	0	0	2	14786.08
SHAREEF DANCER (USA)	37	131	15	17	49	104083.51
SHARPEN UP	33	97	11	15	26	81754.03
SHARPO	50	241	18	26	56	183259.93
SHEER GRIT	4	5	0	0	1	240.00
SHERNAZAR	8	18	0	0	5	2422.00
SHIMATOREE (USA)	1	3	0	0	1	632.80
SHIRLEY HEIGHTS	50	158	17	24	55	362792.31
SHOW–A–LEG	3	17	0	0	1	341.60
SHY GROOM (USA)	26	95	3	4	16	20774.37
SIBERIAN EXPRESS (USA)	8	24	2	2	8	18599.33
SICYOS (USA)	6	18	0	0	2	577.73
SILENT CAL (USA)	1	8	0	0	2	372.00
SILLY PRICES	4	26	1	2	5	16241.00
SILVER HAWK (USA)	2	4	1	1	0	2427.00
SIMPLY GREAT (FR)	47	256	15	22	78	139607.61
SIR IVOR	23	76	6	9	22	65591.94
SIR TRISTRAM	2	12	0	0	2	956.00
SKYLINER	28	115	9	12	20	51934.44
SLEW O' GOLD (USA)	3	6	1	1	3	150494.80
SLIM JIM	1	2	0	0	1	192.00
SLIPPERED	3	5	0	0	1	266.67
SMACKOVER	9	39	1	2	4	5983.60
SMARTSET	6	13	1	1	1	1266.67
SMOGGY	3	20	2	7	1	40059.17
SMOOTH STEPPER	15	38	3	4	8	9261.68
SOLAR WIND (USA)	1	4	0	0	2	268.33
SOLFORD (USA)	10	42	4	5	7	20404.96
SOLO DANCER (GER)	1	8	0	0	2	950.00
SOME HAND	5	20	4	4	1	19412.50
SOMETHINGFABULOUS (USA)	1	7	1	1	2	535.00
SONG	50	284	11	17	52	135197.39
SONNEN GOLD	13	64	2	6	15	29716.50
SON OF SHAKA	2	18	1	4	3	23995.50
SOUDNO	2	6	1	1	3	1578.34
SOUL SINGER	1	8	1	1	1	2144.00
SOVEREIGN DANCER (USA)	3	8	1	1	3	14959.46
SPARKLER	5	13	1	1	2	7083.00
SPARKLING BOY	10	53	3	4	5	13003.40
SPECTACULAR BID (USA)	5	23	3	4	9	20546.46
SPEND A BUCK (USA)	1	2	0	0	2	4132.00
SPIN OF A COIN	1	4	1	2	1	5362.80
SPORTIN' LIFE (USA)	2	10	1	1	7	3248.34
SPRING HEIGHTS	2	5	0	0	2	1008.00
STALWART (USA)	2	14	1	1	4	17268.34
STANFORD	38	199	5	8	40	52404.08
STAR APPEAL	43	239	14	23	46	113817.28
STARCH REDUCED	16	102	3	5	14	16199.00
STAR DE NASKRA (USA)	4	27	4	5	8	25827.90
STATE DINNER (USA)	2	7	1	1	2	847.34
STEP TOGETHER (USA)	2	23	1	1	10	3112.52
STETCHWORTH (USA)	8	33	1	1	12	5423.67
STOP THE MUSIC (USA)	3	12	2	2	3	9353.50
STORM BIRD (CAN)	18	65	6	14	21	197854.82
ST PADDY	1	10	1	1	2	3926.40
STRADAVINSKY	2	12	0	0	4	415.84

Stallions Earnings – Continued

STALLIONS	RNRS	STARTS	WNRS	WINS	PLACES	TOTAL
STRONG GALE	45	147	10	10	38	29961.52
STUBBS GAZETTE	2	15	1	2	3	2406.68
SUMMING (USA)	2	11	2	2	7	49314.70
SUNLEY BUILDS	4	17	0	0	1	222.00
SUNNY CLIME (USA)	1	15	1	2	4	6924.80
SUPER CONCORDE (USA)	7	38	3	3	16	20603.20
SUPERLATIVE	41	177	8	11	41	79400.76
SUPER SLIP	3	4	0	0	2	216.67
SWAN'S ROCK	3	6	0	0	1	50.00
SWEET MONDAY	16	83	5	10	13	39429.80
SWING EASY (USA)	30	160	7	11	32	63809.90
TACHYPOUS	16	51	3	3	10	12439.80
TAMPERO (FR)	7	51	1	2	17	8523.13
TANFIRION	21	82	7	7	22	22783.21
TAP ON WOOD	33	183	9	15	48	82975.21
TARBOOSH (USA)	1	6	1	1	1	1812.50
TAUFAN (USA)	77	391	29	50	101	216537.79
TEENOSO (USA)	19	55	2	2	11	13895.30
TELSMOSS	1	9	1	3	2	9740.60
TENDER KING	50	255	14	20	50	108618.95
TESORO MIO	1	5	0	0	2	216.67
THATCHING	66	315	23	35	80	203110.54
THATCH (USA)	5	36	2	4	9	21066.10
TICKLED PINK	15	90	3	5	15	20627.40
TILT UP (USA)	1	13	1	3	4	17089.00
TIME FOR A CHANGE (USA)	1	2	0	0	1	992.00
TIMELESS MOMENT (USA)	1	11	0	0	5	2181.80
TINA'S PET	43	221	17	31	47	141855.95
TOLD (USA)	2	9	0	0	3	4350.00
TOLOMEO	15	91	3	6	29	51539.43
TOPSIDER (USA)	25	92	11	19	30	169094.34
TOP VILLE	24	79	5	6	23	50308.00
TORENAGA	6	22	1	1	3	1105.01
TORUS	26	62	2	2	15	5621.69
TOUCHING WOOD (USA)	41	209	17	22	56	88661.05
TOUCH PAPER	4	13	0	0	2	194.17
TOWER WALK	18	62	1	1	6	4844.50
TOWN AND COUNTRY	17	68	3	5	14	31605.50
TRACK SPARE	1	3	0	0	2	316.67
TRANSWORLD (USA)	3	22	1	1	5	3812.80
TREBORO (USA)	1	9	0	0	1	4873.50
TRES GATE	1	5	0	0	4	995.01
TRIMMINGHAM	5	12	1	1	1	1268.34
TROJAN FEN	35	185	10	23	42	81160.54
TROMBONE	1	1	1	1	0	862.50
TROY	3	24	0	0	5	11985.40
TRY MY BEST (USA)	29	119	5	7	25	51253.69
TUDORVILLE	1	5	0	0	1	192.00
TUG OF WAR	6	16	1	1	3	1649.17
TULA ROCKET	4	17	1	1	7	2715.02
TUMBLE GOLD	2	4	0	0	1	266.67
TUMBLE WIND (USA)	51	232	7	9	49	69369.14
TWO DAVIDS (USA)	1	6	0	0	1	55.00
TYRANT (USA)	1	2	1	1	1	1826.67
TYRNAVOS	34	140	5	6	12	25776.90
UNCLE POKEY	13	64	2	4	14	21852.50
VACARME (USA)	1	2	0	0	1	400.00
VAGUELY NOBLE	16	45	2	2	15	19080.29
VAIGLY GREAT	54	281	11	16	64	91740.57

Stallions Earnings – Continued

STALLIONS	RNRS	STARTS	WNRS	WINS	PLACES	TOTAL
VAL DE L'ORNE (FR)	1	1	0	0	1	390.00
VALDEZ (USA)	4	15	1	1	4	7022.90
VALIYAR	34	133	6	11	19	51850.40
VAN DER LINDEN (FR)	5	32	0	0	1	285.60
VAYRANN	4	16	1	1	1	2302.00
VERBATIM (USA)	5	30	1	2	10	8179.50
VICE REGENT (CAN)	4	15	1	1	5	31794.50
VICTORIOUS (USA)	1	5	0	0	3	1058.30
VIKING (USA)	23	100	4	5	19	24552.42
VIRGINIA BOY	1	7	1	2	0	6254.00
VISION (USA)	44	203	12	18	58	135968.23
VITIGES (FR)	3	7	1	2	0	43617.67
VIVADARI	2	3	0	0	1	68.33
WARPATH	8	36	3	3	7	14367.80
WASSL	30	126	6	9	32	59395.30
WATER BANK (USA)	1	4	0	0	1	299.60
WATTLEFIELD	6	28	1	1	1	3544.60
WELL DECORATED (USA)	4	9	0	0	1	101.67
WELSH CAPTAIN	12	93	5	9	18	42434.74
WELSH CHANTER	6	20	1	1	2	6190.00
WELSH PAGEANT	12	60	4	5	15	35613.60
WELSH SAINT	30	155	5	11	43	83122.48
WELSH TERM	10	37	2	2	17	35907.03
WHAT A GUEST	22	97	3	6	19	32435.04
WHAT LUCK (USA)	1	7	0	0	3	1162.00
WHISTLING DEER	23	75	2	4	15	22795.02
WHISTLING TOP	2	5	1	1	2	656.33
WHITSTEAD	1	2	0	0	1	228.00
WIND AND WUTHERING (USA)	3	9	0	0	2	585.00
WINDJAMMER (USA)	19	143	7	9	24	38385.90
WOLF POWER (SAF)	3	16	1	1	1	3895.00
WOLLOW	1	10	1	4	4	13721.50
WOLVER HEIGHTS	3	8	0	0	1	392.00
WOLVER HOLLOW	17	76	3	4	12	13627.00
WOLVERLIFE	42	206	14	20	44	78371.93
THE WONDER (FR)	2	8	1	1	0	3260.25
WORKBOY	11	51	1	1	8	6859.30
WRENS HILL	3	7	0	0	1	20.00
YASHGAN	6	24	1	1	6	3145.83
YA ZAMAN (USA)	17	89	2	4	15	17042.63
YOUNG EMPEROR	1	14	1	1	4	10738.50
YOUNG GENERATION	46	241	9	15	52	356862.61
YOUTH (USA)	5	28	3	6	8	20788.90
YUKON (USA)	1	1	0	0	1	448.00
ZINO	2	7	0	0	2	340.33

STATISTICS BY KIND PERMISSION OF WEATHERBYS

Weekend winners begin with Raceform

The following entry was received too late for inclusion in the appropriate section of Horses in Training.

MR W. J. PEARCE, Hambleton

Postal: **Hambleton House, Sutton Bank, Hambleton, N. Yorkshire, YO7 2HA.**
Phone:**(0845) 597373 FAX (0845) 597643**

1 **BOLD HABIT**, 5, ch g Homing—Our Mother **Mr Roger Jelley**
2 **GREY RUM**, 5, gr g Absalom—Cuba Libre **Hambleton Thoroughbred Racing Plc.**
3 **HAGGS TAVERN**, 5, b h Tower Walk—Nonsensical **Mr Willie Smith**
4 **LONG ARM OF TH'LAW**, 4, ro g Longleat (USA)—Burglar Tip **Mr E. K. Geddes**
5 **LUCKY HUMBUG**, 7, ch g Lucky Wednesday—Be My Sweet **Hambleton Thoroughbred Racing Plc.**
6 **MR WADDILOVE**, 4, b c Bold Lad (IRE)—Friendly Sound **Mr G. W. Squire**
7 **RIEVAULX**, 4, b g Petorius—Sister Sala **Hambleton Thoroughbred Racing Plc.**
8 **SHARLIE'S WIMPY**, 11, ch g Tumble Wind (USA)—Sweet Sharlie **Mr Roger Jelley**
9 **SIMPLY FIRST CLASS**, 4, b g Tower Walk—Duchy **J B S Mailing Services Ltd.**
10 **SOLA MIA**, 4, b f Tolomeo—Be My Sweet **Mrs P. A. Barratt**
11 **SPANISH HARLEM**, 4, br c King of Spain—Luscinia **Hambleton Thoroughbred Racing Plc.**
12 **WHATS YOURS CALLED**, 4, ch f Windjammer (USA)—Thorganby Melody **Mrs Lorraine Hunt**

THREE-YEAR-OLDS

13 **CRYPTIC GIRL**, b f Tower Walk—Lucky Saran **Mr Brian Rust**
14 **DORIS GIRL**, gr f Absalom—Targos Delight **Mr David M. Gransby**
15 **ENCHANTING HABIT**, b c Enchantment—Miss Worth **Mr Chris Cobbett**
16 **FIRST BLESSED**, b f Music Boy—Blessit **Mrs M. J. Russell**
17 **FLASH OF GENIUS**, b c Formidable (USA)—Lucent **Hambleton Thoroughbred Racing Plc.**
18 **FRANCISCAN**, b c Godswalk (USA)—Athenian Primrose **Hambleton Thoroughbred Racing Plc.**
19 **LUCKY BARNES**, b c Lucky Wednesday—Hutton Barns **Mike Clynes Associates Ltd.**
20 **MARTINI'S COURIER**, br c Lucky Wednesday—Be My Sweet **Martini Cars (Cheshunt) Ltd.**
21 **MORNING JOY**, b f Mummy's Pet—Satellite **Mr N. B. Mason**
22 **ORIENTAL NATIVE (USA)**, ch g Raise A Native—Etoile d'Orient **Hambleton Thoroughbred Racing Plc**
23 **PREMIER DEVELOPER**, b c Precocious—Arderelle (FR) **Premier Properties Plc.**
24 **PREMIER TOUCH**, b c Petorius—Fingers **Premier Properties Plc.**
25 **PUNDLES PET**, b c Petong—Goody Goody **Mr David M. Gransby**
26 **REXY BOY**, b c Dunbeath (USA)—Coca **Mr David M. Gransby**
27 **TEMPESTOSA**, b f Northern Tempest (USA)—Lucky Candy **Hambleton Lodge Equine Premix Ltd.**
28 **TOSHIBA COMET**, b c Noalto—Silk Lady **Mr P. A. Judd**
29 **VICEROY**, b c Indian King (USA)—Bold Polly **Hambleton Thoroughbred Racing Plc.**

TWO-YEAR-OLDS

30 **ARALDO BLU (IRE)**, b c 22/4 Heraldiste—Lisahunny (Pitskelly) **Hambleton Lodge Equine Premix**
31 B c 15/2 Today and Tomorrow—Baby Bunting (Pyjama Hunt) **Mr B. O'Brien**
32 B c 13/3 Petorius—Be A Dancer (Be Friendly) **Mrs H. A. Inskip**
33 B f 14/3 Taufan (USA)—Bellinzona (Northfields (USA)) **Hambleton Thoroughbred Racing Plc.**
34 B c 8/2 Doulab (USA)—Enchanted (Song) **Hambleton Thoroughbred Racing Plc.**
35 B c 18/1 Full of Hope—Espanita (Riboboy (USA)) **Mr B. O'Brien**
36 **H. M. GEAR**, b c 9/5 Mansingh (USA)—Huntergirl (Huntercombe) **H. M. Gear Ltd.**
37 **MARTIN'S EXECUTIVE**, b c 13/5 King of Spain—Wigeon (Divine Gift) **Martini Cars (Cheshunt) Ltd.**
38 **MERCHANT OF VENICE**, b c 17/3 Precocious—Silka (ITY) (Lypheor) **Hambleton Thoroughbred Racing Plc.**
39 B/br c 22/2 Sure Blade (USA)—Monaco Melody (Tudor Melody) **Hambleton Thoroughbred Racing Plc.**
40 Ch c 8/3 Bay Express—My Bushbaby (Hul a Hul) **Mr N. B. Mason**
41 B f 14/3 Full of Hope—My Mutzie (Vilgora) **Mr B. O'Brien**
42 **PREMIER CHOICE (IRE)**, b c 17/3 Petorius—Numidia (Sallust) **Mr Roger Jelley**
43 **PREMIER ROYALE (IRE)**, b c 29/2 Indian King (USA)—Rince Si (Malinowski (USA)) **Premier Properties Plc.**
44 **PRIME VENUE (IRE)**, b c 29/3 Godswalk (USA)—Friendly Sound (Be Friendly) **N. B. Mason (Amusements Ltd.)**
45 ch c 24/4 Stanford—Royal Home (Royal Palace) **Mr R. Trewhellar**
46 gr c 16/2 Today and Tomorrow—Runager (Lochnager) **Mr B. O'Brien**
47 **SAINT BENE'T (IRE)**, b c 13/3 Glenstal (USA)—Basilea (FR) (Frere Basile (FR)) **Hambleton Thoroughbred Racing Plc.**
48 **SHEPHERD'S SONG**, b c 20/4 Elegant Air—Littleton Song (Song) **Mr Robert Macgregor**
49 B c 26/1 Lucky Wednesday—Starkist (So Blessed) **Mrs H. A. Inskip**
50 Br c 24/5 Precocious—Top Bloom (Thatch (USA)) **Mrs H. A. Inskip**
51 **TOSHIBA COMET TOO (IRE)** ch c 25/2 Gorytus (USA)—No Jargon (Nonoalco (USA) **Toshiba Comet**
52 B c 6/4 Enchantment—Wessex Kingdom (Vaigly Great) **Mrs H. A. Inskip**

Jockey (Flat): D. Nicholls (8-5)